STATS™ 1994 Player Profiles

STATS, Inc.

Published by STATS Publishing
A division of Sports Team Analysis & Tracking Systems, Inc.
Dr. Richard Cramer, Chairman • John Dewan, President

Cover by John Grimwade, New York, NY

Photos by Tony Inzerillo, Bensenville, IL

First Edition: November, 1993

Printed in the United States of America

ISBN 1-8840-6402-7

**This book is dedicated to
the memory of Tim Crews and Steve Olin.**

As much as we love baseball, life transcends it.

Acknowledgments

Hi. My name is Allan Spear, and although you may not have ever heard of me, I was the production assistant for the Player Profiles book. Many long days and longer nights in early October were required to have this book completed, printed and in your hands by November 1, and fortunately there are many talented people here at STATS to help get the job done.

Dr. Richard Cramer is the Chairman and founder of STATS, as well as the brains behind the computer system which manages all this information.

John Dewan is the President and CEO. In addition to managing STATS into an Inc. 500 company, he developed the original concept for the Profiles book and each fall works his fingers almost to the bone to produce new and improved editions of our books.

Rob McQuown did almost all of the core programming for the book. Michael Canter assisted on the programming and redesigned the shading for this edition. Bob Mecca created the Leader Board section, and with help from Kevin Davis, ensured the accuracy of all the data.

Thanks to the rest of the STATS staff whose work every day during the baseball season made this book possible.

Vice President Art Ashley, Vice President Sue Dewan, Director of Marketing Ross Schaufelberger and Director of Sports Operations Steve Moyer were all instrumental in STATS' continued growth. Art keeps our computer system from crashing, Sue is manager of the Systems Department, Ross is in charge of client services, and Steve rules the Reporter Network, the group of individuals who originally collected the data.

Others helping out on the baseball side include Jules Aquino, Michael Coulter, Jason Gumbs, Chuck Miller, Jim Musso and Don Zminda. The systems department includes Stefan Kretschmann and Jeff Schinski. Mike Hammer and Kenn Ruby have made sure football was not forgotten while everyone else was concentrating on baseball, and Stephanie Armstrong, Shawna Hawkins, Alissa Hudson, Marge Morra, and Debbi Spence keep the administrative side of the office running smoothly.

David Pinto, who also assisted in data verification, spends his time working at ESPN to bring the STATS touch right into your living room and Craig Wright continues to use his talents to oversee our Major League Operations. If you bought this book in a bookstore, Steve Heinecke was the reason it got there.

Without their dedication, this book would be full of blank pages.

— Allan Spear, Senior Statistician

Table of Contents

Introduction....1

1993 Player Profiles....3

1993 Team and League Profiles....474

Leader Boards....497

About STATS, Inc.....508

Glossary....510

Introduction

Welcome to the second edition of the Player Profiles book, easily the best edition of this book we have ever published!

For those of you asking "How could you have possibly improved this book from last season?", take a look. First of all, we have added both team and league profiles to compliment the player profiles. Now you can see how well Frank Viola did in September last year (pretty well), contrast that to the rest of the Boston staff (hmmm...), then compare those totals to how the American League and Major League stack up.

We have altered the Leader Boards, putting in minimums for each category.

We also changed the format of the profiles themselves. Instead of shading the "Last 5 Years" section, we are now shading just the header lines. We thought this significantly improved the readability. We have also added the player's age to the top of the profile.

For you longtime STATS Publishing readers, we even changed the "About STATS, Inc." section, bringing it into the 1990's.

Lastly, as you probably noticed already, we have drastically improved the cover. This is probably the only book on the market right now with both John Kruk and Randy Johnson on the cover, and that right there is reason enough to buy the book. All the stats in here are just a bonus.

So, what hasn't changed about this book? Plenty. On these pages you will still find statistical breakdowns for all 1,104 players who appeared in the majors last year, from Jim Abbott to Bob Zupcic. Even Paul Fletcher, who threw six pitches for the Phillies in July. We still have 120 categories in the Leader Boards section, and we kept the Glossary which has all the necessary abbreviations and category descriptions.

How did these changes come to be? All the ideas came from readers who thought they could make this a better book. And they were right. If there is something you would like to see, let us know. We made a bunch of changes this year and there is no reason why we can't do the same thing again next year.

— ***John Dewan and Allan Spear***

Jim Abbott — Yankees

Age 26 – Pitches Left (groundball pitcher)

	ERA	W	L	Sv	G	GS	IP	BB	SO	Avg	H	2B	3B	HR	RBI	OBP	SLG	CG	ShO	Sup	QS	#P/S	SB	CS	GB	FB	G/F
1993 Season	4.37	11	14	0	32	32	214.0	73	95	.271	221	39	0	22	104	.332	.400	4	1	5.00	20	96	16	6	399	187	2.13
Career (1989-1993)	3.66	58	66	0	157	157	1061.0	360	603	.269	1087	164	11	77	414	.330	.372	24	5	4.21	98	102	86	45	1835	919	2.00

1993 Season

	ERA	W	L	Sv	G	GS	IP	H	HR	BB	SO
Home	3.12	8	6	0	15	15	112.1	94	12	30	55
Away	5.75	3	8	0	17	17	101.2	127	10	43	40
Day	4.24	6	4	0	12	12	80.2	70	7	35	40
Night	4.46	5	10	0	20	20	133.1	151	15	38	55
Grass	4.02	9	11	0	25	25	170.1	163	17	58	81
Turf	5.77	2	3	0	7	7	43.2	58	5	15	14
April	3.72	1	4	0	5	5	36.1	39	2	6	15
May	4.89	3	1	0	6	6	38.2	39	5	15	20
June	4.15	1	2	0	4	4	26.0	24	1	12	12
July	3.41	3	1	0	5	5	34.1	30	4	13	16
August	5.18	1	3	0	6	6	40.0	49	4	11	19
September/October	4.66	2	3	0	6	6	38.2	40	6	16	13
Starter	4.37	11	14	0	32	32	214.0	221	22	73	95
Reliever	0.00	0	0	0	0	0	0.0	0	0	0	0
0-3 Days Rest	0.00	0	0	0	0	0	0.0	0	0	0	0
4 Days Rest	4.41	8	6	0	18	18	118.1	116	10	45	58
5+ Days Rest	4.33	3	8	0	14	14	95.2	105	12	28	37
Pre-All Star	4.29	5	8	0	17	17	113.1	115	9	40	50
Post-All Star	4.47	6	6	0	15	15	100.2	106	13	33	45

	Avg	AB	H	2B	3B	HR	RBI	BB	SO	OBP	SLG
vs. Left	.283	106	30	7	0	0	7	12	8	.364	.349
vs. Right	.270	708	191	32	0	22	97	61	87	.327	.408
Inning 1-6	.269	674	181	33	0	17	87	60	78	.329	.393
Inning 7+	.286	140	40	6	0	5	17	13	17	.348	.436
None on	.251	474	119	23	0	8	8	43	55	.316	.350
Runners on	.300	340	102	16	0	14	96	30	40	.355	.471
Scoring Posn	.302	182	55	9	0	8	82	19	26	.361	.484
Close & Late	.355	62	22	4	0	1	9	4	5	.388	.468
None on/out	.257	206	53	12	0	5	5	24	19	.335	.388
vs. 1st Batr (relief)	.000	0	0	0	0	0	0	0	0	.000	.000
First Inning Pitched	.211	114	24	4	0	2	12	18	21	.316	.298
First 75 Pitches	.266	616	164	29	0	15	72	54	68	.326	.386
Pitch 76-90	.291	117	34	9	0	1	15	9	15	.344	.393
Pitch 91-105	.311	61	19	1	0	5	15	7	8	.377	.574
Pitch 106+	.200	20	4	0	0	1	2	3	4	.304	.350
First Pitch	.309	149	46	5	0	7	26	4	0	.325	.483
Ahead in Count	.241	352	85	15	0	7	32	0	81	.245	.344
Behind in Count	.283	159	45	9	0	5	28	42	0	.433	.434
Two Strikes	.211	298	63	10	0	6	28	27	95	.276	.305

Career (1989-1993)

	ERA	W	L	Sv	G	GS	IP	H	HR	BB	SO
Home	3.64	27	33	0	77	77	534.0	549	43	159	296
Away	3.69	31	33	0	80	80	527.0	538	34	201	307
Day	3.38	20	18	0	44	44	292.2	279	20	102	176
Night	3.77	38	48	0	113	113	768.1	808	57	258	427
Grass	3.57	47	52	0	129	129	876.1	878	66	291	503
Turf	4.09	11	14	0	28	28	184.2	209	11	69	100
April	3.89	3	14	0	21	21	136.1	154	6	41	72
May	3.79	14	9	0	29	29	187.2	178	14	75	104
June	3.97	9	9	0	25	25	170.0	169	12	63	98
July	2.75	11	9	0	24	24	170.1	164	11	39	107
August	4.06	12	11	0	29	29	190.2	209	14	70	110
September/October	3.54	9	14	0	29	29	206.0	213	20	72	112
Starter	3.66	58	66	0	157	157	1061.0	1087	77	360	603
Reliever	0.00	0	0	0	0	0	0.0	0	0	0	0
0-3 Days Rest	2.49	2	1	0	4	4	25.1	24	2	10	24
4 Days Rest	3.60	35	34	0	90	90	612.0	619	40	196	359
5+ Days Rest	3.82	21	31	0	63	63	423.2	444	35	154	220
Pre-All Star	3.76	29	37	0	85	85	560.0	570	35	197	325
Post-All Star	3.56	29	29	0	72	72	501.0	517	42	163	278

	Avg	AB	H	2B	3B	HR	RBI	BB	SO	OBP	SLG
vs. Left	.300	609	183	38	2	8	73	63	92	.367	.409
vs. Right	.263	3431	904	126	9	69	341	297	511	.323	.366
Inning 1-6	.263	3333	875	134	10	57	345	304	507	.325	.360
Inning 7+	.300	707	212	30	1	20	69	56	96	.353	.430
None on	.266	2344	624	99	5	40	40	201	340	.328	.364
Runners on	.273	1696	463	65	6	37	374	159	263	.334	.384
Scoring Posn	.262	898	235	35	4	20	332	114	159	.339	.376
Close & Late	.320	347	111	9	1	8	42	28	39	.370	.421
None on/out	.276	1049	289	48	3	21	21	85	135	.332	.387
vs. 1st Batr (relief)	.000	0	0	0	0	0	0	0	0	.000	.000
First Inning Pitched	.253	584	148	26	1	9	65	69	88	.334	.348
First 75 Pitches	.255	2887	736	110	6	50	274	262	435	.318	.349
Pitch 76-90	.305	545	166	27	2	9	61	46	72	.362	.411
Pitch 91-105	.316	377	119	16	2	10	55	33	57	.370	.448
Pitch 106+	.286	231	66	11	1	8	24	19	39	.340	.446
First Pitch	.338	675	228	31	2	18	91	18	0	.354	.470
Ahead in Count	.219	1826	399	54	4	26	145	0	526	.222	.295
Behind in Count	.313	837	262	46	3	22	113	204	0	.446	.454
Two Strikes	.197	1684	331	45	3	21	122	136	603	.259	.264

Pitcher vs. Batter (career)

Pitches Best Vs.	Avg	AB	H	2B	3B	HR	RBI	BB	SO	OBP	SLG
Chris James	.000	15	0	0	0	0	0	0	3	.000	.000
Michael Huff	.000	13	0	0	0	0	0	1	2	.071	.000
Joey Cora	.000	12	0	0	0	0	0	1	1	.077	.000
Mike Bordick	.000	10	0	0	0	0	0	1	2	.091	.000
Scott Fletcher	.045	22	1	0	0	0	1	0	1	.045	.045

Pitches Worst Vs.	Avg	AB	H	2B	3B	HR	RBI	BB	SO	OBP	SLG
Chris Hoiles	.786	14	11	2	0	1	5	2	0	.765	1.143
Mike Devereaux	.565	23	13	2	0	1	2	6	2	.655	.783
George Brett	.531	32	17	2	0	3	11	4	6	.583	.875
Dave Henderson	.455	22	10	1	0	5	8	3	4	.500	1.182
Mark McGwire	.435	23	10	0	0	4	7	4	3	.519	.957

Kurt Abbott — Athletics

Age 25 – Bats Right

	Avg	G	AB	R	H	2B	3B	HR	RBI	BB	SO	HBP	GDP	SB	CS	OBP	SLG	IBB	SH	SF	#Pit	#P/PA	GB	FB	G/F
1993 Season	.246	20	61	11	15	1	0	3	9	3	20	0	3	2	0	.281	.410	0	3	0	261	3.90	16	14	1.14

1993 Season

	Avg	AB	H	2B	3B	HR	RBI	BB	SO	OBP	SLG
vs. Left	.231	26	6	0	0	2	3	1	9	.259	.462
vs. Right	.257	35	9	1	0	1	6	2	11	.297	.371
Scoring Posn	.389	18	7	0	0	1	6	0	7	.389	.556
Close & Late	.333	9	3	0	0	0	2	0	4	.333	.333

Paul Abbott — Indians

Age 26 – Pitches Right (flyball pitcher)

	ERA	W	L	Sv	G	GS	IP	BB	SO	Avg	H	2B	3B	HR	RBI	OBP	SLG	CG	ShO	Sup	QS	#P/S	SB	CS	GB	FB	G/F
1993 Season	6.38	0	1	0	5	5	18.1	11	7	.260	19	5	1	5	13	.357	.562	0	0	3.93	0	66	3	0	27	19	1.42
Career (1990-1993)	5.25	3	7	0	33	15	111.1	80	88	.258	106	26	5	11	63	.378	.426	0	0	3.96	4	80	21	3	118	129	0.91

1993 Season

	ERA	W	L	Sv	G	GS	IP	H	HR	BB	SO
Home	3.72	0	0	0	3	3	9.2	7	1	7	5
Away	9.35	0	1	0	2	2	8.2	12	4	4	2

	Avg	AB	H	2B	3B	HR	RBI	BB	SO	OBP	SLG
vs. Left	.244	41	10	2	1	1	5	8	5	.367	.415
vs. Right	.281	32	9	3	0	4	8	3	2	.343	.750

Juan Agosto — Astros

Age 36 – Pitches Left (groundball pitcher)

	ERA	W	L	Sv	G	GS	IP	BB	SO	Avg	H	2B	3B	HR	RBI	OBP	SLG	GF	IR	IRS	Hld	SvOp	SB	CS	GB	FB	G/F
1993 Season	6.00	0	0	0	6	0	6.0	0	3	.308	8	1	0	1	6	.308	.462	3	4	4	1	0	1	0	10	5	2.00
Last Five Years	4.40	20	20	7	270	1	317.1	122	158	.279	338	56	9	14	180	.351	.375	66	180	63	40	22	30	6	580	244	2.38

1993 Season

	ERA	W	L	Sv	G	GS	IP	H	HR	BB	SO
Home	0.00	0	0	0	3	0	2.2	3	0	0	1
Away	10.80	0	0	0	3	0	3.1	5	1	0	2

	Avg	AB	H	2B	3B	HR	RBI	BB	SO	OBP	SLG
vs. Left	.333	12	4	1	0	1	3	0	1	.333	.667
vs. Right	.286	14	4	0	0	0	3	0	2	.286	.286

Last Five Years

	ERA	W	L	Sv	G	GS	IP	H	HR	BB	SO
Home	4.10	14	10	5	136	0	162.1	164	6	67	95
Away	4.70	6	10	2	134	1	155.0	174	8	55	63
Day	4.43	5	6	1	72	1	91.1	103	5	31	46
Night	4.38	15	14	6	198	0	226.0	235	9	91	112
Grass	5.65	4	6	0	75	1	79.2	98	3	32	31
Turf	3.98	16	14	7	195	0	237.2	240	11	90	127
April	4.73	2	3	1	44	0	45.2	50	2	27	25
May	3.52	7	3	1	51	0	71.2	68	2	13	30
June	4.57	4	4	1	59	0	61.0	74	1	25	32
July	6.24	1	6	0	45	1	57.2	70	6	24	28
August	3.40	2	2	1	33	0	39.2	44	1	10	23
September/October	3.67	4	2	3	38	0	41.2	32	2	23	20
Starter	6.75	0	0	0	1	1	2.2	5	0	0	1
Reliever	4.38	20	20	7	269	0	314.2	333	14	122	157
0 Days rest	3.57	7	8	1	101	0	111.0	114	4	35	56
1 or 2 Days rest	4.89	10	8	6	99	0	116.0	131	6	50	59
3+ Days rest	4.72	3	4	0	69	0	87.2	88	4	37	42
Pre-All Star	4.56	13	13	3	169	1	199.1	221	9	71	97
Post-All Star	4.12	7	7	4	101	0	118.0	117	5	51	61

	Avg	AB	H	2B	3B	HR	RBI	BB	SO	OBP	SLG
vs. Left	.259	390	101	21	3	2	63	36	70	.338	.344
vs. Right	.289	820	237	35	6	12	116	86	88	.358	.390
Inning 1-6	.312	269	84	17	3	4	53	28	33	.377	.442
Inning 7+	.270	941	254	39	6	10	126	94	125	.344	.356
None on	.277	600	166	30	3	2	2	55	72	.341	.347
Runners on	.282	610	172	26	6	12	177	67	86	.360	.403
Scoring Posn	.311	376	117	18	5	6	161	56	53	.400	.434
Close & Late	.272	383	104	14	0	3	48	43	48	.355	.332
None on/out	.303	287	87	14	1	1	1	23	39	.359	.369
vs. 1st Batr (relief)	.298	238	71	13	3	2	36	23	31	.360	.403
First Inning Pitched	.299	824	246	42	8	9	146	80	101	.365	.402
First 15 Pitches	.313	789	247	42	9	8	132	76	86	.379	.420
Pitch 16-30	.219	311	68	12	0	5	38	35	45	.300	.305
Pitch 31-45	.200	80	16	1	0	0	7	11	18	.316	.213
Pitch 46+	.233	30	7	1	0	1	3	0	9	.233	.367
First Pitch	.306	206	63	13	2	2	37	21	0	.385	.417
Ahead in Count	.214	485	104	14	3	4	53	0	133	.225	.280
Behind in Count	.358	316	113	22	3	5	50	71	0	.476	.494
Two Strikes	.191	456	87	10	3	4	49	30	158	.249	.252

Pitcher vs. Batter (since 1984)

Pitches Best Vs.	Avg	AB	H	2B	3B	HR	RBI	BB	SO	OBP	SLG
Terry Pendleton	.083	12	1	0	0	0	0	1	0	.154	.083
Eddie Murray	.118	17	2	0	0	0	1	3	1	.250	.118
Mark Grace	.143	14	2	0	0	0	2	0	1	.143	.143
Brett Butler	.160	25	4	0	0	0	0	2	1	.222	.160
Dave Martinez	.182	11	2	0	0	0	0	0	3	.182	.182

Pitches Worst Vs.	Avg	AB	H	2B	3B	HR	RBI	BB	SO	OBP	SLG
Eric Davis	.556	9	5	0	0	1	2	2	3	.636	.889
Spike Owen	.545	11	6	2	1	1	3	0	0	.545	1.182
John Kruk	.417	12	5	2	0	0	3	1	2	.462	.583
Dave Justice	.385	13	5	0	0	1	5	1	1	.429	.615
Howard Johnson	.357	14	5	1	0	1	6	2	3	.412	.643

Rick Aguilera — Twins

Age 32 – Pitches Right (flyball pitcher)

	ERA	W	L	Sv	G	GS	IP	BB	SO	Avg	H	2B	3B	HR	RBI	OBP	SLG	GF	IR	IRS	Hld	SvOp	SB	CS	GB	FB	G/F
1993 Season	3.11	4	3	34	65	0	72.1	14	59	.223	60	11	2	9	31	.263	.379	61	21	6	0	40	4	0	86	89	0.97
Last Five Years	2.78	24	28	156	295	11	418.1	118	370	.225	349	62	9	32	171	.283	.338	236	155	40	1	189	28	5	460	468	0.98

1993 Season

	ERA	W	L	Sv	G	GS	IP	H	HR	BB	SO
Home	2.97	2	1	15	30	0	36.1	25	5	2	28
Away	3.25	2	2	19	35	0	36.0	35	4	12	31
Day	3.10	1	1	13	26	0	29.0	23	5	6	31
Night	3.12	3	2	21	39	0	43.1	37	4	8	28
Grass	3.60	2	2	16	30	0	30.0	29	4	12	26
Turf	2.76	2	1	18	35	0	42.1	31	5	2	33
April	3.60	0	0	5	9	0	10.0	8	1	3	10
May	2.92	1	0	7	12	0	12.1	13	1	5	10
June	0.00	0	0	10	13	0	13.0	2	0	1	10
July	5.79	0	2	5	10	0	9.1	13	2	3	7
August	2.70	0	1	1	8	0	10.0	6	1	1	5
September/October	4.08	3	0	6	13	0	17.2	18	4	1	17
Starter	0.00	0	0	0	0	0	0.0	0	0	0	0
Reliever	3.11	4	3	34	65	0	72.1	60	9	14	59
0 Days rest	1.69	1	1	13	15	0	16.0	9	2	2	11
1 or 2 Days rest	4.05	3	2	16	28	0	33.1	31	5	10	28
3+ Days rest	2.74	0	0	5	22	0	23.0	20	2	2	20
Pre-All Star	2.58	1	1	23	37	0	38.1	29	2	11	31
Post-All Star	3.71	3	2	11	28	0	34.0	31	7	3	28

	Avg	AB	H	2B	3B	HR	RBI	BB	SO	OBP	SLG
vs. Left	.200	145	29	5	2	3	13	8	30	.247	.324
vs. Right	.250	124	31	6	0	6	18	6	29	.282	.444
Inning 1-6	.000	0	0	0	0	0	0	0	0	.000	.000
Inning 7+	.223	269	60	11	2	9	31	14	59	.263	.379
None on	.194	170	33	6	0	5	5	7	42	.230	.318
Runners on	.273	99	27	5	2	4	26	7	17	.318	.485
Scoring Posn	.263	57	15	4	0	1	17	6	12	.328	.386
Close & Late	.250	168	42	8	1	6	24	10	32	.294	.417
None on/out	.152	66	10	2	0	1	1	2	12	.176	.227
vs. 1st Batr (relief)	.177	62	11	2	0	2	5	2	16	.200	.306
First Inning Pitched	.220	227	50	8	2	8	25	13	53	.264	.379
First 15 Pitches	.222	207	46	7	1	7	21	11	48	.264	.367
Pitch 16-30	.193	57	11	2	1	2	8	3	10	.233	.368
Pitch 31-45	.500	4	2	2	0	0	1	0	1	.500	1.000
Pitch 46+	1.000	1	1	0	0	0	1	0	0	1.000	1.000
First Pitch	.289	45	13	3	0	2	6	2	0	.313	.489
Ahead in Count	.191	141	27	4	1	2	11	0	54	.197	.277
Behind in Count	.175	40	7	2	0	1	4	7	0	.298	.300
Two Strikes	.167	138	23	5	0	4	13	5	59	.201	.290

Last Five Years

	ERA	W	L	Sv	G	GS	IP	H	HR	BB	SO
Home	2.76	14	11	74	150	5	208.1	160	19	51	198
Away	2.79	10	17	82	145	6	210.0	189	13	67	172
Day	2.23	11	6	50	111	4	165.1	134	13	47	147
Night	3.13	13	22	106	184	7	253.0	215	19	71	223
Grass	2.87	13	16	70	130	4	185.0	155	15	58	169
Turf	2.70	11	12	86	165	7	233.1	194	17	60	201
April	3.35	1	4	18	39	0	48.1	45	4	14	50
May	1.64	3	4	35	56	0	77.0	59	2	24	77
June	2.10	4	3	35	58	0	64.1	47	3	21	54
July	4.00	5	9	25	52	0	63.0	59	8	19	61
August	3.32	3	5	18	41	6	76.0	67	7	18	56

	Avg	AB	H	2B	3B	HR	RBI	BB	SO	OBP	SLG
vs. Left	.228	800	182	23	8	11	77	71	189	.292	.318
vs. Right	.222	751	167	39	1	21	94	47	181	.273	.361
Inning 1-6	.263	300	79	18	4	5	37	21	64	.315	.400
Inning 7+	.216	1251	270	44	5	27	134	97	306	.275	.324
None on	.216	861	186	33	4	16	16	49	214	.264	.319
Runners on	.236	690	163	29	5	16	155	69	156	.306	.362
Scoring Posn	.228	416	95	18	1	11	133	57	106	.320	.356
Close & Late	.221	797	176	29	3	18	104	72	194	.286	.332
None on/out	.198	353	70	14	1	6	6	23	83	.255	.295
vs. 1st Batr (relief)	.193	259	50	12	0	4	24	20	65	.258	.286
First Inning Pitched	.226	882	199	34	6	23	108	69	214	.284	.356

Last Five Years

	ERA	W	L	Sv	G	GS	IP	H	HR	BB	SO
September/October	2.61	8	3	25	49	5	89.2	72	8	22	72
Starter	3.21	3	5	0	11	11	75.2	71	5	17	57
Reliever	2.68	21	23	156	284	0	342.2	278	27	101	313
0 Days rest	3.12	5	7	47	64	0	66.1	57	6	23	52
1 or 2 Days rest	2.93	9	13	72	119	0	150.2	125	16	45	140
3+ Days rest	2.15	7	3	37	101	0	125.2	96	5	33	121
Pre-All Star	2.43	10	13	98	172	0	214.2	173	10	70	201
Post-All Star	3.14	14	15	58	123	11	203.2	176	22	48	169

	Avg	AB	H	2B	3B	HR	RBI	BB	SO	OBP	SLG
First 15 Pitches	.229	872	200	36	5	19	91	67	212	.287	.347
Pitch 16-30	.216	357	77	9	1	6	42	29	95	.279	.297
Pitch 31-45	.230	135	31	7	1	3	20	11	30	.288	.363
Pitch 46+	.219	187	41	10	2	4	18	11	33	.266	.358
First Pitch	.270	215	58	12	3	5	21	14	0	.319	.423
Ahead in Count	.170	796	135	23	3	12	65	0	335	.176	.251
Behind in Count	.324	272	88	15	0	8	45	51	0	.429	.467
Two Strikes	.155	811	126	22	4	11	63	51	370	.209	.233

Pitcher vs. Batter (career)

Pitches Best Vs.	Avg	AB	H	2B	3B	HR	RBI	BB	SO	OBP	SLG
Lou Whitaker	.000	11	0	0	0	0	0	1	2	.083	.000
Tom Brunansky	.000	11	0	0	0	0	0	0	5	.000	.000
Mike Aldrete	.003	10	1	0	0	0	0	2	4	.167	.083
Dave Henderson	.071	14	1	0	0	0	0	0	8	.071	.071
Scott Fletcher	.118	17	2	0	0	0	1	0	3	.118	.118

Pitches Worst Vs.	Avg	AB	H	2B	3B	HR	RBI	BB	SO	OBP	SLG
Jim Eisenreich	.583	12	7	1	1	0	0	0	1	.583	.833
Paul Molitor	.455	11	5	1	0	1	5	1	1	.500	.818
Lance Parrish	.385	13	5	2	0	1	5	1	4	.429	.769
Greg Vaughn	.364	11	4	1	0	1	4	1	4	.417	.727
Sid Bream	.333	15	5	3	0	1	4	1	1	.353	.733

Scott Aldred — Expos

Age 26 – Pitches Left (flyball pitcher)

	ERA	W	L	Sv	G	GS	IP	BB	SO	Avg	H	2B	3B	HR	RBI	OBP	SLG	GF	IR	IRS	Hld	SvOp	SB	CS	GB	FB	G/F
1993 Season	9.00	1	0	0	8	0	12.0	10	9	.365	19	5	0	2	14	.476	.577	2	7	4	0	1	2	1	18	16	1.13
Career (1990-1993)	6.05	7	14	0	39	27	148.2	83	85	.293	170	30	2	23	92	.383	.471	2	12	6	0	1	17	7	178	187	0.95

1993 Season

	ERA	W	L	Sv	G	GS	IP	H	HR	BB	SO
Home	14.14	1	0	0	5	0	7.0	14	2	6	6
Away	1.80	0	0	0	3	0	5.0	5	0	4	3

	Avg	AB	H	2B	3B	HR	RBI	BB	SO	OBP	SLG
vs. Left	.429	7	3	0	0	1	4	2	2	.556	.857
vs. Right	.356	45	16	5	0	1	10	8	7	.463	.533

Mike Aldrete — Athletics

Age 33 – Bats Left (groundball hitter)

	Avg	G	AB	R	H	2B	3B	HR	RBI	BB	SO	HBP	GDP	SB	CS	OBP	SLG	IBB	SH	SF	#Pit	#P/PA	GB	FB	G/F
1993 Season	.267	95	255	40	68	13	1	10	33	34	45	0	7	1	1	.353	.443	2	3	0	1133	3.88	99	61	1.62
Last Five Years	.247	364	750	98	185	34	4	13	83	129	147	2	14	4	9	.357	.355	5	5	5	3548	3.98	313	168	1.86

1993 Season

	Avg	AB	H	2B	3B	HR	RBI	BB	SO	OBP	SLG
vs. Left	.138	29	4	0	0	2	4	5	6	.265	.345
vs. Right	.283	226	64	13	1	8	29	29	39	.365	.456
Home	.233	133	31	2	0	5	13	15	28	.311	.361
Away	.303	122	37	11	1	5	20	19	17	.397	.533
First Pitch	.313	32	10	3	0	2	8	1	0	.333	.594
Ahead in Count	.460	50	23	6	0	5	16	15	0	.585	.880
Behind in Count	.191	110	21	4	0	1	5	0	36	.191	.255
Two Strikes	.175	114	20	4	0	0	4	18	45	.288	.211

	Avg	AB	H	2B	3B	HR	RBI	BB	SO	OBP	SLG
Scoring Posn	.333	54	18	5	0	3	22	10	7	.438	.593
Close & Late	.216	37	8	1	0	2	5	7	8	.341	.405
None on/out	.238	63	15	2	1	2	2	11	14	.351	.397
Batting #6	.285	151	43	7	0	9	26	15	24	.349	.510
Batting #7	.273	33	9	3	0	0	2	2	10	.314	.364
Other	.225	71	16	3	1	1	5	17	11	.375	.338
Pre-All Star	.273	88	24	5	0	3	9	9	16	.340	.432
Post-All Star	.263	167	44	8	1	7	24	25	29	.359	.449

Last Five Years

	Avg	AB	H	2B	3B	HR	RBI	BB	SO	OBP	SLG
vs. Left	.149	67	10	1	1	2	8	12	17	.272	.284
vs. Right	.256	683	175	33	3	11	75	117	130	.365	.362
Groundball	.226	239	54	10	2	3	22	41	45	.343	.322
Flyball	.312	157	49	8	1	5	22	25	32	.407	.471
Home	.238	362	86	10	3	5	34	72	70	.365	.323
Away	.255	388	99	24	1	8	49	57	77	.349	.384
Day	.245	253	62	11	1	2	22	47	54	.363	.320
Night	.247	497	123	23	3	11	61	82	93	.353	.372
Grass	.252	452	114	17	2	12	56	62	90	.340	.378
Turf	.238	298	71	17	2	1	27	67	57	.379	.319
First Pitch	.324	74	24	6	0	2	12	2	0	.338	.486
Ahead in Count	.349	175	61	11	2	6	41	70	0	.534	.537
Behind in Count	.195	323	63	14	0	3	21	0	118	.197	.266
Two Strikes	.159	353	56	11	1	0	15	55	147	.273	.195

	Avg	AB	H	2B	3B	HR	RBI	BB	SO	OBP	SLG
Scoring Posn	.244	180	44	11	1	3	65	37	41	.371	.367
Close & Late	.224	174	39	4	1	3	18	28	37	.332	.310
None on/out	.262	183	48	5	2	5	5	29	30	.363	.393
Batting #5	.219	151	33	5	1	2	13	30	25	.344	.305
Batting #6	.268	284	76	15	0	9	39	43	48	.366	.415
Other	.241	315	76	14	3	2	31	56	74	.355	.324
April	.143	35	5	0	0	0	3	6	9	.279	.143
May	.211	76	16	2	0	0	4	14	19	.330	.237
June	.265	151	40	11	1	2	15	28	25	.383	.391
July	.275	160	44	8	2	4	19	27	31	.380	.425
August	.269	167	45	7	1	6	26	20	33	.348	.431
September/October	.217	161	35	6	0	1	16	34	30	.348	.273
Pre-All Star	.247	328	81	17	2	5	32	58	66	.362	.357
Post-All Star	.246	422	104	17	2	8	51	71	81	.353	.353

Batter vs. Pitcher (career)

Hits Best Against	Avg	AB	H	2B	3B	HR	RBI	BB	SO	OBP	SLG
Scott Erickson	.600	10	6	1	0	0	0	1	1	.636	.700
Danny Cox	.500	16	8	0	0	1	2	4	3	.600	.688
John Smoltz	.500	8	4	1	1	0	1	3	0	.636	.875
Scott Sanderson	.462	13	6	2	0	1	1	1	2	.500	.846
Les Lancaster	.400	10	4	3	0	0	4	1	2	.455	.700

Hits Worst Against	Avg	AB	H	2B	3B	HR	RBI	BB	SO	OBP	SLG
Fernando Valenzuela	.000	8	0	0	0	0	1	3	2	.250	.000
Rick Aguilera	.063	16	1	0	0	0	0	2	4	.167	.063
Greg Harris	.111	9	1	0	0	0	0	2	2	.273	.111
Kevin Brown	.143	14	2	0	0	0	0	0	2	.143	.143
John Burkett	.167	12	2	0	0	0	2	1	1	.231	.167

Luis Alicea — Cardinals

Age 28 – Bats Both

	Avg	G	AB	R	H	2B	3B	HR	RBI	BB	SO	HBP	GDP	SB	CS	OBP	SLG	IBB	SH	SF	#Pit	#P/PA	GB	FB	G/F
1993 Season	.279	115	362	50	101	19	3	3	46	47	54	4	10	11	1	.362	.373	2	1	7	1623	3.86	120	103	1.17
Last Five Years	.258	256	695	81	179	31	14	5	78	82	113	8	15	13	7	.338	.364	3	3	11	2993	3.75	229	216	1.06

1993 Season

	Avg	AB	H	2B	3B	HR	RBI	BB	SO	OBP	SLG
vs. Left	.367	79	29	5	0	1	9	9	4	.432	.468
vs. Right	.254	283	72	14	3	2	37	38	50	.343	.346

	Avg	AB	H	2B	3B	HR	RBI	BB	SO	OBP	SLG
Scoring Posn	.338	77	26	6	3	2	43	18	12	.431	.571
Close & Late	.319	69	22	4	1	0	15	14	9	.425	.406

1993 Season

	Avg	AB	H	2B	3B	HR	RBI	BB	SO	OBP	SLG		Avg	AB	H	2B	3B	HR	RBI	BB	SO	OBP	SLG
Groundball	.270	115	31	7	1	0	14	13	20	.338	.348	None on/out	.226	106	24	3	0	0	0	15	19	.322	.255
Flyball	.354	65	23	6	0	1	4	10	8	.447	.492	Batting #1	.259	143	37	7	0	0	7	10	22	.308	.308
Home	.287	202	58	7	2	2	25	24	26	.361	.371	Batting #7	.299	144	43	10	2	2	26	30	18	.421	.438
Away	.269	160	43	12	1	1	21	23	28	.364	.375	Other	.280	75	21	2	1	1	13	7	14	.337	.373
Day	.237	118	28	4	2	0	11	17	20	.333	.305	April	.318	22	7	0	0	0	4	3	2	.400	.318
Night	.299	244	73	15	1	3	35	30	34	.376	.406	May	.333	51	17	1	1	0	9	8	4	.419	.392
Grass	.262	84	22	3	0	1	6	13	15	.364	.333	June	.304	46	14	4	0	1	6	5	10	.373	.457
Turf	.284	278	79	16	3	2	40	34	39	.361	.385	July	.291	79	23	5	1	0	6	12	17	.387	.380
First Pitch	.300	30	9	0	0	0	4	1	0	.343	.300	August	.265	98	26	3	0	2	17	14	10	.348	.357
Ahead in Count	.359	117	42	15	1	2	23	20	0	.449	.556	September/October	.212	66	14	6	1	0	4	5	11	.284	.333
Behind in Count	.208	154	32	3	2	1	14	0	48	.210	.273	Pre-All Star	.314	153	48	6	2	1	22	17	21	.379	.399
Two Strikes	.189	164	31	3	2	1	18	26	54	.299	.250	Post-All Star	.254	209	53	13	1	2	24	30	33	.350	.354

1993 By Position

Position	Avg	AB	H	2B	3B	HR	RBI	BB	SO	OBP	SLG	G	GS	Innings	PO	A	E	DP	Fld Pct	Rng Fctr	In Zone	Outs	Zone Rtg	MLB Zone
As Pinch Hitter	.353	17	6	1	0	0	4	4	3	.455	.412	22	0	---	---	---	---	---	---	---	---	---	---	---
As 2b	.271	329	89	18	3	3	39	42	50	.355	.371	96	87	779.2	202	280	11	61	.978	5.56	313	284	.907	.895

Last Five Years

	Avg	AB	H	2B	3B	HR	RBI	BB	SO	OBP	SLG		Avg	AB	H	2B	3B	HR	RBI	BB	SO	OBP	SLG
vs. Left	.322	180	58	10	3	1	21	16	17	.380	.428	Scoring Posn	.274	157	43	9	6	2	68	26	28	.362	.446
vs. Right	.235	515	121	21	11	4	57	66	96	.324	.342	Close & Late	.242	153	37	6	2	1	21	28	27	.358	.327
Groundball	.229	258	59	11	5	0	26	25	39	.293	.310	None on/out	.209	187	39	6	1	0	0	24	35	.305	.251
Flyball	.347	124	43	8	3	2	13	20	23	.446	.508	Batting #1	.261	153	40	7	1	0	8	10	26	.308	.320
Home	.275	375	103	14	12	4	43	45	51	.355	.408	Batting #7	.242	273	66	13	6	2	38	39	42	.341	.355
Away	.238	320	76	17	2	1	35	37	62	.318	.313	Other	.271	269	73	11	7	3	32	33	45	.352	.398
Day	.248	222	55	8	7	2	23	28	41	.336	.374	April	.182	66	12	1	0	0	6	6	11	.243	.197
Night	.262	473	124	23	7	3	55	54	72	.339	.359	May	.342	114	39	3	7	1	21	14	9	.422	.518
Grass	.212	165	35	6	0	1	11	21	35	.302	.267	June	.310	58	18	6	0	1	6	7	13	.385	.466
Turf	.272	530	144	25	14	4	67	61	78	.349	.394	July	.268	127	34	6	2	0	8	16	25	.352	.346
First Pitch	.333	69	23	3	0	0	9	2	0	.359	.377	August	.243	189	46	6	3	2	21	28	28	.339	.339
Ahead in Count	.312	215	67	20	4	2	28	40	0	.416	.470	September/October	.213	141	30	9	2	1	16	11	27	.276	.326
Behind in Count	.187	289	54	5	6	2	27	0	96	.190	.266	Pre-All Star	.284	278	79	11	8	2	36	28	38	.351	.403
Two Strikes	.163	300	49	4	6	2	27	40	113	.266	.237	Post-All Star	.240	417	100	20	6	3	42	54	75	.329	.338

Batter vs. Pitcher (career)

Hits Best Against	Avg	AB	H	2B	3B	HR	RBI	BB	SO	OBP	SLG	Hits Worst Against	Avg	AB	H	2B	3B	HR	RBI	BB	SO	OBP	SLG
Jose Rijo	.462	13	6	0	1	0	1	3	2	.563	.615	Ken Hill	.071	14	1	0	0	0	2	3	1	.235	.071
Curt Schilling	.417	12	5	2	1	0	5	0	2	.417	.750	Anthony Young	.083	12	1	1	0	0	0	0	1	.083	.167
Steve Avery	.400	10	4	1	1	0	5	1	0	.455	.700	Sid Fernandez	.111	9	1	1	0	0	1	1	2	.182	.222
Bobby Ojeda	.357	14	5	0	1	0	0	2	1	.438	.500	Mark Portugal	.133	15	2	0	0	0	0	1	3	.188	.133
Randy Tomlin	.333	9	3	2	0	0	0	2	0	.455	.556	Doug Drabek	.133	15	2	0	0	0	1	4	3	.316	.133

Andy Allanson — Giants

Age 32 – Bats Right (flyball hitter)

	Avg	G	AB	R	H	2B	3B	HR	RBI	BB	SO	HBP	GDP	SB	CS	OBP	SLG	IBB	SH	SF	#Pit	#P/PA	GB	FB	G/F
1993 Season	.167	13	24	3	4	1	0	0	2	1	2	0	1	0	0	.200	.208	0	1	0	104	4.00	11	5	2.20
Last Five Years	.233	193	523	49	122	21	1	4	35	32	82	4	12	7	6	.281	.300	2	11	3	2070	3.61	170	172	0.99

1993 Season

	Avg	AB	H	2B	3B	HR	RBI	BB	SO	OBP	SLG		Avg	AB	H	2B	3B	HR	RBI	BB	SO	OBP	SLG
vs. Left	.167	12	2	0	0	0	0	1	0	.231	.167	Scoring Posn	.143	7	1	1	0	0	2	1	1	.250	.286
vs. Right	.167	12	2	1	0	0	2	0	2	.167	.250	Close & Late	.000	3	0	0	0	0	0	0	0	.000	.000

Last Five Years

	Avg	AB	H	2B	3B	HR	RBI	BB	SO	OBP	SLG		Avg	AB	H	2B	3B	HR	RBI	BB	SO	OBP	SLG
vs. Left	.241	228	55	11	1	0	13	12	37	.281	.298	Scoring Posn	.190	121	23	4	0	1	27	11	25	.263	.248
vs. Right	.227	295	67	10	0	4	22	20	45	.281	.302	Close & Late	.280	75	21	3	0	2	5	3	12	.308	.400
Groundball	.269	134	36	10	0	1	16	7	19	.310	.366	None on/out	.222	126	28	3	0	2	2	7	16	.263	.294
Flyball	.205	112	23	3	0	1	6	8	22	.264	.259	Batting #8	.216	342	74	14	1	2	16	20	53	.267	.281
Home	.212	236	50	7	0	1	15	19	32	.275	.254	Batting #9	.269	160	43	7	0	2	18	12	24	.316	.350
Away	.251	287	72	14	1	3	20	13	50	.286	.338	Other	.238	21	5	0	0	0	1	0	5	.238	.238
Day	.215	177	38	11	0	2	12	12	29	.271	.311	April	.223	94	21	7	0	0	5	3	13	.247	.298
Night	.243	346	84	10	1	2	23	20	53	.286	.295	May	.233	120	28	5	0	1	9	7	16	.281	.300
Grass	.229	441	101	19	0	4	33	27	72	.278	.299	June	.191	68	13	1	0	1	4	3	10	.247	.250
Turf	.256	82	21	2	1	0	2	5	10	.295	.305	July	.207	87	18	4	1	1	5	7	17	.271	.310
First Pitch	.276	76	21	3	0	1	7	1	0	.300	.355	August	.297	91	27	3	0	0	11	8	17	.347	.330
Ahead in Count	.272	103	28	6	0	1	11	17	0	.372	.359	September/October	.238	63	15	1	0	1	1	4	9	.284	.302
Behind in Count	.211	246	52	6	1	1	12	0	69	.217	.256	Pre-All Star	.233	318	74	16	1	2	20	15	43	.274	.308
Two Strikes	.167	239	40	7	0	0	4	14	82	.219	.197	Post-All Star	.234	205	48	5	0	2	15	17	39	.292	.288

Batter vs. Pitcher (career)

Hits Best Against	Avg	AB	H	2B	3B	HR	RBI	BB	SO	OBP	SLG	Hits Worst Against	Avg	AB	H	2B	3B	HR	RBI	BB	SO	OBP	SLG
Chuck Crim	.500	12	6	2	0	0	4	0	2	.500	.667	Dave Stewart	.067	15	1	0	0	0	0	1	1	.125	.067
Bob Welch	.455	11	5	0	0	1	2	0	2	.455	.727	Bobby Witt	.071	14	1	0	0	0	1	0	4	.071	.071
Charlie Leibrandt	.429	14	6	1	0	0	2	1	1	.438	.500	Dan Plesac	.111	9	1	0	0	0	1	2	3	.273	.111
Jeff Ballard	.400	10	4	1	0	0	0	2	1	.500	.500	Jimmy Key	.167	24	4	1	0	0	0	0	3	.167	.208
Roger Clemens	.333	15	5	2	0	1	2	2	5	.412	.667	Bret Saberhagen	.174	23	4	0	0	0	1	0	2	.174	.174

Roberto Alomar — Blue Jays

Age 26 – Bats Both (groundball hitter)

	Avg	G	AB	R	H	2B	3B	HR	RBI	BB	SO	HBP	GDP	SB	CS	OBP	SLG	IBB	SH	SF	#Pit	#P/PA	GB	FB	G/F
1993 Season	.326	153	589	109	192	35	6	17	93	80	67	5	13	55	15	.408	.492	5	4	5	2602	3.81	224	181	1.24
Last Five Years	.302	771	3006	464	909	157	31	47	354	325	353	17	52	223	59	.371	.422	18	48	25	12914	3.77	1238	799	1.55

1993 Season

	Avg	AB	H	2B	3B	HR	RBI	BB	SO	OBP	SLG		Avg	AB	H	2B	3B	HR	RBI	BB	SO	OBP	SLG
vs. Left	.241	166	40	8	1	4	24	12	29	.297	.373	Scoring Posn	.320	147	47	6	3	5	74	25	16	.410	.503
vs. Right	.359	423	152	27	5	13	69	68	38	.449	.539	Close & Late	.274	84	23	3	1	3	16	9	14	.344	.440
Groundball	.360	89	32	3	2	3	20	7	7	.418	.539	None on/out	.319	135	43	4	1	4	4	13	11	.378	.452
Flyball	.393	84	33	3	0	5	17	14	10	.475	.607	Batting #2	.314	401	126	24	4	13	59	52	50	.393	.491
Home	.325	289	94	18	4	8	38	40	30	.409	.498	Batting #3	.420	100	42	8	2	2	21	15	6	.496	.600
Away	.327	300	98	17	2	9	55	40	37	.407	.487	Other	.273	88	24	3	0	2	13	13	11	.375	.375
Day	.283	184	52	12	1	5	32	26	24	.375	.440	April	.302	86	26	4	1	1	8	13	11	.400	.407
Night	.346	405	140	23	5	12	61	54	43	.423	.516	May	.259	108	28	3	1	3	18	15	13	.344	.389
Grass	.339	239	81	13	2	8	41	28	25	.411	.510	June	.369	103	38	5	0	5	15	10	10	.431	.563
Turf	.317	350	111	22	4	9	52	52	42	.406	.480	July	.309	97	30	8	2	2	12	10	14	.374	.495
First Pitch	.381	84	32	3	1	4	19	3	0	.404	.583	August	.360	111	40	8	0	3	20	12	13	.423	.514
Ahead in Count	.338	142	48	13	1	3	12	44	0	.497	.507	September/October	.357	84	30	7	2	3	20	20	6	.481	.595
Behind in Count	.285	242	69	12	1	3	31	0	52	.286	.380	Pre-All Star	.308	325	100	15	2	10	43	43	39	.390	.458
Two Strikes	.264	258	68	11	3	6	47	33	67	.345	.399	Post-All Star	.348	264	92	20	4	7	50	37	28	.430	.534

1993 By Position

Position	Avg	AB	H	2B	3B	HR	RBI	BB	SO	OBP	SLG	G	GS	Innings	PO	A	E	DP	Fld Pct	Rng Fctr	In Zone	Outs	Zone Rtg	MLB Zone
As 2b	.325	587	191	35	6	17	93	80	67	.408	.492	151	151	1305.1	253	439	14	92	.980	4.77	511	441	.863	.895

Last Five Years

	Avg	AB	H	2B	3B	HR	RBI	BB	SO	OBP	SLG		Avg	AB	H	2B	3B	HR	RBI	BB	SO	OBP	SLG
vs. Left	.261	912	238	48	5	21	111	86	147	.329	.394	Scoring Posn	.309	718	222	37	10	12	294	88	89	.377	.439
vs. Right	.320	2094	671	109	26	26	243	239	206	.389	.435	Close & Late	.302	467	141	21	4	7	66	62	69	.384	.409
Groundball	.296	878	260	53	5	7	93	80	103	.357	.392	None on/out	.318	661	210	38	7	15	15	71	66	.386	.464
Flyball	.310	670	208	29	7	15	76	79	85	.383	.442	Batting #1	.325	292	95	12	2	6	28	29	39	.387	.442
Home	.317	1454	461	73	22	26	197	173	153	.389	.451	Batting #2	.297	2288	680	116	24	36	266	252	269	.368	.416
Away	.289	1552	448	84	9	21	157	152	200	.353	.395	Other	.315	426	134	29	5	5	60	44	45	.378	.441
Day	.291	906	264	62	7	13	122	102	104	.363	.418	April	.293	434	127	19	2	5	45	42	48	.354	.380
Night	.307	2100	645	95	24	34	232	223	249	.374	.424	May	.300	534	160	23	6	11	68	57	60	.368	.427
Grass	.293	1607	471	73	11	20	173	149	190	.353	.390	June	.301	495	149	30	6	8	58	55	52	.374	.434
Turf	.313	1399	438	84	20	27	181	176	163	.391	.460	July	.298	493	147	30	6	3	48	53	64	.365	.402
First Pitch	.378	328	124	18	5	10	56	10	0	.394	.555	August	.302	569	172	30	6	9	61	56	78	.365	.424
Ahead in Count	.354	655	232	42	7	13	82	185	0	.495	.499	September/October	.320	481	154	25	5	11	74	62	51	.399	.462
Behind in Count	.250	1384	346	52	8	14	140	0	302	.254	.329	Pre-All Star	.297	1616	480	86	16	26	183	171	183	.366	.418
Two Strikes	.235	1333	313	54	12	15	145	129	353	.304	.327	Post-All Star	.309	1390	429	71	15	21	171	154	170	.377	.427

Batter vs. Pitcher (career)

Hits Best Against	Avg	AB	H	2B	3B	HR	RBI	BB	SO	OBP	SLG	Hits Worst Against	Avg	AB	H	2B	3B	HR	RBI	BB	SO	OBP	SLG
Jaime Navarro	.550	20	11	2	1	0	0	0	0	.550	.750	Charlie Hough	.063	16	1	0	0	0	2	2	1	.158	.063
Jack McDowell	.526	19	10	0	0	1	3	4	5	.609	.684	Dan Plesac	.077	13	1	0	0	0	1	1	2	.143	.077
Scott Sanderson	.524	21	11	2	1	1	5	3	3	.560	.857	Bill Krueger	.083	12	1	0	0	0	0	1	0	.154	.083
Julio Valera	.417	12	5	0	0	2	4	1	1	.462	.917	Trevor Wilson	.091	11	1	0	0	0	0	0	1	.091	.091
Neal Heaton	.381	21	8	3	0	2	4	2	4	.435	.810	Mike Mussina	.100	10	1	0	0	0	0	1	0	.182	.100

Sandy Alomar Jr. — Indians

Age 28 – Bats Right

	Avg	G	AB	R	H	2B	3B	HR	RBI	BB	SO	HBP	GDP	SB	CS	OBP	SLG	IBB	SH	SF	#Pit	#P/PA	GB	FB	G/F
1993 Season	.270	64	215	24	58	7	1	6	32	11	28	6	3	3	1	.318	.395	0	1	4	846	3.57	75	75	1.00
Last Five Years	.263	343	1162	117	306	59	3	18	137	60	133	17	25	10	9	.306	.366	7	11	11	4261	3.38	436	390	1.12

1993 Season

	Avg	AB	H	2B	3B	HR	RBI	BB	SO	OBP	SLG		Avg	AB	H	2B	3B	HR	RBI	BB	SO	OBP	SLG
vs. Left	.283	60	17	1	1	1	9	3	9	.318	.383	Scoring Posn	.262	61	16	4	1	0	23	6	16	.338	.361
vs. Right	.265	155	41	6	0	5	23	8	19	.318	.400	Close & Late	.391	46	18	1	0	2	8	1	2	.440	.543
Home	.293	92	27	5	0	3	16	5	11	.337	.446	None on/out	.233	60	14	0	0	3	3	3	3	.281	.383
Away	.252	123	31	2	1	3	16	6	17	.303	.358	Batting #8	.147	34	5	0	0	1	2	6	5	.310	.235
First Pitch	.258	31	8	1	0	0	5	0	0	.265	.290	Batting #9	.310	171	53	7	1	5	28	5	21	.339	.450
Ahead in Count	.306	49	15	0	1	1	6	5	0	.370	.408	Other	.000	10	0	0	0	0	2	0	2	.000	.000
Behind in Count	.227	88	20	4	0	2	10	0	25	.250	.341	Pre-All Star	.125	56	7	0	0	1	4	7	11	.242	.179
Two Strikes	.236	89	21	2	0	5	11	6	28	.296	.427	Post-All Star	.321	159	51	7	1	5	28	4	17	.347	.472

Last Five Years

	Avg	AB	H	2B	3B	HR	RBI	BB	SO	OBP	SLG		Avg	AB	H	2B	3B	HR	RBI	BB	SO	OBP	SLG
vs. Left	.287	282	81	11	1	3	31	21	32	.337	.365	Scoring Posn	.250	312	78	20	1	2	113	26	43	.312	.340
vs. Right	.256	880	225	48	2	15	106	39	101	.296	.366	Close & Late	.287	237	68	10	1	5	34	11	25	.328	.401
Groundball	.239	348	83	13	1	1	30	19	42	.284	.290	None on/out	.289	287	83	10	1	6	6	12	29	.329	.394
Flyball	.235	260	61	11	1	5	24	13	38	.281	.342	Batting #8	.270	366	99	20	0	7	49	27	39	.323	.383
Home	.278	564	157	29	0	10	67	36	61	.324	.383	Batting #9	.288	354	102	17	1	6	47	11	38	.322	.393
Away	.249	598	149	30	3	8	70	24	72	.290	.349	Other	.238	442	105	22	2	5	41	22	56	.280	.330
Day	.266	334	89	15	0	5	45	19	44	.316	.356	April	.214	234	50	11	0	3	24	16	37	.276	.299
Night	.262	828	217	44	3	13	92	41	89	.302	.370	May	.241	141	34	6	1	2	17	7	24	.285	.340
Grass	.271	970	263	50	3	16	113	53	107	.316	.378	June	.254	193	49	4	1	1	14	8	23	.286	.301
Turf	.224	192	43	9	0	2	24	7	26	.257	.302	July	.282	206	58	14	0	2	22	11	10	.326	.379
First Pitch	.235	179	42	10	0	5	28	5	0	.267	.374	August	.313	211	66	11	1	6	35	8	19	.342	.460

Last Five Years

	Avg	AB	H	2B	3B	HR	RBI	BB	SO	OBP	SLG		Avg	AB	H	2B	3B	HR	RBI	BB	SO	OBP	SLG
Ahead in Count	.347	242	84	11	3	3	32	38	0	.436	.455	September/October	.277	177	49	13	0	4	25	10	20	.321	.418
Behind in Count	.237	531	126	31	0	7	52	0	119	.246	.335	Pre-All Star	.250	637	159	28	2	6	62	36	88	.298	.328
Two Strikes	.201	467	94	16	0	8	43	15	133	.235	.287	Post-All Star	.280	525	147	31	1	12	75	24	45	.316	.411

Batter vs. Pitcher (career)

Hits Best Against	Avg	AB	H	2B	3B	HR	RBI	BB	SO	OBP	SLG	Hits Worst Against	Avg	AB	H	2B	3B	HR	RBI	BB	SO	OBP	SLG
Rick Sutcliffe	.455	11	5	1	0	0	0	0	1	.455	.545	Bob Milacki	.000	13	0	0	0	0	0	0	1	.000	.000
Melido Perez	.438	16	7	3	0	0	6	0	0	.438	.625	Randy Johnson	.000	9	0	0	0	0	0	4	1	.308	.000
Mike Boddicker	.429	14	6	1	0	0	3	0	0	.429	.500	Mark Eichhorn	.091	11	1	0	0	0	2	0	3	.091	.091
Greg Harris	.400	15	6	2	0	1	2	1	2	.438	.733	Juan Guzman	.133	15	2	0	0	0	1	0	3	.133	.133
Scott Sanderson	.313	16	5	2	0	1	2	0	3	.313	.625	Jeff Montgomery	.182	11	2	0	0	0	1	0	4	.182	.182

Moises Alou — Expos

Age 27 – Bats Right

	Avg	G	AB	R	H	2B	3B	HR	RBI	BB	SO	HBP	GDP	SB	CS	OBP	SLG	IBB	SH	SF	#Pit	#P/PA	GB	FB	G/F
1993 Season	.286	136	482	70	138	29	6	18	85	38	53	5	9	17	6	.340	.483	9	3	7	1704	3.19	181	159	1.14
Career (1990-1993)	.282	267	843	127	238	57	9	27	141	63	102	6	15	33	8	.332	.467	9	9	12	3075	3.30	298	282	1.06

1993 Season

	Avg	AB	H	2B	3B	HR	RBI	BB	SO	OBP	SLG		Avg	AB	H	2B	3B	HR	RBI	BB	SO	OBP	SLG
vs. Left	.268	164	44	10	2	5	24	11	10	.320	.445	Scoring Posn	.293	147	43	13	1	4	67	24	19	.383	.476
vs. Right	.296	318	94	19	4	13	61	27	43	.350	.503	Close & Late	.250	68	17	2	1	1	10	16	13	.384	.353
Groundball	.236	144	34	4	1	2	16	9	18	.294	.319	None on/out	.300	100	30	8	3	5	5	4	16	.340	.590
Flyball	.304	92	28	10	0	5	22	6	8	.343	.576	Batting #5	.258	217	56	14	3	2	28	15	28	.308	.378
Home	.252	222	56	8	1	10	47	20	27	.310	.432	Batting #6	.301	123	37	9	1	9	31	17	13	.383	.610
Away	.315	260	82	21	5	8	38	18	26	.366	.527	Other	.317	142	45	6	2	7	26	6	12	.351	.535
Day	.295	156	46	12	1	3	21	11	19	.341	.442	April	.298	84	25	4	2	2	10	6	9	.337	.464
Night	.282	326	92	17	5	15	64	27	34	.340	.503	May	.322	90	29	6	0	1	13	6	7	.374	.422
Grass	.292	161	47	12	2	4	18	12	20	.343	.466	June	.180	89	16	4	0	4	15	9	8	.260	.360
Turf	.283	321	91	17	4	14	67	26	33	.339	.492	July	.323	99	32	9	1	7	24	8	12	.374	.646
First Pitch	.376	101	38	8	3	4	15	7	0	.423	.634	August	.279	104	29	4	2	3	20	8	17	.322	.442
Ahead in Count	.307	114	35	8	1	7	31	19	0	.400	.579	September/October	.438	16	7	2	1	1	3	1	0	.526	.875
Behind in Count	.251	183	46	6	2	6	24	0	41	.262	.404	Pre-All Star	.272	298	81	16	2	13	50	24	28	.328	.470
Two Strikes	.220	164	36	6	2	3	18	12	53	.271	.335	Post-All Star	.310	184	57	13	4	5	35	14	25	.360	.505

1993 By Position

Position	Avg	AB	H	2B	3B	HR	RBI	BB	SO	OBP	SLG	G	GS	Innings	PO	A	E	DP	Fld Pct	Rng Fctr	In Zone	Outs	Zone Rtg	MLB Zone
As lf	.296	351	104	22	5	16	68	25	39	.349	.524	102	91	796.1	178	6	2	1	.989	2.08	205	172	.839	.818
As cf	.333	27	9	1	0	1	6	3	1	.364	.481	12	7	67.2	23	2	0	0	1.000	3.33	28	23	.821	.820
As rf	.238	101	24	6	1	1	11	10	13	.304	.347	34	25	236.2	53	3	2	1	.966	2.13	67	51	.761	.826

Career (1990-1993)

	Avg	AB	H	2B	3B	HR	RBI	BB	SO	OBP	SLG		Avg	AB	H	2B	3B	HR	RBI	BB	SO	OBP	SLG
vs. Left	.274	317	87	21	3	7	38	18	25	.317	.426	Scoring Posn	.291	261	76	21	2	9	114	35	33	.367	.490
vs. Right	.287	526	151	36	6	20	103	45	77	.341	.492	Close & Late	.255	137	35	6	2	4	24	19	24	.340	.416
Groundball	.265	272	72	16	2	4	39	23	33	.327	.382	None on/out	.322	171	55	16	4	7	7	9	26	.363	.585
Flyball	.275	178	49	16	1	9	40	9	24	.307	.528	Batting #3	.286	311	89	21	3	9	47	24	37	.336	.460
Home	.282	383	108	22	4	16	82	31	49	.331	.486	Batting #5	.258	244	63	16	3	4	38	15	32	.303	.398
Away	.283	460	130	35	5	11	59	32	53	.333	.452	Other	.299	288	86	20	3	14	56	24	33	.352	.535
Day	.305	275	84	25	1	6	37	19	34	.349	.469	April	.323	93	30	6	2	2	11	6	11	.356	.495
Night	.271	568	154	32	8	21	104	44	68	.324	.467	May	.305	141	43	10	1	2	17	12	14	.365	.433
Grass	.277	253	70	21	2	5	28	22	32	.333	.435	June	.244	168	41	10	1	7	37	15	16	.303	.440
Turf	.285	590	168	36	7	22	113	41	70	.332	.481	July	.297	148	44	14	1	7	29	10	19	.342	.547
First Pitch	.358	165	59	15	4	7	29	7	0	.384	.624	August	.255	192	49	10	2	5	28	16	31	.308	.406
Ahead in Count	.305	190	58	12	1	8	39	31	0	.397	.505	September/October	.307	101	31	7	2	4	19	4	11	.346	.535
Behind in Count	.246	349	86	15	3	8	43	0	81	.254	.375	Pre-All Star	.288	469	135	33	4	17	81	37	50	.339	.484
Two Strikes	.229	315	72	14	3	6	36	25	102	.286	.349	Post-All Star	.275	374	103	24	5	10	60	26	52	.324	.447

Batter vs. Pitcher (career)

Hits Best Against	Avg	AB	H	2B	3B	HR	RBI	BB	SO	OBP	SLG	Hits Worst Against	Avg	AB	H	2B	3B	HR	RBI	BB	SO	OBP	SLG
Andy Benes	.455	11	5	4	0	1	4	0	1	.455	1.091	Terry Mulholland	.158	19	3	0	0	1	2	1	1	.200	.316
Curt Schilling	.333	15	5	1	1	0	2	2	0	.389	.533	Steve Avery	.176	17	3	1	0	0	1	0	0	.167	.235
Greg Swindell	.308	13	4	1	0	0	1	0	2	.308	.385	Jose Rijo	.200	10	2	0	0	0	0	1	3	.273	.200
												Joe Magrane	.200	10	2	0	0	0	1	1	0	.273	.200
												Mike Morgan	.214	14	3	0	0	0	4	0	0	.188	.214

Wilson Alvarez — White Sox

Age 24 – Pitches Left

	ERA	W	L	Sv	G	GS	IP	BB	SO	Avg	H	2B	3B	HR	RBI	OBP	SLG	CG	ShO	Sup	QS	#P/S	SB	CS	GB	FB	G/F
1993 Season	2.95	15	8	0	31	31	207.2	122	155	.230	168	28	1	14	66	.344	.329	1	1	4.25	20	114	21	17	242	219	1.11
Career (1989-1993)	3.73	23	14	1	76	50	364.1	218	253	.244	321	48	2	37	145	.354	.368	3	2	5.36	26	105	30	29	442	409	1.08

1993 Season

	ERA	W	L	Sv	G	GS	IP	H	HR	BB	SO		Avg	AB	H	2B	3B	HR	RBI	BB	SO	OBP	SLG
Home	3.38	7	5	0	16	16	106.2	89	9	69	86	vs. Left	.258	89	23	2	0	1	9	25	20	.432	.315
Away	2.50	8	3	0	15	15	101.0	79	5	53	69	vs. Right	.227	640	145	26	1	13	57	97	135	.330	.331
Day	4.09	3	3	0	9	9	55.0	48	8	35	34	Inning 1-6	.219	602	132	24	0	11	51	97	140	.331	.314
Night	2.53	12	5	0	22	22	152.2	120	6	87	121	Inning 7+	.283	127	36	4	1	3	15	25	15	.404	.402
Grass	2.96	13	8	0	28	28	191.2	155	14	110	150	None on	.246	418	103	19	1	8	8	72	97	.361	.354

1993 Season

	ERA	W	L	Sv	G	GS	IP	H	HR	BB	SO
Turf	2.81	2	0	0	3	3	16.0	13	0	12	5
April	2.37	1	0	0	3	3	19.0	18	1	9	14
May	3.64	4	1	0	6	6	42.0	35	5	30	31
June	3.12	2	3	0	6	6	43.1	37	2	20	36
July	3.75	1	2	0	6	6	36.0	33	1	30	16
August	4.18	2	2	0	4	4	23.2	22	3	13	26
September/October	1.03	5	0	0	6	6	43.2	23	2	20	32
Starter	2.95	15	8	0	31	31	207.2	168	14	122	155
Reliever	0.00	0	0	0	0	0	0.0	0	0	0	0
0-3 Days Rest	0.00	0	0	0	0	0	0.0	0	0	0	0
4 Days Rest	3.39	7	6	0	17	17	111.2	96	9	68	72
5+ Days Rest	2.44	8	2	0	14	14	96.0	72	5	54	83
Pre-All Star	3.32	8	5	0	17	17	119.1	105	9	60	84
Post-All Star	2.45	7	3	0	14	14	88.1	63	5	59	71

	Avg	AB	H	2B	3B	HR	RBI	BB	SO	OBP	SLG
Runners on	.209	311	65	9	0	6	58	50	58	.321	.296
Scoring Posn	.201	159	32	7	0	2	48	40	36	.357	.283
Close & Late	.215	65	14	1	0	1	6	15	6	.373	.277
None on/out	.253	198	50	4	1	6	6	23	45	.333	.374
vs. 1st Batr (relief)	.000	0	0	0	0	0	0	0	0	.000	.000
First Inning Pitched	.248	113	28	4	0	3	12	17	28	.356	.363
First 75 Pitches	.224	446	100	15	0	8	37	75	106	.341	.312
Pitch 76-90	.189	90	17	3	0	1	7	13	21	.286	.256
Pitch 91-105	.264	87	23	4	0	2	7	18	18	.396	.379
Pitch 106+	.264	106	28	6	1	3	15	16	10	.360	.425
First Pitch	.291	79	23	4	0	2	6	7	0	.360	.418
Ahead in Count	.173	365	63	9	0	2	18	0	124	.177	.214
Behind in Count	.310	126	30	7	1	5	10	60	0	.524	.500
Two Strikes	.182	396	72	10	0	4	28	55	155	.283	.237

Rich Amaral — Mariners

Age 32 – Bats Right

	Avg	G	AB	R	H	2B	3B	HR	RBI	BB	SO	HBP	GDP	SB	CS	OBP	SLG	IBB	SH	SF	#Pit	#P/PA	GB	FB	G/F
1993 Season	.290	110	373	53	108	24	1	1	44	33	54	3	5	19	11	.348	.367	0	7	5	1448	3.44	139	99	1.40
Career (1991-1993)	.272	159	489	64	133	27	1	2	51	39	75	4	10	23	13	.328	.344	0	11	5	1902	3.47	181	133	1.36

1993 Season

	Avg	AB	H	2B	3B	HR	RBI	BB	SO	OBP	SLG
vs. Left	.372	148	55	14	1	0	21	10	12	.411	.480
vs. Right	.236	225	53	10	0	1	23	23	42	.307	.293
Groundball	.311	61	19	4	0	0	7	9	8	.394	.377
Flyball	.157	70	11	3	0	0	6	8	15	.241	.200
Home	.264	178	47	9	1	0	19	24	26	.353	.326
Away	.313	195	61	15	0	1	25	9	28	.343	.405
Day	.250	108	27	6	0	0	11	9	20	.311	.306
Night	.306	265	81	18	1	1	33	24	34	.363	.392
Grass	.306	157	48	10	0	1	18	6	25	.331	.389
Turf	.278	216	60	14	1	0	26	27	29	.359	.352
First Pitch	.283	60	17	7	0	0	9	0	0	.297	.400
Ahead in Count	.379	95	36	7	1	1	16	13	0	.445	.505
Behind in Count	.220	150	33	8	0	0	14	0	49	.219	.273
Two Strikes	.210	138	29	6	0	0	12	20	54	.308	.254

	Avg	AB	H	2B	3B	HR	RBI	BB	SO	OBP	SLG
Scoring Posn	.337	83	28	6	1	0	39	8	11	.375	.434
Close & Late	.281	64	18	2	0	0	12	7	10	.347	.313
None on/out	.276	127	35	8	0	0	0	10	16	.328	.339
Batting #1	.354	158	56	13	1	0	22	15	20	.408	.449
Batting #9	.221	131	29	6	0	1	12	8	25	.262	.290
Other	.274	84	23	5	0	0	10	10	9	.364	.333
April	.324	71	23	7	0	0	6	5	11	.377	.423
May	.330	97	32	6	0	1	13	10	17	.393	.423
June	.219	64	14	4	0	0	5	6	10	.296	.281
July	.260	77	20	2	0	0	8	9	8	.337	.286
August	.250	16	4	1	0	0	2	0	1	.235	.313
September/October	.313	48	15	4	1	0	10	3	7	.340	.438
Pre-All Star	.292	267	78	17	0	1	27	27	41	.360	.367
Post-All Star	.283	106	30	7	1	0	17	6	13	.316	.368

1993 By Position

Position	Avg	AB	H	2B	3B	HR	RBI	BB	SO	OBP	SLG	G	GS	Innings	PO	A	E	DP	Fld Pct	Rng Fctr	In Zone	Outs	Zone Rtg	MLB Zone
As 2b	.303	261	79	15	0	1	24	28	38	.375	.372	77	72	617.2	151	206	9	47	.975	5.20	229	192	.838	.895
As 3b	.227	44	10	4	0	0	5	3	7	.277	.318	19	10	108.0	5	30	1	7	.972	2.92	33	34	1.030	.834
As ss	.216	37	8	1	0	0	6	1	6	.225	.243	14	9	85.0	20	34	0	14	1.000	5.72	40	37	.925	.880

Ruben Amaro — Phillies

Age 29 – Bats Both

	Avg	G	AB	R	H	2B	3B	HR	RBI	BB	SO	HBP	GDP	SB	CS	OBP	SLG	IBB	SH	SF	#Pit	#P/PA	GB	FB	G/F
1993 Season	.333	25	48	7	16	2	2	1	6	6	5	0	1	0	0	.400	.521	0	3	1	202	3.48	18	15	1.20
Career (1991-1993)	.231	161	445	50	103	18	8	8	42	46	62	9	13	11	5	.314	.362	2	7	3	1861	3.64	172	126	1.37

1993 Season

	Avg	AB	H	2B	3B	HR	RBI	BB	SO	OBP	SLG
vs. Left	.500	28	14	2	2	1	5	4	1	.563	.821
vs. Right	.100	20	2	0	0	0	1	2	4	.174	.100
Scoring Posn	.333	12	4	0	1	0	4	3	0	.438	.500
Close & Late	.500	8	4	0	0	1	2	0	1	.500	.875

Career (1991-1993)

	Avg	AB	H	2B	3B	HR	RBI	BB	SO	OBP	SLG
vs. Left	.285	186	53	10	5	3	22	23	15	.373	.441
vs. Right	.193	259	50	8	3	5	20	23	47	.271	.305
Groundball	.239	205	49	13	5	5	20	20	32	.320	.424
Flyball	.264	87	23	2	1	2	10	8	9	.347	.379
Home	.200	190	38	7	4	5	17	18	30	.282	.358
Away	.255	255	65	11	4	3	25	28	32	.338	.365
Day	.203	143	29	2	3	3	14	15	22	.286	.322
Night	.245	302	74	16	5	5	28	31	40	.327	.381
Grass	.250	132	33	5	1	1	10	19	12	.355	.326
Turf	.224	313	70	13	7	7	32	27	50	.296	.377
First Pitch	.282	78	22	2	2	1	7	2	0	.333	.397
Ahead in Count	.294	85	25	9	2	3	9	23	0	.444	.553
Behind in Count	.188	181	34	5	0	1	15	0	48	.198	.232
Two Strikes	.188	192	36	4	2	3	19	21	62	.273	.276

	Avg	AB	H	2B	3B	HR	RBI	BB	SO	OBP	SLG
Scoring Posn	.192	104	20	4	3	0	30	17	15	.304	.288
Close & Late	.228	79	18	2	0	2	5	9	16	.315	.329
None on/out	.267	120	32	7	3	2	2	10	16	.348	.425
Batting #1	.177	147	26	6	2	5	10	15	22	.274	.347
Batting #7	.248	105	26	4	4	2	15	8	15	.301	.419
Other	.264	193	51	8	2	1	17	23	25	.351	.342
April	.138	65	9	3	0	3	7	10	9	.273	.323
May	.239	46	11	2	0	0	5	6	9	.327	.283
June	.284	95	27	5	3	2	11	14	15	.387	.463
July	.209	67	14	0	1	1	4	3	7	.250	.284
August	.292	24	7	0	1	0	0	2	5	.346	.375
September/October	.236	148	35	8	3	2	15	11	17	.303	.372
Pre-All Star	.228	268	61	10	4	6	27	33	38	.322	.362
Post-All Star	.237	177	42	8	4	2	15	13	24	.301	.362

Batter vs. Pitcher (career)

Hits Best Against	Avg	AB	H	2B	3B	HR	RBI	BB	SO	OBP	SLG
Dwight Gooden	.417	12	5	2	0	0	0	1	1	.462	.583
Sid Fernandez	.400	10	4	1	0	0	0	3	0	.538	.500
Donovan Osborne	.333	12	4	0	2	0	2	0	2	.333	.667

Hits Worst Against	Avg	AB	H	2B	3B	HR	RBI	BB	SO	OBP	SLG
Doug Drabek	.077	13	1	1	0	0	0	1	4	.143	.154
Rheal Cormier	.111	9	1	1	0	0	0	2	1	.273	.222
Mike Morgan	.125	16	2	0	0	0	0	0	4	.125	.125
Zane Smith	.200	15	3	0	1	1	2	4	2	.368	.533

Larry Andersen — Phillies

Age 41 – Pitches Right (groundball pitcher)

	ERA	W	L	Sv	G	GS	IP	BB	SO	Avg	H	2B	3B	HR	RBI	OBP	SLG	GF	IR	IRS	Hld	SvOp	SB	CS	GB	FB	G/F
1993 Season	2.92	3	2	0	64	0	61.2	21	67	.233	54	5	3	4	26	.299	.332	13	48	14	25	4	4	1	73	63	1.16
Last Five Years	2.17	16	13	25	261	0	327.0	93	320	.218	261	25	6	10	126	.274	.274	74	176	61	63	39	40	9	431	269	1.60

1993 Season

	ERA	W	L	Sv	G	GS	IP	H	HR	BB	SO
Home	1.14	1	0	0	32	0	31.2	28	0	12	33
Away	4.80	2	2	0	32	0	30.0	26	4	9	34
Day	3.86	0	0	0	19	0	16.1	16	3	6	22
Night	2.58	3	2	0	45	0	45.1	38	1	15	45
Grass	5.94	1	0	0	18	0	16.2	15	3	5	12
Turf	1.80	2	2	0	46	0	45.0	39	1	16	55
April	1.93	1	0	0	11	0	9.1	11	1	4	11
May	10.13	1	1	0	4	0	2.2	3	0	1	0
June	0.00	1	0	0	11	0	11.1	5	0	3	13
July	2.40	0	0	0	13	0	15.0	11	2	8	10
August	5.68	0	1	0	13	0	12.2	13	0	5	18
September/October	2.53	0	0	0	12	0	10.2	11	1	0	15
Starter	0.00	0	0	0	0	0	0.0	0	0	0	0
Reliever	2.92	3	2	0	64	0	61.2	54	4	21	67
0 Days rest	1.76	1	0	0	19	0	15.1	15	1	4	12
1 or 2 Days rest	3.90	1	2	0	29	0	27.2	25	2	12	33
3+ Days rest	2.41	1	0	0	16	0	18.2	14	1	5	22
Pre-All Star	1.74	3	1	0	32	0	31.0	25	1	12	31
Post-All Star	4.11	0	1	0	32	0	30.2	29	3	9	36

	Avg	AB	H	2B	3B	HR	RBI	BB	SO	OBP	SLG
vs. Left	.291	86	25	1	1	2	14	4	23	.330	.395
vs. Right	.199	146	29	4	2	2	12	17	44	.282	.295
Inning 1-6	.000	0	0	0	0	0	0	0	0	.000	.000
Inning 7+	.233	232	54	5	3	4	26	21	67	.299	.332
None on	.242	128	31	4	1	3	3	12	34	.312	.359
Runners on	.221	104	23	1	2	1	23	9	33	.283	.298
Scoring Posn	.220	59	13	1	2	0	21	6	18	.292	.305
Close & Late	.223	148	33	2	1	1	18	15	48	.299	.270
None on/out	.137	51	7	1	0	1	1	6	13	.228	.216
vs. 1st Batr (relief)	.121	58	7	1	0	0	6	6	18	.203	.138
First Inning Pitched	.213	188	40	4	3	3	24	19	59	.288	.314
First 15 Pitches	.225	169	38	4	2	2	19	13	48	.284	.308
Pitch 16-30	.271	59	16	1	1	2	7	8	19	.358	.424
Pitch 31-45	.000	4	0	0	0	0	0	0	0	.000	.000
Pitch 46+	.000	0	0	0	0	0	0	0	0	.000	.000
First Pitch	.308	13	4	0	1	0	0	1	0	.357	.462
Ahead in Count	.163	123	20	2	2	2	12	0	56	.163	.260
Behind in Count	.310	42	13	0	0	0	5	8	0	.431	.310
Two Strikes	.156	128	20	2	1	3	15	12	67	.229	.258

Last Five Years

	ERA	W	L	Sv	G	GS	IP	H	HR	BB	SO
Home	1.39	11	3	15	144	0	180.2	139	2	44	187
Away	3.14	5	10	10	117	0	146.1	122	8	49	133
Day	2.87	5	2	7	65	0	84.2	80	3	27	87
Night	1.93	11	11	18	196	0	242.1	181	7	66	233
Grass	2.76	6	3	15	117	0	147.0	114	5	37	123
Turf	1.70	10	10	10	144	0	180.0	147	5	56	197
April	1.00	4	0	2	40	0	45.0	36	1	14	33
May	2.19	2	3	2	30	0	37.0	24	0	15	29
June	1.68	4	1	2	50	0	64.1	51	1	15	64
July	3.45	3	4	6	48	0	62.2	51	4	20	56
August	3.26	2	5	7	44	0	58.0	54	3	21	70
September/October	1.20	1	0	6	49	0	60.0	45	1	8	68
Starter	0.00	0	0	0	0	0	0.0	0	0	0	0
Reliever	2.17	16	13	25	261	0	327.0	261	10	93	320
0 Days rest	1.49	6	4	3	56	0	66.2	55	3	14	55
1 or 2 Days rest	3.06	7	6	5	121	0	144.1	137	3	57	145
3+ Days rest	1.47	3	3	17	84	0	116.0	69	4	22	120
Pre-All Star	2.15	11	5	7	141	0	175.2	138	3	56	157
Post-All Star	2.20	5	8	18	120	0	151.1	123	7	37	163

	Avg	AB	H	2B	3B	HR	RBI	BB	SO	OBP	SLG
vs. Left	.263	574	151	12	3	7	73	52	113	.324	.331
vs. Right	.177	621	110	13	3	3	53	41	207	.226	.222
Inning 1-6	.230	100	23	1	0	0	18	3	21	.245	.240
Inning 7+	.217	1095	238	24	6	10	108	90	299	.277	.278
None on	.218	664	145	12	3	8	8	50	181	.275	.282
Runners on	.218	531	116	13	3	2	118	43	139	.273	.266
Scoring Posn	.214	332	71	11	2	0	112	31	87	.273	.259
Close & Late	.230	618	142	11	2	4	76	57	165	.296	.273
None on/out	.197	279	55	4	1	2	2	26	79	.266	.240
vs. 1st Batr (relief)	.202	243	49	5	1	0	35	13	71	.242	.230
First Inning Pitched	.219	816	179	14	5	8	104	55	215	.268	.278
First 15 Pitches	.221	739	163	14	4	6	79	48	184	.269	.275
Pitch 16-30	.228	360	82	6	1	4	36	38	112	.298	.283
Pitch 31-45	.149	87	13	4	1	0	6	7	22	.213	.218
Pitch 46+	.333	9	3	1	0	0	5	0	2	.333	.444
First Pitch	.258	89	23	3	2	1	9	14	0	.356	.371
Ahead in Count	.188	676	127	10	4	6	68	0	273	.189	.241
Behind in Count	.257	179	46	1	0	1	19	38	0	.385	.279
Two Strikes	.162	679	110	10	3	6	62	41	320	.210	.212

Pitcher vs. Batter (since 1984)

Pitches Best Vs.	Avg	AB	H	2B	3B	HR	RBI	BB	SO	OBP	SLG
Benito Santiago	.071	14	1	0	0	0	2	1	3	.133	.071
Eddie Murray	.083	12	1	0	0	0	1	1	4	.154	.083
Ryne Sandberg	.091	33	3	0	0	0	3	0	8	.088	.091
Shawon Dunston	.118	17	2	0	0	0	1	1	5	.167	.118
Jeff Blauser	.125	16	2	0	0	0	0	0	6	.125	.125

Pitches Worst Vs.	Avg	AB	H	2B	3B	HR	RBI	BB	SO	OBP	SLG
Brett Butler	.625	8	5	0	0	0	1	3	2	.727	.625
Wally Backman	.500	16	8	1	0	0	2	1	1	.529	.563
Ozzie Smith	.438	16	7	1	0	0	5	6	2	.565	.500
Gerald Perry	.357	14	5	2	0	1	3	1	0	.375	.714
Dale Murphy	.346	26	9	1	0	3	8	1	6	.370	.731

Brady Anderson — Orioles

Age 30 – Bats Left

	Avg	G	AB	R	H	2B	3B	HR	RBI	BB	SO	HBP	GDP	SB	CS	OBP	SLG	IBB	SH	SF	#Pit	#P/PA	GB	FB	G/F
1993 Season	.263	142	560	87	147	36	8	13	66	82	99	10	4	24	12	.363	.425	4	6	6	2816	4.24	178	179	0.99
Last Five Years	.250	597	1939	295	484	93	25	43	213	292	332	32	16	120	39	.353	.390	26	36	23	9448	4.07	647	603	1.07

1993 Season

	Avg	AB	H	2B	3B	HR	RBI	BB	SO	OBP	SLG
vs. Left	.259	170	44	10	0	2	17	32	38	.390	.353
vs. Right	.264	390	103	26	8	11	49	50	61	.350	.456
Groundball	.350	100	35	11	1	3	13	20	16	.463	.570
Flyball	.149	114	17	6	0	2	7	10	22	.246	.254
Home	.242	265	64	17	2	2	31	40	50	.344	.343
Away	.281	295	83	19	6	11	35	42	49	.381	.498
Day	.289	173	50	15	2	6	21	24	31	.380	.503
Night	.251	387	97	21	6	7	45	58	68	.356	.390
Grass	.264	466	123	30	7	8	54	71	82	.369	.410
Turf	.255	94	24	6	1	5	12	11	17	.333	.500
First Pitch	.256	43	11	4	1	1	7	3	0	.298	.465
Ahead in Count	.338	142	48	13	1	5	20	55	0	.523	.549
Behind in Count	.221	217	48	8	1	4	19	0	77	.242	.323
Two Strikes	.220	273	60	13	3	5	25	24	99	.294	.344

	Avg	AB	H	2B	3B	HR	RBI	BB	SO	OBP	SLG
Scoring Posn	.260	127	33	9	1	0	48	24	26	.375	.346
Close & Late	.306	85	26	6	3	2	13	14	15	.396	.518
None on/out	.260	219	57	10	3	10	10	26	37	.344	.470
Batting #1	.264	542	143	35	8	13	62	80	95	.365	.430
Batting #8	.267	15	4	1	0	0	4	2	3	.353	.333
Other	.000	3	0	0	0	0	0	0	1	.000	.000
April	.287	87	25	7	1	2	11	12	17	.376	.460
May	.180	111	20	5	1	2	7	15	19	.283	.297
June	.256	78	20	8	1	3	10	10	12	.356	.500
July	.239	71	17	4	0	3	8	10	17	.341	.423
August	.319	91	29	6	1	1	17	20	16	.436	.440
September/October	.295	122	36	6	4	2	13	15	18	.383	.459
Pre-All Star	.237	291	69	21	3	7	32	39	51	.334	.402
Post-All Star	.290	269	78	15	5	6	34	43	48	.393	.450

1993 By Position

Position	Avg	AB	H	2B	3B	HR	RBI	BB	SO	OBP	SLG	G	GS	Innings	PO	A	E	DP	Fld Pct	Rng Fctr	In Zone	Outs	Zone Rtg	MLB Zone
As lf	.267	483	129	33	7	13	59	77	85	.373	.445	126	123	1080.0	247	5	2	0	.992	2.10	291	234	.804	.818
As cf	.219	64	14	1	1	0	5	2	12	.261	.266	18	13	134.2	44	2	0	0	1.000	3.07	51	43	.843	.829

Last Five Years

	Avg	AB	H	2B	3B	HR	RBI	BB	SO	OBP	SLG		Avg	AB	H	2B	3B	HR	RBI	BB	SO	OBP	SLG
vs. Left	.211	512	108	20	5	8	54	92	108	.341	.316	Scoring Posn	.268	422	113	21	6	6	163	90	78	.386	.389
vs. Right	.263	1427	376	73	20	35	159	200	224	.358	.416	Close & Late	.281	288	81	14	6	4	35	44	48	.374	.413
Groundball	.299	491	147	27	4	10	56	61	61	.381	.432	None on/out	.237	748	177	34	10	22	22	89	116	.325	.397
Flyball	.182	418	76	17	2	7	36	69	78	.310	.282	Batting #1	.258	1576	406	80	23	39	169	237	262	.360	.412
Home	.235	950	223	43	8	21	110	138	171	.338	.363	Batting #2	.211	209	44	11	1	4	29	35	33	.335	.330
Away	.264	989	261	50	17	22	103	154	161	.368	.416	Other	.221	154	34	2	1	0	15	20	37	.311	.247
Day	.283	569	161	35	13	14	65	79	93	.376	.464	April	.279	290	81	23	8	5	41	49	54	.394	.466
Night	.236	1070	[illegible]	50	12	29	140	213	239	.344	.359	May	.208	395	82	18	1	12	43	47	68	.298	.349
Grass	.245	1605	394	72	16	34	172	233	278	.347	.374	June	.241	282	68	17	2	8	27	43	44	.348	.401
Turf	.269	334	90	21	9	9	41	59	54	.382	.467	July	.283	286	81	11	3	7	32	46	47	.389	.416
First Pitch	.253	178	45	7	2	4	18	15	0	.308	.382	August	.244	307	75	9	4	6	38	62	45	.370	.358
Ahead in Count	.327	471	154	34	4	16	76	190	0	.519	.518	September/October	.256	379	97	15	7	5	32	45	74	.340	.372
Behind in Count	.200	815	163	26	10	12	60	0	272	.220	.301	Pre-All Star	.244	1055	257	61	11	27	125	157	178	.350	.399
Two Strikes	.203	951	193	32	15	18	85	87	332	.279	.325	Post-All Star	.257	884	227	32	14	16	88	135	154	.358	.379

Batter vs. Pitcher (career)

Hits Best Against	Avg	AB	H	2B	3B	HR	RBI	BB	SO	OBP	SLG	Hits Worst Against	Avg	AB	H	2B	3B	HR	RBI	BB	SO	OBP	SLG
Kevin Tapani	.500	14	7	0	0	2	5	2	3	.563	.929	Dave Stieb	.000	15	0	0	0	0	0	3	6	.167	.000
Hipolito Pichardo	.500	10	5	0	1	1	1	1	0	.545	1.000	Rod Nichols	.000	11	0	0	0	0	0	0	4	.000	.000
Mike Henneman	.455	11	5	1	0	1	5	3	0	.571	.818	Jack McDowell	.095	21	2	0	0	0	0	2	3	.174	.095
Roger Clemens	.412	17	7	4	0	1	2	2	3	.474	.824	Teddy Higuera	.100	10	1	0	0	0	0	1	2	.182	.100
Erik Hanson	.400	25	10	6	0	1	7	3	5	.448	.760	Curt Young	.133	15	2	0	0	0	0	0	2	.133	.133

Brian Anderson — Angels

Age 22 – Pitches Left

	ERA	W	L	Sv	G	GS	IP	BB	SO	Avg	H	2B	3B	HR	RBI	OBP	SLG	GF	IR	IRS	Hld	SvOp	SB	CS	GB	FB	G/F
1993 Season	3.97	0	0	0	4	1	11.1	2	4	.256	11	3	1	1	6	.289	.442	3	2	1	0	0	1	0	8	22	0.36

1993 Season

	ERA	W	L	Sv	G	GS	IP	H	HR	BB	SO		Avg	AB	H	2B	3B	HR	RBI	BB	SO	OBP	SLG
Home	2.70	0	0	0	2	0	3.1	2	1	0	1	vs. Left	.167	6	1	0	0	0	1	0	0	.167	.167
Away	4.50	0	0	0	2	1	8.0	9	0	2	3	vs. Right	.270	37	10	3	1	1	5	2	4	.308	.486

Mike Anderson — Reds

Age 27 – Pitches Right

	ERA	W	L	Sv	G	GS	IP	BB	SO	Avg	H	2B	3B	HR	RBI	OBP	SLG	GF	IR	IRS	Hld	SvOp	SB	CS	GB	FB	G/F
1993 Season	18.56	0	0	0	3	0	5.1	3	4	.444	12	0	0	3	10	.500	.778	0	4	0	0	0	0	0	9	8	1.13

1993 Season

	ERA	W	L	Sv	G	GS	IP	H	HR	BB	SO		Avg	AB	H	2B	3B	HR	RBI	BB	SO	OBP	SLG
Home	27.00	0	0	0	2	0	3.0	9	2	3	2	vs. Left	.500	14	7	0	0	3	9	2	3	.563	1.143
Away	7.71	0	0	0	1	0	2.1	3	1	0	2	vs. Right	.385	13	5	0	0	0	1	1	1	.429	.385

Eric Anthony — Astros

Age 26 – Bats Left

	Avg	G	AB	R	H	2B	3B	HR	RBI	BB	SO	HBP	GDP	SB	CS	OBP	SLG	IBB	SH	SF	#Pit	#P/PA	GB	FB	G/F
1993 Season	.249	145	486	70	121	19	4	15	66	49	88	2	9	3	5	.319	.397	2	0	2	2035	3.77	205	122	1.68
Career (1989-1993)	.224	430	1344	159	301	50	5	49	189	137	321	5	22	14	9	.295	.378	13	1	14	5678	3.78	497	359	1.38

1993 Season

	Avg	AB	H	2B	3B	HR	RBI	BB	SO	OBP	SLG		Avg	AB	H	2B	3B	HR	RBI	BB	SO	OBP	SLG
vs. Left	.247	158	39	4	1	5	25	16	38	.314	.380	Scoring Posn	.228	127	29	3	1	4	44	12	24	.296	.362
vs. Right	.250	328	82	15	3	10	41	33	50	.321	.405	Close & Late	.218	78	17	1	0	3	14	7	15	.279	.346
Groundball	.197	173	34	7	2	5	20	16	34	.265	.347	None on/out	.237	118	28	4	1	6	6	14	20	.323	.441
Flyball	.304	56	17	2	0	3	11	9	16	.394	.500	Batting #4	.272	327	89	15	4	12	49	36	57	.346	.453
Home	.255	251	64	11	3	5	31	25	46	.326	.382	Batting #5	.204	93	19	2	0	2	9	6	15	.253	.290
Away	.243	235	57	8	1	10	35	24	42	.312	.413	Other	.197	66	13	2	0	1	8	7	16	.274	.273
Day	.222	144	32	5	2	3	19	16	21	.300	.347	April	.338	80	27	6	1	2	13	8	11	.398	.513
Night	.260	342	89	14	2	12	47	33	67	.327	.418	May	.260	96	25	4	0	2	13	10	17	.327	.365
Grass	.209	148	31	3	0	8	24	13	26	.273	.392	June	.217	83	18	1	1	1	6	6	17	.270	.289
Turf	.266	338	90	16	4	7	42	36	62	.339	.399	July	.239	88	21	2	0	4	12	10	15	.313	.398
First Pitch	.324	68	22	4	2	2	13	1	0	.333	.529	August	.244	90	22	2	2	6	16	10	18	.333	.511
Ahead in Count	.302	126	38	7	1	3	15	24	0	.408	.444	September/October	.163	49	8	4	0	0	6	5	10	.241	.245
Behind in Count	.184	190	35	2	1	5	23	0	72	.188	.284	Pre-All Star	.263	297	78	12	2	7	39	27	52	.323	.387
Two Strikes	.175	212	37	3	1	7	25	24	88	.258	.297	Post-All Star	.228	189	43	7	2	8	27	22	36	.313	.413

1993 By Position

Position	Avg	AB	H	2B	3B	HR	RBI	BB	SO	OBP	SLG	G	GS	Innings	PO	A	E	DP	Fld Pct	Rng Fctr	In Zone	Outs	Zone Rtg	MLB Zone
As Pinch Hitter	.125	16	2	0	0	0	0	0	3	.125	.125	17	0	---	---	---	---	---	---	---	---	---	---	---
As cf	.306	72	22	3	0	2	15	2	16	.324	.431	23	19	146.2	32	1	1	0	.971	2.03	40	32	.800	.829
As rf	.244	398	97	16	4	13	51	47	69	.325	.402	121	106	948.0	201	5	2	0	.990	1.96	236	196	.831	.826

Career (1989-1993)

	Avg	AB	H	2B	3B	HR	RBI	BB	SO	OBP	SLG
vs. Left	.218	432	94	13	1	13	64	41	116	.285	.343
vs. Right	.227	912	207	37	4	36	125	96	205	.300	.395
Groundball	.216	458	99	17	2	16	68	43	102	.282	.367
Flyball	.205	263	54	8	0	14	46	35	79	.299	.395
Home	.238	642	153	26	4	21	87	60	148	.305	.389
Away	.211	702	148	24	1	28	102	77	173	.286	.368
Day	.208	395	82	17	3	13	54	36	86	.271	.365
Night	.231	949	219	33	2	36	135	101	235	.305	.384
Grass	.199	417	83	9	0	22	69	39	99	.265	.379
Turf	.235	927	218	41	5	27	120	98	222	.309	.378
First Pitch	.311	180	56	16	2	8	39	8	0	.337	.556
Ahead in Count	.277	285	79	12	1	11	41	61	0	.401	.442
Behind in Count	.164	592	97	10	2	15	66	0	258	.168	.264
Two Strikes	.144	658	95	9	1	17	70	67	321	.223	.239

	Avg	AB	H	2B	3B	HR	RBI	BB	SO	OBP	SLG
Scoring Posn	.225	355	80	16	1	10	127	44	87	.304	.361
Close & Late	.236	242	57	5	0	11	42	25	62	.305	.393
None on/out	.199	332	66	6	1	11	11	36	71	.281	.322
Batting #4	.261	537	140	24	4	21	90	54	101	.328	.438
Batting #5	.201	313	63	8	1	14	47	27	75	.263	.367
Other	.198	494	98	18	0	14	52	56	145	.280	.320
April	.309	97	30	6	1	2	13	10	15	.374	.454
May	.256	250	64	13	0	8	40	28	55	.330	.404
June	.212	293	62	11	2	8	31	27	82	.276	.345
July	.201	264	53	8	0	12	40	23	66	.260	.367
August	.209	211	44	5	2	10	36	25	47	.298	.393
September/October	.210	229	48	7	0	9	29	24	56	.286	.358
Pre-All Star	.233	748	174	31	3	24	102	74	182	.300	.378
Post-All Star	.213	596	127	19	2	25	87	63	139	.289	.378

Batter vs. Pitcher (career)

Hits Best Against	Avg	AB	H	2B	3B	HR	RBI	BB	SO	OBP	SLG
Jose DeLeon	.455	11	5	2	0	0	4	1	3	.500	.636
Les Lancaster	.444	9	4	1	0	0	2	2	0	.545	.556
Bob Walk	.429	14	6	1	0	2	4	1	5	.467	.929
Rheal Cormier	.417	12	5	1	0	1	4	2	2	.500	.750
Mike Bielecki	.400	10	4	0	0	1	1	1	3	.455	.700

Hits Worst Against	Avg	AB	H	2B	3B	HR	RBI	BB	SO	OBP	SLG
Trevor Wilson	.077	13	1	0	0	0	0	0	5	.077	.077
Ken Hill	.100	20	2	0	0	0	0	3	3	.217	.100
Dwight Gooden	.120	25	3	1	0	1	6	1	10	.143	.280
Doug Drabek	.154	13	2	0	0	0	1	0	2	.154	.154
Tom Browning	.182	11	2	0	0	0	0	1	3	.250	.182

Kevin Appier — Royals

Age 26 – Pitches Right

	ERA	W	L	Sv	G	GS	IP	BB	SO	Avg	H	2B	3B	HR	RBI	OBP	SLG	CG	ShO	Sup	QS	#P/S	SB	CS	GB	FB	G/F
1993 Season	2.56	18	8	0	34	34	238.2	81	186	.212	183	39	3	8	63	.279	.292	5	1	4.49	29	110	11	8	290	237	1.22
Career (1989-1993)	2.95	59	38	0	136	124	862.0	276	631	.237	768	139	11	47	274	.297	.331	17	7	4.45	86	105	55	28	1126	930	1.21

1993 Season

	ERA	W	L	Sv	G	GS	IP	H	HR	BB	SO
Home	2.39	8	5	0	17	17	116.2	84	4	39	90
Away	2.73	10	3	0	17	17	122.0	99	4	42	96
Day	2.59	6	4	0	14	14	93.2	81	0	31	76
Night	2.54	12	4	0	20	20	145.0	102	8	50	110
Grass	2.94	8	3	0	14	14	98.0	84	4	35	83
Turf	2.30	10	5	0	20	20	140.2	99	4	46	103
April	3.70	2	3	0	6	6	41.1	37	1	16	34
May	3.28	3	1	0	5	5	35.2	38	1	16	28
June	2.23	4	0	0	6	6	44.1	30	3	12	33
July	2.43	2	1	0	5	5	29.2	17	2	9	30
August	2.89	3	1	0	6	6	43.2	36	1	11	25
September/October	1.02	4	2	0	6	6	44.0	25	0	17	36
Starter	2.56	18	8	0	34	34	238.2	183	8	81	186
Reliever	0.00	0	0	0	0	0	0.0	0	0	0	0
0-3 Days Rest	0.00	0	0	0	0	0	0.0	0	0	0	0
4 Days Rest	2.55	10	6	0	21	21	151.2	119	7	47	122
5+ Days Rest	2.59	8	2	0	13	13	87.0	64	1	34	64
Pre-All Star	3.00	10	4	0	19	19	129.0	109	5	47	105
Post-All Star	2.05	8	4	0	15	15	109.2	74	3	34	81

	Avg	AB	H	2B	3B	HR	RBI	BB	SO	OBP	SLG
vs. Left	.240	438	105	19	1	5	37	47	82	.311	.322
vs. Right	.184	425	78	20	2	3	26	34	104	.245	.261
Inning 1-6	.198	688	136	30	3	5	47	66	152	.266	.272
Inning 7+	.269	175	47	9	0	3	16	15	34	.328	.371
None on	.193	539	104	21	1	6	6	49	120	.260	.269
Runners on	.244	324	79	18	2	2	57	32	66	.309	.330
Scoring Posn	.213	178	38	9	2	0	50	19	38	.282	.287
Close & Late	.248	109	27	4	0	1	10	11	16	.320	.312
None on/out	.164	226	37	8	0	2	2	21	46	.235	.226
vs. 1st Batr (relief)	.000	0	0	0	0	0	0	0	0	.000	.000
First Inning Pitched	.147	116	17	3	2	2	7	9	26	.208	.259
First 75 Pitches	.195	560	109	24	3	4	33	48	120	.257	.270
Pitch 76-90	.235	102	24	6	0	2	10	10	22	.304	.353
Pitch 91-105	.208	101	21	5	0	1	8	11	32	.283	.287
Pitch 106+	.290	100	29	4	0	1	12	12	12	.368	.360
First Pitch	.287	94	27	2	0	2	4	2	0	.302	.372
Ahead in Count	.166	447	74	17	1	2	26	0	151	.164	.221
Behind in Count	.296	159	47	13	1	1	15	33	0	.415	.409
Two Strikes	.156	441	69	16	2	3	26	46	186	.235	.222

Career (1989-1993)

	ERA	W	L	Sv	G	GS	IP	H	HR	BB	SO
Home	2.76	29	20	0	64	59	407.1	344	18	120	307
Away	3.13	30	18	0	72	65	454.2	424	29	156	324
Day	2.54	18	11	0	41	38	247.2	234	10	95	183
Night	3.12	41	27	0	95	86	614.1	534	37	181	448
Grass	3.18	25	16	0	60	53	370.1	351	25	132	275
Turf	2.78	34	22	0	76	71	491.2	417	22	144	356
April	2.96	3	8	0	17	15	100.1	87	5	37	74
May	3.09	10	4	0	24	16	139.2	140	9	45	88
June	3.57	11	8	0	28	26	171.2	158	15	54	116
July	2.78	13	3	0	23	23	155.2	127	4	41	131
August	2.80	14	6	0	23	23	157.2	134	9	49	115
September/October	2.43	8	9	0	21	21	137.0	122	5	50	107
Starter	2.90	59	37	0	124	124	837.1	734	44	266	608
Reliever	4.74	0	1	0	12	0	24.2	34	3	10	23
0-3 Days Rest	4.25	2	2	0	5	5	29.2	33	1	10	20
4 Days Rest	2.59	32	20	0	68	68	470.0	393	25	153	352
5+ Days Rest	3.23	25	15	0	51	51	337.2	308	18	103	236
Pre-All Star	3.27	30	21	0	78	66	465.0	431	29	154	324
Post-All Star	2.58	29	17	0	58	58	397.0	337	18	122	307

	Avg	AB	H	2B	3B	HR	RBI	BB	SO	OBP	SLG
vs. Left	.247	1566	387	69	7	30	156	166	261	.316	.358
vs. Right	.228	1671	381	70	4	17	118	110	370	.278	.305
Inning 1-6	.236	2656	627	113	9	40	228	224	533	.295	.331
Inning 7+	.243	581	141	26	2	7	46	52	98	.308	.330
None on	.228	1916	437	75	8	26	26	166	375	.292	.316
Runners on	.251	1321	331	64	3	21	248	110	256	.305	.351
Scoring Posn	.222	721	160	32	3	7	209	78	157	.292	.304
Close & Late	.205	341	70	9	1	4	28	30	55	.271	.273
None on/out	.222	833	185	37	4	11	11	73	155	.286	.316
vs. 1st Batr (relief)	.100	10	1	1	0	0	2	1	3	.167	.200
First Inning Pitched	.223	493	110	25	3	10	55	50	90	.291	.347
First 75 Pitches	.240	2260	543	105	9	30	189	182	435	.296	.335
Pitch 76-90	.227	384	87	13	0	10	35	36	78	.296	.339
Pitch 91-105	.196	326	64	10	1	6	26	32	79	.267	.288
Pitch 106+	.277	267	74	11	1	1	24	26	39	.343	.337
First Pitch	.311	418	130	22	2	10	45	11	0	.326	.445
Ahead in Count	.183	1554	285	50	4	13	89	0	533	.185	.246
Behind in Count	.319	680	217	43	4	13	72	129	0	.427	.451
Two Strikes	.166	1517	252	46	3	12	93	136	631	.235	.224

Pitcher vs. Batter (career)

Pitches Best Vs.	Avg	AB	H	2B	3B	HR	RBI	BB	SO	OBP	SLG
Tino Martinez	.000	14	0	0	0	0	1	4	4	.222	.000
Kevin Maas	.000	9	0	0	0	0	0	3	6	.250	.000
Gary Gaetti	.077	13	1	0	0	0	0	0	6	.077	.077
Glenn Davis	.077	13	1	0	0	0	0	0	4	.077	.077

Pitches Worst Vs.	Avg	AB	H	2B	3B	HR	RBI	BB	SO	OBP	SLG
Darryl Hamilton	.615	13	8	0	0	0	0	2	1	.667	.615
Carlton Fisk	.467	15	7	1	0	1	1	2	3	.529	.733
Leo Gomez	.450	20	9	1	0	2	4	2	4	.500	.800
Gary DiSarcina	.429	14	6	1	0	1	4	3	1	.529	.714

Pitcher vs. Batter (career)																						
Pitches Best Vs.	Avg	AB	H	2B	3B	HR	RBI	BB	SO	OBP	SLG	**Pitches Worst Vs.**	Avg	AB	H	2B	3B	HR	RBI	BB	SO	OBP	SLG
Tim Naehring	.083	12	1	0	0	0	1	0	3	.083	.083	Phil Plantier	.400	10	4	3	0	0	0	3	2	.538	.700

Luis Aquino — Marlins

Age 29 – Pitches Right

	ERA	W	L	Sv	G	GS	IP	BB	SO	Avg	H	2B	3B	HR	RBI	OBP	SLG	GF	IR	IRS	Hld	SvOp	SB	CS	GB	FB	G/F
1993 Season	3.42	6	8	0	38	13	110.2	40	67	.276	115	23	2	6	37	.345	.384	5	10	1	3	1	10	5	146	117	1.25
Last Five Years	3.55	27	27	3	145	63	545.0	169	254	.267	555	105	8	33	219	.325	.373	18	61	23	5	6	28	21	762	672	1.13

1993 Season

	ERA	W	L	Sv	G	GS	IP	H	HR	BB	SO
Home	2.62	3	3	0	21	4	44.2	48	3	21	33
Away	3.95	3	5	0	17	9	66.0	67	3	19	34
Starter	3.36	4	6	0	13	13	80.1	81	5	25	46
Reliever	3.56	2	2	0	25	0	30.1	34	1	15	21
0 Days rest	2.45	0	1	0	5	0	3.2	3	0	6	1
1 or 2 Days rest	3.86	2	0	0	12	0	14.0	12	1	7	13
3+ Days rest	3.55	0	1	0	8	0	12.2	19	0	2	7
Pre-All Star	3.28	4	6	0	16	12	79.2	81	4	26	45
Post-All Star	3.77	2	2	0	22	1	31.0	34	2	14	22

	Avg	AB	H	2B	3B	HR	RBI	BB	SO	OBP	SLG
vs. Left	.257	237	61	10	1	5	16	21	34	.320	.371
vs. Right	.300	180	54	13	1	1	21	19	33	.376	.400
Scoring Posn	.252	103	26	8	0	1	29	17	21	.358	.359
Close & Late	.306	72	22	3	0	1	5	7	15	.386	.389
None on/out	.280	107	30	6	2	1	1	7	19	.336	.402
First Pitch	.292	65	19	3	0	0	6	1	0	.294	.338
Ahead in Count	.232	181	42	11	1	3	20	0	58	.240	.354
Behind in Count	.337	92	31	5	1	2	6	20	0	.465	.478
Two Strikes	.229	170	39	5	1	3	14	19	67	.314	.324

Last Five Years

	ERA	W	L	Sv	G	GS	IP	H	HR	BB	SO
Home	3.10	13	10	1	70	26	250.0	239	14	80	118
Away	3.94	14	17	2	75	37	295.0	316	19	89	136
Day	2.50	7	4	2	37	13	136.2	116	6	46	70
Night	3.90	20	23	1	108	50	408.1	439	27	123	184
Grass	3.42	15	15	2	77	33	278.2	294	17	88	153
Turf	3.68	12	12	1	68	30	266.1	261	16	81	101
April	4.40	4	2	0	22	4	61.1	67	8	24	27
May	2.77	2	3	0	24	6	78.0	67	2	23	48
June	3.47	4	4	1	19	10	85.2	89	6	27	43
July	2.38	10	6	2	22	15	124.2	111	4	29	54
August	3.99	4	6	0	28	15	103.2	110	7	38	48
September/October	4.81	3	6	0	30	13	91.2	111	6	28	34
Starter	3.78	19	24	0	63	63	376.0	391	23	107	161
Reliever	3.04	8	3	3	82	0	169.0	164	10	62	93
0 Days rest	1.80	2	1	0	11	0	20.0	18	0	12	6
1 or 2 Days rest	2.08	3	0	1	25	0	47.2	34	1	21	36
3+ Days rest	3.73	3	2	2	46	0	101.1	112	9	29	51
Pre-All Star	3.53	11	13	1	71	25	262.2	262	17	84	136
Post-All Star	3.57	16	14	2	74	38	282.1	293	16	85	118

	Avg	AB	H	2B	3B	HR	RBI	BB	SO	OBP	SLG
vs. Left	.272	1012	275	51	6	15	100	94	121	.333	.378
vs. Right	.262	1068	280	54	2	18	119	75	133	.317	.367
Inning 1-6	.273	1601	437	86	7	27	186	120	181	.326	.386
Inning 7+	.246	479	118	19	1	6	33	49	73	.321	.328
None on	.261	1192	311	59	6	14	14	84	154	.314	.356
Runners on	.275	888	244	46	2	19	205	85	100	.339	.395
Scoring Posn	.255	495	126	27	1	9	175	62	65	.332	.368
Close & Late	.276	221	61	9	0	4	18	25	40	.356	.371
None on/out	.250	509	127	27	4	2	2	41	61	.310	.330
vs. 1st Batr (relief)	.300	70	21	6	0	1	14	8	11	.383	.429
First Inning Pitched	.282	522	147	25	2	9	78	54	78	.354	.389
First 15 Pitches	.291	460	134	19	2	8	56	43	61	.356	.393
Pitch 16-30	.277	419	116	26	0	3	39	36	55	.336	.360
Pitch 31-45	.233	365	85	16	4	5	37	26	42	.283	.340
Pitch 46+	.263	836	220	44	2	17	87	64	96	.319	.382
First Pitch	.322	326	105	18	2	5	53	14	0	.356	.436
Ahead in Count	.212	867	184	35	4	12	78	0	213	.217	.303
Behind in Count	.292	511	149	26	2	8	45	92	0	.401	.397
Two Strikes	.208	799	166	32	3	10	67	63	254	.268	.293

Pitcher vs. Batter (career)

Pitches Best Vs.	Avg	AB	H	2B	3B	HR	RBI	BB	SO	OBP	SLG	**Pitches Worst Vs.**	Avg	AB	H	2B	3B	HR	RBI	BB	SO	OBP	SLG
Manuel Lee	.000	14	0	0	0	0	1	1	3	.067	.000	Frank Thomas	.545	11	6	1	0	3	6	2	0	.615	1.455
Alan Trammell	.059	17	1	0	0	0	0	1	0	.111	.059	Lance Johnson	.462	13	6	2	2	0	2	1	0	.500	.923
Paul Molitor	.071	14	1	0	0	0	0	0	3	.071	.071	Dan Pasqua	.400	15	6	1	0	2	3	1	2	.438	.867
Fred McGriff	.091	11	1	0	0	0	0	1	2	.167	.091	George Bell	.385	13	5	0	0	2	2	0	0	.385	.846
Luis Rivera	.100	20	2	1	0	0	0	0	2	.100	.150	Chili Davis	.364	11	4	1	0	2	5	3	3	.467	1.000

Alex Arias — Marlins

Age 26 – Bats Right (groundball hitter)

	Avg	G	AB	R	H	2B	3B	HR	RBI	BB	SO	HBP	GDP	SB	CS	OBP	SLG	IBB	SH	SF	#Pit	#P/PA	GB	FB	G/F
1993 Season	.269	96	249	27	67	5	1	2	20	27	18	3	5	1	1	.344	.321	0	1	3	1079	3.81	118	59	2.00
Career (1992-1993)	.276	128	348	41	96	11	1	2	27	38	31	5	9	1	1	.353	.330	0	2	3	1525	3.85	160	79	2.03

1993 Season

	Avg	AB	H	2B	3B	HR	RBI	BB	SO	OBP	SLG
vs. Left	.284	81	23	2	0	0	8	9	4	.366	.309
vs. Right	.262	168	44	3	1	2	12	18	14	.333	.327
Home	.276	105	29	1	0	1	8	11	8	.356	.314
Away	.264	144	38	4	1	1	12	16	10	.335	.326
First Pitch	.412	17	7	0	0	0	1	0	0	.444	.412
Ahead in Count	.254	63	16	1	0	1	8	18	0	.410	.317
Behind in Count	.207	116	24	3	0	0	8	0	16	.212	.233
Two Strikes	.226	106	24	1	1	1	7	9	18	.293	.283

	Avg	AB	H	2B	3B	HR	RBI	BB	SO	OBP	SLG
Scoring Posn	.224	58	13	0	0	0	17	7	2	.304	.224
Close & Late	.156	45	7	0	0	1	3	10	5	.309	.222
None on/out	.299	67	20	2	1	0	0	6	8	.365	.358
Batting #2	.273	44	12	1	0	0	5	3	4	.313	.295
Batting #7	.313	96	30	3	1	1	11	15	8	.417	.396
Other	.229	109	25	1	0	1	4	9	6	.286	.266
Pre-All Star	.276	170	47	5	1	1	17	18	11	.352	.335
Post-All Star	.253	79	20	0	0	1	3	9	7	.326	.291

Marcos Armas — Athletics

Age 24 – Bats Right

	Avg	G	AB	R	H	2B	3B	HR	RBI	BB	SO	HBP	GDP	SB	CS	OBP	SLG	IBB	SH	SF	#Pit	#P/PA	GB	FB	G/F
1993 Season	.194	15	31	7	6	2	0	1	1	1	12	1	0	1	0	.242	.355	0	0	0	140	4.24	6	7	0.86

1993 Season

	Avg	AB	H	2B	3B	HR	RBI	BB	SO	OBP	SLG		Avg	AB	H	2B	3B	HR	RBI	BB	SO	OBP	SLG
vs. Left	.235	17	4	1	0	1	1	0	7	.278	.471	Scoring Posn	.125	8	1	0	0	0	0	0	5	.125	.125
vs. Right	.143	14	2	1	0	0	0	1	5	.200	.214	Close & Late	.167	6	1	0	0	1	1	0	2	.167	.667

Jack Armstrong — Marlins

Age 29 – Pitches Right

	ERA	W	L	Sv	G	GS	IP	BB	SO	Avg	H	2B	3B	HR	RBI	OBP	SLG	CG	ShO	Sup	QS	#P/S	SB	CS	GB	FB	G/F
1993 Season	4.49	9	17	0	36	33	196.1	78	118	.271	210	35	6	29	98	.339	.443	0	0	3.53	17	95	18	3	285	239	1.19
Last Five Years	4.48	36	57	0	136	115	711.1	279	458	.266	735	127	20	91	359	.335	.426	4	1	4.18	53	92	65	27	940	868	1.08

1993 Season

	ERA	W	L	Sv	G	GS	IP	H	HR	BB	SO		Avg	AB	H	2B	3B	HR	RBI	BB	SO	OBP	SLG
Home	4.73	5	13	0	20	19	118.0	125	17	42	80	vs. Left	.288	416	120	23	2	22	60	57	55	.373	.512
Away	4.14	4	4	0	16	14	78.1	85	12	36	38	vs. Right	.250	360	90	12	4	7	38	21	63	.296	.364
Day	2.68	4	2	0	7	6	40.1	32	3	15	31	Inning 1-6	.268	691	185	30	6	26	88	70	107	.336	.441
Night	4.96	5	15	0	29	27	156.0	178	26	63	87	Inning 7+	.294	85	25	5	0	3	10	8	11	.362	.459
Grass	4.61	7	15	0	28	26	154.1	164	24	59	92	None on	.275	454	125	15	4	18	18	40	69	.339	.445
Turf	4.07	2	2	0	8	7	42.0	46	5	19	26	Runners on	.264	322	85	20	2	11	80	38	49	.338	.441
April	3.62	2	2	0	5	5	32.1	33	0	11	30	Scoring Posn	.227	163	37	7	0	4	56	29	22	.333	.344
May	4.08	2	2	0	6	6	39.2	38	8	12	23	Close & Late	.280	50	14	2	0	0	2	6	7	.357	.320
June	4.83	1	5	0	6	6	31.2	32	4	9	16	None on/out	.284	208	59	3	2	9	9	10	34	.323	.447
July	4.88	2	1	0	5	5	27.2	33	6	9	16	vs. 1st Batr (relief)	.000	3	0	0	0	0	0	0	0	.000	.000
August	5.40	0	4	0	6	6	35.0	41	7	21	18	First Inning Pitched	.313	150	47	9	2	8	28	18	25	.380	.560
September/October	4.20	2	3	0	8	5	30.0	33	4	16	15	First 75 Pitches	.276	569	157	25	5	21	78	63	89	.349	.448
Starter	4.59	8	17	0	33	33	192.0	206	29	74	116	Pitch 76-90	.261	111	29	5	1	5	9	9	15	.317	.459
Reliever	0.00	1	0	0	3	0	4.1	4	0	4	2	Pitch 91-105	.260	73	19	4	0	2	8	4	8	.308	.397
0-3 Days Rest	4.50	0	1	0	1	1	6.0	6	0	1	3	Pitch 106+	.217	23	5	1	0	1	3	2	6	.280	.391
4 Days Rest	5.56	4	11	0	21	21	115.0	142	24	45	76	First Pitch	.375	112	42	9	0	7	21	3	0	.381	.643
5+ Days Rest	3.04	4	5	0	11	11	71.0	58	5	28	37	Ahead in Count	.211	331	70	15	2	4	26	0	101	.220	.305
Pre-All Star	4.49	6	9	0	19	19	112.1	119	15	35	75	Behind in Count	.296	179	53	4	2	12	31	40	0	.420	.542
Post-All Star	4.50	3	8	0	17	14	84.0	91	14	43	43	Two Strikes	.211	323	68	14	3	3	25	35	118	.292	.300

Last Five Years

	ERA	W	L	Sv	G	GS	IP	H	HR	BB	SO		Avg	AB	H	2B	3B	HR	RBI	BB	SO	OBP	SLG
Home	4.91	22	31	0	69	58	353.2	364	50	145	235	vs. Left	.276	1469	405	75	12	52	208	184	190	.356	.449
Away	4.05	14	26	0	67	57	357.2	371	41	134	223	vs. Right	.256	1289	330	52	8	39	151	95	268	.308	.400
Day	4.03	12	14	0	34	28	169.2	169	15	72	132	Inning 1-6	.266	2436	649	118	15	83	330	250	405	.335	.429
Night	4.62	24	43	0	102	87	541.2	566	76	207	326	Inning 7+	.267	322	86	9	5	8	29	29	53	.331	.401
Grass	4.46	18	35	0	78	63	405.2	427	60	152	257	None on	.247	1638	405	68	11	51	51	158	284	.317	.396
Turf	4.50	18	22	0	58	52	305.2	308	31	127	201	Runners on	.295	1120	330	59	9	40	308	121	174	.359	.471
April	3.27	7	6	0	16	16	99.0	94	9	30	74	Scoring Posn	.283	626	177	28	4	21	249	89	99	.361	.441
May	3.76	10	9	0	26	25	162.2	149	15	63	95	Close & Late	.259	139	36	4	4	0	8	10	25	.313	.345
June	4.75	5	13	0	23	22	130.2	138	19	54	92	None on/out	.252	726	183	25	4	29	29	54	131	.309	.417
July	5.93	6	12	0	23	19	115.1	142	18	37	67	vs. 1st Batr (relief)	.200	20	4	1	0	1	2	1	6	.238	.400
August	5.38	3	8	0	18	14	85.1	88	16	50	47	First Inning Pitched	.301	538	162	27	4	22	112	70	86	.377	.489
September/October	4.11	5	9	0	30	19	118.1	124	14	45	83	First 75 Pitches	.262	2132	559	101	14	68	279	225	362	.333	.418
Starter	4.67	32	57	0	115	115	664.2	703	87	256	418	Pitch 76-90	.275	346	95	15	1	15	42	34	55	.340	.454
Reliever	1.74	4	0	0	21	0	46.2	32	4	23	40	Pitch 91-105	.277	195	54	10	2	3	23	16	27	.332	.395
0-3 Days Rest	3.52	0	3	0	6	6	30.2	22	2	14	21	Pitch 106+	.318	85	27	1	3	5	15	4	14	.352	.576
4 Days Rest	4.70	17	33	0	67	67	396.1	431	54	147	249	First Pitch	.346	425	147	31	0	25	79	13	0	.364	.595
5+ Days Rest	4.77	15	21	0	42	42	237.2	250	31	95	148	Ahead in Count	.194	1133	220	39	6	18	100	0	389	.201	.287
Pre-All Star	4.19	26	32	0	74	72	442.0	445	52	159	293	Behind in Count	.315	691	218	28	10	34	120	143	0	.428	.533
Post-All Star	4.95	10	25	0	62	43	269.1	290	39	120	165	Two Strikes	.182	1126	205	40	6	16	84	123	458	.265	.271

Pitcher vs. Batter (career)

Pitches Best Vs.	Avg	AB	H	2B	3B	HR	RBI	BB	SO	OBP	SLG	Pitches Worst Vs.	Avg	AB	H	2B	3B	HR	RBI	BB	SO	OBP	SLG
Tim Raines	.063	16	1	0	0	0	1	1	2	.118	.063	Jay Bell	.545	11	6	0	1	0	1	2	1	.615	.727
Candy Maldonado	.083	12	1	0	0	0	0	2	6	.214	.083	Eddie Murray	.538	13	7	1	0	2	4	1	1	.571	1.077
Derrick May	.091	11	1	1	0	0	2	1	2	.154	.182	Rick Wilkins	.500	8	4	1	0	2	3	3	0	.636	1.375
Kirt Manwaring	.154	13	2	1	0	0	2	0	3	.154	.231	Darren Daulton	.444	18	8	2	1	4	9	1	2	.474	1.333
Jose Lind	.167	12	2	1	0	0	0	0	2	.167	.250	Ron Gant	.346	26	9	0	0	5	9	1	5	.370	.923

Rene Arocha — Cardinals

Age 28 – Pitches Right (groundball pitcher)

	ERA	W	L	Sv	G	GS	IP	BB	SO	Avg	H	2B	3B	HR	RBI	OBP	SLG	CG	ShO	Sup	QS	#P/S	SB	CS	GB	FB	G/F
1993 Season	3.78	11	8	0	32	29	188.0	31	96	.271	197	36	7	20	83	.302	.422	1	0	4.84	16	87	14	8	310	198	1.57

1993 Season

	ERA	W	L	Sv	G	GS	IP	H	HR	BB	SO		Avg	AB	H	2B	3B	HR	RBI	BB	SO	OBP	SLG
Home	3.43	6	3	0	17	15	99.2	101	8	14	57	vs. Left	.313	352	110	16	5	9	44	19	35	.348	.463
Away	4.18	5	5	0	15	14	88.1	96	12	17	39	vs. Right	.232	375	87	20	2	11	39	12	61	.258	.384
Day	4.30	2	5	0	11	9	60.2	61	9	8	35	Inning 1-6	.277	643	178	35	6	18	76	29	89	.309	.434
Night	3.53	9	3	0	21	20	127.1	136	11	23	61	Inning 7+	.226	84	19	1	1	2	7	2	7	.241	.333
Grass	4.16	4	3	0	11	10	62.2	66	9	13	25	None on	.263	456	120	22	6	11	11	14	59	.285	.410
Turf	3.59	7	5	0	21	19	125.1	131	11	18	71	Runners on	.284	271	77	14	1	9	72	17	37	.328	.443
April	1.66	3	0	0	3	3	21.2	15	1	1	11	Scoring Posn	.274	164	45	8	1	5	61	17	22	.344	.427
May	3.28	1	0	0	5	3	24.2	20	3	4	15	Close & Late	.229	48	11	1	1	1	4	1	6	.240	.354
June	4.45	2	2	0	5	5	28.1	33	1	5	12	None on/out	.256	195	50	9	3	2	2	6	24	.279	.364
July	3.96	2	1	0	6	6	36.1	44	7	3	21	vs. 1st Batr (relief)	.000	3	0	0	0	0	0	0	1	.000	.000
August	4.10	2	2	0	6	6	41.2	46	3	6	15	First Inning Pitched	.312	125	39	6	0	2	15	9	14	.360	.408
September/October	4.33	1	3	0	7	6	35.1	39	5	12	22	First 75 Pitches	.274	606	166	30	5	17	66	27	86	.307	.424
Starter	3.68	11	7	0	29	29	181.0	191	19	29	90	Pitch 76-90	.213	75	16	4	0	2	10	3	8	.238	.347
Reliever	6.43	0	1	0	3	0	7.0	6	1	2	6	Pitch 91-105	.375	32	12	2	2	0	5	1	1	.382	.563
0-3 Days Rest	3.86	0	0	0	1	1	7.0	6	1	1	6	Pitch 106+	.214	14	3	0	0	1	2	0	1	.214	.429
4 Days Rest	3.94	5	6	0	19	19	114.1	125	13	21	55	First Pitch	.343	140	48	7	1	6	24	2	0	.354	.536

	ERA	W	L	Sv	G	GS	IP	H	HR	BB	SO		Avg	AB	H	2B	3B	HR	RBI	BB	SO	OBP	SLG
1993 Season																							
5+ Days Rest	3.17	6	1	0	9	9	59.2	60	5	7	29	Ahead in Count	.212	292	62	10	3	4	20	0	87	.214	.308
Pre-All Star	3.47	6	3	0	15	13	85.2	83	7	11	44	Behind in Count	.304	171	52	11	1	8	21	12	0	.348	.520
Post-All Star	4.05	5	5	0	17	16	102.1	114	13	20	52	Two Strikes	.201	283	57	10	3	4	23	17	96	.245	.300

Andy Ashby — Padres

Age 26 – Pitches Right (groundball pitcher)

	ERA	W	L	Sv	G	GS	IP	BB	SO	Avg	H	2B	3B	HR	RBI	OBP	SLG	CG	ShO	Sup	QS	#P/S	SB	CS	GB	FB	G/F
1993 Season	6.80	3	10	1	32	21	123.0	56	77	.333	168	29	3	19	90	.399	.516	0	0	5.49	7	89	11	1	232	102	2.27
Career (1991-1993)	6.77	5	18	1	50	37	202.0	96	127	.310	251	45	7	30	141	.384	.494	0	0	4.90	10	83	15	4	348	177	1.97

	ERA	W	L	Sv	G	GS	IP	H	HR	BB	SO		Avg	AB	H	2B	3B	HR	RBI	BB	SO	OBP	SLG
1993 Season																							
Home	6.00	2	3	0	16	11	66.0	80	11	30	44	vs. Left	.307	274	84	7	2	7	41	31	35	.380	.423
Away	7.74	1	7	1	16	10	57.0	88	8	26	33	vs. Right	.365	230	84	22	1	12	49	25	42	.422	.626
Starter	6.53	3	10	0	21	21	111.2	149	17	48	72	Scoring Posn	.365	159	58	14	2	4	73	25	25	.440	.553
Reliever	9.53	0	0	1	11	0	11.1	19	2	8	5	Close & Late	.208	24	5	0	0	0	0	2	3	.269	.208
0-3 Days Rest	0.00	0	0	0	0	0	0.0	0	0	0	0	None on/out	.395	119	47	10	1	8	8	15	12	.471	.697
4 Days Rest	7.68	1	7	0	13	13	65.2	101	10	28	49	First Pitch	.342	76	26	3	0	1	13	3	0	.363	.421
5+ Days Rest	4.89	2	3	0	8	8	46.0	48	7	20	23	Ahead in Count	.256	207	53	11	0	6	27	0	60	.263	.396
Pre-All Star	8.50	0	4	1	20	9	54.0	89	5	32	33	Behind in Count	.477	130	62	9	1	11	32	35	0	.588	.815
Post-All Star	5.48	3	6	0	12	12	69.0	79	14	24	44	Two Strikes	.218	206	45	10	1	5	25	18	77	.291	.350

Billy Ashley — Dodgers

Age 23 – Bats Right

	Avg	G	AB	R	H	2B	3B	HR	RBI	BB	SO	HBP	GDP	SB	CS	OBP	SLG	IBB	SH	SF	#Pit	#P/PA	GB	FB	G/F
1993 Season	.243	14	37	0	9	0	0	0	0	2	11	0	0	0	0	.282	.243	0	0	0	128	3.28	12	8	1.50
Career (1992-1993)	.227	43	132	6	30	5	0	2	6	7	45	0	2	0	0	.266	.311	0	0	0	515	3.71	36	33	1.09

	Avg	AB	H	2B	3B	HR	RBI	BB	SO	OBP	SLG		Avg	AB	H	2B	3B	HR	RBI	BB	SO	OBP	SLG
1993 Season																							
vs. Left	.200	10	2	0	0	0	0	1	4	.273	.200	Scoring Posn	.000	8	0	0	0	0	0	1	3	.111	.000
vs. Right	.259	27	7	0	0	0	0	1	7	.286	.259	Close & Late	.250	4	1	0	0	0	0	1	2	.400	.250

Paul Assenmacher — Yankees

Age 33 – Pitches Left

	ERA	W	L	Sv	G	GS	IP	BB	SO	Avg	H	2B	3B	HR	RBI	OBP	SLG	GF	IR	IRS	Hld	SvOp	SB	CS	GB	FB	G/F
1993 Season	3.38	4	3	0	72	0	56.0	22	45	.257	54	9	0	5	26	.330	.371	21	63	15	17	5	4	1	81	51	1.59
Last Five Years	3.43	25	21	33	354	1	406.1	143	403	.246	375	63	7	34	191	.312	.364	96	281	82	74	65	32	16	483	379	1.27

	ERA	W	L	Sv	G	GS	IP	H	HR	BB	SO		Avg	AB	H	2B	3B	HR	RBI	BB	SO	OBP	SLG
1993 Season																							
Home	3.34	2	1	0	43	0	32.1	29	2	11	29	vs. Left	.239	92	22	1	0	4	14	9	25	.314	.380
Away	3.42	2	2	0	29	0	23.2	25	3	11	16	vs. Right	.271	118	32	8	0	1	12	13	20	.344	.364
Day	2.65	2	0	0	40	0	34.0	31	3	8	28	Inning 1-6	.000	2	0	0	0	0	0	0	0	.000	.000
Night	4.50	2	3	0	32	0	22.0	23	2	14	17	Inning 7+	.260	208	54	9	0	5	26	22	45	.333	.375
Grass	3.40	4	3	0	59	0	45.0	42	3	17	39	None on	.239	113	27	6	0	2	2	10	26	.306	.345
Turf	3.27	0	0	0	13	0	11.0	12	2	5	6	Runners on	.278	97	27	3	0	3	24	12	19	.358	.402
April	3.24	1	0	0	9	0	8.1	11	2	1	6	Scoring Posn	.328	58	19	2	0	1	20	11	10	.435	.414
May	6.30	0	1	0	14	0	10.0	11	1	5	8	Close & Late	.287	94	27	2	0	2	14	10	21	.356	.372
June	2.25	1	0	0	14	0	12.0	13	0	6	10	None on/out	.235	51	12	3	0	1	1	3	13	.278	.353
July	2.16	0	0	0	10	0	8.1	10	2	1	10	vs. 1st Batr (relief)	.254	67	17	3	0	1	12	4	14	.296	.343
August	1.13	2	0	0	12	0	8.0	0	0	1	7	First Inning Pitched	.267	180	48	8	0	4	24	18	37	.337	.378
September/October	4.82	0	2	0	13	0	9.1	9	0	8	4	First 15 Pitches	.270	174	47	8	0	4	23	16	36	.335	.385
Starter	0.00	0	0	0	0	0	0.0	0	0	0	0	Pitch 16-30	.206	34	7	1	0	1	3	6	8	.325	.324
Reliever	3.38	4	3	0	72	0	56.0	54	5	22	45	Pitch 31-45	.000	2	0	0	0	0	0	0	1	.000	.000
0 Days rest	4.11	1	1	0	24	0	15.1	20	2	7	13	Pitch 46+	.000	0	0	0	0	0	0	0	0	.000	.000
1 or 2 Days rest	3.86	3	2	0	28	0	21.0	18	2	12	23	First Pitch	.265	34	9	2	0	0	3	3	0	.324	.324
3+ Days rest	2.29	0	0	0	20	0	19.2	16	1	3	9	Ahead in Count	.196	102	20	2	0	1	7	0	36	.196	.245
Pre-All Star	3.60	2	1	0	41	0	35.0	39	4	13	30	Behind in Count	.462	39	18	4	0	3	14	13	0	.596	.795
Post-All Star	3.00	2	2	0	31	0	21.0	15	1	9	15	Two Strikes	.190	100	19	3	0	1	8	6	45	.236	.250
Last Five Years																							
Home	3.26	17	10	16	198	0	226.1	202	17	67	227	vs. Left	.218	523	114	16	2	9	67	41	162	.280	.308
Away	3.65	8	11	17	156	1	180.0	173	17	76	176	vs. Right	.261	1000	261	47	5	25	124	102	241	.329	.393
Day	3.19	16	5	19	181	0	220.1	205	19	73	233	Inning 1-6	.216	134	29	5	1	3	27	16	44	.298	.336
Night	3.73	9	16	14	173	1	186.0	170	15	70	170	Inning 7+	.249	1389	346	58	6	31	164	127	359	.314	.366
Grass	3.24	21	16	25	267	0	311.1	276	25	97	319	None on	.255	805	205	35	3	20	20	52	203	.301	.380
Turf	4.07	4	5	8	87	1	95.0	99	9	46	84	Runners on	.237	718	170	28	4	14	171	91	200	.324	.345
April	1.68	2	2	3	47	0	59.0	35	5	16	60	Scoring Posn	.242	451	109	20	1	8	152	77	128	.352	.344
May	3.53	3	4	4	63	0	71.1	68	6	22	63	Close & Late	.248	847	210	39	2	17	109	81	233	.315	.359
June	5.37	3	3	7	70	1	63.2	77	4	39	65	None on/out	.243	350	85	17	1	10	10	22	92	.288	.383
July	3.52	4	3	5	56	0	61.1	65	6	15	70	vs. 1st Batr (relief)	.196	271	53	7	1	11	44	24	79	.265	.351
August	1.89	8	1	6	53	0	71.1	47	8	16	74	First Inning Pitched	.251	878	220	40	4	22	131	100	219	.327	.380
September/October	4.41	5	8	8	65	0	79.2	83	5	35	71	First 15 Pitches	.254	957	243	42	4	24	133	94	236	.321	.381
Starter	36.00	0	0	0	1	1	1.0	4	1	2	1	Pitch 16-30	.240	437	105	19	3	6	44	37	125	.300	.339
Reliever	3.35	25	21	33	353	0	405.1	371	33	141	402	Pitch 31-45	.200	110	22	2	0	3	11	9	36	.279	.300
0 Days rest	3.79	10	10	11	113	0	116.1	112	9	48	121	Pitch 46+	.263	19	5	0	0	1	3	3	6	.364	.421

Last Five Years

	ERA	W	L	Sv	G	GS	IP	H	HR	BB	SO
1 or 2 Days rest	3.47	11	9	12	149	0	171.1	156	15	62	171
3+ Days rest	2.75	4	2	10	91	0	117.2	103	9	31	110
Pre-All Star	3.64	10	11	14	204	1	217.2	206	18	84	214
Post-All Star	3.20	15	10	19	150	0	188.2	169	16	59	189

	Avg	AB	H	2B	3B	HR	RBI	BB	SO	OBP	SLG
First Pitch	.333	222	74	16	2	10	37	25	0	.402	.559
Ahead in Count	.179	801	143	25	4	8	69	0	353	.180	.250
Behind in Count	.365	260	95	12	1	11	60	74	0	.504	.546
Two Strikes	.157	792	124	24	3	6	58	43	403	.201	.217

Pitcher vs. Batter (career)

Pitches Best Vs.	Avg	AB	H	2B	3B	HR	RBI	BB	SO	OBP	SLG
Glenn Wilson	.000	11	0	0	0	0	0	0	4	.000	.000
Milt Thompson	.053	19	1	1	0	0	1	1	2	.100	.105
Paul O'Neill	.071	14	1	0	0	0	1	1	7	.133	.071
Keith Miller	.083	12	1	0	0	0	0	1	8	.154	.083
Jeff King	.091	11	1	0	0	0	1	0	2	.091	.091

Pitches Worst Vs.	Avg	AB	H	2B	3B	HR	RBI	BB	SO	OBP	SLG
Brett Butler	.692	13	9	1	0	0	4	1	2	.714	.769
Lenny Dykstra	.571	14	8	2	0	1	4	0	3	.533	.929
Kevin McReynolds	.500	20	10	4	0	1	6	2	3	.545	.850
Jay Bell	.455	11	5	1	1	1	2	1	2	.500	1.000
Barry Larkin	.400	10	4	1	0	1	2	3	2	.538	.800

Pedro Astacio — Dodgers

Age 24 – Pitches Right (groundball pitcher)

	ERA	W	L	Sv	G	GS	IP	BB	SO	Avg	H	2B	3B	HR	RBI	OBP	SLG	CG	ShO	Sup	QS	#P/S	SB	CS	GB	FB	G/F
1993 Season	3.57	14	9	0	31	31	186.1	68	122	.239	165	32	2	14	63	.309	.353	3	2	4.73	16	92	19	12	278	195	1.43
Career (1992-1993)	3.09	19	14	0	42	42	268.1	88	165	.244	245	40	4	15	81	.307	.337	7	6	4.19	26	95	24	15	414	272	1.52

1993 Season

	ERA	W	L	Sv	G	GS	IP	H	HR	BB	SO
Home	3.34	6	3	0	16	16	97.0	94	4	38	62
Away	3.83	8	6	0	15	15	89.1	71	10	30	60
Day	3.38	4	2	0	8	8	45.1	39	5	17	27
Night	3.64	10	7	0	23	23	141.0	126	9	51	95
Grass	3.81	8	7	0	22	22	132.1	127	11	49	83
Turf	3.00	6	2	0	9	9	54.0	38	3	19	39
April	3.00	1	2	0	4	4	24.0	21	1	11	14
May	4.97	2	1	0	5	5	25.1	32	2	7	15
June	4.17	3	1	0	6	6	36.2	34	3	9	15
July	6.92	1	2	0	5	5	26.0	28	5	16	17
August	2.67	3	1	0	5	5	27.0	20	2	13	20
September/October	1.33	4	2	0	6	6	47.1	30	1	12	41
Starter	3.57	14	9	0	31	31	186.1	165	14	68	122
Reliever	0.00	0	0	0	0	0	0.0	0	0	0	0
0-3 Days Rest	27.00	0	1	0	1	1	2.0	4	2	4	2
4 Days Rest	3.69	2	4	0	9	9	53.2	51	3	20	34
5+ Days Rest	3.17	12	4	0	21	21	130.2	110	9	44	86
Pre-All Star	4.69	7	5	0	17	17	94.0	95	9	36	50
Post-All Star	2.44	7	4	0	14	14	92.1	70	5	32	72

	Avg	AB	H	2B	3B	HR	RBI	BB	SO	OBP	SLG
vs. Left	.240	391	94	18	0	9	40	36	67	.303	.355
vs. Right	.238	298	71	14	2	5	23	32	55	.317	.349
Inning 1-6	.237	617	146	27	1	12	59	62	112	.307	.342
Inning 7+	.264	72	19	5	1	2	4	6	10	.325	.444
None on	.249	429	107	25	2	7	7	36	71	.312	.366
Runners on	.223	260	58	7	0	7	56	32	51	.305	.331
Scoring Posn	.239	138	33	3	0	4	49	19	33	.319	.348
Close & Late	.294	34	10	2	0	1	3	3	5	.342	.441
None on/out	.253	186	47	15	1	4	4	16	30	.319	.409
vs. 1st Batr (relief)	.000	0	0	0	0	0	0	0	0	.000	.000
First Inning Pitched	.237	114	27	7	0	6	20	16	14	.326	.456
First 75 Pitches	.247	542	134	26	1	12	57	50	93	.311	.365
Pitch 76-90	.250	68	17	2	1	1	2	8	13	.346	.353
Pitch 91-105	.149	47	7	2	0	1	3	4	10	.212	.255
Pitch 106+	.219	32	7	2	0	0	1	6	6	.342	.281
First Pitch	.324	102	33	3	0	6	20	2	0	.333	.529
Ahead in Count	.183	241	44	10	1	5	15	0	98	.189	.295
Behind in Count	.256	180	46	9	0	2	20	33	0	.370	.339
Two Strikes	.140	265	37	6	1	1	9	33	122	.236	.181

Rich Aude — Pirates

Age 22 – Bats Right

	Avg	G	AB	R	H	2B	3B	HR	RBI	BB	SO	HBP	GDP	SB	CS	OBP	SLG	IBB	SH	SF	#Pit	#P/PA	GB	FB	G/F
1993 Season	.115	13	26	1	3	1	0	0	4	1	7	0	0	0	0	.148	.154	0	0	0	99	3.67	11	5	2.20

1993 Season

	Avg	AB	H	2B	3B	HR	RBI	BB	SO	OBP	SLG
vs. Left	.214	14	3	1	0	0	4	0	3	.214	.286
vs. Right	.000	12	0	0	0	0	0	1	4	.077	.000
Scoring Posn	.250	12	3	1	0	0	4	1	2	.308	.333
Close & Late	.200	5	1	0	0	0	2	0	1	.200	.200

Brad Ausmus — Padres

Age 25 – Bats Right (groundball hitter)

	Avg	G	AB	R	H	2B	3B	HR	RBI	BB	SO	HBP	GDP	SB	CS	OBP	SLG	IBB	SH	SF	#Pit	#P/PA	GB	FB	G/F
1993 Season	.256	49	160	18	41	8	1	5	12	6	28	0	2	2	0	.283	.413	0	0	0	596	3.57	55	36	1.53

1993 Season

	Avg	AB	H	2B	3B	HR	RBI	BB	SO	OBP	SLG
vs. Left	.295	44	13	3	1	1	4	3	7	.340	.477
vs. Right	.241	116	28	5	0	4	8	3	21	.261	.388
Home	.325	80	26	6	1	4	9	2	15	.341	.575
Away	.188	80	15	2	0	1	3	4	13	.226	.250
First Pitch	.458	24	11	4	0	0	2	0	0	.458	.625
Ahead in Count	.321	28	9	1	0	3	5	4	0	.406	.679
Behind in Count	.183	82	15	2	1	2	4	0	25	.183	.305
Two Strikes	.145	76	11	2	1	2	4	2	28	.167	.276
Scoring Posn	.219	32	7	3	0	1	7	1	7	.242	.406
Close & Late	.190	21	4	1	0	0	1	1	7	.227	.238
None on/out	.304	46	14	3	0	1	1	1	8	.319	.435
Batting #7	.250	4	1	1	0	0	0	0	1	.250	.500
Batting #8	.252	155	39	7	1	5	11	6	27	.280	.406
Other	1.000	1	1	0	0	0	1	0	0	1.000	1.000
Pre-All Star	.000	0	0	0	0	0	0	0	0	.000	.000
Post-All Star	.256	160	41	8	1	5	12	6	28	.283	.413

James Austin — Brewers

Age 30 – Pitches Right (flyball pitcher)

	ERA	W	L	Sv	G	GS	IP	BB	SO	Avg	H	2B	3B	HR	RBI	OBP	SLG	GF	IR	IRS	Hld	SvOp	SB	CS	GB	FB	G/F
1993 Season	3.82	1	2	0	31	0	33.0	13	15	.230	28	4	0	3	13	.309	.336	8	26	6	4	2	0	1	34	46	0.74
Career (1991-1993)	3.06	6	4	0	83	0	100.0	56	48	.211	74	15	0	6	36	.329	.306	21	77	20	13	3	2	5	91	143	0.64

1993 Season

	ERA	W	L	Sv	G	GS	IP	H	HR	BB	SO
Home	2.53	1	1	0	18	0	21.1	13	3	6	10
Away	6.17	0	1	0	13	0	11.2	15	0	7	5
Starter	0.00	0	0	0	0	0	0.0	0	0	0	0
Reliever	3.82	1	2	0	31	0	33.0	28	3	13	15

	Avg	AB	H	2B	3B	HR	RBI	BB	SO	OBP	SLG
vs. Left	.297	37	11	2	0	1	4	1	3	.316	.432
vs. Right	.200	85	17	2	0	2	9	12	12	.306	.294
Scoring Posn	.167	36	6	1	0	0	9	6	4	.302	.194
Close & Late	.258	62	16	3	0	1	8	11	5	.378	.355

1993 Season

	ERA	W	L	Sv	G	GS	IP	H	HR	BB	SO
0 Days rest	0.87	0	0	0	8	0	10.1	6	1	2	6
1 or 2 Days rest	3.55	1	1	0	11	0	12.2	10	1	5	2
3+ Days rest	7.20	0	1	0	12	0	10.0	12	1	6	7
Pre-All Star	3.69	1	2	0	29	0	31.2	24	3	12	15
Post-All Star	6.75	0	0	0	2	0	1.1	4	0	1	0

	Avg	AB	H	2B	3B	HR	RBI	BB	SO	OBP	SLG
None on/out	.286	28	8	2	0	0	0	2	4	.333	.357
First Pitch	.474	19	9	0	0	0	1	1	0	.524	.474
Ahead in Count	.151	53	8	2	0	0	5	0	13	.151	.189
Behind in Count	.200	30	6	1	0	1	3	6	0	.333	.333
Two Strikes	.133	60	8	3	0	0	5	6	15	.212	.183

Steve Avery — Braves

Age 24 – Pitches Left

	ERA	W	L	Sv	G	GS	IP	BB	SO	Avg	H	2B	3B	HR	RBI	OBP	SLG	CG	ShO	Sup	QS	#P/S	SB	CS	GB	FB	G/F
1993 Season	2.94	18	6	0	35	35	223.1	43	125	.261	216	35	3	14	74	.295	.362	3	1	5.04	25	89	32	14	318	219	1.45
Career (1990-1993)	3.49	50	36	0	126	125	766.1	224	466	.256	742	124	16	56	300	.309	.368	9	5	4.59	71	92	115	47	1110	808	1.37

1993 Season

	ERA	W	L	Sv	G	GS	IP	H	HR	BB	SO
Home	2.85	9	2	0	18	18	116.2	120	7	17	59
Away	3.04	9	4	0	17	17	106.2	96	7	26	66
Day	2.00	7	2	0	11	11	76.2	67	4	13	48
Night	3.44	11	4	0	24	24	146.2	149	10	30	77
Grass	2.72	14	4	0	28	28	185.1	180	11	29	96
Turf	4.03	4	2	0	7	7	38.0	36	3	14	29
April	2.75	1	2	0	5	5	36.0	34	2	6	18
May	3.53	4	0	0	6	6	35.2	37	0	9	22
June	2.16	4	0	0	6	6	41.2	38	1	4	23
July	4.26	2	1	0	5	5	25.1	37	3	6	14
August	2.22	4	1	0	6	6	44.2	34	3	9	19
September/October	3.38	3	2	0	7	7	40.0	36	5	9	29
Starter	2.94	18	6	0	35	35	223.1	216	14	43	125
Reliever	0.00	0	0	0	0	0	0.0	0	0	0	0
0-3 Days Rest	9.39	1	1	0	2	2	7.2	12	2	4	8
4 Days Rest	2.93	13	4	0	26	26	165.2	151	11	32	89
5+ Days Rest	1.98	4	1	0	7	7	50.0	53	1	7	28
Pre-All Star	3.46	9	3	0	19	19	117.0	122	5	21	66
Post-All Star	2.37	9	3	0	16	16	106.1	94	9	22	59

	Avg	AB	H	2B	3B	HR	RBI	BB	SO	OBP	SLG
vs. Left	.231	143	33	6	0	2	12	11	32	.286	.315
vs. Right	.268	684	183	29	3	12	62	32	93	.297	.371
Inning 1-6	.265	703	186	31	3	12	67	38	104	.299	.368
Inning 7+	.242	124	30	4	0	2	7	5	21	.271	.323
None on	.254	531	135	24	3	8	8	25	86	.288	.356
Runners on	.274	296	81	11	0	6	66	18	39	.307	.372
Scoring Posn	.245	163	40	5	0	3	57	13	24	.288	.331
Close & Late	.263	95	25	4	0	2	6	5	14	.300	.368
None on/out	.258	225	58	14	2	5	5	10	33	.289	.404
vs. 1st Batr (relief)	.000	0	0	0	0	0	0	0	0	.000	.000
First Inning Pitched	.277	130	36	5	0	2	16	7	13	.314	.362
First 75 Pitches	.264	670	177	28	2	13	62	28	95	.292	.370
Pitch 76-90	.267	90	24	5	1	1	8	11	17	.337	.378
Pitch 91-105	.204	54	11	2	0	0	3	3	8	.246	.241
Pitch 106+	.308	13	4	0	0	0	1	1	5	.357	.308
First Pitch	.318	132	42	2	1	1	9	2	0	.326	.371
Ahead in Count	.194	382	74	18	1	5	30	0	112	.192	.285
Behind in Count	.316	177	56	8	1	8	22	29	0	.409	.508
Two Strikes	.189	370	70	17	1	1	28	12	125	.212	.249

Career (1990-1993)

	ERA	W	L	Sv	G	GS	IP	H	HR	BB	SO
Home	3.21	27	15	0	63	63	389.1	392	25	106	229
Away	3.77	23	21	0	63	62	377.0	350	31	118	237
Day	3.52	16	10	0	34	33	204.1	198	19	52	130
Night	3.48	34	26	0	92	92	562.0	544	37	172	336
Grass	3.11	40	24	0	94	93	587.1	559	37	160	336
Turf	4.73	10	12	0	32	32	179.0	183	19	64	130
April	2.88	4	5	0	13	13	84.1	73	5	24	43
May	3.37	10	4	0	19	19	117.2	116	6	46	74
June	3.28	9	5	0	20	20	123.1	126	7	33	70
July	3.51	8	6	0	24	24	146.1	135	10	48	78
August	3.93	11	9	0	24	24	146.2	158	11	42	98
September/October	3.65	8	7	0	26	25	148.0	134	17	31	103
Starter	3.46	50	35	0	125	125	764.1	737	56	224	466
Reliever	13.50	0	1	0	1	0	2.0	5	0	0	0
0-3 Days Rest	5.49	2	3	0	8	8	39.1	39	6	19	19
4 Days Rest	3.27	38	22	0	89	89	560.2	519	43	156	336
5+ Days Rest	3.61	10	10	0	28	28	164.1	179	7	49	111
Pre-All Star	3.36	25	18	0	60	60	369.2	361	21	121	217
Post-All Star	3.61	25	18	0	66	65	396.2	381	35	103	249

	Avg	AB	H	2B	3B	HR	RBI	BB	SO	OBP	SLG
vs. Left	.228	523	119	16	3	8	52	48	122	.291	.315
vs. Right	.263	2371	623	108	13	48	248	176	344	.312	.380
Inning 1-6	.254	2487	631	108	15	49	259	196	411	.307	.368
Inning 7+	.273	407	111	16	1	7	41	28	55	.320	.369
None on	.242	1768	428	80	10	29	29	131	278	.296	.348
Runners on	.279	1126	314	44	6	27	271	93	188	.328	.401
Scoring Posn	.255	662	169	26	1	12	229	68	126	.314	.352
Close & Late	.260	258	67	9	1	3	26	20	34	.312	.337
None on/out	.263	768	202	42	6	17	17	56	117	.314	.400
vs. 1st Batr (relief)	.000	1	0	0	0	0	0	0	0	.000	.000
First Inning Pitched	.274	478	131	19	3	11	61	44	76	.333	.395
First 75 Pitches	.251	2237	561	97	15	45	226	160	377	.300	.368
Pitch 76-90	.274	350	96	13	1	7	35	34	50	.336	.377
Pitch 91-105	.282	213	60	12	0	1	26	21	24	.343	.352
Pitch 106+	.266	94	25	2	0	3	13	9	15	.333	.383
First Pitch	.314	465	146	20	3	11	60	6	0	.321	.441
Ahead in Count	.202	1337	270	52	6	16	103	0	407	.202	.286
Behind in Count	.334	611	204	36	4	22	98	127	0	.444	.514
Two Strikes	.182	1311	239	43	5	10	87	91	466	.235	.246

Pitcher vs. Batter (career)

Pitches Best Vs.	Avg	AB	H	2B	3B	HR	RBI	BB	SO	OBP	SLG
Gerald Perry	.000	11	0	0	0	0	0	2	1	.154	.000
Dave Gallagher	.000	10	0	0	0	0	0	1	1	.091	.000
Mike Benjamin	.000	9	0	0	0	0	0	2	1	.182	.000
Jose Offerman	.059	17	1	0	0	0	0	0	1	.059	.059
Scott Servais	.083	12	1	0	0	0	0	0	0	.083	.083

Pitches Worst Vs.	Avg	AB	H	2B	3B	HR	RBI	BB	SO	OBP	SLG
Royce Clayton	.533	15	8	2	1	0	2	0	4	.500	.800
Gary Sheffield	.500	14	7	0	0	1	3	0	0	.500	.714
Eric Yelding	.455	11	5	3	0	0	2	3	1	.571	.727
Lenny Dykstra	.444	9	4	2	0	1	3	4	1	.615	1.000
Luis Alicea	.400	10	4	1	1	0	5	1	0	.455	.700

Bobby Ayala — Reds

Age 24 – Pitches Right (groundball pitcher)

	ERA	W	L	Sv	G	GS	IP	BB	SO	Avg	H	2B	3B	HR	RBI	OBP	SLG	GF	IR	IRS	Hld	SvOp	SB	CS	GB	FB	G/F
1993 Season	5.60	7	10	3	43	9	98.0	45	65	.274	106	15	2	16	66	.358	.447	8	23	6	6	5	9	1	155	94	1.65
Career (1992-1993)	5.31	9	11	3	48	14	127.0	58	88	.279	139	25	2	17	78	.362	.440	8	23	6	6	5	11	4	208	112	1.86

1993 Season

	ERA	W	L	Sv	G	GS	IP	H	HR	BB	SO
Home	5.02	4	7	1	23	5	57.1	61	8	21	38
Away	6.42	3	3	2	20	4	40.2	45	8	24	27
Starter	8.41	2	6	0	9	9	40.2	60	9	23	29
Reliever	3.61	5	4	3	34	0	57.1	46	7	22	36
0 Days rest	3.60	0	1	2	4	0	5.0	4	0	3	1
1 or 2 Days rest	3.79	4	2	1	20	0	35.2	30	4	14	28

	Avg	AB	H	2B	3B	HR	RBI	BB	SO	OBP	SLG
vs. Left	.270	185	50	8	1	6	21	26	36	.367	.422
vs. Right	.277	202	56	7	1	10	45	19	29	.350	.470
Scoring Posn	.244	119	29	5	0	6	51	22	19	.357	.437
Close & Late	.207	87	18	1	0	3	8	11	17	.297	.322
None on/out	.269	93	25	2	0	3	3	7	19	.333	.387
First Pitch	.382	76	29	3	0	6	21	3	0	.420	.658

1993 Season	ERA	W	L	Sv	G	GS	IP	H	HR	BB	SO		Avg	AB	H	2B	3B	HR	RBI	BB	SO	OBP	SLG
3+ Days rest	3.24	1	1	0	10	0	16.2	12	3	5	7	Ahead in Count	.233	150	35	4	2	5	27	0	54	.247	.387
Pre-All Star	3.89	3	4	3	23	0	39.1	32	4	18	23	Behind in Count	.303	89	27	6	0	3	10	19	0	.427	.472
Post-All Star	6.75	4	6	0	20	9	58.2	74	12	27	42	Two Strikes	.187	150	28	3	1	6	27	23	65	.303	.340

Bob Ayrault — Dodgers

Age 28 – Pitches Right (flyball pitcher)

	ERA	W	L	Sv	G	GS	IP	BB	SO	Avg	H	2B	3B	HR	RBI	OBP	SLG	GF	IR	IRS	Hld	SvOp	SB	CS	GB	FB	G/F
1993 Season	5.40	3	1	0	24	0	30.0	16	15	.303	36	7	2	2	26	.384	.445	9	28	11	1	2	4	0	26	53	0.49
Career (1992-1993)	4.05	5	3	0	54	0	73.1	33	42	.250	68	16	4	2	46	.330	.360	16	44	19	1	2	7	0	71	103	0.69

1993 Season	ERA	W	L	Sv	G	GS	IP	H	HR	BB	SO		Avg	AB	H	2B	3B	HR	RBI	BB	SO	OBP	SLG
Home	2.81	2	0	0	14	0	16.0	11	0	7	9	vs. Left	.317	41	13	3	0	0	4	8	2	.420	.390
Away	8.36	1	1	0	10	0	14.0	25	2	9	6	vs. Right	.295	78	23	4	2	2	22	8	13	.364	.474

Wally Backman — Mariners

Age 34 – Bats Left (groundball hitter)

	Avg	G	AB	R	H	2B	3B	HR	RBI	BB	SO	HBP	GDP	SB	CS	OBP	SLG	IBB	SH	SF	#Pit	#P/PA	GB	FB	G/F
1993 Season	.138	10	29	2	4	0	0	0	0	1	8	0	0	0	0	.167	.138	0	1	0	129	4.16	13	5	2.60
Last Five Years	.255	337	876	123	223	43	5	3	75	111	145	2	14	11	6	.337	.325	2	8	7	3801	3.79	408	163	2.50

1993 Season	Avg	AB	H	2B	3B	HR	RBI	BB	SO	OBP	SLG		Avg	AB	H	2B	3B	HR	RBI	BB	SO	OBP	SLG
vs. Left	.000	0	0	0	0	0	0	0	0	.000	.000	Scoring Posn	.000	9	0	0	0	0	0	0	4	.000	.000
vs. Right	.138	29	4	0	0	0	0	1	8	.167	.138	Close & Late	.200	5	1	0	0	0	0	1	0	.333	.200

Last Five Years	Avg	AB	H	2B	3B	HR	RBI	BB	SO	OBP	SLG		Avg	AB	H	2B	3B	HR	RBI	BB	SO	OBP	SLG
vs. Left	.212	113	24	4	1	0	15	15	19	.308	.265	Scoring Posn	.279	183	51	11	2	0	67	28	35	.362	.361
vs. Right	.261	763	199	39	4	3	60	96	126	.342	.334	Close & Late	.226	146	33	9	0	0	17	25	31	.335	.288
Groundball	.274	270	74	9	3	2	32	31	37	.351	.352	None on/out	.248	310	77	14	0	3	3	37	47	.329	.323
Flyball	.218	156	34	6	0	0	10	29	37	.337	.256	Batting #1	.280	475	133	26	3	3	39	55	71	.353	.366
Home	.270	419	113	25	3	0	39	57	67	.356	.344	Batting #2	.257	202	52	9	1	0	15	27	34	.346	.312
Away	.241	457	110	18	2	3	36	54	78	.320	.309	Other	.191	199	38	8	1	0	21	29	40	.293	.241
Day	.262	260	68	9	3	1	17	27	40	.330	.331	April	.297	185	55	6	2	0	18	17	29	.358	.351
Night	.252	616	155	34	2	2	58	84	105	.340	.323	May	.255	153	39	8	0	1	16	17	29	.327	.327
Grass	.264	277	73	13	1	3	28	31	49	.334	.350	June	.225	209	47	12	1	2	20	22	31	.297	.321
Turf	.250	599	150	30	4	0	47	80	96	.339	.314	July	.260	100	26	5	0	0	5	20	25	.377	.310
First Pitch	.398	88	35	8	1	1	14	1	0	.404	.545	August	.200	100	20	6	0	0	5	20	15	.339	.260
Ahead in Count	.297	249	74	12	2	0	20	66	0	.439	.361	September/October	.279	129	36	6	2	0	11	15	16	.349	.357
Behind in Count	.191	376	72	15	2	1	28	0	122	.194	.250	Pre-All Star	.259	607	157	29	3	3	57	65	105	.329	.331
Two Strikes	.187	396	74	17	2	1	33	43	145	.267	.247	Post-All Star	.245	269	66	14	2	0	18	46	40	.354	.312

Batter vs. Pitcher (since 1984)																							
Hits Best Against	Avg	AB	H	2B	3B	HR	RBI	BB	SO	OBP	SLG	**Hits Worst Against**	Avg	AB	H	2B	3B	HR	RBI	BB	SO	OBP	SLG
Doug Drabek	.500	18	9	0	0	0	0	1	4	.526	.500	Melido Perez	.000	9	0	0	0	0	0	3	4	.250	.000
Larry Andersen	.500	16	8	1	0	0	2	1	1	.529	.563	Fernando Valenzuela	.071	14	1	0	0	0	0	1	3	.133	.071
Shawn Boskie	.417	12	5	2	0	0	0	0	2	.417	.583	Craig Lefferts	.083	12	1	0	0	0	0	1	4	.154	.083
Ramon Martinez	.357	14	5	3	0	0	4	3	2	.444	.571	Mark Portugal	.100	10	1	0	0	0	0	1	0	.182	.100
Jack Armstrong	.357	14	5	0	0	0	0	7	0	.571	.357	Tim Belcher	.154	13	2	0	0	0	1	0	4	.143	.154

Carlos Baerga — Indians

Age 25 – Bats Both (groundball hitter)

	Avg	G	AB	R	H	2B	3B	HR	RBI	BB	SO	HBP	GDP	SB	CS	OBP	SLG	IBB	SH	SF	#Pit	#P/PA	GB	FB	G/F
1993 Season	.321	154	624	105	200	28	6	21	114	34	68	6	17	15	4	.355	.486	7	3	13	2337	3.44	276	157	1.76
Career (1990-1993)	.301	581	2186	323	657	105	11	59	335	133	275	29	48	28	10	.344	.440	24	10	30	8221	3.44	968	534	1.81

1993 Season	Avg	AB	H	2B	3B	HR	RBI	BB	SO	OBP	SLG		Avg	AB	H	2B	3B	HR	RBI	BB	SO	OBP	SLG
vs. Left	.315	219	69	5	3	6	33	7	25	.345	.447	Scoring Posn	.341	167	57	4	3	7	92	18	26	.385	.527
vs. Right	.323	405	131	23	3	15	81	27	43	.360	.506	Close & Late	.292	96	28	2	0	3	13	9	9	.358	.406
Groundball	.333	90	30	6	0	2	22	6	7	.360	.467	None on/out	.325	123	40	5	2	5	5	5	8	.357	.520
Flyball	.244	123	30	9	0	1	10	3	19	.271	.341	Total	.321	624	200	28	6	21	114	34	68	.355	.486
Home	.331	299	99	11	3	8	60	15	35	.356	.468	Batting #3	.321	624	200	28	6	21	114	34	68	.355	.486
Away	.311	325	101	17	3	13	54	19	33	.353	.502	Other	.000	0	0	0	0	0	0	0	0	.000	.000
Day	.340	197	67	7	3	8	44	11	24	.375	.528	April	.286	91	26	5	0	4	14	3	13	.313	.473
Night	.311	427	133	21	3	13	70	23	44	.345	.466	May	.274	106	29	4	4	2	22	5	12	.304	.443
Grass	.318	531	169	22	5	18	97	30	59	.354	.480	June	.333	108	36	6	1	7	24	4	14	.353	.602
Turf	.333	93	31	6	1	3	17	4	9	.360	.516	July	.337	104	35	4	0	3	15	6	10	.384	.462
First Pitch	.337	83	28	3	1	3	18	5	0	.374	.506	August	.341	123	42	5	1	4	23	11	11	.390	.496
Ahead in Count	.399	173	69	9	2	11	37	14	0	.440	.665	September/October	.348	92	32	4	0	1	16	5	8	.373	.424
Behind in Count	.273	271	74	11	2	4	39	0	59	.274	.373	Pre-All Star	.296	348	103	17	5	15	63	15	44	.328	.503
Two Strikes	.244	250	61	9	1	4	32	15	68	.287	.336	Post-All Star	.351	276	97	11	1	6	51	19	24	.387	.464

1993 By Position																									
Position	Avg	AB	H	2B	3B	HR	RBI	BB	SO	OBP	SLG	G	GS	Innings	PO	A	E	DP	Fld Pct	Rng Fctr	In Zone	Outs	Zone Rtg	MLB Zone
As 2b	.318	606	193	27	5	21	110	32	66	.353	.483	150	148	1303.2	347	444	17	106	.979	5.46	501	445	.888	.895

Career (1990-1993)	Avg	AB	H	2B	3B	HR	RBI	BB	SO	OBP	SLG		Avg	AB	H	2B	3B	HR	RBI	BB	SO	OBP	SLG
vs. Left	.323	651	210	26	3	14	104	19	80	.349	.436	Scoring Posn	.304	586	178	18	4	20	269	60	83	.362	.451
vs. Right	.291	1535	447	79	8	45	231	114	195	.343	.441	Close & Late	.275	389	107	21	0	8	48	32	55	.338	.391
Groundball	.285	551	157	31	3	8	85	37	78	.332	.396	None on/out	.292	431	126	21	2	12	12	25	42	.338	.434
Flyball	.278	492	137	25	1	13	60	31	75	.331	.413	Batting #3	.305	1834	560	88	9	49	283	98	227	.345	.443
Home	.322	1077	347	51	6	22	170	62	124	.361	.442	Batting #5	.310	87	27	3	1	2	11	7	9	.371	.437
Away	.280	1109	310	54	5	37	165	71	151	.329	.437	Other	.264	265	70	14	1	8	41	28	39	.332	.415
Day	.299	689	206	23	4	21	117	53	92	.354	.435	April	.274	274	75	9	1	9	32	13	30	.309	.412
Night	.301	1497	451	82	7	38	218	80	183	.340	.442	May	.285	375	107	12	5	7	63	22	38	.329	.400
Grass	.307	1854	569	86	9	54	293	113	222	.349	.450	June	.288	351	101	21	1	17	58	27	51	.339	.499
Turf	.265	332	88	19	2	5	42	20	53	.319	.380	July	.318	337	107	17	1	9	43	21	43	.363	.454
First Pitch	.328	274	90	11	1	7	48	20	0	.382	.453	August	.312	414	129	21	1	11	69	21	55	.352	.447
Ahead in Count	.371	553	205	37	6	25	108	67	0	.439	.595	September/October	.317	435	138	25	2	6	70	29	58	.362	.425
Behind in Count	.272	1001	272	40	3	19	129	0	243	.278	.375	Pre-All Star	.288	1120	323	48	7	39	169	71	136	.335	.448
Two Strikes	.237	898	213	36	2	16	100	44	275	.277	.335	Post-All Star	.313	1066	334	57	4	20	166	62	139	.355	.431

Batter vs. Pitcher (career)

Hits Best Against	Avg	AB	H	2B	3B	HR	RBI	BB	SO	OBP	SLG	Hits Worst Against	Avg	AB	H	2B	3B	HR	RBI	BB	SO	OBP	SLG
Nolan Ryan	.600	10	6	0	0	1	2	2	0	.667	.900	Dave Stieb	.000	9	0	0	0	0	0	2	0	.182	.000
Bob Welch	.560	25	14	3	0	1	3	0	1	.560	.800	Alex Fernandez	.083	12	1	0	0	0	0	0	3	.083	.083
Bill Gullickson	.520	25	13	4	0	2	9	0	1	.481	.920	Bill Krueger	.091	11	1	0	0	0	0	0	2	.091	.091
Willie Banks	.455	11	5	1	0	1	4	1	0	.500	.818	Alan Mills	.091	11	1	0	0	0	0	2	2	.231	.091
Scott Kamieniecki	.385	13	5	1	0	2	5	2	2	.467	.923	Erik Hanson	.143	21	3	0	0	0	1	0	3	.143	.143

Kevin Baez — Mets

Age 27 – Bats Right

	Avg	G	AB	R	H	2B	3B	HR	RBI	BB	SO	HBP	GDP	SB	CS	OBP	SLG	IBB	SH	SF	#Pit	#P/PA	GB	FB	G/F
1993 Season	.183	52	126	10	23	9	0	0	7	13	17	0	1	0	0	.259	.254	1	4	0	463	3.24	40	41	0.98
Career (1990-1993)	.179	63	151	10	27	10	0	0	7	13	17	0	4	0	0	.244	.245	1	4	0	537	3.20	52	50	1.04

1993 Season

	Avg	AB	H	2B	3B	HR	RBI	BB	SO	OBP	SLG		Avg	AB	H	2B	3B	HR	RBI	BB	SO	OBP	SLG
vs. Left	.180	50	9	5	0	0	4	3	8	.226	.280	Scoring Posn	.130	23	3	1	0	0	7	4	6	.259	.174
vs. Right	.184	76	14	4	0	0	3	10	9	.279	.237	Close & Late	.188	16	3	1	0	0	0	3	4	.316	.250
Home	.143	63	9	3	0	0	3	2	10	.169	.190	None on/out	.097	31	3	1	0	0	0	3	4	.176	.129
Away	.222	63	14	6	0	0	4	11	7	.338	.317	Batting #2	.208	48	10	3	0	0	3	1	6	.224	.271
First Pitch	.139	36	5	5	0	0	0	1	0	.162	.278	Batting #8	.173	75	13	6	0	0	4	12	9	.287	.253
Ahead in Count	.310	29	9	2	0	0	5	5	0	.412	.379	Other	.000	3	0	0	0	0	0	0	2	.000	.000
Behind in Count	.143	42	6	1	0	0	1	0	16	.143	.167	Pre-All Star	.182	11	2	1	0	0	2	0	2	.182	.273
Two Strikes	.146	41	6	0	0	0	1	7	17	.271	.146	Post-All Star	.183	115	21	8	0	0	5	13	15	.266	.252

Jeff Bagwell — Astros

Age 26 – Bats Right

	Avg	G	AB	R	H	2B	3B	HR	RBI	BB	SO	HBP	GDP	SB	CS	OBP	SLG	IBB	SH	SF	#Pit	#P/PA	GB	FB	G/F
1993 Season	.320	142	535	76	171	37	4	20	88	62	73	3	21	13	4	.388	.516	6	0	9	2178	3.58	198	157	1.26
Career (1991-1993)	.295	460	1675	242	494	97	14	53	266	221	286	28	50	30	14	.380	.464	24	3	29	7282	3.72	575	497	1.16

1993 Season

	Avg	AB	H	2B	3B	HR	RBI	BB	SO	OBP	SLG		Avg	AB	H	2B	3B	HR	RBI	BB	SO	OBP	SLG
vs. Left	.318	179	57	17	1	10	36	30	20	.408	.592	Scoring Posn	.291	127	37	6	1	4	63	22	19	.377	.449
vs. Right	.320	356	114	20	3	10	52	32	53	.376	.478	Close & Late	.226	84	19	5	0	2	9	8	14	.290	.357
Groundball	.331	181	60	15	0	6	32	16	28	.385	.514	None on/out	.324	111	36	8	2	5	5	5	15	.353	.568
Flyball	.240	75	18	5	0	5	14	10	9	.326	.507	Batting #3	.318	519	165	36	4	20	84	61	72	.386	.518
Home	.330	267	88	17	2	9	43	37	32	.409	.509	Batting #4	.357	14	5	1	0	0	2	0	0	.400	.429
Away	.310	268	83	20	2	11	45	25	41	.365	.522	Other	.500	2	1	0	0	0	2	1	1	.667	.500
Day	.272	162	44	7	0	8	26	17	26	.344	.463	April	.314	86	27	7	1	3	15	13	11	.404	.523
Night	.340	373	127	30	4	12	62	45	47	.406	.539	May	.412	102	42	6	0	7	25	14	13	.467	.676
Grass	.337	166	56	12	2	9	34	15	26	.382	.596	June	.240	96	23	4	1	2	8	8	11	.292	.365
Turf	.312	369	115	25	2	11	54	47	47	.390	.480	July	.289	114	33	7	1	4	21	10	14	.349	.474
First Pitch	.376	85	32	5	1	6	18	5	0	.409	.671	August	.352	108	38	10	1	4	15	13	21	.419	.574
Ahead in Count	.402	132	53	13	2	5	25	28	0	.500	.644	September/October	.276	29	8	3	0	0	4	4	3	.382	.379
Behind in Count	.262	210	55	13	0	6	27	0	61	.266	.410	Pre-All Star	.324	330	107	20	2	14	58	42	39	.393	.524
Two Strikes	.225	213	48	12	0	7	30	29	73	.317	.380	Post-All Star	.312	205	64	17	2	6	30	20	34	.378	.502

1993 By Position

Position	Avg	AB	H	2B	3B	HR	RBI	BB	SO	OBP	SLG	G	GS	Innings	PO	A	E	DP	Fld Pct	Rng Fctr	In Zone	Outs	Zone Rtg	MLB Zone
As 1b	.319	533	170	37	4	20	86	61	73	.386	.516	141	138	1229.2	1197	111	9	105	.993	---	241	217	.900	.834

Career (1991-1993)

	Avg	AB	H	2B	3B	HR	RBI	BB	SO	OBP	SLG		Avg	AB	H	2B	3B	HR	RBI	BB	SO	OBP	SLG
vs. Left	.309	595	184	40	4	27	107	101	88	.406	.526	Scoring Posn	.284	457	130	17	5	14	206	85	90	.388	.435
vs. Right	.287	1080	310	57	10	26	159	120	198	.366	.431	Close & Late	.316	269	85	19	2	12	50	49	46	.431	.535
Groundball	.293	587	172	34	5	16	102	64	102	.373	.450	None on/out	.299	368	110	27	3	10	10	38	66	.374	.470
Flyball	.254	327	83	15	1	14	49	52	54	.358	.434	Batting #3	.296	1112	329	64	10	40	184	138	174	.376	.479
Home	.293	835	245	53	7	23	126	115	134	.384	.456	Batting #4	.295	336	99	22	3	8	53	55	51	.402	.449
Away	.296	840	249	44	7	30	140	106	152	.377	.473	Other	.291	227	66	11	1	5	29	28	61	.370	.414
Day	.287	449	129	22	2	18	71	52	76	.363	.465	April	.278	223	62	14	2	7	35	35	47	.377	.453
Night	.298	1226	365	75	12	35	195	169	210	.387	.464	May	.297	296	88	13	1	14	55	36	62	.378	.490
Grass	.315	496	156	18	5	21	97	67	89	.393	.498	June	.283	297	84	16	2	7	32	38	44	.360	.421

Career (1991-1993)	Avg	AB	H	2B	3B	HR	RBI	BB	SO	OBP	SLG
Turf	.287	1179	338	79	9	32	169	154	197	.375	.450
First Pitch	.352	227	80	14	2	15	53	20	0	.406	.630
Ahead in Count	.365	417	152	34	6	17	70	96	0	.482	.597
Behind in Count	.235	711	167	28	4	12	89	0	236	.248	.336
Two Strikes	.226	736	166	36	4	18	104	106	286	.328	.359
July	.281	285	80	16	5	10	49	38	47	.367	.477
August	.289	318	92	21	4	7	51	46	50	.382	.447
September/October	.344	256	88	17	0	8	44	28	36	.423	.504
Pre-All Star	.293	919	269	49	9	31	145	126	170	.378	.467
Post-All Star	.298	756	225	48	5	22	121	95	116	.383	.462

Batter vs. Pitcher (career)

Hits Best Against	Avg	AB	H	2B	3B	HR	RBI	BB	SO	OBP	SLG
Roger McDowell	.538	13	7	1	0	1	4	0	1	.500	.846
Bob Walk	.500	14	7	1	0	1	2	1	3	.533	.786
Norm Charlton	.500	8	4	1	0	1	2	3	1	.636	1.000
Randy Myers	.455	11	5	3	0	2	5	0	3	.455	1.273
Andy Benes	.417	24	10	3	0	2	3	6	2	.516	.792

Hits Worst Against	Avg	AB	H	2B	3B	HR	RBI	BB	SO	OBP	SLG
Frank Castillo	.000	15	0	0	0	0	0	1	1	.063	.000
Jeff Fassero	.000	8	0	0	0	0	0	3	0	.273	.000
Rich Rodriguez	.100	10	1	0	0	0	0	2	4	.250	.100
Donovan Osborne	.111	9	1	0	0	0	3	1	2	.182	.111
Jose DeLeon	.125	16	2	0	0	0	1	2	3	.222	.125

Cory Bailey — Red Sox

Age 23 – Pitches Right (groundball pitcher)

	ERA	W	L	Sv	G	GS	IP	BB	SO	Avg	H	2B	3B	HR	RBI	OBP	SLG	GF	IR	IRS	Hld	SvOp	SB	CS	GB	FB	G/F
1993 Season	3.45	0	1	0	11	0	15.2	12	11	.231	12	1	1	0	8	.369	.288	5	10	4	0	0	3	2	21	12	1.75

1993 Season

	ERA	W	L	Sv	G	GS	IP	H	HR	BB	SO
Home	2.70	0	1	0	8	0	13.1	11	0	9	10
Away	7.71	0	0	0	3	0	2.1	1	0	3	1

	Avg	AB	H	2B	3B	HR	RBI	BB	SO	OBP	SLG
vs. Left	.333	18	6	1	1	0	4	7	3	.520	.500
vs. Right	.176	34	6	0	0	0	4	5	8	.275	.176

Harold Baines — Orioles

Age 35 – Bats Left (groundball hitter)

	Avg	G	AB	R	H	2B	3B	HR	RBI	BB	SO	HBP	GDP	SB	CS	OBP	SLG	IBB	SH	SF	#Pit	#P/PA	GB	FB	G/F
1993 Season	.313	118	416	64	130	22	0	20	78	57	52	0	14	0	0	.390	.510	9	1	6	1655	3.45	171	120	1.43
Last Five Years	.291	680	2302	323	669	109	3	88	381	328	339	2	69	1	10	.376	.455	60	1	28	9330	3.51	933	599	1.56

1993 Season

	Avg	AB	H	2B	3B	HR	RBI	BB	SO	OBP	SLG
vs. Left	.260	96	25	4	0	4	18	10	16	.330	.427
vs. Right	.328	320	105	18	0	16	60	47	36	.408	.534
Groundball	.268	82	22	2	0	2	9	10	10	.340	.366
Flyball	.288	80	23	2	0	6	18	15	15	.396	.538
Home	.345	197	68	11	0	12	46	32	24	.431	.584
Away	.283	219	62	11	0	8	32	25	28	.352	.443
Day	.333	114	38	7	0	5	20	18	15	.421	.526
Night	.305	302	92	15	0	15	58	39	37	.379	.503
Grass	.310	355	110	18	0	17	66	51	39	.393	.504
Turf	.328	61	20	4	0	3	12	6	13	.377	.541
First Pitch	.456	79	36	6	0	6	25	6	0	.483	.759
Ahead in Count	.303	99	30	5	0	4	16	35	0	.481	.475
Behind in Count	.261	153	40	7	0	7	23	0	46	.256	.444
Two Strikes	.239	155	37	6	0	6	22	16	52	.306	.394
Scoring Posn	.333	111	37	9	0	5	57	19	13	.412	.550
Close & Late	.278	54	15	4	0	2	9	7	9	.349	.463
None on/out	.310	116	36	6	0	5	5	13	17	.380	.491
Batting #4	.314	385	121	20	0	20	74	55	49	.395	.522
Batting #5	.286	21	6	2	0	0	2	1	2	.318	.381
Other	.300	10	3	0	0	0	2	1	1	.364	.300
April	.298	57	17	3	0	0	6	5	12	.349	.351
May	.348	23	8	3	0	0	2	8	4	.516	.478
June	.292	89	26	5	0	4	19	8	10	.347	.483
July	.392	74	29	4	0	6	22	10	11	.448	.689
August	.250	80	20	2	0	3	10	16	7	.371	.388
September/October	.323	93	30	5	0	7	19	10	8	.388	.602
Pre-All Star	.307	202	62	12	0	5	32	27	32	.385	.441
Post-All Star	.318	214	68	10	0	15	46	30	20	.395	.575

1993 By Position

Position	Avg	AB	H	2B	3B	HR	RBI	BB	SO	OBP	SLG	G	GS	Innings	PO	A	E	DP	Fld Pct	Rng Fctr	In Zone	Outs	Zone Rtg	MLB Zone
As Designated Hitter	.313	415	130	22	0	20	78	57	52	.391	.511	116	110	---	---	---	---	---	---	---	---	---	---	---

Last Five Years

	Avg	AB	H	2B	3B	HR	RBI	BB	SO	OBP	SLG
vs. Left	.265	479	127	19	0	16	85	52	98	.336	.405
vs. Right	.297	1823	542	90	3	72	296	276	241	.385	.468
Groundball	.305	619	189	29	1	14	91	85	83	.386	.423
Flyball	.267	479	128	19	0	20	85	91	90	.378	.432
Home	.291	1102	321	54	1	47	218	164	170	.377	.470
Away	.290	1200	348	55	2	41	163	164	169	.374	.442
Day	.327	679	222	37	2	29	116	96	100	.406	.515
Night	.275	1623	447	72	1	59	265	232	239	.363	.430
Grass	.291	1928	562	91	1	78	338	281	278	.378	.461
Turf	.286	374	107	18	2	10	43	47	61	.362	.425
First Pitch	.390	477	186	26	1	26	96	34	0	.427	.612
Ahead in Count	.364	535	195	39	0	28	114	161	0	.506	.594
Behind in Count	.203	852	173	29	1	19	95	0	277	.205	.306
Two Strikes	.198	884	175	34	2	21	111	120	339	.292	.312
Scoring Posn	.283	608	172	26	0	24	287	129	93	.393	.444
Close & Late	.252	325	82	16	0	13	45	57	60	.362	.422
None on/out	.278	551	153	27	0	18	18	60	84	.349	.425
Batting #3	.300	604	181	33	1	22	98	88	94	.385	.467
Batting #4	.280	1258	352	59	1	53	220	189	157	.370	.455
Other	.309	440	136	17	1	13	63	51	88	.380	.441
April	.255	337	86	16	1	7	42	40	63	.334	.371
May	.320	344	110	20	0	8	56	58	48	.411	.448
June	.303	422	128	20	1	24	86	64	63	.392	.526
July	.344	369	127	20	1	16	73	47	58	.413	.534
August	.250	396	99	13	0	14	50	57	49	.342	.389
September/October	.274	434	119	20	0	19	74	62	58	.361	.452
Pre-All Star	.297	1231	366	65	2	45	209	175	196	.382	.463
Post-All Star	.283	1071	303	44	1	43	172	153	143	.369	.446

Batter vs. Pitcher (since 1984)

Hits Best Against	Avg	AB	H	2B	3B	HR	RBI	BB	SO	OBP	SLG
Edwin Nunez	.583	12	7	2	0	2	7	1	2	.615	1.250
Eric Plunk	.556	9	5	0	0	0	0	4	2	.692	.556
Ben McDonald	.462	13	6	1	0	2	5	2	1	.533	1.000
Bill Gullickson	.429	14	6	1	0	2	4	1	1	.467	.929
Nolan Ryan	.364	22	8	1	0	4	6	3	4	.440	.955

Hits Worst Against	Avg	AB	H	2B	3B	HR	RBI	BB	SO	OBP	SLG
Mike Mussina	.000	10	0	0	0	0	0	1	3	.091	.000
Kenny Rogers	.077	13	1	0	0	0	0	1	3	.143	.077
Joe Grahe	.077	13	1	0	0	0	2	4	1	.294	.077
Mark Langston	.139	36	5	0	0	1	3	0	12	.139	.222
Bud Black	.143	28	4	0	0	0	2	1	3	.161	.143

Steve Balboni — Rangers

Age 37 – Bats Right (flyball hitter)

	Avg	G	AB	R	H	2B	3B	HR	RBI	BB	SO	HBP	GDP	SB	CS	OBP	SLG	IBB	SH	SF	#Pit	#P/PA	GB	FB	G/F
1993 Season	.600	2	5	0	3	0	0	0	0	0	2	0	0	0	0	.600	.600	0	0	0	18	3.60	0	2	0.00
Last Five Years	.219	228	571	57	125	18	2	34	93	60	160	6	14	0	0	.296	.436	7	1	8	2474	3.83	141	206	0.68

1993 Season

	Avg	AB	H	2B	3B	HR	RBI	BB	SO	OBP	SLG		Avg	AB	H	2B	3B	HR	RBI	BB	SO	OBP	SLG
vs. Left	.000	0	0	0	0	0	0	0	0	.000	.000	Scoring Posn	.000	0	0	0	0	0	0	0	0	.000	.000
vs. Right	.600	5	3	0	0	0	0	0	2	.600	.600	Close & Late	.000	0	0	0	0	0	0	0	0	.000	.000

Last Five Years

	Avg	AB	H	2B	3B	HR	RBI	BB	SO	OBP	SLG		Avg	AB	H	2B	3B	HR	RBI	BB	SO	OBP	SLG
vs. Left	.231	355	82	13	1	27	73	44	92	.317	.501	Scoring Posn	.210	167	35	5	0	3	49	18	42	.282	.293
vs. Right	.199	216	43	5	1	7	20	16	68	.261	.329	Close & Late	.241	108	26	2	0	6	15	14	34	.328	.426
Groundball	.260	146	38	5	0	5	23	17	38	.337	.397	None on/out	.150	133	20	3	0	6	6	17	46	.252	.308
Flyball	.200	120	24	4	1	10	20	14	39	.285	.500	Batting #4	.196	387	76	13	1	24	67	38	106	.269	.421
Home	.231	255	59	8	0	15	42	28	77	.310	.439	Batting #5	.244	119	29	4	1	7	17	14	29	.326	.471
Away	.209	316	66	10	2	19	51	32	83	.285	.434	Other	.308	65	20	1	0	3	9	8	25	.395	.462
Day	.217	175	38	7	0	6	17	19	43	.289	.360	April	.167	78	13	3	1	1	10	4	15	.207	.269
Night	.220	396	87	11	2	28	76	41	117	.299	.470	May	.266	79	21	2	0	8	18	10	24	.358	.595
Grass	.215	460	99	16	1	24	68	50	131	.296	.411	June	.266	109	29	3	0	8	22	13	28	.339	.514
Turf	.234	111	26	2	1	10	25	10	29	.296	.541	July	.212	99	21	5	0	6	14	12	27	.301	.444
First Pitch	.290	69	20	3	0	5	17	4	0	.333	.551	August	.169	77	13	0	0	5	14	11	29	.286	.364
Ahead in Count	.252	103	26	4	0	10	19	32	0	.430	.583	September/October	.217	129	28	5	1	6	15	10	37	.271	.411
Behind in Count	.172	290	50	5	1	12	35	0	142	.178	.321	Pre-All Star	.228	298	68	10	1	17	50	29	75	.299	.440
Two Strikes	.182	303	55	6	1	15	38	22	160	.238	.356	Post-All Star	.209	273	57	8	1	17	43	31	85	.294	.432

Batter vs. Pitcher (since 1984)

Hits Best Against	Avg	AB	H	2B	3B	HR	RBI	BB	SO	OBP	SLG	**Hits Worst Against**	Avg	AB	H	2B	3B	HR	RBI	BB	SO	OBP	SLG
Chuck Finley	.438	16	7	3	0	1	1	0	2	.438	.813	Bud Black	.000	13	0	0	0	0	0	1	6	.071	.000
Bob McClure	.364	11	4	1	0	2	3	0	5	.364	1.000	Edwin Nunez	.000	12	0	0	0	0	0	0	7	.000	.000
Greg Hibbard	.357	14	5	2	0	2	5	1	2	.400	.929	Jose Guzman	.083	12	1	0	0	0	1	3	7	.267	.083
Bill Swift	.333	12	4	1	0	0	1	1	4	.385	.417	Dan Plesac	.083	12	1	0	0	0	0	0	8	.083	.083
Neal Heaton	.313	16	5	0	0	0	0	1	3	.353	.313	Dave Stewart	.107	28	3	1	1	0	2	1	10	.133	.214

Jeff Ballard — Pirates

Age 30 – Pitches Left

	ERA	W	L	Sv	G	GS	IP	BB	SO	Avg	H	2B	3B	HR	RBI	OBP	SLG	GF	IR	IRS	Hld	SvOp	SB	CS	GB	FB	G/F
1993 Season	4.86	4	1	0	25	5	53.2	15	16	.332	70	12	2	3	25	.380	.450	4	7	1	3	0	2	1	105	47	2.23
Last Five Years	4.47	30	32	0	130	79	526.0	142	165	.296	615	120	10	57	250	.343	.446	11	33	6	10	0	25	25	816	637	1.28

1993 Season

	ERA	W	L	Sv	G	GS	IP	H	HR	BB	SO		Avg	AB	H	2B	3B	HR	RBI	BB	SO	OBP	SLG
Home	4.18	0	1	0	15	3	32.1	38	0	11	10	vs. Left	.328	61	20	3	0	0	6	6	8	.382	.377
Away	5.91	4	0	0	10	2	21.1	32	3	4	6	vs. Right	.333	150	50	9	2	3	19	9	8	.379	.480
Starter	4.21	1	1	0	5	5	25.2	35	0	6	6	Scoring Posn	.309	55	17	3	2	1	22	5	2	.361	.491
Reliever	5.46	3	0	0	20	0	28.0	35	3	9	10	Close & Late	.227	22	5	1	0	1	2	1	1	.250	.409
0 Days rest	9.82	0	0	0	3	0	3.2	7	0	0	0	None on/out	.333	54	18	4	0	1	1	1	4	.345	.463
1 or 2 Days rest	4.76	1	0	0	8	0	11.1	11	0	4	5	First Pitch	.243	37	9	2	0	1	4	3	0	.317	.378
3+ Days rest	4.85	2	0	0	9	0	13.0	17	3	5	5	Ahead in Count	.115	61	7	1	0	0	1	0	12	.115	.131
Pre-All Star	2.79	1	0	0	3	1	9.2	10	0	1	4	Behind in Count	.457	70	32	5	1	1	15	7	0	.506	.600
Post-All Star	5.32	3	1	0	22	4	44.0	60	3	14	12	Two Strikes	.197	71	14	2	1	1	5	5	16	.250	.296

Last Five Years

	ERA	W	L	Sv	G	GS	IP	H	HR	BB	SO		Avg	AB	H	2B	3B	HR	RBI	BB	SO	OBP	SLG
Home	4.15	10	18	0	63	38	254.0	288	22	68	89	vs. Left	.271	424	115	14	2	9	45	31	66	.322	.377
Away	4.76	20	14	0	67	41	272.0	327	35	74	76	vs. Right	.302	1654	500	106	8	48	205	111	99	.348	.463
Day	4.71	9	8	0	31	18	133.2	146	14	30	35	Inning 1-6	.294	1697	499	99	9	47	209	111	130	.339	.446
Night	4.38	21	24	0	99	61	392.1	469	43	112	130	Inning 7+	.304	381	116	21	1	10	41	31	35	.357	.444
Grass	4.56	25	27	0	93	63	406.1	475	47	112	131	None on	.288	1231	354	67	5	29	29	60	93	.325	.421
Turf	4.14	5	5	0	37	16	119.2	140	10	30	34	Runners on	.308	847	261	53	5	28	221	82	72	.367	.482
April	3.10	7	5	0	14	14	93.0	83	11	17	27	Scoring Posn	.291	461	134	26	3	16	185	68	51	.375	.464
May	3.49	5	7	0	17	16	90.1	99	9	25	26	Close & Late	.255	145	37	8	0	2	13	12	16	.308	.352
June	7.49	2	8	0	16	16	79.1	125	12	31	30	None on/out	.301	545	164	32	1	16	16	28	39	.340	.451
July	4.28	5	5	0	30	14	101.0	110	8	21	24	vs. 1st Batr (relief)	.196	46	9	1	0	1	2	4	9	.255	.283
August	5.20	5	2	0	26	9	83.0	110	10	22	30	First Inning Pitched	.298	463	138	32	1	8	70	40	50	.360	.423
September/October	3.63	6	5	0	27	10	79.1	88	7	26	28	First 15 Pitches	.287	435	125	26	1	10	47	29	40	.335	.421
Starter	4.35	26	31	0	79	79	455.0	533	50	115	136	Pitch 16-30	.312	382	119	18	3	6	44	28	32	.365	.421
Reliever	5.20	4	1	0	51	0	71.0	82	7	27	29	Pitch 31-45	.301	349	105	22	3	16	50	20	29	.337	.519
0 Days rest	4.15	0	1	0	8	0	13.0	14	0	3	2	Pitch 46+	.292	912	266	54	3	25	109	65	64	.339	.440
1 or 2 Days rest	6.35	2	0	0	22	0	28.1	32	2	11	15	First Pitch	.299	344	103	23	3	11	57	14	0	.329	.480
3+ Days rest	4.55	2	0	0	21	0	29.2	36	5	13	12	Ahead in Count	.235	767	180	33	1	15	58	0	138	.240	.339
Pre-All Star	4.38	17	22	0	58	51	302.1	348	34	79	95	Behind in Count	.340	577	196	36	3	19	77	83	0	.422	.511
Post-All Star	4.59	13	10	0	72	28	223.2	267	23	63	70	Two Strikes	.203	700	142	27	1	12	52	45	165	.257	.296

Pitcher vs. Batter (career)

Pitches Best Vs.	Avg	AB	H	2B	3B	HR	RBI	BB	SO	OBP	SLG	**Pitches Worst Vs.**	Avg	AB	H	2B	3B	HR	RBI	BB	SO	OBP	SLG
Lou Whitaker	.063	16	1	0	0	0	1	0	5	.063	.063	Kirby Puckett	.563	16	9	2	0	1	3	1	0	.556	.875
Terry Steinbach	.063	16	1	0	0	0	0	1	1	.118	.063	Ron Karkovice	.556	9	5	0	0	1	3	2	1	.636	.889
Mike Gallego	.067	15	1	1	0	0	0	0	1	.067	.133	Jay Buhner	.467	15	7	1	1	1	2	1	1	.500	.867
Omar Vizquel	.083	12	1	0	0	0	1	1	0	.154	.083	Dave Valle	.458	24	11	0	0	3	10	3	1	.500	.833
Felix Fermin	.143	14	2	1	0	0	2	1	0	.200	.214	Rob Deer	.353	17	6	0	0	2	4	4	3	.476	.706

Scott Bankhead — Red Sox

Age 30 – Pitches Right (flyball pitcher)

	ERA	W	L	Sv	G	GS	IP	BB	SO	Avg	H	2B	3B	HR	RBI	OBP	SLG	GF	IR	IRS	Hld	SvOp	SB	CS	GB	FB	G/F
1993 Season	3.50	2	1	0	40	0	64.1	29	47	.250	59	11	0	7	32	.327	.386	4	28	11	4	2	3	2	75	74	1.01
Last Five Years	3.76	29	19	1	148	46	419.0	149	278	.249	394	72	16	40	175	.314	.391	16	65	18	18	7	36	11	479	549	0.87

1993 Season

	ERA	W	L	Sv	G	GS	IP	H	HR	BB	SO
Home	3.19	0	0	0	20	0	31.0	31	3	14	26
Away	3.78	2	1	0	20	0	33.1	28	4	15	21
Starter	0.00	0	0	0	0	0	0.0	0	0	0	0
Reliever	3.50	2	1	0	40	0	64.1	59	7	29	47
0 Days rest	0.00	0	0	0	1	0	1.2	0	0	1	2
1 or 2 Days rest	3.15	0	1	0	15	0	20.0	23	1	13	20
3+ Days rest	3.80	2	0	0	24	0	42.2	36	6	15	25
Pre-All Star	4.17	1	1	0	21	0	36.2	34	5	14	25
Post-All Star	2.60	1	0	0	19	0	27.2	25	2	15	22

	Avg	AB	H	2B	3B	HR	RBI	BB	SO	OBP	SLG
vs. Left	.264	106	28	6	0	2	13	15	19	.352	.377
vs. Right	.238	130	31	5	0	5	19	14	28	.306	.392
Scoring Posn	.302	53	16	4	0	2	26	12	12	.406	.491
Close & Late	.239	46	11	1	0	0	2	3	14	.286	.261
None on/out	.241	58	14	3	0	2	2	7	8	.323	.397
First Pitch	.367	30	11	3	0	1	3	3	0	.424	.567
Ahead in Count	.170	100	17	4	0	1	12	0	41	.168	.240
Behind in Count	.290	62	18	2	0	4	11	10	0	.378	.516
Two Strikes	.182	110	20	3	0	2	15	16	47	.281	.264

Last Five Years

	ERA	W	L	Sv	G	GS	IP	H	HR	BB	SO
Home	3.89	14	7	0	77	24	206.0	207	19	70	137
Away	3.63	15	12	1	71	22	213.0	187	21	79	141
Day	3.95	5	6	0	46	9	116.1	105	15	42	83
Night	3.69	24	13	1	102	37	302.2	289	25	107	195
Grass	3.67	11	8	1	67	17	179.0	167	19	69	121
Turf	3.83	18	11	0	81	29	240.0	227	21	80	157
April	4.91	5	6	1	23	11	80.2	90	10	25	51
May	3.59	5	4	0	24	9	67.2	63	7	25	48
June	2.90	7	3	0	26	9	77.2	60	4	21	50
July	4.07	5	1	0	22	6	59.2	53	10	15	34
August	4.20	1	3	0	24	5	55.2	59	4	26	44
September/October	3.01	6	2	0	29	6	77.2	69	5	37	51
Starter	4.06	16	13	0	46	46	266.0	262	27	86	173
Reliever	3.24	13	6	1	102	0	153.0	132	13	63	105
0 Days rest	1.04	1	0	0	7	0	8.2	6	0	2	10
1 or 2 Days rest	3.31	4	3	1	39	0	49.0	47	3	25	35
3+ Days rest	3.40	8	3	0	56	0	95.1	79	10	36	60
Pre-All Star	3.70	20	14	1	82	31	252.2	232	24	78	164
Post-All Star	3.84	9	5	0	66	15	166.1	162	16	71	114

	Avg	AB	H	2B	3B	HR	RBI	BB	SO	OBP	SLG
vs. Left	.247	787	194	41	6	19	84	74	129	.309	.386
vs. Right	.252	794	200	31	10	21	91	75	149	.318	.395
Inning 1-6	.252	1122	283	52	12	29	131	95	195	.309	.398
Inning 7+	.242	459	111	20	4	11	44	54	83	.324	.375
None on	.235	959	225	38	11	21	21	71	158	.291	.363
Runners on	.272	622	169	34	5	19	154	78	120	.346	.434
Scoring Posn	.254	351	89	19	3	9	125	59	73	.348	.402
Close & Late	.233	219	51	10	0	4	16	27	43	.323	.333
None on/out	.206	402	83	13	4	8	8	32	63	.270	.318
vs. 1st Batr (relief)	.253	95	24	6	0	3	14	5	16	.284	.411
First Inning Pitched	.247	511	126	23	4	13	70	59	109	.322	.384
First 15 Pitches	.267	450	120	20	4	12	53	40	76	.327	.409
Pitch 16-30	.199	331	66	13	2	11	40	46	73	.294	.350
Pitch 31-45	.284	243	69	18	4	5	25	18	33	.335	.453
Pitch 46+	.250	557	139	21	6	12	57	45	96	.305	.373
First Pitch	.322	239	77	12	2	9	29	9	0	.344	.502
Ahead in Count	.200	684	137	27	3	8	52	0	236	.207	.284
Behind in Count	.274	336	92	18	6	14	50	65	0	.384	.488
Two Strikes	.195	717	140	26	6	8	59	74	278	.274	.282

Pitcher vs. Batter (career)

Pitches Best Vs.	Avg	AB	H	2B	3B	HR	RBI	BB	SO	OBP	SLG
Kevin Seitzer	.000	11	0	0	0	0	0	2	2	.154	.000
Mickey Tettleton	.059	17	1	0	0	0	1	1	4	.105	.059
Dick Schofield	.111	18	2	0	0	0	2	2	4	.190	.111
Tony Fernandez	.129	31	4	0	0	0	0	1	3	.156	.129
Julio Franco	.136	22	3	0	0	0	1	1	2	.174	.136

Pitches Worst Vs.	Avg	AB	H	2B	3B	HR	RBI	BB	SO	OBP	SLG
Mike Gallego	.583	12	7	2	0	0	1	3	1	.667	.750
Walt Weiss	.545	11	6	1	1	1	4	1	0	.583	1.091
Dave Winfield	.474	19	9	4	0	2	6	3	3	.545	1.000
George Bell	.433	30	13	4	0	5	7	0	2	.433	1.067
Rafael Palmeiro	.429	14	6	1	0	2	3	2	1	.500	.929

Willie Banks — Twins

Age 25 – Pitches Right

	ERA	W	L	Sv	G	GS	IP	BB	SO	Avg	H	2B	3B	HR	RBI	OBP	SLG	CG	ShO	Sup	QS	#P/S	SB	CS	GB	FB	G/F
1993 Season	4.04	11	12	0	31	30	171.1	78	138	.280	186	38	1	17	70	.356	.417	0	0	4.57	12	95	6	6	243	169	1.44
Career (1991-1993)	4.61	16	17	0	52	45	259.2	127	191	.282	287	55	4	24	123	.362	.415	0	0	4.44	18	93	16	10	368	274	1.34

1993 Season

	ERA	W	L	Sv	G	GS	IP	H	HR	BB	SO
Home	3.65	7	7	0	19	19	106.0	111	9	47	81
Away	4.68	4	5	0	12	11	65.1	75	8	31	57
Day	4.74	1	4	0	9	9	49.1	54	5	22	40
Night	3.76	10	8	0	22	21	122.0	132	12	56	98
Grass	5.10	2	4	0	8	8	42.1	52	4	25	38
Turf	3.70	9	8	0	23	22	129.0	134	13	53	100
April	2.66	2	1	0	4	4	23.2	25	2	10	21
May	5.73	2	1	0	5	4	22.0	31	2	9	14
June	5.40	1	2	0	5	5	26.2	29	4	13	22
July	3.54	2	3	0	5	5	28.0	24	2	10	17
August	3.55	1	2	0	6	6	38.0	40	4	14	35
September/October	3.82	3	3	0	6	6	33.0	37	3	22	29
Starter	3.83	11	12	0	30	30	169.1	178	16	78	138
Reliever	22.50	0	0	0	1	0	2.0	8	1	0	0
0-3 Days Rest	3.60	1	0	0	1	1	5.0	6	1	1	5
4 Days Rest	4.76	2	10	0	15	15	79.1	92	7	40	55
5+ Days Rest	2.96	8	2	0	14	14	85.0	80	8	37	78
Pre-All Star	4.58	5	7	0	17	16	88.1	99	9	37	65
Post-All Star	3.47	6	5	0	14	14	83.0	87	8	41	73

	Avg	AB	H	2B	3B	HR	RBI	BB	SO	OBP	SLG
vs. Left	.290	393	114	21	1	10	37	43	80	.358	.425
vs. Right	.265	272	72	17	0	7	33	35	58	.353	.404
Inning 1-6	.276	605	167	34	1	15	61	69	129	.350	.410
Inning 7+	.317	60	19	4	0	2	9	9	9	.414	.483
None on	.294	364	107	22	0	10	10	44	69	.370	.437
Runners on	.262	301	79	16	1	7	60	34	69	.339	.392
Scoring Posn	.241	158	38	7	0	5	54	26	39	.347	.380
Close & Late	.250	32	8	3	0	0	2	5	8	.368	.344
None on/out	.287	164	47	8	0	5	5	22	23	.371	.427
vs. 1st Batr (relief)	.000	1	0	0	0	0	0	0	0	.000	.000
First Inning Pitched	.283	120	34	5	0	3	17	7	29	.318	.400
First 75 Pitches	.279	519	145	29	1	14	57	55	112	.347	.420
Pitch 76-90	.292	72	21	5	0	2	7	9	11	.370	.444
Pitch 91-105	.306	49	15	1	0	1	2	9	7	.424	.388
Pitch 106+	.200	25	5	3	0	0	4	5	8	.355	.320
First Pitch	.345	87	30	6	1	5	16	1	0	.352	.609
Ahead in Count	.197	279	55	8	0	7	21	0	111	.202	.301
Behind in Count	.407	182	74	18	0	4	24	52	0	.536	.571
Two Strikes	.175	308	54	10	0	6	21	25	138	.239	.266

Bret Barberie — Marlins

Age 26 – Bats Both

	Avg	G	AB	R	H	2B	3B	HR	RBI	BB	SO	HBP	GDP	SB	CS	OBP	SLG	IBB	SH	SF	#Pit	#P/PA	GB	FB	G/F
1993 Season	.277	99	375	45	104	16	2	5	33	33	58	7	7	2	4	.344	.371	2	5	3	1581	3.73	136	102	1.33
Career (1991-1993)	.274	267	796	87	218	39	4	8	75	100	142	17	15	11	9	.364	.363	7	7	8	3602	3.88	283	212	1.33

1993 Season

	Avg	AB	H	2B	3B	HR	RBI	BB	SO	OBP	SLG		Avg	AB	H	2B	3B	HR	RBI	BB	SO	OBP	SLG
vs. Left	.312	109	34	6	0	2	3	9	15	.370	.422	Scoring Posn	.258	89	23	3	0	1	26	11	16	.349	.326
vs. Right	.263	266	70	10	2	3	30	24	43	.334	.350	Close & Late	.320	75	24	4	0	0	6	6	13	.378	.373
Groundball	.258	124	32	6	1	0	5	14	16	.338	.323	None on/out	.329	73	24	6	0	2	2	4	11	.372	.493
Flyball	.400	75	30	4	0	1	6	6	12	.452	.493	Batting #2	.298	255	76	12	2	4	24	28	42	.375	.408
Home	.226	199	45	8	1	2	15	18	31	.305	.307	Batting #3	.203	69	14	2	0	0	8	4	7	.269	.232
Away	.335	176	59	8	1	3	18	15	27	.391	.443	Other	.275	51	14	2	0	1	1	1	9	.288	.373
Day	.326	86	28	6	0	1	10	8	10	.396	.430	April	.286	35	10	0	0	0	1	6	6	.390	.286
Night	.263	289	76	10	2	4	23	25	48	.329	.353	May	.250	12	3	0	0	0	0	1	2	.357	.250
Grass	.246	293	72	11	2	4	30	31	46	.327	.338	June	.312	93	29	5	1	1	8	14	16	.407	.419
Turf	.390	82	32	5	0	1	3	2	12	.412	.488	July	.154	26	4	0	0	1	2	1	5	.185	.269
First Pitch	.372	43	16	1	0	0	6	0	0	.391	.395	August	.333	108	36	7	1	3	12	6	13	.381	.500
Ahead in Count	.366	101	37	6	1	3	9	20	0	.476	.535	September/October	.218	101	22	4	0	0	10	5	16	.264	.257
Behind in Count	.220	141	31	5	1	1	9	0	42	.229	.291	Pre-All Star	.300	140	42	5	1	1	9	21	24	.399	.371
Two Strikes	.173	162	28	6	1	2	10	13	58	.239	.259	Post-All Star	.264	235	62	11	1	4	24	12	34	.310	.370

1993 By Position

Position	Avg	AB	H	2B	3B	HR	RBI	BB	SO	OBP	SLG	G	GS	Innings	PO	A	E	DP	Fld Pct	Rng Fctr	In Zone	Outs	Zone Rtg	MLB Zone
As 2b	.279	373	104	16	2	5	33	33	56	.346	.373	97	96	844.1	200	301	9	61	.982	5.34	330	303	.918	.895

Career (1991-1993)

	Avg	AB	H	2B	3B	HR	RBI	BB	SO	OBP	SLG		Avg	AB	H	2B	3B	HR	RBI	BB	SO	OBP	SLG
vs. Left	.258	213	55	12	0	3	15	24	38	.342	.357	Scoring Posn	.251	191	48	11	0	1	62	36	41	.371	.325
vs. Right	.280	583	163	27	4	5	60	76	104	.372	.365	Close & Late	.285	172	49	11	0	1	17	17	37	.359	.366
Groundball	.291	296	86	16	3	0	18	47	52	.395	.365	None on/out	.293	191	56	12	1	4	4	10	28	.341	.429
Flyball	.329	164	54	10	0	2	16	21	32	.409	.427	Batting #2	.287	387	111	20	2	4	31	47	63	.372	.380
Home	.253	372	94	12	1	4	34	50	61	.351	.323	Batting #3	.297	111	33	5	1	0	13	14	12	.394	.360
Away	.292	424	124	27	3	4	41	50	81	.375	.399	Other	.248	298	74	14	1	4	31	39	67	.342	.342
Day	.260	246	64	16	1	2	25	34	52	.357	.358	April	.248	105	26	4	0	0	2	20	24	.373	.286
Night	.280	550	154	23	3	6	50	66	90	.367	.365	May	.262	42	11	0	0	0	5	7	12	.392	.262
Grass	.246	414	102	18	3	5	41	45	79	.330	.341	June	.276	123	34	7	1	1	14	18	23	.377	.374
Turf	.304	382	116	21	1	3	34	55	63	.399	.387	July	.233	86	20	5	0	2	12	12	17	.337	.360
First Pitch	.340	97	33	3	0	1	9	4	0	.375	.402	August	.300	210	63	10	2	5	20	14	38	.358	.438
Ahead in Count	.363	201	73	14	1	5	21	49	0	.488	.517	September/October	.278	230	64	13	1	0	22	29	28	.362	.343
Behind in Count	.205	308	63	10	2	1	22	0	108	.226	.260	Pre-All Star	.256	312	80	14	1	2	26	50	69	.369	.327
Two Strikes	.183	361	66	14	3	2	27	48	142	.294	.255	Post-All Star	.285	484	138	25	3	6	49	50	73	.360	.386

Batter vs. Pitcher (career)

Hits Best Against	Avg	AB	H	2B	3B	HR	RBI	BB	SO	OBP	SLG	Hits Worst Against	Avg	AB	H	2B	3B	HR	RBI	BB	SO	OBP	SLG
David Cone	.500	8	4	1	0	0	2	4	2	.667	.625	Andy Benes	.071	14	1	0	0	0	0	2	2	.188	.071
Greg Swindell	.417	12	5	0	0	1	1	0	3	.417	.667	Ben Rivera	.077	13	1	0	0	0	0	0	4	.077	.077
Bob Tewksbury	.400	15	6	1	0	0	0	3	1	.500	.467	Darryl Kile	.111	9	1	0	0	0	0	2	2	.273	.111
Bret Saberhagen	.364	11	4	0	0	1	4	2	2	.462	.636	Mike Morgan	.154	13	2	0	0	0	0	2	1	.267	.154
Bill Swift	.364	11	4	2	0	0	1	1	0	.417	.545	Dwight Gooden	.167	12	2	0	0	0	0	2	1	.286	.167

Brian Barnes — Expos

Age 27 – Pitches Left

	ERA	W	L	Sv	G	GS	IP	BB	SO	Avg	H	2B	3B	HR	RBI	OBP	SLG	GF	IR	IRS	Hld	SvOp	SB	CS	GB	FB	G/F
1993 Season	4.41	2	6	3	52	8	100.0	48	60	.274	105	23	3	9	57	.353	.420	8	32	13	1	5	8	3	109	134	0.81
Career (1990-1993)	3.85	14	21	3	105	56	388.0	185	265	.239	342	65	7	36	165	.328	.370	10	34	15	1	5	46	18	460	420	1.10

1993 Season

	ERA	W	L	Sv	G	GS	IP	H	HR	BB	SO		Avg	AB	H	2B	3B	HR	RBI	BB	SO	OBP	SLG
Home	4.05	1	2	3	24	4	53.1	54	4	20	34	vs. Left	.352	88	31	8	1	2	16	17	12	.453	.534
Away	4.82	1	4	0	28	4	46.2	51	5	28	26	vs. Right	.251	295	74	15	2	7	41	31	48	.320	.386
Starter	4.35	1	3	0	8	8	39.1	42	3	20	24	Scoring Posn	.258	128	33	8	0	3	47	21	18	.355	.391
Reliever	4.45	1	3	3	44	0	60.2	63	6	28	36	Close & Late	.171	82	14	3	0	0	7	12	14	.277	.207
0 Days rest	3.09	0	1	0	8	0	11.2	11	0	4	4	None on/out	.306	85	26	6	1	1	1	12	13	.392	.435
1 or 2 Days rest	4.81	0	1	2	17	0	24.1	24	4	7	21	First Pitch	.440	50	22	4	0	1	9	2	0	.462	.580
3+ Days rest	4.74	1	1	1	19	0	24.2	28	2	17	11	Ahead in Count	.206	175	36	10	0	1	19	0	55	.203	.280
Pre-All Star	4.65	2	4	3	28	8	71.2	76	7	34	38	Behind in Count	.330	100	33	8	3	7	24	27	0	.469	.680
Post-All Star	3.81	0	2	0	24	0	28.1	29	2	14	22	Two Strikes	.180	161	29	7	0	0	14	19	60	.265	.224

Career (1990-1993)

	ERA	W	L	Sv	G	GS	IP	H	HR	BB	SO		Avg	AB	H	2B	3B	HR	RBI	BB	SO	OBP	SLG
Home	3.45	7	10	3	49	26	195.2	159	15	80	146	vs. Left	.273	275	75	17	3	9	39	48	47	.385	.455
Away	4.26	7	11	0	56	30	192.1	183	21	105	119	vs. Right	.231	1156	267	48	4	27	126	137	218	.314	.349
Day	3.39	5	5	1	33	13	109.0	92	8	53	79	Inning 1-6	.238	1171	279	51	6	33	133	158	220	.331	.377
Night	4.03	9	16	2	72	43	279.0	250	28	132	186	Inning 7+	.242	260	63	14	1	3	32	27	45	.313	.338
Grass	3.76	5	3	0	34	16	105.1	103	10	54	60	None on	.231	831	192	36	3	18	18	98	153	.317	.347
Turf	3.88	9	18	3	71	40	282.2	239	26	131	205	Runners on	.250	600	150	29	4	18	147	87	112	.343	.402
April	4.70	1	0	2	10	0	15.1	16	2	6	5	Scoring Posn	.238	365	87	17	1	10	122	53	77	.333	.373
May	5.06	0	3	1	14	6	42.2	42	3	23	29	Close & Late	.184	125	23	5	0	0	10	17	25	.282	.224
June	3.91	2	4	0	13	13	73.2	70	7	36	52	None on/out	.244	365	89	18	1	9	9	42	61	.327	.373
July	3.66	3	3	0	20	10	71.1	65	10	31	50	vs. 1st Batr (relief)	.275	40	11	2	1	0	6	6	7	.362	.375

Career (1990-1993)	ERA	W	L	Sv	G	GS	IP	H	HR	BB	SO		Avg	AB	H	2B	3B	HR	RBI	BB	SO	OBP	SLG
August	3.08	3	5	0	20	11	79.0	60	7	36	53	First Inning Pitched	.214	359	77	17	1	7	43	52	69	.314	.326
September/October	3.91	5	6	0	28	16	106.0	89	7	53	76	First 15 Pitches	.232	319	74	17	1	8	29	42	60	.322	.367
Starter	3.82	13	18	0	56	56	320.2	275	30	156	220	Pitch 16-30	.246	281	69	13	1	7	40	30	54	.316	.374
Reliever	4.01	1	3	3	49	0	67.1	67	6	29	45	Pitch 31-45	.260	208	54	14	1	2	18	24	43	.346	.365
0 Days rest	3.09	0	1	0	8	0	11.2	11	0	4	4	Pitch 46+	.233	623	145	21	4	19	78	89	108	.330	.371
1 or 2 Days rest	4.18	0	1	2	20	0	28.0	25	4	7	25	First Pitch	.352	193	68	13	0	8	31	3	0	.364	.544
3+ Days rest	4.23	1	1	1	21	0	27.2	31	2	18	16	Ahead in Count	.175	613	107	19	1	6	51	0	232	.177	.238
Pre-All Star	4.39	3	9	3	44	23	160.0	156	16	80	103	Behind in Count	.313	390	122	22	6	20	67	112	0	.467	.554
Post-All Star	3.47	11	12	0	61	33	228.0	186	20	105	162	Two Strikes	.149	624	93	17	0	6	43	70	265	.238	.205

Pitcher vs. Batter (career)

Pitches Best Vs.	Avg	AB	H	2B	3B	HR	RBI	BB	SO	OBP	SLG	Pitches Worst Vs.	Avg	AB	H	2B	3B	HR	RBI	BB	SO	OBP	SLG
Chico Walker	.067	15	1	0	0	0	0	1	3	.125	.067	Charlie Hayes	.526	19	10	4	0	2	5	0	2	.526	1.053
George Bell	.091	11	1	0	0	0	1	1	4	.167	.091	Eddie Murray	.500	10	5	1	0	1	6	1	0	.545	.900
Wes Chamberlain	.095	21	2	0	0	0	0	3	8	.208	.095	Barry Bonds	.500	10	5	2	0	2	2	2	0	.583	1.300
Eric Davis	.100	10	1	0	0	0	0	2	1	.250	.100	Darren Daulton	.417	12	5	1	0	1	3	2	3	.500	.750
Dickie Thon	.125	16	2	0	0	0	0	0	4	.125	.125	Tony Gwynn	.364	11	4	0	2	0	0	2	0	.462	.727

Skeeter Barnes — Tigers

Age 37 – Bats Right (flyball hitter)

	Avg	G	AB	R	H	2B	3B	HR	RBI	BB	SO	HBP	GDP	SB	CS	OBP	SLG	IBB	SH	SF	#Pit	#P/PA	GB	FB	G/F
1993 Season	.281	84	160	24	45	8	1	2	27	11	19	0	2	5	5	.318	.381	0	4	5	647	3.59	59	50	1.18
Last Five Years	.279	259	487	80	136	29	4	10	69	30	61	2	7	18	14	.319	.417	2	8	8	1871	3.50	158	164	0.96

1993 Season

	Avg	AB	H	2B	3B	HR	RBI	BB	SO	OBP	SLG		Avg	AB	H	2B	3B	HR	RBI	BB	SO	OBP	SLG
vs. Left	.278	97	27	6	1	1	19	8	14	.327	.392	Scoring Posn	.294	51	15	3	0	0	24	7	6	.349	.353
vs. Right	.286	63	18	2	0	1	8	3	5	.304	.365	Close & Late	.400	15	6	1	0	0	4	4	1	.526	.467
Home	.263	80	21	3	1	2	12	4	7	.291	.400	None on/out	.313	32	10	2	0	0	0	0	6	.313	.375
Away	.300	80	24	5	0	0	15	7	12	.344	.363	Batting #7	.279	61	17	2	0	0	7	3	6	.303	.311
First Pitch	.235	17	4	0	0	1	1	0	0	.235	.412	Batting #8	.262	42	11	3	0	1	7	2	7	.295	.405
Ahead in Count	.341	44	15	5	1	0	11	6	0	.404	.500	Other	.298	57	17	3	1	1	13	6	6	.348	.439
Behind in Count	.257	70	18	2	0	0	9	0	14	.250	.286	Pre-All Star	.254	71	18	2	1	1	10	6	9	.304	.352
Two Strikes	.224	67	15	2	0	1	8	5	19	.270	.299	Post-All Star	.303	89	27	6	0	1	17	5	10	.330	.404

Last Five Years

	Avg	AB	H	2B	3B	HR	RBI	BB	SO	OBP	SLG		Avg	AB	H	2B	3B	HR	RBI	BB	SO	OBP	SLG
vs. Left	.269	301	81	17	4	7	49	20	41	.314	.422	Scoring Posn	.315	124	39	3	3	3	58	13	16	.359	.460
vs. Right	.296	186	55	12	0	3	20	10	20	.327	.409	Close & Late	.273	66	18	5	0	0	8	5	9	.319	.348
Groundball	.267	131	35	5	1	4	23	9	17	.315	.412	None on/out	.250	108	27	6	0	1	1	2	15	.277	.333
Flyball	.292	120	35	9	2	1	17	6	16	.313	.425	Batting #7	.284	134	38	8	0	2	18	5	15	.310	.388
Home	.277	220	61	11	3	6	34	11	26	.309	.436	Batting #8	.250	112	28	5	1	1	11	8	14	.306	.339
Away	.281	267	75	18	1	4	35	19	35	.326	.401	Other	.290	241	70	16	3	7	40	17	32	.330	.469
Day	.291	148	43	8	0	3	20	9	20	.323	.405	April	.294	17	5	1	0	0	3	3	1	.364	.353
Night	.274	339	93	21	4	7	49	21	41	.317	.422	May	.193	57	11	3	0	1	7	4	5	.246	.298
Grass	.276	399	110	27	4	8	56	27	52	.319	.424	June	.265	68	18	1	3	3	13	2	7	.292	.500
Turf	.295	88	26	2	0	2	13	3	9	.319	.386	July	.281	114	32	9	0	3	15	4	16	.308	.439
First Pitch	.156	64	10	2	0	1	3	2	0	.194	.234	August	.340	106	36	5	0	3	16	7	17	.377	.472
Ahead in Count	.454	130	59	16	2	5	31	12	0	.490	.723	September/October	.272	125	34	10	1	0	15	10	15	.319	.368
Behind in Count	.230	204	47	9	0	3	20	0	48	.231	.319	Pre-All Star	.255	192	49	9	3	6	33	12	20	.297	.427
Two Strikes	.201	199	40	9	1	4	21	16	61	.260	.317	Post-All Star	.295	295	87	20	1	4	36	18	41	.333	.410

Batter vs. Pitcher (since 1984)

Hits Best Against	Avg	AB	H	2B	3B	HR	RBI	BB	SO	OBP	SLG	Hits Worst Against	Avg	AB	H	2B	3B	HR	RBI	BB	SO	OBP	SLG
Randy Johnson	.333	15	5	1	0	1	3	3	5	.444	.600	Chuck Finley	.154	13	2	1	0	0	0	0	3	.154	.231
Joe Hesketh	.333	12	4	1	0	1	3	0	3	.333	.667	Matt Young	.182	11	2	0	0	0	0	1	4	.250	.182
Wilson Alvarez	.308	13	4	1	0	1	1	1	4	.357	.615	Dave Fleming	.182	11	2	0	0	1	2	0	2	.182	.455
												Mark Langston	.214	14	3	1	1	0	2	0	1	.200	.429

Kevin Bass — Astros

Age 35 – Bats Both

	Avg	G	AB	R	H	2B	3B	HR	RBI	BB	SO	HBP	GDP	SB	CS	OBP	SLG	IBB	SH	SF	#Pit	#P/PA	GB	FB	G/F
1993 Season	.284	111	229	31	65	18	0	3	37	26	31	1	4	7	1	.359	.402	3	2	0	927	3.59	93	60	1.55
Last Five Years	.267	518	1519	181	405	79	14	34	192	128	227	9	31	41	20	.325	.404	20	8	11	5960	3.56	602	434	1.39

1993 Season

	Avg	AB	H	2B	3B	HR	RBI	BB	SO	OBP	SLG		Avg	AB	H	2B	3B	HR	RBI	BB	SO	OBP	SLG
vs. Left	.225	80	18	9	0	2	15	9	13	.303	.413	Scoring Posn	.391	64	25	9	0	2	34	6	8	.443	.625
vs. Right	.315	149	47	9	0	1	22	17	18	.389	.396	Close & Late	.226	62	14	2	0	0	5	8	14	.314	.258
Home	.270	100	27	7	0	2	20	9	17	.336	.400	None on/out	.235	51	12	3	0	0	0	3	8	.278	.294
Away	.295	129	38	11	0	1	17	17	14	.377	.403	Batting #5	.333	63	21	4	0	1	11	12	8	.440	.444
First Pitch	.214	28	6	0	0	0	2	2	0	.267	.214	Batting #6	.269	52	14	7	0	1	12	3	7	.321	.462
Ahead in Count	.421	57	24	5	0	2	16	12	0	.522	.614	Other	.263	114	30	7	0	1	14	11	16	.328	.351
Behind in Count	.237	93	22	11	0	0	11	0	23	.245	.355	Pre-All Star	.261	115	30	10	0	1	18	6	17	.303	.374
Two Strikes	.184	87	16	7	0	0	6	12	31	.290	.264	Post-All Star	.307	114	35	8	0	2	19	20	14	.410	.430

Last Five Years

	Avg	AB	H	2B	3B	HR	RBI	BB	SO	OBP	SLG		Avg	AB	H	2B	3B	HR	RBI	BB	SO	OBP	SLG
vs. Left	.239	510	122	39	1	19	77	28	77	.281	.431	Scoring Posn	.279	402	112	23	3	10	157	57	62	.361	.425
vs. Right	.280	1009	283	40	13	15	115	100	150	.347	.390	Close & Late	.259	320	83	11	4	8	48	33	56	.326	.394

Last Five Years

	Avg	AB	H	2B	3B	HR	RBI	BB	SO	OBP	SLG
Groundball	.267	551	147	29	7	12	69	48	77	.327	.410
Flyball	.266	319	85	15	3	7	42	22	45	.317	.398
Home	.262	766	201	41	5	19	104	64	130	.320	.403
Away	.271	753	204	38	9	15	88	64	97	.331	.405
Day	.256	516	132	19	6	14	68	34	94	.306	.397
Night	.272	1003	273	60	8	20	124	94	133	.335	.408
Grass	.263	885	233	37	8	24	107	77	148	.323	.405
Turf	.271	634	172	42	6	10	85	51	79	.328	.404
First Pitch	.274	175	48	8	0	2	20	15	0	.337	.354
Ahead in Count	.333	411	137	25	3	15	73	57	0	.413	.518
Behind in Count	.214	625	134	33	7	8	61	0	186	.218	.328
Two Strikes	.214	594	127	28	5	10	50	53	227	.281	.328

	Avg	AB	H	2B	3B	HR	RBI	BB	SO	OBP	SLG
None on/out	.272	349	95	18	6	7	7	18	45	.312	.418
Batting #5	.274	482	132	24	3	10	70	46	55	.336	.398
Batting #6	.260	339	88	23	4	7	40	30	53	.321	.413
Other	.265	698	185	32	7	17	82	52	119	.319	.404
April	.255	298	76	16	4	4	32	26	49	.314	.376
May	.269	338	91	20	4	8	43	20	40	.313	.423
June	.247	150	37	7	0	4	25	13	21	.309	.373
July	.260	127	33	3	0	4	17	12	24	.321	.378
August	.274	252	69	14	0	9	33	19	39	.325	.437
September/October	.280	354	99	19	6	5	42	38	54	.353	.410
Pre-All Star	.261	852	222	46	8	17	106	61	121	.311	.393
Post-All Star	.274	667	183	33	6	17	86	67	106	.342	.418

Batter vs. Pitcher (since 1984)

Hits Best Against	Avg	AB	H	2B	3B	HR	RBI	BB	SO	OBP	SLG
Goose Gossage	.727	11	8	1	0	0	3	0	1	.727	.818
Mike Maddux	.600	10	6	1	1	0	2	2	1	.667	.900
Neal Heaton	.474	19	9	3	0	3	7	1	0	.500	1.105
Shawn Hillegas	.455	11	5	1	0	1	3	1	2	.500	.818
Randy Myers	.357	14	5	0	0	2	3	2	2	.438	.786

Hits Worst Against	Avg	AB	H	2B	3B	HR	RBI	BB	SO	OBP	SLG
Norm Charlton	.056	18	1	1	0	0	1	0	5	.053	.111
Todd Worrell	.091	11	1	0	0	0	1	0	1	.091	.091
Lee Smith	.105	19	2	0	0	0	0	0	5	.105	.105
Bob Tewksbury	.118	17	2	0	0	0	0	0	1	.118	.118
Danny Cox	.120	25	3	0	0	0	1	2	3	.179	.120

Richard Batchelor — Cardinals

Age 27 – Pitches Right

	ERA	W	L	Sv	G	GS	IP	BB	SO	Avg	H	2B	3B	HR	RBI	OBP	SLG	GF	IR	IRS	Hld	SvOp	SB	CS	GB	FB	G/F
1993 Season	8.10	0	0	0	9	0	10.0	3	4	.359	14	2	0	1	6	.386	.487	2	3	2	1	0	2	0	17	6	2.83

1993 Season

	ERA	W	L	Sv	G	GS	IP	H	HR	BB	SO
Home	11.57	0	0	0	3	0	2.1	2	0	2	1
Away	7.04	0	0	0	6	0	7.2	12	1	1	3

	Avg	AB	H	2B	3B	HR	RBI	BB	SO	OBP	SLG
vs. Left	.368	19	7	1	0	1	5	1	2	.381	.579
vs. Right	.350	20	7	1	0	0	1	2	2	.391	.400

Kim Batiste — Phillies

Age 26 – Bats Right

	Avg	G	AB	R	H	2B	3B	HR	RBI	BB	SO	HBP	GDP	SB	CS	OBP	SLG	IBB	SH	SF	#Pit	#P/PA	GB	FB	G/F
1993 Season	.282	79	156	14	44	7	1	5	29	3	29	1	3	0	1	.298	.436	2	0	1	505	3.14	49	47	1.04
Career (1991-1993)	.245	133	319	25	78	11	1	6	40	8	55	1	10	0	2	.262	.342	4	2	4	1066	3.19	121	90	1.34

1993 Season

	Avg	AB	H	2B	3B	HR	RBI	BB	SO	OBP	SLG
vs. Left	.349	43	15	1	1	4	11	1	9	.356	.698
vs. Right	.257	113	29	6	0	1	18	2	20	.276	.336
Home	.300	80	24	5	0	1	15	0	13	.300	.400
Away	.263	76	20	2	1	4	14	3	16	.296	.474
First Pitch	.400	25	10	3	0	1	6	1	0	.423	.640
Ahead in Count	.586	29	17	2	1	2	9	1	0	.600	.931
Behind in Count	.167	84	14	2	0	2	13	0	28	.174	.262
Two Strikes	.113	71	8	1	0	0	4	1	29	.125	.127

	Avg	AB	H	2B	3B	HR	RBI	BB	SO	OBP	SLG
Scoring Posn	.311	45	14	2	0	1	21	2	11	.333	.422
Close & Late	.138	29	4	0	0	2	8	0	11	.138	.345
None on/out	.250	40	10	3	0	1	1	1	6	.268	.400
Batting #7	.319	69	22	2	1	1	13	0	15	.319	.420
Batting #8	.286	63	18	4	0	2	10	2	12	.303	.444
Other	.167	24	4	1	0	2	6	1	2	.231	.458
Pre-All Star	.276	134	37	6	1	4	23	2	26	.290	.425
Post-All Star	.318	22	7	1	0	1	6	1	3	.348	.500

Danny Bautista — Tigers

Age 22 – Bats Right

	Avg	G	AB	R	H	2B	3B	HR	RBI	BB	SO	HBP	GDP	SB	CS	OBP	SLG	IBB	SH	SF	#Pit	#P/PA	GB	FB	G/F
1993 Season	.311	17	61	6	19	3	0	1	9	1	10	0	1	3	1	.317	.410	0	0	1	194	3.08	22	17	1.29

1993 Season

	Avg	AB	H	2B	3B	HR	RBI	BB	SO	OBP	SLG
vs. Left	.167	18	3	0	0	1	2	0	2	.167	.333
vs. Right	.372	43	16	3	0	0	7	1	8	.378	.442

	Avg	AB	H	2B	3B	HR	RBI	BB	SO	OBP	SLG
Scoring Posn	.286	21	6	1	0	0	8	0	5	.273	.333
Close & Late	.500	10	5	0	0	1	4	0	2	.500	.800

Jose Bautista — Cubs

Age 29 – Pitches Right

	ERA	W	L	Sv	G	GS	IP	BB	SO	Avg	H	2B	3B	HR	RBI	OBP	SLG	GF	IR	IRS	Hld	SvOp	SB	CS	GB	FB	G/F
1993 Season	2.82	10	3	2	58	7	111.2	27	63	.250	105	19	2	11	47	.301	.383	14	38	15	7	2	5	2	156	106	1.47
Last Five Years	4.18	14	8	2	100	17	221.2	54	111	.268	230	36	9	33	124	.315	.446	26	71	28	12	2	12	5	297	263	1.13

1993 Season

	ERA	W	L	Sv	G	GS	IP	H	HR	BB	SO
Home	2.32	5	0	1	31	2	54.1	45	5	16	29
Away	3.30	5	3	1	27	5	57.1	60	6	11	34
Starter	3.80	4	2	0	7	7	42.2	47	5	9	24
Reliever	2.22	6	1	2	51	0	69.0	58	6	18	39
0 Days rest	2.01	3	0	0	17	0	22.1	18	3	8	13
1 or 2 Days rest	1.74	2	1	2	21	0	31.0	25	2	8	18
3+ Days rest	3.45	1	0	0	13	0	15.2	15	1	2	8
Pre-All Star	2.83	4	2	0	27	3	54.0	55	5	12	34
Post-All Star	2.81	6	1	2	31	4	57.2	50	6	15	29

	Avg	AB	H	2B	3B	HR	RBI	BB	SO	OBP	SLG
vs. Left	.232	185	43	8	0	3	19	19	25	.311	.324
vs. Right	.264	235	62	11	2	8	28	8	38	.293	.430
Scoring Posn	.266	109	29	5	0	4	39	8	19	.314	.422
Close & Late	.179	106	19	3	0	2	6	10	15	.269	.264
None on/out	.220	100	22	4	1	3	3	8	11	.284	.370
First Pitch	.243	74	18	0	1	3	7	2	0	.266	.392
Ahead in Count	.251	199	50	12	0	6	27	0	55	.261	.402
Behind in Count	.343	70	24	3	1	2	9	14	0	.452	.500
Two Strikes	.235	170	40	9	0	3	23	11	63	.288	.341

Billy Bean — Padres

Age 30 – Bats Left

	Avg	G	AB	R	H	2B	3B	HR	RBI	BB	SO	HBP	GDP	SB	CS	OBP	SLG	IBB	SH	SF	#Pit	#P/PA	GB	FB	G/F
1993 Season	.260	88	177	19	46	9	0	5	32	6	29	2	4	2	4	.284	.395	1	2	5	630	3.28	55	59	0.93
Last Five Years	.232	148	259	26	60	13	0	5	35	12	42	4	4	2	6	.271	.340	1	2	5	957	3.39	88	85	1.04

1993 Season

	Avg	AB	H	2B	3B	HR	RBI	BB	SO	OBP	SLG
vs. Left	.200	15	3	1	0	0	2	0	2	.188	.267
vs. Right	.265	162	43	8	0	5	30	6	27	.293	.407
Home	.268	82	22	3	0	4	17	3	13	.295	.451
Away	.253	95	24	6	0	1	15	3	16	.275	.347
First Pitch	.345	29	10	2	0	3	12	1	0	.344	.724
Ahead in Count	.327	52	17	3	0	0	7	3	0	.357	.385
Behind in Count	.191	68	13	3	0	1	8	0	22	.211	.279
Two Strikes	.091	66	6	1	0	1	7	2	29	.141	.152

	Avg	AB	H	2B	3B	HR	RBI	BB	SO	OBP	SLG
Scoring Posn	.410	39	16	5	0	2	26	1	6	.391	.692
Close & Late	.256	39	10	1	0	1	11	3	10	.311	.359
None on/out	.186	43	8	1	0	0	0	2	10	.239	.209
Batting #1	.262	42	11	3	0	0	2	0	7	.289	.333
Batting #3	.205	39	8	2	0	0	3	2	6	.244	.256
Other	.281	96	27	4	0	5	27	4	16	.298	.479
Pre-All Star	.239	67	16	4	0	0	5	2	10	.264	.299
Post-All Star	.273	110	30	5	0	5	27	4	19	.297	.455

Rod Beck — Giants

Age 25 – Pitches Right (flyball pitcher)

	ERA	W	L	Sv	G	GS	IP	BB	SO	Avg	H	2B	3B	HR	RBI	OBP	SLG	GF	IR	IRS	Hld	SvOp	SB	CS	GB	FB	G/F
1993 Season	2.16	3	1	48	76	0	79.1	13	86	.201	57	5	0	11	26	.241	.335	71	35	7	0	52	1	0	63	94	0.67
Career (1991-1993)	2.37	7	5	66	172	0	223.2	41	211	.214	172	24	3	19	77	.255	.322	123	90	21	5	76	5	7	218	240	0.91

1993 Season

	ERA	W	L	Sv	G	GS	IP	H	HR	BB	SO
Home	1.62	3	0	21	38	0	39.0	27	5	8	42
Away	2.68	0	1	27	38	0	40.1	30	6	5	44
Day	1.73	1	0	26	40	0	41.2	31	5	8	49
Night	2.63	2	1	22	36	0	37.2	26	6	5	37
Grass	1.71	3	0	39	60	0	63.0	42	8	12	67
Turf	3.86	0	1	9	16	0	16.1	15	3	1	19
April	2.35	2	1	7	14	0	15.1	9	1	2	20
May	0.82	0	0	6	11	0	11.0	7	1	1	12
June	0.84	0	0	10	11	0	10.2	10	0	2	15
July	1.46	0	0	7	11	0	12.1	7	2	1	13
August	4.15	0	0	8	13	0	13.0	12	3	5	12
September/October	2.65	1	0	10	16	0	17.0	12	4	2	14
Starter	0.00	0	0	0	0	0	0.0	0	0	0	0
Reliever	2.16	3	1	48	76	0	79.1	57	11	13	86
0 Days rest	1.65	2	0	19	27	0	27.1	18	4	6	31
1 or 2 Days rest	2.70	1	1	18	31	0	33.1	28	4	7	35
3+ Days rest	1.93	0	0	11	18	0	18.2	11	3	0	20
Pre-All Star	1.79	2	1	24	39	0	40.1	30	4	5	50
Post-All Star	2.54	1	0	24	37	0	39.0	27	7	8	36

	Avg	AB	H	2B	3B	HR	RBI	BB	SO	OBP	SLG
vs. Left	.180	161	29	2	0	6	13	11	56	.231	.304
vs. Right	.228	123	28	3	0	5	13	2	30	.254	.374
Inning 1-6	.000	0	0	0	0	0	0	0	0	.000	.000
Inning 7+	.201	284	57	5	0	11	26	13	86	.241	.335
None on	.228	162	37	4	0	6	6	7	50	.273	.364
Runners on	.164	122	20	1	0	5	20	6	36	.198	.295
Scoring Posn	.138	58	8	0	0	2	13	5	23	.197	.241
Close & Late	.165	176	29	2	0	3	16	12	59	.227	.227
None on/out	.212	66	14	1	0	1	1	3	16	.268	.273
vs. 1st Batr (relief)	.159	69	11	1	0	1	4	5	21	.224	.217
First Inning Pitched	.213	267	57	5	0	11	26	12	76	.253	.356
First 15 Pitches	.217	235	51	5	0	10	22	9	64	.249	.366
Pitch 16-30	.122	49	6	0	0	1	4	4	22	.204	.184
Pitch 31-45	.000	0	0	0	0	0	0	0	0	.000	.000
Pitch 46+	.000	0	0	0	0	0	0	0	0	.000	.000
First Pitch	.205	39	8	3	0	1	3	3	0	.279	.359
Ahead in Count	.156	160	25	0	0	4	8	0	75	.166	.231
Behind in Count	.326	46	15	1	0	5	13	5	0	.377	.674
Two Strikes	.166	157	26	0	0	5	9	5	86	.200	.261

Career (1991-1993)

	ERA	W	L	Sv	G	GS	IP	H	HR	BB	SO
Home	2.33	5	4	31	84	0	108.1	88	7	16	108
Away	2.42	2	1	35	88	0	115.1	84	12	25	103
Day	2.02	1	0	34	76	0	89.0	67	6	14	100
Night	2.61	6	5	32	96	0	134.2	105	13	27	111
Grass	2.06	5	4	55	126	0	161.1	125	12	27	159
Turf	3.18	2	1	11	46	0	62.1	47	7	14	52
April	1.11	2	1	8	22	0	32.1	17	1	5	36
May	4.37	0	1	7	27	0	35.0	34	4	3	38
June	1.57	0	2	12	20	0	23.0	21	1	5	24
July	1.72	1	1	12	28	0	36.2	26	3	4	43
August	2.18	0	0	12	34	0	41.1	31	3	14	31
September/October	2.77	4	0	15	41	0	55.1	43	7	10	39
Starter	0.00	0	0	0	0	0	0.0	0	0	0	0
Reliever	2.37	7	5	66	172	0	223.2	172	19	41	211
0 Days rest	2.79	2	0	25	39	0	38.2	29	4	9	41
1 or 2 Days rest	2.34	4	4	28	85	0	123.0	103	10	27	111
3+ Days rest	2.18	1	1	13	48	0	62.0	40	5	5	59
Pre-All Star	2.54	2	5	32	79	0	102.2	84	8	14	115
Post-All Star	2.23	5	0	34	93	0	121.0	88	11	27	96

	Avg	AB	H	2B	3B	HR	RBI	BB	SO	OBP	SLG
vs. Left	.202	430	87	14	2	12	36	23	122	.245	.328
vs. Right	.227	375	85	10	1	7	41	18	89	.266	.315
Inning 1-6	.246	142	35	6	1	0	20	12	32	.314	.303
Inning 7+	.207	663	137	18	2	19	57	29	179	.241	.326
None on	.218	467	102	12	2	14	14	17	125	.252	.343
Runners on	.207	338	70	12	1	5	63	24	86	.259	.293
Scoring Posn	.216	199	43	7	1	2	55	18	57	.276	.291
Close & Late	.185	395	73	10	1	6	33	22	112	.231	.261
None on/out	.229	192	44	3	0	4	4	7	40	.267	.307
vs. 1st Batr (relief)	.193	161	31	2	0	3	12	8	41	.233	.261
First Inning Pitched	.206	596	123	19	1	15	63	30	149	.248	.317
First 15 Pitches	.204	555	113	19	2	15	49	25	136	.240	.326
Pitch 16-30	.228	215	49	5	1	4	22	12	64	.273	.316
Pitch 31-45	.286	35	10	0	0	0	6	4	11	.366	.286
Pitch 46+	.000	0	0	0	0	0	0	0	0	.000	.000
First Pitch	.239	109	26	7	1	3	8	7	0	.291	.404
Ahead in Count	.178	437	78	8	2	5	28	0	185	.182	.240
Behind in Count	.299	137	41	6	0	9	28	17	0	.377	.540
Two Strikes	.160	420	67	7	2	5	25	17	211	.197	.221

Pitcher vs. Batter (career)

Pitches Best Vs.	Avg	AB	H	2B	3B	HR	RBI	BB	SO	OBP	SLG
Terry Pendleton	.083	12	1	0	0	0	0	0	4	.083	.083

Pitches Worst Vs.	Avg	AB	H	2B	3B	HR	RBI	BB	SO	OBP	SLG
Luis Gonzalez	.308	13	4	0	0	0	0	1	3	.357	.308

Rich Becker — Twins

Age 22 – Bats Both

	Avg	G	AB	R	H	2B	3B	HR	RBI	BB	SO	HBP	GDP	SB	CS	OBP	SLG	IBB	SH	SF	#Pit	#P/PA	GB	FB	G/F
1993 Season	.286	3	7	3	2	2	0	0	0	5	4	0	0	1	1	.583	.571	0	0	0	58	4.83	1	0	0.00

1993 Season

	Avg	AB	H	2B	3B	HR	RBI	BB	SO	OBP	SLG
vs. Left	.333	3	1	1	0	0	0	1	2	.500	.667
vs. Right	.250	4	1	1	0	0	0	4	2	.625	.500

	Avg	AB	H	2B	3B	HR	RBI	BB	SO	OBP	SLG
Scoring Posn	.000	1	0	0	0	0	0	1	0	.500	.000
Close & Late	.500	2	1	1	0	0	0	1	1	.667	1.000

Steve Bedrosian — Braves

Age 36 – Pitches Right (flyball pitcher)

	ERA	W	L	Sv	G	GS	IP	BB	SO	Avg	H	2B	3B	HR	RBI	OBP	SLG	GF	IR	IRS	Hld	SvOp	SB	CS	GB	FB	G/F
1993 Season	1.63	5	2	0	49	0	49.2	14	33	.194	34	7	0	4	24	.256	.303	12	36	16	4	0	6	2	45	67	0.67
Last Five Years	3.43	22	21	46	241	0	291.0	132	178	.219	232	39	2	33	138	.307	.353	87	143	40	16	60	41	6	296	420	0.70

1993 Season

	ERA	W	L	Sv	G	GS	IP	H	HR	BB	SO
Home	1.32	2	1	0	28	0	27.1	22	0	5	20
Away	2.01	3	1	0	21	0	22.1	12	4	9	13
Starter	0.00	0	0	0	0	0	0.0	0	0	0	0
Reliever	1.63	5	2	0	49	0	49.2	34	4	14	33
0 Days rest	0.75	0	1	0	14	0	12.0	8	0	1	10
1 or 2 Days rest	2.45	3	1	0	17	0	14.2	13	3	5	10
3+ Days rest	1.57	2	0	0	18	0	23.0	13	1	8	13
Pre-All Star	1.96	0	2	0	23	0	23.0	17	2	9	13
Post-All Star	1.35	5	0	0	26	0	26.2	17	2	5	20

	Avg	AB	H	2B	3B	HR	RBI	BB	SO	OBP	SLG
vs. Left	.203	74	15	2	0	2	12	5	16	.256	.311
vs. Right	.188	101	19	5	0	2	12	9	17	.257	.297
Scoring Posn	.226	53	12	4	0	0	20	8	13	.318	.302
Close & Late	.233	30	7	1	0	1	4	2	7	.294	.367
None on/out	.275	40	11	3	0	2	2	2	6	.326	.500
First Pitch	.300	30	9	2	0	2	6	1	0	.323	.567
Ahead in Count	.129	93	12	2	0	2	10	0	28	.143	.215
Behind in Count	.231	26	6	1	0	0	3	5	0	.355	.269
Two Strikes	.103	87	9	2	0	2	8	8	33	.182	.195

Last Five Years

	ERA	W	L	Sv	G	GS	IP	H	HR	BB	SO
Home	3.26	14	10	27	131	0	165.2	126	16	72	109
Away	3.66	8	11	19	110	0	125.1	106	17	60	69
Day	4.06	8	6	15	86	0	99.2	88	14	41	69
Night	3.10	14	15	31	155	0	191.1	144	19	91	109
Grass	2.63	15	10	33	143	0	174.2	132	14	54	111
Turf	4.64	7	11	13	98	0	116.1	100	19	78	67
April	5.30	3	7	5	34	0	37.1	33	8	20	20
May	2.64	1	2	9	37	0	47.2	31	5	26	27
June	3.04	3	4	7	41	0	50.1	39	5	20	32
July	3.40	4	2	5	42	0	55.2	49	5	24	37
August	3.57	5	4	7	45	0	53.0	46	5	24	31
September/October	3.06	6	2	13	42	0	47.0	34	5	18	31
Starter	0.00	0	0	0	0	0	0.0	0	0	0	0
Reliever	3.43	22	21	46	241	0	291.0	232	33	132	178
0 Days rest	4.20	1	9	11	52	0	49.1	39	6	32	34
1 or 2 Days rest	3.67	13	9	24	121	0	154.2	128	19	60	92
3+ Days rest	2.59	8	3	11	68	0	87.0	65	8	40	52
Pre-All Star	3.60	7	13	22	126	0	152.2	120	21	72	93
Post-All Star	3.25	15	8	24	115	0	138.1	112	12	60	85

	Avg	AB	H	2B	3B	HR	RBI	BB	SO	OBP	SLG
vs. Left	.235	528	124	20	2	18	77	80	91	.336	.383
vs. Right	.203	531	108	19	0	15	61	52	87	.277	.324
Inning 1-6	.211	90	19	3	0	3	14	6	15	.255	.344
Inning 7+	.220	969	213	36	2	30	124	126	163	.311	.354
None on	.213	564	120	20	1	19	19	59	95	.292	.353
Runners on	.226	495	112	19	1	14	119	73	83	.323	.354
Scoring Posn	.225	315	71	10	1	12	110	60	60	.343	.378
Close & Late	.223	439	98	16	1	12	60	69	75	.331	.346
None on/out	.210	238	50	11	1	8	8	27	33	.296	.366
vs. 1st Batr (relief)	.197	188	37	5	1	6	20	20	26	.277	.330
First Inning Pitched	.225	672	151	25	2	18	88	81	111	.309	.348
First 15 Pitches	.221	684	151	29	2	22	87	82	113	.305	.365
Pitch 16-30	.209	297	62	8	0	7	35	34	49	.294	.306
Pitch 31-45	.243	70	17	2	0	3	14	15	12	.376	.400
Pitch 46+	.250	8	2	0	0	1	2	1	4	.333	.625
First Pitch	.256	172	44	8	1	6	22	17	0	.321	.419
Ahead in Count	.187	492	92	15	0	11	54	0	146	.194	.285
Behind in Count	.277	184	51	14	1	8	35	66	0	.467	.495
Two Strikes	.171	491	84	9	0	13	47	49	178	.250	.269

Pitcher vs. Batter (since 1984)

Pitches Best Vs.	Avg	AB	H	2B	3B	HR	RBI	BB	SO	OBP	SLG
Rafael Palmeiro	.000	10	0	0	0	0	0	2	1	.167	.000
Tom Foley	.083	12	1	0	0	0	2	0	3	.083	.083
Glenn Wilson	.100	10	1	0	0	0	1	2	3	.250	.100
Jose Uribe	.105	19	2	1	0	0	0	1	5	.150	.158
Tim Wallach	.161	31	5	0	0	0	2	2	8	.212	.161

Pitches Worst Vs.	Avg	AB	H	2B	3B	HR	RBI	BB	SO	OBP	SLG
Sid Bream	.538	13	7	2	0	1	2	2	2	.600	.923
Craig Biggio	.538	13	7	1	0	1	4	1	0	.571	.846
Chili Davis	.455	11	5	0	0	1	2	1	2	.500	.727
Barry Bonds	.375	16	6	1	0	3	6	8	3	.583	1.000
Andy Van Slyke	.350	20	7	0	0	2	7	5	4	.462	.650

Tim Belcher — White Sox

Age 32 – Pitches Right (flyball pitcher)

	ERA	W	L	Sv	G	GS	IP	BB	SO	Avg	H	2B	3B	HR	RBI	OBP	SLG	CG	ShO	Sup	QS	#P/S	SB	CS	GB	FB	G/F
1993 Season	4.44	12	11	0	34	33	208.2	74	135	.250	198	33	7	19	90	.319	.381	5	3	4.96	16	98	11	8	235	269	0.87
Last Five Years	3.53	61	55	1	165	154	1028.2	357	742	.237	906	144	25	83	383	.303	.352	24	15	4.19	92	101	67	50	1190	1216	0.98

1993 Season

	ERA	W	L	Sv	G	GS	IP	H	HR	BB	SO
Home	4.74	8	4	0	19	19	114.0	119	14	42	74
Away	4.09	4	7	0	15	14	94.2	79	5	32	61
Day	4.96	2	3	0	9	8	49.0	57	7	16	29
Night	4.28	10	8	0	25	25	159.2	141	12	58	106
Grass	3.26	4	7	0	15	14	96.2	84	7	29	50
Turf	5.46	8	4	0	19	19	112.0	114	12	45	85
April	5.65	1	3	0	5	5	28.2	33	1	11	14
May	2.20	1	1	0	5	5	32.2	20	1	14	29
June	3.05	4	1	0	6	6	44.1	40	5	5	25
July	7.76	3	1	0	6	6	31.1	41	4	17	33
August	4.28	3	2	0	5	5	33.2	30	4	11	19
September/October	4.50	0	3	0	7	6	38.0	34	4	16	15
Starter	4.46	12	11	0	33	33	207.2	198	19	74	134
Reliever	0.00	0	0	0	1	0	1.0	0	0	0	1
0-3 Days Rest	0.00	0	0	0	0	0	0.0	0	0	0	0
4 Days Rest	4.58	9	7	0	22	22	137.2	138	13	49	86
5+ Days Rest	4.24	3	4	0	11	11	70.0	60	6	25	48
Pre-All Star	4.05	7	5	0	18	18	115.2	107	7	35	80
Post-All Star	4.94	5	6	0	16	15	93.0	91	12	39	55

	Avg	AB	H	2B	3B	HR	RBI	BB	SO	OBP	SLG
vs. Left	.259	394	102	18	3	8	50	48	52	.342	.381
vs. Right	.241	398	96	15	4	11	40	26	83	.295	.382
Inning 1-6	.246	668	164	31	6	17	82	65	121	.316	.386
Inning 7+	.274	124	34	2	1	2	8	9	14	.333	.355
None on	.221	480	106	18	2	11	11	45	87	.290	.335
Runners on	.295	312	92	15	5	8	79	29	48	.362	.452
Scoring Posn	.280	175	49	10	1	4	64	16	32	.343	.417
Close & Late	.356	45	16	1	1	0	4	3	4	.396	.422
None on/out	.214	201	43	10	1	5	5	23	33	.298	.348
vs. 1st Batr (relief)	.000	1	0	0	0	0	0	0	1	.000	.000
First Inning Pitched	.220	118	26	6	1	2	13	13	22	.293	.339
First 75 Pitches	.231	584	135	26	6	15	62	55	106	.302	.373
Pitch 76-90	.364	107	39	6	0	1	14	10	15	.429	.449
Pitch 91-105	.234	64	15	1	0	2	10	6	9	.296	.344
Pitch 106+	.243	37	9	0	1	1	4	3	5	.300	.378
First Pitch	.276	123	34	11	0	4	22	2	0	.302	.463
Ahead in Count	.209	364	76	10	2	7	29	0	116	.217	.305
Behind in Count	.317	164	52	6	5	5	25	43	0	.459	.506
Two Strikes	.188	352	66	8	1	7	23	29	135	.255	.276

Last Five Years

	ERA	W	L	Sv	G	GS	IP	H	HR	BB	SO
Home	3.15	42	22	0	84	79	560.1	484	49	173	426
Away	3.98	19	33	1	81	75	468.1	422	34	184	316
Day	3.93	12	16	1	52	44	279.2	287	23	103	191
Night	3.38	49	39	0	113	110	749.0	619	60	254	551

	Avg	AB	H	2B	3B	HR	RBI	BB	SO	OBP	SLG
vs. Left	.253	2128	539	87	13	36	196	234	372	.328	.357
vs. Right	.216	1700	367	57	12	47	187	123	370	.272	.346
Inning 1-6	.233	3111	725	110	22	73	329	295	630	.301	.353
Inning 7+	.252	717	181	34	3	10	54	62	112	.315	.350

Last Five Years

	ERA	W	L	Sv	G	GS	IP	H	HR	BB	SO
Grass	2.93	36	29	0	96	89	617.1	526	47	188	441
Turf	4.42	25	26	1	69	65	411.1	380	36	169	301
April	3.66	8	11	0	24	24	160.0	142	9	43	115
May	3.02	11	9	0	26	26	169.2	135	12	67	134
June	3.37	10	9	1	31	28	195.0	175	19	65	134
July	4.15	13	10	0	34	27	186.1	185	14	75	131
August	3.75	9	10	0	25	25	161.0	148	15	56	115
September/October	3.16	10	6	0	25	24	156.2	121	14	51	113
Starter	3.50	60	52	0	154	154	1008.0	884	80	348	725
Reliever	4.79	1	3	1	11	0	20.2	22	3	9	17
0-3 Days Rest	3.23	2	2	0	6	6	39.0	36	3	17	27
4 Days Rest	3.31	40	27	0	95	95	633.2	539	49	200	467
5+ Days Rest	3.89	18	23	0	53	53	335.1	309	28	131	231
Pre-All Star	3.43	34	31	1	95	85	584.1	516	43	200	422
Post-All Star	3.65	27	24	0	70	69	444.1	390	40	157	320

	Avg	AB	H	2B	3B	HR	RBI	BB	SO	OBP	SLG
None on	.225	2344	527	86	10	51	51	197	451	.287	.335
Runners on	.255	1484	379	58	15	32	332	160	291	.328	.379
Scoring Posn	.241	837	202	37	9	19	289	95	183	.314	.375
Close & Late	.255	369	94	18	2	4	31	35	54	.317	.347
None on/out	.221	1006	222	37	7	26	26	88	165	.285	.349
vs. 1st Batr (relief)	.125	8	1	0	0	0	1	3	2	.364	.125
First Inning Pitched	.245	604	148	23	6	10	77	70	148	.324	.353
First 75 Pitches	.234	2713	634	100	21	59	262	250	563	.300	.351
Pitch 76-90	.280	496	139	25	2	16	68	45	71	.342	.435
Pitch 91-105	.198	344	68	9	1	4	30	34	66	.270	.265
Pitch 106+	.236	275	65	10	1	4	23	28	42	.305	.324
First Pitch	.301	559	168	33	6	23	81	12	0	.322	.504
Ahead in Count	.189	1842	349	47	9	22	131	0	625	.194	.261
Behind in Count	.293	723	212	29	8	24	111	187	0	.434	.455
Two Strikes	.170	1804	307	40	6	24	113	158	742	.240	.239

Pitcher vs. Batter (career)

Pitches Best Vs.	Avg	AB	H	2B	3B	HR	RBI	BB	SO	OBP	SLG
Sammy Sosa	.000	13	0	0	0	0	0	0	1	.000	.000
Mitch Webster	.059	17	1	0	0	0	0	1	5	.111	.059
Kirt Manwaring	.091	11	1	0	0	0	0	0	2	.091	.091
Jose Uribe	.095	21	2	0	0	0	0	0	4	.095	.095
Tom Brunansky	.100	10	1	0	0	0	2	0	3	.091	.100

Pitches Worst Vs.	Avg	AB	H	2B	3B	HR	RBI	BB	SO	OBP	SLG
Jose Vizcaino	.615	13	8	1	1	0	4	1	2	.643	.846
Bob Melvin	.583	12	7	0	0	1	2	0	3	.583	.833
Dave Clark	.438	16	7	3	0	2	8	0	1	.438	1.000
Kevin McReynolds	.389	18	7	0	1	3	7	2	1	.450	1.000
Eric Karros	.357	14	5	2	0	2	6	1	2	.400	.929

Stan Belinda — Royals

Age 27 – Pitches Right (flyball pitcher)

	ERA	W	L	Sv	G	GS	IP	BB	SO	Avg	H	2B	3B	HR	RBI	OBP	SLG	GF	IR	IRS	Hld	SvOp	SB	CS	GB	FB	G/F
1993 Season	3.88	4	2	19	63	0	69.2	17	55	.247	65	11	2	6	39	.296	.373	44	29	9	8	23	17	2	88	80	1.10
Career (1989-1993)	3.59	20	16	61	245	0	288.0	112	248	.223	234	38	8	28	147	.299	.354	140	136	49	25	80	51	7	297	354	0.84

1993 Season

	ERA	W	L	Sv	G	GS	IP	H	HR	BB	SO
Home	4.67	4	1	8	30	0	34.2	34	3	7	27
Away	3.09	0	1	11	33	0	35.0	31	3	10	28
Day	3.91	1	0	4	21	0	25.1	27	2	7	29
Night	3.86	3	2	15	42	0	44.1	38	4	10	26
Grass	3.63	0	1	8	21	0	22.1	19	3	3	16
Turf	3.99	4	1	11	42	0	47.1	46	3	14	39
April	2.70	0	0	5	9	0	10.0	7	2	1	9
May	3.14	1	0	5	11	0	14.1	13	0	4	13
June	1.80	2	0	4	10	0	10.0	6	1	2	1
July	7.88	0	1	5	10	0	8.0	9	1	4	7
August	3.24	1	1	0	15	0	16.2	12	1	1	16
September/October	5.91	0	0	0	8	0	10.2	18	1	5	9
Starter	0.00	0	0	0	0	0	0.0	0	0	0	0
Reliever	3.88	4	2	19	63	0	69.2	65	6	17	55
0 Days rest	5.23	1	0	5	12	0	10.1	7	1	3	8
1 or 2 Days rest	2.49	2	1	9	34	0	43.1	40	2	6	35
3+ Days rest	6.75	1	1	5	17	0	16.0	18	3	8	12
Pre-All Star	2.41	3	0	17	35	0	37.1	27	3	10	26
Post-All Star	5.57	1	2	2	28	0	32.1	38	3	7	29

	Avg	AB	H	2B	3B	HR	RBI	BB	SO	OBP	SLG
vs. Left	.303	119	36	5	2	5	18	10	21	.362	.504
vs. Right	.201	144	29	6	0	1	21	7	34	.240	.264
Inning 1-6	.600	10	6	0	0	0	5	3	1	.692	.600
Inning 7+	.233	253	59	11	2	6	34	14	54	.277	.364
None on	.226	133	30	7	2	3	3	8	31	.275	.376
Runners on	.269	130	35	4	0	3	36	9	24	.317	.369
Scoring Posn	.288	80	23	2	0	3	36	8	16	.352	.425
Close & Late	.220	146	33	8	1	3	24	6	30	.258	.356
None on/out	.278	54	15	3	1	3	3	6	8	.361	.537
vs. 1st Batr (relief)	.259	58	15	3	1	3	6	5	8	.317	.500
First Inning Pitched	.257	214	55	10	1	6	34	15	45	.306	.397
First 15 Pitches	.258	186	48	7	2	5	27	13	36	.308	.398
Pitch 16-30	.215	65	14	4	0	1	10	4	15	.268	.323
Pitch 31-45	.111	9	1	0	0	0	2	0	4	.111	.111
Pitch 46+	.667	3	2	0	0	0	0	0	0	.667	.667
First Pitch	.324	37	12	5	1	1	7	4	0	.390	.595
Ahead in Count	.168	107	18	1	0	3	10	0	47	.176	.262
Behind in Count	.299	67	20	3	1	1	9	7	0	.355	.418
Two Strikes	.231	117	27	2	0	4	17	6	55	.274	.350

Career (1989-1993)

	ERA	W	L	Sv	G	GS	IP	H	HR	BB	SO
Home	3.49	9	6	31	116	0	142.0	125	9	47	120
Away	3.70	11	10	30	129	0	146.0	109	19	65	128
Day	4.70	4	5	18	69	0	84.1	83	10	40	79
Night	3.14	16	11	43	176	0	203.2	151	18	72	169
Grass	4.18	4	6	15	68	0	75.1	58	13	31	60
Turf	3.39	16	10	46	177	0	212.2	176	15	81	188
April	3.04	1	1	12	21	0	26.2	14	3	8	27
May	4.76	5	2	9	38	0	45.1	41	5	18	40
June	1.18	5	2	13	44	0	45.2	28	1	17	37
July	4.67	2	4	13	45	0	52.0	41	10	28	43
August	3.39	1	4	8	51	0	61.0	49	5	21	57
September/October	4.08	6	3	6	46	0	57.1	61	4	20	44
Starter	0.00	0	0	0	0	0	0.0	0	0	0	0
Reliever	3.59	20	16	61	245	0	288.0	234	28	112	248
0 Days rest	4.43	4	5	14	42	0	42.2	40	6	18	35
1 or 2 Days rest	3.02	10	6	32	132	0	170.0	131	14	57	148
3+ Days rest	4.42	6	5	15	71	0	75.1	63	8	37	65
Pre-All Star	2.69	11	6	40	121	0	137.0	90	10	54	121
Post-All Star	4.41	9	10	21	124	0	151.0	144	18	58	127

	Avg	AB	H	2B	3B	HR	RBI	BB	SO	OBP	SLG
vs. Left	.227	484	110	19	2	14	57	56	96	.309	.362
vs. Right	.219	566	124	19	6	14	90	56	152	.290	.348
Inning 1-6	.293	41	12	0	0	0	14	11	10	.418	.293
Inning 7+	.220	1009	222	38	8	28	133	101	238	.293	.357
None on	.198	572	113	20	6	12	12	56	152	.275	.316
Runners on	.253	478	121	18	2	16	135	56	96	.326	.400
Scoring Posn	.240	317	76	9	2	13	125	46	69	.328	.404
Close & Late	.215	633	136	28	5	15	91	66	144	.290	.346
None on/out	.204	235	48	10	3	8	8	23	63	.278	.374
vs. 1st Batr (relief)	.196	214	42	9	2	9	28	28	54	.286	.383
First Inning Pitched	.227	780	177	32	7	19	117	84	178	.301	.359
First 15 Pitches	.224	689	154	27	6	17	89	70	159	.295	.354
Pitch 16-30	.216	306	66	9	2	9	45	33	74	.293	.346
Pitch 31-45	.231	52	12	2	0	2	13	9	15	.355	.385
Pitch 46+	.667	3	2	0	0	0	0	0	0	.667	.667
First Pitch	.305	128	39	12	1	4	30	14	0	.367	.508
Ahead in Count	.166	530	88	13	2	8	48	0	217	.171	.243
Behind in Count	.296	203	60	8	3	8	32	52	0	.433	.483
Two Strikes	.171	545	93	10	3	14	58	45	248	.236	.277

Pitcher vs. Batter (career)

Pitches Best Vs.	Avg	AB	H	2B	3B	HR	RBI	BB	SO	OBP	SLG
Charlie Hayes	.083	12	1	0	0	0	1	0	0	.083	.083
Tim Wallach	.167	18	3	1	0	0	2	2	3	.250	.222
Andres Galarraga	.167	18	3	0	0	0	1	0	7	.167	.167

Pitches Worst Vs.	Avg	AB	H	2B	3B	HR	RBI	BB	SO	OBP	SLG
Barry Larkin	.444	9	4	0	1	0	3	1	0	.455	.667
Andre Dawson	.385	13	5	0	0	4	10	0	1	.385	1.308
Ryne Sandberg	.385	13	5	0	0	1	3	1	2	.429	.615

Pitcher vs. Batter (career)																						
Pitches Best Vs.	Avg	AB	H	2B	3B	HR	RBI	BB	SO	OBP	SLG	**Pitches Worst Vs.**	Avg	AB	H	2B	3B	HR	RBI	BB	SO	OBP	SLG
Terry Pendleton	.167	12	2	0	0	1	3	0	3	.167	.417												
Todd Zeile	.167	12	2	1	0	1	4	4	2	.375	.500												

Derek Bell — Padres

Age 25 – Bats Right (groundball hitter)

	Avg	G	AB	R	H	2B	3B	HR	RBI	BB	SO	HBP	GDP	SB	CS	OBP	SLG	IBB	SH	SF	#Pit	#P/PA	GB	FB	G/F
1993 Season	.262	150	542	73	142	19	1	21	72	23	122	12	7	26	5	.303	.417	5	0	8	1978	3.38	221	111	1.99
Career (1991-1993)	.253	229	731	101	185	25	4	23	88	44	161	18	13	36	9	.308	.393	6	2	9	2779	3.46	299	164	1.82

1993 Season

	Avg	AB	H	2B	3B	HR	RBI	BB	SO	OBP	SLG		Avg	AB	H	2B	3B	HR	RBI	BB	SO	OBP	SLG
vs. Left	.299	177	53	6	0	11	30	10	31	.342	.520	Scoring Posn	.259	139	36	2	0	5	47	11	31	.335	.381
vs. Right	.244	365	89	13	1	10	42	13	91	.284	.367	Close & Late	.218	101	22	2	0	2	9	6	25	.288	.297
Groundball	.231	182	42	9	1	8	28	9	37	.285	.423	None on/out	.299	137	41	8	0	5	5	6	20	.338	.407
Flyball	.268	97	26	2	0	6	14	4	26	.301	.464	Batting #5	.293	229	67	10	0	11	32	11	53	.332	.480
Home	.252	274	69	9	0	12	34	17	60	.309	.416	Batting #6	.264	140	37	3	0	5	17	5	40	.307	.393
Away	.272	268	73	10	1	9	38	6	62	.296	.418	Other	.220	173	38	6	1	5	23	7	29	.261	.353
Day	.195	169	33	9	0	4	14	5	38	.239	.320	April	.274	73	20	3	0	5	11	7	25	.346	.521
Night	.292	373	109	10	1	17	58	18	84	.331	.461	May	.330	103	34	2	0	5	17	2	19	.358	.495
Grass	.262	416	109	16	1	19	62	20	86	.306	.442	June	.208	101	21	2	0	3	11	5	28	.259	.317
Turf	.262	126	33	3	0	2	10	3	36	.290	.333	July	.204	93	19	4	1	1	8	2	20	.232	.301
First Pitch	.398	98	39	6	0	9	24	5	0	.426	.735	August	.283	92	26	5	0	4	17	4	20	.320	.467
Ahead in Count	.323	96	31	3	0	4	17	4	0	.347	.479	September/October	.275	80	22	3	0	3	8	3	10	.310	.425
Behind in Count	.188	272	51	4	1	5	23	0	109	.215	.265	Pre-All Star	.265	310	82	8	1	13	42	14	79	.307	.423
Two Strikes	.151	258	39	7	0	5	15	14	122	.214	.236	Post-All Star	.259	232	60	11	0	8	30	9	43	.297	.409

1993 By Position

Position	Avg	AB	H	2B	3B	HR	RBI	BB	SO	OBP	SLG	G	GS	Innings	PO	A	E	DP	Fld Pct	Rng Fctr	In Zone	Outs	Zone Rtg	MLB Zone
As 3b	.382	68	26	2	0	4	11	3	8	.411	.588	19	18	152.0	12	28	9	3	.816	2.37	35	30	.857	.834
As cf	.260	447	116	17	1	17	60	19	107	.301	.416	120	117	1019.0	317	8	8	4	.976	2.87	365	312	.855	.829

Eric Bell — Astros

Age 30 – Pitches Left

	ERA	W	L	Sv	G	GS	IP	BB	SO	Avg	H	2B	3B	HR	RBI	OBP	SLG	GF	IR	IRS	Hld	SvOp	SB	CS	GB	FB	G/F
1993 Season	6.14	0	1	0	10	0	7.1	2	2	.313	10	1	0	0	5	.353	.344	2	10	2	1	0	2	0	11	13	0.85
Last Five Years	4.20	4	3	0	27	1	40.2	16	19	.247	37	6	0	1	19	.325	.307	7	21	3	4	0	8	1	55	50	1.10

1993 Season

	ERA	W	L	Sv	G	GS	IP	H	HR	BB	SO		Avg	AB	H	2B	3B	HR	RBI	BB	SO	OBP	SLG
Home	6.75	0	1	0	8	0	6.2	10	0	1	1	vs. Left	.500	8	4	0	0	0	0	1	1	.556	.500
Away	0.00	0	0	0	2	0	0.2	0	0	1	1	vs. Right	.250	24	6	1	0	0	5	1	1	.280	.292

George Bell — White Sox

Age 34 – Bats Right (flyball hitter)

	Avg	G	AB	R	H	2B	3B	HR	RBI	BB	SO	HBP	GDP	SB	CS	OBP	SLG	IBB	SH	SF	#Pit	#P/PA	GB	FB	G/F
1993 Season	.217	102	410	36	89	17	2	13	64	13	49	4	14	1	1	.243	.363	2	0	9	1493	3.42	136	172	0.79
Last Five Years	.267	701	2770	328	739	137	4	102	452	141	348	21	85	15	14	.302	.430	26	0	49	10350	3.47	858	1073	0.80

1993 Season

	Avg	AB	H	2B	3B	HR	RBI	BB	SO	OBP	SLG		Avg	AB	H	2B	3B	HR	RBI	BB	SO	OBP	SLG
vs. Left	.193	109	21	4	0	3	12	4	17	.217	.312	Scoring Posn	.218	124	27	2	1	7	56	3	19	.226	.419
vs. Right	.226	301	68	13	2	10	52	9	32	.252	.382	Close & Late	.226	53	12	0	1	1	6	1	4	.250	.321
Groundball	.236	89	21	3	0	3	15	1	7	.250	.371	None on/out	.190	105	20	6	0	2	2	2	13	.213	.305
Flyball	.213	80	17	5	0	4	15	5	10	.253	.425	Batting #4	.221	258	57	11	2	4	32	11	29	.254	.326
Home	.224	201	45	8	2	7	38	6	25	.249	.388	Batting #5	.218	133	29	6	0	8	30	2	17	.234	.444
Away	.211	209	44	9	0	6	26	7	24	.238	.340	Other	.158	19	3	0	0	1	2	0	3	.158	.316
Day	.250	132	33	6	1	5	27	1	11	.248	.424	April	.186	86	16	4	0	0	8	6	8	.247	.233
Night	.201	278	56	11	1	8	37	12	38	.241	.335	May	.262	103	27	3	1	4	18	2	8	.275	.427
Grass	.231	364	84	15	2	13	62	10	40	.253	.390	June	.229	105	24	7	1	2	16	3	15	.241	.371
Turf	.109	46	5	2	0	0	2	3	9	.163	.152	July	.217	23	5	0	0	1	4	0	2	.217	.348
First Pitch	.171	41	7	1	0	1	6	2	0	.205	.268	August	.000	0	0	0	0	0	0	0	0	.000	.000
Ahead in Count	.231	117	27	6	1	6	23	8	0	.278	.453	September/October	.183	93	17	3	0	6	18	2	16	.212	.409
Behind in Count	.202	198	40	8	1	5	26	0	47	.207	.328	Pre-All Star	.228	298	68	14	2	6	42	11	31	.255	.349
Two Strikes	.196	168	33	8	1	5	25	3	49	.215	.345	Post-All Star	.188	112	21	3	0	7	22	2	18	.212	.402

1993 By Position

Position	Avg	AB	H	2B	3B	HR	RBI	BB	SO	OBP	SLG	G	GS	Innings	PO	A	E	DP	Fld Pct	Rng Fctr	In Zone	Outs	Zone Rtg	MLB Zone
As Designated Hitter	.217	410	89	17	2	13	64	13	49	.243	.363	102	102	---	---	---	---	---	---	---	---	---	---	---

Last Five Years

	Avg	AB	H	2B	3B	HR	RBI	BB	SO	OBP	SLG		Avg	AB	H	2B	3B	HR	RBI	BB	SO	OBP	SLG
vs. Left	.271	786	213	38	1	39	135	57	93	.318	.471	Scoring Posn	.277	806	223	39	2	33	356	55	122	.310	.453
vs. Right	.265	1984	526	99	3	63	317	84	255	.296	.413	Close & Late	.251	438	110	17	2	16	65	27	68	.294	.409
Groundball	.283	718	203	38	1	21	108	31	93	.314	.426	None on/out	.245	686	168	32	1	29	29	28	85	.278	.421
Flyball	.264	674	178	35	0	34	116	38	90	.303	.467	Batting #4	.263	1874	492	87	3	65	294	100	242	.300	.416
Home	.265	1370	363	63	4	51	234	66	174	.300	.428	Batting #5	.265	667	177	35	0	25	108	32	90	.302	.430
Away	.269	1400	376	74	0	51	218	75	174	.304	.431	Other	.306	229	70	15	1	12	50	9	16	.324	.537
Day	.266	900	239	44	3	30	143	46	114	.302	.421	April	.262	420	110	18	0	16	61	17	43	.293	.419

Last Five Years

	Avg	AB	H	2B	3B	HR	RBI	BB	SO	OBP	SLG
Night	.267	1870	500	93	1	72	309	95	234	.303	.434
Grass	.267	1788	477	86	2	70	315	90	221	.301	.435
Turf	.267	982	262	51	2	32	137	51	127	.305	.421
First Pitch	.305	269	82	16	0	12	59	14	0	.341	.498
Ahead in Count	.279	699	195	41	1	35	131	84	0	.353	.491
Behind in Count	.242	1347	326	58	2	38	186	0	306	.245	.373
Two Strikes	.217	1163	252	38	2	27	136	36	348	.244	.322

	Avg	AB	H	2B	3B	HR	RBI	BB	SO	OBP	SLG
May	.249	494	123	16	1	19	82	29	61	.292	.401
June	.284	542	154	33	1	22	98	31	77	.319	.470
July	.266	395	105	23	0	12	62	21	50	.307	.415
August	.306	418	128	26	2	18	77	23	50	.338	.507
September/October	.238	501	119	21	0	15	72	20	67	.268	.369
Pre-All Star	.270	1591	429	78	2	61	268	85	192	.307	.436
Post-All Star	.263	1179	310	59	2	41	184	56	156	.296	.421

Batter vs. Pitcher (since 1984)

Hits Best Against	Avg	AB	H	2B	3B	HR	RBI	BB	SO	OBP	SLG
Mark Knudson	.455	11	5	0	0	2	4	1	0	.500	1.000
Neal Heaton	.444	27	12	4	0	4	10	0	0	.444	1.037
Scott Bankhead	.433	30	13	4	0	5	7	0	2	.433	1.067
Tom Browning	.364	11	4	0	0	3	4	2	2	.462	1.182
Trevor Wilson	.333	9	3	1	0	2	4	2	0	.417	1.111

Hits Worst Against	Avg	AB	H	2B	3B	HR	RBI	BB	SO	OBP	SLG
Paul Gibson	.000	11	0	0	0	0	1	2	2	.143	.000
Alan Mills	.071	14	1	0	0	0	0	1	1	.133	.071
John Dopson	.083	12	1	0	0	0	1	1	4	.143	.083
Rod Nichols	.083	12	1	1	0	0	2	0	0	.071	.167
Jack McDowell	.091	11	1	0	0	0	1	0	2	.083	.091

Jay Bell — Pirates

Age 28 – Bats Right

	Avg	G	AB	R	H	2B	3B	HR	RBI	BB	SO	HBP	GDP	SB	CS	OBP	SLG	IBB	SH	SF	#Pit	#P/PA	GB	FB	G/F
1993 Season	.310	154	604	102	187	32	9	9	51	77	122	6	16	16	10	.392	.437	6	13	1	2786	3.97	222	147	1.51
Last Five Years	.273	707	2698	411	736	141	33	43	252	268	480	18	66	48	30	.341	.397	7	111	14	11719	3.77	944	798	1.18

1993 Season

	Avg	AB	H	2B	3B	HR	RBI	BB	SO	OBP	SLG
vs. Left	.342	190	65	14	2	3	21	33	30	.449	.484
vs. Right	.295	414	122	18	7	6	30	44	92	.364	.415
Groundball	.310	200	62	7	1	2	14	19	45	.376	.385
Flyball	.256	90	23	9	1	2	8	14	22	.356	.444
Home	.322	286	92	19	3	3	22	49	57	.424	.441
Away	.299	318	95	13	6	6	29	28	65	.362	.434
Day	.329	164	54	14	1	3	13	23	28	.418	.482
Night	.302	440	133	18	8	6	38	54	94	.383	.420
Grass	.333	207	69	10	4	5	20	18	42	.390	.493
Turf	.297	397	118	22	5	4	31	59	80	.393	.408
First Pitch	.421	57	24	3	0	2	9	5	0	.460	.579
Ahead in Count	.380	129	49	10	1	4	13	40	0	.532	.566
Behind in Count	.266	278	74	9	7	2	16	0	101	.277	.371
Two Strikes	.226	297	67	9	5	2	18	32	122	.309	.310

	Avg	AB	H	2B	3B	HR	RBI	BB	SO	OBP	SLG
Scoring Posn	.274	117	32	6	1	0	38	27	26	.411	.342
Close & Late	.268	97	26	3	1	0	11	18	29	.383	.320
None on/out	.295	112	33	5	3	4	4	13	23	.368	.500
Total	.310	604	187	32	9	9	51	77	122	.392	.437
Batting #2	.310	604	187	32	9	9	51	77	122	.392	.437
Other	.000	0	0	0	0	0	0	0	0	.000	.000
April	.326	86	28	5	2	1	6	7	16	.376	.465
May	.300	110	33	11	1	1	10	10	27	.358	.445
June	.326	95	31	3	1	2	11	18	20	.435	.442
July	.273	110	30	5	2	1	7	6	18	.322	.382
August	.386	114	44	8	1	2	13	13	22	.453	.526
September/October	.236	89	21	0	2	2	4	23	19	.404	.348
Pre-All Star	.298	339	101	22	4	5	30	36	72	.366	.431
Post-All Star	.325	265	86	10	5	4	21	41	50	.424	.445

1993 By Position

Position	Avg	AB	H	2B	3B	HR	RBI	BB	SO	OBP	SLG	G	GS	Innings	PO	A	E	DP	Fld Pct	Rng Fctr	In Zone	Outs	Zone Rtg	MLB Zone
As ss	.310	604	187	32	9	9	51	77	122	.392	.437	154	153	1349.0	259	525	11	103	.986	5.23	651	555	.853	.880

Last Five Years

	Avg	AB	H	2B	3B	HR	RBI	BB	SO	OBP	SLG
vs. Left	.302	980	296	63	16	13	96	129	152	.385	.439
vs. Right	.256	1718	440	78	17	30	156	139	328	.314	.374
Groundball	.271	966	262	47	10	10	76	83	163	.333	.372
Flyball	.244	542	132	30	5	13	56	58	126	.315	.389
Home	.282	1319	372	80	15	17	110	146	240	.356	.404
Away	.264	1379	364	61	18	26	142	122	240	.327	.391
Day	.291	729	212	51	8	13	75	67	130	.354	.436
Night	.266	1969	524	90	25	30	177	201	350	.336	.383
Grass	.274	727	199	35	12	13	71	58	131	.329	.409
Turf	.272	1971	537	106	21	30	181	210	349	.345	.393
First Pitch	.323	313	101	20	6	7	43	6	0	.336	.492
Ahead in Count	.328	536	176	34	7	14	59	162	0	.485	.496
Behind in Count	.236	1301	307	53	16	14	92	0	412	.240	.334
Two Strikes	.211	1306	275	49	15	14	96	99	480	.269	.303

	Avg	AB	H	2B	3B	HR	RBI	BB	SO	OBP	SLG
Scoring Posn	.299	551	165	32	11	8	195	70	96	.373	.441
Close & Late	.272	430	117	16	8	5	50	52	91	.349	.381
None on/out	.270	500	135	22	8	14	14	54	88	.342	.430
Batting #2	.277	2610	722	137	32	42	243	265	464	.346	.402
Batting #8	.148	81	12	4	0	0	5	3	14	.176	.198
Other	.286	7	2	0	1	1	4	0	2	.286	1.000
April	.242	318	77	13	3	2	23	34	55	.317	.321
May	.275	407	112	32	3	8	46	38	77	.336	.428
June	.295	397	117	18	8	7	39	48	77	.373	.433
July	.269	475	128	23	3	9	43	28	61	.312	.387
August	.291	549	160	30	6	7	46	40	106	.342	.406
September/October	.257	552	142	25	10	10	55	80	104	.357	.393
Pre-All Star	.269	1281	345	72	14	19	120	128	232	.336	.392
Post-All Star	.276	1417	391	69	19	24	132	140	248	.345	.402

Batter vs. Pitcher (career)

Hits Best Against	Avg	AB	H	2B	3B	HR	RBI	BB	SO	OBP	SLG
Mike Bielecki	.632	19	12	4	2	0	5	2	3	.667	1.053
Jimmy Jones	.600	15	9	1	0	2	5	1	2	.625	1.067
Jack Armstrong	.545	11	6	0	1	0	1	2	1	.615	.727
Paul Assenmacher	.455	11	5	1	1	1	2	1	2	.500	1.000
Randy Myers	.333	12	4	1	1	1	6	3	4	.467	.833

Hits Worst Against	Avg	AB	H	2B	3B	HR	RBI	BB	SO	OBP	SLG
Lee Smith	.000	10	0	0	0	0	0	1	5	.091	.000
Mike Maddux	.067	15	1	0	0	0	0	0	1	.067	.067
Darryl Kile	.067	15	1	0	0	0	0	0	2	.067	.067
Rich Rodriguez	.071	14	1	0	0	0	0	0	5	.071	.071
Xavier Hernandez	.083	12	1	0	0	0	0	0	4	.083	.083

Juan Bell — Brewers

Age 26 – Bats Both

	Avg	G	AB	R	H	2B	3B	HR	RBI	BB	SO	HBP	GDP	SB	CS	OBP	SLG	IBB	SH	SF	#Pit	#P/PA	GB	FB	G/F
1993 Season	.228	115	351	47	80	12	3	5	36	41	76	2	4	6	7	.311	.322	0	5	1	1537	3.84	110	90	1.22
Career (1989-1993)	.205	274	713	88	146	24	6	7	59	67	158	3	6	12	7	.274	.285	5	9	5	2976	3.73	237	187	1.27

1993 Season

	Avg	AB	H	2B	3B	HR	RBI	BB	SO	OBP	SLG
vs. Left	.271	144	39	6	0	3	13	14	28	.344	.375
vs. Right	.198	207	41	6	3	2	23	27	48	.289	.285
Groundball	.250	76	19	5	0	1	9	8	16	.329	.355

	Avg	AB	H	2B	3B	HR	RBI	BB	SO	OBP	SLG
Scoring Posn	.269	93	25	3	0	1	32	14	23	.361	.333
Close & Late	.186	43	8	1	0	0	3	4	14	.271	.209
None on/out	.196	102	20	4	0	0	0	13	21	.293	.235

1993 Season

	Avg	AB	H	2B	3B	HR	RBI	BB	SO	OBP	SLG
Flyball	.145	62	9	0	0	1	7	8	14	.250	.194
Home	.275	193	53	10	3	2	19	29	41	.369	.389
Away	.171	158	27	2	0	3	17	12	35	.237	.241
Day	.242	128	31	2	0	4	19	12	27	.307	.352
Night	.220	223	49	10	3	1	17	29	49	.314	.305
Grass	.248	270	67	7	2	4	30	33	57	.331	.333
Turf	.160	81	13	5	1	1	6	8	19	.244	.284
First Pitch	.341	44	15	4	0	0	9	0	0	.348	.432
Ahead in Count	.237	97	23	3	0	2	11	23	0	.383	.330
Behind in Count	.178	157	28	2	3	2	12	0	65	.184	.268
Two Strikes	.180	172	31	1	3	3	13	18	76	.262	.273

	Avg	AB	H	2B	3B	HR	RBI	BB	SO	OBP	SLG
Batting #8	.213	122	26	7	2	1	14	12	21	.289	.328
Batting #9	.270	100	27	4	1	2	9	17	24	.376	.390
Other	.209	129	27	1	0	2	13	12	31	.280	.264
April	.195	41	8	4	1	0	5	2	8	.250	.341
May	.208	24	5	2	0	0	2	3	4	.296	.292
June	.270	74	20	2	1	1	5	9	15	.353	.365
July	.261	46	12	0	0	3	8	9	11	.382	.457
August	.258	89	23	3	1	1	9	11	21	.340	.348
September/October	.156	77	12	1	0	0	7	7	17	.226	.169
Pre-All Star	.224	161	36	8	2	2	15	19	32	.311	.335
Post-All Star	.232	190	44	4	1	3	21	22	44	.311	.311

1993 By Position

Position	Avg	AB	H	2B	3B	HR	RBI	BB	SO	OBP	SLG	G	GS	Innings	PO	A	E	DP	Fld Pct	Rng Fctr	In Zone	Outs	Zone Rtg	MLB Zone
As 2b	.224	152	34	3	1	2	14	15	36	.293	.296	47	44	389.2	115	115	4	34	.983	5.31	126	121	.960	.895
As ss	.237	194	46	9	2	3	22	23	37	.323	.351	62	56	484.1	100	166	16	31	.943	4.94	218	181	.830	.880

Career (1989-1993)

	Avg	AB	H	2B	3B	HR	RBI	BB	SO	OBP	SLG
vs. Left	.220	255	56	9	0	3	16	21	57	.287	.290
vs. Right	.197	458	90	15	6	4	43	46	101	.267	.282
Groundball	.199	191	38	8	0	1	13	14	43	.257	.257
Flyball	.152	145	22	4	1	1	10	17	32	.247	.214
Home	.225	373	84	16	6	3	34	45	82	.308	.324
Away	.182	340	62	8	0	4	25	22	76	.235	.241
Day	.183	224	41	5	0	4	20	16	56	.237	.259
Night	.215	489	105	19	6	3	39	51	102	.291	.297
Grass	.211	474	100	15	4	4	40	43	106	.276	.285
Turf	.192	239	46	9	2	3	19	24	52	.270	.285
First Pitch	.278	108	30	8	1	0	13	3	0	.307	.370
Ahead in Count	.234	171	40	6	1	2	17	34	0	.357	.316
Behind in Count	.152	323	49	5	3	2	19	0	134	.154	.204
Two Strikes	.152	356	54	3	3	4	19	30	158	.219	.211

	Avg	AB	H	2B	3B	HR	RBI	BB	SO	OBP	SLG
Scoring Posn	.207	169	35	5	1	1	51	32	40	.329	.266
Close & Late	.170	106	18	2	0	1	6	7	26	.226	.217
None on/out	.206	189	39	7	1	1	1	14	42	.265	.270
Batting #8	.209	263	55	10	3	2	22	29	46	.291	.293
Batting #9	.207	300	62	13	3	3	24	24	73	.264	.300
Other	.193	150	29	1	0	2	13	14	39	.265	.240
April	.182	55	10	4	1	0	5	2	10	.224	.291
May	.175	40	7	3	0	0	2	3	9	.233	.250
June	.245	98	24	3	1	1	8	11	22	.324	.327
July	.215	107	23	1	0	4	11	10	26	.282	.336
August	.232	207	48	9	4	1	20	17	45	.288	.329
September/October	.165	206	34	4	0	1	13	24	46	.253	.199
Pre-All Star	.198	222	44	10	2	2	19	21	47	.272	.288
Post-All Star	.208	491	102	14	4	5	40	46	111	.275	.283

Batter vs. Pitcher (career)

Hits Best Against	Avg	AB	H	2B	3B	HR	RBI	BB	SO	OBP	SLG

Hits Worst Against	Avg	AB	H	2B	3B	HR	RBI	BB	SO	OBP	SLG
Danny Darwin	.091	11	1	1	0	0	0	0	2	.091	.182

Albert Belle — Indians

Age 27 – Bats Right

	Avg	G	AB	R	H	2B	3B	HR	RBI	BB	SO	HBP	GDP	SB	CS	OBP	SLG	IBB	SH	SF	#Pit	#P/PA	GB	FB	G/F
1993 Season	.290	159	594	93	172	36	3	38	129	76	96	8	18	23	12	.370	.552	13	1	14	2563	3.70	197	196	1.01
Career (1989-1993)	.270	506	1881	257	507	98	10	108	376	166	384	19	65	36	17	.330	.505	20	3	29	7585	3.61	632	579	1.09

1993 Season

	Avg	AB	H	2B	3B	HR	RBI	BB	SO	OBP	SLG
vs. Left	.327	162	53	11	0	12	39	26	25	.412	.617
vs. Right	.275	432	119	25	3	26	90	50	71	.353	.528
Groundball	.325	83	27	6	0	3	15	14	17	.437	.506
Flyball	.290	107	31	7	1	10	28	13	15	.363	.654
Home	.306	271	83	11	2	20	66	42	36	.399	.583
Away	.276	323	89	25	1	18	63	34	60	.344	.526
Day	.337	205	69	15	0	15	42	22	27	.403	.629
Night	.265	389	103	21	3	23	87	54	69	.353	.512
Grass	.287	495	142	29	2	33	107	67	80	.371	.554
Turf	.303	99	30	7	1	5	22	9	16	.363	.545
First Pitch	.297	118	35	7	1	3	22	10	0	.348	.449
Ahead in Count	.397	141	56	8	0	20	46	31	0	.497	.879
Behind in Count	.222	198	44	11	2	7	33	0	66	.228	.404
Two Strikes	.232	250	58	15	2	12	44	35	96	.331	.452

	Avg	AB	H	2B	3B	HR	RBI	BB	SO	OBP	SLG
Scoring Posn	.302	159	48	10	1	11	90	37	29	.408	.585
Close & Late	.333	81	27	5	1	7	26	17	12	.444	.679
None on/out	.257	148	38	13	1	4	4	9	21	.308	.439
Batting #2	.000	3	0	0	0	0	0	0	1	.000	.000
Batting #4	.291	591	172	36	3	38	129	76	95	.372	.555
Other	.000	0	0	0	0	0	0	0	0	.000	.000
April	.302	86	26	5	0	8	21	6	16	.365	.640
May	.276	105	29	6	0	7	23	14	14	.372	.533
June	.298	84	25	8	2	5	19	12	16	.386	.619
July	.341	91	31	4	0	9	25	17	12	.432	.681
August	.282	117	33	7	0	5	22	15	17	.360	.470
September/October	.252	111	28	6	1	4	19	12	21	.315	.432
Pre-All Star	.298	315	94	22	2	23	72	38	52	.381	.600
Post-All Star	.280	279	78	14	1	15	57	38	44	.358	.498

1993 By Position

Position	Avg	AB	H	2B	3B	HR	RBI	BB	SO	OBP	SLG	G	GS	Innings	PO	A	E	DP	Fld Pct	Rng Fctr	In Zone	Outs	Zone Rtg	MLB Zone
As lf	.284	563	160	36	3	33	118	71	94	.365	.535	150	149	1324.2	338	16	5	7	.986	2.41	395	319	.808	.818

Career (1989-1993)

	Avg	AB	H	2B	3B	HR	RBI	BB	SO	OBP	SLG
vs. Left	.287	499	143	34	1	32	113	48	99	.344	.551
vs. Right	.263	1382	364	64	9	76	263	118	285	.325	.488
Groundball	.254	441	112	17	1	13	65	44	105	.326	.385
Flyball	.280	425	119	26	3	36	94	37	81	.336	.609
Home	.272	920	250	46	4	47	191	87	180	.336	.484
Away	.267	961	257	52	6	61	185	79	204	.325	.524
Day	.287	595	171	42	3	33	123	51	117	.347	.534
Night	.261	1286	336	56	7	75	253	115	267	.323	.491
Grass	.266	1600	425	83	7	92	317	145	325	.327	.499
Turf	.292	281	82	15	3	16	59	21	59	.347	.537
First Pitch	.314	350	110	25	1	25	91	15	0	.342	.606

	Avg	AB	H	2B	3B	HR	RBI	BB	SO	OBP	SLG
Scoring Posn	.289	505	146	34	3	32	265	69	112	.362	.558
Close & Late	.255	294	75	10	2	15	70	32	71	.325	.456
None on/out	.264	469	124	26	4	19	19	31	88	.317	.458
Batting #4	.273	1594	435	86	6	94	324	153	319	.338	.511
Batting #6	.299	127	38	5	3	6	25	8	27	.341	.528
Other	.213	160	34	7	1	8	27	5	38	.238	.419
April	.260	246	64	12	0	17	46	18	58	.324	.516
May	.286	297	85	17	2	19	62	33	57	.361	.549
June	.257	218	56	12	2	12	38	19	41	.321	.495
July	.289	322	93	12	2	22	74	30	59	.345	.543
August	.259	401	104	20	1	21	73	33	86	.315	.471

Career (1989-1993)

	Avg	AB	H	2B	3B	HR	RBI	BB	SO	OBP	SLG
Ahead in Count	.357	398	142	16	2	41	104	57	0	.433	.716
Behind in Count	.215	752	162	37	5	21	97	0	297	.218	.362
Two Strikes	.196	841	165	39	5	24	111	94	384	.280	.340

	Avg	AB	H	2B	3B	HR	RBI	BB	SO	OBP	SLG
September/October	.264	397	105	25	3	17	83	33	83	.319	.471
Pre-All Star	.275	868	239	46	4	55	168	77	174	.339	.528
Post-All Star	.265	1013	268	52	6	53	208	89	210	.323	.485

Batter vs. Pitcher (career)

Hits Best Against	Avg	AB	H	2B	3B	HR	RBI	BB	SO	OBP	SLG
Cal Eldred	.545	11	6	0	1	2	4	2	0	.615	1.273
Todd Stottlemyre	.500	22	11	2	0	2	7	2	4	.542	.864
David Wells	.462	13	6	2	0	1	5	1	1	.467	.846
Ron Darling	.417	12	5	1	0	1	5	1	2	.462	.750
Arthur Rhodes	.400	10	4	2	0	2	7	2	2	.500	1.200

Hits Worst Against	Avg	AB	H	2B	3B	HR	RBI	BB	SO	OBP	SLG
Melido Perez	.000	16	0	0	0	0	0	5	6	.238	.000
Frank Viola	.059	17	1	1	0	0	3	1	4	.095	.118
Kevin Tapani	.059	17	1	0	0	0	2	2	5	.158	.059
Jim Abbott	.105	19	2	0	0	0	1	2	5	.182	.105
Kevin Appier	.115	26	3	1	0	0	2	0	10	.111	.154

Rafael Belliard — Braves

Age 32 – Bats Right (groundball hitter)

	Avg	G	AB	R	H	2B	3B	HR	RBI	BB	SO	HBP	GDP	SB	CS	OBP	SLG	IBB	SH	SF	#Pit	#P/PA	GB	FB	G/F
1993 Season	.228	91	79	6	18	5	0	0	6	4	13	3	1	0	0	.291	.291	0	3	0	268	3.01	41	13	3.15
Last Five Years	.227	498	925	82	210	27	3	0	61	53	154	9	14	9	6	.275	.263	8	27	1	3064	3.02	446	166	2.69

1993 Season

	Avg	AB	H	2B	3B	HR	RBI	BB	SO	OBP	SLG
vs. Left	.118	17	2	0	0	0	2	1	3	.167	.118
vs. Right	.258	62	16	5	0	0	4	3	10	.324	.339

	Avg	AB	H	2B	3B	HR	RBI	BB	SO	OBP	SLG
Scoring Posn	.167	24	4	1	0	0	5	2	4	.259	.208
Close & Late	.100	10	1	0	0	0	0	0	2	.100	.100

Last Five Years

	Avg	AB	H	2B	3B	HR	RBI	BB	SO	OBP	SLG
vs. Left	.226	230	52	5	0	0	16	10	37	.258	.248
vs. Right	.227	695	158	22	3	0	45	43	117	.281	.268
Groundball	.240	321	77	6	1	0	24	16	44	.280	.265
Flyball	.185	216	40	5	0	0	9	13	37	.235	.208
Home	.219	439	96	11	2	0	28	27	61	.272	.253
Away	.235	486	114	16	1	0	33	26	93	.279	.272
Day	.240	287	69	9	1	0	20	20	37	.294	.279
Night	.221	638	141	18	2	0	41	33	117	.267	.255
Grass	.226	579	131	18	2	0	35	32	91	.273	.264
Turf	.228	346	79	9	1	0	26	21	63	.280	.260
First Pitch	.329	219	72	7	1	0	24	7	0	.350	.370
Ahead in Count	.282	117	33	7	1	0	11	37	0	.462	.359
Behind in Count	.163	472	77	10	1	0	21	0	144	.172	.189
Two Strikes	.125	384	48	2	1	0	14	9	154	.154	.135

	Avg	AB	H	2B	3B	HR	RBI	BB	SO	OBP	SLG
Scoring Posn	.227	220	50	7	1	0	58	16	33	.282	.268
Close & Late	.241	112	27	1	0	0	4	4	23	.274	.250
None on/out	.201	214	43	5	1	0	0	14	39	.253	.234
Batting #2	.221	86	19	2	0	0	5	6	9	.280	.244
Batting #8	.226	782	177	23	3	0	51	42	134	.272	.263
Other	.246	57	14	2	0	0	5	5	11	.317	.281
April	.255	165	42	6	0	0	13	10	25	.305	.291
May	.218	193	42	6	1	0	15	11	33	.260	.259
June	.217	175	38	2	0	0	8	8	23	.258	.229
July	.209	129	27	5	1	0	12	9	20	.261	.264
August	.239	113	27	1	1	0	5	5	22	.283	.265
September/October	.227	150	34	7	0	0	8	10	31	.288	.273
Pre-All Star	.230	573	132	15	1	0	38	31	87	.274	.260
Post-All Star	.222	352	78	12	2	0	23	22	67	.277	.267

Batter vs. Pitcher (since 1984)

Hits Best Against	Avg	AB	H	2B	3B	HR	RBI	BB	SO	OBP	SLG
Mike Bielecki	.417	12	5	1	0	0	2	1	2	.462	.500
Terry Mulholland	.417	12	5	1	1	0	2	1	1	.462	.667

Hits Worst Against	Avg	AB	H	2B	3B	HR	RBI	BB	SO	OBP	SLG
Ramon Martinez	.071	14	1	0	0	0	0	1	2	.133	.071
Danny Cox	.077	13	1	0	0	0	0	2	3	.200	.077
Jose Rijo	.077	13	1	0	0	0	0	1	2	.143	.077
Fernando Valenzuela	.143	14	2	0	0	0	2	0	0	.143	.143
Jimmy Jones	.143	14	2	0	0	0	0	0	4	.143	.143

Freddie Benavides — Rockies

Age 28 – Bats Right (groundball hitter)

	Avg	G	AB	R	H	2B	3B	HR	RBI	BB	SO	HBP	GDP	SB	CS	OBP	SLG	IBB	SH	SF	#Pit	#P/PA	GB	FB	G/F
1993 Season	.286	74	213	20	61	10	3	3	26	6	27	0	4	3	2	.305	.404	1	3	1	710	3.18	97	37	2.62
Career (1991-1993)	.265	172	449	45	119	21	4	4	46	17	76	2	8	4	3	.294	.356	6	6	2	1569	3.30	193	86	2.24

1993 Season

	Avg	AB	H	2B	3B	HR	RBI	BB	SO	OBP	SLG
vs. Left	.356	59	21	3	1	1	5	1	4	.367	.492
vs. Right	.260	154	40	7	2	2	21	5	23	.281	.370
Home	.387	93	36	6	2	3	21	3	11	.406	.591
Away	.208	120	25	4	1	0	5	3	16	.226	.258
First Pitch	.340	47	16	5	0	1	3	1	0	.354	.511
Ahead in Count	.308	52	16	2	1	0	7	4	0	.357	.385
Behind in Count	.241	87	21	1	2	2	16	0	24	.239	.368
Two Strikes	.253	79	20	1	2	1	14	1	27	.259	.354

	Avg	AB	H	2B	3B	HR	RBI	BB	SO	OBP	SLG
Scoring Posn	.364	44	16	0	2	1	23	3	5	.396	.523
Close & Late	.395	38	15	1	1	2	11	1	3	.410	.632
None on/out	.254	67	17	6	0	1	1	1	8	.265	.388
Batting #7	.275	40	11	0	0	1	4	0	7	.275	.350
Batting #8	.275	109	30	7	2	1	12	6	15	.310	.404
Other	.313	64	20	3	1	1	10	0	5	.313	.438
Pre-All Star	.224	85	19	4	0	0	10	2	9	.239	.271
Post-All Star	.328	128	42	6	3	3	16	4	18	.348	.492

Andy Benes — Padres

Age 26 – Pitches Right (flyball pitcher)

	ERA	W	L	Sv	G	GS	IP	BB	SO	Avg	H	2B	3B	HR	RBI	OBP	SLG	CG	ShO	Sup	QS	#P/S	SB	CS	GB	FB	G/F
1993 Season	3.78	15	15	0	34	34	230.2	86	179	.232	200	37	7	23	90	.303	.371	4	2	4.10	20	106	21	7	250	272	0.92
Career (1989-1993)	3.44	59	54	0	143	142	944.0	306	721	.241	852	134	29	85	341	.302	.367	12	5	3.63	94	103	77	35	1051	1083	0.97

1993 Season

	ERA	W	L	Sv	G	GS	IP	H	HR	BB	SO
Home	3.47	6	7	0	15	15	103.2	87	13	33	93
Away	4.04	9	8	0	19	19	127.0	113	10	53	86
Day	2.51	5	2	0	9	9	64.2	46	2	17	58
Night	4.28	10	13	0	25	25	166.0	154	21	69	121
Grass	3.39	12	10	0	24	24	164.2	137	19	59	143
Turf	4.77	3	5	0	10	10	66.0	63	4	27	36

	Avg	AB	H	2B	3B	HR	RBI	BB	SO	OBP	SLG
vs. Left	.242	433	105	17	5	10	39	52	69	.327	.374
vs. Right	.221	429	95	20	2	13	51	34	110	.278	.368
Inning 1-6	.212	712	151	26	6	19	71	68	155	.282	.346
Inning 7+	.327	150	49	11	1	4	19	18	24	.398	.493
None on	.233	523	122	24	6	14	14	43	118	.294	.382
Runners on	.230	339	78	13	1	9	76	43	61	.315	.354

1993 Season

	ERA	W	L	Sv	G	GS	IP	H	HR	BB	SO
April	2.72	4	1	0	5	5	36.1	29	1	11	24
May	2.70	3	2	0	6	6	43.1	36	3	9	34
June	2.38	1	3	0	6	6	41.2	30	4	13	38
July	2.89	3	1	0	5	5	37.1	24	4	12	30
August	7.90	3	3	0	6	6	35.1	42	7	21	26
September/October	4.66	1	5	0	6	6	36.2	39	4	20	27
Starter	3.78	15	15	0	34	34	230.2	200	23	86	179
Reliever	0.00	0	0	0	0	0	0.0	0	0	0	0
0-3 Days Rest	0.00	0	0	0	0	0	0.0	0	0	0	0
4 Days Rest	3.61	13	12	0	28	28	189.2	159	21	70	158
5+ Days Rest	4.61	2	3	0	6	6	41.0	41	2	16	21
Pre-All Star	2.57	9	6	0	19	19	136.1	102	9	39	107
Post-All Star	5.53	6	9	0	15	15	94.1	98	14	47	72

	Avg	AB	H	2B	3B	HR	RBI	BB	SO	OBP	SLG
Scoring Posn	.221	190	42	9	1	6	68	35	34	.339	.374
Close & Late	.301	83	25	5	0	1	9	10	15	.379	.398
None on/out	.248	234	58	11	1	9	9	17	53	.302	.419
vs. 1st Batr (relief)	.000	0	0	0	0	0	0	0	0	.000	.000
First Inning Pitched	.186	118	22	3	0	1	10	16	25	.279	.237
First 75 Pitches	.214	598	128	23	3	12	50	50	134	.275	.323
Pitch 76-90	.205	112	23	6	2	4	15	15	19	.302	.402
Pitch 91-105	.343	105	36	5	2	6	18	10	18	.407	.600
Pitch 106+	.277	47	13	3	0	1	7	11	8	.407	.404
First Pitch	.337	104	35	5	1	5	16	5	0	.369	.548
Ahead in Count	.195	452	88	14	4	11	45	0	151	.197	.316
Behind in Count	.281	153	43	12	0	5	21	46	0	.445	.458
Two Strikes	.157	428	67	11	4	9	33	35	179	.222	.264

Career (1989-1993)

	ERA	W	L	Sv	G	GS	IP	H	HR	BB	SO
Home	3.72	28	24	0	70	69	459.2	441	47	148	384
Away	3.18	31	30	0	73	73	484.1	411	38	158	337
Day	2.71	20	9	0	41	41	275.1	232	21	77	241
Night	3.74	39	45	0	102	101	668.2	620	64	229	480
Grass	3.38	44	36	0	105	104	692.0	634	67	218	549
Turf	3.61	15	18	0	38	38	252.0	218	18	88	172
April	3.62	8	7	0	18	18	114.1	108	8	38	103
May	3.39	11	9	0	23	23	159.1	140	15	42	116
June	3.42	5	9	0	24	24	160.2	147	14	54	118
July	2.92	7	8	0	19	19	132.1	115	11	39	98
August	4.64	15	8	0	27	26	165.0	148	19	66	111
September/October	2.80	13	13	0	32	32	212.1	194	18	67	175
Starter	3.42	59	54	0	142	142	942.0	850	85	304	720
Reliever	13.50	0	0	0	1	0	2.0	2	0	2	1
0-3 Days Rest	7.20	1	1	0	2	2	10.0	15	0	4	7
4 Days Rest	3.37	38	38	0	94	94	632.2	568	51	208	509
5+ Days Rest	3.40	20	15	0	46	46	299.1	267	34	92	204
Pre-All Star	3.44	26	28	0	72	72	484.2	436	40	154	375
Post-All Star	3.45	33	26	0	71	70	459.1	416	45	152	346

	Avg	AB	H	2B	3B	HR	RBI	BB	SO	OBP	SLG
vs. Left	.248	2002	496	72	21	46	193	192	363	.315	.374
vs. Right	.232	1536	356	62	8	39	148	114	358	.285	.359
Inning 1-6	.232	3019	701	107	24	71	288	257	632	.293	.354
Inning 7+	.291	519	151	27	5	14	53	49	89	.352	.443
None on	.236	2161	510	78	22	54	54	168	443	.293	.367
Runners on	.248	1377	342	56	7	31	287	138	278	.315	.367
Scoring Posn	.230	770	177	33	6	14	245	95	166	.311	.343
Close & Late	.281	313	88	13	2	6	29	32	60	.348	.393
None on/out	.249	953	237	31	10	31	31	67	177	.301	.400
vs. 1st Batr (relief)	.000	1	0	0	0	0	0	0	0	.000	.000
First Inning Pitched	.206	515	106	16	1	8	39	56	117	.286	.287
First 75 Pitches	.224	2507	561	88	20	54	211	202	536	.282	.339
Pitch 76-90	.297	481	143	25	3	12	61	47	77	.361	.437
Pitch 91-105	.279	351	98	10	6	13	47	32	70	.340	.453
Pitch 106+	.251	199	50	11	0	6	22	25	38	.333	.397
First Pitch	.315	496	156	21	4	14	57	17	0	.339	.458
Ahead in Count	.187	1740	325	45	14	35	141	0	610	.190	.289
Behind in Count	.317	657	208	41	3	24	82	163	0	.450	.498
Two Strikes	.168	1731	291	45	13	28	111	125	721	.225	.258

Pitcher vs. Batter (career)

Pitches Best Vs.	Avg	AB	H	2B	3B	HR	RBI	BB	SO	OBP	SLG
Chico Walker	.000	13	0	0	0	0	0	0	4	.000	.000
Mike Felder	.071	14	1	0	0	0	0	2	3	.188	.071
Bret Barberie	.071	14	1	0	0	0	0	2	2	.188	.071
Steve Buechele	.083	12	1	0	0	0	0	0	5	.083	.083
Sammy Sosa	.083	12	1	0	0	0	0	0	4	.083	.083

Pitches Worst Vs.	Avg	AB	H	2B	3B	HR	RBI	BB	SO	OBP	SLG
Jeff Reed	.476	21	10	1	0	2	6	3	3	.520	.810
Moises Alou	.455	11	5	4	0	1	4	0	1	.455	1.091
Tommy Gregg	.438	16	7	3	0	0	0	4	5	.550	.625
Jeff Bagwell	.417	24	10	3	0	2	3	6	2	.516	.792
Kevin Mitchell	.346	26	9	3	1	4	7	2	8	.393	1.000

Mike Benjamin — Giants

Age 28 – Bats Right

	Avg	G	AB	R	H	2B	3B	HR	RBI	BB	SO	HBP	GDP	SB	CS	OBP	SLG	IBB	SH	SF	#Pit	#P/PA	GB	FB	G/F
1993 Season	.199	63	146	22	29	7	0	4	16	9	23	4	3	0	0	.264	.329	2	6	0	561	3.40	41	46	0.89
Career (1989-1993)	.175	193	389	51	68	15	2	9	30	23	75	6	7	5	0	.231	.293	6	12	2	1418	3.28	127	125	1.02

1993 Season

	Avg	AB	H	2B	3B	HR	RBI	BB	SO	OBP	SLG
vs. Left	.316	38	12	4	0	3	8	1	2	.333	.658
vs. Right	.157	108	17	3	0	1	8	8	21	.242	.213
Home	.197	71	14	4	0	3	10	5	13	.250	.380
Away	.200	75	15	3	0	1	6	4	10	.277	.280
First Pitch	.167	24	4	0	0	0	1	2	0	.231	.167
Ahead in Count	.176	34	6	2	0	3	8	3	0	.282	.500
Behind in Count	.200	70	14	4	0	0	3	0	21	.222	.257
Two Strikes	.197	66	13	2	0	1	5	4	23	.254	.273

	Avg	AB	H	2B	3B	HR	RBI	BB	SO	OBP	SLG
Scoring Posn	.294	34	10	4	0	1	9	5	3	.385	.500
Close & Late	.167	30	5	0	0	0	1	0	6	.167	.167
None on/out	.212	33	7	1	0	0	0	2	4	.278	.242
Batting #2	.130	23	3	0	0	1	2	2	5	.200	.261
Batting #8	.212	113	24	6	0	3	14	7	16	.282	.345
Other	.200	10	2	1	0	0	0	0	2	.200	.300
Pre-All Star	.212	113	24	6	0	4	14	7	14	.282	.372
Post-All Star	.152	33	5	1	0	0	2	2	9	.200	.182

Todd Benzinger — Giants

Age 31 – Bats Both

	Avg	G	AB	R	H	2B	3B	HR	RBI	BB	SO	HBP	GDP	SB	CS	OBP	SLG	IBB	SH	SF	#Pit	#P/PA	GB	FB	G/F
1993 Season	.288	86	177	25	51	7	2	6	26	13	35	0	2	0	0	.332	.452	1	1	3	682	3.52	58	59	0.98
Last Five Years	.253	615	1890	199	479	83	14	35	230	118	344	9	23	12	21	.297	.368	23	9	26	7032	3.43	669	592	1.13

1993 Season

	Avg	AB	H	2B	3B	HR	RBI	BB	SO	OBP	SLG
vs. Left	.486	37	18	1	1	2	11	4	5	.512	.730
vs. Right	.236	140	33	6	1	4	15	9	30	.280	.379
Home	.194	72	14	2	0	0	6	3	16	.218	.222
Away	.352	105	37	5	2	6	20	10	19	.409	.610
First Pitch	.367	30	11	1	1	2	7	1	0	.375	.667
Ahead in Count	.421	38	16	1	1	1	5	8	0	.522	.579
Behind in Count	.198	81	16	4	0	2	9	0	31	.198	.321
Two Strikes	.171	82	14	4	0	2	9	4	35	.209	.293

	Avg	AB	H	2B	3B	HR	RBI	BB	SO	OBP	SLG
Scoring Posn	.220	50	11	2	0	2	20	8	10	.311	.380
Close & Late	.213	47	10	3	0	0	4	2	9	.240	.277
None on/out	.382	34	13	0	1	1	1	1	7	.400	.529
Batting #5	.255	51	13	1	1	1	5	1	11	.269	.373
Batting #6	.356	45	16	1	0	3	13	4	6	.400	.578
Other	.272	81	22	5	1	2	8	8	18	.330	.432
Pre-All Star	.250	72	18	2	1	0	7	4	13	.286	.306
Post-All Star	.314	105	33	5	1	6	19	9	22	.362	.552

Last Five Years

	Avg	AB	H	2B	3B	HR	RBI	BB	SO	OBP	SLG
vs. Left	.272	709	193	27	3	13	83	34	75	.301	.374
vs. Right	.242	1181	286	56	11	22	147	84	269	.294	.364
Groundball	.272	677	184	32	4	15	94	37	116	.308	.397
Flyball	.245	441	108	20	6	8	54	32	85	.293	.372
Home	.259	927	240	51	8	13	108	54	147	.299	.373
Away	.248	963	239	32	6	22	122	64	197	.294	.362
Day	.248	604	150	23	4	9	62	49	118	.304	.344
Night	.256	1286	329	60	10	26	168	69	226	.293	.379
Grass	.243	774	188	30	3	15	83	51	148	.289	.348
Turf	.261	1116	291	53	11	20	147	67	196	.302	.382
First Pitch	.389	306	119	18	5	11	55	16	0	.417	.588
Ahead in Count	.295	390	115	18	3	9	55	59	0	.385	.426
Behind in Count	.187	859	161	31	4	7	64	0	296	.189	.257
Two Strikes	.170	822	140	24	5	11	78	37	344	.206	.252

	Avg	AB	H	2B	3B	HR	RBI	BB	SO	OBP	SLG
Scoring Posn	.234	530	124	24	4	12	196	55	114	.299	.362
Close & Late	.208	355	74	10	4	5	43	32	68	.272	.301
None on/out	.278	439	122	16	2	3	3	26	77	.320	.344
Batting #5	.256	738	189	33	6	14	100	42	134	.294	.374
Batting #6	.234	448	105	13	2	5	57	29	82	.283	.306
Other	.263	704	185	37	6	16	73	47	128	.308	.401
April	.244	234	57	11	2	1	27	16	38	.284	.321
May	.242	306	74	12	3	5	47	21	49	.282	.350
June	.254	370	94	17	1	9	41	25	78	.305	.378
July	.247	296	73	13	1	5	29	15	53	.283	.348
August	.260	358	93	15	5	8	45	15	62	.293	.397
September/October	.270	326	88	15	2	7	41	26	64	.327	.393
Pre-All Star	.245	983	241	44	6	15	119	66	179	.289	.348
Post-All Star	.262	907	238	39	8	20	111	52	165	.305	.389

Batter vs. Pitcher (career)

Hits Best Against	Avg	AB	H	2B	3B	HR	RBI	BB	SO	OBP	SLG
Derek Lilliquist	.688	16	11	0	0	0	0	1	1	.706	.688
Teddy Higuera	.500	16	8	3	0	0	6	2	2	.526	.688
David Cone	.444	9	4	0	1	0	0	2	2	.545	.667
Mark Langston	.438	16	7	1	0	1	3	2	4	.500	.688
Jay Howell	.375	8	3	1	0	1	4	1	3	.364	.875

Hits Worst Against	Avg	AB	H	2B	3B	HR	RBI	BB	SO	OBP	SLG
Greg W. Harris	.042	24	1	0	0	0	1	0	7	.042	.042
Bob Tewksbury	.071	14	1	0	0	0	0	1	3	.133	.071
John Smoltz	.083	12	1	0	0	0	0	2	3	.214	.083
Kevin Gross	.100	10	1	0	0	0	2	0	1	.091	.100
Terry Mulholland	.118	17	2	0	0	0	1	1	2	.167	.118

Jason Bere — White Sox

Age 23 – Pitches Right

	ERA	W	L	Sv	G	GS	IP	BB	SO	Avg	H	2B	3B	HR	RBI	OBP	SLG	CG	ShO	Sup	QS	#P/S	SB	CS	GB	FB	G/F
1993 Season	3.47	12	5	0	24	24	142.2	81	129	.210	109	14	1	12	50	.322	.311	1	0	6.06	16	104	9	8	158	142	1.11

1993 Season

	ERA	W	L	Sv	G	GS	IP	H	HR	BB	SO
Home	2.84	6	3	0	12	12	69.2	44	7	39	64
Away	4.07	6	2	0	12	12	73.0	65	5	42	65
Starter	3.47	12	5	0	24	24	142.2	109	12	81	129
Reliever	0.00	0	0	0	0	0	0.0	0	0	0	0
0-3 Days Rest	0.00	0	0	0	0	0	0.0	0	0	0	0
4 Days Rest	3.83	6	3	0	14	14	80.0	58	7	50	68
5+ Days Rest	3.02	6	2	0	10	10	62.2	51	5	31	61
Pre-All Star	5.96	4	3	0	9	9	48.1	43	5	38	44
Post-All Star	2.19	8	2	0	15	15	94.1	66	7	43	85

	Avg	AB	H	2B	3B	HR	RBI	BB	SO	OBP	SLG
vs. Left	.212	264	56	7	0	2	18	54	51	.348	.261
vs. Right	.209	254	53	7	1	10	32	27	78	.293	.362
Scoring Posn	.179	112	20	2	0	1	31	22	30	.309	.223
Close & Late	.412	17	7	1	0	0	3	2	2	.474	.471
None on/out	.252	123	31	3	0	5	5	29	31	.399	.398
First Pitch	.254	67	17	2	1	1	8	0	0	.275	.358
Ahead in Count	.161	230	37	4	0	4	14	0	104	.167	.230
Behind in Count	.283	113	32	5	0	5	15	45	0	.487	.460
Two Strikes	.153	261	40	3	0	4	18	36	129	.254	.211

Sean Bergman — Tigers

Age 24 – Pitches Right (groundball pitcher)

	ERA	W	L	Sv	G	GS	IP	BB	SO	Avg	H	2B	3B	HR	RBI	OBP	SLG	CG	ShO	Sup	QS	#P/S	SB	CS	GB	FB	G/F
1993 Season	5.67	1	4	0	9	6	39.2	23	19	.294	47	3	2	6	27	.382	.450	1	0	4.54	0	86	4	0	71	45	1.58

1993 Season

	ERA	W	L	Sv	G	GS	IP	H	HR	BB	SO
Home	5.87	0	3	0	4	4	23.0	26	3	14	12
Away	5.40	1	1	0	5	2	16.2	21	3	9	7

	Avg	AB	H	2B	3B	HR	RBI	BB	SO	OBP	SLG
vs. Left	.297	64	19	0	2	4	14	10	6	.395	.547
vs. Right	.292	96	28	3	0	2	13	13	13	.373	.385

Geronimo Berroa — Marlins

Age 29 – Bats Right

	Avg	G	AB	R	H	2B	3B	HR	RBI	BB	SO	HBP	GDP	SB	CS	OBP	SLG	IBB	SH	SF	#Pit	#P/PA	GB	FB	G/F
1993 Season	.118	14	34	3	4	1	0	0	0	2	7	0	2	0	0	.167	.147	0	0	0	145	4.03	11	11	1.00
Career (1989-1993)	.233	115	189	12	44	6	0	2	9	12	41	1	5	0	2	.282	.296	2	0	0	731	3.62	72	51	1.41

1993 Season

	Avg	AB	H	2B	3B	HR	RBI	BB	SO	OBP	SLG
vs. Left	.188	16	3	0	0	0	0	2	5	.278	.188
vs. Right	.056	18	1	1	0	0	0	0	2	.056	.111
Scoring Posn	.000	9	0	0	0	0	0	1	2	.100	.000
Close & Late	.000	5	0	0	0	0	0	1	2	.167	.000

Sean Berry — Expos

Age 28 – Bats Right (flyball hitter)

	Avg	G	AB	R	H	2B	3B	HR	RBI	BB	SO	HBP	GDP	SB	CS	OBP	SLG	IBB	SH	SF	#Pit	#P/PA	GB	FB	G/F
1993 Season	.261	122	299	50	78	15	2	14	49	41	70	2	4	12	2	.348	.465	6	3	6	1289	3.67	90	93	0.97
Career (1990-1993)	.251	185	439	62	110	20	3	15	58	49	109	3	6	14	3	.326	.412	6	3	6	1875	3.75	131	135	0.97

1993 Season

	Avg	AB	H	2B	3B	HR	RBI	BB	SO	OBP	SLG
vs. Left	.232	95	22	3	1	3	9	17	15	.348	.379
vs. Right	.275	204	56	12	1	11	40	24	55	.347	.505
Groundball	.245	98	24	3	0	3	13	8	21	.296	.367
Flyball	.167	42	7	1	0	1	5	11	12	.345	.262
Home	.261	134	35	5	0	5	22	23	34	.362	.410
Away	.261	165	43	10	2	9	27	18	36	.335	.509
Day	.256	90	23	4	1	6	22	13	21	.346	.522
Night	.263	209	55	11	1	8	27	28	49	.349	.440
Grass	.267	101	27	5	1	6	13	15	22	.368	.515
Turf	.258	198	51	10	1	8	36	26	48	.338	.439

	Avg	AB	H	2B	3B	HR	RBI	BB	SO	OBP	SLG
Scoring Posn	.213	89	19	5	0	3	34	16	25	.321	.371
Close & Late	.197	61	12	0	0	0	8	4	21	.254	.197
None on/out	.286	70	20	4	1	4	4	8	11	.359	.543
Batting #6	.404	57	23	6	1	6	18	10	4	.485	.860
Batting #7	.273	77	21	3	0	2	11	10	25	.344	.390
Other	.206	165	34	6	1	6	20	21	41	.300	.364
April	.160	25	4	0	0	0	4	8	6	.371	.160
May	.235	17	4	0	0	1	4	0	4	.278	.412
June	.302	43	13	2	0	4	9	7	8	.392	.628
July	.292	72	21	2	0	1	8	7	19	.346	.361

1993 Season

	Avg	AB	H	2B	3B	HR	RBI	BB	SO	OBP	SLG		Avg	AB	H	2B	3B	HR	RBI	BB	SO	OBP	SLG
First Pitch	.114	35	4	0	0	1	6	6	0	.256	.200	August	.211	76	16	5	1	5	15	9	20	.291	.500
Ahead in Count	.271	59	16	4	0	5	15	18	0	.430	.593	September/October	.303	66	20	6	1	3	9	10	13	.390	.561
Behind in Count	.279	154	43	6	2	5	18	0	61	.278	.442	Pre-All Star	.279	111	31	3	0	6	23	19	26	.382	.468
Two Strikes	.236	144	34	6	2	6	18	17	70	.319	.431	Post-All Star	.250	188	47	12	2	8	26	22	44	.325	.463

1993 By Position

Position	Avg	AB	H	2B	3B	HR	RBI	BB	SO	OBP	SLG	G	GS	Innings	PO	A	E	DP	Fld Pct	Rng Fctr	In Zone	Outs	Zone Rtg	MLB Zone
As Pinch Hitter	.233	30	7	1	0	1	7	2	10	.303	.367	33	0	---	---	---	---	---	---	---	---	---	---	---
As 3b	.264	269	71	14	2	13	42	39	60	.352	.476	96	73	686.1	66	153	15	13	.936	2.87	217	179	.825	.834

Damon Berryhill — Braves

Age 30 – Bats Both

	Avg	G	AB	R	H	2B	3B	HR	RBI	BB	SO	HBP	GDP	SB	CS	OBP	SLG	IBB	SH	SF	#Pit	#P/PA	GB	FB	G/F
1993 Season	.245	115	335	24	82	18	2	8	43	21	64	2	7	0	0	.291	.382	1	2	3	1282	3.53	108	103	1.05
Last Five Years	.234	387	1189	101	278	58	3	29	150	70	241	6	29	2	4	.277	.361	11	6	13	4548	3.54	391	378	1.03

1993 Season

	Avg	AB	H	2B	3B	HR	RBI	BB	SO	OBP	SLG		Avg	AB	H	2B	3B	HR	RBI	BB	SO	OBP	SLG
vs. Left	.272	81	22	5	1	2	14	6	13	.315	.432	Scoring Posn	.242	95	23	5	0	2	33	9	18	.299	.358
vs. Right	.236	254	60	13	1	6	29	15	51	.283	.366	Close & Late	.203	59	12	3	0	2	6	4	15	.254	.356
Groundball	.258	120	31	3	0	1	12	8	23	.302	.308	None on/out	.205	73	15	4	1	0	0	5	10	.266	.288
Flyball	.212	52	11	5	1	0	7	4	8	.259	.346	Batting #7	.252	309	78	17	2	8	39	20	59	.297	.398
Home	.275	171	47	10	1	6	26	9	35	.306	.450	Batting #9	.125	16	2	1	0	0	2	0	3	.176	.188
Away	.213	164	35	8	1	2	17	12	29	.275	.311	Other	.200	10	2	0	0	0	2	1	2	.273	.200
Day	.213	80	17	5	0	1	6	6	15	.273	.313	April	.325	40	13	4	0	2	6	3	7	.364	.575
Night	.255	255	65	13	2	7	37	15	49	.297	.404	May	.132	38	5	2	0	0	3	2	6	.175	.184
Grass	.249	253	63	14	1	8	35	16	47	.290	.407	June	.295	44	13	4	1	2	7	3	8	.340	.568
Turf	.232	82	19	4	1	0	8	5	17	.292	.305	July	.233	60	14	2	0	1	7	1	11	.246	.317
First Pitch	.338	71	24	5	0	4	14	1	0	.342	.577	August	.219	73	16	2	1	1	6	10	12	.321	.315
Ahead in Count	.308	52	16	5	0	2	10	4	0	.357	.519	September/October	.263	80	21	4	0	2	14	2	20	.282	.388
Behind in Count	.164	159	26	5	0	2	11	0	54	.173	.233	Pre-All Star	.257	144	37	12	1	5	19	9	26	.299	.458
Two Strikes	.151	152	23	4	1	1	12	16	64	.240	.211	Post-All Star	.236	191	45	6	1	3	24	12	38	.285	.325

1993 By Position

Position	Avg	AB	H	2B	3B	HR	RBI	BB	SO	OBP	SLG	G	GS	Innings	PO	A	E	DP	Fld Pct	Rng Fctr	In Zone	Outs	Zone Rtg	MLB Zone
As Pinch Hitter	.167	12	2	1	0	0	2	1	2	.231	.250	13	0	---	---	---	---	---	---	---	---	---	---	---
As c	.248	323	80	17	2	8	41	20	62	.293	.387	105	85	774.0	570	52	6	3	.990	---	---	---	---	---

Last Five Years

	Avg	AB	H	2B	3B	HR	RBI	BB	SO	OBP	SLG		Avg	AB	H	2B	3B	HR	RBI	BB	SO	OBP	SLG
vs. Left	.255	306	78	14	1	7	44	17	42	.289	.376	Scoring Posn	.267	326	87	19	0	7	120	31	70	.321	.390
vs. Right	.227	883	200	44	2	22	106	53	199	.273	.356	Close & Late	.209	225	47	9	1	4	18	15	57	.262	.311
Groundball	.249	498	124	16	0	12	69	28	90	.286	.353	None on/out	.243	268	65	15	1	6	6	13	47	.283	.373
Flyball	.205	234	48	14	1	5	24	19	58	.264	.338	Batting #6	.243	387	94	20	0	10	41	20	84	.281	.372
Home	.266	575	153	33	2	18	87	32	128	.304	.424	Batting #7	.248	500	124	28	3	15	74	32	93	.292	.406
Away	.204	614	125	25	1	11	63	38	113	.252	.301	Other	.199	302	60	10	0	4	35	18	64	.247	.272
Day	.231	429	99	26	0	7	51	32	95	.282	.340	April	.240	125	30	7	0	6	16	8	24	.284	.440
Night	.236	760	179	32	3	22	99	38	146	.274	.372	May	.226	257	58	14	0	7	33	8	50	.247	.362
Grass	.241	852	205	42	2	23	115	48	173	.281	.376	June	.264	193	51	12	1	2	29	12	43	.306	.368
Turf	.217	337	73	16	1	6	35	22	68	.268	.323	July	.190	205	39	6	0	4	20	11	39	.237	.278
First Pitch	.315	219	69	16	1	8	37	8	0	.335	.507	August	.249	181	45	6	1	5	16	18	29	.320	.376
Ahead in Count	.321	212	68	14	0	8	36	18	0	.371	.500	September/October	.241	228	55	13	1	5	36	13	56	.280	.373
Behind in Count	.165	575	95	20	0	10	54	0	208	.172	.252	Pre-All Star	.240	651	156	36	1	17	87	33	130	.276	.376
Two Strikes	.157	555	87	17	1	10	57	42	241	.219	.245	Post-All Star	.227	538	122	22	2	12	63	37	111	.278	.342

Batter vs. Pitcher (career)

Hits Best Against	Avg	AB	H	2B	3B	HR	RBI	BB	SO	OBP	SLG	Hits Worst Against	Avg	AB	H	2B	3B	HR	RBI	BB	SO	OBP	SLG
Ken Hill	.333	12	4	3	0	0	1	0	1	.333	.583	Omar Olivares	.077	13	1	0	0	0	2	2	3	.188	.077
Doug Drabek	.308	39	12	3	0	1	7	3	7	.357	.462	Orel Hershiser	.107	28	3	0	0	0	3	1	4	.138	.107
Roger McDowell	.308	13	4	1	0	0	2	3	0	.438	.385	Sid Fernandez	.125	16	2	0	0	0	2	2	3	.222	.125
												Mike Morgan	.133	15	2	0	0	0	1	1	1	.188	.133
												Mike Maddux	.167	12	2	0	0	0	2	0	2	.167	.167

Dante Bichette — Rockies

Age 30 – Bats Right

	Avg	G	AB	R	H	2B	3B	HR	RBI	BB	SO	HBP	GDP	SB	CS	OBP	SLG	IBB	SH	SF	#Pit	#P/PA	GB	FB	G/F
1993 Season	.310	141	538	93	167	43	5	21	89	28	99	7	7	14	8	.348	.526	2	0	8	1843	3.17	180	149	1.21
Last Five Years	.270	544	1857	236	502	110	11	59	257	88	383	14	41	54	25	.305	.437	10	4	21	6791	3.42	631	528	1.20

1993 Season

	Avg	AB	H	2B	3B	HR	RBI	BB	SO	OBP	SLG		Avg	AB	H	2B	3B	HR	RBI	BB	SO	OBP	SLG
vs. Left	.286	119	34	11	1	4	18	10	22	.346	.496	Scoring Posn	.308	143	44	6	2	4	64	11	31	.359	.462
vs. Right	.317	419	133	32	4	17	71	18	77	.348	.535	Close & Late	.313	83	26	6	0	8	21	3	13	.352	.675
Groundball	.310	197	61	17	0	7	33	5	41	.332	.503	None on/out	.298	94	28	7	2	1	1	3	15	.320	.447
Flyball	.316	95	30	8	1	2	13	7	18	.368	.484	Batting #3	.323	359	116	32	3	15	63	15	67	.353	.554
Home	.373	260	97	29	5	11	51	13	37	.408	.650	Batting #4	.263	99	26	6	2	4	12	5	19	.306	.485
Away	.252	278	70	14	0	10	38	15	62	.291	.410	Other	.313	80	25	5	0	2	14	8	13	.375	.450
Day	.263	167	44	13	0	5	21	6	34	.294	.431	April	.314	70	22	5	0	3	14	5	11	.359	.514

1993 Season

	Avg	AB	H	2B	3B	HR	RBI	BB	SO	OBP	SLG
Night	.332	371	123	30	5	16	68	22	65	.371	.569
Grass	.319	401	128	33	5	15	63	22	69	.359	.539
Turf	.285	137	39	10	0	6	26	6	30	.313	.489
First Pitch	.431	109	47	10	3	4	21	1	0	.431	.688
Ahead in Count	.278	79	22	5	1	5	17	14	0	.383	.557
Behind in Count	.233	279	65	17	0	9	35	0	93	.242	.391
Two Strikes	.204	230	47	15	0	6	24	13	99	.253	.348

	Avg	AB	H	2B	3B	HR	RBI	BB	SO	OBP	SLG
May	.303	99	30	5	2	3	15	11	18	.369	.485
June	.313	96	30	12	0	2	13	3	20	.327	.500
July	.324	102	33	11	1	7	21	4	20	.352	.657
August	.309	110	34	8	2	4	15	4	23	.339	.527
September/October	.295	61	18	2	0	2	11	1	7	.338	.426
Pre-All Star	.309	301	93	26	2	10	52	21	56	.352	.508
Post-All Star	.312	237	74	17	3	11	37	7	43	.343	.549

1993 By Position

Position	Avg	AB	H	2B	3B	HR	RBI	BB	SO	OBP	SLG	G	GS	Innings	PO	A	E	DP	Fld Pct	Rng Fctr	In Zone	Outs	Zone Rtg	MLB Zone
As rf	.316	507	160	40	5	20	83	24	95	.350	.533	134	125	1122.0	284	14	9	3	.971	2.39	336	268	.798	.826

Last Five Years

	Avg	AB	H	2B	3B	HR	RBI	BB	SO	OBP	SLG
vs. Left	.266	624	166	38	6	20	89	41	133	.312	.442
vs. Right	.273	1233	336	72	5	39	168	47	250	.301	.434
Groundball	.290	531	154	38	2	16	86	20	101	.316	.460
Flyball	.266	394	105	21	2	10	50	17	86	.300	.406
Home	.283	870	246	57	9	30	139	44	163	.320	.472
Away	.259	987	256	53	2	29	118	44	220	.292	.405
Day	.272	589	160	32	2	21	81	30	125	.309	.440
Night	.270	1268	342	78	9	38	176	58	258	.303	.435
Grass	.271	1517	411	86	11	49	210	72	303	.307	.439
Turf	.268	340	91	24	0	10	47	16	80	.298	.426
First Pitch	.350	317	111	19	4	12	62	7	0	.362	.549
Ahead in Count	.334	293	98	25	4	16	54	34	0	.407	.611
Behind in Count	.203	936	190	40	2	18	94	0	340	.207	.308
Two Strikes	.175	864	151	34	0	14	74	46	383	.218	.263

	Avg	AB	H	2B	3B	HR	RBI	BB	SO	OBP	SLG
Scoring Posn	.255	475	121	21	5	15	192	32	111	.296	.415
Close & Late	.283	322	91	12	2	14	55	13	68	.317	.463
None on/out	.278	399	111	23	4	8	8	15	86	.308	.416
Batting #3	.323	371	120	33	3	15	63	16	71	.354	.550
Batting #6	.277	506	140	33	4	17	64	22	99	.306	.458
Other	.247	980	242	44	4	27	130	50	213	.286	.383
April	.280	300	84	18	0	10	47	14	53	.311	.440
May	.264	421	111	21	3	13	54	27	89	.308	.420
June	.258	314	81	26	2	10	48	16	70	.291	.449
July	.296	291	86	18	1	14	49	12	64	.321	.509
August	.261	272	71	17	3	6	28	13	63	.307	.412
September/October	.266	259	69	10	2	6	31	6	44	.290	.390
Pre-All Star	.268	1125	302	71	5	36	170	60	234	.304	.436
Post-All Star	.273	732	200	39	6	23	87	28	149	.306	.437

Batter vs. Pitcher (career)

Hits Best Against	Avg	AB	H	2B	3B	HR	RBI	BB	SO	OBP	SLG
Curt Young	.625	8	5	0	0	2	3	4	1	.750	1.375
Doug Drabek	.538	13	7	2	0	0	2	0	1	.538	.692
Jose Guzman	.467	15	7	1	0	0	1	1	2	.500	.533
Frank Viola	.429	14	6	3	0	1	4	0	1	.400	.857
Tommy Greene	.357	14	5	2	1	1	3	0	2	.333	.857

Hits Worst Against	Avg	AB	H	2B	3B	HR	RBI	BB	SO	OBP	SLG
Mike Moore	.000	9	0	0	0	0	0	2	2	.182	.000
Jimmy Key	.063	16	1	0	0	0	1	0	2	.059	.063
Nolan Ryan	.071	14	1	0	0	0	0	0	6	.071	.071
Todd Stottlemyre	.091	11	1	0	0	0	0	0	2	.091	.091
Danny Darwin	.154	13	2	0	0	0	0	0	5	.154	.154

Mike Bielecki — Orioles

Age 34 – Pitches Right

	ERA	W	L	Sv	G	GS	IP	BB	SO	Avg	H	2B	3B	HR	RBI	OBP	SLG	CG	ShO	Sup	QS	#P/S	SB	CS	GB	FB	G/F
1993 Season	5.90	4	5	0	13	13	68.2	23	38	.310	90	18	0	8	36	.363	.455	0	0	5.90	2	93	14	1	107	87	1.23
Last Five Years	4.09	45	38	1	142	114	703.1	257	425	.265	713	141	28	57	289	.330	.402	5	4	4.76	54	93	61	28	1010	747	1.35

1993 Season

	ERA	W	L	Sv	G	GS	IP	H	HR	BB	SO
Home	4.23	3	1	0	8	8	44.2	53	5	12	21
Away	9.00	1	4	0	5	5	24.0	37	3	11	17
Starter	5.90	4	5	0	13	13	68.2	90	8	23	38
Reliever	0.00	0	0	0	0	0	0.0	0	0	0	0
0-3 Days Rest	0.00	0	0	0	0	0	0.0	0	0	0	0
4 Days Rest	5.40	3	3	0	7	7	38.1	46	6	15	19
5+ Days Rest	6.53	1	2	0	6	6	30.1	44	2	8	19
Pre-All Star	5.90	4	5	0	13	13	68.2	90	8	23	38
Post-All Star	0.00	0	0	0	0	0	0.0	0	0	0	0

	Avg	AB	H	2B	3B	HR	RBI	BB	SO	OBP	SLG
vs. Left	.312	141	44	7	0	4	20	14	22	.372	.447
vs. Right	.309	149	46	11	0	4	16	9	16	.354	.463
Scoring Posn	.341	82	28	3	0	2	29	13	12	.423	.451
Close & Late	.667	3	2	0	0	0	0	0	0	.667	.667
None on/out	.307	75	23	10	0	1	1	2	8	.333	.480
First Pitch	.385	39	15	2	0	0	5	0	0	.375	.436
Ahead in Count	.193	119	23	8	0	0	4	0	33	.207	.261
Behind in Count	.395	76	30	5	0	4	15	13	0	.478	.618
Two Strikes	.203	123	25	8	0	2	8	9	38	.269	.317

Last Five Years

	ERA	W	L	Sv	G	GS	IP	H	HR	BB	SO
Home	3.88	23	20	0	72	60	368.2	358	34	126	228
Away	4.33	22	18	1	70	54	334.2	355	23	131	197
Day	4.57	21	20	1	68	53	336.2	345	31	132	202
Night	3.66	24	18	0	74	61	366.2	368	26	125	223
Grass	4.14	31	30	0	102	85	511.0	508	44	188	317
Turf	3.98	14	8	1	40	29	192.1	205	13	69	108
April	3.65	8	8	0	22	19	118.1	114	12	42	76
May	3.51	11	6	0	30	24	146.0	147	8	55	88
June	5.03	4	11	0	29	20	127.0	137	12	54	81
July	4.42	8	4	0	22	17	106.0	114	7	33	61
August	4.50	7	2	0	19	19	110.0	108	14	38	64
September/October	3.47	7	7	1	20	15	96.0	93	4	35	55
Starter	4.17	41	35	0	114	114	654.2	672	56	235	397
Reliever	3.14	4	3	1	28	0	48.2	41	1	22	28
0-3 Days Rest	4.28	7	2	0	14	14	75.2	73	7	40	49
4 Days Rest	4.21	23	23	0	64	64	369.2	390	36	123	218
5+ Days Rest	4.04	11	10	0	36	36	209.1	209	13	72	130
Pre-All Star	4.17	26	27	0	88	70	429.1	442	36	165	273
Post-All Star	3.97	19	11	1	54	44	274.0	271	21	92	152

	Avg	AB	H	2B	3B	HR	RBI	BB	SO	OBP	SLG
vs. Left	.271	1480	401	76	14	32	148	167	219	.344	.406
vs. Right	.258	1209	312	65	14	25	141	90	206	.311	.397
Inning 1-6	.271	2332	633	128	25	47	255	221	354	.334	.408
Inning 7+	.224	357	80	13	3	10	34	36	71	.298	.361
None on	.267	1575	421	89	16	39	39	124	236	.323	.418
Runners on	.262	1114	292	52	12	18	250	133	189	.339	.379
Scoring Posn	.274	638	175	30	7	8	217	101	109	.368	.381
Close & Late	.228	171	39	6	1	5	23	23	40	.321	.363
None on/out	.284	700	199	40	5	17	17	58	97	.343	.429
vs. 1st Batr (relief)	.222	27	6	3	0	1	7	1	5	.250	.444
First Inning Pitched	.273	520	142	29	7	13	72	69	78	.359	.431
First 75 Pitches	.268	2085	558	111	24	42	231	200	319	.332	.404
Pitch 76-90	.253	316	80	19	1	8	36	25	45	.309	.396
Pitch 91-105	.255	196	50	8	3	4	13	18	33	.321	.388
Pitch 106+	.272	92	25	3	0	3	9	14	28	.368	.402
First Pitch	.295	359	106	17	6	4	38	22	0	.332	.409
Ahead in Count	.213	1139	243	42	9	12	99	0	366	.217	.298
Behind in Count	.315	683	215	49	11	24	87	134	0	.426	.524
Two Strikes	.210	1169	246	44	9	19	99	99	425	.275	.312

Pitches Best Vs.	Avg	AB	H	2B	3B	HR	RBI	BB	SO	OBP	SLG	Pitches Worst Vs.	Avg	AB	H	2B	3B	HR	RBI	BB	SO	OBP	SLG
Pitcher vs. Batter (career)																							
Glenn Davis	.000	16	0	0	0	0	1	2	3	.111	.000	Jay Bell	.632	19	12	4	2	0	5	2	3	.667	1.053
Spike Owen	.042	24	1	0	0	0	0	1	5	.080	.042	Steve Finley	.571	14	8	1	2	1	2	1	1	.600	1.143
Barry Bonds	.063	32	2	1	0	0	2	6	8	.211	.094	Otis Nixon	.545	11	6	0	1	0	2	1	3	.583	.727
Alfredo Griffin	.083	12	1	1	0	0	0	0	0	.083	.167	Juan Samuel	.474	19	9	2	0	2	8	2	2	.478	.895
Todd Benzinger	.125	16	2	1	0	0	0	1	2	.176	.188	Kevin Mitchell	.333	15	5	1	2	2	6	0	1	.333	1.067

Craig Biggio — Astros

Age 28 – Bats Right

	Avg	G	AB	R	H	2B	3B	HR	RBI	BB	SO	HBP	GDP	SB	CS	OBP	SLG	IBB	SH	SF	#Pit	#P/PA	GB	FB	G/F
1993 Season	.287	155	610	98	175	41	5	21	64	77	93	10	10	15	17	.373	.474	7	4	5	2630	3.72	211	197	1.07
Last Five Years	.279	750	2767	390	773	141	16	48	251	326	402	28	35	118	52	.359	.394	28	29	16	11517	3.64	1040	781	1.33

1993 Season

	Avg	AB	H	2B	3B	HR	RBI	BB	SO	OBP	SLG		Avg	AB	H	2B	3B	HR	RBI	BB	SO	OBP	SLG
vs. Left	.295	183	54	11	2	8	19	32	22	.408	.508	Scoring Posn	.287	115	33	7	1	3	41	20	19	.392	.443
vs. Right	.283	427	121	30	3	13	45	45	71	.357	.459	Close & Late	.244	86	21	5	0	2	8	16	13	.387	.372
Groundball	.300	217	65	16	4	7	22	28	34	.388	.507	None on/out	.271	251	68	13	3	9	9	26	36	.346	.454
Flyball	.312	77	24	2	1	4	13	16	14	.433	.519	Total	.287	610	175	41	5	21	64	77	93	.373	.474
Home	.285	295	84	19	2	8	30	46	50	.389	.444	Batting #1	.287	610	175	41	5	21	64	77	93	.373	.474
Away	.289	315	91	22	3	13	34	31	43	.358	.502	Other	.000	0	0	0	0	0	0	0	0	.000	.000
Day	.276	185	51	9	3	7	15	17	27	.348	.470	April	.250	80	20	5	1	1	4	14	10	.362	.375
Night	.292	425	124	32	2	14	49	60	66	.384	.475	May	.324	105	34	9	0	6	10	11	16	.398	.581
Grass	.289	204	59	14	3	9	23	25	31	.371	.520	June	.212	104	22	7	1	5	11	11	15	.297	.442
Turf	.286	406	116	27	2	12	41	52	62	.374	.451	July	.291	103	30	7	1	1	11	13	18	.388	.408
First Pitch	.359	78	28	5	3	4	11	6	0	.407	.654	August	.318	110	35	10	0	5	20	15	12	.394	.545
Ahead in Count	.340	106	36	8	0	4	14	43	0	.530	.528	September/October	.315	108	34	3	2	3	8	13	22	.395	.463
Behind in Count	.244	312	76	16	1	7	28	0	84	.261	.369	Pre-All Star	.267	330	88	25	3	12	26	43	47	.357	.470
Two Strikes	.196	276	54	11	1	7	23	28	93	.279	.319	Post-All Star	.311	280	87	16	2	9	38	34	46	.392	.479

1993 By Position

Position	Avg	AB	H	2B	3B	HR	RBI	BB	SO	OBP	SLG	G	GS	Innings	PO	A	E	DP	Fld Pct	Rng Fctr	In Zone	Outs	Zone Rtg	MLB Zone
As 2b	.287	610	175	41	5	21	64	77	93	.373	.474	155	155	1352.1	307	447	14	89	.982	5.02	496	460	.927	.895

Last Five Years

	Avg	AB	H	2B	3B	HR	RBI	BB	SO	OBP	SLG		Avg	AB	H	2B	3B	HR	RBI	BB	SO	OBP	SLG
vs. Left	.268	927	248	42	6	15	72	144	103	.368	.374	Scoring Posn	.282	599	169	26	2	8	193	104	105	.386	.372
vs. Right	.285	1840	525	99	10	33	179	182	299	.354	.404	Close & Late	.252	477	120	21	2	5	49	65	76	.351	.335
Groundball	.293	953	279	54	7	12	91	117	134	.374	.402	None on/out	.259	846	219	44	9	19	19	92	110	.336	.400
Flyball	.275	582	160	23	2	14	62	76	100	.361	.393	Batting #1	.278	1358	377	78	9	31	121	194	204	.373	.417
Home	.285	1371	391	79	10	19	122	174	206	.369	.399	Batting #2	.291	481	140	22	2	8	46	43	72	.350	.395
Away	.274	1396	382	62	6	29	129	152	196	.349	.389	Other	.276	928	256	41	5	9	84	89	126	.343	.360
Day	.301	727	219	37	6	18	77	81	91	.378	.443	April	.290	328	95	14	2	5	19	42	53	.371	.390
Night	.272	2040	554	104	10	30	174	245	311	.353	.376	May	.302	483	146	30	1	11	50	49	82	.368	.437
Grass	.266	865	230	32	4	19	76	86	117	.336	.378	June	.259	482	125	24	1	12	41	63	63	.348	.388
Turf	.285	1902	543	109	12	29	175	240	285	.370	.401	July	.287	467	134	21	4	4	42	47	60	.364	.375
First Pitch	.329	359	118	22	3	11	38	24	0	.377	.499	August	.284	496	141	27	4	8	53	71	58	.375	.403
Ahead in Count	.328	503	165	35	4	13	65	198	0	.517	.491	September/October	.258	511	132	25	4	8	46	54	86	.334	.370
Behind in Count	.231	1345	311	45	5	9	92	0	349	.240	.292	Pre-All Star	.280	1448	406	76	6	28	119	172	222	.359	.399
Two Strikes	.199	1220	243	44	5	13	80	103	402	.268	.275	Post-All Star	.278	1319	367	65	10	20	132	154	180	.360	.388

Batter vs. Pitcher (career)

Hits Best Against	Avg	AB	H	2B	3B	HR	RBI	BB	SO	OBP	SLG	Hits Worst Against	Avg	AB	H	2B	3B	HR	RBI	BB	SO	OBP	SLG
Andy Ashby	.615	13	8	1	2	1	4	2	3	.667	1.231	Kelly Downs	.000	11	0	0	0	0	1	0	2	.000	.000
Rich Rodriguez	.545	11	6	3	0	0	2	3	0	.643	.818	Kent Mercker	.000	9	0	0	0	0	1	2	1	.182	.000
Donovan Osborne	.545	11	6	1	0	1	2	1	2	.583	.909	Randy Myers	.067	15	1	0	0	0	0	0	3	.067	.067
Steve Bedrosian	.538	13	7	1	0	1	4	1	0	.571	.846	Neal Heaton	.071	14	1	0	0	0	0	0	0	.071	.071
John Wetteland	.455	11	5	0	0	2	6	3	4	.571	1.000	Bret Saberhagen	.091	11	1	0	0	0	0	0	3	.091	.091

Bud Black — Giants

Age 37 – Pitches Left

	ERA	W	L	Sv	G	GS	IP	BB	SO	Avg	H	2B	3B	HR	RBI	OBP	SLG	CG	ShO	Sup	QS	#P/S	SB	CS	GB	FB	G/F
1993 Season	3.56	8	2	0	16	16	93.2	33	45	.256	89	10	2	13	36	.321	.409	0	0	6.82	6	88	9	8	112	118	0.95
Last Five Years	3.69	55	52	0	143	141	914.0	276	425	.250	862	135	22	94	339	.306	.384	16	9	4.21	82	96	57	49	1288	1104	1.17

1993 Season

	ERA	W	L	Sv	G	GS	IP	H	HR	BB	SO		Avg	AB	H	2B	3B	HR	RBI	BB	SO	OBP	SLG
Home	3.96	4	2	0	7	7	38.2	43	5	16	21	vs. Left	.294	51	15	2	0	1	4	3	2	.333	.392
Away	3.27	4	0	0	9	9	55.0	46	8	17	24	vs. Right	.250	296	74	8	2	12	32	30	43	.319	.412
Starter	3.56	8	2	0	16	16	93.2	89	13	33	45	Scoring Posn	.215	65	14	1	0	3	23	11	14	.321	.369
Reliever	0.00	0	0	0	0	0	0.0	0	0	0	0	Close & Late	.000	6	0	0	0	0	0	1	1	.143	.000
0-3 Days Rest	0.00	0	0	0	0	0	0.0	0	0	0	0	None on/out	.312	93	29	4	2	2	2	7	6	.360	.462
4 Days Rest	4.20	4	1	0	8	8	49.1	44	10	17	31	First Pitch	.241	54	13	0	0	3	6	1	0	.268	.407
5+ Days Rest	2.84	4	1	0	8	8	44.1	45	3	16	14	Ahead in Count	.201	139	28	5	1	1	7	0	34	.207	.273
Pre-All Star	3.54	8	1	0	14	14	84.0	76	12	32	43	Behind in Count	.306	85	26	2	0	6	15	18	0	.415	.541
Post-All Star	3.72	0	1	0	2	2	9.2	13	1	1	2	Two Strikes	.177	130	23	3	1	1	10	14	45	.255	.238

Last Five Years

	ERA	W	L	Sv	G	GS	IP	H	HR	BB	SO		Avg	AB	H	2B	3B	HR	RBI	BB	SO	OBP	SLG
Home	3.29	33	28	0	73	71	481.0	451	47	135	224	vs. Left	.246	631	155	19	1	20	67	48	64	.296	.374

Last Five Years

	ERA	W	L	Sv	G	GS	IP	H	HR	BB	SO
Away	4.14	22	24	0	70	70	433.0	411	47	141	201
Day	2.98	21	12	0	44	44	286.2	270	30	85	151
Night	4.02	34	40	0	99	97	627.1	592	64	191	274
Grass	3.52	47	40	0	115	114	748.1	693	69	226	356
Turf	4.45	8	12	0	28	27	165.2	169	25	50	69
April	4.25	5	7	0	16	16	101.2	94	11	33	42
May	2.92	13	8	0	28	27	194.0	155	18	59	88
June	3.73	11	5	0	26	26	169.0	171	17	62	77
July	3.24	13	7	0	26	26	172.1	154	16	45	81
August	5.08	5	13	0	23	23	125.2	152	14	37	66
September/October	3.63	8	12	0	24	23	151.1	136	18	40	71
Starter	3.71	53	52	0	141	141	907.2	859	93	274	423
Reliever	1.42	2	0	0	2	0	6.1	3	1	2	2
0-3 Days Rest	4.70	1	3	0	4	4	23.0	23	1	3	11
4 Days Rest	3.46	34	27	0	87	87	575.1	538	63	184	283
5+ Days Rest	4.10	18	22	0	50	50	309.1	298	29	87	129
Pre-All Star	3.37	35	21	0	80	79	539.1	482	54	169	240
Post-All Star	4.16	20	31	0	63	62	374.2	380	40	107	185

	Avg	AB	H	2B	3B	HR	RBI	BB	SO	OBP	SLG
vs. Right	.251	2815	707	116	21	74	272	228	361	.308	.386
Inning 1-6	.251	2928	735	124	18	77	295	236	359	.307	.385
Inning 7+	.245	518	127	11	4	17	44	40	66	.300	.380
None on	.249	2188	545	87	13	56	56	140	257	.297	.378
Runners on	.252	1258	317	48	9	38	283	136	168	.321	.395
Scoring Posn	.234	683	160	27	7	18	233	85	102	.313	.373
Close & Late	.227	273	62	5	4	6	24	21	33	.284	.341
None on/out	.248	930	231	34	3	18	18	59	90	.293	.349
vs. 1st Batr (relief)	.000	2	0	0	0	0	0	0	0	.000	.000
First Inning Pitched	.234	529	124	24	4	14	50	32	56	.278	.374
First 75 Pitches	.254	2651	674	114	19	65	259	203	318	.307	.385
Pitch 76-90	.255	415	106	12	0	15	45	33	57	.312	.393
Pitch 91-105	.242	252	61	7	3	11	26	15	34	.286	.425
Pitch 106+	.164	128	21	2	0	3	9	25	16	.301	.250
First Pitch	.283	576	163	28	5	15	71	17	0	.304	.427
Ahead in Count	.212	1385	294	42	7	20	81	0	351	.216	.296
Behind in Count	.302	807	244	41	4	32	109	142	0	.401	.482
Two Strikes	.191	1379	264	39	7	29	93	117	425	.256	.293

Pitcher vs. Batter (since 1984)

Pitches Best Vs.	Avg	AB	H	2B	3B	HR	RBI	BB	SO	OBP	SLG
Jose Lind	.000	14	0	0	0	0	0	0	1	.000	.000
Steve Balboni	.000	13	0	0	0	0	0	1	6	.071	.000
Dave Henderson	.000	13	0	0	0	0	1	0	0	.000	.000
Kurt Stillwell	.000	12	0	0	0	0	0	0	5	.000	.000
B.J. Surhoff	.000	10	0	0	0	0	1	0	0	.000	.000

Pitches Worst Vs.	Avg	AB	H	2B	3B	HR	RBI	BB	SO	OBP	SLG
Ruben Sierra	.667	21	14	4	0	2	7	1	0	.682	1.143
Juan Samuel	.526	19	10	1	1	2	3	2	0	.571	1.000
Tim Hulett	.500	20	10	3	0	2	5	2	2	.545	.950
Darrin Jackson	.500	14	7	2	0	1	4	0	1	.500	.857
Pete Incaviglia	.458	24	11	3	0	4	8	2	5	.500	1.083

Willie Blair — Rockies

Age 28 – Pitches Right

	ERA	W	L	Sv	G	GS	IP	BB	SO	Avg	H	2B	3B	HR	RBI	OBP	SLG	GF	IR	IRS	Hld	SvOp	SB	CS	GB	FB	G/F
1993 Season	4.75	6	10	0	46	18	146.0	42	84	.306	184	30	6	20	90	.350	.476	5	18	8	3	0	8	4	209	178	1.17
Career (1990-1993)	4.65	16	25	0	113	37	329.1	105	188	.290	382	69	13	36	195	.342	.445	15	60	23	5	1	20	11	460	394	1.17

1993 Season

	ERA	W	L	Sv	G	GS	IP	H	HR	BB	SO
Home	5.96	2	3	0	21	6	54.1	80	12	18	27
Away	4.03	4	7	0	25	12	91.2	104	8	24	57
Starter	5.03	4	10	0	18	18	111.0	150	15	27	60
Reliever	3.86	2	0	0	28	0	35.0	34	5	15	24
0 Days rest	0.00	0	0	0	5	0	4.0	4	1	2	1
1 or 2 Days rest	4.74	1	0	0	19	0	24.2	28	4	10	18
3+ Days rest	2.84	1	0	0	4	0	6.1	2	0	3	5
Pre-All Star	5.31	3	6	0	30	10	83.0	107	13	21	51
Post-All Star	4.00	3	4	0	16	8	63.0	77	7	21	33

	Avg	AB	H	2B	3B	HR	RBI	BB	SO	OBP	SLG
vs. Left	.282	308	87	17	4	8	47	26	44	.336	.442
vs. Right	.331	293	97	13	2	12	43	16	40	.365	.512
Scoring Posn	.229	153	35	9	2	7	68	22	23	.311	.451
Close & Late	.377	69	26	5	1	3	15	6	11	.427	.609
None on/out	.295	146	43	8	1	4	4	8	22	.331	.445
First Pitch	.389	108	42	9	3	8	35	4	0	.409	.750
Ahead in Count	.235	243	57	7	0	2	17	0	72	.240	.288
Behind in Count	.336	140	47	13	2	2	18	19	0	.402	.500
Two Strikes	.234	231	54	3	0	5	21	19	84	.296	.312

Career (1990-1993)

	ERA	W	L	Sv	G	GS	IP	H	HR	BB	SO
Home	4.76	9	8	0	60	14	145.2	175	16	53	86
Away	4.56	7	17	0	53	23	183.2	207	20	52	102
Day	5.72	4	10	0	45	13	118.0	143	14	40	64
Night	4.05	12	15	0	68	24	211.1	239	22	65	124
Grass	5.29	7	17	0	64	25	202.1	256	29	59	113
Turf	3.61	9	8	0	49	12	127.0	126	7	46	75
April	2.84	0	0	0	17	0	19.0	15	1	11	13
May	4.70	1	3	0	18	6	51.2	58	3	14	41
June	5.45	2	10	0	16	12	77.2	104	12	24	38
July	4.07	4	5	0	19	5	55.1	61	5	21	28
August	4.64	3	5	0	19	8	66.0	81	11	15	30
September/October	4.68	6	2	0	24	6	59.2	63	4	20	38
Starter	5.24	7	20	0	37	37	209.2	272	25	63	116
Reliever	3.61	9	5	0	76	0	119.2	110	11	42	72
0 Days rest	2.25	1	1	0	8	0	8.0	6	3	4	3
1 or 2 Days rest	4.85	5	2	0	35	0	52.0	54	6	17	30
3+ Days rest	2.72	3	2	0	33	0	59.2	50	2	21	39
Pre-All Star	4.84	5	15	0	57	20	167.1	201	18	53	105
Post-All Star	4.44	11	10	0	56	17	162.0	181	18	52	83

	Avg	AB	H	2B	3B	HR	RBI	BB	SO	OBP	SLG
vs. Left	.280	664	186	37	7	14	89	60	94	.339	.420
vs. Right	.301	652	196	32	6	22	106	45	94	.345	.469
Inning 1-6	.287	1009	290	54	10	30	152	77	141	.338	.450
Inning 7+	.300	307	92	15	3	6	43	28	47	.356	.427
None on	.275	735	202	36	4	16	16	56	117	.331	.400
Runners on	.310	581	180	33	9	20	179	49	71	.355	.501
Scoring Posn	.270	318	86	23	4	12	153	40	46	.336	.481
Close & Late	.329	140	46	7	2	4	24	14	20	.387	.493
None on/out	.263	323	85	15	1	8	8	24	45	.316	.390
vs. 1st Batr (relief)	.212	66	14	2	0	1	13	7	14	.293	.288
First Inning Pitched	.243	378	92	15	4	10	66	33	57	.301	.384
First 15 Pitches	.228	347	79	15	4	6	44	31	46	.288	.346
Pitch 16-30	.259	259	67	11	2	6	39	30	46	.334	.386
Pitch 31-45	.359	209	75	12	1	9	42	12	28	.391	.555
Pitch 46+	.321	501	161	31	6	15	70	32	68	.364	.497
First Pitch	.378	217	82	20	5	11	58	8	0	.398	.668
Ahead in Count	.222	550	122	15	2	6	46	0	163	.227	.289
Behind in Count	.333	306	102	24	3	9	53	53	0	.423	.520
Two Strikes	.211	531	112	11	3	6	43	44	188	.275	.277

Pitcher vs. Batter (career)

Pitches Best Vs.	Avg	AB	H	2B	3B	HR	RBI	BB	SO	OBP	SLG
Jeff Gardner	.000	14	0	0	0	0	0	0	5	.000	.000
Terry Pendleton	.091	11	1	0	0	1	1	0	3	.091	.364
Brett Butler	.143	14	2	1	0	0	2	0	0	.143	.214
Cory Snyder	.154	13	2	1	0	0	1	0	2	.154	.231
Tony Gwynn	.167	12	2	0	0	0	1	0	1	.167	.167

Pitches Worst Vs.	Avg	AB	H	2B	3B	HR	RBI	BB	SO	OBP	SLG
Jody Reed	.571	14	8	1	0	2	5	0	2	.571	1.071
Mickey Morandini	.545	11	6	1	1	0	1	0	1	.545	.818
Jose Offerman	.500	12	6	4	0	0	1	1	0	.538	.833
Dave Hollins	.400	10	4	1	0	0	2	2	3	.500	.500
Eric Karros	.385	13	5	1	0	2	4	0	1	.385	.923

Lance Blankenship — Athletics

Age 30 – Bats Right

	Avg	G	AB	R	H	2B	3B	HR	RBI	BB	SO	HBP	GDP	SB	CS	OBP	SLG	IBB	SH	SF	#Pit	#P/PA	GB	FB	G/F
1993 Season	.190	94	252	43	48	8	1	2	23	67	64	2	9	13	5	.363	.254	0	6	1	1446	4.41	80	67	1.19
Last Five Years	.223	451	1047	175	233	48	3	9	92	200	217	11	27	54	17	.351	.300	2	25	6	5263	4.08	350	303	1.16

1993 Season

	Avg	AB	H	2B	3B	HR	RBI	BB	SO	OBP	SLG
vs. Left	.145	83	12	3	0	0	5	24	28	.336	.181
vs. Right	.213	169	36	5	1	2	18	43	36	.377	.290
Groundball	.220	50	11	1	0	0	4	12	15	.371	.240
Flyball	.258	62	16	2	0	2	7	18	10	.425	.387
Home	.210	124	26	6	0	2	16	36	39	.385	.306
Away	.172	128	22	2	1	0	7	31	25	.342	.203
Day	.183	109	20	5	0	1	13	30	30	.362	.257
Night	.196	143	28	3	1	1	10	37	34	.365	.252
Grass	.176	199	35	6	0	2	19	53	54	.350	.236
Turf	.245	53	13	2	1	0	4	14	10	.412	.321
First Pitch	.333	6	2	0	0	0	2	0	0	.333	.333
Ahead in Count	.286	56	16	3	0	1	11	35	0	.560	.393
Behind in Count	.138	130	18	4	0	1	6	0	53	.145	.192
Two Strikes	.128	148	19	4	1	1	8	32	64	.286	.189

	Avg	AB	H	2B	3B	HR	RBI	BB	SO	OBP	SLG
Scoring Posn	.273	66	18	2	0	1	22	24	15	.462	.348
Close & Late	.186	43	8	2	0	0	5	17	12	.417	.233
None on/out	.179	67	12	3	1	1	1	18	16	.353	.299
Batting #1	.092	65	6	1	0	0	2	18	18	.289	.108
Batting #9	.232	155	36	5	1	2	18	38	39	.385	.316
Other	.188	32	6	2	0	0	3	11	7	.409	.250
April	.256	43	11	3	0	1	5	10	12	.396	.395
May	.211	71	15	4	0	0	6	16	19	.360	.268
June	.241	58	14	1	1	1	0	21	12	.450	.345
July	.098	51	5	0	0	0	3	13	13	.281	.098
August	.103	29	3	0	0	0	1	7	8	.278	.103
September/October	.000	0	0	0	0	0	0	0	0	.000	.000
Pre-All Star	.212	189	40	8	1	2	19	53	49	.388	.296
Post-All Star	.127	63	8	0	0	0	4	14	15	.286	.127

1993 By Position

Position	Avg	AB	H	2B	3B	HR	RBI	BB	SO	OBP	SLG	G	GS	Innings	PO	A	E	DP	Fld Pct	Rng Fctr	In Zone	Outs	Zone Rtg	MLB Zone
As 2b	.211	57	12	3	0	1	5	12	15	.348	.316	19	18	157.1	32	56	4	11	.957	5.03	65	57	.877	.895
As lf	.145	55	8	2	0	0	2	13	18	.309	.182	17	15	136.1	45	0	0	0	1.000	2.97	49	45	.918	.818
As cf	.207	121	25	3	1	1	14	37	29	.398	.273	49	40	358.2	113	1	1	0	.991	2.86	137	112	.818	.829

Last Five Years

	Avg	AB	H	2B	3B	HR	RBI	BB	SO	OBP	SLG
vs. Left	.206	350	72	15	0	2	30	73	69	.347	.266
vs. Right	.231	697	161	33	3	7	62	127	148	.354	.317
Groundball	.245	274	67	15	0	2	24	54	60	.372	.321
Flyball	.254	248	63	10	0	4	31	47	42	.370	.343
Home	.220	508	112	25	2	4	50	105	113	.357	.301
Away	.224	539	121	23	1	5	42	95	104	.345	.299
Day	.209	446	93	18	1	3	34	80	99	.335	.274
Night	.233	601	140	30	2	6	58	120	118	.363	.319
Grass	.222	869	193	42	2	7	80	168	185	.352	.299
Turf	.225	178	40	6	1	2	12	32	32	.347	.303
First Pitch	.292	65	19	5	0	0	6	2	0	.343	.369
Ahead in Count	.295	288	85	15	1	5	39	97	0	.473	.406
Behind in Count	.153	476	73	16	0	2	25	0	187	.160	.200
Two Strikes	.148	515	76	19	1	4	32	101	217	.289	.212

	Avg	AB	H	2B	3B	HR	RBI	BB	SO	OBP	SLG
Scoring Posn	.211	270	57	6	0	1	73	60	53	.356	.244
Close & Late	.214	168	36	8	0	1	12	43	37	.377	.280
None on/out	.194	252	49	10	2	4	4	51	54	.334	.298
Batting #1	.179	195	35	9	1	0	17	48	46	.346	.236
Batting #9	.238	462	110	23	1	6	42	91	91	.369	.331
Other	.226	390	88	16	1	3	33	61	80	.333	.295
April	.228	189	43	6	0	4	24	30	38	.330	.323
May	.237	207	49	13	0	0	16	46	44	.379	.300
June	.217	253	55	13	2	3	21	46	56	.344	.320
July	.174	138	24	4	0	0	11	26	30	.309	.203
August	.202	109	22	6	0	1	9	20	22	.336	.284
September/October	.265	151	40	6	1	1	11	32	27	.397	.338
Pre-All Star	.222	695	154	34	2	7	65	133	153	.350	.306
Post-All Star	.224	352	79	14	1	2	27	67	64	.354	.287

Batter vs. Pitcher (career)

Hits Best Against	Avg	AB	H	2B	3B	HR	RBI	BB	SO	OBP	SLG
Nolan Ryan	.556	9	5	1	0	0	2	3	1	.667	.667
Greg Cadaret	.333	6	2	0	0	0	1	5	0	.636	.333

Hits Worst Against	Avg	AB	H	2B	3B	HR	RBI	BB	SO	OBP	SLG
Greg Harris	.000	10	0	0	0	0	0	1	2	.091	.000
Wilson Alvarez	.000	9	0	0	0	0	1	3	6	.231	.000
Roger Clemens	.077	13	1	0	0	0	0	2	5	.200	.077
Tom Gordon	.083	12	1	1	0	0	0	1	3	.154	.167
Jaime Navarro	.143	21	3	1	0	0	1	2	2	.217	.190

Jeff Blauser — Braves

Age 28 – Bats Right

	Avg	G	AB	R	H	2B	3B	HR	RBI	BB	SO	HBP	GDP	SB	CS	OBP	SLG	IBB	SH	SF	#Pit	#P/PA	GB	FB	G/F
1993 Season	.305	161	597	110	182	29	2	15	73	85	109	16	13	16	6	.401	.436	0	5	7	2831	3.99	211	169	1.25
Last Five Years	.276	670	2134	329	590	110	13	60	258	258	421	28	30	34	24	.359	.425	9	27	17	9505	3.86	680	664	1.02

1993 Season

	Avg	AB	H	2B	3B	HR	RBI	BB	SO	OBP	SLG
vs. Left	.283	145	41	8	2	5	16	22	25	.374	.469
vs. Right	.312	452	141	21	0	10	57	63	84	.410	.425
Groundball	.354	212	75	12	2	1	25	28	34	.429	.443
Flyball	.244	86	21	2	0	4	12	20	26	.391	.407
Home	.277	282	78	12	1	4	27	48	55	.396	.369
Away	.330	315	104	17	1	11	46	37	54	.407	.495
Day	.327	150	49	8	1	4	17	18	25	.409	.473
Night	.298	447	133	21	1	11	56	67	84	.399	.423
Grass	.314	456	143	21	1	13	52	71	81	.417	.450
Turf	.277	141	39	8	1	2	21	14	28	.350	.390
First Pitch	.431	72	31	1	0	3	11	0	0	.446	.569
Ahead in Count	.355	152	54	7	1	7	25	44	0	.493	.553
Behind in Count	.209	235	49	7	1	3	15	0	87	.239	.285
Two Strikes	.217	276	60	13	1	3	25	41	109	.336	.304

	Avg	AB	H	2B	3B	HR	RBI	BB	SO	OBP	SLG
Scoring Posn	.302	139	42	8	0	1	50	27	28	.406	.381
Close & Late	.272	92	25	2	0	2	17	10	20	.361	.359
None on/out	.259	108	28	4	0	2	2	12	19	.339	.352
Batting #2	.310	561	174	29	2	15	71	80	101	.406	.449
Batting #3	.242	33	8	0	0	0	2	5	7	.342	.242
Other	.000	3	0	0	0	0	0	0	1	.250	.000
April	.330	94	31	4	0	0	6	13	15	.414	.372
May	.344	93	32	6	0	3	16	15	15	.451	.505
June	.276	87	24	6	1	2	9	17	16	.402	.437
July	.258	97	25	0	0	5	14	17	18	.376	.412
August	.350	103	36	7	1	4	10	11	17	.432	.553
September/October	.276	123	34	6	0	1	18	12	28	.345	.350
Pre-All Star	.311	312	97	16	1	6	34	49	52	.416	.426
Post-All Star	.298	285	85	13	1	9	39	36	57	.385	.446

1993 By Position

Position	Avg	AB	H	2B	3B	HR	RBI	BB	SO	OBP	SLG	G	GS	Innings	PO	A	E	DP	Fld Pct	Rng Fctr	In Zone	Outs	Zone Rtg	MLB Zone
As ss	.306	595	182	29	2	15	73	85	108	.403	.437	161	159	1321.2	189	425	19	85	.970	4.18	510	460	.902	.880

Last Five Years

	Avg	AB	H	2B	3B	HR	RBI	BB	SO	OBP	SLG
vs. Left	.291	748	218	49	8	25	99	108	130	.379	.479
vs. Right	.268	1386	372	61	5	35	159	150	291	.349	.395
Groundball	.310	741	230	44	5	13	86	80	121	.379	.436
Flyball	.238	499	119	26	5	17	57	65	124	.329	.413
Home	.274	1019	279	51	6	24	118	139	194	.368	.406
Away	.279	1115	311	59	7	36	140	119	227	.351	.441
Day	.275	531	146	20	5	16	63	61	110	.357	.422
Night	.277	1603	444	90	8	44	195	197	311	.360	.425
Grass	.277	1593	442	80	9	50	194	205	303	.366	.433
Turf	.274	541	148	30	4	10	64	53	118	.340	.399
First Pitch	.377	265	100	17	1	10	37	6	0	.399	.562
Ahead in Count	.358	497	178	32	5	25	90	142	0	.497	.594
Behind in Count	.191	962	184	37	5	16	73	0	348	.204	.290
Two Strikes	.179	1029	184	38	5	16	80	107	421	.263	.272

	Avg	AB	H	2B	3B	HR	RBI	BB	SO	OBP	SLG
Scoring Posn	.296	469	139	29	4	9	182	84	103	.397	.433
Close & Late	.231	386	89	13	3	13	53	35	91	.303	.381
None on/out	.276	475	131	28	2	16	16	35	80	.327	.444
Batting #2	.292	1060	310	61	5	31	122	149	199	.386	.447
Batting #6	.251	355	89	13	3	12	49	40	70	.327	.406
Other	.266	719	191	36	5	17	87	69	152	.335	.401
April	.257	280	72	10	2	2	22	22	52	.314	.329
May	.292	267	78	19	4	9	43	39	59	.390	.494
June	.274	376	103	26	3	9	49	45	71	.357	.431
July	.249	362	90	11	1	14	49	54	73	.348	.401
August	.298	406	121	20	1	14	41	48	69	.379	.456
September/October	.284	443	126	24	2	12	54	50	97	.363	.429
Pre-All Star	.276	1034	285	58	9	28	132	119	204	.356	.430
Post-All Star	.277	1100	305	52	4	32	126	139	217	.362	.419

Batter vs. Pitcher (career)

Hits Best Against	Avg	AB	H	2B	3B	HR	RBI	BB	SO	OBP	SLG
Mike Harkey	.600	10	6	1	0	2	2	1	1	.636	1.300
Eric Hillman	.500	12	6	0	0	1	2	1	0	.538	.750
Jose Guzman	.455	11	5	0	0	1	3	1	2	.500	.727
Mark Portugal	.389	18	7	0	0	3	5	3	3	.476	.889
Frank Castillo	.308	13	4	2	0	2	2	0	3	.308	.923

Hits Worst Against	Avg	AB	H	2B	3B	HR	RBI	BB	SO	OBP	SLG
Danny Darwin	.000	14	0	0	0	0	0	3	5	.176	.000
Jose DeLeon	.083	12	1	0	0	0	0	1	5	.154	.083
Dennis Cook	.091	11	1	0	0	0	0	0	1	.091	.091
Andy Benes	.100	30	3	0	0	0	1	3	7	.176	.100
Larry Andersen	.125	16	2	0	0	0	0	0	6	.125	.125

Greg Blosser — Red Sox

Age 23 – Bats Left

	Avg	G	AB	R	H	2B	3B	HR	RBI	BB	SO	HBP	GDP	SB	CS	OBP	SLG	IBB	SH	SF	#Pit	#P/PA	GB	FB	G/F
1993 Season	.071	17	28	1	2	1	0	0	1	2	7	0	0	1	0	.133	.107	0	0	0	124	4.13	7	8	0.88

1993 Season

	Avg	AB	H	2B	3B	HR	RBI	BB	SO	OBP	SLG
vs. Left	.000	0	0	0	0	0	0	0	0	.000	.000
vs. Right	.071	28	2	1	0	0	1	2	7	.133	.107

	Avg	AB	H	2B	3B	HR	RBI	BB	SO	OBP	SLG
Scoring Posn	.000	6	0	0	0	0	1	0	2	.000	.000
Close & Late	.000	5	0	0	0	0	0	1	2	.167	.000

Mike Blowers — Mariners

Age 29 – Bats Right (groundball hitter)

	Avg	G	AB	R	H	2B	3B	HR	RBI	BB	SO	HBP	GDP	SB	CS	OBP	SLG	IBB	SH	SF	#Pit	#P/PA	GB	FB	G/F
1993 Season	.280	127	379	55	106	23	3	15	57	44	98	2	12	1	5	.357	.475	3	3	1	1708	3.98	134	92	1.46
Career (1989-1993)	.245	234	669	83	164	30	3	22	84	69	184	3	20	2	5	.318	.398	4	5	1	2929	3.92	236	151	1.56

1993 Season

	Avg	AB	H	2B	3B	HR	RBI	BB	SO	OBP	SLG
vs. Left	.357	154	55	14	2	10	34	17	24	.424	.669
vs. Right	.227	225	51	9	1	5	23	27	74	.311	.342
Groundball	.388	49	19	3	0	3	9	3	11	.423	.633
Flyball	.198	81	16	5	1	3	10	11	12	.293	.395
Home	.265	185	49	9	1	8	23	32	53	.379	.454
Away	.294	194	57	14	2	7	34	12	45	.333	.495
Day	.269	108	29	8	1	2	12	10	30	.333	.417
Night	.284	271	77	15	2	13	45	34	68	.366	.498
Grass	.305	154	47	12	2	6	25	10	35	.345	.526
Turf	.262	225	59	11	1	9	32	34	63	.364	.440
First Pitch	.200	45	9	3	0	1	2	2	0	.234	.333
Ahead in Count	.405	74	30	4	2	8	25	18	0	.522	.838
Behind in Count	.239	184	44	12	0	4	21	0	81	.246	.370
Two Strikes	.217	198	43	10	1	3	22	24	98	.305	.323

	Avg	AB	H	2B	3B	HR	RBI	BB	SO	OBP	SLG
Scoring Posn	.311	103	32	3	1	6	46	23	23	.438	.534
Close & Late	.392	51	20	7	0	2	10	8	12	.475	.647
None on/out	.310	87	27	6	0	3	3	4	21	.341	.483
Batting #6	.262	122	32	7	1	6	17	13	31	.338	.484
Batting #7	.235	136	32	7	1	2	11	19	35	.327	.346
Other	.347	121	42	9	1	7	29	12	32	.410	.612
April	.258	31	8	0	1	0	2	3	6	.324	.323
May	.313	67	21	10	0	3	17	6	15	.370	.597
June	.220	59	13	4	1	1	5	9	19	.319	.373
July	.324	34	11	1	0	2	5	6	7	.439	.529
August	.319	72	23	4	0	5	15	5	14	.364	.583
September/October	.259	116	30	4	1	4	13	15	37	.348	.414
Pre-All Star	.274	168	46	15	2	6	27	22	42	.359	.494
Post-All Star	.284	211	60	8	1	9	30	22	56	.355	.460

1993 By Position

Position	Avg	AB	H	2B	3B	HR	RBI	BB	SO	OBP	SLG	G	GS	Innings	PO	A	E	DP	Fld Pct	Rng Fctr	In Zone	Outs	Zone Rtg	MLB Zone
As 3b	.279	369	103	22	3	15	53	42	97	.355	.477	117	103	928.2	65	224	15	13	.951	2.80	305	247	.810	.834

Mike Boddicker — Brewers

Age 36 – Pitches Right

	ERA	W	L	Sv	G	GS	IP	BB	SO	Avg	H	2B	3B	HR	RBI	OBP	SLG	CG	ShO	Sup	QS	#P/S	SB	CS	GB	FB	G/F
1993 Season	5.67	3	5	0	10	10	54.0	15	24	.338	77	10	2	6	33	.387	.478	1	0	5.50	2	85	6	3	87	69	1.26
Last Five Years	4.06	48	40	3	137	115	761.0	251	438	.271	799	154	20	59	326	.336	.397	9	2	4.86	55	98	65	31	1129	842	1.34

1993 Season

	ERA	W	L	Sv	G	GS	IP	H	HR	BB	SO
Home	5.09	3	2	0	7	7	35.1	47	3	13	14
Away	6.75	0	3	0	3	3	18.2	30	3	2	10

	Avg	AB	H	2B	3B	HR	RBI	BB	SO	OBP	SLG
vs. Left	.392	130	51	6	1	6	20	7	9	.429	.592
vs. Right	.265	98	26	4	1	0	13	8	15	.333	.327

Last Five Years

	ERA	W	L	Sv	G	GS	IP	H	HR	BB	SO
Home	4.14	29	25	0	73	64	421.2	465	25	124	238
Away	3.95	19	15	3	64	51	339.1	334	34	127	200
Day	4.15	13	13	2	39	32	199.1	215	18	73	122
Night	4.02	35	27	1	98	83	561.2	584	41	178	316
Grass	4.06	34	24	3	91	80	508.0	546	42	175	318
Turf	4.06	14	16	0	46	35	253.0	253	17	76	120

	Avg	AB	H	2B	3B	HR	RBI	BB	SO	OBP	SLG
vs. Left	.290	1561	452	82	15	34	186	122	156	.346	.427
vs. Right	.250	1386	347	72	5	25	140	129	282	.325	.364
Inning 1-6	.279	2474	690	144	18	53	298	213	365	.342	.416
Inning 7+	.230	473	109	10	2	6	28	38	73	.304	.298
None on	.273	1669	456	99	13	33	33	134	247	.334	.407
Runners on	.268	1278	343	55	7	26	293	117	191	.339	.383

Last Five Years

	ERA	W	L	Sv	G	GS	IP	H	HR	BB	SO
April	4.60	5	10	0	21	17	103.2	110	4	36	57
May	4.51	10	7	1	28	22	157.2	164	14	60	94
June	3.87	9	8	1	28	22	151.1	154	10	40	76
July	4.49	7	4	1	21	19	116.1	131	11	39	59
August	2.60	8	6	0	19	17	128.0	129	12	34	83
September/October	4.41	9	5	0	20	18	104.0	111	8	42	69
Starter	4.09	46	40	0	115	115	712.1	755	56	230	409
Reliever	3.51	2	0	3	22	0	48.2	44	3	21	29
0-3 Days Rest	5.35	2	3	0	6	6	33.2	33	4	16	22
4 Days Rest	4.07	32	22	0	70	70	431.0	458	41	133	260
5+ Days Rest	3.96	12	15	0	39	39	247.2	264	11	81	127
Pre-All Star	4.27	27	27	3	85	67	457.0	466	32	151	253
Post-All Star	3.73	21	13	0	52	48	304.0	[illegible]	27	100	185

	Avg	AB	H	2B	3B	HR	RBI	BB	SO	OBP	SLG
Scoring Posn	.258	747	193	33	6	11	254	77	129	.336	.363
Close & Late	.205	215	44	4	0	3	15	17	35	.276	.265
None on/out	.276	756	209	43	5	16	16	56	107	.332	.410
vs. 1st Batr (relief)	.300	20	6	2	0	0	5	2	3	.364	.400
First Inning Pitched	.248	505	125	30	3	13	64	49	77	.319	.396
First 75 Pitches	.274	2194	601	125	14	46	240	193	323	.339	.407
Pitch 76-90	.283	332	94	15	2	7	45	23	48	.342	.404
Pitch 91-105	.254	252	64	7	3	3	25	19	39	.320	.341
Pitch 106+	.237	169	40	7	1	3	16	16	28	.309	.343
First Pitch	.329	414	136	22	1	13	57	13	0	.359	.481
Ahead in Count	.198	1169	231	47	6	10	92	0	356	.210	.274
Behind in Count	.341	782	267	48	9	24	119	119	0	.432	.518
Two Strikes	.183	1221	223	56	5	9	92	119	438	.263	.259

Pitcher vs. Batter (since 1984)

Pitches Best Vs.	Avg	AB	H	2B	3B	HR	RBI	BB	SO	OBP	SLG
Pat Borders	.000	12	0	0	0	0	0	1	3	.077	.000
Mike Felder	.063	16	1	0	0	0	1	1	0	.118	.063
Steve Finley	.071	14	1	0	0	0	0	2	0	.188	.071
Mike Greenwell	.083	12	1	0	0	0	1	0	0	.077	.083
Cecil Espy	.091	11	1	0	0	0	0	0	2	.091	.091

Pitches Worst Vs.	Avg	AB	H	2B	3B	HR	RBI	BB	SO	OBP	SLG
Darryl Hamilton	.545	11	6	1	1	0	1	1	0	.583	.818
Lance Johnson	.522	23	12	0	2	0	7	0	1	.522	.696
Fred McGriff	.480	25	12	2	0	2	3	1	3	.500	.800
Geno Petralli	.444	36	16	4	0	2	3	4	5	.500	.722
Jay Buhner	.429	14	6	4	0	1	3	3	4	.529	.929

Joe Boever — Tigers

Age 33 – Pitches Right

	ERA	W	L	Sv	G	GS	IP	BB	SO	Avg	H	2B	3B	HR	RBI	OBP	SLG	GF	IR	IRS	Hld	SvOp	SB	CS	GB	FB	G/F
1993 Season	3.61	6	3	3	61	0	102.1	44	63	.260	101	22	3	9	55	.336	.401	22	36	14	9	5	4	3	131	134	0.98
Last Five Years	3.41	19	31	40	343	0	482.2	228	362	.248	449	80	10	34	230	.332	.359	109	193	57	30	62	45	19	573	570	1.01

1993 Season

	ERA	W	L	Sv	G	GS	IP	H	HR	BB	SO
Home	3.21	5	2	1	30	0	47.2	50	3	18	27
Away	3.95	1	1	2	31	0	54.2	51	6	26	36
Day	2.94	3	2	1	29	0	52.0	48	3	20	29
Night	4.29	3	1	2	32	0	50.1	53	6	24	34
Grass	3.65	6	3	3	54	0	86.1	89	8	37	50
Turf	3.38	0	0	0	7	0	16.0	12	1	7	13
April	3.97	0	0	0	7	0	11.1	15	0	7	6
May	4.50	1	1	0	11	0	20.0	24	1	7	9
June	1.23	1	1	0	9	0	22.0	13	1	8	15
July	5.23	2	0	0	11	0	20.2	28	4	7	13
August	5.14	0	0	0	10	0	14.0	12	2	8	12
September/October	1.88	2	1	3	13	0	14.1	9	1	7	8
Starter	0.00	0	0	0	0	0	0.0	0	0	0	0
Reliever	3.61	6	3	3	61	0	102.1	101	9	44	63
0 Days rest	7.11	1	1	2	12	0	12.2	17	1	6	11
1 or 2 Days rest	4.00	3	2	0	27	0	45.0	47	4	23	25
3+ Days rest	2.22	2	0	1	22	0	44.2	37	4	15	27
Pre-All Star	3.14	4	2	0	32	0	63.0	65	3	24	35
Post-All Star	4.35	2	1	3	29	0	39.1	36	6	20	28

	Avg	AB	H	2B	3B	HR	RBI	BB	SO	OBP	SLG
vs. Left	.291	172	50	12	1	4	30	21	20	.365	.442
vs. Right	.235	217	51	10	2	5	25	23	43	.312	.369
Inning 1-6	.230	126	29	7	1	3	18	11	24	.293	.373
Inning 7+	.274	263	72	15	2	6	37	33	39	.355	.414
None on	.279	219	61	13	2	5	5	13	28	.319	.425
Runners on	.235	170	40	9	1	4	50	31	35	.354	.371
Scoring Posn	.273	99	27	6	1	2	45	25	21	.402	.414
Close & Late	.333	66	22	4	1	1	14	4	5	.378	.470
None on/out	.268	97	26	3	2	3	3	5	12	.304	.433
vs. 1st Batr (relief)	.268	56	15	3	2	1	9	5	6	.328	.446
First Inning Pitched	.249	205	51	11	3	3	34	28	36	.333	.376
First 15 Pitches	.277	195	54	11	3	3	27	20	32	.339	.410
Pitch 16-30	.259	116	30	6	0	2	14	16	14	.353	.362
Pitch 31-45	.220	50	11	3	0	3	8	5	15	.291	.460
Pitch 46+	.214	28	6	2	0	1	6	3	2	.313	.393
First Pitch	.234	64	15	3	1	2	10	5	0	.296	.406
Ahead in Count	.243	181	44	10	0	3	20	0	55	.250	.348
Behind in Count	.293	75	22	6	1	2	12	23	0	.455	.480
Two Strikes	.219	183	40	7	0	4	22	16	63	.289	.322

Last Five Years

	ERA	W	L	Sv	G	GS	IP	H	HR	BB	SO
Home	3.00	14	14	16	185	0	266.2	246	13	115	197
Away	3.92	5	17	24	158	0	216.0	203	21	113	165
Day	4.15	5	9	12	107	0	154.0	159	14	77	113
Night	3.07	14	22	28	236	0	328.2	290	20	151	249
Grass	3.86	13	18	20	176	0	249.1	247	22	120	185
Turf	2.93	6	13	20	167	0	233.1	202	12	108	177
April	2.91	2	3	5	44	0	68.0	57	4	36	54
May	3.28	6	7	9	64	0	90.2	86	5	38	63
June	4.38	2	5	6	56	0	86.1	80	6	54	65
July	2.81	4	2	9	58	0	77.0	76	5	31	46
August	4.26	2	7	4	60	0	80.1	80	9	41	66
September/October	2.69	3	7	7	61	0	80.1	70	5	28	68
Starter	0.00	0	0	0	0	0	0.0	0	0	0	0
Reliever	3.41	19	31	40	343	0	482.2	449	34	228	362
0 Days rest	3.92	4	13	16	88	0	114.2	108	8	53	100
1 or 2 Days rest	3.02	10	14	17	171	0	244.1	236	18	111	172
3+ Days rest	3.71	5	4	7	84	0	123.2	105	8	64	90
Pre-All Star	3.47	12	17	24	184	0	274.2	252	16	138	198
Post-All Star	3.33	7	14	16	159	0	208.0	197	18	90	164

	Avg	AB	H	2B	3B	HR	RBI	BB	SO	OBP	SLG
vs. Left	.245	886	217	36	6	12	116	135	169	.344	.340
vs. Right	.250	927	232	44	4	22	114	93	193	.319	.378
Inning 1-6	.230	339	78	12	2	8	49	33	69	.299	.348
Inning 7+	.252	1474	371	68	8	26	181	195	293	.339	.362
None on	.263	944	248	40	5	24	24	91	177	.328	.392
Runners on	.231	869	201	40	5	10	206	137	185	.335	.323
Scoring Posn	.241	514	124	30	3	6	189	114	111	.372	.346
Close & Late	.249	702	175	33	3	13	83	103	140	.346	.360
None on/out	.254	422	107	15	4	12	12	33	72	.309	.393
vs. 1st Batr (relief)	.243	309	75	14	5	7	33	28	50	.310	.388
First Inning Pitched	.243	1139	277	51	7	17	157	146	228	.327	.345
First 15 Pitches	.254	1036	263	42	7	16	117	111	181	.324	.354
Pitch 16-30	.242	546	132	26	2	12	74	93	119	.353	.363
Pitch 31-45	.230	178	41	10	1	5	31	18	54	.303	.382
Pitch 46+	.245	53	13	2	0	1	8	6	8	.333	.340
First Pitch	.291	258	75	17	1	3	41	32	0	.367	.399
Ahead in Count	.196	888	174	27	2	10	80	0	308	.198	.265
Behind in Count	.319	339	108	22	4	13	59	109	0	.480	.522
Two Strikes	.179	893	160	25	1	12	86	84	362	.252	.250

Pitcher vs. Batter (career)

Pitches Best Vs.	Avg	AB	H	2B	3B	HR	RBI	BB	SO	OBP	SLG
Jose Uribe	.000	11	0	0	0	0	0	0	2	.000	.000
Spike Owen	.067	15	1	0	0	0	1	0	3	.063	.067
Tom Foley	.091	11	1	0	0	0	0	1	5	.167	.091
Joe Oliver	.091	11	1	0	0	0	0	1	3	.167	.091
Mike Felder	.100	10	1	0	0	0	1	0	1	.091	.100

Pitches Worst Vs.	Avg	AB	H	2B	3B	HR	RBI	BB	SO	OBP	SLG
Eddie Murray	.556	9	5	1	0	1	6	3	0	.667	1.000
Felix Jose	.545	11	6	3	0	1	4	3	0	.643	1.091
Billy Hatcher	.500	14	7	2	0	1	3	2	0	.563	.857
Paul O'Neill	.467	15	7	6	0	0	4	5	2	.600	.867
Hubie Brooks	.375	8	3	2	0	1	3	2	3	.455	1.000

Tim Bogar — Mets

Age 27 – Bats Right

	Avg	G	AB	R	H	2B	3B	HR	RBI	BB	SO	HBP	GDP	SB	CS	OBP	SLG	IBB	SH	SF	#Pit	#P/PA	GB	FB	G/F
1993 Season	.244	78	205	19	50	13	0	3	25	14	29	3	2	0	1	.300	.351	2	1	1	750	3.35	79	60	1.32

1993 Season

	Avg	AB	H	2B	3B	HR	RBI	BB	SO	OBP	SLG
vs. Left	.243	70	17	5	0	1	7	5	9	.293	.357
vs. Right	.244	135	33	8	0	2	18	9	20	.304	.348
Home	.204	98	20	4	0	1	9	5	17	.257	.276
Away	.280	107	30	9	0	2	16	9	12	.339	.421
First Pitch	.257	35	9	1	0	0	3	2	0	.297	.286
Ahead in Count	.239	46	11	1	0	2	6	6	0	.340	.391
Behind in Count	.189	90	17	5	0	0	7	0	26	.196	.244
Two Strikes	.200	90	18	5	0	0	9	6	29	.255	.256

	Avg	AB	H	2B	3B	HR	RBI	BB	SO	OBP	SLG
Scoring Posn	.315	54	17	5	0	1	23	3	7	.367	.463
Close & Late	.171	35	6	1	0	0	3	2	5	.211	.200
None on/out	.220	59	13	3	0	1	1	3	6	.258	.322
Batting #2	.800	5	4	2	0	2	4	0	0	.800	2.400
Batting #8	.233	189	44	10	0	1	19	14	27	.295	.302
Other	.182	11	2	1	0	0	2	0	2	.182	.273
Pre-All Star	.277	130	36	9	0	1	15	8	18	.326	.369
Post-All Star	.187	75	14	4	0	2	10	6	11	.256	.320

Wade Boggs — Yankees

Age 36 – Bats Left (groundball hitter)

	Avg	G	AB	R	H	2B	3B	HR	RBI	BB	SO	HBP	GDP	SB	CS	OBP	SLG	IBB	SH	SF	#Pit	#P/PA	GB	FB	G/F
1993 Season	.302	143	560	83	169	26	1	2	59	74	49	0	10	0	1	.378	.363	4	1	9	2705	4.20	232	154	1.51
Last Five Years	.306	741	2860	440	875	185	19	26	277	431	231	12	69	4	12	.395	.411	86	1	34	13589	4.07	1270	693	1.83

1993 Season

	Avg	AB	H	2B	3B	HR	RBI	BB	SO	OBP	SLG
vs. Left	.262	168	44	8	1	1	25	18	18	.323	.339
vs. Right	.319	392	125	18	0	1	34	56	31	.401	.372
Groundball	.356	101	36	6	0	1	10	12	8	.421	.446
Flyball	.281	114	32	6	0	0	14	13	12	.341	.333
Home	.314	271	85	13	0	1	24	33	23	.383	.373
Away	.291	289	84	13	1	1	35	41	26	.373	.353
Day	.267	195	52	7	0	0	20	19	22	.327	.303
Night	.321	365	117	19	1	2	39	55	27	.404	.395
Grass	.304	471	143	22	1	2	53	63	44	.379	.367
Turf	.292	89	26	4	0	0	6	11	5	.370	.337
First Pitch	.333	21	7	2	0	0	0	3	0	.417	.429
Ahead in Count	.339	165	56	11	1	2	26	36	0	.451	.455
Behind in Count	.261	245	64	8	0	0	20	0	40	.258	.294
Two Strikes	.264	276	73	9	0	0	22	35	49	.344	.297

	Avg	AB	H	2B	3B	HR	RBI	BB	SO	OBP	SLG
Scoring Posn	.291	127	37	4	0	1	57	21	14	.369	.346
Close & Late	.297	74	22	0	0	1	7	10	8	.372	.338
None on/out	.248	157	39	6	0	1	1	27	11	.359	.306
Batting #1	.316	253	80	11	0	0	23	35	21	.397	.360
Batting #2	.272	213	58	11	0	2	27	27	24	.347	.352
Other	.330	94	31	4	1	0	9	12	4	.398	.394
April	.300	70	21	5	0	0	7	13	11	.405	.371
May	.296	108	32	3	0	0	15	13	7	.363	.324
June	.323	99	32	6	1	1	11	9	4	.369	.434
July	.304	79	24	6	0	1	8	10	8	.382	.418
August	.326	92	30	2	0	0	4	16	9	.422	.348
September/October	.268	112	30	4	0	0	14	13	10	.341	.304
Pre-All Star	.292	301	88	15	1	2	36	39	26	.366	.369
Post-All Star	.313	259	81	11	0	0	23	35	23	.392	.355

1993 By Position

Position	Avg	AB	H	2B	3B	HR	RBI	BB	SO	OBP	SLG	G	GS	Innings	PO	A	E	DP	Fld Pct	Rng Fctr	In Zone	Outs	Zone Rtg	MLB Zone
As 3b	.299	522	156	23	0	2	52	70	45	.377	.354	134	129	1122.2	74	311	12	29	.970	3.09	388	342	.881	.834

Last Five Years

	Avg	AB	H	2B	3B	HR	RBI	BB	SO	OBP	SLG
vs. Left	.275	932	256	48	7	5	106	93	104	.340	.357
vs. Right	.321	1928	619	137	12	21	171	338	127	.420	.437
Groundball	.320	740	237	50	2	9	78	97	49	.397	.430
Flyball	.287	648	186	43	7	6	59	95	74	.376	.403
Home	.338	1383	468	121	10	16	141	237	110	.433	.475
Away	.276	1477	407	64	9	10	136	194	121	.358	.351
Day	.300	970	291	52	2	8	89	136	85	.384	.382
Night	.309	1890	584	133	17	18	188	295	146	.400	.426
Grass	.310	2401	744	164	19	25	243	367	198	.399	.425
Turf	.285	459	131	21	0	1	34	64	33	.372	.338
First Pitch	.365	115	42	13	0	0	9	56	0	.580	.478
Ahead in Count	.359	804	289	66	6	13	97	212	0	.490	.505
Behind in Count	.247	1265	312	58	4	5	93	0	190	.248	.311
Two Strikes	.254	1358	345	64	7	7	99	143	231	.325	.327

	Avg	AB	H	2B	3B	HR	RBI	BB	SO	OBP	SLG
Scoring Posn	.319	583	186	31	3	5	239	173	55	.456	.408
Close & Late	.295	434	128	21	2	3	37	68	50	.390	.373
None on/out	.298	946	282	68	4	9	9	105	66	.370	.407
Batting #1	.307	1748	537	118	12	15	145	286	141	.403	.414
Batting #3	.313	881	276	56	7	9	103	114	62	.391	.423
Other	.268	231	62	11	0	2	29	31	28	.348	.342
April	.296	378	112	26	0	4	35	77	37	.413	.397
May	.295	475	140	32	5	6	55	72	40	.383	.421
June	.309	498	154	33	5	9	60	74	29	.397	.450
July	.335	457	153	38	6	2	43	70	37	.419	.457
August	.314	548	172	26	2	3	39	66	44	.388	.385
September/October	.286	504	144	30	1	2	45	72	44	.375	.361
Pre-All Star	.303	1485	450	101	12	20	163	248	120	.400	.428
Post-All Star	.309	1375	425	84	7	6	114	183	111	.390	.393

Batter vs. Pitcher (since 1984)

Hits Best Against	Avg	AB	H	2B	3B	HR	RBI	BB	SO	OBP	SLG
Bill Gullickson	.667	9	6	2	1	0	1	2	0	.727	1.111
Carl Willis	.583	12	7	1	0	0	4	3	0	.667	.667
Mark Leiter	.500	10	5	1	1	0	1	4	1	.643	.800
Mark Williamson	.438	16	7	1	0	1	3	2	1	.500	.688
Jeff Russell	.385	13	5	2	0	1	1	4	1	.529	.769

Hits Worst Against	Avg	AB	H	2B	3B	HR	RBI	BB	SO	OBP	SLG
Matt Young	.091	22	2	0	0	0	3	1	5	.130	.091
Bob MacDonald	.091	11	1	0	0	0	0	1	2	.167	.091
Randy Johnson	.125	16	2	0	0	0	0	1	8	.176	.125
Rick Sutcliffe	.133	15	2	0	0	0	1	0	2	.133	.133
Mike Mussina	.133	15	2	1	0	0	0	0	1	.133	.200

Brian Bohanon — Rangers

Age 25 – Pitches Left

	ERA	W	L	Sv	G	GS	IP	BB	SO	Avg	H	2B	3B	HR	RBI	OBP	SLG	GF	IR	IRS	Hld	SvOp	SB	CS	GB	FB	G/F
1993 Season	4.76	4	4	0	36	8	92.2	46	45	.296	107	22	1	8	53	.377	.429	4	33	11	1	1	8	7	140	95	1.47
Career (1990-1993)	5.35	9	11	0	76	32	233.2	112	123	.291	270	48	4	25	147	.367	.432	8	53	21	1	1	14	12	346	285	1.21

1993 Season

	ERA	W	L	Sv	G	GS	IP	H	HR	BB	SO
Home	4.35	4	2	0	20	5	51.2	57	6	23	26
Away	5.27	0	2	0	16	3	41.0	50	2	23	19
Starter	5.50	1	3	0	8	8	37.2	44	4	16	17
Reliever	4.25	3	1	0	28	0	55.0	63	4	30	28

	Avg	AB	H	2B	3B	HR	RBI	BB	SO	OBP	SLG
vs. Left	.319	91	29	3	0	2	19	15	12	.426	.418
vs. Right	.289	270	78	19	1	6	34	31	33	.360	.433
Scoring Posn	.290	100	29	7	1	1	38	13	19	.361	.410
Close & Late	.190	21	4	0	0	1	3	7	1	.393	.333

1993 Season	ERA	W	L	Sv	G	GS	IP	H	HR	BB	SO
0 Days rest	0.00	0	0	0	1	0	1.0	0	0	1	1
1 or 2 Days rest	4.95	2	1	0	12	0	20.0	28	3	6	9
3+ Days rest	3.97	1	0	0	15	0	34.0	35	1	23	18
Pre-All Star	3.88	3	1	0	20	4	46.1	44	4	25	21
Post-All Star	5.63	1	3	0	16	4	46.1	63	4	21	24

1993 Season	Avg	AB	H	2B	3B	HR	RBI	BB	SO	OBP	SLG
None on/out	.288	80	23	5	0	1	1	13	8	.394	.388
First Pitch	.463	54	25	6	1	1	11	3	0	.492	.667
Ahead in Count	.225	151	34	5	0	3	18	0	38	.227	.318
Behind in Count	.390	77	30	4	0	4	17	23	0	.530	.597
Two Strikes	.233	150	35	9	0	3	18	20	45	.326	.353

Frank Bolick — Expos

Age 28 – Bats Both (flyball hitter)

	Avg	G	AB	R	H	2B	3B	HR	RBI	BB	SO	HBP	GDP	SB	CS	OBP	SLG	IBB	SH	SF	#Pit	#P/PA	GB	FB	G/F
1993 Season	.211	95	213	25	45	13	0	4	24	23	37	4	4	1	0	.298	.329	2	0	2	949	3.92	68	76	0.89

1993 Season	Avg	AB	H	2B	3B	HR	RBI	BB	SO	OBP	SLG
vs. Left	.237	59	14	3	0	2	8	8	8	.333	.390
vs. Right	.201	154	31	10	0	2	16	15	29	.283	.305
Home	.193	109	21	8	0	2	11	14	22	.299	.321
Away	.231	104	24	5	0	2	13	9	15	.296	.337
First Pitch	.250	16	4	1	0	0	0	2	0	.333	.313
Ahead in Count	.232	69	16	5	0	4	15	11	0	.333	.478
Behind in Count	.159	82	13	3	0	0	5	0	33	.198	.195
Two Strikes	.168	95	16	4	0	0	7	10	37	.252	.211

1993 Season	Avg	AB	H	2B	3B	HR	RBI	BB	SO	OBP	SLG
Scoring Posn	.159	69	11	0	0	1	18	12	15	.294	.203
Close & Late	.204	49	10	1	0	1	4	4	9	.278	.286
None on/out	.258	62	16	6	0	0	0	2	9	.303	.355
Batting #4	.200	30	6	1	0	1	3	5	4	.368	.333
Batting #5	.210	105	22	7	0	3	18	16	21	.315	.362
Other	.218	78	17	5	0	0	3	2	12	.238	.282
Pre-All Star	.228	171	39	12	0	4	24	22	30	.327	.368
Post-All Star	.143	42	6	1	0	0	0	1	7	.163	.167

Rodney Bolton — White Sox

Age 25 – Pitches Right

	ERA	W	L	Sv	G	GS	IP	BB	SO	Avg	H	2B	3B	HR	RBI	OBP	SLG	CG	ShO	Sup	QS	#P/S	SB	CS	GB	FB	G/F
1993 Season	7.44	2	6	0	9	8	42.1	16	17	.314	55	6	2	4	32	.367	.440	0	0	4.46	1	77	2	0	71	49	1.45

1993 Season	ERA	W	L	Sv	G	GS	IP	H	HR	BB	SO
Home	5.89	1	2	0	4	4	18.1	20	1	5	8
Away	8.63	1	4	0	5	4	24.0	35	3	11	9

1993 Season	Avg	AB	H	2B	3B	HR	RBI	BB	SO	OBP	SLG
vs. Left	.337	92	31	4	2	1	19	8	8	.386	.457
vs. Right	.289	83	24	2	0	3	13	8	9	.347	.422

Tom Bolton — Tigers

Age 32 – Pitches Left (groundball pitcher)

	ERA	W	L	Sv	G	GS	IP	BB	SO	Avg	H	2B	3B	HR	RBI	OBP	SLG	GF	IR	IRS	Hld	SvOp	SB	CS	GB	FB	G/F
1993 Season	4.47	6	6	0	43	8	102.2	45	66	.282	113	22	2	5	55	.363	.384	9	33	15	2	0	7	5	154	103	1.50
Last Five Years	4.53	28	29	0	130	56	425.0	190	254	.281	467	78	9	37	209	.358	.406	24	65	26	2	0	26	13	694	406	1.71

1993 Season	ERA	W	L	Sv	G	GS	IP	H	HR	BB	SO
Home	4.01	3	1	0	20	4	51.2	56	1	20	42
Away	4.94	3	5	0	23	4	51.0	57	4	25	24
Starter	3.98	5	2	0	8	8	40.2	39	1	12	20
Reliever	4.79	1	4	0	35	0	62.0	74	4	33	46
0 Days rest	8.22	0	1	0	5	0	7.2	10	1	6	5
1 or 2 Days rest	2.96	1	2	0	12	0	27.1	21	1	9	22
3+ Days rest	5.67	0	1	0	18	0	27.0	43	2	18	19
Pre-All Star	5.13	1	3	0	25	3	47.1	56	2	19	31
Post-All Star	3.90	5	3	0	18	5	55.1	57	3	26	35

1993 Season	Avg	AB	H	2B	3B	HR	RBI	BB	SO	OBP	SLG
vs. Left	.266	94	25	5	0	2	13	12	20	.361	.383
vs. Right	.287	307	88	17	2	3	42	33	46	.363	.384
Scoring Posn	.310	116	36	8	1	2	50	22	26	.418	.448
Close & Late	.306	36	11	0	2	2	9	7	3	.444	.583
None on/out	.337	101	34	4	0	1	1	5	14	.368	.406
First Pitch	.314	51	16	6	0	1	9	7	0	.400	.490
Ahead in Count	.241	145	35	3	0	0	10	0	50	.257	.262
Behind in Count	.286	119	34	5	0	3	19	26	0	.415	.403
Two Strikes	.232	164	38	6	1	1	18	12	66	.292	.299

Last Five Years	ERA	W	L	Sv	G	GS	IP	H	HR	BB	SO
Home	3.93	16	11	0	62	26	226.2	240	19	85	143
Away	5.22	12	18	0	68	30	198.1	227	18	105	111
Day	4.33	10	12	0	44	19	139.1	159	10	58	86
Night	4.63	18	17	0	86	37	285.2	308	27	132	168
Grass	4.35	23	23	0	102	44	339.0	381	29	148	206
Turf	5.23	5	6	0	28	12	86.0	86	8	42	48
April	2.70	3	1	0	11	3	30.0	28	1	9	12
May	6.14	4	4	0	21	8	51.1	61	8	30	38
June	5.16	2	5	0	23	6	61.0	83	5	25	39
July	2.71	5	5	0	27	9	93.0	97	6	45	57
August	4.99	8	8	0	25	20	124.1	122	12	53	67
September/October	5.23	6	6	0	23	10	65.1	76	5	28	41
Starter	4.71	22	24	0	56	56	303.2	333	30	131	169
Reliever	4.08	6	5	0	74	0	121.1	134	7	59	85
0 Days rest	8.31	0	1	0	6	0	8.2	11	1	7	6
1 or 2 Days rest	3.79	2	2	0	25	0	40.1	40	2	16	32
3+ Days rest	3.73	4	2	0	43	0	72.1	83	4	36	47
Pre-All Star	4.57	10	11	0	69	19	175.1	210	15	81	109
Post-All Star	4.51	18	18	0	61	37	249.2	257	22	109	145

Last Five Years	Avg	AB	H	2B	3B	HR	RBI	BB	SO	OBP	SLG
vs. Left	.257	366	94	16	2	6	44	34	63	.325	.361
vs. Right	.288	1293	373	62	7	31	165	156	191	.367	.419
Inning 1-6	.273	1251	341	55	5	26	161	145	197	.351	.387
Inning 7+	.309	408	126	23	4	11	48	45	57	.380	.466
None on	.272	907	247	38	5	17	17	91	139	.342	.381
Runners on	.293	752	220	40	4	20	192	99	115	.376	.436
Scoring Posn	.292	415	121	21	2	11	168	72	76	.390	.431
Close & Late	.331	151	50	7	2	5	20	23	13	.429	.503
None on/out	.301	429	129	18	3	11	11	35	61	.353	.434
vs. 1st Batr (relief)	.286	63	18	4	2	2	14	10	12	.378	.508
First Inning Pitched	.276	449	124	26	4	7	73	54	74	.358	.399
First 15 Pitches	.281	370	104	18	4	3	42	48	57	.369	.376
Pitch 16-30	.276	315	87	12	2	11	56	43	53	.367	.432
Pitch 31-45	.288	264	76	10	0	6	28	29	38	.364	.394
Pitch 46+	.282	710	200	38	3	17	83	70	106	.346	.415
First Pitch	.346	214	74	14	0	12	42	13	0	.380	.579
Ahead in Count	.228	672	153	17	4	6	51	0	204	.234	.292
Behind in Count	.337	445	150	25	2	13	76	102	0	.458	.490
Two Strikes	.207	667	138	21	2	8	56	74	254	.290	.280

Pitcher vs. Batter (career)

Pitches Best Vs.	Avg	AB	H	2B	3B	HR	RBI	BB	SO	OBP	SLG
Bill Pecota	.091	11	1	0	0	0	1	0	2	.091	.091
Fred McGriff	.111	9	1	0	0	0	1	2	3	.273	.111
Devon White	.143	14	2	1	0	0	0	1	5	.200	.214
Robin Ventura	.176	17	3	0	0	0	0	1	3	.222	.176
Luis Polonia	.182	11	2	0	0	0	1	0	2	.182	.182

Pitches Worst Vs.	Avg	AB	H	2B	3B	HR	RBI	BB	SO	OBP	SLG
Greg Vaughn	.571	7	4	0	0	0	1	4	0	.727	.571
Julio Franco	.500	12	6	1	0	1	1	4	3	.625	.833
Mike Stanley	.500	10	5	1	1	1	2	2	2	.583	1.100
Paul Molitor	.417	12	5	0	0	1	3	5	2	.588	.667
Ivan Calderon	.417	12	5	1	0	2	4	0	1	.417	1.000

Barry Bonds — Giants

Age 29 – Bats Left (flyball hitter)

	Avg	G	AB	R	H	2B	3B	HR	RBI	BB	SO	HBP	GDP	SB	CS	OBP	SLG	IBB	SH	SF	#Pit	#P/PA	GB	FB	G/F
1993 Season	.336	159	539	129	181	38	4	46	123	126	79	2	11	29	12	.458	.677	43	0	7	2406	3.57	158	210	0.75
Last Five Years	.296	762	2621	533	777	168	23	157	514	546	397	15	44	195	56	.416	.558	137	1	37	11975	3.72	818	971	0.84

1993 Season

	Avg	AB	H	2B	3B	HR	RBI	BB	SO	OBP	SLG
vs. Left	.326	218	71	15	2	15	45	39	29	.423	.619
vs. Right	.343	321	110	23	2	31	78	87	50	.481	.717
Groundball	.364	162	59	8	1	14	45	35	20	.470	.685
Flyball	.330	88	29	5	0	10	23	22	18	.460	.727
Home	.312	266	83	17	0	21	58	42	36	.403	.613
Away	.359	273	98	21	4	25	65	84	43	.507	.740
Day	.312	263	82	19	2	24	61	55	34	.430	.673
Night	.359	276	99	19	2	22	62	71	45	.484	.681
Grass	.333	408	136	24	2	36	91	93	61	.453	.667
Turf	.344	131	45	14	2	10	32	33	18	.476	.710
First Pitch	.380	79	30	4	0	8	24	37	0	.568	.734
Ahead in Count	.420	157	66	14	0	17	38	53	0	.561	.834
Behind in Count	.303	195	59	16	1	15	48	0	58	.303	.626
Two Strikes	.238	202	48	11	2	10	32	36	79	.350	.460

	Avg	AB	H	2B	3B	HR	RBI	BB	SO	OBP	SLG
Scoring Posn	.358	123	44	10	1	9	70	64	18	.559	.675
Close & Late	.370	81	30	4	0	11	24	11	12	.436	.827
None on/out	.286	154	44	12	3	10	10	17	24	.357	.597
Batting #4	.295	78	23	7	0	7	21	15	9	.411	.654
Batting #5	.344	404	139	29	4	31	86	100	60	.471	.666
Other	.333	57	19	2	0	8	16	11	10	.435	.789
April	.431	72	31	8	2	7	25	21	12	.553	.889
May	.367	98	36	6	2	7	16	20	19	.475	.684
June	.280	93	26	5	0	7	19	18	14	.393	.559
July	.308	91	28	5	0	10	22	19	9	.432	.692
August	.353	85	30	4	0	8	19	24	15	.486	.682
September/October	.300	100	30	10	0	7	22	24	10	.429	.610
Pre-All Star	.348	299	104	24	4	24	71	67	47	.466	.696
Post-All Star	.321	240	77	14	0	22	52	59	32	.449	.654

1993 By Position

Position	Avg	AB	H	2B	3B	HR	RBI	BB	SO	OBP	SLG	G	GS	Innings	PO	A	E	DP	Fld Pct	Rng Fctr	In Zone	Outs	Zone Rtg	MLB Zone
As If	.338	536	181	38	4	46	123	126	77	.461	.681	157	156	1370.0	310	7	5	0	.984	2.08	340	287	.844	.818

Last Five Years

	Avg	AB	H	2B	3B	HR	RBI	BB	SO	OBP	SLG
vs. Left	.299	1059	317	75	10	56	210	188	168	.404	.548
vs. Right	.294	1562	460	93	13	101	304	358	229	.423	.565
Groundball	.316	904	286	55	7	44	159	166	125	.420	.539
Flyball	.263	562	148	32	2	43	125	128	108	.398	.557
Home	.277	1256	348	71	7	69	227	253	199	.396	.510
Away	.314	1365	429	97	16	88	287	293	198	.433	.602
Day	.286	863	247	53	7	55	169	189	130	.411	.555
Night	.301	1758	530	115	16	102	345	357	267	.418	.559
Grass	.308	992	306	62	7	63	195	189	144	.415	.576
Turf	.289	1629	471	106	16	94	319	357	253	.416	.547
First Pitch	.335	376	126	26	3	29	96	96	0	.466	.652
Ahead in Count	.346	745	258	51	7	66	175	256	0	.509	.699
Behind in Count	.243	949	231	54	6	36	164	0	304	.247	.427
Two Strikes	.220	1053	232	59	6	38	155	180	397	.333	.396

	Avg	AB	H	2B	3B	HR	RBI	BB	SO	OBP	SLG
Scoring Posn	.330	624	206	42	7	40	343	228	85	.491	.612
Close & Late	.289	432	125	28	3	20	67	99	77	.417	.507
None on/out	.282	751	212	53	11	35	35	116	113	.381	.522
Batting #1	.250	480	120	23	7	16	51	79	77	.355	.427
Batting #5	.307	1628	499	108	12	95	337	340	243	.424	.563
Other	.308	513	158	37	4	46	126	127	77	.443	.665
April	.301	355	107	26	4	23	73	51	62	.390	.592
May	.298	467	139	28	5	26	90	87	67	.414	.546
June	.289	394	114	27	4	20	66	91	55	.421	.530
July	.321	446	143	26	6	30	106	93	62	.432	.608
August	.276	457	126	23	0	28	85	115	77	.415	.510
September/October	.295	502	148	38	4	30	94	109	74	.416	.566
Pre-All Star	.297	1369	406	94	16	76	265	255	201	.408	.555
Post-All Star	.296	1252	371	74	7	81	249	291	196	.424	.561

Batter vs. Pitcher (career)

Hits Best Against	Avg	AB	H	2B	3B	HR	RBI	BB	SO	OBP	SLG
Marvin Freeman	.571	7	4	2	0	0	0	4	0	.727	.857
Brian Barnes	.500	10	5	2	0	2	2	2	0	.583	1.300
Tommy Greene	.467	15	7	1	0	3	9	5	3	.571	1.133
Bill Sampen	.429	7	3	0	0	2	4	4	1	.636	1.286
Andy Ashby	.364	11	4	1	0	3	3	1	0	.417	1.273

Hits Worst Against	Avg	AB	H	2B	3B	HR	RBI	BB	SO	OBP	SLG
Jeff Brantley	.000	13	0	0	0	0	0	1	5	.071	.000
Cris Carpenter	.000	9	0	0	0	0	0	3	3	.250	.000
Chuck McElroy	.056	18	1	1	0	0	1	1	3	.100	.111
Steve Cooke	.077	13	1	1	0	0	0	1	1	.143	.154
Charlie Leibrandt	.133	15	2	0	0	0	1	0	5	.133	.133

Ricky Bones — Brewers

Age 25 – Pitches Right

	ERA	W	L	Sv	G	GS	IP	BB	SO	Avg	H	2B	3B	HR	RBI	OBP	SLG	CG	ShO	Sup	QS	#P/S	SB	CS	GB	FB	G/F
1993 Season	4.86	11	11	0	32	31	203.2	63	63	.278	222	41	11	28	100	.334	.461	3	0	5.79	14	98	20	5	292	274	1.07
Career (1991-1993)	4.75	24	27	0	74	70	421.0	129	159	.271	448	75	17	58	204	.327	.442	3	0	5.32	31	90	36	8	634	542	1.17

1993 Season

	ERA	W	L	Sv	G	GS	IP	H	HR	BB	SO
Home	4.75	4	6	0	11	11	72.0	83	11	22	20
Away	4.92	7	5	0	21	20	131.2	139	17	41	43
Day	6.51	3	5	0	10	10	56.2	80	11	21	17
Night	4.22	8	6	0	22	21	147.0	142	17	42	46
Grass	5.56	6	11	0	25	24	150.2	182	24	50	48
Turf	2.89	5	0	0	7	7	53.0	40	4	13	15
April	6.75	1	1	0	3	3	14.2	24	0	7	10
May	5.32	1	1	0	5	4	23.2	25	6	9	8
June	3.86	2	3	0	6	6	42.0	34	6	6	11
July	4.46	2	2	0	6	6	40.1	46	7	16	7
August	4.40	3	2	0	6	6	45.0	47	3	13	15
September/October	5.92	2	2	0	6	6	38.0	46	6	12	12
Starter	4.91	11	11	0	31	31	201.2	222	28	63	63
Reliever	0.00	0	0	0	1	0	2.0	0	0	0	0
0-3 Days Rest	5.40	1	3	0	5	5	31.2	35	6	7	10
4 Days Rest	3.84	8	5	0	15	15	105.1	104	13	30	33
5+ Days Rest	6.40	2	3	0	11	11	64.2	83	9	26	20
Pre-All Star	4.31	6	5	0	16	15	96.0	96	13	26	33
Post-All Star	5.35	5	6	0	16	16	107.2	126	15	37	30

	Avg	AB	H	2B	3B	HR	RBI	BB	SO	OBP	SLG
vs. Left	.256	390	100	21	6	12	46	27	12	.303	.433
vs. Right	.298	410	122	20	5	16	54	36	51	.363	.488
Inning 1-6	.291	688	200	36	10	26	94	61	49	.352	.485
Inning 7+	.196	112	22	5	1	2	6	2	14	.216	.313
None on	.263	494	130	30	7	20	20	34	37	.315	.474
Runners on	.301	306	92	11	4	8	80	29	26	.363	.441
Scoring Posn	.265	181	48	5	3	6	72	19	19	.336	.425
Close & Late	.196	46	9	2	0	0	1	1	8	.213	.239
None on/out	.272	213	58	18	4	7	7	13	14	.317	.493
vs. 1st Batr (relief)	.000	1	0	0	0	0	0	0	0	.000	.000
First Inning Pitched	.280	132	37	6	2	6	21	8	7	.329	.492
First 75 Pitches	.290	590	171	30	6	24	85	51	42	.349	.483
Pitch 76-90	.241	112	27	4	4	2	9	9	7	.309	.402
Pitch 91-105	.286	70	20	7	1	2	6	2	11	.301	.500
Pitch 106+	.143	28	4	0	0	0	0	1	3	.172	.143
First Pitch	.271	144	39	9	3	4	18	3	0	.285	.458
Ahead in Count	.224	299	67	11	2	10	26	0	55	.239	.375
Behind in Count	.396	197	78	12	4	10	41	32	0	.474	.650
Two Strikes	.194	283	55	11	2	6	21	28	63	.274	.311

Career (1991-1993)

	ERA	W	L	Sv	G	GS	IP	H	HR	BB	SO
Home	4.13	13	13	0	34	33	205.0	205	22	57	81
Away	5.33	11	14	0	40	37	216.0	243	36	72	78
Day	4.98	8	10	0	25	24	141.0	157	26	44	58
Night	4.63	16	17	0	49	46	280.0	291	32	85	101
Grass	4.97	17	23	0	60	56	328.0	362	43	105	134
Turf	3.97	7	4	0	14	14	93.0	86	15	24	25
April	4.10	2	1	0	8	7	37.1	41	3	11	21
May	5.33	1	3	0	10	9	52.1	50	11	18	22
June	4.67	5	5	0	11	11	71.1	66	14	18	18
July	4.90	4	5	0	11	11	68.0	87	9	23	18
August	4.22	5	7	0	16	14	98.0	94	11	29	45
September/October	5.17	7	6	0	18	18	94.0	110	10	30	35
Starter	4.84	24	27	0	70	70	410.2	440	57	127	154
Reliever	0.87	0	0	0	4	0	10.1	8	1	2	5
0-3 Days Rest	4.93	2	3	0	6	6	38.1	39	7	7	13
4 Days Rest	4.66	13	16	0	36	36	216.1	233	27	68	83
5+ Days Rest	5.08	9	8	0	28	28	156.0	168	23	52	58
Pre-All Star	4.63	11	10	0	33	31	188.2	189	30	54	68
Post-All Star	4.84	13	17	0	41	39	232.1	259	28	75	91

	Avg	AB	H	2B	3B	HR	RBI	BB	SO	OBP	SLG
vs. Left	.262	808	212	37	9	23	87	59	47	.313	.416
vs. Right	.279	845	236	38	8	35	117	70	112	.341	.467
Inning 1-6	.279	1463	408	66	16	54	193	122	135	.337	.457
Inning 7+	.211	190	40	9	1	4	11	7	24	.245	.332
None on	.259	1019	264	51	12	38	38	75	92	.316	.445
Runners on	.290	634	184	24	5	20	166	54	67	.346	.438
Scoring Posn	.262	347	91	10	4	11	141	38	43	.332	.409
Close & Late	.195	87	17	4	0	2	3	3	13	.222	.310
None on/out	.251	435	109	29	6	14	14	31	34	.308	.441
vs. 1st Batr (relief)	.000	2	0	0	0	0	1	1	1	.250	.000
First Inning Pitched	.259	290	75	11	2	10	37	22	26	.322	.414
First 75 Pitches	.275	1293	355	56	12	49	167	106	122	.333	.460
Pitch 76 00	.249	209	52	10	4	5	23	17	17	.316	.407
Pitch 91-105	.306	111	34	9	1	4	13	4	15	.322	.514
Pitch 106+	.175	40	7	0	0	0	1	2	5	.214	.175
First Pitch	.285	284	81	12	4	11	35	3	0	.294	.472
Ahead in Count	.243	647	157	21	5	19	66	0	133	.256	.379
Behind in Count	.329	389	128	27	4	17	67	67	0	.422	.550
Two Strikes	.222	626	139	21	6	15	55	59	159	.297	.347

Pitcher vs. Batter (career)

Pitches Best Vs.	Avg	AB	H	2B	3B	HR	RBI	BB	SO	OBP	SLG
Brian McRae	.077	13	1	0	0	0	1	0	1	.071	.077
Bernie Williams	.083	12	1	0	0	0	1	0	0	.083	.083
Mike Greenwell	.091	11	1	1	0	0	1	0	0	.083	.182
Brian Harper	.154	13	2	0	0	0	0	1	2	.214	.154
Felix Jose	.182	11	2	0	0	0	0	0	2	.182	.182

Pitches Worst Vs.	Avg	AB	H	2B	3B	HR	RBI	BB	SO	OBP	SLG
Lance Johnson	.636	11	7	0	0	0	0	1	0	.667	.636
Pedro Munoz	.583	12	7	3	1	1	2	0	0	.583	1.250
Luis Polonia	.545	11	6	1	0	0	1	2	0	.571	.636
Kevin McReynolds	.455	11	5	0	0	3	5	0	1	.417	1.273
Billy Hatcher	.357	14	5	1	0	2	4	1	2	.400	.857

Bobby Bonilla — Mets

Age 31 – Bats Both (flyball hitter)

	Avg	G	AB	R	H	2B	3B	HR	RBI	BB	SO	HBP	GDP	SB	CS	OBP	SLG	IBB	SH	SF	#Pit	#P/PA	GB	FB	G/F
1993 Season	.265	139	502	81	133	21	3	34	87	72	96	0	12	3	3	.352	.522	11	0	8	2256	3.88	135	169	0.80
Last Five Years	.277	747	2758	453	764	164	26	127	463	349	432	5	57	21	21	.355	.493	58	0	40	11364	3.61	888	982	0.90

1993 Season

	Avg	AB	H	2B	3B	HR	RBI	BB	SO	OBP	SLG
vs. Left	.277	155	43	5	1	10	32	12	15	.325	.516
vs. Right	.259	347	90	16	2	24	55	60	81	.363	.524
Groundball	.251	171	43	6	1	5	17	23	31	.337	.386
Flyball	.307	88	27	5	0	10	20	12	17	.390	.705
Home	.275	240	66	8	2	18	54	27	37	.341	.550
Away	.256	262	67	13	1	16	33	45	59	.362	.496
Day	.260	200	52	9	1	12	30	22	37	.330	.495
Night	.268	302	81	12	2	22	57	50	59	.366	.540
Grass	.268	380	102	17	2	26	75	52	66	.350	.529
Turf	.254	122	31	4	1	8	12	20	30	.359	.500
First Pitch	.259	85	22	7	1	3	10	8	0	.319	.471
Ahead in Count	.342	120	41	5	1	12	33	28	0	.460	.700
Behind in Count	.224	192	43	7	1	10	22	0	72	.222	.427
Two Strikes	.204	225	46	6	1	13	27	36	96	.309	.413

	Avg	AB	H	2B	3B	HR	RBI	BB	SO	OBP	SLG
Scoring Posn	.257	109	28	3	1	5	48	22	24	.360	.440
Close & Late	.241	83	20	3	0	6	14	18	20	.369	.494
None on/out	.306	147	45	4	2	11	11	15	26	.370	.585
Batting #3	.176	17	3	0	0	0	0	2	5	.263	.176
Batting #4	.264	481	127	21	3	33	85	68	91	.350	.526
Other	.750	4	3	0	0	1	2	2	0	.833	1.500
April	.234	77	18	4	0	4	16	12	8	.330	.442
May	.243	103	25	1	0	9	17	11	26	.313	.515
June	.283	106	30	7	2	5	15	10	18	.345	.528
July	.255	94	24	7	0	4	13	18	22	.365	.457
August	.302	96	29	1	1	9	21	19	16	.410	.615
September/October	.269	26	7	1	0	3	5	2	6	.321	.654
Pre-All Star	.255	322	82	14	2	20	55	42	60	.336	.497
Post-All Star	.283	180	51	7	1	14	32	30	36	.380	.567

1993 By Position

Position	Avg	AB	H	2B	3B	HR	RBI	BB	SO	OBP	SLG	G	GS	Innings	PO	A	E	DP	Fld Pct	Rng Fctr	In Zone	Outs	Zone Rtg	MLB Zone
As 3b	.289	180	52	4	1	15	36	25	35	.367	.572	52	50	426.0	40	101	11	6	.928	2.98	138	101	.732	.834
As rf	.248	302	75	17	2	17	48	44	56	.341	.487	85	83	712.2	147	8	5	1	.969	1.96	171	142	.830	.826

Last Five Years

	Avg	AB	H	2B	3B	HR	RBI	BB	SO	OBP	SLG
vs. Left	.258	1063	274	54	5	50	178	102	113	.318	.459
vs. Right	.289	1695	490	110	21	77	285	247	319	.377	.515
Groundball	.276	988	273	55	10	29	146	109	146	.344	.440
Flyball	.269	590	159	33	8	35	99	87	86	.364	.531
Home	.278	1327	369	83	13	58	220	166	180	.355	.491
Away	.276	1431	395	81	13	69	243	183	252	.354	.495
Day	.275	888	244	54	6	47	148	88	138	.337	.508
Night	.278	1870	520	110	20	80	315	261	294	.363	.487
Grass	.266	1162	309	52	10	64	205	134	198	.339	.493
Turf	.285	1596	455	112	16	63	258	215	234	.366	.494
First Pitch	.338	535	181	50	9	23	106	41	0	.381	.594
Ahead in Count	.343	664	228	48	6	39	138	141	0	.453	.610
Behind in Count	.207	1035	214	41	10	39	132	0	339	.207	.379
Two Strikes	.197	1143	225	45	7	45	150	159	432	.292	.367

	Avg	AB	H	2B	3B	HR	RBI	BB	SO	OBP	SLG
Scoring Posn	.281	716	201	43	7	26	317	148	117	.387	.469
Close & Late	.244	442	108	17	1	22	71	81	84	.356	.437
None on/out	.309	732	226	46	11	40	40	60	101	.363	.566
Batting #4	.280	2362	662	146	26	107	397	293	362	.355	.500
Batting #5	.266	241	64	13	0	15	45	33	36	.355	.506
Other	.245	155	38	5	0	5	21	23	34	.343	.374
April	.278	414	115	22	1	17	80	45	57	.347	.459
May	.276	485	134	24	5	26	78	58	80	.350	.507
June	.258	469	121	38	7	16	68	63	77	.343	.471
July	.257	495	127	28	2	21	72	60	83	.333	.448
August	.316	475	150	27	5	33	97	71	61	.399	.602
September/October	.279	420	117	25	6	14	68	52	74	.354	.467
Pre-All Star	.269	1545	416	93	14	67	251	186	250	.345	.478
Post-All Star	.287	1213	348	71	12	60	212	163	182	.367	.514

Batter vs. Pitcher (career)

Hits Best Against	Avg	AB	H	2B	3B	HR	RBI	BB	SO	OBP	SLG
Shawn Boskie	.571	14	8	1	1	1	3	1	0	.600	1.000
Pete Smith	.529	17	9	2	0	3	8	4	3	.591	1.176
Tommy Greene	.450	20	9	4	0	1	5	6	2	.577	.800

Hits Worst Against	Avg	AB	H	2B	3B	HR	RBI	BB	SO	OBP	SLG
Danny Darwin	.067	15	1	0	0	0	1	1	2	.125	.067
Charlie Hough	.083	12	1	0	0	0	0	1	3	.154	.083
John Wetteland	.083	12	1	0	0	0	1	0	2	.083	.083

Batter vs. Pitcher (career)																							
Hits Best Against	Avg	AB	H	2B	3B	HR	RBI	BB	SO	OBP	SLG	**Hits Worst Against**	Avg	AB	H	2B	3B	HR	RBI	BB	SO	OBP	SLG
Tom Browning	.409	44	18	4	1	10	20	1	2	.404	1.227	Craig Lefferts	.087	23	2	0	0	0	3	0	4	.083	.087
Jeff Fassero	.333	9	3	0	0	2	4	2	0	.455	1.000	Bud Black	.095	21	2	1	0	0	1	0	0	.095	.143

Bret Boone — Mariners

Age 25 – Bats Right

	Avg	G	AB	R	H	2B	3B	HR	RBI	BB	SO	HBP	GDP	SB	CS	OBP	SLG	IBB	SH	SF	#Pit	#P/PA	GB	FB	G/F
1993 Season	.251	76	271	31	68	12	2	12	38	17	52	4	6	2	3	.301	.443	1	6	4	1056	3.50	108	83	1.30
Career (1992-1993)	.233	109	400	46	93	16	2	16	53	21	86	5	10	3	4	.277	.403	1	7	4	1569	3.59	154	111	1.39

1993 Season																							
	Avg	AB	H	2B	3B	HR	RBI	BB	SO	OBP	SLG		Avg	AB	H	2B	3B	HR	RBI	BB	SO	OBP	SLG
vs. Left	.266	79	21	4	1	4	11	9	19	.337	.494	Scoring Posn	.245	53	13	1	0	1	21	5	8	.302	.321
vs. Right	.245	192	47	8	1	8	27	8	33	.285	.422	Close & Late	.326	46	15	5	0	0	4	2	9	.367	.435
Home	.259	135	35	8	1	7	19	7	29	.301	.489	None on/out	.242	62	15	1	0	1	1	2	16	.266	.306
Away	.243	136	33	4	1	5	19	10	23	.300	.397	Batting #2	.247	150	37	5	1	7	21	10	26	.292	.433
First Pitch	.472	36	17	4	0	3	11	1	0	.475	.833	Batting #6	.235	51	12	4	0	3	10	4	9	.293	.490
Ahead in Count	.327	55	18	1	2	6	11	6	0	.393	.745	Other	.271	70	19	3	1	2	7	3	17	.325	.429
Behind in Count	.138	116	16	4	0	1	10	0	43	.157	.198	Pre-All Star	.235	51	12	2	0	2	5	4	13	.310	.392
Two Strikes	.129	124	16	3	0	2	13	10	52	.199	.202	Post-All Star	.255	220	56	10	2	10	33	13	39	.298	.455

Pedro Borbon — Braves

Age 26 – Pitches Left

	ERA	W	L	Sv	G	GS	IP	BB	SO	Avg	H	2B	3B	HR	RBI	OBP	SLG	GF	IR	IRS	Hld	SvOp	SB	CS	GB	FB	G/F
1993 Season	21.60	0	0	0	3	0	1.2	3	2	.429	3	1	0	0	1	.600	.571	0	3	0	0	0	0	0	0	2	0.00
Career (1992-1993)	15.00	0	1	0	5	0	3.0	4	3	.385	5	2	0	0	2	.529	.538	2	4	0	0	0	0	0	3	3	1.00

1993 Season																						
	ERA	W	L	Sv	G	GS	IP	H	HR	BB	SO		Avg	AB	H	2B	3B	HR	RBI	BB	SO	OBP	SLG
Home	21.60	0	0	0	3	0	1.2	3	0	3	2	vs. Left	.000	2	0	0	0	0	0	3	1	.600	.000
Away	0.00	0	0	0	0	0	0.0	0	0	0	0	vs. Right	.600	5	3	1	0	0	1	0	1	.600	.800

Pat Borders — Blue Jays

Age 31 – Bats Right

	Avg	G	AB	R	H	2B	3B	HR	RBI	BB	SO	HBP	GDP	SB	CS	OBP	SLG	IBB	SH	SF	#Pit	#P/PA	GB	FB	G/F
1993 Season	.254	138	488	38	124	30	0	9	55	20	66	2	18	2	2	.285	.371	2	7	3	1796	3.45	205	128	1.60
Last Five Years	.256	600	1846	165	472	108	5	45	222	93	288	6	61	5	5	.291	.393	10	16	16	6851	3.47	706	537	1.31

1993 Season																							
	Avg	AB	H	2B	3B	HR	RBI	BB	SO	OBP	SLG		Avg	AB	H	2B	3B	HR	RBI	BB	SO	OBP	SLG
vs. Left	.244	119	29	8	0	2	16	6	15	.278	.361	Scoring Posn	.221	131	29	8	0	1	43	10	18	.276	.305
vs. Right	.257	369	95	22	0	7	39	14	51	.287	.374	Close & Late	.296	71	21	6	0	1	11	5	15	.338	.423
Groundball	.277	65	18	5	0	1	9	2	9	.304	.400	None on/out	.274	124	34	8	0	2	2	3	13	.291	.387
Flyball	.265	68	18	4	0	1	3	3	11	.306	.368	Batting #8	.239	318	76	16	0	7	35	12	41	.269	.355
Home	.239	247	59	10	0	6	33	10	32	.273	.352	Batting #9	.285	165	47	14	0	2	20	8	23	.316	.406
Away	.270	241	65	20	0	3	22	10	34	.296	.390	Other	.200	5	1	0	0	0	0	0	2	.200	.200
Day	.216	148	32	7	0	4	12	5	31	.245	.345	April	.195	77	15	5	0	0	3	3	13	.222	.260
Night	.271	340	92	23	0	5	43	15	35	.302	.382	May	.274	84	23	3	0	5	15	3	8	.299	.488
Grass	.271	181	49	9	0	3	16	10	22	.307	.370	June	.245	94	23	6	0	1	8	3	7	.280	.340
Turf	.244	307	75	21	0	6	39	10	44	.271	.371	July	.234	64	15	3	0	1	10	0	12	.234	.328
First Pitch	.293	92	27	5	0	4	14	1	0	.298	.478	August	.319	91	29	7	0	0	5	4	10	.344	.396
Ahead in Count	.336	107	36	5	0	3	15	14	0	.410	.467	September/October	.244	78	19	6	0	2	14	7	16	.306	.397
Behind in Count	.186	199	37	13	0	1	17	0	58	.189	.266	Pre-All Star	.232	285	66	16	0	6	30	9	35	.258	.351
Two Strikes	.139	202	28	11	0	0	12	5	66	.163	.193	Post-All Star	.286	203	58	14	0	3	25	11	31	.321	.399

1993 By Position																									
Position	Avg	AB	H	2B	3B	HR	RBI	BB	SO	OBP	SLG	G	GS	Innings	PO	A	E	DP	Fld Pct	Rng Fctr	In Zone	Outs	Zone Rtg	MLB Zone
As c	.254	488	124	30	0	9	55	20	66	.285	.371	138	134	1182.0	868	80	13	11	.986	---	---	---	---	---

Last Five Years																							
	Avg	AB	H	2B	3B	HR	RBI	BB	SO	OBP	SLG		Avg	AB	H	2B	3B	HR	RBI	BB	SO	OBP	SLG
vs. Left	.260	743	193	49	3	15	91	54	106	.309	.394	Scoring Posn	.235	451	106	26	1	9	165	43	68	.296	.357
vs. Right	.253	1103	279	59	2	30	131	39	182	.279	.392	Close & Late	.258	325	84	20	0	7	39	19	68	.301	.385
Groundball	.268	444	119	25	2	10	58	18	74	.296	.401	None on/out	.279	451	126	28	2	13	13	14	63	.301	.437
Flyball	.242	372	90	25	1	11	35	22	68	.286	.403	Batting #7	.266	410	109	28	0	12	49	23	62	.305	.422
Home	.249	893	222	54	2	26	119	47	120	.288	.401	Batting #8	.249	897	223	47	2	24	109	49	130	.288	.386
Away	.262	953	250	54	3	19	103	46	168	.295	.385	Other	.260	539	140	33	3	9	64	21	96	.287	.382
Day	.222	589	131	34	1	16	59	23	117	.251	.365	April	.242	269	65	15	1	7	21	15	49	.280	.383
Night	.271	1257	341	74	4	29	163	70	171	.310	.406	May	.255	337	86	15	1	11	36	15	57	.286	.404
Grass	.265	739	196	34	3	15	84	42	126	.302	.380	June	.253	296	75	19	1	6	36	12	32	.288	.385
Turf	.249	1107	276	74	2	30	138	51	162	.284	.401	July	.285	281	80	20	0	8	51	16	41	.323	.441
First Pitch	.312	321	100	16	1	13	38	6	0	.321	.489	August	.283	332	94	21	0	5	35	13	51	.308	.392
Ahead in Count	.314	430	135	27	3	19	87	53	0	.387	.523	September/October	.218	331	72	18	2	8	43	22	58	.265	.356
Behind in Count	.189	788	149	37	0	6	63	0	257	.189	.259	Pre-All Star	.245	1003	246	55	3	25	105	50	159	.282	.381
Two Strikes	.176	767	135	38	1	5	49	32	288	.210	.248	Post-All Star	.268	843	226	53	2	20	117	43	129	.302	.407

Batter vs. Pitcher (career)																							
Hits Best Against	Avg	AB	H	2B	3B	HR	RBI	BB	SO	OBP	SLG	**Hits Worst Against**	Avg	AB	H	2B	3B	HR	RBI	BB	SO	OBP	SLG
Todd Burns	.500	12	6	3	0	0	3	1	2	.538	.750	Mike Boddicker	.000	12	0	0	0	0	0	1	3	.077	.000
Jamie Moyer	.500	10	5	0	1	1	2	1	1	.545	1.000	Kirk McCaskill	.059	17	1	0	1	0	2	0	2	.059	.176

Batter vs. Pitcher (career)

Hits Best Against	Avg	AB	H	2B	3B	HR	RBI	BB	SO	OBP	SLG	Hits Worst Against	Avg	AB	H	2B	3B	HR	RBI	BB	SO	OBP	SLG
Scott Sanderson	.438	16	7	2	0	1	1	0	2	.438	.750	Alex Fernandez	.059	17	1	0	0	0	0	0	5	.059	.059
Bill Gullickson	.412	17	7	0	0	3	4	0	2	.412	.941	Bobby Witt	.077	13	1	0	0	0	0	0	0	.077	.077
Paul Gibson	.400	10	4	2	0	1	3	5	0	.563	.900	Bud Black	.125	16	2	0	0	0	0	0	3	.125	.125

Mike Bordick — Athletics

Age 28 – Bats Right (groundball hitter)

	Avg	G	AB	R	H	2B	3B	HR	RBI	BB	SO	HBP	GDP	SB	CS	OBP	SLG	IBB	SH	SF	#Pit	#P/PA	GB	FB	G/F
1993 Season	.249	159	546	60	136	21	2	3	48	60	58	11	9	10	10	.332	.311	2	10	6	2339	3.70	232	150	1.55
Career (1990-1993)	.265	428	1299	143	344	45	7	6	117	115	158	23	22	25	20	.333	.324	4	36	12	5489	3.70	556	349	1.59

1993 Season

	Avg	AB	H	2B	3B	HR	RBI	BB	SO	OBP	SLG		Avg	AB	H	2B	3B	HR	RBI	BB	SO	OBP	SLG
vs. Left	.265	162	43	10	0	1	11	19	20	.351	.346	Scoring Posn	.274	117	32	3	0	1	43	25	15	.397	.325
vs. Right	.242	384	93	11	2	2	37	41	38	.324	.207	Close & Late	.195	87	17	0	0	0	5	16	13	.339	.195
Groundball	.246	114	28	6	0	1	11	14	16	.358	.325	None on/out	.196	143	28	5	0	0	0	12	10	.281	.231
Flyball	.204	108	22	3	0	0	8	11	13	.287	.231	Batting #8	.242	244	59	11	1	2	19	27	28	.325	.320
Home	.250	280	70	12	0	2	20	25	25	.324	.314	Batting #9	.299	107	32	3	1	0	13	13	5	.389	.346
Away	.248	266	66	9	2	1	28	35	33	.341	.308	Other	.231	195	45	7	0	1	16	20	25	.309	.282
Day	.229	223	51	8	1	1	18	21	23	.301	.287	April	.236	55	13	2	0	1	4	6	6	.333	.327
Night	.263	323	85	13	1	2	30	39	35	.353	.328	May	.261	92	24	4	1	0	7	11	10	.349	.326
Grass	.252	453	114	17	2	3	32	43	45	.328	.318	June	.264	91	24	4	0	1	9	13	8	.358	.341
Turf	.237	93	22	4	0	0	16	17	13	.351	.280	July	.295	95	28	4	0	0	10	5	9	.330	.337
First Pitch	.200	70	14	1	0	0	4	2	0	.243	.214	August	.288	104	30	3	1	1	7	17	10	.403	.365
Ahead in Count	.295	139	41	11	0	0	15	33	0	.433	.374	September/October	.156	109	17	4	0	0	11	8	15	.223	.193
Behind in Count	.209	220	46	5	1	0	9	0	50	.227	.241	Pre-All Star	.250	276	69	10	1	2	25	33	26	.338	.315
Two Strikes	.205	220	45	3	2	2	20	25	58	.295	.264	Post-All Star	.248	270	67	11	1	1	23	27	32	.327	.307

1993 By Position

Position	Avg	AB	H	2B	3B	HR	RBI	BB	SO	OBP	SLG	G	GS	Innings	PO	A	E	DP	Fld Pct	Rng Fctr	In Zone	Outs	Zone Rtg	MLB Zone
As ss	.252	540	136	21	2	3	48	59	56	.334	.315	159	154	1374.0	280	416	13	106	.982	4.56	505	435	.861	.880

Career (1990-1993)

	Avg	AB	H	2B	3B	HR	RBI	BB	SO	OBP	SLG		Avg	AB	H	2B	3B	HR	RBI	BB	SO	OBP	SLG
vs. Left	.280	357	100	16	2	2	32	35	40	.349	.353	Scoring Posn	.283	325	92	10	2	2	108	39	41	.359	.345
vs. Right	.259	942	244	29	5	4	85	80	118	.326	.313	Close & Late	.222	176	39	3	2	0	15	23	26	.324	.261
Groundball	.285	309	88	10	1	1	27	29	37	.361	.333	None on/out	.249	334	83	12	1	2	2	25	33	.312	.308
Flyball	.242	285	69	12	1	1	24	28	40	.318	.302	Batting #8	.275	626	172	22	5	5	59	57	75	.342	.350
Home	.261	631	165	21	5	5	52	51	70	.329	.334	Batting #9	.268	380	102	13	2	0	38	33	43	.340	.313
Away	.268	668	179	24	2	1	65	64	88	.336	.314	Other	.239	293	70	10	0	1	20	25	40	.302	.283
Day	.269	502	135	15	4	4	48	38	57	.327	.339	April	.292	137	40	4	0	1	14	11	17	.351	.343
Night	.262	797	209	30	3	2	69	77	101	.336	.315	May	.304	181	55	6	2	1	15	17	18	.366	.376
Grass	.257	1073	276	34	7	6	82	84	130	.320	.319	June	.247	178	44	8	1	2	17	21	21	.332	.337
Turf	.301	226	68	11	0	0	35	31	28	.390	.350	July	.274	252	69	12	1	0	23	12	32	.312	.329
First Pitch	.307	140	43	3	0	0	15	3	0	.331	.329	August	.271	269	73	5	2	1	17	34	29	.368	.316
Ahead in Count	.323	297	96	16	2	1	30	69	0	.455	.401	September/October	.223	282	63	10	1	1	31	20	41	.284	.277
Behind in Count	.217	558	121	20	4	1	35	0	133	.233	.272	Pre-All Star	.279	591	165	23	3	4	58	55	68	.345	.349
Two Strikes	.208	566	118	15	4	3	41	43	158	.274	.265	Post-All Star	.253	708	179	22	4	2	59	60	90	.322	.304

Batter vs. Pitcher (career)

Hits Best Against	Avg	AB	H	2B	3B	HR	RBI	BB	SO	OBP	SLG	Hits Worst Against	Avg	AB	H	2B	3B	HR	RBI	BB	SO	OBP	SLG
Charles Nagy	.467	15	7	0	0	0	1	1	2	.500	.467	Mark Leiter	.000	11	0	0	0	0	0	0	2	.000	.000
Alex Fernandez	.429	14	6	0	1	0	1	1	2	.467	.571	Jim Abbott	.000	10	0	0	0	0	0	1	2	.091	.000
Charlie Hough	.364	11	4	1	0	0	0	2	1	.462	.455	Jaime Navarro	.063	16	1	0	1	0	0	1	1	.118	.188
Joe Grahe	.333	12	4	1	1	0	1	1	2	.385	.583	Ben McDonald	.083	12	1	0	0	0	0	1	3	.154	.083
Bob Wickman	.333	9	3	0	0	1	3	2	1	.455	.667	Jack Morris	.100	10	1	0	0	0	1	1	2	.167	.100

Chris Bosio — Mariners

Age 31 – Pitches Right

	ERA	W	L	Sv	G	GS	IP	BB	SO	Avg	H	2B	3B	HR	RBI	OBP	SLG	CG	ShO	Sup	QS	#P/S	SB	CS	GB	FB	G/F
1993 Season	3.45	9	9	1	29	24	164.1	59	119	.229	138	24	4	14	59	.303	.352	3	1	4.22	12	96	8	6	241	141	1.71
Last Five Years	3.40	58	44	1	147	142	967.2	247	605	.247	904	138	19	81	355	.298	.362	24	7	4.83	82	95	52	25	1401	969	1.45

1993 Season

	ERA	W	L	Sv	G	GS	IP	H	HR	BB	SO		Avg	AB	H	2B	3B	HR	RBI	BB	SO	OBP	SLG
Home	2.95	6	6	1	17	12	94.2	68	7	31	65	vs. Left	.258	299	77	10	4	8	33	35	51	.336	.398
Away	4.13	3	3	0	12	12	69.2	70	7	28	54	vs. Right	.201	303	61	14	0	6	26	24	68	.269	.307
Day	5.60	0	3	0	7	5	35.1	40	7	16	37	Inning 1-6	.214	495	106	19	4	8	47	48	102	.290	.317
Night	2.86	9	6	1	22	19	129.0	98	7	43	82	Inning 7+	.299	107	32	5	0	6	12	11	17	.361	.514
Grass	3.88	2	3	0	9	9	51.0	52	3	22	44	None on	.225	373	84	14	1	8	8	33	77	.292	.332
Turf	3.26	7	6	1	20	15	113.1	86	11	37	75	Runners on	.236	229	54	10	3	6	51	26	42	.319	.384
April	2.67	2	1	0	5	5	33.2	24	0	10	29	Scoring Posn	.211	123	26	6	2	3	43	13	24	.289	.366
May	0.00	0	0	0	1	0	3.0	1	0	1	3	Close & Late	.356	59	21	3	0	4	9	4	10	.397	.610
June	5.56	0	2	0	3	3	11.1	14	2	7	11	None on/out	.270	163	44	5	0	5	5	14	29	.328	.393
July	6.21	2	2	1	8	4	29.0	33	4	9	20	vs. 1st Batr (relief)	.250	4	1	0	0	0	0	1	2	.400	.250
August	3.40	3	2	0	6	6	45.0	35	5	19	28	First Inning Pitched	.175	103	18	3	1	1	8	11	26	.261	.252
September/October	1.91	2	2	0	6	6	42.1	31	3	13	28	First 75 Pitches	.204	436	89	16	4	8	41	45	92	.285	.314
Starter	3.40	8	9	0	24	24	156.1	132	12	57	108	Pitch 76-90	.266	79	21	3	0	5	14	4	15	.306	.494
Reliever	4.50	1	0	1	5	0	8.0	6	2	2	11	Pitch 91-105	.328	61	20	3	0	0	1	5	5	.379	.377

1993 Season

	ERA	W	L	Sv	G	GS	IP	H	HR	BB	SO
0-3 Days Rest	1.29	1	1	0	2	2	14.0	4	0	7	8
4 Days Rest	4.13	4	4	0	13	13	85.0	82	10	26	70
5+ Days Rest	2.83	3	4	0	9	9	57.1	46	2	24	30
Pre-All Star	3.81	3	4	1	14	9	59.0	47	5	20	54
Post-All Star	3.25	6	5	0	15	15	105.1	91	9	39	65

	Avg	AB	H	2B	3B	HR	RBI	BB	SO	OBP	SLG
Pitch 106+	.308	26	8	2	0	1	3	5	7	.406	.500
First Pitch	.284	81	23	2	0	0	5	3	0	.314	.309
Ahead in Count	.190	258	49	12	1	4	21	0	96	.202	.291
Behind in Count	.296	152	45	7	3	4	17	37	0	.432	.461
Two Strikes	.150	254	38	5	1	5	21	19	119	.217	.236

Last Five Years

	ERA	W	L	Sv	G	GS	IP	H	HR	BB	SO
Home	3.25	31	25	1	80	75	526.2	496	40	126	330
Away	3.59	27	19	0	67	67	441.0	408	41	121	275
Day	3.10	16	16	0	49	47	327.2	296	33	86	223
Night	3.56	42	28	1	98	95	640.0	608	48	161	382
Grass	3.35	47	32	0	114	114	764.2	725	61	191	475
Turf	3.59	11	12	1	33	28	203.0	179	20	56	130
April	2.32	14	4	0	25	25	170.2	132	7	48	106
May	3.98	5	11	0	25	24	165.0	175	22	30	109
June	4.52	6	10	0	24	24	149.1	154	13	47	94
July	3.48	10	8	1	27	23	160.1	157	14	46	96
August	3.29	12	6	0	24	24	172.1	158	12	44	107
September/October	2.94	11	5	0	22	22	150.0	128	13	32	93
Starter	3.39	57	44	0	142	142	959.2	898	79	245	594
Reliever	4.50	1	0	1	5	0	8.0	6	2	2	11
0-3 Days Rest	3.60	2	6	0	10	10	70.0	65	9	17	43
4 Days Rest	3.43	43	23	0	91	91	622.0	592	50	165	402
5+ Days Rest	3.26	12	15	0	41	41	267.2	241	20	63	149
Pre-All Star	3.55	28	27	1	83	78	525.0	501	46	133	338
Post-All Star	3.23	30	17	0	64	64	442.2	403	35	114	267

	Avg	AB	H	2B	3B	HR	RBI	BB	SO	OBP	SLG
vs. Left	.261	1869	488	68	13	42	187	136	242	.313	.379
vs. Right	.232	1790	416	70	6	39	168	111	363	.282	.344
Inning 1-6	.242	3005	728	111	17	68	302	206	527	.294	.358
Inning 7+	.269	654	176	27	2	13	53	41	78	.314	.376
None on	.236	2243	530	78	10	45	45	138	362	.284	.340
Runners on	.264	1416	374	60	9	36	310	109	243	.319	.395
Scoring Posn	.242	748	181	29	6	17	257	65	141	.301	.365
Close & Late	.272	316	86	13	1	7	24	20	42	.316	.386
None on/out	.248	972	241	38	6	19	19	58	145	.292	.358
vs. 1st Batr (relief)	.250	4	1	0	0	0	0	1	2	.400	.250
First Inning Pitched	.207	535	111	19	1	8	43	42	106	.270	.292
First 75 Pitches	.244	2759	672	103	16	62	270	177	479	.292	.360
Pitch 76-90	.252	445	112	19	3	14	51	34	66	.307	.402
Pitch 91-105	.257	303	78	7	0	3	23	21	34	.311	.310
Pitch 106+	.276	152	42	9	0	2	11	15	26	.343	.375
First Pitch	.310	600	186	23	2	13	71	4	0	.321	.420
Ahead in Count	.205	1574	322	50	8	25	115	0	519	.210	.294
Behind in Count	.306	846	259	45	5	26	105	144	0	.406	.463
Two Strikes	.167	1463	245	33	7	19	94	99	605	.222	.239

Pitcher vs. Batter (career)

Pitches Best Vs.	Avg	AB	H	2B	3B	HR	RBI	BB	SO	OBP	SLG
Dave Clark	.000	12	0	0	0	0	0	0	5	.000	.000
John Valentin	.000	10	0	0	0	0	0	1	4	.091	.000
Willie Wilson	.045	22	1	0	0	0	2	0	6	.043	.045
Tony Pena	.053	19	1	0	0	0	1	0	2	.053	.053
Juan Gonzalez	.053	19	1	0	0	0	0	1	7	.100	.053

Pitches Worst Vs.	Avg	AB	H	2B	3B	HR	RBI	BB	SO	OBP	SLG
Harold Reynolds	.538	26	14	2	0	0	1	2	1	.571	.615
Dion James	.500	20	10	3	0	0	3	2	2	.545	.650
Don Slaught	.417	12	5	1	0	1	2	0	2	.417	.750
Felix Jose	.385	13	5	1	0	2	5	1	2	.429	.923
Kirk Gibson	.375	16	6	3	0	1	2	3	3	.474	.750

Shawn Boskie — Cubs

Age 27 – Pitches Right

	ERA	W	L	Sv	G	GS	IP	BB	SO	Avg	H	2B	3B	HR	RBI	OBP	SLG	GF	IR	IRS	Hld	SvOp	SB	CS	GB	FB	G/F
1993 Season	3.43	5	3	0	39	2	65.2	21	39	.258	63	11	2	7	28	.333	.406	10	28	6	6	3	4	1	86	65	1.32
Career (1990-1993)	4.48	19	29	0	105	55	384.0	140	189	.278	408	86	10	43	176	.345	.439	14	44	7	6	3	16	10	513	461	1.11

1993 Season

	ERA	W	L	Sv	G	GS	IP	H	HR	BB	SO
Home	2.72	4	1	0	22	1	39.2	33	6	14	23
Away	4.50	1	2	0	17	1	26.0	30	1	7	16
Starter	6.75	1	1	0	2	2	10.2	11	1	5	8
Reliever	2.78	4	2	0	37	0	55.0	52	6	16	31
0 Days rest	2.70	1	0	0	8	0	10.0	9	1	4	9
1 or 2 Days rest	2.94	3	2	0	21	0	33.2	32	4	8	16
3+ Days rest	2.38	0	0	0	8	0	11.1	11	1	4	6
Pre-All Star	4.19	1	1	0	8	2	19.1	20	1	6	11
Post-All Star	3.11	4	2	0	31	0	46.1	43	6	15	28

	Avg	AB	H	2B	3B	HR	RBI	BB	SO	OBP	SLG
vs. Left	.218	110	24	4	0	3	9	12	18	.306	.336
vs. Right	.291	134	39	7	2	4	19	9	21	.356	.463
Scoring Posn	.156	64	10	2	1	0	15	12	13	.304	.219
Close & Late	.238	42	10	0	1	3	7	6	8	.360	.500
None on/out	.333	60	20	4	0	1	1	5	4	.403	.450
First Pitch	.235	34	8	4	1	0	4	2	0	.278	.412
Ahead in Count	.212	113	24	2	0	1	4	0	29	.246	.257
Behind in Count	.362	47	17	4	0	3	11	8	0	.464	.638
Two Strikes	.213	108	23	3	0	2	6	11	39	.309	.296

Career (1990-1993)

	ERA	W	L	Sv	G	GS	IP	H	HR	BB	SO
Home	4.50	12	14	0	60	28	204.0	224	29	80	92
Away	4.45	7	15	0	45	27	180.0	184	14	60	97
Day	4.16	12	14	0	63	28	222.2	233	31	73	104
Night	4.91	7	15	0	42	27	161.1	175	12	67	85
Grass	4.77	14	22	0	80	38	270.0	303	34	110	128
Turf	3.79	5	7	0	25	17	114.0	105	9	30	61
April	3.33	5	2	0	9	7	48.2	45	5	16	25
May	4.78	2	7	0	14	14	84.2	95	7	25	39
June	5.22	4	7	0	17	15	79.1	82	5	34	45
July	3.39	4	5	0	23	10	79.2	76	6	25	32
August	1.82	3	2	0	19	1	39.2	36	3	13	25
September/October	7.62	1	6	0	23	8	52.0	74	17	27	23
Starter	4.87	12	26	0	55	55	303.0	334	33	112	142
Reliever	3.00	7	3	0	50	0	81.0	74	10	28	47
0 Days rest	1.65	1	0	0	10	0	16.1	11	1	6	15
1 or 2 Days rest	3.19	4	3	0	23	0	36.2	34	6	12	17
3+ Days rest	3.54	2	0	0	17	0	28.0	29	3	10	15
Pre-All Star	4.48	12	18	0	49	40	241.0	253	19	88	120
Post-All Star	4.47	7	11	0	56	15	143.0	155	24	52	69

	Avg	AB	H	2B	3B	HR	RBI	BB	SO	OBP	SLG
vs. Left	.290	810	235	53	8	25	102	107	95	.372	.468
vs. Right	.264	656	173	33	2	18	74	33	94	.309	.402
Inning 1-6	.278	1202	334	75	9	33	147	106	160	.338	.438
Inning 7+	.280	264	74	11	1	10	29	34	29	.377	.443
None on	.279	845	236	54	4	25	25	72	117	.341	.441
Runners on	.277	621	172	32	6	18	151	68	72	.350	.435
Scoring Posn	.244	356	87	17	4	8	119	47	46	.327	.382
Close & Late	.254	118	30	5	1	6	15	20	15	.380	.466
None on/out	.313	377	118	29	4	12	12	35	44	.379	.507
vs. 1st Batr (relief)	.209	43	9	1	0	1	7	5	6	.320	.302
First Inning Pitched	.268	358	96	16	0	11	49	43	55	.351	.405
First 15 Pitches	.259	313	81	12	0	7	25	29	42	.332	.364
Pitch 16-30	.297	283	84	18	2	12	46	28	46	.361	.502
Pitch 31-45	.268	220	59	15	1	6	30	25	29	.344	.427
Pitch 46+	.283	650	184	41	7	18	75	58	72	.344	.451
First Pitch	.345	223	77	18	2	10	40	13	0	.376	.578
Ahead in Count	.220	623	137	30	3	9	55	0	160	.232	.321
Behind in Count	.331	329	109	24	3	13	46	73	0	.453	.541
Two Strikes	.223	618	138	29	3	11	59	54	189	.290	.333

Pitcher vs. Batter (career)

Pitches Best Vs.	Avg	AB	H	2B	3B	HR	RBI	BB	SO	OBP	SLG
Jose Uribe	.000	11	0	0	0	0	0	0	2	.000	.000

Pitches Worst Vs.	Avg	AB	H	2B	3B	HR	RBI	BB	SO	OBP	SLG
Terry Pendleton	.615	13	8	4	0	1	1	1	1	.643	1.154

Pitcher vs. Batter (career)

Pitches Best Vs.	Avg	AB	H	2B	3B	HR	RBI	BB	SO	OBP	SLG	Pitches Worst Vs.	Avg	AB	H	2B	3B	HR	RBI	BB	SO	OBP	SLG
Ken Caminiti	.077	13	1	0	0	0	0	0	1	.077	.077	Paul O'Neill	.600	10	6	1	0	2	2	2	1	.667	1.300
Dave Martinez	.080	25	2	0	0	0	0	3	4	.179	.080	Bernard Gilkey	.600	10	6	1	0	2	3	1	1	.636	1.300
Alfredo Griffin	.091	11	1	0	0	0	0	0	0	.091	.091	Bobby Bonilla	.571	14	8	1	1	1	3	1	0	.600	1.000
Andres Galarraga	.133	15	2	0	0	0	0	0	2	.133	.133	Andy Van Slyke	.462	13	6	0	1	2	3	1	2	.467	1.077

Daryl Boston — Rockies

Age 31 – Bats Left

	Avg	G	AB	R	H	2B	3B	HR	RBI	BB	SO	HBP	GDP	SB	CS	OBP	SLG	IBB	SH	SF	#Pit	#P/PA	GB	FB	G/F
1993 Season	.261	124	291	46	76	15	1	14	40	26	57	2	5	1	6	.325	.464	1	0	1	1217	3.80	86	93	0.92
Last Five Years	.263	612	1420	222	373	69	13	46	164	146	240	7	20	54	29	.333	.427	12	4	7	6022	3.80	463	459	1.01

1993 Season

	Avg	AB	H	2B	3B	HR	RBI	BB	SO	OBP	SLG		Avg	AB	H	2B	3B	HR	RBI	BB	SO	OBP	SLG
vs. Left	.231	13	3	0	0	1	4	0	4	.286	.462	Scoring Posn	.186	86	16	4	0	3	26	5	14	.228	.337
vs. Right	.263	278	73	15	1	13	36	26	53	.327	.464	Close & Late	.174	46	8	2	0	0	2	4	11	.255	.217
Home	.279	136	38	7	1	3	18	16	27	.359	.412	None on/out	.382	68	26	6	1	7	7	5	11	.425	.809
Away	.245	155	38	8	0	11	22	10	30	.293	.510	Batting #3	.264	125	33	5	0	6	18	8	22	.311	.448
First Pitch	.300	40	12	1	0	5	10	0	0	.300	.700	Batting #5	.233	60	14	2	0	4	8	8	14	.333	.467
Ahead in Count	.368	76	28	5	1	4	15	14	0	.467	.618	Other	.274	106	29	8	1	4	14	10	21	.336	.481
Behind in Count	.218	119	26	7	0	4	9	0	49	.225	.378	Pre-All Star	.231	156	36	6	0	5	15	17	26	.314	.365
Two Strikes	.145	131	19	3	0	4	7	12	57	.217	.260	Post-All Star	.296	135	40	9	1	9	25	9	31	.338	.578

Last Five Years

	Avg	AB	H	2B	3B	HR	RBI	BB	SO	OBP	SLG		Avg	AB	H	2B	3B	HR	RBI	BB	SO	OBP	SLG
vs. Left	.236	178	42	8	1	3	19	12	42	.294	.343	Scoring Posn	.261	337	88	14	3	13	120	45	53	.345	.436
vs. Right	.267	1242	331	61	12	43	145	134	198	.338	.439	Close & Late	.241	249	60	16	3	6	24	34	52	.339	.402
Groundball	.294	483	142	22	7	15	68	37	72	.345	.462	None on/out	.295	387	114	23	4	16	16	36	62	.356	.499
Flyball	.210	281	59	12	0	9	24	29	68	.287	.349	Batting #1	.260	331	86	23	4	7	26	36	56	.332	.417
Home	.262	711	186	36	9	17	77	76	126	.334	.409	Batting #7	.293	280	82	11	1	10	48	40	47	.381	.446
Away	.264	709	187	33	4	29	87	70	114	.332	.444	Other	.253	809	205	35	8	29	90	70	137	.316	.424
Day	.258	457	118	23	4	15	60	49	72	.332	.425	April	.245	147	36	2	2	1	13	18	26	.337	.306
Night	.265	963	255	46	9	31	104	97	168	.333	.428	May	.226	234	53	10	3	9	25	20	30	.290	.410
Grass	.262	1087	285	53	11	35	128	107	180	.329	.428	June	.267	210	56	19	1	7	31	21	38	.338	.467
Turf	.264	333	88	16	2	11	36	39	60	.344	.423	July	.251	231	58	14	1	5	18	17	44	.301	.385
First Pitch	.371	175	65	7	2	10	33	6	0	.390	.606	August	.292	336	98	11	2	11	31	27	55	.344	.435
Ahead in Count	.319	367	117	25	1	20	62	81	0	.439	.556	September/October	.275	262	72	13	4	13	46	43	47	.375	.504
Behind in Count	.200	610	122	22	4	10	40	0	200	.204	.298	Pre-All Star	.250	661	165	37	6	20	73	66	108	.322	.415
Two Strikes	.176	660	116	23	5	10	38	56	240	.242	.271	Post-All Star	.274	759	208	32	7	26	91	80	132	.342	.437

Batter vs. Pitcher (career)

Hits Best Against	Avg	AB	H	2B	3B	HR	RBI	BB	SO	OBP	SLG	Hits Worst Against	Avg	AB	H	2B	3B	HR	RBI	BB	SO	OBP	SLG
Bryn Smith	.700	10	7	1	1	0	3	3	0	.769	1.000	Mike Moore	.087	23	2	2	0	0	2	0	6	.083	.174
Bob Walk	.545	11	6	1	0	2	9	3	0	.643	1.182	Ramon Martinez	.095	21	2	0	0	0	1	4	2	.231	.095
Pedro Astacio	.417	12	5	1	0	1	2	1	2	.462	.750	Tim Belcher	.100	10	1	0	0	0	0	1	2	.182	.100
Omar Olivares	.381	21	8	1	1	1	3	2	1	.417	.667	Tommy Greene	.154	13	2	0	0	0	0	2	2	.267	.154
Kevin Gross	.313	16	5	0	0	2	4	2	4	.389	.688	Bret Saberhagen	.167	18	3	1	0	0	0	1	4	.211	.222

Kent Bottenfield — Rockies

Age 25 – Pitches Right

	ERA	W	L	Sv	G	GS	IP	BB	SO	Avg	H	2B	3B	HR	RBI	OBP	SLG	CG	ShO	Sup	QS	#P/S	SB	CS	GB	FB	G/F
1993 Season	5.07	5	10	0	37	25	159.2	71	63	.294	179	35	3	24	90	.372	.480	1	0	3.78	11	84	16	6	231	193	1.20
Career (1992-1993)	4.59	6	12	1	47	29	192.0	82	77	.282	205	40	4	25	99	.357	.451	1	0	3.94	13	83	19	6	279	232	1.20

1993 Season

	ERA	W	L	Sv	G	GS	IP	H	HR	BB	SO		Avg	AB	H	2B	3B	HR	RBI	BB	SO	OBP	SLG
Home	5.28	2	3	0	18	12	76.2	93	11	35	27	vs. Left	.325	286	93	19	1	11	33	38	22	.405	.514
Away	4.88	3	7	0	19	13	83.0	86	13	36	36	vs. Right	.267	322	86	16	2	13	57	33	41	.341	.450
Starter	5.32	5	9	0	25	25	135.1	152	21	56	54	Scoring Posn	.291	182	53	13	1	5	67	25	24	.376	.456
Reliever	3.70	0	1	0	12	0	24.1	27	3	15	9	Close & Late	.300	40	12	2	0	2	6	4	3	.378	.500
0-3 Days Rest	1.29	0	1	0	1	1	7.0	7	1	2	3	None on/out	.361	155	56	10	0	8	8	19	15	.441	.581
4 Days Rest	6.61	3	5	0	16	16	80.1	98	12	34	35	First Pitch	.312	109	34	3	1	4	15	1	0	.324	.468
5+ Days Rest	3.75	2	3	0	8	8	48.0	47	8	20	16	Ahead in Count	.247	247	61	16	0	7	31	0	52	.256	.397
Pre-All Star	4.12	2	5	0	23	11	83.0	93	11	33	33	Behind in Count	.364	143	52	8	2	9	29	48	0	.526	.636
Post-All Star	6.10	3	5	0	14	14	76.2	86	13	38	30	Two Strikes	.247	243	60	15	0	8	30	22	63	.311	.407

Denis Boucher — Expos

Age 26 – Pitches Left

	ERA	W	L	Sv	G	GS	IP	BB	SO	Avg	H	2B	3B	HR	RBI	OBP	SLG	CG	ShO	Sup	QS	#P/S	SB	CS	GB	FB	G/F
1993 Season	1.91	3	1	0	5	5	28.1	3	14	.229	24	4	2	1	7	.243	.333	0	0	3.81	2	83	1	2	25	38	0.66
Career (1991-1993)	5.23	6	10	0	25	24	127.1	47	60	.290	146	30	4	22	70	.349	.496	0	0	4.24	8	87	4	4	170	159	1.07

1993 Season

	ERA	W	L	Sv	G	GS	IP	H	HR	BB	SO		Avg	AB	H	2B	3B	HR	RBI	BB	SO	OBP	SLG
Home	1.99	2	1	0	4	4	22.2	18	1	3	11	vs. Left	.263	19	5	2	1	0	4	1	4	.273	.474
Away	1.59	1	0	0	1	1	5.2	6	0	0	3	vs. Right	.221	86	19	2	1	1	3	2	10	.236	.302

Rafael Bournigal — Dodgers

Age 28 – Bats Right

	Avg	G	AB	R	H	2B	3B	HR	RBI	BB	SO	HBP	GDP	SB	CS	OBP	SLG	IBB	SH	SF	#Pit	#P/PA	GB	FB	G/F
1993 Season	.500	8	18	0	9	1	0	0	3	0	2	0	0	0	0	.500	.556	0	0	0	40	2.22	9	2	4.50
Career (1992-1993)	.316	18	38	1	12	2	0	0	3	1	4	1	0	0	0	.350	.368	0	0	0	98	2.45	19	9	2.11

1993 Season

	Avg	AB	H	2B	3B	HR	RBI	BB	SO	OBP	SLG
vs. Left	.500	4	2	0	0	0	0	0	0	.500	.500
vs. Right	.500	14	7	1	0	0	3	0	2	.500	.571

	Avg	AB	H	2B	3B	HR	RBI	BB	SO	OBP	SLG
Scoring Posn	.750	4	3	0	0	0	3	0	0	.750	.750
Close & Late	.000	0	0	0	0	0	0	0	0	.000	.000

Ryan Bowen — Marlins

Age 26 – Pitches Right (groundball pitcher)

	ERA	W	L	Sv	G	GS	IP	BB	SO	Avg	H	2B	3B	HR	RBI	OBP	SLG	CG	ShO	Sup	QS	#P/S	SB	CS	GB	FB	G/F
1993 Season	4.42	8	12	0	27	27	156.2	87	98	.263	156	28	3	11	66	.358	.375	2	1	4.08	13	91	15	7	254	140	1.81
Career (1991-1993)	5.46	14	23	0	52	49	262.0	153	169	.274	277	50	4	23	135	.371	.400	2	1	4.60	18	88	32	11	424	248	1.71

1993 Season

	ERA	W	L	Sv	G	GS	IP	H	HR	BB	SO
Home	4.47	4	7	0	15	15	88.2	95	8	40	61
Away	4.37	4	5	0	12	12	68.0	61	3	47	37
Starter	4.42	8	12	0	27	27	156.2	156	11	87	98
Reliever	0.00	0	0	0	0	0	0.0	0	0	0	0
0-3 Days Rest	0.00	0	0	0	0	0	0.0	0	0	0	0
4 Days Rest	4.12	6	8	0	15	15	89.2	83	6	55	62
5+ Days Rest	4.84	2	4	0	12	12	67.0	73	5	32	36
Pre-All Star	4.28	4	9	0	18	18	109.1	106	9	62	70
Post-All Star	4.75	4	3	0	9	9	47.1	50	2	25	28

	Avg	AB	H	2B	3B	HR	RBI	BB	SO	OBP	SLG
vs. Left	.278	302	84	13	1	5	35	46	46	.372	.377
vs. Right	.247	292	72	15	2	6	31	41	52	.342	.373
Scoring Posn	.228	167	38	4	0	2	53	26	30	.328	.287
Close & Late	.209	43	9	3	0	0	3	7	4	.320	.279
None on/out	.252	151	38	8	0	6	6	18	22	.335	.424
First Pitch	.308	104	32	3	0	0	14	5	0	.354	.337
Ahead in Count	.223	247	55	7	1	5	22	0	78	.222	.320
Behind in Count	.293	147	43	7	0	4	17	50	0	.472	.422
Two Strikes	.170	241	41	7	1	3	16	32	98	.267	.245

Jeff Branson — Reds

Age 27 – Bats Left (groundball hitter)

	Avg	G	AB	R	H	2B	3B	HR	RBI	BB	SO	HBP	GDP	SB	CS	OBP	SLG	IBB	SH	SF	#Pit	#P/PA	GB	FB	G/F
1993 Season	.241	125	381	40	92	15	1	3	22	19	73	0	4	4	1	.275	.310	2	8	4	1451	3.52	154	83	1.86
Career (1992-1993)	.254	197	496	52	126	22	2	3	37	24	89	0	8	4	2	.286	.325	4	10	5	1872	3.50	200	111	1.80

1993 Season

	Avg	AB	H	2B	3B	HR	RBI	BB	SO	OBP	SLG
vs. Left	.253	91	23	5	0	1	3	4	22	.281	.341
vs. Right	.238	290	69	10	1	2	19	15	51	.273	.300
Groundball	.263	133	35	4	0	1	6	6	19	.293	.316
Flyball	.188	64	12	4	0	0	2	2	18	.209	.250
Home	.232	185	43	11	0	2	8	9	33	.265	.324
Away	.250	196	49	4	1	1	14	10	40	.284	.296
Day	.220	100	22	4	1	1	7	5	28	.255	.310
Night	.249	281	70	11	0	2	15	14	45	.282	.310
Grass	.246	122	30	1	1	1	8	7	28	.287	.295
Turf	.239	259	62	14	0	2	14	12	45	.269	.317
First Pitch	.273	77	21	2	1	1	4	1	0	.275	.364
Ahead in Count	.338	77	26	7	0	1	7	8	0	.395	.468
Behind in Count	.210	167	35	4	0	1	8	0	61	.208	.251
Two Strikes	.182	176	32	6	0	1	6	10	73	.225	.233

	Avg	AB	H	2B	3B	HR	RBI	BB	SO	OBP	SLG
Scoring Posn	.181	83	15	2	0	0	17	8	19	.242	.205
Close & Late	.231	52	12	0	0	0	2	3	14	.273	.231
None on/out	.243	115	28	3	1	2	2	4	18	.269	.339
Batting #2	.276	127	35	6	0	1	8	8	30	.319	.346
Batting #8	.221	136	30	2	0	0	6	2	18	.229	.235
Other	.229	118	27	7	1	2	8	9	25	.279	.356
April	.333	15	5	1	0	0	0	1	2	.375	.400
May	.414	29	12	4	0	0	3	1	8	.433	.552
June	.293	58	17	1	0	1	3	3	12	.323	.362
July	.211	90	19	5	1	0	3	8	15	.273	.289
August	.232	95	22	3	0	2	9	3	19	.253	.326
September/October	.181	94	17	1	0	0	4	3	17	.204	.191
Pre-All Star	.296	135	40	9	1	1	7	8	28	.331	.400
Post-All Star	.211	246	52	6	0	2	15	11	45	.243	.260

1993 By Position

Position	Avg	AB	H	2B	3B	HR	RBI	BB	SO	OBP	SLG	G	GS	Innings	PO	A	E	DP	Fld Pct	Rng Fctr	In Zone	Outs	Zone Rtg	MLB Zone
As Pinch Hitter	.353	17	6	0	0	0	1	1	4	.389	.353	20	0	---	---	---	---	---	---	---	---	---	---	---
As 2b	.261	142	37	9	1	1	7	8	30	.298	.359	45	36	330.2	80	105	5	29	.974	5.04	115	95	.826	.895
As 3b	.250	40	10	0	0	0	2	3	8	.295	.250	14	8	92.0	7	16	1	0	.958	2.25	21	15	.714	.834
As ss	.213	178	38	6	0	2	12	7	30	.241	.281	59	46	426.1	88	138	5	28	.978	4.77	179	157	.877	.880

Jeff Brantley — Giants

Age 30 – Pitches Right (flyball pitcher)

	ERA	W	L	Sv	G	GS	IP	BB	SO	Avg	H	2B	3B	HR	RBI	OBP	SLG	GF	IR	IRS	Hld	SvOp	SB	CS	GB	FB	G/F
1993 Season	4.28	5	6	0	53	12	113.2	46	76	.259	112	15	3	19	49	.336	.439	9	18	6	10	3	1	5	125	162	0.77
Last Five Years	3.14	29	19	41	290	17	484.2	213	373	.242	435	62	5	48	193	.326	.362	112	165	48	44	56	41	14	553	588	0.94

1993 Season

	ERA	W	L	Sv	G	GS	IP	H	HR	BB	SO
Home	3.58	3	2	0	27	5	60.1	51	10	20	41
Away	5.06	2	4	0	26	7	53.1	61	9	26	35
Starter	4.86	3	5	0	12	12	63.0	76	13	25	30
Reliever	3.55	2	1	0	41	0	50.2	36	6	21	46
0 Days rest	3.12	0	0	0	9	0	8.2	7	0	5	9
1 or 2 Days rest	4.40	1	1	0	21	0	28.2	22	4	10	26
3+ Days rest	2.03	1	0	0	11	0	13.1	7	2	6	11
Pre-All Star	4.63	4	5	0	23	12	72.0	86	14	30	41
Post-All Star	3.67	1	1	0	30	0	41.2	26	5	16	35

	Avg	AB	H	2B	3B	HR	RBI	BB	SO	OBP	SLG
vs. Left	.285	221	63	13	2	11	26	33	30	.374	.511
vs. Right	.231	212	49	2	1	8	23	13	46	.295	.363
Scoring Posn	.189	90	17	1	0	3	28	13	19	.284	.300
Close & Late	.180	61	11	1	0	3	7	9	14	.286	.344
None on/out	.250	112	28	3	0	6	6	9	20	.306	.438
First Pitch	.222	63	14	2	0	2	6	2	0	.250	.349
Ahead in Count	.245	188	46	6	0	8	18	0	62	.262	.404
Behind in Count	.309	94	29	5	3	7	17	27	0	.459	.649
Two Strikes	.208	202	42	5	0	7	19	17	76	.277	.337

Last Five Years

	ERA	W	L	Sv	G	GS	IP	H	HR	BB	SO
Home	2.76	17	7	19	137	8	235.0	200	21	93	185
Away	3.50	12	12	22	153	9	249.2	235	27	120	188

	Avg	AB	H	2B	3B	HR	RBI	BB	SO	OBP	SLG
vs. Left	.250	983	246	44	2	23	90	141	185	.343	.369
vs. Right	.232	813	189	18	3	25	103	72	188	.306	.354

Last Five Years

	ERA	W	L	Sv	G	GS	IP	H	HR	BB	SO
Day	2.69	17	5	13	120	9	204.0	182	21	92	153
Night	3.46	12	14	28	170	8	280.2	253	27	121	220
Grass	3.08	22	13	26	216	14	362.2	337	36	152	282
Turf	3.32	7	6	15	74	3	122.0	98	12	61	91
April	3.45	2	3	4	41	4	73.0	60	6	38	52
May	2.65	4	4	11	51	6	95.0	87	12	40	58
June	3.22	7	4	6	49	2	81.0	84	12	33	50
July	3.68	7	2	11	51	0	73.1	66	7	26	63
August	2.79	4	4	5	55	1	87.0	70	7	52	74
September/October	3.23	5	2	4	43	4	75.1	68	4	24	76
Starter	4.09	6	6	0	17	17	88.0	93	13	33	61
Reliever	2.93	23	13	41	273	0	396.2	342	35	180	312
0 Days rest	3.04	6	2	10	51	0	68.0	60	6	24	61
1 or 2 Days rest	3.16	11	8	23	149	0	227.2	202	20	107	170
3+ Days rest	2.32	6	3	8	73	0	101.0	80	9	49	81
Pre-All Star	3.10	17	11	25	159	12	273.1	254	32	118	183
Post-All Star	3.19	12	8	16	131	5	211.1	181	16	95	190

	Avg	AB	H	2B	3B	HR	RBI	BB	SO	OBP	SLG
Inning 1-6	.255	592	151	25	4	20	72	67	112	.334	.412
Inning 7+	.236	1204	284	37	1	28	121	146	261	.323	.338
None on	.243	979	238	40	0	34	34	103	213	.323	.388
Runners on	.241	817	197	22	5	14	159	110	160	.331	.332
Scoring Posn	.202	494	100	11	0	10	144	79	117	.309	.285
Close & Late	.232	685	159	21	0	13	62	100	141	.332	.320
None on/out	.228	425	97	15	0	15	15	42	84	.302	.369
vs. 1st Batr (relief)	.200	235	47	6	1	6	24	28	54	.289	.311
First Inning Pitched	.225	958	216	23	3	23	116	126	224	.318	.328
First 15 Pitches	.238	822	196	23	3	21	92	97	173	.321	.350
Pitch 16-30	.234	543	127	19	1	12	46	73	116	.331	.339
Pitch 31-45	.253	221	56	13	0	4	30	26	49	.337	.367
Pitch 46+	.207	210	56	7	1	11	25	17	35	.323	.467
First Pitch	.253	225	57	8	1	5	24	24	0	.328	.364
Ahead in Count	.204	867	177	27	0	15	61	0	315	.215	.287
Behind in Count	.297	353	105	15	4	20	62	95	0	.445	.533
Two Strikes	.163	900	147	19	0	15	65	94	373	.249	.234

Pitcher vs. Batter (career)

Pitches Best Vs.	Avg	AB	H	2B	3B	HR	RBI	BB	SO	OBP	SLG
Barry Bonds	.000	13	0	0	0	0	0	1	5	.071	.000
Bobby Bonilla	.077	13	1	0	0	0	0	2	3	.200	.077
Darren Daulton	.083	12	1	0	0	0	1	1	0	.154	.083
Dave Hollins	.111	9	1	0	0	0	1	1	2	.182	.111
Barry Larkin	.133	15	2	0	0	0	0	0	1	.133	.133

Pitches Worst Vs.	Avg	AB	H	2B	3B	HR	RBI	BB	SO	OBP	SLG
Tony Gwynn	.600	20	12	1	0	0	1	4	0	.667	.650
Ryne Sandberg	.500	10	5	1	0	1	3	3	3	.615	.900
Howard Johnson	.455	11	5	0	0	1	3	4	2	.563	.727
John Kruk	.400	10	4	0	0	1	1	5	1	.600	.700
Paul O'Neill	.364	11	4	0	0	2	6	6	1	.588	.909

Sid Bream — Braves

Age 33 – Bats Left (flyball hitter)

	Avg	G	AB	R	H	2B	3B	HR	RBI	BB	SO	HBP	GDP	SB	CS	OBP	SLG	IBB	SH	SF	#Pit	#P/PA	GB	FB	G/F
1993 Season	.260	117	277	33	72	14	1	9	35	31	43	0	6	4	2	.332	.415	3	1	2	1100	3.54	96	87	1.10
Last Five Years	.261	499	1339	137	349	77	4	45	212	162	200	3	23	18	13	.338	.425	15	14	15	5517	3.60	445	459	0.97

1993 Season

	Avg	AB	H	2B	3B	HR	RBI	BB	SO	OBP	SLG
vs. Left	.276	29	8	3	0	0	5	1	7	.290	.379
vs. Right	.258	248	64	11	1	9	30	30	36	.337	.419
Home	.232	125	29	5	0	5	9	14	15	.309	.392
Away	.283	152	43	9	1	4	26	17	28	.351	.434
First Pitch	.340	50	17	4	0	2	9	2	0	.365	.540
Ahead in Count	.319	69	22	5	0	5	12	24	0	.495	.609
Behind in Count	.193	114	22	4	1	0	6	0	37	.193	.246
Two Strikes	.204	113	23	4	1	2	11	5	43	.237	.310

	Avg	AB	H	2B	3B	HR	RBI	BB	SO	OBP	SLG
Scoring Posn	.250	68	17	3	0	2	24	10	10	.338	.382
Close & Late	.185	54	10	1	1	2	9	10	9	.313	.352
None on/out	.297	64	19	4	0	2	2	6	9	.357	.453
Batting #6	.251	243	61	13	1	8	28	24	39	.316	.412
Batting #9	.263	19	5	0	0	1	5	4	2	.391	.421
Other	.400	15	6	1	0	0	2	3	2	.500	.467
Pre-All Star	.243	239	58	12	1	8	27	24	41	.311	.402
Post-All Star	.368	38	14	2	0	1	8	7	2	.457	.500

Last Five Years

	Avg	AB	H	2B	3B	HR	RBI	BB	SO	OBP	SLG
vs. Left	.240	208	50	17	1	4	33	12	40	.283	.389
vs. Right	.264	1131	299	60	3	41	179	150	160	.348	.431
Groundball	.280	454	127	28	2	11	72	63	53	.365	.423
Flyball	.234	291	68	16	1	14	52	34	51	.311	.440
Home	.264	607	160	32	1	20	98	74	79	.342	.418
Away	.258	732	189	45	3	25	114	88	121	.335	.430
Day	.283	375	106	21	3	11	72	44	61	.357	.443
Night	.252	964	243	56	1	34	140	118	139	.331	.418
Grass	.246	797	196	42	2	24	118	89	122	.318	.394
Turf	.282	542	153	35	2	21	94	73	78	.368	.470
First Pitch	.317	202	64	10	0	7	36	8	0	.343	.470
Ahead in Count	.285	368	105	25	1	13	62	104	0	.442	.465
Behind in Count	.211	525	111	31	2	12	76	0	170	.211	.347
Two Strikes	.211	530	112	27	2	18	82	47	200	.272	.372

	Avg	AB	H	2B	3B	HR	RBI	BB	SO	OBP	SLG
Scoring Posn	.277	376	104	23	1	12	156	63	55	.371	.439
Close & Late	.229	205	47	11	1	5	30	27	28	.316	.366
None on/out	.265	309	82	18	1	10	10	32	44	.334	.427
Batting #5	.256	469	120	30	1	14	77	52	67	.328	.414
Batting #6	.258	749	193	41	3	26	112	88	115	.334	.425
Other	.298	121	36	6	0	5	23	22	18	.400	.471
April	.223	247	55	17	0	4	23	31	46	.309	.340
May	.278	270	75	19	0	12	51	42	49	.375	.481
June	.285	242	69	9	3	6	36	17	31	.327	.421
July	.257	175	45	8	0	9	31	19	22	.327	.457
August	.315	162	51	15	0	7	38	22	18	.392	.537
September/October	.222	243	54	9	1	7	33	31	34	.308	.354
Pre-All Star	.262	833	218	48	3	26	119	99	136	.339	.420
Post-All Star	.259	506	131	29	1	19	93	63	64	.338	.433

Batter vs. Pitcher (since 1984)

Hits Best Against	Avg	AB	H	2B	3B	HR	RBI	BB	SO	OBP	SLG
Steve Bedrosian	.538	13	7	2	0	1	2	2	2	.600	.923
Mike Maddux	.529	17	9	1	1	0	3	5	3	.636	.706
Bill Sampen	.500	10	5	0	0	1	3	0	2	.455	.800
Randy Myers	.444	9	4	2	0	1	4	2	3	.462	1.000
Omar Olivares	.357	14	5	1	0	2	5	2	1	.389	.857

Hits Worst Against	Avg	AB	H	2B	3B	HR	RBI	BB	SO	OBP	SLG
Tom Browning	.000	10	0	0	0	0	0	2	2	.167	.000
Sid Fernandez	.063	16	1	0	0	0	0	1	3	.118	.063
Mark Gardner	.100	10	1	0	0	0	0	1	1	.182	.100
Jim Deshaies	.133	15	2	0	0	0	1	0	2	.133	.133
Paul Assenmacher	.143	14	2	0	0	0	0	0	4	.143	.143

Bill Brennan — Cubs

Age 31 – Pitches Right (groundball pitcher)

	ERA	W	L	Sv	G	GS	IP	BB	SO	Avg	H	2B	3B	HR	RBI	OBP	SLG	GF	IR	IRS	Hld	SvOp	SB	CS	GB	FB	G/F
1993 Season	4.20	2	1	0	8	1	15.0	8	11	.291	16	2	0	2	10	.385	.436	0	9	4	0	0	1	3	22	12	1.83

1993 Season

	ERA	W	L	Sv	G	GS	IP	H	HR	BB	SO
Home	1.93	1	0	0	3	0	4.2	3	0	3	2
Away	5.23	1	1	0	5	1	10.1	13	2	5	9

	Avg	AB	H	2B	3B	HR	RBI	BB	SO	OBP	SLG
vs. Left	.333	30	10	1	0	2	5	7	7	.459	.567
vs. Right	.240	25	6	1	0	0	5	1	4	.286	.280

George Brett — Royals

Age 41 – Bats Left

	Avg	G	AB	R	H	2B	3B	HR	RBI	BB	SO	HBP	GDP	SB	CS	OBP	SLG	IBB	SH	SF	#Pit	#P/PA	GB	FB	G/F
1993 Season	.266	145	560	69	149	31	3	19	75	39	67	3	20	7	5	.312	.434	9	0	10	2027	3.31	234	161	1.45
Last Five Years	.284	694	2658	350	755	177	20	62	364	247	321	12	90	40	17	.343	.436	53	1	38	9980	3.38	1066	794	1.34

1993 Season

	Avg	AB	H	2B	3B	HR	RBI	BB	SO	OBP	SLG
vs. Left	.209	187	39	7	2	2	19	7	18	.246	.299
vs. Right	.295	373	110	24	1	17	56	32	49	.344	.501
Groundball	.357	84	30	8	0	2	11	9	17	.419	.524
Flyball	.302	116	35	8	0	3	9	8	8	.349	.448
Home	.269	275	74	17	3	7	32	17	28	.313	.429
Away	.263	285	75	14	0	12	43	22	39	.311	.439
Day	.296	179	53	13	1	9	30	15	23	.347	.531
Night	.252	381	96	18	2	10	45	24	44	.295	.388
Grass	.265	234	62	10	0	11	35	18	33	.311	.449
Turf	.267	326	87	21	3	8	40	21	34	.313	.423
First Pitch	.279	104	29	8	0	2	15	8	0	.328	.413
Ahead in Count	.270	152	41	7	3	11	29	16	0	.337	.572
Behind in Count	.263	217	57	14	0	3	17	0	57	.261	.369
Two Strikes	.221	199	44	12	0	1	16	15	67	.269	.296

	Avg	AB	H	2B	3B	HR	RBI	BB	SO	OBP	SLG
Scoring Posn	.214	145	31	8	0	3	50	20	20	.291	.331
Close & Late	.260	100	26	4	0	3	8	10	10	.321	.390
None on/out	.320	100	32	10	0	3	3	3	7	.346	.510
Batting #3	.264	550	145	28	3	19	71	38	66	.309	.429
Batting #5	.500	4	2	1	0	0	3	1	0	.600	.750
Other	.333	6	2	2	0	0	1	0	1	.333	.667
April	.220	82	18	5	0	1	8	4	9	.250	.317
May	.245	94	23	5	0	3	14	7	10	.294	.394
June	.299	97	29	7	0	3	15	8	10	.346	.464
July	.310	71	22	5	1	5	13	3	8	.342	.620
August	.248	109	27	5	1	2	8	10	18	.306	.367
September/October	.280	107	30	4	1	5	17	7	12	.331	.477
Pre-All Star	.252	290	73	18	0	7	37	21	31	.297	.386
Post-All Star	.281	270	76	13	3	12	38	18	36	.328	.485

1993 By Position

Position	Avg	AB	H	2B	3B	HR	RBI	BB	SO	OBP	SLG	G	GS	Innings	PO	A	E	DP	Fld Pct	Rng Fctr	In Zone	Outs	Zone Rtg	MLB Zone
As Designated Hitter	.265	555	147	29	3	19	74	39	66	.311	.431	140	139	---	---	---	---	---	---	---	---	---	---	---

Last Five Years

	Avg	AB	H	2B	3B	HR	RBI	BB	SO	OBP	SLG
vs. Left	.252	892	225	50	8	11	109	67	113	.308	.363
vs. Right	.300	1766	530	127	12	51	255	180	208	.361	.472
Groundball	.309	631	195	40	1	13	84	70	81	.377	.437
Flyball	.292	643	188	51	3	17	95	56	68	.350	.460
Home	.281	1347	379	84	16	17	177	124	136	.341	.405
Away	.287	1311	376	93	4	45	187	123	185	.346	.467
Day	.296	709	210	56	5	24	113	65	90	.352	.491
Night	.280	1949	545	121	15	38	251	182	231	.340	.416
Grass	.282	1055	298	72	3	38	154	97	151	.341	.464
Turf	.285	1603	457	105	17	24	210	150	170	.345	.417
First Pitch	.311	495	154	40	2	9	75	34	0	.353	.455
Ahead in Count	.323	675	218	47	9	32	115	117	0	.418	.561
Behind in Count	.240	1013	243	57	6	15	100	0	267	.241	.352
Two Strikes	.209	964	201	49	4	11	83	84	321	.271	.302

	Avg	AB	H	2B	3B	HR	RBI	BB	SO	OBP	SLG
Scoring Posn	.278	654	182	41	2	10	276	128	80	.381	.393
Close & Late	.250	412	103	17	1	12	48	59	45	.342	.383
None on/out	.285	515	147	40	2	14	14	30	58	.327	.452
Batting #3	.284	2149	611	140	14	54	310	210	269	.346	.438
Batting #5	.284	370	105	25	4	5	35	27	34	.337	.414
Other	.281	139	39	12	2	3	19	10	18	.322	.460
April	.216	343	74	13	0	5	32	37	46	.292	.297
May	.281	313	88	18	3	5	36	31	42	.346	.406
June	.260	439	114	36	1	6	59	37	46	.313	.387
July	.313	501	157	42	4	20	82	46	55	.370	.533
August	.298	534	159	37	8	10	76	54	64	.358	.453
September/October	.309	528	163	31	4	16	79	42	68	.360	.473
Pre-All Star	.256	1262	323	80	5	20	150	120	151	.319	.375
Post-All Star	.309	1396	432	97	15	42	214	127	170	.365	.491

Batter vs. Pitcher (since 1984)

Hits Best Against	Avg	AB	H	2B	3B	HR	RBI	BB	SO	OBP	SLG
Julio Valera	.727	11	8	1	1	0	2	0	0	.727	1.000
Danny Darwin	.526	19	10	3	0	2	4	6	3	.615	1.000
Jose Rijo	.500	12	6	1	0	2	7	5	2	.647	1.083
Edwin Nunez	.417	12	5	1	0	2	5	1	1	.462	1.000
Jeff Russell	.400	15	6	0	0	3	10	5	2	.500	1.000

Hits Worst Against	Avg	AB	H	2B	3B	HR	RBI	BB	SO	OBP	SLG
Rick Sutcliffe	.000	12	0	0	0	0	0	0	0	.000	.000
Steve Ontiveros	.056	18	1	0	0	0	0	0	4	.056	.056
Chuck Crim	.077	13	1	0	0	0	0	1	3	.143	.077
John Smiley	.091	11	1	0	0	0	0	0	1	.091	.091
Scott Radinsky	.111	18	2	0	0	0	0	0	3	.111	.111

Billy Brewer — Royals

Age 26 – Pitches Left (flyball pitcher)

	ERA	W	L	Sv	G	GS	IP	BB	SO	Avg	H	2B	3B	HR	RBI	OBP	SLG	GF	IR	IRS	Hld	SvOp	SB	CS	GB	FB	G/F
1993 Season	3.46	2	2	0	46	0	39.0	20	28	.230	31	4	1	6	16	.327	.407	14	39	4	5	2	5	2	39	43	0.91

1993 Season

	ERA	W	L	Sv	G	GS	IP	H	HR	BB	SO
Home	3.10	1	2	0	25	0	20.1	16	1	9	10
Away	3.86	1	0	0	21	0	18.2	15	5	11	18
Starter	0.00	0	0	0	0	0	0.0	0	0	0	0
Reliever	3.46	2	2	0	46	0	39.0	31	6	20	28
0 Days rest	0.00	0	0	0	6	0	3.1	2	0	1	3
1 or 2 Days rest	4.98	1	2	0	25	0	21.2	18	4	16	15
3+ Days rest	1.93	1	0	0	15	0	14.0	11	2	3	10
Pre-All Star	2.84	1	1	0	22	0	19.0	15	2	8	8
Post-All Star	4.05	1	1	0	24	0	20.0	16	4	12	20

	Avg	AB	H	2B	3B	HR	RBI	BB	SO	OBP	SLG
vs. Left	.183	60	11	0	0	3	11	9	14	.286	.333
vs. Right	.267	75	20	4	1	3	5	11	14	.360	.467
Scoring Posn	.143	42	6	2	0	0	9	10	9	.302	.190
Close & Late	.136	44	6	0	0	1	5	7	13	.255	.205
None on/out	.516	31	16	1	1	4	4	8	2	.615	1.000
First Pitch	.267	15	4	0	0	1	3	3	0	.368	.467
Ahead in Count	.210	62	13	3	0	1	4	0	20	.210	.306
Behind in Count	.281	32	9	0	1	1	3	11	0	.465	.438
Two Strikes	.159	63	10	2	0	1	5	6	28	.232	.238

Rod Brewer — Cardinals

Age 28 – Bats Left

	Avg	G	AB	R	H	2B	3B	HR	RBI	BB	SO	HBP	GDP	SB	CS	OBP	SLG	IBB	SH	SF	#Pit	#P/PA	GB	FB	G/F
1993 Season	.286	110	147	15	42	8	0	2	20	17	26	1	5	1	0	.359	.381	5	2	2	585	3.46	53	45	1.18
Career (1990-1993)	.278	172	288	30	80	15	0	2	33	25	47	2	7	1	1	.336	.351	5	2	3	1092	3.41	106	84	1.26

1993 Season

	Avg	AB	H	2B	3B	HR	RBI	BB	SO	OBP	SLG
vs. Left	.267	15	4	1	0	0	0	2	3	.353	.333
vs. Right	.288	132	38	7	0	2	20	15	23	.360	.386
Home	.324	74	24	3	0	0	5	7	11	.386	.365
Away	.247	73	18	5	0	2	15	10	15	.333	.397

	Avg	AB	H	2B	3B	HR	RBI	BB	SO	OBP	SLG
Scoring Posn	.333	36	12	4	0	0	18	10	8	.458	.444
Close & Late	.316	38	12	2	0	0	6	6	6	.400	.368
None on/out	.318	44	14	3	0	1	1	2	10	.348	.455
Batting #7	.282	71	20	6	0	1	10	11	15	.386	.408

1993 Season

	Avg	AB	H	2B	3B	HR	RBI	BB	SO	OBP	SLG
First Pitch	.417	24	10	1	0	0	3	2	0	.444	.458
Ahead in Count	.211	19	4	0	0	1	3	9	0	.464	.368
Behind in Count	.222	81	18	5	0	0	10	0	24	.229	.284
Two Strikes	.230	74	17	4	0	0	8	6	26	.288	.284

	Avg	AB	H	2B	3B	HR	RBI	BB	SO	OBP	SLG
Batting #9	.282	39	11	2	0	1	5	4	6	.349	.410
Other	.297	37	11	0	0	0	5	2	5	.317	.297
Pre-All Star	.262	84	22	5	0	0	12	8	16	.319	.321
Post-All Star	.317	63	20	3	0	2	8	9	10	.411	.460

Greg Briley — Marlins

Age 29 – Bats Left (groundball hitter)

	Avg	G	AB	R	H	2B	3B	HR	RBI	BB	SO	HBP	GDP	SB	CS	OBP	SLG	IBB	SH	SF	#Pit	#P/PA	GB	FB	G/F
1993 Season	.194	120	170	17	33	6	0	3	12	12	42	1	4	6	2	.250	.282	0	1	1	672	3.63	72	35	2.06
Last Five Years	.253	585	1482	166	375	73	9	28	131	119	254	8	30	65	24	.309	.371	1	4	15	5978	3.67	609	378	1.61

1993 Season

	Avg	AB	H	2B	3B	HR	RBI	BB	SO	OBP	SLG
vs. Left	.214	14	3	0	0	1	3	0	4	.214	.429
vs. Right	.192	156	30	6	0	2	9	12	38	.253	.269
Home	.165	85	14	1	0	2	7	8	25	.234	.247
Away	.224	85	19	5	0	1	5	4	17	.267	.318
First Pitch	.387	31	12	2	0	1	3	0	0	.387	.548
Ahead in Count	.188	32	6	2	0	0	2	4	0	.270	.250
Behind in Count	.117	77	9	2	0	2	4	0	38	.128	.221
Two Strikes	.123	81	10	2	0	1	4	8	42	.211	.185

	Avg	AB	H	2B	3B	HR	RBI	BB	SO	OBP	SLG
Scoring Posn	.194	36	7	1	0	0	6	4	11	.268	.222
Close & Late	.152	46	7	2	0	1	5	5	14	.250	.261
None on/out	.143	42	6	2	0	0	0	0	10	.163	.190
Batting #6	.154	39	6	1	0	0	0	1	12	.175	.179
Batting #9	.203	69	14	2	0	1	7	6	15	.276	.275
Other	.210	62	13	3	0	2	5	5	15	.265	.355
Pre-All Star	.246	118	29	6	0	3	10	7	29	.294	.373
Post-All Star	.077	52	4	0	0	0	2	5	13	.155	.077

Last Five Years

	Avg	AB	H	2B	3B	HR	RBI	BB	SO	OBP	SLG
vs. Left	.250	144	36	6	2	2	22	11	34	.308	.361
vs. Right	.253	1338	339	67	7	26	109	108	220	.309	.372
Groundball	.252	420	106	20	2	7	38	31	69	.306	.360
Flyball	.265	321	85	21	3	7	30	25	48	.316	.414
Home	.236	695	164	26	3	14	63	59	114	.295	.342
Away	.268	787	211	47	6	14	68	60	140	.322	.396
Day	.236	399	94	14	2	9	34	26	71	.285	.348
Night	.259	1083	281	59	7	19	97	93	183	.318	.380
Grass	.247	681	168	31	6	11	53	59	135	.308	.358
Turf	.258	801	207	42	3	17	78	60	119	.310	.382
First Pitch	.277	188	52	11	1	3	15	0	0	.280	.394
Ahead in Count	.315	400	126	24	4	10	53	72	0	.417	.470
Behind in Count	.190	616	117	21	4	8	33	0	216	.194	.276
Two Strikes	.180	634	114	21	4	9	41	47	254	.238	.268

	Avg	AB	H	2B	3B	HR	RBI	BB	SO	OBP	SLG
Scoring Posn	.232	315	73	9	5	5	93	31	61	.288	.340
Close & Late	.255	278	71	15	3	3	26	16	61	.300	.363
None on/out	.241	352	85	17	1	5	5	20	60	.290	.338
Batting #2	.244	626	153	28	7	17	72	59	111	.309	.393
Batting #7	.254	283	72	17	1	2	20	18	40	.296	.343
Other	.262	573	150	28	1	9	39	42	103	.315	.361
April	.222	176	39	12	0	1	13	15	26	.289	.307
May	.264	269	71	12	0	5	27	14	43	.300	.364
June	.243	284	69	15	1	8	26	16	61	.282	.387
July	.279	204	57	9	3	6	25	20	34	.346	.441
August	.235	281	66	13	3	5	21	26	49	.302	.356
September/October	.272	268	73	12	2	3	19	28	41	.338	.366
Pre-All Star	.244	770	188	40	1	14	68	48	136	.290	.353
Post-All Star	.263	712	187	33	8	14	63	71	118	.329	.390

Batter vs. Pitcher (career)

Hits Best Against	Avg	AB	H	2B	3B	HR	RBI	BB	SO	OBP	SLG
Jose Mesa	.636	11	7	2	0	0	0	0	0	.636	.818
Pete Harnisch	.435	23	10	4	0	1	4	4	0	.519	.739
Mike Boddicker	.414	29	12	2	0	0	3	2	2	.452	.483
Kirk McCaskill	.407	27	11	1	0	1	2	5	4	.500	.556
Dave Johnson	.333	12	4	1	0	2	5	0	1	.308	.917

Hits Worst Against	Avg	AB	H	2B	3B	HR	RBI	BB	SO	OBP	SLG
Scott Sanderson	.000	21	0	0	0	0	0	0	3	.000	.000
Tim Leary	.091	22	2	1	0	0	0	2	1	.167	.136
Bob Milacki	.091	11	1	1	0	0	0	0	4	.091	.182
Bill Wegman	.143	14	2	0	0	0	1	0	4	.143	.143
Duane Ward	.167	12	2	0	0	0	1	0	6	.167	.167

Brad Brink — Phillies

Age 29 – Pitches Right

	ERA	W	L	Sv	G	GS	IP	BB	SO	Avg	H	2B	3B	HR	RBI	OBP	SLG	GF	IR	IRS	Hld	SvOp	SB	CS	GB	FB	G/F
1993 Season	3.00	0	0	0	2	0	6.0	3	8	.143	3	1	0	1	2	.250	.333	1	0	0	0	0	0	0	4	6	0.67
Career (1992-1993)	3.99	0	4	0	10	7	47.1	16	24	.290	56	9	2	3	25	.348	.404	1	0	0	0	0	3	2	65	64	1.02

1993 Season

	ERA	W	L	Sv	G	GS	IP	H	HR	BB	SO
Home	4.50	0	0	0	1	0	2.0	2	0	0	3
Away	2.25	0	0	0	1	0	4.0	1	1	3	5

	Avg	AB	H	2B	3B	HR	RBI	BB	SO	OBP	SLG
vs. Left	.133	15	2	1	0	0	1	2	5	.235	.200
vs. Right	.167	6	1	0	0	1	1	1	3	.286	.667

John Briscoe — Athletics

Age 26 – Pitches Right

	ERA	W	L	Sv	G	GS	IP	BB	SO	Avg	H	2B	3B	HR	RBI	OBP	SLG	GF	IR	IRS	Hld	SvOp	SB	CS	GB	FB	G/F
1993 Season	8.03	1	0	0	17	0	24.2	26	24	.277	26	6	0	2	16	.426	.404	6	9	3	0	0	0	2	30	29	1.03
Career (1991-1993)	7.49	1	1	0	30	2	45.2	45	37	.286	50	11	0	5	35	.426	.434	15	15	8	0	0	0	3	55	54	1.02

1993 Season

	ERA	W	L	Sv	G	GS	IP	H	HR	BB	SO
Home	4.76	0	0	0	6	0	11.1	7	2	10	14
Away	10.80	1	0	0	11	0	13.1	19	0	16	10

	Avg	AB	H	2B	3B	HR	RBI	BB	SO	OBP	SLG
vs. Left	.405	42	17	4	0	0	9	13	9	.536	.500
vs. Right	.173	52	9	2	0	2	7	13	15	.333	.327

Bernardo Brito — Twins

Age 30 – Bats Right

	Avg	G	AB	R	H	2B	3B	HR	RBI	BB	SO	HBP	GDP	SB	CS	OBP	SLG	IBB	SH	SF	#Pit	#P/PA	GB	FB	G/F
1993 Season	.241	27	54	8	13	2	0	4	9	1	20	0	1	0	0	.255	.500	0	0	0	244	4.44	12	13	0.92
Career (1992-1993)	.221	35	68	9	15	3	0	4	11	1	24	0	1	0	1	.229	.441	0	0	1	289	4.13	17	17	1.00

1993 Season

	Avg	AB	H	2B	3B	HR	RBI	BB	SO	OBP	SLG
vs. Left	.333	33	11	2	0	4	9	1	9	.353	.758
vs. Right	.095	21	2	0	0	0	0	0	11	.095	.095

	Avg	AB	H	2B	3B	HR	RBI	BB	SO	OBP	SLG
Scoring Posn	.167	12	2	1	0	1	4	1	7	.231	.500
Close & Late	.000	8	0	0	0	0	0	0	5	.000	.000

Doug Brocail — Padres

Age 27 – Pitches Right

	ERA	W	L	Sv	G	GS	IP	BB	SO	Avg	H	2B	3B	HR	RBI	OBP	SLG	CG	ShO	Sup	QS	#P/S	SB	CS	GB	FB	G/F
1993 Season	4.56	4	13	0	24	24	128.1	42	70	.283	143	25	4	16	65	.338	.443	0	0	4.00	7	87	10	4	177	145	1.22
Career (1992-1993)	4.74	4	13	0	27	27	142.1	47	85	.284	160	30	4	18	73	.339	.448	0	0	3.86	7	86	10	4	194	162	1.20

1993 Season

	ERA	W	L	Sv	G	GS	IP	H	HR	BB	SO
Home	4.67	2	5	0	11	11	61.2	67	6	17	36
Away	4.46	2	8	0	13	13	66.2	76	10	25	34
Starter	4.56	4	13	0	24	24	128.1	143	16	42	70
Reliever	0.00	0	0	0	0	0	0.0	0	0	0	0
0-3 Days Rest	2.84	0	2	0	2	2	12.2	15	0	7	5
4 Days Rest	4.70	1	7	0	12	12	69.0	75	8	16	44
5+ Days Rest	4.82	3	4	0	10	10	46.2	53	8	19	21
Pre-All Star	3.60	2	4	0	9	9	50.0	53	6	13	31
Post-All Star	5.17	2	9	0	15	15	78.1	90	10	29	39

	Avg	AB	H	2B	3B	HR	RBI	BB	SO	OBP	SLG
vs. Left	.292	243	71	11	2	8	35	30	30	.367	.453
vs. Right	.274	263	72	14	2	8	30	12	40	.309	.433
Scoring Posn	.213	127	27	4	3	4	49	13	16	.285	.386
Close & Late	.250	16	4	1	1	0	3	1	1	.278	.438
None on/out	.262	130	34	10	0	2	2	7	15	.299	.385
First Pitch	.354	79	28	2	2	4	19	2	0	.365	.582
Ahead in Count	.220	205	45	6	0	4	17	0	56	.224	.307
Behind in Count	.405	121	49	13	1	8	24	24	0	.500	.727
Two Strikes	.196	219	43	6	1	4	17	16	70	.256	.288

Jeff Bronkey — Rangers

Age 28 – Pitches Right (groundball pitcher)

	ERA	W	L	Sv	G	GS	IP	BB	SO	Avg	H	2B	3B	HR	RBI	OBP	SLG	GF	IR	IRS	Hld	SvOp	SB	CS	GB	FB	G/F
1993 Season	4.00	1	1	1	21	0	36.0	11	18	.285	39	8	0	4	22	.338	.431	6	24	8	2	3	0	1	75	28	2.68

1993 Season

	ERA	W	L	Sv	G	GS	IP	H	HR	BB	SO
Home	3.79	0	0	1	9	0	19.0	24	2	6	8
Away	4.24	1	1	0	12	0	17.0	15	2	5	10

	Avg	AB	H	2B	3B	HR	RBI	BB	SO	OBP	SLG
vs. Left	.283	46	13	1	0	1	7	3	7	.320	.370
vs. Right	.286	91	26	7	0	3	15	8	11	.347	.462

Hubie Brooks — Royals

Age 37 – Bats Right

	Avg	G	AB	R	H	2B	3B	HR	RBI	BB	SO	HBP	GDP	SB	CS	OBP	SLG	IBB	SH	SF	#Pit	#P/PA	GB	FB	G/F
1993 Season	.286	75	168	14	48	12	0	1	24	11	27	1	5	0	1	.331	.375	1	0	1	648	3.58	62	50	1.24
Last Five Years	.255	561	1941	220	495	94	3	59	271	139	351	15	50	14	21	.306	.398	24	0	24	7444	3.51	726	574	1.26

1993 Season

	Avg	AB	H	2B	3B	HR	RBI	BB	SO	OBP	SLG
vs. Left	.327	110	36	10	0	1	13	7	12	.368	.445
vs. Right	.207	58	12	2	0	0	11	4	15	.266	.241
Home	.286	84	24	8	0	0	13	5	12	.330	.381
Away	.286	84	24	4	0	1	11	6	15	.333	.369
First Pitch	.250	24	6	1	0	0	2	1	0	.308	.292
Ahead in Count	.308	39	12	4	0	0	7	6	0	.400	.410
Behind in Count	.243	74	18	4	0	1	10	0	23	.243	.338
Two Strikes	.230	74	17	4	0	1	10	4	27	.266	.324

	Avg	AB	H	2B	3B	HR	RBI	BB	SO	OBP	SLG
Scoring Posn	.296	54	16	4	0	0	21	5	11	.350	.370
Close & Late	.286	42	12	1	0	0	7	3	13	.326	.310
None on/out	.212	33	7	3	0	0	0	1	8	.235	.303
Batting #5	.324	34	11	1	0	0	5	1	4	.351	.353
Batting #6	.171	41	7	4	0	0	3	4	7	.244	.268
Other	.323	93	30	7	0	1	16	6	16	.364	.430
Pre-All Star	.275	102	28	5	0	0	11	5	16	.315	.324
Post-All Star	.303	66	20	7	0	1	13	6	11	.356	.455

Last Five Years

	Avg	AB	H	2B	3B	HR	RBI	BB	SO	OBP	SLG
vs. Left	.263	692	182	40	0	22	95	61	107	.324	.416
vs. Right	.251	1249	313	54	3	37	176	78	244	.297	.388
Groundball	.267	656	175	32	2	16	93	59	99	.327	.395
Flyball	.269	454	122	18	1	16	66	28	83	.315	.419
Home	.261	941	246	47	2	22	127	79	163	.319	.386
Away	.249	1000	249	47	1	37	144	60	188	.294	.409
Day	.251	514	129	28	2	20	69	36	89	.305	.430
Night	.256	1427	366	66	1	39	202	103	262	.307	.386
Grass	.244	1168	285	46	3	38	168	80	212	.293	.386
Turf	.272	773	210	48	0	21	103	59	139	.327	.415
First Pitch	.324	216	70	7	1	11	35	10	0	.353	.519
Ahead in Count	.322	419	135	28	1	16	73	69	0	.419	.508
Behind in Count	.211	985	208	42	1	21	118	0	318	.214	.320
Two Strikes	.196	909	178	36	0	22	104	51	351	.242	.308

	Avg	AB	H	2B	3B	HR	RBI	BB	SO	OBP	SLG
Scoring Posn	.255	529	135	26	1	15	210	74	108	.340	.393
Close & Late	.269	335	90	12	1	11	49	29	80	.329	.409
None on/out	.248	500	124	29	0	16	16	14	81	.273	.402
Batting #4	.254	716	182	32	0	24	97	51	120	.306	.399
Batting #5	.258	782	202	39	2	23	118	51	150	.305	.402
Other	.251	443	111	23	1	12	56	37	81	.309	.388
April	.273	330	90	18	0	14	52	20	54	.310	.455
May	.231	403	93	12	2	10	42	18	76	.268	.345
June	.265	336	89	18	1	11	53	36	54	.338	.423
July	.229	319	73	12	0	7	41	21	57	.280	.332
August	.264	265	70	18	0	8	34	19	53	.315	.423
September/October	.278	288	80	16	0	9	49	25	57	.336	.427
Pre-All Star	.250	1174	294	51	3	37	161	83	201	.302	.394
Post-All Star	.262	767	201	43	0	22	110	56	150	.313	.404

Batter vs. Pitcher (since 1984)

Hits Best Against	Avg	AB	H	2B	3B	HR	RBI	BB	SO	OBP	SLG
Rick Honeycutt	.579	19	11	0	0	0	1	2	0	.619	.579
Jeff Parrett	.500	10	5	2	0	0	6	0	0	.455	.700
Tom Glavine	.440	25	11	2	0	1	6	2	4	.481	.640
Ken Dayley	.400	10	4	0	1	0	5	3	2	.538	.600
Joe Boever	.375	8	3	2	0	1	3	2	3	.455	1.000

Hits Worst Against	Avg	AB	H	2B	3B	HR	RBI	BB	SO	OBP	SLG
Randy Myers	.077	13	1	0	0	0	0	0	5	.077	.077
Steve Avery	.091	11	1	0	0	0	1	1	2	.167	.091
Todd Worrell	.095	21	2	0	0	0	0	2	5	.174	.095
Bill Wegman	.100	10	1	0	0	0	0	1	1	.182	.100
Lee Smith	.118	17	2	1	0	0	0	0	7	.118	.176

Jerry Brooks — Dodgers

Age 27 – Bats Right

	Avg	G	AB	R	H	2B	3B	HR	RBI	BB	SO	HBP	GDP	SB	CS	OBP	SLG	IBB	SH	SF	#Pit	#P/PA	GB	FB	G/F
1993 Season	.222	9	9	2	2	1	0	1	1	0	2	0	0	0	0	.222	.667	0	0	0	26	2.89	3	3	1.00

1993 Season

	Avg	AB	H	2B	3B	HR	RBI	BB	SO	OBP	SLG
vs. Left	.000	3	0	0	0	0	0	0	1	.000	.000
vs. Right	.333	6	2	1	0	1	1	0	1	.333	1.000

	Avg	AB	H	2B	3B	HR	RBI	BB	SO	OBP	SLG
Scoring Posn	.000	2	0	0	0	0	0	0	0	.000	.000
Close & Late	1.000	1	1	1	0	0	0	0	0	1.000	2.000

Scott Brosius — Athletics

Age 27 – Bats Right (flyball hitter)

	Avg	G	AB	R	H	2B	3B	HR	RBI	BB	SO	HBP	GDP	SB	CS	OBP	SLG	IBB	SH	SF	#Pit	#P/PA	GB	FB	G/F
1993 Season	.249	70	213	26	53	10	1	6	25	14	37	1	6	6	0	.296	.390	0	3	2	895	3.84	65	77	0.84
Career (1991-1993)	.239	144	368	48	88	17	1	12	42	20	61	3	8	12	1	.282	.389	1	4	3	1496	3.76	116	134	0.87

1993 Season

	Avg	AB	H	2B	3B	HR	RBI	BB	SO	OBP	SLG
vs. Left	.210	81	17	4	0	3	11	5	14	.261	.370
vs. Right	.273	132	36	6	1	3	14	9	23	.317	.402
Home	.208	106	22	3	0	3	10	10	15	.274	.321
Away	.290	107	31	7	1	3	15	4	22	.319	.458
First Pitch	.368	19	7	1	0	1	4	0	0	.368	.579
Ahead in Count	.283	46	13	4	1	2	6	9	0	.393	.543
Behind in Count	.196	97	19	2	0	1	9	0	32	.194	.247
Two Strikes	.221	104	23	3	0	2	10	5	37	.255	.308

	Avg	AB	H	2B	3B	HR	RBI	BB	SO	OBP	SLG
Scoring Posn	.255	55	14	2	0	3	21	5	10	.306	.455
Close & Late	.273	33	9	5	0	0	2	2	6	.333	.424
None on/out	.212	52	11	2	1	0	0	1	9	.226	.288
Batting #7	.151	73	11	1	1	1	4	4	16	.195	.233
Batting #8	.317	60	19	2	0	3	11	2	10	.328	.500
Other	.288	80	23	7	0	2	10	8	11	.360	.450
Pre-All Star	.160	75	12	2	0	2	3	5	16	.213	.267
Post-All Star	.297	138	41	8	1	4	22	9	21	.040	.457

Terry Bross — Giants

Age 28 – Pitches Right

	ERA	W	L	Sv	G	GS	IP	BB	SO	Avg	H	2B	3B	HR	RBI	OBP	SLG	GF	IR	IRS	Hld	SvOp	SB	CS	GB	FB	G/F
1993 Season	9.00	0	0	0	2	0	2.0	1	1	.333	3	0	0	1	6	.400	.667	1	4	4	0	0	0	0	3	5	0.60
Career (1991-1993)	3.00	0	0	0	10	0	12.0	4	6	.227	10	1	0	2	8	.292	.386	5	7	4	0	0	0	0	16	17	0.94

1993 Season

	ERA	W	L	Sv	G	GS	IP	H	HR	BB	SO
Home	9.00	0	0	0	2	0	2.0	3	1	1	1
Away	0.00	0	0	0	0	0	0.0	0	0	0	0

	Avg	AB	H	2B	3B	HR	RBI	BB	SO	OBP	SLG
vs. Left	.333	3	1	0	0	0	1	1	1	.500	.333
vs. Right	.333	6	2	0	0	1	5	0	0	.333	.833

Scott Brow — Blue Jays

Age 25 – Pitches Right

	ERA	W	L	Sv	G	GS	IP	BB	SO	Avg	H	2B	3B	HR	RBI	OBP	SLG	CG	ShO	Sup	QS	#P/S	SB	CS	GB	FB	G/F
1993 Season	6.00	1	1	0	6	3	18.0	10	7	.275	19	2	0	2	12	.366	.391	0	0	11.00	0	92	2	0	29	24	1.21

1993 Season

	ERA	W	L	Sv	G	GS	IP	H	HR	BB	SO
Home	5.73	0	1	0	4	2	11.0	14	1	6	3
Away	6.43	1	0	0	2	1	7.0	5	1	4	4

	Avg	AB	H	2B	3B	HR	RBI	BB	SO	OBP	SLG
vs. Left	.205	39	8	1	0	0	5	7	5	.319	.231
vs. Right	.367	30	11	1	0	2	7	3	2	.429	.600

Jarvis Brown — Padres

Age 27 – Bats Right

	Avg	G	AB	R	H	2B	3B	HR	RBI	BB	SO	HBP	GDP	SB	CS	OBP	SLG	IBB	SH	SF	#Pit	#P/PA	GB	FB	G/F
1993 Season	.233	47	133	21	31	9	2	0	8	15	26	6	4	3	3	.335	.331	0	2	1	593	3.78	41	34	1.21
Career (1991-1993)	.216	120	185	39	40	9	2	0	8	19	38	7	4	12	6	.311	.286	0	3	1	805	3.74	59	47	1.26

1993 Season

	Avg	AB	H	2B	3B	HR	RBI	BB	SO	OBP	SLG
vs. Left	.263	38	10	3	1	0	1	5	9	.349	.395
vs. Right	.221	95	21	6	1	0	7	10	17	.330	.305
Home	.148	54	8	3	1	0	1	3	13	.217	.241
Away	.291	79	23	6	1	0	7	12	13	.411	.392
First Pitch	.563	16	9	1	2	0	2	0	0	.563	.875
Ahead in Count	.387	31	12	2	0	0	2	5	0	.486	.452
Behind in Count	.094	64	6	3	0	0	4	0	21	.145	.141
Two Strikes	.085	59	5	3	0	0	2	10	26	.257	.136

	Avg	AB	H	2B	3B	HR	RBI	BB	SO	OBP	SLG
Scoring Posn	.214	28	6	2	1	0	8	3	7	.324	.357
Close & Late	.100	20	2	1	0	0	0	3	5	.250	.150
None on/out	.213	61	13	4	0	0	0	6	9	.314	.279
Batting #1	.246	118	29	9	1	0	7	15	20	.360	.339
Batting #5	.000	4	0	0	0	0	1	0	1	.000	.000
Other	.182	11	2	0	1	0	0	0	5	.182	.364
Pre-All Star	.000	0	0	0	0	0	0	0	0	.000	.000
Post-All Star	.233	133	31	9	2	0	8	15	26	.335	.331

Kevin Brown — Rangers

Age 29 – Pitches Right (groundball pitcher)

	ERA	W	L	Sv	G	GS	IP	BB	SO	Avg	H	2B	3B	HR	RBI	OBP	SLG	CG	ShO	Sup	QS	#P/S	SB	CS	GB	FB	G/F
1993 Season	3.59	15	12	0	34	34	233.0	74	142	.252	228	41	4	14	87	.319	.353	12	3	4.67	20	107	10	10	406	187	2.17
Last Five Years	3.64	69	54	0	156	156	1080.1	370	603	.258	1065	179	11	65	429	.324	.354	36	6	4.76	99	104	35	42	2082	768	2.71

1993 Season

	ERA	W	L	Sv	G	GS	IP	H	HR	BB	SO
Home	2.46	9	5	0	17	17	124.1	104	6	34	94
Away	4.89	6	7	0	17	17	108.2	124	8	40	48
Day	3.62	5	2	0	9	9	54.2	56	2	19	21
Night	3.58	10	10	0	25	25	178.1	172	12	55	121
Grass	3.40	13	11	0	31	31	214.1	203	13	71	136
Turf	5.79	2	1	0	3	3	18.2	25	1	3	6
April	1.14	2	1	0	4	4	31.2	28	1	7	23
May	2.52	2	2	0	6	6	50.0	37	3	9	24
June	5.46	2	3	0	5	5	29.2	36	4	13	15
July	6.23	2	1	0	6	6	34.2	42	2	18	25
August	5.26	2	4	0	6	6	39.1	50	2	16	26
September/October	1.89	5	1	0	7	7	47.2	35	2	11	29
Starter	3.59	15	12	0	34	34	233.0	228	14	74	142
Reliever	0.00	0	0	0	0	0	0.0	0	0	0	0
0-3 Days Rest	2.53	2	3	0	5	5	32.0	27	1	11	21
4 Days Rest	3.24	9	4	0	17	17	125.0	115	8	41	89
5+ Days Rest	4.62	4	5	0	12	12	76.0	86	5	22	32

	Avg	AB	H	2B	3B	HR	RBI	BB	SO	OBP	SLG
vs. Left	.254	512	130	22	2	9	52	50	75	.324	.357
vs. Right	.251	391	98	19	2	5	35	24	67	.311	.348
Inning 1-6	.268	706	189	34	3	11	78	61	102	.335	.371
Inning 7+	.198	197	39	7	1	3	9	13	40	.260	.289
None on	.250	533	133	25	3	8	8	35	91	.303	.353
Runners on	.257	370	95	16	1	6	79	39	51	.340	.354
Scoring Posn	.239	209	50	7	1	3	67	21	33	.331	.325
Close & Late	.197	61	12	4	0	2	4	2	11	.242	.361
None on/out	.221	231	51	11	0	3	3	14	46	.268	.307
vs. 1st Batr (relief)	.000	0	0	0	0	0	0	0	0	.000	.000
First Inning Pitched	.312	141	44	9	1	3	22	18	20	.409	.454
First 75 Pitches	.273	598	163	28	3	9	63	49	89	.337	.375
Pitch 76-90	.208	120	25	6	0	3	12	9	18	.269	.333
Pitch 91-105	.200	100	20	3	0	0	4	4	14	.252	.230
Pitch 106+	.235	85	20	4	1	2	8	12	21	.333	.376
First Pitch	.344	125	43	10	0	1	17	3	0	.366	.448
Ahead in Count	.194	403	78	8	2	4	27	0	120	.203	.253

1993 Season

	ERA	W	L	Sv	G	GS	IP	H	HR	BB	SO
Pre-All Star	3.21	6	6	0	17	17	123.1	115	8	36	70
Post-All Star	4.02	9	6	0	17	17	109.2	113	6	38	72

	Avg	AB	H	2B	3B	HR	RBI	BB	SO	OBP	SLG
Behind in Count	.298	198	59	13	2	5	22	38	0	.421	.460
Two Strikes	.180	383	69	11	2	4	22	33	142	.254	.251

Last Five Years

	ERA	W	L	Sv	G	GS	IP	H	HR	BB	SO
Home	3.01	36	21	0	74	74	526.0	490	33	172	319
Away	4.24	33	33	0	82	82	554.1	575	32	198	284
Day	4.69	12	13	0	36	36	226.2	245	11	96	107
Night	3.36	57	41	0	120	120	853.2	820	54	274	496
Grass	3.57	57	46	0	130	130	901.2	879	56	315	511
Turf	3.98	12	8	0	26	26	178.2	186	9	55	92
April	3.23	13	4	0	21	21	145.0	131	7	51	83
May	3.52	12	10	0	28	28	199.2	190	8	67	93
June	3.11	15	10	0	28	28	205.1	172	10	66	109
July	4.14	10	11	0	28	28	195.2	198	19	70	116
August	4.07	9	11	0	27	27	179.1	215	9	69	103
September/October	3.77	10	8	0	24	24	155.1	159	12	47	99
Starter	3.64	69	54	0	156	156	1080.1	1065	65	370	603
Reliever	0.00	0	0	0	0	0	0.0	0	0	0	0
0-3 Days Rest	2.31	2	4	0	7	7	46.2	36	1	18	27
4 Days Rest	3.63	42	29	0	89	89	632.0	626	41	207	348
5+ Days Rest	3.81	25	21	0	60	60	401.2	403	23	145	228
Pre-All Star	3.37	44	27	0	87	87	619.2	559	31	212	321
Post-All Star	4.01	25	27	0	69	69	460.2	506	34	158	282

	Avg	AB	H	2B	3B	HR	RBI	BB	SO	OBP	SLG
vs. Left	.255	2098	536	96	5	35	211	213	292	.325	.356
vs. Right	.260	2033	529	83	6	30	218	157	311	.322	.351
Inning 1-6	.257	3287	845	140	7	45	346	304	474	.325	.345
Inning 7+	.261	844	220	39	4	20	83	66	129	.317	.387
None on	.252	2354	594	103	8	35	35	198	354	.316	.347
Runners on	.265	1777	471	76	3	30	394	172	249	.333	.362
Scoring Posn	.255	984	251	40	3	17	347	115	158	.335	.354
Close & Late	.286	434	124	23	3	14	56	40	55	.348	.449
None on/out	.248	1052	261	44	3	11	11	81	165	.306	.327
vs. 1st Batr (relief)	.000	0	0	0	0	0	0	0	0	.000	.000
First Inning Pitched	.267	584	156	30	1	8	84	78	91	.360	.363
First 75 Pitches	.257	2842	730	121	6	36	287	257	417	.323	.342
Pitch 76-90	.258	542	140	23	3	13	59	43	73	.319	.384
Pitch 91-105	.244	442	108	22	0	5	36	33	62	.305	.328
Pitch 106+	.285	305	87	13	2	11	47	37	51	.358	.449
First Pitch	.318	651	207	42	2	10	87	14	0	.338	.435
Ahead in Count	.203	1735	352	51	6	16	127	0	516	.212	.267
Behind in Count	.312	990	309	52	2	24	139	206	0	.431	.441
Two Strikes	.181	1637	297	50	7	15	106	150	603	.258	.248

Pitcher vs. Batter (career)

Pitches Best Vs.	Avg	AB	H	2B	3B	HR	RBI	BB	SO	OBP	SLG
Ozzie Guillen	.063	32	2	1	0	0	0	0	3	.063	.094
Carlton Fisk	.095	21	2	0	0	0	1	0	5	.095	.095
Devon White	.115	26	3	1	0	0	2	2	5	.179	.154
Billy Hatcher	.143	21	3	0	0	0	0	1	2	.182	.143
Mike Aldrete	.143	14	2	0	0	0	0	0	2	.143	.143

Pitches Worst Vs.	Avg	AB	H	2B	3B	HR	RBI	BB	SO	OBP	SLG
Scott Brosius	.583	12	7	1	0	0	1	0	0	.583	.667
John Olerud	.478	23	11	4	0	1	6	3	4	.538	.783
George Brett	.455	33	15	5	0	2	7	0	2	.455	.788
Joe Orsulak	.400	20	8	3	0	1	7	4	1	.500	.700
Dave Winfield	.370	27	10	0	0	4	7	4	4	.452	.815

Jerry Browne — Athletics

Age 28 – Bats Both

	Avg	G	AB	R	H	2B	3B	HR	RBI	BB	SO	HBP	GDP	SB	CS	OBP	SLG	IBB	SH	SF	#Pit	#P/PA	GB	FB	G/F
1993 Season	.250	76	260	27	65	13	0	2	19	22	17	0	9	4	0	.306	.323	0	2	2	1011	3.53	115	80	1.44
Last Five Years	.272	587	1985	273	540	87	13	17	183	229	196	8	42	35	20	.345	.355	11	56	27	8291	3.60	828	587	1.41

1993 Season

	Avg	AB	H	2B	3B	HR	RBI	BB	SO	OBP	SLG
vs. Left	.267	60	16	2	0	1	3	3	4	.302	.350
vs. Right	.245	200	49	11	0	1	16	19	13	.308	.315
Home	.321	112	36	5	0	1	8	9	9	.372	.393
Away	.196	148	29	8	0	1	11	13	8	.258	.270
First Pitch	.275	40	11	2	0	1	4	0	0	.275	.400
Ahead in Count	.351	57	20	4	0	0	5	15	0	.479	.421
Behind in Count	.214	117	25	6	0	0	7	0	16	.214	.265
Two Strikes	.196	102	20	2	0	0	3	7	17	.248	.216

	Avg	AB	H	2B	3B	HR	RBI	BB	SO	OBP	SLG
Scoring Posn	.200	55	11	2	0	0	17	5	5	.258	.236
Close & Late	.167	48	8	1	0	0	3	4	3	.231	.188
None on/out	.292	72	21	7	0	1	1	7	3	.354	.431
Batting #1	.244	82	20	4	0	0	5	7	3	.303	.293
Batting #2	.275	120	33	6	0	0	6	9	7	.326	.325
Other	.207	58	12	3	0	2	8	6	7	.273	.362
Pre-All Star	.313	32	10	0	0	0	4	4	3	.389	.313
Post-All Star	.241	228	55	13	0	2	15	18	14	.294	.325

Last Five Years

	Avg	AB	H	2B	3B	HR	RBI	BB	SO	OBP	SLG
vs. Left	.271	501	136	22	5	3	45	52	40	.339	.353
vs. Right	.272	1484	404	65	8	14	138	177	156	.348	.355
Groundball	.285	502	143	26	1	5	50	67	52	.367	.371
Flyball	.296	477	141	19	4	5	50	60	51	.370	.384
Home	.297	959	285	43	8	6	87	112	85	.372	.377
Away	.249	1026	255	44	5	11	96	117	111	.321	.333
Day	.271	683	185	24	4	4	62	75	56	.345	.335
Night	.273	1302	355	63	9	13	121	154	140	.346	.365
Grass	.277	1671	463	69	12	16	162	196	162	.351	.361
Turf	.245	314	77	18	1	1	21	33	34	.313	.318
First Pitch	.316	247	78	8	1	3	39	7	0	.331	.393
Ahead in Count	.300	444	133	28	2	2	48	146	0	.464	.385
Behind in Count	.249	855	213	37	6	4	63	0	169	.250	.320
Two Strikes	.225	804	181	25	6	3	48	71	196	.289	.282

	Avg	AB	H	2B	3B	HR	RBI	BB	SO	OBP	SLG
Scoring Posn	.270	422	114	17	3	4	162	70	42	.357	.353
Close & Late	.291	337	98	10	1	4	33	47	38	.374	.362
None on/out	.256	610	156	31	7	5	5	63	72	.326	.354
Batting #1	.283	905	256	44	8	7	67	103	82	.355	.372
Batting #2	.266	785	209	36	2	7	83	98	87	.345	.344
Other	.254	295	75	7	3	3	33	28	27	.316	.329
April	.202	233	47	1	0	1	18	15	25	.245	.219
May	.267	292	78	11	4	1	38	20	37	.312	.342
June	.297	350	104	14	2	3	26	45	24	.378	.374
July	.269	342	92	19	4	4	25	49	33	.361	.383
August	.313	383	120	17	2	6	40	44	36	.383	.415
September/October	.257	385	99	25	1	2	36	56	41	.347	.343
Pre-All Star	.266	974	259	32	10	7	90	101	96	.332	.341
Post-All Star	.278	1011	281	55	3	10	93	128	100	.358	.368

Batter vs. Pitcher (career)

Hits Best Against	Avg	AB	H	2B	3B	HR	RBI	BB	SO	OBP	SLG
Chuck Crim	.636	11	7	1	0	1	1	1	1	.667	1.000
Scott Bankhead	.600	10	6	1	0	0	2	1	0	.636	.700
Mark Knudson	.545	11	6	0	0	0	2	1	0	.583	.545
Pete Harnisch	.538	13	7	2	0	1	4	1	1	.571	.923
Mike Witt	.429	21	9	4	0	1	3	3	1	.500	.762

Hits Worst Against	Avg	AB	H	2B	3B	HR	RBI	BB	SO	OBP	SLG
Greg Harris	.000	14	0	0	0	0	2	2	1	.118	.000
Ben McDonald	.000	10	0	0	0	0	0	2	0	.167	.000
Todd Stottlemyre	.077	13	1	0	0	0	0	1	1	.143	.077
Kirk McCaskill	.083	24	2	0	0	0	3	3	4	.185	.083
Tom Henke	.100	10	1	0	0	0	0	1	2	.182	.100

Tom Browning — Reds

Age 34 – Pitches Left (flyball pitcher)

	ERA	W	L	Sv	G	GS	IP	BB	SO	Avg	H	2B	3B	HR	RBI	OBP	SLG	CG	ShO	Sup	QS	#P/S	SB	CS	GB	FB	G/F
1993 Season	4.74	7	7	0	21	20	114.0	20	53	.333	159	32	3	15	58	.359	.506	0	0	5.37	11	85	5	7	150	161	0.93
Last Five Years	4.02	57	47	0	145	144	908.2	220	418	.276	984	190	24	108	400	.319	.434	12	3	4.56	81	89	64	33	1072	1353	0.79

1993 Season

	ERA	W	L	Sv	G	GS	IP	H	HR	BB	SO
Home	2.84	4	2	0	8	8	50.2	61	4	9	28
Away	6.25	3	5	0	13	12	63.1	98	11	11	25
Starter	4.70	7	7	0	20	20	113.0	157	15	20	53
Reliever	9.00	0	0	0	1	0	1.0	2	0	0	0
0-3 Days Rest	0.00	0	0	0	0	0	0.0	0	0	0	0
4 Days Rest	4.35	4	5	0	14	14	78.2	110	9	15	37
5+ Days Rest	5.50	3	2	0	6	6	34.1	47	6	5	16
Pre-All Star	4.96	6	4	0	16	15	85.1	122	12	19	45
Post-All Star	4.08	1	3	0	5	5	28.2	37	3	1	8

	Avg	AB	H	2B	3B	HR	RBI	BB	SO	OBP	SLG
vs. Left	.250	76	19	4	0	2	6	7	9	.310	.382
vs. Right	.348	402	140	28	3	13	52	13	44	.369	.530
Scoring Posn	.298	114	34	5	1	4	40	10	12	.349	.465
Close & Late	.200	10	2	0	0	0	0	1	0	.273	.200
None on/out	.380	121	46	10	1	3	3	2	17	.395	.554
First Pitch	.432	81	35	6	1	3	9	1	0	.439	.642
Ahead in Count	.301	186	56	12	1	3	19	0	44	.301	.425
Behind in Count	.374	107	40	8	0	7	20	8	0	.415	.045
Two Strikes	.277	177	49	9	0	1	12	11	53	.319	.345

Last Five Years

	ERA	W	L	Sv	G	GS	IP	H	HR	BB	SO
Home	4.03	34	23	0	71	71	459.2	478	65	112	209
Away	4.01	23	24	0	74	73	449.0	506	43	108	209
Day	3.71	17	17	0	45	45	281.2	307	29	77	132
Night	4.16	40	30	0	100	99	627.0	677	79	143	286
Grass	3.65	15	12	0	46	45	285.2	321	24	64	126
Turf	4.19	42	35	0	99	99	623.0	663	84	156	292
April	3.87	12	6	0	24	24	149.0	153	18	29	75
May	4.35	9	13	0	29	29	176.0	195	24	55	77
June	3.32	13	4	0	29	28	181.2	186	13	50	86
July	4.28	8	10	0	24	24	153.2	173	23	25	68
August	2.84	10	4	0	19	19	136.1	133	14	26	61
September/October	5.95	5	10	0	20	20	112.0	144	16	35	51
Starter	4.02	57	47	0	144	144	907.2	982	108	220	418
Reliever	9.00	0	0	0	1	0	1.0	2	0	0	0
0-3 Days Rest	3.92	10	7	0	22	22	133.1	163	14	33	59
4 Days Rest	3.88	31	27	0	85	85	540.1	570	66	132	237
5+ Days Rest	4.38	16	13	0	37	37	234.0	249	28	55	122
Pre-All Star	3.88	37	26	0	91	90	556.0	593	60	147	260
Post-All Star	4.24	20	21	0	54	54	352.2	391	48	73	158

	Avg	AB	H	2B	3B	HR	RBI	BB	SO	OBP	SLG
vs. Left	.248	665	165	36	3	18	82	60	112	.309	.392
vs. Right	.283	2894	819	154	21	90	318	160	306	.321	.444
Inning 1-6	.276	3095	853	164	23	93	358	199	374	.320	.434
Inning 7+	.282	464	131	26	1	15	42	21	44	.312	.440
None on	.273	2158	589	103	11	75	75	110	259	.312	.435
Runners on	.282	1401	395	87	13	33	325	110	159	.330	.433
Scoring Posn	.280	726	203	43	7	13	264	89	89	.349	.412
Close & Late	.261	249	65	14	0	5	19	15	25	.305	.378
None on/out	.288	953	274	42	7	38	38	38	101	.320	.466
vs. 1st Batr (relief)	1.000	1	1	0	0	0	0	0	0	1.000	1.000
First Inning Pitched	.292	575	168	29	4	14	71	34	77	.331	.430
First 75 Pitches	.277	2913	808	153	20	87	323	168	348	.317	.433
Pitch 76-90	.286	413	118	23	3	13	49	26	40	.330	.450
Pitch 91-105	.279	179	50	12	1	8	24	24	22	.361	.492
Pitch 106+	.148	54	8	2	0	0	4	2	8	.175	.185
First Pitch	.314	647	203	45	5	25	72	33	0	.347	.515
Ahead in Count	.247	1560	385	74	7	35	148	0	360	.250	.371
Behind in Count	.310	706	219	39	9	28	109	104	0	.397	.510
Two Strikes	.225	1372	309	50	4	30	120	82	418	.271	.333

Pitcher vs. Batter (career)

Pitches Best Vs.	Avg	AB	H	2B	3B	HR	RBI	BB	SO	OBP	SLG
Sid Bream	.000	10	0	0	0	0	0	2	2	.167	.000
Milt Thompson	.071	14	1	0	0	0	0	1	3	.133	.071
Chico Walker	.077	13	1	0	0	0	0	0	1	.077	.077
Otis Nixon	.091	33	3	0	0	0	4	3	3	.167	.091
Delino DeShields	.100	20	2	0	0	0	1	1	4	.143	.100

Pitches Worst Vs.	Avg	AB	H	2B	3B	HR	RBI	BB	SO	OBP	SLG
Brian Hunter	.545	11	6	0	1	1	3	0	0	.545	1.000
Spike Owen	.500	24	12	4	1	1	2	1	1	.520	.875
Tim Teufel	.458	48	22	3	0	5	8	5	5	.509	.833
Bobby Bonilla	.409	44	18	4	1	10	20	1	2	.404	1.227
George Bell	.364	11	4	0	0	3	4	2	2	.462	1.182

J.T. Bruett — Twins

Age 26 – Bats Left (groundball hitter)

	Avg	G	AB	R	H	2B	3B	HR	RBI	BB	SO	HBP	GDP	SB	CS	OBP	SLG	IBB	SH	SF	#Pit	#P/PA	GB	FB	G/F
1993 Season	.250	17	20	2	5	2	0	0	1	1	4	1	0	0	0	.318	.350	0	0	0	71	3.23	9	3	3.00
Career (1992-1993)	.250	73	96	9	24	6	0	0	3	7	16	2	0	6	3	.314	.313	1	1	0	364	3.43	40	20	2.00

1993 Season

	Avg	AB	H	2B	3B	HR	RBI	BB	SO	OBP	SLG
vs. Left	.000	2	0	0	0	0	0	0	1	.000	.000
vs. Right	.278	18	5	2	0	0	1	1	3	.350	.389

	Avg	AB	H	2B	3B	HR	RBI	BB	SO	OBP	SLG
Scoring Posn	.400	5	2	1	0	0	1	1	1	.500	.600
Close & Late	.000	2	0	0	0	0	0	0	0	.000	.000

Jacob Brumfield — Reds

Age 29 – Bats Right (flyball hitter)

	Avg	G	AB	R	H	2B	3B	HR	RBI	BB	SO	HBP	GDP	SB	CS	OBP	SLG	IBB	SH	SF	#Pit	#P/PA	GB	FB	G/F
1993 Season	.268	103	272	40	73	17	3	6	23	21	47	1	1	20	8	.321	.419	4	3	2	1093	3.66	88	91	0.97
Career (1992-1993)	.255	127	302	46	77	17	3	6	25	23	51	2	1	26	8	.310	.391	5	3	2	1211	3.65	98	103	0.95

1993 Season

	Avg	AB	H	2B	3B	HR	RBI	BB	SO	OBP	SLG
vs. Left	.303	89	27	7	0	2	5	5	9	.340	.449
vs. Right	.251	183	46	10	3	4	18	16	38	.312	.404
Home	.217	120	26	7	0	1	8	8	23	.264	.300
Away	.309	152	47	10	3	5	15	13	24	.365	.513
First Pitch	.262	42	11	2	1	1	5	3	0	.326	.429
Ahead in Count	.338	68	23	6	0	1	5	9	0	.410	.471
Behind in Count	.198	106	21	5	1	3	6	0	36	.196	.349
Two Strikes	.222	126	28	4	2	4	12	9	47	.272	.381

	Avg	AB	H	2B	3B	HR	RBI	BB	SO	OBP	SLG
Scoring Posn	.278	54	15	2	1	0	15	7	12	.349	.352
Close & Late	.327	49	16	2	1	2	5	2	9	.353	.531
None on/out	.294	85	25	8	0	4	4	4	11	.326	.529
Batting #1	.258	93	24	6	0	1	3	5	12	.296	.355
Batting #8	.289	90	26	7	2	2	9	10	14	.359	.478
Other	.258	89	23	4	1	3	11	6	21	.305	.427
Pre-All Star	.329	73	24	6	0	3	8	9	13	.402	.534
Post-All Star	.246	199	49	11	3	3	15	12	34	.290	.377

Mike Brumley — Angels

Age 31 – Bats Both (groundball hitter)

	Avg	G	AB	R	H	2B	3B	HR	RBI	BB	SO	HBP	GDP	SB	CS	OBP	SLG	IBB	SH	SF	#Pit	#P/PA	GB	FB	G/F
1993 Season	.300	8	10	1	3	0	0	0	2	1	3	0	0	0	1	.364	.300	0	0	0	49	4.45	4	2	2.00
Last Five Years	.211	227	488	69	103	15	6	1	25	35	92	1	9	12	5	.265	.273	0	11	1	1846	3.44	194	111	1.75

1993 Season

	Avg	AB	H	2B	3B	HR	RBI	BB	SO	OBP	SLG		Avg	AB	H	2B	3B	HR	RBI	BB	SO	OBP	SLG
vs. Left	.000	2	0	0	0	0	0	0	1	.000	.000	Scoring Posn	.500	2	1	0	0	0	2	0	0	.500	.500
vs. Right	.375	8	3	0	0	0	2	1	2	.444	.375	Close & Late	.250	4	1	0	0	0	2	0	1	.250	.250

Last Five Years

	Avg	AB	H	2B	3B	HR	RBI	BB	SO	OBP	SLG		Avg	AB	H	2B	3B	HR	RBI	BB	SO	OBP	SLG
vs. Left	.243	144	35	5	1	1	8	6	26	.273	.313	Scoring Posn	.173	127	22	3	0	0	21	6	30	.209	.197
vs. Right	.198	344	68	10	5	0	17	29	66	.261	.256	Close & Late	.203	79	16	2	2	0	3	7	15	.267	.278
Groundball	.227	154	35	4	3	0	9	10	26	.274	.292	None on/out	.195	118	23	5	0	0	0	8	17	.252	.237
Flyball	.196	102	20	6	1	0	5	5	29	.234	.275	Batting #8	.171	35	6	0	1	1	5	3	4	.237	.314
Home	.212	241	51	10	3	1	15	13	43	.252	.290	Batting #9	.207	391	81	10	5	0	17	26	77	.258	.258
Away	.211	247	52	5	3	0	10	22	49	.277	.255	Other	.258	62	16	5	0	0	3	6	11	.324	.339
Day	.215	172	37	3	1	0	8	15	32	.278	.244	April	.152	46	7	1	1	0	3	4	2	.216	.217
Night	.209	316	66	12	5	1	17	20	60	.257	.288	May	.209	115	24	2	5	0	6	8	22	.260	.313
Grass	.210	338	71	11	2	1	19	25	66	.264	.263	June	.242	62	15	3	0	0	3	7	12	.329	.290
Turf	.213	150	32	4	4	0	6	10	26	.267	.293	July	.230	61	14	2	0	0	0	1	14	.242	.262
First Pitch	.234	94	22	1	2	1	7	0	0	.234	.319	August	.252	107	27	6	0	0	4	7	25	.298	.308
Ahead in Count	.298	114	34	8	1	0	7	20	0	.403	.386	September/October	.165	97	16	1	0	1	9	8	17	.229	.206
Behind in Count	.161	199	32	5	1	0	6	0	79	.165	.196	Pre-All Star	.203	232	47	6	6	0	12	19	37	.265	.280
Two Strikes	.148	210	31	4	2	0	7	15	92	.208	.186	Post-All Star	.219	256	56	9	0	1	13	16	55	.265	.266

Greg Brummett — Twins

Age 27 – Pitches Right

	ERA	W	L	Sv	G	GS	IP	BB	SO	Avg	H	2B	3B	HR	RBI	OBP	SLG	CG	ShO	Sup	QS	#P/S	SB	CS	GB	FB	G/F
1993 Season	5.08	4	4	0	13	13	72.2	28	30	.297	82	9	2	12	40	.356	.475	0	0	5.70	6	84	12	1	97	95	1.02

1993 Season

	ERA	W	L	Sv	G	GS	IP	H	HR	BB	SO		Avg	AB	H	2B	3B	HR	RBI	BB	SO	OBP	SLG
Home	4.69	2	2	0	7	7	40.1	45	6	17	15	vs. Left	.348	132	46	5	1	6	24	21	11	.427	.538
Away	5.57	2	2	0	6	6	32.1	37	6	11	15	vs. Right	.250	144	36	4	1	6	16	7	19	.283	.417
Starter	5.08	4	4	0	13	13	72.2	82	12	28	30	Scoring Posn	.286	70	20	1	0	3	27	13	8	.375	.429
Reliever	0.00	0	0	0	0	0	0.0	0	0	0	0	Close & Late	.250	8	2	0	0	0	0	1	0	.333	.250
0-3 Days Rest	0.00	0	0	0	0	0	0.0	0	0	0	0	None on/out	.329	73	24	6	1	4	4	7	7	.388	.603
4 Days Rest	6.19	1	2	0	6	6	32.0	41	7	12	14	First Pitch	.238	42	10	1	1	4	9	1	0	.250	.595
5+ Days Rest	4.20	3	2	0	7	7	40.2	41	5	16	16	Ahead in Count	.234	111	26	3	0	4	15	0	26	.230	.369
Pre-All Star	2.95	1	2	0	3	3	18.1	18	1	3	8	Behind in Count	.413	75	31	5	1	2	10	21	0	.536	.587
Post-All Star	5.80	3	2	0	10	10	54.1	64	11	25	22	Two Strikes	.221	104	23	1	0	4	13	6	30	.259	.346

Tom Brunansky — Brewers

Age 33 – Bats Right (flyball hitter)

	Avg	G	AB	R	H	2B	3B	HR	RBI	BB	SO	HBP	GDP	SB	CS	OBP	SLG	IBB	SH	SF	#Pit	#P/PA	GB	FB	G/F
1993 Season	.183	80	224	20	41	7	3	6	29	25	59	0	6	3	4	.265	.321	0	2	0	1045	4.16	49	79	0.62
Last Five Years	.241	666	2215	254	533	118	15	73	331	265	449	9	49	16	30	.320	.406	14	4	29	9780	3.88	602	811	0.74

1993 Season

	Avg	AB	H	2B	3B	HR	RBI	BB	SO	OBP	SLG		Avg	AB	H	2B	3B	HR	RBI	BB	SO	OBP	SLG
vs. Left	.178	101	18	4	2	3	14	15	23	.284	.347	Scoring Posn	.184	76	14	2	0	0	19	7	18	.253	.211
vs. Right	.187	123	23	3	1	3	15	10	36	.248	.301	Close & Late	.233	30	7	0	0	2	5	5	6	.343	.433
Home	.180	100	18	3	2	2	17	11	29	.261	.310	None on/out	.196	46	9	0	2	1	1	5	10	.275	.348
Away	.185	124	23	4	1	4	12	14	30	.268	.331	Batting #5	.149	74	11	4	1	0	6	14	17	.284	.230
First Pitch	.143	21	3	0	0	1	4	0	0	.143	.286	Batting #6	.176	74	13	2	0	1	9	3	17	.208	.243
Ahead in Count	.244	45	11	2	1	2	7	14	0	.424	.467	Other	.224	76	17	1	2	5	14	8	25	.298	.487
Behind in Count	.109	110	12	1	2	1	5	0	50	.109	.182	Pre-All Star	.176	187	33	7	3	3	22	22	49	.263	.294
Two Strikes	.148	122	18	4	1	1	11	11	59	.218	.221	Post-All Star	.216	37	8	0	0	3	7	3	10	.275	.459

Last Five Years

	Avg	AB	H	2B	3B	HR	RBI	BB	SO	OBP	SLG		Avg	AB	H	2B	3B	HR	RBI	BB	SO	OBP	SLG
vs. Left	.242	774	187	40	6	31	116	101	120	.325	.429	Scoring Posn	.236	649	153	35	6	25	256	92	135	.321	.424
vs. Right	.240	1441	346	78	9	42	215	164	329	.318	.394	Close & Late	.244	360	88	24	1	9	53	60	82	.348	.392
Groundball	.268	667	179	37	1	23	113	84	127	.349	.430	None on/out	.232	526	122	25	4	13	13	50	101	.301	.369
Flyball	.232	542	126	28	4	21	78	62	110	.309	.415	Batting #4	.250	820	205	45	6	30	129	98	166	.328	.429
Home	.275	1066	293	77	10	39	189	124	198	.348	.476	Batting #6	.239	742	177	44	5	24	116	77	143	.309	.408
Away	.209	1149	240	41	5	34	142	141	251	.295	.342	Other	.231	653	151	29	4	19	86	90	140	.324	.375
Day	.234	744	174	32	2	27	114	73	152	.302	.391	April	.203	251	51	11	1	7	30	34	43	.297	.339
Night	.244	1471	359	86	13	46	217	192	297	.330	.414	May	.225	405	91	16	2	15	69	51	79	.308	.385
Grass	.239	1515	362	75	10	55	235	190	298	.323	.411	June	.267	412	110	38	4	9	55	48	82	.345	.444
Turf	.244	700	171	43	5	18	96	75	151	.316	.397	July	.224	424	95	19	4	17	70	49	97	.302	.408
First Pitch	.304	286	87	16	1	12	51	5	0	.313	.493	August	.272	367	100	17	3	13	52	46	75	.356	.441
Ahead in Count	.307	511	157	34	6	28	101	142	0	.453	.562	September/October	.242	356	86	17	1	12	55	37	73	.309	.396
Behind in Count	.179	974	174	44	6	15	103	0	370	.182	.282	Pre-All Star	.236	1214	287	74	8	35	180	151	236	.319	.397
Two Strikes	.189	1054	199	50	4	23	120	113	449	.270	.309	Post-All Star	.246	1001	246	44	7	38	151	114	213	.322	.418

Batter vs. Pitcher (since 1984)

Hits Best Against	Avg	AB	H	2B	3B	HR	RBI	BB	SO	OBP	SLG	**Hits Worst Against**	Avg	AB	H	2B	3B	HR	RBI	BB	SO	OBP	SLG
Mark Eichhorn	.389	18	7	3	0	1	8	3	1	.476	.722	Rick Aguilera	.000	11	0	0	0	0	0	0	5	.000	.000

Batter vs. Pitcher (since 1984)																						
Hits Best Against	Avg	AB	H	2B	3B	HR	RBI	BB	SO	OBP	SLG	Hits Worst Against	Avg	AB	H	2B	3B	HR	RBI	BB	SO	OBP	SLG
Kevin Gross	.385	13	5	0	2	1	3	3	3	.500	.923	Nolan Ryan	.000	9	0	0	0	0	1	1	5	.091	.000
David Wells	.381	21	8	2	0	3	5	0	2	.381	.905	Gene Nelson	.063	16	1	0	0	0	0	1	4	.118	.063
Alex Fernandez	.381	21	8	0	1	3	7	0	6	.381	.905	Sid Fernandez	.063	16	1	0	0	0	0	1	3	.118	.063
Jose Rijo	.333	18	6	2	0	2	4	2	5	.400	.778	Mike Henneman	.071	14	1	0	0	0	0	0	5	.071	.071

Steve Buechele — Cubs

Age 32 – Bats Right

	Avg	G	AB	R	H	2B	3B	HR	RBI	BB	SO	HBP	GDP	SB	CS	OBP	SLG	IBB	SH	SF	#Pit	#P/PA	GB	FB	G/F
1993 Season	.272	133	460	53	125	27	2	15	65	48	87	5	12	1	1	.345	.437	5	4	3	1938	3.73	162	123	1.32
Last Five Years	.253	676	2251	269	569	104	11	69	303	212	459	26	62	4	12	.323	.401	16	28	12	9607	3.80	753	647	1.16

1993 Season

	Avg	AB	H	2B	3B	HR	RBI	BB	SO	OBP	SLG		Avg	AB	H	2B	3B	HR	RBI	BB	SO	OBP	SLG
vs. Left	.281	128	36	9	0	5	14	19	18	.378	.469	Scoring Posn	.283	120	34	7	0	3	45	16	19	.369	.417
vs. Right	.268	332	89	18	2	10	51	29	60	.332	.425	Close & Late	.242	62	15	2	1	0	9	8	23	.329	.306
Groundball	.242	153	37	6	1	6	28	17	35	.324	.412	None on/out	.305	118	36	10	0	4	4	8	19	.354	.492
Flyball	.271	70	19	1	0	2	9	5	12	.329	.371	Batting #6	.247	223	55	11	2	7	27	19	43	.306	.408
Home	.281	224	63	12	1	8	29	25	38	.359	.451	Batting #7	.321	84	27	5	0	1	14	14	19	.414	.417
Away	.263	236	62	15	1	7	36	23	49	.332	.424	Other	.281	153	43	11	0	7	24	15	25	.360	.490
Day	.272	232	63	10	1	7	22	24	37	.342	.414	April	.250	80	20	4	1	2	9	7	17	.310	.400
Night	.272	228	62	17	1	8	43	24	50	.347	.461	May	.241	87	21	7	1	4	14	3	16	.272	.483
Grass	.280	354	99	20	2	12	50	39	64	.358	.449	June	.186	43	8	3	0	0	3	2	6	.234	.256
Turf	.245	106	26	7	0	3	15	9	23	.302	.396	July	.308	65	20	5	0	2	8	5	15	.361	.477
First Pitch	.378	45	17	4	0	2	10	4	0	.429	.600	August	.273	88	24	3	0	3	16	15	17	.385	.409
Ahead in Count	.327	98	32	10	0	7	22	23	0	.459	.643	September/October	.330	97	32	5	0	4	15	16	16	.430	.505
Behind in Count	.201	239	48	11	1	4	21	0	79	.209	.305	Pre-All Star	.234	235	55	15	2	6	29	12	46	.274	.391
Two Strikes	.181	221	40	5	0	3	19	21	87	.256	.244	Post-All Star	.311	225	70	12	0	9	36	36	41	.413	.484

1993 By Position

Position	Avg	AB	H	2B	3B	HR	RBI	BB	SO	OBP	SLG	G	GS	Innings	PO	A	E	DP	Fld Pct	Rng Fctr	In Zone	Outs	Zone Rtg	MLB Zone
As 3b	.276	449	124	27	2	15	65	45	86	.347	.445	129	126	1082.0	79	232	8	22	.975	2.59	295	257	.871	.834

Last Five Years

	Avg	AB	H	2B	3B	HR	RBI	BB	SO	OBP	SLG		Avg	AB	H	2B	3B	HR	RBI	BB	SO	OBP	SLG
vs. Left	.285	694	198	47	2	29	95	89	120	.369	.484	Scoring Posn	.271	605	164	30	6	15	224	82	127	.362	.415
vs. Right	.238	1557	371	57	9	40	208	123	339	.301	.364	Close & Late	.234	380	89	13	3	5	44	36	104	.306	.324
Groundball	.227	709	161	21	5	16	89	66	161	.301	.339	None on/out	.269	554	149	36	1	18	18	36	99	.318	.435
Flyball	.251	458	115	22	0	22	74	48	85	.328	.443	Batting #6	.246	769	189	32	5	22	106	75	157	.316	.386
Home	.255	1114	284	44	6	33	131	108	218	.327	.394	Batting #8	.245	531	130	24	1	13	70	49	115	.315	.367
Away	.251	1137	285	60	5	36	172	104	241	.319	.407	Other	.263	951	250	48	5	34	127	88	187	.333	.431
Day	.251	641	161	27	4	20	74	63	113	.324	.399	April	.254	311	79	16	3	11	46	32	62	.331	.431
Night	.253	1610	408	77	7	49	229	149	346	.322	.401	May	.274	368	101	23	1	16	55	31	78	.333	.473
Grass	.257	1581	406	76	8	51	211	141	311	.324	.412	June	.199	367	73	15	1	5	37	38	76	.276	.286
Turf	.243	670	163	28	3	18	92	71	148	.319	.375	July	.293	362	106	16	3	13	50	29	67	.350	.461
First Pitch	.294	235	69	12	3	7	40	11	0	.336	.460	August	.246	419	103	19	2	13	67	37	86	.316	.394
Ahead in Count	.332	467	155	35	3	26	88	119	0	.466	.587	September/October	.252	424	107	15	1	11	48	45	90	.331	.370
Behind in Count	.208	1136	236	40	3	22	117	0	392	.217	.306	Pre-All Star	.248	1163	288	60	5	36	153	104	243	.313	.401
Two Strikes	.175	1123	197	28	0	19	93	82	459	.238	.251	Post-All Star	.258	1088	281	44	6	33	150	108	216	.333	.401

Batter vs. Pitcher (career)

Hits Best Against	Avg	AB	H	2B	3B	HR	RBI	BB	SO	OBP	SLG	Hits Worst Against	Avg	AB	H	2B	3B	HR	RBI	BB	SO	OBP	SLG
John Habyan	.500	10	5	1	0	0	2	1	2	.545	.600	Mike Jackson	.000	12	0	0	0	0	0	1	3	.077	.000
Bret Saberhagen	.462	26	12	2	0	1	3	0	3	.462	.654	Duane Ward	.000	10	0	0	0	0	0	2	6	.167	.000
Tim Leary	.462	13	6	1	1	2	6	2	1	.533	1.154	Bill Wegman	.059	17	1	0	0	0	2	1	2	.111	.059
Pete Harnisch	.364	11	4	0	0	2	4	2	4	.462	.909	Mike Henneman	.059	17	1	0	0	0	2	1	6	.111	.059
Lee Guetterman	.333	18	6	2	1	2	6	2	2	.400	.889	Andy Benes	.083	12	1	0	0	0	0	0	5	.083	.083

Damon Buford — Orioles

Age 24 – Bats Right

	Avg	G	AB	R	H	2B	3B	HR	RBI	BB	SO	HBP	GDP	SB	CS	OBP	SLG	IBB	SH	SF	#Pit	#P/PA	GB	FB	G/F
1993 Season	.228	53	79	18	18	5	0	2	9	9	19	1	1	2	2	.315	.367	0	1	0	339	3.77	21	19	1.11

1993 Season

	Avg	AB	H	2B	3B	HR	RBI	BB	SO	OBP	SLG		Avg	AB	H	2B	3B	HR	RBI	BB	SO	OBP	SLG
vs. Left	.217	23	5	3	0	0	1	0	8	.250	.348	Scoring Posn	.313	16	5	1	0	0	6	4	6	.450	.375
vs. Right	.232	56	13	2	0	2	8	9	11	.338	.375	Close & Late	.125	16	2	1	0	0	1	0	3	.125	.188

Jay Buhner — Mariners

Age 29 – Bats Right (flyball hitter)

	Avg	G	AB	R	H	2B	3B	HR	RBI	BB	SO	HBP	GDP	SB	CS	OBP	SLG	IBB	SH	SF	#Pit	#P/PA	GB	FB	G/F
1993 Season	.272	158	563	91	153	28	3	27	98	100	144	2	12	2	5	.379	.476	11	2	8	2618	3.88	177	166	1.07
Last Five Years	.258	556	1879	267	485	85	11	95	320	260	512	20	40	5	18	.351	.467	19	5	22	8433	3.86	540	588	0.92

1993 Season

	Avg	AB	H	2B	3B	HR	RBI	BB	SO	OBP	SLG		Avg	AB	H	2B	3B	HR	RBI	BB	SO	OBP	SLG
vs. Left	.320	172	55	10	0	9	32	35	44	.435	.535	Scoring Posn	.278	151	42	7	0	6	65	44	37	.424	.444
vs. Right	.251	391	98	18	3	18	66	65	100	.353	.450	Close & Late	.304	79	24	5	1	2	10	19	13	.426	.468
Groundball	.326	92	30	3	0	5	20	11	18	.390	.522	None on/out	.302	159	48	10	2	7	7	23	40	.390	.522
Flyball	.339	124	42	10	1	10	30	20	40	.428	.677	Batting #4	.254	370	94	18	1	18	67	66	97	.365	.454

1993 Season

	Avg	AB	H	2B	3B	HR	RBI	BB	SO	OBP	SLG		Avg	AB	H	2B	3B	HR	RBI	BB	SO	OBP	SLG
Home	.273	275	75	17	2	13	53	59	74	.402	.491	Batting #5	.329	143	47	8	2	7	25	23	27	.419	.559
Away	.271	288	78	11	1	14	45	41	70	.355	.462	Other	.240	50	12	2	0	2	6	11	20	.371	.400
Day	.287	167	48	9	1	7	27	28	33	.392	.479	April	.321	81	26	3	0	2	16	14	18	.412	.432
Night	.265	396	105	19	2	20	71	72	111	.373	.475	May	.270	100	27	3	1	9	19	9	26	.327	.590
Grass	.285	228	65	8	1	12	32	31	48	.365	.487	June	.300	90	27	5	1	4	15	19	23	.422	.511
Turf	.263	335	88	20	2	15	66	69	96	.388	.469	July	.283	92	26	4	0	4	18	19	18	.404	.457
First Pitch	.431	72	31	7	1	5	24	9	0	.482	.764	August	.179	84	15	3	1	4	11	21	27	.343	.381
Ahead in Count	.308	117	36	7	0	8	24	49	0	.509	.573	September/October	.276	116	32	10	0	4	19	18	32	.370	.466
Behind in Count	.206	257	53	7	1	8	31	0	114	.210	.335	Pre-All Star	.296	307	91	12	2	17	59	49	73	.392	.515
Two Strikes	.170	282	48	9	1	7	31	42	144	.280	.284	Post-All Star	.242	256	62	16	1	10	39	51	71	.364	.430

1993 By Position

Position	Avg	AB	H	2B	3B	HR	RBI	BB	SO	OBP	SLG	G	GS	Innings	PO	A	E	DP	Fld Pct	Rng Fctr	In Zone	Outs	Zone Rtg	MLB Zone
As Designated Hitter	.171	35	6	2	0	2	5	4	7	.250	.400	10	9	---	---	---	---	---	---	---	---	---	---	---
As rf	.278	526	146	26	3	24	92	96	136	.387	.475	148	146	1286.1	263	8	6	2	.978	1.90	336	256	.762	.826

Last Five Years

	Avg	AB	H	2B	3B	HR	RBI	BB	SO	OBP	SLG		Avg	AB	H	2B	3B	HR	RBI	BB	SO	OBP	SLG
vs. Left	.271	582	158	31	2	34	104	96	141	.379	.507	Scoring Posn	.277	494	137	24	5	22	214	101	123	.392	.480
vs. Right	.252	1297	327	54	9	61	216	164	371	.338	.449	Close & Late	.253	312	79	12	2	13	46	51	77	.353	.429
Groundball	.279	456	127	15	3	21	91	44	116	.343	.463	None on/out	.293	454	133	24	3	21	21	57	114	.374	.498
Flyball	.238	407	97	23	2	20	63	61	117	.342	.452	Batting #5	.271	557	151	31	2	24	77	67	144	.353	.463
Home	.254	922	234	48	7	45	157	150	266	.362	.467	Batting #6	.240	645	155	23	5	29	107	87	189	.334	.426
Away	.262	957	251	37	4	50	163	110	246	.340	.466	Other	.264	677	179	31	4	42	136	106	179	.364	.508
Day	.282	525	148	30	2	32	91	70	143	.369	.530	April	.266	199	53	8	1	7	28	34	54	.369	.422
Night	.249	1354	337	55	9	63	229	190	369	.344	.442	May	.257	222	57	4	2	15	45	31	57	.346	.495
Grass	.276	725	200	22	3	45	130	89	174	.355	.501	June	.245	383	94	16	3	21	75	47	104	.333	.467
Turf	.247	1154	285	63	8	50	190	171	338	.348	.445	July	.283	272	77	9	1	20	52	37	70	.369	.544
First Pitch	.370	262	97	15	5	19	77	15	0	.404	.683	August	.244	356	87	20	4	17	59	53	111	.347	.466
Ahead in Count	.323	371	120	28	1	25	81	130	0	.495	.606	September/October	.262	447	117	28	0	15	61	58	116	.352	.425
Behind in Count	.196	851	167	27	3	31	106	0	398	.204	.344	Pre-All Star	.257	913	235	31	6	54	175	126	244	.348	.482
Two Strikes	.163	951	155	27	2	30	98	115	512	.258	.290	Post-All Star	.259	966	250	54	5	41	145	134	268	.353	.452

Batter vs. Pitcher (career)

Hits Best Against	Avg	AB	H	2B	3B	HR	RBI	BB	SO	OBP	SLG	Hits Worst Against	Avg	AB	H	2B	3B	HR	RBI	BB	SO	OBP	SLG
Matt Young	.556	9	5	0	0	1	3	2	3	.636	.889	Jeff Reardon	.000	10	0	0	0	0	0	1	2	.091	.000
Storm Davis	.500	14	7	1	1	1	4	2	3	.563	.929	Chris Haney	.000	9	0	0	0	0	0	2	5	.182	.000
Jeff Ballard	.467	15	7	1	1	1	2	1	1	.500	.867	Brian Bohanon	.000	7	0	0	0	0	1	3	1	.273	.000
Curt Young	.455	11	5	1	0	1	4	5	1	.588	.818	Bill Gullickson	.048	21	1	0	0	0	0	3	6	.167	.048
Mike Boddicker	.429	14	6	4	0	1	3	3	4	.529	.929	Todd Stottlemyre	.111	18	2	0	0	0	1	0	4	.111	.111

Scott Bullett — Pirates

Age 25 – Bats Left

	Avg	G	AB	R	H	2B	3B	HR	RBI	BB	SO	HBP	GDP	SB	CS	OBP	SLG	IBB	SH	SF	#Pit	#P/PA	GB	FB	G/F
1993 Season	.200	23	55	2	11	0	2	0	4	3	15	0	1	3	2	.237	.273	0	0	1	237	4.02	17	14	1.21
Career (1991-1993)	.186	34	59	4	11	0	2	0	4	3	18	1	1	4	3	.234	.254	0	0	1	263	4.11	18	14	1.29

1993 Season

	Avg	AB	H	2B	3B	HR	RBI	BB	SO	OBP	SLG		Avg	AB	H	2B	3B	HR	RBI	BB	SO	OBP	SLG
vs. Left	.100	10	1	0	0	0	0	1	2	.182	.100	Scoring Posn	.158	19	3	0	1	0	4	0	7	.150	.263
vs. Right	.222	45	10	0	2	0	4	2	13	.250	.311	Close & Late	.250	12	3	0	0	0	0	0	4	.250	.250

Jim Bullinger — Cubs

Age 28 – Pitches Right

	ERA	W	L	Sv	G	GS	IP	BB	SO	Avg	H	2B	3B	HR	RBI	OBP	SLG	GF	IR	IRS	Hld	SvOp	SB	CS	GB	FB	G/F
1993 Season	4.32	1	0	1	15	0	16.2	9	10	.277	18	5	1	1	8	.360	.431	6	7	0	3	1	1	1	26	15	1.73
Career (1992-1993)	4.60	3	8	8	54	9	101.2	63	46	.241	90	14	6	10	52	.352	.390	21	28	5	7	8	9	3	155	109	1.42

1993 Season

	ERA	W	L	Sv	G	GS	IP	H	HR	BB	SO		Avg	AB	H	2B	3B	HR	RBI	BB	SO	OBP	SLG
Home	5.40	1	0	0	6	0	6.2	6	0	4	1	vs. Left	.360	25	9	3	0	1	6	7	3	.485	.600
Away	3.60	0	0	1	9	0	10.0	12	1	5	9	vs. Right	.225	40	9	2	1	0	2	2	7	.262	.325

Dave Burba — Giants

Age 27 – Pitches Right

	ERA	W	L	Sv	G	GS	IP	BB	SO	Avg	H	2B	3B	HR	RBI	OBP	SLG	GF	IR	IRS	Hld	SvOp	SB	CS	GB	FB	G/F
1993 Season	4.25	10	3	0	54	5	95.1	37	88	.265	95	12	1	14	53	.336	.421	9	35	12	10	0	10	3	100	111	0.90
Career (1990-1993)	4.40	14	12	1	105	18	210.2	84	155	.269	217	34	5	24	114	.340	.413	26	59	21	10	1	16	5	256	253	1.01

1993 Season

	ERA	W	L	Sv	G	GS	IP	H	HR	BB	SO		Avg	AB	H	2B	3B	HR	RBI	BB	SO	OBP	SLG
Home	3.39	5	1	0	30	4	58.1	53	6	22	54	vs. Left	.320	150	48	4	0	6	24	14	25	.381	.467
Away	5.59	5	2	0	24	1	37.0	42	8	15	34	vs. Right	.225	209	47	8	1	8	29	23	63	.303	.388
Starter	5.32	3	1	0	5	5	23.2	32	3	10	21	Scoring Posn	.299	87	26	1	1	4	39	20	29	.423	.471
Reliever	3.89	7	2	0	49	0	71.2	63	11	27	67	Close & Late	.224	49	11	2	1	1	6	6	9	.298	.367
0 Days rest	4.70	0	1	0	8	0	7.2	7	1	5	7	None on/out	.333	93	31	3	0	5	5	3	16	.361	.527
1 or 2 Days rest	3.90	5	1	0	22	0	30.0	35	6	16	27	First Pitch	.404	52	21	2	0	5	13	5	0	.466	.731
3+ Days rest	3.71	2	0	0	19	0	34.0	21	4	6	33	Ahead in Count	.177	164	29	4	0	3	16	0	70	.181	.256
Pre-All Star	3.96	6	2	0	30	3	50.0	51	6	15	43	Behind in Count	.242	66	16	3	0	1	11	17	0	.388	.333

1993 Season	ERA	W	L	Sv	G	GS	IP	H	HR	BB	SO		Avg	AB	H	2B	3B	HR	RBI	BB	SO	OBP	SLG
Post-All Star	4.57	4	1	0	24	2	45.1	44	8	22	45	Two Strikes	.168	185	31	2	0	3	17	15	88	.236	.227

Enrique Burgos — Royals

Age 28 – Pitches Left

	ERA	W	L	Sv	G	GS	IP	BB	SO	Avg	H	2B	3B	HR	RBI	OBP	SLG	GF	IR	IRS	Hld	SvOp	SB	CS	GB	FB	G/F
1993 Season	9.00	0	1	0	5	0	5.0	6	6	.238	5	1	0	0	1	.429	.286	3	2	1	0	0	1	0	8	4	2.00

1993 Season	ERA	W	L	Sv	G	GS	IP	H	HR	BB	SO		Avg	AB	H	2B	3B	HR	RBI	BB	SO	OBP	SLG
Home	0.00	0	0	0	2	0	1.1	2	0	1	3	vs. Left	.000	0	0	0	0	0	0	1	0	1.000	.000
Away	12.27	0	1	0	3	0	3.2	3	0	5	3	vs. Right	.238	21	5	1	0	0	1	5	6	.407	.286

John Burkett — Giants

Age 29 – Pitches Right

	ERA	W	L	Sv	G	GS	IP	BB	SO	Avg	H	2B	3B	HR	RBI	OBP	SLG	CG	ShO	Sup	QS	#P/S	SB	CS	GB	FB	G/F
1993 Season	3.65	22	7	0	34	34	231.2	40	145	.255	224	30	7	18	90	.294	.366	2	1	5.52	24	95	14	14	328	244	1.34
Last Five Years	3.86	61	34	1	135	132	832.0	206	501	.263	842	128	18	68	352	.312	.378	10	3	5.03	75	92	66	44	1232	887	1.39

1993 Season	ERA	W	L	Sv	G	GS	IP	H	HR	BB	SO		Avg	AB	H	2B	3B	HR	RBI	BB	SO	OBP	SLG
Home	2.66	9	3	0	16	16	121.2	104	7	12	87	vs. Left	.282	464	131	16	4	8	50	22	71	.318	.386
Away	4.75	13	4	0	18	18	110.0	120	11	28	58	vs. Right	.224	415	93	14	3	10	40	18	74	.269	.345
Day	3.24	9	4	0	17	17	122.1	118	7	25	78	Inning 1-6	.251	728	183	23	6	13	74	35	119	.293	.353
Night	4.12	13	3	0	17	17	109.1	106	11	15	67	Inning 7+	.272	151	41	7	1	5	16	5	26	.299	.430
Grass	3.56	15	5	0	25	25	174.1	164	14	28	118	None on	.240	551	132	20	3	6	6	23	98	.276	.319
Turf	3.92	7	2	0	9	9	57.1	60	4	12	27	Runners on	.280	328	92	10	4	12	84	17	47	.324	.445
April	2.62	5	0	0	5	5	34.1	26	3	6	23	Scoring Posn	.282	170	48	2	2	7	68	13	31	.340	.441
May	3.92	2	1	0	6	6	41.1	40	2	9	24	Close & Late	.258	66	17	3	0	2	7	2	11	.290	.394
June	2.70	5	1	0	6	6	43.1	38	3	3	28	None on/out	.241	232	56	11	2	1	1	10	41	.282	.319
July	3.44	3	2	0	5	5	34.0	36	2	9	21	vs. 1st Batr (relief)	.000	0	0	0	0	0	0	0	0	.000	.000
August	6.21	3	2	0	6	6	37.2	48	6	5	26	First Inning Pitched	.231	121	28	1	2	2	10	9	16	.290	.322
September/October	3.07	4	1	0	6	6	41.0	36	2	8	23	First 75 Pitches	.246	668	164	22	6	11	62	32	104	.289	.346
Starter	3.65	22	7	0	34	34	231.2	224	18	40	145	Pitch 76-90	.271	129	35	6	1	3	16	3	25	.288	.403
Reliever	0.00	0	0	0	0	0	0.0	0	0	0	0	Pitch 91-105	.288	59	17	1	0	4	11	4	12	.344	.508
0-3 Days Rest	5.11	2	0	0	2	2	12.1	13	2	1	10	Pitch 106+	.348	23	8	1	0	0	1	1	4	.375	.391
4 Days Rest	3.29	15	3	0	21	21	150.1	136	12	24	92	First Pitch	.348	161	56	6	1	2	20	4	0	.387	.435
5+ Days Rest	4.17	5	4	0	11	11	69.0	75	4	15	43	Ahead in Count	.157	388	61	6	2	5	22	0	138	.166	.222
Pre-All Star	3.28	13	3	0	19	19	131.2	122	9	23	82	Behind in Count	.353	167	59	10	2	5	25	13	0	.398	.527
Post-All Star	4.14	9	4	0	15	15	100.0	102	9	17	63	Two Strikes	.154	363	56	9	1	6	19	23	145	.209	.234

Last Five Years	ERA	W	L	Sv	G	GS	IP	H	HR	BB	SO		Avg	AB	H	2B	3B	HR	RBI	BB	SO	OBP	SLG
Home	3.30	31	13	0	64	64	437.0	397	34	87	282	vs. Left	.283	1851	523	86	12	43	221	124	262	.328	.412
Away	4.49	30	21	1	71	68	395.0	445	34	119	219	vs. Right	.237	1348	319	42	6	25	131	82	239	.290	.332
Day	3.33	29	16	0	63	61	397.2	382	29	101	237	Inning 1-6	.263	2733	720	105	17	55	307	181	437	.314	.375
Night	4.35	32	18	1	72	71	434.1	460	39	105	264	Inning 7+	.262	466	122	23	1	13	45	25	64	.300	.399
Grass	3.62	45	24	1	99	96	624.1	608	50	146	385	None on	.252	1895	478	66	6	37	37	106	312	.297	.352
Turf	4.59	16	10	0	36	36	207.2	234	18	60	116	Runners on	.279	1304	364	62	12	31	315	100	189	.332	.416
April	3.61	10	3	0	16	16	102.1	93	6	27	63	Scoring Posn	.288	705	203	26	8	17	267	72	121	.351	.420
May	3.69	8	3	0	23	23	144.0	144	11	41	86	Close & Late	.268	209	56	9	0	7	27	12	28	.310	.411
June	3.23	10	7	0	24	23	147.2	133	13	38	89	None on/out	.268	833	223	35	3	15	15	44	124	.308	.371
July	3.47	10	5	0	23	22	145.1	148	10	36	85	vs. 1st Batr (relief)	.000	1	0	0	0	0	1	2	0	.667	.000
August	4.99	11	8	0	23	23	139.0	158	15	27	76	First Inning Pitched	.250	505	126	12	4	9	59	44	86	.317	.343
September/October	4.16	12	8	1	26	25	153.2	166	13	37	102	First 75 Pitches	.263	2486	654	99	17	49	274	159	390	.312	.376
Starter	3.88	61	34	0	132	132	827.1	840	68	204	500	Pitch 76-90	.278	392	109	18	1	11	50	27	61	.325	.413
Reliever	0.00	0	0	1	3	0	4.2	2	0	2	1	Pitch 91-105	.255	216	55	7	0	7	21	12	33	.300	.384
0-3 Days Rest	4.20	8	5	0	20	20	124.1	126	12	38	83	Pitch 106+	.229	105	24	4	0	1	7	8	17	.283	.295
4 Days Rest	3.52	39	17	0	74	74	481.0	461	41	103	296	First Pitch	.327	571	187	29	3	14	75	16	0	.356	.462
5+ Days Rest	4.50	14	12	0	38	38	222.0	253	15	63	121	Ahead in Count	.183	1363	249	29	7	18	91	0	448	.189	.254
Pre-All Star	3.45	33	15	0	71	70	450.2	425	35	119	277	Behind in Count	.336	658	221	41	6	16	106	96	0	.420	.489
Post-All Star	4.34	28	19	1	64	62	381.1	417	33	87	224	Two Strikes	.179	1329	238	29	5	21	85	94	501	.238	.256

Pitcher vs. Batter (career)

Pitches Best Vs.	Avg	AB	H	2B	3B	HR	RBI	BB	SO	OBP	SLG	Pitches Worst Vs.	Avg	AB	H	2B	3B	HR	RBI	BB	SO	OBP	SLG
Cory Snyder	.000	12	0	0	0	0	0	1	7	.077	.000	Deion Sanders	.600	15	9	1	2	0	3	0	2	.600	.933
Kevin McReynolds	.083	12	1	0	0	0	0	0	0	.083	.083	Ryne Sandberg	.533	15	8	0	0	1	1	1	1	.563	.733
Andres Galarraga	.083	12	1	0	0	0	0	0	1	.083	.083	John Kruk	.444	27	12	3	1	2	4	2	7	.483	.852
Joe Oliver	.083	12	1	0	0	0	0	0	3	.083	.083	Gary Sheffield	.417	12	5	1	0	3	6	1	0	.462	1.250
Orlando Merced	.100	20	2	0	0	0	1	1	4	.143	.100	Jerald Clark	.412	17	7	1	2	1	4	1	1	.444	.882

Ellis Burks — White Sox

Age 29 – Bats Right

	Avg	G	AB	R	H	2B	3B	HR	RBI	BB	SO	HBP	GDP	SB	CS	OBP	SLG	IBB	SH	SF	#Pit	#P/PA	GB	FB	G/F
1993 Season	.275	146	499	75	137	24	4	17	74	60	97	4	11	6	9	.352	.441	2	3	8	2286	3.98	165	153	1.08
Last Five Years	.278	591	2195	328	611	117	24	72	310	208	360	17	49	47	38	.343	.452	12	9	19	9421	3.85	768	676	1.14

1993 Season	Avg	AB	H	2B	3B	HR	RBI	BB	SO	OBP	SLG		Avg	AB	H	2B	3B	HR	RBI	BB	SO	OBP	SLG
vs. Left	.281	153	43	4	1	8	28	25	24	.380	.477	Scoring Posn	.252	119	30	10	0	4	57	16	27	.331	.437

1993 Season	Avg	AB	H	2B	3B	HR	RBI	BB	SO	OBP	SLG		Avg	AB	H	2B	3B	HR	RBI	BB	SO	OBP	SLG
vs. Right	.272	346	94	20	3	9	46	35	73	.339	.425	Close & Late	.268	71	19	5	0	1	11	11	20	.357	.380
Groundball	.284	95	27	3	2	4	20	12	23	.369	.484	None on/out	.273	121	33	5	1	2	2	15	20	.353	.380
Flyball	.157	102	16	4	1	2	7	10	23	.239	.275	Batting #5	.284	155	44	11	0	5	21	13	31	.339	.452
Home	.298	238	71	15	3	7	40	31	46	.383	.475	Batting #6	.276	250	69	9	4	8	37	31	49	.355	.440
Away	.253	261	66	9	1	10	34	29	51	.323	.410	Other	.255	94	24	4	0	4	16	16	17	.363	.426
Day	.265	113	30	4	1	4	19	20	22	.380	.425	April	.338	71	24	3	3	1	9	7	13	.400	.507
Night	.277	386	107	20	3	13	55	40	75	.343	.446	May	.253	75	19	1	1	5	14	8	18	.326	.493
Grass	.275	415	114	20	4	15	67	52	77	.355	.451	June	.256	86	22	4	0	3	15	10	15	.333	.407
Turf	.274	84	23	4	0	2	7	8	20	.337	.393	July	.303	89	27	5	0	5	14	10	15	.370	.528
First Pitch	.220	41	9	0	1	0	2	2	0	.256	.268	August	.298	94	28	8	0	3	16	7	18	.352	.479
Ahead in Count	.368	144	53	8	2	8	33	33	0	.480	.618	September/October	.202	84	17	3	0	0	6	18	18	.337	.238
Behind in Count	.203	212	43	8	1	5	20	0	86	.215	.321	Pre-All Star	.295	264	78	9	4	11	45	31	48	.369	.485
Two Strikes	.208	236	49	9	1	7	23	25	97	.282	.343	Post-All Star	.251	235	59	15	0	6	29	29	49	.333	.391

1993 By Position																			Fld	Rng	In		Zone	MLB
Position	Avg	AB	H	2B	3B	HR	RBI	BB	SO	OBP	SLG	G	GS	Innings	PO	A	E	DP	Pct	Fctr	Zone	Outs	Rtg	Zone
As cf	.188	69	13	3	0	3	8	11	11	.300	.362	21	20	162.0	49	2	0	0	1.000	2.83	52	46	.885	.829
As rf	.287	425	122	21	4	14	66	49	85	.360	.454	132	113	1046.0	265	4	6	1	.978	2.31	307	253	.824	.826

Last Five Years	Avg	AB	H	2B	3B	HR	RBI	BB	SO	OBP	SLG		Avg	AB	H	2B	3B	HR	RBI	BB	SO	OBP	SLG
vs. Left	.272	646	176	34	7	23	95	79	89	.351	.454	Scoring Posn	.267	602	161	34	6	21	244	71	114	.338	.449
vs. Right	.281	1549	435	83	17	49	215	129	271	.339	.451	Close & Late	.252	349	88	21	4	9	45	38	77	.329	.413
Groundball	.287	568	163	24	9	16	84	47	102	.346	.445	None on/out	.273	510	139	23	7	19	19	46	70	.338	.457
Flyball	.248	496	123	30	4	14	56	41	81	.308	.409	Batting #4	.265	453	120	19	6	14	61	43	77	.328	.426
Home	.291	1079	314	67	14	35	160	103	161	.355	.476	Batting #6	.280	657	184	40	5	20	100	63	108	.344	.447
Away	.266	1116	297	50	10	37	150	105	199	.330	.428	Other	.283	1085	307	58	13	38	149	102	175	.348	.465
Day	.273	659	180	32	6	18	104	78	105	.354	.422	April	.260	369	96	20	6	6	40	43	65	.347	.396
Night	.281	1536	431	85	18	54	206	130	255	.338	.465	May	.286	458	131	23	9	17	64	43	73	.346	.487
Grass	.276	1847	510	95	20	60	263	175	299	.340	.447	June	.263	407	107	23	2	20	60	33	60	.318	.477
Turf	.290	348	101	22	4	12	47	33	61	.357	.480	July	.303	254	77	15	2	10	38	24	44	.369	.496
First Pitch	.291	230	67	14	3	4	26	7	0	.321	.430	August	.297	441	131	25	4	13	71	38	70	.354	.460
Ahead in Count	.324	553	179	28	9	28	111	113	0	.435	.559	September/October	.259	266	69	11	1	6	37	27	48	.326	.376
Behind in Count	.229	923	211	41	9	24	95	0	299	.236	.371	Pre-All Star	.277	1315	364	70	17	46	183	128	204	.343	.461
Two Strikes	.209	989	207	36	4	26	101	86	360	.275	.333	Post-All Star	.281	880	247	47	7	26	127	80	156	.343	.439

Batter vs. Pitcher (career)																							
Hits Best Against	Avg	AB	H	2B	3B	HR	RBI	BB	SO	OBP	SLG	**Hits Worst Against**	Avg	AB	H	2B	3B	HR	RBI	BB	SO	OBP	SLG
Matt Young	.556	9	5	0	0	1	2	3	2	.667	.889	Tim Leary	.059	17	1	0	0	0	0	1	5	.111	.059
Bill Wegman	.500	16	8	1	0	1	5	4	2	.600	.750	Bill Krueger	.059	17	1	0	0	0	0	2	2	.158	.059
Erik Hanson	.481	27	13	1	0	3	8	2	4	.517	.852	Rich DeLucia	.100	10	1	0	0	0	1	0	3	.091	.100
Jeff Russell	.450	20	9	2	0	2	6	2	3	.500	.850	Jimmy Key	.111	36	4	1	0	0	1	3	7	.179	.139
Al Leiter	.375	8	3	1	0	1	5	3	1	.545	.875	Lee Guetterman	.133	15	2	0	0	0	0	0	0	.133	.133

Jeromy Burnitz — Mets

Age 25 – Bats Left (flyball hitter)

	Avg	G	AB	R	H	2B	3B	HR	RBI	BB	SO	HBP	GDP	SB	CS	OBP	SLG	IBB	SH	SF	#Pit	#P/PA	GB	FB	G/F
1993 Season	.243	86	263	49	64	10	6	13	38	38	66	1	2	3	6	.339	.475	4	2	2	1224	4.00	62	84	0.74

1993 Season	Avg	AB	H	2B	3B	HR	RBI	BB	SO	OBP	SLG		Avg	AB	H	2B	3B	HR	RBI	BB	SO	OBP	SLG
vs. Left	.242	33	8	1	2	1	3	4	6	.324	.485	Scoring Posn	.273	66	18	2	2	4	26	10	13	.359	.545
vs. Right	.243	230	56	9	4	12	35	34	60	.341	.474	Close & Late	.240	50	12	3	2	1	7	8	14	.339	.440
Home	.255	141	36	5	4	6	17	15	33	.325	.475	None on/out	.242	66	16	4	2	5	5	8	17	.324	.591
Away	.230	122	28	5	2	7	21	23	33	.354	.475	Batting #5	.259	112	29	5	1	6	21	19	29	.364	.482
First Pitch	.448	29	13	4	2	5	14	4	0	.529	1.241	Batting #7	.183	82	15	2	4	5	12	10	22	.280	.488
Ahead in Count	.438	48	21	2	3	4	14	20	0	.594	.854	Other	.290	69	20	3	1	2	5	9	15	.367	.449
Behind in Count	.140	129	18	2	1	4	7	0	54	.140	.264	Pre-All Star	.288	52	15	3	1	4	12	7	13	.377	.615
Two Strikes	.147	143	21	4	0	2	6	14	66	.223	.217	Post-All Star	.232	211	49	7	5	9	26	31	53	.329	.441

Todd Burns — Cardinals

Age 30 – Pitches Right (flyball pitcher)

	ERA	W	L	Sv	G	GS	IP	BB	SO	Avg	H	2B	3B	HR	RBI	OBP	SLG	GF	IR	IRS	Hld	SvOp	SB	CS	GB	FB	G/F
1993 Season	5.08	0	8	0	49	5	95.2	41	45	.260	95	20	5	14	60	.333	.456	13	45	16	8	5	3	3	113	145	0.78
Last Five Years	3.56	13	21	12	186	19	387.0	141	195	.241	346	76	13	35	172	.309	.385	36	141	44	27	22	9	17	458	531	0.86

1993 Season	ERA	W	L	Sv	G	GS	IP	H	HR	BB	SO		Avg	AB	H	2B	3B	HR	RBI	BB	SO	OBP	SLG
Home	3.92	0	2	0	21	2	39.0	31	4	13	13	vs. Left	.230	139	32	10	1	4	19	14	16	.305	.403
Away	5.88	0	6	0	28	3	56.2	64	10	28	32	vs. Right	.278	227	63	10	4	10	41	27	29	.350	.489
Starter	7.62	0	4	0	5	5	26.0	32	2	14	10	Scoring Posn	.288	104	30	8	2	1	46	17	12	.373	.433
Reliever	4.13	0	4	0	44	0	69.2	63	12	27	35	Close & Late	.367	60	22	7	3	2	16	11	4	.440	.683
0 Days rest	6.75	0	1	0	7	0	14.2	15	5	7	5	None on/out	.224	76	17	3	2	2	2	10	9	.322	.395
1 or 2 Days rest	3.65	0	2	0	21	0	24.2	24	3	9	12	First Pitch	.286	49	14	2	0	2	4	8	0	.386	.449
3+ Days rest	3.26	0	1	0	16	0	30.1	24	4	11	18	Ahead in Count	.168	155	26	4	2	6	20	0	41	.175	.335
Pre-All Star	4.65	0	4	0	23	5	62.0	63	6	28	34	Behind in Count	.360	86	31	10	2	2	23	19	0	.467	.593
Post-All Star	5.88	0	4	0	26	0	33.2	32	8	13	11	Two Strikes	.160	144	23	2	2	6	14	14	45	.242	.326

Last Five Years	ERA	W	L	Sv	G	GS	IP	H	HR	BB	SO		Avg	AB	H	2B	3B	HR	RBI	BB	SO	OBP	SLG
Home	2.82	8	6	8	90	8	185.0	146	15	56	88	vs. Left	.220	590	130	29	8	9	47	62	64	.298	.342
Away	4.23	5	15	4	96	11	202.0	200	20	85	107	vs. Right	.255	846	216	47	5	26	125	79	131	.316	.415
Day	3.04	5	6	7	60	3	115.1	89	4	42	66	Inning 1-6	.241	684	165	40	7	17	89	66	98	.309	.395
Night	3.78	8	15	5	126	16	271.2	257	31	99	129	Inning 7+	.241	752	181	36	6	18	83	75	97	.309	.376
Grass	3.57	11	13	11	146	17	317.1	284	31	114	157	None on	.241	792	191	42	8	23	23	75	114	.312	.402
Turf	3.49	2	8	1	40	2	69.2	62	4	27	38	Runners on	.241	644	155	34	5	12	149	66	81	.306	.365
April	3.35	1	0	1	22	0	45.2	41	3	15	24	Scoring Posn	.247	372	92	22	3	5	129	52	47	.328	.363
May	2.90	4	2	2	21	5	62.0	54	4	14	31	Close & Late	.275	298	82	17	4	10	41	42	38	.359	.460
June	3.57	3	6	2	31	6	75.2	63	8	35	38	None on/out	.258	349	90	20	4	9	9	30	51	.322	.415
July	3.60	3	5	4	41	6	90.0	80	5	31	50	vs. 1st Batr (relief)	.299	144	43	10	2	4	19	16	26	.377	.479
August	5.51	1	4	1	36	0	50.2	47	9	24	29	First Inning Pitched	.267	606	162	30	5	16	108	72	93	.345	.413
September/October	2.71	1	4	2	35	2	63.0	61	6	22	23	First 15 Pitches	.277	574	159	31	4	15	93	61	80	.347	.423
Starter	3.89	4	8	0	19	19	115.2	106	7	35	53	Pitch 16-30	.189	350	66	12	5	5	27	41	50	.272	.294
Reliever	3.42	9	13	12	167	0	271.1	240	28	106	142	Pitch 31-45	.203	202	41	9	2	8	19	13	26	.257	.386
0 Days rest	5.52	0	2	3	18	0	31.0	28	8	18	16	Pitch 46+	.258	310	80	24	2	7	33	26	39	.313	.416
1 or 2 Days rest	3.41	4	8	4	71	0	105.2	90	9	40	63	First Pitch	.253	186	47	8	4	3	16	16	0	.312	.387
3+ Days rest	2.94	5	3	5	78	0	134.2	122	11	48	63	Ahead in Count	.193	616	119	20	2	12	51	0	162	.198	.291
Pre-All Star	3.25	8	10	7	92	14	224.0	189	18	77	121	Behind in Count	.324	364	118	33	5	13	71	76	0	.434	.549
Post-All Star	3.98	5	11	5	94	5	163.0	157	17	64	74	Two Strikes	.164	593	97	14	2	13	47	49	195	.231	.260

Pitcher vs. Batter (career)

Pitches Best Vs.	Avg	AB	H	2B	3B	HR	RBI	BB	SO	OBP	SLG	Pitches Worst Vs.	Avg	AB	H	2B	3B	HR	RBI	BB	SO	OBP	SLG
Mickey Tettleton	.000	16	0	0	0	0	0	2	6	.111	.000	Pat Borders	.500	12	6	3	0	0	3	1	2	.538	.750
Rob Deer	.063	16	1	1	0	0	0	2	8	.167	.125	Scott Fletcher	.455	11	5	2	0	0	2	3	1	.571	.636
Mike Devereaux	.091	11	1	0	0	0	0	1	3	.167	.091	Ruben Sierra	.421	19	8	2	0	1	1	3	1	.500	.684
Brian Harper	.100	10	1	0	0	0	1	0	0	.091	.100	Tony Phillips	.417	12	5	1	0	1	2	1	1	.462	.750
Cory Snyder	.167	12	2	0	0	0	1	0	2	.167	.167	Kirby Puckett	.333	12	4	2	0	1	1	2	2	.429	.750

Randy Bush — Twins

Age 35 – Bats Left

	Avg	G	AB	R	H	2B	3B	HR	RBI	BB	SO	HBP	GDP	SB	CS	OBP	SLG	IBB	SH	SF	#Pit	#P/PA	GB	FB	G/F
1993 Season	.156	35	45	1	7	2	0	0	3	7	13	0	3	0	0	.269	.200	1	0	0	193	3.71	18	11	1.64
Last Five Years	.252	442	964	113	243	45	6	28	120	111	175	14	31	6	14	.336	.398	15	0	7	3867	3.53	318	305	1.04

1993 Season

	Avg	AB	H	2B	3B	HR	RBI	BB	SO	OBP	SLG		Avg	AB	H	2B	3B	HR	RBI	BB	SO	OBP	SLG
vs. Left	.000	1	0	0	0	0	0	0	0	.000	.000	Scoring Posn	.231	13	3	0	0	0	3	4	3	.412	.231
vs. Right	.159	44	7	2	0	0	3	7	13	.275	.205	Close & Late	.167	12	2	0	0	0	1	5	4	.412	.167

Last Five Years

	Avg	AB	H	2B	3B	HR	RBI	BB	SO	OBP	SLG		Avg	AB	H	2B	3B	HR	RBI	BB	SO	OBP	SLG
vs. Left	.171	35	6	4	0	0	4	0	15	.189	.286	Scoring Posn	.245	249	61	11	2	6	88	56	48	.377	.378
vs. Right	.255	929	237	41	6	28	116	111	160	.341	.403	Close & Late	.249	185	46	6	1	5	22	27	39	.355	.373
Groundball	.253	281	71	13	1	5	30	32	40	.336	.359	None on/out	.211	213	45	8	2	5	5	21	47	.288	.338
Flyball	.217	180	39	6	3	8	22	24	43	.311	.417	Batting #2	.265	196	52	8	0	5	22	20	34	.339	.383
Home	.258	446	115	21	3	12	53	60	77	.355	.399	Batting #6	.254	355	90	18	4	12	43	32	59	.327	.428
Away	.247	518	128	24	3	16	67	51	98	.319	.398	Other	.245	413	101	19	2	11	55	59	82	.341	.380
Day	.242	293	71	11	2	14	40	37	63	.339	.437	April	.176	142	25	6	1	3	14	18	24	.270	.296
Night	.256	671	172	34	4	14	80	74	112	.334	.382	May	.238	172	41	10	0	6	28	18	29	.311	.401
Grass	.251	383	96	19	2	13	51	41	70	.328	.413	June	.267	116	31	2	3	5	20	12	24	.351	.466
Turf	.253	581	147	26	4	15	69	70	105	.341	.389	July	.267	180	48	9	0	5	15	22	29	.354	.400
First Pitch	.314	140	44	10	2	5	24	10	0	.368	.521	August	.307	179	55	12	1	6	27	22	31	.392	.486
Ahead in Count	.325	243	79	15	2	11	47	47	0	.432	.539	September/October	.246	175	43	6	1	3	16	19	38	.327	.343
Behind in Count	.191	409	78	12	2	6	30	0	145	.208	.274	Pre-All Star	.229	480	110	20	4	14	64	54	88	.311	.375
Two Strikes	.170	383	65	8	1	7	28	51	175	.280	.251	Post-All Star	.275	484	133	25	2	14	56	57	87	.361	.421

Batter vs. Pitcher (since 1984)

Hits Best Against	Avg	AB	H	2B	3B	HR	RBI	BB	SO	OBP	SLG	Hits Worst Against	Avg	AB	H	2B	3B	HR	RBI	BB	SO	OBP	SLG
Bobby Thigpen	.667	9	6	2	0	1	6	3	0	.750	1.222	Mark Eichhorn	.056	18	1	1	0	0	2	0	3	.056	.111
Gene Nelson	.545	11	6	1	0	1	3	1	2	.583	.909	Storm Davis	.061	33	2	1	0	0	2	3	11	.139	.091
Mike Morgan	.478	23	11	2	0	2	8	3	1	.538	.826	Mike Jackson	.100	10	1	0	0	0	0	2	2	.250	.100
Tim Leary	.471	17	8	2	0	1	2	2	2	.526	.765	Tom Henke	.125	24	3	0	0	0	0	3	12	.222	.125
Mike Schooler	.385	13	5	0	0	2	7	1	2	.429	.846	Eric Plunk	.167	12	2	0	0	0	1	1	1	.231	.167

Chris Bushing — Reds

Age 26 – Pitches Right

	ERA	W	L	Sv	G	GS	IP	BB	SO	Avg	H	2B	3B	HR	RBI	OBP	SLG	GF	IR	IRS	Hld	SvOp	SB	CS	GB	FB	G/F
1993 Season	12.46	0	0	0	6	0	4.1	4	3	.450	9	3	1	1	6	.520	.850	2	4	1	0	0	0	0	8	7	1.14

1993 Season

	ERA	W	L	Sv	G	GS	IP	H	HR	BB	SO		Avg	AB	H	2B	3B	HR	RBI	BB	SO	OBP	SLG
Home	18.00	0	0	0	3	0	2.0	7	1	0	1	vs. Left	.333	6	2	1	0	1	2	2	0	.444	1.000
Away	7.71	0	0	0	3	0	2.1	2	0	4	2	vs. Right	.500	14	7	2	1	0	4	2	3	.563	.786

Mike Butcher — Angels

Age 29 – Pitches Right (flyball pitcher)

	ERA	W	L	Sv	G	GS	IP	BB	SO	Avg	H	2B	3B	HR	RBI	OBP	SLG	GF	IR	IRS	Hld	SvOp	SB	CS	GB	FB	G/F
1993 Season	2.86	1	0	8	23	0	28.1	15	24	.204	21	4	0	2	15	.309	.301	11	21	5	3	10	4	0	29	35	0.83
Career (1992-1993)	3.05	3	2	8	42	0	56.0	28	48	.235	50	6	0	5	30	.331	.333	17	43	16	3	11	7	0	57	73	0.78

1993 Season

	ERA	W	L	Sv	G	GS	IP	H	HR	BB	SO
Home	3.46	1	0	3	10	0	13.0	10	1	7	7
Away	2.35	0	0	5	13	0	15.1	11	1	8	17

	Avg	AB	H	2B	3B	HR	RBI	BB	SO	OBP	SLG
vs. Left	.182	44	8	2	0	1	3	5	13	.294	.295
vs. Right	.220	59	13	2	0	1	12	10	11	.319	.305

Brett Butler — Dodgers

Age 37 – Bats Left (groundball hitter)

	Avg	G	AB	R	H	2B	3B	HR	RBI	BB	SO	HBP	GDP	SB	CS	OBP	SLG	IBB	SH	SF	#Pit	#P/PA	GB	FB	G/F
1993 Season	.298	156	607	80	181	21	10	1	42	86	69	5	6	39	19	.387	.371	1	14	4	2836	3.96	260	99	2.63
Last Five Years	.299	788	2991	486	894	90	39	13	199	438	346	18	20	200	103	.390	.368	10	62	17	14043	3.98	1326	560	2.37

1993 Season

	Avg	AB	H	2B	3B	HR	RBI	BB	SO	OBP	SLG
vs. Left	.330	206	68	5	2	0	17	28	18	.407	.374
vs. Right	.282	401	113	16	8	1	25	58	51	.378	.369
Groundball	.315	149	47	4	3	0	3	28	15	.433	.383
Flyball	.323	96	31	7	2	0	8	15	15	.404	.438
Home	.347	291	101	10	4	0	22	49	32	.441	.409
Away	.253	316	80	11	6	1	20	37	37	.336	.335
Day	.270	163	44	5	5	0	7	20	17	.353	.362
Night	.309	444	137	16	5	1	35	66	52	.400	.374
Grass	.311	463	144	14	6	1	34	72	54	.404	.374
Turf	.257	144	37	7	4	0	8	14	15	.331	.361
First Pitch	.403	72	29	3	2	0	6	1	0	.411	.500
Ahead in Count	.344	122	42	10	2	1	16	44	0	.515	.484
Behind in Count	.247	271	67	5	3	0	10	0	58	.255	.288
Two Strikes	.221	289	64	6	3	0	10	41	69	.321	.263

	Avg	AB	H	2B	3B	HR	RBI	BB	SO	OBP	SLG
Scoring Posn	.322	121	39	4	3	0	40	20	13	.411	.405
Close & Late	.337	104	35	6	4	1	9	19	12	.444	.500
None on/out	.302	258	78	8	5	1	1	29	35	.375	.384
Batting #1	.301	584	176	20	10	1	41	78	65	.385	.375
Batting #2	.227	22	5	1	0	0	1	8	3	.452	.273
Other	.000	1	0	0	0	0	0	0	1	.000	.000
April	.329	82	27	3	1	0	5	17	9	.450	.390
May	.308	107	33	4	1	0	11	9	11	.356	.364
June	.315	108	34	4	1	0	12	8	14	.359	.370
July	.269	104	28	3	4	0	4	17	8	.369	.375
August	.253	99	25	4	3	0	2	15	13	.373	.354
September/October	.318	107	34	3	0	1	8	20	14	.425	.374
Pre-All Star	.303	346	105	13	3	0	29	39	39	.373	.358
Post-All Star	.291	261	76	8	7	1	13	47	30	.406	.387

1993 By Position

Position	Avg	AB	H	2B	3B	HR	RBI	BB	SO	OBP	SLG	G	GS	Innings	PO	A	E	DP	Fld Pct	Rng Fctr	In Zone	Outs	Zone Rtg	MLB Zone
As cf	.299	606	181	21	10	1	42	86	68	.388	.371	155	154	1381.2	369	6	0	0	1.000	2.44	424	361	.851	.829

Last Five Years

	Avg	AB	H	2B	3B	HR	RBI	BB	SO	OBP	SLG
vs. Left	.297	1130	336	22	12	3	83	171	152	.390	.346
vs. Right	.300	1861	558	68	27	10	116	267	194	.389	.382
Groundball	.291	966	281	21	8	2	50	140	105	.386	.335
Flyball	.310	649	201	20	11	4	44	102	90	.403	.393
Home	.321	1461	469	46	15	8	109	236	144	.415	.389
Away	.278	1530	425	44	24	5	90	202	202	.365	.348
Day	.275	983	270	31	6	7	66	132	129	.362	.340
Night	.311	2008	624	59	33	6	133	306	217	.403	.382
Grass	.309	2234	690	73	26	11	159	333	243	.398	.380
Turf	.269	757	204	17	13	2	40	105	103	.365	.334
First Pitch	.349	358	125	10	3	1	32	8	0	.366	.402
Ahead in Count	.365	611	223	26	14	4	56	244	0	.543	.473
Behind in Count	.251	1346	338	35	12	1	67	0	286	.254	.297
Two Strikes	.240	1448	347	33	14	4	69	186	346	.328	.290

	Avg	AB	H	2B	3B	HR	RBI	BB	SO	OBP	SLG
Scoring Posn	.286	560	160	17	11	1	179	96	67	.383	.361
Close & Late	.309	492	152	17	6	4	40	83	77	.410	.392
None on/out	.296	1269	375	37	16	7	7	172	146	.382	.366
Batting #1	.294	2733	803	81	35	11	178	387	321	.382	.361
Batting #2	.350	246	86	9	4	2	21	48	23	.459	.443
Other	.417	12	5	0	0	0	0	3	2	.533	.417
April	.330	421	139	17	6	4	31	63	44	.418	.428
May	.248	496	123	10	3	0	28	70	71	.344	.280
June	.295	501	148	16	5	1	39	72	61	.383	.353
July	.322	510	164	12	12	3	42	74	50	.407	.410
August	.299	512	153	18	8	3	35	76	60	.395	.383
September/October	.303	551	167	17	5	2	24	83	60	.395	.363
Pre-All Star	.292	1602	468	46	15	7	115	231	191	.382	.353
Post-All Star	.307	1389	426	44	24	6	84	207	155	.399	.386

Batter vs. Pitcher (since 1984)

Hits Best Against	Avg	AB	H	2B	3B	HR	RBI	BB	SO	OBP	SLG
Paul Assenmacher	.692	13	9	1	0	0	4	1	2	.714	.769
Ryan Bowen	.667	9	6	1	0	0	1	4	1	.714	.778
Larry Andersen	.625	8	5	0	0	0	1	3	2	.727	.625
Craig Lefferts	.545	11	6	0	0	1	1	1	1	.583	.818
Chuck McElroy	.500	6	3	1	0	0	1	6	2	.750	.667

Hits Worst Against	Avg	AB	H	2B	3B	HR	RBI	BB	SO	OBP	SLG
Frank Castillo	.053	19	1	0	0	0	0	1	2	.100	.053
Bill Wegman	.056	18	1	1	0	0	1	0	0	.056	.111
Mike Stanton	.100	10	1	0	0	0	1	2	1	.250	.100
Willie Blair	.143	14	2	1	0	0	2	0	0	.143	.214
Juan Agosto	.160	25	4	0	0	0	0	2	1	.222	.160

Rob Butler — Blue Jays

Age 24 – Bats Left (groundball hitter)

	Avg	G	AB	R	H	2B	3B	HR	RBI	BB	SO	HBP	GDP	SB	CS	OBP	SLG	IBB	SH	SF	#Pit	#P/PA	GB	FB	G/F
1993 Season	.271	17	48	8	13	4	0	0	2	7	12	1	0	2	2	.375	.354	0	0	0	211	3.77	21	7	3.00

1993 Season

	Avg	AB	H	2B	3B	HR	RBI	BB	SO	OBP	SLG
vs. Left	.294	17	5	2	0	0	1	2	4	.400	.412
vs. Right	.258	31	8	2	0	0	1	5	8	.361	.323

	Avg	AB	H	2B	3B	HR	RBI	BB	SO	OBP	SLG
Scoring Posn	.167	12	2	0	0	0	2	0	5	.167	.167
Close & Late	.000	4	0	0	0	0	0	2	1	.333	.000

Francisco Cabrera — Braves

Age 27 – Bats Right

	Avg	G	AB	R	H	2B	3B	HR	RBI	BB	SO	HBP	GDP	SB	CS	OBP	SLG	IBB	SH	SF	#Pit	#P/PA	GB	FB	G/F
1993 Season	.241	70	83	8	20	3	0	4	11	8	21	0	2	0	0	.308	.422	1	0	0	365	4.01	31	20	1.55
Career (1989-1993)	.254	196	351	32	89	17	1	17	62	21	69	0	11	2	1	.294	.453	1	0	2	1374	3.67	128	111	1.15

1993 Season

	Avg	AB	H	2B	3B	HR	RBI	BB	SO	OBP	SLG
vs. Left	.280	50	14	3	0	4	10	7	13	.368	.580

	Avg	AB	H	2B	3B	HR	RBI	BB	SO	OBP	SLG
Scoring Posn	.160	25	4	0	0	1	7	5	9	.300	.280

1993 Season	Avg	AB	H	2B	3B	HR	RBI	BB	SO	OBP	SLG		Avg	AB	H	2B	3B	HR	RBI	BB	SO	OBP	SLG
vs. Right	.182	33	6	0	0	0	1	1	8	.206	.182	Close & Late	.148	27	4	1	0	0	1	2	10	.207	.185

Greg Cadaret — Royals

Age 32 – Pitches Left

	ERA	W	L	Sv	G	GS	IP	BB	SO	Avg	H	2B	3B	HR	RBI	OBP	SLG	GF	IR	IRS	Hld	SvOp	SB	CS	GB	FB	G/F
1993 Season	4.31	3	2	1	47	0	48.0	30	25	.293	54	8	0	3	30	.398	.386	18	22	7	5	1	3	3	80	37	2.16
Last Five Years	4.04	25	25	8	261	35	514.2	284	363	.268	518	98	11	38	257	.362	.389	53	194	64	37	17	43	40	726	491	1.48

1993 Season

	ERA	W	L	Sv	G	GS	IP	H	HR	BB	SO		Avg	AB	H	2B	3B	HR	RBI	BB	SO	OBP	SLG
Home	2.60	1	2	1	26	0	27.2	29	1	10	12	vs. Left	.333	63	21	2	0	0	8	7	6	.408	.365
Away	6.64	2	0	0	21	0	20.1	25	2	20	13	vs. Right	.273	121	33	6	0	3	22	23	19	.393	.397
Starter	0.00	0	0	0	0	0	0.0	0	0	0	0	Scoring Posn	.333	54	18	2	0	1	24	13	6	.463	.426
Reliever	4.31	3	2	1	47	0	48.0	54	3	30	25	Close & Late	.351	57	20	1	0	1	10	10	5	.404	.421
0 Days rest	0.77	1	0	1	8	0	11.2	9	0	4	2	None on/out	.267	45	12	1	0	1	1	3	4	.340	.356
1 or 2 Days rest	7.71	0	0	0	19	0	16.1	21	3	15	13	First Pitch	.304	23	7	2	0	0	0	4	0	.429	.391
3+ Days rest	3.60	2	2	0	20	0	20.0	24	0	11	10	Ahead in Count	.219	64	14	0	0	0	5	0	20	.231	.219
Pre-All Star	5.23	2	1	1	33	0	31.0	39	3	22	21	Behind in Count	.419	62	26	4	0	2	18	12	0	.514	.581
Post-All Star	2.65	1	1	0	14	0	17.0	15	0	8	4	Two Strikes	.211	71	15	2	0	1	8	14	25	.349	.282

Last Five Years

	ERA	W	L	Sv	G	GS	IP	H	HR	BB	SO		Avg	AB	H	2B	3B	HR	RBI	BB	SO	OBP	SLG
Home	3.68	16	10	1	131	19	276.0	263	18	149	194	vs. Left	.256	511	131	23	1	7	60	59	83	.336	.346
Away	4.45	9	15	7	130	16	238.2	255	20	135	169	vs. Right	.273	1420	387	75	10	31	197	225	280	.371	.405
Day	4.51	11	12	5	88	15	199.2	203	16	114	148	Inning 1-6	.259	1102	285	53	5	26	154	152	208	.349	.387
Night	3.74	14	13	3	173	20	315.0	315	22	170	215	Inning 7+	.281	829	233	45	6	12	103	132	155	.380	.393
Grass	4.27	20	17	5	188	29	398.0	391	31	229	291	None on	.264	990	261	52	4	21	21	133	186	.355	.388
Turf	3.24	5	8	3	73	6	116.2	127	7	55	72	Runners on	.273	941	257	46	7	17	236	151	177	.370	.391
April	3.68	4	5	0	37	7	71.0	62	3	39	53	Scoring Posn	.278	568	158	24	5	11	211	111	118	.388	.396
May	3.90	2	6	2	48	8	87.2	87	9	61	46	Close & Late	.285	358	102	14	4	4	45	68	68	.400	.380
June	4.43	4	3	0	51	2	85.1	95	9	45	61	None on/out	.267	453	121	29	1	12	12	62	77	.363	.415
July	4.22	4	4	2	40	5	81.0	91	6	34	46	vs. 1st Batr (relief)	.219	160	35	8	0	1	25	35	28	.364	.288
August	3.96	8	4	1	42	9	116.0	111	8	59	97	First Inning Pitched	.256	714	183	35	3	14	122	111	148	.357	.373
September/October	4.03	3	3	3	43	4	73.2	72	3	46	60	First 15 Pitches	.273	670	183	34	2	10	94	102	113	.371	.375
Starter	4.77	11	14	0	35	35	203.2	227	22	104	140	Pitch 16-30	.248	399	99	22	2	9	61	71	101	.359	.381
Reliever	3.56	14	11	8	226	0	311.0	291	16	180	223	Pitch 31-45	.222	248	55	8	1	3	23	40	47	.325	.298
0 Days rest	0.90	2	0	3	40	0	60.1	39	0	22	41	Pitch 46+	.295	614	181	34	6	16	79	71	102	.370	.448
1 or 2 Days rest	4.81	6	6	2	110	0	149.2	164	15	107	102	First Pitch	.330	233	77	15	2	5	35	16	0	.374	.476
3+ Days rest	3.30	6	5	3	76	0	101.0	88	1	51	80	Ahead in Count	.206	782	161	32	3	7	80	0	284	.209	.281
Pre-All Star	4.32	11	16	2	151	18	271.0	284	25	162	172	Behind in Count	.332	500	166	26	5	17	95	138	0	.470	.506
Post-All Star	3.73	14	9	6	110	17	243.2	234	13	122	191	Two Strikes	.188	899	169	35	4	9	80	128	363	.290	.266

Pitcher vs. Batter (career)

Pitches Best Vs.	Avg	AB	H	2B	3B	HR	RBI	BB	SO	OBP	SLG	Pitches Worst Vs.	Avg	AB	H	2B	3B	HR	RBI	BB	SO	OBP	SLG
Kent Hrbek	.059	17	1	0	0	0	2	3	3	.200	.059	Edgar Martinez	.778	9	7	4	0	0	1	2	0	.818	1.222
Cecil Fielder	.100	10	1	1	0	0	0	1	3	.182	.200	Gary Gaetti	.733	15	11	2	0	1	7	4	1	.750	1.067
Albert Belle	.111	9	1	0	0	0	1	1	2	.182	.111	Dave Winfield	.545	11	6	2	0	0	3	3	1	.600	.727
Devon White	.115	26	3	0	0	1	3	1	4	.148	.231	Tony Fernandez	.500	10	5	1	1	1	4	1	1	.500	1.100
Junior Felix	.167	12	2	0	0	0	0	0	4	.167	.167	Paul Molitor	.385	13	5	2	0	1	5	5	2	.556	.769

Ivan Calderon — White Sox

Age 32 – Bats Right

	Avg	G	AB	R	H	2B	3B	HR	RBI	BB	SO	HBP	GDP	SB	CS	OBP	SLG	IBB	SH	SF	#Pit	#P/PA	GB	FB	G/F
1993 Season	.209	82	239	26	50	10	2	1	22	21	33	1	13	4	2	.274	.280	1	2	2	919	3.47	105	67	1.57
Last Five Years	.275	579	2108	282	580	124	18	51	282	182	292	9	70	75	37	.331	.424	20	5	27	7990	3.43	821	628	1.31

1993 Season

	Avg	AB	H	2B	3B	HR	RBI	BB	SO	OBP	SLG		Avg	AB	H	2B	3B	HR	RBI	BB	SO	OBP	SLG
vs. Left	.127	63	8	2	0	0	2	5	8	.188	.159	Scoring Posn	.238	63	15	5	1	0	21	8	6	.324	.349
vs. Right	.239	176	42	8	2	1	20	16	25	.304	.324	Close & Late	.238	42	10	1	1	0	5	2	3	.289	.310
Home	.191	89	17	5	2	0	12	8	11	.258	.292	None on/out	.214	56	12	2	0	0	0	4	12	.267	.250
Away	.220	150	33	5	0	1	10	13	22	.283	.273	Batting #5	.211	38	8	3	1	0	7	4	7	.279	.342
First Pitch	.261	46	12	4	2	0	11	1	0	.286	.435	Batting #6	.217	115	25	2	1	1	8	11	17	.283	.278
Ahead in Count	.276	58	16	3	0	1	4	6	0	.344	.379	Other	.198	86	17	5	0	0	7	6	9	.258	.256
Behind in Count	.179	95	17	2	0	0	6	0	24	.179	.200	Pre-All Star	.222	189	42	7	2	1	17	19	25	.295	.296
Two Strikes	.109	92	10	2	0	0	3	14	33	.226	.130	Post-All Star	.160	50	8	3	0	0	5	2	8	.189	.220

Last Five Years

	Avg	AB	H	2B	3B	HR	RBI	BB	SO	OBP	SLG		Avg	AB	H	2B	3B	HR	RBI	BB	SO	OBP	SLG
vs. Left	.306	686	210	47	8	21	92	69	77	.369	.490	Scoring Posn	.285	544	155	30	6	18	224	61	67	.343	.461
vs. Right	.260	1422	370	77	10	30	190	113	215	.313	.392	Close & Late	.278	349	97	20	2	8	41	36	53	.346	.415
Groundball	.276	558	154	27	5	8	62	50	83	.338	.385	None on/out	.270	445	120	29	2	11	11	38	65	.329	.418
Flyball	.250	472	118	25	2	15	66	39	67	.302	.407	Batting #3	.289	1319	381	87	10	31	179	130	178	.351	.440
Home	.274	984	270	58	14	17	130	88	136	.332	.414	Batting #4	.244	332	81	15	4	12	50	18	48	.288	.422
Away	.276	1124	310	66	4	34	152	94	156	.331	.432	Other	.258	457	118	22	4	8	53	34	66	.306	.376
Day	.279	577	161	36	5	12	82	50	83	.336	.421	April	.231	333	77	19	0	9	50	29	53	.295	.369
Night	.274	1531	419	88	13	39	200	132	209	.330	.425	May	.302	410	124	23	4	11	67	36	54	.354	.459
Grass	.283	1386	392	82	15	32	187	110	180	.334	.433	June	.296	365	108	25	4	9	45	36	52	.356	.460
Turf	.260	722	188	42	3	19	95	72	112	.326	.406	July	.284	285	81	12	4	4	35	25	34	.341	.396

Last Five Years

	Avg	AB	H	2B	3B	HR	RBI	BB	SO	OBP	SLG		Avg	AB	H	2B	3B	HR	RBI	BB	SO	OBP	SLG
First Pitch	.314	423	133	24	6	12	69	12	0	.336	.485	August	.283	364	103	26	2	11	47	22	48	.323	.456
Ahead in Count	.342	468	160	34	5	16	85	80	0	.430	.538	September/October	.248	351	87	19	4	7	38	34	51	.315	.385
Behind in Count	.210	841	177	36	6	15	85	0	233	.212	.321	Pre-All Star	.274	1192	327	69	9	29	168	107	169	.332	.420
Two Strikes	.213	844	180	35	4	16	80	84	292	.283	.321	Post-All Star	.276	916	253	55	9	22	114	75	123	.331	.428

Batter vs. Pitcher (career)

Hits Best Against	Avg	AB	H	2B	3B	HR	RBI	BB	SO	OBP	SLG	Hits Worst Against	Avg	AB	H	2B	3B	HR	RBI	BB	SO	OBP	SLG
Tom Bolton	.417	12	5	1	0	2	4	0	1	.417	1.000	Mark Eichhorn	.000	11	0	0	0	0	0	0	5	.000	.000
Dennis Rasmussen	.400	15	6	0	0	3	6	2	3	.471	1.000	Mike Witt	.071	28	2	0	0	0	1	2	6	.129	.071
Teddy Higuera	.391	23	9	3	1	1	7	3	5	.462	.739	Todd Stottlemyre	.071	14	1	1	0	0	0	0	4	.071	.143
Mark Gubicza	.375	16	6	3	0	2	4	0	3	.375	.938	Lee Smith	.100	10	1	0	0	0	0	1	3	.182	.100
Melido Perez	.364	11	4	2	1	0	2	3	3	.500	.727	Scott Sanderson	.125	16	2	0	0	0	0	0	0	.125	.125

Ken Caminiti — Astros

Age 31 – Bats Both

	Avg	G	AB	R	H	2B	3B	HR	RBI	BB	SO	HBP	GDP	SB	CS	OBP	SLG	IBB	SH	SF	#Pit	#P/PA	GB	FB	G/F
1993 Season	.262	143	543	75	142	31	0	13	75	49	88	0	15	8	5	.321	.390	10	1	3	2145	3.60	188	160	1.18
Last Five Years	.260	744	2749	331	716	143	10	53	340	238	431	9	69	35	19	.319	.378	46	12	19	10523	3.48	982	800	1.23

1993 Season

	Avg	AB	H	2B	3B	HR	RBI	BB	SO	OBP	SLG		Avg	AB	H	2B	3B	HR	RBI	BB	SO	OBP	SLG
vs. Left	.246	187	46	14	0	5	36	21	22	.319	.401	Scoring Posn	.264	163	43	13	0	3	61	24	28	.353	.399
vs. Right	.270	356	96	17	0	8	39	28	66	.322	.385	Close & Late	.288	80	23	6	0	2	9	7	12	.345	.438
Groundball	.273	172	47	12	0	3	29	13	27	.321	.395	None on/out	.246	138	34	6	0	2	2	7	19	.283	.333
Flyball	.286	84	24	7	0	4	19	11	18	.365	.512	Batting #4	.237	173	41	6	0	1	18	19	33	.309	.289
Home	.257	288	74	19	0	5	45	22	46	.308	.375	Batting #5	.272	356	97	25	0	12	56	28	55	.325	.444
Away	.267	255	68	12	0	8	30	27	42	.336	.408	Other	.286	14	4	0	0	0	1	2	0	.375	.286
Day	.276	156	43	11	0	3	22	19	25	.352	.404	April	.226	84	19	6	0	3	15	7	14	.286	.405
Night	.256	387	99	20	0	10	53	30	63	.308	.385	May	.260	104	27	7	0	5	21	3	16	.280	.471
Grass	.264	174	46	7	0	7	23	20	26	.338	.425	June	.265	98	26	7	0	1	8	5	15	.301	.367
Turf	.260	369	96	24	0	6	52	29	62	.313	.374	July	.253	79	20	4	0	0	12	6	14	.299	.304
First Pitch	.253	95	24	4	0	1	12	8	0	.311	.326	August	.238	84	20	3	0	2	8	12	14	.330	.345
Ahead in Count	.344	131	45	10	0	4	22	22	0	.438	.511	September/October	.319	94	30	4	0	2	11	16	15	.418	.426
Behind in Count	.221	213	47	13	0	6	29	0	71	.219	.366	Pre-All Star	.260	327	85	23	0	9	52	21	52	.304	.413
Two Strikes	.209	225	47	12	0	5	21	19	88	.269	.329	Post-All Star	.264	216	57	8	0	4	23	28	36	.346	.356

1993 By Position

Position	Avg	AB	H	2B	3B	HR	RBI	BB	SO	OBP	SLG	G	GS	Innings	PO	A	E	DP	Fld Pct	Rng Fctr	In Zone	Outs	Zone Rtg	MLB Zone
As 3b	.262	542	142	31	0	13	75	49	88	.322	.391	143	142	1236.2	123	262	24	22	.941	2.80	352	295	.838	.834

Last Five Years

	Avg	AB	H	2B	3B	HR	RBI	BB	SO	OBP	SLG		Avg	AB	H	2B	3B	HR	RBI	BB	SO	OBP	SLG
vs. Left	.283	1032	292	62	5	27	160	77	136	.331	.431	Scoring Posn	.271	763	207	45	2	15	277	112	129	.358	.394
vs. Right	.247	1717	424	81	5	26	180	161	295	.313	.345	Close & Late	.263	483	127	18	3	10	47	44	95	.324	.375
Groundball	.262	942	247	48	4	19	117	77	140	.319	.382	None on/out	.278	669	186	40	3	10	10	36	95	.319	.392
Flyball	.260	565	147	36	4	19	86	59	97	.332	.439	Batting #5	.259	1116	289	66	2	26	147	104	173	.323	.392
Home	.275	1401	385	88	5	26	190	120	224	.331	.400	Batting #6	.283	481	136	20	3	15	55	34	75	.330	.430
Away	.246	1348	331	55	5	27	150	118	207	.307	.354	Other	.253	1152	291	57	5	12	138	100	183	.311	.342
Day	.265	762	202	40	5	11	85	73	132	.328	.374	April	.264	349	92	21	0	8	43	27	58	.319	.393
Night	.259	1987	514	103	5	42	255	165	299	.316	.379	May	.256	441	113	17	2	11	57	34	56	.310	.379
Grass	.249	839	209	30	4	19	87	74	127	.310	.362	June	.256	496	127	28	1	8	56	38	80	.305	.365
Turf	.265	1910	507	113	6	34	253	164	304	.324	.384	July	.278	449	125	23	4	7	65	38	58	.335	.394
First Pitch	.308	487	150	27	1	9	68	33	0	.355	.423	August	.249	489	122	32	2	8	62	54	92	.324	.372
Ahead in Count	.317	652	207	42	4	19	99	112	0	.417	.482	September/October	.261	525	137	22	1	11	57	47	87	.323	.370
Behind in Count	.206	1114	230	46	2	17	113	0	355	.207	.297	Pre-All Star	.261	1426	372	74	6	29	176	111	209	.314	.382
Two Strikes	.199	1119	223	49	3	15	105	89	431	.258	.289	Post-All Star	.260	1323	344	69	4	24	164	127	222	.325	.373

Batter vs. Pitcher (career)

Hits Best Against	Avg	AB	H	2B	3B	HR	RBI	BB	SO	OBP	SLG	Hits Worst Against	Avg	AB	H	2B	3B	HR	RBI	BB	SO	OBP	SLG
Bobby Ojeda	.611	18	11	2	0	1	4	4	1	.682	.889	Chris Hammond	.077	26	2	0	0	0	2	0	4	.077	.077
Pete Schourek	.500	12	6	0	0	2	5	2	1	.571	1.000	Shawn Boskie	.077	13	1	0	0	0	0	0	1	.077	.077
Mitch Williams	.417	12	5	0	0	1	3	3	4	.533	.667	Jeff Innis	.083	12	1	0	0	0	0	0	1	.083	.083
Mark Grant	.400	10	4	0	0	2	7	1	2	.455	1.000	Jay Howell	.125	16	2	0	0	0	0	0	6	.125	.125
Trevor Wilson	.360	25	9	3	0	3	11	3	0	.414	.840	Chris Nabholz	.125	16	2	0	0	0	1	0	1	.125	.125

Kevin Campbell — Athletics

Age 29 – Pitches Right (flyball pitcher)

	ERA	W	L	Sv	G	GS	IP	BB	SO	Avg	H	2B	3B	HR	RBI	OBP	SLG	GF	IR	IRS	Hld	SvOp	SB	CS	GB	FB	G/F
1993 Season	7.31	0	0	0	11	0	16.0	11	9	.313	20	5	0	1	12	.416	.438	4	8	0	0	0	0	2	19	17	1.12
Career (1991-1993)	4.93	3	3	1	57	5	104.0	70	63	.254	99	20	1	9	51	.369	.380	12	45	8	6	2	3	7	122	130	0.94

1993 Season

	ERA	W	L	Sv	G	GS	IP	H	HR	BB	SO		Avg	AB	H	2B	3B	HR	RBI	BB	SO	OBP	SLG
Home	4.76	0	0	0	4	0	5.2	4	0	3	5	vs. Left	.417	24	10	1	0	0	3	5	4	.517	.458
Away	8.71	0	0	0	7	0	10.1	16	1	8	4	vs. Right	.250	40	10	4	0	1	9	6	5	.354	.425

Willie Canate — Blue Jays

Age 22 – Bats Right

	Avg	G	AB	R	H	2B	3B	HR	RBI	BB	SO	HBP	GDP	SB	CS	OBP	SLG	IBB	SH	SF	#Pit	#P/PA	GB	FB	G/F
1993 Season	.213	38	47	12	10	0	0	1	3	6	15	1	2	1	1	.309	.277	0	2	1	215	3.77	13	12	1.08

1993 Season

	Avg	AB	H	2B	3B	HR	RBI	BB	SO	OBP	SLG		Avg	AB	H	2B	3B	HR	RBI	BB	SO	OBP	SLG
vs. Left	.222	18	4	0	0	0	1	1	9	.250	.222	Scoring Posn	.182	11	2	0	0	0	2	1	3	.286	.182
vs. Right	.207	29	6	0	0	1	2	5	6	.343	.310	Close & Late	.200	5	1	0	0	1	1	0	0	.200	.800

Casey Candaele — Astros

Age 33 – Bats Both

	Avg	G	AB	R	H	2B	3B	HR	RBI	BB	SO	HBP	GDP	SB	CS	OBP	SLG	IBB	SH	SF	#Pit	#P/PA	GB	FB	G/F
1993 Season	.240	75	121	18	29	8	0	1	7	10	14	0	0	2	3	.298	.331	0	0	0	507	3.87	49	34	1.44
Last Five Years	.252	491	1164	111	293	48	14	9	97	105	141	4	14	25	12	.314	.340	15	12	9	4490	3.47	455	325	1.40

1993 Season

	Avg	AB	H	2B	3B	HR	RBI	BB	SO	OBP	SLG		Avg	AB	H	2B	3B	HR	RBI	BB	SO	OBP	SLG
vs. Left	.268	41	11	1	0	1	2	4	4	.333	.366	Scoring Posn	.207	29	6	3	0	0	6	1	5	.233	.310
vs. Right	.225	80	18	7	0	0	5	6	10	.279	.313	Close & Late	.323	31	10	3	0	0	2	2	5	.364	.419
Home	.196	56	11	3	0	0	3	5	5	.262	.250	None on/out	.256	43	11	3	0	0	0	4	3	.319	.326
Away	.277	65	18	5	0	1	4	5	9	.329	.400	Batting #1	.314	35	11	4	0	1	4	2	2	.351	.514
First Pitch	.100	10	1	0	0	0	1	0	0	.100	.100	Batting #9	.170	47	8	1	0	0	0	5	8	.250	.191
Ahead in Count	.385	26	10	4	0	1	4	6	0	.500	.654	Other	.256	39	10	3	0	0	3	3	4	.310	.333
Behind in Count	.200	60	12	3	0	0	2	0	14	.200	.250	Pre-All Star	.234	64	15	5	0	0	2	7	7	.310	.313
Two Strikes	.237	59	14	2	0	0	2	4	14	.286	.271	Post-All Star	.246	57	14	3	0	1	5	3	7	.283	.351

Last Five Years

	Avg	AB	H	2B	3B	HR	RBI	BB	SO	OBP	SLG		Avg	AB	H	2B	3B	HR	RBI	BB	SO	OBP	SLG
vs. Left	.294	453	133	18	3	5	34	45	42	.358	.380	Scoring Posn	.256	273	70	12	5	2	87	32	47	.329	.359
vs. Right	.225	711	160	30	11	4	63	60	99	.285	.315	Close & Late	.281	274	77	15	4	1	33	29	33	.348	.376
Groundball	.252	397	100	10	5	2	34	27	43	.300	.317	None on/out	.240	317	76	15	2	2	2	34	38	.317	.319
Flyball	.197	254	50	10	1	3	18	31	35	.280	.280	Batting #2	.258	194	50	5	3	1	18	15	22	.313	.330
Home	.255	576	147	23	11	3	57	63	65	.329	.349	Batting #8	.274	383	105	23	6	3	33	39	44	.340	.389
Away	.248	588	146	25	3	6	40	42	76	.298	.332	Other	.235	587	138	20	5	5	46	51	75	.297	.312
Day	.257	319	82	18	4	4	28	29	38	.320	.376	April	.224	125	28	3	3	2	12	8	17	.267	.344
Night	.250	845	211	30	10	5	69	76	103	.311	.327	May	.208	212	44	9	1	0	11	19	27	.273	.259
Grass	.268	358	96	15	1	5	32	24	47	.313	.358	June	.254	193	49	7	3	3	17	22	28	.332	.368
Turf	.244	806	197	33	13	4	65	81	94	.314	.333	July	.280	207	58	11	4	3	14	23	24	.350	.415
First Pitch	.282	177	50	9	0	0	16	9	0	.312	.333	August	.259	185	48	10	2	0	18	14	22	.310	.335
Ahead in Count	.272	246	67	13	6	6	36	67	0	.424	.447	September/October	.273	242	66	8	1	1	25	19	23	.328	.326
Behind in Count	.214	523	112	14	5	2	26	0	126	.219	.272	Pre-All Star	.224	603	135	22	7	7	47	53	82	.285	.318
Two Strikes	.217	483	105	10	6	1	30	25	141	.259	.269	Post-All Star	.282	561	158	26	7	2	50	52	59	.344	.364

Batter vs. Pitcher (career)

Hits Best Against	Avg	AB	H	2B	3B	HR	RBI	BB	SO	OBP	SLG	Hits Worst Against	Avg	AB	H	2B	3B	HR	RBI	BB	SO	OBP	SLG
Bob Patterson	.583	12	7	2	0	0	1	0	0	.583	.750	John Smoltz	.056	18	1	0	0	0	1	3	1	.190	.056
Fernando Valenzuela	.476	21	10	2	0	2	4	2	1	.522	.857	Bob Tewksbury	.071	14	1	1	0	0	0	1	4	.133	.143
Jamie Moyer	.462	13	6	4	0	0	0	1	0	.500	.769	Bob Walk	.083	12	1	0	0	0	0	1	0	.154	.083
Bobby Ojeda	.444	27	12	1	1	1	2	2	3	.483	.667	Bryn Smith	.091	11	1	0	0	0	0	1	1	.167	.091
Ramon Martinez	.400	10	4	0	0	0	2	2	3	.500	.400	Mike Jackson	.100	10	1	0	0	0	1	0	1	.091	.100

John Candelaria — Pirates

Age 40 – Pitches Left

	ERA	W	L	Sv	G	GS	IP	BB	SO	Avg	H	2B	3B	HR	RBI	OBP	SLG	GF	IR	IRS	Hld	SvOp	SB	CS	GB	FB	G/F
1993 Season	8.24	0	3	1	24	0	19.2	9	17	.313	25	5	2	2	18	.385	.500	6	15	5	4	3	1	1	21	25	0.84
Last Five Years	4.39	13	20	13	202	9	223.2	69	192	.267	229	43	11	28	128	.318	.440	42	191	48	42	23	10	8	265	252	1.05

1993 Season

	ERA	W	L	Sv	G	GS	IP	H	HR	BB	SO		Avg	AB	H	2B	3B	HR	RBI	BB	SO	OBP	SLG
Home	8.74	0	3	1	11	0	11.1	12	2	8	7	vs. Left	.290	31	9	2	0	0	4	1	12	.333	.355
Away	7.56	0	0	0	13	0	8.1	13	0	1	10	vs. Right	.327	49	16	3	2	2	14	8	5	.414	.592

Last Five Years

	ERA	W	L	Sv	G	GS	IP	H	HR	BB	SO		Avg	AB	H	2B	3B	HR	RBI	BB	SO	OBP	SLG
Home	4.54	6	11	9	94	4	111.0	108	15	33	97	vs. Left	.219	270	59	9	3	2	31	17	94	.263	.296
Away	4.23	7	9	4	108	5	112.2	121	13	36	95	vs. Right	.289	589	170	34	8	26	97	52	98	.342	.506
Day	2.14	4	1	4	52	2	63.0	52	4	14	51	Inning 1-6	.261	291	76	13	4	12	39	20	54	.309	.457
Night	5.27	9	19	9	150	7	160.2	177	24	55	141	Inning 7+	.269	568	153	30	7	16	89	49	138	.322	.431
Grass	4.64	9	12	5	124	6	126.0	123	17	44	123	None on	.274	471	129	30	3	17	17	24	93	.313	.459
Turf	4.05	4	8	8	78	3	97.2	106	11	25	69	Runners on	.258	388	100	13	8	11	111	45	99	.322	.418
April	4.04	4	4	3	35	5	69.0	63	9	16	51	Scoring Posn	.244	242	59	9	8	6	98	35	62	.320	.421
May	4.62	4	1	4	35	2	39.0	40	8	9	35	Close & Late	.270	318	86	18	5	7	57	36	86	.337	.425
June	3.51	3	4	2	39	0	33.1	30	2	11	29	None on/out	.239	205	49	13	0	6	6	7	47	.271	.390
July	2.92	2	2	2	31	0	24.2	20	1	8	25	vs. 1st Batr (relief)	.247	170	42	6	3	4	34	10	48	.285	.388
August	7.22	0	6	1	28	2	28.2	41	4	15	20	First Inning Pitched	.248	455	113	23	7	12	81	40	112	.303	.409
September/October	4.34	0	3	1	34	0	29.0	35	4	10	32	First 15 Pitches	.267	472	126	29	6	15	82	41	102	.321	.449
Starter	5.06	3	5	0	9	9	53.1	57	9	14	37	Pitch 16-30	.232	194	45	6	1	2	14	12	59	.271	.304
Reliever	4.17	10	15	13	193	0	170.1	172	19	55	155	Pitch 31-45	.253	83	21	3	1	5	13	8	13	.315	.494
0 Days rest	3.26	2	4	2	44	0	30.1	27	1	12	30	Pitch 46+	.336	110	37	5	3	6	19	8	18	.387	.600
1 or 2 Days rest	5.23	4	7	5	80	0	74.0	86	14	29	63	First Pitch	.278	115	32	4	2	3	17	11	0	.336	.426
3+ Days rest	3.41	4	4	6	69	0	66.0	59	4	14	62	Ahead in Count	.209	422	88	18	3	7	37	0	176	.209	.315

Last Five Years

	ERA	W	L	Sv	G	GS	IP	H	HR	BB	SO
Pre-All Star	3.87	11	9	9	122	7	149.0	136	19	39	121
Post-All Star	5.42	2	11	4	80	2	74.2	93	9	30	71

	Avg	AB	H	2B	3B	HR	RBI	BB	SO	OBP	SLG
Behind in Count	.380	192	73	16	2	12	46	28	0	.451	.672
Two Strikes	.161	391	63	13	1	7	35	30	192	.218	.253

Pitcher vs. Batter (since 1984)

Pitches Best Vs.	Avg	AB	H	2B	3B	HR	RBI	BB	SO	OBP	SLG
Kirby Puckett	.091	22	2	1	0	0	4	4	6	.222	.136
Dale Sveum	.091	11	1	0	0	0	0	2	3	.231	.091
Will Clark	.143	14	2	0	0	0	1	1	6	.200	.143
Lou Whitaker	.167	12	2	0	0	0	3	1	4	.200	.167
Don Slaught	.182	11	2	0	0	0	0	0	3	.182	.182

Pitches Worst Vs.	Avg	AB	H	2B	3B	HR	RBI	BB	SO	OBP	SLG
Scott Fletcher	.579	19	11	2	1	0	1	3	0	.636	.789
Glenn Wilson	.526	19	10	2	0	2	3	1	3	.550	.947
Carlton Fisk	.417	12	5	0	0	3	9	3	1	.533	1.167
Dave Valle	.400	10	4	2	0	1	3	1	0	.455	.900
Barry Bonds	.400	10	4	3	1	0	4	1	1	.455	.900

Tom Candiotti — Dodgers

Age 36 – Pitches Right

	ERA	W	L	Sv	G	GS	IP	BB	SO	Avg	H	2B	3B	HR	RBI	OBP	SLG	CG	ShO	Sup	QS	#P/S	SB	CS	GB	FB	G/F
1993 Season	3.12	8	10	0	33	32	213.2	71	155	.241	192	33	4	12	75	.305	.338	2	0	2.53	22	106	25	6	275	226	1.22
Last Five Years	3.09	60	59	0	161	156	1063.1	317	726	.242	966	161	22	70	365	.299	.346	21	3	3.61	105	107	123	31	1475	1078	1.37

1993 Season

	ERA	W	L	Sv	G	GS	IP	H	HR	BB	SO
Home	1.95	5	3	0	16	15	115.2	90	5	33	84
Away	4.50	3	7	0	17	17	98.0	102	7	38	71
Day	3.07	3	3	0	9	8	55.2	41	3	27	44
Night	3.13	5	7	0	24	24	158.0	151	9	44	111
Grass	2.44	6	5	0	23	22	155.0	133	6	49	114
Turf	4.91	2	5	0	10	10	58.2	59	6	22	41
April	6.55	0	3	0	4	4	22.0	24	3	13	16
May	2.61	3	1	0	6	6	41.1	39	0	12	32
June	1.80	0	1	0	5	5	35.0	24	2	11	33
July	1.49	3	0	0	6	6	42.1	26	2	13	29
August	1.46	2	0	0	5	5	37.0	33	2	7	26
September/October	6.50	0	5	0	7	6	36.0	46	3	15	19
Starter	2.97	8	10	0	32	32	212.1	188	11	70	155
Reliever	27.00	0	0	0	1	0	1.1	4	1	1	0
0-3 Days Rest	3.27	0	0	0	2	2	11.0	10	0	3	6
4 Days Rest	2.01	4	3	0	12	12	89.2	70	4	28	58
5+ Days Rest	3.71	4	7	0	18	18	111.2	108	7	39	91
Pre-All Star	3.02	3	5	0	18	18	116.1	99	5	39	93
Post-All Star	3.24	5	5	0	15	14	97.1	93	7	32	62

	Avg	AB	H	2B	3B	HR	RBI	BB	SO	OBP	SLG
vs. Left	.231	415	96	15	2	5	39	46	75	.305	.313
vs. Right	.251	382	96	18	2	7	36	25	80	.304	.364
Inning 1-6	.256	673	172	30	3	11	70	62	132	.320	.358
Inning 7+	.161	124	20	3	1	1	5	9	23	.216	.226
None on	.222	477	106	15	3	8	8	37	94	.285	.317
Runners on	.269	320	86	18	1	4	67	34	61	.332	.369
Scoring Posn	.235	183	43	9	1	2	60	27	39	.323	.328
Close & Late	.155	97	15	2	1	0	3	9	17	.226	.196
None on/out	.216	208	45	7	0	3	3	13	40	.266	.293
vs. 1st Batr (relief)	1.000	1	1	0	0	0	0	0	0	1.000	1.000
First Inning Pitched	.286	133	38	6	2	1	20	22	23	.387	.383
First 75 Pitches	.257	538	138	23	2	12	60	50	105	.321	.374
Pitch 76-90	.234	107	25	5	1	0	7	5	21	.272	.299
Pitch 91-105	.176	74	13	2	0	0	2	8	15	.265	.203
Pitch 106+	.205	78	16	3	1	0	6	8	14	.276	.269
First Pitch	.259	108	28	4	1	2	16	1	0	.268	.370
Ahead in Count	.224	362	81	10	2	4	21	0	115	.228	.296
Behind in Count	.313	144	45	7	1	3	18	37	0	.451	.438
Two Strikes	.198	388	77	13	1	5	30	33	155	.264	.276

Last Five Years

	ERA	W	L	Sv	G	GS	IP	H	HR	BB	SO
Home	2.90	31	24	0	78	74	527.1	484	31	147	361
Away	3.27	29	35	0	83	82	536.0	482	39	170	365
Day	3.25	24	16	0	47	45	310.1	279	20	102	228
Night	3.02	36	43	0	114	111	753.0	687	50	215	498
Grass	3.06	45	44	0	119	114	790.2	715	55	220	533
Turf	3.17	15	15	0	42	42	272.2	251	15	97	193
April	3.85	10	5	0	19	19	128.2	117	14	43	101
May	2.94	15	8	0	27	27	187.0	169	7	56	124
June	2.81	7	14	0	29	28	192.1	176	15	58	132
July	2.18	11	9	0	28	25	185.2	139	11	54	128
August	2.63	10	7	0	27	27	184.2	161	13	46	133
September/October	4.38	7	16	0	31	30	185.0	204	10	60	108
Starter	3.06	59	59	0	156	156	1054.0	953	68	313	717
Reliever	6.75	1	0	0	5	0	9.1	13	2	4	9
0-3 Days Rest	3.98	0	4	0	10	10	61.0	56	7	16	38
4 Days Rest	2.85	38	30	0	83	83	591.1	518	40	165	385
5+ Days Rest	3.23	21	25	0	63	63	401.2	379	21	132	294
Pre-All Star	3.10	34	30	0	85	82	560.2	504	41	173	400
Post-All Star	3.08	26	29	0	76	74	502.2	462	29	144	326

	Avg	AB	H	2B	3B	HR	RBI	BB	SO	OBP	SLG
vs. Left	.244	2069	505	69	17	31	187	194	323	.308	.339
vs. Right	.239	1927	461	92	5	39	178	123	403	.290	.353
Inning 1-6	.243	3302	802	138	16	59	314	263	613	.301	.348
Inning 7+	.236	694	164	23	6	11	51	54	113	.292	.334
None on	.239	2440	583	104	15	42	42	167	460	.292	.345
Runners on	.246	1556	383	57	7	28	323	150	266	.310	.346
Scoring Posn	.237	916	217	33	5	18	295	116	163	.318	.343
Close & Late	.224	411	92	13	3	4	30	37	72	.291	.299
None on/out	.230	1050	242	45	6	16	16	60	203	.274	.330
vs. 1st Batr (relief)	.400	5	2	0	0	0	1	0	1	.400	.400
First Inning Pitched	.265	633	168	30	5	8	80	71	116	.342	.367
First 75 Pitches	.242	2713	656	107	13	50	255	219	491	.301	.346
Pitch 76-90	.242	488	118	20	2	8	35	29	88	.285	.340
Pitch 91-105	.236	411	97	20	3	4	25	35	79	.298	.328
Pitch 106+	.247	384	95	14	4	8	50	34	68	.309	.367
First Pitch	.299	492	147	24	2	10	58	10	0	.316	.417
Ahead in Count	.190	1710	325	48	7	19	106	0	570	.195	.260
Behind in Count	.313	903	283	55	6	24	116	156	0	.412	.467
Two Strikes	.186	1831	341	58	9	23	126	150	726	.251	.265

Pitcher vs. Batter (since 1984)

Pitches Best Vs.	Avg	AB	H	2B	3B	HR	RBI	BB	SO	OBP	SLG
Spike Owen	.034	29	1	0	0	0	0	2	2	.097	.034
Darren Lewis	.059	17	1	1	0	0	0	0	2	.059	.118
Edgar Martinez	.083	12	1	0	0	0	0	1	5	.154	.083
Bill Spiers	.100	20	2	0	0	0	3	1	5	.136	.100
Alvaro Espinoza	.118	17	2	0	0	0	0	0	5	.118	.118

Pitches Worst Vs.	Avg	AB	H	2B	3B	HR	RBI	BB	SO	OBP	SLG
Alfredo Griffin	.700	10	7	1	0	0	0	1	1	.727	.800
George Bell	.529	34	18	6	0	2	8	3	4	.568	.882
Rafael Palmeiro	.438	16	7	2	0	1	2	1	2	.471	.750
Mike Greenwell	.429	35	15	3	0	3	10	4	0	.487	.771
Kirk Gibson	.412	17	7	1	2	1	4	2	1	.474	.882

Jose Canseco — Rangers

Age 29 – Bats Right (flyball hitter)

	Avg	G	AB	R	H	2B	3B	HR	RBI	BB	SO	HBP	GDP	SB	CS	OBP	SLG	IBB	SH	SF	#Pit	#P/PA	GB	FB	G/F
1993 Season	.255	60	231	30	59	14	1	10	46	16	62	3	6	6	6	.308	.455	2	0	3	1051	4.15	70	68	1.03
Last Five Years	.262	529	1950	342	511	84	5	134	413	252	569	25	51	63	32	.350	.516	24	0	24	9167	4.07	530	583	0.91

1993 Season

	Avg	AB	H	2B	3B	HR	RBI	BB	SO	OBP	SLG
vs. Left	.237	38	9	0	0	3	9	4	9	.302	.474
vs. Right	.259	193	50	14	1	7	37	12	53	.310	.451

	Avg	AB	H	2B	3B	HR	RBI	BB	SO	OBP	SLG
Scoring Posn	.338	65	22	5	0	4	38	5	14	.370	.600
Close & Late	.182	33	6	2	0	0	6	3	12	.263	.242

1993 Season

	Avg	AB	H	2B	3B	HR	RBI	BB	SO	OBP	SLG
Home	.291	110	32	7	1	6	20	6	27	.331	.536
Away	.223	121	27	7	0	4	26	10	35	.289	.380
First Pitch	.389	18	7	1	0	3	6	2	0	.450	.944
Ahead in Count	.422	45	19	5	0	4	14	8	0	.519	.800
Behind in Count	.202	119	24	7	1	2	17	0	47	.211	.328
Two Strikes	.164	134	22	6	1	3	17	6	62	.203	.291

	Avg	AB	H	2B	3B	HR	RBI	BB	SO	OBP	SLG
None on/out	.257	35	9	3	1	1	1	2	8	.297	.486
Batting #3	.254	205	52	11	1	9	39	13	55	.305	.449
Batting #6	.304	23	7	3	0	1	7	3	6	.370	.565
Other	.000	3	0	0	0	0	0	0	1	.000	.000
Pre-All Star	.255	231	59	14	1	10	46	16	62	.308	.455
Post-All Star	.000	0	0	0	0	0	0	0	0	.000	.000

Last Five Years

	Avg	AB	H	2B	3B	HR	RBI	BB	SO	OBP	SLG
vs. Left	.259	441	114	16	1	37	92	69	137	.364	.551
vs. Right	.263	1509	397	68	4	97	321	183	432	.346	.506
Groundball	.264	569	150	24	2	34	122	61	160	.338	.492
Flyball	.257	444	114	16	1	30	89	58	137	.342	.500
Home	.266	902	240	35	2	63	171	128	270	.361	.519
Away	.259	1048	271	49	3	71	242	124	299	.341	.514
Day	.289	667	193	39	4	45	156	87	210	.377	.562
Night	.248	1283	318	45	1	89	257	165	359	.336	.493
Grass	.266	1623	431	70	4	110	341	219	467	.357	.517
Turf	.245	327	80	14	1	24	72	33	102	.314	.514
First Pitch	.383	175	67	7	1	22	60	12	0	.437	.811
Ahead in Count	.381	409	156	23	3	50	147	118	0	.517	.819
Behind in Count	.196	978	192	40	1	37	123	0	454	.203	.353
Two Strikes	.168	1102	185	34	1	34	119	116	569	.249	.293

	Avg	AB	H	2B	3B	HR	RBI	BB	SO	OBP	SLG
Scoring Posn	.285	557	159	24	1	37	284	81	165	.367	.531
Close & Late	.232	293	68	14	0	18	69	31	92	.309	.464
None on/out	.275	357	98	15	2	28	28	46	94	.362	.563
Batting #3	.261	1832	478	75	5	127	388	234	539	.348	.515
Batting #5	.264	53	14	3	0	3	10	12	14	.409	.491
Other	.292	65	19	6	0	4	15	6	16	.342	.569
April	.267	307	82	13	0	19	63	51	83	.374	.495
May	.262	381	100	15	1	25	78	46	114	.338	.504
June	.256	250	64	12	0	22	52	24	63	.336	.568
July	.282	298	84	13	1	28	74	34	70	.359	.614
August	.247	352	87	14	0	19	69	45	123	.337	.449
September/October	.260	362	94	17	3	21	77	52	116	.358	.497
Pre-All Star	.264	996	263	43	2	71	211	126	272	.350	.525
Post-All Star	.260	954	248	41	3	63	202	126	297	.351	.507

Batter vs. Pitcher (career)

Hits Best Against	Avg	AB	H	2B	3B	HR	RBI	BB	SO	OBP	SLG
Dave Johnson	.600	10	6	1	0	2	3	3	2	.692	1.300
Jaime Navarro	.500	14	7	1	0	1	9	4	3	.611	.786
Todd Stottlemyre	.423	26	11	0	0	8	15	4	6	.500	1.346
Bill Gullickson	.364	11	4	0	1	2	3	2	2	.462	1.091
Bob Milacki	.357	14	5	0	0	3	6	1	3	.353	1.000

Hits Worst Against	Avg	AB	H	2B	3B	HR	RBI	BB	SO	OBP	SLG
Duane Ward	.000	17	0	0	0	0	2	0	10	.000	.000
Charles Nagy	.000	12	0	0	0	0	0	2	2	.143	.000
Mike Jackson	.000	11	0	0	0	0	0	2	3	.154	.000
Erik Hanson	.043	23	1	0	0	0	0	3	11	.154	.043
Mike Mussina	.071	14	1	0	0	0	1	0	2	.071	.071

Ozzie Canseco — Cardinals

Age 29 – Bats Right (flyball hitter)

	Avg	G	AB	R	H	2B	3B	HR	RBI	BB	SO	HBP	GDP	SB	CS	OBP	SLG	IBB	SH	SF	#Pit	#P/PA	GB	FB	G/F
1993 Season	.176	6	17	0	3	0	0	0	0	1	3	0	0	0	0	.222	.176	0	0	0	55	3.06	5	6	0.83
Career (1990-1993)	.200	24	65	8	13	6	0	0	4	9	17	0	1	0	0	.297	.292	0	0	0	314	4.24	18	20	0.90

1993 Season

	Avg	AB	H	2B	3B	HR	RBI	BB	SO	OBP	SLG
vs. Left	.222	9	2	0	0	0	0	0	2	.222	.222
vs. Right	.125	8	1	0	0	0	0	1	1	.222	.125

	Avg	AB	H	2B	3B	HR	RBI	BB	SO	OBP	SLG
Scoring Posn	.250	4	1	0	0	0	0	0	2	.250	.250
Close & Late	.333	3	1	0	0	0	0	1	0	.500	.333

Paul Carey — Orioles

Age 26 – Bats Right (groundball hitter)

	Avg	G	AB	R	H	2B	3B	HR	RBI	BB	SO	HBP	GDP	SB	CS	OBP	SLG	IBB	SH	SF	#Pit	#P/PA	GB	FB	G/F
1993 Season	.213	18	47	1	10	1	0	0	3	5	14	0	4	0	0	.288	.234	0	0	0	201	3.87	20	8	2.50

1993 Season

	Avg	AB	H	2B	3B	HR	RBI	BB	SO	OBP	SLG
vs. Left	.000	2	0	0	0	0	0	0	1	.000	.000
vs. Right	.222	45	10	1	0	0	3	5	13	.300	.244

	Avg	AB	H	2B	3B	HR	RBI	BB	SO	OBP	SLG
Scoring Posn	.308	13	4	1	0	0	3	1	0	.357	.385
Close & Late	.500	10	5	1	0	0	2	1	1	.545	.600

Cris Carpenter — Rangers

Age 29 – Pitches Right (flyball pitcher)

	ERA	W	L	Sv	G	GS	IP	BB	SO	Avg	H	2B	3B	HR	RBI	OBP	SLG	GF	IR	IRS	Hld	SvOp	SB	CS	GB	FB	G/F
1993 Season	3.50	4	2	1	56	0	69.1	25	53	.248	64	13	2	5	34	.320	.372	17	45	14	14	4	5	1	78	75	1.04
Last Five Years	3.46	23	14	2	228	5	299.1	100	187	.235	261	58	8	27	149	.301	.375	58	167	54	35	14	28	11	354	378	0.94

1993 Season

	ERA	W	L	Sv	G	GS	IP	H	HR	BB	SO
Home	4.19	3	1	1	29	0	38.2	39	3	15	33
Away	2.64	1	1	0	27	0	30.2	25	2	10	20
Starter	0.00	0	0	0	0	0	0.0	0	0	0	0
Reliever	3.50	4	2	1	56	0	69.1	64	5	25	53
0 Days rest	0.00	1	0	0	7	0	6.0	4	0	2	4
1 or 2 Days rest	3.57	2	0	1	29	0	40.1	36	2	17	33
3+ Days rest	4.30	1	2	0	20	0	23.0	24	3	6	16
Pre-All Star	3.00	0	1	0	28	0	36.0	29	1	12	25
Post-All Star	4.05	4	1	1	28	0	33.1	35	4	13	28

	Avg	AB	H	2B	3B	HR	RBI	BB	SO	OBP	SLG
vs. Left	.327	110	36	11	1	3	20	14	13	.395	.527
vs. Right	.189	148	28	2	1	2	14	11	40	.259	.257
Scoring Posn	.196	92	18	6	0	0	27	8	24	.264	.261
Close & Late	.262	122	32	5	1	4	18	10	22	.326	.418
None on/out	.298	57	17	2	2	1	1	4	9	.344	.456
First Pitch	.429	35	15	3	0	0	9	2	0	.463	.514
Ahead in Count	.192	125	24	7	1	0	9	0	47	.202	.264
Behind in Count	.280	50	14	2	1	2	8	14	0	.438	.480
Two Strikes	.175	126	22	5	1	1	8	9	53	.237	.254

Last Five Years

	ERA	W	L	Sv	G	GS	IP	H	HR	BB	SO
Home	3.91	10	6	2	110	4	154.1	138	12	53	99
Away	2.98	13	8	0	118	1	145.0	123	15	47	88
Day	2.87	8	5	0	59	3	78.1	69	6	23	46
Night	3.67	15	9	2	169	2	221.0	192	21	77	141
Grass	2.95	8	4	1	88	0	109.2	99	10	35	77
Turf	3.75	15	10	1	140	5	189.2	162	17	65	110

	Avg	AB	H	2B	3B	HR	RBI	BB	SO	OBP	SLG
vs. Left	.259	545	141	40	3	12	76	61	74	.331	.409
vs. Right	.213	564	120	18	5	15	73	39	113	.271	.342
Inning 1-6	.241	324	78	18	3	3	46	25	51	.296	.343
Inning 7+	.233	785	183	40	5	24	103	75	136	.303	.389
None on	.225	609	137	28	5	16	16	39	105	.274	.366
Runners on	.248	500	124	30	3	11	133	61	82	.332	.386

Last Five Years

	ERA	W	L	Sv	G	GS	IP	H	HR	BB	SO
April	2.45	4	3	0	41	2	58.2	43	5	15	31
May	4.02	5	4	1	45	1	53.2	50	3	19	32
June	3.76	3	2	0	39	0	55.0	45	4	23	34
July	4.25	0	4	0	33	0	48.2	43	8	13	34
August	3.72	4	0	1	35	0	38.2	35	2	18	29
September/October	2.62	7	1	0	35	2	44.2	45	5	12	27
Starter	3.00	1	2	0	5	5	27.0	30	1	7	12
Reliever	3.50	22	12	2	223	0	272.1	231	26	93	175
0 Days rest	1.50	9	1	0	47	0	48.0	31	4	11	23
1 or 2 Days rest	4.19	10	9	2	125	0	152.2	140	15	60	105
3+ Days rest	3.39	3	2	0	51	0	71.2	60	7	22	47
Pre-All Star	3.19	12	9	1	138	3	186.0	149	12	61	110
Post-All Star	3.89	11	5	1	90	2	113.1	112	15	39	77

	Avg	AB	H	2B	3B	HR	RBI	BB	SO	OBP	SLG
Scoring Posn	.211	350	74	19	3	4	113	50	62	.309	.317
Close & Late	.248	399	99	24	3	15	61	43	72	.325	.436
None on/out	.241	257	62	9	4	7	7	16	38	.288	.389
vs. 1st Batr (relief)	.261	199	52	6	2	6	32	18	35	.323	.402
First Inning Pitched	.247	705	174	36	7	18	113	65	133	.313	.394
First 15 Pitches	.261	655	171	37	6	18	98	56	116	.322	.418
Pitch 16-30	.176	301	53	11	2	6	33	31	47	.256	.286
Pitch 31-45	.237	93	22	9	0	2	11	8	17	.294	.398
Pitch 46+	.250	60	15	1	0	1	7	5	7	.313	.317
First Pitch	.281	171	48	9	0	6	33	25	0	.369	.439
Ahead in Count	.175	527	92	21	3	4	48	0	164	.181	.249
Behind in Count	.295	241	71	17	3	12	47	43	0	.404	.539
Two Strikes	.174	512	89	23	3	5	46	32	187	.229	.260

Pitcher vs. Batter (career)

Pitches Best Vs.	Avg	AB	H	2B	3B	HR	RBI	BB	SO	OBP	SLG
Barry Bonds	.000	9	0	0	0	0	0	3	3	.250	.000
Eric Davis	.083	12	1	0	0	0	0	0	2	.083	.083
Ricky Jordan	.100	10	1	0	0	0	0	1	0	.182	.100
Spike Owen	.182	11	2	1	0	0	1	0	1	.182	.273
Dave Martinez	.182	11	2	0	0	0	0	1	1	.250	.182

Pitches Worst Vs.	Avg	AB	H	2B	3B	HR	RBI	BB	SO	OBP	SLG
Mark Grace	.538	13	7	1	0	0	1	1	0	.571	.615
Shawon Dunston	.500	12	6	1	1	0	4	0	2	.500	.750
John Kruk	.455	11	5	1	0	1	4	0	1	.417	.818
Dwight Smith	.455	11	5	3	0	0	1	1	2	.500	.727
Tim Raines	.429	7	3	0	1	0	1	4	0	.636	.714

Chuck Carr — Marlins

Age 25 – Bats Both (groundball hitter)

	Avg	G	AB	R	H	2B	3B	HR	RBI	BB	SO	HBP	GDP	SB	CS	OBP	SLG	IBB	SH	SF	#Pit	#P/PA	GB	FB	G/F
1993 Season	.267	142	551	75	147	19	2	4	41	49	74	2	6	58	22	.327	.330	0	7	4	2157	3.52	221	135	1.64
Career (1990-1993)	.260	180	628	84	163	22	2	4	45	58	84	2	6	70	24	.322	.320	0	10	4	2451	3.49	255	157	1.62

1993 Season

	Avg	AB	H	2B	3B	HR	RBI	BB	SO	OBP	SLG
vs. Left	.254	173	44	9	1	2	15	13	33	.309	.353
vs. Right	.272	378	103	10	1	2	26	36	41	.335	.320
Groundball	.239	176	42	4	1	0	12	11	25	.286	.273
Flyball	.226	106	24	3	0	2	13	12	16	.298	.311
Home	.284	271	77	8	0	3	20	28	36	.349	.347
Away	.250	280	70	11	2	1	21	21	38	.305	.314
Day	.261	119	31	1	1	0	3	12	13	.333	.286
Night	.269	432	116	18	1	4	38	37	61	.325	.343
Grass	.280	410	115	12	1	3	28	40	55	.341	.337
Turf	.227	141	32	7	1	1	13	9	19	.283	.312
First Pitch	.364	110	40	4	0	1	8	0	0	.364	.427
Ahead in Count	.345	116	40	6	1	1	7	29	0	.476	.440
Behind in Count	.183	229	42	5	0	1	18	0	64	.187	.218
Two Strikes	.160	231	37	6	0	2	20	20	74	.230	.212

	Avg	AB	H	2B	3B	HR	RBI	BB	SO	OBP	SLG
Scoring Posn	.239	113	27	2	0	2	37	16	21	.328	.310
Close & Late	.356	90	32	4	0	0	9	7	20	.400	.400
None on/out	.293	246	72	8	1	1	1	19	29	.343	.346
Batting #1	.268	549	147	19	2	4	41	49	73	.328	.332
Batting #9	.000	2	0	0	0	0	0	0	1	.000	.000
Other	.000	0	0	0	0	0	0	0	0	.000	.000
April	.226	62	14	4	0	0	0	4	9	.273	.290
May	.288	104	30	5	0	1	18	15	20	.388	.365
June	.237	97	23	4	1	1	12	7	14	.278	.330
July	.259	54	14	2	0	0	2	2	5	.286	.296
August	.303	119	36	3	0	2	6	7	12	.341	.378
September/October	.261	115	30	1	1	0	3	14	14	.341	.287
Pre-All Star	.255	263	67	13	1	2	30	26	43	.322	.335
Post-All Star	.278	288	80	6	1	2	11	23	31	.331	.326

1993 By Position

Position	Avg	AB	H	2B	3B	HR	RBI	BB	SO	OBP	SLG	G	GS	Innings	PO	A	E	DP	Fld Pct	Rng Fctr	In Zone	Outs	Zone Rtg	MLB Zone
As cf	.267	550	147	19	2	4	41	49	73	.327	.331	139	133	1180.2	393	7	6	2	.985	3.05	458	374	.817	.829

Mark Carreon — Giants

Age 30 – Bats Right

	Avg	G	AB	R	H	2B	3B	HR	RBI	BB	SO	HBP	GDP	SB	CS	OBP	SLG	IBB	SH	SF	#Pit	#P/PA	GB	FB	G/F
1993 Season	.327	78	150	22	49	9	1	7	33	13	16	1	8	1	0	.373	.540	2	0	5	624	3.69	57	52	1.10
Last Five Years	.265	435	1061	124	281	44	2	37	137	74	145	7	36	9	5	.314	.415	6	2	10	4274	3.70	366	352	1.04

1993 Season

	Avg	AB	H	2B	3B	HR	RBI	BB	SO	OBP	SLG
vs. Left	.350	100	35	8	0	6	25	11	14	.409	.610
vs. Right	.280	50	14	1	1	1	8	2	2	.296	.400
Home	.280	82	23	6	1	2	12	8	10	.344	.451
Away	.382	68	26	3	0	5	21	5	6	.408	.647
First Pitch	.333	15	5	2	0	0	2	1	0	.375	.467
Ahead in Count	.326	46	15	3	0	2	11	6	0	.389	.522
Behind in Count	.311	61	19	3	1	2	11	0	14	.313	.492
Two Strikes	.276	58	16	2	1	2	11	6	16	.343	.448

	Avg	AB	H	2B	3B	HR	RBI	BB	SO	OBP	SLG
Scoring Posn	.385	39	15	4	1	2	24	7	2	.442	.692
Close & Late	.297	37	11	1	0	0	3	3	2	.341	.324
None on/out	.333	27	9	2	0	1	1	1	4	.357	.519
Batting #6	.316	79	25	4	1	3	18	5	10	.356	.506
Batting #9	.276	29	8	1	0	0	4	3	3	.333	.310
Other	.381	42	16	4	0	4	11	5	3	.429	.762
Pre-All Star	.354	82	29	3	0	5	17	8	10	.400	.573
Post-All Star	.294	68	20	6	1	2	16	5	6	.338	.500

Last Five Years

	Avg	AB	H	2B	3B	HR	RBI	BB	SO	OBP	SLG
vs. Left	.261	568	148	25	0	23	74	39	71	.310	.426
vs. Right	.270	493	133	19	2	14	63	35	74	.319	.402
Groundball	.298	312	93	20	1	6	42	16	27	.332	.426
Flyball	.216	264	57	8	0	9	24	19	58	.273	.348
Home	.249	539	134	26	2	15	59	44	78	.310	.388
Away	.282	522	147	18	0	22	78	30	67	.318	.443
Day	.271	421	114	19	2	15	55	24	56	.311	.432
Night	.261	640	167	25	0	22	82	50	89	.316	.403
Grass	.260	792	206	35	2	28	100	54	111	.310	.415
Turf	.279	269	75	9	0	9	37	20	34	.326	.413

	Avg	AB	H	2B	3B	HR	RBI	BB	SO	OBP	SLG
Scoring Posn	.256	297	76	14	1	6	96	23	41	.308	.370
Close & Late	.271	218	59	4	0	9	23	14	33	.315	.413
None on/out	.271	229	62	11	1	13	13	14	34	.313	.498
Batting #6	.245	379	93	10	1	8	52	19	56	.284	.340
Batting #7	.293	157	46	4	0	7	17	18	28	.369	.452
Other	.270	525	142	30	1	22	68	37	61	.319	.457
April	.293	147	43	7	0	8	20	17	23	.367	.503
May	.280	186	52	9	1	8	27	10	35	.318	.468
June	.256	160	41	3	0	6	17	9	23	.297	.388
July	.207	193	40	9	1	7	27	18	22	.274	.373

Last Five Years

	Avg	AB	H	2B	3B	HR	RBI	BB	SO	OBP	SLG		Avg	AB	H	2B	3B	HR	RBI	BB	SO	OBP	SLG
First Pitch	.307	127	39	6	0	5	21	5	0	.341	.472	August	.233	163	38	5	0	2	15	7	23	.272	.301
Ahead in Count	.274	296	81	15	1	11	41	37	0	.358	.443	September/October	.316	212	67	11	0	6	31	13	19	.355	.453
Behind in Count	.237	438	104	15	1	10	40	0	123	.239	.345	Pre-All Star	.272	562	153	23	1	27	75	45	87	.327	.461
Two Strikes	.238	445	106	15	1	12	44	32	145	.289	.357	Post-All Star	.257	499	128	21	1	10	62	29	58	.299	.363

Batter vs. Pitcher (career)

Hits Best Against	Avg	AB	H	2B	3B	HR	RBI	BB	SO	OBP	SLG	Hits Worst Against	Avg	AB	H	2B	3B	HR	RBI	BB	SO	OBP	SLG
Neal Heaton	.636	11	7	0	0	2	5	0	0	.636	1.182	Scott Sanderson	.083	12	1	0	0	1	2	0	4	.083	.333
Mark Langston	.500	14	7	2	0	0	1	3	1	.588	.643	John Smiley	.133	30	4	0	0	2	2	0	4	.133	.333
Zane Smith	.429	14	6	2	0	0	4	0	1	.429	.571	Tom Glavine	.143	14	2	0	0	0	0	1	1	.200	.143
Rheal Cormier	.429	14	6	1	0	1	3	0	0	.429	.714	Tom Browning	.154	13	2	1	0	0	1	0	0	.154	.231
Randy Tomlin	.364	11	4	0	0	1	1	1	0	.417	.636	Terry Mulholland	.176	17	3	0	0	0	0	0	1	.176	.176

Matias Carrillo — Marlins

Age 31 – Bats Left

	Avg	G	AB	R	H	2B	3B	HR	RBI	BB	SO	HBP	GDP	SB	CS	OBP	SLG	IBB	SH	SF	#Pit	#P/PA	GB	FB	G/F
1993 Season	.255	24	55	4	14	6	0	0	3	1	7	1	5	0	0	.281	.364	0	1	0	188	3.24	21	14	1.50

1993 Season

	Avg	AB	H	2B	3B	HR	RBI	BB	SO	OBP	SLG		Avg	AB	H	2B	3B	HR	RBI	BB	SO	OBP	SLG
vs. Left	.400	5	2	0	0	0	0	1	1	.500	.400	Scoring Posn	.167	12	2	1	0	0	3	0	1	.167	.250
vs. Right	.240	50	12	6	0	0	3	0	6	.255	.360	Close & Late	.231	13	3	1	0	0	1	1	2	.286	.308

Joe Carter — Blue Jays

Age 34 – Bats Right (flyball hitter)

	Avg	G	AB	R	H	2B	3B	HR	RBI	BB	SO	HBP	GDP	SB	CS	OBP	SLG	IBB	SH	SF	#Pit	#P/PA	GB	FB	G/F
1993 Season	.254	155	603	92	153	33	5	33	121	47	113	9	10	8	3	.312	.489	5	0	10	2556	3.82	127	258	0.49
Last Five Years	.253	799	3148	441	796	164	20	159	568	219	539	45	49	75	28	.307	.469	47	3	45	12625	3.65	818	1261	0.65

1993 Season

	Avg	AB	H	2B	3B	HR	RBI	BB	SO	OBP	SLG		Avg	AB	H	2B	3B	HR	RBI	BB	SO	OBP	SLG
vs. Left	.296	162	48	6	1	10	34	12	28	.341	.531	Scoring Posn	.273	187	51	10	1	11	92	22	43	.345	.513
vs. Right	.238	441	105	27	4	23	87	35	85	.302	.474	Close & Late	.227	88	20	2	1	3	9	6	15	.284	.375
Groundball	.272	103	28	4	0	7	20	4	19	.306	.515	None on/out	.283	145	41	8	2	12	12	5	18	.316	.614
Flyball	.235	81	19	4	1	5	16	11	24	.320	.494	Batting #3	.240	25	6	1	0	0	4	2	4	.296	.280
Home	.250	312	78	18	3	21	66	21	58	.304	.529	Batting #4	.255	577	147	32	5	33	117	45	109	.314	.499
Away	.258	291	75	15	2	12	55	26	55	.321	.447	Other	.000	1	0	0	0	0	0	0	0	.000	.000
Day	.238	202	48	11	1	15	42	15	46	.298	.525	April	.277	83	23	6	1	6	25	4	18	.304	.590
Night	.262	401	105	22	4	18	79	32	67	.320	.471	May	.313	115	36	10	2	7	16	2	20	.336	.617
Grass	.257	226	58	14	1	12	44	20	44	.318	.487	June	.230	87	20	5	1	5	22	13	20	.349	.483
Turf	.252	377	95	19	4	21	77	27	69	.309	.491	July	.219	105	23	6	0	1	18	8	19	.274	.305
First Pitch	.324	74	24	12	0	7	19	3	0	.383	.770	August	.243	111	27	2	0	9	21	10	23	.306	.505
Ahead in Count	.346	104	36	4	1	8	26	25	0	.470	.635	September/October	.235	102	24	4	1	5	19	10	13	.304	.441
Behind in Count	.194	310	60	14	2	7	44	0	100	.197	.319	Pre-All Star	.265	324	86	21	4	18	65	20	65	.317	.522
Two Strikes	.190	305	58	12	3	10	38	19	113	.242	.348	Post-All Star	.240	279	67	12	1	15	56	27	48	.308	.452

1993 By Position

Position	Avg	AB	H	2B	3B	HR	RBI	BB	SO	OBP	SLG	G	GS	Innings	PO	A	E	DP	Fld Pct	Rng Fctr	In Zone	Outs	Zone Rtg	MLB Zone
As lf	.282	216	61	16	3	13	48	10	43	.318	.565	55	55	465.2	104	1	4	0	.963	2.03	129	98	.760	.818
As rf	.233	373	87	17	2	18	71	37	66	.308	.434	96	96	825.2	184	6	4	0	.979	2.07	224	175	.781	.826

Last Five Years

	Avg	AB	H	2B	3B	HR	RBI	BB	SO	OBP	SLG		Avg	AB	H	2B	3B	HR	RBI	BB	SO	OBP	SLG
vs. Left	.268	897	240	47	2	42	144	65	138	.314	.465	Scoring Posn	.272	920	250	44	10	43	404	116	185	.351	.482
vs. Right	.247	2251	556	117	18	117	424	154	401	.304	.471	Close & Late	.211	512	108	13	4	16	71	40	96	.272	.346
Groundball	.247	859	212	42	3	35	133	60	147	.302	.425	None on/out	.272	651	177	39	4	41	41	25	82	.306	.533
Flyball	.252	650	164	42	7	28	111	52	119	.313	.468	Batting #3	.259	1569	406	81	11	84	272	104	265	.310	.485
Home	.252	1585	400	83	10	93	303	98	286	.303	.493	Batting #4	.247	1307	323	69	9	65	242	93	245	.304	.463
Away	.253	1563	396	81	10	66	265	121	253	.311	.445	Other	.246	272	67	14	0	10	54	22	29	.302	.408
Day	.235	997	234	53	3	49	166	60	190	.286	.441	April	.265	423	112	26	1	16	77	21	69	.301	.444
Night	.261	2151	562	111	17	110	402	159	349	.316	.482	May	.276	544	150	32	5	26	92	30	88	.323	.496
Grass	.245	1744	427	84	9	76	291	126	286	.299	.434	June	.266	512	136	31	5	35	106	40	99	.330	.551
Turf	.263	1404	369	80	11	83	277	93	253	.316	.513	July	.231	520	120	28	2	22	87	47	86	.298	.419
First Pitch	.340	382	130	35	4	32	102	21	0	.382	.704	August	.243	568	138	27	2	36	112	40	96	.297	.488
Ahead in Count	.325	600	195	34	4	37	144	111	0	.427	.580	September/October	.241	581	140	20	5	24	94	41	101	.291	.417
Behind in Count	.198	1599	317	67	8	58	208	0	477	.208	.359	Pre-All Star	.261	1650	430	96	12	82	299	104	280	.312	.482
Two Strikes	.185	1484	275	57	10	55	178	74	539	.229	.348	Post-All Star	.244	1498	366	68	8	77	269	115	259	.301	.455

Batter vs. Pitcher (since 1984)

Hits Best Against	Avg	AB	H	2B	3B	HR	RBI	BB	SO	OBP	SLG	Hits Worst Against	Avg	AB	H	2B	3B	HR	RBI	BB	SO	OBP	SLG
Mark Knudson	.571	14	8	0	0	4	7	0	0	.571	1.429	Jeff Montgomery	.000	12	0	0	0	0	1	0	3	.000	.000
Tim Leary	.556	18	10	2	0	4	7	0	3	.500	1.333	Todd Stottlemyre	.000	11	0	0	0	0	0	0	2	.000	.000
Ben McDonald	.455	22	10	2	1	4	11	0	1	.455	1.182	Rich DeLucia	.000	11	0	0	0	0	0	0	5	.000	.000
Bob Tewksbury	.455	11	5	0	0	2	3	1	0	.500	1.000	Bobby Thigpen	.063	16	1	1	0	0	2	0	5	.063	.125
Nolan Ryan	.353	17	6	3	1	2	7	2	6	.421	1.000	Alex Fernandez	.087	23	2	0	0	0	1	1	5	.120	.087

Chuck Cary — White Sox

Age 34 – Pitches Left (flyball pitcher)

	ERA	W	L	Sv	G	GS	IP	BB	SO	Avg	H	2B	3B	HR	RBI	OBP	SLG	GF	IR	IRS	Hld	SvOp	SB	CS	GB	FB	G/F
1993 Season	5.23	1	0	0	16	0	20.2	11	10	.286	22	6	1	1	17	.379	.429	4	14	8	1	0	0	2	34	15	2.27
Last Five Years	4.25	12	22	0	76	47	330.0	127	257	.251	316	73	9	41	161	.319	.420	5	31	18	1	0	27	14	338	455	0.74

1993 Season

	ERA	W	L	Sv	G	GS	IP	H	HR	BB	SO
Home	3.68	1	0	0	12	0	14.2	13	1	9	7
Away	9.00	0	0	0	4	0	6.0	9	0	2	3

	Avg	AB	H	2B	3B	HR	RBI	BB	SO	OBP	SLG
vs. Left	.250	32	8	3	0	0	6	4	4	.375	.344
vs. Right	.311	45	14	3	1	1	11	7	6	.382	.489

Last Five Years

	ERA	W	L	Sv	G	GS	IP	H	HR	BB	SO
Home	3.39	9	7	0	42	23	188.2	162	21	61	148
Away	5.41	3	15	0	34	24	141.1	154	20	66	109
Day	3.59	2	4	0	21	11	82.2	72	10	37	62
Night	4.48	10	18	0	55	36	247.1	244	31	90	195
Grass	3.66	11	19	0	67	40	292.2	259	34	107	232
Turf	8.92	1	3	0	9	7	37.1	57	7	20	25
April	7.59	1	2	0	6	3	21.1	24	1	16	12
May	4.16	2	4	0	16	9	62.2	58	7	29	56
June	4.97	2	4	0	12	8	54.1	61	8	20	32
July	2.61	1	3	0	9	8	58.2	49	5	21	41
August	4.64	4	5	0	20	12	77.2	80	15	24	58
September/October	3.58	2	4	0	13	7	55.1	44	5	17	58
Starter	4.25	11	21	0	47	47	277.1	268	36	102	219
Reliever	4.27	1	1	0	29	0	52.2	48	5	25	38
0 Days rest	3.52	1	0	0	6	0	7.2	4	0	3	3
1 or 2 Days rest	3.00	0	0	0	7	0	9.0	7	1	3	8
3+ Days rest	4.75	0	1	0	16	0	36.0	37	4	19	27
Pre-All Star	4.97	5	10	0	36	21	145.0	150	17	67	103
Post-All Star	3.70	7	12	0	40	26	185.0	166	24	60	154

	Avg	AB	H	2B	3B	HR	RBI	BB	SO	OBP	SLG
vs. Left	.266	248	66	14	2	8	40	29	41	.346	.435
vs. Right	.247	1013	250	59	7	33	121	98	216	.312	.417
Inning 1-6	.261	1025	268	61	8	37	146	99	209	.325	.445
Inning 7+	.203	236	48	12	1	4	15	28	48	.294	.314
None on	.236	749	177	46	7	21	21	74	162	.308	.401
Runners on	.271	512	139	27	2	20	140	53	95	.335	.449
Scoring Posn	.296	297	88	20	2	15	128	45	62	.380	.529
Close & Late	.247	81	20	6	0	0	2	17	16	.384	.321
None on/out	.234	320	75	21	4	7	7	28	65	.300	.391
vs. 1st Batr (relief)	.286	21	6	2	1	0	7	5	6	.448	.476
First Inning Pitched	.257	272	70	16	3	9	48	29	61	.329	.438
First 15 Pitches	.262	237	62	14	2	8	35	24	49	.332	.439
Pitch 16-30	.236	229	54	19	1	7	26	18	52	.287	.419
Pitch 31-45	.247	186	46	10	1	4	27	21	36	.324	.376
Pitch 46+	.253	609	154	30	5	22	73	64	120	.324	.427
First Pitch	.313	192	60	10	3	8	31	8	0	.338	.521
Ahead in Count	.189	541	102	19	0	14	51	0	220	.193	.301
Behind in Count	.319	298	95	30	3	14	50	55	0	.421	.581
Two Strikes	.174	564	98	18	2	14	55	62	257	.256	.287

Pitcher vs. Batter (career)

Pitches Best Vs.	Avg	AB	H	2B	3B	HR	RBI	BB	SO	OBP	SLG
Luis Rivera	.000	12	0	0	0	0	0	1	4	.077	.000
Ozzie Guillen	.077	13	1	0	0	0	0	1	2	.143	.077
Lance Johnson	.100	10	1	0	0	0	1	2	3	.231	.100
Mike Devereaux	.118	17	2	1	0	0	1	0	5	.118	.176
Gary Gaetti	.143	14	2	0	0	0	1	0	3	.133	.143

Pitches Worst Vs.	Avg	AB	H	2B	3B	HR	RBI	BB	SO	OBP	SLG
Chili Davis	.444	9	4	0	0	2	2	2	3	.545	1.111
Greg Gagne	.385	13	5	2	0	1	3	0	1	.357	.769
Ellis Burks	.385	13	5	2	0	1	3	1	1	.429	.769
Mike Greenwell	.357	14	5	0	0	1	4	2	0	.438	.571
Jim Eisenreich	.308	13	4	2	1	0	1	1	2	.357	.615

Larry Casian — Twins

Age 28 – Pitches Left

	ERA	W	L	Sv	G	GS	IP	BB	SO	Avg	H	2B	3B	HR	RBI	OBP	SLG	GF	IR	IRS	Hld	SvOp	SB	CS	GB	FB	G/F
1993 Season	3.02	5	3	1	54	0	56.2	14	31	.268	59	12	0	1	24	.311	.336	8	47	10	15	3	1	0	77	75	1.03
Career (1990-1993)	3.81	8	4	1	80	3	104.0	26	50	.292	120	29	0	7	46	.334	.414	14	65	11	18	3	1	0	148	129	1.15

1993 Season

	ERA	W	L	Sv	G	GS	IP	H	HR	BB	SO
Home	4.18	2	0	0	25	0	23.2	24	1	8	8
Away	2.18	3	3	1	29	0	33.0	35	0	6	23
Starter	0.00	0	0	0	0	0	0.0	0	0	0	0
Reliever	3.02	5	3	1	54	0	56.2	59	1	14	31
0 Days rest	4.63	0	2	1	15	0	11.2	14	0	2	6
1 or 2 Days rest	1.26	3	1	0	27	0	28.2	26	1	7	17
3+ Days rest	4.96	2	0	0	12	0	16.1	19	0	5	8
Pre-All Star	1.11	2	1	0	21	0	24.1	28	0	4	14
Post-All Star	4.45	3	2	1	33	0	32.1	31	1	10	17

	Avg	AB	H	2B	3B	HR	RBI	BB	SO	OBP	SLG
vs. Left	.289	76	22	4	0	1	13	1	12	.296	.382
vs. Right	.257	144	37	8	0	0	11	13	19	.318	.313
Scoring Posn	.345	58	20	5	0	0	21	5	4	.388	.431
Close & Late	.235	98	23	2	0	1	8	6	11	.280	.286
None on/out	.189	53	10	4	0	0	0	3	13	.232	.264
First Pitch	.323	31	10	2	0	1	4	2	0	.364	.484
Ahead in Count	.181	105	19	3	0	0	4	0	26	.181	.210
Behind in Count	.413	46	19	5	0	0	13	6	0	.464	.522
Two Strikes	.177	96	17	4	0	0	4	6	31	.225	.219

Pedro Castellano — Rockies

Age 24 – Bats Right

	Avg	G	AB	R	H	2B	3B	HR	RBI	BB	SO	HBP	GDP	SB	CS	OBP	SLG	IBB	SH	SF	#Pit	#P/PA	GB	FB	G/F
1993 Season	.183	34	71	12	13	2	0	3	7	8	16	0	1	1	1	.266	.338	0	0	0	332	4.20	25	18	1.39

1993 Season

	Avg	AB	H	2B	3B	HR	RBI	BB	SO	OBP	SLG
vs. Left	.333	9	3	0	0	0	1	2	3	.455	.333
vs. Right	.161	62	10	2	0	3	6	6	13	.235	.339
Scoring Posn	.143	21	3	0	0	0	3	1	5	.182	.143
Close & Late	.250	12	3	0	0	1	3	1	1	.308	.500

Vinny Castilla — Rockies

Age 26 – Bats Right

	Avg	G	AB	R	H	2B	3B	HR	RBI	BB	SO	HBP	GDP	SB	CS	OBP	SLG	IBB	SH	SF	#Pit	#P/PA	GB	FB	G/F
1993 Season	.255	105	337	36	86	9	7	9	30	13	45	2	10	2	5	.283	.404	4	0	5	1043	2.92	140	102	1.37
Career (1991-1993)	.254	126	358	38	91	10	7	9	31	14	51	3	10	2	5	.284	.397	5	1	5	1109	2.91	144	109	1.32

1993 Season

	Avg	AB	H	2B	3B	HR	RBI	BB	SO	OBP	SLG
vs. Left	.333	87	29	4	2	3	8	5	11	.370	.529
vs. Right	.228	250	57	5	5	6	22	8	34	.253	.360
Groundball	.261	119	31	4	1	3	10	2	15	.274	.387
Flyball	.190	58	11	2	0	2	3	3	6	.226	.328
Home	.305	167	51	5	6	5	19	11	19	.346	.497

	Avg	AB	H	2B	3B	HR	RBI	BB	SO	OBP	SLG
Scoring Posn	.179	78	14	1	3	2	22	10	15	.266	.346
Close & Late	.206	34	7	2	0	1	3	3	4	.256	.353
None on/out	.369	84	31	2	1	4	4	1	10	.376	.560
Batting #7	.209	129	27	4	1	2	9	6	20	.246	.302
Batting #8	.282	142	40	4	5	5	14	6	18	.309	.486

1993 Season

	Avg	AB	H	2B	3B	HR	RBI	BB	SO	OBP	SLG
Away	.206	170	35	4	1	4	11	2	26	.217	.312
Day	.278	108	30	3	3	5	15	2	16	.292	.500
Night	.245	229	56	6	4	4	15	11	29	.279	.358
Grass	.278	259	72	8	7	8	28	13	34	.309	.456
Turf	.179	78	14	1	0	1	2	0	11	.190	.231
First Pitch	.266	79	21	1	3	3	8	2	0	.269	.468
Ahead in Count	.329	79	26	3	2	2	7	7	0	.375	.494
Behind in Count	.179	134	24	4	2	3	11	0	42	.178	.306
Two Strikes	.149	114	17	2	1	2	6	4	45	.176	.237

	Avg	AB	H	2B	3B	HR	RBI	BB	SO	OBP	SLG
Other	.288	66	19	1	1	2	7	1	7	.299	.424
April	.273	22	6	0	2	1	2	2	4	.320	.591
May	.400	60	24	2	2	0	4	2	3	.429	.500
June	.262	84	22	2	2	4	11	2	13	.279	.476
July	.167	54	9	2	0	0	1	1	8	.179	.204
August	.250	72	18	2	1	4	10	2	11	.263	.472
September/October	.156	45	7	1	0	0	2	4	6	.235	.178
Pre-All Star	.297	202	60	5	6	5	18	7	25	.321	.455
Post-All Star	.193	135	26	4	1	4	12	6	20	.228	.326

1993 By Position

Position	Avg	AB	H	2B	3B	HR	RBI	BB	SO	OBP	SLG	G	GS	Innings	PO	A	E	DP	Fld Pct	Rng Fctr	In Zone	Outs	Zone Rtg	MLB Zone
As ss	.257	335	86	0	7	9	00	10	45	.205	.400	104	92	810.0	140	282	11	67	.975	4.69	314	279	.889	.880

Frank Castillo — Cubs

Age 25 – Pitches Right

	ERA	W	L	Sv	G	GS	IP	BB	SO	Avg	H	2B	3B	HR	RBI	OBP	SLG	CG	ShO	Sup	QS	#P/S	SB	CS	GB	FB	G/F
1993 Season	4.84	5	8	0	29	25	141.1	39	84	.293	162	28	6	20	75	.348	.474	2	0	5.09	13	82	7	12	180	159	1.13
Career (1991-1993)	4.10	21	26	0	80	76	458.1	135	292	.256	448	93	12	44	188	.313	.399	6	0	4.10	42	91	32	25	582	488	1.19

1993 Season

	ERA	W	L	Sv	G	GS	IP	H	HR	BB	SO
Home	4.54	2	4	0	13	13	71.1	79	12	20	46
Away	5.14	3	4	0	16	12	70.0	83	8	19	38
Starter	4.82	5	8	0	25	25	136.1	156	19	38	81
Reliever	5.40	0	0	0	4	0	5.0	6	1	1	3
0-3 Days Rest	3.00	0	1	0	1	1	6.0	8	1	1	3
4 Days Rest	6.39	1	7	0	14	14	69.0	91	9	24	41
5+ Days Rest	3.23	4	0	0	10	10	61.1	57	9	13	37
Pre-All Star	4.79	2	6	0	16	15	82.2	98	9	27	52
Post-All Star	4.91	3	2	0	13	10	58.2	64	11	12	32

	Avg	AB	H	2B	3B	HR	RBI	BB	SO	OBP	SLG
vs. Left	.287	268	77	13	2	14	45	25	37	.350	.507
vs. Right	.298	285	85	15	4	6	30	14	47	.345	.442
Scoring Posn	.288	139	40	5	1	7	56	16	25	.363	.489
Close & Late	.310	29	9	2	1	1	4	1	4	.355	.552
None on/out	.338	145	49	9	3	5	5	8	16	.385	.545
First Pitch	.299	97	29	6	2	3	11	2	0	.320	.495
Ahead in Count	.258	248	64	8	0	8	25	0	70	.276	.387
Behind in Count	.407	108	44	10	2	6	23	18	0	.496	.704
Two Strikes	.218	229	50	7	0	6	18	19	84	.287	.328

Career (1991-1993)

	ERA	W	L	Sv	G	GS	IP	H	HR	BB	SO
Home	3.92	11	14	0	40	40	243.1	227	28	69	171
Away	4.31	10	12	0	40	36	215.0	221	16	66	121
Day	3.71	13	13	0	41	40	245.0	220	24	75	160
Night	4.56	8	13	0	39	36	213.1	228	20	60	132
Grass	4.03	15	22	0	57	55	332.2	321	34	96	231
Turf	4.30	6	4	0	23	21	125.2	127	10	39	61
April	4.03	0	3	0	8	8	44.2	38	6	16	28
May	2.16	4	3	0	10	9	58.1	52	2	18	44
June	5.14	4	5	0	12	12	70.0	79	8	19	37
July	3.45	6	4	0	17	17	107.0	104	6	29	68
August	4.22	4	5	0	15	15	89.2	81	11	21	49
September/October	5.28	3	6	0	18	15	88.2	94	11	32	66
Starter	4.09	21	26	0	76	76	453.1	442	43	134	289
Reliever	5.40	0	0	0	4	0	5.0	6	1	1	3
0-3 Days Rest	4.62	1	1	0	6	6	37.0	42	3	9	22
4 Days Rest	4.65	12	21	0	46	46	263.1	274	24	88	167
5+ Days Rest	3.00	8	4	0	24	24	153.0	126	16	37	100
Pre-All Star	3.80	9	13	0	36	35	213.1	209	20	66	137
Post-All Star	4.37	12	13	0	44	41	245.0	239	24	69	155

	Avg	AB	H	2B	3B	HR	RBI	BB	SO	OBP	SLG
vs. Left	.259	992	257	45	5	30	116	101	160	.327	.405
vs. Right	.253	756	191	48	7	14	72	34	132	.294	.390
Inning 1-6	.252	1528	385	83	11	40	168	117	261	.308	.399
Inning 7+	.286	220	63	10	1	4	20	18	31	.347	.395
None on	.245	1079	264	57	9	27	27	58	188	.290	.389
Runners on	.275	669	184	36	3	17	161	77	104	.348	.414
Scoring Posn	.268	388	104	17	2	11	142	64	60	.367	.407
Close & Late	.306	121	37	5	1	2	12	10	21	.361	.413
None on/out	.266	463	123	28	6	12	12	32	66	.320	.430
vs. 1st Batr (relief)	.000	3	0	0	0	0	0	0	0	.250	.000
First Inning Pitched	.256	301	77	12	2	6	30	25	53	.318	.369
First 75 Pitches	.256	1362	348	70	9	37	146	99	232	.310	.402
Pitch 76-90	.218	216	47	12	2	3	22	19	34	.280	.333
Pitch 91-105	.323	130	42	9	1	3	14	11	20	.385	.477
Pitch 106+	.275	40	11	2	0	1	6	6	6	.367	.400
First Pitch	.287	268	77	17	4	7	30	9	0	.314	.459
Ahead in Count	.217	806	175	37	0	13	67	0	249	.223	.311
Behind in Count	.333	339	113	24	3	15	55	77	0	.457	.555
Two Strikes	.187	793	148	30	2	10	54	49	292	.238	.267

Pitcher vs. Batter (career)

Pitches Best Vs.	Avg	AB	H	2B	3B	HR	RBI	BB	SO	OBP	SLG
Jeff Bagwell	.000	15	0	0	0	0	0	1	1	.063	.000
Brett Butler	.053	19	1	0	0	0	0	1	2	.100	.053
Milt Thompson	.083	12	1	0	0	0	0	2	3	.214	.083
Willie McGee	.091	11	1	0	0	0	0	1	1	.167	.091
Lenny Harris	.154	13	2	0	0	0	1	0	4	.143	.154

Pitches Worst Vs.	Avg	AB	H	2B	3B	HR	RBI	BB	SO	OBP	SLG
Lenny Dykstra	.600	10	6	1	0	3	4	1	0	.636	1.600
Eddie Murray	.588	17	10	2	0	1	8	1	1	.579	.882
Eric Karros	.538	13	7	2	1	0	0	0	3	.538	.846
Andy Van Slyke	.526	19	10	0	1	2	5	1	3	.550	.947
John Kruk	.412	17	7	3	0	3	5	4	4	.524	1.118

Tony Castillo — Blue Jays

Age 31 – Pitches Left

	ERA	W	L	Sv	G	GS	IP	BB	SO	Avg	H	2B	3B	HR	RBI	OBP	SLG	GF	IR	IRS	Hld	SvOp	SB	CS	GB	FB	G/F
1993 Season	3.38	3	2	0	51	0	50.2	22	28	.242	44	4	2	4	23	.320	.352	10	45	11	13	1	4	1	74	50	1.48
Last Five Years	4.05	11	6	2	149	6	186.2	67	125	.285	208	31	2	13	107	.342	.387	23	128	37	23	4	26	5	276	193	1.43

1993 Season

	ERA	W	L	Sv	G	GS	IP	H	HR	BB	SO
Home	4.91	3	2	0	26	0	29.1	27	4	15	15
Away	1.27	0	0	0	25	0	21.1	17	0	7	13
Starter	0.00	0	0	0	0	0	0.0	0	0	0	0
Reliever	3.38	3	2	0	51	0	50.2	44	4	22	28
0 Days rest	0.00	2	0	0	10	0	7.1	3	0	2	5
1 or 2 Days rest	4.28	0	1	0	27	0	27.1	24	2	11	16
3+ Days rest	3.38	1	1	0	14	0	16.0	17	2	9	7
Pre-All Star	2.22	1	0	0	24	0	28.1	21	2	13	12

	Avg	AB	H	2B	3B	HR	RBI	BB	SO	OBP	SLG
vs. Left	.213	61	13	1	1	1	9	1	7	.222	.311
vs. Right	.256	121	31	3	1	3	14	21	21	.364	.372
Scoring Posn	.207	58	12	2	0	1	19	9	5	.304	.293
Close & Late	.224	67	15	2	0	1	10	7	9	.293	.299
None on/out	.256	43	11	2	0	1	1	4	6	.319	.372
First Pitch	.238	21	5	0	0	2	6	3	0	.320	.524
Ahead in Count	.244	82	20	2	1	0	9	0	26	.241	.293
Behind in Count	.227	44	10	2	0	1	6	12	0	.393	.341

1993 Season

	ERA	W	L	Sv	G	GS	IP	H	HR	BB	SO
Post-All Star	4.84	2	2	0	27	0	22.1	23	2	9	16

	Avg	AB	H	2B	3B	HR	RBI	BB	SO	OBP	SLG
Two Strikes	.207	82	17	2	1	1	8	7	28	.267	.293

Last Five Years

	ERA	W	L	Sv	G	GS	IP	H	HR	BB	SO
Home	4.67	4	3	1	67	3	88.2	103	10	33	62
Away	3.49	7	3	1	82	3	98.0	105	3	34	63
Day	4.05	2	1	1	37	1	46.2	51	2	13	30
Night	4.05	9	5	1	112	5	140.0	157	11	54	95
Grass	3.99	4	4	1	89	4	112.2	138	7	37	87
Turf	4.14	7	2	1	60	2	74.0	70	6	30	38
April	5.31	1	1	1	16	0	20.1	19	0	10	12
May	3.68	2	0	0	24	0	29.1	35	2	10	22
June	4.67	1	1	0	20	0	27.0	31	3	9	20
July	3.94	2	0	1	12	1	16.0	20	1	4	7
August	3.59	3	1	0	38	2	42.2	44	3	13	32
September/October	3.86	2	3	0	39	3	51.1	59	4	21	32
Starter	1.50	3	0	0	6	6	30.0	28	1	9	15
Reliever	4.54	8	6	2	143	0	156.2	180	12	58	110
0 Days rest	5.14	4	1	0	32	0	28.0	38	3	10	19
1 or 2 Days rest	4.96	3	4	1	68	0	78.0	89	6	27	65
3+ Days rest	3.55	1	1	1	43	0	50.2	53	3	21	26
Pre-All Star	4.26	4	2	1	62	0	80.1	87	5	31	55
Post-All Star	3.89	7	4	1	87	6	106.1	121	8	36	70

	Avg	AB	H	2B	3B	HR	RBI	BB	SO	OBP	SLG
vs. Left	.257	222	57	9	1	4	35	10	46	.288	.360
vs. Right	.298	507	151	22	1	9	72	57	79	.365	.398
Inning 1-6	.304	349	106	19	1	5	51	28	56	.352	.407
Inning 7+	.268	380	102	12	1	8	56	39	69	.334	.368
None on	.289	357	103	15	2	6	6	28	55	.342	.392
Runners on	.282	372	105	16	0	7	101	39	70	.343	.382
Scoring Posn	.280	225	63	10	0	4	93	30	44	.350	.378
Close & Late	.239	138	33	4	0	2	20	17	26	.316	.312
None on/out	.284	169	48	8	0	3	3	9	21	.320	.385
vs. 1st Batr (relief)	.239	113	27	4	0	1	16	8	23	.282	.301
First Inning Pitched	.265	396	105	12	1	8	60	31	73	.314	.361
First 15 Pitches	.258	383	99	12	1	8	59	34	63	.311	.358
Pitch 16-30	.317	199	63	10	1	3	25	22	37	.387	.422
Pitch 31-45	.317	82	26	7	0	2	20	4	14	.352	.476
Pitch 46+	.308	65	20	2	0	0	3	7	11	.375	.338
First Pitch	.413	109	45	8	0	4	26	12	0	.467	.596
Ahead in Count	.226	328	74	12	1	4	41	0	111	.226	.305
Behind in Count	.315	165	52	8	0	1	25	33	0	.421	.382
Two Strikes	.201	328	66	9	1	7	37	22	125	.251	.299

Pitcher vs. Batter (career)

Pitches Best Vs.	Avg	AB	H	2B	3B	HR	RBI	BB	SO	OBP	SLG
Paul O'Neill	.200	10	2	0	0	0	2	1	4	.273	.200

Pitches Worst Vs.	Avg	AB	H	2B	3B	HR	RBI	BB	SO	OBP	SLG

Andujar Cedeno — Astros

Age 24 – Bats Right

	Avg	G	AB	R	H	2B	3B	HR	RBI	BB	SO	HBP	GDP	SB	CS	OBP	SLG	IBB	SH	SF	#Pit	#P/PA	GB	FB	G/F
1993 Season	.283	149	505	69	143	24	4	11	56	48	97	3	17	9	7	.346	.412	9	4	5	2026	3.56	186	128	1.45
Career (1990-1993)	.246	294	984	111	242	50	8	22	105	71	247	7	21	15	10	.299	.380	12	5	7	3967	3.68	331	237	1.40

1993 Season

	Avg	AB	H	2B	3B	HR	RBI	BB	SO	OBP	SLG
vs. Left	.341	164	56	7	2	4	18	14	21	.400	.482
vs. Right	.255	341	87	17	2	7	38	34	76	.320	.378
Groundball	.294	180	53	12	2	4	21	8	28	.321	.450
Flyball	.221	68	15	2	1	4	7	13	16	.346	.456
Home	.308	247	76	14	2	6	27	26	55	.377	.453
Away	.260	258	67	10	2	5	29	22	42	.316	.372
Day	.288	160	46	8	2	4	24	11	29	.337	.438
Night	.281	345	97	16	2	7	32	37	68	.350	.400
Grass	.272	169	46	7	2	5	20	16	31	.333	.426
Turf	.289	336	97	17	2	6	36	32	66	.352	.405
First Pitch	.361	97	35	8	1	2	13	6	0	.400	.526
Ahead in Count	.417	84	35	5	2	3	8	20	0	.529	.631
Behind in Count	.205	224	46	4	1	5	23	0	82	.210	.299
Two Strikes	.182	220	40	7	0	5	22	22	97	.260	.282

	Avg	AB	H	2B	3B	HR	RBI	BB	SO	OBP	SLG
Scoring Posn	.252	143	36	6	1	1	43	16	24	.325	.329
Close & Late	.265	83	22	3	0	1	10	9	15	.337	.337
None on/out	.333	126	42	5	0	6	6	10	26	.382	.516
Batting #7	.313	166	52	12	2	4	24	16	30	.371	.482
Batting #8	.268	239	64	8	1	4	19	28	51	.346	.360
Other	.270	100	27	4	1	3	13	4	16	.302	.420
April	.292	65	19	5	1	0	7	6	13	.347	.400
May	.309	94	29	7	1	2	9	7	19	.363	.468
June	.346	78	27	2	2	2	13	7	12	.402	.500
July	.232	95	22	4	0	1	8	8	12	.295	.305
August	.262	84	22	1	0	1	6	12	18	.351	.310
September/October	.270	89	24	5	0	5	13	8	23	.327	.494
Pre-All Star	.319	279	89	17	4	5	35	22	51	.371	.462
Post-All Star	.239	226	54	7	0	6	21	26	46	.315	.350

1993 By Position

Position	Avg	AB	H	2B	3B	HR	RBI	BB	SO	OBP	SLG	G	GS	Innings	PO	A	E	DP	Fld Pct	Rng Fctr	In Zone	Outs	Zone Rtg	MLB Zone
As ss	.281	501	141	24	4	11	55	48	97	.345	.411	149	146	1224.1	153	373	25	77	.955	3.87	451	365	.809	.880

Career (1990-1993)

	Avg	AB	H	2B	3B	HR	RBI	BB	SO	OBP	SLG
vs. Left	.276	312	86	16	4	4	32	22	65	.326	.391
vs. Right	.232	672	156	34	4	18	73	49	182	.287	.375
Groundball	.231	364	84	20	3	6	39	15	87	.266	.352
Flyball	.260	181	47	7	3	10	24	20	53	.333	.497
Home	.254	511	130	31	5	12	56	44	138	.317	.405
Away	.237	473	112	19	3	10	49	27	109	.280	.353
Day	.259	286	74	14	3	7	38	12	67	.294	.402
Night	.241	698	168	36	5	15	67	59	180	.302	.371
Grass	.259	305	79	13	3	10	37	20	70	.307	.420
Turf	.240	679	163	37	5	12	68	51	177	.296	.362
First Pitch	.309	165	51	12	2	5	22	9	0	.350	.497
Ahead in Count	.342	146	50	9	2	4	16	25	0	.442	.514
Behind in Count	.190	506	96	19	2	8	37	0	212	.195	.283
Two Strikes	.165	498	82	18	2	9	41	37	247	.227	.263

	Avg	AB	H	2B	3B	HR	RBI	BB	SO	OBP	SLG
Scoring Posn	.223	265	59	10	3	4	80	28	63	.297	.328
Close & Late	.241	158	38	8	0	4	15	15	39	.306	.367
None on/out	.266	237	63	10	0	8	8	13	64	.307	.409
Batting #7	.270	437	118	27	5	12	56	28	111	.314	.437
Batting #8	.221	398	88	16	2	5	30	37	101	.293	.309
Other	.242	149	36	7	1	5	19	6	35	.274	.403
April	.236	106	25	7	2	0	7	8	29	.293	.340
May	.271	155	42	11	1	3	14	12	40	.331	.413
June	.346	78	27	2	2	2	13	7	12	.402	.500
July	.235	115	27	5	1	1	10	9	18	.294	.322
August	.252	226	57	10	1	6	27	19	58	.308	.385
September/October	.211	304	64	15	1	10	34	16	90	.253	.365
Pre-All Star	.283	381	108	23	5	6	40	29	88	.340	.417
Post-All Star	.222	603	134	27	3	16	65	42	159	.273	.357

Batter vs. Pitcher (career)

Hits Best Against	Avg	AB	H	2B	3B	HR	RBI	BB	SO	OBP	SLG
Tom Glavine	.417	12	5	0	1	1	2	3	3	.533	.833
Jack Armstrong	.400	10	4	0	0	0	1	1	1	.455	.400
Greg Maddux	.333	15	5	1	0	0	4	1	3	.353	.400
John Smoltz	.318	22	7	3	0	0	1	1	9	.348	.455

Hits Worst Against	Avg	AB	H	2B	3B	HR	RBI	BB	SO	OBP	SLG
Mike Morgan	.067	15	1	1	0	0	1	0	6	.067	.133
Greg W. Harris	.067	15	1	0	0	0	0	3	5	.222	.067
Bruce Hurst	.100	10	1	0	0	0	1	2	4	.250	.100
Curt Schilling	.100	10	1	0	0	0	0	1	2	.182	.100
John Burkett	.133	15	2	0	0	0	0	0	6	.133	.133

Domingo Cedeno — Blue Jays

Age 25 – Bats Both (groundball hitter)

	Avg	G	AB	R	H	2B	3B	HR	RBI	BB	SO	HBP	GDP	SB	CS	OBP	SLG	IBB	SH	SF	#Pit	#P/PA	GB	FB	G/F
1993 Season	.174	15	46	5	8	0	0	0	7	1	10	0	2	1	0	.188	.174	0	2	1	181	3.62	19	10	1.90

1993 Season

	Avg	AB	H	2B	3B	HR	RBI	BB	SO	OBP	SLG
vs. Left	.273	11	3	0	0	0	1	0	3	.273	.273
vs. Right	.143	35	5	0	0	0	6	1	7	.162	.143
Scoring Posn	.500	10	5	0	0	0	7	0	1	.455	.500
Close & Late	.250	8	2	0	0	0	1	0	0	.250	.250

Wes Chamberlain — Phillies

Age 28 – Bats Right

	Avg	G	AB	R	H	2B	3B	HR	RBI	BB	SO	HBP	GDP	SB	CS	OBP	SLG	IBB	SH	SF	#Pit	#P/PA	GB	FB	G/F
1993 Season	.282	96	284	34	80	20	2	12	45	17	51	1	7	2	1	.320	.493	3	0	4	1089	3.56	106	78	1.36
Career (1990-1993)	.259	291	988	120	256	57	5	36	140	59	188	4	22	19	5	.302	.436	5	2	8	3654	3.45	347	286	1.21

1993 Season

	Avg	AB	H	2B	3B	HR	RBI	BB	SO	OBP	SLG
vs. Left	.328	134	44	9	1	9	25	10	23	.374	.612
vs. Right	.240	150	36	11	1	3	20	7	28	.270	.387
Home	.310	168	52	13	1	5	30	6	25	.335	.488
Away	.241	116	28	7	1	7	15	11	26	.300	.500
First Pitch	.462	39	18	7	0	2	9	3	0	.488	.795
Ahead in Count	.274	62	17	4	1	4	9	9	0	.356	.565
Behind in Count	.236	148	35	7	1	3	21	0	48	.235	.358
Two Strikes	.234	128	30	5	0	4	20	5	51	.261	.367
Scoring Posn	.263	76	20	2	1	3	32	9	10	.326	.434
Close & Late	.238	42	10	2	0	0	3	2	11	.283	.286
None on/out	.338	77	26	6	0	4	4	3	13	.363	.571
Batting #6	.282	124	35	10	1	6	26	6	16	.313	.524
Batting #7	.290	138	40	9	1	6	18	10	28	.336	.500
Other	.227	22	5	1	0	0	1	1	7	.261	.273
Pre-All Star	.274	168	46	14	1	8	25	10	25	.311	.512
Post-All Star	.293	116	34	6	1	4	20	7	26	.333	.466

Career (1990-1993)

	Avg	AB	H	2B	3B	HR	RBI	BB	SO	OBP	SLG
vs. Left	.288	403	116	26	2	20	68	31	63	.339	.511
vs. Right	.239	585	140	31	3	16	72	28	125	.275	.385
Groundball	.254	398	101	25	5	15	55	21	65	.295	.455
Flyball	.270	174	47	7	0	9	25	13	45	.317	.466
Home	.284	550	156	34	2	17	81	26	97	.317	.445
Away	.228	438	100	23	3	19	59	33	91	.283	.425
Day	.259	301	78	22	0	11	47	17	60	.297	.442
Night	.259	687	178	35	5	25	93	42	128	.304	.434
Grass	.236	267	63	16	0	13	35	14	54	.275	.442
Turf	.268	721	193	41	5	23	105	45	134	.312	.434
First Pitch	.352	176	62	18	0	9	33	5	0	.373	.608
Ahead in Count	.347	193	67	17	1	12	32	33	0	.439	.632
Behind in Count	.212	491	104	16	4	11	64	0	157	.213	.328
Two Strikes	.185	444	82	16	2	11	56	21	188	.221	.304
Scoring Posn	.255	255	65	9	2	12	102	26	45	.322	.447
Close & Late	.231	173	40	8	0	2	16	9	38	.276	.312
None on/out	.277	220	61	13	1	8	8	9	41	.309	.455
Batting #3	.234	342	80	15	3	9	37	29	66	.298	.374
Batting #6	.268	317	85	21	1	15	58	14	56	.300	.483
Other	.277	329	91	21	1	12	45	16	66	.308	.456
April	.243	140	34	8	0	5	16	3	25	.264	.407
May	.220	82	18	8	0	4	11	7	17	.275	.463
June	.333	120	40	9	1	4	14	5	14	.362	.525
July	.278	205	57	13	1	7	36	9	41	.310	.454
August	.266	218	58	10	2	10	39	20	44	.328	.468
September/October	.220	223	49	9	1	6	24	15	47	.270	.350
Pre-All Star	.271	398	108	29	1	15	52	15	67	.299	.462
Post-All Star	.251	590	148	28	4	21	88	44	121	.304	.419

Batter vs. Pitcher (career)

Hits Best Against	Avg	AB	H	2B	3B	HR	RBI	BB	SO	OBP	SLG
John Smiley	.400	15	6	0	0	2	6	0	3	.400	.800
Mike Bielecki	.385	13	5	1	1	0	2	0	0	.385	.615
Pete Schourek	.333	9	3	0	0	1	2	1	2	.364	.667
Doug Drabek	.308	13	4	0	0	0	2	0	5	.308	.308

Hits Worst Against	Avg	AB	H	2B	3B	HR	RBI	BB	SO	OBP	SLG
Omar Olivares	.000	11	0	0	0	0	0	0	2	.000	.000
Brian Barnes	.095	21	2	0	0	0	0	3	8	.208	.095
Tom Glavine	.143	14	2	0	0	0	1	0	2	.143	.143
Andy Benes	.167	12	2	0	0	0	0	0	5	.167	.167
Anthony Young	.167	12	2	0	0	0	2	0	1	.167	.167

Norm Charlton — Mariners

Age 31 – Pitches Left (groundball pitcher)

	ERA	W	L	Sv	G	GS	IP	BB	SO	Avg	H	2B	3B	HR	RBI	OBP	SLG	GF	IR	IRS	Hld	SvOp	SB	CS	GB	FB	G/F
1993 Season	2.34	1	3	18	34	0	34.2	17	48	.179	22	3	0	4	20	.277	.301	29	13	9	1	21	3	0	38	28	1.36
Last Five Years	2.83	28	22	47	262	27	474.0	187	430	.227	391	64	10	32	184	.307	.332	98	104	41	28	63	54	18	637	400	1.59

1993 Season

	ERA	W	L	Sv	G	GS	IP	H	HR	BB	SO
Home	0.90	1	1	10	17	0	20.0	8	2	5	32
Away	4.30	0	2	8	17	0	14.2	14	2	12	16
Starter	0.00	0	0	0	0	0	0.0	0	0	0	0
Reliever	2.34	1	3	18	34	0	34.2	22	4	17	48
0 Days rest	0.00	0	0	4	5	0	5.0	3	0	2	8
1 or 2 Days rest	3.07	0	1	8	14	0	14.2	11	2	8	15
3+ Days rest	2.40	1	2	6	15	0	15.0	8	2	7	25
Pre-All Star	2.61	1	2	17	30	0	31.0	21	4	14	44
Post-All Star	0.00	0	1	1	4	0	3.2	1	0	3	4

	Avg	AB	H	2B	3B	HR	RBI	BB	SO	OBP	SLG
vs. Left	.095	21	2	0	0	0	3	5	9	.269	.095
vs. Right	.196	102	20	3	0	4	17	12	39	.278	.343
Scoring Posn	.257	35	9	0	0	2	17	6	12	.357	.429
Close & Late	.181	83	15	2	0	3	17	13	35	.289	.313
None on/out	.129	31	4	2	0	0	0	1	14	.156	.194
First Pitch	.214	14	3	1	0	1	2	0	0	.214	.500
Ahead in Count	.121	58	7	0	0	1	6	0	38	.121	.172
Behind in Count	.286	21	6	2	0	0	3	5	0	.407	.381
Two Strikes	.116	69	8	0	0	2	10	12	48	.247	.203

Last Five Years

	ERA	W	L	Sv	G	GS	IP	H	HR	BB	SO
Home	2.89	11	11	25	128	14	224.0	180	17	87	197
Away	2.77	17	11	22	134	13	250.0	211	15	100	233
Day	3.32	6	10	12	81	10	143.2	125	11	47	138
Night	2.62	22	12	35	181	17	330.1	266	21	140	292
Grass	2.47	13	9	12	79	5	135.0	108	8	59	116
Turf	2.97	15	13	35	183	22	339.0	283	24	128	314
April	2.58	2	3	10	39	4	69.2	48	4	32	71
May	3.76	7	4	11	53	5	81.1	82	9	30	74
June	3.22	7	0	14	48	2	72.2	60	4	26	63

	Avg	AB	H	2B	3B	HR	RBI	BB	SO	OBP	SLG
vs. Left	.221	376	83	14	2	6	53	50	91	.326	.316
vs. Right	.229	1346	308	50	8	26	131	137	339	.301	.336
Inning 1-6	.240	628	151	22	3	15	71	74	102	.326	.357
Inning 7+	.219	1094	240	42	7	17	113	113	328	.295	.317
None on	.213	991	211	37	7	17	17	101	253	.292	.316
Runners on	.246	731	180	27	3	15	167	86	177	.326	.353
Scoring Posn	.237	456	108	18	2	9	148	62	123	.324	.344
Close & Late	.220	617	136	23	4	12	75	74	187	.306	.329
None on/out	.244	434	106	23	3	8	8	43	104	.315	.366

Last Five Years

	ERA	W	L	Sv	G	GS	IP	H	HR	BB	SO
July	2.60	3	8	8	38	4	72.2	60	4	23	61
August	2.29	4	2	3	43	6	94.1	72	5	41	82
September/October	2.59	5	5	1	41	6	83.1	69	6	35	79
Starter	3.24	9	10	0	27	27	169.1	148	13	70	97
Reliever	2.60	19	12	47	235	0	304.2	243	19	117	333
0 Days rest	1.98	3	4	12	52	0	63.2	45	1	22	74
1 or 2 Days rest	3.30	11	4	22	117	0	158.1	145	11	60	155
3+ Days rest	1.74	5	4	13	66	0	82.2	53	7	35	104
Pre-All Star	3.28	16	11	40	155	11	244.0	213	18	94	235
Post-All Star	2.35	12	11	7	107	16	230.0	178	14	93	195

	Avg	AB	H	2B	3B	HR	RBI	BB	SO	OBP	SLG
vs. 1st Batr (relief)	.287	209	60	15	2	5	31	21	57	.353	.450
First Inning Pitched	.231	876	202	40	3	16	121	98	240	.312	.338
First 15 Pitches	.239	790	189	36	4	15	90	90	196	.323	.352
Pitch 16-30	.221	426	94	14	3	6	47	45	127	.297	.310
Pitch 31-45	.184	179	33	4	1	5	16	15	46	.246	.302
Pitch 46+	.229	327	75	10	2	6	31	37	61	.314	.327
First Pitch	.337	285	96	19	2	4	46	14	0	.376	.460
Ahead in Count	.158	773	122	14	2	10	59	0	361	.162	.220
Behind in Count	.294	337	99	19	3	11	41	94	0	.452	.466
Two Strikes	.133	774	103	15	2	8	55	78	430	.214	.189

Pitcher vs. Batter (career)

Pitches Best Vs.	Avg	AB	H	2B	3B	HR	RBI	BB	SO	OBP	SLG
Lenny Dykstra	.000	10	0	0	0	0	0	1	4	.091	.000
Tom Pagnozzi	.000	10	0	0	0	0	0	1	2	.091	.000
Kevin Bass	.056	18	1	1	0	0	1	0	5	.053	.111
Dickie Thon	.083	12	1	0	0	0	0	1	3	.154	.083
Robby Thompson	.091	11	1	0	0	0	1	0	4	.091	.091

Pitches Worst Vs.	Avg	AB	H	2B	3B	HR	RBI	BB	SO	OBP	SLG
Terry Pendleton	.500	18	9	1	1	1	6	1	1	.526	.833
Jay Bell	.500	14	7	0	0	1	2	0	0	.500	.714
Jeff Bagwell	.500	8	4	1	0	1	2	3	1	.636	1.000
Jose Oquendo	.417	12	5	1	0	1	3	3	0	.533	.750
Lonnie Smith	.412	17	7	1	1	2	3	2	4	.474	.941

Mike Christopher — Indians

Age 30 – Pitches Right (flyball pitcher)

	ERA	W	L	Sv	G	GS	IP	BB	SO	Avg	H	2B	3B	HR	RBI	OBP	SLG	GF	IR	IRS	Hld	SvOp	SB	CS	GB	FB	G/F
1993 Season	3.86	0	0	0	9	0	11.2	2	8	.286	14	1	0	3	6	.314	.490	3	4	0	0	0	1	0	15	16	0.94
Career (1991-1993)	2.94	0	0	0	22	0	33.2	15	23	.258	33	6	2	5	15	.333	.453	9	17	4	2	0	3	2	39	44	0.89

1993 Season

	ERA	W	L	Sv	G	GS	IP	H	HR	BB	SO
Home	3.52	0	0	0	5	0	7.2	8	1	2	6
Away	4.50	0	0	0	4	0	4.0	6	2	0	2

	Avg	AB	H	2B	3B	HR	RBI	BB	SO	OBP	SLG
vs. Left	.391	23	9	1	0	2	2	1	3	.417	.696
vs. Right	.192	26	5	0	0	1	4	1	5	.222	.308

Archi Cianfrocco — Padres

Age 27 – Bats Right

	Avg	G	AB	R	H	2B	3B	HR	RBI	BB	SO	HBP	GDP	SB	CS	OBP	SLG	IBB	SH	SF	#Pit	#P/PA	GB	FB	G/F
1993 Season	.243	96	296	30	72	11	2	12	48	17	69	3	9	2	0	.287	.416	1	2	5	1194	3.69	107	76	1.41
Career (1992-1993)	.242	182	528	55	128	16	4	18	78	28	135	4	11	5	0	.282	.390	1	3	7	2126	3.72	174	132	1.32

1993 Season

	Avg	AB	H	2B	3B	HR	RBI	BB	SO	OBP	SLG
vs. Left	.282	78	22	5	0	2	15	5	16	.310	.423
vs. Right	.229	218	50	6	2	10	33	12	53	.278	.413
Home	.266	154	41	7	2	6	21	8	32	.305	.455
Away	.218	142	31	4	0	6	27	9	37	.266	.373
First Pitch	.184	38	7	2	0	3	11	0	0	.184	.474
Ahead in Count	.370	54	20	3	0	2	8	5	0	.410	.537
Behind in Count	.182	154	28	2	2	3	15	0	63	.191	.279
Two Strikes	.169	142	24	2	2	3	17	12	69	.236	.275

	Avg	AB	H	2B	3B	HR	RBI	BB	SO	OBP	SLG
Scoring Posn	.325	77	25	4	1	4	39	5	19	.360	.558
Close & Late	.269	52	14	3	0	2	6	4	13	.333	.442
None on/out	.226	53	12	0	1	2	2	3	8	.268	.377
Batting #6	.200	75	15	1	1	1	15	3	17	.232	.280
Batting #7	.298	114	34	5	0	5	16	5	24	.322	.474
Other	.215	107	23	5	1	6	17	9	28	.288	.449
Pre-All Star	.186	70	13	3	0	3	8	4	17	.227	.357
Post-All Star	.261	226	59	8	2	9	40	13	52	.305	.434

Dave Clark — Pirates

Age 31 – Bats Left (groundball hitter)

	Avg	G	AB	R	H	2B	3B	HR	RBI	BB	SO	HBP	GDP	SB	CS	OBP	SLG	IBB	SH	SF	#Pit	#P/PA	GB	FB	G/F
1993 Season	.271	110	277	43	75	11	2	11	46	38	58	1	10	1	0	.358	.444	5	0	2	1144	3.60	125	58	2.16
Last Five Years	.257	330	744	90	191	27	4	26	103	83	170	1	21	8	3	.330	.409	11	1	6	3038	3.64	329	143	2.30

1993 Season

	Avg	AB	H	2B	3B	HR	RBI	BB	SO	OBP	SLG
vs. Left	.250	16	4	0	0	2	4	4	8	.400	.625
vs. Right	.272	261	71	11	2	9	42	34	50	.356	.433
Home	.273	143	39	5	2	8	29	19	29	.356	.503
Away	.269	134	36	6	0	3	17	19	29	.361	.381
First Pitch	.400	50	20	2	1	2	15	3	0	.434	.600
Ahead in Count	.365	63	23	2	1	3	11	22	0	.535	.571
Behind in Count	.168	107	18	3	0	3	12	0	43	.167	.280
Two Strikes	.116	121	14	2	0	3	13	13	58	.201	.207

	Avg	AB	H	2B	3B	HR	RBI	BB	SO	OBP	SLG
Scoring Posn	.289	83	24	4	0	1	31	20	20	.419	.373
Close & Late	.263	57	15	1	0	2	7	8	15	.354	.386
None on/out	.258	62	16	3	0	3	3	8	9	.343	.452
Batting #5	.287	167	48	4	2	7	30	23	31	.373	.461
Batting #6	.308	65	20	5	0	2	9	7	12	.375	.477
Other	.156	45	7	2	0	2	7	8	15	.283	.333
Pre-All Star	.250	116	29	8	0	2	17	17	23	.348	.371
Post-All Star	.286	161	46	3	2	9	29	21	35	.366	.497

Last Five Years

	Avg	AB	H	2B	3B	HR	RBI	BB	SO	OBP	SLG
vs. Left	.194	31	6	0	0	2	4	4	18	.286	.387
vs. Right	.259	713	185	27	4	24	99	79	152	.332	.410
Groundball	.269	212	57	7	0	6	30	27	45	.350	.387
Flyball	.286	175	50	5	2	11	25	18	41	.351	.526
Home	.267	393	105	16	4	17	64	44	90	.339	.458
Away	.245	351	86	11	0	9	39	39	80	.319	.353
Day	.236	280	66	12	1	10	38	33	66	.314	.393
Night	.269	464	125	15	3	16	65	50	104	.339	.418
Grass	.253	435	110	17	2	11	51	42	105	.319	.377
Turf	.262	309	81	10	2	15	52	41	65	.345	.453
First Pitch	.328	116	38	5	1	5	25	7	0	.360	.517
Ahead in Count	.398	166	66	9	2	6	30	41	0	.517	.584
Behind in Count	.159	314	50	6	1	7	29	0	139	.158	.252

	Avg	AB	H	2B	3B	HR	RBI	BB	SO	OBP	SLG
Scoring Posn	.242	207	50	8	1	3	71	43	57	.363	.333
Close & Late	.257	167	43	3	1	5	23	23	43	.344	.377
None on/out	.244	180	44	7	0	9	9	14	33	.299	.433
Batting #5	.255	306	78	7	3	9	42	37	66	.335	.386
Batting #6	.273	176	48	9	0	6	18	17	35	.337	.426
Other	.248	262	65	11	1	11	43	29	69	.319	.424
April	.272	81	22	4	0	2	5	8	19	.344	.395
May	.190	100	19	0	0	5	14	14	20	.287	.340
June	.200	135	27	6	1	3	17	16	33	.283	.326
July	.339	124	42	11	0	4	25	16	27	.408	.524
August	.243	177	43	4	1	6	22	14	44	.297	.379
September/October	.299	127	38	2	2	6	20	15	27	.371	.488
Pre-All Star	.234	367	86	18	1	11	47	44	79	.316	.379

Last Five Years

	Avg	AB	H	2B	3B	HR	RBI	BB	SO	OBP	SLG		Avg	AB	H	2B	3B	HR	RBI	BB	SO	OBP	SLG
Two Strikes	.137	343	47	5	1	7	28	34	170	.214	.219	Post-All Star	.279	377	105	9	3	15	56	39	91	.344	.438

Batter vs. Pitcher (career)

Hits Best Against	Avg	AB	H	2B	3B	HR	RBI	BB	SO	OBP	SLG	Hits Worst Against	Avg	AB	H	2B	3B	HR	RBI	BB	SO	OBP	SLG
Tim Belcher	.438	16	7	3	0	2	8	0	1	.438	1.000	Chris Bosio	.000	12	0	0	0	0	0	0	5	.000	.000
Kevin Gross	.429	14	6	0	0	1	4	1	1	.467	.643	Dave Stewart	.059	17	1	1	0	0	1	0	4	.059	.118
Dwight Gooden	.417	12	5	0	0	0	1	4	0	.563	.417	Dennis Martinez	.100	10	1	0	0	0	1	4	2	.357	.100
Mike Moore	.333	18	6	2	0	0	0	1	3	.368	.444	Bobby Witt	.111	9	1	0	0	0	0	2	1	.273	.111
John Smoltz	.333	15	5	0	0	0	3	1	4	.353	.333	Jack Morris	.222	18	4	0	0	0	1	1	3	.263	.222

Jerald Clark — Rockies

Age 30 – Bats Right

	Avg	G	AB	R	H	2B	3B	HR	RBI	BB	SO	HBP	GDP	SB	CS	OBP	SLG	IBB	SH	SF	#Pit	#P/PA	GB	FB	G/F
1993 Season	.282	140	478	65	135	26	6	13	67	20	60	10	12	9	6	.324	.444	2	3	1	1648	3.22	174	140	1.18
Last Five Years	.252	473	1485	153	374	70	13	41	190	81	280	20	32	14	8	.298	.399	7	5	9	5424	3.39	492	428	1.15

1993 Season

	Avg	AB	H	2B	3B	HR	RBI	BB	SO	OBP	SLG		Avg	AB	H	2B	3B	HR	RBI	BB	SO	OBP	SLG
vs. Left	.276	116	32	9	1	2	15	5	15	.323	.422	Scoring Posn	.312	125	39	11	1	5	57	10	14	.360	.536
vs. Right	.285	362	103	17	5	11	52	15	45	.325	.450	Close & Late	.284	74	21	2	0	4	16	1	7	.289	.473
Groundball	.271	155	42	10	1	3	20	4	17	.315	.406	None on/out	.246	114	28	7	0	3	3	4	18	.295	.386
Flyball	.232	82	19	4	0	1	11	3	14	.264	.317	Batting #5	.237	76	18	3	1	3	18	2	9	.272	.421
Home	.322	227	73	16	3	8	40	17	26	.387	.524	Batting #6	.303	307	93	17	4	7	37	14	41	.342	.453
Away	.247	251	62	10	3	5	27	3	34	.262	.371	Other	.253	95	24	6	1	3	12	4	10	.311	.432
Day	.299	154	46	10	4	6	23	9	18	.353	.532	April	.211	57	12	4	1	2	4	3	8	.262	.421
Night	.275	324	89	16	2	7	44	11	42	.310	.401	May	.267	86	23	5	0	3	12	3	14	.337	.430
Grass	.287	359	103	22	4	11	54	19	44	.338	.462	June	.373	75	28	5	1	0	7	6	11	.427	.467
Turf	.269	119	32	4	2	2	13	1	16	.281	.387	July	.173	52	9	2	0	1	6	2	5	.214	.269
First Pitch	.338	80	27	6	3	3	15	2	0	.369	.600	August	.306	98	30	4	2	3	17	3	13	.333	.480
Ahead in Count	.364	88	32	8	2	4	16	10	0	.430	.636	September/October	.300	110	33	6	2	4	21	3	9	.319	.500
Behind in Count	.246	228	56	7	0	3	25	0	57	.259	.316	Pre-All Star	.277	242	67	15	2	6	27	12	35	.332	.430
Two Strikes	.255	184	47	7	0	2	15	8	60	.297	.326	Post-All Star	.288	236	68	11	4	7	40	8	25	.316	.458

1993 By Position

Position	Avg	AB	H	2B	3B	HR	RBI	BB	SO	OBP	SLG	G	GS	Innings	PO	A	E	DP	Fld Pct	Rng Fctr	In Zone	Outs	Zone Rtg	MLB Zone
As Pinch Hitter	.250	16	4	1	0	0	1	0	4	.250	.313	16	0	---	---	---	---	---	---	---	---	---	---	---
As 1b	.314	118	37	6	2	3	18	4	17	.341	.475	37	29	271.2	284	15	5	29	.984	---	60	48	.800	.834
As lf	.269	279	75	15	3	6	29	13	35	.321	.409	80	76	660.0	160	7	7	1	.960	2.28	196	152	.776	.818
As rf	.292	65	19	4	1	4	19	3	4	.324	.569	17	16	140.0	31	0	0	0	1.000	1.99	34	31	.912	.826

Last Five Years

	Avg	AB	H	2B	3B	HR	RBI	BB	SO	OBP	SLG		Avg	AB	H	2B	3B	HR	RBI	BB	SO	OBP	SLG
vs. Left	.238	463	110	22	4	14	51	24	89	.281	.393	Scoring Posn	.262	370	97	17	5	13	149	25	59	.312	.441
vs. Right	.258	1022	264	48	9	27	139	57	191	.305	.402	Close & Late	.231	268	62	8	1	9	45	9	54	.256	.369
Groundball	.275	539	148	28	4	14	75	25	86	.315	.419	None on/out	.245	376	92	20	1	6	6	19	77	.290	.351
Flyball	.235	285	67	13	2	9	38	13	72	.276	.389	Batting #6	.264	602	159	30	5	16	68	30	113	.307	.410
Home	.257	735	189	37	6	28	112	46	125	.311	.438	Batting #7	.249	437	109	21	7	11	57	20	85	.288	.405
Away	.247	750	185	33	7	13	78	35	155	.285	.361	Other	.238	446	106	19	1	14	65	31	82	.296	.379
Day	.259	455	118	22	5	13	53	30	80	.312	.415	April	.221	222	49	9	1	9	25	20	45	.294	.392
Night	.249	1030	256	48	8	28	137	51	200	.291	.392	May	.235	234	55	12	0	3	20	9	49	.283	.325
Grass	.260	1101	286	55	10	37	161	62	205	.306	.429	June	.300	217	65	15	2	5	27	21	30	.369	.456
Turf	.229	384	88	15	3	4	29	19	75	.275	.315	July	.258	229	59	11	2	6	31	13	44	.299	.402
First Pitch	.340	235	80	17	4	8	45	7	0	.367	.549	August	.264	250	66	10	3	6	29	8	40	.297	.400
Ahead in Count	.314	271	85	16	4	14	46	26	0	.375	.557	September/October	.240	333	80	13	5	12	58	10	72	.261	.417
Behind in Count	.197	730	144	26	3	7	65	0	250	.208	.270	Pre-All Star	.258	753	194	40	3	22	88	55	137	.319	.406
Two Strikes	.171	645	110	23	2	5	44	48	280	.237	.236	Post-All Star	.246	732	180	30	10	19	102	26	143	.275	.392

Batter vs. Pitcher (career)

Hits Best Against	Avg	AB	H	2B	3B	HR	RBI	BB	SO	OBP	SLG	Hits Worst Against	Avg	AB	H	2B	3B	HR	RBI	BB	SO	OBP	SLG
Doug Drabek	.533	15	8	2	0	1	1	2	1	.588	.867	Donovan Osborne	.000	14	0	0	0	0	0	1	3	.067	.000
John Burkett	.412	17	7	1	2	1	4	1	1	.444	.882	Charlie Leibrandt	.000	11	0	0	0	0	0	0	1	.000	.000
Randy Tomlin	.385	13	5	1	0	1	2	0	0	.385	.692	John Smoltz	.071	14	1	0	0	0	1	0	5	.071	.071
Bobby Ojeda	.353	17	6	0	1	2	5	1	4	.389	.824	Tommy Greene	.091	11	1	0	0	0	0	0	4	.091	.091
Bud Black	.333	12	4	0	0	2	6	2	3	.429	.833	Danny Jackson	.118	17	2	0	0	0	1	0	5	.118	.118

Mark Clark — Indians

Age 26 – Pitches Right

	ERA	W	L	Sv	G	GS	IP	BB	SO	Avg	H	2B	3B	HR	RBI	OBP	SLG	CG	ShO	Sup	QS	#P/S	SB	CS	GB	FB	G/F
1993 Season	4.28	7	5	0	26	15	109.1	25	57	.279	119	21	3	18	53	.320	.469	1	0	4.69	8	90	8	10	148	132	1.12
Career (1991-1993)	4.33	11	16	0	53	37	245.0	72	114	.267	253	41	7	33	108	.317	.430	2	1	4.19	19	85	30	13	332	311	1.07

1993 Season

	ERA	W	L	Sv	G	GS	IP	H	HR	BB	SO		Avg	AB	H	2B	3B	HR	RBI	BB	SO	OBP	SLG
Home	3.43	3	4	0	13	8	57.2	56	9	14	26	vs. Left	.320	200	64	10	1	8	24	8	24	.349	.500
Away	5.23	4	1	0	13	7	51.2	63	9	11	31	vs. Right	.243	226	55	11	2	10	29	17	33	.295	.442
Starter	4.15	7	5	0	15	15	89.0	94	13	19	47	Scoring Posn	.266	94	25	6	0	2	34	10	14	.333	.394
Reliever	4.87	0	0	0	11	0	20.1	25	5	6	10	Close & Late	.125	16	2	1	0	0	1	0	2	.125	.188
0-3 Days Rest	0.00	0	0	0	0	0	0.0	0	0	0	0	None on/out	.250	112	28	2	1	5	5	5	12	.288	.420
4 Days Rest	5.29	3	2	0	6	6	34.0	39	5	7	22	First Pitch	.345	55	19	4	1	4	12	1	0	.357	.673

1993 Season

	ERA	W	L	Sv	G	GS	IP	H	HR	BB	SO
5+ Days Rest	3.44	4	3	0	9	9	55.0	55	8	12	25
Pre-All Star	5.70	4	3	0	20	9	66.1	89	14	15	35
Post-All Star	2.09	3	2	0	6	6	43.0	30	4	10	22

	Avg	AB	H	2B	3B	HR	RBI	BB	SO	OBP	SLG
Ahead in Count	.207	184	38	8	1	5	22	0	49	.211	.342
Behind in Count	.317	101	32	7	0	4	10	13	0	.391	.505
Two Strikes	.197	183	36	4	1	6	14	11	57	.246	.328

Phil Clark — Padres

Age 26 – Bats Right

	Avg	G	AB	R	H	2B	3B	HR	RBI	BB	SO	HBP	GDP	SB	CS	OBP	SLG	IBB	SH	SF	#Pit	#P/PA	GB	FB	G/F
1993 Season	.313	102	240	33	75	17	0	9	33	8	31	5	2	2	0	.345	.496	2	1	2	828	3.23	86	71	1.21
Career (1992-1993)	.330	125	294	36	97	21	0	10	38	14	40	5	4	3	0	.368	.503	3	2	2	1052	3.32	108	81	1.33

1993 Season

	Avg	AB	H	2B	3B	HR	RBI	BB	SO	OBP	SLG
vs. Left	.323	133	43	11	0	4	17	8	14	.368	.496
vs. Right	.299	107	32	6	0	5	16	0	17	.315	.495
Home	.328	116	38	4	0	6	21	5	15	.365	.517
Away	.298	124	37	13	0	3	12	3	16	.326	.476
First Pitch	.359	39	14	2	0	2	8	2	0	.395	.564
Ahead in Count	.284	67	19	6	0	3	8	4	0	.324	.507
Behind in Count	.247	93	23	4	0	1	13	0	28	.260	.323
Two Strikes	.200	80	16	4	0	2	8	2	31	.229	.325

	Avg	AB	H	2B	3B	HR	RBI	BB	SO	OBP	SLG
Scoring Posn	.265	68	18	4	0	2	26	2	8	.278	.412
Close & Late	.289	45	13	2	0	2	6	1	8	.313	.467
None on/out	.286	56	16	3	0	2	2	2	11	.322	.446
Batting #5	.284	109	31	6	0	5	19	4	16	.313	.477
Batting #7	.381	42	16	4	0	3	6	1	6	.409	.690
Other	.315	89	28	7	0	1	8	3	9	.354	.427
Pre-All Star	.311	122	38	9	0	2	10	3	14	.344	.434
Post-All Star	.314	118	37	8	0	7	23	5	17	.346	.559

Will Clark — Giants

Age 30 – Bats Left (flyball hitter)

	Avg	G	AB	R	H	2B	3B	HR	RBI	BB	SO	HBP	GDP	SB	CS	OBP	SLG	IBB	SH	SF	#Pit	#P/PA	GB	FB	G/F
1993 Season	.283	132	491	82	139	27	2	14	73	63	68	6	10	2	2	.367	.432	6	1	6	2084	3.68	146	174	0.84
Last Five Years	.303	737	2757	430	836	162	24	101	468	323	441	20	33	34	16	.375	.489	64	1	42	11261	3.58	840	900	0.93

1993 Season

	Avg	AB	H	2B	3B	HR	RBI	BB	SO	OBP	SLG
vs. Left	.269	182	49	6	1	1	28	17	22	.335	.330
vs. Right	.291	309	90	21	1	13	45	46	46	.386	.492
Groundball	.302	149	45	10	0	6	20	16	22	.373	.490
Flyball	.286	84	24	3	0	1	8	5	8	.337	.357
Home	.249	257	64	12	1	5	31	38	39	.349	.362
Away	.321	234	75	15	1	9	42	25	29	.389	.509
Day	.265	249	66	16	1	7	36	32	42	.355	.422
Night	.302	242	73	11	1	7	37	31	26	.380	.442
Grass	.277	394	109	22	2	10	58	52	54	.365	.419
Turf	.309	97	30	5	0	4	15	11	14	.380	.485
First Pitch	.365	85	31	9	1	4	21	6	0	.398	.635
Ahead in Count	.336	119	40	5	0	4	19	31	0	.474	.479
Behind in Count	.246	199	49	8	0	4	21	0	52	.255	.347
Two Strikes	.212	203	43	7	0	5	18	26	68	.308	.320

	Avg	AB	H	2B	3B	HR	RBI	BB	SO	OBP	SLG
Scoring Posn	.227	141	32	7	2	1	51	16	23	.294	.326
Close & Late	.290	69	20	3	1	3	11	7	9	.364	.493
None on/out	.341	91	31	7	0	4	4	7	13	.406	.549
Batting #3	.285	484	138	27	2	14	73	61	68	.368	.436
Batting #5	.200	5	1	0	0	0	0	1	0	.333	.200
Other	.000	2	0	0	0	0	0	1	0	.333	.000
April	.198	91	18	4	0	1	10	10	13	.277	.275
May	.277	94	26	5	0	1	12	14	12	.373	.362
June	.295	88	26	9	0	3	18	16	15	.402	.500
July	.299	97	29	4	0	4	13	11	14	.384	.464
August	.286	63	18	2	2	3	14	3	6	.324	.524
September/October	.379	58	22	3	0	2	6	9	8	.456	.534
Pre-All Star	.281	313	88	20	0	7	46	45	45	.371	.412
Post-All Star	.287	178	51	7	2	7	27	18	23	.361	.466

1993 By Position

Position	Avg	AB	H	2B	3B	HR	RBI	BB	SO	OBP	SLG	G	GS	Innings	PO	A	E	DP	Fld Pct	Rng Fctr	In Zone	Outs	Zone Rtg	MLB Zone
As 1b	.284	489	139	27	2	14	73	62	68	.368	.434	129	129	1113.1	1079	86	14	114	.988	---	207	165	.797	.834

Last Five Years

	Avg	AB	H	2B	3B	HR	RBI	BB	SO	OBP	SLG
vs. Left	.293	1048	307	47	10	29	199	89	161	.349	.440
vs. Right	.310	1709	529	115	14	72	269	234	280	.391	.520
Groundball	.304	936	285	49	6	36	153	131	154	.389	.485
Flyball	.303	595	180	37	3	25	102	48	91	.358	.501
Home	.303	1383	419	92	11	50	223	178	222	.379	.494
Away	.303	1374	417	70	13	51	245	145	219	.371	.485
Day	.302	1131	342	80	12	42	184	146	191	.383	.506
Night	.304	1626	494	82	12	59	284	177	250	.370	.478
Grass	.308	2050	631	124	18	72	345	249	330	.381	.491
Turf	.290	707	205	38	6	29	123	74	111	.357	.484
First Pitch	.360	478	172	36	5	20	98	48	0	.415	.582
Ahead in Count	.392	592	232	40	4	30	127	161	0	.514	.625
Behind in Count	.234	1185	277	50	7	29	153	0	353	.238	.361
Two Strikes	.214	1186	254	49	11	32	136	109	441	.283	.355

	Avg	AB	H	2B	3B	HR	RBI	BB	SO	OBP	SLG
Scoring Posn	.313	721	226	40	9	29	349	135	129	.403	.515
Close & Late	.284	429	122	20	6	17	82	65	83	.378	.478
None on/out	.292	518	151	27	5	17	17	43	79	.356	.461
Batting #3	.305	2732	832	162	24	100	464	317	437	.376	.491
Batting #4	.100	10	1	0	0	0	1	0	2	.091	.100
Other	.200	15	3	0	0	1	3	6	2	.409	.400
April	.309	421	130	25	6	13	77	58	61	.392	.489
May	.269	498	134	22	2	21	79	61	86	.350	.448
June	.321	446	143	25	4	18	89	60	63	.395	.516
July	.303	475	144	26	2	17	74	45	86	.367	.474
August	.309	479	148	36	6	19	89	46	70	.371	.528
September/October	.313	438	137	28	4	13	60	53	75	.381	.484
Pre-All Star	.301	1536	463	78	13	60	271	201	240	.380	.486
Post-All Star	.305	1221	373	84	11	41	197	122	201	.369	.493

Batter vs. Pitcher (career)

Hits Best Against	Avg	AB	H	2B	3B	HR	RBI	BB	SO	OBP	SLG
Todd Worrell	.600	10	6	2	0	1	3	3	2	.692	1.100
Derek Lilliquist	.526	19	10	3	0	2	3	1	2	.550	1.000
Jimmy Jones	.500	20	10	3	1	2	7	4	2	.583	1.050
Mark Davis	.471	17	8	2	2	1	11	0	3	.471	1.000
Ted Power	.467	15	7	1	0	2	5	3	1	.556	.933

Hits Worst Against	Avg	AB	H	2B	3B	HR	RBI	BB	SO	OBP	SLG
Chris Nabholz	.000	17	0	0	0	0	1	1	1	.056	.000
Mike Harkey	.000	15	0	0	0	0	0	2	3	.118	.000
Frank DiPino	.000	11	0	0	0	0	0	4	1	.267	.000
Norm Charlton	.105	19	2	0	0	0	0	2	5	.190	.105
Jamie Moyer	.133	15	2	0	0	0	0	1	3	.188	.133

Royce Clayton — Giants

Age 24 – Bats Right (groundball hitter)

	Avg	G	AB	R	H	2B	3B	HR	RBI	BB	SO	HBP	GDP	SB	CS	OBP	SLG	IBB	SH	SF	#Pit	#P/PA	GB	FB	G/F
1993 Season	.282	153	549	54	155	21	5	6	70	38	91	5	16	11	10	.331	.372	2	8	7	2095	3.45	220	141	1.56
Career (1991-1993)	.257	260	896	85	230	29	9	10	96	65	160	5	28	19	14	.308	.343	5	11	9	3526	3.58	372	220	1.69

1993 Season

	Avg	AB	H	2B	3B	HR	RBI	BB	SO	OBP	SLG		Avg	AB	H	2B	3B	HR	RBI	BB	SO	OBP	SLG
vs. Left	.247	170	42	10	0	2	16	9	29	.283	.341	Scoring Posn	.254	173	44	3	2	1	63	15	34	.310	.312
vs. Right	.298	379	113	11	5	4	54	29	62	.352	.385	Close & Late	.177	79	14	2	0	0	2	4	22	.217	.203
Groundball	.277	177	49	4	0	2	20	11	26	.326	.333	None on/out	.311	132	41	11	1	3	3	13	14	.377	.477
Flyball	.272	81	22	2	3	1	16	6	15	.318	.407	Batting #6	.330	100	33	4	0	2	17	5	15	.358	.430
Home	.305	266	81	12	2	5	34	16	44	.346	.421	Batting #7	.274	430	118	17	5	4	53	31	72	.326	.365
Away	.261	283	74	9	3	1	36	22	47	.316	.325	Other	.211	19	4	0	0	0	0	2	4	.286	.211
Day	.265	268	71	7	2	3	32	16	47	.308	.340	April	.264	91	24	1	1	0	9	0	18	.261	.297
Night	.299	281	84	14	3	3	38	22	44	.352	.402	May	.311	90	28	3	2	1	13	10	12	.385	.422
Grass	.285	421	120	17	4	6	48	30	70	.335	.387	June	.271	96	26	3	0	1	11	3	14	.293	.333
Turf	.273	128	35	4	1	0	22	8	21	.317	.320	July	.333	87	29	6	1	2	21	10	12	.394	.494
First Pitch	.330	103	34	6	2	1	15	2	0	.343	.456	August	.209	86	18	4	1	0	8	4	20	.258	.279
Ahead in Count	.313	96	30	4	0	3	13	24	0	.446	.448	September/October	.303	99	30	4	0	2	8	11	15	.375	.404
Behind in Count	.249	273	68	10	3	2	35	0	81	.249	.330	Pre-All Star	.301	316	95	10	3	3	47	17	48	.336	.380
Two Strikes	.211	251	53	7	2	1	23	12	91	.248	.267	Post-All Star	.258	233	60	11	2	3	23	21	43	.323	.361

1993 By Position

Position	Avg	AB	H	2B	3B	HR	RBI	BB	SO	OBP	SLG	G	GS	Innings	PO	A	E	DP	Fld Pct	Rng Fctr	In Zone	Outs	Zone Rtg	MLB Zone
As ss	.283	548	155	21	5	6	70	38	90	.331	.372	153	151	1328.2	251	450	27	103	.963	4.75	546	458	.839	.880

Career (1991-1993)

	Avg	AB	H	2B	3B	HR	RBI	BB	SO	OBP	SLG		Avg	AB	H	2B	3B	HR	RBI	BB	SO	OBP	SLG
vs. Left	.247	271	67	14	2	2	20	20	51	.297	.336	Scoring Posn	.231	260	60	4	5	2	85	24	48	.292	.308
vs. Right	.261	625	163	15	7	8	76	45	109	.312	.346	Close & Late	.184	141	26	2	0	0	4	11	36	.243	.199
Groundball	.231	350	81	9	2	4	33	20	58	.277	.303	None on/out	.293	215	63	12	1	5	5	20	31	.356	.428
Flyball	.256	133	34	3	4	2	19	14	27	.322	.383	Batting #7	.268	488	131	20	5	5	58	36	91	.321	.361
Home	.279	451	126	15	4	8	51	31	71	.326	.384	Batting #8	.219	237	52	3	3	3	20	22	39	.285	.295
Away	.234	445	104	14	5	2	45	34	89	.289	.301	Other	.275	171	47	6	1	2	18	7	30	.302	.357
Day	.247	409	101	9	4	5	44	30	66	.300	.325	April	.242	165	40	2	3	0	15	7	33	.270	.291
Night	.265	487	129	20	5	5	52	35	94	.315	.357	May	.270	148	40	7	2	3	21	16	24	.343	.405
Grass	.263	680	179	22	7	9	68	51	115	.316	.356	June	.245	143	35	4	1	2	13	7	23	.280	.329
Turf	.236	216	51	7	2	1	28	14	45	.282	.301	July	.333	87	29	6	1	2	21	10	12	.394	.494
First Pitch	.315	146	46	6	4	3	22	5	0	.335	.473	August	.240	121	29	4	1	0	11	8	23	.295	.289
Ahead in Count	.265	162	43	7	0	4	15	33	0	.388	.383	September/October	.246	232	57	6	1	3	15	17	45	.299	.319
Behind in Count	.217	442	96	13	4	3	43	0	141	.217	.285	Pre-All Star	.267	495	132	16	6	6	63	34	84	.313	.360
Two Strikes	.194	427	83	10	3	2	32	27	160	.243	.246	Post-All Star	.244	401	98	13	3	4	33	31	76	.301	.322

Batter vs. Pitcher (career)

Hits Best Against	Avg	AB	H	2B	3B	HR	RBI	BB	SO	OBP	SLG	Hits Worst Against	Avg	AB	H	2B	3B	HR	RBI	BB	SO	OBP	SLG
Steve Avery	.533	15	8	2	1	0	2	0	4	.500	.800	Orel Hershiser	.111	18	2	0	0	0	0	1	1	.158	.111
Kevin Gross	.500	12	6	2	0	0	1	0	1	.500	.667	Mark Portugal	.154	13	2	0	0	0	0	0	2	.154	.154
Darryl Kile	.455	11	5	0	0	1	3	0	1	.455	.727	Greg Maddux	.182	11	2	0	0	0	0	1	1	.250	.182
Armando Reynoso	.429	7	3	0	0	1	3	2	0	.455	.857	Tom Glavine	.182	11	2	1	0	0	0	1	1	.250	.273
Steve Cooke	.417	12	5	2	0	1	1	1	1	.462	.833	Doug Drabek	.235	17	4	0	0	1	5	0	4	.235	.412

Roger Clemens — Red Sox

Age 31 – Pitches Right (groundball pitcher)

	ERA	W	L	Sv	G	GS	IP	BB	SO	Avg	H	2B	3B	HR	RBI	OBP	SLG	CG	ShO	Sup	QS	#P/S	SB	CS	GB	FB	G/F
1993 Season	4.46	11	14	0	29	29	191.2	67	160	.244	175	31	5	17	91	.315	.372	2	1	3.66	14	109	16	7	274	155	1.77
Last Five Years	2.85	85	52	0	162	162	1191.1	341	1048	.229	1005	182	24	70	374	.288	.329	41	17	4.44	113	116	96	66	1621	985	1.65

1993 Season

	ERA	W	L	Sv	G	GS	IP	H	HR	BB	SO		Avg	AB	H	2B	3B	HR	RBI	BB	SO	OBP	SLG
Home	5.14	6	8	0	16	16	105.0	106	9	38	92	vs. Left	.260	404	105	19	3	8	44	51	84	.346	.381
Away	3.63	5	6	0	13	13	86.2	69	8	29	68	vs. Right	.223	314	70	12	2	9	47	16	76	.273	.360
Day	4.60	4	4	0	9	9	60.2	58	6	21	57	Inning 1-6	.248	614	152	29	4	16	84	57	129	.319	.386
Night	4.40	7	10	0	20	20	131.0	117	11	46	103	Inning 7+	.221	104	23	2	1	1	7	10	31	.289	.288
Grass	4.66	8	12	0	24	24	162.1	154	17	53	148	None on	.223	440	98	19	2	9	9	36	96	.286	.336
Turf	3.38	3	2	0	5	5	29.1	21	0	14	12	Runners on	.277	278	77	12	3	8	82	31	64	.358	.428
April	1.64	3	1	0	5	5	38.1	28	3	10	29	Scoring Posn	.278	151	42	8	0	4	68	24	34	.383	.411
May	3.80	3	3	0	6	6	42.2	34	3	16	48	Close & Late	.159	63	10	1	0	1	2	5	17	.221	.222
June	6.65	1	2	0	4	4	23.0	26	3	6	21	None on/out	.234	184	43	6	0	2	2	17	44	.302	.299
July	2.17	2	1	0	4	4	29.0	25	0	6	23	vs. 1st Batr (relief)	.000	0	0	0	0	0	0	0	0	.000	.000
August	7.02	1	4	0	6	6	33.1	38	6	15	22	First Inning Pitched	.236	106	25	4	1	1	15	15	22	.333	.321
September/October	7.11	1	3	0	4	4	25.1	24	2	14	17	First 75 Pitches	.248	488	121	25	3	10	53	35	104	.310	.373
Starter	4.46	11	14	0	29	29	191.2	175	17	67	160	Pitch 76-90	.221	86	19	3	1	4	14	15	22	.333	.419
Reliever	0.00	0	0	0	0	0	0.0	0	0	0	0	Pitch 91-105	.221	77	17	0	1	2	15	8	17	.287	.325
0-3 Days Rest	10.45	0	2	0	2	2	10.1	18	3	4	6	Pitch 106+	.269	67	18	3	0	1	9	9	17	.355	.358
4 Days Rest	4.51	6	9	0	17	17	115.2	109	9	45	97	First Pitch	.255	98	25	3	0	3	13	2	0	.302	.378
5+ Days Rest	3.43	5	3	0	10	10	65.2	48	5	18	57	Ahead in Count	.200	325	65	13	1	7	30	0	142	.209	.311
Pre-All Star	3.63	7	6	0	15	15	104.0	88	9	32	98	Behind in Count	.351	134	47	6	1	4	33	26	0	.448	.500
Post-All Star	5.44	4	8	0	14	14	87.2	87	8	35	62	Two Strikes	.168	352	59	13	2	6	32	39	160	.253	.267

Last Five Years

	ERA	W	L	Sv	G	GS	IP	H	HR	BB	SO
Home	2.96	42	24	0	81	81	593.1	537	35	173	541
Away	2.74	43	28	0	81	81	598.0	468	35	168	507
Day	2.42	28	14	0	52	52	390.1	318	16	100	336
Night	3.06	57	38	0	110	110	801.0	687	54	241	712
Grass	2.98	71	45	0	137	137	1003.0	865	61	288	925
Turf	2.15	14	7	0	25	25	188.1	140	9	53	123
April	1.70	17	5	0	25	25	190.1	129	8	46	182
May	3.09	17	10	0	30	30	227.0	171	12	60	202
June	3.07	11	10	0	25	25	178.2	177	14	55	155
July	2.79	11	9	0	27	27	196.2	171	11	64	162
August	2.99	18	7	0	31	31	222.2	196	16	62	195
September/October	3.43	11	11	0	24	24	176.0	161	9	54	152
Starter	2.85	85	52	0	162	162	1191.1	1005	70	341	1048
Reliever	0.00	0	0	0	0	0	0.0	0	0	0	0
0-3 Days Rest	6.25	1	3	0	5	5	31.2	37	5	12	26
4 Days Rest	2.91	59	38	0	114	114	837.1	730	52	257	753
5+ Days Rest	2.35	25	11	0	43	43	322.1	238	13	72	269
Pre-All Star	2.72	48	27	0	88	88	652.0	533	40	181	586
Post-All Star	3.00	37	25	0	74	74	539.1	472	30	160	462

	Avg	AB	H	2B	3B	HR	RBI	BB	SO	OBP	SLG
vs. Left	.236	2360	558	102	13	31	187	212	510	.301	.330
vs. Right	.220	2034	447	80	11	39	187	129	538	.273	.327
Inning 1-6	.231	3469	800	152	18	56	319	264	825	.289	.333
Inning 7+	.222	925	205	30	6	14	55	77	223	.285	.312
None on	.227	2697	613	105	10	45	45	177	657	.280	.324
Runners on	.231	1697	392	77	14	25	329	164	391	.301	.337
Scoring Posn	.219	928	203	37	8	10	278	115	223	.303	.308
Close & Late	.198	504	100	16	3	5	26	47	117	.273	.272
None on/out	.232	1157	269	42	3	16	16	80	273	.286	.315
vs. 1st Batr (relief)	.000	0	0	0	0	0	0	0	0	.000	.000
First Inning Pitched	.258	613	158	29	5	7	65	60	142	.327	.356
First 75 Pitches	.234	2751	644	125	14	39	227	192	666	.289	.332
Pitch 76-90	.196	570	112	20	4	11	46	53	123	.266	.304
Pitch 91-105	.232	514	119	19	2	9	47	40	116	.289	.329
Pitch 106+	.233	559	130	18	4	11	54	56	143	.306	.338
First Pitch	.296	564	167	30	4	13	65	23	0	.337	.433
Ahead in Count	.177	2093	371	67	6	26	132	0	869	.185	.252
Behind in Count	.302	828	250	47	7	15	110	142	0	.399	.430
Two Strikes	.158	2241	355	69	7	22	128	175	1048	.221	.225

Pitcher vs. Batter (career)

Pitches Best Vs.	Avg	AB	H	2B	3B	HR	RBI	BB	SO	OBP	SLG
Ron Tingley	.000	11	0	0	0	0	0	0	5	.000	.000
Tim Teufel	.000	10	0	0	0	0	1	1	3	.083	.000
Cecil Fielder	.043	23	1	0	0	0	1	2	12	.120	.043
Greg Vaughn	.056	18	1	0	0	0	0	0	10	.056	.056
Cory Snyder	.087	23	2	0	0	0	0	0	12	.087	.087

Pitches Worst Vs.	Avg	AB	H	2B	3B	HR	RBI	BB	SO	OBP	SLG
Gary Sheffield	.533	15	8	1	0	0	2	1	1	.563	.600
Reggie Jefferson	.500	14	7	3	0	0	2	0	5	.500	.714
Brady Anderson	.412	17	7	4	0	1	2	2	3	.474	.824
Ken Griffey Jr	.400	30	12	5	0	1	6	8	4	.526	.667
Eddie Murray	.346	26	9	2	0	2	3	4	2	.433	.654

Craig Colbert — Giants

Age 29 – Bats Right

	Avg	G	AB	R	H	2B	3B	HR	RBI	BB	SO	HBP	GDP	SB	CS	OBP	SLG	IBB	SH	SF	#Pit	#P/PA	GB	FB	G/F
1993 Season	.162	23	37	2	6	2	0	1	5	3	13	0	0	0	0	.225	.297	1	0	0	152	3.80	10	9	1.11
Career (1992-1993)	.215	72	163	12	35	7	2	2	21	12	35	0	8	1	0	.266	.319	1	2	2	599	3.35	59	40	1.48

1993 Season

	Avg	AB	H	2B	3B	HR	RBI	BB	SO	OBP	SLG
vs. Left	.136	22	3	2	0	0	2	1	6	.174	.227
vs. Right	.200	15	3	0	0	1	3	2	7	.294	.400
Scoring Posn	.400	10	4	1	0	1	5	1	4	.455	.800
Close & Late	.000	9	0	0	0	0	0	0	4	.000	.000

Greg Colbrunn — Expos

Age 24 – Bats Right

	Avg	G	AB	R	H	2B	3B	HR	RBI	BB	SO	HBP	GDP	SB	CS	OBP	SLG	IBB	SH	SF	#Pit	#P/PA	GB	FB	G/F
1993 Season	.255	70	153	15	39	9	0	4	23	6	33	1	1	4	2	.282	.392	1	1	3	607	3.70	52	52	1.00
Career (1992-1993)	.262	122	321	27	84	17	0	6	41	12	67	3	2	7	4	.289	.371	2	1	7	1251	3.64	108	98	1.10

1993 Season

	Avg	AB	H	2B	3B	HR	RBI	BB	SO	OBP	SLG
vs. Left	.324	74	24	4	0	4	17	2	14	.333	.541
vs. Right	.190	79	15	5	0	0	6	4	19	.235	.253
Home	.233	73	17	5	0	2	14	4	12	.275	.384
Away	.275	80	22	4	0	2	9	2	21	.289	.400
First Pitch	.214	14	3	0	0	0	5	0	0	.200	.214
Ahead in Count	.333	33	11	4	0	3	8	3	0	.389	.727
Behind in Count	.237	76	18	4	0	0	5	0	30	.244	.289
Two Strikes	.205	73	15	3	0	0	2	3	33	.244	.247
Scoring Posn	.225	40	9	2	0	3	21	4	10	.292	.500
Close & Late	.167	30	5	1	0	0	1	2	5	.219	.200
None on/out	.244	41	10	2	0	0	0	0	10	.244	.293
Batting #6	.243	37	9	3	0	1	8	1	9	.256	.405
Batting #7	.325	40	13	2	0	2	10	0	6	.326	.525
Other	.224	76	17	4	0	1	5	5	18	.272	.316
Pre-All Star	.255	153	39	9	0	4	23	6	33	.282	.392
Post-All Star	.000	0	0	0	0	0	0	0	0	.000	.000

Alex Cole — Rockies

Age 28 – Bats Left (groundball hitter)

	Avg	G	AB	R	H	2B	3B	HR	RBI	BB	SO	HBP	GDP	SB	CS	OBP	SLG	IBB	SH	SF	#Pit	#P/PA	GB	FB	G/F
1993 Season	.256	126	348	50	89	9	4	0	24	43	58	2	6	30	13	.339	.305	3	4	2	1473	3.69	129	78	1.65
Career (1990-1993)	.275	416	1264	195	348	35	18	0	73	157	210	5	20	113	45	.356	.331	6	9	6	5529	3.84	502	252	1.99

1993 Season

	Avg	AB	H	2B	3B	HR	RBI	BB	SO	OBP	SLG
vs. Left	.143	21	3	1	1	0	3	1	9	.182	.286
vs. Right	.263	327	86	8	3	0	21	42	49	.349	.306
Groundball	.244	123	30	3	3	0	9	16	22	.331	.317
Flyball	.231	52	12	1	0	0	3	5	12	.305	.250
Home	.235	179	42	4	4	0	18	20	31	.315	.302
Away	.278	169	47	5	0	0	6	23	27	.365	.308
Day	.248	125	31	4	1	0	7	16	24	.331	.296
Night	.260	223	58	5	3	0	17	27	34	.344	.309
Grass	.258	275	71	8	4	0	22	30	46	.333	.316
Turf	.247	73	18	1	0	0	2	13	12	.360	.260
First Pitch	.392	51	20	0	2	0	7	1	0	.407	.471
Ahead in Count	.312	93	29	3	1	0	3	27	0	.467	.366
Behind in Count	.165	139	23	5	1	0	10	0	52	.171	.216
Two Strikes	.152	145	22	5	1	0	10	15	58	.236	.200
Scoring Posn	.315	73	23	4	1	0	23	12	15	.409	.397
Close & Late	.239	46	11	0	1	0	5	6	8	.321	.283
None on/out	.240	100	24	2	2	0	0	9	16	.303	.300
Batting #1	.229	118	27	2	1	0	6	16	18	.319	.263
Batting #2	.282	149	42	2	3	0	12	18	24	.361	.336
Other	.247	81	20	5	0	0	6	9	16	.330	.309
April	.309	68	21	1	2	0	3	8	10	.382	.382
May	.213	80	17	3	0	0	6	7	14	.284	.250
June	.269	52	14	2	1	0	10	10	9	.375	.346
July	.268	41	11	2	0	0	2	5	7	.348	.317
August	.284	74	21	1	1	0	1	8	9	.354	.324
September/October	.152	33	5	0	0	0	2	5	9	.282	.152
Pre-All Star	.264	220	58	7	3	0	21	27	35	.344	.323
Post-All Star	.242	128	31	2	1	0	3	16	23	.331	.273

1993 By Position																								
Position	Avg	AB	H	2B	3B	HR	RBI	BB	SO	OBP	SLG	G	GS	Innings	PO	A	E	DP	Fld Pct	Rng Fctr	In Zone	Outs	Zone Rtg	MLB Zone
As Pinch Hitter	.214	28	6	1	0	0	1	2	8	.267	.250	31	0	---	---	---	---	---	---	---	---	---	---	---
As cf	.259	320	83	8	4	0	23	41	50	.345	.309	93	85	749.2	218	5	4	1	.982	2.68	274	218	.796	.829

Career (1990-1993)																							
	Avg	AB	H	2B	3B	HR	RBI	BB	SO	OBP	SLG		Avg	AB	H	2B	3B	HR	RBI	BB	SO	OBP	SLG
vs. Left	.293	184	54	6	5	0	18	31	41	.400	.380	Scoring Posn	.279	244	68	6	3	0	68	38	47	.372	.328
vs. Right	.272	1080	294	29	13	0	55	126	169	.348	.323	Close & Late	.254	205	52	3	2	0	17	25	38	.339	.288
Groundball	.294	435	128	11	7	0	27	50	80	.368	.352	None on/out	.267	449	120	13	6	0	0	70	73	.366	.323
Flyball	.242	244	59	5	2	0	12	36	46	.342	.279	Batting #1	.282	941	265	27	15	0	51	122	150	.364	.342
Home	.279	619	173	17	12	0	54	88	111	.371	.346	Batting #2	.270	196	53	3	3	0	14	22	31	.344	.316
Away	.271	645	175	18	6	0	19	69	99	.341	.318	Other	.236	127	30	5	0	0	8	13	29	.317	.276
Day	.270	370	100	9	3	0	20	52	68	.358	.311	April	.281	153	43	5	3	0	5	16	25	.345	.353
Night	.277	894	248	26	15	0	53	105	142	.356	.340	May	.231	147	34	4	0	0	11	15	24	.309	.259
Grass	.273	927	253	26	10	0	57	118	148	.356	.323	June	.270	141	38	3	1	0	14	24	21	.373	.305
Turf	.282	337	95	9	8	0	16	39	62	.356	.356	July	.273	187	51	4	4	0	13	28	34	.367	.337
First Pitch	.393	183	72	4	4	0	14	4	0	.411	.459	August	.309	298	92	10	6	0	13	35	55	.383	.383
Ahead in Count	.344	305	105	9	10	0	23	79	0	.475	.439	September/October	.266	338	90	9	4	0	17	40	51	.344	.317
Behind in Count	.189	497	94	11	4	0	23	0	171	.194	.227	Pre-All Star	.264	496	131	13	6	0	35	61	81	.346	.315
Two Strikes	.175	555	97	13	3	0	21	74	210	.275	.209	Post-All Star	.283	768	217	22	12	0	38	96	129	.363	.342

Batter vs. Pitcher (career)																							
Hits Best Against	Avg	AB	H	2B	3B	HR	RBI	BB	SO	OBP	SLG	Hits Worst Against	Avg	AB	H	2B	3B	HR	RBI	BB	SO	OBP	SLG
Todd Stottlemyre	.636	11	7	1	0	0	0	0	1	.636	.727	Bill Wegman	.077	13	1	0	0	0	1	2	1	.200	.077
Scott Erickson	.571	14	8	0	0	0	0	1	0	.600	.571	Jose Guzman	.083	12	1	1	0	0	0	0	4	.083	.167
Ramon Martinez	.400	10	4	1	0	0	0	3	1	.538	.500	Charlie Hough	.200	10	2	0	0	0	0	1	1	.273	.200
Kevin Brown	.357	14	5	2	0	0	1	1	4	.400	.500	Ben Rivera	.200	10	2	0	0	0	0	1	0	.273	.200
Jack Morris	.333	12	4	0	0	0	1	4	1	.500	.333	Dwight Gooden	.214	14	3	0	0	0	0	1	1	.267	.214

Vince Coleman — Mets

Age 32 – Bats Both (groundball hitter)

	Avg	G	AB	R	H	2B	3B	HR	RBI	BB	SO	HBP	GDP	SB	CS	OBP	SLG	IBB	SH	SF	#Pit	#P/PA	GB	FB	G/F
1993 Season	.279	92	373	64	104	14	8	2	25	21	58	0	2	38	13	.316	.375	1	3	2	1449	3.63	132	84	1.57
Last Five Years	.271	504	1940	313	526	71	32	13	130	172	324	6	16	241	63	.331	.361	5	17	6	7861	3.67	774	434	1.78

1993 Season																							
	Avg	AB	H	2B	3B	HR	RBI	BB	SO	OBP	SLG		Avg	AB	H	2B	3B	HR	RBI	BB	SO	OBP	SLG
vs. Left	.290	100	29	5	3	1	6	7	17	.333	.430	Scoring Posn	.224	67	15	1	0	0	22	7	15	.289	.239
vs. Right	.275	273	75	9	5	1	19	14	41	.309	.355	Close & Late	.197	61	12	3	1	0	2	2	14	.219	.279
Groundball	.295	129	38	7	2	0	6	5	19	.319	.380	None on/out	.310	155	48	9	6	2	2	9	23	.348	.484
Flyball	.151	73	11	2	2	0	3	4	13	.195	.233	Batting #1	.279	369	103	14	8	2	25	21	57	.316	.377
Home	.284	190	54	6	4	2	16	13	39	.328	.389	Batting #9	.333	3	1	0	0	0	0	0	1	.333	.333
Away	.273	183	50	8	4	0	9	8	19	.302	.361	Other	.000	1	0	0	0	0	0	0	0	.000	.000
Day	.268	142	38	9	1	1	9	12	17	.325	.366	April	.258	93	24	3	2	0	6	4	12	.289	.333
Night	.286	231	66	5	7	1	16	9	41	.310	.381	May	.236	110	26	5	2	1	8	10	14	.298	.345
Grass	.290	307	89	9	7	2	23	17	51	.325	.384	June	.303	89	27	3	2	1	8	4	18	.333	.416
Turf	.227	66	15	5	1	0	2	4	7	.271	.333	July	.333	81	27	3	2	0	3	3	14	.353	.420
First Pitch	.349	43	15	1	0	0	0	1	0	.364	.372	August	.000	0	0	0	0	0	0	0	0	.000	.000
Ahead in Count	.355	76	27	4	3	0	10	15	0	.462	.487	September/October	.000	0	0	0	0	0	0	0	0	.000	.000
Behind in Count	.225	178	40	5	5	2	10	0	54	.222	.343	Pre-All Star	.274	336	92	12	7	2	24	20	54	.313	.369
Two Strikes	.186	167	31	5	2	2	6	5	58	.208	.275	Post-All Star	.324	37	12	2	1	0	1	1	4	.342	.432

1993 By Position																								
Position	Avg	AB	H	2B	3B	HR	RBI	BB	SO	OBP	SLG	G	GS	Innings	PO	A	E	DP	Fld Pct	Rng Fctr	In Zone	Outs	Zone Rtg	MLB Zone
As lf	.278	370	103	14	8	2	25	21	58	.316	.376	90	88	744.1	162	5	3	0	.982	2.02	192	156	.813	.818

Last Five Years																							
	Avg	AB	H	2B	3B	HR	RBI	BB	SO	OBP	SLG		Avg	AB	H	2B	3B	HR	RBI	BB	SO	OBP	SLG
vs. Left	.256	720	184	39	10	10	54	50	129	.305	.379	Scoring Posn	.245	396	97	15	7	3	118	45	77	.321	.341
vs. Right	.280	1220	342	32	22	3	76	122	195	.347	.350	Close & Late	.234	312	73	11	2	2	22	28	56	.298	.301
Groundball	.281	726	204	32	8	3	47	59	112	.336	.360	None on/out	.280	838	235	40	15	6	6	77	152	.344	.385
Flyball	.228	443	101	18	6	6	32	38	76	.290	.336	Batting #1	.273	1898	519	71	31	12	127	170	316	.334	.362
Home	.274	952	261	35	16	10	76	95	159	.341	.376	Batting #9	.133	15	2	0	1	0	0	1	4	.188	.267
Away	.268	988	265	36	16	3	54	77	165	.322	.346	Other	.185	27	5	0	0	1	3	1	4	.214	.296
Day	.269	595	160	22	10	6	40	55	94	.331	.370	April	.284	352	100	16	7	0	23	31	51	.341	.369
Night	.272	1345	366	49	22	7	90	117	230	.332	.357	May	.276	398	110	11	7	3	29	43	69	.348	.362
Grass	.261	934	244	25	11	5	60	89	168	.325	.328	June	.273	455	124	22	7	5	35	33	79	.324	.385
Turf	.280	1006	282	46	21	8	70	83	156	.338	.392	July	.281	270	76	8	3	2	14	25	44	.340	.356
First Pitch	.357	266	95	15	8	2	25	4	0	.370	.496	August	.278	299	83	10	6	2	22	31	44	.350	.371
Ahead in Count	.306	369	113	19	6	2	40	104	0	.457	.407	September/October	.199	166	33	4	2	1	7	9	37	.240	.265
Behind in Count	.228	955	218	26	17	6	42	0	294	.231	.310	Pre-All Star	.276	1295	358	51	22	8	94	116	214	.336	.368
Two Strikes	.210	909	191	23	13	8	38	63	324	.263	.290	Post-All Star	.260	645	168	20	10	5	36	56	110	.322	.346

Batter vs. Pitcher (career)																							
Hits Best Against	Avg	AB	H	2B	3B	HR	RBI	BB	SO	OBP	SLG	Hits Worst Against	Avg	AB	H	2B	3B	HR	RBI	BB	SO	OBP	SLG
John Burkett	.583	12	7	0	0	0	0	2	0	.643	.583	Randy Tomlin	.043	23	1	0	0	0	0	0	5	.043	.043
Mark Portugal	.545	11	6	1	1	0	0	1	2	.583	.818	Dennis Rasmussen	.083	12	1	0	0	0	0	0	5	.083	.083
Tim Belcher	.500	22	11	0	1	0	1	3	5	.560	.591	Greg W. Harris	.083	12	1	0	0	0	0	1	2	.154	.083
Barry Jones	.500	10	5	1	1	0	3	1	1	.545	.800	Pete Harnisch	.091	11	1	1	0	0	0	0	3	.091	.182

Batter vs. Pitcher (career)																						
Hits Best Against	Avg	AB	H	2B	3B	HR	RBI	BB	SO	OBP	SLG	Hits Worst Against	Avg	AB	H	2B	3B	HR	RBI	BB	SO	OBP	SLG
Mark Grant	.467	15	7	2	0	0	0	3	1	.556	.600	Bob Welch	.095	21	2	0	0	0	1	1	9	.136	.095

Darnell Coles — Blue Jays

Age 32 – Bats Right (flyball hitter)

	Avg	G	AB	R	H	2B	3B	HR	RBI	BB	SO	HBP	GDP	SB	CS	OBP	SLG	IBB	SH	SF	#Pit	#P/PA	GB	FB	G/F
1993 Season	.253	64	194	26	49	9	1	4	26	16	29	4	3	1	1	.319	.371	1	1	2	803	3.70	57	67	0.85
Last Five Years	.251	365	1099	119	276	48	7	20	123	62	145	11	22	7	9	.296	.362	4	7	9	4284	3.61	356	384	0.93

1993 Season

	Avg	AB	H	2B	3B	HR	RBI	BB	SO	OBP	SLG		Avg	AB	H	2B	3B	HR	RBI	BB	SO	OBP	SLG
vs. Left	.213	61	13	1	0	0	5	8	9	.310	.230	Scoring Posn	.245	53	13	1	0	2	20	4	9	.300	.377
vs. Right	.271	133	36	8	1	4	21	8	20	.324	.436	Close & Late	.310	29	9	0	1	0	4	4	7	.412	.379
Home	.300	90	27	4	1	3	16	9	15	.376	.467	None on/out	.234	47	11	2	0	0	0	6	6	.333	.277
Away	.212	104	22	5	0	1	10	7	14	.270	.288	Batting #7	.239	67	16	4	1	1	8	3	9	.282	.373
First Pitch	.440	25	11	3	0	2	7	1	0	.483	.800	Batting #8	.250	56	14	3	0	0	8	2	13	.283	.304
Ahead in Count	.280	50	14	3	0	2	9	8	0	.383	.460	Other	.268	71	19	2	0	3	10	11	7	.376	.423
Behind in Count	.165	85	14	2	0	0	5	0	25	.174	.188	Pre-All Star	.240	104	25	3	1	2	13	14	12	.328	.346
Two Strikes	.153	85	13	1	0	0	6	7	29	.226	.165	Post-All Star	.267	90	24	6	0	2	13	2	17	.309	.400

Last Five Years

	Avg	AB	H	2B	3B	HR	RBI	BB	SO	OBP	SLG		Avg	AB	H	2B	3B	HR	RBI	BB	SO	OBP	SLG
vs. Left	.251	443	111	23	4	4	44	28	54	.295	.348	Scoring Posn	.236	271	64	10	1	5	94	20	37	.289	.336
vs. Right	.252	656	165	25	3	16	79	34	91	.296	.372	Close & Late	.279	183	51	6	3	3	20	13	27	.333	.393
Groundball	.217	244	53	9	3	3	28	12	31	.253	.316	None on/out	.236	246	58	8	1	3	3	18	30	.291	.313
Flyball	.229	231	53	7	1	5	23	13	41	.278	.333	Batting #5	.283	286	81	13	2	10	43	13	31	.317	.448
Home	.275	524	144	23	4	11	69	34	61	.325	.397	Batting #7	.223	211	47	9	2	3	22	11	33	.265	.327
Away	.230	575	132	25	3	9	54	28	84	.268	.330	Other	.246	602	148	26	3	7	58	38	81	.296	.334
Day	.287	296	85	16	3	2	28	17	42	.328	.382	April	.222	144	32	6	1	2	15	9	14	.273	.319
Night	.238	803	191	32	4	18	95	45	103	.284	.355	May	.242	256	62	13	2	4	36	10	27	.272	.355
Grass	.234	483	113	16	2	7	43	23	73	.272	.319	June	.296	125	37	6	1	2	12	6	27	.326	.408
Turf	.265	616	163	32	5	13	80	39	72	.314	.396	July	.275	189	52	8	3	5	30	19	17	.340	.429
First Pitch	.327	153	50	10	0	2	17	2	0	.344	.431	August	.253	229	58	10	0	5	20	11	33	.298	.362
Ahead in Count	.284	268	76	11	2	7	35	33	0	.364	.418	September/October	.224	156	35	5	0	2	10	7	27	.271	.295
Behind in Count	.201	498	100	16	2	7	48	0	126	.208	.283	Pre-All Star	.251	577	145	28	5	9	71	33	72	.294	.364
Two Strikes	.179	481	86	15	3	4	36	25	145	.225	.247	Post-All Star	.251	522	131	20	2	11	52	29	73	.297	.360

Batter vs. Pitcher (since 1984)

Hits Best Against	Avg	AB	H	2B	3B	HR	RBI	BB	SO	OBP	SLG	Hits Worst Against	Avg	AB	H	2B	3B	HR	RBI	BB	SO	OBP	SLG
Jack Morris	.600	10	6	1	0	0	1	1	2	.636	.700	Greg Harris	.000	13	0	0	0	0	0	0	7	.000	.000
Mike Moore	.467	15	7	1	1	3	10	3	0	.556	1.267	Dave Righetti	.000	12	0	0	0	0	0	2	4	.143	.000
Charlie Hough	.462	13	6	1	0	1	6	3	1	.529	.769	Doug Drabek	.000	11	0	0	0	0	0	0	2	.000	.000
Bill Wegman	.455	11	5	2	0	1	3	3	3	.571	.909	Dave Stieb	.077	13	1	0	0	0	2	1	1	.143	.077
Jamie Moyer	.375	16	6	1	0	3	5	1	2	.412	1.000	Jimmy Key	.107	28	3	0	0	0	2	2	2	.167	.107

David Cone — Royals

Age 31 – Pitches Right (flyball pitcher)

	ERA	W	L	Sv	G	GS	IP	BB	SO	Avg	H	2B	3B	HR	RBI	OBP	SLG	CG	ShO	Sup	QS	#P/S	SB	CS	GB	FB	G/F
1993 Season	3.33	11	14	0	34	34	254.0	114	191	.223	205	43	4	20	89	.312	.343	6	1	2.94	24	122	32	13	268	327	0.82
Last Five Years	3.23	70	56	0	168	165	1167.2	437	1116	.225	970	163	38	89	401	.299	.342	31	12	4.25	111	114	158	55	1214	1278	0.95

1993 Season

	ERA	W	L	Sv	G	GS	IP	H	HR	BB	SO		Avg	AB	H	2B	3B	HR	RBI	BB	SO	OBP	SLG
Home	4.05	4	6	0	17	17	126.2	116	10	65	86	vs. Left	.226	500	113	16	3	14	52	66	81	.319	.354
Away	2.62	7	8	0	17	17	127.1	89	10	49	105	vs. Right	.219	420	92	27	1	6	37	48	110	.304	.331
Day	2.55	3	4	0	9	9	67.0	43	4	25	57	Inning 1-6	.204	712	145	32	3	15	63	90	157	.298	.320
Night	3.61	8	10	0	25	25	187.0	162	16	89	134	Inning 7+	.288	208	60	11	1	5	26	24	34	.365	.423
Grass	2.71	5	7	0	13	13	99.2	72	7	36	82	None on	.225	542	122	26	2	14	14	65	111	.316	.358
Turf	3.73	6	7	0	21	21	154.1	133	13	78	109	Runners on	.220	378	83	17	2	6	75	49	80	.308	.323
April	3.79	0	4	0	5	5	35.2	34	3	15	26	Scoring Posn	.178	225	40	7	0	2	60	36	55	.287	.236
May	2.15	3	1	0	6	6	46.0	25	3	25	39	Close & Late	.307	140	43	9	1	4	17	17	18	.386	.471
June	4.75	2	3	0	5	5	36.0	33	3	17	24	None on/out	.247	247	61	13	2	9	9	20	49	.314	.425
July	3.15	2	2	0	6	6	45.2	36	5	21	30	vs. 1st Batr (relief)	.000	0	0	0	0	0	0	0	0	.000	.000
August	3.50	3	1	0	6	6	43.2	44	4	15	36	First Inning Pitched	.231	121	28	10	0	2	15	12	21	.296	.364
September/October	3.06	1	3	0	6	6	47.0	33	2	21	36	First 75 Pitches	.212	566	120	30	2	13	50	64	111	.298	.341
Starter	3.33	11	14	0	34	34	254.0	205	20	114	191	Pitch 76-90	.242	91	22	2	0	4	13	19	23	.368	.396
Reliever	0.00	0	0	0	0	0	0.0	0	0	0	0	Pitch 91-105	.210	119	25	6	2	1	7	11	25	.277	.319
0-3 Days Rest	0.00	0	0	0	0	0	0.0	0	0	0	0	Pitch 106+	.264	144	38	5	0	2	19	20	32	.358	.340
4 Days Rest	3.65	7	10	0	23	23	170.1	149	12	72	137	First Pitch	.311	106	33	10	0	6	18	2	0	.330	.575
5+ Days Rest	2.69	4	4	0	11	11	83.2	56	8	42	54	Ahead in Count	.186	441	82	14	1	4	32	0	151	.195	.249
Pre-All Star	3.53	6	8	0	18	18	132.2	105	11	65	100	Behind in Count	.245	192	47	11	2	8	30	53	0	.407	.448
Post-All Star	3.12	5	6	0	16	16	121.1	100	9	49	91	Two Strikes	.166	439	73	12	1	5	29	59	191	.270	.232

Last Five Years

	ERA	W	L	Sv	G	GS	IP	H	HR	BB	SO		Avg	AB	H	2B	3B	HR	RBI	BB	SO	OBP	SLG
Home	3.57	33	27	0	83	82	585.1	513	48	226	567	vs. Left	.231	2466	569	95	28	54	228	273	524	.310	.358
Away	2.89	37	29	0	85	83	582.1	457	41	211	549	vs. Right	.217	1844	401	68	10	35	173	164	592	.284	.322
Day	3.48	20	21	0	55	53	364.1	312	28	115	355	Inning 1-6	.217	3443	748	130	29	71	330	352	937	.293	.334
Night	3.11	50	35	0	113	112	803.1	658	61	322	761	Inning 7+	.256	867	222	33	9	18	71	85	179	.322	.377
Grass	3.32	43	38	0	100	100	704.1	592	59	238	706	None on	.227	2567	583	104	22	52	52	246	651	.299	.346

Last Five Years

	ERA	W	L	Sv	G	GS	IP	H	HR	BB	SO
Turf	3.09	27	18	0	68	65	463.1	378	30	199	410
April	4.00	6	10	0	23	23	155.1	150	8	68	135
May	2.80	11	8	0	27	26	186.1	138	15	65	177
June	3.68	10	8	0	26	25	168.2	153	12	58	163
July	3.03	17	5	0	29	29	214.0	162	29	83	217
August	3.49	13	11	0	30	30	211.2	200	12	69	188
September/October	2.68	13	14	0	33	32	231.2	167	13	94	236
Starter	3.24	70	56	0	165	165	1163.2	967	89	435	1112
Reliever	0.00	0	0	0	3	0	4.0	3	0	2	4
0-3 Days Rest	1.63	6	2	0	9	9	66.1	44	6	12	67
4 Days Rest	3.42	34	35	0	90	90	636.0	551	51	240	615
5+ Days Rest	3.22	30	19	0	66	66	461.1	372	32	183	430
Pre-All Star	3.37	34	26	0	86	84	587.2	499	45	229	551
Post-All Star	3.09	36	30	0	82	81	580.0	471	44	208	565

	Avg	AB	H	2B	3B	HR	RBI	BB	SO	OBP	SLG
Runners on	.222	1743	387	59	16	37	349	191	465	.299	.338
Scoring Posn	.199	1034	206	31	8	22	295	142	307	.294	.309
Close & Late	.250	456	114	18	6	9	41	51	97	.325	.375
None on/out	.249	1144	285	47	15	30	30	84	267	.305	.395
vs. 1st Batr (relief)	.000	3	0	0	0	0	0	0	0	.000	.000
First Inning Pitched	.229	630	144	30	3	16	72	64	174	.307	.362
First 75 Pitches	.226	2747	621	108	23	56	257	275	736	.301	.343
Pitch 76-90	.215	489	105	20	5	13	56	54	124	.292	.356
Pitch 91-105	.206	504	104	17	6	10	35	41	110	.267	.323
Pitch 106+	.246	570	140	18	4	10	53	67	146	.324	.344
First Pitch	.340	533	181	38	6	27	81	10	0	.354	.585
Ahead in Count	.170	2130	363	55	17	14	129	0	926	.177	.232
Behind in Count	.301	800	241	37	12	28	110	215	0	.446	.403
Two Strikes	.150	2265	340	53	15	18	122	210	1116	.226	.211

Pitcher vs. Batter (career)

Pitches Best Vs.	Avg	AB	H	2B	3B	HR	RBI	BB	SO	OBP	SLG
Chris James	.000	21	0	0	0	0	1	0	5	.000	.000
Danny Tartabull	.000	12	0	0	0	0	0	2	3	.143	.000
Charlie Hayes	.053	19	1	1	0	0	1	0	7	.053	.105
Jose Offerman	.059	17	1	0	0	0	0	0	6	.059	.059
Stan Javier	.077	13	1	0	0	0	1	0	5	.071	.077

Pitches Worst Vs.	Avg	AB	H	2B	3B	HR	RBI	BB	SO	OBP	SLG
Deion Sanders	.600	10	6	0	0	1	1	1	1	.636	.900
Bret Barberie	.500	8	4	1	0	0	2	4	2	.667	.625
Dwight Smith	.462	13	6	1	1	1	3	2	1	.533	.923
Mo Vaughn	.400	15	6	2	0	1	1	3	2	.500	.733
Robin Ventura	.364	11	4	1	0	2	3	4	2	.533	1.000

Jeff Conine — Marlins

Age 28 – Bats Right

	Avg	G	AB	R	H	2B	3B	HR	RBI	BB	SO	HBP	GDP	SB	CS	OBP	SLG	IBB	SH	SF	#Pit	#P/PA	GB	FB	G/F
1993 Season	.292	162	595	75	174	24	3	12	79	52	135	5	14	2	2	.351	.403	2	0	6	2461	3.74	180	161	1.12
Career (1990-1993)	.286	199	706	88	202	31	5	12	90	62	163	5	16	2	2	.345	.395	3	0	6	2896	3.72	206	195	1.06

1993 Season

	Avg	AB	H	2B	3B	HR	RBI	BB	SO	OBP	SLG
vs. Left	.299	167	50	7	2	5	28	20	36	.366	.455
vs. Right	.290	428	124	17	1	7	51	32	99	.345	.383
Groundball	.327	196	64	7	2	2	25	17	30	.379	.413
Flyball	.279	111	31	6	1	2	14	7	35	.325	.405
Home	.296	307	91	11	0	5	41	21	71	.340	.381
Away	.288	288	83	13	3	7	38	31	64	.362	.427
Day	.281	128	36	5	0	3	14	17	36	.367	.391
Night	.296	467	138	19	3	9	65	35	99	.346	.407
Grass	.288	462	133	21	0	10	59	38	105	.341	.398
Turf	.308	133	41	3	3	2	20	14	30	.384	.421
First Pitch	.390	118	46	3	1	4	25	1	0	.398	.534
Ahead in Count	.422	109	46	8	1	6	26	16	0	.492	.679
Behind in Count	.190	269	51	9	0	2	19	0	119	.197	.245
Two Strikes	.167	269	45	9	1	1	17	35	135	.268	.219

	Avg	AB	H	2B	3B	HR	RBI	BB	SO	OBP	SLG
Scoring Posn	.311	148	46	4	0	6	66	17	31	.376	.459
Close & Late	.225	102	23	2	1	3	18	9	27	.283	.353
None on/out	.224	125	28	7	1	1	1	11	33	.287	.320
Batting #3	.292	267	78	10	2	5	31	24	51	.349	.401
Batting #6	.272	125	34	4	0	3	18	18	33	.366	.376
Other	.305	203	62	10	1	4	30	10	51	.344	.424
April	.321	78	25	2	0	0	7	9	20	.386	.346
May	.258	89	23	3	1	2	11	18	22	.383	.382
June	.292	96	28	6	1	3	15	10	25	.369	.469
July	.358	106	38	5	0	2	15	4	20	.382	.462
August	.286	112	32	4	1	3	20	3	23	.305	.420
September/October	.246	114	28	4	0	2	11	8	25	.298	.333
Pre-All Star	.283	307	87	14	2	7	43	38	78	.365	.410
Post-All Star	.302	288	87	10	1	5	36	14	57	.336	.396

1993 By Position

Position	Avg	AB	H	2B	3B	HR	RBI	BB	SO	OBP	SLG	G	GS	Innings	PO	A	E	DP	Fld Pct	Rng Fctr	In Zone	Outs	Zone Rtg	MLB Zone
As 1b	.259	54	14	1	0	3	8	5	14	.322	.444	43	11	152.2	151	14	0	11	1.000	---	40	41	1.025	.834
As lf	.296	537	159	23	3	9	70	47	120	.355	.400	147	143	1212.1	252	11	2	0	.992	1.95	323	233	.721	.818

Jim Converse — Mariners

Age 22 – Pitches Right (groundball pitcher)

	ERA	W	L	Sv	G	GS	IP	BB	SO	Avg	H	2B	3B	HR	RBI	OBP	SLG	CG	ShO	Sup	QS	#P/S	SB	CS	GB	FB	G/F
1993 Season	5.31	1	3	0	4	4	20.1	14	10	.295	23	7	0	0	12	.398	.385	0	0	1.77	2	87	2	2	35	17	2.06

1993 Season

	ERA	W	L	Sv	G	GS	IP	H	HR	BB	SO
Home	6.75	1	2	0	3	3	13.1	17	0	13	3
Away	2.57	0	1	0	1	1	7.0	6	0	1	7

	Avg	AB	H	2B	3B	HR	RBI	BB	SO	OBP	SLG
vs. Left	.326	46	15	5	0	0	5	9	5	.436	.435
vs. Right	.250	32	8	2	0	0	7	5	5	.342	.313

Andy Cook — Yankees

Age 26 – Pitches Right

	ERA	W	L	Sv	G	GS	IP	BB	SO	Avg	H	2B	3B	HR	RBI	OBP	SLG	GF	IR	IRS	Hld	SvOp	SB	CS	GB	FB	G/F
1993 Season	5.06	0	1	0	4	0	5.1	7	4	.200	4	1	0	1	2	.407	.400	3	1	0	0	0	0	0	7	7	1.00

1993 Season

	ERA	W	L	Sv	G	GS	IP	H	HR	BB	SO
Home	8.10	0	1	0	2	0	3.1	3	1	7	2
Away	0.00	0	0	0	2	0	2.0	1	0	0	2

	Avg	AB	H	2B	3B	HR	RBI	BB	SO	OBP	SLG
vs. Left	.125	8	1	0	0	0	0	5	1	.462	.125
vs. Right	.250	12	3	1	0	1	2	2	3	.357	.583

Dennis Cook — Indians

Age 31 – Pitches Left (flyball pitcher)

	ERA	W	L	Sv	G	GS	IP	BB	SO	Avg	H	2B	3B	HR	RBI	OBP	SLG	GF	IR	IRS	Hld	SvOp	SB	CS	GB	FB	G/F
1993 Season	5.67	5	5	0	25	6	54.0	16	34	.295	62	17	4	9	33	.348	.543	2	13	4	2	2	1	5	55	77	0.71
Last Five Years	3.91	27	24	1	147	66	506.2	167	269	.257	495	99	13	76	243	.317	.441	12	86	33	8	5	31	29	591	717	0.82

1993 Season

	ERA	W	L	Sv	G	GS	IP	H	HR	BB	SO		Avg	AB	H	2B	3B	HR	RBI	BB	SO	OBP	SLG
Home	4.56	3	3	0	12	2	25.2	28	4	5	19	vs. Left	.259	54	14	4	0	2	10	2	10	.276	.444
Away	6.67	2	2	0	13	4	28.1	34	5	11	15	vs. Right	.308	156	48	13	4	7	23	14	24	.372	.577
Starter	7.43	1	3	0	6	6	26.2	32	4	11	16	Scoring Posn	.405	42	17	6	0	2	24	5	6	.449	.690
Reliever	3.95	4	2	0	19	0	27.1	30	5	5	18	Close & Late	.387	31	12	3	0	1	2	2	4	.441	.581
0 Days rest	0.00	0	0	0	1	0	0.2	1	0	0	0	None on/out	.276	58	16	5	3	1	1	1	10	.288	.517
1 or 2 Days rest	3.29	1	2	0	9	0	13.2	13	2	1	7	First Pitch	.586	29	17	5	2	3	8	1	0	.625	1.207
3+ Days rest	4.85	3	0	0	9	0	13.0	16	3	4	11	Ahead in Count	.115	96	11	5	1	2	12	0	30	.113	.250
Pre-All Star	5.74	5	5	0	24	6	53.1	60	9	16	34	Behind in Count	.333	42	14	1	1	3	8	10	0	.453	.619
Post-All Star	0.00	0	0	0	1	0	0.2	2	0	0	0	Two Strikes	.155	103	16	7	0	1	9	5	34	.193	.252

Last Five Years

	ERA	W	L	Sv	G	GS	IP	H	HR	BB	SO		Avg	AB	H	2B	3B	HR	RBI	BB	SO	OBP	SLG
Home	3.57	17	12	1	74	35	290.0	257	47	87	165	vs. Left	.251	375	94	18	3	14	55	31	52	.309	.427
Away	4.36	10	12	0	73	31	216.2	238	29	80	104	vs. Right	.259	1548	401	81	10	62	188	136	217	.319	.444
Day	3.72	11	10	0	55	28	208.1	206	33	69	117	Inning 1-6	.262	1584	415	87	12	65	214	134	226	.320	.455
Night	4.04	16	14	1	92	38	298.1	289	43	98	152	Inning 7+	.236	339	80	12	1	11	29	33	43	.303	.375
Grass	4.23	14	14	0	81	37	261.2	272	47	87	154	None on	.245	1243	304	61	8	48	48	79	178	.292	.422
Turf	3.56	13	10	1	66	29	245.0	223	29	80	115	Runners on	.281	680	191	38	5	28	195	88	91	.358	.475
April	3.40	4	2	0	12	7	50.1	44	7	11	16	Scoring Posn	.281	402	113	21	3	16	161	58	48	.361	.468
May	4.74	5	5	0	21	12	79.2	83	13	20	41	Close & Late	.314	140	44	4	1	4	15	19	15	.395	.443
June	3.90	5	4	0	26	12	97.0	92	15	42	62	None on/out	.236	508	120	32	4	18	18	36	66	.289	.421
July	2.91	6	4	1	36	11	105.0	96	11	29	63	vs. 1st Batr (relief)	.333	66	22	3	0	1	20	9	11	.392	.424
August	5.33	3	5	0	22	11	74.1	86	14	40	35	First Inning Pitched	.258	484	125	28	4	18	84	46	67	.319	.444
September/October	3.50	4	4	0	30	13	100.1	94	16	25	52	First 15 Pitches	.273	443	121	27	4	18	76	38	56	.327	.474
Starter	4.16	19	20	0	66	66	376.0	383	61	118	199	Pitch 16-30	.223	382	85	16	1	15	41	34	63	.290	.387
Reliever	3.17	8	4	1	81	0	130.2	112	15	49	70	Pitch 31-45	.236	301	71	18	4	9	27	25	49	.296	.412
0 Days rest	4.50	0	0	0	17	0	24.0	23	3	10	11	Pitch 46+	.274	797	218	38	4	34	99	70	101	.332	.459
1 or 2 Days rest	2.44	5	3	1	32	0	55.1	44	4	23	25	First Pitch	.307	267	82	16	2	16	49	16	0	.356	.562
3+ Days rest	3.33	3	1	0	32	0	51.1	45	8	16	34	Ahead in Count	.187	866	162	29	6	20	70	0	228	.186	.304
Pre-All Star	3.86	15	14	1	73	35	268.0	254	39	81	147	Behind in Count	.319	405	129	29	4	21	71	90	0	.439	.565
Post-All Star	3.96	12	10	0	74	31	238.2	241	37	86	122	Two Strikes	.194	844	164	35	5	21	70	60	269	.248	.322

Pitcher vs. Batter (career)

Pitches Best Vs.	Avg	AB	H	2B	3B	HR	RBI	BB	SO	OBP	SLG	Pitches Worst Vs.	Avg	AB	H	2B	3B	HR	RBI	BB	SO	OBP	SLG
Jeff Blauser	.091	11	1	0	0	0	0	0	1	.091	.091	Greg Litton	.615	13	8	1	0	1	2	0	0	.615	.923
Juan Gonzalez	.100	10	1	1	0	0	0	1	3	.182	.200	Lonnie Smith	.412	17	7	1	0	3	6	0	1	.412	1.000
Candy Maldonado	.111	9	1	0	0	0	0	2	3	.273	.111	Joe Carter	.364	11	4	1	0	1	1	4	0	.533	.727
Kevin McReynolds	.133	15	2	0	0	0	1	2	3	.235	.133	Dan Gladden	.364	11	4	2	0	1	1	2	3	.462	.818
Willie McGee	.182	11	2	0	0	0	1	0	1	.167	.182	Darryl Strawberry	.333	9	3	0	0	1	2	3	0	.500	.667

Mike Cook — Orioles

Age 30 – Pitches Right

	ERA	W	L	Sv	G	GS	IP	BB	SO	Avg	H	2B	3B	HR	RBI	OBP	SLG	GF	IR	IRS	Hld	SvOp	SB	CS	GB	FB	G/F
1993 Season	0.00	0	0	0	2	0	3.0	2	3	.091	1	0	0	0	2	.231	.091	0	2	2	0	0	0	0	4	4	1.00
Last Five Years	4.44	0	1	0	17	0	24.1	19	18	.247	23	3	1	1	20	.374	.333	0	11	8	1	0	3	0	34	29	1.17

1993 Season

	ERA	W	L	Sv	G	GS	IP	H	HR	BB	SO		Avg	AB	H	2B	3B	HR	RBI	BB	SO	OBP	SLG
Home	0.00	0	0	0	2	0	3.0	1	0	2	3	vs. Left	.200	5	1	0	0	0	0	1	1	.333	.200
Away	0.00	0	0	0	0	0	0.0	0	0	0	0	vs. Right	.000	6	0	0	0	0	2	1	2	.143	.000

Steve Cooke — Pirates

Age 24 – Pitches Left

	ERA	W	L	Sv	G	GS	IP	BB	SO	Avg	H	2B	3B	HR	RBI	OBP	SLG	CG	ShO	Sup	QS	#P/S	SB	CS	GB	FB	G/F
1993 Season	3.89	10	10	0	32	32	210.2	59	132	.258	207	58	6	22	94	.310	.428	3	1	4.87	20	102	22	9	284	257	1.11
Career (1992-1993)	3.85	12	10	1	43	32	233.2	63	142	.258	229	64	6	24	101	.307	.425	3	1	4.70	20	102	22	9	313	284	1.10

1993 Season

	ERA	W	L	Sv	G	GS	IP	H	HR	BB	SO		Avg	AB	H	2B	3B	HR	RBI	BB	SO	OBP	SLG
Home	4.41	5	5	0	16	16	104.0	105	10	30	55	vs. Left	.265	136	36	7	3	2	20	12	25	.325	.404
Away	3.38	5	5	0	16	16	106.2	102	12	29	77	vs. Right	.257	665	171	51	3	20	74	47	107	.306	.433
Day	4.40	4	4	0	11	11	71.2	80	11	16	46	Inning 1-6	.250	687	172	48	4	17	81	57	117	.308	.406
Night	3.63	6	6	0	21	21	139.0	127	11	43	86	Inning 7+	.307	114	35	10	2	5	13	2	15	.319	.561
Grass	2.54	4	2	0	11	11	74.1	65	8	21	55	None on	.260	480	125	40	2	13	13	36	71	.316	.433
Turf	4.62	6	8	0	21	21	136.1	142	14	38	77	Runners on	.255	321	82	18	4	9	81	23	61	.300	.421
April	4.56	0	1	0	4	4	23.2	25	3	9	11	Scoring Posn	.258	186	48	14	2	4	67	21	39	.324	.419
May	3.12	3	1	0	6	6	43.1	38	5	12	29	Close & Late	.261	69	18	6	1	2	7	2	11	.282	.464
June	2.87	2	1	0	5	5	37.2	28	1	12	30	None on/out	.258	213	55	22	1	9	9	16	28	.313	.498
July	4.99	0	3	0	5	5	30.2	32	3	11	18	vs. 1st Batr (relief)	.000	0	0	0	0	0	0	0	0	.000	.000
August	4.78	3	2	0	6	6	37.2	49	6	5	22	First Inning Pitched	.224	116	26	4	0	2	9	11	18	.291	.310
September/October	3.58	2	2	0	6	6	37.2	35	4	10	22	First 75 Pitches	.246	565	139	34	4	10	57	48	95	.307	.373
Starter	3.89	10	10	0	32	32	210.2	207	22	59	132	Pitch 76-90	.266	124	33	16	1	4	18	6	18	.293	.508
Reliever	0.00	0	0	0	0	0	0.0	0	0	0	0	Pitch 91-105	.284	67	19	3	0	6	11	4	10	.324	.597
0-3 Days Rest	0.00	0	0	0	0	0	0.0	0	0	0	0	Pitch 106+	.356	45	16	5	1	2	8	1	9	.370	.644

1993 Season	ERA	W	L	Sv	G	GS	IP	H	HR	BB	SO
4 Days Rest	3.98	5	6	0	17	17	113.0	114	11	28	63
5+ Days Rest	3.78	5	4	0	15	15	97.2	93	11	31	69
Pre-All Star	3.64	5	4	0	17	17	118.2	108	10	37	77
Post-All Star	4.21	5	6	0	15	15	92.0	99	12	22	55

1993 Season	Avg	AB	H	2B	3B	HR	RBI	BB	SO	OBP	SLG
First Pitch	.327	101	33	10	1	4	15	2	0	.343	.564
Ahead in Count	.171	328	56	15	2	5	24	0	115	.175	.274
Behind in Count	.323	217	70	22	3	7	36	27	0	.391	.548
Two Strikes	.176	341	60	15	1	7	26	30	132	.246	.287

Scott Cooper — Red Sox

Age 26 – Bats Left

	Avg	G	AB	R	H	2B	3B	HR	RBI	BB	SO	HBP	GDP	SB	CS	OBP	SLG	IBB	SH	SF	#Pit	#P/PA	GB	FB	G/F
1993 Season	.279	156	526	67	147	29	3	9	63	58	81	5	8	5	2	.355	.397	15	4	3	2125	3.56	163	165	0.99
Career (1990-1993)	.285	295	899	107	256	54	5	14	103	97	117	5	13	6	3	.356	.403	15	6	5	3600	3.55	311	278	1.12

1993 Season

	Avg	AB	H	2B	3B	HR	RBI	BB	SO	OBP	SLG
vs. Left	.257	144	37	5	2	2	17	10	25	.321	.361
vs. Right	.288	382	110	24	1	7	46	48	56	.367	.411
Groundball	.333	84	28	8	1	1	13	5	9	.371	.488
Flyball	.336	125	42	8	2	0	13	11	19	.401	.432
Home	.325	255	83	19	1	3	31	30	37	.396	.443
Away	.236	271	64	10	2	6	32	28	44	.316	.354
Day	.268	164	44	9	1	2	18	26	22	.373	.372
Night	.285	362	103	20	2	7	45	32	59	.346	.409
Grass	.291	437	127	23	2	7	50	49	67	.365	.400
Turf	.225	89	20	6	1	2	13	9	14	.303	.382
First Pitch	.292	72	21	5	0	3	11	14	0	.404	.486
Ahead in Count	.352	145	51	9	1	1	19	20	0	.431	.448
Behind in Count	.230	213	49	13	2	2	18	0	69	.237	.338
Two Strikes	.198	207	41	7	1	1	19	24	81	.284	.256

	Avg	AB	H	2B	3B	HR	RBI	BB	SO	OBP	SLG
Scoring Posn	.311	132	41	7	0	3	53	25	23	.413	.432
Close & Late	.192	78	15	5	1	0	6	15	14	.319	.282
None on/out	.236	123	29	8	1	1	1	3	16	.254	.341
Batting #6	.318	151	48	13	0	5	28	18	17	.386	.503
Batting #7	.276	304	84	14	3	4	32	34	51	.356	.382
Other	.211	71	15	2	0	0	3	6	13	.282	.239
April	.350	80	28	4	0	2	16	7	17	.402	.475
May	.280	82	23	3	1	0	6	7	12	.359	.341
June	.267	90	24	6	0	2	12	15	12	.371	.400
July	.253	95	24	4	0	3	7	11	13	.330	.389
August	.215	79	17	5	2	1	10	9	15	.303	.367
September/October	.310	100	31	7	0	1	12	9	12	.363	.410
Pre-All Star	.282	287	81	14	1	6	36	33	45	.362	.401
Post-All Star	.276	239	66	15	2	3	27	25	36	.346	.393

1993 By Position

Position	Avg	AB	H	2B	3B	HR	RBI	BB	SO	OBP	SLG	G	GS	Innings	PO	A	E	DP	Fld Pct	Rng Fctr	In Zone	Outs	Zone Rtg	MLB Zone
As 3b	.279	520	145	28	3	9	63	57	80	.354	.396	154	145	1304.1	111	245	24	20	.937	2.46	340	268	.788	.834

Career (1990-1993)

	Avg	AB	H	2B	3B	HR	RBI	BB	SO	OBP	SLG
vs. Left	.272	191	52	8	3	3	24	18	32	.346	.393
vs. Right	.288	708	204	46	2	11	79	79	85	.359	.405
Groundball	.347	173	60	17	1	1	23	12	20	.389	.474
Flyball	.305	243	74	13	2	3	26	25	30	.375	.412
Home	.326	436	142	29	3	5	48	46	55	.390	.440
Away	.246	463	114	25	2	9	55	51	62	.324	.367
Day	.299	284	85	20	1	4	34	37	31	.382	.419
Night	.278	615	171	34	4	10	69	60	86	.344	.395
Grass	.293	765	224	43	4	12	86	81	98	.361	.407
Turf	.239	134	32	11	1	2	17	16	19	.325	.381
First Pitch	.295	132	39	10	1	3	17	14	0	.362	.455
Ahead in Count	.375	253	95	20	2	4	35	41	0	.461	.518
Behind in Count	.228	342	78	18	2	3	31	0	98	.232	.319
Two Strikes	.201	338	68	10	1	3	35	42	117	.291	.263

	Avg	AB	H	2B	3B	HR	RBI	BB	SO	OBP	SLG
Scoring Posn	.310	210	65	10	0	3	87	35	35	.400	.400
Close & Late	.263	160	42	14	2	0	17	22	23	.350	.375
None on/out	.271	203	55	17	2	2	2	7	23	.295	.404
Batting #6	.306	170	52	14	0	5	29	22	20	.381	.476
Batting #7	.264	447	118	20	4	5	45	53	60	.346	.360
Other	.305	282	86	20	1	4	29	22	37	.356	.426
April	.322	90	29	4	0	2	18	9	19	.380	.433
May	.269	119	32	5	1	0	9	12	13	.351	.328
June	.269	167	45	13	0	2	20	20	19	.346	.383
July	.254	134	34	5	0	3	12	18	22	.342	.358
August	.242	132	32	10	2	1	13	13	22	.315	.371
September/October	.327	257	84	17	2	6	31	25	22	.385	.479
Pre-All Star	.272	437	119	23	1	6	54	49	62	.348	.371
Post-All Star	.297	462	137	31	4	8	49	48	55	.363	.433

Batter vs. Pitcher (career)

Hits Best Against	Avg	AB	H	2B	3B	HR	RBI	BB	SO	OBP	SLG
Mike Mussina	.700	10	7	1	0	1	2	2	0	.750	1.100
John Doherty	.600	10	6	4	0	0	2	2	0	.667	1.000
Bill Gullickson	.500	16	8	0	0	2	5	2	2	.556	.875
Ron Darling	.462	13	6	1	0	0	1	3	0	.563	.538
Dave Stewart	.333	15	5	3	0	1	2	4	3	.450	.733

Hits Worst Against	Avg	AB	H	2B	3B	HR	RBI	BB	SO	OBP	SLG
Jose Mesa	.083	12	1	0	0	0	1	2	3	.214	.083
Chris Bosio	.100	10	1	1	0	0	0	2	1	.250	.200
Kevin Appier	.133	15	2	0	0	0	0	3	2	.278	.133
Jaime Navarro	.158	19	3	1	0	0	0	1	0	.200	.211
David Cone	.182	11	2	0	0	0	1	2	1	.308	.182

Joey Cora — White Sox

Age 29 – Bats Both

	Avg	G	AB	R	H	2B	3B	HR	RBI	BB	SO	HBP	GDP	SB	CS	OBP	SLG	IBB	SH	SF	#Pit	#P/PA	GB	FB	G/F
1993 Season	.268	153	579	95	155	15	13	2	51	67	63	9	14	20	8	.351	.349	0	19	4	2552	3.76	207	153	1.35
Last Five Years	.260	384	1048	176	273	28	17	2	81	116	106	18	18	50	20	.341	.325	2	29	10	4539	3.72	395	278	1.42

1993 Season

	Avg	AB	H	2B	3B	HR	RBI	BB	SO	OBP	SLG
vs. Left	.255	161	41	4	1	0	8	19	19	.337	.292
vs. Right	.273	418	114	11	12	2	43	48	44	.356	.371
Groundball	.264	106	28	2	4	0	8	14	14	.344	.358
Flyball	.313	128	40	6	2	0	7	18	15	.409	.391
Home	.262	279	73	6	7	0	24	34	29	.350	.333
Away	.273	300	82	9	6	2	27	33	34	.351	.363
Day	.250	168	42	3	3	0	11	17	16	.324	.304
Night	.275	411	113	12	10	2	40	50	47	.361	.367
Grass	.263	476	125	11	10	2	41	61	49	.355	.340
Turf	.291	103	30	4	3	0	10	6	14	.330	.388
First Pitch	.267	75	20	2	1	1	4	0	0	.286	.360
Ahead in Count	.314	153	48	1	6	1	25	29	0	.418	.418
Behind in Count	.212	245	52	9	1	0	11	0	54	.228	.257

	Avg	AB	H	2B	3B	HR	RBI	BB	SO	OBP	SLG
Scoring Posn	.294	126	37	3	3	0	43	15	10	.372	.365
Close & Late	.216	74	16	3	1	0	4	8	10	.293	.284
None on/out	.183	131	24	1	4	1	1	18	15	.296	.275
Batting #1	.270	159	43	4	5	0	16	18	15	.345	.358
Batting #2	.269	416	112	11	8	2	35	47	46	.353	.349
Other	.000	4	0	0	0	0	0	2	2	.333	.000
April	.325	83	27	4	2	0	7	11	11	.404	.422
May	.236	89	21	2	2	0	9	14	9	.340	.303
June	.278	97	27	2	1	1	7	14	10	.383	.351
July	.272	92	25	5	2	0	10	11	8	.362	.370
August	.254	114	29	2	2	1	11	6	17	.293	.333
September/October	.250	104	26	0	4	0	7	11	8	.336	.327
Pre-All Star	.269	308	83	9	5	1	25	42	34	.363	.341

1993 Season

	Avg	AB	H	2B	3B	HR	RBI	BB	SO	OBP	SLG		Avg	AB	H	2B	3B	HR	RBI	BB	SO	OBP	SLG
Two Strikes	.207	241	50	7	3	0	10	38	63	.327	.261	Post-All Star	.266	271	72	6	8	1	26	25	29	.336	.358

1993 By Position

Position	Avg	AB	H	2B	3B	HR	RBI	BB	SO	OBP	SLG	G	GS	Innings	PO	A	E	DP	Fld Pct	Rng Fctr	In Zone	Outs	Zone Rtg	MLB Zone
As 2b	.268	571	153	15	13	2	51	66	61	.351	.350	151	145	1299.0	293	410	19	85	.974	4.87	474	408	.861	.895

Last Five Years

	Avg	AB	H	2B	3B	HR	RBI	BB	SO	OBP	SLG		Avg	AB	H	2B	3B	HR	RBI	BB	SO	OBP	SLG
vs. Left	.265	275	73	6	1	0	13	31	32	.345	.295	Scoring Posn	.251	235	59	5	3	0	71	30	20	.333	.298
vs. Right	.259	773	200	22	16	2	68	85	74	.340	.336	Close & Late	.208	154	32	4	1	0	6	15	19	.285	.247
Groundball	.279	247	69	6	5	0	19	23	24	.341	.344	None on/out	.225	275	62	7	6	1	1	33	28	.324	.305
Flyball	.300	230	69	10	3	0	10	35	27	.408	.370	Batting #1	.271	255	69	10	6	0	20	32	24	.355	.357
Home	.270	497	134	13	9	0	40	56	44	.356	.332	Batting #2	.268	471	126	12	8	2	39	54	49	.352	.340
Away	.252	551	139	15	8	2	41	60	62	.329	.319	Other	.242	322	78	6	3	0	22	30	33	.314	.280
Day	.242	326	79	7	4	0	20	33	30	.320	.288	April	.295	112	33	5	2	0	8	14	12	.378	.375
Night	.269	722	194	21	13	2	61	83	76	.351	.342	May	.236	144	34	4	2	0	12	20	16	.333	.292
Grass	.260	860	224	23	14	2	65	105	84	.350	.327	June	.279	183	51	4	3	1	13	19	19	.362	.350
Turf	.261	188	49	5	3	0	16	11	22	.300	.319	July	.256	172	44	8	3	0	15	16	13	.332	.337
First Pitch	.257	148	38	3	2	1	11	1	0	.277	.324	August	.232	190	44	2	2	1	20	16	28	.289	.279
Ahead in Count	.316	253	80	4	8	1	34	52	0	.431	.407	September/October	.271	247	67	5	5	0	13	31	18	.360	.332
Behind in Count	.209	450	94	16	1	0	18	0	92	.225	.249	Pre-All Star	.266	489	130	16	7	1	35	56	52	.351	.333
Two Strikes	.215	441	95	13	4	0	18	62	106	.323	.263	Post-All Star	.256	559	143	12	10	1	46	60	54	.333	.318

Batter vs. Pitcher (career)

Hits Best Against	Avg	AB	H	2B	3B	HR	RBI	BB	SO	OBP	SLG	Hits Worst Against	Avg	AB	H	2B	3B	HR	RBI	BB	SO	OBP	SLG
Danny Darwin	.400	15	6	3	0	0	0	1	2	.438	.600	Jim Abbott	.000	12	0	0	0	0	0	1	1	.077	.000
Juan Guzman	.400	10	4	1	0	0	0	1	1	.455	.500	Kelly Downs	.000	11	0	0	0	0	1	1	0	.083	.000
Cal Eldred	.364	11	4	2	0	0	2	0	2	.364	.545	Mark Leiter	.083	12	1	0	0	0	0	1	1	.154	.083
John Dopson	.333	9	3	0	1	0	2	1	1	.333	.556	Bob Welch	.091	22	2	0	0	0	1	2	4	.167	.091
Jaime Navarro	.308	13	4	0	2	0	1	0	1	.308	.615	Jeff Montgomery	.100	10	1	0	0	0	0	1	1	.182	.100

Wil Cordero — Expos

Age 22 – Bats Right

	Avg	G	AB	R	H	2B	3B	HR	RBI	BB	SO	HBP	GDP	SB	CS	OBP	SLG	IBB	SH	SF	#Pit	#P/PA	GB	FB	G/F
1993 Season	.248	138	475	56	118	32	2	10	58	34	60	7	12	12	3	.308	.387	8	4	1	1871	3.59	189	143	1.32
Career (1992-1993)	.260	183	601	73	156	36	3	12	66	43	91	8	14	12	3	.317	.389	8	5	1	2441	3.71	237	166	1.43

1993 Season

	Avg	AB	H	2B	3B	HR	RBI	BB	SO	OBP	SLG		Avg	AB	H	2B	3B	HR	RBI	BB	SO	OBP	SLG
vs. Left	.243	148	36	11	2	1	14	14	18	.315	.365	Scoring Posn	.263	118	31	9	1	3	44	18	15	.367	.432
vs. Right	.251	327	82	21	0	9	44	20	42	.304	.398	Close & Late	.235	81	19	5	0	4	13	4	9	.279	.444
Groundball	.241	141	34	10	1	0	10	7	21	.285	.326	None on/out	.236	123	29	8	0	2	2	6	12	.277	.350
Flyball	.294	85	25	5	0	4	16	7	8	.355	.494	Batting #7	.238	164	39	11	1	1	13	11	23	.294	.335
Home	.225	213	48	16	1	8	26	17	35	.288	.423	Batting #8	.284	162	46	10	0	6	26	13	18	.348	.457
Away	.267	262	70	16	1	2	32	17	25	.324	.359	Other	.221	149	33	11	1	3	19	10	19	.278	.369
Day	.192	151	29	8	0	0	17	7	27	.231	.245	April	.235	81	19	7	1	2	10	7	12	.295	.420
Night	.275	324	89	24	2	10	41	27	33	.342	.454	May	.255	98	25	9	0	2	10	3	11	.282	.408
Grass	.268	153	41	6	0	2	24	12	15	.333	.346	June	.220	82	18	5	0	0	4	8	12	.312	.280
Turf	.239	322	77	26	2	8	34	22	45	.295	.407	July	.262	61	16	0	1	2	10	8	10	.357	.393
First Pitch	.280	25	7	3	0	1	4	7	0	.438	.520	August	.261	69	18	6	0	1	7	3	6	.301	.391
Ahead in Count	.270	148	40	14	2	1	20	16	0	.341	.412	September/October	.262	84	22	5	0	3	17	5	9	.311	.429
Behind in Count	.195	220	43	9	0	5	20	0	56	.216	.305	Pre-All Star	.237	279	66	21	1	5	25	23	39	.305	.373
Two Strikes	.199	201	40	8	0	7	28	11	60	.260	.343	Post-All Star	.265	196	52	11	1	5	33	11	21	.311	.408

1993 By Position

Position	Avg	AB	H	2B	3B	HR	RBI	BB	SO	OBP	SLG	G	GS	Innings	PO	A	E	DP	Fld Pct	Rng Fctr	In Zone	Outs	Zone Rtg	MLB Zone
As ss	.250	464	116	31	2	10	58	34	56	.310	.390	134	129	1114.0	160	368	33	61	.941	4.27	462	390	.844	.880

Rheal Cormier — Cardinals

Age 27 – Pitches Left

	ERA	W	L	Sv	G	GS	IP	BB	SO	Avg	H	2B	3B	HR	RBI	OBP	SLG	CG	ShO	Sup	QS	#P/S	SB	CS	GB	FB	G/F
1993 Season	4.33	7	6	0	38	21	145.1	27	75	.284	163	39	3	18	70	.319	.456	1	0	5.39	11	81	3	2	228	156	1.46
Career (1991-1993)	3.99	21	21	0	80	61	399.0	68	230	.276	431	89	7	38	167	.309	.415	6	0	4.31	33	85	15	9	620	417	1.49

1993 Season

	ERA	W	L	Sv	G	GS	IP	H	HR	BB	SO		Avg	AB	H	2B	3B	HR	RBI	BB	SO	OBP	SLG
Home	2.17	4	1	0	15	8	66.1	56	6	8	33	vs. Left	.207	145	30	3	0	3	10	8	23	.248	.290
Away	6.15	3	5	0	23	13	79.0	107	12	19	42	vs. Right	.310	429	133	36	3	15	60	19	52	.342	.513
Starter	4.22	6	5	0	21	21	121.2	131	17	21	60	Scoring Posn	.238	143	34	5	2	5	50	12	16	.302	.406
Reliever	4.94	1	1	0	17	0	23.2	32	1	6	15	Close & Late	.289	45	13	6	0	0	5	5	6	.373	.422
0-3 Days Rest	3.00	0	1	0	2	2	12.0	12	2	1	4	None on/out	.358	151	54	14	0	5	5	5	24	.382	.550
4 Days Rest	5.52	2	4	0	11	11	58.2	71	11	10	24	First Pitch	.336	113	38	12	2	5	17	3	0	.361	.611
5+ Days Rest	3.00	4	0	0	8	8	51.0	48	4	10	32	Ahead in Count	.211	246	52	9	1	4	22	0	68	.217	.305
Pre-All Star	4.44	5	5	0	23	13	81.0	91	10	14	40	Behind in Count	.368	133	49	13	0	6	23	10	0	.410	.602
Post-All Star	4.20	2	1	0	15	8	64.1	72	8	13	35	Two Strikes	.213	225	48	10	1	5	20	14	75	.263	.333

Career (1991-1993)	ERA	W	L	Sv	G	GS	IP	H	HR	BB	SO		Avg	AB	H	2B	3B	HR	RBI	BB	SO	OBP	SLG
Home	3.40	15	7	0	37	29	198.2	211	13	30	97	vs. Left	.231	325	75	13	1	4	24	14	58	.267	.314
Away	4.58	6	14	0	43	32	200.1	220	25	38	133	vs. Right	.288	1236	356	76	6	34	143	54	172	.320	.442
Day	3.41	9	5	0	25	20	132.0	144	13	15	69	Inning 1-6	.268	1321	354	71	6	31	142	55	203	.300	.401
Night	4.28	12	16	0	55	41	267.0	287	25	53	161	Inning 7+	.321	240	77	18	1	7	25	13	27	.358	.492
Grass	4.06	3	9	0	23	19	119.2	127	16	23	77	None on	.270	928	251	57	2	18	18	35	153	.301	.394
Turf	3.96	18	12	0	57	42	279.1	304	22	45	153	Runners on	.284	633	180	32	5	20	149	33	77	.320	.445
April	4.24	1	5	0	8	8	46.2	54	4	13	31	Scoring Posn	.253	360	91	19	3	11	125	28	51	.308	.414
May	5.52	1	3	0	17	9	58.2	64	6	10	28	Close & Late	.348	112	39	8	0	2	14	8	13	.397	.473
June	4.26	4	2	0	10	8	44.1	51	7	10	21	None on/out	.297	411	122	31	0	10	10	14	66	.325	.445
July	4.96	2	4	0	14	6	45.1	67	5	6	30	vs. 1st Batr (relief)	.412	17	7	1	0	1	1	2	1	.474	.647
August	2.96	4	4	0	13	13	85.0	74	6	15	39	First Inning Pitched	.277	296	82	15	3	5	30	14	46	.307	.399
September/October	3.40	9	3	0	18	17	119.0	121	10	14	81	First 75 Pitches	.273	1302	355	72	7	33	139	58	195	.307	.415
Starter	3.01	20	20	0	61	61	373.1	396	35	62	215	Pitch 76-90	.299	157	47	7	0	4	19	4	24	.317	.420
Reliever	5.26	1	1	0	19	0	25.2	35	3	6	15	Pitch 91-105	.288	73	21	5	0	1	8	3	5	.316	.397
0-3 Days Rest	2.19	2	1	0	4	4	24.2	24	3	2	11	Pitch 106+	.276	29	8	5	0	0	1	3	6	.344	.448
4 Days Rest	3.80	8	11	0	31	31	194.1	198	19	32	105	First Pitch	.340	306	104	23	4	13	48	6	0	.358	.569
5+ Days Rest	4.32	10	8	0	26	26	154.1	174	13	28	99	Ahead in Count	.214	651	139	23	2	5	56	0	198	.222	.278
Pre-All Star	4.53	7	12	0	39	28	167.0	188	19	34	97	Behind in Count	.328	351	115	31	0	12	42	33	0	.381	.519
Post-All Star	3.61	14	9	0	41	33	232.0	243	19	34	133	Two Strikes	.201	596	120	21	2	8	51	29	230	.244	.284

Pitcher vs. Batter (career)

Pitches Best Vs.	Avg	AB	H	2B	3B	HR	RBI	BB	SO	OBP	SLG	Pitches Worst Vs.	Avg	AB	H	2B	3B	HR	RBI	BB	SO	OBP	SLG
John Kruk	.077	13	1	0	0	0	2	2	2	.200	.077	Delino DeShields	.462	13	6	0	0	1	3	3	4	.563	.692
Darren Daulton	.091	11	1	0	0	0	0	0	4	.091	.091	Mark Carreon	.429	14	6	1	0	1	3	0	0	.429	.714
Gary Sheffield	.100	10	1	0	0	0	0	1	1	.182	.100	Matt D. Williams	.417	12	5	0	0	2	3	0	1	.417	.917
Archi Cianfrocco	.100	10	1	0	0	0	1	1	4	.182	.100	Eric Anthony	.417	12	5	1	0	1	4	2	2	.500	.750
Kevin McReynolds	.154	13	2	0	0	0	1	0	0	.143	.154	Jeff King	.385	13	5	1	0	1	3	1	0	.429	.692

Rod Correia — Angels

Age 26 – Bats Right (groundball hitter)

	Avg	G	AB	R	H	2B	3B	HR	RBI	BB	SO	HBP	GDP	SB	CS	OBP	SLG	IBB	SH	SF	#Pit	#P/PA	GB	FB	G/F
1993 Season	.266	64	128	12	34	5	0	0	9	6	20	4	1	2	4	.319	.305	0	5	0	475	3.32	54	30	1.80

1993 Season

	Avg	AB	H	2B	3B	HR	RBI	BB	SO	OBP	SLG		Avg	AB	H	2B	3B	HR	RBI	BB	SO	OBP	SLG
vs. Left	.326	43	14	3	0	0	0	4	4	.396	.395	Scoring Posn	.231	26	6	1	0	0	9	3	6	.333	.269
vs. Right	.235	85	20	2	0	0	9	2	16	.278	.259	Close & Late	.125	8	1	0	0	0	0	0	1	.125	.125
Home	.267	60	16	2	0	0	4	2	9	.313	.300	None on/out	.263	38	10	2	0	0	0	1	5	.282	.316
Away	.265	68	18	3	0	0	5	4	11	.324	.309	Batting #8	.500	16	8	1	0	0	0	1	1	.556	.563
First Pitch	.077	13	1	0	0	0	2	0	0	.143	.077	Batting #9	.219	96	21	2	0	0	9	4	17	.265	.240
Ahead in Count	.366	41	15	1	0	0	2	5	0	.447	.390	Other	.313	16	5	2	0	0	0	1	2	.389	.438
Behind in Count	.291	55	16	2	0	0	4	0	19	.316	.327	Pre-All Star	.500	4	2	0	0	0	2	0	1	.500	.500
Two Strikes	.234	47	11	1	0	0	4	1	20	.280	.255	Post-All Star	.258	124	32	5	0	0	7	6	19	.313	.298

Jim Corsi — Marlins

Age 32 – Pitches Right (groundball pitcher)

	ERA	W	L	Sv	G	GS	IP	BB	SO	Avg	H	2B	3B	HR	RBI	OBP	SLG	GF	IR	IRS	Hld	SvOp	SB	CS	GB	FB	G/F
1993 Season	6.64	0	2	0	15	0	20.1	10	7	.337	28	2	1	1	13	.404	.422	6	9	2	1	0	2	0	38	16	2.38
Last Five Years	3.09	5	11	0	116	0	180.1	61	100	.259	174	17	3	11	80	.319	.343	37	72	24	11	3	18	8	329	127	2.59

1993 Season

	ERA	W	L	Sv	G	GS	IP	H	HR	BB	SO		Avg	AB	H	2B	3B	HR	RBI	BB	SO	OBP	SLG
Home	3.18	0	0	0	7	0	11.1	11	0	6	5	vs. Left	.354	48	17	2	1	0	7	5	3	.415	.438
Away	11.00	0	2	0	8	0	9.0	17	1	4	2	vs. Right	.314	35	11	0	0	1	6	5	4	.390	.400

Last Five Years

	ERA	W	L	Sv	G	GS	IP	H	HR	BB	SO		Avg	AB	H	2B	3B	HR	RBI	BB	SO	OBP	SLG
Home	3.13	5	5	0	55	0	89.0	77	7	26	52	vs. Left	.287	331	95	11	2	6	35	29	42	.345	.387
Away	3.05	0	6	0	61	0	91.1	97	4	35	48	vs. Right	.232	340	79	6	1	5	45	32	58	.294	.300
Day	2.21	2	0	0	25	0	40.2	29	1	17	30	Inning 1-6	.263	217	57	7	1	3	30	23	33	.328	.346
Night	3.35	3	11	0	91	0	139.2	145	10	44	70	Inning 7+	.258	454	117	10	2	8	50	38	67	.315	.341
Grass	2.45	5	6	0	69	0	106.1	101	5	41	55	None on	.261	357	93	6	1	4	4	31	58	.321	.317
Turf	4.01	0	5	0	47	0	74.0	73	6	20	45	Runners on	.258	314	81	11	2	7	76	30	42	.316	.373
April	4.50	0	2	0	5	0	10.0	14	0	3	1	Scoring Posn	.269	171	46	5	2	2	61	24	26	.347	.357
May	5.64	0	2	0	17	0	22.1	25	4	7	14	Close & Late	.323	155	50	5	1	5	26	17	24	.390	.465
June	1.96	1	2	0	21	0	41.1	34	0	15	17	None on/out	.272	158	43	3	0	4	4	15	18	.335	.367
July	3.66	0	2	0	25	0	39.1	41	3	13	20	vs. 1st Batr (relief)	.192	104	20	2	0	0	9	9	13	.254	.212
August	3.31	2	2	0	23	0	32.2	33	3	11	25	First Inning Pitched	.274	402	110	11	2	3	55	40	61	.336	.333
September/October	1.56	2	1	0	25	0	34.2	27	1	12	23	First 15 Pitches	.273	373	102	11	1	3	48	32	53	.327	.332
Starter	0.00	0	0	0	0	0	0.0	0	0	0	0	Pitch 16-30	.267	202	54	3	2	5	21	21	33	.336	.376
Reliever	3.09	5	11	0	116	0	180.1	174	11	61	100	Pitch 31-45	.169	77	13	2	0	2	7	5	12	.220	.273
0 Days rest	3.38	1	1	0	10	0	18.2	17	2	7	10	Pitch 46+	.263	19	5	1	0	1	4	3	2	.364	.474
1 or 2 Days rest	3.27	1	6	0	50	0	77.0	73	4	28	39	First Pitch	.300	90	27	2	1	0	10	8	0	.356	.344
3+ Days rest	2.87	3	4	0	56	0	84.2	84	5	26	51	Ahead in Count	.227	273	62	9	1	4	31	0	72	.225	.311
Pre-All Star	4.10	1	8	0	52	0	85.2	90	6	29	35	Behind in Count	.311	148	46	4	0	5	25	28	0	.416	.439
Post-All Star	2.19	4	3	0	64	0	94.2	84	5	32	65	Two Strikes	.193	275	53	6	1	4	20	25	100	.259	.265

Tim Costo — Reds

Age 25 – Bats Right

	Avg	G	AB	R	H	2B	3B	HR	RBI	BB	SO	HBP	GDP	SB	CS	OBP	SLG	IBB	SH	SF	#Pit	#P/PA	GB	FB	G/F
1993 Season	.224	31	98	13	22	5	0	3	12	4	17	0	1	0	0	.250	.367	0	0	2	357	3.43	35	28	1.25
Career (1992-1993)	.224	43	134	16	30	7	0	3	14	9	23	0	5	0	0	.267	.343	0	0	3	496	3.40	50	38	1.32

1993 Season

	Avg	AB	H	2B	3B	HR	RBI	BB	SO	OBP	SLG		Avg	AB	H	2B	3B	HR	RBI	BB	SO	OBP	SLG
vs. Left	.316	38	12	2	0	2	7	1	1	.333	.526	Scoring Posn	.217	23	5	2	0	1	9	1	4	.231	.435
vs. Right	.167	60	10	3	0	1	5	3	16	.200	.267	Close & Late	.222	9	2	1	0	0	2	1	1	.300	.333

Henry Cotto — Marlins

Age 33 – Bats Right

	Avg	G	AB	R	H	2B	3B	HR	RBI	BB	SO	HBP	GDP	SB	CS	OBP	SLG	IBB	SH	SF	#Pit	#P/PA	GB	FB	G/F
1993 Season	.250	108	240	25	60	8	0	5	21	5	40	2	3	16	5	.269	.346	0	2	2	907	3.61	89	68	1.31
Last Five Years	.265	509	1361	186	360	50	8	29	137	63	212	12	29	86	17	.301	.377	8	13	7	4876	3.35	540	361	1.50

1993 Season

	Avg	AB	H	2B	3B	HR	RBI	BB	SO	OBP	SLG		Avg	AB	H	2B	3B	HR	RBI	BB	SO	OBP	SLG
vs. Left	.282	149	42	5	0	2	12	5	27	.301	.356	Scoring Posn	.185	54	10	0	0	0	13	2	12	.207	.185
vs. Right	.198	91	18	3	0	3	9	0	13	.215	.330	Close & Late	.277	47	13	0	0	1	5	2	6	.314	.340
Home	.259	116	30	6	0	1	10	3	21	.279	.336	None on/out	.238	63	15	2	0	1	1	0	9	.250	.317
Away	.242	124	30	2	0	4	11	2	19	.260	.355	Batting #1	.274	62	17	1	0	2	8	1	8	.286	.387
First Pitch	.346	26	9	1	0	0	4	0	0	.346	.385	Batting #2	.258	89	23	4	0	2	8	3	17	.280	.371
Ahead in Count	.339	59	20	3	0	2	6	3	0	.371	.492	Other	.225	89	20	3	0	1	5	1	15	.247	.292
Behind in Count	.210	119	25	3	0	2	8	0	31	.221	.286	Pre-All Star	.221	145	32	4	0	4	12	3	27	.242	.331
Two Strikes	.195	118	23	2	0	2	6	2	40	.215	.263	Post-All Star	.295	95	28	4	0	1	9	2	13	.310	.368

Last Five Years

	Avg	AB	H	2B	3B	HR	RBI	BB	SO	OBP	SLG		Avg	AB	H	2B	3B	HR	RBI	BB	SO	OBP	SLG
vs. Left	.286	765	219	28	5	17	84	46	113	.328	.403	Scoring Posn	.258	306	79	6	4	4	93	26	43	.314	.343
vs. Right	.237	596	141	22	3	12	53	17	99	.267	.344	Close & Late	.238	248	59	3	2	5	21	12	41	.282	.327
Groundball	.284	328	93	15	2	4	28	14	58	.319	.378	None on/out	.247	352	87	14	0	8	8	15	54	.284	.355
Flyball	.268	310	83	18	0	5	36	17	50	.306	.374	Batting #1	.271	369	100	12	3	5	30	18	60	.306	.360
Home	.260	628	163	25	3	12	68	37	90	.309	.366	Batting #2	.255	635	162	28	3	11	61	35	95	.300	.361
Away	.269	733	197	25	5	17	69	26	122	.295	.386	Other	.275	357	98	10	2	13	46	10	57	.299	.423
Day	.262	370	97	15	3	6	34	11	71	.288	.368	April	.278	158	44	8	0	3	15	6	23	.303	.386
Night	.265	991	263	35	5	23	103	52	141	.306	.380	May	.261	276	72	3	0	7	24	14	50	.301	.348
Grass	.279	596	166	23	4	14	57	25	98	.309	.401	June	.294	228	67	8	3	6	29	14	35	.341	.434
Turf	.254	765	194	27	4	15	80	38	114	.295	.358	July	.243	296	72	15	2	5	28	8	39	.271	.358
First Pitch	.361	191	69	14	1	4	32	5	0	.376	.508	August	.274	164	45	4	0	4	19	10	28	.316	.372
Ahead in Count	.355	327	116	15	3	12	40	31	0	.414	.529	September/October	.251	239	60	12	3	4	22	11	37	.289	.377
Behind in Count	.196	621	122	12	2	9	41	0	182	.204	.266	Pre-All Star	.268	792	212	23	3	19	80	36	126	.304	.376
Two Strikes	.174	568	99	10	2	6	35	24	212	.212	.231	Post-All Star	.260	569	148	27	5	10	57	27	86	.298	.378

Batter vs. Pitcher (career)

Hits Best Against	Avg	AB	H	2B	3B	HR	RBI	BB	SO	OBP	SLG	Hits Worst Against	Avg	AB	H	2B	3B	HR	RBI	BB	SO	OBP	SLG
Jack Morris	.500	16	8	2	0	1	1	0	2	.500	.813	Dave Stewart	.067	15	1	0	0	0	0	1	6	.125	.067
John Farrell	.429	21	9	1	0	1	3	0	2	.429	.619	Mark Guthrie	.071	14	1	0	0	0	0	0	6	.071	.071
Rick Honeycutt	.400	10	4	0	0	1	2	1	1	.417	.700	Joe Hesketh	.111	18	2	1	0	0	0	0	3	.111	.167
Curt Young	.391	23	9	1	0	2	5	0	2	.391	.696	Bruce Hurst	.133	15	2	0	0	0	0	0	5	.133	.133
Greg Cadaret	.385	13	5	0	0	1	1	3	1	.500	.615	Mark Langston	.139	36	5	0	0	0	3	0	7	.135	.139

Danny Cox — Blue Jays

Age 34 – Pitches Right

	ERA	W	L	Sv	G	GS	IP	BB	SO	Avg	H	2B	3B	HR	RBI	OBP	SLG	GF	IR	IRS	Hld	SvOp	SB	CS	GB	FB	G/F
1993 Season	3.12	7	6	2	44	0	83.2	29	84	.230	73	12	0	8	32	.293	.343	13	27	10	10	6	7	3	101	75	1.35
Last Five Years	4.09	16	15	5	92	24	248.2	95	178	.252	237	40	4	27	126	.318	.389	23	50	19	13	11	23	11	338	258	1.31

1993 Season

	ERA	W	L	Sv	G	GS	IP	H	HR	BB	SO		Avg	AB	H	2B	3B	HR	RBI	BB	SO	OBP	SLG
Home	3.21	3	1	0	20	0	42.0	36	7	16	44	vs. Left	.254	138	35	9	0	5	19	19	35	.342	.428
Away	3.02	4	5	2	24	0	41.2	37	1	13	40	vs. Right	.211	180	38	3	0	3	13	10	49	.253	.278
Starter	0.00	0	0	0	0	0	0.0	0	0	0	0	Scoring Posn	.284	81	23	3	0	4	28	15	22	.392	.469
Reliever	3.12	7	6	2	44	0	83.2	73	8	29	84	Close & Late	.231	147	34	5	0	3	12	19	36	.317	.327
0 Days rest	9.00	0	1	0	1	0	2.0	4	0	1	3	None on/out	.222	81	18	3	0	2	2	3	18	.250	.333
1 or 2 Days rest	1.29	6	0	0	17	0	35.0	22	1	10	35	First Pitch	.250	32	8	1	0	0	2	3	0	.314	.281
3+ Days rest	4.24	1	5	2	26	0	46.2	47	7	18	46	Ahead in Count	.182	137	25	4	0	2	9	0	65	.182	.255
Pre-All Star	2.47	5	4	1	27	0	54.2	44	4	19	53	Behind in Count	.303	76	23	3	0	4	12	14	0	.407	.500
Post-All Star	4.34	2	2	1	17	0	29.0	29	4	10	31	Two Strikes	.185	157	29	7	0	3	13	12	84	.243	.287

Last Five Years

	ERA	W	L	Sv	G	GS	IP	H	HR	BB	SO		Avg	AB	H	2B	3B	HR	RBI	BB	SO	OBP	SLG
Home	3.87	8	7	2	46	12	128.0	117	16	51	97	vs. Left	.272	456	124	26	2	15	73	63	70	.356	.436
Away	4.33	8	8	3	46	12	120.2	120	11	44	81	vs. Right	.233	485	113	14	2	12	53	32	108	.280	.344
Day	3.93	4	5	1	30	6	68.2	61	9	28	49	Inning 1-6	.257	569	146	24	3	19	86	60	94	.325	.409
Night	4.15	12	10	4	62	18	180.0	176	18	67	129	Inning 7+	.245	372	91	16	1	8	40	35	84	.306	.358
Grass	3.54	8	3	2	34	8	89.0	75	7	30	65	None on	.234	547	128	21	1	15	15	52	100	.301	.358
Turf	4.40	8	12	3	58	16	159.2	162	20	65	113	Runners on	.277	394	109	19	3	12	111	43	78	.341	.431
April	3.02	3	1	0	14	6	47.2	42	4	14	40	Scoring Posn	.289	246	71	12	2	9	101	32	50	.356	.463
May	3.95	5	3	1	17	6	57.0	49	6	24	42	Close & Late	.230	222	51	11	0	3	22	27	50	.308	.320
June	5.40	2	2	0	10	3	26.2	27	1	14	20	None on/out	.227	233	53	8	0	5	5	19	31	.286	.326

Last Five Years

	ERA	W	L	Sv	G	GS	IP	H	HR	BB	SO
July	5.82	0	5	0	8	3	21.2	30	5	13	10
August	3.97	4	3	2	19	6	56.2	54	8	15	33
September/October	3.92	2	1	2	24	0	39.0	35	3	15	33
Starter	4.75	6	8	0	24	24	125.0	130	15	53	68
Reliever	3.42	10	7	5	68	0	123.2	107	12	42	110
0 Days rest	9.00	0	1	0	1	0	2.0	4	0	1	3
1 or 2 Days rest	1.88	9	1	2	31	0	57.1	38	2	18	51
3+ Days rest	4.62	1	5	3	36	0	64.1	65	10	23	56
Pre-All Star	3.87	10	8	1	45	16	142.0	129	11	59	107
Post-All Star	4.39	6	7	4	47	8	106.2	108	16	36	71

	Avg	AB	H	2B	3B	HR	RBI	BB	SO	OBP	SLG
vs. 1st Batr (relief)	.169	65	11	0	0	3	16	1	16	.176	.308
First Inning Pitched	.232	328	76	13	1	8	50	33	75	.299	.351
First 15 Pitches	.239	293	70	14	1	7	32	28	61	.303	.365
Pitch 16-30	.204	240	49	8	0	5	28	23	53	.271	.300
Pitch 31-45	.294	163	48	8	1	3	17	11	25	.337	.411
Pitch 46+	.286	245	70	10	2	12	49	33	39	.366	.490
First Pitch	.228	114	26	7	0	0	12	7	0	.266	.289
Ahead in Count	.199	386	77	11	0	4	25	0	145	.200	.259
Behind in Count	.326	239	78	11	3	14	54	46	0	.431	.573
Two Strikes	.183	409	75	15	1	3	33	42	178	.259	.247

Pitcher vs. Batter (since 1984)

Pitches Best Vs.	Avg	AB	H	2B	3B	HR	RBI	BB	SO	OBP	SLG
Gary Redus	.059	17	1	0	0	0	1	0	2	.059	.059
Rafael Belliard	.077	13	1	0	0	0	0	2	3	.200	.077
Kevin Bass	.120	25	3	0	0	0	1	2	3	.179	.120
Mike LaValliere	.154	13	2	0	0	0	1	1	2	.214	.154
Mariano Duncan	.154	13	2	0	0	0	0	0	2	.154	.154

Pitches Worst Vs.	Avg	AB	H	2B	3B	HR	RBI	BB	SO	OBP	SLG
Gerald Perry	.550	20	11	2	0	0	2	2	1	.601	.650
Mike Aldrete	.500	16	8	0	0	1	2	4	3	.600	.688
Matt D. Williams	.455	11	5	1	0	3	5	1	0	.500	1.364
Otis Nixon	.444	9	4	1	0	0	0	3	1	.583	.556
Rafael Palmeiro	.417	12	5	3	0	1	2	2	1	.500	.917

Chuck Crim — Angels

Age 32 – Pitches Right (groundball pitcher)

	ERA	W	L	Sv	G	GS	IP	BB	SO	Avg	H	2B	3B	HR	RBI	OBP	SLG	GF	IR	IRS	Hld	SvOp	SB	CS	GB	FB	G/F
1993 Season	5.87	2	2	0	11	0	15.1	5	10	.298	17	2	0	2	10	.369	.439	3	7	0	2	0	3	0	22	15	1.47
Last Five Years	4.01	29	25	22	277	0	397.0	118	177	.280	434	55	8	36	228	.333	.395	73	234	82	59	38	35	9	692	412	1.68

1993 Season

	ERA	W	L	Sv	G	GS	IP	H	HR	BB	SO
Home	7.88	2	0	0	7	0	8.0	10	1	2	5
Away	3.68	0	2	0	4	0	7.1	7	1	3	5

	Avg	AB	H	2B	3B	HR	RBI	BB	SO	OBP	SLG
vs. Left	.308	26	8	0	0	1	4	1	4	.379	.423
vs. Right	.290	31	9	2	0	1	6	4	6	.361	.452

Last Five Years

	ERA	W	L	Sv	G	GS	IP	H	HR	BB	SO
Home	4.05	15	9	13	143	0	204.2	221	14	55	88
Away	3.98	14	16	9	134	0	192.1	213	22	63	89
Day	4.77	13	11	7	90	0	117.0	125	13	43	48
Night	3.70	16	14	15	187	0	280.0	309	23	75	129
Grass	3.76	25	20	18	236	0	337.1	362	27	100	142
Turf	5.43	4	5	4	41	0	59.2	72	9	18	35
April	3.76	6	4	5	45	0	67.0	61	5	25	23
May	5.37	6	6	2	56	0	68.2	84	5	20	40
June	5.76	4	7	5	47	0	65.2	85	8	22	24
July	2.17	6	2	2	38	0	62.1	55	2	12	31
August	3.93	4	2	4	44	0	66.1	73	11	19	26
September/October	2.96	3	4	4	47	0	67.0	76	5	20	33
Starter	0.00	0	0	0	0	0	0.0	0	0	0	0
Reliever	4.01	29	25	22	277	0	397.0	434	36	118	177
0 Days rest	5.63	7	5	6	66	0	84.2	114	13	26	40
1 or 2 Days rest	3.54	17	15	15	142	0	213.1	219	17	66	92
3+ Days rest	3.64	5	5	1	69	0	99.0	101	6	26	45
Pre-All Star	4.65	18	17	12	158	0	224.2	249	18	72	106
Post-All Star	3.19	11	8	10	119	0	172.1	185	18	46	71

	Avg	AB	H	2B	3B	HR	RBI	BB	SO	OBP	SLG
vs. Left	.269	644	173	23	1	14	86	51	68	.325	.373
vs. Right	.287	908	261	32	7	22	142	67	109	.338	.411
Inning 1-6	.281	256	72	8	0	10	62	19	32	.338	.430
Inning 7+	.279	1296	362	47	8	26	166	99	145	.332	.388
None on	.254	823	209	34	5	20	20	43	96	.296	.380
Runners on	.309	729	225	21	3	16	208	75	81	.372	.412
Scoring Posn	.305	446	136	12	3	12	193	67	50	.388	.426
Close & Late	.280	625	175	20	3	16	94	56	72	.338	.398
None on/out	.270	359	97	21	2	10	10	15	40	.303	.423
vs. 1st Batr (relief)	.315	254	80	11	2	9	53	15	37	.348	.480
First Inning Pitched	.296	909	269	36	4	19	177	74	105	.348	.407
First 15 Pitches	.291	899	262	34	4	19	143	60	98	.336	.402
Pitch 16-30	.252	444	112	16	3	10	59	39	44	.316	.369
Pitch 31-45	.285	172	49	4	0	5	21	16	27	.354	.395
Pitch 46+	.297	37	11	1	1	2	5	3	8	.366	.541
First Pitch	.288	292	84	12	0	6	36	18	0	.335	.390
Ahead in Count	.238	609	145	14	3	9	74	0	147	.246	.315
Behind in Count	.320	375	120	20	1	10	71	53	0	.398	.459
Two Strikes	.217	581	126	11	5	13	70	45	177	.281	.320

Pitcher vs. Batter (career)

Pitches Best Vs.	Avg	AB	H	2B	3B	HR	RBI	BB	SO	OBP	SLG
Cory Snyder	.063	16	1	0	0	0	0	0	5	.063	.063
Lou Whitaker	.067	15	1	0	0	0	1	1	0	.125	.067
George Brett	.077	13	1	0	0	0	0	1	3	.143	.077
Brian Harper	.083	12	1	0	0	0	2	0	0	.077	.083
Manuel Lee	.133	15	2	0	0	0	2	0	4	.133	.133

Pitches Worst Vs.	Avg	AB	H	2B	3B	HR	RBI	BB	SO	OBP	SLG
Jerry Browne	.636	11	7	1	0	1	1	1	1	.667	1.000
Cal Ripken	.529	17	9	1	0	1	6	1	1	.556	.765
Frank Thomas	.500	12	6	0	0	1	5	1	1	.538	.750
Gary Gaetti	.438	16	7	2	0	1	4	2	1	.500	.750
Fred McGriff	.333	9	3	1	0	1	2	2	1	.455	.778

Tripp Cromer — Cardinals

Age 26 – Bats Right

	Avg	G	AB	R	H	2B	3B	HR	RBI	BB	SO	HBP	GDP	SB	CS	OBP	SLG	IBB	SH	SF	#Pit	#P/PA	GB	FB	G/F
1993 Season	.087	10	23	1	2	0	0	0	0	1	6	0	0	0	0	.125	.087	0	0	0	75	3.13	11	4	2.75

1993 Season

	Avg	AB	H	2B	3B	HR	RBI	BB	SO	OBP	SLG
vs. Left	.182	11	2	0	0	0	0	1	1	.250	.182
vs. Right	.000	12	0	0	0	0	0	0	5	.000	.000
Scoring Posn	.167	6	1	0	0	0	0	1	1	.286	.167
Close & Late	.500	2	1	0	0	0	0	0	1	.500	.500

John Cummings — Mariners

Age 25 – Pitches Left (groundball pitcher)

	ERA	W	L	Sv	G	GS	IP	BB	SO	Avg	H	2B	3B	HR	RBI	OBP	SLG	CG	ShO	Sup	QS	#P/S	SB	CS	GB	FB	G/F
1993 Season	6.02	0	6	0	10	8	46.1	16	19	.316	59	7	0	6	30	.372	.449	1	0	1.94	2	86	2	4	77	47	1.64

1993 Season

	ERA	W	L	Sv	G	GS	IP	H	HR	BB	SO
Home	8.86	0	3	0	5	4	21.1	30	4	9	8
Away	3.60	0	3	0	5	4	25.0	29	2	7	11

	Avg	AB	H	2B	3B	HR	RBI	BB	SO	OBP	SLG
vs. Left	.244	41	10	1	0	2	8	5	1	.340	.415
vs. Right	.336	146	49	6	0	4	22	11	18	.381	.459

Midre Cummings — Pirates

Age 22 – Bats Left

	Avg	G	AB	R	H	2B	3B	HR	RBI	BB	SO	HBP	GDP	SB	CS	OBP	SLG	IBB	SH	SF	#Pit	#P/PA	GB	FB	G/F
1993 Season	.111	13	36	5	4	1	0	0	3	4	9	0	1	0	0	.195	.139	0	0	1	133	3.24	13	11	1.18

1993 Season

	Avg	AB	H	2B	3B	HR	RBI	BB	SO	OBP	SLG		Avg	AB	H	2B	3B	HR	RBI	BB	SO	OBP	SLG
vs. Left	.077	13	1	0	0	0	0	0	4	.077	.077	Scoring Posn	.077	13	1	1	0	0	3	2	5	.188	.154
vs. Right	.130	23	3	1	0	0	3	4	5	.250	.174	Close & Late	.143	7	1	0	0	0	0	0	3	.143	.143

Chad Curtis — Angels

Age 25 – Bats Right (groundball hitter)

	Avg	G	AB	R	H	2B	3B	HR	RBI	BB	SO	HBP	GDP	SB	CS	OBP	SLG	IBB	SH	SF	#Pit	#P/PA	GB	FB	G/F
1993 Season	.285	152	583	94	166	25	3	6	59	70	89	4	16	48	24	.361	.369	2	7	7	2523	3.76	248	149	1.66
Career (1992-1993)	.273	291	1024	153	280	41	5	16	105	121	160	10	26	91	42	.352	.370	4	12	11	4406	3.74	437	256	1.71

1993 Season

	Avg	AB	H	2B	3B	HR	RBI	BB	SO	OBP	SLG		Avg	AB	H	2B	3B	HR	RBI	BB	SO	OBP	SLG
vs. Left	.324	148	48	8	2	2	11	21	19	.408	.446	Scoring Posn	.273	143	39	7	0	0	50	14	27	.327	.322
vs. Right	.271	435	118	17	1	4	48	49	70	.345	.343	Close & Late	.305	95	29	3	0	0	6	12	12	.383	.337
Groundball	.314	105	33	6	1	1	5	17	11	.424	.419	None on/out	.362	105	38	6	1	4	4	16	9	.451	.552
Flyball	.302	129	39	3	0	1	14	15	19	.374	.349	Batting #2	.283	580	164	25	2	6	59	70	89	.360	.364
Home	.310	303	94	17	1	3	35	30	44	.374	.403	Batting #9	1.000	2	2	0	1	0	0	0	0	1.000	2.000
Away	.257	280	72	8	2	3	24	40	45	.349	.332	Other	.000	1	0	0	0	0	0	0	0	.000	.000
Day	.292	171	50	9	0	2	23	23	26	.376	.380	April	.294	68	20	2	0	0	6	8	7	.367	.324
Night	.282	412	116	16	3	4	36	47	63	.355	.364	May	.350	100	35	7	1	2	16	20	13	.463	.500
Grass	.289	484	140	20	1	4	50	57	76	.363	.360	June	.241	87	21	4	0	0	7	16	14	.362	.287
Turf	.263	99	26	5	2	2	9	13	13	.354	.414	July	.272	103	28	4	0	3	9	7	17	.318	.398
First Pitch	.420	88	37	9	0	3	22	0	0	.424	.625	August	.316	117	37	3	0	0	12	10	20	.367	.342
Ahead in Count	.302	129	39	5	1	2	15	41	0	.468	.403	September/October	.231	108	25	5	2	1	9	9	18	.286	.343
Behind in Count	.227	260	59	4	1	0	15	0	72	.227	.250	Pre-All Star	.296	301	89	16	1	3	31	46	39	.392	.385
Two Strikes	.223	256	57	4	1	0	15	29	89	.301	.246	Post-All Star	.273	282	77	9	2	3	28	24	50	.327	.351

1993 By Position

Position	Avg	AB	H	2B	3B	HR	RBI	BB	SO	OBP	SLG	G	GS	Innings	PO	A	E	DP	Fld Pct	Rng Fctr	In Zone	Outs	Zone Rtg	MLB Zone
As cf	.284	578	164	25	3	6	59	70	89	.361	.369	151	150	1314.1	426	13	9	4	.980	3.01	471	412	.875	.829

Career (1992-1993)

	Avg	AB	H	2B	3B	HR	RBI	BB	SO	OBP	SLG		Avg	AB	H	2B	3B	HR	RBI	BB	SO	OBP	SLG
vs. Left	.300	270	81	14	3	8	33	47	37	.401	.463	Scoring Posn	.253	249	63	10	1	4	88	24	44	.314	.349
vs. Right	.264	754	199	27	2	8	72	74	123	.334	.337	Close & Late	.275	171	47	5	0	2	11	24	25	.367	.339
Groundball	.266	214	57	7	1	1	11	29	29	.361	.322	None on/out	.318	198	63	9	2	6	6	31	22	.418	.475
Flyball	.294	265	78	8	1	6	36	30	47	.368	.400	Batting #2	.279	750	209	29	3	9	73	88	114	.356	.361
Home	.292	504	147	23	2	8	55	54	76	.364	.393	Batting #5	.241	137	33	7	0	2	13	17	27	.329	.336
Away	.256	520	133	18	3	8	50	67	84	.342	.348	Other	.277	137	38	5	2	5	19	16	19	.359	.453
Day	.262	282	74	11	0	5	34	39	41	.357	.355	April	.305	95	29	4	1	0	10	12	10	.378	.368
Night	.278	742	206	30	5	11	71	82	119	.351	.376	May	.300	160	48	9	2	4	19	28	23	.408	.456
Grass	.274	851	233	33	2	11	81	96	136	.349	.356	June	.260	169	44	6	0	2	21	24	25	.357	.331
Turf	.272	173	47	8	3	5	24	25	24	.371	.439	July	.251	191	48	8	0	7	18	17	32	.319	.403
First Pitch	.342	158	54	10	0	5	32	2	0	.357	.500	August	.277	202	56	5	0	1	19	23	38	.348	.317
Ahead in Count	.326	215	70	9	2	7	32	62	0	.477	.484	September/October	.266	207	55	9	2	2	18	17	32	.325	.357
Behind in Count	.226	477	108	12	2	2	31	0	135	.229	.273	Pre-All Star	.280	507	142	25	3	9	57	70	70	.371	.394
Two Strikes	.227	480	109	9	2	3	31	57	160	.310	.273	Post-All Star	.267	517	138	16	2	7	48	51	90	.334	.346

Batter vs. Pitcher (career)

Hits Best Against	Avg	AB	H	2B	3B	HR	RBI	BB	SO	OBP	SLG	Hits Worst Against	Avg	AB	H	2B	3B	HR	RBI	BB	SO	OBP	SLG
Wilson Alvarez	.500	14	7	1	0	0	2	3	2	.588	.571	Kelly Downs	.000	7	0	0	0	0	0	5	1	.417	.000
Ben McDonald	.500	10	5	1	0	0	2	1	1	.545	.600	Bill Gullickson	.077	13	1	0	0	0	0	0	1	.077	.077
Jack Morris	.455	11	5	2	0	1	5	1	1	.500	.909	Danny Darwin	.100	10	1	0	0	0	0	1	3	.182	.100
Todd Stottlemyre	.385	13	5	2	0	1	2	1	1	.429	.769	Jaime Navarro	.133	15	2	0	0	0	0	0	4	.133	.133
Erik Hanson	.357	14	5	0	1	1	2	2	0	.438	.714	Bob Welch	.167	12	2	0	0	0	0	0	1	.167	.167

Milt Cuyler — Tigers

Age 25 – Bats Both (groundball hitter)

	Avg	G	AB	R	H	2B	3B	HR	RBI	BB	SO	HBP	GDP	SB	CS	OBP	SLG	IBB	SH	SF	#Pit	#P/PA	GB	FB	G/F
1993 Season	.213	82	249	46	53	11	7	0	19	19	53	3	2	13	2	.276	.313	0	4	1	977	3.54	81	65	1.25
Career (1990-1993)	.242	344	1066	170	258	40	16	6	88	86	217	12	11	63	19	.305	.326	0	26	4	4304	3.60	396	216	1.83

1993 Season

	Avg	AB	H	2B	3B	HR	RBI	BB	SO	OBP	SLG		Avg	AB	H	2B	3B	HR	RBI	BB	SO	OBP	SLG
vs. Left	.182	77	14	2	1	0	8	6	14	.241	.234	Scoring Posn	.161	62	10	2	1	0	16	5	14	.232	.226
vs. Right	.227	172	39	9	6	0	11	13	39	.291	.349	Close & Late	.281	32	9	2	3	0	3	2	7	.324	.531
Home	.220	127	28	4	3	0	11	10	21	.286	.299	None on/out	.175	63	11	4	1	0	0	3	14	.224	.270
Away	.205	122	25	7	4	0	8	9	32	.265	.328	Batting #8	.235	17	4	1	0	0	1	4	2	.381	.294
First Pitch	.268	41	11	2	0	0	3	0	0	.286	.317	Batting #9	.198	222	44	8	6	0	15	14	48	.254	.288
Ahead in Count	.229	48	11	4	2	0	4	9	0	.351	.396	Other	.500	10	5	2	1	0	3	1	3	.545	.900
Behind in Count	.178	118	21	2	3	0	4	0	45	.192	.246	Pre-All Star	.215	237	51	10	7	0	19	14	51	.264	.316
Two Strikes	.185	108	20	3	4	0	7	10	53	.267	.287	Post-All Star	.167	12	2	1	0	0	0	5	2	.444	.250

Career (1990-1993)

	Avg	AB	H	2B	3B	HR	RBI	BB	SO	OBP	SLG		Avg	AB	H	2B	3B	HR	RBI	BB	SO	OBP	SLG
vs. Left	.256	297	76	11	2	2	27	22	44	.315	.327	Scoring Posn	.216	259	56	10	5	3	81	20	63	.276	.328

Career (1990-1993)

	Avg	AB	H	2B	3B	HR	RBI	BB	SO	OBP	SLG
vs. Right	.237	769	182	29	14	4	61	64	173	.301	.326
Groundball	.216	328	71	9	4	0	30	26	70	.279	.268
Flyball	.268	231	62	14	4	4	21	18	41	.325	.416
Home	.223	515	115	14	6	2	37	53	95	.306	.285
Away	.260	551	143	26	10	4	51	33	122	.303	.365
Day	.254	338	86	16	6	2	40	27	66	.319	.355
Night	.236	728	172	24	10	4	48	59	151	.298	.313
Grass	.231	872	201	30	13	4	72	76	182	.299	.308
Turf	.294	194	57	10	3	2	16	10	35	.332	.407
First Pitch	.326	172	56	8	1	2	19	0	0	.331	.419
Ahead in Count	.265	230	61	16	7	1	17	48	0	.389	.409
Behind in Count	.195	457	89	8	5	2	32	0	180	.210	.247
Two Strikes	.164	456	75	9	6	0	22	38	217	.240	.211

	Avg	AB	H	2B	3B	HR	RBI	BB	SO	OBP	SLG
Close & Late	.230	148	34	7	3	2	10	8	33	.288	.358
None on/out	.243	276	67	11	4	1	1	24	57	.308	.322
Batting #1	.257	171	44	7	3	1	8	17	38	.335	.351
Batting #9	.239	863	206	30	13	5	72	63	174	.296	.321
Other	.250	32	8	3	0	0	8	6	5	.359	.344
April	.217	166	36	8	2	1	16	9	34	.264	.307
May	.258	217	56	3	6	2	25	19	39	.322	.355
June	.225	253	57	11	3	3	18	10	49	.266	.328
July	.226	168	38	6	0	0	8	22	40	.318	.262
August	.216	111	24	6	2	0	7	14	25	.315	.306
September/October	.311	151	47	6	3	0	14	12	30	.364	.391
Pre-All Star	.232	729	169	25	11	6	63	43	151	.281	.321
Post-All Star	.264	337	89	15	5	0	25	43	66	.353	.338

Batter vs. Pitcher (career)

Hits Best Against	Avg	AB	H	2B	3B	HR	RBI	BB	SO	OBP	SLG
Juan Guzman	.364	11	4	1	0	0	0	2	2	.462	.455
Mike Boddicker	.357	14	5	0	0	0	4	0	1	.357	.357
Mike Moore	.333	12	4	2	0	0	4	1	3	.385	.500
Russ Swan	.333	12	4	0	0	0	1	1	1	.385	.333
Charles Nagy	.333	12	4	0	1	0	0	0	3	.333	.500

Hits Worst Against	Avg	AB	H	2B	3B	HR	RBI	BB	SO	OBP	SLG
Tim Leary	.000	15	0	0	0	0	1	0	2	.000	.000
Erik Hanson	.071	14	1	0	0	0	0	2	5	.188	.071
Mark Langston	.083	12	1	0	0	0	0	0	1	.083	.083
Chuck Finley	.083	12	1	0	0	0	2	1	3	.143	.083
Kevin Brown	.133	15	2	0	0	0	1	3	4	.278	.133

Omar Daal — Dodgers

Age 22 – Pitches Left (groundball pitcher)

	ERA	W	L	Sv	G	GS	IP	BB	SO	Avg	H	2B	3B	HR	RBI	OBP	SLG	GF	IR	IRS	Hld	SvOp	SB	CS	GB	FB	G/F
1993 Season	5.09	2	3	0	47	0	35.1	21	19	.277	36	4	1	5	27	.373	.438	12	48	13	7	1	1	1	62	27	2.30

1993 Season

	ERA	W	L	Sv	G	GS	IP	H	HR	BB	SO
Home	5.74	0	3	0	22	0	15.2	18	3	10	8
Away	4.58	2	0	0	25	0	19.2	18	2	11	11
Starter	0.00	0	0	0	0	0	0.0	0	0	0	0
Reliever	5.09	2	3	0	47	0	35.1	36	5	21	19
0 Days rest	11.88	1	1	0	17	0	8.1	18	2	7	4
1 or 2 Days rest	3.18	1	1	0	16	0	17.0	14	2	10	4
3+ Days rest	2.70	0	1	0	14	0	10.0	4	1	4	11
Pre-All Star	3.94	1	1	0	27	0	16.0	14	2	9	10
Post-All Star	6.05	1	2	0	20	0	19.1	22	3	12	9

	Avg	AB	H	2B	3B	HR	RBI	BB	SO	OBP	SLG
vs. Left	.230	74	17	2	0	2	16	11	12	.326	.338
vs. Right	.339	56	19	2	1	3	11	10	7	.433	.571
Scoring Posn	.319	47	15	1	0	2	21	10	8	.424	.468
Close & Late	.382	34	13	2	0	1	8	4	5	.447	.529
None on/out	.194	31	6	2	0	0	0	5	4	.306	.258
First Pitch	.375	16	6	0	0	2	4	2	0	.444	.750
Ahead in Count	.204	49	10	0	0	2	7	0	15	.200	.327
Behind in Count	.343	35	12	4	0	1	12	9	0	.477	.543
Two Strikes	.184	49	9	0	0	0	4	10	19	.311	.184

Ron Darling — Athletics

Age 33 – Pitches Right

	ERA	W	L	Sv	G	GS	IP	BB	SO	Avg	H	2B	3B	HR	RBI	OBP	SLG	CG	ShO	Sup	QS	#P/S	SB	CS	GB	FB	G/F
1993 Season	5.16	5	9	0	31	29	178.0	72	95	.281	198	39	4	22	97	.349	.441	3	0	4.15	12	97	14	11	251	242	1.04
Last Five Years	4.16	49	57	0	162	145	922.0	329	575	.263	930	171	28	98	424	.327	.410	12	3	4.35	83	95	98	42	1232	1043	1.18

1993 Season

	ERA	W	L	Sv	G	GS	IP	H	HR	BB	SO
Home	4.75	3	6	0	16	16	94.2	94	14	38	60
Away	5.62	2	3	0	15	13	83.1	104	8	34	35
Day	4.58	2	4	0	9	9	53.0	50	6	24	33
Night	5.40	3	5	0	22	20	125.0	148	16	48	62
Grass	5.06	4	8	0	26	24	144.0	157	19	60	79
Turf	5.56	1	1	0	5	5	34.0	41	3	12	16
April	5.54	0	1	0	3	3	13.0	10	1	7	6
May	6.83	0	2	0	6	6	29.0	33	5	13	18
June	5.68	1	1	0	5	5	31.2	41	4	10	17
July	4.58	3	0	0	7	5	35.1	45	2	19	10
August	3.77	1	3	0	6	6	43.0	44	7	13	24
September/October	5.54	0	2	0	4	4	26.0	25	3	10	20
Starter	5.16	5	9	0	29	29	171.0	189	22	69	94
Reliever	5.14	0	0	0	2	0	7.0	9	0	3	1
0-3 Days Rest	3.43	2	1	0	3	3	21.0	24	0	4	9
4 Days Rest	5.91	2	5	0	14	14	77.2	87	14	35	42
5+ Days Rest	4.85	1	3	0	12	12	72.1	78	8	30	43
Pre-All Star	6.04	2	4	0	16	16	85.0	95	12	40	44
Post-All Star	4.35	3	5	0	15	13	93.0	103	10	32	51

	Avg	AB	H	2B	3B	HR	RBI	BB	SO	OBP	SLG
vs. Left	.276	352	97	16	3	12	48	40	41	.349	.440
vs. Right	.286	353	101	23	1	10	49	32	54	.349	.442
Inning 1-6	.288	626	180	35	3	22	89	62	83	.354	.458
Inning 7+	.228	79	18	4	1	0	8	10	12	.311	.304
None on	.291	409	119	27	3	9	9	29	58	.342	.438
Runners on	.267	296	79	12	1	13	88	43	37	.357	.446
Scoring Posn	.268	168	45	8	0	7	73	31	23	.374	.440
Close & Late	.259	27	7	0	1	0	2	2	5	.310	.333
None on/out	.283	184	52	11	2	4	4	6	23	.309	.429
vs. 1st Batr (relief)	.500	2	1	1	0	0	0	0	0	.500	1.000
First Inning Pitched	.312	125	39	10	1	5	27	22	14	.411	.528
First 75 Pitches	.297	525	156	32	3	19	81	53	68	.365	.478
Pitch 76-90	.224	85	19	2	0	1	3	9	13	.295	.282
Pitch 91-105	.268	56	15	2	1	1	5	3	5	.305	.393
Pitch 106+	.205	39	8	3	0	1	8	7	9	.319	.359
First Pitch	.306	111	34	3	0	5	16	4	0	.336	.468
Ahead in Count	.218	262	57	14	1	2	21	0	80	.226	.302
Behind in Count	.351	194	68	18	2	9	38	37	0	.451	.603
Two Strikes	.204	279	57	10	0	4	30	31	95	.287	.283

Last Five Years

	ERA	W	L	Sv	G	GS	IP	H	HR	BB	SO
Home	4.02	26	29	0	79	72	465.2	441	49	162	289
Away	4.30	23	28	0	83	73	456.1	489	49	167	286
Day	4.02	14	18	0	49	42	264.1	263	30	102	151
Night	4.21	35	39	0	113	103	657.2	667	68	227	424
Grass	4.15	40	44	0	124	112	714.1	712	84	246	458
Turf	4.20	9	13	0	38	33	207.2	218	14	83	117
April	4.78	4	9	0	20	19	101.2	105	11	42	64
May	4.61	6	7	0	26	24	144.1	139	22	53	103
June	4.81	10	7	0	27	24	151.2	164	12	49	84

	Avg	AB	H	2B	3B	HR	RBI	BB	SO	OBP	SLG
vs. Left	.266	1879	499	90	15	44	216	193	292	.334	.400
vs. Right	.260	1660	431	81	13	54	208	136	283	.319	.422
Inning 1-6	.266	3055	814	151	25	82	376	287	494	.331	.413
Inning 7+	.240	484	116	20	3	16	48	42	81	.305	.393
None on	.256	2107	540	102	16	57	57	160	341	.314	.401
Runners on	.272	1432	390	69	12	41	367	169	234	.346	.423
Scoring Posn	.262	848	222	39	9	23	317	124	159	.349	.410
Close & Late	.223	202	45	6	3	4	16	20	37	.302	.342
None on/out	.255	927	236	33	6	21	21	49	153	.298	.371

Last Five Years

	ERA	W	L	Sv	G	GS	IP	H	HR	BB	SO
July	3.66	10	11	0	30	26	177.0	183	18	65	96
August	3.79	12	9	0	29	28	183.0	198	21	56	110
September/October	3.72	7	14	0	30	24	164.1	141	14	64	118
Starter	4.16	48	55	0	145	145	885.2	894	94	316	551
Reliever	4.21	1	2	0	17	0	36.1	36	4	13	24
0-3 Days Rest	4.12	3	3	0	6	6	39.1	45	3	12	18
4 Days Rest	4.34	27	33	0	84	84	510.2	523	52	190	320
5+ Days Rest	3.89	18	19	0	55	55	335.2	326	39	114	213
Pre-All Star	4.69	23	26	0	82	75	447.1	455	51	170	274
Post-All Star	3.66	26	31	0	80	70	474.2	475	47	159	301

	Avg	AB	H	2B	3B	HR	RBI	BB	SO	OBP	SLG
vs. 1st Batr (relief)	.214	14	3	1	0	1	4	1	4	.235	.500
First Inning Pitched	.261	617	161	28	4	14	97	74	109	.341	.387
First 75 Pitches	.270	2710	733	135	23	70	337	250	425	.334	.415
Pitch 76-90	.243	428	104	23	2	13	38	44	85	.313	.397
Pitch 91-105	.259	282	73	9	3	12	34	18	43	.303	.440
Pitch 106+	.168	119	20	4	0	3	15	17	22	.275	.277
First Pitch	.316	553	175	37	4	20	85	19	0	.342	.506
Ahead in Count	.193	1434	277	45	6	18	112	0	486	.202	.271
Behind in Count	.338	915	309	62	11	38	154	159	0	.430	.554
Two Strikes	.179	1462	262	41	4	23	111	151	575	.259	.260

Pitcher vs. Batter (since 1984)

Pitches Best Vs.	Avg	AB	H	2B	3B	HR	RBI	BB	SO	OBP	SLG
Mark Grace	.042	24	1	1	0	0	2	4	1	.179	.083
Brian McRae	.056	18	1	0	0	0	1	1	6	.105	.056
Gary Gaetti	.083	12	1	0	0	0	0	0	2	.083	.083
Gerald Young	.083	12	1	0	0	0	1	1	3	.154	.083
Doug Dascenzo	.100	10	1	0	0	0	0	1	1	.182	.100

Pitches Worst Vs.	Avg	AB	H	2B	3B	HR	RBI	BB	SO	OBP	SLG
Danny Tartabull	.500	22	11	1	1	1	6	1	4	.522	.773
Lenny Dykstra	.500	10	5	2	0	0	1	2	1	.583	.700
Jeff King	.455	11	5	1	0	1	3	1	2	.500	.818
Juan Gonzalez	.429	14	6	1	0	2	5	2	3	.500	.929
Greg Vaughn	.350	20	7	1	0	3	5	4	1	.458	.850

Danny Darwin — Red Sox

Age 38 – Pitches Right (flyball pitcher)

	ERA	W	L	Sv	G	GS	IP	BB	SO	Avg	H	2B	3B	HR	RBI	OBP	SLG	CG	ShO	Sup	QS	#P/S	SB	CS	GB	FB	G/F
1993 Season	3.26	15	11	0	34	34	229.1	49	130	.230	196	45	3	31	83	.272	.399	2	1	4.55	23	91	11	5	234	339	0.69
Last Five Years	3.21	49	34	12	213	78	743.1	181	509	.235	654	133	13	76	278	.284	.375	7	1	4.13	51	96	57	24	701	1044	0.67

1993 Season

	ERA	W	L	Sv	G	GS	IP	H	HR	BB	SO
Home	3.38	8	3	0	15	15	101.1	93	13	18	61
Away	3.16	7	8	0	19	19	128.0	103	18	31	69
Day	3.09	7	2	0	11	11	70.0	59	5	23	45
Night	3.33	8	9	0	23	23	159.1	137	26	26	85
Grass	2.88	15	9	0	31	31	212.2	170	26	44	120
Turf	8.10	0	2	0	3	3	16.2	26	5	5	10
April	8.20	0	4	0	4	4	18.2	27	8	5	3
May	1.33	5	0	0	6	6	40.2	24	1	6	26
June	2.88	2	3	0	6	6	40.2	34	5	10	19
July	3.25	2	1	0	5	5	36.0	35	4	7	19
August	2.23	4	1	0	6	6	44.1	33	3	10	26
September/October	4.22	2	2	0	7	7	49.0	43	10	11	37
Starter	3.26	15	11	0	34	34	229.1	196	31	49	130
Reliever	0.00	0	0	0	0	0	0.0	0	0	0	0
0-3 Days Rest	2.35	1	0	0	2	2	15.1	8	2	3	10
4 Days Rest	3.50	9	7	0	21	21	139.0	124	22	30	86
5+ Days Rest	3.00	5	4	0	11	11	75.0	64	7	16	34
Pre-All Star	3.05	8	7	0	18	18	115.0	96	15	25	55
Post-All Star	3.46	7	4	0	16	16	114.1	100	16	24	75

	Avg	AB	H	2B	3B	HR	RBI	BB	SO	OBP	SLG
vs. Left	.251	475	119	28	3	19	52	32	52	.295	.442
vs. Right	.204	377	77	17	0	12	31	17	78	.242	.345
Inning 1-6	.225	723	163	36	2	27	72	39	117	.266	.393
Inning 7+	.256	129	33	9	1	4	11	10	13	.305	.434
None on	.233	563	131	33	2	21	21	24	78	.268	.410
Runners on	.225	289	65	12	1	10	62	25	52	.279	.377
Scoring Posn	.219	160	35	5	1	5	50	19	31	.287	.356
Close & Late	.256	78	20	6	0	3	9	5	10	.294	.449
None on/out	.278	241	67	20	1	9	9	8	29	.304	.481
vs. 1st Batr (relief)	.000	0	0	0	0	0	0	0	0	.000	.000
First Inning Pitched	.237	131	31	6	0	3	12	4	25	.265	.351
First 75 Pitches	.227	696	158	35	2	24	69	35	102	.265	.386
Pitch 76-90	.212	104	22	6	1	4	9	10	22	.276	.404
Pitch 91-105	.311	45	14	2	0	3	5	3	5	.347	.556
Pitch 106+	.286	7	2	2	0	0	0	1	1	.375	.571
First Pitch	.289	159	46	10	2	6	22	6	0	.312	.491
Ahead in Count	.204	407	83	19	0	12	34	0	113	.206	.339
Behind in Count	.218	147	32	10	0	6	16	28	0	.339	.408
Two Strikes	.173	352	61	13	0	13	27	15	130	.209	.321

Last Five Years

	ERA	W	L	Sv	G	GS	IP	H	HR	BB	SO
Home	3.26	29	13	6	109	38	372.2	346	30	86	276
Away	3.16	20	21	6	104	40	370.2	308	46	95	233
Day	3.15	18	11	3	67	27	245.2	211	20	68	182
Night	3.24	31	23	9	146	51	497.2	443	56	113	327
Grass	3.34	31	27	7	117	59	496.0	438	59	113	337
Turf	2.95	18	7	5	96	19	247.1	216	17	68	172
April	4.36	5	6	1	33	7	84.2	83	12	21	61
May	2.39	9	1	2	42	8	101.2	80	8	28	67
June	3.92	9	12	5	49	12	133.1	130	20	31	84
July	2.60	10	3	1	32	15	131.1	108	8	29	93
August	2.36	11	3	0	28	17	144.2	111	10	32	107
September/October	3.84	5	9	3	29	19	147.2	142	18	40	97
Starter	3.31	31	25	0	78	78	522.0	466	58	123	327
Reliever	2.97	18	9	12	135	0	221.1	188	18	58	182
0-3 Days Rest	3.10	1	0	0	3	3	20.1	15	2	6	13
4 Days Rest	3.22	22	18	0	53	53	365.2	320	45	83	240
5+ Days Rest	3.57	8	7	0	22	22	136.0	131	11	34	74
Pre-All Star	3.40	27	20	8	137	32	365.1	331	44	88	243
Post-All Star	3.02	22	14	4	76	46	378.0	323	32	93	266

	Avg	AB	H	2B	3B	HR	RBI	BB	SO	OBP	SLG
vs. Left	.258	1493	385	85	10	33	145	110	237	.309	.395
vs. Right	.209	1286	269	48	3	43	133	71	272	.256	.351
Inning 1-6	.231	1809	417	90	9	53	185	107	324	.275	.378
Inning 7+	.244	970	237	43	4	23	93	74	185	.300	.368
None on	.236	1693	400	86	6	50	50	90	300	.280	.383
Runners on	.234	1086	254	47	7	26	228	91	209	.290	.362
Scoring Posn	.223	636	142	26	5	14	195	70	129	.294	.346
Close & Late	.225	511	115	22	1	11	47	42	99	.285	.337
None on/out	.257	728	187	45	2	21	21	31	124	.290	.411
vs. 1st Batr (relief)	.200	120	24	5	1	2	21	9	34	.258	.308
First Inning Pitched	.232	745	173	32	5	15	95	40	150	.275	.349
First 75 Pitches	.232	2311	536	103	11	59	229	144	428	.279	.363
Pitch 76-90	.249	237	59	14	2	7	25	22	43	.313	.414
Pitch 91-105	.234	158	37	6	0	9	18	10	26	.278	.443
Pitch 106+	.301	73	22	10	0	1	6	5	12	.354	.479
First Pitch	.287	457	131	22	3	17	67	23	0	.324	.460
Ahead in Count	.197	1424	280	53	4	29	118	0	450	.200	.301
Behind in Count	.270	426	115	25	3	15	55	88	0	.394	.448
Two Strikes	.175	1310	229	51	3	25	98	68	509	.219	.276

Pitcher vs. Batter (since 1984)

Pitches Best Vs.	Avg	AB	H	2B	3B	HR	RBI	BB	SO	OBP	SLG
Jeff Blauser	.000	14	0	0	0	0	0	3	5	.176	.000
Frank Thomas	.000	12	0	0	0	0	0	2	1	.143	.000
Jose Lind	.000	11	0	0	0	0	0	0	3	.000	.000
Curt Wilkerson	.000	10	0	0	0	0	1	1	1	.083	.000
Harold Reynolds	.053	19	1	1	0	0	1	0	1	.053	.105

Pitches Worst Vs.	Avg	AB	H	2B	3B	HR	RBI	BB	SO	OBP	SLG
George Brett	.526	19	10	3	0	2	4	6	3	.615	1.000
Andre Dawson	.500	14	7	1	0	2	4	3	3	.556	1.000
Chad Kreuter	.462	13	6	2	0	2	4	1	3	.500	1.077
Ken Griffey Jr	.462	13	6	0	1	2	5	0	1	.462	1.077
Howard Johnson	.409	22	9	1	0	3	8	3	4	.462	.864

Doug Dascenzo — Rangers

Age 30 – Bats Both (groundball hitter)

	Avg	G	AB	R	H	2B	3B	HR	RBI	BB	SO	HBP	GDP	SB	CS	OBP	SLG	IBB	SH	SF	#Pit	#P/PA	GB	FB	G/F
1993 Season	.199	76	146	20	29	5	1	2	10	8	22	0	1	2	0	.239	.288	0	3	1	605	3.83	57	40	1.43
Last Five Years	.237	493	1141	144	270	39	10	5	86	93	111	3	12	43	24	.294	.301	6	21	9	4245	3.35	499	282	1.77

1993 Season

	Avg	AB	H	2B	3B	HR	RBI	BB	SO	OBP	SLG
vs. Left	.237	59	14	3	0	0	5	0	7	.233	.288
vs. Right	.172	87	15	2	1	2	5	8	15	.242	.287
Home	.215	65	14	4	1	0	3	4	9	.261	.308
Away	.185	81	15	1	0	2	7	4	13	.221	.272
First Pitch	.158	19	3	0	0	0	1	0	0	.158	.158
Ahead in Count	.111	27	3	0	0	1	1	2	0	.172	.222
Behind in Count	.186	59	11	1	0	0	4	0	20	.183	.203
Two Strikes	.215	65	14	2	1	1	4	6	22	.282	.323

	Avg	AB	H	2B	3B	HR	RBI	BB	SO	OBP	SLG
Scoring Posn	.226	31	7	1	0	0	7	3	5	.286	.258
Close & Late	.250	28	7	1	0	0	0	3	3	.323	.286
None on/out	.228	57	13	4	0	0	0	4	10	.279	.298
Batting #1	.173	75	13	3	0	1	5	6	11	.232	.253
Batting #8	.346	26	9	1	1	0	2	2	5	.393	.462
Other	.156	45	7	1	0	1	3	0	6	.156	.244
Pre-All Star	.177	113	20	4	1	2	8	6	19	.217	.283
Post-All Star	.273	33	9	1	0	0	2	2	3	.314	.303

Last Five Years

	Avg	AB	H	2B	3B	HR	RBI	BB	SO	OBP	SLG
vs. Left	.256	512	131	23	1	1	47	26	36	.290	.311
vs. Right	.221	629	139	16	9	4	39	67	75	.296	.294
Groundball	.276	406	112	16	3	1	31	31	33	.328	.337
Flyball	.162	271	44	10	1	0	19	22	26	.223	.207
Home	.239	585	140	22	8	1	40	48	57	.298	.309
Away	.234	556	130	17	2	4	46	45	54	.289	.293
Day	.227	559	127	18	4	2	42	42	61	.282	.284
Night	.246	582	143	21	6	3	44	51	50	.305	.318
Grass	.246	829	204	28	9	3	62	63	86	.300	.312
Turf	.212	312	66	11	1	2	24	30	25	.277	.272
First Pitch	.278	248	69	8	0	1	17	3	0	.286	.323
Ahead in Count	.245	237	58	6	3	2	22	53	0	.380	.321
Behind in Count	.196	460	90	14	5	0	28	0	102	.196	.248
Two Strikes	.207	434	90	14	6	2	31	35	111	.268	.281

	Avg	AB	H	2B	3B	HR	RBI	BB	SO	OBP	SLG
Scoring Posn	.233	253	59	4	0	0	74	23	21	.290	.249
Close & Late	.274	215	59	9	2	0	22	23	19	.343	.335
None on/out	.238	399	95	22	3	1	1	31	44	.295	.316
Batting #1	.244	657	160	24	4	3	48	50	56	.296	.306
Batting #8	.267	135	36	5	2	0	8	15	16	.336	.333
Other	.212	349	74	10	4	2	30	28	39	.273	.281
April	.241	112	27	4	0	2	12	10	8	.303	.330
May	.191	204	39	4	1	1	18	10	23	.228	.235
June	.230	248	57	11	3	1	14	20	27	.289	.310
July	.227	185	42	7	1	0	12	17	18	.291	.276
August	.273	172	47	10	3	0	11	12	12	.319	.366
September/October	.264	220	58	3	2	1	19	24	23	.336	.309
Pre-All Star	.222	645	143	23	5	4	49	51	68	.279	.291
Post-All Star	.256	496	127	16	5	1	37	42	43	.313	.315

Batter vs. Pitcher (career)

Hits Best Against	Avg	AB	H	2B	3B	HR	RBI	BB	SO	OBP	SLG
Frank Viola	.471	17	8	0	0	0	5	0	3	.444	.471
Dennis Rasmussen	.412	17	7	3	0	0	2	0	2	.412	.588
Dennis Martinez	.389	18	7	0	0	0	0	2	1	.450	.389
Ken Hill	.333	12	4	1	0	0	0	2	3	.429	.417
Rob Dibble	.333	9	3	0	1	0	3	2	2	.455	.556

Hits Worst Against	Avg	AB	H	2B	3B	HR	RBI	BB	SO	OBP	SLG
Jose Rijo	.000	13	0	0	0	0	0	1	3	.071	.000
Bob Walk	.083	12	1	1	0	0	0	0	0	.083	.167
Jose Melendez	.091	11	1	0	0	0	0	1	3	.167	.091
Jim Deshaies	.100	20	2	0	0	0	0	1	2	.143	.100
Derek Lilliquist	.100	10	1	0	0	0	1	0	0	.091	.100

Jack Daugherty — Reds

Age 33 – Bats Both

	Avg	G	AB	R	H	2B	3B	HR	RBI	BB	SO	HBP	GDP	SB	CS	OBP	SLG	IBB	SH	SF	#Pit	#P/PA	GB	FB	G/F
1993 Season	.226	50	62	7	14	2	0	2	9	11	15	0	0	0	0	.338	.355	0	0	1	294	3.97	13	23	0.57
Last Five Years	.258	344	749	79	193	38	6	10	86	76	129	4	10	5	2	.325	.364	2	6	12	3071	3.62	276	206	1.34

1993 Season

	Avg	AB	H	2B	3B	HR	RBI	BB	SO	OBP	SLG
vs. Left	.600	5	3	0	0	0	1	0	1	.600	.600
vs. Right	.193	57	11	2	0	2	8	11	14	.319	.333

	Avg	AB	H	2B	3B	HR	RBI	BB	SO	OBP	SLG
Scoring Posn	.250	16	4	0	0	1	7	4	5	.381	.438
Close & Late	.100	20	2	1	0	0	1	3	6	.208	.150

Last Five Years

	Avg	AB	H	2B	3B	HR	RBI	BB	SO	OBP	SLG
vs. Left	.261	165	43	6	2	1	17	15	38	.324	.339
vs. Right	.257	584	150	32	4	9	69	61	91	.325	.372
Groundball	.285	221	63	9	3	3	27	22	29	.350	.394
Flyball	.246	171	42	7	1	2	17	18	41	.316	.333
Home	.276	387	107	18	4	8	45	40	60	.346	.406
Away	.238	362	86	20	2	2	41	36	69	.302	.320
Day	.276	181	50	11	2	3	20	27	32	.364	.409
Night	.252	568	143	27	4	7	66	49	97	.311	.350
Grass	.255	584	149	29	4	7	61	62	98	.327	.354
Turf	.267	165	44	9	2	3	25	14	31	.315	.400
First Pitch	.300	130	39	8	1	2	12	1	0	.301	.423
Ahead in Count	.343	178	61	16	2	2	31	41	0	.462	.489
Behind in Count	.183	312	57	8	3	1	22	0	111	.188	.237
Two Strikes	.203	315	64	10	2	2	24	34	129	.283	.267

	Avg	AB	H	2B	3B	HR	RBI	BB	SO	OBP	SLG
Scoring Posn	.217	184	40	8	0	1	65	23	40	.294	.277
Close & Late	.217	166	36	9	0	2	15	20	40	.297	.307
None on/out	.264	182	48	7	0	2	2	24	34	.350	.335
Batting #1	.192	120	23	4	2	1	9	7	22	.229	.283
Batting #2	.294	194	57	12	2	2	21	16	23	.346	.407
Other	.260	435	113	22	2	7	56	53	84	.341	.368
April	.149	74	11	2	0	0	5	9	13	.238	.176
May	.239	159	38	9	0	0	16	14	17	.296	.296
June	.310	58	18	6	1	0	9	2	13	.339	.448
July	.326	132	43	11	0	4	20	13	23	.384	.500
August	.255	102	26	5	1	1	7	8	20	.313	.353
September/October	.254	224	57	5	4	5	29	30	43	.341	.379
Pre-All Star	.257	334	86	22	1	2	35	26	46	.308	.347
Post-All Star	.258	415	107	16	5	8	51	50	83	.338	.378

Batter vs. Pitcher (career)

Hits Best Against	Avg	AB	H	2B	3B	HR	RBI	BB	SO	OBP	SLG
Jack Morris	.462	13	6	2	0	0	3	2	1	.533	.615
Randy Johnson	.333	12	4	0	0	0	0	1	5	.385	.333

Hits Worst Against	Avg	AB	H	2B	3B	HR	RBI	BB	SO	OBP	SLG
Mike Moore	.200	10	2	1	0	1	1	1	1	.273	.600
Erik Hanson	.200	10	2	0	1	0	1	1	2	.273	.400
Mike Boddicker	.231	13	3	0	0	0	0	1	3	.286	.231

Darren Daulton — Phillies

Age 32 – Bats Left (flyball hitter)

	Avg	G	AB	R	H	2B	3B	HR	RBI	BB	SO	HBP	GDP	SB	CS	OBP	SLG	IBB	SH	SF	#Pit	#P/PA	GB	FB	G/F
1993 Season	.257	147	510	90	131	35	4	24	105	117	111	2	2	5	0	.392	.482	12	0	8	2556	4.01	148	173	0.86
Last Five Years	.244	655	2107	297	515	121	12	83	357	370	410	14	19	30	4	.357	.431	44	6	24	9738	3.86	653	718	0.91

1993 Season

	Avg	AB	H	2B	3B	HR	RBI	BB	SO	OBP	SLG
vs. Left	.213	188	40	10	1	8	29	38	45	.346	.404
vs. Right	.283	322	91	25	3	16	76	79	66	.418	.528
Groundball	.279	179	50	13	3	10	50	43	33	.412	.553
Flyball	.178	90	16	6	0	3	6	16	23	.308	.344
Home	.260	262	68	16	3	10	55	48	56	.375	.458
Away	.254	248	63	19	1	14	50	69	55	.409	.508
Day	.261	119	31	10	1	6	28	29	31	.403	.513
Night	.256	391	100	25	3	18	77	88	80	.389	.473
Grass	.259	158	41	14	1	11	37	48	31	.424	.570
Turf	.256	352	90	21	3	13	68	69	80	.377	.443
First Pitch	.364	44	16	5	0	3	13	9	0	.446	.682
Ahead in Count	.328	131	43	10	2	10	39	60	0	.536	.664
Behind in Count	.211	223	47	12	1	6	32	0	88	.211	.354
Two Strikes	.170	241	41	13	2	3	31	48	111	.307	.278

	Avg	AB	H	2B	3B	HR	RBI	BB	SO	OBP	SLG
Scoring Posn	.239	159	38	9	2	7	79	56	33	.424	.453
Close & Late	.284	81	23	6	0	4	14	29	22	.473	.506
None on/out	.265	117	31	9	0	7	7	18	24	.368	.521
Batting #4	.275	51	14	4	0	0	7	9	14	.393	.353
Batting #5	.254	456	116	31	4	24	96	107	95	.392	.498
Other	.333	3	1	0	0	0	2	1	2	.500	.333
April	.234	64	15	3	0	5	15	23	16	.438	.516
May	.260	96	25	6	1	9	30	22	20	.395	.625
June	.256	90	23	7	1	1	16	13	24	.349	.389
July	.259	81	21	7	1	3	17	23	15	.415	.481
August	.253	79	20	5	1	4	14	18	16	.388	.494
September/October	.270	100	27	7	0	2	13	18	20	.378	.400
Pre-All Star	.244	287	70	19	2	15	65	66	66	.383	.481
Post-All Star	.274	223	61	16	2	9	40	51	45	.404	.484

1993 By Position

Position	Avg	AB	H	2B	3B	HR	RBI	BB	SO	OBP	SLG	G	GS	Innings	PO	A	E	DP	Fld Pct	Rng Fctr	In Zone	Outs	Zone Rtg	MLB Zone
As c	.256	508	130	35	4	24	103	115	110	.390	.482	147	144	1287.0	986	67	9	18	.992	---	---	---	---	---

Last Five Years

	Avg	AB	H	2B	3B	HR	RBI	BB	SO	OBP	SLG
vs. Left	.227	657	149	38	2	23	96	110	153	.342	.396
vs. Right	.252	1450	366	83	10	60	261	260	257	.364	.448
Groundball	.286	772	221	48	8	34	150	132	133	.388	.501
Flyball	.184	429	79	22	0	14	58	63	89	.292	.333
Home	.247	1039	257	64	8	42	185	183	204	.360	.446
Away	.242	1068	258	57	4	41	172	187	206	.355	.418
Day	.233	520	121	26	1	20	80	82	112	.336	.402
Night	.248	1587	394	95	11	63	277	288	298	.364	.441
Grass	.242	607	147	33	2	25	102	110	119	.359	.427
Turf	.245	1500	368	88	10	58	255	260	291	.357	.433
First Pitch	.315	238	75	23	2	10	50	27	0	.383	.555
Ahead in Count	.311	517	161	32	4	31	119	175	0	.484	.569
Behind in Count	.197	893	176	41	3	22	112	0	320	.200	.324
Two Strikes	.167	970	162	38	5	18	105	157	410	.285	.272

	Avg	AB	H	2B	3B	HR	RBI	BB	SO	OBP	SLG
Scoring Posn	.268	563	151	36	3	22	257	146	101	.408	.460
Close & Late	.234	389	91	19	0	11	58	61	99	.340	.368
None on/out	.218	491	107	29	0	19	19	63	93	.314	.393
Batting #5	.244	708	173	43	7	41	156	155	147	.377	.499
Batting #7	.228	381	87	19	2	14	57	50	79	.322	.399
Other	.250	1018	255	59	3	28	144	165	184	.356	.397
April	.234	291	68	16	2	11	56	58	69	.362	.416
May	.243	300	73	19	2	13	55	61	61	.371	.450
June	.231	333	77	18	1	13	56	58	62	.341	.408
July	.240	400	96	21	3	18	71	72	73	.355	.443
August	.242	418	101	22	2	20	61	63	79	.345	.447
September/October	.274	365	100	25	2	8	58	58	66	.375	.419
Pre-All Star	.227	1068	242	58	5	40	181	201	217	.347	.403
Post-All Star	.263	1039	273	63	7	43	176	169	193	.368	.461

Batter vs. Pitcher (since 1984)

Hits Best Against	Avg	AB	H	2B	3B	HR	RBI	BB	SO	OBP	SLG
Bill Swift	.500	14	7	3	0	2	5	1	2	.533	1.143
Jack Armstrong	.444	18	8	2	1	4	9	1	2	.474	1.333
Butch Henry	.444	9	4	2	0	1	4	2	0	.545	1.000
Donovan Osborne	.444	9	4	1	0	1	4	3	2	.583	.889
Mike Stanton	.400	10	4	2	0	1	1	2	3	.500	.900

Hits Worst Against	Avg	AB	H	2B	3B	HR	RBI	BB	SO	OBP	SLG
Bobby Ojeda	.000	11	0	0	0	0	0	0	5	.000	.000
Bill Landrum	.000	11	0	0	0	0	1	0	3	.000	.000
Bob Patterson	.077	13	1	0	0	0	0	1	2	.143	.077
Chuck McElroy	.091	11	1	0	0	0	1	0	5	.083	.091
Rheal Cormier	.091	11	1	0	0	0	0	0	4	.091	.091

Butch Davis — Rangers

Age 36 – Bats Right

	Avg	G	AB	R	H	2B	3B	HR	RBI	BB	SO	HBP	GDP	SB	CS	OBP	SLG	IBB	SH	SF	#Pit	#P/PA	GB	FB	G/F
1993 Season	.245	62	159	24	39	10	4	3	20	5	28	1	0	3	1	.273	.415	1	5	0	561	3.30	60	44	1.36
Last Five Years	.241	68	166	25	40	11	4	3	20	5	31	1	0	3	1	.267	.410	1	5	0	583	3.29	62	45	1.38

1993 Season

	Avg	AB	H	2B	3B	HR	RBI	BB	SO	OBP	SLG
vs. Left	.255	55	14	2	2	2	8	3	11	.305	.473
vs. Right	.240	104	25	8	2	1	12	2	17	.255	.385
Home	.265	68	18	4	3	0	10	3	11	.296	.412
Away	.231	91	21	6	1	3	10	2	17	.255	.418
First Pitch	.400	30	12	3	1	1	7	1	0	.419	.667
Ahead in Count	.241	29	7	1	0	2	4	2	0	.290	.483
Behind in Count	.200	75	15	4	2	0	5	0	22	.211	.307
Two Strikes	.176	68	12	3	3	0	6	2	28	.211	.309

	Avg	AB	H	2B	3B	HR	RBI	BB	SO	OBP	SLG
Scoring Posn	.317	41	13	3	2	1	16	3	2	.364	.561
Close & Late	.182	22	4	1	0	0	1	3	4	.280	.227
None on/out	.175	40	7	3	0	1	1	1	7	.195	.325
Batting #2	.156	45	7	2	2	1	5	0	6	.156	.356
Batting #8	.300	40	12	4	1	1	8	2	8	.333	.525
Other	.270	74	20	4	1	1	7	3	14	.308	.392
Pre-All Star	.237	97	23	5	4	2	12	4	18	.275	.433
Post-All Star	.258	62	16	5	0	1	8	1	10	.270	.387

Chili Davis — Angels

Age 34 – Bats Both

	Avg	G	AB	R	H	2B	3B	HR	RBI	BB	SO	HBP	GDP	SB	CS	OBP	SLG	IBB	SH	SF	#Pit	#P/PA	GB	FB	G/F
1993 Season	.243	152	573	74	139	32	0	27	112	71	135	1	18	4	1	.327	.440	12	0	0	2432	3.77	191	159	1.20
Last Five Years	.268	710	2523	360	676	134	5	102	419	361	526	5	73	17	14	.358	.446	52	3	22	10825	3.71	920	688	1.34

1993 Season

	Avg	AB	H	2B	3B	HR	RBI	BB	SO	OBP	SLG
vs. Left	.260	131	34	7	0	8	31	13	32	.326	.496
vs. Right	.238	442	105	25	0	19	81	58	103	.327	.423
Groundball	.245	102	25	5	0	3	18	9	22	.306	.382
Flyball	.234	137	32	8	0	8	26	13	35	.305	.467

	Avg	AB	H	2B	3B	HR	RBI	BB	SO	OBP	SLG
Scoring Posn	.325	163	53	16	0	9	81	28	31	.427	.589
Close & Late	.278	90	25	4	0	3	11	19	20	.409	.422
None on/out	.135	141	19	4	0	0	0	16	40	.223	.163
Batting #4	.242	553	134	30	0	26	106	68	130	.326	.438

1993 Season

	Avg	AB	H	2B	3B	HR	RBI	BB	SO	OBP	SLG		Avg	AB	H	2B	3B	HR	RBI	BB	SO	OBP	SLG
Home	.269	283	76	17	0	13	59	36	62	.353	.466	Batting #5	.263	19	5	2	0	1	6	2	5	.333	.526
Away	.217	290	63	15	0	14	53	35	73	.302	.414	Other	.000	1	0	0	0	0	0	1	0	.500	.000
Day	.280	175	49	11	0	13	44	23	43	.364	.566	April	.232	56	13	4	0	1	12	3	14	.283	.357
Night	.226	398	90	21	0	14	68	48	92	.311	.384	May	.216	97	21	5	0	3	17	20	27	.350	.361
Grass	.250	476	119	26	0	22	94	59	115	.334	.443	June	.241	108	26	8	0	6	27	5	18	.274	.481
Turf	.206	97	20	6	0	5	18	12	20	.294	.423	July	.255	102	26	5	0	4	19	19	19	.372	.422
First Pitch	.338	77	26	4	0	4	20	10	0	.414	.545	August	.229	109	25	5	0	5	16	13	33	.311	.413
Ahead in Count	.325	120	39	12	0	7	33	31	0	.464	.600	September/October	.277	101	28	5	0	8	21	11	24	.348	.564
Behind in Count	.144	263	38	10	0	7	30	0	112	.148	.262	Pre-All Star	.238	298	71	18	0	12	64	41	65	.332	.419
Two Strikes	.153	287	44	7	0	9	32	30	135	.236	.272	Post-All Star	.247	275	68	14	0	15	48	30	70	.321	.462

1993 By Position

Position	Avg	AB	H	2B	3B	HR	RBI	BB	SO	OBP	SLG	G	GS	Innings	PO	A	E	DP	Fld Pct	Rng Fctr	In Zone	Outs	Zone Rtg	MLB Zone
As Designated Hitter	.243	572	139	32	0	27	112	70	135	.327	.441	150	150	---	---	---	---	---	---	---	---	---	---	---

Last Five Years

	Avg	AB	H	2B	3B	HR	RBI	BB	SO	OBP	SLG		Avg	AB	H	2B	3B	HR	RBI	BB	SO	OBP	SLG
vs. Left	.257	752	193	34	1	35	133	86	166	.329	.444	Scoring Posn	.289	703	203	48	0	31	313	144	154	.401	.489
vs. Right	.273	1771	483	100	4	67	286	275	360	.370	.447	Close & Late	.275	382	105	21	0	10	53	72	90	.387	.408
Groundball	.286	604	173	31	3	18	105	71	112	.359	.437	None on/out	.250	593	148	32	2	22	22	66	119	.325	.422
Flyball	.263	593	156	27	2	31	96	78	143	.347	.472	Batting #4	.251	1161	291	58	1	51	203	165	243	.343	.434
Home	.279	1285	358	72	5	49	220	195	249	.372	.457	Batting #5	.302	728	220	50	3	27	109	116	152	.398	.490
Away	.257	1238	318	62	0	53	199	166	277	.343	.435	Other	.260	634	165	26	1	24	107	80	131	.339	.418
Day	.263	677	178	34	1	26	120	101	146	.356	.431	April	.254	339	86	15	1	10	48	48	75	.348	.392
Night	.270	1846	498	100	4	76	299	260	380	.359	.452	May	.278	468	130	29	2	15	78	64	87	.360	.444
Grass	.261	1643	429	77	2	63	274	222	354	.348	.425	June	.260	465	121	23	0	28	92	59	85	.342	.490
Turf	.281	880	247	57	3	39	145	139	172	.376	.485	July	.253	400	101	19	0	16	66	61	75	.348	.420
First Pitch	.345	411	142	32	2	20	79	40	0	.401	.579	August	.271	458	124	28	0	15	69	67	114	.364	.430
Ahead in Count	.335	556	186	39	0	26	110	151	0	.473	.545	September/October	.290	393	114	20	2	18	66	62	90	.386	.489
Behind in Count	.193	1049	202	34	3	31	133	0	413	.195	.319	Pre-All Star	.260	1418	368	70	3	57	233	198	269	.348	.434
Two Strikes	.183	1153	211	32	2	36	144	167	526	.286	.308	Post-All Star	.279	1105	308	64	2	45	186	163	257	.370	.462

Batter vs. Pitcher (since 1984)

Hits Best Against	Avg	AB	H	2B	3B	HR	RBI	BB	SO	OBP	SLG	Hits Worst Against	Avg	AB	H	2B	3B	HR	RBI	BB	SO	OBP	SLG
Mark Knudson	.538	13	7	2	0	1	5	2	2	.600	.923	Jesse Orosco	.000	14	0	0	0	0	0	4	7	.222	.000
Chuck Cary	.444	9	4	0	0	2	2	2	3	.545	1.111	Al Leiter	.000	12	0	0	0	0	0	0	6	.000	.000
Pat Hentgen	.385	13	5	1	0	3	5	3	3	.500	1.154	Steve Farr	.083	12	1	0	0	0	1	2	4	.200	.083
Alex Fernandez	.375	8	3	2	0	1	3	3	3	.545	1.000	Jamie Moyer	.133	15	2	0	0	0	0	0	5	.133	.133
Luis Aquino	.364	11	4	1	0	2	5	3	3	.467	1.000	Jose Bautista	.143	14	2	0	0	0	0	0	2	.143	.143

Eric Davis — Tigers

Age 32 – Bats Right

	Avg	G	AB	R	H	2B	3B	HR	RBI	BB	SO	HBP	GDP	SB	CS	OBP	SLG	IBB	SH	SF	#Pit	#P/PA	GB	FB	G/F
1993 Season	.237	131	451	71	107	18	1	20	68	55	106	1	12	35	7	.319	.415	7	0	4	1971	3.86	142	139	1.02
Last Five Years	.252	554	1918	289	483	76	6	94	320	267	485	12	46	110	20	.343	.445	32	0	22	8450	3.81	658	528	1.25

1993 Season

	Avg	AB	H	2B	3B	HR	RBI	BB	SO	OBP	SLG		Avg	AB	H	2B	3B	HR	RBI	BB	SO	OBP	SLG
vs. Left	.219	137	30	6	0	4	19	22	26	.323	.350	Scoring Posn	.228	114	26	5	1	4	47	23	29	.352	.395
vs. Right	.245	314	77	12	1	16	49	33	80	.317	.443	Close & Late	.209	91	19	2	0	4	11	11	24	.294	.363
Groundball	.227	128	29	4	0	4	13	13	29	.294	.352	None on/out	.229	96	22	7	0	6	6	5	22	.267	.490
Flyball	.315	73	23	3	0	4	17	10	13	.393	.521	Batting #3	.173	191	33	6	0	7	24	26	47	.269	.314
Home	.250	232	58	6	0	10	39	34	46	.342	.405	Batting #6	.281	153	43	7	1	9	25	16	42	.347	.516
Away	.224	219	49	12	1	10	29	21	60	.293	.425	Other	.290	107	31	5	0	4	19	13	17	.369	.449
Day	.212	132	28	7	1	6	18	13	35	.281	.417	April	.253	87	22	1	0	1	10	8	19	.320	.299
Night	.248	319	79	11	0	14	50	42	71	.334	.414	May	.172	64	11	3	0	3	11	10	17	.280	.359
Grass	.235	370	87	14	1	16	58	52	87	.326	.408	June	.228	57	13	3	0	3	12	10	14	.338	.439
Turf	.247	81	20	4	0	4	10	3	19	.282	.444	July	.276	98	27	6	0	3	10	8	22	.327	.429
First Pitch	.295	44	13	5	0	0	6	6	0	.385	.409	August	.214	70	15	4	0	4	10	5	16	.267	.443
Ahead in Count	.304	102	31	4	0	9	25	24	0	.433	.608	September/October	.253	75	19	1	1	6	15	14	18	.371	.533
Behind in Count	.211	199	42	6	1	4	23	0	83	.209	.312	Pre-All Star	.249	249	62	10	0	9	38	30	61	.329	.398
Two Strikes	.193	218	42	5	0	9	27	25	106	.273	.339	Post-All Star	.223	202	45	8	1	11	30	25	45	.307	.436

1993 By Position

Position	Avg	AB	H	2B	3B	HR	RBI	BB	SO	OBP	SLG	G	GS	Innings	PO	A	E	DP	Fld Pct	Rng Fctr	In Zone	Outs	Zone Rtg	MLB Zone
As lf	.234	364	85	16	0	13	46	40	86	.308	.385	101	92	849.1	216	7	2	2	.991	2.36	244	211	.865	.818
As cf	.264	72	19	1	1	7	20	10	18	.354	.597	21	20	171.1	57	0	1	0	.983	2.99	60	56	.933	.829

Last Five Years

	Avg	AB	H	2B	3B	HR	RBI	BB	SO	OBP	SLG		Avg	AB	H	2B	3B	HR	RBI	BB	SO	OBP	SLG
vs. Left	.246	637	157	30	1	29	103	114	146	.360	.433	Scoring Posn	.260	504	131	26	2	24	221	115	122	.390	.462
vs. Right	.254	1281	326	46	5	65	217	153	339	.335	.450	Close & Late	.236	330	78	11	0	17	61	47	80	.332	.424
Groundball	.253	652	165	24	3	23	102	87	165	.342	.405	None on/out	.258	434	112	16	1	28	28	34	106	.313	.493
Flyball	.271	398	108	19	1	24	62	58	99	.366	.505	Batting #3	.234	606	142	18	1	31	90	89	160	.333	.421
Home	.252	902	227	31	2	44	157	145	215	.353	.437	Batting #4	.256	909	233	41	3	43	159	125	214	.345	.450
Away	.252	1016	256	45	4	50	163	122	270	.335	.452	Other	.268	403	108	17	2	20	71	53	111	.355	.469
Day	.239	577	138	23	4	25	78	60	162	.313	.423	April	.256	317	81	12	1	12	48	43	79	.342	.413
Night	.257	1341	345	53	2	69	242	207	323	.356	.454	May	.215	260	56	12	0	12	43	41	73	.325	.400

Last Five Years

	Avg	AB	H	2B	3B	HR	RBI	BB	SO	OBP	SLG		Avg	AB	H	2B	3B	HR	RBI	BB	SO	OBP	SLG
Grass	.253	985	249	39	3	45	160	131	247	.342	.436	June	.275	306	84	10	2	20	65	49	72	.375	.516
Turf	.251	933	234	37	3	49	160	136	238	.344	.454	July	.236	428	101	15	1	14	53	57	107	.327	.374
First Pitch	.350	240	84	16	1	17	56	21	0	.402	.638	August	.253	300	76	14	1	16	48	31	78	.323	.467
Ahead in Count	.330	458	151	24	1	33	104	128	0	.471	.603	September/October	.277	307	85	13	1	20	63	46	76	.370	.521
Behind in Count	.182	813	148	17	2	21	85	0	378	.187	.285	Pre-All Star	.246	1032	254	38	3	49	172	147	262	.341	.431
Two Strikes	.163	907	148	19	1	30	101	110	485	.256	.286	Post-All Star	.258	886	229	38	3	45	148	120	223	.347	.460

Batter vs. Pitcher (career)

Hits Best Against	Avg	AB	H	2B	3B	HR	RBI	BB	SO	OBP	SLG	Hits Worst Against	Avg	AB	H	2B	3B	HR	RBI	BB	SO	OBP	SLG
John Smoltz	.500	26	13	2	0	4	6	5	3	.581	1.038	Todd Worrell	.000	12	0	0	0	0	0	3	2	.200	.000
Les Lancaster	.500	8	4	0	0	2	6	2	3	.500	1.250	Ken Hill	.000	9	0	0	0	0	2	3	5	.231	.000
Frank DiPino	.455	11	5	2	0	1	5	5	2	.625	.909	Cris Carpenter	.083	12	1	0	0	0	0	0	2	.083	.083
Mark Grant	.450	20	9	1	0	4	9	5	4	.560	1.100	Chris Nabholz	.091	11	1	1	0	0	2	0	3	.091	.182
Butch Henry	.429	7	3	2	0	1	4	4	1	.583	1.143	Bryan Hickerson	.100	10	1	0	0	0	1	1	6	.182	.100

Glenn Davis — Orioles

Age 33 – Bats Right (flyball hitter)

	Avg	G	AB	R	H	2B	3B	HR	RBI	BB	SO	HBP	GDP	SB	CS	OBP	SLG	IBB	SH	SF	#Pit	#P/PA	GB	FB	G/F
1993 Season	.177	30	113	8	20	3	0	1	9	7	29	1	2	0	1	.230	.230	0	1	1	476	3.87	32	42	0.76
Last Five Years	.256	436	1595	214	408	68	8	80	238	175	300	23	30	17	6	.336	.459	36	2	13	6504	3.60	522	550	0.95

1993 Season

	Avg	AB	H	2B	3B	HR	RBI	BB	SO	OBP	SLG		Avg	AB	H	2B	3B	HR	RBI	BB	SO	OBP	SLG
vs. Left	.222	36	8	0	0	0	1	3	10	.282	.222	Scoring Posn	.172	29	5	1	0	0	8	1	9	.194	.207
vs. Right	.156	77	12	3	0	1	8	4	19	.205	.234	Close & Late	.050	20	1	0	0	0	1	0	6	.050	.050

Last Five Years

	Avg	AB	H	2B	3B	HR	RBI	BB	SO	OBP	SLG		Avg	AB	H	2B	3B	HR	RBI	BB	SO	OBP	SLG
vs. Left	.261	459	120	18	1	34	79	57	68	.349	.527	Scoring Posn	.249	406	101	24	3	13	144	83	88	.370	.419
vs. Right	.254	1136	288	50	7	46	159	118	232	.330	.431	Close & Late	.224	277	62	9	1	12	36	32	62	.304	.394
Groundball	.262	507	133	14	4	21	66	58	77	.342	.430	None on/out	.247	453	112	16	1	23	23	31	84	.305	.439
Flyball	.284	348	99	19	3	24	73	49	70	.374	.563	Batting #4	.249	1432	357	62	6	74	214	165	268	.334	.456
Home	.271	786	213	39	5	28	89	79	156	.344	.440	Batting #5	.309	123	38	5	1	4	13	9	23	.356	.463
Away	.241	809	195	29	3	52	149	96	144	.327	.477	Other	.325	40	13	1	1	2	11	1	9	.341	.550
Day	.224	450	101	17	5	16	55	56	110	.319	.391	April	.281	281	79	15	0	18	46	29	66	.362	.527
Night	.268	1145	307	51	3	64	183	119	190	.342	.486	May	.214	295	63	10	1	12	46	21	61	.269	.376
Grass	.250	840	210	29	5	42	122	75	163	.317	.446	June	.230	226	52	6	2	15	33	27	50	.314	.473
Turf	.262	755	198	39	3	38	116	100	137	.355	.473	July	.327	162	53	9	0	9	29	24	22	.414	.549
First Pitch	.325	212	69	10	1	18	44	11	0	.361	.637	August	.246	236	58	11	1	12	33	30	42	.331	.453
Ahead in Count	.306	314	96	15	1	27	66	84	0	.451	.618	September/October	.261	395	103	17	4	14	51	44	59	.347	.430
Behind in Count	.220	751	165	22	6	22	83	0	246	.232	.353	Pre-All Star	.241	851	205	32	3	46	129	83	184	.316	.448
Two Strikes	.180	738	133	18	6	15	66	61	300	.249	.282	Post-All Star	.273	744	203	36	5	34	109	92	116	.358	.472

Batter vs. Pitcher (career)

Hits Best Against	Avg	AB	H	2B	3B	HR	RBI	BB	SO	OBP	SLG	Hits Worst Against	Avg	AB	H	2B	3B	HR	RBI	BB	SO	OBP	SLG
Dennis Martinez	.481	27	13	0	0	6	12	3	2	.516	1.148	Mike Bielecki	.000	16	0	0	0	0	1	2	3	.111	.000
Jeff Parrett	.455	11	5	2	0	2	4	4	3	.600	1.182	Kevin Appier	.077	13	1	0	0	0	0	0	4	.077	.077
Neal Heaton	.409	22	9	4	0	2	5	2	2	.440	.864	Jose Rijo	.083	24	2	1	0	0	1	0	4	.083	.125
Danny Jackson	.400	15	6	0	0	2	4	5	1	.550	.800	Jose DeLeon	.091	11	1	0	0	0	0	0	5	.091	.091
Mark Grant	.357	14	5	1	0	2	5	2	1	.438	.857	Dave Fleming	.091	11	1	0	0	0	0	0	1	.091	.091

Mark Davis — Padres

Age 33 – Pitches Left

	ERA	W	L	Sv	G	GS	IP	BB	SO	Avg	H	2B	3B	HR	RBI	OBP	SLG	GF	IR	IRS	Hld	SvOp	SB	CS	GB	FB	G/F
1993 Season	4.26	1	5	4	60	0	69.2	44	70	.285	79	12	3	10	44	.384	.458	13	38	13	5	7	8	2	92	59	1.56
Last Five Years	4.26	15	21	55	239	14	346.2	207	316	.253	335	63	8	40	208	.354	.404	60	186	57	15	67	36	7	419	371	1.13

1993 Season

	ERA	W	L	Sv	G	GS	IP	H	HR	BB	SO		Avg	AB	H	2B	3B	HR	RBI	BB	SO	OBP	SLG
Home	4.14	1	3	2	32	0	37.0	37	5	23	39	vs. Left	.255	94	24	3	1	5	15	13	28	.346	.468
Away	4.41	0	2	2	28	0	32.2	42	5	21	31	vs. Right	.301	183	55	9	2	5	29	31	42	.403	.454
Day	4.76	1	1	2	19	0	22.2	27	4	14	26	Inning 1-6	.316	57	18	0	1	5	13	6	11	.381	.614
Night	4.02	0	4	2	41	0	47.0	52	6	30	44	Inning 7+	.277	220	61	12	2	5	31	38	59	.385	.418
Grass	4.42	0	3	2	35	0	38.2	47	6	24	40	None on	.319	119	38	7	1	7	7	21	29	.421	.571
Turf	4.06	1	2	2	25	0	31.0	32	4	20	30	Runners on	.259	158	41	5	2	3	37	23	41	.355	.373
April	2.08	0	0	0	7	0	8.2	3	0	9	6	Scoring Posn	.252	107	27	4	1	3	36	18	26	.357	.393
May	8.31	1	2	0	8	0	8.2	16	0	9	11	Close & Late	.284	95	27	3	1	2	18	18	26	.400	.400
June	3.95	0	0	0	9	0	13.2	14	3	4	10	None on/out	.291	55	16	4	0	3	3	13	13	.426	.527
July	4.91	0	0	3	9	0	11.0	14	4	6	17	vs. 1st Batr (relief)	.271	48	13	2	1	3	7	12	10	.417	.542
August	5.40	0	3	0	12	0	10.0	15	0	9	7	First Inning Pitched	.281	199	56	7	3	7	38	34	48	.387	.452
September/October	2.55	0	0	1	15	0	17.2	17	3	7	19	First 15 Pitches	.304	171	52	7	2	9	31	26	35	.397	.526
Starter	0.00	0	0	0	0	0	0.0	0	0	0	0	Pitch 16-30	.244	86	21	4	1	1	10	15	28	.356	.349
Reliever	4.26	1	5	4	60	0	69.2	79	10	44	70	Pitch 31-45	.250	16	4	1	0	0	3	3	7	.368	.313
0 Days rest	6.75	0	1	1	14	0	16.0	19	3	12	16	Pitch 46+	.500	4	2	0	0	0	0	0	0	.500	.500
1 or 2 Days rest	4.40	0	4	1	27	0	28.2	37	4	20	26	First Pitch	.438	32	14	2	0	1	3	6	0	.526	.594
3+ Days rest	2.52	1	0	2	19	0	25.0	23	3	12	28	Ahead in Count	.170	147	25	3	1	1	15	0	66	.174	.224
Pre-All Star	5.03	1	2	0	26	0	34.0	39	5	24	32	Behind in Count	.407	54	22	3	1	4	14	18	0	.556	.722
Post-All Star	3.53	0	3	4	34	0	35.2	40	5	20	38	Two Strikes	.201	144	29	4	1	3	14	20	70	.303	.306

Last Five Years

	ERA	W	L	Sv	G	GS	IP	H	HR	BB	SO
Home	4.19	10	7	28	122	7	176.0	169	16	105	161
Away	4.32	5	14	27	117	7	170.2	166	24	102	155
Day	5.04	2	6	18	76	4	105.1	104	13	73	107
Night	3.92	13	15	37	163	10	241.1	231	27	134	209
Grass	3.81	7	10	38	132	6	186.2	180	26	96	171
Turf	4.78	8	11	17	107	8	160.0	155	14	111	145
April	5.07	0	3	15	33	3	49.2	46	7	32	42
May	4.80	5	4	8	42	1	50.2	63	3	42	56
June	4.42	3	6	4	43	1	53.0	50	7	26	50
July	6.46	0	2	7	28	3	39.0	43	11	32	35
August	3.88	3	4	7	39	3	62.2	58	4	30	46
September/October	2.75	4	2	14	54	3	91.2	75	8	45	87
Starter	6.61	4	0	0	14	14	64.0	65	10	49	29
Reliever	3.73	11	15	55	225	0	282.2	270	30	158	287
0 Days rest	3.19	4	3	18	51	0	59.1	53	4	34	71
1 or 2 Days rest	4.20	3	9	27	102	0	124.1	129	14	74	118
3+ Days rest	3.45	4	3	10	72	0	99.0	88	12	50	98
Pre-All Star	5.24	8	15	28	126	7	165.0	178	21	115	156
Post-All Star	3.37	7	6	27	113	7	181.2	157	19	92	160

	Avg	AB	H	2B	3B	HR	RBI	BB	SO	OBP	SLG
vs. Left	.261	310	81	13	2	8	46	42	77	.358	.394
vs. Right	.251	1013	254	50	6	32	162	165	239	.353	.407
Inning 1-6	.258	391	101	18	3	16	70	77	69	.374	.442
Inning 7+	.251	932	234	45	5	24	138	130	247	.345	.387
None on	.259	613	159	33	3	21	21	87	139	.357	.426
Runners on	.248	710	176	30	5	19	187	120	177	.352	.385
Scoring Posn	.235	438	103	16	3	13	168	86	119	.352	.374
Close & Late	.255	357	91	10	3	9	57	47	99	.345	.375
None on/out	.237	274	65	11	1	10	10	46	69	.353	.394
vs. 1st Batr (relief)	.218	188	41	8	2	5	25	32	57	.338	.362
First Inning Pitched	.237	767	182	32	4	17	135	138	202	.354	.356
First 15 Pitches	.247	644	159	28	3	18	97	99	156	.349	.384
Pitch 16-30	.249	377	94	20	1	11	56	62	105	.354	.395
Pitch 31-45	.241	145	35	6	2	2	21	25	28	.351	.352
Pitch 46+	.299	157	47	9	2	9	34	21	27	.378	.554
First Pitch	.359	145	52	12	1	6	23	11	0	.409	.579
Ahead in Count	.182	693	126	16	1	10	64	0	284	.186	.251
Behind in Count	.322	283	91	22	3	15	77	113	0	.510	.580
Two Strikes	.167	670	112	14	2	11	64	83	316	.261	.243

Pitcher vs. Batter (since 1984)

Pitches Best Vs.	Avg	AB	H	2B	3B	HR	RBI	BB	SO	OBP	SLG
Tim Wallach	.000	11	0	0	0	0	0	1	5	.083	.000
Tim Teufel	.000	8	0	0	0	0	0	3	3	.273	.000
Fred McGriff	.000	8	0	0	0	0	1	3	3	.273	.000
Alfredo Griffin	.100	10	1	0	0	0	0	1	3	.182	.100
Kevin McReynolds	.111	27	3	0	0	0	0	2	7	.172	.111

Pitches Worst Vs.	Avg	AB	H	2B	3B	HR	RBI	BB	SO	OBP	SLG
Ozzie Smith	.500	20	10	1	0	1	2	3	2	.565	.700
Will Clark	.471	17	8	2	2	1	11	0	3	.471	1.000
Howard Johnson	.455	11	5	0	0	2	5	2	4	.538	1.000
Dickie Thon	.400	10	4	0	1	2	4	3	2	.538	1.200
Dale Murphy	.393	28	11	0	0	4	10	6	4	.486	.821

Storm Davis — Tigers

Age 32 – Pitches Right

	ERA	W	L	Sv	G	GS	IP	BB	SO	Avg	H	2B	3B	HR	RBI	OBP	SLG	GF	IR	IRS	Hld	SvOp	SB	CS	GB	FB	G/F
1993 Season	5.05	2	8	4	43	8	98.0	48	73	.250	93	18	3	9	53	.338	.387	12	28	6	3	5	15	3	145	88	1.65
Last Five Years	4.52	38	37	10	194	70	583.0	233	332	.278	628	104	13	53	298	.345	.405	58	110	28	12	15	37	17	848	662	1.28

1993 Season

	ERA	W	L	Sv	G	GS	IP	H	HR	BB	SO
Home	4.52	1	4	3	24	5	63.2	65	7	22	46
Away	6.03	1	4	1	19	3	34.1	28	2	26	27
Starter	5.98	1	4	0	8	8	40.2	45	4	21	24
Reliever	4.40	1	4	4	35	0	57.1	48	5	27	49
0 Days rest	2.16	0	0	1	5	0	8.1	6	1	1	9
1 or 2 Days rest	4.75	1	3	1	18	0	30.1	21	2	16	26
3+ Days rest	4.82	0	1	2	12	0	18.2	21	2	10	14
Pre-All Star	6.18	2	6	0	19	8	62.2	68	5	33	37
Post-All Star	3.06	0	2	4	24	0	35.1	25	4	15	36

	Avg	AB	H	2B	3B	HR	RBI	BB	SO	OBP	SLG
vs. Left	.232	177	41	8	0	3	26	32	39	.346	.328
vs. Right	.267	195	52	10	3	6	27	16	34	.330	.441
Scoring Posn	.281	114	32	3	0	3	46	21	18	.384	.386
Close & Late	.316	57	18	3	0	2	12	9	8	.409	.474
None on/out	.250	92	23	5	3	2	2	6	21	.296	.435
First Pitch	.283	46	13	3	0	3	12	6	0	.377	.543
Ahead in Count	.189	159	30	7	2	3	17	0	54	.193	.314
Behind in Count	.385	78	30	3	1	0	12	18	0	.495	.449
Two Strikes	.185	178	33	8	1	4	18	24	73	.281	.309

Last Five Years

	ERA	W	L	Sv	G	GS	IP	H	HR	BB	SO
Home	4.25	22	18	4	104	38	328.0	343	28	113	177
Away	4.87	16	19	6	90	32	255.0	285	25	120	155
Day	5.40	13	16	5	72	25	208.1	245	23	100	116
Night	4.04	25	21	5	122	45	374.2	383	30	133	216
Grass	4.60	26	24	9	127	43	367.2	390	40	160	220
Turf	4.39	12	13	1	67	27	215.1	238	13	73	112
April	4.82	6	10	0	24	17	104.2	120	7	40	55
May	5.95	3	9	0	28	17	101.1	116	12	51	51
June	3.93	6	5	3	36	6	84.2	78	7	34	49
July	4.35	6	3	2	32	11	93.0	103	8	31	51
August	3.43	11	6	3	43	13	128.2	132	11	43	75
September/October	4.97	6	4	2	31	6	70.2	79	8	34	51
Starter	4.53	29	26	0	70	70	379.1	422	35	145	197
Reliever	4.51	9	11	10	124	0	203.2	206	18	88	135
0 Days rest	5.33	1	4	1	19	0	25.1	26	2	12	17
1 or 2 Days rest	3.15	8	4	6	61	0	114.1	101	4	47	72
3+ Days rest	6.61	0	3	3	44	0	64.0	79	12	29	46
Pre-All Star	4.84	16	25	3	97	43	322.0	342	30	136	174
Post-All Star	4.14	22	12	7	97	27	261.0	286	23	97	158

	Avg	AB	H	2B	3B	HR	RBI	BB	SO	OBP	SLG
vs. Left	.277	1090	302	50	7	25	150	146	177	.360	.405
vs. Right	.278	1172	326	54	6	28	148	87	155	.330	.406
Inning 1-6	.284	1548	440	77	10	34	202	152	205	.347	.413
Inning 7+	.263	714	188	27	3	19	96	81	127	.340	.389
None on	.283	1208	342	67	10	32	32	108	174	.344	.435
Runners on	.271	1054	286	37	3	21	266	125	158	.345	.372
Scoring Posn	.281	620	174	25	2	12	242	91	84	.364	.385
Close & Late	.269	290	78	7	0	9	44	37	38	.352	.386
None on/out	.305	554	169	33	5	17	17	45	76	.359	.475
vs. 1st Batr (relief)	.225	102	23	2	1	3	18	17	17	.333	.353
First Inning Pitched	.289	698	202	25	5	16	115	82	111	.363	.408
First 15 Pitches	.282	614	173	22	3	14	61	66	89	.350	.396
Pitch 16-30	.271	512	139	28	4	12	84	53	77	.342	.412
Pitch 31-45	.277	358	99	16	2	7	56	31	51	.333	.391
Pitch 46+	.279	778	217	38	4	20	97	83	115	.347	.415
First Pitch	.304	329	100	17	1	11	50	20	0	.343	.462
Ahead in Count	.233	975	227	44	3	11	104	0	267	.236	.318
Behind in Count	.322	506	163	26	4	15	79	106	0	.436	.478
Two Strikes	.236	981	232	41	6	15	102	107	332	.313	.336

Pitcher vs. Batter (since 1984)

Pitches Best Vs.	Avg	AB	H	2B	3B	HR	RBI	BB	SO	OBP	SLG
Pete Incaviglia	.056	18	1	0	0	0	0	3	5	.190	.056
Randy Bush	.061	33	2	1	0	0	2	3	11	.139	.091
Larry Sheets	.083	12	1	0	0	0	1	0	3	.083	.083
Brian Harper	.143	21	3	2	0	0	3	0	1	.136	.238
Dave Winfield	.182	22	4	0	0	0	2	0	2	.174	.182

Pitches Worst Vs.	Avg	AB	H	2B	3B	HR	RBI	BB	SO	OBP	SLG
Felix Fermin	.529	17	9	3	0	1	2	0	0	.529	.882
Jay Buhner	.500	14	7	1	1	1	4	2	3	.563	.929
Billy Ripken	.462	13	6	1	1	0	0	1	0	.500	.692
Tony Phillips	.400	25	10	1	0	2	8	6	3	.516	.680
Greg Myers	.375	8	3	3	0	0	1	2	1	.455	.750

Andre Dawson — Red Sox

Age 39 – Bats Right

	Avg	G	AB	R	H	2B	3B	HR	RBI	BB	SO	HBP	GDP	SB	CS	OBP	SLG	IBB	SH	SF	#Pit	#P/PA	GB	FB	G/F
1993 Season	.273	121	461	44	126	29	1	13	67	17	49	13	18	2	1	.313	.425	4	0	7	1708	3.43	183	150	1.22
Last Five Years	.278	678	2511	307	698	123	18	114	438	146	326	25	69	36	15	.320	.477	49	0	34	9139	3.36	934	809	1.15

1993 Season

	Avg	AB	H	2B	3B	HR	RBI	BB	SO	OBP	SLG
vs. Left	.317	126	40	9	1	7	22	5	14	.353	.571
vs. Right	.257	335	86	20	0	6	45	12	35	.298	.370
Groundball	.290	62	18	4	0	1	9	2	3	.333	.403
Flyball	.351	114	40	16	1	3	14	1	9	.368	.588
Home	.304	247	75	19	1	8	45	10	23	.340	.486
Away	.238	214	51	10	0	5	22	7	26	.283	.355
Day	.248	165	41	9	0	6	23	6	17	.284	.412
Night	.287	296	85	20	1	7	44	11	32	.329	.432
Grass	.276	391	108	26	1	11	61	15	39	.318	.432
Turf	.257	70	18	3	0	2	6	2	10	.289	.386
First Pitch	.317	60	19	6	0	2	10	3	0	.379	.517
Ahead in Count	.375	104	39	9	1	5	20	9	0	.431	.625
Behind in Count	.220	223	49	11	0	5	27	0	43	.228	.336
Two Strikes	.238	189	45	8	0	5	24	5	49	.276	.360

	Avg	AB	H	2B	3B	HR	RBI	BB	SO	OBP	SLG
Scoring Posn	.313	128	40	8	0	6	60	7	13	.354	.516
Close & Late	.303	76	23	4	0	2	10	0	6	.303	.434
None on/out	.271	107	29	8	0	4	4	3	9	.316	.458
Batting #3	.300	80	24	7	0	1	6	2	6	.348	.425
Batting #4	.272	353	96	20	1	12	55	15	37	.312	.436
Other	.214	28	6	2	0	0	6	0	6	.214	.286
April	.237	76	18	3	0	1	10	2	10	.286	.316
May	.242	33	8	1	0	0	9	0	2	.235	.273
June	.227	97	22	5	1	2	11	3	15	.257	.361
July	.330	97	32	6	0	5	20	7	8	.383	.546
August	.305	105	32	11	0	3	10	5	9	.348	.495
September/October	.264	53	14	3	0	2	7	0	5	.298	.434
Pre-All Star	.242	248	60	9	1	6	37	6	30	.273	.359
Post-All Star	.310	213	66	20	0	7	30	11	19	.359	.502

1993 By Position

Position	Avg	AB	H	2B	3B	HR	RBI	BB	SO	OBP	SLG	G	GS	Innings	PO	A	E	DP	Fld Pct	Rng Fctr	In Zone	Outs	Zone Rtg	MLB Zone
As Designated Hitter	.266	380	101	22	1	13	56	14	38	.308	.432	97	97	---	---	---	---	---	---	---	---	---	---	---
As rf	.299	77	23	6	0	0	8	3	10	.329	.377	20	20	160.0	42	0	0	0	1.000	2.36	47	42	.894	.826

Last Five Years

	Avg	AB	H	2B	3B	HR	RBI	BB	SO	OBP	SLG
vs. Left	.298	839	250	47	5	46	157	50	98	.336	.530
vs. Right	.268	1672	448	76	13	68	281	96	228	.312	.451
Groundball	.262	814	213	31	9	33	133	42	98	.301	.443
Flyball	.307	590	181	40	2	37	103	36	72	.346	.569
Home	.293	1263	370	68	8	63	238	86	150	.340	.509
Away	.263	1248	328	55	10	51	200	60	176	.299	.446
Day	.295	1224	361	59	12	66	240	86	151	.343	.525
Night	.262	1287	337	64	6	48	198	60	175	.298	.433
Grass	.285	1843	526	90	13	89	344	116	229	.330	.493
Turf	.257	668	172	33	5	25	94	30	97	.292	.434
First Pitch	.324	361	117	25	4	25	83	30	0	.377	.623
Ahead in Count	.321	533	171	26	4	37	130	61	0	.392	.593
Behind in Count	.236	1227	290	53	6	35	162	0	294	.239	.375
Two Strikes	.225	1065	240	38	5	29	126	37	326	.256	.352

	Avg	AB	H	2B	3B	HR	RBI	BB	SO	OBP	SLG
Scoring Posn	.295	691	204	39	4	30	321	88	93	.366	.493
Close & Late	.273	455	124	15	1	22	67	28	65	.318	.455
None on/out	.240	626	150	30	3	26	26	24	89	.278	.422
Batting #4	.278	1900	529	95	13	86	326	116	234	.321	.478
Batting #5	.275	495	136	19	5	24	92	27	77	.315	.479
Other	.284	116	33	9	0	4	20	3	15	.320	.466
April	.281	352	99	17	3	15	68	19	44	.322	.474
May	.316	351	111	18	6	20	74	17	39	.347	.573
June	.248	419	104	21	1	14	55	26	56	.294	.403
July	.278	424	118	18	1	21	77	34	57	.333	.474
August	.267	490	131	26	4	17	69	28	65	.311	.441
September/October	.284	475	135	23	3	27	95	22	65	.320	.516
Pre-All Star	.282	1283	362	62	10	61	228	77	158	.325	.489
Post-All Star	.274	1228	336	61	8	53	210	69	168	.315	.466

Batter vs. Pitcher (since 1984)

Hits Best Against	Avg	AB	H	2B	3B	HR	RBI	BB	SO	OBP	SLG
Jesse Orosco	.600	10	6	1	0	1	3	1	1	.636	1.000
Mark Grant	.571	21	12	2	1	3	9	1	0	.591	1.190
Danny Darwin	.500	14	7	1	0	2	4	3	3	.556	1.000
Stan Belinda	.385	13	5	0	0	4	10	0	1	.385	1.308
Pete Smith	.368	19	7	2	0	4	8	0	1	.350	1.105

Hits Worst Against	Avg	AB	H	2B	3B	HR	RBI	BB	SO	OBP	SLG
Danny Jackson	.071	14	1	0	0	0	0	0	3	.071	.071
Pete Harnisch	.071	14	1	1	0	0	2	0	3	.063	.143
John Smoltz	.074	27	2	0	0	1	1	0	9	.074	.185
Jay Howell	.091	11	1	0	0	0	0	0	3	.091	.091
Bill Sampen	.091	11	1	0	0	0	0	1	2	.167	.091

Ken Dayley — Dodgers

Age 35 – Pitches Left (flyball pitcher)

	ERA	W	L	Sv	G	GS	IP	BB	SO	Avg	H	2B	3B	HR	RBI	OBP	SLG	GF	IR	IRS	Hld	SvOp	SB	CS	GB	FB	G/F
1993 Season	0.00	0	0	0	2	0	0.2	4	2	.333	1	1	0	0	0	.714	.667	0	2	0	0	0	0	0	0	1	0.00
Last Five Years	3.28	8	7	14	139	0	153.2	69	96	.236	134	26	4	8	65	.316	.338	20	110	30	36	24	11	5	180	193	0.93

1993 Season

	ERA	W	L	Sv	G	GS	IP	H	HR	BB	SO
Home	0.00	0	0	0	1	0	0.0	1	0	1	0
Away	0.00	0	0	0	1	0	0.2	0	0	3	2

	Avg	AB	H	2B	3B	HR	RBI	BB	SO	OBP	SLG
vs. Left	.000	2	0	0	0	0	0	1	2	.333	.000
vs. Right	1.000	1	1	1	0	0	0	3	0	1.000	2.000

Last Five Years

	ERA	W	L	Sv	G	GS	IP	H	HR	BB	SO
Home	3.33	5	2	8	69	0	78.1	78	3	31	48
Away	3.23	3	5	6	70	0	75.1	56	5	38	48
Day	2.87	2	3	3	47	0	53.1	47	3	24	37
Night	3.50	6	4	11	92	0	100.1	87	5	45	59
Grass	2.87	1	3	2	37	0	37.2	31	2	21	18
Turf	3.41	7	4	12	102	0	116.0	103	6	48	78
April	1.59	1	0	3	22	0	17.0	16	1	8	6
May	2.25	3	2	0	22	0	24.0	27	1	7	19
June	5.23	0	1	3	28	0	31.0	35	2	13	24
July	3.20	1	0	2	17	0	19.2	13	1	10	9
August	1.20	1	0	3	22	0	30.0	16	2	9	19
September/October	5.06	2	4	3	28	0	32.0	27	1	22	19
Starter	0.00	0	0	0	0	0	0.0	0	0	0	0
Reliever	3.28	8	7	14	139	0	153.2	134	8	69	96
0 Days rest	4.08	0	1	4	21	0	17.2	18	2	10	15
1 or 2 Days rest	3.39	5	5	9	83	0	93.0	78	3	38	55

	Avg	AB	H	2B	3B	HR	RBI	BB	SO	OBP	SLG
vs. Left	.237	219	52	10	0	4	26	20	41	.302	.338
vs. Right	.235	349	82	16	4	4	39	49	55	.325	.338
Inning 1-6	.132	68	9	1	0	0	2	12	16	.263	.147
Inning 7+	.250	500	125	25	4	8	63	57	80	.324	.364
None on	.215	297	64	12	2	5	5	30	57	.287	.320
Runners on	.258	271	70	14	2	3	60	39	39	.346	.358
Scoring Posn	.275	149	41	10	1	2	54	34	28	.398	.396
Close & Late	.261	226	59	11	2	4	36	27	29	.339	.381
None on/out	.146	123	18	3	1	0	0	15	26	.239	.187
vs. 1st Batr (relief)	.205	117	24	2	1	0	12	19	21	.312	.239
First Inning Pitched	.229	385	88	17	3	4	47	52	68	.318	.319
First 15 Pitches	.244	365	89	18	4	4	44	47	61	.327	.348
Pitch 16-30	.190	163	31	6	0	2	13	20	30	.279	.264
Pitch 31-45	.378	37	14	2	0	2	8	2	4	.400	.595
Pitch 46+	.000	3	0	0	0	0	0	0	1	.000	.000
First Pitch	.280	82	23	4	0	2	13	15	0	.388	.402

Last Five Years

	ERA	W	L	Sv	G	GS	IP	H	HR	BB	SO
3+ Days rest	2.72	3	1	1	35	0	43.0	38	3	21	26
Pre-All Star	3.46	4	3	8	77	0	78.0	80	5	30	54
Post-All Star	3.09	4	4	6	62	0	75.2	54	3	39	42

	Avg	AB	H	2B	3B	HR	RBI	BB	SO	OBP	SLG
Ahead in Count	.174	247	43	8	1	2	19	0	82	.175	.239
Behind in Count	.269	145	39	9	2	1	18	33	0	.400	.379
Two Strikes	.171	251	43	6	2	2	21	21	96	.235	.235

Pitcher vs. Batter (since 1984)

Pitches Best Vs.	Avg	AB	H	2B	3B	HR	RBI	BB	SO	OBP	SLG
Ryne Sandberg	.000	10	0	0	0	0	0	4	1	.286	.000
Juan Samuel	.000	7	0	0	0	0	0	4	2	.364	.000
Robby Thompson	.083	12	1	1	0	0	2	0	2	.083	.167
Billy Doran	.091	11	1	1	0	0	1	0	2	.091	.182
Bobby Bonilla	.095	21	2	0	0	0	1	3	3	.208	.095

Pitches Worst Vs.	Avg	AB	H	2B	3B	HR	RBI	BB	SO	OBP	SLG
Tim Raines	.409	22	9	3	0	1	5	7	2	.552	.682
Hubie Brooks	.400	10	4	0	1	0	5	3	2	.538	.600
Andy Van Slyke	.333	21	7	1	1	0	5	1	5	.364	.476
Kevin Bass	.333	15	5	0	0	2	4	0	2	.333	.733
Gary Redus	.333	9	3	0	1	0	0	3	1	.500	.556

Steve Decker — Marlins

Age 28 – Bats Right (flyball hitter)

	Avg	G	AB	R	H	2B	3B	HR	RBI	BB	SO	HBP	GDP	SB	CS	OBP	SLG	IBB	SH	SF	#Pit	#P/PA	GB	FB	G/F
1993 Season	.000	8	15	0	0	0	0	0	1	3	3	0	2	0	0	.158	.000	0	0	1	86	4.53	4	9	0.44
Career (1990-1993)	.206	117	345	19	71	10	1	8	34	26	64	4	10	0	1	.266	.310	1	3	5	1512	3.95	100	129	0.78

1993 Season

	Avg	AB	H	2B	3B	HR	RBI	BB	SO	OBP	SLG
vs. Left	.000	7	0	0	0	0	1	3	1	.273	.000
vs. Right	.000	8	0	0	0	0	0	0	2	.000	.000

	Avg	AB	H	2B	3B	HR	RBI	BB	SO	OBP	SLG
Scoring Posn	.000	5	0	0	0	0	1	3	2	.333	.000
Close & Late	.000	4	0	0	0	0	0	2	0	.333	.000

Career (1990-1993)

	Avg	AB	H	2B	3B	HR	RBI	BB	SO	OBP	SLG
vs. Left	.217	129	28	3	1	4	16	7	17	.250	.349
vs. Right	.199	216	43	7	0	4	18	19	47	.275	.287
Groundball	.204	103	21	1	0	4	10	9	16	.278	.330
Flyball	.160	81	13	1	0	3	9	7	18	.233	.284
Home	.212	165	35	5	1	5	23	14	26	.279	.345
Away	.200	180	36	5	0	3	11	12	38	.254	.278
Day	.221	131	29	5	1	2	18	13	28	.307	.321
Night	.196	214	42	5	0	6	16	13	36	.239	.304
Grass	.207	271	56	9	1	8	32	20	44	.264	.336
Turf	.203	74	15	1	0	0	2	6	20	.274	.216
First Pitch	.320	25	8	3	0	0	4	0	0	.308	.440
Ahead in Count	.227	75	17	2	0	2	9	17	0	.362	.333
Behind in Count	.183	164	30	3	0	2	10	0	48	.198	.238
Two Strikes	.149	175	26	5	1	1	14	9	64	.194	.206

	Avg	AB	H	2B	3B	HR	RBI	BB	SO	OBP	SLG
Scoring Posn	.161	87	14	1	1	1	23	11	21	.243	.230
Close & Late	.169	65	11	1	0	2	5	6	13	.239	.277
None on/out	.175	80	14	3	0	2	2	5	9	.233	.288
Batting #6	.205	39	8	1	0	2	4	0	8	.205	.385
Batting #7	.217	263	57	9	1	6	30	25	49	.287	.327
Other	.140	43	6	0	0	0	0	1	7	.178	.140
April	.211	71	15	1	0	4	9	10	18	.301	.394
May	.129	62	8	2	0	1	5	2	10	.154	.210
June	.255	51	13	3	0	0	5	2	11	.304	.314
July	.240	25	6	1	0	0	2	3	3	.333	.280
August	.000	0	0	0	0	0	0	0	0	.000	.000
September/October	.213	136	29	3	1	3	13	9	22	.267	.316
Pre-All Star	.202	193	39	7	0	5	20	15	39	.260	.316
Post-All Star	.211	152	32	3	1	3	14	11	25	.273	.303

Batter vs. Pitcher (career)

Hits Best Against	Avg	AB	H	2B	3B	HR	RBI	BB	SO	OBP	SLG

Hits Worst Against	Avg	AB	H	2B	3B	HR	RBI	BB	SO	OBP	SLG
Andy Benes	.182	11	2	1	0	1	1	3	5	.357	.545

Rob Deer — Red Sox

Age 33 – Bats Right (flyball hitter)

	Avg	G	AB	R	H	2B	3B	HR	RBI	BB	SO	HBP	GDP	SB	CS	OBP	SLG	IBB	SH	SF	#Pit	#P/PA	GB	FB	G/F
1993 Season	.210	128	466	66	98	17	1	21	55	58	169	5	6	5	2	.303	.386	1	0	3	2204	4.14	99	138	0.72
Last Five Years	.210	636	2213	325	465	84	7	131	317	322	780	16	25	16	18	.313	.432	14	0	11	10614	4.14	441	706	0.62

1993 Season

	Avg	AB	H	2B	3B	HR	RBI	BB	SO	OBP	SLG
vs. Left	.281	121	34	7	1	9	21	22	40	.397	.579
vs. Right	.186	345	64	10	0	12	34	36	129	.267	.319
Groundball	.233	90	21	4	0	6	20	14	28	.346	.478
Flyball	.232	95	22	4	0	5	7	13	46	.336	.432
Home	.214	192	41	7	0	12	34	33	66	.330	.438
Away	.208	274	57	10	1	9	21	25	103	.281	.350
Day	.270	174	47	9	1	11	29	24	54	.355	.523
Night	.175	292	51	8	0	10	26	34	115	.271	.305
Grass	.211	361	76	13	1	17	46	53	129	.316	.393
Turf	.210	105	22	4	0	4	9	5	40	.252	.362
First Pitch	.306	49	15	4	0	4	10	1	0	.340	.633
Ahead in Count	.357	84	30	6	1	7	18	21	0	.491	.702
Behind in Count	.129	232	30	4	0	5	12	0	135	.136	.211
Two Strikes	.109	265	29	5	0	6	19	36	169	.217	.196

	Avg	AB	H	2B	3B	HR	RBI	BB	SO	OBP	SLG
Scoring Posn	.173	133	23	4	0	4	34	24	47	.302	.293
Close & Late	.278	79	22	4	0	7	18	12	26	.380	.595
None on/out	.216	102	22	3	0	8	8	9	43	.286	.480
Batting #5	.222	158	35	8	1	7	21	22	54	.324	.418
Batting #7	.147	136	20	4	0	5	9	17	55	.255	.287
Other	.250	172	43	5	0	9	25	19	60	.321	.436
April	.205	88	18	5	0	6	16	10	33	.286	.466
May	.239	71	17	4	0	2	8	12	24	.345	.380
June	.205	44	9	0	0	3	6	6	16	.300	.409
July	.232	82	19	2	0	2	6	5	32	.286	.329
August	.160	75	12	1	0	2	6	8	27	.259	.253
September/October	.217	106	23	5	1	6	13	17	37	.331	.453
Pre-All Star	.218	243	53	10	0	11	30	31	86	.308	.395
Post-All Star	.202	223	45	7	1	10	25	27	83	.297	.377

1993 By Position

Position	Avg	AB	H	2B	3B	HR	RBI	BB	SO	OBP	SLG	G	GS	Innings	PO	A	E	DP	Fld Pct	Rng Fctr	In Zone	Outs	Zone Rtg	MLB Zone
As rf	.210	443	93	17	1	20	52	56	160	.304	.388	120	114	1030.1	287	7	8	3	.974	2.57	330	286	.867	.826

Last Five Years

	Avg	AB	H	2B	3B	HR	RBI	BB	SO	OBP	SLG
vs. Left	.261	632	165	26	2	56	112	103	193	.366	.574
vs. Right	.190	1581	300	58	5	75	205	219	587	.292	.375
Groundball	.225	581	131	25	2	34	99	86	185	.329	.451
Flyball	.198	505	100	21	2	35	69	74	207	.304	.455
Home	.208	1031	214	39	3	63	158	171	362	.325	.435
Away	.212	1182	251	45	4	68	159	151	418	.303	.430

	Avg	AB	H	2B	3B	HR	RBI	BB	SO	OBP	SLG
Scoring Posn	.202	570	115	18	0	32	186	123	207	.342	.402
Close & Late	.232	353	82	19	0	23	57	54	137	.338	.482
None on/out	.228	543	124	22	0	38	38	62	184	.310	.479
Batting #6	.198	768	152	19	1	53	115	113	269	.302	.432
Batting #7	.208	476	99	19	2	25	58	67	171	.312	.414
Other	.221	969	214	46	4	53	144	142	340	.323	.441

Last Five Years

	Avg	AB	H	2B	3B	HR	RBI	BB	SO	OBP	SLG
Day	.214	753	161	34	2	46	117	115	258	.320	.448
Night	.208	1460	304	50	5	85	200	207	522	.310	.424
Grass	.214	1819	390	72	6	111	266	276	632	.321	.444
Turf	.190	394	75	12	1	20	51	46	148	.276	.378
First Pitch	.289	225	65	13	1	16	41	5	0	.315	.569
Ahead in Count	.340	415	141	22	2	47	96	133	0	.504	.742
Behind in Count	.151	1130	171	28	4	49	116	0	619	.154	.313
Two Strikes	.127	1268	161	34	3	41	113	177	780	.235	.256

	Avg	AB	H	2B	3B	HR	RBI	BB	SO	OBP	SLG
April	.208	332	69	16	2	25	64	53	122	.323	.494
May	.214	415	89	15	1	29	64	72	153	.330	.465
June	.210	396	83	11	0	27	65	49	125	.299	.442
July	.225	342	77	11	1	19	42	39	121	.308	.430
August	.180	327	59	10	2	16	38	47	126	.288	.370
September/October	.219	401	88	21	1	15	44	62	133	.327	.389
Pre-All Star	.212	1267	268	46	3	84	200	189	440	.317	.451
Post-All Star	.208	946	197	38	4	47	117	133	340	.309	.406

Batter vs. Pitcher (career)

Hits Best Against	Avg	AB	H	2B	3B	HR	RBI	BB	SO	OBP	SLG
Bob Milacki	.467	15	7	2	1	1	4	3	3	.556	.933
Lee Guetterman	.429	7	3	1	0	2	3	4	1	.636	1.429
Paul Gibson	.385	13	5	2	0	2	3	3	4	.500	1.000
Donn Pall	.385	13	5	0	0	3	9	0	4	.385	1.077
Danny Jackson	.364	11	4	0	0	2	7	4	4	.500	.909

Hits Worst Against	Avg	AB	H	2B	3B	HR	RBI	BB	SO	OBP	SLG
Nolan Ryan	.000	14	0	0	0	0	0	0	10	.000	.000
Mike Jackson	.000	12	0	0	0	0	0	1	8	.077	.000
Bill Gullickson	.000	11	0	0	0	0	1	1	7	.083	.000
Dan Plesac	.000	11	0	0	0	0	0	0	5	.000	.000
Jose Bautista	.083	12	1	0	0	0	1	0	4	.083	.083

Jose DeLeon — White Sox

Age 33 – Pitches Right (flyball pitcher)

	ERA	W	L	Sv	G	GS	IP	BB	SO	Avg	H	2B	3B	HR	RBI	OBP	SLG	GF	IR	IRS	Hld	SvOp	SB	CS	GB	FB	G/F
1993 Season	2.98	3	0	0	35	3	57.1	30	40	.218	44	7	1	7	23	.333	.366	7	13	4	7	2	5	8	54	76	0.71
Last Five Years	3.51	33	48	0	163	117	764.2	305	602	.228	640	128	22	60	286	.307	.353	10	21	4	7	2	62	49	761	973	0.78

1993 Season

	ERA	W	L	Sv	G	GS	IP	H	HR	BB	SO
Home	2.62	1	0	0	19	1	34.1	28	2	17	24
Away	3.52	2	0	0	16	2	23.0	16	5	13	16
Starter	2.81	0	0	0	3	3	16.0	11	2	5	13
Reliever	3.05	3	0	0	32	0	41.1	33	5	25	27
0 Days rest	7.20	0	0	0	5	0	5.0	7	2	3	2
1 or 2 Days rest	3.18	1	0	0	13	0	17.0	13	1	4	12
3+ Days rest	1.86	2	0	0	14	0	19.1	13	2	18	13
Pre-All Star	3.38	3	0	0	22	2	40.0	33	4	22	27
Post-All Star	2.08	0	0	0	13	1	17.1	11	3	8	13

	Avg	AB	H	2B	3B	HR	RBI	BB	SO	OBP	SLG
vs. Left	.264	91	24	6	1	3	10	15	16	.382	.451
vs. Right	.180	111	20	1	0	4	13	15	24	.292	.297
Scoring Posn	.218	55	12	1	0	4	20	12	13	.366	.455
Close & Late	.179	39	7	2	0	2	3	4	2	.289	.385
None on/out	.245	49	12	3	0	2	2	7	10	.351	.429
First Pitch	.269	26	7	1	1	1	4	3	0	.387	.500
Ahead in Count	.180	89	16	2	0	1	5	0	36	.202	.236
Behind in Count	.286	49	14	4	0	3	8	13	0	.435	.551
Two Strikes	.137	102	14	2	0	3	9	14	40	.246	.245

Last Five Years

	ERA	W	L	Sv	G	GS	IP	H	HR	BB	SO
Home	3.27	17	22	0	86	62	410.0	338	27	156	309
Away	3.78	16	26	0	77	55	354.2	302	33	149	293
Day	3.70	11	15	0	50	38	246.0	220	19	84	201
Night	3.42	22	33	0	113	79	518.2	420	41	221	401
Grass	3.39	7	16	0	49	30	212.1	175	18	75	173
Turf	3.55	26	32	0	114	87	552.1	465	42	230	429
April	2.92	10	5	0	27	19	126.1	88	12	51	95
May	4.31	6	9	0	26	24	144.0	142	10	58	121
June	3.61	6	11	0	33	20	139.2	121	9	56	123
July	3.12	5	10	0	29	18	132.2	118	9	54	95
August	3.45	4	6	0	25	20	133.0	95	10	46	111
September/October	3.54	2	7	0	23	16	89.0	76	10	40	57
Starter	3.53	30	48	0	117	117	702.0	591	55	268	560
Reliever	3.30	3	0	0	46	0	62.2	49	5	37	42
0 Days rest	7.50	0	0	0	6	0	6.0	10	2	3	3
1 or 2 Days rest	3.42	1	0	0	17	0	23.2	16	1	7	16
3+ Days rest	2.45	2	0	0	23	0	33.0	23	2	27	23
Pre-All Star	3.64	22	28	0	97	68	447.2	387	34	181	369
Post-All Star	3.32	11	20	0	66	49	317.0	253	26	124	233

	Avg	AB	H	2B	3B	HR	RBI	BB	SO	OBP	SLG
vs. Left	.259	1578	408	82	18	35	177	199	253	.343	.400
vs. Right	.188	1232	232	46	4	25	109	106	349	.259	.293
Inning 1-6	.228	2368	540	106	18	50	246	251	525	.304	.351
Inning 7+	.226	442	100	22	4	10	40	54	77	.318	.362
None on	.214	1684	360	71	17	36	36	185	353	.298	.340
Runners on	.249	1126	280	57	5	24	250	120	249	.319	.372
Scoring Posn	.233	661	154	35	4	12	212	83	148	.315	.352
Close & Late	.215	205	44	11	3	5	19	25	35	.309	.371
None on/out	.215	722	155	34	4	15	15	89	150	.303	.335
vs. 1st Batr (relief)	.171	35	6	1	0	3	6	8	8	.348	.457
First Inning Pitched	.238	580	138	30	4	13	73	86	132	.342	.371
First 15 Pitches	.246	483	119	23	3	12	38	70	99	.349	.381
Pitch 16-30	.211	493	104	22	5	8	60	51	112	.286	.325
Pitch 31-45	.245	432	106	20	5	10	44	42	91	.318	.384
Pitch 46+	.222	1402	311	63	9	30	144	142	300	.295	.344
First Pitch	.319	395	126	26	4	9	51	17	0	.361	.473
Ahead in Count	.169	1338	226	38	10	10	91	0	532	.174	.235
Behind in Count	.308	623	192	50	8	29	99	170	0	.454	.554
Two Strikes	.147	1344	197	28	8	14	87	118	602	.218	.211

Pitcher vs. Batter (since 1984)

Pitches Best Vs.	Avg	AB	H	2B	3B	HR	RBI	BB	SO	OBP	SLG
Cal Ripken	.000	10	0	0	0	0	0	3	4	.231	.000
Danny Cox	.000	10	0	0	0	0	0	1	7	.091	.000
Tom Brunansky	.000	8	0	0	0	0	1	2	5	.182	.000
Glenn Davis	.091	11	1	0	0	0	0	0	5	.091	.091
Eric Yelding	.091	11	1	0	0	0	0	0	5	.091	.091

Pitches Worst Vs.	Avg	AB	H	2B	3B	HR	RBI	BB	SO	OBP	SLG
Kirby Puckett	.571	14	8	1	0	2	3	0	2	.571	1.071
Terry Pendleton	.542	24	13	3	2	0	3	3	2	.593	.833
Luis Polonia	.538	13	7	0	1	0	1	1	0	.571	.692
John Kruk	.481	27	13	3	0	1	10	5	5	.563	.704
Barry Bonds	.406	32	13	1	0	5	11	7	5	.513	.906

Carlos Delgado — Blue Jays

Age 22 – Bats Left

	Avg	G	AB	R	H	2B	3B	HR	RBI	BB	SO	HBP	GDP	SB	CS	OBP	SLG	IBB	SH	SF	#Pit	#P/PA	GB	FB	G/F
1993 Season	.000	2	1	0	0	0	0	0	0	1	0	0	0	0	0	.500	.000	0	0	0	11	5.50	0	1	0.00

1993 Season

	Avg	AB	H	2B	3B	HR	RBI	BB	SO	OBP	SLG
vs. Left	.000	0	0	0	0	0	0	0	0	.000	.000
vs. Right	.000	1	0	0	0	0	0	1	0	.500	.000

	Avg	AB	H	2B	3B	HR	RBI	BB	SO	OBP	SLG
Scoring Posn	.000	0	0	0	0	0	0	0	0	.000	.000
Close & Late	.000	0	0	0	0	0	0	0	0	.000	.000

Rich DeLucia — Mariners

Age 29 – Pitches Right (flyball pitcher)

	ERA	W	L	Sv	G	GS	IP	BB	SO	Avg	H	2B	3B	HR	RBI	OBP	SLG	GF	IR	IRS	Hld	SvOp	SB	CS	GB	FB	G/F
1993 Season	4.64	3	6	0	30	1	42.2	23	48	.272	46	6	1	5	29	.361	.408	11	26	12	6	4	2	2	33	54	0.61
Career (1990-1993)	4.81	19	27	1	97	48	344.1	145	232	.266	352	71	7	51	184	.338	.447	17	47	20	9	7	11	14	360	498	0.72

1993 Season

	ERA	W	L	Sv	G	GS	IP	H	HR	BB	SO
Home	5.32	2	2	0	18	0	22.0	25	2	12	28
Away	3.92	1	4	0	12	1	20.2	21	3	11	20
Starter	13.50	0	1	0	1	1	2.0	4	0	4	0
Reliever	4.20	3	5	0	29	0	40.2	42	5	19	48
0 Days rest	7.71	0	0	0	3	0	2.1	4	1	2	4
1 or 2 Days rest	4.22	3	2	0	14	0	21.1	23	2	10	26
3+ Days rest	3.71	0	3	0	12	0	17.0	15	2	7	18
Pre-All Star	4.82	2	5	0	26	1	37.1	36	5	22	44
Post-All Star	3.38	1	1	0	4	0	5.1	10	0	1	4

	Avg	AB	H	2B	3B	HR	RBI	BB	SO	OBP	SLG
vs. Left	.333	75	25	5	1	3	16	12	15	.420	.547
vs. Right	.223	94	21	1	0	2	13	11	33	.311	.298
Scoring Posn	.310	58	18	1	1	3	25	6	19	.369	.517
Close & Late	.277	94	26	4	1	3	18	13	31	.367	.436
None on/out	.342	38	13	3	0	1	1	5	8	.419	.500
First Pitch	.211	19	4	0	0	1	4	2	0	.286	.368
Ahead in Count	.225	80	18	2	0	1	10	0	28	.232	.288
Behind in Count	.536	28	15	3	1	3	12	10	0	.658	1.036
Two Strikes	.152	99	15	1	0	1	7	11	48	.234	.192

Career (1990-1993)

	ERA	W	L	Sv	G	GS	IP	H	HR	BB	SO
Home	4.72	13	8	1	50	21	171.2	180	28	62	117
Away	4.90	6	19	0	47	27	172.2	172	23	83	115
Day	6.63	3	12	0	31	15	95.0	111	12	47	66
Night	4.11	16	15	1	66	33	249.1	241	39	98	166
Grass	5.14	4	17	0	39	21	138.1	138	19	69	88
Turf	4.59	15	10	1	58	27	206.0	214	32	76	144
April	5.16	4	4	0	14	7	52.1	55	10	25	38
May	4.85	4	4	0	20	6	55.2	61	6	25	50
June	5.32	3	6	0	19	11	64.1	68	11	38	44
July	4.76	4	4	0	16	8	56.2	61	5	19	38
August	3.62	2	2	0	7	5	32.1	30	7	6	14
September/October	4.66	2	7	1	21	11	83.0	77	12	32	48
Starter	5.08	15	22	0	48	48	265.2	278	41	108	150
Reliever	3.89	4	5	1	49	0	78.2	74	10	37	82
0 Days rest	2.70	0	0	0	5	0	10.0	10	2	4	10
1 or 2 Days rest	5.40	3	2	0	21	0	30.0	36	2	15	34
3+ Days rest	3.03	1	3	1	23	0	38.2	28	6	18	38
Pre-All Star	5.08	12	15	0	57	27	187.2	197	27	95	143
Post-All Star	4.48	7	12	1	40	21	156.2	155	24	50	89

	Avg	AB	H	2B	3B	HR	RBI	BB	SO	OBP	SLG
vs. Left	.297	617	183	32	6	19	79	88	75	.381	.460
vs. Right	.240	704	169	39	1	32	105	57	157	.299	.435
Inning 1-6	.263	989	260	55	6	33	137	115	157	.339	.431
Inning 7+	.277	332	92	16	1	18	47	30	75	.337	.494
None on	.253	795	201	40	4	31	31	70	136	.315	.430
Runners on	.287	526	151	31	3	20	153	75	96	.371	.471
Scoring Posn	.276	294	81	14	2	11	129	52	61	.368	.449
Close & Late	.320	150	48	7	1	9	28	16	39	.387	.560
None on/out	.266	353	94	16	3	16	16	25	54	.317	.465
vs. 1st Batr (relief)	.310	42	13	2	0	2	14	6	11	.408	.500
First Inning Pitched	.296	348	103	21	2	11	77	51	84	.382	.463
First 15 Pitches	.300	257	77	19	1	7	32	34	57	.380	.463
Pitch 16-30	.261	234	61	9	1	9	47	33	46	.347	.423
Pitch 31-45	.261	226	59	10	3	9	37	19	45	.324	.451
Pitch 46+	.257	604	155	33	2	26	68	59	84	.321	.447
First Pitch	.285	165	47	8	2	10	26	6	0	.310	.539
Ahead in Count	.221	538	119	19	0	10	54	0	172	.225	.312
Behind in Count	.321	296	95	18	2	21	55	76	0	.451	.608
Two Strikes	.191	608	116	24	1	15	57	62	232	.265	.308

Pitcher vs. Batter (career)

Pitches Best Vs.	Avg	AB	H	2B	3B	HR	RBI	BB	SO	OBP	SLG
Joe Carter	.000	11	0	0	0	0	0	0	5	.000	.000
Travis Fryman	.000	10	0	0	0	0	0	2	3	.167	.000
Carlton Fisk	.077	13	1	0	0	0	2	0	3	.077	.077
Ellis Burks	.100	10	1	0	0	0	1	0	3	.091	.100
Mark McGwire	.118	17	2	1	0	0	0	1	3	.167	.176

Pitches Worst Vs.	Avg	AB	H	2B	3B	HR	RBI	BB	SO	OBP	SLG
Chili Davis	.455	11	5	0	0	1	2	2	2	.538	.727
Dave Henderson	.417	12	5	1	0	2	4	1	0	.462	1.000
Sam Horn	.375	8	3	0	0	1	2	5	2	.615	.750
Cecil Fielder	.333	12	4	0	0	3	11	2	2	.429	1.083
Jose Canseco	.313	16	5	1	0	3	3	1	4	.353	.938

Drew Denson — White Sox

Age 28 – Bats Right (groundball hitter)

	Avg	G	AB	R	H	2B	3B	HR	RBI	BB	SO	HBP	GDP	SB	CS	OBP	SLG	IBB	SH	SF	#Pit	#P/PA	GB	FB	G/F
1993 Season	.200	4	5	0	1	0	0	0	0	0	2	0	0	0	0	.200	.200	0	0	0	18	3.60	0	2	0.00
Career (1989-1993)	.244	16	41	1	10	1	0	0	5	3	11	0	0	1	0	.295	.268	0	0	0	165	3.75	13	9	1.44

1993 Season

	Avg	AB	H	2B	3B	HR	RBI	BB	SO	OBP	SLG
vs. Left	.000	2	0	0	0	0	0	0	1	.000	.000
vs. Right	.333	3	1	0	0	0	0	0	1	.333	.333

	Avg	AB	H	2B	3B	HR	RBI	BB	SO	OBP	SLG
Scoring Posn	.333	3	1	0	0	0	0	0	2	.333	.333
Close & Late	.000	3	0	0	0	0	0	0	2	.000	.000

Jim Deshaies — Giants

Age 34 – Pitches Left (flyball pitcher)

	ERA	W	L	Sv	G	GS	IP	BB	SO	Avg	H	2B	3B	HR	RBI	OBP	SLG	CG	ShO	Sup	QS	#P/S	SB	CS	GB	FB	G/F
1993 Season	4.39	13	15	0	32	31	184.1	57	85	.264	183	39	4	26	81	.323	.444	1	0	4.30	16	95	8	18	192	286	0.67
Last Five Years	3.85	44	56	0	143	142	876.1	325	501	.246	797	162	21	87	333	.316	.389	10	3	3.72	77	99	83	57	902	1225	0.74

1993 Season

	ERA	W	L	Sv	G	GS	IP	H	HR	BB	SO
Home	3.81	8	6	0	15	15	89.2	84	9	22	41
Away	4.94	5	9	0	17	16	94.2	99	17	35	44
Day	3.82	6	5	0	13	12	77.2	76	6	19	43
Night	4.81	7	10	0	19	19	106.2	107	20	38	42
Grass	5.42	3	8	0	14	13	73.0	83	11	31	35
Turf	3.72	10	7	0	18	18	111.1	100	15	26	50
April	2.36	4	1	0	5	5	34.1	29	1	11	13
May	6.16	2	3	0	6	6	30.2	34	5	8	19
June	3.34	3	1	0	5	5	32.1	28	6	12	10
July	6.55	2	3	0	6	6	34.1	39	7	13	20
August	3.79	0	5	0	5	5	35.2	29	5	7	18
September/October	4.24	2	2	0	5	4	17.0	24	2	6	5
Starter	4.36	13	15	0	31	31	183.2	181	25	56	84
Reliever	13.50	0	0	0	1	0	0.2	2	1	1	1
0-3 Days Rest	2.77	1	1	0	2	2	13.0	6	2	7	8

	Avg	AB	H	2B	3B	HR	RBI	BB	SO	OBP	SLG
vs. Left	.230	122	28	4	1	3	6	10	13	.309	.352
vs. Right	.271	572	155	35	3	23	75	47	72	.326	.463
Inning 1-6	.265	630	167	37	4	24	77	51	75	.322	.451
Inning 7+	.250	64	16	2	0	2	4	6	10	.329	.375
None on	.254	441	112	21	2	18	18	33	52	.313	.433
Runners on	.281	253	71	18	2	8	63	24	33	.339	.462
Scoring Posn	.266	128	34	9	1	2	47	13	19	.322	.398
Close & Late	.200	35	7	1	0	1	2	4	6	.293	.314
None on/out	.255	192	49	9	1	9	9	11	20	.299	.453
vs. 1st Batr (relief)	1.000	1	1	0	0	1	2	0	0	1.000	4.000
First Inning Pitched	.270	122	33	8	0	6	18	10	13	.326	.484
First 75 Pitches	.271	524	142	32	4	20	67	40	60	.326	.462
Pitch 76-90	.288	80	23	1	0	4	9	8	10	.352	.450
Pitch 91-105	.182	66	12	5	0	1	3	7	8	.260	.303
Pitch 106+	.250	24	6	1	0	1	2	2	7	.333	.417

1993 Season

	ERA	W	L	Sv	G	GS	IP	H	HR	BB	SO
4 Days Rest	4.21	7	7	0	17	17	104.2	108	9	30	42
5+ Days Rest	4.91	5	7	0	12	12	66.0	67	14	19	34
Pre-All Star	4.50	9	6	0	18	18	108.0	107	15	34	47
Post-All Star	4.24	4	9	0	14	13	76.1	76	11	23	38

	Avg	AB	H	2B	3B	HR	RBI	BB	SO	OBP	SLG
First Pitch	.333	96	32	9	2	3	15	0	0	.343	.563
Ahead in Count	.238	261	62	13	0	8	24	0	69	.244	.379
Behind in Count	.324	182	59	10	2	12	24	25	0	.402	.599
Two Strikes	.215	288	62	13	0	8	24	32	85	.297	.344

Last Five Years

	ERA	W	L	Sv	G	GS	IP	H	HR	BB	SO
Home	3.39	24	20	0	66	66	421.2	357	35	147	245
Away	4.28	20	36	0	77	76	454.2	440	52	178	256
Day	3.74	14	12	0	39	38	238.0	222	21	74	152
Night	3.89	30	44	0	104	104	638.1	575	66	251	349
Grass	4.32	14	26	0	55	54	320.2	322	35	126	179
Turf	3.58	30	30	0	88	88	555.2	475	52	199	322
April	3.15	7	5	0	19	19	120.0	104	6	42	61
May	4.74	9	9	0	24	24	142.1	136	13	62	72
June	4.40	7	6	0	22	22	133.0	127	21	59	70
July	3.92	7	10	0	25	25	149.1	131	18	58	94
August	4.12	5	17	0	27	27	177.0	161	17	62	116
September/October	2.73	9	9	0	26	25	154.2	138	12	42	88
Starter	3.84	44	56	0	142	142	875.2	795	86	324	500
Reliever	13.50	0	0	0	1	0	0.2	2	1	1	1
0-3 Days Rest	2.77	1	1	0	2	2	13.0	6	2	7	8
4 Days Rest	3.71	31	36	0	95	95	592.2	531	50	221	349
5+ Days Rest	4.20	12	19	0	45	45	270.0	258	34	96	143
Pre-All Star	4.12	25	24	0	73	73	443.1	408	49	187	240
Post-All Star	3.58	19	32	0	70	69	433.0	389	38	138	261

	Avg	AB	H	2B	3B	HR	RBI	BB	SO	OBP	SLG
vs. Left	.277	520	144	27	4	9	49	84	81	.380	.396
vs. Right	.240	2721	653	135	17	78	284	241	420	.302	.388
Inning 1-6	.248	2848	706	146	20	79	311	291	445	.319	.396
Inning 7+	.232	393	91	16	1	8	22	34	56	.293	.338
None on	.235	2001	471	89	11	58	58	180	293	.303	.378
Runners on	.263	1240	326	73	10	29	275	145	208	.335	.408
Scoring Posn	.253	688	174	38	6	14	228	107	135	.343	.387
Close & Late	.230	200	46	6	0	4	11	23	29	.310	.320
None on/out	.254	877	223	43	4	33	33	75	116	.317	.425
vs. 1st Batr (relief)	1.000	1	1	0	0	1	2	0	0	1.000	4.000
First Inning Pitched	.266	537	143	32	2	17	76	58	77	.336	.428
First 75 Pitches	.248	2369	587	125	17	64	250	235	364	.318	.396
Pitch 76-90	.267	389	104	17	2	10	42	38	61	.329	.398
Pitch 91-105	.214	295	63	12	1	8	29	29	47	.286	.342
Pitch 106+	.229	188	43	8	1	5	12	23	29	.312	.362
First Pitch	.309	489	151	37	6	12	61	16	0	.334	.483
Ahead in Count	.216	1246	269	49	5	23	96	0	370	.221	.319
Behind in Count	.280	743	208	46	8	28	98	171	0	.413	.476
Two Strikes	.189	1410	266	51	4	24	103	136	501	.261	.282

Pitcher vs. Batter (career)

Pitches Best Vs.	Avg	AB	H	2B	3B	HR	RBI	BB	SO	OBP	SLG
Luis Rivera	.000	12	0	0	0	0	0	0	5	.000	.000
Billy Hatcher	.045	22	1	0	0	0	0	1	2	.087	.045
Tim Raines	.095	21	2	0	0	0	1	0	2	.091	.095
Mike Sharperson	.105	19	2	0	0	0	0	0	1	.105	.105
Charlie Hayes	.105	19	2	0	0	0	1	0	4	.100	.105

Pitches Worst Vs.	Avg	AB	H	2B	3B	HR	RBI	BB	SO	OBP	SLG
Don Slaught	.583	12	7	3	0	0	3	3	1	.625	.833
Barry Larkin	.444	36	16	2	0	5	8	2	2	.474	.917
Randy Ready	.429	14	6	2	0	1	7	6	1	.571	.786
Lenny Dykstra	.429	7	3	0	1	0	1	4	0	.636	.714
Andre Dawson	.423	26	11	4	1	2	5	1	2	.444	.885

Delino DeShields — Expos

Age 25 – Bats Left (groundball hitter)

	Avg	G	AB	R	H	2B	3B	HR	RBI	BB	SO	HBP	GDP	SB	CS	OBP	SLG	IBB	SH	SF	#Pit	#P/PA	GB	FB	G/F
1993 Season	.295	123	481	75	142	17	7	2	29	72	64	3	5	43	10	.389	.372	3	4	2	2277	4.05	207	127	1.63
Career (1990-1993)	.277	538	2073	309	575	79	25	23	181	287	419	12	31	187	70	.367	.373	12	22	12	9795	4.07	857	445	1.93

1993 Season

	Avg	AB	H	2B	3B	HR	RBI	BB	SO	OBP	SLG
vs. Left	.311	161	50	8	3	2	13	24	22	.407	.435
vs. Right	.288	320	92	9	4	0	16	48	42	.379	.341
Groundball	.311	151	47	9	1	1	17	26	18	.413	.404
Flyball	.239	67	16	1	1	0	3	14	10	.373	.284
Home	.333	234	78	9	4	2	14	41	29	.435	.432
Away	.259	247	64	8	3	0	15	31	35	.343	.316
Day	.406	133	54	6	3	0	10	24	20	.497	.496
Night	.253	348	88	11	4	2	19	48	44	.346	.325
Grass	.256	160	41	4	0	0	11	16	21	.322	.281
Turf	.315	321	101	13	7	2	18	56	43	.420	.417
First Pitch	.386	44	17	1	1	0	5	3	0	.426	.455
Ahead in Count	.308	143	44	5	1	0	10	38	0	.454	.357
Behind in Count	.255	192	49	9	4	0	8	0	54	.262	.344
Two Strikes	.242	223	54	10	2	0	8	31	64	.336	.305

	Avg	AB	H	2B	3B	HR	RBI	BB	SO	OBP	SLG
Scoring Posn	.252	111	28	2	1	0	25	23	17	.375	.288
Close & Late	.318	85	27	1	1	0	10	10	16	.381	.353
None on/out	.326	190	62	10	3	1	1	26	25	.416	.426
Batting #1	.300	423	127	15	6	2	25	59	55	.388	.378
Batting #2	.259	58	15	2	1	0	4	13	9	.397	.328
Other	.000	0	0	0	0	0	0	0	0	.000	.000
April	.273	55	15	4	0	1	5	13	8	.412	.400
May	.276	105	29	4	0	1	5	20	16	.394	.343
June	.243	107	26	2	1	0	3	12	16	.325	.280
July	.393	117	46	4	3	0	10	8	10	.432	.479
August	.306	36	11	1	2	0	2	6	4	.405	.444
September/October	.246	61	15	2	1	0	4	13	10	.382	.311
Pre-All Star	.292	312	91	12	2	2	14	47	45	.387	.362
Post-All Star	.302	169	51	5	5	0	15	25	19	.393	.391

1993 By Position

Position	Avg	AB	H	2B	3B	HR	RBI	BB	SO	OBP	SLG	G	GS	Innings	PO	A	E	DP	Fld Pct	Rng Fctr	In Zone	Outs	Zone Rtg	MLB Zone
As 2b	.295	481	142	17	7	2	29	72	64	.389	.372	123	123	1073.2	244	381	11	74	.983	5.24	420	384	.914	.895

Career (1990-1993)

	Avg	AB	H	2B	3B	HR	RBI	BB	SO	OBP	SLG
vs. Left	.275	728	200	25	8	9	65	105	161	.371	.368
vs. Right	.279	1345	375	54	17	14	116	182	258	.364	.375
Groundball	.278	701	195	28	9	8	68	100	133	.370	.378
Flyball	.237	434	103	13	6	3	31	60	100	.331	.316
Home	.296	969	287	42	11	9	75	140	190	.388	.390
Away	.261	1104	288	37	14	14	106	147	229	.348	.358
Day	.305	580	177	25	5	4	55	84	131	.391	.386
Night	.267	1493	398	54	20	19	126	203	288	.357	.368
Grass	.254	619	157	19	6	7	60	80	131	.337	.338
Turf	.287	1454	418	60	19	16	121	207	288	.379	.388
First Pitch	.336	211	71	8	1	3	24	7	0	.365	.427
Ahead in Count	.356	528	188	27	11	11	74	145	0	.493	.511
Behind in Count	.201	854	172	26	8	0	38	0	330	.205	.251

	Avg	AB	H	2B	3B	HR	RBI	BB	SO	OBP	SLG
Scoring Posn	.273	440	120	23	5	3	152	87	93	.384	.368
Close & Late	.267	374	100	12	4	3	46	51	90	.353	.345
None on/out	.289	793	229	24	10	11	11	86	141	.364	.386
Batting #1	.282	1626	459	62	21	22	139	222	312	.371	.387
Batting #2	.271	362	98	14	4	0	29	50	76	.356	.331
Other	.212	85	18	3	0	1	13	15	31	.340	.282
April	.291	289	84	14	3	5	21	43	59	.383	.412
May	.247	381	94	14	2	6	25	67	82	.361	.341
June	.286	367	105	12	7	2	31	57	79	.383	.373
July	.338	385	130	17	4	3	34	41	56	.401	.426
August	.281	338	95	13	6	4	41	38	57	.360	.391
September/October	.214	313	67	9	3	3	29	41	86	.306	.291
Pre-All Star	.285	1156	330	45	13	15	85	180	244	.383	.386

Career (1990-1993)

	Avg	AB	H	2B	3B	HR	RBI	BB	SO	OBP	SLG
Two Strikes	.201	1025	206	29	7	1	45	132	419	.293	.246
Post-All Star	.267	917	245	34	12	8	96	107	175	.346	.357

Batter vs. Pitcher (career)

Hits Best Against	Avg	AB	H	2B	3B	HR	RBI	BB	SO	OBP	SLG
Tim Belcher	.556	9	5	0	0	0	2	3	1	.667	.556
Joe Magrane	.500	14	7	1	0	1	2	3	1	.588	.786
Bret Saberhagen	.462	13	6	1	1	0	1	4	3	.588	.692
Rheal Cormier	.462	13	6	0	0	1	3	3	4	.563	.692
Steve Cooke	.417	12	5	1	2	0	2	1	1	.462	.833

Hits Worst Against	Avg	AB	H	2B	3B	HR	RBI	BB	SO	OBP	SLG
Tom Candiotti	.000	8	0	0	0	0	0	3	2	.273	.000
Denny Neagle	.091	11	1	0	0	0	0	2	2	.231	.091
Tom Browning	.100	20	2	0	0	0	1	1	4	.143	.100
Bryn Smith	.167	18	3	0	0	0	0	0	5	.167	.167
Frank Tanana	.167	12	2	0	0	0	0	0	2	.167	.167

John DeSilva — Dodgers

Age 26 – Pitches Right

	ERA	W	L	Sv	G	GS	IP	BB	SO	Avg	H	2B	3B	HR	RBI	OBP	SLG	GF	IR	IRS	Hld	SvOp	SB	CS	GB	FB	G/F
1993 Season	7.11	0	0	0	4	0	6.1	1	6	.320	8	3	0	0	5	.333	.440	3	2	0	0	0	0	0	7	8	0.88

1993 Season

	ERA	W	L	Sv	G	GS	IP	H	HR	BB	SO
Home	6.75	0	0	0	1	0	1.1	2	0	0	0
Away	7.20	0	0	0	3	0	5.0	6	0	1	6

	Avg	AB	H	2B	3B	HR	RBI	BB	SO	OBP	SLG
vs. Left	.222	9	2	0	0	0	1	1	1	.273	.222
vs. Right	.375	16	6	3	0	0	4	0	5	.375	.563

Orestes Destrade — Marlins

Age 32 – Bats Both (flyball hitter)

	Avg	G	AB	R	H	2B	3B	HR	RBI	BB	SO	HBP	GDP	SB	CS	OBP	SLG	IBB	SH	SF	#Pit	#P/PA	GB	FB	G/F
1993 Season	.255	153	569	61	145	20	3	20	87	58	130	3	17	0	2	.324	.406	8	1	6	2299	3.61	170	175	0.97

1993 Season

	Avg	AB	H	2B	3B	HR	RBI	BB	SO	OBP	SLG
vs. Left	.294	177	52	5	3	6	28	13	39	.344	.458
vs. Right	.237	392	93	15	0	14	59	45	91	.315	.383
Groundball	.255	188	48	9	2	6	25	18	46	.327	.420
Flyball	.254	114	29	4	0	4	17	10	26	.305	.395
Home	.266	282	75	13	2	9	46	33	60	.343	.422
Away	.244	287	70	7	1	11	41	25	70	.305	.390
Day	.281	121	34	4	1	6	26	13	29	.350	.479
Night	.248	448	111	16	2	14	61	45	101	.317	.386
Grass	.235	425	100	16	2	15	69	52	101	.320	.388
Turf	.313	144	45	4	1	5	18	6	29	.338	.458
First Pitch	.333	93	31	3	1	4	16	2	0	.347	.516
Ahead in Count	.364	154	56	11	2	7	35	29	0	.459	.597
Behind in Count	.137	227	31	2	0	5	20	0	108	.142	.211
Two Strikes	.133	240	32	3	0	6	18	27	130	.222	.221

	Avg	AB	H	2B	3B	HR	RBI	BB	SO	OBP	SLG
Scoring Posn	.303	152	46	9	1	4	64	26	42	.395	.454
Close & Late	.239	88	21	3	1	0	10	14	23	.340	.295
None on/out	.181	144	26	2	1	5	5	9	34	.234	.313
Batting #4	.259	367	95	14	3	12	55	30	80	.314	.411
Batting #5	.237	198	47	5	0	7	29	26	49	.327	.369
Other	.750	4	3	1	0	1	3	2	1	.833	1.750
April	.273	88	24	3	1	1	11	11	12	.350	.364
May	.202	99	20	3	0	2	13	5	20	.248	.293
June	.316	98	31	5	2	4	16	8	24	.358	.531
July	.215	93	20	6	0	2	14	7	24	.277	.344
August	.301	93	28	1	0	8	16	14	24	.393	.570
September/October	.224	98	22	2	0	3	17	13	26	.316	.337
Pre-All Star	.250	324	81	13	3	7	43	26	67	.306	.373
Post-All Star	.261	245	64	7	0	13	44	32	63	.346	.449

1993 By Position

Position	Avg	AB	H	2B	3B	HR	RBI	BB	SO	OBP	SLG	G	GS	Innings	PO	A	E	DP	Fld Pct	Rng Fctr	In Zone	Outs	Zone Rtg	MLB Zone
As 1b	.255	568	145	20	3	20	87	57	129	.323	.407	152	151	1281.2	1310	89	19	108	.987	---	278	232	.835	.834

Mike Devereaux — Orioles

Age 31 – Bats Right

	Avg	G	AB	R	H	2B	3B	HR	RBI	BB	SO	HBP	GDP	SB	CS	OBP	SLG	IBB	SH	SF	#Pit	#P/PA	GB	FB	G/F
1993 Season	.250	131	527	72	132	31	3	14	75	43	99	1	13	3	3	.306	.400	0	2	4	2236	3.88	205	153	1.34
Last Five Years	.260	666	2546	333	662	119	28	77	336	198	416	9	57	64	43	.313	.419	3	15	24	10684	3.83	914	830	1.10

1993 Season

	Avg	AB	H	2B	3B	HR	RBI	BB	SO	OBP	SLG
vs. Left	.276	156	43	9	1	5	23	19	29	.352	.442
vs. Right	.240	371	89	22	2	9	52	24	70	.286	.383
Groundball	.258	89	23	7	0	1	11	5	19	.295	.371
Flyball	.231	91	21	6	1	3	15	8	21	.297	.418
Home	.263	247	65	20	2	8	48	27	41	.331	.457
Away	.239	280	67	11	1	6	27	16	58	.283	.350
Day	.260	154	40	5	2	5	23	5	23	.286	.416
Night	.247	373	92	26	1	9	52	38	76	.314	.394
Grass	.244	446	109	28	2	13	68	38	80	.303	.404
Turf	.284	81	23	3	1	1	7	5	19	.326	.383
First Pitch	.194	36	7	1	0	0	2	0	0	.194	.222
Ahead in Count	.303	132	40	10	0	6	26	20	0	.390	.515
Behind in Count	.211	256	54	10	2	5	29	0	85	.212	.324
Two Strikes	.195	256	50	7	2	5	25	23	99	.262	.297

	Avg	AB	H	2B	3B	HR	RBI	BB	SO	OBP	SLG
Scoring Posn	.291	158	46	12	2	4	61	9	25	.322	.468
Close & Late	.197	76	15	3	0	1	9	7	12	.262	.276
None on/out	.257	101	26	10	0	2	2	11	19	.336	.416
Batting #3	.247	287	71	10	1	9	47	27	58	.308	.383
Batting #5	.258	120	31	13	0	4	16	12	24	.326	.467
Other	.250	120	30	8	2	1	12	4	17	.280	.375
April	.229	96	22	6	2	1	11	2	13	.245	.365
May	.346	26	9	2	0	0	3	1	5	.393	.423
June	.248	105	26	10	0	3	12	13	20	.331	.429
July	.302	106	32	5	1	3	17	8	21	.348	.453
August	.216	111	24	5	0	4	17	13	19	.294	.369
September/October	.229	83	19	3	0	3	15	6	21	.278	.373
Pre-All Star	.253	273	69	21	2	5	32	17	45	.298	.399
Post-All Star	.248	254	63	10	1	9	43	26	54	.314	.402

1993 By Position

Position	Avg	AB	H	2B	3B	HR	RBI	BB	SO	OBP	SLG	G	GS	Innings	PO	A	E	DP	Fld Pct	Rng Fctr	In Zone	Outs	Zone Rtg	MLB Zone
As cf	.250	527	132	31	3	14	75	43	99	.306	.400	130	130	1130.0	310	8	4	3	.988	2.53	376	303	.806	.829

Last Five Years

	Avg	AB	H	2B	3B	HR	RBI	BB	SO	OBP	SLG
vs. Left	.287	840	241	42	11	30	106	73	122	.343	.470
vs. Right	.247	1706	421	77	17	47	230	125	294	.298	.394
Groundball	.262	614	161	34	6	17	83	62	94	.327	.420

	Avg	AB	H	2B	3B	HR	RBI	BB	SO	OBP	SLG
Scoring Posn	.268	639	171	38	11	21	262	49	99	.311	.460
Close & Late	.239	402	96	9	2	14	54	32	72	.293	.376
None on/out	.253	655	166	35	6	19	19	56	107	.315	.412

Last Five Years

	Avg	AB	H	2B	3B	HR	RBI	BB	SO	OBP	SLG
Flyball	.241	536	129	30	6	16	71	40	106	.295	.409
Home	.253	1227	310	59	15	42	177	108	193	.312	.428
Away	.267	1319	352	60	13	35	159	90	223	.314	.412
Day	.255	694	177	28	6	18	75	43	110	.300	.390
Night	.262	1852	485	91	22	59	261	155	306	.318	.430
Grass	.256	2133	546	97	25	71	288	171	353	.311	.425
Turf	.281	413	116	22	3	6	48	27	63	.325	.392
First Pitch	.256	203	52	9	1	7	31	2	0	.262	.414
Ahead in Count	.315	615	194	35	6	29	101	103	0	.410	.533
Behind in Count	.217	1204	261	44	16	24	124	0	349	.219	.340
Two Strikes	.213	1238	264	38	16	24	113	93	416	.269	.328

	Avg	AB	H	2B	3B	HR	RBI	BB	SO	OBP	SLG
Batting #1	.262	791	207	37	11	20	73	67	141	.320	.412
Batting #2	.269	662	178	30	13	21	115	40	84	.308	.449
Other	.253	1093	277	52	4	36	148	91	191	.310	.407
April	.233	300	70	15	4	8	31	23	41	.289	.390
May	.284	292	83	22	2	9	39	22	45	.334	.466
June	.265	468	124	23	7	13	57	41	70	.322	.427
July	.286	479	137	17	7	15	66	38	84	.337	.445
August	.239	503	120	20	5	16	74	47	80	.304	.394
September/October	.254	504	128	22	3	16	69	27	96	.292	.405
Pre-All Star	.262	1226	321	66	14	34	146	93	182	.313	.422
Post-All Star	.258	1320	341	53	14	43	190	105	234	.313	.417

Batter vs. Pitcher (career)

Hits Best Against	Avg	AB	H	2B	3B	HR	RBI	BB	SO	OBP	SLG
Jim Abbott	.565	23	13	2	0	1	2	6	2	.655	.783
Dave Fleming	.500	16	8	2	0	2	6	3	1	.579	1.000
Bobby Thigpen	.500	14	7	3	0	0	5	0	4	.500	.714
Bill Krueger	.476	21	10	1	0	2	2	0	2	.476	.810
Jeff Johnson	.364	11	4	0	1	1	4	1	1	.417	.818

Hits Worst Against	Avg	AB	H	2B	3B	HR	RBI	BB	SO	OBP	SLG
Bobby Witt	.063	16	1	0	0	0	0	1	2	.118	.063
Tom Henke	.067	15	1	0	0	0	0	1	6	.125	.067
Bret Saberhagen	.077	13	1	0	0	0	1	0	3	.077	.077
Wilson Alvarez	.100	20	2	0	0	0	0	0	5	.100	.100
Curt Young	.105	19	2	0	0	0	0	1	2	.150	.105

Mark Dewey — Pirates

Age 29 – Pitches Right (groundball pitcher)

	ERA	W	L	Sv	G	GS	IP	BB	SO	Avg	H	2B	3B	HR	RBI	OBP	SLG	GF	IR	IRS	Hld	SvOp	SB	CS	GB	FB	G/F
1993 Season	2.36	1	2	7	21	0	26.2	10	14	.157	14	5	1	0	12	.257	.236	17	12	5	0	12	2	0	35	32	1.09
Career (1990-1993)	3.27	3	3	7	55	0	82.2	25	49	.239	73	13	3	3	37	.300	.330	28	30	13	2	13	5	4	130	81	1.60

1993 Season

	ERA	W	L	Sv	G	GS	IP	H	HR	BB	SO
Home	1.69	1	0	1	8	0	10.2	6	0	1	9
Away	2.81	0	2	6	13	0	16.0	8	0	9	5

	Avg	AB	H	2B	3B	HR	RBI	BB	SO	OBP	SLG
vs. Left	.194	36	7	2	0	0	7	6	5	.295	.250
vs. Right	.132	53	7	3	1	0	5	4	9	.230	.226

Alex Diaz — Brewers

Age 25 – Bats Both (groundball hitter)

	Avg	G	AB	R	H	2B	3B	HR	RBI	BB	SO	HBP	GDP	SB	CS	OBP	SLG	IBB	SH	SF	#Pit	#P/PA	GB	FB	G/F
1993 Season	.319	32	69	9	22	2	0	0	1	0	12	0	3	5	3	.319	.348	0	3	0	196	2.72	30	9	3.33
Career (1992-1993)	.295	54	78	14	23	2	0	0	2	0	12	0	3	8	5	.295	.321	0	3	0	218	2.69	32	15	2.13

1993 Season

	Avg	AB	H	2B	3B	HR	RBI	BB	SO	OBP	SLG
vs. Left	.382	34	13	2	0	0	0	0	6	.382	.441
vs. Right	.257	35	9	0	0	0	1	0	6	.257	.257

	Avg	AB	H	2B	3B	HR	RBI	BB	SO	OBP	SLG
Scoring Posn	.235	17	4	0	0	0	1	0	5	.235	.235
Close & Late	.467	15	7	1	0	0	1	0	3	.467	.533

Mario Diaz — Rangers

Age 32 – Bats Right (groundball hitter)

	Avg	G	AB	R	H	2B	3B	HR	RBI	BB	SO	HBP	GDP	SB	CS	OBP	SLG	IBB	SH	SF	#Pit	#P/PA	GB	FB	G/F
1993 Season	.273	71	205	24	56	10	1	2	24	8	13	1	6	1	0	.297	.361	0	7	5	786	3.48	105	47	2.23
Last Five Years	.241	254	514	59	124	19	1	4	55	31	43	1	15	1	2	.282	.305	1	17	7	1934	3.39	229	146	1.57

1993 Season

	Avg	AB	H	2B	3B	HR	RBI	BB	SO	OBP	SLG
vs. Left	.333	51	17	4	0	1	6	4	4	.375	.471
vs. Right	.253	154	39	6	1	1	18	4	9	.270	.325
Home	.238	105	25	2	0	1	9	4	7	.268	.286
Away	.310	100	31	8	1	1	15	4	6	.327	.440
First Pitch	.200	35	7	0	0	0	4	0	0	.216	.200
Ahead in Count	.333	42	14	5	0	0	9	3	0	.370	.452
Behind in Count	.267	90	24	3	1	2	11	0	11	.258	.389
Two Strikes	.238	84	20	2	0	1	10	5	13	.272	.298

	Avg	AB	H	2B	3B	HR	RBI	BB	SO	OBP	SLG
Scoring Posn	.319	47	15	2	0	0	21	0	4	.302	.362
Close & Late	.400	20	8	0	0	0	3	1	1	.429	.400
None on/out	.291	55	16	4	1	1	1	1	3	.304	.455
Batting #2	.271	48	13	3	0	1	7	3	2	.296	.396
Batting #9	.298	104	31	2	0	1	13	3	10	.318	.346
Other	.226	53	12	5	1	0	4	2	1	.255	.358
Pre-All Star	.313	67	21	5	1	1	11	0	5	.313	.463
Post-All Star	.254	138	35	5	0	1	13	8	8	.289	.312

Last Five Years

	Avg	AB	H	2B	3B	HR	RBI	BB	SO	OBP	SLG
vs. Left	.258	194	50	9	0	1	22	16	16	.311	.320
vs. Right	.231	320	74	10	1	3	33	15	27	.264	.297
Groundball	.274	113	31	6	0	1	8	6	10	.311	.354
Flyball	.227	97	22	3	0	1	9	5	8	.260	.289
Home	.226	239	54	7	0	2	21	16	18	.273	.280
Away	.255	275	70	12	1	2	34	15	25	.290	.327
Day	.231	104	24	8	0	1	11	6	7	.270	.337
Night	.244	410	100	11	1	3	44	25	36	.285	.298
Grass	.258	392	101	16	0	4	48	25	31	.299	.329
Turf	.189	122	23	3	1	0	7	6	12	.227	.230
First Pitch	.233	90	21	1	0	1	12	1	0	.247	.278
Ahead in Count	.295	112	33	7	0	0	20	18	0	.386	.357
Behind in Count	.213	216	46	7	1	2	18	0	39	.209	.282
Two Strikes	.201	204	41	3	0	1	18	12	43	.241	.230

	Avg	AB	H	2B	3B	HR	RBI	BB	SO	OBP	SLG
Scoring Posn	.252	131	33	2	0	0	47	7	8	.281	.267
Close & Late	.347	75	26	1	0	0	6	4	10	.380	.360
None on/out	.211	123	26	7	1	1	1	8	12	.260	.309
Batting #8	.218	147	32	10	1	0	10	7	7	.252	.299
Batting #9	.259	247	64	6	0	2	29	15	29	.302	.308
Other	.233	120	28	3	0	2	16	9	7	.278	.308
April	.171	35	6	0	0	1	4	2	1	.216	.257
May	.259	54	14	4	0	1	11	5	2	.322	.389
June	.288	80	23	2	0	1	8	5	5	.329	.350
July	.266	109	29	6	1	0	12	4	14	.284	.339
August	.179	134	24	5	0	1	12	5	14	.213	.239
September/October	.275	102	28	2	0	0	8	10	7	.330	.294
Pre-All Star	.274	197	54	10	1	3	28	12	11	.316	.381
Post-All Star	.221	317	70	9	0	1	27	19	32	.262	.259

Batter vs. Pitcher (career)

Hits Best Against	Avg	AB	H	2B	3B	HR	RBI	BB	SO	OBP	SLG
Alex Fernandez	.500	10	5	0	0	0	1	1	0	.545	.500

Hits Worst Against	Avg	AB	H	2B	3B	HR	RBI	BB	SO	OBP	SLG

Rob Dibble — Reds

Age 30 – Pitches Right

	ERA	W	L	Sv	G	GS	IP	BB	SO	Avg	H	2B	3B	HR	RBI	OBP	SLG	GF	IR	IRS	Hld	SvOp	SB	CS	GB	FB	G/F
1993 Season	6.48	1	4	19	45	0	41.2	42	49	.225	34	2	2	8	33	.400	.424	37	19	7	0	28	13	2	40	42	0.95
Last Five Years	2.87	25	22	88	317	0	391.1	171	560	.196	273	43	8	23	171	.265	.288	172	215	55	44	119	76	14	356	304	1.17

1993 Season

	ERA	W	L	Sv	G	GS	IP	H	HR	BB	SO
Home	8.71	0	0	9	21	0	20.2	18	5	24	21
Away	4.29	1	4	10	24	0	21.0	16	3	18	28
Starter	0.00	0	0	0	0	0	0.0	0	0	0	0
Reliever	6.48	1	4	19	45	0	41.2	34	8	42	49
0 Days rest	5.63	0	1	5	9	0	8.0	8	3	8	11
1 or 2 Days rest	7.36	1	2	8	19	0	18.1	16	3	20	23
3+ Days rest	5.87	0	1	6	17	0	15.1	10	2	14	15
Pre-All Star	2.78	1	0	12	23	0	22.2	12	2	22	28
Post-All Star	10.89	0	4	7	22	0	19.0	22	6	20	21

	Avg	AB	H	2B	3B	HR	RBI	BB	SO	OBP	SLG
vs. Left	.247	73	18	2	0	5	15	31	20	.476	.479
vs. Right	.205	78	16	0	2	3	18	11	29	.311	.372
Scoring Posn	.222	54	12	0	2	2	25	18	20	.417	.407
Close & Late	.225	89	20	2	1	5	25	30	24	.425	.438
None on/out	.179	28	5	1	0	0	0	9	6	.395	.214
First Pitch	.417	12	5	0	0	2	4	0	0	.462	.917
Ahead in Count	.118	85	10	1	0	2	5	0	41	.118	.200
Behind in Count	.485	33	16	1	2	4	21	26	0	.712	1.000
Two Strikes	.098	82	8	1	0	1	4	16	49	.253	.146

Last Five Years

	ERA	W	L	Sv	G	GS	IP	H	HR	BB	SO
Home	3.12	11	8	49	153	0	187.2	131	12	92	272
Away	2.65	14	14	39	164	0	203.2	142	11	79	288
Day	2.37	10	3	24	88	0	117.2	74	7	58	167
Night	3.09	15	19	64	229	0	273.2	199	16	113	393
Grass	2.90	7	9	22	99	0	127.1	95	9	48	171
Turf	2.86	18	13	66	218	0	264.0	178	14	123	389
April	2.47	4	0	14	45	0	51.0	39	1	26	73
May	2.33	3	3	14	48	0	58.0	39	1	28	91
June	2.32	4	5	21	64	0	81.1	45	5	35	121
July	2.60	2	2	11	45	0	55.1	39	3	28	65
August	3.06	7	7	14	61	0	82.1	53	8	30	121
September/October	4.41	5	5	14	54	0	63.1	58	5	24	89
Starter	0.00	0	0	0	0	0	0.0	0	0	0	0
Reliever	2.87	25	22	88	317	0	391.1	273	23	171	560
0 Days rest	3.29	4	6	24	71	0	76.2	61	6	34	113
1 or 2 Days rest	2.51	17	14	43	169	0	222.1	139	11	90	328
3+ Days rest	3.41	4	2	21	77	0	92.1	73	6	47	119
Pre-All Star	2.44	11	9	55	175	0	210.0	138	10	98	308
Post-All Star	3.38	14	13	33	142	0	181.1	135	13	73	252

	Avg	AB	H	2B	3B	HR	RBI	BB	SO	OBP	SLG
vs. Left	.193	719	139	25	3	11	80	116	300	.304	.282
vs. Right	.199	673	134	18	5	12	91	55	260	.263	.294
Inning 1-6	.102	49	5	0	0	1	6	7	21	.203	.163
Inning 7+	.200	1343	268	43	8	22	165	164	539	.288	.293
None on	.188	714	134	20	5	12	12	82	306	.275	.280
Runners on	.205	678	139	23	3	11	159	89	254	.295	.296
Scoring Posn	.193	492	95	16	3	8	151	67	194	.285	.287
Close & Late	.221	842	186	28	5	17	129	106	325	.309	.327
None on/out	.193	300	58	11	1	4	4	37	116	.286	.277
vs. 1st Batr (relief)	.207	276	57	8	1	6	33	32	110	.289	.308
First Inning Pitched	.200	1005	201	30	7	21	149	133	395	.294	.306
First 15 Pitches	.207	869	180	26	4	20	101	102	334	.292	.315
Pitch 16-30	.174	432	75	11	3	3	56	57	181	.270	.234
Pitch 31-45	.182	88	16	6	1	0	13	12	45	.275	.273
Pitch 46+	.667	3	2	0	0	0	1	0	0	.667	.667
First Pitch	.431	137	59	7	2	8	35	16	0	.500	.686
Ahead in Count	.131	834	109	20	1	6	62	0	482	.130	.179
Behind in Count	.325	203	66	10	4	6	44	81	0	.512	.502
Two Strikes	.106	846	90	20	0	3	56	72	560	.176	.141

Pitcher vs. Batter (career)

Pitches Best Vs.	Avg	AB	H	2B	3B	HR	RBI	BB	SO	OBP	SLG
Darryl Strawberry	.000	10	0	0	0	0	0	2	6	.167	.000
Matt D. Williams	.067	15	1	0	0	0	0	0	9	.067	.067
Ricky Jordan	.083	12	1	1	0	0	1	1	3	.154	.167
Craig Biggio	.133	15	2	0	0	0	2	1	7	.188	.133
Dale Murphy	.150	20	3	0	0	0	2	0	11	.150	.150

Pitches Worst Vs.	Avg	AB	H	2B	3B	HR	RBI	BB	SO	OBP	SLG
Willie McGee	.455	11	5	0	0	0	1	2	2	.538	.455
Ozzie Smith	.429	14	6	0	0	0	4	1	2	.467	.429
Juan Samuel	.400	10	4	1	0	1	7	0	4	.364	.800
Will Clark	.333	15	5	2	0	0	0	0	6	.333	.467
Doug Dascenzo	.333	9	3	0	1	0	3	2	2	.455	.556

Frank DiPino — Royals

Age 37 – Pitches Left (groundball pitcher)

	ERA	W	L	Sv	G	GS	IP	BB	SO	Avg	H	2B	3B	HR	RBI	OBP	SLG	GF	IR	IRS	Hld	SvOp	SB	CS	GB	FB	G/F
1993 Season	6.89	1	1	0	11	0	15.2	6	5	.328	21	8	1	2	12	.392	.578	5	6	2	0	0	0	0	27	21	1.29
Last Five Years	3.63	15	3	3	149	0	196.0	60	106	.264	195	41	8	16	110	.316	.406	32	128	45	12	8	7	5	330	182	1.81

1993 Season

	ERA	W	L	Sv	G	GS	IP	H	HR	BB	SO
Home	4.35	0	0	0	6	0	10.1	12	1	3	2
Away	11.81	1	1	0	5	0	5.1	9	1	3	3

	Avg	AB	H	2B	3B	HR	RBI	BB	SO	OBP	SLG
vs. Left	.333	12	4	3	0	0	3	2	1	.467	.583
vs. Right	.327	52	17	5	1	2	9	4	4	.373	.577

Last Five Years

	ERA	W	L	Sv	G	GS	IP	H	HR	BB	SO
Home	2.90	7	2	3	76	0	102.1	96	8	33	54
Away	4.42	8	1	0	73	0	93.2	99	8	27	52
Day	3.41	5	0	1	49	0	58.0	62	5	16	34
Night	3.72	10	3	2	100	0	138.0	133	11	44	72
Grass	4.30	6	1	0	42	0	52.1	57	4	14	27
Turf	3.38	9	2	3	107	0	143.2	138	12	46	79
April	1.98	1	0	0	19	0	27.1	21	2	6	6
May	4.01	3	0	0	22	0	24.2	28	4	6	11
June	6.16	4	2	0	26	0	30.2	36	3	15	18
July	3.69	2	0	2	24	0	39.0	41	4	9	23
August	4.00	2	1	1	23	0	27.0	26	1	9	13
September/October	2.47	3	0	0	35	0	47.1	43	2	15	35
Starter	0.00	0	0	0	0	0	0.0	0	0	0	0
Reliever	3.63	15	3	3	149	0	196.0	195	16	60	106
0 Days rest	4.63	2	1	1	32	0	44.2	48	4	14	22
1 or 2 Days rest	3.55	9	2	1	74	0	99.0	97	9	29	51
3+ Days rest	2.92	4	0	1	43	0	52.1	50	3	17	33
Pre-All Star	4.09	10	2	0	78	0	101.1	108	11	32	42
Post-All Star	3.14	5	1	3	71	0	94.2	87	5	28	64

	Avg	AB	H	2B	3B	HR	RBI	BB	SO	OBP	SLG
vs. Left	.252	290	73	14	1	2	36	21	44	.302	.328
vs. Right	.272	449	122	27	7	14	74	39	62	.325	.457
Inning 1-6	.259	297	77	19	2	7	48	21	44	.304	.407
Inning 7+	.267	442	118	22	6	9	62	39	62	.324	.405
None on	.254	398	101	17	3	6	6	29	59	.306	.357
Runners on	.276	341	94	24	5	10	104	31	47	.327	.463
Scoring Posn	.278	209	58	14	3	6	88	28	29	.345	.459
Close & Late	.272	114	31	5	1	3	24	14	18	.341	.412
None on/out	.251	175	44	7	2	4	4	9	24	.288	.383
vs. 1st Batr (relief)	.264	129	34	9	4	4	29	11	21	.306	.488
First Inning Pitched	.265	438	116	24	8	11	84	41	66	.320	.432
First 15 Pitches	.274	430	118	22	7	12	77	39	56	.329	.442
Pitch 16-30	.230	217	50	12	1	3	24	12	39	.272	.336
Pitch 31-45	.343	70	24	7	0	1	9	8	8	.410	.486
Pitch 46+	.136	22	3	0	0	0	0	1	3	.174	.136
First Pitch	.270	115	31	8	0	4	16	19	0	.368	.443
Ahead in Count	.249	333	83	20	6	2	48	0	92	.251	.363
Behind in Count	.281	160	45	8	0	7	26	22	0	.368	.463
Two Strikes	.256	324	83	19	5	3	47	19	106	.295	.373

Pitcher vs. Batter (since 1984)

Pitches Best Vs.	Avg	AB	H	2B	3B	HR	RBI	BB	SO	OBP	SLG
Will Clark	.000	11	0	0	0	0	0	4	1	.267	.000
Tony Gwynn	.056	18	1	0	0	0	2	1	2	.100	.056
Tim Wallach	.077	13	1	0	0	0	0	2	5	.200	.077
Mike LaValliere	.111	18	2	1	0	0	2	0	4	.111	.167
John Kruk	.111	18	2	0	0	0	1	0	9	.111	.111

Pitches Worst Vs.	Avg	AB	H	2B	3B	HR	RBI	BB	SO	OBP	SLG
Glenn Wilson	.667	12	8	1	0	2	5	3	0	.733	1.250
Candy Maldonado	.615	13	8	0	0	1	5	1	2	.643	.846
Paul O'Neill	.545	11	6	3	1	0	5	3	3	.643	1.000
Eric Davis	.455	11	5	2	0	1	5	5	2	.625	.909
Howard Johnson	.350	20	7	0	0	4	6	4	5	.458	.950

Jerry DiPoto — Indians

Age 26 – Pitches Right (groundball pitcher)

	ERA	W	L	Sv	G	GS	IP	BB	SO	Avg	H	2B	3B	HR	RBI	OBP	SLG	GF	IR	IRS	Hld	SvOp	SB	CS	GB	FB	G/F
1993 Season	2.40	4	4	11	46	0	56.1	30	41	.270	57	7	0	0	23	.361	.303	26	30	10	6	17	1	0	105	32	3.28

1993 Season

	ERA	W	L	Sv	G	GS	IP	H	HR	BB	SO
Home	1.65	1	2	5	21	0	27.1	33	0	15	27
Away	3.10	3	2	6	25	0	29.0	24	0	15	14
Starter	0.00	0	0	0	0	0	0.0	0	0	0	0
Reliever	2.40	4	4	11	46	0	56.1	57	0	30	41
0 Days rest	1.29	2	1	6	18	0	21.0	17	0	9	15
1 or 2 Days rest	2.66	1	3	5	19	0	23.2	22	0	16	19
3+ Days rest	3.86	1	0	0	9	0	11.2	18	0	5	7
Pre-All Star	5.14	0	0	0	7	0	7.0	10	0	4	2
Post-All Star	2.01	4	4	11	39	0	49.1	47	0	26	39

	Avg	AB	H	2B	3B	HR	RBI	BB	SO	OBP	SLG
vs. Left	.271	85	23	0	0	0	5	18	12	.394	.271
vs. Right	.270	126	34	7	0	0	18	12	29	.336	.325
Scoring Posn	.250	76	19	3	0	0	23	13	13	.359	.289
Close & Late	.271	140	38	6	0	0	18	19	23	.358	.314
None on/out	.372	43	16	1	0	0	0	8	9	.471	.395
First Pitch	.304	23	7	2	0	0	2	6	0	.448	.391
Ahead in Count	.190	100	19	2	0	0	9	0	34	.196	.210
Behind in Count	.366	41	15	1	0	0	5	14	0	.518	.390
Two Strikes	.152	99	15	0	0	0	8	10	41	.234	.152

Gary DiSarcina — Angels

Age 26 – Bats Right (groundball hitter)

	Avg	G	AB	R	H	2B	3B	HR	RBI	BB	SO	HBP	GDP	SB	CS	OBP	SLG	IBB	SH	SF	#Pit	#P/PA	GB	FB	G/F
1993 Season	.238	126	416	44	99	20	1	3	45	15	38	6	13	5	7	.273	.313	0	5	3	1517	3.41	180	122	1.48
Career (1989-1993)	.236	321	1048	105	247	42	2	6	90	41	102	15	31	15	14	.273	.297	0	13	6	3643	3.24	457	282	1.62

1993 Season

	Avg	AB	H	2B	3B	HR	RBI	BB	SO	OBP	SLG
vs. Left	.210	119	25	4	0	0	7	3	10	.234	.244
vs. Right	.249	297	74	16	1	3	38	12	28	.288	.340
Groundball	.313	83	26	6	1	1	15	2	6	.337	.446
Flyball	.167	96	16	5	0	0	5	5	11	.216	.219
Home	.250	216	54	8	1	2	28	7	19	.279	.324
Away	.225	200	45	12	0	1	17	8	19	.265	.300
Day	.239	113	27	6	1	1	9	4	12	.283	.336
Night	.238	303	72	14	0	2	36	11	26	.269	.304
Grass	.231	355	82	16	1	3	36	13	35	.268	.307
Turf	.279	61	17	4	0	0	9	2	3	.302	.344
First Pitch	.322	59	19	2	0	1	8	0	0	.333	.407
Ahead in Count	.250	104	26	9	0	2	14	8	0	.298	.394
Behind in Count	.251	175	44	7	1	0	16	0	34	.271	.303
Two Strikes	.205	156	32	4	0	0	12	7	38	.253	.231

	Avg	AB	H	2B	3B	HR	RBI	BB	SO	OBP	SLG
Scoring Posn	.267	116	31	6	0	1	40	5	5	.307	.345
Close & Late	.176	74	13	1	0	0	7	2	8	.218	.189
None on/out	.227	97	22	6	1	0	0	5	11	.272	.309
Batting #8	.216	199	43	9	0	1	20	6	15	.240	.276
Batting #9	.268	194	52	10	1	2	25	9	21	.313	.361
Other	.174	23	4	1	0	0	0	0	2	.208	.217
April	.227	66	15	4	0	1	6	1	8	.239	.333
May	.231	91	21	3	0	1	12	4	5	.265	.297
June	.281	89	25	6	1	1	15	5	11	.316	.404
July	.229	96	22	4	0	0	9	4	8	.282	.271
August	.216	74	16	3	0	0	3	1	6	.247	.257
September/October	.000	0	0	0	0	0	0	0	0	.000	.000
Pre-All Star	.260	289	75	15	1	3	39	11	24	.286	.349
Post-All Star	.189	127	24	5	0	0	6	4	14	.243	.228

1993 By Position

Position	Avg	AB	H	2B	3B	HR	RBI	BB	SO	OBP	SLG	G	GS	Innings	PO	A	E	DP	Fld Pct	Rng Fctr	In Zone	Outs	Zone Rtg	MLB Zone
As ss	.239	415	99	20	1	3	45	15	37	.273	.313	126	124	1072.1	194	364	14	79	.976	4.68	417	382	.916	.880

Career (1989-1993)

	Avg	AB	H	2B	3B	HR	RBI	BB	SO	OBP	SLG
vs. Left	.209	263	55	9	0	0	12	9	24	.239	.243
vs. Right	.245	785	192	33	2	6	78	32	78	.284	.315
Groundball	.277	242	67	13	1	1	23	8	24	.307	.351
Flyball	.173	260	45	7	0	1	14	15	30	.229	.212
Home	.227	520	118	18	1	4	53	20	46	.264	.288
Away	.244	528	129	24	1	2	37	21	56	.281	.305
Day	.241	290	70	15	1	3	21	16	29	.290	.331
Night	.234	758	177	27	1	3	69	25	73	.266	.284
Grass	.227	874	198	32	1	5	72	36	86	.267	.283
Turf	.282	174	49	10	1	1	18	5	16	.306	.368
First Pitch	.303	185	56	10	0	2	18	0	0	.312	.389
Ahead in Count	.257	237	61	16	1	4	23	19	0	.313	.384
Behind in Count	.203	454	92	14	1	0	32	0	93	.217	.238
Two Strikes	.181	376	68	9	0	0	26	22	102	.236	.205

	Avg	AB	H	2B	3B	HR	RBI	BB	SO	OBP	SLG
Scoring Posn	.239	251	60	10	0	1	79	15	22	.296	.291
Close & Late	.143	182	26	2	0	1	14	11	23	.204	.170
None on/out	.246	248	61	13	1	0	0	12	22	.286	.306
Batting #8	.232	285	66	12	0	1	24	8	26	.253	.284
Batting #9	.237	641	152	26	2	5	56	32	66	.284	.307
Other	.238	122	29	4	0	0	10	1	10	.260	.270
April	.266	128	34	7	0	1	9	7	17	.307	.344
May	.210	200	42	5	0	1	17	11	18	.255	.250
June	.256	195	50	11	2	3	22	7	18	.288	.379
July	.222	180	40	6	0	0	16	8	16	.267	.256
August	.232	177	41	7	0	1	18	2	15	.255	.288
September/October	.238	168	40	6	0	0	8	6	18	.277	.274
Pre-All Star	.242	599	145	26	2	5	55	27	58	.278	.317
Post-All Star	.227	449	102	16	0	1	35	14	44	.266	.269

Batter vs. Pitcher (career)

Hits Best Against	Avg	AB	H	2B	3B	HR	RBI	BB	SO	OBP	SLG
Dave Fleming	.545	11	6	2	0	0	2	0	0	.545	.727
Melido Perez	.500	14	7	1	0	1	6	3	0	.588	.786
Wilson Alvarez	.455	11	5	2	0	0	2	1	1	.500	.636
Kevin Appier	.429	14	6	1	0	1	4	3	1	.529	.714
Erik Hanson	.313	16	5	2	0	1	2	1	0	.353	.625

Hits Worst Against	Avg	AB	H	2B	3B	HR	RBI	BB	SO	OBP	SLG
Dave Stewart	.000	12	0	0	0	0	0	1	3	.077	.000
Kenny Rogers	.000	11	0	0	0	0	0	0	0	.000	.000
Kevin Tapani	.067	15	1	0	0	0	0	0	3	.067	.067
Jaime Navarro	.071	14	1	0	0	0	1	0	0	.071	.071
Todd Stottlemyre	.091	11	1	0	0	0	0	0	0	.091	.091

Steve Dixon — Cardinals

Age 24 – Pitches Left

	ERA	W	L	Sv	G	GS	IP	BB	SO	Avg	H	2B	3B	HR	RBI	OBP	SLG	GF	IR	IRS	Hld	SvOp	SB	CS	GB	FB	G/F
1993 Season	33.75	0	0	0	4	0	2.2	5	2	.538	7	2	0	1	7	.667	.923	0	3	1	0	0	0	0	3	3	1.00

1993 Season

	ERA	W	L	Sv	G	GS	IP	H	HR	BB	SO
Home	0.00	0	0	0	1	0	0.0	0	0	1	0
Away	33.75	0	0	0	3	0	2.2	7	1	4	2

	Avg	AB	H	2B	3B	HR	RBI	BB	SO	OBP	SLG
vs. Left	.400	5	2	1	0	0	5	3	1	.625	.600
vs. Right	.625	8	5	1	0	1	2	2	1	.700	1.125

John Doherty — Tigers

Age 27 – Pitches Right (groundball pitcher)

	ERA	W	L	Sv	G	GS	IP	BB	SO	Avg	H	2B	3B	HR	RBI	OBP	SLG	CG	ShO	Sup	QS	#P/S	SB	CS	GB	FB	G/F
1993 Season	4.44	14	11	0	32	31	184.2	48	63	.286	205	34	4	19	88	.333	.423	3	2	5.85	14	86	7	12	373	142	2.63
Career (1992-1993)	4.22	21	15	3	79	42	300.2	73	100	.286	336	47	5	23	139	.331	.393	3	2	6.17	21	84	11	16	621	224	2.77

1993 Season

	ERA	W	L	Sv	G	GS	IP	H	HR	BB	SO
Home	4.76	6	6	0	17	17	96.1	110	13	31	36
Away	4.08	8	5	0	15	14	88.1	95	6	17	27
Day	6.18	4	8	0	15	14	71.1	94	10	24	20
Night	3.34	10	3	0	17	17	113.1	111	9	24	43
Grass	4.67	12	10	0	28	28	163.2	183	17	47	58
Turf	2.57	2	1	0	4	3	21.0	22	2	1	5
April	2.08	3	1	0	5	5	34.2	30	5	7	9
May	5.09	1	1	0	4	4	23.0	28	4	11	7
June	3.18	3	1	0	4	4	22.2	21	0	9	8
July	6.06	2	3	0	7	6	35.2	48	4	3	11
August	6.07	2	4	0	6	6	29.2	31	3	13	10
September/October	4.15	3	1	0	6	6	39.0	47	3	5	18
Starter	4.47	14	11	0	31	31	183.1	203	19	47	63
Reliever	0.00	0	0	0	1	0	1.1	2	0	1	0
0-3 Days Rest	2.57	2	1	0	3	3	21.0	16	3	7	6
4 Days Rest	5.86	7	9	0	20	20	109.0	140	13	27	39
5+ Days Rest	2.36	5	1	0	8	8	53.1	47	3	13	18
Pre-All Star	3.80	8	5	0	16	16	97.0	104	11	27	28
Post-All Star	5.13	6	6	0	16	15	87.2	101	8	21	35

	Avg	AB	H	2B	3B	HR	RBI	BB	SO	OBP	SLG
vs. Left	.308	389	120	19	3	12	42	24	36	.347	.465
vs. Right	.258	329	85	15	1	7	46	24	27	.317	.374
Inning 1-6	.283	615	174	27	3	18	82	45	54	.334	.424
Inning 7+	.301	103	31	7	1	1	6	3	9	.327	.417
None on	.277	441	122	18	2	12	12	20	41	.313	.408
Runners on	.300	277	83	16	2	7	76	28	22	.363	.448
Scoring Posn	.324	148	48	8	2	7	73	20	14	.402	.547
Close & Late	.333	57	19	3	0	1	6	1	4	.356	.439
None on/out	.262	191	50	5	1	4	4	9	24	.302	.361
vs. 1st Batr (relief)	1.000	1	1	1	0	0	1	0	0	1.000	2.000
First Inning Pitched	.276	123	34	9	1	3	14	8	13	.321	.439
First 75 Pitches	.280	586	164	29	3	15	69	41	52	.330	.416
Pitch 76-90	.262	65	17	1	0	2	7	3	6	.294	.369
Pitch 91-105	.380	50	19	3	1	2	11	3	2	.415	.600
Pitch 106+	.294	17	5	1	0	0	1	1	3	.333	.353
First Pitch	.277	101	28	3	0	2	5	4	0	.311	.366
Ahead in Count	.252	286	72	12	2	7	33	0	55	.261	.381
Behind in Count	.310	187	58	13	2	6	32	32	0	.407	.497
Two Strikes	.269	268	72	10	2	8	42	12	63	.303	.410

Chris Donnels — Astros

Age 28 – Bats Left (groundball hitter)

	Avg	G	AB	R	H	2B	3B	HR	RBI	BB	SO	HBP	GDP	SB	CS	OBP	SLG	IBB	SH	SF	#Pit	#P/PA	GB	FB	G/F
1993 Season	.257	88	179	18	46	14	2	2	24	19	33	0	6	2	0	.327	.391	0	0	1	762	3.83	80	36	2.22
Career (1991-1993)	.224	170	389	33	87	20	2	2	35	50	77	0	7	4	1	.311	.301	1	2	1	1706	3.86	164	83	1.98

1993 Season

	Avg	AB	H	2B	3B	HR	RBI	BB	SO	OBP	SLG
vs. Left	.242	33	8	2	1	0	1	5	3	.342	.364
vs. Right	.260	146	38	12	1	2	23	14	30	.323	.397
Home	.200	70	14	5	0	0	8	7	13	.273	.271
Away	.294	109	32	9	2	2	16	12	20	.361	.468
First Pitch	.200	20	4	1	0	0	2	0	0	.200	.250
Ahead in Count	.349	43	15	6	0	0	7	13	0	.491	.488
Behind in Count	.231	78	18	4	1	1	9	0	26	.231	.346
Two Strikes	.198	81	16	3	1	1	10	6	33	.253	.296

	Avg	AB	H	2B	3B	HR	RBI	BB	SO	OBP	SLG
Scoring Posn	.241	54	13	3	0	1	19	4	12	.288	.352
Close & Late	.138	29	4	2	0	0	2	4	5	.242	.207
None on/out	.148	27	4	2	0	0	0	6	6	.303	.222
Batting #6	.264	91	24	6	2	0	8	10	16	.337	.374
Batting #7	.179	28	5	3	0	0	3	5	5	.303	.286
Other	.283	60	17	5	0	2	13	4	12	.323	.467
Pre-All Star	.244	45	11	3	0	0	6	5	13	.320	.311
Post-All Star	.261	134	35	11	2	2	18	14	20	.329	.418

John Dopson — Red Sox

Age 30 – Pitches Right (groundball pitcher)

	ERA	W	L	Sv	G	GS	IP	BB	SO	Avg	H	2B	3B	HR	RBI	OBP	SLG	CG	ShO	Sup	QS	#P/S	SB	CS	GB	FB	G/F
1993 Season	4.97	7	11	0	34	28	155.2	59	89	.281	170	34	6	16	77	.343	.437	1	1	5.15	9	83	11	5	294	114	2.58
Last Five Years	4.29	26	30	0	93	85	485.0	176	248	.272	510	88	10	49	215	.334	.408	3	1	4.66	36	84	57	18	907	391	2.32

1993 Season

	ERA	W	L	Sv	G	GS	IP	H	HR	BB	SO
Home	4.64	5	3	0	19	15	85.1	91	8	33	46
Away	5.37	2	8	0	15	13	70.1	79	8	26	43
Starter	4.83	7	9	0	28	28	149.0	162	16	55	86
Reliever	8.10	0	2	0	6	0	6.2	8	0	4	3
0-3 Days Rest	0.00	0	0	0	0	0	0.0	0	0	0	0
4 Days Rest	5.15	4	6	0	18	18	94.1	104	8	36	49
5+ Days Rest	4.28	3	3	0	10	10	54.2	58	8	19	37
Pre-All Star	4.24	7	5	0	18	18	102.0	104	10	35	70
Post-All Star	6.37	0	6	0	16	10	53.2	66	6	24	19

	Avg	AB	H	2B	3B	HR	RBI	BB	SO	OBP	SLG
vs. Left	.302	308	93	16	5	9	45	31	37	.365	.474
vs. Right	.260	296	77	18	1	7	32	28	52	.320	.399
Scoring Posn	.275	138	38	5	1	2	55	26	19	.376	.370
Close & Late	.400	20	8	2	1	1	4	2	3	.455	.750
None on/out	.297	165	49	14	2	8	8	12	24	.345	.552
First Pitch	.351	97	34	10	3	3	21	5	0	.371	.608
Ahead in Count	.248	250	62	12	1	4	27	0	71	.253	.352
Behind in Count	.317	139	44	6	2	7	19	38	0	.461	.540
Two Strikes	.197	244	48	10	0	2	19	16	89	.252	.262

Last Five Years

	ERA	W	L	Sv	G	GS	IP	H	HR	BB	SO
Home	3.85	16	13	0	54	49	285.0	293	24	104	144
Away	4.91	10	17	0	39	36	200.0	217	25	72	104
Day	4.11	11	8	0	35	30	159.2	176	20	63	68
Night	4.37	15	22	0	58	55	325.1	334	29	113	180
Grass	4.19	24	24	0	82	76	430.0	448	44	157	220
Turf	5.07	2	6	0	11	9	55.0	62	5	19	28
April	2.39	4	2	0	12	11	71.2	51	4	23	58

	Avg	AB	H	2B	3B	HR	RBI	BB	SO	OBP	SLG
vs. Left	.271	910	247	35	7	20	101	87	99	.333	.391
vs. Right	.273	964	263	53	3	29	114	89	149	.335	.424
Inning 1-6	.263	1663	438	73	7	41	188	158	227	.327	.390
Inning 7+	.341	211	72	15	3	8	27	18	21	.392	.555
None on	.274	1094	300	48	6	31	31	104	159	.338	.414
Runners on	.269	780	210	40	4	18	184	72	89	.328	.400
Scoring Posn	.264	451	119	22	2	7	152	50	54	.329	.368

Last Five Years

	ERA	W	L	Sv	G	GS	IP	H	HR	BB	SO
May	4.17	5	7	0	15	15	86.1	97	8	27	43
June	4.33	9	4	0	17	17	95.2	93	12	40	44
July	4.32	4	1	0	16	16	85.1	98	7	32	40
August	5.03	0	8	0	14	11	62.2	79	7	31	26
September/October	5.40	4	8	0	19	15	83.1	92	11	23	37
Starter	4.24	25	28	0	85	85	471.2	496	49	170	241
Reliever	6.08	1	2	0	8	0	13.1	14	0	6	7
0-3 Days Rest	1.46	1	0	0	2	2	12.1	10	2	2	8
4 Days Rest	4.44	16	15	0	48	48	265.2	284	30	107	135
5+ Days Rest	4.14	8	13	0	35	35	193.2	202	17	61	98
Pre-All Star	3.86	21	14	0	51	50	293.2	294	29	101	162
Post-All Star	4.94	5	16	0	42	35	191.1	216	20	75	86

	Avg	AB	H	2B	3B	HR	RBI	BB	SO	OBP	SLG
Close & Late	.356	87	31	7	1	3	13	7	7	.400	.563
None on/out	.264	489	129	28	4	13	13	51	66	.333	.417
vs. 1st Batr (relief)	.167	6	1	0	0	0	0	2	3	.375	.167
First Inning Pitched	.273	348	95	14	1	8	39	32	45	.331	.388
First 75 Pitches	.267	1567	418	72	7	35	177	143	206	.327	.389
Pitch 76-90	.319	182	58	11	1	9	25	25	23	.396	.538
Pitch 91-105	.258	93	24	2	2	4	10	6	15	.314	.452
Pitch 106+	.313	32	10	3	0	1	3	2	4	.353	.500
First Pitch	.345	284	98	14	4	10	48	7	0	.356	.528
Ahead in Count	.217	784	170	31	1	14	74	0	209	.219	.313
Behind in Count	.320	453	145	22	4	17	57	105	0	.444	.499
Two Strikes	.184	734	135	23	1	10	57	63	248	.252	.259

Pitcher vs. Batter (career)

Pitches Best Vs.	Avg	AB	H	2B	3B	HR	RBI	BB	SO	OBP	SLG
Brady Anderson	.067	15	1	1	0	0	0	2	1	.176	.133
George Bell	.083	12	1	0	0	0	1	1	4	.143	.083
Steve Sax	.087	23	2	0	0	0	0	3	1	.192	.087
Bobby Kelly	.100	10	1	0	0	0	0	1	0	.182	.100
Don Mattingly	.158	19	3	0	0	0	0	1	0	.200	.158

Pitches Worst Vs.	Avg	AB	H	2B	3B	HR	RBI	BB	SO	OBP	SLG
Troy Neel	.571	14	8	2	0	2	6	0	1	.571	1.143
Devon White	.538	13	7	0	0	2	4	0	1	.538	1.000
Omar Vizquel	.462	13	6	1	1	0	2	0	1	.462	.692
Bobby Bonilla	.400	10	4	1	0	1	3	3	1	.538	.800
Juan Samuel	.333	12	4	0	2	1	3	0	1	.333	.917

Billy Doran — Brewers

Age 36 – Bats Both

	Avg	G	AB	R	H	2B	3B	HR	RBI	BB	SO	HBP	GDP	SB	CS	OBP	SLG	IBB	SH	SF	#Pit	#P/PA	GB	FB	G/F
1993 Season	.217	28	60	7	13	4	0	0	6	6	3	0	3	1	0	.284	.283	1	0	1	240	3.58	26	18	1.44
Last Five Years	.254	539	1718	230	437	86	8	29	183	254	203	2	29	58	20	.349	.364	15	7	14	7277	3.65	629	575	1.09

1993 Season

	Avg	AB	H	2B	3B	HR	RBI	BB	SO	OBP	SLG
vs. Left	.200	40	8	3	0	0	5	4	1	.267	.275
vs. Right	.250	20	5	1	0	0	1	2	2	.318	.300
Scoring Posn	.333	12	4	1	0	0	5	2	0	.400	.417
Close & Late	.133	15	2	1	0	0	1	1	2	.188	.200

Last Five Years

	Avg	AB	H	2B	3B	HR	RBI	BB	SO	OBP	SLG
vs. Left	.235	527	124	30	2	10	53	100	55	.354	.357
vs. Right	.263	1191	313	56	6	19	130	154	148	.346	.368
Groundball	.245	609	149	30	2	7	58	78	62	.330	.335
Flyball	.239	389	93	19	0	10	47	61	53	.340	.365
Home	.271	842	228	43	5	16	98	132	87	.367	.391
Away	.239	876	209	43	3	13	85	122	116	.330	.339
Day	.266	526	140	38	3	7	60	64	64	.345	.390
Night	.249	1192	297	48	5	22	123	190	139	.350	.353
Grass	.247	554	137	29	2	8	51	75	61	.334	.350
Turf	.258	1164	300	57	6	21	132	179	142	.355	.371
First Pitch	.293	276	81	17	1	3	28	9	0	.314	.395
Ahead in Count	.326	457	149	26	2	14	72	148	0	.488	.484
Behind in Count	.191	643	123	26	4	4	46	0	161	.193	.263
Two Strikes	.179	663	119	32	3	9	52	91	203	.278	.278

	Avg	AB	H	2B	3B	HR	RBI	BB	SO	OBP	SLG
Scoring Posn	.249	413	103	19	2	6	144	83	47	.365	.349
Close & Late	.221	308	68	12	1	6	39	52	47	.331	.325
None on/out	.264	390	103	18	1	9	9	59	55	.361	.385
Batting #2	.268	355	95	25	2	7	33	76	45	.393	.408
Batting #3	.238	470	112	19	1	8	62	54	56	.316	.334
Other	.258	893	230	42	5	14	88	124	102	.346	.363
April	.248	282	70	19	1	3	32	39	32	.335	.355
May	.269	305	82	17	2	7	46	37	35	.346	.407
June	.288	299	86	11	1	6	36	49	33	.386	.391
July	.222	306	68	12	1	8	32	38	45	.307	.346
August	.206	301	62	13	2	3	20	59	37	.335	.292
September/October	.307	225	69	14	1	2	17	32	21	.393	.404
Pre-All Star	.262	969	254	51	4	17	121	135	115	.350	.376
Post-All Star	.244	749	183	35	4	12	62	119	88	.347	.350

Batter vs. Pitcher (since 1984)

Hits Best Against	Avg	AB	H	2B	3B	HR	RBI	BB	SO	OBP	SLG
Tommy Greene	.545	11	6	0	0	0	1	0	1	.545	.545
Tom Glavine	.480	25	12	1	0	0	3	8	1	.606	.520
Mike Maddux	.400	15	6	2	0	1	2	4	2	.526	.733
John Wetteland	.400	10	4	0	0	1	5	2	1	.500	.700
Mark Grant	.308	13	4	0	1	1	3	3	2	.438	.692

Hits Worst Against	Avg	AB	H	2B	3B	HR	RBI	BB	SO	OBP	SLG
Jose Rijo	.056	18	1	0	0	0	0	3	5	.190	.056
Rob Murphy	.077	13	1	0	0	0	2	3	0	.250	.077
Ken Dayley	.091	11	1	1	0	0	1	0	2	.091	.182
Jamie Moyer	.091	11	1	0	0	0	0	2	1	.231	.091
Norm Charlton	.100	10	1	0	0	0	0	1	3	.182	.100

Brian Dorsett — Reds

Age 33 – Bats Right (flyball hitter)

	Avg	G	AB	R	H	2B	3B	HR	RBI	BB	SO	HBP	GDP	SB	CS	OBP	SLG	IBB	SH	SF	#Pit	#P/PA	GB	FB	G/F
1993 Season	.254	25	63	7	16	4	0	2	12	3	14	0	1	0	0	.288	.413	0	0	0	258	3.91	15	17	0.88
Last Five Years	.227	58	132	12	30	7	0	2	17	6	24	0	3	0	0	.261	.326	0	0	0	503	3.64	35	42	0.83

1993 Season

	Avg	AB	H	2B	3B	HR	RBI	BB	SO	OBP	SLG
vs. Left	.333	24	8	2	0	1	4	2	6	.385	.542
vs. Right	.205	39	8	2	0	1	8	1	8	.225	.333
Scoring Posn	.267	15	4	2	0	0	8	0	3	.267	.400
Close & Late	.429	7	3	1	0	0	2	0	1	.429	.571

Kelly Downs — Athletics

Age 33 – Pitches Right

	ERA	W	L	Sv	G	GS	IP	BB	SO	Avg	H	2B	3B	HR	RBI	OBP	SLG	GF	IR	IRS	Hld	SvOp	SB	CS	GB	FB	G/F
1993 Season	5.64	5	10	0	42	12	119.2	60	66	.287	135	20	0	14	69	.368	.419	12	26	3	1	1	13	4	167	135	1.24
Last Five Years	4.30	28	31	0	155	67	521.1	229	279	.257	509	95	6	43	244	.336	.376	24	67	18	4	3	57	21	713	622	1.15

1993 Season

	ERA	W	L	Sv	G	GS	IP	H	HR	BB	SO
Home	4.35	3	3	0	23	6	68.1	68	4	32	42
Away	7.36	2	7	0	19	6	51.1	67	10	28	24
Starter	7.02	0	6	0	12	12	59.0	70	9	29	33
Reliever	4.30	5	4	0	30	0	60.2	65	5	31	33

	Avg	AB	H	2B	3B	HR	RBI	BB	SO	OBP	SLG
vs. Left	.320	225	72	7	0	7	32	38	20	.417	.444
vs. Right	.257	245	63	13	0	7	37	22	46	.320	.396
Scoring Posn	.279	129	36	5	0	6	57	28	16	.398	.457
Close & Late	.289	45	13	2	0	0	3	8	7	.389	.333

1993 Season

	ERA	W	L	Sv	G	GS	IP	H	HR	BB	SO		Avg	AB	H	2B	3B	HR	RBI	BB	SO	OBP	SLG
0 Days rest	2.45	0	0	0	2	0	3.2	4	0	2	2	None on/out	.264	110	29	4	0	3	3	14	11	.357	.382
1 or 2 Days rest	6.75	1	3	0	11	0	16.0	20	2	14	7	First Pitch	.346	78	27	2	0	2	12	8	0	.407	.449
3+ Days rest	3.51	4	1	0	17	0	41.0	41	3	15	24	Ahead in Count	.231	199	46	9	0	4	22	0	60	.234	.337
Pre-All Star	6.06	2	3	0	23	7	65.1	79	5	40	37	Behind in Count	.319	116	37	4	0	4	20	30	0	.456	.457
Post-All Star	5.13	3	7	0	19	5	54.1	56	9	20	29	Two Strikes	.196	179	35	11	0	4	19	22	66	.286	.324

Last Five Years

	ERA	W	L	Sv	G	GS	IP	H	HR	BB	SO		Avg	AB	H	2B	3B	HR	RBI	BB	SO	OBP	SLG
Home	3.80	17	9	0	76	32	262.2	225	16	113	146	vs. Left	.283	1039	294	53	6	19	129	125	100	.358	.400
Away	4.80	11	22	0	79	35	258.2	284	27	116	133	vs. Right	.229	940	215	42	0	24	115	104	179	.311	.350
Day	3.93	9	8	0	60	21	199.0	178	14	74	103	Inning 1-6	.263	1554	409	72	5	36	204	181	211	.343	.385
Night	4.52	19	23	0	95	46	322.1	331	29	155	176	Inning 7+	.235	425	100	23	1	7	40	48	68	.311	.344
Grass	3.90	26	24	0	116	53	413.1	383	20	101	210	None on	.258	1087	280	49	3	19	19	110	150	.330	.361
Turf	5.50	2	7	0	39	14	108.0	126	14	38	69	Runners on	.257	892	229	46	3	24	225	119	129	.343	.396
April	4.39	4	6	0	18	13	82.0	88	4	35	37	Scoring Posn	.235	515	121	21	2	13	189	92	79	.345	.359
May	4.74	3	4	0	23	11	74.0	81	6	44	45	Close & Late	.232	177	41	5	0	1	13	25	24	.327	.277
June	5.24	2	1	0	22	4	44.2	45	4	26	23	None on/out	.258	493	127	21	0	8	8	53	51	.336	.349
July	3.80	5	5	0	19	11	73.1	68	7	21	43	vs. 1st Batr (relief)	.235	81	19	4	0	2	11	4	13	.273	.358
August	3.95	6	9	0	35	14	116.1	113	13	57	57	First Inning Pitched	.277	574	159	34	1	14	97	72	83	.360	.413
September/October	4.26	8	6	0	38	14	131.0	114	9	46	74	First 15 Pitches	.272	514	140	31	1	11	65	59	66	.350	.401
Starter	4.56	14	27	0	67	67	353.1	358	29	157	173	Pitch 16-30	.253	438	111	22	1	10	65	48	72	.328	.377
Reliever	3.75	14	4	0	88	0	168.0	151	14	72	106	Pitch 31-45	.240	337	81	18	2	7	39	39	40	.317	.368
0 Days rest	3.94	2	0	0	10	0	16.0	20	2	10	8	Pitch 46+	.257	690	177	24	2	15	75	83	101	.339	.362
1 or 2 Days rest	4.39	4	3	0	38	0	69.2	65	6	33	51	First Pitch	.269	350	94	17	1	6	46	25	0	.317	.374
3+ Days rest	3.17	8	1	0	40	0	82.1	66	6	29	47	Ahead in Count	.205	800	164	30	2	11	72	0	228	.213	.289
Pre-All Star	4.61	9	13	0	69	32	226.1	246	14	109	120	Behind in Count	.313	469	147	27	2	17	74	113	0	.446	.488
Post-All Star	4.06	19	18	0	86	35	295.0	263	29	120	159	Two Strikes	.196	757	148	33	2	9	72	91	279	.286	.280

Pitcher vs. Batter (career)

Pitches Best Vs.	Avg	AB	H	2B	3B	HR	RBI	BB	SO	OBP	SLG	Pitches Worst Vs.	Avg	AB	H	2B	3B	HR	RBI	BB	SO	OBP	SLG
Joey Cora	.000	11	0	0	0	0	1	1	0	.083	.000	Chris Sabo	.545	11	6	3	0	1	3	1	0	.583	1.091
Craig Biggio	.000	11	0	0	0	0	1	0	2	.000	.000	Mike LaValliere	.478	23	11	3	0	0	3	5	1	.571	.609
Alfredo Griffin	.077	26	2	1	0	0	0	0	2	.077	.115	Andres Galarraga	.440	25	11	2	0	3	6	1	5	.462	.880
Willie McGee	.083	12	1	0	0	0	1	0	2	.083	.083	Darnell Coles	.400	10	4	2	0	0	0	1	2	.455	.600
Darren Daulton	.083	12	1	0	0	0	0	1	2	.154	.083	Ron Gant	.350	20	7	2	0	1	5	4	5	.458	.600

Doug Drabek — Astros

Age 31 – Pitches Right (groundball pitcher)

	ERA	W	L	Sv	G	GS	IP	BB	SO	Avg	H	2B	3B	HR	RBI	OBP	SLG	CG	ShO	Sup	QS	#P/S	SB	CS	GB	FB	G/F
1993 Season	3.79	9	18	0	34	34	237.2	60	157	.267	242	41	4	18	97	.312	.381	7	2	3.64	22	98	28	7	382	206	1.85
Last Five Years	3.03	75	61	0	171	170	1204.2	301	730	.247	1110	184	21	87	392	.295	.355	39	16	4.27	118	102	117	54	1819	1160	1.57

1993 Season

	ERA	W	L	Sv	G	GS	IP	H	HR	BB	SO		Avg	AB	H	2B	3B	HR	RBI	BB	SO	OBP	SLG
Home	3.04	5	8	0	19	19	142.1	136	5	35	100	vs. Left	.288	459	132	25	3	11	59	35	60	.337	.427
Away	4.91	4	10	0	15	15	95.1	106	13	25	57	vs. Right	.246	447	110	16	1	7	38	25	97	.287	.333
Day	3.32	5	4	0	12	12	86.2	90	6	19	67	Inning 1-6	.271	739	200	36	4	16	86	50	121	.315	.395
Night	4.05	4	14	0	22	22	151.0	152	12	41	90	Inning 7+	.251	167	42	5	0	2	11	10	36	.298	.317
Grass	5.82	4	5	0	10	10	60.1	81	9	19	33	None on	.246	558	137	20	3	10	10	24	90	.278	.346
Turf	3.10	5	13	0	24	24	177.1	161	9	41	124	Runners on	.302	348	105	21	1	8	87	36	67	.363	.437
April	1.98	2	3	0	5	5	41.0	28	1	8	31	Scoring Posn	.274	208	57	9	1	7	77	33	46	.367	.428
May	3.71	3	2	0	6	6	43.2	48	1	9	25	Close & Late	.248	117	29	1	0	2	8	7	30	.296	.308
June	4.17	1	3	0	6	6	41.0	41	4	10	19	None on/out	.235	238	56	3	2	4	4	13	33	.275	.315
July	3.98	1	4	0	6	6	40.2	40	2	12	29	vs. 1st Batr (relief)	.000	0	0	0	0	0	0	0	0	.000	.000
August	4.13	0	3	0	5	5	32.2	35	3	10	29	First Inning Pitched	.267	131	35	5	1	1	15	18	28	.356	.344
September/October	4.89	2	3	0	6	6	38.2	50	7	11	24	First 75 Pitches	.271	680	184	33	4	15	75	43	112	.313	.397
Starter	3.79	9	18	0	34	34	237.2	242	18	60	157	Pitch 76-90	.273	121	33	4	0	2	13	9	21	.326	.355
Reliever	0.00	0	0	0	0	0	0.0	0	0	0	0	Pitch 91-105	.231	78	18	3	0	1	6	4	17	.265	.308
0-3 Days Rest	2.00	1	0	0	1	1	9.0	6	1	1	11	Pitch 106+	.259	27	7	1	0	0	3	4	7	.355	.296
4 Days Rest	3.26	7	9	0	20	20	146.1	139	7	33	91	First Pitch	.281	171	48	8	2	3	24	10	0	.322	.404
5+ Days Rest	4.92	1	9	0	13	13	82.1	97	10	26	55	Ahead in Count	.202	386	78	11	1	4	24	0	137	.205	.267
Pre-All Star	3.52	7	9	0	19	19	140.2	133	7	29	87	Behind in Count	.359	198	71	14	1	9	35	31	0	.438	.576
Post-All Star	4.18	2	9	0	15	15	97.0	109	11	31	70	Two Strikes	.187	369	69	7	1	5	19	19	157	.227	.252

Last Five Years

	ERA	W	L	Sv	G	GS	IP	H	HR	BB	SO		Avg	AB	H	2B	3B	HR	RBI	BB	SO	OBP	SLG
Home	2.55	41	27	0	86	85	640.0	553	40	153	420	vs. Left	.265	2564	680	123	13	47	231	198	330	.317	.378
Away	3.59	34	34	0	85	85	564.2	557	47	148	310	vs. Right	.223	1929	430	61	8	40	161	103	400	.265	.325
Day	2.97	25	14	0	50	49	339.1	320	23	81	206	Inning 1-6	.249	3657	909	153	19	75	337	239	597	.295	.362
Night	3.06	50	47	0	121	121	865.1	790	64	220	524	Inning 7+	.240	836	201	31	2	12	55	62	133	.293	.325
Grass	4.92	17	23	0	47	47	291.0	328	34	89	155	None on	.242	2817	683	109	14	56	56	154	469	.283	.351
Turf	2.43	58	38	0	124	123	913.2	782	53	212	575	Runners on	.255	1676	427	75	7	31	336	147	261	.314	.363
April	2.59	11	12	0	25	25	174.0	143	9	48	92	Scoring Posn	.230	980	225	36	4	21	300	119	170	.310	.339
May	2.97	10	10	0	27	27	193.2	177	14	46	116	Close & Late	.225	529	119	14	0	7	31	45	94	.288	.291
June	3.25	10	9	0	29	29	196.2	196	18	57	123	None on/out	.248	1207	299	47	6	22	22	58	197	.282	.351
July	3.35	15	10	0	29	29	207.0	192	16	61	125	vs. 1st Batr (relief)	.000	1	0	0	0	0	0	0	0	.000	.000
August	2.91	12	10	0	30	29	210.2	193	18	45	133	First Inning Pitched	.267	660	176	33	2	14	69	48	100	.317	.386
September/October	3.07	17	10	0	31	31	222.2	209	12	44	141	First 75 Pitches	.248	3251	806	133	16	64	274	195	523	.291	.358
Starter	3.04	74	61	0	170	170	1202.2	1108	87	301	730	Pitch 76-90	.238	568	135	21	4	11	55	49	93	.301	.347

Last Five Years

	ERA	W	L	Sv	G	GS	IP	H	HR	BB	SO		Avg	AB	H	2B	3B	HR	RBI	BB	SO	OBP	SLG
Reliever	0.00	1	0	0	1	0	2.0	2	0	0	0	Pitch 91-105	.250	436	109	13	1	9	39	29	70	.296	.346
0-3 Days Rest	1.73	2	1	0	3	3	26.0	23	2	3	22	Pitch 106+	.252	238	60	17	0	3	24	28	44	.326	.361
4 Days Rest	2.87	53	36	0	113	113	807.0	729	46	189	487	First Pitch	.302	706	213	36	7	18	84	27	0	.331	.449
5+ Days Rest	3.51	19	24	0	54	54	369.2	356	39	109	221	Ahead in Count	.196	1990	390	58	4	26	112	0	628	.199	.268
Pre-All Star	2.94	37	34	0	91	91	640.1	584	44	165	378	Behind in Count	.298	987	294	52	7	29	120	155	0	.390	.453
Post-All Star	3.14	38	27	0	80	79	564.1	526	43	136	352	Two Strikes	.179	1926	344	53	4	29	101	118	730	.227	.255

Pitcher vs. Batter (career)

Pitches Best Vs.	Avg	AB	H	2B	3B	HR	RBI	BB	SO	OBP	SLG	Pitches Worst Vs.	Avg	AB	H	2B	3B	HR	RBI	BB	SO	OBP	SLG
Darnell Coles	.000	11	0	0	0	0	0	0	2	.000	.000	Fred McGriff	.615	13	8	0	0	2	4	3	1	.647	1.077
Curt Wilkerson	.000	11	0	0	0	0	0	0	4	.000	.000	Dante Bichette	.538	13	7	2	0	0	2	0	1	.538	.692
Benito Santiago	.045	22	1	0	1	0	3	1	4	.087	.136	Jerald Clark	.533	15	8	2	0	1	1	2	1	.588	.867
Geronimo Pena	.071	14	1	0	0	0	1	0	4	.071	.071	Kurt Stillwell	.400	10	4	2	1	0	2	1	1	.455	.800
Mike Morgan	.083	12	1	0	0	0	0	0	5	.083	.083	Eric Karros	.400	10	4	1	0	2	5	2	1	.462	1.100

Brian Drahman — White Sox

Age 27 – Pitches Right

	ERA	W	L	Sv	G	GS	IP	BB	SO	Avg	H	2B	3B	HR	RBI	OBP	SLG	GF	IR	IRS	Hld	SvOp	SB	CS	GB	FB	G/F
1993 Season	0.00	0	0	1	5	0	5.1	2	3	.333	7	1	0	0	1	.391	.381	4	2	1	0	1	0	0	7	3	2.33
Career (1991-1993)	2.72	3	2	1	38	0	43.0	17	22	.217	34	5	1	4	24	.291	.338	14	39	12	4	3	1	1	57	49	1.16

1993 Season

	ERA	W	L	Sv	G	GS	IP	H	HR	BB	SO		Avg	AB	H	2B	3B	HR	RBI	BB	SO	OBP	SLG
Home	0.00	0	0	0	1	0	1.0	0	0	0	1	vs. Left	.333	9	3	0	0	0	0	1	0	.400	.333
Away	0.00	0	0	1	4	0	4.1	7	0	2	2	vs. Right	.333	12	4	1	0	0	1	1	3	.385	.417

Mike Draper — Mets

Age 27 – Pitches Right (groundball pitcher)

	ERA	W	L	Sv	G	GS	IP	BB	SO	Avg	H	2B	3B	HR	RBI	OBP	SLG	GF	IR	IRS	Hld	SvOp	SB	CS	GB	FB	G/F
1993 Season	4.25	1	1	0	29	1	42.1	14	16	.327	53	13	1	2	26	.370	.457	11	18	10	2	2	7	1	65	41	1.59

1993 Season

	ERA	W	L	Sv	G	GS	IP	H	HR	BB	SO		Avg	AB	H	2B	3B	HR	RBI	BB	SO	OBP	SLG
Home	3.38	0	0	0	16	1	26.2	32	1	12	11	vs. Left	.384	73	28	9	0	0	8	10	6	.447	.507
Away	5.74	1	1	0	13	0	15.2	21	1	2	5	vs. Right	.281	89	25	4	1	2	18	4	10	.302	.416
Starter	9.00	0	0	0	1	1	3.0	5	0	3	2	Scoring Posn	.291	55	16	1	1	1	20	8	5	.353	.400
Reliever	3.89	1	1	0	28	0	39.1	48	2	11	14	Close & Late	.471	17	8	1	0	1	5	2	0	.526	.706
0 Days rest	3.18	0	0	0	5	0	5.2	11	0	3	0	None on/out	.294	34	10	3	0	0	0	4	4	.368	.382
1 or 2 Days rest	3.00	0	0	0	9	0	12.0	13	1	4	5	First Pitch	.219	32	7	1	0	0	4	3	0	.270	.250
3+ Days rest	4.57	1	1	0	14	0	21.2	24	1	4	9	Ahead in Count	.328	64	21	7	1	1	10	0	15	.318	.516
Pre-All Star	4.10	0	1	0	26	0	37.1	48	2	11	14	Behind in Count	.429	42	18	4	0	1	9	4	0	.478	.595
Post-All Star	5.40	1	0	0	3	1	5.0	5	0	3	2	Two Strikes	.304	56	17	5	1	1	10	7	16	.375	.482

Steve Dreyer — Rangers

Age 24 – Pitches Right

	ERA	W	L	Sv	G	GS	IP	BB	SO	Avg	H	2B	3B	HR	RBI	OBP	SLG	CG	ShO	Sup	QS	#P/S	SB	CS	GB	FB	G/F
1993 Season	5.71	3	3	0	10	6	41.0	20	23	.291	48	10	0	7	19	.371	.479	0	0	7.46	2	87	2	2	61	46	1.33

1993 Season

	ERA	W	L	Sv	G	GS	IP	H	HR	BB	SO		Avg	AB	H	2B	3B	HR	RBI	BB	SO	OBP	SLG
Home	3.38	3	1	0	5	4	26.2	24	4	10	17	vs. Left	.266	79	21	4	0	3	8	16	10	.389	.430
Away	10.05	0	2	0	5	2	14.1	24	3	10	6	vs. Right	.314	86	27	6	0	4	11	4	13	.352	.523

Rob Ducey — Rangers

Age 29 – Bats Left (flyball hitter)

	Avg	G	AB	R	H	2B	3B	HR	RBI	BB	SO	HBP	GDP	SB	CS	OBP	SLG	IBB	SH	SF	#Pit	#P/PA	GB	FB	G/F
1993 Season	.282	27	85	15	24	6	3	2	9	10	17	0	1	2	3	.351	.494	2	2	2	410	4.14	25	24	1.04
Last Five Years	.240	180	362	42	87	21	5	3	29	37	105	1	5	9	9	.309	.351	3	4	4	1623	3.98	89	98	0.91

1993 Season

	Avg	AB	H	2B	3B	HR	RBI	BB	SO	OBP	SLG		Avg	AB	H	2B	3B	HR	RBI	BB	SO	OBP	SLG
vs. Left	.182	11	2	0	1	0	1	0	4	.167	.364	Scoring Posn	.250	20	5	2	0	0	6	5	5	.370	.350
vs. Right	.297	74	22	6	2	2	8	10	13	.376	.514	Close & Late	.286	7	2	0	0	0	1	3	0	.500	.286

Mariano Duncan — Phillies

Age 31 – Bats Right (groundball hitter)

	Avg	G	AB	R	H	2B	3B	HR	RBI	BB	SO	HBP	GDP	SB	CS	OBP	SLG	IBB	SH	SF	#Pit	#P/PA	GB	FB	G/F
1993 Season	.282	124	496	68	140	26	4	11	73	12	88	4	13	6	5	.304	.417	0	4	2	1744	3.37	215	92	2.34
Last Five Years	.275	585	2096	284	576	110	24	44	239	73	371	21	41	56	24	.304	.413	4	20	13	7590	3.41	863	502	1.72

1993 Season

	Avg	AB	H	2B	3B	HR	RBI	BB	SO	OBP	SLG		Avg	AB	H	2B	3B	HR	RBI	BB	SO	OBP	SLG
vs. Left	.273	198	54	11	1	6	24	5	29	.291	.429	Scoring Posn	.316	152	48	9	2	2	60	0	31	.316	.441
vs. Right	.289	298	86	15	3	5	49	7	59	.312	.409	Close & Late	.276	76	21	6	0	3	14	0	14	.273	.474
Groundball	.287	181	52	9	0	3	22	4	37	.305	.387	None on/out	.333	90	30	4	0	5	5	5	12	.375	.544
Flyball	.354	82	29	7	1	3	27	1	16	.365	.573	Batting #2	.279	390	109	20	3	8	55	10	68	.304	.408
Home	.289	211	61	8	3	5	28	5	44	.315	.427	Batting #8	.292	72	21	3	1	3	15	1	16	.297	.486
Away	.277	285	79	18	1	6	45	7	44	.295	.411	Other	.294	34	10	3	0	0	3	1	4	.314	.382
Day	.295	122	36	6	0	4	22	4	23	.326	.443	April	.255	55	14	3	0	0	4	2	8	.293	.309
Night	.278	374	104	20	4	7	51	8	65	.296	.409	May	.200	90	18	3	0	4	13	3	22	.223	.367
Grass	.256	180	46	7	1	4	27	3	30	.270	.372	June	.302	96	29	3	3	2	14	3	14	.333	.458
Turf	.297	316	94	19	3	7	46	9	58	.322	.443	July	.349	63	22	2	0	1	12	1	10	.359	.429
First Pitch	.333	75	25	4	1	4	15	0	0	.333	.573	August	.276	98	27	7	1	1	17	2	20	.297	.398
Ahead in Count	.382	102	39	7	1	2	20	4	0	.402	.529	September/October	.319	94	30	8	0	3	13	1	14	.326	.500
Behind in Count	.232	241	56	12	1	4	27	0	78	.244	.340	Pre-All Star	.262	248	65	11	3	6	32	8	44	.291	.403
Two Strikes	.182	214	39	8	0	3	18	8	88	.226	.262	Post-All Star	.302	248	75	15	1	5	41	4	44	.316	.431

1993 By Position

Position	Avg	AB	H	2B	3B	HR	RBI	BB	SO	OBP	SLG	G	GS	Innings	PO	A	E	DP	Fld Pct	Rng Fctr	In Zone	Outs	Zone Rtg	MLB Zone
As Pinch Hitter	.400	10	4	0	0	1	5	0	3	.400	.700	10	0	---	---	---	---	---	---	---	---	---	---	---
As 2b	.280	279	78	17	3	5	36	8	51	.304	.416	65	61	544.2	109	168	9	29	.969	4.58	200	177	.885	.895
As ss	.280	207	58	9	1	5	32	4	34	.298	.406	59	49	447.2	71	136	12	21	.945	4.16	180	141	.783	.880

Last Five Years

	Avg	AB	H	2B	3B	HR	RBI	BB	SO	OBP	SLG		Avg	AB	H	2B	3B	HR	RBI	BB	SO	OBP	SLG
vs. Left	.314	856	269	56	10	21	103	31	132	.341	.477	Scoring Posn	.289	512	148	27	8	10	191	12	101	.306	.432
vs. Right	.248	1240	307	54	14	23	136	42	239	.279	.369	Close & Late	.262	340	89	14	1	5	40	11	72	.291	.353
Groundball	.278	798	222	50	5	8	76	25	139	.302	.383	None on/out	.284	464	132	24	6	13	13	21	73	.322	.446
Flyball	.277	444	123	25	8	13	70	16	85	.308	.457	Batting #2	.270	1092	295	60	9	24	125	37	190	.297	.408
Home	.277	1014	281	51	12	25	112	39	184	.309	.425	Batting #7	.256	293	75	16	4	4	33	8	42	.283	.379
Away	.273	1082	295	59	12	19	127	34	187	.300	.402	Other	.290	711	206	34	11	16	81	28	139	.323	.436
Day	.285	555	158	24	10	14	70	24	95	.319	.440	April	.300	250	75	20	1	5	28	11	42	.344	.448
Night	.271	1541	418	86	14	30	169	49	276	.299	.404	May	.233	378	88	15	5	6	41	10	68	.254	.347
Grass	.265	663	176	37	9	11	80	18	125	.293	.398	June	.275	367	101	17	6	7	39	12	56	.310	.411
Turf	.279	1433	400	73	15	33	159	55	246	.309	.420	July	.276	304	84	15	2	5	28	10	59	.300	.388
First Pitch	.314	306	96	14	5	9	51	0	0	.314	.480	August	.300	387	116	20	7	9	56	17	66	.332	.457
Ahead in Count	.357	414	148	29	11	13	61	36	0	.410	.575	September/October	.273	410	112	23	3	12	47	13	80	.296	.432
Behind in Count	.224	1019	228	43	6	18	90	0	326	.233	.331	Pre-All Star	.267	1082	289	57	12	21	117	34	181	.298	.400
Two Strikes	.196	923	181	34	4	13	78	35	371	.233	.284	Post-All Star	.283	1014	287	53	12	23	122	39	190	.311	.427

Batter vs. Pitcher (career)

Hits Best Against	Avg	AB	H	2B	3B	HR	RBI	BB	SO	OBP	SLG	Hits Worst Against	Avg	AB	H	2B	3B	HR	RBI	BB	SO	OBP	SLG
Lee Smith	.500	16	8	0	2	1	7	0	1	.500	.938	Rick Sutcliffe	.000	14	0	0	0	0	0	0	4	.000	.000
Trevor Wilson	.444	27	12	3	1	1	5	0	1	.444	.741	Les Lancaster	.000	11	0	0	0	0	0	0	1	.000	.000
Dennis Rasmussen	.421	19	8	3	0	1	4	0	3	.421	.737	Bill Swift	.067	15	1	0	0	0	1	0	3	.067	.067
Mark Portugal	.400	10	4	1	0	1	1	1	1	.455	.800	Jim Gott	.077	13	1	0	0	0	1	1	2	.133	.077
Derek Lilliquist	.400	10	4	1	0	1	2	1	1	.455	.800	Mike Maddux	.083	12	1	0	0	0	1	1	5	.154	.083

Shawon Dunston — Cubs

Age 31 – Bats Right (flyball hitter)

	Avg	G	AB	R	H	2B	3B	HR	RBI	BB	SO	HBP	GDP	SB	CS	OBP	SLG	IBB	SH	SF	#Pit	#P/PA	GB	FB	G/F
1993 Season	.400	7	10	3	4	2	0	0	2	0	1	0	0	0	0	.400	.600	0	0	0	33	3.30	2	5	0.40
Last Five Years	.270	451	1591	195	429	69	22	38	180	71	251	8	25	67	25	.300	.412	21	14	21	5518	3.24	526	527	1.00

1993 Season

	Avg	AB	H	2B	3B	HR	RBI	BB	SO	OBP	SLG		Avg	AB	H	2B	3B	HR	RBI	BB	SO	OBP	SLG
vs. Left	.429	7	3	2	0	0	2	0	0	.429	.714	Scoring Posn	1.000	2	2	1	0	0	2	0	0	1.000	1.500
vs. Right	.333	3	1	0	0	0	0	0	1	.333	.333	Close & Late	1.000	2	2	1	0	0	1	0	0	1.000	1.500

Last Five Years

	Avg	AB	H	2B	3B	HR	RBI	BB	SO	OBP	SLG		Avg	AB	H	2B	3B	HR	RBI	BB	SO	OBP	SLG
vs. Left	.288	552	159	22	10	16	70	24	70	.315	.451	Scoring Posn	.263	361	95	14	9	9	138	30	66	.308	.427
vs. Right	.260	1039	270	47	12	22	110	47	181	.293	.392	Close & Late	.308	295	91	13	3	6	33	13	48	.345	.434
Groundball	.285	561	160	29	9	10	63	23	77	.311	.422	None on/out	.296	416	123	21	3	10	10	20	63	.333	.433
Flyball	.251	375	94	19	5	13	50	17	65	.285	.432	Batting #7	.267	857	229	37	12	23	92	35	133	.292	.419
Home	.285	761	217	35	9	17	85	34	115	.319	.422	Batting #8	.287	341	98	16	5	12	51	21	57	.335	.469
Away	.255	830	212	34	13	21	95	37	136	.284	.404	Other	.260	393	102	16	5	3	37	15	61	.288	.349
Day	.289	810	234	41	7	23	98	40	136	.323	.442	April	.256	246	63	10	2	5	16	16	36	.299	.374
Night	.250	781	195	28	15	15	82	31	115	.277	.382	May	.260	281	73	12	2	10	33	13	43	.294	.423
Grass	.275	1113	306	52	12	29	130	48	182	.306	.421	June	.254	256	65	12	5	7	39	8	50	.283	.422
Turf	.257	478	123	17	10	9	50	23	69	.288	.391	July	.291	254	74	10	4	7	30	16	41	.331	.445
First Pitch	.340	235	80	14	3	9	41	18	0	.388	.540	August	.324	287	93	14	6	5	38	11	41	.346	.467
Ahead in Count	.316	269	85	9	7	12	41	41	0	.402	.535	September/October	.228	267	61	11	3	4	24	7	40	.247	.337
Behind in Count	.237	810	192	32	9	14	73	0	228	.238	.351	Pre-All Star	.257	874	225	38	9	26	102	41	147	.292	.411
Two Strikes	.203	660	134	23	8	7	49	11	251	.216	.294	Post-All Star	.285	717	204	31	13	12	78	30	104	.311	.414

Batter vs. Pitcher (career)																							
Hits Best Against	Avg	AB	H	2B	3B	HR	RBI	BB	SO	OBP	SLG	**Hits Worst Against**	Avg	AB	H	2B	3B	HR	RBI	BB	SO	OBP	SLG
Cris Carpenter	.500	12	6	1	1	0	4	0	2	.500	.750	Nolan Ryan	.080	25	2	0	0	0	1	1	12	.115	.080
John Burkett	.364	11	4	0	0	1	2	0	1	.364	.636	Steve Avery	.083	12	1	0	0	0	0	1	4	.154	.083
Mike Maddux	.333	18	6	3	0	1	2	2	6	.400	.667	Larry Andersen	.118	17	2	0	0	0	1	1	5	.167	.118
Mike Morgan	.333	15	5	2	0	1	2	2	1	.412	.667	Ken Hill	.125	16	2	0	0	0	1	0	5	.125	.125
Craig Lefferts	.333	15	5	0	0	2	5	0	3	.333	.733	Todd Worrell	.133	15	2	0	0	0	2	0	4	.133	.133

Lenny Dykstra — Phillies

Age 31 – Bats Left

	Avg	G	AB	R	H	2B	3B	HR	RBI	BB	SO	HBP	GDP	SB	CS	OBP	SLG	IBB	SH	SF	#Pit	#P/PA	GB	FB	G/F
1993 Season	.305	161	637	143	194	44	6	19	66	129	64	2	8	37	12	.420	.482	9	0	5	3027	3.92	215	208	1.03
Last Five Years	.294	604	2329	416	684	142	18	44	209	355	217	16	22	154	38	.388	.427	29	7	17	10228	3.75	883	713	1.24

1993 Season																							
	Avg	AB	H	2B	3B	HR	RBI	BB	SO	OBP	SLG		Avg	AB	H	2B	3B	HR	RBI	BB	SO	OBP	SLG
vs. Left	.281	217	61	14	2	2	18	48	29	.414	.392	Scoring Posn	.230	135	31	6	1	3	46	34	17	.377	.356
vs. Right	.317	420	133	30	4	17	48	81	35	.424	.529	Close & Late	.310	84	26	5	0	5	16	24	10	.463	.548
Groundball	.287	216	62	16	3	4	19	47	18	.417	.444	None on/out	.319	260	83	23	3	8	8	51	31	.433	.523
Flyball	.354	96	34	8	2	6	20	23	14	.479	.667	Total	.305	637	194	44	6	19	66	129	64	.420	.482
Home	.300	307	92	25	3	12	36	69	29	.425	.518	Batting #1	.305	637	194	44	6	19	66	129	64	.420	.482
Away	.309	330	102	19	3	7	30	60	35	.416	.448	Other	.000	0	0	0	0	0	0	0	0	.000	.000
Day	.313	176	55	14	2	3	14	39	16	.437	.466	April	.216	88	19	5	1	3	3	20	6	.361	.398
Night	.302	461	139	30	4	16	52	90	48	.414	.488	May	.296	115	34	9	0	0	7	15	8	.382	.374
Grass	.317	205	65	9	1	6	18	36	20	.424	.459	June	.337	104	35	9	0	4	9	26	12	.466	.538
Turf	.299	432	129	35	5	13	48	93	44	.419	.493	July	.374	107	40	8	0	5	16	23	11	.485	.589
First Pitch	.342	79	27	9	1	1	10	7	0	.386	.519	August	.269	104	28	6	3	4	11	26	12	.409	.500
Ahead in Count	.354	161	57	15	1	9	24	68	0	.543	.627	September/October	.319	119	38	7	2	3	20	19	15	.410	.487
Behind in Count	.221	263	58	6	2	6	18	0	56	.226	.327	Pre-All Star	.295	349	103	26	1	10	27	72	31	.416	.461
Two Strikes	.256	285	73	10	3	8	25	54	64	.375	.396	Post-All Star	.316	288	91	18	5	9	39	57	33	.425	.507

1993 By Position																							
Position	Avg	AB	H	2B	3B	HR	RBI	BB	SO	OBP	SLG	G	GS	Innings	PO	A	E	DP	Fld Pct	Rng Fctr	In Zone	Outs	Zone Rtg	MLB Zone
As cf	.305	636	194	44	6	19	66	129	64	.421	.483	160	160	1422.1	469	2	10	0	.979	2.98	530	449	.847	.829

Last Five Years																							
	Avg	AB	H	2B	3B	HR	RBI	BB	SO	OBP	SLG		Avg	AB	H	2B	3B	HR	RBI	BB	SO	OBP	SLG
vs. Left	.283	810	229	38	9	9	71	127	98	.382	.385	Scoring Posn	.299	425	127	22	3	4	152	101	45	.423	.393
vs. Right	.300	1519	455	104	9	35	138	228	119	.392	.449	Close & Late	.325	363	118	21	0	8	56	71	38	.434	.449
Groundball	.268	867	232	46	9	10	66	120	86	.359	.376	None on/out	.272	1002	273	58	10	21	21	147	97	.369	.413
Flyball	.309	466	144	37	3	16	64	84	54	.413	.504	Batting #1	.294	2294	674	138	17	44	206	348	211	.388	.426
Home	.303	1135	344	70	8	31	109	201	103	.407	.461	Batting #2	.278	18	5	2	1	0	2	3	3	.391	.500
Away	.285	1194	340	72	10	13	100	154	114	.370	.394	Other	.294	17	5	2	0	0	1	4	3	.409	.412
Day	.290	641	186	47	4	9	53	104	52	.392	.418	April	.288	313	90	27	4	6	24	52	19	.394	.457
Night	.295	1688	498	95	14	35	156	251	165	.387	.430	May	.306	399	122	24	1	5	38	57	33	.397	.409
Grass	.276	702	194	41	6	10	60	104	70	.373	.395	June	.322	388	125	27	1	9	37	66	35	.420	.466
Turf	.301	1627	490	101	12	34	149	251	147	.395	.441	July	.318	434	138	23	2	8	40	73	43	.418	.435
First Pitch	.295	353	104	29	3	6	47	12	0	.316	.445	August	.265	476	126	30	7	10	34	62	49	.349	.420
Ahead in Count	.342	590	202	39	7	21	60	193	0	.506	.539	September/October	.260	319	83	11	3	6	36	45	38	.350	.370
Behind in Count	.240	917	220	33	6	6	56	0	186	.245	.309	Pre-All Star	.305	1201	366	83	6	23	113	200	96	.406	.441
Two Strikes	.239	964	230	38	7	12	67	138	217	.335	.330	Post-All Star	.282	1128	318	59	12	21	96	155	121	.369	.411

Batter vs. Pitcher (career)																							
Hits Best Against	Avg	AB	H	2B	3B	HR	RBI	BB	SO	OBP	SLG	**Hits Worst Against**	Avg	AB	H	2B	3B	HR	RBI	BB	SO	OBP	SLG
Frank Castillo	.600	10	6	1	0	3	4	1	0	.636	1.600	Norm Charlton	.000	10	0	0	0	0	0	1	4	.091	.000
Ken Hill	.571	21	12	2	0	1	1	6	0	.667	.810	Joe Magrane	.074	27	2	0	0	0	0	2	1	.138	.074
Paul Assenmacher	.571	14	8	2	0	1	4	0	3	.533	.929	Mike Harkey	.091	11	1	0	0	0	0	1	2	.167	.091
Rich Rodriguez	.500	8	4	0	0	1	3	3	1	.636	.875	Craig Lefferts	.111	18	2	1	0	0	0	1	4	.158	.167
Steve Avery	.444	9	4	2	0	1	3	4	1	.615	1.000	John Franco	.125	16	2	0	0	0	1	0	4	.125	.125

Damion Easley — Angels

Age 24 – Bats Right (groundball hitter)

	Avg	G	AB	R	H	2B	3B	HR	RBI	BB	SO	HBP	GDP	SB	CS	OBP	SLG	IBB	SH	SF	#Pit	#P/PA	GB	FB	G/F
1993 Season	.313	73	230	33	72	13	2	2	22	28	35	3	5	6	6	.392	.413	2	1	2	962	3.64	101	57	1.77
Career (1992-1993)	.291	120	381	47	111	18	2	3	34	36	61	6	7	15	11	.359	.373	2	3	3	1567	3.65	155	101	1.53

1993 Season																							
	Avg	AB	H	2B	3B	HR	RBI	BB	SO	OBP	SLG		Avg	AB	H	2B	3B	HR	RBI	BB	SO	OBP	SLG
vs. Left	.361	72	26	7	0	1	3	5	9	.418	.500	Scoring Posn	.255	55	14	1	0	1	18	8	15	.358	.327
vs. Right	.291	158	46	6	2	1	19	23	26	.380	.373	Close & Late	.239	46	11	2	0	0	6	5	9	.314	.283
Home	.302	129	39	7	2	0	12	15	21	.381	.388	None on/out	.377	61	23	3	1	1	1	5	4	.424	.508
Away	.327	101	33	6	0	2	10	13	14	.405	.446	Batting #7	.324	108	35	6	1	1	9	10	20	.383	.426
First Pitch	.371	35	13	5	0	1	6	2	0	.410	.600	Batting #8	.317	60	19	2	1	1	11	9	5	.414	.433
Ahead in Count	.400	65	26	6	0	1	3	10	0	.480	.538	Other	.290	62	18	5	0	0	2	9	10	.384	.371
Behind in Count	.217	92	20	2	1	0	8	0	28	.234	.261	Pre-All Star	.307	199	61	12	2	2	20	20	31	.374	.417
Two Strikes	.182	88	16	1	1	0	10	16	35	.318	.216	Post-All Star	.355	31	11	1	0	0	2	8	4	.488	.387

Dennis Eckersley — Athletics

Age 39 – Pitches Right (flyball pitcher)

	ERA	W	L	Sv	G	GS	IP	BB	SO	Avg	H	2B	3B	HR	RBI	OBP	SLG	GF	IR	IRS	Hld	SvOp	SB	CS	GB	FB	G/F
1993 Season	4.16	2	4	36	64	0	67.0	13	80	.261	67	8	4	7	43	.299	.405	52	32	13	0	46	12	2	50	83	0.60
Last Five Years	2.24	22	11	211	314	0	354.0	40	388	.202	262	40	8	30	125	.228	.315	237	147	37	1	240	33	6	291	419	0.69

1993 Season

	ERA	W	L	Sv	G	GS	IP	H	HR	BB	SO
Home	3.08	1	3	19	36	0	38.0	31	4	8	53
Away	5.59	1	1	17	28	0	29.0	36	3	5	27
Day	2.30	1	2	16	27	0	27.1	19	3	2	31
Night	5.45	1	2	20	37	0	39.2	48	4	11	49
Grass	3.88	1	4	28	53	0	55.2	54	5	12	72
Turf	5.56	1	0	8	11	0	11.1	13	2	1	8
April	5.19	0	1	2	9	0	8.2	10	0	4	12
May	4.91	1	0	7	12	0	11.0	10	1	2	10
June	3.09	1	0	7	10	0	11.2	11	1	1	13
July	3.09	0	0	7	10	0	11.2	8	1	1	16
August	3.29	0	1	6	12	0	13.2	16	1	4	18
September/October	6.10	0	2	7	11	0	10.1	12	3	1	11
Starter	0.00	0	0	0	0	0	0.0	0	0	0	0
Reliever	4.16	2	4	36	64	0	67.0	67	7	13	80
0 Days rest	1.86	0	1	18	22	0	19.1	16	2	2	21
1 or 2 Days rest	3.42	1	2	12	22	0	26.1	20	2	5	31
3+ Days rest	7.17	1	1	6	20	0	21.1	31	3	6	28
Pre-All Star	3.72	2	1	21	36	0	36.1	32	2	8	43
Post-All Star	4.70	0	3	15	28	0	30.2	35	5	5	37

	Avg	AB	H	2B	3B	HR	RBI	BB	SO	OBP	SLG
vs. Left	.323	130	42	7	3	5	34	9	25	.364	.538
vs. Right	.197	127	25	1	1	2	9	4	55	.231	.268
Inning 1-6	.000	0	0	0	0	0	0	0	0	.000	.000
Inning 7+	.261	257	67	8	4	7	43	13	80	.299	.405
None on	.228	136	31	1	2	4	4	5	43	.261	.353
Runners on	.298	121	36	7	2	3	39	8	37	.341	.463
Scoring Posn	.307	75	23	3	1	1	31	6	24	.357	.413
Close & Late	.262	195	51	7	3	6	39	10	62	.301	.421
None on/out	.276	58	16	0	2	1	1	2	12	.300	.397
vs. 1st Batr (relief)	.279	61	17	1	2	1	6	2	17	.297	.410
First Inning Pitched	.270	226	61	7	4	5	38	11	69	.307	.403
First 15 Pitches	.286	199	57	6	4	7	31	8	59	.316	.462
Pitch 16-30	.173	52	9	2	0	0	10	3	19	.228	.212
Pitch 31-45	.167	6	1	0	0	0	2	2	2	.375	.167
Pitch 46+	.000	0	0	0	0	0	0	0	0	.000	.000
First Pitch	.350	40	14	2	0	2	9	4	0	.409	.550
Ahead in Count	.203	148	30	5	2	1	14	0	77	.211	.284
Behind in Count	.432	37	16	0	1	3	14	3	0	.475	.730
Two Strikes	.189	148	28	4	2	1	15	6	80	.229	.264

Last Five Years

	ERA	W	L	Sv	G	GS	IP	H	HR	BB	SO
Home	2.17	18	6	99	164	0	186.1	130	16	29	222
Away	2.31	4	5	112	150	0	167.2	132	14	11	166
Day	1.66	11	5	86	132	0	146.0	97	11	17	163
Night	2.64	11	6	125	182	0	208.0	165	19	23	225
Grass	2.14	21	10	171	265	0	298.2	216	25	38	333
Turf	2.77	1	1	40	49	0	55.1	46	5	2	55
April	1.80	3	2	32	46	0	50.0	34	2	6	53
May	2.33	3	0	37	51	0	54.0	46	6	3	65
June	2.05	2	1	34	44	0	52.2	43	3	7	50
July	2.45	1	2	30	48	0	55.0	32	7	6	67
August	1.71	6	2	42	61	0	68.1	55	2	12	73
September/October	2.92	7	4	36	64	0	74.0	52	10	6	80
Starter	0.00	0	0	0	0	0	0.0	0	0	0	0
Reliever	2.24	22	11	211	314	0	354.0	262	30	40	388
0 Days rest	1.33	5	1	72	87	0	88.0	60	4	9	96
1 or 2 Days rest	2.38	10	8	91	134	0	158.2	112	16	20	176
3+ Days rest	2.77	7	2	48	93	0	107.1	90	10	11	116
Pre-All Star	1.98	8	3	113	154	0	172.2	133	12	18	186
Post-All Star	2.48	14	8	98	160	0	181.1	129	18	22	202

	Avg	AB	H	2B	3B	HR	RBI	BB	SO	OBP	SLG
vs. Left	.240	645	155	24	4	15	79	26	135	.270	.360
vs. Right	.165	649	107	16	4	15	46	14	253	.185	.271
Inning 1-6	.000	0	0	0	0	0	0	0	0	.000	.000
Inning 7+	.202	1294	262	40	8	30	125	40	388	.228	.315
None on	.203	760	154	24	6	16	16	15	231	.222	.313
Runners on	.202	534	108	16	2	14	109	25	157	.236	.318
Scoring Posn	.203	310	63	9	1	6	88	21	95	.251	.297
Close & Late	.195	886	173	27	6	18	101	30	276	.223	.300
None on/out	.218	298	65	10	3	6	6	4	81	.231	.332
vs. 1st Batr (relief)	.216	305	66	10	3	5	24	5	89	.229	.318
First Inning Pitched	.202	1063	215	31	7	22	100	30	307	.226	.307
First 15 Pitches	.216	982	212	32	7	26	89	24	274	.236	.342
Pitch 16-30	.157	281	44	7	0	3	29	12	102	.193	.214
Pitch 31-45	.194	31	6	1	1	1	7	4	12	.286	.387
Pitch 46+	.000	0	0	0	0	0	0	0	0	.000	.000
First Pitch	.318	170	54	8	0	4	17	12	0	.363	.435
Ahead in Count	.160	815	130	23	5	15	50	0	356	.164	.255
Behind in Count	.341	126	43	6	2	6	31	10	0	.387	.563
Two Strikes	.137	776	106	15	4	10	44	17	388	.158	.205

Pitcher vs. Batter (since 1984)

Pitches Best Vs.	Avg	AB	H	2B	3B	HR	RBI	BB	SO	OBP	SLG
Lance Parrish	.000	12	0	0	0	0	0	0	5	.000	.000
Cecil Fielder	.071	14	1	0	0	0	2	1	10	.133	.071
Mike Macfarlane	.091	11	1	0	0	0	1	0	4	.091	.091
Kirby Puckett	.105	19	2	0	1	0	1	0	5	.100	.211
Dan Gladden	.143	14	2	0	0	0	0	0	5	.143	.143

Pitches Worst Vs.	Avg	AB	H	2B	3B	HR	RBI	BB	SO	OBP	SLG
Jim Eisenreich	.500	10	5	2	0	0	1	1	3	.545	.700
Tim Raines	.429	21	9	2	0	0	2	1	3	.455	.524
Gene Larkin	.400	15	6	4	0	0	3	0	0	.400	.667
Tim Wallach	.357	14	5	1	0	0	0	2	2	.438	.429
Tom Brunansky	.333	12	4	2	0	1	3	0	2	.333	.750

Tom Edens — Astros

Age 33 – Pitches Right (groundball pitcher)

	ERA	W	L	Sv	G	GS	IP	BB	SO	Avg	H	2B	3B	HR	RBI	OBP	SLG	GF	IR	IRS	Hld	SvOp	SB	CS	GB	FB	G/F
1993 Season	3.12	1	1	0	38	0	49.0	19	21	.263	47	6	1	4	26	.332	.374	20	27	10	3	1	4	1	78	51	1.53
Last Five Years	3.64	13	11	5	133	12	247.1	98	137	.254	235	34	7	15	108	.327	.354	43	101	29	16	8	30	13	376	236	1.59

1993 Season

	ERA	W	L	Sv	G	GS	IP	H	HR	BB	SO
Home	3.15	0	0	0	17	0	20.0	19	2	6	7
Away	3.10	1	1	0	21	0	29.0	28	2	13	14
Starter	0.00	0	0	0	0	0	0.0	0	0	0	0
Reliever	3.12	1	1	0	38	0	49.0	47	4	19	21
0 Days rest	0.00	0	0	0	4	0	4.0	4	0	0	1
1 or 2 Days rest	3.07	0	1	0	11	0	14.2	12	3	4	6
3+ Days rest	3.56	1	0	0	23	0	30.1	31	1	15	14
Pre-All Star	2.53	0	1	0	20	0	21.1	25	0	8	9
Post-All Star	3.58	1	0	0	18	0	27.2	22	4	11	12

	Avg	AB	H	2B	3B	HR	RBI	BB	SO	OBP	SLG
vs. Left	.267	75	20	3	1	1	8	13	10	.375	.373
vs. Right	.260	104	27	3	0	3	18	6	11	.297	.375
Scoring Posn	.315	54	17	3	0	1	22	9	4	.406	.426
Close & Late	.269	26	7	0	0	1	3	4	4	.367	.385
None on/out	.200	40	8	0	1	1	1	3	6	.256	.325
First Pitch	.207	29	6	1	0	0	7	4	0	.303	.241
Ahead in Count	.172	58	10	1	0	0	4	0	20	.169	.190
Behind in Count	.308	52	16	1	1	2	7	8	0	.400	.481
Two Strikes	.203	74	15	3	0	1	8	7	21	.268	.284

Last Five Years

	ERA	W	L	Sv	G	GS	IP	H	HR	BB	SO
Home	4.65	8	5	2	63	4	112.1	116	6	43	64
Away	2.80	5	6	3	70	8	135.0	119	9	55	73
Day	2.76	3	2	2	45	2	88.0	65	6	32	54
Night	4.12	10	9	3	88	10	159.1	170	9	66	83

	Avg	AB	H	2B	3B	HR	RBI	BB	SO	OBP	SLG
vs. Left	.262	390	102	11	6	4	39	39	66	.329	.351
vs. Right	.248	537	133	23	1	11	69	59	71	.326	.356
Inning 1-6	.280	528	148	26	6	8	74	48	76	.341	.398
Inning 7+	.218	399	87	8	1	7	34	50	61	.309	.296

Last Five Years

	ERA	W	L	Sv	G	GS	IP	H	HR	BB	SO
Grass	3.75	6	8	1	63	9	141.2	142	10	54	66
Turf	3.49	7	3	4	70	3	105.2	93	5	44	71
April	3.86	1	0	0	6	0	11.2	14	0	5	11
May	3.32	2	1	1	17	0	21.2	26	0	13	10
June	2.49	2	0	1	26	0	43.1	33	0	15	23
July	3.83	3	2	2	31	0	47.0	40	6	19	24
August	3.48	1	2	1	27	5	64.2	55	4	24	39
September/October	4.58	4	6	0	26	7	59.0	67	5	22	30
Starter	4.25	4	4	0	12	12	59.1	69	5	21	33
Reliever	3.45	9	7	5	121	0	188.0	166	10	77	104
0 Days rest	1.71	1	0	0	16	0	21.0	17	0	11	11
1 or 2 Days rest	4.52	2	5	5	54	0	83.2	77	4	35	47
3+ Days rest	2.81	6	2	0	51	0	83.1	72	6	31	46
Pre-All Star	2.36	7	2	2	64	0	99.1	85	0	41	51
Post-All Star	4.50	6	9	3	69	12	148.0	150	15	57	86

	Avg	AB	H	2B	3B	HR	RBI	BB	SO	OBP	SLG
None on	.255	505	129	20	5	9	9	45	82	.316	.368
Runners on	.251	422	106	14	2	6	99	53	55	.340	.336
Scoring Posn	.267	262	70	10	1	3	91	44	40	.371	.347
Close & Late	.226	159	36	4	0	2	11	21	30	.324	.289
None on/out	.258	221	57	6	4	6	6	17	31	.311	.403
vs. 1st Batr (relief)	.255	106	27	3	0	2	16	11	14	.331	.340
First Inning Pitched	.275	426	117	15	4	8	68	49	60	.352	.385
First 15 Pitches	.286	374	107	11	5	8	57	41	47	.359	.406
Pitch 16-30	.194	273	53	8	0	4	23	32	48	.279	.267
Pitch 31-45	.259	135	35	3	1	2	12	13	23	.329	.341
Pitch 46+	.276	145	40	12	1	1	16	12	19	.333	.393
First Pitch	.279	136	38	7	0	0	21	7	0	.319	.331
Ahead in Count	.198	359	71	7	1	2	29	0	113	.205	.240
Behind in Count	.300	227	68	12	4	8	33	48	0	.421	.493
Two Strikes	.191	414	79	9	2	4	35	43	137	.272	.251

Pitcher vs. Batter (career)

Pitches Best Vs.	Avg	AB	H	2B	3B	HR	RBI	BB	SO	OBP	SLG
Candy Maldonado	.083	12	1	0	1	0	1	0	3	.083	.250
Randy Milligan	.200	10	2	0	0	0	0	3	1	.385	.200
Robin Ventura	.200	10	2	0	0	0	2	1	0	.273	.200
Mike Devereaux	.222	9	2	1	0	1	2	2	2	.364	.667

Pitches Worst Vs.	Avg	AB	H	2B	3B	HR	RBI	BB	SO	OBP	SLG
Scott Fletcher	.500	10	5	0	0	0	2	1	0	.545	.500
Cal Ripken	.417	12	5	3	0	0	4	0	0	.417	.667
Kelly Gruber	.333	9	3	2	0	0	2	1	2	.364	.556

Jim Edmonds — Angels

Age 24 – Bats Left

	Avg	G	AB	R	H	2B	3B	HR	RBI	BB	SO	HBP	GDP	SB	CS	OBP	SLG	IBB	SH	SF	#Pit	#P/PA	GB	FB	G/F
1993 Season	.246	18	61	5	15	4	1	0	4	2	16	0	1	0	2	.270	.344	1	0	0	264	4.19	18	12	1.50

1993 Season

	Avg	AB	H	2B	3B	HR	RBI	BB	SO	OBP	SLG
vs. Left	.222	9	2	0	0	0	0	1	4	.300	.222
vs. Right	.250	52	13	4	1	0	4	1	12	.264	.365
Scoring Posn	.308	13	4	1	0	0	3	1	5	.357	.385
Close & Late	.000	4	0	0	0	0	0	0	1	.000	.000

Mark Eichhorn — Blue Jays

Age 33 – Pitches Right (groundball pitcher)

	ERA	W	L	Sv	G	GS	IP	BB	SO	Avg	H	2B	3B	HR	RBI	OBP	SLG	GF	IR	IRS	Hld	SvOp	SB	CS	GB	FB	G/F
1993 Season	2.72	3	1	0	54	0	72.2	22	47	.272	76	15	2	3	45	.330	.373	16	48	20	5	2	8	3	134	56	2.39
Last Five Years	3.01	17	18	16	294	0	395.0	102	275	.262	393	70	10	16	211	.312	.354	105	249	88	47	30	30	15	680	292	2.33

1993 Season

	ERA	W	L	Sv	G	GS	IP	H	HR	BB	SO
Home	3.38	2	1	0	29	0	42.2	45	3	16	33
Away	1.80	1	0	0	25	0	30.0	31	0	6	14
Starter	0.00	0	0	0	0	0	0.0	0	0	0	0
Reliever	2.72	3	1	0	54	0	72.2	76	3	22	47
0 Days rest	1.46	1	0	0	10	0	12.1	15	0	1	8
1 or 2 Days rest	3.94	2	1	0	21	0	29.2	35	2	13	18
3+ Days rest	2.05	0	0	0	23	0	30.2	26	1	8	21
Pre-All Star	2.94	2	0	0	32	0	52.0	57	2	12	38
Post-All Star	2.18	1	1	0	22	0	20.2	19	1	10	9

	Avg	AB	H	2B	3B	HR	RBI	BB	SO	OBP	SLG
vs. Left	.326	132	43	4	1	2	19	10	17	.382	.417
vs. Right	.224	147	33	11	1	1	26	12	30	.284	.333
Scoring Posn	.273	99	27	9	0	0	39	18	22	.383	.364
Close & Late	.200	55	11	5	0	1	10	8	6	.302	.345
None on/out	.258	62	16	2	1	1	1	0	7	.258	.371
First Pitch	.378	37	14	3	0	0	4	7	0	.500	.459
Ahead in Count	.195	123	24	5	0	0	14	0	38	.194	.236
Behind in Count	.359	64	23	6	1	3	20	10	0	.447	.625
Two Strikes	.165	121	20	3	0	0	11	5	47	.197	.190

Last Five Years

	ERA	W	L	Sv	G	GS	IP	H	HR	BB	SO
Home	3.24	10	10	6	145	0	194.2	199	10	48	142
Away	2.79	7	8	10	149	0	200.1	194	6	54	133
Day	2.91	6	7	4	89	0	126.2	135	5	32	94
Night	3.05	11	11	12	205	0	268.1	258	11	70	181
Grass	2.95	10	16	11	213	0	283.1	275	10	67	191
Turf	3.14	7	2	5	81	0	111.2	118	6	35	84
April	3.15	1	3	4	39	0	68.2	68	1	12	41
May	1.77	2	5	5	48	0	76.1	63	3	18	53
June	1.48	3	1	5	53	0	61.0	65	3	6	49
July	3.92	4	3	1	53	0	66.2	72	2	24	52
August	4.22	4	4	1	56	0	70.1	72	3	29	48
September/October	3.63	3	2	0	45	0	52.0	53	4	13	32
Starter	0.00	0	0	0	0	0	0.0	0	0	0	0
Reliever	3.01	17	18	16	294	0	395.0	393	16	102	275
0 Days rest	3.12	5	3	5	68	0	80.2	87	2	24	55
1 or 2 Days rest	3.32	8	10	9	140	0	190.0	191	9	51	141
3+ Days rest	2.46	4	5	2	86	0	124.1	115	5	27	79
Pre-All Star	2.37	6	11	14	158	0	228.0	220	8	47	159
Post-All Star	3.88	11	7	2	136	0	167.0	173	8	55	116

	Avg	AB	H	2B	3B	HR	RBI	BB	SO	OBP	SLG
vs. Left	.310	670	208	31	6	9	92	51	104	.363	.415
vs. Right	.223	828	185	39	4	7	119	51	171	.270	.306
Inning 1-6	.323	220	71	13	4	3	59	16	41	.359	.459
Inning 7+	.252	1278	322	57	6	13	152	86	234	.304	.336
None on	.254	760	193	30	4	8	8	29	120	.285	.336
Runners on	.271	738	200	40	6	8	203	73	155	.337	.374
Scoring Posn	.255	518	132	28	1	7	192	59	120	.328	.353
Close & Late	.251	569	143	28	2	5	72	52	106	.316	.334
None on/out	.256	328	84	19	2	4	4	9	48	.282	.363
vs. 1st Batr (relief)	.258	275	71	19	0	5	47	13	50	.295	.382
First Inning Pitched	.265	978	259	47	6	14	170	65	191	.313	.368
First 15 Pitches	.265	942	250	44	7	10	137	50	161	.306	.359
Pitch 16-30	.235	451	106	19	2	6	49	41	96	.300	.326
Pitch 31-45	.366	93	34	6	1	0	22	9	15	.427	.452
Pitch 46+	.250	12	3	1	0	0	3	2	3	.357	.333
First Pitch	.284	204	58	13	2	1	26	19	0	.349	.382
Ahead in Count	.207	706	146	22	3	5	75	0	238	.211	.268
Behind in Count	.318	311	99	21	1	5	62	50	0	.410	.441
Two Strikes	.177	638	113	13	3	8	63	33	275	.220	.245

Pitcher vs. Batter (since 1984)

Pitches Best Vs.	Avg	AB	H	2B	3B	HR	RBI	BB	SO	OBP	SLG
Cecil Fielder	.000	16	0	0	0	0	3	1	5	.056	.000
Ivan Calderon	.000	11	0	0	0	0	0	0	5	.000	.000
Randy Bush	.056	18	1	1	0	0	2	0	3	.056	.111
Steve Buechele	.063	16	1	0	0	0	0	1	3	.118	.063

Pitches Worst Vs.	Avg	AB	H	2B	3B	HR	RBI	BB	SO	OBP	SLG
Wally Joyner	.600	10	6	1	0	0	2	1	1	.636	.700
Larry Sheets	.545	11	6	2	0	0	3	0	1	.545	.727
Dale Sveum	.500	14	7	1	0	1	6	0	1	.500	.786
Mickey Tettleton	.400	15	6	0	0	4	7	2	5	.444	1.200

Pitcher vs. Batter (since 1984)											
Pitches Best Vs.	Avg	AB	H	2B	3B	HR	RBI	BB	SO	OBP	SLG
Sandy Alomar Jr	.091	11	1	0	0	0	2	0	3	.091	.091

Pitches Worst Vs.	Avg	AB	H	2B	3B	HR	RBI	BB	SO	OBP	SLG
Tom Brunansky	.389	18	7	3	0	1	8	3	1	.476	.722

Dave Eiland — Padres

Age 27 – Pitches Right (groundball pitcher)

	ERA	W	L	Sv	G	GS	IP	BB	SO	Avg	H	2B	3B	HR	RBI	OBP	SLG	CG	ShO	Sup	QS	#P/S	SB	CS	GB	FB	G/F
1993 Season	5.21	0	3	0	10	9	48.1	17	14	.297	58	11	0	5	28	.353	.431	0	0	4.28	3	80	8	3	102	45	2.27
Last Five Years	5.16	5	14	0	46	40	212.2	63	69	.296	253	53	10	23	126	.346	.463	0	0	4.53	11	74	21	7	413	208	1.99

1993 Season

	ERA	W	L	Sv	G	GS	IP	H	HR	BB	SO
Home	5.95	0	1	0	4	4	19.2	25	1	8	6
Away	4.71	0	2	0	6	5	28.2	33	4	9	8

	Avg	AB	H	2B	3B	HR	RBI	BB	SO	OBP	SLG
vs. Left	.314	102	32	6	0	0	15	13	5	.385	.373
vs. Right	.280	93	26	5	0	5	13	4	9	.316	.495

Last Five Years

	ERA	W	L	Sv	G	GS	IP	H	HR	BB	SO
Home	5.27	4	6	0	25	23	114.1	131	12	34	44
Away	5.03	1	8	0	21	17	98.1	122	11	29	25
Day	8.20	2	5	0	16	13	63.2	99	13	17	10
Night	3.87	3	9	0	30	27	149.0	154	10	46	59
Grass	5.35	5	12	0	42	36	188.1	225	20	56	63
Turf	3.70	0	2	0	4	4	24.1	28	3	7	6
April	4.28	1	3	0	13	13	67.1	67	3	22	22
May	7.08	0	5	0	11	10	40.2	64	7	13	10
June	3.62	1	1	0	4	4	27.1	23	2	11	8
July	7.88	0	2	0	4	4	16.0	26	3	4	6
August	9.64	0	2	0	4	2	14.0	24	3	7	5
September/October	3.42	3	1	0	10	7	47.1	49	5	6	18
Starter	5.14	5	14	0	40	40	201.1	236	18	60	67
Reliever	5.56	0	0	0	6	0	11.1	17	5	3	2
0-3 Days Rest	0.00	0	0	0	0	0	0.0	0	0	0	0
4 Days Rest	5.45	3	6	0	22	22	105.2	132	10	31	32
5+ Days Rest	4.80	2	8	0	18	18	95.2	104	8	29	35
Pre-All Star	5.07	2	10	0	31	30	147.1	171	13	49	43
Post-All Star	5.37	3	4	0	15	10	65.1	82	10	14	26

	Avg	AB	H	2B	3B	HR	RBI	BB	SO	OBP	SLG
vs. Left	.302	463	140	29	8	9	63	38	24	.352	.458
vs. Right	.289	391	113	24	2	14	63	25	45	.339	.468
Inning 1-6	.301	791	238	50	9	20	122	59	64	.351	.463
Inning 7+	.238	63	15	3	1	3	4	4	5	.284	.460
None on	.280	486	136	28	2	14	14	34	39	.331	.432
Runners on	.318	368	117	25	8	9	112	29	30	.366	.503
Scoring Posn	.313	224	70	15	4	2	86	22	21	.369	.442
Close & Late	.261	23	6	2	1	0	1	2	1	.320	.435
None on/out	.299	224	67	18	1	7	7	13	15	.346	.482
vs. 1st Batr (relief)	.333	6	2	0	0	2	4	0	0	.333	1.333
First Inning Pitched	.279	183	51	11	3	5	27	19	15	.347	.454
First 75 Pitches	.301	762	229	49	7	22	118	54	58	.349	.470
Pitch 76-90	.265	68	18	3	2	0	7	7	9	.329	.368
Pitch 91-105	.190	21	4	1	0	1	1	2	2	.261	.381
Pitch 106+	.667	3	2	0	1	0	0	0	0	.667	1.333
First Pitch	.385	122	47	14	0	7	23	3	0	.406	.672
Ahead in Count	.299	385	115	26	3	5	53	0	57	.302	.421
Behind in Count	.260	204	53	9	3	8	32	39	0	.376	.451
Two Strikes	.273	304	83	13	3	5	33	20	69	.323	.385

Jim Eisenreich — Phillies

Age 35 – Bats Left (groundball hitter)

	Avg	G	AB	R	H	2B	3B	HR	RBI	BB	SO	HBP	GDP	SB	CS	OBP	SLG	IBB	SH	SF	#Pit	#P/PA	GB	FB	G/F
1993 Season	.318	153	362	51	115	17	4	7	54	26	36	1	6	5	0	.363	.445	5	3	2	1334	3.39	151	86	1.76
Last Five Years	.292	677	2061	254	601	114	24	25	239	149	202	3	38	60	31	.337	.407	21	11	19	7318	3.26	895	576	1.55

1993 Season

	Avg	AB	H	2B	3B	HR	RBI	BB	SO	OBP	SLG
vs. Left	.293	58	17	2	1	1	11	6	11	.354	.414
vs. Right	.322	304	98	15	3	6	43	20	25	.365	.451
Groundball	.282	131	37	4	0	3	18	11	12	.343	.382
Flyball	.365	52	19	3	2	0	9	6	7	.424	.500
Home	.327	156	51	7	2	3	24	10	15	.371	.455
Away	.311	206	64	10	2	4	30	16	21	.357	.437
Day	.261	88	23	3	0	0	13	2	10	.275	.295
Night	.336	274	92	14	4	7	41	24	26	.390	.493
Grass	.323	127	41	6	1	3	19	8	13	.358	.457
Turf	.315	235	74	11	3	4	35	18	23	.366	.438
First Pitch	.327	52	17	4	0	4	10	5	0	.386	.635
Ahead in Count	.404	89	36	7	1	1	20	15	0	.490	.539
Behind in Count	.243	148	36	2	2	0	11	0	32	.247	.284
Two Strikes	.252	131	33	2	3	1	14	6	36	.290	.336

	Avg	AB	H	2B	3B	HR	RBI	BB	SO	OBP	SLG
Scoring Posn	.303	122	37	4	1	3	47	14	12	.370	.426
Close & Late	.268	71	19	2	0	0	10	6	8	.321	.296
None on/out	.260	77	20	4	2	1	1	4	12	.296	.403
Batting #6	.339	248	84	12	3	6	43	22	26	.392	.484
Batting #7	.311	45	14	2	0	0	5	2	2	.340	.356
Other	.246	69	17	3	1	1	6	2	8	.268	.362
April	.320	25	8	1	1	0	5	3	2	.393	.440
May	.371	35	13	5	0	0	5	3	1	.421	.514
June	.351	77	27	5	2	2	18	5	9	.390	.545
July	.310	84	26	0	0	1	9	2	6	.326	.345
August	.282	71	20	3	1	4	9	3	9	.320	.521
September/October	.300	70	21	3	0	0	8	10	9	.378	.343
Pre-All Star	.345	171	59	11	3	2	31	13	13	.391	.480
Post-All Star	.293	191	56	6	1	5	23	13	23	.338	.414

1993 By Position

Position	Avg	AB	H	2B	3B	HR	RBI	BB	SO	OBP	SLG	G	GS	Innings	PO	A	E	DP	Fld Pct	Rng Fctr	In Zone	Outs	Zone Rtg	MLB Zone
As Pinch Hitter	.143	21	3	0	0	0	1	1	3	.182	.143	25	0	---	---	---	---	---	---	---	---	---	---	---
As rf	.323	337	109	17	4	7	51	25	33	.370	.460	133	78	809.0	216	6	1	0	.996	2.47	241	212	.880	.826

Last Five Years

	Avg	AB	H	2B	3B	HR	RBI	BB	SO	OBP	SLG
vs. Left	.277	483	134	21	5	5	67	29	66	.316	.373
vs. Right	.296	1578	467	93	19	20	172	120	136	.344	.417
Groundball	.282	632	178	32	6	4	63	46	50	.330	.370
Flyball	.289	467	135	30	9	7	56	40	67	.340	.437
Home	.289	973	281	48	17	12	120	77	84	.339	.410
Away	.294	1088	320	66	7	13	119	72	118	.336	.403
Day	.316	548	173	36	7	5	78	35	45	.353	.434
Night	.283	1513	428	78	17	20	161	114	157	.332	.397
Grass	.300	824	247	52	4	8	82	53	96	.340	.402
Turf	.286	1237	354	62	20	17	157	96	106	.335	.410
First Pitch	.325	416	135	34	6	10	52	14	0	.344	.507
Ahead in Count	.340	536	182	32	10	5	88	82	0	.424	.465
Behind in Count	.261	605	158	24	5	4	61	0	101	.259	.337

	Avg	AB	H	2B	3B	HR	RBI	BB	SO	OBP	SLG
Scoring Posn	.277	575	159	24	6	8	212	61	60	.337	.381
Close & Late	.271	369	100	16	7	5	39	32	48	.325	.393
None on/out	.311	530	165	44	6	7	7	33	59	.352	.457
Batting #5	.283	714	202	47	12	11	86	39	74	.318	.429
Batting #6	.298	627	187	29	4	8	73	55	64	.353	.396
Other	.294	720	212	38	8	6	80	55	64	.342	.394
April	.286	231	66	14	4	4	30	14	31	.323	.433
May	.314	347	109	27	2	2	42	32	36	.370	.421
June	.290	396	115	20	3	4	43	33	33	.343	.386
July	.280	386	108	19	7	1	36	24	30	.321	.373
August	.319	310	99	17	4	10	47	19	26	.358	.497
September/October	.266	391	104	17	4	4	41	27	46	.310	.361
Pre-All Star	.294	1132	333	68	13	10	126	88	111	.343	.404

Last Five Years	Avg	AB	H	2B	3B	HR	RBI	BB	SO	OBP	SLG		Avg	AB	H	2B	3B	HR	RBI	BB	SO	OBP	SLG
Two Strikes	.235	673	158	23	6	5	50	50	202	.288	.309	Post-All Star	.288	929	268	46	11	15	113	61	91	.330	.410

Batter vs. Pitcher (since 1984)

Hits Best Against	Avg	AB	H	2B	3B	HR	RBI	BB	SO	OBP	SLG	Hits Worst Against	Avg	AB	H	2B	3B	HR	RBI	BB	SO	OBP	SLG
Rick Aguilera	.583	12	7	1	1	0	0	0	1	.583	.833	David Wells	.091	11	1	0	0	0	0	0	0	.091	.091
Dennis Eckersley	.500	10	5	2	0	0	1	1	3	.545	.700	Mike Mussina	.091	11	1	1	0	0	0	0	1	.091	.182
Lee Guetterman	.462	13	6	2	0	0	0	2	1	.533	.615	Nolan Ryan	.105	19	2	0	0	0	1	3	5	.217	.105
Mike Boddicker	.429	21	9	4	0	1	1	0	3	.429	.762	Mark Williamson	.188	16	3	0	0	0	1	0	1	.176	.188
Pete Harnisch	.385	13	5	2	2	0	1	3	1	.500	.846	Scott Bankhead	.200	10	2	0	0	0	1	0	1	.182	.200

Cal Eldred — Brewers

Age 26 – Pitches Right (flyball pitcher)

	ERA	W	L	Sv	G	GS	IP	BB	SO	Avg	H	2B	3B	HR	RBI	OBP	SLG	CG	ShO	Sup	QS	#P/S	SB	CS	GB	FB	G/F
1993 Season	4.01	16	16	0	36	36	258.0	91	180	.239	232	47	7	32	110	.308	.401	8	1	4.74	21	118	21	9	288	348	0.83
Career (1991-1993)	3.44	29	18	0	53	53	374.1	120	252	.234	328	58	10	38	131	.297	.371	10	2	5.19	34	115	32	14	420	515	0.82

1993 Season

	ERA	W	L	Sv	G	GS	IP	H	HR	BB	SO		Avg	AB	H	2B	3B	HR	RBI	BB	SO	OBP	SLG
Home	2.91	11	6	0	19	19	148.2	118	11	37	97	vs. Left	.245	507	124	27	6	12	53	52	75	.320	.393
Away	5.52	5	10	0	17	17	109.1	114	21	54	83	vs. Right	.234	462	108	20	1	20	57	39	105	.294	.411
Day	4.36	6	4	0	12	12	84.2	78	10	25	58	Inning 1-6	.242	764	185	39	6	23	90	78	152	.316	.399
Night	3.84	10	12	0	24	24	173.1	154	22	66	122	Inning 7+	.229	205	47	8	1	9	20	13	28	.276	.410
Grass	3.80	16	14	0	33	33	239.1	211	29	80	163	None on	.243	602	146	33	5	18	18	45	104	.302	.404
Turf	6.75	0	2	0	3	3	18.2	21	3	11	17	Runners on	.234	367	86	14	2	14	92	46	76	.317	.398
April	3.73	3	2	0	5	5	31.1	23	2	10	26	Scoring Posn	.212	212	45	6	1	8	77	31	47	.304	.363
May	3.67	3	3	0	6	6	41.2	46	4	10	29	Close & Late	.239	109	26	3	1	6	15	7	13	.286	.450
June	3.48	3	3	0	6	6	44.0	39	8	13	21	None on/out	.244	258	63	16	2	4	4	17	48	.299	.368
July	5.40	2	3	0	7	7	46.2	49	9	20	33	vs. 1st Batr (relief)	.000	0	0	0	0	0	0	0	0	.000	.000
August	3.54	4	1	0	6	6	48.1	41	5	19	36	First Inning Pitched	.254	138	35	8	2	5	20	12	26	.325	.449
September/October	4.11	1	4	0	6	6	46.0	34	4	19	35	First 75 Pitches	.247	583	144	28	6	16	62	58	113	.320	.398
Starter	4.01	16	16	0	36	36	258.0	232	32	91	180	Pitch 76-90	.276	134	37	8	0	7	28	14	20	.340	.493
Reliever	0.00	0	0	0	0	0	0.0	0	0	0	0	Pitch 91-105	.221	122	27	8	0	3	9	6	22	.265	.361
0-3 Days Rest	4.18	1	3	0	4	4	28.0	24	4	8	11	Pitch 106+	.185	130	24	3	1	6	11	13	25	.257	.362
4 Days Rest	4.39	11	12	0	24	24	170.1	165	22	60	124	First Pitch	.318	132	42	7	1	5	13	2	0	.338	.500
5+ Days Rest	2.87	4	1	0	8	8	59.2	43	6	23	45	Ahead in Count	.156	449	70	14	3	9	33	0	152	.161	.261
Pre-All Star	3.85	10	8	0	20	20	135.2	129	17	42	89	Behind in Count	.340	200	68	15	2	11	40	37	0	.440	.600
Post-All Star	4.19	6	8	0	16	16	122.1	103	15	49	91	Two Strikes	.163	490	80	13	3	12	44	52	180	.244	.276

Scott Erickson — Twins

Age 26 – Pitches Right (groundball pitcher)

	ERA	W	L	Sv	G	GS	IP	BB	SO	Avg	H	2B	3B	HR	RBI	OBP	SLG	CG	ShO	Sup	QS	#P/S	SB	CS	GB	FB	G/F
1993 Season	5.19	8	19	0	34	34	218.2	71	116	.305	266	43	8	17	119	.359	.431	1	0	4.94	12	100	28	4	415	194	2.14
Career (1990-1993)	3.78	49	43	0	117	115	747.2	276	378	.268	760	127	20	57	313	.336	.387	12	6	5.02	62	96	61	24	1386	621	2.23

1993 Season

	ERA	W	L	Sv	G	GS	IP	H	HR	BB	SO		Avg	AB	H	2B	3B	HR	RBI	BB	SO	OBP	SLG
Home	5.30	4	11	0	19	19	127.1	150	9	43	80	vs. Left	.342	474	162	31	7	7	57	44	55	.392	.481
Away	5.03	4	8	0	15	15	91.1	116	8	28	36	vs. Right	.261	398	104	12	1	10	62	27	61	.320	.372
Day	5.50	2	6	0	8	8	52.1	68	5	7	33	Inning 1-6	.299	759	227	36	8	16	105	59	104	.350	.431
Night	5.09	6	13	0	26	26	166.1	198	12	64	83	Inning 7+	.345	113	39	7	0	1	14	12	12	.419	.434
Grass	4.65	3	4	0	10	10	60.0	75	6	21	20	None on	.299	462	138	27	4	10	10	40	69	.360	.439
Turf	5.39	5	15	0	24	24	158.2	191	11	50	96	Runners on	.312	410	128	16	4	7	109	31	47	.359	.422
April	9.60	0	3	0	3	3	15.0	21	3	6	7	Scoring Posn	.315	248	78	11	2	6	102	24	34	.369	.448
May	4.20	2	3	0	6	6	40.2	34	4	9	22	Close & Late	.333	66	22	5	0	0	8	8	9	.416	.409
June	5.98	2	3	0	7	7	43.2	58	2	17	25	None on/out	.336	217	73	18	1	5	5	17	28	.390	.498
July	4.74	2	3	0	6	6	38.0	47	6	17	18	vs. 1st Batr (relief)	.000	0	0	0	0	0	0	0	0	.000	.000
August	4.60	2	4	0	6	6	43.0	57	0	9	21	First Inning Pitched	.285	130	37	2	0	3	20	17	22	.359	.369
September/October	4.70	0	3	0	6	6	38.1	49	2	13	23	First 75 Pitches	.288	636	183	27	5	12	79	52	88	.341	.403
Starter	5.19	8	19	0	34	34	218.2	266	17	71	116	Pitch 76-90	.336	113	38	8	3	5	22	5	15	.369	.593
Reliever	0.00	0	0	0	0	0	0.0	0	0	0	0	Pitch 91-105	.363	80	29	7	0	0	10	9	9	.433	.450
0-3 Days Rest	4.59	2	2	0	5	5	33.1	38	2	10	19	Pitch 106+	.372	43	16	1	0	0	8	5	4	.451	.395
4 Days Rest	5.25	5	14	0	24	24	154.1	187	15	52	79	First Pitch	.284	141	40	5	1	1	13	1	0	.311	.355
5+ Days Rest	5.52	1	3	0	5	5	31.0	41	0	9	18	Ahead in Count	.257	339	87	13	4	4	47	0	93	.261	.354
Pre-All Star	5.68	5	9	0	18	18	109.1	131	11	35	58	Behind in Count	.368	234	86	16	3	9	38	36	0	.444	.577
Post-All Star	4.69	3	10	0	16	16	109.1	135	6	36	58	Two Strikes	.211	298	63	8	2	3	33	34	116	.300	.282

Career (1990-1993)

	ERA	W	L	Sv	G	GS	IP	H	HR	BB	SO		Avg	AB	H	2B	3B	HR	RBI	BB	SO	OBP	SLG
Home	4.01	29	22	0	65	64	426.0	453	31	132	232	vs. Left	.288	1525	439	76	14	26	161	157	152	.353	.407
Away	3.47	20	21	0	52	51	321.2	307	26	144	146	vs. Right	.245	1312	321	51	6	31	152	119	226	.316	.364
Day	3.24	21	15	0	43	43	286.0	280	14	88	146	Inning 1-6	.264	2415	638	107	17	43	264	228	329	.331	.376
Night	4.11	28	28	0	74	72	461.2	480	43	188	232	Inning 7+	.289	422	122	20	3	14	49	48	49	.366	.450
Grass	2.90	18	12	0	39	38	245.1	220	18	116	106	None on	.269	1584	426	80	10	33	33	164	221	.344	.395
Turf	4.21	31	31	0	78	77	502.1	540	39	160	272	Runners on	.267	1253	334	47	10	24	280	112	157	.326	.377
April	4.74	2	8	0	12	12	76.0	77	6	31	31	Scoring Posn	.260	697	181	23	6	15	249	82	105	.330	.374
May	3.21	10	4	0	17	17	115.0	101	10	32	69	Close & Late	.290	238	69	12	3	5	26	24	31	.358	.429
June	3.82	11	6	0	20	20	132.0	137	8	50	76	None on/out	.280	724	203	46	2	19	19	70	93	.350	.428

Career (1990-1993)

	ERA	W	L	Sv	G	GS	IP	H	HR	BB	SO		Avg	AB	H	2B	3B	HR	RBI	BB	SO	OBP	SLG
July	3.91	6	6	0	21	19	122.0	134	17	54	53	vs. 1st Batr (relief)	1.000	1	1	0	0	0	0	1	0	1.000	1.000
August	4.74	7	12	0	22	22	131.0	156	7	45	61	First Inning Pitched	.264	436	115	16	1	10	52	50	62	.336	.374
September/October	2.88	13	7	0	25	25	171.2	155	9	64	88	First 75 Pitches	.264	2117	559	87	12	40	227	202	286	.331	.373
Starter	3.76	49	43	0	115	115	742.0	752	55	270	377	Pitch 76-90	.282	344	97	21	6	11	47	34	47	.351	.474
Reliever	6.35	0	0	0	2	0	5.2	8	2	6	1	Pitch 91-105	.269	234	63	12	1	3	24	19	29	.329	.368
0-3 Days Rest	4.47	2	3	0	7	7	44.1	51	4	14	25	Pitch 106+	.289	142	41	7	1	3	15	21	16	.386	.415
4 Days Rest	3.96	32	28	0	73	73	466.1	482	38	177	241	First Pitch	.308	458	141	19	3	12	67	6	0	.325	.441
5+ Days Rest	3.23	15	12	0	35	35	231.1	219	13	79	111	Ahead in Count	.215	1079	232	46	7	12	89	0	305	.224	.304
Pre-All Star	3.82	24	19	0	54	54	351.0	353	28	124	189	Behind in Count	.309	812	251	37	7	24	102	155	0	.417	.461
Post-All Star	3.74	25	24	0	63	61	396.2	407	29	152	189	Two Strikes	.184	996	183	37	5	9	68	115	378	.276	.258

Pitcher vs. Batter (career)

Pitches Best Vs.	Avg	AB	H	2B	3B	HR	RBI	BB	SO	OBP	SLG	Pitches Worst Vs.	Avg	AB	H	2B	3B	HR	RBI	BB	SO	OBP	SLG
Dave Valle	.000	14	0	0	0	0	1	4	5	.222	.000	Mike Aldrete	.600	10	6	1	0	0	0	1	1	.636	.700
Kevin Seitzer	.000	12	0	0	0	0	1	0	0	.000	.000	Ken Griffey Jr	.538	26	14	5	0	1	4	4	0	.563	.846
Bob Melvin	.000	9	0	0	0	0	2	1	2	.091	.000	Tino Martinez	.500	12	6	2	0	1	4	2	1	.533	.917
Glenn Davis	.100	10	1	0	0	0	0	1	4	.182	.100	Greg Vaughn	.455	11	5	0	0	2	3	2	3	.538	1.000
Pat Borders	.105	19	2	1	0	0	1	0	4	.105	.158	Mark McGwire	.444	18	8	2	0	3	7	3	3	.524	1.056

Alvaro Espinoza — Indians

Age 32 – Bats Right (groundball hitter)

	Avg	G	AB	R	H	2B	3B	HR	RBI	BB	SO	HBP	GDP	SB	CS	OBP	SLG	IBB	SH	SF	#Pit	#P/PA	GB	FB	G/F
1993 Season	.278	129	263	34	73	15	0	4	27	8	36	1	7	2	2	.298	.380	0	8	3	919	3.25	92	75	1.23
Last Five Years	.259	573	1684	167	436	73	5	11	121	54	207	9	44	10	8	.284	.328	1	51	10	5400	2.99	678	446	1.52

1993 Season

	Avg	AB	H	2B	3B	HR	RBI	BB	SO	OBP	SLG		Avg	AB	H	2B	3B	HR	RBI	BB	SO	OBP	SLG
vs. Left	.345	113	39	9	0	2	12	4	13	.364	.478	Scoring Posn	.300	70	21	5	0	1	24	2	7	.307	.414
vs. Right	.227	150	34	6	0	2	15	4	23	.248	.307	Close & Late	.370	46	17	2	0	1	8	1	3	.367	.478
Home	.218	124	27	5	0	3	14	4	17	.244	.331	None on/out	.349	63	22	5	0	3	3	1	6	.369	.571
Away	.331	139	46	10	0	1	13	4	19	.347	.424	Batting #7	.250	168	42	11	0	1	14	8	19	.285	.333
First Pitch	.298	47	14	3	0	0	4	0	0	.298	.362	Batting #8	.297	64	19	2	0	2	7	0	12	.292	.422
Ahead in Count	.310	42	13	2	0	1	5	7	0	.392	.429	Other	.387	31	12	2	0	1	6	0	5	.387	.548
Behind in Count	.262	130	34	7	0	0	9	0	34	.267	.315	Pre-All Star	.333	147	49	8	0	3	20	3	16	.346	.449
Two Strikes	.279	104	29	5	0	3	12	1	36	.292	.413	Post-All Star	.207	116	24	7	0	1	7	5	20	.238	.293

Last Five Years

	Avg	AB	H	2B	3B	HR	RBI	BB	SO	OBP	SLG		Avg	AB	H	2B	3B	HR	RBI	BB	SO	OBP	SLG
vs. Left	.309	580	179	28	1	4	48	28	52	.340	.381	Scoring Posn	.267	356	95	16	1	2	107	12	40	.287	.334
vs. Right	.233	1104	257	45	4	7	73	26	155	.254	.300	Close & Late	.272	250	68	8	1	2	21	10	24	.297	.336
Groundball	.225	409	92	17	2	2	28	15	46	.255	.291	None on/out	.249	394	98	19	2	5	5	9	43	.269	.345
Flyball	.263	353	93	13	0	4	26	8	54	.281	.334	Batting #8	.263	692	182	31	2	5	54	19	88	.284	.335
Home	.249	838	209	36	4	5	59	29	90	.276	.320	Batting #9	.240	462	111	15	3	2	27	18	49	.274	.299
Away	.268	846	227	37	1	6	62	25	117	.292	.336	Other	.270	530	143	27	0	4	40	17	70	.292	.343
Day	.242	512	124	19	3	5	37	21	57	.275	.320	April	.293	188	55	11	1	1	22	10	25	.327	.378
Night	.266	1172	312	54	2	6	84	33	150	.288	.331	May	.221	258	57	8	0	1	14	8	29	.244	.264
Grass	.255	1424	363	61	4	8	101	49	175	.282	.320	June	.266	304	81	13	1	4	23	9	34	.288	.355
Turf	.281	260	73	12	1	3	20	5	32	.296	.369	July	.281	310	87	12	2	2	23	16	35	.317	.352
First Pitch	.304	408	124	21	2	2	37	0	0	.308	.380	August	.266	342	91	12	1	3	22	3	36	.276	.333
Ahead in Count	.304	280	85	17	1	4	26	37	0	.382	.414	September/October	.230	282	65	17	0	0	17	8	48	.259	.291
Behind in Count	.212	777	165	21	1	1	36	0	196	.217	.246	Pre-All Star	.267	855	228	35	3	6	64	29	97	.291	.336
Two Strikes	.207	608	126	18	2	4	33	17	207	.234	.263	Post-All Star	.251	829	208	38	2	5	57	25	110	.276	.320

Batter vs. Pitcher (career)

Hits Best Against	Avg	AB	H	2B	3B	HR	RBI	BB	SO	OBP	SLG	Hits Worst Against	Avg	AB	H	2B	3B	HR	RBI	BB	SO	OBP	SLG
Teddy Higuera	.550	20	11	0	0	0	1	1	2	.571	.550	Shawn Hillegas	.071	14	1	0	0	0	0	0	7	.071	.071
Scott Sanderson	.545	11	6	1	0	0	1	0	0	.545	.636	Mike Witt	.083	12	1	0	0	0	0	0	4	.083	.083
Bret Saberhagen	.529	17	9	2	1	0	1	0	0	.529	.765	Tom Gordon	.091	11	1	0	0	0	2	1	4	.167	.091
Frank Tanana	.480	25	12	3	0	0	1	1	3	.500	.600	Tom Candiotti	.118	17	2	0	0	0	0	0	5	.118	.118
Jack McDowell	.333	12	4	0	0	1	1	3	1	.467	.583	Curt Young	.143	14	2	0	0	0	0	0	1	.143	.143

Cecil Espy — Reds

Age 31 – Bats Both (groundball hitter)

	Avg	G	AB	R	H	2B	3B	HR	RBI	BB	SO	HBP	GDP	SB	CS	OBP	SLG	IBB	SH	SF	#Pit	#P/PA	GB	FB	G/F
1993 Season	.233	40	60	6	14	2	0	0	5	14	13	0	2	2	2	.368	.267	0	0	2	315	4.14	25	13	1.92
Last Five Years	.244	389	882	109	215	25	10	5	68	82	189	2	8	68	30	.307	.312	4	15	7	3668	3.71	342	192	1.78

1993 Season

	Avg	AB	H	2B	3B	HR	RBI	BB	SO	OBP	SLG		Avg	AB	H	2B	3B	HR	RBI	BB	SO	OBP	SLG
vs. Left	.231	13	3	0	0	0	1	1	2	.267	.231	Scoring Posn	.176	17	3	1	0	0	4	5	7	.333	.235
vs. Right	.234	47	11	2	0	0	4	13	11	.393	.277	Close & Late	.269	26	7	1	0	0	2	3	7	.345	.308

Last Five Years

	Avg	AB	H	2B	3B	HR	RBI	BB	SO	OBP	SLG		Avg	AB	H	2B	3B	HR	RBI	BB	SO	OBP	SLG
vs. Left	.220	209	46	3	0	4	16	17	37	.275	.292	Scoring Posn	.222	216	48	7	1	1	62	17	55	.271	.278
vs. Right	.251	673	169	22	10	1	52	65	152	.317	.318	Close & Late	.230	187	43	5	1	0	15	26	40	.322	.267
Groundball	.248	274	68	9	3	1	25	28	59	.317	.314	None on/out	.252	305	77	7	8	2	2	33	55	.327	.348
Flyball	.243	222	54	5	2	1	19	21	47	.306	.297	Batting #1	.240	566	136	12	7	3	34	45	118	.297	.302
Home	.264	432	114	12	7	3	38	37	91	.319	.345	Batting #9	.219	128	28	3	2	0	13	16	33	.303	.273

Last Five Years	Avg	AB	H	2B	3B	HR	RBI	BB	SO	OBP	SLG		Avg	AB	H	2B	3B	HR	RBI	BB	SO	OBP	SLG
Away	.224	450	101	13	3	2	30	45	98	.296	.280	Other	.271	188	51	10	1	2	21	21	38	.340	.367
Day	.233	202	47	3	4	1	12	18	50	.297	.302	April	.283	152	43	5	4	0	16	15	33	.345	.368
Night	.247	680	168	22	6	4	56	64	139	.310	.315	May	.208	173	36	5	0	0	8	18	35	.283	.237
Grass	.255	522	133	13	7	2	31	45	109	.315	.318	June	.238	185	44	3	0	3	15	16	38	.297	.303
Turf	.228	360	82	12	3	3	37	37	80	.296	.303	July	.218	110	24	2	2	1	9	8	30	.277	.300
First Pitch	.325	126	41	5	1	2	17	3	0	.336	.429	August	.241	145	35	5	1	1	13	11	30	.291	.310
Ahead in Count	.280	132	37	4	2	0	11	47	0	.464	.341	September/October	.282	117	33	5	3	0	7	14	23	.356	.376
Behind in Count	.183	447	82	9	4	3	31	0	162	.186	.242	Pre-All Star	.235	550	129	13	4	4	41	53	115	.302	.295
Two Strikes	.172	442	76	7	5	2	21	32	189	.229	.224	Post-All Star	.259	332	86	12	6	1	27	29	74	.316	.340

Batter vs. Pitcher (since 1984)

Hits Best Against	Avg	AB	H	2B	3B	HR	RBI	BB	SO	OBP	SLG	Hits Worst Against	Avg	AB	H	2B	3B	HR	RBI	BB	SO	OBP	SLG
Roger Clemens	.421	19	8	1	0	0	2	1	5	.450	.474	Mike Moore	.071	14	1	1	0	0	1	2	5	.188	.143
Scott Bankhead	.316	19	6	1	0	0	1	1	4	.350	.368	Mike Boddicker	.091	11	1	0	0	0	0	0	2	.091	.091
												Mike Witt	.167	12	2	1	0	0	0	0	3	.167	.250
												Dave Stewart	.208	24	5	1	0	0	3	0	8	.208	.250
												Tom Candiotti	.231	13	3	0	0	0	0	0	4	.231	.231

Mark Ettles — Padres

Age 27 – Pitches Right

	ERA	W	L	Sv	G	GS	IP	BB	SO	Avg	H	2B	3B	HR	RBI	OBP	SLG	GF	IR	IRS	Hld	SvOp	SB	CS	GB	FB	G/F
1993 Season	6.50	1	0	0	14	0	18.0	4	9	.307	23	3	0	4	21	.333	.507	5	9	5	1	0	0	0	26	25	1.04

1993 Season

	ERA	W	L	Sv	G	GS	IP	H	HR	BB	SO		Avg	AB	H	2B	3B	HR	RBI	BB	SO	OBP	SLG
Home	5.63	0	0	0	7	0	8.0	9	1	2	4	vs. Left	.448	29	13	1	0	3	11	3	1	.485	.793
Away	7.20	1	0	0	7	0	10.0	14	3	2	5	vs. Right	.217	46	10	2	0	1	10	1	8	.229	.326

Carl Everett — Marlins

Age 24 – Bats Both

	Avg	G	AB	R	H	2B	3B	HR	RBI	BB	SO	HBP	GDP	SB	CS	OBP	SLG	IBB	SH	SF	#Pit	#P/PA	GB	FB	G/F
1993 Season	.105	11	19	0	2	0	0	0	0	1	9	0	0	1	0	.150	.105	0	0	0	95	4.75	4	3	1.33

1993 Season

	Avg	AB	H	2B	3B	HR	RBI	BB	SO	OBP	SLG		Avg	AB	H	2B	3B	HR	RBI	BB	SO	OBP	SLG
vs. Left	.000	5	0	0	0	0	0	0	1	.000	.000	Scoring Posn	.000	4	0	0	0	0	0	1	0	.200	.000
vs. Right	.143	14	2	0	0	0	0	1	8	.200	.143	Close & Late	.333	3	1	0	0	0	0	1	2	.500	.333

Hector Fajardo — Rangers

Age 23 – Pitches Right (flyball pitcher)

	ERA	W	L	Sv	G	GS	IP	BB	SO	Avg	H	2B	3B	HR	RBI	OBP	SLG	GF	IR	IRS	Hld	SvOp	SB	CS	GB	FB	G/F
1993 Season	0.00	0	0	0	1	0	0.2	0	1	.000	0	0	0	0	0	.000	.000	1	1	0	0	0	0	0	0	1	0.00
Career (1991-1993)	6.58	0	2	0	7	5	26.0	11	24	.330	35	6	1	2	10	.388	.462	2	1	0	0	0	7	2	28	32	0.88

1993 Season

	ERA	W	L	Sv	G	GS	IP	H	HR	BB	SO		Avg	AB	H	2B	3B	HR	RBI	BB	SO	OBP	SLG
Home	0.00	0	0	0	1	0	0.2	0	0	0	1	vs. Left	.000	0	0	0	0	0	0	0	0	.000	.000
Away	0.00	0	0	0	0	0	0.0	0	0	0	0	vs. Right	.000	2	0	0	0	0	0	0	1	.000	.000

Rikkert Faneyte — Giants

Age 25 – Bats Right

	Avg	G	AB	R	H	2B	3B	HR	RBI	BB	SO	HBP	GDP	SB	CS	OBP	SLG	IBB	SH	SF	#Pit	#P/PA	GB	FB	G/F
1993 Season	.133	7	15	2	2	0	0	0	0	2	4	0	0	0	0	.235	.133	0	0	0	56	3.29	4	5	0.80

1993 Season

	Avg	AB	H	2B	3B	HR	RBI	BB	SO	OBP	SLG		Avg	AB	H	2B	3B	HR	RBI	BB	SO	OBP	SLG
vs. Left	.222	9	2	0	0	0	0	0	2	.222	.222	Scoring Posn	.250	4	1	0	0	0	0	0	1	.250	.250
vs. Right	.000	6	0	0	0	0	0	2	2	.250	.000	Close & Late	.000	2	0	0	0	0	0	1	1	.333	.000

Paul Faries — Giants

Age 29 – Bats Right (groundball hitter)

	Avg	G	AB	R	H	2B	3B	HR	RBI	BB	SO	HBP	GDP	SB	CS	OBP	SLG	IBB	SH	SF	#Pit	#P/PA	GB	FB	G/F
1993 Season	.222	15	36	6	8	2	1	0	4	1	4	0	1	2	0	.237	.333	0	1	1	127	3.26	18	8	2.25
Career (1990-1993)	.201	96	214	26	43	7	2	0	14	20	34	2	6	5	2	.273	.252	0	7	2	862	3.52	96	46	2.09

1993 Season

	Avg	AB	H	2B	3B	HR	RBI	BB	SO	OBP	SLG		Avg	AB	H	2B	3B	HR	RBI	BB	SO	OBP	SLG
vs. Left	.154	13	2	1	0	0	0	1	0	.214	.231	Scoring Posn	.231	13	3	1	1	0	4	1	3	.267	.462
vs. Right	.261	23	6	1	1	0	4	0	4	.250	.391	Close & Late	.000	1	0	0	0	0	0	0	0	.000	.000

Monty Fariss — Marlins

Age 26 – Bats Right

	Avg	G	AB	R	H	2B	3B	HR	RBI	BB	SO	HBP	GDP	SB	CS	OBP	SLG	IBB	SH	SF	#Pit	#P/PA	GB	FB	G/F
1993 Season	.172	18	29	3	5	2	1	0	2	5	13	0	2	0	0	.294	.310	0	0	0	170	5.00	8	6	1.33
Career (1991-1993)	.217	104	226	22	49	10	2	4	29	29	75	2	5	0	2	.311	.332	0	2	0	1049	4.05	68	51	1.33

1993 Season

	Avg	AB	H	2B	3B	HR	RBI	BB	SO	OBP	SLG		Avg	AB	H	2B	3B	HR	RBI	BB	SO	OBP	SLG
vs. Left	.158	19	3	1	1	0	2	4	9	.304	.316	Scoring Posn	.125	8	1	0	0	0	1	2	4	.300	.125
vs. Right	.200	10	2	1	0	0	0	1	4	.273	.300	Close & Late	.000	3	0	0	0	0	0	1	3	.250	.000

Steve Farr — Yankees

Age 37 – Pitches Right

	ERA	W	L	Sv	G	GS	IP	BB	SO	Avg	H	2B	3B	HR	RBI	OBP	SLG	GF	IR	IRS	Hld	SvOp	SB	CS	GB	FB	G/F
1993 Season	4.21	2	2	25	49	0	47.0	28	39	.253	44	10	2	8	36	.356	.471	37	28	17	1	31	4	1	51	54	0.94
Last Five Years	2.63	24	21	97	267	8	359.1	137	286	.234	309	53	6	25	149	.311	.340	147	133	46	13	120	24	10	429	385	1.11

1993 Season

	ERA	W	L	Sv	G	GS	IP	H	HR	BB	SO		Avg	AB	H	2B	3B	HR	RBI	BB	SO	OBP	SLG
Home	5.23	0	2	14	23	0	20.2	20	4	14	15	vs. Left	.293	75	22	4	2	3	12	11	9	.391	.520
Away	3.42	2	0	11	26	0	26.1	24	4	14	24	vs. Right	.222	99	22	6	0	5	24	17	30	.331	.434
Starter	0.00	0	0	0	0	0	0.0	0	0	0	0	Scoring Posn	.327	52	17	4	0	4	30	13	13	.443	.635
Reliever	4.21	2	2	25	49	0	47.0	44	8	28	39	Close & Late	.224	125	28	6	1	2	22	20	30	.327	.336
0 Days rest	2.35	1	1	4	8	0	7.2	5	1	2	7	None on/out	.184	38	7	1	0	0	0	4	9	.262	.211
1 or 2 Days rest	4.07	0	1	14	25	0	24.1	22	3	19	18	First Pitch	.150	20	3	2	0	0	2	4	0	.308	.250
3+ Days rest	5.40	1	0	7	16	0	15.0	17	4	7	14	Ahead in Count	.173	81	14	3	1	0	5	0	28	.181	.235
Pre-All Star	3.19	1	2	18	31	0	31.0	27	4	19	29	Behind in Count	.481	27	13	3	0	5	15	8	0	.583	1.148
Post-All Star	6.19	1	0	7	18	0	16.0	17	4	9	10	Two Strikes	.210	100	21	4	1	3	15	16	39	.322	.360

Last Five Years

	ERA	W	L	Sv	G	GS	IP	H	HR	BB	SO		Avg	AB	H	2B	3B	HR	RBI	BB	SO	OBP	SLG
Home	2.42	15	9	59	140	4	190.0	147	10	64	149	vs. Left	.247	603	149	23	4	8	54	74	104	.338	.338
Away	2.87	9	12	38	127	4	169.1	162	15	73	137	vs. Right	.223	718	160	30	2	17	95	63	182	.288	.341
Day	2.94	8	7	24	72	3	110.1	95	6	43	88	Inning 1-6	.219	233	51	7	1	3	18	21	51	.290	.296
Night	2.49	16	14	73	195	5	249.0	214	19	94	198	Inning 7+	.237	1088	258	46	5	22	131	116	235	.315	.349
Grass	2.96	9	14	71	171	3	209.2	187	21	86	166	None on	.243	742	180	34	4	13	13	52	158	.298	.352
Turf	2.16	15	7	26	96	5	149.2	122	4	51	120	Runners on	.223	579	129	19	2	12	136	85	128	.326	.325
April	3.38	1	4	15	39	0	42.2	41	5	17	38	Scoring Posn	.213	347	74	10	1	10	126	61	89	.334	.334
May	1.88	6	4	15	50	0	62.1	51	4	28	52	Close & Late	.225	590	133	21	1	10	79	75	135	.316	.315
June	2.49	1	2	25	50	2	65.0	47	3	21	56	None on/out	.245	318	78	17	1	4	4	18	62	.292	.343
July	2.73	5	3	11	41	1	52.2	46	4	23	46	vs. 1st Batr (relief)	.222	230	51	8	0	4	20	25	52	.304	.309
August	3.39	4	5	16	46	0	66.1	58	5	21	43	First Inning Pitched	.222	877	195	34	3	17	116	99	197	.306	.326
September/October	2.18	7	3	15	41	5	70.1	66	4	27	51	First 15 Pitches	.227	752	171	30	3	14	84	72	166	.302	.331
Starter	1.48	6	1	0	8	8	48.2	41	2	14	34	Pitch 16-30	.245	322	79	11	1	8	42	43	73	.334	.360
Reliever	2.81	18	20	97	259	0	310.2	268	23	123	252	Pitch 31-45	.231	134	31	8	1	0	10	11	30	.297	.306
0 Days rest	2.81	6	3	19	39	0	41.2	39	3	10	31	Pitch 46+	.248	113	28	4	1	3	13	11	17	.320	.381
1 or 2 Days rest	2.91	7	14	46	132	0	164.0	142	13	79	128	First Pitch	.294	160	47	9	2	2	23	17	0	.366	.413
3+ Days rest	2.66	5	3	32	88	0	105.0	87	7	34	93	Ahead in Count	.177	685	121	16	3	8	49	0	227	.189	.244
Pre-All Star	2.35	9	10	58	151	3	187.1	151	13	73	165	Behind in Count	.324	207	67	14	0	11	40	57	0	.466	.551
Post-All Star	2.93	15	11	39	116	5	172.0	158	12	64	121	Two Strikes	.168	714	120	19	3	10	61	62	286	.242	.245

Pitcher vs. Batter (career)

Pitches Best Vs.	Avg	AB	H	2B	3B	HR	RBI	BB	SO	OBP	SLG	Pitches Worst Vs.	Avg	AB	H	2B	3B	HR	RBI	BB	SO	OBP	SLG
Mickey Tettleton	.067	15	1	0	0	0	0	2	10	.176	.067	Larry Sheets	.545	11	6	3	0	1	1	1	2	.583	1.091
Kelly Gruber	.077	13	1	0	0	0	0	0	3	.077	.077	Harold Reynolds	.500	22	11	2	1	0	0	2	2	.542	.682
Chili Davis	.083	12	1	0	0	0	1	2	4	.200	.083	Ruben Sierra	.500	20	10	1	0	1	3	2	6	.545	.700
Jody Reed	.091	11	1	0	0	0	0	1	1	.167	.091	Luis Polonia	.471	17	8	4	0	0	0	2	2	.526	.706
Dave Winfield	.130	23	3	0	0	0	1	1	3	.167	.130	Don Mattingly	.400	15	6	1	0	2	4	2	0	.471	.867

John Farrell — Angels

Age 31 – Pitches Right

	ERA	W	L	Sv	G	GS	IP	BB	SO	Avg	H	2B	3B	HR	RBI	OBP	SLG	CG	ShO	Sup	QS	#P/S	SB	CS	GB	FB	G/F
1993 Season	7.35	3	12	0	21	17	90.2	44	45	.301	110	23	2	22	70	.385	.556	0	0	3.87	5	84	14	3	120	126	0.95
Last Five Years	4.64	16	31	0	69	65	395.1	148	221	.268	414	75	9	46	193	.336	.417	8	2	4.26	29	96	40	10	542	496	1.09

1993 Season

	ERA	W	L	Sv	G	GS	IP	H	HR	BB	SO		Avg	AB	H	2B	3B	HR	RBI	BB	SO	OBP	SLG
Home	8.69	2	6	0	9	8	39.1	53	10	24	24	vs. Left	.323	189	61	16	1	10	34	28	22	.412	.577
Away	6.31	1	6	0	12	9	51.1	57	12	20	21	vs. Right	.278	176	49	7	1	12	36	16	23	.355	.534
Starter	7.12	3	11	0	17	17	84.2	102	19	44	41	Scoring Posn	.298	94	28	5	1	8	50	19	14	.419	.628
Reliever	10.50	0	1	0	4	0	6.0	8	3	0	4	Close & Late	.400	15	6	0	0	1	4	2	0	.471	.600
0-3 Days Rest	0.00	0	0	0	0	0	0.0	0	0	0	0	None on/out	.312	93	29	7	0	6	6	7	10	.373	.581
4 Days Rest	6.26	2	4	0	9	9	50.1	56	10	23	24	First Pitch	.267	45	12	2	0	3	6	1	0	.298	.511
5+ Days Rest	8.39	1	7	0	8	8	34.1	46	9	21	17	Ahead in Count	.285	144	41	9	1	6	22	0	39	.309	.486
Pre-All Star	7.09	2	8	0	12	12	59.2	69	13	33	29	Behind in Count	.280	107	30	6	1	10	31	28	0	.423	.636
Post-All Star	7.84	1	4	0	9	5	31.0	41	9	11	16	Two Strikes	.291	148	43	11	1	5	22	15	45	.360	.480

Last Five Years

	ERA	W	L	Sv	G	GS	IP	H	HR	BB	SO		Avg	AB	H	2B	3B	HR	RBI	BB	SO	OBP	SLG
Home	4.48	8	14	0	30	29	176.2	189	17	66	105	vs. Left	.265	811	215	45	5	20	100	88	99	.338	.407
Away	4.77	8	17	0	39	36	218.2	225	29	82	116	vs. Right	.271	734	199	30	4	26	93	60	122	.334	.429
Day	5.36	5	14	0	26	24	132.2	153	20	54	79	Inning 1-6	.267	1326	354	68	9	39	168	128	191	.336	.420
Night	4.28	11	17	0	43	41	262.2	261	26	94	142	Inning 7+	.274	219	60	7	0	7	25	20	30	.338	.402
Grass	4.81	13	27	0	52	51	303.1	320	36	114	182	None on	.251	906	227	44	6	25	25	80	121	.318	.395
Turf	4.11	3	4	0	17	14	92.0	94	10	34	39	Runners on	.293	639	187	31	3	21	168	68	100	.361	.449
April	4.97	4	5	0	11	11	63.1	59	4	31	33	Scoring Posn	.265	378	100	19	2	12	146	47	65	.342	.421
May	4.85	4	8	0	18	18	111.1	115	15	40	52	Close & Late	.337	101	34	4	0	4	15	5	10	.368	.495
June	5.43	2	7	0	12	12	64.2	78	8	26	29	None on/out	.273	399	109	28	3	13	13	31	48	.333	.456
July	3.72	2	2	0	6	6	36.1	40	2	16	21	vs. 1st Batr (relief)	.750	4	3	0	0	2	2	0	0	.750	2.250
August	4.76	2	6	0	9	9	56.2	56	10	18	43	First Inning Pitched	.238	265	63	12	2	10	36	27	46	.314	.411
September/October	3.57	2	3	0	13	9	63.0	66	7	17	43	First 75 Pitches	.266	1177	313	61	9	32	137	98	170	.328	.415

Last Five Years	ERA	W	L	Sv	G	GS	IP	H	HR	BB	SO		Avg	AB	H	2B	3B	HR	RBI	BB	SO	OBP	SLG
Starter	4.55	16	30	0	65	65	389.1	406	43	148	217	Pitch 76-90	.274	164	45	5	0	7	25	28	17	.374	.433
Reliever	10.50	0	1	0	4	0	6.0	8	3	0	4	Pitch 91-105	.289	121	35	4	0	6	23	14	14	.363	.471
0-3 Days Rest	0.00	1	0	0	1	1	9.0	5	0	2	5	Pitch 106+	.253	83	21	5	0	1	8	8	20	.319	.349
4 Days Rest	4.80	10	14	0	37	37	225.0	234	24	82	123	First Pitch	.311	244	76	15	2	7	33	5	0	.324	.475
5+ Days Rest	4.46	5	16	0	27	27	155.1	167	19	64	89	Ahead in Count	.222	662	147	28	4	11	57	0	190	.234	.326
Pre-All Star	5.05	10	21	0	43	43	249.1	266	29	103	116	Behind in Count	.303	370	112	15	3	18	70	86	0	.429	.505
Post-All Star	3.95	6	10	0	26	22	146.0	148	17	45	105	Two Strikes	.223	663	148	35	3	11	62	57	221	.291	.335

Pitcher vs. Batter (career)

Pitches Best Vs.	Avg	AB	H	2B	3B	HR	RBI	BB	SO	OBP	SLG	Pitches Worst Vs.	Avg	AB	H	2B	3B	HR	RBI	BB	SO	OBP	SLG
Danny Tartabull	.059	17	1	0	0	0	0	0	6	.059	.059	Mike Gallego	.500	10	5	1	0	0	0	2	1	.583	.600
Scott Fletcher	.067	15	1	0	0	0	0	1	2	.125	.067	Dan Gladden	.480	25	12	5	0	1	5	1	1	.481	.800
Rob Deer	.077	13	1	0	0	0	2	3	7	.250	.077	Lou Whitaker	.438	16	7	1	0	3	6	1	1	.471	1.063
Jay Buhner	.100	10	1	0	0	0	0	1	3	.182	.100	Edgar Martinez	.400	15	6	1	0	1	2	1	0	.438	.667
Stan Javier	.154	13	2	0	0	0	0	0	6	.154	.154	Cecil Fielder	.364	11	4	1	0	2	7	0	4	.364	1.000

Jeff Fassero — Expos

Age 31 – Pitches Left (groundball pitcher)

	ERA	W	L	Sv	G	GS	IP	BB	SO	Avg	H	2B	3B	HR	RBI	OBP	SLG	GF	IR	IRS	Hld	SvOp	SB	CS	GB	FB	G/F
1993 Season	2.29	12	5	1	56	15	149.2	54	140	.216	119	18	1	7	49	.284	.290	10	24	10	6	3	12	4	239	101	2.37
Career (1991-1993)	2.48	22	17	10	177	15	290.2	105	245	.222	239	37	8	9	101	.292	.297	62	113	33	25	21	27	7	480	204	2.35

1993 Season

	ERA	W	L	Sv	G	GS	IP	H	HR	BB	SO		Avg	AB	H	2B	3B	HR	RBI	BB	SO	OBP	SLG
Home	2.00	7	1	1	26	6	67.2	47	3	27	64	vs. Left	.183	115	21	4	0	1	14	15	29	.273	.243
Away	2.52	5	4	0	30	9	82.0	72	4	27	76	vs. Right	.225	436	98	14	1	6	35	39	111	.287	.303
Starter	2.29	7	4	0	15	15	94.1	81	4	29	89	Scoring Posn	.239	117	28	2	0	1	36	20	35	.340	.282
Reliever	2.28	5	1	1	41	0	55.1	38	3	25	51	Close & Late	.245	94	23	2	0	1	11	12	23	.330	.298
0 Days rest	2.16	2	1	0	16	0	16.2	16	1	6	18	None on/out	.207	145	30	4	0	0	0	8	35	.248	.234
1 or 2 Days rest	3.22	1	0	1	14	0	22.1	14	2	15	14	First Pitch	.319	91	29	5	0	1	17	0	0	.312	.407
3+ Days rest	1.10	2	0	0	11	0	16.1	8	0	4	19	Ahead in Count	.123	268	33	6	0	1	12	0	125	.123	.157
Pre-All Star	2.21	5	1	1	41	1	57.0	40	3	28	52	Behind in Count	.278	108	30	4	0	2	11	25	0	.410	.370
Post-All Star	2.33	7	4	0	15	14	92.2	79	4	26	88	Two Strikes	.111	262	29	5	1	1	10	29	140	.199	.149

Career (1991-1993)

	ERA	W	L	Sv	G	GS	IP	H	HR	BB	SO		Avg	AB	H	2B	3B	HR	RBI	BB	SO	OBP	SLG
Home	2.63	15	6	4	88	6	136.2	105	4	61	114	vs. Left	.227	278	63	8	3	2	37	26	72	.293	.299
Away	2.34	7	11	6	89	9	154.0	134	5	44	131	vs. Right	.221	797	176	29	5	7	64	79	173	.291	.296
Day	3.44	3	8	2	56	4	81.0	79	3	31	65	Inning 1-6	.216	399	86	16	1	5	34	38	102	.283	.298
Night	2.10	19	9	8	121	11	209.2	160	6	74	180	Inning 7+	.226	676	153	21	7	4	67	67	143	.297	.296
Grass	1.98	3	6	4	42	6	82.0	71	3	21	71	None on	.215	600	129	25	3	2	2	48	136	.274	.277
Turf	2.67	19	11	6	135	9	208.2	168	6	84	174	Runners on	.232	475	110	12	5	7	99	57	109	.313	.322
April	4.44	1	1	0	21	0	26.1	24	1	15	12	Scoring Posn	.231	295	68	7	2	3	84	44	75	.327	.298
May	1.96	5	3	0	26	0	36.2	22	1	11	35	Close & Late	.230	369	85	9	3	2	41	41	76	.309	.287
June	1.74	3	2	4	38	0	51.2	34	3	22	44	None on/out	.232	267	62	10	2	0	0	18	56	.281	.285
July	1.92	2	1	2	28	4	51.2	43	0	18	48	vs. 1st Batr (relief)	.204	142	29	5	1	1	12	17	33	.284	.275
August	1.90	6	5	2	32	6	66.1	58	3	20	55	First Inning Pitched	.237	557	132	19	4	4	70	58	114	.309	.307
September/October	3.72	5	5	2	32	5	58.0	58	1	19	51	First 15 Pitches	.247	538	133	20	4	4	56	53	111	.314	.322
Starter	2.29	7	4	0	15	15	94.1	81	4	29	89	Pitch 16-30	.196	250	49	7	2	1	25	23	60	.267	.252
Reliever	2.57	15	13	10	162	0	196.1	158	5	76	156	Pitch 31-45	.167	102	17	2	2	0	4	9	27	.234	.225
0 Days rest	3.22	8	5	4	50	0	58.2	53	2	24	45	Pitch 46+	.216	185	40	8	0	4	16	20	47	.293	.324
1 or 2 Days rest	2.24	4	6	4	70	0	84.1	67	3	38	61	First Pitch	.268	183	49	8	1	1	27	6	0	.292	.339
3+ Days rest	2.36	3	2	2	42	0	53.1	38	0	14	50	Ahead in Count	.155	510	79	13	3	1	30	0	219	.156	.198
Pre-All Star	2.53	9	7	4	96	1	128.0	94	5	55	104	Behind in Count	.265	211	56	9	1	2	20	50	0	.403	.346
Post-All Star	2.43	13	10	6	81	14	162.2	145	4	50	141	Two Strikes	.154	506	78	11	2	2	27	49	245	.230	.196

Pitcher vs. Batter (career)

Pitches Best Vs.	Avg	AB	H	2B	3B	HR	RBI	BB	SO	OBP	SLG	Pitches Worst Vs.	Avg	AB	H	2B	3B	HR	RBI	BB	SO	OBP	SLG
Mark Lemke	.000	10	0	0	0	0	0	1	0	.091	.000	Steve Finley	.455	11	5	0	1	0	5	1	1	.500	.636
Orlando Merced	.000	9	0	0	0	0	0	2	3	.182	.000	Eddie Murray	.417	12	5	3	0	0	2	0	0	.417	.667
Jeff Bagwell	.000	8	0	0	0	0	0	3	0	.273	.000	Jay Bell	.417	12	5	0	0	0	4	5	1	.588	.417
Andy Van Slyke	.083	12	1	1	0	0	1	1	5	.154	.167	Lenny Dykstra	.400	10	4	1	0	0	3	2	2	.500	.500
Fred McGriff	.083	12	1	0	0	0	1	1	5	.154	.083	Bobby Bonilla	.333	9	3	0	0	2	4	2	0	.455	1.000

Mike Felder — Mariners

Age 31 – Bats Both (groundball hitter)

	Avg	G	AB	R	H	2B	3B	HR	RBI	BB	SO	HBP	GDP	SB	CS	OBP	SLG	IBB	SH	SF	#Pit	#P/PA	GB	FB	G/F
1993 Season	.211	109	342	31	72	7	5	1	20	22	34	2	2	15	9	.262	.269	2	7	1	1344	3.59	132	113	1.17
Last Five Years	.254	624	1564	214	397	48	19	11	111	118	149	5	11	96	33	.307	.330	7	29	9	6190	3.59	656	435	1.51

1993 Season

	Avg	AB	H	2B	3B	HR	RBI	BB	SO	OBP	SLG		Avg	AB	H	2B	3B	HR	RBI	BB	SO	OBP	SLG
vs. Left	.190	63	12	1	1	0	2	5	6	.271	.238	Scoring Posn	.175	80	14	1	1	0	17	7	6	.256	.213
vs. Right	.215	279	60	6	4	1	18	17	28	.259	.276	Close & Late	.160	75	12	2	0	0	5	6	11	.220	.187
Groundball	.191	47	9	1	1	0	1	5	7	.269	.255	None on/out	.155	84	13	3	2	0	0	5	11	.202	.238
Flyball	.175	63	11	0	3	0	5	6	7	.243	.270	Batting #1	.176	119	21	2	1	0	7	4	9	.210	.210
Home	.234	167	39	4	3	0	10	12	17	.287	.293	Batting #2	.215	158	34	3	3	1	8	11	19	.265	.291
Away	.189	175	33	3	2	1	10	10	17	.237	.246	Other	.262	65	17	2	1	0	5	7	6	.342	.323
Day	.223	94	21	3	1	1	5	10	14	.308	.309	April	.253	75	19	3	0	1	6	7	8	.325	.333

1993 Season

	Avg	AB	H	2B	3B	HR	RBI	BB	SO	OBP	SLG
Night	.206	248	51	4	4	0	15	12	20	.242	.254
Grass	.188	133	25	2	2	1	7	10	14	.250	.256
Turf	.225	209	47	5	3	0	13	12	20	.269	.278
First Pitch	.263	38	10	2	1	1	5	2	0	.300	.447
Ahead in Count	.241	87	21	2	0	0	4	10	0	.327	.264
Behind in Count	.165	139	23	0	3	0	5	0	30	.165	.209
Two Strikes	.140	136	19	0	1	0	5	10	34	.197	.154

	Avg	AB	H	2B	3B	HR	RBI	BB	SO	OBP	SLG
May	.235	102	24	0	4	0	5	6	9	.284	.314
June	.161	56	9	2	0	0	4	3	6	.200	.196
July	.237	38	9	1	0	0	2	3	5	.293	.263
August	.200	20	4	0	0	0	0	0	0	.200	.200
September/October	.137	51	7	1	1	0	3	3	6	.185	.196
Pre-All Star	.218	238	52	5	4	1	15	17	24	.275	.286
Post-All Star	.192	104	20	2	1	0	5	5	10	.229	.231

1993 By Position

Position	Avg	AB	H	2B	3B	HR	RBI	BB	SO	OBP	SLG	G	GS	Innings	PO	A	E	DP	Fld Pct	Rng Fctr	In Zone	Outs	Zone Rtg	MLB Zone
As Pinch Hitter	.130	23	3	0	0	0	3	2	2	.200	.130	26	0	---	---	---	---	---	---	---	---	---	---	---
As lf	.220	296	65	6	5	1	17	16	30	.261	.284	89	69	656.1	133	9	2	0	.986	1.95	164	130	.793	.818

Last Five Years

	Avg	AB	H	2B	3B	HR	RBI	BB	SO	OBP	SLG
vs. Left	.269	439	118	15	4	4	32	32	35	.319	.349
vs. Right	.248	1125	279	33	15	7	79	86	114	.302	.323
Groundball	.263	463	122	11	6	1	31	34	47	.312	.320
Flyball	.252	326	82	15	6	6	32	26	31	.307	.390
Home	.246	748	184	21	9	3	45	53	71	.297	.310
Away	.261	816	213	27	10	8	66	65	78	.315	.348
Day	.224	558	125	13	5	7	38	48	64	.289	.303
Night	.270	1006	272	35	14	4	73	70	85	.317	.345
Grass	.250	1095	274	29	12	8	74	80	109	.302	.321
Turf	.262	469	123	19	7	3	37	38	40	.317	.352
First Pitch	.324	176	57	10	3	5	24	6	0	.353	.500
Ahead in Count	.289	350	101	11	3	4	38	74	0	.411	.371
Behind in Count	.206	704	145	14	7	2	30	0	128	.206	.254
Two Strikes	.187	691	129	11	5	1	26	38	149	.229	.221

	Avg	AB	H	2B	3B	HR	RBI	BB	SO	OBP	SLG
Scoring Posn	.238	332	79	12	5	2	95	36	30	.309	.322
Close & Late	.222	334	74	10	3	3	33	38	42	.302	.296
None on/out	.251	521	131	19	3	6	6	35	52	.300	.334
Batting #1	.255	835	213	28	11	8	52	56	81	.303	.344
Batting #2	.246	268	66	7	6	2	20	19	22	.298	.340
Other	.256	461	118	13	2	1	39	43	46	.318	.299
April	.291	172	50	4	0	1	10	15	19	.349	.331
May	.261	299	78	5	12	1	27	19	29	.304	.368
June	.234	338	79	13	1	0	17	29	29	.295	.278
July	.243	255	62	10	1	3	19	18	23	.293	.325
August	.263	213	56	7	2	4	17	11	15	.300	.371
September/October	.251	287	72	9	3	2	21	26	34	.313	.324
Pre-All Star	.250	879	220	27	13	2	56	68	86	.305	.317
Post-All Star	.258	685	177	21	6	9	55	50	63	.309	.346

Batter vs. Pitcher (career)

Hits Best Against	Avg	AB	H	2B	3B	HR	RBI	BB	SO	OBP	SLG
Alex Fernandez	.455	11	5	1	0	0	0	0	1	.455	.545
John Smoltz	.389	18	7	1	1	0	2	1	2	.421	.556
Frank Tanana	.364	11	4	0	1	0	1	1	0	.385	.545
Dave Johnson	.364	11	4	2	0	1	3	2	1	.462	.818
Terry Mulholland	.333	12	4	1	0	1	1	0	2	.333	.667

Hits Worst Against	Avg	AB	H	2B	3B	HR	RBI	BB	SO	OBP	SLG
Paul Gibson	.000	15	0	0	0	0	0	1	3	.063	.000
Greg Harris	.000	9	0	0	0	0	1	1	2	.091	.000
Mike Boddicker	.063	16	1	0	0	0	1	1	0	.118	.063
Lee Guetterman	.091	11	1	0	0	0	0	0	0	.091	.091
Joe Boever	.100	10	1	0	0	0	1	0	1	.091	.100

Junior Felix — Marlins

Age 26 – Bats Both (groundball hitter)

	Avg	G	AB	R	H	2B	3B	HR	RBI	BB	SO	HBP	GDP	SB	CS	OBP	SLG	IBB	SH	SF	#Pit	#P/PA	GB	FB	G/F
1993 Season	.238	57	214	25	51	11	1	7	22	10	50	1	6	2	1	.276	.397	1	0	0	805	3.58	81	48	1.69
Career (1989-1993)	.257	499	1831	255	470	80	23	42	231	132	433	11	29	48	34	.308	.394	8	7	19	7200	3.60	705	409	1.72

1993 Season

	Avg	AB	H	2B	3B	HR	RBI	BB	SO	OBP	SLG
vs. Left	.250	68	17	4	0	4	11	2	11	.271	.485
vs. Right	.233	146	34	7	1	3	11	8	39	.277	.356
Home	.277	83	23	3	1	3	7	8	23	.348	.446
Away	.214	131	28	8	0	4	15	2	27	.226	.366
First Pitch	.361	36	13	5	0	0	1	1	0	.378	.500
Ahead in Count	.340	47	16	1	0	5	14	5	0	.404	.681
Behind in Count	.149	94	14	3	1	2	5	0	41	.158	.266
Two Strikes	.074	94	7	0	1	2	5	4	50	.121	.160

	Avg	AB	H	2B	3B	HR	RBI	BB	SO	OBP	SLG
Scoring Posn	.228	57	13	2	0	4	18	3	15	.279	.474
Close & Late	.324	34	11	2	1	1	3	3	7	.395	.529
None on/out	.262	42	11	1	1	1	1	1	9	.279	.405
Batting #2	.229	96	22	5	0	5	14	7	26	.288	.438
Batting #6	.250	52	13	1	0	1	4	1	9	.264	.327
Other	.242	66	16	5	1	1	4	2	15	.265	.394
Pre-All Star	.238	214	51	11	1	7	22	10	50	.276	.397
Post-All Star	.000	0	0	0	0	0	0	0	0	.000	.000

Career (1989-1993)

	Avg	AB	H	2B	3B	HR	RBI	BB	SO	OBP	SLG
vs. Left	.236	522	123	26	5	18	75	35	138	.284	.408
vs. Right	.265	1309	347	54	18	24	156	97	295	.317	.389
Groundball	.276	497	137	19	10	11	70	32	92	.318	.421
Flyball	.225	449	101	16	4	11	53	34	133	.285	.352
Home	.257	874	225	30	16	21	95	74	195	.319	.400
Away	.256	957	245	50	7	21	136	58	238	.297	.389
Day	.265	565	150	27	7	16	85	33	123	.308	.423
Night	.253	1266	320	53	16	26	146	99	310	.307	.382
Grass	.265	1105	293	47	10	28	148	76	273	.312	.402
Turf	.244	726	177	33	13	14	83	56	160	.301	.383
First Pitch	.368	288	106	17	2	14	50	6	0	.387	.587
Ahead in Count	.363	405	147	30	8	14	84	78	0	.460	.580
Behind in Count	.167	801	134	20	8	9	65	0	368	.172	.246
Two Strikes	.142	853	121	17	8	8	55	49	433	.192	.209

	Avg	AB	H	2B	3B	HR	RBI	BB	SO	OBP	SLG
Scoring Posn	.260	473	123	17	5	12	186	40	111	.314	.393
Close & Late	.215	284	61	7	3	8	26	19	81	.269	.345
None on/out	.286	483	138	21	9	13	13	35	122	.335	.447
Batting #1	.262	507	133	20	10	9	61	40	112	.316	.394
Batting #3	.243	408	99	18	3	7	53	28	100	.291	.353
Other	.260	916	238	42	10	26	117	64	221	.310	.413
April	.267	307	82	14	4	11	59	20	68	.321	.446
May	.267	405	108	17	4	12	42	27	95	.311	.417
June	.285	358	102	20	3	6	48	30	82	.337	.408
July	.225	222	50	9	5	4	26	21	51	.294	.365
August	.222	275	61	10	3	4	26	16	73	.266	.324
September/October	.254	264	67	10	4	5	30	18	64	.301	.379
Pre-All Star	.268	1169	313	55	13	32	165	84	272	.318	.419
Post-All Star	.237	662	157	25	10	10	66	48	161	.290	.350

Batter vs. Pitcher (career)

Hits Best Against	Avg	AB	H	2B	3B	HR	RBI	BB	SO	OBP	SLG
Kirk McCaskill	.556	9	5	0	0	1	2	2	0	.636	.889
Charlie Hough	.444	9	4	2	0	1	1	3	1	.583	1.000
Frank Tanana	.389	18	7	4	0	1	1	3	2	.476	.778
Bob Welch	.368	19	7	0	0	1	1	2	2	.429	.526
Bob Milacki	.364	11	4	2	1	0	1	0	0	.364	.727

Hits Worst Against	Avg	AB	H	2B	3B	HR	RBI	BB	SO	OBP	SLG
Bill Krueger	.000	16	0	0	0	0	0	0	7	.000	.000
Bret Saberhagen	.063	16	1	0	0	0	1	2	7	.167	.063
Alex Fernandez	.063	16	1	0	0	0	0	0	6	.063	.063
Todd Stottlemyre	.091	11	1	0	0	0	1	1	3	.154	.091
Jaime Navarro	.118	17	2	0	0	0	0	2	5	.211	.118

Felix Fermin — Indians

Age 30 – Bats Right (groundball hitter)

	Avg	G	AB	R	H	2B	3B	HR	RBI	BB	SO	HBP	GDP	SB	CS	OBP	SLG	IBB	SH	SF	#Pit	#P/PA	GB	FB	G/F
1993 Season	.263	140	480	48	126	16	2	2	45	24	14	4	12	4	5	.303	.317	1	5	1	1578	3.07	257	113	2.27
Last Five Years	.256	652	2017	202	516	58	9	3	150	135	100	12	63	18	16	.305	.298	2	72	12	7030	3.13	1093	401	2.73

1993 Season

	Avg	AB	H	2B	3B	HR	RBI	BB	SO	OBP	SLG		Avg	AB	H	2B	3B	HR	RBI	BB	SO	OBP	SLG
vs. Left	.293	157	46	9	2	1	15	6	2	.323	.395	Scoring Posn	.312	125	39	4	1	1	44	8	3	.356	.384
vs. Right	.248	323	80	7	0	1	30	18	12	.293	.279	Close & Late	.369	65	24	4	0	1	7	7	0	.446	.477
Groundball	.218	78	17	3	0	0	4	5	1	.274	.256	None on/out	.212	99	21	5	1	1	1	7	2	.271	.313
Flyball	.193	88	17	2	0	0	5	2	1	.220	.216	Batting #2	.220	109	24	3	0	0	9	6	3	.259	.248
Home	.230	226	52	6	2	0	21	14	5	.277	.274	Batting #8	.275	335	92	12	2	2	33	16	10	.314	.340
Away	.291	254	74	10	0	2	24	10	9	.326	.354	Other	.278	36	10	1	0	0	3	2	1	.333	.306
Day	.233	146	34	3	0	1	12	8	4	.277	.274	April	.264	72	19	2	0	0	7	6	1	.329	.292
Night	.275	334	92	13	2	1	33	16	10	.314	.335	May	.281	89	25	3	0	0	8	3	4	.304	.315
Grass	.256	406	104	10	2	1	36	18	12	.292	.298	June	.221	77	17	1	0	0	3	6	3	.286	.234
Turf	.297	74	22	6	0	1	9	6	2	.358	.419	July	.293	82	24	4	1	1	7	4	1	.341	.402
First Pitch	.200	90	18	1	0	0	8	1	0	.226	.211	August	.222	99	22	3	0	0	7	3	2	.243	.253
Ahead in Count	.316	114	36	4	2	0	10	23	0	.431	.386	September/October	.311	61	19	3	1	1	13	2	3	.333	.443
Behind in Count	.239	184	44	8	0	0	17	0	13	.246	.283	Pre-All Star	.263	266	70	9	0	1	23	16	8	.312	.308
Two Strikes	.215	144	31	4	0	1	15	0	14	.224	.264	Post-All Star	.262	214	56	7	2	1	22	8	6	.290	.327

1993 By Position

Position	Avg	AB	H	2B	3B	HR	RBI	BB	SO	OBP	SLG	G	GS	Innings	PO	A	E	DP	Fld Pct	Rng Fctr	In Zone	Outs	Zone Rtg	MLB Zone
As ss	.263	480	126	16	2	2	45	24	14	.303	.317	140	137	1186.1	211	344	23	86	.960	4.21	446	372	.834	.880

Last Five Years

	Avg	AB	H	2B	3B	HR	RBI	BB	SO	OBP	SLG		Avg	AB	H	2B	3B	HR	RBI	BB	SO	OBP	SLG
vs. Left	.276	580	160	19	3	1	50	50	19	.334	.324	Scoring Posn	.261	494	129	14	3	1	144	42	27	.317	.308
vs. Right	.248	1437	356	39	6	2	100	85	81	.293	.287	Close & Late	.267	285	76	9	0	1	17	26	14	.339	.309
Groundball	.244	545	133	12	2	1	32	34	26	.292	.279	None on/out	.256	472	121	11	2	2	2	33	19	.308	.301
Flyball	.230	409	94	13	3	0	34	36	19	.296	.276	Batting #2	.236	551	130	15	4	0	36	45	31	.298	.278
Home	.259	978	253	34	8	1	82	71	46	.310	.313	Batting #9	.252	933	235	27	2	1	71	61	47	.298	.288
Away	.253	1039	263	24	1	2	68	64	54	.300	.284	Other	.283	533	151	16	3	2	43	29	22	.324	.336
Day	.258	625	161	13	1	2	41	43	37	.307	.291	April	.230	226	52	3	1	1	20	19	9	.291	.265
Night	.255	1392	355	45	8	1	109	92	63	.303	.301	May	.263	323	85	11	2	0	24	15	15	.299	.310
Grass	.251	1709	429	46	8	2	123	114	82	.301	.291	June	.242	376	91	9	0	0	15	23	18	.289	.266
Turf	.282	308	87	12	1	1	27	21	18	.327	.338	July	.252	381	96	11	3	1	27	22	18	.297	.304
First Pitch	.271	413	112	11	1	0	26	2	0	.279	.303	August	.266	354	94	13	1	0	35	21	15	.307	.308
Ahead in Count	.260	404	105	11	3	0	31	94	0	.396	.302	September/October	.275	357	98	11	2	1	29	35	25	.339	.325
Behind in Count	.232	854	198	27	4	1	58	0	94	.239	.276	Pre-All Star	.250	1035	259	27	4	2	69	60	45	.294	.290
Two Strikes	.222	680	151	15	2	2	45	39	100	.269	.259	Post-All Star	.262	982	257	31	5	1	81	75	55	.315	.307

Batter vs. Pitcher (career)

Hits Best Against	Avg	AB	H	2B	3B	HR	RBI	BB	SO	OBP	SLG	Hits Worst Against	Avg	AB	H	2B	3B	HR	RBI	BB	SO	OBP	SLG
Mark Guthrie	.909	11	10	1	0	0	3	0	1	.909	1.000	Charlie Hough	.067	15	1	1	0	0	0	1	1	.125	.133
Terry Leach	.636	11	7	3	0	0	1	0	0	.636	.909	Nolan Ryan	.077	13	1	0	0	0	0	1	1	.143	.077
Bobby Witt	.571	21	12	2	0	0	5	4	0	.640	.667	Juan Guzman	.091	11	1	0	0	0	0	0	1	.091	.091
Storm Davis	.529	17	9	3	0	1	2	0	0	.529	.882	Hipolito Pichardo	.091	11	1	0	0	0	0	0	0	.091	.091
Tim Leary	.500	10	5	0	0	0	1	1	0	.545	.500	David Cone	.100	10	1	0	0	0	1	0	1	.091	.100

Alex Fernandez — White Sox

Age 24 – Pitches Right

	ERA	W	L	Sv	G	GS	IP	BB	SO	Avg	H	2B	3B	HR	RBI	OBP	SLG	CG	ShO	Sup	QS	#P/S	SB	CS	GB	FB	G/F
1993 Season	3.13	18	9	0	34	34	247.1	67	169	.240	221	40	4	27	85	.295	.381	3	1	5.57	23	112	5	11	284	293	0.97
Career (1990-1993)	3.88	40	38	0	110	108	714.1	239	470	.256	695	113	15	70	291	.319	.387	12	3	4.49	64	105	36	30	865	862	1.00

1993 Season

	ERA	W	L	Sv	G	GS	IP	H	HR	BB	SO		Avg	AB	H	2B	3B	HR	RBI	BB	SO	OBP	SLG
Home	2.79	9	4	0	16	16	119.1	99	13	30	79	vs. Left	.260	442	115	27	1	15	43	34	82	.312	.428
Away	3.45	9	5	0	18	18	128.0	122	14	37	90	vs. Right	.222	477	106	13	3	12	42	33	87	.280	.338
Day	3.79	5	4	0	11	11	78.1	70	12	25	58	Inning 1-6	.240	755	181	31	4	23	72	56	141	.295	.383
Night	2.82	13	5	0	23	23	169.0	151	15	42	111	Inning 7+	.244	164	40	9	0	4	13	11	28	.295	.372
Grass	3.38	14	8	0	26	26	184.0	167	21	49	127	None on	.244	554	135	26	3	18	18	44	98	.305	.399
Turf	2.42	4	1	0	8	8	63.1	54	6	18	42	Runners on	.236	365	86	14	1	9	67	23	71	.281	.353
April	2.17	3	2	0	5	5	37.1	23	2	8	28	Scoring Posn	.215	177	38	8	0	2	49	19	38	.286	.294
May	3.93	2	1	0	5	5	34.1	33	4	10	25	Close & Late	.258	93	24	7	0	3	8	6	16	.303	.430
June	2.72	3	1	0	6	6	46.1	39	5	20	33	None on/out	.261	245	64	16	2	8	8	18	36	.314	.441
July	3.25	4	1	0	6	6	44.1	36	7	15	30	vs. 1st Batr (relief)	.000	0	0	0	0	0	0	0	0	.000	.000
August	3.38	4	1	0	6	6	42.2	39	4	6	25	First Inning Pitched	.225	129	29	8	1	0	6	9	23	.284	.302
September/October	3.40	2	3	0	6	6	42.1	51	5	8	28	First 75 Pitches	.236	597	141	24	2	17	46	41	115	.289	.369
Starter	3.13	18	9	0	34	34	247.1	221	27	67	169	Pitch 76-90	.190	121	23	4	0	4	8	13	23	.274	.322
Reliever	0.00	0	0	0	0	0	0.0	0	0	0	0	Pitch 91-105	.294	109	32	7	1	2	14	6	16	.330	.431
0-3 Days Rest	0.00	0	0	0	0	0	0.0	0	0	0	0	Pitch 106+	.272	92	25	5	1	4	17	7	15	.323	.478
4 Days Rest	2.95	13	5	0	24	24	174.0	154	17	49	114	First Pitch	.314	118	37	9	0	4	20	4	0	.339	.492
5+ Days Rest	3.56	5	4	0	10	10	73.1	67	10	18	55	Ahead in Count	.169	419	71	14	1	5	22	0	140	.175	.243
Pre-All Star	2.77	10	4	0	18	18	133.1	108	12	45	92	Behind in Count	.320	197	63	10	1	11	21	25	0	.395	.548
Post-All Star	3.55	8	5	0	16	16	114.0	113	15	22	77	Two Strikes	.164	428	70	14	2	6	21	38	169	.237	.248

Career (1990-1993)

	ERA	W	L	Sv	G	GS	IP	H	HR	BB	SO
Home	3.82	20	19	0	54	52	353.1	318	32	112	216
Away	3.94	20	19	0	56	56	361.0	377	38	127	254
Day	4.66	8	11	0	27	27	170.0	175	19	59	128
Night	3.64	32	27	0	83	81	544.1	520	51	180	342
Grass	4.15	31	36	0	91	89	575.0	563	59	192	379
Turf	2.78	9	2	0	19	19	139.1	132	11	47	91
April	4.41	6	6	0	14	13	81.2	78	8	34	63
May	3.92	3	6	0	15	15	101.0	91	9	41	68
June	4.06	6	6	0	17	17	115.1	107	8	43	79
July	3.64	6	1	0	15	14	94.0	86	14	27	56
August	4.41	9	8	0	24	24	147.0	157	10	35	90
September/October	3.18	10	11	0	25	25	175.1	176	21	59	114
Starter	3.90	40	38	0	108	108	711.2	694	70	238	468
Reliever	0.00	0	0	0	2	0	2.2	1	0	1	2
0-3 Days Rest	4.91	0	1	0	2	2	11.0	13	1	5	10
4 Days Rest	3.99	30	23	0	73	73	476.0	470	42	161	301
5+ Days Rest	3.65	10	14	0	33	33	224.2	211	27	72	157
Pre-All Star	4.02	17	18	0	50	49	324.2	300	27	128	220
Post-All Star	3.76	23	20	0	60	59	389.2	395	43	111	250

	Avg	AB	H	2B	3B	HR	RBI	BB	SO	OBP	SLG
vs. Left	.257	1299	334	69	5	31	136	112	220	.316	.390
vs. Right	.256	1411	361	44	10	39	155	127	250	.322	.384
Inning 1-6	.261	2278	595	98	14	57	261	209	399	.326	.392
Inning 7+	.231	432	100	15	1	13	30	30	71	.282	.361
None on	.246	1595	392	66	10	46	46	135	271	.310	.386
Runners on	.272	1115	303	47	5	24	245	104	199	.332	.387
Scoring Posn	.255	580	148	24	1	10	205	73	110	.333	.352
Close & Late	.237	249	59	8	0	7	18	16	43	.283	.353
None on/out	.255	699	178	34	5	17	17	63	103	.322	.391
vs. 1st Batr (relief)	.000	2	0	0	0	0	0	0	0	.000	.000
First Inning Pitched	.245	428	105	20	3	4	38	37	90	.307	.334
First 75 Pitches	.260	1832	477	82	13	43	194	160	323	.323	.390
Pitch 76-90	.225	346	78	9	0	10	29	33	57	.294	.338
Pitch 91-105	.289	294	85	14	1	7	35	24	48	.343	.415
Pitch 106+	.231	238	55	8	1	10	33	22	42	.295	.399
First Pitch	.350	354	124	21	2	12	57	5	0	.361	.523
Ahead in Count	.199	1225	244	42	5	16	78	0	390	.207	.281
Behind in Count	.299	588	176	33	4	24	79	107	0	.403	.491
Two Strikes	.184	1233	227	32	7	18	83	127	470	.264	.265

Pitcher vs. Batter (career)

Pitches Best Vs.	Avg	AB	H	2B	3B	HR	RBI	BB	SO	OBP	SLG
Kirk Gibson	.000	14	0	0	0	0	0	1	7	.067	.000
Pat Borders	.059	17	1	0	0	0	0	0	5	.059	.059
Junior Felix	.063	16	1	0	0	0	0	0	6	.063	.063
Doug Strange	.077	13	1	0	0	0	0	0	2	.077	.077
Carlos Baerga	.083	12	1	0	0	0	0	0	3	.083	.083

Pitches Worst Vs.	Avg	AB	H	2B	3B	HR	RBI	BB	SO	OBP	SLG
Joe Orsulak	.467	15	7	1	2	0	2	0	0	.467	.800
Mike Gallego	.462	13	6	2	0	1	4	0	2	.462	.846
Tom Brunansky	.381	21	8	0	1	3	7	0	6	.381	.905
Chili Davis	.375	8	3	2	0	1	3	3	3	.545	1.000
Kevin Seitzer	.375	8	3	0	0	2	3	3	1	.545	1.125

Sid Fernandez — Mets

Age 31 – Pitches Left (flyball pitcher)

	ERA	W	L	Sv	G	GS	IP	BB	SO	Avg	H	2B	3B	HR	RBI	OBP	SLG	CG	ShO	Sup	QS	#P/S	SB	CS	GB	FB	G/F
1993 Season	2.93	5	6	0	18	18	119.2	36	81	.192	82	11	0	17	38	.260	.338	1	1	3.53	12	94	13	4	82	177	0.46
Last Five Years	2.97	43	39	0	123	120	777.0	254	684	.202	567	107	23	72	248	.271	.334	14	6	4.36	83	100	64	24	561	1090	0.51

1993 Season

	ERA	W	L	Sv	G	GS	IP	H	HR	BB	SO
Home	3.24	2	2	0	8	8	58.1	40	9	14	49
Away	2.64	3	4	0	10	10	61.1	42	8	22	32
Starter	2.93	5	6	0	18	18	119.2	82	17	36	81
Reliever	0.00	0	0	0	0	0	0.0	0	0	0	0
0-3 Days Rest	0.00	0	0	0	0	0	0.0	0	0	0	0
4 Days Rest	3.21	4	3	0	12	12	75.2	54	10	25	44
5+ Days Rest	2.45	1	3	0	6	6	44.0	28	7	11	37
Pre-All Star	4.13	1	0	0	5	5	28.1	27	5	6	24
Post-All Star	2.56	4	6	0	13	13	91.1	55	12	30	57

	Avg	AB	H	2B	3B	HR	RBI	BB	SO	OBP	SLG
vs. Left	.185	81	15	2	0	2	5	12	16	.298	.284
vs. Right	.194	345	67	9	0	15	33	24	65	.250	.351
Scoring Posn	.268	71	19	0	0	2	20	9	17	.346	.352
Close & Late	.186	43	8	2	0	2	4	0	6	.205	.372
None on/out	.197	122	24	4	0	4	4	5	20	.228	.328
First Pitch	.281	64	18	1	0	5	7	0	0	.303	.531
Ahead in Count	.143	210	30	4	0	4	15	0	74	.146	.219
Behind in Count	.253	87	22	6	0	6	9	19	0	.387	.529
Two Strikes	.161	193	31	2	0	5	17	17	81	.232	.249

Last Five Years

	ERA	W	L	Sv	G	GS	IP	H	HR	BB	SO
Home	2.54	25	14	0	60	60	411.0	271	37	121	391
Away	3.44	18	25	0	63	60	366.0	296	35	133	293
Day	3.38	10	12	0	35	35	218.1	177	23	81	195
Night	2.80	33	27	0	88	85	558.2	390	49	173	489
Grass	2.85	32	22	0	85	84	556.2	396	57	168	503
Turf	3.27	11	17	0	38	36	220.1	171	15	86	181
April	4.09	6	4	0	19	17	103.1	76	10	45	92
May	2.50	5	7	0	16	15	97.1	77	12	28	85
June	3.31	6	3	0	15	15	89.2	76	12	32	86
July	2.76	8	6	0	20	20	124.0	86	10	39	116
August	2.91	9	9	0	29	29	195.0	147	19	54	157
September/October	2.58	9	10	0	24	24	167.2	105	9	56	148
Starter	2.96	43	39	0	120	120	771.0	563	71	253	680
Reliever	3.00	0	0	0	3	0	6.0	4	1	1	4
0-3 Days Rest	2.12	1	0	0	3	3	17.0	12	1	4	17
4 Days Rest	2.80	29	20	0	74	74	486.0	346	45	157	415
5+ Days Rest	3.32	13	19	0	43	43	268.0	205	25	92	248
Pre-All Star	3.24	20	15	0	55	52	325.0	246	37	117	290
Post-All Star	2.77	23	24	0	68	68	452.0	321	35	137	394

	Avg	AB	H	2B	3B	HR	RBI	BB	SO	OBP	SLG
vs. Left	.209	511	107	20	6	8	50	54	147	.290	.319
vs. Right	.201	2292	460	87	17	64	198	200	537	.266	.337
Inning 1-6	.197	2406	473	86	22	59	221	225	613	.267	.324
Inning 7+	.237	397	94	21	1	13	27	29	71	.295	.393
None on	.194	1857	361	70	14	43	43	143	483	.257	.317
Runners on	.218	946	206	37	9	29	205	111	201	.297	.368
Scoring Posn	.225	494	111	20	3	13	162	68	118	.308	.356
Close & Late	.271	177	48	9	0	6	14	8	32	.312	.424
None on/out	.204	780	159	23	6	22	22	45	188	.249	.333
vs. 1st Batr (relief)	.500	2	1	0	0	0	0	0	0	.667	.500
First Inning Pitched	.206	447	92	14	4	13	53	49	112	.286	.342
First 75 Pitches	.191	1982	378	68	16	45	168	191	529	.264	.309
Pitch 76-90	.217	360	78	17	5	14	42	29	71	.278	.408
Pitch 91-105	.238	269	64	9	2	10	24	13	49	.276	.398
Pitch 106+	.245	192	47	13	0	3	14	21	35	.321	.359
First Pitch	.283	360	102	23	5	15	52	10	0	.310	.500
Ahead in Count	.155	1478	229	42	8	20	91	0	586	.159	.235
Behind in Count	.274	508	139	28	7	26	62	127	0	.418	.510
Two Strikes	.142	1491	211	34	6	19	80	116	684	.207	.211

Pitcher vs. Batter (since 1984)

Pitches Best Vs.	Avg	AB	H	2B	3B	HR	RBI	BB	SO	OBP	SLG
Luis Rivera	.000	12	0	0	0	0	0	2	3	.143	.000
Jim Lindeman	.000	10	0	0	0	0	1	1	3	.091	.000
Chris Sabo	.037	27	1	1	0	0	0	2	6	.103	.074
Charlie Hayes	.048	21	1	0	0	0	0	2	7	.130	.048
Tom Brunansky	.063	16	1	0	0	0	0	1	3	.118	.063

Pitches Worst Vs.	Avg	AB	H	2B	3B	HR	RBI	BB	SO	OBP	SLG
Mariano Duncan	.405	42	17	6	2	0	5	3	5	.435	.643
Lance Parrish	.389	18	7	1	0	2	4	3	4	.476	.778
Tim Teufel	.333	12	4	0	0	2	4	1	2	.385	.833
Tim Raines	.324	37	12	2	0	3	5	8	5	.435	.622
Kevin Mitchell	.320	25	8	2	0	4	5	1	5	.346	.880

Tony Fernandez — Blue Jays

Age 32 – Bats Both (groundball hitter)

	Avg	G	AB	R	H	2B	3B	HR	RBI	BB	SO	HBP	GDP	SB	CS	OBP	SLG	IBB	SH	SF	#Pit	#P/PA	GB	FB	G/F
1993 Season	.279	142	526	65	147	23	11	5	64	56	45	1	17	21	10	.348	.394	3	8	3	1993	3.36	226	133	1.70
Last Five Years	.272	743	2914	378	792	134	46	28	269	267	302	15	59	112	58	.334	.378	12	28	23	11319	3.49	1190	770	1.55

1993 Season

	Avg	AB	H	2B	3B	HR	RBI	BB	SO	OBP	SLG		Avg	AB	H	2B	3B	HR	RBI	BB	SO	OBP	SLG
vs. Left	.248	165	41	8	2	0	14	23	7	.339	.321	Scoring Posn	.311	148	46	5	6	2	57	26	20	.407	.466
vs. Right	.294	361	106	15	9	5	50	33	38	.353	.427	Close & Late	.293	92	27	4	0	1	13	12	12	.375	.370
Groundball	.297	118	35	4	1	1	15	8	13	.341	.373	None on/out	.240	100	24	2	0	1	1	6	6	.283	.290
Flyball	.272	81	22	3	2	1	9	19	9	.410	.395	Batting #6	.262	225	59	12	5	3	27	20	19	.321	.400
Home	.271	255	69	10	7	1	31	31	20	.351	.376	Batting #7	.338	148	50	8	4	1	23	11	11	.381	.466
Away	.288	271	78	13	4	4	33	25	25	.346	.410	Other	.248	153	38	3	2	1	14	25	15	.356	.314
Day	.235	162	38	6	1	1	21	22	13	.330	.302	April	.203	69	14	1	1	0	8	15	6	.349	.246
Night	.299	364	109	17	10	4	43	34	32	.357	.434	May	.191	68	13	3	1	1	6	8	7	.273	.309
Grass	.275	280	77	15	5	4	39	30	20	.344	.407	June	.330	106	35	7	4	2	16	9	12	.383	.528
Turf	.285	246	70	8	6	1	25	26	25	.353	.378	July	.278	90	25	2	0	1	8	9	5	.343	.333
First Pitch	.304	115	35	6	3	1	14	2	0	.314	.435	August	.266	109	29	4	3	0	15	7	12	.308	.358
Ahead in Count	.326	144	47	10	1	1	17	36	0	.459	.431	September/October	.369	84	31	6	2	1	11	8	3	.424	.524
Behind in Count	.217	180	39	5	6	1	23	0	34	.221	.328	Pre-All Star	.265	275	73	11	6	3	31	36	26	.350	.382
Two Strikes	.163	172	28	3	3	2	16	18	45	.245	.250	Post-All Star	.295	251	74	12	5	2	33	20	19	.346	.406

1993 By Position

Position	Avg	AB	H	2B	3B	HR	RBI	BB	SO	OBP	SLG	G	GS	Innings	PO	A	E	DP	Fld Pct	Rng Fctr	In Zone	Outs	Zone Rtg	MLB Zone
As ss	.279	526	147	23	11	5	64	56	45	.348	.394	142	142	1235.1	279	410	13	88	.981	5.02	489	429	.877	.880

Last Five Years

	Avg	AB	H	2B	3B	HR	RBI	BB	SO	OBP	SLG		Avg	AB	H	2B	3B	HR	RBI	BB	SO	OBP	SLG
vs. Left	.260	943	245	40	7	6	79	104	71	.332	.336	Scoring Posn	.293	642	188	26	15	9	234	78	78	.364	.422
vs. Right	.278	1971	547	94	39	22	190	163	231	.334	.398	Close & Late	.296	449	133	14	6	2	37	47	40	.363	.367
Groundball	.267	876	234	34	12	5	66	68	90	.321	.350	None on/out	.269	788	212	35	10	7	7	67	70	.331	.365
Flyball	.263	547	144	24	12	5	55	63	57	.339	.378	Batting #1	.258	925	239	40	8	7	59	83	104	.323	.342
Home	.279	1424	398	68	27	9	129	146	151	.347	.384	Batting #2	.265	1300	345	60	22	13	118	127	148	.330	.375
Away	.264	1490	394	66	19	19	140	121	151	.320	.372	Other	.302	689	208	34	16	8	92	57	50	.354	.433
Day	.260	865	225	36	8	9	80	85	100	.328	.351	April	.269	346	93	10	4	3	40	32	45	.337	.347
Night	.277	2049	567	98	38	19	189	182	202	.336	.389	May	.252	504	127	25	6	6	40	53	59	.324	.361
Grass	.270	1617	437	72	21	21	147	161	176	.337	.380	June	.300	533	160	27	11	5	51	58	58	.370	.420
Turf	.274	1297	355	62	25	7	122	106	126	.330	.376	July	.220	478	105	20	6	4	35	37	48	.274	.312
First Pitch	.326	549	179	32	11	4	56	6	0	.333	.446	August	.269	525	141	23	13	3	55	43	50	.324	.379
Ahead in Count	.314	770	242	42	20	8	71	146	0	.419	.452	September/October	.314	528	166	29	6	7	48	44	42	.366	.432
Behind in Count	.225	1110	250	41	11	8	95	0	255	.232	.304	Pre-All Star	.272	1551	422	69	23	14	139	160	175	.342	.373
Two Strikes	.208	1098	228	36	6	11	89	111	302	.285	.281	Post-All Star	.271	1363	370	65	23	14	130	107	127	.323	.384

Batter vs. Pitcher (since 1984)

Hits Best Against	Avg	AB	H	2B	3B	HR	RBI	BB	SO	OBP	SLG	Hits Worst Against	Avg	AB	H	2B	3B	HR	RBI	BB	SO	OBP	SLG
Greg Cadaret	.500	10	5	1	1	1	4	1	1	.500	1.100	Bobby Thigpen	.000	12	0	0	0	0	0	1	1	.077	.000
Mark Knudson	.462	13	6	1	1	0	0	1	1	.500	.692	Chris Nabholz	.000	12	0	0	0	0	1	1	0	.077	.000
Mike Henneman	.444	9	4	0	1	1	4	3	0	.583	1.000	Alex Fernandez	.000	11	0	0	0	0	0	3	0	.214	.000
Curt Schilling	.429	14	6	2	1	0	2	2	3	.500	.714	Dwight Gooden	.118	17	2	0	0	0	0	1	4	.167	.118
Paul Gibson	.421	19	8	2	2	1	8	6	2	.560	.895	Scott Bankhead	.129	31	4	0	0	0	0	1	3	.156	.129

Mike Fetters — Brewers

Age 29 – Pitches Right (groundball pitcher)

	ERA	W	L	Sv	G	GS	IP	BB	SO	Avg	H	2B	3B	HR	RBI	OBP	SLG	GF	IR	IRS	Hld	SvOp	SB	CS	GB	FB	G/F
1993 Season	3.34	3	3	0	45	0	59.1	22	23	.278	59	6	3	4	42	.344	.392	14	41	19	8	0	6	7	100	49	2.04
Career (1989-1993)	3.52	11	10	3	141	6	237.2	95	129	.265	232	27	4	21	137	.344	.378	43	134	51	17	7	22	17	403	178	2.26

1993 Season

	ERA	W	L	Sv	G	GS	IP	H	HR	BB	SO		Avg	AB	H	2B	3B	HR	RBI	BB	SO	OBP	SLG
Home	2.97	2	1	0	26	0	36.1	34	2	11	15	vs. Left	.233	90	21	0	3	2	16	12	10	.317	.367
Away	3.91	1	2	0	19	0	23.0	25	2	11	8	vs. Right	.311	122	38	6	0	2	26	10	13	.365	.410
Starter	0.00	0	0	0	0	0	0.0	0	0	0	0	Scoring Posn	.328	64	21	3	2	1	37	7	5	.377	.484
Reliever	3.34	3	3	0	45	0	59.1	59	4	22	23	Close & Late	.220	82	18	1	1	1	9	10	10	.304	.293
0 Days rest	5.40	0	0	0	8	0	8.1	8	2	3	3	None on/out	.318	44	14	1	0	1	1	2	8	.348	.409
1 or 2 Days rest	2.14	3	1	0	15	0	21.0	15	1	10	7	First Pitch	.286	35	10	1	0	1	13	3	0	.341	.400
3+ Days rest	3.60	0	2	0	22	0	30.0	36	1	9	13	Ahead in Count	.194	67	13	2	1	1	9	0	14	.188	.299
Pre-All Star	3.97	2	1	0	30	0	34.0	33	3	15	10	Behind in Count	.359	64	23	1	1	2	10	14	0	.468	.500
Post-All Star	2.49	1	2	0	15	0	25.1	26	1	7	13	Two Strikes	.137	73	10	3	0	1	6	5	23	.190	.219

Career (1989-1993)

	ERA	W	L	Sv	G	GS	IP	H	HR	BB	SO		Avg	AB	H	2B	3B	HR	RBI	BB	SO	OBP	SLG
Home	2.73	6	3	2	71	0	108.2	98	8	38	51	vs. Left	.277	379	105	10	4	11	63	46	43	.357	.412
Away	4.19	5	7	1	70	6	129.0	134	13	57	78	vs. Right	.257	495	127	17	0	10	74	49	86	.335	.352
Day	5.13	4	3	0	44	4	72.0	87	9	24	35	Inning 1-6	.320	338	108	13	2	9	72	38	47	.393	.450
Night	2.82	7	7	3	97	2	165.2	145	12	71	94	Inning 7+	.231	536	124	14	2	12	65	57	82	.314	.332
Grass	3.60	9	7	3	120	3	197.2	198	19	77	105	None on	.252	444	112	16	0	10	10	46	68	.331	.356
Turf	3.15	2	3	0	21	3	40.0	34	2	18	24	Runners on	.279	430	120	11	4	11	127	49	61	.358	.400
April	3.00	0	0	0	12	0	9.0	9	0	5	6	Scoring Posn	.291	258	75	8	3	6	115	36	38	.379	.415
May	2.81	1	0	0	15	1	25.2	19	2	6	13	Close & Late	.203	197	40	3	1	6	33	29	34	.319	.320
June	3.69	3	2	1	28	0	46.1	44	6	19	17	None on/out	.254	193	49	3	0	4	4	17	28	.318	.332
July	3.75	4	4	1	31	1	60.0	59	5	19	37	vs. 1st Batr (relief)	.330	115	38	5	2	1	27	18	13	.425	.435

Career (1989-1993)

	ERA	W	L	Sv	G	GS	IP	H	HR	BB	SO
August	3.17	2	2	0	28	1	48.1	53	2	23	24
September/October	3.91	1	2	1	27	3	48.1	48	6	23	32
Starter	6.84	0	4	0	6	6	25.0	39	4	13	16
Reliever	3.13	11	6	3	135	0	212.2	193	17	82	113
0 Days rest	8.31	2	0	0	17	0	21.2	24	5	9	14
1 or 2 Days rest	2.29	7	3	2	44	0	63.0	43	3	20	33
3+ Days rest	2.67	2	3	1	74	0	128.0	126	9	53	66
Pre-All Star	3.62	7	3	1	69	1	104.1	95	9	37	49
Post-All Star	3.44	4	7	2	72	5	133.1	137	12	58	80

	Avg	AB	H	2B	3B	HR	RBI	BB	SO	OBP	SLG
First Inning Pitched	.271	435	118	16	4	8	95	50	66	.349	.382
First 15 Pitches	.264	421	111	16	4	8	80	48	60	.346	.378
Pitch 16-30	.223	233	52	6	0	6	27	26	40	.311	.326
Pitch 31-45	.296	115	34	3	0	4	15	7	14	.341	.426
Pitch 46+	.333	105	35	2	0	3	15	14	15	.417	.438
First Pitch	.279	122	34	5	0	3	25	4	0	.313	.393
Ahead in Count	.214	346	74	11	1	6	38	0	103	.222	.303
Behind in Count	.329	231	76	5	2	8	43	56	0	.461	.472
Two Strikes	.198	354	70	12	0	8	38	35	129	.275	.299

Pitcher vs. Batter (career)

Pitches Best Vs.	Avg	AB	H	2B	3B	HR	RBI	BB	SO	OBP	SLG
Mark McGwire	.200	10	2	0	0	0	0	2	2	.333	.200
Mickey Tettleton	.222	9	2	0	0	1	1	2	1	.364	.556

Pitches Worst Vs.	Avg	AB	H	2B	3B	HR	RBI	BB	SO	OBP	SLG
Ruben Sierra	.364	11	4	0	0	1	3	1	0	.417	.636

Cecil Fielder — Tigers

Age 30 – Bats Right (flyball hitter)

	Avg	G	AB	R	H	2B	3B	HR	RBI	BB	SO	HBP	GDP	SB	CS	OBP	SLG	IBB	SH	SF	#Pit	#P/PA	GB	FB	G/F
1993 Season	.267	154	573	80	153	23	0	30	117	90	125	4	22	0	1	.368	.464	15	0	5	2659	3.96	186	174	1.07
Last Five Years	.262	630	2364	366	620	95	1	160	506	331	609	17	68	0	2	.354	.506	46	0	21	10669	3.90	667	717	0.93

1993 Season

	Avg	AB	H	2B	3B	HR	RBI	BB	SO	OBP	SLG
vs. Left	.324	142	46	11	0	8	35	38	25	.462	.570
vs. Right	.248	431	107	12	0	22	82	52	100	.333	.429
Groundball	.296	125	37	8	0	4	22	12	25	.367	.456
Flyball	.274	117	32	4	0	12	28	17	25	.360	.615
Home	.283	283	80	12	0	20	67	44	63	.381	.537
Away	.252	290	73	11	0	10	50	46	62	.354	.393
Day	.276	199	55	8	0	11	46	35	46	.390	.482
Night	.262	374	98	15	0	19	71	55	79	.356	.455
Grass	.269	484	130	17	0	27	101	76	101	.368	.471
Turf	.258	89	23	6	0	3	16	14	24	.365	.427
First Pitch	.370	73	27	9	0	7	17	10	0	.446	.781
Ahead in Count	.413	109	45	9	0	9	41	39	0	.567	.743
Behind in Count	.199	266	53	5	0	9	34	0	94	.203	.320
Two Strikes	.161	298	48	4	0	7	28	40	125	.259	.245

	Avg	AB	H	2B	3B	HR	RBI	BB	SO	OBP	SLG
Scoring Posn	.292	195	57	8	0	10	90	40	41	.407	.487
Close & Late	.214	70	15	3	0	2	10	12	15	.333	.343
None on/out	.283	127	36	2	0	8	8	17	24	.372	.488
Batting #4	.267	572	153	23	0	30	117	89	125	.367	.465
Batting #5	.000	1	0	0	0	0	0	1	0	.500	.000
Other	.000	0	0	0	0	0	0	0	0	.000	.000
April	.271	85	23	3	0	2	17	13	21	.367	.376
May	.250	92	23	3	0	7	16	18	22	.381	.511
June	.286	98	28	3	0	10	32	20	18	.403	.622
July	.278	108	30	7	0	7	24	15	23	.363	.537
August	.273	99	27	4	0	3	17	15	21	.368	.404
September/October	.242	91	22	3	0	1	11	9	20	.317	.308
Pre-All Star	.274	314	86	12	0	23	77	59	68	.390	.532
Post-All Star	.259	259	67	11	0	7	40	31	57	.339	.382

1993 By Position

Position	Avg	AB	H	2B	3B	HR	RBI	BB	SO	OBP	SLG	G	GS	Innings	PO	A	E	DP	Fld Pct	Rng Fctr	In Zone	Outs	Zone Rtg	MLB Zone
As Designated Hitter	.277	130	36	7	0	6	28	29	24	.407	.469	36	35	---	---	---	---	---	---	---	---	---	---	---
As 1b	.264	443	117	16	0	24	89	61	101	.355	.463	119	118	962.1	971	76	10	84	.991	---	160	120	.750	.834

Last Five Years

	Avg	AB	H	2B	3B	HR	RBI	BB	SO	OBP	SLG
vs. Left	.310	613	190	36	0	55	151	124	146	.427	.638
vs. Right	.246	1751	430	59	1	105	355	207	463	.327	.460
Groundball	.262	653	171	23	0	33	109	67	164	.338	.449
Flyball	.244	550	134	18	1	47	135	84	152	.342	.536
Home	.268	1155	310	52	0	90	270	173	282	.366	.547
Away	.256	1209	310	43	1	70	236	158	327	.343	.467
Day	.244	762	186	24	0	56	180	108	195	.341	.496
Night	.271	1602	434	71	1	104	326	223	414	.361	.511
Grass	.263	2005	527	76	0	141	433	289	501	.357	.512
Turf	.259	359	93	19	1	19	73	42	108	.337	.476
First Pitch	.375	301	113	24	0	30	88	27	0	.426	.754
Ahead in Count	.389	473	184	37	0	55	160	142	0	.528	.816
Behind in Count	.188	1097	206	18	1	46	164	0	482	.192	.332
Two Strikes	.167	1216	203	22	1	44	152	152	609	.261	.295

	Avg	AB	H	2B	3B	HR	RBI	BB	SO	OBP	SLG
Scoring Posn	.277	703	195	29	1	44	334	142	178	.394	.509
Close & Late	.255	337	86	9	0	13	58	51	89	.355	.398
None on/out	.264	602	159	18	0	44	44	59	154	.333	.513
Batting #3	.182	66	12	1	0	4	9	8	27	.276	.379
Batting #4	.262	2210	580	88	1	144	468	312	556	.355	.499
Other	.318	88	28	6	0	12	29	11	26	.396	.795
April	.259	305	79	9	0	19	74	34	71	.338	.475
May	.272	371	101	25	0	26	70	60	103	.377	.550
June	.276	416	115	14	0	34	111	67	109	.376	.555
July	.256	418	107	17	0	31	91	52	112	.338	.519
August	.261	418	109	22	1	26	90	60	111	.354	.505
September/October	.250	436	109	8	0	24	70	58	103	.339	.433
Pre-All Star	.271	1239	336	52	0	90	292	182	321	.366	.531
Post-All Star	.252	1125	284	43	1	70	214	149	288	.341	.479

Batter vs. Pitcher (career)

Hits Best Against	Avg	AB	H	2B	3B	HR	RBI	BB	SO	OBP	SLG
Ken Patterson	.625	8	5	0	0	3	8	3	3	.727	1.750
Pat Hentgen	.545	11	6	0	0	4	7	0	2	.545	1.636
Ben McDonald	.412	17	7	0	0	3	4	3	4	.500	.941
Rich DeLucia	.333	12	4	0	0	3	11	2	2	.429	1.083
Matt Young	.313	16	5	0	0	4	11	5	5	.476	1.063

Hits Worst Against	Avg	AB	H	2B	3B	HR	RBI	BB	SO	OBP	SLG
Mark Eichhorn	.000	16	0	0	0	0	3	1	5	.056	.000
Roger Clemens	.043	23	1	0	0	0	1	2	12	.120	.043
Dennis Eckersley	.071	14	1	0	0	0	2	1	10	.133	.071
Rick Sutcliffe	.083	12	1	0	0	0	1	0	0	.083	.083
Gene Nelson	.087	23	2	0	0	0	1	1	5	.125	.087

Chuck Finley — Angels

Age 31 – Pitches Left

	ERA	W	L	Sv	G	GS	IP	BB	SO	Avg	H	2B	3B	HR	RBI	OBP	SLG	CG	ShO	Sup	QS	#P/S	SB	CS	GB	FB	G/F
1993 Season	3.15	16	14	0	35	35	251.1	82	187	.253	243	38	1	22	93	.314	.364	13	2	4.37	25	112	21	9	333	267	1.25
Last Five Years	3.17	75	53	0	161	161	1118.2	444	815	.250	1041	182	12	99	390	.324	.371	37	8	4.49	108	110	89	71	1429	1232	1.16

1993 Season

	ERA	W	L	Sv	G	GS	IP	H	HR	BB	SO
Home	2.79	8	5	0	16	16	122.2	106	13	32	104
Away	3.50	8	9	0	19	19	128.2	137	9	50	83
Day	3.73	4	6	0	12	12	82.0	94	8	28	63

	Avg	AB	H	2B	3B	HR	RBI	BB	SO	OBP	SLG
vs. Left	.313	128	40	7	0	2	10	14	22	.381	.414
vs. Right	.244	831	203	31	1	20	83	68	165	.303	.356
Inning 1-6	.256	762	195	33	1	20	81	69	147	.319	.381

1993 Season

	ERA	W	L	Sv	G	GS	IP	H	HR	BB	SO
Night	2.87	12	8	0	23	23	169.1	149	14	54	124
Grass	3.12	13	11	0	29	29	207.2	199	19	65	160
Turf	3.30	3	3	0	6	6	43.2	44	3	17	27
April	3.47	2	1	0	5	5	36.1	28	5	18	29
May	2.72	3	3	0	6	6	39.2	45	4	13	30
June	1.91	4	1	0	5	5	37.2	33	0	6	27
July	4.63	3	3	0	7	7	46.2	52	7	13	37
August	2.43	2	2	0	5	5	37.0	31	1	12	31
September/October	3.33	2	4	0	7	7	54.0	54	5	20	33
Starter	3.15	16	14	0	35	35	251.1	243	22	82	187
Reliever	0.00	0	0	0	0	0	0.0	0	0	0	0
0-3 Days Rest	2.45	1	0	0	1	1	7.1	9	0	2	8
4 Days Rest	3.48	12	10	0	26	26	186.1	186	20	61	141
5+ Days Rest	2.18	3	4	0	8	8	57.2	48	2	19	38
Pre-All Star	2.87	10	6	0	19	19	135.0	127	11	45	104
Post-All Star	3.48	6	8	0	16	16	116.1	116	11	37	83

	Avg	AB	H	2B	3B	HR	RBI	BB	SO	OBP	SLG
Inning 7+	.244	197	48	5	0	2	12	13	40	.292	.299
None on	.258	555	143	23	1	13	13	45	116	.316	.373
Runners on	.248	404	100	15	0	9	80	37	71	.312	.351
Scoring Posn	.237	224	53	7	0	6	74	23	44	.310	.348
Close & Late	.245	102	25	3	0	0	5	9	20	.306	.275
None on/out	.293	246	72	10	0	7	7	20	50	.348	.419
vs. 1st Batr (relief)	.000	0	0	0	0	0	0	0	0	.000	.000
First Inning Pitched	.250	136	34	7	0	4	19	18	23	.338	.390
First 75 Pitches	.258	617	159	29	1	16	66	55	120	.320	.386
Pitch 76-90	.241	116	28	4	0	2	12	11	19	.310	.328
Pitch 91-105	.222	108	24	4	0	2	7	7	27	.267	.315
Pitch 106+	.271	118	32	1	0	2	8	9	21	.328	.331
First Pitch	.300	130	39	8	0	6	19	1	0	.299	.500
Ahead in Count	.180	401	72	9	0	5	25	0	157	.189	.239
Behind in Count	.336	241	81	18	1	8	31	39	0	.427	.519
Two Strikes	.146	425	62	6	0	3	21	42	187	.227	.181

Last Five Years

	ERA	W	L	Sv	G	GS	IP	H	HR	BB	SO
Home	2.68	39	24	0	81	81	598.0	524	53	206	469
Away	3.73	36	29	0	80	80	520.2	517	46	238	346
Day	3.79	19	18	0	48	48	318.1	331	34	137	230
Night	2.92	56	35	0	113	113	800.1	710	65	307	585
Grass	3.17	59	47	0	136	136	947.2	890	87	371	724
Turf	3.16	16	6	0	25	25	171.0	151	12	73	91
April	2.58	13	5	0	20	20	132.1	104	13	54	88
May	3.56	15	9	0	28	28	187.1	194	18	73	143
June	3.43	13	12	0	29	29	194.0	190	16	68	152
July	3.36	14	7	0	29	29	214.1	204	22	76	154
August	3.06	9	9	0	25	25	176.1	154	15	74	130
September/October	2.86	11	11	0	30	30	214.1	195	15	99	148
Starter	3.17	75	53	0	161	161	1118.2	1041	99	444	815
Reliever	0.00	0	0	0	0	0	0.0	0	0	0	0
0-3 Days Rest	5.66	4	1	0	6	6	35.0	32	4	19	25
4 Days Rest	3.04	45	29	0	99	99	710.2	670	61	278	527
5+ Days Rest	3.18	26	23	0	56	56	373.0	339	34	147	263
Pre-All Star	3.32	45	29	0	87	87	585.2	550	54	227	437
Post-All Star	3.01	30	24	0	74	74	533.0	491	45	217	378

	Avg	AB	H	2B	3B	HR	RBI	BB	SO	OBP	SLG
vs. Left	.278	544	151	22	1	7	36	57	83	.347	.360
vs. Right	.246	3613	890	160	11	92	354	387	732	.321	.373
Inning 1-6	.248	3346	829	150	11	80	329	366	671	.323	.371
Inning 7+	.261	811	212	32	1	19	61	78	144	.327	.374
None on	.258	2433	627	112	8	64	64	266	476	.333	.389
Runners on	.240	1724	414	70	4	35	326	178	339	.311	.346
Scoring Posn	.231	926	214	36	3	18	284	117	201	.313	.335
Close & Late	.254	473	120	20	1	8	35	48	94	.322	.351
None on/out	.257	1097	282	43	5	27	27	99	204	.322	.379
vs. 1st Batr (relief)	.000	0	0	0	0	0	0	0	0	.000	.000
First Inning Pitched	.246	594	146	25	2	16	69	73	110	.330	.375
First 75 Pitches	.253	2704	685	123	10	70	274	298	527	.329	.384
Pitch 76-90	.241	522	126	25	1	9	45	56	95	.318	.345
Pitch 91-105	.232	466	108	20	1	7	30	36	106	.286	.324
Pitch 106+	.262	465	122	14	0	13	41	54	87	.341	.376
First Pitch	.303	565	171	32	1	20	71	6	0	.309	.469
Ahead in Count	.191	1824	349	51	4	25	104	0	683	.197	.265
Behind in Count	.312	987	308	61	3	34	122	238	0	.445	.483
Two Strikes	.171	1923	329	49	5	30	119	200	815	.252	.249

Pitcher vs. Batter (career)

Pitches Best Vs.	Avg	AB	H	2B	3B	HR	RBI	BB	SO	OBP	SLG
Terry Shumpert	.000	14	0	0	0	0	0	0	1	.000	.000
Greg Vaughn	.050	20	1	0	0	0	1	2	8	.136	.050
Steve Lyons	.083	12	1	0	0	0	0	0	5	.083	.083
Milt Cuyler	.083	12	1	0	0	0	2	1	3	.143	.083
Tim Hulett	.091	11	1	0	0	0	0	1	5	.167	.091

Pitches Worst Vs.	Avg	AB	H	2B	3B	HR	RBI	BB	SO	OBP	SLG
Mark Whiten	.500	16	8	3	1	0	1	2	3	.556	.813
Terry Steinbach	.474	38	18	3	0	4	17	1	4	.487	.868
Candy Maldonado	.444	18	8	2	0	2	6	2	3	.500	.889
Steve Balboni	.438	16	7	3	0	1	1	0	2	.438	.813
Shane Mack	.436	39	17	6	2	2	3	5	7	.500	.846

Steve Finley — Astros

Age 29 – Bats Left (groundball hitter)

	Avg	G	AB	R	H	2B	3B	HR	RBI	BB	SO	HBP	GDP	SB	CS	OBP	SLG	IBB	SH	SF	#Pit	#P/PA	GB	FB	G/F
1993 Season	.266	142	545	69	145	15	13	8	44	28	65	3	8	19	6	.304	.385	1	6	3	2025	3.46	233	151	1.54
Career (1989-1993)	.274	686	2429	318	665	93	42	26	215	175	276	11	37	136	45	.323	.379	16	48	18	9384	3.50	1047	616	1.70

1993 Season

	Avg	AB	H	2B	3B	HR	RBI	BB	SO	OBP	SLG
vs. Left	.268	164	44	6	3	2	16	5	16	.297	.378
vs. Right	.265	381	101	9	10	6	28	23	49	.307	.388
Groundball	.238	172	41	5	4	1	10	12	23	.292	.331
Flyball	.263	76	20	2	4	1	9	5	5	.313	.434
Home	.246	252	62	5	7	1	20	11	29	.280	.333
Away	.283	293	83	10	6	7	24	17	36	.325	.430
Day	.258	178	46	3	2	3	9	13	17	.314	.348
Night	.270	367	99	12	11	5	35	15	48	.299	.403
Grass	.270	196	53	7	5	5	15	13	22	.316	.434
Turf	.264	349	92	8	8	3	29	15	43	.297	.358
First Pitch	.412	68	28	5	0	0	8	1	0	.429	.485
Ahead in Count	.293	123	36	3	5	2	11	18	0	.387	.447
Behind in Count	.201	249	50	6	3	4	16	0	59	.202	.297
Two Strikes	.169	213	36	4	2	4	13	9	65	.204	.263

	Avg	AB	H	2B	3B	HR	RBI	BB	SO	OBP	SLG
Scoring Posn	.292	113	33	2	5	1	35	5	14	.314	.425
Close & Late	.306	85	26	2	2	3	10	4	6	.348	.482
None on/out	.261	111	29	3	4	0	0	8	14	.317	.360
Batting #2	.258	469	121	12	11	6	35	25	58	.298	.369
Batting #8	.313	64	20	1	2	0	5	3	6	.343	.391
Other	.333	12	4	2	0	2	4	0	1	.333	1.000
April	.222	63	14	1	0	1	3	7	7	.315	.286
May	.262	65	17	2	2	0	3	4	2	.310	.354
June	.226	84	19	2	2	0	1	5	9	.270	.298
July	.313	99	31	5	3	1	11	3	10	.333	.455
August	.274	113	31	2	2	2	12	4	15	.299	.381
September/October	.273	121	33	3	4	4	14	5	22	.299	.463
Pre-All Star	.245	253	62	6	6	2	14	18	21	.301	.340
Post-All Star	.284	292	83	9	7	6	30	10	44	.307	.425

1993 By Position

Position	Avg	AB	H	2B	3B	HR	RBI	BB	SO	OBP	SLG	G	GS	Innings	PO	A	E	DP	Fld Pct	Rng Fctr	In Zone	Outs	Zone Rtg	MLB Zone
As cf	.264	542	143	14	13	8	44	28	65	.302	.382	140	131	1166.2	327	11	4	4	.988	2.61	380	312	.821	.829

Career (1989-1993)

	Avg	AB	H	2B	3B	HR	RBI	BB	SO	OBP	SLG
vs. Left	.249	726	181	23	9	6	66	37	94	.289	.331
vs. Right	.284	1703	484	70	33	20	149	138	182	.338	.399

	Avg	AB	H	2B	3B	HR	RBI	BB	SO	OBP	SLG
Scoring Posn	.280	517	145	14	14	6	179	52	71	.338	.397
Close & Late	.286	374	107	12	2	6	43	29	42	.337	.377

Career (1989-1993)	Avg	AB	H	2B	3B	HR	RBI	BB	SO	OBP	SLG
Groundball	.279	775	216	23	16	6	60	64	81	.335	.373
Flyball	.276	490	135	23	8	7	52	34	52	.321	.398
Home	.261	1207	315	44	25	7	95	87	150	.312	.356
Away	.286	1222	350	49	17	19	120	88	126	.335	.401
Day	.261	666	174	26	7	6	44	56	60	.320	.348
Night	.279	1763	491	67	35	20	171	119	216	.324	.390
Grass	.273	1153	315	49	13	13	99	77	137	.318	.372
Turf	.274	1276	350	44	29	13	116	98	139	.328	.385
First Pitch	.354	311	110	11	4	2	47	10	0	.373	.434
Ahead in Count	.332	515	171	28	14	7	57	113	0	.453	.482
Behind in Count	.218	1120	244	36	16	12	72	0	242	.221	.311
Two Strikes	.207	1017	211	32	14	10	65	51	276	.247	.296

	Avg	AB	H	2B	3B	HR	RBI	BB	SO	OBP	SLG
None on/out	.274	614	168	26	12	3	3	41	74	.321	.370
Batting #1	.286	651	186	28	10	9	58	39	79	.325	.401
Batting #2	.270	1571	424	56	29	15	133	120	170	.323	.371
Other	.266	207	55	9	3	2	24	16	27	.317	.367
April	.248	294	73	9	5	3	23	25	38	.310	.344
May	.272	404	110	23	9	4	32	28	40	.319	.403
June	.254	413	105	17	7	3	29	36	36	.317	.351
July	.297	390	116	12	7	3	33	23	44	.339	.387
August	.280	393	110	16	5	3	45	32	46	.334	.369
September/October	.282	535	151	16	9	10	53	31	72	.319	.402
Pre-All Star	.263	1242	327	52	23	12	102	99	132	.319	.371
Post-All Star	.285	1187	338	41	19	14	113	76	144	.327	.387

Batter vs. Pitcher (career)

Hits Best Against	Avg	AB	H	2B	3B	HR	RBI	BB	SO	OBP	SLG
Mike Bielecki	.571	14	8	1	2	1	2	1	1	.600	1.143
Charlie Hough	.458	24	11	3	0	1	4	0	0	.440	.708
Jeff Fassero	.455	11	5	0	1	0	5	1	1	.500	.636
Jack Morris	.400	10	4	0	1	0	0	3	2	.538	.600
Roger McDowell	.400	10	4	0	2	0	2	2	0	.462	.800

Hits Worst Against	Avg	AB	H	2B	3B	HR	RBI	BB	SO	OBP	SLG
Rich Rodriguez	.000	10	0	0	0	0	0	1	1	.091	.000
Greg Swindell	.048	21	1	1	0	0	0	1	4	.091	.095
Bob Welch	.063	16	1	0	0	0	0	1	0	.118	.063
Mike Boddicker	.071	14	1	0	0	0	0	2	0	.188	.071
Zane Smith	.143	14	2	0	0	0	0	0	3	.143	.143

Carlton Fisk — White Sox

Age 46 – Bats Right (flyball hitter)

	Avg	G	AB	R	H	2B	3B	HR	RBI	BB	SO	HBP	GDP	SB	CS	OBP	SLG	IBB	SH	SF	#Pit	#P/PA	GB	FB	G/F
1993 Season	.189	25	53	2	10	0	0	1	4	2	11	1	0	0	1	.228	.245	0	1	1	214	3.69	16	18	0.89
Last Five Years	.264	461	1528	168	403	75	3	53	232	154	268	19	48	12	5	.336	.421	25	1	11	6310	3.68	498	502	0.99

1993 Season

	Avg	AB	H	2B	3B	HR	RBI	BB	SO	OBP	SLG
vs. Left	.290	31	9	0	0	1	3	0	3	.290	.387
vs. Right	.045	22	1	0	0	0	1	2	8	.154	.045
Scoring Posn	.091	11	1	0	0	0	3	1	5	.154	.091
Close & Late	.111	9	1	0	0	0	0	1	3	.200	.111

Last Five Years

	Avg	AB	H	2B	3B	HR	RBI	BB	SO	OBP	SLG
vs. Left	.280	522	146	26	1	19	83	49	70	.343	.443
vs. Right	.255	1006	257	49	2	34	149	105	198	.333	.410
Groundball	.276	421	116	24	0	6	51	31	71	.333	.375
Flyball	.291	330	96	15	0	19	65	36	57	.360	.509
Home	.271	733	199	41	1	20	117	89	115	.354	.412
Away	.257	795	204	34	2	33	115	65	153	.320	.429
Day	.240	279	67	12	0	10	34	29	46	.312	.391
Night	.269	1249	336	63	3	43	198	125	222	.342	.428
Grass	.271	1286	348	64	3	41	191	134	212	.344	.421
Turf	.227	242	55	11	0	12	41	20	56	.293	.421
First Pitch	.351	174	61	15	0	8	29	12	0	.394	.575
Ahead in Count	.301	329	99	24	1	16	72	81	0	.440	.526
Behind in Count	.220	715	157	23	0	17	85	0	236	.234	.323
Two Strikes	.191	700	134	20	2	12	65	53	268	.253	.277

	Avg	AB	H	2B	3B	HR	RBI	BB	SO	OBP	SLG
Scoring Posn	.258	430	111	20	2	13	169	62	79	.354	.405
Close & Late	.260	273	71	18	0	11	52	33	65	.342	.447
None on/out	.269	353	95	19	0	14	14	26	64	.328	.442
Batting #4	.250	420	105	26	0	16	68	36	68	.317	.426
Batting #5	.291	604	176	29	1	26	96	66	99	.365	.472
Other	.242	504	122	20	2	11	68	52	101	.319	.355
April	.296	162	48	8	0	3	18	9	28	.341	.401
May	.232	177	41	7	0	4	21	24	36	.332	.339
June	.263	289	76	9	1	9	41	29	56	.333	.394
July	.269	271	73	16	1	9	44	23	40	.327	.435
August	.277	314	87	19	1	15	55	30	52	.346	.487
September/October	.248	315	78	16	0	13	53	39	56	.339	.422
Pre-All Star	.264	716	189	30	1	20	96	68	138	.333	.392
Post-All Star	.264	812	214	45	2	33	136	86	130	.340	.446

Batter vs. Pitcher (since 1984)

Hits Best Against	Avg	AB	H	2B	3B	HR	RBI	BB	SO	OBP	SLG
Greg Swindell	.478	23	11	1	0	4	9	1	3	.500	1.043
Eric Plunk	.462	13	6	0	0	2	6	2	2	.533	.923
Pete Harnisch	.429	7	3	1	0	1	2	4	1	.636	1.000
John Candelaria	.417	12	5	0	0	3	9	3	1	.533	1.167
Tom Gordon	.385	13	5	1	0	2	4	4	3	.529	.923

Hits Worst Against	Avg	AB	H	2B	3B	HR	RBI	BB	SO	OBP	SLG
Rich DeLucia	.077	13	1	0	0	0	2	0	3	.077	.077
Steve Ontiveros	.091	11	1	0	0	0	2	1	1	.167	.091
Kevin Brown	.095	21	2	0	0	0	1	0	5	.095	.095
Curt Young	.097	31	3	0	0	0	1	1	4	.121	.097
Jose Rijo	.100	10	1	0	0	0	0	1	2	.182	.100

John Flaherty — Red Sox

Age 26 – Bats Right (flyball hitter)

	Avg	G	AB	R	H	2B	3B	HR	RBI	BB	SO	HBP	GDP	SB	CS	OBP	SLG	IBB	SH	SF	#Pit	#P/PA	GB	FB	G/F
1993 Season	.120	13	25	3	3	2	0	0	2	2	6	1	0	0	0	.214	.200	0	1	0	108	3.72	4	14	0.29
Career (1992-1993)	.176	48	91	6	16	4	0	0	4	5	13	1	0	0	0	.224	.220	0	2	1	362	3.62	29	33	0.88

1993 Season

	Avg	AB	H	2B	3B	HR	RBI	BB	SO	OBP	SLG
vs. Left	.286	7	2	2	0	0	2	1	2	.375	.571
vs. Right	.056	18	1	0	0	0	0	1	4	.150	.056
Scoring Posn	.111	9	1	1	0	0	2	0	3	.200	.222
Close & Late	.000	1	0	0	0	0	0	0	0	.500	.000

Dave Fleming — Mariners

Age 24 – Pitches Left

	ERA	W	L	Sv	G	GS	IP	BB	SO	Avg	H	2B	3B	HR	RBI	OBP	SLG	CG	ShO	Sup	QS	#P/S	SB	CS	GB	FB	G/F
1993 Season	4.36	12	5	0	26	26	167.1	67	75	.290	189	35	2	15	75	.357	.419	1	1	5.16	14	103	8	12	237	217	1.09
Career (1991-1993)	3.92	30	15	0	68	62	413.1	130	198	.271	433	94	7	31	169	.329	.397	8	5	4.64	36	103	27	27	587	511	1.15

1993 Season

	ERA	W	L	Sv	G	GS	IP	H	HR	BB	SO
Home	4.48	5	1	0	12	12	72.1	89	6	29	35
Away	4.26	7	4	0	14	14	95.0	100	9	38	40
Day	3.65	3	0	0	7	7	44.1	54	2	20	23
Night	4.61	9	5	0	19	19	123.0	135	13	47	52

	Avg	AB	H	2B	3B	HR	RBI	BB	SO	OBP	SLG
vs. Left	.258	128	33	6	2	4	19	5	14	.297	.430
vs. Right	.298	524	156	29	0	11	56	62	61	.371	.416
Inning 1-6	.275	557	153	27	2	14	67	59	68	.345	.406
Inning 7+	.379	95	36	8	0	1	8	8	7	.433	.495

1993 Season

	ERA	W	L	Sv	G	GS	IP	H	HR	BB	SO
Grass	4.52	4	3	0	9	9	61.2	66	7	26	28
Turf	4.26	8	2	0	17	17	105.2	123	8	41	47
April	0.00	0	0	0	0	0	0.0	0	0	0	0
May	8.64	0	0	0	2	2	8.1	14	1	4	6
June	2.51	3	1	0	6	6	43.0	34	3	14	15
July	5.49	3	0	0	6	6	39.1	52	4	10	13
August	4.64	3	1	0	5	5	33.0	39	4	18	21
September/October	4.12	3	3	0	7	7	43.2	50	3	21	20
Starter	4.36	12	5	0	26	26	167.1	189	15	67	75
Reliever	0.00	0	0	0	0	0	0.0	0	0	0	0
0-3 Days Rest	0.00	0	0	0	0	0	0.0	0	0	0	0
4 Days Rest	4.10	7	5	0	18	18	116.1	126	9	50	49
5+ Days Rest	4.94	5	0	0	8	8	51.0	63	6	17	26
Pre-All Star	3.92	4	1	0	10	10	64.1	67	5	19	25
Post-All Star	4.63	8	4	0	16	16	103.0	122	10	48	50

	Avg	AB	H	2B	3B	HR	RBI	BB	SO	OBP	SLG
None on	.295	370	109	19	1	9	9	28	43	.349	.424
Runners on	.284	282	80	16	1	6	66	39	32	.367	.411
Scoring Posn	.230	152	35	7	1	4	59	29	22	.342	.368
Close & Late	.327	49	16	4	0	1	5	4	2	.377	.469
None on/out	.315	168	53	7	0	4	4	14	21	.372	.429
vs. 1st Batr (relief)	.000	0	0	0	0	0	0	0	0	.000	.000
First Inning Pitched	.313	96	30	6	1	2	15	16	9	.393	.458
First 75 Pitches	.284	455	129	20	2	12	56	49	52	.355	.415
Pitch 76-90	.217	83	18	5	0	3	9	8	13	.290	.386
Pitch 91-105	.360	75	27	6	0	0	5	6	7	.407	.440
Pitch 106+	.385	39	15	4	0	0	5	4	3	.442	.487
First Pitch	.388	103	40	5	1	3	16	5	0	.417	.544
Ahead in Count	.254	260	66	12	1	4	22	0	62	.258	.354
Behind in Count	.289	152	44	8	0	4	24	34	0	.418	.421
Two Strikes	.261	253	66	14	1	3	21	28	75	.334	.360

Career (1991-1993)

	ERA	W	L	Sv	G	GS	IP	H	HR	BB	SO
Home	3.72	13	6	0	32	28	193.1	203	15	59	94
Away	4.09	17	9	0	36	34	220.0	230	16	71	104
Day	4.95	5	5	0	18	16	100.0	130	7	37	52
Night	3.59	25	10	0	50	46	313.1	303	24	93	146
Grass	4.28	12	6	0	26	25	153.2	165	14	49	78
Turf	3.71	18	9	0	42	37	259.2	268	17	81	120
April	6.53	2	1	0	4	4	20.2	25	2	9	15
May	2.96	5	0	0	8	8	51.2	52	2	24	22
June	2.85	6	3	0	12	12	82.0	74	4	24	35
July	3.99	5	1	0	11	11	79.0	85	8	13	29
August	3.51	6	3	0	15	11	84.2	81	9	26	49
September/October	5.10	6	7	0	18	16	95.1	116	6	34	48
Starter	3.89	30	15	0	62	62	407.1	429	31	129	197
Reliever	6.00	0	0	0	6	0	6.0	4	0	1	1
0-3 Days Rest	7.11	1	0	0	2	2	6.1	11	0	2	3
4 Days Rest	3.67	17	11	0	40	40	265.0	278	20	94	126
5+ Days Rest	4.17	12	4	0	20	20	136.0	140	11	33	68
Pre-All Star	3.46	15	4	0	28	28	182.1	180	11	60	81
Post-All Star	4.29	15	11	0	40	34	231.0	253	20	70	117

	Avg	AB	H	2B	3B	HR	RBI	BB	SO	OBP	SLG
vs. Left	.255	278	71	17	3	6	33	17	38	.308	.403
vs. Right	.275	1318	362	77	4	25	136	113	160	.334	.396
Inning 1-6	.262	1304	342	74	4	26	146	112	169	.324	.385
Inning 7+	.312	292	91	20	3	5	23	18	29	.356	.452
None on	.274	930	255	55	4	18	18	61	111	.323	.400
Runners on	.267	666	178	39	3	13	151	69	87	.338	.393
Scoring Posn	.239	380	91	19	3	6	128	45	51	.320	.353
Close & Late	.283	127	36	8	1	3	10	10	12	.336	.433
None on/out	.284	412	117	23	1	8	8	30	50	.337	.403
vs. 1st Batr (relief)	.000	5	0	0	0	0	0	0	0	.000	.000
First Inning Pitched	.273	249	68	12	2	5	30	26	33	.343	.398
First 75 Pitches	.265	1104	293	64	5	21	126	95	141	.328	.389
Pitch 76-90	.261	207	54	10	0	6	20	16	26	.314	.396
Pitch 91-105	.308	172	53	11	1	2	12	10	18	.346	.419
Pitch 106+	.292	113	33	9	1	2	11	9	13	.344	.442
First Pitch	.342	231	79	16	3	5	33	8	0	.364	.502
Ahead in Count	.226	619	140	22	1	8	41	0	155	.233	.304
Behind in Count	.284	398	113	30	2	10	61	70	0	.390	.445
Two Strikes	.223	636	142	28	2	10	45	52	198	.287	.321

Pitcher vs. Batter (career)

Pitches Best Vs.	Avg	AB	H	2B	3B	HR	RBI	BB	SO	OBP	SLG
Chris Hoiles	.077	13	1	0	0	0	0	0	2	.077	.077
Dickie Thon	.091	11	1	0	0	0	0	2	3	.231	.091
Glenn Davis	.091	11	1	0	0	0	0	0	1	.091	.091
John Olerud	.100	10	1	0	0	0	1	1	1	.167	.100
Brian Harper	.154	13	2	0	0	0	2	0	1	.143	.154

Pitches Worst Vs.	Avg	AB	H	2B	3B	HR	RBI	BB	SO	OBP	SLG
Paul Molitor	.875	8	7	0	0	0	2	2	0	.818	.875
Robin Yount	.600	10	6	2	0	0	1	3	1	.692	.800
Mike Devereaux	.500	16	8	2	0	2	6	3	1	.579	1.000
Steve Sax	.500	14	7	4	0	0	1	1	0	.533	.786
Mike Macfarlane	.429	14	6	3	0	2	2	2	2	.500	1.071

Huck Flener — Blue Jays

Age 25 – Pitches Left

	ERA	W	L	Sv	G	GS	IP	BB	SO	Avg	H	2B	3B	HR	RBI	OBP	SLG	GF	IR	IRS	Hld	SvOp	SB	CS	GB	FB	G/F
1993 Season	4.05	0	0	0	6	0	6.2	4	2	.269	7	2	1	0	3	.367	.423	1	3	0	2	0	1	0	13	9	1.44

1993 Season

	ERA	W	L	Sv	G	GS	IP	H	HR	BB	SO
Home	0.00	0	0	0	2	0	1.1	2	0	1	0
Away	5.06	0	0	0	4	0	5.1	5	0	3	2

	Avg	AB	H	2B	3B	HR	RBI	BB	SO	OBP	SLG
vs. Left	.267	15	4	2	0	0	2	0	1	.267	.400
vs. Right	.273	11	3	0	1	0	1	4	1	.467	.455

Darrin Fletcher — Expos

Age 27 – Bats Left (flyball hitter)

	Avg	G	AB	R	H	2B	3B	HR	RBI	BB	SO	HBP	GDP	SB	CS	OBP	SLG	IBB	SH	SF	#Pit	#P/PA	GB	FB	G/F
1993 Season	.255	133	396	33	101	20	1	9	60	34	40	6	7	0	0	.320	.379	2	5	4	1625	3.65	133	145	0.92
Career (1989-1993)	.246	278	785	55	193	39	3	13	101	55	89	8	17	0	3	.299	.353	5	8	8	3142	3.64	267	272	0.98

1993 Season

	Avg	AB	H	2B	3B	HR	RBI	BB	SO	OBP	SLG
vs. Left	.260	77	20	3	0	2	11	11	11	.356	.377
vs. Right	.254	319	81	17	1	7	49	23	29	.311	.379
Groundball	.296	115	34	7	1	3	20	8	9	.352	.452
Flyball	.263	57	15	2	0	0	8	7	8	.348	.298
Home	.257	183	47	12	0	5	30	17	16	.322	.404
Away	.254	213	54	8	1	4	30	17	24	.319	.357
Day	.235	115	27	4	0	1	10	4	18	.273	.296
Night	.263	281	74	16	1	8	50	30	22	.339	.413
Grass	.271	133	36	2	1	3	19	13	13	.347	.368
Turf	.247	263	65	18	0	6	41	21	27	.307	.384
First Pitch	.294	51	15	3	1	0	6	1	0	.315	.392
Ahead in Count	.272	114	31	4	0	4	19	23	0	.394	.412
Behind in Count	.241	158	38	6	0	3	21	0	35	.253	.335
Two Strikes	.258	155	40	8	0	4	26	10	40	.308	.387

	Avg	AB	H	2B	3B	HR	RBI	BB	SO	OBP	SLG
Scoring Posn	.244	127	31	9	0	3	51	19	14	.342	.386
Close & Late	.309	68	21	6	1	0	10	6	9	.390	.426
None on/out	.205	83	17	3	1	4	4	3	9	.233	.410
Batting #5	.276	181	50	11	0	4	28	13	15	.332	.403
Batting #6	.246	126	31	5	0	4	18	10	14	.307	.381
Other	.225	89	20	4	1	1	14	11	11	.317	.326
April	.327	49	16	4	0	1	9	4	4	.377	.469
May	.196	51	10	0	0	0	3	2	5	.226	.196
June	.196	46	9	2	0	1	11	8	5	.327	.304
July	.349	83	29	4	0	3	13	13	5	.439	.506
August	.275	91	25	4	0	3	16	4	12	.320	.418
September/October	.158	76	12	6	1	1	8	3	9	.202	.303
Pre-All Star	.260	173	45	7	0	3	26	19	15	.335	.353
Post-All Star	.251	223	56	13	1	6	34	15	25	.309	.399

1993 By Position

Position	Avg	AB	H	2B	3B	HR	RBI	BB	SO	OBP	SLG	G	GS	Innings	PO	A	E	DP	Fld Pct	Rng Fctr	In Zone	Outs	Zone Rtg	MLB Zone
As Pinch Hitter	.438	16	7	1	0	1	6	3	2	.526	.688	20	0	---	---	---	---	---	---	---	---	---	---	---
As c	.247	380	94	19	1	8	54	31	38	.311	.366	127	105	918.1	620	40	8	3	.988	---	---	---	---	---

Career (1989-1993)

	Avg	AB	H	2B	3B	HR	RBI	BB	SO	OBP	SLG		Avg	AB	H	2B	3B	HR	RBI	BB	SO	OBP	SLG
vs. Left	.265	117	31	6	0	2	16	14	20	.346	.368	Scoring Posn	.229	227	52	14	0	4	84	30	33	.317	.344
vs. Right	.243	668	162	33	3	11	85	41	69	.290	.350	Close & Late	.246	142	35	11	1	0	13	10	23	.308	.338
Groundball	.292	271	79	17	1	4	38	14	24	.331	.406	None on/out	.253	182	46	9	1	5	5	4	14	.269	.396
Flyball	.215	135	29	5	0	1	15	11	26	.275	.274	Batting #5	.285	253	72	14	1	4	39	19	22	.337	.395
Home	.240	342	82	19	1	7	46	25	37	.291	.363	Batting #7	.224	228	51	10	1	2	21	15	26	.273	.303
Away	.251	443	111	20	2	6	55	30	52	.306	.345	Other	.230	304	70	15	1	7	41	21	41	.286	.355
Day	.262	221	58	13	1	3	27	16	27	.318	.371	April	.266	94	25	5	0	2	15	6	11	.314	.383
Night	.239	564	135	26	2	10	74	39	62	.292	.346	May	.215	107	23	4	0	1	12	3	12	.236	.280
Grass	.275	247	68	8	2	5	34	22	24	.345	.385	June	.192	99	19	4	0	1	14	11	12	.279	.263
Turf	.232	538	125	31	1	8	67	33	65	.277	.338	July	.331	136	45	7	1	3	18	16	12	.404	.463
First Pitch	.239	113	27	4	1	0	8	3	0	.261	.292	August	.252	131	33	5	0	3	21	8	17	.303	.359
Ahead in Count	.258	198	51	11	2	4	27	38	0	.377	.394	September/October	.220	218	48	14	2	3	21	11	25	.260	.344
Behind in Count	.237	338	80	113	0	6	38	0	78	.244	.328	Pre-All Star	.239	352	84	15	0	5	46	28	38	.299	.324
Two Strikes	.246	329	81	16	0	7	46	14	89	.282	.359	Post-All Star	.252	433	109	24	3	8	55	27	51	.299	.376

Batter vs. Pitcher (career)

Hits Best Against	Avg	AB	H	2B	3B	HR	RBI	BB	SO	OBP	SLG	Hits Worst Against	Avg	AB	H	2B	3B	HR	RBI	BB	SO	OBP	SLG
Omar Olivares	.500	12	6	2	0	0	2	0	1	.500	.667	Curt Schilling	.000	22	0	0	0	0	2	0	3	.000	.000
Bob Walk	.417	12	5	1	0	2	6	0	1	.417	1.000	Bill Swift	.133	15	2	0	0	0	0	0	1	.133	.133
Bob Tewksbury	.368	19	7	0	0	0	2	0	2	.350	.368	Greg Maddux	.200	20	4	1	0	0	5	0	3	.182	.250
Doug Drabek	.318	22	7	2	0	1	3	0	1	.318	.545	Greg W. Harris	.200	15	3	2	0	0	3	1	0	.250	.333
Jose Rijo	.308	13	4	2	0	0	1	1	2	.357	.462	Ben Rivera	.200	15	3	1	0	0	1	2	0	.294	.267

Paul Fletcher — Phillies

Age 27 – Pitches Right

	ERA	W	L	Sv	G	GS	IP	BB	SO	Avg	H	2B	3B	HR	RBI	OBP	SLG	GF	IR	IRS	Hld	SvOp	SB	CS	GB	FB	G/F
1993 Season	0.00	0	0	0	1	0	0.1	0	0	.000	0	0	0	0	0	.000	.000	0	1	0	0	0	0	0	0	0	0.00

1993 Season

	ERA	W	L	Sv	G	GS	IP	H	HR	BB	SO		Avg	AB	H	2B	3B	HR	RBI	BB	SO	OBP	SLG
Home	0.00	0	0	0	1	0	0.1	0	0	0	0	vs. Left	.000	0	0	0	0	0	0	0	0	.000	.000
Away	0.00	0	0	0	0	0	0.0	0	0	0	0	vs. Right	.000	1	0	0	0	0	0	0	0	.000	.000

Scott Fletcher — Red Sox

Age 35 – Bats Right

	Avg	G	AB	R	H	2B	3B	HR	RBI	BB	SO	HBP	GDP	SB	CS	OBP	SLG	IBB	SH	SF	#Pit	#P/PA	GB	FB	G/F
1993 Season	.285	121	480	81	137	31	5	5	45	37	35	5	12	16	3	.341	.402	1	6	3	1767	3.33	217	118	1.84
Last Five Years	.256	627	2169	279	555	102	14	14	223	193	217	21	41	36	19	.320	.335	6	40	20	8273	3.39	899	605	1.49

1993 Season

	Avg	AB	H	2B	3B	HR	RBI	BB	SO	OBP	SLG		Avg	AB	H	2B	3B	HR	RBI	BB	SO	OBP	SLG
vs. Left	.268	123	33	8	1	3	17	4	8	.292	.423	Scoring Posn	.289	97	28	6	2	0	39	7	7	.345	.392
vs. Right	.291	357	104	23	4	2	28	33	27	.357	.395	Close & Late	.239	71	17	3	0	0	6	5	8	.299	.282
Groundball	.333	87	29	5	1	1	9	7	4	.383	.448	None on/out	.302	192	58	17	3	2	2	20	16	.374	.453
Flyball	.304	115	35	8	2	1	11	11	10	.367	.435	Batting #1	.288	472	136	31	5	5	44	37	33	.344	.407
Home	.284	250	71	18	0	2	22	21	21	.348	.380	Batting #2	.250	4	1	0	0	0	0	0	1	.250	.250
Away	.287	230	66	13	5	3	23	16	14	.333	.426	Other	.000	4	0	0	0	0	1	0	1	.000	.000
Day	.281	167	47	12	1	1	16	12	12	.330	.383	April	.250	52	13	2	2	1	3	4	4	.328	.423
Night	.288	313	90	19	4	4	29	25	23	.347	.412	May	.304	79	24	8	0	2	11	12	6	.389	.481
Grass	.287	408	117	26	2	4	35	30	31	.340	.390	June	.250	44	11	1	0	1	3	3	5	.298	.341
Turf	.278	72	20	5	3	1	10	7	4	.346	.472	July	.299	107	32	5	1	0	13	7	6	.348	.364
First Pitch	.367	79	29	5	1	1	11	0	0	.373	.494	August	.302	106	32	12	1	0	7	3	6	.327	.434
Ahead in Count	.295	132	39	11	2	3	15	18	0	.380	.477	September/October	.272	92	25	3	1	1	8	8	8	.330	.359
Behind in Count	.211	175	37	10	1	0	8	0	28	.219	.280	Pre-All Star	.290	217	63	14	3	4	23	24	17	.364	.438
Two Strikes	.210	167	35	10	2	0	7	19	35	.298	.293	Post-All Star	.281	263	74	17	2	1	22	13	18	.320	.373

1993 By Position

Position	Avg	AB	H	2B	3B	HR	RBI	BB	SO	OBP	SLG	G	GS	Innings	PO	A	E	DP	Fld Pct	Rng Fctr	In Zone	Outs	Zone Rtg	MLB Zone
As 2b	.288	472	136	31	5	5	44	37	33	.344	.407	116	115	982.1	217	370	11	68	.982	5.38	419	379	.905	.895

Last Five Years

	Avg	AB	H	2B	3B	HR	RBI	BB	SO	OBP	SLG		Avg	AB	H	2B	3B	HR	RBI	BB	SO	OBP	SLG
vs. Left	.269	665	179	33	3	4	58	58	61	.332	.346	Scoring Posn	.276	532	147	30	3	4	202	55	60	.341	.367
vs. Right	.250	1504	376	69	11	10	165	135	156	.315	.330	Close & Late	.237	359	85	12	0	2	40	34	46	.308	.287
Groundball	.265	528	140	14	3	5	57	43	49	.324	.331	None on/out	.236	594	140	33	4	4	4	52	65	.302	.325
Flyball	.273	512	140	32	4	4	65	43	58	.333	.375	Batting #1	.285	487	139	32	5	5	46	38	37	.341	.402
Home	.262	1075	282	53	4	5	112	97	106	.327	.333	Batting #2	.231	635	147	24	2	1	46	80	73	.317	.280
Away	.250	1094	273	49	10	9	111	96	111	.313	.337	Other	.257	1047	269	46	7	8	131	75	107	.312	.337
Day	.264	611	161	31	5	2	59	59	49	.327	.340	April	.268	272	73	12	5	2	32	42	31	.371	.371
Night	.253	1558	394	71	9	12	164	134	168	.317	.333	May	.237	396	94	16	3	4	32	40	47	.306	.323
Grass	.257	1835	472	87	9	13	183	162	188	.320	.336	June	.259	328	85	18	1	2	26	30	32	.330	.338
Turf	.249	334	83	15	5	1	40	31	29	.319	.332	July	.253	328	83	15	2	2	40	22	27	.300	.329
First Pitch	.297	323	96	17	3	4	40	0	0	.314	.406	August	.278	421	117	25	1	0	47	31	33	.331	.342

Last Five Years

	Avg	AB	H	2B	3B	HR	RBI	BB	SO	OBP	SLG
Ahead in Count	.303	585	177	37	6	5	76	109	0	.411	.412
Behind in Count	.231	700	162	32	2	5	67	0	127	.233	.304
Two Strikes	.178	807	144	26	5	3	48	80	217	.255	.234

	Avg	AB	H	2B	3B	HR	RBI	BB	SO	OBP	SLG
September/October	.243	424	103	16	2	4	46	28	47	.295	.318
Pre-All Star	.252	1116	281	51	11	8	99	124	120	.330	.339
Post-All Star	.260	1053	274	51	3	6	124	69	97	.309	.331

Batter vs. Pitcher (since 1984)

Hits Best Against	Avg	AB	H	2B	3B	HR	RBI	BB	SO	OBP	SLG
John Candelaria	.579	19	11	2	1	0	1	3	0	.636	.789
Dave Johnson	.545	11	6	1	1	0	1	1	0	.583	.818
Scott Sanderson	.516	31	16	2	1	2	12	0	2	.516	.839
Todd Burns	.455	11	5	2	0	0	2	3	1	.571	.636
Pat Hentgen	.333	9	3	0	1	1	1	2	0	.455	.889

Hits Worst Against	Avg	AB	H	2B	3B	HR	RBI	BB	SO	OBP	SLG
Jim Abbott	.045	22	1	0	0	0	1	0	1	.045	.045
John Farrell	.067	15	1	0	0	0	0	1	2	.125	.067
Mark Williamson	.083	12	1	1	0	0	2	1	0	.154	.167
Rick Aguilera	.118	17	2	0	0	0	1	0	3	.118	.118
Bill Wegman	.143	21	3	0	0	0	1	2	0	.217	.143

Cliff Floyd — Expos

Age 21 – Bats Left

	Avg	G	AB	R	H	2B	3B	HR	RBI	BB	SO	HBP	GDP	SB	CS	OBP	SLG	IBB	SH	SF	#Pit	#P/PA	GB	FB	G/F
1993 Season	.226	10	31	3	7	0	0	1	2	0	9	0	0	0	0	.226	.323	0	0	0	103	3.32	9	8	1.13

1993 Season

	Avg	AB	H	2B	3B	HR	RBI	BB	SO	OBP	SLG
vs. Left	.000	2	0	0	0	0	0	0	0	.000	.000
vs. Right	.241	29	7	0	0	1	2	0	9	.241	.345

	Avg	AB	H	2B	3B	HR	RBI	BB	SO	OBP	SLG
Scoring Posn	.400	5	2	0	0	0	0	0	2	.400	.400
Close & Late	.000	3	0	0	0	0	0	0	1	.000	.000

Tom Foley — Pirates

Age 34 – Bats Left

	Avg	G	AB	R	H	2B	3B	HR	RBI	BB	SO	HBP	GDP	SB	CS	OBP	SLG	IBB	SH	SF	#Pit	#P/PA	GB	FB	G/F
1993 Season	.253	86	194	18	49	11	1	3	22	11	26	0	4	0	0	.287	.366	1	2	4	711	3.37	83	55	1.51
Last Five Years	.221	439	1016	82	225	46	6	10	93	90	152	5	20	7	4	.284	.308	13	11	14	3931	3.46	374	316	1.18

1993 Season

	Avg	AB	H	2B	3B	HR	RBI	BB	SO	OBP	SLG
vs. Left	.417	12	5	1	0	0	1	0	1	.417	.500
vs. Right	.242	182	44	10	1	3	21	11	25	.279	.357
Home	.272	81	22	5	1	1	12	4	8	.299	.395
Away	.239	113	27	6	0	2	10	7	18	.279	.345
First Pitch	.225	40	9	0	1	0	3	1	0	.238	.275
Ahead in Count	.321	53	17	3	0	1	9	7	0	.393	.434
Behind in Count	.228	79	18	5	0	2	7	0	25	.225	.367
Two Strikes	.233	73	17	5	0	2	7	3	26	.260	.384

	Avg	AB	H	2B	3B	HR	RBI	BB	SO	OBP	SLG
Scoring Posn	.196	46	9	4	0	1	18	3	9	.226	.348
Close & Late	.245	49	12	2	1	1	8	1	8	.250	.388
None on/out	.304	46	14	4	1	1	1	2	6	.333	.500
Batting #1	.256	43	11	2	0	1	4	3	4	.304	.372
Batting #8	.245	49	12	2	0	0	9	2	7	.255	.286
Other	.255	102	26	7	1	2	9	6	15	.296	.402
Pre-All Star	.236	110	26	7	1	2	17	6	17	.267	.373
Post-All Star	.274	84	23	4	0	1	5	5	9	.315	.357

Last Five Years

	Avg	AB	H	2B	3B	HR	RBI	BB	SO	OBP	SLG
vs. Left	.239	92	22	4	1	0	7	3	17	.265	.304
vs. Right	.220	924	203	42	5	10	86	87	135	.286	.308
Groundball	.228	391	89	18	1	4	31	30	45	.288	.309
Flyball	.178	225	40	7	1	2	21	23	50	.249	.244
Home	.211	512	108	23	4	5	43	37	69	.264	.301
Away	.232	504	117	23	2	5	50	53	83	.304	.315
Day	.238	294	70	13	3	2	28	24	35	.295	.323
Night	.215	722	155	33	3	8	65	66	117	.280	.302
Grass	.257	280	72	12	2	3	22	30	42	.327	.346
Turf	.208	736	153	34	4	7	71	60	110	.268	.293
First Pitch	.216	185	40	7	1	2	16	7	0	.240	.297
Ahead in Count	.281	221	62	12	3	2	29	58	0	.426	.389
Behind in Count	.193	441	85	16	2	4	28	0	131	.195	.265
Two Strikes	.168	423	71	16	2	3	28	23	152	.211	.236

	Avg	AB	H	2B	3B	HR	RBI	BB	SO	OBP	SLG
Scoring Posn	.234	252	59	13	2	5	85	35	43	.317	.361
Close & Late	.225	218	49	10	2	2	21	21	46	.292	.317
None on/out	.241	232	56	11	3	2	2	10	34	.279	.341
Batting #2	.233	292	68	15	1	5	30	32	45	.313	.342
Batting #8	.226	323	73	15	2	0	32	27	47	.280	.285
Other	.209	401	84	16	3	5	31	31	60	.267	.302
April	.236	123	29	7	0	3	19	11	16	.290	.366
May	.209	187	39	8	3	0	16	14	27	.262	.283
June	.240	204	49	11	1	1	23	30	31	.333	.319
July	.253	174	44	10	2	3	15	10	29	.302	.385
August	.195	159	31	5	0	2	14	12	23	.251	.264
September/October	.195	169	33	5	0	1	6	13	26	.255	.243
Pre-All Star	.237	595	141	32	5	7	69	58	84	.302	.343
Post-All Star	.200	421	84	14	1	3	24	32	68	.259	.259

Batter vs. Pitcher (since 1984)

Hits Best Against	Avg	AB	H	2B	3B	HR	RBI	BB	SO	OBP	SLG
Les Lancaster	.385	13	5	1	0	1	3	1	2	.400	.692
Ron Darling	.348	46	16	1	0	2	9	3	4	.388	.500
Bill Gullickson	.333	21	7	2	1	0	2	2	2	.391	.524
Craig Lefferts	.333	12	4	0	0	0	0	0	2	.333	.333
Greg Maddux	.327	52	17	2	0	0	5	5	7	.386	.365

Hits Worst Against	Avg	AB	H	2B	3B	HR	RBI	BB	SO	OBP	SLG
Jose Rijo	.067	15	1	0	0	0	1	0	4	.067	.067
Fernando Valenzuela	.077	13	1	0	0	0	0	0	4	.077	.077
Steve Bedrosian	.083	12	1	0	0	0	2	0	3	.083	.083
Omar Olivares	.083	12	1	0	0	0	0	0	1	.083	.083
Joe Boever	.091	11	1	0	0	0	0	1	5	.167	.091

Tony Fossas — Red Sox

Age 36 – Pitches Left (groundball pitcher)

	ERA	W	L	Sv	G	GS	IP	BB	SO	Avg	H	2B	3B	HR	RBI	OBP	SLG	GF	IR	IRS	Hld	SvOp	SB	CS	GB	FB	G/F
1993 Season	5.18	1	1	0	71	0	40.0	15	39	.242	38	7	0	4	20	.314	.363	19	60	11	13	2	3	0	50	49	1.02
Last Five Years	4.06	9	10	4	278	0	217.0	89	153	.263	219	37	5	16	138	.338	.377	63	284	82	66	12	16	5	344	187	1.84

1993 Season

	ERA	W	L	Sv	G	GS	IP	H	HR	BB	SO
Home	3.68	1	1	0	36	0	22.0	17	1	9	21
Away	7.00	0	0	0	35	0	18.0	21	3	6	18
Day	1.80	0	0	0	22	0	10.0	5	0	3	11
Night	6.30	1	1	0	49	0	30.0	33	4	12	28
Grass	4.29	1	1	0	61	0	35.2	32	2	14	34
Turf	12.46	0	0	0	10	0	4.1	6	2	1	5
April	5.40	0	0	0	6	0	3.1	3	0	1	3
May	0.00	0	0	0	11	0	5.0	3	0	3	6

	Avg	AB	H	2B	3B	HR	RBI	BB	SO	OBP	SLG
vs. Left	.129	70	9	2	0	0	7	6	22	.215	.157
vs. Right	.333	87	29	5	0	4	13	9	17	.396	.529
Inning 1-6	.000	7	0	0	0	0	0	0	1	.000	.000
Inning 7+	.253	150	38	7	0	4	20	15	38	.327	.380
None on	.211	76	16	2	0	3	3	7	20	.286	.355
Runners on	.272	81	22	5	0	1	17	8	19	.341	.370
Scoring Posn	.261	46	12	3	0	0	15	5	14	.340	.326
Close & Late	.210	62	13	2	0	2	8	9	17	.310	.339

1993 Season

	ERA	W	L	Sv	G	GS	IP	H	HR	BB	SO
June	6.75	0	0	0	10	0	6.2	9	3	2	6
July	9.00	1	0	0	11	0	4.0	3	0	3	5
August	4.70	0	0	0	14	0	7.2	8	0	1	7
September/October	5.40	0	1	0	19	0	13.1	12	1	5	12
Starter	0.00	0	0	0	0	0	0.0	0	0	0	0
Reliever	5.18	1	1	0	71	0	40.0	38	4	15	39
0 Days rest	5.54	0	0	0	28	0	13.0	12	0	3	12
1 or 2 Days rest	6.88	1	1	0	25	0	17.0	20	3	10	15
3+ Days rest	1.80	0	0	0	18	0	10.0	6	1	2	12
Pre-All Star	5.06	0	0	0	30	0	16.0	16	3	7	16
Post-All Star	5.25	1	1	0	41	0	24.0	22	1	8	23

	Avg	AB	H	2B	3B	HR	RBI	BB	SO	OBP	SLG
None on/out	.306	36	11	1	0	3	3	5	12	.405	.583
vs. 1st Batr (relief)	.200	65	13	3	0	2	10	5	19	.268	.338
First Inning Pitched	.250	136	34	7	0	4	19	13	34	.318	.390
First 15 Pitches	.238	130	31	6	0	3	17	10	32	.296	.354
Pitch 16-30	.227	22	5	1	0	1	2	3	5	.346	.409
Pitch 31-45	.500	2	1	0	0	0	0	2	0	.750	.500
Pitch 46+	.333	3	1	0	0	0	1	0	2	.333	.333
First Pitch	.529	17	9	3	0	2	8	1	0	.579	1.059
Ahead in Count	.154	78	12	3	0	1	5	0	34	.154	.231
Behind in Count	.194	31	6	0	0	1	4	9	0	.366	.290
Two Strikes	.179	78	14	2	0	1	7	5	39	.229	.244

Last Five Years

	ERA	W	L	Sv	G	GS	IP	H	HR	BB	SO
Home	2.90	5	3	3	142	0	118.0	104	0	45	87
Away	5.45	4	7	1	136	0	99.0	115	10	44	66
Day	3.14	2	4	2	87	0	77.1	76	3	33	53
Night	4.58	7	6	2	191	0	139.2	143	13	56	100
Grass	3.68	8	8	4	239	0	188.1	183	13	79	133
Turf	6.59	1	2	0	39	0	28.2	36	3	10	20
April	6.20	1	4	0	27	0	20.1	22	2	9	13
May	3.62	0	1	0	41	0	27.1	26	3	12	13
June	3.25	2	0	1	47	0	44.1	43	7	15	38
July	4.91	3	1	0	53	0	36.2	39	2	21	29
August	4.76	3	3	1	52	0	39.2	45	1	13	31
September/October	2.96	0	1	2	58	0	48.2	44	1	19	29
Starter	0.00	0	0	0	0	0	0.0	0	0	0	0
Reliever	4.06	9	10	4	278	0	217.0	219	16	89	153
0 Days rest	3.05	3	2	2	98	0	76.2	68	2	28	52
1 or 2 Days rest	5.44	4	5	2	103	0	86.0	102	11	31	59
3+ Days rest	3.31	2	3	0	77	0	54.1	49	3	30	42
Pre-All Star	3.96	4	5	1	127	0	100.0	100	12	41	72
Post-All Star	4.15	5	5	3	151	0	117.0	119	4	48	81

	Avg	AB	H	2B	3B	HR	RBI	BB	SO	OBP	SLG
vs. Left	.193	331	64	11	0	4	47	27	92	.263	.263
vs. Right	.309	501	155	26	5	12	91	62	61	.386	.453
Inning 1-6	.232	112	26	5	0	1	23	13	23	.310	.304
Inning 7+	.268	720	193	32	5	15	115	76	130	.342	.389
None on	.243	358	87	14	4	8	8	34	61	.317	.372
Runners on	.278	474	132	23	1	8	130	55	92	.353	.382
Scoring Posn	.272	313	85	16	1	4	122	45	65	.362	.367
Close & Late	.241	228	55	11	2	4	42	33	46	.343	.360
None on/out	.238	168	40	4	2	4	4	20	37	.326	.357
vs. 1st Batr (relief)	.204	245	50	11	0	2	44	19	59	.270	.273
First Inning Pitched	.261	651	170	31	4	12	118	67	127	.333	.376
First 15 Pitches	.261	633	165	29	4	10	104	59	120	.327	.367
Pitch 16-30	.250	160	40	8	1	4	26	24	25	.351	.388
Pitch 31-45	.417	24	10	0	0	2	6	5	3	.517	.667
Pitch 46+	.267	15	4	0	0	0	2	1	5	.313	.267
First Pitch	.385	135	52	9	1	5	39	19	0	.462	.578
Ahead in Count	.169	362	61	10	1	5	39	0	140	.174	.243
Behind in Count	.316	190	60	13	2	3	40	40	0	.438	.453
Two Strikes	.171	340	58	9	2	7	42	30	153	.242	.271

Pitcher vs. Batter (career)

Pitches Best Vs.	Avg	AB	H	2B	3B	HR	RBI	BB	SO	OBP	SLG
Kent Hrbek	.083	12	1	0	0	0	1	2	3	.214	.083
Ken Griffey Jr	.125	16	2	0	0	0	1	1	4	.176	.125
George Brett	.167	18	3	1	0	0	2	3	2	.286	.222
Wally Joyner	.167	12	2	0	0	1	6	0	5	.167	.417
Tony Phillips	.214	14	3	1	0	0	1	0	3	.214	.286

Pitches Worst Vs.	Avg	AB	H	2B	3B	HR	RBI	BB	SO	OBP	SLG
Lou Whitaker	.455	11	5	2	0	0	4	0	0	.455	.636
Mickey Tettleton	.333	12	4	1	0	2	5	1	3	.385	.917

Kevin Foster — Phillies

Age 25 – Pitches Right

	ERA	W	L	Sv	G	GS	IP	BB	SO	Avg	H	2B	3B	HR	RBI	OBP	SLG	CG	ShO	Sup	QS	#P/S	SB	CS	GB	FB	G/F
1993 Season	14.85	0	1	0	2	1	6.2	7	6	.394	13	3	0	3	10	.500	.758	0	0	1.35	0	103	2	0	12	12	1.00

1993 Season

	ERA	W	L	Sv	G	GS	IP	H	HR	BB	SO
Home	10.13	0	0	0	1	0	2.2	4	0	3	3
Away	18.00	0	1	0	1	1	4.0	9	3	4	3

	Avg	AB	H	2B	3B	HR	RBI	BB	SO	OBP	SLG
vs. Left	.458	24	11	2	0	3	10	6	4	.567	.917
vs. Right	.222	9	2	1	0	0	0	1	2	.300	.333

Steve Foster — Reds

Age 27 – Pitches Right

	ERA	W	L	Sv	G	GS	IP	BB	SO	Avg	H	2B	3B	HR	RBI	OBP	SLG	GF	IR	IRS	Hld	SvOp	SB	CS	GB	FB	G/F
1993 Season	1.75	2	2	0	17	0	25.2	5	16	.235	23	3	1	1	10	.279	.316	7	4	2	5	0	0	0	29	31	0.94
Career (1991-1993)	2.41	3	3	2	59	1	89.2	22	61	.244	82	12	4	6	32	.291	.357	19	30	9	9	3	1	1	122	93	1.31

1993 Season

	ERA	W	L	Sv	G	GS	IP	H	HR	BB	SO
Home	1.35	1	0	0	9	0	13.1	10	0	3	8
Away	2.19	1	2	0	8	0	12.1	13	1	2	8

	Avg	AB	H	2B	3B	HR	RBI	BB	SO	OBP	SLG
vs. Left	.209	43	9	2	0	1	3	3	12	.261	.326
vs. Right	.255	55	14	1	1	0	7	2	4	.293	.309

Eric Fox — Athletics

Age 30 – Bats Both

	Avg	G	AB	R	H	2B	3B	HR	RBI	BB	SO	HBP	GDP	SB	CS	OBP	SLG	IBB	SH	SF	#Pit	#P/PA	GB	FB	G/F
1993 Season	.143	29	56	5	8	1	0	1	5	2	7	0	0	0	2	.172	.214	0	3	0	228	3.74	27	12	2.25
Career (1992-1993)	.211	80	199	29	42	6	2	4	18	15	36	0	1	3	6	.265	.322	0	9	1	845	3.77	70	56	1.25

1993 Season

	Avg	AB	H	2B	3B	HR	RBI	BB	SO	OBP	SLG
vs. Left	.125	16	2	0	0	1	4	1	3	.176	.313
vs. Right	.150	40	6	1	0	0	1	1	4	.171	.175

	Avg	AB	H	2B	3B	HR	RBI	BB	SO	OBP	SLG
Scoring Posn	.059	17	1	0	0	1	5	0	1	.059	.235
Close & Late	.444	9	4	0	0	1	4	0	0	.444	.778

John Franco — Mets

Age 33 – Pitches Left (groundball pitcher)

	ERA	W	L	Sv	G	GS	IP	BB	SO	Avg	H	2B	3B	HR	RBI	OBP	SLG	GF	IR	IRS	Hld	SvOp	SB	CS	GB	FB	G/F
1993 Season	5.20	4	3	10	35	0	36.1	19	29	.313	46	4	0	6	28	.393	.463	30	12	6	0	17	4	0	68	22	3.09
Last Five Years	3.03	24	25	120	233	0	273.0	105	210	.261	274	36	5	16	130	.328	.351	156	95	33	2	147	18	9	475	183	2.60

1993 Season

	ERA	W	L	Sv	G	GS	IP	H	HR	BB	SO
Home	3.31	1	0	6	15	0	16.1	14	3	7	11
Away	6.75	3	3	4	20	0	20.0	32	3	12	18
Starter	0.00	0	0	0	0	0	0.0	0	0	0	0
Reliever	5.20	4	3	10	35	0	36.1	46	6	19	29
0 Days rest	13.50	0	1	1	2	0	1.1	1	1	2	2
1 or 2 Days rest	6.64	3	1	4	17	0	20.1	30	3	11	15
3+ Days rest	2.45	1	1	5	16	0	14.2	15	2	6	12
Pre-All Star	3.20	2	0	4	19	0	19.2	20	4	10	10
Post-All Star	7.56	2	3	6	16	0	16.2	26	2	9	19

	Avg	AB	H	2B	3B	HR	RBI	BB	SO	OBP	SLG
vs. Left	.317	41	13	1	0	2	9	4	10	.378	.488
vs. Right	.311	106	33	3	0	4	19	15	19	.398	.453
Scoring Posn	.311	45	14	2	0	1	21	9	4	.429	.422
Close & Late	.322	87	28	3	0	3	18	17	16	.434	.460
None on/out	.290	31	9	1	0	0	0	3	7	.353	.323
First Pitch	.150	20	3	0	0	0	2	2	0	.227	.150
Ahead in Count	.236	55	13	1	0	3	10	0	26	.250	.418
Behind in Count	.404	47	19	3	0	2	10	9	0	.500	.596
Two Strikes	.204	54	11	1	0	2	10	8	29	.313	.333

Last Five Years

	ERA	W	L	Sv	G	GS	IP	H	HR	BB	SO
Home	2.96	14	11	66	122	0	142.2	143	6	52	107
Away	3.11	10	14	54	111	0	130.1	131	10	53	103
Day	3.01	10	10	36	85	0	104.2	99	7	45	89
Night	3.05	14	15	84	148	0	168.1	175	9	60	121
Grass	2.24	13	11	72	143	0	164.2	152	10	59	124
Turf	4.24	11	14	48	90	0	108.1	122	6	46	86
April	1.43	2	1	24	32	0	37.2	17	1	11	27
May	1.02	6	2	19	35	0	44.1	36	1	15	32
June	2.96	6	5	19	47	0	51.2	60	2	25	35
July	3.47	3	3	24	37	0	46.2	49	6	13	40
August	2.16	3	4	21	44	0	50.0	51	3	18	38
September/October	7.17	4	10	13	38	0	42.2	61	3	23	38
Starter	0.00	0	0	0	0	0	0.0	0	0	0	0
Reliever	3.03	24	25	120	233	0	273.0	274	16	105	210
0 Days rest	3.60	4	5	23	37	0	40.0	46	4	14	40
1 or 2 Days rest	2.42	12	10	58	111	0	133.2	124	4	55	98
3+ Days rest	3.62	8	10	39	85	0	99.1	104	8	36	72
Pre-All Star	2.05	15	9	73	128	0	149.0	130	7	56	112
Post-All Star	4.21	9	16	47	105	0	124.0	144	9	49	98

	Avg	AB	H	2B	3B	HR	RBI	BB	SO	OBP	SLG
vs. Left	.266	229	61	8	2	2	31	26	49	.342	.345
vs. Right	.260	819	213	28	3	14	98	79	161	.324	.353
Inning 1-6	.000	0	0	0	0	0	0	0	0	.000	.000
Inning 7+	.261	1048	274	36	5	16	129	105	210	.328	.351
None on	.259	517	134	15	1	9	9	41	113	.314	.344
Runners on	.264	531	140	21	4	7	120	64	97	.341	.358
Scoring Posn	.250	324	81	14	2	4	109	50	58	.347	.343
Close & Late	.258	718	185	22	4	10	91	74	145	.326	.341
None on/out	.247	231	57	9	0	3	3	14	43	.290	.325
vs. 1st Batr (relief)	.218	211	46	9	0	0	10	16	37	.271	.261
First Inning Pitched	.256	823	211	29	5	10	101	83	168	.323	.340
First 15 Pitches	.247	692	171	24	5	10	68	63	133	.308	.340
Pitch 16-30	.281	288	81	10	0	5	45	33	64	.357	.368
Pitch 31-45	.328	67	22	2	0	1	17	9	13	.408	.403
Pitch 46+	.000	1	0	0	0	0	0	0	0	.000	.000
First Pitch	.319	141	45	7	1	2	20	15	0	.382	.426
Ahead in Count	.186	457	85	8	1	4	37	0	181	.187	.234
Behind in Count	.322	255	82	15	3	7	44	51	0	.434	.486
Two Strikes	.183	486	89	6	1	3	42	39	210	.243	.218

Pitcher vs. Batter (career)

Pitches Best Vs.	Avg	AB	H	2B	3B	HR	RBI	BB	SO	OBP	SLG
Tom Pagnozzi	.000	13	0	0	0	0	0	2	5	.133	.000
Jose Lind	.083	12	1	0	0	0	0	0	1	.083	.083
Darren Daulton	.091	11	1	1	0	0	0	1	5	.167	.182
Lenny Dykstra	.125	16	2	0	0	0	1	0	4	.125	.125
Bobby Thompson	.143	14	2	0	0	0	1	2	1	.250	.143

Pitches Worst Vs.	Avg	AB	H	2B	3B	HR	RBI	BB	SO	OBP	SLG
Mariano Duncan	.500	16	8	1	0	0	0	2	4	.556	.563
Terry Pendleton	.467	15	7	1	0	0	2	1	1	.500	.533
Kevin McReynolds	.385	13	5	1	0	1	4	2	1	.467	.692
Todd Zeile	.385	13	5	0	0	1	1	1	3	.429	.615
Kevin Mitchell	.333	12	4	0	0	1	1	6	2	.556	.583

Julio Franco — Rangers

Age 32 – Bats Right (groundball hitter)

	Avg	G	AB	R	H	2B	3B	HR	RBI	BB	SO	HBP	GDP	SB	CS	OBP	SLG	IBB	SH	SF	#Pit	#P/PA	GB	FB	G/F
1993 Season	.289	144	532	85	154	31	3	14	84	62	95	1	16	9	3	.360	.438	4	5	7	2506	4.13	217	111	1.95
Last Five Years	.307	632	2358	388	725	123	12	55	331	290	342	7	71	98	26	.382	.440	28	8	17	10330	3.85	997	542	1.84

1993 Season

	Avg	AB	H	2B	3B	HR	RBI	BB	SO	OBP	SLG
vs. Left	.265	102	27	5	1	3	18	10	21	.330	.422
vs. Right	.295	430	127	26	2	11	66	52	74	.368	.442
Groundball	.284	102	29	7	2	3	20	10	21	.339	.480
Flyball	.323	96	31	5	0	6	23	12	15	.394	.563
Home	.330	264	87	21	3	6	45	32	42	.400	.500
Away	.250	268	67	10	0	8	39	30	53	.321	.377
Day	.311	119	37	11	0	3	22	12	19	.368	.479
Night	.283	413	117	20	3	11	62	50	76	.358	.426
Grass	.301	445	134	30	3	11	70	53	75	.374	.456
Turf	.230	87	20	1	0	3	14	9	20	.293	.345
First Pitch	.386	44	17	4	0	0	12	2	0	.396	.477
Ahead in Count	.342	111	38	7	1	3	17	33	0	.483	.505
Behind in Count	.230	256	59	15	2	5	26	0	85	.230	.363
Two Strikes	.234	291	68	16	1	6	38	27	95	.298	.357

	Avg	AB	H	2B	3B	HR	RBI	BB	SO	OBP	SLG
Scoring Posn	.338	148	50	8	1	4	68	18	27	.393	.486
Close & Late	.243	74	18	3	2	2	11	7	18	.301	.419
None on/out	.302	129	39	10	0	2	2	11	27	.362	.426
Batting #2	.258	244	63	15	0	10	39	29	47	.335	.443
Batting #5	.324	213	69	13	2	3	30	30	33	.405	.446
Other	.293	75	22	3	1	1	15	3	15	.313	.400
April	.286	77	22	5	1	1	9	6	15	.337	.416
May	.265	98	26	9	0	4	16	4	22	.291	.480
June	.190	42	8	2	0	1	4	7	6	.300	.310
July	.278	108	30	3	0	5	21	19	19	.386	.444
August	.333	99	33	6	0	2	14	19	13	.445	.455
September/October	.324	108	35	6	2	1	20	7	20	.350	.444
Pre-All Star	.271	262	71	18	1	9	41	25	50	.332	.450
Post-All Star	.307	270	83	13	2	5	43	37	45	.387	.426

1993 By Position

Position	Avg	AB	H	2B	3B	HR	RBI	BB	SO	OBP	SLG	G	GS	Innings	PO	A	E	DP	Fld Pct	Rng Fctr	In Zone	Outs	Zone Rtg	MLB Zone
As Designated Hitter	.289	529	153	31	3	14	83	61	94	.360	.439	140	140	---	---	---	---	---	---	---	---	---	---	---

Last Five Years

	Avg	AB	H	2B	3B	HR	RBI	BB	SO	OBP	SLG
vs. Left	.308	636	196	37	5	20	97	82	95	.385	.476
vs. Right	.307	1722	529	86	7	35	234	208	247	.382	.426
Groundball	.290	638	185	32	4	16	90	81	87	.368	.428
Flyball	.308	513	158	28	2	15	80	64	76	.384	.458
Home	.335	1192	399	74	10	28	171	152	165	.409	.484

	Avg	AB	H	2B	3B	HR	RBI	BB	SO	OBP	SLG
Scoring Posn	.333	603	201	31	4	15	265	108	94	.427	.473
Close & Late	.305	367	112	17	2	8	42	47	60	.383	.428
None on/out	.292	565	165	31	1	11	11	45	87	.345	.409
Batting #2	.321	673	216	34	2	18	97	98	99	.406	.458
Batting #5	.310	971	301	52	7	19	134	116	135	.381	.437

Last Five Years

	Avg	AB	H	2B	3B	HR	RBI	BB	SO	OBP	SLG
Away	.280	1166	326	49	2	27	160	138	177	.355	.395
Day	.285	445	127	27	2	8	66	61	63	.374	.409
Night	.313	1913	598	96	10	47	265	229	279	.384	.447
Grass	.316	1962	620	108	11	48	280	246	281	.392	.456
Turf	.265	396	105	15	1	7	51	44	61	.337	.361
First Pitch	.351	208	73	9	2	3	26	12	0	.381	.457
Ahead in Count	.376	591	222	39	3	18	105	173	0	.513	.543
Behind in Count	.244	1078	263	43	6	17	104	0	296	.247	.342
Two Strikes	.242	1118	271	52	5	23	130	99	342	.306	.360

	Avg	AB	H	2B	3B	HR	RBI	BB	SO	OBP	SLG
Other	.291	714	208	37	3	18	100	76	108	.361	.427
April	.268	321	86	16	1	7	50	28	45	.327	.389
May	.326	405	132	29	1	14	66	46	70	.394	.506
June	.304	438	133	22	3	11	57	54	67	.378	.443
July	.291	402	117	17	1	8	56	53	53	.374	.398
August	.326	390	127	17	2	7	54	62	45	.419	.433
September/October	.323	402	130	22	4	8	48	47	62	.390	.458
Pre-All Star	.299	1294	387	72	5	36	192	143	201	.368	.446
Post-All Star	.318	1064	338	51	7	19	139	147	141	.400	.432

Batter vs. Pitcher (since 1984)

Hits Best Against	Avg	AB	H	2B	3B	HR	RBI	BB	SO	OBP	SLG
Bobby Thigpen	.643	14	9	2	0	1	1	0	1	.643	1.000
Scott Sanderson	.500	18	9	1	0	2	4	3	0	.571	.889
Tom Bolton	.500	12	6	1	0	1	1	4	3	.625	.833
Erik Hanson	.471	17	8	0	0	1	2	3	1	.550	.647
Dan Plesac	.455	11	5	0	0	1	1	2	1	.538	.727

Hits Worst Against	Avg	AB	H	2B	3B	HR	RBI	BB	SO	OBP	SLG
Tom Henke	.118	17	2	0	0	0	1	1	2	.167	.118
Chuck Crim	.136	22	3	0	0	0	3	2	1	.208	.136
Scott Bankhead	.136	22	3	0	0	0	1	1	2	.174	.136
Ron Darling	.167	12	2	0	0	0	2	1	2	.231	.167
Eric Plunk	.200	15	3	0	0	0	3	1	3	.235	.200

Lou Frazier — Expos

Age 29 – Bats Both (groundball hitter)

	Avg	G	AB	R	H	2B	3B	HR	RBI	BB	SO	HBP	GDP	SB	CS	OBP	SLG	IBB	SH	SF	#Pit	#P/PA	GB	FB	G/F
1993 Season	.286	112	189	27	54	7	1	1	16	16	24	0	3	17	2	.340	.349	0	5	1	790	3.74	89	42	2.12

1993 Season

	Avg	AB	H	2B	3B	HR	RBI	BB	SO	OBP	SLG
vs. Left	.295	61	18	2	0	1	4	4	9	.338	.377
vs. Right	.281	128	36	5	1	0	12	12	15	.340	.336
Home	.350	103	36	4	1	1	12	7	11	.387	.437
Away	.209	86	18	3	0	0	4	9	13	.284	.244
First Pitch	.214	28	6	0	0	0	4	0	0	.214	.214
Ahead in Count	.390	41	16	1	0	1	4	9	0	.500	.488
Behind in Count	.244	82	20	3	0	0	6	0	20	.244	.280
Two Strikes	.225	89	20	3	1	0	7	7	24	.278	.281

	Avg	AB	H	2B	3B	HR	RBI	BB	SO	OBP	SLG
Scoring Posn	.292	48	14	1	0	0	14	4	4	.340	.313
Close & Late	.292	48	14	3	0	0	5	7	7	.375	.354
None on/out	.265	49	13	2	1	0	0	5	6	.333	.347
Batting #1	.234	47	11	1	1	0	3	3	7	.275	.298
Batting #2	.317	63	20	3	0	1	5	7	6	.386	.413
Other	.291	79	23	3	0	0	8	6	11	.341	.329
Pre-All Star	.340	106	36	5	0	1	8	11	10	.402	.415
Post-All Star	.217	83	18	2	1	0	8	5	14	.258	.265

Scott Fredrickson — Rockies

Age 26 – Pitches Right (groundball pitcher)

	ERA	W	L	Sv	G	GS	IP	BB	SO	Avg	H	2B	3B	HR	RBI	OBP	SLG	GF	IR	IRS	Hld	SvOp	SB	CS	GB	FB	G/F
1993 Season	6.21	0	1	0	25	0	29.0	17	20	.287	33	4	1	3	20	.378	.417	4	20	5	2	0	1	2	39	23	1.70

1993 Season

	ERA	W	L	Sv	G	GS	IP	H	HR	BB	SO
Home	5.79	0	1	0	16	0	18.2	17	1	11	16
Away	6.97	0	0	0	9	0	10.1	16	2	6	4
Starter	0.00	0	0	0	0	0	0.0	0	0	0	0
Reliever	6.21	0	1	0	25	0	29.0	33	3	17	20
0 Days rest	13.50	0	0	0	5	0	3.1	8	0	4	4
1 or 2 Days rest	4.35	0	1	0	10	0	10.1	11	0	7	9
3+ Days rest	5.87	0	0	0	10	0	15.1	14	3	6	7
Pre-All Star	5.47	0	1	0	22	0	24.2	23	3	15	18
Post-All Star	10.38	0	0	0	3	0	4.1	10	0	2	2

	Avg	AB	H	2B	3B	HR	RBI	BB	SO	OBP	SLG
vs. Left	.212	52	11	0	1	0	5	10	8	.339	.250
vs. Right	.349	63	22	4	0	3	15	7	12	.411	.556
Scoring Posn	.289	45	13	2	0	0	16	5	6	.346	.333
Close & Late	.222	9	2	0	0	0	1	4	2	.462	.222
None on/out	.333	24	8	2	0	0	0	5	6	.448	.417
First Pitch	.438	16	7	1	1	0	6	1	0	.444	.625
Ahead in Count	.178	45	8	2	0	1	5	0	17	.174	.289
Behind in Count	.313	32	10	1	0	2	5	10	0	.476	.531
Two Strikes	.224	49	11	1	0	0	4	6	20	.304	.245

Marvin Freeman — Braves

Age 31 – Pitches Right (groundball pitcher)

	ERA	W	L	Sv	G	GS	IP	BB	SO	Avg	H	2B	3B	HR	RBI	OBP	SLG	GF	IR	IRS	Hld	SvOp	SB	CS	GB	FB	G/F
1993 Season	6.08	2	0	0	21	0	23.2	10	25	.261	24	5	1	1	16	.340	.370	5	10	3	1	0	3	3	32	17	1.88
Last Five Years	3.85	11	7	5	139	4	187.0	74	138	.235	165	23	4	15	98	.315	.343	31	90	32	27	8	17	13	321	133	2.41

1993 Season

	ERA	W	L	Sv	G	GS	IP	H	HR	BB	SO
Home	14.40	0	0	0	10	0	10.0	20	1	9	10
Away	0.00	2	0	0	11	0	13.2	4	0	1	15

	Avg	AB	H	2B	3B	HR	RBI	BB	SO	OBP	SLG
vs. Left	.286	28	8	1	1	1	7	7	3	.429	.500
vs. Right	.250	64	16	4	0	0	9	3	22	.294	.313

Last Five Years

	ERA	W	L	Sv	G	GS	IP	H	HR	BB	SO
Home	3.49	5	4	3	71	1	98.0	88	8	37	70
Away	4.25	6	3	2	68	3	89.0	77	7	37	68
Day	5.43	3	0	1	40	2	56.1	52	6	19	38
Night	3.17	8	7	4	99	2	130.2	113	9	55	100
Grass	3.46	9	3	3	99	2	138.0	117	10	47	98
Turf	4.96	2	4	2	40	2	49.0	48	5	27	40
April	3.13	2	1	0	17	1	23.0	18	1	18	15
May	5.06	1	1	3	30	0	37.1	41	3	17	29
June	5.40	0	2	0	17	3	31.2	33	5	10	19
July	3.96	2	2	1	27	0	36.1	31	3	12	30
August	4.03	3	0	1	23	0	22.1	24	2	9	17
September/October	1.49	3	1	0	25	0	36.1	18	1	8	28
Starter	6.75	0	1	0	4	4	16.0	17	3	8	9
Reliever	3.58	11	6	5	135	0	171.0	148	12	66	129
0 Days rest	1.99	2	2	1	24	0	31.2	23	1	11	22

	Avg	AB	H	2B	3B	HR	RBI	BB	SO	OBP	SLG
vs. Left	.252	305	77	7	3	8	43	46	36	.353	.374
vs. Right	.222	397	88	16	1	7	55	28	102	.284	.320
Inning 1-6	.250	308	77	9	3	7	47	34	60	.338	.367
Inning 7+	.223	394	88	14	1	8	51	40	78	.297	.325
None on	.220	386	85	13	1	8	8	36	74	.293	.321
Runners on	.253	316	80	10	3	7	90	38	64	.341	.370
Scoring Posn	.243	202	49	8	3	2	78	29	40	.349	.342
Close & Late	.211	180	38	7	0	3	19	23	37	.300	.300
None on/out	.231	169	39	3	0	5	5	15	29	.297	.337
vs. 1st Batr (relief)	.210	124	26	2	0	1	15	9	24	.267	.250
First Inning Pitched	.235	452	106	15	4	6	73	42	93	.310	.325
First 15 Pitches	.233	425	99	13	1	6	53	39	82	.305	.311
Pitch 16-30	.261	203	53	9	3	7	39	27	39	.353	.438
Pitch 31-45	.179	39	7	0	0	1	3	5	12	.273	.256
Pitch 46+	.171	35	6	1	0	1	3	3	5	.256	.286

Last Five Years

	ERA	W	L	Sv	G	GS	IP	H	HR	BB	SO
1 or 2 Days rest	2.68	6	2	4	64	0	80.2	63	5	32	63
3+ Days rest	5.68	3	2	0	47	0	58.2	62	6	23	44
Pre-All Star	4.40	3	5	3	74	4	106.1	104	10	48	71
Post-All Star	3.12	8	2	2	65	0	80.2	61	5	26	67

	Avg	AB	H	2B	3B	HR	RBI	BB	SO	OBP	SLG
First Pitch	.313	96	30	5	0	3	18	8	0	.365	.458
Ahead in Count	.191	345	66	12	3	3	36	0	120	.202	.270
Behind in Count	.279	147	41	5	1	5	31	46	0	.456	.429
Two Strikes	.176	319	56	10	1	2	26	20	138	.230	.232

Pitcher vs. Batter (career)

Pitches Best Vs.	Avg	AB	H	2B	3B	HR	RBI	BB	SO	OBP	SLG
Barry Larkin	.000	13	0	0	0	0	1	0	0	.000	.000
Robby Thompson	.077	13	1	1	0	0	1	1	3	.143	.154
Jose Lind	.182	11	2	0	0	0	1	1	2	.250	.182
Mark Grace	.200	15	3	0	0	0	1	0	2	.200	.200
Howard Johnson	.200	10	2	1	0	0	0	1	0	.273	.300

Pitches Worst Vs.	Avg	AB	H	2B	3B	HR	RBI	BB	SO	OBP	SLG
Barry Bonds	.571	7	4	2	0	0	0	4	0	.727	.857
Doug Dascenzo	.333	9	3	0	0	0	0	2	1	.455	.333

Steve Frey — Angels

Age 30 – Pitches Left

	ERA	W	L	Sv	G	GS	IP	BB	SO	Avg	H	2B	3B	HR	RBI	OBP	SLG	GF	IR	IRS	Hld	SvOp	SB	CS	GB	FB	G/F
1993 Season	2.98	2	3	13	55	0	48.1	26	22	.230	41	8	1	1	26	.337	.303	28	49	14	7	16	3	1	63	58	1.09
Career (1989-1993)	3.51	17	10	27	208	0	210.1	111	111	.250	196	31	2	18	98	.345	.364	74	151	37	21	32	17	8	272	266	1.02

1993 Season

	ERA	W	L	Sv	G	GS	IP	H	HR	BB	SO
Home	2.61	2	2	7	32	0	31.0	26	1	16	15
Away	3.63	0	1	6	23	0	17.1	15	0	10	7
Starter	0.00	0	0	0	0	0	0.0	0	0	0	0
Reliever	2.98	2	3	13	55	0	48.1	41	1	26	22
0 Days rest	1.88	1	2	6	19	0	14.1	7	1	9	7
1 or 2 Days rest	1.35	1	1	5	17	0	20.0	17	0	9	8
3+ Days rest	6.43	0	0	2	19	0	14.0	17	0	8	7
Pre-All Star	1.82	2	0	10	35	0	29.2	27	0	18	12
Post-All Star	4.82	0	3	3	20	0	18.2	14	1	8	10

	Avg	AB	H	2B	3B	HR	RBI	BB	SO	OBP	SLG
vs. Left	.208	53	11	4	1	0	6	13	8	.386	.321
vs. Right	.240	125	30	4	0	1	20	13	14	.312	.296
Scoring Posn	.222	72	16	1	0	0	23	12	8	.337	.236
Close & Late	.214	103	22	4	0	1	18	20	12	.344	.282
None on/out	.235	34	8	3	0	0	0	5	6	.333	.324
First Pitch	.296	27	8	0	0	0	7	0	0	.286	.296
Ahead in Count	.178	73	13	3	0	0	5	0	15	.189	.219
Behind in Count	.297	37	11	3	0	0	5	13	0	.480	.378
Two Strikes	.162	74	12	1	1	0	8	13	22	.295	.203

Career (1989-1993)

	ERA	W	L	Sv	G	GS	IP	H	HR	BB	SO
Home	2.70	9	4	16	108	0	106.2	96	7	49	57
Away	4.34	8	6	11	100	0	103.2	100	11	62	54
Day	3.84	7	3	9	66	0	68.0	71	7	34	42
Night	3.35	10	7	18	142	0	142.1	125	11	77	69
Grass	4.13	6	8	15	116	0	109.0	104	11	60	49
Turf	2.84	11	2	12	92	0	101.1	92	7	51	62
April	3.28	2	1	5	32	0	35.2	26	4	17	19
May	2.77	2	1	3	50	0	48.2	41	2	27	29
June	2.51	4	1	7	28	0	28.2	29	1	14	15
July	3.00	5	2	1	37	0	33.0	35	3	22	14
August	7.42	2	5	4	31	0	30.1	42	7	17	15
September/October	2.65	2	0	7	30	0	34.0	23	1	14	19
Starter	0.00	0	0	0	0	0	0.0	0	0	0	0
Reliever	3.51	17	10	27	208	0	210.1	196	18	111	111
0 Days rest	2.04	2	2	10	42	0	39.2	26	4	18	19
1 or 2 Days rest	2.43	9	6	13	84	0	89.0	69	8	49	43
3+ Days rest	5.40	6	2	4	82	0	81.2	101	6	44	49
Pre-All Star	2.81	10	3	16	125	0	128.1	111	7	73	70
Post-All Star	4.61	7	7	11	83	0	82.0	85	11	38	41

	Avg	AB	H	2B	3B	HR	RBI	BB	SO	OBP	SLG
vs. Left	.244	250	61	11	1	8	39	39	50	.354	.392
vs. Right	.253	534	135	20	1	10	59	72	61	.341	.350
Inning 1-6	.327	104	34	6	1	3	24	13	13	.412	.490
Inning 7+	.238	680	162	25	1	15	74	98	98	.335	.344
None on	.244	369	90	16	2	12	12	54	58	.348	.396
Runners on	.255	415	106	15	0	6	86	57	53	.342	.335
Scoring Posn	.227	255	58	6	0	2	74	44	34	.334	.275
Close & Late	.227	374	85	13	0	7	37	64	49	.339	.318
None on/out	.249	173	43	6	1	5	5	21	26	.340	.382
vs. 1st Batr (relief)	.292	178	52	10	0	5	29	22	23	.374	.433
First Inning Pitched	.253	593	150	27	1	14	81	79	85	.344	.373
First 15 Pitches	.261	522	136	24	0	15	72	69	68	.351	.393
Pitch 16-30	.214	210	45	6	2	1	20	36	36	.327	.276
Pitch 31-45	.349	43	15	1	0	2	6	6	4	.429	.512
Pitch 46+	.000	9	0	0	0	0	0	0	3	.000	.000
First Pitch	.274	117	32	3	0	3	20	13	0	.338	.376
Ahead in Count	.206	296	61	13	0	4	25	0	82	.214	.291
Behind in Count	.316	187	59	10	1	6	27	52	0	.461	.476
Two Strikes	.191	330	63	11	1	6	33	46	111	.295	.285

Pitcher vs. Batter (career)

Pitches Best Vs.	Avg	AB	H	2B	3B	HR	RBI	BB	SO	OBP	SLG

Pitches Worst Vs.	Avg	AB	H	2B	3B	HR	RBI	BB	SO	OBP	SLG
Barry Bonds	.500	12	6	1	0	1	6	1	1	.538	.833

Todd Frohwirth — Orioles

Age 31 – Pitches Right (groundball pitcher)

	ERA	W	L	Sv	G	GS	IP	BB	SO	Avg	H	2B	3B	HR	RBI	OBP	SLG	GF	IR	IRS	Hld	SvOp	SB	CS	GB	FB	G/F
1993 Season	3.83	6	7	3	70	0	96.1	44	50	.256	91	10	1	7	46	.342	.349	30	79	20	14	7	16	4	149	88	1.69
Last Five Years	2.91	18	14	10	236	0	362.1	138	225	.235	311	48	6	17	167	.311	.319	63	241	77	46	20	46	13	630	271	2.32

1993 Season

	ERA	W	L	Sv	G	GS	IP	H	HR	BB	SO
Home	3.92	6	1	1	37	0	57.1	51	4	24	30
Away	3.69	0	6	2	33	0	39.0	40	3	20	20
Day	4.32	2	1	2	20	0	25.0	26	4	15	11
Night	3.66	4	6	1	50	0	71.1	65	3	29	39
Grass	3.58	6	5	1	61	0	88.0	82	5	39	45
Turf	6.48	0	2	2	9	0	8.1	9	2	5	5
April	1.29	0	1	1	9	0	14.0	4	0	6	9
May	4.91	2	3	1	13	0	14.2	18	1	9	8
June	1.62	2	0	0	12	0	16.2	11	0	8	8
July	10.22	0	0	0	11	0	12.1	19	4	5	6
August	1.71	2	3	1	15	0	21.0	20	0	9	8
September/October	5.09	0	0	0	10	0	17.2	19	2	7	11
Starter	0.00	0	0	0	0	0	0.0	0	0	0	0
Reliever	3.83	6	7	3	70	0	96.1	91	7	44	50

	Avg	AB	H	2B	3B	HR	RBI	BB	SO	OBP	SLG
vs. Left	.267	116	31	3	1	4	18	18	9	.370	.414
vs. Right	.251	239	60	7	0	3	28	26	41	.327	.318
Inning 1-6	.250	48	12	2	0	0	8	4	8	.321	.292
Inning 7+	.257	307	79	8	1	7	38	40	42	.345	.358
None on	.250	160	40	5	1	3	3	19	26	.333	.350
Runners on	.262	195	51	5	0	4	43	25	24	.348	.349
Scoring Posn	.231	121	28	2	0	1	36	22	17	.349	.273
Close & Late	.245	139	34	3	0	1	12	22	17	.350	.288
None on/out	.346	78	27	3	1	0	0	8	11	.407	.410
vs. 1st Batr (relief)	.322	59	19	3	0	1	10	11	9	.429	.424
First Inning Pitched	.251	207	52	6	0	4	31	24	33	.326	.338
First 15 Pitches	.271	203	55	7	0	3	26	21	32	.338	.350
Pitch 16-30	.219	105	23	3	1	4	15	17	10	.339	.381
Pitch 31-45	.286	42	12	0	0	0	5	5	7	.367	.286

1993 Season

	ERA	W	L	Sv	G	GS	IP	H	HR	BB	SO
0 Days rest	4.30	1	2	1	19	0	23.0	23	1	12	11
1 or 2 Days rest	3.31	4	2	1	32	0	51.2	44	2	21	23
3+ Days rest	4.57	1	3	1	19	0	21.2	24	4	11	16
Pre-All Star	3.75	4	4	2	39	0	50.1	42	4	23	27
Post-All Star	3.91	2	3	1	31	0	46.0	49	3	21	23

	Avg	AB	H	2B	3B	HR	RBI	BB	SO	OBP	SLG
Pitch 46+	.200	5	1	0	0	0	0	1	1	.333	.200
First Pitch	.277	47	13	1	0	1	11	7	0	.370	.362
Ahead in Count	.196	158	31	3	1	1	12	0	40	.205	.247
Behind in Count	.329	76	25	5	0	2	10	24	0	.495	.474
Two Strikes	.123	138	17	1	0	1	9	13	50	.208	.152

Last Five Years

	ERA	W	L	Sv	G	GS	IP	H	HR	BB	SO
Home	3.00	12	3	4	124	0	207.0	174	12	64	127
Away	2.78	6	11	6	112	0	155.1	137	5	74	98
Day	4.58	6	4	4	68	0	96.1	99	9	51	61
Night	2.30	12	10	6	168	0	266.0	212	8	87	164
Grass	2.78	15	10	8	167	0	262.2	231	10	99	149
Turf	3.25	3	4	2	69	0	99.2	80	7	39	76
April	1.86	1	2	2	25	0	29.0	12	0	17	22
May	4.74	2	3	2	34	0	38.0	47	3	20	26
June	1.56	5	1	0	38	0	63.1	54	2	26	37
July	4.08	3	3	2	44	0	75.0	70	6	20	41
August	2.26	5	3	2	53	0	83.2	69	3	32	52
September/October	3.07	2	2	2	42	0	73.1	59	3	23	47
Starter	0.00	0	0	0	0	0	0.0	0	0	0	0
Reliever	2.91	18	14	10	236	0	362.1	311	17	138	225
0 Days rest	2.89	4	4	2	58	0	84.0	76	1	32	45
1 or 2 Days rest	2.51	11	3	5	113	0	182.2	149	6	66	117
3+ Days rest	3.67	3	7	3	65	0	95.2	86	10	40	63
Pre-All Star	2.75	8	7	5	112	0	157.0	133	8	69	99
Post-All Star	3.02	10	7	5	124	0	205.1	178	9	69	126

	Avg	AB	H	2B	3B	HR	RBI	BB	SO	OBP	SLG
vs. Left	.268	489	131	19	5	8	70	65	55	.358	.376
vs. Right	.216	833	180	29	1	9	97	73	170	.282	.286
Inning 1-6	.226	297	67	14	1	2	49	23	54	.283	.300
Inning 7+	.238	1025	244	34	5	15	118	115	171	.319	.325
None on	.223	681	152	23	4	8	8	59	125	.289	.304
Runners on	.248	641	159	25	2	9	159	79	100	.334	.335
Scoring Posn	.246	427	105	15	1	6	147	66	77	.360	.328
Close & Late	.221	457	101	14	2	3	47	61	81	.316	.280
None on/out	.236	296	70	8	4	1	1	25	55	.302	.301
vs. 1st Batr (relief)	.257	206	53	8	1	3	39	25	34	.339	.350
First Inning Pitched	.250	717	179	25	2	11	124	79	120	.326	.336
First 15 Pitches	.248	703	174	25	2	8	104	67	114	.314	.323
Pitch 16-30	.226	376	85	17	3	8	42	44	59	.314	.351
Pitch 31-45	.230	183	42	3	1	1	16	17	35	.304	.273
Pitch 46+	.167	60	10	3	0	0	5	10	17	.286	.217
First Pitch	.256	195	50	9	1	4	35	16	0	.313	.374
Ahead in Count	.168	591	99	13	3	3	55	0	186	.174	.215
Behind in Count	.316	294	93	16	1	5	42	75	0	.460	.429
Two Strikes	.140	549	77	9	1	3	37	47	225	.214	.177

Pitcher vs. Batter (career)

Pitches Best Vs.	Avg	AB	H	2B	3B	HR	RBI	BB	SO	OBP	SLG
Kirby Puckett	.000	16	0	0	0	0	0	1	4	.059	.000
Ruben Sierra	.000	11	0	0	0	0	0	0	0	.000	.000
Billy Hatcher	.077	13	1	0	0	0	1	0	2	.077	.077
Jose Canseco	.091	11	1	0	0	0	1	1	2	.167	.091
Chuck Knoblauch	.143	14	2	0	0	0	0	0	1	.143	.143

Pitches Worst Vs.	Avg	AB	H	2B	3B	HR	RBI	BB	SO	OBP	SLG
Candy Maldonado	.455	11	5	2	0	0	1	0	2	.455	.636
Cecil Fielder	.364	11	4	0	0	0	3	0	1	.364	.364
Danny Tartabull	.308	13	4	1	0	1	4	0	1	.308	.615

Travis Fryman — Tigers

Age 25 – Bats Right (flyball hitter)

	Avg	G	AB	R	H	2B	3B	HR	RBI	BB	SO	HBP	GDP	SB	CS	OBP	SLG	IBB	SH	SF	#Pit	#P/PA	GB	FB	G/F
1993 Season	.300	151	607	98	182	37	5	22	97	77	128	4	8	9	4	.379	.486	1	1	6	2735	3.94	163	190	0.86
Career (1990-1993)	.277	527	2055	282	570	115	13	72	311	179	472	14	37	32	16	.337	.451	2	13	18	8777	3.85	542	617	0.88

1993 Season

	Avg	AB	H	2B	3B	HR	RBI	BB	SO	OBP	SLG
vs. Left	.265	166	44	7	1	9	29	23	32	.349	.482
vs. Right	.313	441	138	30	4	13	68	54	96	.390	.488
Groundball	.325	126	41	8	2	6	24	17	25	.400	.563
Flyball	.280	125	35	5	0	6	20	16	29	.361	.464
Home	.316	285	90	20	2	13	45	42	53	.402	.537
Away	.286	322	92	17	3	9	52	35	75	.358	.441
Day	.324	222	72	16	2	8	33	16	47	.372	.523
Night	.286	385	110	21	3	14	64	61	81	.383	.465
Grass	.292	517	151	30	5	18	74	67	109	.374	.474
Turf	.344	90	31	7	0	4	23	10	19	.408	.556
First Pitch	.365	74	27	4	0	3	12	1	0	.385	.541
Ahead in Count	.349	146	51	9	3	10	40	31	0	.456	.658
Behind in Count	.236	259	61	13	1	2	20	0	106	.235	.317
Two Strikes	.207	276	57	9	2	5	20	45	128	.318	.308

	Avg	AB	H	2B	3B	HR	RBI	BB	SO	OBP	SLG
Scoring Posn	.333	183	61	12	2	7	74	27	44	.410	.536
Close & Late	.324	71	23	5	0	1	11	12	20	.417	.437
None on/out	.302	116	35	9	1	2	2	13	18	.382	.448
Batting #2	.333	9	3	0	0	0	3	0	3	.333	.333
Batting #3	.299	598	179	37	5	22	94	76	125	.379	.488
Other	.000	0	0	0	0	0	0	1	0	1.000	.000
April	.341	91	31	6	1	4	21	10	23	.406	.560
May	.253	99	25	2	2	2	13	9	26	.313	.374
June	.228	101	23	4	0	4	13	11	19	.301	.386
July	.345	110	38	11	2	3	17	13	22	.416	.564
August	.313	112	35	8	0	5	20	17	18	.408	.518
September/October	.319	94	30	6	0	4	13	17	20	.425	.511
Pre-All Star	.275	331	91	16	3	11	55	36	74	.343	.441
Post-All Star	.330	276	91	21	2	11	42	41	54	.421	.540

1993 By Position

Position	Avg	AB	H	2B	3B	HR	RBI	BB	SO	OBP	SLG	G	GS	Innings	PO	A	E	DP	Fld Pct	Rng Fctr	In Zone	Outs	Zone Rtg	MLB Zone
As 3b	.331	272	90	21	2	11	42	40	53	.421	.544	69	68	599.0	44	118	4	10	.976	2.43	143	122	.853	.834
As ss	.275	331	91	16	3	11	55	36	74	.343	.441	81	81	721.1	126	262	19	60	.953	4.84	319	274	.859	.880

Career (1990-1993)

	Avg	AB	H	2B	3B	HR	RBI	BB	SO	OBP	SLG
vs. Left	.287	564	162	30	4	26	95	54	121	.350	.493
vs. Right	.274	1491	408	85	9	46	216	125	351	.332	.435
Groundball	.289	547	158	31	4	15	85	37	116	.336	.442
Flyball	.263	509	134	24	0	22	78	45	116	.327	.440
Home	.264	973	257	47	7	35	135	98	225	.334	.435
Away	.289	1082	313	68	6	37	176	81	247	.339	.466
Day	.287	686	197	38	6	22	94	52	159	.338	.456
Night	.272	1369	373	77	7	50	217	127	313	.336	.449
Grass	.279	1752	488	92	12	61	247	153	397	.338	.449
Turf	.271	303	82	23	1	11	64	26	75	.330	.462
First Pitch	.342	275	94	13	2	15	53	2	0	.348	.567
Ahead in Count	.374	439	164	38	4	27	102	75	0	.464	.663

	Avg	AB	H	2B	3B	HR	RBI	BB	SO	OBP	SLG
Scoring Posn	.290	587	170	41	5	15	227	55	150	.345	.453
Close & Late	.257	268	69	15	1	8	40	27	75	.324	.410
None on/out	.294	378	111	26	4	11	11	29	73	.347	.471
Batting #3	.277	1194	331	66	9	40	176	116	266	.343	.448
Batting #6	.263	205	54	11	1	8	28	14	44	.314	.444
Other	.282	656	185	38	3	24	107	49	162	.332	.459
April	.290	231	67	8	2	9	38	22	45	.353	.459
May	.253	296	75	12	2	10	50	24	77	.306	.409
June	.263	327	86	20	2	11	49	21	72	.309	.437
July	.290	365	106	28	3	15	55	31	89	.347	.507
August	.292	424	124	23	2	14	55	38	94	.354	.455
September/October	.272	412	112	24	2	13	64	43	95	.345	.434

Career (1990-1993)

	Avg	AB	H	2B	3B	HR	RBI	BB	SO	OBP	SLG
Behind in Count	.212	959	203	37	4	18	102	0	392	.214	.315
Two Strikes	.177	1002	177	32	4	16	93	102	472	.254	.264

	Avg	AB	H	2B	3B	HR	RBI	BB	SO	OBP	SLG
Pre-All Star	.268	978	262	48	6	34	157	78	224	.322	.434
Post-All Star	.286	1077	308	67	7	38	154	101	248	.350	.467

Batter vs. Pitcher (career)

Hits Best Against	Avg	AB	H	2B	3B	HR	RBI	BB	SO	OBP	SLG
Kevin Tapani	.643	14	9	1	0	1	2	0	1	.643	.929
Mike Moore	.467	15	7	2	0	1	4	1	2	.500	.800
Randy Johnson	.375	16	6	0	0	3	7	4	5	.500	.938
Joe Hesketh	.364	11	4	0	1	2	4	1	4	.417	1.091
Bill Krueger	.333	12	4	1	0	2	2	0	3	.333	.917

Hits Worst Against	Avg	AB	H	2B	3B	HR	RBI	BB	SO	OBP	SLG
Carl Willis	.000	12	0	0	0	0	1	0	2	.000	.000
Rich DeLucia	.000	10	0	0	0	0	0	2	3	.167	.000
Melido Perez	.050	20	1	0	0	0	0	0	7	.050	.050
Donn Pall	.091	11	1	0	0	0	1	0	0	.091	.091
Tom Henke	.100	10	1	0	0	0	1	0	7	.091	.100

Gary Gaetti — Royals

Age 35 – Bats Right

	Avg	G	AB	R	H	2B	3B	HR	RBI	BB	SO	HBP	GDP	SB	CS	OBP	SLG	IBB	SH	SF	#Pit	#P/PA	GB	FB	G/F
1993 Season	.245	102	331	40	81	20	1	14	50	21	87	8	5	1	3	.300	.438	0	2	7	1299	3.52	92	106	0.87
Last Five Years	.239	668	2448	263	585	93	13	79	324	136	458	28	61	21	12	.283	.384	13	6	32	8993	3.39	816	805	1.01

1993 Season

	Avg	AB	H	2B	3B	HR	RBI	BB	SO	OBP	SLG
vs. Left	.278	97	27	7	0	7	20	13	27	.365	.567
vs. Right	.231	234	54	13	1	7	30	8	60	.270	.385
Groundball	.133	45	6	0	0	1	7	4	14	.259	.200
Flyball	.250	72	18	5	1	4	12	2	19	.263	.514
Home	.286	168	48	17	0	6	28	12	42	.342	.494
Away	.202	163	33	3	1	8	22	9	45	.256	.380
Day	.216	97	21	5	1	4	17	8	28	.269	.412
Night	.256	234	60	15	0	10	33	13	59	.313	.449
Grass	.213	150	32	5	0	6	19	9	38	.271	.367
Turf	.271	181	49	15	1	8	31	12	49	.323	.497
First Pitch	.273	55	15	4	1	2	11	0	0	.283	.491
Ahead in Count	.362	58	21	10	0	3	11	15	0	.480	.690
Behind in Count	.171	170	29	2	0	7	19	0	76	.199	.306
Two Strikes	.150	160	24	2	0	3	12	6	87	.202	.219

	Avg	AB	H	2B	3B	HR	RBI	BB	SO	OBP	SLG
Scoring Posn	.238	84	20	4	0	2	31	6	22	.290	.357
Close & Late	.229	70	16	3	0	2	8	3	23	.282	.357
None on/out	.237	76	18	5	1	1	1	5	16	.293	.368
Batting #5	.247	93	23	8	0	4	14	6	27	.311	.462
Batting #6	.257	148	38	9	1	7	20	10	41	.307	.473
Other	.222	90	20	3	0	3	16	5	19	.277	.356
April	.222	18	4	1	0	0	2	2	5	.286	.278
May	.167	30	5	1	0	0	2	3	7	.242	.200
June	.231	26	6	2	0	1	2	1	5	.286	.423
July	.346	78	27	8	1	2	14	7	16	.414	.551
August	.205	88	18	4	0	5	11	1	28	.211	.420
September/October	.231	91	21	4	0	6	19	7	26	.306	.473
Pre-All Star	.238	101	24	7	0	3	15	11	22	.316	.396
Post-All Star	.248	230	57	13	1	11	35	10	65	.292	.457

1993 By Position

Position	Avg	AB	H	2B	3B	HR	RBI	BB	SO	OBP	SLG	G	GS	Innings	PO	A	E	DP	Fld Pct	Rng Fctr	In Zone	Outs	Zone Rtg	MLB Zone
As 1b	.298	57	17	7	0	2	8	5	15	.344	.526	24	15	139.1	134	12	1	13	.993	---	26	20	.769	.834
As 3b	.241	249	60	13	1	12	38	12	66	.293	.446	79	66	600.2	51	140	6	15	.970	2.86	163	144	.883	.834

Last Five Years

	Avg	AB	H	2B	3B	HR	RBI	BB	SO	OBP	SLG
vs. Left	.241	698	168	30	2	28	103	58	112	.301	.410
vs. Right	.238	1750	417	63	11	51	221	78	346	.276	.374
Groundball	.214	626	134	13	4	16	92	39	114	.271	.324
Flyball	.233	546	127	20	5	22	74	31	99	.275	.408
Home	.259	1214	315	49	6	43	172	65	224	.302	.416
Away	.219	1234	270	44	7	36	152	71	234	.265	.353
Day	.246	684	168	22	3	29	121	30	133	.278	.414
Night	.236	1764	417	71	10	50	203	106	325	.285	.373
Grass	.240	1437	345	48	5	47	174	86	272	.287	.379
Turf	.237	1011	240	45	8	32	150	50	186	.277	.393
First Pitch	.298	483	144	20	2	17	70	8	0	.314	.453
Ahead in Count	.291	450	131	25	5	20	91	77	0	.393	.502
Behind in Count	.192	1139	219	34	4	26	108	0	401	.202	.298
Two Strikes	.165	1058	175	26	4	19	82	50	458	.212	.251

	Avg	AB	H	2B	3B	HR	RBI	BB	SO	OBP	SLG
Scoring Posn	.253	616	156	23	2	23	243	57	126	.311	.409
Close & Late	.220	405	89	11	2	13	50	20	67	.257	.353
None on/out	.233	610	142	23	3	17	17	24	94	.269	.364
Batting #4	.229	628	144	16	4	25	96	37	108	.273	.387
Batting #5	.230	977	225	40	6	27	125	53	180	.275	.366
Other	.256	843	216	37	3	27	103	46	170	.300	.403
April	.260	308	80	11	3	10	39	19	62	.301	.412
May	.242	434	105	20	3	13	66	21	71	.276	.392
June	.243	399	97	9	1	15	50	21	68	.290	.383
July	.265	437	116	24	2	11	68	31	77	.317	.405
August	.202	441	89	14	2	17	43	20	96	.240	.358
September/October	.228	429	98	15	2	13	58	24	84	.280	.364
Pre-All Star	.250	1286	321	46	8	41	175	72	229	.292	.393
Post-All Star	.227	1162	264	47	5	38	149	64	229	.274	.374

Batter vs. Pitcher (since 1984)

Hits Best Against	Avg	AB	H	2B	3B	HR	RBI	BB	SO	OBP	SLG
Greg Cadaret	.733	15	11	2	0	1	7	4	1	.750	1.067
Scott Kamieniecki	.545	11	6	0	0	0	0	1	1	.583	.545
Chuck Crim	.438	16	7	2	0	1	4	2	1	.500	.750
Greg Harris	.435	23	10	4	0	1	6	2	7	.462	.739
Mark Leiter	.429	14	6	2	0	1	1	0	1	.429	.786

Hits Worst Against	Avg	AB	H	2B	3B	HR	RBI	BB	SO	OBP	SLG
Tim Leary	.048	21	1	0	0	0	1	1	3	.091	.048
Jeff Russell	.048	21	1	0	0	0	1	0	6	.045	.048
Kevin Appier	.077	13	1	0	0	0	0	0	6	.077	.077
Ron Darling	.083	12	1	0	0	0	0	0	2	.083	.083
Donn Pall	.091	11	1	0	0	0	0	0	1	.091	.091

Greg Gagne — Royals

Age 32 – Bats Right

	Avg	G	AB	R	H	2B	3B	HR	RBI	BB	SO	HBP	GDP	SB	CS	OBP	SLG	IBB	SH	SF	#Pit	#P/PA	GB	FB	G/F
1993 Season	.280	159	540	66	151	32	3	10	57	33	93	0	7	10	12	.319	.406	1	4	4	2089	3.60	160	174	0.92
Last Five Years	.261	731	2235	278	583	129	16	41	224	119	404	8	48	46	40	.298	.388	1	36	17	8445	3.50	713	712	1.00

1993 Season

	Avg	AB	H	2B	3B	HR	RBI	BB	SO	OBP	SLG
vs. Left	.314	137	43	12	0	2	20	12	26	.364	.445
vs. Right	.268	403	108	20	3	8	37	21	67	.303	.392
Groundball	.318	85	27	5	0	0	8	4	7	.348	.376
Flyball	.310	116	36	6	0	6	21	3	24	.328	.517
Home	.305	269	82	20	1	3	31	16	38	.340	.420
Away	.255	271	69	12	2	7	26	17	55	.298	.391
Day	.250	148	37	7	1	5	23	8	28	.287	.412

	Avg	AB	H	2B	3B	HR	RBI	BB	SO	OBP	SLG
Scoring Posn	.295	122	36	9	1	3	47	12	22	.348	.459
Close & Late	.237	114	27	4	1	2	11	3	20	.256	.342
None on/out	.304	138	42	8	1	3	3	9	26	.347	.442
Batting #8	.237	236	56	8	1	3	24	13	54	.277	.318
Batting #9	.264	91	24	4	2	1	7	7	12	.316	.385
Other	.333	213	71	20	0	6	26	13	27	.365	.512
April	.194	67	13	1	1	1	5	7	10	.270	.284

1993 Season

	Avg	AB	H	2B	3B	HR	RBI	BB	SO	OBP	SLG		Avg	AB	H	2B	3B	HR	RBI	BB	SO	OBP	SLG
Night	.291	392	114	25	2	5	34	25	65	.331	.403	May	.321	84	27	4	1	1	9	3	13	.345	.429
Grass	.262	206	54	10	2	7	25	11	41	.298	.432	June	.266	94	25	3	0	1	8	8	18	.320	.330
Turf	.290	334	97	22	1	3	32	22	52	.331	.389	July	.344	96	33	9	0	2	15	2	15	.350	.500
First Pitch	.393	84	33	7	1	5	18	0	0	.388	.679	August	.284	102	29	10	1	3	10	5	18	.318	.490
Ahead in Count	.327	98	32	4	2	2	18	17	0	.419	.469	September/October	.247	97	24	5	0	2	10	8	19	.302	.361
Behind in Count	.224	268	60	14	0	2	19	0	89	.223	.299	Pre-All Star	.277	278	77	11	2	3	24	18	46	.319	.363
Two Strikes	.212	241	51	14	0	3	18	16	93	.260	.307	Post-All Star	.282	262	74	21	1	7	33	15	47	.319	.450

1993 By Position

Position	Avg	AB	H	2B	3B	HR	RBI	BB	SO	OBP	SLG	G	GS	Innings	PO	A	E	DP	Fld Pct	Rng Fctr	In Zone	Outs	Zone Rtg	MLB Zone
As ss	.280	539	151	32	3	10	57	33	93	.319	.406	159	148	1331.0	265	451	10	95	.986	4.84	507	462	.911	.880

Last Five Years

	Avg	AB	H	2B	3B	HR	RBI	BB	SO	OBP	SLG		Avg	AB	H	2B	3B	HR	RBI	BB	SO	OBP	SLG
vs. Left	.278	655	182	49	0	13	72	47	112	.326	.437	Scoring Posn	.247	531	131	27	4	9	175	45	106	.299	.363
vs. Right	.254	1580	401	80	8	28	152	72	292	.287	.368	Close & Late	.251	343	86	14	4	3	25	13	68	.281	.341
Groundball	.267	577	154	33	4	7	52	30	69	.304	.374	None on/out	.277	535	148	36	5	10	10	25	92	.309	.419
Flyball	.262	470	123	25	6	14	50	20	118	.294	.430	Batting #8	.241	532	128	27	5	10	53	32	109	.285	.367
Home	.271	1082	293	72	8	15	112	63	186	.312	.394	Batting #9	.254	1291	328	69	9	20	128	63	239	.290	.368
Away	.252	1153	290	57	8	26	112	56	218	.286	.382	Other	.308	412	127	33	2	11	43	24	56	.343	.478
Day	.263	665	175	41	5	15	73	31	129	.297	.408	April	.262	302	79	15	2	7	27	28	46	.326	.394
Night	.260	1570	408	88	11	26	151	88	275	.299	.380	May	.282	408	115	22	4	7	44	23	70	.322	.407
Grass	.256	890	228	47	6	21	86	44	162	.290	.393	June	.223	417	93	21	4	7	41	22	78	.261	.343
Turf	.264	1345	355	82	10	20	138	75	242	.304	.384	July	.257	381	98	21	0	5	38	11	76	.276	.352
First Pitch	.330	376	124	32	5	11	47	0	0	.332	.529	August	.296	389	115	33	4	9	40	19	66	.331	.470
Ahead in Count	.288	459	132	24	4	8	56	78	0	.387	.410	September/October	.246	338	83	17	2	6	34	16	68	.278	.361
Behind in Count	.203	1028	209	46	3	15	78	0	369	.206	.298	Pre-All Star	.255	1247	318	66	10	22	121	75	217	.297	.377
Two Strikes	.192	982	189	44	5	13	79	41	404	.226	.287	Post-All Star	.268	988	265	63	6	19	103	44	187	.300	.402

Batter vs. Pitcher (since 1984)

Hits Best Against	Avg	AB	H	2B	3B	HR	RBI	BB	SO	OBP	SLG	Hits Worst Against	Avg	AB	H	2B	3B	HR	RBI	BB	SO	OBP	SLG
Brian Bohanon	.600	10	6	2	0	0	2	0	1	.545	.800	Frank Viola	.000	11	0	0	0	0	0	1	5	.083	.000
Charles Nagy	.529	17	9	3	0	0	1	0	2	.529	.706	Mike Morgan	.077	13	1	1	0	0	0	0	0	.077	.154
Bill Krueger	.444	18	8	3	0	1	3	0	3	.444	.778	Dave Johnson	.091	11	1	0	0	0	0	1	3	.167	.091
Greg Hibbard	.438	16	7	3	0	1	2	0	0	.438	.813	David Wells	.100	20	2	0	0	0	0	2	5	.182	.100
Mark Leiter	.429	14	6	2	0	1	3	0	3	.429	.786	Jeff Montgomery	.100	10	1	0	0	0	0	1	1	.182	.100

Jay Gainer — Rockies

Age 27 – Bats Left

	Avg	G	AB	R	H	2B	3B	HR	RBI	BB	SO	HBP	GDP	SB	CS	OBP	SLG	IBB	SH	SF	#Pit	#P/PA	GB	FB	G/F
1993 Season	.171	23	41	4	7	0	0	3	6	4	12	0	0	1	1	.244	.390	0	0	0	164	3.64	10	14	0.71

1993 Season

	Avg	AB	H	2B	3B	HR	RBI	BB	SO	OBP	SLG		Avg	AB	H	2B	3B	HR	RBI	BB	SO	OBP	SLG
vs. Left	.000	3	0	0	0	0	0	1	1	.250	.000	Scoring Posn	.100	10	1	0	0	1	4	1	3	.182	.400
vs. Right	.184	38	7	0	0	3	6	3	11	.244	.421	Close & Late	.111	9	1	0	0	0	0	1	4	.200	.111

Andres Galarraga — Rockies

Age 33 – Bats Right (groundball hitter)

	Avg	G	AB	R	H	2B	3B	HR	RBI	BB	SO	HBP	GDP	SB	CS	OBP	SLG	IBB	SH	SF	#Pit	#P/PA	GB	FB	G/F
1993 Season	.370	120	470	71	174	35	4	22	98	24	73	6	9	2	4	.403	.602	12	0	6	1503	2.97	184	112	1.64
Last Five Years	.271	629	2321	284	630	121	9	84	342	146	555	33	49	34	20	.321	.440	35	0	17	8732	3.47	844	542	1.56

1993 Season

	Avg	AB	H	2B	3B	HR	RBI	BB	SO	OBP	SLG		Avg	AB	H	2B	3B	HR	RBI	BB	SO	OBP	SLG
vs. Left	.350	117	41	6	1	6	25	6	16	.383	.573	Scoring Posn	.422	128	54	14	0	7	76	17	22	.477	.695
vs. Right	.377	353	133	29	3	16	73	18	57	.410	.612	Close & Late	.358	53	19	5	0	0	7	5	14	.414	.453
Groundball	.331	166	55	12	1	7	28	9	29	.365	.542	None on/out	.305	131	40	6	2	6	6	1	25	.311	.519
Flyball	.451	71	32	5	1	7	17	7	8	.500	.845	Batting #3	.286	77	22	4	0	3	11	3	12	.329	.455
Home	.402	266	107	20	3	13	64	15	33	.430	.647	Batting #4	.388	392	152	31	4	19	87	21	61	.419	.633
Away	.328	204	67	15	1	9	34	9	40	.368	.544	Other	.000	1	0	0	0	0	0	0	0	.000	.000
Day	.362	163	59	12	1	6	38	9	22	.400	.558	April	.412	85	35	8	0	4	25	5	9	.435	.647
Night	.375	307	115	23	3	16	60	15	51	.405	.625	May	.360	50	18	4	0	1	13	2	7	.385	.500
Grass	.356	379	135	25	3	16	80	21	58	.389	.565	June	.420	100	42	8	2	6	21	6	19	.458	.720
Turf	.429	91	39	10	1	6	18	3	15	.464	.758	July	.351	74	26	5	1	4	11	5	13	.407	.608
First Pitch	.462	119	55	17	2	5	31	12	0	.511	.765	August	.231	39	9	2	0	2	5	1	9	.273	.436
Ahead in Count	.584	89	52	7	1	6	26	6	0	.611	.888	September/October	.361	122	44	8	1	5	23	5	16	.385	.566
Behind in Count	.223	184	41	8	1	7	30	0	65	.228	.391	Pre-All Star	.391	271	106	24	3	13	65	14	42	.424	.646
Two Strikes	.182	170	31	6	1	5	20	6	73	.212	.318	Post-All Star	.342	199	68	11	1	9	33	10	31	.375	.543

1993 By Position

Position	Avg	AB	H	2B	3B	HR	RBI	BB	SO	OBP	SLG	G	GS	Innings	PO	A	E	DP	Fld Pct	Rng Fctr	In Zone	Outs	Zone Rtg	MLB Zone
As 1b	.372	468	174	35	4	22	98	24	73	.405	.605	119	119	1007.1	1016	100	11	88	.990	---	215	178	.828	.834

Last Five Years

	Avg	AB	H	2B	3B	HR	RBI	BB	SO	OBP	SLG		Avg	AB	H	2B	3B	HR	RBI	BB	SO	OBP	SLG
vs. Left	.289	761	220	40	4	38	133	47	178	.332	.502	Scoring Posn	.262	633	166	31	2	21	247	77	176	.343	.417
vs. Right	.263	1560	410	81	5	46	209	99	377	.316	.410	Close & Late	.253	434	110	21	0	11	55	33	116	.311	.378

Last Five Years	Avg	AB	H	2B	3B	HR	RBI	BB	SO	OBP	SLG		Avg	AB	H	2B	3B	HR	RBI	BB	SO	OBP	SLG
Groundball	.260	861	224	49	4	24	101	59	186	.313	.410	None on/out	.271	538	146	33	4	18	18	23	121	.309	.448
Flyball	.277	512	142	28	1	27	81	34	148	.330	.494	Batting #3	.253	628	159	31	0	26	94	45	173	.315	.427
Home	.285	1149	328	70	6	39	186	75	264	.335	.459	Batting #4	.322	734	236	50	4	29	132	36	139	.359	.519
Away	.258	1172	302	51	3	45	156	71	291	.308	.422	Other	.245	959	235	40	5	29	116	65	243	.298	.388
Day	.253	676	171	33	3	24	96	56	165	.316	.417	April	.279	308	86	17	0	9	52	28	72	.348	.422
Night	.279	1645	459	88	6	60	246	90	390	.324	.449	May	.275	342	94	17	0	11	57	18	77	.315	.421
Grass	.290	867	251	40	4	36	145	51	193	.331	.469	June	.292	384	112	26	3	12	49	24	91	.345	.469
Turf	.261	1454	379	81	5	48	197	95	362	.316	.422	July	.274	427	117	22	3	19	62	31	100	.331	.473
First Pitch	.358	383	137	35	2	14	69	25	0	.405	.569	August	.219	415	91	13	0	14	48	20	108	.265	.352
Ahead in Count	.373	477	178	29	1	27	100	50	0	.432	.608	September/October	.292	445	130	26	3	19	74	25	107	.331	.492
Behind in Count	.196	1055	207	40	5	24	109	0	472	.207	.312	Pre-All Star	.280	1176	329	71	4	38	178	81	273	.335	.444
Two Strikes	.162	1061	172	33	3	24	97	64	555	.216	.267	Post-All Star	.263	1145	301	50	5	46	164	65	282	.307	.436

Batter vs. Pitcher (career)

Hits Best Against	Avg	AB	H	2B	3B	HR	RBI	BB	SO	OBP	SLG	Hits Worst Against	Avg	AB	H	2B	3B	HR	RBI	BB	SO	OBP	SLG
Greg Swindell	.545	11	6	2	0	1	5	1	2	.583	1.000	John Burkett	.083	12	1	0	0	0	0	0	1	.083	.083
Dennis Rasmussen	.500	10	5	1	0	2	4	2	1	.583	1.200	Randy Tomlin	.083	12	1	0	0	0	0	0	4	.083	.083
Kelly Downs	.440	25	11	2	0	3	6	1	5	.462	.880	Jeff Innis	.118	17	2	0	0	0	0	0	3	.118	.118
Dennis Martinez	.389	18	7	3	0	2	7	1	4	.421	.889	Wally Whitehurst	.133	15	2	0	0	0	0	0	2	.133	.133
Chris Hammond	.333	12	4	0	1	2	5	1	0	.385	1.000	Shawn Boskie	.133	15	2	0	0	0	0	0	2	.133	.133

Dave Gallagher — Mets

Age 33 – Bats Right

	Avg	G	AB	R	H	2B	3B	HR	RBI	BB	SO	HBP	GDP	SB	CS	OBP	SLG	IBB	SH	SF	#Pit	#P/PA	GB	FB	G/F
1993 Season	.274	99	201	34	55	12	2	6	28	20	18	0	7	1	1	.338	.443	1	7	1	798	3.48	77	58	1.33
Last Five Years	.268	516	1373	172	368	66	6	9	132	116	168	6	32	13	18	.325	.345	2	43	11	5736	3.70	512	425	1.20

1993 Season

	Avg	AB	H	2B	3B	HR	RBI	BB	SO	OBP	SLG		Avg	AB	H	2B	3B	HR	RBI	BB	SO	OBP	SLG
vs. Left	.259	143	37	7	2	4	15	11	13	.312	.420	Scoring Posn	.375	48	18	3	1	1	22	8	3	.456	.542
vs. Right	.310	58	18	5	0	2	13	9	5	.397	.500	Close & Late	.239	46	11	3	1	0	9	6	4	.321	.348
Home	.240	100	24	6	2	1	5	11	11	.315	.370	None on/out	.333	39	13	3	0	1	1	3	2	.381	.487
Away	.307	101	31	6	0	5	23	9	7	.360	.515	Batting #4	.189	37	7	3	0	1	3	5	5	.286	.351
First Pitch	.321	28	9	0	0	1	4	1	0	.345	.429	Batting #5	.250	64	16	2	1	2	11	7	6	.324	.406
Ahead in Count	.388	67	26	6	0	4	18	10	0	.468	.657	Other	.320	100	32	7	1	3	14	8	7	.367	.500
Behind in Count	.191	68	13	3	2	1	4	0	13	.191	.338	Pre-All Star	.307	101	31	9	1	2	15	10	9	.366	.475
Two Strikes	.182	66	12	2	2	0	5	9	18	.276	.273	Post-All Star	.240	100	24	3	1	4	13	10	9	.309	.410

Last Five Years

	Avg	AB	H	2B	3B	HR	RBI	BB	SO	OBP	SLG		Avg	AB	H	2B	3B	HR	RBI	BB	SO	OBP	SLG
vs. Left	.271	657	178	31	5	4	63	53	68	.325	.352	Scoring Posn	.271	336	91	15	2	2	118	40	46	.339	.345
vs. Right	.265	716	190	35	1	5	69	63	100	.326	.338	Close & Late	.216	250	54	12	1	0	23	26	22	.290	.272
Groundball	.309	382	118	23	1	5	37	30	42	.360	.414	None on/out	.286	384	110	20	0	2	2	30	39	.338	.354
Flyball	.244	266	65	14	2	2	29	30	30	.318	.335	Batting #1	.256	434	111	14	0	0	27	32	58	.308	.288
Home	.260	669	174	31	3	3	53	64	75	.323	.329	Batting #2	.295	359	106	22	1	3	33	38	42	.361	.387
Away	.276	704	194	35	3	6	79	52	93	.327	.359	Other	.260	580	151	30	5	6	72	46	68	.316	.360
Day	.262	416	109	16	3	6	37	40	40	.323	.358	April	.294	160	47	8	2	1	26	20	10	.364	.388
Night	.271	957	259	50	3	3	95	76	128	.327	.339	May	.310	197	61	9	0	2	17	22	21	.377	.386
Grass	.269	1122	302	51	4	6	103	102	135	.330	.338	June	.286	262	75	14	0	1	20	16	33	.327	.351
Turf	.263	251	66	15	2	3	29	14	33	.306	.375	July	.262	244	64	10	1	3	23	20	41	.325	.348
First Pitch	.311	148	46	3	0	1	19	1	0	.310	.351	August	.221	276	61	10	2	1	22	15	36	.264	.283
Ahead in Count	.312	359	112	22	2	6	51	58	0	.406	.435	September/October	.256	234	60	15	1	1	24	23	27	.323	.342
Behind in Count	.229	568	130	25	3	12	44	0	141	.233	.294	Pre-All Star	.289	698	202	37	2	4	67	66	77	.349	.365
Two Strikes	.217	585	127	20	3	1	44	56	168	.287	.267	Post-All Star	.246	675	166	29	4	5	65	50	91	.301	.323

Batter vs. Pitcher (career)

Hits Best Against	Avg	AB	H	2B	3B	HR	RBI	BB	SO	OBP	SLG	Hits Worst Against	Avg	AB	H	2B	3B	HR	RBI	BB	SO	OBP	SLG
Danny Jackson	.588	17	10	2	0	1	3	4	1	.667	.882	Steve Avery	.000	10	0	0	0	0	0	1	1	.091	.000
Scott Bankhead	.462	13	6	0	1	0	3	1	0	.500	.615	Chris Bosio	.091	11	1	1	0	0	1	1	2	.167	.182
Greg Hibbard	.462	13	6	2	0	0	2	3	1	.563	.615	Roger Clemens	.100	10	1	0	0	0	0	1	4	.182	.100
Bob Milacki	.455	11	5	0	0	0	1	2	2	.538	.455	Jack Morris	.125	16	2	0	0	0	1	0	2	.125	.125
Steve Cooke	.438	16	7	2	0	1	4	0	0	.438	.750	David Wells	.154	13	2	0	0	0	0	0	1	.154	.154

Mike Gallego — Yankees

Age 33 – Bats Right

	Avg	G	AB	R	H	2B	3B	HR	RBI	BB	SO	HBP	GDP	SB	CS	OBP	SLG	IBB	SH	SF	#Pit	#P/PA	GB	FB	G/F
1993 Season	.283	119	403	63	114	20	1	10	54	50	65	4	16	3	2	.364	.412	0	3	5	1728	3.72	151	117	1.29
Last Five Years	.248	604	1804	235	447	69	10	31	181	207	264	23	52	21	22	.331	.349	3	41	14	7621	3.65	686	523	1.31

1993 Season

	Avg	AB	H	2B	3B	HR	RBI	BB	SO	OBP	SLG		Avg	AB	H	2B	3B	HR	RBI	BB	SO	OBP	SLG
vs. Left	.305	151	46	9	0	5	17	17	13	.376	.464	Scoring Posn	.237	114	27	7	0	2	45	13	21	.303	.351
vs. Right	.270	252	68	11	1	5	37	33	52	.356	.381	Close & Late	.217	60	13	1	0	2	7	3	10	.266	.333
Groundball	.333	57	19	4	1	1	6	9	7	.441	.491	None on/out	.271	96	26	7	0	4	4	12	14	.358	.469
Flyball	.209	91	19	1	0	1	9	7	14	.265	.253	Batting #1	.304	46	14	3	1	1	4	7	1	.396	.478
Home	.302	192	58	11	0	5	20	27	31	.394	.438	Batting #8	.300	233	70	13	0	7	33	33	39	.384	.446
Away	.265	211	56	9	1	5	34	23	34	.336	.389	Other	.242	124	30	4	0	2	17	10	25	.312	.323
Day	.321	137	44	5	1	2	20	26	23	.435	.416	April	.438	16	7	0	0	2	4	0	4	.438	.813
Night	.263	266	70	15	0	8	34	24	42	.323	.410	May	.302	53	16	4	0	1	8	13	5	.456	.434

1993 Season

	Avg	AB	H	2B	3B	HR	RBI	BB	SO	OBP	SLG
Grass	.290	348	101	16	1	8	45	42	56	.368	.411
Turf	.236	55	13	4	0	2	9	8	9	.338	.418
First Pitch	.343	70	24	5	0	2	6	0	0	.343	.500
Ahead in Count	.383	94	36	8	0	5	22	36	0	.547	.628
Behind in Count	.209	163	34	4	0	1	13	0	55	.212	.252
Two Strikes	.191	173	33	4	1	2	18	14	65	.254	.260

	Avg	AB	H	2B	3B	HR	RBI	BB	SO	OBP	SLG
June	.327	49	16	5	0	1	7	2	10	.346	.490
July	.250	92	23	0	0	1	9	8	13	.314	.283
August	.313	99	31	8	1	2	13	9	15	.367	.475
September/October	.223	94	21	3	0	3	13	18	18	.348	.351
Pre-All Star	.301	153	46	9	0	4	23	18	23	.381	.438
Post-All Star	.272	250	68	11	1	6	31	32	42	.353	.396

1993 By Position

Position	Avg	AB	H	2B	3B	HR	RBI	BB	SO	OBP	SLG	G	GS	Innings	PO	A	E	DP	Fld Pct	Rng Fctr	In Zone	Outs	Zone Rtg	MLB Zone
As 2b	.234	145	34	8	0	4	18	19	31	.325	.372	52	41	364.1	83	143	5	37	.978	5.58	153	147	.961	.895
As 3b	.351	97	34	3	1	3	11	8	7	.407	.495	27	24	214.2	18	53	2	5	.973	2.98	61	60	.984	.834
As ss	.288	160	46	9	0	3	25	23	27	.374	.400	55	46	400.2	69	172	6	35	.976	5.41	190	168	.884	.880

Last Five Years

	Avg	AB	H	2B	3B	HR	RBI	BB	SO	OBP	SLG
vs. Left	.264	564	149	28	2	11	52	69	67	.345	.379
vs. Right	.240	1240	298	41	8	20	129	138	197	.324	.335
Groundball	.248	496	123	22	4	3	43	43	67	.325	.327
Flyball	.222	379	84	12	0	10	38	52	57	.316	.332
Home	.262	864	226	32	7	15	79	115	115	.353	.367
Away	.235	940	221	37	3	16	102	92	149	.310	.332
Day	.255	619	158	21	5	9	66	91	95	.357	.349
Night	.244	1185	289	48	5	22	115	116	169	.316	.349
Grass	.254	1522	386	55	9	24	146	176	213	.336	.349
Turf	.216	282	61	14	1	7	35	31	51	.301	.348
First Pitch	.294	303	89	15	2	6	25	2	0	.310	.416
Ahead in Count	.307	456	140	23	3	10	48	114	0	.446	.436
Behind in Count	.183	732	134	18	2	6	62	0	234	.191	.238
Two Strikes	.180	756	136	18	4	12	73	91	264	.271	.262

	Avg	AB	H	2B	3B	HR	RBI	BB	SO	OBP	SLG
Scoring Posn	.229	424	97	17	3	4	142	50	61	.315	.311
Close & Late	.272	272	74	9	2	6	28	21	45	.331	.386
None on/out	.219	471	103	18	1	14	14	58	68	.307	.350
Batting #8	.274	643	176	30	3	19	72	75	115	.352	.418
Batting #9	.225	901	203	27	6	8	78	96	114	.308	.295
Other	.262	260	68	12	1	4	31	36	35	.355	.362
April	.277	166	46	7	1	3	17	21	24	.356	.386
May	.254	307	78	17	3	5	40	43	40	.357	.378
June	.239	330	79	9	1	4	26	34	49	.311	.309
July	.245	359	88	12	2	7	42	30	46	.313	.348
August	.263	293	77	15	2	6	29	30	36	.334	.389
September/October	.226	349	79	9	1	6	27	49	69	.328	.309
Pre-All Star	.252	920	232	34	6	15	97	106	125	.335	.351
Post-All Star	.243	884	215	35	4	16	84	101	139	.326	.346

Batter vs. Pitcher (career)

Hits Best Against	Avg	AB	H	2B	3B	HR	RBI	BB	SO	OBP	SLG
Scott Bankhead	.583	12	7	2	0	0	1	3	1	.667	.750
John Farrell	.500	10	5	1	0	0	0	2	1	.583	.600
Joe Hesketh	.500	8	4	1	0	0	0	3	0	.636	.625
Alex Fernandez	.462	13	6	2	0	1	4	0	2	.462	.846
Wilson Alvarez	.364	11	4	2	0	0	2	2	2	.462	.545

Hits Worst Against	Avg	AB	H	2B	3B	HR	RBI	BB	SO	OBP	SLG
Bill Krueger	.000	9	0	0	0	0	0	2	2	.182	.000
Mark Gubicza	.053	19	1	0	0	0	0	3	3	.182	.053
Jeff Ballard	.067	15	1	1	0	0	0	0	1	.067	.133
Bob Milacki	.067	15	1	0	0	0	0	1	1	.125	.067
Ben McDonald	.067	15	1	0	0	0	0	2	5	.176	.067

Ron Gant — Braves

Age 29 – Bats Right (flyball hitter)

	Avg	G	AB	R	H	2B	3B	HR	RBI	BB	SO	HBP	GDP	SB	CS	OBP	SLG	IBB	SH	SF	#Pit	#P/PA	GB	FB	G/F
1993 Season	.274	157	606	113	166	27	4	36	117	67	117	2	14	26	9	.345	.510	2	0	7	2626	3.85	178	204	0.87
Last Five Years	.262	691	2546	421	668	126	19	126	411	253	471	16	38	134	56	.330	.475	15	3	24	10696	3.76	788	893	0.88

1993 Season

	Avg	AB	H	2B	3B	HR	RBI	BB	SO	OBP	SLG
vs. Left	.295	149	44	6	1	8	34	23	13	.385	.510
vs. Right	.267	457	122	21	3	28	83	44	104	.331	.510
Groundball	.275	207	57	6	3	11	39	30	44	.365	.493
Flyball	.255	106	27	5	1	6	21	7	19	.304	.491
Home	.279	301	84	13	2	17	55	35	53	.352	.505
Away	.269	305	82	14	2	19	62	32	64	.337	.515
Day	.209	158	33	3	2	6	22	18	44	.287	.367
Night	.297	448	133	24	2	30	95	49	73	.365	.560
Grass	.276	464	128	19	4	26	92	54	85	.348	.502
Turf	.268	142	38	8	0	10	25	13	32	.333	.535
First Pitch	.368	76	28	4	0	7	28	1	0	.383	.697
Ahead in Count	.393	135	53	11	1	15	28	34	0	.509	.822
Behind in Count	.208	269	56	9	3	8	39	0	91	.207	.353
Two Strikes	.189	286	54	9	3	7	35	32	117	.270	.315

	Avg	AB	H	2B	3B	HR	RBI	BB	SO	OBP	SLG
Scoring Posn	.301	173	52	14	1	12	89	23	38	.369	.601
Close & Late	.253	95	24	5	1	7	20	6	17	.291	.547
None on/out	.244	123	30	1	0	11	11	15	24	.326	.520
Batting #3	.272	316	86	7	2	18	66	35	63	.341	.478
Batting #5	.286	196	56	16	2	14	36	18	46	.346	.602
Other	.255	94	24	4	0	4	15	14	8	.355	.426
April	.207	87	18	3	0	4	8	10	19	.286	.379
May	.309	94	29	6	1	7	23	13	15	.389	.617
June	.283	99	28	10	1	6	17	9	22	.343	.586
July	.273	110	30	5	1	8	21	12	20	.350	.555
August	.262	107	28	0	0	6	21	9	21	.314	.430
September/October	.303	109	33	3	1	5	27	14	20	.378	.486
Pre-All Star	.261	318	83	21	2	20	55	39	63	.340	.528
Post-All Star	.288	288	83	6	2	16	62	28	54	.350	.490

1993 By Position

Position	Avg	AB	H	2B	3B	HR	RBI	BB	SO	OBP	SLG	G	GS	Innings	PO	A	E	DP	Fld Pct	Rng Fctr	In Zone	Outs	Zone Rtg	MLB Zone
As lf	.274	605	166	27	4	36	117	66	116	.344	.511	155	155	1384.1	270	5	11	1	.962	1.79	314	263	.838	.818

Last Five Years

	Avg	AB	H	2B	3B	HR	RBI	BB	SO	OBP	SLG
vs. Left	.266	773	206	48	4	34	141	95	107	.346	.471
vs. Right	.261	1773	462	78	15	92	270	158	364	.323	.477
Groundball	.271	865	234	37	7	41	134	88	144	.340	.472
Flyball	.237	617	146	31	4	31	94	67	121	.313	.451
Home	.275	1239	341	59	9	68	212	123	219	.343	.502
Away	.250	1307	327	67	10	58	199	130	252	.318	.450
Day	.236	643	152	20	5	28	94	77	152	.321	.414
Night	.271	1903	516	106	14	98	317	176	319	.333	.496
Grass	.265	1890	501	82	14	98	313	186	344	.332	.479
Turf	.255	656	167	44	5	28	98	67	127	.324	.465
First Pitch	.338	343	116	24	5	28	95	11	0	.364	.682

	Avg	AB	H	2B	3B	HR	RBI	BB	SO	OBP	SLG
Scoring Posn	.260	697	181	47	6	24	281	91	133	.337	.448
Close & Late	.214	384	82	16	1	16	56	38	76	.286	.385
None on/out	.292	596	174	27	1	47	47	45	93	.344	.577
Batting #3	.277	1114	309	52	7	52	182	115	189	.345	.477
Batting #4	.249	469	117	23	4	26	95	52	88	.329	.482
Other	.251	963	242	51	8	48	134	86	194	.313	.470
April	.205	332	68	15	2	13	41	40	76	.293	.380
May	.275	487	134	27	3	27	86	43	81	.333	.509
June	.269	420	113	30	4	21	58	34	71	.330	.510
July	.271	413	112	20	3	21	67	32	79	.326	.487
August	.259	397	103	14	3	20	66	47	74	.336	.461

Last Five Years

	Avg	AB	H	2B	3B	HR	RBI	BB	SO	OBP	SLG
Ahead in Count	.369	578	213	48	6	48	127	148	0	.495	.721
Behind in Count	.192	1128	217	38	8	31	120	0	365	.195	.323
Two Strikes	.181	1214	220	36	5	32	121	94	471	.242	.298

	Avg	AB	H	2B	3B	HR	RBI	BB	SO	OBP	SLG
September/October	.278	497	138	20	4	24	93	57	90	.351	.479
Pre-All Star	.257	1371	352	80	10	68	208	127	256	.322	.478
Post-All Star	.269	1175	316	46	9	58	203	126	215	.339	.471

Batter vs. Pitcher (career)

Hits Best Against	Avg	AB	H	2B	3B	HR	RBI	BB	SO	OBP	SLG
Jeff Innis	.545	11	6	2	0	0	3	1	0	.583	.727
Bruce Ruffin	.450	20	9	4	1	1	7	3	2	.522	.900
Omar Olivares	.444	18	8	3	0	2	3	4	3	.545	.944
Eric Hillman	.444	9	4	1	0	1	3	1	1	.455	.889
Bryan Hickerson	.385	13	5	2	0	2	5	2	2	.467	1.000

Hits Worst Against	Avg	AB	H	2B	3B	HR	RBI	BB	SO	OBP	SLG
Jose Guzman	.000	10	0	0	0	0	0	1	4	.091	.000
Anthony Young	.000	8	0	0	0	0	0	3	2	.273	.000
Scott Scudder	.000	7	0	0	0	0	0	4	2	.364	.000
Sid Fernandez	.118	17	2	0	0	0	2	2	5	.200	.118
Tom Candiotti	.143	14	2	0	0	0	2	1	5	.188	.143

Rich Garces — Twins

Age 23 – Pitches Right

	ERA	W	L	Sv	G	GS	IP	BB	SO	Avg	H	2B	3B	HR	RBI	OBP	SLG	GF	IR	IRS	Hld	SvOp	SB	CS	GB	FB	G/F
1993 Season	0.00	0	0	0	3	0	4.0	2	3	.250	4	0	0	0	1	.333	.250	1	1	0	0	0	0	0	8	3	2.67
Career (1990-1993)	0.93	0	0	2	8	0	9.2	6	4	.222	8	0	0	0	2	.333	.222	4	1	0	0	2	3	0	17	9	1.89

1993 Season

	ERA	W	L	Sv	G	GS	IP	H	HR	BB	SO
Home	0.00	0	0	0	1	0	1.0	0	0	1	1
Away	0.00	0	0	0	2	0	3.0	4	0	1	2

	Avg	AB	H	2B	3B	HR	RBI	BB	SO	OBP	SLG
vs. Left	.500	8	4	0	0	0	1	1	1	.556	.500
vs. Right	.000	8	0	0	0	0	0	1	2	.111	.000

Carlos Garcia — Pirates

Age 26 – Bats Right

	Avg	G	AB	R	H	2B	3B	HR	RBI	BB	SO	HBP	GDP	SB	CS	OBP	SLG	IBB	SH	SF	#Pit	#P/PA	GB	FB	G/F
1993 Season	.269	141	546	77	147	25	5	12	47	31	67	9	9	18	11	.316	.399	2	6	5	2074	3.47	232	158	1.47
Career (1990-1993)	.266	179	613	84	163	26	7	12	52	32	86	9	11	18	11	.309	.390	2	7	7	2311	3.46	251	173	1.45

1993 Season

	Avg	AB	H	2B	3B	HR	RBI	BB	SO	OBP	SLG
vs. Left	.304	191	58	15	2	4	15	10	17	.337	.466
vs. Right	.251	355	89	10	3	8	32	21	50	.306	.363
Groundball	.255	165	42	7	2	2	12	7	14	.290	.358
Flyball	.191	89	17	2	1	2	8	5	14	.247	.303
Home	.256	285	73	9	4	7	25	14	44	.294	.389
Away	.284	261	74	16	1	5	22	17	23	.340	.410
Day	.314	153	48	6	1	3	10	8	10	.358	.425
Night	.252	393	99	19	4	9	37	23	57	.300	.389
Grass	.303	165	50	9	1	5	18	13	14	.369	.461
Turf	.255	381	97	16	4	7	29	18	53	.292	.373
First Pitch	.304	56	17	1	0	3	6	2	0	.355	.482
Ahead in Count	.303	142	43	7	1	5	15	19	0	.393	.472
Behind in Count	.207	241	50	9	2	0	10	0	61	.219	.261
Two Strikes	.205	210	43	10	1	2	9	10	67	.246	.290

	Avg	AB	H	2B	3B	HR	RBI	BB	SO	OBP	SLG
Scoring Posn	.230	113	26	4	0	1	34	11	15	.292	.292
Close & Late	.242	95	23	3	1	0	7	7	16	.298	.295
None on/out	.277	202	56	11	0	5	5	8	23	.315	.406
Batting #1	.276	377	104	12	3	10	32	16	44	.314	.403
Batting #8	.246	142	35	11	2	2	11	10	17	.303	.394
Other	.296	27	8	2	0	0	4	5	6	.406	.370
April	.254	67	17	4	0	1	7	3	10	.301	.358
May	.250	72	18	5	2	1	6	7	10	.316	.417
June	.230	74	17	4	1	1	4	5	9	.275	.351
July	.257	109	28	5	0	3	8	6	15	.299	.385
August	.331	118	39	4	1	4	14	6	13	.385	.483
September/October	.264	106	28	3	1	2	8	4	10	.295	.368
Pre-All Star	.264	258	68	17	3	4	19	16	34	.312	.399
Post-All Star	.274	288	79	8	2	8	28	15	33	.321	.399

1993 By Position

Position	Avg	AB	H	2B	3B	HR	RBI	BB	SO	OBP	SLG	G	GS	Innings	PO	A	E	DP	Fld Pct	Rng Fctr	In Zone	Outs	Zone Rtg	MLB Zone
As 2b	.269	542	146	25	5	12	46	30	66	.316	.400	140	132	1186.0	294	344	11	83	.983	4.84	403	331	.821	.895

Mike Gardiner — Tigers

Age 28 – Pitches Right

	ERA	W	L	Sv	G	GS	IP	BB	SO	Avg	H	2B	3B	HR	RBI	OBP	SLG	GF	IR	IRS	Hld	SvOp	SB	CS	GB	FB	G/F
1993 Season	4.93	2	3	0	34	2	49.1	26	25	.271	52	10	2	3	28	.356	.391	4	27	4	4	2	4	2	68	54	1.26
Career (1990-1993)	5.05	15	25	0	89	45	322.2	136	201	.270	340	54	12	34	169	.341	.413	8	50	9	4	2	18	10	446	367	1.22

1993 Season

	ERA	W	L	Sv	G	GS	IP	H	HR	BB	SO
Home	4.50	1	3	0	18	2	28.0	29	0	18	14
Away	5.48	1	0	0	16	0	21.1	23	3	8	11
Starter	9.00	1	1	0	2	2	6.0	8	0	3	3
Reliever	4.36	1	2	0	32	0	43.1	44	3	23	22
0 Days rest	3.48	0	0	0	5	0	10.1	11	1	6	8
1 or 2 Days rest	7.16	0	2	0	14	0	16.1	23	2	12	9
3+ Days rest	2.16	1	0	0	13	0	16.2	10	0	5	5
Pre-All Star	5.00	1	3	0	22	2	36.0	38	3	18	21
Post-All Star	4.72	1	0	0	12	0	13.1	14	0	8	4

	Avg	AB	H	2B	3B	HR	RBI	BB	SO	OBP	SLG
vs. Left	.261	92	24	5	1	2	14	11	14	.343	.402
vs. Right	.280	100	28	5	1	1	14	15	11	.368	.380
Scoring Posn	.209	67	14	2	0	1	25	17	8	.356	.284
Close & Late	.235	34	8	1	0	0	1	4	2	.316	.265
None on/out	.357	42	15	2	2	1	1	4	5	.413	.571
First Pitch	.217	23	5	1	1	1	2	3	0	.308	.478
Ahead in Count	.236	89	21	1	0	0	8	0	24	.242	.247
Behind in Count	.366	41	15	6	0	1	11	10	0	.481	.585
Two Strikes	.271	96	26	2	0	1	11	13	25	.360	.323

Career (1990-1993)

	ERA	W	L	Sv	G	GS	IP	H	HR	BB	SO
Home	4.98	7	11	0	43	24	162.2	178	13	74	94
Away	5.12	8	14	0	46	21	160.0	162	21	62	107
Day	5.03	4	8	0	30	13	105.2	103	11	45	64
Night	5.06	11	17	0	59	32	217.0	237	23	91	137
Grass	4.52	12	15	0	62	34	247.0	248	26	101	156
Turf	6.78	3	10	0	27	11	75.2	92	8	35	45
April	3.62	2	1	0	11	2	27.1	22	1	11	26
May	3.74	2	3	0	10	7	45.2	42	1	17	27
June	5.27	3	8	0	20	11	82.0	89	10	37	54

	Avg	AB	H	2B	3B	HR	RBI	BB	SO	OBP	SLG
vs. Left	.265	586	155	27	8	10	66	58	95	.329	.389
vs. Right	.275	673	185	27	4	24	103	78	106	.350	.434
Inning 1-6	.271	1089	295	50	10	32	156	118	179	.341	.423
Inning 7+	.265	170	45	4	2	2	13	18	22	.340	.347
None on	.248	698	173	31	5	15	15	68	121	.316	.371
Runners on	.298	561	167	23	7	19	154	68	80	.371	.465
Scoring Posn	.270	311	84	13	5	7	126	51	48	.364	.412
Close & Late	.288	80	23	3	0	1	7	10	13	.374	.363
None on/out	.271	310	84	11	3	10	10	39	49	.352	.423

Career (1990-1993)	ERA	W	L	Sv	G	GS	IP	H	HR	BB	SO
July	7.26	1	6	0	10	5	31.0	45	5	20	12
August	5.27	3	1	0	9	6	42.2	44	9	12	29
September/October	5.07	4	6	0	29	14	94.0	98	8	39	53
Starter	5.32	12	21	0	45	45	247.0	267	28	98	162
Reliever	4.16	3	4	0	44	0	75.2	73	6	38	39
0 Days rest	3.38	0	0	0	6	0	10.2	12	1	6	9
1 or 2 Days rest	5.09	1	2	0	16	0	23.0	26	2	16	11
3+ Days rest	3.86	2	2	0	22	0	42.0	35	3	16	19
Pre-All Star	4.93	7	14	0	45	22	166.0	171	14	73	110
Post-All Star	5.17	8	11	0	44	23	156.2	169	20	63	91

	Avg	AB	H	2B	3B	HR	RBI	BB	SO	OBP	SLG
vs. 1st Batr (relief)	.143	35	5	0	1	0	3	8	3	.295	.200
First Inning Pitched	.216	306	66	8	3	7	51	33	52	.293	.330
First 15 Pitches	.203	261	53	8	3	7	32	26	37	.275	.337
Pitch 16-30	.270	237	64	6	0	8	35	35	48	.364	.397
Pitch 31-45	.303	201	61	10	6	4	31	17	27	.356	.473
Pitch 46+	.289	560	162	30	3	15	71	58	89	.356	.434
First Pitch	.306	180	55	6	2	7	26	6	0	.328	.478
Ahead in Count	.243	551	134	20	4	11	56	0	162	.243	.354
Behind in Count	.295	258	76	14	3	7	37	66	0	.435	.453
Two Strikes	.210	576	121	19	2	10	59	64	201	.289	.302

Pitcher vs. Batter (career)

Pitches Best Vs.	Avg	AB	H	2B	3B	HR	RBI	BB	SO	OBP	SLG
Sam Horn	.000	10	0	0	0	0	0	2	2	.167	.000
B.J. Surhoff	.083	12	1	1	0	0	0	1	0	.154	.167
Robin Yount	.091	11	1	0	0	0	1	2	3	.231	.091
Jay Buhner	.091	11	1	0	0	0	0	2	5	.231	.091
Greg Vaughn	.100	10	1	0	0	0	1	0	1	.091	.100

Pitches Worst Vs.	Avg	AB	H	2B	3B	HR	RBI	BB	SO	OBP	SLG
Frank Thomas	.643	14	9	1	0	2	5	2	1	.688	1.143
Dave Winfield	.444	9	4	2	0	0	2	3	0	.583	.667
Omar Vizquel	.400	10	4	0	1	0	2	1	0	.455	.600
Leo Gomez	.400	10	4	1	0	1	2	3	3	.538	.800
Mark McGwire	.333	9	3	0	0	3	7	3	3	.462	1.333

Jeff Gardner — Padres

Age 30 – Bats Left (groundball hitter)

	Avg	G	AB	R	H	2B	3B	HR	RBI	BB	SO	HBP	GDP	SB	CS	OBP	SLG	IBB	SH	SF	#Pit	#P/PA	GB	FB	G/F
1993 Season	.262	140	404	53	106	21	7	1	24	45	69	1	3	2	6	.337	.356	0	1	1	1747	3.87	164	70	2.34
Career (1991-1993)	.248	168	460	56	114	21	7	1	25	50	83	1	3	2	6	.322	.330	0	1	2	1994	3.88	181	87	2.08

1993 Season

	Avg	AB	H	2B	3B	HR	RBI	BB	SO	OBP	SLG
vs. Left	.174	23	4	1	0	0	0	6	7	.345	.217
vs. Right	.268	381	102	20	7	1	24	39	62	.336	.365
Groundball	.298	151	45	11	2	0	11	14	19	.358	.397
Flyball	.190	58	11	3	0	0	4	6	13	.262	.241
Home	.236	199	47	7	3	1	11	22	41	.314	.317
Away	.288	205	59	14	4	0	13	23	28	.360	.395
Day	.254	134	34	9	1	0	6	17	28	.342	.336
Night	.267	270	72	12	6	1	18	28	41	.334	.367
Grass	.256	317	81	16	4	1	18	34	55	.329	.341
Turf	.287	87	25	5	3	0	6	11	14	.367	.414
First Pitch	.333	57	19	5	1	0	3	0	0	.333	.456
Ahead in Count	.238	84	20	4	2	0	5	23	0	.398	.333
Behind in Count	.209	182	38	6	3	1	11	0	60	.209	.291
Two Strikes	.207	188	39	6	2	1	11	22	69	.290	.277

	Avg	AB	H	2B	3B	HR	RBI	BB	SO	OBP	SLG
Scoring Posn	.275	80	22	5	1	0	21	9	20	.344	.363
Close & Late	.203	74	15	3	0	0	6	9	14	.298	.243
None on/out	.278	115	32	9	2	1	1	17	15	.371	.417
Batting #1	.301	166	50	11	3	1	11	16	32	.366	.422
Batting #2	.217	161	35	8	2	0	6	21	24	.308	.292
Other	.273	77	21	2	2	0	7	8	13	.337	.351
April	.255	47	12	4	1	0	3	2	9	.286	.383
May	.296	81	24	6	1	0	4	10	11	.370	.395
June	.221	77	17	3	1	0	1	11	13	.326	.286
July	.368	68	25	4	1	1	8	6	13	.419	.500
August	.269	67	18	3	1	0	2	6	12	.329	.343
September/October	.156	64	10	1	2	0	6	10	11	.270	.234
Pre-All Star	.261	234	61	16	3	0	13	23	38	.328	.355
Post-All Star	.265	170	45	5	4	1	11	22	31	.349	.359

1993 By Position

Position	Avg	AB	H	2B	3B	HR	RBI	BB	SO	OBP	SLG	G	GS	Innings	PO	A	E	DP	Fld Pct	Rng Fctr	In Zone	Outs	Zone Rtg	MLB Zone
As Pinch Hitter	.118	17	2	0	0	0	1	2	4	.200	.118	22	0	---	---	---	---	---	---	---	---	---	---	---
As 2b	.270	385	104	21	7	1	23	43	64	.345	.369	133	96	907.2	212	295	9	47	.983	5.03	322	301	.935	.895

Mark Gardner — Royals

Age 32 – Pitches Right (flyball pitcher)

	ERA	W	L	Sv	G	GS	IP	BB	SO	Avg	H	2B	3B	HR	RBI	OBP	SLG	CG	ShO	Sup	QS	#P/S	SB	CS	GB	FB	G/F
1993 Season	6.19	4	6	0	17	16	91.2	36	54	.272	92	26	2	17	58	.343	.512	0	0	5.30	5	92	8	11	96	133	0.72
Career (1989-1993)	4.29	32	39	0	111	103	618.2	243	449	.246	565	107	13	64	275	.323	.387	3	3	3.97	56	96	72	46	700	757	0.92

1993 Season

	ERA	W	L	Sv	G	GS	IP	H	HR	BB	SO
Home	6.30	3	2	0	7	7	40.0	47	7	13	18
Away	6.10	1	4	0	10	9	51.2	45	10	23	36
Starter	6.02	4	6	0	16	16	89.2	91	17	33	53
Reliever	13.50	0	0	0	1	0	2.0	1	0	3	1
0-3 Days Rest	0.00	0	0	0	0	0	0.0	0	0	0	0
4 Days Rest	5.86	2	1	0	6	6	35.1	42	6	7	18
5+ Days Rest	6.13	2	5	0	10	10	54.1	49	11	26	35
Pre-All Star	6.02	4	6	0	16	16	89.2	91	17	33	53
Post-All Star	13.50	0	0	0	1	0	2.0	1	0	3	1

	Avg	AB	H	2B	3B	HR	RBI	BB	SO	OBP	SLG
vs. Left	.311	164	51	10	1	7	24	18	20	.376	.512
vs. Right	.236	174	41	16	1	10	34	18	34	.312	.511
Scoring Posn	.391	69	27	8	1	3	42	13	10	.456	.667
Close & Late	.429	7	3	0	0	1	1	2	2	.556	.857
None on/out	.270	100	27	6	0	11	11	7	16	.318	.660
First Pitch	.385	39	15	4	0	4	10	0	0	.395	.795
Ahead in Count	.218	147	32	11	1	2	18	0	42	.220	.347
Behind in Count	.389	72	28	10	1	7	21	18	0	.500	.847
Two Strikes	.212	151	32	7	1	5	23	18	54	.298	.371

Career (1989-1993)

	ERA	W	L	Sv	G	GS	IP	H	HR	BB	SO
Home	3.66	18	15	0	53	49	299.2	270	23	106	238
Away	4.88	14	24	0	58	54	319.0	295	41	137	211
Day	4.76	7	18	0	33	33	181.1	193	25	71	145
Night	4.10	25	21	0	78	70	437.1	372	39	172	304
Grass	5.14	7	15	0	34	33	184.0	185	29	76	128
Turf	3.93	25	24	0	77	70	434.2	380	35	167	321
April	4.08	4	4	0	12	11	68.1	58	6	28	51
May	3.77	4	7	0	23	21	121.2	118	11	47	102
June	4.61	9	9	0	22	22	130.2	127	20	48	72
July	2.26	8	7	0	18	18	127.2	89	7	42	99
August	4.75	5	5	0	16	16	89.0	88	6	35	65

	Avg	AB	H	2B	3B	HR	RBI	BB	SO	OBP	SLG
vs. Left	.250	1326	332	58	11	33	150	156	229	.330	.385
vs. Right	.240	971	233	49	2	31	125	87	220	.312	.390
Inning 1-6	.242	2029	491	98	9	56	252	213	394	.319	.382
Inning 7+	.276	268	74	9	4	8	23	30	55	.348	.429
None on	.220	142[illegible]	314	57	6	40	40	128	284	.289	.353
Runners on	.288	871	[illegible]51	50	7	24	235	115	165	.374	.444
Scoring Posn	.286	528	151	28	5	15	202	84	112	.383	.443
Close & Late	.281	153	43	3	3	4	13	22	34	.371	.418
None on/out	.239	615	147	26	3	24	24	54	115	.306	.408
vs. 1st Batr (relief)	.000	7	0	0	0	0	1	0	0	.000	.000
First Inning Pitched	.278	418	116	21	2	9	65	55	78	.367	.402

Career (1989-1993)

	ERA	W	L	Sv	G	GS	IP	H	HR	BB	SO
September/October	7.41	2	7	0	20	15	81.1	85	14	43	60
Starter	4.26	31	38	0	103	103	606.0	554	64	239	444
Reliever	5.68	1	1	0	8	0	12.2	11	0	4	5
0-3 Days Rest	7.88	0	2	0	2	2	8.0	11	3	4	7
4 Days Rest	3.52	20	15	0	57	57	353.1	302	35	135	263
5+ Days Rest	5.22	11	21	0	44	44	244.2	241	26	100	174
Pre-All Star	3.91	21	23	0	64	61	368.1	342	40	142	257
Post-All Star	4.85	11	16	0	47	42	250.1	223	24	101	192

	Avg	AB	H	2B	3B	HR	RBI	BB	SO	OBP	SLG
First 75 Pitches	.242	1707	413	84	6	44	208	178	347	.320	.376
Pitch 76-90	.238	302	72	13	4	12	38	32	50	.311	.427
Pitch 91-105	.294	197	58	7	3	7	22	16	26	.347	.467
Pitch 106+	.242	91	22	3	0	1	7	17	26	.361	.308
First Pitch	.292	284	83	11	2	9	31	7	0	.323	.440
Ahead in Count	.198	1059	210	37	7	16	97	0	351	.204	.292
Behind in Count	.308	506	156	41	2	23	87	132	0	.452	.534
Two Strikes	.175	1085	190	34	8	19	99	104	449	.251	.274

Pitcher vs. Batter (career)

Pitches Best Vs.	Avg	AB	H	2B	3B	HR	RBI	BB	SO	OBP	SLG
Curt Wilkerson	.091	11	1	0	0	0	0	1	3	.167	.091
Jose Oquendo	.091	11	1	0	0	0	1	2	2	.214	.091
Sid Bream	.100	10	1	0	0	0	0	1	1	.182	.100
Eric Yelding	.154	13	2	0	0	0	0	0	4	.154	.154
Gary Varsho	.167	12	2	0	0	0	0	0	1	.167	.167

Pitches Worst Vs.	Avg	AB	H	2B	3B	HR	RBI	BB	SO	OBP	SLG
Greg Olson	.556	9	5	0	0	0	3	2	2	.636	.556
Tony Gwynn	.471	17	8	0	2	0	3	1	0	.500	.706
Dwight Smith	.429	14	6	1	1	1	3	2	2	.471	.857
Felix Jose	.357	14	5	1	0	2	4	3	4	.471	.857
Andre Dawson	.348	23	8	4	0	3	10	0	5	.348	.913

Brent Gates — Athletics

Age 24 – Bats Both (groundball hitter)

	Avg	G	AB	R	H	2B	3B	HR	RBI	BB	SO	HBP	GDP	SB	CS	OBP	SLG	IBB	SH	SF	#Pit	#P/PA	GB	FB	G/F
1993 Season	.290	139	535	64	155	29	2	7	69	56	75	4	17	7	3	.357	.391	4	6	8	2308	3.79	213	131	1.63

1993 Season

	Avg	AB	H	2B	3B	HR	RBI	BB	SO	OBP	SLG
vs. Left	.256	172	44	9	0	2	18	20	24	.337	.343
vs. Right	.306	363	111	20	2	5	51	36	51	.366	.413
Groundball	.306	108	33	8	0	1	9	4	8	.333	.407
Flyball	.303	119	36	7	0	2	24	14	19	.375	.412
Home	.264	258	68	9	0	4	36	25	39	.328	.345
Away	.314	277	87	20	2	3	33	31	36	.383	.433
Day	.276	199	55	8	0	2	21	23	34	.351	.347
Night	.298	336	100	21	2	5	48	33	41	.360	.417
Grass	.271	435	118	20	1	6	54	42	62	.336	.363
Turf	.370	100	37	9	1	1	15	14	13	.443	.510
First Pitch	.353	51	18	2	0	1	7	3	0	.382	.451
Ahead in Count	.265	113	30	7	1	3	16	36	0	.441	.425
Behind in Count	.287	247	71	13	1	2	32	0	60	.291	.372
Two Strikes	.268	257	69	14	0	2	31	17	75	.314	.346

	Avg	AB	H	2B	3B	HR	RBI	BB	SO	OBP	SLG
Scoring Posn	.266	143	38	7	1	1	56	20	21	.343	.350
Close & Late	.278	90	25	6	0	1	18	13	19	.365	.378
None on/out	.327	104	34	6	0	1	1	11	12	.397	.413
Batting #2	.319	288	92	16	0	5	35	31	33	.387	.427
Batting #5	.291	127	37	10	2	2	22	9	20	.333	.449
Other	.217	120	26	3	0	0	12	16	22	.309	.242
April	.000	0	0	0	0	0	0	0	0	.000	.000
May	.276	87	24	4	0	2	10	14	11	.375	.391
June	.294	102	30	6	0	1	18	9	19	.350	.382
July	.276	116	32	1	0	1	10	13	16	.354	.310
August	.277	112	31	8	1	2	13	7	11	.314	.420
September/October	.322	118	38	10	1	1	18	13	18	.389	.449
Pre-All Star	.291	234	68	11	0	3	32	30	36	.370	.376
Post-All Star	.289	301	87	18	2	4	37	26	39	.345	.402

1993 By Position

Position	Avg	AB	H	2B	3B	HR	RBI	BB	SO	OBP	SLG	G	GS	Innings	PO	A	E	DP	Fld Pct	Rng Fctr	In Zone	Outs	Zone Rtg	MLB Zone
As 2b	.289	532	154	29	2	7	68	55	74	.356	.391	139	135	1210.1	281	430	14	87	.981	5.29	522	440	.843	.895

Bob Geren — Padres

Age 32 – Bats Right

	Avg	G	AB	R	H	2B	3B	HR	RBI	BB	SO	HBP	GDP	SB	CS	OBP	SLG	IBB	SH	SF	#Pit	#P/PA	GB	FB	G/F
1993 Season	.214	58	145	8	31	6	0	3	6	13	28	0	4	0	0	.278	.317	4	4	0	559	3.45	50	42	1.19
Last Five Years	.234	297	755	62	177	21	1	22	76	47	176	6	26	0	1	.284	.352	5	19	3	2986	3.60	248	212	1.17

1993 Season

	Avg	AB	H	2B	3B	HR	RBI	BB	SO	OBP	SLG
vs. Left	.280	75	21	5	0	3	5	5	10	.325	.467
vs. Right	.143	70	10	1	0	0	1	8	18	.231	.157
Home	.203	74	15	3	0	1	1	5	15	.253	.284
Away	.225	71	16	3	0	2	5	8	13	.304	.352
First Pitch	.261	23	6	1	0	0	0	4	0	.370	.304
Ahead in Count	.256	39	10	1	0	2	3	6	0	.356	.436
Behind in Count	.167	66	11	2	0	0	1	0	26	.167	.197
Two Strikes	.155	58	9	4	0	0	2	3	28	.197	.224

	Avg	AB	H	2B	3B	HR	RBI	BB	SO	OBP	SLG
Scoring Posn	.065	46	3	0	0	0	2	6	12	.173	.065
Close & Late	.080	25	2	0	0	0	0	1	7	.115	.080
None on/out	.375	32	12	2	0	2	2	3	3	.429	.625
Batting #7	.222	9	2	0	0	0	1	1	2	.300	.222
Batting #8	.214	126	27	5	0	3	5	11	23	.277	.325
Other	.200	10	2	1	0	0	0	1	3	.273	.300
Pre-All Star	.219	128	28	5	0	2	5	12	25	.286	.305
Post-All Star	.176	17	3	1	0	1	1	1	3	.222	.412

Last Five Years

	Avg	AB	H	2B	3B	HR	RBI	BB	SO	OBP	SLG
vs. Left	.266	361	96	15	0	11	36	23	64	.313	.399
vs. Right	.206	394	81	6	1	11	40	24	112	.256	.310
Groundball	.244	197	48	4	0	7	20	12	44	.289	.371
Flyball	.263	175	46	9	0	8	25	12	46	.318	.451
Home	.222	410	91	13	0	10	33	20	98	.260	.327
Away	.249	345	86	8	1	12	43	27	78	.310	.383
Day	.293	232	68	7	1	8	29	8	49	.324	.435
Night	.208	523	109	14	0	14	47	39	127	.266	.315
Grass	.225	632	142	16	1	14	50	36	153	.272	.320
Turf	.285	123	35	5	0	8	26	11	23	.341	.520
First Pitch	.234	111	26	2	0	3	12	4	0	.267	.333
Ahead in Count	.280	164	46	6	1	7	17	30	0	.395	.457
Behind in Count	.196	357	70	10	0	8	30	0	150	.202	.291
Two Strikes	.166	362	60	10	0	7	32	11	176	.195	.251

	Avg	AB	H	2B	3B	HR	RBI	BB	SO	OBP	SLG
Scoring Posn	.215	191	41	6	0	5	51	16	44	.271	.325
Close & Late	.209	134	28	2	0	3	12	5	36	.241	.291
None on/out	.253	190	48	3	1	6	6	6	41	.279	.374
Batting #7	.286	161	46	4	1	6	16	10	40	.337	.435
Batting #8	.222	464	103	15	0	11	44	28	110	.270	.325
Other	.215	130	28	2	0	5	16	9	26	.264	.346
April	.279	61	17	4	0	1	5	2	14	.302	.393
May	.193	171	33	3	0	6	12	15	44	.265	.316
June	.250	128	32	4	0	3	13	5	32	.284	.352
July	.264	148	39	5	0	4	15	7	31	.299	.378
August	.259	158	41	4	1	7	25	11	30	.306	.430
September/October	.169	89	15	1	0	1	6	7	25	.245	.213
Pre-All Star	.239	423	101	14	0	11	35	25	100	.287	.350
Post-All Star	.229	332	76	7	1	11	41	22	76	.279	.355

Batter vs. Pitcher (career)																							
Hits Best Against	Avg	AB	H	2B	3B	HR	RBI	BB	SO	OBP	SLG	**Hits Worst Against**	Avg	AB	H	2B	3B	HR	RBI	BB	SO	OBP	SLG
Jimmy Key	.455	11	5	0	0	0	2	1	2	.500	.455	Tom Candiotti	.100	10	1	0	0	0	0	1	3	.182	.100
												Mark Langston	.158	19	3	0	0	0	3	0	4	.158	.158
												Frank Tanana	.167	12	2	0	0	0	0	1	4	.231	.167
												Jeff Ballard	.231	13	3	1	0	0	1	0	1	.231	.308
												Greg Hibbard	.235	17	4	0	0	0	1	0	3	.235	.235

Kirk Gibson — Tigers

Age 37 – Bats Left

	Avg	G	AB	R	H	2B	3B	HR	RBI	BB	SO	HBP	GDP	SB	CS	OBP	SLG	IBB	SH	SF	#Pit	#P/PA	GB	FB	G/F
1993 Season	.261	116	403	62	105	18	6	13	62	44	87	4	2	15	6	.337	.432	4	0	3	1759	3.87	127	112	1.13
Last Five Years	.242	424	1489	243	361	63	14	48	188	190	322	15	21	74	16	.332	.400	12	2	9	6589	3.86	477	448	1.06

1993 Season																							
	Avg	AB	H	2B	3B	HR	RBI	BB	SO	OBP	SLG		Avg	AB	H	2B	3B	HR	RBI	BB	SO	OBP	SLG
vs. Left	.275	40	11	2	0	0	8	1	12	.326	.325	Scoring Posn	.243	111	27	6	1	1	44	13	17	.331	.342
vs. Right	.259	363	94	16	6	13	54	43	75	.338	.444	Close & Late	.226	53	12	2	0	1	4	7	14	.328	.321
Groundball	.376	93	35	5	0	6	27	6	12	.414	.624	None on/out	.276	87	24	3	1	4	4	13	22	.370	.471
Flyball	.230	87	20	2	1	2	10	11	21	.316	.345	Batting #5	.240	287	69	11	4	7	45	37	65	.328	.380
Home	.254	197	50	8	5	5	30	22	42	.326	.421	Batting #6	.346	81	28	5	1	5	11	4	14	.376	.617
Away	.267	206	55	10	1	8	32	22	45	.348	.442	Other	.229	35	8	2	1	1	6	3	8	.325	.429
Day	.254	142	36	9	2	0	11	15	39	.331	.345	April	.407	59	24	6	0	3	15	14	13	.520	.661
Night	.264	261	69	9	4	13	51	29	48	.340	.479	May	.270	74	20	1	2	3	10	12	18	.372	.459
Grass	.226	328	74	11	5	7	47	36	72	.302	.354	June	.115	78	9	3	1	1	9	3	23	.146	.218
Turf	.413	75	31	7	1	6	15	8	15	.488	.773	July	.328	67	22	5	1	3	5	3	9	.366	.567
First Pitch	.378	45	17	3	2	1	11	2	0	.420	.600	August	.261	88	23	3	1	3	17	5	19	.316	.420
Ahead in Count	.330	106	35	4	1	6	19	31	0	.475	.557	September/October	.189	37	7	0	1	0	6	7	5	.311	.243
Behind in Count	.186	167	31	8	2	2	16	0	77	.195	.293	Pre-All Star	.247	235	58	13	3	7	34	30	57	.335	.417
Two Strikes	.152	191	29	7	1	1	18	11	87	.202	.215	Post-All Star	.280	168	47	5	3	6	28	14	30	.341	.452

1993 By Position																									
Position	Avg	AB	H	2B	3B	HR	RBI	BB	SO	OBP	SLG	G	GS	Innings	PO	A	E	DP	Fld Pct	Rng Fctr	In Zone	Outs	Zone Rtg	MLB Zone
As Designated Hitter	.248	278	69	13	4	7	40	36	62	.333	.399	76	75	---	---	---	---	---	---	---	---	---	---	---
As Pinch Hitter	.182	11	2	1	0	0	3	1	3	.308	.273	13	0	---	---	---	---	---	---	---	---	---	---	---
As cf	.301	113	34	4	2	6	19	7	21	.352	.531	30	27	234.0	74	0	1	0	.987	2.85	93	72	.774	.829

Last Five Years																							
	Avg	AB	H	2B	3B	HR	RBI	BB	SO	OBP	SLG		Avg	AB	H	2B	3B	HR	RBI	BB	SO	OBP	SLG
vs. Left	.199	376	75	12	3	9	44	41	99	.295	.319	Scoring Posn	.236	343	81	15	4	8	124	63	69	.356	.373
vs. Right	.257	1113	286	51	11	39	144	149	223	.345	.428	Close & Late	.214	243	52	8	4	4	30	35	65	.319	.329
Groundball	.265	460	122	18	4	21	78	60	79	.356	.459	None on/out	.234	334	78	13	4	12	12	33	75	.316	.404
Flyball	.237	325	77	12	2	11	39	48	80	.333	.388	Batting #2	.262	511	134	30	5	14	59	69	101	.357	.423
Home	.235	744	175	26	13	15	85	98	150	.327	.366	Batting #5	.237	346	82	11	5	11	55	44	78	.324	.393
Away	.250	745	186	37	1	33	103	92	172	.338	.435	Other	.229	632	145	22	4	23	74	77	143	.317	.386
Day	.215	474	102	20	4	11	51	52	114	.300	.344	April	.288	229	66	9	1	13	40	34	48	.384	.507
Night	.255	1015	259	43	10	37	137	138	208	.347	.427	May	.250	196	49	7	3	5	17	27	40	.341	.393
Grass	.233	935	218	38	7	31	122	121	206	.324	.388	June	.191	346	66	12	3	14	50	39	76	.271	.364
Turf	.258	554	143	25	7	17	66	69	116	.346	.421	July	.273	278	76	19	2	5	26	24	43	.337	.410
First Pitch	.339	189	64	13	4	6	32	9	0	.374	.545	August	.281	267	75	9	4	11	41	34	64	.371	.468
Ahead in Count	.314	350	110	20	5	19	58	92	0	.455	.563	September/October	.168	173	29	7	1	0	14	32	51	.308	.220
Behind in Count	.164	669	110	17	2	9	48	0	274	.174	.236	Pre-All Star	.234	853	200	33	7	32	115	106	177	.320	.402
Two Strikes	.148	701	104	18	2	11	54	89	322	.250	.227	Post-All Star	.253	636	161	30	7	16	73	84	145	.348	.398

Batter vs. Pitcher (since 1984)																							
Hits Best Against	Avg	AB	H	2B	3B	HR	RBI	BB	SO	OBP	SLG	**Hits Worst Against**	Avg	AB	H	2B	3B	HR	RBI	BB	SO	OBP	SLG
Charlie Leibrandt	.500	12	6	2	0	1	3	0	1	.500	.917	Alex Fernandez	.000	14	0	0	0	0	0	1	7	.067	.000
Eric Plunk	.500	12	6	0	0	3	5	3	3	.600	1.250	Todd Stottlemyre	.000	10	0	0	0	0	0	3	4	.231	.000
Kirk McCaskill	.440	25	11	3	0	4	6	8	6	.576	1.040	Cal Eldred	.000	9	0	0	0	0	1	2	1	.182	.000
Tom Candiotti	.412	17	7	1	2	1	4	2	1	.474	.882	Jimmy Key	.083	24	2	0	0	0	0	4	9	.214	.083
Scott Sanderson	.357	14	5	1	0	2	6	2	4	.438	.857	Matt Young	.091	11	1	1	0	0	1	0	5	.091	.182

Paul Gibson — Yankees

Age 34 – Pitches Left

	ERA	W	L	Sv	G	GS	IP	BB	SO	Avg	H	2B	3B	HR	RBI	OBP	SLG	GF	IR	IRS	Hld	SvOp	SB	CS	GB	FB	G/F
1993 Season	3.48	3	1	0	28	0	44.0	11	37	.265	45	9	1	5	30	.304	.418	10	30	14	1	1	5	0	51	48	1.06
Last Five Years	4.24	17	21	11	245	14	431.1	185	271	.275	455	87	12	43	236	.348	.419	67	225	78	27	22	42	20	536	520	1.03

1993 Season																							
	ERA	W	L	Sv	G	GS	IP	H	HR	BB	SO		Avg	AB	H	2B	3B	HR	RBI	BB	SO	OBP	SLG
Home	3.80	1	1	0	13	0	21.1	19	5	5	18	vs. Left	.224	67	15	5	0	1	11	5	14	.270	.343
Away	3.18	2	0	0	15	0	22.2	26	0	6	19	vs. Right	.291	103	30	4	1	4	19	6	23	.327	.466
Starter	0.00	0	0	0	0	0	0.0	0	0	0	0	Scoring Posn	.346	52	18	5	1	1	25	1	11	.339	.538
Reliever	3.48	3	1	0	28	0	44.0	45	5	11	37	Close & Late	.296	27	8	0	0	1	7	1	9	.321	.407
0 Days rest	0.00	0	0	0	2	0	1.2	2	0	0	2	None on/out	.243	37	9	1	0	1	1	2	11	.282	.351
1 or 2 Days rest	4.29	3	1	0	13	0	21.0	25	2	4	13	First Pitch	.250	20	5	0	0	1	6	0	0	.250	.400
3+ Days rest	2.95	0	0	0	13	0	21.1	18	3	7	22	Ahead in Count	.200	75	15	1	0	0	9	0	31	.195	.213
Pre-All Star	4.15	1	1	0	12	0	13.0	18	1	5	14	Behind in Count	.341	44	15	4	1	3	8	8	0	.434	.682
Post-All Star	3.19	2	0	0	16	0	31.0	27	4	6	23	Two Strikes	.197	76	15	2	0	1	9	3	37	.222	.263

Last Five Years	ERA	W	L	Sv	G	GS	IP	H	HR	BB	SO
Home	3.41	11	9	6	118	7	226.2	210	15	89	155
Away	5.14	6	12	5	127	7	204.2	245	28	96	116
Day	3.59	6	5	3	72	5	140.1	144	9	58	93
Night	4.55	11	16	8	173	9	291.0	311	34	127	178
Grass	3.90	16	17	7	188	13	343.2	354	32	134	212
Turf	5.54	1	4	4	57	1	87.2	101	11	51	59
April	3.70	3	2	1	31	1	48.2	52	4	25	32
May	3.38	3	4	5	49	4	93.1	86	7	43	68
June	5.35	2	5	1	44	1	65.2	81	5	29	39
July	4.21	2	2	1	41	6	94.0	89	10	39	51
August	4.91	2	7	1	42	1	69.2	81	12	25	43
September/October	4.05	5	1	2	38	1	60.0	66	5	24	38
Starter	4.61	1	5	0	14	14	82.0	88	7	32	43
Reliever	4.15	16	16	11	231	0	349.1	367	36	153	228
0 Days rest	4.34	1	2	1	46	0	58.0	70	6	26	39
1 or 2 Days rest	4.01	10	7	9	112	0	170.2	171	14	81	104
3+ Days rest	4.25	5	7	1	73	0	120.2	126	16	46	85
Pre-All Star	4.19	8	12	8	137	8	229.2	244	20	109	154
Post-All Star	4.28	9	9	3	108	6	201.2	211	23	76	117

Last Five Years	Avg	AB	H	2B	3B	HR	RBI	BB	SO	OBP	SLG
vs. Left	.288	486	140	20	4	16	85	51	62	.353	.444
vs. Right	.269	1171	315	67	8	27	151	134	209	.346	.409
Inning 1-6	.282	755	213	53	2	19	124	84	113	.355	.433
Inning 7+	.268	902	242	34	10	24	112	101	158	.342	.408
None on	.275	855	235	48	3	23	23	86	144	.344	.419
Runners on	.274	802	220	39	9	20	213	99	127	.352	.420
Scoring Posn	.279	477	133	23	5	9	179	81	76	.374	.405
Close & Late	.280	386	108	10	3	13	50	35	65	.339	.422
None on/out	.295	383	113	24	2	11	11	41	61	.368	.454
vs. 1st Batr (relief)	.341	205	70	13	4	3	49	17	26	.383	.488
First Inning Pitched	.286	758	217	39	5	24	141	92	127	.362	.446
First 15 Pitches	.288	694	200	39	5	20	119	76	108	.356	.445
Pitch 16-30	.233	421	98	16	2	10	45	53	94	.323	.352
Pitch 31-45	.296	247	73	13	3	6	26	25	38	.359	.445
Pitch 46+	.285	295	84	19	2	7	46	31	31	.356	.434
First Pitch	.327	220	72	10	3	8	46	25	0	.398	.509
Ahead in Count	.216	759	164	31	3	11	61	0	235	.219	.308
Behind in Count	.338	373	126	26	5	12	68	92	0	.465	.531
Two Strikes	.197	752	148	31	2	12	72	66	271	.264	.291

Pitcher vs. Batter (career)

Pitches Best Vs.	Avg	AB	H	2B	3B	HR	RBI	BB	SO	OBP	SLG
Mike Felder	.000	15	0	0	0	0	0	1	3	.063	.000
George Bell	.000	11	0	0	0	0	1	2	2	.143	.000
Devon White	.077	13	1	1	0	0	1	1	4	.143	.154
Dave Henderson	.091	11	1	0	0	0	1	1	2	.167	.091
Kelly Gruber	.118	17	2	0	0	0	0	1	0	.167	.118

Pitches Worst Vs.	Avg	AB	H	2B	3B	HR	RBI	BB	SO	OBP	SLG
Ken Griffey Jr	.615	13	8	2	0	2	2	3	0	.688	1.231
Steve Sax	.545	11	6	2	0	0	1	0	0	.545	.727
Tony Fernandez	.421	19	8	2	2	1	8	6	2	.560	.895
Pat Borders	.400	10	4	2	0	1	3	5	0	.563	.900
Rob Deer	.385	13	5	2	0	2	3	3	4	.500	1.000

Benji Gil — Rangers

Age 21 – Bats Right (flyball hitter)

	Avg	G	AB	R	H	2B	3B	HR	RBI	BB	SO	HBP	GDP	SB	CS	OBP	SLG	IBB	SH	SF	#Pit	#P/PA	GB	FB	G/F
1993 Season	.123	22	57	3	7	0	0	0	2	5	22	0	0	1	2	.194	.123	0	4	0	246	3.73	9	12	0.75

1993 Season

	Avg	AB	H	2B	3B	HR	RBI	BB	SO	OBP	SLG
vs. Left	.222	9	2	0	0	0	0	1	4	.300	.222
vs. Right	.104	48	5	0	0	0	2	4	18	.173	.104
Scoring Posn	.176	17	3	0	0	0	2	1	8	.222	.176
Close & Late	.000	3	0	0	0	0	0	0	2	.000	.000

Bernard Gilkey — Cardinals

Age 27 – Bats Right

	Avg	G	AB	R	H	2B	3B	HR	RBI	BB	SO	HBP	GDP	SB	CS	OBP	SLG	IBB	SH	SF	#Pit	#P/PA	GB	FB	G/F
1993 Season	.305	137	557	99	170	40	5	16	70	56	66	4	16	15	10	.370	.481	2	0	5	2235	3.59	204	193	1.06
Career (1990-1993)	.285	367	1273	194	363	71	13	29	136	142	156	6	36	53	31	.357	.430	3	4	11	5074	3.53	483	422	1.14

1993 Season

	Avg	AB	H	2B	3B	HR	RBI	BB	SO	OBP	SLG
vs. Left	.343	137	47	8	2	4	22	11	15	.396	.518
vs. Right	.293	420	123	32	3	12	48	45	51	.362	.469
Groundball	.330	176	58	15	3	4	26	16	20	.390	.517
Flyball	.278	90	25	1	0	3	9	7	13	.333	.389
Home	.325	265	86	21	3	7	35	23	26	.380	.506
Away	.288	292	84	19	2	9	35	33	40	.361	.459
Day	.324	170	55	14	2	4	16	14	17	.385	.500
Night	.297	387	115	26	3	12	54	42	49	.363	.473
Grass	.295	176	52	12	1	6	23	21	26	.368	.477
Turf	.310	381	118	28	4	10	47	35	40	.371	.483
First Pitch	.274	95	26	4	1	3	12	1	0	.290	.432
Ahead in Count	.351	154	54	10	2	4	23	30	0	.457	.519
Behind in Count	.293	191	56	15	1	5	24	0	57	.294	.461
Two Strikes	.259	205	53	11	2	6	20	25	66	.338	.420

	Avg	AB	H	2B	3B	HR	RBI	BB	SO	OBP	SLG
Scoring Posn	.311	135	42	8	1	5	56	18	16	.384	.496
Close & Late	.293	99	29	7	1	2	14	12	14	.377	.444
None on/out	.342	196	67	14	3	8	8	18	19	.403	.566
Batting #1	.311	395	123	32	4	11	47	42	49	.380	.496
Batting #5	.290	69	20	5	1	1	9	5	8	.338	.435
Other	.290	93	27	3	0	4	14	9	9	.349	.452
April	.339	56	19	5	1	0	3	9	10	.424	.464
May	.279	68	19	3	1	1	6	7	8	.347	.397
June	.336	107	36	13	1	4	16	7	15	.379	.589
July	.333	102	34	4	0	5	17	9	12	.387	.520
August	.257	101	26	7	1	3	17	13	9	.347	.436
September/October	.293	123	36	8	1	3	11	11	12	.353	.447
Pre-All Star	.327	275	90	23	3	6	30	28	41	.389	.498
Post-All Star	.284	282	80	17	2	10	40	28	25	.351	.465

1993 By Position

Position	Avg	AB	H	2B	3B	HR	RBI	BB	SO	OBP	SLG	G	GS	Innings	PO	A	E	DP	Fld Pct	Rng Fctr	In Zone	Outs	Zone Rtg	MLB Zone
As lf	.302	539	163	39	5	15	66	49	65	.362	.477	132	130	1141.1	223	19	8	2	.968	1.91	285	213	.747	.818

Career (1990-1993)

	Avg	AB	H	2B	3B	HR	RBI	BB	SO	OBP	SLG
vs. Left	.299	479	143	22	6	8	51	51	50	.367	.420
vs. Right	.277	794	220	49	7	21	85	91	106	.351	.436
Groundball	.297	448	133	27	5	7	49	41	52	.355	.426
Flyball	.269	223	60	7	3	6	18	33	34	.364	.408
Home	.281	643	181	37	7	12	66	62	67	.345	.417
Away	.289	630	182	34	6	17	70	80	89	.369	.443
Day	.293	372	109	24	3	9	35	32	42	.354	.446
Night	.282	901	254	47	10	20	101	110	114	.358	.423
Grass	.292	318	93	17	3	10	41	42	51	.374	.459
Turf	.283	955	270	54	10	19	95	100	105	.351	.420
First Pitch	.321	240	77	12	1	5	29	2	0	.328	.442

	Avg	AB	H	2B	3B	HR	RBI	BB	SO	OBP	SLG
Scoring Posn	.303	284	86	15	5	7	108	53	40	.401	.465
Close & Late	.294	238	70	15	1	6	30	33	33	.380	.441
None on/out	.304	425	129	26	5	14	14	35	42	.361	.487
Batting #1	.272	794	216	48	10	16	78	93	96	.350	.418
Batting #6	.329	164	54	10	1	6	18	10	19	.366	.512
Other	.295	315	93	13	2	7	40	39	41	.368	.416
April	.294	180	53	9	2	1	10	24	30	.376	.383
May	.249	173	43	7	2	3	15	25	20	.343	.364
June	.330	191	63	16	3	4	24	14	27	.375	.508
July	.275	229	63	8	1	6	30	23	33	.341	.397
August	.228	228	52	13	1	6	31	28	25	.315	.373

Career (1990-1993)	Avg	AB	H	2B	3B	HR	RBI	BB	SO	OBP	SLG		Avg	AB	H	2B	3B	HR	RBI	BB	SO	OBP	SLG
Ahead in Count	.329	353	116	20	5	13	52	75	0	.445	.524	September/October	.327	272	89	18	4	9	26	28	21	.389	.522
Behind in Count	.244	442	108	25	4	6	31	0	130	.248	.360	Pre-All Star	.295	610	180	35	7	9	55	69	89	.366	.420
Two Strikes	.202	451	91	17	5	8	33	65	156	.303	.315	Post-All Star	.276	663	183	36	6	20	81	73	67	.348	.439

Batter vs. Pitcher (career)																							
Hits Best Against	Avg	AB	H	2B	3B	HR	RBI	BB	SO	OBP	SLG	Hits Worst Against	Avg	AB	H	2B	3B	HR	RBI	BB	SO	OBP	SLG
Greg Swindell	.700	10	7	0	0	0	2	1	0	.727	.700	Mitch Williams	.100	10	1	0	0	0	0	1	2	.182	.100
Chris Hammond	.632	19	12	2	0	0	4	4	0	.696	.737	John Burkett	.125	16	2	0	0	0	0	0	2	.125	.125
Shawn Boskie	.600	10	6	1	0	2	3	1	1	.636	1.300	Darryl Kile	.143	14	2	0	0	0	0	3	1	.294	.143
Terry Mulholland	.500	24	12	1	2	1	4	2	0	.538	.833	Randy Tomlin	.148	27	4	2	0	0	2	2	4	.207	.222
Bob Walk	.444	9	4	1	0	1	2	3	0	.583	.889	Bruce Hurst	.167	12	2	0	0	0	1	1	1	.214	.167

Joe Girardi — Rockies

Age 29 – Bats Right (groundball hitter)

	Avg	G	AB	R	H	2B	3B	HR	RBI	BB	SO	HBP	GDP	SB	CS	OBP	SLG	IBB	SH	SF	#Pit	#P/PA	GB	FB	G/F
1993 Season	.290	86	310	35	90	14	5	3	31	24	41	3	6	6	6	.346	.397	0	12	1	1118	3.19	140	66	2.12
Career (1989-1993)	.269	390	1203	108	324	53	8	6	101	77	161	9	31	16	12	.316	.342	20	18	7	4004	3.05	547	281	1.95

1993 Season	Avg	AB	H	2B	3B	HR	RBI	BB	SO	OBP	SLG		Avg	AB	H	2B	3B	HR	RBI	BB	SO	OBP	SLG
vs. Left	.295	78	23	5	2	1	5	7	7	.349	.449	Scoring Posn	.286	70	20	4	2	0	25	7	14	.346	.400
vs. Right	.289	232	67	9	3	2	26	17	34	.345	.379	Close & Late	.234	47	11	1	1	0	3	3	9	.294	.298
Groundball	.287	101	29	6	5	0	9	6	17	.330	.446	None on/out	.288	66	19	4	1	1	1	1	5	.299	.424
Flyball	.227	66	15	3	0	1	5	6	13	.292	.318	Batting #2	.319	141	45	8	3	2	13	14	21	.390	.461
Home	.327	147	48	8	3	2	19	13	21	.385	.463	Batting #7	.253	99	25	3	2	0	12	5	13	.288	.323
Away	.258	163	42	6	2	1	12	11	20	.311	.337	Other	.286	70	20	3	0	1	6	5	7	.333	.371
Day	.318	107	34	7	3	1	10	7	10	.362	.467	April	.280	75	21	5	1	0	6	2	14	.299	.373
Night	.276	203	56	7	2	2	21	17	31	.338	.360	May	.272	92	25	3	1	1	11	5	7	.306	.359
Grass	.299	221	66	11	4	3	26	20	29	.361	.425	June	.000	4	0	0	0	0	0	0	1	.000	.000
Turf	.270	89	24	3	1	0	5	4	12	.309	.326	July	.000	0	0	0	0	0	0	0	0	.000	.000
First Pitch	.258	66	17	4	0	2	8	0	0	.269	.409	August	.291	55	16	2	2	1	7	5	7	.350	.455
Ahead in Count	.284	81	23	5	2	0	5	14	0	.385	.395	September/October	.333	84	28	4	1	1	7	12	12	.434	.440
Behind in Count	.246	118	29	3	1	0	15	0	39	.258	.288	Pre-All Star	.269	171	46	8	2	1	17	7	22	.296	.357
Two Strikes	.184	98	18	2	0	1	10	10	41	.273	.235	Post-All Star	.317	139	44	6	3	2	14	17	19	.403	.446

1993 By Position																							
Position	Avg	AB	H	2B	3B	HR	RBI	BB	SO	OBP	SLG	G	GS	Innings	PO	A	E	DP	Fld Pct	Rng Fctr	In Zone	Outs	Zone Rtg	MLB Zone
As c	.292	308	90	14	5	3	31	22	40	.344	.399	84	80	707.2	479	45	6	7	.989	---	---	---	---	---

Career (1989-1993)	Avg	AB	H	2B	3B	HR	RBI	BB	SO	OBP	SLG		Avg	AB	H	2B	3B	HR	RBI	BB	SO	OBP	SLG
vs. Left	.293	441	129	28	4	2	38	26	45	.329	.388	Scoring Posn	.271	273	74	14	2	1	88	34	49	.346	.348
vs. Right	.256	762	195	25	4	4	63	51	116	.309	.315	Close & Late	.274	212	58	6	2	0	12	10	35	.309	.321
Groundball	.278	439	122	18	6	1	38	18	61	.315	.353	None on/out	.260	288	75	13	1	2	2	9	34	.290	.333
Flyball	.240	288	69	16	2	1	19	17	55	.281	.319	Batting #7	.245	318	78	6	3	1	29	19	44	.289	.292
Home	.287	588	169	23	5	4	65	42	81	.336	.364	Batting #8	.268	624	167	37	2	2	54	38	79	.313	.343
Away	.252	615	155	30	3	2	36	35	80	.297	.320	Other	.303	261	79	10	3	3	18	20	38	.358	.398
Day	.274	581	159	28	4	3	55	35	72	.316	.351	April	.269	216	58	8	1	0	13	5	31	.292	.315
Night	.265	622	165	25	4	3	46	42	89	.317	.333	May	.265	238	63	9	2	2	26	23	28	.330	.345
Grass	.275	837	230	32	6	6	82	61	108	.327	.349	June	.272	147	40	6	1	2	11	4	23	.296	.367
Turf	.257	366	94	21	2	0	19	16	53	.292	.325	July	.298	124	37	6	0	0	11	6	7	.323	.347
First Pitch	.282	280	79	18	1	4	31	8	0	.301	.396	August	.247	255	63	12	3	1	21	19	33	.299	.329
Ahead in Count	.306	242	74	12	3	0	13	35	0	.392	.380	September/October	.283	223	63	12	1	1	19	20	39	.352	.359
Behind in Count	.235	510	120	16	1	1	42	0	153	.246	.276	Pre-All Star	.268	637	171	26	4	4	52	35	83	.310	.341
Two Strikes	.185	432	80	9	0	1	31	24	161	.235	.213	Post-All Star	.270	566	153	27	4	2	49	42	78	.324	.343

Batter vs. Pitcher (career)																							
Hits Best Against	Avg	AB	H	2B	3B	HR	RBI	BB	SO	OBP	SLG	Hits Worst Against	Avg	AB	H	2B	3B	HR	RBI	BB	SO	OBP	SLG
Bruce Ruffin	.500	12	6	2	0	1	4	1	2	.538	.917	Bob Tewksbury	.063	16	1	0	0	0	0	0	1	.063	.063
Mark Portugal	.458	24	11	3	0	0	5	0	1	.458	.583	Dwight Gooden	.067	15	1	0	0	0	1	2	2	.176	.067
Jose Rijo	.455	11	5	1	0	1	2	1	1	.500	.818	Bud Black	.154	13	2	0	0	0	2	1	1	.214	.154
Trevor Wilson	.357	14	5	1	0	0	0	1	1	.400	.429	Frank Viola	.188	16	3	0	0	0	2	0	2	.188	.188
Orel Hershiser	.333	15	5	1	0	0	0	1	1	.375	.400	Ramon Martinez	.200	15	3	0	0	0	1	0	3	.200	.200

Dan Gladden — Tigers

Age 36 – Bats Right

	Avg	G	AB	R	H	2B	3B	HR	RBI	BB	SO	HBP	GDP	SB	CS	OBP	SLG	IBB	SH	SF	#Pit	#P/PA	GB	FB	G/F
1993 Season	.267	91	356	52	95	16	2	13	56	21	50	3	14	8	5	.312	.433	0	4	2	1376	3.56	136	112	1.21
Last Five Years	.268	587	2229	307	598	100	21	39	236	136	294	21	60	75	32	.314	.384	6	20	22	8556	3.52	796	707	1.13

1993 Season	Avg	AB	H	2B	3B	HR	RBI	BB	SO	OBP	SLG		Avg	AB	H	2B	3B	HR	RBI	BB	SO	OBP	SLG
vs. Left	.261	138	36	6	0	8	20	8	13	.304	.478	Scoring Posn	.282	103	29	1	0	6	43	3	13	.303	.466
vs. Right	.271	218	59	10	2	5	36	13	37	.316	.404	Close & Late	.258	31	8	0	0	2	8	2	4	.294	.452
Groundball	.261	69	18	1	0	2	12	7	4	.321	.362	None on/out	.233	73	17	5	1	2	2	7	12	.300	.411
Flyball	.254	63	16	5	0	2	7	6	13	.319	.429	Batting #2	.279	201	56	13	0	9	35	9	28	.315	.478
Home	.251	167	42	8	0	11	35	12	21	.302	.497	Batting #9	.284	67	19	2	1	1	12	5	9	.333	.388
Away	.280	189	53	8	2	2	21	9	29	.320	.376	Other	.227	88	20	1	1	3	9	7	13	.289	.364
Day	.277	130	36	3	2	5	21	10	12	.333	.446	April	.313	16	5	2	1	0	3	0	0	.278	.563

1993 Season

	Avg	AB	H	2B	3B	HR	RBI	BB	SO	OBP	SLG
Night	.261	226	59	13	0	8	35	11	38	.298	.425
Grass	.269	308	83	14	2	11	50	21	41	.316	.435
Turf	.250	48	12	2	0	2	6	0	9	.280	.417
First Pitch	.362	47	17	6	0	0	4	0	0	.362	.489
Ahead in Count	.290	69	20	1	0	5	21	16	0	.419	.522
Behind in Count	.211	166	35	3	2	7	22	0	46	.225	.380
Two Strikes	.193	145	28	1	1	3	10	5	50	.235	.276

	Avg	AB	H	2B	3B	HR	RBI	BB	SO	OBP	SLG
May	.000	0	0	0	0	0	0	0	0	.000	.000
June	.256	78	20	3	0	3	8	6	11	.310	.410
July	.271	70	19	5	0	2	9	2	6	.301	.429
August	.278	108	30	4	1	6	25	10	18	.339	.500
September/October	.250	84	21	2	0	2	11	3	15	.292	.345
Pre-All Star	.268	142	38	9	1	5	20	6	16	.298	.451
Post-All Star	.266	214	57	7	1	8	36	15	34	.320	.421

1993 By Position

Position	Avg	AB	H	2B	3B	HR	RBI	BB	SO	OBP	SLG	G	GS	Innings	PO	A	E	DP	Fld Pct	Rng Fctr	In Zone	Outs	Zone Rtg	MLB Zone
As lf	.273	278	76	13	2	11	51	14	39	.311	.453	69	67	592.1	149	8	3	1	.981	2.39	174	145	.833	.818
As cf	.227	66	15	3	0	2	5	6	9	.301	.364	18	17	149.2	47	1	0	0	1.000	2.89	55	47	.855	.829

Last Five Years

	Avg	AB	H	2B	3B	HR	RBI	BB	SO	OBP	SLG
vs. Left	.276	700	193	35	6	18	84	50	76	.325	.420
vs. Right	.265	1529	405	65	15	21	152	86	218	.308	.368
Groundball	.305	609	186	31	10	9	70	43	65	.352	.433
Flyball	.241	468	113	22	3	9	45	28	74	.283	.359
Home	.269	1073	289	51	12	20	118	78	125	.322	.395
Away	.267	1156	309	49	9	19	118	58	169	.305	.375
Day	.262	646	169	25	4	12	59	47	85	.317	.368
Night	.271	1583	429	75	17	27	177	89	209	.312	.391
Grass	.256	1221	312	53	7	25	132	74	172	.299	.372
Turf	.284	1008	286	47	14	14	104	62	122	.331	.400
First Pitch	.337	368	124	27	2	3	42	3	0	.344	.446
Ahead in Count	.328	534	175	26	9	16	76	82	0	.417	.500
Behind in Count	.189	931	176	22	9	14	74	0	255	.199	.277
Two Strikes	.189	899	170	24	5	11	55	47	294	.237	.264

	Avg	AB	H	2B	3B	HR	RBI	BB	SO	OBP	SLG
Scoring Posn	.257	548	141	19	5	14	192	31	74	.291	.387
Close & Late	.263	297	78	15	1	6	44	28	39	.326	.380
None on/out	.266	707	188	33	6	13	13	45	88	.320	.385
Batting #1	.266	1235	329	53	14	16	118	73	148	.312	.371
Batting #2	.293	549	161	30	2	16	72	28	73	.331	.443
Other	.243	445	108	17	5	7	46	35	73	.297	.351
April	.245	314	77	16	2	5	33	19	22	.295	.357
May	.298	342	102	19	4	7	38	17	49	.333	.439
June	.298	393	117	15	3	6	32	32	49	.354	.397
July	.262	271	71	15	1	3	33	17	36	.307	.358
August	.255	470	120	17	6	13	69	29	65	.301	.400
September/October	.253	439	111	18	5	5	31	22	73	.291	.351
Pre-All Star	.280	1141	319	55	9	20	115	70	133	.325	.396
Post-All Star	.256	1088	279	45	12	19	121	66	161	.301	.372

Batter vs. Pitcher (since 1984)

Hits Best Against	Avg	AB	H	2B	3B	HR	RBI	BB	SO	OBP	SLG
Jaime Navarro	.563	16	9	2	0	0	2	0	1	.563	.688
Ted Power	.545	11	6	2	0	1	5	3	0	.643	1.000
Donn Pall	.500	12	6	2	0	0	2	0	0	.500	.667
John Farrell	.480	25	12	5	0	1	5	1	1	.481	.800
Dennis Cook	.364	11	4	2	0	1	1	2	3	.462	.818

Hits Worst Against	Avg	AB	H	2B	3B	HR	RBI	BB	SO	OBP	SLG
Arthur Rhodes	.000	11	0	0	0	0	0	0	0	.000	.000
Lee Guetterman	.071	14	1	0	0	0	0	0	2	.071	.071
Juan Guzman	.071	14	1	0	0	0	0	0	5	.071	.071
Tom Henke	.100	10	1	0	0	0	1	1	3	.182	.100
Jeff Russell	.129	31	4	0	0	0	2	0	8	.125	.129

Tom Glavine — Braves

Age 28 – Pitches Left

	ERA	W	L	Sv	G	GS	IP	BB	SO	Avg	H	2B	3B	HR	RBI	OBP	SLG	CG	ShO	Sup	QS	#P/S	SB	CS	GB	FB	G/F
1993 Season	3.20	22	6	0	36	36	239.1	90	120	.259	236	50	4	16	77	.327	.376	4	2	5.72	28	99	9	5	338	295	1.15
Last Five Years	3.26	86	45	0	165	165	1111.1	347	660	.248	1038	192	21	77	384	.305	.359	27	12	5.05	108	100	74	45	1619	1178	1.37

1993 Season

	ERA	W	L	Sv	G	GS	IP	H	HR	BB	SO
Home	3.18	13	3	0	20	20	135.2	136	9	51	63
Away	3.21	9	3	0	16	16	103.2	100	7	39	57
Day	4.06	5	1	0	8	8	51.0	56	6	20	28
Night	2.96	17	5	0	28	28	188.1	180	10	70	92
Grass	3.70	15	5	0	27	27	175.1	193	12	67	93
Turf	1.83	7	1	0	9	9	64.0	43	4	23	27
April	2.81	3	0	0	5	5	32.0	24	0	22	7
May	3.27	4	1	0	6	6	41.1	35	3	14	24
June	2.61	2	2	0	5	5	38.0	42	3	13	15
July	2.58	4	1	0	7	7	45.1	40	2	17	20
August	5.09	3	1	0	6	6	35.1	40	5	16	23
September/October	3.04	6	1	0	7	7	47.1	55	3	8	31
Starter	3.20	22	6	0	36	36	239.1	236	16	90	120
Reliever	0.00	0	0	0	0	0	0.0	0	0	0	0
0-3 Days Rest	3.32	2	1	0	3	3	21.2	17	2	5	16
4 Days Rest	3.65	16	4	0	26	26	170.0	174	12	64	76
5+ Days Rest	1.51	4	1	0	7	7	47.2	45	2	21	28
Pre-All Star	2.90	10	4	0	19	19	130.1	119	7	51	55
Post-All Star	3.55	12	2	0	17	17	109.0	117	9	39	65

	Avg	AB	H	2B	3B	HR	RBI	BB	SO	OBP	SLG
vs. Left	.275	167	46	10	0	1	14	20	28	.353	.353
vs. Right	.256	743	190	40	4	15	63	70	92	.321	.381
Inning 1-6	.268	766	205	45	4	13	69	81	97	.338	.388
Inning 7+	.215	144	31	5	0	3	8	9	23	.261	.313
None on	.273	523	143	26	3	11	11	43	70	.330	.398
Runners on	.240	387	93	24	1	5	66	47	50	.323	.346
Scoring Posn	.225	200	45	14	1	2	57	32	29	.329	.335
Close & Late	.209	91	19	2	0	2	5	8	13	.273	.297
None on/out	.282	238	67	12	1	8	8	17	29	.329	.441
vs. 1st Batr (relief)	.000	0	0	0	0	0	0	0	0	.000	.000
First Inning Pitched	.268	138	37	7	1	2	13	13	20	.331	.377
First 75 Pitches	.268	663	178	40	3	11	56	67	83	.337	.388
Pitch 76-90	.259	116	30	6	1	3	15	15	13	.344	.405
Pitch 91-105	.177	96	17	3	0	1	2	7	17	.233	.240
Pitch 106+	.314	35	11	1	0	1	4	1	7	.333	.429
First Pitch	.287	164	47	16	0	6	18	4	0	.304	.494
Ahead in Count	.193	347	67	12	2	3	20	0	104	.198	.265
Behind in Count	.315	238	75	15	1	6	28	52	0	.435	.462
Two Strikes	.184	342	63	11	1	0	17	34	120	.262	.222

Last Five Years

	ERA	W	L	Sv	G	GS	IP	H	HR	BB	SO
Home	3.27	47	23	0	85	85	580.0	551	49	168	317
Away	3.24	39	22	0	80	80	531.1	487	28	179	343
Day	4.19	20	14	0	45	45	281.1	306	22	100	180
Night	2.94	66	31	0	120	120	830.0	732	55	247	480
Grass	3.36	62	31	0	118	118	793.2	780	63	233	464
Turf	3.00	24	14	0	47	47	317.2	258	14	114	196
April	2.70	12	5	0	23	23	160.0	137	8	44	86
May	2.77	17	5	0	28	28	192.0	161	14	54	120
June	3.44	14	9	0	28	28	198.2	195	16	58	120
July	2.91	15	5	0	27	27	185.2	167	14	57	106

	Avg	AB	H	2B	3B	HR	RBI	BB	SO	OBP	SLG
vs. Left	.258	775	200	33	4	8	68	86	157	.332	.342
vs. Right	.245	3415	838	159	17	69	316	261	503	.299	.363
Inning 1-6	.248	3460	858	160	19	60	328	309	560	.310	.357
Inning 7+	.247	730	180	32	2	17	56	38	100	.284	.366
None on	.243	2559	621	109	11	54	54	162	409	.289	.357
Runners on	.256	1631	417	83	10	23	330	185	251	.329	.361
Scoring Posn	.251	871	219	46	7	13	295	147	147	.354	.365
Close & Late	.252	404	102	20	2	5	32	25	55	.295	.349
None on/out	.245	1099	269	53	5	22	22	67	162	.291	.362
vs. 1st Batr (relief)	.000	0	0	0	0	0	0	0	0	.000	.000

Last Five Years	ERA	W	L	Sv	G	GS	IP	H	HR	BB	SO		Avg	AB	H	2B	3B	HR	RBI	BB	SO	OBP	SLG
August	4.24	12	13	0	31	31	189.0	200	14	69	113	First Inning Pitched	.284	638	181	34	8	9	87	67	110	.351	.404
September/October	3.39	16	8	0	28	28	186.0	178	11	65	115	First 75 Pitches	.246	3020	742	149	17	53	273	257	487	.305	.359
Starter	3.26	86	45	0	165	165	1111.1	1038	77	347	660	Pitch 76-90	.241	556	134	21	2	12	49	42	71	.293	.351
Reliever	0.00	0	0	0	0	0	0.0	0	0	0	0	Pitch 91-105	.256	407	104	14	1	7	43	30	71	.306	.346
0-3 Days Rest	3.66	4	5	0	12	12	78.2	73	5	18	49	Pitch 106+	.280	207	58	8	1	5	19	18	31	.338	.401
4 Days Rest	3.36	60	27	0	105	105	704.0	661	45	238	414	First Pitch	.281	670	188	48	0	11	60	21	0	.301	.401
5+ Days Rest	2.93	22	13	0	48	48	328.2	304	27	91	197	Ahead in Count	.191	1746	333	54	9	28	117	0	562	.194	.280
Pre-All Star	2.89	48	21	0	88	88	614.1	549	41	168	360	Behind in Count	.324	990	321	62	6	27	132	189	0	.430	.481
Post-All Star	3.71	38	24	0	77	77	497.0	489	36	179	300	Two Strikes	.174	1749	304	46	11	21	115	137	660	.237	.249

Pitcher vs. Batter (career)

Pitches Best Vs.	Avg	AB	H	2B	3B	HR	RBI	BB	SO	OBP	SLG	Pitches Worst Vs.	Avg	AB	H	2B	3B	HR	RBI	BB	SO	OBP	SLG
Stan Javier	.000	12	0	0	0	0	0	3	2	.200	.000	Robby Thompson	.452	42	19	7	1	3	6	4	6	.500	.881
Tim Belcher	.000	11	0	0	0	0	0	0	5	.000	.000	Gregg Jefferies	.450	20	9	1	0	2	5	0	2	.450	.800
Paul O'Neill	.050	20	1	0	0	0	0	0	7	.050	.050	Andujar Cedeno	.417	12	5	0	1	1	2	3	3	.533	.833
Mark Parent	.050	20	1	0	0	0	0	0	2	.050	.050	Kevin Mitchell	.353	34	12	3	0	3	8	4	6	.421	.706
Sammy Sosa	.091	11	1	0	0	0	1	0	2	.091	.091	Tim Wallach	.352	54	19	4	1	5	11	5	2	.407	.741

Jerry Goff — Pirates

Age 30 – Bats Left (flyball hitter)

	Avg	G	AB	R	H	2B	3B	HR	RBI	BB	SO	HBP	GDP	SB	CS	OBP	SLG	IBB	SH	SF	#Pit	#P/PA	GB	FB	G/F
1993 Season	.297	14	37	5	11	2	0	2	6	8	9	0	0	0	0	.422	.514	1	1	0	153	3.33	9	12	0.75
Career (1990-1993)	.239	69	159	19	38	3	0	5	13	29	48	0	0	0	2	.356	.352	5	2	0	715	3.76	39	42	0.93

1993 Season

	Avg	AB	H	2B	3B	HR	RBI	BB	SO	OBP	SLG		Avg	AB	H	2B	3B	HR	RBI	BB	SO	OBP	SLG
vs. Left	.333	3	1	0	0	0	1	0	2	.333	.333	Scoring Posn	.500	8	4	2	0	0	4	6	1	.714	.750
vs. Right	.294	34	10	2	0	2	5	8	7	.429	.529	Close & Late	.286	7	2	0	0	0	1	1	2	.375	.286

Greg Gohr — Tigers

Age 26 – Pitches Right (flyball pitcher)

	ERA	W	L	Sv	G	GS	IP	BB	SO	Avg	H	2B	3B	HR	RBI	OBP	SLG	GF	IR	IRS	Hld	SvOp	SB	CS	GB	FB	G/F
1993 Season	5.96	0	0	0	16	0	22.2	14	23	.289	26	4	2	1	15	.393	.411	9	10	3	1	1	1	0	23	25	0.92

1993 Season

	ERA	W	L	Sv	G	GS	IP	H	HR	BB	SO		Avg	AB	H	2B	3B	HR	RBI	BB	SO	OBP	SLG
Home	2.70	0	0	0	10	0	13.1	11	0	5	13	vs. Left	.324	37	12	1	2	0	5	6	11	.419	.459
Away	10.61	0	0	0	6	0	9.1	15	1	9	10	vs. Right	.264	53	14	3	0	1	10	8	12	.375	.377

Chris Gomez — Tigers

Age 23 – Bats Right (flyball hitter)

	Avg	G	AB	R	H	2B	3B	HR	RBI	BB	SO	HBP	GDP	SB	CS	OBP	SLG	IBB	SH	SF	#Pit	#P/PA	GB	FB	G/F
1993 Season	.250	46	128	11	32	7	1	0	11	9	17	1	2	2	2	.304	.320	0	3	0	479	3.40	40	41	0.98

1993 Season

	Avg	AB	H	2B	3B	HR	RBI	BB	SO	OBP	SLG		Avg	AB	H	2B	3B	HR	RBI	BB	SO	OBP	SLG
vs. Left	.154	52	8	1	1	0	3	4	5	.214	.212	Scoring Posn	.259	27	7	1	1	0	8	3	7	.355	.370
vs. Right	.316	76	24	6	0	0	8	5	12	.366	.395	Close & Late	.222	9	2	0	0	0	0	2	1	.364	.222
Home	.196	56	11	3	1	0	5	4	6	.262	.286	None on/out	.100	30	3	2	0	0	0	2	5	.156	.167
Away	.292	72	21	4	0	0	6	5	11	.338	.347	Batting #7	.250	4	1	0	1	0	2	0	1	.250	.750
First Pitch	.263	19	5	1	0	0	1	0	0	.263	.316	Batting #9	.248	121	30	7	0	0	9	9	15	.305	.306
Ahead in Count	.286	28	8	2	0	0	4	6	0	.429	.357	Other	.333	3	1	0	0	0	0	0	1	.333	.333
Behind in Count	.151	53	8	3	0	0	2	0	15	.151	.208	Pre-All Star	.000	0	0	0	0	0	0	0	0	.000	.000
Two Strikes	.222	45	10	2	1	0	4	3	17	.271	.311	Post-All Star	.250	128	32	7	1	0	11	9	17	.304	.320

Leo Gomez — Orioles

Age 27 – Bats Right (flyball hitter)

	Avg	G	AB	R	H	2B	3B	HR	RBI	BB	SO	HBP	GDP	SB	CS	OBP	SLG	IBB	SH	SF	#Pit	#P/PA	GB	FB	G/F
1993 Season	.197	71	244	30	48	7	0	10	25	32	60	3	2	0	1	.295	.348	1	3	2	1176	4.13	56	89	0.63
Career (1990-1993)	.238	338	1142	135	272	48	2	43	135	143	227	13	29	3	5	.325	.397	5	14	17	5358	4.03	286	455	0.63

1993 Season

	Avg	AB	H	2B	3B	HR	RBI	BB	SO	OBP	SLG		Avg	AB	H	2B	3B	HR	RBI	BB	SO	OBP	SLG
vs. Left	.224	67	15	3	0	2	6	7	16	.303	.358	Scoring Posn	.188	64	12	2	0	2	15	7	18	.270	.313
vs. Right	.186	177	33	4	0	8	19	25	44	.293	.345	Close & Late	.282	39	11	0	0	2	6	7	11	.404	.436
Home	.200	110	22	2	0	7	15	13	27	.296	.409	None on/out	.176	51	9	2	0	2	2	6	14	.263	.333
Away	.194	134	26	5	0	3	10	19	33	.295	.299	Batting #5	.234	64	15	0	0	5	8	8	15	.324	.469
First Pitch	.237	38	9	2	0	3	6	1	0	.256	.526	Batting #6	.194	93	18	5	0	3	11	13	28	.306	.344
Ahead in Count	.250	48	12	3	0	2	7	12	0	.403	.438	Other	.172	87	15	2	0	2	6	11	17	.263	.264
Behind in Count	.137	95	13	0	0	2	6	0	46	.144	.200	Pre-All Star	.201	239	48	7	0	10	25	32	59	.301	.356
Two Strikes	.118	127	15	1	0	1	4	19	60	.242	.150	Post-All Star	.000	5	0	0	0	0	0	0	1	.000	.000

Career (1990-1993)

	Avg	AB	H	2B	3B	HR	RBI	BB	SO	OBP	SLG		Avg	AB	H	2B	3B	HR	RBI	BB	SO	OBP	SLG
vs. Left	.234	303	71	14	0	12	39	44	54	.331	.399	Scoring Posn	.205	273	56	9	0	9	88	38	61	.293	.337
vs. Right	.240	839	201	34	2	31	96	99	173	.324	.396	Close & Late	.223	184	41	6	0	9	23	23	45	.310	.402
Groundball	.252	325	82	14	0	11	36	37	55	.334	.397	None on/out	.218	248	54	8	1	8	8	27	56	.302	.355
Flyball	.175	234	41	7	0	8	26	32	59	.275	.308	Batting #6	.234	209	49	12	0	10	30	32	49	.347	.435
Home	.238	559	133	24	2	20	63	71	101	.327	.395	Batting #7	.238	608	145	28	2	21	75	76	120	.323	.395

Career (1990-1993)

	Avg	AB	H	2B	3B	HR	RBI	BB	SO	OBP	SLG		Avg	AB	H	2B	3B	HR	RBI	BB	SO	OBP	SLG
Away	.238	583	139	24	0	23	72	72	126	.324	.398	Other	.240	325	78	8	0	12	30	35	58	.316	.375
Day	.238	315	75	12	0	13	38	31	65	.306	.400	April	.285	158	45	11	0	2	16	23	26	.377	.392
Night	.238	827	197	36	2	30	97	112	162	.333	.395	May	.258	178	46	6	0	10	23	20	46	.337	.461
Grass	.239	955	228	41	2	37	115	114	183	.322	.402	June	.213	230	49	7	1	6	24	37	43	.328	.330
Turf	.235	187	44	7	0	6	20	29	44	.344	.369	July	.211	199	42	12	0	8	30	22	39	.291	.392
First Pitch	.239	142	34	5	1	6	16	5	0	.281	.415	August	.225	169	38	5	1	12	25	22	35	.323	.479
Ahead in Count	.285	242	69	16	0	8	34	60	0	.423	.450	September/October	.250	208	52	7	0	5	17	19	38	.307	.356
Behind in Count	.198	491	97	15	1	16	45	0	177	.200	.330	Pre-All Star	.246	637	157	31	1	20	71	90	128	.344	.392
Two Strikes	.170	565	96	19	1	12	46	78	227	.271	.271	Post-All Star	.228	505	115	17	1	23	64	53	99	.302	.402

Batter vs. Pitcher (career)

Hits Best Against	Avg	AB	H	2B	3B	HR	RBI	BB	SO	OBP	SLG	Hits Worst Against	Avg	AB	H	2B	3B	HR	RBI	BB	SO	OBP	SLG
Erik Hanson	.500	14	7	0	0	1	2	5	5	.632	.714	Randy Johnson	.000	8	0	0	0	0	0	5	4	.385	.000
Hipolito Pichardo	.455	11	5	1	0	1	2	1	2	.500	.818	Charlie Hough	.083	12	1	0	0	0	0	3	0	.267	.083
Kevin Appier	.450	20	9	1	0	2	4	2	4	.500	.800	Mark Leiter	.091	11	1	0	0	0	0	1	6	.167	.091
Mike Gardiner	.400	10	4	1	0	1	2	3	3	.538	.800	Duane Ward	.111	9	1	0	0	0	1	2	2	.273	.111
Chuck Finley	.389	18	7	2	0	2	7	1	5	.381	.833	Charles Nagy	.154	13	2	0	0	0	0	0	3	.154	.154

Pat Gomez — Padres

Age 26 – Pitches Left (groundball pitcher)

	ERA	W	L	Sv	G	GS	IP	BB	SO	Avg	H	2B	3B	HR	RBI	OBP	SLG	GF	IR	IRS	Hld	SvOp	SB	CS	GB	FB	G/F
1993 Season	5.12	1	2	0	27	1	31.2	19	26	.294	35	6	1	2	19	.380	.412	6	21	8	1	0	0	3	48	26	1.85

1993 Season

	ERA	W	L	Sv	G	GS	IP	H	HR	BB	SO		Avg	AB	H	2B	3B	HR	RBI	BB	SO	OBP	SLG
Home	2.84	1	1	0	12	1	12.2	14	0	8	13	vs. Left	.268	41	11	1	0	0	5	0	8	.256	.293
Away	6.63	0	1	0	15	0	19.0	21	2	11	13	vs. Right	.308	78	24	5	1	2	14	19	18	.434	.474
Starter	9.00	0	1	0	1	1	3.0	6	0	3	1	Scoring Posn	.250	40	10	1	0	1	16	7	10	.333	.350
Reliever	4.71	1	1	0	26	0	28.2	29	2	16	25	Close & Late	.313	16	5	0	0	0	1	2	2	.368	.313
0 Days rest	1.42	0	0	0	3	0	6.1	4	0	5	6	None on/out	.269	26	7	3	0	0	0	2	5	.321	.385
1 or 2 Days rest	7.62	0	1	0	13	0	13.0	18	1	7	10	First Pitch	.429	14	6	0	0	0	2	2	0	.471	.429
3+ Days rest	2.89	1	0	0	10	0	9.1	7	1	4	9	Ahead in Count	.180	50	9	2	0	0	3	0	23	.176	.220
Pre-All Star	5.12	1	2	0	27	1	31.2	35	2	19	26	Behind in Count	.375	32	12	2	0	1	8	9	0	.488	.531
Post-All Star	0.00	0	0	0	0	0	0.0	0	0	0	0	Two Strikes	.182	55	10	4	1	0	5	8	26	.281	.291

Larry Gonzales — Angels

Age 27 – Bats Right

	Avg	G	AB	R	H	2B	3B	HR	RBI	BB	SO	HBP	GDP	SB	CS	OBP	SLG	IBB	SH	SF	#Pit	#P/PA	GB	FB	G/F
1993 Season	.500	2	2	0	1	0	0	0	1	1	0	0	0	0	0	.667	.500	0	0	0	14	4.67	1	0	0.00

1993 Season

	Avg	AB	H	2B	3B	HR	RBI	BB	SO	OBP	SLG		Avg	AB	H	2B	3B	HR	RBI	BB	SO	OBP	SLG
vs. Left	.500	2	1	0	0	0	1	1	0	.667	.500	Scoring Posn	1.000	1	1	0	0	0	1	0	0	1.000	1.000
vs. Right	.000	0	0	0	0	0	0	0	0	.000	.000	Close & Late	.000	0	0	0	0	0	0	0	0	.000	.000

Rene Gonzales — Angels

Age 32 – Bats Right (groundball hitter)

	Avg	G	AB	R	H	2B	3B	HR	RBI	BB	SO	HBP	GDP	SB	CS	OBP	SLG	IBB	SH	SF	#Pit	#P/PA	GB	FB	G/F
1993 Season	.251	117	335	34	84	17	0	2	31	49	45	1	12	5	5	.346	.319	2	2	2	1474	3.79	139	86	1.62
Last Five Years	.244	430	1051	126	256	44	2	12	98	126	157	9	43	18	14	.328	.324	3	25	5	4414	3.63	433	258	1.68

1993 Season

	Avg	AB	H	2B	3B	HR	RBI	BB	SO	OBP	SLG		Avg	AB	H	2B	3B	HR	RBI	BB	SO	OBP	SLG
vs. Left	.295	112	33	9	0	1	8	16	14	.388	.402	Scoring Posn	.304	79	24	2	0	1	29	18	14	.430	.367
vs. Right	.229	223	51	8	0	1	23	33	31	.326	.278	Close & Late	.217	46	10	1	0	1	6	10	7	.357	.304
Groundball	.262	61	16	2	0	0	3	7	7	.338	.295	None on/out	.253	83	21	5	0	0	0	10	10	.333	.313
Flyball	.259	81	21	7	0	1	9	10	10	.337	.383	Batting #6	.238	143	34	7	0	0	7	18	17	.327	.287
Home	.230	178	41	10	0	1	16	23	23	.320	.303	Batting #7	.233	73	17	5	0	0	10	14	12	.352	.301
Away	.274	157	43	7	0	1	15	26	22	.375	.338	Other	.277	119	33	5	0	2	14	17	16	.365	.370
Day	.263	99	26	5	0	1	13	16	12	.362	.343	April	.241	58	14	3	0	0	6	10	11	.357	.293
Night	.246	236	58	12	0	1	18	33	33	.339	.309	May	.282	71	20	2	0	1	10	15	9	.407	.352
Grass	.259	282	73	15	0	2	29	43	39	.357	.333	June	.167	36	6	2	0	0	0	5	5	.268	.222
Turf	.208	53	11	2	0	0	2	6	6	.288	.245	July	.316	57	18	4	0	0	5	4	6	.361	.386
First Pitch	.286	49	14	2	0	1	5	1	0	.300	.388	August	.289	38	11	4	0	0	3	5	4	.372	.395
Ahead in Count	.300	80	24	10	0	1	11	24	0	.462	.463	September/October	.200	75	15	2	0	1	7	10	10	.291	.267
Behind in Count	.189	148	28	3	0	0	9	0	41	.188	.209	Pre-All Star	.253	190	48	9	0	1	18	31	29	.359	.316
Two Strikes	.191	141	27	3	0	0	10	24	45	.311	.213	Post-All Star	.248	145	36	8	0	1	13	18	16	.329	.324

1993 By Position

Position	Avg	AB	H	2B	3B	HR	RBI	BB	SO	OBP	SLG	G	GS	Innings	PO	A	E	DP	Fld Pct	Rng Fctr	In Zone	Outs	Zone Rtg	MLB Zone
As 1b	.257	70	18	6	0	0	3	7	6	.325	.343	31	19	176.1	163	10	2	24	.989	---	30	25	.833	.834
As 3b	.243	247	60	8	0	2	26	37	34	.341	.300	79	73	646.2	64	154	10	21	.956	3.03	200	173	.865	.834

Last Five Years

	Avg	AB	H	2B	3B	HR	RBI	BB	SO	OBP	SLG		Avg	AB	H	2B	3B	HR	RBI	BB	SO	OBP	SLG
vs. Left	.247	287	71	14	1	4	30	46	45	.358	.345	Scoring Posn	.269	238	64	9	2	4	87	44	42	.381	.374
vs. Right	.242	764	185	30	1	8	68	80	112	.317	.315	Close & Late	.228	162	37	3	0	3	16	28	26	.346	.302
Groundball	.232	276	64	10	0	2	17	30	32	.307	.290	None on/out	.268	250	67	12	0	2	2	24	37	.337	.340
Flyball	.276	254	70	13	1	5	39	30	37	.357	.394	Batting #6	.262	302	79	16	1	2	21	43	43	.357	.341

Last Five Years

	Avg	AB	H	2B	3B	HR	RBI	BB	SO	OBP	SLG
Home	.248	508	126	27	0	9	51	64	69	.336	.354
Away	.239	543	130	17	2	3	47	62	88	.321	.295
Day	.226	340	77	19	1	4	39	43	50	.313	.324
Night	.252	711	179	25	1	8	59	83	107	.335	.323
Grass	.252	824	208	38	2	11	88	102	121	.335	.343
Turf	.211	227	48	6	0	1	10	24	36	.304	.251
First Pitch	.297	158	47	5	0	2	14	2	0	.306	.367
Ahead in Count	.265	230	61	19	1	5	29	62	0	.423	.422
Behind in Count	.201	477	96	14	0	2	33	0	137	.210	.243
Two Strikes	.185	449	83	10	1	3	30	62	157	.290	.232

	Avg	AB	H	2B	3B	HR	RBI	BB	SO	OBP	SLG
Batting #9	.205	297	61	8	1	2	22	28	51	.281	.259
Other	.257	452	116	20	0	8	55	55	63	.339	.354
April	.226	146	33	6	0	4	16	25	28	.339	.349
May	.271	236	64	7	1	4	34	31	32	.359	.360
June	.216	176	38	11	0	2	14	20	21	.303	.313
July	.284	197	56	9	0	1	13	22	26	.355	.345
August	.243	169	41	8	1	0	14	14	29	.308	.302
September/October	.189	127	24	3	0	1	7	14	21	.278	.236
Pre-All Star	.246	641	158	27	1	11	71	81	94	.334	.343
Post-All Star	.239	410	98	17	1	1	27	45	63	.319	.293

Batter vs. Pitcher (career)

Hits Best Against	Avg	AB	H	2B	3B	HR	RBI	BB	SO	OBP	SLG
Melido Perez	.583	12	7	1	0	0	2	2	3	.643	.667
Matt Young	.500	8	4	0	0	0	0	3	0	.636	.500
Randy Johnson	.467	15	7	1	0	1	2	5	2	.600	.733
Kevin Brown	.444	9	4	0	0	0	0	2	0	.545	.444
Dave Stieb	.385	13	5	1	0	1	4	0	1	.385	.692

Hits Worst Against	Avg	AB	H	2B	3B	HR	RBI	BB	SO	OBP	SLG
Frank Tanana	.063	16	1	0	0	0	0	2	4	.167	.063
Roger Clemens	.136	22	3	1	0	0	0	0	4	.136	.182
Mike Moore	.143	21	3	1	0	0	0	1	1	.182	.190
Bob Welch	.200	15	3	0	0	0	0	1	4	.250	.200
Jack Morris	.214	14	3	0	0	0	3	0	4	.214	.214

Juan Gonzalez — Rangers

Age 24 – Bats Right (flyball hitter)

	Avg	G	AB	R	H	2B	3B	HR	RBI	BB	SO	HBP	GDP	SB	CS	OBP	SLG	IBB	SH	SF	#Pit	#P/PA	GB	FB	G/F
1993 Season	.310	140	536	105	166	33	1	46	118	37	99	13	11	4	1	.368	.632	7	0	1	1981	3.37	170	164	1.04
Career (1989-1993)	.274	486	1815	277	497	101	5	121	348	122	395	25	43	8	7	.326	.535	15	2	13	7019	3.55	546	608	0.90

1993 Season

	Avg	AB	H	2B	3B	HR	RBI	BB	SO	OBP	SLG
vs. Left	.333	108	36	8	0	9	20	7	20	.374	.657
vs. Right	.304	428	130	25	1	37	98	30	79	.367	.626
Groundball	.346	104	36	10	0	7	24	5	19	.376	.644
Flyball	.306	108	33	4	1	13	32	8	15	.377	.722
Home	.330	273	90	17	0	24	58	19	54	.386	.656
Away	.289	263	76	16	1	22	60	18	45	.349	.608
Day	.282	117	33	7	1	8	27	9	24	.361	.564
Night	.317	419	133	26	0	38	91	28	75	.370	.652
Grass	.307	460	141	25	1	37	102	34	85	.366	.607
Turf	.329	76	25	8	0	9	16	3	14	.378	.789
First Pitch	.398	88	35	11	0	9	25	5	0	.436	.830
Ahead in Count	.357	129	46	10	0	14	42	17	0	.432	.760
Behind in Count	.252	234	59	9	1	17	37	0	82	.280	.517
Two Strikes	.213	216	46	5	0	14	31	15	99	.283	.431

	Avg	AB	H	2B	3B	HR	RBI	BB	SO	OBP	SLG
Scoring Posn	.308	159	49	9	0	16	76	17	33	.383	.667
Close & Late	.324	74	24	6	0	6	18	3	17	.359	.649
None on/out	.369	141	52	12	1	9	9	7	21	.426	.660
Batting #4	.308	535	165	33	1	46	117	37	99	.367	.632
Batting #9	1.000	1	1	0	0	0	1	0	0	1.000	1.000
Other	.000	0	0	0	0	0	0	0	0	.000	.000
April	.321	78	25	4	0	7	12	6	17	.391	.641
May	.348	66	23	7	0	7	17	7	8	.434	.773
June	.313	96	30	6	0	6	22	6	15	.353	.563
July	.349	106	37	6	1	10	29	9	17	.402	.708
August	.252	111	28	3	0	10	22	5	24	.314	.550
September/October	.291	79	23	7	0	6	16	4	18	.333	.608
Pre-All Star	.320	284	91	19	1	23	60	24	46	.386	.637
Post-All Star	.298	252	75	14	0	23	58	13	53	.347	.627

1993 By Position

Position	Avg	AB	H	2B	3B	HR	RBI	BB	SO	OBP	SLG	G	GS	Innings	PO	A	E	DP	Fld Pct	Rng Fctr	In Zone	Outs	Zone Rtg	MLB Zone
As Designated Hitter	.220	41	9	2	0	2	5	2	9	.256	.415	10	10	---	---	---	---	---	---	---	---	---	---	---
As lf	.316	494	156	31	1	44	112	35	90	.376	.650	129	129	1100.0	265	5	4	0	.985	2.21	302	245	.811	.818

Career (1989-1993)

	Avg	AB	H	2B	3B	HR	RBI	BB	SO	OBP	SLG
vs. Left	.282	461	130	24	0	27	80	38	104	.334	.510
vs. Right	.271	1354	367	77	5	94	268	84	291	.323	.544
Groundball	.317	448	142	29	0	31	92	25	92	.355	.589
Flyball	.253	427	108	21	2	35	105	28	100	.308	.557
Home	.284	913	259	55	3	54	161	57	218	.334	.528
Away	.264	902	238	46	2	67	187	65	177	.318	.542
Day	.282	323	91	19	2	21	73	22	69	.345	.548
Night	.272	1492	406	82	3	100	275	100	326	.322	.532
Grass	.275	1515	417	79	4	100	288	104	333	.327	.531
Turf	.267	300	80	22	1	21	60	18	62	.319	.557
First Pitch	.359	209	75	17	0	20	49	12	0	.412	.727
Ahead in Count	.357	412	147	34	1	41	117	61	0	.440	.743
Behind in Count	.222	873	194	34	3	36	123	0	331	.229	.392
Two Strikes	.186	833	155	27	3	31	96	49	395	.235	.337

	Avg	AB	H	2B	3B	HR	RBI	BB	SO	OBP	SLG
Scoring Posn	.272	544	148	24	1	33	223	53	129	.336	.502
Close & Late	.259	286	74	17	0	20	52	21	72	.320	.528
None on/out	.277	411	114	28	2	21	21	19	79	.325	.509
Batting #4	.284	835	237	46	1	66	164	56	176	.341	.578
Batting #5	.276	453	125	25	1	28	91	24	102	.314	.521
Other	.256	527	135	30	3	27	93	42	117	.313	.478
April	.302	182	55	9	0	12	32	12	38	.352	.549
May	.304	273	83	23	1	15	55	25	49	.368	.560
June	.286	294	84	11	1	21	63	29	66	.347	.544
July	.282	291	82	15	1	25	70	17	68	.326	.598
August	.270	344	93	16	1	31	71	19	78	.319	.593
September/October	.232	431	100	27	1	17	57	20	96	.278	.418
Pre-All Star	.295	854	252	49	3	54	171	74	173	.355	.549
Post-All Star	.255	961	245	52	2	67	177	48	222	.299	.522

Batter vs. Pitcher (career)

Hits Best Against	Avg	AB	H	2B	3B	HR	RBI	BB	SO	OBP	SLG
Matt Young	.500	12	6	3	0	1	1	0	3	.500	1.000
Mark Gubicza	.462	13	6	2	0	1	5	0	2	.462	.846
Ron Darling	.429	14	6	1	0	2	5	2	3	.500	.929
David Wells	.385	13	5	0	0	2	6	2	1	.467	.846
Charlie Hough	.333	12	4	1	0	2	4	1	2	.385	.917

Hits Worst Against	Avg	AB	H	2B	3B	HR	RBI	BB	SO	OBP	SLG
Arthur Rhodes	.000	12	0	0	0	0	1	0	6	.000	.000
Chris Bosio	.053	19	1	0	0	0	0	1	7	.100	.053
Greg Harris	.077	13	1	0	0	0	1	1	3	.143	.077
Danny Darwin	.077	13	1	0	0	0	0	1	2	.143	.077
Rich Monteleone	.077	13	1	1	0	0	0	0	3	.077	.154

Luis Gonzalez — Astros

Age 26 – Bats Left

	Avg	G	AB	R	H	2B	3B	HR	RBI	BB	SO	HBP	GDP	SB	CS	OBP	SLG	IBB	SH	SF	#Pit	#P/PA	GB	FB	G/F
1993 Season	.300	154	540	82	162	34	3	15	72	47	83	10	9	20	9	.361	.457	7	3	10	2098	3.44	179	170	1.05
Career (1990-1993)	.267	425	1421	174	380	83	15	38	196	113	241	20	24	37	23	.327	.427	15	5	16	5504	3.49	461	450	1.02

1993 Season

	Avg	AB	H	2B	3B	HR	RBI	BB	SO	OBP	SLG
vs. Left	.302	172	52	10	0	3	21	13	28	.369	.413
vs. Right	.299	368	110	24	3	12	51	34	55	.357	.478
Groundball	.349	186	65	16	1	6	26	13	23	.403	.543
Flyball	.267	86	23	5	0	1	14	8	16	.354	.360
Home	.291	265	77	15	1	8	40	19	43	.341	.445
Away	.309	275	85	19	2	7	32	28	40	.379	.469
Day	.298	168	50	16	3	6	23	16	26	.360	.536
Night	.301	372	112	18	0	9	49	31	57	.361	.422
Grass	.315	178	56	14	2	6	24	17	27	.378	.517
Turf	.293	362	106	20	1	9	48	30	56	.352	.428
First Pitch	.350	100	35	4	1	7	27	6	0	.384	.620
Ahead in Count	.426	122	52	10	1	3	17	24	0	.517	.598
Behind in Count	.219	219	48	12	1	2	23	0	69	.237	.311
Two Strikes	.199	226	45	9	1	3	19	17	83	.268	.288

	Avg	AB	H	2B	3B	HR	RBI	BB	SO	OBP	SLG
Scoring Posn	.265	147	39	8	1	4	55	22	25	.348	.415
Close & Late	.310	84	26	6	0	1	9	5	15	.356	.417
None on/out	.373	110	41	6	2	3	3	7	15	.420	.545
Batting #2	.274	117	32	6	1	3	13	13	13	.361	.419
Batting #6	.305	223	68	16	2	8	36	12	37	.350	.502
Other	.310	200	62	12	0	4	23	22	33	.372	.430
April	.315	73	23	4	0	4	13	4	6	.381	.534
May	.200	90	18	3	1	3	9	9	12	.282	.356
June	.286	70	20	3	0	1	7	8	11	.359	.371
July	.368	95	35	8	1	4	16	11	11	.431	.600
August	.310	100	31	8	1	0	9	6	24	.346	.410
September/October	.313	112	35	8	0	3	18	9	19	.365	.464
Pre-All Star	.272	268	73	13	2	11	38	27	34	.352	.459
Post-All Star	.327	272	89	21	1	4	34	20	49	.370	.456

1993 By Position

Position	Avg	AB	H	2B	3B	HR	RBI	BB	SO	OBP	SLG	G	GS	Innings	PO	A	E	DP	Fld Pct	Rng Fctr	In Zone	Outs	Zone Rtg	MLB Zone
As Pinch Hitter	.500	6	3	0	0	0	1	2	0	.625	.500	10	0	---	---	---	---	---	---	---	---	---	---	---
As lf	.298	534	159	34	3	15	71	45	83	.357	.457	149	142	1247.2	346	10	8	2	.978	2.58	383	316	.825	.818

Career (1990-1993)

	Avg	AB	H	2B	3B	HR	RBI	BB	SO	OBP	SLG
vs. Left	.269	375	101	23	3	5	47	32	70	.340	.387
vs. Right	.267	1046	279	60	12	33	149	81	171	.322	.442
Groundball	.278	486	135	27	5	15	68	30	66	.326	.447
Flyball	.278	288	80	18	4	12	49	29	59	.359	.493
Home	.260	703	183	41	8	16	97	55	121	.317	.410
Away	.274	718	197	42	7	22	99	58	120	.336	.444
Day	.264	398	105	27	5	13	49	35	63	.327	.455
Night	.269	1023	275	56	10	25	147	78	178	.327	.416
Grass	.280	461	129	25	5	15	68	34	77	.335	.453
Turf	.261	960	251	58	10	23	128	79	164	.323	.415
First Pitch	.328	256	84	12	3	14	52	11	0	.362	.563
Ahead in Count	.353	329	116	22	4	9	51	49	0	.436	.526
Behind in Count	.202	590	119	31	5	9	64	0	202	.213	.317
Two Strikes	.187	588	110	25	5	10	57	51	241	.260	.298

	Avg	AB	H	2B	3B	HR	RBI	BB	SO	OBP	SLG
Scoring Posn	.262	393	103	21	3	11	150	51	81	.342	.415
Close & Late	.300	237	71	14	2	4	33	19	43	.360	.426
None on/out	.297	286	85	16	4	11	11	19	42	.347	.497
Batting #4	.225	396	89	22	3	13	54	29	86	.283	.394
Batting #6	.289	401	116	24	6	12	61	27	62	.341	.469
Other	.280	624	175	37	6	13	81	57	93	.345	.421
April	.207	184	38	9	1	5	20	12	36	.277	.348
May	.236	229	54	13	4	9	34	15	37	.284	.445
June	.272	224	61	14	1	7	31	24	33	.348	.438
July	.309	217	67	13	4	7	34	25	34	.383	.502
August	.301	259	78	13	4	4	33	14	51	.342	.429
September/October	.266	308	82	21	1	6	44	23	50	.320	.399
Pre-All Star	.248	722	179	41	9	25	102	68	118	.320	.434
Post-All Star	.288	699	201	42	6	13	94	45	123	.334	.421

Batter vs. Pitcher (career)

Hits Best Against	Avg	AB	H	2B	3B	HR	RBI	BB	SO	OBP	SLG
Mike Harkey	.583	12	7	1	1	2	6	0	2	.583	1.333
Dwight Gooden	.500	16	8	4	0	1	3	1	2	.529	.938
Pete Schourek	.500	14	7	2	0	0	4	1	1	.533	.643
Mike Bielecki	.500	10	5	0	1	0	2	1	1	.545	.700
Jose DeLeon	.333	12	4	0	0	2	3	0	2	.333	.833

Hits Worst Against	Avg	AB	H	2B	3B	HR	RBI	BB	SO	OBP	SLG
Mike Stanton	.000	8	0	0	0	0	1	3	3	.250	.000
Ken Hill	.083	24	2	0	1	0	3	1	5	.120	.167
Bryn Smith	.083	12	1	0	0	0	1	0	3	.083	.083
Pedro Astacio	.091	11	1	0	0	0	0	1	4	.167	.091
Randy Tomlin	.143	14	2	0	0	0	1	0	2	.143	.143

Dwight Gooden — Mets

Age 29 – Pitches Right (groundball pitcher)

	ERA	W	L	Sv	G	GS	IP	BB	SO	Avg	H	2B	3B	HR	RBI	OBP	SLG	CG	ShO	Sup	QS	#P/S	SB	CS	GB	FB	G/F
1993 Season	3.45	12	15	0	29	29	208.2	61	149	.242	188	34	4	16	81	.302	.357	7	2	4.57	18	106	26	10	292	167	1.75
Last Five Years	3.55	63	46	1	140	138	955.2	304	768	.248	892	159	25	58	372	.308	.354	15	4	4.99	89	106	173	59	1388	772	1.80

1993 Season

	ERA	W	L	Sv	G	GS	IP	H	HR	BB	SO
Home	2.78	8	10	0	19	19	139.0	117	12	38	94
Away	4.78	4	5	0	10	10	69.2	71	4	23	55
Day	2.54	6	5	0	11	11	85.0	65	3	35	52
Night	4.08	6	10	0	18	18	123.2	123	13	26	97
Grass	3.11	11	13	0	25	25	185.0	161	13	55	131
Turf	6.08	1	2	0	4	4	23.2	27	3	6	18
April	2.68	2	3	0	5	5	37.0	25	2	14	14
May	2.72	3	1	0	6	6	49.2	44	3	15	29
June	3.86	2	3	0	5	5	35.0	35	2	12	27
July	3.72	3	3	0	6	6	46.0	46	3	11	41
August	4.39	2	5	0	7	7	41.0	38	6	9	38
September/October	0.00	0	0	0	0	0	0.0	0	0	0	0
Starter	3.45	12	15	0	29	29	208.2	188	16	61	149
Reliever	0.00	0	0	0	0	0	0.0	0	0	0	0
0-3 Days Rest	1.13	1	0	0	1	1	8.0	4	1	1	9
4 Days Rest	4.32	8	11	0	20	20	141.2	145	12	39	103
5+ Days Rest	1.68	3	4	0	8	8	59.0	39	3	21	37
Pre-All Star	3.34	8	9	0	19	19	145.2	131	8	43	91
Post-All Star	3.71	4	6	0	10	10	63.0	57	8	18	58

	Avg	AB	H	2B	3B	HR	RBI	BB	SO	OBP	SLG
vs. Left	.247	396	98	18	1	9	37	34	70	.307	.366
vs. Right	.236	382	90	16	3	7	44	27	79	.296	.348
Inning 1-6	.251	626	157	27	4	14	73	49	121	.309	.374
Inning 7+	.204	152	31	7	0	2	8	12	28	.271	.289
None on	.237	468	111	20	2	12	12	33	93	.293	.365
Runners on	.248	310	77	14	2	4	69	28	56	.314	.345
Scoring Posn	.217	203	44	9	1	3	64	19	41	.291	.315
Close & Late	.200	85	17	4	0	2	5	10	16	.292	.318
None on/out	.251	199	50	12	1	3	3	16	38	.310	.367
vs. 1st Batr (relief)	.000	0	0	0	0	0	0	0	0	.000	.000
First Inning Pitched	.322	118	38	7	0	0	22	12	17	.385	.381
First 75 Pitches	.258	532	137	24	3	12	61	38	101	.310	.382
Pitch 76-90	.205	88	18	3	0	2	8	11	17	.304	.307
Pitch 91-105	.259	81	21	4	1	1	8	7	15	.326	.370
Pitch 106+	.156	77	12	3	0	1	4	5	16	.217	.234
First Pitch	.296	125	37	6	1	6	19	0	0	.297	.504
Ahead in Count	.163	349	57	10	3	2	22	0	118	.182	.226
Behind in Count	.335	170	57	13	0	8	28	32	0	.438	.553
Two Strikes	.131	336	44	8	2	2	18	29	149	.214	.185

Last Five Years

	ERA	W	L	Sv	G	GS	IP	H	HR	BB	SO
Home	3.33	39	22	0	76	76	534.2	473	35	165	426
Away	3.83	24	24	1	64	62	421.0	419	23	139	342
Day	3.60	21	19	1	50	49	340.1	311	19	120	266
Night	3.52	42	27	0	90	89	615.1	581	39	184	502
Grass	3.38	54	31	1	105	104	736.0	666	45	237	574
Turf	4.14	9	15	0	35	34	219.2	226	13	67	194
April	2.84	12	7	0	24	24	167.2	121	8	60	135
May	3.62	11	12	0	29	29	204.0	205	12	69	159
June	4.41	12	9	0	28	28	189.2	191	13	64	140
July	3.09	12	6	0	20	20	140.0	129	8	40	123
August	4.27	9	9	0	23	23	141.1	142	12	45	121
September/October	2.71	7	3	1	16	14	113.0	104	5	26	90
Starter	3.57	63	46	0	138	138	948.2	887	58	302	762
Reliever	1.29	0	0	1	2	0	7.0	5	0	2	6
0-3 Days Rest	5.11	1	1	0	2	2	12.1	13	2	3	14
4 Days Rest	3.64	45	26	0	94	94	652.1	622	38	202	516
5+ Days Rest	3.33	17	19	0	42	42	284.0	252	18	97	232
Pre-All Star	3.70	39	32	0	89	89	617.1	569	38	203	484
Post-All Star	3.27	24	14	1	51	49	338.1	323	20	101	284

	Avg	AB	H	2B	3B	HR	RBI	BB	SO	OBP	SLG
vs. Left	.248	2010	499	93	9	31	192	197	395	.315	.350
vs. Right	.247	1591	393	66	16	27	180	107	373	.300	.360
Inning 1-6	.251	2987	749	141	21	48	325	255	641	.312	.360
Inning 7+	.233	614	143	18	4	10	47	49	127	.291	.324
None on	.247	2072	512	97	14	34	34	183	440	.312	.357
Runners on	.249	1529	380	62	11	24	338	121	328	.303	.351
Scoring Posn	.237	964	228	37	6	13	299	92	228	.302	.328
Close & Late	.214	336	72	7	0	7	29	27	72	.272	.298
None on/out	.267	918	245	54	4	14	14	75	182	.326	.380
vs. 1st Batr (relief)	.500	2	1	0	0	0	0	0	0	.500	.500
First Inning Pitched	.259	528	137	29	4	5	65	52	106	.326	.358
First 75 Pitches	.254	2499	635	122	20	40	260	200	526	.312	.367
Pitch 76-90	.253	451	114	18	1	9	47	44	94	.321	.357
Pitch 91-105	.218	381	83	13	3	5	38	32	81	.278	.307
Pitch 106+	.222	270	60	6	1	4	27	28	67	.298	.296
First Pitch	.297	569	169	26	6	16	80	12	0	.314	.448
Ahead in Count	.188	1668	313	57	14	13	118	0	646	.195	.262
Behind in Count	.337	739	249	47	5	23	113	130	0	.435	.507
Two Strikes	.164	1689	277	56	10	12	117	162	768	.241	.230

Pitcher vs. Batter (career)

Pitches Best Vs.	Avg	AB	H	2B	3B	HR	RBI	BB	SO	OBP	SLG
Eric Karros	.000	11	0	0	0	0	0	0	2	.000	.000
Chico Walker	.063	16	1	0	0	0	0	1	1	.118	.063
Gary Redus	.067	15	1	1	0	0	1	1	5	.118	.133
Joe Girardi	.067	15	1	0	0	0	1	2	2	.176	.067
Jose Oquendo	.077	26	2	0	0	0	0	1	3	.111	.077

Pitches Worst Vs.	Avg	AB	H	2B	3B	HR	RBI	BB	SO	OBP	SLG
Luis Gonzalez	.500	16	8	4	0	1	3	1	2	.529	.938
Randy Ready	.500	12	6	1	1	0	0	1	2	.538	.750
Ray Lankford	.440	25	11	2	0	2	7	5	4	.533	.760
Reggie Sanders	.375	8	3	0	0	1	3	2	3	.455	.750
Orestes Destrade	.333	9	3	2	0	1	4	2	3	.455	.889

Tom Goodwin — Dodgers

Age 25 – Bats Left (groundball hitter)

	Avg	G	AB	R	H	2B	3B	HR	RBI	BB	SO	HBP	GDP	SB	CS	OBP	SLG	IBB	SH	SF	#Pit	#P/PA	GB	FB	G/F
1993 Season	.294	30	17	6	5	1	0	0	1	1	4	0	1	1	2	.333	.353	0	0	0	64	3.56	9	2	4.50
Career (1991-1993)	.237	103	97	24	23	2	1	0	4	7	14	0	1	9	6	.288	.278	0	0	0	367	3.53	36	23	1.57

1993 Season

	Avg	AB	H	2B	3B	HR	RBI	BB	SO	OBP	SLG
vs. Left	.000	1	0	0	0	0	0	0	0	.000	.000
vs. Right	.313	16	5	1	0	0	1	1	4	.353	.375
Scoring Posn	.400	5	2	0	0	0	1	0	2	.400	.400
Close & Late	.600	5	3	0	0	0	1	0	2	.600	.600

Keith Gordon — Reds

Age 25 – Bats Right

	Avg	G	AB	R	H	2B	3B	HR	RBI	BB	SO	HBP	GDP	SB	CS	OBP	SLG	IBB	SH	SF	#Pit	#P/PA	GB	FB	G/F
1993 Season	.167	3	6	0	1	0	0	0	0	0	2	0	0	0	0	.167	.167	0	0	0	16	2.67	1	1	1.00

1993 Season

	Avg	AB	H	2B	3B	HR	RBI	BB	SO	OBP	SLG
vs. Left	.000	1	0	0	0	0	0	0	0	.000	.000
vs. Right	.200	5	1	0	0	0	0	0	2	.200	.200
Scoring Posn	.000	2	0	0	0	0	0	0	0	.000	.000
Close & Late	.500	2	1	0	0	0	0	0	1	.500	.500

Tom Gordon — Royals

Age 26 – Pitches Right

	ERA	W	L	Sv	G	GS	IP	BB	SO	Avg	H	2B	3B	HR	RBI	OBP	SLG	GF	IR	IRS	Hld	SvOp	SB	CS	GB	FB	G/F
1993 Season	3.58	12	6	1	48	14	155.2	77	143	.223	125	27	3	11	64	.315	.340	18	23	11	2	6	15	9	215	126	1.71
Last Five Years	3.84	56	50	3	214	87	789.2	404	736	.234	684	115	24	63	343	.328	.355	42	92	38	9	19	44	36	1025	740	1.39

1993 Season

	ERA	W	L	Sv	G	GS	IP	H	HR	BB	SO
Home	2.38	6	1	1	23	5	72.0	45	5	31	64
Away	4.63	6	5	0	25	9	83.2	80	6	46	79
Starter	3.36	8	4	0	14	14	93.2	79	6	40	80
Reliever	3.92	4	2	1	34	0	62.0	46	5	37	63
0 Days rest	5.40	1	0	0	2	0	5.0	5	1	3	6
1 or 2 Days rest	2.12	2	1	1	18	0	29.2	20	2	16	34
3+ Days rest	5.60	1	1	0	14	0	27.1	21	2	18	23
Pre-All Star	3.66	4	2	1	32	0	59.0	41	5	35	60
Post-All Star	3.54	8	4	0	16	14	96.2	84	6	42	83

	Avg	AB	H	2B	3B	HR	RBI	BB	SO	OBP	SLG
vs. Left	.228	294	67	11	2	6	30	41	72	.319	.340
vs. Right	.217	267	58	16	1	5	34	36	71	.310	.341
Scoring Posn	.221	149	33	7	1	3	51	26	45	.326	.342
Close & Late	.273	88	24	6	1	3	18	11	26	.354	.466
None on/out	.226	137	31	12	1	1	1	16	29	.307	.350
First Pitch	.289	45	13	5	0	0	7	4	0	.340	.400
Ahead in Count	.158	234	37	6	2	1	14	0	106	.160	.214
Behind in Count	.282	142	40	7	0	8	31	41	0	.438	.500
Two Strikes	.129	272	35	7	2	1	14	32	143	.221	.180

Last Five Years

	ERA	W	L	Sv	G	GS	IP	H	HR	BB	SO
Home	3.27	31	23	2	111	43	415.0	334	24	194	377
Away	4.47	25	27	1	103	44	374.2	350	39	210	359
Day	3.38	21	16	0	60	27	239.2	214	21	106	220
Night	4.04	35	34	3	154	60	550.0	470	42	298	516
Grass	4.88	15	22	1	78	33	274.2	275	34	148	264
Turf	3.29	41	28	2	136	54	515.0	409	29	256	472
April	3.01	7	4	0	31	9	104.2	87	7	51	112
May	4.31	7	10	2	38	15	127.1	103	11	67	110
June	4.08	9	7	0	37	10	106.0	97	11	56	107
July	4.04	9	10	0	34	14	133.2	123	11	80	124

	Avg	AB	H	2B	3B	HR	RBI	BB	SO	OBP	SLG
vs. Left	.245	1468	359	51	12	23	156	207	339	.337	.343
vs. Right	.224	1454	325	64	12	40	187	197	397	.319	.367
Inning 1-6	.237	1964	466	79	20	42	234	273	464	.330	.362
Inning 7+	.228	958	218	36	4	21	109	131	272	.323	.339
None on	.235	1621	381	68	13	38	38	210	405	.325	.363
Runners on	.233	1301	303	47	11	25	305	194	331	.331	.344
Scoring Posn	.246	771	190	33	9	16	276	120	209	.344	.375
Close & Late	.251	458	115	21	3	8	56	61	137	.344	.362
None on/out	.229	717	164	32	7	16	16	87	177	.314	.360
vs. 1st Batr (relief)	.192	104	20	6	1	1	22	20	26	.325	.298

Last Five Years

	ERA	W	L	Sv	G	GS	IP	H	HR	BB	SO
August	2.86	15	9	1	31	19	167.0	132	12	64	159
September/October	4.77	9	10	0	43	20	151.0	142	11	86	124
Starter	4.11	32	34	0	87	87	525.0	491	46	265	453
Reliever	3.30	24	16	3	127	0	264.2	193	17	139	283
0 Days rest	2.42	3	1	0	12	0	26.0	16	2	9	34
1 or 2 Days rest	3.15	11	7	2	62	0	120.0	99	9	62	127
3+ Days rest	3.64	10	8	1	53	0	118.2	78	6	68	122
Pre-All Star	3.88	25	26	2	119	37	382.1	321	32	202	372
Post-All Star	3.80	31	24	1	95	50	407.1	363	31	202	364

	Avg	AB	H	2B	3B	HR	RBI	BB	SO	OBP	SLG
First Inning Pitched	.207	728	151	30	4	11	108	121	211	.319	.305
First 15 Pitches	.205	595	122	26	4	9	64	91	156	.310	.308
Pitch 16-30	.211	592	125	13	3	10	70	94	174	.320	.294
Pitch 31-45	.278	468	130	19	3	6	62	75	113	.379	.370
Pitch 46+	.242	1267	307	57	14	38	147	144	293	.320	.399
First Pitch	.327	346	113	16	4	9	69	16	0	.356	.474
Ahead in Count	.176	1369	241	36	9	19	95	0	578	.180	.257
Behind in Count	.300	630	189	34	5	23	111	256	0	.499	.479
Two Strikes	.141	1456	205	36	9	16	83	132	736	.214	.211

Pitcher vs. Batter (career)

Pitches Best Vs.	Avg	AB	H	2B	3B	HR	RBI	BB	SO	OBP	SLG
Robin Ventura	.000	16	0	0	0	0	0	4	5	.200	.000
Bobby Kelly	.000	13	0	0	0	0	1	0	6	.000	.000
Dave Henderson	.000	12	0	0	0	0	0	1	9	.077	.000
Geno Petralli	.000	11	0	0	0	0	0	3	2	.214	.000
Kevin Maas	.000	11	0	0	0	0	0	1	5	.083	.000

Pitches Worst Vs.	Avg	AB	H	2B	3B	HR	RBI	BB	SO	OBP	SLG
Kevin Reimer	.467	15	7	2	0	2	4	2	4	.529	1.000
Alan Trammell	.429	14	6	1	0	2	3	3	1	.529	.929
Sam Horn	.400	10	4	1	0	1	3	2	3	.500	.800
Carlton Fisk	.385	13	5	1	0	2	4	4	3	.529	.923
Ken Griffey Jr	.375	24	9	1	0	4	8	3	3	.444	.917

Goose Gossage — Athletics

Age 42 – Pitches Right

	ERA	W	L	Sv	G	GS	IP	BB	SO	Avg	H	2B	3B	HR	RBI	OBP	SLG	GF	IR	IRS	Hld	SvOp	SB	CS	GB	FB	G/F
1993 Season	4.53	4	5	1	39	0	47.2	26	40	.266	49	9	3	6	34	.357	.446	12	29	13	8	4	6	1	63	48	1.31
Last Five Years	3.47	11	10	7	155	0	184.0	91	124	.239	160	27	5	17	103	.333	.370	41	117	43	22	16	15	10	227	212	1.07

1993 Season

	ERA	W	L	Sv	G	GS	IP	H	HR	BB	SO
Home	4.03	3	1	1	17	0	22.1	21	2	14	17
Away	4.97	1	4	0	22	0	25.1	28	4	12	23
Starter	0.00	0	0	0	0	0	0.0	0	0	0	0
Reliever	4.53	4	5	1	39	0	47.2	49	6	26	40
0 Days rest	37.80	0	0	0	2	0	1.2	10	1	3	1
1 or 2 Days rest	4.58	2	4	1	18	0	19.2	19	3	11	14
3+ Days rest	2.39	2	1	0	19	0	26.1	20	2	12	25
Pre-All Star	3.45	4	4	1	23	0	28.2	24	2	19	19
Post-All Star	6.16	0	1	0	16	0	19.0	25	4	7	21

	Avg	AB	H	2B	3B	HR	RBI	BB	SO	OBP	SLG
vs. Left	.246	69	17	5	0	0	9	15	14	.384	.319
vs. Right	.278	115	32	4	3	6	25	11	26	.339	.522
Scoring Posn	.339	56	19	1	0	3	27	8	13	.418	.518
Close & Late	.247	85	21	4	1	1	12	14	19	.347	.353
None on/out	.143	42	6	1	1	1	1	2	11	.182	.286
First Pitch	.214	14	3	1	0	0	1	2	0	.313	.286
Ahead in Count	.211	95	20	2	2	0	11	0	34	.216	.274
Behind in Count	.306	36	11	2	0	3	12	15	0	.500	.611
Two Strikes	.206	97	20	2	3	3	13	9	40	.271	.381

Last Five Years

	ERA	W	L	Sv	G	GS	IP	H	HR	BB	SO
Home	2.67	6	2	5	71	0	87.2	74	8	40	65
Away	4.20	5	8	2	84	0	96.1	86	9	51	59
Day	4.03	3	2	0	46	0	58.0	58	6	20	43
Night	3.21	8	8	7	109	0	126.0	102	11	71	81
Grass	3.43	10	7	6	123	0	144.1	124	15	72	109
Turf	3.63	1	3	1	32	0	39.2	36	2	19	15
April	1.03	4	1	1	28	0	35.0	15	2	17	24
May	3.46	3	1	2	36	0	41.2	30	4	28	33
June	3.43	3	4	1	31	0	39.1	38	3	19	20
July	6.89	0	4	2	30	0	32.2	42	6	17	25
August	4.64	0	0	1	17	0	21.1	24	2	8	15
September/October	0.00	1	0	0	13	0	14.0	11	0	2	7
Starter	0.00	0	0	0	0	0	0.0	0	0	0	0
Reliever	3.47	11	10	7	155	0	184.0	160	17	91	124
0 Days rest	8.85	2	1	0	18	0	20.1	28	4	12	10
1 or 2 Days rest	2.81	5	6	4	72	0	86.1	70	8	41	58
3+ Days rest	2.79	4	3	3	65	0	77.1	62	5	38	56
Pre-All Star	2.94	10	8	4	103	0	125.2	95	9	69	84
Post-All Star	4.63	1	2	3	52	0	58.1	65	8	22	40

	Avg	AB	H	2B	3B	HR	RBI	BB	SO	OBP	SLG
vs. Left	.237	270	64	14	1	2	27	45	39	.346	.319
vs. Right	.240	400	96	13	4	15	76	46	85	.325	.405
Inning 1-6	.333	69	23	3	2	4	23	10	11	.413	.609
Inning 7+	.228	601	137	24	3	13	80	81	113	.324	.343
None on	.217	337	73	17	2	7	7	48	58	.323	.341
Runners on	.261	333	87	10	3	10	96	43	66	.344	.399
Scoring Posn	.275	200	55	4	1	6	83	35	40	.379	.395
Close & Late	.238	235	56	11	1	7	42	44	54	.364	.383
None on/out	.224	143	32	6	1	4	4	16	25	.319	.364
vs. 1st Batr (relief)	.262	107	28	5	1	5	19	13	22	.363	.467
First Inning Pitched	.251	379	95	15	4	14	77	47	74	.339	.422
First 15 Pitches	.272	430	117	19	5	16	82	58	73	.365	.451
Pitch 16-30	.191	194	37	7	0	1	19	29	38	.294	.242
Pitch 31-45	.100	40	4	1	0	0	2	4	13	.182	.125
Pitch 46+	.333	6	2	0	0	0	0	0	0	.333	.333
First Pitch	.291	86	25	3	0	3	13	7	0	.351	.430
Ahead in Count	.190	321	61	9	2	1	29	0	113	.198	.240
Behind in Count	.284	148	42	10	1	9	41	48	0	.457	.547
Two Strikes	.172	309	53	7	3	4	28	36	124	.261	.252

Pitcher vs. Batter (since 1984)

Pitches Best Vs.	Avg	AB	H	2B	3B	HR	RBI	BB	SO	OBP	SLG
Gerald Perry	.100	10	1	0	0	0	2	0	2	.091	.100
Dale Murphy	.130	23	3	0	0	1	6	0	6	.130	.261
Darryl Strawberry	.167	12	2	0	0	0	3	2	5	.286	.167
Billy Doran	.200	10	2	0	0	0	0	1	1	.273	.200
Tony Pena	.211	19	4	0	0	0	3	1	1	.238	.211

Pitches Worst Vs.	Avg	AB	H	2B	3B	HR	RBI	BB	SO	OBP	SLG
Kevin Bass	.727	11	8	1	0	0	3	0	1	.727	.818
Andy Van Slyke	.545	11	6	0	0	1	4	0	1	.545	.818
Lenny Dykstra	.417	12	5	0	1	0	3	0	0	.417	.583
Hubie Brooks	.400	15	6	0	0	1	4	0	5	.400	.600
Terry Pendleton	.385	13	5	2	0	0	2	0	0	.385	.538

Jim Gott — Dodgers

Age 34 – Pitches Right (groundball pitcher)

	ERA	W	L	Sv	G	GS	IP	BB	SO	Avg	H	2B	3B	HR	RBI	OBP	SLG	GF	IR	IRS	Hld	SvOp	SB	CS	GB	FB	G/F
1993 Season	2.32	4	8	25	62	0	77.2	17	67	.248	71	8	0	6	30	.291	.339	45	35	12	7	29	4	2	97	73	1.33
Last Five Years	2.63	14	19	36	236	0	304.1	125	260	.237	266	29	4	20	106	.313	.324	123	117	37	29	46	20	9	426	250	1.70

1993 Season

	ERA	W	L	Sv	G	GS	IP	H	HR	BB	SO
Home	3.19	2	4	12	31	0	42.1	44	5	10	39
Away	1.27	2	4	13	31	0	35.1	27	1	7	28
Day	0.59	3	1	6	12	0	15.1	8	0	2	14
Night	2.74	1	7	19	50	0	62.1	63	6	15	53
Grass	2.71	3	7	19	50	0	63.0	62	6	17	51

	Avg	AB	H	2B	3B	HR	RBI	BB	SO	OBP	SLG
vs. Left	.222	153	34	4	0	5	18	9	41	.264	.346
vs. Right	.278	133	37	4	0	1	12	8	26	.322	.331
Inning 1-6	.000	0	0	0	0	0	0	0	0	.000	.000
Inning 7+	.248	286	71	8	0	6	30	17	67	.291	.339
None on	.236	161	38	7	0	2	2	5	37	.259	.317

1993 Season

	ERA	W	L	Sv	G	GS	IP	H	HR	BB	SO
Turf	0.61	1	1	6	12	0	14.2	9	0	0	16
April	0.00	0	0	2	8	0	12.1	8	0	7	9
May	3.07	2	1	4	11	0	14.2	14	1	2	14
June	3.94	0	4	7	15	0	16.0	16	2	3	13
July	1.65	2	0	5	12	0	16.1	13	1	1	15
August	2.03	0	2	6	10	0	13.1	14	0	3	11
September/October	3.60	0	1	1	6	0	5.0	6	2	1	5
Starter	0.00	0	0	0	0	0	0.0	0	0	0	0
Reliever	2.32	4	8	25	62	0	77.2	71	6	17	67
0 Days rest	0.40	0	0	10	20	0	22.1	18	0	7	17
1 or 2 Days rest	3.93	3	5	9	25	0	34.1	33	4	6	29
3+ Days rest	1.71	1	3	6	17	0	21.0	20	2	4	21
Pre-All Star	2.09	3	5	16	40	0	51.2	44	3	12	44
Post-All Star	2.77	1	3	9	22	0	26.0	27	3	5	23

	Avg	AB	H	2B	3B	HR	RBI	BB	SO	OBP	SLG
Runners on	.264	125	33	1	0	4	28	12	30	.329	.368
Scoring Posn	.260	73	19	0	0	3	26	10	15	.341	.384
Close & Late	.272	224	61	7	0	6	30	15	53	.315	.384
None on/out	.254	67	17	4	0	1	1	2	11	.275	.358
vs. 1st Batr (relief)	.233	60	14	2	0	0	2	2	10	.258	.267
First Inning Pitched	.275	207	57	6	0	5	25	11	47	.312	.377
First 15 Pitches	.255	200	51	6	0	4	20	8	42	.284	.345
Pitch 16-30	.203	69	14	1	0	2	10	8	20	.286	.304
Pitch 31-45	.357	14	5	1	0	0	0	1	4	.400	.429
Pitch 46+	.333	3	1	0	0	0	0	0	1	.333	.333
First Pitch	.366	41	15	3	0	1	9	3	0	.400	.512
Ahead in Count	.199	146	29	1	0	3	13	0	59	.204	.267
Behind in Count	.365	52	19	2	0	2	7	5	0	.414	.519
Two Strikes	.177	141	25	0	0	3	12	9	67	.232	.241

Last Five Years

	ERA	W	L	Sv	G	GS	IP	H	HR	BB	SO
Home	2.63	6	8	16	115	0	154.0	126	11	67	144
Away	2.63	8	11	20	121	0	150.1	140	9	58	116
Day	1.88	5	2	9	55	0	72.0	65	4	32	59
Night	2.87	9	17	27	181	0	232.1	201	16	93	201
Grass	2.60	10	15	28	175	0	232.1	200	16	104	191
Turf	2.75	4	4	8	61	0	72.0	66	4	21	69
April	1.21	0	1	4	29	0	37.1	28	0	18	29
May	3.05	2	1	5	30	0	38.1	33	1	14	38
June	3.81	2	9	7	47	0	54.1	56	7	28	47
July	1.91	3	1	7	43	0	56.2	48	3	19	41
August	1.69	4	3	11	47	0	69.1	47	5	25	57
September/October	4.28	3	4	2	40	0	48.1	54	4	21	48
Starter	0.00	0	0	0	0	0	0.0	0	0	0	0
Reliever	2.63	14	19	36	236	0	304.1	266	20	125	260
0 Days rest	1.51	2	0	15	67	0	83.1	58	5	39	68
1 or 2 Days rest	2.97	8	14	13	107	0	142.1	130	9	51	125
3+ Days rest	3.20	4	5	8	62	0	78.2	78	6	35	67
Pre-All Star	2.60	5	12	20	123	0	152.1	134	9	69	133
Post-All Star	2.66	9	7	16	113	0	152.0	132	11	56	127

	Avg	AB	H	2B	3B	HR	RBI	BB	SO	OBP	SLG
vs. Left	.240	574	138	16	4	11	52	74	137	.327	.340
vs. Right	.234	547	128	13	0	9	54	51	123	.299	.307
Inning 1-6	.185	108	20	1	0	4	10	16	25	.286	.306
Inning 7+	.243	1013	246	28	4	16	96	109	235	.317	.326
None on	.242	619	150	22	1	8	8	48	142	.297	.320
Runners on	.231	502	116	7	3	12	98	77	118	.332	.329
Scoring Posn	.208	307	64	3	3	6	85	61	77	.334	.296
Close & Late	.237	558	132	17	2	12	68	69	135	.321	.339
None on/out	.277	267	74	15	0	4	4	27	53	.344	.378
vs. 1st Batr (relief)	.274	215	59	10	0	1	16	19	43	.331	.335
First Inning Pitched	.244	776	189	20	3	13	85	93	184	.324	.327
First 15 Pitches	.248	725	180	23	2	11	71	78	161	.320	.331
Pitch 16-30	.203	325	66	4	1	7	28	42	88	.296	.286
Pitch 31-45	.293	58	17	2	1	2	7	5	9	.349	.466
Pitch 46+	.231	13	3	0	0	0	0	0	2	.231	.231
First Pitch	.294	136	40	5	1	3	19	26	0	.404	.412
Ahead in Count	.172	564	97	5	1	7	36	0	230	.173	.222
Behind in Count	.357	230	82	13	0	6	31	47	0	.463	.491
Two Strikes	.157	559	88	4	2	7	31	52	260	.230	.209

Pitcher vs. Batter (since 1984)

Pitches Best Vs.	Avg	AB	H	2B	3B	HR	RBI	BB	SO	OBP	SLG
Casey Candaele	.071	14	1	0	0	0	0	3	2	.235	.071
Kevin Mitchell	.077	13	1	0	0	0	0	1	2	.143	.077
Mariano Duncan	.077	13	1	0	0	0	1	1	2	.133	.077
Kurt Stillwell	.091	11	1	0	0	0	0	0	3	.091	.091
Ozzie Smith	.143	14	2	0	0	0	1	0	2	.133	.143

Pitches Worst Vs.	Avg	AB	H	2B	3B	HR	RBI	BB	SO	OBP	SLG
Paul O'Neill	.455	11	5	1	0	0	5	1	1	.500	.545
Juan Samuel	.417	12	5	1	0	1	3	0	2	.417	.750
Milt Thompson	.400	10	4	0	1	0	2	1	2	.455	.600
Eric Davis	.357	14	5	2	0	2	4	3	5	.471	.929
Dave Justice	.333	9	3	0	1	0	1	3	2	.500	.556

Mauro Gozzo — Mets

Age 28 – Pitches Right (groundball pitcher)

	ERA	W	L	Sv	G	GS	IP	BB	SO	Avg	H	2B	3B	HR	RBI	OBP	SLG	GF	IR	IRS	Hld	SvOp	SB	CS	GB	FB	G/F
1993 Season	2.57	0	1	1	10	0	14.0	5	6	.212	11	1	0	1	4	.281	.288	5	0	0	2	1	1	0	23	16	1.44
Career (1989-1993)	5.89	4	2	1	25	5	55.0	23	22	.296	64	17	1	4	31	.362	.440	6	4	2	3	2	3	0	96	55	1.75

1993 Season

	ERA	W	L	Sv	G	GS	IP	H	HR	BB	SO
Home	1.13	0	1	0	5	0	8.0	6	0	3	2
Away	4.50	0	0	1	5	0	6.0	5	1	2	4

	Avg	AB	H	2B	3B	HR	RBI	BB	SO	OBP	SLG
vs. Left	.300	30	9	1	0	1	4	4	2	.382	.433
vs. Right	.091	22	2	0	0	0	0	1	4	.130	.091

Mark Grace — Cubs

Age 30 – Bats Left (groundball hitter)

	Avg	G	AB	R	H	2B	3B	HR	RBI	BB	SO	HBP	GDP	SB	CS	OBP	SLG	IBB	SH	SF	#Pit	#P/PA	GB	FB	G/F
1993 Season	.325	155	594	86	193	39	4	14	98	71	32	1	25	8	4	.393	.475	14	1	9	2173	3.21	239	158	1.51
Last Five Years	.305	772	2915	391	889	164	18	53	396	352	217	13	67	46	22	.378	.428	47	11	35	11263	3.39	1190	785	1.52

1993 Season

	Avg	AB	H	2B	3B	HR	RBI	BB	SO	OBP	SLG
vs. Left	.352	193	68	14	1	6	41	21	12	.412	.528
vs. Right	.312	401	125	25	3	8	57	50	20	.383	.449
Groundball	.301	216	65	12	2	3	31	25	15	.371	.417
Flyball	.295	78	23	2	0	0	9	11	5	.378	.321
Home	.353	300	106	19	2	5	52	37	18	.421	.480
Away	.296	294	87	20	2	9	46	34	14	.364	.469
Day	.337	315	106	16	2	5	48	36	20	.400	.448
Night	.312	279	87	23	2	9	50	35	12	.384	.505
Grass	.346	451	156	33	4	11	79	54	27	.412	.510
Turf	.259	143	37	6	0	3	19	17	5	.331	.364
First Pitch	.346	127	44	12	1	2	21	12	0	.397	.504
Ahead in Count	.359	198	71	11	3	6	42	39	0	.458	.535
Behind in Count	.251	175	44	10	0	2	16	0	26	.254	.343
Two Strikes	.252	163	41	8	0	3	16	20	32	.335	.356

	Avg	AB	H	2B	3B	HR	RBI	BB	SO	OBP	SLG
Scoring Posn	.336	152	51	9	2	3	73	30	10	.424	.480
Close & Late	.453	86	39	7	0	5	24	16	5	.529	.709
None on/out	.350	100	35	6	0	3	3	11	8	.414	.500
Batting #3	.328	497	163	30	4	13	85	61	26	.397	.483
Batting #4	.313	96	30	9	0	1	13	10	6	.374	.438
Other	.000	1	0	0	0	0	0	0	0	.000	.000
April	.325	83	27	6	0	3	16	9	2	.379	.506
May	.364	99	36	8	2	1	22	11	6	.416	.515
June	.302	106	32	9	0	4	18	12	8	.370	.500
July	.301	83	25	4	0	1	6	10	3	.376	.386
August	.336	119	40	6	0	2	15	14	5	.410	.437
September/October	.317	104	33	6	2	3	21	15	8	.397	.500
Pre-All Star	.332	307	102	24	2	9	60	35	18	.393	.511
Post-All Star	.317	287	91	15	2	5	38	36	14	.393	.436

1993 By Position																							
Position	Avg	AB	H	2B	3B	HR	RBI	BB	SO	OBP	SLG	G	GS	Innings	PO	A	E	DP	Fld Pct	Rng Fctr	In Zone	Outs	Zone Rtg	MLB Zone
As 1b	.325	593	193	39	4	14	98	71	32	.393	.476	154	153	1350.1	1455	109	5	136	.997	---	268	232	.866	.834

Last Five Years

	Avg	AB	H	2B	3B	HR	RBI	BB	SO	OBP	SLG		Avg	AB	H	2B	3B	HR	RBI	BB	SO	OBP	SLG
vs. Left	.294	1014	298	53	7	18	146	99	103	.357	.413	Scoring Posn	.309	726	224	48	6	7	315	139	59	.407	.420
vs. Right	.311	1901	591	111	11	35	250	253	114	.389	.436	Close & Late	.332	479	159	18	1	12	74	80	35	.429	.449
Groundball	.308	1062	327	60	7	13	148	134	71	.384	.414	None on/out	.297	579	172	26	2	16	16	54	42	.358	.432
Flyball	.282	652	184	32	2	8	69	76	59	.357	.374	Batting #3	.303	1813	550	108	10	36	264	206	133	.373	.434
Home	.318	1473	468	87	5	27	214	197	109	.396	.439	Batting #4	.307	443	136	25	3	9	65	65	39	.395	.438
Away	.292	1442	421	77	13	26	182	155	108	.360	.417	Other	.308	659	203	31	5	8	67	81	45	.382	.407
Day	.310	1534	475	84	8	31	219	202	120	.389	.435	April	.283	367	104	22	2	8	51	59	19	.381	.420
Night	.300	1381	414	80	10	22	177	150	97	.366	.420	May	.306	520	159	30	5	6	76	52	48	.367	.417
Grass	.311	2119	660	122	12	39	302	260	169	.384	.436	June	.324	441	143	27	2	6	56	53	30	.394	.435
Turf	.288	796	229	42	6	14	94	92	48	.362	.408	July	.292	463	135	29	2	10	51	56	29	.368	.428
First Pitch	.332	608	202	35	5	11	96	34	0	.366	.461	August	.326	576	188	27	3	16	83	63	47	.394	.467
Ahead in Count	.342	827	283	54	9	19	141	196	0	.464	.498	September/October	.292	548	160	29	4	7	79	69	44	.367	.398
Behind in Count	.254	953	242	45	4	13	94	0	172	.255	.350	Pre-All Star	.303	1474	446	87	10	25	203	186	110	.378	.426
Two Strikes	.248	945	234	43	3	17	94	119	217	.331	.353	Post-All Star	.307	1441	443	77	8	28	193	166	107	.378	.430

Batter vs. Pitcher (career)

Hits Best Against	Avg	AB	H	2B	3B	HR	RBI	BB	SO	OBP	SLG	Hits Worst Against	Avg	AB	H	2B	3B	HR	RBI	BB	SO	OBP	SLG
Joe Boever	.556	9	5	1	0	0	4	4	1	.692	.667	Ron Darling	.042	24	1	1	0	0	2	4	1	.179	.083
Craig Lefferts	.500	10	5	2	0	0	1	3	0	.615	.700	Mitch Williams	.077	13	1	0	0	0	0	0	2	.077	.077
Andy Ashby	.462	13	6	1	1	1	6	3	0	.563	.923	Jimmy Jones	.083	12	1	0	0	0	1	2	0	.200	.083
Randy Myers	.429	14	6	0	2	1	6	1	3	.467	.929	Jay Howell	.091	11	1	0	0	0	0	0	2	.091	.091
John Smoltz	.354	48	17	5	1	5	8	7	3	.436	.813	Juan Agosto	.143	14	2	0	0	0	2	0	1	.143	.143

Joe Grahe — Angels

Age 26 – Pitches Right (groundball pitcher)

	ERA	W	L	Sv	G	GS	IP	BB	SO	Avg	H	2B	3B	HR	RBI	OBP	SLG	GF	IR	IRS	Hld	SvOp	SB	CS	GB	FB	G/F
1993 Season	2.86	4	1	11	45	0	56.2	25	31	.251	54	8	1	5	33	.331	.367	32	38	12	3	13	4	0	107	41	2.61
Career (1990-1993)	3.97	15	18	32	117	25	267.2	120	135	.267	274	52	6	15	137	.349	.373	65	63	18	5	37	23	11	485	221	2.19

1993 Season

	ERA	W	L	Sv	G	GS	IP	H	HR	BB	SO		Avg	AB	H	2B	3B	HR	RBI	BB	SO	OBP	SLG
Home	3.54	3	1	7	21	0	28.0	27	3	9	17	vs. Left	.317	82	26	6	0	1	5	10	10	.391	.427
Away	2.20	1	0	4	24	0	28.2	27	2	16	14	vs. Right	.211	133	28	2	1	4	28	15	21	.294	.331
Starter	0.00	0	0	0	0	0	0.0	0	0	0	0	Scoring Posn	.266	64	17	2	1	1	25	11	8	.367	.375
Reliever	2.86	4	1	11	45	0	56.2	54	5	25	31	Close & Late	.228	92	21	5	0	2	13	12	18	.318	.348
0 Days rest	3.38	1	0	0	7	0	8.0	6	1	8	3	None on/out	.186	43	8	1	0	0	0	2	6	.239	.209
1 or 2 Days rest	1.42	2	0	5	20	0	25.1	24	1	10	13	First Pitch	.152	33	5	1	0	1	5	3	0	.243	.273
3+ Days rest	4.24	1	1	6	18	0	23.1	24	3	7	15	Ahead in Count	.245	94	23	2	1	0	7	0	30	.245	.287
Pre-All Star	3.57	2	1	6	18	0	22.2	22	3	10	13	Behind in Count	.302	53	16	5	0	2	15	15	0	.444	.509
Post-All Star	2.38	2	0	5	27	0	34.0	32	2	15	18	Two Strikes	.184	87	16	2	0	0	3	7	31	.245	.207

Career (1990-1993)

	ERA	W	L	Sv	G	GS	IP	H	HR	BB	SO		Avg	AB	H	2B	3B	HR	RBI	BB	SO	OBP	SLG
Home	4.24	7	10	21	58	11	136.0	138	10	55	67	vs. Left	.311	463	144	30	3	6	55	48	56	.380	.428
Away	3.69	8	8	11	59	14	131.2	136	5	65	68	vs. Right	.230	564	130	22	3	9	82	72	79	.324	.328
Day	3.28	6	4	12	38	6	79.2	75	2	34	39	Inning 1-6	.297	563	167	37	4	7	87	69	71	.381	.414
Night	4.26	9	14	20	79	19	188.0	199	13	86	96	Inning 7+	.231	464	107	15	2	8	50	51	64	.310	.323
Grass	3.74	14	17	31	102	23	248.0	250	14	104	127	None on	.246	544	134	24	0	8	8	52	75	.317	.335
Turf	6.86	1	1	1	15	2	19.2	24	1	16	8	Runners on	.290	483	140	28	6	7	129	68	60	.383	.416
April	6.05	3	3	2	10	5	38.2	46	3	18	19	Scoring Posn	.272	287	78	19	4	4	114	53	41	.387	.408
May	3.63	1	1	4	13	2	22.1	18	3	14	11	Close & Late	.208	279	58	10	0	5	27	35	39	.299	.297
June	3.86	1	1	3	15	1	28.0	28	1	9	22	None on/out	.247	239	59	12	0	1	1	22	30	.321	.310
July	2.39	2	0	8	18	0	26.1	25	2	10	10	vs. 1st Batr (relief)	.240	75	18	2	0	2	12	13	11	.363	.347
August	4.01	3	8	6	31	9	76.1	83	3	34	34	First Inning Pitched	.265	389	103	19	3	8	67	51	53	.356	.391
September/October	3.55	5	5	9	30	8	76.0	74	3	35	39	First 15 Pitches	.256	351	90	15	1	6	40	41	41	.340	.356
Starter	5.40	7	14	0	25	25	136.2	160	8	69	65	Pitch 16-30	.270	230	62	13	2	3	38	30	31	.359	.383
Reliever	2.47	8	4	32	92	0	131.0	114	7	51	70	Pitch 31-45	.256	125	32	4	0	1	13	13	21	.326	.312
0 Days rest	3.71	1	1	6	15	0	17.0	15	1	17	6	Pitch 46+	.280	321	90	20	3	5	46	36	42	.361	.408
1 or 2 Days rest	1.17	5	1	16	41	0	61.2	47	3	19	30	First Pitch	.273	154	42	8	0	4	23	4	0	.304	.403
3+ Days rest	3.61	2	2	10	36	0	52.1	52	3	15	34	Ahead in Count	.218	418	91	12	2	3	38	0	117	.233	.278
Pre-All Star	4.67	5	5	10	42	8	96.1	100	8	44	56	Behind in Count	.326	258	84	16	2	4	48	72	0	.469	.450
Post-All Star	3.57	10	13	22	75	17	171.1	174	7	76	79	Two Strikes	.187	407	76	12	1	2	28	44	135	.272	.236

Pitcher vs. Batter (career)

Pitches Best Vs.	Avg	AB	H	2B	3B	HR	RBI	BB	SO	OBP	SLG	Pitches Worst Vs.	Avg	AB	H	2B	3B	HR	RBI	BB	SO	OBP	SLG
Harold Baines	.077	13	1	0	0	0	2	4	1	.294	.077	B.J. Surhoff	.556	9	5	1	0	0	2	3	0	.667	.667
Mark McGwire	.133	15	2	0	0	0	0	5	1	.350	.133	Paul Molitor	.385	13	5	0	0	1	2	2	0	.467	.615
Rickey Henderson	.143	14	2	1	0	0	0	4	3	.333	.214	Lou Whitaker	.364	11	4	3	0	1	2	0	2	.364	.909
Dave Henderson	.154	13	2	1	0	0	0	0	4	.154	.231	Robin Ventura	.357	14	5	2	0	0	2	3	0	.471	.500
Cecil Fielder	.200	15	3	0	0	0	1	4	5	.368	.200	Mike Bordick	.333	12	4	1	1	0	1	1	2	.385	.583

Jeff Granger — Royals

Age 22 – Pitches Left

	ERA	W	L	Sv	G	GS	IP	BB	SO	Avg	H	2B	3B	HR	RBI	OBP	SLG	GF	IR	IRS	Hld	SvOp	SB	CS	GB	FB	G/F
1993 Season	27.00	0	0	0	1	0	1.0	2	1	.500	3	0	0	0	3	.625	.500	0	0	0	0	0	0	0	2	1	2.00

1993 Season

	ERA	W	L	Sv	G	GS	IP	H	HR	BB	SO		Avg	AB	H	2B	3B	HR	RBI	BB	SO	OBP	SLG
Home	0.00	0	0	0	0	0	0.0	0	0	0	0	vs. Left	1.000	1	1	0	0	0	0	0	0	1.000	1.000
Away	27.00	0	0	0	1	0	1.0	3	0	2	1	vs. Right	.400	5	2	0	0	0	3	2	1	.571	.400

Mark Grant — Rockies

Age 30 – Pitches Right

	ERA	W	L	Sv	G	GS	IP	BB	SO	Avg	H	2B	3B	HR	RBI	OBP	SLG	GF	IR	IRS	Hld	SvOp	SB	CS	GB	FB	G/F
1993 Season	7.46	0	1	1	20	0	25.1	11	14	.337	34	8	0	4	22	.395	.535	9	16	4	0	2	1	1	45	24	1.88
Last Five Years	4.21	12	10	6	152	11	314.0	102	194	.287	347	71	6	30	168	.343	.430	34	109	44	8	11	22	11	456	340	1.34

1993 Season

	ERA	W	L	Sv	G	GS	IP	H	HR	BB	SO		Avg	AB	H	2B	3B	HR	RBI	BB	SO	OBP	SLG
Home	9.53	0	1	1	10	0	11.1	15	2	10	9	vs. Left	.395	38	15	2	0	0	6	4	6	.442	.447
Away	5.79	0	0	0	10	0	14.0	19	2	1	5	vs. Right	.302	63	19	6	0	4	16	7	8	.366	.587

Last Five Years

	ERA	W	L	Sv	G	GS	IP	H	HR	BB	SO		Avg	AB	H	2B	3B	HR	RBI	BB	SO	OBP	SLG
Home	4.89	5	5	5	79	5	151.0	171	20	57	106	vs. Left	.298	584	174	33	4	11	71	54	93	.357	.425
Away	3.59	7	5	1	73	6	163.0	176	10	45	88	vs. Right	.277	625	173	38	2	19	97	48	101	.329	.435
Day	4.23	3	3	2	55	5	127.2	133	15	45	80	Inning 1-6	.294	637	187	37	3	16	102	54	93	.349	.436
Night	4.20	9	7	4	97	6	186.1	214	15	57	114	Inning 7+	.280	572	160	34	3	14	66	48	101	.336	.423
Grass	5.07	7	5	6	107	6	204.1	223	26	74	127	None on	.279	657	183	36	2	14	14	45	108	.328	.403
Turf	2.63	5	5	0	45	5	109.2	124	4	28	67	Runners on	.297	552	164	35	4	16	154	57	86	.360	.462
April	5.20	0	0	0	17	0	27.2	30	4	11	21	Scoring Posn	.255	330	84	20	2	8	126	46	54	.339	.400
May	2.23	2	1	0	19	0	36.1	35	1	12	17	Close & Late	.322	143	46	7	0	5	22	18	24	.405	.476
June	5.21	1	2	1	25	0	38.0	42	6	14	27	None on/out	.302	298	90	17	0	8	8	14	51	.338	.440
July	5.00	3	3	0	33	6	77.1	96	8	29	39	vs. 1st Batr (relief)	.220	127	28	7	1	4	23	8	20	.264	.386
August	4.16	3	3	2	28	4	67.0	76	6	23	40	First Inning Pitched	.291	533	155	31	5	17	100	44	90	.342	.463
September/October	3.46	3	1	3	30	1	67.2	68	5	13	50	First 15 Pitches	.295	509	150	33	5	17	77	38	77	.341	.479
Starter	4.88	2	4	0	11	11	62.2	84	5	21	29	Pitch 16-30	.272	357	97	15	0	8	50	28	66	.326	.381
Reliever	4.05	10	6	6	141	0	251.1	263	25	81	165	Pitch 31-45	.272	162	44	14	1	2	23	20	30	.353	.407
0 Days rest	3.89	2	1	1	20	0	37.0	41	4	12	30	Pitch 46+	.309	181	56	9	0	3	18	16	21	.372	.409
1 or 2 Days rest	5.54	3	4	5	67	0	112.0	126	16	42	75	First Pitch	.271	207	56	15	2	4	21	21	0	.332	.420
3+ Days rest	2.46	5	1	0	54	0	102.1	96	5	27	60	Ahead in Count	.237	498	118	18	3	7	58	0	161	.243	.327
Pre-All Star	3.89	4	4	1	71	3	136.1	141	13	54	83	Behind in Count	.352	281	99	20	1	12	54	40	0	.431	.559
Post-All Star	4.46	8	6	5	81	8	177.2	206	17	48	111	Two Strikes	.225	485	109	17	1	6	49	41	194	.288	.301

Pitcher vs. Batter (career)

Pitches Best Vs.	Avg	AB	H	2B	3B	HR	RBI	BB	SO	OBP	SLG	Pitches Worst Vs.	Avg	AB	H	2B	3B	HR	RBI	BB	SO	OBP	SLG
Ozzie Smith	.100	20	2	0	0	0	2	3	2	.217	.100	Andre Dawson	.571	21	12	2	1	3	9	1	0	.591	1.190
Matt D. Williams	.143	14	2	0	0	0	1	0	4	.133	.143	Eddie Murray	.500	8	4	0	0	2	6	3	0	.636	1.250
Jose Oquendo	.167	12	2	0	0	0	0	1	4	.231	.167	Eric Davis	.450	20	9	1	0	4	9	5	4	.560	1.100
Hubie Brooks	.182	11	2	0	0	0	2	0	1	.182	.182	Kevin Mitchell	.400	20	8	2	0	3	6	3	4	.478	.950
Gerald Young	.182	11	2	0	0	0	0	0	2	.182	.182	Ken Caminiti	.400	10	4	0	0	2	7	1	2	.455	1.000

Mark Grater — Tigers

Age 30 – Pitches Right

	ERA	W	L	Sv	G	GS	IP	BB	SO	Avg	H	2B	3B	HR	RBI	OBP	SLG	GF	IR	IRS	Hld	SvOp	SB	CS	GB	FB	G/F
1993 Season	5.40	0	0	0	6	0	5.0	4	4	.286	6	0	0	0	6	.400	.286	1	6	5	1	0	0	0	7	2	3.50
Career (1991-1993)	3.38	0	0	0	9	0	8.0	6	4	.324	11	0	0	0	7	.425	.324	3	10	6	1	0	0	1	16	3	5.33

1993 Season

	ERA	W	L	Sv	G	GS	IP	H	HR	BB	SO		Avg	AB	H	2B	3B	HR	RBI	BB	SO	OBP	SLG
Home	2.45	0	0	0	3	0	3.2	4	0	3	1	vs. Left	.429	7	3	0	0	0	2	1	0	.500	.429
Away	13.50	0	0	0	3	0	1.1	2	0	1	3	vs. Right	.214	14	3	0	0	0	4	3	4	.353	.214

Craig Grebeck — White Sox

Age 29 – Bats Right (flyball hitter)

	Avg	G	AB	R	H	2B	3B	HR	RBI	BB	SO	HBP	GDP	SB	CS	OBP	SLG	IBB	SH	SF	#Pit	#P/PA	GB	FB	G/F
1993 Season	.226	72	190	25	43	5	0	1	12	26	26	0	9	1	2	.319	.268	0	7	0	842	3.78	80	47	1.70
Career (1990-1993)	.248	326	820	93	203	45	6	11	87	102	124	6	19	2	8	.333	.357	0	24	7	3636	3.79	258	275	0.94

1993 Season

	Avg	AB	H	2B	3B	HR	RBI	BB	SO	OBP	SLG		Avg	AB	H	2B	3B	HR	RBI	BB	SO	OBP	SLG
vs. Left	.222	117	26	3	0	0	6	11	16	.289	.248	Scoring Posn	.268	41	11	2	0	0	11	10	3	.412	.317
vs. Right	.233	73	17	2	0	1	6	15	10	.364	.301	Close & Late	.250	24	6	2	0	0	3	4	3	.357	.333
Home	.274	106	29	4	0	0	8	14	14	.358	.311	None on/out	.256	43	11	1	0	1	1	5	7	.333	.349
Away	.167	84	14	1	0	1	4	12	12	.271	.214	Batting #2	.185	65	12	1	0	0	2	8	7	.274	.200
First Pitch	.395	38	15	3	0	1	5	0	0	.395	.553	Batting #9	.242	99	24	2	0	1	7	15	15	.342	.293
Ahead in Count	.333	36	12	1	0	0	5	12	0	.500	.361	Other	.269	26	7	2	0	0	3	3	4	.345	.346
Behind in Count	.143	77	11	1	0	0	2	0	19	.143	.156	Pre-All Star	.233	90	21	0	0	1	5	12	13	.324	.267
Two Strikes	.132	76	10	1	0	0	2	14	26	.267	.145	Post-All Star	.220	100	22	5	0	0	7	14	13	.316	.270

Career (1990-1993)

	Avg	AB	H	2B	3B	HR	RBI	BB	SO	OBP	SLG		Avg	AB	H	2B	3B	HR	RBI	BB	SO	OBP	SLG
vs. Left	.244	406	99	22	3	5	40	43	64	.316	.350	Scoring Posn	.257	191	49	15	0	2	68	33	31	.363	.366
vs. Right	.251	414	104	23	3	6	47	59	60	.349	.365	Close & Late	.225	142	32	7	1	1	17	17	18	.309	.310

Career (1990-1993)

	Avg	AB	H	2B	3B	HR	RBI	BB	SO	OBP	SLG		Avg	AB	H	2B	3B	HR	RBI	BB	SO	OBP	SLG
Groundball	.271	218	59	10	1	1	15	20	31	.335	.339	None on/out	.244	213	52	8	1	4	4	20	38	.309	.347
Flyball	.273	187	51	9	2	6	30	28	35	.370	.439	Batting #8	.236	182	43	9	1	3	15	18	32	.309	.346
Home	.264	406	107	23	2	6	49	53	59	.347	.374	Batting #9	.243	296	72	15	2	4	35	40	43	.337	.348
Away	.232	414	96	22	4	5	38	49	65	.318	.341	Other	.257	342	88	21	3	4	37	44	49	.341	.371
Day	.241	220	53	10	1	2	25	31	27	.329	.323	April	.224	58	13	2	0	2	9	5	7	.281	.362
Night	.250	600	150	35	5	9	62	71	97	.334	.370	May	.230	165	38	8	0	1	15	19	21	.312	.297
Grass	.256	687	176	39	5	9	79	86	104	.341	.367	June	.236	182	43	11	1	3	14	14	28	.289	.357
Turf	.203	133	27	6	1	2	8	16	20	.289	.308	July	.297	148	44	9	2	3	20	18	19	.376	.446
First Pitch	.341	135	46	11	1	4	28	0	0	.343	.526	August	.254	134	34	8	2	1	17	14	22	.329	.366
Ahead in Count	.295	176	52	15	1	6	31	58	0	.473	.494	September/October	.233	133	31	7	1	1	12	32	27	.386	.323
Behind in Count	.201	344	69	15	1	0	16	0	104	.202	.250	Pre-All Star	.236	478	113	24	3	6	42	46	68	.303	.337
Two Strikes	.146	355	52	8	1	1	16	44	124	.241	.183	Post-All Star	.263	342	90	21	3	5	45	56	56	.371	.386

Batter vs. Pitcher (career)

Hits Best Against	Avg	AB	H	2B	3B	HR	RBI	BB	SO	OBP	SLG	Hits Worst Against	Avg	AB	H	2B	3B	HR	RBI	BB	SO	OBP	SLG
Matt Young	.571	14	8	1	0	0	2	2	4	.625	.643	Randy Johnson	.000	13	0	0	0	0	0	2	4	.133	.000
Kenny Rogers	.500	10	5	1	0	2	7	2	2	.583	1.200	Mark Langston	.048	21	1	0	0	0	1	2	4	.130	.048
David Wells	.375	16	6	1	0	1	1	0	2	.375	.625	Erik Hanson	.091	11	1	0	0	0	0	1	2	.167	.091
Frank Tanana	.353	17	6	1	0	0	2	2	2	.421	.412	Jimmy Key	.208	24	5	1	0	0	3	1	2	.231	.250
Frank Viola	.333	12	4	0	0	0	0	1	0	.385	.333	Jim Abbott	.217	23	5	1	0	0	0	3	3	.308	.261

Shawn Green — Blue Jays Age 21 – Bats Left

	Avg	G	AB	R	H	2B	3B	HR	RBI	BB	SO	HBP	GDP	SB	CS	OBP	SLG	IBB	SH	SF	#Pit	#P/PA	GB	FB	G/F
1993 Season	.000	3	6	0	0	0	0	0	0	0	1	0	0	0	0	.000	.000	0	0	0	19	3.17	2	3	0.67

1993 Season

	Avg	AB	H	2B	3B	HR	RBI	BB	SO	OBP	SLG		Avg	AB	H	2B	3B	HR	RBI	BB	SO	OBP	SLG
vs. Left	.000	1	0	0	0	0	0	0	0	.000	.000	Scoring Posn	.000	3	0	0	0	0	0	0	0	.000	.000
vs. Right	.000	5	0	0	0	0	0	0	1	.000	.000	Close & Late	.000	0	0	0	0	0	0	0	0	.000	.000

Tyler Green — Phillies Age 24 – Pitches Right

	ERA	W	L	Sv	G	GS	IP	BB	SO	Avg	H	2B	3B	HR	RBI	OBP	SLG	CG	ShO	Sup	QS	#P/S	SB	CS	GB	FB	G/F
1993 Season	7.36	0	0	0	3	2	7.1	5	7	.444	16	2	0	1	6	.512	.583	0	0	7.36	0	65	0	1	13	6	2.17

1993 Season

	ERA	W	L	Sv	G	GS	IP	H	HR	BB	SO		Avg	AB	H	2B	3B	HR	RBI	BB	SO	OBP	SLG
Home	7.94	0	0	0	2	1	5.2	11	1	4	4	vs. Left	.462	13	6	0	0	1	4	2	4	.533	.692
Away	5.40	0	0	0	1	1	1.2	5	0	1	3	vs. Right	.435	23	10	2	0	0	2	3	3	.500	.522

Tommy Greene — Phillies Age 27 – Pitches Right (flyball pitcher)

	ERA	W	L	Sv	G	GS	IP	BB	SO	Avg	H	2B	3B	HR	RBI	OBP	SLG	CG	ShO	Sup	QS	#P/S	SB	CS	GB	FB	G/F
1993 Season	3.42	16	4	0	31	30	200.0	62	167	.233	175	36	4	12	70	.291	.340	7	2	6.89	17	106	18	5	218	236	0.92
Career (1989-1993)	3.82	36	19	0	99	82	549.2	194	398	.242	499	99	12	49	222	.306	.372	11	5	5.32	45	100	52	21	643	687	0.94

1993 Season

	ERA	W	L	Sv	G	GS	IP	H	HR	BB	SO		Avg	AB	H	2B	3B	HR	RBI	BB	SO	OBP	SLG
Home	2.99	10	0	0	17	16	114.1	87	6	37	99	vs. Left	.235	358	84	16	1	5	34	42	75	.314	.327
Away	3.99	6	4	0	14	14	85.2	88	6	25	68	vs. Right	.232	393	91	20	3	7	36	20	92	.269	.351
Day	2.97	4	0	0	6	5	36.1	28	2	12	28	Inning 1-6	.232	604	140	25	4	10	58	55	141	.296	.336
Night	3.52	12	4	0	25	25	163.2	147	10	50	139	Inning 7+	.238	147	35	11	0	2	12	7	26	.271	.354
Grass	2.52	4	1	0	8	8	53.2	51	3	12	40	None on	.229	459	105	20	3	9	9	32	103	.282	.344
Turf	3.75	12	3	0	23	22	146.1	124	9	50	127	Runners on	.240	292	70	16	1	3	61	30	64	.304	.332
April	2.45	2	0	0	5	4	29.1	19	1	8	28	Scoring Posn	.244	168	41	12	1	1	56	24	38	.327	.345
May	1.45	5	0	0	5	5	43.1	27	2	8	35	Close & Late	.234	47	11	6	0	1	9	3	5	.280	.426
June	6.98	2	2	0	6	6	29.2	41	3	13	26	None on/out	.241	199	48	11	1	5	5	12	44	.284	.382
July	3.52	3	1	0	5	5	30.2	28	2	10	22	vs. 1st Batr (relief)	.000	1	0	0	0	0	0	0	1	.000	.000
August	5.32	0	0	0	4	4	22.0	30	2	7	18	First Inning Pitched	.287	122	35	6	1	3	22	13	23	.350	.426
September/October	2.60	4	1	0	6	6	45.0	30	2	16	38	First 75 Pitches	.232	496	115	19	2	9	45	46	110	.296	.333
Starter	3.47	16	4	0	30	30	197.1	174	12	62	166	Pitch 76-90	.270	100	27	6	1	3	12	8	21	.330	.440
Reliever	0.00	0	0	0	1	0	2.2	1	0	0	1	Pitch 91-105	.237	76	18	6	1	0	9	3	18	.263	.342
0-3 Days Rest	1.29	1	0	0	1	1	7.0	2	1	1	8	Pitch 106+	.190	79	15	5	0	0	4	5	18	.235	.253
4 Days Rest	4.33	8	2	0	16	16	99.2	104	6	32	74	First Pitch	.264	91	24	6	2	1	12	2	0	.281	.407
5+ Days Rest	2.68	7	2	0	13	13	90.2	68	5	29	84	Ahead in Count	.203	365	74	16	2	4	23	0	147	.204	.290
Pre-All Star	3.51	11	2	0	18	17	115.1	99	7	35	96	Behind in Count	.248	153	38	7	0	2	16	32	0	.370	.333
Post-All Star	3.30	5	2	0	13	13	84.2	76	5	27	71	Two Strikes	.177	373	66	17	2	4	28	28	167	.235	.265

Career (1989-1993)

	ERA	W	L	Sv	G	GS	IP	H	HR	BB	SO		Avg	AB	H	2B	3B	HR	RBI	BB	SO	OBP	SLG
Home	3.26	21	6	0	51	43	295.2	248	22	103	230	vs. Left	.268	1094	293	56	8	27	125	132	191	.345	.408
Away	4.46	15	13	0	48	39	254.0	251	27	91	168	vs. Right	.212	972	206	43	4	22	97	62	207	.259	.332
Day	4.06	10	5	0	22	18	119.2	94	15	53	93	Inning 1-6	.245	1740	426	80	11	44	196	170	340	.311	.379
Night	3.75	26	14	0	77	64	430.0	405	34	141	305	Inning 7+	.224	326	73	19	1	5	26	24	58	.276	.334
Grass	4.13	8	4	0	27	21	135.0	130	16	48	86	None on	.234	1254	293	53	5	33	33	109	259	.298	.363
Turf	3.71	28	15	0	72	61	414.2	369	33	146	312	Runners on	.254	812	206	46	7	16	189	85	139	.317	.387
April	4.65	4	1	0	18	9	79.1	70	5	36	54	Scoring Posn	.260	453	118	29	5	7	160	59	87	.331	.393
May	1.36	9	0	0	12	9	79.2	44	2	23	68	Close & Late	.225	120	27	9	0	2	15	10	23	.285	.350

Career (1989-1993)	ERA	W	L	Sv	G	GS	IP	H	HR	BB	SO		Avg	AB	H	2B	3B	HR	RBI	BB	SO	OBP	SLG
June	5.00	4	3	0	15	14	81.0	91	11	28	63	None on/out	.233	536	125	25	2	12	12	46	110	.295	.354
July	3.78	5	4	0	11	11	66.2	60	7	25	46	vs. 1st Batr (relief)	.200	15	3	0	0	0	3	0	2	.188	.200
August	4.90	2	4	0	13	13	71.2	82	9	26	52	First Inning Pitched	.249	361	90	18	3	8	60	47	65	.330	.382
September/October	3.57	12	7	0	30	26	171.1	152	15	56	115	First 75 Pitches	.243	1464	356	72	9	35	162	148	275	.312	.376
Starter	3.75	35	19	0	82	82	511.1	463	46	177	382	Pitch 76-90	.266	256	68	10	1	9	30	24	52	.329	.418
Reliever	4.70	1	0	0	17	0	38.1	36	3	17	16	Pitch 91-105	.220	191	42	8	2	4	18	11	42	.260	.346
0-3 Days Rest	0.95	2	0	0	3	3	19.0	10	2	8	14	Pitch 106+	.213	155	33	9	0	1	12	11	29	.260	.290
4 Days Rest	4.41	18	15	0	49	49	302.1	300	29	102	212	First Pitch	.259	286	74	17	3	6	34	7	0	.275	.402
5+ Days Rest	2.98	15	4	0	30	30	190.0	153	15	67	156	Ahead in Count	.191	964	184	33	3	10	60	0	353	.192	.262
Pre-All Star	3.86	19	6	0	49	36	263.2	230	21	96	198	Behind in Count	.320	428	137	33	4	18	78	107	0	.449	.542
Post-All Star	3.78	17	13	0	50	46	286.0	269	28	98	200	Two Strikes	.174	1009	176	33	5	17	74	80	398	.236	.268

Pitcher vs. Batter (career)

Pitches Best Vs.	Avg	AB	H	2B	3B	HR	RBI	BB	SO	OBP	SLG	Pitches Worst Vs.	Avg	AB	H	2B	3B	HR	RBI	BB	SO	OBP	SLG
Jose Lind	.000	13	0	0	0	0	1	1	1	.007	.000	Felix Jose	.571	14	8	4	1	0	4	2	2	.556	1.000
Eric Karros	.000	13	0	0	0	0	0	0	3	.000	.000	Barry Bonds	.467	15	7	1	0	3	9	5	3	.571	1.133
Todd Hundley	.077	13	1	0	0	0	0	0	2	.077	.077	Bobby Bonilla	.450	20	9	4	0	1	5	6	2	.577	.800
Jerald Clark	.091	11	1	0	0	0	0	0	4	.091	.091	Darryl Strawberry	.375	8	3	0	0	1	2	3	1	.545	.750
Eric Young	.100	10	1	0	0	0	0	1	2	.182	.100	Rick Wilkins	.375	8	3	0	0	1	1	3	2	.545	.750

Willie Greene — Reds

Age 22 – Bats Left

	Avg	G	AB	R	H	2B	3B	HR	RBI	BB	SO	HBP	GDP	SB	CS	OBP	SLG	IBB	SH	SF	#Pit	#P/PA	GB	FB	G/F
1993 Season	.160	15	50	7	8	1	1	2	5	2	19	0	1	0	0	.189	.340	0	0	1	203	3.83	17	11	1.55
Career (1992-1993)	.231	44	143	17	33	6	3	4	18	12	42	0	2	0	2	.287	.399	0	0	2	564	3.59	43	40	1.08

1993 Season

	Avg	AB	H	2B	3B	HR	RBI	BB	SO	OBP	SLG		Avg	AB	H	2B	3B	HR	RBI	BB	SO	OBP	SLG
vs. Left	.063	16	1	0	0	1	2	0	10	.059	.250	Scoring Posn	.000	10	0	0	0	0	2	1	6	.083	.000
vs. Right	.206	34	7	1	1	1	3	2	9	.250	.382	Close & Late	.000	5	0	0	0	0	0	0	1	.000	.000

Mike Greenwell — Red Sox

Age 30 – Bats Left

	Avg	G	AB	R	H	2B	3B	HR	RBI	BB	SO	HBP	GDP	SB	CS	OBP	SLG	IBB	SH	SF	#Pit	#P/PA	GB	FB	G/F
1993 Season	.315	146	540	77	170	38	6	13	72	54	46	4	17	5	4	.379	.480	12	2	3	1875	3.11	213	166	1.28
Last Five Years	.299	646	2452	327	734	132	18	52	341	236	187	16	76	43	24	.362	.431	46	3	19	8561	3.14	1057	730	1.45

1993 Season

	Avg	AB	H	2B	3B	HR	RBI	BB	SO	OBP	SLG		Avg	AB	H	2B	3B	HR	RBI	BB	SO	OBP	SLG
vs. Left	.304	161	49	7	2	5	26	11	14	.362	.466	Scoring Posn	.355	121	43	8	2	5	58	22	8	.449	.579
vs. Right	.319	379	121	31	4	8	46	43	32	.387	.485	Close & Late	.386	83	32	3	0	3	17	10	7	.457	.530
Groundball	.381	84	32	7	1	1	10	5	5	.416	.524	None on/out	.275	109	30	7	3	0	0	4	8	.307	.394
Flyball	.279	122	34	6	1	7	19	16	12	.367	.516	Batting #2	.441	118	52	9	2	4	15	11	6	.488	.653
Home	.332	247	82	21	4	6	38	27	18	.401	.522	Batting #3	.273	381	104	26	4	8	50	40	35	.346	.425
Away	.300	293	88	17	2	7	34	27	28	.361	.444	Other	.341	41	14	3	0	1	7	3	5	.386	.488
Day	.331	175	58	9	3	2	26	20	16	.405	.451	April	.306	85	26	7	3	2	18	7	8	.366	.529
Night	.307	365	112	29	3	11	46	34	30	.367	.493	May	.316	57	18	5	0	0	6	4	3	.355	.404
Grass	.307	440	135	30	5	10	52	48	36	.377	.466	June	.289	97	28	5	0	4	17	13	11	.369	.464
Turf	.350	100	35	8	1	3	20	6	10	.389	.540	July	.270	89	24	6	1	3	13	15	11	.383	.461
First Pitch	.416	137	57	11	2	6	19	8	0	.452	.657	August	.307	101	31	8	0	0	5	4	4	.340	.386
Ahead in Count	.336	149	50	15	3	1	24	29	0	.439	.497	September/October	.387	111	43	7	2	4	13	11	9	.443	.595
Behind in Count	.232	177	41	4	1	4	17	0	36	.243	.333	Pre-All Star	.302	275	83	19	3	7	47	31	26	.374	.469
Two Strikes	.201	164	33	4	1	4	15	17	46	.279	.311	Post-All Star	.328	265	87	19	3	6	25	23	20	.385	.491

1993 By Position

Position	Avg	AB	H	2B	3B	HR	RBI	BB	SO	OBP	SLG	G	GS	Innings	PO	A	E	DP	Fld Pct	Rng Fctr	In Zone	Outs	Zone Rtg	MLB Zone
As Designated Hitter	.324	34	11	2	1	2	6	2	5	.368	.618	10	9	---	---	---	---	---	---	---	---	---	---	---
As lf	.316	503	159	36	5	11	66	51	41	.381	.473	134	130	1125.0	263	6	2	1	.993	2.15	315	254	.806	.818

Last Five Years

	Avg	AB	H	2B	3B	HR	RBI	BB	SO	OBP	SLG		Avg	AB	H	2B	3B	HR	RBI	BB	SO	OBP	SLG
vs. Left	.263	791	224	31	6	14	115	49	68	.331	.391	Scoring Posn	.282	670	189	35	6	10	274	100	55	.369	.397
vs. Right	.307	1661	510	101	12	38	226	187	119	.376	.451	Close & Late	.321	371	119	14	4	8	53	44	30	.400	.445
Groundball	.309	624	193	30	3	10	95	47	47	.358	.415	None on/out	.276	550	152	28	5	10	10	30	36	.316	.400
Flyball	.277	531	147	23	2	17	72	57	34	.350	.424	Batting #3	.270	767	207	39	7	13	81	88	64	.349	.390
Home	.311	1177	366	81	9	23	183	127	83	.378	.454	Batting #4	.308	701	216	45	1	17	119	67	60	.369	.448
Away	.289	1275	368	51	9	29	158	109	104	.347	.411	Other	.316	984	311	48	10	22	141	81	63	.368	.452
Day	.316	791	250	46	4	13	107	82	63	.384	.434	April	.271	377	102	13	5	11	47	42	34	.351	.419
Night	.291	1661	484	86	14	39	234	154	124	.351	.430	May	.285	400	114	21	1	4	51	49	30	.361	.373
Grass	.301	2060	620	117	13	41	286	206	149	.365	.430	June	.302	493	149	19	1	8	76	41	41	.356	.394
Turf	.291	392	114	15	5	11	55	30	38	.346	.439	July	.292	384	112	20	3	12	46	37	27	.358	.453
First Pitch	.347	577	200	30	2	17	94	28	0	.377	.494	August	.315	387	122	27	2	6	57	25	24	.355	.442
Ahead in Count	.343	635	218	46	8	20	106	124	0	.447	.535	September/October	.328	411	135	32	6	11	64	42	31	.391	.516
Behind in Count	.236	856	202	32	6	9	92	0	160	.244	.319	Pre-All Star	.288	1398	403	59	7	27	193	147	112	.358	.398
Two Strikes	.221	759	168	26	6	9	73	73	187	.292	.307	Post-All Star	.314	1054	331	73	11	25	148	89	75	.368	.475

Batter vs. Pitcher (career)

Hits Best Against	Avg	AB	H	2B	3B	HR	RBI	BB	SO	OBP	SLG	Hits Worst Against	Avg	AB	H	2B	3B	HR	RBI	BB	SO	OBP	SLG
Jeff Russell	.615	13	8	1	0	2	11	2	2	.667	1.154	Kenny Rogers	.063	16	1	1	0	0	0	0	3	.063	.125

Batter vs. Pitcher (career)																						
Hits Best Against	Avg	AB	H	2B	3B	HR	RBI	BB	SO	OBP	SLG	**Hits Worst Against**	Avg	AB	H	2B	3B	HR	RBI	BB	SO	OBP	SLG
Juan Guzman	.600	10	6	1	1	0	5	2	0	.667	.900	Mike Boddicker	.083	12	1	0	0	0	1	0	0	.077	.083
Lee Guetterman	.533	15	8	0	1	1	4	2	2	.588	.867	Bryan Harvey	.091	11	1	0	0	0	1	0	2	.083	.091
Jose Bautista	.500	18	9	1	1	4	7	2	0	.550	1.333	Ricky Bones	.091	11	1	1	0	0	1	0	0	.083	.182
Bill Gullickson	.429	14	6	3	1	1	3	1	0	.467	1.000	Jose Mesa	.129	31	4	0	0	0	2	1	2	.156	.129

Ken Greer — Mets

Age 27 – Pitches Right

	ERA	W	L	Sv	G	GS	IP	BB	SO	Avg	H	2B	3B	HR	RBI	OBP	SLG	GF	IR	IRS	Hld	SvOp	SB	CS	GB	FB	G/F
1993 Season	0.00	1	0	0	1	0	1.0	0	2	.000	0	0	0	0	0	.000	.000	1	0	0	0	0	0	0	0	1	0.00

1993 Season																						
	ERA	W	L	Sv	G	GS	IP	H	HR	BB	SO		Avg	AB	H	2B	3B	HR	RBI	BB	SO	OBP	SLG
Home	0.00	1	0	0	1	0	1.0	0	0	0	2	vs. Left	.000	1	0	0	0	0	0	0	1	.000	.000
Away	0.00	0	0	0	0	0	0.0	0	0	0	0	vs. Right	.000	2	0	0	0	0	0	0	1	.000	.000

Tommy Gregg — Reds

Age 30 – Bats Left

	Avg	G	AB	R	H	2B	3B	HR	RBI	BB	SO	HBP	GDP	SB	CS	OBP	SLG	IBB	SH	SF	#Pit	#P/PA	GB	FB	G/F
1993 Season	.167	10	12	1	2	0	0	0	1	0	0	0	0	0	0	.154	.167	0	0	1	51	3.92	7	5	1.40
Last Five Years	.240	326	653	57	157	29	2	13	61	51	115	2	9	10	9	.296	.351	8	3	3	2558	3.59	240	200	1.20

1993 Season																						
	Avg	AB	H	2B	3B	HR	RBI	BB	SO	OBP	SLG		Avg	AB	H	2B	3B	HR	RBI	BB	SO	OBP	SLG
vs. Left	.000	0	0	0	0	0	0	0	0	.000	.000	Scoring Posn	.000	2	0	0	0	0	1	0	0	.000	.000
vs. Right	.167	12	2	0	0	0	1	0	0	.154	.167	Close & Late	.333	3	1	0	0	0	0	0	0	.333	.333

Last Five Years																						
	Avg	AB	H	2B	3B	HR	RBI	BB	SO	OBP	SLG		Avg	AB	H	2B	3B	HR	RBI	BB	SO	OBP	SLG
vs. Left	.176	85	15	1	0	0	2	8	30	.247	.188	Scoring Posn	.229	157	36	5	1	5	50	20	28	.315	.369
vs. Right	.250	568	142	28	2	13	59	43	85	.304	.375	Close & Late	.218	133	29	5	0	4	14	14	32	.293	.346
Groundball	.236	212	50	5	1	3	20	13	39	.286	.311	None on/out	.209	134	28	6	1	2	2	5	27	.237	.313
Flyball	.228	162	37	9	0	4	12	22	31	.321	.358	Batting #5	.218	188	41	10	1	1	16	14	34	.271	.298
Home	.245	322	79	13	1	6	34	21	49	.292	.348	Batting #6	.260	123	32	6	0	3	8	7	20	.300	.382
Away	.236	331	78	16	1	7	27	30	66	.300	.353	Other	.246	342	84	13	1	9	37	30	61	.309	.368
Day	.306	147	45	13	1	2	17	14	21	.362	.449	April	.258	66	17	5	0	1	8	6	13	.315	.379
Night	.221	506	112	16	1	11	44	37	94	.277	.322	May	.083	24	2	1	0	1	1	5	3	.267	.250
Grass	.241	497	120	19	2	10	50	34	85	.290	.348	June	.236	148	35	6	0	0	9	12	17	.298	.277
Turf	.237	156	37	10	0	3	11	17	30	.314	.359	July	.243	111	27	2	1	4	14	7	21	.288	.387
First Pitch	.367	98	36	6	0	4	16	4	0	.394	.551	August	.265	166	44	10	1	4	16	8	29	.297	.410
Ahead in Count	.313	128	40	11	0	7	19	21	0	.409	.563	September/October	.232	138	32	5	0	3	13	13	32	.296	.333
Behind in Count	.171	321	55	6	1	2	14	0	103	.174	.215	Pre-All Star	.231	260	60	14	0	3	22	24	34	.300	.319
Two Strikes	.162	303	49	6	2	1	17	24	115	.222	.205	Post-All Star	.247	393	97	15	2	10	39	27	81	.294	.372

Batter vs. Pitcher (career)																						
Hits Best Against	Avg	AB	H	2B	3B	HR	RBI	BB	SO	OBP	SLG	**Hits Worst Against**	Avg	AB	H	2B	3B	HR	RBI	BB	SO	OBP	SLG
Andy Benes	.438	16	7	3	0	0	0	4	5	.550	.625	Ron Darling	.071	14	1	0	0	1	3	1	4	.133	.286
Mike Morgan	.364	22	8	1	0	0	1	0	1	.364	.409	Scott Scudder	.077	13	1	0	0	0	1	1	3	.143	.077
Greg Maddux	.364	11	4	0	0	0	2	0	2	.364	.364	David Cone	.091	11	1	1	0	0	0	2	2	.231	.182
Ramon Martinez	.350	20	7	2	0	1	1	1	3	.381	.600	Tim Belcher	.176	17	3	0	0	0	1	2	1	.263	.176
Jose Rijo	.333	12	4	2	0	0	1	0	1	.333	.500	Doug Drabek	.211	19	4	1	0	0	0	2	1	.286	.263

Ken Griffey Jr. — Mariners

Age 24 – Bats Left

	Avg	G	AB	R	H	2B	3B	HR	RBI	BB	SO	HBP	GDP	SB	CS	OBP	SLG	IBB	SH	SF	#Pit	#P/PA	GB	FB	G/F
1993 Season	.309	156	582	113	180	38	3	45	109	96	91	6	14	17	9	.408	.617	25	0	7	2464	3.57	175	198	0.88
Career (1989-1993)	.303	734	2747	424	832	170	15	132	453	318	404	16	54	77	38	.375	.520	81	5	27	10967	3.52	951	837	1.14

1993 Season																						
	Avg	AB	H	2B	3B	HR	RBI	BB	SO	OBP	SLG		Avg	AB	H	2B	3B	HR	RBI	BB	SO	OBP	SLG
vs. Left	.318	211	67	14	0	13	36	24	38	.394	.569	Scoring Posn	.239	142	34	6	2	7	58	45	31	.407	.458
vs. Right	.305	371	113	24	3	32	73	72	53	.416	.644	Close & Late	.305	95	29	5	1	3	15	17	19	.412	.474
Groundball	.276	87	24	4	0	6	15	14	17	.375	.529	None on/out	.305	128	39	9	0	11	11	5	19	.336	.633
Flyball	.341	126	43	11	1	10	23	23	18	.444	.683	Batting #2	.333	24	8	3	1	0	2	1	1	.360	.542
Home	.332	274	91	21	1	21	60	59	46	.455	.646	Batting #3	.308	558	172	35	2	45	107	95	90	.410	.620
Away	.289	308	89	17	2	24	49	37	45	.363	.591	Other	.000	0	0	0	0	0	0	0	0	.000	.000
Day	.319	160	51	7	1	16	32	29	24	.426	.675	April	.280	82	23	5	0	7	18	14	21	.388	.598
Night	.306	422	129	31	2	29	77	67	67	.401	.595	May	.288	104	30	8	1	3	12	14	12	.372	.471
Grass	.277	235	65	10	1	20	39	26	37	.347	.583	June	.353	102	36	7	0	10	22	13	12	.427	.716
Turf	.331	347	115	28	2	25	70	70	54	.446	.640	July	.330	106	35	5	2	10	26	13	19	.403	.698
First Pitch	.341	91	31	9	0	7	23	23	0	.474	.670	August	.333	75	25	4	0	9	13	20	12	.479	.747
Ahead in Count	.413	143	59	14	1	14	34	43	0	.542	.818	September/October	.274	113	31	9	0	6	18	22	15	.393	.513
Behind in Count	.214	238	51	8	1	15	31	0	74	.216	.445	Pre-All Star	.317	325	103	22	2	22	60	49	51	.407	.600
Two Strikes	.193	238	46	7	1	18	35	30	91	.285	.458	Post-All Star	.300	257	77	16	1	23	49	47	40	.410	.638

1993 By Position																								
Position	Avg	AB	H	2B	3B	HR	RBI	BB	SO	OBP	SLG	G	GS	Innings	PO	A	E	DP	Fld Pct	Rng Fctr	In Zone	Outs	Zone Rtg	MLB Zone
As Designated Hitter	.309	68	21	5	0	5	13	13	18	.422	.603	19	19	---	---	---	---	---	---	---	---	---	---	---
As cf	.309	514	159	33	3	40	96	83	73	.406	.619	139	137	1208.1	316	8	3	2	.991	2.41	396	307	.775	.829

Career (1989-1993)	Avg	AB	H	2B	3B	HR	RBI	BB	SO	OBP	SLG		Avg	AB	H	2B	3B	HR	RBI	BB	SO	OBP	SLG
vs. Left	.308	880	271	54	1	38	131	81	167	.371	.501	Scoring Posn	.303	704	213	43	5	28	305	149	133	.414	.497
vs. Right	.300	1867	561	116	14	94	322	237	237	.377	.529	Close & Late	.274	424	116	19	3	14	60	67	92	.373	.432
Groundball	.320	649	208	43	4	23	101	74	81	.389	.505	None on/out	.279	574	160	27	4	29	29	31	69	.318	.491
Flyball	.311	627	195	41	2	36	111	71	96	.380	.555	Batting #3	.308	1971	608	132	11	102	349	238	279	.383	.542
Home	.315	1356	427	96	7	71	247	175	187	.394	.553	Batting #5	.290	458	133	25	2	18	60	48	60	.357	.472
Away	.291	1391	405	74	8	61	206	143	217	.356	.487	Other	.286	318	91	13	2	12	44	32	65	.350	.453
Day	.319	730	233	38	5	40	121	88	119	.393	.549	April	.309	392	121	19	1	19	62	44	65	.376	.508
Night	.297	2017	599	132	10	92	332	230	285	.369	.509	May	.306	490	150	33	2	25	73	51	70	.370	.535
Grass	.292	1075	314	51	6	50	170	112	167	.358	.490	June	.284	426	121	29	0	20	65	57	60	.369	.493
Turf	.310	1672	518	119	9	82	283	206	237	.386	.539	July	.332	470	156	31	4	24	90	46	72	.390	.568
First Pitch	.374	438	164	30	3	31	110	58	0	.447	.669	August	.318	444	141	31	3	26	72	59	64	.400	.577
Ahead in Count	.374	617	231	48	1	36	118	158	0	.498	.630	September/October	.272	525	143	27	5	18	91	61	73	.350	.446
Behind in Count	.234	1177	276	59	6	42	133	0	342	.236	.402	Pre-All Star	.300	1465	440	88	4	71	224	170	222	.372	.511
Two Strikes	.211	1165	246	48	6	44	140	93	404	.270	.376	Post-All Star	.306	1282	392	82	11	61	229	148	182	.379	.530

Batter vs. Pitcher (career)

Hits Best Against	Avg	AB	H	2B	3B	HR	RBI	BB	SO	OBP	SLG	Hits Worst Against	Avg	AB	H	2B	3B	HR	RBI	BB	SO	OBP	SLG
Bob Milacki	.667	9	6	1	0	0	3	2	0	.727	.778	Arthur Rhodes	.000	11	0	0	0	0	0	1	2	.083	.000
Paul Gibson	.615	13	8	2	0	2	2	3	0	.688	1.231	Scott Radinsky	.071	14	1	1	0	0	0	0	6	.071	.143
Scott Erickson	.538	26	14	5	0	1	4	4	0	.563	.846	Greg Hibbard	.077	13	1	0	0	0	1	0	2	.071	.077
Danny Darwin	.462	13	6	0	1	2	5	0	1	.462	1.077	Bret Saberhagen	.083	12	1	0	0	0	0	2	3	.214	.083
John Doherty	.400	10	4	1	0	2	4	2	2	.500	1.100	Tony Fossas	.125	16	2	0	0	0	1	1	4	.176	.125

Alfredo Griffin — Blue Jays

Age 37 – Bats Both

	Avg	G	AB	R	H	2B	3B	HR	RBI	BB	SO	HBP	GDP	SB	CS	OBP	SLG	IBB	SH	SF	#Pit	#P/PA	GB	FB	G/F
1993 Season	.211	46	95	15	20	3	0	0	3	3	13	0	3	0	0	.235	.242	0	4	0	332	3.25	43	22	1.95
Last Five Years	.232	495	1562	150	362	54	7	1	104	92	203	3	21	24	15	.274	.277	18	31	12	5429	3.19	619	425	1.46

1993 Season

	Avg	AB	H	2B	3B	HR	RBI	BB	SO	OBP	SLG		Avg	AB	H	2B	3B	HR	RBI	BB	SO	OBP	SLG
vs. Left	.148	27	4	0	0	0	1	0	6	.148	.148	Scoring Posn	.231	26	6	2	0	0	3	1	2	.259	.308
vs. Right	.235	68	16	3	0	0	2	3	7	.268	.279	Close & Late	.214	14	3	1	0	0	1	1	4	.267	.286

Last Five Years

	Avg	AB	H	2B	3B	HR	RBI	BB	SO	OBP	SLG		Avg	AB	H	2B	3B	HR	RBI	BB	SO	OBP	SLG
vs. Left	.251	550	138	12	2	1	34	36	83	.297	.285	Scoring Posn	.242	368	89	12	3	0	102	32	54	.297	.291
vs. Right	.221	1012	224	42	5	0	70	56	120	.261	.273	Close & Late	.236	267	63	9	0	0	13	13	44	.274	.270
Groundball	.275	512	141	22	2	0	36	21	50	.302	.326	None on/out	.209	436	91	11	3	1	1	29	55	.258	.255
Flyball	.210	338	71	10	1	1	22	23	55	.262	.254	Batting #1	.237	291	69	13	1	0	17	19	34	.283	.289
Home	.229	742	170	25	2	0	49	46	90	.272	.268	Batting #8	.238	975	232	30	6	1	72	61	132	.282	.284
Away	.234	820	192	29	5	1	55	46	113	.276	.285	Other	.206	296	61	11	0	0	15	12	37	.235	.243
Day	.235	490	115	21	2	0	34	26	65	.276	.286	April	.234	222	52	13	1	0	13	11	23	.268	.302
Night	.230	1072	247	33	5	1	70	66	138	.273	.273	May	.248	206	51	6	1	0	16	16	24	.302	.286
Grass	.227	1066	242	35	3	0	65	60	149	.267	.265	June	.261	303	79	8	2	1	21	14	47	.292	.310
Turf	.242	496	120	19	4	1	39	32	54	.288	.302	July	.230	265	61	10	1	0	18	17	28	.277	.275
First Pitch	.302	324	98	17	1	1	34	7	0	.311	.370	August	.212	250	53	8	0	0	13	15	35	.257	.244
Ahead in Count	.254	283	72	13	1	0	18	38	0	.341	.307	September/October	.209	316	66	9	2	0	23	19	46	.252	.250
Behind in Count	.193	731	141	19	3	0	38	0	177	.195	.227	Pre-All Star	.244	824	201	31	4	1	59	48	104	.284	.295
Two Strikes	.159	610	97	14	1	0	23	36	203	.209	.185	Post-All Star	.218	738	161	23	3	0	45	44	99	.262	.257

Batter vs. Pitcher (since 1984)

Hits Best Against	Avg	AB	H	2B	3B	HR	RBI	BB	SO	OBP	SLG	Hits Worst Against	Avg	AB	H	2B	3B	HR	RBI	BB	SO	OBP	SLG
Tom Candiotti	.700	10	7	1	0	0	0	1	1	.727	.800	Kelly Downs	.077	26	2	1	0	0	0	0	2	.077	.115
Matt Young	.545	11	6	0	1	0	0	0	1	.545	.727	Mike Bielecki	.083	12	1	1	0	0	0	0	0	.083	.167
Bud Black	.500	20	10	2	1	0	0	0	2	.500	.700	Scott Scudder	.083	12	1	0	0	0	1	1	0	.143	.083
Mike Boddicker	.444	36	16	4	0	0	5	2	2	.474	.556	Shawn Boskie	.091	11	1	0	0	0	0	0	0	.091	.091
Mark Eichhorn	.308	13	4	2	0	1	3	1	1	.357	.692	Mark Davis	.100	10	1	0	0	0	0	1	3	.182	.100

Jason Grimsley — Indians

Age 26 – Pitches Right (groundball pitcher)

	ERA	W	L	Sv	G	GS	IP	BB	SO	Avg	H	2B	3B	HR	RBI	OBP	SLG	CG	ShO	Sup	QS	#P/S	SB	CS	GB	FB	G/F
1993 Season	5.31	3	4	0	10	6	42.1	20	27	.302	52	6	0	3	18	.378	.390	0	0	4.25	3	98	7	1	71	41	1.73
Career (1989-1993)	4.58	8	16	0	37	33	179.0	123	117	.256	172	28	5	10	65	.374	.357	0	0	3.92	12	90	26	7	292	154	1.90

1993 Season

	ERA	W	L	Sv	G	GS	IP	H	HR	BB	SO		Avg	AB	H	2B	3B	HR	RBI	BB	SO	OBP	SLG
Home	7.65	1	3	0	5	3	20.0	29	1	9	13	vs. Left	.281	64	18	3	0	1	6	8	10	.361	.375
Away	3.22	2	1	0	5	3	22.1	23	2	11	14	vs. Right	.315	108	34	3	0	2	12	12	17	.388	.398

Marquis Grissom — Expos

Age 27 – Bats Right

	Avg	G	AB	R	H	2B	3B	HR	RBI	BB	SO	HBP	GDP	SB	CS	OBP	SLG	IBB	SH	SF	#Pit	#P/PA	GB	FB	G/F
1993 Season	.298	157	630	104	188	27	2	19	95	52	76	3	10	53	10	.351	.438	6	0	8	2549	3.68	270	202	1.34
Career (1989-1993)	.277	588	2203	334	610	105	19	43	231	167	307	9	34	230	42	.329	.400	14	12	13	8636	3.59	923	639	1.44

1993 Season

	Avg	AB	H	2B	3B	HR	RBI	BB	SO	OBP	SLG		Avg	AB	H	2B	3B	HR	RBI	BB	SO	OBP	SLG
vs. Left	.307	192	59	13	1	7	28	16	24	.362	.495	Scoring Posn	.259	185	48	9	1	6	77	16	18	.310	.416
vs. Right	.295	438	129	14	1	12	67	36	52	.346	.413	Close & Late	.347	98	34	8	0	1	21	9	18	.398	.459

1993 Season

	Avg	AB	H	2B	3B	HR	RBI	BB	SO	OBP	SLG
Groundball	.282	195	55	6	0	2	27	19	23	.349	.344
Flyball	.282	103	29	4	1	6	20	5	13	.312	.515
Home	.319	307	98	13	0	9	50	23	32	.366	.450
Away	.279	323	90	14	2	10	45	29	44	.336	.427
Day	.273	194	53	6	2	5	26	13	28	.317	.402
Night	.310	436	135	21	0	14	69	39	48	.365	.454
Grass	.272	191	52	10	1	6	26	18	28	.336	.429
Turf	.310	439	136	17	1	13	69	34	48	.357	.442
First Pitch	.242	66	16	3	0	3	9	5	0	.315	.424
Ahead in Count	.354	181	64	8	1	5	36	33	0	.443	.492
Behind in Count	.274	252	69	10	1	6	30	0	63	.273	.393
Two Strikes	.264	250	66	9	1	5	28	14	76	.305	.368

	Avg	AB	H	2B	3B	HR	RBI	BB	SO	OBP	SLG
None on/out	.358	148	53	6	1	4	4	10	14	.399	.493
Batting #1	.370	138	51	4	0	7	25	11	13	.411	.551
Batting #3	.280	490	137	23	2	12	69	41	63	.335	.408
Other	.000	2	0	0	0	0	1	0	0	.000	.000
April	.294	85	25	3	0	4	17	9	10	.362	.471
May	.326	92	30	6	1	2	17	7	11	.376	.478
June	.276	105	29	6	1	4	13	10	13	.336	.467
July	.224	107	24	4	0	2	13	10	17	.298	.318
August	.325	117	38	3	0	3	18	10	14	.372	.427
September/October	.339	124	42	5	0	4	17	6	11	.364	.476
Pre-All Star	.285	326	93	16	2	11	53	28	42	.340	.448
Post-All Star	.313	304	95	11	0	8	42	24	34	.362	.428

1993 By Position

Position	Avg	AB	H	2B	3B	HR	RBI	BB	SO	OBP	SLG	G	GS	Innings	PO	A	E	DP	Fld Pct	Rng Fctr	In Zone	Outs	Zone Rtg	MLB Zone
As cf	.299	629	188	27	2	19	94	52	76	.351	.439	157	156	1357.0	416	8	7	3	.984	2.81	491	412	.839	.829

Career (1989-1993)

	Avg	AB	H	2B	3B	HR	RBI	BB	SO	OBP	SLG
vs. Left	.276	830	229	50	8	18	87	74	118	.336	.420
vs. Right	.277	1373	381	55	11	25	144	93	189	.324	.388
Groundball	.279	788	220	32	6	8	71	59	89	.332	.365
Flyball	.243	460	112	16	3	12	48	37	78	.298	.370
Home	.284	1039	295	51	7	22	117	78	143	.335	.410
Away	.271	1164	315	54	12	21	114	89	164	.323	.392
Day	.255	647	165	22	6	15	72	48	114	.307	.377
Night	.286	1556	445	83	13	28	159	119	193	.337	.410
Grass	.264	629	166	24	6	9	58	44	96	.314	.364
Turf	.282	1574	444	81	13	34	173	123	211	.334	.415
First Pitch	.289	263	76	15	3	11	35	10	0	.322	.494
Ahead in Count	.316	582	184	35	4	11	73	105	0	.416	.447
Behind in Count	.243	938	228	37	9	10	74	0	260	.247	.334
Two Strikes	.229	927	212	35	9	11	71	50	307	.270	.321

	Avg	AB	H	2B	3B	HR	RBI	BB	SO	OBP	SLG
Scoring Posn	.274	555	152	29	2	13	186	59	78	.340	.404
Close & Late	.257	397	102	15	2	7	53	33	65	.313	.358
None on/out	.298	557	166	27	7	13	13	41	79	.347	.442
Batting #1	.297	619	184	31	9	13	60	43	79	.342	.439
Batting #2	.270	770	208	40	6	10	63	56	118	.322	.377
Other	.268	814	218	34	4	20	108	68	110	.324	.393
April	.264	288	76	18	1	8	40	25	39	.323	.417
May	.291	378	110	16	3	8	38	26	57	.339	.413
June	.287	324	93	20	3	4	32	34	42	.355	.404
July	.235	378	89	12	4	5	41	27	60	.291	.328
August	.272	360	98	17	5	9	38	25	47	.317	.422
September/October	.303	475	144	22	3	9	42	30	62	.345	.419
Pre-All Star	.273	1136	310	58	8	21	122	94	164	.328	.393
Post-All Star	.281	1067	300	47	11	22	109	73	143	.329	.408

Batter vs. Pitcher (career)

Hits Best Against	Avg	AB	H	2B	3B	HR	RBI	BB	SO	OBP	SLG
Curt Schilling	.519	27	14	2	0	1	6	0	2	.519	.704
Jeff Innis	.500	14	7	1	0	1	2	0	1	.500	.786
Bruce Hurst	.480	25	12	0	0	1	4	3	3	.536	.600
Greg Swindell	.438	16	7	0	1	4	7	0	2	.438	1.313
Trevor Wilson	.350	20	7	1	0	3	4	2	1	.409	.850

Hits Worst Against	Avg	AB	H	2B	3B	HR	RBI	BB	SO	OBP	SLG
Pat Rapp	.000	11	0	0	0	0	0	0	2	.000	.000
Mitch Williams	.063	16	1	1	0	0	0	2	1	.167	.125
Bill Swift	.077	13	1	0	0	0	0	0	1	.077	.077
Mike Maddux	.091	11	1	0	0	0	0	0	4	.091	.091
Kelly Downs	.154	13	2	0	0	0	0	0	3	.154	.154

Buddy Groom — Tigers

Age 28 – Pitches Left (groundball pitcher)

	ERA	W	L	Sv	G	GS	IP	BB	SO	Avg	H	2B	3B	HR	RBI	OBP	SLG	GF	IR	IRS	Hld	SvOp	SB	CS	GB	FB	G/F
1993 Season	6.14	0	2	0	19	3	36.2	13	15	.322	48	12	0	4	23	.375	.483	8	4	1	1	0	4	2	56	46	1.22
Career (1992-1993)	5.97	0	7	1	31	10	75.1	35	30	.321	96	22	2	8	47	.389	.488	11	11	4	1	2	4	4	119	77	1.55

1993 Season

	ERA	W	L	Sv	G	GS	IP	H	HR	BB	SO
Home	5.51	0	0	0	9	2	16.1	24	1	6	10
Away	6.64	0	2	0	10	1	20.1	24	3	7	5

	Avg	AB	H	2B	3B	HR	RBI	BB	SO	OBP	SLG
vs. Left	.279	43	12	3	0	2	5	3	5	.319	.488
vs. Right	.340	106	36	9	0	2	18	10	10	.397	.481

Kevin Gross — Dodgers

Age 33 – Pitches Right

	ERA	W	L	Sv	G	GS	IP	BB	SO	Avg	H	2B	3B	HR	RBI	OBP	SLG	CG	ShO	Sup	QS	#P/S	SB	CS	GB	FB	G/F
1993 Season	4.14	13	13	0	33	32	202.1	74	150	.282	224	26	3	15	95	.344	.379	3	0	5.87	16	98	18	10	322	173	1.86
Last Five Years	3.98	51	61	3	175	129	887.1	354	672	.262	888	131	19	65	373	.333	.370	13	7	4.36	72	98	116	43	1243	840	1.48

1993 Season

	ERA	W	L	Sv	G	GS	IP	H	HR	BB	SO
Home	3.29	8	5	0	17	16	109.1	98	6	35	75
Away	5.13	5	8	0	16	16	93.0	126	9	39	75
Day	3.95	2	1	0	7	7	43.1	46	0	16	33
Night	4.19	11	12	0	26	25	159.0	178	15	58	117
Grass	3.77	12	8	0	27	26	169.2	181	10	61	122
Turf	6.06	1	5	0	6	6	32.2	43	5	13	28
April	6.67	2	2	0	6	5	27.0	32	1	15	20
May	3.86	2	2	0	5	5	32.2	37	0	11	27
June	1.78	2	2	0	5	5	35.1	28	2	8	31
July	5.28	1	3	0	5	5	30.2	43	3	13	21
August	5.35	2	3	0	6	6	33.2	45	5	16	21
September/October	2.93	4	1	0	6	6	43.0	39	4	11	30
Starter	4.09	13	12	0	32	32	200.1	223	15	72	149
Reliever	9.00	0	1	0	1	0	2.0	1	0	2	1
0-3 Days Rest	4.50	1	0	0	1	1	8.0	8	0	3	5
4 Days Rest	3.80	5	5	0	13	13	87.2	98	8	28	61
5+ Days Rest	4.30	7	7	0	18	18	104.2	117	7	41	83

	Avg	AB	H	2B	3B	HR	RBI	BB	SO	OBP	SLG
vs. Left	.277	394	109	10	1	7	45	54	74	.363	.360
vs. Right	.287	401	115	16	2	8	50	20	76	.325	.397
Inning 1-6	.290	696	202	21	3	15	88	60	138	.349	.394
Inning 7+	.222	99	22	5	0	0	7	14	12	.316	.273
None on	.282	426	120	14	2	12	12	40	80	.349	.408
Runners on	.282	369	104	12	1	3	83	34	70	.339	.344
Scoring Posn	.278	205	57	6	1	2	80	26	45	.350	.346
Close & Late	.282	39	11	3	0	0	4	8	5	.396	.359
None on/out	.286	192	55	7	1	4	4	22	34	.366	.396
vs. 1st Batr (relief)	.000	0	0	0	0	0	0	1	0	1.000	.000
First Inning Pitched	.336	134	45	2	1	1	24	22	25	.430	.388
First 75 Pitches	.291	597	174	16	3	12	73	54	119	.352	.389
Pitch 76-90	.204	98	20	6	0	2	10	10	17	.278	.327
Pitch 91-105	.297	74	22	3	0	0	9	6	11	.346	.338
Pitch 106+	.308	26	8	1	0	1	3	4	3	.400	.462
First Pitch	.333	114	38	1	0	3	12	4	0	.358	.421
Ahead in Count	.219	370	81	7	2	2	36	0	124	.223	.265

1993 Season

	ERA	W	L	Sv	G	GS	IP	H	HR	BB	SO
Pre-All Star	4.39	7	7	0	18	17	106.2	118	5	39	86
Post-All Star	3.86	6	6	0	15	15	95.2	106	10	35	64

	Avg	AB	H	2B	3B	HR	RBI	BB	SO	OBP	SLG
Behind in Count	.348	161	56	9	1	5	26	38	0	.471	.509
Two Strikes	.192	343	66	7	1	2	29	32	150	.265	.236

Last Five Years

	ERA	W	L	Sv	G	GS	IP	H	HR	BB	SO
Home	3.62	29	26	1	82	63	447.0	414	25	158	337
Away	4.33	22	35	2	93	66	440.1	474	40	196	335
Day	3.17	13	12	0	45	31	229.2	208	8	84	171
Night	4.26	38	49	3	130	98	657.2	680	57	270	501
Grass	3.78	31	35	3	107	73	526.1	529	34	202	396
Turf	4.26	20	26	0	68	56	361.0	359	31	152	276
April	4.92	8	11	0	24	22	124.1	146	7	57	94
May	3.39	13	7	0	29	23	167.1	151	9	53	145
June	4.04	7	13	2	29	22	156.0	144	13	56	117
July	3.58	8	10	1	27	18	125.2	127	7	67	98
August	4.67	7	12	0	35	23	154.1	161	17	68	110
September/October	3.44	10	8	0	31	21	159.2	159	12	53	110
Starter	4.11	44	54	0	129	129	801.1	798	59	319	599
Reliever	2.72	7	7	3	46	0	86.0	90	6	35	73
0-3 Days Rest	4.21	4	4	0	8	8	51.1	44	4	17	44
4 Days Rest	3.87	24	29	0	67	67	439.0	417	34	167	326
5+ Days Rest	4.43	16	21	0	54	54	311.0	337	21	135	229
Pre-All Star	4.18	31	34	3	91	73	489.0	493	32	189	384
Post-All Star	3.73	20	27	0	84	56	398.1	395	33	165	288

	Avg	AB	H	2B	3B	HR	RBI	BB	SO	OBP	SLG
vs. Left	.276	1823	504	78	14	35	221	246	343	.362	.392
vs. Right	.246	1563	384	53	5	30	152	108	329	.298	.344
Inning 1-6	.263	2754	723	110	17	54	317	288	563	.333	.374
Inning 7+	.261	632	165	21	2	11	56	66	109	.334	.353
None on	.260	1929	501	68	8	43	43	176	393	.325	.370
Runners on	.266	1457	387	63	11	22	330	178	279	.343	.369
Scoring Posn	.257	855	220	34	9	14	304	133	186	.350	.367
Close & Late	.292	318	93	13	0	5	31	31	66	.358	.381
None on/out	.285	861	245	34	4	20	20	88	166	.354	.403
vs. 1st Batr (relief)	.350	40	14	3	0	2	4	6	8	.435	.575
First Inning Pitched	.288	645	186	25	4	10	96	103	123	.386	.386
First 75 Pitches	.266	2552	680	95	13	49	278	263	525	.336	.371
Pitch 76-90	.250	396	99	21	5	10	58	47	69	.330	.404
Pitch 91-105	.254	284	72	8	1	3	19	22	48	.308	.320
Pitch 106+	.240	154	37	7	0	3	18	22	30	.337	.344
First Pitch	.336	503	169	26	2	14	70	25	0	.373	.479
Ahead in Count	.190	1512	288	37	8	10	122	0	551	.193	.245
Behind in Count	.349	724	253	38	6	28	113	181	0	.476	.535
Two Strikes	.169	1508	255	40	9	9	112	147	672	.244	.225

Pitcher vs. Batter (since 1984)

Pitches Best Vs.	Avg	AB	H	2B	3B	HR	RBI	BB	SO	OBP	SLG
Phil Plantier	.000	12	0	0	0	0	0	1	5	.077	.000
Bob Melvin	.000	10	0	0	0	0	0	1	4	.091	.000
Reggie Sanders	.071	14	1	0	0	0	0	2	5	.188	.071
Craig Biggio	.086	35	3	0	0	0	2	2	8	.135	.086
Todd Benzinger	.100	10	1	0	0	0	2	0	1	.091	.100

Pitches Worst Vs.	Avg	AB	H	2B	3B	HR	RBI	BB	SO	OBP	SLG
Rick Wilkins	.571	14	8	3	0	2	4	1	2	.600	1.214
Charlie Hayes	.563	16	9	1	0	2	3	1	0	.588	1.000
Rafael Palmeiro	.429	14	6	2	1	1	5	3	0	.529	.929
Eric Davis	.385	26	10	2	1	3	5	6	6	.500	.885
Tom Brunansky	.385	13	5	0	2	1	3	3	3	.500	.923

Kip Gross — Dodgers

Age 29 – Pitches Right (groundball pitcher)

	ERA	W	L	Sv	G	GS	IP	BB	SO	Avg	H	2B	3B	HR	RBI	OBP	SLG	GF	IR	IRS	Hld	SvOp	SB	CS	GB	FB	G/F
1993 Season	0.60	0	0	0	10	0	15.0	4	12	.236	13	2	0	0	2	.288	.273	0	3	1	3	0	2	1	11	19	0.58
Career (1990-1993)	3.31	7	5	0	60	10	130.2	56	69	.283	144	19	2	9	57	.352	.381	15	27	12	6	0	13	6	211	127	1.66

1993 Season

	ERA	W	L	Sv	G	GS	IP	H	HR	BB	SO
Home	1.13	0	0	0	6	0	8.0	6	0	3	7
Away	0.00	0	0	0	4	0	7.0	7	0	1	5

	Avg	AB	H	2B	3B	HR	RBI	BB	SO	OBP	SLG
vs. Left	.208	24	5	0	0	0	1	2	8	.269	.208
vs. Right	.258	31	8	2	0	0	1	2	4	.303	.323

Kelly Gruber — Angels

Age 32 – Bats Right

	Avg	G	AB	R	H	2B	3B	HR	RBI	BB	SO	HBP	GDP	SB	CS	OBP	SLG	IBB	SH	SF	#Pit	#P/PA	GB	FB	G/F
1993 Season	.277	18	65	10	18	3	0	3	9	2	11	1	2	0	0	.309	.462	0	2	0	249	3.56	22	20	1.10
Last Five Years	.264	536	2077	285	548	97	15	83	308	137	307	22	50	43	21	.312	.445	10	7	27	7497	3.30	748	705	1.06

1993 Season

	Avg	AB	H	2B	3B	HR	RBI	BB	SO	OBP	SLG
vs. Left	.304	23	7	1	0	1	5	0	4	.304	.478
vs. Right	.262	42	11	2	0	2	4	2	7	.311	.452

	Avg	AB	H	2B	3B	HR	RBI	BB	SO	OBP	SLG
Scoring Posn	.250	16	4	1	0	1	7	2	5	.333	.500
Close & Late	.111	9	1	0	0	1	1	0	2	.111	.444

Last Five Years

	Avg	AB	H	2B	3B	HR	RBI	BB	SO	OBP	SLG
vs. Left	.291	574	167	29	5	27	90	40	81	.333	.500
vs. Right	.253	1503	381	68	10	56	218	97	226	.304	.424
Groundball	.245	599	147	26	3	17	92	39	76	.300	.384
Flyball	.263	472	124	20	8	23	72	36	75	.315	.485
Home	.274	1034	283	43	9	47	157	61	152	.318	.469
Away	.254	1043	265	54	6	36	151	76	155	.307	.421
Day	.245	632	155	26	6	24	95	46	97	.302	.419
Night	.272	1445	393	71	9	59	213	91	210	.317	.456
Grass	.250	836	209	47	5	32	126	64	118	.308	.433
Turf	.273	1241	339	50	10	51	182	73	189	.316	.453
First Pitch	.281	413	116	23	0	17	40	7	0	.300	.460
Ahead in Count	.317	404	128	26	5	23	92	65	0	.406	.577
Behind in Count	.230	955	220	31	6	31	123	0	271	.238	.373
Two Strikes	.189	859	162	28	6	20	101	64	307	.249	.305

	Avg	AB	H	2B	3B	HR	RBI	BB	SO	OBP	SLG
Scoring Posn	.269	551	148	25	6	24	227	46	82	.320	.466
Close & Late	.248	335	83	15	3	10	56	19	62	.292	.400
None on/out	.245	457	112	19	4	11	11	17	54	.280	.376
Batting #3	.274	1017	279	56	7	46	168	73	148	.324	.479
Batting #5	.243	419	102	21	2	17	57	22	64	.283	.425
Other	.261	641	167	20	6	20	83	42	95	.312	.404
April	.302	298	90	13	3	16	57	22	48	.353	.527
May	.260	296	77	18	2	13	43	27	45	.324	.466
June	.280	422	118	19	2	17	59	26	55	.326	.455
July	.241	291	70	8	0	12	36	16	45	.286	.392
August	.213	348	74	18	2	5	32	16	52	.251	.319
September/October	.282	422	119	21	6	20	81	30	62	.330	.502
Pre-All Star	.276	1075	297	50	7	46	161	78	153	.329	.464
Post-All Star	.250	1002	251	47	8	37	147	59	154	.294	.424

Batter vs. Pitcher (career)

Hits Best Against	Avg	AB	H	2B	3B	HR	RBI	BB	SO	OBP	SLG
Jeff Reardon	.500	12	6	2	0	1	2	2	1	.571	.917
Jeff Russell	.429	14	6	1	0	2	6	0	0	.400	.929
Mark Knudson	.429	14	6	0	1	1	4	0	1	.400	.786
Bob Welch	.412	17	7	2	0	1	2	4	2	.500	.706
Charles Nagy	.400	20	8	3	0	2	6	2	2	.455	.850

Hits Worst Against	Avg	AB	H	2B	3B	HR	RBI	BB	SO	OBP	SLG
Steve Farr	.077	13	1	0	0	0	0	0	3	.077	.077
Jose Guzman	.077	13	1	0	0	0	0	0	4	.077	.077
Mark Langston	.080	25	2	0	0	0	0	1	10	.115	.080
Tim Leary	.083	12	1	0	0	0	1	1	3	.154	.083
Nolan Ryan	.091	22	2	0	0	0	1	1	6	.130	.091

Eddie Guardado — Twins

Age 23 – Pitches Left (flyball pitcher)

	ERA	W	L	Sv	G	GS	IP	BB	SO	Avg	H	2B	3B	HR	RBI	OBP	SLG	CG	ShO	Sup	QS	#P/S	SB	CS	GB	FB	G/F
1993 Season	6.18	3	8	0	19	16	94.2	36	46	.319	123	34	5	13	64	.376	.535	0	0	4.75	5	94	12	5	106	164	0.65

1993 Season

	ERA	W	L	Sv	G	GS	IP	H	HR	BB	SO
Home	6.39	1	3	0	9	7	43.2	64	6	15	21
Away	6.00	2	5	0	10	9	51.0	59	7	21	25
Starter	6.08	3	8	0	16	16	87.1	109	13	32	42
Reliever	7.36	0	0	0	3	0	7.1	14	0	4	4
0-3 Days Rest	6.75	0	1	0	1	1	5.1	6	1	0	2
4 Days Rest	7.11	1	5	0	7	7	38.0	53	4	13	13
5+ Days Rest	5.11	2	2	0	8	8	44.0	50	8	19	27
Pre-All Star	6.10	1	2	0	6	6	31.0	39	4	14	12
Post-All Star	6.22	2	6	0	13	10	63.2	84	9	22	34

	Avg	AB	H	2B	3B	HR	RBI	BB	SO	OBP	SLG
vs. Left	.318	88	28	6	3	2	15	4	12	.348	.523
vs. Right	.320	297	95	28	2	11	49	32	34	.384	.539
Scoring Posn	.388	98	38	9	3	3	50	9	10	.427	.633
Close & Late	.500	14	7	2	1	0	6	0	3	.500	.786
None on/out	.242	95	23	6	0	2	2	9	13	.308	.368
First Pitch	.500	50	25	4	0	4	11	1	0	.509	.820
Ahead in Count	.264	182	48	11	2	3	23	0	39	.264	.396
Behind in Count	.337	92	31	9	3	4	21	16	0	.427	.630
Two Strikes	.306	180	55	15	1	4	22	19	46	.372	.467

Mark Gubicza — Royals

Age 31 – Pitches Right (groundball pitcher)

	ERA	W	L	Sv	G	GS	IP	BB	SO	Avg	H	2B	3B	HR	RBI	OBP	SLG	GF	IR	IRS	Hld	SvOp	SB	CS	GB	FB	G/F
1993 Season	4.66	5	8	2	49	6	104.1	43	80	.307	128	24	3	2	62	.370	.393	12	33	15	8	3	11	2	178	72	2.47
Last Five Years	4.09	40	44	2	145	102	697.2	222	494	.279	759	131	16	35	311	.335	.378	12	33	15	8	3	53	22	1188	529	2.25

1993 Season

	ERA	W	L	Sv	G	GS	IP	H	HR	BB	SO
Home	5.02	4	4	2	30	3	61.0	75	1	27	49
Away	4.15	1	4	0	19	3	43.1	53	1	16	31
Starter	7.03	0	4	0	6	6	32.0	47	1	12	19
Reliever	3.61	5	4	2	43	0	72.1	81	1	31	61
0 Days rest	0.00	0	0	0	0	0	0.0	0	0	0	0
1 or 2 Days rest	3.66	4	2	2	29	0	51.2	54	1	22	43
3+ Days rest	3.48	1	2	0	14	0	20.2	27	0	9	18
Pre-All Star	4.50	2	6	0	26	6	72.0	81	1	26	53
Post-All Star	5.01	3	2	2	23	0	32.1	47	1	17	27

	Avg	AB	H	2B	3B	HR	RBI	BB	SO	OBP	SLG
vs. Left	.311	190	59	12	2	1	33	23	33	.382	.411
vs. Right	.304	227	69	12	1	1	29	20	47	.359	.379
Scoring Posn	.323	133	43	11	3	2	61	19	31	.392	.496
Close & Late	.292	144	42	7	1	0	17	21	26	.382	.354
None on/out	.295	95	28	3	0	0	0	5	14	.330	.326
First Pitch	.339	59	20	4	0	0	13	7	0	.391	.407
Ahead in Count	.250	164	41	4	2	1	19	0	55	.257	.317
Behind in Count	.398	108	43	13	1	1	25	15	0	.464	.565
Two Strikes	.227	194	44	6	1	1	19	21	80	.304	.284

Last Five Years

	ERA	W	L	Sv	G	GS	IP	H	HR	BB	SO
Home	4.00	24	20	2	81	54	375.1	400	11	121	253
Away	4.19	16	24	0	64	48	322.1	359	24	101	241
Day	3.84	11	12	1	41	27	194.2	213	7	63	138
Night	4.19	29	32	1	104	75	503.0	546	28	159	356
Grass	4.13	9	18	0	49	36	248.1	273	19	73	191
Turf	4.07	31	26	2	96	66	449.1	486	16	149	303
April	4.89	3	10	0	18	18	106.2	132	1	44	64
May	3.59	9	10	0	30	24	178.0	164	7	55	120
June	3.52	10	8	0	32	22	163.2	175	10	41	118
July	4.45	7	4	1	24	14	95.0	108	10	30	75
August	3.22	7	4	1	23	13	95.0	99	1	28	74
September/October	6.52	4	8	0	18	11	59.1	81	6	24	43
Starter	4.14	35	40	0	102	102	625.1	678	34	191	433
Reliever	3.61	5	4	2	43	0	72.1	81	1	31	61
0 Days rest	0.00	0	0	0	0	0	0.0	0	0	0	0
1 or 2 Days rest	3.66	4	2	2	29	0	51.2	54	1	22	43
3+ Days rest	3.48	1	2	0	14	0	20.2	27	0	9	18
Pre-All Star	3.82	25	30	0	90	70	488.0	516	20	147	335
Post-All Star	4.72	15	14	2	55	32	209.2	243	15	75	159

	Avg	AB	H	2B	3B	HR	RBI	BB	SO	OBP	SLG
vs. Left	.270	1331	360	65	9	16	138	131	227	.337	.369
vs. Right	.288	1386	399	66	7	19	173	91	267	.332	.387
Inning 1-6	.281	2160	607	105	11	28	253	171	392	.336	.379
Inning 7+	.273	557	152	26	5	7	58	51	102	.330	.375
None on	.274	1509	414	69	9	18	18	113	280	.328	.368
Runners on	.286	1208	345	62	7	17	293	109	214	.343	.391
Scoring Posn	.272	713	194	38	7	13	272	82	148	.340	.400
Close & Late	.263	327	86	17	2	2	30	36	57	.335	.346
None on/out	.285	685	195	35	7	10	10	32	109	.320	.400
vs. 1st Batr (relief)	.342	38	13	2	2	0	9	4	4	.405	.500
First Inning Pitched	.288	553	159	27	2	3	74	49	113	.349	.360
First 15 Pitches	.291	475	138	21	2	3	43	34	83	.341	.362
Pitch 16-30	.247	481	119	33	2	5	55	45	101	.317	.356
Pitch 31-45	.289	402	116	17	1	6	48	35	77	.346	.381
Pitch 46+	.284	1359	386	60	11	21	165	108	233	.336	.391
First Pitch	.328	430	141	27	3	12	85	22	0	.353	.488
Ahead in Count	.206	1086	224	35	10	6	87	0	390	.216	.273
Behind in Count	.384	661	254	53	1	12	101	102	0	.462	.522
Two Strikes	.193	1160	224	34	8	6	80	98	494	.260	.252

Pitcher vs. Batter (career)

Pitches Best Vs.	Avg	AB	H	2B	3B	HR	RBI	BB	SO	OBP	SLG
Dick Schofield	.000	27	0	0	0	0	0	1	5	.036	.000
Stan Javier	.000	11	0	0	0	0	0	0	1	.000	.000
Geno Petralli	.050	20	1	0	0	0	1	2	7	.130	.050
Mike Gallego	.053	19	1	0	0	0	0	3	3	.182	.053
Mark McLemore	.063	16	1	0	0	0	1	0	2	.063	.063

Pitches Worst Vs.	Avg	AB	H	2B	3B	HR	RBI	BB	SO	OBP	SLG
Fred McGriff	.500	20	10	3	0	4	4	3	3	.565	1.250
Edgar Martinez	.467	15	7	2	0	1	3	1	3	.500	.800
Juan Gonzalez	.462	13	6	2	0	1	5	0	2	.462	.846
Randy Milligan	.417	12	5	1	1	2	7	1	4	.462	1.167
Ivan Calderon	.375	16	6	3	0	2	4	0	3	.375	.938

Lee Guetterman — Cardinals

Age 35 – Pitches Left (groundball pitcher)

	ERA	W	L	Sv	G	GS	IP	BB	SO	Avg	H	2B	3B	HR	RBI	OBP	SLG	GF	IR	IRS	Hld	SvOp	SB	CS	GB	FB	G/F
1993 Season	2.93	3	3	1	40	0	46.0	16	19	.240	41	4	4	1	25	.309	.327	14	30	11	4	4	5	0	84	37	2.27
Last Five Years	3.77	26	24	24	296	0	396.0	120	173	.267	402	59	13	29	201	.321	.381	94	234	69	45	36	26	9	748	344	2.17

1993 Season

	ERA	W	L	Sv	G	GS	IP	H	HR	BB	SO
Home	2.49	3	1	0	19	0	21.2	16	1	5	12
Away	3.33	0	2	1	21	0	24.1	25	0	11	7
Starter	0.00	0	0	0	0	0	0.0	0	0	0	0
Reliever	2.93	3	3	1	40	0	46.0	41	1	16	19
0 Days rest	5.87	0	2	1	8	0	7.2	8	0	5	2
1 or 2 Days rest	2.22	3	0	0	24	0	28.1	25	0	7	15
3+ Days rest	2.70	0	1	0	8	0	10.0	8	1	4	2
Pre-All Star	3.52	1	0	0	5	0	7.2	7	0	3	3
Post-All Star	2.82	2	3	1	35	0	38.1	34	1	13	16

	Avg	AB	H	2B	3B	HR	RBI	BB	SO	OBP	SLG
vs. Left	.234	47	11	0	0	1	4	7	7	.345	.298
vs. Right	.242	124	30	4	4	0	21	9	12	.294	.339
Scoring Posn	.242	62	15	2	2	0	24	13	6	.372	.339
Close & Late	.228	79	18	0	3	1	12	7	11	.291	.342
None on/out	.316	38	12	1	0	1	1	0	5	.316	.421
First Pitch	.148	27	4	0	0	1	3	5	0	.281	.259
Ahead in Count	.243	74	18	2	2	0	6	0	17	.240	.324
Behind in Count	.267	45	12	1	2	0	11	7	0	.370	.378
Two Strikes	.219	64	14	0	2	0	6	4	19	.265	.281

Last Five Years

	ERA	W	L	Sv	G	GS	IP	H	HR	BB	SO
Home	3.79	20	11	14	153	0	225.1	225	16	65	106
Away	3.74	6	13	10	143	0	170.2	177	13	55	67
Day	3.28	11	7	7	92	0	118.0	119	9	39	41
Night	3.98	15	17	17	204	0	278.0	283	20	81	132
Grass	3.61	21	18	21	233	0	316.2	321	21	99	143
Turf	4.42	5	6	3	63	0	79.1	81	8	21	30
April	3.43	1	1	3	28	0	44.2	44	4	12	24
May	2.73	3	2	7	42	0	56.0	45	4	17	21
June	3.48	5	2	2	49	0	64.2	73	1	17	24
July	4.64	7	8	5	56	0	77.2	88	10	27	29
August	4.37	4	5	4	65	0	78.1	85	5	25	35
September/October	3.50	6	6	3	56	0	74.2	67	5	22	40
Starter	0.00	0	0	0	0	0	0.0	0	0	0	0
Reliever	3.77	26	24	24	296	0	396.0	402	29	120	173
0 Days rest	3.46	7	5	8	75	0	93.2	96	7	26	38
1 or 2 Days rest	3.13	11	9	11	141	0	192.2	176	13	60	89
3+ Days rest	5.17	8	10	5	80	0	109.2	130	9	34	46
Pre-All Star	3.23	12	6	16	140	0	196.0	194	13	54	85
Post-All Star	4.32	14	18	8	156	0	198.0	208	16	66	88

	Avg	AB	H	2B	3B	HR	RBI	BB	SO	OBP	SLG
vs. Left	.235	439	103	13	3	6	42	41	65	.306	.319
vs. Right	.280	1066	299	46	10	23	159	79	108	.327	.407
Inning 1-6	.244	168	41	9	0	4	27	19	31	.317	.369
Inning 7+	.270	1337	361	50	13	25	174	101	142	.321	.383
None on	.271	778	211	28	6	14	14	39	86	.310	.377
Runners on	.263	727	191	31	7	15	187	81	87	.331	.387
Scoring Posn	.248	451	112	19	6	12	175	70	60	.340	.397
Close & Late	.271	613	166	15	7	20	91	51	67	.326	.416
None on/out	.288	337	97	14	0	7	7	8	34	.308	.392
vs. 1st Batr (relief)	.235	268	63	11	1	3	39	19	35	.281	.317
First Inning Pitched	.260	942	245	30	10	17	140	78	103	.314	.367
First 15 Pitches	.264	905	239	30	9	18	118	70	95	.315	.377
Pitch 16-30	.276	427	118	18	3	7	52	28	55	.325	.382
Pitch 31-45	.222	126	28	8	1	2	17	15	18	.303	.349
Pitch 46+	.362	47	17	3	0	2	14	7	5	.444	.553
First Pitch	.294	211	62	8	0	5	33	26	0	.368	.403
Ahead in Count	.223	637	142	21	6	6	59	0	152	.224	.303
Behind in Count	.326	383	125	16	5	14	67	49	0	.401	.504
Two Strikes	.198	585	116	16	6	1	53	44	173	.254	.251

Pitcher vs. Batter (career)

Pitches Best Vs.	Avg	AB	H	2B	3B	HR	RBI	BB	SO	OBP	SLG
Dan Gladden	.071	14	1	0	0	0	0	0	2	.071	.071
Mike Felder	.091	11	1	0	0	0	0	0	0	.091	.091
Nelson Liriano	.100	10	1	0	0	0	2	2	1	.250	.100
Ellis Burks	.133	15	2	0	0	0	0	0	0	.133	.133
B.J. Surhoff	.154	13	2	0	0	0	1	0	1	.143	.154

Pitches Worst Vs.	Avg	AB	H	2B	3B	HR	RBI	BB	SO	OBP	SLG
Dave Winfield	.900	10	9	0	1	1	4	1	0	.909	1.400
Mike Greenwell	.533	15	8	0	1	1	4	2	2	.588	.867
Rob Deer	.429	7	3	1	0	2	3	4	1	.636	1.429
Chili Davis	.364	11	4	0	0	2	3	0	1	.364	.909
Steve Buechele	.333	18	6	2	1	2	6	2	2	.400	.889

Ozzie Guillen — White Sox

Age 30 – Bats Left (groundball hitter)

	Avg	G	AB	R	H	2B	3B	HR	RBI	BB	SO	HBP	GDP	SB	CS	OBP	SLG	IBB	SH	SF	#Pit	#P/PA	GB	FB	G/F
1993 Season	.280	134	457	44	128	23	4	4	50	10	41	0	6	5	4	.292	.374	0	13	6	1429	2.94	205	109	1.88
Last Five Years	.269	615	2134	225	574	88	19	9	218	63	169	1	28	76	53	.287	.341	12	53	22	6542	2.88	936	591	1.58

1993 Season

	Avg	AB	H	2B	3B	HR	RBI	BB	SO	OBP	SLG
vs. Left	.231	130	30	4	2	0	6	2	11	.241	.292
vs. Right	.300	327	98	19	2	4	44	8	30	.312	.407
Groundball	.299	87	26	4	0	1	10	1	10	.303	.379
Flyball	.238	105	25	4	1	0	8	1	14	.241	.295
Home	.297	212	63	10	1	3	22	5	19	.309	.396
Away	.265	245	65	13	3	1	28	5	22	.277	.355
Day	.282	124	35	5	0	2	19	4	6	.302	.371
Night	.279	333	93	18	4	2	31	6	35	.288	.375
Grass	.278	378	105	18	2	4	40	8	29	.290	.368
Turf	.291	79	23	5	2	0	10	2	12	.301	.405
First Pitch	.253	91	23	4	0	2	16	0	0	.242	.363
Ahead in Count	.344	93	32	7	1	0	10	9	0	.402	.441
Behind in Count	.242	207	50	9	2	1	17	0	39	.239	.319
Two Strikes	.253	154	39	7	2	1	13	1	41	.256	.344

	Avg	AB	H	2B	3B	HR	RBI	BB	SO	OBP	SLG
Scoring Posn	.304	112	34	3	2	1	42	2	12	.300	.393
Close & Late	.273	77	21	3	0	0	8	3	11	.296	.312
None on/out	.283	106	30	5	0	0	0	4	6	.309	.330
Total	.280	457	128	23	4	4	50	10	41	.292	.374
Batting #9	.280	457	128	23	4	4	50	10	41	.292	.374
Other	.000	0	0	0	0	0	0	0	0	.000	.000
April	.200	70	14	1	1	0	8	3	4	.230	.243
May	.278	54	15	3	0	1	8	2	4	.293	.389
June	.310	87	27	4	1	0	7	2	6	.322	.379
July	.301	83	25	6	0	3	13	2	11	.318	.482
August	.247	73	18	5	1	0	6	0	11	.240	.342
September/October	.322	90	29	4	1	0	8	1	5	.330	.389
Pre-All Star	.276	246	68	11	2	3	31	8	18	.295	.374
Post-All Star	.284	211	60	12	2	1	19	2	23	.288	.374

1993 By Position

Position	Avg	AB	H	2B	3B	HR	RBI	BB	SO	OBP	SLG	G	GS	Innings	PO	A	E	DP	Fld Pct	Rng Fctr	In Zone	Outs	Zone Rtg	MLB Zone
As ss	.280	454	127	23	4	4	49	10	40	.291	.374	133	128	1131.0	189	361	16	82	.972	4.38	397	379	.955	.880

Last Five Years

	Avg	AB	H	2B	3B	HR	RBI	BB	SO	OBP	SLG
vs. Left	.241	725	175	22	5	1	61	12	69	.253	.290
vs. Right	.283	1409	399	66	14	8	157	51	100	.305	.367
Groundball	.272	556	151	19	3	3	65	18	43	.291	.333
Flyball	.275	466	128	17	6	1	37	12	40	.290	.343
Home	.272	1015	276	39	12	5	101	27	79	.288	.349
Away	.266	1119	298	49	7	4	117	36	90	.287	.333
Day	.279	570	159	22	4	3	64	22	42	.304	.347
Night	.265	1564	415	66	15	6	154	41	127	.281	.338
Grass	.265	1813	481	74	15	9	177	51	140	.283	.338
Turf	.290	321	93	14	4	0	41	12	29	.313	.358
First Pitch	.277	516	143	25	3	5	76	3	0	.276	.366
Ahead in Count	.289	353	102	20	3	1	42	36	0	.353	.371
Behind in Count	.249	963	240	32	9	2	75	0	156	.248	.307
Two Strikes	.234	719	168	24	7	1	49	16	169	.249	.291

	Avg	AB	H	2B	3B	HR	RBI	BB	SO	OBP	SLG
Scoring Posn	.290	544	158	26	7	4	201	26	38	.312	.386
Close & Late	.281	413	116	20	2	1	47	22	43	.316	.346
None on/out	.252	503	127	23	1	0	0	14	48	.273	.302
Batting #1	.251	215	54	5	3	0	13	7	22	.275	.302
Batting #9	.275	1693	466	78	15	9	190	46	128	.292	.355
Other	.239	226	54	5	1	0	15	10	19	.268	.270
April	.247	332	82	12	4	0	32	13	25	.272	.307
May	.293	365	107	12	4	1	29	13	31	.313	.356
June	.263	372	98	14	4	0	34	5	24	.270	.323
July	.291	358	104	15	2	3	43	9	30	.309	.369
August	.248	347	86	20	4	3	42	10	28	.264	.354
September/October	.269	360	97	15	1	2	38	13	31	.293	.333
Pre-All Star	.269	1177	317	43	12	3	109	35	90	.287	.334
Post-All Star	.269	957	257	45	7	6	109	28	79	.287	.349

Batter vs. Pitcher (career)

Hits Best Against	Avg	AB	H	2B	3B	HR	RBI	BB	SO	OBP	SLG
David Wells	.545	11	6	0	1	0	0	1	1	.583	.727
Steve Ontiveros	.533	15	8	2	0	0	1	0	2	.533	.667
Mark Knudson	.533	15	8	1	0	0	0	1	1	.563	.600
Bill Gullickson	.500	10	5	1	0	0	2	1	0	.545	.600

Hits Worst Against	Avg	AB	H	2B	3B	HR	RBI	BB	SO	OBP	SLG
Matt Young	.048	21	1	0	0	0	0	0	6	.048	.048
Kevin Brown	.063	32	2	1	0	0	0	0	3	.063	.094
Kenny Rogers	.071	14	1	0	0	0	2	0	0	.071	.071
Chuck Cary	.077	13	1	0	0	0	0	1	2	.143	.077

Batter vs. Pitcher (career)

Hits Best Against	Avg	AB	H	2B	3B	HR	RBI	BB	SO	OBP	SLG	Hits Worst Against	Avg	AB	H	2B	3B	HR	RBI	BB	SO	OBP	SLG
John Farrell	.364	11	4	3	0	0	2	2	0	.462	.636	Eric Plunk	.083	12	1	0	0	0	1	1	0	.143	.083

Bill Gullickson — Tigers

Age 35 – Pitches Right (flyball pitcher)

	ERA	W	L	Sv	G	GS	IP	BB	SO	Avg	H	2B	3B	HR	RBI	OBP	SLG	CG	ShO	Sup	QS	#P/S	SB	CS	GB	FB	G/F
1993 Season	5.37	13	9	0	28	28	159.1	44	70	.291	186	37	5	28	91	.336	.496	2	0	6.95	11	84	13	5	179	236	0.76
Last Five Years	4.29	57	45	0	129	129	800.2	199	298	.283	891	163	26	106	381	.324	.452	12	2	5.38	64	88	71	30	1076	1077	1.00

1993 Season

	ERA	W	L	Sv	G	GS	IP	H	HR	BB	SO
Home	5.02	7	7	0	17	17	95.0	112	17	25	38
Away	5.88	6	2	0	11	11	64.1	74	11	19	32
Starter	5.37	13	9	0	28	28	159.1	186	28	44	70
Reliever	0.00	0	0	0	0	0	0.0	0	0	0	0
0-3 Days Rest	6.55	1	0	0	2	2	11.0	12	4	2	3
4 Days Rest	5.11	9	8	0	21	21	118.0	137	18	34	53
5+ Days Rest	5.93	3	1	0	5	5	30.1	37	6	8	14
Pre-All Star	5.23	5	4	0	12	12	72.1	86	11	22	29
Post-All Star	5.48	8	5	0	16	16	87.0	100	17	22	41

	Avg	AB	H	2B	3B	HR	RBI	BB	SO	OBP	SLG
vs. Left	.329	316	104	24	4	13	52	23	25	.373	.554
vs. Right	.254	323	82	13	1	15	39	21	45	.300	.440
Scoring Posn	.271	140	38	9	1	3	53	14	16	.331	.414
Close & Late	.333	33	11	2	0	2	4	3	4	.389	.576
None on/out	.283	166	47	11	1	5	5	10	17	.324	.452
First Pitch	.441	111	49	12	0	8	20	0	0	.447	.766
Ahead in Count	.234	265	62	11	3	9	29	0	58	.234	.400
Behind in Count	.302	162	49	8	2	7	28	28	0	.399	.506
Two Strikes	.175	228	40	8	2	5	21	16	70	.231	.294

Last Five Years

	ERA	W	L	Sv	G	GS	IP	H	HR	BB	SO
Home	4.51	31	27	0	71	71	443.1	499	70	104	162
Away	4.03	26	18	0	58	58	357.1	392	36	95	136
Day	4.33	17	15	0	45	45	276.2	315	37	74	99
Night	4.28	40	30	0	84	84	524.0	576	69	125	199
Grass	4.51	37	30	0	85	85	535.1	597	80	130	197
Turf	3.87	20	15	0	44	44	265.1	294	26	69	101
April	4.28	6	3	0	12	12	67.1	75	9	17	28
May	3.86	10	6	0	22	22	133.0	150	10	32	49
June	3.47	11	9	0	23	23	158.0	168	14	41	66
July	5.66	9	9	0	22	22	130.1	160	25	37	40
August	3.30	14	6	0	25	25	163.2	154	21	35	58
September/October	5.46	7	12	0	25	25	148.1	184	27	37	57
Starter	4.29	57	45	0	129	129	800.2	891	106	199	298
Reliever	0.00	0	0	0	0	0	0.0	0	0	0	0
0-3 Days Rest	3.51	3	0	0	4	4	25.2	27	5	2	10
4 Days Rest	4.24	37	32	0	91	91	571.1	647	67	142	203
5+ Days Rest	4.55	17	13	0	34	34	203.2	217	34	55	85
Pre-All Star	3.89	30	20	0	65	65	412.1	454	40	107	158
Post-All Star	4.73	27	25	0	64	64	388.1	437	66	92	140

	Avg	AB	H	2B	3B	HR	RBI	BB	SO	OBP	SLG
vs. Left	.298	1685	502	97	15	58	213	119	111	.343	.477
vs. Right	.265	1466	389	66	11	48	168	80	187	.302	.424
Inning 1-6	.279	2687	751	145	23	87	328	166	263	.320	.448
Inning 7+	.302	464	140	18	3	19	53	33	35	.347	.476
None on	.286	1896	543	100	14	66	66	103	184	.326	.458
Runners on	.277	1255	348	63	12	40	315	96	114	.322	.442
Scoring Posn	.277	675	187	33	4	19	248	77	65	.338	.422
Close & Late	.321	215	69	9	1	9	28	18	20	.373	.498
None on/out	.277	829	230	42	6	24	24	45	84	.316	.429
vs. 1st Batr (relief)	.000	0	0	0	0	0	0	0	0	.000	.000
First Inning Pitched	.295	501	148	26	7	18	69	37	37	.344	.483
First 75 Pitches	.275	2495	687	133	22	79	289	150	236	.315	.441
Pitch 76-90	.299	375	112	23	3	13	49	24	37	.342	.480
Pitch 91-105	.345	200	69	5	1	10	32	20	19	.403	.530
Pitch 106+	.284	81	23	2	0	4	11	5	6	.326	.457
First Pitch	.305	538	164	34	3	23	73	23	0	.333	.507
Ahead in Count	.255	1266	323	55	10	29	143	0	261	.255	.383
Behind in Count	.299	813	243	46	11	35	97	121	0	.386	.512
Two Strikes	.234	1092	256	52	6	22	111	55	298	.270	.353

Pitcher vs. Batter (since 1984)

Pitches Best Vs.	Avg	AB	H	2B	3B	HR	RBI	BB	SO	OBP	SLG	Pitches Worst Vs.	Avg	AB	H	2B	3B	HR	RBI	BB	SO	OBP	SLG
Manuel Lee	.000	13	0	0	0	0	0	2	1	.133	.000	Wade Boggs	.667	9	6	2	1	0	1	2	0	.727	1.111
Rob Deer	.000	11	0	0	0	0	1	1	7	.083	.000	Rafael Palmeiro	.471	17	8	1	0	4	7	0	1	.471	1.235
B.J. Surhoff	.077	13	1	0	0	0	1	1	0	.133	.077	Barry Bonds	.467	15	7	3	1	1	4	2	0	.529	1.000
Chad Curtis	.077	13	1	0	0	0	0	0	1	.077	.077	Bobby Kelly	.455	11	5	1	0	2	7	1	3	.462	1.091
Jim Thome	.091	11	1	0	0	0	0	0	2	.091	.091	Jose Canseco	.364	11	4	0	1	2	3	2	2	.462	1.091

Mark Guthrie — Twins

Age 28 – Pitches Left

	ERA	W	L	Sv	G	GS	IP	BB	SO	Avg	H	2B	3B	HR	RBI	OBP	SLG	GF	IR	IRS	Hld	SvOp	SB	CS	GB	FB	G/F
1993 Season	4.71	2	1	0	22	0	21.0	16	15	.267	20	4	0	2	15	.387	.400	2	21	9	8	1	4	3	26	24	1.08
Career (1989-1993)	3.91	20	22	7	154	41	396.0	140	302	.274	415	68	7	35	169	.334	.397	30	96	28	32	10	41	28	546	401	1.36

1993 Season

	ERA	W	L	Sv	G	GS	IP	H	HR	BB	SO
Home	5.11	1	1	0	12	0	12.1	14	2	10	8
Away	4.15	1	0	0	10	0	8.2	6	0	6	7

	Avg	AB	H	2B	3B	HR	RBI	BB	SO	OBP	SLG
vs. Left	.148	27	4	1	0	0	2	3	6	.233	.185
vs. Right	.333	48	16	3	0	2	13	13	9	.460	.521

Career (1989-1993)

	ERA	W	L	Sv	G	GS	IP	H	HR	BB	SO
Home	4.04	8	10	4	74	21	194.0	204	19	68	168
Away	3.79	12	12	3	80	20	202.0	211	16	72	134
Day	2.73	7	6	3	56	10	125.1	114	11	40	95
Night	4.46	13	16	4	98	31	270.2	301	24	100	207
Grass	3.18	10	6	3	56	14	147.0	147	8	46	96
Turf	4.34	10	16	4	98	27	249.0	268	27	94	206
April	7.11	1	3	0	24	3	31.2	37	7	23	23
May	2.93	8	1	1	29	7	76.2	71	4	30	64
June	7.62	1	5	0	16	8	41.1	63	8	20	30
July	1.97	3	2	3	26	4	64.0	61	2	14	54
August	3.95	3	5	1	27	8	82.0	87	9	29	63
September/October	3.32	4	6	2	32	11	100.1	96	5	24	68
Starter	4.60	13	17	0	41	41	236.2	274	21	77	158
Reliever	2.88	7	5	7	113	0	159.1	141	14	63	144
0 Days rest	1.80	0	1	1	10	0	10.0	5	0	2	11
1 or 2 Days rest	3.23	2	2	4	59	0	78.0	71	7	34	69

	Avg	AB	H	2B	3B	HR	RBI	BB	SO	OBP	SLG
vs. Left	.285	344	98	12	1	7	36	20	60	.322	.387
vs. Right	.271	1171	317	56	6	28	133	120	242	.337	.401
Inning 1-6	.284	989	281	43	5	25	121	81	172	.337	.414
Inning 7+	.255	526	134	25	2	10	48	59	130	.329	.367
None on	.294	836	246	45	3	19	19	75	156	.353	.423
Runners on	.249	679	169	23	4	16	150	65	146	.311	.365
Scoring Posn	.249	389	97	13	1	7	123	50	95	.329	.342
Close & Late	.281	263	74	15	2	7	31	31	64	.357	.433
None on/out	.302	377	114	20	3	6	6	26	73	.347	.419
vs. 1st Batr (relief)	.260	104	27	5	0	2	20	7	22	.304	.365
First Inning Pitched	.244	483	118	21	2	14	66	54	114	.316	.383
First 15 Pitches	.262	442	116	19	2	12	53	45	94	.327	.396
Pitch 16-30	.270	319	86	15	1	11	39	35	79	.339	.426
Pitch 31-45	.276	221	61	8	1	3	25	13	35	.315	.362
Pitch 46+	.285	533	152	26	3	9	52	47	94	.345	.396
First Pitch	.305	203	62	16	2	3	30	11	0	.341	.448

Career (1989-1993)

	ERA	W	L	Sv	G	GS	IP	H	HR	BB	SO
3+ Days rest	2.65	5	2	2	44	0	71.1	65	7	27	64
Pre-All Star	4.66	10	10	2	77	18	166.0	182	20	78	131
Post-All Star	3.37	10	12	5	77	23	230.0	233	15	62	171

	Avg	AB	H	2B	3B	HR	RBI	BB	SO	OBP	SLG
Ahead in Count	.201	683	137	20	0	10	51	0	256	.201	.274
Behind in Count	.397	340	135	18	4	12	66	71	0	.494	.579
Two Strikes	.192	697	134	25	0	10	44	57	302	.253	.271

Pitcher vs. Batter (career)

Pitches Best Vs.	Avg	AB	H	2B	3B	HR	RBI	BB	SO	OBP	SLG
Greg Vaughn	.000	11	0	0	0	0	0	1	3	.083	.000
Henry Cotto	.071	14	1	0	0	0	0	0	6	.071	.071
Manuel Lee	.071	14	1	0	0	0	0	1	4	.133	.071
Carlton Fisk	.133	15	2	0	0	0	2	2	8	.235	.133
Paul Molitor	.143	14	2	0	0	0	1	0	3	.143	.143

Pitches Worst Vs.	Avg	AB	H	2B	3B	HR	RBI	BB	SO	OBP	SLG
Felix Fermin	.909	11	10	1	0	0	3	0	1	.909	1.000
Danny Tartabull	.545	11	6	0	0	2	5	6	2	.706	1.091
Glenallen Hill	.538	13	7	2	0	1	4	0	3	.538	.923
Ken Griffey Jr	.500	16	8	0	0	1	2	2	3	.556	.688
Dave Valle	.462	13	6	0	0	1	4	0	2	.462	.692

Ricky Gutierrez — Padres

Age 24 – Bats Right (groundball hitter)

	Avg	G	AB	R	H	2B	3B	HR	RBI	BB	SO	HBP	GDP	SB	CS	OBP	SLG	IBB	SH	SF	#Pit	#P/PA	GB	FB	G/F
1993 Season	.251	133	438	76	110	10	5	5	26	50	97	5	7	4	3	.334	.331	2	1	1	1966	3.97	188	63	2.98

1993 Season

	Avg	AB	H	2B	3B	HR	RBI	BB	SO	OBP	SLG
vs. Left	.277	159	44	3	1	3	12	22	32	.365	.365
vs. Right	.237	279	66	7	4	2	14	28	65	.316	.312
Groundball	.238	143	34	4	0	1	4	16	30	.319	.287
Flyball	.189	90	17	1	2	1	7	9	19	.275	.278
Home	.257	230	59	2	1	5	16	24	58	.335	.339
Away	.245	208	51	8	4	0	10	26	39	.333	.322
Day	.254	122	31	3	2	3	11	17	28	.352	.385
Night	.250	316	79	7	3	2	15	33	69	.327	.310
Grass	.263	346	91	8	2	5	23	39	81	.346	.341
Turf	.207	92	19	2	3	0	3	11	16	.288	.293
First Pitch	.250	40	10	2	1	0	2	1	0	.268	.350
Ahead in Count	.337	83	28	2	2	4	10	24	0	.486	.554
Behind in Count	.200	230	46	2	2	1	10	0	85	.214	.239
Two Strikes	.198	232	46	3	1	1	11	25	97	.282	.233

	Avg	AB	H	2B	3B	HR	RBI	BB	SO	OBP	SLG
Scoring Posn	.210	100	21	0	1	0	17	17	20	.322	.230
Close & Late	.321	78	25	1	1	0	4	13	23	.424	.359
None on/out	.281	121	34	3	2	1	1	12	30	.360	.364
Batting #1	.264	144	38	6	0	1	8	17	31	.346	.326
Batting #2	.244	172	42	3	2	3	11	18	41	.323	.337
Other	.246	122	30	1	3	1	7	15	25	.336	.328
April	.364	33	12	0	0	0	1	4	9	.447	.364
May	.229	35	8	1	0	0	0	4	3	.308	.257
June	.284	88	25	1	1	1	7	6	25	.330	.352
July	.263	99	26	3	4	2	8	18	21	.376	.434
August	.239	92	22	5	0	0	3	12	15	.336	.293
September/October	.187	91	17	0	0	2	7	6	24	.253	.253
Pre-All Star	.270	196	53	5	3	1	10	20	44	.341	.342
Post-All Star	.236	242	57	5	2	4	16	30	53	.329	.322

1993 By Position

Position	Avg	AB	H	2B	3B	HR	RBI	BB	SO	OBP	SLG	G	GS	Innings	PO	A	E	DP	Fld Pct	Rng Fctr	In Zone	Outs	Zone Rtg	MLB Zone
As Pinch Hitter	.250	8	2	0	0	0	0	2	3	.400	.250	12	0	---	---	---	---	---	---	---	---	---	---	---
As ss	.251	419	105	9	5	5	26	46	92	.330	.332	117	106	939.0	190	286	14	55	.971	4.56	352	307	.872	.880

Jose Guzman — Cubs

Age 31 – Pitches Right

	ERA	W	L	Sv	G	GS	IP	BB	SO	Avg	H	2B	3B	HR	RBI	OBP	SLG	CG	ShO	Sup	QS	#P/S	SB	CS	GB	FB	G/F
1993 Season	4.34	12	10	0	30	30	191.0	74	163	.258	188	39	5	25	83	.327	.428	2	1	5.09	16	103	19	10	249	181	1.38
Last Five Years	3.71	41	28	0	88	88	584.2	231	467	.257	569	124	10	52	220	.328	.392	12	2	5.26	56	106	47	38	771	567	1.36

1993 Season

	ERA	W	L	Sv	G	GS	IP	H	HR	BB	SO
Home	4.32	8	5	0	18	18	114.2	112	19	40	99
Away	4.36	4	5	0	12	12	76.1	76	6	34	64
Day	2.71	7	4	0	13	13	86.1	70	6	31	74
Night	5.68	5	6	0	17	17	104.2	118	19	43	89
Grass	4.30	10	6	0	23	23	148.2	146	22	48	131
Turf	4.46	2	4	0	7	7	42.1	42	3	26	32
April	2.81	3	2	0	5	5	32.0	24	2	16	19
May	5.63	1	2	0	6	6	32.0	37	7	11	29
June	4.66	3	2	0	6	6	38.2	41	6	15	32
July	3.31	2	1	0	5	5	32.2	26	3	12	30
August	4.25	2	2	0	6	6	42.1	43	5	16	39
September/October	6.75	1	1	0	2	2	13.1	17	2	4	14
Starter	4.34	12	10	0	30	30	191.0	188	25	74	163
Reliever	0.00	0	0	0	0	0	0.0	0	0	0	0
0-3 Days Rest	5.40	0	1	0	1	1	6.2	7	1	3	8
4 Days Rest	4.92	5	8	0	18	18	109.2	111	15	48	88
5+ Days Rest	3.38	7	1	0	11	11	74.2	70	9	23	67
Pre-All Star	4.46	7	7	0	19	19	113.0	116	17	47	91
Post-All Star	4.15	5	3	0	11	11	78.0	72	8	27	72

	Avg	AB	H	2B	3B	HR	RBI	BB	SO	OBP	SLG
vs. Left	.271	395	107	24	4	16	48	44	77	.343	.473
vs. Right	.243	334	81	15	1	9	35	30	86	.307	.374
Inning 1-6	.248	644	160	29	5	24	75	66	149	.318	.421
Inning 7+	.329	85	28	10	0	1	8	8	14	.389	.482
None on	.241	456	110	25	2	16	16	37	99	.301	.410
Runners on	.286	273	78	14	3	9	67	37	64	.367	.458
Scoring Posn	.274	164	45	8	3	5	56	24	42	.358	.451
Close & Late	.225	40	9	2	0	0	3	6	7	.333	.275
None on/out	.221	190	42	9	1	7	7	16	37	.285	.389
vs. 1st Batr (relief)	.000	0	0	0	0	0	0	0	0	.000	.000
First Inning Pitched	.274	117	32	8	2	2	11	9	26	.323	.427
First 75 Pitches	.255	513	131	25	5	17	59	50	116	.322	.423
Pitch 76-90	.296	98	29	4	0	7	15	11	25	.364	.551
Pitch 91-105	.200	70	14	6	0	0	5	9	12	.293	.286
Pitch 106+	.292	48	14	4	0	1	4	4	10	.358	.438
First Pitch	.319	94	30	5	0	6	14	5	0	.356	.564
Ahead in Count	.171	310	53	10	0	5	22	0	139	.169	.252
Behind in Count	.347	173	60	13	4	8	26	39	0	.467	.607
Two Strikes	.174	339	59	14	1	8	28	30	163	.240	.292

Last Five Years

	ERA	W	L	Sv	G	GS	IP	H	HR	BB	SO
Home	4.20	19	15	0	42	42	278.1	282	36	98	220
Away	3.26	22	13	0	46	46	306.1	287	16	133	247
Day	2.95	12	5	0	24	24	161.2	138	8	73	140
Night	4.00	29	23	0	64	64	423.0	431	44	158	327
Grass	3.65	35	21	0	71	71	478.1	463	46	174	378
Turf	3.98	6	7	0	17	17	106.1	106	6	57	89
April	2.62	5	4	0	10	10	65.1	50	3	27	41
May	4.55	3	4	0	14	14	85.0	95	9	33	64
June	4.26	9	6	0	17	17	112.0	117	17	42	87

	Avg	AB	H	2B	3B	HR	RBI	BB	SO	OBP	SLG
vs. Left	.266	1077	287	71	6	28	122	120	194	.339	.422
vs. Right	.247	1141	282	53	4	24	98	111	273	.317	.364
Inning 1-6	.252	1873	472	103	10	46	195	204	396	.327	.391
Inning 7+	.281	345	97	21	0	6	25	27	71	.334	.394
None on	.261	1305	341	77	4	38	38	128	275	.329	.414
Runners on	.250	913	228	47	6	14	182	103	192	.326	.360
Scoring Posn	.230	526	121	24	6	6	156	68	118	.314	.333
Close & Late	.257	187	48	8	0	1	14	16	38	.317	.316
None on/out	.252	571	144	36	2	17	17	52	103	.317	.412

Last Five Years

	ERA	W	L	Sv	G	GS	IP	H	HR	BB	SO
July	3.29	6	5	0	15	15	98.1	92	6	47	85
August	3.51	9	5	0	18	18	120.2	123	12	39	108
September/October	3.75	9	4	0	14	14	103.1	92	5	43	82
Starter	3.71	41	28	0	88	88	584.2	569	52	231	467
Reliever	0.00	0	0	0	0	0	0.0	0	0	0	0
0-3 Days Rest	4.67	1	2	0	3	3	17.1	21	1	8	17
4 Days Rest	3.49	24	14	0	52	52	348.0	332	30	139	272
5+ Days Rest	3.98	16	12	0	33	33	219.1	216	21	84	178
Pre-All Star	3.91	18	17	0	46	46	292.2	296	32	114	222
Post-All Star	3.51	23	11	0	42	42	292.0	273	20	117	245

	Avg	AB	H	2B	3B	HR	RBI	BB	SO	OBP	SLG
vs. 1st Batr (relief)	.000	0	0	0	0	0	0	0	0	.000	.000
First Inning Pitched	.266	334	89	23	5	6	31	30	72	.324	.419
First 75 Pitches	.255	1503	383	89	10	32	152	164	309	.329	.391
Pitch 76-90	.276	308	85	14	0	15	44	26	58	.334	.468
Pitch 91-105	.260	227	59	10	0	3	14	27	54	.340	.344
Pitch 106+	.233	180	42	11	0	2	10	14	46	.292	.328
First Pitch	.322	323	104	20	1	10	38	6	0	.337	.483
Ahead in Count	.173	934	162	31	1	10	55	0	394	.174	.241
Behind in Count	.331	523	173	36	6	21	75	127	0	.460	.543
Two Strikes	.172	993	171	43	2	11	64	98	467	.247	.253

Pitcher vs. Batter (career)

Pitches Best Vs.	Avg	AB	H	2B	3B	HR	RBI	BB	SO	OBP	SLG
Dan Pasqua	.000	10	0	0	0	0	0	2	2	.167	.000
Ron Gant	.000	10	0	0	0	0	0	1	4	.091	.000
Darryl Hamilton	.059	17	1	0	0	0	1	0	1	.059	.059
Kelly Gruber	.077	13	1	0	0	0	0	0	4	.077	.077
Tony Pena	.083	12	1	0	0	0	0	0	1	.083	.083

Pitches Worst Vs.	Avg	AB	H	2B	3B	HR	RBI	BB	SO	OBP	SLG
Pat Listach	.545	11	6	1	0	0	2	1	1	.583	.636
Jeff Blauser	.455	11	5	0	0	1	3	1	2	.500	.727
Danny Tartabull	.375	40	15	2	1	3	7	4	11	.432	.700
Kent Hrbek	.344	32	11	3	0	3	6	6	4	.447	.719
Frank Thomas	.333	9	3	0	0	1	3	2	0	.455	.667

Juan Guzman — Blue Jays

Age 27 – Pitches Right

	ERA	W	L	Sv	G	GS	IP	BB	SO	Avg	H	2B	3B	HR	RBI	OBP	SLG	CG	ShO	Sup	QS	#P/S	SB	CS	GB	FB	G/F
1993 Season	3.99	14	3	0	33	33	221.0	110	194	.252	211	35	1	17	85	.338	.358	2	1	6.19	20	115	25	17	254	227	1.12
Career (1991-1993)	3.28	40	11	0	84	84	540.1	248	482	.224	444	72	4	29	178	.310	.308	4	1	5.70	53	108	63	31	602	558	1.08

1993 Season

	ERA	W	L	Sv	G	GS	IP	H	HR	BB	SO
Home	3.43	7	1	0	15	15	99.2	102	5	43	89
Away	4.45	7	2	0	18	18	121.1	109	12	67	105
Day	4.11	7	0	0	13	13	85.1	88	6	44	74
Night	3.91	7	3	0	20	20	135.2	123	11	66	120
Grass	4.83	5	2	0	14	14	91.1	83	9	52	80
Turf	3.40	9	1	0	19	19	129.2	128	8	58	114
April	4.60	3	0	0	5	5	31.1	34	2	17	28
May	5.71	1	0	0	6	6	34.2	37	4	19	27
June	3.79	3	1	0	5	5	35.2	29	2	16	35
July	3.46	0	2	0	6	6	39.0	45	2	23	34
August	3.60	3	0	0	5	5	35.0	30	3	16	38
September/October	3.18	4	0	0	6	6	45.1	36	4	19	32
Starter	3.99	14	3	0	33	33	221.0	211	17	110	194
Reliever	0.00	0	0	0	0	0	0.0	0	0	0	0
0-3 Days Rest	0.00	0	0	0	0	0	0.0	0	0	0	0
4 Days Rest	4.30	9	3	0	22	22	144.1	143	12	71	127
5+ Days Rest	3.40	5	0	0	11	11	76.2	68	5	39	67
Pre-All Star	4.74	7	2	0	18	18	114.0	119	8	60	98
Post-All Star	3.20	7	1	0	15	15	107.0	92	9	50	96

	Avg	AB	H	2B	3B	HR	RBI	BB	SO	OBP	SLG
vs. Left	.280	428	120	18	1	7	41	65	73	.371	.376
vs. Right	.223	408	91	17	0	10	44	45	121	.302	.338
Inning 1-6	.248	710	176	31	1	17	75	93	168	.334	.366
Inning 7+	.278	126	35	4	0	0	10	17	26	.361	.310
None on	.255	467	119	19	0	7	7	57	108	.337	.340
Runners on	.249	369	92	16	1	10	78	53	86	.339	.379
Scoring Posn	.225	200	45	7	0	3	58	31	55	.320	.305
Close & Late	.250	68	17	2	0	0	4	12	9	.358	.279
None on/out	.224	205	46	7	0	2	2	29	45	.323	.288
vs. 1st Batr (relief)	.000	0	0	0	0	0	0	0	0	.000	.000
First Inning Pitched	.256	125	32	7	1	2	15	17	33	.340	.376
First 75 Pitches	.236	529	125	19	1	14	52	70	127	.325	.355
Pitch 76-90	.301	123	37	6	0	3	15	11	25	.353	.423
Pitch 91-105	.240	96	23	5	0	0	9	15	22	.339	.292
Pitch 106+	.295	88	26	5	0	0	9	14	20	.394	.352
First Pitch	.265	113	30	3	0	2	15	2	0	.271	.345
Ahead in Count	.225	373	84	14	1	4	27	0	160	.231	.300
Behind in Count	.337	169	57	10	0	6	29	47	0	.473	.503
Two Strikes	.165	399	66	15	0	2	21	61	194	.276	.218

Career (1991-1993)

	ERA	W	L	Sv	G	GS	IP	H	HR	BB	SO
Home	3.35	19	4	0	39	39	247.1	216	12	107	226
Away	3.23	21	7	0	45	45	293.0	228	17	141	256
Day	3.31	14	4	0	31	31	195.2	168	11	97	178
Night	3.26	26	7	0	53	53	344.2	276	18	151	304
Grass	3.33	15	5	0	33	33	213.1	165	13	107	190
Turf	3.25	25	6	0	51	51	327.0	279	16	141	292
April	3.14	6	0	0	10	10	66.0	57	3	34	67
May	3.77	4	0	0	11	11	71.2	60	5	31	53
June	3.19	9	4	0	14	14	93.0	69	4	36	84
July	2.70	3	3	0	16	16	100.0	87	4	49	95
August	4.04	5	1	0	13	13	78.0	65	6	41	80
September/October	3.14	13	3	0	20	20	131.2	106	7	57	103
Starter	3.28	40	11	0	84	84	540.1	444	29	248	482
Reliever	0.00	0	0	0	0	0	0.0	0	0	0	0
0-3 Days Rest	3.13	2	1	0	4	4	23.0	23	0	7	10
4 Days Rest	3.61	20	6	0	45	45	287.0	247	16	137	263
5+ Days Rest	2.89	18	4	0	35	35	230.1	174	13	104	209
Pre-All Star	3.26	21	6	0	42	42	276.0	224	13	120	245
Post-All Star	3.30	19	5	0	42	42	264.1	220	16	128	237

	Avg	AB	H	2B	3B	HR	RBI	BB	SO	OBP	SLG
vs. Left	.238	989	235	31	2	9	72	135	180	.327	.300
vs. Right	.210	996	209	41	2	20	106	113	302	.293	.315
Inning 1-6	.223	1712	382	63	4	28	160	210	426	.308	.314
Inning 7+	.227	273	62	9	0	1	18	38	56	.323	.271
None on	.222	1135	252	40	0	13	13	141	280	.311	.292
Runners on	.226	850	192	32	4	16	165	107	202	.309	.329
Scoring Posn	.210	472	99	14	2	7	133	70	125	.304	.292
Close & Late	.194	144	28	2	0	1	9	25	30	.312	.229
None on/out	.217	502	109	15	0	6	6	64	112	.309	.283
vs. 1st Batr (relief)	.000	0	0	0	0	0	0	0	0	.000	.000
First Inning Pitched	.232	310	72	15	2	4	34	48	86	.332	.332
First 75 Pitches	.215	1332	287	44	3	25	124	166	323	.303	.309
Pitch 76-90	.258	271	70	13	1	3	26	22	67	.311	.347
Pitch 91-105	.196	219	43	6	0	1	14	29	51	.288	.237
Pitch 106+	.270	163	44	9	0	0	14	31	41	.388	.325
First Pitch	.289	253	73	10	1	4	32	4	0	.296	.383
Ahead in Count	.177	943	167	25	2	10	58	0	395	.182	.240
Behind in Count	.316	383	121	22	1	8	49	106	0	.460	.441
Two Strikes	.142	1018	145	26	1	6	54	138	482	.246	.188

Pitcher vs. Batter (career)

Pitches Best Vs.	Avg	AB	H	2B	3B	HR	RBI	BB	SO	OBP	SLG
Dave Henderson	.000	13	0	0	0	0	0	0	7	.000	.000
Brent Mayne	.000	11	0	0	0	0	0	1	4	.083	.000
Robin Yount	.059	17	1	0	0	0	1	1	8	.111	.059
Dan Gladden	.071	14	1	0	0	0	0	0	5	.071	.071
Felix Fermin	.091	11	1	0	0	0	0	0	1	.091	.091

Pitches Worst Vs.	Avg	AB	H	2B	3B	HR	RBI	BB	SO	OBP	SLG
Mike Greenwell	.600	10	6	1	1	0	5	2	0	.667	.900
Wally Joyner	.467	15	7	1	1	1	3	2	1	.529	.867
Frank Thomas	.455	11	5	0	0	1	3	4	2	.600	.727
Don Mattingly	.444	18	8	1	0	1	4	1	1	.474	.667
Mike Aldrete	.417	12	5	0	0	0	1	8	1	.650	.417

Chris Gwynn — Royals

Age 29 – Bats Left

	Avg	G	AB	R	H	2B	3B	HR	RBI	BB	SO	HBP	GDP	SB	CS	OBP	SLG	IBB	SH	SF	#Pit	#P/PA	GB	FB	G/F
1993 Season	.300	103	287	36	86	14	4	1	25	24	34	1	7	0	1	.354	.387	5	2	2	1088	3.44	124	73	1.70
Last Five Years	.280	364	719	91	201	28	9	12	83	46	104	2	16	2	2	.320	.394	8	6	11	2714	3.46	290	201	1.44

1993 Season

	Avg	AB	H	2B	3B	HR	RBI	BB	SO	OBP	SLG
vs. Left	.176	17	3	1	0	0	2	0	2	.176	.235
vs. Right	.307	270	83	13	4	1	23	24	32	.364	.396
Home	.333	132	44	9	3	0	15	11	15	.385	.447
Away	.271	155	42	5	1	1	10	13	19	.327	.335
First Pitch	.420	50	21	5	1	0	7	4	0	.446	.560
Ahead in Count	.316	57	18	3	2	0	7	10	0	.418	.439
Behind in Count	.202	129	26	3	1	1	6	0	27	.208	.264
Two Strikes	.198	116	23	6	1	0	4	10	34	.268	.267

	Avg	AB	H	2B	3B	HR	RBI	BB	SO	OBP	SLG
Scoring Posn	.225	71	16	3	1	0	23	13	14	.337	.296
Close & Late	.283	53	15	3	0	0	5	8	10	.377	.340
None on/out	.443	70	31	7	1	0	0	2	3	.458	.571
Batting #5	.286	105	30	5	1	1	7	8	15	.333	.381
Batting #6	.289	90	26	4	1	0	9	7	4	.343	.356
Other	.326	92	30	5	2	0	9	9	15	.386	.424
Pre-All Star	.304	181	55	10	2	1	22	10	18	.340	.398
Post-All Star	.292	106	31	4	2	0	3	14	16	.375	.368

Last Five Years

	Avg	AB	H	2B	3B	HR	RBI	BB	SO	OBP	SLG
vs. Left	.179	67	12	2	1	1	7	3	14	.214	.284
vs. Right	.290	652	189	26	8	11	76	43	90	.331	.405
Groundball	.291	158	46	8	3	0	20	10	30	.329	.380
Flyball	.254	185	47	10	3	4	21	8	23	.286	.405
Home	.304	313	95	13	5	3	31	19	44	.341	.406
Away	.261	406	106	15	4	9	52	27	60	.304	.384
Day	.303	241	73	10	3	2	22	18	35	.347	.394
Night	.268	478	128	18	6	10	61	28	69	.306	.393
Grass	.285	403	115	9	4	9	42	27	62	.329	.395
Turf	.272	316	86	19	5	3	41	19	42	.309	.392
First Pitch	.397	121	48	9	3	1	13	5	0	.411	.545
Ahead in Count	.368	152	56	7	2	7	34	19	0	.429	.579
Behind in Count	.176	324	57	8	3	3	20	0	86	.180	.247
Two Strikes	.166	308	51	9	4	1	13	20	104	.221	.231

	Avg	AB	H	2B	3B	HR	RBI	BB	SO	OBP	SLG
Scoring Posn	.247	178	44	6	1	5	71	22	34	.316	.376
Close & Late	.242	157	38	7	4	2	21	13	23	.295	.376
None on/out	.313	179	56	9	3	2	2	5	21	.332	.430
Batting #5	.289	159	46	5	1	2	12	15	24	.347	.371
Batting #6	.289	149	43	4	2	1	15	9	11	.329	.362
Other	.273	411	112	19	6	9	56	22	69	.306	.414
April	.302	86	26	3	0	0	13	3	14	.326	.337
May	.294	194	57	9	3	1	22	12	26	.332	.387
June	.269	130	35	8	2	4	17	9	17	.312	.454
July	.246	134	33	3	2	3	16	10	18	.293	.366
August	.310	84	26	3	1	3	11	5	13	.352	.476
September/October	.264	91	24	2	1	1	4	7	16	.313	.341
Pre-All Star	.287	450	129	20	6	5	54	26	63	.323	.391
Post-All Star	.268	269	72	8	3	7	29	20	41	.315	.398

Batter vs. Pitcher (career)

Hits Best Against	Avg	AB	H	2B	3B	HR	RBI	BB	SO	OBP	SLG
Mark Leiter	.500	10	5	1	1	0	1	0	1	.455	.800
Jack Morris	.429	14	6	1	1	0	3	0	0	.429	.643
Danny Darwin	.357	14	5	3	0	0	0	0	2	.357	.571
John Smoltz	.357	14	5	1	0	0	0	1	2	.400	.429

Hits Worst Against	Avg	AB	H	2B	3B	HR	RBI	BB	SO	OBP	SLG
Bryn Smith	.214	14	3	0	0	0	0	0	2	.214	.214
Juan Guzman	.222	9	2	0	0	0	0	3	0	.417	.222

Tony Gwynn — Padres

Age 34 – Bats Left (groundball hitter)

	Avg	G	AB	R	H	2B	3B	HR	RBI	BB	SO	HBP	GDP	SB	CS	OBP	SLG	IBB	SH	SF	#Pit	#P/PA	GB	FB	G/F
1993 Season	.358	122	489	70	175	41	3	7	59	36	19	1	18	14	1	.398	.497	11	1	7	1705	3.19	210	108	1.94
Last Five Years	.327	683	2716	377	888	151	34	25	296	216	107	3	67	82	39	.374	.435	67	19	26	9805	3.29	1285	607	2.12

1993 Season

	Avg	AB	H	2B	3B	HR	RBI	BB	SO	OBP	SLG
vs. Left	.359	192	69	14	1	3	20	11	6	.393	.490
vs. Right	.357	297	106	27	2	4	39	25	13	.401	.502
Groundball	.281	167	47	8	2	2	18	14	6	.332	.389
Flyball	.437	87	38	9	0	3	14	3	2	.451	.644
Home	.382	254	97	20	2	4	32	20	14	.421	.524
Away	.332	235	78	21	1	3	27	16	5	.373	.468
Day	.352	165	58	14	1	5	23	8	6	.382	.539
Night	.361	324	117	27	2	2	36	28	13	.406	.475
Grass	.380	371	141	32	2	5	49	31	16	.422	.518
Turf	.288	118	34	9	1	2	10	5	3	.320	.432
First Pitch	.351	74	26	6	0	3	11	6	0	.381	.554
Ahead in Count	.447	132	59	17	1	3	21	21	0	.516	.659
Behind in Count	.289	187	54	11	1	1	15	0	15	.293	.374
Two Strikes	.322	146	47	10	0	1	17	9	19	.365	.411

	Avg	AB	H	2B	3B	HR	RBI	BB	SO	OBP	SLG
Scoring Posn	.368	87	32	10	1	1	49	16	4	.436	.540
Close & Late	.371	89	33	9	0	2	18	8	2	.416	.539
None on/out	.339	121	41	7	2	2	2	12	7	.403	.479
Batting #2	.348	158	55	9	2	2	15	8	4	.376	.468
Batting #3	.396	217	86	23	0	4	33	15	6	.430	.558
Other	.298	114	34	9	1	1	11	13	9	.367	.421
April	.295	95	28	5	1	1	8	6	3	.330	.400
May	.342	111	38	8	0	0	8	8	3	.385	.414
June	.286	56	16	6	1	1	9	5	7	.344	.482
July	.381	105	40	10	1	3	16	7	4	.420	.581
August	.448	105	47	10	0	2	14	10	2	.487	.600
September/October	.353	17	6	2	0	0	4	0	0	.333	.471
Pre-All Star	.331	299	99	22	3	3	29	21	15	.372	.455
Post-All Star	.400	190	76	19	0	4	30	15	4	.438	.563

1993 By Position

Position	Avg	AB	H	2B	3B	HR	RBI	BB	SO	OBP	SLG	G	GS	Innings	PO	A	E	DP	Fld Pct	Rng Fctr	In Zone	Outs	Zone Rtg	MLB Zone
As rf	.361	485	175	41	3	7	59	36	18	.401	.501	121	119	1012.1	242	8	5	2	.980	2.22	264	234	.886	.826

Last Five Years

	Avg	AB	H	2B	3B	HR	RBI	BB	SO	OBP	SLG
vs. Left	.312	1036	323	41	10	11	106	62	42	.350	.403
vs. Right	.336	1680	565	110	24	14	190	154	65	.388	.455
Groundball	.327	953	312	47	12	5	108	80	41	.378	.418
Flyball	.304	566	172	31	6	9	58	41	20	.348	.428
Home	.326	1321	431	69	16	14	139	113	60	.376	.435
Away	.328	1395	457	82	18	11	157	103	47	.372	.436
Day	.310	815	253	42	12	8	85	60	35	.355	.421
Night	.334	1901	635	109	22	17	211	156	72	.382	.441
Grass	.324	1979	641	108	22	18	202	170	83	.375	.428
Turf	.335	737	247	43	12	7	94	46	24	.372	.455
First Pitch	.369	363	134	27	2	4	47	37	0	.421	.488
Ahead in Count	.338	715	242	41	11	11	91	110	0	.421	.473

	Avg	AB	H	2B	3B	HR	RBI	BB	SO	OBP	SLG
Scoring Posn	.337	588	198	41	11	4	250	110	30	.425	.464
Close & Late	.340	453	154	23	3	6	55	48	19	.400	.444
None on/out	.308	556	171	19	7	6	6	32	22	.347	.399
Batting #2	.325	808	263	42	6	11	67	60	25	.370	.433
Batting #3	.330	1731	572	98	25	13	215	141	71	.378	.438
Other	.299	177	53	11	3	1	14	15	11	.352	.412
April	.323	452	146	24	8	4	39	33	16	.365	.438
May	.345	531	183	36	9	7	68	44	13	.395	.486
June	.337	486	164	26	5	5	59	44	30	.388	.442
July	.290	496	144	25	6	5	44	38	21	.340	.395
August	.354	522	185	26	3	4	56	42	22	.399	.439
September/October	.288	229	66	14	3	0	30	15	5	.327	.376

Last Five Years

	Avg	AB	H	2B	3B	HR	RBI	BB	SO	OBP	SLG
Behind in Count	.307	1076	330	60	12	7	108	0	97	.307	.404
Two Strikes	.297	860	255	37	10	5	86	50	107	.336	.380

	Avg	AB	H	2B	3B	HR	RBI	BB	SO	OBP	SLG
Pre-All Star	.335	1622	544	93	24	17	179	131	67	.382	.454
Post-All Star	.314	1094	344	58	10	8	117	85	40	.361	.408

Batter vs. Pitcher (since 1984)

Hits Best Against	Avg	AB	H	2B	3B	HR	RBI	BB	SO	OBP	SLG
Jeff Brantley	.600	20	12	1	0	0	1	4	0	.667	.650
Jeff Parrett	.529	17	9	1	0	0	2	4	1	.619	.588
Mark Gardner	.471	17	8	0	2	0	3	1	0	.500	.706
John Smoltz	.465	43	20	2	2	2	9	1	1	.477	.744
Curt Schilling	.438	16	7	3	0	1	3	0	1	.438	.813

Hits Worst Against	Avg	AB	H	2B	3B	HR	RBI	BB	SO	OBP	SLG
Frank DiPino	.056	18	1	0	0	0	2	1	2	.100	.056
Omar Olivares	.059	17	1	0	0	1	2	1	0	.111	.235
Charlie Hough	.100	10	1	1	0	0	1	0	1	.091	.200
Denny Neagle	.100	10	1	0	0	0	0	1	0	.182	.100
Willie Blair	.167	12	2	0	0	0	1	0	1	.167	.167

Dave Haas — Tigers

Age 28 – Pitches Right

	ERA	W	L	Sv	G	GS	IP	BB	SO	Avg	H	2B	3B	HR	RBI	OBP	SLG	GF	IR	IRS	Hld	SvOp	SB	CS	GB	FB	G/F
1993 Season	6.11	1	2	0	20	0	28.0	8	17	.375	45	4	0	9	22	.411	.633	5	17	6	2	0	1	0	43	34	1.26
Career (1991-1993)	4.84	7	5	0	43	11	100.1	36	52	.303	121	14	1	18	59	.361	.479	6	30	12	2	1	2	2	151	119	1.27

1993 Season

	ERA	W	L	Sv	G	GS	IP	H	HR	BB	SO
Home	7.20	1	2	0	11	0	15.0	26	7	4	12
Away	4.85	0	0	0	9	0	13.0	19	2	4	5

	Avg	AB	H	2B	3B	HR	RBI	BB	SO	OBP	SLG
vs. Left	.426	47	20	1	0	2	6	4	7	.471	.574
vs. Right	.342	73	25	3	0	7	16	4	10	.372	.671

John Habyan — Royals

Age 30 – Pitches Right (groundball pitcher)

	ERA	W	L	Sv	G	GS	IP	BB	SO	Avg	H	2B	3B	HR	RBI	OBP	SLG	GF	IR	IRS	Hld	SvOp	SB	CS	GB	FB	G/F
1993 Season	4.15	2	1	1	48	0	56.1	20	39	.272	59	12	2	6	32	.331	.429	23	33	9	7	3	6	0	86	54	1.59
Last Five Years	3.24	11	9	10	176	0	227.2	63	157	.263	226	46	8	14	112	.315	.384	60	123	45	43	20	15	1	352	196	1.80

1993 Season

	ERA	W	L	Sv	G	GS	IP	H	HR	BB	SO
Home	2.54	2	0	1	22	0	28.1	19	1	4	20
Away	5.79	0	1	0	26	0	28.0	40	5	16	19
Starter	0.00	0	0	0	0	0	0.0	0	0	0	0
Reliever	4.15	2	1	1	48	0	56.1	59	6	20	39
0 Days rest	4.09	1	0	1	8	0	11.0	13	0	3	7
1 or 2 Days rest	1.66	0	0	0	17	0	21.2	19	1	8	17
3+ Days rest	6.46	1	1	0	23	0	23.2	27	5	9	15
Pre-All Star	3.82	1	1	1	31	0	37.2	38	5	15	26
Post-All Star	4.82	1	0	0	17	0	18.2	21	1	5	13

	Avg	AB	H	2B	3B	HR	RBI	BB	SO	OBP	SLG
vs. Left	.241	79	19	4	2	3	13	6	11	.287	.456
vs. Right	.290	138	40	8	0	3	19	14	28	.355	.413
Scoring Posn	.343	67	23	4	0	4	28	11	12	.425	.582
Close & Late	.289	76	22	4	1	3	15	5	16	.329	.487
None on/out	.283	46	13	5	2	1	1	5	6	.353	.543
First Pitch	.423	26	11	1	1	0	3	4	0	.500	.538
Ahead in Count	.247	97	24	6	0	2	10	0	31	.242	.371
Behind in Count	.293	58	17	3	0	4	17	8	0	.379	.552
Two Strikes	.129	85	11	4	0	1	5	8	39	.202	.212

Last Five Years

	ERA	W	L	Sv	G	GS	IP	H	HR	BB	SO
Home	2.59	10	3	6	83	0	114.2	110	4	25	75
Away	3.90	1	6	4	93	0	113.0	116	10	38	82
Day	3.78	6	4	4	53	0	69.0	73	3	13	49
Night	3.01	5	5	6	123	0	158.2	153	11	50	108
Grass	2.98	11	7	9	143	0	187.0	170	12	52	125
Turf	4.43	0	2	1	33	0	40.2	56	2	11	32
April	1.59	1	2	2	26	0	34.0	32	2	12	25
May	2.79	5	1	1	32	0	51.2	34	3	13	32
June	3.73	2	2	0	32	0	31.1	37	2	9	20
July	2.75	1	2	6	29	0	39.1	42	1	10	29
August	5.16	0	2	0	27	0	29.2	35	4	9	27
September/October	3.89	2	0	1	30	0	41.2	46	2	10	24
Starter	0.00	0	0	0	0	0	0.0	0	0	0	0
Reliever	3.24	11	9	10	176	0	227.2	226	14	63	157
0 Days rest	4.50	3	1	2	32	0	36.0	43	1	12	29
1 or 2 Days rest	2.80	4	4	6	76	0	99.2	97	6	27	71
3+ Days rest	3.23	4	4	2	68	0	92.0	86	7	24	57
Pre-All Star	2.55	8	6	8	101	0	134.0	120	7	36	90
Post-All Star	4.23	3	3	2	75	0	93.2	106	7	27	67

	Avg	AB	H	2B	3B	HR	RBI	BB	SO	OBP	SLG
vs. Left	.292	332	97	20	4	5	46	23	38	.334	.422
vs. Right	.244	528	129	26	4	9	66	40	119	.303	.360
Inning 1-6	.222	167	37	9	0	1	21	17	26	.303	.293
Inning 7+	.273	693	189	37	8	13	91	46	131	.318	.405
None on	.244	451	110	17	3	5	5	26	84	.290	.328
Runners on	.284	409	116	29	5	9	107	37	73	.341	.445
Scoring Posn	.287	254	73	18	5	8	99	34	46	.368	.492
Close & Late	.279	416	116	14	5	8	60	29	79	.327	.394
None on/out	.263	190	50	7	3	3	3	14	26	.314	.379
vs. 1st Batr (relief)	.270	159	43	7	3	4	24	15	33	.337	.428
First Inning Pitched	.256	566	145	34	4	10	85	50	114	.318	.383
First 15 Pitches	.261	564	147	33	7	8	69	43	108	.314	.387
Pitch 16-30	.281	221	62	12	1	6	36	20	39	.343	.425
Pitch 31-45	.215	65	14	1	0	0	7	0	8	.224	.231
Pitch 46+	.300	10	3	0	0	0	0	0	2	.300	.300
First Pitch	.300	130	39	4	1	0	12	9	0	.355	.346
Ahead in Count	.210	400	84	22	1	4	40	0	131	.213	.300
Behind in Count	.362	207	75	15	4	9	47	35	0	.451	.604
Two Strikes	.143	363	52	16	0	4	31	19	157	.189	.220

Pitcher vs. Batter (career)

Pitches Best Vs.	Avg	AB	H	2B	3B	HR	RBI	BB	SO	OBP	SLG
Lou Whitaker	.083	12	1	0	0	0	0	3	0	.267	.083
Paul Molitor	.083	12	1	0	0	0	0	1	4	.154	.083
Tony Phillips	.083	12	1	0	0	0	0	1	1	.154	.083
Rob Deer	.133	15	2	0	0	0	1	1	5	.188	.133
Ruben Sierra	.167	12	2	0	0	0	3	0	3	.143	.167

Pitches Worst Vs.	Avg	AB	H	2B	3B	HR	RBI	BB	SO	OBP	SLG
Dave Winfield	.667	12	8	3	0	0	4	2	1	.714	.917
Steve Buechele	.500	10	5	1	0	0	2	1	2	.545	.600
Devon White	.417	12	5	1	0	0	1	0	1	.417	.500
Harold Reynolds	.400	15	6	2	0	0	4	1	1	.438	.533
Joe Carter	.333	12	4	0	1	2	4	0	4	.333	1.000

Chip Hale — Twins

Age 29 – Bats Left

	Avg	G	AB	R	H	2B	3B	HR	RBI	BB	SO	HBP	GDP	SB	CS	OBP	SLG	IBB	SH	SF	#Pit	#P/PA	GB	FB	G/F
1993 Season	.333	69	186	25	62	6	1	3	27	18	17	6	3	2	1	.408	.425	0	2	1	793	3.72	66	52	1.27
Career (1989-1993)	.298	98	255	31	76	9	1	3	33	19	24	6	3	2	1	.354	.376	0	3	5	1025	3.56	96	74	1.30

1993 Season

	Avg	AB	H	2B	3B	HR	RBI	BB	SO	OBP	SLG
vs. Left	.143	7	1	0	0	0	1	1	2	.333	.143
vs. Right	.341	179	61	6	1	3	26	17	15	.411	.436

	Avg	AB	H	2B	3B	HR	RBI	BB	SO	OBP	SLG
Scoring Posn	.326	46	15	1	0	1	23	6	5	.429	.413
Close & Late	.289	38	11	1	0	0	8	6	5	.417	.316

1993 Season

	Avg	AB	H	2B	3B	HR	RBI	BB	SO	OBP	SLG		Avg	AB	H	2B	3B	HR	RBI	BB	SO	OBP	SLG
Home	.353	85	30	3	1	1	13	15	8	.466	.447	None on/out	.294	34	10	1	0	0	0	1	3	.351	.324
Away	.317	101	32	3	0	2	14	3	9	.352	.406	Batting #2	.326	92	30	4	1	1	13	6	8	.376	.424
First Pitch	.500	28	14	2	1	0	8	0	0	.500	.643	Batting #6	.360	25	9	0	0	2	3	3	2	.467	.600
Ahead in Count	.326	46	15	1	0	1	7	12	0	.475	.413	Other	.333	69	23	2	0	0	11	9	7	.425	.362
Behind in Count	.313	80	25	3	0	2	10	0	14	.341	.425	Pre-All Star	.299	87	26	3	1	1	9	7	6	.367	.391
Two Strikes	.296	81	24	3	0	2	10	6	17	.360	.407	Post-All Star	.364	99	36	3	0	2	18	11	11	.442	.455

Bob Hamelin — Royals

Age 26 – Bats Left (flyball hitter)

	Avg	G	AB	R	H	2B	3B	HR	RBI	BB	SO	HBP	GDP	SB	CS	OBP	SLG	IBB	SH	SF	#Pit	#P/PA	GB	FB	G/F
1993 Season	.224	16	49	2	11	3	0	2	5	6	15	0	2	0	0	.309	.408	0	0	0	235	4.27	12	14	0.86

1993 Season

	Avg	AB	H	2B	3B	HR	RBI	BB	SO	OBP	SLG		Avg	AB	H	2B	3B	HR	RBI	BB	SO	OBP	SLG
vs. Left	.400	5	2	0	0	0	2	0	2	.400	.400	Scoring Posn	.182	11	2	0	0	0	3	0	3	.182	.182
vs. Right	.205	44	9	3	0	2	3	6	13	.300	.409	Close & Late	.182	11	2	1	0	0	0	3	4	.357	.273

Darryl Hamilton — Brewers

Age 29 – Bats Left (groundball hitter)

	Avg	G	AB	R	H	2B	3B	HR	RBI	BB	SO	HBP	GDP	SB	CS	OBP	SLG	IBB	SH	SF	#Pit	#P/PA	GB	FB	G/F
1993 Season	.310	135	520	74	161	21	1	9	48	45	62	3	9	21	13	.367	.406	5	4	1	2327	4.06	196	135	1.45
Last Five Years	.305	474	1551	232	473	60	14	16	185	132	154	4	30	88	36	.359	.393	7	18	11	6621	3.86	652	356	1.83

1993 Season

	Avg	AB	H	2B	3B	HR	RBI	BB	SO	OBP	SLG		Avg	AB	H	2B	3B	HR	RBI	BB	SO	OBP	SLG
vs. Left	.264	182	48	3	1	1	10	13	25	.316	.308	Scoring Posn	.313	112	35	4	0	0	35	20	16	.422	.348
vs. Right	.334	338	113	18	0	8	38	32	37	.394	.459	Close & Late	.349	83	29	5	1	1	9	9	10	.413	.470
Groundball	.219	105	23	4	1	1	9	8	14	.274	.305	None on/out	.326	175	57	9	1	5	5	9	23	.362	.474
Flyball	.370	100	37	5	0	3	11	13	13	.447	.510	Batting #1	.326	304	99	13	1	4	27	30	38	.387	.414
Home	.317	262	83	9	1	5	28	30	30	.388	.416	Batting #3	.312	109	34	7	0	2	14	9	11	.364	.431
Away	.302	258	78	12	0	4	20	15	32	.345	.395	Other	.262	107	28	1	0	3	7	6	13	.313	.355
Day	.273	187	51	6	0	2	13	13	22	.322	.337	April	.346	78	27	1	0	0	7	5	8	.393	.359
Night	.330	333	110	15	1	7	35	32	40	.392	.444	May	.304	56	17	3	0	1	3	8	6	.385	.411
Grass	.319	423	135	14	1	8	42	39	55	.380	.414	June	.314	105	33	5	0	1	11	7	11	.357	.390
Turf	.268	97	26	7	0	1	6	6	7	.311	.371	July	.327	98	32	5	0	2	8	8	12	.377	.439
First Pitch	.385	26	10	1	0	0	3	3	0	.467	.423	August	.296	98	29	3	1	4	12	7	13	.355	.469
Ahead in Count	.349	109	38	5	0	5	17	26	0	.471	.532	September/October	.271	85	23	4	0	1	7	10	12	.347	.353
Behind in Count	.268	250	67	8	1	2	18	0	54	.274	.332	Pre-All Star	.326	273	89	11	0	2	23	24	27	.381	.388
Two Strikes	.281	253	71	12	0	2	21	16	62	.326	.352	Post-All Star	.291	247	72	10	1	7	25	21	35	.352	.425

1993 By Position

Position	Avg	AB	H	2B	3B	HR	RBI	BB	SO	OBP	SLG	G	GS	Innings	PO	A	E	DP	Fld Pct	Rng Fctr	In Zone	Outs	Zone Rtg	MLB Zone
As lf	.299	107	32	6	0	1	6	11	11	.364	.383	31	26	234.2	73	3	0	0	1.000	2.91	81	70	.864	.818
As cf	.288	156	45	4	1	3	17	5	25	.309	.385	49	33	317.2	113	2	2	1	.983	3.26	123	109	.886	.829
As rf	.333	252	84	11	0	5	25	28	26	.406	.437	70	64	537.1	156	5	1	0	.994	2.70	187	151	.807	.826

Last Five Years

	Avg	AB	H	2B	3B	HR	RBI	BB	SO	OBP	SLG		Avg	AB	H	2B	3B	HR	RBI	BB	SO	OBP	SLG
vs. Left	.259	367	95	9	3	1	34	29	47	.315	.308	Scoring Posn	.326	396	129	12	4	3	165	47	37	.392	.399
vs. Right	.319	1184	378	51	11	15	151	103	107	.372	.419	Close & Late	.361	233	84	11	3	2	29	26	25	.423	.459
Groundball	.266	413	110	10	2	2	56	31	38	.315	.315	None on/out	.299	398	119	22	3	5	5	22	45	.337	.407
Flyball	.326	316	103	14	2	7	47	33	26	.388	.449	Batting #1	.314	407	128	18	2	4	35	39	50	.373	.398
Home	.308	762	235	31	9	7	90	80	75	.373	.400	Batting #2	.303	476	144	16	6	6	63	36	40	.353	.399
Away	.302	789	238	29	5	9	95	52	79	.344	.385	Other	.301	668	201	26	6	6	87	57	64	.353	.385
Day	.273	506	138	16	4	5	55	40	43	.326	.350	April	.279	179	50	3	1	1	20	19	20	.350	.324
Night	.321	1045	335	44	10	11	130	92	111	.374	.413	May	.267	131	35	6	0	2	10	12	12	.326	.359
Grass	.304	1280	389	50	10	13	155	109	134	.358	.389	June	.333	261	87	13	2	1	31	18	23	.375	.410
Turf	.310	271	84	10	4	3	30	23	20	.363	.410	July	.319	304	97	18	3	4	36	24	38	.364	.438
First Pitch	.380	121	46	6	3	1	16	5	0	.411	.504	August	.305	344	105	13	4	5	50	26	27	.355	.410
Ahead in Count	.314	338	106	14	1	7	45	83	0	.448	.423	September/October	.298	332	99	7	4	3	38	33	34	.362	.370
Behind in Count	.262	710	186	23	4	6	77	0	124	.261	.331	Pre-All Star	.306	673	206	28	3	5	73	58	64	.360	.379
Two Strikes	.261	687	179	28	6	6	81	44	154	.304	.345	Post-All Star	.304	878	267	32	11	11	112	74	90	.358	.403

Batter vs. Pitcher (career)

Hits Best Against	Avg	AB	H	2B	3B	HR	RBI	BB	SO	OBP	SLG	Hits Worst Against	Avg	AB	H	2B	3B	HR	RBI	BB	SO	OBP	SLG
Kevin Appier	.615	13	8	0	0	0	0	2	1	.667	.615	Jeff Montgomery	.000	12	0	0	0	0	0	1	0	.077	.000
Mike Boddicker	.545	11	6	1	1	0	1	1	0	.583	.818	Jose Guzman	.059	17	1	0	0	0	1	0	1	.059	.059
Bill Gullickson	.400	10	4	1	0	1	3	2	0	.500	.800	Roger Clemens	.150	20	3	0	0	0	3	0	1	.143	.150
Scott Kamieniecki	.389	18	7	3	0	1	3	3	0	.476	.722	Alex Fernandez	.154	13	2	1	0	0	1	0	3	.154	.231
Bret Saberhagen	.364	11	4	1	0	1	4	1	5	.417	.727	Kirk McCaskill	.182	11	2	0	0	0	0	0	1	.182	.182

Chris Hammond — Marlins

Age 28 – Pitches Left (groundball pitcher)

	ERA	W	L	Sv	G	GS	IP	BB	SO	Avg	H	2B	3B	HR	RBI	OBP	SLG	CG	ShO	Sup	QS	#P/S	SB	CS	GB	FB	G/F
1993 Season	4.66	11	12	0	32	32	191.0	66	108	.277	207	30	6	18	92	.336	.406	1	0	4.38	16	91	5	6	310	198	1.57
Career (1990-1993)	4.43	25	31	0	83	79	449.1	181	241	.268	461	70	16	37	203	.339	.392	1	0	3.93	39	86	21	14	748	449	1.67

1993 Season

	ERA	W	L	Sv	G	GS	IP	H	HR	BB	SO
Home	4.91	5	5	0	14	14	80.2	95	8	24	52
Away	4.49	6	7	0	18	18	110.1	112	10	42	56
Day	3.48	4	2	0	8	8	51.2	50	3	16	28
Night	5.10	7	10	0	24	24	139.1	157	15	50	80
Grass	4.50	9	8	0	24	24	142.0	157	15	44	81
Turf	5.14	2	4	0	8	8	49.0	50	3	22	27
April	5.04	0	3	0	5	5	25.0	30	5	11	9
May	4.88	3	1	0	5	5	31.1	24	6	13	17
June	2.53	6	0	0	6	6	42.2	48	0	11	22
July	4.71	1	2	0	5	5	28.2	32	2	12	11
August	8.23	0	3	0	5	5	27.1	39	2	7	21
September/October	4.00	1	3	0	6	6	36.0	34	3	12	28
Starter	4.66	11	12	0	32	32	191.0	207	18	66	108
Reliever	0.00	0	0	0	0	0	0.0	0	0	0	0
0-3 Days Rest	0.00	0	0	0	0	0	0.0	0	0	0	0
4 Days Rest	4.32	7	6	0	21	21	127.0	131	11	39	73
5+ Days Rest	5.34	4	6	0	11	11	64.0	76	7	27	35
Pre-All Star	3.91	10	4	0	18	18	112.2	115	12	38	52
Post-All Star	5.74	1	8	0	14	14	78.1	92	6	28	56

	Avg	AB	H	2B	3B	HR	RBI	BB	SO	OBP	SLG
vs. Left	.266	128	34	6	2	3	10	22	23	.377	.414
vs. Right	.279	619	173	24	4	15	82	44	85	.326	.404
Inning 1-6	.277	672	186	26	6	16	82	58	96	.335	.405
Inning 7+	.280	75	21	4	0	2	10	8	12	.345	.413
None on	.228	438	100	12	3	8	8	37	68	.290	.324
Runners on	.346	309	107	18	3	10	84	29	40	.400	.521
Scoring Posn	.344	186	64	8	2	4	64	17	28	.395	.473
Close & Late	.275	40	11	3	0	1	5	3	10	.326	.425
None on/out	.246	191	47	2	2	4	4	18	20	.311	.340
vs. 1st Batr (relief)	.000	0	0	0	0	0	0	0	0	.000	.000
First Inning Pitched	.293	123	36	5	1	4	13	9	23	.343	.447
First 75 Pitches	.263	601	158	20	6	16	65	47	89	.317	.396
Pitch 76-90	.330	88	29	6	0	0	16	10	11	.398	.398
Pitch 91-105	.313	48	15	3	0	1	6	7	7	.400	.438
Pitch 106+	.500	10	5	1	0	1	5	2	1	.538	.900
First Pitch	.333	111	37	4	4	3	18	0	0	.333	.523
Ahead in Count	.226	314	71	12	1	4	31	0	94	.225	.309
Behind in Count	.293	181	53	8	0	3	22	45	0	.436	.387
Two Strikes	.223	318	71	11	1	6	35	21	108	.271	.321

Career (1990-1993)

	ERA	W	L	Sv	G	GS	IP	H	HR	BB	SO
Home	4.54	13	13	0	41	38	216.0	230	19	88	123
Away	4.32	12	18	0	42	41	233.1	231	18	93	118
Day	3.59	10	8	0	27	23	145.1	134	12	49	75
Night	4.83	15	23	0	56	56	304.0	327	25	132	166
Grass	4.44	11	11	0	33	32	186.2	203	17	62	105
Turf	4.42	14	20	0	50	47	262.2	258	20	119	136
April	3.36	5	4	0	13	12	72.1	68	7	26	38
May	4.58	5	5	0	14	13	76.2	62	8	36	35
June	3.87	10	4	0	17	17	100.0	106	5	44	49
July	4.94	2	6	0	16	15	78.1	94	6	36	40
August	6.35	2	8	0	13	13	66.2	83	7	23	40
September/October	3.58	1	4	0	10	9	55.1	48	4	16	39
Starter	4.46	25	31	0	79	79	442.1	457	37	178	237
Reliever	2.57	0	0	0	4	0	7.0	4	0	3	4
0-3 Days Rest	3.75	1	1	0	2	2	12.0	13	0	4	6
4 Days Rest	4.10	16	17	0	45	45	257.0	249	23	85	142
5+ Days Rest	5.04	8	13	0	32	32	173.1	195	14	89	89
Pre-All Star	3.85	22	14	0	49	47	280.1	263	22	113	138
Post-All Star	5.38	3	17	0	34	32	169.0	198	15	68	103

	Avg	AB	H	2B	3B	HR	RBI	BB	SO	OBP	SLG
vs. Left	.256	356	91	13	6	11	41	51	58	.352	.419
vs. Right	.271	1363	370	57	10	26	162	130	183	.335	.385
Inning 1-6	.266	1585	421	62	14	34	190	162	227	.335	.387
Inning 7+	.299	134	40	8	2	3	13	19	14	.383	.455
None on	.233	1027	239	33	10	15	15	100	159	.303	.328
Runners on	.321	692	222	37	6	22	188	81	82	.391	.487
Scoring Posn	.321	390	125	17	5	8	147	57	57	.404	.451
Close & Late	.311	74	23	5	1	2	7	10	11	.393	.486
None on/out	.243	448	109	11	6	9	9	41	54	.308	.355
vs. 1st Batr (relief)	.250	4	1	0	0	0	0	0	1	.250	.250
First Inning Pitched	.283	318	90	14	2	8	38	34	50	.354	.415
First 75 Pitches	.263	1436	377	51	14	32	159	140	209	.330	.384
Pitch 76-90	.296	186	55	13	2	3	32	24	21	.374	.435
Pitch 91-105	.271	85	23	5	0	1	7	14	10	.374	.365
Pitch 106+	.500	12	6	1	0	1	5	3	1	.563	.833
First Pitch	.337	255	86	15	5	8	41	9	0	.363	.529
Ahead in Count	.221	697	154	23	7	10	63	0	206	.223	.317
Behind in Count	.276	438	121	18	2	9	55	110	0	.423	.388
Two Strikes	.209	718	150	21	5	12	72	61	241	.273	.302

Pitcher vs. Batter (career)

Pitches Best Vs.	Avg	AB	H	2B	3B	HR	RBI	BB	SO	OBP	SLG
Ken Caminiti	.077	26	2	0	0	0	2	0	4	.077	.077
Mark Grace	.091	11	1	0	0	0	1	2	1	.231	.091
Charlie O'Brien	.100	10	1	0	0	0	1	1	1	.182	.100
Mariano Duncan	.100	10	1	0	0	0	1	1	1	.182	.100
Eric Yelding	.154	13	2	0	0	0	0	0	0	.154	.154

Pitches Worst Vs.	Avg	AB	H	2B	3B	HR	RBI	BB	SO	OBP	SLG
Bernard Gilkey	.632	19	12	2	0	0	4	4	0	.696	.737
Robby Thompson	.500	16	8	2	0	0	2	3	0	.579	.625
Barry Bonds	.385	26	10	2	0	2	5	3	5	.448	.692
Gary Redus	.368	19	7	2	2	0	2	4	2	.478	.684
Andres Galarraga	.333	12	4	0	1	2	5	1	0	.385	1.000

Jeffrey Hammonds — Orioles

Age 23 – Bats Right (flyball hitter)

	Avg	G	AB	R	H	2B	3B	HR	RBI	BB	SO	HBP	GDP	SB	CS	OBP	SLG	IBB	SH	SF	#Pit	#P/PA	GB	FB	G/F
1993 Season	.305	33	105	10	32	8	0	3	19	2	16	0	3	4	0	.312	.467	1	1	2	358	3.25	29	38	0.76

1993 Season

	Avg	AB	H	2B	3B	HR	RBI	BB	SO	OBP	SLG
vs. Left	.279	43	12	3	0	2	7	0	7	.273	.488
vs. Right	.323	62	20	5	0	1	12	2	9	.338	.452

	Avg	AB	H	2B	3B	HR	RBI	BB	SO	OBP	SLG
Scoring Posn	.438	32	14	3	0	2	18	1	4	.429	.719
Close & Late	.385	13	5	1	0	0	0	1	3	.429	.462

Mike Hampton — Mariners

Age 21 – Pitches Left

	ERA	W	L	Sv	G	GS	IP	BB	SO	Avg	H	2B	3B	HR	RBI	OBP	SLG	GF	IR	IRS	Hld	SvOp	SB	CS	GB	FB	G/F
1993 Season	9.53	1	3	1	13	3	17.0	17	8	.368	28	6	1	3	17	.479	.592	2	4	1	2	1	4	0	26	20	1.30

1993 Season

	ERA	W	L	Sv	G	GS	IP	H	HR	BB	SO
Home	12.60	1	2	0	6	2	10.0	21	3	8	5
Away	5.14	0	1	1	7	1	7.0	7	0	9	3

	Avg	AB	H	2B	3B	HR	RBI	BB	SO	OBP	SLG
vs. Left	.345	29	10	1	1	2	6	1	2	.367	.655
vs. Right	.383	47	18	5	0	1	11	16	6	.531	.553

Chris Haney — Royals

Age 25 – Pitches Left

	ERA	W	L	Sv	G	GS	IP	BB	SO	Avg	H	2B	3B	HR	RBI	OBP	SLG	CG	ShO	Sup	QS	#P/S	SB	CS	GB	FB	G/F
1993 Season	6.02	9	9	0	23	23	124.0	53	65	.286	141	25	2	13	76	.356	.424	1	1	5.37	8	94	7	4	179	145	1.23
Career (1991-1993)	5.05	16	22	0	55	52	288.2	122	170	.274	310	66	7	30	159	.346	.424	3	3	4.43	19	91	24	14	413	346	1.19

1993 Season

	ERA	W	L	Sv	G	GS	IP	H	HR	BB	SO
Home	6.36	3	7	0	13	13	69.1	85	8	21	30
Away	5.60	6	2	0	10	10	54.2	56	5	32	35
Starter	6.02	9	9	0	23	23	124.0	141	13	53	65
Reliever	0.00	0	0	0	0	0	0.0	0	0	0	0
0-3 Days Rest	0.00	0	0	0	0	0	0.0	0	0	0	0
4 Days Rest	6.68	4	7	0	13	13	67.1	75	7	33	35
5+ Days Rest	5.24	5	2	0	10	10	56.2	66	6	20	30
Pre-All Star	6.08	5	2	0	10	10	53.1	58	6	19	31
Post-All Star	5.99	4	7	0	13	13	70.2	83	7	34	34

	Avg	AB	H	2B	3B	HR	RBI	BB	SO	OBP	SLG
vs. Left	.277	83	23	3	0	1	14	10	5	.362	.349
vs. Right	.288	410	118	22	2	12	62	43	60	.355	.439
Scoring Posn	.344	122	42	7	2	3	64	20	17	.436	.508
Close & Late	.316	19	6	1	0	1	4	0	1	.316	.526
None on/out	.258	128	33	8	0	5	5	10	15	.312	.438
First Pitch	.373	51	19	5	0	0	6	2	0	.400	.471
Ahead in Count	.234	214	50	4	1	5	31	0	56	.239	.332
Behind in Count	.302	129	39	6	1	2	17	29	0	.430	.411
Two Strikes	.235	217	51	7	0	6	30	22	65	.300	.350

Career (1991-1993)

	ERA	W	L	Sv	G	GS	IP	H	HR	BB	SO
Home	5.11	8	13	0	29	28	156.2	170	15	48	83
Away	4.98	8	9	0	26	24	132.0	140	15	74	87
Day	5.14	4	3	0	13	13	70.0	73	8	39	38
Night	5.02	12	19	0	42	39	218.2	237	22	83	132
Grass	4.96	5	4	0	14	14	74.1	77	10	41	43
Turf	5.08	11	18	0	41	38	214.1	233	20	81	127
April	4.50	2	1	0	4	3	20.0	20	2	5	12
May	5.16	2	2	0	6	5	29.2	32	4	9	17
June	6.20	2	3	0	9	8	45.0	46	8	15	32
July	4.68	4	4	0	9	9	50.0	57	3	19	28
August	3.30	4	3	0	12	12	71.0	64	3	37	37
September/October	6.41	2	9	0	15	15	73.0	91	10	37	44
Starter	5.02	16	22	0	52	52	281.1	303	29	119	161
Reliever	6.14	0	0	0	3	0	7.1	7	1	3	9
0-3 Days Rest	15.75	0	1	0	1	1	4.0	8	1	1	0
4 Days Rest	5.69	6	11	0	23	23	123.1	139	11	60	72
5+ Days Rest	4.21	10	10	0	28	28	154.0	156	17	58	89
Pre-All Star	5.70	7	8	0	22	19	107.1	116	15	36	68
Post-All Star	4.67	9	14	0	33	33	181.1	194	15	86	102

	Avg	AB	H	2B	3B	HR	RBI	BB	SO	OBP	SLG
vs. Left	.244	209	51	10	3	3	32	25	33	.336	.364
vs. Right	.281	923	259	56	4	27	127	97	137	.348	.438
Inning 1-6	.278	1025	285	59	7	27	149	115	151	.352	.428
Inning 7+	.234	107	25	7	0	3	10	7	19	.284	.383
None on	.260	645	168	37	3	17	17	63	96	.330	.406
Runners on	.292	487	142	29	4	13	142	59	74	.365	.448
Scoring Posn	.297	279	83	16	4	6	126	44	42	.388	.448
Close & Late	.250	32	8	1	0	2	5	1	4	.273	.469
None on/out	.261	284	74	15	0	9	9	27	41	.329	.408
vs. 1st Batr (relief)	.667	3	2	2	0	0	2	0	0	.667	1.333
First Inning Pitched	.296	216	64	15	2	10	43	37	34	.400	.523
First 75 Pitches	.281	881	248	54	3	25	123	99	137	.355	.435
Pitch 76-90	.236	140	33	8	3	3	21	10	14	.288	.400
Pitch 91-105	.263	80	21	3	1	1	10	10	11	.344	.363
Pitch 106+	.258	31	8	1	0	1	5	3	8	.324	.387
First Pitch	.280	132	37	8	0	2	20	4	0	.300	.386
Ahead in Count	.224	496	111	19	3	9	55	0	148	.230	.329
Behind in Count	.323	285	92	19	2	5	37	73	0	.460	.456
Two Strikes	.215	498	107	21	2	13	55	45	170	.282	.343

Pitcher vs. Batter (career)

Pitches Best Vs.	Avg	AB	H	2B	3B	HR	RBI	BB	SO	OBP	SLG
Jay Buhner	.000	9	0	0	0	0	0	2	5	.182	.000
Billy Hatcher	.167	12	2	2	0	0	0	1	0	.231	.333
Dickie Thon	.182	11	2	1	0	0	2	0	1	.182	.273

Pitches Worst Vs.	Avg	AB	H	2B	3B	HR	RBI	BB	SO	OBP	SLG
Andre Dawson	.417	12	5	0	0	1	3	2	0	.500	.667
Ken Griffey Jr	.333	9	3	1	0	0	0	3	1	.500	.444

Dave Hansen — Dodgers

Age 25 – Bats Left

	Avg	G	AB	R	H	2B	3B	HR	RBI	BB	SO	HBP	GDP	SB	CS	OBP	SLG	IBB	SH	SF	#Pit	#P/PA	GB	FB	G/F
1993 Season	.362	84	105	13	38	3	0	4	30	21	13	0	0	0	1	.465	.505	3	0	1	458	3.61	45	22	2.05
Career (1990-1993)	.250	274	509	46	127	18	0	11	58	57	77	1	9	1	3	.325	.350	6	0	3	2141	3.75	199	138	1.44

1993 Season

	Avg	AB	H	2B	3B	HR	RBI	BB	SO	OBP	SLG
vs. Left	.000	2	0	0	0	0	0	0	1	.000	.000
vs. Right	.369	103	38	3	0	4	30	21	12	.472	.515
Home	.375	48	18	0	0	2	13	11	3	.492	.500
Away	.351	57	20	3	0	2	17	10	10	.441	.509
First Pitch	.368	19	7	0	0	1	6	2	0	.409	.526
Ahead in Count	.375	32	12	1	0	1	12	12	0	.545	.500
Behind in Count	.278	36	10	1	0	0	4	0	9	.278	.306
Two Strikes	.279	43	12	2	0	0	5	7	13	.380	.326

	Avg	AB	H	2B	3B	HR	RBI	BB	SO	OBP	SLG
Scoring Posn	.526	38	20	3	0	1	24	11	6	.620	.684
Close & Late	.406	32	13	2	0	3	19	7	5	.513	.750
None on/out	.333	18	6	0	0	1	1	2	1	.400	.500
Batting #3	.452	31	14	1	0	1	9	3	2	.500	.581
Batting #9	.410	39	16	1	0	1	12	7	5	.500	.513
Other	.229	35	8	1	0	2	9	11	6	.404	.429
Pre-All Star	.294	34	10	0	0	1	8	4	7	.368	.382
Post-All Star	.394	71	28	3	0	3	22	17	6	.506	.563

Career (1990-1993)

	Avg	AB	H	2B	3B	HR	RBI	BB	SO	OBP	SLG
vs. Left	.182	55	10	3	0	0	1	4	12	.233	.236
vs. Right	.258	454	117	15	0	11	57	53	65	.335	.363
Groundball	.242	165	40	6	0	2	19	22	20	.332	.315
Flyball	.276	127	35	9	0	5	18	14	25	.352	.465
Home	.261	264	69	6	0	3	25	29	34	.336	.318
Away	.237	245	58	12	0	8	33	28	43	.313	.384
Day	.201	159	32	5	0	4	24	22	26	.293	.308
Night	.271	350	95	13	0	7	34	35	51	.339	.369
Grass	.255	369	94	10	0	7	43	43	50	.333	.339
Turf	.236	140	33	8	0	4	15	14	27	.303	.379
First Pitch	.250	88	22	1	0	1	11	5	0	.295	.295
Ahead in Count	.281	114	32	6	0	4	21	32	0	.435	.439
Behind in Count	.174	207	36	5	0	2	9	0	63	.173	.227
Two Strikes	.218	238	52	8	0	3	16	20	77	.278	.290

	Avg	AB	H	2B	3B	HR	RBI	BB	SO	OBP	SLG
Scoring Posn	.281	121	34	5	0	2	42	22	22	.384	.372
Close & Late	.240	121	29	5	0	3	22	13	26	.311	.355
None on/out	.266	139	37	6	0	4	4	9	19	.311	.396
Batting #7	.279	140	39	7	0	4	10	17	22	.361	.414
Batting #8	.191	136	26	4	0	2	11	9	22	.238	.265
Other	.266	233	62	7	0	5	37	31	33	.351	.361
April	.140	43	6	1	0	1	3	2	7	.178	.233
May	.255	55	14	3	0	2	6	9	5	.359	.418
June	.222	54	12	2	0	2	8	10	7	.344	.370
July	.299	97	29	4	0	2	14	5	16	.330	.402
August	.241	116	28	4	0	1	12	14	17	.323	.302
September/October	.264	144	38	4	0	3	15	17	25	.342	.354
Pre-All Star	.237	198	47	7	0	5	21	22	26	.314	.348
Post-All Star	.257	311	80	11	0	6	37	35	51	.331	.350

Batter vs. Pitcher (career)

Hits Best Against	Avg	AB	H	2B	3B	HR	RBI	BB	SO	OBP	SLG
John Burkett	.500	10	5	0	0	1	6	0	2	.455	.800

Hits Worst Against	Avg	AB	H	2B	3B	HR	RBI	BB	SO	OBP	SLG
Darryl Kile	.071	14	1	1	0	0	0	1	0	.133	.143

Batter vs. Pitcher (career)

Hits Best Against	Avg	AB	H	2B	3B	HR	RBI	BB	SO	OBP	SLG	Hits Worst Against	Avg	AB	H	2B	3B	HR	RBI	BB	SO	OBP	SLG
Bill Swift	.375	16	6	0	0	0	2	0	1	.375	.375	Greg W. Harris	.083	12	1	0	0	0	1	1	4	.154	.083

Erik Hanson — Mariners

Age 29 – Pitches Right (groundball pitcher)

	ERA	W	L	Sv	G	GS	IP	BB	SO	Avg	H	2B	3B	HR	RBI	OBP	SLG	CG	ShO	Sup	QS	#P/S	SB	CS	GB	FB	G/F
1993 Season	3.47	11	12	0	31	30	215.0	60	163	.263	215	49	7	17	79	.315	.402	7	0	4.52	22	108	15	13	329	196	1.68
Last Five Years	3.71	54	51	0	139	137	925.2	273	704	.259	914	170	23	69	356	.314	.379	21	3	4.55	88	105	61	44	1359	846	1.61

1993 Season

	ERA	W	L	Sv	G	GS	IP	H	HR	BB	SO
Home	2.79	6	5	0	17	17	119.1	115	8	26	99
Away	4.33	5	7	0	14	13	95.2	100	9	34	64
Day	2.87	4	3	0	8	8	59.2	62	5	14	44
Night	3.71	7	9	0	23	22	155.1	153	12	46	119
Grass	4.69	4	7	0	12	11	80.2	89	9	29	54
Turf	2.75	7	5	0	19	19	134.1	126	8	31	109
April	1.53	3	0	0	5	5	35.1	31	1	13	28
May	2.28	2	2	0	6	6	47.1	44	3	4	44
June	6.19	0	4	0	5	4	32.0	43	5	16	21
July	3.54	3	2	0	6	6	40.2	40	4	9	22
August	4.41	2	3	0	5	5	34.2	32	4	10	28
September/October	3.60	1	1	0	4	4	25.0	25	0	8	20
Starter	3.32	11	11	0	30	30	209.0	206	16	57	161
Reliever	9.00	0	1	0	1	0	6.0	9	1	3	2
0-3 Days Rest	0.00	1	0	0	1	1	7.0	4	0	2	7
4 Days Rest	2.86	7	6	0	19	19	138.2	139	9	28	108
5+ Days Rest	4.69	3	5	0	10	10	63.1	63	7	27	46
Pre-All Star	2.92	7	6	0	19	18	138.2	138	10	36	107
Post-All Star	4.48	4	6	0	12	12	76.1	77	7	24	56

	Avg	AB	H	2B	3B	HR	RBI	BB	SO	OBP	SLG
vs. Left	.229	428	98	23	3	4	33	33	95	.283	.325
vs. Right	.299	391	117	26	4	13	46	27	68	.351	.486
Inning 1-6	.270	673	182	41	5	11	66	49	130	.321	.395
Inning 7+	.226	146	33	8	2	6	13	11	33	.288	.432
None on	.257	506	130	37	5	9	9	32	105	.304	.403
Runners on	.272	313	85	12	2	8	70	28	58	.333	.399
Scoring Posn	.253	194	49	7	1	8	69	19	39	.320	.423
Close & Late	.325	80	26	7	2	5	12	8	14	.389	.650
None on/out	.244	213	52	16	2	2	2	14	39	.291	.366
vs. 1st Batr (relief)	.000	0	0	0	0	0	0	1	0	1.000	.000
First Inning Pitched	.248	113	28	8	0	2	7	9	20	.303	.372
First 75 Pitches	.265	551	146	33	4	9	45	42	109	.317	.388
Pitch 76-90	.302	106	32	8	1	4	24	7	17	.345	.509
Pitch 91-105	.231	91	21	4	1	2	5	7	15	.300	.363
Pitch 106+	.225	71	16	4	1	2	5	4	22	.276	.394
First Pitch	.286	119	34	8	1	2	11	3	0	.303	.420
Ahead in Count	.173	347	60	13	0	2	23	0	135	.182	.228
Behind in Count	.377	191	72	17	3	10	33	32	0	.463	.654
Two Strikes	.164	377	62	15	1	3	25	25	163	.220	.233

Last Five Years

	ERA	W	L	Sv	G	GS	IP	H	HR	BB	SO
Home	3.73	28	24	0	71	71	468.0	483	39	122	365
Away	3.70	26	27	0	68	66	457.2	431	30	151	339
Day	3.57	13	12	0	35	34	219.1	229	17	70	153
Night	3.76	41	39	0	104	103	706.1	685	52	203	551
Grass	3.64	21	23	0	57	55	380.2	351	27	130	289
Turf	3.77	33	28	0	82	82	545.0	563	42	143	415
April	2.99	10	6	0	24	24	156.2	146	9	56	125
May	4.05	9	12	0	26	26	166.2	178	14	48	136
June	4.31	7	11	0	19	18	131.2	140	15	48	93
July	3.65	11	9	0	23	22	155.1	146	12	38	106
August	4.64	5	8	0	22	22	143.2	144	12	39	107
September/October	2.88	12	5	0	25	25	171.2	160	7	44	137
Starter	3.68	53	50	0	137	137	916.2	903	68	270	701
Reliever	7.00	1	1	0	2	0	9.0	11	1	3	3
0-3 Days Rest	0.89	2	0	0	3	3	20.1	13	0	8	18
4 Days Rest	3.75	31	29	0	80	80	545.0	552	39	150	411
5+ Days Rest	3.74	20	21	0	54	54	351.1	338	29	112	272
Pre-All Star	3.67	31	31	0	78	76	514.2	517	42	164	394
Post-All Star	3.77	23	20	0	61	61	411.0	397	27	109	310

	Avg	AB	H	2B	3B	HR	RBI	BB	SO	OBP	SLG
vs. Left	.229	1839	422	86	13	26	174	134	387	.281	.333
vs. Right	.291	1690	492	84	10	43	182	139	317	.348	.429
Inning 1-6	.265	2914	772	144	19	57	312	225	564	.319	.386
Inning 7+	.231	615	142	26	4	12	44	48	140	.287	.345
None on	.247	2166	534	99	13	40	40	142	443	.296	.360
Runners on	.279	1363	380	71	10	29	316	131	261	.341	.409
Scoring Posn	.261	755	197	34	9	19	278	88	162	.333	.405
Close & Late	.258	299	77	16	4	8	31	26	65	.317	.418
None on/out	.228	927	211	46	5	15	15	59	180	.275	.337
vs. 1st Batr (relief)	.000	1	0	0	0	0	0	1	0	.500	.000
First Inning Pitched	.250	523	131	30	1	10	40	37	85	.302	.369
First 75 Pitches	.266	2463	654	125	13	50	252	191	472	.320	.388
Pitch 76-90	.273	439	120	22	6	9	61	35	74	.326	.412
Pitch 91-105	.216	352	76	11	2	7	21	26	93	.276	.318
Pitch 106+	.233	275	64	12	2	3	22	21	65	.289	.324
First Pitch	.305	537	164	31	5	14	54	10	0	.323	.460
Ahead in Count	.170	1369	233	38	7	11	90	0	586	.175	.232
Behind in Count	.359	898	322	69	5	32	138	129	0	.436	.553
Two Strikes	.165	1580	261	44	8	16	115	134	704	.233	.234

Pitcher vs. Batter (career)

Pitches Best Vs.	Avg	AB	H	2B	3B	HR	RBI	BB	SO	OBP	SLG	Pitches Worst Vs.	Avg	AB	H	2B	3B	HR	RBI	BB	SO	OBP	SLG
Sam Horn	.000	21	0	0	0	0	0	2	8	.087	.000	Leo Gomez	.500	14	7	0	0	1	2	5	5	.632	.714
Jose Canseco	.043	23	1	0	0	0	0	3	11	.154	.043	Stan Javier	.500	12	6	1	1	0	2	2	1	.571	.750
Scott Livingstone	.063	16	1	0	0	0	1	0	4	.059	.063	Ellis Burks	.481	27	13	1	0	3	8	2	4	.517	.852
Pat Kelly	.083	12	1	0	0	0	0	0	3	.083	.083	Bo Jackson	.455	11	5	0	0	4	6	2	5	.538	1.545
Randy Velarde	.091	11	1	0	0	0	0	0	3	.091	.091	Frank Thomas	.450	20	9	1	0	2	4	7	3	.593	.800

Mike Harkey — Cubs

Age 27 – Pitches Right

	ERA	W	L	Sv	G	GS	IP	BB	SO	Avg	H	2B	3B	HR	RBI	OBP	SLG	CG	ShO	Sup	QS	#P/S	SB	CS	GB	FB	G/F
1993 Season	5.26	10	10	0	28	28	157.1	43	67	.305	187	23	8	17	86	.349	.451	1	0	5.43	13	81	7	6	216	187	1.16
Last Five Years	4.04	26	18	0	66	66	387.2	123	197	.266	395	62	16	38	171	.324	.406	3	1	5.13	35	88	20	15	564	443	1.27

1993 Season

	ERA	W	L	Sv	G	GS	IP	H	HR	BB	SO
Home	4.86	4	6	0	14	14	79.2	93	12	24	38
Away	5.68	6	4	0	14	14	77.2	94	5	19	29
Starter	5.26	10	10	0	28	28	157.1	187	17	43	67
Reliever	0.00	0	0	0	0	0	0.0	0	0	0	0
0-3 Days Rest	2.84	0	0	0	1	1	6.1	9	1	1	5
4 Days Rest	6.08	4	8	0	14	14	77.0	94	9	21	30
5+ Days Rest	4.62	6	2	0	13	13	74.0	84	7	21	32
Pre-All Star	4.44	6	3	0	13	13	75.0	86	6	22	30
Post-All Star	6.01	4	7	0	15	15	82.1	101	11	21	37

	Avg	AB	H	2B	3B	HR	RBI	BB	SO	OBP	SLG
vs. Left	.279	305	85	10	3	9	46	27	37	.337	.420
vs. Right	.330	309	102	13	5	8	40	16	30	.361	.482
Scoring Posn	.359	131	47	8	3	2	65	14	15	.403	.511
Close & Late	.375	16	6	0	0	0	2	4	4	.476	.375
None on/out	.276	170	47	2	0	9	9	8	17	.313	.447
First Pitch	.368	106	39	4	3	5	14	4	0	.396	.604
Ahead in Count	.214	262	56	3	2	3	34	0	57	.216	.275
Behind in Count	.411	146	60	9	3	7	27	20	0	.476	.658
Two Strikes	.187	241	45	4	2	3	28	19	67	.247	.257

Last Five Years

	ERA	W	L	Sv	G	GS	IP	H	HR	BB	SO
Home	3.58	11	9	0	31	31	193.2	205	22	62	98
Away	4.50	15	9	0	35	35	194.0	190	16	61	99
Day	3.96	16	12	0	42	42	254.1	258	26	74	135
Night	4.18	10	6	0	24	24	133.1	137	12	49	62
Grass	3.62	21	11	0	48	48	296.0	298	32	84	148
Turf	5.40	5	7	0	18	18	91.2	97	6	39	49
April	3.20	5	3	0	10	10	56.1	49	4	21	37
May	5.88	5	2	0	12	12	64.1	89	10	22	27
June	3.46	0	2	0	6	6	39.0	33	2	13	21
July	3.99	7	5	0	13	13	76.2	80	6	19	41
August	3.40	7	3	0	17	17	108.2	102	14	32	50
September/October	4.64	2	3	0	8	8	42.2	42	2	16	21
Starter	4.04	26	18	0	66	66	387.2	395	38	123	197
Reliever	0.00	0	0	0	0	0	0.0	0	0	0	0
0-3 Days Rest	4.32	3	2	0	6	6	33.1	37	1	10	20
4 Days Rest	4.00	12	11	0	34	34	209.1	200	24	65	104
5+ Days Rest	4.03	11	5	0	26	26	145.0	158	13	48	73
Pre-All Star	4.19	12	8	0	31	31	180.1	189	18	59	92
Post-All Star	3.91	14	10	0	35	35	207.1	206	20	64	105

	Avg	AB	H	2B	3B	HR	RBI	BB	SO	OBP	SLG
vs. Left	.254	834	212	35	8	20	95	77	115	.317	.387
vs. Right	.282	650	183	27	8	18	76	46	82	.333	.431
Inning 1-6	.271	1330	361	57	15	35	161	108	184	.328	.416
Inning 7+	.221	154	34	5	1	3	10	15	13	.287	.325
None on	.253	920	233	36	10	30	30	62	125	.304	.412
Runners on	.287	564	162	26	6	8	141	61	72	.354	.397
Scoring Posn	.278	316	88	16	4	3	124	48	43	.364	.383
Close & Late	.268	82	22	2	1	2	7	12	7	.358	.390
None on/out	.246	402	99	10	4	17	17	23	55	.295	.418
vs. 1st Batr (relief)	.000	0	0	0	0	0	0	0	0	.000	.000
First Inning Pitched	.308	266	82	8	0	6	41	15	29	.350	.406
First 75 Pitches	.268	1207	323	50	13	30	139	94	163	.323	.405
Pitch 76-90	.294	143	42	9	2	5	22	15	25	.360	.490
Pitch 91-105	.244	82	20	2	1	2	8	8	8	.308	.366
Pitch 106+	.192	52	10	1	0	1	2	6	3	.276	.269
First Pitch	.309	230	71	8	5	10	28	10	0	.342	.517
Ahead in Count	.207	641	133	16	4	7	54	0	175	.214	.278
Behind in Count	.328	360	118	17	7	15	55	68	0	.430	.539
Two Strikes	.194	614	119	19	4	7	52	45	197	.252	.272

Pitcher vs. Batter (career)

Pitches Best Vs.	Avg	AB	H	2B	3B	HR	RBI	BB	SO	OBP	SLG
Will Clark	.000	15	0	0	0	0	0	2	3	.118	.000
Lenny Dykstra	.091	11	1	0	0	0	0	1	2	.167	.091
John Kruk	.091	11	1	1	0	0	0	0	1	.091	.182
Jeff Conine	.091	11	1	1	0	0	0	0	1	.091	.182
Orestes Destrade	.111	9	1	0	0	0	1	1	0	.182	.111

Pitches Worst Vs.	Avg	AB	H	2B	3B	HR	RBI	BB	SO	OBP	SLG
Jeff Blauser	.600	10	6	1	0	2	2	1	1	.636	1.300
Luis Gonzalez	.583	12	7	1	1	2	6	0	2	.583	1.333
Kevin Mitchell	.500	10	5	1	0	1	3	1	2	.545	.900
Paul O'Neill	.500	10	5	0	0	2	4	3	0	.615	1.100
Matt D. Williams	.438	16	7	0	0	3	5	0	2	.438	1.000

Pete Harnisch — Astros

Age 27 – Pitches Right (flyball pitcher)

	ERA	W	L	Sv	G	GS	IP	BB	SO	Avg	H	2B	3B	HR	RBI	OBP	SLG	CG	ShO	Sup	QS	#P/S	SB	CS	GB	FB	G/F
1993 Season	2.98	16	9	0	33	33	217.2	79	185	.214	171	32	4	20	75	.289	.340	5	4	5.17	24	104	15	6	240	263	0.91
Last Five Years	3.53	53	48	0	149	148	933.0	376	713	.232	808	151	24	79	339	.308	.357	14	6	4.51	87	102	101	28	1022	1140	0.90

1993 Season

	ERA	W	L	Sv	G	GS	IP	H	HR	BB	SO
Home	2.52	9	5	0	18	18	128.2	92	14	38	117
Away	3.64	7	4	0	15	15	89.0	79	6	41	68
Day	3.06	5	2	0	10	10	61.2	49	3	26	47
Night	2.94	11	7	0	23	23	156.0	122	17	53	138
Grass	2.54	4	2	0	8	8	49.2	35	2	19	41
Turf	3.11	12	7	0	25	25	168.0	136	18	60	144
April	3.30	2	0	0	5	5	30.0	22	2	19	21
May	3.26	3	2	0	6	6	38.2	34	4	10	35
June	5.02	1	3	0	5	5	28.2	33	5	7	32
July	3.24	4	2	0	6	6	41.2	31	4	16	36
August	2.47	2	1	0	6	6	40.0	28	4	14	29
September/October	1.16	4	1	0	5	5	38.2	23	1	13	32
Starter	2.98	16	9	0	33	33	217.2	171	20	79	185
Reliever	0.00	0	0	0	0	0	0.0	0	0	0	0
0-3 Days Rest	0.00	1	0	0	1	1	9.0	1	0	3	10
4 Days Rest	3.27	10	7	0	19	19	124.0	106	13	36	113
5+ Days Rest	2.87	5	2	0	13	13	84.2	64	7	40	62
Pre-All Star	3.70	8	6	0	19	19	119.1	104	14	44	106
Post-All Star	2.11	8	3	0	14	14	98.1	67	6	35	79

	Avg	AB	H	2B	3B	HR	RBI	BB	SO	OBP	SLG
vs. Left	.238	428	102	12	4	13	38	55	87	.328	.376
vs. Right	.186	370	69	20	0	7	37	24	98	.241	.297
Inning 1-6	.223	687	153	28	4	18	71	68	157	.297	.354
Inning 7+	.162	111	18	4	0	2	4	11	28	.238	.252
None on	.205	484	99	16	3	14	14	48	119	.282	.337
Runners on	.229	314	72	16	1	6	61	31	66	.299	.344
Scoring Posn	.224	183	41	12	1	2	52	20	41	.295	.333
Close & Late	.167	48	8	2	0	2	4	4	14	.231	.333
None on/out	.211	213	45	3	3	10	10	17	47	.273	.394
vs. 1st Batr (relief)	.000	0	0	0	0	0	0	0	0	.000	.000
First Inning Pitched	.212	118	25	5	2	1	13	13	25	.288	.314
First 75 Pitches	.222	559	124	25	4	14	54	54	133	.294	.356
Pitch 76-90	.210	105	22	3	0	2	10	14	23	.308	.295
Pitch 91-105	.205	83	17	2	0	4	10	7	20	.264	.373
Pitch 106+	.157	51	8	2	0	0	1	4	9	.232	.196
First Pitch	.306	111	34	7	0	2	16	5	0	.339	.423
Ahead in Count	.158	393	62	11	1	5	21	0	147	.163	.229
Behind in Count	.294	153	45	10	1	9	24	29	0	.413	.549
Two Strikes	.146	404	59	10	3	7	24	45	185	.235	.238

Last Five Years

	ERA	W	L	Sv	G	GS	IP	H	HR	BB	SO
Home	2.99	33	20	0	77	76	509.1	399	39	162	415
Away	4.18	20	28	0	72	72	423.2	409	40	214	298
Day	3.76	12	10	0	36	36	215.1	193	20	98	169
Night	3.46	41	38	0	113	112	717.2	615	59	278	544
Grass	3.60	25	23	0	66	65	394.2	351	35	188	290
Turf	3.48	28	25	0	83	83	538.1	457	44	188	423
April	2.79	6	4	0	20	20	122.2	96	8	64	84
May	3.91	9	9	0	24	24	154.1	134	12	51	108
June	3.58	6	10	0	22	22	138.1	123	18	53	116
July	4.20	9	8	0	27	26	167.0	155	17	66	119
August	3.27	8	11	0	30	30	190.0	168	16	86	156
September/October	3.30	15	6	0	26	26	160.2	132	8	56	130
Starter	3.53	53	48	0	148	148	932.2	808	79	376	712
Reliever	0.00	0	0	0	1	0	0.1	0	0	0	1
0-3 Days Rest	2.61	4	2	0	7	7	48.1	35	3	20	36
4 Days Rest	3.66	31	31	0	85	85	538.2	496	46	215	392
5+ Days Rest	3.46	18	15	0	56	56	345.2	277	30	141	284
Pre-All Star	3.48	23	27	0	75	75	472.2	405	44	188	349
Post-All Star	3.58	30	21	0	74	73	460.1	403	35	188	364

	Avg	AB	H	2B	3B	HR	RBI	BB	SO	OBP	SLG
vs. Left	.249	1967	490	84	20	46	192	235	344	.332	.382
vs. Right	.209	1519	318	67	4	33	147	141	369	.277	.324
Inning 1-6	.232	3033	705	131	20	68	302	323	626	.308	.356
Inning 7+	.227	453	103	20	4	11	37	53	87	.308	.362
None on	.223	2067	460	78	17	50	50	215	435	.301	.349
Runners on	.245	1419	348	73	7	29	289	161	278	.319	.368
Scoring Posn	.227	814	185	44	4	14	247	121	172	.319	.343
Close & Late	.197	254	50	9	3	6	18	32	53	.285	.327
None on/out	.229	919	210	33	7	25	25	84	182	.297	.361
vs. 1st Batr (relief)	.000	1	0	0	0	0	0	0	1	.000	.000
First Inning Pitched	.234	552	129	24	4	6	59	71	109	.317	.324
First 75 Pitches	.229	2452	561	110	14	50	232	253	518	.303	.346
Pitch 76-90	.244	450	110	20	5	12	48	54	80	.325	.391
Pitch 91-105	.244	336	82	12	3	12	36	34	77	.315	.405
Pitch 106+	.222	248	55	9	2	5	23	35	38	.319	.335
First Pitch	.291	488	142	34	2	10	64	16	0	.316	.430
Ahead in Count	.191	1745	333	55	9	22	119	0	606	.195	.270
Behind in Count	.284	640	182	36	4	33	91	186	0	.445	.508
Two Strikes	.172	1747	301	53	14	23	110	173	713	.250	.258

Pitcher vs. Batter (career)																							
Pitches Best Vs.	Avg	AB	H	2B	3B	HR	RBI	BB	SO	OBP	SLG	**Pitches Worst Vs.**	Avg	AB	H	2B	3B	HR	RBI	BB	SO	OBP	SLG
Todd Hundley	.000	13	0	0	0	0	0	1	1	.071	.000	Kent Hrbek	.556	9	5	2	0	2	7	2	0	.636	1.444
Walt Weiss	.000	9	0	0	0	0	0	2	2	.182	.000	Jerry Browne	.538	13	7	2	0	1	4	1	1	.571	.923
Ruben Sierra	.067	15	1	0	0	0	1	1	3	.118	.067	Don Slaught	.455	11	5	2	0	2	7	1	1	.500	1.182
Andre Dawson	.071	14	1	1	0	0	2	0	3	.063	.143	Carlton Fisk	.429	7	3	1	0	1	2	4	1	.636	1.000
Mitch Webster	.071	14	1	0	0	0	0	1	3	.133	.071	Steve Buechele	.364	11	4	0	0	2	4	2	4	.462	.909

Brian Harper — Twins

Age 34 – Bats Right

	Avg	G	AB	R	H	2B	3B	HR	RBI	BB	SO	HBP	GDP	SB	CS	OBP	SLG	IBB	SH	SF	#Pit	#P/PA	GB	FB	G/F
1993 Season	.304	147	530	52	161	26	1	12	73	29	29	9	15	1	3	.347	.425	9	0	5	1873	3.27	173	201	0.86
Last Five Years	.307	670	2337	268	718	145	5	45	326	101	116	35	75	7	12	.341	.431	24	7	29	8096	3.23	870	821	1.06

1993 Season																							
	Avg	AB	H	2B	3B	HR	RBI	BB	SO	OBP	SLG		Avg	AB	H	2B	3B	HR	RBI	BB	SO	OBP	SLG
vs. Left	.333	123	41	9	1	5	25	8	9	.373	.545	Scoring Posn	.358	134	48	5	0	1	56	13	8	.417	.418
vs. Right	.295	407	120	17	0	7	48	21	20	.339	.388	Close & Late	.306	98	30	4	0	3	14	7	9	.346	.439
Groundball	.286	105	30	7	0	1	14	4	8	.324	.381	None on/out	.309	139	43	8	1	6	6	5	5	.347	.511
Flyball	.295	105	31	5	0	4	16	7	5	.345	.457	Batting #5	.291	261	76	9	1	6	35	17	14	.346	.402
Home	.325	255	83	17	1	6	42	19	13	.374	.471	Batting #6	.318	245	78	16	0	5	32	10	13	.349	.445
Away	.284	275	78	9	0	6	31	10	16	.322	.382	Other	.292	24	7	1	0	1	6	2	2	.346	.458
Day	.336	152	51	11	1	3	24	11	7	.393	.480	April	.319	69	22	5	0	0	8	3	2	.347	.391
Night	.291	378	110	15	0	9	49	18	22	.328	.402	May	.299	87	26	4	0	3	16	4	6	.344	.448
Grass	.275	204	56	7	0	4	20	9	13	.317	.368	June	.326	86	28	3	0	4	12	5	4	.379	.500
Turf	.322	326	105	19	1	8	53	20	16	.366	.460	July	.298	94	28	5	0	3	17	2	7	.323	.447
First Pitch	.342	79	27	7	1	1	13	7	0	.398	.494	August	.330	103	34	6	0	2	12	9	3	.381	.447
Ahead in Count	.364	132	48	7	0	7	23	17	0	.430	.576	September/October	.253	91	23	3	1	0	8	6	7	.307	.308
Behind in Count	.250	220	55	9	0	1	26	0	23	.271	.305	Pre-All Star	.310	281	87	14	0	9	46	13	14	.349	.456
Two Strikes	.225	187	42	8	0	0	20	5	29	.270	.267	Post-All Star	.297	249	74	12	1	3	27	16	15	.346	.390

1993 By Position																									
Position	Avg	AB	H	2B	3B	HR	RBI	BB	SO	OBP	SLG	G	GS	Innings	PO	A	E	DP	Fld Pct	Rng Fctr	In Zone	Outs	Zone Rtg	MLB Zone
As Pinch Hitter	.625	8	5	1	0	1	5	2	1	.700	1.125	10	0	---	---	---	---	---	---	---	---	---	---	---
As c	.300	493	148	23	1	11	64	26	24	.343	.418	134	129	1124.2	736	61	10	6	.988	---	---	---	---	---

Last Five Years																							
	Avg	AB	H	2B	3B	HR	RBI	BB	SO	OBP	SLG		Avg	AB	H	2B	3B	HR	RBI	BB	SO	OBP	SLG
vs. Left	.311	647	201	49	3	15	93	40	39	.350	.465	Scoring Posn	.317	643	204	35	0	10	266	48	38	.363	.418
vs. Right	.306	1690	517	96	2	30	233	61	77	.338	.418	Close & Late	.309	385	119	14	1	10	62	21	20	.345	.429
Groundball	.321	614	197	43	1	9	88	22	31	.349	.438	None on/out	.313	543	170	38	1	15	15	18	13	.346	.470
Flyball	.280	525	147	20	0	13	79	20	24	.314	.392	Batting #5	.302	881	266	55	3	14	116	39	44	.338	.419
Home	.316	1124	355	72	4	18	159	61	57	.353	.435	Batting #6	.313	970	304	55	1	21	140	39	46	.345	.437
Away	.299	1213	363	73	1	27	167	40	59	.330	.428	Other	.305	486	148	35	1	10	70	23	26	.341	.442
Day	.328	619	203	48	1	14	101	29	34	.366	.477	April	.303	277	84	18	0	6	40	15	9	.348	.433
Night	.300	1718	515	97	4	31	225	72	82	.332	.415	May	.310	374	116	29	0	9	74	15	20	.341	.460
Grass	.293	908	266	55	0	21	131	36	49	.325	.423	June	.314	398	125	20	1	7	46	16	22	.349	.422
Turf	.316	1429	452	90	5	24	195	65	67	.351	.437	July	.324	410	133	27	0	6	55	14	19	.349	.434
First Pitch	.348	362	126	32	1	7	58	19	0	.386	.500	August	.306	457	140	27	2	11	66	17	21	.333	.446
Ahead in Count	.365	575	210	48	2	17	101	59	0	.420	.544	September/October	.285	421	120	24	2	6	45	24	25	.332	.394
Behind in Count	.268	1013	271	47	2	12	123	0	99	.281	.353	Pre-All Star	.312	1189	371	75	1	26	185	51	58	.347	.442
Two Strikes	.256	820	210	40	2	5	90	23	116	.292	.328	Post-All Star	.302	1148	347	70	4	19	141	50	58	.336	.420

Batter vs. Pitcher (since 1984)																							
Hits Best Against	Avg	AB	H	2B	3B	HR	RBI	BB	SO	OBP	SLG	**Hits Worst Against**	Avg	AB	H	2B	3B	HR	RBI	BB	SO	OBP	SLG
Dan Plesac	.545	11	6	0	0	3	8	1	0	.583	1.364	Chuck Crim	.083	12	1	0	0	0	2	0	0	.077	.083
Frank Viola	.500	10	5	1	0	1	1	3	0	.615	.900	Duane Ward	.091	11	1	1	0	0	0	0	1	.091	.182
Edwin Nunez	.455	11	5	1	0	1	3	2	1	.538	.818	Melido Perez	.100	20	2	0	0	1	4	0	0	.100	.250
Todd Stottlemyre	.438	16	7	0	1	1	6	0	0	.412	.750	Todd Burns	.100	10	1	0	0	0	1	0	0	.091	.100
Bob Welch	.414	29	12	2	0	2	6	3	4	.469	.690	Dave Fleming	.154	13	2	0	0	0	2	0	1	.143	.154

Donald Harris — Rangers

Age 26 – Bats Right (groundball hitter)

	Avg	G	AB	R	H	2B	3B	HR	RBI	BB	SO	HBP	GDP	SB	CS	OBP	SLG	IBB	SH	SF	#Pit	#P/PA	GB	FB	G/F
1993 Season	.197	40	76	10	15	2	0	1	8	5	18	1	0	0	1	.253	.263	0	3	1	330	3.84	33	16	2.06
Career (1991-1993)	.205	82	117	17	24	3	0	2	11	6	36	1	0	2	1	.248	.282	0	3	1	476	3.72	41	24	1.71

1993 Season																							
	Avg	AB	H	2B	3B	HR	RBI	BB	SO	OBP	SLG		Avg	AB	H	2B	3B	HR	RBI	BB	SO	OBP	SLG
vs. Left	.225	40	9	0	0	0	4	3	7	.295	.225	Scoring Posn	.158	19	3	0	0	0	6	1	5	.190	.158
vs. Right	.167	36	6	2	0	1	4	2	11	.205	.306	Close & Late	.000	4	0	0	0	0	0	0	1	.000	.000

Gene Harris — Padres

Age 29 – Pitches Right (groundball pitcher)

	ERA	W	L	Sv	G	GS	IP	BB	SO	Avg	H	2B	3B	HR	RBI	OBP	SLG	GF	IR	IRS	Hld	SvOp	SB	CS	GB	FB	G/F
1993 Season	3.03	6	6	23	59	0	59.1	37	39	.256	57	4	1	3	26	.361	.323	48	31	9	1	31	10	0	102	34	3.00
Career (1989-1993)	4.40	9	15	25	135	7	194.1	117	138	.259	189	31	5	16	103	.360	.380	67	80	21	6	36	25	3	303	158	1.92

1993 Season																							
	ERA	W	L	Sv	G	GS	IP	H	HR	BB	SO		Avg	AB	H	2B	3B	HR	RBI	BB	SO	OBP	SLG
Home	2.78	5	3	8	30	0	32.1	27	2	14	20	vs. Left	.265	113	30	3	0	1	10	18	18	.371	.319

1993 Season

	ERA	W	L	Sv	G	GS	IP	H	HR	BB	SO
Away	3.33	1	3	15	29	0	27.0	30	1	23	19
Starter	0.00	0	0	0	0	0	0.0	0	0	0	0
Reliever	3.03	6	6	23	59	0	59.1	57	3	37	39
0 Days rest	3.45	2	2	6	15	0	15.2	17	0	10	8
1 or 2 Days rest	3.38	2	3	9	22	0	21.1	21	3	13	15
3+ Days rest	2.42	2	1	8	22	0	22.1	19	0	14	16
Pre-All Star	3.31	4	3	15	35	0	35.1	32	1	18	26
Post-All Star	2.63	2	3	8	24	0	24.0	25	2	19	13

	Avg	AB	H	2B	3B	HR	RBI	BB	SO	OBP	SLG
vs. Right	.245	110	27	1	1	2	16	19	21	.351	.327
Scoring Posn	.272	81	22	1	0	0	23	19	17	.402	.284
Close & Late	.261	161	42	1	1	3	20	29	29	.373	.335
None on/out	.245	49	12	1	0	1	1	4	4	.302	.327
First Pitch	.326	46	15	2	0	1	6	2	0	.360	.435
Ahead in Count	.179	95	17	0	0	1	6	0	32	.179	.211
Behind in Count	.341	41	14	1	1	0	11	20	0	.557	.415
Two Strikes	.144	97	14	1	0	1	6	15	39	.259	.186

Career (1989-1993)

	ERA	W	L	Sv	G	GS	IP	H	HR	BB	SO
Home	3.75	8	5	9	65	4	105.2	91	7	55	71
Away	5.18	1	10	16	70	3	88.2	98	9	62	67
Day	4.45	3	5	10	43	2	64.2	65	6	34	43
Night	4.37	6	10	15	92	5	129.2	124	10	83	95
Grass	4.27	6	8	18	73	2	84.1	86	8	45	69
Turf	4.50	3	7	7	62	5	110.0	103	8	72	69
April	3.86	2	1	5	29	0	39.2	27	2	26	31
May	6.43	2	1	3	21	0	28.0	25	6	19	17
June	3.46	1	3	5	28	4	54.2	50	0	20	44
July	8.10	1	7	4	20	3	26.2	48	6	21	17
August	2.89	2	1	4	18	0	18.2	16	1	15	11
September/October	2.36	1	2	4	19	0	26.2	23	1	16	18
Starter	7.76	1	3	0	7	7	29.0	40	3	12	12
Reliever	3.81	8	12	25	128	0	165.1	149	13	105	126
0 Days rest	4.03	2	2	6	19	0	22.1	23	0	14	12
1 or 2 Days rest	3.94	4	7	9	49	0	59.1	48	8	42	44
3+ Days rest	3.66	2	3	10	60	0	83.2	78	5	49	70
Pre-All Star	4.26	6	7	16	85	5	133.0	115	8	75	97
Post-All Star	4.70	3	8	9	50	2	61.1	74	8	42	41

	Avg	AB	H	2B	3B	HR	RBI	BB	SO	OBP	SLG
vs. Left	.263	342	90	20	1	5	39	63	51	.379	.371
vs. Right	.254	389	99	11	4	11	64	54	87	.344	.388
Inning 1-6	.248	210	52	11	1	3	32	34	39	.351	.352
Inning 7+	.263	521	137	20	4	13	71	83	99	.364	.392
None on	.255	361	92	16	4	11	11	49	68	.347	.413
Runners on	.262	370	97	15	1	5	92	68	70	.373	.349
Scoring Posn	.255	247	63	9	1	3	85	50	48	.373	.336
Close & Late	.277	238	66	4	2	7	34	45	47	.394	.399
None on/out	.277	166	46	10	3	4	4	23	22	.365	.446
vs. 1st Batr (relief)	.275	109	30	9	1	2	16	7	16	.316	.431
First Inning Pitched	.251	418	105	17	3	13	63	69	84	.357	.400
First 15 Pitches	.259	378	98	18	4	7	43	52	65	.347	.384
Pitch 16-30	.223	220	49	5	0	7	32	40	50	.346	.341
Pitch 31-45	.294	85	25	4	1	2	16	15	19	.396	.435
Pitch 46+	.354	48	17	4	0	0	12	10	4	.459	.438
First Pitch	.306	134	41	5	0	3	22	9	0	.352	.410
Ahead in Count	.183	317	58	7	3	4	25	0	114	.187	.262
Behind in Count	.390	141	55	11	1	5	33	61	0	.569	.589
Two Strikes	.155	330	51	10	4	6	29	47	138	.264	.264

Greg Harris — Red Sox

Age 38 – Pitches Right (groundball pitcher)

	ERA	W	L	Sv	G	GS	IP	BB	SO	Avg	H	2B	3B	HR	RBI	OBP	SLG	GF	IR	IRS	Hld	SvOp	SB	CS	GB	FB	G/F
1993 Season	3.77	6	7	8	80	0	112.1	60	103	.232	95	15	2	7	54	.341	.329	24	75	18	17	18	5	4	157	80	1.96
Last Five Years	3.58	38	41	15	296	53	680.2	324	496	.241	605	110	15	47	291	.330	.352	64	218	67	47	35	35	28	981	597	1.64

1993 Season

	ERA	W	L	Sv	G	GS	IP	H	HR	BB	SO
Home	4.77	3	5	5	39	0	54.2	53	5	30	45
Away	2.81	3	2	3	41	0	57.2	42	2	30	58
Day	4.50	0	4	2	28	0	40.0	29	4	21	46
Night	3.36	6	3	6	52	0	72.1	66	3	39	57
Grass	3.66	5	7	8	65	0	93.1	78	6	46	81
Turf	4.26	1	0	0	15	0	19.0	17	1	14	22
April	2.57	0	0	0	9	0	14.0	10	1	7	9
May	1.86	1	0	0	16	0	19.1	14	2	10	21
June	3.98	2	3	2	14	0	20.1	14	0	12	16
July	1.40	3	0	2	12	0	19.1	11	1	7	19
August	3.93	0	1	0	14	0	18.1	16	2	10	18
September/October	8.14	0	3	4	15	0	21.0	30	1	14	20
Starter	0.00	0	0	0	0	0	0.0	0	0	0	0
Reliever	3.77	6	7	8	80	0	112.1	95	7	60	103
0 Days rest	3.58	1	3	3	26	0	32.2	25	1	15	31
1 or 2 Days rest	4.91	3	3	5	40	0	55.0	54	5	31	53
3+ Days rest	1.46	2	1	0	14	0	24.2	16	1	14	19
Pre-All Star	2.45	4	3	3	44	0	62.1	43	3	32	57
Post-All Star	5.40	2	4	5	36	0	50.0	52	4	28	46

	Avg	AB	H	2B	3B	HR	RBI	BB	SO	OBP	SLG
vs. Left	.253	198	50	9	2	2	29	31	44	.353	.348
vs. Right	.212	212	45	6	0	5	25	29	59	.329	.311
Inning 1-6	.192	26	5	0	0	0	2	5	6	.323	.192
Inning 7+	.234	384	90	15	2	7	52	55	97	.342	.339
None on	.206	194	40	9	0	2	2	23	49	.306	.284
Runners on	.255	216	55	6	2	5	52	37	54	.370	.370
Scoring Posn	.219	146	32	3	1	3	46	27	40	.348	.315
Close & Late	.260	231	60	11	1	3	33	29	59	.356	.355
None on/out	.209	91	19	5	0	1	1	3	22	.250	.297
vs. 1st Batr (relief)	.271	70	19	5	1	1	9	4	13	.338	.414
First Inning Pitched	.219	242	53	8	2	4	38	29	66	.312	.318
First 15 Pitches	.232	211	49	9	2	3	33	26	54	.331	.336
Pitch 16-30	.205	127	26	3	0	2	11	21	33	.329	.276
Pitch 31-45	.302	53	16	3	0	1	6	9	10	.413	.415
Pitch 46+	.211	19	4	0	0	1	4	4	6	.333	.368
First Pitch	.372	43	16	2	0	1	9	13	0	.525	.488
Ahead in Count	.190	200	38	10	1	1	19	0	82	.204	.265
Behind in Count	.318	88	28	3	0	5	19	22	0	.460	.523
Two Strikes	.150	213	32	7	0	1	13	25	103	.248	.197

Last Five Years

	ERA	W	L	Sv	G	GS	IP	H	HR	BB	SO
Home	4.04	20	18	11	150	23	323.0	300	29	165	249
Away	3.17	18	23	4	146	30	357.2	305	18	159	247
Day	3.53	16	12	5	100	15	211.1	167	13	114	178
Night	3.61	22	29	10	196	38	469.1	438	34	210	318
Grass	3.65	32	30	14	222	44	516.0	465	37	239	375
Turf	3.39	6	11	1	74	9	164.2	140	10	85	121
April	2.53	5	3	0	33	5	78.1	56	7	38	60
May	3.56	4	8	1	54	10	116.1	109	6	47	79
June	3.21	8	6	2	57	11	129.0	97	3	65	89
July	3.25	8	9	4	50	11	130.1	114	8	54	86
August	3.03	9	4	2	48	9	124.2	106	12	54	104
September/October	6.00	4	11	6	54	7	102.0	123	11	66	78
Starter	4.14	19	20	0	53	53	313.0	305	23	125	210
Reliever	3.11	19	21	15	243	0	367.2	300	24	199	286
0 Days rest	2.98	4	3	5	74	0	96.2	73	4	63	76
1 or 2 Days rest	3.29	7	11	8	108	0	175.1	150	14	78	136
3+ Days rest	2.92	8	7	2	61	0	95.2	77	6	58	74

	Avg	AB	H	2B	3B	HR	RBI	BB	SO	OBP	SLG
vs. Left	.232	1173	272	53	8	16	127	160	213	.325	.332
vs. Right	.248	1342	333	57	7	31	164	164	283	.334	.370
Inning 1-6	.244	1271	310	65	6	23	139	143	242	.320	.359
Inning 7+	.237	1244	295	45	9	24	152	181	254	.340	.346
None on	.228	1379	314	62	8	28	28	160	271	.314	.345
Runners on	.256	1136	291	48	7	19	263	164	225	.349	.361
Scoring Posn	.244	671	164	24	6	10	232	124	145	.359	.343
Close & Late	.234	619	145	19	5	6	63	88	130	.338	.310
None on/out	.227	608	138	26	4	16	16	66	110	.313	.362
vs. 1st Batr (relief)	.246	175	43	8	3	5	30	15	27	.318	.411
First Inning Pitched	.229	804	184	32	5	17	119	106	176	.323	.345
First 15 Pitches	.232	826	192	35	6	19	119	104	156	.325	.358
Pitch 16-30	.247	604	149	23	4	12	60	92	151	.348	.358
Pitch 31-45	.221	376	83	13	1	2	23	34	72	.285	.277
Pitch 46+	.255	709	181	39	4	14	89	94	117	.344	.381
First Pitch	.275	327	90	11	0	6	46	37	0	.359	.364
Ahead in Count	.192	1143	220	45	5	13	90	0	422	.200	.275

Last Five Years

	ERA	W	L	Sv	G	GS	IP	H	HR	BB	SO
Pre-All Star	3.14	19	18	5	159	29	355.1	290	18	164	254
Post-All Star	4.07	19	23	10	137	24	325.1	315	29	160	242

	Avg	AB	H	2B	3B	HR	RBI	BB	SO	OBP	SLG
Behind in Count	.308	595	183	34	7	22	105	157	0	.448	.499
Two Strikes	.174	1174	204	46	4	12	85	129	496	.258	.250

Pitcher vs. Batter (since 1984)

Pitches Best Vs.	Avg	AB	H	2B	3B	HR	RBI	BB	SO	OBP	SLG
Jerry Browne	.000	14	0	0	0	0	2	2	1	.118	.000
Darnell Coles	.000	13	0	0	0	0	0	0	7	.000	.000
Lance Blankenship	.000	10	0	0	0	0	0	1	2	.091	.000
Mike Felder	.000	9	0	0	0	0	1	1	2	.091	.000
Jose Canseco	.059	17	1	0	0	0	1	2	10	.158	.059

Pitches Worst Vs.	Avg	AB	H	2B	3B	HR	RBI	BB	SO	OBP	SLG
George Bell	.455	22	10	2	0	2	7	1	2	.478	.818
Gary Sheffield	.444	9	4	1	0	1	3	2	0	.545	.889
Dan Pasqua	.400	10	4	2	1	0	1	2	2	.500	.800
Bobby Kelly	.333	15	5	1	1	2	3	0	2	.333	.933
Mark McGwire	.318	22	7	0	0	4	7	5	4	.429	.864

Greg W. Harris — Rockies

Age 30 – Pitches Right

	ERA	W	L	Sv	G	GS	IP	BB	SO	Avg	H	2B	3B	HR	RBI	OBP	SLG	CG	ShO	Sup	QS	#P/S	SB	CS	GB	FB	G/F
1993 Season	4.59	11	17	0	35	35	225.1	69	123	.271	239	45	9	33	116	.328	.455	4	0	3.91	18	96	22	10	315	244	1.29
Last Five Years	3.35	40	47	15	204	83	728.2	232	487	.243	666	109	14	76	294	.304	.376	8	2	3.52	48	94	70	30	994	729	1.36

1993 Season

	ERA	W	L	Sv	G	GS	IP	H	HR	BB	SO
Home	3.68	6	7	0	18	18	120.0	121	16	33	66
Away	5.64	5	10	0	17	17	105.1	118	17	36	57
Day	3.62	5	4	0	11	11	69.2	74	5	25	38
Night	5.03	6	13	0	24	24	155.2	165	28	44	85
Grass	4.06	9	12	0	27	27	179.2	181	26	52	102
Turf	6.70	2	5	0	8	8	45.2	58	7	17	21
April	5.23	1	4	0	5	5	31.0	33	5	8	14
May	3.32	4	2	0	6	6	40.2	42	5	12	24
June	3.50	2	2	0	6	6	43.2	47	4	11	27
July	3.76	3	2	0	6	6	40.2	37	6	9	20
August	6.27	1	4	0	6	6	37.1	42	8	12	25
September/October	6.19	0	3	0	6	6	32.0	38	5	17	13
Starter	4.59	11	17	0	35	35	225.1	239	33	69	123
Reliever	0.00	0	0	0	0	0	0.0	0	0	0	0
0-3 Days Rest	8.31	0	1	0	1	1	4.1	8	1	0	5
4 Days Rest	4.18	9	12	0	28	28	187.1	196	26	52	97
5+ Days Rest	6.42	2	4	0	6	6	33.2	35	6	17	21
Pre-All Star	3.99	8	9	0	19	19	128.2	134	17	35	68
Post-All Star	5.40	3	8	0	16	16	96.2	105	16	34	55

	Avg	AB	H	2B	3B	HR	RBI	BB	SO	OBP	SLG
vs. Left	.272	463	126	19	4	16	60	40	63	.331	.434
vs. Right	.270	418	113	26	5	17	56	29	60	.324	.478
Inning 1-6	.269	747	201	38	7	26	98	63	108	.330	.443
Inning 7+	.284	134	38	7	2	7	18	6	15	.314	.522
None on	.276	536	148	26	4	22	22	30	72	.317	.463
Runners on	.264	345	91	19	5	11	94	39	51	.344	.443
Scoring Posn	.255	204	52	12	2	5	76	32	28	.361	.407
Close & Late	.292	65	19	2	1	3	11	4	4	.333	.492
None on/out	.267	240	64	8	1	15	15	10	34	.299	.496
vs. 1st Batr (relief)	.000	0	0	0	0	0	0	0	0	.000	.000
First Inning Pitched	.322	149	48	6	1	7	29	17	18	.399	.517
First 75 Pitches	.272	655	178	33	5	20	83	56	92	.334	.429
Pitch 76-90	.219	114	25	5	3	8	18	3	19	.239	.526
Pitch 91-105	.326	86	28	6	1	4	10	8	11	.383	.558
Pitch 106+	.308	26	8	1	0	1	5	2	1	.357	.462
First Pitch	.305	141	43	10	3	6	21	5	0	.329	.546
Ahead in Count	.222	374	83	17	3	8	30	0	104	.232	.348
Behind in Count	.360	211	76	13	3	10	42	30	0	.440	.592
Two Strikes	.181	343	62	12	1	7	28	34	123	.260	.283

Last Five Years

	ERA	W	L	Sv	G	GS	IP	H	HR	BB	SO
Home	2.81	23	20	4	97	42	371.1	331	37	110	256
Away	3.90	17	27	11	107	41	357.1	335	39	122	231
Day	3.34	18	14	4	64	27	234.1	206	13	90	146
Night	3.35	22	33	11	140	56	494.1	460	63	142	341
Grass	2.90	32	31	10	149	61	550.0	485	53	164	371
Turf	4.74	8	16	5	55	22	178.2	181	23	68	116
April	2.84	5	6	0	26	13	101.1	86	11	20	60
May	3.69	7	7	6	36	12	112.1	105	16	45	86
June	3.09	5	5	1	31	7	84.1	78	6	34	62
July	3.86	5	10	1	31	14	116.2	109	13	34	69
August	3.61	8	9	2	36	18	144.2	134	14	44	102
September/October	2.98	10	10	5	44	19	169.1	154	16	55	108
Starter	3.79	27	34	0	83	83	527.2	515	66	153	327
Reliever	2.19	13	13	15	121	0	201.0	151	10	79	160
0-3 Days Rest	2.27	2	2	0	5	5	31.2	29	3	11	27
4 Days Rest	3.56	19	20	0	53	53	351.1	340	42	97	209
5+ Days Rest	4.67	6	12	0	25	25	144.2	146	21	45	91
Pre-All Star	3.30	18	20	8	103	35	327.1	296	37	107	216
Post-All Star	3.39	22	27	7	101	48	401.1	370	39	125	271

	Avg	AB	H	2B	3B	HR	RBI	BB	SO	OBP	SLG
vs. Left	.256	1563	400	57	7	43	169	136	253	.316	.384
vs. Right	.226	1176	266	52	7	33	125	96	234	.289	.366
Inning 1-6	.259	1805	467	78	9	57	210	140	306	.314	.407
Inning 7+	.213	934	199	31	5	19	84	92	181	.286	.318
None on	.244	1689	412	71	5	49	49	100	302	.289	.379
Runners on	.242	1050	254	38	9	27	245	132	185	.327	.372
Scoring Posn	.225	612	138	22	4	13	205	106	120	.338	.338
Close & Late	.209	564	118	17	2	7	52	67	114	.294	.284
None on/out	.235	720	169	32	1	25	25	38	130	.276	.386
vs. 1st Batr (relief)	.213	108	23	6	1	2	16	8	27	.267	.343
First Inning Pitched	.248	726	180	25	4	17	94	76	145	.320	.364
First 75 Pitches	.240	2238	538	89	9	51	228	195	407	.304	.357
Pitch 76-90	.240	254	61	8	3	17	39	13	39	.277	.496
Pitch 91-105	.298	171	51	11	2	5	17	19	30	.368	.474
Pitch 106+	.211	76	16	1	0	3	10	5	11	.259	.342
First Pitch	.298	456	136	22	3	18	66	26	0	.333	.478
Ahead in Count	.180	1199	216	36	5	14	81	0	412	.186	.254
Behind in Count	.319	618	197	34	6	31	97	114	0	.424	.544
Two Strikes	.173	1171	202	31	3	14	79	89	487	.234	.240

Pitcher vs. Batter (career)

Pitches Best Vs.	Avg	AB	H	2B	3B	HR	RBI	BB	SO	OBP	SLG
Matt D. Williams	.000	20	0	0	0	0	0	0	3	.000	.000
Todd Benzinger	.042	24	1	0	0	0	1	0	7	.042	.042
Gerald Young	.071	14	1	0	0	0	0	0	1	.071	.071
Vince Coleman	.083	12	1	0	0	0	0	1	2	.154	.083
Dave Hansen	.083	12	1	0	0	0	1	1	4	.154	.083

Pitches Worst Vs.	Avg	AB	H	2B	3B	HR	RBI	BB	SO	OBP	SLG
Larry Walker	.478	23	11	1	0	3	7	5	3	.571	.913
Eric Karros	.462	13	6	0	0	2	3	2	2	.533	.923
Paul O'Neill	.440	25	11	1	0	2	4	2	3	.481	.720
Jeff Bagwell	.400	10	4	0	0	1	2	4	1	.571	.700
Darryl Strawberry	.360	25	9	1	0	3	8	5	3	.452	.760

Lenny Harris — Dodgers

Age 29 – Bats Left (groundball hitter)

	Avg	G	AB	R	H	2B	3B	HR	RBI	BB	SO	HBP	GDP	SB	CS	OBP	SLG	IBB	SH	SF	#Pit	#P/PA	GB	FB	G/F
1993 Season	.238	107	160	20	38	6	1	2	11	15	15	0	4	3	1	.303	.325	4	1	0	569	3.23	78	39	2.00
Last Five Years	.273	639	1702	204	465	59	7	10	134	125	135	9	53	63	30	.325	.334	14	23	5	5935	3.18	872	378	2.31

1993 Season

	Avg	AB	H	2B	3B	HR	RBI	BB	SO	OBP	SLG
vs. Left	.333	15	5	1	0	0	1	0	1	.333	.400
vs. Right	.228	145	33	5	1	2	10	15	14	.300	.317

	Avg	AB	H	2B	3B	HR	RBI	BB	SO	OBP	SLG
Scoring Posn	.387	31	12	0	1	0	9	7	3	.500	.452
Close & Late	.320	50	16	1	0	0	3	5	7	.382	.340

1993 Season

	Avg	AB	H	2B	3B	HR	RBI	BB	SO	OBP	SLG		Avg	AB	H	2B	3B	HR	RBI	BB	SO	OBP	SLG
Home	.284	67	19	4	0	0	3	3	7	.314	.343	None on/out	.190	42	8	1	0	2	2	3	3	.244	.357
Away	.204	93	19	2	1	2	8	12	8	.295	.312	Batting #8	.272	81	22	3	1	1	7	10	7	.352	.370
First Pitch	.188	32	6	0	0	0	3	3	0	.257	.188	Batting #9	.158	38	6	1	0	1	3	2	6	.200	.263
Ahead in Count	.378	37	14	5	1	1	4	8	0	.489	.649	Other	.244	41	10	2	0	0	1	3	2	.295	.293
Behind in Count	.167	66	11	0	0	1	4	0	14	.167	.212	Pre-All Star	.248	109	27	4	1	0	9	13	11	.328	.303
Two Strikes	.125	56	7	0	0	1	3	4	15	.183	.179	Post-All Star	.216	51	11	2	0	2	2	2	4	.245	.373

Last Five Years

	Avg	AB	H	2B	3B	HR	RBI	BB	SO	OBP	SLG		Avg	AB	H	2B	3B	HR	RBI	BB	SO	OBP	SLG
vs. Left	.218	248	54	3	1	1	19	16	29	.280	.250	Scoring Posn	.283	357	101	12	4	3	118	31	36	.336	.364
vs. Right	.283	1454	411	56	6	9	115	109	106	.333	.348	Close & Late	.279	294	82	6	0	0	18	32	31	.355	.299
Groundball	.272	592	161	19	1	3	52	22	45	.300	.323	None on/out	.261	471	123	10	2	3	3	29	29	.305	.310
Flyball	.279	358	100	15	1	1	28	37	33	.353	.335	Batting #1	.290	431	125	19	3	2	29	26	34	.332	.362
Home	.270	833	225	28	3	2	57	54	66	.317	.318	Batting #2	.278	349	97	11	0	2	23	32	26	.341	.327
Away	.276	869	240	31	4	8	77	71	69	.333	.349	Other	.264	922	243	29	4	6	82	67	75	.316	.323
Day	.258	511	132	13	2	5	45	46	52	.322	.321	April	.267	161	43	1	1	0	12	11	8	.312	.286
Night	.280	1191	333	46	5	5	89	79	83	.327	.339	May	.302	252	76	11	2	0	16	24	30	.365	.361
Grass	.277	1179	327	38	6	7	97	81	94	.324	.338	June	.279	359	100	12	2	3	30	21	29	.320	.348
Turf	.264	523	138	21	1	3	37	44	41	.328	.325	July	.237	317	75	13	1	1	24	21	20	.290	.293
First Pitch	.328	369	121	13	2	4	45	7	0	.342	.407	August	.287	282	81	11	0	2	23	18	19	.332	.348
Ahead in Count	.293	386	113	23	3	1	36	76	0	.409	.376	September/October	.272	331	90	11	1	4	29	30	29	.334	.347
Behind in Count	.234	637	149	14	0	3	30	0	111	.237	.270	Pre-All Star	.271	912	247	26	5	4	68	65	74	.320	.323
Two Strikes	.231	575	133	9	0	4	30	40	135	.284	.268	Post-All Star	.276	790	218	33	2	6	66	60	61	.331	.346

Batter vs. Pitcher (career)

Hits Best Against	Avg	AB	H	2B	3B	HR	RBI	BB	SO	OBP	SLG	Hits Worst Against	Avg	AB	H	2B	3B	HR	RBI	BB	SO	OBP	SLG
Bob Tewksbury	.583	12	7	2	0	0	1	0	0	.583	.750	Doug Drabek	.080	25	2	1	0	0	0	1	2	.115	.120
Joe Boever	.556	9	5	2	0	0	1	2	0	.636	.778	Scott Scudder	.100	10	1	0	0	0	0	2	1	.250	.100
Omar Olivares	.455	11	5	1	0	0	1	1	1	.500	.545	Curt Schilling	.154	13	2	0	0	0	2	1	1	.214	.154
Jose Rijo	.412	34	14	2	0	1	1	2	2	.444	.559	Frank Castillo	.154	13	2	0	0	0	1	0	4	.143	.154
Tommy Greene	.308	13	4	1	0	1	5	3	0	.438	.615	Dennis Martinez	.179	28	5	0	0	0	0	0	3	.179	.179

Mike Hartley — Twins

Age 32 – Pitches Right (flyball pitcher)

	ERA	W	L	Sv	G	GS	IP	BB	SO	Avg	H	2B	3B	HR	RBI	OBP	SLG	GF	IR	IRS	Hld	SvOp	SB	CS	GB	FB	G/F
1993 Season	4.00	1	2	1	53	0	81.0	36	57	.281	86	23	0	4	44	.363	.395	21	54	19	6	3	11	4	83	106	0.78
Career (1989-1993)	3.63	18	13	4	194	6	304.2	136	253	.240	274	54	7	27	144	.328	.371	60	121	44	22	14	46	8	315	363	0.87

1993 Season

	ERA	W	L	Sv	G	GS	IP	H	HR	BB	SO		Avg	AB	H	2B	3B	HR	RBI	BB	SO	OBP	SLG
Home	4.60	1	2	1	28	0	45.0	51	3	18	34	vs. Left	.246	138	34	9	0	2	16	18	22	.327	.355
Away	3.25	0	0	0	25	0	36.0	35	1	18	23	vs. Right	.310	168	52	14	0	2	28	18	35	.393	.429
Starter	0.00	0	0	0	0	0	0.0	0	0	0	0	Scoring Posn	.257	105	27	12	0	0	38	19	18	.354	.371
Reliever	4.00	1	2	1	53	0	81.0	86	4	36	57	Close & Late	.250	48	12	4	0	0	8	9	7	.371	.333
0 Days rest	5.65	1	1	0	13	0	14.1	12	2	8	7	None on/out	.227	66	15	5	0	1	1	5	17	.301	.348
1 or 2 Days rest	2.97	0	0	0	21	0	39.1	42	2	10	28	First Pitch	.375	48	18	4	0	0	9	2	0	.411	.458
3+ Days rest	4.61	0	1	1	19	0	27.1	32	0	18	22	Ahead in Count	.235	132	31	9	0	2	16	0	49	.237	.348
Pre-All Star	4.86	0	2	1	32	0	50.0	52	2	26	33	Behind in Count	.333	81	27	8	0	1	12	15	0	.444	.469
Post-All Star	2.61	1	0	0	21	0	31.0	34	2	10	24	Two Strikes	.206	131	27	8	0	2	16	19	57	.312	.313

Career (1989-1993)

	ERA	W	L	Sv	G	GS	IP	H	HR	BB	SO		Avg	AB	H	2B	3B	HR	RBI	BB	SO	OBP	SLG
Home	3.38	11	5	2	99	3	160.0	142	14	62	148	vs. Left	.233	567	132	23	5	9	53	80	111	.328	.339
Away	3.92	7	8	2	95	3	144.2	132	13	74	105	vs. Right	.248	573	142	31	2	18	91	56	142	.328	.403
Day	4.04	5	5	2	61	1	89.0	90	9	39	71	Inning 1-6	.233	403	94	18	3	9	55	47	79	.319	.360
Night	3.46	13	8	2	133	5	215.2	184	18	97	182	Inning 7+	.244	737	180	36	4	18	89	89	174	.333	.377
Grass	3.20	10	7	2	92	5	163.0	131	13	78	129	None on	.233	613	143	23	2	14	14	66	138	.321	.346
Turf	4.13	8	6	2	102	1	141.2	143	14	58	124	Runners on	.249	527	131	31	5	13	130	70	115	.336	.400
April	3.44	0	1	1	22	0	34.0	26	4	17	32	Scoring Posn	.224	352	79	24	4	8	117	58	84	.332	.384
May	3.58	1	1	1	39	0	50.1	46	5	28	42	Close & Late	.239	238	57	12	2	3	33	41	50	.361	.345
June	4.59	5	2	1	32	0	51.0	54	3	24	44	None on/out	.230	269	62	14	1	5	5	24	58	.305	.346
July	4.15	2	3	0	34	0	47.2	48	4	24	47	vs. 1st Batr (relief)	.238	160	38	16	0	3	28	20	38	.328	.394
August	2.98	6	2	1	33	3	66.1	54	4	26	46	First Inning Pitched	.242	629	152	35	4	16	96	75	144	.327	.386
September/October	3.25	4	4	0	34	3	55.1	46	7	17	42	First 15 Pitches	.248	568	141	34	4	14	70	63	120	.327	.396
Starter	2.52	3	2	0	6	6	35.2	21	2	12	23	Pitch 16-30	.238	332	79	11	2	7	47	43	90	.341	.346
Reliever	3.78	15	11	4	188	0	269.0	253	25	124	230	Pitch 31-45	.247	146	36	6	0	5	21	16	28	.319	.390
0 Days rest	4.02	3	3	1	42	0	56.0	47	7	34	38	Pitch 46+	.191	94	18	3	1	1	6	14	15	.303	.277
1 or 2 Days rest	3.69	3	5	1	79	0	114.2	117	11	43	94	First Pitch	.304	171	52	9	0	3	24	16	0	.378	.409
3+ Days rest	3.75	9	3	2	67	0	98.1	89	7	47	98	Ahead in Count	.197	539	106	22	4	11	63	0	208	.204	.314
Pre-All Star	3.94	7	7	3	107	0	157.2	150	14	83	134	Behind in Count	.303	241	73	14	2	11	37	67	0	.457	.515
Post-All Star	3.31	11	6	1	87	6	147.0	124	13	53	119	Two Strikes	.164	561	92	18	3	9	59	53	253	.244	.255

Pitcher vs. Batter (career)

Pitches Best Vs.	Avg	AB	H	2B	3B	HR	RBI	BB	SO	OBP	SLG	Pitches Worst Vs.	Avg	AB	H	2B	3B	HR	RBI	BB	SO	OBP	SLG
Marquis Grissom	.100	10	1	0	0	0	0	2	3	.250	.100	Spike Owen	.364	11	4	2	0	0	3	1	2	.385	.545
Dave Magadan	.125	8	1	0	0	0	0	4	2	.417	.125	Gregg Jefferies	.364	11	4	0	0	0	0	2	1	.462	.364
Kevin McReynolds	.143	7	1	0	0	1	3	4	1	.455	.571	Ron Gant	.333	9	3	1	1	0	4	2	2	.455	.667
Delino DeShields	.167	12	2	0	0	0	0	0	4	.167	.167												
Andres Galarraga	.200	10	2	0	0	1	2	2	2	.333	.500												

Bryan Harvey — Marlins

Age 31 – Pitches Right

	ERA	W	L	Sv	G	GS	IP	BB	SO	Avg	H	2B	3B	HR	RBI	OBP	SLG	GF	IR	IRS	Hld	SvOp	SB	CS	GB	FB	G/F
1993 Season	1.70	1	5	45	59	0	69.0	13	73	.186	45	1	0	4	21	.222	.240	54	28	9	0	49	15	0	72	70	1.03
Last Five Years	2.44	10	20	154	256	0	295.2	117	368	.189	199	22	1	24	110	.266	.280	186	142	36	1	180	38	3	300	263	1.14

1993 Season

	ERA	W	L	Sv	G	GS	IP	H	HR	BB	SO
Home	1.11	1	1	24	32	0	40.2	23	3	9	43
Away	2.54	0	4	21	27	0	28.1	22	1	4	30
Starter	0.00	0	0	0	0	0	0.0	0	0	0	0
Reliever	1.70	1	5	45	59	0	69.0	45	4	13	73
0 Days rest	0.00	0	0	11	11	0	10.2	4	0	2	13
1 or 2 Days rest	1.62	1	3	21	27	0	33.1	19	1	8	37
3+ Days rest	2.52	0	2	13	21	0	25.0	22	3	3	23
Pre-All Star	1.63	1	2	25	33	0	38.2	26	3	7	47
Post-All Star	1.78	0	3	20	26	0	30.1	19	1	6	26

	Avg	AB	H	2B	3B	HR	RBI	BB	SO	OBP	SLG
vs. Left	.132	121	16	1	0	0	5	9	43	.191	.140
vs. Right	.240	121	29	0	0	4	16	4	30	.254	.339
Scoring Posn	.169	59	10	0	0	1	16	4	18	.203	.220
Close & Late	.174	207	36	1	0	3	19	12	64	.213	.222
None on/out	.281	57	16	0	0	1	1	2	13	.305	.333
First Pitch	.406	32	13	1	0	2	6	2	0	.441	.625
Ahead in Count	.134	142	19	0	0	1	5	0	64	.133	.155
Behind in Count	.167	36	6	0	0	1	7	8	0	.292	.250
Two Strikes	.124	145	18	0	0	1	7	3	73	.141	.145

Last Five Years

	ERA	W	L	Sv	G	GS	IP	H	HR	BB	SO
Home	2.44	8	7	78	134	0	162.1	119	15	61	193
Away	2.43	2	13	76	122	0	133.1	80	9	56	175
Day	1.49	1	2	42	65	0	78.1	48	5	26	99
Night	2.77	9	18	112	191	0	217.1	151	19	91	269
Grass	2.63	9	17	132	221	0	256.2	170	22	107	320
Turf	1.15	1	3	22	35	0	39.0	29	2	10	48
April	2.27	2	3	23	42	0	47.2	39	4	18	58
May	2.73	3	4	26	50	0	62.2	50	5	21	70
June	1.74	0	2	26	41	0	46.2	25	4	21	63
July	3.40	4	6	20	38	0	39.2	32	4	18	51
August	0.71	0	1	28	38	0	50.2	19	3	14	65
September/October	3.91	1	4	31	47	0	48.1	34	4	25	61
Starter	0.00	0	0	0	0	0	0.0	0	0	0	0
Reliever	2.44	10	20	154	256	0	295.2	199	24	117	368
0 Days rest	0.57	2	0	40	45	0	47.1	22	2	12	43
1 or 2 Days rest	3.11	5	15	72	115	0	136.0	98	9	65	190
3+ Days rest	2.40	3	5	42	96	0	112.1	79	13	40	135
Pre-All Star	2.18	5	10	83	144	0	169.0	119	13	64	206
Post-All Star	2.77	5	10	71	112	0	126.2	80	11	53	162

	Avg	AB	H	2B	3B	HR	RBI	BB	SO	OBP	SLG
vs. Left	.171	549	94	15	1	10	56	66	200	.257	.257
vs. Right	.208	506	105	7	0	14	54	51	168	.276	.304
Inning 1-6	.000	0	0	0	0	0	0	0	0	.000	.000
Inning 7+	.189	1055	199	22	1	24	110	117	368	.266	.280
None on	.200	539	108	8	0	16	16	45	182	.262	.304
Runners on	.176	516	91	14	1	8	94	72	186	.271	.254
Scoring Posn	.157	312	49	6	1	6	87	59	117	.280	.240
Close & Late	.192	714	137	15	0	14	83	76	251	.266	.272
None on/out	.202	223	45	5	0	6	6	20	70	.267	.305
vs. 1st Batr (relief)	.233	227	53	7	0	7	21	26	70	.311	.357
First Inning Pitched	.192	847	163	18	1	17	96	98	288	.273	.276
First 15 Pitches	.204	732	149	13	1	18	72	68	239	.268	.298
Pitch 16-30	.152	282	43	8	0	5	28	41	112	.258	.234
Pitch 31-45	.179	39	7	1	0	1	10	8	17	.306	.282
Pitch 46+	.000	2	0	0	0	0	0	0	0	.000	.000
First Pitch	.302	116	35	4	0	4	15	11	0	.359	.440
Ahead in Count	.130	629	82	8	0	6	38	0	324	.129	.172
Behind in Count	.321	140	45	5	0	10	40	54	0	.490	.571
Two Strikes	.116	637	74	7	0	5	37	52	368	.182	.151

Pitcher vs. Batter (career)

Pitches Best Vs.	Avg	AB	H	2B	3B	HR	RBI	BB	SO	OBP	SLG
Kent Hrbek	.000	10	0	0	0	0	0	1	3	.091	.000
Mike Greenwell	.091	11	1	0	0	0	1	0	2	.083	.091
Carlton Fisk	.100	10	1	0	0	0	0	2	5	.250	.100
Kirby Puckett	.100	10	1	0	0	0	0	1	4	.182	.100
Harold Reynolds	.182	11	2	0	0	0	0	0	6	.182	.182

Pitches Worst Vs.	Avg	AB	H	2B	3B	HR	RBI	BB	SO	OBP	SLG
Tony Fernandez	.333	9	3	2	0	0	0	2	0	.455	.556

Bill Haselman — Mariners

Age 28 – Bats Right (groundball hitter)

	Avg	G	AB	R	H	2B	3B	HR	RBI	BB	SO	HBP	GDP	SB	CS	OBP	SLG	IBB	SH	SF	#Pit	#P/PA	GB	FB	G/F
1993 Season	.255	58	137	21	35	8	0	5	16	12	19	1	5	2	1	.316	.423	0	2	2	542	3.52	62	37	1.68
Career (1990-1993)	.249	73	169	22	42	8	0	5	19	13	31	1	6	2	1	.303	.385	0	2	2	665	3.56	73	43	1.70

1993 Season

	Avg	AB	H	2B	3B	HR	RBI	BB	SO	OBP	SLG
vs. Left	.280	50	14	4	0	1	8	2	3	.302	.420
vs. Right	.241	87	21	4	0	4	8	10	16	.323	.425
Home	.254	63	16	3	0	3	10	8	11	.333	.444
Away	.257	74	19	5	0	2	6	4	8	.300	.405
First Pitch	.269	26	7	3	0	0	2	0	0	.296	.385
Ahead in Count	.423	26	11	3	0	3	6	2	0	.464	.885
Behind in Count	.188	64	12	2	0	1	2	0	15	.185	.266
Two Strikes	.129	62	8	2	0	1	3	10	19	.250	.210

	Avg	AB	H	2B	3B	HR	RBI	BB	SO	OBP	SLG
Scoring Posn	.158	38	6	3	0	0	10	4	5	.227	.237
Close & Late	.194	31	6	2	0	1	3	3	10	.265	.355
None on/out	.250	36	9	3	0	1	1	3	4	.308	.417
Batting #5	.417	12	5	0	0	1	3	3	2	.500	.667
Batting #8	.268	97	26	8	0	4	12	8	10	.327	.474
Other	.143	28	4	0	0	0	1	1	7	.172	.143
Pre-All Star	.274	84	23	6	0	4	13	9	13	.344	.488
Post-All Star	.226	53	12	2	0	1	3	3	6	.268	.321

Billy Hatcher — Red Sox

Age 33 – Bats Right (groundball hitter)

	Avg	G	AB	R	H	2B	3B	HR	RBI	BB	SO	HBP	GDP	SB	CS	OBP	SLG	IBB	SH	SF	#Pit	#P/PA	GB	FB	G/F
1993 Season	.287	136	508	71	146	24	3	9	57	28	46	11	14	14	7	.336	.400	4	11	4	1869	3.33	212	154	1.38
Last Five Years	.262	666	2344	290	614	115	16	25	207	139	257	29	42	83	41	.309	.357	16	25	16	8506	3.33	988	652	1.52

1993 Season

	Avg	AB	H	2B	3B	HR	RBI	BB	SO	OBP	SLG
vs. Left	.232	138	32	7	0	1	14	7	11	.269	.304
vs. Right	.308	370	114	17	3	8	43	21	35	.360	.435
Groundball	.198	81	16	2	0	1	5	3	10	.253	.259
Flyball	.380	121	46	8	2	5	24	4	10	.402	.603
Home	.295	261	77	13	2	5	35	16	23	.344	.418
Away	.279	247	69	11	1	4	22	12	23	.327	.381
Day	.308	146	45	10	1	2	24	14	10	.386	.432

	Avg	AB	H	2B	3B	HR	RBI	BB	SO	OBP	SLG
Scoring Posn	.336	119	40	6	1	4	48	10	11	.385	.504
Close & Late	.338	68	23	4	1	2	11	3	7	.378	.515
None on/out	.256	125	32	4	2	1	1	4	12	.285	.344
Batting #1	.230	122	28	4	0	2	11	4	12	.277	.311
Batting #2	.298	312	93	16	2	7	40	20	28	.348	.429
Other	.338	74	25	4	1	0	6	4	6	.378	.419
April	.226	62	14	3	0	0	3	4	6	.284	.274

1993 Season

	Avg	AB	H	2B	3B	HR	RBI	BB	SO	OBP	SLG		Avg	AB	H	2B	3B	HR	RBI	BB	SO	OBP	SLG
Night	.279	362	101	14	2	7	33	14	36	.314	.387	May	.375	104	39	4	1	2	13	5	8	.407	.490
Grass	.286	440	126	21	3	9	54	26	41	.338	.409	June	.271	96	26	6	0	3	14	7	8	.340	.427
Turf	.294	68	20	3	0	0	3	2	5	.324	.338	July	.361	97	35	8	0	3	20	5	8	.400	.536
First Pitch	.360	86	31	3	0	2	12	3	0	.385	.465	August	.227	97	22	3	2	1	7	6	10	.283	.330
Ahead in Count	.304	125	38	11	1	3	14	17	0	.389	.480	September/October	.192	52	10	0	0	0	0	1	6	.222	.192
Behind in Count	.245	216	53	9	2	3	22	0	39	.271	.347	Pre-All Star	.316	294	93	15	1	7	38	18	24	.366	.446
Two Strikes	.222	189	42	6	1	2	13	8	46	.279	.296	Post-All Star	.248	214	53	9	2	2	19	10	22	.293	.336

1993 By Position

Position	Avg	AB	H	2B	3B	HR	RBI	BB	SO	OBP	SLG	G	GS	Innings	PO	A	E	DP	Fld Pct	Rng Fctr	In Zone	Outs	Zone Rtg	MLB Zone
As cf	.291	499	145	24	3	9	56	28	46	.339	.405	129	125	1098.1	279	6	2	1	.993	2.34	353	278	.788	.829

Last Five Years

	Avg	AB	H	2B	3B	HR	RBI	BB	SO	OBP	SLG		Avg	AB	H	2B	3B	HR	RBI	BB	SO	OBP	SLG
vs. Left	.253	809	205	37	4	7	60	46	78	.293	.335	Scoring Posn	.274	551	151	25	4	5	175	43	66	.324	.361
vs. Right	.266	1535	409	78	12	18	147	93	179	.318	.368	Close & Late	.279	383	107	15	4	4	38	20	56	.321	.371
Groundball	.250	719	180	26	5	5	53	42	74	.295	.321	None on/out	.244	706	172	35	5	8	8	41	86	.292	.341
Flyball	.273	535	146	29	5	7	53	31	66	.317	.385	Batting #1	.234	942	220	47	6	8	65	54	106	.284	.322
Home	.267	1145	306	66	9	10	103	82	118	.320	.367	Batting #2	.285	821	234	40	8	13	88	52	86	.333	.401
Away	.257	1199	308	49	7	15	104	57	139	.299	.347	Other	.275	581	160	28	2	4	54	33	65	.317	.351
Day	.253	644	163	39	3	9	72	53	57	.318	.365	April	.252	306	77	10	2	3	28	13	38	.287	.327
Night	.265	1700	451	76	13	16	135	86	200	.306	.354	May	.301	356	107	15	3	3	31	21	41	.347	.385
Grass	.265	1169	310	50	8	18	118	70	126	.313	.368	June	.278	431	120	28	6	8	43	30	48	.332	.427
Turf	.259	1175	304	65	8	7	89	69	131	.306	.346	July	.291	423	123	25	0	5	47	30	48	.338	.385
First Pitch	.298	409	122	15	2	4	41	10	0	.318	.374	August	.230	430	99	23	3	6	34	26	46	.283	.340
Ahead in Count	.275	528	145	34	4	9	53	83	0	.373	.405	September/October	.221	398	88	14	2	0	24	19	36	.265	.266
Behind in Count	.231	1052	243	47	8	7	79	0	233	.242	.311	Pre-All Star	.283	1213	343	59	11	17	119	77	136	.331	.392
Two Strikes	.207	900	186	35	6	6	59	41	257	.252	.279	Post-All Star	.240	1131	271	56	5	8	88	62	121	.286	.319

Batter vs. Pitcher (career)

Hits Best Against	Avg	AB	H	2B	3B	HR	RBI	BB	SO	OBP	SLG	Hits Worst Against	Avg	AB	H	2B	3B	HR	RBI	BB	SO	OBP	SLG
Bill Landrum	.600	15	9	0	2	0	4	1	0	.625	.867	Ben McDonald	.000	13	0	0	0	0	0	1	5	.071	.000
Joe Boever	.500	14	7	2	0	1	3	2	0	.563	.857	Randy Johnson	.000	10	0	0	0	0	1	1	5	.091	.000
Chuck Finley	.500	14	7	3	0	0	3	1	0	.533	.714	Jim Deshaies	.045	22	1	0	0	0	0	1	2	.087	.045
Ted Power	.474	19	9	1	0	1	2	1	1	.500	.684	Dennis Martinez	.063	16	1	0	0	0	0	1	1	.118	.063
Ricky Bones	.357	14	5	1	0	2	4	1	2	.400	.857	Todd Frohwirth	.077	13	1	0	0	0	1	0	2	.077	.077

Hilly Hathaway — Angels

Age 24 – Pitches Left (groundball pitcher)

	ERA	W	L	Sv	G	GS	IP	BB	SO	Avg	H	2B	3B	HR	RBI	OBP	SLG	CG	ShO	Sup	QS	#P/S	SB	CS	GB	FB	G/F
1993 Season	5.02	4	3	0	11	11	57.1	26	11	.326	71	11	0	6	32	.405	.459	0	0	6.12	6	80	7	3	103	63	1.63
Career (1992-1993)	5.29	4	3	0	13	12	63.0	29	12	.326	79	12	0	7	37	.404	.463	0	0	6.14	6	80	7	3	114	73	1.56

1993 Season

	ERA	W	L	Sv	G	GS	IP	H	HR	BB	SO		Avg	AB	H	2B	3B	HR	RBI	BB	SO	OBP	SLG
Home	4.72	2	2	0	6	6	34.1	41	4	19	6	vs. Left	.250	44	11	3	0	0	4	4	2	.340	.318
Away	5.48	2	1	0	5	5	23.0	30	2	7	5	vs. Right	.345	174	60	8	0	6	28	22	9	.421	.494

Charlie Hayes — Rockies

Age 29 – Bats Right

	Avg	G	AB	R	H	2B	3B	HR	RBI	BB	SO	HBP	GDP	SB	CS	OBP	SLG	IBB	SH	SF	#Pit	#P/PA	GB	FB	G/F
1993 Season	.305	157	573	89	175	45	2	25	98	43	82	5	25	11	6	.355	.522	6	1	8	2208	3.50	181	181	1.00
Last Five Years	.264	680	2407	257	635	122	6	73	317	126	398	11	68	24	19	.301	.410	13	8	24	9018	3.50	842	745	1.13

1993 Season

	Avg	AB	H	2B	3B	HR	RBI	BB	SO	OBP	SLG		Avg	AB	H	2B	3B	HR	RBI	BB	SO	OBP	SLG
vs. Left	.338	142	48	14	0	5	21	6	21	.367	.542	Scoring Posn	.318	148	47	12	0	10	77	17	23	.374	.601
vs. Right	.295	431	127	31	2	20	77	37	61	.351	.515	Close & Late	.319	72	23	8	0	1	13	7	13	.378	.472
Groundball	.258	190	49	13	0	5	31	12	22	.302	.405	None on/out	.291	141	41	16	0	7	7	6	20	.320	.553
Flyball	.269	104	28	7	2	1	9	4	15	.300	.404	Batting #4	.279	122	34	8	1	6	21	8	24	.321	.508
Home	.338	296	100	23	2	17	66	24	36	.387	.601	Batting #5	.317	350	111	28	1	15	59	26	47	.366	.531
Away	.271	277	75	22	0	8	32	19	46	.319	.437	Other	.297	101	30	9	0	4	18	9	11	.353	.505
Day	.293	188	55	12	1	7	29	15	29	.345	.479	April	.317	82	26	5	0	5	18	6	4	.359	.561
Night	.312	385	120	33	1	18	69	28	53	.359	.543	May	.240	104	25	8	0	3	13	9	18	.302	.404
Grass	.304	438	133	32	2	20	78	34	61	.355	.523	June	.381	84	32	6	0	4	18	10	14	.449	.595
Turf	.311	135	42	13	0	5	20	9	21	.354	.519	July	.330	100	33	6	1	5	16	2	16	.343	.560
First Pitch	.375	104	39	11	2	5	16	5	0	.414	.663	August	.226	93	21	7	0	3	9	4	13	.255	.398
Ahead in Count	.349	129	45	14	0	6	30	21	0	.435	.597	September/October	.345	110	38	13	1	5	24	12	17	.415	.618
Behind in Count	.263	244	69	16	0	10	37	0	72	.283	.471	Pre-All Star	.311	309	96	22	0	13	54	25	40	.362	.508
Two Strikes	.224	245	55	13	0	10	36	17	82	.278	.400	Post-All Star	.299	264	79	23	2	12	44	18	42	.345	.538

1993 By Position

Position	Avg	AB	H	2B	3B	HR	RBI	BB	SO	OBP	SLG	G	GS	Innings	PO	A	E	DP	Fld Pct	Rng Fctr	In Zone	Outs	Zone Rtg	MLB Zone
As 3b	.307	567	174	45	2	25	97	43	81	.356	.526	154	151	1301.1	123	290	20	21	.954	2.86	376	312	.830	.834

Last Five Years

	Avg	AB	H	2B	3B	HR	RBI	BB	SO	OBP	SLG		Avg	AB	H	2B	3B	HR	RBI	BB	SO	OBP	SLG
vs. Left	.274	780	214	48	0	21	97	34	115	.306	.417	Scoring Posn	.263	590	155	30	1	20	238	41	103	.303	.419

Last Five Years

	Avg	AB	H	2B	3B	HR	RBI	BB	SO	OBP	SLG
vs. Right	.259	1627	421	74	6	52	220	92	283	.298	.407
Groundball	.254	816	207	34	3	15	89	46	126	.294	.358
Flyball	.241	536	129	19	2	16	64	20	98	.268	.373
Home	.264	1227	324	66	5	36	180	67	194	.302	.414
Away	.264	1180	311	56	1	37	137	59	204	.299	.407
Day	.260	703	183	36	4	21	87	37	126	.297	.413
Night	.265	1704	452	86	2	52	230	89	272	.302	.410
Grass	.269	1204	324	60	4	48	174	73	198	.311	.445
Turf	.259	1203	311	62	2	25	143	53	200	.290	.376
First Pitch	.325	467	152	29	2	16	59	9	0	.344	.499
Ahead in Count	.316	449	142	28	2	19	75	52	0	.381	.514
Behind in Count	.209	1099	230	47	0	21	112	0	343	.212	.309
Two Strikes	.195	1085	212	44	1	23	121	62	398	.239	.301

	Avg	AB	H	2B	3B	HR	RBI	BB	SO	OBP	SLG
Close & Late	.276	410	113	23	1	12	49	21	81	.312	.424
None on/out	.268	586	157	36	2	25	25	22	87	.294	.464
Batting #6	.261	727	190	43	2	18	86	34	114	.295	.400
Batting #8	.276	485	134	17	1	15	58	29	88	.315	.408
Other	.260	1195	311	62	3	40	173	63	196	.298	.418
April	.282	301	85	13	0	9	46	12	37	.310	.415
May	.239	389	93	19	1	13	41	25	69	.285	.393
June	.290	352	102	17	1	10	47	25	67	.338	.429
July	.240	413	99	17	1	15	60	18	78	.272	.395
August	.252	523	132	32	1	14	57	17	75	.275	.398
September/October	.289	429	124	24	2	12	66	29	72	.335	.438
Pre-All Star	.264	1194	315	55	2	35	148	68	200	.305	.401
Post-All Star	.264	1213	320	67	4	38	169	58	198	.297	.420

Batter vs. Pitcher (career)

Hits Best Against	Avg	AB	H	2B	3B	HR	RBI	BB	SO	OBP	SLG
Randy Tomlin	.600	10	6	1	0	0	1	1	1	.636	.700
Kevin Gross	.563	16	9	1	0	2	3	1	0	.588	1.000
Rick Reed	.556	18	10	1	0	2	6	0	3	.556	.944
Brian Barnes	.526	19	10	4	0	2	5	0	2	.526	1.053
Bob Walk	.438	16	7	4	0	0	3	2	0	.500	.688

Hits Worst Against	Avg	AB	H	2B	3B	HR	RBI	BB	SO	OBP	SLG
Sid Fernandez	.048	21	1	0	0	0	0	2	7	.130	.048
David Cone	.053	19	1	1	0	0	1	0	7	.053	.105
Stan Belinda	.083	12	1	0	0	0	1	0	0	.083	.083
Bill Landrum	.091	11	1	0	0	0	0	0	2	.091	.091
Ted Power	.100	10	1	0	0	0	1	0	4	.091	.100

Neal Heaton — Yankees

Age 34 – Pitches Left

	ERA	W	L	Sv	G	GS	IP	BB	SO	Avg	H	2B	3B	HR	RBI	OBP	SLG	GF	IR	IRS	Hld	SvOp	SB	CS	GB	FB	G/F
1993 Season	6.00	1	0	0	18	0	27.0	11	15	.301	34	5	0	6	28	.375	.504	9	16	11	2	0	2	0	45	31	1.45
Last Five Years	3.68	25	20	0	164	43	431.0	148	215	.258	419	77	6	46	193	.324	.398	25	61	26	17	5	47	18	615	512	1.20

1993 Season

	ERA	W	L	Sv	G	GS	IP	H	HR	BB	SO
Home	5.84	1	0	0	8	0	12.1	15	3	5	6
Away	6.14	0	0	0	10	0	14.2	19	3	6	9

	Avg	AB	H	2B	3B	HR	RBI	BB	SO	OBP	SLG
vs. Left	.250	32	8	1	0	0	6	4	6	.385	.281
vs. Right	.321	81	26	4	0	6	22	7	9	.371	.593

Last Five Years

	ERA	W	L	Sv	G	GS	IP	H	HR	BB	SO
Home	3.52	12	11	0	79	23	219.2	214	19	85	108
Away	3.83	13	9	0	85	20	211.1	205	27	63	107
Day	4.04	6	4	0	43	11	111.1	122	16	40	49
Night	3.55	19	16	0	121	32	319.2	297	30	108	166
Grass	4.58	5	8	0	58	10	123.2	131	21	41	64
Turf	3.31	20	12	0	106	33	307.1	288	25	107	151
April	3.68	6	3	0	27	8	80.2	72	8	32	37
May	4.00	5	5	0	35	11	99.0	92	12	31	43
June	4.41	5	3	0	35	7	79.2	96	12	24	32
July	4.58	2	5	0	24	5	57.0	61	7	29	29
August	1.92	3	3	0	22	5	56.1	44	2	19	31
September/October	2.93	4	1	0	21	7	58.1	54	5	13	43
Starter	3.48	16	16	0	43	43	246.0	237	27	74	108
Reliever	3.94	9	4	0	121	0	185.0	182	19	74	107
0 Days rest	3.33	2	1	0	17	0	27.0	27	3	8	11
1 or 2 Days rest	4.98	3	1	0	45	0	72.1	76	10	27	45
3+ Days rest	3.26	4	2	0	59	0	85.2	79	6	39	51
Pre-All Star	4.04	16	12	0	107	27	278.2	285	34	98	121
Post-All Star	3.01	9	8	0	57	16	152.1	134	12	50	94

	Avg	AB	H	2B	3B	HR	RBI	BB	SO	OBP	SLG
vs. Left	.248	375	93	15	0	7	36	33	64	.316	.344
vs. Right	.261	1247	326	62	6	39	157	115	151	.326	.415
Inning 1-6	.256	1128	289	54	6	32	136	101	154	.321	.400
Inning 7+	.263	494	130	23	0	14	57	47	61	.330	.395
None on	.250	941	235	46	2	31	31	76	113	.314	.402
Runners on	.270	681	184	31	4	15	162	72	102	.336	.394
Scoring Posn	.261	417	109	18	2	8	140	52	64	.336	.372
Close & Late	.277	188	52	12	0	5	21	22	29	.357	.420
None on/out	.275	422	116	24	0	17	17	27	43	.326	.453
vs. 1st Batr (relief)	.274	113	31	3	0	1	11	4	10	.308	.327
First Inning Pitched	.245	563	138	23	1	15	79	62	82	.322	.369
First 15 Pitches	.248	536	133	26	1	11	57	54	66	.319	.362
Pitch 16-30	.224	389	87	18	2	10	45	34	69	.297	.357
Pitch 31-45	.296	230	68	7	0	8	28	25	31	.369	.430
Pitch 46+	.281	467	131	26	3	17	63	35	49	.327	.458
First Pitch	.291	289	84	15	1	10	40	14	0	.325	.453
Ahead in Count	.215	679	146	22	1	15	69	0	182	.224	.317
Behind in Count	.303	373	113	26	2	12	47	84	0	.429	.480
Two Strikes	.191	627	120	19	0	10	67	50	215	.259	.270

Pitcher vs. Batter (since 1984)

Pitches Best Vs.	Avg	AB	H	2B	3B	HR	RBI	BB	SO	OBP	SLG
Craig Biggio	.071	14	1	0	0	0	0	0	0	.071	.071
Lonnie Smith	.111	18	2	0	0	0	1	2	2	.200	.111
Dave Henderson	.118	17	2	0	0	0	3	2	4	.200	.118
Andy Van Slyke	.167	12	2	0	0	0	0	0	3	.167	.167
Harold Reynolds	.182	11	2	0	0	0	0	0	1	.182	.182

Pitches Worst Vs.	Avg	AB	H	2B	3B	HR	RBI	BB	SO	OBP	SLG
Mark Carreon	.636	11	7	0	0	2	5	0	0	.636	1.182
Kevin Bass	.474	19	9	3	0	3	7	1	0	.500	1.105
Paul Molitor	.467	15	7	3	1	1	3	2	2	.500	1.000
George Bell	.444	27	12	4	0	4	10	0	0	.444	1.037
Barry Bonds	.400	10	4	2	0	1	2	1	1	.455	.900

Eric Helfand — Athletics

Age 25 – Bats Left

	Avg	G	AB	R	H	2B	3B	HR	RBI	BB	SO	HBP	GDP	SB	CS	OBP	SLG	IBB	SH	SF	#Pit	#P/PA	GB	FB	G/F
1993 Season	.231	8	13	1	3	0	0	0	1	0	1	0	0	0	0	.231	.231	0	0	0	40	3.08	5	3	1.67

1993 Season

	Avg	AB	H	2B	3B	HR	RBI	BB	SO	OBP	SLG
vs. Left	1.000	1	1	0	0	0	0	0	0	1.000	1.000
vs. Right	.167	12	2	0	0	0	1	0	1	.167	.167

	Avg	AB	H	2B	3B	HR	RBI	BB	SO	OBP	SLG
Scoring Posn	.667	3	2	0	0	0	1	0	0	.667	.667
Close & Late	.000	2	0	0	0	0	0	0	0	.000	.000

Scott Hemond — Athletics

Age 28 – Bats Right (flyball hitter)

	Avg	G	AB	R	H	2B	3B	HR	RBI	BB	SO	HBP	GDP	SB	CS	OBP	SLG	IBB	SH	SF	#Pit	#P/PA	GB	FB	G/F
1993 Season	.256	91	215	31	55	16	0	6	26	32	55	1	2	14	5	.353	.414	0	6	1	989	3.88	49	66	0.74
Career (1989-1993)	.244	150	291	45	71	18	0	6	29	37	80	1	4	16	7	.329	.368	0	6	2	1302	3.86	69	85	0.81

1993 Season

	Avg	AB	H	2B	3B	HR	RBI	BB	SO	OBP	SLG		Avg	AB	H	2B	3B	HR	RBI	BB	SO	OBP	SLG
vs. Left	.299	77	23	7	0	2	7	15	25	.409	.468	Scoring Posn	.212	52	11	6	0	1	17	10	16	.333	.385
vs. Right	.232	138	32	9	0	4	19	17	30	.321	.384	Close & Late	.294	34	10	2	0	1	4	8	11	.442	.441
Home	.247	97	24	5	0	3	9	18	23	.365	.392	None on/out	.340	50	17	5	0	0	0	9	10	.450	.440
Away	.263	118	31	11	0	3	17	14	32	.343	.432	Batting #8	.235	34	8	2	0	0	3	2	13	.278	.294
First Pitch	.480	25	12	4	0	1	4	0	0	.480	.760	Batting #9	.274	157	43	12	0	6	22	26	33	.380	.465
Ahead in Count	.286	42	12	2	0	2	9	17	0	.483	.476	Other	.167	24	4	2	0	0	1	4	9	.276	.250
Behind in Count	.142	106	15	5	0	1	6	0	47	.150	.217	Pre-All Star	.197	66	13	4	0	0	4	9	19	.293	.258
Two Strikes	.138	109	15	6	0	2	7	15	55	.248	.248	Post-All Star	.282	149	42	12	0	6	22	23	36	.379	.483

Dave Henderson — Athletics

Age 35 – Bats Right (flyball hitter)

	Avg	G	AB	R	H	2B	3B	HR	RBI	BB	SO	HBP	GDP	SB	CS	OBP	SLG	IBB	SH	SF	#Pit	#P/PA	GB	FB	G/F
1993 Season	.220	107	382	37	84	19	0	20	53	32	113	0	1	0	3	.275	.427	0	0	8	1715	4.06	83	144	0.58
Last Five Years	.253	556	2046	266	518	105	3	80	283	186	478	8	27	17	15	.315	.425	5	3	18	8748	3.87	534	695	0.77

1993 Season

	Avg	AB	H	2B	3B	HR	RBI	BB	SO	OBP	SLG		Avg	AB	H	2B	3B	HR	RBI	BB	SO	OBP	SLG
vs. Left	.225	142	32	6	0	11	29	14	36	.291	.500	Scoring Posn	.161	112	18	4	0	3	33	9	43	.209	.277
vs. Right	.217	240	52	13	0	9	24	18	77	.265	.383	Close & Late	.216	74	16	3	0	2	8	8	22	.286	.338
Groundball	.227	75	17	4	0	0	6	7	23	.282	.280	None on/out	.250	84	21	7	0	7	7	10	25	.330	.583
Flyball	.179	84	15	5	0	2	8	5	21	.222	.310	Batting #2	.271	107	29	5	0	6	12	8	25	.322	.486
Home	.194	211	41	9	0	7	27	14	66	.239	.336	Batting #4	.198	116	23	5	0	7	16	9	35	.250	.422
Away	.251	171	43	10	0	13	26	18	47	.318	.538	Other	.201	159	32	9	0	7	25	15	53	.263	.390
Day	.185	151	28	7	0	8	19	13	55	.243	.391	April	.179	39	7	0	0	2	6	6	16	.283	.333
Night	.242	231	56	12	0	12	34	19	58	.296	.450	May	.238	84	20	4	0	6	8	4	20	.273	.500
Grass	.206	344	71	15	0	16	46	26	105	.257	.390	June	.000	16	0	0	0	0	1	2	5	.105	.000
Turf	.342	38	13	4	0	4	7	6	8	.432	.763	July	.216	74	16	4	0	4	13	7	29	.274	.432
First Pitch	.392	51	20	7	0	3	10	0	0	.385	.706	August	.202	89	18	5	0	2	10	6	26	.247	.326
Ahead in Count	.316	76	24	7	0	4	12	14	0	.413	.566	September/October	.288	80	23	6	0	6	15	7	17	.341	.588
Behind in Count	.147	177	26	4	0	7	17	0	83	.144	.288	Pre-All Star	.192	172	33	6	0	10	19	14	56	.250	.401
Two Strikes	.128	211	27	3	0	9	23	18	113	.195	.270	Post-All Star	.243	210	51	13	0	10	34	18	57	.295	.448

1993 By Position

Position	Avg	AB	H	2B	3B	HR	RBI	BB	SO	OBP	SLG	G	GS	Innings	PO	A	E	DP	Fld Pct	Rng Fctr	In Zone	Outs	Zone Rtg	MLB Zone
As Designated Hitter	.160	100	16	3	0	4	14	11	35	.237	.310	28	26	---	---	---	---	---	---	---	---	---	---	---
As cf	.243	218	53	13	0	11	28	16	61	.290	.454	60	57	484.2	168	5	1	1	.994	3.21	203	165	.813	.829
As rf	.222	54	12	2	0	4	9	4	16	.271	.481	14	13	119.2	35	2	1	2	.974	2.78	44	33	.750	.826

Last Five Years

	Avg	AB	H	2B	3B	HR	RBI	BB	SO	OBP	SLG		Avg	AB	H	2B	3B	HR	RBI	BB	SO	OBP	SLG
vs. Left	.300	614	184	37	0	35	105	55	115	.357	.531	Scoring Posn	.245	554	136	27	1	13	188	60	159	.311	.368
vs. Right	.233	1432	334	68	3	45	178	131	363	.297	.379	Close & Late	.250	328	82	14	1	8	39	24	78	.301	.372
Groundball	.265	581	154	32	0	16	75	47	116	.318	.403	None on/out	.269	446	120	28	0	21	21	33	92	.321	.473
Flyball	.253	434	110	21	1	18	60	41	99	.321	.431	Batting #2	.263	818	215	41	1	36	117	65	174	.321	.447
Home	.256	1043	267	44	1	43	147	85	246	.311	.424	Batting #5	.237	427	101	20	0	15	55	44	94	.308	.389
Away	.250	1003	251	61	2	37	136	101	232	.319	.426	Other	.252	801	202	44	2	29	111	77	210	.313	.421
Day	.250	756	189	36	2	35	111	65	187	.307	.442	April	.289	273	79	13	2	15	44	39	67	.377	.516
Night	.255	1290	329	69	1	45	172	121	291	.320	.415	May	.261	379	99	20	1	18	58	26	73	.311	.462
Grass	.258	1770	457	84	3	71	252	158	412	.318	.429	June	.230	309	71	14	0	14	43	31	68	.298	.411
Turf	.221	276	61	21	0	9	31	28	66	.295	.395	July	.251	371	93	18	0	9	40	36	90	.316	.372
First Pitch	.352	250	88	21	0	10	39	3	0	.364	.556	August	.249	370	92	23	0	11	49	25	87	.298	.400
Ahead in Count	.350	412	144	33	3	30	96	108	0	.482	.663	September/October	.244	344	84	17	0	13	49	29	93	.301	.407
Behind in Count	.188	990	186	34	0	25	90	0	384	.191	.298	Pre-All Star	.249	1075	268	53	3	49	152	109	243	.319	.441
Two Strikes	.173	1065	184	36	0	28	101	74	478	.227	.285	Post-All Star	.257	971	250	52	0	31	131	77	235	.311	.407

Batter vs. Pitcher (since 1984)

Hits Best Against	Avg	AB	H	2B	3B	HR	RBI	BB	SO	OBP	SLG	Hits Worst Against	Avg	AB	H	2B	3B	HR	RBI	BB	SO	OBP	SLG
Bill Swift	.615	13	8	1	0	0	2	1	0	.600	.692	Bud Black	.000	13	0	0	0	0	1	0	0	.000	.000
Mark Knudson	.600	10	6	2	0	0	1	2	3	.667	.800	Juan Guzman	.000	13	0	0	0	0	0	0	7	.000	.000
Jim Abbott	.455	22	10	1	0	5	8	3	4	.500	1.182	Tom Gordon	.000	12	0	0	0	0	0	1	9	.077	.000
Rich DeLucia	.417	12	5	1	0	2	4	1	0	.462	1.000	Dave Righetti	.000	10	0	0	0	0	1	0	0	.000	.000
Dave Johnson	.357	14	5	1	0	2	4	0	4	.357	.857	Rick Aguilera	.071	14	1	0	0	0	0	0	8	.071	.071

Rickey Henderson — Blue Jays

Age 35 – Bats Right

	Avg	G	AB	R	H	2B	3B	HR	RBI	BB	SO	HBP	GDP	SB	CS	OBP	SLG	IBB	SH	SF	#Pit	#P/PA	GB	FB	G/F
1993 Season	.289	134	481	114	139	22	2	21	59	120	65	4	9	53	8	.432	.474	7	1	4	2628	4.31	173	154	1.12
Last Five Years	.288	671	2377	528	684	116	12	94	280	536	322	24	42	301	61	.421	.465	26	3	16	12719	4.30	822	787	1.04

1993 Season

	Avg	AB	H	2B	3B	HR	RBI	BB	SO	OBP	SLG		Avg	AB	H	2B	3B	HR	RBI	BB	SO	OBP	SLG
vs. Left	.315	130	41	4	0	12	16	35	23	.461	.623	Scoring Posn	.237	114	27	5	1	3	39	33	21	.401	.377
vs. Right	.279	351	98	18	2	9	43	85	42	.421	.419	Close & Late	.243	74	18	3	2	2	11	15	13	.367	.419

1993 Season

	Avg	AB	H	2B	3B	HR	RBI	BB	SO	OBP	SLG
Groundball	.329	85	28	5	0	3	14	23	8	.473	.494
Flyball	.341	91	31	6	1	6	13	28	15	.500	.626
Home	.283	251	71	12	1	10	26	60	39	.422	.458
Away	.296	230	68	10	1	11	33	60	26	.442	.491
Day	.290	183	53	10	0	6	14	54	25	.458	.443
Night	.289	298	86	12	2	15	45	66	40	.415	.493
Grass	.315	336	106	17	1	17	43	88	41	.458	.524
Turf	.228	145	33	5	1	4	16	32	24	.369	.359
First Pitch	.381	21	8	2	0	0	3	7	0	.533	.476
Ahead in Count	.299	127	38	9	0	10	22	66	0	.536	.606
Behind in Count	.246	1012	249	33	3	19	79	0	256	.256	.341
Two Strikes	.254	252	64	5	2	7	22	47	65	.374	.373

	Avg	AB	H	2B	3B	HR	RBI	BB	SO	OBP	SLG
None on/out	.323	186	60	7	0	14	14	46	32	.462	.586
Batting #1	.294	466	137	22	2	21	59	112	64	.432	.485
Batting #3	.154	13	2	0	0	0	0	5	0	.389	.154
Other	.000	2	0	0	0	0	0	3	1	.600	.000
April	.286	63	18	4	0	3	11	17	5	.444	.492
May	.309	68	21	4	1	2	8	21	18	.478	.485
June	.313	96	30	3	0	4	13	29	11	.472	.469
July	.385	91	35	8	0	8	15	18	12	.477	.736
August	.208	77	16	1	1	1	4	20	12	.374	.286
September/October	.221	86	19	2	0	3	8	15	7	.340	.349
Pre-All Star	.307	261	80	13	1	12	39	74	39	.462	.502
Post-All Star	.268	220	59	9	1	9	20	46	26	.395	.441

1993 By Position

Position	Avg	AB	H	2B	3B	HR	RBI	BB	SO	OBP	SLG	G	GS	Innings	PO	A	E	DP	Fld Pct	Rng Fctr	In Zone	Outs	Zone Rtg	MLB Zone
As Designated Hitter	.292	48	14	3	0	2	3	17	15	.477	.479	16	13	---	---	---	---	---	---	---	---	---	---	---
As lf	.289	433	125	19	2	19	56	103	50	.426	.473	118	118	1006.0	258	6	7	0	.974	2.36	291	252	.866	.818

Last Five Years

	Avg	AB	H	2B	3B	HR	RBI	BB	SO	OBP	SLG
vs. Left	.293	656	192	33	2	35	76	144	95	.421	.509
vs. Right	.286	1721	492	83	10	59	204	392	227	.421	.449
Groundball	.313	659	206	37	6	23	85	135	83	.433	.492
Flyball	.300	477	143	25	2	26	65	119	75	.443	.524
Home	.289	1172	339	55	6	43	134	274	152	.425	.456
Away	.286	1205	345	61	6	51	146	262	170	.417	.474
Day	.283	812	230	42	3	33	95	205	117	.431	.464
Night	.290	1565	454	74	9	61	185	331	205	.416	.466
Grass	.291	1940	565	94	10	78	228	438	258	.424	.471
Turf	.272	437	119	22	2	16	52	98	64	.410	.442
First Pitch	.280	125	35	7	0	6	22	20	0	.376	.480
Ahead in Count	.329	660	217	44	4	53	115	324	0	.550	.648
Behind in Count	.265	672	178	33	3	16	58	0	140	.272	.394
Two Strikes	.253	1255	318	43	7	20	93	192	322	.357	.347

	Avg	AB	H	2B	3B	HR	RBI	BB	SO	OBP	SLG
Scoring Posn	.245	503	123	16	3	19	184	173	88	.436	.402
Close & Late	.284	334	95	12	5	14	61	87	53	.432	.476
None on/out	.303	992	301	53	5	48	48	191	129	.418	.512
Batting #1	.289	2346	678	116	12	94	279	524	315	.421	.469
Batting #3	.188	16	3	0	0	0	0	6	1	.409	.188
Other	.200	15	3	0	0	0	1	6	6	.429	.200
April	.283	322	91	22	1	10	38	67	44	.408	.450
May	.294	425	125	24	2	15	48	109	64	.441	.466
June	.299	384	115	14	2	12	44	104	42	.449	.440
July	.329	395	130	22	3	23	61	73	52	.434	.575
August	.266	421	112	16	1	16	45	91	62	.402	.423
September/October	.258	430	111	18	3	18	44	92	58	.394	.440
Pre-All Star	.297	1254	372	66	5	47	155	302	171	.434	.470
Post-All Star	.278	1123	312	50	7	47	125	234	151	.406	.460

Batter vs. Pitcher (since 1984)

Hits Best Against	Avg	AB	H	2B	3B	HR	RBI	BB	SO	OBP	SLG
Rick Sutcliffe	.583	12	7	0	0	1	3	7	2	.737	.833
Mark Portugal	.500	8	4	1	0	1	3	2	0	.545	1.000
Ben McDonald	.429	21	9	2	0	2	4	8	1	.586	.810
Mike Morgan	.400	10	4	0	0	2	2	1	2	.455	1.000
Todd Stottlemyre	.364	11	4	0	0	2	2	7	2	.611	.909

Hits Worst Against	Avg	AB	H	2B	3B	HR	RBI	BB	SO	OBP	SLG
Steve Ontiveros	.077	13	1	0	0	0	0	0	1	.077	.077
Julio Valera	.091	11	1	0	0	0	0	1	3	.167	.091
John Smiley	.100	10	1	0	0	0	0	1	1	.182	.100
Greg Hibbard	.100	10	1	0	0	0	0	1	1	.182	.100
Juan Guzman	.143	14	2	1	0	0	0	0	2	.143	.214

Tom Henke — Rangers

Age 36 – Pitches Right (flyball pitcher)

	ERA	W	L	Sv	G	GS	IP	BB	SO	Avg	H	2B	3B	HR	RBI	OBP	SLG	GF	IR	IRS	Hld	SvOp	SB	CS	GB	FB	G/F
1993 Season	2.91	5	5	40	66	0	74.1	27	79	.205	55	6	0	7	30	.278	.306	60	36	9	0	47	3	2	89	70	1.27
Last Five Years	2.30	18	16	158	297	0	344.0	104	369	.203	252	48	4	29	125	.264	.318	211	132	36	8	181	19	6	344	358	0.96

1993 Season

	ERA	W	L	Sv	G	GS	IP	H	HR	BB	SO
Home	1.62	5	1	27	38	0	44.1	28	4	5	50
Away	4.80	0	4	13	28	0	30.0	27	3	22	29
Day	5.59	0	1	8	18	0	19.1	18	3	11	17
Night	1.96	5	4	32	48	0	55.0	37	4	16	62
Grass	2.67	5	5	34	58	0	67.1	50	6	21	73
Turf	5.14	0	0	6	8	0	7.0	5	1	6	6
April	0.00	1	0	4	8	0	9.0	3	0	2	10
May	2.30	3	1	5	13	0	15.2	14	1	6	12
June	5.23	0	1	6	11	0	10.1	9	1	4	11
July	5.40	0	1	7	10	0	10.0	11	1	3	16
August	1.93	1	1	9	11	0	14.0	5	2	2	17
September/October	2.93	0	1	9	13	0	15.1	13	2	10	13
Starter	0.00	0	0	0	0	0	0.0	0	0	0	0
Reliever	2.91	5	5	40	66	0	74.1	55	7	27	79
0 Days rest	0.69	1	0	10	13	0	13.0	6	1	6	10
1 or 2 Days rest	3.57	3	4	19	32	0	35.1	30	4	12	37
3+ Days rest	3.12	1	1	11	21	0	26.0	19	2	9	32
Pre-All Star	3.05	4	2	17	35	0	38.1	30	2	14	38
Post-All Star	2.75	1	3	23	31	0	36.0	25	5	13	41

	Avg	AB	H	2B	3B	HR	RBI	BB	SO	OBP	SLG
vs. Left	.205	132	27	4	0	3	14	16	36	.289	.303
vs. Right	.206	136	28	2	0	4	16	11	43	.267	.309
Inning 1-6	.000	0	0	0	0	0	0	0	0	.000	.000
Inning 7+	.205	268	55	6	0	7	30	27	79	.278	.306
None on	.188	154	29	2	0	3	3	10	43	.238	.260
Runners on	.228	114	26	4	0	4	27	17	36	.326	.368
Scoring Posn	.215	65	14	2	0	3	24	11	18	.325	.385
Close & Late	.210	205	43	6	0	6	24	23	62	.290	.327
None on/out	.188	64	12	0	0	2	2	2	16	.212	.281
vs. 1st Batr (relief)	.302	63	19	0	0	2	5	3	19	.333	.397
First Inning Pitched	.224	223	50	6	0	7	30	21	63	.290	.345
First 15 Pitches	.216	194	42	5	0	6	22	16	51	.275	.335
Pitch 16-30	.180	61	11	1	0	1	8	8	23	.278	.246
Pitch 31-45	.154	13	2	0	0	0	0	2	5	.267	.154
Pitch 46+	.000	0	0	0	0	0	0	1	0	1.000	.000
First Pitch	.375	40	15	2	0	1	8	3	0	.419	.500
Ahead in Count	.162	136	22	2	0	2	9	0	57	.159	.221
Behind in Count	.250	36	9	1	0	1	5	10	0	.404	.361
Two Strikes	.134	149	20	1	0	2	6	14	79	.207	.181

Last Five Years

	ERA	W	L	Sv	G	GS	IP	H	HR	BB	SO
Home	2.21	15	2	83	148	0	170.2	120	19	42	189
Away	2.39	3	14	75	149	0	173.1	132	10	62	180
Day	3.03	2	5	36	85	0	92.0	78	9	43	87
Night	2.04	16	11	122	212	0	252.0	174	20	61	282
Grass	2.30	8	15	79	152	0	180.1	135	13	56	196

	Avg	AB	H	2B	3B	HR	RBI	BB	SO	OBP	SLG
vs. Left	.197	619	122	26	3	15	72	65	171	.271	.321
vs. Right	.208	625	130	22	1	14	53	39	198	.257	.314
Inning 1-6	.214	14	3	2	0	0	2	2	5	.313	.357
Inning 7+	.202	1230	249	46	4	29	123	102	364	.264	.317
None on	.204	724	148	30	2	12	12	44	212	.251	.301

Last Five Years

	ERA	W	L	Sv	G	GS	IP	H	HR	BB	SO
Turf	2.31	10	1	79	145	0	163.2	117	16	48	173
April	2.97	3	4	12	36	0	33.1	31	4	14	30
May	2.43	6	2	18	46	0	55.2	34	7	22	52
June	1.85	3	1	27	51	0	58.1	33	2	15	59
July	2.62	1	3	34	53	0	58.1	47	3	16	70
August	2.14	2	3	35	55	0	71.1	51	8	11	89
September/October	2.15	3	3	32	56	0	67.0	56	5	26	69
Starter	0.00	0	0	0	0	0	0.0	0	0	0	0
Reliever	2.30	18	16	158	297	0	344.0	252	29	104	369
0 Days rest	2.01	2	3	36	57	0	58.1	45	7	19	69
1 or 2 Days rest	2.16	10	8	84	145	0	166.1	118	14	41	171
3+ Days rest	2.64	6	5	38	95	0	119.1	89	8	44	129
Pre-All Star	2.25	13	7	69	152	0	167.2	108	14	56	161
Post-All Star	2.35	5	9	89	145	0	176.1	144	15	48	208

	Avg	AB	H	2B	3B	HR	RBI	BB	SO	OBP	SLG
Runners on	.200	520	104	18	2	17	113	60	157	.282	.340
Scoring Posn	.203	316	64	12	2	11	98	45	92	.298	.358
Close & Late	.211	736	155	29	3	22	97	56	230	.266	.348
None on/out	.226	305	69	10	1	6	6	13	82	.258	.325
vs. 1st Batr (relief)	.258	283	73	10	1	10	29	11	77	.287	.406
First Inning Pitched	.205	1008	207	41	4	25	112	79	292	.263	.328
First 15 Pitches	.204	893	182	38	4	22	85	64	251	.256	.329
Pitch 16-30	.199	276	55	8	0	5	32	26	95	.269	.283
Pitch 31-45	.208	72	15	2	0	2	8	13	21	.337	.319
Pitch 46+	.000	3	0	0	0	0	0	1	2	.250	.000
First Pitch	.306	186	57	11	1	6	24	11	0	.347	.473
Ahead in Count	.156	673	105	19	1	7	47	0	316	.158	.218
Behind in Count	.260	169	44	9	0	7	21	45	0	.412	.438
Two Strikes	.139	698	97	17	2	7	40	48	369	.195	.199

Pitcher vs. Batter (since 1984)

Pitches Best Vs.	Avg	AB	H	2B	3B	HR	RBI	BB	SO	OBP	SLG
Dick Schofield	.000	11	0	0	0	0	0	1	4	.083	.000
Mike Devereaux	.067	15	1	0	0	0	0	1	6	.125	.067
Lou Whitaker	.074	27	2	0	0	0	0	1	6	.107	.074
Larry Sheets	.083	12	1	0	0	0	0	1	5	.154	.083
Travis Fryman	.100	10	1	0	0	0	1	0	7	.091	.100

Pitches Worst Vs.	Avg	AB	H	2B	3B	HR	RBI	BB	SO	OBP	SLG
Jody Reed	.556	9	5	1	0	0	1	2	0	.636	.667
Mike Greenwell	.417	12	5	1	0	1	6	1	3	.462	.750
Don Mattingly	.333	21	7	1	0	2	5	2	4	.391	.667
Wally Joyner	.333	15	5	1	0	1	1	2	4	.412	.600
Luis Polonia	.333	12	4	2	1	0	3	1	2	.385	.667

Mike Henneman — Tigers

Age 32 – Pitches Right (groundball pitcher)

	ERA	W	L	Sv	G	GS	IP	BB	SO	Avg	H	2B	3B	HR	RBI	OBP	SLG	GF	IR	IRS	Hld	SvOp	SB	CS	GB	FB	G/F
1993 Season	2.64	5	3	24	63	0	71.2	32	58	.251	69	11	3	4	31	.331	.356	50	42	9	2	29	0	0	101	69	1.46
Last Five Years	3.25	36	21	99	312	0	417.2	170	296	.254	399	67	10	20	173	.327	.347	206	170	38	13	121	16	6	615	384	1.60

1993 Season

	ERA	W	L	Sv	G	GS	IP	H	HR	BB	SO
Home	3.41	3	1	7	27	0	31.2	26	4	15	27
Away	2.03	2	2	17	36	0	40.0	43	0	17	31
Day	1.83	2	1	7	20	0	19.2	16	0	12	14
Night	2.94	3	2	17	43	0	52.0	53	4	20	44
Grass	2.40	5	1	20	50	0	56.1	44	4	23	47
Turf	3.52	0	2	4	13	0	15.1	25	0	9	11
April	1.69	0	0	5	10	0	10.2	11	0	5	7
May	1.26	1	0	5	13	0	14.1	10	2	8	9
June	2.61	0	1	2	11	0	10.1	9	1	4	10
July	2.35	1	0	5	10	0	15.1	15	0	4	10
August	4.50	1	2	4	11	0	12.0	16	0	4	12
September/October	4.00	2	0	3	8	0	9.0	8	1	7	10
Starter	0.00	0	0	0	0	0	0.0	0	0	0	0
Reliever	2.64	5	3	24	63	0	71.2	69	4	32	58
0 Days rest	0.45	0	0	10	19	0	20.0	19	0	12	10
1 or 2 Days rest	1.98	3	2	7	23	0	27.1	27	2	9	26
3+ Days rest	5.18	2	1	7	21	0	24.1	23	2	11	22
Pre-All Star	1.48	2	1	14	39	0	42.2	34	3	18	32
Post-All Star	4.34	3	2	10	24	0	29.0	35	1	14	26

	Avg	AB	H	2B	3B	HR	RBI	BB	SO	OBP	SLG
vs. Left	.285	130	37	7	2	3	21	20	20	.377	.438
vs. Right	.221	145	32	4	1	1	10	12	38	.288	.283
Inning 1-6	.000	0	0	0	0	0	0	0	0	.000	.000
Inning 7+	.251	275	69	11	3	4	31	32	58	.331	.356
None on	.275	120	33	6	2	3	3	10	23	.331	.433
Runners on	.232	155	36	5	1	1	28	22	35	.331	.297
Scoring Posn	.214	98	21	2	1	1	28	14	22	.313	.286
Close & Late	.271	181	49	7	1	3	25	22	36	.353	.370
None on/out	.340	53	18	3	2	2	2	6	8	.407	.585
vs. 1st Batr (relief)	.281	57	16	3	1	1	4	5	12	.333	.421
First Inning Pitched	.246	207	51	7	2	3	26	27	43	.336	.343
First 15 Pitches	.246	187	46	7	2	2	18	21	36	.325	.337
Pitch 16-30	.268	71	19	4	1	1	8	11	18	.366	.394
Pitch 31-45	.235	17	4	0	0	1	5	0	4	.235	.412
Pitch 46+	.000	0	0	0	0	0	0	0	0	.000	.000
First Pitch	.298	47	14	4	2	1	4	8	0	.411	.532
Ahead in Count	.209	139	29	1	0	2	10	0	54	.214	.259
Behind in Count	.310	42	13	4	0	0	7	10	0	.434	.405
Two Strikes	.178	118	21	1	0	3	12	14	58	.269	.263

Last Five Years

	ERA	W	L	Sv	G	GS	IP	H	HR	BB	SO
Home	3.16	24	8	49	166	0	222.1	192	14	78	174
Away	3.36	12	13	50	146	0	195.1	207	6	92	122
Day	3.33	11	8	31	98	0	132.1	130	6	63	80
Night	3.22	25	13	68	214	0	285.1	269	14	107	216
Grass	3.17	34	15	81	263	0	354.2	332	19	138	260
Turf	3.71	2	6	18	49	0	63.0	67	1	32	36
April	2.77	2	1	16	44	0	52.0	48	0	22	35
May	3.24	8	7	19	56	0	75.0	69	5	32	41
June	2.67	5	3	18	60	0	81.0	65	6	36	62
July	5.38	8	7	17	55	0	75.1	85	4	36	54
August	2.50	6	3	15	51	0	72.0	73	3	24	53
September/October	2.74	7	0	14	46	0	62.1	59	2	20	51
Starter	0.00	0	0	0	0	0	0.0	0	0	0	0
Reliever	3.25	36	21	99	312	0	417.2	399	20	170	296
0 Days rest	1.06	8	2	29	79	0	93.2	75	1	39	57
1 or 2 Days rest	3.60	22	13	45	144	0	205.0	219	10	76	154
3+ Days rest	4.39	6	6	25	89	0	119.0	105	9	55	85
Pre-All Star	2.93	16	15	61	180	0	239.2	209	13	102	158
Post-All Star	3.69	20	6	38	132	0	178.0	190	7	68	138

	Avg	AB	H	2B	3B	HR	RBI	BB	SO	OBP	SLG
vs. Left	.275	699	192	39	5	6	75	98	97	.362	.371
vs. Right	.237	874	207	28	5	14	98	72	199	.298	.328
Inning 1-6	.351	37	13	2	0	0	10	6	8	.432	.405
Inning 7+	.251	1536	386	65	10	20	163	164	288	.324	.346
None on	.255	804	205	32	5	12	12	63	150	.313	.352
Runners on	.252	769	194	35	5	8	161	107	146	.341	.342
Scoring Posn	.232	465	108	18	4	5	150	83	102	.339	.320
Close & Late	.255	905	231	37	3	13	107	108	176	.335	.346
None on/out	.262	351	92	12	5	3	3	26	59	.315	.350
vs. 1st Batr (relief)	.251	279	70	9	1	2	14	28	58	.319	.312
First Inning Pitched	.251	1054	265	42	5	11	124	109	203	.322	.332
First 15 Pitches	.238	975	232	35	5	10	89	93	187	.304	.315
Pitch 16-30	.283	474	134	27	4	8	58	62	88	.370	.407
Pitch 31-45	.241	112	27	4	0	1	23	12	19	.312	.304
Pitch 46+	.500	12	6	1	1	1	3	3	2	.600	1.000
First Pitch	.295	224	66	13	4	3	30	49	0	.421	.429
Ahead in Count	.214	779	167	22	2	11	65	0	261	.219	.290
Behind in Count	.281	288	81	14	1	4	48	62	0	.402	.378
Two Strikes	.197	747	147	23	3	9	58	59	296	.259	.272

Pitcher vs. Batter (career)

Pitches Best Vs.	Avg	AB	H	2B	3B	HR	RBI	BB	SO	OBP	SLG
Fred McGriff	.000	16	0	0	0	0	1	1	4	.059	.000
Don Slaught	.000	10	0	0	0	0	0	1	3	.091	.000
Tom Brunansky	.071	14	1	0	0	0	0	0	5	.071	.071
Pete Incaviglia	.077	13	1	0	0	0	1	0	3	.071	.077

Pitches Worst Vs.	Avg	AB	H	2B	3B	HR	RBI	BB	SO	OBP	SLG
Luis Polonia	.600	10	6	0	0	0	2	1	0	.636	.600
Harold Reynolds	.529	17	9	3	1	1	5	2	3	.579	1.000
Brady Anderson	.455	11	5	1	0	1	5	3	0	.571	.818
Tony Fernandez	.444	9	4	0	1	1	4	3	0	.583	1.000

Pitcher vs. Batter (career)																						
Pitches Best Vs.	Avg	AB	H	2B	3B	HR	RBI	BB	SO	OBP	SLG	Pitches Worst Vs.	Avg	AB	H	2B	3B	HR	RBI	BB	SO	OBP	SLG
Dave Winfield	.083	12	1	0	0	0	0	0	5	.083	.083	Kent Hrbek	.417	12	5	1	0	1	4	3	2	.533	.750

Butch Henry — Expos

Age 25 – Pitches Left

	ERA	W	L	Sv	G	GS	IP	BB	SO	Avg	H	2B	3B	HR	RBI	OBP	SLG	CG	ShO	Sup	QS	#P/S	SB	CS	GB	FB	G/F
1993 Season	6.12	3	9	0	30	16	103.0	28	47	.317	135	25	2	15	69	.356	.491	1	0	4.63	5	84	9	4	169	128	1.32
Career (1992-1993)	4.82	9	18	0	58	44	268.2	69	143	.298	320	63	7	31	138	.337	.456	3	1	3.85	15	86	19	11	410	311	1.32

1993 Season

	ERA	W	L	Sv	G	GS	IP	H	HR	BB	SO		Avg	AB	H	2B	3B	HR	RBI	BB	SO	OBP	SLG
Home	7.45	1	4	0	16	8	48.1	77	10	12	19	vs. Left	.343	99	34	11	1	2	16	7	10	.383	.535
Away	4.94	2	5	0	14	8	54.2	58	5	16	28	vs. Right	.309	327	101	14	1	13	53	21	37	.347	.477
Starter	6.37	3	8	0	16	16	83.1	112	15	20	34	Scoring Posn	.369	111	41	6	1	3	53	11	15	.411	.523
Reliever	5.03	0	1	0	14	0	19.2	23	0	8	13	Close & Late	.429	14	6	1	0	0	2	2	5	.500	.500
0-3 Days Rest	1.50	0	0	0	1	1	6.0	7	1	0	0	None on/out	.292	106	31	9	0	2	2	6	9	.330	.434
4 Days Rest	5.98	2	6	0	10	10	55.2	72	9	18	24	First Pitch	.329	70	23	7	1	1	18	2	0	.342	.500
5+ Days Rest	8.72	1	2	0	5	5	21.2	33	5	2	10	Ahead in Count	.286	175	50	9	0	3	19	0	41	.287	.389
Pre-All Star	6.59	2	8	0	20	15	84.2	117	14	24	39	Behind in Count	.346	107	37	5	1	6	20	14	0	.415	.579
Post-All Star	3.93	1	1	0	10	1	18.1	18	1	4	8	Two Strikes	.290	169	49	9	0	4	16	12	47	.335	.414

Career (1992-1993)

	ERA	W	L	Sv	G	GS	IP	H	HR	BB	SO		Avg	AB	H	2B	3B	HR	RBI	BB	SO	OBP	SLG
Home	4.75	4	7	0	30	22	136.1	168	17	31	70	vs. Left	.317	240	76	21	1	4	29	19	24	.364	.463
Away	4.90	5	11	0	28	22	132.1	152	14	38	73	vs. Right	.292	835	244	42	6	27	109	50	119	.330	.454
Day	3.10	5	3	0	21	13	98.2	103	6	20	64	Inning 1-6	.295	921	272	54	5	29	121	56	117	.334	.459
Night	5.82	4	15	0	37	31	170.0	217	25	49	79	Inning 7+	.312	154	48	9	2	2	17	13	26	.359	.435
Grass	5.92	3	9	0	26	19	111.0	151	14	34	56	None on	.302	636	192	41	4	18	18	33	86	.337	.464
Turf	4.05	6	9	0	32	25	157.2	169	17	35	87	Runners on	.292	439	128	22	3	13	120	36	57	.337	.444
April	4.09	1	4	0	9	8	50.2	56	7	15	27	Scoring Posn	.304	240	73	10	1	7	101	29	31	.364	.442
May	7.09	2	6	0	13	12	66.0	89	8	17	32	Close & Late	.304	56	17	4	0	1	4	3	11	.333	.429
June	4.79	1	3	0	10	8	41.1	50	3	18	18	None on/out	.272	276	75	20	2	5	5	16	35	.312	.413
July	4.31	1	2	0	10	8	48.0	60	5	10	32	vs. 1st Batr (relief)	.429	14	6	2	0	0	1	0	2	.429	.571
August	3.33	3	2	0	7	7	46.0	49	7	6	26	First Inning Pitched	.287	223	64	13	2	2	33	17	28	.333	.390
September/October	3.78	1	1	0	9	1	16.2	16	1	3	8	First 75 Pitches	.290	886	257	51	6	25	111	55	115	.329	.446
Starter	4.81	9	17	0	44	44	249.0	297	31	61	130	Pitch 76-90	.365	104	38	5	1	4	16	7	15	.398	.548
Reliever	5.03	0	1	0	14	0	19.2	23	0	8	13	Pitch 91-105	.322	59	19	7	0	1	8	3	7	.355	.492
0-3 Days Rest	1.50	0	0	0	1	1	6.0	7	1	0	0	Pitch 106+	.231	26	6	0	0	1	3	4	6	.333	.346
4 Days Rest	4.53	5	12	0	26	26	147.0	172	17	44	75	First Pitch	.308	182	56	14	3	3	28	9	0	.338	.467
5+ Days Rest	5.44	4	5	0	17	17	96.0	118	13	17	55	Ahead in Count	.221	485	107	20	1	4	40	0	130	.221	.291
Pre-All Star	5.51	5	14	0	38	33	183.0	232	21	56	97	Behind in Count	.393	229	90	17	2	11	39	38	0	.471	.629
Post-All Star	3.36	4	4	0	20	11	85.2	88	10	13	46	Two Strikes	.228	451	103	19	1	8	33	22	143	.263	.328

Pitcher vs. Batter (career)

Pitches Best Vs.	Avg	AB	H	2B	3B	HR	RBI	BB	SO	OBP	SLG	Pitches Worst Vs.	Avg	AB	H	2B	3B	HR	RBI	BB	SO	OBP	SLG
Mark Grace	.125	16	2	1	0	0	0	0	0	.125	.188	Dave Hollins	.833	12	10	3	0	4	8	2	2	.800	2.083
Eric Karros	.133	15	2	0	0	0	0	0	3	.133	.133	Darren Lewis	.556	9	5	1	0	0	0	2	0	.636	.667
Mariano Duncan	.143	14	2	0	0	0	1	0	2	.133	.143	Fred McGriff	.462	13	6	1	0	1	5	2	0	.533	.769
Tim Teufel	.154	13	2	1	0	0	2	0	0	.154	.231	Darren Daulton	.444	9	4	2	0	1	4	2	0	.545	1.000
Tom Pagnozzi	.182	11	2	1	0	0	0	0	3	.182	.273	Eric Davis	.429	7	3	2	0	1	4	4	1	.583	1.143

Doug Henry — Brewers

Age 30 – Pitches Right

	ERA	W	L	Sv	G	GS	IP	BB	SO	Avg	H	2B	3B	HR	RBI	OBP	SLG	GF	IR	IRS	Hld	SvOp	SB	CS	GB	FB	G/F
1993 Season	5.56	4	4	17	54	0	55.0	25	38	.300	67	13	2	7	38	.373	.471	41	27	10	0	24	4	0	79	65	1.22
Career (1991-1993)	3.87	7	9	61	154	0	156.0	63	118	.248	147	33	4	14	85	.319	.388	122	71	22	4	73	8	4	181	180	1.01

1993 Season

	ERA	W	L	Sv	G	GS	IP	H	HR	BB	SO		Avg	AB	H	2B	3B	HR	RBI	BB	SO	OBP	SLG
Home	7.20	3	2	7	30	0	30.0	40	7	14	21	vs. Left	.314	102	32	4	1	2	13	13	20	.393	.431
Away	3.60	1	2	10	24	0	25.0	27	0	11	17	vs. Right	.289	121	35	9	1	5	25	12	18	.355	.504
Starter	0.00	0	0	0	0	0	0.0	0	0	0	0	Scoring Posn	.247	73	18	2	0	2	29	15	17	.359	.356
Reliever	5.56	4	4	17	54	0	55.0	67	7	25	38	Close & Late	.310	126	39	8	2	4	25	13	25	.373	.500
0 Days rest	4.50	0	1	3	8	0	6.0	11	0	1	4	None on/out	.360	50	18	5	1	1	1	3	6	.407	.560
1 or 2 Days rest	6.39	1	2	9	23	0	25.1	34	4	17	21	First Pitch	.406	32	13	3	0	2	11	8	0	.512	.688
3+ Days rest	4.94	3	1	5	23	0	23.2	22	3	7	13	Ahead in Count	.165	91	15	3	0	1	3	0	30	.189	.231
Pre-All Star	4.58	2	2	16	35	0	35.1	38	5	10	26	Behind in Count	.426	47	20	4	0	1	11	9	0	.518	.574
Post-All Star	7.32	2	2	1	19	0	19.2	29	2	15	12	Two Strikes	.152	99	15	2	1	1	7	8	38	.218	.222

Career (1991-1993)

	ERA	W	L	Sv	G	GS	IP	H	HR	BB	SO		Avg	AB	H	2B	3B	HR	RBI	BB	SO	OBP	SLG
Home	3.89	4	3	33	82	0	83.1	76	10	31	69	vs. Left	.231	268	62	14	1	3	28	37	51	.322	.325
Away	3.84	3	6	28	72	0	72.2	71	4	32	49	vs. Right	.262	325	85	19	3	11	57	26	67	.317	.440
Day	3.15	2	1	22	54	0	54.1	45	4	22	34	Inning 1-6	.320	50	16	5	0	1	9	6	7	.407	.480
Night	4.25	5	8	39	100	0	101.2	102	10	41	84	Inning 7+	.241	543	131	28	4	13	76	57	111	.311	.379
Grass	3.38	7	7	55	135	0	136.0	120	12	50	107	None on	.243	329	80	20	1	6	6	19	66	.289	.365
Turf	7.20	0	2	6	19	0	20.0	27	2	13	11	Runners on	.254	264	67	13	3	8	79	44	52	.353	.417
April	7.94	0	0	9	17	0	17.0	27	2	9	8	Scoring Posn	.277	159	44	7	1	6	70	34	32	.388	.447
May	1.90	1	1	7	23	0	23.2	18	1	9	16	Close & Late	.246	342	84	19	3	5	52	39	80	.320	.363
June	1.19	0	2	11	23	0	22.2	14	1	5	23	None on/out	.236	140	33	9	1	3	3	9	27	.287	.379

Career (1991-1993)	ERA	W	L	Sv	G	GS	IP	H	HR	BB	SO
July	4.74	3	1	10	25	0	24.2	24	4	11	17
August	5.44	3	3	10	36	0	41.1	43	6	22	34
September/October	2.03	0	2	14	30	0	26.2	21	0	7	20
Starter	0.00	0	0	0	0	0	0.0	0	0	0	0
Reliever	3.87	7	9	61	154	0	156.0	147	14	63	118
0 Days rest	2.33	2	2	22	39	0	38.2	32	1	18	27
1 or 2 Days rest	3.90	2	6	27	61	0	62.1	62	6	29	46
3+ Days rest	4.91	3	1	12	54	0	55.0	53	7	16	45
Pre-All Star	3.67	3	3	32	72	0	73.2	69	7	25	55
Post-All Star	4.04	4	6	29	82	0	82.1	78	7	38	63

	Avg	AB	H	2B	3B	HR	RBI	BB	SO	OBP	SLG
vs. 1st Batr (relief)	.275	138	38	11	0	4	20	15	25	.346	.442
First Inning Pitched	.257	505	130	29	3	13	78	54	95	.329	.404
First 15 Pitches	.266	433	115	25	2	10	61	44	82	.334	.402
Pitch 16-30	.192	130	25	7	1	4	20	14	28	.269	.354
Pitch 31-45	.269	26	7	1	1	0	4	5	7	.364	.385
Pitch 46+	.000	4	0	0	0	0	0	0	1	.000	.000
First Pitch	.317	82	26	5	1	2	16	13	0	.398	.476
Ahead in Count	.165	261	43	9	0	2	16	0	96	.173	.222
Behind in Count	.352	122	43	10	1	5	29	25	0	.463	.574
Two Strikes	.160	293	47	9	1	2	21	25	118	.227	.218

Dwayne Henry — Mariners

Age 32 – Pitches Right (flyball pitcher)

	ERA	W	L	Sv	G	GS	IP	BB	SO	Avg	H	2B	3B	HR	RBI	OBP	SLG	GF	IR	IRS	Hld	SvOp	SB	CS	GB	FB	G/F
1993 Season	6.44	2	2	2	34	1	58.2	39	37	.273	62	16	4	6	46	.379	.458	16	23	6	0	2	3	2	61	88	0.69
Last Five Years	4.38	10	11	5	192	1	261.0	152	210	.236	225	50	10	22	152	.340	.378	66	126	51	11	9	21	11	258	339	0.76

1993 Season	ERA	W	L	Sv	G	GS	IP	H	HR	BB	SO
Home	6.12	2	2	0	18	0	32.1	33	5	25	21
Away	6.84	0	0	2	16	1	26.1	29	1	14	16
Starter	12.46	0	0	0	1	1	4.1	9	1	0	1
Reliever	5.96	2	2	2	33	0	54.1	53	5	39	36
0 Days rest	4.35	1	1	0	6	0	10.1	10	0	11	9
1 or 2 Days rest	7.32	0	1	1	10	0	19.2	18	4	9	9
3+ Days rest	5.55	1	0	1	17	0	24.1	25	1	19	18
Pre-All Star	6.56	2	2	1	24	1	46.2	52	5	29	21
Post-All Star	6.00	0	0	1	10	0	12.0	10	1	10	16

	Avg	AB	H	2B	3B	HR	RBI	BB	SO	OBP	SLG
vs. Left	.281	89	25	6	4	2	21	21	12	.420	.506
vs. Right	.268	138	37	10	0	4	25	18	25	.350	.428
Scoring Posn	.313	80	25	8	1	1	38	15	18	.404	.475
Close & Late	.158	19	3	2	0	0	1	5	2	.360	.263
None on/out	.250	48	12	4	1	1	1	7	8	.357	.438
First Pitch	.176	34	6	2	0	0	8	4	0	.256	.235
Ahead in Count	.252	103	26	7	3	3	21	0	31	.252	.466
Behind in Count	.364	44	16	2	1	2	8	18	0	.540	.591
Two Strikes	.234	107	25	9	2	3	20	17	37	.344	.439

Last Five Years	ERA	W	L	Sv	G	GS	IP	H	HR	BB	SO
Home	4.13	8	5	2	101	0	143.2	117	15	85	125
Away	4.68	2	6	3	91	1	117.1	108	7	67	85
Day	5.03	1	5	3	53	0	62.2	63	4	37	54
Night	4.17	9	6	2	139	1	198.1	162	18	115	156
Grass	4.77	2	5	2	81	1	105.2	94	9	53	84
Turf	4.11	8	6	3	111	0	155.1	131	13	99	126
April	4.43	2	2	3	34	0	44.2	36	3	23	25
May	4.39	3	2	0	34	1	53.1	48	6	34	33
June	5.73	1	1	0	28	0	37.2	38	3	27	24
July	3.09	2	0	0	23	0	32.0	25	2	16	30
August	4.53	2	4	1	37	0	49.2	49	3	28	48
September/October	3.92	0	2	1	36	0	43.2	29	5	24	50
Starter	12.46	0	0	0	1	1	4.1	9	1	0	1
Reliever	4.24	10	11	5	191	0	256.2	216	21	152	209
0 Days rest	4.53	2	4	1	44	0	59.2	56	4	40	51
1 or 2 Days rest	4.56	4	6	2	74	0	100.2	78	12	60	80
3+ Days rest	3.74	4	1	2	73	0	96.1	82	5	52	78
Pre-All Star	4.97	6	5	3	99	1	141.1	131	13	84	85
Post-All Star	3.69	4	6	2	93	0	119.2	94	9	68	125

	Avg	AB	H	2B	3B	HR	RBI	BB	SO	OBP	SLG
vs. Left	.240	442	106	25	9	10	74	88	91	.368	.405
vs. Right	.232	513	119	25	1	12	78	64	119	.316	.355
Inning 1-6	.256	262	67	16	5	8	56	38	52	.351	.447
Inning 7+	.228	693	158	34	5	14	96	114	158	.337	.352
None on	.203	508	103	21	6	11	11	76	121	.308	.333
Runners on	.273	447	122	29	4	11	141	76	89	.376	.430
Scoring Posn	.284	289	82	23	3	4	123	59	65	.397	.426
Close & Late	.240	246	59	14	1	5	39	44	56	.355	.366
None on/out	.212	222	47	9	2	7	7	28	45	.303	.365
vs. 1st Batr (relief)	.233	163	38	12	0	4	30	24	33	.332	.380
First Inning Pitched	.233	588	137	32	4	13	104	100	138	.342	.367
First 15 Pitches	.241	522	126	27	3	14	86	75	110	.335	.385
Pitch 16-30	.213	296	63	18	3	5	38	55	77	.337	.345
Pitch 31-45	.231	104	24	3	1	3	20	16	20	.341	.365
Pitch 46+	.364	33	12	2	3	0	8	6	3	.450	.606
First Pitch	.295	122	36	9	0	1	21	16	0	.371	.393
Ahead in Count	.175	458	80	13	6	9	51	0	173	.178	.288
Behind in Count	.344	186	64	14	3	9	46	70	0	.521	.597
Two Strikes	.147	496	73	14	5	10	55	66	210	.251	.256

Pitcher vs. Batter (career)

Pitches Best Vs.	Avg	AB	H	2B	3B	HR	RBI	BB	SO	OBP	SLG

Pitches Worst Vs.	Avg	AB	H	2B	3B	HR	RBI	BB	SO	OBP	SLG
Eddie Murray	.455	11	5	1	0	1	3	2	0	.538	.818

Pat Hentgen — Blue Jays

Age 25 – Pitches Right (flyball pitcher)

	ERA	W	L	Sv	G	GS	IP	BB	SO	Avg	H	2B	3B	HR	RBI	OBP	SLG	CG	ShO	Sup	QS	#P/S	SB	CS	GB	FB	G/F
1993 Season	3.87	19	9	0	34	32	216.1	74	122	.258	215	35	7	27	91	.322	.414	3	0	6.07	16	105	16	6	263	291	0.90
Career (1991-1993)	4.11	24	11	0	65	35	274.0	109	164	.256	269	48	8	35	116	.329	.417	3	0	5.88	17	102	22	6	319	377	0.85

1993 Season	ERA	W	L	Sv	G	GS	IP	H	HR	BB	SO
Home	4.77	7	6	0	18	16	111.1	116	20	38	56
Away	2.91	12	3	0	16	16	105.0	99	7	36	66
Day	4.39	8	2	0	11	10	65.2	64	9	24	37
Night	3.64	11	7	0	23	22	150.2	151	18	50	85
Grass	3.13	10	3	0	14	14	89.0	92	6	31	58
Turf	4.38	9	6	0	20	18	127.1	123	21	43	64
April	2.20	3	1	0	5	3	28.2	18	2	11	15
May	3.25	3	1	0	6	6	36.0	35	4	13	25
June	3.44	5	0	0	6	6	36.2	38	3	12	16
July	6.19	1	3	0	5	5	32.0	34	4	11	16
August	3.77	4	2	0	6	6	45.1	45	7	14	19
September/October	4.30	3	2	0	6	6	37.2	45	7	13	31
Starter	3.88	19	8	0	32	32	208.2	208	27	67	117
Reliever	3.52	0	1	0	2	0	7.2	7	0	7	5
0-3 Days Rest	0.00	1	0	0	1	1	5.0	3	0	2	3

	Avg	AB	H	2B	3B	HR	RBI	BB	SO	OBP	SLG
vs. Left	.284	426	121	20	4	11	45	33	49	.339	.427
vs. Right	.230	408	94	15	3	16	46	41	73	.304	.400
Inning 1-6	.257	708	182	29	7	25	83	55	108	.314	.424
Inning 7+	.262	126	33	6	0	2	8	19	14	.363	.357
None on	.263	472	124	24	7	17	17	46	67	.335	.451
Runners on	.251	362	91	11	0	10	74	28	55	.305	.365
Scoring Posn	.219	201	44	3	0	6	63	15	35	.270	.323
Close & Late	.258	62	16	3	0	1	2	10	8	.370	.355
None on/out	.278	212	59	10	5	10	10	19	30	.349	.514
vs. 1st Batr (relief)	.000	1	0	0	0	0	0	0	0	.000	.000
First Inning Pitched	.254	126	32	4	2	3	17	14	22	.329	.389
First 75 Pitches	.267	589	157	25	7	18	69	49	93	.327	.424
Pitch 76-90	.273	110	30	6	0	7	13	9	13	.328	.518
Pitch 91-105	.155	84	13	2	0	1	3	9	11	.234	.214
Pitch 106+	.294	51	15	2	0	1	6	7	5	.390	.392

1993 Season

	ERA	W	L	Sv	G	GS	IP	H	HR	BB	SO		Avg	AB	H	2B	3B	HR	RBI	BB	SO	OBP	SLG
4 Days Rest	4.36	12	5	0	20	20	126.0	132	19	43	76	First Pitch	.310	113	35	5	5	5	12	0	0	.325	.575
5+ Days Rest	3.36	6	3	0	11	11	77.2	73	8	22	38	Ahead in Count	.219	370	81	14	0	6	33	0	99	.227	.305
Pre-All Star	3.54	11	4	0	19	17	112.0	107	11	40	63	Behind in Count	.312	189	59	10	1	10	27	44	0	.438	.534
Post-All Star	4.23	8	5	0	15	15	104.1	108	16	34	59	Two Strikes	.211	375	79	13	1	9	33	30	122	.272	.323

Gil Heredia — Expos

Age 28 – Pitches Right (groundball pitcher)

	ERA	W	L	Sv	G	GS	IP	BB	SO	Avg	H	2B	3B	HR	RBI	OBP	SLG	GF	IR	IRS	Hld	SvOp	SB	CS	GB	FB	G/F
1993 Season	3.92	4	2	2	20	9	57.1	14	40	.293	66	9	1	4	22	.339	.396	2	8	0	1	3	7	0	115	32	3.59
Career (1991-1993)	4.00	6	7	2	47	18	135.0	41	75	.272	137	20	2	12	60	.328	.391	7	21	7	2	3	14	5	254	97	2.62

1993 Season

	ERA	W	L	Sv	G	GS	IP	H	HR	BB	SO		Avg	AB	H	2B	3B	HR	RBI	BB	SO	OBP	SLG
Home	5.85	2	1	0	8	3	20.0	30	2	7	12	vs. Left	.244	123	30	5	1	2	14	11	19	.304	.350
Away	2.89	2	1	2	12	6	37.1	36	2	7	28	vs. Right	.353	102	36	4	0	2	8	3	21	.383	.451

Carlos Hernandez — Dodgers

Age 27 – Bats Right (groundball hitter)

	Avg	G	AB	R	H	2B	3B	HR	RBI	BB	SO	HBP	GDP	SB	CS	OBP	SLG	IBB	SH	SF	#Pit	#P/PA	GB	FB	G/F
1993 Season	.253	50	99	6	25	5	0	2	7	2	11	0	0	0	0	.267	.364	0	1	0	306	3.00	48	20	2.40
Career (1990-1993)	.252	144	306	20	77	11	0	5	26	13	39	5	10	1	1	.291	.337	1	1	3	1023	3.12	127	77	1.65

1993 Season

	Avg	AB	H	2B	3B	HR	RBI	BB	SO	OBP	SLG		Avg	AB	H	2B	3B	HR	RBI	BB	SO	OBP	SLG
vs. Left	.267	30	8	1	0	1	1	1	3	.290	.400	Scoring Posn	.190	21	4	0	0	0	5	0	3	.190	.190
vs. Right	.246	69	17	4	0	1	6	1	8	.257	.348	Close & Late	.115	26	3	0	0	1	2	1	7	.148	.231

Cesar Hernandez — Reds

Age 27 – Bats Right (groundball hitter)

	Avg	G	AB	R	H	2B	3B	HR	RBI	BB	SO	HBP	GDP	SB	CS	OBP	SLG	IBB	SH	SF	#Pit	#P/PA	GB	FB	G/F
1993 Season	.083	27	24	3	2	0	0	0	1	1	8	0	0	1	2	.120	.083	0	1	0	92	3.54	9	4	2.25
Career (1992-1993)	.213	61	75	9	16	4	0	0	5	1	18	0	1	4	3	.224	.267	0	1	0	288	3.74	25	16	1.56

1993 Season

	Avg	AB	H	2B	3B	HR	RBI	BB	SO	OBP	SLG		Avg	AB	H	2B	3B	HR	RBI	BB	SO	OBP	SLG
vs. Left	.000	10	0	0	0	0	0	1	4	.091	.000	Scoring Posn	.000	4	0	0	0	0	1	0	1	.000	.000
vs. Right	.143	14	2	0	0	0	1	0	4	.143	.143	Close & Late	.200	5	1	0	0	0	1	1	2	.333	.200

Jeremy Hernandez — Indians

Age 27 – Pitches Right (groundball pitcher)

	ERA	W	L	Sv	G	GS	IP	BB	SO	Avg	H	2B	3B	HR	RBI	OBP	SLG	GF	IR	IRS	Hld	SvOp	SB	CS	GB	FB	G/F
1993 Season	3.63	6	7	8	70	0	111.2	34	70	.274	116	15	4	14	58	.324	.428	31	50	18	9	13	4	6	174	100	1.74
Career (1991-1993)	3.43	7	11	11	105	0	162.2	50	104	.268	163	20	5	18	75	.319	.406	49	67	21	13	17	7	7	259	141	1.84

1993 Season

	ERA	W	L	Sv	G	GS	IP	H	HR	BB	SO		Avg	AB	H	2B	3B	HR	RBI	BB	SO	OBP	SLG
Home	3.66	5	3	5	40	0	64.0	68	7	18	35	vs. Left	.276	192	53	7	0	8	25	20	27	.340	.438
Away	3.59	1	4	3	30	0	47.2	48	7	16	35	vs. Right	.273	231	63	8	4	6	33	14	43	.310	.420
Day	3.99	2	2	2	18	0	38.1	32	3	11	19	Inning 1-6	.190	58	11	1	1	1	5	3	14	.222	.293
Night	3.44	4	5	6	52	0	73.1	84	11	23	51	Inning 7+	.288	365	105	14	3	13	53	31	56	.340	.449
Grass	3.56	5	4	8	57	0	91.0	93	10	28	51	None on	.263	232	61	5	2	10	10	17	37	.313	.431
Turf	3.92	1	3	0	13	0	20.2	23	4	6	19	Runners on	.288	191	55	10	2	4	48	17	33	.336	.424
April	6.00	0	2	0	9	0	15.0	22	2	2	8	Scoring Posn	.343	102	35	4	2	3	45	12	15	.392	.510
May	3.72	0	0	0	12	0	19.1	19	0	5	18	Close & Late	.254	185	47	8	0	7	23	16	30	.310	.411
June	1.08	1	1	4	14	0	25.0	13	2	5	12	None on/out	.294	102	30	1	0	5	5	8	15	.345	.451
July	5.14	1	1	3	11	0	14.0	16	5	5	7	vs. 1st Batr (relief)	.354	65	23	1	1	3	14	5	12	.400	.538
August	2.82	2	0	1	12	0	22.1	23	3	4	14	First Inning Pitched	.282	238	67	8	3	8	39	22	42	.336	.441
September/October	5.06	2	3	0	12	0	16.0	23	2	13	11	First 15 Pitches	.281	217	61	6	2	8	29	15	38	.325	.438
Starter	0.00	0	0	0	0	0	0.0	0	0	0	0	Pitch 16-30	.243	152	37	6	2	4	21	16	24	.310	.388
Reliever	3.63	6	7	8	70	0	111.2	116	14	34	70	Pitch 31-45	.354	48	17	3	0	2	8	3	6	.385	.542
0 Days rest	4.18	2	1	2	16	0	23.2	24	2	4	16	Pitch 46+	.167	6	1	0	0	0	0	0	2	.167	.167
1 or 2 Days rest	3.52	1	4	6	38	0	64.0	68	8	26	40	First Pitch	.354	48	17	0	0	2	10	5	0	.407	.479
3+ Days rest	3.38	3	2	0	16	0	24.0	24	4	4	14	Ahead in Count	.209	187	39	2	1	3	18	0	59	.206	.278
Pre-All Star	3.11	1	4	6	40	0	66.2	62	5	13	42	Behind in Count	.339	112	38	8	1	6	16	15	0	.417	.589
Post-All Star	4.40	5	3	2	30	0	45.0	54	9	21	28	Two Strikes	.208	192	40	5	3	4	22	14	70	.257	.328

Roberto Hernandez — White Sox

Age 29 – Pitches Right

	ERA	W	L	Sv	G	GS	IP	BB	SO	Avg	H	2B	3B	HR	RBI	OBP	SLG	GF	IR	IRS	Hld	SvOp	SB	CS	GB	FB	G/F
1993 Season	2.29	3	4	38	70	0	78.2	20	71	.228	66	6	2	6	33	.276	.324	67	39	13	0	44	2	4	96	67	1.43
Career (1991-1993)	2.51	11	7	50	122	3	164.2	47	145	.214	129	21	2	11	69	.274	.311	95	80	29	6	60	8	8	189	156	1.21

1993 Season

	ERA	W	L	Sv	G	GS	IP	H	HR	BB	SO		Avg	AB	H	2B	3B	HR	RBI	BB	SO	OBP	SLG
Home	2.77	2	3	18	36	0	39.0	37	3	7	31	vs. Left	.231	117	27	3	0	2	13	14	33	.311	.308
Away	1.82	1	1	20	34	0	39.2	29	3	13	40	vs. Right	.225	173	39	3	2	4	20	6	38	.250	.335
Day	2.18	1	0	10	20	0	20.2	23	1	4	17	Inning 1-6	.000	0	0	0	0	0	0	0	0	.000	.000
Night	2.33	2	4	28	50	0	58.0	43	5	16	54	Inning 7+	.228	290	66	6	2	6	33	20	71	.276	.324

1993 Season

	ERA	W	L	Sv	G	GS	IP	H	HR	BB	SO
Grass	2.53	2	4	30	58	0	64.0	54	6	17	61
Turf	1.23	1	0	8	12	0	14.2	12	0	3	10
April	1.93	0	0	3	8	0	9.1	3	0	6	9
May	2.92	1	1	5	11	0	12.1	13	1	3	14
June	3.14	0	2	6	12	0	14.1	14	2	3	12
July	1.50	0	1	8	13	0	12.0	9	2	3	8
August	0.68	0	0	8	13	0	13.1	5	0	0	9
September/October	3.12	2	0	8	13	0	17.1	22	1	5	19
Starter	0.00	0	0	0	0	0	0.0	0	0	0	0
Reliever	2.29	3	4	38	70	0	78.2	66	6	20	71
0 Days rest	0.96	1	1	10	15	0	18.2	13	1	9	17
1 or 2 Days rest	2.80	2	2	23	41	0	45.0	42	4	9	39
3+ Days rest	2.40	0	1	5	14	0	15.0	11	1	2	15
Pre-All Star	2.36	1	3	17	37	0	42.0	35	3	14	39
Post-All Star	2.21	2	1	21	33	0	36.2	31	3	6	32

	Avg	AB	H	2B	3B	HR	RBI	BB	SO	OBP	SLG
None on	.210	157	33	3	1	3	3	10	40	.257	.299
Runners on	.248	133	33	3	1	3	30	10	31	.297	.353
Scoring Posn	.224	76	17	1	1	0	23	8	14	.291	.263
Close & Late	.218	174	38	2	2	5	24	16	44	.281	.339
None on/out	.172	64	11	1	0	1	1	4	19	.221	.234
vs. 1st Batr (relief)	.227	66	15	2	0	2	12	4	15	.271	.348
First Inning Pitched	.219	242	53	5	2	6	32	16	61	.265	.331
First 15 Pitches	.219	210	46	5	1	5	23	11	49	.257	.324
Pitch 16-30	.266	64	17	1	0	1	7	7	18	.338	.328
Pitch 31-45	.200	15	3	0	1	0	3	2	3	.278	.333
Pitch 46+	.000	1	0	0	0	0	0	0	1	.000	.000
First Pitch	.289	38	11	2	1	0	4	0	0	.289	.395
Ahead in Count	.155	155	24	0	0	3	12	0	68	.154	.213
Behind in Count	.326	43	14	3	0	1	5	7	0	.420	.465
Two Strikes	.163	153	25	1	1	4	15	13	71	.226	.261

Xavier Hernandez — Astros

Age 28 – Pitches Right

	ERA	W	L	Sv	G	GS	IP	BB	SO	Avg	H	2B	3B	HR	RBI	OBP	SLG	GF	IR	IRS	Hld	SvOp	SB	CS	GB	FB	G/F
1993 Season	2.61	4	5	9	72	0	96.2	28	101	.212	75	19	1	6	43	.269	.322	29	48	14	22	17	9	2	104	94	1.11
Career (1989-1993)	3.31	18	14	19	222	7	355.2	134	283	.230	307	57	4	27	154	.302	.340	72	140	40	37	34	35	11	495	338	1.46

1993 Season

	ERA	W	L	Sv	G	GS	IP	H	HR	BB	SO
Home	2.88	1	2	5	37	0	50.0	35	2	16	54
Away	2.31	3	3	4	35	0	46.2	40	4	12	47
Day	2.01	0	1	3	25	0	31.1	21	2	14	30
Night	2.89	4	4	6	47	0	65.1	54	4	14	71
Grass	2.59	2	3	3	23	0	31.1	28	4	6	31
Turf	2.62	2	2	6	49	0	65.1	47	2	22	70
April	2.19	1	0	1	9	0	12.1	12	0	5	14
May	2.95	1	1	0	14	0	18.1	12	2	5	19
June	5.14	0	1	2	13	0	14.0	13	1	5	8
July	2.00	0	0	2	13	0	18.0	15	1	3	18
August	2.37	1	2	2	13	0	19.0	14	2	4	22
September/October	1.20	1	1	2	10	0	15.0	9	0	6	20
Starter	0.00	0	0	0	0	0	0.0	0	0	0	0
Reliever	2.61	4	5	9	72	0	96.2	75	6	28	101
0 Days rest	1.69	2	0	4	23	0	32.0	19	2	6	35
1 or 2 Days rest	2.96	0	4	5	32	0	45.2	37	4	16	43
3+ Days rest	3.32	2	1	0	17	0	19.0	19	0	6	23
Pre-All Star	3.06	2	2	4	40	0	50.0	41	3	15	48
Post-All Star	2.12	2	3	5	32	0	46.2	34	3	13	53

	Avg	AB	H	2B	3B	HR	RBI	BB	SO	OBP	SLG
vs. Left	.220	168	37	7	1	6	22	17	52	.293	.381
vs. Right	.204	186	38	12	0	0	21	11	49	.247	.269
Inning 1-6	.316	19	6	1	0	0	5	1	3	.333	.368
Inning 7+	.206	335	69	18	1	6	38	27	98	.266	.319
None on	.204	196	40	9	0	4	4	11	61	.246	.311
Runners on	.222	158	35	10	1	2	39	17	40	.296	.335
Scoring Posn	.235	102	24	7	1	0	33	13	30	.319	.324
Close & Late	.243	226	55	15	1	5	32	18	62	.302	.385
None on/out	.173	81	14	3	0	1	1	5	27	.221	.247
vs. 1st Batr (relief)	.242	66	16	5	0	1	8	4	16	.278	.364
First Inning Pitched	.247	239	59	16	1	6	35	18	56	.296	.397
First 15 Pitches	.244	221	54	13	0	6	25	14	54	.286	.385
Pitch 16-30	.168	113	19	6	1	0	17	12	38	.254	.239
Pitch 31-45	.100	20	2	0	0	0	1	2	9	.182	.100
Pitch 46+	.000	0	0	0	0	0	0	0	0	.000	.000
First Pitch	.230	61	14	3	0	1	10	3	0	.258	.328
Ahead in Count	.126	167	21	7	0	0	11	0	95	.126	.168
Behind in Count	.308	78	24	6	0	3	11	16	0	.427	.500
Two Strikes	.121	165	20	4	1	0	11	9	101	.167	.158

Career (1989-1993)

	ERA	W	L	Sv	G	GS	IP	H	HR	BB	SO
Home	2.54	10	6	11	106	3	177.1	129	8	53	143
Away	4.09	8	8	8	116	4	178.1	178	19	81	140
Day	3.23	4	4	4	62	1	97.2	77	11	43	80
Night	3.35	14	10	15	160	6	258.0	230	16	91	203
Grass	3.69	6	6	6	74	2	114.2	112	14	50	93
Turf	3.14	12	8	13	148	5	241.0	195	13	84	190
April	1.65	3	1	1	27	1	43.2	32	0	18	35
May	6.32	2	5	0	40	4	68.1	73	13	25	49
June	3.23	3	2	5	40	1	75.1	71	4	33	47
July	4.41	1	1	3	33	0	49.0	47	6	15	33
August	2.17	3	2	2	35	0	49.2	36	3	16	55
September/October	1.55	6	3	8	47	1	69.2	48	1	27	64
Starter	6.00	0	6	0	7	7	36.0	37	5	25	24
Reliever	3.01	18	8	19	215	0	319.2	270	22	109	259
0 Days rest	2.62	6	1	9	55	0	75.2	57	4	28	70
1 or 2 Days rest	2.54	7	6	10	96	0	138.0	111	7	50	117
3+ Days rest	3.91	5	1	0	64	0	106.0	102	11	31	72
Pre-All Star	4.21	8	8	8	120	6	205.0	195	21	84	143
Post-All Star	2.09	10	6	11	102	1	150.2	112	6	50	140

	Avg	AB	H	2B	3B	HR	RBI	BB	SO	OBP	SLG
vs. Left	.236	658	155	25	4	13	72	89	141	.328	.345
vs. Right	.225	675	152	32	0	14	82	45	142	.276	.335
Inning 1-6	.239	440	105	20	1	11	57	53	76	.321	.364
Inning 7+	.226	893	202	37	3	16	97	81	207	.293	.328
None on	.225	723	163	32	0	13	13	64	153	.292	.324
Runners on	.236	610	144	25	4	14	141	70	130	.314	.359
Scoring Posn	.217	373	81	13	3	7	121	57	86	.317	.324
Close & Late	.236	449	106	22	2	6	52	44	111	.307	.334
None on/out	.214	304	65	15	0	5	5	28	66	.280	.313
vs. 1st Batr (relief)	.239	197	47	7	0	3	28	13	39	.279	.320
First Inning Pitched	.230	730	168	28	2	19	100	76	156	.302	.352
First 15 Pitches	.230	716	165	24	1	16	74	62	148	.293	.334
Pitch 16-30	.225	386	87	22	2	7	52	45	90	.309	.347
Pitch 31-45	.239	134	32	7	1	2	17	13	30	.311	.351
Pitch 46+	.237	97	23	4	0	2	11	14	15	.330	.340
First Pitch	.275	247	68	9	2	5	36	20	0	.333	.389
Ahead in Count	.168	595	100	22	0	8	57	0	262	.172	.245
Behind in Count	.282	298	84	14	1	10	34	75	0	.424	.436
Two Strikes	.146	560	82	15	1	5	43	39	283	.204	.204

Pitcher vs. Batter (career)

Pitches Best Vs.	Avg	AB	H	2B	3B	HR	RBI	BB	SO	OBP	SLG
Jay Bell	.083	12	1	0	0	0	0	0	4	.083	.083
Otis Nixon	.100	10	1	0	0	0	1	0	1	.091	.100
Eric Karros	.100	10	1	0	0	0	1	1	5	.182	.100
Paul O'Neill	.133	15	2	0	0	0	2	4	3	.316	.133
Bip Roberts	.133	15	2	0	0	0	0	1	5	.188	.133

Pitches Worst Vs.	Avg	AB	H	2B	3B	HR	RBI	BB	SO	OBP	SLG
Jeff Blauser	.538	13	7	1	0	0	5	1	2	.571	.615
Tony Gwynn	.455	11	5	1	0	0	1	1	1	.500	.545
Matt D. Williams	.385	13	5	2	0	1	6	0	2	.385	.769
Will Clark	.364	11	4	0	0	0	1	3	0	.500	.364
Robby Thompson	.308	13	4	2	0	0	4	1	1	.357	.462

Orel Hershiser — Dodgers

Age 35 – Pitches Right (groundball pitcher)

	ERA	W	L	Sv	G	GS	IP	BB	SO	Avg	H	2B	3B	HR	RBI	OBP	SLG	CG	ShO	Sup	QS	#P/S	SB	CS	GB	FB	G/F
1993 Season	3.59	12	14	0	33	33	215.2	72	141	.246	201	42	6	17	95	.311	.375	5	1	5.05	21	93	10	10	366	176	2.08
Last Five Years	3.21	45	47	0	126	124	820.1	254	538	.249	774	147	13	45	289	.310	.349	14	5	4.26	81	93	45	28	1408	673	2.09

1993 Season

	ERA	W	L	Sv	G	GS	IP	H	HR	BB	SO
Home	3.17	4	8	0	16	16	99.1	88	7	38	70
Away	3.95	8	6	0	17	17	116.1	113	10	34	71
Day	4.23	5	7	0	12	12	78.2	77	5	29	53
Night	3.22	7	7	0	21	21	137.0	124	12	43	88
Grass	3.13	12	10	0	27	27	181.1	153	13	56	121
Turf	6.03	0	4	0	6	6	34.1	48	4	16	20
April	2.70	3	2	0	5	5	36.2	30	1	12	20
May	5.06	2	2	0	5	5	26.2	25	2	11	25
June	3.92	1	3	0	6	6	41.1	44	4	17	27
July	2.57	2	2	0	5	5	35.0	34	1	11	17
August	4.50	2	3	0	6	6	38.0	35	6	11	27
September/October	3.08	2	2	0	6	6	38.0	33	3	10	25
Starter	3.59	12	14	0	33	33	215.2	201	17	72	141
Reliever	0.00	0	0	0	0	0	0.0	0	0	0	0
0-3 Days Rest	2.00	1	0	0	1	1	9.0	9	0	0	5
4 Days Rest	2.88	5	6	0	13	13	84.1	65	2	28	49
5+ Days Rest	4.19	6	8	0	19	19	122.1	127	15	44	87
Pre-All Star	3.56	7	8	0	18	18	118.2	116	7	44	79
Post-All Star	3.62	5	6	0	15	15	97.0	85	10	28	62

	Avg	AB	H	2B	3B	HR	RBI	BB	SO	OBP	SLG
vs. Left	.242	434	105	25	4	5	44	51	68	.320	.353
vs. Right	.251	383	96	17	2	12	51	21	73	.300	.399
Inning 1-6	.247	677	167	33	6	14	82	55	118	.308	.375
Inning 7+	.243	140	34	9	0	3	13	17	23	.327	.371
None on	.217	502	109	24	1	13	13	32	89	.271	.347
Runners on	.292	315	92	18	5	4	82	40	52	.371	.419
Scoring Posn	.296	206	61	14	4	3	76	34	34	.394	.447
Close & Late	.219	73	16	6	0	1	8	13	15	.345	.342
None on/out	.236	216	51	8	1	7	7	14	34	.289	.380
vs. 1st Batr (relief)	.000	0	0	0	0	0	0	0	0	.000	.000
First Inning Pitched	.279	136	38	9	1	1	21	11	23	.347	.382
First 75 Pitches	.241	630	152	29	6	13	68	47	106	.299	.368
Pitch 76-90	.233	90	21	6	0	2	13	10	16	.310	.367
Pitch 91-105	.269	67	18	1	0	2	7	8	15	.355	.373
Pitch 106+	.333	30	10	6	0	0	7	7	4	.447	.533
First Pitch	.286	154	44	15	2	3	24	10	0	.327	.468
Ahead in Count	.194	350	68	7	2	5	28	0	123	.208	.269
Behind in Count	.323	186	60	15	2	7	31	35	0	.429	.538
Two Strikes	.159	320	51	7	1	3	20	27	141	.233	.216

Last Five Years

	ERA	W	L	Sv	G	GS	IP	H	HR	BB	SO
Home	2.98	24	24	0	65	65	426.0	393	21	128	260
Away	3.47	21	23	0	61	59	394.1	381	24	126	278
Day	3.38	17	17	0	42	41	282.1	279	13	79	177
Night	3.13	28	30	0	84	83	538.0	495	32	175	361
Grass	3.14	39	35	0	99	98	649.2	601	36	193	423
Turf	3.48	6	12	0	27	26	170.2	173	9	61	115
April	3.15	9	7	0	19	19	131.1	111	4	39	87
May	3.75	8	6	0	17	17	105.2	95	6	38	77
June	2.90	7	9	0	23	22	155.0	149	11	54	108
July	3.63	7	7	0	22	21	134.0	145	5	43	69
August	3.50	8	7	0	23	23	149.1	140	11	39	94
September/October	2.54	6	11	0	22	22	145.0	134	8	41	103
Starter	3.24	45	47	0	124	124	811.1	768	45	251	526
Reliever	1.00	0	0	0	2	0	9.0	6	0	3	12
0-3 Days Rest	2.08	2	0	0	2	2	17.1	15	0	3	9
4 Days Rest	2.88	24	22	0	65	65	432.0	400	16	115	268
5+ Days Rest	3.73	19	25	0	57	57	362.0	353	29	133	249
Pre-All Star	3.26	27	25	0	67	65	439.0	420	22	143	301
Post-All Star	3.16	18	22	0	59	59	381.1	354	23	111	237

	Avg	AB	H	2B	3B	HR	RBI	BB	SO	OBP	SLG
vs. Left	.262	1669	438	79	11	24	155	177	245	.334	.366
vs. Right	.234	1435	336	68	2	21	134	77	293	.280	.328
Inning 1-6	.251	2645	664	124	12	39	259	198	467	.307	.351
Inning 7+	.240	459	110	23	1	6	30	56	71	.326	.333
None on	.244	1817	443	83	7	32	32	115	307	.294	.350
Runners on	.257	1287	331	64	6	13	257	139	231	.330	.347
Scoring Posn	.241	755	182	38	4	8	233	112	162	.339	.334
Close & Late	.229	266	61	14	0	4	22	40	46	.334	.327
None on/out	.261	811	212	36	4	16	16	47	132	.306	.375
vs. 1st Batr (relief)	.000	2	0	0	0	0	0	0	0	.000	.000
First Inning Pitched	.282	504	142	29	1	5	59	37	76	.338	.373
First 75 Pitches	.250	2439	610	111	12	36	220	173	423	.304	.350
Pitch 76-90	.235	361	85	21	0	5	41	38	67	.308	.335
Pitch 91-105	.255	188	48	3	0	3	15	21	32	.332	.319
Pitch 106+	.267	116	31	12	1	1	13	22	16	.386	.414
First Pitch	.288	542	156	32	2	13	67	37	0	.337	.426
Ahead in Count	.200	1332	266	49	5	12	89	0	472	.208	.271
Behind in Count	.312	693	216	42	4	18	98	128	0	.418	.462
Two Strikes	.165	1257	208	39	3	7	66	89	538	.226	.218

Pitcher vs. Batter (since 1984)

Pitches Best Vs.	Avg	AB	H	2B	3B	HR	RBI	BB	SO	OBP	SLG
Spike Owen	.000	13	0	0	0	0	0	2	2	.133	.000
Junior Ortiz	.000	11	0	0	0	0	1	0	0	.000	.000
Randy Ready	.000	11	0	0	0	0	0	1	1	.083	.000
Darren Lewis	.105	19	2	0	0	0	2	1	1	.150	.105
Damon Berryhill	.107	28	3	0	0	0	3	1	4	.138	.107

Pitches Worst Vs.	Avg	AB	H	2B	3B	HR	RBI	BB	SO	OBP	SLG
Jose Vizcaino	.455	11	5	1	1	0	0	1	1	.500	.727
Steve Finley	.400	25	10	0	1	1	1	5	2	.500	.600
Kurt Stillwell	.391	23	9	3	1	0	2	3	2	.462	.609
Orestes Destrade	.364	11	4	2	0	1	3	0	4	.364	.818
Deion Sanders	.348	23	8	1	1	2	3	1	3	.375	.739

Joe Hesketh — Red Sox

Age 35 – Pitches Left (groundball pitcher)

	ERA	W	L	Sv	G	GS	IP	BB	SO	Avg	H	2B	3B	HR	RBI	OBP	SLG	GF	IR	IRS	Hld	SvOp	SB	CS	GB	FB	G/F
1993 Season	5.06	3	4	1	28	5	53.1	29	34	.294	62	15	0	4	33	.376	.422	8	17	8	0	1	4	2	90	52	1.73
Last Five Years	4.25	30	27	10	185	49	463.1	191	336	.273	489	110	8	50	228	.341	.426	33	107	43	10	15	35	17	675	440	1.53

1993 Season

	ERA	W	L	Sv	G	GS	IP	H	HR	BB	SO
Home	2.17	2	1	1	12	2	29.0	27	0	15	18
Away	8.51	1	3	0	16	3	24.1	35	4	14	16
Starter	8.44	1	3	0	5	5	21.1	29	2	15	13
Reliever	2.81	2	1	1	23	0	32.0	33	2	14	21
0 Days rest	13.50	0	0	0	2	0	0.2	4	1	0	0
1 or 2 Days rest	0.96	0	0	1	6	0	9.1	5	1	3	6
3+ Days rest	3.27	2	1	0	15	0	22.0	24	0	11	15
Pre-All Star	6.53	3	4	0	20	5	40.0	52	3	24	28
Post-All Star	0.68	0	0	1	8	0	13.1	10	1	5	6

	Avg	AB	H	2B	3B	HR	RBI	BB	SO	OBP	SLG
vs. Left	.203	69	14	3	0	1	8	6	13	.263	.290
vs. Right	.338	142	48	12	0	3	25	23	21	.428	.486
Scoring Posn	.319	69	22	4	0	1	29	11	15	.402	.420
Close & Late	.250	4	1	0	0	0	0	2	1	.500	.250
None on/out	.326	46	15	4	0	1	1	8	6	.426	.478
First Pitch	.467	30	14	4	0	1	8	2	0	.500	.700
Ahead in Count	.237	97	23	3	0	0	11	0	28	.237	.268
Behind in Count	.435	46	20	6	0	3	12	15	0	.565	.761
Two Strikes	.189	90	17	3	0	0	8	12	34	.284	.222

Last Five Years

	ERA	W	L	Sv	G	GS	IP	H	HR	BB	SO
Home	3.79	15	12	5	93	22	228.0	245	21	103	173
Away	4.70	15	15	5	92	27	235.1	244	29	88	163
Day	3.36	14	9	1	66	19	190.1	186	18	72	130
Night	4.88	16	18	9	119	30	273.0	303	32	119	206

	Avg	AB	H	2B	3B	HR	RBI	BB	SO	OBP	SLG
vs. Left	.250	384	96	19	1	10	55	42	84	.324	.383
vs. Right	.279	1410	393	91	7	40	173	149	252	.346	.438
Inning 1-6	.278	1227	341	76	6	39	155	116	225	.338	.445
Inning 7+	.261	567	148	34	2	11	73	75	111	.347	.386

Last Five Years

	ERA	W	L	Sv	G	GS	IP	H	HR	BB	SO		Avg	AB	H	2B	3B	HR	RBI	BB	SO	OBP	SLG
Grass	3.97	20	19	5	119	39	342.1	361	33	144	242	None on	.284	985	280	67	4	30	30	93	168	.348	.452
Turf	5.06	10	8	5	66	10	121.0	128	17	47	94	Runners on	.258	809	209	43	4	20	198	98	168	.333	.396
April	4.44	6	1	1	26	6	52.2	53	2	31	32	Scoring Posn	.252	477	120	23	1	13	174	74	110	.343	.386
May	4.96	5	7	2	38	7	89.0	95	7	41	68	Close & Late	.245	184	45	9	1	6	28	27	34	.344	.402
June	5.19	2	4	4	39	7	76.1	81	13	36	61	None on/out	.281	445	125	31	3	15	15	38	77	.339	.465
July	4.29	5	7	1	32	9	79.2	94	11	24	53	vs. 1st Batr (relief)	.235	119	28	8	0	3	25	12	24	.303	.378
August	4.20	6	4	1	27	10	81.1	91	11	27	56	First Inning Pitched	.260	599	156	32	0	13	91	69	120	.334	.379
September/October	2.56	6	4	1	23	10	84.1	75	6	32	66	First 15 Pitches	.276	558	154	33	1	15	78	62	93	.347	.419
Starter	4.14	18	18	0	49	49	280.1	301	29	95	196	Pitch 16-30	.255	373	95	20	0	10	40	34	91	.318	.389
Reliever	4.43	12	9	10	136	0	183.0	188	21	96	140	Pitch 31-45	.270	248	67	18	1	8	33	28	50	.342	.448
0 Days rest	5.25	1	1	2	25	0	24.0	28	2	12	20	Pitch 46+	.281	615	173	39	6	17	77	67	102	.350	.447
1 or 2 Days rest	4.95	4	4	6	47	0	60.0	60	6	36	47	First Pitch	.313	256	80	14	2	8	45	15	0	.347	.477
3+ Days rest	3.91	7	4	2	64	0	99.0	100	13	48	73	Ahead in Count	.205	795	163	37	2	10	80	0	282	.206	.294
Pre-All Star	4.95	15	15	7	113	22	240.0	253	26	120	174	Behind in Count	.386	409	158	41	3	22	77	98	0	.499	.663
Post-All Star	3.51	16	12	3	72	27	223.1	236	24	71	162	Two Strikes	.178	774	138	30	2	10	51	70	330	.253	.265

Pitcher vs. Batter (career)

Pitches Best Vs.	Avg	AB	H	2B	3B	HR	RBI	BB	SO	OBP	SLG	Pitches Worst Vs.	Avg	AB	H	2B	3B	HR	RBI	BB	SO	OBP	SLG
Rob Deer	.000	10	0	0	0	0	0	3	4	.231	.000	Kevin Mitchell	.600	15	9	2	0	1	3	2	2	.647	.933
Lance Parrish	.083	12	1	0	0	0	0	1	4	.154	.083	Shane Mack	.571	14	8	1	0	2	5	2	1	.625	1.071
Chris James	.091	11	1	0	0	0	0	0	2	.091	.091	Frank Thomas	.556	9	5	2	0	2	4	5	3	.714	1.444
Henry Cotto	.111	18	2	1	0	0	0	0	3	.111	.167	Kent Hrbek	.455	11	5	2	0	1	5	2	3	.500	.909
Don Mattingly	.118	17	2	0	0	0	4	1	3	.150	.118	Travis Fryman	.364	11	4	0	1	2	4	1	4	.417	1.091

Phil Hiatt — Royals

Age 25 – Bats Right (flyball hitter)

	Avg	G	AB	R	H	2B	3B	HR	RBI	BB	SO	HBP	GDP	SB	CS	OBP	SLG	IBB	SH	SF	#Pit	#P/PA	GB	FB	G/F
1993 Season	.218	81	238	30	52	12	1	7	36	16	82	7	8	6	3	.285	.366	0	0	2	1000	3.80	62	64	0.97

1993 Season

	Avg	AB	H	2B	3B	HR	RBI	BB	SO	OBP	SLG		Avg	AB	H	2B	3B	HR	RBI	BB	SO	OBP	SLG
vs. Left	.250	80	20	5	0	2	12	7	28	.307	.388	Scoring Posn	.209	67	14	5	0	2	24	6	24	.276	.373
vs. Right	.203	158	32	7	1	5	24	9	54	.274	.354	Close & Late	.216	37	8	0	0	3	9	8	16	.362	.459
Home	.260	127	33	8	0	4	21	6	43	.304	.417	None on/out	.196	51	10	0	0	1	1	1	13	.226	.255
Away	.171	111	19	4	1	3	15	10	39	.264	.306	Batting #7	.216	139	30	8	1	5	22	10	46	.290	.396
First Pitch	.200	35	7	0	1	2	6	0	0	.216	.429	Batting #8	.213	94	20	4	0	2	14	3	35	.250	.319
Ahead in Count	.405	42	17	4	0	1	9	9	0	.510	.571	Other	.400	5	2	0	0	0	0	3	1	.625	.400
Behind in Count	.153	124	19	5	0	2	12	0	70	.192	.242	Pre-All Star	.224	205	46	12	1	7	34	13	68	.288	.395
Two Strikes	.104	135	14	4	0	1	10	7	82	.159	.156	Post-All Star	.182	33	6	0	0	0	2	3	14	.270	.182

Greg Hibbard — Cubs

Age 29 – Pitches Left (groundball pitcher)

	ERA	W	L	Sv	G	GS	IP	BB	SO	Avg	H	2B	3B	HR	RBI	OBP	SLG	CG	ShO	Sup	QS	#P/S	SB	CS	GB	FB	G/F
1993 Season	3.96	15	11	0	31	31	191.0	47	82	.286	209	54	3	19	84	.327	.446	1	0	4.76	16	84	2	10	348	160	2.18
Career (1989-1993)	3.82	56	45	1	150	144	909.1	257	369	.270	936	166	21	75	370	.321	.395	11	1	4.34	72	89	37	38	1585	847	1.87

1993 Season

	ERA	W	L	Sv	G	GS	IP	H	HR	BB	SO		Avg	AB	H	2B	3B	HR	RBI	BB	SO	OBP	SLG
Home	4.24	7	6	0	17	17	102.0	104	12	25	40	vs. Left	.274	117	32	4	0	5	18	10	17	.338	.436
Away	3.64	8	5	0	14	14	89.0	105	7	22	42	vs. Right	.288	614	177	50	3	14	66	37	65	.325	.448
Day	4.78	5	7	0	16	16	92.1	102	13	22	38	Inning 1-6	.289	643	186	49	3	18	78	38	73	.327	.459
Night	3.19	10	4	0	15	15	98.2	107	6	25	44	Inning 7+	.261	88	23	5	0	1	6	9	9	.330	.352
Grass	4.27	11	8	0	24	24	141.1	157	15	31	61	None on	.292	438	128	30	2	10	10	27	52	.338	.438
Turf	3.08	4	3	0	7	7	49.2	52	4	16	21	Runners on	.276	293	81	24	1	9	74	20	30	.313	.457
April	5.83	1	2	0	5	5	29.1	32	8	9	7	Scoring Posn	.303	152	46	15	0	4	61	17	19	.352	.480
May	2.52	4	1	0	5	5	35.2	30	0	5	15	Close & Late	.205	39	8	2	0	1	3	3	4	.262	.333
June	2.70	2	1	0	3	3	16.2	15	0	4	5	None on/out	.335	194	65	18	2	4	4	9	19	.374	.510
July	4.55	1	3	0	6	6	29.2	37	3	10	18	vs. 1st Batr (relief)	.000	0	0	0	0	0	0	0	0	.000	.000
August	3.38	2	4	0	6	6	40.0	39	2	10	14	First Inning Pitched	.236	110	26	5	0	3	11	9	13	.295	.364
September/October	4.54	5	0	0	6	6	39.2	56	6	9	23	First 75 Pitches	.294	616	181	46	3	17	74	38	68	.333	.461
Starter	3.96	15	11	0	31	31	191.0	209	19	47	82	Pitch 76-90	.221	77	17	5	0	1	3	5	7	.268	.325
Reliever	0.00	0	0	0	0	0	0.0	0	0	0	0	Pitch 91-105	.276	29	8	2	0	0	3	3	6	.344	.345
0-3 Days Rest	0.00	0	1	0	1	1	6.0	3	1	3	2	Pitch 106+	.333	9	3	1	0	1	4	1	1	.400	.778
4 Days Rest	3.38	11	6	0	19	19	122.1	133	12	33	46	First Pitch	.273	139	38	12	0	3	21	7	0	.306	.424
5+ Days Rest	5.46	4	4	0	11	11	62.2	73	6	11	34	Ahead in Count	.242	265	64	17	0	7	26	0	76	.241	.385
Pre-All Star	3.99	7	6	0	16	16	97.0	98	11	22	35	Behind in Count	.311	190	59	14	1	7	23	28	0	.397	.505
Post-All Star	3.93	8	5	0	15	15	94.0	111	8	25	47	Two Strikes	.215	260	56	18	0	5	22	12	82	.248	.342

Career (1989-1993)

	ERA	W	L	Sv	G	GS	IP	H	HR	BB	SO		Avg	AB	H	2B	3B	HR	RBI	BB	SO	OBP	SLG
Home	3.41	30	22	1	77	75	480.1	453	40	139	186	vs. Left	.252	481	121	17	1	11	59	36	63	.312	.360
Away	4.28	26	23	0	73	69	429.0	483	35	118	183	vs. Right	.273	2983	815	149	20	64	311	221	306	.323	.401
Day	4.56	16	14	0	45	45	268.1	274	32	72	119	Inning 1-6	.272	2989	814	149	21	66	345	222	322	.323	.402
Night	3.51	40	31	1	105	99	641.0	662	43	185	250	Inning 7+	.257	475	122	17	0	9	25	35	47	.314	.349
Grass	3.70	47	35	1	124	119	757.1	760	62	210	306	None on	.262	2089	548	87	10	44	44	154	232	.317	.377
Turf	4.44	9	10	0	26	25	152.0	176	13	47	63	Runners on	.282	1375	388	79	11	31	326	103	137	.329	.423
April	3.32	9	3	0	16	16	105.2	91	12	35	38	Scoring Posn	.286	713	204	51	8	14	278	68	73	.340	.439
May	3.62	8	9	0	25	24	159.1	156	13	45	63	Close & Late	.253	289	73	13	0	5	16	21	29	.311	.349

Career (1989-1993)

	ERA	W	L	Sv	G	GS	IP	H	HR	BB	SO
June	3.87	8	8	0	25	25	155.2	171	17	35	57
July	4.46	7	7	0	27	27	151.1	158	15	48	74
August	3.71	10	13	1	28	27	169.2	171	7	52	61
September/October	3.81	14	5	0	29	25	167.2	189	11	42	76
Starter	3.88	55	45	0	144	144	892.2	924	75	256	360
Reliever	0.54	1	0	1	6	0	16.2	12	0	1	9
0-3 Days Rest	1.51	2	2	0	6	6	41.2	32	2	12	20
4 Days Rest	3.96	35	21	0	82	82	520.2	537	50	156	205
5+ Days Rest	4.06	18	22	0	56	56	330.1	355	23	88	135
Pre-All Star	3.62	27	24	0	76	75	480.1	477	47	131	187
Post-All Star	4.05	29	21	1	74	69	429.0	459	28	126	182

	Avg	AB	H	2B	3B	HR	RBI	BB	SO	OBP	SLG
None on/out	.259	926	240	43	7	20	20	58	89	.306	.386
vs. 1st Batr (relief)	.000	6	0	0	0	0	0	0	0	.000	.000
First Inning Pitched	.229	547	125	18	2	11	52	47	76	.293	.329
First 75 Pitches	.273	2769	756	132	18	60	306	201	289	.322	.399
Pitch 76-90	.258	411	106	18	2	9	32	28	48	.309	.377
Pitch 91-105	.261	203	53	13	1	4	21	21	26	.333	.394
Pitch 106+	.259	81	21	3	0	2	11	7	6	.333	.370
First Pitch	.286	583	167	26	3	9	66	10	0	.301	.388
Ahead in Count	.217	1342	291	39	8	23	116	0	319	.220	.309
Behind in Count	.326	896	292	62	5	32	119	159	0	.427	.513
Two Strikes	.205	1285	264	44	8	18	95	88	369	.260	.294

Pitcher vs. Batter (career)

Pitches Best Vs.	Avg	AB	H	2B	3B	HR	RBI	BB	SO	OBP	SLG
Randy Velarde	.063	16	1	1	0	0	2	0	2	.063	.125
Gary Gaetti	.077	26	2	0	0	0	0	1	1	.111	.077
Ken Griffey Jr	.077	13	1	0	0	0	1	0	2	.071	.077
Pete O'Brien	.083	12	1	0	0	0	0	0	1	.083	.083
Luis Sojo	.091	11	1	0	0	0	1	0	1	.091	.091

Pitches Worst Vs.	Avg	AB	H	2B	3B	HR	RBI	BB	SO	OBP	SLG
Carlos Baerga	.500	22	11	0	0	2	7	2	2	.500	.773
Lance Parrish	.500	18	9	0	0	2	3	2	1	.550	.833
Mickey Tettleton	.500	16	8	3	0	2	4	1	3	.529	1.063
Steve Balboni	.357	14	5	2	0	2	5	1	2	.400	.929
Mike Macfarlane	.333	9	3	0	0	2	3	2	0	.455	1.000

Bryan Hickerson — Giants

Age 30 – Pitches Left

	ERA	W	L	Sv	G	GS	IP	BB	SO	Avg	H	2B	3B	HR	RBI	OBP	SLG	GF	IR	IRS	Hld	SvOp	SB	CS	GB	FB	G/F
1993 Season	4.26	7	5	0	47	15	120.1	39	69	.291	137	21	1	14	51	.344	.430	5	11	4	6	0	4	6	163	146	1.12
Career (1991-1993)	3.74	14	10	0	125	22	257.2	77	180	.270	264	51	2	24	102	.322	.400	17	56	15	15	5	11	16	312	300	1.04

1993 Season

	ERA	W	L	Sv	G	GS	IP	H	HR	BB	SO
Home	4.00	4	3	0	23	8	63.0	63	7	15	40
Away	4.55	3	2	0	24	7	57.1	74	7	24	29
Starter	4.63	7	3	0	15	15	79.2	94	12	24	49
Reliever	3.54	0	2	0	32	0	40.2	43	2	15	20
0 Days rest	2.45	0	1	0	2	0	3.2	5	0	2	0
1 or 2 Days rest	6.16	0	1	0	18	0	19.0	25	2	9	8
3+ Days rest	1.00	0	0	0	12	0	18.0	13	0	4	12
Pre-All Star	4.66	3	1	0	31	5	56.0	63	7	21	28
Post-All Star	3.92	4	4	0	16	10	64.1	74	7	18	41

	Avg	AB	H	2B	3B	HR	RBI	BB	SO	OBP	SLG
vs. Left	.241	108	26	1	0	1	10	6	16	.274	.278
vs. Right	.307	362	111	20	1	13	41	33	53	.365	.475
Scoring Posn	.284	102	29	6	0	1	34	9	11	.330	.373
Close & Late	.250	64	16	0	0	0	3	5	6	.300	.250
None on/out	.336	122	41	11	1	5	5	10	20	.391	.566
First Pitch	.321	84	27	3	0	4	9	3	0	.345	.500
Ahead in Count	.204	206	42	2	1	2	14	0	65	.205	.252
Behind in Count	.375	112	42	9	0	6	20	19	0	.462	.616
Two Strikes	.208	192	40	3	1	2	12	17	69	.274	.266

Career (1991-1993)

	ERA	W	L	Sv	G	GS	IP	H	HR	BB	SO
Home	3.94	7	7	0	60	11	125.2	119	13	26	96
Away	3.55	7	3	0	65	11	132.0	145	11	51	84
Day	4.16	5	6	0	51	11	114.2	114	13	33	81
Night	3.40	9	4	0	74	11	143.0	150	11	44	99
Grass	3.71	8	10	0	92	17	189.0	192	17	48	133
Turf	3.80	6	0	0	33	5	68.2	72	7	29	47
April	5.57	1	1	0	19	0	21.0	26	3	9	15
May	2.57	1	1	0	22	0	28.0	22	1	9	18
June	3.78	1	0	0	18	3	33.1	30	3	10	20
July	4.13	6	1	0	18	5	48.0	46	7	10	28
August	4.02	3	5	0	26	4	62.2	68	7	17	50
September/October	3.06	2	2	0	22	10	64.2	72	3	22	49
Starter	3.92	9	5	0	22	22	114.2	129	14	36	74
Reliever	3.59	5	5	0	103	0	143.0	135	10	41	106
0 Days rest	1.27	2	1	0	15	0	28.1	15	1	4	28
1 or 2 Days rest	4.48	3	3	0	53	0	70.1	76	4	24	45
3+ Days rest	3.65	0	1	0	35	0	44.1	44	5	13	33
Pre-All Star	3.68	6	2	0	64	5	102.2	101	10	32	66
Post-All Star	3.77	8	8	0	61	17	155.0	163	14	45	114

	Avg	AB	H	2B	3B	HR	RBI	BB	SO	OBP	SLG
vs. Left	.237	257	61	7	1	2	20	16	41	.277	.296
vs. Right	.282	720	203	44	1	22	82	61	139	.338	.438
Inning 1-6	.292	631	184	34	2	18	72	51	108	.344	.437
Inning 7+	.231	346	80	17	0	6	30	26	72	.281	.332
None on	.274	559	153	35	2	14	14	45	120	.330	.419
Runners on	.266	418	111	16	0	10	88	32	60	.312	.376
Scoring Posn	.259	224	58	11	0	4	74	19	36	.306	.362
Close & Late	.235	187	44	7	0	3	18	17	35	.293	.321
None on/out	.285	249	71	18	1	7	7	18	48	.336	.450
vs. 1st Batr (relief)	.163	92	15	2	0	1	9	5	17	.196	.217
First Inning Pitched	.266	421	112	21	1	12	55	32	79	.315	.406
First 15 Pitches	.262	409	107	21	1	11	43	29	77	.308	.399
Pitch 16-30	.295	224	66	12	0	4	24	18	45	.346	.402
Pitch 31-45	.237	131	31	6	1	2	13	15	23	.313	.344
Pitch 46+	.282	213	60	12	0	7	22	15	35	.330	.437
First Pitch	.329	161	53	9	0	6	17	7	0	.355	.497
Ahead in Count	.197	452	89	13	2	5	31	0	167	.198	.268
Behind in Count	.339	218	74	16	0	8	36	39	0	.436	.523
Two Strikes	.201	437	88	13	2	5	30	31	180	.255	.275

Pitcher vs. Batter (career)

Pitches Best Vs.	Avg	AB	H	2B	3B	HR	RBI	BB	SO	OBP	SLG
Eric Davis	.100	10	1	0	0	0	1	1	6	.182	.100
Paul O'Neill	.100	10	1	0	0	0	0	1	2	.182	.100
Ken Caminiti	.200	10	2	0	0	0	2	1	1	.250	.200
Dave Justice	.214	14	3	1	0	0	3	1	1	.267	.286
Jose Offerman	.222	9	2	0	0	0	0	2	0	.364	.222

Pitches Worst Vs.	Avg	AB	H	2B	3B	HR	RBI	BB	SO	OBP	SLG
Terry Pendleton	.692	13	9	1	0	1	3	0	0	.692	1.000
Fred McGriff	.667	9	6	2	0	0	1	1	1	.636	.889
Brett Butler	.545	11	6	1	0	0	2	2	1	.571	.636
Craig Biggio	.400	10	4	1	0	1	2	4	1	.571	.800
Ron Gant	.385	13	5	2	0	2	5	2	2	.467	1.000

Kevin Higgins — Padres

Age 27 – Bats Left (groundball hitter)

	Avg	G	AB	R	H	2B	3B	HR	RBI	BB	SO	HBP	GDP	SB	CS	OBP	SLG	IBB	SH	SF	#Pit	#P/PA	GB	FB	G/F
1993 Season	.221	71	181	17	40	4	1	0	13	16	17	3	6	0	1	.294	.254	0	1	1	740	3.66	69	44	1.57

1993 Season

	Avg	AB	H	2B	3B	HR	RBI	BB	SO	OBP	SLG
vs. Left	.250	16	4	0	0	0	2	0	2	.250	.250
vs. Right	.218	165	36	4	1	0	11	16	15	.297	.255
Home	.228	92	21	2	1	0	3	6	9	.297	.272
Away	.213	89	19	2	0	0	10	10	8	.290	.236

	Avg	AB	H	2B	3B	HR	RBI	BB	SO	OBP	SLG
Scoring Posn	.200	45	9	2	0	0	13	5	8	.302	.244
Close & Late	.256	39	10	1	0	0	3	8	4	.388	.282
None on/out	.271	48	13	1	0	0	0	2	4	.300	.292
Batting #7	.233	86	20	2	0	0	5	6	7	.295	.256

1993 Season

	Avg	AB	H	2B	3B	HR	RBI	BB	SO	OBP	SLG
First Pitch	.211	19	4	1	0	0	1	0	0	.211	.263
Ahead in Count	.229	48	11	0	1	0	4	10	0	.377	.271
Behind in Count	.191	89	17	3	0	0	7	0	16	.200	.225
Two Strikes	.176	74	13	2	0	0	2	6	17	.238	.203

	Avg	AB	H	2B	3B	HR	RBI	BB	SO	OBP	SLG
Batting #8	.243	74	18	2	1	0	6	7	9	.309	.297
Other	.095	21	2	0	0	0	2	3	1	.240	.095
Pre-All Star	.245	94	23	1	0	0	7	10	7	.321	.255
Post-All Star	.195	87	17	3	1	0	6	6	10	.263	.253

Teddy Higuera — Brewers

Age 35 – Pitches Left (flyball pitcher)

	ERA	W	L	Sv	G	GS	IP	BB	SO	Avg	H	2B	3B	HR	RBI	OBP	SLG	CG	ShO	Sup	QS	#P/S	SB	CS	GB	FB	G/F
1993 Season	7.20	1	3	0	8	8	30.0	16	27	.333	43	16	2	4	23	.408	.581	0	0	6.60	0	68	3	1	31	41	0.76
Last Five Years	4.00	24	21	0	64	63	371.2	124	280	.261	372	74	4	31	162	.321	.383	6	2	4.82	28	90	41	10	381	466	0.82

1993 Season

	ERA	W	L	Sv	G	GS	IP	H	HR	BB	SO
Home	4.67	1	2	0	5	5	17.1	20	2	10	15
Away	10.66	0	1	0	3	3	12.2	23	2	6	12

	Avg	AB	H	2B	3B	HR	RBI	BB	SO	OBP	SLG
vs. Left	.154	13	2	1	0	0	1	1	5	.200	.231
vs. Right	.353	116	41	15	2	4	22	15	22	.432	.621

Last Five Years

	ERA	W	L	Sv	G	GS	IP	H	HR	BB	SO
Home	3.41	17	9	0	37	36	216.1	192	22	69	171
Away	4.81	7	12	0	27	27	155.1	180	9	55	109
Day	3.09	5	6	0	17	17	105.0	94	4	35	87
Night	4.35	19	15	0	47	46	266.2	278	27	89	193
Grass	3.81	21	17	0	54	53	314.0	310	27	102	236
Turf	4.99	3	4	0	10	10	57.2	62	4	22	44
April	0.00	2	0	0	3	3	20.1	9	0	9	16
May	4.93	2	3	0	9	8	45.2	49	4	18	30
June	3.12	6	3	0	16	16	86.2	74	3	29	69
July	3.97	5	5	0	11	11	70.1	73	6	16	54
August	3.46	5	3	0	12	12	75.1	67	8	24	51
September/October	6.14	4	7	0	13	13	73.1	100	10	28	60
Starter	3.97	24	21	0	63	63	369.2	368	30	124	277
Reliever	9.00	0	0	0	1	0	2.0	4	1	0	3
0-3 Days Rest	0.00	0	0	0	0	0	0.0	0	0	0	0
4 Days Rest	3.17	15	10	0	32	32	210.1	193	14	58	167
5+ Days Rest	5.03	9	11	0	31	31	159.1	175	16	66	110
Pre-All Star	3.30	12	7	0	31	30	174.1	150	9	61	134
Post-All Star	4.61	12	14	0	33	33	197.1	222	22	63	146

	Avg	AB	H	2B	3B	HR	RBI	BB	SO	OBP	SLG
vs. Left	.231	260	60	8	1	3	26	13	52	.268	.304
vs. Right	.267	1167	312	66	3	28	136	111	228	.333	.401
Inning 1-6	.260	1263	328	66	4	24	147	109	248	.321	.375
Inning 7+	.268	164	44	8	0	7	15	15	32	.328	.445
None on	.240	821	197	38	3	18	18	72	181	.307	.359
Runners on	.289	606	175	36	1	13	144	52	99	.341	.416
Scoring Posn	.267	333	89	17	1	2	113	35	65	.329	.342
Close & Late	.248	101	25	5	0	1	6	9	21	.304	.327
None on/out	.252	361	91	18	1	9	9	34	75	.320	.382
vs. 1st Batr (relief)	1.000	1	1	1	0	0	0	0	0	1.000	2.000
First Inning Pitched	.259	247	64	10	2	4	31	25	44	.328	.364
First 75 Pitches	.250	1101	275	59	4	19	106	93	219	.310	.362
Pitch 76-90	.346	179	62	12	0	5	39	14	33	.389	.497
Pitch 91-105	.237	97	23	1	0	5	12	13	16	.342	.402
Pitch 106+	.240	50	12	2	0	2	5	4	12	.291	.400
First Pitch	.274	237	65	14	1	5	32	4	0	.294	.405
Ahead in Count	.222	648	144	24	2	11	64	0	222	.223	.316
Behind in Count	.364	272	99	27	1	9	42	64	0	.484	.570
Two Strikes	.192	639	123	18	2	9	57	56	280	.257	.269

Pitcher vs. Batter (career)

Pitches Best Vs.	Avg	AB	H	2B	3B	HR	RBI	BB	SO	OBP	SLG
Luis Polonia	.000	10	0	0	0	0	0	1	3	.091	.000
Ruben Sierra	.059	17	1	0	0	0	0	0	2	.059	.059
Dave Valle	.074	27	2	1	0	0	1	4	5	.188	.111
Brady Anderson	.100	10	1	0	0	0	0	1	2	.182	.100
Willie Wilson	.118	34	4	1	0	0	0	1	3	.143	.147

Pitches Worst Vs.	Avg	AB	H	2B	3B	HR	RBI	BB	SO	OBP	SLG
Alvaro Espinoza	.550	20	11	0	0	0	1	1	2	.571	.550
Todd Benzinger	.500	16	8	3	0	0	6	2	2	.526	.688
Ivan Calderon	.391	23	9	3	1	1	7	3	5	.462	.739
Mark McGwire	.333	18	6	1	1	2	6	2	5	.400	.833
Cecil Fielder	.323	31	10	3	0	4	8	1	11	.344	.806

Glenallen Hill — Cubs

Age 29 – Bats Right

	Avg	G	AB	R	H	2B	3B	HR	RBI	BB	SO	HBP	GDP	SB	CS	OBP	SLG	IBB	SH	SF	#Pit	#P/PA	GB	FB	G/F
1993 Season	.264	97	261	33	69	14	2	15	47	17	71	1	4	8	3	.307	.506	1	1	4	977	3.44	77	74	1.04
Career (1989-1993)	.249	374	1163	151	290	49	8	54	160	81	272	5	27	33	17	.299	.445	1	2	8	4394	3.49	369	357	1.03

1993 Season

	Avg	AB	H	2B	3B	HR	RBI	BB	SO	OBP	SLG
vs. Left	.275	153	42	6	1	12	33	11	36	.317	.562
vs. Right	.250	108	27	8	1	3	14	6	35	.293	.426
Home	.229	96	22	5	1	5	20	6	27	.279	.458
Away	.285	165	47	9	1	10	27	11	44	.324	.533
First Pitch	.367	60	22	2	0	3	10	1	0	.377	.550
Ahead in Count	.395	38	15	3	1	3	13	9	0	.480	.763
Behind in Count	.188	128	24	8	1	8	20	0	62	.192	.453
Two Strikes	.178	129	23	7	0	7	17	7	71	.221	.395

	Avg	AB	H	2B	3B	HR	RBI	BB	SO	OBP	SLG
Scoring Posn	.288	73	21	2	1	3	30	7	19	.333	.466
Close & Late	.286	35	10	2	0	2	7	3	13	.350	.514
None on/out	.238	63	15	4	1	4	4	1	18	.262	.524
Batting #6	.229	83	19	2	0	5	16	7	25	.290	.434
Batting #7	.265	68	18	4	2	3	11	4	15	.306	.515
Other	.291	110	32	8	0	7	20	6	31	.322	.555
Pre-All Star	.239	134	32	6	2	5	17	7	33	.273	.425
Post-All Star	.291	127	37	8	0	10	30	10	38	.343	.591

Career (1989-1993)

	Avg	AB	H	2B	3B	HR	RBI	BB	SO	OBP	SLG
vs. Left	.259	528	137	25	5	29	80	42	111	.314	.491
vs. Right	.241	635	153	24	3	25	80	39	161	.287	.406
Groundball	.314	283	89	19	1	11	46	27	57	.375	.505
Flyball	.189	249	47	7	1	13	35	17	75	.242	.382
Home	.254	543	138	28	2	23	74	37	113	.305	.440
Away	.245	620	152	21	6	31	86	44	159	.294	.448
Day	.233	377	88	21	1	15	48	23	96	.280	.414
Night	.257	786	202	28	7	39	112	58	176	.308	.459
Grass	.252	798	201	30	6	36	113	52	190	.299	.440
Turf	.244	365	89	19	2	18	47	29	82	.299	.455
First Pitch	.354	226	80	12	1	8	29	1	0	.362	.522
Ahead in Count	.332	226	75	10	1	14	43	38	0	.420	.571
Behind in Count	.158	525	83	17	4	20	58	0	228	.162	.320

	Avg	AB	H	2B	3B	HR	RBI	BB	SO	OBP	SLG
Scoring Posn	.267	277	74	11	3	10	104	28	68	.326	.437
Close & Late	.219	196	43	5	0	9	21	12	58	.274	.383
None on/out	.251	291	73	14	3	16	16	18	68	.304	.485
Batting #6	.224	312	70	12	3	14	43	22	78	.277	.417
Batting #7	.249	253	63	8	3	13	38	20	58	.307	.458
Other	.263	598	157	29	2	27	79	39	136	.307	.453
April	.283	173	49	10	1	4	18	8	39	.312	.422
May	.148	155	23	5	2	5	16	8	44	.190	.303
June	.284	169	48	9	2	9	26	13	26	.342	.521
July	.276	199	55	7	0	11	29	17	43	.336	.477
August	.219	269	59	11	3	10	34	25	67	.285	.394
September/October	.283	198	56	7	0	15	37	10	53	.316	.545
Pre-All Star	.248	560	139	26	5	24	70	34	122	.293	.441

Career (1989-1993)

	Avg	AB	H	2B	3B	HR	RBI	BB	SO	OBP	SLG
Two Strikes	.153	531	81	16	2	18	53	42	272	.216	.292
Post-All Star	.250	603	151	23	3	30	90	47	150	.305	.448

Batter vs. Pitcher (career)

Hits Best Against	Avg	AB	H	2B	3B	HR	RBI	BB	SO	OBP	SLG
Mark Guthrie	.538	13	7	2	0	1	4	0	3	.538	.923
Kirk McCaskill	.500	8	4	0	0	0	2	5	1	.692	.500
Greg Hibbard	.381	21	8	2	2	0	3	3	2	.458	.667
Joe Hesketh	.333	12	4	1	0	1	2	0	0	.333	.667
Roger Clemens	.313	16	5	0	0	1	2	1	7	.353	.500

Hits Worst Against	Avg	AB	H	2B	3B	HR	RBI	BB	SO	OBP	SLG
Bret Saberhagen	.063	16	1	0	0	0	0	0	7	.063	.063
Jamie Moyer	.071	14	1	1	0	0	0	2	4	.188	.143
Matt Young	.100	10	1	0	0	0	0	1	2	.182	.100
Dave Fleming	.167	12	2	1	0	0	3	0	0	.167	.250
Mark Langston	.192	26	5	0	0	1	3	0	11	.192	.308

Ken Hill — Expos

Age 28 – Pitches Right (groundball pitcher)

	ERA	W	L	Sv	G	GS	IP	BB	SO	Avg	H	2B	3B	HR	RBI	OBP	SLG	CG	ShO	Sup	QS	#P/S	SB	CS	GB	FB	G/F
1993 Season	3.23	9	7	0	28	28	183.2	74	90	.238	163	42	2	7	68	.315	.336	2	0	4.56	16	100	21	8	307	181	1.70
Last Five Years	3.50	48	47	0	141	138	858.1	348	531	.239	762	145	24	51	320	.315	.347	8	4	4.16	85	94	98	40	1310	834	1.57

1993 Season

	ERA	W	L	Sv	G	GS	IP	H	HR	BB	SO
Home	3.12	4	4	0	15	15	101.0	89	5	39	40
Away	3.38	5	3	0	13	13	82.2	74	2	35	50
Day	2.58	3	2	0	7	7	52.1	40	5	16	20
Night	3.49	6	5	0	21	21	131.1	123	2	58	70
Grass	4.14	2	3	0	7	7	41.1	42	2	13	25
Turf	2.97	7	4	0	21	21	142.1	121	5	61	65
April	1.80	4	0	0	5	5	40.0	23	0	12	23
May	3.15	2	0	0	5	5	34.1	28	3	15	14
June	3.20	0	2	0	4	4	25.1	24	0	13	8
July	2.41	1	0	0	3	3	18.2	15	0	7	13
August	3.31	1	3	0	6	6	35.1	37	2	16	18
September/October	5.70	1	2	0	5	5	30.0	36	2	11	14
Starter	3.23	9	7	0	28	28	183.2	163	7	74	90
Reliever	0.00	0	0	0	0	0	0.0	0	0	0	0
0-3 Days Rest	0.00	0	0	0	0	0	0.0	0	0	0	0
4 Days Rest	3.16	6	4	0	13	13	88.1	81	5	34	44
5+ Days Rest	3.30	3	3	0	15	15	95.1	82	2	40	46
Pre-All Star	2.62	6	2	0	14	14	99.2	75	3	40	45
Post-All Star	3.96	3	5	0	14	14	84.0	88	4	34	45

	Avg	AB	H	2B	3B	HR	RBI	BB	SO	OBP	SLG
vs. Left	.234	376	88	26	2	4	35	49	43	.322	.346
vs. Right	.244	308	75	16	0	3	33	25	47	.307	.325
Inning 1-6	.230	582	134	31	1	6	57	70	80	.316	.318
Inning 7+	.284	102	29	11	1	1	11	4	10	.308	.441
None on	.242	388	94	22	1	5	5	37	47	.313	.343
Runners on	.233	296	69	20	1	2	63	37	43	.318	.328
Scoring Posn	.220	182	40	12	0	2	57	26	24	.310	.319
Close & Late	.236	55	13	6	0	1	4	1	7	.246	.400
None on/out	.244	176	43	14	1	1	1	15	13	.311	.352
vs. 1st Batr (relief)	.000	0	0	0	0	0	0	0	0	.000	.000
First Inning Pitched	.238	101	24	6	1	1	12	13	12	.330	.347
First 75 Pitches	.219	502	110	27	1	4	39	51	68	.297	.301
Pitch 76-90	.326	86	28	2	0	2	15	19	9	.443	.419
Pitch 91-105	.273	66	18	10	1	0	10	3	8	.300	.455
Pitch 106+	.233	30	7	3	0	1	4	1	5	.250	.433
First Pitch	.309	110	34	9	0	1	11	7	0	.345	.418
Ahead in Count	.157	299	47	12	1	0	15	0	80	.164	.204
Behind in Count	.331	145	48	11	1	5	29	36	0	.457	.524
Two Strikes	.143	293	42	10	1	1	17	31	90	.231	.195

Last Five Years

	ERA	W	L	Sv	G	GS	IP	H	HR	BB	SO
Home	3.55	20	21	0	67	66	408.0	369	17	169	226
Away	3.46	28	26	0	74	72	450.1	393	34	179	305
Day	2.91	18	17	0	49	49	318.1	267	21	111	196
Night	3.85	30	30	0	92	89	540.0	495	30	237	335
Grass	3.25	14	13	0	38	37	238.0	201	17	78	159
Turf	3.60	34	34	0	103	101	620.1	561	34	270	372
April	2.47	9	4	0	20	17	124.0	99	4	40	63
May	3.14	8	4	0	22	22	143.1	120	12	58	91
June	3.33	8	7	0	21	21	127.0	117	5	58	72
July	3.93	9	5	0	21	21	126.0	105	8	56	88
August	3.78	7	13	0	25	25	145.1	141	9	61	93
September/October	4.06	7	14	0	32	32	192.2	180	13	75	124
Starter	3.44	48	47	0	138	138	854.2	754	50	345	529
Reliever	17.18	0	0	0	3	0	3.2	8	1	3	2
0-3 Days Rest	4.00	2	1	0	6	6	36.0	43	3	13	24
4 Days Rest	3.34	26	29	0	76	76	482.1	433	30	185	306
5+ Days Rest	3.53	20	17	0	56	56	336.1	278	17	147	199
Pre-All Star	3.08	28	15	0	69	66	429.1	364	26	171	251
Post-All Star	3.92	20	32	0	72	72	429.0	398	25	177	280

	Avg	AB	H	2B	3B	HR	RBI	BB	SO	OBP	SLG
vs. Left	.242	1795	434	78	16	25	164	224	270	.326	.345
vs. Right	.235	1395	328	67	8	26	156	124	261	.302	.351
Inning 1-6	.234	2778	651	128	19	40	279	310	470	.313	.337
Inning 7+	.269	412	111	17	5	11	41	38	61	.335	.415
None on	.238	1829	435	83	11	32	32	194	301	.316	.348
Runners on	.240	1361	327	62	13	19	288	154	230	.315	.347
Scoring Posn	.233	801	187	35	6	14	257	119	141	.325	.345
Close & Late	.290	231	67	10	3	8	29	23	38	.357	.463
None on/out	.241	817	197	38	6	16	16	86	113	.320	.361
vs. 1st Batr (relief)	.333	3	1	0	0	0	0	0	0	.333	.333
First Inning Pitched	.238	517	123	24	4	10	69	81	95	.342	.358
First 75 Pitches	.230	2445	563	109	16	34	231	262	412	.307	.330
Pitch 76-90	.289	402	116	15	4	11	54	52	59	.366	.428
Pitch 91-105	.252	246	62	17	4	4	28	20	44	.317	.402
Pitch 106+	.216	97	21	4	0	2	7	14	16	.313	.320
First Pitch	.311	521	162	31	1	9	60	15	0	.332	.426
Ahead in Count	.171	1429	245	35	11	15	103	0	465	.176	.243
Behind in Count	.322	681	219	53	8	19	111	192	0	.466	.507
Two Strikes	.155	1396	217	40	9	17	98	139	531	.234	.234

Pitcher vs. Batter (career)

Pitches Best Vs.	Avg	AB	H	2B	3B	HR	RBI	BB	SO	OBP	SLG
Dale Murphy	.000	12	0	0	0	0	1	1	3	.077	.000
Eric Davis	.000	9	0	0	0	0	2	3	5	.231	.000
Robby Thompson	.071	14	1	0	0	0	0	1	2	.133	.071
Shawon Dunston	.125	16	2	0	0	0	1	0	5	.125	.125
Steve Buechele	.143	14	2	0	0	0	0	0	4	.143	.143

Pitches Worst Vs.	Avg	AB	H	2B	3B	HR	RBI	BB	SO	OBP	SLG
Tim Raines	.714	14	10	3	1	0	4	7	1	.810	1.071
Jeff Kent	.583	12	7	0	0	2	6	0	1	.583	1.083
Lenny Dykstra	.571	21	12	2	0	1	1	6	0	.667	.810
Lonnie Smith	.545	11	6	3	0	0	2	4	0	.667	.818
Rick Wilkins	.533	15	8	3	0	1	4	2	2	.556	.933

Milt Hill — Reds

Age 28 – Pitches Right

	ERA	W	L	Sv	G	GS	IP	BB	SO	Avg	H	2B	3B	HR	RBI	OBP	SLG	GF	IR	IRS	Hld	SvOp	SB	CS	GB	FB	G/F
1993 Season	5.65	3	0	0	19	0	28.2	9	23	.301	34	7	1	5	21	.344	.513	2	16	5	0	0	2	2	42	33	1.27
Career (1991-1993)	4.28	4	1	1	55	0	82.0	22	53	.278	85	18	3	7	45	.321	.425	15	42	12	1	2	7	6	117	92	1.27

1993 Season

	ERA	W	L	Sv	G	GS	IP	H	HR	BB	SO
Home	3.45	2	0	0	9	0	15.2	17	2	2	11
Away	8.31	1	0	0	10	0	13.0	17	3	7	12

	Avg	AB	H	2B	3B	HR	RBI	BB	SO	OBP	SLG
vs. Left	.250	48	12	1	1	2	7	4	8	.302	.438
vs. Right	.338	65	22	6	0	3	14	5	15	.375	.569

Shawn Hillegas — Athletics

Age 29 – Pitches Right (flyball pitcher)

	ERA	W	L	Sv	G	GS	IP	BB	SO	Avg	H	2B	3B	HR	RBI	OBP	SLG	CG	ShO	Sup	QS	#P/S	SB	CS	GB	FB	G/F
1993 Season	6.97	3	6	0	18	11	60.2	33	29	.317	78	14	4	8	43	.404	.504	0	0	5.49	2	79	2	4	87	81	1.07
Last Five Years	5.02	14	29	10	152	36	360.2	172	225	.275	385	70	15	40	204	.355	.433	1	1	4.34	8	86	31	21	463	470	0.99

1993 Season

	ERA	W	L	Sv	G	GS	IP	H	HR	BB	SO
Home	4.97	3	1	0	8	5	29.0	38	3	13	17
Away	8.81	0	5	0	10	6	31.2	40	5	20	12
Starter	7.80	2	5	0	11	11	47.1	61	8	29	22
Reliever	4.05	1	1	0	7	0	13.1	17	0	4	7
0-3 Days Rest	10.38	0	1	0	1	1	4.1	5	1	5	4
4 Days Rest	12.21	0	1	0	4	4	14.0	22	2	11	8
5+ Days Rest	5.28	2	3	0	6	6	29.0	34	5	13	10
Pre-All Star	7.06	3	6	0	16	11	58.2	75	8	31	29
Post-All Star	4.50	0	0	0	2	0	2.0	3	0	2	0

	Avg	AB	H	2B	3B	HR	RBI	BB	SO	OBP	SLG
vs. Left	.326	138	45	10	3	5	23	15	10	.391	.551
vs. Right	.306	108	33	4	1	3	20	18	19	.419	.444
Scoring Posn	.303	66	20	2	0	3	35	11	5	.392	.470
Close & Late	.250	8	2	0	1	0	0	3	1	.455	.500
None on/out	.283	60	17	4	2	3	3	8	8	.377	.567
First Pitch	.385	39	15	2	1	1	9	1	0	.415	.564
Ahead in Count	.214	84	18	3	1	1	11	0	23	.230	.310
Behind in Count	.344	64	22	6	0	3	13	17	0	.481	.578
Two Strikes	.237	93	22	3	1	2	12	15	29	.351	.355

Last Five Years

	ERA	W	L	Sv	G	GS	IP	H	HR	BB	SO
Home	4.02	12	10	6	82	17	195.0	189	16	85	138
Away	6.19	2	19	4	70	19	165.2	196	24	87	87
Day	7.09	2	9	1	47	12	99.0	117	13	59	62
Night	4.23	12	20	9	105	24	261.2	268	27	113	163
Grass	4.35	14	21	8	128	29	306.1	305	31	138	190
Turf	8.78	0	8	2	24	7	54.1	80	9	34	35
April	4.63	1	5	0	11	8	44.2	42	5	23	27
May	6.46	1	6	4	26	9	71.0	83	11	33	45
June	4.84	5	6	2	29	4	67.0	70	8	41	42
July	4.83	5	5	2	37	5	76.1	85	8	35	46
August	5.36	1	5	1	25	4	50.1	62	5	24	37
September/October	3.51	1	2	1	24	6	51.1	43	3	16	28
Starter	6.28	5	17	0	36	36	177.2	223	23	80	93
Reliever	3.79	9	12	10	116	0	183.0	162	17	92	132
0-3 Days Rest	7.59	0	2	0	2	2	10.2	16	1	8	7
4 Days Rest	8.73	0	7	0	14	14	66.0	96	10	38	40
5+ Days Rest	4.54	5	8	0	20	20	101.0	111	12	34	46
Pre-All Star	5.03	9	19	7	80	23	218.1	235	26	107	135
Post-All Star	5.00	5	10	3	72	13	142.1	150	14	65	90

	Avg	AB	H	2B	3B	HR	RBI	BB	SO	OBP	SLG
vs. Left	.305	685	209	37	9	14	92	87	93	.382	.447
vs. Right	.247	713	176	33	6	26	112	85	132	.329	.419
Inning 1-6	.296	854	253	50	11	29	150	100	127	.370	.482
Inning 7+	.243	544	132	20	4	11	54	72	98	.331	.355
None on	.267	768	205	35	11	21	21	81	115	.339	.423
Runners on	.286	630	180	35	4	19	183	91	110	.373	.444
Scoring Posn	.272	383	104	17	2	14	165	64	70	.365	.436
Close & Late	.257	257	66	9	2	6	30	43	44	.359	.377
None on/out	.243	338	82	14	5	13	13	32	53	.310	.429
vs. 1st Batr (relief)	.228	92	21	5	1	2	17	21	20	.371	.370
First Inning Pitched	.257	509	131	19	10	14	101	76	89	.350	.417
First 75 Pitches	.262	1240	325	58	14	35	179	152	207	.343	.416
Pitch 76-90	.367	79	29	9	0	2	8	12	12	.451	.557
Pitch 91-105	.418	55	23	2	1	2	12	7	4	.484	.600
Pitch 106+	.333	24	8	1	0	1	5	1	2	.360	.500
First Pitch	.359	195	70	11	2	6	35	10	0	.392	.528
Ahead in Count	.220	599	132	18	5	10	64	0	175	.227	.317
Behind in Count	.357	311	111	21	3	20	72	78	0	.478	.637
Two Strikes	.197	629	124	19	7	7	61	84	225	.294	.283

Pitcher vs. Batter (career)

Pitches Best Vs.	Avg	AB	H	2B	3B	HR	RBI	BB	SO	OBP	SLG
Alvaro Espinoza	.071	14	1	0	0	0	0	0	7	.071	.071
Chili Davis	.100	10	1	0	0	0	2	2	1	.231	.100
Greg Gagne	.100	10	1	0	0	0	2	2	4	.250	.100
Glenn Davis	.100	10	1	0	0	0	1	1	1	.182	.100
Wade Boggs	.188	16	3	0	0	0	1	2	1	.278	.188

Pitches Worst Vs.	Avg	AB	H	2B	3B	HR	RBI	BB	SO	OBP	SLG
Don Mattingly	.600	15	9	0	0	3	5	2	0	.611	1.200
Bobby Kelly	.545	11	6	3	0	0	2	0	2	.545	.818
Kevin Bass	.455	11	5	1	0	1	3	1	2	.500	.818
Devon White	.429	14	6	2	1	0	2	2	0	.500	.714
Ken Griffey Jr	.429	14	6	1	1	1	3	2	1	.500	.857

Eric Hillman — Mets

Age 28 – Pitches Left (groundball pitcher)

	ERA	W	L	Sv	G	GS	IP	BB	SO	Avg	H	2B	3B	HR	RBI	OBP	SLG	CG	ShO	Sup	QS	#P/S	SB	CS	GB	FB	G/F
1993 Season	3.97	2	9	0	27	22	145.0	24	60	.299	173	28	5	12	72	.326	.427	3	1	3.85	13	88	11	8	282	126	2.24
Career (1992-1993)	4.33	4	11	0	38	30	197.1	34	76	.304	240	38	6	21	101	.333	.447	3	1	4.06	16	85	15	13	387	176	2.20

1993 Season

	ERA	W	L	Sv	G	GS	IP	H	HR	BB	SO
Home	4.21	1	4	0	11	9	66.1	78	5	12	30
Away	3.78	1	5	0	16	13	78.2	95	7	12	30
Starter	3.91	2	8	0	22	22	138.0	162	11	23	57
Reliever	5.14	0	1	0	5	0	7.0	11	1	1	3
0-3 Days Rest	1.26	0	1	0	2	2	14.1	12	0	0	6
4 Days Rest	4.06	1	4	0	13	13	82.0	96	6	21	35
5+ Days Rest	4.54	1	3	0	7	7	41.2	54	5	2	16
Pre-All Star	5.03	0	3	0	11	6	39.1	53	3	10	17
Post-All Star	3.58	2	6	0	16	16	105.2	120	9	14	43

	Avg	AB	H	2B	3B	HR	RBI	BB	SO	OBP	SLG
vs. Left	.280	125	35	3	2	1	16	8	18	.326	.360
vs. Right	.304	454	138	25	3	11	56	16	42	.326	.445
Scoring Posn	.338	148	50	4	2	2	55	8	14	.357	.432
Close & Late	.415	65	27	3	0	2	10	1	7	.412	.554
None on/out	.331	151	50	11	1	5	5	7	8	.369	.517
First Pitch	.400	105	42	8	1	5	22	2	0	.396	.638
Ahead in Count	.258	229	59	12	1	3	22	0	53	.266	.358
Behind in Count	.293	150	44	4	2	3	19	13	0	.350	.407
Two Strikes	.242	198	48	8	0	2	17	9	60	.276	.313

Sterling Hitchcock — Yankees

Age 23 – Pitches Left (flyball pitcher)

	ERA	W	L	Sv	G	GS	IP	BB	SO	Avg	H	2B	3B	HR	RBI	OBP	SLG	CG	ShO	Sup	QS	#P/S	SB	CS	GB	FB	G/F
1993 Season	4.65	1	2	0	6	6	31.0	14	26	.271	32	7	0	4	17	.348	.432	0	0	4.94	1	91	3	2	31	38	0.82
Career (1992-1993)	5.73	1	4	0	9	9	44.0	20	32	.307	55	12	0	6	29	.379	.475	0	0	5.11	2	91	4	3	49	61	0.80

1993 Season

	ERA	W	L	Sv	G	GS	IP	H	HR	BB	SO
Home	4.41	0	1	0	3	3	16.1	14	2	8	17
Away	4.91	1	1	0	3	3	14.2	18	2	6	9

	Avg	AB	H	2B	3B	HR	RBI	BB	SO	OBP	SLG
vs. Left	.286	21	6	0	0	0	3	5	2	.407	.286
vs. Right	.268	97	26	7	0	4	14	9	24	.333	.464

Denny Hocking — Twins

Age 24 – Bats Both

	Avg	G	AB	R	H	2B	3B	HR	RBI	BB	SO	HBP	GDP	SB	CS	OBP	SLG	IBB	SH	SF	#Pit	#P/PA	GB	FB	G/F
1993 Season	.139	15	36	7	5	1	0	0	0	6	8	0	1	1	0	.262	.167	0	0	0	168	4.00	11	11	1.00

1993 Season

	Avg	AB	H	2B	3B	HR	RBI	BB	SO	OBP	SLG		Avg	AB	H	2B	3B	HR	RBI	BB	SO	OBP	SLG
vs. Left	.167	6	1	0	0	0	0	1	0	.286	.167	Scoring Posn	.000	5	0	0	0	0	0	2	2	.286	.000
vs. Right	.133	30	4	1	0	0	0	5	8	.257	.167	Close & Late	.143	7	1	0	0	0	0	2	4	.333	.143

Trevor Hoffman — Padres

Age 26 – Pitches Right (flyball pitcher)

	ERA	W	L	Sv	G	GS	IP	BB	SO	Avg	H	2B	3B	HR	RBI	OBP	SLG	GF	IR	IRS	Hld	SvOp	SB	CS	GB	FB	G/F
1993 Season	3.90	4	6	5	67	0	90.0	39	79	.234	80	16	4	10	40	.310	.392	26	45	6	15	8	7	1	85	124	0.69

1993 Season

	ERA	W	L	Sv	G	GS	IP	H	HR	BB	SO		Avg	AB	H	2B	3B	HR	RBI	BB	SO	OBP	SLG
Home	3.40	2	3	1	34	0	45.0	45	3	15	36	vs. Left	.222	158	35	3	3	6	23	27	38	.332	.392
Away	4.40	2	3	4	33	0	45.0	35	7	24	43	vs. Right	.245	184	45	13	1	4	17	12	41	.290	.391
Day	3.37	0	4	1	24	0	34.2	23	5	19	34	Inning 1-6	.222	18	4	2	1	1	4	0	3	.200	.611
Night	4.23	4	2	4	43	0	55.1	57	5	20	45	Inning 7+	.235	324	76	14	3	9	36	39	76	.316	.380
Grass	3.28	2	3	4	51	0	68.2	57	7	25	59	None on	.250	184	46	8	4	7	7	21	37	.330	.451
Turf	5.91	2	3	1	16	0	21.1	23	3	14	20	Runners on	.215	158	34	8	0	3	33	18	42	.287	.323
April	3.09	1	0	1	10	0	11.2	6	2	7	7	Scoring Posn	.182	99	18	2	0	2	28	15	28	.277	.263
May	4.15	1	1	0	10	0	13.0	13	1	9	9	Close & Late	.228	193	44	10	2	3	20	25	43	.317	.347
June	5.79	0	1	1	11	0	14.0	16	2	4	11	None on/out	.271	85	23	5	2	3	3	6	15	.326	.482
July	3.68	1	1	0	10	0	14.2	11	1	10	19	vs. 1st Batr (relief)	.226	62	14	3	1	2	3	4	14	.269	.403
August	3.38	0	2	2	14	0	18.2	17	0	5	13	First Inning Pitched	.238	223	53	11	1	8	31	27	52	.318	.404
September/October	3.50	1	1	1	12	0	18.0	17	4	4	20	First 15 Pitches	.232	207	48	11	1	8	24	20	49	.297	.411
Starter	0.00	0	0	0	0	0	0.0	0	0	0	0	Pitch 16-30	.268	97	26	3	2	1	11	15	20	.366	.371
Reliever	3.90	4	6	5	67	0	90.0	80	10	39	79	Pitch 31-45	.171	35	6	2	1	1	5	4	8	.250	.371
0 Days rest	6.14	0	0	1	8	0	7.1	8	1	2	3	Pitch 46+	.000	3	0	0	0	0	0	0	2	.000	.000
1 or 2 Days rest	3.30	4	4	3	45	0	62.2	56	5	26	60	First Pitch	.310	42	13	2	1	1	7	12	0	.455	.476
3+ Days rest	4.95	0	2	1	14	0	20.0	16	4	11	16	Ahead in Count	.197	178	35	7	2	4	17	0	66	.200	.326
Pre-All Star	4.74	2	3	2	35	0	43.2	42	5	24	34	Behind in Count	.298	57	17	5	0	2	8	15	0	.432	.491
Post-All Star	3.11	2	3	3	32	0	46.1	38	5	15	45	Two Strikes	.181	182	33	6	2	4	14	12	79	.235	.302

Chris Hoiles — Orioles

Age 29 – Bats Right (flyball hitter)

	Avg	G	AB	R	H	2B	3B	HR	RBI	BB	SO	HBP	GDP	SB	CS	OBP	SLG	IBB	SH	SF	#Pit	#P/PA	GB	FB	G/F
1993 Season	.310	126	419	80	130	28	0	29	82	69	94	9	10	1	1	.416	.585	4	3	3	2128	4.23	98	166	0.59
Career (1989-1993)	.272	358	1142	172	311	57	1	61	160	159	230	12	29	1	5	.365	.484	8	4	7	5337	4.03	296	445	0.67

1993 Season

	Avg	AB	H	2B	3B	HR	RBI	BB	SO	OBP	SLG		Avg	AB	H	2B	3B	HR	RBI	BB	SO	OBP	SLG
vs. Left	.318	110	35	9	0	8	25	25	22	.442	.618	Scoring Posn	.277	101	28	4	0	6	46	21	28	.406	.495
vs. Right	.307	309	95	19	0	21	57	44	72	.406	.573	Close & Late	.260	73	19	5	0	4	14	7	20	.349	.493
Groundball	.386	83	32	8	0	6	18	8	13	.469	.699	None on/out	.291	79	23	5	0	4	4	15	21	.404	.506
Flyball	.228	79	18	5	0	4	12	10	24	.315	.443	Batting #6	.304	184	56	10	0	12	36	27	43	.406	.554
Home	.322	205	66	13	0	16	46	38	46	.433	.620	Batting #7	.369	122	45	13	0	11	24	18	26	.458	.746
Away	.299	214	64	15	0	13	36	31	48	.399	.551	Other	.257	113	29	5	0	6	22	24	25	.390	.460
Day	.278	90	25	5	0	8	15	19	28	.412	.600	April	.220	59	13	3	0	2	4	8	18	.333	.373
Night	.319	329	105	23	0	21	67	50	66	.417	.581	May	.288	80	23	7	0	5	12	14	26	.402	.563
Grass	.320	359	115	24	0	25	74	58	81	.419	.596	June	.350	80	28	5	0	7	18	11	13	.429	.675
Turf	.250	60	15	4	0	4	8	11	13	.400	.517	July	.301	83	25	4	0	5	20	15	12	.426	.530
First Pitch	.333	24	8	0	0	3	6	3	0	.452	.708	August	.269	26	7	1	0	1	3	3	6	.333	.423
Ahead in Count	.438	112	49	11	0	14	36	32	0	.565	.911	September/October	.374	91	34	8	0	9	25	18	19	.482	.758
Behind in Count	.229	175	40	10	0	5	22	0	68	.242	.371	Pre-All Star	.300	253	76	17	0	18	46	39	60	.403	.581
Two Strikes	.237	215	51	12	0	9	29	34	94	.347	.419	Post-All Star	.325	166	54	11	0	11	36	30	34	.436	.590

1993 By Position

Position	Avg	AB	H	2B	3B	HR	RBI	BB	SO	OBP	SLG	G	GS	Innings	PO	A	E	DP	Fld Pct	Rng Fctr	In Zone	Outs	Zone Rtg	MLB Zone
As c	.314	411	129	27	0	29	82	66	89	.417	.591	124	117	1039.2	696	64	5	11	.993	---	---	---	---	---

Career (1989-1993)

	Avg	AB	H	2B	3B	HR	RBI	BB	SO	OBP	SLG		Avg	AB	H	2B	3B	HR	RBI	BB	SO	OBP	SLG
vs. Left	.267	341	91	15	0	18	38	54	52	.366	.469	Scoring Posn	.236	258	61	11	0	11	95	50	67	.358	.407
vs. Right	.275	801	220	42	1	43	122	105	178	.365	.491	Close & Late	.225	191	43	6	0	13	36	19	50	.304	.461
Groundball	.336	283	95	17	0	21	56	35	52	.418	.618	None on/out	.264	261	69	12	1	17	17	33	53	.347	.513
Flyball	.200	240	48	8	0	8	22	28	62	.281	.333	Batting #6	.270	296	80	13	0	18	46	52	69	.387	.497
Home	.278	558	155	28	0	30	81	82	106	.374	.489	Batting #8	.264	420	111	22	0	15	42	36	83	.322	.424
Away	.267	584	156	29	1	31	79	77	124	.357	.479	Other	.282	426	120	22	1	28	72	71	78	.389	.535
Day	.243	268	65	11	0	19	39	38	67	.339	.496	April	.244	160	39	8	0	7	15	20	39	.337	.425
Night	.281	874	246	46	1	42	121	121	163	.373	.481	May	.272	213	58	11	1	12	27	47	48	.405	.502
Grass	.277	962	266	46	1	55	138	135	193	.368	.498	June	.274	201	55	9	0	13	34	26	35	.358	.512
Turf	.250	180	45	11	0	6	22	24	37	.351	.411	July	.304	158	48	8	0	8	30	18	24	.385	.506
First Pitch	.308	120	37	6	0	7	19	4	0	.344	.533	August	.236	161	38	7	0	4	14	13	34	.291	.354
Ahead in Count	.386	277	107	21	1	27	66	75	0	.515	.762	September/October	.293	249	73	14	0	17	40	35	50	.384	.554
Behind in Count	.196	489	96	16	0	13	42	0	178	.206	.309	Pre-All Star	.268	631	169	31	1	37	90	101	128	.373	.496
Two Strikes	.190	546	104	18	0	19	51	80	230	.298	.328	Post-All Star	.278	511	142	26	0	24	70	58	102	.355	.470

Batter vs. Pitcher (career)																							
Hits Best Against	Avg	AB	H	2B	3B	HR	RBI	BB	SO	OBP	SLG	**Hits Worst Against**	Avg	AB	H	2B	3B	HR	RBI	BB	SO	OBP	SLG
Jim Abbott	.786	14	11	2	0	1	5	2	0	.765	1.143	Matt Young	.000	7	0	0	0	0	0	4	1	.364	.000
Jack McDowell	.476	21	10	2	1	1	3	2	2	.522	.810	Dave Fleming	.077	13	1	0	0	0	0	0	2	.077	.077
Randy Johnson	.400	10	4	0	0	1	1	3	3	.538	.700	Todd Stottlemyre	.100	10	1	0	0	0	0	1	1	.182	.100
Erik Hanson	.375	16	6	3	0	0	1	5	2	.524	.563	Jack Morris	.143	14	2	0	0	0	0	1	3	.200	.143
Chuck Finley	.333	21	7	1	0	1	3	3	6	.400	.524	Mark Langston	.200	10	2	0	0	0	0	1	2	.273	.200

Dave Hollins — Phillies

Age 28 – Bats Both

	Avg	G	AB	R	H	2B	3B	HR	RBI	BB	SO	HBP	GDP	SB	CS	OBP	SLG	IBB	SH	SF	#Pit	#P/PA	GB	FB	G/F
1993 Season	.273	143	543	104	148	30	4	18	93	85	109	5	15	2	3	.372	.442	5	0	7	2468	3.86	191	148	1.29
Career (1990-1993)	.267	427	1394	240	372	68	10	56	222	188	273	28	26	12	10	.362	.451	13	0	14	6208	3.82	475	419	1.13

1993 Season																							
	Avg	AB	H	2B	3B	HR	RBI	BB	SO	OBP	SLG		Avg	AB	H	2B	3B	HR	RBI	BB	SO	OBP	SLG
vs. Left	.323	195	63	14	3	8	34	13	33	.369	.549	Scoring Posn	.294	170	50	14	1	5	70	37	40	.412	.476
vs. Right	.244	348	85	16	1	10	59	72	76	.373	.382	Close & Late	.232	82	19	2	1	3	16	11	24	.323	.390
Groundball	.238	181	43	6	1	8	30	22	41	.322	.414	None on/out	.250	128	32	3	0	2	2	15	29	.333	.320
Flyball	.229	96	22	5	0	3	14	13	19	.318	.375	Total	.273	543	148	30	4	18	93	85	109	.372	.442
Home	.271	262	71	13	1	9	39	44	49	.378	.431	Batting #4	.273	543	148	30	4	18	93	85	109	.372	.442
Away	.274	281	77	17	3	9	54	41	60	.366	.452	Other	.000	0	0	0	0	0	0	0	0	.000	.000
Day	.294	153	45	12	0	4	24	28	35	.404	.451	April	.282	85	24	6	0	2	17	13	21	.374	.424
Night	.264	390	103	18	4	14	69	57	74	.359	.438	May	.317	104	33	8	1	6	26	15	20	.408	.587
Grass	.303	185	56	14	2	6	38	28	35	.397	.497	June	.189	37	7	2	0	1	5	10	11	.347	.324
Turf	.257	358	92	16	2	12	55	57	74	.359	.413	July	.241	112	27	2	2	2	13	11	17	.315	.348
First Pitch	.418	79	33	9	1	1	20	4	0	.440	.595	August	.295	95	28	7	0	4	15	18	20	.417	.495
Ahead in Count	.359	128	46	9	2	10	32	44	0	.514	.695	September/October	.264	110	29	5	1	3	17	18	20	.362	.409
Behind in Count	.173	220	38	3	0	4	24	0	84	.190	.241	Pre-All Star	.277	274	76	18	1	9	53	42	61	.373	.449
Two Strikes	.176	244	43	5	0	3	23	37	109	.297	.234	Post-All Star	.268	269	72	12	3	9	40	43	48	.371	.435

1993 By Position																									
Position	Avg	AB	H	2B	3B	HR	RBI	BB	SO	OBP	SLG	G	GS	Innings	PO	A	E	DP	Fld Pct	Rng Fctr	In Zone	Outs	Zone Rtg	MLB Zone
As 3b	.273	543	148	30	4	18	93	85	109	.372	.442	143	143	1214.2	73	215	27	8	.914	2.13	293	231	.788	.834

Career (1990-1993)																							
	Avg	AB	H	2B	3B	HR	RBI	BB	SO	OBP	SLG		Avg	AB	H	2B	3B	HR	RBI	BB	SO	OBP	SLG
vs. Left	.320	531	170	31	8	31	96	43	98	.379	.584	Scoring Posn	.280	400	112	24	2	13	152	80	78	.400	.448
vs. Right	.234	863	202	37	2	25	126	145	175	.353	.368	Close & Late	.216	232	50	6	2	8	35	27	56	.312	.362
Groundball	.255	545	139	21	2	22	90	61	114	.341	.422	None on/out	.240	296	71	13	0	4	4	30	69	.320	.324
Flyball	.223	264	59	15	2	9	33	38	64	.330	.398	Batting #3	.281	501	141	26	4	21	75	65	96	.379	.475
Home	.259	671	174	38	4	28	101	106	131	.371	.453	Batting #4	.274	584	160	32	4	20	102	90	116	.372	.445
Away	.274	723	198	30	6	28	121	82	142	.353	.448	Other	.230	309	71	10	2	15	45	33	61	.313	.421
Day	.285	390	111	22	2	20	73	57	84	.383	.505	April	.237	186	44	8	0	5	33	28	42	.353	.360
Night	.260	1004	261	46	8	36	149	131	189	.354	.429	May	.301	206	62	15	2	10	38	32	39	.403	.539
Grass	.290	411	119	21	4	18	81	48	84	.373	.491	June	.237	173	41	5	1	7	21	23	35	.322	.399
Turf	.257	983	253	47	6	38	141	140	189	.358	.433	July	.270	281	76	12	5	12	47	29	57	.355	.477
First Pitch	.358	193	69	15	2	8	40	9	0	.396	.580	August	.268	220	59	12	0	10	32	36	45	.379	.459
Ahead in Count	.343	324	111	23	4	21	69	99	0	.492	.633	September/October	.274	328	90	16	2	12	51	40	55	.356	.445
Behind in Count	.209	589	123	15	3	18	71	0	215	.235	.336	Pre-All Star	.251	668	168	31	4	23	102	90	142	.349	.413
Two Strikes	.187	632	118	13	0	18	71	77	273	.293	.293	Post-All Star	.281	726	204	37	6	33	120	98	131	.374	.485

Batter vs. Pitcher (career)																							
Hits Best Against	Avg	AB	H	2B	3B	HR	RBI	BB	SO	OBP	SLG	**Hits Worst Against**	Avg	AB	H	2B	3B	HR	RBI	BB	SO	OBP	SLG
Butch Henry	.833	12	10	3	0	4	8	2	2	.800	2.083	Jose Rijo	.083	12	1	0	0	0	1	0	4	.083	.083
Bruce Hurst	.500	14	7	1	0	2	5	4	3	.611	1.000	Bob Walk	.091	11	1	0	0	0	0	2	2	.231	.091
John Smoltz	.429	7	3	2	0	0	3	3	0	.545	.714	Jimmy Jones	.100	10	1	0	0	0	1	2	1	.250	.100
Bud Black	.417	12	5	0	1	1	1	0	1	.417	.833	Jeff Brantley	.111	9	1	0	0	0	1	1	2	.182	.111
Pete Harnisch	.316	19	6	1	0	2	2	4	4	.435	.684	Randy Tomlin	.125	16	2	0	0	0	1	1	3	.176	.125

Brad Holman — Mariners

Age 26 – Pitches Right

	ERA	W	L	Sv	G	GS	IP	BB	SO	Avg	H	2B	3B	HR	RBI	OBP	SLG	GF	IR	IRS	Hld	SvOp	SB	CS	GB	FB	G/F
1993 Season	3.72	1	3	3	19	0	36.1	16	17	.208	27	6	0	1	12	.318	.277	9	23	3	2	3	1	0	48	35	1.37

1993 Season																							
	ERA	W	L	Sv	G	GS	IP	H	HR	BB	SO		Avg	AB	H	2B	3B	HR	RBI	BB	SO	OBP	SLG
Home	6.61	0	2	0	11	0	16.1	18	1	8	10	vs. Left	.208	53	11	1	0	1	5	6	6	.288	.283
Away	1.35	1	1	3	8	0	20.0	9	0	8	7	vs. Right	.208	77	16	5	0	0	7	10	11	.337	.273

Darren Holmes — Rockies

Age 28 – Pitches Right

	ERA	W	L	Sv	G	GS	IP	BB	SO	Avg	H	2B	3B	HR	RBI	OBP	SLG	GF	IR	IRS	Hld	SvOp	SB	CS	GB	FB	G/F
1993 Season	4.05	3	3	25	62	0	66.2	20	60	.222	56	9	2	6	30	.285	.345	51	13	6	2	29	3	2	101	60	1.68
Career (1990-1993)	4.09	8	12	34	157	0	202.2	69	169	.253	196	33	5	14	98	.316	.362	86	104	29	7	43	12	8	289	205	1.41

1993 Season																							
	ERA	W	L	Sv	G	GS	IP	H	HR	BB	SO		Avg	AB	H	2B	3B	HR	RBI	BB	SO	OBP	SLG
Home	5.65	3	2	13	35	0	36.2	36	3	14	37	vs. Left	.228	136	31	5	2	1	13	13	22	.305	.316
Away	2.10	0	1	12	27	0	30.0	20	3	6	23	vs. Right	.216	116	25	4	0	5	17	7	38	.260	.379
Day	5.40	0	1	11	21	0	20.0	20	4	4	20	Inning 1-6	.000	2	0	0	0	0	0	1	0	.500	.000

1993 Season	ERA	W	L	Sv	G	GS	IP	H	HR	BB	SO		Avg	AB	H	2B	3B	HR	RBI	BB	SO	OBP	SLG
Night	3.47	3	2	14	41	0	46.2	36	2	16	40	Inning 7+	.224	250	56	9	2	6	30	19	60	.281	.348
Grass	5.08	3	3	20	50	0	51.1	46	6	17	48	None on	.212	151	32	3	2	2	2	8	31	.261	.298
Turf	0.59	0	0	5	12	0	15.1	10	0	3	12	Runners on	.238	101	24	6	0	4	28	12	29	.319	.416
April	18.56	0	2	1	7	0	5.1	12	0	7	6	Scoring Posn	.218	55	12	4	0	1	22	9	15	.328	.345
May	5.19	0	1	2	10	0	8.2	8	2	3	7	Close & Late	.214	145	31	6	1	4	18	13	34	.278	.352
June	2.61	0	0	2	8	0	10.1	7	1	2	9	None on/out	.217	60	13	1	0	0	0	2	13	.266	.233
July	4.30	1	0	5	13	0	14.2	12	2	2	14	vs. 1st Batr (relief)	.255	55	14	1	0	0	2	5	8	.339	.273
August	1.35	0	0	9	12	0	13.1	8	0	4	12	First Inning Pitched	.227	220	50	8	2	6	29	18	51	.292	.364
September/October	1.26	2	0	6	12	0	14.1	9	1	2	12	First 15 Pitches	.242	194	47	6	2	6	22	12	45	.293	.387
Starter	0.00	0	0	0	0	0	0.0	0	0	0	0	Pitch 16-30	.152	46	7	3	0	0	7	7	13	.264	.217
Reliever	4.05	3	3	25	62	0	66.2	56	6	20	60	Pitch 31-45	.250	8	2	0	0	0	1	0	2	.250	.250
0 Days rest	1.15	0	0	9	16	0	15.2	16	0	4	13	Pitch 46+	.000	4	0	0	0	0	0	1	0	.200	.000
1 or 2 Days rest	6.03	2	3	10	29	0	31.1	27	5	12	34	First Pitch	.200	25	5	0	0	1	3	1	0	.231	.320
3+ Days rest	3.20	1	0	6	17	0	19.2	13	1	4	13	Ahead in Count	.215	130	28	5	0	2	12	0	50	.227	.300
Pre-All Star	6.16	0	3	8	31	0	30.2	33	4	12	28	Behind in Count	.271	59	16	3	0	2	11	5	0	.328	.424
Post-All Star	2.25	3	0	17	31	0	36.0	23	2	8	32	Two Strikes	.190	137	26	5	0	2	14	14	60	.265	.270

Career (1990-1993)	ERA	W	L	Sv	G	GS	IP	H	HR	BB	SO		Avg	AB	H	2B	3B	HR	RBI	BB	SO	OBP	SLG
Home	5.01	6	6	17	83	0	106.0	114	8	34	92	vs. Left	.250	384	96	19	2	3	39	35	69	.317	.333
Away	3.07	2	6	17	74	0	96.2	82	6	35	77	vs. Right	.255	392	100	14	3	11	59	34	100	.315	.390
Day	3.98	1	4	14	54	0	72.1	72	7	22	62	Inning 1-6	.258	159	41	6	1	3	31	25	46	.362	.365
Night	4.14	7	8	20	103	0	130.1	124	7	47	107	Inning 7+	.251	617	155	27	4	11	67	44	123	.303	.361
Grass	4.89	8	11	25	126	0	158.1	165	13	57	133	None on	.249	406	101	13	3	5	5	21	80	.289	.333
Turf	1.22	0	1	9	31	0	44.1	31	1	12	36	Runners on	.257	370	95	20	2	9	93	48	89	.343	.395
April	6.64	1	3	1	13	0	20.1	24	0	12	20	Scoring Posn	.228	219	50	11	1	5	81	37	57	.336	.356
May	2.70	2	2	4	23	0	33.1	36	4	9	27	Close & Late	.230	317	73	12	3	7	36	26	62	.289	.353
June	4.50	0	2	2	27	0	32.0	34	3	10	24	None on/out	.311	177	55	7	1	3	3	9	31	.351	.412
July	8.24	2	2	6	28	0	31.2	36	4	9	26	vs. 1st Batr (relief)	.248	137	34	5	1	2	14	13	29	.320	.343
August	2.30	0	1	11	25	0	31.1	24	1	8	26	First Inning Pitched	.238	520	124	22	4	8	63	48	121	.306	.342
September/October	2.33	3	2	10	41	0	54.0	42	2	21	46	First 15 Pitches	.255	463	118	20	4	8	47	33	102	.309	.367
Starter	0.00	0	0	0	0	0	0.0	0	0	0	0	Pitch 16-30	.218	202	44	8	1	1	27	24	51	.298	.282
Reliever	4.09	8	12	34	157	0	202.2	196	14	69	169	Pitch 31-45	.302	86	26	3	0	4	18	10	15	.378	.477
0 Days rest	4.08	1	4	11	34	0	39.2	43	2	17	35	Pitch 46+	.320	25	8	2	0	1	6	2	1	.370	.520
1 or 2 Days rest	4.53	5	8	13	69	0	89.1	92	9	31	76	First Pitch	.326	95	31	2	1	1	10	6	0	.366	.400
3+ Days rest	3.54	2	0	10	54	0	73.2	61	3	21	58	Ahead in Count	.219	370	81	16	1	3	34	0	139	.228	.292
Pre-All Star	4.56	3	7	11	74	0	98.2	105	9	34	85	Behind in Count	.310	174	54	9	1	7	35	24	0	.390	.494
Post-All Star	3.63	5	5	23	83	0	104.0	91	5	35	84	Two Strikes	.213	403	86	20	1	4	45	39	169	.283	.298

Mark Holzemer — Angels

Age 24 – Pitches Left

	ERA	W	L	Sv	G	GS	IP	BB	SO	Avg	H	2B	3B	HR	RBI	OBP	SLG	CG	ShO	Sup	QS	#P/S	SB	CS	GB	FB	G/F
1993 Season	8.87	0	3	0	5	4	23.1	13	10	.340	34	8	0	2	23	.431	.480	0	0	4.63	0	98	2	1	32	25	1.28

1993 Season	ERA	W	L	Sv	G	GS	IP	H	HR	BB	SO		Avg	AB	H	2B	3B	HR	RBI	BB	SO	OBP	SLG
Home	6.92	0	1	0	2	2	13.0	16	0	6	4	vs. Left	.296	27	8	1	0	0	4	6	2	.457	.333
Away	11.32	0	2	0	3	2	10.1	18	2	7	6	vs. Right	.356	73	26	7	0	2	19	7	8	.420	.534

Rick Honeycutt — Athletics

Age 40 – Pitches Left (groundball pitcher)

	ERA	W	L	Sv	G	GS	IP	BB	SO	Avg	H	2B	3B	HR	RBI	OBP	SLG	GF	IR	IRS	Hld	SvOp	SB	CS	GB	FB	G/F
1993 Season	2.81	1	4	1	52	0	41.2	20	21	.211	30	4	1	2	14	.305	.296	7	35	8	20	3	2	3	58	42	1.38
Last Five Years	2.89	8	16	23	276	0	258.1	98	169	.226	210	27	6	14	105	.301	.313	34	191	50	103	40	15	10	385	235	1.64

1993 Season	ERA	W	L	Sv	G	GS	IP	H	HR	BB	SO		Avg	AB	H	2B	3B	HR	RBI	BB	SO	OBP	SLG
Home	2.14	0	2	1	26	0	21.0	13	1	8	12	vs. Left	.255	55	14	1	1	1	8	6	6	.328	.364
Away	3.48	1	2	0	26	0	20.2	17	1	12	9	vs. Right	.184	87	16	3	0	1	6	14	15	.291	.253
Starter	0.00	0	0	0	0	0	0.0	0	0	0	0	Scoring Posn	.182	33	6	1	0	1	12	8	4	.311	.303
Reliever	2.81	1	4	1	52	0	41.2	30	2	20	21	Close & Late	.240	96	23	2	1	0	8	17	15	.347	.281
0 Days rest	3.18	0	2	0	13	0	11.1	8	0	6	7	None on/out	.250	36	9	1	1	0	0	2	3	.289	.333
1 or 2 Days rest	1.66	0	1	1	25	0	21.2	13	0	6	13	First Pitch	.063	16	1	1	0	0	3	6	0	.304	.125
3+ Days rest	5.19	1	1	0	14	0	8.2	9	2	8	1	Ahead in Count	.213	75	16	1	1	0	2	0	18	.221	.253
Pre-All Star	3.32	0	2	1	26	0	21.2	16	1	10	11	Behind in Count	.269	26	7	1	0	1	3	6	0	.406	.423
Post-All Star	2.25	1	2	0	26	0	20.0	14	1	10	10	Two Strikes	.197	71	14	1	0	0	2	8	21	.284	.211

Last Five Years	ERA	W	L	Sv	G	GS	IP	H	HR	BB	SO		Avg	AB	H	2B	3B	HR	RBI	BB	SO	OBP	SLG
Home	2.41	3	8	15	137	0	130.2	98	5	44	86	vs. Left	.199	347	69	9	1	5	33	32	63	.271	.274
Away	3.38	5	8	8	139	0	127.2	112	9	54	83	vs. Right	.241	584	141	18	5	9	72	66	106	.318	.336
Day	2.46	2	6	10	103	0	106.0	82	9	40	76	Inning 1-6	.208	53	11	1	0	4	19	2	9	.263	.453
Night	3.19	6	10	13	173	0	152.1	128	5	58	93	Inning 7+	.227	878	199	26	6	10	86	96	160	.303	.304
Grass	2.82	6	13	22	230	0	217.1	172	13	81	146	None on	.218	472	103	7	5	4	4	44	85	.292	.280
Turf	3.29	2	3	1	46	0	41.0	38	1	17	23	Runners on	.233	459	107	20	1	10	101	54	84	.309	.346
April	2.65	1	3	2	32	0	37.1	22	4	10	28	Scoring Posn	.225	236	53	7	0	5	88	40	47	.325	.318
May	2.50	2	2	6	46	0	39.2	27	1	18	26	Close & Late	.217	539	117	14	4	5	55	65	97	.301	.286

Last Five Years

	ERA	W	L	Sv	G	GS	IP	H	HR	BB	SO
June	2.23	0	1	5	39	0	44.1	35	3	7	29
July	4.15	3	3	4	51	0	47.2	50	2	25	33
August	3.65	1	5	5	58	0	44.1	41	1	18	30
September/October	2.00	1	2	1	50	0	45.0	35	3	20	23
Starter	0.00	0	0	0	0	0	0.0	0	0	0	0
Reliever	2.89	8	16	23	276	0	258.1	210	14	98	169
0 Days rest	2.87	1	5	9	61	0	53.1	42	4	20	34
1 or 2 Days rest	2.81	4	7	9	135	0	131.1	110	2	49	78
3+ Days rest	3.05	3	4	5	80	0	73.2	58	8	29	57
Pre-All Star	2.74	3	8	15	132	0	138.0	99	8	41	99
Post-All Star	3.07	5	8	8	144	0	120.1	111	6	57	70

	Avg	AB	H	2B	3B	HR	RBI	BB	SO	OBP	SLG
None on/out	.230	204	47	5	4	2	2	10	42	.270	.324
vs. 1st Batr (relief)	.194	253	49	6	3	5	27	11	47	.233	.300
First Inning Pitched	.229	725	166	22	5	11	89	70	137	.298	.319
First 15 Pitches	.232	710	165	21	5	12	84	60	126	.294	.327
Pitch 16-30	.198	187	37	5	0	2	17	33	35	.318	.257
Pitch 31-45	.267	30	8	1	1	0	4	5	7	.361	.367
Pitch 46+	.000	4	0	0	0	0	0	0	1	.000	.000
First Pitch	.234	128	30	6	0	1	11	15	0	.313	.305
Ahead in Count	.193	441	85	10	4	3	27	0	142	.204	.254
Behind in Count	.337	178	60	8	1	7	41	48	0	.468	.511
Two Strikes	.167	419	70	7	3	2	22	35	169	.242	.212

Pitcher vs. Batter (since 1984)

Pitches Best Vs.	Avg	AB	H	2B	3B	HR	RBI	BB	SO	OBP	SLG
Lou Whitaker	.000	14	0	0	0	0	1	4	3	.211	.000
Fred McGriff	.000	12	0	0	0	0	1	0	5	.000	.000
Manuel Lee	.000	12	0	0	0	0	0	2	3	.143	.000
Bip Roberts	.000	11	0	0	0	0	0	1	2	.083	.000
Rafael Palmeiro	.100	20	2	0	0	0	0	0	2	.100	.100

Pitches Worst Vs.	Avg	AB	H	2B	3B	HR	RBI	BB	SO	OBP	SLG
Hubie Brooks	.579	19	11	0	0	0	1	2	0	.619	.579
Kevin Mitchell	.538	13	7	2	0	2	3	0	0	.538	1.154
Kevin McReynolds	.469	32	15	2	0	1	5	3	3	.514	.625
Ozzie Smith	.412	17	7	3	0	0	0	3	2	.500	.588
Henry Cotto	.400	10	4	0	0	1	2	1	1	.417	.700

John Hope — Pirates

Age 23 – Pitches Right

	ERA	W	L	Sv	G	GS	IP	BB	SO	Avg	H	2B	3B	HR	RBI	OBP	SLG	CG	ShO	Sup	QS	#P/S	SB	CS	GB	FB	G/F
1993 Season	4.03	0	2	0	7	7	38.0	8	8	.313	47	11	2	2	19	.354	.453	0	0	3.08	2	75	3	2	60	50	1.20

1993 Season

	ERA	W	L	Sv	G	GS	IP	H	HR	BB	SO
Home	4.43	0	1	0	4	4	22.1	30	1	6	6
Away	3.45	0	1	0	3	3	15.2	17	1	2	2

	Avg	AB	H	2B	3B	HR	RBI	BB	SO	OBP	SLG
vs. Left	.303	66	20	2	0	0	7	7	3	.370	.333
vs. Right	.321	84	27	9	2	2	12	1	5	.341	.548

Sam Horn — Indians

Age 30 – Bats Left (flyball hitter)

	Avg	G	AB	R	H	2B	3B	HR	RBI	BB	SO	HBP	GDP	SB	CS	OBP	SLG	IBB	SH	SF	#Pit	#P/PA	GB	FB	G/F
1993 Season	.455	12	33	8	15	1	0	4	8	1	5	1	1	0	0	.472	.848	0	0	1	130	3.61	8	11	0.73
Last Five Years	.241	308	812	97	196	42	1	46	137	103	242	5	31	0	0	.329	.466	8	0	5	3602	3.89	218	235	0.93

1993 Season

	Avg	AB	H	2B	3B	HR	RBI	BB	SO	OBP	SLG
vs. Left	.000	4	0	0	0	0	0	1	1	.200	.000
vs. Right	.517	29	15	1	0	4	8	0	4	.516	.966
Scoring Posn	.286	7	2	0	0	0	3	0	1	.250	.286
Close & Late	.667	3	2	0	0	0	1	1	1	.750	.667

Last Five Years

	Avg	AB	H	2B	3B	HR	RBI	BB	SO	OBP	SLG
vs. Left	.068	44	3	0	0	1	1	3	17	.146	.136
vs. Right	.251	768	193	42	1	45	136	100	225	.339	.484
Groundball	.253	241	61	11	0	14	42	36	61	.350	.473
Flyball	.272	162	44	12	1	10	32	22	56	.364	.543
Home	.246	406	100	19	1	24	63	62	121	.350	.475
Away	.236	406	96	23	0	22	74	41	121	.307	.456
Day	.244	250	61	11	1	16	45	26	72	.323	.488
Night	.240	562	135	31	0	30	92	77	170	.331	.456
Grass	.241	685	165	35	1	41	116	87	209	.328	.474
Turf	.244	127	31	7	0	5	21	16	33	.331	.417
First Pitch	.281	128	36	7	0	10	27	5	0	.308	.570
Ahead in Count	.368	136	50	13	0	14	33	48	0	.527	.772
Behind in Count	.185	395	73	11	1	16	54	0	197	.192	.339
Two Strikes	.157	427	67	15	1	14	50	49	242	.247	.295

	Avg	AB	H	2B	3B	HR	RBI	BB	SO	OBP	SLG
Scoring Posn	.236	216	51	14	0	12	87	32	64	.331	.468
Close & Late	.228	136	31	6	0	5	27	17	45	.323	.382
None on/out	.213	202	43	8	1	12	12	17	62	.277	.441
Batting #4	.232	466	108	31	1	21	69	54	137	.314	.438
Batting #6	.272	151	41	3	0	11	29	16	47	.339	.510
Other	.241	195	47	8	0	14	39	33	58	.354	.497
April	.245	139	34	5	0	6	26	24	53	.356	.410
May	.207	145	30	6	1	6	18	12	45	.272	.386
June	.270	122	33	14	0	6	17	20	35	.378	.533
July	.224	125	28	4	0	10	23	20	38	.327	.496
August	.170	106	18	4	0	3	9	16	22	.279	.292
September/October	.303	175	53	9	0	15	44	11	49	.349	.611
Pre-All Star	.241	452	109	26	1	23	72	59	148	.332	.456
Post-All Star	.242	360	87	16	0	23	65	44	94	.324	.478

Batter vs. Pitcher (career)

Hits Best Against	Avg	AB	H	2B	3B	HR	RBI	BB	SO	OBP	SLG
Bill Wegman	.500	16	8	2	0	2	4	2	0	.556	1.000
Bill Gullickson	.421	19	8	2	0	3	5	1	5	.450	1.000
Bret Saberhagen	.421	19	8	1	0	4	9	0	7	.421	1.105
Tom Gordon	.400	10	4	1	0	1	3	2	3	.500	.800
Rich DeLucia	.375	8	3	0	0	1	2	5	2	.615	.750

Hits Worst Against	Avg	AB	H	2B	3B	HR	RBI	BB	SO	OBP	SLG
Erik Hanson	.000	21	0	0	0	0	0	2	8	.087	.000
Bobby Witt	.000	10	0	0	0	0	1	2	7	.154	.000
Mike Gardiner	.000	10	0	0	0	0	0	2	2	.167	.000
Kevin Appier	.091	11	1	0	0	0	0	1	6	.167	.091
Alex Fernandez	.100	10	1	0	0	0	0	1	3	.182	.100

Vince Horsman — Athletics

Age 27 – Pitches Left

	ERA	W	L	Sv	G	GS	IP	BB	SO	Avg	H	2B	3B	HR	RBI	OBP	SLG	GF	IR	IRS	Hld	SvOp	SB	CS	GB	FB	G/F
1993 Season	5.40	2	0	0	40	0	25.0	15	17	.255	25	2	0	2	16	.371	.337	5	35	7	10	0	2	1	40	20	2.00
Career (1991-1993)	3.36	4	1	1	102	0	72.1	39	37	.249	66	6	0	5	35	.351	.328	16	89	20	21	2	2	3	106	74	1.43

1993 Season

	ERA	W	L	Sv	G	GS	IP	H	HR	BB	SO
Home	7.30	1	0	0	19	0	12.1	15	1	7	10
Away	3.55	1	0	0	21	0	12.2	10	1	8	7
Starter	0.00	0	0	0	0	0	0.0	0	0	0	0
Reliever	5.40	2	0	0	40	0	25.0	25	2	15	17
0 Days rest	9.53	1	0	0	17	0	11.1	17	2	6	9
1 or 2 Days rest	2.35	1	0	0	13	0	7.2	4	0	8	6

	Avg	AB	H	2B	3B	HR	RBI	BB	SO	OBP	SLG
vs. Left	.304	46	14	1	0	0	4	8	7	.418	.326
vs. Right	.212	52	11	1	0	2	12	7	10	.328	.346
Scoring Posn	.306	36	11	2	0	2	16	7	7	.432	.528
Close & Late	.200	25	5	0	0	1	4	2	4	.259	.320
None on/out	.174	23	4	0	0	0	0	1	4	.208	.174
First Pitch	.400	10	4	0	0	0	0	1	0	.500	.400

1993 Season

	ERA	W	L	Sv	G	GS	IP	H	HR	BB	SO
3+ Days rest	1.50	0	0	0	10	0	6.0	4	0	1	2
Pre-All Star	6.75	1	0	0	10	0	5.1	5	1	2	3
Post-All Star	5.03	1	0	0	30	0	19.2	20	1	13	14

	Avg	AB	H	2B	3B	HR	RBI	BB	SO	OBP	SLG
Ahead in Count	.174	46	8	0	0	0	1	0	15	.191	.174
Behind in Count	.407	27	11	1	0	2	13	8	0	.543	.667
Two Strikes	.156	45	7	0	0	0	2	6	17	.255	.156

Career (1991-1993)

	ERA	W	L	Sv	G	GS	IP	H	HR	BB	SO
Home	4.39	1	1	0	57	0	41.0	38	4	21	20
Away	2.01	3	0	1	45	0	31.1	28	1	18	17
Day	3.60	1	0	0	38	0	25.0	30	1	15	12
Night	3.23	3	1	1	64	0	47.1	36	4	24	25
Grass	4.03	2	1	0	88	0	60.1	58	5	33	35
Turf	0.00	2	0	1	14	0	12.0	8	0	6	2
April	0.00	1	0	1	10	0	10.2	8	0	4	5
May	6.75	0	0	0	9	0	5.1	9	2	3	3
June	3.00	1	0	0	18	0	15.0	10	1	4	6
July	5.91	1	0	0	19	0	10.2	15	1	12	5
August	1.98	0	0	0	19	0	13.2	8	1	6	7
September/October	4.24	1	1	0	27	0	17.0	16	0	10	11
Starter	0.00	0	0	0	0	0	0.0	0	0	0	0
Reliever	3.36	4	1	1	102	0	72.1	66	5	39	37
0 Days rest	7.00	3	1	0	32	0	18.0	26	3	10	11
1 or 2 Days rest	2.48	1	0	1	36	0	29.0	20	2	18	17
3+ Days rest	1.78	0	0	0	34	0	25.1	20	0	11	9
Pre-All Star	2.97	3	0	1	43	0	33.1	33	4	12	16
Post-All Star	3.69	1	1	0	59	0	39.0	33	1	27	21

	Avg	AB	H	2B	3B	HR	RBI	BB	SO	OBP	SLG
vs. Left	.244	123	30	1	0	1	17	21	16	.356	.276
vs. Right	.254	142	36	5	0	4	18	18	21	.346	.373
Inning 1-6	.311	90	28	3	0	3	19	14	13	.415	.444
Inning 7+	.217	175	38	3	0	2	16	25	24	.317	.269
None on	.250	136	34	4	0	1	1	11	17	.311	.301
Runners on	.248	129	32	2	0	4	34	28	20	.388	.357
Scoring Posn	.259	85	22	2	0	4	34	16	16	.379	.424
Close & Late	.167	54	9	0	0	1	7	9	9	.281	.222
None on/out	.259	58	15	1	0	1	1	3	7	.295	.328
vs. 1st Batr (relief)	.283	92	26	1	0	1	12	6	9	.333	.326
First Inning Pitched	.255	231	59	6	0	4	34	35	31	.359	.333
First 15 Pitches	.261	218	57	5	0	5	32	30	29	.357	.353
Pitch 16-30	.214	42	9	1	0	0	3	9	7	.353	.238
Pitch 31-45	.000	5	0	0	0	0	0	0	1	.000	.000
Pitch 46+	.000	0	0	0	0	0	0	0	0	.000	.000
First Pitch	.269	26	7	0	0	0	0	5	0	.406	.269
Ahead in Count	.216	102	22	1	0	1	8	0	27	.223	.255
Behind in Count	.269	78	21	2	0	3	18	19	0	.408	.410
Two Strikes	.182	110	20	1	0	2	12	15	37	.280	.245

Steve Hosey — Giants

Age 25 – Bats Right

	Avg	G	AB	R	H	2B	3B	HR	RBI	BB	SO	HBP	GDP	SB	CS	OBP	SLG	IBB	SH	SF	#Pit	#P/PA	GB	FB	G/F
1993 Season	.500	3	2	0	1	1	0	0	1	1	1	0	0	0	0	.667	1.000	0	0	0	14	4.67	0	1	0.00
Career (1992-1993)	.259	24	58	6	15	2	0	1	7	1	16	0	1	1	1	.262	.345	0	0	2	252	4.13	17	16	1.06

1993 Season

	Avg	AB	H	2B	3B	HR	RBI	BB	SO	OBP	SLG
vs. Left	.500	2	1	1	0	0	1	1	1	.667	1.000
vs. Right	.000	0	0	0	0	0	0	0	0	.000	.000

	Avg	AB	H	2B	3B	HR	RBI	BB	SO	OBP	SLG
Scoring Posn	.000	1	0	0	0	0	0	0	1	.000	.000
Close & Late	.500	2	1	1	0	0	1	0	1	.500	1.000

Charlie Hough — Marlins

Age 46 – Pitches Right

	ERA	W	L	Sv	G	GS	IP	BB	SO	Avg	H	2B	3B	HR	RBI	OBP	SLG	CG	ShO	Sup	QS	#P/S	SB	CS	GB	FB	G/F
1993 Season	4.27	9	16	0	34	34	204.1	71	126	.259	202	42	2	20	91	.325	.395	0	0	3.22	21	95	19	14	272	240	1.13
Last Five Years	4.13	47	63	0	154	152	980.2	445	517	.242	887	151	22	112	431	.327	.386	18	2	3.98	82	103	105	41	1314	1222	1.08

1993 Season

	ERA	W	L	Sv	G	GS	IP	H	HR	BB	SO
Home	4.18	5	6	0	18	18	114.0	105	10	45	69
Away	4.38	4	10	0	16	16	90.1	97	10	26	57
Day	2.60	2	2	0	7	7	45.0	39	4	16	26
Night	4.74	7	14	0	27	27	159.1	163	16	55	100
Grass	3.73	8	9	0	24	24	154.1	141	14	54	95
Turf	5.94	1	7	0	10	10	50.0	61	6	17	31
April	3.73	2	2	0	5	5	31.1	32	1	7	22
May	6.55	0	4	0	6	6	34.1	40	3	10	20
June	2.48	1	2	0	5	5	32.2	28	2	15	24
July	3.47	2	3	0	6	6	36.1	30	6	8	15
August	5.09	3	3	0	6	6	35.1	41	6	13	23
September/October	4.19	1	2	0	6	6	34.1	31	2	18	22
Starter	4.27	9	16	0	34	34	204.1	202	20	71	126
Reliever	0.00	0	0	0	0	0	0.0	0	0	0	0
0-3 Days Rest	3.86	0	1	0	1	1	7.0	7	0	3	4
4 Days Rest	4.35	5	8	0	21	21	126.1	118	10	49	73
5+ Days Rest	4.18	4	7	0	12	12	71.0	77	10	19	49
Pre-All Star	4.33	4	10	0	19	19	116.1	116	10	37	73
Post-All Star	4.19	5	6	0	15	15	88.0	86	10	34	53

	Avg	AB	H	2B	3B	HR	RBI	BB	SO	OBP	SLG
vs. Left	.248	383	95	17	1	11	43	35	56	.310	.384
vs. Right	.270	396	107	25	1	9	48	36	70	.339	.407
Inning 1-6	.252	701	177	40	2	18	82	65	118	.321	.392
Inning 7+	.321	78	25	2	0	2	9	6	8	.365	.423
None on	.258	466	120	26	0	10	10	38	83	.319	.378
Runners on	.262	313	82	16	2	10	81	33	43	.333	.422
Scoring Posn	.237	190	45	8	1	2	61	25	27	.324	.321
Close & Late	.292	65	19	1	0	1	6	4	7	.329	.354
None on/out	.260	204	53	9	0	3	3	17	34	.323	.348
vs. 1st Batr (relief)	.000	0	0	0	0	0	0	0	0	.000	.000
First Inning Pitched	.290	131	38	7	0	6	23	14	21	.372	.481
First 75 Pitches	.259	599	155	34	2	16	73	51	96	.321	.402
Pitch 76-90	.228	92	21	3	0	2	6	8	16	.294	.326
Pitch 91-105	.271	59	16	4	0	1	5	7	8	.348	.390
Pitch 106+	.345	29	10	1	0	1	7	5	6	.441	.483
First Pitch	.314	102	32	8	0	5	17	2	0	.345	.539
Ahead in Count	.220	369	81	16	0	6	30	0	98	.223	.312
Behind in Count	.287	164	47	10	1	3	22	41	0	.425	.415
Two Strikes	.213	352	75	15	0	10	35	28	126	.273	.341

Last Five Years

	ERA	W	L	Sv	G	GS	IP	H	HR	BB	SO
Home	4.04	26	29	0	76	76	497.1	459	53	203	260
Away	4.23	21	34	0	78	76	483.1	428	59	242	257
Day	3.09	12	11	0	38	36	253.0	197	23	104	138
Night	4.49	35	52	0	116	116	727.2	690	89	341	379
Grass	4.03	43	42	0	120	118	779.1	692	89	358	412
Turf	4.51	4	21	0	34	34	201.1	195	23	87	105
April	4.81	5	7	0	18	17	106.2	108	12	48	63
May	4.65	7	11	0	27	26	160.2	152	14	78	83
June	3.38	12	10	0	28	28	197.0	146	28	89	107
July	3.72	3	14	0	25	25	169.1	147	23	71	80
August	4.69	13	12	0	29	29	178.1	181	21	88	97

	Avg	AB	H	2B	3B	HR	RBI	BB	SO	OBP	SLG
vs. Left	.240	1690	406	66	10	42	176	205	218	.323	.366
vs. Right	.243	1980	481	85	12	70	255	240	299	.331	.404
Inning 1-6	.240	3093	742	129	19	91	368	381	450	.326	.382
Inning 7+	.251	577	145	22	3	21	63	64	67	.330	.409
None on	.239	2183	521	101	6	70	70	247	321	.322	.387
Runners on	.246	1487	366	50	16	42	361	198	196	.334	.386
Scoring Posn	.226	831	188	22	8	15	290	147	120	.335	.326
Close & Late	.272	290	79	13	1	11	35	41	34	.365	.438
None on/out	.240	966	232	45	4	25	25	92	126	.312	.373
vs. 1st Batr (relief)	.000	2	0	0	0	0	0	0	1	.000	.000
First Inning Pitched	.246	565	139	24	2	15	89	92	97	.357	.375

Last Five Years

	ERA	W	L	Sv	G	GS	IP	H	HR	BB	SO
September/October	3.90	7	9	0	27	27	168.2	153	14	71	87
Starter	4.12	47	63	0	152	152	975.0	883	112	440	512
Reliever	6.35	0	0	0	2	0	5.2	4	0	5	5
0-3 Days Rest	3.53	2	4	0	6	6	43.1	37	4	16	24
4 Days Rest	3.93	29	30	0	84	84	540.0	471	56	255	299
5+ Days Rest	4.43	16	29	0	62	62	391.2	375	52	169	189
Pre-All Star	4.17	25	34	0	82	80	524.2	453	63	244	282
Post-All Star	4.09	22	29	0	72	72	456.0	434	49	201	235

	Avg	AB	H	2B	3B	HR	RBI	BB	SO	OBP	SLG
First 75 Pitches	.246	2544	625	110	16	75	309	297	380	.328	.390
Pitch 76-90	.240	462	111	19	2	10	36	50	58	.317	.355
Pitch 91-105	.198	344	68	9	1	5	30	59	37	.317	.273
Pitch 106+	.259	320	83	13	3	22	56	39	42	.348	.525
First Pitch	.280	479	134	26	0	14	63	5	0	.302	.422
Ahead in Count	.201	1557	313	52	11	34	147	0	405	.206	.314
Behind in Count	.288	891	257	43	7	41	131	275	0	.454	.490
Two Strikes	.193	1564	302	49	7	35	146	163	517	.273	.301

Pitcher vs. Batter (since 1984)

Pitches Best Vs.	Avg	AB	H	2B	3B	HR	RBI	BB	SO	OBP	SLG
Roberto Alomar	.063	16	1	0	0	0	2	2	1	.158	.063
Felix Fermin	.067	15	1	1	0	0	0	1	1	.125	.133
Otis Nixon	.071	14	1	0	0	0	1	2	0	.176	.071
Bobby Bonilla	.083	12	1	0	0	0	0	1	3	.154	.083
Luis Polonia	.115	26	3	0	0	0	1	1	2	.148	.115

Pitches Worst Vs.	Avg	AB	H	2B	3B	HR	RBI	BB	SO	OBP	SLG
Cecil Fielder	.545	11	6	3	0	0	4	2	1	.571	.818
Junior Felix	.444	9	4	2	0	1	1	3	1	.583	1.000
Rob Deer	.429	14	6	0	0	2	9	3	3	.529	.857
Al Martin	.364	11	4	1	0	2	4	2	2	.462	1.000
Juan Gonzalez	.333	12	4	1	0	2	4	1	2	.385	.917

Wayne Housie — Brewers

Age 29 – Bats Both (flyball hitter)

	Avg	G	AB	R	H	2B	3B	HR	RBI	BB	SO	HBP	GDP	SB	CS	OBP	SLG	IBB	SH	SF	#Pit	#P/PA	GB	FB	G/F
1993 Season	.188	18	16	2	3	1	0	0	1	1	1	0	0	0	0	.235	.250	0	0	0	55	3.24	6	4	1.50
Career (1991-1993)	.208	29	24	4	5	2	0	0	1	2	4	0	1	1	0	.269	.292	0	1	0	86	3.19	7	7	1.00

1993 Season

	Avg	AB	H	2B	3B	HR	RBI	BB	SO	OBP	SLG
vs. Left	.250	4	1	0	0	0	1	0	0	.250	.250
vs. Right	.167	12	2	1	0	0	0	1	1	.231	.250
Scoring Posn	.200	5	1	0	0	0	1	1	1	.333	.200
Close & Late	.250	4	1	1	0	0	0	0	0	.250	.500

Chris Howard — Mariners

Age 28 – Bats Right (flyball hitter)

	Avg	G	AB	R	H	2B	3B	HR	RBI	BB	SO	HBP	GDP	SB	CS	OBP	SLG	IBB	SH	SF	#Pit	#P/PA	GB	FB	G/F
1993 Season	.000	4	1	0	0	0	0	0	0	0	0	0	0	0	0	.000	.000	0	0	0	3	3.00	1	0	0.00
Career (1991-1993)	.143	13	7	1	1	1	0	0	0	1	2	0	0	0	0	.250	.286	0	0	0	25	3.13	1	3	0.33

1993 Season

	Avg	AB	H	2B	3B	HR	RBI	BB	SO	OBP	SLG
vs. Left	.000	0	0	0	0	0	0	0	0	.000	.000
vs. Right	.000	1	0	0	0	0	0	0	0	.000	.000
Scoring Posn	.000	1	0	0	0	0	0	0	0	.000	.000
Close & Late	.000	1	0	0	0	0	0	0	0	.000	.000

Chris Howard — White Sox

Age 28 – Pitches Left

	ERA	W	L	Sv	G	GS	IP	BB	SO	Avg	H	2B	3B	HR	RBI	OBP	SLG	GF	IR	IRS	Hld	SvOp	SB	CS	GB	FB	G/F
1993 Season	0.00	1	0	0	3	0	2.1	3	1	.286	2	0	0	0	1	.500	.286	0	2	1	0	0	0	1	3	2	1.50

1993 Season

	ERA	W	L	Sv	G	GS	IP	H	HR	BB	SO
Home	0.00	0	0	0	1	0	0.2	0	0	1	0
Away	0.00	1	0	0	2	0	1.2	2	0	2	1

	Avg	AB	H	2B	3B	HR	RBI	BB	SO	OBP	SLG
vs. Left	.250	4	1	0	0	0	0	2	0	.500	.250
vs. Right	.333	3	1	0	0	0	1	1	1	.500	.333

Dave Howard — Royals

Age 27 – Bats Both

	Avg	G	AB	R	H	2B	3B	HR	RBI	BB	SO	HBP	GDP	SB	CS	OBP	SLG	IBB	SH	SF	#Pit	#P/PA	GB	FB	G/F
1993 Season	.333	15	24	5	8	0	1	0	2	2	5	0	0	1	0	.370	.417	0	2	1	102	3.52	12	3	4.00
Career (1991-1993)	.225	183	479	44	108	13	3	2	37	33	93	1	4	7	6	.274	.278	0	19	5	1913	3.56	166	127	1.31

1993 Season

	Avg	AB	H	2B	3B	HR	RBI	BB	SO	OBP	SLG
vs. Left	.000	0	0	0	0	0	0	0	0	.000	.000
vs. Right	.333	24	8	0	1	0	2	2	5	.370	.417
Scoring Posn	.200	5	1	0	0	0	2	0	2	.167	.200
Close & Late	.500	4	2	0	0	0	2	0	2	.400	.500

Career (1991-1993)

	Avg	AB	H	2B	3B	HR	RBI	BB	SO	OBP	SLG
vs. Left	.217	152	33	4	1	1	12	8	27	.255	.276
vs. Right	.229	327	75	9	2	1	25	25	66	.283	.278
Groundball	.254	114	29	4	1	0	10	8	15	.303	.307
Flyball	.167	132	22	2	1	1	8	12	28	.236	.220
Home	.231	251	58	6	2	1	23	22	51	.289	.283
Away	.219	228	50	7	1	1	14	11	42	.257	.272
Day	.228	127	29	1	1	0	8	7	21	.268	.252
Night	.224	352	79	12	2	2	29	26	72	.276	.287
Grass	.229	175	40	4	1	0	9	8	31	.265	.263
Turf	.224	304	68	9	2	2	28	25	62	.279	.286
First Pitch	.242	99	24	2	1	0	9	0	0	.240	.283
Ahead in Count	.313	67	21	2	1	1	8	16	0	.435	.418
Behind in Count	.171	228	39	4	0	0	11	0	84	.173	.189
Two Strikes	.177	226	40	4	1	1	10	17	93	.233	.217

	Avg	AB	H	2B	3B	HR	RBI	BB	SO	OBP	SLG
Scoring Posn	.242	124	30	3	0	2	36	8	17	.277	.315
Close & Late	.229	70	16	5	0	1	7	3	13	.257	.343
None on/out	.214	117	25	2	3	0	0	8	25	.264	.282
Batting #8	.191	131	25	3	0	1	13	10	27	.246	.237
Batting #9	.239	310	74	9	3	1	24	21	60	.286	.297
Other	.237	38	9	1	0	0	0	2	6	.275	.263
April	.081	37	3	0	0	0	3	3	7	.150	.081
May	.235	17	4	0	0	0	1	2	4	.316	.235
June	.188	32	6	0	1	0	2	3	7	.250	.250
July	.231	104	24	4	0	1	10	6	17	.277	.298
August	.306	160	49	9	0	1	18	11	29	.347	.381
September/October	.171	129	22	0	2	0	3	8	29	.217	.202
Pre-All Star	.152	92	14	0	1	0	8	8	20	.216	.174
Post-All Star	.243	387	94	13	2	2	29	25	73	.288	.302

Batter vs. Pitcher (career)

Hits Best Against	Avg	AB	H	2B	3B	HR	RBI	BB	SO	OBP	SLG

Hits Worst Against	Avg	AB	H	2B	3B	HR	RBI	BB	SO	OBP	SLG
Dave Stewart	.083	12	1	0	0	0	2	1	3	.143	.083

Batter vs. Pitcher (career)																							
Hits Best Against	Avg	AB	H	2B	3B	HR	RBI	BB	SO	OBP	SLG	Hits Worst Against	Avg	AB	H	2B	3B	HR	RBI	BB	SO	OBP	SLG
												Randy Johnson	.182	11	2	1	0	0	1	0	5	.182	.273

Thomas Howard — Reds

Age 29 – Bats Both (groundball hitter)

	Avg	G	AB	R	H	2B	3B	HR	RBI	BB	SO	HBP	GDP	SB	CS	OBP	SLG	IBB	SH	SF	#Pit	#P/PA	GB	FB	G/F
1993 Season	.254	112	319	48	81	15	3	7	36	24	63	0	9	10	7	.302	.386	0	0	5	1300	3.74	135	72	1.88
Career (1990-1993)	.262	360	1005	119	263	44	8	13	90	65	191	1	18	35	23	.305	.360	5	14	8	3896	3.56	413	214	1.93

1993 Season

	Avg	AB	H	2B	3B	HR	RBI	BB	SO	OBP	SLG		Avg	AB	H	2B	3B	HR	RBI	BB	SO	OBP	SLG
vs. Left	.156	109	17	1	0	1	8	9	34	.213	.193	Scoring Posn	.260	77	20	4	1	3	32	8	16	.311	.455
vs. Right	.305	210	64	14	3	6	28	15	29	.350	.486	Close & Late	.182	55	10	3	0	0	9	5	15	.242	.236
Groundball	.213	75	16	3	0	2	5	7	9	.277	.333	None on/out	.301	93	28	9	1	1	1	7	13	.350	.452
Flyball	.288	59	17	3	2	1	7	2	14	.302	.458	Batting #1	.318	132	42	8	3	5	15	12	19	.375	.538
Home	.252	143	36	6	1	5	17	16	23	.321	.413	Batting #2	.206	131	27	3	0	2	16	7	33	.241	.275
Away	.256	176	45	9	2	2	19	8	40	.285	.364	Other	.214	56	12	4	0	0	5	5	11	.270	.286
Day	.273	110	30	6	1	2	13	6	17	.303	.400	April	.283	53	15	3	0	2	12	2	10	.304	.453
Night	.244	209	51	9	2	5	23	18	46	.301	.378	May	.203	59	12	0	0	0	2	3	13	.242	.203
Grass	.240	196	47	8	2	3	19	14	38	.284	.347	June	.211	19	4	2	0	0	4	2	5	.261	.316
Turf	.276	123	34	7	1	4	17	10	25	.331	.447	July	.250	32	8	1	0	0	3	4	11	.333	.281
First Pitch	.361	36	13	3	0	1	8	0	0	.333	.528	August	.264	53	14	2	0	4	9	4	9	.305	.528
Ahead in Count	.242	62	15	2	2	2	10	13	0	.368	.435	September/October	.272	103	28	7	3	1	6	9	15	.330	.427
Behind in Count	.228	171	39	8	1	4	15	0	56	.227	.357	Pre-All Star	.235	153	36	6	0	2	21	8	37	.268	.314
Two Strikes	.194	160	31	5	1	3	10	11	63	.244	.294	Post-All Star	.271	166	45	9	3	5	15	16	26	.332	.452

1993 By Position

Position	Avg	AB	H	2B	3B	HR	RBI	BB	SO	OBP	SLG	G	GS	Innings	PO	A	E	DP	Fld Pct	Rng Fctr	In Zone	Outs	Zone Rtg	MLB Zone
As Pinch Hitter	.207	29	6	4	0	0	3	3	8	.281	.345	32	0	---	---	---	---	---	---	---	---	---	---	---
As lf	.292	106	31	5	3	4	13	8	13	.336	.509	36	23	228.1	59	2	1	0	.984	2.40	57	50	.877	.818
As cf	.250	76	19	3	0	2	7	8	17	.318	.368	23	17	171.0	50	3	0	2	1.000	2.79	59	48	.814	.829
As rf	.241	87	21	3	0	1	12	5	22	.280	.310	28	20	183.2	46	2	2	0	.960	2.35	53	41	.774	.826

Career (1990-1993)

	Avg	AB	H	2B	3B	HR	RBI	BB	SO	OBP	SLG		Avg	AB	H	2B	3B	HR	RBI	BB	SO	OBP	SLG
vs. Left	.226	257	58	4	1	4	21	20	66	.278	.296	Scoring Posn	.273	242	66	9	1	5	78	24	58	.328	.380
vs. Right	.274	748	205	40	7	9	69	45	125	.315	.382	Close & Late	.223	202	45	9	0	2	25	12	39	.263	.297
Groundball	.275	276	76	8	4	3	29	20	33	.326	.366	None on/out	.258	279	72	18	2	1	1	16	46	.298	.348
Flyball	.251	223	56	11	3	3	16	9	48	.277	.368	Batting #1	.282	337	95	19	5	6	25	22	55	.326	.421
Home	.263	486	128	15	4	10	49	36	89	.313	.372	Batting #2	.265	385	102	15	1	3	40	17	78	.292	.332
Away	.260	519	135	29	4	3	41	29	102	.297	.349	Other	.233	283	66	10	2	4	25	26	58	.297	.325
Day	.277	332	92	16	2	5	27	21	48	.319	.383	April	.314	105	33	5	0	2	14	5	17	.342	.419
Night	.254	673	171	28	6	8	63	44	143	.298	.349	May	.223	166	37	3	2	0	8	6	34	.247	.265
Grass	.262	738	193	30	6	8	65	45	137	.302	.351	June	.276	170	47	9	1	1	17	13	20	.326	.359
Turf	.262	267	70	14	2	5	25	20	54	.313	.386	July	.256	160	41	5	0	1	8	15	41	.320	.306
First Pitch	.444	151	67	11	1	4	24	5	0	.450	.609	August	.277	177	49	9	1	5	23	8	33	.305	.424
Ahead in Count	.282	188	53	8	3	4	22	25	0	.364	.420	September/October	.247	227	56	13	4	4	20	18	46	.302	.392
Behind in Count	.198	515	102	18	2	5	35	0	169	.198	.270	Pre-All Star	.262	508	133	18	3	3	43	30	90	.301	.327
Two Strikes	.172	472	81	11	2	3	25	34	191	.226	.222	Post-All Star	.262	497	130	26	5	10	47	35	101	.309	.394

Batter vs. Pitcher (career)

Hits Best Against	Avg	AB	H	2B	3B	HR	RBI	BB	SO	OBP	SLG	Hits Worst Against	Avg	AB	H	2B	3B	HR	RBI	BB	SO	OBP	SLG
Les Lancaster	.545	11	6	4	0	1	3	0	2	.545	1.182	Rick Sutcliffe	.000	10	0	0	0	0	1	0	1	.000	.000
Jack Morris	.500	12	6	1	0	1	5	0	1	.500	.833	Dennis Martinez	.154	13	2	0	0	1	1	2	1	.267	.385
Mike Moore	.462	13	6	0	0	1	3	0	0	.462	.692	Randy Johnson	.167	12	2	0	0	0	2	2	4	.286	.167
Kevin Brown	.455	11	5	1	0	0	1	0	1	.455	.545	Dwight Gooden	.182	11	2	0	0	0	0	1	3	.250	.182
John Smiley	.417	12	5	1	0	1	3	0	4	.417	.750	Chris Bosio	.182	11	2	0	0	0	0	0	2	.182	.182

Steve Howe — Yankees

Age 36 – Pitches Left (groundball pitcher)

	ERA	W	L	Sv	G	GS	IP	BB	SO	Avg	H	2B	3B	HR	RBI	OBP	SLG	GF	IR	IRS	Hld	SvOp	SB	CS	GB	FB	G/F
1993 Season	4.97	3	5	4	51	0	50.2	10	19	.297	58	11	0	7	31	.338	.462	19	59	13	10	7	1	1	88	44	2.00
Last Five Years	3.20	9	6	13	108	0	121.0	20	65	.238	106	19	0	9	49	.278	.342	39	109	23	22	17	2	1	192	111	1.73

1993 Season

	ERA	W	L	Sv	G	GS	IP	H	HR	BB	SO		Avg	AB	H	2B	3B	HR	RBI	BB	SO	OBP	SLG
Home	5.71	1	2	1	18	0	17.1	25	3	3	4	vs. Left	.242	62	15	1	0	1	6	3	9	.288	.306
Away	4.59	2	3	3	33	0	33.1	33	4	7	15	vs. Right	.323	133	43	10	0	6	25	7	10	.361	.534
Starter	0.00	0	0	0	0	0	0.0	0	0	0	0	Scoring Posn	.291	55	16	4	0	1	22	6	5	.349	.418
Reliever	4.97	3	5	4	51	0	50.2	58	7	10	19	Close & Late	.297	64	19	4	0	5	18	6	6	.356	.594
0 Days rest	2.45	1	0	1	9	0	7.1	5	1	1	2	None on/out	.333	48	16	2	0	2	2	1	8	.360	.500
1 or 2 Days rest	3.13	2	3	3	27	0	31.2	28	3	7	11	First Pitch	.371	35	13	2	0	0	7	4	0	.439	.429
3+ Days rest	11.57	0	2	0	15	0	11.2	25	3	2	6	Ahead in Count	.228	79	18	6	0	2	8	0	17	.238	.380
Pre-All Star	6.57	2	3	3	26	0	24.2	29	4	7	7	Behind in Count	.308	52	16	1	0	3	11	4	0	.362	.500
Post-All Star	3.46	1	2	1	25	0	26.0	29	3	3	12	Two Strikes	.221	68	15	6	0	3	8	2	19	.254	.441

Jay Howell — Braves

Age 38 – Pitches Right (flyball pitcher)

	ERA	W	L	Sv	G	GS	IP	BB	SO	Avg	H	2B	3B	HR	RBI	OBP	SLG	GF	IR	IRS	Hld	SvOp	SB	CS	GB	FB	G/F
1993 Season	2.31	3	3	0	54	0	58.1	16	37	.229	48	6	0	3	23	.278	.300	22	25	11	7	3	5	5	78	61	1.28
Last Five Years	2.12	20	19	64	240	0	301.2	87	227	.225	247	36	4	16	100	.284	.308	118	101	39	15	83	28	11	341	346	0.99

1993 Season

	ERA	W	L	Sv	G	GS	IP	H	HR	BB	SO		Avg	AB	H	2B	3B	HR	RBI	BB	SO	OBP	SLG
Home	1.82	2	1	0	35	0	39.2	33	2	9	25	vs. Left	.233	90	21	2	0	0	6	4	16	.263	.256
Away	3.38	1	2	0	19	0	18.2	15	1	7	12	vs. Right	.225	120	27	4	0	3	17	12	21	.289	.333
Starter	0.00	0	0	0	0	0	0.0	0	0	0	0	Scoring Posn	.289	45	13	3	0	1	20	6	10	.345	.422
Reliever	2.31	3	3	0	54	0	58.1	48	3	16	37	Close & Late	.240	50	12	2	0	0	8	3	7	.273	.280
0 Days rest	3.38	0	2	0	14	0	16.0	16	0	3	10	None on/out	.170	53	9	1	0	0	0	2	6	.200	.189
1 or 2 Days rest	3.10	1	1	0	20	0	20.1	17	2	6	15	First Pitch	.226	31	7	1	0	0	3	2	0	.265	.258
3+ Days rest	0.82	2	0	0	20	0	22.0	15	1	7	12	Ahead in Count	.182	110	20	1	0	3	11	0	35	.182	.273
Pre-All Star	2.64	1	2	0	28	0	30.2	28	1	8	14	Behind in Count	.378	37	14	2	0	0	6	10	0	.490	.432
Post-All Star	1.95	2	1	0	26	0	27.2	20	2	8	23	Two Strikes	.175	103	18	3	0	3	12	4	37	.206	.291

Last Five Years

	ERA	W	L	Sv	G	GS	IP	H	HR	BB	SO		Avg	AB	H	2B	3B	HR	RBI	BB	SO	OBP	SLG
Home	2.01	14	11	32	134	0	175.0	137	7	46	134	vs. Left	.220	587	129	20	3	7	50	47	129	.283	.300
Away	2.27	6	8	32	106	0	126.2	110	9	41	93	vs. Right	.230	512	118	16	1	9	50	40	98	.286	.318
Day	1.66	4	4	25	73	0	92.0	74	5	23	69	Inning 1-6	.256	39	10	1	0	0	4	4	8	.318	.282
Night	2.32	16	15	39	167	0	209.2	173	11	64	158	Inning 7+	.224	1060	237	35	4	16	96	83	219	.283	.309
Grass	1.98	17	12	51	186	0	236.0	187	10	63	183	None on	.219	643	141	23	1	13	13	36	126	.267	.319
Turf	2.60	3	7	13	54	0	65.2	60	6	24	44	Runners on	.232	456	106	13	3	3	87	51	101	.307	.294
April	2.23	3	4	3	26	0	36.1	38	0	11	24	Scoring Posn	.232	276	64	6	3	3	83	39	64	.322	.308
May	2.12	1	5	16	39	0	46.2	36	3	13	27	Close & Late	.238	610	145	18	3	8	66	55	122	.306	.316
June	1.69	4	2	10	49	0	64.0	47	3	19	53	None on/out	.241	274	66	9	1	8	8	13	48	.280	.369
July	2.40	3	2	10	38	0	48.2	37	4	17	38	vs. 1st Batr (relief)	.237	215	51	8	0	6	20	19	36	.303	.358
August	1.35	4	5	15	49	0	60.0	45	3	13	43	First Inning Pitched	.214	782	167	24	3	12	79	61	160	.273	.298
September/October	3.33	5	1	10	39	0	46.0	44	3	14	42	First 15 Pitches	.229	755	173	23	2	13	74	55	140	.284	.317
Starter	0.00	0	0	0	0	0	0.0	0	0	0	0	Pitch 16-30	.215	297	64	10	2	3	25	28	76	.284	.293
Reliever	2.12	20	19	64	240	0	301.2	247	16	87	227	Pitch 31-45	.217	46	10	3	0	0	1	4	10	.294	.283
0 Days rest	2.59	7	6	12	51	0	59.0	46	2	12	41	Pitch 46+	.000	1	0	0	0	0	0	0	1	.000	.000
1 or 2 Days rest	1.92	6	6	31	101	0	131.0	107	7	38	105	First Pitch	.278	169	47	7	0	2	19	16	0	.339	.355
3+ Days rest	2.10	7	7	21	88	0	111.2	94	7	37	81	Ahead in Count	.185	542	100	12	2	7	34	0	205	.195	.253
Pre-All Star	2.02	8	11	30	126	0	160.1	135	6	48	115	Behind in Count	.282	206	58	9	2	5	25	41	0	.397	.417
Post-All Star	2.23	12	8	34	114	0	141.1	112	10	39	112	Two Strikes	.168	529	89	12	2	7	35	30	227	.215	.238

Pitcher vs. Batter (since 1984)

Pitches Best Vs.	Avg	AB	H	2B	3B	HR	RBI	BB	SO	OBP	SLG	Pitches Worst Vs.	Avg	AB	H	2B	3B	HR	RBI	BB	SO	OBP	SLG
Tim Wallach	.000	9	0	0	0	0	1	1	1	.091	.000	Paul O'Neill	.727	11	8	2	1	2	10	2	1	.769	1.636
Andre Dawson	.091	11	1	0	0	0	0	0	3	.091	.091	Harold Baines	.400	10	4	0	0	0	0	1	3	.455	.400
Mark Grace	.091	11	1	0	0	0	0	0	2	.091	.091	Mike Pagliarulo	.385	13	5	2	0	0	3	1	3	.429	.538
Robby Thompson	.118	17	2	0	0	0	3	0	9	.111	.118	Todd Benzinger	.375	8	3	1	0	1	4	1	3	.364	.875
Ken Caminiti	.125	16	2	0	0	0	0	0	6	.125	.125	Dale Murphy	.308	13	4	1	0	1	2	1	3	.357	.615

Dann Howitt — Mariners

Age 30 – Bats Left

	Avg	G	AB	R	H	2B	3B	HR	RBI	BB	SO	HBP	GDP	SB	CS	OBP	SLG	IBB	SH	SF	#Pit	#P/PA	GB	FB	G/F
1993 Season	.211	32	76	6	16	3	1	2	8	4	18	0	0	0	0	.250	.355	0	0	0	291	3.64	27	24	1.13
Career (1989-1993)	.184	105	228	21	42	8	3	5	22	16	53	0	7	1	1	.234	.311	1	1	4	931	3.74	81	70	1.16

1993 Season

	Avg	AB	H	2B	3B	HR	RBI	BB	SO	OBP	SLG		Avg	AB	H	2B	3B	HR	RBI	BB	SO	OBP	SLG
vs. Left	.000	3	0	0	0	0	0	0	2	.000	.000	Scoring Posn	.105	19	2	0	0	1	6	0	2	.105	.263
vs. Right	.219	73	16	3	1	2	8	4	16	.260	.370	Close & Late	.083	12	1	0	0	0	0	0	4	.083	.083

Kent Hrbek — Twins

Age 34 – Bats Left

	Avg	G	AB	R	H	2B	3B	HR	RBI	BB	SO	HBP	GDP	SB	CS	OBP	SLG	IBB	SH	SF	#Pit	#P/PA	GB	FB	G/F
1993 Season	.242	123	392	60	95	11	1	25	83	71	57	1	12	4	2	.357	.467	6	3	4	1711	3.63	159	124	1.28
Last Five Years	.267	619	2115	304	565	94	2	107	393	331	241	9	63	21	10	.366	.465	31	11	21	8646	3.48	847	684	1.24

1993 Season

	Avg	AB	H	2B	3B	HR	RBI	BB	SO	OBP	SLG		Avg	AB	H	2B	3B	HR	RBI	BB	SO	OBP	SLG
vs. Left	.224	58	13	1	0	3	14	12	12	.352	.397	Scoring Posn	.206	126	26	2	1	7	55	31	23	.354	.405
vs. Right	.246	334	82	10	1	22	69	59	45	.358	.479	Close & Late	.333	60	20	5	0	0	5	14	3	.459	.417
Groundball	.303	76	23	2	0	4	15	19	9	.438	.487	None on/out	.216	97	21	4	0	5	5	13	12	.309	.412
Flyball	.253	83	21	2	1	7	26	17	8	.379	.554	Batting #3	.111	18	2	0	0	1	2	7	3	.360	.278
Home	.249	193	48	7	1	12	45	35	28	.364	.482	Batting #4	.257	335	86	10	1	24	80	53	46	.356	.507
Away	.236	199	47	4	0	13	38	36	29	.350	.452	Other	.179	39	7	1	0	0	1	11	8	.360	.205
Day	.254	138	35	4	0	9	31	25	19	.361	.478	April	.303	66	20	4	1	3	14	10	9	.395	.530
Night	.236	254	60	7	1	16	52	46	38	.354	.461	May	.219	64	14	1	0	5	13	16	10	.366	.469
Grass	.257	140	36	3	0	12	33	26	17	.369	.536	June	.129	31	4	0	0	1	2	3	5	.206	.226
Turf	.234	252	59	8	1	13	50	45	40	.350	.429	July	.240	75	18	1	0	4	17	10	10	.330	.413
First Pitch	.268	71	19	2	0	8	18	6	0	.325	.634	August	.221	95	21	2	0	5	17	17	16	.339	.400
Ahead in Count	.292	113	33	3	0	11	34	39	0	.465	.611	September/October	.295	61	18	3	0	7	20	15	7	.434	.689
Behind in Count	.172	134	23	4	1	3	12	0	46	.178	.284	Pre-All Star	.238	193	46	5	1	11	37	32	28	.343	.446
Two Strikes	.190	147	28	6	1	4	23	26	57	.312	.327	Post-All Star	.246	199	49	6	0	14	46	39	29	.370	.487

1993 By Position

Position	Avg	AB	H	2B	3B	HR	RBI	BB	SO	OBP	SLG	G	GS	Innings	PO	A	E	DP	Fld Pct	Rng Fctr	In Zone	Outs	Zone Rtg	MLB Zone
As Pinch Hitter	.125	8	1	0	0	0	0	3	2	.364	.125	11	0	---	---	---	---	---	---	---	---	---	---	---
As 1b	.243	379	92	11	1	24	81	68	55	.356	.467	115	109	944.2	941	80	5	99	.995	---	188	160	.851	.834

Last Five Years

	Avg	AB	H	2B	3B	HR	RBI	BB	SO	OBP	SLG		Avg	AB	H	2B	3B	HR	RBI	BB	SO	OBP	SLG
vs. Left	.270	507	137	16	0	18	90	69	75	.358	.408	Scoring Posn	.258	612	158	27	1	29	278	136	81	.384	.448
vs. Right	.266	1608	428	78	2	89	303	262	166	.368	.483	Close & Late	.312	308	96	19	0	12	49	50	31	.404	.490
Groundball	.266	552	147	22	0	23	93	91	63	.371	.431	None on/out	.240	504	121	26	0	24	24	66	59	.330	.435
Flyball	.306	444	136	28	1	27	97	76	48	.405	.556	Batting #4	.269	1559	420	70	1	83	310	246	168	.367	.475
Home	.279	1060	296	52	1	58	225	163	108	.373	.494	Batting #7	.262	168	44	9	0	7	19	27	27	.371	.440
Away	.255	1055	269	42	1	49	168	168	133	.358	.436	Other	.260	388	101	15	1	17	64	58	46	.358	.436
Day	.252	627	158	24	0	29	109	92	67	.346	.429	April	.267	266	71	16	1	13	60	41	33	.368	.481
Night	.274	1488	407	70	2	78	284	239	174	.374	.481	May	.281	356	100	16	1	17	53	68	33	.394	.475
Grass	.256	788	202	34	0	39	135	134	95	.365	.448	June	.268	299	80	20	0	13	48	45	35	.361	.465
Turf	.274	1327	363	60	2	68	258	197	146	.366	.476	July	.270	422	114	16	0	22	80	62	48	.367	.464
First Pitch	.321	470	151	24	0	29	98	20	0	.348	.557	August	.248	463	115	15	0	24	84	58	64	.329	.436
Ahead in Count	.291	578	168	28	1	40	135	173	0	.450	.550	September/October	.275	309	85	11	0	18	68	57	28	.385	.485
Behind in Count	.229	698	160	23	1	23	96	0	199	.233	.364	Pre-All Star	.272	1054	287	55	2	49	188	174	119	.375	.468
Two Strikes	.204	727	148	29	1	16	90	131	241	.326	.312	Post-All Star	.262	1061	278	39	0	58	205	157	122	.356	.463

Batter vs. Pitcher (since 1984)

Hits Best Against	Avg	AB	H	2B	3B	HR	RBI	BB	SO	OBP	SLG	Hits Worst Against	Avg	AB	H	2B	3B	HR	RBI	BB	SO	OBP	SLG
Pete Harnisch	.556	9	5	2	0	2	7	2	0	.636	1.444	Bryan Harvey	.000	10	0	0	0	0	0	1	3	.091	.000
Dennis Martinez	.545	11	6	2	0	1	3	1	0	.583	1.000	Dan Plesac	.000	8	0	0	0	0	2	1	1	.091	.000
Dave Johnson	.545	11	6	3	0	2	2	3	0	.643	1.364	Greg Cadaret	.059	17	1	0	0	0	2	3	3	.200	.059
Doug Jones	.500	14	7	2	0	2	5	1	1	.533	1.071	Edwin Nunez	.063	16	1	0	0	0	1	3	3	.211	.063
Joe Hesketh	.455	11	5	2	0	1	5	2	3	.500	.909	Charles Nagy	.067	15	1	0	0	0	0	2	4	.176	.067

Michael Huff — White Sox

Age 30 – Bats Right

	Avg	G	AB	R	H	2B	3B	HR	RBI	BB	SO	HBP	GDP	SB	CS	OBP	SLG	IBB	SH	SF	#Pit	#P/PA	GB	FB	G/F
1993 Season	.182	43	44	4	8	2	0	1	6	9	15	1	0	1	0	.321	.295	0	1	2	249	4.37	11	16	0.69
Career (1989-1993)	.230	217	427	63	98	18	2	5	41	59	93	9	9	16	7	.331	.316	3	10	6	2020	3.95	147	112	1.31

1993 Season

	Avg	AB	H	2B	3B	HR	RBI	BB	SO	OBP	SLG		Avg	AB	H	2B	3B	HR	RBI	BB	SO	OBP	SLG
vs. Left	.188	16	3	1	0	1	1	2	5	.278	.438	Scoring Posn	.286	7	2	1	0	0	5	4	2	.462	.429
vs. Right	.179	28	5	1	0	0	5	7	10	.342	.214	Close & Late	.000	6	0	0	0	0	1	2	2	.222	.000

Career (1989-1993)

	Avg	AB	H	2B	3B	HR	RBI	BB	SO	OBP	SLG		Avg	AB	H	2B	3B	HR	RBI	BB	SO	OBP	SLG
vs. Left	.225	244	55	11	1	5	19	28	44	.312	.340	Scoring Posn	.274	95	26	5	1	0	36	18	20	.370	.347
vs. Right	.235	183	43	7	1	0	22	31	49	.356	.284	Close & Late	.250	84	21	3	1	0	7	8	20	.326	.310
Groundball	.205	132	27	3	1	0	13	21	22	.331	.242	None on/out	.234	124	29	6	1	2	2	21	22	.354	.347
Flyball	.188	85	16	3	0	1	7	11	22	.286	.259	Batting #1	.224	174	39	6	1	2	9	27	29	.335	.305
Home	.226	212	48	10	2	1	20	27	46	.328	.307	Batting #7	.231	91	21	4	1	2	14	12	25	.336	.363
Away	.233	215	50	8	0	4	21	32	47	.335	.326	Other	.235	162	38	8	0	1	18	20	39	.324	.302
Day	.176	136	24	4	1	0	4	21	36	.300	.221	April	.250	60	15	4	1	0	7	11	12	.361	.350
Night	.254	291	74	14	1	5	37	38	57	.346	.361	May	.250	108	27	6	0	1	11	19	27	.370	.333
Grass	.233	348	81	15	2	2	34	49	80	.335	.305	June	.229	70	16	1	0	2	4	7	10	.299	.329
Turf	.215	79	17	3	0	3	7	10	13	.315	.367	July	.136	22	3	1	0	0	3	3	6	.231	.182
First Pitch	.356	45	16	2	1	0	4	1	0	.362	.444	August	.286	63	18	3	1	2	12	7	11	.375	.460
Ahead in Count	.259	85	22	6	1	1	13	34	0	.471	.388	September/October	.183	104	19	3	0	0	4	12	27	.286	.212
Behind in Count	.180	211	38	7	0	1	15	0	70	.203	.227	Pre-All Star	.240	242	58	11	1	3	22	37	50	.344	.331
Two Strikes	.166	229	38	8	0	4	14	23	93	.257	.253	Post-All Star	.216	185	40	7	1	2	19	22	43	.315	.297

Batter vs. Pitcher (career)

Hits Best Against	Avg	AB	H	2B	3B	HR	RBI	BB	SO	OBP	SLG	Hits Worst Against	Avg	AB	H	2B	3B	HR	RBI	BB	SO	OBP	SLG
Bill Krueger	.400	10	4	1	0	0	1	0	3	.364	.500	Jim Abbott	.000	13	0	0	0	0	0	1	2	.071	.000
Chuck Finley	.333	9	3	1	0	0	0	4	2	.538	.444	Frank Tanana	.077	13	1	0	0	0	0	1	2	.143	.077
												David Wells	.091	11	1	0	0	0	1	1	1	.154	.091
												Jimmy Key	.188	16	3	2	0	0	0	0	1	.188	.313

Keith Hughes — Reds

Age 30 – Bats Left

	Avg	G	AB	R	H	2B	3B	HR	RBI	BB	SO	HBP	GDP	SB	CS	OBP	SLG	IBB	SH	SF	#Pit	#P/PA	GB	FB	G/F
1993 Season	.000	3	4	0	0	0	0	0	0	0	0	0	0	0	0	.000	.000	0	0	0	12	3.00	3	1	3.00
Last Five Years	.000	11	13	0	0	0	0	0	0	0	4	0	0	0	0	.000	.000	0	0	0	38	2.92	4	4	1.00

1993 Season

	Avg	AB	H	2B	3B	HR	RBI	BB	SO	OBP	SLG		Avg	AB	H	2B	3B	HR	RBI	BB	SO	OBP	SLG
vs. Left	.000	0	0	0	0	0	0	0	0	.000	.000	Scoring Posn	.000	1	0	0	0	0	0	0	0	.000	.000
vs. Right	.000	4	0	0	0	0	0	0	0	.000	.000	Close & Late	.000	0	0	0	0	0	0	0	0	.000	.000

Tim Hulett — Orioles

Age 34 – Bats Right

	Avg	G	AB	R	H	2B	3B	HR	RBI	BB	SO	HBP	GDP	SB	CS	OBP	SLG	IBB	SH	SF	#Pit	#P/PA	GB	FB	G/F
1993 Season	.300	85	260	40	78	15	0	2	23	23	56	3	5	1	2	.361	.381	1	1	2	1133	3.92	92	57	1.61
Last Five Years	.265	307	858	108	227	43	3	17	96	71	194	5	20	2	4	.323	.381	2	4	3	3747	3.98	262	242	1.08

1993 Season

	Avg	AB	H	2B	3B	HR	RBI	BB	SO	OBP	SLG
vs. Left	.288	104	30	6	0	0	7	6	18	.324	.346
vs. Right	.306	156	48	9	0	2	16	17	38	.384	.404
Home	.333	126	42	9	0	2	9	13	28	.393	.452
Away	.269	134	36	6	0	0	14	10	28	.331	.313
First Pitch	.375	16	6	1	0	0	0	0	0	.375	.438
Ahead in Count	.406	69	28	5	0	0	6	15	0	.506	.478
Behind in Count	.250	140	35	5	0	2	12	0	47	.254	.329
Two Strikes	.212	132	28	5	0	1	9	8	56	.266	.273

	Avg	AB	H	2B	3B	HR	RBI	BB	SO	OBP	SLG
Scoring Posn	.271	70	19	5	0	1	22	9	14	.346	.386
Close & Late	.190	42	8	1	0	0	2	4	15	.250	.214
None on/out	.364	55	20	4	0	0	0	6	11	.426	.436
Batting #7	.313	99	31	3	0	2	14	11	25	.381	.404
Batting #8	.333	60	20	6	0	0	4	6	12	.412	.433
Other	.267	101	27	6	0	0	5	6	19	.308	.327
Pre-All Star	.298	94	28	7	0	0	6	7	17	.353	.372
Post-All Star	.301	166	50	8	0	2	17	16	39	.366	.386

Last Five Years

	Avg	AB	H	2B	3B	HR	RBI	BB	SO	OBP	SLG
vs. Left	.240	342	82	15	1	8	40	23	69	.289	.360
vs. Right	.281	516	145	28	2	9	56	48	125	.346	.395
Groundball	.289	190	55	12	0	3	20	9	33	.320	.400
Flyball	.291	203	59	11	2	6	30	15	54	.342	.453
Home	.298	376	112	21	2	8	40	37	87	.361	.428
Away	.239	482	115	22	1	9	56	34	107	.294	.344
Day	.262	237	62	13	2	3	25	15	60	.310	.371
Night	.266	621	165	30	1	14	71	56	134	.328	.385
Grass	.276	713	197	32	3	15	79	62	158	.335	.393
Turf	.207	145	30	11	0	2	17	9	36	.263	.324
First Pitch	.277	65	18	2	0	3	6	1	0	.309	.446
Ahead in Count	.320	222	71	15	1	2	22	42	0	.426	.423
Behind in Count	.219	415	91	13	0	10	47	0	162	.220	.323
Two Strikes	.207	440	91	18	0	9	46	28	194	.257	.309

	Avg	AB	H	2B	3B	HR	RBI	BB	SO	OBP	SLG
Scoring Posn	.288	219	63	14	2	4	80	21	52	.346	.425
Close & Late	.247	154	38	4	1	4	14	11	37	.293	.364
None on/out	.265	189	50	8	1	5	5	11	44	.305	.397
Batting #7	.283	230	65	13	1	4	30	17	58	.332	.400
Batting #8	.309	162	50	8	1	2	19	13	35	.371	.407
Other	.240	466	112	22	1	11	47	41	101	.303	.363
April	.286	63	18	4	0	1	6	4	15	.328	.397
May	.288	118	34	7	1	4	16	8	24	.339	.466
June	.253	146	37	4	0	2	11	14	29	.323	.322
July	.253	154	39	10	1	2	15	10	32	.307	.370
August	.281	196	55	7	0	4	26	21	49	.350	.378
September/October	.243	181	44	11	1	4	22	14	45	.296	.381
Pre-All Star	.266	380	101	18	2	8	40	30	76	.324	.387
Post-All Star	.264	478	126	25	1	9	56	41	118	.323	.377

Batter vs. Pitcher (since 1984)

Hits Best Against	Avg	AB	H	2B	3B	HR	RBI	BB	SO	OBP	SLG
Bud Black	.500	20	10	3	0	2	5	2	2	.545	.950
Cal Eldred	.500	12	6	1	1	0	0	1	3	.538	.750
Jack McDowell	.409	22	9	3	0	0	4	2	5	.458	.545
Neal Heaton	.368	19	7	1	2	1	4	2	1	.429	.789
Jose Rijo	.364	11	4	3	0	0	1	0	2	.364	.636

Hits Worst Against	Avg	AB	H	2B	3B	HR	RBI	BB	SO	OBP	SLG
Chuck Finley	.091	11	1	0	0	0	0	1	5	.167	.091
Bruce Hurst	.188	16	3	0	0	0	0	2	3	.278	.188
John Candelaria	.200	15	3	0	0	0	4	0	3	.200	.200
Mark Langston	.219	32	7	1	0	0	1	0	7	.212	.250
Kirk McCaskill	.222	18	4	0	0	0	2	0	4	.222	.222

David Hulse — Rangers

Age 26 – Bats Left (groundball hitter)

	Avg	G	AB	R	H	2B	3B	HR	RBI	BB	SO	HBP	GDP	SB	CS	OBP	SLG	IBB	SH	SF	#Pit	#P/PA	GB	FB	G/F
1993 Season	.290	114	407	71	118	9	10	1	29	26	57	1	9	29	9	.333	.369	1	5	2	1555	3.53	187	75	2.49
Career (1992-1993)	.293	146	499	85	146	13	10	1	31	29	75	1	9	32	10	.331	.365	1	7	2	1877	3.49	223	88	2.53

1993 Season

	Avg	AB	H	2B	3B	HR	RBI	BB	SO	OBP	SLG
vs. Left	.257	35	9	1	1	0	5	4	7	.350	.343
vs. Right	.293	372	109	8	9	1	24	22	50	.331	.371
Groundball	.192	78	15	1	1	0	3	1	7	.210	.231
Flyball	.276	87	24	2	4	0	7	9	15	.340	.391
Home	.276	199	55	5	6	0	15	11	29	.313	.362
Away	.303	208	63	4	4	1	14	15	28	.351	.375
Day	.340	106	36	3	4	1	7	9	11	.393	.472
Night	.272	301	82	6	6	0	22	17	46	.310	.332
Grass	.301	356	107	9	8	1	29	23	52	.343	.379
Turf	.216	51	11	0	2	0	0	3	5	.259	.294
First Pitch	.295	61	18	2	1	1	2	1	0	.302	.410
Ahead in Count	.302	63	19	1	0	0	7	12	0	.413	.317
Behind in Count	.250	200	50	3	5	0	13	0	51	.252	.315
Two Strikes	.218	179	39	2	5	0	8	13	57	.271	.285

	Avg	AB	H	2B	3B	HR	RBI	BB	SO	OBP	SLG
Scoring Posn	.304	79	24	1	1	0	27	7	8	.352	.342
Close & Late	.375	48	18	2	2	0	6	1	3	.388	.500
None on/out	.270	152	41	5	2	0	0	11	19	.319	.329
Batting #1	.289	381	110	9	10	1	27	24	52	.331	.373
Batting #9	.300	10	3	0	0	0	0	0	0	.300	.300
Other	.313	16	5	0	0	0	2	2	5	.389	.313
April	.184	38	7	0	1	0	1	5	9	.273	.237
May	.308	104	32	4	4	0	4	4	9	.333	.423
June	.300	80	24	2	2	0	7	7	11	.356	.375
July	.282	78	22	2	3	0	5	5	10	.325	.385
August	.308	52	16	1	0	0	5	2	8	.339	.327
September/October	.309	55	17	0	0	1	7	3	10	.345	.364
Pre-All Star	.290	269	78	7	8	0	13	19	35	.336	.375
Post-All Star	.290	138	40	2	2	1	16	7	22	.327	.355

1993 By Position

Position	Avg	AB	H	2B	3B	HR	RBI	BB	SO	OBP	SLG	G	GS	Innings	PO	A	E	DP	Fld Pct	Rng Fctr	In Zone	Outs	Zone Rtg	MLB Zone
As cf	.283	400	113	9	9	1	26	26	57	.326	.358	112	96	851.2	244	3	3	1	.988	2.61	284	233	.820	.829

Mike Humphreys — Yankees

Age 27 – Bats Right (flyball hitter)

	Avg	G	AB	R	H	2B	3B	HR	RBI	BB	SO	HBP	GDP	SB	CS	OBP	SLG	IBB	SH	SF	#Pit	#P/PA	GB	FB	G/F
1993 Season	.171	25	35	6	6	2	1	1	6	4	11	0	0	2	1	.250	.371	0	0	1	173	4.32	6	13	0.46
Career (1991-1993)	.176	54	85	15	15	2	1	1	9	13	19	0	2	4	1	.283	.259	0	1	1	421	4.21	19	36	0.53

1993 Season

	Avg	AB	H	2B	3B	HR	RBI	BB	SO	OBP	SLG
vs. Left	.115	26	3	2	1	0	2	4	10	.226	.269
vs. Right	.333	9	3	0	0	1	4	0	1	.333	.667

	Avg	AB	H	2B	3B	HR	RBI	BB	SO	OBP	SLG
Scoring Posn	.250	8	2	0	0	1	5	0	3	.222	.625
Close & Late	.143	7	1	0	0	0	2	2	3	.333	.143

Todd Hundley — Mets

Age 25 – Bats Both

	Avg	G	AB	R	H	2B	3B	HR	RBI	BB	SO	HBP	GDP	SB	CS	OBP	SLG	IBB	SH	SF	#Pit	#P/PA	GB	FB	G/F
1993 Season	.228	130	417	40	95	17	2	11	53	23	62	2	10	1	1	.269	.357	7	2	4	1488	3.32	163	122	1.34
Career (1990-1993)	.213	310	902	85	192	40	3	19	94	54	170	7	22	4	1	.261	.327	11	11	7	3408	3.47	325	265	1.23

1993 Season

	Avg	AB	H	2B	3B	HR	RBI	BB	SO	OBP	SLG
vs. Left	.259	54	14	2	0	0	5	5	14	.344	.296
vs. Right	.223	363	81	15	2	11	48	18	48	.257	.366
Groundball	.298	131	39	8	1	4	17	11	15	.350	.466
Flyball	.108	74	8	2	0	0	6	4	12	.175	.135
Home	.258	209	54	13	0	5	27	9	22	.294	.392
Away	.197	208	41	4	2	6	26	14	40	.244	.322
Day	.248	145	36	9	0	4	16	7	16	.286	.393
Night	.217	272	59	8	2	7	37	16	46	.260	.338
Grass	.233	326	76	15	1	9	45	19	42	.277	.368
Turf	.209	91	19	2	1	2	8	4	20	.240	.319
First Pitch	.277	65	18	2	1	4	17	5	0	.329	.523
Ahead in Count	.288	111	32	5	0	3	18	9	0	.342	.414
Behind in Count	.163	184	30	4	1	2	8	0	59	.168	.228
Two Strikes	.146	164	24	5	1	3	10	9	62	.194	.244

	Avg	AB	H	2B	3B	HR	RBI	BB	SO	OBP	SLG
Scoring Posn	.276	105	29	2	1	3	43	10	16	.333	.400
Close & Late	.179	84	15	2	1	2	12	9	16	.255	.298
None on/out	.227	88	20	4	0	4	4	3	9	.261	.409
Batting #7	.215	158	34	5	1	3	19	10	15	.259	.316
Batting #8	.197	137	27	4	1	5	19	9	27	.257	.350
Other	.279	122	34	8	0	3	15	4	20	.297	.418
April	.226	53	12	3	1	3	11	5	12	.317	.491
May	.243	70	17	2	0	2	8	3	11	.274	.357
June	.192	78	15	2	1	2	8	4	13	.229	.321
July	.173	75	13	2	0	1	7	7	7	.238	.240
August	.215	65	14	3	0	1	7	3	10	.246	.308
September/October	.316	76	24	5	0	2	12	1	9	.325	.461
Pre-All Star	.234	235	55	9	2	8	33	16	38	.286	.391
Post-All Star	.220	182	40	8	0	3	20	7	24	.246	.313

1993 By Position

Position	Avg	AB	H	2B	3B	HR	RBI	BB	SO	OBP	SLG	G	GS	Innings	PO	A	E	DP	Fld Pct	Rng Fctr	In Zone	Outs	Zone Rtg	MLB Zone
As Pinch Hitter	.200	15	3	1	0	0	2	3	2	.333	.267	19	0	---	---	---	---	---	---	---	---	---	---	---
As c	.229	402	92	16	2	11	51	20	60	.266	.361	123	105	942.2	592	63	8	6	.988	---	---	---	---	---

Career (1990-1993)

	Avg	AB	H	2B	3B	HR	RBI	BB	SO	OBP	SLG
vs. Left	.198	207	41	7	0	4	18	14	63	.263	.290
vs. Right	.217	695	151	33	3	15	76	40	107	.260	.338
Groundball	.235	327	77	18	1	5	27	24	62	.287	.343
Flyball	.175	166	29	7	0	4	15	8	30	.226	.289
Home	.233	442	103	22	1	8	48	26	71	.282	.342
Away	.193	460	89	18	2	11	46	28	99	.241	.313
Day	.222	284	63	13	0	7	26	17	53	.269	.342
Night	.209	618	129	27	3	12	68	37	117	.257	.320
Grass	.217	658	143	31	2	13	71	42	113	.269	.330
Turf	.201	244	49	9	1	6	23	12	57	.239	.320
First Pitch	.242	149	36	8	1	4	24	9	0	.286	.389
Ahead in Count	.268	205	55	12	0	4	28	29	0	.356	.385
Behind in Count	.146	412	60	10	2	6	24	0	158	.156	.223
Two Strikes	.156	405	63	14	2	10	29	17	170	.197	.274

	Avg	AB	H	2B	3B	HR	RBI	BB	SO	OBP	SLG
Scoring Posn	.226	221	50	6	2	5	77	23	47	.302	.339
Close & Late	.219	187	41	10	1	3	18	17	39	.290	.332
None on/out	.201	219	44	9	0	6	6	8	35	.232	.324
Batting #7	.198	324	64	10	2	4	30	20	56	.242	.278
Batting #8	.212	372	79	20	1	10	45	26	70	.276	.352
Other	.238	206	49	10	0	5	19	8	44	.263	.359
April	.194	93	18	3	1	5	13	8	22	.279	.409
May	.196	148	29	5	0	3	13	11	28	.261	.291
June	.197	137	27	7	1	5	21	5	23	.224	.372
July	.212	151	32	8	0	2	11	11	24	.262	.305
August	.219	137	30	8	0	1	8	8	30	.265	.299
September/October	.237	236	56	9	1	3	28	11	43	.271	.322
Pre-All Star	.206	433	89	19	2	14	53	29	81	.262	.356
Post-All Star	.220	469	103	21	1	5	41	25	89	.259	.301

Batter vs. Pitcher (career)

Hits Best Against	Avg	AB	H	2B	3B	HR	RBI	BB	SO	OBP	SLG
Mike Morgan	.429	21	9	3	0	1	2	2	1	.478	.714
Tom Candiotti	.364	11	4	0	0	0	0	0	0	.364	.364
Frank Castillo	.333	15	5	0	0	2	7	0	1	.333	.733
Greg Maddux	.303	33	10	2	0	0	2	0	6	.303	.364

Hits Worst Against	Avg	AB	H	2B	3B	HR	RBI	BB	SO	OBP	SLG
Pete Harnisch	.000	13	0	0	0	0	0	1	1	.071	.000
Tommy Greene	.077	13	1	0	0	0	0	0	2	.077	.077
Doug Drabek	.125	16	2	1	0	0	2	1	2	.176	.188
Andy Benes	.158	19	3	1	0	0	1	0	3	.158	.211
Curt Schilling	.200	20	4	0	0	0	1	0	6	.200	.200

Brian Hunter — Braves

Age 26 – Bats Right (flyball hitter)

	Avg	G	AB	R	H	2B	3B	HR	RBI	BB	SO	HBP	GDP	SB	CS	OBP	SLG	IBB	SH	SF	#Pit	#P/PA	GB	FB	G/F
1993 Season	.138	37	80	4	11	3	1	0	8	2	15	0	1	0	0	.153	.200	1	0	3	315	3.71	19	41	0.46
Career (1991-1993)	.231	236	589	70	136	32	4	26	99	40	113	1	9	1	4	.275	.431	4	1	13	2334	3.62	153	237	0.65

1993 Season

	Avg	AB	H	2B	3B	HR	RBI	BB	SO	OBP	SLG
vs. Left	.161	56	9	3	1	0	6	2	11	.183	.250
vs. Right	.083	24	2	0	0	0	2	0	4	.080	.083

	Avg	AB	H	2B	3B	HR	RBI	BB	SO	OBP	SLG
Scoring Posn	.200	20	4	2	0	0	8	1	4	.208	.300
Close & Late	.250	8	2	0	0	0	2	1	2	.300	.250

Career (1991-1993)

	Avg	AB	H	2B	3B	HR	RBI	BB	SO	OBP	SLG
vs. Left	.253	332	84	17	2	18	60	24	51	.295	.479
vs. Right	.202	257	52	15	2	8	39	16	62	.249	.370
Groundball	.233	193	45	12	2	5	30	15	33	.282	.394
Flyball	.200	150	30	3	1	10	20	11	41	.256	.433
Home	.259	294	76	14	2	16	62	27	55	.315	.483
Away	.203	295	60	18	2	10	37	13	58	.233	.380
Day	.250	144	36	11	0	7	13	12	32	.308	.472
Night	.225	445	100	21	4	19	86	28	81	.265	.418
Grass	.234	431	101	22	3	21	75	34	84	.285	.445
Turf	.222	158	35	10	1	5	24	6	29	.247	.392
First Pitch	.326	89	29	9	0	7	22	4	0	.340	.663
Ahead in Count	.321	131	42	10	1	13	39	24	0	.421	.710
Behind in Count	.173	272	47	11	2	4	29	0	94	.170	.272
Two Strikes	.146	287	42	9	2	3	26	12	113	.178	.223

	Avg	AB	H	2B	3B	HR	RBI	BB	SO	OBP	SLG
Scoring Posn	.263	167	44	14	1	4	68	13	30	.295	.431
Close & Late	.202	99	20	8	1	7	23	9	24	.261	.515
None on/out	.216	134	29	5	1	10	10	10	27	.271	.493
Batting #6	.209	359	75	15	3	16	58	25	63	.254	.401
Batting #7	.234	107	25	9	0	2	16	4	22	.265	.374
Other	.293	123	36	8	1	8	25	11	28	.343	.569
April	.078	51	4	2	0	2	4	2	15	.111	.235
May	.308	65	20	4	2	2	11	6	11	.351	.523
June	.248	101	25	5	1	7	24	5	17	.273	.525
July	.203	133	27	6	1	4	22	3	17	.217	.353
August	.240	146	35	8	0	6	22	14	31	.307	.418
September/October	.269	93	25	7	0	5	16	10	22	.337	.505
Pre-All Star	.219	260	57	12	4	12	45	14	48	.251	.435
Post-All Star	.240	329	79	20	0	14	54	26	65	.294	.429

Batter vs. Pitcher (career)

Hits Best Against	Avg	AB	H	2B	3B	HR	RBI	BB	SO	OBP	SLG
Tom Browning	.545	11	6	0	1	1	3	0	0	.545	1.000
Donovan Osborne	.545	11	6	0	0	2	2	0	1	.545	1.091
Terry Mulholland	.385	13	5	1	0	1	1	1	0	.429	.692
Frank Viola	.364	11	4	1	0	1	5	0	3	.364	.727
Danny Jackson	.313	16	5	1	0	1	4	2	0	.389	.563

Hits Worst Against	Avg	AB	H	2B	3B	HR	RBI	BB	SO	OBP	SLG
Mitch Williams	.222	9	2	0	0	1	3	1	2	.273	.556

Bruce Hurst — Rockies

Age 36 – Pitches Left (groundball pitcher)

	ERA	W	L	Sv	G	GS	IP	BB	SO	Avg	H	2B	3B	HR	RBI	OBP	SLG	CG	ShO	Sup	QS	#P/S	SB	CS	GB	FB	G/F
1993 Season	7.62	0	2	0	5	5	13.0	6	9	.283	15	1	0	1	11	.356	.358	0	0	7.62	0	43	3	1	18	16	1.13
Last Five Years	3.29	55	39	0	134	134	920.1	245	622	.244	841	137	10	77	317	.294	.356	29	10	4.03	89	97	66	38	1289	859	1.50

1993 Season

	ERA	W	L	Sv	G	GS	IP	H	HR	BB	SO
Home	5.40	0	2	0	4	4	10.0	9	1	4	7
Away	15.00	0	0	0	1	1	3.0	6	0	2	2

	Avg	AB	H	2B	3B	HR	RBI	BB	SO	OBP	SLG
vs. Left	.200	5	1	0	0	0	2	1	1	.333	.200
vs. Right	.292	48	14	1	0	1	9	5	8	.358	.375

Last Five Years

	ERA	W	L	Sv	G	GS	IP	H	HR	BB	SO
Home	3.21	28	20	0	72	72	499.0	419	48	137	370
Away	3.38	27	19	0	62	62	421.1	422	29	108	252
Day	3.31	9	9	0	28	28	204.0	196	15	55	135
Night	3.28	46	30	0	106	106	716.1	645	62	190	487
Grass	3.22	43	25	0	100	100	696.1	613	61	190	480
Turf	3.50	12	14	0	34	34	224.0	228	16	55	142
April	3.78	6	6	0	18	18	126.1	105	17	32	95
May	3.55	11	8	0	25	25	172.1	167	14	52	123
June	2.98	10	8	0	24	24	163.0	154	12	39	111
July	3.50	11	6	0	23	23	164.2	154	17	45	107
August	3.15	10	4	0	22	22	151.2	137	9	43	90
September/October	2.78	7	7	0	22	22	142.1	124	8	34	96
Starter	3.29	55	39	0	134	134	920.1	841	77	245	622
Reliever	0.00	0	0	0	0	0	0.0	0	0	0	0
0-3 Days Rest	9.00	0	1	0	1	1	4.0	5	0	3	3
4 Days Rest	3.08	38	23	0	85	85	602.1	526	41	164	419
5+ Days Rest	3.61	17	15	0	48	48	314.0	310	36	78	200
Pre-All Star	3.48	29	24	0	74	74	512.2	476	51	137	363
Post-All Star	3.05	26	15	0	60	60	407.2	365	26	108	259

	Avg	AB	H	2B	3B	HR	RBI	BB	SO	OBP	SLG
vs. Left	.250	607	152	21	3	18	73	54	123	.311	.384
vs. Right	.242	2842	689	116	7	59	244	191	499	.290	.350
Inning 1-6	.246	2803	689	114	8	62	271	205	531	.297	.359
Inning 7+	.235	646	152	23	2	15	46	40	91	.281	.347
None on	.238	2115	503	72	4	53	53	152	407	.290	.351
Runners on	.253	1334	338	65	6	24	264	93	215	.300	.365
Scoring Posn	.253	719	182	33	2	11	220	64	123	.310	.350
Close & Late	.262	344	90	11	2	9	32	21	45	.306	.384
None on/out	.226	900	203	33	3	27	27	75	169	.286	.359
vs. 1st Batr (relief)	.000	0	0	0	0	0	0	0	0	.000	.000
First Inning Pitched	.239	498	119	22	1	7	49	44	104	.299	.329
First 75 Pitches	.243	2505	608	101	8	53	229	183	474	.294	.353
Pitch 76-90	.262	454	119	20	0	14	46	31	76	.309	.399
Pitch 91-105	.241	328	79	11	2	6	29	18	48	.280	.341
Pitch 106+	.216	162	35	5	0	4	13	13	24	.278	.321
First Pitch	.304	583	177	24	1	13	68	14	0	.319	.415
Ahead in Count	.203	1671	340	53	2	29	118	0	546	.204	.290
Behind in Count	.300	657	197	29	5	24	84	141	0	.423	.469
Two Strikes	.171	1512	258	44	2	26	98	88	622	.217	.254

Pitcher vs. Batter (since 1984)

Pitches Best Vs.	Avg	AB	H	2B	3B	HR	RBI	BB	SO	OBP	SLG
Stan Javier	.118	17	2	0	0	0	0	1	2	.167	.118
Darryl Strawberry	.125	24	3	0	0	0	1	1	3	.160	.125
Kent Hrbek	.125	16	2	1	0	0	0	0	4	.125	.188
Ruben Sierra	.130	23	3	0	0	0	0	0	7	.130	.130
Henry Cotto	.133	15	2	0	0	0	0	0	5	.133	.133

Pitches Worst Vs.	Avg	AB	H	2B	3B	HR	RBI	BB	SO	OBP	SLG
Dave Hollins	.500	14	7	1	0	2	5	4	3	.611	1.000
Reggie Sanders	.500	14	7	2	0	1	3	0	3	.500	.857
Barry Bonds	.462	26	12	3	0	3	4	8	4	.588	.923
Lance Parrish	.385	13	5	0	0	3	7	3	4	.500	1.077
Kevin Mitchell	.333	21	7	1	0	5	8	5	2	.462	1.095

Butch Huskey — Mets

Age 22 – Bats Right

	Avg	G	AB	R	H	2B	3B	HR	RBI	BB	SO	HBP	GDP	SB	CS	OBP	SLG	IBB	SH	SF	#Pit	#P/PA	GB	FB	G/F
1993 Season	.146	13	41	2	6	1	0	0	3	1	13	0	0	0	0	.159	.171	1	0	2	147	3.34	6	20	0.30

1993 Season

	Avg	AB	H	2B	3B	HR	RBI	BB	SO	OBP	SLG
vs. Left	.067	15	1	0	0	0	0	0	4	.067	.067
vs. Right	.192	26	5	1	0	0	3	1	9	.207	.231

	Avg	AB	H	2B	3B	HR	RBI	BB	SO	OBP	SLG
Scoring Posn	.000	9	0	0	0	0	2	1	1	.083	.000
Close & Late	.167	6	1	0	0	0	0	0	3	.167	.167

Jeff Huson — Rangers

Age 29 – Bats Left

	Avg	G	AB	R	H	2B	3B	HR	RBI	BB	SO	HBP	GDP	SB	CS	OBP	SLG	IBB	SH	SF	#Pit	#P/PA	GB	FB	G/F
1993 Season	.133	23	45	3	6	1	1	0	2	0	10	0	0	0	0	.133	.200	0	1	0	158	3.43	17	9	1.89
Last Five Years	.230	442	1101	146	253	40	9	6	82	132	145	3	27	41	13	.311	.299	5	28	10	4774	3.75	434	307	1.41

1993 Season

	Avg	AB	H	2B	3B	HR	RBI	BB	SO	OBP	SLG
vs. Left	.222	9	2	1	1	0	1	0	2	.222	.556
vs. Right	.111	36	4	0	0	0	1	0	8	.111	.111

	Avg	AB	H	2B	3B	HR	RBI	BB	SO	OBP	SLG
Scoring Posn	.077	13	1	0	0	0	1	0	4	.077	.077
Close & Late	.000	8	0	0	0	0	0	0	3	.000	.000

Last Five Years

	Avg	AB	H	2B	3B	HR	RBI	BB	SO	OBP	SLG
vs. Left	.214	126	27	5	1	1	9	13	27	.291	.294
vs. Right	.232	975	226	35	8	5	73	119	118	.314	.299
Groundball	.212	339	72	11	5	0	17	31	37	.279	.274
Flyball	.245	233	57	8	1	0	20	30	37	.332	.288
Home	.212	543	115	18	4	1	40	64	80	.296	.265
Away	.247	558	138	22	5	5	42	68	65	.326	.332
Day	.232	250	58	10	1	1	18	32	34	.318	.292
Night	.229	851	195	30	8	5	64	100	111	.309	.301
Grass	.241	875	211	32	8	5	72	100	121	.318	.313

	Avg	AB	H	2B	3B	HR	RBI	BB	SO	OBP	SLG
Scoring Posn	.210	243	51	8	3	1	68	35	40	.303	.280
Close & Late	.215	177	38	3	1	0	7	24	27	.310	.243
None on/out	.224	317	71	15	1	1	1	41	45	.315	.287
Batting #1	.209	349	73	8	3	0	22	32	49	.276	.249
Batting #9	.247	377	93	14	3	4	36	46	52	.327	.332
Other	.232	375	87	18	3	2	24	54	44	.327	.312
April	.269	134	36	4	2	0	13	15	21	.338	.328
May	.229	227	52	17	3	1	11	26	32	.313	.344
June	.268	183	49	4	2	1	13	25	22	.354	.328

Last Five Years

	Avg	AB	H	2B	3B	HR	RBI	BB	SO	OBP	SLG		Avg	AB	H	2B	3B	HR	RBI	BB	SO	OBP	SLG
Turf	.186	226	42	8	1	1	10	32	24	.285	.243	July	.239	213	51	8	2	3	18	25	27	.318	.338
First Pitch	.269	134	36	4	2	1	15	4	0	.282	.351	August	.213	202	43	6	0	1	16	26	27	.300	.257
Ahead in Count	.271	262	71	13	1	1	20	70	0	.425	.340	September/October	.155	142	22	1	0	0	11	15	16	.234	.162
Behind in Count	.179	486	87	11	4	3	27	0	125	.183	.237	Pre-All Star	.246	598	147	27	7	2	39	77	82	.332	.324
Two Strikes	.173	486	84	14	4	3	30	57	145	.259	.237	Post-All Star	.211	503	106	13	2	4	43	55	63	.286	.268

Batter vs. Pitcher (career)

Hits Best Against	Avg	AB	H	2B	3B	HR	RBI	BB	SO	OBP	SLG	Hits Worst Against	Avg	AB	H	2B	3B	HR	RBI	BB	SO	OBP	SLG
Jack McDowell	.381	21	8	2	0	0	2	2	3	.435	.476	Todd Stottlemyre	.000	9	0	0	0	0	0	2	1	.182	.000
Jaime Navarro	.375	16	6	0	2	0	3	2	1	.444	.625	Alex Fernandez	.000	9	0	0	0	0	1	3	1	.231	.000
Rick Sutcliffe	.357	14	5	1	1	0	2	2	1	.438	.571	Kevin Tapani	.048	21	1	1	0	0	1	0	3	.048	.095
Storm Davis	.333	9	3	1	0	0	1	2	2	.455	.444	Dave Stewart	.091	11	1	0	0	0	0	0	0	.091	.091
Charlie Hough	.308	13	4	0	0	1	1	1	0	.357	.538	Bob Welch	.100	10	1	0	0	0	1	1	1	.182	.100

Mark Hutton — Yankees

Age 24 – Pitches Right (groundball pitcher)

	ERA	W	L	Sv	G	GS	IP	BB	SO	Avg	H	2B	3B	HR	RBI	OBP	SLG	CG	ShO	Sup	QS	#P/S	SB	CS	GB	FB	G/F
1993 Season	5.73	1	1	0	7	4	22.0	17	12	.293	24	5	0	2	15	.412	.427	0	0	6.55	1	87	4	1	37	20	1.85

1993 Season

	ERA	W	L	Sv	G	GS	IP	H	HR	BB	SO		Avg	AB	H	2B	3B	HR	RBI	BB	SO	OBP	SLG
Home	2.08	1	0	0	3	2	13.0	9	0	8	7	vs. Left	.292	48	14	3	0	1	6	7	5	.382	.417
Away	11.00	0	1	0	4	2	9.0	15	2	9	5	vs. Right	.294	34	10	2	0	1	9	10	7	.447	.441

Mike Ignasiak — Brewers

Age 28 – Pitches Right (flyball pitcher)

	ERA	W	L	Sv	G	GS	IP	BB	SO	Avg	H	2B	3B	HR	RBI	OBP	SLG	GF	IR	IRS	Hld	SvOp	SB	CS	GB	FB	G/F
1993 Season	3.65	1	1	0	27	0	37.0	21	28	.241	32	4	1	2	20	.350	.331	4	26	8	3	2	1	3	34	39	0.87
Career (1991-1993)	4.17	3	2	0	31	1	49.2	29	38	.222	39	4	2	4	26	.337	.335	4	28	8	3	2	3	3	46	56	0.82

1993 Season

	ERA	W	L	Sv	G	GS	IP	H	HR	BB	SO		Avg	AB	H	2B	3B	HR	RBI	BB	SO	OBP	SLG
Home	2.63	0	0	0	16	0	24.0	15	1	14	19	vs. Left	.318	44	14	2	0	1	9	11	4	.456	.432
Away	5.54	1	1	0	11	0	13.0	17	1	7	9	vs. Right	.202	89	18	2	1	1	11	10	24	.290	.281
Starter	0.00	0	0	0	0	0	0.0	0	0	0	0	Scoring Posn	.243	37	9	0	0	1	17	8	6	.383	.324
Reliever	3.65	1	1	0	27	0	37.0	32	2	21	28	Close & Late	.226	31	7	0	0	0	4	5	9	.342	.226
0 Days rest	3.27	0	0	0	6	0	11.0	7	0	7	4	None on/out	.200	30	6	1	1	0	0	3	7	.273	.300
1 or 2 Days rest	4.15	1	1	0	11	0	13.0	12	2	4	16	First Pitch	.364	22	8	1	0	0	3	4	0	.462	.409
3+ Days rest	3.46	0	0	0	10	0	13.0	13	0	10	8	Ahead in Count	.196	56	11	1	1	1	8	0	21	.211	.304
Pre-All Star	6.59	0	0	0	9	0	13.2	15	1	8	6	Behind in Count	.235	34	8	1	0	1	7	11	0	.426	.353
Post-All Star	1.93	1	1	0	18	0	23.1	17	1	13	22	Two Strikes	.169	59	10	2	0	1	7	6	28	.246	.254

Pete Incaviglia — Phillies

Age 30 – Bats Right

	Avg	G	AB	R	H	2B	3B	HR	RBI	BB	SO	HBP	GDP	SB	CS	OBP	SLG	IBB	SH	SF	#Pit	#P/PA	GB	FB	G/F
1993 Season	.274	116	368	60	101	16	3	24	89	21	82	6	9	1	1	.318	.530	1	0	7	1436	3.57	125	106	1.18
Last Five Years	.244	612	2036	236	496	104	9	91	337	159	555	25	51	12	17	.304	.438	8	1	19	8079	3.61	633	548	1.16

1993 Season

	Avg	AB	H	2B	3B	HR	RBI	BB	SO	OBP	SLG		Avg	AB	H	2B	3B	HR	RBI	BB	SO	OBP	SLG
vs. Left	.278	162	45	7	2	13	42	9	34	.318	.586	Scoring Posn	.304	125	38	4	1	7	66	8	35	.338	.520
vs. Right	.272	206	56	9	1	11	47	12	48	.319	.485	Close & Late	.154	65	10	1	0	1	12	7	17	.227	.215
Groundball	.286	112	32	8	1	8	23	7	26	.325	.589	None on/out	.318	85	27	8	0	7	7	5	8	.363	.659
Flyball	.300	50	15	1	1	1	12	6	11	.373	.420	Batting #5	.227	75	17	0	0	2	15	6	21	.306	.307
Home	.278	205	57	7	2	15	47	12	47	.324	.551	Batting #6	.302	182	55	10	3	14	52	7	35	.330	.621
Away	.270	163	44	9	1	9	42	9	35	.311	.503	Other	.261	111	29	6	0	8	22	8	26	.309	.532
Day	.252	115	29	3	1	7	26	5	30	.276	.478	April	.261	46	12	0	0	3	14	1	15	.292	.457
Night	.285	253	72	13	2	17	63	16	52	.337	.553	May	.294	68	20	6	2	5	18	2	12	.315	.662
Grass	.281	96	27	6	1	7	28	4	18	.308	.583	June	.273	77	21	3	0	5	21	4	20	.314	.506
Turf	.272	272	74	10	2	17	61	17	64	.322	.511	July	.173	52	9	2	0	2	5	2	14	.232	.327
First Pitch	.313	67	21	5	1	4	13	0	0	.313	.597	August	.368	68	25	3	0	8	21	10	12	.449	.765
Ahead in Count	.372	86	32	3	0	13	43	11	0	.426	.860	September/October	.246	57	14	2	1	1	10	2	9	.262	.368
Behind in Count	.178	152	27	4	2	3	19	0	65	.206	.289	Pre-All Star	.259	216	56	10	2	13	53	9	53	.301	.505
Two Strikes	.168	167	28	5	1	3	20	10	82	.231	.263	Post-All Star	.296	152	45	6	1	11	36	12	29	.343	.566

1993 By Position

Position	Avg	AB	H	2B	3B	HR	RBI	BB	SO	OBP	SLG	G	GS	Innings	PO	A	E	DP	Fld Pct	Rng Fctr	In Zone	Outs	Zone Rtg	MLB Zone
As Pinch Hitter	.250	24	6	1	0	0	5	2	9	.296	.292	27	0	---	---	---	---	---	---	---	---	---	---	---
As lf	.278	317	88	15	3	23	78	19	68	.323	.562	89	80	690.2	152	3	5	0	.969	2.02	178	143	.803	.818

Last Five Years

	Avg	AB	H	2B	3B	HR	RBI	BB	SO	OBP	SLG		Avg	AB	H	2B	3B	HR	RBI	BB	SO	OBP	SLG
vs. Left	.249	746	186	42	5	34	123	64	186	.313	.456	Scoring Posn	.244	585	143	32	2	21	231	55	176	.311	.414
vs. Right	.240	1290	310	62	4	57	214	95	369	.298	.427	Close & Late	.194	376	73	20	0	11	54	29	114	.249	.335
Groundball	.247	639	158	26	6	29	116	49	163	.306	.443	None on/out	.250	452	113	30	2	24	24	31	107	.305	.485
Flyball	.241	423	102	24	1	13	52	40	137	.309	.395	Batting #5	.242	463	112	19	1	17	74	42	128	.318	.397
Home	.256	1035	265	51	4	55	184	93	289	.323	.472	Batting #6	.250	891	223	50	5	50	167	68	234	.306	.486
Away	.231	1001	231	53	5	36	153	66	266	.284	.402	Other	.236	682	161	35	3	24	96	49	193	.291	.402
Day	.224	490	110	17	2	21	76	50	141	.300	.396	April	.237	321	76	14	1	12	52	16	106	.283	.399

Last Five Years	Avg	AB	H	2B	3B	HR	RBI	BB	SO	OBP	SLG		Avg	AB	H	2B	3B	HR	RBI	BB	SO	OBP	SLG
Night	.250	1546	386	87	7	70	261	109	414	.305	.451	May	.241	390	94	24	3	16	65	25	105	.289	.441
Grass	.238	1270	302	66	5	59	203	112	353	.304	.437	June	.252	330	83	16	1	14	57	23	87	.306	.433
Turf	.253	766	194	38	4	32	134	47	202	.303	.439	July	.259	320	83	21	0	19	63	29	79	.326	.503
First Pitch	.313	339	106	24	3	21	68	2	0	.315	.587	August	.229	315	72	10	1	16	45	32	89	.308	.419
Ahead in Count	.343	411	141	30	0	31	112	83	0	.453	.642	September/October	.244	360	88	19	3	14	55	34	89	.312	.431
Behind in Count	.177	938	166	38	4	21	98	0	459	.191	.293	Pre-All Star	.244	1126	275	61	5	47	186	74	319	.298	.433
Two Strikes	.147	992	146	38	4	22	99	71	555	.214	.260	Post-All Star	.243	910	221	43	4	44	151	85	236	.311	.444

Batter vs. Pitcher (career)

Hits Best Against	Avg	AB	H	2B	3B	HR	RBI	BB	SO	OBP	SLG	Hits Worst Against	Avg	AB	H	2B	3B	HR	RBI	BB	SO	OBP	SLG
Randy Tomlin	.538	13	7	3	0	1	5	0	1	.538	1.000	Bob Welch	.056	18	1	0	0	0	0	1	7	.105	.056
Bob Milacki	.462	13	6	3	0	3	8	2	3	.533	1.385	Storm Davis	.056	18	1	0	0	0	0	3	5	.190	.056
Bud Black	.458	24	11	3	0	4	8	2	5	.500	1.083	Dan Plesac	.056	18	1	0	0	0	2	1	4	.105	.056
Dave Righetti	.364	11	4	2	0	2	6	3	4	.500	1.091	Mike Henneman	.077	13	1	0	0	0	1	0	3	.071	.077
Greg Cadaret	.364	11	4	2	0	1	6	1	3	.417	.818	Doug Drabek	.083	12	1	0	0	0	0	1	4	.154	.083

Jeff Innis — Mets

Age 31 – Pitches Right (groundball pitcher)

	ERA	W	L	Sv	G	GS	IP	BB	SO	Avg	H	2B	3B	HR	RBI	OBP	SLG	GF	IR	IRS	Hld	SvOp	SB	CS	GB	FB	G/F
1993 Season	4.11	2	3	3	67	0	76.2	38	36	.278	81	16	1	5	36	.372	.392	30	34	9	6	5	9	3	132	58	2.28
Last Five Years	3.11	9	18	5	259	0	315.1	115	150	.251	289	46	7	17	130	.323	.347	99	170	51	29	14	35	13	607	209	2.90

1993 Season

	ERA	W	L	Sv	G	GS	IP	H	HR	BB	SO		Avg	AB	H	2B	3B	HR	RBI	BB	SO	OBP	SLG
Home	3.51	1	0	1	33	0	41.0	40	4	21	18	vs. Left	.296	115	34	4	0	1	12	19	11	.409	.357
Away	4.79	1	3	2	34	0	35.2	41	1	17	18	vs. Right	.267	176	47	12	1	4	24	19	25	.347	.415
Day	4.45	1	1	0	23	0	28.1	30	3	9	14	Inning 1-6	.333	42	14	3	0	0	10	3	2	.391	.405
Night	3.91	1	2	3	44	0	48.1	51	2	29	22	Inning 7+	.269	249	67	13	1	5	26	35	34	.369	.390
Grass	4.70	2	2	1	49	0	59.1	66	5	31	28	None on	.305	141	43	9	0	3	3	14	15	.380	.433
Turf	2.08	0	1	2	18	0	17.1	15	0	7	8	Runners on	.253	150	38	7	1	2	33	24	21	.365	.353
April	3.86	0	1	0	9	0	11.2	12	1	2	5	Scoring Posn	.274	95	26	6	0	2	32	21	13	.417	.400
May	4.72	0	1	1	13	0	13.1	19	1	7	4	Close & Late	.236	89	21	2	0	3	9	13	12	.340	.360
June	5.40	0	0	0	11	0	10.0	10	2	5	7	None on/out	.299	67	20	4	0	2	2	6	10	.373	.448
July	7.20	1	0	0	11	0	10.0	16	1	7	7	vs. 1st Batr (relief)	.242	62	15	5	0	1	7	2	9	.284	.371
August	1.93	0	1	2	12	0	14.0	8	0	5	6	First Inning Pitched	.270	222	60	11	1	4	29	24	29	.351	.383
September/October	3.06	1	0	0	11	0	17.2	16	0	12	7	First 15 Pitches	.277	206	57	10	0	4	23	24	27	.362	.383
Starter	0.00	0	0	0	0	0	0.0	0	0	0	0	Pitch 16-30	.286	70	20	4	1	1	6	11	7	.398	.414
Reliever	4.11	2	3	3	67	0	76.2	81	5	38	36	Pitch 31-45	.267	15	4	2	0	0	7	3	2	.389	.400
0 Days rest	8.80	1	1	1	14	0	15.1	22	1	9	8	Pitch 46+	.000	0	0	0	0	0	0	0	0	.000	.000
1 or 2 Days rest	3.69	1	2	2	36	0	39.0	43	4	19	18	First Pitch	.333	51	17	5	0	0	5	10	0	.443	.431
3+ Days rest	1.61	0	0	0	17	0	22.1	16	0	10	10	Ahead in Count	.175	120	21	2	0	3	14	0	31	.202	.267
Pre-All Star	5.01	1	2	1	39	0	41.1	52	5	19	21	Behind in Count	.389	72	28	6	0	2	14	17	0	.505	.556
Post-All Star	3.06	1	1	2	28	0	35.1	29	0	19	15	Two Strikes	.195	113	22	3	0	2	13	11	36	.283	.274

Last Five Years

	ERA	W	L	Sv	G	GS	IP	H	HR	BB	SO		Avg	AB	H	2B	3B	HR	RBI	BB	SO	OBP	SLG
Home	2.81	5	10	3	134	0	169.2	142	11	61	84	vs. Left	.282	489	138	23	2	8	62	64	50	.370	.387
Away	3.46	4	8	2	125	0	145.2	147	6	54	66	vs. Right	.228	663	151	23	5	9	68	51	100	.287	.318
Day	3.26	2	7	0	87	0	105.0	101	8	32	54	Inning 1-6	.230	196	45	8	1	1	30	14	22	.280	.296
Night	3.04	7	11	5	172	0	210.1	188	9	83	96	Inning 7+	.255	956	244	38	6	16	100	101	128	.331	.358
Grass	3.32	7	13	3	189	0	233.1	214	16	86	114	None on	.256	624	160	24	4	13	13	41	80	.307	.370
Turf	2.52	2	5	2	70	0	82.0	75	1	29	36	Runners on	.244	528	129	22	3	4	117	74	70	.340	.320
April	3.94	3	4	0	28	0	32.0	31	4	9	21	Scoring Posn	.232	345	80	13	2	3	111	63	50	.349	.307
May	3.34	1	1	1	31	0	35.0	36	3	16	11	Close & Late	.276	417	115	18	4	8	51	50	54	.360	.396
June	3.00	1	3	1	49	0	54.0	49	2	20	31	None on/out	.279	272	76	10	1	6	6	19	41	.331	.390
July	3.58	2	5	1	54	0	75.1	72	4	24	37	vs. 1st Batr (relief)	.241	237	57	9	1	5	33	15	39	.291	.350
August	2.73	0	2	2	50	0	52.2	45	2	17	26	First Inning Pitched	.233	791	184	29	3	12	95	69	113	.298	.322
September/October	2.44	2	3	0	47	0	66.1	56	2	29	24	First 15 Pitches	.240	780	187	32	3	13	84	64	108	.303	.338
Starter	0.00	0	0	0	0	0	0.0	0	0	0	0	Pitch 16-30	.283	307	87	12	4	4	34	38	35	.364	.388
Reliever	3.11	9	18	5	259	0	315.1	289	17	115	150	Pitch 31-45	.230	61	14	2	0	0	12	13	7	.364	.262
0 Days rest	4.17	2	5	1	75	0	86.1	98	3	35	44	Pitch 46+	.250	4	1	0	0	0	0	0	0	.250	.250
1 or 2 Days rest	3.22	4	8	4	114	0	142.1	138	7	54	64	First Pitch	.312	186	58	10	1	2	26	18	0	.371	.409
3+ Days rest	1.87	3	5	0	70	0	86.2	53	7	26	42	Ahead in Count	.189	491	93	12	1	6	46	0	132	.197	.255
Pre-All Star	3.40	7	10	3	129	0	150.2	146	13	55	78	Behind in Count	.305	298	91	16	3	7	39	58	0	.424	.450
Post-All Star	2.84	2	8	2	130	0	164.2	143	4	60	72	Two Strikes	.174	443	77	9	1	5	36	38	150	.244	.233

Pitcher vs. Batter (career)

Pitches Best Vs.	Avg	AB	H	2B	3B	HR	RBI	BB	SO	OBP	SLG	Pitches Worst Vs.	Avg	AB	H	2B	3B	HR	RBI	BB	SO	OBP	SLG
Ken Caminiti	.083	12	1	0	0	0	0	0	1	.083	.083	Ron Gant	.545	11	6	2	0	0	3	1	0	.583	.727
Hal Morris	.111	9	1	0	0	0	1	1	0	.182	.111	Marquis Grissom	.500	14	7	1	0	1	2	0	1	.500	.786
Andres Galarraga	.118	17	2	0	0	0	0	0	3	.118	.118	Andy Van Slyke	.444	9	4	1	0	1	2	1	1	.455	.889
Matt D. Williams	.167	12	2	0	0	0	1	1	2	.231	.167	Don Slaught	.364	11	4	2	0	0	4	0	1	.333	.545
Barry Bonds	.200	10	2	0	0	0	0	1	1	.273	.200	Jay Bell	.308	13	4	2	1	0	0	4	0	.471	.615

Bo Jackson — White Sox

Age 31 – Bats Right

	Avg	G	AB	R	H	2B	3B	HR	RBI	BB	SO	HBP	GDP	SB	CS	OBP	SLG	IBB	SH	SF	#Pit	#P/PA	GB	FB	G/F
1993 Season	.232	85	284	32	66	9	0	16	45	23	106	0	5	0	2	.289	.433	1	0	1	1221	3.96	92	50	1.84
Last Five Years	.254	354	1275	200	324	44	7	79	242	118	431	5	28	41	21	.317	.485	12	0	11	5336	3.79	411	277	1.48

1993 Season

	Avg	AB	H	2B	3B	HR	RBI	BB	SO	OBP	SLG
vs. Left	.203	133	27	1	0	9	22	11	50	.264	.414
vs. Right	.258	151	39	8	0	7	23	12	56	.311	.450
Home	.228	145	33	5	0	9	25	10	49	.277	.448
Away	.237	139	33	4	0	7	20	13	57	.301	.417
First Pitch	.342	38	13	1	0	2	10	1	0	.359	.526
Ahead in Count	.354	48	17	1	0	9	21	8	0	.446	.938
Behind in Count	.167	138	23	4	0	3	8	0	82	.167	.261
Two Strikes	.116	155	18	5	0	1	5	14	106	.189	.168

	Avg	AB	H	2B	3B	HR	RBI	BB	SO	OBP	SLG
Scoring Posn	.270	74	20	0	0	5	29	8	23	.337	.473
Close & Late	.258	31	8	1	0	0	5	2	15	.303	.290
None on/out	.258	62	16	3	0	4	4	4	25	.303	.500
Batting #6	.234	137	32	6	0	8	25	9	54	.279	.453
Batting #7	.247	77	19	2	0	3	7	10	27	.333	.390
Other	.214	70	15	1	0	5	13	4	25	.257	.443
Pre-All Star	.229	144	33	5	0	7	19	17	55	.309	.410
Post-All Star	.236	140	33	4	0	9	26	6	51	.267	.457

Last Five Years

	Avg	AB	H	2B	3B	HR	RBI	BB	SO	OBP	SLG
vs. Left	.247	430	106	10	2	28	72	49	151	.326	.474
vs. Right	.258	845	218	34	5	51	170	69	280	.312	.491
Groundball	.274	296	81	8	4	14	55	29	84	.337	.470
Flyball	.226	274	62	5	1	17	50	24	108	.289	.438
Home	.253	625	158	30	4	35	118	56	201	.313	.482
Away	.255	650	166	14	3	44	124	62	230	.321	.489
Day	.253	316	80	11	4	21	63	27	119	.312	.513
Night	.254	959	244	33	3	58	179	91	312	.319	.477
Grass	.256	669	171	18	2	44	127	59	227	.316	.486
Turf	.252	606	153	26	5	35	115	59	204	.319	.485
First Pitch	.344	180	62	5	2	19	62	6	0	.372	.711
Ahead in Count	.363	212	77	10	2	25	67	55	0	.489	.783
Behind in Count	.182	649	118	16	2	22	63	0	346	.183	.314
Two Strikes	.159	693	110	18	3	19	65	55	431	.221	.276

	Avg	AB	H	2B	3B	HR	RBI	BB	SO	OBP	SLG
Scoring Posn	.257	362	93	9	4	29	174	51	116	.341	.544
Close & Late	.267	187	50	3	0	13	32	15	73	.325	.492
None on/out	.268	314	84	13	1	20	20	20	107	.313	.506
Batting #4	.254	690	175	21	5	44	149	69	235	.321	.490
Batting #6	.253	348	88	14	2	20	53	21	118	.296	.477
Other	.257	237	61	9	0	15	40	28	78	.336	.485
April	.302	172	52	10	1	10	27	19	54	.372	.547
May	.259	247	64	7	2	12	35	23	83	.324	.449
June	.239	222	53	7	1	13	34	17	78	.293	.455
July	.261	180	47	4	1	16	56	16	58	.313	.561
August	.227	150	34	2	1	10	28	14	52	.293	.453
September/October	.243	304	74	14	1	18	62	29	106	.313	.474
Pre-All Star	.259	742	192	27	5	44	127	69	248	.320	.487
Post-All Star	.248	533	132	17	2	35	115	49	183	.313	.484

Batter vs. Pitcher (career)

Hits Best Against	Avg	AB	H	2B	3B	HR	RBI	BB	SO	OBP	SLG
Paul Kilgus	.500	14	7	2	0	2	4	0	4	.500	1.071
Erik Hanson	.455	11	5	0	0	4	6	2	5	.538	1.545
Mike Moore	.400	20	8	1	0	2	3	3	4	.478	.750
Kenny Rogers	.400	10	4	0	0	2	5	3	2	.538	1.000
Kirk McCaskill	.385	13	5	0	0	2	8	1	4	.429	.846

Hits Worst Against	Avg	AB	H	2B	3B	HR	RBI	BB	SO	OBP	SLG
Bobby Witt	.000	11	0	0	0	0	0	2	8	.154	.000
David Wells	.000	11	0	0	0	0	0	1	6	.083	.000
Mike Witt	.071	14	1	0	0	0	0	0	8	.071	.071
Chris Bosio	.167	24	4	0	0	0	3	0	7	.167	.167
Bill Swift	.167	12	2	0	0	0	2	0	2	.167	.167

Danny Jackson — Phillies

Age 32 – Pitches Left (groundball pitcher)

	ERA	W	L	Sv	G	GS	IP	BB	SO	Avg	H	2B	3B	HR	RBI	OBP	SLG	CG	ShO	Sup	QS	#P/S	SB	CS	GB	FB	G/F
1993 Season	3.77	12	11	0	32	32	210.1	80	120	.263	214	39	6	12	87	.329	.370	2	1	5.52	22	101	15	7	321	202	1.59
Last Five Years	4.35	33	46	0	125	121	715.1	302	394	.272	755	128	19	47	332	.343	.383	3	1	4.71	61	91	65	30	1196	655	1.83

1993 Season

	ERA	W	L	Sv	G	GS	IP	H	HR	BB	SO
Home	3.86	8	5	0	16	16	109.2	119	7	32	67
Away	3.67	4	6	0	16	16	100.2	95	5	48	53
Day	3.84	3	3	0	11	11	68.0	66	3	35	41
Night	3.73	9	8	0	21	21	142.1	148	9	45	79
Grass	2.84	4	4	0	10	10	66.2	59	2	32	34
Turf	4.20	8	7	0	22	22	143.2	155	10	48	86
April	3.51	2	0	0	5	5	33.1	32	3	12	19
May	3.97	2	2	0	5	5	34.0	30	1	10	18
June	2.91	3	2	0	6	6	43.1	38	2	17	18
July	4.72	2	4	0	6	6	40.0	49	5	20	30
August	1.35	2	1	0	4	4	26.2	25	0	7	16
September/October	5.73	1	2	0	6	6	33.0	40	1	14	19
Starter	3.77	12	11	0	32	32	210.1	214	12	80	120
Reliever	0.00	0	0	0	0	0	0.0	0	0	0	0
0-3 Days Rest	0.00	0	0	0	0	0	0.0	0	0	0	0
4 Days Rest	3.52	8	6	0	18	18	122.2	122	6	43	75
5+ Days Rest	4.11	4	5	0	14	14	87.2	92	6	37	45
Pre-All Star	4.05	7	6	0	18	18	122.1	125	9	42	66
Post-All Star	3.38	5	5	0	14	14	88.0	89	3	38	54

	Avg	AB	H	2B	3B	HR	RBI	BB	SO	OBP	SLG
vs. Left	.294	143	42	5	0	4	19	16	24	.377	.413
vs. Right	.257	670	172	34	6	8	68	64	96	.319	.361
Inning 1-6	.259	699	181	33	4	11	72	69	108	.325	.365
Inning 7+	.289	114	33	6	2	1	15	11	12	.354	.404
None on	.258	438	113	24	2	7	7	45	62	.333	.370
Runners on	.269	375	101	15	4	5	80	35	58	.325	.371
Scoring Posn	.268	209	56	10	1	5	75	24	36	.332	.397
Close & Late	.316	38	12	4	0	1	6	6	2	.400	.500
None on/out	.234	201	47	13	1	4	4	19	25	.306	.368
vs. 1st Batr (relief)	.000	0	0	0	0	0	0	0	0	.000	.000
First Inning Pitched	.230	122	28	6	1	1	11	18	23	.329	.320
First 75 Pitches	.256	590	151	29	4	6	60	58	94	.322	.349
Pitch 76-90	.257	109	28	5	1	3	9	10	11	.328	.404
Pitch 91-105	.309	81	25	2	0	3	12	9	10	.374	.444
Pitch 106+	.303	33	10	3	1	0	6	3	5	.361	.455
First Pitch	.321	140	45	8	2	5	25	2	0	.331	.514
Ahead in Count	.220	382	84	15	2	4	32	0	104	.224	.301
Behind in Count	.309	181	56	10	2	3	20	39	0	.432	.436
Two Strikes	.201	344	69	11	1	4	28	39	120	.285	.273

Last Five Years

	ERA	W	L	Sv	G	GS	IP	H	HR	BB	SO
Home	4.09	19	19	0	64	61	380.1	400	26	143	214
Away	4.65	14	27	0	61	60	335.0	355	21	159	180
Day	4.37	11	19	0	50	49	275.2	300	18	125	148
Night	4.34	22	27	0	75	72	439.2	455	29	177	246
Grass	4.13	12	22	0	55	53	316.1	318	21	146	167
Turf	4.53	21	24	0	70	68	399.0	437	26	156	227
April	5.63	3	10	0	21	21	112.0	132	12	52	53
May	4.18	4	9	0	19	19	116.1	108	3	46	62
June	3.97	12	6	0	25	25	158.2	161	7	71	81
July	3.20	6	8	0	18	18	118.0	109	13	54	68

	Avg	AB	H	2B	3B	HR	RBI	BB	SO	OBP	SLG
vs. Left	.268	474	127	15	3	9	62	62	89	.356	.369
vs. Right	.273	2301	628	113	16	38	270	240	305	.340	.385
Inning 1-6	.267	2487	664	116	16	39	296	278	353	.340	.374
Inning 7+	.316	288	91	12	3	8	36	24	41	.368	.462
None on	.263	1502	395	74	12	21	21	159	206	.337	.370
Runners on	.283	1273	360	54	7	26	311	143	188	.350	.397
Scoring Posn	.282	760	214	34	3	14	276	94	122	.351	.389
Close & Late	.344	154	53	5	1	7	22	13	18	.391	.526
None on/out	.261	679	177	34	4	9	9	85	87	.347	.362
vs. 1st Batr (relief)	.667	3	2	0	0	0	1	1	0	.750	.667

Last Five Years

	ERA	W	L	Sv	G	GS	IP	H	HR	BB	SO
August	4.50	4	4	0	17	16	84.0	90	5	34	52
September/October	4.84	4	9	0	25	22	126.1	155	7	45	78
Starter	4.32	33	46	0	121	121	709.2	744	47	298	390
Reliever	7.94	0	0	0	4	0	5.2	11	0	4	4
0-3 Days Rest	4.78	3	3	0	8	8	43.1	56	2	21	23
4 Days Rest	4.19	19	26	0	70	70	425.1	426	28	182	234
5+ Days Rest	4.48	11	17	0	43	43	241.0	262	17	95	133
Pre-All Star	4.44	21	28	0	72	72	429.1	447	28	186	222
Post-All Star	4.22	12	18	0	53	49	286.0	308	19	116	172

	Avg	AB	H	2B	3B	HR	RBI	BB	SO	OBP	SLG
First Inning Pitched	.266	473	126	20	3	10	66	80	76	.372	.385
First 75 Pitches	.266	2176	579	105	14	30	249	251	315	.341	.369
Pitch 76-90	.285	312	89	12	3	8	42	29	36	.350	.420
Pitch 91-105	.294	211	62	7	0	6	27	16	32	.339	.412
Pitch 106+	.329	76	25	4	2	3	14	6	11	.378	.553
First Pitch	.316	469	148	24	2	10	65	18	0	.341	.439
Ahead in Count	.220	1205	265	47	7	16	121	0	341	.222	.310
Behind in Count	.338	642	217	34	7	15	88	169	0	.474	.483
Two Strikes	.192	1085	208	34	3	12	99	115	394	.270	.262

Pitcher vs. Batter (since 1984)

Pitches Best Vs.	Avg	AB	H	2B	3B	HR	RBI	BB	SO	OBP	SLG
Gary Redus	.000	18	0	0	0	0	1	4	2	.182	.000
Jacob Brumfield	.000	11	0	0	0	0	1	0	2	.000	.000
Archi Cianfrocco	.000	11	0	0	0	0	0	1	4	.083	.000
Andre Dawson	.071	14	1	0	0	0	0	0	3	.071	.071
Jerald Clark	.118	17	2	0	0	0	1	0	5	.118	.118

Pitches Worst Vs.	Avg	AB	H	2B	3B	HR	RBI	BB	SO	OBP	SLG
Geronimo Pena	.600	10	6	2	0	1	3	1	0	.636	1.100
Dave Gallagher	.588	17	10	2	0	1	3	4	1	.667	.882
Felix Jose	.500	12	6	5	0	0	4	0	1	.500	.917
Kent Hrbek	.450	20	9	5	0	1	4	2	4	.500	.850
Bob Deer	.364	11	4	0	0	2	7	4	4	.500	.909

Darrin Jackson — Mets

Age 30 – Bats Right

	Avg	G	AB	R	H	2B	3B	HR	RBI	BB	SO	HBP	GDP	SB	CS	OBP	SLG	IBB	SH	SF	#Pit	#P/PA	GB	FB	G/F
1993 Season	.209	77	263	19	55	9	0	6	26	10	75	0	9	0	2	.237	.312	0	6	1	1026	3.66	82	61	1.34
Last Five Years	.242	482	1492	169	361	54	6	51	174	81	305	6	38	23	12	.282	.389	12	16	12	5640	3.51	473	442	1.07

1993 Season

	Avg	AB	H	2B	3B	HR	RBI	BB	SO	OBP	SLG
vs. Left	.250	84	21	3	0	2	8	3	20	.273	.357
vs. Right	.190	179	34	6	0	4	18	7	55	.220	.291
Home	.230	135	31	6	0	4	14	5	35	.255	.363
Away	.188	128	24	3	0	2	12	5	40	.218	.258
First Pitch	.333	27	9	2	0	0	5	0	0	.321	.407
Ahead in Count	.367	49	18	5	0	5	7	3	0	.404	.776
Behind in Count	.114	149	17	0	0	0	8	0	70	.114	.114
Two Strikes	.095	137	13	1	0	0	5	7	75	.139	.102

	Avg	AB	H	2B	3B	HR	RBI	BB	SO	OBP	SLG
Scoring Posn	.222	63	14	2	0	1	20	4	19	.265	.302
Close & Late	.257	35	9	2	0	1	3	2	10	.297	.400
None on/out	.164	61	10	1	0	1	1	0	20	.164	.230
Batting #6	.238	105	25	6	0	2	15	6	31	.279	.352
Batting #7	.218	78	17	3	0	3	6	3	21	.244	.372
Other	.163	80	13	0	0	1	5	1	23	.173	.200
Pre-All Star	.204	226	46	8	0	6	24	9	66	.234	.319
Post-All Star	.243	37	9	1	0	0	2	1	9	.256	.270

Last Five Years

	Avg	AB	H	2B	3B	HR	RBI	BB	SO	OBP	SLG
vs. Left	.238	585	139	20	4	24	72	37	103	.281	.409
vs. Right	.245	907	222	34	2	27	102	44	202	.282	.376
Groundball	.241	510	123	19	2	17	62	29	103	.280	.386
Flyball	.229	319	73	17	1	14	35	21	68	.282	.420
Home	.255	732	187	27	4	29	96	35	137	.291	.422
Away	.229	760	174	27	2	22	78	46	168	.273	.357
Day	.248	468	116	26	1	18	63	26	102	.287	.423
Night	.239	1024	245	28	5	33	111	55	203	.279	.373
Grass	.261	1063	277	37	6	42	136	55	193	.298	.425
Turf	.196	429	84	17	0	9	38	26	112	.241	.298
First Pitch	.269	223	60	13	1	7	28	7	0	.291	.430
Ahead in Count	.318	277	88	17	0	19	49	39	0	.399	.585
Behind in Count	.183	747	137	16	4	13	50	0	275	.187	.268
Two Strikes	.165	705	116	11	2	14	47	35	305	.206	.245

	Avg	AB	H	2B	3B	HR	RBI	BB	SO	OBP	SLG
Scoring Posn	.261	348	91	17	2	12	129	33	68	.322	.425
Close & Late	.230	248	57	8	1	10	31	18	59	.281	.391
None on/out	.262	404	106	16	2	17	17	13	83	.285	.438
Batting #5	.243	317	77	13	2	7	39	11	59	.268	.363
Batting #6	.255	345	88	17	2	10	45	18	75	.298	.403
Other	.236	830	196	24	2	34	90	52	171	.280	.393
April	.255	196	50	11	1	8	28	13	48	.302	.444
May	.212	293	62	12	0	7	27	18	61	.257	.324
June	.250	224	56	5	2	8	25	11	44	.285	.397
July	.269	156	42	5	2	7	22	6	24	.296	.462
August	.233	210	49	7	1	7	29	11	44	.274	.376
September/October	.247	413	102	14	0	14	43	22	84	.286	.383
Pre-All Star	.242	774	187	29	3	26	90	44	161	.282	.388
Post-All Star	.242	718	174	25	3	25	84	37	144	.281	.390

Batter vs. Pitcher (career)

Hits Best Against	Avg	AB	H	2B	3B	HR	RBI	BB	SO	OBP	SLG
Bud Black	.500	14	7	2	0	1	4	0	1	.500	.857
Roger McDowell	.500	12	6	2	0	0	1	1	2	.538	.667
Donovan Osborne	.467	15	7	0	0	1	2	1	2	.500	.667
Danny Jackson	.417	24	10	1	0	2	5	3	4	.464	.708
John Smoltz	.400	20	8	3	0	1	4	0	4	.400	.700

Hits Worst Against	Avg	AB	H	2B	3B	HR	RBI	BB	SO	OBP	SLG
Randy Tomlin	.000	11	0	0	0	0	0	1	2	.083	.000
Ramon Martinez	.059	17	1	0	0	0	1	0	2	.059	.059
Terry Mulholland	.087	23	2	0	1	0	3	1	5	.125	.174
Randy Myers	.100	10	1	0	0	0	1	2	0	.250	.100
Fernando Valenzuela	.167	12	2	0	0	0	2	1	3	.214	.167

Mike Jackson — Giants

Age 29 – Pitches Right (flyball pitcher)

	ERA	W	L	Sv	G	GS	IP	BB	SO	Avg	H	2B	3B	HR	RBI	OBP	SLG	GF	IR	IRS	Hld	SvOp	SB	CS	GB	FB	G/F
1993 Season	3.03	6	6	1	81	0	77.1	24	70	.204	58	8	1	7	39	.272	.313	17	58	17	34	6	1	1	78	93	0.84
Last Five Years	3.52	28	32	27	348	0	424.2	189	387	.222	343	59	7	35	206	.313	.337	104	265	80	74	53	36	11	446	474	0.94

1993 Season

	ERA	W	L	Sv	G	GS	IP	H	HR	BB	SO
Home	4.32	3	4	1	38	0	33.1	33	5	12	33
Away	2.05	3	2	0	43	0	44.0	25	2	12	37
Day	3.03	4	2	1	41	0	38.2	30	5	11	35
Night	3.03	2	4	0	40	0	38.2	28	2	13	35
Grass	4.09	5	6	1	62	0	55.0	50	7	21	51
Turf	0.40	1	0	0	19	0	22.1	8	0	3	19
April	2.13	1	1	1	16	0	12.2	8	1	4	11
May	1.10	2	0	0	15	0	16.1	9	1	2	13
June	4.15	1	1	0	13	0	13.0	7	1	5	10
July	5.40	1	1	0	11	0	8.1	11	2	3	6
August	6.23	0	2	0	9	0	8.2	8	1	1	7

	Avg	AB	H	2B	3B	HR	RBI	BB	SO	OBP	SLG
vs. Left	.246	126	31	4	1	3	21	13	23	.317	.365
vs. Right	.171	158	27	4	0	4	18	11	47	.236	.272
Inning 1-6	.167	12	2	0	0	0	2	0	4	.167	.167
Inning 7+	.206	272	56	8	1	7	37	24	66	.276	.320
None on	.191	152	29	6	0	1	1	11	39	.255	.250
Runners on	.220	132	29	2	1	6	38	13	31	.291	.386
Scoring Posn	.195	82	16	1	1	5	36	10	20	.284	.415
Close & Late	.218	170	37	5	1	5	28	14	41	.281	.347
None on/out	.217	60	13	1	0	0	0	3	9	.266	.233
vs. 1st Batr (relief)	.227	75	17	3	0	0	8	3	18	.263	.267
First Inning Pitched	.211	237	50	6	1	6	37	17	58	.270	.321

1993 Season

	ERA	W	L	Sv	G	GS	IP	H	HR	BB	SO
September/October	1.96	1	1	0	17	0	18.1	15	1	9	23
Starter	0.00	0	0	0	0	0	0.0	0	0	0	0
Reliever	3.03	6	6	1	81	0	77.1	58	7	24	70
0 Days rest	4.26	2	3	0	31	0	25.1	30	3	5	26
1 or 2 Days rest	3.16	3	2	1	37	0	37.0	21	4	15	33
3+ Days rest	0.60	1	1	0	13	0	15.0	7	0	4	11
Pre-All Star	2.53	5	2	1	49	0	46.1	29	3	12	37
Post-All Star	3.77	1	4	0	32	0	31.0	29	4	12	33

	Avg	AB	H	2B	3B	HR	RBI	BB	SO	OBP	SLG
First 15 Pitches	.223	220	49	6	1	6	35	15	50	.279	.341
Pitch 16-30	.155	58	9	2	0	1	4	7	19	.246	.241
Pitch 31-45	.000	5	0	0	0	0	0	2	1	.286	.000
Pitch 46+	.000	1	0	0	0	0	0	0	0	.000	.000
First Pitch	.286	28	8	1	1	1	7	5	0	.412	.500
Ahead in Count	.171	140	24	3	0	2	14	0	52	.182	.236
Behind in Count	.250	52	13	2	0	1	6	9	0	.355	.346
Two Strikes	.111	144	16	2	0	1	9	10	70	.178	.146

Last Five Years

	ERA	W	L	Sv	G	GS	IP	H	HR	BB	SO
Home	3.64	14	12	12	170	0	215.0	170	19	87	198
Away	3.39	14	20	15	178	0	209.2	173	16	102	189
Day	3.36	8	7	7	116	0	131.1	92	12	62	111
Night	3.59	20	25	20	232	0	293.1	251	23	127	276
Grass	3.75	17	17	13	185	0	211.1	182	19	103	193
Turf	3.29	11	15	14	163	0	213.1	161	16	86	194
April	3.41	3	5	4	51	0	63.1	53	6	20	50
May	2.43	8	2	6	60	0	85.1	59	9	21	75
June	3.59	5	4	12	56	0	72.2	46	8	34	70
July	4.55	5	7	0	58	0	61.1	60	4	34	58
August	3.22	4	7	3	59	0	67.0	48	4	36	57
September/October	4.20	3	7	2	64	0	75.0	77	4	44	77
Starter	0.00	0	0	0	0	0	0.0	0	0	0	0
Reliever	3.52	28	32	27	348	0	424.2	343	35	189	387
0 Days rest	5.00	7	15	7	84	0	90.0	88	9	43	81
1 or 2 Days rest	3.10	14	12	17	177	0	232.1	175	19	100	206
3+ Days rest	3.17	7	5	3	87	0	102.1	80	7	46	100
Pre-All Star	3.07	19	13	22	187	0	243.1	179	24	82	223
Post-All Star	4.12	9	19	5	161	0	181.1	164	11	107	164

	Avg	AB	H	2B	3B	HR	RBI	BB	SO	OBP	SLG
vs. Left	.248	670	166	33	4	18	91	104	120	.351	.390
vs. Right	.202	877	177	26	3	17	115	85	267	.283	.296
Inning 1-6	.271	140	38	8	2	1	28	21	36	.367	.379
Inning 7+	.217	1407	305	51	5	34	178	168	351	.307	.333
None on	.207	832	172	23	3	23	23	69	204	.275	.325
Runners on	.239	715	171	36	4	12	183	120	183	.353	.351
Scoring Posn	.234	465	109	24	1	9	169	97	116	.368	.348
Close & Late	.225	816	184	31	5	17	116	101	210	.318	.338
None on/out	.232	354	82	8	2	12	12	27	77	.290	.367
vs. 1st Batr (relief)	.223	301	67	10	1	4	38	33	85	.304	.302
First Inning Pitched	.228	1087	248	39	6	19	164	126	272	.315	.328
First 15 Pitches	.237	997	236	37	4	20	142	106	236	.317	.342
Pitch 16-30	.190	443	84	19	2	12	49	62	129	.294	.323
Pitch 31-45	.216	88	19	3	1	3	13	17	17	.349	.375
Pitch 46+	.211	19	4	0	0	0	2	4	5	.375	.211
First Pitch	.289	194	56	7	2	6	37	36	0	.409	.438
Ahead in Count	.158	767	121	18	1	9	59	0	319	.172	.219
Behind in Count	.316	282	89	17	2	10	53	93	0	.484	.496
Two Strikes	.139	798	111	19	3	7	63	60	387	.206	.197

Pitcher vs. Batter (career)

Pitches Best Vs.	Avg	AB	H	2B	3B	HR	RBI	BB	SO	OBP	SLG
Paul Molitor	.000	12	0	0	0	0	0	1	4	.077	.000
Rob Deer	.000	12	0	0	0	0	0	1	8	.077	.000
Steve Buechele	.000	12	0	0	0	0	0	1	3	.077	.000
Jose Canseco	.000	11	0	0	0	0	0	2	3	.154	.000
Casey Candaele	.100	10	1	0	0	0	1	0	1	.091	.100

Pitches Worst Vs.	Avg	AB	H	2B	3B	HR	RBI	BB	SO	OBP	SLG
Rafael Palmeiro	.778	9	7	1	0	2	3	2	1	.818	1.556
Chili Davis	.667	9	6	0	0	0	2	5	0	.733	.667
Dave Martinez	.571	7	4	0	0	0	1	3	1	.636	.571
Candy Maldonado	.455	11	5	1	0	2	6	0	3	.455	1.091
Ellis Burks	.308	13	4	0	0	2	4	2	2	.400	.769

John Jaha — Brewers

Age 28 – Bats Right (groundball hitter)

	Avg	G	AB	R	H	2B	3B	HR	RBI	BB	SO	HBP	GDP	SB	CS	OBP	SLG	IBB	SH	SF	#Pit	#P/PA	GB	FB	G/F
1993 Season	.264	153	515	78	136	21	0	19	70	51	109	8	6	13	9	.337	.416	4	4	4	2207	3.79	198	126	1.57
Career (1992-1993)	.256	200	648	95	166	24	1	21	80	63	139	10	7	23	9	.328	.394	5	5	8	2767	3.77	246	163	1.51

1993 Season

	Avg	AB	H	2B	3B	HR	RBI	BB	SO	OBP	SLG
vs. Left	.233	172	40	6	0	6	26	15	36	.296	.372
vs. Right	.280	343	96	15	0	13	44	36	73	.357	.437
Groundball	.330	88	29	7	0	1	11	7	17	.385	.443
Flyball	.284	102	29	5	0	6	13	7	24	.327	.510
Home	.264	254	67	10	0	5	36	22	56	.325	.362
Away	.264	261	69	11	0	14	34	29	53	.349	.467
Day	.216	190	41	7	0	3	21	17	41	.294	.300
Night	.292	325	95	14	0	16	49	34	68	.362	.483
Grass	.260	427	111	16	0	13	57	41	93	.329	.389
Turf	.284	88	25	5	0	6	13	10	16	.376	.545
First Pitch	.429	77	33	5	0	3	15	4	0	.477	.610
Ahead in Count	.350	100	35	8	0	7	17	22	0	.467	.640
Behind in Count	.182	236	43	5	0	2	19	0	93	.193	.229
Two Strikes	.159	246	39	3	0	6	25	25	109	.236	.244

	Avg	AB	H	2B	3B	HR	RBI	BB	SO	OBP	SLG
Scoring Posn	.305	118	36	6	0	2	47	22	25	.407	.407
Close & Late	.312	93	29	3	0	3	9	9	18	.390	.441
None on/out	.252	131	33	7	0	7	7	10	27	.310	.466
Batting #7	.254	169	43	5	0	5	24	15	42	.316	.373
Batting #8	.286	175	50	12	0	4	19	17	31	.352	.423
Other	.251	171	43	4	0	10	27	19	36	.344	.450
April	.217	60	13	1	0	0	4	5	10	.304	.233
May	.273	88	24	3	0	3	12	6	23	.326	.409
June	.221	95	21	4	0	2	5	9	21	.295	.326
July	.270	74	20	6	0	0	10	6	14	.329	.351
August	.287	108	31	5	0	8	20	11	22	.350	.556
September/October	.300	90	27	2	0	6	19	14	19	.402	.522
Pre-All Star	.247	279	69	12	0	5	26	23	58	.315	.344
Post-All Star	.284	236	67	9	0	14	44	28	51	.363	.500

1993 By Position

Position	Avg	AB	H	2B	3B	HR	RBI	BB	SO	OBP	SLG	G	GS	Innings	PO	A	E	DP	Fld Pct	Rng Fctr	In Zone	Outs	Zone Rtg	MLB Zone
As 1b	.267	510	136	21	0	19	70	50	108	.339	.420	150	143	1281.1	1187	128	10	116	.992	---	296	246	.831	.834

Chris James — Rangers

Age 31 – Bats Right

	Avg	G	AB	R	H	2B	3B	HR	RBI	BB	SO	HBP	GDP	SB	CS	OBP	SLG	IBB	SH	SF	#Pit	#P/PA	GB	FB	G/F
1993 Season	.275	73	160	24	44	11	1	9	26	18	40	1	2	2	0	.348	.525	2	1	2	694	3.81	40	54	0.74
Last Five Years	.260	571	1855	197	483	86	13	44	234	107	285	12	44	16	12	.303	.392	12	10	13	6898	3.45	710	550	1.29

1993 Season

	Avg	AB	H	2B	3B	HR	RBI	BB	SO	OBP	SLG
vs. Left	.246	118	29	10	1	8	19	13	27	.316	.551
vs. Right	.357	42	15	1	0	1	7	5	13	.438	.452
Home	.277	65	18	5	1	6	14	5	15	.333	.662
Away	.274	95	26	6	0	3	12	13	25	.358	.432

	Avg	AB	H	2B	3B	HR	RBI	BB	SO	OBP	SLG
Scoring Posn	.255	47	12	1	1	2	18	9	13	.373	.447
Close & Late	.324	37	12	3	0	3	10	5	9	.419	.649
None on/out	.233	43	10	2	0	4	4	3	9	.283	.558
Batting #4	.294	34	10	4	0	0	4	5	8	.375	.412

1993 Season

	Avg	AB	H	2B	3B	HR	RBI	BB	SO	OBP	SLG		Avg	AB	H	2B	3B	HR	RBI	BB	SO	OBP	SLG
First Pitch	.267	15	4	1	0	0	1	2	0	.368	.333	Batting #6	.277	47	13	3	0	4	8	5	10	.340	.596
Ahead in Count	.390	41	16	1	1	7	15	5	0	.447	.976	Other	.266	79	21	4	1	5	14	8	22	.341	.532
Behind in Count	.192	73	14	6	0	1	7	0	32	.192	.315	Pre-All Star	.261	88	23	8	1	4	12	9	19	.333	.511
Two Strikes	.152	79	12	4	0	1	6	11	40	.256	.241	Post-All Star	.292	72	21	3	0	5	14	9	21	.366	.542

Last Five Years

	Avg	AB	H	2B	3B	HR	RBI	BB	SO	OBP	SLG		Avg	AB	H	2B	3B	HR	RBI	BB	SO	OBP	SLG
vs. Left	.271	695	188	34	5	23	99	52	110	.320	.433	Scoring Posn	.272	504	137	20	5	10	187	47	85	.330	.391
vs. Right	.254	1160	295	52	8	21	135	55	175	.292	.367	Close & Late	.239	310	74	12	0	6	32	23	61	.297	.335
Groundball	.273	640	175	31	7	13	80	37	88	.316	.405	None on/out	.224	410	92	13	1	15	15	21	64	.269	.371
Flyball	.267	408	109	26	3	11	52	26	65	.315	.426	Batting #3	.294	282	83	12	4	4	51	12	40	.320	.408
Home	.271	857	232	40	7	23	123	48	119	.312	.414	Batting #5	.280	671	188	31	6	20	82	40	94	.322	.434
Away	.252	998	251	46	6	21	111	59	166	.295	.373	Other	.235	902	212	43	3	20	101	55	151	.284	.356
Day	.287	567	163	36	6	16	86	34	104	.332	.457	April	.253	249	63	11	0	6	30	12	36	.292	.369
Night	.248	1288	320	50	7	28	148	73	181	.290	.363	May	.227	308	70	11	1	5	30	22	50	.284	.318
Grass	.268	1322	354	55	11	30	174	78	194	.310	.394	June	.251	327	82	15	3	5	39	19	55	.291	.361
Turf	.242	533	129	31	2	14	60	29	91	.285	.386	July	.274	354	97	19	4	11	42	19	50	.315	.444
First Pitch	.339	230	78	12	2	9	32	7	0	.360	.526	August	.312	330	103	20	1	10	45	16	52	.345	.470
Ahead in Count	.337	478	161	28	5	25	102	53	0	.401	.573	September/October	.237	287	68	10	4	7	40	19	42	.285	.373
Behind in Count	.196	838	164	26	4	5	59	0	247	.202	.254	Pre-All Star	.249	991	247	42	7	19	122	61	156	.296	.363
Two Strikes	.173	775	134	20	6	5	58	45	285	.223	.234	Post-All Star	.273	864	236	44	6	25	112	46	129	.312	.425

Batter vs. Pitcher (career)

Hits Best Against	Avg	AB	H	2B	3B	HR	RBI	BB	SO	OBP	SLG	Hits Worst Against	Avg	AB	H	2B	3B	HR	RBI	BB	SO	OBP	SLG
Les Lancaster	.500	14	7	0	0	2	6	1	2	.533	.929	David Cone	.000	21	0	0	0	0	1	0	5	.000	.000
Kevin Appier	.500	14	7	0	0	1	2	0	1	.500	.714	Jim Abbott	.000	15	0	0	0	0	0	0	3	.000	.000
Barry Jones	.500	10	5	1	1	0	2	1	1	.545	.800	Charlie Leibrandt	.000	12	0	0	0	0	0	1	2	.077	.000
Neal Heaton	.450	20	9	2	0	2	5	1	1	.476	.850	Jose Rijo	.091	11	1	1	0	0	0	0	0	.091	.182
Zane Smith	.389	18	7	1	1	2	5	1	2	.421	.889	Joe Hesketh	.091	11	1	0	0	0	0	0	2	.091	.091

Dion James — Yankees

Age 31 – Bats Left (groundball hitter)

	Avg	G	AB	R	H	2B	3B	HR	RBI	BB	SO	HBP	GDP	SB	CS	OBP	SLG	IBB	SH	SF	#Pit	#P/PA	GB	FB	G/F
1993 Season	.332	115	343	62	114	21	2	7	36	31	31	2	5	0	0	.390	.466	1	1	1	1344	3.56	132	95	1.39
Last Five Years	.295	403	1151	155	339	62	4	16	115	129	118	5	23	8	10	.367	.397	10	9	5	4559	3.51	487	297	1.64

1993 Season

	Avg	AB	H	2B	3B	HR	RBI	BB	SO	OBP	SLG		Avg	AB	H	2B	3B	HR	RBI	BB	SO	OBP	SLG
vs. Left	.231	26	6	1	0	0	4	3	2	.310	.269	Scoring Posn	.236	72	17	4	0	0	26	14	4	.356	.292
vs. Right	.341	317	108	20	2	7	32	28	29	.397	.483	Close & Late	.318	44	14	0	0	0	5	7	5	.412	.318
Groundball	.228	57	13	2	0	1	7	7	4	.323	.316	None on/out	.363	91	33	6	0	3	3	4	12	.396	.527
Flyball	.319	91	29	6	0	1	7	9	15	.380	.418	Batting #1	.323	65	21	6	1	1	10	4	7	.371	.492
Home	.359	181	65	12	1	5	16	11	14	.394	.519	Batting #2	.363	193	70	12	0	4	15	17	15	.417	.487
Away	.302	162	49	9	1	2	20	20	17	.386	.407	Other	.271	85	23	3	1	2	11	10	9	.344	.400
Day	.436	94	41	8	0	3	12	10	7	.495	.617	April	.500	8	4	0	0	0	2	0	0	.500	.500
Night	.293	249	73	13	2	4	24	21	24	.349	.410	May	.339	59	20	5	1	1	9	3	8	.375	.508
Grass	.330	285	94	19	1	6	32	23	25	.381	.467	June	.243	70	17	4	1	2	9	9	8	.329	.414
Turf	.345	58	20	2	1	1	4	8	6	.433	.466	July	.397	58	23	3	0	1	5	4	5	.435	.500
First Pitch	.455	44	20	3	1	0	5	1	0	.478	.568	August	.391	64	25	4	0	2	7	8	5	.458	.547
Ahead in Count	.417	96	40	6	1	2	14	19	0	.513	.563	September/October	.298	84	25	5	0	1	4	7	5	.359	.393
Behind in Count	.248	137	34	11	0	3	11	0	27	.252	.394	Pre-All Star	.299	154	46	10	2	3	21	14	17	.359	.448
Two Strikes	.240	121	29	4	0	4	9	11	31	.306	.372	Post-All Star	.360	189	68	11	0	4	15	17	14	.415	.481

1993 By Position

Position	Avg	AB	H	2B	3B	HR	RBI	BB	SO	OBP	SLG	G	GS	Innings	PO	A	E	DP	Fld Pct	Rng Fctr	In Zone	Outs	Zone Rtg	MLB Zone
As Pinch Hitter	.409	22	9	0	0	0	3	3	5	.480	.409	27	0	---	---	---	---	---	---	---	---	---	---	---
As lf	.321	274	88	16	1	6	26	25	21	.379	.453	91	71	608.0	124	4	3	1	.977	1.89	152	122	.803	.818
As cf	.362	47	17	5	1	1	7	3	5	.412	.574	14	12	95.0	15	0	2	0	.882	1.42	23	16	.696	.829

Last Five Years

	Avg	AB	H	2B	3B	HR	RBI	BB	SO	OBP	SLG		Avg	AB	H	2B	3B	HR	RBI	BB	SO	OBP	SLG
vs. Left	.208	101	21	5	0	1	11	16	9	.322	.287	Scoring Posn	.245	257	63	9	1	2	87	46	24	.354	.311
vs. Right	.303	1050	318	57	4	15	104	113	109	.371	.408	Close & Late	.230	196	45	4	0	0	14	28	30	.326	.250
Groundball	.280	325	91	17	1	5	38	45	29	.371	.385	None on/out	.289	277	80	12	1	4	4	23	33	.348	.383
Flyball	.267	277	74	13	0	3	21	32	32	.344	.347	Batting #2	.333	403	134	24	0	8	37	37	31	.391	.452
Home	.297	558	166	33	2	8	52	58	65	.363	.407	Batting #3	.314	271	85	16	1	3	35	32	32	.385	.413
Away	.292	593	173	29	2	8	63	71	53	.370	.388	Other	.252	477	120	22	3	5	43	60	55	.336	.342
Day	.341	369	126	20	2	8	44	45	32	.416	.472	April	.257	101	26	4	0	0	7	13	7	.339	.297
Night	.272	782	213	42	2	8	71	84	86	.343	.362	May	.282	216	61	15	1	2	22	28	28	.367	.389
Grass	.292	927	271	49	3	13	90	96	101	.360	.394	June	.239	209	50	11	2	3	18	24	25	.316	.354
Turf	.304	224	68	13	1	3	25	33	17	.394	.411	July	.349	209	73	14	1	5	26	29	18	.431	.498
First Pitch	.383	175	67	6	2	1	24	6	0	.408	.457	August	.308	224	69	10	0	3	20	19	21	.362	.393
Ahead in Count	.337	329	111	23	1	6	46	75	0	.458	.468	September/October	.313	192	60	8	0	3	22	16	19	.370	.401
Behind in Count	.227	441	100	26	1	5	27	0	106	.231	.324	Pre-All Star	.266	576	153	34	3	7	53	69	61	.344	.372
Two Strikes	.226	421	95	19	1	5	24	46	118	.305	.311	Post-All Star	.323	575	186	28	1	9	62	60	57	.390	.423

Batter vs. Pitcher (since 1984)

Hits Best Against	Avg	AB	H	2B	3B	HR	RBI	BB	SO	OBP	SLG	Hits Worst Against	Avg	AB	H	2B	3B	HR	RBI	BB	SO	OBP	SLG
Kevin Tapani	.526	19	10	3	1	2	5	0	2	.526	1.105	Nolan Ryan	.050	20	1	0	0	0	0	2	4	.136	.050

Batter vs. Pitcher (since 1984)																							
Hits Best Against	Avg	AB	H	2B	3B	HR	RBI	BB	SO	OBP	SLG	Hits Worst Against	Avg	AB	H	2B	3B	HR	RBI	BB	SO	OBP	SLG
Todd Stottlemyre	.522	23	12	1	0	0	1	6	1	.621	.565	Bryn Smith	.105	19	2	1	0	0	0	1	5	.150	.158
Chris Bosio	.500	20	10	3	0	0	3	2	2	.545	.650	Jack Morris	.148	27	4	0	0	0	1	5	3	.281	.148
Bob Walk	.455	22	10	6	0	0	4	3	1	.520	.727	Scott Bankhead	.182	11	2	0	0	0	0	1	1	.250	.182
Greg Maddux	.333	12	4	1	1	1	5	2	2	.429	.833	Orel Hershiser	.188	32	6	0	0	0	0	2	5	.235	.188

Stan Javier — Angels

Age 30 – Bats Both (groundball hitter)

	Avg	G	AB	R	H	2B	3B	HR	RBI	BB	SO	HBP	GDP	SB	CS	OBP	SLG	IBB	SH	SF	#Pit	#P/PA	GB	FB	G/F
1993 Season	.291	92	237	33	69	10	4	3	28	27	33	1	7	12	2	.362	.405	1	1	3	1046	3.89	100	51	1.96
Last Five Years	.261	578	1366	198	357	53	17	9	123	151	218	5	27	64	15	.335	.345	6	17	11	5816	3.75	598	290	2.06

1993 Season																							
	Avg	AB	H	2B	3B	HR	RBI	BB	SO	OBP	SLG		Avg	AB	H	2B	3B	HR	RBI	BB	SO	OBP	SLG
vs. Left	.271	85	23	4	1	1	8	12	10	.357	.376	Scoring Posn	.274	62	17	1	3	1	23	4	14	.304	.435
vs. Right	.303	152	46	6	3	2	20	15	23	.365	.421	Close & Late	.264	53	14	0	2	0	6	8	12	.365	.340
Home	.318	88	28	3	1	0	10	12	15	.396	.375	None on/out	.294	68	20	4	0	0	0	6	5	.351	.353
Away	.275	149	41	7	3	3	18	15	18	.341	.423	Batting #1	.218	78	17	3	1	0	10	10	11	.300	.282
First Pitch	.286	28	8	0	2	0	4	1	0	.310	.429	Batting #7	.444	45	20	2	0	1	5	9	6	.527	.556
Ahead in Count	.385	52	20	1	0	1	10	14	0	.507	.462	Other	.281	114	32	5	3	2	13	8	16	.333	.430
Behind in Count	.210	105	22	3	1	0	3	0	32	.217	.257	Pre-All Star	.220	100	22	3	3	0	9	11	15	.295	.310
Two Strikes	.252	115	29	8	2	2	12	12	33	.323	.409	Post-All Star	.343	137	47	7	1	3	19	16	18	.410	.474

Last Five Years																							
	Avg	AB	H	2B	3B	HR	RBI	BB	SO	OBP	SLG		Avg	AB	H	2B	3B	HR	RBI	BB	SO	OBP	SLG
vs. Left	.257	526	135	18	8	3	39	57	78	.329	.338	Scoring Posn	.260	327	85	11	6	2	107	46	54	.341	.349
vs. Right	.264	840	222	35	9	6	84	94	140	.338	.349	Close & Late	.222	288	64	7	5	1	28	38	58	.312	.292
Groundball	.262	401	105	13	8	0	30	39	55	.328	.334	None on/out	.264	363	96	15	4	3	3	40	54	.337	.353
Flyball	.218	285	62	12	5	2	27	33	55	.297	.316	Batting #1	.260	396	103	14	5	2	33	54	56	.346	.336
Home	.263	620	163	23	4	3	58	77	102	.343	.327	Batting #2	.270	263	71	8	4	2	15	27	42	.342	.354
Away	.260	746	194	30	13	6	65	74	116	.328	.359	Other	.259	707	183	31	8	5	75	70	120	.325	.347
Day	.234	466	109	16	6	4	41	47	77	.305	.320	April	.250	128	32	4	3	0	8	10	20	.304	.328
Night	.276	900	248	37	11	5	82	104	141	.350	.358	May	.234	214	50	4	6	1	26	27	35	.322	.322
Grass	.249	925	230	29	9	6	83	112	144	.328	.319	June	.273	275	75	17	4	3	24	27	39	.334	.396
Turf	.288	441	127	24	8	3	40	39	74	.349	.399	July	.222	216	48	6	1	0	14	24	39	.306	.259
First Pitch	.294	197	58	4	4	1	22	4	0	.304	.371	August	.261	253	66	11	1	0	24	30	46	.336	.312
Ahead in Count	.304	273	83	11	5	2	25	90	0	.475	.403	September/October	.307	280	86	11	2	5	27	33	39	.379	.414
Behind in Count	.214	621	133	21	6	2	40	0	192	.218	.277	Pre-All Star	.251	717	180	26	14	4	62	79	109	.326	.343
Two Strikes	.220	646	142	28	7	4	52	54	218	.281	.303	Post-All Star	.273	649	177	27	3	5	61	72	109	.344	.347

Batter vs. Pitcher (career)																							
Hits Best Against	Avg	AB	H	2B	3B	HR	RBI	BB	SO	OBP	SLG	Hits Worst Against	Avg	AB	H	2B	3B	HR	RBI	BB	SO	OBP	SLG
Erik Hanson	.500	12	6	1	1	0	2	2	1	.571	.750	Tom Glavine	.000	12	0	0	0	0	0	3	2	.200	.000
Jack McDowell	.429	14	6	1	0	0	1	2	2	.500	.500	Mark Gubicza	.000	11	0	0	0	0	0	0	1	.000	.000
Danny Jackson	.389	18	7	2	0	0	2	2	2	.450	.500	David Cone	.077	13	1	0	0	0	1	0	5	.071	.077
Dennis Rasmussen	.333	9	3	0	0	1	1	4	1	.538	.667	Frank Tanana	.095	21	2	1	0	0	4	0	4	.095	.143
Tom Gordon	.333	9	3	1	0	0	1	3	2	.500	.444	John Smoltz	.133	15	2	0	0	0	1	0	2	.133	.133

Domingo Jean — Yankees

Age 25 – Pitches Right (groundball pitcher)

	ERA	W	L	Sv	G	GS	IP	BB	SO	Avg	H	2B	3B	HR	RBI	OBP	SLG	CG	ShO	Sup	QS	#P/S	SB	CS	GB	FB	G/F
1993 Season	4.46	1	1	0	10	6	40.1	19	20	.237	37	7	2	7	19	.318	.442	0	0	5.80	3	86	2	0	76	44	1.73

1993 Season																						
	ERA	W	L	Sv	G	GS	IP	H	HR	BB	SO		Avg	AB	H	2B	3B	HR	RBI	BB	SO	OBP	SLG
Home	2.37	1	0	0	4	3	19.0	13	3	8	6	vs. Left	.243	74	18	4	2	2	10	7	11	.305	.432
Away	6.33	0	1	0	6	3	21.1	24	4	11	14	vs. Right	.232	82	19	3	0	5	9	12	9	.330	.451

Gregg Jefferies — Cardinals

Age 26 – Bats Both

	Avg	G	AB	R	H	2B	3B	HR	RBI	BB	SO	HBP	GDP	SB	CS	OBP	SLG	IBB	SH	SF	#Pit	#P/PA	GB	FB	G/F
1993 Season	.342	142	544	89	186	24	3	16	83	62	32	2	15	46	9	.408	.485	7	0	4	2159	3.53	223	175	1.27
Last Five Years	.288	724	2746	382	792	147	13	62	344	237	185	15	80	123	31	.345	.419	23	3	25	10648	3.52	1087	896	1.21

1993 Season																							
	Avg	AB	H	2B	3B	HR	RBI	BB	SO	OBP	SLG		Avg	AB	H	2B	3B	HR	RBI	BB	SO	OBP	SLG
vs. Left	.351	148	52	8	0	8	29	9	6	.394	.568	Scoring Posn	.384	146	56	6	0	4	66	26	10	.469	.507
vs. Right	.338	396	134	16	3	8	54	53	26	.414	.455	Close & Late	.402	87	35	3	0	2	12	11	3	.465	.506
Groundball	.339	168	57	7	0	2	25	21	13	.411	.417	None on/out	.313	83	26	8	0	2	2	6	4	.367	.482
Flyball	.253	95	24	4	0	4	12	10	4	.324	.421	Batting #3	.344	523	180	24	3	16	80	60	31	.410	.493
Home	.341	249	85	10	2	10	43	31	19	.417	.518	Batting #4	.250	20	5	0	0	0	1	1	1	.348	.250
Away	.342	295	101	14	1	6	40	31	13	.401	.458	Other	1.000	1	1	0	0	0	2	1	0	.667	1.000
Day	.329	170	56	11	1	4	25	17	12	.389	.476	April	.263	80	21	0	1	4	13	6	6	.310	.438
Night	.348	374	130	13	2	12	58	45	20	.417	.489	May	.260	96	25	2	0	2	13	11	9	.343	.344
Grass	.349	189	66	10	1	4	25	22	8	.415	.476	June	.444	108	48	10	2	4	16	5	4	.465	.685
Turf	.338	355	120	14	2	12	58	40	24	.405	.490	July	.367	79	29	1	0	2	12	8	5	.425	.456
First Pitch	.413	46	19	3	1	0	10	6	0	.481	.522	August	.350	80	28	6	0	3	9	15	3	.443	.538
Ahead in Count	.308	159	49	5	0	4	25	45	0	.456	.415	September/October	.347	101	35	5	0	1	20	17	5	.445	.426
Behind in Count	.329	210	69	7	2	7	29	0	29	.333	.481	Pre-All Star	.343	327	112	13	3	12	51	26	22	.390	.511
Two Strikes	.302	182	55	11	0	5	27	11	32	.347	.445	Post-All Star	.341	217	74	11	0	4	32	36	10	.434	.447

1993 By Position

Position	Avg	AB	H	2B	3B	HR	RBI	BB	SO	OBP	SLG	G	GS	Innings	PO	A	E	DP	Fld Pct	Rng Fctr	In Zone	Outs	Zone Rtg	MLB Zone
As 1b	.339	542	184	24	3	16	81	61	32	.406	.483	140	139	1184.2	1279	75	9	114	.993	---	215	173	.805	.834

Last Five Years

	Avg	AB	H	2B	3B	HR	RBI	BB	SO	OBP	SLG		Avg	AB	H	2B	3B	HR	RBI	BB	SO	OBP	SLG
vs. Left	.281	897	252	54	3	22	106	52	59	.323	.421	Scoring Posn	.295	685	202	31	5	11	267	86	53	.364	.403
vs. Right	.292	1849	540	93	10	40	238	185	126	.356	.418	Close & Late	.283	459	130	18	0	5	51	45	27	.348	.355
Groundball	.292	863	252	45	4	17	105	70	64	.348	.413	None on/out	.286	619	177	41	1	18	18	48	38	.340	.443
Flyball	.270	641	173	37	2	12	64	58	43	.330	.390	Batting #1	.302	526	159	30	3	18	59	41	34	.354	.473
Home	.307	1321	405	78	9	34	176	139	91	.374	.456	Batting #3	.302	1328	401	68	7	33	182	117	79	.358	.438
Away	.272	1425	387	69	4	28	168	98	94	.318	.385	Other	.260	892	232	49	3	11	103	79	72	.322	.359
Day	.299	875	262	55	5	17	104	66	57	.351	.432	April	.220	354	78	22	1	5	38	32	31	.288	.331
Night	.283	1871	530	92	8	45	240	171	128	.343	.413	May	.282	447	126	28	0	9	55	22	35	.318	.405
Grass	.293	1622	475	96	5	36	188	133	105	.347	.425	June	.337	469	158	31	3	16	69	39	22	.387	.518
Turf	.282	1124	317	51	8	26	156	104	80	.343	.411	July	.304	450	137	19	4	13	69	40	32	.361	.451
First Pitch	.277	296	82	18	2	5	44	19	0	.322	.402	August	.293	467	137	26	0	7	48	45	31	.356	.405
Ahead in Count	.293	777	228	44	0	18	107	172	0	.418	.420	September/October	.279	559	156	22	2	12	65	59	34	.347	.390
Behind in Count	.275	1100	302	48	8	22	127	0	160	.280	.393	Pre-All Star	.288	1419	409	84	4	34	184	107	103	.339	.425
Two Strikes	.259	997	258	53	4	15	103	44	185	.293	.365	Post-All Star	.289	1327	383	63	9	28	160	130	82	.352	.413

Batter vs. Pitcher (career)

Hits Best Against	Avg	AB	H	2B	3B	HR	RBI	BB	SO	OBP	SLG	Hits Worst Against	Avg	AB	H	2B	3B	HR	RBI	BB	SO	OBP	SLG
Jose Mesa	.615	13	8	2	0	1	1	0	0	.615	1.000	Bill Landrum	.077	13	1	1	0	0	0	0	3	.077	.154
Dave Stewart	.556	9	5	1	0	1	1	2	1	.636	1.000	Jack McDowell	.091	11	1	0	0	0	0	1	0	.167	.091
Tim Belcher	.471	17	8	1	1	0	5	0	0	.471	.647	Bryn Smith	.111	18	2	0	0	0	1	0	1	.111	.111
Tom Glavine	.450	20	9	1	0	2	5	0	2	.450	.800	Frank DiPino	.182	11	2	0	0	0	1	0	0	.182	.182
Ted Power	.417	12	5	1	0	2	4	1	0	.462	1.000	Melido Perez	.200	10	2	0	0	0	2	0	0	.182	.200

Reggie Jefferson — Indians

Age 25 – Bats Both (groundball hitter)

	Avg	G	AB	R	H	2B	3B	HR	RBI	BB	SO	HBP	GDP	SB	CS	OBP	SLG	IBB	SH	SF	#Pit	#P/PA	GB	FB	G/F
1993 Season	.249	113	366	35	91	11	2	10	34	28	78	5	7	1	3	.310	.372	7	3	1	1446	3.59	161	76	2.12
Career (1991-1993)	.252	168	563	54	142	20	4	14	53	33	119	6	10	1	3	.300	.377	7	3	2	2165	3.57	237	121	1.96

1993 Season

	Avg	AB	H	2B	3B	HR	RBI	BB	SO	OBP	SLG		Avg	AB	H	2B	3B	HR	RBI	BB	SO	OBP	SLG
vs. Left	.196	107	21	4	0	1	9	9	26	.283	.262	Scoring Posn	.209	86	18	2	0	3	26	14	19	.324	.337
vs. Right	.270	259	70	7	2	9	25	19	52	.321	.417	Close & Late	.246	61	15	2	0	2	5	7	9	.333	.377
Groundball	.262	61	16	0	0	1	6	3	15	.308	.311	None on/out	.207	92	19	3	0	2	2	5	18	.255	.304
Flyball	.178	73	13	1	1	3	6	10	17	.286	.342	Batting #6	.221	235	52	6	1	5	17	14	50	.271	.319
Home	.250	172	43	3	1	4	14	14	39	.314	.349	Batting #7	.301	83	25	2	1	4	11	5	21	.352	.494
Away	.247	194	48	8	1	6	20	14	39	.307	.392	Other	.292	48	14	3	0	1	6	9	7	.414	.417
Day	.261	115	30	5	1	3	13	6	25	.298	.400	April	.291	79	23	4	1	3	9	5	23	.333	.481
Night	.243	251	61	6	1	7	21	22	53	.315	.359	May	.169	59	10	1	0	0	2	5	9	.242	.186
Grass	.265	313	83	10	2	9	31	26	63	.330	.396	June	.300	80	24	2	0	4	9	6	15	.356	.475
Turf	.151	53	8	1	0	1	3	2	15	.182	.226	July	.120	50	6	1	0	1	3	2	12	.170	.200
First Pitch	.286	63	18	2	1	4	10	5	0	.338	.540	August	.277	83	23	2	1	2	9	5	17	.326	.398
Ahead in Count	.286	84	24	1	0	2	7	4	0	.322	.369	September/October	.333	15	5	1	0	0	2	5	2	.524	.400
Behind in Count	.184	163	30	2	1	3	12	0	67	.194	.264	Pre-All Star	.246	236	58	7	1	8	22	17	53	.304	.386
Two Strikes	.199	171	34	5	1	3	10	19	78	.283	.292	Post-All Star	.254	130	33	4	1	2	12	11	25	.322	.346

1993 By Position

Position	Avg	AB	H	2B	3B	HR	RBI	BB	SO	OBP	SLG	G	GS	Innings	PO	A	E	DP	Fld Pct	Rng Fctr	In Zone	Outs	Zone Rtg	MLB Zone
As Designated Hitter	.256	316	81	10	2	10	31	21	69	.308	.396	88	79	---	---	---	---	---	---	---	---	---	---	---
As Pinch Hitter	.176	17	3	0	0	1	4	3	4	.333	.353	21	0	---	---	---	---	---	---	---	---	---	---	---
As 1b	.190	42	8	1	0	0	1	4	7	.277	.214	15	13	111.0	113	10	3	10	.976	---	23	18	.783	.834

Doug Jennings — Cubs

Age 29 – Bats Left (flyball hitter)

	Avg	G	AB	R	H	2B	3B	HR	RBI	BB	SO	HBP	GDP	SB	CS	OBP	SLG	IBB	SH	SF	#Pit	#P/PA	GB	FB	G/F
1993 Season	.250	42	52	8	13	3	1	2	8	3	10	2	0	0	0	.316	.462	0	0	0	193	3.39	11	22	0.50
Last Five Years	.199	118	221	27	44	10	3	4	22	22	62	4	2	0	4	.280	.326	0	2	3	983	3.90	53	75	0.71

1993 Season

	Avg	AB	H	2B	3B	HR	RBI	BB	SO	OBP	SLG		Avg	AB	H	2B	3B	HR	RBI	BB	SO	OBP	SLG
vs. Left	.250	4	1	0	0	0	1	0	0	.250	.250	Scoring Posn	.364	11	4	1	1	1	7	3	2	.533	.909
vs. Right	.250	48	12	3	1	2	7	3	10	.321	.479	Close & Late	.176	17	3	1	1	0	2	2	4	.300	.353

Miguel Jimenez — Athletics

Age 24 – Pitches Right (flyball pitcher)

	ERA	W	L	Sv	G	GS	IP	BB	SO	Avg	H	2B	3B	HR	RBI	OBP	SLG	CG	ShO	Sup	QS	#P/S	SB	CS	GB	FB	G/F
1993 Season	4.00	1	0	0	5	4	27.0	16	13	.262	27	4	0	5	12	.367	.447	0	0	6.00	3	100	1	1	24	43	0.56

1993 Season

	ERA	W	L	Sv	G	GS	IP	H	HR	BB	SO		Avg	AB	H	2B	3B	HR	RBI	BB	SO	OBP	SLG
Home	4.91	1	0	0	2	2	11.0	13	2	7	3	vs. Left	.304	56	17	2	0	2	6	8	4	.391	.446
Away	3.38	0	0	0	3	2	16.0	14	3	9	10	vs. Right	.213	47	10	2	0	3	6	8	9	.339	.447

Dave Johnson — Tigers

Age 34 – Pitches Right (flyball pitcher)

	ERA	W	L	Sv	G	GS	IP	BB	SO	Avg	H	2B	3B	HR	RBI	OBP	SLG	GF	IR	IRS	Hld	SvOp	SB	CS	GB	FB	G/F
1993 Season	12.96	1	1	0	6	0	8.1	5	7	.342	13	1	0	3	13	.435	.605	2	4	2	0	0	0	0	12	14	0.86
Last Five Years	5.03	22	25	0	72	57	361.2	100	139	.295	426	81	6	62	189	.344	.489	6	17	13	0	0	4	13	453	546	0.83

1993 Season

	ERA	W	L	Sv	G	GS	IP	H	HR	BB	SO
Home	15.63	1	1	0	5	0	6.1	10	3	5	6
Away	4.50	0	0	0	1	0	2.0	3	0	0	1

	Avg	AB	H	2B	3B	HR	RBI	BB	SO	OBP	SLG
vs. Left	.421	19	8	0	0	3	10	5	3	.520	.895
vs. Right	.263	19	5	1	0	0	3	0	4	.333	.316

Last Five Years

	ERA	W	L	Sv	G	GS	IP	H	HR	BB	SO
Home	4.74	11	14	0	38	27	190.0	220	30	54	80
Away	5.35	11	11	0	34	30	171.2	206	32	46	59
Day	3.91	7	4	0	21	19	119.2	129	19	35	45
Night	5.58	15	21	0	51	38	242.0	297	43	65	94
Grass	5.13	20	23	0	63	48	312.1	371	54	90	126
Turf	4.38	2	2	0	9	9	49.1	55	8	10	13
April	6.80	3	4	0	8	8	42.1	58	8	16	12
May	5.40	2	3	0	13	5	46.2	62	9	8	26
June	3.23	4	1	0	6	6	39.0	43	6	8	5
July	5.12	3	2	0	8	7	45.2	44	11	8	23
August	5.20	8	7	0	16	14	81.1	96	11	21	35
September/October	4.64	2	8	0	21	17	106.2	123	17	39	38
Starter	4.89	19	24	0	57	57	331.1	386	54	94	122
Reliever	6.53	3	1	0	15	0	30.1	40	8	6	17
0 Days rest	9.64	0	0	0	2	0	4.2	9	2	1	4
1 or 2 Days rest	7.20	1	0	0	2	0	5.0	7	1	0	1
3+ Days rest	5.66	2	1	0	11	0	20.2	24	5	5	12
Pre-All Star	5.44	10	8	0	29	21	137.1	175	26	32	48
Post-All Star	4.77	12	17	0	43	36	224.1	251	36	68	91

	Avg	AB	H	2B	3B	HR	RBI	BB	SO	OBP	SLG
vs. Left	.333	718	239	50	5	32	103	61	54	.382	.550
vs. Right	.258	724	187	31	1	30	86	39	85	.306	.428
Inning 1-6	.298	1207	360	74	5	48	161	85	118	.347	.487
Inning 7+	.281	235	66	7	1	14	28	15	21	.331	.498
None on	.299	869	260	59	4	38	38	56	88	.344	.507
Runners on	.290	573	166	22	2	24	151	44	51	.344	.461
Scoring Posn	.269	308	83	12	2	7	116	26	36	.323	.390
Close & Late	.304	69	21	2	0	5	6	7	4	.368	.551
None on/out	.286	378	108	24	1	15	15	24	31	.333	.474
vs. 1st Batr (relief)	.214	14	3	1	0	0	1	1	4	.267	.286
First Inning Pitched	.351	291	102	19	2	19	62	23	35	.399	.625
First 15 Pitches	.351	262	92	21	2	14	48	15	28	.391	.607
Pitch 16-30	.288	257	74	12	0	15	31	18	34	.343	.510
Pitch 31-45	.275	251	69	15	1	7	37	12	29	.304	.426
Pitch 46+	.284	672	191	33	3	26	73	55	48	.341	.458
First Pitch	.328	241	79	18	2	12	37	4	0	.339	.568
Ahead in Count	.242	557	135	22	2	17	55	0	128	.251	.381
Behind in Count	.339	384	130	23	1	20	61	59	0	.427	.560
Two Strikes	.231	506	117	23	3	15	49	37	139	.290	.377

Pitcher vs. Batter (career)

Pitches Best Vs.	Avg	AB	H	2B	3B	HR	RBI	BB	SO	OBP	SLG
Greg Gagne	.091	11	1	0	0	0	0	1	3	.167	.091
Ozzie Guillen	.091	11	1	1	0	0	0	0	0	.091	.182
Carlos Quintana	.091	11	1	0	0	0	0	1	0	.167	.091
Luis Rivera	.125	16	2	0	0	0	0	0	0	.125	.125
Mike Gallego	.154	13	2	0	0	0	2	0	0	.154	.154

Pitches Worst Vs.	Avg	AB	H	2B	3B	HR	RBI	BB	SO	OBP	SLG
Dan Pasqua	.667	9	6	1	0	3	6	2	1	.727	1.778
Jose Canseco	.600	10	6	1	0	2	3	3	2	.692	1.300
Kent Hrbek	.545	11	6	3	0	2	2	3	0	.643	1.364
Scott Fletcher	.545	11	6	1	1	0	1	1	0	.583	.818
Lou Whitaker	.529	17	9	0	0	2	4	0	2	.529	.882

Erik Johnson — Giants

Age 28 – Bats Right

	Avg	G	AB	R	H	2B	3B	HR	RBI	BB	SO	HBP	GDP	SB	CS	OBP	SLG	IBB	SH	SF	#Pit	#P/PA	GB	FB	G/F
1993 Season	.400	4	5	1	2	2	0	0	0	0	1	0	0	0	0	.400	.800	0	0	0	16	3.20	1	1	1.00

1993 Season

	Avg	AB	H	2B	3B	HR	RBI	BB	SO	OBP	SLG
vs. Left	.500	2	1	1	0	0	0	0	0	.500	1.000
vs. Right	.333	3	1	1	0	0	0	0	1	.333	.667

	Avg	AB	H	2B	3B	HR	RBI	BB	SO	OBP	SLG
Scoring Posn	.000	2	0	0	0	0	0	0	1	.000	.000
Close & Late	1.000	1	1	1	0	0	0	0	0	1.000	2.000

Howard Johnson — Mets

Age 33 – Bats Both (flyball hitter)

	Avg	G	AB	R	H	2B	3B	HR	RBI	BB	SO	HBP	GDP	SB	CS	OBP	SLG	IBB	SH	SF	#Pit	#P/PA	GB	FB	G/F
1993 Season	.238	72	235	32	56	8	2	7	26	43	43	0	3	6	4	.354	.379	3	0	2	1104	3.94	58	87	0.67
Last Five Years	.255	635	2310	381	588	139	12	111	377	322	468	4	25	133	41	.342	.469	40	0	35	9928	3.72	532	902	0.59

1993 Season

	Avg	AB	H	2B	3B	HR	RBI	BB	SO	OBP	SLG
vs. Left	.162	68	11	3	0	0	2	10	12	.269	.206
vs. Right	.269	167	45	5	2	7	24	33	31	.386	.449
Home	.207	116	24	4	0	3	12	18	25	.313	.319
Away	.269	119	32	4	2	4	14	25	18	.390	.437
First Pitch	.300	20	6	0	0	2	2	3	0	.391	.600
Ahead in Count	.300	70	21	2	1	2	11	21	0	.457	.443
Behind in Count	.115	96	11	2	1	0	4	0	35	.113	.156
Two Strikes	.155	97	15	1	1	3	9	19	43	.291	.278

	Avg	AB	H	2B	3B	HR	RBI	BB	SO	OBP	SLG
Scoring Posn	.250	52	13	1	1	0	16	13	14	.388	.308
Close & Late	.298	47	14	1	0	0	5	6	12	.370	.319
None on/out	.250	64	16	2	1	3	3	9	11	.342	.453
Batting #2	.218	55	12	1	0	2	4	12	8	.358	.345
Batting #5	.245	139	34	6	0	4	17	28	26	.367	.374
Other	.244	41	10	1	2	1	5	3	9	.295	.439
Pre-All Star	.234	209	49	7	2	6	25	37	41	.347	.373
Post-All Star	.269	26	7	1	0	1	1	6	2	.406	.423

Last Five Years

	Avg	AB	H	2B	3B	HR	RBI	BB	SO	OBP	SLG
vs. Left	.236	832	196	45	2	31	111	119	200	.328	.406
vs. Right	.265	1478	392	94	10	80	266	203	268	.350	.505
Groundball	.278	820	228	50	6	38	146	103	161	.355	.493
Flyball	.241	460	111	29	1	22	74	76	98	.346	.452
Home	.247	1127	278	55	5	58	184	146	228	.329	.459
Away	.262	1183	310	84	7	53	193	176	240	.355	.479
Day	.260	799	208	53	3	42	144	105	145	.342	.492
Night	.251	1511	380	86	9	69	233	217	323	.342	.457
Grass	.251	1648	414	93	8	78	260	225	325	.338	.459
Turf	.263	662	174	46	4	33	117	97	143	.354	.494
First Pitch	.340	329	112	26	3	20	84	22	0	.375	.620
Ahead in Count	.301	564	170	43	4	32	115	168	0	.456	.562

	Avg	AB	H	2B	3B	HR	RBI	BB	SO	OBP	SLG
Scoring Posn	.281	563	158	45	1	21	255	121	123	.389	.476
Close & Late	.255	388	99	20	2	16	64	61	104	.354	.441
None on/out	.283	590	167	31	4	39	39	54	117	.343	.547
Batting #3	.270	814	220	50	2	41	138	100	165	.346	.488
Batting #5	.234	564	132	24	4	27	91	96	109	.339	.434
Other	.253	932	236	65	6	43	148	126	194	.341	.474
April	.242	339	82	16	0	18	63	48	71	.332	.448
May	.238	454	108	22	3	19	67	69	100	.333	.425
June	.263	419	110	31	5	25	73	53	78	.341	.539
July	.266	429	114	28	1	15	60	75	71	.371	.441
August	.263	323	85	21	2	16	51	33	62	.332	.489
September/October	.257	346	89	21	1	18	63	44	86	.338	.480

Last Five Years

	Avg	AB	H	2B	3B	HR	RBI	BB	SO	OBP	SLG
Behind in Count	.191	940	180	46	2	27	96	0	361	.190	.331
Two Strikes	.169	1004	170	34	4	36	109	118	468	.254	.319

	Avg	AB	H	2B	3B	HR	RBI	BB	SO	OBP	SLG
Pre-All Star	.251	1368	344	79	8	67	227	193	272	.339	.468
Post-All Star	.259	942	244	60	4	44	150	129	196	.346	.471

Batter vs. Pitcher (since 1984)

Hits Best Against	Avg	AB	H	2B	3B	HR	RBI	BB	SO	OBP	SLG
Scott Scudder	.833	6	5	3	0	2	6	4	0	.818	2.333
Todd Worrell	.556	9	5	0	0	4	8	6	1	.733	1.889
Mark Davis	.455	11	5	0	0	2	5	2	4	.538	1.000
Derek Lilliquist	.417	12	5	1	0	2	3	0	0	.417	1.000
Frank DiPino	.350	20	7	0	0	4	6	4	5	.458	.950

Hits Worst Against	Avg	AB	H	2B	3B	HR	RBI	BB	SO	OBP	SLG
Kelly Downs	.063	16	1	0	0	0	1	3	2	.211	.063
John Smiley	.091	44	4	1	0	0	1	1	12	.111	.114
Chris Nabholz	.100	10	1	0	0	0	1	1	3	.167	.100
Tom Browning	.103	39	4	0	0	2	6	1	9	.122	.256
Bob Welch	.133	15	2	0	0	0	1	1	5	.188	.133

Jeff Johnson — Yankees

Age 27 – Pitches Left (groundball pitcher)

	ERA	W	L	Sv	G	GS	IP	BB	SO	Avg	H	2B	3B	HR	RBI	OBP	SLG	CG	ShO	Sup	QS	#P/S	SB	CS	GB	FB	G/F
1993 Season	30.38	0	2	0	2	2	2.2	2	0	.600	12	3	0	1	9	.636	.900	0	0	0.00	0	41	1	1	9	7	1.29
Career (1991-1993)	6.52	8	16	0	38	33	182.1	58	76	.320	239	41	7	20	125	.372	.473	0	0	4.15	12	83	23	7	328	204	1.61

1993 Season

	ERA	W	L	Sv	G	GS	IP	H	HR	BB	SO
Home	0.00	0	0	0	0	0	0.0	0	0	0	0
Away	30.38	0	2	0	2	2	2.2	12	1	2	0

	Avg	AB	H	2B	3B	HR	RBI	BB	SO	OBP	SLG
vs. Left	.250	4	1	1	0	0	0	1	0	.400	.500
vs. Right	.688	16	11	2	0	1	9	1	0	.706	1.000

Career (1991-1993)

	ERA	W	L	Sv	G	GS	IP	H	HR	BB	SO
Home	5.85	3	8	0	17	15	95.1	121	9	20	38
Away	7.24	5	8	0	21	18	87.0	118	11	38	38
Day	6.27	2	5	0	12	10	56.0	67	8	17	20
Night	6.63	6	11	0	26	23	126.1	172	12	41	56
Grass	6.24	5	12	0	30	26	147.0	190	14	46	69
Turf	7.64	3	4	0	8	7	35.1	49	6	12	7
April	6.52	1	2	0	4	4	19.1	21	2	12	6
May	2.08	0	0	0	2	0	4.1	5	0	2	0
June	6.58	2	6	0	11	11	53.1	74	6	16	15
July	3.44	3	0	0	6	5	36.2	39	2	6	15
August	10.87	1	5	0	6	6	25.2	43	4	7	16
September/October	6.91	1	3	0	9	7	43.0	57	6	15	24
Starter	6.51	8	16	0	33	33	170.0	222	20	54	72
Reliever	6.57	0	0	0	5	0	12.1	17	0	4	4
0-3 Days Rest	0.00	0	0	0	0	0	0.0	0	0	0	0
4 Days Rest	7.89	4	12	0	23	23	110.2	165	14	35	45
5+ Days Rest	3.94	4	4	0	10	10	59.1	57	6	19	27
Pre-All Star	6.11	3	8	0	19	16	88.1	112	9	32	25
Post-All Star	6.89	5	8	0	19	17	94.0	127	11	26	51

	Avg	AB	H	2B	3B	HR	RBI	BB	SO	OBP	SLG
vs. Left	.263	95	25	5	1	2	15	11	11	.355	.400
vs. Right	.328	653	214	36	6	18	110	47	65	.375	.484
Inning 1-6	.323	668	216	36	6	18	115	50	69	.375	.476
Inning 7+	.288	80	23	5	1	2	10	8	7	.348	.450
None on	.291	409	119	16	2	10	10	26	40	.341	.413
Runners on	.354	339	120	25	5	10	115	32	36	.408	.546
Scoring Posn	.374	198	74	13	2	7	102	21	23	.427	.566
Close & Late	.355	31	11	1	0	2	4	2	1	.394	.581
None on/out	.312	189	59	10	0	6	6	14	19	.363	.460
vs. 1st Batr (relief)	.400	5	2	1	0	0	2	0	0	.400	.600
First Inning Pitched	.357	157	56	12	0	2	34	11	12	.400	.471
First 75 Pitches	.317	631	200	36	5	14	101	47	62	.367	.456
Pitch 76-90	.329	85	28	4	1	5	17	9	6	.402	.576
Pitch 91-105	.367	30	11	1	1	1	7	2	6	.400	.567
Pitch 106+	.000	2	0	0	0	0	0	0	2	.000	.000
First Pitch	.411	129	53	7	2	1	14	0	0	.415	.519
Ahead in Count	.242	277	67	11	0	6	39	0	64	.254	.347
Behind in Count	.418	196	82	16	3	8	44	34	0	.500	.653
Two Strikes	.237	283	67	12	1	6	42	24	76	.305	.350

Pitcher vs. Batter (career)

Pitches Best Vs.	Avg	AB	H	2B	3B	HR	RBI	BB	SO	OBP	SLG
Joe Carter	.143	14	2	0	0	0	0	1	4	.200	.143
Mark Whiten	.167	12	2	0	1	0	0	0	2	.167	.333

Pitches Worst Vs.	Avg	AB	H	2B	3B	HR	RBI	BB	SO	OBP	SLG
Devon White	.455	11	5	1	0	1	3	1	2	.462	.818
Kirby Puckett	.444	9	4	1	0	1	3	2	1	.545	.889
Roberto Alomar	.400	15	6	0	0	2	5	0	3	.400	.800
Mike Devereaux	.364	11	4	0	1	1	4	1	1	.417	.818
Shane Mack	.333	12	4	2	0	1	4	0	1	.333	.750

Lance Johnson — White Sox

Age 30 – Bats Left (groundball hitter)

	Avg	G	AB	R	H	2B	3B	HR	RBI	BB	SO	HBP	GDP	SB	CS	OBP	SLG	IBB	SH	SF	#Pit	#P/PA	GB	FB	G/F
1993 Season	.311	147	540	75	168	18	14	0	47	36	33	0	10	35	7	.354	.396	1	3	0	1783	3.08	265	110	2.41
Last Five Years	.288	665	2416	318	695	73	50	4	210	146	193	3	56	154	57	.328	.364	9	23	12	8050	3.10	1191	492	2.42

1993 Season

	Avg	AB	H	2B	3B	HR	RBI	BB	SO	OBP	SLG
vs. Left	.272	147	40	5	2	0	9	10	16	.318	.333
vs. Right	.326	393	128	13	12	0	38	26	17	.368	.420
Groundball	.257	101	26	2	2	0	8	8	6	.312	.317
Flyball	.287	129	37	6	5	0	11	5	9	.313	.411
Home	.320	259	83	5	6	0	19	20	14	.369	.386
Away	.302	281	85	13	8	0	28	16	19	.340	.406
Day	.261	165	43	5	5	0	11	13	15	.315	.352
Night	.333	375	125	13	9	0	36	23	18	.372	.416
Grass	.302	444	134	13	9	0	31	29	25	.345	.372
Turf	.354	96	34	5	5	0	16	7	8	.398	.510
First Pitch	.407	140	57	3	5	0	9	1	0	.411	.500
Ahead in Count	.297	118	35	3	4	0	18	24	0	.415	.390
Behind in Count	.269	175	47	8	2	0	16	0	30	.269	.337
Two Strikes	.285	158	45	5	4	0	12	11	33	.331	.367

	Avg	AB	H	2B	3B	HR	RBI	BB	SO	OBP	SLG
Scoring Posn	.364	118	43	6	5	0	45	6	4	.395	.500
Close & Late	.274	84	23	4	3	0	9	8	6	.337	.393
None on/out	.320	122	39	2	2	0	0	7	5	.357	.369
Batting #2	.326	132	43	3	3	0	12	7	9	.360	.394
Batting #7	.310	400	124	15	11	0	35	29	23	.357	.403
Other	.125	8	1	0	0	0	0	0	1	.125	.125
April	.337	83	28	4	1	0	11	3	7	.360	.410
May	.306	98	30	1	3	0	7	7	9	.352	.378
June	.272	92	25	1	2	0	5	8	3	.330	.326
July	.320	100	32	4	5	0	7	7	8	.364	.460
August	.333	90	30	5	1	0	11	6	2	.375	.411
September/October	.299	77	23	3	2	0	6	5	4	.341	.390
Pre-All Star	.311	315	98	7	9	0	26	19	21	.350	.390
Post-All Star	.311	225	70	11	5	0	21	17	12	.360	.404

1993 By Position

Position	Avg	AB	H	2B	3B	HR	RBI	BB	SO	OBP	SLG	G	GS	Innings	PO	A	E	DP	Fld Pct	Rng Fctr	In Zone	Outs	Zone Rtg	MLB Zone
As cf	.312	538	168	18	14	0	47	36	33	.355	.398	146	136	1238.0	425	7	9	1	.980	3.14	465	405	.871	.829

Last Five Years

	Avg	AB	H	2B	3B	HR	RBI	BB	SO	OBP	SLG
vs. Left	.274	683	187	16	9	0	54	41	81	.315	.324
vs. Right	.293	1733	508	57	41	4	156	105	112	.332	.380
Groundball	.265	641	170	10	12	0	48	40	56	.309	.318
Flyball	.294	564	166	22	17	2	57	29	45	.327	.404
Home	.286	1168	334	30	24	2	98	76	83	.328	.358
Away	.289	1248	361	43	26	2	112	70	110	.327	.370
Day	.280	665	186	19	15	0	49	48	64	.327	.353
Night	.291	1751	509	54	35	4	161	98	129	.328	.368
Grass	.286	2028	579	53	39	4	165	121	162	.325	.356
Turf	.299	388	116	20	11	0	45	25	31	.341	.407
First Pitch	.339	620	210	17	19	1	49	5	0	.343	.432
Ahead in Count	.288	520	150	14	11	1	62	98	0	.400	.363
Behind in Count	.244	868	212	24	13	1	66	0	174	.245	.305
Two Strikes	.236	787	186	18	17	0	47	41	193	.274	.302

	Avg	AB	H	2B	3B	HR	RBI	BB	SO	OBP	SLG
Scoring Posn	.304	559	170	20	16	1	199	43	38	.350	.403
Close & Late	.241	410	99	10	8	0	34	31	44	.295	.305
None on/out	.285	610	174	16	12	2	2	32	40	.321	.361
Batting #2	.299	488	146	13	7	0	38	24	38	.333	.355
Batting #7	.292	890	260	26	25	2	71	64	51	.340	.384
Other	.278	1038	289	34	18	2	101	58	104	.314	.352
April	.286	280	80	9	2	0	24	10	28	.310	.332
May	.267	390	104	7	3	1	27	22	37	.306	.308
June	.284	373	106	12	7	0	31	23	25	.323	.354
July	.294	408	120	8	12	1	38	20	34	.326	.380
August	.278	449	125	14	10	2	46	29	30	.322	.367
September/October	.310	516	160	23	16	0	44	42	39	.362	.417
Pre-All Star	.276	1188	328	30	18	1	98	61	102	.311	.334
Post-All Star	.299	1228	367	43	32	3	112	85	91	.344	.393

Batter vs. Pitcher (career)

Hits Best Against	Avg	AB	H	2B	3B	HR	RBI	BB	SO	OBP	SLG
Ricky Bones	.636	11	7	0	0	0	0	1	0	.667	.636
Mike Boddicker	.522	23	12	0	2	0	7	0	1	.522	.696
Rich DeLucia	.500	18	9	0	2	0	3	1	0	.526	.722
Rick Sutcliffe	.500	12	6	0	1	0	1	1	0	.538	.667
Luis Aquino	.462	13	6	2	2	0	2	1	0	.500	.923

Hits Worst Against	Avg	AB	H	2B	3B	HR	RBI	BB	SO	OBP	SLG
Roger Pavlik	.083	12	1	0	0	0	0	1	2	.154	.083
Rick Honeycutt	.091	11	1	0	0	0	1	2	2	.231	.091
Todd Stottlemyre	.100	30	3	0	1	0	0	2	0	.156	.167
Chuck Cary	.100	10	1	0	0	0	1	2	3	.231	.100
Roger Clemens	.147	34	5	0	0	0	0	0	6	.147	.147

Randy Johnson — Mariners

Age 30 – Pitches Left

	ERA	W	L	Sv	G	GS	IP	BB	SO	Avg	H	2B	3B	HR	RBI	OBP	SLG	CG	ShO	Sup	QS	#P/S	SB	CS	GB	FB	G/F
1993 Season	3.24	19	8	1	35	34	255.1	99	308	.203	185	37	3	22	88	.290	.322	10	3	5.43	23	124	28	12	263	238	1.11
Last Five Years	3.82	65	56	1	161	159	1047.1	611	1101	.215	811	156	13	89	424	.330	.334	25	8	4.71	96	115	148	50	1116	1048	1.06

1993 Season

	ERA	W	L	Sv	G	GS	IP	H	HR	BB	SO
Home	2.86	11	3	1	20	19	151.0	102	12	53	193
Away	3.80	8	5	0	15	15	104.1	83	10	46	115
Day	3.05	5	2	0	10	10	79.2	56	6	34	98
Night	3.33	14	6	1	25	24	175.2	129	16	65	210
Grass	4.86	5	4	0	11	11	70.1	59	7	42	79
Turf	2.63	14	4	1	24	23	185.0	126	15	57	229
April	2.97	3	1	0	5	5	39.1	33	4	15	44
May	2.45	3	2	0	6	6	44.0	29	4	18	48
June	3.11	4	1	0	6	6	46.1	31	4	19	65
July	7.36	0	3	0	5	5	29.1	28	3	16	30
August	3.45	4	1	1	7	6	44.1	36	5	16	54
September/October	1.73	5	0	0	6	6	52.0	28	2	15	67
Starter	3.26	19	8	0	34	34	254.0	184	22	98	304
Reliever	0.00	0	0	1	1	0	1.1	1	0	1	4
0-3 Days Rest	1.00	1	0	0	1	1	9.0	3	1	1	11
4 Days Rest	3.47	12	8	0	25	25	184.1	131	17	76	218
5+ Days Rest	2.97	6	0	0	8	8	60.2	50	4	21	75
Pre-All Star	3.30	10	5	0	19	19	144.2	107	14	58	171
Post-All Star	3.17	9	3	1	16	15	110.2	78	8	41	137

	Avg	AB	H	2B	3B	HR	RBI	BB	SO	OBP	SLG
vs. Left	.183	71	13	4	0	0	6	4	27	.256	.239
vs. Right	.204	842	172	33	3	22	82	95	281	.293	.329
Inning 1-6	.206	698	144	25	3	14	64	66	223	.285	.311
Inning 7+	.191	215	41	12	0	8	24	33	85	.306	.358
None on	.189	566	107	24	2	16	16	57	185	.276	.323
Runners on	.225	347	78	13	1	6	72	42	123	.312	.320
Scoring Posn	.244	205	50	9	1	3	65	26	86	.325	.341
Close & Late	.159	107	17	5	0	3	16	14	50	.266	.290
None on/out	.197	238	47	13	2	5	5	27	74	.298	.332
vs. 1st Batr (relief)	1.000	1	1	0	0	0	2	0	0	1.000	1.000
First Inning Pitched	.167	114	19	6	1	1	11	11	38	.254	.263
First 75 Pitches	.207	540	112	20	3	11	53	53	185	.290	.317
Pitch 76-90	.255	110	28	5	0	6	10	9	27	.322	.464
Pitch 91-105	.196	112	22	2	0	4	16	13	37	.283	.321
Pitch 106+	.152	151	23	10	0	1	9	24	59	.271	.238
First Pitch	.267	86	23	5	1	3	11	1	0	.292	.453
Ahead in Count	.135	504	68	13	1	9	33	0	279	.148	.218
Behind in Count	.306	160	49	11	1	5	22	43	0	.458	.481
Two Strikes	.133	543	72	11	1	9	35	55	308	.218	.206

Last Five Years

	ERA	W	L	Sv	G	GS	IP	H	HR	BB	SO
Home	3.29	35	24	1	81	80	546.1	384	36	295	600
Away	4.38	30	32	0	80	79	501.0	427	53	316	501
Day	4.03	17	8	0	40	40	261.1	201	23	157	286
Night	3.74	48	48	1	121	119	786.0	610	66	454	815
Grass	4.49	25	22	0	60	60	381.0	316	41	256	383
Turf	3.43	40	34	1	101	99	666.1	495	48	355	718
April	3.76	10	7	0	22	21	139.0	117	19	74	130
May	4.39	8	13	0	28	28	170.0	131	10	120	175
June	3.27	14	4	0	23	23	151.1	102	12	99	165
July	3.99	8	14	0	28	28	187.0	155	17	116	184
August	3.58	16	8	1	30	29	201.1	153	18	97	214
September/October	3.85	9	10	0	30	30	198.2	153	13	105	233
Starter	3.82	65	56	0	159	159	1045.0	809	89	610	1096
Reliever	0.00	0	0	1	2	0	2.1	2	0	1	5
0-3 Days Rest	3.27	1	1	0	2	2	11.0	6	1	4	13
4 Days Rest	4.01	39	32	0	98	98	637.0	489	62	388	667
5+ Days Rest	3.54	25	23	0	59	59	397.0	314	26	218	416
Pre-All Star	3.82	33	28	0	82	81	525.1	406	48	323	525
Post-All Star	3.81	32	28	1	79	78	522.0	405	41	288	576

	Avg	AB	H	2B	3B	HR	RBI	BB	SO	OBP	SLG
vs. Left	.195	400	78	16	0	5	47	46	113	.286	.273
vs. Right	.218	3369	733	140	13	84	377	565	988	.335	.342
Inning 1-6	.217	3134	680	130	12	74	373	510	892	.331	.337
Inning 7+	.206	635	131	26	1	15	51	101	209	.321	.321
None on	.206	2154	444	86	10	54	54	348	619	.325	.331
Runners on	.227	1615	367	70	3	35	370	263	482	.336	.339
Scoring Posn	.227	971	220	43	2	19	327	171	319	.338	.334
Close & Late	.188	346	65	12	1	7	33	56	128	.308	.289
None on/out	.225	959	216	43	6	22	22	163	270	.347	.351
vs. 1st Batr (relief)	1.000	2	2	0	0	0	2	0	0	1.000	1.000
First Inning Pitched	.204	544	111	30	3	8	61	87	163	.319	.314
First 75 Pitches	.216	2388	515	99	9	58	269	382	690	.330	.338
Pitch 76-90	.236	450	106	21	2	16	56	82	114	.357	.398
Pitch 91-105	.201	433	87	15	1	9	55	60	132	.299	.303
Pitch 106+	.207	498	103	21	1	6	44	87	165	.331	.289
First Pitch	.320	406	130	22	1	15	71	4	0	.331	.490
Ahead in Count	.146	1944	284	54	4	28	146	0	960	.158	.221
Behind in Count	.308	727	224	44	6	29	117	325	0	.521	.505
Two Strikes	.134	2076	278	53	4	27	152	281	1101	.244	.202

Pitcher vs. Batter (career)

Pitches Best Vs.	Avg	AB	H	2B	3B	HR	RBI	BB	SO	OBP	SLG
Craig Grebeck	.000	13	0	0	0	0	0	2	4	.133	.000
Kevin McReynolds	.000	10	0	0	0	0	0	1	4	.091	.000
Billy Hatcher	.000	10	0	0	0	0	1	1	5	.091	.000

Pitches Worst Vs.	Avg	AB	H	2B	3B	HR	RBI	BB	SO	OBP	SLG
Jody Reed	.500	10	5	4	0	0	0	6	3	.688	.900
Rene Gonzales	.467	15	7	1	0	1	2	5	2	.600	.733
Ellis Burks	.400	15	6	1	0	2	6	2	5	.471	.867

Pitcher vs. Batter (career)																							
Pitches Best Vs.	Avg	AB	H	2B	3B	HR	RBI	BB	SO	OBP	SLG	Pitches Worst Vs.	Avg	AB	H	2B	3B	HR	RBI	BB	SO	OBP	SLG
Ed Sprague	.056	18	1	1	0	0	0	0	9	.056	.111	Travis Fryman	.375	16	6	0	0	3	7	4	5	.500	.938
Rafael Palmeiro	.059	17	1	0	0	0	0	0	2	.059	.059	Bill Pecota	.364	11	4	1	0	2	2	5	0	.563	1.000

Joel Johnston — Pirates

Age 27 – Pitches Right (flyball pitcher)

	ERA	W	L	Sv	G	GS	IP	BB	SO	Avg	H	2B	3B	HR	RBI	OBP	SLG	GF	IR	IRS	Hld	SvOp	SB	CS	GB	FB	G/F
1993 Season	3.38	2	4	2	33	0	53.1	19	31	.203	38	10	1	7	18	.277	.380	16	14	2	5	3	2	1	57	72	0.79
Career (1991-1993)	2.87	3	4	2	51	0	78.1	30	52	.183	50	11	1	9	22	.264	.330	18	28	3	8	3	3	2	86	102	0.84

1993 Season																						
	ERA	W	L	Sv	G	GS	IP	H	HR	BB	SO		Avg	AB	H	2B	3B	HR	RBI	BB	SO	OBP	SLG
Home	3.93	2	4	2	20	0	36.2	28	6	13	23	vs. Left	.227	75	17	5	0	4	10	10	9	.318	.453
Away	2.16	0	0	0	13	0	16.2	10	1	6	8	vs. Right	.188	112	21	5	1	3	8	9	22	.248	.330
Starter	0.00	0	0	0	0	0	0.0	0	0	0	0	Scoring Posn	.243	37	9	3	0	0	10	9	8	.391	.324
Reliever	3.38	2	4	2	33	0	53.1	38	7	19	31	Close & Late	.250	96	24	5	0	4	12	12	16	.333	.427
0 Days rest	5.40	0	0	0	2	0	5.0	6	0	2	5	None on/out	.192	52	10	2	1	3	3	3	11	.236	.442
1 or 2 Days rest	3.49	2	3	2	23	0	38.2	27	7	10	21	First Pitch	.194	31	6	1	0	1	2	3	0	.265	.323
3+ Days rest	1.86	0	1	0	8	0	9.2	5	0	7	5	Ahead in Count	.174	86	15	4	0	1	6	0	29	.174	.256
Pre-All Star	0.00	0	0	0	3	0	4.2	3	0	2	4	Behind in Count	.318	44	14	4	0	4	8	9	0	.434	.682
Post-All Star	3.70	2	4	2	30	0	48.2	35	7	17	27	Two Strikes	.155	84	13	3	0	2	7	7	31	.220	.262

John Johnstone — Marlins

Age 25 – Pitches Right

	ERA	W	L	Sv	G	GS	IP	BB	SO	Avg	H	2B	3B	HR	RBI	OBP	SLG	GF	IR	IRS	Hld	SvOp	SB	CS	GB	FB	G/F
1993 Season	5.91	0	2	0	7	0	10.2	7	5	.340	16	4	0	1	7	.426	.489	3	3	0	0	0	1	0	16	16	1.00

1993 Season																						
	ERA	W	L	Sv	G	GS	IP	H	HR	BB	SO		Avg	AB	H	2B	3B	HR	RBI	BB	SO	OBP	SLG
Home	8.53	0	2	0	5	0	6.1	11	0	5	1	vs. Left	.348	23	8	2	0	1	5	5	1	.464	.565
Away	2.08	0	0	0	2	0	4.1	5	1	2	4	vs. Right	.333	24	8	2	0	0	2	2	4	.385	.417

Barry Jones — White Sox

Age 31 – Pitches Right (groundball pitcher)

	ERA	W	L	Sv	G	GS	IP	BB	SO	Avg	H	2B	3B	HR	RBI	OBP	SLG	GF	IR	IRS	Hld	SvOp	SB	CS	GB	FB	G/F
1993 Season	8.59	0	1	0	6	0	7.1	3	7	.412	14	1	0	2	9	.459	.618	1	2	2	1	0	1	1	12	8	1.50
Last Five Years	3.70	25	22	16	231	0	270.0	112	145	.262	259	40	5	17	153	.336	.364	73	165	61	45	37	23	10	428	248	1.73

1993 Season																						
	ERA	W	L	Sv	G	GS	IP	H	HR	BB	SO		Avg	AB	H	2B	3B	HR	RBI	BB	SO	OBP	SLG
Home	7.50	0	0	0	5	0	6.0	11	1	3	6	vs. Left	.636	11	7	0	0	2	5	1	2	.667	1.182
Away	13.50	0	1	0	1	0	1.1	3	1	0	1	vs. Right	.304	23	7	1	0	0	4	2	5	.360	.348

Last Five Years																						
	ERA	W	L	Sv	G	GS	IP	H	HR	BB	SO		Avg	AB	H	2B	3B	HR	RBI	BB	SO	OBP	SLG
Home	3.41	14	8	7	117	0	142.1	138	5	53	84	vs. Left	.298	447	133	22	3	7	66	59	46	.376	.407
Away	4.02	11	14	9	114	0	127.2	121	12	59	61	vs. Right	.232	542	126	18	2	10	87	53	99	.302	.328
Day	2.66	4	1	8	64	0	71.0	60	5	25	35	Inning 1-6	.230	61	14	4	0	1	15	9	10	.324	.344
Night	4.07	21	21	8	167	0	199.0	199	12	87	110	Inning 7+	.264	928	245	36	5	16	138	103	135	.337	.365
Grass	4.07	14	12	6	130	0	152.2	144	12	68	87	None on	.229	494	113	18	0	7	7	52	78	.306	.308
Turf	3.22	11	10	10	101	0	117.1	115	5	44	58	Runners on	.295	495	146	22	5	10	146	60	67	.365	.420
April	3.02	4	3	2	43	0	56.2	50	5	22	21	Scoring Posn	.302	321	97	17	3	5	134	47	46	.378	.421
May	4.33	8	4	1	43	0	54.0	57	6	22	29	Close & Late	.273	590	161	21	3	9	92	70	81	.350	.364
June	3.29	5	5	4	34	0	41.0	39	2	15	27	None on/out	.238	210	50	7	0	4	4	28	30	.328	.329
July	4.58	2	5	2	35	0	39.1	43	2	19	22	vs. 1st Batr (relief)	.271	203	55	9	1	3	31	19	27	.335	.369
August	1.71	3	1	3	29	0	31.2	21	1	11	18	First Inning Pitched	.258	722	186	28	4	10	125	80	111	.329	.349
September/October	4.75	3	4	4	47	0	47.1	49	1	23	28	First 15 Pitches	.256	694	178	30	3	11	109	78	98	.330	.356
Starter	0.00	0	0	0	0	0	0.0	0	0	0	0	Pitch 16-30	.270	248	67	9	2	6	35	29	37	.344	.395
Reliever	3.70	25	22	16	231	0	270.0	259	17	112	145	Pitch 31-45	.289	45	13	1	0	0	8	5	10	.373	.311
0 Days rest	6.02	1	4	3	44	0	40.1	51	7	16	19	Pitch 46+	.500	2	1	0	0	0	1	0	0	.500	.500
1 or 2 Days rest	3.46	18	14	7	134	0	169.0	151	7	66	85	First Pitch	.318	154	49	6	0	4	40	19	0	.388	.435
3+ Days rest	2.82	6	4	6	53	0	60.2	57	3	30	41	Ahead in Count	.225	414	93	17	2	2	47	0	115	.228	.290
Pre-All Star	3.94	18	14	7	134	0	166.2	167	14	68	87	Behind in Count	.299	231	69	10	0	8	37	58	0	.438	.446
Post-All Star	3.31	7	8	9	97	0	103.1	92	3	44	58	Two Strikes	.180	394	71	12	1	3	38	35	145	.247	.239

Pitcher vs. Batter (career)																							
Pitches Best Vs.	Avg	AB	H	2B	3B	HR	RBI	BB	SO	OBP	SLG	Pitches Worst Vs.	Avg	AB	H	2B	3B	HR	RBI	BB	SO	OBP	SLG
Juan Samuel	.214	14	3	1	0	1	4	0	4	.214	.500	Kurt Stillwell	.545	11	6	1	0	0	2	0	1	.545	.636
Andre Dawson	.231	13	3	1	0	1	3	0	3	.231	.538	Vince Coleman	.500	10	5	1	1	0	3	1	1	.545	.800
												Chris James	.500	10	5	1	1	0	2	1	1	.545	.800
												Andres Galarraga	.400	15	6	3	0	1	5	0	2	.400	.800
												Ryne Sandberg	.375	8	3	0	1	0	2	3	2	.500	.625

Bobby Jones — Mets

Age 24 – Pitches Right

	ERA	W	L	Sv	G	GS	IP	BB	SO	Avg	H	2B	3B	HR	RBI	OBP	SLG	CG	ShO	Sup	QS	#P/S	SB	CS	GB	FB	G/F
1993 Season	3.65	2	4	0	9	9	61.2	22	35	.262	61	18	1	6	27	.327	.425	0	0	3.06	6	107	3	2	79	79	1.00

1993 Season

	ERA	W	L	Sv	G	GS	IP	H	HR	BB	SO		Avg	AB	H	2B	3B	HR	RBI	BB	SO	OBP	SLG
Home	3.54	0	3	0	4	4	28.0	27	3	14	20	vs. Left	.224	125	28	7	1	1	7	17	21	.317	.320
Away	3.74	2	1	0	5	5	33.2	34	3	8	15	vs. Right	.306	108	33	11	0	5	20	5	14	.339	.546
Starter	3.65	2	4	0	9	9	61.2	61	6	22	35	Scoring Posn	.242	66	16	4	0	1	21	10	8	.346	.348
Reliever	0.00	0	0	0	0	0	0.0	0	0	0	0	Close & Late	.222	18	4	1	0	0	1	3	3	.333	.278
0-3 Days Rest	0.00	0	0	0	0	0	0.0	0	0	0	0	None on/out	.290	62	18	8	1	3	3	5	7	.343	.597
4 Days Rest	1.38	1	0	0	4	4	32.2	21	1	11	19	First Pitch	.342	38	13	4	0	1	2	2	0	.375	.526
5+ Days Rest	6.21	1	4	0	5	5	29.0	40	5	11	16	Ahead in Count	.196	92	18	6	0	2	9	0	29	.211	.326
Pre-All Star	0.00	0	0	0	0	0	0.0	0	0	0	0	Behind in Count	.349	63	22	6	1	2	11	11	0	.440	.571
Post-All Star	3.65	2	4	0	9	9	61.2	61	6	22	35	Two Strikes	.192	104	20	6	0	2	7	9	35	.270	.308

Chipper Jones — Braves

Age 22 – Bats Both

	Avg	G	AB	R	H	2B	3B	HR	RBI	BB	SO	HBP	GDP	SB	CS	OBP	SLG	IBB	SH	SF	#Pit	#P/PA	GB	FB	G/F
1993 Season	.667	8	3	2	2	1	0	0	0	1	1	0	0	0	0	.750	1.000	0	0	0	17	4.25	1	0	0.00

1993 Season

	Avg	AB	H	2B	3B	HR	RBI	BB	SO	OBP	SLG		Avg	AB	H	2B	3B	HR	RBI	BB	SO	OBP	SLG
vs. Left	1.000	1	1	0	0	0	0	1	0	1.000	1.000	Scoring Posn	.000	1	0	0	0	0	0	0	1	.000	.000
vs. Right	.500	2	1	1	0	0	0	0	1	.500	1.000	Close & Late	.000	0	0	0	0	0	0	0	0	.000	.000

Chris Jones — Rockies

Age 28 – Bats Right (groundball hitter)

	Avg	G	AB	R	H	2B	3B	HR	RBI	BB	SO	HBP	GDP	SB	CS	OBP	SLG	IBB	SH	SF	#Pit	#P/PA	GB	FB	G/F
1993 Season	.273	86	209	29	57	11	4	6	31	10	48	0	6	9	4	.305	.450	1	5	1	784	3.48	83	47	1.77
Career (1991-1993)	.263	192	361	50	95	14	7	9	41	19	100	0	9	14	5	.298	.416	1	8	2	1410	3.62	132	71	1.86

1993 Season

	Avg	AB	H	2B	3B	HR	RBI	BB	SO	OBP	SLG		Avg	AB	H	2B	3B	HR	RBI	BB	SO	OBP	SLG
vs. Left	.299	97	29	7	2	2	13	2	22	.313	.474	Scoring Posn	.304	56	17	2	0	3	23	4	11	.344	.500
vs. Right	.250	112	28	4	2	4	18	8	26	.298	.429	Close & Late	.293	41	12	3	1	1	8	2	6	.326	.488
Home	.260	104	27	5	3	2	15	7	18	.304	.423	None on/out	.282	39	11	2	1	0	0	0	9	.282	.385
Away	.286	105	30	6	1	4	16	3	30	.306	.476	Batting #2	.386	44	17	6	1	0	6	0	11	.378	.568
First Pitch	.316	38	12	2	0	2	13	1	0	.325	.526	Batting #6	.224	49	11	2	0	2	9	1	11	.240	.388
Ahead in Count	.484	31	15	5	1	1	6	3	0	.529	.806	Other	.250	116	29	3	3	4	16	9	26	.304	.431
Behind in Count	.223	112	25	4	3	2	9	0	43	.223	.366	Pre-All Star	.330	100	33	6	2	5	20	2	23	.340	.580
Two Strikes	.175	103	18	2	3	2	7	6	48	.220	.311	Post-All Star	.220	109	24	5	2	1	11	8	25	.274	.330

Doug Jones — Astros

Age 37 – Pitches Right (groundball pitcher)

	ERA	W	L	Sv	G	GS	IP	BB	SO	Avg	H	2B	3B	HR	RBI	OBP	SLG	GF	IR	IRS	Hld	SvOp	SB	CS	GB	FB	G/F
1993 Season	4.54	4	10	26	71	0	85.1	21	66	.298	102	11	0	7	50	.344	.392	60	20	9	1	34	2	0	131	80	1.64
Last Five Years	3.17	31	41	144	312	4	425.1	90	327	.262	427	75	7	28	198	.304	.368	223	158	51	1	180	14	6	613	391	1.57

1993 Season

	ERA	W	L	Sv	G	GS	IP	H	HR	BB	SO		Avg	AB	H	2B	3B	HR	RBI	BB	SO	OBP	SLG
Home	5.00	3	4	8	30	0	36.0	43	5	8	25	vs. Left	.273	165	45	5	0	2	21	12	25	.335	.339
Away	4.20	1	6	18	41	0	49.1	59	2	13	41	vs. Right	.322	177	57	6	0	5	29	9	41	.353	.441
Day	3.00	2	4	11	29	0	36.0	33	2	7	25	Inning 1-6	.000	6	0	0	0	0	0	0	1	.000	.000
Night	5.66	2	6	15	42	0	49.1	69	5	14	41	Inning 7+	.304	336	102	11	0	7	50	21	65	.350	.399
Grass	5.61	1	5	12	28	0	33.2	47	1	8	25	None on	.254	185	47	6	0	1	1	9	36	.292	.303
Turf	3.83	3	5	14	43	0	51.2	55	6	13	41	Runners on	.350	157	55	5	0	6	49	12	30	.401	.497
April	1.72	1	0	4	11	0	15.2	11	2	2	15	Scoring Posn	.359	92	33	4	0	3	43	10	20	.427	.500
May	4.58	1	4	7	14	0	17.2	20	3	3	12	Close & Late	.318	195	62	5	0	5	35	16	34	.374	.421
June	9.95	1	2	2	10	0	12.2	27	0	3	8	None on/out	.275	80	22	2	0	1	1	4	16	.310	.338
July	4.26	0	2	5	13	0	12.2	13	1	6	10	vs. 1st Batr (relief)	.324	68	22	3	0	1	4	2	12	.352	.412
August	2.16	1	2	5	13	0	16.2	13	1	3	11	First Inning Pitched	.293	263	77	9	0	6	40	14	53	.338	.395
September/October	6.30	0	0	3	10	0	10.0	18	0	4	10	First 15 Pitches	.289	232	67	8	0	6	27	9	44	.324	.401
Starter	0.00	0	0	0	0	0	0.0	0	0	0	0	Pitch 16-30	.326	89	29	3	0	0	20	12	17	.404	.360
Reliever	4.54	4	10	26	71	0	85.1	102	7	21	66	Pitch 31-45	.286	21	6	0	0	1	3	0	5	.286	.429
0 Days rest	4.38	1	5	11	21	0	24.2	31	4	6	23	Pitch 46+	.000	0	0	0	0	0	0	0	0	.000	.000
1 or 2 Days rest	4.46	3	3	10	29	0	38.1	45	2	12	26	First Pitch	.391	46	18	2	0	1	10	6	0	.473	.500
3+ Days rest	4.84	0	2	5	21	0	22.1	26	1	3	17	Ahead in Count	.251	183	46	6	0	3	23	0	61	.258	.333
Pre-All Star	5.44	3	6	13	39	0	49.2	64	6	9	37	Behind in Count	.421	57	24	2	0	3	14	13	0	.514	.614
Post-All Star	3.28	1	4	13	32	0	35.2	38	1	12	29	Two Strikes	.219	169	37	6	0	2	19	2	66	.236	.290

Last Five Years

	ERA	W	L	Sv	G	GS	IP	H	HR	BB	SO		Avg	AB	H	2B	3B	HR	RBI	BB	SO	OBP	SLG
Home	3.42	20	21	64	158	2	218.1	208	14	44	165	vs. Left	.259	839	217	43	3	16	101	53	139	.305	.374
Away	2.91	11	20	80	154	2	207.0	219	14	46	162	vs. Right	.266	790	210	32	4	12	97	37	188	.302	.362
Day	1.79	7	9	52	96	0	120.2	91	6	22	88	Inning 1-6	.238	105	25	5	0	0	6	6	21	.277	.286
Night	3.72	24	32	92	216	4	304.2	336	22	68	239	Inning 7+	.264	1524	402	70	7	28	192	84	306	.305	.374
Grass	3.24	19	26	92	185	4	258.1	262	14	51	191	None on	.272	828	225	45	1	10	10	38	160	.308	.365
Turf	3.07	12	15	52	127	0	167.0	165	14	39	136	Runners on	.252	801	202	30	6	18	188	52	167	.299	.372
April	1.97	3	4	26	47	0	59.1	57	6	8	56	Scoring Posn	.267	475	127	23	5	10	170	39	102	.322	.400
May	3.84	5	10	30	59	0	75.0	75	9	16	52	Close & Late	.272	1000	272	50	7	17	141	57	200	.315	.387

Last Five Years

	ERA	W	L	Sv	G	GS	IP	H	HR	BB	SO
June	3.94	6	8	20	53	0	64.0	79	1	13	41
July	2.96	6	7	20	51	0	67.0	55	6	18	47
August	3.65	3	7	25	48	0	61.2	55	5	14	44
September/October	2.75	8	5	23	54	4	98.1	106	1	21	87
Starter	3.77	3	1	0	4	4	31.0	40	0	6	24
Reliever	3.13	28	40	144	308	0	394.1	387	28	84	303
0 Days rest	2.51	7	12	47	81	0	100.1	97	9	18	89
1 or 2 Days rest	3.24	15	15	70	140	0	189.0	183	11	47	129
3+ Days rest	3.51	6	13	27	87	0	105.0	107	8	19	85
Pre-All Star	3.22	17	23	82	178	0	223.1	233	17	42	165
Post-All Star	3.12	14	18	62	134	4	202.0	194	11	48	162

	Avg	AB	H	2B	3B	HR	RBI	BB	SO	OBP	SLG
None on/out	.261	360	94	21	0	5	5	17	69	.298	.361
vs. 1st Batr (relief)	.266	286	76	14	0	5	28	14	50	.306	.367
First Inning Pitched	.265	1107	293	49	3	22	142	59	234	.306	.374
First 15 Pitches	.276	1005	277	47	3	24	113	47	196	.313	.400
Pitch 16-30	.233	437	102	15	3	3	61	35	90	.288	.302
Pitch 31-45	.229	96	22	4	0	1	13	5	22	.275	.302
Pitch 46+	.286	91	26	9	1	0	11	3	19	.309	.407
First Pitch	.399	198	79	9	1	6	40	23	0	.469	.545
Ahead in Count	.202	912	184	37	2	11	85	0	293	.204	.283
Behind in Count	.340	265	90	17	2	9	45	47	0	.435	.521
Two Strikes	.187	824	154	38	1	4	68	20	327	.210	.250

Pitcher vs. Batter (since 1984)

Pitches Best Vs.	Avg	AB	H	2B	3B	HR	RBI	BB	SO	OBP	SLG
Kurt Stillwell	.000	9	0	0	0	0	0	2	3	.182	.000
Fred McGriff	.067	15	1	0	0	0	1	1	3	.125	.067
Ruben Sierra	.071	14	1	0	0	0	0	0	2	.071	.071
Dan Pasqua	.077	13	1	0	0	0	1	0	5	.077	.077
Paul Molitor	.100	20	2	0	0	0	0	0	3	.100	.100

Pitches Worst Vs.	Avg	AB	H	2B	3B	HR	RBI	BB	SO	OBP	SLG
Cal Ripken	.556	18	10	3	0	1	6	2	2	.600	.889
Kent Hrbek	.500	14	7	2	0	2	5	1	1	.533	1.071
Greg Vaughn	.500	12	6	4	0	1	3	0	1	.500	1.083
Mark McGwire	.467	15	7	1	0	1	5	2	3	.529	.733
Nelson Liriano	.400	10	4	0	0	1	2	3	0	.500	.700

Jimmy Jones — Expos

Age 30 – Pitches Right (groundball pitcher)

	ERA	W	L	Sv	G	GS	IP	BB	SO	Avg	H	2B	3B	HR	RBI	OBP	SLG	CG	ShO	Sup	QS	#P/S	SB	CS	GB	FB	G/F
1993 Season	6.35	4	1	0	12	6	39.2	9	21	.285	47	12	0	6	27	.322	.467	0	0	6.13	2	71	5	0	72	42	1.71
Last Five Years	4.80	23	18	0	91	64	412.1	138	228	.280	453	79	10	43	210	.338	.421	1	1	4.65	26	83	53	14	716	354	2.02

1993 Season

	ERA	W	L	Sv	G	GS	IP	H	HR	BB	SO
Home	4.50	2	0	0	4	2	18.0	15	3	5	9
Away	7.89	2	1	0	8	4	21.2	32	3	4	12

	Avg	AB	H	2B	3B	HR	RBI	BB	SO	OBP	SLG
vs. Left	.321	78	25	7	0	4	15	7	6	.376	.564
vs. Right	.253	87	22	5	0	2	12	2	15	.270	.379

Last Five Years

	ERA	W	L	Sv	G	GS	IP	H	HR	BB	SO
Home	3.87	12	7	0	47	33	228.0	215	18	78	131
Away	5.96	11	11	0	44	31	184.1	238	25	60	97
Day	5.06	7	4	0	28	19	121.0	155	9	38	74
Night	4.70	16	14	0	63	45	291.1	298	34	100	154
Grass	5.96	7	7	0	44	26	176.2	225	26	59	90
Turf	3.93	16	11	0	47	38	235.2	228	17	79	138
April	3.06	6	1	0	8	7	47.0	40	3	11	27
May	4.38	4	3	0	17	14	86.1	82	9	29	54
June	5.45	5	5	0	21	20	104.0	124	10	33	48
July	5.22	2	6	0	16	12	70.2	90	7	25	41
August	4.89	4	2	0	17	9	70.0	77	11	27	41
September/October	5.24	2	1	0	12	2	34.1	40	3	13	17
Starter	4.77	19	17	0	64	64	351.0	375	35	114	200
Reliever	4.99	4	1	0	27	0	61.1	78	8	24	28
0-3 Days Rest	1.38	0	0	0	2	2	13.0	13	0	2	8
4 Days Rest	5.27	10	9	0	34	34	176.0	193	24	61	97
5+ Days Rest	4.50	9	8	0	28	28	162.0	169	11	51	95
Pre-All Star	4.68	16	12	0	53	46	267.1	281	26	82	146
Post-All Star	5.03	7	6	0	38	18	145.0	172	17	56	82

	Avg	AB	H	2B	3B	HR	RBI	BB	SO	OBP	SLG
vs. Left	.299	915	274	45	8	24	115	87	114	.362	.445
vs. Right	.254	704	179	34	2	19	95	51	114	.307	.389
Inning 1-6	.278	1351	375	65	8	35	177	120	189	.338	.415
Inning 7+	.291	268	78	14	2	8	33	18	39	.342	.448
None on	.274	925	253	44	2	25	25	72	137	.330	.406
Runners on	.288	694	200	35	8	18	185	66	91	.349	.439
Scoring Posn	.301	385	116	22	4	8	155	49	53	.376	.442
Close & Late	.181	83	15	1	1	0	3	4	17	.236	.217
None on/out	.288	413	119	26	1	12	12	28	57	.338	.443
vs. 1st Batr (relief)	.360	25	9	1	0	1	5	1	2	.370	.520
First Inning Pitched	.326	356	116	20	1	7	65	49	44	.406	.447
First 75 Pitches	.285	1398	398	67	7	37	172	126	197	.344	.422
Pitch 76-90	.228	149	34	10	2	3	27	7	18	.266	.383
Pitch 91-105	.250	60	15	2	0	2	8	4	12	.328	.383
Pitch 106+	.500	12	6	0	1	1	3	1	1	.571	.917
First Pitch	.335	266	89	13	4	11	47	4	0	.343	.538
Ahead in Count	.232	671	156	30	2	15	67	0	194	.240	.350
Behind in Count	.308	399	123	19	2	15	66	75	0	.418	.479
Two Strikes	.216	630	136	30	3	13	62	59	228	.286	.335

Pitcher vs. Batter (career)

Pitches Best Vs.	Avg	AB	H	2B	3B	HR	RBI	BB	SO	OBP	SLG
Dave Magadan	.000	8	0	0	0	0	0	4	0	.333	.000
Robby Thompson	.053	19	1	0	0	0	0	3	3	.182	.053
Mark Grace	.083	12	1	0	0	0	1	2	0	.200	.083
Tom Foley	.125	16	2	1	0	0	2	0	2	.118	.188
Rafael Belliard	.143	14	2	0	0	0	0	0	4	.143	.143

Pitches Worst Vs.	Avg	AB	H	2B	3B	HR	RBI	BB	SO	OBP	SLG
Hal Morris	.636	11	7	0	0	1	2	0	0	.636	.909
Jay Bell	.600	15	9	1	0	2	5	1	2	.625	1.067
Will Clark	.500	20	10	3	1	2	7	4	2	.583	1.050
Orlando Merced	.467	15	7	2	0	2	4	2	3	.529	1.000
Andy Van Slyke	.448	29	13	1	2	3	10	3	2	.485	.931

Tim Jones — Cardinals

Age 31 – Bats Left

	Avg	G	AB	R	H	2B	3B	HR	RBI	BB	SO	HBP	GDP	SB	CS	OBP	SLG	IBB	SH	SF	#Pit	#P/PA	GB	FB	G/F
1993 Season	.262	29	61	13	16	6	0	0	1	9	8	1	0	2	2	.366	.361	0	2	0	269	3.68	19	15	1.27
Last Five Years	.229	221	433	43	99	25	1	1	25	41	71	3	4	11	9	.298	.298	4	9	3	1664	3.40	159	123	1.29

1993 Season

	Avg	AB	H	2B	3B	HR	RBI	BB	SO	OBP	SLG
vs. Left	.143	7	1	0	0	0	0	0	1	.143	.143
vs. Right	.278	54	15	6	0	0	1	9	7	.391	.389
Scoring Posn	.125	8	1	0	0	0	0	0	1	.125	.125
Close & Late	.083	12	1	0	0	0	0	1	4	.154	.083

Last Five Years

	Avg	AB	H	2B	3B	HR	RBI	BB	SO	OBP	SLG
vs. Left	.193	83	16	5	0	0	7	8	13	.263	.253
vs. Right	.237	350	83	20	1	1	18	33	58	.306	.309
Groundball	.229	166	38	5	0	1	12	15	27	.290	.277
Flyball	.234	77	18	8	0	0	5	9	17	.322	.338
Home	.223	175	39	10	0	1	11	15	29	.283	.297
Away	.233	258	60	15	1	0	14	26	42	.308	.298
Scoring Posn	.179	106	19	5	0	0	21	14	19	.274	.226
Close & Late	.183	82	15	4	0	0	6	7	13	.247	.232
None on/out	.242	99	24	3	0	0	0	9	18	.318	.273
Batting #2	.286	91	26	3	0	0	5	12	15	.371	.319
Batting #8	.217	235	51	17	1	1	13	21	40	.282	.311
Other	.206	107	22	5	0	0	7	8	16	.267	.252

Last Five Years	Avg	AB	H	2B	3B	HR	RBI	BB	SO	OBP	SLG		Avg	AB	H	2B	3B	HR	RBI	BB	SO	OBP	SLG
Day	.270	178	48	20	0	1	11	14	28	.321	.399	April	.189	90	17	3	0	0	3	8	10	.253	.222
Night	.200	255	51	5	1	0	14	27	43	.282	.227	May	.094	32	3	2	0	0	2	5	9	.237	.156
Grass	.206	170	35	9	1	0	3	18	29	.292	.271	June	.243	70	17	4	0	0	6	5	11	.289	.300
Turf	.243	263	64	16	0	1	22	23	42	.302	.316	July	.169	71	12	0	0	0	0	4	17	.213	.169
First Pitch	.276	87	24	5	0	0	6	3	0	.315	.333	August	.274	73	20	6	0	1	8	13	13	.384	.397
Ahead in Count	.313	115	36	10	1	1	7	19	0	.410	.443	September/October	.309	97	30	10	1	0	6	6	11	.358	.433
Behind in Count	.120	158	19	4	0	0	3	0	62	.125	.146	Pre-All Star	.191	225	43	9	0	0	11	21	37	.261	.231
Two Strikes	.128	156	20	6	0	0	5	18	71	.222	.167	Post-All Star	.269	208	56	16	1	1	14	20	34	.338	.370

Batter vs. Pitcher (career)

Hits Best Against	Avg	AB	H	2B	3B	HR	RBI	BB	SO	OBP	SLG	Hits Worst Against	Avg	AB	H	2B	3B	HR	RBI	BB	SO	OBP	SLG
Greg Maddux	.333	12	4	0	0	0	0	0	1	.333	.333	John Burkett	.154	13	2	0	0	0	0	0	1	.154	.154
												David Cone	.158	19	3	1	0	0	0	1	6	.200	.211
												Doug Drabek	.235	17	4	0	0	0	2	0	3	.235	.235

Todd Jones — Astros

Age 26 – Pitches Right (groundball pitcher)

	ERA	W	L	Sv	G	GS	IP	BB	SO	Avg	H	2B	3B	HR	RBI	OBP	SLG	GF	IR	IRS	Hld	SvOp	SB	CS	GB	FB	G/F
1993 Season	3.13	1	2	2	27	0	37.1	15	25	.214	28	4	0	4	10	.297	.336	8	8	1	6	3	2	3	67	23	2.91

1993 Season

	ERA	W	L	Sv	G	GS	IP	H	HR	BB	SO		Avg	AB	H	2B	3B	HR	RBI	BB	SO	OBP	SLG
Home	1.42	1	1	1	12	0	19.0	10	1	6	14	vs. Left	.194	62	12	2	0	0	2	7	11	.282	.226
Away	4.91	0	1	1	15	0	18.1	18	3	9	11	vs. Right	.232	69	16	2	0	4	8	8	14	.312	.435
Starter	0.00	0	0	0	0	0	0.0	0	0	0	0	Scoring Posn	.192	26	5	0	0	1	6	3	2	.290	.308
Reliever	3.13	1	2	2	27	0	37.1	28	4	15	25	Close & Late	.327	52	17	2	0	3	8	8	9	.417	.538
0 Days rest	4.76	0	0	0	3	0	5.2	4	2	3	2	None on/out	.171	35	6	1	0	0	0	3	10	.237	.200
1 or 2 Days rest	3.55	1	1	0	11	0	12.2	10	1	5	10	First Pitch	.231	13	3	1	0	0	1	1	0	.267	.308
3+ Days rest	2.37	0	1	2	13	0	19.0	14	1	7	13	Ahead in Count	.190	63	12	1	0	3	5	0	21	.190	.349
Pre-All Star	0.00	0	0	0	1	0	2.2	2	0	1	2	Behind in Count	.242	33	8	1	0	1	4	7	0	.375	.364
Post-All Star	3.37	1	2	2	26	0	34.2	26	4	14	23	Two Strikes	.194	67	13	2	0	2	4	7	25	.270	.313

Brian Jordan — Cardinals

Age 27 – Bats Right

	Avg	G	AB	R	H	2B	3B	HR	RBI	BB	SO	HBP	GDP	SB	CS	OBP	SLG	IBB	SH	SF	#Pit	#P/PA	GB	FB	G/F
1993 Season	.309	67	223	33	69	10	6	10	44	12	35	4	6	6	6	.351	.543	0	0	3	863	3.57	85	71	1.20
Career (1992-1993)	.262	122	416	50	109	19	10	15	66	22	83	5	12	13	8	.305	.464	1	0	3	1584	3.55	162	115	1.41

1993 Season

	Avg	AB	H	2B	3B	HR	RBI	BB	SO	OBP	SLG		Avg	AB	H	2B	3B	HR	RBI	BB	SO	OBP	SLG
vs. Left	.365	63	23	4	2	7	18	5	7	.412	.825	Scoring Posn	.344	64	22	3	1	2	31	7	11	.416	.516
vs. Right	.288	160	46	6	4	3	26	7	28	.328	.431	Close & Late	.316	38	12	1	0	2	3	2	8	.350	.500
Home	.299	137	41	6	5	4	27	7	20	.342	.504	None on/out	.196	46	9	1	1	1	1	2	8	.229	.326
Away	.326	86	28	4	1	6	17	5	15	.366	.605	Batting #5	.394	66	26	4	2	5	19	4	8	.431	.742
First Pitch	.424	33	14	1	2	3	11	0	0	.429	.848	Batting #6	.308	91	28	5	3	2	18	6	19	.366	.495
Ahead in Count	.407	54	22	4	3	2	14	4	0	.450	.704	Other	.227	66	15	1	1	3	7	2	8	.246	.409
Behind in Count	.237	97	23	3	1	3	12	0	30	.253	.381	Pre-All Star	.277	94	26	3	3	3	19	7	17	.327	.468
Two Strikes	.202	89	18	2	1	3	9	8	35	.280	.348	Post-All Star	.333	129	43	7	3	7	25	5	18	.370	.597

Ricky Jordan — Phillies

Age 29 – Bats Right

	Avg	G	AB	R	H	2B	3B	HR	RBI	BB	SO	HBP	GDP	SB	CS	OBP	SLG	IBB	SH	SF	#Pit	#P/PA	GB	FB	G/F
1993 Season	.289	90	159	21	46	4	1	5	18	8	32	1	2	0	0	.324	.421	1	0	2	589	3.46	67	37	1.81
Last Five Years	.277	521	1583	187	439	87	7	35	220	63	226	13	49	9	5	.306	.407	14	0	22	5250	3.12	637	433	1.47

1993 Season

	Avg	AB	H	2B	3B	HR	RBI	BB	SO	OBP	SLG		Avg	AB	H	2B	3B	HR	RBI	BB	SO	OBP	SLG
vs. Left	.275	69	19	0	1	2	7	6	13	.329	.391	Scoring Posn	.213	47	10	0	0	2	14	1	9	.220	.340
vs. Right	.300	90	27	4	0	3	11	2	19	.319	.444	Close & Late	.300	40	12	1	0	1	4	2	6	.318	.400
Home	.317	82	26	2	1	3	13	5	16	.352	.476	None on/out	.267	30	8	1	0	1	1	3	9	.333	.400
Away	.260	77	20	2	0	2	5	3	16	.293	.364	Batting #3	.287	101	29	2	1	5	13	3	20	.314	.475
First Pitch	.333	24	8	1	0	2	7	1	0	.346	.625	Batting #9	.295	44	13	1	0	0	4	5	10	.353	.318
Ahead in Count	.290	31	9	1	1	0	1	6	0	.405	.387	Other	.286	14	4	1	0	0	1	0	2	.286	.357
Behind in Count	.266	79	21	2	0	3	8	0	27	.272	.405	Pre-All Star	.319	72	23	3	0	4	9	5	18	.372	.528
Two Strikes	.203	69	14	0	0	2	6	1	32	.222	.290	Post-All Star	.264	87	23	1	1	1	9	3	14	.283	.333

Last Five Years

	Avg	AB	H	2B	3B	HR	RBI	BB	SO	OBP	SLG		Avg	AB	H	2B	3B	HR	RBI	BB	SO	OBP	SLG
vs. Left	.314	646	203	44	3	15	88	38	74	.350	.461	Scoring Posn	.260	446	116	19	3	9	170	33	76	.306	.377
vs. Right	.252	937	236	43	4	20	132	25	152	.275	.370	Close & Late	.274	303	83	13	1	4	44	18	48	.319	.363
Groundball	.277	555	154	35	2	4	66	23	83	.310	.369	None on/out	.290	369	107	15	0	12	12	10	45	.311	.428
Flyball	.273	362	99	22	2	9	61	11	60	.299	.420	Batting #4	.279	592	165	35	3	8	76	24	71	.310	.389
Home	.283	767	217	34	4	19	115	21	109	.302	.412	Batting #5	.295	420	124	26	2	17	80	17	44	.324	.488
Away	.272	816	222	53	3	16	105	42	117	.310	.403	Other	.263	571	150	26	2	10	64	22	111	.290	.368
Day	.293	502	147	30	3	14	84	15	65	.314	.448	April	.283	180	51	12	1	3	26	14	27	.337	.411

Last Five Years

	Avg	AB	H	2B	3B	HR	RBI	BB	SO	OBP	SLG
Night	.270	1081	292	57	4	21	136	48	161	.303	.389
Grass	.277	426	118	27	1	12	62	15	63	.302	.430
Turf	.277	1157	321	60	6	23	158	48	163	.308	.399
First Pitch	.343	286	98	20	1	14	64	6	0	.359	.566
Ahead in Count	.304	313	95	23	3	4	40	38	0	.373	.435
Behind in Count	.245	767	188	36	2	15	90	0	202	.250	.356
Two Strikes	.205	616	126	17	2	7	58	14	226	.223	.273

	Avg	AB	H	2B	3B	HR	RBI	BB	SO	OBP	SLG
May	.254	303	77	10	1	8	42	8	41	.274	.373
June	.257	265	68	21	0	5	29	18	38	.306	.392
July	.254	279	71	11	1	6	39	8	50	.280	.366
August	.289	253	73	15	3	8	50	6	27	.308	.466
September/October	.327	303	99	18	1	5	34	9	43	.344	.442
Pre-All Star	.262	862	226	47	3	21	110	43	131	.298	.397
Post-All Star	.295	721	213	40	4	14	110	20	95	.317	.420

Batter vs. Pitcher (career)

Hits Best Against	Avg	AB	H	2B	3B	HR	RBI	BB	SO	OBP	SLG
Charlie Leibrandt	.583	12	7	1	0	1	3	1	0	.615	.917
Tom Browning	.500	18	9	1	0	1	4	0	0	.474	.722
John Burkett	.417	12	5	0	0	1	1	1	3	.462	.667
Ramon Martinez	.412	17	7	2	0	1	4	0	1	.412	.706
Jose DeLeon	.368	19	7	2	0	2	6	0	2	.368	.789

Hits Worst Against	Avg	AB	H	2B	3B	HR	RBI	BB	SO	OBP	SLG
Rob Dibble	.083	12	1	1	0	0	1	1	3	.154	.167
Bob Walk	.100	10	1	0	0	0	1	1	1	.167	.100
Cris Carpenter	.100	10	1	0	0	0	0	1	0	.182	.100
Doug Drabek	.111	18	2	1	0	0	1	0	8	.111	.167
Ken Hill	.143	14	2	0	0	0	0	0	1	.143	.143

Terry Jorgensen — Twins

Age 27 – Bats Right (groundball hitter)

	Avg	G	AB	R	H	2B	3B	HR	RBI	BB	SO	HBP	GDP	SB	CS	OBP	SLG	IBB	SH	SF	#Pit	#P/PA	GB	FB	G/F
1993 Season	.224	59	152	15	34	7	0	1	12	10	21	0	7	1	0	.270	.289	0	0	1	576	3.53	58	44	1.32
Career (1989-1993)	.240	91	233	21	56	9	0	1	19	17	37	1	12	2	2	.292	.292	0	0	2	897	3.55	96	59	1.63

1993 Season

	Avg	AB	H	2B	3B	HR	RBI	BB	SO	OBP	SLG
vs. Left	.273	66	18	3	0	1	6	7	7	.342	.364
vs. Right	.186	86	16	4	0	0	6	3	14	.211	.233
Home	.247	85	21	4	0	0	7	6	12	.293	.294
Away	.194	67	13	3	0	1	5	4	9	.239	.284
First Pitch	.167	24	4	0	0	0	0	0	0	.167	.167
Ahead in Count	.323	31	10	3	0	1	6	3	0	.382	.516
Behind in Count	.191	68	13	3	0	0	5	0	16	.191	.235
Two Strikes	.180	61	11	1	0	0	4	7	21	.261	.197

	Avg	AB	H	2B	3B	HR	RBI	BB	SO	OBP	SLG
Scoring Posn	.209	43	9	1	0	1	11	5	7	.286	.302
Close & Late	.273	22	6	2	0	0	2	2	2	.333	.364
None on/out	.257	35	9	3	0	0	0	1	4	.278	.343
Batting #7	.091	22	2	0	0	0	0	3	7	.200	.091
Batting #8	.231	104	24	6	0	0	8	5	12	.264	.288
Other	.308	26	8	1	0	1	4	2	2	.357	.462
Pre-All Star	.203	64	13	3	0	0	4	4	10	.250	.250
Post-All Star	.239	88	21	4	0	1	8	6	11	.284	.318

Felix Jose — Royals

Age 29 – Bats Both (groundball hitter)

	Avg	G	AB	R	H	2B	3B	HR	RBI	BB	SO	HBP	GDP	SB	CS	OBP	SLG	IBB	SH	SF	#Pit	#P/PA	GB	FB	G/F
1993 Season	.253	149	499	64	126	24	3	6	43	36	95	1	5	31	13	.303	.349	5	1	2	1884	3.50	209	103	2.03
Last Five Years	.278	580	2059	252	573	104	13	39	252	154	402	9	37	91	44	.330	.398	21	3	9	7772	3.48	850	447	1.90

1993 Season

	Avg	AB	H	2B	3B	HR	RBI	BB	SO	OBP	SLG
vs. Left	.094	64	6	1	0	0	4	3	15	.134	.109
vs. Right	.276	435	120	23	3	6	39	33	80	.327	.384
Groundball	.246	65	16	4	0	0	1	8	10	.329	.308
Flyball	.209	110	23	3	1	2	13	6	25	.250	.309
Home	.269	238	64	16	1	2	24	21	34	.327	.370
Away	.238	261	62	8	2	4	19	15	61	.281	.330
Day	.278	162	45	7	0	1	16	11	29	.324	.340
Night	.240	337	81	17	3	5	27	25	66	.293	.353
Grass	.250	204	51	6	2	3	16	10	51	.287	.343
Turf	.254	295	75	18	1	3	27	26	44	.314	.353
First Pitch	.311	103	32	8	1	4	13	2	0	.324	.524
Ahead in Count	.365	74	27	5	1	0	12	18	0	.479	.459
Behind in Count	.199	231	46	8	1	0	9	0	82	.203	.242
Two Strikes	.177	232	41	8	1	1	8	16	95	.230	.233

	Avg	AB	H	2B	3B	HR	RBI	BB	SO	OBP	SLG
Scoring Posn	.245	102	25	4	0	2	34	13	17	.325	.343
Close & Late	.210	81	17	3	0	1	5	7	15	.273	.284
None on/out	.260	173	45	9	2	0	0	15	34	.323	.335
Batting #1	.262	347	91	20	3	5	29	22	64	.307	.380
Batting #4	.206	68	14	1	0	1	7	8	14	.289	.265
Other	.250	84	21	3	0	0	7	6	17	.297	.286
April	.224	67	15	4	0	1	7	7	12	.297	.328
May	.294	85	25	3	0	0	8	4	14	.330	.329
June	.298	94	28	7	2	1	11	6	14	.340	.447
July	.190	79	15	1	1	0	3	6	14	.247	.228
August	.239	88	21	5	0	2	6	7	20	.295	.364
September/October	.256	86	22	4	0	2	8	6	21	.301	.372
Pre-All Star	.270	274	74	15	2	2	26	19	43	.319	.361
Post-All Star	.231	225	52	9	1	4	17	17	52	.284	.333

1993 By Position

Position	Avg	AB	H	2B	3B	HR	RBI	BB	SO	OBP	SLG	G	GS	Innings	PO	A	E	DP	Fld Pct	Rng Fctr	In Zone	Outs	Zone Rtg	MLB Zone
As Pinch Hitter	.222	9	2	1	0	0	0	2	3	.364	.333	11	0	---	---	---	---	---	---	---	---	---	---	---
As cf	.250	32	8	0	0	0	3	3	4	.333	.250	10	8	72.0	19	1	0	1	1.000	2.50	21	19	.905	.829
As rf	.253	454	115	23	3	6	40	31	87	.300	.357	136	113	1027.0	218	5	7	2	.970	1.95	265	213	.804	.826

Last Five Years

	Avg	AB	H	2B	3B	HR	RBI	BB	SO	OBP	SLG
vs. Left	.301	632	190	37	5	10	86	49	125	.351	.422
vs. Right	.268	1427	383	67	8	29	166	105	277	.321	.388
Groundball	.300	590	177	31	3	9	71	39	104	.345	.408
Flyball	.284	429	122	23	4	13	70	40	93	.346	.448
Home	.274	1017	279	51	8	22	141	85	185	.332	.405
Away	.282	1042	294	53	5	17	111	69	217	.328	.392
Day	.275	662	182	31	4	13	94	43	126	.320	.393
Night	.280	1397	391	73	9	26	158	111	276	.335	.401
Grass	.269	865	233	38	4	12	94	47	185	.310	.364
Turf	.285	1194	340	66	9	27	158	107	217	.344	.423

	Avg	AB	H	2B	3B	HR	RBI	BB	SO	OBP	SLG
Scoring Posn	.294	534	157	33	4	10	205	55	109	.359	.427
Close & Late	.284	345	98	16	1	9	41	31	82	.344	.414
None on/out	.287	547	157	31	2	6	6	38	104	.334	.384
Batting #4	.266	410	109	14	2	9	54	42	84	.336	.376
Batting #5	.306	605	185	40	6	11	70	41	123	.349	.446
Other	.267	1044	279	50	5	19	128	71	195	.316	.379
April	.286	220	63	17	2	5	31	21	33	.350	.450
May	.301	349	105	15	2	6	52	34	70	.364	.407
June	.281	360	101	24	3	4	45	20	64	.318	.397
July	.252	345	87	13	1	6	30	26	76	.308	.348

Last Five Years

	Avg	AB	H	2B	3B	HR	RBI	BB	SO	OBP	SLG		Avg	AB	H	2B	3B	HR	RBI	BB	SO	OBP	SLG
First Pitch	.355	392	139	27	3	17	76	15	0	.380	.569	August	.283	389	110	19	0	5	34	24	84	.329	.370
Ahead in Count	.324	340	110	22	3	9	45	79	0	.448	.485	September/October	.270	396	107	16	5	13	60	29	75	.319	.434
Behind in Count	.227	982	223	42	4	5	80	0	350	.228	.293	Pre-All Star	.282	1041	294	61	7	15	132	81	189	.335	.398
Two Strikes	.214	963	206	39	5	9	75	60	402	.261	.293	Post-All Star	.274	1018	279	43	6	24	120	73	213	.324	.399

Batter vs. Pitcher (career)

Hits Best Against	Avg	AB	H	2B	3B	HR	RBI	BB	SO	OBP	SLG	Hits Worst Against	Avg	AB	H	2B	3B	HR	RBI	BB	SO	OBP	SLG
Chris Nabholz	.636	11	7	2	0	0	3	1	3	.667	.818	Greg Maddux	.000	16	0	0	0	0	0	1	7	.059	.000
Tommy Greene	.571	14	8	4	1	0	4	2	2	.556	1.000	Ben McDonald	.083	12	1	0	0	0	1	3	6	.267	.083
Joe Boever	.545	11	6	3	0	1	4	3	0	.643	1.091	Jose Mesa	.091	11	1	0	0	0	0	0	2	.091	.091
Danny Jackson	.500	12	6	5	0	0	4	0	1	.500	.917	Alex Fernandez	.118	17	2	1	0	0	0	0	4	.118	.176
Chris Bosio	.385	13	5	1	0	2	5	1	2	.429	.923	Randy Myers	.182	11	2	0	0	0	0	0	4	.182	.182

Wally Joyner — Royals

Age 32 – Bats Left (flyball hitter)

	Avg	G	AB	R	H	2B	3B	HR	RBI	BB	SO	HBP	GDP	SB	CS	OBP	SLG	IBB	SH	SF	#Pit	#P/PA	GB	FB	G/F
1993 Season	.292	141	497	83	145	36	3	15	65	66	67	3	6	5	9	.375	.467	13	2	5	2094	3.65	154	171	0.90
Last Five Years	.283	675	2523	341	715	151	10	69	347	260	275	15	61	23	17	.351	.433	32	6	25	10010	3.54	864	903	0.96

1993 Season

	Avg	AB	H	2B	3B	HR	RBI	BB	SO	OBP	SLG		Avg	AB	H	2B	3B	HR	RBI	BB	SO	OBP	SLG
vs. Left	.259	166	43	12	0	2	20	18	21	.340	.367	Scoring Posn	.279	129	36	8	1	2	46	27	24	.395	.403
vs. Right	.308	331	102	24	3	13	45	48	46	.392	.517	Close & Late	.325	83	27	5	0	3	14	16	15	.440	.494
Groundball	.348	69	24	6	1	2	9	8	6	.410	.551	None on/out	.300	130	39	10	1	8	8	7	11	.341	.577
Flyball	.270	100	27	6	1	7	17	16	16	.373	.560	Batting #4	.320	178	57	14	2	7	29	21	24	.388	.539
Home	.320	256	82	25	3	4	35	29	28	.389	.488	Batting #5	.235	187	44	11	1	3	18	26	28	.332	.353
Away	.261	241	63	11	0	11	30	37	39	.360	.444	Other	.333	132	44	11	0	5	18	19	15	.418	.530
Day	.234	158	37	9	1	3	15	24	25	.332	.361	April	.266	79	21	7	0	0	3	16	6	.389	.354
Night	.319	339	108	27	2	12	50	42	42	.396	.516	May	.322	87	28	4	0	6	18	15	15	.423	.575
Grass	.263	186	49	8	0	9	25	29	29	.361	.452	June	.282	103	29	7	0	1	7	9	14	.342	.379
Turf	.309	311	96	28	3	6	40	37	38	.384	.476	July	.376	93	35	9	2	6	26	12	11	.443	.710
First Pitch	.337	86	29	9	1	3	12	8	0	.392	.570	August	.243	111	27	7	1	1	7	8	16	.295	.351
Ahead in Count	.365	126	46	14	0	2	15	29	0	.487	.524	September/October	.208	24	5	2	0	1	4	6	5	.367	.417
Behind in Count	.199	186	37	7	2	2	14	0	49	.200	.290	Pre-All Star	.294	299	88	21	1	9	36	43	35	.384	.462
Two Strikes	.209	206	43	9	1	4	19	29	67	.307	.320	Post-All Star	.288	198	57	15	2	6	29	23	32	.360	.475

1993 By Position

Position	Avg	AB	H	2B	3B	HR	RBI	BB	SO	OBP	SLG	G	GS	Innings	PO	A	E	DP	Fld Pct	Rng Fctr	In Zone	Outs	Zone Rtg	MLB Zone
As 1b	.292	496	145	36	3	15	64	65	67	.374	.468	140	134	1194.0	1116	145	7	115	.994	---	276	241	.873	.834

Last Five Years

	Avg	AB	H	2B	3B	HR	RBI	BB	SO	OBP	SLG		Avg	AB	H	2B	3B	HR	RBI	BB	SO	OBP	SLG
vs. Left	.255	859	219	48	1	17	117	63	111	.311	.373	Scoring Posn	.296	636	188	40	3	14	265	99	76	.384	.434
vs. Right	.298	1664	496	103	9	52	230	197	164	.370	.465	Close & Late	.269	409	110	22	0	13	61	43	45	.338	.418
Groundball	.316	576	182	32	3	16	88	51	49	.372	.465	None on/out	.261	597	156	33	2	22	22	45	52	.314	.434
Flyball	.286	615	176	33	5	23	93	68	80	.358	.468	Batting #3	.269	813	219	53	3	21	109	80	92	.333	.419
Home	.282	1227	346	77	6	28	164	124	121	.349	.423	Batting #4	.299	817	244	49	3	27	124	76	87	.362	.465
Away	.285	1296	369	74	4	41	183	136	154	.353	.443	Other	.282	893	252	49	4	21	114	104	96	.357	.417
Day	.268	637	171	35	2	18	84	78	77	.347	.414	April	.272	389	106	27	0	5	38	52	42	.355	.380
Night	.288	1886	544	116	8	51	263	182	198	.352	.440	May	.329	435	143	22	1	21	81	55	42	.404	.529
Grass	.271	1634	442	85	4	52	224	172	178	.339	.423	June	.278	508	141	33	2	6	59	38	60	.329	.386
Turf	.307	889	273	66	6	17	123	88	97	.372	.452	July	.289	454	131	30	2	14	79	41	57	.349	.456
First Pitch	.307	414	127	27	3	15	54	17	0	.336	.495	August	.259	437	113	21	4	16	57	37	47	.320	.435
Ahead in Count	.329	680	224	57	1	26	115	132	0	.436	.531	September/October	.270	300	81	18	1	7	33	37	27	.349	.407
Behind in Count	.233	981	229	38	5	13	100	0	226	.239	.322	Pre-All Star	.291	1509	439	95	4	36	208	157	163	.358	.431
Two Strikes	.225	977	220	47	4	15	101	108	275	.305	.328	Post-All Star	.272	1014	276	56	6	33	139	103	112	.340	.437

Batter vs. Pitcher (career)

Hits Best Against	Avg	AB	H	2B	3B	HR	RBI	BB	SO	OBP	SLG	Hits Worst Against	Avg	AB	H	2B	3B	HR	RBI	BB	SO	OBP	SLG
Eric Plunk	.625	16	10	2	0	3	8	3	1	.684	1.313	Bud Black	.083	24	2	1	0	0	2	1	0	.115	.125
Mark Eichhorn	.600	10	6	1	0	0	2	1	1	.636	.700	Jose DeLeon	.100	10	1	0	0	0	1	2	3	.231	.100
Eric Bell	.556	9	5	1	0	1	5	2	1	.636	1.000	Greg Hibbard	.158	19	3	0	0	0	0	0	0	.158	.158
Juan Guzman	.467	15	7	1	1	1	3	2	1	.529	.867	Danny Jackson	.167	12	2	0	0	0	0	0	4	.167	.167
Danny Darwin	.308	13	4	0	1	2	3	2	1	.375	.923	Gregg Olson	.167	12	2	0	0	0	2	0	3	.154	.167

Jeff Juden — Astros

Age 23 – Pitches Right

	ERA	W	L	Sv	G	GS	IP	BB	SO	Avg	H	2B	3B	HR	RBI	OBP	SLG	GF	IR	IRS	Hld	SvOp	SB	CS	GB	FB	G/F
1993 Season	5.40	0	1	0	2	0	5.0	4	7	.222	4	1	0	1	3	.348	.444	1	0	0	0	0	1	0	3	6	0.50
Career (1991-1993)	5.87	0	3	0	6	3	23.0	11	18	.264	23	4	0	4	16	.333	.448	1	0	0	0	0	4	1	31	27	1.15

1993 Season

	ERA	W	L	Sv	G	GS	IP	H	HR	BB	SO		Avg	AB	H	2B	3B	HR	RBI	BB	SO	OBP	SLG
Home	0.00	0	0	0	1	0	2.0	1	0	2	3	vs. Left	.400	10	4	1	0	1	2	3	4	.538	.800
Away	9.00	0	1	0	1	0	3.0	3	1	2	4	vs. Right	.000	8	0	0	0	0	1	1	3	.100	.000

Dave Justice — Braves

Age 28 – Bats Left (flyball hitter)

	Avg	G	AB	R	H	2B	3B	HR	RBI	BB	SO	HBP	GDP	SB	CS	OBP	SLG	IBB	SH	SF	#Pit	#P/PA	GB	FB	G/F
1993 Season	.270	157	585	90	158	15	4	40	120	78	90	3	10	3	5	.357	.515	12	0	4	2539	3.79	171	212	0.81
Career (1989-1993)	.270	553	1955	318	527	85	12	111	360	289	357	9	18	26	24	.364	.496	34	1	16	8753	3.86	553	669	0.83

1993 Season

	Avg	AB	H	2B	3B	HR	RBI	BB	SO	OBP	SLG		Avg	AB	H	2B	3B	HR	RBI	BB	SO	OBP	SLG
vs. Left	.294	177	52	5	0	11	36	18	27	.362	.508	Scoring Posn	.290	169	49	3	0	12	78	36	30	.412	.521
vs. Right	.260	408	106	10	4	29	84	60	63	.354	.517	Close & Late	.242	91	22	0	2	7	15	13	18	.343	.516
Groundball	.266	188	50	6	0	12	39	24	29	.347	.489	None on/out	.257	148	38	5	0	7	7	11	16	.313	.432
Flyball	.240	104	25	2	0	6	18	24	16	.392	.433	Batting #4	.243	202	49	7	2	13	42	25	29	.332	.490
Home	.272	290	79	6	1	18	57	32	40	.348	.486	Batting #5	.267	318	85	5	2	21	60	46	51	.359	.494
Away	.268	295	79	9	3	22	63	46	50	.365	.542	Other	.369	65	24	3	0	6	18	7	10	.425	.692
Day	.373	150	56	6	2	14	38	27	19	.466	.720	April	.157	89	14	3	0	4	11	13	21	.272	.326
Night	.234	435	102	9	2	26	82	51	71	.317	.444	May	.282	103	29	4	1	8	22	6	14	.330	.573
Grass	.273	461	126	11	4	34	98	54	71	.351	.536	June	.236	89	21	0	1	4	12	11	12	.317	.393
Turf	.258	124	32	4	0	6	22	24	19	.377	.435	July	.357	08	35	4	0	8	27	18	8	.453	.643
First Pitch	.400	85	34	2	1	6	21	9	0	.457	.659	August	.277	94	26	0	0	11	24	14	13	.370	.628
Ahead in Count	.294	119	35	3	1	14	37	39	0	.460	.689	September/October	.295	112	33	4	2	5	24	16	22	.380	.500
Behind in Count	.201	264	53	7	1	12	29	0	75	.204	.371	Pre-All Star	.242	322	78	10	2	20	58	37	50	.324	.472
Two Strikes	.214	276	59	3	2	12	37	30	90	.293	.370	Post-All Star	.304	263	80	5	2	20	62	41	40	.395	.567

1993 By Position

Position	Avg	AB	H	2B	3B	HR	RBI	BB	SO	OBP	SLG	G	GS	Innings	PO	A	E	DP	Fld Pct	Rng Fctr	In Zone	Outs	Zone Rtg	MLB Zone
As rf	.270	585	158	15	4	40	120	78	90	.357	.515	157	157	1394.1	324	9	5	1	.985	2.15	371	308	.830	.826

Career (1989-1993)

	Avg	AB	H	2B	3B	HR	RBI	BB	SO	OBP	SLG		Avg	AB	H	2B	3B	HR	RBI	BB	SO	OBP	SLG
vs. Left	.299	632	189	28	2	33	124	66	102	.366	.506	Scoring Posn	.293	543	159	28	3	32	246	131	105	.424	.532
vs. Right	.255	1323	338	57	10	78	236	223	255	.363	.491	Close & Late	.253	296	75	11	3	16	46	41	70	.345	.473
Groundball	.301	647	195	29	4	39	136	89	110	.385	.539	None on/out	.222	510	113	21	2	24	24	44	97	.286	.412
Flyball	.248	444	110	24	3	19	68	76	87	.359	.444	Batting #4	.262	1082	283	49	9	62	210	172	193	.363	.495
Home	.271	972	263	48	7	59	183	141	183	.362	.516	Batting #5	.277	585	162	24	3	29	100	74	105	.358	.477
Away	.269	983	264	37	5	52	177	148	174	.365	.475	Other	.285	288	82	12	0	20	50	43	59	.377	.535
Day	.274	503	138	17	4	30	96	91	76	.383	.503	April	.168	185	31	7	0	6	21	25	48	.269	.303
Night	.268	1452	389	68	8	81	264	198	281	.357	.493	May	.292	373	109	22	1	19	71	42	63	.369	.509
Grass	.276	1462	403	65	12	89	275	204	276	.364	.519	June	.247	336	83	11	4	14	53	52	64	.347	.429
Turf	.252	493	124	20	0	22	85	85	81	.362	.426	July	.289	263	76	11	1	13	43	40	40	.381	.487
First Pitch	.354	254	90	9	3	20	67	26	0	.415	.650	August	.282	355	100	15	2	29	76	44	62	.361	.580
Ahead in Count	.342	409	140	24	2	39	94	144	0	.511	.697	September/October	.289	443	128	19	4	30	96	86	80	.401	.553
Behind in Count	.204	877	179	34	3	31	113	0	289	.205	.356	Pre-All Star	.255	988	252	46	6	44	162	135	191	.347	.447
Two Strikes	.194	939	182	25	5	29	126	118	357	.284	.324	Post-All Star	.284	967	275	39	6	67	198	154	166	.381	.545

Batter vs. Pitcher (career)

Hits Best Against	Avg	AB	H	2B	3B	HR	RBI	BB	SO	OBP	SLG	Hits Worst Against	Avg	AB	H	2B	3B	HR	RBI	BB	SO	OBP	SLG
Ryan Bowen	.556	9	5	1	1	1	3	4	1	.692	1.222	Mike Maddux	.000	7	0	0	0	0	1	4	2	.333	.000
Kevin Gross	.429	14	6	0	0	2	5	4	3	.500	.857	Mitch Williams	.091	11	1	0	0	0	0	1	4	.167	.091
Greg Swindell	.400	10	4	0	0	2	2	1	1	.455	1.000	Pete Harnisch	.094	32	3	1	0	1	2	3	8	.171	.219
Curt Schilling	.375	16	6	1	0	3	8	6	5	.545	1.000	Danny Darwin	.100	10	1	0	0	0	0	2	5	.250	.100
Anthony Young	.364	11	4	0	0	2	4	1	2	.417	.909	Jose DeLeon	.125	16	2	1	0	0	1	0	6	.125	.188

Jeff Kaiser — Mets

Age 33 – Pitches Left

	ERA	W	L	Sv	G	GS	IP	BB	SO	Avg	H	2B	3B	HR	RBI	OBP	SLG	GF	IR	IRS	Hld	SvOp	SB	CS	GB	FB	G/F
1993 Season	7.88	0	0	0	9	0	8.0	5	9	.323	10	4	0	1	6	.405	.548	3	4	1	0	0	4	1	10	6	1.67
Last Five Years	6.14	0	2	2	30	0	29.1	22	26	.308	37	7	2	5	29	.407	.525	7	31	11	0	3	6	2	42	30	1.40

1993 Season

	ERA	W	L	Sv	G	GS	IP	H	HR	BB	SO		Avg	AB	H	2B	3B	HR	RBI	BB	SO	OBP	SLG
Home	13.50	0	0	0	2	0	2.0	2	0	2	1	vs. Left	.357	14	5	2	0	1	3	1	4	.400	.714
Away	6.00	0	0	0	7	0	6.0	8	1	3	8	vs. Right	.294	17	5	2	0	0	3	4	5	.409	.412

Scott Kamieniecki — Yankees

Age 30 – Pitches Right

	ERA	W	L	Sv	G	GS	IP	BB	SO	Avg	H	2B	3B	HR	RBI	OBP	SLG	CG	ShO	Sup	QS	#P/S	SB	CS	GB	FB	G/F
1993 Season	4.08	10	7	1	30	20	154.1	59	72	.277	163	25	5	17	71	.343	.423	2	0	5.07	11	104	7	10	249	153	1.63
Career (1991-1993)	4.19	20	25	1	67	57	397.2	155	194	.270	410	75	9	38	175	.340	.407	6	0	4.66	30	104	40	18	600	431	1.39

1993 Season

	ERA	W	L	Sv	G	GS	IP	H	HR	BB	SO		Avg	AB	H	2B	3B	HR	RBI	BB	SO	OBP	SLG
Home	3.84	8	2	0	18	13	103.0	104	10	36	56	vs. Left	.284	285	81	14	3	9	33	28	38	.348	.449
Away	4.56	2	5	1	12	7	51.1	59	7	23	16	vs. Right	.270	304	82	11	2	8	38	31	34	.338	.398
Starter	3.80	10	6	0	20	20	130.1	134	12	50	61	Scoring Posn	.314	121	38	5	0	4	51	20	12	.401	.455
Reliever	5.63	0	1	1	10	0	24.0	29	5	9	11	Close & Late	.290	31	9	0	0	1	3	8	5	.436	.387
0-3 Days Rest	0.00	0	0	0	0	0	0.0	0	0	0	0	None on/out	.285	151	43	5	0	5	5	15	18	.349	.417
4 Days Rest	4.21	5	3	0	10	10	62.0	65	5	24	28	First Pitch	.382	76	29	3	2	5	14	6	0	.422	.671

1993 Season

	ERA	W	L	Sv	G	GS	IP	H	HR	BB	SO		Avg	AB	H	2B	3B	HR	RBI	BB	SO	OBP	SLG
5+ Days Rest	3.42	5	3	0	10	10	68.1	69	7	26	33	Ahead in Count	.223	256	57	8	2	6	24	0	61	.230	.340
Pre-All Star	4.17	3	3	1	18	8	73.1	76	8	31	27	Behind in Count	.316	152	48	9	1	3	24	30	0	.424	.447
Post-All Star	4.00	7	4	0	12	12	81.0	87	9	28	45	Two Strikes	.222	252	56	7	1	4	19	23	72	.291	.306

Career (1991-1993)

	ERA	W	L	Sv	G	GS	IP	H	HR	BB	SO		Avg	AB	H	2B	3B	HR	RBI	BB	SO	OBP	SLG
Home	3.91	16	8	0	37	32	225.1	223	22	83	117	vs. Left	.279	738	206	37	6	19	81	76	102	.346	.423
Away	4.54	4	17	1	30	25	172.1	187	16	72	77	vs. Right	.262	779	204	38	3	19	94	79	92	.335	.392
Day	3.92	6	5	1	19	16	119.1	109	9	44	54	Inning 1-6	.265	1255	333	65	8	30	140	127	170	.334	.402
Night	4.30	14	20	0	48	41	278.1	301	29	111	140	Inning 7+	.294	262	77	10	1	8	35	28	24	.367	.431
Grass	4.17	18	23	1	62	52	367.0	374	36	145	180	None on	.269	888	239	40	4	25	25	75	112	.330	.408
Turf	4.40	2	2	0	5	5	30.2	36	2	10	14	Runners on	.272	629	171	35	5	13	150	80	82	.354	.405
April	2.30	0	0	1	4	2	15.2	14	1	8	3	Scoring Posn	.278	352	98	18	1	8	131	58	51	.372	.403
May	3.97	1	3	0	13	6	56.2	55	3	26	24	Close & Late	.349	109	38	7	1	3	17	18	13	.445	.514
June	5.03	4	5	0	13	12	78.2	90	8	30	38	None on/out	.285	396	113	17	0	13	13	31	51	.340	.427
July	3.90	7	6	0	15	15	101.2	101	12	30	54	vs. 1st Batr (relief)	.500	8	4	0	0	1	5	1	1	.500	.875
August	3.89	5	5	0	11	11	74.0	66	8	30	31	First Inning Pitched	.282	255	72	11	0	11	47	28	35	.355	.455
September/October	4.56	3	6	0	11	11	71.0	84	6	31	44	First 75 Pitches	.269	1080	291	53	8	27	125	111	136	.338	.408
Starter	4.09	20	24	0	57	57	373.2	381	33	146	183	Pitch 76-90	.276	181	50	11	0	5	19	19	30	.353	.420
Reliever	5.63	0	1	1	10	0	24.0	29	5	9	11	Pitch 91-105	.237	173	41	5	1	5	17	15	19	.298	.364
0-3 Days Rest	0.00	0	0	0	0	0	0.0	0	0	0	0	Pitch 106+	.337	83	28	6	0	1	14	10	9	.423	.446
4 Days Rest	4.71	9	12	0	30	30	187.1	198	21	75	103	First Pitch	.310	203	63	10	2	9	27	13	0	.357	.512
5+ Days Rest	3.48	11	12	0	27	27	186.1	183	12	71	80	Ahead in Count	.248	650	161	25	3	14	67	0	151	.254	.360
Pre-All Star	4.21	8	10	1	35	25	186.0	192	16	75	82	Behind in Count	.294	378	111	24	2	9	50	85	0	.419	.439
Post-All Star	4.17	12	15	0	32	32	211.2	218	22	80	112	Two Strikes	.226	654	148	24	3	10	58	57	194	.294	.318

Pitcher vs. Batter (career)

Pitches Best Vs.	Avg	AB	H	2B	3B	HR	RBI	BB	SO	OBP	SLG	Pitches Worst Vs.	Avg	AB	H	2B	3B	HR	RBI	BB	SO	OBP	SLG
Wally Joyner	.091	11	1	0	0	0	1	3	0	.267	.091	Lou Whitaker	.500	12	6	2	0	1	3	1	1	.538	.917
Harold Reynolds	.133	15	2	0	0	0	2	0	1	.133	.133	Frank Thomas	.455	11	5	1	0	1	2	3	1	.571	.818
Billy Hatcher	.154	13	2	0	0	0	1	1	0	.200	.154	Mark McGwire	.417	12	5	2	0	2	5	1	2	.462	1.083
Dave Valle	.167	12	2	0	0	0	0	1	1	.231	.167	Kenny Lofton	.400	10	4	0	1	1	3	1	1	.455	.900
Tim Raines	.182	11	2	0	0	0	0	0	1	.182	.182	Carlos Baerga	.385	13	5	1	0	2	5	2	2	.467	.923

Ron Karkovice — White Sox

Age 30 – Bats Right (flyball hitter)

	Avg	G	AB	R	H	2B	3B	HR	RBI	BB	SO	HBP	GDP	SB	CS	OBP	SLG	IBB	SH	SF	#Pit	#P/PA	GB	FB	G/F
1993 Season	.228	128	403	60	92	17	1	20	54	29	126	6	12	2	2	.287	.424	1	11	4	1667	3.68	88	129	0.68
Last Five Years	.240	465	1277	175	307	61	4	47	170	100	365	13	18	14	6	.300	.405	4	38	10	5194	3.61	312	382	0.82

1993 Season

	Avg	AB	H	2B	3B	HR	RBI	BB	SO	OBP	SLG		Avg	AB	H	2B	3B	HR	RBI	BB	SO	OBP	SLG
vs. Left	.198	121	24	5	0	7	18	12	39	.281	.413	Scoring Posn	.185	92	17	5	0	3	29	13	28	.282	.337
vs. Right	.241	282	68	12	1	13	36	17	87	.290	.429	Close & Late	.156	64	10	2	1	2	5	0	25	.169	.313
Groundball	.278	72	20	3	0	3	7	3	21	.325	.444	None on/out	.342	111	38	7	0	8	8	5	31	.371	.622
Flyball	.203	79	16	4	0	4	14	2	30	.238	.405	Batting #7	.250	4	1	0	0	1	2	0	1	.250	1.000
Home	.217	189	41	9	0	6	20	9	51	.261	.360	Batting #8	.228	399	91	17	1	19	52	29	125	.288	.419
Away	.238	214	51	8	1	14	34	20	75	.310	.481	Other	.000	0	0	0	0	0	0	0	0	.000	.000
Day	.214	117	25	5	1	5	15	8	43	.276	.402	April	.217	60	13	3	0	2	10	7	20	.294	.367
Night	.234	286	67	12	0	15	39	21	83	.292	.434	May	.234	77	18	5	0	3	9	4	18	.274	.416
Grass	.235	332	78	14	0	18	44	21	100	.291	.440	June	.373	51	19	3	1	6	13	2	15	.407	.824
Turf	.197	71	14	3	1	2	10	8	26	.272	.352	July	.167	60	10	0	0	1	3	4	18	.231	.217
First Pitch	.262	65	17	1	0	3	10	1	0	.279	.415	August	.209	86	18	3	0	5	12	4	29	.250	.419
Ahead in Count	.250	72	18	1	0	4	10	14	0	.368	.431	September/October	.203	69	14	3	0	3	7	8	26	.304	.377
Behind in Count	.195	195	38	12	1	9	26	0	109	.211	.405	Pre-All Star	.258	209	54	11	1	12	33	15	61	.310	.493
Two Strikes	.140	207	29	7	0	10	19	14	126	.201	.319	Post-All Star	.196	194	38	6	0	8	21	14	65	.263	.351

1993 By Position

Position	Avg	AB	H	2B	3B	HR	RBI	BB	SO	OBP	SLG	G	GS	Innings	PO	A	E	DP	Fld Pct	Rng Fctr	In Zone	Outs	Zone Rtg	MLB Zone
As c	.229	401	92	17	1	20	54	28	125	.287	.426	127	118	1038.2	769	60	5	3	.994	---	---	---	---	---

Last Five Years

	Avg	AB	H	2B	3B	HR	RBI	BB	SO	OBP	SLG		Avg	AB	H	2B	3B	HR	RBI	BB	SO	OBP	SLG
vs. Left	.238	441	105	22	2	17	63	44	128	.310	.413	Scoring Posn	.236	322	76	13	1	9	114	45	101	.328	.366
vs. Right	.242	836	202	39	2	30	107	56	237	.295	.401	Close & Late	.240	217	52	8	1	4	14	12	67	.288	.341
Groundball	.241	319	77	16	0	8	26	23	90	.302	.367	None on/out	.290	328	95	22	0	14	14	14	85	.321	.485
Flyball	.208	307	64	12	0	10	44	17	98	.255	.345	Batting #7	.242	264	64	16	0	6	31	25	63	.315	.371
Home	.226	611	138	31	2	11	59	45	162	.284	.337	Batting #8	.256	667	171	32	4	33	102	48	199	.311	.465
Away	.254	666	169	30	2	36	111	55	203	.314	.467	Other	.208	346	72	13	0	8	37	27	103	.267	.315
Day	.239	457	109	26	2	16	67	31	150	.294	.409	April	.247	162	40	6	0	4	22	17	45	.319	.358
Night	.241	820	198	35	2	31	103	69	215	.303	.402	May	.215	237	51	9	0	6	26	17	61	.266	.329
Grass	.243	1068	260	49	3	38	141	84	300	.303	.402	June	.288	156	45	8	1	11	23	11	48	.347	.564
Turf	.225	209	47	12	1	9	29	16	65	.283	.421	July	.233	202	47	14	0	5	21	14	46	.291	.376
First Pitch	.293	184	54	9	1	6	27	2	0	.313	.451	August	.246	264	65	13	2	11	42	19	81	.302	.436
Ahead in Count	.302	258	78	15	1	12	47	47	0	.409	.508	September/October	.230	256	59	11	1	10	36	22	84	.295	.398
Behind in Count	.180	611	110	22	2	19	59	0	307	.189	.316	Pre-All Star	.242	611	148	25	1	23	77	51	168	.303	.399

Last Five Years

	Avg	AB	H	2B	3B	HR	RBI	BB	SO	OBP	SLG
Two Strikes	.144	626	90	20	1	23	60	50	365	.211	.289
Post-All Star	.239	666	159	36	3	24	93	49	197	.298	.410

Batter vs. Pitcher (career)

Hits Best Against	Avg	AB	H	2B	3B	HR	RBI	BB	SO	OBP	SLG
Jeff Ballard	.556	9	5	0	0	1	3	2	1	.636	.889
Jack Morris	.429	14	6	1	0	1	2	0	3	.429	.714
Jim Abbott	.385	13	5	0	0	2	5	3	2	.500	.846
David West	.364	11	4	1	0	1	5	1	2	.417	.727
Ron Darling	.333	12	4	2	0	1	5	0	5	.333	.750

Hits Worst Against	Avg	AB	H	2B	3B	HR	RBI	BB	SO	OBP	SLG
Matt Young	.000	12	0	0	0	0	0	0	7	.000	.000
Jaime Navarro	.000	12	0	0	0	0	0	0	6	.000	.000
Ben McDonald	.000	12	0	0	0	0	0	0	3	.000	.000
Dave Stewart	.071	14	1	0	0	0	0	2	4	.188	.071
Greg Swindell	.077	13	1	0	0	0	0	1	7	.143	.077

Eric Karros — Dodgers

Age 26 – Bats Right

	Avg	G	AB	R	H	2B	3B	HR	RBI	BB	SO	HBP	GDP	SB	CS	OBP	SLG	IBB	SH	SF	#Pit	#P/PA	GB	FB	G/F
1993 Season	.247	158	610	74	153	27	2	23	80	34	82	2	17	0	1	.287	.409	1	0	3	2300	3.50	228	199	1.15
Career (1991-1993)	.250	321	1178	137	294	58	3	43	169	72	191	4	32	2	5	.293	.413	4	0	8	4514	3.58	402	382	1.05

1993 Season

	Avg	AB	H	2B	3B	HR	RBI	BB	SO	OBP	SLG
vs. Left	.312	170	53	14	1	5	27	8	20	.343	.494
vs. Right	.223	449	100	13	1	18	53	26	62	.267	.376
Groundball	.246	171	42	5	0	4	16	10	18	.287	.345
Flyball	.216	97	21	5	0	2	12	4	14	.248	.330
Home	.231	303	70	11	1	13	42	20	33	.279	.403
Away	.263	316	83	16	1	10	38	14	49	.295	.415
Day	.274	168	46	12	2	5	19	11	28	.322	.458
Night	.237	451	107	15	0	18	61	23	54	.274	.390
Grass	.242	476	115	22	2	19	62	27	64	.283	.416
Turf	.266	143	38	5	0	4	18	7	18	.300	.385
First Pitch	.278	90	25	5	0	6	20	1	0	.301	.533
Ahead in Count	.326	144	47	9	0	10	30	13	0	.380	.597
Behind in Count	.212	278	59	9	1	4	16	0	71	.211	.295
Two Strikes	.189	264	50	9	0	4	14	20	82	.246	.269

	Avg	AB	H	2B	3B	HR	RBI	BB	SO	OBP	SLG
Scoring Posn	.253	178	45	7	0	8	63	15	27	.310	.427
Close & Late	.182	121	22	3	0	4	9	6	19	.227	.306
None on/out	.274	157	43	8	1	9	9	6	21	.301	.510
Batting #4	.222	248	55	14	0	10	36	16	29	.272	.399
Batting #5	.237	152	36	4	1	6	23	6	21	.266	.395
Other	.283	219	62	9	1	7	21	12	32	.319	.429
April	.230	87	20	3	0	2	13	7	12	.284	.333
May	.302	96	29	5	1	2	4	7	13	.350	.438
June	.308	104	32	6	0	4	12	3	14	.333	.481
July	.210	105	22	7	0	3	14	5	9	.252	.362
August	.204	103	21	2	0	7	19	5	15	.241	.427
September/October	.234	124	29	4	1	5	18	7	19	.271	.403
Pre-All Star	.276	333	92	15	1	9	37	19	43	.316	.408
Post-All Star	.213	286	61	12	1	14	43	15	39	.253	.409

1993 By Position

Position	Avg	AB	H	2B	3B	HR	RBI	BB	SO	OBP	SLG	G	GS	Innings	PO	A	E	DP	Fld Pct	Rng Fctr	In Zone	Outs	Zone Rtg	MLB Zone
As 1b	.248	618	153	27	2	23	80	34	82	.288	.409	157	157	1373.2	1337	146	12	118	.992	---	314	261	.831	.834

Career (1991-1993)

	Avg	AB	H	2B	3B	HR	RBI	BB	SO	OBP	SLG
vs. Left	.285	393	112	24	1	13	59	25	50	.326	.450
vs. Right	.232	785	182	34	2	30	110	47	141	.277	.395
Groundball	.261	356	93	12	0	9	37	20	50	.302	.371
Flyball	.210	252	53	14	1	8	41	16	50	.257	.369
Home	.243	560	136	26	2	19	78	44	81	.298	.398
Away	.256	618	158	32	1	24	91	28	110	.289	.427
Day	.265	347	92	21	2	11	44	19	64	.305	.432
Night	.243	831	202	37	1	32	125	53	127	.288	.406
Grass	.249	876	218	46	3	32	125	58	141	.296	.418
Turf	.252	302	76	12	0	11	44	14	50	.284	.401
First Pitch	.293	157	46	11	0	8	26	3	0	.315	.516
Ahead in Count	.333	267	89	14	0	18	53	34	0	.409	.588
Behind in Count	.199	534	106	19	2	10	45	0	163	.197	.298
Two Strikes	.183	515	94	16	0	11	39	35	191	.234	.278

	Avg	AB	H	2B	3B	HR	RBI	BB	SO	OBP	SLG
Scoring Posn	.244	353	86	18	1	12	129	37	62	.313	.402
Close & Late	.213	221	47	10	0	8	26	16	43	.269	.367
None on/out	.284	292	83	16	1	12	12	11	35	.310	.469
Batting #4	.233	588	137	35	0	21	95	44	96	.286	.400
Batting #5	.244	295	72	9	2	10	37	13	48	.275	.390
Other	.288	295	85	14	1	12	37	15	47	.325	.464
April	.246	122	30	5	0	4	19	9	17	.293	.385
May	.286	154	44	8	1	6	16	10	26	.327	.468
June	.290	210	61	11	0	7	21	9	34	.320	.443
July	.228	224	51	12	1	9	34	9	27	.267	.411
August	.215	209	45	10	0	10	40	16	37	.271	.407
September/October	.243	259	63	12	1	7	39	19	50	.292	.378
Pre-All Star	.268	596	160	28	2	19	70	31	88	.304	.418
Post-All Star	.230	582	134	30	1	24	99	41	103	.282	.409

Batter vs. Pitcher (career)

Hits Best Against	Avg	AB	H	2B	3B	HR	RBI	BB	SO	OBP	SLG
Frank Castillo	.538	13	7	2	1	0	0	0	3	.538	.846
Greg W. Harris	.462	13	6	0	0	2	3	2	2	.533	.923
Doug Drabek	.400	10	4	1	0	2	5	2	1	.462	1.100
Willie Blair	.385	13	5	1	0	2	4	0	1	.385	.923
Tim Belcher	.357	14	5	2	0	2	6	1	2	.400	.929

Hits Worst Against	Avg	AB	H	2B	3B	HR	RBI	BB	SO	OBP	SLG
Greg Maddux	.000	13	0	0	0	0	1	1	3	.071	.000
Tommy Greene	.000	13	0	0	0	0	0	0	3	.000	.000
Dwight Gooden	.000	11	0	0	0	0	0	0	2	.000	.000
Xavier Hernandez	.100	10	1	0	0	0	1	1	5	.182	.100
Butch Henry	.133	15	2	0	0	0	0	0	3	.133	.133

Steve Karsay — Athletics

Age 22 – Pitches Right (flyball pitcher)

	ERA	W	L	Sv	G	GS	IP	BB	SO	Avg	H	2B	3B	HR	RBI	OBP	SLG	CG	ShO	Sup	QS	#P/S	SB	CS	GB	FB	G/F
1993 Season	4.04	3	3	0	8	8	49.0	16	33	.258	49	8	2	4	22	.319	.384	0	0	4.78	4	100	5	2	53	64	0.83

1993 Season

	ERA	W	L	Sv	G	GS	IP	H	HR	BB	SO
Home	3.62	1	2	0	4	4	27.1	27	2	8	16
Away	4.57	2	1	0	4	4	21.2	22	2	8	17

	Avg	AB	H	2B	3B	HR	RBI	BB	SO	OBP	SLG
vs. Left	.262	103	27	4	2	1	14	11	17	.330	.369
vs. Right	.253	87	22	4	0	3	8	5	16	.305	.402

Bobby Kelly — Reds

Age 29 – Bats Right

	Avg	G	AB	R	H	2B	3B	HR	RBI	BB	SO	HBP	GDP	SB	CS	OBP	SLG	IBB	SH	SF	#Pit	#P/PA	GB	FB	G/F
1993 Season	.319	78	320	44	102	17	3	9	35	17	43	2	10	21	5	.354	.475	0	0	3	1212	3.53	139	78	1.78
Last Five Years	.286	655	2468	343	706	120	14	63	279	177	453	21	59	158	48	.337	.423	9	15	18	9790	3.61	901	669	1.35

1993 Season

	Avg	AB	H	2B	3B	HR	RBI	BB	SO	OBP	SLG
vs. Left	.250	96	24	6	1	3	8	3	12	.280	.427
vs. Right	.348	224	78	11	2	6	27	14	31	.384	.496
Groundball	.366	123	45	7	0	3	12	6	14	.394	.496
Flyball	.328	58	19	5	1	2	5	1	6	.350	.552
Home	.296	152	45	3	2	4	20	9	24	.337	.421
Away	.339	168	57	14	1	5	15	8	19	.369	.524
Day	.310	84	26	5	2	3	11	4	8	.348	.524
Night	.322	236	76	12	1	6	24	13	35	.356	.458
Grass	.350	100	35	10	1	4	11	5	11	.381	.590
Turf	.305	220	67	7	2	5	24	12	32	.342	.423
First Pitch	.308	39	12	2	0	0	2	0	0	.300	.359
Ahead in Count	.357	70	25	3	1	3	9	9	0	.425	.557
Behind in Count	.269	145	39	8	0	4	17	0	33	.277	.407
Two Strikes	.246	138	34	7	0	2	14	8	43	.291	.341

	Avg	AB	H	2B	3B	HR	RBI	BB	SO	OBP	SLG
Scoring Posn	.278	79	22	2	0	1	26	10	7	.355	.342
Close & Late	.256	43	11	1	0	0	5	2	5	.292	.279
None on/out	.372	78	29	7	1	3	3	1	8	.380	.603
Batting #2	.306	147	45	5	2	3	14	8	19	.340	.429
Batting #5	.364	99	36	6	1	4	18	6	16	.402	.566
Other	.284	74	21	6	0	2	3	3	8	.316	.446
April	.272	81	22	2	2	2	7	3	12	.298	.420
May	.328	122	40	8	0	3	9	9	12	.371	.467
June	.339	109	37	6	1	3	18	5	17	.373	.495
July	.375	8	3	1	0	1	1	0	2	.375	.875
August	.000	0	0	0	0	0	0	0	0	.000	.000
September/October	.000	0	0	0	0	0	0	0	0	.000	.000
Pre-All Star	.319	320	102	17	3	9	35	17	43	.354	.475
Post-All Star	.000	0	0	0	0	0	0	0	0	.000	.000

1993 By Position

Position	Avg	AB	H	2B	3B	HR	RBI	BB	SO	OBP	SLG	G	GS	Innings	PO	A	E	DP	Fld Pct	Rng Fctr	In Zone	Outs	Zone Rtg	MLB Zone
As cf	.319	320	102	17	3	9	35	17	43	.354	.475	78	77	663.1	197	3	1	1	.995	2.71	230	186	.809	.829

Last Five Years

	Avg	AB	H	2B	3B	HR	RBI	BB	SO	OBP	SLG
vs. Left	.302	765	231	36	3	24	88	67	126	.359	.451
vs. Right	.279	1703	475	84	11	39	191	110	327	.326	.410
Groundball	.299	740	221	31	5	22	88	43	127	.339	.443
Flyball	.296	530	157	35	2	18	60	50	111	.362	.472
Home	.295	1200	354	62	6	28	138	88	197	.346	.427
Away	.278	1268	352	58	8	35	141	89	256	.328	.419
Day	.298	709	211	40	5	19	95	52	125	.348	.449
Night	.281	1759	495	80	9	44	184	125	328	.332	.412
Grass	.285	1898	540	99	8	50	211	143	346	.338	.424
Turf	.291	570	166	21	6	13	68	34	107	.332	.418
First Pitch	.332	361	120	19	2	7	55	8	0	.347	.454
Ahead in Count	.340	483	164	33	4	18	71	95	0	.450	.536
Behind in Count	.231	1201	278	44	4	29	107	0	397	.239	.347
Two Strikes	.225	1167	263	47	3	24	106	73	453	.275	.332

	Avg	AB	H	2B	3B	HR	RBI	BB	SO	OBP	SLG
Scoring Posn	.273	568	155	29	2	10	206	54	95	.336	.384
Close & Late	.269	420	113	16	2	14	60	34	88	.328	.417
None on/out	.287	652	187	39	4	23	23	31	121	.325	.465
Batting #1	.281	627	176	34	3	20	55	37	122	.324	.440
Batting #3	.291	506	147	30	2	13	76	42	89	.345	.435
Other	.287	1335	383	56	9	30	148	98	242	.340	.410
April	.311	360	112	18	4	6	47	25	65	.356	.433
May	.290	504	146	26	2	13	52	36	92	.338	.427
June	.275	477	131	18	4	13	51	22	97	.312	.411
July	.302	325	98	18	1	9	45	24	60	.350	.446
August	.292	394	115	22	1	11	35	34	76	.354	.437
September/October	.255	408	104	18	2	11	49	36	63	.319	.390
Pre-All Star	.291	1474	429	71	10	35	167	91	281	.334	.424
Post-All Star	.279	994	277	49	4	28	112	86	172	.341	.421

Batter vs. Pitcher (career)

Hits Best Against	Avg	AB	H	2B	3B	HR	RBI	BB	SO	OBP	SLG
Curt Young	.600	10	6	1	0	1	1	1	2	.636	1.000
Shawn Hillegas	.545	11	6	3	0	0	2	0	2	.545	.818
Bill Gullickson	.455	11	5	1	0	2	7	1	3	.462	1.091
Bill Krueger	.417	12	5	1	0	1	2	2	2	.500	.750
Greg Harris	.333	15	5	1	1	2	3	0	2	.333	.933

Hits Worst Against	Avg	AB	H	2B	3B	HR	RBI	BB	SO	OBP	SLG
Tom Gordon	.000	13	0	0	0	0	1	0	6	.000	.000
Jack McDowell	.000	9	0	0	0	0	0	2	5	.182	.000
Chris Bosio	.077	13	1	0	0	0	0	0	4	.077	.077
Danny Jackson	.083	12	1	0	0	0	0	2	4	.214	.083
John Dopson	.100	10	1	0	0	0	0	1	0	.182	.100

Pat Kelly — Yankees

Age 26 – Bats Right (flyball hitter)

	Avg	G	AB	R	H	2B	3B	HR	RBI	BB	SO	HBP	GDP	SB	CS	OBP	SLG	IBB	SH	SF	#Pit	#P/PA	GB	FB	G/F
1993 Season	.273	127	406	49	111	24	1	7	51	24	68	5	9	14	11	.317	.389	0	10	6	1542	3.42	121	119	1.02
Career (1991-1993)	.250	329	1022	122	255	58	7	17	101	64	192	20	20	34	17	.303	.370	1	18	11	3979	3.50	293	319	0.92

1993 Season

	Avg	AB	H	2B	3B	HR	RBI	BB	SO	OBP	SLG
vs. Left	.283	145	41	8	0	3	17	9	20	.333	.400
vs. Right	.268	261	70	16	1	4	34	15	48	.309	.383
Groundball	.231	78	18	5	0	0	8	3	12	.256	.295
Flyball	.308	91	28	6	1	5	18	5	7	.343	.560
Home	.263	186	49	9	1	4	19	13	26	.319	.387
Away	.282	220	62	15	0	3	32	11	42	.316	.391
Day	.292	130	38	9	1	2	25	10	22	.347	.423
Night	.264	276	73	15	0	5	26	14	46	.303	.373
Grass	.270	348	94	17	1	6	40	20	55	.316	.376
Turf	.293	58	17	7	0	1	11	4	13	.328	.466
First Pitch	.280	82	23	5	0	2	11	0	0	.286	.415
Ahead in Count	.415	82	34	8	0	3	13	10	0	.473	.622
Behind in Count	.201	174	35	8	1	1	17	0	60	.215	.276
Two Strikes	.190	163	31	7	1	2	18	14	68	.268	.282

	Avg	AB	H	2B	3B	HR	RBI	BB	SO	OBP	SLG
Scoring Posn	.271	118	32	10	0	1	41	7	32	.319	.381
Close & Late	.333	63	21	6	0	0	8	4	13	.368	.429
None on/out	.261	92	24	4	0	3	3	8	11	.320	.402
Batting #2	.000	2	0	0	0	0	0	0	1	.000	.000
Batting #9	.273	403	110	24	1	6	50	24	67	.317	.382
Other	1.000	1	1	0	0	1	1	0	0	1.000	4.000
April	.246	69	17	4	0	2	9	3	8	.270	.391
May	.264	72	19	2	0	2	8	3	9	.303	.375
June	.288	80	23	7	0	1	15	8	16	.359	.413
July	.310	71	22	2	1	2	9	4	12	.355	.451
August	.212	85	18	5	0	0	6	6	16	.269	.271
September/October	.414	29	12	4	0	0	4	0	7	.400	.552
Pre-All Star	.271	251	68	13	0	5	33	16	41	.320	.382
Post-All Star	.277	155	43	11	1	2	18	8	27	.313	.400

1993 By Position

Position	Avg	AB	H	2B	3B	HR	RBI	BB	SO	OBP	SLG	G	GS	Innings	PO	A	E	DP	Fld Pct	Rng Fctr	In Zone	Outs	Zone Rtg	MLB Zone
As 2b	.275	404	111	24	1	7	51	24	67	.319	.391	125	119	1051.2	246	369	14	86	.978	5.26	399	370	.927	.895

Career (1991-1993)

	Avg	AB	H	2B	3B	HR	RBI	BB	SO	OBP	SLG		Avg	AB	H	2B	3B	HR	RBI	BB	SO	OBP	SLG
vs. Left	.260	358	93	18	1	7	31	22	58	.307	.374	Scoring Posn	.230	244	56	15	0	2	75	19	67	.297	.316
vs. Right	.244	664	162	40	6	10	70	42	134	.301	.367	Close & Late	.265	155	41	14	1	1	17	11	30	.316	.387
Groundball	.218	248	54	14	2	1	21	11	39	.265	.302	None on/out	.277	235	65	13	0	4	4	17	35	.328	.383
Flyball	.282	234	66	20	4	7	33	16	41	.342	.491	Batting #1	.250	8	2	0	0	1	1	0	2	.250	.625
Home	.246	512	126	26	5	10	48	39	91	.308	.375	Batting #9	.251	1008	253	58	7	16	100	64	189	.306	.370
Away	.253	510	129	32	2	7	53	25	101	.299	.365	Other	.000	6	0	0	0	0	0	0	1	.000	.000
Day	.249	325	81	19	4	7	46	25	69	.315	.397	April	.232	99	23	6	0	2	9	8	17	.291	.354
Night	.250	697	174	39	3	10	55	39	123	.298	.357	May	.253	170	43	12	2	4	22	11	35	.321	.418
Grass	.250	864	216	46	5	15	84	57	159	.309	.367	June	.246	187	46	8	1	4	20	11	37	.302	.364
Turf	.247	158	39	12	2	2	17	7	33	.274	.386	July	.244	225	55	11	2	4	22	13	41	.290	.364
First Pitch	.288	198	57	15	0	6	20	0	0	.304	.455	August	.254	236	60	10	2	3	22	16	41	.304	.352
Ahead in Count	.359	192	69	17	3	4	25	18	0	.410	.542	September/October	.267	105	28	11	0	0	6	5	21	.316	.371
Behind in Count	.186	436	81	16	4	3	32	0	163	.207	.261	Pre-All Star	.246	532	131	29	3	10	53	35	103	.307	.368
Two Strikes	.174	431	75	13	4	6	40	46	192	.268	.265	Post-All Star	.253	490	124	29	4	7	48	29	89	.300	.371

Batter vs. Pitcher (career)

Hits Best Against	Avg	AB	H	2B	3B	HR	RBI	BB	SO	OBP	SLG	Hits Worst Against	Avg	AB	H	2B	3B	HR	RBI	BB	SO	OBP	SLG
Mike Moore	.636	11	7	1	0	0	3	0	2	.636	.727	Bill Wegman	.083	12	1	0	0	0	0	0	0	.083	.083
Dave Stewart	.400	10	4	0	1	1	3	1	3	.455	.900	Erik Hanson	.083	12	1	0	0	0	0	0	3	.083	.083
Mark Langston	.357	14	5	0	0	0	1	2	2	.438	.357	Todd Stottlemyre	.130	23	3	0	1	0	2	1	4	.167	.217
Ron Darling	.333	15	5	3	0	0	2	2	2	.412	.533	Kevin Tapani	.133	15	2	0	0	0	0	1	1	.188	.133
Mark Gubicza	.333	12	4	1	0	1	2	0	2	.333	.667	Ben McDonald	.167	12	2	0	0	0	0	1	1	.231	.167

Jeff Kent — Mets

Age 26 – Bats Right (flyball hitter)

	Avg	G	AB	R	H	2B	3B	HR	RBI	BB	SO	HBP	GDP	SB	CS	OBP	SLG	IBB	SH	SF	#Pit	#P/PA	GB	FB	G/F
1993 Season	.270	140	496	65	134	24	0	21	80	30	88	8	11	4	4	.320	.446	2	6	4	1852	3.40	137	154	0.89
Career (1992-1993)	.258	242	801	117	207	45	2	32	130	57	164	15	16	6	7	.317	.439	2	6	8	3162	3.56	220	248	0.89

1993 Season

	Avg	AB	H	2B	3B	HR	RBI	BB	SO	OBP	SLG		Avg	AB	H	2B	3B	HR	RBI	BB	SO	OBP	SLG
vs. Left	.230	148	34	9	0	0	11	10	22	.277	.291	Scoring Posn	.314	121	38	5	0	7	59	13	25	.379	.529
vs. Right	.287	348	100	15	0	21	69	20	66	.338	.511	Close & Late	.208	101	21	2	0	4	12	6	27	.252	.347
Groundball	.326	172	56	8	0	8	33	8	27	.364	.512	None on/out	.283	106	30	7	0	2	2	2	15	.303	.406
Flyball	.154	78	12	2	0	2	7	5	19	.202	.256	Batting #6	.283	378	107	18	0	17	62	22	66	.326	.466
Home	.275	247	68	13	0	9	41	13	44	.319	.437	Batting #7	.194	67	13	3	0	2	11	3	12	.270	.328
Away	.265	249	66	11	0	12	39	17	44	.320	.454	Other	.275	51	14	3	0	2	7	5	10	.339	.451
Day	.269	175	47	10	0	9	22	12	32	.330	.480	April	.213	61	13	2	0	1	5	5	19	.290	.295
Night	.271	321	87	14	0	12	58	18	56	.314	.427	May	.257	70	18	7	0	2	9	4	13	.316	.443
Grass	.266	398	106	19	0	17	66	24	71	.316	.442	June	.231	78	18	2	0	3	13	0	11	.244	.372
Turf	.286	98	28	5	0	4	14	6	17	.333	.459	July	.323	96	31	4	0	6	19	6	15	.359	.552
First Pitch	.181	83	15	4	0	1	8	2	0	.207	.265	August	.330	97	32	5	0	4	14	10	13	.393	.505
Ahead in Count	.391	92	36	5	0	10	29	19	0	.500	.772	September/October	.234	94	22	4	0	5	20	5	17	.287	.436
Behind in Count	.232	233	54	8	0	6	28	0	74	.243	.343	Pre-All Star	.257	253	65	13	0	7	34	10	52	.298	.391
Two Strikes	.202	213	43	7	0	5	26	9	88	.237	.305	Post-All Star	.284	243	69	11	0	14	46	20	36	.342	.502

1993 By Position

Position	Avg	AB	H	2B	3B	HR	RBI	BB	SO	OBP	SLG	G	GS	Innings	PO	A	E	DP	Fld Pct	Rng Fctr	In Zone	Outs	Zone Rtg	MLB Zone
As 2b	.277	447	124	23	0	19	72	30	82	.331	.456	127	124	1070.2	250	312	18	67	.969	4.72	371	330	.889	.895
As 3b	.205	44	9	1	0	1	6	0	4	.213	.295	12	12	101.1	9	28	3	4	.925	3.29	40	32	.800	.834

Career (1992-1993)

	Avg	AB	H	2B	3B	HR	RBI	BB	SO	OBP	SLG		Avg	AB	H	2B	3B	HR	RBI	BB	SO	OBP	SLG
vs. Left	.225	240	54	14	0	3	25	20	42	.282	.321	Scoring Posn	.289	211	61	12	2	12	101	20	46	.355	.536
vs. Right	.273	561	153	31	2	29	105	37	122	.331	.490	Close & Late	.242	149	36	7	0	8	24	7	41	.285	.450
Groundball	.291	265	77	13	1	12	46	12	50	.332	.483	None on/out	.298	178	53	14	0	4	4	9	34	.335	.444
Flyball	.190	158	30	7	1	3	19	10	43	.238	.304	Batting #6	.282	440	124	24	0	18	68	27	80	.328	.459
Home	.261	414	108	27	1	13	61	31	83	.319	.425	Batting #7	.205	171	35	7	0	7	31	13	36	.285	.368
Away	.256	387	99	18	1	19	69	26	81	.315	.455	Other	.253	190	48	14	2	7	31	17	48	.321	.458
Day	.236	263	62	17	0	11	28	18	55	.294	.426	April	.225	80	18	5	0	2	8	9	24	.319	.363
Night	.270	538	145	28	2	21	102	39	109	.328	.446	May	.263	80	21	9	0	2	10	6	15	.330	.450
Grass	.266	542	144	26	2	24	95	32	112	.317	.454	June	.245	139	34	6	1	5	22	8	25	.301	.410
Turf	.243	259	63	19	0	8	35	25	52	.316	.409	July	.267	161	43	7	0	8	33	11	31	.313	.460
First Pitch	.230	122	28	7	1	2	14	2	0	.252	.352	August	.291	158	46	7	1	8	26	11	31	.343	.500
Ahead in Count	.362	141	51	11	1	12	42	32	0	.483	.709	September/October	.246	183	45	11	0	7	31	12	38	.303	.421
Behind in Count	.207	.401	83	13	0	11	51	0	142	.218	.322	Pre-All Star	.253	380	96	23	1	10	49	25	82	.310	.397
Two Strikes	.194	381	74	19	0	12	49	23	164	.244	.339	Post-All Star	.264	421	111	22	1	22	81	32	82	.323	.477

Batter vs. Pitcher (career)

Hits Best Against	Avg	AB	H	2B	3B	HR	RBI	BB	SO	OBP	SLG	Hits Worst Against	Avg	AB	H	2B	3B	HR	RBI	BB	SO	OBP	SLG
Ken Hill	.583	12	7	0	0	2	6	0	1	.583	1.083	Greg Maddux	.071	14	1	0	0	0	0	0	6	.071	.071
Doug Drabek	.417	12	5	2	0	0	0	3	1	.533	.583	Chris Nabholz	.167	12	2	0	0	0	0	1	4	.231	.167
												Danny Jackson	.214	14	3	0	0	0	2	0	0	.214	.214
												Charlie Hough	.222	9	2	0	0	0	1	1	3	.273	.222
												Tim Pugh	.222	9	2	1	0	0	0	2	2	.364	.333

Keith Kessinger — Reds

Age 27 – Bats Both

	Avg	G	AB	R	H	2B	3B	HR	RBI	BB	SO	HBP	GDP	SB	CS	OBP	SLG	IBB	SH	SF	#Pit	#P/PA	GB	FB	G/F
1993 Season	.259	11	27	4	7	1	0	1	3	4	4	0	1	0	0	.344	.407	0	0	1	105	3.28	10	10	1.00

1993 Season

	Avg	AB	H	2B	3B	HR	RBI	BB	SO	OBP	SLG
vs. Left	.600	5	3	1	0	0	0	0	1	.600	.800
vs. Right	.182	22	4	0	0	1	3	4	3	.296	.318

	Avg	AB	H	2B	3B	HR	RBI	BB	SO	OBP	SLG
Scoring Posn	.500	2	1	0	0	0	2	1	1	.500	.500
Close & Late	.333	6	2	1	0	0	0	0	2	.333	.500

Jimmy Key — Yankees

Age 33 – Pitches Left

	ERA	W	L	Sv	G	GS	IP	BB	SO	Avg	H	2B	3B	HR	RBI	OBP	SLG	CG	ShO	Sup	QS	#P/S	SB	CS	GB	FB	G/F
1993 Season	3.00	18	6	0	34	34	236.2	43	173	.246	219	35	4	26	81	.279	.382	4	2	6.01	25	106	15	6	354	234	1.51
Last Five Years	3.49	73	52	0	160	160	1033.1	195	621	.258	1026	201	16	100	385	.293	.392	15	7	5.21	98	99	50	25	1462	1177	1.24

1993 Season

	ERA	W	L	Sv	G	GS	IP	H	HR	BB	SO
Home	2.75	8	2	0	14	14	104.2	89	12	17	80
Away	3.20	10	4	0	20	20	132.0	130	14	26	93
Day	4.50	3	2	0	8	8	56.0	62	9	6	43
Night	2.54	15	4	0	26	26	180.2	157	17	37	130
Grass	2.84	16	5	0	30	30	212.0	189	24	36	152
Turf	4.38	2	1	0	4	4	24.2	30	2	7	21
April	0.93	3	0	0	5	5	38.2	22	2	5	24
May	2.82	2	2	0	6	6	44.2	39	5	4	40
June	3.08	5	0	0	6	6	38.0	39	3	9	28
July	3.50	2	2	0	6	6	43.2	41	8	6	25
August	5.06	3	1	0	5	5	32.0	40	5	5	22
September/October	2.95	3	1	0	6	6	39.2	38	3	14	34
Starter	3.00	18	6	0	34	34	236.2	219	26	43	173
Reliever	0.00	0	0	0	0	0	0.0	0	0	0	0
0-3 Days Rest	0.00	0	0	0	0	0	0.0	0	0	0	0
4 Days Rest	2.95	12	4	0	22	22	155.2	143	15	30	129
5+ Days Rest	3.11	6	2	0	12	12	81.0	76	11	13	44
Pre-All Star	2.31	11	2	0	19	19	136.1	111	12	21	101
Post-All Star	3.95	7	4	0	15	15	100.1	108	14	22	72

	Avg	AB	H	2B	3B	HR	RBI	BB	SO	OBP	SLG
vs. Left	.260	131	34	3	0	6	13	6	26	.292	.420
vs. Right	.244	758	185	32	4	20	68	37	147	.277	.376
Inning 1-6	.249	748	186	27	4	20	63	39	147	.284	.376
Inning 7+	.234	141	33	8	0	6	18	4	26	.253	.418
None on	.257	568	146	29	3	19	19	24	101	.288	.419
Runners on	.227	321	73	6	1	7	62	19	72	.264	.318
Scoring Posn	.225	169	38	3	1	3	53	13	40	.267	.308
Close & Late	.268	56	15	3	0	3	8	1	7	.276	.482
None on/out	.252	242	61	12	1	9	9	8	44	.279	.421
vs. 1st Batr (relief)	.000	0	0	0	0	0	0	0	0	.000	.000
First Inning Pitched	.240	125	30	6	1	1	13	9	27	.287	.328
First 75 Pitches	.238	605	144	21	3	16	50	34	121	.275	.362
Pitch 76-90	.264	140	37	9	0	4	10	2	18	.280	.414
Pitch 91-105	.330	88	29	3	1	4	16	6	18	.368	.523
Pitch 106+	.161	56	9	2	0	2	5	1	16	.175	.304
First Pitch	.270	111	30	10	0	1	9	1	0	.272	.387
Ahead in Count	.165	369	61	10	0	6	16	0	146	.168	.241
Behind in Count	.320	225	72	8	1	11	31	22	0	.376	.511
Two Strikes	.178	411	73	9	1	9	24	20	173	.215	.270

Last Five Years

	ERA	W	L	Sv	G	GS	IP	H	HR	BB	SO
Home	3.54	36	26	0	83	83	528.2	529	50	108	325
Away	3.44	37	26	0	77	77	504.2	497	50	87	296
Day	4.13	17	19	0	50	50	307.0	336	34	55	187
Night	3.22	56	33	0	110	110	726.1	690	66	140	434
Grass	3.36	37	23	0	76	76	511.2	491	53	89	315
Turf	3.62	36	29	0	84	84	521.2	535	47	106	306
April	2.71	12	3	0	23	23	156.0	130	10	24	88
May	3.35	13	9	0	28	28	188.0	179	20	33	111
June	3.52	10	9	0	25	25	161.0	178	13	29	90
July	3.99	8	14	0	26	26	176.0	187	25	31	86
August	3.94	13	10	0	27	27	162.0	166	17	33	100
September/October	3.40	17	7	0	31	31	190.1	186	15	45	146
Starter	3.49	73	52	0	160	160	1033.1	1026	100	195	621
Reliever	0.00	0	0	0	0	0	0.0	0	0	0	0
0-3 Days Rest	1.29	1	0	0	1	1	7.0	6	0	1	2
4 Days Rest	3.57	42	35	0	100	100	646.0	653	63	119	395
5+ Days Rest	3.41	30	17	0	59	59	380.1	367	37	75	224
Pre-All Star	3.13	39	24	0	84	84	564.1	540	48	97	318
Post-All Star	3.93	34	28	0	76	76	469.0	486	52	98	303

	Avg	AB	H	2B	3B	HR	RBI	BB	SO	OBP	SLG
vs. Left	.227	612	139	17	1	12	54	26	108	.259	.317
vs. Right	.264	3360	887	184	15	88	331	169	513	.299	.406
Inning 1-6	.258	3441	889	177	16	79	335	174	552	.294	.388
Inning 7+	.258	531	137	24	0	21	50	21	69	.286	.422
None on	.250	2478	620	127	10	62	62	106	391	.284	.385
Runners on	.272	1494	406	74	6	38	323	89	230	.307	.406
Scoring Posn	.248	774	192	35	5	19	270	69	130	.298	.380
Close & Late	.295	241	71	12	0	9	24	10	27	.319	.456
None on/out	.249	1066	265	56	5	29	29	35	156	.274	.392
vs. 1st Batr (relief)	.000	0	0	0	0	0	0	0	0	.000	.000
First Inning Pitched	.272	613	167	36	3	12	65	37	102	.312	.400
First 75 Pitches	.259	2906	753	151	14	64	270	138	462	.292	.387
Pitch 76-90	.236	533	126	26	1	15	52	27	82	.274	.373
Pitch 91-105	.289	370	107	18	1	15	48	22	48	.328	.465
Pitch 106+	.245	163	40	6	0	6	15	8	29	.285	.393
First Pitch	.286	521	149	31	1	12	53	8	0	.295	.418
Ahead in Count	.196	1670	328	71	4	28	132	0	511	.198	.294
Behind in Count	.326	988	322	60	6	31	108	106	0	.389	.493
Two Strikes	.198	1776	351	65	5	38	140	81	621	.233	.304

Pitcher vs. Batter (career)

Pitches Best Vs.	Avg	AB	H	2B	3B	HR	RBI	BB	SO	OBP	SLG
John Jaha	.000	12	0	0	0	0	0	0	4	.000	.000
Dante Bichette	.063	16	1	0	0	0	1	0	2	.059	.063
Eddie Murray	.083	24	2	0	0	0	1	1	4	.120	.083
Darnell Coles	.107	28	3	0	0	0	2	2	2	.167	.107
Mike Pagliarulo	.111	18	2	0	0	0	0	1	7	.158	.111

Pitches Worst Vs.	Avg	AB	H	2B	3B	HR	RBI	BB	SO	OBP	SLG
Carlos Baerga	.481	27	13	3	0	1	2	0	2	.481	.704
Tony Pena	.467	30	14	2	0	2	6	0	1	.467	.733
Rickey Henderson	.412	85	35	4	1	9	14	13	8	.485	.800
Tino Martinez	.364	11	4	0	0	2	4	0	1	.364	.909
Mo Vaughn	.364	11	4	0	0	3	4	1	1	.417	1.182

Mark Kiefer — Brewers

Age 25 – Pitches Right

	ERA	W	L	Sv	G	GS	IP	BB	SO	Avg	H	2B	3B	HR	RBI	OBP	SLG	GF	IR	IRS	Hld	SvOp	SB	CS	GB	FB	G/F
1993 Season	0.00	0	0	1	6	0	9.1	5	7	.097	3	0	0	0	3	.243	.097	4	6	3	0	2	1	0	8	13	0.62

1993 Season

	ERA	W	L	Sv	G	GS	IP	H	HR	BB	SO
Home	0.00	0	0	0	2	0	2.1	1	0	1	3
Away	0.00	0	0	1	4	0	7.0	2	0	4	4

	Avg	AB	H	2B	3B	HR	RBI	BB	SO	OBP	SLG
vs. Left	.083	12	1	0	0	0	0	1	2	.214	.083
vs. Right	.105	19	2	0	0	0	3	4	5	.261	.105

John Kiely — Tigers

Age 29 – Pitches Right

	ERA	W	L	Sv	G	GS	IP	BB	SO	Avg	H	2B	3B	HR	RBI	OBP	SLG	GF	IR	IRS	Hld	SvOp	SB	CS	GB	FB	G/F
1993 Season	7.71	0	2	0	8	0	11.2	13	5	.295	13	3	0	2	11	.466	.500	5	6	2	0	0	0	0	21	9	2.33
Career (1991-1993)	4.17	4	5	0	54	0	73.1	50	24	.260	70	17	0	4	43	.375	.368	28	50	20	7	1	2	1	116	79	1.47

1993 Season

	ERA	W	L	Sv	G	GS	IP	H	HR	BB	SO
Home	10.80	0	0	0	3	0	3.1	3	1	6	2
Away	6.48	0	2	0	5	0	8.1	10	1	7	3

	Avg	AB	H	2B	3B	HR	RBI	BB	SO	OBP	SLG
vs. Left	.154	13	2	0	0	1	3	4	0	.353	.385
vs. Right	.355	31	11	3	0	1	8	9	5	.512	.548

Darryl Kile — Astros

Age 25 – Pitches Right

	ERA	W	L	Sv	G	GS	IP	BB	SO	Avg	H	2B	3B	HR	RBI	OBP	SLG	CG	ShO	Sup	QS	#P/S	SB	CS	GB	FB	G/F
1993 Season	3.51	15	8	0	32	26	171.2	69	141	.239	152	21	4	12	66	.324	.341	4	2	6.45	14	105	9	5	207	164	1.26
Career (1991-1993)	3.69	27	29	0	91	70	450.2	216	331	.247	420	75	15	36	185	.338	.373	6	2	4.87	40	96	27	11	586	479	1.22

1993 Season

	ERA	W	L	Sv	G	GS	IP	H	HR	BB	SO
Home	2.35	9	4	0	16	13	92.0	66	6	32	83
Away	4.86	6	4	0	16	13	79.2	86	6	37	58
Day	1.95	2	2	0	5	4	32.1	24	3	10	29
Night	3.88	13	6	0	27	22	139.1	128	9	59	112
Grass	4.98	4	3	0	11	9	56.0	56	4	27	39
Turf	2.80	11	5	0	21	17	115.2	96	8	42	102
April	3.60	1	0	0	4	2	10.0	7	1	7	7
May	3.22	2	1	0	6	3	22.1	17	1	10	14
June	1.16	5	0	0	5	4	31.0	26	2	11	23
July	4.50	3	2	0	6	6	36.0	39	4	11	31
August	4.24	3	2	0	5	5	34.0	28	2	13	29
September/October	3.99	1	3	0	6	6	38.1	35	2	17	37
Starter	3.60	14	8	0	26	26	165.0	145	11	65	140
Reliever	1.35	1	0	0	6	0	6.2	7	1	4	1
0-3 Days Rest	0.79	2	0	0	2	2	11.1	10	0	5	13
4 Days Rest	3.76	7	4	0	11	11	76.2	65	7	26	71
5+ Days Rest	3.86	5	4	0	13	13	77.0	70	4	34	56
Pre-All Star	2.26	10	1	0	17	11	79.2	64	5	30	55
Post-All Star	4.60	5	7	0	15	15	92.0	88	7	39	86

	Avg	AB	H	2B	3B	HR	RBI	BB	SO	OBP	SLG
vs. Left	.236	330	78	8	2	8	36	44	59	.326	.345
vs. Right	.241	307	74	13	2	4	30	25	82	.322	.336
Inning 1-6	.235	523	123	18	4	9	55	58	116	.326	.337
Inning 7+	.254	114	29	3	0	3	11	11	25	.317	.360
None on	.240	362	87	11	4	7	7	42	88	.334	.351
Runners on	.236	275	65	10	0	5	59	27	53	.311	.327
Scoring Posn	.245	139	34	5	0	2	49	16	27	.317	.324
Close & Late	.294	34	10	0	0	1	3	2	12	.333	.382
None on/out	.222	171	38	6	2	6	6	14	35	.285	.386
vs. 1st Batr (relief)	.750	4	3	0	0	1	1	2	0	.833	1.500
First Inning Pitched	.254	114	29	3	1	2	13	11	20	.341	.351
First 75 Pitches	.237	438	104	14	4	8	45	46	100	.324	.342
Pitch 76-90	.216	74	16	3	0	1	5	10	17	.333	.297
Pitch 91-105	.266	64	17	2	0	2	10	8	13	.333	.391
Pitch 106+	.246	61	15	2	0	1	6	5	11	.303	.328
First Pitch	.224	85	19	5	0	1	9	1	0	.253	.318
Ahead in Count	.159	270	43	5	0	5	24	0	122	.183	.233
Behind in Count	.349	172	60	6	2	5	23	31	0	.450	.494
Two Strikes	.159	309	49	7	2	6	25	37	141	.261	.252

Career (1991-1993)

	ERA	W	L	Sv	G	GS	IP	H	HR	BB	SO
Home	3.01	16	14	0	45	36	233.1	195	9	113	183
Away	4.43	11	15	0	46	34	217.1	225	27	103	148
Day	3.97	3	9	0	19	15	90.2	85	11	44	68
Night	3.63	24	20	0	72	55	360.0	335	25	172	263
Grass	4.29	6	8	0	28	21	138.1	129	16	64	95
Turf	3.43	21	21	0	63	49	312.1	291	20	152	236
April	3.75	3	3	0	16	8	57.2	47	5	29	45
May	4.37	2	4	0	17	8	57.2	62	5	38	29
June	2.18	7	2	0	14	11	74.1	58	5	40	46
July	4.23	5	6	0	12	11	61.2	69	8	22	53
August	4.45	5	7	0	15	15	89.0	89	7	39	66
September/October	3.43	5	7	0	17	17	110.1	95	6	48	92
Starter	3.54	26	27	0	70	70	419.1	381	30	193	322
Reliever	5.74	1	2	0	21	0	31.1	39	6	23	9
0-3 Days Rest	1.27	2	1	0	5	5	28.1	20	0	12	22
4 Days Rest	3.69	13	14	0	32	32	197.1	177	19	97	158
5+ Days Rest	3.72	11	12	0	33	33	193.2	184	11	84	142
Pre-All Star	3.25	15	9	0	50	30	213.0	190	18	111	138
Post-All Star	4.09	12	20	0	41	40	237.2	230	18	105	193

	Avg	AB	H	2B	3B	HR	RBI	BB	SO	OBP	SLG
vs. Left	.251	944	237	42	9	20	104	146	168	.351	.378
vs. Right	.243	754	183	33	6	16	81	70	163	.321	.366
Inning 1-6	.239	1446	346	63	10	29	151	182	286	.331	.357
Inning 7+	.294	252	74	12	5	7	34	34	45	.377	.464
None on	.247	915	226	43	9	21	21	125	199	.345	.383
Runners on	.248	783	194	32	6	15	164	91	132	.329	.361
Scoring Posn	.223	458	102	17	2	9	139	68	87	.318	.328
Close & Late	.264	87	23	3	2	2	10	11	21	.343	.414
None on/out	.244	426	104	22	7	13	13	54	91	.332	.420
vs. 1st Batr (relief)	.357	14	5	0	1	1	1	7	2	.571	.714
First Inning Pitched	.244	332	81	14	3	6	41	53	61	.356	.358
First 75 Pitches	.248	1294	321	55	11	27	141	162	254	.338	.370
Pitch 76-90	.249	189	47	13	3	6	22	26	42	.350	.444
Pitch 91-105	.264	140	37	5	1	2	13	15	21	.331	.357
Pitch 106+	.200	75	15	2	0	1	9	13	14	.311	.267
First Pitch	.283	272	77	17	1	5	27	7	0	.314	.408
Ahead in Count	.171	683	117	18	4	12	59	0	291	.183	.262
Behind in Count	.307	437	134	25	7	11	54	124	0	.458	.471
Two Strikes	.170	740	126	19	4	12	58	85	331	.263	.255

Pitcher vs. Batter (career)

Pitches Best Vs.	Avg	AB	H	2B	3B	HR	RBI	BB	SO	OBP	SLG
Jay Bell	.067	15	1	0	0	0	0	0	2	.067	.067
Dave Hansen	.071	14	1	1	0	0	0	1	0	.133	.143
Felix Jose	.111	9	1	0	0	0	0	2	2	.273	.111
Benito Santiago	.133	15	2	0	0	0	0	0	3	.133	.133
Jeff Blauser	.158	19	3	0	0	0	1	1	4	.200	.158

Pitches Worst Vs.	Avg	AB	H	2B	3B	HR	RBI	BB	SO	OBP	SLG
Willie McGee	.588	17	10	2	0	0	3	3	3	.650	.706
Kevin Mitchell	.500	10	5	1	0	2	5	3	0	.571	1.200
Ray Lankford	.467	15	7	3	0	1	4	3	3	.556	.867
Eddie Murray	.400	15	6	2	0	1	4	4	3	.526	.733
Ryne Sandberg	.375	8	3	2	0	1	4	3	1	.500	1.000

Paul Kilgus — Cardinals

Age 32 – Pitches Left (groundball pitcher)

	ERA	W	L	Sv	G	GS	IP	BB	SO	Avg	H	2B	3B	HR	RBI	OBP	SLG	GF	IR	IRS	Hld	SvOp	SB	CS	GB	FB	G/F
1993 Season	0.63	1	0	1	22	1	28.2	8	21	.180	18	3	0	1	2	.248	.240	7	14	1	7	1	4	2	34	32	1.06
Last Five Years	4.24	7	12	4	106	24	252.2	88	121	.268	261	49	8	20	122	.331	.396	25	61	17	12	4	12	10	426	262	1.63

1993 Season

	ERA	W	L	Sv	G	GS	IP	H	HR	BB	SO
Home	1.42	0	0	0	9	0	6.1	5	0	3	4
Away	0.40	1	0	1	13	1	22.1	13	1	5	17

	Avg	AB	H	2B	3B	HR	RBI	BB	SO	OBP	SLG
vs. Left	.160	25	4	2	0	1	1	3	8	.276	.360
vs. Right	.187	75	14	1	0	0	1	5	13	.238	.200

Last Five Years

	ERA	W	L	Sv	G	GS	IP	H	HR	BB	SO
Home	4.77	3	6	1	53	13	134.0	146	14	45	56
Away	3.64	4	6	3	53	11	118.2	115	6	43	65
Day	3.72	2	4	1	42	11	111.1	116	7	37	45
Night	4.65	5	8	3	64	13	141.1	145	13	51	76
Grass	3.89	4	9	2	70	19	196.2	192	17	65	95
Turf	5.46	3	3	2	36	5	56.0	69	3	23	26
April	4.37	2	2	0	19	5	59.2	63	9	21	23
May	3.78	2	3	0	16	6	52.1	51	1	17	21
June	6.19	2	5	2	30	5	48.0	57	4	19	24
July	3.86	1	2	1	15	4	42.0	42	1	12	22
August	21.60	0	0	0	4	0	1.2	6	1	2	0
September/October	2.39	0	0	1	22	4	49.0	42	4	17	31
Starter	4.53	6	10	0	24	24	129.0	141	8	42	56
Reliever	3.93	1	2	4	82	0	123.2	120	12	46	65
0 Days rest	2.00	0	0	1	9	0	9.0	7	1	2	8
1 or 2 Days rest	4.52	0	2	1	43	0	63.2	64	7	27	37
3+ Days rest	3.53	1	0	2	30	0	51.0	49	4	17	20
Pre-All Star	4.75	6	10	3	70	16	168.2	181	14	60	73
Post-All Star	3.21	1	2	1	36	8	84.0	80	6	28	48

	Avg	AB	H	2B	3B	HR	RBI	BB	SO	OBP	SLG
vs. Left	.238	231	55	12	2	6	38	24	32	.322	.385
vs. Right	.277	744	206	37	6	14	84	64	89	.334	.399
Inning 1-6	.259	637	165	30	8	10	78	54	78	.319	.378
Inning 7+	.284	338	96	19	0	10	44	34	43	.353	.429
None on	.263	537	141	22	3	10	10	41	70	.322	.371
Runners on	.274	438	120	27	5	10	112	47	51	.342	.427
Scoring Posn	.264	239	63	14	3	6	98	38	30	.357	.423
Close & Late	.284	102	29	4	0	4	12	9	9	.345	.441
None on/out	.250	240	60	9	1	7	7	14	30	.302	.383
vs. 1st Batr (relief)	.282	71	20	6	0	1	9	7	7	.358	.408
First Inning Pitched	.298	346	103	22	2	5	61	37	48	.364	.416
First 15 Pitches	.282	305	86	19	1	3	31	32	33	.352	.380
Pitch 16-30	.252	222	56	8	2	9	46	21	40	.317	.428
Pitch 31-45	.252	155	39	5	0	2	9	12	18	.310	.323
Pitch 46+	.273	293	80	17	5	6	36	23	30	.331	.427
First Pitch	.285	158	45	14	0	2	25	10	0	.326	.411
Ahead in Count	.214	384	82	10	2	3	35	0	102	.223	.273
Behind in Count	.307	274	84	18	2	10	38	46	0	.406	.496
Two Strikes	.200	355	71	9	3	2	29	32	121	.274	.259

Pitcher vs. Batter (career)

Pitches Best Vs.	Avg	AB	H	2B	3B	HR	RBI	BB	SO	OBP	SLG
Kevin Seitzer	.091	11	1	1	0	0	0	1	2	.167	.182
Steve Balboni	.118	17	2	0	0	1	4	0	6	.118	.294
Benito Santiago	.154	13	2	0	0	0	0	0	3	.154	.154
Ozzie Guillen	.182	11	2	0	0	0	1	0	1	.182	.182
B.J. Surhoff	.182	11	2	0	0	0	0	1	2	.250	.182

Pitches Worst Vs.	Avg	AB	H	2B	3B	HR	RBI	BB	SO	OBP	SLG
Larry Sheets	.600	10	6	0	0	2	5	1	0	.636	1.200
Mark McGwire	.556	9	5	2	0	2	4	4	0	.692	1.444
Bo Jackson	.500	14	7	2	0	2	4	0	4	.500	1.071
Gary Redus	.364	11	4	2	1	0	2	1	1	.417	.727
Wally Joyner	.333	15	5	1	0	2	5	1	0	.375	.800

Jeff King — Pirates

Age 29 – Bats Right (flyball hitter)

	Avg	G	AB	R	H	2B	3B	HR	RBI	BB	SO	HBP	GDP	SB	CS	OBP	SLG	IBB	SH	SF	#Pit	#P/PA	GB	FB	G/F
1993 Season	.295	158	611	82	180	35	3	9	98	59	54	4	17	8	6	.356	.406	4	1	8	2428	3.55	239	212	1.13
Career (1989-1993)	.252	523	1786	231	450	87	10	46	253	141	209	10	43	22	18	.306	.389	12	13	25	7039	3.56	646	657	0.98

1993 Season

	Avg	AB	H	2B	3B	HR	RBI	BB	SO	OBP	SLG
vs. Left	.324	188	61	12	1	4	34	18	13	.383	.463
vs. Right	.281	423	119	23	2	5	64	41	41	.345	.381
Groundball	.325	194	63	11	2	2	38	22	13	.399	.433
Flyball	.277	101	28	8	0	4	19	8	9	.321	.475
Home	.306	297	91	18	3	4	60	30	25	.366	.428
Away	.283	314	89	17	0	5	38	29	29	.347	.385
Day	.299	157	47	13	1	2	31	14	8	.351	.433
Night	.293	454	133	22	2	7	67	45	46	.358	.396
Grass	.230	196	45	9	0	1	20	21	22	.305	.291
Turf	.325	415	135	26	3	8	78	38	32	.381	.460
First Pitch	.388	80	31	5	1	2	17	4	0	.407	.550
Ahead in Count	.280	157	44	11	0	5	29	26	0	.384	.446
Behind in Count	.272	254	69	9	1	2	35	0	47	.273	.339
Two Strikes	.268	220	59	11	1	1	26	29	54	.353	.341

	Avg	AB	H	2B	3B	HR	RBI	BB	SO	OBP	SLG
Scoring Posn	.303	178	54	12	2	2	86	25	13	.383	.427
Close & Late	.257	105	27	4	0	0	11	11	15	.339	.295
None on/out	.333	174	58	14	0	3	3	11	10	.376	.466
Batting #4	.279	448	125	29	2	4	68	48	38	.349	.379
Batting #5	.361	97	35	5	1	5	26	9	6	.409	.588
Other	.303	66	20	1	0	0	4	2	10	.329	.318
April	.261	88	23	4	0	0	7	13	8	.356	.307
May	.216	102	22	5	0	2	18	5	9	.261	.324
June	.362	105	38	5	1	3	17	9	13	.409	.514
July	.320	103	33	5	0	2	18	11	6	.393	.427
August	.301	103	31	8	2	1	22	8	7	.345	.447
September/October	.300	110	33	8	0	1	16	13	11	.368	.400
Pre-All Star	.291	337	98	15	1	7	51	31	32	.352	.404
Post-All Star	.299	274	82	20	2	2	47	28	22	.362	.409

1993 By Position

Position	Avg	AB	H	2B	3B	HR	RBI	BB	SO	OBP	SLG	G	GS	Innings	PO	A	E	DP	Fld Pct	Rng Fctr	In Zone	Outs	Zone Rtg	MLB Zone
As 3b	.296	605	179	34	3	9	98	57	53	.356	.407	156	155	1366.2	105	354	17	27	.964	3.02	467	394	.844	.834

Career (1989-1993)

	Avg	AB	H	2B	3B	HR	RBI	BB	SO	OBP	SLG
vs. Left	.263	778	205	45	7	20	114	69	74	.321	.416
vs. Right	.243	1008	245	42	3	26	139	72	135	.295	.368
Groundball	.246	602	148	25	5	11	84	37	62	.294	.359
Flyball	.260	366	95	22	2	17	58	30	43	.312	.470
Home	.260	905	235	46	6	25	147	71	99	.312	.407
Away	.244	881	215	41	4	21	106	70	110	.300	.371
Day	.263	502	132	27	2	13	80	40	55	.314	.402
Night	.248	1284	318	60	8	33	173	101	154	.303	.384
Grass	.234	478	112	24	1	8	54	43	67	.296	.339
Turf	.258	1308	338	63	9	38	199	98	142	.310	.407
First Pitch	.275	233	64	14	2	6	36	9	0	.305	.429
Ahead in Count	.285	431	123	24	3	22	82	68	0	.379	.508

	Avg	AB	H	2B	3B	HR	RBI	BB	SO	OBP	SLG
Scoring Posn	.253	517	131	22	7	7	194	54	71	.318	.364
Close & Late	.218	316	69	10	1	6	37	27	42	.286	.313
None on/out	.283	463	131	29	0	15	15	19	36	.313	.443
Batting #4	.274	482	132	31	3	5	73	49	42	.341	.382
Batting #6	.258	520	134	30	3	14	69	39	72	.307	.408
Other	.235	784	184	26	4	27	111	53	95	.284	.381
April	.227	247	56	5	3	2	23	31	29	.314	.296
May	.223	264	59	13	0	8	35	13	28	.261	.364
June	.254	272	69	10	3	7	36	21	35	.311	.390
July	.286	245	70	14	0	7	37	24	22	.353	.429
August	.265	359	95	23	3	12	62	20	44	.298	.446
September/October	.253	399	101	22	1	10	60	32	51	.305	.388

Career (1989-1993)	Avg	AB	H	2B	3B	HR	RBI	BB	SO	OBP	SLG		Avg	AB	H	2B	3B	HR	RBI	BB	SO	OBP	SLG
Behind in Count	.228	772	176	29	3	12	93	0	170	.230	.320	Pre-All Star	.242	851	206	30	6	20	107	69	98	.301	.362
Two Strikes	.203	698	142	24	4	10	64	63	209	.272	.292	Post-All Star	.261	935	244	57	4	26	146	72	111	.311	.414

Batter vs. Pitcher (career)																							
Hits Best Against	Avg	AB	H	2B	3B	HR	RBI	BB	SO	OBP	SLG	Hits Worst Against	Avg	AB	H	2B	3B	HR	RBI	BB	SO	OBP	SLG
Charlie Hough	.500	10	5	1	0	0	2	2	1	.583	.600	John Wetteland	.000	13	0	0	0	0	0	1	5	.071	.000
Ron Darling	.455	11	5	1	0	1	3	1	2	.500	.818	Mel Rojas	.000	12	0	0	0	0	0	1	1	.077	.000
Steve Avery	.400	20	8	3	0	1	6	2	3	.435	.700	Jose Rijo	.091	11	1	0	0	0	1	0	4	.083	.091
Rheal Cormier	.385	13	5	1	0	1	3	1	0	.429	.692	Paul Assenmacher	.091	11	1	0	0	0	1	0	2	.091	.091
Steve Wilson	.333	15	5	1	0	2	4	2	2	.412	.800	Mike Maddux	.091	11	1	0	0	0	0	0	1	.091	.091

Kevin King — Mariners

Age 25 – Pitches Left

	ERA	W	L	Sv	G	GS	IP	BB	SO	Avg	H	2B	3B	HR	RBI	OBP	SLG	GF	IR	IRS	Hld	SvOp	SB	CS	GB	FB	G/F
1993 Season	6.17	0	1	0	13	0	11.2	4	8	.231	9	3	0	3	10	.304	.538	3	15	4	4	1	1	0	15	11	1.36

1993 Season	ERA	W	L	Sv	G	GS	IP	H	HR	BB	SO		Avg	AB	H	2B	3B	HR	RBI	BB	SO	OBP	SLG
Home	0.00	0	0	0	6	0	4.1	0	0	1	2	vs. Left	.286	14	4	2	0	1	4	2	3	.412	.643
Away	9.82	0	1	0	7	0	7.1	9	3	3	6	vs. Right	.200	25	5	1	0	2	6	2	5	.241	.480

Wayne Kirby — Indians

Age 30 – Bats Left (groundball hitter)

	Avg	G	AB	R	H	2B	3B	HR	RBI	BB	SO	HBP	GDP	SB	CS	OBP	SLG	IBB	SH	SF	#Pit	#P/PA	GB	FB	G/F
1993 Season	.269	131	458	71	123	19	5	6	60	37	58	3	8	17	5	.323	.371	2	7	6	1807	3.54	182	118	1.54
Career (1991-1993)	.260	173	519	84	135	22	5	7	66	42	66	3	11	18	10	.315	.362	2	8	7	2039	3.52	208	135	1.54

1993 Season	Avg	AB	H	2B	3B	HR	RBI	BB	SO	OBP	SLG		Avg	AB	H	2B	3B	HR	RBI	BB	SO	OBP	SLG
vs. Left	.231	108	25	3	1	0	9	12	21	.320	.278	Scoring Posn	.300	120	36	5	3	4	53	11	16	.343	.492
vs. Right	.280	350	98	16	4	6	51	25	37	.325	.400	Close & Late	.231	65	15	4	1	0	8	8	14	.307	.323
Groundball	.284	67	19	2	2	0	13	7	13	.355	.373	None on/out	.177	96	17	2	0	0	0	8	13	.248	.198
Flyball	.253	75	19	3	0	3	10	7	9	.313	.413	Batting #1	.250	64	16	1	2	0	10	5	11	.324	.328
Home	.289	232	67	10	3	4	29	19	29	.342	.409	Batting #2	.282	380	107	18	3	6	50	29	45	.329	.392
Away	.248	226	56	9	2	2	31	18	29	.304	.332	Other	.000	14	0	0	0	0	0	3	2	.176	.000
Day	.255	149	38	5	3	2	24	10	16	.303	.369	April	.000	0	0	0	0	0	0	0	0	.000	.000
Night	.275	309	85	14	2	4	36	27	42	.333	.372	May	.333	81	27	3	1	0	10	2	8	.345	.395
Grass	.267	393	105	14	5	6	51	34	50	.326	.374	June	.273	88	24	6	0	2	12	10	12	.343	.409
Turf	.277	65	18	5	0	0	9	3	8	.309	.354	July	.256	82	21	4	1	2	14	8	7	.319	.402
First Pitch	.357	56	20	0	0	1	8	2	0	.367	.411	August	.250	104	26	1	3	2	15	9	15	.319	.375
Ahead in Count	.320	100	32	8	1	1	13	25	0	.456	.450	September/October	.243	103	25	5	0	0	9	8	16	.297	.291
Behind in Count	.205	220	45	8	4	3	31	0	55	.205	.318	Pre-All Star	.296	196	58	9	1	3	28	13	21	.336	.398
Two Strikes	.180	200	36	7	3	3	26	10	58	.221	.290	Post-All Star	.248	262	65	10	4	3	32	24	37	.314	.351

1993 By Position																								
Position	Avg	AB	H	2B	3B	HR	RBI	BB	SO	OBP	SLG	G	GS	Innings	PO	A	E	DP	Fld Pct	Rng Fctr	In Zone	Outs	Zone Rtg	MLB Zone
As Pinch Hitter	.000	10	0	0	0	0	0	1	2	.091	.000	12	0	---	---	---	---	---	---	---	---	---	---	---
As cf	.233	60	14	2	1	0	7	5	11	.303	.300	15	12	120.0	38	4	0	0	1.000	3.15	46	38	.826	.829
As rf	.276	380	105	16	4	6	50	30	43	.329	.387	113	98	859.1	225	13	5	5	.979	2.49	242	213	.880	.826

Ryan Klesko — Braves

Age 23 – Bats Left

	Avg	G	AB	R	H	2B	3B	HR	RBI	BB	SO	HBP	GDP	SB	CS	OBP	SLG	IBB	SH	SF	#Pit	#P/PA	GB	FB	G/F
1993 Season	.353	22	17	3	6	1	0	2	5	3	4	0	0	0	0	.450	.765	1	0	0	75	3.75	3	6	0.50
Career (1992-1993)	.194	35	31	3	6	1	0	2	6	3	9	1	0	0	0	.286	.419	1	0	0	125	3.57	7	10	0.70

1993 Season	Avg	AB	H	2B	3B	HR	RBI	BB	SO	OBP	SLG		Avg	AB	H	2B	3B	HR	RBI	BB	SO	OBP	SLG
vs. Left	.000	1	0	0	0	0	0	1	1	.500	.000	Scoring Posn	.400	5	2	1	0	1	4	2	0	.571	1.200
vs. Right	.375	16	6	1	0	2	5	2	3	.444	.813	Close & Late	.455	11	5	1	0	1	3	1	3	.500	.818

Joe Klink — Marlins

Age 32 – Pitches Left

	ERA	W	L	Sv	G	GS	IP	BB	SO	Avg	H	2B	3B	HR	RBI	OBP	SLG	GF	IR	IRS	Hld	SvOp	SB	CS	GB	FB	G/F
1993 Season	5.02	0	2	0	59	0	37.2	24	22	.266	37	8	1	0	22	.367	.338	10	56	14	9	0	5	3	60	34	1.76
Last Five Years	3.88	10	5	3	161	0	139.1	63	75	.254	131	22	3	5	59	.339	.337	39	133	25	29	5	11	5	198	150	1.32

1993 Season	ERA	W	L	Sv	G	GS	IP	H	HR	BB	SO		Avg	AB	H	2B	3B	HR	RBI	BB	SO	OBP	SLG
Home	4.05	0	0	0	32	0	20.0	14	0	13	13	vs. Left	.216	74	16	2	0	0	6	13	12	.333	.243
Away	6.11	0	2	0	27	0	17.2	23	0	11	9	vs. Right	.323	65	21	6	1	0	16	11	10	.405	.446
Starter	0.00	0	0	0	0	0	0.0	0	0	0	0	Scoring Posn	.293	58	17	4	0	0	22	12	13	.397	.362
Reliever	5.02	0	2	0	59	0	37.2	37	0	24	22	Close & Late	.235	51	12	2	0	0	2	10	7	.361	.275
0 Days rest	8.31	0	0	0	15	0	8.2	13	0	5	5	None on/out	.321	28	9	2	0	0	0	4	1	.406	.393
1 or 2 Days rest	5.59	0	0	0	21	0	9.2	9	0	9	4	First Pitch	.333	15	5	1	1	0	1	3	0	.444	.533
3+ Days rest	3.26	0	2	0	23	0	19.1	15	0	10	13	Ahead in Count	.254	67	17	3	0	0	9	0	18	.250	.299
Pre-All Star	3.79	0	1	0	28	0	19.0	14	0	10	10	Behind in Count	.375	32	12	3	0	0	8	12	0	.545	.469
Post-All Star	6.27	0	1	0	31	0	18.2	23	0	14	12	Two Strikes	.190	63	12	2	0	0	8	9	22	.288	.222

Last Five Years

	ERA	W	L	Sv	G	GS	IP	H	HR	BB	SO
Home	3.12	4	1	1	82	0	69.1	54	1	24	37
Away	4.63	6	4	2	79	0	70.0	77	4	39	38
Day	3.05	1	2	2	48	0	44.1	30	1	17	29
Night	4.26	9	3	1	113	0	95.0	101	4	46	46
Grass	3.36	8	3	3	130	0	112.2	98	5	46	61
Turf	6.08	2	2	0	31	0	26.2	33	0	17	14
April	3.32	0	2	1	19	0	19.0	13	1	8	10
May	3.04	4	1	1	29	0	26.2	19	2	6	10
June	3.31	1	0	0	21	0	16.1	18	1	11	10
July	1.90	2	0	0	23	0	23.2	22	1	2	14
August	5.79	2	2	0	35	0	28.0	29	0	16	11
September/October	5.26	1	0	1	34	0	25.2	30	0	20	20
Starter	0.00	0	0	0	0	0	0.0	0	0	0	0
Reliever	3.88	10	5	3	161	0	139.1	131	5	63	75
0 Days rest	6.57	3	0	2	34	0	24.2	28	0	11	19
1 or 2 Days rest	3.29	7	3	1	70	0	63.0	61	3	30	28
3+ Days rest	3.31	0	2	0	57	0	51.2	42	2	22	28
Pre-All Star	3.00	5	3	2	74	0	66.0	54	4	25	31
Post-All Star	4.66	5	2	1	87	0	73.1	77	1	38	44

	Avg	AB	H	2B	3B	HR	RBI	BB	SO	OBP	SLG
vs. Left	.229	223	51	7	1	3	19	26	38	.315	.309
vs. Right	.273	293	80	15	2	2	40	37	37	.357	.358
Inning 1-6	.366	82	30	6	2	0	24	14	17	.460	.488
Inning 7+	.233	434	101	16	1	5	35	49	58	.314	.309
None on	.265	245	65	10	2	3	3	18	34	.323	.359
Runners on	.244	271	66	12	1	2	56	45	41	.352	.317
Scoring Posn	.243	177	43	7	1	1	52	33	28	.360	.311
Close & Late	.229	166	38	6	0	2	13	23	23	.326	.301
None on/out	.302	116	35	4	1	2	2	7	13	.347	.405
vs. 1st Batr (relief)	.252	143	36	5	0	0	9	13	18	.316	.287
First Inning Pitched	.254	421	107	15	2	4	52	51	59	.340	.328
First 15 Pitches	.257	404	104	15	3	4	37	41	53	.331	.339
Pitch 16-30	.250	100	25	6	0	1	20	21	19	.380	.340
Pitch 31-45	.167	12	2	1	0	0	2	1	3	.231	.250
Pitch 46+	.000	0	0	0	0	0	0	0	0	.000	.000
First Pitch	.383	60	23	4	1	1	6	7	0	.464	.533
Ahead in Count	.211	228	48	8	1	1	20	0	62	.213	.268
Behind in Count	.310	116	36	7	1	3	27	30	0	.452	.466
Two Strikes	.192	219	42	8	1	0	17	26	75	.279	.237

Joe Kmak — Brewers

Age 31 – Bats Right (groundball hitter)

	Avg	G	AB	R	H	2B	3B	HR	RBI	BB	SO	HBP	GDP	SB	CS	OBP	SLG	IBB	SH	SF	#Pit	#P/PA	GB	FB	G/F
1993 Season	.218	51	110	9	24	5	0	0	7	14	13	2	2	6	2	.317	.264	0	1	0	485	3.82	52	24	2.17

1993 Season

	Avg	AB	H	2B	3B	HR	RBI	BB	SO	OBP	SLG
vs. Left	.221	68	15	2	0	0	3	7	8	.303	.250
vs. Right	.214	42	9	3	0	0	4	7	5	.340	.286
Home	.213	47	10	2	0	0	3	6	6	.315	.255
Away	.222	63	14	3	0	0	4	8	7	.319	.270
First Pitch	.385	13	5	1	0	0	2	0	0	.385	.462
Ahead in Count	.161	31	5	1	0	0	2	9	0	.366	.194
Behind in Count	.234	47	11	3	0	0	2	0	10	.250	.298
Two Strikes	.191	47	9	3	0	0	2	5	13	.283	.255

	Avg	AB	H	2B	3B	HR	RBI	BB	SO	OBP	SLG
Scoring Posn	.316	19	6	1	0	0	6	5	2	.458	.368
Close & Late	.250	12	3	1	0	0	1	1	0	.308	.333
None on/out	.222	27	6	1	0	0	0	5	4	.364	.259
Batting #6	.000	1	0	0	0	0	0	0	0	.000	.000
Batting #9	.220	109	24	5	0	0	7	14	13	.320	.266
Other	.000	0	0	0	0	0	0	0	0	.000	.000
Pre-All Star	.218	110	24	5	0	0	7	14	13	.317	.264
Post-All Star	.000	0	0	0	0	0	0	0	0	.000	.000

Chuck Knoblauch — Twins

Age 25 – Bats Right (groundball hitter)

	Avg	G	AB	R	H	2B	3B	HR	RBI	BB	SO	HBP	GDP	SB	CS	OBP	SLG	IBB	SH	SF	#Pit	#P/PA	GB	FB	G/F
1993 Season	.277	153	602	82	167	27	4	2	41	65	44	9	11	29	11	.354	.346	1	4	5	2370	3.46	277	158	1.75
Career (1991-1993)	.285	459	1767	264	504	70	16	5	147	212	144	18	27	88	29	.364	.351	2	7	22	7170	3.54	807	479	1.68

1993 Season

	Avg	AB	H	2B	3B	HR	RBI	BB	SO	OBP	SLG
vs. Left	.269	156	42	9	0	0	10	10	13	.321	.327
vs. Right	.280	446	125	18	4	2	31	55	31	.365	.352
Groundball	.256	117	30	6	1	1	9	7	12	.304	.350
Flyball	.302	126	38	6	1	0	11	10	13	.360	.365
Home	.298	312	93	12	1	2	22	33	21	.369	.362
Away	.255	290	74	15	3	0	19	32	23	.337	.328
Day	.320	178	57	9	1	1	15	21	11	.398	.399
Night	.259	424	110	18	3	1	26	44	33	.335	.323
Grass	.265	223	59	11	2	0	15	25	15	.346	.332
Turf	.285	379	108	16	2	2	26	40	29	.358	.354
First Pitch	.300	110	33	11	0	0	7	1	0	.313	.400
Ahead in Count	.263	160	42	3	2	2	8	40	0	.409	.344
Behind in Count	.275	229	63	9	2	0	16	0	37	.288	.332
Two Strikes	.244	201	49	4	2	0	14	24	44	.336	.284

	Avg	AB	H	2B	3B	HR	RBI	BB	SO	OBP	SLG
Scoring Posn	.262	126	33	7	1	0	37	15	10	.351	.333
Close & Late	.236	89	21	3	0	0	7	14	7	.333	.270
None on/out	.247	194	48	5	1	0	0	13	15	.298	.284
Batting #1	.272	320	87	13	2	0	16	38	24	.358	.325
Batting #2	.287	275	79	13	2	2	24	26	20	.352	.371
Other	.143	7	1	1	0	0	1	1	0	.250	.286
April	.197	76	15	4	0	0	4	16	9	.344	.250
May	.348	92	32	6	1	0	10	10	8	.430	.435
June	.236	106	25	1	1	0	6	9	5	.293	.264
July	.313	96	30	6	0	1	8	8	3	.371	.406
August	.306	108	33	7	1	1	7	14	8	.387	.417
September/October	.258	124	32	3	1	0	6	8	11	.308	.298
Pre-All Star	.278	306	85	13	2	1	25	37	23	.364	.343
Post-All Star	.277	296	82	14	2	1	16	28	21	.343	.348

1993 By Position

Position	Avg	AB	H	2B	3B	HR	RBI	BB	SO	OBP	SLG	G	GS	Innings	PO	A	E	DP	Fld Pct	Rng Fctr	In Zone	Outs	Zone Rtg	MLB Zone
As 2b	.277	589	163	26	4	2	40	63	44	.353	.345	148	147	1273.0	298	426	9	99	.988	5.12	486	424	.872	.895

Career (1991-1993)

	Avg	AB	H	2B	3B	HR	RBI	BB	SO	OBP	SLG
vs. Left	.278	428	119	23	3	1	25	41	34	.347	.353
vs. Right	.288	1339	385	47	13	4	122	171	110	.369	.351
Groundball	.301	439	132	17	4	2	40	38	35	.355	.371
Flyball	.295	387	114	16	2	2	34	55	43	.381	.362
Home	.304	888	270	29	8	3	71	112	62	.382	.365
Away	.266	879	234	41	8	2	76	100	82	.344	.338
Day	.315	514	162	23	7	1	52	67	40	.396	.393
Night	.273	1253	342	47	9	4	95	145	104	.350	.334
Grass	.275	677	186	30	4	1	56	72	53	.347	.335
Turf	.292	1090	318	40	12	4	91	140	91	.374	.361
First Pitch	.316	294	93	20	1	0	28	1	0	.319	.391
Ahead in Count	.314	417	131	16	6	4	42	139	0	.483	.410

	Avg	AB	H	2B	3B	HR	RBI	BB	SO	OBP	SLG
Scoring Posn	.276	388	107	13	6	0	135	57	40	.359	.340
Close & Late	.260	262	68	10	1	0	26	30	22	.334	.305
None on/out	.288	500	144	18	3	2	2	44	39	.353	.348
Batting #1	.274	669	183	25	8	1	39	78	66	.353	.339
Batting #2	.294	1070	315	44	8	4	106	130	78	.372	.362
Other	.214	28	6	1	0	0	2	4	0	.313	.250
April	.273	231	63	7	2	1	21	32	25	.359	.333
May	.317	281	89	19	2	0	28	37	23	.401	.399
June	.258	291	75	6	3	0	24	40	14	.349	.299
July	.288	292	84	15	4	1	26	29	20	.350	.377
August	.293	328	96	15	2	2	21	30	36	.353	.369
September/October	.282	344	97	8	3	1	27	44	26	.369	.331

Career (1991-1993)

	Avg	AB	H	2B	3B	HR	RBI	BB	SO	OBP	SLG
Behind in Count	.253	746	186	21	7	0	50	0	122	.257	.300
Two Strikes	.250	645	161	18	7	0	47	72	144	.329	.299

	Avg	AB	H	2B	3B	HR	RBI	BB	SO	OBP	SLG
Pre-All Star	.287	899	258	38	7	2	83	118	68	.372	.352
Post-All Star	.283	868	246	32	9	3	64	94	76	.355	.351

Batter vs. Pitcher (career)

Hits Best Against	Avg	AB	H	2B	3B	HR	RBI	BB	SO	OBP	SLG
Bob Welch	.467	15	7	1	0	0	2	2	0	.529	.533
Frank Viola	.462	13	6	1	0	0	0	2	0	.533	.538
Mark Gubicza	.438	16	7	0	1	0	4	1	1	.471	.563
Mike Mussina	.400	20	8	1	0	1	1	2	1	.455	.600
Joe Hesketh	.364	11	4	2	1	0	1	1	2	.417	.727

Hits Worst Against	Avg	AB	H	2B	3B	HR	RBI	BB	SO	OBP	SLG
Mike Magnante	.000	11	0	0	0	0	0	1	1	.083	.000
Charles Nagy	.091	11	1	0	0	0	1	0	0	.083	.091
Jose Mesa	.100	10	1	0	0	0	1	2	1	.231	.100
Todd Frohwirth	.143	14	2	0	0	0	0	0	1	.143	.143
Nolan Ryan	.167	18	3	0	0	0	0	0	4	.167	.167

Randy Knorr — Blue Jays

Age 25 – Bats Right

	Avg	G	AB	R	H	2B	3B	HR	RBI	BB	SO	HBP	GDP	SB	CS	OBP	SLG	IBB	SH	SF	#Pit	#P/PA	GB	FB	G/F
1993 Season	.248	39	101	11	25	3	2	4	20	9	29	0	2	0	0	.309	.406	0	2	0	413	3.69	30	25	1.20
Career (1991-1993)	.248	50	121	12	30	3	2	5	22	11	35	0	2	0	0	.311	.430	1	2	0	488	3.64	34	32	1.06

1993 Season

	Avg	AB	H	2B	3B	HR	RBI	BB	SO	OBP	SLG
vs. Left	.229	35	8	1	1	1	7	4	10	.308	.400
vs. Right	.258	66	17	2	1	3	13	5	19	.310	.455

	Avg	AB	H	2B	3B	HR	RBI	BB	SO	OBP	SLG
Scoring Posn	.310	29	9	2	0	2	14	3	10	.375	.586
Close & Late	.222	9	2	0	1	0	1	1	3	.300	.444

Kurt Knudsen — Tigers

Age 27 – Pitches Right (flyball pitcher)

	ERA	W	L	Sv	G	GS	IP	BB	SO	Avg	H	2B	3B	HR	RBI	OBP	SLG	GF	IR	IRS	Hld	SvOp	SB	CS	GB	FB	G/F
1993 Season	4.78	3	2	2	30	0	37.2	16	29	.281	41	5	0	9	28	.361	.500	7	27	11	6	4	2	3	43	48	0.90
Career (1992-1993)	4.65	5	5	7	78	1	108.1	57	80	.270	111	18	1	18	71	.362	.450	21	69	24	14	11	8	8	93	152	0.61

1993 Season

	ERA	W	L	Sv	G	GS	IP	H	HR	BB	SO
Home	5.28	0	1	1	11	0	15.1	18	3	6	10
Away	4.43	3	1	1	19	0	22.1	23	6	10	19
Starter	0.00	0	0	0	0	0	0.0	0	0	0	0
Reliever	4.78	3	2	2	30	0	37.2	41	9	16	29
0 Days rest	1.17	0	0	0	8	0	7.2	7	1	2	5
1 or 2 Days rest	4.30	2	1	0	12	0	14.2	14	4	6	11
3+ Days rest	7.04	1	1	2	10	0	15.1	20	4	8	13
Pre-All Star	4.30	1	1	1	21	0	23.0	26	7	8	17
Post-All Star	5.52	2	1	1	9	0	14.2	15	2	8	12

	Avg	AB	H	2B	3B	HR	RBI	BB	SO	OBP	SLG
vs. Left	.392	51	20	2	0	5	15	8	6	.475	.725
vs. Right	.221	95	21	3	0	4	13	8	23	.296	.379
Scoring Posn	.263	38	10	2	0	2	18	5	7	.354	.474
Close & Late	.231	39	9	0	0	1	2	2	8	.262	.308
None on/out	.286	35	10	1	0	2	2	4	9	.375	.486
First Pitch	.350	20	7	1	0	1	3	2	0	.435	.550
Ahead in Count	.250	72	18	1	0	3	11	0	26	.263	.389
Behind in Count	.360	25	9	1	0	4	7	6	0	.484	.880
Two Strikes	.214	70	15	2	0	4	16	8	29	.305	.414

Mark Knudson — Rockies

Age 33 – Pitches Right

	ERA	W	L	Sv	G	GS	IP	BB	SO	Avg	H	2B	3B	HR	RBI	OBP	SLG	GF	IR	IRS	Hld	SvOp	SB	CS	GB	FB	G/F
1993 Season	22.24	0	0	0	4	0	5.2	5	3	.471	16	1	1	4	15	.538	.912	2	4	2	0	0	0	0	16	9	1.78
Last Five Years	4.55	19	17	0	86	41	332.2	89	129	.280	367	66	10	41	163	.326	.439	5	31	15	2	2	17	16	517	422	1.23

1993 Season

	ERA	W	L	Sv	G	GS	IP	H	HR	BB	SO
Home	24.30	0	0	0	3	0	3.1	9	3	4	2
Away	19.29	0	0	0	1	0	2.1	7	1	1	1

	Avg	AB	H	2B	3B	HR	RBI	BB	SO	OBP	SLG
vs. Left	.364	11	4	0	1	1	4	3	2	.500	.818
vs. Right	.522	23	12	1	0	3	11	2	1	.560	.957

Last Five Years

	ERA	W	L	Sv	G	GS	IP	H	HR	BB	SO
Home	4.45	8	9	0	42	19	161.2	175	18	48	70
Away	4.63	11	8	0	44	22	171.0	192	23	41	59
Day	4.70	9	7	0	30	20	130.1	144	10	40	51
Night	4.45	10	10	0	56	21	202.1	223	31	49	78
Grass	4.33	18	12	0	72	35	284.2	303	35	79	119
Turf	5.81	1	5	0	14	6	48.0	64	6	10	10
April	3.55	4	1	0	11	6	45.2	46	5	13	14
May	6.11	1	3	0	19	7	66.1	94	13	21	25
June	5.31	3	4	0	18	5	61.0	70	8	18	34
July	3.61	3	2	0	17	8	57.1	64	6	15	23
August	4.38	5	4	0	14	9	63.2	63	7	12	22
September/October	3.49	3	3	0	7	6	38.2	30	2	10	11
Starter	4.42	16	13	0	41	41	232.1	257	26	59	78
Reliever	4.84	3	4	0	45	0	100.1	110	15	30	51
0 Days rest	0.00	1	0	0	3	0	6.1	2	0	0	3
1 or 2 Days rest	6.80	1	3	0	23	0	43.2	64	8	16	16
3+ Days rest	3.75	1	1	0	19	0	50.1	44	7	14	32
Pre-All Star	5.12	8	9	0	52	21	190.0	235	29	62	79
Post-All Star	3.79	11	8	0	34	20	142.2	132	12	27	50

	Avg	AB	H	2B	3B	HR	RBI	BB	SO	OBP	SLG
vs. Left	.278	633	176	37	6	16	69	43	59	.321	.431
vs. Right	.281	680	191	29	4	25	94	46	70	.330	.446
Inning 1-6	.285	952	271	52	6	31	126	72	87	.334	.450
Inning 7+	.266	361	96	14	4	10	37	17	42	.302	.410
None on	.291	776	226	47	6	25	25	45	76	.333	.464
Runners on	.263	537	141	19	4	16	138	44	53	.316	.402
Scoring Posn	.282	291	82	11	2	10	121	33	30	.343	.436
Close & Late	.351	114	40	7	2	2	16	4	15	.380	.500
None on/out	.275	338	93	20	3	8	8	19	35	.314	.423
vs. 1st Batr (relief)	.244	41	10	2	0	0	5	4	4	.311	.293
First Inning Pitched	.300	337	101	18	3	12	61	35	37	.365	.478
First 15 Pitches	.306	281	86	14	3	10	40	24	27	.362	.484
Pitch 16-30	.238	261	62	15	0	7	26	18	31	.288	.375
Pitch 31-45	.297	219	65	12	1	7	28	18	19	.346	.457
Pitch 46+	.279	552	154	25	6	17	69	29	52	.316	.438
First Pitch	.323	220	71	12	1	8	27	2	0	.327	.495
Ahead in Count	.239	497	119	16	1	13	53	0	107	.247	.354
Behind in Count	.289	356	103	22	5	14	53	50	0	.373	.497
Two Strikes	.236	488	115	22	2	10	45	36	129	.293	.350

Pitcher vs. Batter (career)

Pitches Best Vs.	Avg	AB	H	2B	3B	HR	RBI	BB	SO	OBP	SLG
Willie Wilson	.100	10	1	0	0	0	0	1	5	.182	.100
Tony Phillips	.143	14	2	1	0	0	1	2	1	.250	.214
Kevin Seitzer	.182	11	2	0	0	0	0	1	1	.250	.182
Mark McGwire	.200	15	3	0	0	0	0	1	5	.250	.200
Lou Whitaker	.200	10	2	0	0	0	0	1	2	.273	.200

Pitches Worst Vs.	Avg	AB	H	2B	3B	HR	RBI	BB	SO	OBP	SLG
Kirby Puckett	.727	11	8	1	0	1	3	1	1	.750	1.091
Joe Carter	.571	14	8	0	0	4	7	0	0	.571	1.429
Ruben Sierra	.556	9	5	2	0	3	7	0	0	.455	1.778
Chili Davis	.538	13	7	2	0	1	5	2	2	.600	.923
George Bell	.455	11	5	0	0	2	4	1	0	.500	1.000

Brian Koelling — Reds

Age 25 – Bats Right

	Avg	G	AB	R	H	2B	3B	HR	RBI	BB	SO	HBP	GDP	SB	CS	OBP	SLG	IBB	SH	SF	#Pit	#P/PA	GB	FB	G/F
1993 Season	.067	7	15	2	1	0	0	0	0	0	2	1	0	0	0	.125	.067	0	0	0	50	3.13	4	6	0.67

1993 Season

	Avg	AB	H	2B	3B	HR	RBI	BB	SO	OBP	SLG		Avg	AB	H	2B	3B	HR	RBI	BB	SO	OBP	SLG
vs. Left	.125	8	1	0	0	0	0	0	0	.125	.125	Scoring Posn	.000	1	0	0	0	0	0	0	0	.000	.000
vs. Right	.000	7	0	0	0	0	0	0	2	.125	.000	Close & Late	.000	0	0	0	0	0	0	0	0	.000	.000

Kevin Koslofski — Royals

Age 27 – Bats Left

	Avg	G	AB	R	H	2B	3B	HR	RBI	BB	SO	HBP	GDP	SB	CS	OBP	SLG	IBB	SH	SF	#Pit	#P/PA	GB	FB	G/F
1993 Season	.269	15	26	4	7	0	0	1	2	4	5	1	1	0	1	.387	.385	0	1	0	128	4.00	4	12	0.33
Career (1992-1993)	.252	70	159	24	40	0	2	4	15	16	28	2	3	2	2	.326	.352	0	4	1	621	3.41	55	49	1.12

1993 Season

	Avg	AB	H	2B	3B	HR	RBI	BB	SO	OBP	SLG		Avg	AB	H	2B	3B	HR	RBI	BB	SO	OBP	SLG
vs. Left	.250	4	1	0	0	0	0	0	2	.250	.250	Scoring Posn	.333	9	3	0	0	0	1	1	1	.400	.333
vs. Right	.273	22	6	0	0	1	2	4	3	.407	.409	Close & Late	.667	6	4	0	0	1	2	1	0	.714	1.167

Tom Kramer — Indians

Age 26 – Pitches Right (flyball pitcher)

	ERA	W	L	Sv	G	GS	IP	BB	SO	Avg	H	2B	3B	HR	RBI	OBP	SLG	GF	IR	IRS	Hld	SvOp	SB	CS	GB	FB	G/F
1993 Season	4.02	7	3	0	39	16	121.0	59	71	.269	126	24	2	19	61	.352	.450	6	19	10	3	2	6	7	116	180	0.64
Career (1991-1993)	4.51	7	3	0	43	16	125.2	65	75	.278	136	27	3	20	72	.361	.467	7	24	15	3	2	6	7	122	188	0.65

1993 Season

	ERA	W	L	Sv	G	GS	IP	H	HR	BB	SO		Avg	AB	H	2B	3B	HR	RBI	BB	SO	OBP	SLG
Home	4.42	3	1	0	15	9	55.0	53	9	28	41	vs. Left	.234	235	55	8	0	10	32	32	29	.328	.396
Away	3.68	4	2	0	24	7	66.0	73	10	31	30	vs. Right	.303	234	71	16	2	9	29	27	42	.375	.504
Starter	4.34	5	2	0	16	16	83.0	78	14	39	47	Scoring Posn	.219	128	28	3	1	4	40	25	22	.346	.352
Reliever	3.32	2	1	0	23	0	38.0	48	5	20	24	Close & Late	.194	36	7	2	0	1	3	8	4	.356	.333
0 Days rest	0.00	0	0	0	1	0	1.1	1	0	2	2	None on/out	.318	110	35	9	0	4	4	17	12	.414	.509
1 or 2 Days rest	4.03	0	1	0	14	0	22.1	29	5	7	12	First Pitch	.373	51	19	3	0	3	8	7	0	.448	.608
3+ Days rest	2.51	2	0	0	8	0	14.1	18	0	11	10	Ahead in Count	.181	182	33	8	1	5	21	0	59	.189	.319
Pre-All Star	3.87	3	2	0	25	9	74.1	70	12	29	50	Behind in Count	.307	127	39	6	1	5	19	32	0	.444	.488
Post-All Star	4.24	4	1	0	14	7	46.2	56	7	30	21	Two Strikes	.202	208	42	8	1	6	23	20	71	.277	.337

Chad Kreuter — Tigers

Age 29 – Bats Both

	Avg	G	AB	R	H	2B	3B	HR	RBI	BB	SO	HBP	GDP	SB	CS	OBP	SLG	IBB	SH	SF	#Pit	#P/PA	GB	FB	G/F
1993 Season	.286	119	374	59	107	23	3	15	51	49	92	3	5	2	1	.371	.484	4	2	3	1754	4.07	108	99	1.09
Last Five Years	.241	298	748	99	180	36	3	22	78	104	180	3	17	2	3	.333	.385	5	12	7	3508	4.01	232	205	1.13

1993 Season

	Avg	AB	H	2B	3B	HR	RBI	BB	SO	OBP	SLG		Avg	AB	H	2B	3B	HR	RBI	BB	SO	OBP	SLG
vs. Left	.209	110	23	4	0	5	17	17	32	.313	.382	Scoring Posn	.216	97	21	6	1	4	35	18	26	.336	.423
vs. Right	.318	264	84	19	3	10	34	32	60	.395	.527	Close & Late	.279	61	17	7	0	1	8	10	19	.380	.443
Groundball	.293	75	22	5	0	1	3	9	16	.376	.400	None on/out	.287	87	25	2	2	3	3	8	17	.347	.460
Flyball	.333	84	28	6	0	5	18	7	19	.398	.583	Batting #7	.305	141	43	11	2	3	12	18	36	.385	.475
Home	.283	198	56	11	1	9	27	21	53	.354	.485	Batting #8	.279	129	36	7	0	8	24	21	33	.386	.519
Away	.290	176	51	12	2	6	24	28	39	.388	.483	Other	.269	104	28	5	1	4	15	10	23	.330	.452
Day	.315	143	45	9	1	5	24	16	30	.393	.497	April	.431	51	22	6	1	3	10	6	7	.492	.765
Night	.268	231	62	14	2	10	27	33	62	.357	.476	May	.324	71	23	4	0	2	8	10	16	.407	.465
Grass	.291	306	89	20	2	12	42	38	75	.371	.487	June	.250	72	18	6	2	0	2	7	14	.316	.389
Turf	.265	68	18	3	1	3	9	11	17	.367	.471	July	.149	67	10	2	0	3	7	8	21	.237	.313
First Pitch	.378	45	17	1	0	0	5	4	0	.429	.400	August	.276	58	16	2	0	3	13	11	17	.400	.466
Ahead in Count	.430	79	34	7	3	7	14	22	0	.554	.861	September/October	.327	55	18	3	0	4	11	7	17	.406	.600
Behind in Count	.164	336	55	13	0	6	30	0	149	.167	.256	Pre-All Star	.303	231	70	17	3	7	24	25	51	.372	.494
Two Strikes	.188	197	37	12	0	5	19	23	92	.270	.325	Post-All Star	.259	143	37	6	0	8	27	24	41	.368	.469

1993 By Position

Position	Avg	AB	H	2B	3B	HR	RBI	BB	SO	OBP	SLG	G	GS	Innings	PO	A	E	DP	Fld Pct	Rng Fctr	In Zone	Outs	Zone Rtg	MLB Zone
As Pinch Hitter	.500	8	4	2	0	1	7	3	2	.636	1.125	11	0	---	---	---	---	---	---	---	---	---	---	---
As c	.282	365	103	21	3	14	44	46	90	.365	.471	112	99	897.0	518	67	7	10	.988	---	---	---	---	---

Last Five Years

	Avg	AB	H	2B	3B	HR	RBI	BB	SO	OBP	SLG		Avg	AB	H	2B	3B	HR	RBI	BB	SO	OBP	SLG
vs. Left	.193	228	44	10	0	9	30	41	58	.314	.355	Scoring Posn	.202	173	35	12	1	5	56	29	43	.310	.370
vs. Right	.262	520	136	26	3	13	48	63	122	.342	.398	Close & Late	.265	102	27	8	0	1	10	17	30	.367	.373
Groundball	.271	155	42	9	0	1	8	25	30	.374	.348	None on/out	.239	176	42	5	2	5	5	22	40	.323	.375
Flyball	.244	197	48	8	0	8	24	18	51	.312	.406	Batting #8	.232	272	63	14	0	9	35	35	70	.318	.382
Home	.250	376	94	15	1	13	41	53	99	.341	.399	Batting #9	.210	243	51	7	0	9	26	40	59	.320	.350
Away	.231	372	86	21	2	9	37	51	81	.325	.371	Other	.283	233	66	15	3	4	17	29	51	.364	.425
Day	.275	236	65	12	1	7	28	33	51	.370	.424	April	.261	92	24	7	1	3	12	12	17	.346	.457
Night	.225	512	115	24	2	15	50	71	129	.316	.367	May	.270	115	31	6	0	3	10	14	27	.349	.400
Grass	.242	631	153	31	2	17	67	90	156	.337	.379	June	.227	163	37	10	2	2	10	17	31	.298	.350
Turf	.231	117	27	5	1	5	11	14	24	.313	.419	July	.167	138	23	5	0	3	8	23	40	.284	.268
First Pitch	.272	103	28	3	0	1	8	5	0	.306	.330	August	.270	122	33	2	0	5	18	18	34	.369	.410

Last Five Years

	Avg	AB	H	2B	3B	HR	RBI	BB	SO	OBP	SLG
Ahead in Count	.375	160	60	11	3	10	24	41	0	.498	.669
Behind in Count	.207	227	47	8	2	7	27	0	80	.211	.352
Two Strikes	.164	385	63	16	0	8	29	58	180	.272	.268

	Avg	AB	H	2B	3B	HR	RBI	BB	SO	OBP	SLG
September/October	.271	118	32	6	0	6	20	20	31	.373	.475
Pre-All Star	.234	435	102	24	3	10	36	47	97	.309	.372
Post-All Star	.249	313	78	12	0	12	42	57	83	.364	.403

Batter vs. Pitcher (career)

Hits Best Against	Avg	AB	H	2B	3B	HR	RBI	BB	SO	OBP	SLG
Kevin Appier	.500	8	4	0	0	0	2	2	4	.545	.500
Danny Darwin	.462	13	6	2	0	2	4	1	3	.500	1.077
Dave Stewart	.400	10	4	0	0	1	4	1	2	.455	.700

Hits Worst Against	Avg	AB	H	2B	3B	HR	RBI	BB	SO	OBP	SLG
Scott Bankhead	.111	9	1	0	0	1	1	2	2	.273	.444
Randy Johnson	.167	12	2	1	0	1	1	0	5	.167	.500
Dave Fleming	.182	11	2	1	0	0	0	0	2	.182	.273
Mark Langston	.200	15	3	2	0	0	1	2	7	.278	.333
Kevin Brown	.214	14	3	1	0	0	1	1	4	.267	.286

Bill Krueger — Tigers

Age 36 – Pitches Left

	ERA	W	L	Sv	G	GS	IP	BB	SO	Avg	H	2B	3B	HR	RBI	OBP	SLG	GF	IR	IRS	Hld	SvOp	SB	CS	GB	FB	G/F
1993 Season	3.40	6	4	0	32	7	82.0	30	60	.285	90	14	1	6	38	.351	.392	7	25	6	6	3	11	4	110	79	1.39
Last Five Years	3.94	36	30	3	167	83	658.1	230	386	.277	706	117	14	58	295	.337	.402	16	82	30	10	6	64	23	906	782	1.16

1993 Season

	ERA	W	L	Sv	G	GS	IP	H	HR	BB	SO
Home	1.69	4	0	0	12	3	42.2	39	3	10	29
Away	5.26	2	4	0	20	4	39.1	51	3	20	31
Starter	3.52	3	2	0	7	7	38.1	45	3	12	31
Reliever	3.30	3	2	0	25	0	43.2	45	3	18	29
0 Days rest	7.50	0	1	0	4	0	6.0	6	1	3	4
1 or 2 Days rest	2.61	2	0	0	10	0	20.2	19	1	4	19
3+ Days rest	2.65	1	1	0	11	0	17.0	20	1	11	6
Pre-All Star	3.46	5	3	0	23	4	54.2	67	3	22	28
Post-All Star	3.29	1	1	0	9	3	27.1	23	3	8	32

	Avg	AB	H	2B	3B	HR	RBI	BB	SO	OBP	SLG
vs. Left	.296	71	21	3	0	3	14	4	8	.333	.465
vs. Right	.282	245	69	11	1	3	24	26	52	.356	.371
Scoring Posn	.295	78	23	3	0	3	33	17	12	.431	.449
Close & Late	.341	41	14	2	0	1	8	3	3	.400	.463
None on/out	.329	73	24	2	1	0	0	7	8	.388	.384
First Pitch	.425	40	17	6	0	0	5	3	0	.489	.575
Ahead in Count	.183	126	23	2	0	4	16	0	50	.181	.294
Behind in Count	.370	81	30	5	0	1	11	17	0	.475	.469
Two Strikes	.195	154	30	3	0	5	19	10	60	.242	.312

Last Five Years

	ERA	W	L	Sv	G	GS	IP	H	HR	BB	SO
Home	3.78	19	15	1	76	41	326.1	335	31	109	210
Away	4.09	17	15	2	91	42	332.0	371	27	121	176
Day	3.75	8	7	0	43	18	146.1	163	12	54	76
Night	3.99	28	23	3	124	65	512.0	543	46	176	310
Grass	3.67	22	18	1	109	50	416.2	442	32	145	256
Turf	4.39	14	12	2	58	33	241.2	264	26	85	130
April	2.34	7	1	0	16	8	69.1	68	2	18	38
May	3.96	6	4	1	40	9	122.2	134	14	47	69
June	3.31	12	8	0	33	20	149.2	151	13	55	79
July	2.98	6	3	0	25	16	120.2	116	11	44	70
August	6.27	2	9	2	22	14	84.2	104	8	31	53
September/October	5.01	3	5	0	31	16	111.1	133	10	35	77
Starter	4.12	29	23	0	83	83	471.2	528	46	152	246
Reliever	3.47	7	7	3	84	0	186.2	178	12	78	140
0 Days rest	7.50	0	1	0	4	0	6.0	6	1	3	4
1 or 2 Days rest	3.13	4	3	1	39	0	86.1	84	6	28	68
3+ Days rest	3.53	3	3	2	41	0	94.1	88	5	47	68
Pre-All Star	3.50	26	14	1	97	42	378.0	387	33	135	209
Post-All Star	4.53	10	16	2	70	41	280.1	319	25	95	177

	Avg	AB	H	2B	3B	HR	RBI	BB	SO	OBP	SLG
vs. Left	.277	502	139	24	3	7	60	32	79	.322	.378
vs. Right	.277	2049	567	93	11	51	235	198	307	.341	.408
Inning 1-6	.288	2054	591	96	13	47	255	187	296	.348	.416
Inning 7+	.231	497	115	21	1	11	40	43	90	.293	.344
None on	.276	1457	402	64	4	39	39	94	216	.323	.406
Runners on	.278	1094	304	53	10	19	256	136	170	.355	.397
Scoring Posn	.267	622	166	26	6	14	231	99	105	.362	.395
Close & Late	.270	211	57	8	0	5	21	17	34	.326	.379
None on/out	.287	651	187	24	3	18	18	40	82	.333	.416
vs. 1st Batr (relief)	.351	74	26	4	2	2	18	9	13	.417	.541
First Inning Pitched	.299	613	183	30	3	13	107	62	111	.364	.421
First 15 Pitches	.290	548	159	25	2	9	60	38	100	.341	.392
Pitch 16-30	.262	516	135	21	2	10	71	47	77	.326	.368
Pitch 31-45	.320	440	141	22	3	12	57	39	55	.372	.466
Pitch 46+	.259	1047	271	49	7	27	107	106	154	.326	.396
First Pitch	.345	435	150	28	1	10	54	9	0	.358	.483
Ahead in Count	.196	909	178	22	3	14	74	0	340	.202	.273
Behind in Count	.325	714	232	46	7	22	101	123	0	.421	.501
Two Strikes	.204	1016	207	31	2	18	95	98	386	.275	.291

Pitcher vs. Batter (since 1984)

Pitches Best Vs.	Avg	AB	H	2B	3B	HR	RBI	BB	SO	OBP	SLG
Junior Felix	.000	16	0	0	0	0	0	0	7	.000	.000
Mike Gallego	.000	9	0	0	0	0	0	2	2	.182	.000
Ellis Burks	.059	17	1	0	0	0	0	2	2	.158	.059
Roberto Alomar	.083	12	1	0	0	0	0	1	0	.154	.083
Carlos Baerga	.091	11	1	0	0	0	0	0	2	.091	.091

Pitches Worst Vs.	Avg	AB	H	2B	3B	HR	RBI	BB	SO	OBP	SLG
Mike Greenwell	.600	20	12	2	1	0	5	1	1	.619	.800
Shane Mack	.556	9	5	1	1	1	9	2	0	.636	1.222
Mike Devereaux	.476	21	10	1	0	2	2	0	2	.476	.810
Danny Tartabull	.333	15	5	0	0	3	9	2	5	.412	.933
Ken Griffey Jr	.333	12	4	1	0	2	4	2	3	.429	.917

John Kruk — Phillies

Age 33 – Bats Left (groundball hitter)

	Avg	G	AB	R	H	2B	3B	HR	RBI	BB	SO	HBP	GDP	SB	CS	OBP	SLG	IBB	SH	SF	#Pit	#P/PA	GB	FB	G/F
1993 Season	.316	150	535	100	169	33	5	14	85	111	87	0	10	6	2	.430	.475	10	0	5	2488	3.82	227	113	2.01
Last Five Years	.305	700	2380	375	727	128	29	60	358	383	398	2	53	29	12	.399	.459	52	4	25	10443	3.74	973	524	1.86

1993 Season

	Avg	AB	H	2B	3B	HR	RBI	BB	SO	OBP	SLG
vs. Left	.292	185	54	6	1	5	30	27	39	.377	.416
vs. Right	.329	350	115	27	4	9	55	84	48	.456	.506
Groundball	.326	175	57	10	1	6	27	41	29	.447	.497
Flyball	.302	96	29	6	0	3	15	17	17	.407	.458
Home	.327	257	84	14	4	8	47	54	34	.441	.506
Away	.306	278	85	19	1	6	38	57	53	.420	.446
Day	.326	132	43	6	2	6	25	24	23	.427	.538
Night	.313	403	126	27	3	8	60	87	64	.431	.454
Grass	.313	179	56	8	0	5	25	30	33	.410	.441
Turf	.317	356	113	25	5	9	60	81	54	.440	.492
First Pitch	.329	79	26	3	0	3	14	9	0	.393	.481

	Avg	AB	H	2B	3B	HR	RBI	BB	SO	OBP	SLG
Scoring Posn	.279	165	46	10	2	3	68	50	29	.436	.418
Close & Late	.329	85	28	4	1	4	18	23	14	.468	.541
None on/out	.434	99	43	10	1	4	4	16	14	.513	.677
Batting #3	.318	529	168	33	5	14	84	109	85	.431	.478
Batting #9	.200	5	1	0	0	0	1	1	2	.286	.200
Other	.000	1	0	0	0	0	0	1	0	.500	.000
April	.343	70	24	7	0	5	15	15	9	.459	.657
May	.385	91	35	7	0	0	16	27	12	.517	.462
June	.304	92	28	6	1	2	13	22	16	.439	.457
July	.365	85	31	3	1	2	13	21	14	.491	.494
August	.263	99	26	4	1	4	12	11	17	.333	.444

1993 Season

	Avg	AB	H	2B	3B	HR	RBI	BB	SO	OBP	SLG
Ahead in Count	.462	132	61	10	4	8	29	62	0	.634	.780
Behind in Count	.237	215	51	14	1	2	22	0	69	.235	.340
Two Strikes	.238	223	53	13	0	2	26	40	87	.348	.323

	Avg	AB	H	2B	3B	HR	RBI	BB	SO	OBP	SLG
September/October	.255	98	25	6	2	1	16	15	19	.348	.388
Pre-All Star	.350	294	103	22	2	9	51	73	44	.477	.531
Post-All Star	.274	241	66	11	3	5	34	38	43	.369	.407

1993 By Position

Position	Avg	AB	H	2B	3B	HR	RBI	BB	SO	OBP	SLG	G	GS	Innings	PO	A	E	DP	Fld Pct	Rng Fctr	In Zone	Outs	Zone Rtg	MLB Zone
As 1b	.318	528	168	33	5	14	84	110	85	.433	.479	144	138	1243.1	1149	69	8	79	.993	---	215	183	.851	.834

Last Five Years

	Avg	AB	H	2B	3B	HR	RBI	BB	SO	OBP	SLG
vs. Left	.286	815	233	33	7	12	105	103	157	.362	.388
vs. Right	.316	1565	494	95	22	48	253	280	241	.417	.496
Groundball	.319	852	272	43	7	22	125	137	134	.411	.464
Flyball	.299	492	147	21	6	11	73	77	97	.391	.433
Home	.309	1193	369	65	15	31	199	189	179	.400	.467
Away	.302	1187	358	63	14	29	159	194	219	.397	.452
Day	.306	605	185	29	9	20	94	95	109	.397	.483
Night	.305	1775	542	99	20	40	264	288	289	.399	.451
Grass	.291	701	204	26	7	23	93	116	135	.390	.447
Turf	.311	1679	523	102	22	37	265	267	263	.402	.465
First Pitch	.324	346	112	19	8	12	63	27	0	.370	.529
Ahead in Count	.404	612	247	50	7	27	126	194	0	.544	.641
Behind in Count	.240	935	324	35	6	11	96	0	315	.237	.325
Two Strikes	.227	994	226	36	8	12	100	149	398	.325	.316

	Avg	AB	H	2B	3B	HR	RBI	BB	SO	OBP	SLG
Scoring Posn	.278	661	184	31	7	16	279	164	123	.410	.419
Close & Late	.303	390	118	14	5	10	60	85	70	.424	.441
None on/out	.340	544	185	38	3	13	13	65	87	.411	.493
Batting #3	.303	943	286	52	12	25	145	158	155	.399	.463
Batting #4	.324	845	274	52	9	23	133	132	149	.412	.489
Other	.282	592	167	24	8	12	80	93	94	.377	.410
April	.304	335	102	14	2	11	67	48	44	.388	.457
May	.323	368	119	21	4	8	54	73	64	.430	.467
June	.302	437	132	24	8	8	63	67	66	.393	.449
July	.300	323	97	17	3	10	46	73	66	.427	.464
August	.299	445	133	20	3	11	59	70	66	.391	.431
September/October	.305	472	144	32	9	12	69	52	92	.371	.487
Pre-All Star	.307	1271	390	64	15	32	201	220	200	.406	.456
Post-All Star	.304	1109	337	64	14	28	157	163	198	.390	.463

Batter vs. Pitcher (career)

Hits Best Against	Avg	AB	H	2B	3B	HR	RBI	BB	SO	OBP	SLG
Ted Power	.556	18	10	3	1	0	6	2	0	.600	.833
Eric Hillman	.545	11	6	0	0	1	4	1	2	.538	.818
Roger Mason	.500	8	4	0	1	1	1	4	0	.667	1.125
Jeff Parrett	.444	9	4	0	0	1	2	3	1	.583	.778
Frank Castillo	.412	17	7	3	0	3	5	4	4	.524	1.118

Hits Worst Against	Avg	AB	H	2B	3B	HR	RBI	BB	SO	OBP	SLG
Lee Smith	.000	15	0	0	0	0	0	1	6	.063	.000
Rich Rodriguez	.000	9	0	0	0	0	0	2	1	.182	.000
Rheal Cormier	.077	13	1	0	0	0	2	2	2	.200	.077
Mike Harkey	.091	11	1	1	0	0	0	0	1	.091	.182
Frank DiPino	.111	18	2	0	0	0	1	0	9	.111	.111

Steve Lake — Cubs

Age 37 – Bats Right

	Avg	G	AB	R	H	2B	3B	HR	RBI	BB	SO	HBP	GDP	SB	CS	OBP	SLG	IBB	SH	SF	#Pit	#P/PA	GB	FB	G/F
1993 Season	.225	44	120	11	27	6	0	5	13	4	19	0	8	0	0	.250	.400	3	2	0	367	2.91	34	45	0.76
Last Five Years	.239	209	566	39	135	19	2	9	46	22	85	1	20	0	0	.267	.327	9	7	2	1754	2.93	198	179	1.11

1993 Season

	Avg	AB	H	2B	3B	HR	RBI	BB	SO	OBP	SLG
vs. Left	.192	78	15	4	0	3	6	3	10	.222	.359
vs. Right	.286	42	12	2	0	2	7	1	9	.302	.476
Home	.163	49	8	2	0	1	4	2	8	.196	.265
Away	.268	71	19	4	0	4	9	2	11	.288	.493
First Pitch	.346	26	9	0	0	4	6	3	0	.414	.808
Ahead in Count	.095	21	2	1	0	0	0	1	0	.136	.143
Behind in Count	.237	59	14	4	0	0	6	0	18	.237	.305
Two Strikes	.205	44	9	2	0	1	5	0	19	.205	.318

	Avg	AB	H	2B	3B	HR	RBI	BB	SO	OBP	SLG
Scoring Posn	.276	29	8	1	0	0	7	3	3	.344	.310
Close & Late	.250	8	2	0	0	0	1	0	3	.250	.250
None on/out	.267	30	8	3	0	2	2	1	4	.290	.567
Batting #6	.000	2	0	0	0	0	0	0	0	.000	.000
Batting #8	.228	114	26	6	0	5	12	4	18	.254	.412
Other	.250	4	1	0	0	0	1	0	1	.250	.250
Pre-All Star	.241	58	14	3	0	2	6	1	10	.254	.397
Post-All Star	.210	62	13	3	0	3	7	3	9	.246	.403

Last Five Years

	Avg	AB	H	2B	3B	HR	RBI	BB	SO	OBP	SLG
vs. Left	.242	392	95	14	2	5	30	16	52	.273	.327
vs. Right	.230	174	40	5	0	4	16	6	33	.256	.328
Groundball	.223	197	44	9	1	3	20	7	18	.254	.325
Flyball	.284	148	42	2	0	5	13	3	30	.298	.399
Home	.225	271	61	8	2	3	19	9	34	.252	.303
Away	.251	295	74	11	0	6	27	13	51	.282	.349
Day	.240	225	54	5	1	4	18	13	37	.280	.324
Night	.238	341	81	14	1	5	28	9	48	.259	.328
Grass	.203	197	40	6	0	5	17	7	38	.230	.310
Turf	.257	369	95	13	2	4	29	15	47	.287	.336
First Pitch	.372	129	48	4	0	4	16	7	0	.401	.496
Ahead in Count	.155	103	16	3	1	1	3	6	0	.200	.233
Behind in Count	.200	255	51	10	1	3	22	0	80	.203	.282
Two Strikes	.178	197	35	8	0	3	12	8	85	.214	.264

	Avg	AB	H	2B	3B	HR	RBI	BB	SO	OBP	SLG
Scoring Posn	.260	127	33	3	0	0	33	14	24	.329	.283
Close & Late	.231	78	18	3	0	0	2	4	13	.268	.269
None on/out	.281	135	38	5	1	5	5	5	25	.312	.444
Batting #7	.288	104	30	3	0	1	6	3	23	.306	.346
Batting #8	.224	437	98	15	2	8	38	19	59	.258	.323
Other	.280	25	7	1	0	0	2	0	3	.280	.320
April	.245	98	24	3	0	2	8	5	9	.282	.337
May	.241	112	27	3	0	1	4	4	20	.271	.295
June	.238	126	30	6	0	1	9	2	15	.250	.310
July	.241	87	21	1	1	3	12	6	18	.287	.379
August	.186	70	13	1	0	1	6	4	12	.230	.243
September/October	.274	73	20	5	1	1	7	1	11	.284	.411
Pre-All Star	.237	372	88	12	0	5	25	12	51	.262	.309
Post-All Star	.242	194	47	7	2	4	21	10	34	.278	.361

Batter vs. Pitcher (since 1984)

Hits Best Against	Avg	AB	H	2B	3B	HR	RBI	BB	SO	OBP	SLG
Zane Smith	.423	26	11	1	0	0	4	2	0	.464	.462
Neal Heaton	.333	12	4	0	0	0	1	0	1	.308	.333
Danny Jackson	.313	16	5	1	0	0	1	1	1	.353	.375
Ron Darling	.308	13	4	0	0	0	3	0	3	.308	.308

Hits Worst Against	Avg	AB	H	2B	3B	HR	RBI	BB	SO	OBP	SLG
Bobby Ojeda	.083	24	2	0	0	1	3	2	1	.148	.208
Tom Glavine	.111	18	2	2	0	0	1	1	4	.158	.222
Frank Viola	.182	11	2	0	0	0	0	0	1	.182	.182
Jim Deshaies	.208	24	5	0	0	0	4	1	3	.240	.208
Fernando Valenzuela	.231	13	3	0	0	0	2	0	5	.231	.231

Tim Laker — Expos

Age 24 – Bats Right (groundball hitter)

	Avg	G	AB	R	H	2B	3B	HR	RBI	BB	SO	HBP	GDP	SB	CS	OBP	SLG	IBB	SH	SF	#Pit	#P/PA	GB	FB	G/F
1993 Season	.198	43	86	3	17	2	1	0	7	2	16	1	2	2	0	.222	.244	0	3	1	328	3.53	32	26	1.23
Career (1992-1993)	.205	71	132	11	27	5	1	0	11	4	30	1	3	3	1	.232	.258	0	3	1	498	3.53	51	32	1.59

1993 Season

	Avg	AB	H	2B	3B	HR	RBI	BB	SO	OBP	SLG		Avg	AB	H	2B	3B	HR	RBI	BB	SO	OBP	SLG
vs. Left	.227	44	10	1	0	0	6	0	7	.222	.250	Scoring Posn	.167	18	3	1	0	0	6	1	5	.200	.222
vs. Right	.167	42	7	1	1	0	1	2	9	.222	.238	Close & Late	.091	11	1	0	0	0	0	0	2	.091	.091

Tom Lampkin — Brewers

Age 30 – Bats Left (groundball hitter)

	Avg	G	AB	R	H	2B	3B	HR	RBI	BB	SO	HBP	GDP	SB	CS	OBP	SLG	IBB	SH	SF	#Pit	#P/PA	GB	FB	G/F
1993 Season	.198	73	162	22	32	8	0	4	25	20	26	0	2	7	3	.280	.321	3	2	4	683	3.63	68	51	1.33
Last Five Years	.203	146	300	33	61	11	2	5	32	33	45	1	4	9	4	.281	.303	4	2	4	1225	3.60	133	86	1.55

1993 Season

	Avg	AB	H	2B	3B	HR	RBI	BB	SO	OBP	SLG		Avg	AB	H	2B	3B	HR	RBI	BB	SO	OBP	SLG
vs. Left	.114	35	4	2	0	1	5	4	6	.205	.257	Scoring Posn	.242	33	8	4	0	1	18	10	8	.383	.455
vs. Right	.220	127	28	6	0	3	20	16	20	.299	.339	Close & Late	.176	34	6	1	0	0	2	8	7	.326	.206
Home	.178	73	13	3	0	1	7	8	13	.256	.260	None on/out	.186	43	8	0	0	0	0	4	7	.255	.186
Away	.213	89	19	5	0	3	18	12	13	.298	.371	Batting #7	.122	41	5	0	0	0	3	4	6	.196	.122
First Pitch	.263	19	5	2	0	1	4	1	0	.300	.526	Batting #9	.250	40	10	5	0	1	9	3	5	.295	.450
Ahead in Count	.310	42	13	1	0	1	9	15	0	.475	.405	Other	.210	81	17	3	0	3	13	13	15	.313	.358
Behind in Count	.095	74	7	2	0	1	4	0	23	.092	.162	Pre-All Star	.186	70	13	4	0	1	12	9	11	.272	.286
Two Strikes	.114	70	8	3	0	0	4	4	26	.160	.157	Post-All Star	.207	92	19	4	0	3	13	11	15	.286	.348

Les Lancaster — Cardinals

Age 32 – Pitches Right

	ERA	W	L	Sv	G	GS	IP	BB	SO	Avg	H	2B	3B	HR	RBI	OBP	SLG	GF	IR	IRS	Hld	SvOp	SB	CS	GB	FB	G/F
1993 Season	2.93	4	1	0	50	0	61.1	21	36	.242	56	14	1	5	35	.307	.377	12	49	19	5	0	3	3	76	75	1.01
Last Five Years	3.87	29	19	17	252	18	485.2	176	294	.263	488	87	7	42	269	.327	.386	76	214	91	23	31	29	24	654	547	1.20

1993 Season

	ERA	W	L	Sv	G	GS	IP	H	HR	BB	SO		Avg	AB	H	2B	3B	HR	RBI	BB	SO	OBP	SLG
Home	5.04	0	0	0	23	0	25.0	25	4	10	17	vs. Left	.237	97	23	7	1	1	7	12	16	.321	.361
Away	1.49	4	1	0	27	0	36.1	31	1	11	19	vs. Right	.246	134	33	7	0	4	28	9	20	.297	.388
Starter	0.00	0	0	0	0	0	0.0	0	0	0	0	Scoring Posn	.293	75	22	4	1	3	32	10	11	.372	.493
Reliever	2.93	4	1	0	50	0	61.1	56	5	21	36	Close & Late	.204	49	10	2	0	0	4	6	7	.291	.245
0 Days rest	2.33	1	0	0	17	0	27.0	24	3	8	15	None on/out	.146	48	7	1	0	0	0	2	7	.180	.167
1 or 2 Days rest	4.35	2	1	0	21	0	20.2	21	1	10	15	First Pitch	.290	31	9	3	1	1	5	4	0	.371	.548
3+ Days rest	1.98	1	0	0	12	0	13.2	11	1	3	6	Ahead in Count	.175	97	17	2	0	0	4	0	29	.184	.196
Pre-All Star	2.98	3	0	0	39	0	48.1	46	4	18	28	Behind in Count	.316	57	18	7	0	2	18	9	0	.403	.544
Post-All Star	2.77	1	1	0	11	0	13.0	10	1	3	8	Two Strikes	.175	97	17	2	0	1	4	8	36	.245	.227

Last Five Years

	ERA	W	L	Sv	G	GS	IP	H	HR	BB	SO		Avg	AB	H	2B	3B	HR	RBI	BB	SO	OBP	SLG
Home	4.22	15	8	7	130	10	255.2	263	23	87	159	vs. Left	.269	886	238	48	3	12	91	116	137	.353	.370
Away	3.48	14	11	10	122	8	230.0	225	19	89	135	vs. Right	.258	968	250	39	4	30	178	60	157	.302	.400
Day	4.02	15	9	9	113	10	219.1	219	23	72	159	Inning 1-6	.265	803	213	44	3	24	138	68	109	.322	.417
Night	3.75	14	10	8	139	8	266.1	269	19	104	135	Inning 7+	.262	1051	275	43	4	18	131	108	185	.331	.362
Grass	4.07	23	14	10	170	15	349.2	365	30	126	213	None on	.256	995	255	47	4	20	20	78	166	.313	.372
Turf	3.38	6	5	7	82	3	136.0	123	12	50	81	Runners on	.271	859	233	40	3	22	249	98	128	.343	.402
April	5.22	4	2	0	39	0	60.1	66	6	29	30	Scoring Posn	.283	520	147	27	3	19	234	71	83	.361	.456
May	3.79	6	2	2	41	4	78.1	82	10	26	47	Close & Late	.276	456	126	16	2	7	64	48	81	.344	.366
June	3.57	5	3	3	42	4	95.2	95	6	43	56	None on/out	.244	427	104	12	2	8	8	28	68	.292	.337
July	4.58	8	4	3	40	7	98.1	101	9	30	58	vs. 1st Batr (relief)	.276	217	60	5	3	5	46	13	30	.318	.396
August	3.51	2	5	5	37	0	59.0	67	5	14	44	First Inning Pitched	.261	831	217	36	4	19	158	83	136	.325	.383
September/October	2.87	4	3	4	53	3	94.0	77	6	34	59	First 15 Pitches	.263	775	204	34	3	18	130	70	113	.322	.385
Starter	4.54	8	5	0	18	18	109.0	118	12	34	62	Pitch 16-30	.266	489	130	25	3	10	65	43	99	.323	.391
Reliever	3.68	21	14	17	234	0	376.2	370	30	142	232	Pitch 31-45	.205	264	54	9	0	6	26	33	48	.293	.307
0 Days rest	3.24	6	5	3	59	0	80.2	81	6	26	60	Pitch 46+	.307	326	100	19	1	8	48	30	34	.372	.445
1 or 2 Days rest	4.42	12	8	12	111	0	183.1	199	16	82	122	First Pitch	.321	296	95	16	4	9	57	29	0	.380	.493
3+ Days rest	2.80	3	1	2	64	0	112.2	90	8	34	50	Ahead in Count	.195	806	157	27	2	8	70	0	245	.201	.263
Pre-All Star	4.35	17	10	6	139	11	273.1	283	27	115	158	Behind in Count	.359	379	136	26	1	12	81	77	0	.461	.528
Post-All Star	3.26	12	9	11	113	7	212.1	205	15	61	136	Two Strikes	.189	815	154	28	0	12	78	70	294	.256	.267

Pitcher vs. Batter (career)

Pitches Best Vs.	Avg	AB	H	2B	3B	HR	RBI	BB	SO	OBP	SLG	Pitches Worst Vs.	Avg	AB	H	2B	3B	HR	RBI	BB	SO	OBP	SLG
Mariano Duncan	.000	11	0	0	0	0	0	0	1	.000	.000	Thomas Howard	.545	11	6	4	0	1	3	0	2	.545	1.182
Barry Larkin	.000	10	0	0	0	0	1	1	1	.083	.000	Chris James	.500	14	7	0	0	2	6	1	2	.533	.929
Jose Lind	.111	18	2	0	0	0	0	0	4	.111	.111	Eric Davis	.500	8	4	0	0	2	6	2	3	.500	1.250
Steve Sax	.143	14	2	0	0	0	1	0	0	.143	.143	Bobby Bonilla	.500	8	4	1	0	0	1	8	3	.706	.625
Billy Hatcher	.167	12	2	0	0	0	0	0	2	.167	.167	Darryl Strawberry	.391	23	9	1	1	2	4	4	5	.481	.783

Bill Landrum — Reds

Age 35 – Pitches Right (groundball pitcher)

	ERA	W	L	Sv	G	GS	IP	BB	SO	Avg	H	2B	3B	HR	RBI	OBP	SLG	GF	IR	IRS	Hld	SvOp	SB	CS	GB	FB	G/F
1993 Season	3.74	0	2	0	18	0	21.2	6	14	.231	18	6	1	1	10	.286	.372	6	11	2	2	0	4	1	34	14	2.43
Last Five Years	2.79	14	13	56	207	0	270.2	83	156	.246	250	31	7	14	112	.302	.331	96	111	34	12	67	29	7	408	271	1.51

1993 Season

	ERA	W	L	Sv	G	GS	IP	H	HR	BB	SO
Home	5.19	0	0	0	7	0	8.2	8	0	3	5
Away	2.77	0	2	0	11	0	13.0	10	1	3	9

	Avg	AB	H	2B	3B	HR	RBI	BB	SO	OBP	SLG
vs. Left	.225	40	9	4	1	0	2	5	8	.311	.375
vs. Right	.237	38	9	2	0	1	8	1	6	.256	.368

Last Five Years

	ERA	W	L	Sv	G	GS	IP	H	HR	BB	SO
Home	3.24	7	6	27	102	0	130.2	122	4	40	73
Away	2.38	7	7	29	105	0	140.0	128	10	43	83
Day	3.42	2	6	12	57	0	76.1	66	5	26	52
Night	2.55	12	7	44	150	0	194.1	184	9	57	104
Grass	2.69	5	4	16	54	0	73.2	60	9	18	43
Turf	2.83	9	9	40	153	0	197.0	190	5	65	113
April	1.55	1	0	5	38	0	46.1	33	2	14	34
May	2.72	2	4	11	45	0	56.1	48	3	13	25
June	2.36	3	1	19	33	0	45.2	50	0	13	28
July	3.72	1	3	7	32	0	46.0	44	3	18	27
August	2.86	2	4	8	33	0	44.0	40	3	14	28
September/October	3.90	5	1	6	26	0	32.1	35	3	11	14
Starter	0.00	0	0	0	0	0	0.0	0	0	0	0
Reliever	2.79	14	13	56	207	0	270.2	250	14	83	156
0 Days rest	3.32	2	2	17	40	0	40.2	38	1	16	20
1 or 2 Days rest	2.47	6	9	28	97	0	138.1	131	9	40	76
3+ Days rest	3.04	6	2	11	70	0	91.2	81	4	27	60
Pre-All Star	2.18	7	6	38	124	0	160.2	141	7	46	95
Post-All Star	3.68	7	7	18	83	0	110.0	109	7	37	61

	Avg	AB	H	2B	3B	HR	RBI	BB	SO	OBP	SLG
vs. Left	.245	519	127	18	4	7	52	48	67	.308	.335
vs. Right	.247	498	123	13	3	7	60	35	89	.296	.327
Inning 1-6	.224	76	17	1	1	0	9	5	16	.265	.263
Inning 7+	.248	941	233	30	6	14	103	78	140	.305	.337
None on	.244	549	134	13	5	9	9	29	83	.283	.335
Runners on	.248	468	116	18	2	5	103	54	73	.323	.327
Scoring Posn	.259	294	76	15	2	1	95	46	44	.353	.333
Close & Late	.243	456	111	14	2	4	49	48	73	.314	.309
None on/out	.263	236	62	5	2	5	5	11	31	.298	.364
vs. 1st Batr (relief)	.279	190	53	5	2	4	17	13	20	.325	.389
First Inning Pitched	.240	705	169	18	5	9	82	49	111	.288	.318
First 15 Pitches	.241	676	163	19	5	9	67	43	100	.286	.324
Pitch 16-30	.270	278	75	11	1	4	35	28	43	.336	.360
Pitch 31-45	.204	54	11	1	1	1	10	11	8	.348	.315
Pitch 46+	.111	9	1	0	0	0	0	1	5	.200	.111
First Pitch	.288	146	42	7	1	1	17	20	0	.381	.370
Ahead in Count	.198	455	90	13	2	6	45	0	143	.197	.275
Behind in Count	.288	236	68	7	0	3	28	38	0	.384	.356
Two Strikes	.189	438	83	14	2	5	38	25	156	.232	.265

Pitcher vs. Batter (career)

Pitches Best Vs.	Avg	AB	H	2B	3B	HR	RBI	BB	SO	OBP	SLG
Darren Daulton	.000	11	0	0	0	0	1	0	3	.000	.000
Tom Pagnozzi	.000	11	0	0	0	0	0	0	2	.000	.000
Gregg Jefferies	.077	13	1	1	0	0	0	0	3	.077	.154
Ken Caminiti	.091	11	1	0	0	0	2	1	1	.167	.091
Charlie Hayes	.091	11	1	0	0	0	0	0	2	.091	.091

Pitches Worst Vs.	Avg	AB	H	2B	3B	HR	RBI	BB	SO	OBP	SLG
Dave Magadan	.714	7	5	0	0	0	0	4	0	.818	.714
Billy Hatcher	.600	15	9	0	2	0	4	1	0	.625	.867
Dave Martinez	.500	10	5	1	0	0	1	1	1	.545	.600
Kevin McReynolds	.467	15	7	1	0	0	4	0	1	.467	.533
Jerome Walton	.364	11	4	0	0	2	3	1	3	.417	.909

Ced Landrum — Mets

Age 30 – Bats Left

	Avg	G	AB	R	H	2B	3B	HR	RBI	BB	SO	HBP	GDP	SB	CS	OBP	SLG	IBB	SH	SF	#Pit	#P/PA	GB	FB	G/F
1993 Season	.263	22	19	2	5	1	0	0	1	0	5	0	0	0	0	.263	.316	0	1	0	67	3.35	4	5	0.80
Career (1991-1993)	.238	78	105	30	25	3	1	0	7	10	23	0	2	27	5	.304	.286	0	4	0	421	3.54	34	23	1.48

1993 Season

	Avg	AB	H	2B	3B	HR	RBI	BB	SO	OBP	SLG
vs. Left	.000	0	0	0	0	0	0	0	0	.000	.000
vs. Right	.263	19	5	1	0	0	1	0	5	.263	.316

	Avg	AB	H	2B	3B	HR	RBI	BB	SO	OBP	SLG
Scoring Posn	.250	4	1	0	0	0	1	0	2	.250	.250
Close & Late	.250	8	2	1	0	0	0	0	2	.250	.375

Mark Langston — Angels

Age 33 – Pitches Left

	ERA	W	L	Sv	G	GS	IP	BB	SO	Avg	H	2B	3B	HR	RBI	OBP	SLG	CG	ShO	Sup	QS	#P/S	SB	CS	GB	FB	G/F
1993 Season	3.20	16	11	0	35	35	256.1	85	196	.234	220	39	1	22	89	.295	.347	7	0	4.00	23	109	10	12	326	262	1.24
Last Five Years	3.37	74	64	0	168	168	1204.2	471	983	.233	1029	186	19	95	437	.308	.349	36	8	4.01	110	112	86	69	1448	1281	1.13

1993 Season

	ERA	W	L	Sv	G	GS	IP	H	HR	BB	SO
Home	3.66	9	5	0	18	18	135.1	118	16	43	112
Away	2.68	7	6	0	17	17	121.0	102	6	42	84
Day	3.02	4	3	0	9	9	59.2	57	2	18	49
Night	3.25	12	8	0	26	26	196.2	163	20	67	147
Grass	3.19	15	8	0	30	30	220.1	182	21	72	175
Turf	3.25	1	3	0	5	5	36.0	38	1	13	21
April	2.50	3	0	0	5	5	36.0	24	1	12	36
May	2.25	2	1	0	6	6	44.0	36	3	14	36
June	3.09	4	1	0	6	6	43.2	41	3	16	30
July	3.69	1	3	0	5	5	39.0	35	4	12	22
August	2.44	4	1	0	6	6	44.1	33	5	17	35
September/October	4.93	2	5	0	7	7	49.1	51	6	14	37
Starter	3.20	16	11	0	35	35	256.1	220	22	85	196
Reliever	0.00	0	0	0	0	0	0.0	0	0	0	0
0-3 Days Rest	0.00	1	0	0	1	1	6.0	5	0	2	7
4 Days Rest	3.63	11	9	0	26	26	188.2	176	18	60	136
5+ Days Rest	2.19	4	2	0	8	8	61.2	39	4	23	53
Pre-All Star	2.82	9	3	0	19	19	140.2	121	9	46	114
Post-All Star	3.66	7	8	0	16	16	115.2	99	13	39	82

	Avg	AB	H	2B	3B	HR	RBI	BB	SO	OBP	SLG
vs. Left	.176	136	24	3	0	2	11	11	29	.238	.243
vs. Right	.243	806	196	36	1	20	78	74	167	.305	.365
Inning 1-6	.234	753	176	36	1	15	74	65	166	.293	.344
Inning 7+	.233	189	44	3	0	7	15	20	30	.306	.360
None on	.216	569	123	23	0	15	15	61	134	.293	.336
Runners on	.260	373	97	16	1	7	74	24	62	.299	.365
Scoring Posn	.272	191	52	12	0	3	64	13	33	.307	.382
Close & Late	.230	139	32	2	0	3	9	14	23	.301	.309
None on/out	.243	247	60	13	0	6	6	23	59	.310	.368
vs. 1st Batr (relief)	.000	0	0	0	0	0	0	0	0	.000	.000
First Inning Pitched	.254	134	34	7	0	2	15	8	34	.294	.351
First 75 Pitches	.231	632	146	28	1	12	54	50	142	.286	.335
Pitch 76-90	.208	125	26	7	0	3	20	11	18	.268	.336
Pitch 91-105	.264	110	29	2	0	4	9	12	19	.336	.391
Pitch 106+	.253	75	19	2	0	3	6	12	17	.356	.400
First Pitch	.302	162	49	8	0	5	15	1	0	.311	.444
Ahead in Count	.172	430	74	11	0	5	31	0	169	.171	.233
Behind in Count	.279	201	56	11	1	8	25	49	0	.415	.463
Two Strikes	.159	429	68	13	0	4	32	35	196	.220	.217

Last Five Years

	ERA	W	L	Sv	G	GS	IP	H	HR	BB	SO
Home	3.74	38	31	0	86	86	626.0	553	61	224	526
Away	2.97	36	33	0	82	82	578.2	476	34	247	457
Day	4.00	16	19	0	46	46	299.0	275	18	125	271
Night	3.16	58	45	0	122	122	905.2	754	77	346	712
Grass	3.37	55	47	0	127	127	907.1	762	77	348	741
Turf	3.36	19	17	0	41	41	297.1	267	18	123	242
April	3.81	10	6	0	22	22	144.0	127	9	52	125
May	3.11	14	9	0	29	29	217.0	169	15	79	170
June	2.77	16	9	0	28	28	211.1	183	19	83	175
July	4.22	10	16	0	29	29	206.2	193	21	82	158
August	3.48	13	10	0	29	29	199.0	168	17	93	151
September/October	3.02	11	14	0	31	31	226.2	189	14	82	204
Starter	3.37	74	64	0	168	168	1204.2	1029	95	471	983
Reliever	0.00	0	0	0	0	0	0.0	0	0	0	0
0-3 Days Rest	3.29	4	2	0	7	7	52.0	38	5	15	47
4 Days Rest	3.44	42	43	0	104	104	754.0	656	62	296	611
5+ Days Rest	3.25	28	19	0	57	57	398.2	335	28	160	325
Pre-All Star	3.39	43	29	0	89	89	639.2	548	48	247	519
Post-All Star	3.35	31	35	0	79	79	565.0	481	47	224	464

	Avg	AB	H	2B	3B	HR	RBI	BB	SO	OBP	SLG
vs. Left	.193	626	121	23	4	7	49	61	136	.269	.276
vs. Right	.240	3786	908	163	15	88	388	410	847	.314	.361
Inning 1-6	.235	3526	827	157	17	70	367	375	802	.309	.348
Inning 7+	.228	886	202	29	2	25	70	96	181	.304	.350
None on	.224	2633	589	101	11	58	58	303	593	.306	.336
Runners on	.247	1779	440	85	8	37	379	168	390	.310	.366
Scoring Posn	.255	932	238	46	5	20	335	108	233	.326	.380
Close & Late	.225	524	118	19	1	13	45	54	108	.297	.340
None on/out	.236	1138	268	46	3	21	21	126	258	.314	.337
vs. 1st Batr (relief)	.000	0	0	0	0	0	0	0	0	.000	.000
First Inning Pitched	.246	589	145	28	0	14	69	71	140	.327	.365
First 75 Pitches	.231	2890	669	122	12	58	278	295	659	.303	.342
Pitch 76-90	.252	563	142	30	3	15	76	63	112	.326	.396
Pitch 91-105	.232	482	112	20	1	9	40	50	102	.308	.334
Pitch 106+	.222	477	106	14	3	13	43	63	110	.311	.346
First Pitch	.283	643	182	34	2	18	70	10	0	.296	.426
Ahead in Count	.164	1984	326	63	6	17	132	0	831	.167	.228
Behind in Count	.327	1026	336	54	7	44	157	252	0	.458	.522
Two Strikes	.153	2082	319	62	9	24	142	209	983	.231	.226

Pitcher vs. Batter (career)

Pitches Best Vs.	Avg	AB	H	2B	3B	HR	RBI	BB	SO	OBP	SLG
Scott Leius	.000	10	0	0	0	0	0	2	2	.167	.000
Craig Grebeck	.048	21	1	0	0	0	1	2	4	.130	.048
Keith Miller	.063	16	1	1	0	0	0	0	3	.063	.125
Kelly Gruber	.080	25	2	0	0	0	0	1	10	.115	.080
Milt Cuyler	.083	12	1	0	0	0	0	0	1	.083	.083

Pitches Worst Vs.	Avg	AB	H	2B	3B	HR	RBI	BB	SO	OBP	SLG
Bob Zupcic	.538	13	7	3	0	0	0	2	3	.600	.769
Rich Amaral	.533	15	8	2	0	1	3	0	2	.533	.867
Mark Carreon	.500	14	7	2	0	0	1	3	1	.588	.643
Kevin Mitchell	.467	15	7	2	0	1	4	0	2	.467	.800
Frank Thomas	.370	27	10	1	0	2	5	13	5	.575	.630

Ray Lankford — Cardinals

Age 27 – Bats Left

	Avg	G	AB	R	H	2B	3B	HR	RBI	BB	SO	HBP	GDP	SB	CS	OBP	SLG	IBB	SH	SF	#Pit	#P/PA	GB	FB	G/F
1993 Season	.238	127	407	64	97	17	3	7	45	81	111	3	5	14	14	.366	.346	7	1	3	2143	4.33	144	91	1.58
Career (1990-1993)	.265	470	1697	246	450	90	25	39	212	207	399	9	16	108	60	.346	.417	14	7	11	7712	3.99	554	455	1.22

1993 Season

	Avg	AB	H	2B	3B	HR	RBI	BB	SO	OBP	SLG
vs. Left	.207	116	24	1	1	0	7	26	38	.357	.233
vs. Right	.251	291	73	16	2	7	38	55	73	.370	.392
Groundball	.264	125	33	6	0	2	17	26	26	.392	.360
Flyball	.195	87	17	2	2	2	9	15	31	.314	.333
Home	.249	197	49	9	1	6	26	40	46	.375	.396
Away	.229	210	48	8	2	1	19	41	65	.358	.300
Day	.199	136	27	7	2	0	12	22	50	.306	.279
Night	.258	271	70	10	1	7	33	59	61	.395	.380
Grass	.200	140	28	4	0	1	9	23	42	.315	.250
Turf	.258	267	69	13	3	6	36	58	69	.392	.397
First Pitch	.424	33	14	1	0	0	7	2	0	.444	.455
Ahead in Count	.360	89	32	5	2	4	18	38	0	.543	.596
Behind in Count	.167	203	34	6	1	0	12	0	92	.176	.207
Two Strikes	.169	237	40	7	1	1	15	41	111	.296	.219

	Avg	AB	H	2B	3B	HR	RBI	BB	SO	OBP	SLG
Scoring Posn	.246	126	31	5	0	3	41	33	37	.399	.357
Close & Late	.205	73	15	4	2	1	1	12	22	.318	.356
None on/out	.275	109	30	6	3	3	3	13	27	.358	.468
Batting #4	.259	166	43	6	1	1	19	35	43	.392	.325
Batting #5	.209	86	18	6	0	1	8	20	24	.361	.314
Other	.232	155	36	5	2	5	18	26	44	.341	.387
April	.230	74	17	1	1	1	7	11	14	.329	.311
May	.308	91	28	1	1	1	15	20	27	.429	.374
June	.261	69	18	5	0	1	7	15	24	.407	.377
July	.229	48	11	4	1	0	5	11	12	.383	.354
August	.185	65	12	3	0	3	6	16	16	.346	.369
September/October	.183	60	11	3	0	1	5	8	18	.271	.283
Pre-All Star	.267	240	64	8	2	3	29	46	66	.388	.354
Post-All Star	.198	167	33	9	1	4	16	35	45	.337	.335

1993 By Position

Position	Avg	AB	H	2B	3B	HR	RBI	BB	SO	OBP	SLG	G	GS	Innings	PO	A	E	DP	Fld Pct	Rng Fctr	In Zone	Outs	Zone Rtg	MLB Zone
As cf	.241	399	96	16	3	7	45	81	109	.370	.348	121	112	1011.2	312	6	7	0	.978	2.83	369	308	.835	.829

Career (1990-1993)

	Avg	AB	H	2B	3B	HR	RBI	BB	SO	OBP	SLG
vs. Left	.243	597	145	26	11	4	66	73	159	.330	.343
vs. Right	.277	1100	305	64	14	35	146	134	240	.355	.456
Groundball	.303	557	169	29	5	17	76	67	108	.380	.465
Flyball	.235	378	89	17	12	7	47	40	108	.310	.399
Home	.268	837	224	40	15	25	119	105	178	.348	.441
Away	.263	860	226	50	10	14	93	102	221	.344	.393
Day	.232	479	111	29	8	9	51	62	124	.319	.382
Night	.278	1218	339	61	17	30	161	145	275	.357	.430
Grass	.264	474	125	29	5	7	54	54	118	.340	.390
Turf	.266	1223	325	61	20	32	158	153	281	.348	.427
First Pitch	.363	168	61	11	5	4	30	9	0	.397	.560
Ahead in Count	.344	363	125	24	9	17	75	103	0	.484	.601
Behind in Count	.201	821	165	33	5	12	65	0	335	.206	.297
Two Strikes	.192	884	170	35	7	10	69	95	399	.274	.282

	Avg	AB	H	2B	3B	HR	RBI	BB	SO	OBP	SLG
Scoring Posn	.289	454	131	25	11	12	172	80	111	.392	.471
Close & Late	.257	315	81	12	4	7	34	41	88	.346	.387
None on/out	.261	486	127	18	7	13	13	37	117	.315	.407
Batting #1	.269	561	151	26	10	13	60	54	133	.337	.421
Batting #3	.287	670	192	41	13	21	107	68	143	.351	.481
Other	.230	466	107	23	2	5	45	85	123	.349	.320
April	.252	218	55	4	4	3	14	29	40	.348	.349
May	.287	289	83	12	2	4	38	33	65	.359	.384
June	.261	264	69	15	6	4	32	37	64	.356	.409
July	.287	223	64	18	3	5	31	26	56	.361	.462
August	.238	323	77	18	5	7	41	31	84	.305	.390
September/October	.268	380	102	23	5	16	56	51	90	.353	.482
Pre-All Star	.266	834	222	37	12	13	91	103	186	.350	.386
Post-All Star	.264	863	228	53	13	26	121	104	213	.343	.446

Batter vs. Pitcher (career)

Hits Best Against	Avg	AB	H	2B	3B	HR	RBI	BB	SO	OBP	SLG
Mitch Williams	.500	10	5	1	1	0	2	3	3	.615	.800
Kevin Gross	.467	15	7	3	0	1	4	1	3	.500	.867
Darryl Kile	.467	15	7	3	0	1	4	3	3	.556	.867
Dwight Gooden	.440	25	11	2	0	2	7	5	4	.533	.760

Hits Worst Against	Avg	AB	H	2B	3B	HR	RBI	BB	SO	OBP	SLG
Bob Walk	.000	13	0	0	0	0	1	5	2	.263	.000
Randy Tomlin	.125	16	2	1	0	0	0	0	5	.125	.188
Frank Castillo	.136	22	3	1	0	0	0	0	5	.136	.182
Zane Smith	.167	18	3	0	0	0	0	1	5	.211	.167

Batter vs. Pitcher (career)																						
Hits Best Against	Avg	AB	H	2B	3B	HR	RBI	BB	SO	OBP	SLG	Hits Worst Against	Avg	AB	H	2B	3B	HR	RBI	BB	SO	OBP	SLG
Ken Hill	.389	18	7	2	0	2	4	6	2	.542	.833	Bobby Ojeda	.188	16	3	0	0	0	1	0	7	.188	.188

Mike Lansing — Expos

Age 26 – Bats Right (groundball hitter)

	Avg	G	AB	R	H	2B	3B	HR	RBI	BB	SO	HBP	GDP	SB	CS	OBP	SLG	IBB	SH	SF	#Pit	#P/PA	GB	FB	G/F
1993 Season	.287	141	491	64	141	29	1	3	45	46	56	5	16	23	5	.352	.369	2	10	3	1958	3.53	218	124	1.76

1993 Season

	Avg	AB	H	2B	3B	HR	RBI	BB	SO	OBP	SLG		Avg	AB	H	2B	3B	HR	RBI	BB	SO	OBP	SLG
vs. Left	.247	150	37	6	0	1	12	15	20	.315	.307	Scoring Posn	.270	122	33	9	0	2	41	18	19	.366	.393
vs. Right	.305	341	104	23	1	2	33	31	36	.369	.396	Close & Late	.298	84	25	5	0	0	6	10	11	.368	.357
Groundball	.329	140	46	7	0	1	17	18	17	.409	.400	None on/out	.298	114	34	7	1	0	0	7	10	.339	.377
Flyball	.315	73	23	4	0	0	4	5	10	.363	.370	Batting #2	.273	238	65	15	1	1	23	26	24	.349	.357
Home	.261	261	68	15	1	1	23	25	28	.331	.337	Batting #8	.352	71	25	2	0	0	5	9	10	.432	.380
Away	.317	230	73	14	0	2	22	21	28	.376	.404	Other	.280	182	51	12	0	2	17	11	22	.323	.379
Day	.309	162	50	12	0	3	14	12	23	.360	.438	April	.342	76	26	6	0	3	15	4	9	.375	.539
Night	.277	329	91	17	1	0	31	34	33	.349	.334	May	.278	90	25	5	1	0	4	11	10	.371	.356
Grass	.349	129	45	8	0	2	14	8	16	.384	.457	June	.203	79	16	4	0	0	6	7	8	.270	.253
Turf	.265	362	96	21	1	1	31	38	40	.342	.337	July	.297	74	22	4	0	0	3	11	10	.388	.351
First Pitch	.329	70	23	6	0	0	4	1	0	.347	.414	August	.273	88	24	3	0	0	7	5	9	.319	.307
Ahead in Count	.348	138	48	11	1	2	18	30	0	.465	.486	September/October	.333	84	28	7	0	0	10	8	10	.391	.417
Behind in Count	.209	201	42	7	0	0	14	0	49	.217	.244	Pre-All Star	.272	276	75	17	1	3	26	28	30	.344	.373
Two Strikes	.249	189	47	7	0	1	17	15	56	.304	.302	Post-All Star	.307	215	66	12	0	0	19	18	26	.363	.363

1993 By Position

Position	Avg	AB	H	2B	3B	HR	RBI	BB	SO	OBP	SLG	G	GS	Innings	PO	A	E	DP	Fld Pct	Rng Fctr	In Zone	Outs	Zone Rtg	MLB Zone
As 2b	.355	76	27	4	0	3	13	5	9	.395	.526	25	15	148.2	35	52	4	11	.956	5.27	53	45	.849	.895
As 3b	.254	264	67	16	1	0	20	25	31	.324	.322	81	74	617.0	50	162	13	19	.942	3.09	200	181	.905	.834
As ss	.313	147	46	9	0	0	12	15	15	.380	.374	51	34	342.2	51	123	7	23	.961	4.57	137	124	.905	.880

Barry Larkin — Reds

Age 30 – Bats Right (groundball hitter)

	Avg	G	AB	R	H	2B	3B	HR	RBI	BB	SO	HBP	GDP	SB	CS	OBP	SLG	IBB	SH	SF	#Pit	#P/PA	GB	FB	G/F
1993 Season	.315	100	384	57	121	20	3	8	51	51	33	1	13	14	1	.394	.445	6	1	3	1655	3.76	180	104	1.73
Last Five Years	.310	618	2320	353	719	118	23	51	301	238	227	17	54	93	21	.375	.447	23	15	24	9504	3.64	1037	661	1.57

1993 Season

	Avg	AB	H	2B	3B	HR	RBI	BB	SO	OBP	SLG		Avg	AB	H	2B	3B	HR	RBI	BB	SO	OBP	SLG
vs. Left	.358	95	34	9	0	4	21	17	7	.448	.579	Scoring Posn	.321	109	35	4	0	2	40	27	8	.446	.413
vs. Right	.301	289	87	11	3	4	30	34	26	.375	.401	Close & Late	.286	56	16	0	1	0	4	9	9	.385	.321
Groundball	.333	150	50	9	1	3	25	19	13	.404	.467	None on/out	.311	61	19	3	1	1	1	1	4	.323	.443
Flyball	.175	63	11	1	0	1	6	12	10	.316	.238	Batting #2	.345	84	29	2	1	5	15	8	5	.402	.571
Home	.292	195	57	7	1	4	27	27	20	.379	.400	Batting #3	.304	289	88	17	2	3	36	43	27	.393	.408
Away	.339	189	64	13	2	4	24	24	13	.409	.492	Other	.364	11	4	1	0	0	0	0	1	.364	.455
Day	.297	101	30	5	2	6	19	19	6	.398	.564	April	.305	82	25	3	1	0	8	12	5	.400	.366
Night	.322	283	91	15	1	2	32	32	27	.392	.403	May	.342	111	38	7	0	3	20	15	8	.417	.486
Grass	.327	101	33	8	2	3	15	15	8	.407	.535	June	.287	101	29	3	1	2	11	11	13	.354	.396
Turf	.311	283	88	12	1	5	36	36	25	.389	.413	July	.329	76	25	5	0	3	11	9	4	.395	.513
First Pitch	.207	29	6	0	0	0	3	4	0	.303	.207	August	.286	14	4	2	1	0	1	4	3	.444	.571
Ahead in Count	.402	107	43	7	2	3	20	39	0	.558	.589	September/October	.000	0	0	0	0	0	0	0	0	.000	.000
Behind in Count	.212	165	35	7	0	2	10	0	31	.214	.291	Pre-All Star	.319	342	109	17	2	8	48	43	27	.393	.450
Two Strikes	.248	165	41	9	0	3	17	8	33	.286	.358	Post-All Star	.286	42	12	3	1	0	3	8	6	.400	.405

1993 By Position

Position	Avg	AB	H	2B	3B	HR	RBI	BB	SO	OBP	SLG	G	GS	Innings	PO	A	E	DP	Fld Pct	Rng Fctr	In Zone	Outs	Zone Rtg	MLB Zone
As ss	.315	384	121	20	3	8	51	51	33	.394	.445	99	98	845.2	159	281	16	58	.965	4.68	335	295	.881	.880

Last Five Years

	Avg	AB	H	2B	3B	HR	RBI	BB	SO	OBP	SLG		Avg	AB	H	2B	3B	HR	RBI	BB	SO	OBP	SLG
vs. Left	.329	754	248	50	11	24	109	112	53	.413	.520	Scoring Posn	.314	592	186	21	9	9	240	104	66	.405	.426
vs. Right	.301	1566	471	68	12	27	192	126	174	.355	.411	Close & Late	.297	353	105	13	7	3	44	43	45	.373	.399
Groundball	.320	831	266	46	11	14	116	72	83	.375	.452	None on/out	.287	491	141	24	4	11	11	33	47	.337	.420
Flyball	.280	468	131	21	5	10	52	56	56	.359	.410	Batting #2	.294	476	140	23	5	19	53	37	46	.349	.483
Home	.306	1133	347	53	10	33	175	129	118	.379	.458	Batting #3	.315	1554	490	80	16	27	216	176	149	.384	.440
Away	.313	1187	372	65	13	18	126	109	109	.371	.436	Other	.307	290	89	15	2	5	32	25	32	.366	.424
Day	.286	650	186	20	7	18	83	76	63	.363	.422	April	.284	331	94	9	4	6	40	33	34	.358	.390
Night	.319	1670	533	98	16	33	218	162	164	.380	.456	May	.338	417	141	20	6	6	61	39	38	.394	.458
Grass	.296	675	200	40	8	11	70	52	67	.347	.428	June	.313	528	165	25	1	16	71	52	59	.372	.455
Turf	.316	1645	519	78	15	40	231	186	160	.386	.454	July	.314	388	122	30	3	11	44	37	36	.376	.492
First Pitch	.309	233	72	8	3	4	33	17	0	.358	.421	August	.294	357	105	19	6	7	45	47	34	.377	.440
Ahead in Count	.365	646	236	40	9	22	101	166	0	.492	.557	September/October	.308	299	92	15	3	5	40	30	26	.368	.428
Behind in Count	.265	993	263	44	7	13	96	0	189	.269	.363	Pre-All Star	.312	1446	451	68	13	34	192	142	139	.375	.447
Two Strikes	.247	970	240	36	7	14	100	51	227	.287	.342	Post-All Star	.307	874	268	50	10	17	109	96	88	.375	.445

Batter vs. Pitcher (career)																						
Hits Best Against	Avg	AB	H	2B	3B	HR	RBI	BB	SO	OBP	SLG	Hits Worst Against	Avg	AB	H	2B	3B	HR	RBI	BB	SO	OBP	SLG
Randy Tomlin	.692	13	9	4	1	0	2	0	0	.692	1.154	Marvin Freeman	.000	13	0	0	0	0	1	0	0	.000	.000
Andy Ashby	.455	11	5	1	0	1	3	2	1	.538	.818	Les Lancaster	.000	10	0	0	0	0	1	1	1	.083	.000

Batter vs. Pitcher (career)

Hits Best Against	Avg	AB	H	2B	3B	HR	RBI	BB	SO	OBP	SLG	Hits Worst Against	Avg	AB	H	2B	3B	HR	RBI	BB	SO	OBP	SLG
Jim Deshaies	.444	36	16	2	0	5	8	2	2	.474	.917	John Wetteland	.091	11	1	1	0	0	2	0	0	.091	.182
Paul Assenmacher	.400	10	4	1	0	1	2	3	2	.538	.800	Jeff Brantley	.133	15	2	0	0	0	0	0	1	.133	.133
Frank Seminara	.400	10	4	0	1	2	5	0	2	.364	1.200	Bill Swift	.182	11	2	0	0	0	1	0	1	.182	.182

Gene Larkin — Twins

Age 31 – Bats Both

	Avg	G	AB	R	H	2B	3B	HR	RBI	BB	SO	HBP	GDP	SB	CS	OBP	SLG	IBB	SH	SF	#Pit	#P/PA	GB	FB	G/F
1993 Season	.264	56	144	17	38	7	1	1	19	21	16	2	5	0	1	.357	.347	3	2	4	562	3.25	59	47	1.26
Last Five Years	.266	524	1583	196	421	90	8	20	168	175	192	21	41	19	11	.343	.371	20	15	20	6345	3.50	579	513	1.13

1993 Season

	Avg	AB	H	2B	3B	HR	RBI	BB	SO	OBP	SLG		Avg	AB	H	2B	3B	HR	RBI	BB	SO	OBP	SLG
vs. Left	.263	38	10	2	0	0	3	2	1	.310	.316	Scoring Posn	.229	35	8	2	0	1	19	9	3	.367	.371
vs. Right	.264	106	28	5	1	1	16	19	15	.372	.358	Close & Late	.379	29	11	4	0	1	7	2	3	.419	.621
Home	.235	81	19	3	1	1	13	12	7	.330	.333	None on/out	.357	42	15	3	0	0	0	3	6	.400	.429
Away	.302	63	19	4	0	0	6	9	9	.392	.365	Batting #1	.289	45	13	2	1	0	5	8	5	.407	.378
First Pitch	.235	34	8	1	0	0	3	2	0	.308	.265	Batting #7	.302	53	16	3	0	0	5	7	7	.387	.358
Ahead in Count	.351	37	13	1	1	0	5	11	0	.480	.432	Other	.196	46	9	2	0	1	9	6	4	.273	.304
Behind in Count	.273	55	15	4	0	1	9	0	12	.268	.400	Pre-All Star	.258	120	31	6	1	0	13	20	12	.366	.325
Two Strikes	.218	55	12	3	0	1	10	8	16	.313	.327	Post-All Star	.292	24	7	1	0	1	6	1	4	.308	.458

Last Five Years

	Avg	AB	H	2B	3B	HR	RBI	BB	SO	OBP	SLG		Avg	AB	H	2B	3B	HR	RBI	BB	SO	OBP	SLG
vs. Left	.290	458	133	34	3	2	46	47	42	.361	.391	Scoring Posn	.243	416	101	23	3	6	145	62	64	.339	.356
vs. Right	.256	1125	288	56	5	18	122	128	150	.336	.363	Close & Late	.262	271	71	16	1	2	31	27	40	.340	.351
Groundball	.272	460	125	24	4	1	43	44	52	.341	.348	None on/out	.283	381	108	25	2	2	2	40	41	.355	.375
Flyball	.243	337	82	18	3	6	38	49	36	.346	.368	Batting #6	.273	352	96	19	1	7	39	43	38	.356	.392
Home	.273	803	219	44	3	14	96	89	84	.345	.387	Batting #7	.265	520	138	25	1	5	44	58	63	.342	.346
Away	.259	780	202	46	5	6	72	86	108	.341	.354	Other	.263	711	187	46	6	8	85	74	91	.337	.378
Day	.296	524	155	38	4	5	47	77	49	.386	.412	April	.283	276	78	23	1	3	30	19	28	.332	.406
Night	.251	1059	266	52	4	15	121	98	143	.321	.350	May	.265	310	82	17	0	6	46	52	40	.376	.377
Grass	.264	588	155	35	4	5	56	67	78	.346	.362	June	.247	271	67	11	2	2	25	33	43	.341	.325
Turf	.267	995	266	55	4	15	112	108	114	.341	.376	July	.254	205	52	4	2	1	9	25	26	.341	.307
First Pitch	.319	248	79	14	1	3	26	13	0	.359	.419	August	.275	262	72	16	2	4	30	23	27	.333	.397
Ahead in Count	.349	450	157	46	2	10	65	88	0	.448	.527	September/October	.270	259	70	19	1	4	28	23	28	.326	.398
Behind in Count	.213	583	124	16	3	3	47	0	153	.226	.266	Pre-All Star	.263	935	246	54	4	12	105	116	121	.352	.368
Two Strikes	.187	566	106	10	3	6	54	72	192	.288	.247	Post-All Star	.270	648	175	36	4	8	63	59	71	.330	.375

Batter vs. Pitcher (career)

Hits Best Against	Avg	AB	H	2B	3B	HR	RBI	BB	SO	OBP	SLG	Hits Worst Against	Avg	AB	H	2B	3B	HR	RBI	BB	SO	OBP	SLG
Doug Jones	.556	9	5	0	0	0	3	2	0	.636	.556	Jeff Montgomery	.000	12	0	0	0	0	0	1	5	.077	.000
Bud Black	.529	17	9	1	0	1	2	1	1	.556	.765	Tom Henke	.000	8	0	0	0	0	0	4	1	.333	.000
Tim Leary	.500	14	7	1	0	1	4	1	3	.533	.786	Randy Johnson	.067	15	1	0	0	0	1	4	2	.250	.067
Bill Krueger	.400	10	4	2	0	0	1	2	0	.500	.600	Ben McDonald	.100	10	1	0	0	0	0	1	3	.182	.100
Melido Perez	.333	21	7	0	1	2	8	4	4	.423	.714	Bobby Witt	.111	18	2	0	0	0	2	4	6	.261	.111

Mike LaValliere — White Sox

Age 33 – Bats Left

	Avg	G	AB	R	H	2B	3B	HR	RBI	BB	SO	HBP	GDP	SB	CS	OBP	SLG	IBB	SH	SF	#Pit	#P/PA	GB	FB	G/F
1993 Season	.255	38	102	6	26	2	0	0	8	4	14	0	1	0	1	.278	.275	0	7	2	437	3.80	30	33	0.91
Last Five Years	.275	405	1200	95	330	51	3	10	132	154	106	5	29	2	10	.356	.348	33	16	13	4765	3.43	459	393	1.17

1993 Season

	Avg	AB	H	2B	3B	HR	RBI	BB	SO	OBP	SLG		Avg	AB	H	2B	3B	HR	RBI	BB	SO	OBP	SLG
vs. Left	.357	14	5	1	0	0	2	0	2	.357	.429	Scoring Posn	.243	37	9	0	0	0	8	1	7	.250	.243
vs. Right	.239	88	21	1	0	0	6	4	12	.266	.250	Close & Late	.091	11	1	0	0	0	0	0	0	.091	.091

Last Five Years

	Avg	AB	H	2B	3B	HR	RBI	BB	SO	OBP	SLG		Avg	AB	H	2B	3B	HR	RBI	BB	SO	OBP	SLG
vs. Left	.278	180	50	7	2	2	34	21	29	.358	.372	Scoring Posn	.267	330	88	15	3	4	124	67	39	.381	.367
vs. Right	.275	1020	280	44	1	8	98	133	77	.356	.343	Close & Late	.199	156	31	7	0	1	14	37	17	.357	.263
Groundball	.271	409	111	16	2	2	43	59	33	.361	.335	None on/out	.293	287	84	18	0	0	0	31	16	.366	.355
Flyball	.273	271	74	12	1	4	32	35	22	.356	.369	Batting #7	.278	939	261	45	3	8	112	130	79	.365	.358
Home	.302	580	175	21	2	6	73	88	50	.392	.376	Batting #8	.268	138	37	4	0	0	13	8	16	.304	.297
Away	.250	620	155	30	1	4	59	66	56	.321	.321	Other	.260	123	32	2	0	2	7	16	11	.343	.325
Day	.292	363	106	16	1	3	44	42	34	.365	.366	April	.242	153	37	4	1	1	22	16	8	.312	.301
Night	.268	837	224	35	2	7	88	112	72	.353	.339	May	.304	138	42	4	1	1	13	26	11	.410	.370
Grass	.255	377	96	18	0	3	31	37	39	.322	.326	June	.265	162	43	7	0	2	16	21	12	.348	.346
Turf	.284	823	234	33	3	7	101	117	67	.371	.357	July	.290	255	74	10	0	1	23	27	24	.361	.341
First Pitch	.286	224	64	11	2	2	21	19	0	.347	.379	August	.296	233	69	13	0	3	31	32	28	.378	.391
Ahead in Count	.320	294	94	14	0	3	38	94	0	.480	.398	September/October	.251	259	65	13	1	2	27	32	23	.333	.332
Behind in Count	.231	445	103	9	0	3	33	0	90	.232	.272	Pre-All Star	.280	543	152	19	2	4	58	73	43	.364	.344
Two Strikes	.217	433	94	9	1	1	37	35	106	.277	.249	Post-All Star	.271	657	178	32	1	6	74	81	63	.350	.350

Batter vs. Pitcher (career)

Hits Best Against	Avg	AB	H	2B	3B	HR	RBI	BB	SO	OBP	SLG	Hits Worst Against	Avg	AB	H	2B	3B	HR	RBI	BB	SO	OBP	SLG
John Smoltz	.550	20	11	2	0	1	3	5	0	.640	.800	Bob Welch	.083	12	1	0	0	0	1	1	0	.154	.083
Omar Olivares	.545	11	6	0	0	0	1	2	0	.615	.545	Frank DiPino	.111	18	2	1	0	0	2	0	4	.111	.167
Frank Castillo	.500	16	8	1	0	0	1	2	0	.556	.563	Bob Tewksbury	.138	29	4	1	0	0	1	1	1	.167	.172
Kelly Downs	.478	23	11	3	0	0	3	5	1	.571	.609	Danny Cox	.154	13	2	0	0	0	1	1	2	.214	.154

Batter vs. Pitcher (career)												Batter vs. Pitcher (career)										
Hits Best Against	Avg	AB	H	2B	3B	HR	RBI	BB	SO	OBP	SLG	**Hits Worst Against**	Avg	AB	H	2B	3B	HR	RBI	BB	SO	OBP	SLG
Jack Armstrong	.444	9	4	0	0	0	0	3	0	.583	.444	Andy Benes	.176	17	3	0	0	0	0	1	1	.222	.176

Tim Layana — Giants

Age 30 – Pitches Right (groundball pitcher)

	ERA	W	L	Sv	G	GS	IP	BB	SO	Avg	H	2B	3B	HR	RBI	OBP	SLG	GF	IR	IRS	Hld	SvOp	SB	CS	GB	FB	G/F
1993 Season	22.50	0	0	0	1	0	2.0	1	1	.538	7	2	0	1	5	.571	.923	0	1	0	0	0	2	0	5	4	1.25
Career (1990-1993)	4.56	5	5	2	78	0	102.2	56	68	.261	101	22	0	9	54	.355	.388	26	41	13	4	3	16	6	174	89	1.96

1993 Season

	ERA	W	L	Sv	G	GS	IP	H	HR	BB	SO		Avg	AB	H	2B	3B	HR	RBI	BB	SO	OBP	SLG
Home	22.50	0	0	0	1	0	2.0	7	1	1	1	vs. Left	.800	5	4	1	0	1	4	0	0	.800	1.600
Away	0.00	0	0	0	0	0	0.0	0	0	0	0	vs. Right	.375	8	3	1	0	0	1	1	1	.444	.500

Career (1990-1993)

	ERA	W	L	Sv	G	GS	IP	H	HR	BB	SO		Avg	AB	H	2B	3B	HR	RBI	BB	SO	OBP	SLG
Home	5.49	4	2	1	40	0	57.1	60	6	29	31	vs. Left	.286	175	50	14	0	4	30	29	28	.388	.434
Away	3.38	1	3	1	38	0	45.1	41	3	27	37	vs. Right	.241	212	51	8	0	5	24	27	40	.326	.349
Day	7.43	0	2	1	24	0	26.2	36	3	20	14	Inning 1-6	.263	156	41	14	0	5	27	26	31	.373	.449
Night	3.55	5	3	1	54	0	76.0	65	6	36	54	Inning 7+	.260	231	60	8	0	4	27	30	37	.342	.346
Grass	5.76	0	3	0	22	0	25.0	33	2	19	20	None on	.277	202	56	14	0	4	4	26	38	.360	.406
Turf	4.17	5	2	2	56	0	77.2	68	7	37	48	Runners on	.243	185	45	8	0	5	50	30	30	.350	.368
April	8.18	2	0	0	9	0	11.0	15	2	11	4	Scoring Posn	.230	126	29	4	0	4	46	27	23	.367	.357
May	1.42	1	0	0	7	0	6.1	9	0	4	5	Close & Late	.300	60	18	3	0	0	4	13	8	.425	.350
June	1.86	0	0	1	10	0	19.1	17	1	5	14	None on/out	.333	90	30	7	0	2	2	8	14	.388	.478
July	3.60	1	2	0	24	0	30.0	24	2	11	17	vs. 1st Batr (relief)	.333	66	22	2	0	2	5	10	13	.416	.455
August	6.41	1	1	1	15	0	19.2	19	3	13	15	First Inning Pitched	.272	257	70	13	0	7	40	46	55	.382	.405
September/October	6.06	0	2	0	13	0	16.1	17	1	12	13	First 15 Pitches	.265	230	61	12	0	6	30	34	47	.360	.396
Starter	0.00	0	0	0	0	0	0.0	0	0	0	0	Pitch 16-30	.233	116	27	6	0	1	14	19	19	.343	.310
Reliever	4.56	5	5	2	78	0	102.2	101	9	56	68	Pitch 31-45	.325	40	13	4	0	2	10	3	2	.372	.575
0 Days rest	0.42	1	0	0	19	0	21.2	9	0	9	19	Pitch 46+	.000	1	0	0	0	0	0	0	0	.000	.000
1 or 2 Days rest	5.08	2	3	2	32	0	44.1	44	3	27	26	First Pitch	.258	66	17	3	0	2	9	5	0	.319	.394
3+ Days rest	6.38	2	2	0	27	0	36.2	48	6	20	23	Ahead in Count	.177	158	28	8	0	2	11	0	60	.176	.266
Pre-All Star	3.15	3	1	1	31	0	45.2	44	3	20	28	Behind in Count	.433	97	42	9	0	3	27	33	0	.568	.619
Post-All Star	5.68	2	4	1	47	0	57.0	57	6	36	40	Two Strikes	.169	160	27	5	0	4	15	17	68	.249	.275

Terry Leach — White Sox

Age 40 – Pitches Right (groundball pitcher)

	ERA	W	L	Sv	G	GS	IP	BB	SO	Avg	H	2B	3B	HR	RBI	OBP	SLG	GF	IR	IRS	Hld	SvOp	SB	CS	GB	FB	G/F
1993 Season	2.81	0	0	1	14	0	16.0	2	3	.250	15	3	0	0	4	.281	.300	8	8	1	2	1	0	0	23	19	1.21
Last Five Years	3.26	14	18	3	210	3	333.2	97	139	.264	335	66	9	12	162	.317	.358	80	165	57	19	9	34	8	542	348	1.56

1993 Season

	ERA	W	L	Sv	G	GS	IP	H	HR	BB	SO		Avg	AB	H	2B	3B	HR	RBI	BB	SO	OBP	SLG
Home	2.70	0	0	0	7	0	6.2	8	0	1	0	vs. Left	.227	22	5	0	0	0	1	0	2	.227	.227
Away	2.89	0	0	1	7	0	9.1	7	0	1	3	vs. Right	.263	38	10	3	0	0	3	2	1	.310	.342

Last Five Years

	ERA	W	L	Sv	G	GS	IP	H	HR	BB	SO		Avg	AB	H	2B	3B	HR	RBI	BB	SO	OBP	SLG
Home	2.50	6	0	1	103	1	169.1	159	4	38	72	vs. Left	.301	548	165	33	5	4	68	52	29	.359	.401
Away	4.05	8	18	2	107	2	164.1	176	8	59	67	vs. Right	.235	723	170	33	4	8	94	45	110	.285	.325
Day	3.54	2	7	0	60	1	89.0	97	5	25	38	Inning 1-6	.298	383	114	24	2	5	77	28	40	.342	.410
Night	3.16	12	11	3	150	2	244.2	238	7	72	101	Inning 7+	.249	888	221	42	7	7	85	69	99	.306	.336
Grass	3.16	9	15	1	111	2	168.0	166	6	53	66	None on	.240	699	168	36	4	5	5	42	81	.287	.325
Turf	3.37	5	3	2	99	1	165.2	169	6	44	73	Runners on	.292	572	167	30	5	7	157	55	58	.352	.399
April	1.66	1	1	1	28	0	43.1	29	1	7	12	Scoring Posn	.274	390	107	20	4	5	147	46	44	.344	.385
May	3.00	2	0	0	40	0	54.0	49	2	14	25	Close & Late	.282	323	91	18	4	2	41	28	33	.344	.381
June	3.97	1	4	0	39	0	65.2	75	1	17	17	None on/out	.218	294	64	9	1	2	2	18	39	.270	.276
July	3.02	3	6	2	32	2	59.2	63	3	22	29	vs. 1st Batr (relief)	.211	180	38	3	1	2	30	8	24	.259	.272
August	2.03	3	2	0	30	0	57.2	46	4	9	24	First Inning Pitched	.255	647	165	27	5	4	100	51	74	.312	.331
September/October	5.57	4	5	0	41	1	53.1	73	1	28	32	First 15 Pitches	.256	707	181	33	5	3	93	49	78	.306	.330
Starter	7.71	1	2	0	3	3	14.0	23	1	5	10	Pitch 16-30	.271	354	96	22	2	6	39	30	34	.327	.395
Reliever	3.07	13	16	3	207	0	319.2	312	11	92	129	Pitch 31-45	.208	130	27	8	1	1	6	12	19	.280	.308
0 Days rest	2.67	1	2	0	20	0	27.0	29	1	12	15	Pitch 46+	.388	80	31	3	1	2	24	6	8	.427	.525
1 or 2 Days rest	3.42	5	9	1	97	0	139.1	139	5	39	55	First Pitch	.326	230	75	16	2	3	31	24	0	.387	.452
3+ Days rest	2.82	7	5	2	90	0	153.1	144	5	41	59	Ahead in Count	.210	557	117	22	3	4	60	0	126	.215	.282
Pre-All Star	3.00	5	8	1	116	1	186.0	174	5	47	68	Behind in Count	.301	279	84	16	3	2	43	38	0	.384	.401
Post-All Star	3.60	9	10	2	94	2	147.2	161	7	50	71	Two Strikes	.211	479	101	21	2	6	55	33	139	.263	.301

Pitcher vs. Batter (since 1984)

Pitches Best Vs.	Avg	AB	H	2B	3B	HR	RBI	BB	SO	OBP	SLG	**Pitches Worst Vs.**	Avg	AB	H	2B	3B	HR	RBI	BB	SO	OBP	SLG
Glenn Davis	.000	10	0	0	0	0	1	3	1	.231	.000	Felix Fermin	.636	11	7	3	0	0	1	0	0	.636	.909
Bob Melvin	.091	11	1	0	0	0	2	1	2	.167	.091	Don Mattingly	.583	12	7	0	1	0	2	0	0	.583	.750
Luis Rivera	.091	11	1	0	0	0	0	0	0	.091	.091	Dave Martinez	.455	11	5	2	0	1	2	0	2	.455	.909
Andres Galarraga	.133	15	2	0	0	0	0	2	2	.235	.133	Steve Lyons	.444	9	4	2	0	0	2	2	0	.545	.667
Mike Devereaux	.200	15	3	0	0	0	1	0	3	.200	.200	Randy Milligan	.400	10	4	1	0	2	4	1	1	.455	1.100

Tim Leary — Mariners

Age 35 – Pitches Right

	ERA	W	L	Sv	G	GS	IP	BB	SO	Avg	H	2B	3B	HR	RBI	OBP	SLG	CG	ShO	Sup	QS	#P/S	SB	CS	GB	FB	G/F
1993 Season	5.05	11	9	0	33	27	169.1	58	68	.300	202	38	7	21	86	.362	.470	0	0	5.95	13	87	10	9	300	176	1.70
Last Five Years	4.70	40	62	0	151	130	846.0	348	458	.275	890	164	20	88	393	.349	.420	12	1	4.19	59	95	84	35	1329	895	1.48

1993 Season

	ERA	W	L	Sv	G	GS	IP	H	HR	BB	SO
Home	4.97	5	3	0	14	11	67.0	82	7	22	25
Away	5.10	6	6	0	19	16	102.1	120	14	36	43
Day	5.93	4	3	0	12	9	57.2	69	10	20	18
Night	4.59	7	6	0	21	18	111.2	133	11	38	50
Grass	4.61	6	4	0	15	13	82.0	91	10	29	35
Turf	5.46	5	5	0	18	14	87.1	111	11	29	33
April	7.43	0	1	0	6	1	13.1	17	0	8	9
May	3.83	3	1	0	6	6	40.0	40	4	11	14
June	4.02	3	1	0	5	5	31.1	35	2	4	9
July	5.31	2	1	0	4	4	20.1	25	3	8	7
August	9.75	0	3	0	6	5	24.0	38	5	12	7
September/October	3.35	3	2	0	6	6	40.1	47	7	15	22
Starter	4.90	11	8	0	27	27	159.2	192	21	53	61
Reliever	7.45	0	1	0	6	0	9.2	10	0	5	7
0-3 Days Rest	8.44	0	0	0	1	1	5.1	10	0	0	2
4 Days Rest	4.57	6	4	0	14	14	86.2	106	14	29	35
5+ Days Rest	5.05	5	4	0	12	12	67.2	76	7	24	24
Pre-All Star	4.47	7	3	0	18	13	90.2	99	8	24	35
Post-All Star	5.72	4	6	0	15	14	78.2	103	13	34	33

	Avg	AB	H	2B	3B	HR	RBI	BB	SO	OBP	SLG
vs. Left	.331	347	115	29	3	9	38	33	34	.392	.510
vs. Right	.266	327	87	9	4	12	48	25	34	.330	.428
Inning 1-6	.305	573	175	37	4	17	74	42	52	.360	.473
Inning 7+	.267	101	27	1	3	4	12	16	16	.370	.455
None on	.302	384	116	23	3	16	16	28	39	.354	.503
Runners on	.297	290	86	15	4	5	70	30	29	.371	.428
Scoring Posn	.266	173	46	10	1	4	63	25	16	.373	.405
Close & Late	.371	35	13	0	2	2	5	8	5	.488	.657
None on/out	.316	174	55	8	2	7	7	15	19	.374	.506
vs. 1st Batr (relief)	.400	5	2	0	0	0	0	1	0	.500	.400
First Inning Pitched	.328	131	43	10	2	5	22	19	12	.429	.550
First 75 Pitches	.308	575	177	36	6	18	72	44	55	.363	.485
Pitch 76-90	.234	64	15	1	0	1	11	7	9	.329	.297
Pitch 91-105	.308	26	8	1	1	2	3	5	1	.419	.654
Pitch 106+	.222	9	2	0	0	0	0	2	3	.364	.222
First Pitch	.269	119	32	8	0	2	9	4	0	.298	.387
Ahead in Count	.236	258	61	10	3	8	29	0	58	.239	.391
Behind in Count	.393	168	66	13	3	5	24	34	0	.505	.595
Two Strikes	.231	225	52	10	2	7	29	20	68	.297	.387

Last Five Years

	ERA	W	L	Sv	G	GS	IP	H	HR	BB	SO
Home	4.62	14	29	0	68	59	382.0	399	39	165	219
Away	4.77	26	33	0	83	71	464.0	491	49	183	239
Day	5.59	12	17	0	49	42	257.2	284	29	114	149
Night	4.31	28	45	0	102	88	588.1	606	59	234	309
Grass	4.57	22	39	0	93	79	519.2	535	57	224	287
Turf	4.91	18	23	0	58	51	326.1	355	31	124	171
April	4.07	7	5	0	22	17	121.2	113	11	41	81
May	3.82	9	13	0	27	27	184.0	176	18	75	102
June	4.70	8	12	0	28	27	172.1	185	19	53	67
July	7.36	5	9	0	23	17	95.1	130	7	49	51
August	5.50	5	11	0	28	20	129.1	136	16	68	77
September/October	3.89	6	12	0	23	22	143.1	150	17	62	80
Starter	4.54	39	58	0	130	130	808.1	844	84	325	435
Reliever	8.12	1	4	0	21	0	37.2	46	4	23	23
0-3 Days Rest	7.58	0	2	0	4	4	19.0	30	1	8	12
4 Days Rest	4.44	23	37	0	78	78	485.0	512	49	203	263
5+ Days Rest	4.52	16	19	0	48	48	304.1	302	34	114	160
Pre-All Star	4.51	25	35	0	85	79	514.2	527	52	191	269
Post-All Star	5.00	15	27	0	66	51	331.1	363	36	157	189

	Avg	AB	H	2B	3B	HR	RBI	BB	SO	OBP	SLG
vs. Left	.288	1670	481	98	14	47	205	185	213	.359	.448
vs. Right	.261	1567	409	66	6	41	188	163	245	.338	.389
Inning 1-6	.272	2739	744	138	16	71	333	285	377	.344	.411
Inning 7+	.293	498	146	26	4	17	60	63	81	.375	.464
None on	.270	1857	502	87	10	54	54	178	267	.339	.415
Runners on	.281	1380	388	77	10	34	339	170	191	.361	.425
Scoring Posn	.257	777	200	43	6	22	299	133	126	.364	.413
Close & Late	.276	246	68	9	3	6	29	36	43	.372	.411
None on/out	.281	827	232	36	4	29	29	89	111	.357	.439
vs. 1st Batr (relief)	.389	18	7	0	0	1	2	3	4	.476	.556
First Inning Pitched	.310	506	157	30	5	15	82	71	77	.399	.478
First 75 Pitches	.274	2554	701	125	18	64	288	247	350	.342	.413
Pitch 76-90	.279	362	101	19	1	14	65	56	54	.378	.453
Pitch 91-105	.292	202	59	15	1	8	29	26	31	.377	.495
Pitch 106+	.244	119	29	5	0	2	11	19	23	.350	.336
First Pitch	.305	548	167	31	2	15	75	22	0	.343	.451
Ahead in Count	.217	1276	277	52	6	23	110	0	399	.222	.321
Behind in Count	.338	832	281	55	5	30	114	183	0	.458	.524
Two Strikes	.196	1234	242	44	7	25	125	143	458	.280	.304

Pitcher vs. Batter (since 1984)

Pitches Best Vs.	Avg	AB	H	2B	3B	HR	RBI	BB	SO	OBP	SLG
Milt Cuyler	.000	15	0	0	0	0	1	0	2	.000	.000
Greg Vaughn	.000	11	0	0	0	0	1	2	3	.143	.000
Gary Gaetti	.048	21	1	0	0	0	1	1	3	.091	.048
Spike Owen	.056	18	1	0	0	0	1	1	1	.105	.056
David Hulse	.083	12	1	0	0	0	0	0	0	.083	.083

Pitches Worst Vs.	Avg	AB	H	2B	3B	HR	RBI	BB	SO	OBP	SLG
Luis Rivera	.615	13	8	2	0	1	3	1	0	.643	1.000
Cory Snyder	.583	12	7	0	0	2	8	0	2	.583	1.083
Joe Carter	.556	18	10	2	0	4	7	0	3	.500	1.333
Mike Macfarlane	.545	11	6	3	0	2	6	1	1	.583	1.364
Steve Buechele	.462	13	6	1	1	2	6	2	1	.533	1.154

Derek Lee — Twins

Age 27 – Bats Left

	Avg	G	AB	R	H	2B	3B	HR	RBI	BB	SO	HBP	GDP	SB	CS	OBP	SLG	IBB	SH	SF	#Pit	#P/PA	GB	FB	G/F
1993 Season	.152	15	33	3	5	1	0	0	4	1	4	0	0	0	0	.176	.182	0	0	0	131	3.85	13	13	1.00

1993 Season

	Avg	AB	H	2B	3B	HR	RBI	BB	SO	OBP	SLG
vs. Left	.000	0	0	0	0	0	0	0	0	.000	.000
vs. Right	.152	33	5	1	0	0	4	1	4	.176	.182
Scoring Posn	.200	10	2	1	0	0	4	0	0	.200	.300
Close & Late	.000	6	0	0	0	0	1	0	1	.000	.000

Manuel Lee — Rangers

Age 29 – Bats Both (groundball hitter)

	Avg	G	AB	R	H	2B	3B	HR	RBI	BB	SO	HBP	GDP	SB	CS	OBP	SLG	IBB	SH	SF	#Pit	#P/PA	GB	FB	G/F
1993 Season	.220	73	205	31	45	3	1	1	12	22	39	2	2	2	4	.300	.259	3	9	1	928	3.88	87	32	2.72
Last Five Years	.245	555	1737	193	426	52	11	13	155	142	369	4	37	22	11	.302	.310	4	29	12	7226	3.76	735	333	2.21

1993 Season

	Avg	AB	H	2B	3B	HR	RBI	BB	SO	OBP	SLG
vs. Left	.233	43	10	1	0	0	1	3	8	.298	.256
vs. Right	.216	162	35	2	1	1	11	19	31	.301	.259
Home	.263	76	20	2	1	0	6	11	15	.352	.316
Away	.194	129	25	1	0	1	6	11	24	.268	.225
First Pitch	.250	24	6	0	0	0	2	2	0	.357	.250
Ahead in Count	.333	36	12	1	0	0	2	12	0	.500	.361
Scoring Posn	.235	51	12	0	0	0	9	8	9	.344	.235
Close & Late	.217	23	5	0	0	0	0	2	5	.280	.217
None on/out	.238	42	10	1	0	0	0	5	6	.319	.262
Batting #8	.111	36	4	0	0	0	2	6	5	.233	.111
Batting #9	.233	163	38	3	1	1	10	16	34	.309	.282
Other	.500	6	3	0	0	0	0	0	0	.500	.500

1993 Season

	Avg	AB	H	2B	3B	HR	RBI	BB	SO	OBP	SLG
Behind in Count	.165	103	17	1	1	1	5	0	35	.165	.223
Two Strikes	.152	112	17	2	1	0	2	8	39	.208	.188

	Avg	AB	H	2B	3B	HR	RBI	BB	SO	OBP	SLG
Pre-All Star	.164	73	12	0	0	0	3	7	10	.244	.164
Post-All Star	.250	132	33	3	1	1	9	15	29	.331	.311

Last Five Years

	Avg	AB	H	2B	3B	HR	RBI	BB	SO	OBP	SLG
vs. Left	.257	622	160	26	4	7	64	45	116	.308	.346
vs. Right	.239	1115	266	26	7	6	91	97	253	.299	.291
Groundball	.240	471	113	13	2	1	37	34	103	.290	.282
Flyball	.261	360	94	9	5	4	33	37	86	.328	.347
Home	.246	789	194	26	6	4	68	76	169	.311	.309
Away	.245	948	232	26	5	9	87	66	200	.294	.311
Day	.238	499	119	12	3	5	42	38	103	.293	.305
Night	.248	1238	307	40	8	8	113	104	266	.306	.313
Grass	.257	803	206	23	6	6	75	60	164	.308	.323
Turf	.236	934	220	29	5	7	80	82	205	.296	.300
First Pitch	.323	220	71	10	0	3	38	3	0	.338	.409
Ahead in Count	.299	321	96	10	3	2	32	96	0	.452	.368
Behind in Count	.188	867	163	21	5	6	56	0	329	.189	.245
Two Strikes	.170	878	149	18	7	5	46	43	369	.210	.223

	Avg	AB	H	2B	3B	HR	RBI	BB	SO	OBP	SLG
Scoring Posn	.263	426	112	16	2	3	138	33	91	.311	.331
Close & Late	.213	286	61	5	1	1	22	31	63	.291	.248
None on/out	.255	431	110	15	2	3	3	38	91	.316	.320
Batting #8	.235	633	149	19	4	7	58	42	144	.281	.311
Batting #9	.253	965	244	30	5	6	88	91	197	.318	.313
Other	.237	139	33	3	2	0	9	9	28	.284	.288
April	.250	280	70	9	1	0	22	31	59	.326	.289
May	.256	227	58	3	3	8	24	17	48	.308	.401
June	.267	322	86	15	2	1	33	21	65	.311	.335
July	.190	300	57	4	1	1	22	18	68	.234	.220
August	.239	348	83	10	2	2	31	24	75	.286	.296
September/October	.277	260	72	11	2	1	23	31	54	.355	.346
Pre-All Star	.253	925	234	29	7	9	83	76	194	.310	.329
Post-All Star	.236	812	192	23	4	4	72	66	175	.293	.289

Batter vs. Pitcher (career)

Hits Best Against	Avg	AB	H	2B	3B	HR	RBI	BB	SO	OBP	SLG
Danny Darwin	.556	9	5	0	0	0	0	2	1	.636	.556
Tom Candiotti	.500	12	6	0	1	0	3	0	1	.462	.667
Dave Righetti	.471	17	8	0	0	0	4	1	2	.500	.471
Chuck Finley	.435	23	10	1	0	0	3	3	2	.500	.478
Mike Witt	.400	10	4	2	0	0	3	0	1	.364	.600

Hits Worst Against	Avg	AB	H	2B	3B	HR	RBI	BB	SO	OBP	SLG
Luis Aquino	.000	14	0	0	0	0	1	1	3	.067	.000
Bill Gullickson	.000	13	0	0	0	0	0	2	1	.133	.000
Rick Honeycutt	.000	12	0	0	0	0	0	2	3	.143	.000
Charles Nagy	.067	15	1	0	0	0	0	2	5	.176	.067
Mark Guthrie	.071	14	1	0	0	0	0	1	4	.133	.071

Craig Lefferts — Rangers

Age 36 – Pitches Left

	ERA	W	L	Sv	G	GS	IP	BB	SO	Avg	H	2B	3B	HR	RBI	OBP	SLG	GF	IR	IRS	Hld	SvOp	SB	CS	GB	FB	G/F
1993 Season	6.05	3	9	0	52	8	83.1	28	58	.304	102	10	2	17	59	.357	.499	9	38	8	11	0	4	4	100	107	0.93
Last Five Years	3.74	27	36	66	264	40	534.1	127	341	.269	551	79	12	62	261	.310	.410	93	167	45	27	84	39	22	673	591	1.14

1993 Season

	ERA	W	L	Sv	G	GS	IP	H	HR	BB	SO
Home	5.51	1	3	0	21	3	32.2	37	5	13	24
Away	6.39	2	6	0	31	5	50.2	65	12	15	34
Starter	8.54	1	5	0	8	8	39.0	55	11	12	26
Reliever	3.86	2	4	0	44	0	44.1	47	6	16	32
0 Days rest	2.70	1	0	0	8	0	6.2	9	2	1	1
1 or 2 Days rest	3.86	0	2	0	25	0	23.1	25	2	7	14
3+ Days rest	4.40	1	2	0	11	0	14.1	13	2	8	17
Pre-All Star	6.97	2	7	0	26	8	60.2	74	14	16	42
Post-All Star	3.57	1	2	0	26	0	22.2	28	3	12	16

	Avg	AB	H	2B	3B	HR	RBI	BB	SO	OBP	SLG
vs. Left	.253	87	22	3	0	2	11	6	17	.309	.356
vs. Right	.323	248	80	7	2	15	48	22	41	.374	.548
Scoring Posn	.342	76	26	1	1	3	40	14	10	.430	.500
Close & Late	.328	58	19	0	1	1	9	5	8	.381	.414
None on/out	.313	83	26	4	1	5	5	5	15	.352	.566
First Pitch	.360	50	18	1	0	2	8	2	0	.385	.500
Ahead in Count	.183	142	26	3	1	3	16	0	46	.186	.282
Behind in Count	.507	75	38	5	0	6	18	16	0	.593	.813
Two Strikes	.162	136	22	2	2	4	17	10	58	.218	.294

Last Five Years

	ERA	W	L	Sv	G	GS	IP	H	HR	BB	SO
Home	3.39	12	18	31	128	19	263.0	256	27	55	174
Away	4.08	15	18	35	136	21	271.1	295	35	72	167
Day	3.27	10	12	22	84	13	187.1	168	22	34	126
Night	3.99	17	24	44	180	27	347.0	383	40	93	215
Grass	3.83	20	31	48	197	31	407.0	416	45	100	272
Turf	3.46	7	5	18	67	9	127.1	135	17	27	69
April	4.60	5	7	10	35	9	76.1	82	12	16	48
May	3.88	5	7	18	41	9	109.0	109	15	31	75
June	3.62	7	6	11	50	5	97.0	93	7	19	53
July	2.81	6	4	9	47	6	93.0	88	7	27	64
August	4.08	2	6	12	51	6	86.0	102	11	17	38
September/October	3.58	2	6	6	40	5	73.0	77	10	17	63
Starter	4.55	15	17	0	40	40	235.1	269	30	53	130
Reliever	3.10	12	19	66	224	0	299.0	282	32	74	211
0 Days rest	3.38	2	3	13	42	0	48.0	47	9	18	26
1 or 2 Days rest	2.83	7	8	37	115	0	162.0	143	15	24	117
3+ Days rest	3.44	3	8	16	67	0	89.0	92	8	32	68
Pre-All Star	4.01	19	24	40	143	26	320.2	325	39	75	197
Post-All Star	3.33	8	12	26	121	14	213.2	226	23	52	144

	Avg	AB	H	2B	3B	HR	RBI	BB	SO	OBP	SLG
vs. Left	.235	446	105	11	3	8	51	23	91	.274	.327
vs. Right	.278	1605	446	68	9	54	210	104	250	.320	.432
Inning 1-6	.286	900	257	40	5	28	122	54	144	.324	.434
Inning 7+	.255	1151	294	39	7	34	139	73	197	.299	.390
None on	.271	1143	310	49	4	35	35	59	189	.308	.413
Runners on	.265	908	241	30	8	27	226	68	152	.313	.405
Scoring Posn	.255	510	130	14	5	13	187	50	96	.313	.378
Close & Late	.248	665	165	17	3	16	88	44	100	.295	.355
None on/out	.289	502	145	18	1	15	15	21	80	.319	.418
vs. 1st Batr (relief)	.260	204	53	6	1	3	24	13	44	.299	.343
First Inning Pitched	.253	870	220	33	7	22	123	62	166	.301	.383
First 15 Pitches	.268	851	228	39	5	25	113	52	150	.308	.414
Pitch 16-30	.247	507	125	14	4	14	51	33	86	.294	.373
Pitch 31-45	.253	233	59	8	0	7	30	12	46	.286	.378
Pitch 46+	.302	460	139	18	3	16	67	30	59	.343	.459
First Pitch	.347	323	112	17	2	9	53	14	0	.371	.495
Ahead in Count	.206	953	196	28	6	18	90	0	298	.207	.304
Behind in Count	.329	389	128	19	1	18	58	70	0	.430	.522
Two Strikes	.185	868	161	25	6	13	73	41	341	.222	.273

Pitcher vs. Batter (since 1984)

Pitches Best Vs.	Avg	AB	H	2B	3B	HR	RBI	BB	SO	OBP	SLG
Wally Backman	.083	12	1	0	0	0	0	1	4	.154	.083
Darren Daulton	.083	12	1	0	0	0	0	1	4	.154	.083
Bobby Bonilla	.087	23	2	0	0	0	3	0	4	.083	.087
Don Slaught	.091	11	1	0	0	0	0	0	0	.091	.091
Glenn Wilson	.105	19	2	0	0	0	1	0	2	.105	.105

Pitches Worst Vs.	Avg	AB	H	2B	3B	HR	RBI	BB	SO	OBP	SLG
Brett Butler	.545	11	6	0	0	1	1	1	1	.583	.818
Tim Raines	.500	20	10	3	1	1	5	3	2	.542	.900
Andre Dawson	.500	16	8	1	0	1	6	2	0	.526	.750
Mark Grace	.500	10	5	2	0	0	1	3	0	.615	.700
Mike Sharperson	.400	10	4	0	0	2	5	2	1	.500	1.000

Phil Leftwich — Angels

Age 25 – Pitches Right

	ERA	W	L	Sv	G	GS	IP	BB	SO	Avg	H	2B	3B	HR	RBI	OBP	SLG	CG	ShO	Sup	QS	#P/S	SB	CS	GB	FB	G/F
1993 Season	3.79	4	6	0	12	12	80.2	27	31	.262	81	15	1	5	33	.326	.366	1	0	5.24	8	103	4	4	116	106	1.09

1993 Season

	ERA	W	L	Sv	G	GS	IP	H	HR	BB	SO
Home	2.96	2	4	0	7	7	51.2	46	1	12	23
Away	5.28	2	2	0	5	5	29.0	35	4	15	8
Starter	3.79	4	6	0	12	12	80.2	81	5	27	31
Reliever	0.00	0	0	0	0	0	0.0	0	0	0	0
0-3 Days Rest	0.00	0	0	0	0	0	0.0	0	0	0	0
4 Days Rest	3.62	4	3	0	8	8	54.2	52	3	17	21
5+ Days Rest	4.15	0	3	0	4	4	26.0	29	2	10	10
Pre-All Star	0.00	0	0	0	0	0	0.0	0	0	0	0
Post-All Star	3.79	4	6	0	12	12	80.2	81	5	27	31

	Avg	AB	H	2B	3B	HR	RBI	BB	SO	OBP	SLG
vs. Left	.242	161	39	4	1	2	19	17	12	.315	.317
vs. Right	.284	148	42	11	0	3	14	10	19	.340	.419
Scoring Posn	.281	64	18	1	1	1	27	13	5	.405	.375
Close & Late	.154	26	4	1	0	0	1	2	2	.214	.192
None on/out	.244	78	19	5	0	1	1	5	10	.289	.346
First Pitch	.277	47	13	0	1	2	7	0	0	.277	.447
Ahead in Count	.266	124	33	8	0	1	14	0	29	.276	.355
Behind in Count	.278	79	22	4	0	1	8	16	0	.400	.367
Two Strikes	.248	125	31	7	0	2	13	11	31	.317	.352

Charlie Leibrandt — Rangers

Age 37 – Pitches Left

	ERA	W	L	Sv	G	GS	IP	BB	SO	Avg	H	2B	3B	HR	RBI	OBP	SLG	CG	ShO	Sup	QS	#P/S	SB	CS	GB	FB	G/F
1993 Season	4.55	9	10	0	26	26	150.1	45	89	.284	169	40	4	15	73	.336	.440	1	0	5.93	12	92	19	5	201	183	1.10
Last Five Years	3.88	53	52	0	151	144	896.1	232	470	.268	932	186	22	64	374	.316	.390	15	6	4.76	77	94	117	44	1242	1041	1.19

1993 Season

	ERA	W	L	Sv	G	GS	IP	H	HR	BB	SO
Home	4.74	1	6	0	12	12	68.1	79	8	25	40
Away	4.39	8	4	0	14	14	82.0	90	7	20	49
Starter	4.55	9	10	0	26	26	150.1	169	15	45	89
Reliever	0.00	0	0	0	0	0	0.0	0	0	0	0
0-3 Days Rest	0.00	0	0	0	0	0	0.0	0	0	0	0
4 Days Rest	5.38	5	6	0	15	15	85.1	102	8	29	47
5+ Days Rest	3.46	4	4	0	11	11	65.0	67	7	16	42
Pre-All Star	3.89	9	4	0	19	19	118.0	127	12	32	70
Post-All Star	6.96	0	6	0	7	7	32.1	42	3	13	19

	Avg	AB	H	2B	3B	HR	RBI	BB	SO	OBP	SLG
vs. Left	.384	86	33	9	1	2	12	4	10	.418	.581
vs. Right	.267	509	136	31	3	13	61	41	79	.323	.417
Scoring Posn	.272	151	41	12	2	4	57	25	20	.370	.457
Close & Late	.344	32	11	3	0	1	3	1	3	.364	.531
None on/out	.316	155	49	14	1	2	2	9	25	.361	.458
First Pitch	.352	91	32	10	1	2	12	4	0	.371	.549
Ahead in Count	.200	230	46	6	0	4	16	0	69	.213	.278
Behind in Count	.424	151	64	14	2	8	32	23	0	.500	.702
Two Strikes	.167	251	42	8	1	3	22	18	89	.228	.243

Last Five Years

	ERA	W	L	Sv	G	GS	IP	H	HR	BB	SO
Home	3.81	25	26	0	72	68	434.2	468	31	112	205
Away	3.94	28	26	0	79	76	461.2	464	33	120	265
Day	4.49	12	18	0	44	41	242.1	276	18	62	130
Night	3.65	41	34	0	107	103	654.0	656	46	170	340
Grass	3.74	38	38	0	104	102	637.1	650	48	156	343
Turf	4.20	15	14	0	47	42	259.0	282	16	76	127
April	2.81	9	6	0	20	20	128.1	124	5	38	66
May	3.85	8	7	0	24	23	147.1	154	10	26	74
June	3.46	11	8	0	27	27	182.0	183	14	49	75
July	5.59	7	13	0	27	27	153.0	182	13	51	83
August	4.23	9	9	0	23	22	129.2	136	14	26	80
September/October	3.29	9	9	0	30	25	156.0	153	8	42	92
Starter	3.91	53	52	0	144	144	883.1	922	64	229	458
Reliever	1.38	0	0	0	7	0	13.0	10	0	3	12
0-3 Days Rest	4.58	3	4	0	11	11	59.0	63	3	9	36
4 Days Rest	4.24	29	36	0	86	86	520.1	566	42	144	253
5+ Days Rest	3.23	21	12	0	47	47	304.0	293	19	76	169
Pre-All Star	3.63	31	23	0	80	79	508.1	521	36	131	237
Post-All Star	4.20	22	29	0	71	65	388.0	411	28	101	233

	Avg	AB	H	2B	3B	HR	RBI	BB	SO	OBP	SLG
vs. Left	.279	678	189	35	5	8	73	36	87	.320	.381
vs. Right	.266	2794	743	151	17	56	301	196	383	.315	.392
Inning 1-6	.269	2953	793	162	20	57	339	204	423	.317	.395
Inning 7+	.268	519	139	24	2	7	35	28	47	.307	.362
None on	.268	2071	555	99	12	31	31	104	274	.306	.372
Runners on	.269	1401	377	87	10	33	343	128	196	.329	.416
Scoring Posn	.267	802	214	52	6	18	293	97	109	.340	.414
Close & Late	.248	230	57	8	0	2	14	19	19	.305	.309
None on/out	.262	910	238	49	4	16	16	43	116	.299	.377
vs. 1st Batr (relief)	.429	7	3	0	0	0	0	0	2	.429	.429
First Inning Pitched	.277	581	161	35	0	9	74	49	79	.336	.384
First 75 Pitches	.270	2608	705	148	19	52	304	180	364	.319	.401
Pitch 76-90	.238	433	103	19	1	5	30	22	60	.277	.321
Pitch 91-105	.282	280	79	12	1	3	19	19	33	.332	.364
Pitch 106+	.298	151	45	7	1	4	21	11	13	.344	.437
First Pitch	.309	534	165	35	4	8	66	12	0	.321	.434
Ahead in Count	.208	1446	301	59	11	17	95	0	376	.216	.299
Behind in Count	.334	778	260	50	5	23	122	114	0	.417	.500
Two Strikes	.199	1444	287	59	9	15	102	105	470	.257	.283

Pitcher vs. Batter (since 1984)

Pitches Best Vs.	Avg	AB	H	2B	3B	HR	RBI	BB	SO	OBP	SLG
Chris James	.000	12	0	0	0	0	0	1	2	.077	.000
Jerald Clark	.000	11	0	0	0	0	0	0	1	.000	.000
Jose Vizcaino	.083	12	1	1	0	0	0	0	0	.083	.167
Dickie Thon	.091	11	1	0	0	0	1	0	1	.083	.091
Barry Bonds	.133	15	2	0	0	0	1	0	5	.133	.133

Pitches Worst Vs.	Avg	AB	H	2B	3B	HR	RBI	BB	SO	OBP	SLG
Ricky Jordan	.583	12	7	1	0	1	3	1	0	.615	.917
Ryne Sandberg	.500	16	8	1	0	2	3	3	1	.579	.938
Larry Walker	.500	14	7	2	1	1	4	1	1	.500	1.000
Kirk Gibson	.500	12	6	2	0	1	3	0	1	.500	.917
Cecil Fielder	.346	26	9	1	0	4	7	5	4	.452	.846

Al Leiter — Blue Jays

Age 28 – Pitches Left

	ERA	W	L	Sv	G	GS	IP	BB	SO	Avg	H	2B	3B	HR	RBI	OBP	SLG	GF	IR	IRS	Hld	SvOp	SB	CS	GB	FB	G/F
1993 Season	4.11	9	6	2	34	12	105.0	56	66	.240	93	5	0	8	44	.339	.314	4	22	5	3	3	7	5	167	90	1.86
Last Five Years	4.58	10	8	2	47	17	147.1	88	98	.238	130	13	0	10	66	.347	.316	7	24	5	3	3	13	8	213	148	1.44

1993 Season

	ERA	W	L	Sv	G	GS	IP	H	HR	BB	SO
Home	4.30	5	2	0	20	6	58.2	61	3	29	35
Away	3.88	4	4	2	14	6	46.1	32	5	27	31
Starter	4.50	6	5	0	12	12	64.0	49	5	38	39
Reliever	3.51	3	1	2	22	0	41.0	44	3	18	27
0 Days rest	5.79	1	0	0	3	0	4.2	6	0	4	2
1 or 2 Days rest	6.35	0	1	0	4	0	5.2	10	0	3	6
3+ Days rest	2.64	2	0	2	15	0	30.2	28	3	11	19
Pre-All Star	4.93	4	5	1	17	10	65.2	57	3	38	38
Post-All Star	2.75	5	1	1	17	2	39.1	36	5	18	28

	Avg	AB	H	2B	3B	HR	RBI	BB	SO	OBP	SLG
vs. Left	.235	102	24	0	0	3	14	12	14	.313	.324
vs. Right	.241	286	69	5	0	5	30	44	52	.348	.311
Scoring Posn	.250	84	21	1	0	0	34	17	17	.383	.262
Close & Late	.295	44	13	2	0	2	4	8	9	.404	.477
None on/out	.213	89	19	1	0	1	1	17	13	.346	.258
First Pitch	.439	41	18	2	0	2	9	2	0	.477	.634
Ahead in Count	.179	162	29	2	0	1	11	0	48	.188	.210
Behind in Count	.301	103	31	0	0	4	12	32	0	.467	.417
Two Strikes	.114	175	20	0	0	1	9	22	66	.220	.131

Mark Leiter — Tigers

Age 31 – Pitches Right (flyball pitcher)

	ERA	W	L	Sv	G	GS	IP	BB	SO	Avg	H	2B	3B	HR	RBI	OBP	SLG	GF	IR	IRS	Hld	SvOp	SB	CS	GB	FB	G/F
1993 Season	4.72	6	6	0	27	13	106.2	44	70	.267	111	12	2	17	56	.338	.428	4	18	5	1	1	8	4	125	140	0.89
Career (1990-1993)	4.53	24	19	1	108	45	379.2	146	269	.265	385	57	13	47	188	.334	.420	20	75	22	6	3	24	20	426	464	0.92

1993 Season

	ERA	W	L	Sv	G	GS	IP	H	HR	BB	SO
Home	4.98	1	4	0	13	4	47.0	48	10	15	33
Away	4.53	5	2	0	14	9	59.2	63	7	29	37
Starter	4.48	5	4	0	13	13	76.1	79	11	33	44
Reliever	5.34	1	2	0	14	0	30.1	32	6	11	26
0 Days rest	0.00	0	0	0	0	0	0.0	0	0	0	0
1 or 2 Days rest	3.52	0	0	0	4	0	7.2	8	1	0	9
3+ Days rest	5.96	1	2	0	10	0	22.2	24	5	11	17
Pre-All Star	4.53	6	5	0	21	13	95.1	98	13	41	60
Post-All Star	6.35	0	1	0	6	0	11.1	13	4	3	10

	Avg	AB	H	2B	3B	HR	RBI	BB	SO	OBP	SLG
vs. Left	.264	216	57	5	2	9	27	28	29	.348	.431
vs. Right	.270	200	54	7	0	8	29	16	41	.326	.425
Scoring Posn	.219	96	21	0	0	2	31	18	20	.339	.281
Close & Late	.305	59	18	0	0	4	10	9	8	.406	.508
None on/out	.269	108	29	4	0	5	5	7	20	.313	.444
First Pitch	.315	54	17	2	0	5	10	3	0	.339	.630
Ahead in Count	.219	192	42	5	1	2	13	0	63	.226	.286
Behind in Count	.271	96	26	2	0	7	19	21	0	.395	.510
Two Strikes	.199	186	37	4	1	4	18	20	70	.279	.296

Career (1990-1993)

	ERA	W	L	Sv	G	GS	IP	H	HR	BB	SO
Home	4.57	10	10	1	58	22	203.0	204	27	80	156
Away	4.48	14	9	0	50	23	176.2	181	20	66	113
Day	5.22	8	6	1	33	12	108.2	117	17	36	83
Night	4.25	16	13	0	75	33	271.0	268	30	110	186
Grass	4.50	21	17	1	92	38	330.0	331	42	122	246
Turf	4.71	3	2	0	16	7	49.2	54	5	24	23
April	5.58	4	3	0	17	1	30.2	27	3	13	25
May	2.36	5	1	0	26	8	91.2	77	8	47	66
June	6.85	4	5	1	16	12	65.2	80	11	36	50
July	5.31	3	4	0	20	10	76.1	87	14	18	45
August	3.68	5	0	0	9	5	36.2	39	5	8	27
September/October	4.35	3	6	0	20	9	78.2	75	6	24	56
Starter	4.51	18	13	0	45	45	261.1	281	32	92	175
Reliever	4.56	6	6	1	63	0	118.1	104	15	54	94
0 Days rest	4.26	0	1	0	5	0	6.1	6	1	5	5
1 or 2 Days rest	2.66	3	1	1	28	0	47.1	35	4	19	42
3+ Days rest	5.98	3	4	0	30	0	64.2	63	10	30	47
Pre-All Star	4.54	13	10	1	66	25	212.1	216	23	102	153
Post-All Star	4.52	11	9	0	42	20	167.1	169	24	44	116

	Avg	AB	H	2B	3B	HR	RBI	BB	SO	OBP	SLG
vs. Left	.272	687	187	27	9	24	88	85	97	.351	.443
vs. Right	.259	764	198	30	4	23	100	61	172	.318	.399
Inning 1-6	.265	1074	285	41	10	34	136	106	205	.334	.417
Inning 7+	.265	377	100	16	3	13	52	40	64	.336	.427
None on	.256	839	215	38	9	26	26	73	163	.321	.416
Runners on	.278	612	170	19	4	21	162	73	106	.351	.425
Scoring Posn	.274	340	93	9	2	6	125	52	61	.360	.365
Close & Late	.269	156	42	4	1	6	23	16	19	.341	.423
None on/out	.251	358	90	13	1	11	11	38	70	.328	.385
vs. 1st Batr (relief)	.184	49	9	2	0	0	10	10	11	.339	.224
First Inning Pitched	.259	378	98	11	4	12	66	43	81	.343	.405
First 15 Pitches	.235	311	73	13	2	7	41	31	55	.313	.357
Pitch 16-30	.281	281	79	6	2	11	36	26	67	.354	.434
Pitch 31-45	.228	228	52	7	1	6	32	26	46	.300	.346
Pitch 46+	.287	631	181	31	8	23	79	63	101	.349	.471
First Pitch	.323	192	62	8	1	9	30	11	0	.359	.516
Ahead in Count	.210	676	142	20	5	8	54	0	233	.219	.290
Behind in Count	.331	284	94	12	4	19	53	64	0	.446	.602
Two Strikes	.199	708	141	21	6	10	62	71	269	.274	.288

Pitcher vs. Batter (career)

Pitches Best Vs.	Avg	AB	H	2B	3B	HR	RBI	BB	SO	OBP	SLG
Mike Bordick	.000	11	0	0	0	0	0	0	2	.000	.000
Ruben Sierra	.077	13	1	1	0	0	2	1	2	.133	.154
Joey Cora	.083	12	1	0	0	0	0	1	1	.154	.083
Leo Gomez	.091	11	1	0	0	0	0	1	6	.167	.091
Brian McRae	.100	20	2	0	0	0	1	1	3	.143	.100

Pitches Worst Vs.	Avg	AB	H	2B	3B	HR	RBI	BB	SO	OBP	SLG
Rafael Palmeiro	.647	17	11	2	0	3	7	4	0	.714	1.294
Tim Raines	.583	12	7	0	0	3	4	3	1	.667	1.333
Wade Boggs	.500	10	5	1	1	0	1	4	1	.643	.800
Kevin Reimer	.462	13	6	0	0	2	2	3	2	.563	.923
Chito Martinez	.364	11	4	0	2	2	6	1	2	.417	1.273

Scott Leius — Twins

Age 28 – Bats Right (groundball hitter)

	Avg	G	AB	R	H	2B	3B	HR	RBI	BB	SO	HBP	GDP	SB	CS	OBP	SLG	IBB	SH	SF	#Pit	#P/PA	GB	FB	G/F
1993 Season	.167	10	18	4	3	0	0	0	2	2	4	0	1	0	0	.227	.167	0	0	2	78	3.55	4	8	0.50
Career (1990-1993)	.258	262	651	93	168	26	4	8	61	68	102	1	17	11	10	.328	.347	1	11	3	2660	3.62	271	165	1.64

1993 Season

	Avg	AB	H	2B	3B	HR	RBI	BB	SO	OBP	SLG
vs. Left	.000	1	0	0	0	0	0	0	0	.000	.000
vs. Right	.176	17	3	0	0	0	2	2	4	.238	.176

	Avg	AB	H	2B	3B	HR	RBI	BB	SO	OBP	SLG
Scoring Posn	.000	3	0	0	0	0	2	0	0	.000	.000
Close & Late	.000	3	0	0	0	0	0	0	1	.000	.000

Career (1990-1993)

	Avg	AB	H	2B	3B	HR	RBI	BB	SO	OBP	SLG
vs. Left	.305	262	80	11	2	4	27	41	31	.398	.408
vs. Right	.226	389	88	15	2	4	34	27	71	.277	.306
Groundball	.247	174	43	7	1	4	21	11	27	.293	.368
Flyball	.254	142	36	3	1	1	12	20	21	.346	.310
Home	.294	333	98	12	3	4	39	37	47	.364	.384
Away	.220	318	70	14	1	4	22	31	55	.289	.308
Day	.246	195	48	7	1	3	20	20	21	.316	.338
Night	.263	456	120	19	3	5	41	48	81	.333	.351
Grass	.226	243	55	10	1	4	18	22	39	.291	.325
Turf	.277	408	113	16	3	4	43	46	63	.349	.360
First Pitch	.371	89	33	4	2	0	9	0	0	.371	.461
Ahead in Count	.298	161	48	5	1	3	17	38	0	.432	.398
Behind in Count	.183	273	50	12	1	3	22	0	86	.185	.267
Two Strikes	.191	272	52	10	1	2	23	30	102	.269	.257

	Avg	AB	H	2B	3B	HR	RBI	BB	SO	OBP	SLG
Scoring Posn	.240	183	44	7	1	0	51	21	35	.314	.290
Close & Late	.268	97	26	5	0	1	7	7	14	.317	.351
None on/out	.265	170	45	8	2	4	4	12	28	.317	.406
Batting #7	.294	126	37	6	1	1	15	10	23	.343	.381
Batting #8	.265	370	98	15	2	5	36	39	57	.337	.357
Other	.213	155	33	5	1	2	10	19	22	.295	.297
April	.245	102	25	2	2	2	14	14	18	.331	.363
May	.230	87	20	2	1	0	5	8	15	.295	.276
June	.291	141	41	8	0	1	11	8	18	.329	.369
July	.324	108	35	7	1	2	15	12	11	.388	.463
August	.221	77	17	4	0	1	5	14	14	.341	.312
September/October	.221	136	30	3	0	2	11	12	26	.289	.287
Pre-All Star	.262	374	98	14	3	3	32	36	57	.325	.340
Post-All Star	.253	277	70	12	1	5	29	32	45	.331	.357

Batter vs. Pitcher (career)

Hits Best Against	Avg	AB	H	2B	3B	HR	RBI	BB	SO	OBP	SLG
Joe Hesketh	.385	13	5	1	1	0	2	0	3	.385	.615
Jack McDowell	.364	11	4	0	0	0	1	2	1	.462	.364
Todd Stottlemyre	.364	11	4	1	0	0	0	0	3	.364	.455

Hits Worst Against	Avg	AB	H	2B	3B	HR	RBI	BB	SO	OBP	SLG
Mark Langston	.000	10	0	0	0	0	0	2	2	.167	.000
Melido Perez	.077	13	1	1	0	0	3	0	4	.077	.154
Randy Johnson	.154	13	2	1	0	0	4	6	3	.421	.231

Batter vs. Pitcher (career)																							
Hits Best Against	Avg	AB	H	2B	3B	HR	RBI	BB	SO	OBP	SLG	**Hits Worst Against**	Avg	AB	H	2B	3B	HR	RBI	BB	SO	OBP	SLG
Chuck Finley	.313	16	5	1	0	0	0	4	0	.450	.375	Frank Tanana	.200	10	2	0	0	0	0	1	0	.273	.200
Rick Sutcliffe	.308	13	4	0	0	0	3	0	0	.308	.308												

Mark Lemke — Braves

Age 28 – Bats Both

	Avg	G	AB	R	H	2B	3B	HR	RBI	BB	SO	HBP	GDP	SB	CS	OBP	SLG	IBB	SH	SF	#Pit	#P/PA	GB	FB	G/F
1993 Season	.252	151	493	52	124	19	2	7	49	65	50	0	20	1	2	.335	.341	13	5	6	1929	3.39	230	123	1.87
Last Five Years	.235	558	1483	152	348	52	9	17	129	170	145	0	45	2	9	.311	.316	29	27	14	5528	3.26	619	438	1.41

1993 Season

	Avg	AB	H	2B	3B	HR	RBI	BB	SO	OBP	SLG		Avg	AB	H	2B	3B	HR	RBI	BB	SO	OBP	SLG
vs. Left	.309	139	43	5	2	5	14	17	6	.382	.482	Scoring Posn	.246	118	29	7	0	1	41	28	8	.375	.331
vs. Right	.229	354	81	14	0	2	35	48	44	.317	.285	Close & Late	.236	89	21	2	0	4	10	10	13	.313	.393
Groundball	.223	175	39	8	1	1	17	23	19	.307	.297	None on/out	.200	120	24	5	1	1	1	10	16	.262	.283
Flyball	.288	80	23	6	0	2	8	12	0	.380	.438	Batting #2	.313	16	5	0	0	0	2	2	2	.389	.313
Home	.256	246	63	8	2	3	27	31	22	.338	.341	Batting #8	.245	465	114	19	1	7	45	61	47	.329	.335
Away	.247	247	61	11	0	4	22	34	28	.332	.340	Other	.417	12	5	0	1	0	2	2	1	.500	.583
Day	.237	135	32	4	2	1	15	23	15	.344	.319	April	.222	63	14	1	0	2	7	13	8	.346	.333
Night	.257	358	92	15	0	6	34	42	35	.332	.349	May	.323	93	30	5	2	3	9	11	13	.394	.516
Grass	.235	371	87	13	2	6	37	52	36	.325	.329	June	.230	87	20	4	0	1	9	10	3	.309	.310
Turf	.303	122	37	6	0	1	12	13	14	.368	.377	July	.297	91	27	5	0	1	10	12	7	.371	.385
First Pitch	.209	110	23	4	1	0	9	8	0	.258	.264	August	.225	89	20	4	0	0	10	9	12	.290	.270
Ahead in Count	.279	104	29	3	0	4	17	46	0	.497	.423	September/October	.186	70	13	0	0	0	4	10	7	.288	.186
Behind in Count	.228	193	44	8	1	1	13	0	44	.224	.295	Pre-All Star	.257	276	71	12	2	7	29	38	28	.344	.391
Two Strikes	.253	190	48	9	0	1	13	11	50	.292	.316	Post-All Star	.244	217	53	7	0	0	20	27	22	.324	.276

1993 By Position

Position	Avg	AB	H	2B	3B	HR	RBI	BB	SO	OBP	SLG	G	GS	Innings	PO	A	E	DP	Fld Pct	Rng Fctr	In Zone	Outs	Zone Rtg	MLB Zone
As 2b	.252	492	124	19	2	7	49	65	50	.336	.341	150	148	1299.2	329	442	14	100	.982	5.34	466	424	.910	.895

Last Five Years

	Avg	AB	H	2B	3B	HR	RBI	BB	SO	OBP	SLG		Avg	AB	H	2B	3B	HR	RBI	BB	SO	OBP	SLG
vs. Left	.270	512	138	22	5	12	58	51	30	.333	.402	Scoring Posn	.244	369	90	17	4	2	110	62	31	.342	.328
vs. Right	.216	971	210	30	4	5	71	119	115	.299	.271	Close & Late	.238	269	64	6	2	5	30	31	32	.314	.331
Groundball	.224	504	113	18	3	3	40	60	59	.304	.290	None on/out	.213	356	76	13	3	6	6	30	37	.275	.317
Flyball	.274	343	94	18	2	7	34	40	31	.349	.399	Batting #2	.242	248	60	9	1	2	29	29	25	.318	.310
Home	.244	738	180	30	3	10	71	80	66	.316	.333	Batting #8	.233	837	195	26	3	11	69	101	92	.313	.311
Away	.226	745	168	22	6	7	58	90	79	.305	.299	Other	.234	398	93	17	5	4	31	40	28	.302	.332
Day	.260	392	102	16	3	2	37	45	38	.331	.332	April	.217	157	34	6	0	2	14	20	21	.300	.293
Night	.225	1091	246	36	6	15	92	125	107	.303	.311	May	.252	258	65	11	3	4	17	30	27	.326	.364
Grass	.239	1102	263	39	7	14	100	132	104	.318	.325	June	.236	191	45	6	2	2	15	23	13	.318	.319
Turf	.223	381	85	13	2	3	29	38	41	.290	.291	July	.248	218	54	9	1	2	27	29	16	.332	.326
First Pitch	.230	326	75	8	2	3	28	20	0	.271	.294	August	.263	289	76	8	0	4	26	27	34	.323	.332
Ahead in Count	.259	363	94	20	2	8	48	113	0	.432	.391	September/October	.200	370	74	12	3	3	30	41	34	.278	.273
Behind in Count	.202	539	109	16	4	1	35	0	132	.200	.252	Pre-All Star	.235	673	158	25	6	9	55	82	66	.315	.330
Two Strikes	.201	507	102	17	0	3	31	35	145	.250	.252	Post-All Star	.235	810	190	27	3	8	74	88	79	.307	.305

Batter vs. Pitcher (career)

Hits Best Against	Avg	AB	H	2B	3B	HR	RBI	BB	SO	OBP	SLG	**Hits Worst Against**	Avg	AB	H	2B	3B	HR	RBI	BB	SO	OBP	SLG
Kevin Gross	.500	10	5	0	0	0	0	3	0	.615	.500	Jeff Fassero	.000	10	0	0	0	0	0	1	0	.091	.000
Wally Whitehurst	.500	10	5	0	2	0	0	1	0	.545	.900	Ryan Bowen	.000	10	0	0	0	0	2	0	2	.000	.000
Curt Schilling	.471	17	8	0	0	2	3	2	2	.526	.824	Greg W. Harris	.000	9	0	0	0	0	0	3	2	.250	.000
Zane Smith	.357	14	5	1	0	0	0	3	0	.471	.429	Omar Olivares	.077	13	1	0	0	0	0	1	2	.143	.077
Bruce Ruffin	.333	12	4	1	0	0	0	3	1	.467	.417	Dwight Gooden	.091	11	1	1	0	0	2	0	1	.083	.182

Mark Leonard — Orioles

Age 29 – Bats Left

	Avg	G	AB	R	H	2B	3B	HR	RBI	BB	SO	HBP	GDP	SB	CS	OBP	SLG	IBB	SH	SF	#Pit	#P/PA	GB	FB	G/F
1993 Season	.067	10	15	1	1	1	0	0	3	3	7	0	0	0	0	.190	.133	0	0	3	91	4.33	5	5	1.00
Career (1990-1993)	.225	140	289	31	65	16	1	7	35	34	71	4	6	0	2	.309	.360	1	1	6	1322	3.96	88	88	1.00

1993 Season

	Avg	AB	H	2B	3B	HR	RBI	BB	SO	OBP	SLG		Avg	AB	H	2B	3B	HR	RBI	BB	SO	OBP	SLG
vs. Left	.000	0	0	0	0	0	0	0	0	.000	.000	Scoring Posn	.000	4	0	0	0	0	3	1	3	.125	.000
vs. Right	.067	15	1	1	0	0	3	3	7	.190	.133	Close & Late	.000	3	0	0	0	0	2	1	2	.167	.000

Curt Leskanic — Rockies

Age 26 – Pitches Right

	ERA	W	L	Sv	G	GS	IP	BB	SO	Avg	H	2B	3B	HR	RBI	OBP	SLG	GF	IR	IRS	Hld	SvOp	SB	CS	GB	FB	G/F
1993 Season	5.37	1	5	0	18	8	57.0	27	30	.266	59	9	0	7	37	.345	.401	1	6	4	0	0	0	1	90	69	1.30

1993 Season

	ERA	W	L	Sv	G	GS	IP	H	HR	BB	SO		Avg	AB	H	2B	3B	HR	RBI	BB	SO	OBP	SLG
Home	4.20	1	1	0	9	4	30.0	30	4	13	19	vs. Left	.305	118	36	6	0	4	20	14	14	.381	.458
Away	6.67	0	4	0	9	4	27.0	29	3	14	11	vs. Right	.221	104	23	3	0	3	17	13	16	.306	.337

Jesse Levis — Indians

Age 26 – Bats Left

	Avg	G	AB	R	H	2B	3B	HR	RBI	BB	SO	HBP	GDP	SB	CS	OBP	SLG	IBB	SH	SF	#Pit	#P/PA	GB	FB	G/F
1993 Season	.175	31	63	7	11	2	0	0	4	2	10	0	0	0	0	.197	.206	0	1	1	238	3.55	23	18	1.28
Career (1992-1993)	.217	59	106	9	23	6	0	1	7	2	15	0	1	0	0	.229	.302	0	1	1	378	3.44	42	28	1.50

1993 Season

	Avg	AB	H	2B	3B	HR	RBI	BB	SO	OBP	SLG		Avg	AB	H	2B	3B	HR	RBI	BB	SO	OBP	SLG
vs. Left	.125	8	1	0	0	0	0	1	2	.222	.125	Scoring Posn	.071	14	1	0	0	0	4	2	2	.176	.071
vs. Right	.182	55	10	2	0	0	4	1	8	.193	.218	Close & Late	.083	12	1	0	0	0	1	0	3	.077	.083

Darren Lewis — Giants

Age 26 – Bats Right (groundball hitter)

	Avg	G	AB	R	H	2B	3B	HR	RBI	BB	SO	HBP	GDP	SB	CS	OBP	SLG	IBB	SH	SF	#Pit	#P/PA	GB	FB	G/F
1993 Season	.253	136	522	84	132	17	7	2	48	30	40	7	4	46	15	.302	.324	0	12	1	1898	3.32	257	115	2.23
Career (1990-1993)	.245	333	1099	167	269	30	11	4	82	102	120	11	10	89	30	.314	.303	0	32	3	4470	3.58	507	246	2.06

1993 Season

	Avg	AB	H	2B	3B	HR	RBI	BB	SO	OBP	SLG		Avg	AB	H	2B	3B	HR	RBI	BB	SO	OBP	SLG
vs. Left	.267	172	46	7	3	0	15	13	16	.321	.343	Scoring Posn	.319	116	37	2	2	2	45	2	7	.333	.422
vs. Right	.246	350	86	10	4	2	33	17	24	.292	.314	Close & Late	.197	66	13	1	1	0	4	4	9	.254	.242
Groundball	.331	151	50	4	3	2	25	4	8	.357	.437	None on/out	.249	189	47	7	2	0	0	15	14	.317	.307
Flyball	.143	91	13	2	3	0	12	8	9	.212	.231	Batting #1	.252	429	108	11	5	1	37	23	30	.299	.308
Home	.256	250	64	12	2	2	26	14	15	.302	.344	Batting #2	.277	83	23	6	2	1	11	6	10	.330	.434
Away	.250	272	68	5	5	0	22	16	25	.301	.305	Other	.100	10	1	0	0	0	0	1	0	.182	.100
Day	.246	260	64	8	3	2	28	15	17	.296	.323	April	.238	63	15	4	2	0	3	5	8	.290	.365
Night	.260	262	68	9	4	0	20	15	23	.307	.324	May	.250	108	27	4	4	1	15	6	8	.302	.389
Grass	.257	393	101	15	6	2	39	23	26	.307	.341	June	.265	102	27	4	0	0	3	9	6	.336	.304
Turf	.240	129	31	2	1	0	9	7	14	.285	.271	July	.300	110	33	3	0	1	15	4	10	.336	.355
First Pitch	.317	82	26	3	0	0	10	0	0	.317	.354	August	.269	26	7	0	0	0	2	1	1	.296	.269
Ahead in Count	.248	125	31	6	3	1	10	15	0	.338	.368	September/October	.204	113	23	2	1	0	10	5	7	.244	.239
Behind in Count	.239	218	52	4	3	1	20	0	36	.252	.298	Pre-All Star	.264	314	83	12	6	1	27	23	26	.324	.350
Two Strikes	.186	194	36	3	3	1	17	15	40	.260	.247	Post-All Star	.236	208	49	5	1	1	21	7	14	.267	.284

1993 By Position

Position	Avg	AB	H	2B	3B	HR	RBI	BB	SO	OBP	SLG	G	GS	Innings	PO	A	E	DP	Fld Pct	Rng Fctr	In Zone	Outs	Zone Rtg	MLB Zone
As Pinch Hitter	.222	9	2	0	0	0	0	1	1	.300	.222	10	0	---	---	---	---	---	---	---	---	---	---	---
As cf	.250	513	130	17	7	2	48	29	39	.302	.326	131	120	1080.2	344	4	0	3	1.000	2.90	371	329	.887	.829

Career (1990-1993)

	Avg	AB	H	2B	3B	HR	RBI	BB	SO	OBP	SLG		Avg	AB	H	2B	3B	HR	RBI	BB	SO	OBP	SLG
vs. Left	.255	380	97	14	4	2	26	39	41	.327	.329	Scoring Posn	.275	236	65	4	2	2	76	17	27	.326	.335
vs. Right	.239	719	172	16	7	2	56	63	79	.308	.289	Close & Late	.231	156	36	4	2	0	12	16	26	.310	.282
Groundball	.268	369	99	9	3	2	39	29	29	.324	.325	None on/out	.243	411	100	9	5	2	2	49	48	.330	.304
Flyball	.198	197	39	4	3	1	23	24	35	.288	.264	Batting #1	.242	901	218	20	9	3	65	82	97	.310	.294
Home	.226	531	120	16	2	3	40	50	49	.299	.281	Batting #2	.277	137	38	9	2	1	13	10	16	.329	.394
Away	.262	568	149	14	9	1	42	52	71	.329	.324	Other	.213	61	13	1	0	0	4	10	7	.342	.230
Day	.239	493	118	10	3	2	42	44	47	.308	.284	April	.286	154	44	6	3	0	9	17	22	.355	.364
Night	.249	606	151	20	8	2	40	58	73	.320	.318	May	.215	195	42	4	4	1	19	12	22	.269	.292
Grass	.235	799	188	23	7	4	60	77	78	.309	.297	June	.235	153	36	6	0	1	7	14	14	.308	.294
Turf	.270	300	81	7	4	0	22	25	42	.329	.320	July	.301	183	55	7	1	1	20	16	21	.366	.366
First Pitch	.268	153	41	4	0	0	15	0	0	.266	.294	August	.259	143	37	1	2	1	10	14	14	.329	.315
Ahead in Count	.253	257	65	11	4	2	18	51	0	.383	.350	September/October	.203	271	55	6	1	0	17	29	27	.285	.232
Behind in Count	.230	474	109	9	4	2	34	0	99	.241	.278	Pre-All Star	.247	554	137	16	7	2	41	47	63	.311	.312
Two Strikes	.196	454	89	8	5	1	28	51	120	.288	.242	Post-All Star	.242	545	132	14	4	2	41	55	57	.317	.294

Batter vs. Pitcher (career)

Hits Best Against	Avg	AB	H	2B	3B	HR	RBI	BB	SO	OBP	SLG	Hits Worst Against	Avg	AB	H	2B	3B	HR	RBI	BB	SO	OBP	SLG
Butch Henry	.556	9	5	1	0	0	0	2	0	.636	.667	Tom Candiotti	.059	17	1	1	0	0	0	0	2	.059	.118
Tom Browning	.471	17	8	1	1	0	3	0	2	.471	.647	Frank Tanana	.100	10	1	0	0	0	0	1	0	.182	.100
Curt Schilling	.438	16	7	0	0	0	0	1	1	.471	.438	Orel Hershiser	.105	19	2	0	0	0	2	1	1	.150	.105
John Smiley	.364	11	4	0	0	0	0	1	0	.417	.364	Rheal Cormier	.133	15	2	0	0	0	0	1	0	.188	.133
Danny Jackson	.350	20	7	0	0	0	2	1	2	.381	.350	Greg W. Harris	.167	12	2	0	0	0	1	0	1	.167	.167

Mark Lewis — Indians

Age 24 – Bats Right (flyball hitter)

	Avg	G	AB	R	H	2B	3B	HR	RBI	BB	SO	HBP	GDP	SB	CS	OBP	SLG	IBB	SH	SF	#Pit	#P/PA	GB	FB	G/F
1993 Season	.250	14	52	6	13	2	0	1	5	0	7	0	1	3	0	.250	.346	0	1	0	170	3.21	12	22	0.55
Career (1991-1993)	.263	220	779	79	205	38	1	6	65	40	121	3	25	9	7	.298	.338	1	4	9	2909	3.48	245	250	0.98

1993 Season

	Avg	AB	H	2B	3B	HR	RBI	BB	SO	OBP	SLG		Avg	AB	H	2B	3B	HR	RBI	BB	SO	OBP	SLG
vs. Left	.235	17	4	2	0	0	3	0	3	.235	.353	Scoring Posn	.154	13	2	0	0	0	3	0	2	.154	.154
vs. Right	.257	35	9	0	0	1	2	0	4	.257	.343	Close & Late	.167	6	1	0	0	0	0	0	2	.167	.167

Career (1991-1993)

	Avg	AB	H	2B	3B	HR	RBI	BB	SO	OBP	SLG		Avg	AB	H	2B	3B	HR	RBI	BB	SO	OBP	SLG
vs. Left	.279	201	56	15	0	2	20	13	28	.318	.383	Scoring Posn	.247	170	42	8	0	0	55	12	30	.283	.294
vs. Right	.258	578	149	23	1	4	45	27	93	.291	.322	Close & Late	.197	147	29	5	0	0	11	11	32	.263	.231
Groundball	.249	189	47	8	1	0	12	8	26	.280	.302	None on/out	.255	153	39	9	1	2	2	11	23	.309	.366
Flyball	.230	204	47	9	0	2	13	13	36	.280	.304	Batting #2	.280	296	83	21	0	2	26	14	48	.313	.372
Home	.272	386	105	20	1	3	36	20	51	.305	.352	Batting #8	.268	224	60	8	0	2	11	7	31	.290	.330

Career (1991-1993)	Avg	AB	H	2B	3B	HR	RBI	BB	SO	OBP	SLG		Avg	AB	H	2B	3B	HR	RBI	BB	SO	OBP	SLG
Away	.254	393	100	18	0	3	29	20	70	.292	.323	Other	.239	259	62	9	1	2	28	19	42	.289	.305
Day	.298	215	64	12	0	0	22	13	28	.330	.353	April	.311	90	28	6	0	1	6	8	14	.360	.411
Night	.250	564	141	26	1	6	43	27	93	.286	.332	May	.326	187	61	10	0	2	26	11	28	.361	.412
Grass	.264	670	177	34	1	6	58	35	104	.299	.345	June	.178	169	30	5	0	0	10	5	21	.200	.207
Turf	.257	109	28	4	0	0	7	5	17	.297	.294	July	.176	102	18	2	1	1	3	5	20	.220	.245
First Pitch	.262	103	27	6	0	0	7	1	0	.271	.320	August	.337	86	29	7	0	1	5	7	15	.394	.453
Ahead in Count	.332	193	64	12	0	2	28	23	0	.400	.425	September/October	.269	145	39	8	0	1	15	4	23	.285	.345
Behind in Count	.197	340	67	6	1	1	15	0	107	.195	.229	Pre-All Star	.263	498	131	23	1	3	44	26	75	.297	.331
Two Strikes	.188	313	59	10	1	2	11	16	121	.227	.246	Post-All Star	.263	281	74	15	0	3	21	14	46	.301	.349

Batter vs. Pitcher (career)

Hits Best Against	Avg	AB	H	2B	3B	HR	RBI	BB	SO	OBP	SLG	Hits Worst Against	Avg	AB	H	2B	3B	HR	RBI	BB	SO	OBP	SLG
Mike Moore	.636	11	7	3	0	0	3	0	1	.636	.909	Greg Hibbard	.091	11	1	1	0	0	0	0	1	.091	.182
Rick Sutcliffe	.364	11	4	0	0	1	2	0	1	.364	.636	Chuck Finley	.150	20	3	0	0	0	0	3	3	.261	.150
Ben McDonald	.364	11	4	1	0	0	1	0	0	.364	.455	Jaime Navarro	.150	20	3	1	0	0	0	0	1	.150	.200
Jack Morris	.308	13	4	1	0	0	2	1	1	.333	.385	Dave Stewart	.182	11	2	0	0	0	0	1	5	.250	.182
												Frank Tanana	.214	14	3	0	0	0	1	1	3	.250	.214

Richie Lewis — Marlins

Age 28 – Pitches Right (flyball pitcher)

	ERA	W	L	Sv	G	GS	IP	BB	SO	Avg	H	2B	3B	HR	RBI	OBP	SLG	GF	IR	IRS	Hld	SvOp	SB	CS	GB	FB	G/F
1993 Season	3.26	6	3	0	57	0	77.1	43	65	.239	68	15	3	7	44	.336	.386	14	55	20	3	2	5	3	83	84	0.99
Career (1992-1993)	3.86	7	4	0	59	2	84.0	50	69	.256	81	18	3	8	52	.354	.407	14	55	20	3	2	8	3	93	94	0.99

1993 Season

	ERA	W	L	Sv	G	GS	IP	H	HR	BB	SO		Avg	AB	H	2B	3B	HR	RBI	BB	SO	OBP	SLG
Home	2.54	4	2	0	30	0	39.0	29	4	23	37	vs. Left	.258	132	34	8	1	4	28	23	28	.367	.424
Away	3.99	2	1	0	27	0	38.1	39	3	20	28	vs. Right	.222	153	34	7	2	3	16	20	37	.309	.353
Starter	0.00	0	0	0	0	0	0.0	0	0	0	0	Scoring Posn	.172	99	17	4	2	2	36	25	27	.333	.313
Reliever	3.26	6	3	0	57	0	77.1	68	7	43	65	Close & Late	.267	86	23	5	2	3	14	15	19	.379	.477
0 Days rest	2.79	2	0	0	10	0	9.2	7	0	6	10	None on/out	.281	64	18	4	0	3	3	8	10	.361	.484
1 or 2 Days rest	3.00	0	3	0	25	0	36.0	35	5	21	31	First Pitch	.282	39	11	2	0	1	6	5	0	.348	.410
3+ Days rest	3.69	4	0	0	22	0	31.2	26	2	16	24	Ahead in Count	.179	123	22	5	1	2	18	0	54	.185	.285
Pre-All Star	2.41	4	0	0	28	0	41.0	29	3	21	35	Behind in Count	.373	75	28	7	1	4	16	20	0	.505	.653
Post-All Star	4.21	2	3	0	29	0	36.1	39	4	22	30	Two Strikes	.132	136	18	2	2	1	12	18	65	.237	.199

Scott Lewis — Angels

Age 28 – Pitches Right

	ERA	W	L	Sv	G	GS	IP	BB	SO	Avg	H	2B	3B	HR	RBI	OBP	SLG	GF	IR	IRS	Hld	SvOp	SB	CS	GB	FB	G/F
1993 Season	4.22	1	2	0	15	4	32.0	12	10	.311	37	5	1	3	17	.364	.445	2	11	6	2	0	1	1	48	39	1.23
Career (1990-1993)	4.78	9	8	0	54	19	147.0	49	74	.286	164	26	1	17	72	.343	.423	9	34	11	7	0	9	7	200	200	1.00

1993 Season

	ERA	W	L	Sv	G	GS	IP	H	HR	BB	SO		Avg	AB	H	2B	3B	HR	RBI	BB	SO	OBP	SLG
Home	3.72	1	0	0	9	3	19.1	20	2	9	4	vs. Left	.317	60	19	1	1	2	8	4	4	.343	.467
Away	4.97	0	2	0	6	1	12.2	17	1	3	6	vs. Right	.305	59	18	4	0	1	9	8	6	.384	.424

Jim Leyritz — Yankees

Age 30 – Bats Right

	Avg	G	AB	R	H	2B	3B	HR	RBI	BB	SO	HBP	GDP	SB	CS	OBP	SLG	IBB	SH	SF	#Pit	#P/PA	GB	FB	G/F
1993 Season	.309	95	259	43	80	14	0	14	53	37	59	8	12	0	0	.410	.525	3	0	1	1269	4.16	82	65	1.26
Career (1990-1993)	.267	282	783	96	209	36	1	26	108	91	147	21	25	2	5	.357	.415	5	2	5	3579	3.97	284	212	1.34

1993 Season

	Avg	AB	H	2B	3B	HR	RBI	BB	SO	OBP	SLG		Avg	AB	H	2B	3B	HR	RBI	BB	SO	OBP	SLG
vs. Left	.289	149	43	9	0	6	22	25	35	.398	.470	Scoring Posn	.333	75	25	5	0	5	41	11	18	.427	.600
vs. Right	.336	110	37	5	0	8	31	12	24	.426	.600	Close & Late	.231	39	9	2	0	1	7	3	13	.333	.359
Home	.350	117	41	6	0	6	23	21	20	.462	.556	None on/out	.309	55	17	3	0	0	0	7	10	.387	.364
Away	.275	142	39	8	0	8	30	16	39	.364	.500	Batting #2	.320	75	24	6	0	3	10	5	18	.363	.520
First Pitch	.429	14	6	2	0	1	5	3	0	.556	.786	Batting #4	.296	54	16	1	0	3	13	10	11	.433	.481
Ahead in Count	.571	56	32	6	0	6	20	18	0	.680	1.000	Other	.308	130	40	7	0	8	30	22	30	.424	.546
Behind in Count	.202	124	25	2	0	3	18	0	47	.225	.290	Pre-All Star	.321	156	50	7	0	9	33	23	37	.428	.538
Two Strikes	.187	139	26	3	0	3	18	16	59	.289	.273	Post-All Star	.291	103	30	7	0	5	20	14	22	.381	.505

Career (1990-1993)

	Avg	AB	H	2B	3B	HR	RBI	BB	SO	OBP	SLG		Avg	AB	H	2B	3B	HR	RBI	BB	SO	OBP	SLG
vs. Left	.274	391	107	23	1	13	51	55	73	.375	.437	Scoring Posn	.258	186	48	9	0	7	81	29	37	.359	.419
vs. Right	.260	392	102	13	0	13	57	36	74	.338	.393	Close & Late	.250	136	34	7	0	2	19	9	25	.331	.346
Groundball	.293	181	53	6	1	6	26	24	32	.386	.436	None on/out	.305	187	57	9	0	3	3	16	25	.369	.401
Flyball	.253	166	42	9	0	6	26	19	42	.347	.416	Batting #6	.192	208	40	6	0	6	23	20	34	.274	.308
Home	.283	374	106	20	1	10	48	51	63	.383	.422	Batting #7	.310	174	54	7	1	6	26	21	31	.395	.466
Away	.252	409	103	16	0	16	60	40	84	.332	.408	Other	.287	401	115	23	0	14	59	50	82	.382	.449
Day	.305	262	80	15	1	11	39	36	47	.404	.496	April	.353	51	18	2	0	5	14	10	11	.468	.686
Night	.248	521	129	21	0	15	69	55	100	.332	.374	May	.276	127	35	7	0	5	22	14	23	.370	.449
Grass	.261	640	167	29	1	18	83	77	125	.355	.394	June	.305	141	43	5	0	6	19	20	23	.392	.468
Turf	.294	143	42	7	0	8	25	14	22	.366	.510	July	.201	159	32	5	0	1	5	21	31	.317	.252
First Pitch	.449	49	22	6	0	1	7	4	0	.509	.633	August	.250	144	36	8	1	1	15	15	28	.335	.340
Ahead in Count	.419	179	75	10	0	15	43	46	0	.535	.726	September/October	.280	161	45	9	0	8	33	11	31	.335	.484
Behind in Count	.174	390	68	10	1	4	39	0	130	.202	.236	Pre-All Star	.279	376	105	14	0	16	57	52	65	.379	.444

Career (1990-1993)	Avg	AB	H	2B	3B	HR	RBI	BB	SO	OBP	SLG		Avg	AB	H	2B	3B	HR	RBI	BB	SO	OBP	SLG
Two Strikes	.148	386	57	9	0	5	42	39	147	.247	.210	Post-All Star	.256	407	104	22	1	10	51	39	82	.336	.388

Batter vs. Pitcher (career)

Hits Best Against	Avg	AB	H	2B	3B	HR	RBI	BB	SO	OBP	SLG	Hits Worst Against	Avg	AB	H	2B	3B	HR	RBI	BB	SO	OBP	SLG
Dave Fleming	.385	13	5	3	0	0	0	0	1	.385	.615	David Wells	.071	14	1	0	0	0	0	2	3	.188	.071
												Frank Tanana	.077	13	1	0	0	0	0	0	1	.077	.077
												Mark Langston	.087	23	2	0	0	0	0	1	8	.125	.087
												Frank Viola	.111	9	1	0	0	0	0	2	1	.273	.111
												Chuck Finley	.167	12	2	0	0	0	0	1	6	.231	.167

Derek Lilliquist — Indians

Age 28 – Pitches Left (flyball pitcher)

	ERA	W	L	Sv	G	GS	IP	BB	SO	Avg	H	2B	3B	HR	RBI	OBP	SLG	GF	IR	IRS	Hld	SvOp	SB	CS	GB	FB	G/F
1993 Season	2.25	4	4	10	56	2	64.0	19	40	.264	64	12	1	5	22	.318	.384	28	42	8	11	13	2	0	55	96	0.57
Career (1989-1993)	3.94	22	30	16	193	52	427.2	117	236	.280	466	89	4	45	184	.327	.419	54	103	22	27	25	24	12	491	602	0.82

1993 Season

	ERA	W	L	Sv	G	GS	IP	H	HR	BB	SO		Avg	AB	H	2B	3B	HR	RBI	BB	SO	OBP	SLG
Home	2.67	3	3	6	29	1	30.1	30	2	10	11	vs. Left	.270	63	17	0	1	0	6	2	13	.299	.302
Away	1.87	1	1	4	27	1	33.2	34	3	9	29	vs. Right	.263	179	47	12	0	5	16	17	27	.325	.413
Starter	3.18	0	0	0	2	2	11.1	13	3	1	5	Scoring Posn	.227	75	17	3	0	1	18	7	9	.286	.307
Reliever	2.05	4	4	10	54	0	52.2	51	2	18	35	Close & Late	.281	114	32	4	0	1	14	11	18	.341	.342
0 Days rest	0.00	0	0	4	9	0	5.0	5	0	1	1	None on/out	.293	58	17	2	1	3	3	3	12	.328	.517
1 or 2 Days rest	2.86	2	1	4	26	0	22.0	23	1	7	17	First Pitch	.290	31	9	2	0	1	2	5	0	.405	.452
3+ Days rest	1.75	2	3	2	19	0	25.2	23	1	10	17	Ahead in Count	.193	135	26	6	1	0	7	0	37	.191	.252
Pre-All Star	1.13	2	1	8	32	0	32.0	20	1	8	25	Behind in Count	.276	29	8	1	0	3	6	10	0	.462	.621
Post-All Star	3.38	2	3	2	24	2	32.0	44	4	11	15	Two Strikes	.233	120	28	6	1	0	9	4	40	.254	.300

Career (1989-1993)

	ERA	W	L	Sv	G	GS	IP	H	HR	BB	SO		Avg	AB	H	2B	3B	HR	RBI	BB	SO	OBP	SLG
Home	3.63	12	17	11	102	26	223.0	235	23	55	120	vs. Left	.268	365	98	15	2	8	40	20	81	.311	.386
Away	4.27	10	13	5	91	26	204.2	231	22	62	116	vs. Right	.283	1301	368	74	2	37	144	97	155	.332	.428
Day	4.72	8	9	7	64	17	131.2	148	17	36	79	Inning 1-6	.292	1114	325	59	4	33	132	68	136	.333	.441
Night	3.59	14	21	9	129	35	296.0	318	28	81	157	Inning 7+	.255	552	141	30	0	12	52	49	100	.316	.375
Grass	4.04	15	26	15	162	40	341.0	370	37	87	192	None on	.264	958	253	51	4	28	28	56	151	.310	.413
Turf	3.53	7	4	1	31	12	86.2	96	8	30	44	Runners on	.301	708	213	38	0	17	156	61	85	.351	.427
April	4.50	1	6	4	26	8	60.0	66	8	15	38	Scoring Posn	.273	410	112	23	0	10	135	47	56	.339	.402
May	3.10	7	8	3	36	12	98.2	84	9	26	46	Close & Late	.266	308	82	13	0	5	32	30	58	.328	.357
June	5.09	4	3	2	30	8	53.0	68	4	14	27	None on/out	.250	416	104	19	2	14	14	28	68	.302	.406
July	4.31	2	2	3	33	6	56.1	70	9	20	33	vs. 1st Batr (relief)	.256	125	32	7	0	2	17	10	20	.304	.360
August	3.89	3	3	3	31	8	71.2	86	8	24	34	First Inning Pitched	.253	586	148	29	0	16	61	51	83	.311	.384
September/October	3.58	5	8	1	37	10	88.0	92	7	18	58	First 15 Pitches	.285	562	160	31	0	16	59	44	70	.336	.425
Starter	4.58	13	22	0	52	52	287.0	343	34	67	138	Pitch 16-30	.243	341	83	17	2	6	27	20	69	.287	.358
Reliever	2.62	9	8	16	141	0	140.2	123	11	50	98	Pitch 31-45	.317	230	73	17	0	5	27	15	31	.358	.457
0 Days rest	3.22	1	2	6	31	0	22.1	22	3	9	11	Pitch 46+	.281	533	150	24	2	18	71	38	66	.331	.435
1 or 2 Days rest	2.11	5	2	8	63	0	59.2	48	5	17	45	First Pitch	.362	282	102	16	0	5	32	18	0	.402	.472
3+ Days rest	2.91	3	4	2	47	0	58.2	53	3	24	42	Ahead in Count	.203	743	151	33	2	11	54	0	212	.207	.297
Pre-All Star	3.90	12	17	9	100	29	223.2	231	23	60	122	Behind in Count	.355	352	125	26	2	15	57	59	0	.446	.568
Post-All Star	3.97	10	13	7	93	23	204.0	235	22	57	114	Two Strikes	.187	670	125	22	2	10	48	40	236	.231	.270

Pitcher vs. Batter (career)

Pitches Best Vs.	Avg	AB	H	2B	3B	HR	RBI	BB	SO	OBP	SLG	Pitches Worst Vs.	Avg	AB	H	2B	3B	HR	RBI	BB	SO	OBP	SLG
Kevin McReynolds	.059	17	1	0	0	0	1	2	2	.158	.059	Todd Benzinger	.688	16	11	0	0	0	0	1	1	.706	.688
Jose Lind	.091	11	1	0	0	0	0	0	1	.091	.091	Willie McGee	.538	13	7	0	1	1	2	1	0	.571	.923
Doug Dascenzo	.100	10	1	0	0	0	1	0	0	.091	.100	Will Clark	.526	19	10	3	0	2	3	1	2	.550	1.000
Gerald Young	.167	12	2	1	0	0	1	1	1	.231	.250	Craig Biggio	.500	10	5	0	0	1	2	1	1	.545	.800
Dave Magadan	.200	10	2	0	0	0	0	1	0	.273	.200	Howard Johnson	.417	12	5	1	0	2	3	0	0	.417	1.000

Jose Lind — Royals

Age 30 – Bats Right (groundball hitter)

	Avg	G	AB	R	H	2B	3B	HR	RBI	BB	SO	HBP	GDP	SB	CS	OBP	SLG	IBB	SH	SF	#Pit	#P/PA	GB	FB	G/F
1993 Season	.248	136	431	33	107	13	2	0	37	13	36	2	7	3	2	.271	.288	0	13	5	1509	3.25	200	117	1.71
Last Five Years	.248	726	2493	222	618	92	17	6	226	143	237	8	73	36	8	.288	.306	48	42	27	9045	3.33	1155	690	1.67

1993 Season

	Avg	AB	H	2B	3B	HR	RBI	BB	SO	OBP	SLG		Avg	AB	H	2B	3B	HR	RBI	BB	SO	OBP	SLG
vs. Left	.257	105	27	6	1	0	8	2	10	.270	.333	Scoring Posn	.267	101	27	2	2	0	34	2	8	.269	.327
vs. Right	.245	326	80	7	1	0	29	11	26	.271	.273	Close & Late	.167	72	12	0	0	0	6	3	5	.197	.167
Groundball	.339	59	20	2	0	0	9	1	1	.350	.373	None on/out	.216	111	24	3	0	0	0	4	13	.250	.243
Flyball	.205	88	18	3	0	0	6	1	7	.217	.239	Batting #8	.248	153	38	2	2	0	13	5	11	.275	.288
Home	.246	207	51	6	2	0	24	6	16	.267	.295	Batting #9	.248	274	68	10	0	0	23	8	25	.268	.285
Away	.250	224	56	7	0	0	13	7	20	.274	.281	Other	.250	4	1	1	0	0	1	0	0	.250	.500
Day	.259	135	35	3	1	0	8	5	18	.289	.296	April	.297	64	19	4	1	0	10	2	3	.328	.391
Night	.243	296	72	10	1	0	29	8	18	.262	.284	May	.160	75	12	1	0	0	5	0	8	.160	.173
Grass	.222	180	40	4	0	0	7	7	15	.250	.244	June	.344	61	21	3	0	0	3	3	6	.375	.393
Turf	.267	251	67	9	2	0	30	6	21	.285	.319	July	.264	72	19	2	1	0	6	1	7	.274	.319
First Pitch	.219	64	14	0	1	0	4	0	0	.227	.250	August	.205	88	18	1	0	0	6	4	7	.242	.216
Ahead in Count	.330	112	37	5	1	0	16	8	0	.369	.393	September/October	.254	71	18	2	0	0	7	3	5	.273	.282
Behind in Count	.201	189	38	4	0	0	14	0	33	.203	.222	Pre-All Star	.266	218	58	8	1	0	19	5	19	.286	.312

1993 Season	Avg	AB	H	2B	3B	HR	RBI	BB	SO	OBP	SLG		Avg	AB	H	2B	3B	HR	RBI	BB	SO	OBP	SLG
Two Strikes	.171	152	26	3	0	0	6	5	36	.201	.191	Post-All Star	.230	213	49	5	1	0	18	8	17	.256	.263

1993 By Position

Position	Avg	AB	H	2B	3B	HR	RBI	BB	SO	OBP	SLG	G	GS	Innings	PO	A	E	DP	Fld Pct	Rng Fctr	In Zone	Outs	Zone Rtg	MLB Zone
As 2b	.247	430	106	13	2	0	35	13	36	.269	.286	136	132	1152.2	269	361	4	75	.994	4.92	407	368	.904	.895

Last Five Years

	Avg	AB	H	2B	3B	HR	RBI	BB	SO	OBP	SLG		Avg	AB	H	2B	3B	HR	RBI	BB	SO	OBP	SLG
vs. Left	.249	860	214	33	7	4	77	64	88	.296	.317	Scoring Posn	.269	635	171	25	8	1	209	68	62	.330	.339
vs. Right	.247	1633	404	59	10	2	149	79	149	.283	.299	Close & Late	.251	443	111	13	1	0	32	25	43	.290	.284
Groundball	.251	816	205	23	7	1	75	52	75	.297	.300	None on/out	.239	532	127	25	2	3	3	19	48	.266	.310
Flyball	.236	539	127	22	4	3	52	29	59	.273	.308	Batting #2	.229	450	103	17	3	2	40	31	49	.278	.293
Home	.244	1239	302	43	11	5	132	75	113	.284	.308	Batting #8	.253	1614	409	63	12	4	148	97	144	.294	.315
Away	.252	1254	316	49	6	1	94	68	124	.291	.303	Other	.247	429	106	12	2	0	38	15	44	.273	.284
Day	.243	687	167	23	7	1	59	46	91	.292	.301	April	.246	345	85	11	2	2	33	22	29	.290	.307
Night	.250	1806	451	69	10	5	167	97	146	.286	.307	May	.258	399	103	21	2	1	49	11	35	.279	.328
Grass	.230	734	169	21	1	0	46	35	69	.266	.262	June	.278	421	117	18	2	2	37	30	40	.325	.344
Turf	.255	1759	449	71	16	6	180	108	168	.297	.324	July	.241	439	106	13	5	1	31	23	39	.280	.301
First Pitch	.273	315	86	10	2	0	34	22	0	.317	.317	August	.204	466	95	15	2	0	30	29	51	.249	.245
Ahead in Count	.313	674	211	29	8	4	77	81	0	.385	.398	September/October	.265	423	112	14	4	0	46	28	43	.309	.317
Behind in Count	.212	1106	235	38	6	2	86	0	219	.214	.263	Pre-All Star	.260	1307	340	53	7	5	128	72	116	.298	.323
Two Strikes	.188	967	182	26	4	1	63	23	237	.207	.226	Post-All Star	.234	1186	278	39	10	1	98	71	121	.277	.287

Batter vs. Pitcher (career)

Hits Best Against	Avg	AB	H	2B	3B	HR	RBI	BB	SO	OBP	SLG	Hits Worst Against	Avg	AB	H	2B	3B	HR	RBI	BB	SO	OBP	SLG
Shawn Boskie	.500	12	6	1	0	0	1	0	0	.500	.583	Bud Black	.000	14	0	0	0	0	0	0	1	.000	.000
Chris Hammond	.429	14	6	1	0	0	2	3	0	.529	.500	Tommy Greene	.000	13	0	0	0	0	1	1	1	.067	.000
Dennis Rasmussen	.412	17	7	2	0	0	3	2	1	.474	.529	Danny Darwin	.000	11	0	0	0	0	0	0	3	.000	.000
Joe Boever	.409	22	9	1	1	0	2	3	1	.480	.545	John Franco	.083	12	1	0	0	0	0	0	1	.083	.083
Joe Hesketh	.364	11	4	2	0	0	1	5	0	.563	.545	Mike Maddux	.091	11	1	0	0	0	1	0	0	.091	.091

Jim Lindeman — Astros

Age 32 – Bats Right (groundball hitter)

	Avg	G	AB	R	H	2B	3B	HR	RBI	BB	SO	HBP	GDP	SB	CS	OBP	SLG	IBB	SH	SF	#Pit	#P/PA	GB	FB	G/F
1993 Season	.348	9	23	2	8	3	0	0	0	0	7	0	0	0	0	.348	.478	0	0	0	78	3.39	8	3	2.67
Last Five Years	.265	188	234	34	62	11	0	3	28	21	63	0	4	0	1	.323	.350	1	3	2	1004	3.86	80	50	1.60

1993 Season

	Avg	AB	H	2B	3B	HR	RBI	BB	SO	OBP	SLG		Avg	AB	H	2B	3B	HR	RBI	BB	SO	OBP	SLG
vs. Left	.222	9	2	0	0	0	0	0	3	.222	.222	Scoring Posn	.000	4	0	0	0	0	0	0	1	.000	.000
vs. Right	.429	14	6	3	0	0	0	0	4	.429	.643	Close & Late	.200	5	1	1	0	0	0	0	3	.200	.400

Doug Lindsey — White Sox

Age 26 – Bats Right

	Avg	G	AB	R	H	2B	3B	HR	RBI	BB	SO	HBP	GDP	SB	CS	OBP	SLG	IBB	SH	SF	#Pit	#P/PA	GB	FB	G/F
1993 Season	.333	4	3	0	1	0	0	0	0	0	1	0	0	0	0	.333	.333	0	0	0	13	4.33	0	1	0.00
Career (1991-1993)	.167	5	6	0	1	0	0	0	0	0	4	0	0	0	0	.167	.167	0	0	0	27	4.50	0	1	0.00

1993 Season

	Avg	AB	H	2B	3B	HR	RBI	BB	SO	OBP	SLG		Avg	AB	H	2B	3B	HR	RBI	BB	SO	OBP	SLG
vs. Left	.000	0	0	0	0	0	0	0	0	.000	.000	Scoring Posn	.000	0	0	0	0	0	0	0	0	.000	.000
vs. Right	.333	3	1	0	0	0	0	0	1	.333	.333	Close & Late	.000	1	0	0	0	0	0	0	0	.000	.000

Doug Linton — Angels

Age 29 – Pitches Right

	ERA	W	L	Sv	G	GS	IP	BB	SO	Avg	H	2B	3B	HR	RBI	OBP	SLG	GF	IR	IRS	Hld	SvOp	SB	CS	GB	FB	G/F
1993 Season	7.36	2	1	0	23	1	36.2	23	23	.305	46	9	2	8	33	.393	.550	6	19	9	0	1	3	2	55	45	1.22
Career (1992-1993)	7.86	3	4	0	31	4	60.2	40	39	.312	77	14	2	13	52	.403	.543	8	24	10	0	1	3	4	84	76	1.11

1993 Season

	ERA	W	L	Sv	G	GS	IP	H	HR	BB	SO		Avg	AB	H	2B	3B	HR	RBI	BB	SO	OBP	SLG
Home	6.04	2	1	0	12	1	28.1	31	3	17	17	vs. Left	.370	54	20	4	1	4	19	12	5	.471	.704
Away	11.88	0	0	0	11	0	8.1	15	5	6	6	vs. Right	.268	97	26	5	1	4	14	11	18	.345	.464

Nelson Liriano — Rockies

Age 30 – Bats Both (groundball hitter)

	Avg	G	AB	R	H	2B	3B	HR	RBI	BB	SO	HBP	GDP	SB	CS	OBP	SLG	IBB	SH	SF	#Pit	#P/PA	GB	FB	G/F
1993 Season	.305	48	151	28	46	6	3	2	15	18	22	0	6	6	4	.376	.424	2	5	1	677	3.87	65	27	2.41
Last Five Years	.262	293	946	130	248	44	15	8	97	99	119	3	24	30	19	.331	.366	2	20	8	3854	3.58	400	224	1.79

1993 Season

	Avg	AB	H	2B	3B	HR	RBI	BB	SO	OBP	SLG		Avg	AB	H	2B	3B	HR	RBI	BB	SO	OBP	SLG
vs. Left	.212	33	7	1	0	0	4	2	8	.257	.242	Scoring Posn	.240	25	6	1	1	0	13	6	2	.375	.360
vs. Right	.331	118	39	5	3	2	11	16	14	.407	.475	Close & Late	.278	18	5	1	0	0	1	4	3	.409	.333
Home	.330	88	29	4	3	0	13	9	13	.388	.443	None on/out	.311	61	19	4	1	1	1	4	14	.354	.459
Away	.270	63	17	2	0	2	2	9	9	.361	.397	Batting #1	.310	84	26	5	3	1	10	7	16	.359	.476
First Pitch	.462	13	6	1	0	0	3	2	0	.533	.538	Batting #8	.320	25	8	0	0	1	3	5	2	.433	.440
Ahead in Count	.286	35	10	1	0	1	4	6	0	.381	.400	Other	.286	42	12	1	0	0	2	6	4	.375	.310
Behind in Count	.284	67	19	3	1	1	5	0	19	.284	.403	Pre-All Star	.257	70	18	0	0	1	6	9	11	.342	.300

1993 Season

	Avg	AB	H	2B	3B	HR	RBI	BB	SO	OBP	SLG		Avg	AB	H	2B	3B	HR	RBI	BB	SO	OBP	SLG
Two Strikes	.263	76	20	2	2	1	6	10	22	.349	.382	Post-All Star	.346	81	28	6	3	1	9	9	11	.407	.531

Last Five Years

	Avg	AB	H	2B	3B	HR	RBI	BB	SO	OBP	SLG		Avg	AB	H	2B	3B	HR	RBI	BB	SO	OBP	SLG
vs. Left	.233	210	49	11	3	0	26	25	42	.311	.314	Scoring Posn	.284	229	65	14	5	1	85	31	36	.358	.402
vs. Right	.270	736	199	33	12	8	71	74	77	.337	.380	Close & Late	.210	167	35	7	1	0	17	19	25	.284	.263
Groundball	.272	265	72	11	5	1	24	23	23	.332	.362	None on/out	.249	253	63	13	1	3	3	25	30	.319	.344
Flyball	.308	172	53	11	2	3	22	24	22	.389	.448	Batting #8	.229	266	61	14	2	2	22	28	34	.306	.320
Home	.272	486	132	23	11	4	64	55	68	.344	.389	Batting #9	.299	268	80	17	2	4	44	26	34	.358	.422
Away	.252	460	116	21	4	4	33	44	51	.318	.341	Other	.260	412	107	13	11	2	31	45	51	.330	.359
Day	.255	286	73	14	5	1	35	29	32	.320	.350	April	.226	106	24	4	2	1	10	13	14	.308	.330
Night	.265	660	175	30	10	7	62	70	87	.336	.373	May	.294	214	63	10	3	2	24	15	24	.333	.397
Grass	.276	417	115	18	7	3	39	36	43	.333	.374	June	.228	158	36	6	0	1	13	11	21	.282	.285
Turf	.251	529	133	26	8	5	58	63	76	.330	.359	July	.223	94	21	6	0	0	8	17	11	.348	.287
First Pitch	.328	137	45	8	2	1	25	2	0	.340	.438	August	.265	155	41	6	3	2	16	14	21	.329	.381
Ahead in Count	.263	270	71	17	2	4	31	59	0	.390	.385	September/October	.288	219	63	12	7	2	26	29	28	.368	.434
Behind in Count	.213	362	77	15	5	2	22	0	103	.214	.298	Pre-All Star	.254	503	128	22	5	4	51	43	62	.312	.342
Two Strikes	.201	383	77	14	5	2	24	38	119	.273	.279	Post-All Star	.271	443	120	22	10	4	46	56	57	.353	.393

Batter vs. Pitcher (career)

Hits Best Against	Avg	AB	H	2B	3B	HR	RBI	BB	SO	OBP	SLG	Hits Worst Against	Avg	AB	H	2B	3B	HR	RBI	BB	SO	OBP	SLG
Doug Jones	.400	10	4	0	0	1	2	3	0	.500	.700	Frank Tanana	.000	10	0	0	0	0	0	1	3	.091	.000
Bill Swift	.357	14	5	2	0	0	0	1	2	.400	.500	Bob Welch	.091	11	1	0	0	0	0	1	3	.167	.091
Jack Morris	.348	23	8	1	0	1	5	2	4	.400	.522	Lee Guetterman	.100	10	1	0	0	0	2	2	1	.250	.100
Melido Perez	.333	15	5	1	1	0	3	3	2	.444	.533	Chris Bosio	.150	20	3	0	0	0	0	1	1	.190	.150
Tom Candiotti	.333	12	4	1	1	0	1	1	3	.385	.583	Kevin Brown	.182	11	2	0	0	0	0	0	1	.182	.182

Pat Listach — Brewers

Age 26 – Bats Both (groundball hitter)

	Avg	G	AB	R	H	2B	3B	HR	RBI	BB	SO	HBP	GDP	SB	CS	OBP	SLG	IBB	SH	SF	#Pit	#P/PA	GB	FB	G/F
1993 Season	.244	98	356	50	87	15	1	3	30	37	70	3	7	18	9	.319	.317	0	5	2	1550	3.85	129	79	1.63
Career (1992-1993)	.273	247	935	143	255	34	7	4	77	92	194	4	10	72	27	.339	.337	0	17	4	4147	3.94	337	177	1.90

1993 Season

	Avg	AB	H	2B	3B	HR	RBI	BB	SO	OBP	SLG		Avg	AB	H	2B	3B	HR	RBI	BB	SO	OBP	SLG
vs. Left	.279	129	36	7	1	2	14	12	21	.343	.395	Scoring Posn	.250	84	21	4	0	1	28	8	25	.316	.333
vs. Right	.225	227	51	8	0	1	16	25	49	.306	.273	Close & Late	.277	65	18	3	0	0	10	4	11	.319	.323
Groundball	.247	77	19	4	0	1	6	2	17	.263	.338	None on/out	.230	122	28	6	1	2	2	11	22	.299	.344
Flyball	.313	64	20	2	0	0	6	9	12	.405	.344	Batting #1	.238	240	57	11	1	2	18	28	50	.320	.317
Home	.247	174	43	7	0	0	16	23	29	.338	.287	Batting #8	.304	56	17	2	0	0	4	2	9	.328	.339
Away	.242	182	44	8	1	3	14	14	41	.299	.346	Other	.217	60	13	2	0	1	8	7	11	.309	.300
Day	.252	143	36	6	0	2	13	18	28	.341	.336	April	.237	59	14	1	0	0	2	7	10	.338	.254
Night	.239	213	51	9	1	1	17	19	42	.303	.305	May	.210	105	22	4	1	1	3	8	28	.265	.295
Grass	.233	292	68	12	1	1	21	33	56	.315	.291	June	.000	1	0	0	0	0	0	0	0	.000	.000
Turf	.297	64	19	3	0	2	9	4	14	.338	.438	July	.170	47	8	1	0	0	1	5	12	.250	.191
First Pitch	.245	49	12	2	0	0	2	0	0	.269	.286	August	.279	104	29	8	0	1	16	15	15	.364	.385
Ahead in Count	.400	80	32	4	0	1	8	19	0	.515	.488	September/October	.350	40	14	1	0	1	8	2	5	.395	.450
Behind in Count	.164	152	25	6	0	2	13	0	58	.170	.243	Pre-All Star	.218	165	36	5	1	1	5	15	38	.291	.279
Two Strikes	.168	173	29	6	0	2	17	18	70	.250	.237	Post-All Star	.267	191	51	10	0	2	25	22	32	.343	.351

1993 By Position

Position	Avg	AB	H	2B	3B	HR	RBI	BB	SO	OBP	SLG	G	GS	Innings	PO	A	E	DP	Fld Pct	Rng Fctr	In Zone	Outs	Zone Rtg	MLB Zone
As ss	.240	341	82	13	1	3	27	36	66	.317	.311	95	89	791.0	128	265	10	52	.975	4.47	319	280	.878	.880

Career (1992-1993)

	Avg	AB	H	2B	3B	HR	RBI	BB	SO	OBP	SLG		Avg	AB	H	2B	3B	HR	RBI	BB	SO	OBP	SLG
vs. Left	.314	277	87	14	4	3	32	20	46	.363	.426	Scoring Posn	.258	229	59	9	1	1	69	23	63	.326	.319
vs. Right	.255	658	168	20	3	1	45	72	148	.329	.299	Close & Late	.318	154	49	8	1	0	22	13	28	.369	.383
Groundball	.259	216	56	5	1	1	20	8	49	.283	.306	None on/out	.264	318	84	10	4	3	3	34	57	.337	.349
Flyball	.291	223	65	7	1	1	22	26	43	.371	.345	Batting #1	.272	683	186	27	5	3	56	68	146	.340	.340
Home	.249	441	110	16	1	0	42	45	82	.320	.290	Batting #9	.245	98	24	1	1	0	7	12	25	.321	.276
Away	.294	494	145	18	6	4	35	47	112	.356	.379	Other	.292	154	45	6	1	1	14	12	23	.347	.364
Day	.278	320	89	13	0	2	30	41	65	.363	.338	April	.276	87	24	2	1	0	3	10	13	.364	.322
Night	.270	615	166	21	7	2	47	51	129	.326	.337	May	.257	210	54	6	2	1	10	19	45	.319	.319
Grass	.268	775	208	29	3	2	58	74	153	.334	.321	June	.238	101	24	1	1	0	9	5	28	.269	.267
Turf	.294	160	47	5	4	2	19	18	41	.365	.413	July	.275	153	42	6	3	0	12	22	39	.366	.353
First Pitch	.392	130	51	9	0	0	11	0	0	.398	.462	August	.295	220	65	13	0	1	26	21	34	.357	.368
Ahead in Count	.356	191	68	6	2	1	23	53	0	.496	.424	September/October	.280	164	46	6	0	2	17	15	35	.344	.354
Behind in Count	.178	409	73	12	3	3	24	0	162	.180	.244	Pre-All Star	.265	441	117	12	6	1	26	43	100	.332	.327
Two Strikes	.202	475	96	14	4	3	33	39	194	.264	.267	Post-All Star	.279	494	138	22	1	3	51	49	94	.346	.346

Batter vs. Pitcher (career)

Hits Best Against	Avg	AB	H	2B	3B	HR	RBI	BB	SO	OBP	SLG	Hits Worst Against	Avg	AB	H	2B	3B	HR	RBI	BB	SO	OBP	SLG
Jose Guzman	.545	11	6	1	0	0	2	1	1	.583	.636	John Doherty	.071	14	1	0	0	0	0	0	4	.071	.071
Bill Gullickson	.455	11	5	1	0	0	1	0	1	.455	.545	Alex Fernandez	.083	12	1	0	0	0	0	2	5	.214	.083
Jack Morris	.417	12	5	2	0	0	0	1	3	.462	.583	Roger Clemens	.091	11	1	0	0	0	0	0	1	.091	.091
Scott Sanderson	.375	8	3	0	0	0	0	3	0	.545	.375	Nolan Ryan	.167	12	2	0	0	0	0	0	3	.167	.167
Jimmy Key	.368	19	7	1	1	0	0	1	3	.400	.526	Danny Darwin	.176	17	3	0	0	0	0	0	4	.176	.176

Greg Litton — Mariners

Age 29 – Bats Right

	Avg	G	AB	R	H	2B	3B	HR	RBI	BB	SO	HBP	GDP	SB	CS	OBP	SLG	IBB	SH	SF	#Pit	#P/PA	GB	FB	G/F
1993 Season	.299	72	174	25	52	17	0	3	25	18	30	1	6	0	1	.366	.448	2	5	1	722	3.63	54	55	0.98
Career (1989-1993)	.245	363	788	76	193	43	5	13	96	58	162	4	18	1	6	.299	.362	2	17	4	3142	3.61	296	210	1.41

1993 Season

	Avg	AB	H	2B	3B	HR	RBI	BB	SO	OBP	SLG
vs. Left	.308	104	32	12	0	2	15	12	14	.379	.481
vs. Right	.286	70	20	5	0	1	10	6	16	.346	.400
Home	.307	88	27	11	0	3	20	11	18	.380	.534
Away	.291	86	25	6	0	0	5	7	12	.351	.360
First Pitch	.333	21	7	6	0	0	4	2	0	.391	.619
Ahead in Count	.385	39	15	4	0	1	8	11	0	.520	.564
Behind in Count	.253	83	21	3	0	1	10	0	27	.259	.325
Two Strikes	.235	81	19	3	0	1	7	5	30	.284	.309

	Avg	AB	H	2B	3B	HR	RBI	BB	SO	OBP	SLG
Scoring Posn	.348	46	16	8	0	1	23	4	4	.392	.587
Close & Late	.300	30	9	1	0	0	3	1	4	.323	.333
None on/out	.262	42	11	3	0	1	1	4	8	.326	.405
Batting #2	.320	50	16	5	0	1	7	2	8	.340	.480
Batting #7	.270	37	10	2	0	1	8	10	9	.426	.405
Other	.299	87	26	10	0	1	10	6	13	.351	.448
Pre-All Star	.344	64	22	4	0	1	9	2	12	.358	.453
Post-All Star	.273	110	30	13	0	2	16	16	18	.370	.445

Career (1989-1993)

	Avg	AB	H	2B	3B	HR	RBI	BB	SO	OBP	SLG
vs. Left	.271	435	118	30	4	10	57	27	72	.314	.428
vs. Right	.212	353	75	13	1	3	39	31	90	.281	.280
Groundball	.243	255	62	15	1	3	29	17	56	.298	.345
Flyball	.230	204	47	9	2	4	21	7	44	.254	.353
Home	.284	356	101	27	5	8	55	30	76	.341	.455
Away	.213	432	92	16	0	5	41	28	86	.263	.285
Day	.291	282	82	17	1	7	43	18	59	.337	.433
Night	.219	506	111	26	4	6	53	40	103	.278	.322
Grass	.248	492	122	23	5	6	53	38	102	.306	.352
Turf	.240	296	71	20	0	7	43	20	60	.286	.378
First Pitch	.321	109	35	9	1	1	17	2	0	.333	.450
Ahead in Count	.266	158	42	8	0	5	23	29	0	.378	.411
Behind in Count	.206	384	79	15	4	5	33	0	142	.207	.305
Two Strikes	.188	372	70	15	4	5	35	27	162	.243	.290

	Avg	AB	H	2B	3B	HR	RBI	BB	SO	OBP	SLG
Scoring Posn	.259	220	57	18	1	3	82	14	45	.304	.391
Close & Late	.276	174	48	9	1	3	26	9	36	.306	.391
None on/out	.301	173	52	8	2	5	5	12	29	.346	.457
Batting #2	.268	183	49	12	0	3	17	8	36	.295	.383
Batting #6	.191	225	43	10	2	2	18	17	47	.247	.280
Other	.266	380	101	21	3	8	61	33	79	.330	.400
April	.185	27	5	1	0	0	3	3	9	.267	.222
May	.205	122	25	5	0	3	10	9	36	.271	.320
June	.253	186	47	8	3	2	23	13	30	.299	.360
July	.259	158	41	7	1	3	21	3	28	.282	.373
August	.211	152	32	8	0	3	11	17	34	.290	.322
September/October	.301	143	43	14	1	2	28	13	25	.354	.455
Pre-All Star	.245	392	96	17	3	6	42	26	85	.296	.349
Post-All Star	.245	396	97	26	2	7	54	32	77	.302	.374

Batter vs. Pitcher (career)

Hits Best Against	Avg	AB	H	2B	3B	HR	RBI	BB	SO	OBP	SLG
Dennis Cook	.615	13	8	1	0	1	2	0	0	.615	.923
Charlie Leibrandt	.467	15	7	2	0	0	2	0	1	.467	.600
Frank Viola	.444	18	8	4	0	0	3	3	4	.524	.667
Norm Charlton	.417	12	5	2	0	0	0	0	2	.417	.583
Greg Maddux	.333	9	3	1	0	0	2	2	5	.455	.444

Hits Worst Against	Avg	AB	H	2B	3B	HR	RBI	BB	SO	OBP	SLG
Zane Smith	.091	11	1	0	0	0	1	0	1	.091	.091
Bruce Hurst	.143	14	2	0	0	0	0	1	2	.200	.143
Fernando Valenzuela	.150	20	3	2	0	0	1	0	4	.150	.250
John Smoltz	.200	10	2	0	0	0	2	1	2	.273	.200
Terry Mulholland	.217	23	5	1	0	0	1	0	4	.217	.261

Scott Livingstone — Tigers

Age 28 – Bats Left

	Avg	G	AB	R	H	2B	3B	HR	RBI	BB	SO	HBP	GDP	SB	CS	OBP	SLG	IBB	SH	SF	#Pit	#P/PA	GB	FB	G/F
1993 Season	.293	98	304	39	89	10	2	2	39	19	32	0	4	1	3	.328	.359	1	1	6	1086	3.29	113	78	1.45
Career (1991-1993)	.288	259	785	101	226	36	2	8	96	50	93	0	12	4	7	.326	.369	2	5	11	2811	3.30	297	207	1.43

1993 Season

	Avg	AB	H	2B	3B	HR	RBI	BB	SO	OBP	SLG
vs. Left	.261	23	6	0	0	0	3	2	2	.320	.261
vs. Right	.295	281	83	10	2	2	36	17	30	.329	.367
Groundball	.235	68	16	2	0	1	4	4	9	.274	.309
Flyball	.304	79	24	3	0	0	16	3	11	.314	.342
Home	.286	161	46	2	2	1	23	9	14	.322	.342
Away	.301	143	43	8	0	1	16	10	18	.335	.378
Day	.304	115	35	3	1	1	18	9	14	.346	.374
Night	.286	189	54	7	1	1	21	10	18	.317	.349
Grass	.296	250	74	5	2	2	32	17	26	.335	.356
Turf	.278	54	15	5	0	0	7	2	6	.298	.370
First Pitch	.367	49	18	1	1	0	6	1	0	.373	.429
Ahead in Count	.241	83	20	4	0	0	9	10	0	.316	.289
Behind in Count	.289	128	37	4	0	1	12	0	31	.285	.344
Two Strikes	.219	105	23	2	0	1	10	8	32	.270	.267

	Avg	AB	H	2B	3B	HR	RBI	BB	SO	OBP	SLG
Scoring Posn	.272	81	22	2	1	0	36	5	6	.293	.321
Close & Late	.357	42	15	2	0	1	8	2	3	.386	.476
None on/out	.242	62	15	1	1	0	0	4	8	.288	.290
Batting #7	.383	47	18	0	0	1	9	3	4	.412	.447
Batting #8	.281	203	57	8	1	1	25	13	23	.320	.345
Other	.259	54	14	2	1	0	5	3	5	.288	.333
April	.340	50	17	1	0	1	8	4	4	.382	.420
May	.281	64	18	3	0	0	8	6	7	.338	.328
June	.234	64	15	2	0	0	4	2	7	.254	.266
July	.226	53	12	3	0	0	4	1	5	.241	.283
August	.395	43	17	0	1	1	12	6	7	.442	.512
September/October	.333	30	10	1	1	0	3	0	2	.333	.433
Pre-All Star	.281	199	56	8	0	1	20	12	21	.318	.337
Post-All Star	.314	105	33	2	2	1	19	7	11	.348	.400

1993 By Position

Position	Avg	AB	H	2B	3B	HR	RBI	BB	SO	OBP	SLG	G	GS	Innings	PO	A	E	DP	Fld Pct	Rng Fctr	In Zone	Outs	Zone Rtg	MLB Zone
As Designated Hitter	.341	85	29	2	1	1	17	7	11	.379	.424	32	27	---	---	---	---	---	---	---	---	---	---	---
As Pinch Hitter	.333	9	3	0	0	0	1	0	0	.333	.333	11	0	---	---	---	---	---	---	---	---	---	---	---
As 3b	.271	214	58	8	1	1	22	12	21	.306	.332	62	59	503.1	33	94	6	6	.955	2.27	111	98	.883	.834

Career (1991-1993)

	Avg	AB	H	2B	3B	HR	RBI	BB	SO	OBP	SLG
vs. Left	.300	80	24	3	0	2	11	8	11	.360	.413
vs. Right	.287	705	202	33	2	6	85	42	82	.322	.365
Groundball	.236	182	43	4	0	2	20	9	20	.271	.291
Flyball	.267	221	59	8	0	3	35	16	28	.310	.344
Home	.266	379	101	12	2	4	54	26	45	.310	.340
Away	.308	406	125	24	0	4	42	24	48	.342	.397
Day	.307	277	85	12	1	4	38	22	34	.352	.401
Night	.278	508	141	24	1	4	58	28	59	.312	.352
Grass	.283	643	182	26	2	8	86	45	77	.325	.367

	Avg	AB	H	2B	3B	HR	RBI	BB	SO	OBP	SLG
Scoring Posn	.265	204	54	5	1	2	88	14	22	.297	.328
Close & Late	.282	110	31	5	0	2	17	6	11	.316	.382
None on/out	.296	189	56	10	1	2	2	11	19	.335	.392
Batting #7	.339	168	57	13	0	2	25	9	15	.367	.452
Batting #8	.281	416	117	17	1	3	53	26	45	.320	.349
Other	.259	201	52	6	1	3	18	15	33	.306	.343
April	.328	64	21	1	0	1	9	5	7	.371	.391
May	.263	99	26	4	0	0	8	6	14	.302	.303
June	.295	129	38	7	0	0	12	11	15	.345	.349

Career (1991-1993)

	Avg	AB	H	2B	3B	HR	RBI	BB	SO	OBP	SLG		Avg	AB	H	2B	3B	HR	RBI	BB	SO	OBP	SLG
Turf	.310	142	44	10	0	0	10	5	16	.331	.380	July	.250	148	37	7	0	0	14	7	14	.282	.297
First Pitch	.285	158	45	5	1	1	17	2	0	.287	.348	August	.289	187	54	8	1	2	30	12	31	.325	.374
Ahead in Count	.315	184	58	12	0	2	27	31	0	.410	.413	September/October	.316	158	50	9	1	5	23	9	12	.349	.481
Behind in Count	.258	318	82	14	0	3	33	0	85	.255	.330	Pre-All Star	.280	346	97	14	0	1	35	23	41	.322	.329
Two Strikes	.224	286	64	7	0	4	31	18	93	.266	.290	Post-All Star	.294	439	129	22	2	7	61	27	52	.330	.401

Batter vs. Pitcher (career)

Hits Best Against	Avg	AB	H	2B	3B	HR	RBI	BB	SO	OBP	SLG	Hits Worst Against	Avg	AB	H	2B	3B	HR	RBI	BB	SO	OBP	SLG
Rick Sutcliffe	.636	11	7	2	0	0	3	0	0	.636	.818	Erik Hanson	.063	16	1	0	0	0	1	0	4	.059	.063
Jose Mesa	.533	15	8	1	0	0	4	2	0	.556	.600	Juan Guzman	.091	11	1	0	0	0	0	0	1	.091	.091
Jack Morris	.500	12	6	1	0	0	1	0	2	.500	.583	Danny Darwin	.143	14	2	0	0	0	2	1	3	.188	.143
Bill Wegman	.462	13	6	0	1	0	0	0	0	.462	.615	Cal Eldred	.176	17	3	0	0	0	0	0	0	.176	.176
Bob Welch	.444	9	4	0	0	0	1	2	1	.500	.444	Kevin Appier	.235	17	4	1	0	0	0	0	3	.235	.294

Graeme Lloyd — Brewers

Age 27 – Pitches Left (groundball pitcher)

	ERA	W	L	Sv	G	GS	IP	BB	SO	Avg	H	2B	3B	HR	RBI	OBP	SLG	GF	IR	IRS	Hld	SvOp	SB	CS	GB	FB	G/F
1993 Season	2.83	3	4	0	55	0	63.2	13	31	.256	64	8	1	5	34	.299	.356	12	65	21	6	4	2	0	114	61	1.87

1993 Season

	ERA	W	L	Sv	G	GS	IP	H	HR	BB	SO
Home	3.42	1	1	0	26	0	26.1	35	2	2	15
Away	2.41	2	3	0	29	0	37.1	29	3	11	16
Starter	0.00	0	0	0	0	0	0.0	0	0	0	0
Reliever	2.83	3	4	0	55	0	63.2	64	5	13	31
0 Days rest	2.93	1	1	0	13	0	15.1	19	2	6	7
1 or 2 Days rest	2.93	2	2	0	24	0	27.2	28	2	4	17
3+ Days rest	2.61	0	1	0	18	0	20.2	17	1	3	7
Pre-All Star	2.38	2	1	0	36	0	45.1	42	5	9	25
Post-All Star	3.93	1	3	0	19	0	18.1	22	0	4	6

	Avg	AB	H	2B	3B	HR	RBI	BB	SO	OBP	SLG
vs. Left	.192	78	15	2	0	2	11	1	12	.213	.295
vs. Right	.285	172	49	6	1	3	23	12	19	.335	.384
Scoring Posn	.300	80	24	3	0	4	33	6	12	.348	.488
Close & Late	.370	81	30	5	1	1	11	7	5	.411	.494
None on/out	.240	50	12	2	1	1	1	3	7	.283	.380
First Pitch	.325	40	13	1	0	2	8	2	0	.378	.500
Ahead in Count	.220	91	20	3	0	2	13	0	24	.228	.319
Behind in Count	.314	70	22	2	1	1	11	7	0	.377	.414
Two Strikes	.221	95	21	3	0	1	11	4	31	.260	.284

Kenny Lofton — Indians

Age 27 – Bats Left (groundball hitter)

	Avg	G	AB	R	H	2B	3B	HR	RBI	BB	SO	HBP	GDP	SB	CS	OBP	SLG	IBB	SH	SF	#Pit	#P/PA	GB	FB	G/F
1993 Season	.325	148	569	116	185	28	8	1	42	81	83	1	8	70	14	.408	.408	6	2	4	2491	3.79	242	103	2.35
Career (1991-1993)	.299	316	1219	221	364	44	16	6	84	154	156	3	15	138	27	.377	.376	9	6	5	5102	3.68	511	230	2.22

1993 Season

	Avg	AB	H	2B	3B	HR	RBI	BB	SO	OBP	SLG		Avg	AB	H	2B	3B	HR	RBI	BB	SO	OBP	SLG
vs. Left	.292	195	57	9	1	0	15	30	36	.388	.349	Scoring Posn	.282	103	29	2	0	1	39	16	14	.371	.330
vs. Right	.342	374	128	19	7	1	27	51	47	.418	.439	Close & Late	.281	89	25	4	0	0	7	14	14	.381	.326
Groundball	.300	70	21	1	1	0	4	17	4	.437	.343	None on/out	.328	229	75	11	5	0	0	32	36	.410	.419
Flyball	.252	107	27	1	1	0	3	16	15	.347	.280	Batting #1	.325	566	184	28	8	1	42	81	83	.408	.408
Home	.313	278	87	12	6	1	15	49	44	.414	.410	Batting #6	.500	2	1	0	0	0	0	0	0	.500	.500
Away	.337	291	98	16	2	0	27	32	39	.401	.405	Other	.000	1	0	0	0	0	0	0	0	.000	.000
Day	.328	198	65	7	2	0	16	29	26	.409	.384	April	.313	80	25	4	3	0	6	12	12	.398	.438
Night	.323	371	120	21	6	1	26	52	57	.407	.420	May	.373	102	38	2	0	0	7	12	13	.443	.392
Grass	.328	467	153	25	8	1	35	71	70	.415	.422	June	.275	102	28	6	4	1	10	14	18	.362	.441
Turf	.314	102	32	3	0	0	7	10	13	.372	.343	July	.291	103	30	7	0	0	8	13	9	.364	.359
First Pitch	.320	75	24	2	0	0	7	4	0	.350	.347	August	.333	90	30	5	1	0	8	12	18	.408	.411
Ahead in Count	.453	161	73	11	2	1	17	42	0	.564	.565	September/October	.370	92	34	4	0	0	3	18	13	.473	.413
Behind in Count	.225	227	51	8	2	0	8	0	75	.224	.278	Pre-All Star	.321	327	105	17	7	1	27	40	47	.396	.425
Two Strikes	.244	250	61	9	4	0	11	35	83	.338	.312	Post-All Star	.331	242	80	11	1	0	15	41	36	.423	.384

1993 By Position

Position	Avg	AB	H	2B	3B	HR	RBI	BB	SO	OBP	SLG	G	GS	Innings	PO	A	E	DP	Fld Pct	Rng Fctr	In Zone	Outs	Zone Rtg	MLB Zone
As cf	.326	567	185	28	8	1	42	81	83	.409	.409	147	143	1245.0	402	11	9	2	.979	2.99	446	389	.872	.829

Career (1991-1993)

	Avg	AB	H	2B	3B	HR	RBI	BB	SO	OBP	SLG		Avg	AB	H	2B	3B	HR	RBI	BB	SO	OBP	SLG
vs. Left	.318	337	107	15	2	0	27	53	59	.413	.374	Scoring Posn	.297	222	66	3	3	3	76	26	28	.366	.378
vs. Right	.291	882	257	29	14	6	57	101	97	.363	.376	Close & Late	.260	204	53	6	0	1	12	29	25	.356	.304
Groundball	.272	224	61	6	1	1	11	39	14	.380	.321	None on/out	.287	495	142	16	7	2	2	68	74	.374	.360
Flyball	.266	289	77	7	4	2	12	44	43	.364	.339	Batting #1	.297	1189	353	44	16	5	78	152	153	.377	.373
Home	.295	589	174	19	10	4	37	87	80	.386	.382	Batting #9	.391	23	9	0	0	1	6	1	1	.417	.522
Away	.302	630	190	25	6	2	47	67	76	.369	.370	Other	.286	7	2	0	0	0	0	1	2	.375	.286
Day	.304	408	124	12	4	1	26	61	50	.395	.360	April	.269	145	39	5	3	0	9	21	17	.363	.345
Night	.296	811	240	32	12	5	58	93	106	.368	.383	May	.336	211	71	4	1	1	18	21	20	.399	.379
Grass	.301	989	298	38	16	6	75	133	120	.384	.390	June	.261	199	52	8	6	1	14	23	23	.338	.377
Turf	.287	230	66	6	0	0	9	21	36	.345	.313	July	.269	197	53	10	1	2	14	22	17	.342	.360
First Pitch	.325	197	64	4	0	1	20	7	0	.346	.360	August	.337	184	62	9	5	2	18	28	30	.423	.473
Ahead in Count	.411	292	120	16	5	3	27	84	0	.541	.531	September/October	.307	283	87	8	0	0	11	39	49	.390	.336
Behind in Count	.215	479	103	12	5	1	22	0	135	.218	.267	Pre-All Star	.292	634	185	24	11	3	47	69	68	.363	.379
Two Strikes	.225	520	117	15	8	1	26	63	156	.311	.290	Post-All Star	.306	585	179	20	5	3	37	85	88	.393	.373

Batter vs. Pitcher (career)

Hits Best Against	Avg	AB	H	2B	3B	HR	RBI	BB	SO	OBP	SLG	Hits Worst Against	Avg	AB	H	2B	3B	HR	RBI	BB	SO	OBP	SLG
Bill Gullickson	.538	13	7	2	0	0	1	2	0	.600	.692	David Cone	.091	11	1	0	0	0	0	1	3	.167	.091
Jack Morris	.526	19	10	1	1	0	1	1	2	.550	.684	Roger Pavlik	.111	9	1	0	0	0	0	2	3	.273	.111

Batter vs. Pitcher (career)																							
Hits Best Against	Avg	AB	H	2B	3B	HR	RBI	BB	SO	OBP	SLG	**Hits Worst Against**	Avg	AB	H	2B	3B	HR	RBI	BB	SO	OBP	SLG
Fernando Valenzuela	.500	8	4	3	0	0	1	3	1	.636	.875	Chris Bosio	.154	13	2	0	0	0	0	1	1	.214	.154
Scott Kamieniecki	.400	10	4	0	1	1	3	1	1	.455	.900	Scott Sanderson	.167	12	2	0	0	0	0	0	0	.167	.167
Bob Welch	.364	11	4	2	1	1	3	0	0	.364	1.000	Erik Hanson	.167	12	2	0	0	0	0	2	0	.286	.167

Tony Longmire — Phillies

Age 25 – Bats Left

	Avg	G	AB	R	H	2B	3B	HR	RBI	BB	SO	HBP	GDP	SB	CS	OBP	SLG	IBB	SH	SF	#Pit	#P/PA	GB	FB	G/F
1993 Season	.231	11	13	1	3	0	0	0	1	0	1	0	0	0	0	.231	.231	0	0	0	49	3.77	6	5	1.20

1993 Season	Avg	AB	H	2B	3B	HR	RBI	BB	SO	OBP	SLG		Avg	AB	H	2B	3B	HR	RBI	BB	SO	OBP	SLG
vs. Left	.000	0	0	0	0	0	0	0	0	.000	.000	Scoring Posn	.333	3	1	0	0	0	1	0	0	.333	.333
vs. Right	.231	13	3	0	0	0	1	0	1	.231	.231	Close & Late	1.000	2	2	0	0	0	1	0	0	1.000	1.000

Brian Looney — Expos

Age 24 – Pitches Left

	ERA	W	L	Sv	G	GS	IP	BB	SO	Avg	H	2B	3B	HR	RBI	OBP	SLG	GF	IR	IRS	Hld	SvOp	SB	CS	GB	FB	G/F
1993 Season	3.00	0	0	0	3	1	6.0	2	7	.308	8	2	0	0	2	.357	.385	1	3	0	0	0	0	0	5	9	0.56

1993 Season	ERA	W	L	Sv	G	GS	IP	H	HR	BB	SO		Avg	AB	H	2B	3B	HR	RBI	BB	SO	OBP	SLG
Home	0.00	0	0	0	1	0	1.2	0	0	0	3	vs. Left	.250	4	1	1	0	0	0	0	1	.250	.500
Away	4.15	0	0	0	2	1	4.1	8	0	2	4	vs. Right	.318	22	7	1	0	0	2	2	6	.375	.364

Albie Lopez — Indians

Age 22 – Pitches Right

	ERA	W	L	Sv	G	GS	IP	BB	SO	Avg	H	2B	3B	HR	RBI	OBP	SLG	CG	ShO	Sup	QS	#P/S	SB	CS	GB	FB	G/F
1993 Season	5.98	3	1	0	9	9	49.2	32	25	.262	49	7	0	7	30	.371	.412	0	0	7.61	5	92	5	3	72	54	1.33

1993 Season	ERA	W	L	Sv	G	GS	IP	H	HR	BB	SO		Avg	AB	H	2B	3B	HR	RBI	BB	SO	OBP	SLG
Home	3.45	3	0	0	5	5	31.1	21	2	19	18	vs. Left	.271	96	26	2	0	3	11	22	11	.412	.385
Away	10.31	0	1	0	4	4	18.1	28	5	13	7	vs. Right	.253	91	23	5	0	4	19	10	14	.324	.440

Javy Lopez — Braves

Age 23 – Bats Right

	Avg	G	AB	R	H	2B	3B	HR	RBI	BB	SO	HBP	GDP	SB	CS	OBP	SLG	IBB	SH	SF	#Pit	#P/PA	GB	FB	G/F
1993 Season	.375	8	16	1	6	1	1	1	2	0	2	1	0	0	0	.412	.750	0	0	0	45	2.65	7	5	1.40
Career (1992-1993)	.375	17	32	4	12	3	1	1	4	0	3	1	0	0	0	.394	.625	0	0	0	79	2.39	12	10	1.20

1993 Season	Avg	AB	H	2B	3B	HR	RBI	BB	SO	OBP	SLG		Avg	AB	H	2B	3B	HR	RBI	BB	SO	OBP	SLG
vs. Left	.500	2	1	0	0	0	0	0	0	.500	.500	Scoring Posn	.000	2	0	0	0	0	0	0	0	.000	.000
vs. Right	.357	14	5	1	1	1	2	0	2	.400	.786	Close & Late	.500	4	2	0	0	1	2	0	1	.500	1.250

Luis Lopez — Padres

Age 23 – Bats Both

	Avg	G	AB	R	H	2B	3B	HR	RBI	BB	SO	HBP	GDP	SB	CS	OBP	SLG	IBB	SH	SF	#Pit	#P/PA	GB	FB	G/F
1993 Season	.116	17	43	1	5	1	0	0	1	0	8	0	0	0	0	.114	.140	0	0	1	143	3.25	16	14	1.14

1993 Season	Avg	AB	H	2B	3B	HR	RBI	BB	SO	OBP	SLG		Avg	AB	H	2B	3B	HR	RBI	BB	SO	OBP	SLG
vs. Left	.111	9	1	0	0	0	1	0	2	.100	.111	Scoring Posn	.143	7	1	0	0	0	1	0	1	.125	.143
vs. Right	.118	34	4	1	0	0	0	0	6	.118	.147	Close & Late	.200	5	1	0	0	0	0	0	1	.200	.200

Torey Lovullo — Angels

Age 28 – Bats Both (flyball hitter)

	Avg	G	AB	R	H	2B	3B	HR	RBI	BB	SO	HBP	GDP	SB	CS	OBP	SLG	IBB	SH	SF	#Pit	#P/PA	GB	FB	G/F
1993 Season	.251	116	367	42	92	20	0	6	30	36	49	1	8	7	6	.318	.354	1	3	2	1456	3.56	123	122	1.01
Last Five Years	.220	167	505	50	111	24	0	7	36	55	76	1	11	7	6	.296	.309	2	7	4	2028	3.55	168	171	0.98

1993 Season	Avg	AB	H	2B	3B	HR	RBI	BB	SO	OBP	SLG		Avg	AB	H	2B	3B	HR	RBI	BB	SO	OBP	SLG
vs. Left	.286	63	18	2	0	1	7	6	3	.352	.365	Scoring Posn	.239	88	21	4	0	2	25	10	11	.310	.352
vs. Right	.243	304	74	18	0	5	23	30	46	.310	.352	Close & Late	.274	73	20	1	0	3	16	10	8	.360	.411
Groundball	.213	75	16	4	0	1	9	9	9	.294	.307	None on/out	.211	90	19	4	0	0	0	8	18	.276	.256
Flyball	.221	68	15	4	0	1	7	10	8	.329	.324	Batting #5	.220	100	22	2	0	1	7	15	13	.316	.270
Home	.243	173	42	9	0	4	16	20	20	.318	.364	Batting #8	.287	94	27	8	0	2	10	15	12	.391	.436
Away	.258	194	50	11	0	2	14	16	29	.318	.345	Other	.249	173	43	10	0	3	13	6	24	.274	.358
Day	.246	122	30	10	0	0	7	11	14	.306	.328	April	.267	15	4	1	0	1	3	1	2	.313	.533
Night	.253	245	62	10	0	6	23	25	35	.324	.367	May	.328	61	20	8	0	1	6	4	10	.379	.508
Grass	.250	280	70	14	0	5	24	30	38	.323	.354	June	.272	81	22	3	0	1	9	8	9	.333	.346
Turf	.253	87	22	6	0	1	6	6	11	.301	.356	July	.202	84	17	1	0	0	4	10	8	.284	.214
First Pitch	.344	64	22	4	0	0	4	1	0	.358	.406	August	.229	35	8	4	0	0	1	1	3	.250	.343
Ahead in Count	.307	101	31	7	0	3	10	22	0	.427	.465	September/October	.231	91	21	3	0	3	7	12	17	.320	.363
Behind in Count	.168	143	24	3	0	0	6	0	42	.168	.189	Pre-All Star	.262	202	53	13	0	3	22	17	26	.320	.371
Two Strikes	.159	138	22	4	0	1	8	13	49	.232	.210	Post-All Star	.236	165	39	7	0	3	8	19	23	.315	.333

1993 By Position																								
Position	Avg	AB	H	2B	3B	HR	RBI	BB	SO	OBP	SLG	G	GS	Innings	PO	A	E	DP	Fld Pct	Rng Fctr	In Zone	Outs	Zone Rtg	MLB Zone
As Pinch Hitter	.417	12	5	0	0	1	3	3	4	.533	.667	15	0	---	---	---	---	---	---	---	---	---	---	---
As 2b	.241	299	72	18	0	3	23	28	36	.306	.331	91	79	723.0	185	220	8	66	.981	5.04	234	217	.927	.895
As 3b	.227	44	10	2	0	1	1	3	8	.277	.341	14	12	101.0	14	25	3	2	.929	3.48	31	27	.871	.834

Larry Luebbers — Reds

Age 24 – Pitches Right

	ERA	W	L	Sv	G	GS	IP	BB	SO	Avg	H	2B	3B	HR	RBI	OBP	SLG	CG	ShO	Sup	QS	#P/S	SB	CS	GB	FB	G/F
1993 Season	4.54	2	5	0	14	14	77.1	38	38	.261	74	12	0	7	40	.345	.377	0	0	3.03	7	89	5	8	102	90	1.13

1993 Season

	ERA	W	L	Sv	G	GS	IP	H	HR	BB	SO		Avg	AB	H	2B	3B	HR	RBI	BB	SO	OBP	SLG
Home	4.07	1	3	0	7	7	42.0	35	3	21	22	vs. Left	.267	146	39	5	0	5	24	21	16	.351	.404
Away	5.09	1	2	0	7	7	35.1	39	4	17	16	vs. Right	.254	138	35	7	0	2	16	17	22	.338	.348
Starter	4.54	2	5	0	14	14	77.1	74	7	38	38	Scoring Posn	.377	61	23	3	0	5	36	11	3	.442	.672
Reliever	0.00	0	0	0	0	0	0.0	0	0	0	0	Close & Late	.471	17	8	3	0	0	2	0	0	.444	.647
0-3 Days Rest	0.00	0	0	0	0	0	0.0	0	0	0	0	None on/out	.297	74	22	4	0	0	0	10	8	.381	.351
4 Days Rest	5.70	1	2	0	5	5	23.2	24	3	15	11	First Pitch	.396	48	19	2	0	0	6	2	0	.412	.438
5+ Days Rest	4.02	1	3	0	9	9	53.2	50	4	23	27	Ahead in Count	.181	105	19	6	0	1	9	0	31	.189	.267
Pre-All Star	3.38	2	0	0	2	2	10.2	12	2	1	5	Behind in Count	.280	75	21	4	0	4	19	23	0	.431	.493
Post-All Star	4.73	0	5	0	12	12	66.2	62	5	37	33	Two Strikes	.195	113	22	5	0	1	9	13	38	.283	.265

Mitch Lyden — Marlins

Age 29 – Bats Right

	Avg	G	AB	R	H	2B	3B	HR	RBI	BB	SO	HBP	GDP	SB	CS	OBP	SLG	IBB	SH	SF	#Pit	#P/PA	GB	FB	G/F
1993 Season	.300	6	10	2	3	0	0	1	1	0	3	0	0	0	0	.300	.600	0	0	0	25	2.50	4	2	2.00

1993 Season

	Avg	AB	H	2B	3B	HR	RBI	BB	SO	OBP	SLG		Avg	AB	H	2B	3B	HR	RBI	BB	SO	OBP	SLG
vs. Left	.500	4	2	0	0	0	0	0	2	.500	.500	Scoring Posn	.000	2	0	0	0	0	0	0	1	.000	.000
vs. Right	.167	6	1	0	0	1	1	0	1	.167	.667	Close & Late	.000	0	0	0	0	0	0	0	0	.000	.000

Scott Lydy — Athletics

Age 25 – Bats Right (flyball hitter)

	Avg	G	AB	R	H	2B	3B	HR	RBI	BB	SO	HBP	GDP	SB	CS	OBP	SLG	IBB	SH	SF	#Pit	#P/PA	GB	FB	G/F
1993 Season	.225	41	102	11	23	5	0	2	7	8	39	1	1	2	0	.288	.333	0	0	0	443	3.99	21	27	0.78

1993 Season

	Avg	AB	H	2B	3B	HR	RBI	BB	SO	OBP	SLG		Avg	AB	H	2B	3B	HR	RBI	BB	SO	OBP	SLG
vs. Left	.213	47	10	2	0	0	2	2	20	.260	.255	Scoring Posn	.179	28	5	1	0	0	4	5	11	.303	.214
vs. Right	.236	55	13	3	0	2	5	6	19	.311	.400	Close & Late	.118	17	2	0	0	0	0	0	9	.118	.118

Steve Lyons — Red Sox

Age 34 – Bats Left (flyball hitter)

	Avg	G	AB	R	H	2B	3B	HR	RBI	BB	SO	HBP	GDP	SB	CS	OBP	SLG	IBB	SH	SF	#Pit	#P/PA	GB	FB	G/F
1993 Season	.130	28	23	4	3	1	0	0	0	2	5	0	0	1	2	.200	.174	0	0	0	97	3.88	3	12	0.25
Last Five Years	.239	396	879	97	210	38	7	7	82	61	157	2	7	22	14	.288	.322	6	20	6	3393	3.51	243	284	0.86

1993 Season

	Avg	AB	H	2B	3B	HR	RBI	BB	SO	OBP	SLG		Avg	AB	H	2B	3B	HR	RBI	BB	SO	OBP	SLG
vs. Left	.111	9	1	0	0	0	0	1	1	.200	.111	Scoring Posn	.000	5	0	0	0	0	0	1	1	.167	.000
vs. Right	.143	14	2	1	0	0	0	1	4	.200	.214	Close & Late	.250	4	1	1	0	0	0	1	0	.400	.500

Last Five Years

	Avg	AB	H	2B	3B	HR	RBI	BB	SO	OBP	SLG		Avg	AB	H	2B	3B	HR	RBI	BB	SO	OBP	SLG
vs. Left	.185	146	27	2	1	1	16	9	40	.231	.233	Scoring Posn	.244	238	58	8	2	3	75	16	46	.285	.332
vs. Right	.250	733	183	36	6	6	66	52	117	.299	.340	Close & Late	.243	185	45	11	0	1	17	13	35	.293	.319
Groundball	.248	254	63	11	1	2	23	15	44	.292	.323	None on/out	.229	192	44	8	2	0	0	15	32	.285	.292
Flyball	.202	203	41	6	4	2	16	15	40	.260	.300	Batting #2	.265	230	61	12	3	0	17	13	39	.305	.343
Home	.205	430	88	17	4	2	28	23	68	.247	.277	Batting #7	.223	206	46	8	3	3	30	11	29	.265	.335
Away	.272	449	122	21	3	5	54	38	89	.327	.365	Other	.233	443	103	18	1	4	35	37	89	.290	.305
Day	.252	282	71	10	2	2	25	21	55	.306	.323	April	.195	113	22	2	1	1	9	9	16	.254	.257
Night	.233	597	139	28	5	5	57	40	102	.280	.322	May	.254	138	35	8	0	3	16	16	29	.329	.377
Grass	.242	749	181	32	7	5	69	50	128	.289	.323	June	.258	151	39	7	1	0	6	9	27	.298	.318
Turf	.223	130	29	6	0	2	13	11	29	.284	.315	July	.253	158	40	9	2	1	13	9	32	.300	.354
First Pitch	.342	155	53	13	3	3	17	4	0	.358	.523	August	.214	140	30	5	1	0	15	8	22	.253	.264
Ahead in Count	.259	166	43	9	1	4	15	28	0	.364	.398	September/October	.246	179	44	7	2	2	23	10	31	.284	.341
Behind in Count	.186	408	76	11	1	0	31	0	141	.188	.218	Pre-All Star	.241	444	107	19	2	4	35	40	79	.302	.320
Two Strikes	.175	400	70	7	2	0	37	28	157	.227	.203	Post-All Star	.237	435	103	19	5	3	47	21	78	.273	.324

Batter vs. Pitcher (career)

Hits Best Against	Avg	AB	H	2B	3B	HR	RBI	BB	SO	OBP	SLG	Hits Worst Against	Avg	AB	H	2B	3B	HR	RBI	BB	SO	OBP	SLG
Jaime Navarro	.467	15	7	0	0	0	1	1	1	.471	.467	Dave Stewart	.037	27	1	1	0	0	0	2	6	.103	.074
Todd Stottlemyre	.455	11	5	2	0	0	0	0	1	.455	.636	Dave Stieb	.040	25	1	1	0	0	0	1	7	.077	.080
Terry Leach	.444	9	4	2	0	0	2	2	0	.545	.667	Frank Viola	.083	12	1	1	0	0	1	0	5	.083	.167
Rod Nichols	.444	9	4	0	1	0	2	2	0	.545	.667	Chuck Finley	.083	12	1	0	0	0	0	0	5	.083	.083
Erik Hanson	.417	12	5	3	0	0	1	1	2	.429	.667	Rick Aguilera	.100	10	1	0	0	0	0	1	3	.182	.100

Kevin Maas — Yankees

Age 29 – Bats Left (flyball hitter)

	Avg	G	AB	R	H	2B	3B	HR	RBI	BB	SO	HBP	GDP	SB	CS	OBP	SLG	IBB	SH	SF	#Pit	#P/PA	GB	FB	G/F
1993 Season	.205	59	151	20	31	4	0	9	25	24	32	1	2	1	1	.316	.411	2	0	1	734	4.15	30	64	0.47
Career (1990-1993)	.232	384	1191	166	276	39	1	64	164	175	299	8	9	10	5	.332	.427	19	0	10	5634	4.07	271	458	0.59

1993 Season

	Avg	AB	H	2B	3B	HR	RBI	BB	SO	OBP	SLG
vs. Left	.300	20	6	1	0	0	0	1	3	.333	.350
vs. Right	.191	131	25	3	0	9	25	23	29	.314	.420
Home	.189	74	14	1	0	7	18	9	15	.286	.486
Away	.221	77	17	3	0	2	7	15	17	.344	.338
First Pitch	.250	16	4	1	0	2	7	0	0	.235	.688
Ahead in Count	.304	46	14	2	0	3	8	14	0	.467	.543
Behind in Count	.129	62	8	1	0	2	6	0	25	.143	.242
Two Strikes	.127	71	9	1	0	2	7	10	32	.244	.225

	Avg	AB	H	2B	3B	HR	RBI	BB	SO	OBP	SLG
Scoring Posn	.300	30	9	0	0	4	18	7	4	.421	.700
Close & Late	.160	25	4	1	0	1	5	0	6	.154	.320
None on/out	.079	38	3	1	0	1	1	4	9	.167	.184
Batting #6	.250	24	6	0	0	1	6	5	7	.400	.375
Batting #7	.238	80	19	3	0	5	12	15	14	.354	.463
Other	.128	47	6	1	0	3	7	4	11	.196	.340
Pre-All Star	.205	146	30	3	0	9	25	24	32	.320	.411
Post-All Star	.200	5	1	1	0	0	0	0	0	.200	.400

Career (1990-1993)

	Avg	AB	H	2B	3B	HR	RBI	BB	SO	OBP	SLG
vs. Left	.208	322	67	9	0	13	43	43	101	.305	.357
vs. Right	.241	869	209	30	1	51	121	132	198	.341	.453
Groundball	.239	343	82	8	0	13	41	40	81	.319	.376
Flyball	.219	279	61	10	1	14	37	35	75	.304	.412
Home	.211	573	121	19	0	34	85	83	136	.314	.422
Away	.251	618	155	20	1	30	79	92	163	.348	.432
Day	.234	342	80	12	0	19	55	55	71	.338	.436
Night	.231	849	196	27	1	45	109	120	228	.329	.424
Grass	.227	995	226	34	0	53	137	149	250	.330	.421
Turf	.255	196	50	5	1	11	27	26	49	.339	.459
First Pitch	.262	130	34	4	0	8	22	4	0	.292	.477
Ahead in Count	.309	288	89	13	0	25	58	87	0	.465	.615
Behind in Count	.166	524	87	15	0	14	45	0	242	.169	.275
Two Strikes	.186	603	112	16	1	24	67	75	299	.279	.335

	Avg	AB	H	2B	3B	HR	RBI	BB	SO	OBP	SLG
Scoring Posn	.199	271	54	6	0	12	98	66	68	.351	.354
Close & Late	.216	218	47	6	0	12	35	33	68	.319	.408
None on/out	.221	294	65	8	1	15	15	36	67	.306	.408
Batting #4	.275	280	77	11	1	16	37	54	67	.397	.493
Batting #7	.240	337	81	12	0	21	52	44	82	.330	.463
Other	.206	574	118	16	0	27	75	77	150	.299	.375
April	.254	130	33	3	1	5	19	36	27	.413	.408
May	.264	220	58	8	0	18	35	36	54	.370	.545
June	.220	223	49	9	0	9	30	23	47	.295	.381
July	.191	209	40	7	0	10	23	30	59	.295	.368
August	.226	217	49	7	0	12	31	23	58	.303	.424
September/October	.245	192	47	5	0	10	26	27	54	.339	.427
Pre-All Star	.241	642	155	24	1	35	92	106	146	.349	.445
Post-All Star	.220	549	121	15	0	29	72	69	153	.311	.406

Batter vs. Pitcher (career)

Hits Best Against	Avg	AB	H	2B	3B	HR	RBI	BB	SO	OBP	SLG
Jose Mesa	.571	14	8	1	0	1	2	0	1	.571	.857
Kirk McCaskill	.421	19	8	2	0	1	2	1	0	.450	.684
Bill Gullickson	.333	9	3	0	0	0	2	2	0	.417	.333
Todd Stottlemyre	.318	22	7	1	0	1	2	4	3	.423	.500
Greg Swindell	.308	13	4	0	0	2	3	0	3	.308	.769

Hits Worst Against	Avg	AB	H	2B	3B	HR	RBI	BB	SO	OBP	SLG
Tom Gordon	.000	11	0	0	0	0	0	1	5	.083	.000
Kevin Appier	.000	9	0	0	0	0	0	3	6	.250	.000
Mark Gubicza	.077	13	1	0	0	1	4	1	5	.143	.308
Alex Fernandez	.091	11	1	0	0	0	1	2	2	.231	.091
Jim Abbott	.100	10	1	1	0	0	1	1	7	.182	.200

Bob MacDonald — Tigers

Age 29 – Pitches Left (flyball pitcher)

	ERA	W	L	Sv	G	GS	IP	BB	SO	Avg	H	2B	3B	HR	RBI	OBP	SLG	GF	IR	IRS	Hld	SvOp	SB	CS	GB	FB	G/F
1993 Season	5.35	3	3	3	68	0	65.2	33	39	.268	67	16	2	8	48	.349	.444	24	56	18	16	6	2	3	70	87	0.80
Career (1990-1993)	4.21	7	6	3	144	0	169.0	76	89	.261	168	35	4	17	106	.337	.407	44	121	42	23	10	11	7	197	226	0.87

1993 Season

	ERA	W	L	Sv	G	GS	IP	H	HR	BB	SO
Home	6.81	3	2	2	38	0	37.0	39	7	24	22
Away	3.45	0	1	1	30	0	28.2	28	1	9	17
Day	6.53	1	0	1	31	0	30.1	30	5	14	15
Night	4.33	2	3	2	37	0	35.1	37	3	19	24
Grass	5.37	3	2	2	55	0	53.2	53	8	29	31
Turf	5.25	0	1	1	13	0	12.0	14	0	4	8
April	2.79	1	0	0	10	0	9.2	9	0	2	3
May	3.21	2	2	1	13	0	14.0	11	1	6	9
June	5.19	0	0	2	11	0	8.2	9	2	4	4
July	7.90	0	1	0	14	0	13.2	18	3	11	7
August	7.20	0	0	0	8	0	10.0	11	2	4	10
September/October	5.59	0	0	0	12	0	9.2	9	0	6	6
Starter	0.00	0	0	0	0	0	0.0	0	0	0	0
Reliever	5.35	3	3	3	68	0	65.2	67	8	33	39
0 Days rest	7.15	1	1	2	22	0	22.2	25	4	13	13
1 or 2 Days rest	4.26	2	2	1	29	0	25.1	25	3	11	18
3+ Days rest	4.58	0	0	0	17	0	17.2	17	1	9	8
Pre-All Star	4.62	3	2	3	40	0	37.0	36	5	15	21
Post-All Star	6.28	0	1	0	28	0	28.2	31	3	18	18

	Avg	AB	H	2B	3B	HR	RBI	BB	SO	OBP	SLG
vs. Left	.222	90	20	4	2	3	12	12	21	.314	.411
vs. Right	.294	160	47	12	0	5	36	21	18	.369	.463
Inning 1-6	.222	36	8	1	0	1	9	2	9	.244	.333
Inning 7+	.276	214	59	15	2	7	39	31	30	.367	.463
None on	.285	123	35	6	2	2	2	15	22	.362	.415
Runners on	.252	127	32	10	0	6	46	18	17	.338	.472
Scoring Posn	.253	75	19	6	0	3	37	13	8	.351	.453
Close & Late	.281	89	25	5	2	2	17	10	15	.353	.449
None on/out	.269	52	14	2	0	0	0	8	8	.367	.308
vs. 1st Batr (relief)	.158	57	9	0	0	0	5	9	11	.265	.158
First Inning Pitched	.281	196	55	13	2	7	42	25	31	.356	.474
First 15 Pitches	.259	166	43	8	2	4	26	21	25	.335	.404
Pitch 16-30	.319	69	22	7	0	4	20	10	9	.400	.594
Pitch 31-45	.154	13	2	1	0	0	2	2	3	.313	.231
Pitch 46+	.000	2	0	0	0	0	0	0	2	.000	.000
First Pitch	.290	31	9	1	0	1	5	5	0	.389	.419
Ahead in Count	.125	96	12	4	0	0	7	0	36	.133	.167
Behind in Count	.394	66	26	7	1	4	25	12	0	.475	.712
Two Strikes	.193	119	23	8	1	2	14	16	39	.287	.328

Career (1990-1993)

	ERA	W	L	Sv	G	GS	IP	H	HR	BB	SO
Home	5.07	4	3	2	77	0	92.1	105	13	45	46
Away	3.17	3	3	1	67	0	76.2	63	4	31	43
Day	4.43	2	1	1	57	0	65.0	56	7	28	31
Night	4.07	5	5	2	87	0	104.0	112	10	48	58
Grass	4.30	5	3	2	81	0	88.0	78	9	44	49
Turf	4.11	2	3	1	63	0	81.0	90	8	32	40
April	2.31	2	0	0	19	0	23.1	18	0	3	12
May	3.04	2	2	1	22	0	26.2	23	2	15	16
June	3.54	1	0	2	29	0	40.2	37	5	15	21
July	6.93	1	2	0	23	0	24.2	31	5	21	14

	Avg	AB	H	2B	3B	HR	RBI	BB	SO	OBP	SLG
vs. Left	.233	232	54	10	2	5	34	26	44	.310	.358
vs. Right	.277	411	114	25	2	12	72	50	45	.352	.436
Inning 1-6	.243	144	35	4	0	2	29	14	23	.303	.313
Inning 7+	.267	499	133	31	4	15	77	62	66	.348	.435
None on	.253	332	84	15	3	7	7	32	44	.321	.380
Runners on	.270	311	84	20	1	10	99	44	45	.354	.437
Scoring Posn	.293	188	55	13	0	6	85	31	24	.382	.457
Close & Late	.244	180	44	7	2	5	32	22	31	.327	.389
None on/out	.218	142	31	3	0	4	4	12	14	.279	.324
vs. 1st Batr (relief)	.181	127	23	2	0	1	15	14	21	.257	.220

Career (1990-1993)

	ERA	W	L	Sv	G	GS	IP	H	HR	BB	SO
August	5.03	1	0	0	26	0	34.0	40	4	13	15
September/October	4.58	0	2	0	25	0	19.2	19	1	9	11
Starter	0.00	0	0	0	0	0	0.0	0	0	0	0
Reliever	4.21	7	6	3	144	0	169.0	168	17	76	89
0 Days rest	6.32	2	2	2	36	0	37.0	44	6	21	19
1 or 2 Days rest	2.84	3	4	1	53	0	57.0	50	4	32	34
3+ Days rest	4.20	2	0	0	55	0	75.0	74	7	23	36
Pre-All Star	3.61	6	2	3	78	0	97.1	89	10	37	54
Post-All Star	5.02	1	4	0	66	0	71.2	79	7	39	35

	Avg	AB	H	2B	3B	HR	RBI	BB	SO	OBP	SLG
First Inning Pitched	.256	434	111	22	3	12	85	53	63	.333	.403
First 15 Pitches	.247	396	98	17	3	10	67	46	53	.322	.381
Pitch 16-30	.289	166	48	10	0	6	28	24	26	.377	.458
Pitch 31-45	.190	58	11	5	1	0	4	5	6	.266	.310
Pitch 46+	.478	23	11	3	0	1	7	1	4	.500	.739
First Pitch	.263	99	26	5	0	5	18	10	0	.330	.465
Ahead in Count	.186	247	46	10	2	1	18	0	79	.191	.255
Behind in Count	.356	174	62	15	1	6	47	27	0	.434	.557
Two Strikes	.182	269	49	13	2	2	21	38	89	.282	.268

Pitcher vs. Batter (career)

Pitches Best Vs.	Avg	AB	H	2B	3B	HR	RBI	BB	SO	OBP	SLG
Wade Boggs	.091	11	1	0	0	0	0	1	2	.167	.091
Don Mattingly	.200	10	2	2	0	0	4	1	1	.273	.400

Pitches Worst Vs.	Avg	AB	H	2B	3B	HR	RBI	BB	SO	OBP	SLG
Rafael Palmeiro	.556	9	5	0	0	0	3	3	0	.667	.556

Mike Macfarlane — Royals

Age 30 – Bats Right (flyball hitter)

	Avg	G	AB	R	H	2B	3B	HR	RBI	BB	SO	HBP	GDP	SB	CS	OBP	SLG	IBB	SH	SF	#Pit	#P/PA	GB	FB	G/F
1993 Season	.273	117	388	55	106	27	0	20	67	40	83	16	8	2	5	.360	.497	2	1	6	1631	3.62	108	142	0.76
Last Five Years	.255	523	1614	190	411	103	9	58	233	119	320	46	37	5	10	.320	.437	6	4	19	6190	3.43	498	539	0.92

1993 Season

	Avg	AB	H	2B	3B	HR	RBI	BB	SO	OBP	SLG
vs. Left	.233	150	35	9	0	4	19	21	34	.341	.373
vs. Right	.298	238	71	18	0	16	48	19	49	.373	.576
Groundball	.317	60	19	3	0	3	13	6	12	.382	.517
Flyball	.241	79	19	4	0	1	10	6	19	.299	.329
Home	.284	197	56	19	0	7	35	23	37	.374	.487
Away	.262	191	50	8	0	13	32	17	46	.344	.508
Day	.324	111	36	8	0	7	22	13	21	.411	.586
Night	.253	277	70	19	0	13	45	27	62	.340	.462
Grass	.268	153	41	6	0	10	27	16	32	.356	.503
Turf	.277	235	65	21	0	10	40	24	51	.362	.494
First Pitch	.389	54	21	4	0	4	14	1	0	.460	.685
Ahead in Count	.302	86	26	8	0	6	15	19	0	.432	.605
Behind in Count	.194	180	35	6	0	5	21	0	76	.219	.311
Two Strikes	.210	181	38	9	0	7	25	20	83	.303	.376

	Avg	AB	H	2B	3B	HR	RBI	BB	SO	OBP	SLG
Scoring Posn	.293	116	34	9	0	5	48	14	22	.385	.500
Close & Late	.277	83	23	5	0	5	14	7	19	.344	.518
None on/out	.279	111	31	8	0	7	7	11	28	.365	.541
Batting #4	.253	269	68	16	0	14	39	28	65	.341	.468
Batting #5	.263	76	20	7	0	4	15	8	13	.374	.513
Other	.419	43	18	4	0	2	13	4	5	.458	.651
April	.233	30	7	0	0	1	4	1	8	.242	.333
May	.338	65	22	6	0	6	20	5	8	.419	.708
June	.246	69	17	4	0	4	14	9	16	.365	.478
July	.240	75	18	3	0	3	9	5	21	.310	.400
August	.256	86	22	8	0	4	9	12	20	.366	.488
September/October	.317	63	20	6	0	2	11	8	10	.397	.508
Pre-All Star	.283	191	54	12	0	11	41	17	40	.363	.518
Post-All Star	.264	197	52	15	0	9	26	23	43	.357	.477

1993 By Position

Position	Avg	AB	H	2B	3B	HR	RBI	BB	SO	OBP	SLG	G	GS	Innings	PO	A	E	DP	Fld Pct	Rng Fctr	In Zone	Outs	Zone Rtg	MLB Zone
As Pinch Hitter	.417	12	5	2	0	0	3	2	4	.467	.583	15	0	---	---	---	---	---	---	---	---	---	---	---
As c	.269	376	101	25	0	20	64	38	79	.356	.495	114	102	917.1	647	65	11	11	.985	---	---	---	---	---

Last Five Years

	Avg	AB	H	2B	3B	HR	RBI	BB	SO	OBP	SLG
vs. Left	.252	611	154	39	5	18	69	49	119	.321	.421
vs. Right	.256	1003	257	64	4	40	164	70	201	.320	.448
Groundball	.273	396	108	23	4	12	62	26	68	.333	.442
Flyball	.230	417	96	23	2	18	64	26	93	.286	.424
Home	.267	760	203	60	6	21	110	59	130	.335	.445
Away	.244	854	208	43	3	37	123	60	190	.307	.431
Day	.281	381	107	24	1	17	57	31	78	.349	.483
Night	.247	1233	304	79	8	41	176	88	242	.311	.423
Grass	.252	659	166	32	3	28	104	49	136	.317	.437
Turf	.257	955	245	71	6	30	129	70	184	.323	.438
First Pitch	.299	281	84	25	1	12	47	3	0	.327	.523
Ahead in Count	.329	350	115	30	4	19	68	59	0	.433	.600
Behind in Count	.190	711	135	26	2	12	66	0	278	.211	.283
Two Strikes	.175	675	118	26	2	14	60	55	320	.252	.281

	Avg	AB	H	2B	3B	HR	RBI	BB	SO	OBP	SLG
Scoring Posn	.246	435	107	25	2	11	167	43	80	.328	.389
Close & Late	.261	303	79	16	4	12	45	26	69	.336	.459
None on/out	.245	429	105	28	3	21	21	25	94	.303	.471
Batting #4	.249	381	95	21	0	23	53	36	88	.329	.486
Batting #7	.268	347	93	22	1	11	48	17	77	.305	.432
Other	.252	886	223	60	8	24	132	66	155	.323	.419
April	.267	172	46	16	1	2	19	13	37	.332	.407
May	.251	323	81	22	2	16	55	23	64	.319	.480
June	.245	335	82	15	3	9	41	17	61	.293	.388
July	.271	262	71	19	0	10	46	21	57	.338	.458
August	.252	254	64	14	0	15	42	24	57	.326	.484
September/October	.250	268	67	17	3	6	30	21	44	.325	.403
Pre-All Star	.255	930	237	62	6	28	127	62	184	.316	.425
Post-All Star	.254	684	174	41	3	30	106	57	136	.326	.455

Batter vs. Pitcher (career)

Hits Best Against	Avg	AB	H	2B	3B	HR	RBI	BB	SO	OBP	SLG
Tim Leary	.545	11	6	3	0	2	6	1	1	.583	1.364
Mark Williamson	.538	13	7	1	0	1	4	1	0	.571	.846
Jason Bere	.500	8	4	0	0	3	6	4	1	.667	1.625
Dave Fleming	.429	14	6	3	0	2	2	2	2	.500	1.071
Greg Hibbard	.333	9	3	0	0	2	3	2	0	.455	1.000

Hits Worst Against	Avg	AB	H	2B	3B	HR	RBI	BB	SO	OBP	SLG
Dave Stewart	.000	11	0	0	0	0	0	1	2	.083	.000
Jamie Moyer	.077	13	1	0	0	0	0	1	4	.143	.077
Jack McDowell	.087	23	2	1	0	0	1	1	5	.125	.130
Dennis Eckersley	.091	11	1	0	0	0	1	0	4	.091	.091
Greg Swindell	.143	21	3	0	0	0	1	0	5	.143	.143

Shane Mack — Twins

Age 30 – Bats Right (groundball hitter)

	Avg	G	AB	R	H	2B	3B	HR	RBI	BB	SO	HBP	GDP	SB	CS	OBP	SLG	IBB	SH	SF	#Pit	#P/PA	GB	FB	G/F
1993 Season	.276	128	503	66	139	30	4	10	61	41	76	4	13	15	5	.335	.412	1	3	2	2013	3.64	235	122	1.93
Last Five Years	.305	552	1858	296	567	98	22	52	254	168	330	30	40	67	32	.370	.466	4	22	9	7292	3.49	810	424	1.91

1993 Season

	Avg	AB	H	2B	3B	HR	RBI	BB	SO	OBP	SLG
vs. Left	.288	118	34	8	1	2	16	4	11	.317	.424
vs. Right	.273	385	105	22	3	8	45	37	65	.340	.408
Groundball	.243	70	17	3	0	1	7	8	10	.321	.329

	Avg	AB	H	2B	3B	HR	RBI	BB	SO	OBP	SLG
Scoring Posn	.327	104	34	7	1	5	51	12	12	.395	.558
Close & Late	.235	81	19	7	0	3	12	8	13	.303	.432
None on/out	.235	166	39	5	0	3	3	8	23	.278	.319

1993 Season

	Avg	AB	H	2B	3B	HR	RBI	BB	SO	OBP	SLG
Flyball	.281	114	32	5	2	6	24	9	20	.349	.518
Home	.289	218	63	17	3	3	25	19	36	.350	.436
Away	.267	285	76	13	1	7	36	22	40	.323	.393
Day	.196	163	32	7	1	4	21	8	25	.236	.325
Night	.315	340	107	23	3	6	40	33	51	.380	.453
Grass	.286	217	62	13	0	6	29	19	31	.347	.429
Turf	.269	286	77	17	4	4	32	22	45	.325	.399
First Pitch	.269	67	18	6	2	3	13	1	0	.306	.552
Ahead in Count	.402	117	47	12	1	1	23	24	0	.504	.547
Behind in Count	.199	231	46	11	0	4	17	0	65	.202	.299
Two Strikes	.176	222	39	6	0	3	18	16	76	.233	.243

	Avg	AB	H	2B	3B	HR	RBI	BB	SO	OBP	SLG
Batting #1	.277	253	70	16	1	3	26	16	35	.324	.383
Batting #6	.277	65	18	3	1	1	6	5	10	.329	.400
Other	.276	185	51	11	2	6	29	20	31	.351	.454
April	.213	80	17	5	0	0	10	3	11	.250	.275
May	.220	50	11	3	0	1	9	1	3	.245	.340
June	.242	91	22	3	3	4	14	15	16	.355	.473
July	.392	102	40	10	0	3	14	11	13	.447	.578
August	.264	125	33	4	1	1	11	7	23	.308	.336
September/October	.291	55	16	5	0	1	3	4	10	.339	.436
Pre-All Star	.265	257	68	16	3	5	36	24	35	.332	.409
Post-All Star	.289	246	71	14	1	5	25	17	41	.337	.415

1993 By Position

Position	Avg	AB	H	2B	3B	HR	RBI	BB	SO	OBP	SLG	G	GS	Innings	PO	A	E	DP	Fld Pct	Rng Fctr	In Zone	Outs	Zone Rtg	MLB Zone
As lf	.260	227	59	14	3	5	33	23	32	.331	.414	64	60	521.0	147	4	5	0	.968	2.61	177	149	.842	.818
As cf	.280	271	76	15	1	5	28	18	44	.330	.399	67	63	578.1	199	4	0	1	1.000	3.16	233	195	.837	.829

Last Five Years

	Avg	AB	H	2B	3B	HR	RBI	BB	SO	OBP	SLG
vs. Left	.329	529	174	40	9	20	96	44	77	.386	.552
vs. Right	.296	1329	393	58	13	32	158	124	253	.364	.431
Groundball	.308	422	130	17	6	10	60	38	89	.373	.448
Flyball	.300	413	124	23	5	17	64	40	75	.372	.504
Home	.318	858	273	53	18	22	121	84	157	.385	.499
Away	.294	1000	294	45	4	30	133	84	173	.357	.437
Day	.288	579	167	31	7	18	85	58	83	.361	.459
Night	.313	1279	400	67	15	34	169	110	247	.375	.468
Grass	.303	769	233	40	1	25	101	71	133	.371	.455
Turf	.307	1089	334	58	21	27	153	97	197	.370	.473
First Pitch	.378	315	119	22	5	17	65	3	0	.399	.641
Ahead in Count	.402	393	158	34	10	15	76	84	0	.507	.654
Behind in Count	.229	841	193	31	3	13	75	0	292	.241	.320
Two Strikes	.181	784	142	23	4	10	68	80	330	.265	.259

	Avg	AB	H	2B	3B	HR	RBI	BB	SO	OBP	SLG
Scoring Posn	.305	429	131	22	4	14	193	55	74	.390	.473
Close & Late	.261	284	74	14	1	6	37	26	57	.323	.380
None on/out	.304	539	164	27	5	16	16	36	88	.358	.462
Batting #1	.297	694	206	34	7	15	78	55	118	.356	.431
Batting #2	.318	264	84	12	2	9	38	27	47	.391	.481
Other	.308	900	277	52	13	28	138	86	165	.375	.488
April	.246	211	52	12	3	4	24	13	37	.309	.389
May	.320	231	74	10	2	8	41	20	30	.384	.485
June	.251	331	83	17	4	13	48	37	61	.330	.444
July	.363	350	127	21	6	11	49	43	62	.432	.551
August	.301	396	119	19	5	8	48	29	78	.357	.434
September/October	.330	339	112	19	2	8	44	26	62	.390	.469
Pre-All Star	.272	871	237	46	9	26	123	84	149	.344	.435
Post-All Star	.334	987	330	52	13	26	131	84	181	.394	.492

Batter vs. Pitcher (career)

Hits Best Against	Avg	AB	H	2B	3B	HR	RBI	BB	SO	OBP	SLG
Joe Hesketh	.571	14	8	1	0	2	5	2	1	.625	1.071
Bill Krueger	.556	9	5	1	1	1	9	2	0	.636	1.222
Ben McDonald	.538	13	7	2	0	2	4	2	1	.600	1.154
Scott Sanderson	.533	15	8	0	0	3	6	1	1	.563	1.133
Chuck Finley	.436	39	17	6	2	2	3	5	7	.500	.846

Hits Worst Against	Avg	AB	H	2B	3B	HR	RBI	BB	SO	OBP	SLG
Bob Wickman	.000	9	0	0	0	0	0	2	4	.182	.000
Alex Fernandez	.120	25	3	0	0	0	1	0	7	.120	.120
Greg Hibbard	.133	15	2	1	0	0	2	1	2	.188	.200
Mike Magnante	.154	13	2	0	0	0	0	0	0	.154	.154
Dave Fleming	.182	11	2	0	0	0	0	0	2	.182	.182

Lonnie Maclin — Cardinals

Age 27 – Bats Left

	Avg	G	AB	R	H	2B	3B	HR	RBI	BB	SO	HBP	GDP	SB	CS	OBP	SLG	IBB	SH	SF	#Pit	#P/PA	GB	FB	G/F
1993 Season	.077	12	13	2	1	0	0	0	1	0	5	0	0	1	0	.071	.077	0	0	1	60	4.29	5	3	1.67

1993 Season

	Avg	AB	H	2B	3B	HR	RBI	BB	SO	OBP	SLG
vs. Left	.000	0	0	0	0	0	0	0	0	.000	.000
vs. Right	.077	13	1	0	0	0	1	0	5	.071	.077
Scoring Posn	.000	2	0	0	0	0	1	0	0	.000	.000
Close & Late	.000	2	0	0	0	0	0	0	0	.000	.000

Greg Maddux — Braves

Age 28 – Pitches Right (groundball pitcher)

	ERA	W	L	Sv	G	GS	IP	BB	SO	Avg	H	2B	3B	HR	RBI	OBP	SLG	CG	ShO	Sup	QS	#P/S	SB	CS	GB	FB	G/F
1993 Season	2.36	20	10	0	36	36	267.0	52	197	.232	228	38	2	14	75	.273	.317	8	1	4.28	29	100	27	6	460	174	2.64
Last Five Years	2.84	89	59	0	178	178	1273.1	341	873	.238	1125	186	23	63	409	.293	.327	39	10	4.29	125	100	102	42	2192	877	2.50

1993 Season

	ERA	W	L	Sv	G	GS	IP	H	HR	BB	SO
Home	2.19	8	4	0	16	16	123.1	97	5	27	93
Away	2.51	12	6	0	20	20	143.2	131	9	25	104
Day	1.91	5	2	0	9	9	66.0	61	1	17	48
Night	2.51	15	8	0	27	27	201.0	167	13	35	149
Grass	2.41	16	6	0	27	27	202.0	168	12	41	148
Turf	2.22	4	4	0	9	9	65.0	60	2	11	49
April	3.09	2	2	0	6	6	43.2	40	5	9	31
May	2.35	3	2	0	6	6	46.0	33	2	11	40
June	2.70	2	2	0	5	5	36.2	35	2	7	21
July	3.17	5	2	0	7	7	48.1	48	3	8	37
August	1.53	4	1	0	6	6	47.0	36	1	6	29
September/October	1.39	4	1	0	6	6	45.1	36	1	11	39
Starter	2.36	20	10	0	36	36	267.0	228	14	52	197
Reliever	0.00	0	0	0	0	0	0.0	0	0	0	0
0-3 Days Rest	0.78	3	0	0	3	3	23.0	14	1	4	21
4 Days Rest	2.66	13	9	0	26	26	186.1	165	11	38	144
5+ Days Rest	2.03	4	1	0	7	7	57.2	49	2	10	32
Pre-All Star	2.83	8	8	0	20	20	146.1	129	10	32	113

	Avg	AB	H	2B	3B	HR	RBI	BB	SO	OBP	SLG
vs. Left	.235	520	122	19	1	5	36	33	97	.280	.304
vs. Right	.228	464	106	19	1	9	39	19	100	.264	.332
Inning 1-6	.237	781	185	28	2	9	62	38	157	.275	.312
Inning 7+	.212	203	43	10	0	5	13	14	40	.265	.335
None on	.240	592	142	26	2	11	11	29	124	.280	.346
Runners on	.219	392	86	12	0	3	64	23	73	.262	.273
Scoring Posn	.210	233	49	6	0	2	57	20	42	.271	.262
Close & Late	.207	135	28	6	0	4	10	11	33	.270	.341
None on/out	.290	262	76	12	1	5	5	13	48	.331	.401
vs. 1st Batr (relief)	.000	0	0	0	0	0	0	0	0	.000	.000
First Inning Pitched	.255	137	35	7	0	2	15	7	35	.295	.350
First 75 Pitches	.229	729	167	23	2	9	53	35	144	.267	.303
Pitch 76-90	.265	132	35	9	0	1	12	5	30	.292	.356
Pitch 91-105	.167	84	14	3	0	3	6	6	19	.228	.310
Pitch 106+	.308	39	12	3	0	1	4	6	4	.400	.462
First Pitch	.275	171	47	9	0	0	19	4	0	.292	.327
Ahead in Count	.177	429	76	15	0	7	21	0	161	.185	.261
Behind in Count	.292	202	59	7	1	3	16	25	0	.368	.381

1993 Season

	ERA	W	L	Sv	G	GS	IP	H	HR	BB	SO
Post-All Star	1.79	12	2	0	16	16	120.2	99	4	20	84

	Avg	AB	H	2B	3B	HR	RBI	BB	SO	OBP	SLG
Two Strikes	.141	411	58	12	0	5	19	23	197	.190	.207

Last Five Years

	ERA	W	L	Sv	G	GS	IP	H	HR	BB	SO
Home	2.80	45	24	0	83	83	616.2	536	29	175	431
Away	2.88	44	35	0	95	95	656.2	589	34	166	442
Day	3.03	37	25	0	75	75	526.0	503	27	165	363
Night	2.71	52	34	0	103	103	747.1	622	36	176	510
Grass	2.91	67	41	0	128	128	916.1	804	51	258	631
Turf	2.67	22	18	0	50	50	357.0	321	12	83	242
April	3.16	11	8	0	23	23	156.2	140	9	37	99
May	2.92	11	13	0	29	29	212.2	173	11	60	146
June	3.27	10	13	0	30	30	200.2	170	10	64	142
July	3.06	19	5	0	30	30	212.0	204	12	58	141
August	2.28	19	9	0	33	33	253.0	213	11	71	166
September/October	2.61	19	11	0	33	33	238.1	225	10	51	179
Starter	2.84	89	59	0	178	178	1273.1	1125	63	341	873
Reliever	0.00	0	0	0	0	0	0.0	0	0	0	0
0-3 Days Rest	2.67	13	5	0	22	22	162.0	141	7	37	109
4 Days Rest	2.84	57	44	0	120	120	849.0	745	42	234	616
5+ Days Rest	2.95	19	10	0	36	36	262.1	239	14	70	148
Pre-All Star	3.20	36	37	0	92	92	633.1	553	34	179	440
Post-All Star	2.49	53	22	0	86	86	640.0	572	29	162	433

	Avg	AB	H	2B	3B	HR	RBI	BB	SO	OBP	SLG
vs. Left	.258	2733	704	111	17	35	248	237	472	.319	.349
vs. Right	.211	1992	421	75	6	28	161	104	401	.256	.297
Inning 1-6	.235	3795	891	154	20	48	337	269	715	.290	.324
Inning 7+	.252	930	234	32	3	15	72	72	158	.307	.341
None on	.229	2847	652	101	8	36	36	183	550	.280	.308
Runners on	.252	1878	473	85	15	27	373	158	323	.312	.356
Scoring Posn	.235	1066	251	42	11	11	319	124	202	.316	.326
Close & Late	.244	529	129	16	2	7	45	51	101	.313	.321
None on/out	.254	1238	315	41	4	19	19	85	218	.309	.340
vs. 1st Batr (relief)	.000	0	0	0	0	0	0	0	0	.000	.000
First Inning Pitched	.245	669	164	33	3	7	63	60	148	.313	.335
First 75 Pitches	.233	3439	800	132	19	42	273	240	643	.287	.319
Pitch 76-90	.244	636	155	27	0	8	64	39	120	.291	.324
Pitch 91-105	.257	412	106	14	1	9	49	33	71	.313	.362
Pitch 106+	.269	238	64	13	3	4	23	29	39	.353	.399
First Pitch	.287	792	227	38	5	13	95	33	0	.319	.396
Ahead in Count	.167	2043	341	43	7	16	108	0	729	.176	.218
Behind in Count	.329	1053	346	66	5	19	122	178	0	.425	.455
Two Strikes	.146	1915	279	38	8	11	98	129	873	.204	.191

Pitcher vs. Batter (career)

Pitches Best Vs.	Avg	AB	H	2B	3B	HR	RBI	BB	SO	OBP	SLG
Felix Jose	.000	16	0	0	0	0	0	1	7	.059	.000
Eric Karros	.000	13	0	0	0	0	1	1	3	.071	.000
Bob Melvin	.000	11	0	0	0	0	0	1	4	.083	.000
Dale Murphy	.059	34	2	0	0	0	0	1	12	.086	.059
Jeff Kent	.071	14	1	0	0	0	0	0	6	.071	.071

Pitches Worst Vs.	Avg	AB	H	2B	3B	HR	RBI	BB	SO	OBP	SLG
Hal Morris	.520	25	13	3	0	0	2	1	1	.538	.640
Bip Roberts	.480	25	12	3	0	0	3	7	4	.594	.600
Luis Gonzalez	.371	35	13	4	0	3	9	3	4	.421	.743
Andy Van Slyke	.362	58	21	6	0	4	11	10	12	.456	.672
Dion James	.333	12	4	1	1	1	5	2	2	.429	.833

Mike Maddux — Mets

Age 32 – Pitches Right (groundball pitcher)

	ERA	W	L	Sv	G	GS	IP	BB	SO	Avg	H	2B	3B	HR	RBI	OBP	SLG	GF	IR	IRS	Hld	SvOp	SB	CS	GB	FB	G/F
1993 Season	3.60	3	8	5	58	0	75.0	27	57	.243	67	13	3	3	38	.313	.344	31	36	12	3	11	9	3	116	51	2.27
Last Five Years	3.34	13	16	16	199	8	317.2	96	211	.247	292	44	8	15	130	.305	.336	75	125	41	23	28	36	17	542	214	2.53

1993 Season

	ERA	W	L	Sv	G	GS	IP	H	HR	BB	SO
Home	3.31	3	3	1	27	0	35.1	36	2	7	27
Away	3.86	0	5	4	31	0	39.2	31	1	20	30
Starter	0.00	0	0	0	0	0	0.0	0	0	0	0
Reliever	3.60	3	8	5	58	0	75.0	67	3	27	57
0 Days rest	1.69	1	1	0	7	0	10.2	4	1	2	7
1 or 2 Days rest	3.51	2	3	5	33	0	41.0	39	1	17	28
3+ Days rest	4.63	0	4	0	18	0	23.1	24	1	8	22
Pre-All Star	4.50	0	6	3	31	0	44.0	43	3	17	31
Post-All Star	2.32	3	2	2	27	0	31.0	24	0	10	26

	Avg	AB	H	2B	3B	HR	RBI	BB	SO	OBP	SLG
vs. Left	.264	125	33	8	1	2	21	17	24	.351	.392
vs. Right	.225	151	34	5	2	1	17	10	33	.279	.305
Scoring Posn	.228	92	21	6	0	0	31	16	24	.330	.293
Close & Late	.283	127	36	7	2	2	25	15	24	.358	.417
None on/out	.254	63	16	3	1	0	0	6	7	.329	.333
First Pitch	.333	36	12	1	0	0	9	6	0	.409	.361
Ahead in Count	.215	130	28	6	1	1	13	0	54	.227	.300
Behind in Count	.265	49	13	3	2	1	10	8	0	.356	.469
Two Strikes	.176	125	22	6	0	0	10	13	57	.255	.224

Last Five Years

	ERA	W	L	Sv	G	GS	IP	H	HR	BB	SO
Home	3.36	11	6	4	100	4	152.2	143	4	39	110
Away	3.33	2	10	12	99	4	165.0	149	11	57	101
Day	3.58	3	2	3	60	2	93.0	85	5	25	54
Night	3.24	10	14	13	139	6	224.2	207	10	71	157
Grass	3.08	11	10	12	142	3	222.1	198	12	69	141
Turf	3.97	2	6	4	57	5	95.1	94	3	27	70
April	3.80	3	2	4	29	1	45.0	42	2	15	23
May	3.54	0	5	0	50	3	86.1	82	4	28	59
June	4.42	1	3	5	34	3	59.0	62	6	16	35
July	1.11	1	1	1	25	0	32.1	23	0	10	18
August	3.99	6	1	2	27	0	38.1	43	2	10	34
September/October	2.38	2	4	4	34	1	56.2	40	1	17	42
Starter	4.00	2	4	0	8	8	36.0	37	3	10	26
Reliever	3.26	11	12	16	191	0	281.2	255	12	86	185
0 Days rest	2.14	2	2	2	27	0	42.0	36	1	12	19
1 or 2 Days rest	2.91	5	4	10	102	0	139.0	114	6	45	96
3+ Days rest	4.20	4	6	4	62	0	100.2	105	5	29	70
Pre-All Star	3.75	4	11	10	122	7	199.1	194	12	62	124
Post-All Star	2.66	9	5	6	77	1	118.1	98	3	34	87

	Avg	AB	H	2B	3B	HR	RBI	BB	SO	OBP	SLG
vs. Left	.252	583	147	20	4	5	65	54	100	.314	.326
vs. Right	.242	600	145	24	4	10	65	42	111	.295	.345
Inning 1-6	.234	406	95	19	2	5	48	30	77	.290	.328
Inning 7+	.254	777	197	25	6	10	82	66	134	.312	.340
None on	.247	651	161	21	6	7	7	36	117	.292	.330
Runners on	.246	532	131	23	2	8	123	60	94	.319	.342
Scoring Posn	.228	337	77	19	1	2	106	51	67	.324	.309
Close & Late	.262	340	89	13	2	4	51	39	59	.337	.347
None on/out	.276	286	79	11	3	7	7	23	39	.334	.409
vs. 1st Batr (relief)	.221	172	38	4	2	2	17	14	30	.282	.302
First Inning Pitched	.245	641	157	22	5	8	81	51	110	.302	.332
First 15 Pitches	.256	657	168	21	7	10	71	40	108	.299	.355
Pitch 16-30	.209	306	64	12	1	3	31	39	58	.300	.284
Pitch 31-45	.236	127	30	6	0	2	15	6	24	.274	.331
Pitch 46+	.323	93	30	5	0	0	13	11	21	.393	.376
First Pitch	.310	200	62	7	0	3	26	13	0	.352	.390
Ahead in Count	.196	515	101	19	2	5	41	0	192	.203	.270
Behind in Count	.282	245	69	10	6	6	41	40	0	.375	.445
Two Strikes	.154	493	76	14	1	2	33	43	211	.226	.199

Pitcher vs. Batter (career)

Pitches Best Vs.	Avg	AB	H	2B	3B	HR	RBI	BB	SO	OBP	SLG
Jay Bell	.067	15	1	0	0	0	0	0	1	.067	.067
Mariano Duncan	.083	12	1	0	0	0	1	1	5	.154	.083
Jose Lind	.091	11	1	0	0	0	1	0	0	.091	.091
Jeff King	.091	11	1	0	0	0	0	0	1	.091	.091
Marquis Grissom	.091	11	1	0	0	0	0	0	4	.091	.091

Pitches Worst Vs.	Avg	AB	H	2B	3B	HR	RBI	BB	SO	OBP	SLG
Kevin Bass	.600	10	6	1	1	0	2	2	1	.667	.900
Lonnie Smith	.556	9	5	1	0	0	1	2	2	.636	.667
Sid Bream	.529	17	9	1	1	0	3	5	3	.636	.706
Robby Thompson	.471	17	8	1	1	2	6	0	2	.471	1.000
Billy Doran	.400	15	6	2	0	1	2	4	2	.526	.733

Dave Magadan — Mariners

Age 31 – Bats Left (groundball hitter)

	Avg	G	AB	R	H	2B	3B	HR	RBI	BB	SO	HBP	GDP	SB	CS	OBP	SLG	IBB	SH	SF	#Pit	#P/PA	GB	FB	G/F
1993 Season	.273	137	455	49	124	23	0	5	50	80	63	1	12	2	1	.378	.356	7	2	6	2169	3.99	164	123	1.33
Last Five Years	.286	631	2019	261	578	105	10	22	242	342	249	6	35	7	3	.387	.381	23	16	27	9616	3.99	772	497	1.55

1993 Season

	Avg	AB	H	2B	3B	HR	RBI	BB	SO	OBP	SLG
vs. Left	.237	118	28	7	0	0	18	19	22	.333	.297
vs. Right	.285	337	96	16	0	5	32	61	41	.394	.377
Groundball	.303	122	37	4	0	3	19	15	12	.374	.410
Flyball	.216	97	21	5	0	0	7	20	10	.347	.268
Home	.286	206	59	15	0	3	28	51	23	.424	.403
Away	.261	249	65	8	0	2	22	29	40	.336	.317
Day	.230	126	29	5	0	0	12	23	15	.347	.270
Night	.289	329	95	18	0	5	38	57	48	.390	.389
Grass	.278	248	69	10	0	5	28	46	37	.388	.379
Turf	.266	207	55	13	0	0	22	34	26	.366	.329
First Pitch	.217	46	10	1	0	1	5	3	0	.255	.304
Ahead in Count	.306	124	38	5	0	2	15	48	0	.491	.395
Behind in Count	.230	191	44	11	0	1	15	0	53	.233	.304
Two Strikes	.264	208	55	13	0	1	20	29	63	.356	.341

	Avg	AB	H	2B	3B	HR	RBI	BB	SO	OBP	SLG
Scoring Posn	.238	130	31	5	0	1	43	29	23	.364	.300
Close & Late	.253	75	19	3	0	2	14	11	13	.345	.373
None on/out	.259	85	22	8	0	0	0	14	6	.364	.353
Batting #3	.287	129	37	4	0	3	17	23	14	.396	.388
Batting #5	.257	136	35	7	0	1	12	28	18	.377	.331
Other	.274	190	52	12	0	1	21	29	31	.367	.353
April	.320	75	24	4	0	1	10	18	10	.457	.413
May	.244	78	19	5	0	1	8	17	8	.371	.346
June	.310	87	27	3	0	2	12	10	13	.378	.414
July	.286	70	20	5	0	0	10	12	8	.381	.357
August	.227	66	15	3	0	0	4	11	11	.333	.273
September/October	.241	79	19	3	0	1	6	12	13	.341	.316
Pre-All Star	.283	269	76	14	0	4	37	53	33	.398	.379
Post-All Star	.258	186	48	9	0	1	13	27	30	.349	.323

1993 By Position

Position	Avg	AB	H	2B	3B	HR	RBI	BB	SO	OBP	SLG	G	GS	Innings	PO	A	E	DP	Fld Pct	Rng Fctr	In Zone	Outs	Zone Rtg	MLB Zone
As Pinch Hitter	.300	10	3	0	0	0	2	1	3	.364	.300	11	0	---	---	---	---	---	---	---	---	---	---	---
As 1b	.229	131	30	6	0	1	13	18	21	.318	.298	43	36	325.2	314	19	3	33	.991	---	56	45	.804	.834
As 3b	.289	305	88	17	0	4	34	60	39	.403	.384	90	87	757.1	66	173	9	18	.964	2.84	236	196	.831	.834

Last Five Years

	Avg	AB	H	2B	3B	HR	RBI	BB	SO	OBP	SLG
vs. Left	.260	649	169	24	2	2	72	87	90	.346	.313
vs. Right	.299	1370	409	81	8	20	170	255	159	.405	.413
Groundball	.286	654	187	29	3	7	78	129	80	.398	.372
Flyball	.269	412	111	25	1	2	51	65	44	.369	.350
Home	.283	956	271	47	5	12	122	184	110	.394	.381
Away	.289	1063	307	58	5	10	120	158	139	.380	.381
Day	.258	643	166	32	4	8	70	116	81	.368	.358
Night	.299	1376	412	73	6	14	172	226	168	.396	.392
Grass	.287	1337	384	59	6	17	161	227	167	.387	.378
Turf	.284	682	194	46	4	5	81	115	82	.386	.386
First Pitch	.323	223	72	16	0	4	25	11	0	.353	.448
Ahead in Count	.337	498	168	31	4	10	77	197	0	.520	.476
Behind in Count	.249	830	207	32	4	6	86	0	190	.249	.319
Two Strikes	.254	914	232	39	5	6	88	131	249	.346	.327

	Avg	AB	H	2B	3B	HR	RBI	BB	SO	OBP	SLG
Scoring Posn	.298	506	151	23	1	7	212	108	66	.405	.389
Close & Late	.273	326	89	10	1	7	46	56	47	.383	.374
None on/out	.285	424	121	22	1	6	6	69	46	.388	.384
Batting #2	.293	894	262	52	6	11	110	152	87	.392	.402
Batting #3	.275	426	117	16	2	7	54	78	62	.386	.371
Other	.285	699	199	37	2	4	78	112	100	.381	.361
April	.289	256	74	13	1	1	26	50	44	.403	.359
May	.284	348	99	14	2	5	35	52	42	.375	.379
June	.303	406	123	21	3	8	59	74	43	.409	.429
July	.299	415	124	24	1	5	52	66	38	.391	.398
August	.262	344	90	16	0	0	36	61	45	.371	.308
September/October	.272	250	68	17	3	3	34	39	37	.365	.400
Pre-All Star	.293	1138	333	52	6	15	135	200	141	.397	.388
Post-All Star	.278	881	245	53	4	7	107	142	108	.374	.371

Batter vs. Pitcher (career)

Hits Best Against	Avg	AB	H	2B	3B	HR	RBI	BB	SO	OBP	SLG
Bill Landrum	.714	7	5	0	0	0	0	4	0	.818	.714
Neal Heaton	.600	10	6	1	0	0	3	1	0	.538	.700
Bill Swift	.600	10	6	1	0	0	3	3	0	.692	.700
Roger McDowell	.444	9	4	1	0	1	5	2	3	.500	.889
John Smoltz	.409	22	9	4	0	0	3	5	0	.519	.591

Hits Worst Against	Avg	AB	H	2B	3B	HR	RBI	BB	SO	OBP	SLG
Jimmy Jones	.000	8	0	0	0	0	0	4	0	.333	.000
Bud Black	.077	13	1	0	0	0	0	1	0	.143	.077
Steve Wilson	.091	11	1	0	0	0	1	0	1	.091	.091
Randy Tomlin	.100	20	2	0	0	0	1	4	1	.250	.100
Jose Rijo	.105	19	2	0	0	0	1	3	5	.227	.105

Mike Magnante — Royals

Age 29 – Pitches Left

	ERA	W	L	Sv	G	GS	IP	BB	SO	Avg	H	2B	3B	HR	RBI	OBP	SLG	CG	ShO	Sup	QS	#P/S	SB	CS	GB	FB	G/F
1993 Season	4.08	1	2	0	7	6	35.1	11	16	.282	37	5	2	3	15	.340	.420	0	0	3.31	3	83	0	4	47	34	1.38
Career (1991-1993)	4.01	5	12	0	89	18	179.2	69	89	.298	207	37	5	11	90	.360	.413	0	0	4.46	6	76	10	9	261	207	1.26

1993 Season

	ERA	W	L	Sv	G	GS	IP	H	HR	BB	SO
Home	1.77	1	0	0	4	3	20.1	18	1	6	9
Away	7.20	0	2	0	3	3	15.0	19	2	5	7

	Avg	AB	H	2B	3B	HR	RBI	BB	SO	OBP	SLG
vs. Left	.360	25	9	1	1	0	3	2	2	.407	.480
vs. Right	.264	106	28	4	1	3	12	9	14	.325	.406

Career (1991-1993)

	ERA	W	L	Sv	G	GS	IP	H	HR	BB	SO
Home	3.43	3	4	0	47	8	99.2	104	3	28	58
Away	4.72	2	8	0	42	10	80.0	103	8	41	31
Day	4.64	0	4	0	22	6	52.1	61	4	20	24
Night	3.75	5	8	0	67	12	127.1	146	7	49	65
Grass	5.65	1	7	0	32	7	57.1	80	8	32	20
Turf	3.24	4	5	0	57	11	122.1	127	3	37	69
April	4.11	0	1	0	10	1	15.1	23	1	9	10
May	11.02	1	3	0	6	5	16.1	35	3	10	8
June	2.39	2	2	0	9	5	37.2	35	1	8	14
July	3.76	0	2	0	15	1	26.1	29	2	11	14
August	2.72	1	1	0	22	3	43.0	41	2	15	22
September/October	4.17	1	3	0	27	3	41.0	44	2	16	21
Starter	5.03	4	7	0	18	18	87.2	112	7	30	31

	Avg	AB	H	2B	3B	HR	RBI	BB	SO	OBP	SLG
vs. Left	.324	170	55	9	2	2	21	19	24	.389	.435
vs. Right	.290	525	152	28	3	9	69	50	65	.350	.406
Inning 1-6	.294	436	128	20	3	9	60	40	51	.352	.415
Inning 7+	.305	259	79	17	2	2	30	29	38	.372	.409
None on	.284	373	106	20	0	6	6	34	49	.346	.386
Runners on	.314	322	101	17	5	5	84	35	40	.375	.444
Scoring Posn	.282	188	53	8	3	5	78	28	30	.366	.436
Close & Late	.369	111	41	5	1	1	16	11	7	.423	.459
None on/out	.316	171	54	10	0	3	3	9	21	.354	.427
vs. 1st Batr (relief)	.258	66	17	4	1	0	13	5	12	.310	.348
First Inning Pitched	.313	291	91	20	2	1	44	36	44	.386	.405
First 75 Pitches	.298	655	195	35	4	9	85	66	86	.360	.405
Pitch 76-90	.250	24	6	1	1	1	3	3	2	.333	.500

Career (1991-1993)

	ERA	W	L	Sv	G	GS	IP	H	HR	BB	SO
Reliever	3.03	1	5	0	71	0	92.0	95	4	39	58
0-3 Days Rest	2.25	0	0	0	1	1	4.0	7	0	2	1
4 Days Rest	7.07	2	4	0	8	8	35.2	49	3	10	9
5+ Days Rest	3.75	2	3	0	9	9	48.0	56	4	18	21
Pre-All Star	5.03	3	6	0	29	12	78.2	105	7	32	33
Post-All Star	3.21	2	6	0	60	6	101.0	102	4	37	56

	Avg	AB	H	2B	3B	HR	RBI	BB	SO	OBP	SLG
Pitch 91-105	.357	14	5	1	0	1	2	0	1	.357	.643
Pitch 106+	.500	2	1	0	0	0	0	0	0	.500	.500
First Pitch	.390	100	39	8	0	3	15	7	0	.426	.560
Ahead in Count	.256	317	81	12	2	3	39	0	79	.258	.334
Behind in Count	.345	142	49	11	1	3	22	44	0	.492	.500
Two Strikes	.235	302	71	9	4	5	34	18	89	.276	.341

Pitcher vs. Batter (career)

Pitches Best Vs.	Avg	AB	H	2B	3B	HR	RBI	BB	SO	OBP	SLG
Chuck Knoblauch	.000	11	0	0	0	0	0	1	1	.083	.000
Shane Mack	.154	13	2	0	0	0	0	0	0	.154	.154

Pitches Worst Vs.	Avg	AB	H	2B	3B	HR	RBI	BB	SO	OBP	SLG
Don Mattingly	.500	10	5	1	0	0	2	2	0	.583	.600
Frank Thomas	.417	12	5	1	0	0	0	1	2	.462	.500
Robin Ventura	.385	13	5	0	0	1	1	2	1	.467	.615
Kirby Puckett	.364	11	4	1	0	0	1	1	0	.417	.455

Joe Magrane — Angels

Age 29 – Pitches Left (groundball pitcher)

	ERA	W	L	Sv	G	GS	IP	BB	SO	Avg	H	2B	3B	HR	RBI	OBP	SLG	CG	ShO	Sup	QS	#P/S	SB	CS	GB	FB	G/F
1993 Season	4.66	11	12	0	30	28	164.0	58	62	.280	175	36	2	19	83	.341	.435	0	0	4.50	14	89	22	13	247	212	1.17
Last Five Years	3.64	40	40	0	100	97	633.1	204	309	.264	632	118	21	36	231	.324	.376	12	5	3.95	65	96	69	41	1030	669	1.54

1993 Season

	ERA	W	L	Sv	G	GS	IP	H	HR	BB	SO
Home	4.50	5	4	0	13	12	70.0	73	4	24	21
Away	4.79	6	8	0	17	16	94.0	102	15	34	41
Day	4.30	4	1	0	7	6	37.2	43	4	9	16
Night	4.77	7	11	0	23	22	126.1	132	15	49	46
Grass	4.15	6	3	0	11	11	69.1	72	11	20	28
Turf	5.04	5	9	0	19	17	94.2	103	8	38	34
April	3.76	1	2	0	4	4	26.1	25	2	6	5
May	4.50	1	3	0	5	5	30.0	33	4	11	13
June	2.47	5	1	0	6	6	40.0	33	2	9	15
July	11.50	1	3	0	5	5	18.0	31	6	9	5
August	7.15	0	2	0	4	2	11.1	15	1	7	4
September/October	3.76	3	1	0	6	6	38.1	38	4	16	20
Starter	4.49	11	11	0	28	28	162.1	170	18	56	62
Reliever	21.60	0	1	0	2	0	1.2	5	1	2	0
0-3 Days Rest	0.00	0	0	0	0	0	0.0	0	0	0	0
4 Days Rest	3.76	9	5	0	17	17	105.1	104	12	33	45
5+ Days Rest	5.84	2	6	0	11	11	57.0	66	6	23	17
Pre-All Star	3.61	8	7	0	17	17	107.1	100	9	30	36
Post-All Star	6.67	3	5	0	13	11	56.2	75	10	28	26

	Avg	AB	H	2B	3B	HR	RBI	BB	SO	OBP	SLG
vs. Left	.277	94	26	2	1	3	10	15	11	.387	.415
vs. Right	.281	531	149	34	1	16	73	43	51	.332	.439
Inning 1-6	.276	554	153	33	2	16	76	53	59	.340	.430
Inning 7+	.310	71	22	3	0	3	7	5	3	.351	.479
None on	.274	361	99	19	2	11	11	37	36	.347	.429
Runners on	.288	264	76	17	0	8	72	21	26	.333	.443
Scoring Posn	.272	158	43	12	0	5	65	16	23	.324	.443
Close & Late	.209	43	9	0	0	0	1	4	2	.271	.209
None on/out	.294	160	47	8	0	4	4	17	12	.362	.419
vs. 1st Batr (relief)	1.000	2	2	0	0	1	1	0	0	1.000	2.500
First Inning Pitched	.322	115	37	5	0	7	24	14	11	.385	.548
First 75 Pitches	.277	487	135	30	0	14	69	46	51	.340	.425
Pitch 76-90	.306	72	22	3	1	2	10	9	6	.378	.458
Pitch 91-105	.275	51	14	3	1	1	2	2	1	.302	.431
Pitch 106+	.267	15	4	0	0	2	2	1	4	.313	.667
First Pitch	.390	100	39	11	0	4	14	3	0	.404	.620
Ahead in Count	.214	243	52	13	1	1	23	0	51	.221	.288
Behind in Count	.310	168	52	8	1	11	31	33	0	.422	.565
Two Strikes	.224	237	53	11	1	1	24	22	62	.291	.291

Last Five Years

	ERA	W	L	Sv	G	GS	IP	H	HR	BB	SO
Home	3.83	18	19	0	50	48	312.1	318	13	94	131
Away	3.45	22	21	0	50	49	321.0	314	23	110	178
Day	4.19	15	6	0	28	26	165.1	182	9	51	106
Night	3.44	25	34	0	72	71	468.0	450	27	153	203
Grass	3.64	12	8	0	25	25	160.2	159	13	48	98
Turf	3.64	28	32	0	75	72	472.2	473	23	156	211
April	5.67	3	8	0	13	13	73.0	86	2	21	32
May	3.20	4	8	0	16	15	104.0	98	6	31	48
June	2.94	11	6	0	18	18	125.1	110	4	39	62
July	4.25	8	6	0	17	17	101.2	109	8	31	54
August	2.86	8	5	0	15	13	100.2	82	7	28	42
September/October	3.64	6	7	0	21	21	128.2	147	9	54	71
Starter	3.57	40	39	0	97	97	630.2	625	35	201	308
Reliever	20.25	0	1	0	3	0	2.2	7	1	3	1
0-3 Days Rest	2.50	3	4	0	8	8	54.0	47	1	14	28
4 Days Rest	3.63	26	25	0	60	60	401.2	400	25	129	196
5+ Days Rest	3.75	11	10	0	29	29	175.0	178	9	58	84
Pre-All Star	3.69	21	25	0	53	52	341.2	328	14	106	157
Post-All Star	3.58	19	15	0	47	45	291.2	304	22	98	152

	Avg	AB	H	2B	3B	HR	RBI	BB	SO	OBP	SLG
vs. Left	.259	390	101	16	3	4	39	49	64	.349	.346
vs. Right	.265	2001	531	102	18	32	192	155	245	.320	.382
Inning 1-6	.261	2011	524	102	17	29	191	176	269	.322	.371
Inning 7+	.284	380	108	16	4	7	40	28	40	.337	.403
None on	.264	1407	371	76	9	21	21	109	184	.323	.375
Runners on	.265	984	261	42	12	15	210	95	125	.327	.378
Scoring Posn	.250	577	144	25	6	6	180	71	86	.322	.345
Close & Late	.289	180	52	6	3	2	20	11	20	.333	.389
None on/out	.266	620	165	31	3	8	8	47	82	.321	.365
vs. 1st Batr (relief)	1.000	3	3	0	0	1	1	0	0	1.000	2.000
First Inning Pitched	.281	384	108	16	6	9	45	33	46	.339	.424
First 75 Pitches	.265	1779	472	93	15	25	174	152	241	.325	.377
Pitch 76-90	.256	312	80	13	1	4	27	31	32	.329	.343
Pitch 91-105	.265	200	53	10	4	4	18	9	20	.296	.415
Pitch 106+	.270	100	27	2	1	3	12	12	16	.354	.400
First Pitch	.315	409	129	23	3	8	40	15	0	.340	.445
Ahead in Count	.207	919	190	41	5	5	72	0	262	.215	.279
Behind in Count	.310	632	196	33	10	15	74	105	0	.408	.465
Two Strikes	.200	918	184	35	3	5	68	84	309	.271	.261

Pitcher vs. Batter (career)

Pitches Best Vs.	Avg	AB	H	2B	3B	HR	RBI	BB	SO	OBP	SLG
Greg Colbrunn	.000	12	0	0	0	0	1	0	4	.000	.000
Lenny Dykstra	.074	27	2	0	0	0	0	2	1	.138	.074
Junior Ortiz	.091	11	1	0	0	0	0	0	0	.091	.091
Billy Hatcher	.100	30	3	0	0	0	0	1	4	.129	.100
Joe Oliver	.133	15	2	0	0	0	0	0	2	.133	.133

Pitches Worst Vs.	Avg	AB	H	2B	3B	HR	RBI	BB	SO	OBP	SLG
Delino DeShields	.500	14	7	1	0	1	2	3	1	.588	.786
Barry Larkin	.474	19	9	1	1	0	5	5	1	.560	.632
Don Slaught	.455	11	5	0	0	1	1	0	1	.455	.727
Gary Redus	.409	22	9	4	2	0	4	1	3	.417	.773
Ron Gant	.368	19	7	1	0	3	4	1	0	.400	.895

Pat Mahomes — Twins

Age 23 – Pitches Right (flyball pitcher)

	ERA	W	L	Sv	G	GS	IP	BB	SO	Avg	H	2B	3B	HR	RBI	OBP	SLG	GF	IR	IRS	Hld	SvOp	SB	CS	GB	FB	G/F
1993 Season	7.71	1	5	0	12	5	37.1	16	23	.309	47	10	4	8	31	.372	.586	4	3	0	0	0	5	3	41	55	0.75
Career (1992-1993)	5.97	4	9	0	26	18	107.0	53	67	.290	120	29	8	13	70	.367	.493	5	3	0	0	0	14	11	112	145	0.77

1993 Season

	ERA	W	L	Sv	G	GS	IP	H	HR	BB	SO		Avg	AB	H	2B	3B	HR	RBI	BB	SO	OBP	SLG
Home	9.77	1	2	0	7	2	15.2	20	4	7	12	vs. Left	.309	81	25	5	2	4	17	8	10	.374	.568
Away	6.23	0	3	0	5	3	21.2	27	4	9	11	vs. Right	.310	71	22	5	2	4	14	8	13	.370	.606

Mike Maksudian — Twins

Age 28 – Bats Left (flyball hitter)

	Avg	G	AB	R	H	2B	3B	HR	RBI	BB	SO	HBP	GDP	SB	CS	OBP	SLG	IBB	SH	SF	#Pit	#P/PA	GB	FB	G/F
1993 Season	.167	5	12	2	2	1	0	0	2	4	2	0	2	0	0	.353	.250	0	0	1	57	3.35	4	6	0.67
Career (1992-1993)	.133	8	15	2	2	1	0	0	2	4	2	0	2	0	0	.300	.200	0	0	1	73	3.65	5	8	0.63

1993 Season

	Avg	AB	H	2B	3B	HR	RBI	BB	SO	OBP	SLG		Avg	AB	H	2B	3B	HR	RBI	BB	SO	OBP	SLG
vs. Left	.000	0	0	0	0	0	0	0	0	.000	.000	Scoring Posn	.000	2	0	0	0	0	1	0	0	.000	.000
vs. Right	.167	12	2	1	0	0	2	4	2	.353	.250	Close & Late	.000	1	0	0	0	0	0	2	0	.667	.000

Candy Maldonado — Indians

Age 33 – Bats Right

	Avg	G	AB	R	H	2B	3B	HR	RBI	BB	SO	HBP	GDP	SB	CS	OBP	SLG	IBB	SH	SF	#Pit	#P/PA	GB	FB	G/F
1993 Season	.208	98	221	19	46	7	0	8	35	24	58	1	5	0	1	.287	.348	2	1	1	966	3.90	70	61	1.15
Last Five Years	.252	605	1933	235	487	102	6	71	285	205	449	22	47	13	9	.328	.421	17	4	17	8217	3.77	610	575	1.06

1993 Season

	Avg	AB	H	2B	3B	HR	RBI	BB	SO	OBP	SLG		Avg	AB	H	2B	3B	HR	RBI	BB	SO	OBP	SLG
vs. Left	.257	105	27	5	0	5	20	12	24	.333	.448	Scoring Posn	.236	72	17	3	0	4	29	15	22	.371	.444
vs. Right	.164	116	19	2	0	3	15	12	34	.246	.259	Close & Late	.173	52	9	2	0	1	10	3	18	.228	.269
Home	.238	105	25	4	0	5	20	8	31	.289	.419	None on/out	.182	33	6	0	0	1	1	4	8	.270	.273
Away	.181	116	21	3	0	3	15	16	27	.286	.284	Batting #6	.167	60	10	1	0	2	6	10	12	.286	.283
First Pitch	.200	25	5	1	0	0	1	1	0	.231	.240	Batting #7	.256	39	10	2	0	1	8	5	15	.341	.385
Ahead in Count	.321	56	18	2	0	5	16	10	0	.424	.625	Other	.213	122	26	4	0	5	21	9	31	.271	.369
Behind in Count	.132	91	12	2	0	0	9	0	46	.141	.154	Pre-All Star	.186	118	22	2	0	3	13	13	34	.273	.280
Two Strikes	.132	106	14	3	0	0	11	13	58	.225	.160	Post-All Star	.233	103	24	5	0	5	22	11	24	.304	.427

Last Five Years

	Avg	AB	H	2B	3B	HR	RBI	BB	SO	OBP	SLG		Avg	AB	H	2B	3B	HR	RBI	BB	SO	OBP	SLG
vs. Left	.276	620	171	30	1	24	91	85	119	.364	.444	Scoring Posn	.247	531	131	31	3	17	199	92	133	.353	.412
vs. Right	.241	1313	316	72	5	47	194	120	330	.311	.411	Close & Late	.232	315	73	13	0	8	43	32	89	.304	.349
Groundball	.270	656	177	36	1	21	100	63	148	.339	.424	None on/out	.245	482	118	22	0	17	17	33	111	.300	.396
Flyball	.251	435	109	20	1	16	47	54	109	.335	.411	Batting #4	.262	650	170	37	2	25	105	53	149	.319	.440
Home	.243	905	220	38	3	33	136	84	227	.310	.401	Batting #6	.247	510	126	27	3	22	76	74	123	.352	.441
Away	.260	1028	267	64	3	38	149	121	222	.343	.439	Other	.247	773	191	38	1	24	104	78	177	.319	.392
Day	.237	637	151	25	2	26	93	60	154	.306	.405	April	.225	275	62	15	0	6	36	27	58	.301	.345
Night	.259	1296	336	77	4	45	192	145	295	.338	.429	May	.248	218	54	13	0	9	31	23	53	.320	.431
Grass	.255	1320	336	67	2	46	195	132	297	.324	.413	June	.239	285	68	19	1	13	48	37	65	.329	.449
Turf	.246	613	151	35	4	25	90	73	152	.336	.439	July	.279	369	103	20	1	11	45	33	76	.340	.428
First Pitch	.333	267	89	16	0	5	36	9	0	.360	.449	August	.246	403	99	18	1	18	60	34	93	.306	.429
Ahead in Count	.356	477	170	32	3	28	107	97	0	.463	.612	September/October	.264	383	101	17	3	14	65	51	104	.361	.433
Behind in Count	.169	799	135	26	2	18	74	0	357	.181	.274	Pre-All Star	.236	903	213	53	2	29	123	93	206	.311	.395
Two Strikes	.151	878	133	34	2	19	88	96	449	.240	.260	Post-All Star	.266	1030	274	49	4	42	162	112	243	.343	.444

Batter vs. Pitcher (since 1984)

Hits Best Against	Avg	AB	H	2B	3B	HR	RBI	BB	SO	OBP	SLG	Hits Worst Against	Avg	AB	H	2B	3B	HR	RBI	BB	SO	OBP	SLG
Frank DiPino	.615	13	8	0	0	1	5	1	2	.643	.846	Kevin Tapani	.000	11	0	0	0	0	0	1	5	.083	.000
Rick Sutcliffe	.455	11	5	1	0	1	3	1	1	.462	.818	Eric Plunk	.083	12	1	0	0	0	2	2	4	.214	.083
Mike Jackson	.455	11	5	1	0	2	6	0	3	.455	1.091	Jack Armstrong	.083	12	1	0	0	0	0	2	6	.214	.083
Chuck Finley	.444	18	8	2	0	2	6	2	3	.500	.889	Sid Fernandez	.120	25	3	0	0	0	1	1	5	.154	.120
Jesse Orosco	.333	9	3	0	0	2	4	1	2	.364	1.000	Chris Bosio	.133	15	2	1	0	0	1	0	3	.133	.200

Carlos Maldonado — Brewers

Age 27 – Pitches Right

	ERA	W	L	Sv	G	GS	IP	BB	SO	Avg	H	2B	3B	HR	RBI	OBP	SLG	GF	IR	IRS	Hld	SvOp	SB	CS	GB	FB	G/F
1993 Season	4.58	2	2	1	29	0	37.1	17	18	.282	40	8	1	2	20	.350	.394	9	17	5	2	1	2	0	52	44	1.18
Career (1990-1993)	5.65	2	2	1	38	0	51.0	30	28	.299	60	14	2	2	30	.381	.418	12	18	5	3	1	3	0	71	62	1.15

1993 Season

	ERA	W	L	Sv	G	GS	IP	H	HR	BB	SO		Avg	AB	H	2B	3B	HR	RBI	BB	SO	OBP	SLG
Home	3.38	0	1	1	13	0	18.2	19	0	4	7	vs. Left	.327	52	17	1	0	2	12	8	6	.397	.462
Away	5.79	2	1	0	16	0	18.2	21	2	13	11	vs. Right	.256	90	23	7	1	0	8	9	12	.320	.356
Starter	0.00	0	0	0	0	0	0.0	0	0	0	0	Scoring Posn	.174	46	8	3	0	1	17	11	5	.311	.304
Reliever	4.58	2	2	1	29	0	37.1	40	2	17	18	Close & Late	.333	39	13	3	0	1	5	8	6	.429	.487
0 Days rest	6.43	0	0	0	6	0	7.0	8	2	4	3	None on/out	.441	34	15	2	0	0	0	1	4	.457	.500
1 or 2 Days rest	5.00	0	0	1	8	0	9.0	13	0	6	3	First Pitch	.346	26	9	1	1	1	7	5	0	.424	.577
3+ Days rest	3.80	2	2	0	15	0	21.1	19	0	7	12	Ahead in Count	.254	59	15	4	0	1	7	0	16	.250	.373
Pre-All Star	6.00	1	1	0	12	0	15.0	15	2	12	8	Behind in Count	.351	37	13	2	0	0	4	5	0	.419	.405
Post-All Star	3.63	1	1	1	17	0	22.1	25	0	5	10	Two Strikes	.212	52	11	3	0	1	5	7	18	.300	.327

Jeff Manto — Phillies

Age 29 – Bats Right (flyball hitter)

	Avg	G	AB	R	H	2B	3B	HR	RBI	BB	SO	HBP	GDP	SB	CS	OBP	SLG	IBB	SH	SF	#Pit	#P/PA	GB	FB	G/F
1993 Season	.056	8	18	0	1	0	0	0	0	0	3	1	0	0	0	.105	.056	0	0	0	66	3.47	4	10	0.40
Career (1990-1993)	.203	85	222	27	45	12	1	4	27	35	43	5	3	2	1	.323	.320	1	1	1	1074	4.07	66	77	0.86

1993 Season

	Avg	AB	H	2B	3B	HR	RBI	BB	SO	OBP	SLG		Avg	AB	H	2B	3B	HR	RBI	BB	SO	OBP	SLG
vs. Left	.125	8	1	0	0	0	0	0	1	.125	.125	Scoring Posn	.000	3	0	0	0	0	0	0	1	.000	.000
vs. Right	.000	10	0	0	0	0	0	0	2	.091	.000	Close & Late	.500	2	1	0	0	0	0	0	0	.500	.500

Kirt Manwaring — Giants

Age 28 – Bats Right (groundball hitter)

	Avg	G	AB	R	H	2B	3B	HR	RBI	BB	SO	HBP	GDP	SB	CS	OBP	SLG	IBB	SH	SF	#Pit	#P/PA	GB	FB	G/F
1993 Season	.275	130	432	48	119	15	1	5	49	41	76	6	14	1	3	.345	.350	13	5	2	1629	3.35	160	112	1.43
Last Five Years	.246	399	1172	102	288	38	9	9	113	90	171	18	33	6	6	.308	.317	14	25	5	4431	3.38	489	300	1.63

1993 Season

	Avg	AB	H	2B	3B	HR	RBI	BB	SO	OBP	SLG		Avg	AB	H	2B	3B	HR	RBI	BB	SO	OBP	SLG
vs. Left	.315	146	46	5	0	2	18	14	32	.379	.390	Scoring Posn	.303	122	37	9	0	0	40	15	21	.392	.377
vs. Right	.255	286	73	10	1	3	31	27	44	.328	.329	Close & Late	.164	61	10	5	0	0	5	2	18	.190	.246
Groundball	.256	133	34	2	0	1	8	10	17	.317	.293	None on/out	.311	119	37	2	1	1	1	11	19	.374	.370
Flyball	.333	66	22	5	0	0	15	7	13	.395	.409	Batting #7	.313	112	35	5	0	3	16	9	14	.374	.438
Home	.270	189	51	7	0	3	19	14	32	.327	.354	Batting #8	.263	319	84	10	1	2	33	32	62	.336	.320
Away	.280	243	68	8	1	2	30	27	44	.359	.346	Other	.000	1	0	0	0	0	0	0	0	.000	.000
Day	.264	197	52	8	1	4	21	24	34	.345	.376	April	.288	59	17	2	1	1	10	4	7	.348	.407
Night	.285	235	67	7	0	1	28	17	42	.345	.328	May	.306	62	19	2	0	0	5	10	10	.411	.339
Grass	.268	317	85	11	0	5	34	31	59	.341	.350	June	.239	67	16	3	0	0	4	3	13	.282	.284
Turf	.296	115	34	4	1	0	15	10	17	.357	.348	July	.377	77	29	3	0	2	14	9	9	.448	.494
First Pitch	.305	82	25	1	1	1	9	9	0	.374	.378	August	.184	87	16	3	0	2	10	6	20	.245	.287
Ahead in Count	.311	90	28	6	0	0	15	18	0	.431	.378	September/October	.275	80	22	2	0	0	6	9	17	.344	.300
Behind in Count	.241	203	49	6	0	2	17	0	72	.254	.300	Pre-All Star	.299	221	66	8	1	1	25	20	33	.368	.357
Two Strikes	.201	179	36	5	0	2	9	14	76	.267	.263	Post-All Star	.251	211	53	7	0	4	24	21	43	.321	.341

1993 By Position

Position	Avg	AB	H	2B	3B	HR	RBI	BB	SO	OBP	SLG	G	GS	Innings	PO	A	E	DP	Fld Pct	Rng Fctr	In Zone	Outs	Zone Rtg	MLB Zone
As c	.275	432	119	15	1	5	49	41	76	.345	.350	130	126	1090.2	739	69	2	12	.998	---	---	---	---	---

Last Five Years

	Avg	AB	H	2B	3B	HR	RBI	BB	SO	OBP	SLG		Avg	AB	H	2B	3B	HR	RBI	BB	SO	OBP	SLG
vs. Left	.280	482	135	16	5	2	42	36	69	.335	.346	Scoring Posn	.266	297	79	17	3	0	99	31	40	.342	.343
vs. Right	.222	690	153	22	4	7	71	54	102	.290	.296	Close & Late	.198	187	37	7	1	2	16	14	34	.257	.278
Groundball	.227	419	95	12	5	1	26	30	47	.291	.286	None on/out	.262	290	76	7	2	4	4	26	39	.335	.341
Flyball	.244	225	55	7	1	0	36	19	48	.313	.284	Batting #7	.235	701	165	25	6	7	68	44	81	.288	.318
Home	.246	549	135	22	4	4	58	30	73	.294	.322	Batting #8	.269	398	107	11	1	2	39	40	81	.343	.317
Away	.246	623	153	16	5	5	55	60	98	.320	.311	Other	.219	73	16	2	2	0	6	6	9	.305	.301
Day	.253	498	126	18	4	8	55	39	65	.316	.353	April	.267	150	40	3	2	1	17	9	17	.323	.333
Night	.240	674	162	20	5	1	58	51	106	.302	.289	May	.285	151	43	6	2	0	14	22	20	.386	.351
Grass	.250	875	219	29	5	8	84	57	130	.304	.322	June	.249	189	47	5	2	1	15	13	28	.300	.312
Turf	.232	297	69	9	4	1	29	33	41	.321	.300	July	.267	210	56	6	2	2	27	16	28	.325	.343
First Pitch	.271	203	55	7	2	2	16	10	0	.315	.355	August	.209	278	58	13	1	4	28	17	47	.262	.306
Ahead in Count	.250	228	57	8	4	0	28	44	0	.374	.320	September/October	.227	194	44	5	0	1	12	13	31	.286	.268
Behind in Count	.232	555	129	14	3	5	50	0	152	.247	.295	Pre-All Star	.267	569	152	16	6	2	54	48	74	.333	.327
Two Strikes	.199	482	96	12	2	4	37	36	171	.265	.257	Post-All Star	.226	603	136	22	3	7	59	42	97	.284	.307

Batter vs. Pitcher (career)

Hits Best Against	Avg	AB	H	2B	3B	HR	RBI	BB	SO	OBP	SLG	Hits Worst Against	Avg	AB	H	2B	3B	HR	RBI	BB	SO	OBP	SLG
Charlie Leibrandt	.526	19	10	2	0	0	2	0	1	.526	.632	Zane Smith	.000	14	0	0	0	0	0	0	1	.000	.000
Steve Avery	.389	18	7	1	0	0	0	2	3	.450	.444	Greg Swindell	.000	11	0	0	0	0	0	2	3	.154	.000
Terry Mulholland	.385	13	5	1	0	1	1	1	2	.429	.692	Dennis Martinez	.083	12	1	0	0	0	1	0	1	.083	.083
Mark Portugal	.375	16	6	0	0	1	2	0	1	.375	.563	John Smoltz	.083	12	1	0	0	0	1	0	3	.083	.083
Bruce Ruffin	.364	11	4	1	0	0	0	1	2	.417	.455	Tim Belcher	.091	11	1	0	0	0	0	0	2	.091	.091

Josias Manzanillo — Mets

Age 26 – Pitches Right

	ERA	W	L	Sv	G	GS	IP	BB	SO	Avg	H	2B	3B	HR	RBI	OBP	SLG	GF	IR	IRS	Hld	SvOp	SB	CS	GB	FB	G/F
1993 Season	6.83	1	1	1	16	1	29.0	19	21	.265	30	10	0	2	28	.372	.407	6	11	7	0	2	2	0	40	33	1.21
Career (1991-1993)	7.20	1	1	1	17	1	30.0	22	22	.271	32	11	0	2	30	.386	.415	7	11	7	0	2	2	0	42	34	1.24

1993 Season

	ERA	W	L	Sv	G	GS	IP	H	HR	BB	SO		Avg	AB	H	2B	3B	HR	RBI	BB	SO	OBP	SLG
Home	9.58	0	1	0	5	1	10.1	9	1	8	4	vs. Left	.277	47	13	3	0	0	11	11	9	.400	.340
Away	5.30	1	0	1	11	0	18.2	21	1	11	17	vs. Right	.258	66	17	7	0	2	17	8	12	.351	.455

Oreste Marrero — Expos

Age 24 – Bats Left (groundball hitter)

	Avg	G	AB	R	H	2B	3B	HR	RBI	BB	SO	HBP	GDP	SB	CS	OBP	SLG	IBB	SH	SF	#Pit	#P/PA	GB	FB	G/F
1993 Season	.210	32	81	10	17	5	1	1	4	14	16	0	0	1	3	.326	.333	0	0	0	339	3.57	35	22	1.59

1993 Season

	Avg	AB	H	2B	3B	HR	RBI	BB	SO	OBP	SLG		Avg	AB	H	2B	3B	HR	RBI	BB	SO	OBP	SLG
vs. Left	.300	10	3	0	0	0	0	1	4	.364	.300	Scoring Posn	.150	20	3	1	0	1	4	6	3	.346	.350

1993 Season	Avg	AB	H	2B	3B	HR	RBI	BB	SO	OBP	SLG		Avg	AB	H	2B	3B	HR	RBI	BB	SO	OBP	SLG
vs. Right	.197	71	14	5	1	1	4	13	12	.321	.338	Close & Late	.222	9	2	1	0	0	0	2	3	.364	.333

Al Martin — Pirates

Age 26 – Bats Left

	Avg	G	AB	R	H	2B	3B	HR	RBI	BB	SO	HBP	GDP	SB	CS	OBP	SLG	IBB	SH	SF	#Pit	#P/PA	GB	FB	G/F
1993 Season	.281	143	480	85	135	26	8	18	64	42	122	1	5	16	9	.338	.481	5	2	3	1923	3.64	155	142	1.09
Career (1992-1993)	.278	155	492	86	137	26	9	18	66	42	127	1	5	16	9	.334	.478	5	2	4	1973	3.65	160	144	1.11

1993 Season	Avg	AB	H	2B	3B	HR	RBI	BB	SO	OBP	SLG		Avg	AB	H	2B	3B	HR	RBI	BB	SO	OBP	SLG
vs. Left	.191	89	17	5	1	1	8	11	27	.277	.303	Scoring Posn	.291	110	32	5	2	3	42	17	32	.377	.455
vs. Right	.302	391	118	21	7	17	56	31	95	.353	.522	Close & Late	.346	78	27	4	0	4	10	6	24	.388	.551
Groundball	.283	152	43	6	3	2	17	9	41	.317	.401	None on/out	.270	141	38	8	6	1	1	12	36	.327	.433
Flyball	.306	72	22	7	2	2	7	9	16	.383	.542	Batting #1	.253	162	41	10	5	2	9	7	32	.281	.414
Home	.273	253	69	12	5	15	44	25	72	.337	.538	Batting #3	.282	117	33	6	0	3	12	16	35	.373	.410
Away	.291	227	66	14	3	3	20	17	50	.340	.419	Other	.303	201	61	10	3	13	43	19	55	.362	.577
Day	.246	118	29	7	1	4	17	8	29	.291	.424	April	.260	73	19	5	3	1	5	1	17	.267	.452
Night	.293	362	106	19	7	14	47	34	93	.353	.500	May	.207	58	12	2	1	1	3	4	13	.254	.328
Grass	.320	153	49	11	1	2	14	12	28	.365	.444	June	.284	81	23	5	1	4	7	9	19	.356	.519
Turf	.263	327	86	15	7	16	50	30	94	.326	.498	July	.289	90	26	5	0	0	8	10	30	.366	.344
First Pitch	.473	74	35	4	3	4	21	3	0	.481	.770	August	.337	92	31	4	1	5	16	9	18	.396	.565
Ahead in Count	.333	99	33	6	4	3	11	16	0	.422	.566	September/October	.279	86	24	5	2	7	25	9	25	.344	.628
Behind in Count	.175	211	37	7	0	10	24	0	96	.179	.351	Pre-All Star	.258	256	66	14	5	6	20	17	60	.304	.422
Two Strikes	.149	228	34	8	1	6	15	23	122	.230	.272	Post-All Star	.308	224	69	12	3	12	44	25	62	.376	.549

1993 By Position																								
Position	Avg	AB	H	2B	3B	HR	RBI	BB	SO	OBP	SLG	G	GS	Innings	PO	A	E	DP	Fld Pct	Rng Fctr	In Zone	Outs	Zone Rtg	MLB Zone
As Pinch Hitter	.357	14	5	0	0	1	1	0	6	.357	.571	14	0	---	---	---	---	---	---	---	---	---	---	---
As lf	.265	249	66	16	6	7	25	24	62	.326	.462	81	62	572.2	133	3	4	0	.971	2.14	154	123	.799	.818
As cf	.305	210	64	10	2	10	38	18	53	.362	.514	63	58	487.1	132	3	3	0	.978	2.49	178	128	.719	.829

Norberto Martin — White Sox

Age 27 – Bats Right

	Avg	G	AB	R	H	2B	3B	HR	RBI	BB	SO	HBP	GDP	SB	CS	OBP	SLG	IBB	SH	SF	#Pit	#P/PA	GB	FB	G/F
1993 Season	.357	8	14	3	5	0	0	0	2	1	1	0	0	0	0	.400	.357	0	0	0	38	2.53	6	2	3.00

1993 Season	Avg	AB	H	2B	3B	HR	RBI	BB	SO	OBP	SLG		Avg	AB	H	2B	3B	HR	RBI	BB	SO	OBP	SLG
vs. Left	.000	1	0	0	0	0	0	0	0	.000	.000	Scoring Posn	.500	4	2	0	0	0	2	0	1	.500	.500
vs. Right	.385	13	5	0	0	0	2	1	1	.429	.385	Close & Late	.600	5	3	0	0	0	1	1	0	.667	.600

Carlos Martinez — Indians

Age 28 – Bats Right

	Avg	G	AB	R	H	2B	3B	HR	RBI	BB	SO	HBP	GDP	SB	CS	OBP	SLG	IBB	SH	SF	#Pit	#P/PA	GB	FB	G/F
1993 Season	.244	80	262	26	64	10	0	5	31	20	29	0	5	1	1	.295	.340	3	0	3	1005	3.53	105	75	1.40
Last Five Years	.265	422	1369	133	363	61	6	24	152	68	190	4	42	9	10	.299	.371	9	9	13	4961	3.39	530	398	1.33

1993 Season	Avg	AB	H	2B	3B	HR	RBI	BB	SO	OBP	SLG		Avg	AB	H	2B	3B	HR	RBI	BB	SO	OBP	SLG
vs. Left	.276	116	32	5	0	2	12	12	14	.336	.371	Scoring Posn	.210	81	17	2	0	2	27	7	10	.264	.309
vs. Right	.219	146	32	5	0	3	19	8	15	.260	.315	Close & Late	.147	34	5	0	0	1	7	1	3	.167	.235
Home	.246	118	29	3	0	2	14	10	14	.302	.322	None on/out	.347	49	17	3	0	2	2	3	5	.385	.531
Away	.243	144	35	7	0	3	17	10	15	.288	.354	Batting #5	.273	121	33	4	0	1	13	13	12	.338	.331
First Pitch	.385	39	15	2	0	1	7	1	0	.400	.513	Batting #6	.220	123	27	5	0	3	13	5	17	.250	.333
Ahead in Count	.203	59	12	2	0	3	7	10	0	.319	.390	Other	.222	18	4	1	0	1	5	2	0	.286	.444
Behind in Count	.200	115	23	3	0	1	11	0	24	.195	.252	Pre-All Star	.268	224	60	9	0	5	28	14	26	.307	.375
Two Strikes	.202	109	22	2	0	0	7	9	29	.261	.220	Post-All Star	.105	38	4	1	0	0	3	6	3	.227	.132

Last Five Years	Avg	AB	H	2B	3B	HR	RBI	BB	SO	OBP	SLG		Avg	AB	H	2B	3B	HR	RBI	BB	SO	OBP	SLG
vs. Left	.273	564	154	23	3	11	62	31	70	.307	.383	Scoring Posn	.258	356	92	16	3	5	130	24	55	.297	.362
vs. Right	.260	805	209	38	3	13	90	37	120	.294	.363	Close & Late	.215	200	43	12	0	3	32	10	34	.249	.320
Groundball	.259	293	76	14	0	3	28	14	44	.291	.338	None on/out	.289	301	87	15	1	9	9	8	39	.312	.435
Flyball	.231	299	69	11	2	2	32	17	43	.269	.301	Batting #5	.259	417	108	18	1	5	43	27	51	.301	.343
Home	.273	674	184	26	4	11	81	36	96	.309	.372	Batting #6	.244	578	141	21	5	12	66	19	77	.267	.360
Away	.258	695	179	35	2	13	71	32	94	.290	.370	Other	.305	374	114	22	0	7	43	22	62	.344	.420
Day	.222	427	95	13	0	12	51	20	68	.258	.337	April	.281	135	38	7	1	2	15	7	17	.317	.393
Night	.285	942	268	48	6	12	101	48	122	.318	.386	May	.206	233	48	9	1	6	29	10	35	.242	.330
Grass	.269	1162	312	53	6	22	141	62	152	.304	.381	June	.262	172	45	6	0	1	16	10	24	.301	.314
Turf	.246	207	51	8	0	2	11	6	38	.274	.314	July	.286	231	66	11	2	6	24	18	30	.333	.429
First Pitch	.307	231	71	13	1	4	37	2	0	.312	.424	August	.289	280	81	11	1	3	26	12	45	.318	.368
Ahead in Count	.290	262	76	10	1	6	23	37	0	.380	.405	September/October	.267	318	85	17	1	6	42	11	39	.290	.384
Behind in Count	.231	662	153	27	2	10	67	0	163	.231	.323	Pre-All Star	.247	583	144	25	2	10	67	32	81	.286	.348
Two Strikes	.195	600	117	19	2	5	46	27	190	.230	.258	Post-All Star	.279	786	219	36	4	14	85	36	109	.309	.388

Batter vs. Pitcher (career)																							
Hits Best Against	Avg	AB	H	2B	3B	HR	RBI	BB	SO	OBP	SLG	**Hits Worst Against**	Avg	AB	H	2B	3B	HR	RBI	BB	SO	OBP	SLG
Bob Milacki	.500	18	9	5	0	1	4	0	2	.500	.944	Bill Gullickson	.100	10	1	0	0	0	0	1	0	.182	.100
Randy Johnson	.452	31	14	1	0	0	3	1	4	.441	.484	Mark Williamson	.143	14	2	0	0	0	1	0	0	.143	.143

Batter vs. Pitcher (career)

Hits Best Against	Avg	AB	H	2B	3B	HR	RBI	BB	SO	OBP	SLG
Jimmy Key	.379	29	11	2	0	1	1	0	3	.379	.552
Wilson Alvarez	.357	14	5	1	0	1	1	1	1	.400	.643
Dave Fleming	.333	12	4	1	1	0	4	1	1	.357	.583

Hits Worst Against	Avg	AB	H	2B	3B	HR	RBI	BB	SO	OBP	SLG
Charlie Leibrandt	.167	12	2	0	0	0	1	0	4	.167	.167
Dave Stieb	.182	11	2	0	0	0	0	0	3	.182	.182
Bud Black	.182	11	2	0	0	0	0	0	3	.182	.182

Chito Martinez — Orioles

Age 28 – Bats Left

	Avg	G	AB	R	H	2B	3B	HR	RBI	BB	SO	HBP	GDP	SB	CS	OBP	SLG	IBB	SH	SF	#Pit	#P/PA	GB	FB	G/F
1993 Season	.000	8	15	0	0	0	0	0	0	4	4	0	0	0	0	.211	.000	2	0	0	71	3.74	6	5	1.20
Career (1991-1993)	.259	158	429	58	111	22	2	18	58	46	102	2	10	1	2	.330	.445	6	0	5	1879	3.90	133	130	1.02

1993 Season

	Avg	AB	H	2B	3B	HR	RBI	BB	SO	OBP	SLG
vs. Left	.000	2	0	0	0	0	0	0	0	.000	.000
vs. Right	.000	13	0	0	0	0	0	4	4	.235	.000

	Avg	AB	H	2B	3B	HR	RBI	BB	SO	OBP	SLG
Scoring Posn	.000	4	0	0	0	0	0	3	1	.429	.000
Close & Late	.000	4	0	0	0	0	0	2	1	.333	.000

Career (1991-1993)

	Avg	AB	H	2B	3B	HR	RBI	BB	SO	OBP	SLG
vs. Left	.257	70	18	3	0	3	10	5	23	.312	.429
vs. Right	.259	359	93	19	2	15	48	41	79	.333	.448
Groundball	.293	116	34	5	0	3	9	5	25	.322	.414
Flyball	.276	98	27	3	2	8	24	18	24	.390	.592
Home	.282	213	60	13	0	10	33	27	50	.359	.484
Away	.236	216	51	9	2	8	25	19	52	.300	.407
Day	.226	133	30	4	0	3	15	16	40	.311	.323
Night	.274	296	81	18	2	15	43	30	62	.338	.500
Grass	.276	366	101	20	2	16	52	40	81	.345	.473
Turf	.159	63	10	2	0	2	6	6	21	.239	.286
First Pitch	.375	48	18	4	0	2	8	5	0	.426	.583
Ahead in Count	.369	103	38	9	2	7	24	23	0	.477	.699
Behind in Count	.175	200	35	6	0	6	17	0	88	.181	.295
Two Strikes	.148	216	32	7	0	9	21	18	102	.218	.306

	Avg	AB	H	2B	3B	HR	RBI	BB	SO	OBP	SLG
Scoring Posn	.257	101	26	4	1	6	42	16	26	.344	.495
Close & Late	.187	75	14	1	0	2	6	9	17	.282	.280
None on/out	.246	114	28	7	0	6	6	11	27	.323	.465
Batting #6	.270	267	72	15	2	11	35	20	63	.321	.464
Batting #7	.200	50	10	1	0	2	9	9	14	.311	.340
Other	.259	112	29	6	0	5	14	17	25	.359	.446
April	.000	28	0	0	0	0	1	9	7	.263	.000
May	.308	39	12	2	0	3	11	8	8	.417	.590
June	.194	31	6	1	1	0	3	3	6	.257	.290
July	.282	85	24	6	0	5	11	8	24	.340	.529
August	.281	135	38	10	0	6	19	11	30	.338	.489
September/October	.279	111	31	3	1	4	13	7	27	.319	.432
Pre-All Star	.200	120	24	4	1	4	18	20	25	.315	.350
Post-All Star	.282	309	87	18	1	14	40	26	77	.336	.482

Batter vs. Pitcher (career)

Hits Best Against	Avg	AB	H	2B	3B	HR	RBI	BB	SO	OBP	SLG
Jack Morris	.400	10	4	0	0	1	3	3	3	.500	.700
Mark Leiter	.364	11	4	0	2	2	6	1	2	.417	1.273

Hits Worst Against	Avg	AB	H	2B	3B	HR	RBI	BB	SO	OBP	SLG

Dave Martinez — Giants

Age 29 – Bats Left

	Avg	G	AB	R	H	2B	3B	HR	RBI	BB	SO	HBP	GDP	SB	CS	OBP	SLG	IBB	SH	SF	#Pit	#P/PA	GB	FB	G/F
1993 Season	.241	91	241	28	58	12	1	5	27	27	39	0	5	6	3	.317	.361	3	0	0	1041	3.88	86	71	1.21
Last Five Years	.271	594	1782	223	483	79	23	29	166	140	252	4	23	70	33	.324	.390	14	21	10	7287	3.72	651	531	1.23

1993 Season

	Avg	AB	H	2B	3B	HR	RBI	BB	SO	OBP	SLG
vs. Left	.259	27	7	2	1	0	1	6	5	.394	.407
vs. Right	.238	214	51	10	0	5	26	21	34	.306	.355
Home	.197	117	23	4	1	1	4	9	19	.254	.274
Away	.282	124	35	8	0	4	23	18	20	.373	.444
First Pitch	.238	21	5	0	0	0	2	3	0	.333	.238
Ahead in Count	.393	61	24	9	0	2	11	13	0	.500	.639
Behind in Count	.161	112	18	2	1	2	8	0	32	.161	.250
Two Strikes	.175	114	20	3	0	3	9	11	39	.248	.281

	Avg	AB	H	2B	3B	HR	RBI	BB	SO	OBP	SLG
Scoring Posn	.270	63	17	4	0	1	23	12	12	.387	.381
Close & Late	.250	32	8	1	0	1	4	9	5	.415	.375
None on/out	.226	62	14	4	0	1	1	5	8	.284	.339
Batting #1	.232	82	19	4	0	2	8	8	12	.300	.354
Batting #6	.320	75	24	4	0	3	12	6	14	.370	.493
Other	.179	84	15	4	1	0	7	13	13	.289	.250
Pre-All Star	.230	100	23	6	0	3	12	13	19	.319	.380
Post-All Star	.248	141	35	6	1	2	15	14	20	.316	.348

Last Five Years

	Avg	AB	H	2B	3B	HR	RBI	BB	SO	OBP	SLG
vs. Left	.237	287	68	13	3	1	29	30	67	.312	.314
vs. Right	.278	1499	416	66	20	28	137	110	185	.327	.404
Groundball	.265	633	168	28	5	8	44	48	91	.316	.363
Flyball	.251	375	94	17	8	5	36	43	47	.325	.379
Home	.256	868	222	34	8	13	70	61	112	.303	.358
Away	.285	918	262	45	15	16	96	79	140	.344	.419
Day	.251	569	143	24	8	14	63	54	97	.317	.395
Night	.280	1217	341	55	15	15	103	86	155	.328	.387
Grass	.260	600	156	24	11	8	54	49	103	.315	.377
Turf	.277	1186	328	55	12	21	112	91	149	.328	.396
First Pitch	.318	201	64	12	4	1	17	9	0	.343	.433
Ahead in Count	.319	530	169	36	9	14	56	78	0	.408	.500
Behind in Count	.223	723	161	22	6	10	54	0	211	.224	.311
Two Strikes	.212	772	164	23	6	11	61	51	252	.260	.301

	Avg	AB	H	2B	3B	HR	RBI	BB	SO	OBP	SLG
Scoring Posn	.258	431	111	21	6	5	133	54	72	.340	.369
Close & Late	.190	294	56	7	3	1	25	27	57	.262	.245
None on/out	.262	451	118	19	5	6	6	33	54	.312	.366
Batting #1	.284	405	115	19	6	9	37	36	62	.341	.427
Batting #2	.261	700	183	27	9	9	61	49	74	.311	.364
Other	.273	681	186	33	8	11	68	55	116	.327	.394
April	.211	204	43	8	1	0	15	19	24	.278	.260
May	.259	216	56	7	5	2	23	21	38	.324	.366
June	.290	365	106	17	7	11	45	22	63	.327	.466
July	.293	341	100	13	2	6	16	22	46	.340	.396
August	.283	371	105	17	5	6	39	32	44	.342	.404
September/October	.256	289	74	17	3	4	28	24	37	.313	.377
Pre-All Star	.264	908	240	42	13	15	92	74	152	.318	.389
Post-All Star	.278	874	243	37	10	14	74	66	100	.330	.391

Batter vs. Pitcher (career)

Hits Best Against	Avg	AB	H	2B	3B	HR	RBI	BB	SO	OBP	SLG
Mike Jackson	.571	7	4	0	0	0	1	3	1	.636	.571
Mike Maddux	.545	11	6	0	0	0	0	4	1	.667	.545
Ryan Bowen	.500	10	5	1	0	0	0	3	1	.615	.600
Terry Leach	.455	11	5	2	0	1	2	0	2	.455	.909
Jose Rijo	.438	16	7	2	0	3	5	0	2	.438	1.125

Hits Worst Against	Avg	AB	H	2B	3B	HR	RBI	BB	SO	OBP	SLG
Shawn Boskie	.080	25	2	0	0	0	0	3	4	.179	.080
Steve Wilson	.100	10	1	0	0	0	0	1	0	.182	.100
Paul Assenmacher	.118	17	2	0	0	0	1	1	8	.167	.118
Ken Hill	.154	26	4	0	0	0	1	1	2	.185	.154
Juan Agosto	.182	11	2	0	0	0	0	0	3	.182	.182

Dennis Martinez — Expos

Age 39 – Pitches Right (groundball pitcher)

	ERA	W	L	Sv	G	GS	IP	BB	SO	Avg	H	2B	3B	HR	RBI	OBP	SLG	CG	ShO	Sup	QS	#P/S	SB	CS	GB	FB	G/F
1993 Season	3.85	15	9	1	35	34	224.2	64	138	.246	211	38	9	27	92	.306	.407	2	0	4.61	22	98	49	6	399	177	2.25
Last Five Years	2.97	71	49	1	164	162	1131.0	284	706	.234	988	163	30	85	369	.287	.347	29	9	4.23	111	101	135	49	1813	1015	1.79

1993 Season

	ERA	W	L	Sv	G	GS	IP	H	HR	BB	SO
Home	3.51	9	2	1	18	17	110.1	105	10	31	71
Away	4.17	6	7	0	17	17	114.1	106	17	33	67
Day	4.96	4	5	1	15	14	85.1	87	13	29	56
Night	3.17	11	4	0	20	20	139.1	124	14	35	82
Grass	4.75	4	6	0	11	11	72.0	68	7	19	43
Turf	3.42	11	3	1	24	23	152.2	143	20	45	95
April	4.70	1	4	0	6	6	30.2	33	3	8	20
May	3.60	2	1	0	5	5	35.0	34	5	12	15
June	2.17	5	0	0	6	6	45.2	34	4	13	29
July	4.35	2	2	1	7	6	39.1	30	5	0	22
August	6.47	2	1	0	5	5	32.0	37	7	12	20
September/October	2.79	3	1	0	6	6	42.0	34	3	13	32
Starter	3.85	15	9	0	34	34	224.1	211	27	64	137
Reliever	0.00	0	0	1	1	0	0.1	0	0	0	1
0-3 Days Rest	5.73	0	2	0	2	2	11.0	12	0	3	3
4 Days Rest	3.53	11	3	0	22	22	145.1	127	20	36	90
5+ Days Rest	4.24	4	4	0	10	10	68.0	72	7	25	44
Pre-All Star	3.32	10	5	1	20	19	124.2	112	13	34	72
Post-All Star	4.50	5	4	0	15	15	100.0	99	14	30	66

	Avg	AB	H	2B	3B	HR	RBI	BB	SO	OBP	SLG
vs. Left	.249	434	108	18	5	13	45	38	61	.312	.403
vs. Right	.244	422	103	20	4	14	47	26	77	.300	.410
Inning 1-6	.238	727	173	36	8	22	80	56	120	.300	.400
Inning 7+	.295	129	38	2	1	5	12	8	18	.341	.442
None on	.279	517	144	24	6	17	17	28	75	.319	.447
Runners on	.198	339	67	14	3	10	75	36	63	.287	.345
Scoring Posn	.174	207	36	8	2	6	61	34	47	.306	.319
Close & Late	.286	70	20	2	1	1	8	4	12	.324	.386
None on/out	.295	227	67	12	2	8	8	15	29	.342	.471
vs. 1st Batr (relief)	.000	1	0	0	0	0	0	0	1	.000	.000
First Inning Pitched	.269	134	36	3	1	6	19	11	22	.329	.440
First 75 Pitches	.230	613	141	27	7	16	60	50	103	.295	.375
Pitch 76-90	.290	131	38	6	1	6	16	6	15	.321	.489
Pitch 91-105	.270	74	20	4	1	5	13	7	14	.349	.554
Pitch 106+	.316	38	12	1	0	0	3	1	6	.350	.342
First Pitch	.303	122	37	9	0	5	20	4	0	.333	.500
Ahead in Count	.207	397	82	12	4	9	32	0	116	.211	.325
Behind in Count	.289	173	50	9	3	10	28	34	0	.410	.549
Two Strikes	.181	376	68	12	4	9	26	26	138	.236	.306

Last Five Years

	ERA	W	L	Sv	G	GS	IP	H	HR	BB	SO
Home	2.83	37	24	1	82	80	573.1	488	43	128	359
Away	3.11	34	25	0	82	82	557.2	500	42	156	347
Day	3.67	17	19	1	52	51	331.1	322	35	86	214
Night	2.68	54	30	0	112	111	799.2	666	50	198	492
Grass	3.26	19	14	0	41	41	278.2	263	19	77	185
Turf	2.87	52	35	1	123	121	852.1	725	66	207	521
April	2.81	8	12	0	26	26	173.0	147	8	49	104
May	2.81	13	6	0	27	27	192.0	175	17	47	111
June	2.37	17	5	0	30	30	220.0	180	14	63	130
July	3.72	12	8	1	29	28	188.2	188	15	43	119
August	3.29	13	9	0	28	27	194.0	165	20	42	136
September/October	2.87	8	9	0	24	24	163.1	133	11	40	106
Starter	2.97	71	48	0	162	162	1128.2	987	84	284	703
Reliever	3.86	0	1	1	2	0	2.1	1	1	0	3
0-3 Days Rest	5.79	1	4	0	6	6	32.2	37	1	9	23
4 Days Rest	2.96	48	30	0	104	104	730.2	646	60	180	463
5+ Days Rest	2.73	22	14	0	52	52	365.1	304	23	95	217
Pre-All Star	2.79	44	26	1	93	92	643.0	571	44	169	379
Post-All Star	3.21	27	23	0	71	70	488.0	417	41	115	327

	Avg	AB	H	2B	3B	HR	RBI	BB	SO	OBP	SLG
vs. Left	.239	2427	581	92	15	46	213	184	397	.293	.347
vs. Right	.227	1795	407	71	15	39	156	100	309	.279	.348
Inning 1-6	.232	3451	800	140	26	59	297	237	593	.285	.339
Inning 7+	.244	771	188	23	4	26	72	47	113	.296	.385
None on	.243	2632	639	106	17	54	54	133	425	.283	.358
Runners on	.219	1590	349	57	13	31	315	151	281	.294	.330
Scoring Posn	.201	945	190	28	9	16	263	123	192	.299	.301
Close & Late	.234	444	104	13	3	13	43	25	66	.286	.365
None on/out	.251	1135	285	42	8	27	27	56	160	.289	.374
vs. 1st Batr (relief)	.000	2	0	0	0	0	0	0	1	.000	.000
First Inning Pitched	.242	604	146	24	4	14	62	50	113	.303	.364
First 75 Pitches	.228	3010	687	114	21	51	233	203	524	.280	.331
Pitch 76-90	.254	566	144	24	6	16	65	38	74	.307	.403
Pitch 91-105	.230	395	91	17	3	10	42	26	66	.288	.365
Pitch 106+	.263	251	66	8	0	8	29	17	42	.322	.390
First Pitch	.297	644	191	40	2	16	78	16	0	.323	.439
Ahead in Count	.196	1933	378	58	11	29	123	0	610	.202	.282
Behind in Count	.259	853	221	40	8	27	100	144	0	.365	.420
Two Strikes	.183	1866	341	51	14	30	121	124	706	.237	.273

Pitcher vs. Batter (since 1984)

Pitches Best Vs.	Avg	AB	H	2B	3B	HR	RBI	BB	SO	OBP	SLG
Mickey Morandini	.045	22	1	0	0	0	0	1	3	.087	.045
Curt Wilkerson	.059	17	1	0	0	0	0	0	7	.059	.059
Otis Nixon	.071	14	1	0	0	0	1	0	0	.071	.071
Mike Morgan	.083	12	1	0	0	0	0	0	3	.083	.083
Kirt Manwaring	.083	12	1	0	0	0	1	0	1	.083	.083

Pitches Worst Vs.	Avg	AB	H	2B	3B	HR	RBI	BB	SO	OBP	SLG
Kent Hrbek	.545	11	6	2	0	1	3	1	0	.583	1.000
Glenn Davis	.481	27	13	0	0	6	12	3	2	.516	1.148
George Brett	.455	11	5	2	0	1	4	1	0	.500	.909
Derrick May	.444	18	8	2	0	2	8	1	1	.474	.889
Andres Galarraga	.389	18	7	3	0	2	7	1	4	.421	.889

Domingo Martinez — Blue Jays

Age 26 – Bats Right (groundball hitter)

	Avg	G	AB	R	H	2B	3B	HR	RBI	BB	SO	HBP	GDP	SB	CS	OBP	SLG	IBB	SH	SF	#Pit	#P/PA	GB	FB	G/F
1993 Season	.286	8	14	2	4	0	0	1	3	1	7	0	0	0	0	.333	.500	0	0	0	57	3.80	1	4	0.25
Career (1992-1993)	.409	15	22	4	9	0	0	2	6	1	8	0	0	0	0	.435	.682	0	0	0	79	3.43	3	5	0.60

1993 Season

	Avg	AB	H	2B	3B	HR	RBI	BB	SO	OBP	SLG
vs. Left	.500	6	3	0	0	1	3	0	2	.500	1.000
vs. Right	.125	8	1	0	0	0	0	1	5	.222	.125

	Avg	AB	H	2B	3B	HR	RBI	BB	SO	OBP	SLG
Scoring Posn	.400	5	2	0	0	0	2	0	2	.400	.400
Close & Late	1.000	1	1	0	0	0	2	0	0	1.000	1.000

Edgar Martinez — Mariners

Age 31 – Bats Right

	Avg	G	AB	R	H	2B	3B	HR	RBI	BB	SO	HBP	GDP	SB	CS	OBP	SLG	IBB	SH	SF	#Pit	#P/PA	GB	FB	G/F
1993 Season	.237	42	135	20	32	7	0	4	13	28	19	0	4	0	0	.366	.378	1	1	1	676	4.10	55	37	1.49
Last Five Years	.305	536	1865	309	568	120	6	49	207	257	240	20	54	17	12	.392	.454	16	7	16	8781	4.05	700	539	1.30

1993 Season

	Avg	AB	H	2B	3B	HR	RBI	BB	SO	OBP	SLG
vs. Left	.111	36	4	1	0	0	3	10	3	.298	.139
vs. Right	.283	99	28	6	0	4	10	18	16	.393	.465
Home	.228	57	13	2	0	1	5	13	4	.371	.316
Away	.244	78	19	5	0	3	8	15	15	.362	.423
First Pitch	.222	9	2	0	0	2	3	0	0	.222	.889

	Avg	AB	H	2B	3B	HR	RBI	BB	SO	OBP	SLG
Scoring Posn	.323	31	10	2	0	1	9	11	2	.488	.484
Close & Late	.261	23	6	1	0	1	4	6	4	.400	.435
None on/out	.118	34	4	1	0	0	0	4	9	.211	.147
Batting #4	.178	45	8	3	0	0	2	12	9	.345	.244
Batting #6	.294	34	10	3	0	2	4	6	3	.400	.559

1993 Season	Avg	AB	H	2B	3B	HR	RBI	BB	SO	OBP	SLG		Avg	AB	H	2B	3B	HR	RBI	BB	SO	OBP	SLG
Ahead in Count	.342	38	13	3	0	2	4	16	0	.537	.579	Other	.250	56	14	1	0	2	7	10	7	.364	.375
Behind in Count	.132	53	7	3	0	0	2	0	15	.132	.189	Pre-All Star	.213	61	13	3	0	1	6	11	10	.329	.311
Two Strikes	.200	65	13	4	0	0	5	12	19	.321	.262	Post-All Star	.257	74	19	4	0	3	7	17	9	.396	.432

Last Five Years	Avg	AB	H	2B	3B	HR	RBI	BB	SO	OBP	SLG		Avg	AB	H	2B	3B	HR	RBI	BB	SO	OBP	SLG
vs. Left	.321	558	179	41	1	13	66	81	56	.406	.468	Scoring Posn	.271	428	116	19	1	14	157	85	46	.389	.418
vs. Right	.298	1307	389	79	5	36	141	176	184	.385	.448	Close & Late	.329	283	93	19	0	8	43	56	42	.442	.481
Groundball	.309	459	142	28	0	11	57	65	59	.399	.442	None on/out	.321	461	148	37	2	14	14	48	61	.389	.501
Flyball	.282	426	120	32	4	10	43	54	64	.363	.446	Batting #2	.332	485	161	40	1	13	58	59	53	.406	.499
Home	.298	896	267	63	3	23	99	132	117	.391	.452	Batting #6	.327	297	97	16	2	10	32	60	38	.440	.495
Away	.311	969	301	57	3	26	108	125	123	.392	.456	Other	.286	1083	310	64	3	26	117	138	149	.371	.423
Day	.295	468	138	26	4	15	57	57	50	.370	.464	April	.289	239	69	15	0	5	27	38	29	.396	.414
Night	.308	1397	430	94	2	34	150	200	190	.399	.451	May	.315	349	110	14	5	14	47	48	45	.400	.504
Grass	.312	741	231	42	3	20	83	102	93	.397	.457	June	.297	353	105	24	0	8	34	41	59	.374	.433
Turf	.300	1124	337	78	3	29	124	155	147	.388	.452	July	.312	343	107	19	1	11	42	44	44	.394	.469
First Pitch	.338	133	45	9	0	5	15	5	0	.371	.519	August	.306	337	103	32	0	9	36	50	34	.397	.481
Ahead in Count	.362	511	185	37	2	18	60	140	0	.497	.548	September/October	.303	244	74	16	0	2	21	36	29	.389	.393
Behind in Count	.259	803	208	45	2	15	75	0	193	.266	.376	Pre-All Star	.297	1040	309	56	5	29	121	138	145	.383	.444
Two Strikes	.255	856	218	50	2	17	87	110	240	.343	.377	Post-All Star	.314	825	259	64	1	20	86	119	95	.403	.467

Batter vs. Pitcher (career)

Hits Best Against	Avg	AB	H	2B	3B	HR	RBI	BB	SO	OBP	SLG	Hits Worst Against	Avg	AB	H	2B	3B	HR	RBI	BB	SO	OBP	SLG
Greg Cadaret	.778	9	7	4	0	0	1	2	0	.818	1.222	Nolan Ryan	.053	19	1	0	0	0	2	1	10	.100	.053
Rick Sutcliffe	.571	14	8	3	1	0	1	3	2	.611	.929	Mike Witt	.083	12	1	0	0	0	0	2	3	.214	.083
Greg Swindell	.500	14	7	0	1	1	1	1	1	.533	.857	Tom Candiotti	.083	12	1	0	0	0	0	1	5	.154	.083
Kenny Rogers	.500	12	6	2	0	0	3	5	1	.647	.667	Bud Black	.091	11	1	0	0	0	0	1	3	.167	.091
Mark Gubicza	.467	15	7	2	0	1	3	1	3	.500	.800	Alex Fernandez	.118	17	2	0	0	0	0	2	0	.211	.118

Pedro Martinez — Dodgers

Age 22 – Pitches Right (flyball pitcher)

	ERA	W	L	Sv	G	GS	IP	BB	SO	Avg	H	2B	3B	HR	RBI	OBP	SLG	GF	IR	IRS	Hld	SvOp	SB	CS	GB	FB	G/F
1993 Season	2.61	10	5	2	65	2	107.0	57	119	.201	76	6	5	5	29	.309	.283	20	33	7	14	3	6	4	91	102	0.89
Career (1992-1993)	2.58	10	6	2	67	3	115.0	58	127	.201	82	9	5	5	31	.303	.284	21	33	7	14	3	6	4	100	110	0.91

1993 Season	ERA	W	L	Sv	G	GS	IP	H	HR	BB	SO		Avg	AB	H	2B	3B	HR	RBI	BB	SO	OBP	SLG
Home	1.93	7	3	2	32	1	51.1	39	3	23	65	vs. Left	.229	218	50	3	3	3	18	25	62	.308	.312
Away	3.23	3	2	0	33	1	55.2	37	2	34	54	vs. Right	.163	160	26	3	2	2	11	32	57	.310	.244
Day	3.72	1	4	1	20	2	38.2	33	2	24	38	Inning 1-6	.233	86	20	3	4	0	9	14	21	.337	.360
Night	1.98	9	1	1	45	0	68.1	43	3	33	81	Inning 7+	.192	292	56	3	1	5	20	43	98	.300	.260
Grass	2.70	9	4	2	49	2	80.0	60	4	39	94	None on	.212	198	42	2	3	3	3	36	58	.345	.298
Turf	2.33	1	1	0	16	0	27.0	16	1	18	25	Runners on	.189	180	34	4	2	2	26	21	61	.267	.267
April	3.55	0	1	0	7	0	12.2	10	1	10	11	Scoring Posn	.165	91	15	1	1	1	23	9	39	.229	.231
May	1.06	2	1	1	11	0	17.0	7	1	7	13	Close & Late	.187	235	44	3	1	4	14	29	82	.284	.260
June	3.44	3	0	0	11	0	18.1	14	1	10	22	None on/out	.220	91	20	2	1	1	1	12	26	.324	.297
July	1.27	3	0	1	13	0	21.1	11	0	10	29	vs. 1st Batr (relief)	.196	56	11	2	0	1	2	6	15	.286	.286
August	4.32	1	1	0	12	0	16.2	18	2	11	21	First Inning Pitched	.206	214	44	5	1	4	18	29	69	.301	.294
September/October	2.57	1	2	0	11	2	21.0	16	0	9	23	First 15 Pitches	.230	191	44	5	2	4	15	21	55	.312	.340
Starter	7.36	0	2	0	2	2	7.1	11	0	4	6	Pitch 16-30	.126	127	16	1	0	0	4	26	47	.276	.134
Reliever	2.26	10	3	2	63	0	99.2	65	5	53	113	Pitch 31-45	.262	42	11	0	2	0	6	8	13	.380	.357
0 Days rest	0.79	5	0	0	14	0	22.2	8	1	10	21	Pitch 46+	.278	18	5	0	1	1	4	2	4	.350	.556
1 or 2 Days rest	1.94	5	2	2	35	0	55.2	37	2	30	63	First Pitch	.351	57	20	3	2	1	4	3	0	.393	.526
3+ Days rest	4.64	0	1	0	14	0	21.1	20	2	13	29	Ahead in Count	.127	165	21	2	2	1	7	0	91	.132	.182
Pre-All Star	2.53	6	2	1	35	0	57.0	37	3	34	56	Behind in Count	.261	69	18	1	0	1	9	27	0	.459	.319
Post-All Star	2.70	4	3	1	30	2	50.0	39	2	23	63	Two Strikes	.113	195	22	1	1	2	9	27	119	.227	.159

Pedro A. Martinez — Padres

Age 25 – Pitches Left (flyball pitcher)

	ERA	W	L	Sv	G	GS	IP	BB	SO	Avg	H	2B	3B	HR	RBI	OBP	SLG	GF	IR	IRS	Hld	SvOp	SB	CS	GB	FB	G/F
1993 Season	2.43	3	1	0	32	0	37.0	13	32	.172	23	5	0	4	11	.250	.299	9	22	5	3	1	3	2	35	41	0.85

1993 Season	ERA	W	L	Sv	G	GS	IP	H	HR	BB	SO		Avg	AB	H	2B	3B	HR	RBI	BB	SO	OBP	SLG
Home	1.54	3	0	0	17	0	23.1	10	3	8	24	vs. Left	.224	49	11	1	0	3	7	4	9	.296	.429
Away	3.95	0	1	0	15	0	13.2	13	1	5	8	vs. Right	.141	85	12	4	0	1	4	9	23	.223	.224
Starter	0.00	0	0	0	0	0	0.0	0	0	0	0	Scoring Posn	.200	30	6	1	0	0	5	6	7	.333	.233
Reliever	2.43	3	1	0	32	0	37.0	23	4	13	32	Close & Late	.094	32	3	1	0	2	3	4	10	.194	.313
0 Days rest	4.32	2	0	0	7	0	8.1	6	2	4	5	None on/out	.138	29	4	1	0	0	0	3	7	.242	.172
1 or 2 Days rest	2.81	0	1	0	13	0	16.0	11	2	4	18	First Pitch	.083	12	1	0	0	0	0	1	0	.214	.083
3+ Days rest	0.71	1	0	0	12	0	12.2	6	0	5	9	Ahead in Count	.117	60	7	1	0	1	4	0	25	.117	.183
Pre-All Star	5.79	0	0	0	6	0	4.2	4	2	1	3	Behind in Count	.167	30	5	0	0	2	3	4	0	.265	.367
Post-All Star	1.95	3	1	0	26	0	32.1	19	2	12	29	Two Strikes	.192	78	15	4	0	1	6	8	32	.267	.282

Ramon Martinez — Dodgers

Age 26 – Pitches Right

	ERA	W	L	Sv	G	GS	IP	BB	SO	Avg	H	2B	3B	HR	RBI	OBP	SLG	CG	ShO	Sup	QS	#P/S	SB	CS	GB	FB	G/F
1993 Season	3.44	10	12	0	32	32	211.2	104	127	.255	202	31	6	15	77	.342	.366	4	3	3.49	20	108	16	11	277	226	1.23
Last Five Years	3.33	61	46	0	138	138	915.2	350	690	.235	803	143	17	77	341	.309	.354	25	13	4.55	87	108	79	48	1069	1059	1.01

1993 Season

	ERA	W	L	Sv	G	GS	IP	H	HR	BB	SO
Home	4.14	5	8	0	17	17	111.0	118	8	48	64
Away	2.68	5	4	0	15	15	100.2	84	7	56	63
Day	2.08	2	4	0	8	8	56.1	40	6	26	35
Night	3.94	8	8	0	24	24	155.1	162	9	78	92
Grass	3.86	6	11	0	26	26	165.2	172	12	83	102
Turf	1.96	4	1	0	6	6	46.0	30	3	21	25
April	3.13	2	3	0	5	5	31.2	23	3	22	24
May	2.68	2	0	0	5	5	37.0	36	2	12	21
June	3.62	2	1	0	5	5	32.1	30	3	14	18
July	3.12	2	2	0	6	6	43.1	40	4	25	19
August	2.37	1	3	0	5	5	38.0	39	1	12	23
September/October	6.44	1	3	0	6	6	29.1	34	2	19	22
Starter	3.44	10	12	0	32	32	211.2	202	15	104	127
Reliever	0.00	0	0	0	0	0	0.0	0	0	0	0
0-3 Days Rest	0.00	0	0	0	0	0	0.0	0	0	0	0
4 Days Rest	4.02	1	6	0	11	11	71.2	77	7	34	46
5+ Days Rest	3.15	9	6	0	21	21	140.0	125	8	70	81
Pre-All Star	3.21	7	4	0	17	17	115.0	102	10	60	71
Post-All Star	3.72	3	8	0	15	15	96.2	100	5	44	56

	Avg	AB	H	2B	3B	HR	RBI	BB	SO	OBP	SLG
vs. Left	.246	414	102	19	3	9	41	76	68	.362	.372
vs. Right	.264	379	100	12	3	6	36	28	59	.319	.359
Inning 1-6	.256	668	171	27	6	13	73	92	108	.347	.373
Inning 7+	.248	125	31	4	0	2	4	12	19	.317	.328
None on	.270	441	119	18	5	10	10	52	70	.351	.401
Runners on	.236	352	83	13	1	5	67	52	57	.332	.321
Scoring Posn	.183	197	36	9	1	1	57	33	33	.297	.254
Close & Late	.254	67	17	1	0	2	2	4	12	.306	.358
None on/out	.289	201	58	10	3	4	4	26	30	.376	.428
vs. 1st Batr (relief)	.000	0	0	0	0	0	0	0	0	.000	.000
First Inning Pitched	.223	112	25	2	1	2	7	13	19	.302	.313
First 75 Pitches	.251	525	132	20	5	8	56	70	88	.339	.354
Pitch 76-90	.325	114	37	7	0	4	13	15	13	.408	.491
Pitch 91-105	.244	82	20	3	1	3	6	11	14	.340	.415
Pitch 106+	.181	72	13	1	0	0	2	8	12	.259	.194
First Pitch	.236	110	26	2	2	1	9	8	0	.286	.318
Ahead in Count	.227	330	75	12	3	6	32	0	106	.228	.336
Behind in Count	.337	181	61	9	0	7	22	57	0	.498	.503
Two Strikes	.182	351	64	10	4	7	28	39	127	.267	.293

Last Five Years

	ERA	W	L	Sv	G	GS	IP	H	HR	BB	SO
Home	3.32	33	24	0	71	71	487.2	418	43	188	394
Away	3.34	28	22	0	67	67	428.0	385	34	162	296
Day	2.90	18	14	0	39	39	257.2	208	25	99	188
Night	3.50	43	32	0	99	99	658.0	595	52	251	502
Grass	3.28	47	35	0	106	106	713.2	624	61	269	540
Turf	3.52	14	11	0	32	32	202.0	179	16	81	150
April	2.81	7	5	0	18	18	118.1	91	8	47	86
May	3.36	13	4	0	22	22	147.1	140	11	55	121
June	2.72	10	6	0	22	22	152.1	132	9	56	123
July	3.02	13	8	0	25	25	169.2	143	15	65	112
August	4.08	8	15	0	27	27	176.1	167	20	61	123
September/October	3.80	10	8	0	24	24	151.2	130	14	66	125
Starter	3.33	61	46	0	138	138	915.2	803	77	350	690
Reliever	0.00	0	0	0	0	0	0.0	0	0	0	0
0-3 Days Rest	3.44	2	1	0	3	3	18.1	14	2	10	20
4 Days Rest	3.66	27	26	0	69	69	452.1	418	45	174	368
5+ Days Rest	2.99	32	19	0	66	66	445.0	371	30	166	302
Pre-All Star	3.04	34	17	0	69	69	462.0	408	35	180	360
Post-All Star	3.63	27	29	0	69	69	453.2	395	42	170	330

	Avg	AB	H	2B	3B	HR	RBI	BB	SO	OBP	SLG
vs. Left	.242	1895	459	90	10	44	193	258	358	.335	.370
vs. Right	.225	1527	344	53	7	33	148	92	332	.274	.334
Inning 1-6	.234	2848	667	121	17	66	304	293	577	.309	.358
Inning 7+	.237	574	136	22	0	11	37	57	113	.308	.333
None on	.230	2020	464	91	11	48	48	199	429	.303	.357
Runners on	.242	1402	339	52	6	29	293	151	261	.317	.350
Scoring Posn	.223	792	177	31	3	14	249	93	159	.306	.323
Close & Late	.211	308	65	11	0	5	16	25	62	.275	.295
None on/out	.248	886	220	39	7	27	27	87	178	.322	.400
vs. 1st Batr (relief)	.000	0	0	0	0	0	0	0	0	.000	.000
First Inning Pitched	.225	515	116	17	4	14	55	54	93	.303	.355
First 75 Pitches	.232	2305	535	100	14	52	245	222	480	.303	.355
Pitch 76-90	.268	444	119	19	2	9	40	50	73	.346	.381
Pitch 91-105	.223	345	77	13	1	9	31	37	69	.299	.345
Pitch 106+	.220	328	72	11	0	7	25	41	68	.309	.317
First Pitch	.276	434	120	16	4	14	56	19	0	.312	.429
Ahead in Count	.185	1554	287	45	5	24	117	0	587	.191	.266
Behind in Count	.320	719	230	46	5	32	105	194	0	.464	.531
Two Strikes	.168	1657	279	50	8	28	128	137	690	.236	.259

Pitcher vs. Batter (career)

Pitches Best Vs.	Avg	AB	H	2B	3B	HR	RBI	BB	SO	OBP	SLG
Spike Owen	.000	10	0	0	0	0	1	2	4	.167	.000
Darrin Jackson	.059	17	1	0	0	0	1	0	2	.059	.059
Lonnie Smith	.071	14	1	0	0	0	1	0	6	.067	.071
Darryl Strawberry	.083	12	1	0	0	0	1	0	4	.083	.083
Frank Castillo	.091	11	1	0	0	0	0	0	2	.091	.091

Pitches Worst Vs.	Avg	AB	H	2B	3B	HR	RBI	BB	SO	OBP	SLG
Barry Bonds	.450	20	9	1	0	2	8	5	2	.560	.800
Mackey Sasser	.438	16	7	2	0	1	1	0	1	.438	.750
Will Clark	.415	41	17	4	0	3	8	4	4	.467	.732
Howard Johnson	.385	26	10	6	0	2	5	7	3	.515	.846
Eddie Murray	.364	11	4	0	0	2	3	3	2	.500	.909

Tino Martinez — Mariners

Age 26 – Bats Left

	Avg	G	AB	R	H	2B	3B	HR	RBI	BB	SO	HBP	GDP	SB	CS	OBP	SLG	IBB	SH	SF	#Pit	#P/PA	GB	FB	G/F
1993 Season	.265	109	408	48	108	25	1	17	60	45	56	5	7	0	3	.343	.456	9	3	3	1762	3.80	131	148	0.89
Career (1990-1993)	.252	305	1048	116	264	50	3	37	140	107	166	7	33	2	4	.321	.411	18	4	14	4465	3.78	362	351	1.03

1993 Season

	Avg	AB	H	2B	3B	HR	RBI	BB	SO	OBP	SLG
vs. Left	.250	132	33	8	1	5	17	10	22	.322	.439
vs. Right	.272	276	75	17	0	12	43	35	34	.352	.464
Groundball	.271	70	19	4	0	7	17	8	11	.366	.629
Flyball	.275	91	25	6	0	2	8	7	13	.330	.407
Home	.238	193	46	10	0	9	26	23	22	.330	.430
Away	.288	215	62	15	1	8	34	22	34	.354	.479
Day	.315	127	40	8	0	11	28	11	12	.367	.638
Night	.242	281	68	17	1	6	32	34	44	.332	.374
Grass	.281	178	50	11	0	8	25	14	28	.335	.478
Turf	.252	230	58	14	1	9	35	31	28	.348	.439
First Pitch	.382	34	13	2	0	2	6	7	0	.512	.618
Ahead in Count	.327	101	33	9	1	6	26	22	0	.440	.614
Behind in Count	.222	185	41	12	0	5	17	0	47	.233	.368
Two Strikes	.215	186	40	9	0	5	21	16	56	.283	.344

	Avg	AB	H	2B	3B	HR	RBI	BB	SO	OBP	SLG
Scoring Posn	.253	95	24	6	0	6	45	17	18	.362	.505
Close & Late	.284	81	23	6	0	5	17	12	14	.372	.543
None on/out	.250	100	25	4	0	4	4	7	13	.306	.410
Batting #5	.242	132	32	7	0	5	18	9	19	.291	.409
Batting #6	.253	162	41	10	0	7	26	24	24	.354	.444
Other	.307	114	35	8	1	5	16	12	13	.383	.526
April	.160	75	12	3	0	4	9	15	9	.308	.360
May	.306	108	33	4	0	6	15	13	18	.387	.509
June	.292	96	28	10	1	3	15	11	12	.364	.510
July	.303	99	30	7	0	4	18	5	12	.343	.495
August	.167	30	5	1	0	0	3	1	5	.194	.200
September/October	.000	0	0	0	0	0	0	0	0	.000	.000
Pre-All Star	.260	315	82	21	1	13	44	40	42	.350	.457
Post-All Star	.280	93	26	4	0	4	16	5	14	.316	.452

1993 By Position																							
Position	Avg	AB	H	2B	3B	HR	RBI	BB	SO	OBP	SLG	G	GS	Innings	PO	A	E	DP	Fld Pct	Rng Fctr	In Zone	Outs	Zone Rtg	MLB Zone
As 1b	.267	390	104	25	1	16	57	36	52	.334	.459	103	103	909.2	933	60	3	87	.997	---	178	151	.848	.834

Career (1990-1993)

	Avg	AB	H	2B	3B	HR	RBI	BB	SO	OBP	SLG
vs. Left	.244	283	69	15	1	9	38	22	53	.305	.399
vs. Right	.255	765	195	35	2	28	102	85	113	.328	.416
Groundball	.245	229	56	7	0	10	37	26	41	.331	.406
Flyball	.266	256	68	11	0	8	28	20	40	.316	.402
Home	.246	499	123	23	0	22	72	53	68	.321	.425
Away	.257	549	141	27	3	15	68	54	98	.322	.399
Day	.262	305	80	12	1	15	47	27	54	.317	.456
Night	.248	743	184	38	2	22	93	80	112	.323	.393
Grass	.275	425	117	21	1	15	53	37	73	.332	.435
Turf	.236	623	147	29	2	22	87	70	93	.314	.395
First Pitch	.348	89	31	5	0	5	11	15	0	.459	.573
Ahead in Count	.315	241	76	16	1	14	53	57	0	.435	.564
Behind in Count	.212	485	103	24	2	13	54	0	137	.216	.351
Two Strikes	.185	480	89	21	1	11	50	36	166	.244	.302

	Avg	AB	H	2B	3B	HR	RBI	BB	SO	OBP	SLG
Scoring Posn	.231	255	59	12	2	9	107	43	50	.331	.400
Close & Late	.286	206	59	12	0	8	32	22	41	.357	.461
None on/out	.269	264	71	13	0	8	8	16	38	.316	.409
Batting #5	.283	286	81	10	0	14	44	29	45	.347	.465
Batting #6	.233	300	70	16	1	8	40	37	56	.318	.373
Other	.245	462	113	24	2	15	56	41	65	.308	.403
April	.219	137	30	5	1	7	18	18	18	.314	.423
May	.294	187	55	11	0	7	25	21	30	.369	.465
June	.268	183	49	12	2	6	32	16	22	.325	.454
July	.244	164	40	8	0	5	22	13	26	.302	.384
August	.245	184	45	7	0	5	23	13	30	.290	.364
September/October	.233	193	45	7	0	7	20	26	40	.321	.378
Pre-All Star	.258	574	148	32	3	20	81	58	78	.329	.429
Post-All Star	.245	474	116	18	0	17	59	49	88	.313	.390

Batter vs. Pitcher (career)

Hits Best Against	Avg	AB	H	2B	3B	HR	RBI	BB	SO	OBP	SLG
Ben McDonald	.500	12	6	2	0	1	1	0	3	.500	.917
Scott Erickson	.500	12	6	2	0	1	4	2	1	.533	.917
Bobby Witt	.500	10	5	1	0	0	1	1	0	.545	.600
Mike Moore	.364	11	4	0	0	1	1	1	1	.417	.636
Jimmy Key	.364	11	4	0	0	2	4	0	1	.364	.909

Hits Worst Against	Avg	AB	H	2B	3B	HR	RBI	BB	SO	OBP	SLG
Kevin Appier	.000	14	0	0	0	0	1	4	4	.222	.000
Nolan Ryan	.100	10	1	0	0	0	0	1	2	.182	.100
Roger Clemens	.136	22	3	0	0	0	1	0	6	.136	.136
Kevin Brown	.154	13	2	0	0	0	0	1	3	.214	.154
Matt Young	.167	12	2	0	0	0	2	1	4	.214	.167

Roger Mason — Phillies

Age 35 – Pitches Right (flyball pitcher)

	ERA	W	L	Sv	G	GS	IP	BB	SO	Avg	H	2B	3B	HR	RBI	OBP	SLG	GF	IR	IRS	Hld	SvOp	SB	CS	GB	FB	G/F
1993 Season	4.06	5	12	0	68	0	99.2	34	71	.244	90	13	1	10	51	.307	.366	29	41	12	10	3	5	5	106	118	0.90
Last Five Years	4.03	13	21	11	159	0	218.2	75	151	.240	193	30	5	23	102	.307	.375	61	106	22	24	16	9	12	251	267	0.94

1993 Season

	ERA	W	L	Sv	G	GS	IP	H	HR	BB	SO
Home	4.18	4	6	0	36	0	60.1	59	5	17	43
Away	3.89	1	6	0	32	0	39.1	31	5	17	28
Day	5.64	2	4	0	23	0	30.1	30	3	13	18
Night	3.37	3	8	0	45	0	69.1	60	7	21	53
Grass	4.07	1	10	0	37	0	55.1	49	5	19	39
Turf	4.06	4	2	0	31	0	44.1	41	5	15	32
April	1.72	0	0	0	11	0	15.2	10	0	6	16
May	2.00	0	2	0	12	0	18.0	13	0	4	9
June	6.14	0	5	0	9	0	14.2	19	1	6	11
July	5.85	2	0	0	14	0	20.0	24	1	6	10
August	3.54	2	4	0	12	0	20.1	9	4	7	17
September/October	5.73	1	1	0	10	0	11.0	15	4	5	8
Starter	0.00	0	0	0	0	0	0.0	0	0	0	0
Reliever	4.06	5	12	0	68	0	99.2	90	10	34	71
0 Days rest	7.50	0	4	0	13	0	18.0	29	2	7	13
1 or 2 Days rest	3.21	4	4	0	38	0	56.0	41	3	19	42
3+ Days rest	3.51	1	4	0	17	0	25.2	20	5	8	16
Pre-All Star	3.97	0	7	0	39	0	59.0	58	1	21	41
Post-All Star	4.20	5	5	0	29	0	40.2	32	9	13	30

	Avg	AB	H	2B	3B	HR	RBI	BB	SO	OBP	SLG
vs. Left	.284	148	42	5	0	3	19	17	30	.351	.378
vs. Right	.217	221	48	8	1	7	32	17	41	.277	.357
Inning 1-6	.271	96	26	3	0	5	19	8	22	.321	.458
Inning 7+	.234	273	64	10	1	5	32	26	49	.303	.333
None on	.223	206	46	8	0	8	8	16	43	.286	.379
Runners on	.270	163	44	5	1	2	43	18	28	.333	.350
Scoring Posn	.307	101	31	3	1	2	42	15	21	.380	.416
Close & Late	.279	147	41	6	0	4	24	18	24	.355	.401
None on/out	.264	91	24	7	0	1	1	2	23	.280	.374
vs. 1st Batr (relief)	.262	65	17	4	0	1	6	3	20	.294	.369
First Inning Pitched	.242	227	55	10	1	9	39	24	45	.315	.414
First 15 Pitches	.227	220	50	8	1	8	31	20	39	.293	.382
Pitch 16-30	.265	117	31	5	0	2	18	12	25	.333	.359
Pitch 31-45	.280	25	7	0	0	0	2	2	6	.321	.280
Pitch 46+	.286	7	2	0	0	0	0	0	1	.286	.286
First Pitch	.321	56	18	2	0	4	14	5	0	.381	.571
Ahead in Count	.225	178	40	6	1	1	20	0	56	.221	.287
Behind in Count	.224	76	17	2	0	3	10	15	0	.348	.368
Two Strikes	.201	169	34	4	1	1	13	14	71	.259	.254

Last Five Years

	ERA	W	L	Sv	G	GS	IP	H	HR	BB	SO
Home	3.84	8	8	6	78	0	122.0	111	11	31	80
Away	4.28	5	13	5	81	0	96.2	82	12	44	71
Day	4.86	6	6	2	49	0	63.0	59	6	29	35
Night	3.70	7	15	9	110	0	155.2	134	17	46	116
Grass	3.99	3	12	3	64	0	90.1	78	6	35	62
Turf	4.07	10	9	8	95	0	128.1	115	17	40	89
April	2.03	1	1	3	19	0	26.2	20	1	15	21
May	2.93	0	4	1	26	0	40.0	30	2	11	20
June	4.91	1	5	2	21	0	29.1	37	2	9	22
July	5.64	2	3	0	23	0	30.1	32	4	12	15
August	3.10	6	4	2	32	0	52.1	31	7	11	36
September/October	5.85	3	4	3	38	0	40.0	43	7	17	37
Starter	0.00	0	0	0	0	0	0.0	0	0	0	0
Reliever	4.03	13	21	11	159	0	218.2	193	23	75	151
0 Days rest	6.12	1	8	5	34	0	42.2	52	7	13	29
1 or 2 Days rest	3.06	11	6	4	82	0	114.2	88	8	38	81
3+ Days rest	4.40	1	7	2	43	0	61.1	53	8	24	41
Pre-All Star	3.65	2	11	6	76	0	111.0	106	5	42	71
Post-All Star	4.43	11	10	5	83	0	107.2	87	18	33	80

	Avg	AB	H	2B	3B	HR	RBI	BB	SO	OBP	SLG
vs. Left	.247	365	90	15	3	6	35	45	65	.325	.353
vs. Right	.234	440	103	15	2	17	67	30	86	.291	.393
Inning 1-6	.247	198	49	5	0	10	34	14	39	.300	.424
Inning 7+	.237	607	144	25	5	13	68	61	112	.309	.359
None on	.232	452	105	19	3	14	14	36	84	.298	.381
Runners on	.249	353	88	11	2	9	88	39	67	.318	.368
Scoring Posn	.262	214	56	7	2	6	81	34	46	.351	.397
Close & Late	.263	388	102	17	3	12	57	43	69	.336	.415
None on/out	.236	195	46	10	1	4	4	10	37	.273	.359
vs. 1st Batr (relief)	.203	148	30	6	1	1	12	9	35	.252	.277
First Inning Pitched	.232	504	117	22	3	16	67	54	96	.310	.383
First 15 Pitches	.223	484	108	20	2	15	54	45	85	.294	.366
Pitch 16-30	.238	239	57	7	2	6	35	23	49	.304	.360
Pitch 31-45	.333	54	18	2	1	1	9	7	15	.391	.463
Pitch 46+	.357	28	10	1	0	1	4	0	2	.379	.500
First Pitch	.317	123	39	5	0	9	30	12	0	.379	.577
Ahead in Count	.221	385	85	14	3	4	35	0	118	.226	.304
Behind in Count	.225	151	34	4	0	6	15	36	0	.372	.371
Two Strikes	.187	386	72	11	4	3	29	27	151	.242	.259

Pitcher vs. Batter (career)																							
Pitches Best Vs.	Avg	AB	H	2B	3B	HR	RBI	BB	SO	OBP	SLG	**Pitches Worst Vs.**	Avg	AB	H	2B	3B	HR	RBI	BB	SO	OBP	SLG
Mariano Duncan	.176	17	3	0	0	1	4	2	5	.263	.353	John Kruk	.500	8	4	0	1	1	1	4	0	.667	1.125
Ron Gant	.182	11	2	0	0	1	2	0	1	.182	.455	Milt Thompson	.400	15	6	1	0	0	0	0	3	.400	.467
Ryne Sandberg	.200	15	3	1	0	1	2	3	6	.333	.467	Terry Pendleton	.400	10	4	0	0	0	3	3	1	.538	.400
Dion James	.222	9	2	1	0	0	0	2	2	.364	.333	Marquis Grissom	.400	10	4	0	0	0	3	1	1	.455	.400
												Tony Gwynn	.313	16	5	0	1	1	2	0	2	.313	.625

Don Mattingly — Yankees

Age 33 – Bats Left

	Avg	G	AB	R	H	2B	3B	HR	RBI	BB	SO	HBP	GDP	SB	CS	OBP	SLG	IBB	SH	SF	#Pit	#P/PA	GB	FB	G/F
1993 Season	.291	134	530	78	154	27	2	17	86	61	42	2	19	0	0	.364	.445	9	0	3	2080	3.49	201	174	1.16
Last Five Years	.287	703	2782	350	799	155	4	68	395	225	177	11	79	9	0	.339	.419	58	0	31	10030	3.29	1027	999	1.03

1993 Season

	Avg	AB	H	2B	3B	HR	RBI	BB	SO	OBP	SLG		Avg	AB	H	2B	3B	HR	RBI	BB	SO	OBP	SLG
vs. Left	.204	201	53	10	0	5	34	23	19	.344	.388	Scoring Posn	.368	125	46	6	1	4	67	27	8	.471	.528
vs. Right	.307	329	101	17	2	12	52	38	23	.377	.480	Close & Late	.307	75	23	4	0	2	17	4	5	.342	.440
Groundball	.287	87	25	5	0	4	14	6	7	.333	.483	None on/out	.215	93	20	4	1	2	2	6	7	.263	.344
Flyball	.333	117	39	3	1	5	14	18	10	.419	.504	Total	.291	530	154	27	2	17	86	61	42	.364	.445
Home	.303	241	73	15	2	8	40	32	17	.386	.481	Batting #3	.291	530	154	27	2	17	86	61	42	.364	.445
Away	.280	289	81	12	0	9	46	29	25	.345	.415	Other	.000	0	0	0	0	0	0	0	0	.000	.000
Day	.318	179	57	11	1	8	31	22	14	.394	.525	April	.233	90	21	5	0	0	7	7	9	.289	.289
Night	.276	351	97	16	1	9	55	39	28	.349	.405	May	.314	51	16	2	0	2	5	4	5	.375	.471
Grass	.296	456	135	22	2	14	71	57	38	.375	.445	June	.333	78	26	3	0	3	11	8	3	.395	.487
Turf	.257	74	19	5	0	3	15	4	4	.295	.446	July	.362	105	38	8	1	5	25	9	8	.414	.600
First Pitch	.377	53	20	0	0	2	14	7	0	.450	.491	August	.265	98	26	3	1	5	26	17	8	.368	.469
Ahead in Count	.262	145	38	7	2	7	34	43	0	.434	.483	September/October	.250	108	27	6	0	2	12	16	9	.347	.361
Behind in Count	.269	223	60	10	0	7	22	0	36	.270	.408	Pre-All Star	.292	260	76	14	0	6	29	22	21	.350	.415
Two Strikes	.281	185	52	13	0	5	21	11	42	.322	.432	Post-All Star	.289	270	78	13	2	11	57	39	21	.377	.474

1993 By Position

Position	Avg	AB	H	2B	3B	HR	RBI	BB	SO	OBP	SLG	G	GS	Innings	PO	A	E	DP	Fld Pct	Rng Fctr	In Zone	Outs	Zone Rtg	MLB Zone
As 1b	.292	506	148	26	2	15	82	61	39	.369	.441	130	126	1118.0	1257	81	3	124	.998	---	195	174	.892	.834

Last Five Years

	Avg	AB	H	2B	3B	HR	RBI	BB	SO	OBP	SLG		Avg	AB	H	2B	3B	HR	RBI	BB	SO	OBP	SLG
vs. Left	.285	995	284	65	1	20	164	77	80	.337	.413	Scoring Posn	.320	691	221	44	1	16	314	109	46	.399	.456
vs. Right	.288	1787	515	90	3	48	231	148	97	.341	.422	Close & Late	.278	435	121	26	0	17	82	49	33	.354	.455
Groundball	.285	708	202	37	0	15	98	60	47	.337	.401	None on/out	.256	551	141	29	2	15	15	22	27	.288	.397
Flyball	.317	606	192	43	2	17	86	61	38	.378	.479	Batting #2	.269	390	105	24	0	9	45	31	23	.322	.400
Home	.306	1310	401	82	2	44	214	123	75	.364	.473	Batting #3	.289	2210	639	119	4	56	328	187	136	.344	.423
Away	.270	1472	398	73	2	24	181	102	102	.317	.372	Other	.302	182	55	12	0	3	22	7	18	.321	.418
Day	.308	863	266	53	1	24	136	97	53	.377	.455	April	.249	381	95	19	0	5	32	42	26	.324	.339
Night	.278	1919	533	102	3	44	259	128	124	.322	.403	May	.296	470	139	29	0	14	74	33	36	.343	.447
Grass	.292	2343	683	129	2	62	340	203	153	.346	.428	June	.304	520	158	22	1	16	71	35	23	.345	.442
Turf	.264	439	116	26	2	6	55	22	24	.300	.374	July	.295	474	140	31	1	9	67	30	28	.337	.422
First Pitch	.360	258	93	16	0	7	56	36	0	.436	.504	August	.288	431	124	30	2	11	79	36	30	.340	.443
Ahead in Count	.314	867	272	46	4	23	140	128	0	.400	.456	September/October	.283	506	143	24	0	13	72	49	34	.344	.407
Behind in Count	.238	1122	267	53	0	25	121	0	155	.240	.352	Pre-All Star	.288	1521	438	81	1	37	197	119	96	.339	.416
Two Strikes	.235	865	203	42	0	16	81	45	177	.273	.339	Post-All Star	.286	1261	361	74	3	31	198	106	81	.341	.423

Batter vs. Pitcher (since 1984)

Hits Best Against	Avg	AB	H	2B	3B	HR	RBI	BB	SO	OBP	SLG	**Hits Worst Against**	Avg	AB	H	2B	3B	HR	RBI	BB	SO	OBP	SLG
Shawn Hillegas	.600	15	9	0	0	3	5	2	0	.611	1.200	Gregg Olson	.091	11	1	0	0	0	0	2	1	.231	.091
Terry Leach	.583	12	7	0	1	0	2	0	0	.583	.750	Brian Bohanon	.091	11	1	0	0	0	0	2	0	.231	.091
John Doherty	.545	11	6	1	0	1	4	0	0	.545	.909	Joe Hesketh	.118	17	2	0	0	0	4	1	3	.150	.118
Bill Gullickson	.500	16	8	2	0	1	6	2	0	.556	.813	Kevin Tapani	.125	32	4	1	0	0	0	1	1	.152	.156
Steve Farr	.400	15	6	1	0	2	4	2	0	.471	.867	Bobby Thigpen	.143	14	2	0	0	0	1	1	0	.200	.143

Tim Mauser — Padres

Age 27 – Pitches Right

	ERA	W	L	Sv	G	GS	IP	BB	SO	Avg	H	2B	3B	HR	RBI	OBP	SLG	GF	IR	IRS	Hld	SvOp	SB	CS	GB	FB	G/F
1993 Season	4.00	0	1	0	36	0	54.0	24	46	.245	51	11	1	6	33	.325	.394	16	34	14	0	0	4	3	67	46	1.46
Career (1991-1993)	4.59	0	1	0	39	0	64.2	27	52	.268	69	15	1	9	43	.339	.440	17	36	14	0	0	4	3	83	62	1.34

1993 Season

	ERA	W	L	Sv	G	GS	IP	H	HR	BB	SO		Avg	AB	H	2B	3B	HR	RBI	BB	SO	OBP	SLG
Home	3.24	0	0	0	16	0	25.0	18	4	10	19	vs. Left	.202	104	21	4	0	3	13	10	26	.270	.327
Away	4.66	0	1	0	20	0	29.0	33	2	14	27	vs. Right	.288	104	30	7	1	3	20	14	20	.378	.462
Starter	0.00	0	0	0	0	0	0.0	0	0	0	0	Scoring Posn	.197	66	13	2	0	3	27	16	17	.349	.364
Reliever	4.00	0	1	0	36	0	54.0	51	6	24	46	Close & Late	.526	19	10	3	0	1	7	5	4	.600	.842
0 Days rest	0.00	0	0	0	5	0	9.0	6	0	3	7	None on/out	.261	46	12	4	1	0	0	2	6	.292	.391
1 or 2 Days rest	5.04	0	1	0	18	0	25.0	27	4	10	25	First Pitch	.257	35	9	1	0	1	3	4	0	.333	.371
3+ Days rest	4.50	0	0	0	13	0	20.0	18	2	11	14	Ahead in Count	.160	94	15	4	0	1	10	0	44	.160	.234
Pre-All Star	5.75	0	0	0	10	0	20.1	23	2	11	18	Behind in Count	.372	43	16	2	1	4	14	14	0	.526	.744
Post-All Star	2.94	0	1	0	26	0	33.2	28	4	13	28	Two Strikes	.170	94	16	5	0	1	10	6	46	.228	.255

Derrick May — Cubs

Age 25 – Bats Left

	Avg	G	AB	R	H	2B	3B	HR	RBI	BB	SO	HBP	GDP	SB	CS	OBP	SLG	IBB	SH	SF	#Pit	#P/PA	GB	FB	G/F
1993 Season	.295	128	465	62	137	25	2	10	77	31	41	1	15	10	3	.336	.422	6	0	6	1582	3.15	188	121	1.55
Career (1990-1993)	.281	284	899	107	253	41	2	20	136	49	89	4	26	16	6	.319	.398	10	2	8	2949	3.07	354	242	1.46

1993 Season

	Avg	AB	H	2B	3B	HR	RBI	BB	SO	OBP	SLG		Avg	AB	H	2B	3B	HR	RBI	BB	SO	OBP	SLG
vs. Left	.247	89	22	3	1	4	22	2	13	.266	.438	Scoring Posn	.328	134	44	11	1	5	67	14	16	.377	.537
vs. Right	.306	376	115	22	1	6	55	29	28	.352	.418	Close & Late	.301	83	25	4	0	2	16	2	9	.310	.422
Groundball	.293	157	46	10	1	2	26	10	12	.337	.408	None on/out	.283	120	34	4	0	3	3	6	8	.323	.392
Flyball	.351	77	27	3	1	2	15	1	7	.354	.494	Batting #4	.306	252	77	12	1	6	44	18	23	.348	.433
Home	.319	248	79	16	1	3	40	16	26	.360	.427	Batting #5	.292	171	50	13	1	3	31	12	13	.337	.433
Away	.267	217	58	9	1	7	37	15	15	.309	.415	Other	.238	42	10	0	0	1	2	1	5	.256	.310
Day	.319	248	79	13	1	4	38	18	21	.364	.427	April	.345	58	20	1	0	3	14	5	5	.400	.517
Night	.267	217	58	12	1	6	39	13	20	.303	.415	May	.286	91	26	6	0	1	15	6	10	.330	.385
Grass	.288	361	104	20	2	5	56	22	33	.327	.396	June	.274	95	26	6	0	3	12	4	4	.297	.432
Turf	.317	104	33	5	0	5	21	9	8	.365	.510	July	.337	101	34	6	0	2	18	9	8	.391	.455
First Pitch	.318	107	34	9	1	2	20	4	0	.336	.477	August	.295	95	28	5	1	1	16	5	8	.320	.400
Ahead in Count	.320	125	40	8	1	3	31	12	0	.374	.472	September/October	.120	25	3	1	1	0	2	2	6	.185	.240
Behind in Count	.240	150	36	5	0	1	10	0	33	.240	.293	Pre-All Star	.300	283	85	15	0	8	46	18	22	.341	.438
Two Strikes	.179	140	25	2	0	2	12	15	41	.258	.236	Post-All Star	.286	182	52	10	2	2	31	13	19	.328	.396

1993 By Position

Position	Avg	AB	H	2B	3B	HR	RBI	BB	SO	OBP	SLG	G	GS	Innings	PO	A	E	DP	Fld Pct	Rng Fctr	In Zone	Outs	Zone Rtg	MLB Zone
As Pinch Hitter	.100	10	1	0	0	0	0	2	2	.250	.100	12	0	---	---	---	---	---	---	---	---	---	---	---
As lf	.296	449	133	24	2	10	77	29	38	.336	.425	121	112	993.1	217	8	7	1	.970	2.04	258	210	.814	.818

Career (1990-1993)

	Avg	AB	H	2B	3B	HR	RBI	BB	SO	OBP	SLG		Avg	AB	H	2B	3B	HR	RBI	BB	SO	OBP	SLG
vs. Left	.251	171	43	5	1	6	32	7	26	.286	.398	Scoring Posn	.310	245	76	17	1	10	116	20	31	.356	.510
vs. Right	.288	728	210	36	1	14	104	42	63	.326	.398	Close & Late	.267	161	43	5	0	6	29	5	18	.288	.410
Groundball	.284	327	93	15	1	4	43	19	34	.327	.373	None on/out	.260	223	58	6	0	5	5	12	15	.301	.354
Flyball	.285	172	49	4	1	5	27	3	16	.296	.407	Batting #4	.302	255	77	12	1	6	44	18	23	.344	.427
Home	.303	495	150	27	1	8	79	30	47	.343	.410	Batting #5	.274	369	101	23	1	7	66	19	37	.309	.398
Away	.255	404	103	14	1	12	57	19	42	.289	.384	Other	.273	275	75	6	0	7	26	12	29	.307	.371
Day	.283	498	141	22	1	8	74	34	48	.329	.380	April	.304	69	21	1	0	3	15	7	6	.372	.449
Night	.279	401	112	19	1	12	62	15	41	.306	.421	May	.264	148	39	8	0	1	17	9	18	.306	.338
Grass	.290	672	195	33	2	11	102	40	63	.330	.394	June	.291	165	48	8	0	6	26	6	11	.312	.448
Turf	.256	227	58	8	0	9	34	9	26	.285	.410	July	.295	129	38	6	0	3	20	11	12	.348	.411
First Pitch	.332	220	73	14	1	7	40	7	0	.348	.500	August	.303	175	53	9	1	2	26	9	18	.342	.400
Ahead in Count	.301	226	68	11	1	5	42	16	0	.343	.425	September/October	.254	213	54	9	1	5	32	7	24	.276	.376
Behind in Count	.227	309	70	11	0	2	29	0	75	.232	.282	Pre-All Star	.280	435	122	19	0	11	64	26	39	.320	.400
Two Strikes	.201	284	57	8	0	5	34	26	89	.268	.282	Post-All Star	.282	464	131	22	2	9	72	23	50	.318	.397

Batter vs. Pitcher (career)

Hits Best Against	Avg	AB	H	2B	3B	HR	RBI	BB	SO	OBP	SLG	Hits Worst Against	Avg	AB	H	2B	3B	HR	RBI	BB	SO	OBP	SLG
Dennis Martinez	.444	18	8	2	0	2	8	1	1	.474	.889	Jack Armstrong	.091	11	1	1	0	0	2	1	2	.154	.182
Curt Schilling	.438	16	7	1	0	0	0	0	1	.438	.500	Bill Swift	.100	10	1	1	0	0	1	2	2	.250	.200
Ken Hill	.435	23	10	5	0	0	6	1	2	.440	.652	Rheal Cormier	.167	12	2	0	0	0	0	0	1	.167	.167
Bob Walk	.400	15	6	2	0	0	4	2	1	.471	.533	John Smoltz	.190	21	4	1	0	0	0	0	2	.190	.238
Greg W. Harris	.308	13	4	2	0	1	4	0	0	.308	.692	Tim Belcher	.214	14	3	0	0	0	1	0	0	.214	.214

Brent Mayne — Royals

Age 26 – Bats Left (groundball hitter)

	Avg	G	AB	R	H	2B	3B	HR	RBI	BB	SO	HBP	GDP	SB	CS	OBP	SLG	IBB	SH	SF	#Pit	#P/PA	GB	FB	G/F
1993 Season	.254	71	205	22	52	9	1	2	22	18	31	1	6	3	2	.317	.337	7	3	0	762	3.36	77	54	1.43
Career (1990-1993)	.243	243	662	62	161	27	1	5	72	55	102	1	17	5	11	.300	.310	11	7	6	2640	3.61	277	157	1.76

1993 Season

	Avg	AB	H	2B	3B	HR	RBI	BB	SO	OBP	SLG		Avg	AB	H	2B	3B	HR	RBI	BB	SO	OBP	SLG
vs. Left	.211	19	4	0	0	0	1	1	6	.250	.211	Scoring Posn	.333	45	15	3	1	0	20	9	11	.444	.444
vs. Right	.258	186	48	9	1	2	21	17	25	.324	.349	Close & Late	.273	33	9	1	0	0	1	3	7	.333	.303
Home	.320	97	31	3	1	0	9	7	12	.371	.371	None on/out	.278	54	15	4	0	1	1	2	6	.304	.407
Away	.194	108	21	6	0	2	13	11	19	.269	.306	Batting #6	.278	108	30	4	0	2	12	10	17	.345	.370
First Pitch	.276	29	8	2	0	2	4	6	0	.400	.552	Batting #7	.220	50	11	4	1	0	7	5	9	.291	.340
Ahead in Count	.298	57	17	3	0	0	10	9	0	.394	.351	Other	.234	47	11	1	0	0	3	3	5	.280	.255
Behind in Count	.152	99	15	2	1	0	6	0	31	.160	.192	Pre-All Star	.262	126	33	6	1	1	12	9	20	.311	.349
Two Strikes	.154	78	12	2	1	0	5	3	31	.185	.205	Post-All Star	.241	79	19	3	0	1	10	9	11	.326	.316

Career (1990-1993)

	Avg	AB	H	2B	3B	HR	RBI	BB	SO	OBP	SLG		Avg	AB	H	2B	3B	HR	RBI	BB	SO	OBP	SLG
vs. Left	.143	63	9	0	0	0	5	6	17	.208	.143	Scoring Posn	.294	163	48	10	1	2	67	22	35	.366	.405
vs. Right	.254	599	152	27	1	5	67	49	85	.310	.327	Close & Late	.262	122	32	2	0	1	9	13	25	.333	.303
Groundball	.247	158	39	9	0	1	18	12	23	.298	.323	None on/out	.250	164	41	6	0	1	1	9	19	.289	.305
Flyball	.206	180	37	7	1	1	19	16	28	.268	.272	Batting #6	.257	191	49	9	0	2	23	17	29	.319	.335
Home	.272	346	94	14	1	2	37	26	48	.322	.335	Batting #7	.236	280	66	15	1	2	31	19	45	.281	.318
Away	.212	316	67	13	0	3	35	29	54	.276	.282	Other	.241	191	46	3	0	1	18	19	28	.307	.272
Day	.258	236	61	12	0	1	25	19	39	.311	.322	April	.256	82	21	3	0	1	9	6	16	.303	.329
Night	.235	426	100	15	1	4	47	36	63	.293	.303	May	.215	65	14	4	1	0	5	3	8	.250	.308
Grass	.203	237	48	8	0	3	26	19	36	.259	.274	June	.330	97	32	4	0	0	10	9	14	.383	.371
Turf	.266	425	113	19	1	2	46	36	66	.323	.329	July	.246	142	35	5	0	0	15	7	19	.282	.282

Career (1990-1993)

	Avg	AB	H	2B	3B	HR	RBI	BB	SO	OBP	SLG
First Pitch	.277	83	23	5	0	2	13	10	0	.344	.410
Ahead in Count	.317	164	52	12	0	0	29	26	0	.404	.390
Behind in Count	.165	309	51	4	1	2	20	0	96	.168	.204
Two Strikes	.159	283	45	3	1	2	20	19	102	.212	.198
August	.198	116	23	6	0	3	18	16	17	.296	.328
September/October	.225	160	36	5	0	1	15	14	28	.284	.275
Pre-All Star	.261	284	74	11	1	1	26	20	41	.307	.317
Post-All Star	.230	378	87	16	0	4	46	35	61	.294	.304

Batter vs. Pitcher (career)

Hits Best Against	Avg	AB	H	2B	3B	HR	RBI	BB	SO	OBP	SLG
Jaime Navarro	.467	15	7	1	0	0	0	1	2	.500	.533
Ben McDonald	.462	13	6	0	0	1	2	1	2	.500	.692
Ron Darling	.444	9	4	1	0	0	0	2	0	.545	.556
Roger Clemens	.389	18	7	0	0	0	2	3	4	.476	.389
Dave Stewart	.357	14	5	1	0	0	2	2	2	.438	.429

Hits Worst Against	Avg	AB	H	2B	3B	HR	RBI	BB	SO	OBP	SLG
Juan Guzman	.000	11	0	0	0	0	0	1	4	.083	.000
Kevin Tapani	.200	20	4	1	0	0	2	1	5	.238	.250

Matt Maysey — Brewers

Age 27 – Pitchos Right (groundball pitcher)

	ERA	W	L	Sv	G	GS	IP	BB	SO	Avg	H	2B	3B	HR	RBI	OBP	SLG	GF	IR	IRS	Hld	SvOp	SB	CS	GB	FB	G/F
1993 Season	5.73	1	2	1	23	0	22.0	13	10	.322	28	5	0	4	20	.408	.517	12	18	7	0	2	3	0	40	21	1.90
Career (1992-1993)	5.55	1	2	1	25	0	24.1	13	11	.327	32	5	0	5	22	.409	.531	13	20	8	0	2	3	1	42	25	1.68

1993 Season

	ERA	W	L	Sv	G	GS	IP	H	HR	BB	SO
Home	7.63	1	1	0	15	0	15.1	25	3	7	6
Away	1.35	0	1	1	8	0	6.2	3	1	6	4

	Avg	AB	H	2B	3B	HR	RBI	BB	SO	OBP	SLG
vs. Left	.306	36	11	2	0	1	9	6	5	.395	.444
vs. Right	.333	51	17	3	0	3	11	7	5	.417	.569

Dave McCarty — Twins

Age 24 – Bats Right

	Avg	G	AB	R	H	2B	3B	HR	RBI	BB	SO	HBP	GDP	SB	CS	OBP	SLG	IBB	SH	SF	#Pit	#P/PA	GB	FB	G/F
1993 Season	.214	98	350	36	75	15	2	2	21	19	80	1	13	2	6	.257	.286	0	1	0	1351	3.64	127	85	1.49

1993 Season

	Avg	AB	H	2B	3B	HR	RBI	BB	SO	OBP	SLG
vs. Left	.206	107	22	3	1	0	3	5	22	.248	.252
vs. Right	.218	243	53	12	1	2	18	14	58	.261	.300
Groundball	.236	55	13	0	0	1	5	2	10	.263	.291
Flyball	.290	69	20	5	2	1	7	9	15	.372	.464
Home	.223	166	37	9	1	2	8	12	37	.279	.325
Away	.207	184	38	6	1	0	13	7	43	.236	.250
Day	.250	96	24	8	1	1	10	5	17	.287	.385
Night	.201	254	51	7	1	1	11	14	63	.245	.248
Grass	.210	157	33	3	1	0	9	7	34	.244	.242
Turf	.218	193	42	12	1	2	12	12	46	.267	.321
First Pitch	.346	52	18	2	1	0	4	0	0	.346	.423
Ahead in Count	.225	71	16	5	0	1	1	10	0	.321	.338
Behind in Count	.168	155	26	5	1	0	10	0	66	.173	.213
Two Strikes	.161	161	26	7	1	0	12	9	80	.206	.217
Scoring Posn	.210	81	17	4	0	0	18	4	23	.247	.259
Close & Late	.232	69	16	3	0	0	2	1	15	.243	.275
None on/out	.206	68	14	3	1	0	0	2	13	.229	.279
Batting #7	.206	107	22	3	1	1	9	6	29	.254	.280
Batting #8	.173	110	19	5	1	1	5	7	27	.222	.264
Other	.256	133	34	7	0	0	7	6	24	.288	.308
April	.000	0	0	0	0	0	0	0	0	.000	.000
May	.353	51	18	6	1	0	5	1	11	.365	.510
June	.229	70	16	0	0	1	2	5	16	.289	.271
July	.203	59	12	2	0	0	3	1	12	.217	.237
August	.115	61	7	2	1	0	0	6	19	.194	.180
September/October	.202	109	22	5	0	1	11	6	22	.243	.275
Pre-All Star	.277	141	39	6	1	1	7	6	31	.311	.355
Post-All Star	.172	209	36	9	1	1	14	13	49	.221	.239

1993 By Position

Position	Avg	AB	H	2B	3B	HR	RBI	BB	SO	OBP	SLG	G	GS	Innings	PO	A	E	DP	Fld Pct	Rng Fctr	In Zone	Outs	Zone Rtg	MLB Zone
As 1b	.191	110	21	2	0	0	5	7	26	.246	.209	36	29	264.0	278	30	2	24	.994	---	62	52	.839	.834
As lf	.170	112	19	6	2	0	5	4	28	.198	.259	38	30	263.0	75	6	3	1	.964	2.77	92	73	.793	.818
As rf	.254	114	29	6	0	2	8	7	24	.298	.360	34	29	265.2	50	2	3	0	.945	1.76	66	51	.773	.826

Kirk McCaskill — White Sox

Age 33 – Pitches Right

	ERA	W	L	Sv	G	GS	IP	BB	SO	Avg	H	2B	3B	HR	RBI	OBP	SLG	GF	IR	IRS	Hld	SvOp	SB	CS	GB	FB	G/F
1993 Season	5.23	4	8	2	30	14	113.2	36	65	.313	144	26	2	12	72	.362	.457	6	14	7	2	2	8	9	170	108	1.57
Last Five Years	3.85	53	61	2	155	139	886.2	328	430	.263	893	138	25	67	388	.329	.378	6	14	7	2	2	39	39	1365	920	1.48

1993 Season

	ERA	W	L	Sv	G	GS	IP	H	HR	BB	SO
Home	3.80	2	2	1	18	5	66.1	71	6	20	38
Away	7.23	2	6	1	12	9	47.1	73	6	16	27
Starter	5.60	4	7	0	14	14	72.1	99	9	22	37
Reliever	4.57	0	1	2	16	0	41.1	45	3	14	28
0 Days rest	0.00	0	0	1	1	0	1.1	0	0	0	2
1 or 2 Days rest	3.60	0	1	0	5	0	10.0	15	0	2	9
3+ Days rest	5.10	0	0	1	10	0	30.0	30	3	12	17
Pre-All Star	6.58	2	7	0	14	12	67.0	94	10	25	31
Post-All Star	3.28	2	1	2	16	2	46.2	50	2	11	34

	Avg	AB	H	2B	3B	HR	RBI	BB	SO	OBP	SLG
vs. Left	.350	200	70	14	2	7	35	21	19	.410	.545
vs. Right	.285	260	74	12	0	5	37	15	46	.324	.388
Scoring Posn	.347	118	41	9	0	3	59	15	10	.412	.500
Close & Late	.296	54	16	4	0	0	10	5	8	.350	.370
None on/out	.302	116	35	8	1	3	3	6	17	.336	.466
First Pitch	.354	79	28	6	0	0	12	5	0	.384	.430
Ahead in Count	.255	196	50	11	0	1	18	0	58	.259	.327
Behind in Count	.376	109	41	6	1	7	29	18	0	.461	.642
Two Strikes	.249	189	47	12	1	2	21	13	65	.297	.354

Last Five Years

	ERA	W	L	Sv	G	GS	IP	H	HR	BB	SO
Home	3.45	29	26	1	81	68	462.0	443	39	154	235
Away	4.28	24	35	1	74	71	424.2	450	28	174	195
Day	2.50	10	8	0	30	24	172.2	145	5	54	90
Night	4.17	43	53	2	125	115	714.0	748	62	274	340
Grass	3.80	45	51	2	133	118	752.1	747	58	278	364
Turf	4.09	8	10	0	22	21	134.1	146	9	50	66
April	2.92	11	9	0	22	22	142.0	126	9	63	65

	Avg	AB	H	2B	3B	HR	RBI	BB	SO	OBP	SLG
vs. Left	.283	1663	470	69	16	40	201	150	168	.342	.416
vs. Right	.245	1729	423	69	9	27	187	178	262	.317	.342
Inning 1-6	.267	2957	789	115	23	60	348	290	370	.333	.382
Inning 7+	.239	435	104	23	2	7	40	38	60	.303	.349
None on	.252	1939	489	77	13	37	37	193	254	.323	.363
Runners on	.278	1453	404	61	12	30	351	135	176	.337	.398
Scoring Posn	.276	765	211	37	9	16	313	93	104	.348	.410

Last Five Years

	ERA	W	L	Sv	G	GS	IP	H	HR	BB	SO
May	3.63	8	8	0	25	25	146.1	158	11	44	72
June	4.26	9	13	0	24	24	139.1	144	16	52	72
July	5.17	5	11	0	27	22	142.2	151	11	68	48
August	3.50	14	10	0	30	26	172.1	177	10	50	88
September/October	3.69	6	10	2	27	20	144.0	137	10	51	85
Starter	3.81	53	60	0	139	139	845.1	848	64	314	402
Reliever	4.57	0	1	2	16	0	41.1	45	3	14	28
0 Days rest	0.00	0	0	1	1	0	1.1	0	0	0	2
1 or 2 Days rest	3.60	0	1	0	5	0	10.0	15	0	2	9
3+ Days rest	5.10	0	0	1	10	0	30.0	30	3	12	17
Pre-All Star	3.92	30	34	0	80	78	475.0	488	42	187	222
Post-All Star	3.76	23	27	2	75	61	411.2	405	25	141	208

	Avg	AB	H	2B	3B	HR	RBI	BB	SO	OBP	SLG
Close & Late	.241	253	61	14	2	5	28	24	34	.310	.372
None on/out	.247	859	212	35	5	16	16	86	106	.319	.355
vs. 1st Batr (relief)	.313	16	5	1	0	1	4	0	2	.313	.563
First Inning Pitched	.266	587	156	19	3	13	74	65	70	.337	.375
First 15 Pitches	.268	507	136	15	2	10	42	42	48	.327	.365
Pitch 16-30	.244	532	130	20	4	13	60	52	90	.309	.370
Pitch 31-45	.264	527	139	18	2	5	51	40	60	.318	.334
Pitch 46+	.267	1826	488	85	17	39	235	194	232	.339	.396
First Pitch	.295	515	152	26	5	9	73	10	0	.310	.417
Ahead in Count	.215	1385	298	46	5	18	124	0	358	.219	.295
Behind in Count	.308	827	255	41	7	24	109	170	0	.425	.462
Two Strikes	.213	1416	302	47	8	21	139	148	430	.291	.302

Pitcher vs. Batter (career)

Pitches Best Vs.	Avg	AB	H	2B	3B	HR	RBI	BB	SO	OBP	SLG
Mike Stanley	.000	11	0	0	0	0	0	1	5	.083	.000
Tony Pena	.053	19	1	0	0	0	1	1	4	.100	.053
Pat Borders	.059	17	1	0	1	0	2	0	2	.059	.176
Randy Velarde	.083	12	1	1	0	0	0	0	1	.083	.167
Robin Ventura	.091	11	1	0	0	0	0	1	2	.167	.091

Pitches Worst Vs.	Avg	AB	H	2B	3B	HR	RBI	BB	SO	OBP	SLG
Junior Felix	.556	9	5	0	0	1	2	2	0	.636	.889
Mo Vaughn	.500	12	6	1	0	1	4	2	0	.571	.833
Kirk Gibson	.440	25	11	3	0	4	6	8	6	.576	1.040
Lance Parrish	.412	17	7	1	0	3	4	0	5	.412	1.000
Chili Davis	.400	10	4	1	0	1	3	2	2	.500	.800

Lloyd McClendon — Pirates

Age 35 – Bats Right (flyball hitter)

	Avg	G	AB	R	H	2B	3B	HR	RBI	BB	SO	HBP	GDP	SB	CS	OBP	SLG	IBB	SH	SF	#Pit	#P/PA	GB	FB	G/F
1993 Season	.221	88	181	21	40	11	1	2	19	23	17	0	4	0	3	.306	.326	1	1	2	765	3.70	71	69	1.03
Last Five Years	.251	402	903	124	227	41	3	26	115	120	117	5	16	10	11	.338	.390	6	3	13	3901	3.74	315	336	0.94

1993 Season

	Avg	AB	H	2B	3B	HR	RBI	BB	SO	OBP	SLG
vs. Left	.254	142	36	10	1	0	14	18	12	.335	.338
vs. Right	.103	39	4	1	0	2	5	5	5	.200	.282
Home	.182	77	14	3	0	1	9	9	6	.264	.260
Away	.250	104	26	8	1	1	10	14	11	.336	.375
First Pitch	.333	27	9	2	0	2	3	1	0	.357	.630
Ahead in Count	.254	59	15	6	0	0	5	14	0	.392	.356
Behind in Count	.194	72	14	3	1	0	10	0	14	.192	.264
Two Strikes	.189	74	14	3	1	0	10	8	17	.265	.257

	Avg	AB	H	2B	3B	HR	RBI	BB	SO	OBP	SLG
Scoring Posn	.203	59	12	4	1	0	16	10	5	.310	.305
Close & Late	.341	44	15	4	1	1	9	9	3	.453	.545
None on/out	.217	46	10	3	0	0	0	6	7	.308	.283
Batting #4	.118	17	2	1	0	0	3	2	1	.211	.176
Batting #5	.235	132	31	8	1	2	14	12	15	.297	.356
Other	.219	32	7	2	0	0	2	9	1	.381	.281
Pre-All Star	.183	93	17	4	0	1	9	9	12	.252	.258
Post-All Star	.261	88	23	7	1	1	10	14	5	.359	.398

Last Five Years

	Avg	AB	H	2B	3B	HR	RBI	BB	SO	OBP	SLG
vs. Left	.278	634	176	33	2	16	83	88	72	.364	.412
vs. Right	.190	269	51	8	1	10	32	32	45	.276	.338
Groundball	.272	305	83	13	1	7	41	45	38	.366	.390
Flyball	.199	191	38	10	0	8	28	20	28	.271	.377
Home	.239	423	101	17	1	15	63	51	59	.322	.390
Away	.263	480	126	24	2	11	52	69	58	.352	.390
Day	.268	362	97	16	1	15	53	45	49	.347	.442
Night	.240	541	130	25	2	11	62	75	68	.332	.355
Grass	.266	455	121	20	1	17	63	56	57	.344	.426
Turf	.237	448	106	21	2	9	52	64	60	.333	.353
First Pitch	.346	130	45	6	0	7	19	4	0	.360	.554
Ahead in Count	.292	264	77	21	2	7	36	68	0	.430	.466
Behind in Count	.198	343	68	11	1	8	40	0	101	.201	.306
Two Strikes	.199	372	74	10	1	8	42	46	117	.287	.296

	Avg	AB	H	2B	3B	HR	RBI	BB	SO	OBP	SLG
Scoring Posn	.233	275	64	9	1	6	89	42	39	.323	.338
Close & Late	.255	188	48	5	1	2	23	22	29	.336	.324
None on/out	.256	211	54	12	0	9	9	27	36	.343	.441
Batting #4	.247	190	47	8	1	4	23	30	25	.348	.363
Batting #5	.237	379	90	20	1	8	44	41	49	.309	.359
Other	.269	334	90	13	1	14	48	49	43	.364	.440
April	.244	86	21	5	0	3	15	8	16	.302	.407
May	.229	170	39	3	0	5	21	27	25	.330	.335
June	.263	209	55	9	0	4	24	24	25	.336	.364
July	.242	124	30	3	1	6	17	26	16	.374	.427
August	.247	146	36	11	1	5	17	16	19	.323	.438
September/October	.274	168	46	10	1	3	21	19	16	.351	.399
Pre-All Star	.242	492	119	17	0	15	63	63	71	.324	.368
Post-All Star	.263	411	108	24	3	11	52	57	46	.355	.416

Batter vs. Pitcher (career)

Hits Best Against	Avg	AB	H	2B	3B	HR	RBI	BB	SO	OBP	SLG
Dennis Rasmussen	.478	23	11	3	0	2	5	3	1	.538	.870
Danny Jackson	.474	19	9	2	0	0	2	6	0	.577	.579
Bud Black	.462	13	6	1	0	0	0	6	2	.632	.538
Craig Lefferts	.429	14	6	0	0	1	3	3	2	.529	.643
Dwight Gooden	.333	9	3	0	0	1	2	2	0	.455	.667

Hits Worst Against	Avg	AB	H	2B	3B	HR	RBI	BB	SO	OBP	SLG
Trevor Wilson	.000	13	0	0	0	0	0	5	1	.278	.000
Chris Nabholz	.071	14	1	0	0	0	0	2	1	.188	.071
Fernando Valenzuela	.091	11	1	0	0	0	1	0	2	.083	.091
John Smiley	.150	20	3	0	0	0	0	2	5	.227	.150
Bruce Hurst	.222	9	2	0	0	0	3	1	0	.273	.222

Bob McClure — Marlins

Age 41 – Pitches Left (flyball pitcher)

	ERA	W	L	Sv	G	GS	IP	BB	SO	Avg	H	2B	3B	HR	RBI	OBP	SLG	GF	IR	IRS	Hld	SvOp	SB	CS	GB	FB	G/F
1993 Season	7.11	1	1	0	14	0	6.1	5	6	.419	13	2	0	2	8	.500	.677	1	11	4	0	2	0	2	8	10	0.80
Last Five Years	3.31	12	5	3	189	0	152.1	61	92	.261	148	23	2	14	80	.333	.383	29	180	42	33	10	6	6	188	194	0.97

1993 Season

	ERA	W	L	Sv	G	GS	IP	H	HR	BB	SO
Home	9.82	0	1	0	7	0	3.2	7	2	3	4
Away	3.38	1	0	0	7	0	2.2	6	0	2	2

	Avg	AB	H	2B	3B	HR	RBI	BB	SO	OBP	SLG
vs. Left	.450	20	9	2	0	1	5	3	3	.522	.700
vs. Right	.364	11	4	0	0	1	3	2	3	.462	.636

Last Five Years

	ERA	W	L	Sv	G	GS	IP	H	HR	BB	SO
Home	3.01	7	1	1	95	0	77.2	79	5	34	44
Away	3.62	5	4	2	94	0	74.2	69	9	27	48
Day	2.76	4	1	1	60	0	49.0	50	5	15	31
Night	3.57	8	4	2	129	0	103.1	98	9	46	61

	Avg	AB	H	2B	3B	HR	RBI	BB	SO	OBP	SLG
vs. Left	.221	249	55	10	1	7	39	30	49	.300	.353
vs. Right	.293	317	93	13	1	7	41	31	43	.360	.407
Inning 1-6	.286	42	12	1	1	0	7	6	4	.360	.357
Inning 7+	.260	524	136	22	1	14	73	55	88	.331	.385

Last Five Years

	ERA	W	L	Sv	G	GS	IP	H	HR	BB	SO
Grass	3.79	8	3	3	99	0	80.2	79	10	32	53
Turf	2.76	4	2	0	90	0	71.2	69	4	29	39
April	4.15	2	1	0	29	0	21.2	24	4	8	14
May	4.42	2	0	1	25	0	18.1	20	2	10	11
June	3.86	0	2	2	28	0	23.1	24	2	10	12
July	3.48	1	1	0	29	0	20.2	23	1	6	13
August	1.05	3	0	0	39	0	34.1	26	3	9	20
September/October	3.97	4	1	0	39	0	34.0	31	2	18	22
Starter	0.00	0	0	0	0	0	0.0	0	0	0	0
Reliever	3.31	12	5	3	189	0	152.1	148	14	61	92
0 Days rest	4.14	1	3	0	46	0	37.0	33	5	18	18
1 or 2 Days rest	3.81	4	1	1	74	0	56.2	68	5	21	27
3+ Days rest	2.30	7	1	2	69	0	58.2	47	4	22	47
Pre-All Star	4.52	4	3	3	92	0	67.2	76	8	30	38
Post-All Star	2.34	8	2	0	97	0	84.2	72	6	31	54

	Avg	AB	H	2B	3B	HR	RBI	BB	SO	OBP	SLG
None on	.262	290	76	13	1	7	7	16	41	.303	.386
Runners on	.261	276	72	10	1	7	73	45	51	.360	.380
Scoring Posn	.246	171	42	9	0	3	63	32	27	.355	.351
Close & Late	.255	212	54	9	1	4	32	27	35	.333	.363
None on/out	.232	125	29	4	1	3	3	10	15	.289	.352
vs. 1st Batr (relief)	.225	160	36	4	1	6	27	21	22	.310	.375
First Inning Pitched	.267	446	119	21	2	11	74	52	68	.341	.397
First 15 Pitches	.272	430	117	22	2	10	68	48	63	.343	.402
Pitch 16-30	.200	100	20	1	0	4	11	10	22	.278	.330
Pitch 31-45	.385	26	10	0	0	0	1	2	6	.414	.385
Pitch 46+	.100	10	1	0	0	0	0	1	1	.250	.100
First Pitch	.324	74	24	2	1	2	16	8	0	.400	.459
Ahead in Count	.244	262	64	12	1	4	28	0	72	.245	.344
Behind in Count	.283	120	34	5	0	4	19	27	0	.407	.425
Two Strikes	.202	262	53	12	1	3	20	26	92	.273	.290

Pitcher vs. Batter (since 1984)

Pitches Best Vs.	Avg	AB	H	2B	3B	HR	RBI	BB	SO	OBP	SLG
John Kruk	.100	10	1	1	0	0	0	1	2	.182	.200
Eddie Murray	.143	14	2	0	0	0	0	1	1	.200	.143
Ozzie Guillen	.167	12	2	0	0	0	2	0	0	.167	.167
Andy Van Slyke	.182	22	4	1	1	0	3	0	3	.174	.318
Barry Bonds	.231	26	6	2	1	0	1	2	1	.286	.385

Pitches Worst Vs.	Avg	AB	H	2B	3B	HR	RBI	BB	SO	OBP	SLG
Don Mattingly	.467	15	7	1	0	0	2	2	2	.529	.533
George Brett	.455	11	5	1	0	0	2	0	0	.455	.545
Tim Teufel	.444	9	4	0	0	1	4	4	2	.615	.778
Darryl Strawberry	.364	22	8	1	2	2	6	3	6	.423	.864
Steve Balboni	.364	11	4	1	0	2	3	0	5	.364	1.000

Ben McDonald — Orioles

Age 26 – Pitches Right

	ERA	W	L	Sv	G	GS	IP	BB	SO	Avg	H	2B	3B	HR	RBI	OBP	SLG	CG	ShO	Sup	QS	#P/S	SB	CS	GB	FB	G/F
1993 Season	3.39	13	14	0	34	34	220.1	86	171	.228	185	32	5	17	76	.304	.342	7	1	3.96	23	104	19	11	326	199	1.64
Career (1989-1993)	3.82	41	40	0	117	105	699.2	242	482	.237	620	113	13	76	277	.303	.377	15	5	4.32	61	103	64	24	944	765	1.23

1993 Season

	ERA	W	L	Sv	G	GS	IP	H	HR	BB	SO
Home	2.72	10	4	0	19	19	132.1	106	9	43	104
Away	4.40	3	10	0	15	15	88.0	79	8	43	67
Day	4.68	0	5	0	7	7	42.1	47	4	18	29
Night	3.08	13	9	0	27	27	178.0	138	13	68	142
Grass	3.05	13	10	0	30	30	203.1	162	13	73	158
Turf	7.41	0	4	0	4	4	17.0	23	4	13	13
April	4.44	2	2	0	5	5	26.1	33	2	15	17
May	4.70	0	3	0	5	5	30.2	28	6	6	21
June	1.69	2	2	0	6	6	37.1	29	1	18	29
July	2.57	4	2	0	6	6	42.0	28	1	14	33
August	4.81	1	2	0	5	5	33.2	38	4	13	25
September/October	3.04	4	3	0	7	7	50.1	29	3	20	46
Starter	3.39	13	14	0	34	34	220.1	185	17	86	171
Reliever	0.00	0	0	0	0	0	0.0	0	0	0	0
0-3 Days Rest	0.00	0	0	0	0	0	0.0	0	0	0	0
4 Days Rest	3.95	7	10	0	21	21	134.1	121	9	50	102
5+ Days Rest	2.51	6	4	0	13	13	86.0	64	8	36	69
Pre-All Star	3.52	5	8	0	18	18	107.1	101	9	43	73
Post-All Star	3.27	8	6	0	16	16	113.0	84	8	43	98

	Avg	AB	H	2B	3B	HR	RBI	BB	SO	OBP	SLG
vs. Left	.230	439	101	17	5	5	37	49	92	.308	.326
vs. Right	.225	373	84	15	0	12	39	37	79	.300	.362
Inning 1-6	.222	680	151	28	5	15	70	77	143	.303	.344
Inning 7+	.258	132	34	4	0	2	6	9	28	.310	.333
None on	.205	516	106	17	2	10	10	45	120	.272	.304
Runners on	.267	296	79	15	3	7	66	41	51	.358	.409
Scoring Posn	.230	165	38	6	2	4	56	30	26	.348	.364
Close & Late	.288	80	23	2	0	1	5	5	15	.329	.350
None on/out	.220	218	48	9	2	5	5	22	45	.295	.349
vs. 1st Batr (relief)	.000	0	0	0	0	0	0	0	0	.000	.000
First Inning Pitched	.210	119	25	2	1	1	11	13	24	.291	.269
First 75 Pitches	.217	549	119	22	5	12	55	62	120	.297	.341
Pitch 76-90	.255	102	26	5	0	3	7	10	16	.333	.392
Pitch 91-105	.238	101	24	3	0	1	12	9	22	.300	.297
Pitch 106+	.267	60	16	2	0	1	2	5	13	.333	.350
First Pitch	.326	86	28	10	0	3	12	0	0	.326	.547
Ahead in Count	.134	337	45	11	0	4	9	0	149	.141	.202
Behind in Count	.343	213	73	9	1	8	37	50	0	.463	.507
Two Strikes	.135	385	52	12	0	5	16	36	171	.213	.205

Career (1989-1993)

	ERA	W	L	Sv	G	GS	IP	H	HR	BB	SO
Home	3.59	21	19	0	63	56	401.2	359	44	115	272
Away	4.14	20	21	0	54	49	298.0	261	32	127	210
Day	5.02	5	12	0	29	25	152.1	157	17	66	108
Night	3.49	36	28	0	88	80	547.1	463	59	176	374
Grass	3.64	36	34	0	104	93	633.1	544	63	215	431
Turf	5.56	5	6	0	13	12	66.1	76	13	27	51
April	5.05	4	3	0	11	11	57.0	66	6	31	40
May	4.73	6	7	0	16	16	97.0	83	17	26	67
June	3.87	3	5	0	12	12	74.1	67	9	27	55
July	3.23	12	6	0	27	21	156.0	131	15	44	112
August	4.32	6	11	0	22	22	145.2	154	16	53	85
September/October	2.97	10	8	0	29	23	169.2	119	13	61	123
Starter	3.81	40	40	0	105	105	682.2	604	74	237	474
Reliever	4.24	1	0	0	12	0	17.0	16	2	5	8
0-3 Days Rest	4.98	2	2	0	4	4	21.2	19	2	8	12
4 Days Rest	4.26	22	29	0	69	69	443.2	415	54	157	301
5+ Days Rest	2.77	16	9	0	32	32	217.1	170	18	72	161
Pre-All Star	4.52	16	17	0	48	46	276.2	258	38	101	188
Post-All Star	3.36	25	23	0	69	59	423.0	362	38	141	294

	Avg	AB	H	2B	3B	HR	RBI	BB	SO	OBP	SLG
vs. Left	.220	1329	293	51	8	29	118	139	255	.294	.336
vs. Right	.254	1286	327	62	5	47	159	103	227	.313	.420
Inning 1-6	.234	2158	504	92	13	58	233	212	408	.303	.369
Inning 7+	.254	457	116	21	0	18	44	30	74	.303	.418
None on	.218	1658	362	65	6	46	46	136	322	.281	.348
Runners on	.270	957	258	48	7	30	231	106	160	.340	.428
Scoring Posn	.252	523	132	24	5	16	191	74	94	.338	.409
Close & Late	.244	246	60	11	0	10	29	18	40	.297	.411
None on/out	.218	706	154	34	5	21	21	55	132	.278	.370
vs. 1st Batr (relief)	.182	11	2	1	0	0	0	1	1	.250	.273
First Inning Pitched	.206	412	85	11	3	10	42	43	73	.283	.320
First 75 Pitches	.232	1811	420	76	13	49	187	174	352	.301	.369
Pitch 76-90	.243	341	83	13	0	8	30	24	50	.295	.352
Pitch 91-105	.248	278	69	17	0	10	41	27	41	.316	.417
Pitch 106+	.259	185	48	7	0	9	19	17	39	.327	.443
First Pitch	.314	344	108	26	1	14	56	6	0	.329	.517
Ahead in Count	.171	1060	181	34	5	18	54	0	407	.177	.263
Behind in Count	.315	695	219	36	3	35	112	127	0	.416	.527
Two Strikes	.159	1159	184	39	4	20	67	109	482	.234	.251

Pitcher vs. Batter (career)

Pitches Best Vs.	Avg	AB	H	2B	3B	HR	RBI	BB	SO	OBP	SLG
Billy Hatcher	.000	13	0	0	0	0	0	1	5	.071	.000
Ron Karkovice	.000	12	0	0	0	0	0	0	3	.000	.000
Jerry Browne	.000	10	0	0	0	0	0	2	0	.167	.000

Pitches Worst Vs.	Avg	AB	H	2B	3B	HR	RBI	BB	SO	OBP	SLG
Steve Sax	.571	14	8	1	1	1	3	0	1	.533	1.000
Shane Mack	.538	13	7	2	0	2	4	2	1	.600	1.154
Harold Baines	.462	13	6	1	0	2	5	2	1	.533	1.000

Pitcher vs. Batter (career)																						
Pitches Best Vs.	Avg	AB	H	2B	3B	HR	RBI	BB	SO	OBP	SLG	Pitches Worst Vs.	Avg	AB	H	2B	3B	HR	RBI	BB	SO	OBP	SLG
Reggie Jefferson	.000	10	0	0	0	0	0	1	1	.091	.000	Joe Carter	.455	22	10	2	1	4	11	0	1	.455	1.182
Ruben Sierra	.050	20	1	0	0	0	0	1	1	.095	.050	Cecil Fielder	.412	17	7	0	0	3	4	3	4	.500	.941

Jack McDowell — White Sox

Age 28 – Pitches Right

	ERA	W	L	Sv	G	GS	IP	BB	SO	Avg	H	2B	3B	HR	RBI	OBP	SLG	CG	ShO	Sup	QS	#P/S	SB	CS	GB	FB	G/F
1993 Season	3.37	22	10	0	34	34	256.2	69	158	.266	261	43	4	20	93	.314	.379	10	4	5.40	21	110	10	15	345	261	1.32
Last Five Years	3.42	73	39	0	136	136	976.0	303	692	.248	909	164	25	80	355	.307	.371	42	8	5.41	87	110	84	52	1135	1091	1.04

1993 Season

	ERA	W	L	Sv	G	GS	IP	H	HR	BB	SO		Avg	AB	H	2B	3B	HR	RBI	BB	SO	OBP	SLG
Home	4.19	9	7	0	18	18	131.0	154	11	32	70	vs. Left	.258	493	127	21	1	8	41	33	82	.302	.353
Away	2.51	13	3	0	16	16	125.2	107	9	37	88	vs. Right	.275	488	134	22	3	12	52	36	76	.326	.406
Day	3.94	5	4	0	9	9	64.0	68	5	19	48	Inning 1-6	.269	752	202	34	4	15	75	56	122	.319	.384
Night	3.18	17	6	0	25	25	192.2	193	15	50	110	Inning 7+	.258	229	59	9	0	5	18	13	36	.300	.362
Grass	3.56	18	9	0	29	29	219.2	229	18	54	129	None on	.279	567	158	26	2	12	12	37	92	.326	.395
Turf	2.19	4	1	0	5	5	37.0	32	2	15	29	Runners on	.249	414	103	17	2	8	81	32	66	.299	.357
April	4.33	5	0	0	5	5	35.1	41	3	14	17	Scoring Posn	.239	222	53	8	2	2	65	20	39	.294	.320
May	4.15	2	4	0	6	6	47.2	46	7	11	30	Close & Late	.244	127	31	3	0	4	11	6	20	.284	.362
June	2.97	5	0	0	5	5	36.1	37	2	10	18	None on/out	.278	255	71	14	0	7	7	13	36	.319	.416
July	3.83	4	2	0	6	6	44.2	48	3	13	29	vs. 1st Batr (relief)	.000	0	0	0	0	0	0	0	0	.000	.000
August	1.74	4	1	0	6	6	51.2	52	1	10	38	First Inning Pitched	.288	125	36	6	1	2	15	12	27	.350	.400
September/October	3.51	2	3	0	6	6	41.0	37	4	11	26	First 75 Pitches	.282	628	177	31	4	14	68	50	96	.334	.411
Starter	3.37	22	10	0	34	34	256.2	261	20	69	158	Pitch 76-90	.207	135	28	3	0	1	4	7	24	.246	.252
Reliever	0.00	0	0	0	0	0	0.0	0	0	0	0	Pitch 91-105	.252	135	34	6	0	2	12	5	19	.284	.341
0-3 Days Rest	0.00	0	0	0	0	0	0.0	0	0	0	0	Pitch 106+	.265	83	22	3	0	3	9	7	19	.322	.410
4 Days Rest	3.25	14	7	0	22	22	171.2	181	12	42	104	First Pitch	.284	155	44	6	0	8	26	5	0	.311	.477
5+ Days Rest	3.60	8	3	0	12	12	85.0	80	8	27	54	Ahead in Count	.223	476	106	14	2	6	42	0	135	.222	.298
Pre-All Star	3.88	13	6	0	19	19	141.2	144	14	43	75	Behind in Count	.304	181	55	16	2	3	10	40	0	.429	.464
Post-All Star	2.74	9	4	0	15	15	115.0	117	6	26	83	Two Strikes	.209	444	93	16	1	4	29	24	158	.249	.277

Last Five Years

	ERA	W	L	Sv	G	GS	IP	H	HR	BB	SO		Avg	AB	H	2B	3B	HR	RBI	BB	SO	OBP	SLG
Home	3.56	37	22	0	73	73	518.1	499	42	160	362	vs. Left	.247	1872	463	79	13	39	164	153	327	.306	.366
Away	3.26	36	17	0	63	63	457.2	410	38	143	330	vs. Right	.248	1798	446	85	12	41	191	150	365	.309	.377
Day	3.62	21	13	0	42	42	301.0	270	28	99	214	Inning 1-6	.251	2886	723	134	22	69	298	248	548	.312	.384
Night	3.33	52	26	0	94	94	675.0	639	52	204	478	Inning 7+	.237	784	186	30	3	11	57	55	144	.290	.325
Grass	3.44	63	33	0	116	116	833.2	772	70	258	603	None on	.245	2221	544	90	17	45	45	172	433	.303	.362
Turf	3.29	10	6	0	20	20	142.1	137	10	45	89	Runners on	.252	1449	365	74	8	35	310	131	259	.313	.386
April	3.70	15	2	0	19	19	126.1	110	16	38	87	Scoring Posn	.243	785	191	41	5	18	253	90	162	.317	.377
May	4.71	5	11	0	22	22	147.0	156	21	50	113	Close & Late	.230	378	87	14	2	6	28	25	82	.282	.325
June	2.55	17	2	0	23	23	169.1	142	9	56	112	None on/out	.238	974	232	42	7	22	22	60	187	.286	.363
July	3.63	12	6	0	21	21	161.0	156	10	45	113	vs. 1st Batr (relief)	.000	0	0	0	0	0	0	0	0	.000	.000
August	2.60	15	7	0	25	25	194.0	174	11	52	136	First Inning Pitched	.270	519	140	26	5	12	63	42	104	.326	.408
September/October	3.68	9	11	0	26	26	178.1	171	13	62	131	First 75 Pitches	.253	2409	609	116	16	59	256	203	449	.313	.388
Starter	3.42	73	39	0	136	136	976.0	909	80	303	692	Pitch 76-90	.234	475	111	19	4	7	29	32	85	.283	.335
Reliever	0.00	0	0	0	0	0	0.0	0	0	0	0	Pitch 91-105	.255	419	107	21	4	9	45	36	75	.319	.389
0-3 Days Rest	2.35	2	0	0	3	3	23.0	18	1	3	8	Pitch 106+	.223	367	82	8	1	5	25	32	83	.287	.292
4 Days Rest	3.23	50	25	0	91	91	665.1	632	47	215	472	First Pitch	.275	541	149	24	2	21	74	15	0	.300	.444
5+ Days Rest	3.94	21	14	0	42	42	287.2	259	32	85	212	Ahead in Count	.213	1815	386	60	12	27	148	0	598	.216	.304
Pre-All Star	3.63	40	18	0	71	71	495.2	459	50	161	343	Behind in Count	.304	698	212	50	8	25	86	156	0	.430	.506
Post-All Star	3.20	33	21	0	65	65	480.1	450	30	142	349	Two Strikes	.187	1746	327	57	11	22	116	132	692	.245	.270

Pitcher vs. Batter (career)

Pitches Best Vs.	Avg	AB	H	2B	3B	HR	RBI	BB	SO	OBP	SLG	Pitches Worst Vs.	Avg	AB	H	2B	3B	HR	RBI	BB	SO	OBP	SLG
Willie Wilson	.000	13	0	0	0	0	0	0	4	.000	.000	Gary Sheffield	.545	11	6	2	0	0	2	2	0	.615	.727
Kurt Stillwell	.000	10	0	0	0	0	1	2	1	.154	.000	Roberto Alomar	.526	19	10	0	0	1	3	4	5	.609	.684
Walt Weiss	.048	21	1	0	0	0	1	0	4	.048	.048	Chris Hoiles	.476	21	10	2	1	1	3	2	2	.522	.810
Billy Ripken	.077	13	1	0	0	0	1	0	2	.077	.077	Joe Orsulak	.458	24	11	2	0	2	5	1	1	.480	.792
George Bell	.091	11	1	0	0	0	1	0	2	.083	.091	Fred McGriff	.400	10	4	1	1	1	1	1	3	.455	1.000

Roger McDowell — Dodgers

Age 33 – Pitches Right (groundball pitcher)

	ERA	W	L	Sv	G	GS	IP	BB	SO	Avg	H	2B	3B	HR	RBI	OBP	SLG	GF	IR	IRS	Hld	SvOp	SB	CS	GB	FB	G/F
1993 Season	2.25	5	3	2	54	0	68.0	30	27	.288	76	9	2	2	32	.364	.360	19	30	9	3	3	8	6	145	40	3.63
Last Five Years	3.03	30	38	71	331	0	431.1	193	213	.274	450	67	9	14	216	.351	.351	152	206	67	21	96	37	16	903	258	3.50

1993 Season

	ERA	W	L	Sv	G	GS	IP	H	HR	BB	SO		Avg	AB	H	2B	3B	HR	RBI	BB	SO	OBP	SLG
Home	2.45	2	1	0	24	0	33.0	40	2	15	12	vs. Left	.315	124	39	6	1	1	20	17	11	.401	.403
Away	2.06	3	2	2	30	0	35.0	36	0	15	15	vs. Right	.264	140	37	3	1	1	12	13	16	.329	.321
Starter	0.00	0	0	0	0	0	0.0	0	0	0	0	Scoring Posn	.247	85	21	3	1	1	26	19	12	.393	.341
Reliever	2.25	5	3	2	54	0	68.0	76	2	30	27	Close & Late	.216	88	19	1	1	0	13	14	10	.327	.250
0 Days rest	1.54	1	0	1	8	0	11.2	10	0	2	6	None on/out	.246	61	15	1	0	0	0	3	5	.281	.262
1 or 2 Days rest	1.88	2	1	1	25	0	28.2	37	2	7	11	First Pitch	.241	54	13	2	2	0	7	6	0	.311	.352
3+ Days rest	2.93	2	2	0	21	0	27.2	29	0	21	10	Ahead in Count	.192	104	20	2	0	1	10	0	23	.208	.240
Pre-All Star	1.42	4	0	2	35	0	44.1	45	1	12	18	Behind in Count	.356	59	21	1	0	1	8	13	0	.472	.424
Post-All Star	3.80	1	3	0	19	0	23.2	31	1	18	9	Two Strikes	.213	89	19	1	0	1	6	11	27	.300	.258

Last Five Years

	ERA	W	L	Sv	G	GS	IP	H	HR	BB	SO
Home	3.15	16	17	32	153	0	197.1	211	7	76	103
Away	2.92	14	21	39	178	0	234.0	239	7	117	110
Day	3.30	7	12	18	96	0	125.1	134	6	62	63
Night	2.91	23	26	53	235	0	306.0	316	8	131	150
Grass	2.83	17	21	34	178	0	235.2	251	10	100	114
Turf	3.27	13	17	37	153	0	195.2	199	4	93	99
April	2.11	7	2	12	44	0	59.2	43	1	22	33
May	3.58	4	8	14	55	0	73.0	86	2	28	32
June	4.00	3	9	7	56	0	69.2	85	2	41	35
July	2.42	2	3	12	51	0	63.1	59	3	28	37
August	3.07	7	8	7	63	0	88.0	89	5	39	41
September/October	2.78	7	8	19	62	0	77.2	88	1	35	35
Starter	0.00	0	0	0	0	0	0.0	0	0	0	0
Reliever	3.03	30	38	71	331	0	431.1	450	14	193	213
0 Days rest	4.11	7	15	25	86	0	105.0	117	4	45	45
1 or 2 Days rest	2.59	17	17	28	162	0	212.0	224	8	93	110
3+ Days rest	2.83	6	6	18	83	0	114.1	109	2	55	58
Pre-All Star	2.97	16	19	37	173	0	230.1	234	5	103	116
Post-All Star	3.09	14	19	34	158	0	201.0	216	9	90	97

	Avg	AB	H	2B	3B	HR	RBI	BB	SO	OBP	SLG
vs. Left	.297	842	250	34	6	11	134	137	89	.396	.391
vs. Right	.250	801	200	33	3	3	82	56	124	.301	.310
Inning 1-6	.291	86	25	3	1	0	14	13	7	.396	.349
Inning 7+	.273	1557	425	64	8	14	202	180	206	.349	.351
None on	.279	780	218	32	5	6	6	66	95	.337	.356
Runners on	.269	863	232	35	4	8	210	127	118	.363	.346
Scoring Posn	.252	576	145	21	3	6	198	112	85	.373	.330
Close & Late	.280	867	243	33	4	8	127	118	109	.366	.355
None on/out	.268	358	96	18	2	0	0	28	50	.323	.330
vs. 1st Batr (relief)	.287	279	80	17	1	0	26	19	40	.333	.355
First Inning Pitched	.275	1041	286	42	6	7	140	118	139	.349	.347
First 15 Pitches	.270	1061	286	43	8	5	114	113	126	.340	.339
Pitch 16-30	.272	481	131	21	1	8	83	65	73	.365	.370
Pitch 31-45	.333	87	29	3	0	1	18	12	11	.402	.402
Pitch 46+	.286	14	4	0	0	0	1	3	3	.412	.286
First Pitch	.262	298	78	15	3	2	37	48	0	.364	.352
Ahead in Count	.238	717	171	28	3	4	78	0	183	.241	.303
Behind in Count	.333	345	115	13	0	7	68	78	0	.457	.432
Two Strikes	.227	644	146	20	2	3	63	66	213	.297	.278

Pitcher vs. Batter (career)

Pitches Best Vs.	Avg	AB	H	2B	3B	HR	RBI	BB	SO	OBP	SLG
Gerald Young	.000	12	0	0	0	0	0	2	2	.143	.000
Gerald Perry	.063	16	1	1	0	0	0	2	3	.167	.125
Dwight Smith	.083	12	1	0	0	0	0	0	0	.083	.083
Juan Samuel	.120	25	3	0	0	0	3	3	3	.207	.120
Andres Galarraga	.150	20	3	0	0	0	0	0	4	.150	.150

Pitches Worst Vs.	Avg	AB	H	2B	3B	HR	RBI	BB	SO	OBP	SLG
Eddie Murray	.600	10	6	2	0	0	2	2	0	.667	.800
Jeff Bagwell	.538	13	7	1	0	1	4	0	1	.500	.846
Andy Van Slyke	.500	24	12	3	0	2	5	2	3	.538	.875
Dave Magadan	.444	9	4	1	0	1	5	2	3	.500	.889
Terry Pendleton	.382	34	13	2	0	4	12	6	5	.475	.794

Chuck McElroy — Cubs

Age 26 – Pitches Left

	ERA	W	L	Sv	G	GS	IP	BB	SO	Avg	H	2B	3B	HR	RBI	OBP	SLG	GF	IR	IRS	Hld	SvOp	SB	CS	GB	FB	G/F
1993 Season	4.56	2	2	0	49	0	47.1	25	31	.280	51	9	0	4	23	.368	.396	11	23	8	4	0	4	2	53	52	1.02
Career (1989-1993)	3.26	12	12	9	219	0	256.2	147	230	.247	233	49	4	17	121	.345	.361	61	148	50	17	17	23	15	279	262	1.06

1993 Season

	ERA	W	L	Sv	G	GS	IP	H	HR	BB	SO
Home	5.47	1	1	0	25	0	26.1	31	3	17	10
Away	3.43	1	1	0	24	0	21.0	20	1	8	21
Starter	0.00	0	0	0	0	0	0.0	0	0	0	0
Reliever	4.56	2	2	0	49	0	47.1	51	4	25	31
0 Days rest	4.05	0	1	0	12	0	13.1	9	2	4	11
1 or 2 Days rest	4.26	0	0	0	21	0	19.0	24	1	13	10
3+ Days rest	5.40	2	1	0	16	0	15.0	18	1	8	10
Pre-All Star	4.75	2	2	0	27	0	30.1	30	4	16	23
Post-All Star	4.24	0	0	0	22	0	17.0	21	0	9	8

	Avg	AB	H	2B	3B	HR	RBI	BB	SO	OBP	SLG
vs. Left	.303	66	20	2	0	2	9	12	10	.405	.424
vs. Right	.267	116	31	7	0	2	14	13	21	.346	.379
Scoring Posn	.306	49	15	2	0	2	19	11	6	.435	.469
Close & Late	.321	28	9	3	0	0	4	3	6	.387	.429
None on/out	.310	42	13	1	0	1	1	5	6	.383	.405
First Pitch	.417	24	10	1	0	0	0	5	0	.517	.458
Ahead in Count	.224	76	17	5	0	0	10	0	24	.234	.289
Behind in Count	.293	41	12	2	0	1	6	14	0	.464	.415
Two Strikes	.195	77	15	4	0	0	6	6	31	.262	.247

Career (1989-1993)

	ERA	W	L	Sv	G	GS	IP	H	HR	BB	SO
Home	3.49	7	7	4	115	0	142.0	137	8	75	122
Away	2.98	5	5	5	104	0	114.2	96	9	72	108
Day	3.01	9	3	7	110	0	134.2	112	8	69	118
Night	3.54	3	9	2	109	0	122.0	121	9	78	112
Grass	2.86	9	7	7	141	0	179.1	153	12	92	147
Turf	4.19	3	5	2	78	0	77.1	80	5	55	83
April	2.27	2	0	3	34	0	35.2	18	1	21	45
May	3.27	3	4	3	32	0	41.1	36	2	21	30
June	3.21	4	2	0	30	0	42.0	42	6	27	35
July	2.83	1	3	1	27	0	35.0	29	4	15	29
August	3.46	1	1	2	37	0	41.2	40	2	23	35
September/October	3.98	1	2	0	59	0	61.0	68	2	40	56
Starter	0.00	0	0	0	0	0	0.0	0	0	0	0
Reliever	3.26	12	12	9	219	0	256.2	233	17	147	230
0 Days rest	3.03	2	4	2	57	0	59.1	47	5	30	56
1 or 2 Days rest	2.91	7	6	4	104	0	127.0	114	6	73	110
3+ Days rest	4.09	3	2	3	58	0	70.1	72	6	44	64
Pre-All Star	2.92	10	6	6	108	0	132.1	104	9	72	120
Post-All Star	3.62	2	6	3	111	0	124.1	129	8	75	110

	Avg	AB	H	2B	3B	HR	RBI	BB	SO	OBP	SLG
vs. Left	.245	319	78	16	1	7	44	47	86	.336	.367
vs. Right	.248	625	155	33	3	10	77	100	144	.349	.358
Inning 1-6	.235	234	55	7	1	4	39	41	55	.349	.325
Inning 7+	.251	710	178	42	3	13	82	106	175	.343	.373
None on	.246	479	118	26	2	10	10	67	117	.339	.372
Runners on	.247	465	115	23	2	7	111	80	113	.351	.351
Scoring Posn	.255	275	70	13	2	6	104	61	69	.377	.382
Close & Late	.256	352	90	25	3	4	43	62	96	.363	.378
None on/out	.255	216	55	13	1	2	2	29	51	.343	.352
vs. 1st Batr (relief)	.317	186	59	14	1	2	32	25	44	.391	.435
First Inning Pitched	.261	652	170	35	4	10	88	95	159	.350	.373
First 15 Pitches	.273	597	163	36	4	10	79	87	131	.361	.397
Pitch 16-30	.213	272	58	12	0	4	30	49	76	.331	.301
Pitch 31-45	.180	61	11	0	0	3	10	6	21	.250	.328
Pitch 46+	.071	14	1	1	0	0	2	5	2	.316	.143
First Pitch	.336	131	44	11	2	2	18	24	0	.425	.496
Ahead in Count	.219	452	99	22	2	5	48	0	189	.219	.310
Behind in Count	.260	181	47	10	0	5	27	66	0	.450	.398
Two Strikes	.195	483	94	22	2	5	48	57	230	.280	.280

Pitcher vs. Batter (career)

Pitches Best Vs.	Avg	AB	H	2B	3B	HR	RBI	BB	SO	OBP	SLG
Barry Bonds	.056	18	1	1	0	0	1	1	3	.100	.111
Darren Daulton	.091	11	1	0	0	0	1	0	5	.083	.091
Todd Zeile	.100	10	1	0	0	0	0	2	0	.250	.100
Orlando Merced	.111	9	1	0	0	0	0	2	1	.273	.111
John Kruk	.167	12	2	0	0	0	0	1	2	.231	.167

Pitches Worst Vs.	Avg	AB	H	2B	3B	HR	RBI	BB	SO	OBP	SLG
Brett Butler	.500	6	3	1	0	0	1	6	2	.750	.667
Bobby Bonilla	.455	11	5	1	0	0	0	2	4	.538	.545
Larry Walker	.417	12	5	1	0	0	3	2	3	.500	.500
Eddie Murray	.375	8	3	0	0	0	3	5	0	.615	.375
Ray Lankford	.308	13	4	0	0	0	1	6	7	.526	.308

Willie McGee — Giants

Age 35 – Bats Both (groundball hitter)

	Avg	G	AB	R	H	2B	3B	HR	RBI	BB	SO	HBP	GDP	SB	CS	OBP	SLG	IBB	SH	SF	#Pit	#P/PA	GB	FB	G/F
1993 Season	.301	130	475	53	143	28	1	4	46	38	67	1	12	10	9	.353	.389	7	3	2	1758	3.39	253	73	3.47
Last Five Years	.303	611	2259	298	685	123	15	15	219	159	367	6	45	79	37	.350	.391	19	16	8	8775	3.58	1185	331	3.58

1993 Season

	Avg	AB	H	2B	3B	HR	RBI	BB	SO	OBP	SLG
vs. Left	.319	144	46	9	0	1	13	7	21	.349	.403
vs. Right	.293	331	97	19	1	3	33	31	46	.354	.384
Groundball	.316	152	48	9	0	2	11	10	19	.358	.414
Flyball	.286	63	18	5	1	1	6	6	9	.348	.444
Home	.318	217	69	12	1	0	14	19	31	.374	.382
Away	.287	258	74	16	0	4	32	19	36	.335	.395
Day	.274	215	59	11	1	3	19	16	32	.325	.377
Night	.323	260	84	17	0	1	27	22	35	.375	.400
Grass	.306	373	114	23	1	2	36	28	48	.354	.389
Turf	.284	102	29	5	0	2	10	10	19	.348	.392
First Pitch	.380	92	35	9	0	2	12	7	0	.424	.543
Ahead in Count	.379	87	33	8	0	1	14	21	0	.500	.506
Behind in Count	.243	210	51	8	0	0	10	0	59	.242	.281
Two Strikes	.220	191	42	6	1	0	10	10	67	.257	.262

	Avg	AB	H	2B	3B	HR	RBI	BB	SO	OBP	SLG
Scoring Posn	.300	120	36	6	1	1	42	19	10	.394	.392
Close & Late	.400	75	30	4	0	1	9	5	10	.438	.493
None on/out	.288	132	38	7	0	0	0	9	21	.333	.341
Batting #1	.282	163	46	6	0	1	8	10	27	.322	.337
Batting #6	.342	187	64	12	1	1	21	14	20	.391	.433
Other	.264	125	33	10	0	2	17	14	20	.336	.392
April	.266	94	25	4	0	0	5	6	17	.310	.309
May	.375	96	36	7	1	1	8	8	9	.419	.500
June	.344	61	21	7	0	0	7	6	7	.397	.459
July	.455	33	15	3	0	1	7	3	3	.500	.636
August	.235	102	24	3	0	2	16	5	14	.278	.324
September/October	.247	89	22	4	0	0	3	10	17	.323	.292
Pre-All Star	.338	275	93	20	1	2	25	23	36	.387	.440
Post-All Star	.250	200	50	8	0	2	21	15	31	.306	.320

1993 By Position

Position	Avg	AB	H	2B	3B	HR	RBI	BB	SO	OBP	SLG	G	GS	Innings	PO	A	E	DP	Fld Pct	Rng Fctr	In Zone	Outs	Zone Rtg	MLB Zone
As rf	.303	468	142	27	1	4	46	37	65	.354	.391	126	120	1041.2	224	10	5	1	.979	2.02	247	213	.862	.826

Last Five Years

	Avg	AB	H	2B	3B	HR	RBI	BB	SO	OBP	SLG
vs. Left	.300	759	228	38	6	8	82	35	139	.331	.398
vs. Right	.305	1500	457	85	9	7	137	124	228	.358	.387
Groundball	.321	766	246	38	9	7	81	49	122	.363	.422
Flyball	.289	433	125	23	4	4	35	32	71	.338	.388
Home	.307	1097	337	60	7	4	101	76	152	.351	.386
Away	.299	1162	348	63	8	11	118	83	215	.348	.396
Day	.328	813	267	44	8	7	87	57	123	.372	.428
Night	.289	1446	418	79	7	8	132	102	244	.337	.370
Grass	.297	1335	397	67	8	8	127	97	212	.345	.378
Turf	.312	924	288	56	7	7	92	62	155	.356	.410
First Pitch	.388	379	147	36	0	6	52	12	0	.408	.530
Ahead in Count	.378	386	146	38	4	3	51	86	0	.488	.521
Behind in Count	.253	1079	273	33	7	4	75	0	318	.255	.308
Two Strikes	.227	1009	229	23	6	3	68	56	367	.270	.271

	Avg	AB	H	2B	3B	HR	RBI	BB	SO	OBP	SLG
Scoring Posn	.315	555	175	33	4	1	188	70	85	.390	.395
Close & Late	.335	388	130	20	1	3	48	25	66	.374	.415
None on/out	.277	573	159	25	2	5	5	34	104	.320	.354
Batting #1	.286	475	136	23	1	2	30	22	79	.321	.352
Batting #2	.299	894	267	52	8	5	82	62	152	.344	.391
Other	.317	890	282	48	6	8	107	75	136	.370	.411
April	.307	322	99	16	2	3	29	25	59	.356	.398
May	.293	478	140	28	5	4	42	27	67	.329	.397
June	.332	361	120	21	2	1	29	37	55	.393	.410
July	.333	243	81	18	0	3	30	15	49	.375	.444
August	.286	448	128	24	2	4	58	23	67	.324	.375
September/October	.287	407	117	16	4	0	31	32	70	.339	.346
Pre-All Star	.315	1240	390	74	9	9	108	97	197	.363	.410
Post-All Star	.289	1019	295	49	6	6	111	62	170	.333	.367

Batter vs. Pitcher (since 1984)

Hits Best Against	Avg	AB	H	2B	3B	HR	RBI	BB	SO	OBP	SLG
Darryl Kile	.588	17	10	2	0	0	3	3	3	.650	.706
Derek Lilliquist	.538	13	7	0	1	1	2	1	0	.571	.923
Paul Assenmacher	.533	15	8	1	0	0	3	1	3	.563	.600
Ted Power	.462	13	6	2	1	0	5	0	2	.462	.769
Bobby Ojeda	.375	40	15	6	1	3	9	1	5	.390	.800

Hits Worst Against	Avg	AB	H	2B	3B	HR	RBI	BB	SO	OBP	SLG
Kelly Downs	.083	12	1	0	0	0	1	0	2	.083	.083
Frank Castillo	.091	11	1	0	0	0	0	1	1	.167	.091
Tim Wakefield	.133	15	2	0	0	0	1	0	4	.133	.133
Norm Charlton	.143	14	2	0	0	0	0	0	6	.143	.143
Dennis Cook	.182	11	2	0	0	0	1	0	1	.167	.182

Kevin McGehee — Orioles

Age 25 – Pitches Right (flyball pitcher)

	ERA	W	L	Sv	G	GS	IP	BB	SO	Avg	H	2B	3B	HR	RBI	OBP	SLG	GF	IR	IRS	Hld	SvOp	SB	CS	GB	FB	G/F
1993 Season	5.94	0	0	0	5	0	16.2	7	7	.281	18	5	1	5	13	.365	.625	1	7	2	0	0	2	0	18	25	0.72

1993 Season

	ERA	W	L	Sv	G	GS	IP	H	HR	BB	SO
Home	4.35	0	0	0	3	0	10.1	9	1	6	2
Away	8.53	0	0	0	2	0	6.1	9	4	1	5

	Avg	AB	H	2B	3B	HR	RBI	BB	SO	OBP	SLG
vs. Left	.150	20	3	1	0	1	2	4	2	.320	.350
vs. Right	.341	44	15	4	1	4	11	3	5	.388	.750

Fred McGriff — Braves

Age 30 – Bats Left

	Avg	G	AB	R	H	2B	3B	HR	RBI	BB	SO	HBP	GDP	SB	CS	OBP	SLG	IBB	SH	SF	#Pit	#P/PA	GB	FB	G/F
1993 Season	.291	151	557	111	162	29	2	37	101	76	106	2	14	5	3	.375	.549	6	0	5	2458	3.84	166	176	0.94
Last Five Years	.285	770	2724	463	776	126	11	174	491	490	589	11	63	29	17	.393	.531	79	2	25	12457	3.83	887	763	1.16

1993 Season

	Avg	AB	H	2B	3B	HR	RBI	BB	SO	OBP	SLG
vs. Left	.274	201	55	9	1	8	30	25	38	.354	.448
vs. Right	.301	356	107	20	1	29	71	51	68	.386	.607
Groundball	.287	178	51	10	0	17	35	20	36	.361	.629
Flyball	.308	104	32	8	2	3	19	17	17	.405	.510
Home	.282	255	72	10	0	15	47	44	47	.387	.498
Away	.298	302	90	19	2	22	54	32	59	.364	.593
Day	.311	167	52	11	0	11	25	18	30	.376	.575
Night	.282	390	110	18	2	26	76	58	76	.374	.538
Grass	.290	417	121	19	1	25	71	53	80	.368	.520
Turf	.293	140	41	10	1	12	30	23	26	.394	.636
First Pitch	.352	88	31	4	0	9	23	5	0	.379	.705

	Avg	AB	H	2B	3B	HR	RBI	BB	SO	OBP	SLG
Scoring Posn	.269	145	39	8	1	6	59	32	30	.393	.462
Close & Late	.309	81	25	4	0	7	17	13	20	.406	.617
None on/out	.307	163	50	9	1	10	10	10	26	.347	.558
Batting #3	.200	20	4	0	0	1	1	2	3	.273	.350
Batting #4	.293	535	157	28	2	36	100	74	103	.378	.555
Other	.500	2	1	1	0	0	0	0	0	.500	1.000
April	.190	79	15	3	0	3	7	11	22	.293	.342
May	.308	104	32	2	0	7	18	14	18	.387	.529
June	.262	84	22	3	1	6	11	15	11	.374	.536
July	.413	80	33	7	1	9	22	4	9	.430	.863
August	.272	103	28	6	0	6	18	8	21	.321	.505

1993 Season

	Avg	AB	H	2B	3B	HR	RBI	BB	SO	OBP	SLG		Avg	AB	H	2B	3B	HR	RBI	BB	SO	OBP	SLG
Ahead in Count	.395	147	58	15	0	15	40	28	0	.491	.803	September/October	.299	107	32	8	0	6	25	24	25	.432	.542
Behind in Count	.192	213	41	4	2	6	25	0	82	.194	.315	Pre-All Star	.275	302	83	11	1	18	46	42	55	.361	.497
Two Strikes	.191	256	49	6	2	6	22	43	106	.307	.301	Post-All Star	.310	255	79	18	1	19	55	34	51	.392	.612

1993 By Position

Position	Avg	AB	H	2B	3B	HR	RBI	BB	SO	OBP	SLG	G	GS	Innings	PO	A	E	DP	Fld Pct	Rng Fctr	In Zone	Outs	Zone Rtg	MLB Zone
As 1b	.290	555	161	28	2	37	101	76	106	.375	.548	150	150	1290.2	1213	89	17	101	.987	---	231	197	.853	.834

Last Five Years

	Avg	AB	H	2B	3B	HR	RBI	BB	SO	OBP	SLG		Avg	AB	H	2B	3B	HR	RBI	BB	SO	OBP	SLG
vs. Left	.268	1010	271	35	8	48	181	144	241	.358	.461	Scoring Posn	.270	684	185	34	5	34	297	211	166	.432	.484
vs. Right	.295	1714	505	91	3	126	310	346	348	.413	.572	Close & Late	.276	410	113	23	1	19	63	84	101	.396	.476
Groundball	.302	852	257	49	2	55	148	156	178	.408	.558	None on/out	.291	757	220	34	4	48	48	87	147	.364	.536
Flyball	.265	528	140	28	3	32	94	100	111	.380	.511	Batting #4	.284	1873	531	88	7	113	341	340	400	.392	.519
Home	.285	1304	372	59	4	86	242	261	261	.405	.535	Batting #5	.294	778	229	37	4	58	140	138	169	.401	.576
Away	.285	1420	404	67	7	88	249	229	328	.382	.527	Other	.219	73	16	1	0	3	10	12	20	.333	.356
Day	.276	807	223	43	3	45	135	127	159	.373	.504	April	.275	385	106	13	2	22	60	79	101	.400	.491
Night	.288	1917	553	83	8	129	356	363	430	.401	.542	May	.294	476	140	24	2	29	82	70	101	.386	.536
Grass	.286	1639	468	76	4	102	286	287	369	.390	.523	June	.266	410	109	18	1	27	79	87	76	.393	.512
Turf	.284	1085	308	50	7	72	205	203	220	.397	.542	July	.304	447	136	20	2	37	86	61	93	.385	.606
First Pitch	.354	396	140	20	2	42	100	55	0	.430	.732	August	.279	484	135	23	3	36	91	88	114	.386	.562
Ahead in Count	.401	700	281	42	4	68	194	176	0	.520	.764	September/October	.287	522	150	28	1	23	93	105	104	.407	.477
Behind in Count	.199	1051	209	34	5	35	122	0	447	.201	.341	Pre-All Star	.282	1431	404	61	5	90	252	256	307	.391	.521
Two Strikes	.181	1251	226	45	5	39	128	247	589	.314	.318	Post-All Star	.288	1293	372	65	6	84	239	234	282	.395	.542

Batter vs. Pitcher (career)

Hits Best Against	Avg	AB	H	2B	3B	HR	RBI	BB	SO	OBP	SLG	Hits Worst Against	Avg	AB	H	2B	3B	HR	RBI	BB	SO	OBP	SLG
Doug Drabek	.615	13	8	0	0	2	4	3	1	.647	1.077	Randy Tomlin	.000	23	0	0	0	0	1	3	8	.111	.000
Trevor Wilson	.529	17	9	1	0	2	6	4	1	.619	.941	Mike Henneman	.000	16	0	0	0	0	1	1	4	.059	.000
Mark Gubicza	.500	20	10	3	0	4	4	3	3	.565	1.250	Rick Honeycutt	.000	12	0	0	0	0	1	0	5	.000	.000
Chris Nabholz	.500	12	6	0	1	2	4	4	1	.625	1.167	Bruce Ruffin	.000	10	0	0	0	0	0	1	5	.091	.000
Melido Perez	.368	19	7	0	1	4	7	2	2	.429	1.105	Doug Jones	.067	15	1	0	0	0	1	1	3	.125	.067

Terry McGriff — Marlins

Age 30 – Bats Right (groundball hitter)

	Avg	G	AB	R	H	2B	3B	HR	RBI	BB	SO	HBP	GDP	SB	CS	OBP	SLG	IBB	SH	SF	#Pit	#P/PA	GB	FB	G/F
1993 Season	.000	3	7	0	0	0	0	0	0	1	2	0	0	0	0	.125	.000	0	0	0	33	4.13	2	3	0.67
Last Five Years	.111	15	27	1	3	0	0	0	2	3	6	0	0	0	0	.200	.111	1	0	0	103	3.43	12	7	1.71

1993 Season

	Avg	AB	H	2B	3B	HR	RBI	BB	SO	OBP	SLG		Avg	AB	H	2B	3B	HR	RBI	BB	SO	OBP	SLG
vs. Left	.000	6	0	0	0	0	0	1	1	.143	.000	Scoring Posn	.000	2	0	0	0	0	0	0	1	.000	.000
vs. Right	.000	1	0	0	0	0	0	0	1	.000	.000	Close & Late	.000	0	0	0	0	0	0	0	0	.000	.000

Mark McGwire — Athletics

Age 30 – Bats Right (flyball hitter)

	Avg	G	AB	R	H	2B	3B	HR	RBI	BB	SO	HBP	GDP	SB	CS	OBP	SLG	IBB	SH	SF	#Pit	#P/PA	GB	FB	G/F
1993 Season	.333	27	84	16	28	6	0	9	24	21	19	1	0	0	1	.467	.726	5	0	1	396	3.70	17	35	0.49
Last Five Years	.237	619	2047	326	486	83	0	145	406	397	450	19	59	5	5	.361	.490	34	2	35	9213	3.69	460	868	0.53

1993 Season

	Avg	AB	H	2B	3B	HR	RBI	BB	SO	OBP	SLG		Avg	AB	H	2B	3B	HR	RBI	BB	SO	OBP	SLG
vs. Left	.455	22	10	3	0	3	12	4	3	.556	1.000	Scoring Posn	.241	29	7	2	0	1	14	9	6	.425	.414
vs. Right	.290	62	18	3	0	6	12	17	16	.438	.629	Close & Late	.333	12	4	0	0	2	5	5	4	.500	.833

Last Five Years

	Avg	AB	H	2B	3B	HR	RBI	BB	SO	OBP	SLG		Avg	AB	H	2B	3B	HR	RBI	BB	SO	OBP	SLG
vs. Left	.259	513	133	24	0	39	121	102	86	.378	.534	Scoring Posn	.257	513	132	20	0	32	255	124	123	.385	.483
vs. Right	.230	1534	353	59	0	106	285	295	364	.355	.476	Close & Late	.249	265	66	6	0	19	65	71	65	.404	.487
Groundball	.238	608	145	21	0	38	109	120	117	.365	.461	None on/out	.244	501	122	23	0	42	42	92	87	.366	.541
Flyball	.221	447	99	16	0	33	81	89	125	.352	.479	Batting #4	.258	1001	258	41	0	81	230	182	202	.369	.541
Home	.228	993	226	40	0	70	197	205	224	.360	.479	Batting #5	.216	547	118	21	0	33	86	126	139	.364	.435
Away	.247	1054	260	43	0	75	209	192	226	.362	.501	Other	.220	499	110	21	0	31	90	89	109	.341	.449
Day	.241	779	188	30	0	67	168	140	164	.357	.538	April	.272	287	78	15	0	25	62	62	54	.402	.585
Night	.235	1268	298	53	0	78	238	257	286	.364	.461	May	.239	394	94	18	0	29	83	92	83	.380	.505
Grass	.237	1711	406	67	0	125	349	338	393	.362	.496	June	.239	356	85	8	0	29	80	62	98	.350	.506
Turf	.238	336	80	16	0	20	57	59	57	.356	.464	July	.219	366	80	15	0	18	59	52	71	.321	.407
First Pitch	.334	374	125	19	0	43	113	15	0	.360	.730	August	.225	325	73	8	0	23	62	68	73	.358	.462
Ahead in Count	.284	455	129	25	0	38	101	209	0	.509	.589	September/October	.238	319	76	19	0	21	60	61	71	.361	.495
Behind in Count	.161	806	130	26	0	33	105	0	335	.163	.316	Pre-All Star	.241	1157	279	46	0	89	249	234	258	.366	.512
Two Strikes	.136	880	120	27	0	27	99	162	450	.270	.259	Post-All Star	.233	890	207	37	0	56	157	163	192	.354	.463

Batter vs. Pitcher (career)

Hits Best Against	Avg	AB	H	2B	3B	HR	RBI	BB	SO	OBP	SLG	Hits Worst Against	Avg	AB	H	2B	3B	HR	RBI	BB	SO	OBP	SLG
Paul Kilgus	.556	9	5	2	0	2	4	4	0	.692	1.444	Jose Mesa	.000	8	0	0	0	0	0	4	5	.333	.000
John Smiley	.500	10	5	2	0	2	2	3	2	.615	1.300	Charles Nagy	.059	17	1	0	0	0	0	5	6	.273	.059
Mark Williamson	.444	18	8	2	0	3	7	4	4	.545	1.056	Greg Hibbard	.063	16	1	0	0	0	1	2	2	.158	.063
Scott Erickson	.444	18	8	2	0	3	7	3	3	.524	1.056	Jeff Russell	.071	14	1	0	0	0	0	1	3	.133	.071
Mike Gardiner	.333	9	3	0	0	3	7	3	3	.462	1.333	Rich DeLucia	.118	17	2	1	0	0	0	1	3	.167	.176

Tim McIntosh — Expos

Age 29 – Bats Right (flyball hitter)

	Avg	G	AB	R	H	2B	3B	HR	RBI	BB	SO	HBP	GDP	SB	CS	OBP	SLG	IBB	SH	SF	#Pit	#P/PA	GB	FB	G/F
1993 Season	.095	21	21	2	2	1	0	0	2	0	7	0	0	0	0	.095	.143	0	0	0	75	3.57	1	10	0.10
Career (1990-1993)	.184	68	114	12	21	5	0	2	10	3	22	2	1	1	3	.217	.281	0	1	1	408	3.37	26	49	0.53

1993 Season

	Avg	AB	H	2B	3B	HR	RBI	BB	SO	OBP	SLG		Avg	AB	H	2B	3B	HR	RBI	BB	SO	OBP	SLG
vs. Left	.154	13	2	1	0	0	2	0	6	.154	.231	Scoring Posn	.143	7	1	1	0	0	2	0	2	.143	.286
vs. Right	.000	8	0	0	0	0	0	0	1	.000	.000	Close & Late	.000	2	0	0	0	0	0	0	0	.000	.000

Jeff McKnight — Mets

Age 31 – Bats Both

	Avg	G	AB	R	H	2B	3B	HR	RBI	BB	SO	HBP	GDP	SB	CS	OBP	SLG	IBB	SH	SF	#Pit	#P/PA	GB	FB	G/F
1993 Season	.256	105	164	19	42	3	1	2	13	13	31	1	3	0	0	.311	.323	0	3	2	699	3.82	62	36	1.72
Career (1989-1993)	.239	187	377	44	90	9	2	5	32	24	64	2	8	1	1	.286	.313	0	6	2	1556	3.79	136	106	1.28

1993 Season

	Avg	AB	H	2B	3B	HR	RBI	BB	SO	OBP	SLG		Avg	AB	H	2B	3B	HR	RBI	BB	SO	OBP	SLG
vs. Left	.171	35	6	0	0	0	1	2	7	.237	.171	Scoring Posn	.152	33	5	0	0	1	11	4	7	.231	.242
vs. Right	.279	129	36	3	1	2	12	11	24	.331	.364	Close & Late	.298	57	17	0	1	0	4	1	11	.300	.333
Home	.259	85	22	1	1	2	9	7	17	.312	.365	None on/out	.368	38	14	2	0	0	0	3	8	.415	.421
Away	.253	79	20	2	0	0	4	6	14	.310	.278	Batting #7	.132	53	7	3	0	0	1	6	10	.220	.189
First Pitch	.300	20	6	1	0	0	0	0	0	.300	.350	Batting #9	.239	46	11	0	1	0	3	2	8	.265	.283
Ahead in Count	.382	34	13	1	1	1	3	7	0	.476	.559	Other	.369	65	24	0	0	2	9	5	13	.417	.462
Behind in Count	.200	75	15	1	0	1	7	0	27	.200	.253	Pre-All Star	.183	60	11	0	0	1	6	8	12	.290	.233
Two Strikes	.175	80	14	1	0	1	7	6	31	.233	.225	Post-All Star	.298	104	31	3	1	1	7	5	19	.324	.375

Mark McLemore — Orioles

Age 29 – Bats Both (groundball hitter)

	Avg	G	AB	R	H	2B	3B	HR	RBI	BB	SO	HBP	GDP	SB	CS	OBP	SLG	IBB	SH	SF	#Pit	#P/PA	GB	FB	G/F
1993 Season	.284	148	581	81	165	27	5	4	72	64	92	1	21	21	15	.353	.368	4	11	6	2487	3.75	235	148	1.59
Last Five Years	.256	330	1033	145	264	40	8	4	117	102	165	2	31	39	22	.321	.321	5	21	9	4304	3.69	412	249	1.65

1993 Season

	Avg	AB	H	2B	3B	HR	RBI	BB	SO	OBP	SLG		Avg	AB	H	2B	3B	HR	RBI	BB	SO	OBP	SLG
vs. Left	.216	162	35	4	1	0	12	12	24	.270	.253	Scoring Posn	.303	152	46	11	1	0	66	24	22	.388	.388
vs. Right	.310	419	130	23	4	4	60	52	68	.383	.413	Close & Late	.264	87	23	3	1	1	9	10	20	.340	.356
Groundball	.250	108	27	3	0	0	11	14	12	.336	.278	None on/out	.209	110	23	1	0	2	2	12	22	.287	.273
Flyball	.319	113	36	10	1	1	16	14	19	.388	.451	Batting #2	.280	493	138	22	5	3	59	58	73	.353	.363
Home	.314	293	92	13	3	2	39	31	47	.377	.399	Batting #3	.333	39	13	2	0	0	3	2	8	.366	.385
Away	.253	288	73	14	2	2	33	33	45	.328	.337	Other	.286	49	14	3	0	1	10	4	11	.340	.408
Day	.288	170	49	12	1	2	17	19	34	.359	.406	April	.311	45	14	3	0	1	10	4	10	.367	.444
Night	.282	411	116	15	4	2	55	45	58	.350	.353	May	.281	114	32	5	1	0	8	9	22	.331	.342
Grass	.268	488	131	21	3	3	59	55	80	.340	.342	June	.308	104	32	5	1	1	18	13	16	.383	.404
Turf	.366	93	34	6	2	1	13	9	12	.422	.505	July	.303	109	33	7	2	0	13	9	9	.353	.404
First Pitch	.360	86	31	4	1	0	3	3	0	.382	.430	August	.295	112	33	6	1	2	14	12	18	.360	.420
Ahead in Count	.382	152	58	8	1	2	22	31	0	.484	.487	September/October	.216	97	21	1	0	0	9	17	17	.330	.227
Behind in Count	.172	215	37	9	1	1	34	0	71	.172	.237	Pre-All Star	.297	310	92	16	2	2	43	28	51	.353	.381
Two Strikes	.180	244	44	11	2	1	34	30	92	.266	.254	Post-All Star	.269	271	73	11	3	2	29	36	41	.353	.354

1993 By Position

Position	Avg	AB	H	2B	3B	HR	RBI	BB	SO	OBP	SLG	G	GS	Innings	PO	A	E	DP	Fld Pct	Rng Fctr	In Zone	Outs	Zone Rtg	MLB Zone
As 2b	.183	82	15	3	0	1	8	11	9	.280	.256	25	20	183.2	53	59	0	19	1.000	5.49	68	58	.853	.895
As rf	.302	484	146	24	5	3	64	51	82	.365	.390	124	120	1064.2	282	13	4	4	.987	2.49	340	271	.797	.826

Last Five Years

	Avg	AB	H	2B	3B	HR	RBI	BB	SO	OBP	SLG		Avg	AB	H	2B	3B	HR	RBI	BB	SO	OBP	SLG
vs. Left	.236	305	72	9	2	0	33	21	49	.285	.279	Scoring Posn	.283	286	81	15	3	0	110	34	44	.352	.357
vs. Right	.264	728	192	31	6	4	84	81	116	.335	.339	Close & Late	.230	178	41	4	1	1	19	21	39	.310	.281
Groundball	.251	239	60	7	1	0	26	25	31	.320	.289	None on/out	.200	200	40	5	0	2	2	24	39	.289	.255
Flyball	.251	223	56	16	1	1	24	23	36	.319	.345	Batting #2	.268	638	171	26	6	3	77	70	95	.339	.342
Home	.265	513	136	19	5	2	59	50	83	.328	.333	Batting #8	.219	137	30	5	1	0	8	12	26	.280	.270
Away	.246	520	128	21	3	2	58	52	82	.314	.310	Other	.244	258	63	9	1	1	32	20	44	.297	.298
Day	.261	330	86	16	3	2	38	31	63	.322	.345	April	.226	208	47	6	1	1	28	19	43	.294	.279
Night	.253	703	178	24	5	2	79	71	102	.321	.310	May	.240	208	50	9	1	0	17	19	29	.300	.293
Grass	.245	816	200	30	6	3	91	82	129	.313	.308	June	.285	144	41	6	1	1	23	16	23	.356	.361
Turf	.295	217	64	10	2	1	26	20	36	.353	.373	July	.315	149	47	9	4	0	20	13	15	.368	.430
First Pitch	.317	164	52	6	1	0	9	4	0	.331	.366	August	.291	127	37	6	1	2	14	12	20	.350	.402
Ahead in Count	.336	262	88	12	3	2	41	50	0	.438	.427	September/October	.213	197	42	4	0	0	15	23	35	.293	.234
Behind in Count	.171	391	67	14	1	1	44	0	132	.173	.220	Pre-All Star	.254	635	161	26	3	2	77	58	103	.315	.313
Two Strikes	.177	430	76	16	2	1	47	48	165	.257	.230	Post-All Star	.259	398	103	14	5	2	40	44	62	.330	.334

Batter vs. Pitcher (career)

Hits Best Against	Avg	AB	H	2B	3B	HR	RBI	BB	SO	OBP	SLG	Hits Worst Against	Avg	AB	H	2B	3B	HR	RBI	BB	SO	OBP	SLG
Todd Stottlemyre	.538	13	7	2	1	0	3	0	0	.538	.846	Mark Gubicza	.063	16	1	0	0	0	1	0	2	.063	.063
John Doherty	.500	10	5	1	0	0	0	1	0	.545	.600	Mark Williamson	.091	11	1	0	0	0	0	1	1	.167	.091
Bobby Witt	.455	11	5	1	1	0	4	3	1	.533	.727	Jim Abbott	.143	14	2	0	0	0	3	0	0	.143	.143
Jaime Navarro	.455	11	5	1	0	0	2	2	1	.538	.545	Bill Wegman	.154	13	2	0	0	0	1	0	3	.154	.154
Greg Harris	.400	10	4	1	1	0	3	1	1	.455	.700	John Dopson	.182	11	2	0	0	0	0	0	1	.182	.182

Greg McMichael — Braves

Age 27 – Pitches Right (groundball pitcher)

	ERA	W	L	Sv	G	GS	IP	BB	SO	Avg	H	2B	3B	HR	RBI	OBP	SLG	GF	IR	IRS	Hld	SvOp	SB	CS	GB	FB	G/F
1993 Season	2.06	2	3	19	74	0	91.2	29	89	.206	68	7	1	3	23	.269	.261	40	22	6	12	21	5	2	130	61	2.13

1993 Season

	ERA	W	L	Sv	G	GS	IP	H	HR	BB	SO
Home	1.61	0	2	8	36	0	44.2	35	2	10	38
Away	2.49	2	1	11	38	0	47.0	33	1	19	51
Day	2.89	1	1	6	22	0	28.0	21	1	11	24
Night	1.70	1	2	13	52	0	63.2	47	2	18	65
Grass	1.73	2	2	15	57	0	73.0	55	3	18	71
Turf	3.38	0	1	4	17	0	18.2	13	0	11	18
April	3.86	0	1	0	8	0	14.0	10	2	4	11
May	1.98	1	2	0	10	0	13.2	17	0	7	15
June	2.45	0	0	0	11	0	14.2	4	0	5	14
July	1.69	0	0	2	17	0	16.0	12	0	3	23
August	0.63	0	0	9	14	0	14.1	10	0	3	14
September/October	1.89	1	0	8	14	0	19.0	15	1	7	12
Starter	0.00	0	0	0	0	0	0.0	0	0	0	0
Reliever	2.06	2	3	19	74	0	91.2	68	3	29	89
0 Days rest	1.85	0	2	5	23	0	24.1	19	2	6	27
1 or 2 Days rest	1.82	2	1	13	38	0	49.1	37	1	15	48
3+ Days rest	3.00	0	0	1	13	0	18.0	12	0	8	14
Pre-All Star	2.81	1	3	0	35	0	48.0	35	2	18	48
Post-All Star	1.24	1	0	19	39	0	43.2	33	1	11	41

	Avg	AB	H	2B	3B	HR	RBI	BB	SO	OBP	SLG
vs. Left	.194	155	30	4	1	1	12	16	37	.269	.252
vs. Right	.217	175	38	3	0	2	11	13	52	.268	.269
Inning 1-6	.250	36	9	1	0	1	6	1	8	.263	.361
Inning 7+	.201	294	59	6	1	2	17	28	81	.269	.248
None on	.200	190	38	6	0	3	3	18	55	.269	.279
Runners on	.214	140	30	1	1	0	20	11	34	.268	.236
Scoring Posn	.222	81	18	1	0	0	19	7	24	.278	.235
Close & Late	.237	186	44	4	0	2	13	14	42	.289	.290
None on/out	.207	82	17	3	0	2	2	8	29	.278	.317
vs. 1st Batr (relief)	.227	66	15	2	0	0	4	6	21	.284	.258
First Inning Pitched	.218	248	54	6	1	1	18	19	68	.271	.262
First 15 Pitches	.218	238	52	6	0	2	14	17	62	.268	.269
Pitch 16-30	.192	78	15	1	1	0	8	10	25	.284	.231
Pitch 31-45	.071	14	1	0	0	1	1	2	2	.188	.286
Pitch 46+	.000	0	0	0	0	0	0	0	0	.000	.000
First Pitch	.289	38	11	2	0	1	2	3	0	.341	.421
Ahead in Count	.134	179	24	1	1	1	11	0	82	.133	.168
Behind in Count	.264	53	14	2	0	1	7	18	0	.444	.358
Two Strikes	.135	171	23	1	1	1	8	8	89	.172	.170

Jim McNamara — Giants

Age 29 – Bats Left (groundball hitter)

	Avg	G	AB	R	H	2B	3B	HR	RBI	BB	SO	HBP	GDP	SB	CS	OBP	SLG	IBB	SH	SF	#Pit	#P/PA	GB	FB	G/F
1993 Season	.143	4	7	0	1	0	0	0	1	0	1	0	0	0	0	.143	.143	0	0	0	18	2.57	3	2	1.50
Career (1992-1993)	.210	34	81	6	17	1	0	1	10	6	26	0	1	0	0	.264	.259	2	2	0	305	3.43	23	14	1.64

1993 Season

	Avg	AB	H	2B	3B	HR	RBI	BB	SO	OBP	SLG
vs. Left	.500	2	1	0	0	0	1	0	1	.500	.500
vs. Right	.000	5	0	0	0	0	0	0	0	.000	.000
Scoring Posn	.333	3	1	0	0	0	1	0	1	.333	.333
Close & Late	.000	1	0	0	0	0	0	0	0	.000	.000

Jeff McNeely — Red Sox

Age 24 – Bats Right

	Avg	G	AB	R	H	2B	3B	HR	RBI	BB	SO	HBP	GDP	SB	CS	OBP	SLG	IBB	SH	SF	#Pit	#P/PA	GB	FB	G/F
1993 Season	.297	21	37	10	11	1	1	0	1	7	9	0	0	6	0	.409	.378	0	0	0	162	3.68	15	4	3.75

1993 Season

	Avg	AB	H	2B	3B	HR	RBI	BB	SO	OBP	SLG
vs. Left	.200	10	2	0	0	0	1	1	1	.273	.200
vs. Right	.333	27	9	1	1	0	0	6	8	.455	.444
Scoring Posn	.200	10	2	0	0	0	1	1	4	.273	.200
Close & Late	.500	4	2	0	0	0	0	1	0	.600	.500

Brian McRae — Royals

Age 26 – Bats Both (groundball hitter)

	Avg	G	AB	R	H	2B	3B	HR	RBI	BB	SO	HBP	GDP	SB	CS	OBP	SLG	IBB	SH	SF	#Pit	#P/PA	GB	FB	G/F
1993 Season	.282	153	627	78	177	28	9	12	69	37	105	4	8	23	14	.325	.413	1	14	3	2627	3.84	265	138	1.92
Career (1990-1993)	.260	500	1957	248	508	87	26	26	208	112	321	12	35	65	33	.302	.370	3	27	14	7798	3.67	800	445	1.80

1993 Season

	Avg	AB	H	2B	3B	HR	RBI	BB	SO	OBP	SLG
vs. Left	.322	199	64	8	4	5	26	3	23	.340	.477
vs. Right	.264	428	113	20	5	7	43	34	82	.318	.383
Groundball	.284	88	25	6	0	2	12	4	12	.319	.420
Flyball	.226	124	28	2	0	1	4	7	23	.273	.266
Home	.287	321	92	14	5	5	39	13	48	.322	.408
Away	.278	306	85	14	4	7	30	24	57	.328	.418
Day	.296	186	55	7	4	5	21	16	32	.361	.457
Night	.277	441	122	21	5	7	48	21	73	.309	.395
Grass	.274	237	65	7	2	4	19	16	40	.318	.371
Turf	.287	390	112	21	7	8	50	21	65	.329	.438
First Pitch	.376	93	35	3	2	1	9	1	0	.385	.484
Ahead in Count	.311	106	33	6	3	4	16	12	0	.378	.538
Behind in Count	.242	281	68	10	3	3	21	0	95	.246	.331
Two Strikes	.235	302	71	12	4	6	34	24	105	.293	.361

	Avg	AB	H	2B	3B	HR	RBI	BB	SO	OBP	SLG
Scoring Posn	.272	147	40	4	4	5	59	11	25	.325	.456
Close & Late	.300	110	33	6	2	3	15	6	15	.336	.473
None on/out	.351	148	52	10	3	1	1	8	21	.385	.480
Batting #1	.311	190	59	10	3	2	13	8	36	.343	.426
Batting #2	.275	422	116	17	6	9	53	26	69	.319	.408
Other	.133	15	2	1	0	1	3	3	0	.278	.400
April	.283	92	26	5	2	1	8	7	17	.333	.413
May	.330	100	33	5	1	0	7	6	10	.370	.400
June	.310	116	36	6	2	2	16	7	16	.347	.448
July	.309	110	34	5	2	4	10	7	26	.361	.500
August	.250	108	27	2	1	3	17	4	17	.281	.370
September/October	.208	101	21	5	1	2	11	6	19	.252	.337
Pre-All Star	.316	348	110	18	5	5	36	21	52	.355	.440
Post-All Star	.240	279	67	10	4	7	33	16	53	.288	.380

1993 By Position

Position	Avg	AB	H	2B	3B	HR	RBI	BB	SO	OBP	SLG	G	GS	Innings	PO	A	E	DP	Fld Pct	Rng Fctr	In Zone	Outs	Zone Rtg	MLB Zone
As cf	.284	624	177	28	9	12	69	37	104	.326	.415	153	150	1345.1	394	4	7	3	.983	2.66	468	386	.825	.829

Career (1990-1993)

	Avg	AB	H	2B	3B	HR	RBI	BB	SO	OBP	SLG
vs. Left	.295	638	188	33	8	11	78	25	73	.325	.423
vs. Right	.243	1319	320	54	18	15	130	87	248	.291	.345
Groundball	.253	450	114	28	5	3	40	15	68	.279	.358

	Avg	AB	H	2B	3B	HR	RBI	BB	SO	OBP	SLG
Scoring Posn	.264	451	119	12	9	10	175	32	83	.309	.397
Close & Late	.265	328	87	14	6	4	39	24	47	.314	.381
None on/out	.290	565	164	37	8	2	2	23	82	.321	.395

Career (1990-1993)

	Avg	AB	H	2B	3B	HR	RBI	BB	SO	OBP	SLG		Avg	AB	H	2B	3B	HR	RBI	BB	SO	OBP	SLG
Flyball	.228	496	113	20	4	5	43	25	83	.271	.315	Batting #1	.257	764	196	27	11	8	67	37	126	.296	.352
Home	.271	977	265	48	17	11	117	55	159	.313	.389	Batting #2	.261	775	202	36	9	13	86	45	126	.301	.381
Away	.248	980	243	39	9	15	91	57	162	.290	.352	Other	.263	418	110	24	6	5	55	30	69	.314	.385
Day	.236	517	122	17	9	11	59	33	90	.285	.368	April	.214	220	47	9	3	3	22	13	37	.255	.323
Night	.268	1440	386	70	17	15	149	79	231	.308	.372	May	.272	305	83	14	4	3	33	27	43	.331	.374
Grass	.250	743	186	23	6	8	63	38	118	.286	.330	June	.287	327	94	15	5	3	37	18	51	.322	.391
Turf	.265	1214	322	64	20	18	145	74	203	.311	.395	July	.281	324	91	13	4	6	32	21	55	.333	.401
First Pitch	.305	302	92	17	3	2	32	2	0	.306	.401	August	.259	359	93	13	5	5	41	16	51	.293	.365
Ahead in Count	.295	386	114	18	9	10	50	51	0	.376	.466	September/October	.237	422	100	23	5	6	43	17	84	.270	.358
Behind in Count	.237	899	213	33	10	7	76	0	281	.244	.319	Pre-All Star	.269	962	259	44	13	11	101	62	150	.313	.376
Two Strikes	.203	903	183	31	10	8	71	59	321	.256	.286	Post-All Star	.250	995	249	43	13	15	107	50	171	.291	.365

Batter vs. Pitcher (career)

Hits Best Against	Avg	AB	H	2B	3B	HR	RBI	BB	SO	OBP	SLG	Hits Worst Against	Avg	AB	H	2B	3B	HR	RBI	BB	SO	OBP	SLG
John Doherty	.636	11	7	2	0	1	5	0	1	.583	1.091	Ron Darling	.056	18	1	0	0	0	1	1	6	.105	.056
Scott Scudder	.556	9	5	0	1	0	2	3	0	.667	.778	Matt Young	.071	14	1	0	0	0	0	0	3	.071	.071
Melido Perez	.538	13	7	2	0	0	3	0	1	.538	.692	Scott Sanderson	.077	13	1	0	0	0	1	0	2	.077	.077
Brian Bohanon	.538	13	7	2	1	0	2	0	0	.538	.846	Ricky Bones	.077	13	1	0	0	0	1	0	1	.071	.077
Kevin Tapani	.484	31	15	4	0	1	7	0	7	.484	.710	Mark Leiter	.100	20	2	0	0	0	1	1	3	.143	.100

Kevin McReynolds — Royals

Age 34 – Bats Right (flyball hitter)

	Avg	G	AB	R	H	2B	3B	HR	RBI	BB	SO	HBP	GDP	SB	CS	OBP	SLG	IBB	SH	SF	#Pit	#P/PA	GB	FB	G/F
1993 Season	.245	110	351	44	86	22	4	11	42	37	56	1	8	2	2	.316	.425	6	1	3	1534	3.90	92	153	0.60
Last Five Years	.260	657	2312	303	601	127	9	86	332	270	285	5	38	39	18	.335	.434	37	2	27	9694	3.71	658	956	0.69

1993 Season

	Avg	AB	H	2B	3B	HR	RBI	BB	SO	OBP	SLG		Avg	AB	H	2B	3B	HR	RBI	BB	SO	OBP	SLG
vs. Left	.222	126	28	8	1	2	12	22	18	.333	.349	Scoring Posn	.274	84	23	2	0	1	30	15	17	.373	.333
vs. Right	.258	225	58	14	3	9	30	15	38	.306	.467	Close & Late	.263	76	20	5	2	1	10	6	12	.317	.421
Groundball	.273	55	15	3	2	0	13	8	7	.354	.400	None on/out	.189	90	17	8	0	1	1	7	17	.247	.311
Flyball	.231	65	15	5	0	2	3	6	10	.292	.400	Batting #6	.301	103	31	10	1	4	13	10	19	.363	.534
Home	.284	194	55	15	3	8	26	16	21	.340	.515	Batting #7	.229	118	27	4	0	4	15	11	17	.293	.364
Away	.197	157	31	7	1	3	16	21	35	.289	.312	Other	.215	130	28	8	3	3	14	16	20	.301	.392
Day	.235	119	28	8	2	5	18	12	22	.308	.462	April	.262	42	11	4	1	2	6	5	4	.340	.548
Night	.250	232	58	14	2	6	24	25	34	.320	.405	May	.250	20	5	3	0	0	0	3	5	.348	.400
Grass	.246	118	29	7	1	3	14	14	25	.323	.398	June	.192	52	10	2	0	1	5	5	12	.263	.288
Turf	.245	233	57	15	3	8	28	23	31	.313	.438	July	.262	84	22	5	1	2	11	11	6	.340	.417
First Pitch	.300	40	12	2	1	1	3	6	0	.383	.475	August	.234	77	18	3	0	4	10	9	13	.322	.429
Ahead in Count	.292	65	19	5	1	4	13	17	0	.434	.585	September/October	.263	76	20	5	2	2	10	4	16	.296	.461
Behind in Count	.228	171	39	12	1	5	20	0	44	.233	.398	Pre-All Star	.248	141	35	11	2	4	16	17	23	.329	.440
Two Strikes	.213	178	38	12	1	6	17	14	56	.273	.393	Post-All Star	.243	210	51	11	2	7	26	20	33	.308	.414

1993 By Position

Position	Avg	AB	H	2B	3B	HR	RBI	BB	SO	OBP	SLG	G	GS	Innings	PO	A	E	DP	Fld Pct	Rng Fctr	In Zone	Outs	Zone Rtg	MLB Zone
As Pinch Hitter	.125	16	2	1	0	0	2	3	7	.263	.188	19	0	---	---	---	---	---	---	---	---	---	---	---
As lf	.254	331	84	21	4	11	40	34	49	.322	.441	104	89	812.1	190	5	2	0	.990	2.16	220	182	.827	.818

Last Five Years

	Avg	AB	H	2B	3B	HR	RBI	BB	SO	OBP	SLG		Avg	AB	H	2B	3B	HR	RBI	BB	SO	OBP	SLG
vs. Left	.268	811	217	46	4	27	102	125	83	.363	.434	Scoring Posn	.280	583	163	30	2	20	241	115	85	.385	.441
vs. Right	.256	1501	384	81	5	59	230	145	202	.319	.434	Close & Late	.275	429	118	22	2	20	67	48	58	.347	.476
Groundball	.259	691	179	33	5	15	103	77	77	.331	.386	None on/out	.229	595	136	34	1	20	20	56	77	.296	.390
Flyball	.251	541	136	31	0	25	69	68	70	.333	.447	Batting #4	.262	817	214	50	2	23	116	103	106	.344	.412
Home	.259	1134	294	61	5	42	155	125	115	.330	.433	Batting #5	.260	883	230	45	6	39	132	96	102	.330	.458
Away	.261	1178	307	66	4	44	177	145	170	.340	.435	Other	.257	612	157	32	1	24	84	71	77	.331	.430
Day	.255	719	183	42	3	28	95	84	112	.333	.438	April	.232	289	67	12	1	10	36	32	31	.307	.384
Night	.262	1593	418	85	6	58	237	186	173	.336	.433	May	.277	372	103	26	0	13	49	55	38	.367	.452
Grass	.259	1368	354	67	3	60	205	147	165	.328	.444	June	.275	415	114	29	0	14	67	56	57	.359	.446
Turf	.262	944	247	60	6	26	127	123	120	.345	.421	July	.255	478	122	30	2	13	67	68	55	.342	.408
First Pitch	.287	286	82	14	2	12	36	18	0	.331	.476	August	.247	376	93	9	3	20	56	30	51	.301	.447
Ahead in Count	.319	545	174	37	2	28	108	148	0	.457	.549	September/October	.267	382	102	21	3	16	57	29	53	.320	.463
Behind in Count	.223	1021	228	51	2	36	135	0	242	.223	.383	Pre-All Star	.266	1229	327	76	2	43	182	169	140	.352	.436
Two Strikes	.225	1003	226	55	3	32	121	94	285	.289	.382	Post-All Star	.253	1083	274	51	7	43	150	101	145	.315	.432

Batter vs. Pitcher (since 1984)

Hits Best Against	Avg	AB	H	2B	3B	HR	RBI	BB	SO	OBP	SLG	Hits Worst Against	Avg	AB	H	2B	3B	HR	RBI	BB	SO	OBP	SLG
Willie Banks	.700	10	7	3	0	2	7	1	0	.727	1.600	Randy Johnson	.000	10	0	0	0	0	0	1	4	.091	.000
Paul Assenmacher	.500	20	10	4	0	1	6	2	3	.545	.850	Derek Lilliquist	.059	17	1	0	0	0	1	2	2	.158	.059
Ricky Bones	.455	11	5	0	0	3	5	0	1	.417	1.273	John Burkett	.083	12	1	0	0	0	0	0	0	.083	.083
Tim Belcher	.389	18	7	0	1	3	7	2	1	.450	1.000	Jim Abbott	.083	12	1	0	0	0	2	1	1	.154	.083
Jeff Parrett	.375	24	9	1	1	3	8	4	2	.464	.875	Jose Rijo	.087	23	2	1	0	0	1	0	4	.083	.130

Rusty Meacham — Royals

Age 26 – Pitches Right

	ERA	W	L	Sv	G	GS	IP	BB	SO	Avg	H	2B	3B	HR	RBI	OBP	SLG	GF	IR	IRS	Hld	SvOp	SB	CS	GB	FB	G/F
1993 Season	5.57	2	2	0	15	0	21.0	5	13	.326	31	6	1	2	19	.375	.474	11	8	6	1	0	1	0	34	28	1.21
Career (1991-1993)	3.59	14	7	2	89	4	150.1	37	91	.264	154	29	4	11	82	.306	.384	32	67	24	17	6	2	1	225	170	1.32

1993 Season

	ERA	W	L	Sv	G	GS	IP	H	HR	BB	SO
Home	5.94	2	1	0	12	0	16.2	24	2	2	12
Away	4.15	0	1	0	3	0	4.1	7	0	3	1

	Avg	AB	H	2B	3B	HR	RBI	BB	SO	OBP	SLG
vs. Left	.400	40	16	4	1	1	10	2	3	.432	.625
vs. Right	.273	55	15	2	0	1	9	3	10	.333	.364

Career (1991-1993)

	ERA	W	L	Sv	G	GS	IP	H	HR	BB	SO
Home	4.70	9	1	1	50	2	84.1	97	9	16	48
Away	2.18	5	6	1	39	2	66.0	57	2	21	43
Day	3.86	3	1	0	17	2	32.2	33	2	9	21
Night	3.52	11	6	2	72	2	117.2	121	9	28	70
Grass	2.86	5	4	1	33	3	63.0	58	5	24	42
Turf	4.12	9	3	1	56	1	87.1	96	6	13	49
April	3.80	1	1	0	14	0	21.1	25	2	5	11
May	0.00	3	0	0	13	0	21.2	11	0	2	15
June	3.58	3	2	0	20	1	32.2	33	3	5	15
July	4.76	2	3	2	21	3	39.2	49	4	14	24
August	2.29	3	1	0	11	0	19.2	21	2	7	13
September/October	7.04	2	0	0	10	0	15.1	15	0	4	13
Starter	6.52	2	1	0	4	4	19.1	27	4	5	12
Reliever	3.16	12	6	2	85	0	131.0	127	7	32	79
0 Days rest	2.92	1	1	0	18	0	24.2	24	1	7	17
1 or 2 Days rest	3.37	6	4	2	45	0	69.1	67	5	20	47
3+ Days rest	2.92	5	1	0	22	0	37.0	36	1	5	15
Pre-All Star	2.79	8	4	1	53	2	90.1	87	6	19	48
Post-All Star	4.80	6	3	1	36	2	60.0	67	5	18	43

	Avg	AB	H	2B	3B	HR	RBI	BB	SO	OBP	SLG
vs. Left	.268	231	62	10	2	5	37	19	29	.320	.394
vs. Right	.261	353	92	19	2	6	45	18	62	.296	.377
Inning 1-6	.299	154	46	9	1	5	29	15	21	.347	.468
Inning 7+	.251	430	108	20	3	6	53	22	70	.290	.353
None on	.236	318	75	17	2	6	6	15	51	.270	.358
Runners on	.297	266	79	12	2	5	76	22	40	.344	.414
Scoring Posn	.266	169	45	7	2	2	69	17	29	.318	.367
Close & Late	.260	258	67	11	1	5	25	12	42	.293	.368
None on/out	.203	133	27	7	1	4	4	8	17	.248	.361
vs. 1st Batr (relief)	.227	75	17	4	0	2	9	6	9	.271	.360
First Inning Pitched	.241	311	75	15	2	5	52	21	50	.284	.350
First 15 Pitches	.250	300	75	14	2	5	42	15	47	.278	.360
Pitch 16-30	.235	162	38	7	1	3	18	14	26	.304	.346
Pitch 31-45	.284	74	21	4	1	0	12	5	14	.329	.365
Pitch 46+	.417	48	20	4	0	3	10	3	4	.451	.688
First Pitch	.259	81	21	4	0	1	11	6	0	.300	.346
Ahead in Count	.237	245	58	10	3	4	35	0	78	.242	.351
Behind in Count	.290	162	47	10	1	3	27	18	0	.357	.420
Two Strikes	.227	238	54	12	2	3	29	13	91	.268	.332

Pitcher vs. Batter (career)

Pitches Best Vs.	Avg	AB	H	2B	3B	HR	RBI	BB	SO	OBP	SLG
Juan Gonzalez	.182	11	2	1	0	0	0	0	5	.182	.273

Pitches Worst Vs.	Avg	AB	H	2B	3B	HR	RBI	BB	SO	OBP	SLG
Shane Mack	.364	11	4	0	0	0	1	2	2	.462	.364
Ivan Rodriguez	.364	11	4	1	0	0	0	0	3	.364	.455

Pat Meares — Twins

Age 25 – Bats Right (groundball hitter)

	Avg	G	AB	R	H	2B	3B	HR	RBI	BB	SO	HBP	GDP	SB	CS	OBP	SLG	IBB	SH	SF	#Pit	#P/PA	GB	FB	G/F
1993 Season	.251	111	346	33	87	14	3	0	33	7	52	1	11	4	5	.266	.309	0	4	3	1144	3.17	156	77	2.03

1993 Season

	Avg	AB	H	2B	3B	HR	RBI	BB	SO	OBP	SLG
vs. Left	.242	95	23	1	0	0	4	4	15	.267	.253
vs. Right	.255	251	64	13	3	0	29	3	37	.266	.331
Groundball	.300	70	21	3	0	0	13	3	8	.324	.343
Flyball	.302	63	19	4	0	0	5	3	11	.333	.365
Home	.287	157	45	8	0	0	16	6	19	.313	.338
Away	.222	189	42	6	3	0	17	1	33	.225	.286
Day	.287	94	27	5	2	0	6	0	18	.284	.383
Night	.238	252	60	9	1	0	27	7	34	.260	.282
Grass	.235	153	36	6	3	0	15	1	24	.239	.314
Turf	.264	193	51	8	0	0	18	6	28	.287	.306
First Pitch	.339	62	21	3	1	0	6	0	0	.339	.419
Ahead in Count	.353	68	24	5	2	0	10	5	0	.397	.485
Behind in Count	.199	161	32	6	0	0	13	0	46	.201	.236
Two Strikes	.184	147	27	6	0	0	8	2	52	.197	.224

	Avg	AB	H	2B	3B	HR	RBI	BB	SO	OBP	SLG
Scoring Posn	.261	69	18	3	2	0	31	2	13	.270	.362
Close & Late	.373	51	19	6	1	0	7	0	9	.373	.529
None on/out	.264	87	23	3	0	0	0	2	10	.281	.299
Batting #2	.167	24	4	0	0	0	1	0	5	.167	.167
Batting #9	.258	302	78	14	3	0	31	7	44	.276	.325
Other	.250	20	5	0	0	0	1	0	3	.238	.250
April	.000	0	0	0	0	0	0	0	0	.000	.000
May	.278	54	15	2	1	0	4	2	11	.298	.352
June	.342	79	27	5	1	0	7	1	11	.358	.430
July	.250	84	21	4	1	0	9	2	18	.264	.321
August	.188	69	13	2	0	0	4	1	8	.200	.217
September/October	.183	60	11	1	0	0	9	1	4	.194	.200
Pre-All Star	.298	168	50	9	2	0	15	5	30	.318	.375
Post-All Star	.208	178	37	5	1	0	18	2	22	.215	.247

1993 By Position

Position	Avg	AB	H	2B	3B	HR	RBI	BB	SO	OBP	SLG	G	GS	Innings	PO	A	E	DP	Fld Pct	Rng Fctr	In Zone	Outs	Zone Rtg	MLB Zone
As ss	.252	345	87	14	3	0	33	7	52	.267	.310	111	103	890.1	168	304	19	71	.961	4.77	394	333	.845	.880

Roberto Mejia — Rockies

Age 22 – Bats Right (flyball hitter)

	Avg	G	AB	R	H	2B	3B	HR	RBI	BB	SO	HBP	GDP	SB	CS	OBP	SLG	IBB	SH	SF	#Pit	#P/PA	GB	FB	G/F
1993 Season	.231	65	229	31	53	14	5	5	20	13	63	1	2	4	1	.275	.402	1	4	1	878	3.54	60	73	0.82

1993 Season

	Avg	AB	H	2B	3B	HR	RBI	BB	SO	OBP	SLG
vs. Left	.306	49	15	4	3	2	9	4	10	.352	.633
vs. Right	.211	180	38	10	2	3	11	9	53	.253	.339
Home	.274	106	29	6	4	3	14	9	26	.333	.491
Away	.195	123	24	8	1	2	6	4	37	.220	.325
First Pitch	.370	27	10	4	0	1	3	1	0	.400	.630
Ahead in Count	.371	35	13	2	2	2	5	7	0	.476	.714
Behind in Count	.145	131	19	6	2	0	6	0	55	.145	.221
Two Strikes	.119	126	15	4	2	0	5	5	63	.153	.183

	Avg	AB	H	2B	3B	HR	RBI	BB	SO	OBP	SLG
Scoring Posn	.148	54	8	4	1	0	12	6	18	.242	.259
Close & Late	.270	37	10	4	1	1	4	3	7	.325	.514
None on/out	.254	59	15	4	2	1	1	1	12	.267	.441
Batting #2	.233	116	27	7	3	1	9	8	36	.286	.371
Batting #8	.250	104	26	7	2	4	11	4	25	.278	.471
Other	.000	9	0	0	0	0	0	1	2	.100	.000
Pre-All Star	.000	0	0	0	0	0	0	0	0	.000	.000
Post-All Star	.231	229	53	14	5	5	20	13	63	.275	.402

Jose Melendez — Red Sox

Age 28 – Pitches Right (flyball pitcher)

	ERA	W	L	Sv	G	GS	IP	BB	SO	Avg	H	2B	3B	HR	RBI	OBP	SLG	GF	IR	IRS	Hld	SvOp	SB	CS	GB	FB	G/F
1993 Season	2.25	2	1	0	9	0	16.0	5	14	.179	10	2	2	2	11	.238	.393	5	14	7	0	1	0	0	14	20	0.70
Career (1990-1993)	3.26	16	13	3	99	12	204.1	52	163	.234	177	28	3	24	92	.283	.374	34	61	26	6	7	5	10	200	260	0.77

1993 Season

	ERA	W	L	Sv	G	GS	IP	H	HR	BB	SO		Avg	AB	H	2B	3B	HR	RBI	BB	SO	OBP	SLG
Home	0.77	2	0	0	5	0	11.2	5	1	2	11	vs. Left	.190	21	4	0	2	0	3	5	3	.333	.381
Away	6.23	0	1	0	4	0	4.1	5	1	3	3	vs. Right	.171	35	6	2	0	2	8	0	11	.167	.400

Career (1990-1993)

	ERA	W	L	Sv	G	GS	IP	H	HR	BB	SO		Avg	AB	H	2B	3B	HR	RBI	BB	SO	OBP	SLG
Home	3.53	9	7	1	50	7	114.2	104	18	25	95	vs. Left	.253	368	93	11	2	12	43	39	72	.319	.391
Away	2.91	7	6	2	49	5	89.2	73	6	27	68	vs. Right	.216	389	84	17	1	12	49	13	91	.247	.357
Day	3.33	5	5	3	26	5	54.0	49	8	11	43	Inning 1-6	.246	399	98	11	2	18	58	24	78	.291	.419
Night	3.23	11	8	0	73	7	150.1	128	16	41	120	Inning 7+	.221	358	79	17	1	6	34	28	85	.275	.324
Grass	3.17	11	12	3	73	9	153.1	132	19	34	120	None on	.225	463	104	19	2	15	15	27	103	.273	.371
Turf	3.53	5	1	0	26	3	51.0	45	5	18	43	Runners on	.248	294	73	9	1	9	77	25	60	.298	.378
April	1.74	3	0	0	13	0	20.2	14	3	3	19	Scoring Posn	.284	155	44	8	1	3	65	20	34	.346	.406
May	4.26	3	3	0	9	4	31.2	25	5	6	21	Close & Late	.222	198	44	9	0	3	20	17	48	.282	.313
June	3.62	4	6	0	24	5	59.2	52	8	17	46	None on/out	.220	191	42	7	1	7	7	8	50	.266	.377
July	1.08	2	2	0	14	0	25.0	17	0	9	21	vs. 1st Batr (relief)	.238	80	19	4	0	3	13	2	19	.241	.400
August	2.56	1	1	2	20	0	31.2	33	3	7	28	First Inning Pitched	.236	326	77	13	2	6	42	17	81	.270	.344
September/October	4.79	3	1	1	19	3	35.2	36	5	10	28	First 15 Pitches	.258	326	84	14	2	7	41	16	73	.289	.377
Starter	4.86	5	6	0	12	12	70.1	69	14	16	41	Pitch 16-30	.199	186	37	8	0	5	17	16	49	.271	.323
Reliever	2.42	11	7	3	87	0	134.0	108	10	36	122	Pitch 31-45	.234	94	22	1	0	4	14	7	20	.282	.372
0 Days rest	2.45	3	1	1	15	0	25.2	23	2	8	24	Pitch 46+	.225	151	34	5	1	8	20	13	21	.289	.430
1 or 2 Days rest	2.35	1	4	1	39	0	53.2	41	2	13	41	First Pitch	.306	108	33	6	0	4	16	12	0	.377	.472
3+ Days rest	2.47	7	2	1	33	0	54.2	44	6	15	57	Ahead in Count	.180	412	74	14	2	8	39	0	150	.184	.282
Pre-All Star	3.26	11	10	0	53	9	121.1	97	16	29	95	Behind in Count	.298	121	36	6	0	6	16	23	0	.404	.496
Post-All Star	3.25	5	3	3	46	3	83.0	80	8	23	68	Two Strikes	.172	379	65	11	1	9	36	17	163	.209	.277

Pitcher vs. Batter (career)

Pitches Best Vs.	Avg	AB	H	2B	3B	HR	RBI	BB	SO	OBP	SLG	Pitches Worst Vs.	Avg	AB	H	2B	3B	HR	RBI	BB	SO	OBP	SLG
Doug Dascenzo	.091	11	1	0	0	0	0	1	3	.167	.091	Andre Dawson	.545	11	6	1	0	0	0	0	2	.545	.636
Paul O'Neill	.100	10	1	0	0	0	0	1	1	.182	.100	Ryne Sandberg	.429	14	6	0	1	1	4	1	1	.467	.786
Ken Caminiti	.111	9	1	0	0	0	1	2	3	.273	.111	Mark Grace	.308	13	4	1	0	1	4	1	1	.333	.615
Steve Finley	.167	6	1	0	0	0	1	4	0	.455	.167												

Bob Melvin — Red Sox

Age 32 – Bats Right (groundball hitter)

	Avg	G	AB	R	H	2B	3B	HR	RBI	BB	SO	HBP	GDP	SB	CS	OBP	SLG	IBB	SH	SF	#Pit	#P/PA	GB	FB	G/F
1993 Season	.222	77	176	13	39	7	0	3	23	7	44	1	2	0	0	.251	.313	0	3	3	667	3.51	64	38	1.68
Last Five Years	.245	366	1053	81	258	46	2	10	121	49	209	1	28	1	5	.276	.321	6	14	14	3804	3.36	412	247	1.67

1993 Season

	Avg	AB	H	2B	3B	HR	RBI	BB	SO	OBP	SLG		Avg	AB	H	2B	3B	HR	RBI	BB	SO	OBP	SLG
vs. Left	.244	41	10	2	0	1	4	3	8	.295	.366	Scoring Posn	.241	58	14	2	0	0	17	4	15	.288	.276
vs. Right	.215	135	29	5	0	2	19	4	36	.238	.296	Close & Late	.296	27	8	1	0	0	6	0	10	.276	.333
Home	.237	76	18	4	0	1	14	3	22	.265	.329	None on/out	.211	38	8	2	0	1	1	0	6	.211	.342
Away	.210	100	21	3	0	2	9	4	22	.240	.300	Batting #8	.216	116	25	6	0	2	16	5	30	.248	.319
First Pitch	.304	23	7	1	0	1	4	0	0	.320	.478	Batting #9	.217	23	5	0	0	0	0	0	8	.217	.217
Ahead in Count	.235	34	8	2	0	1	5	4	0	.308	.382	Other	.243	37	9	1	0	1	7	2	6	.282	.351
Behind in Count	.133	83	11	1	0	1	7	0	41	.133	.181	Pre-All Star	.267	101	27	4	0	1	13	5	25	.303	.337
Two Strikes	.096	83	8	1	0	0	4	3	44	.128	.108	Post-All Star	.160	75	12	3	0	2	10	2	19	.179	.280

Last Five Years

	Avg	AB	H	2B	3B	HR	RBI	BB	SO	OBP	SLG		Avg	AB	H	2B	3B	HR	RBI	BB	SO	OBP	SLG
vs. Left	.290	472	137	31	1	5	50	33	68	.333	.392	Scoring Posn	.275	309	85	11	2	3	107	20	63	.308	.353
vs. Right	.208	581	121	15	1	5	71	16	141	.227	.263	Close & Late	.214	168	36	3	0	1	19	10	39	.251	.250
Groundball	.238	239	57	6	0	3	32	14	46	.277	.301	None on/out	.209	263	55	13	0	1	1	10	52	.238	.270
Flyball	.242	281	68	13	0	1	27	12	63	.269	.299	Batting #7	.247	271	67	14	1	4	32	15	49	.286	.351
Home	.222	500	111	16	1	4	59	20	115	.249	.282	Batting #8	.235	507	119	22	1	5	53	21	113	.262	.312
Away	.266	553	147	30	1	6	62	29	94	.300	.356	Other	.262	275	72	10	0	1	36	13	47	.291	.309
Day	.275	331	91	21	2	4	46	12	56	.297	.387	April	.218	124	27	7	0	1	11	5	34	.244	.298
Night	.231	722	167	25	0	6	75	37	153	.266	.291	May	.298	191	57	9	0	1	25	10	28	.333	.361
Grass	.227	851	193	30	2	9	102	41	170	.260	.298	June	.272	202	55	9	0	2	27	11	42	.308	.347
Turf	.322	202	65	16	0	1	19	8	39	.344	.416	July	.221	136	30	4	1	0	18	4	30	.238	.265
First Pitch	.327	153	50	8	1	2	26	4	0	.342	.431	August	.223	197	44	7	1	3	22	10	35	.257	.315
Ahead in Count	.295	241	71	14	1	3	32	21	0	.347	.398	September/October	.222	203	45	10	0	3	18	9	40	.251	.315
Behind in Count	.178	490	87	17	0	3	40	0	191	.175	.231	Pre-All Star	.272	566	154	28	0	4	72	28	116	.304	.343
Two Strikes	.167	444	74	16	0	0	31	24	209	.208	.203	Post-All Star	.214	487	104	18	2	6	49	21	93	.243	.296

Batter vs. Pitcher (career)

Hits Best Against	Avg	AB	H	2B	3B	HR	RBI	BB	SO	OBP	SLG	Hits Worst Against	Avg	AB	H	2B	3B	HR	RBI	BB	SO	OBP	SLG
Tim Belcher	.583	12	7	0	0	1	2	0	3	.583	.833	Greg Maddux	.000	11	0	0	0	0	0	1	4	.083	.000
Jim Deshaies	.500	14	7	4	0	0	2	1	0	.500	.786	Kevin Gross	.000	10	0	0	0	0	0	1	4	.091	.000
Scott Sanderson	.412	17	7	1	0	1	5	1	1	.444	.647	Scott Erickson	.000	9	0	0	0	0	2	1	2	.091	.000
Bobby Ojeda	.385	13	5	0	1	1	3	2	2	.438	.769	Bud Black	.083	12	1	0	0	0	0	0	3	.083	.083
Juan Guzman	.333	12	4	1	0	1	3	1	3	.385	.667	Terry Leach	.091	11	1	0	0	0	2	1	2	.167	.091

Tony Menendez — Pirates

Age 29 – Pitches Right (flyball pitcher)

	ERA	W	L	Sv	G	GS	IP	BB	SO	Avg	H	2B	3B	HR	RBI	OBP	SLG	GF	IR	IRS	Hld	SvOp	SB	CS	GB	FB	G/F
1993 Season	3.00	2	0	0	14	0	21.0	4	13	.256	20	4	0	4	8	.298	.462	3	10	1	0	0	0	1	20	38	0.53
Career (1992-1993)	2.81	3	0	0	17	0	25.2	4	18	.226	21	4	0	5	9	.263	.430	4	10	1	0	0	0	1	22	45	0.49

1993 Season

	ERA	W	L	Sv	G	GS	IP	H	HR	BB	SO		Avg	AB	H	2B	3B	HR	RBI	BB	SO	OBP	SLG
Home	3.75	1	0	0	7	0	12.0	15	3	2	6	vs. Left	.250	20	5	1	0	3	6	1	4	.273	.750
Away	2.00	1	0	0	7	0	9.0	5	1	2	7	vs. Right	.259	58	15	3	0	1	2	3	9	.306	.362

Orlando Merced — Pirates

Age 27 – Bats Left (groundball hitter)

	Avg	G	AB	R	H	2B	3B	HR	RBI	BB	SO	HBP	GDP	SB	CS	OBP	SLG	IBB	SH	SF	#Pit	#P/PA	GB	FB	G/F
1993 Season	.313	137	447	68	140	26	4	8	70	77	64	1	9	3	3	.414	.443	10	0	2	1957	3.71	185	121	1.53
Career (1990-1993)	.278	416	1287	204	358	72	11	24	180	194	217	4	22	16	11	.372	.407	22	2	8	5790	3.87	528	339	1.56

1993 Season

	Avg	AB	H	2B	3B	HR	RBI	BB	SO	OBP	SLG		Avg	AB	H	2B	3B	HR	RBI	BB	SO	OBP	SLG
vs. Left	.297	111	33	6	3	0	14	16	17	.386	.405	Scoring Posn	.326	138	45	8	1	4	58	35	19	.457	.486
vs. Right	.318	336	107	20	1	8	56	61	47	.423	.455	Close & Late	.321	78	25	4	0	2	12	12	14	.411	.449
Groundball	.269	145	39	3	0	3	18	18	21	.348	.352	None on/out	.360	86	31	5	1	2	2	16	17	.466	.512
Flyball	.300	60	18	3	0	2	11	12	6	.417	.450	Batting #4	.346	133	46	10	0	3	23	25	14	.450	.489
Home	.298	205	61	13	1	3	20	35	27	.401	.415	Batting #5	.346	159	55	7	3	2	27	23	26	.426	.465
Away	.326	242	79	13	3	5	50	42	37	.425	.467	Other	.252	155	39	9	1	3	20	29	24	.370	.381
Day	.298	114	34	7	1	2	16	21	22	.407	.430	April	.343	67	23	3	0	0	10	12	14	.443	.388
Night	.318	333	106	19	3	6	54	56	42	.416	.447	May	.380	71	27	2	0	3	15	13	12	.476	.535
Grass	.314	156	49	6	2	4	36	26	22	.410	.455	June	.329	82	27	5	0	2	15	15	4	.434	.463
Turf	.313	291	91	20	2	4	34	51	42	.416	.436	July	.366	71	26	8	1	1	11	8	11	.430	.549
First Pitch	.380	50	19	3	1	1	10	10	0	.468	.540	August	.250	100	25	7	0	2	14	16	12	.353	.380
Ahead in Count	.423	111	47	6	2	5	30	32	0	.552	.649	September/October	.214	56	12	1	3	0	5	13	11	.357	.339
Behind in Count	.216	190	41	10	0	0	14	0	51	.220	.268	Pre-All Star	.362	265	96	17	1	6	49	46	38	.457	.502
Two Strikes	.222	185	41	11	0	1	17	35	64	.345	.297	Post-All Star	.242	182	44	9	3	2	21	31	26	.350	.357

1993 By Position

Position	Avg	AB	H	2B	3B	HR	RBI	BB	SO	OBP	SLG	G	GS	Innings	PO	A	E	DP	Fld Pct	Rng Fctr	In Zone	Outs	Zone Rtg	MLB Zone
As Pinch Hitter	.600	15	9	2	0	1	5	4	3	.684	.933	19	0	---	---	---	---	---	---	---	---	---	---	---
As 1b	.292	120	35	4	0	2	24	19	14	.383	.375	42	30	275.1	275	20	2	23	.993	---	45	34	.756	.834
As rf	.308	312	96	20	4	5	41	54	47	.411	.446	109	84	766.0	210	11	8	4	.965	2.60	214	185	.864	.826

Career (1990-1993)

	Avg	AB	H	2B	3B	HR	RBI	BB	SO	OBP	SLG		Avg	AB	H	2B	3B	HR	RBI	BB	SO	OBP	SLG
vs. Left	.238	256	61	12	4	0	27	33	43	.328	.316	Scoring Posn	.311	360	112	23	4	12	157	67	58	.413	.497
vs. Right	.288	1031	297	60	7	24	153	161	174	.383	.430	Close & Late	.262	233	61	17	0	6	38	39	49	.366	.412
Groundball	.249	446	111	19	2	5	46	63	89	.341	.334	None on/out	.273	363	99	21	5	3	3	54	66	.368	.383
Flyball	.250	256	64	12	1	8	37	43	41	.361	.398	Batting #1	.276	463	128	25	4	10	58	76	90	.378	.413
Home	.268	608	163	38	4	12	67	100	100	.371	.403	Batting #5	.272	335	91	15	3	4	50	46	53	.357	.370
Away	.287	679	195	34	7	12	113	94	117	.373	.411	Other	.284	489	139	32	4	10	72	72	74	.378	.427
Day	.297	350	104	21	4	7	62	57	62	.394	.440	April	.292	130	38	4	1	0	18	29	26	.422	.338
Night	.271	937	254	51	7	17	118	137	155	.364	.395	May	.335	212	71	17	1	7	34	33	38	.425	.524
Grass	.286	378	108	16	3	7	65	46	64	.361	.399	June	.250	228	57	12	2	5	30	28	30	.332	.386
Turf	.275	909	250	56	8	17	115	148	153	.377	.410	July	.298	238	71	15	2	5	33	28	41	.371	.441
First Pitch	.373	126	47	13	2	1	24	18	0	.442	.532	August	.248	254	63	15	1	3	36	39	44	.346	.350
Ahead in Count	.379	311	118	23	5	10	69	94	0	.521	.582	September/October	.258	225	58	9	4	4	29	37	38	.364	.387
Behind in Count	.188	538	101	22	2	4	43	0	181	.193	.258	Pre-All Star	.304	682	207	44	6	17	105	100	115	.393	.460
Two Strikes	.187	583	109	25	1	8	52	82	217	.288	.274	Post-All Star	.250	605	151	28	5	7	75	94	102	.349	.347

Batter vs. Pitcher (career)

Hits Best Against	Avg	AB	H	2B	3B	HR	RBI	BB	SO	OBP	SLG	Hits Worst Against	Avg	AB	H	2B	3B	HR	RBI	BB	SO	OBP	SLG
Mark Portugal	.526	19	10	2	1	1	7	1	3	.550	.895	Jeff Fassero	.000	9	0	0	0	0	0	2	3	.182	.000
Jose Rijo	.500	18	9	2	0	0	2	1	2	.526	.611	John Burkett	.100	20	2	0	0	0	1	1	4	.143	.100
Jimmy Jones	.467	15	7	2	0	2	4	2	3	.529	1.000	Chuck McElroy	.111	9	1	0	0	0	0	2	1	.273	.111
Ryan Bowen	.455	11	5	2	0	0	1	3	0	.571	.636	David Cone	.125	16	2	0	0	0	1	1	5	.176	.125
Bryn Smith	.400	15	6	2	0	1	7	0	0	.375	.733	Mark Clark	.182	11	2	1	0	0	3	0	1	.167	.273

Henry Mercedes — Athletics

Age 24 – Bats Right (groundball hitter)

	Avg	G	AB	R	H	2B	3B	HR	RBI	BB	SO	HBP	GDP	SB	CS	OBP	SLG	IBB	SH	SF	#Pit	#P/PA	GB	FB	G/F
1993 Season	.213	20	47	5	10	2	0	0	3	2	15	1	0	1	1	.260	.255	0	0	0	188	3.76	19	8	2.38
Career (1992-1993)	.269	29	52	6	14	2	1	0	4	2	16	1	0	1	1	.309	.346	0	0	0	207	3.76	21	10	2.10

1993 Season

	Avg	AB	H	2B	3B	HR	RBI	BB	SO	OBP	SLG		Avg	AB	H	2B	3B	HR	RBI	BB	SO	OBP	SLG
vs. Left	.304	23	7	1	0	0	0	0	6	.304	.348	Scoring Posn	.111	9	1	0	0	0	2	1	2	.200	.111
vs. Right	.125	24	3	1	0	0	3	2	9	.222	.167	Close & Late	.250	4	1	0	0	0	1	1	0	.500	.250

Luis Mercedes — Giants

Age 26 – Bats Right (groundball hitter)

	Avg	G	AB	R	H	2B	3B	HR	RBI	BB	SO	HBP	GDP	SB	CS	OBP	SLG	IBB	SH	SF	#Pit	#P/PA	GB	FB	G/F
1993 Season	.224	28	49	2	11	2	1	0	3	6	7	2	1	1	2	.333	.306	0	2	0	245	4.15	23	11	2.09
Career (1991-1993)	.190	70	153	19	29	6	1	0	9	18	25	3	4	1	3	.286	.242	0	5	1	725	4.03	72	27	2.67

1993 Season

	Avg	AB	H	2B	3B	HR	RBI	BB	SO	OBP	SLG		Avg	AB	H	2B	3B	HR	RBI	BB	SO	OBP	SLG
vs. Left	.241	29	7	2	0	0	0	3	4	.313	.310	Scoring Posn	.077	13	1	0	1	0	3	1	3	.143	.231
vs. Right	.200	20	4	0	1	0	3	3	3	.360	.300	Close & Late	.125	8	1	0	0	0	0	2	0	.364	.125

Kent Mercker — Braves

Age 26 – Pitches Left

	ERA	W	L	Sv	G	GS	IP	BB	SO	Avg	H	2B	3B	HR	RBI	OBP	SLG	GF	IR	IRS	Hld	SvOp	SB	CS	GB	FB	G/F
1993 Season	2.86	3	1	0	43	6	66.0	36	59	.214	52	11	1	2	22	.320	.292	9	20	7	4	3	6	2	78	71	1.10
Career (1989-1993)	3.15	15	13	19	184	11	260.1	136	213	.219	210	39	4	17	106	.320	.322	83	70	28	13	30	34	8	311	283	1.10

1993 Season

	ERA	W	L	Sv	G	GS	IP	H	HR	BB	SO		Avg	AB	H	2B	3B	HR	RBI	BB	SO	OBP	SLG
Home	2.55	2	0	0	23	3	35.1	29	2	20	25	vs. Left	.200	70	14	4	0	0	6	15	21	.341	.257
Away	3.23	1	1	0	20	3	30.2	23	0	16	34	vs. Right	.220	173	38	7	1	2	16	21	38	.311	.306
Starter	3.00	1	1	0	6	6	30.0	23	1	10	23	Scoring Posn	.222	63	14	3	0	0	18	12	20	.347	.270
Reliever	2.75	2	0	0	37	0	36.0	29	1	26	36	Close & Late	.273	33	9	3	0	1	5	6	7	.385	.455
0 Days rest	4.15	1	0	0	8	0	8.2	9	0	6	10	None on/out	.204	54	11	1	1	1	1	11	11	.338	.315
1 or 2 Days rest	5.73	1	0	0	14	0	11.0	10	1	9	10	First Pitch	.222	18	4	1	0	1	3	3	0	.333	.444
3+ Days rest	0.00	0	0	0	15	0	16.1	10	0	11	16	Ahead in Count	.143	119	17	5	0	1	6	0	47	.157	.210
Pre-All Star	2.77	2	0	0	27	0	26.0	23	0	18	27	Behind in Count	.429	49	21	3	0	0	10	15	0	.563	.490
Post-All Star	2.93	1	1	0	16	6	40.0	29	2	18	32	Two Strikes	.127	134	17	5	1	1	8	18	59	.240	.201

Career (1989-1993)

	ERA	W	L	Sv	G	GS	IP	H	HR	BB	SO		Avg	AB	H	2B	3B	HR	RBI	BB	SO	OBP	SLG
Home	3.23	11	4	14	97	4	136.1	114	9	70	102	vs. Left	.223	265	59	11	0	3	25	46	71	.335	.298
Away	3.05	4	9	5	87	7	124.0	96	8	66	111	vs. Right	.218	692	151	28	4	14	81	90	142	.314	.331
Day	2.90	6	5	3	49	2	59.0	60	2	28	52	Inning 1-6	.203	315	64	13	1	4	35	47	77	.313	.289
Night	3.22	9	8	16	135	9	201.1	150	15	108	161	Inning 7+	.227	642	146	26	3	13	71	89	136	.323	.338
Grass	3.22	14	10	15	135	8	192.2	167	14	101	141	None on	.203	507	103	22	4	9	9	78	113	.315	.316
Turf	2.93	1	3	4	49	3	67.2	43	3	35	72	Runners on	.238	450	107	17	0	8	97	58	100	.326	.329
April	3.80	0	1	1	21	0	23.2	16	3	15	19	Scoring Posn	.263	259	68	12	0	6	90	46	63	.374	.378
May	2.06	5	1	2	31	0	39.1	35	3	13	38	Close & Late	.228	351	80	12	1	9	41	53	75	.330	.345
June	1.82	3	1	3	28	0	29.2	20	0	18	31	None on/out	.174	219	38	8	3	2	2	37	47	.298	.265
July	2.15	5	3	6	40	1	58.2	42	4	35	46	vs. 1st Batr (relief)	.174	144	25	5	2	2	16	26	42	.306	.278
August	4.53	0	3	4	30	2	43.2	42	3	17	32	First Inning Pitched	.203	582	118	23	3	8	67	81	141	.304	.294
September/October	4.13	2	4	3	34	8	65.1	55	4	38	47	First 15 Pitches	.203	482	98	20	2	8	45	70	109	.308	.303
Starter	3.31	2	1	0	11	11	51.2	38	1	24	43	Pitch 16-30	.217	263	57	10	1	5	34	36	64	.317	.319
Reliever	3.11	13	12	19	173	0	208.2	172	16	112	170	Pitch 31-45	.309	97	30	4	1	2	16	16	20	.400	.433
0 Days rest	2.90	4	5	8	37	0	40.1	34	4	23	40	Pitch 46+	.217	115	25	5	0	2	11	14	20	.308	.313
1 or 2 Days rest	2.64	5	3	10	74	0	95.1	70	6	48	70	First Pitch	.271	96	26	7	0	3	15	7	0	.320	.438
3+ Days rest	3.82	4	4	1	62	0	73.0	68	6	41	60	Ahead in Count	.159	479	76	17	2	5	31	0	182	.172	.234
Pre-All Star	2.12	10	3	7	92	0	110.1	84	7	54	103	Behind in Count	.310	187	58	9	0	3	33	63	0	.482	.406
Post-All Star	3.90	5	10	12	92	11	150.0	126	10	82	110	Two Strikes	.156	524	82	14	3	10	42	66	213	.258	.252

Pitcher vs. Batter (career)

Pitches Best Vs.	Avg	AB	H	2B	3B	HR	RBI	BB	SO	OBP	SLG	Pitches Worst Vs.	Avg	AB	H	2B	3B	HR	RBI	BB	SO	OBP	SLG
Craig Biggio	.000	9	0	0	0	0	1	2	1	.182	.000	Larry Walker	.556	9	5	2	0	0	3	2	1	.636	.778
Juan Samuel	.100	10	1	0	0	0	0	1	3	.182	.100	Will Clark	.385	13	5	1	0	1	5	1	0	.429	.692
Dave Magadan	.125	8	1	0	0	0	0	3	5	.364	.125	Ray Lankford	.375	8	3	2	0	0	0	3	3	.545	.625
Ken Caminiti	.167	12	2	1	0	0	1	1	2	.231	.250	Ozzie Smith	.333	12	4	1	0	0	3	2	0	.429	.417
Delino DeShields	.182	11	2	0	0	0	1	2	2	.308	.182	Marquis Grissom	.333	12	4	0	0	0	0	0	3	.333	.333

Brett Merriman — Twins

Age 27 – Pitches Right (groundball pitcher)

	ERA	W	L	Sv	G	GS	IP	BB	SO	Avg	H	2B	3B	HR	RBI	OBP	SLG	GF	IR	IRS	Hld	SvOp	SB	CS	GB	FB	G/F
1993 Season	9.67	1	1	0	19	0	27.0	23	14	.343	36	10	1	3	27	.466	.543	10	12	4	1	0	0	1	50	22	2.27

1993 Season

	ERA	W	L	Sv	G	GS	IP	H	HR	BB	SO		Avg	AB	H	2B	3B	HR	RBI	BB	SO	OBP	SLG
Home	8.38	1	0	0	11	0	19.1	24	1	15	12	vs. Left	.426	47	20	5	0	2	14	13	2	.548	.660
Away	12.91	0	1	0	8	0	7.2	12	2	8	2	vs. Right	.276	58	16	5	1	1	13	10	12	.394	.448

Matt Merullo — White Sox

Age 28 – Bats Left (flyball hitter)

	Avg	G	AB	R	H	2B	3B	HR	RBI	BB	SO	HBP	GDP	SB	CS	OBP	SLG	IBB	SH	SF	#Pit	#P/PA	GB	FB	G/F
1993 Season	.050	8	20	1	1	0	0	0	0	0	1	0	1	0	0	.050	.050	0	1	0	50	2.38	4	15	0.27
Career (1989-1993)	.206	143	291	17	60	3	1	6	32	16	41	1	4	0	1	.245	.285	1	4	6	1008	3.17	84	115	0.73

1993 Season

	Avg	AB	H	2B	3B	HR	RBI	BB	SO	OBP	SLG		Avg	AB	H	2B	3B	HR	RBI	BB	SO	OBP	SLG
vs. Left	.000	0	0	0	0	0	0	0	0	.000	.000	Scoring Posn	.000	2	0	0	0	0	0	0	0	.000	.000
vs. Right	.050	20	1	0	0	0	0	0	1	.050	.050	Close & Late	.000	6	0	0	0	0	0	0	0	.000	.000

Jose Mesa — Indians

Age 28 – Pitches Right

	ERA	W	L	Sv	G	GS	IP	BB	SO	Avg	H	2B	3B	HR	RBI	OBP	SLG	CG	ShO	Sup	QS	#P/S	SB	CS	GB	FB	G/F
1993 Season	4.92	10	12	0	34	33	208.2	62	118	.286	232	34	3	21	96	.339	.414	3	0	4.83	14	98	12	14	288	243	1.19
Last Five Years	4.97	26	37	0	92	90	539.2	221	268	.282	589	109	6	48	248	.352	.408	6	2	4.84	39	96	39	28	719	687	1.05

1993 Season

	ERA	W	L	Sv	G	GS	IP	H	HR	BB	SO
Home	4.63	7	5	0	16	16	101.0	113	11	32	55
Away	5.18	3	7	0	18	17	107.2	119	10	30	63
Day	6.39	2	6	0	11	10	56.1	72	6	25	35
Night	4.37	8	6	0	23	23	152.1	160	15	37	83
Grass	4.83	10	10	0	29	28	179.0	194	19	54	98
Turf	5.46	0	2	0	5	5	29.2	38	2	8	20
April	3.91	1	1	0	4	4	25.1	24	4	5	16
May	2.85	4	2	0	7	6	41.0	38	4	12	27
June	4.23	2	2	0	6	6	38.1	36	4	15	16
July	5.50	2	2	0	6	6	34.1	43	3	10	22
August	5.85	0	0	0	6	6	40.0	48	2	12	21
September/October	7.58	1	2	0	5	5	29.2	43	4	8	16
Starter	4.94	10	12	0	33	33	207.2	232	21	62	118
Reliever	0.00	0	0	0	1	0	1.0	0	0	0	0
0-3 Days Rest	3.50	2	1	0	3	3	18.0	19	3	6	9
4 Days Rest	5.44	6	11	0	20	20	125.2	147	12	38	70
5+ Days Rest	4.36	2	0	0	10	10	64.0	66	6	18	39
Pre-All Star	3.76	8	6	0	19	18	115.0	110	12	39	64
Post-All Star	6.34	2	6	0	15	15	93.2	122	9	23	54

	Avg	AB	H	2B	3B	HR	RBI	BB	SO	OBP	SLG
vs. Left	.302	378	114	12	0	7	42	34	44	.360	.389
vs. Right	.273	432	118	22	3	14	54	28	74	.320	.435
Inning 1-6	.279	687	192	26	3	18	84	54	101	.334	.405
Inning 7+	.325	123	40	8	0	3	12	8	17	.366	.463
None on	.283	459	130	22	1	11	11	37	66	.339	.407
Runners on	.291	351	102	12	2	10	85	25	52	.338	.422
Scoring Posn	.268	198	53	8	1	4	71	19	31	.328	.379
Close & Late	.278	72	20	3	0	1	8	6	10	.333	.361
None on/out	.299	211	63	11	0	6	6	15	30	.348	.436
vs. 1st Batr (relief)	.000	1	0	0	0	0	0	0	0	.000	.000
First Inning Pitched	.244	127	31	4	1	4	17	13	22	.315	.386
First 75 Pitches	.269	599	161	21	2	13	65	48	89	.325	.376
Pitch 76-90	.344	93	32	7	0	5	15	6	13	.384	.581
Pitch 91-105	.338	68	23	2	1	2	8	6	9	.395	.485
Pitch 106+	.320	50	16	4	0	1	8	2	7	.346	.460
First Pitch	.423	111	47	8	1	0	14	2	0	.431	.514
Ahead in Count	.254	370	94	12	2	5	37	0	104	.261	.338
Behind in Count	.258	186	48	10	0	6	19	31	0	.361	.409
Two Strikes	.256	355	91	10	2	7	38	29	118	.319	.355

Last Five Years

	ERA	W	L	Sv	G	GS	IP	H	HR	BB	SO
Home	4.77	13	19	0	46	45	264.1	282	23	113	127
Away	5.16	13	18	0	46	45	275.1	307	25	108	141
Day	5.76	5	16	0	30	29	165.2	197	19	68	87
Night	4.62	21	21	0	62	61	374.0	392	29	153	181
Grass	4.97	21	31	0	76	74	443.2	476	40	187	220
Turf	4.97	5	6	0	16	16	96.0	113	8	34	48
April	3.52	3	6	0	11	11	69.0	69	8	19	42
May	4.36	8	7	0	19	18	109.1	115	12	49	50
June	6.35	3	8	0	15	15	79.1	94	8	31	29
July	4.08	3	3	0	10	9	57.1	63	4	19	31
August	5.40	2	5	0	15	15	96.2	100	9	39	50
September/October	5.48	7	8	0	22	22	128.0	148	7	64	66
Starter	4.98	26	37	0	90	90	536.1	587	48	217	268
Reliever	2.70	0	0	0	2	0	3.1	2	0	4	0
0-3 Days Rest	3.50	2	1	0	3	3	18.0	19	3	6	9
4 Days Rest	5.17	15	23	0	50	50	303.0	334	25	125	143
5+ Days Rest	4.85	9	13	0	37	37	215.1	234	20	86	116
Pre-All Star	4.76	15	22	0	48	46	270.1	292	28	110	126
Post-All Star	5.18	11	15	0	44	44	269.1	297	20	111	142

	Avg	AB	H	2B	3B	HR	RBI	BB	SO	OBP	SLG
vs. Left	.296	1055	312	49	0	19	113	113	105	.364	.396
vs. Right	.267	1036	277	60	6	29	135	108	163	.339	.421
Inning 1-6	.279	1842	513	93	6	43	226	195	240	.349	.406
Inning 7+	.305	249	76	16	0	5	22	26	28	.371	.430
None on	.265	1188	315	60	3	25	25	130	145	.341	.384
Runners on	.303	903	274	49	3	23	223	91	123	.366	.441
Scoring Posn	.297	508	151	30	2	12	194	60	69	.363	.435
Close & Late	.265	132	35	6	0	2	11	15	16	.340	.356
None on/out	.285	550	157	30	0	14	14	47	63	.344	.416
vs. 1st Batr (relief)	.000	2	0	0	0	0	0	0	0	.000	.000
First Inning Pitched	.251	342	86	20	1	7	49	47	51	.342	.377
First 75 Pitches	.273	1559	426	76	5	35	179	166	203	.345	.396
Pitch 76-90	.306	255	78	19	0	8	40	25	32	.365	.475
Pitch 91-105	.300	160	48	6	1	3	15	25	21	.396	.406
Pitch 106+	.316	117	37	8	0	2	14	5	12	.344	.436
First Pitch	.343	303	104	20	3	7	44	6	0	.355	.498
Ahead in Count	.251	907	228	40	2	14	90	0	230	.257	.346
Behind in Count	.300	470	141	34	1	12	63	120	0	.438	.453
Two Strikes	.240	895	215	31	2	19	88	95	268	.316	.343

Pitcher vs. Batter (career)

Pitches Best Vs.	Avg	AB	H	2B	3B	HR	RBI	BB	SO	OBP	SLG
Matt Nokes	.000	15	0	0	0	0	0	2	2	.118	.000
Bill Spiers	.000	12	0	0	0	0	1	1	3	.071	.000
Tim Raines	.091	11	1	0	0	0	0	0	0	.091	.091
Felix Jose	.091	11	1	0	0	0	0	0	2	.091	.091
Mike Greenwell	.129	31	4	0	0	0	2	1	2	.156	.129

Pitches Worst Vs.	Avg	AB	H	2B	3B	HR	RBI	BB	SO	OBP	SLG
Greg Briley	.636	11	7	2	0	0	0	0	0	.636	.818
Gregg Jefferies	.615	13	8	2	0	1	1	0	0	.615	1.000
Kevin Maas	.571	14	8	1	0	1	2	0	1	.571	.857
Rickey Henderson	.444	18	8	3	0	0	0	9	0	.630	.611
Pete O'Brien	.385	13	5	0	0	2	5	3	0	.500	.846

Hensley Meulens — Yankees

Age 27 – Bats Right (groundball hitter)

	Avg	G	AB	R	H	2B	3B	HR	RBI	BB	SO	HBP	GDP	SB	CS	OBP	SLG	IBB	SH	SF	#Pit	#P/PA	GB	FB	G/F
1993 Season	.170	30	53	8	9	1	1	2	5	8	19	0	2	0	1	.279	.340	0	0	0	233	3.82	14	13	1.08
Career (1989-1993)	.221	159	457	60	101	16	2	12	46	38	149	7	15	4	2	.290	.344	1	1	2	1931	3.82	155	94	1.65

1993 Season

	Avg	AB	H	2B	3B	HR	RBI	BB	SO	OBP	SLG
vs. Left	.159	44	7	1	0	1	1	7	16	.275	.250
vs. Right	.222	9	2	0	1	1	4	1	3	.300	.778

	Avg	AB	H	2B	3B	HR	RBI	BB	SO	OBP	SLG
Scoring Posn	.154	13	2	0	1	0	3	2	2	.267	.308
Close & Late	.250	4	1	0	1	0	3	1	1	.400	.750

Career (1989-1993)

	Avg	AB	H	2B	3B	HR	RBI	BB	SO	OBP	SLG
vs. Left	.229	258	59	10	1	7	25	21	80	.296	.357
vs. Right	.211	199	42	6	1	5	21	17	69	.282	.327
Groundball	.161	93	15	4	0	1	3	6	34	.235	.237
Flyball	.220	100	22	3	0	4	18	11	31	.295	.370
Home	.228	259	59	12	0	8	24	19	80	.287	.367
Away	.212	198	42	4	2	4	22	19	69	.293	.313
Day	.231	147	34	5	1	1	12	11	39	.288	.299
Night	.216	310	67	11	1	11	34	27	110	.291	.365
Grass	.210	404	85	13	2	9	39	33	126	.280	.319
Turf	.302	53	16	3	0	3	7	5	23	.362	.528
First Pitch	.300	60	18	4	0	0	2	1	0	.333	.367

	Avg	AB	H	2B	3B	HR	RBI	BB	SO	OBP	SLG
Scoring Posn	.224	107	24	3	2	2	34	8	29	.292	.346
Close & Late	.214	56	12	2	1	0	7	3	18	.279	.286
None on/out	.192	125	24	2	0	3	3	10	45	.257	.280
Batting #6	.270	185	50	11	0	7	20	12	53	.335	.443
Batting #7	.198	96	19	4	0	3	6	11	31	.280	.333
Other	.182	176	32	1	2	2	20	15	65	.247	.244
April	.205	44	9	0	1	0	4	3	16	.255	.250
May	.212	66	14	2	0	4	7	4	25	.257	.424
June	.250	64	16	2	1	0	9	6	20	.314	.313
July	.176	68	12	1	0	3	4	5	27	.243	.324
August	.205	78	16	1	0	0	9	6	22	.264	.218

Career (1989-1993)

	Avg	AB	H	2B	3B	HR	RBI	BB	SO	OBP	SLG		Avg	AB	H	2B	3B	HR	RBI	BB	SO	OBP	SLG
Ahead in Count	.368	76	28	1	1	5	16	20	0	.505	.605	September/October	.248	137	34	10	0	5	13	14	39	.340	.431
Behind in Count	.133	248	33	10	0	3	14	0	132	.143	.210	Pre-All Star	.215	195	42	4	2	5	21	14	69	.268	.333
Two Strikes	.138	260	36	7	0	6	19	17	149	.199	.235	Post-All Star	.225	262	59	12	0	7	25	24	80	.305	.351

Batter vs. Pitcher (career)

Hits Best Against	Avg	AB	H	2B	3B	HR	RBI	BB	SO	OBP	SLG	Hits Worst Against	Avg	AB	H	2B	3B	HR	RBI	BB	SO	OBP	SLG
Greg Swindell	.400	10	4	2	0	1	1	1	2	.455	.900	Mark Langston	.067	15	1	0	0	1	1	1	6	.125	.267
Jimmy Key	.364	11	4	1	0	1	2	0	4	.364	.727												
Frank Tanana	.308	13	4	0	0	0	2	1	4	.333	.308												
Jeff Ballard	.308	13	4	0	0	0	1	0	2	.308	.308												

Danny Miceli — Pirates

Age 23 – Pitches Right

	ERA	W	L	Sv	G	GS	IP	BB	SO	Avg	H	2B	3B	HR	RBI	OBP	SLG	GF	IR	IRS	Hld	SvOp	SB	CS	GB	FB	G/F
1993 Season	5.06	0	0	0	9	0	5.1	3	4	.273	6	2	0	0	3	.360	.364	1	8	1	0	0	2	0	3	11	0.27

1993 Season

	ERA	W	L	Sv	G	GS	IP	H	HR	BB	SO		Avg	AB	H	2B	3B	HR	RBI	BB	SO	OBP	SLG
Home	0.00	0	0	0	6	0	3.2	1	0	1	3	vs. Left	.500	6	3	0	0	0	0	2	1	.625	.500
Away	16.20	0	0	0	3	0	1.2	5	0	2	1	vs. Right	.188	16	3	2	0	0	3	1	3	.235	.313

Matt Mieske — Brewers

Age 26 – Bats Right (groundball hitter)

	Avg	G	AB	R	H	2B	3B	HR	RBI	BB	SO	HBP	GDP	SB	CS	OBP	SLG	IBB	SH	SF	#Pit	#P/PA	GB	FB	G/F
1993 Season	.241	23	58	9	14	0	0	3	7	4	14	0	2	0	2	.290	.397	0	1	0	243	3.86	25	10	2.50

1993 Season

	Avg	AB	H	2B	3B	HR	RBI	BB	SO	OBP	SLG		Avg	AB	H	2B	3B	HR	RBI	BB	SO	OBP	SLG
vs. Left	.261	23	6	0	0	2	4	2	4	.320	.522	Scoring Posn	.364	11	4	0	0	1	5	0	1	.364	.636
vs. Right	.229	35	8	0	0	1	3	2	10	.270	.314	Close & Late	.333	6	2	0	0	0	1	0	3	.333	.333

Bob Milacki — Indians

Age 29 – Pitches Right

	ERA	W	L	Sv	G	GS	IP	BB	SO	Avg	H	2B	3B	HR	RBI	OBP	SLG	GF	IR	IRS	Hld	SvOp	SB	CS	GB	FB	G/F
1993 Season	3.38	1	1	0	5	2	16.0	11	7	.302	19	2	1	3	7	.405	.508	0	2	2	0	0	1	0	21	24	0.88
Last Five Years	4.29	36	38	1	123	108	694.0	257	339	.266	710	137	11	75	319	.329	.410	2	22	15	0	1	62	16	974	839	1.16

1993 Season

	ERA	W	L	Sv	G	GS	IP	H	HR	BB	SO		Avg	AB	H	2B	3B	HR	RBI	BB	SO	OBP	SLG
Home	2.35	1	0	0	3	1	7.2	8	1	7	4	vs. Left	.324	34	11	1	1	2	4	8	5	.452	.588
Away	4.32	0	1	0	2	1	8.1	11	2	4	3	vs. Right	.276	29	8	1	0	1	3	3	2	.344	.414

Last Five Years

	ERA	W	L	Sv	G	GS	IP	H	HR	BB	SO		Avg	AB	H	2B	3B	HR	RBI	BB	SO	OBP	SLG
Home	4.63	17	18	0	60	52	330.2	359	38	118	172	vs. Left	.262	1329	348	68	7	29	134	140	173	.331	.389
Away	3.99	19	20	1	63	56	363.1	351	37	139	167	vs. Right	.270	1340	362	69	4	46	185	117	166	.328	.431
Day	3.91	8	8	1	30	25	163.1	147	18	63	82	Inning 1-6	.270	2285	617	123	10	65	289	214	298	.331	.418
Night	4.41	28	30	0	93	83	530.2	563	57	194	257	Inning 7+	.242	384	93	14	1	10	30	43	41	.319	.362
Grass	4.24	30	34	1	105	91	590.2	600	66	228	287	None on	.261	1565	408	83	7	44	44	159	213	.330	.407
Turf	4.62	6	4	0	18	17	103.1	110	9	29	52	Runners on	.274	1104	302	54	4	31	275	98	126	.328	.414
April	3.83	4	3	0	16	15	94.0	79	8	44	37	Scoring Posn	.285	576	164	30	2	14	228	65	65	.348	.417
May	5.12	5	10	0	23	19	117.2	144	14	56	50	Close & Late	.220	182	40	7	0	8	12	27	17	.321	.390
June	4.54	8	6	0	24	24	146.2	160	17	46	84	None on/out	.264	694	183	34	4	23	23	70	88	.333	.424
July	5.59	3	10	0	19	18	96.2	105	16	36	47	vs. 1st Batr (relief)	.571	14	8	2	1	0	8	1	0	.600	.857
August	3.46	6	4	0	12	12	88.1	76	11	17	50	First Inning Pitched	.276	490	135	24	3	13	91	58	61	.352	.416
September/October	3.35	10	5	1	29	20	150.2	146	9	58	71	First 15 Pitches	.282	415	117	22	3	11	61	40	46	.346	.429
Starter	4.32	34	38	0	108	108	650.1	664	71	239	324	Pitch 16-30	.278	425	118	20	0	13	58	53	61	.357	.416
Reliever	3.92	2	0	1	15	0	43.2	46	4	18	15	Pitch 31-45	.268	429	115	26	3	8	52	30	60	.311	.399
0 Days rest	0.00	0	0	0	0	0	0.0	0	0	0	0	Pitch 46+	.257	1400	360	69	5	43	148	134	172	.322	.406
1 or 2 Days rest	4.00	0	0	0	3	0	9.0	11	2	5	3	First Pitch	.277	423	117	26	1	8	47	8	0	.289	.400
3+ Days rest	3.89	2	0	1	12	0	34.2	35	2	13	12	Ahead in Count	.214	1050	225	40	3	21	108	0	277	.215	.318
Pre-All Star	4.84	18	23	0	69	63	383.1	421	44	157	186	Behind in Count	.343	686	235	45	6	30	113	140	0	.451	.557
Post-All Star	3.62	18	15	1	54	45	310.2	289	31	100	153	Two Strikes	.201	1042	209	38	4	19	85	109	339	.277	.299

Pitcher vs. Batter (career)

Pitches Best Vs.	Avg	AB	H	2B	3B	HR	RBI	BB	SO	OBP	SLG	Pitches Worst Vs.	Avg	AB	H	2B	3B	HR	RBI	BB	SO	OBP	SLG
Sandy Alomar Jr	.000	13	0	0	0	0	0	0	1	.000	.000	Ken Griffey Jr	.667	9	6	1	0	0	3	2	0	.727	.778
Alan Trammell	.067	30	2	0	0	0	0	5	5	.200	.067	Rafael Palmeiro	.600	15	9	2	0	2	5	5	0	.700	1.133
Mike Gallego	.067	15	1	0	0	0	0	1	1	.125	.067	Frank Thomas	.500	10	5	0	0	2	5	1	2	.545	1.100
Greg Briley	.091	11	1	1	0	0	0	0	4	.091	.182	Rob Deer	.467	15	7	2	1	1	4	3	3	.556	.933
Bernie Williams	.091	11	1	0	0	0	0	1	0	.167	.091	Pete Incaviglia	.462	13	6	3	0	3	8	2	3	.533	1.385

Sam Militello — Yankees

Age 24 – Pitches Right (flyball pitcher)

	ERA	W	L	Sv	G	GS	IP	BB	SO	Avg	H	2B	3B	HR	RBI	OBP	SLG	CG	ShO	Sup	QS	#P/S	SB	CS	GB	FB	G/F
1993 Season	6.75	1	1	0	3	2	9.1	7	5	.270	10	3	0	1	6	.413	.432	0	0	4.82	0	62	1	0	9	14	0.64
Career (1992-1993)	3.89	4	4	0	12	11	69.1	39	47	.205	53	16	0	7	26	.319	.349	0	0	4.15	6	97	8	0	65	102	0.64

1993 Season

	ERA	W	L	Sv	G	GS	IP	H	HR	BB	SO		Avg	AB	H	2B	3B	HR	RBI	BB	SO	OBP	SLG
Home	10.80	0	0	0	1	0	1.2	1	0	1	0	vs. Left	.333	21	7	2	0	1	3	1	2	.364	.571
Away	5.87	1	1	0	2	2	7.2	9	1	6	5	vs. Right	.188	16	3	1	0	0	3	6	3	.458	.250

Keith Miller — Royals

Age 31 – Bats Right

	Avg	G	AB	R	H	2B	3B	HR	RBI	BB	SO	HBP	GDP	SB	CS	OBP	SLG	IBB	SH	SF	#Pit	#P/PA	GB	FB	G/F
1993 Season	.167	37	108	9	18	3	0	0	3	8	19	1	3	3	1	.229	.194	0	0	1	405	3.43	40	33	1.21
Last Five Years	.260	386	1175	164	306	64	5	10	83	90	182	23	11	55	14	.324	.349	1	6	6	4634	3.56	411	330	1.25

1993 Season

	Avg	AB	H	2B	3B	HR	RBI	BB	SO	OBP	SLG		Avg	AB	H	2B	3B	HR	RBI	BB	SO	OBP	SLG
vs. Left	.071	28	2	0	0	0	0	5	8	.212	.071	Scoring Posn	.083	24	2	1	0	0	3	1	8	.115	.125
vs. Right	.200	80	16	3	0	0	3	3	11	.235	.238	Close & Late	.179	28	5	1	0	0	1	1	6	.233	.214

Last Five Years

	Avg	AB	H	2B	3B	HR	RBI	BB	SO	OBP	SLG		Avg	AB	H	2B	3B	HR	RBI	BB	SO	OBP	SLG
vs. Left	.252	489	123	31	2	2	28	40	88	.310	.335	Scoring Posn	.270	233	63	15	1	0	69	19	43	.338	.343
vs. Right	.267	686	183	33	3	8	55	50	94	.334	.359	Close & Late	.262	191	50	7	0	2	13	20	42	.336	.330
Groundball	.267	318	85	13	2	0	21	24	45	.331	.321	None on/out	.221	407	90	17	2	4	4	39	55	.299	.302
Flyball	.252	313	79	16	1	2	23	16	45	.307	.329	Batting #1	.267	705	188	40	4	6	60	54	102	.330	.360
Home	.259	580	150	27	2	4	40	57	78	.336	.333	Batting #2	.280	311	87	20	1	4	18	18	45	.328	.389
Away	.262	595	156	37	3	6	43	33	104	.312	.365	Other	.195	159	31	4	0	0	5	18	35	.290	.220
Day	.235	379	89	26	0	3	24	28	57	.296	.327	April	.249	169	42	14	0	2	6	17	23	.328	.367
Night	.273	796	217	38	5	7	59	62	125	.337	.359	May	.272	151	41	8	0	2	10	7	26	.308	.364
Grass	.248	625	155	34	0	6	42	52	106	.311	.331	June	.277	177	49	10	2	1	19	15	27	.343	.373
Turf	.275	550	151	30	5	4	41	38	76	.338	.369	July	.328	128	42	9	0	0	10	1	16	.353	.398
First Pitch	.361	194	70	18	3	1	22	0	0	.381	.500	August	.201	199	40	6	0	2	15	15	40	.274	.261
Ahead in Count	.304	273	83	20	1	4	27	55	0	.422	.429	September/October	.262	351	92	17	3	3	23	35	50	.336	.353
Behind in Count	.202	495	100	16	1	2	19	0	165	.212	.251	Pre-All Star	.273	567	155	37	2	5	41	40	83	.331	.372
Two Strikes	.195	493	96	16	1	3	20	34	182	.256	.249	Post-All Star	.248	608	151	27	3	5	42	50	99	.317	.327

Batter vs. Pitcher (career)

Hits Best Against	Avg	AB	H	2B	3B	HR	RBI	BB	SO	OBP	SLG	Hits Worst Against	Avg	AB	H	2B	3B	HR	RBI	BB	SO	OBP	SLG
Bruce Ruffin	.500	16	8	4	1	0	1	4	3	.600	.875	Mark Langston	.063	16	1	1	0	0	0	0	3	.063	.125
Tom Browning	.400	15	6	0	0	0	0	0	3	.400	.400	Paul Assenmacher	.083	12	1	0	0	0	0	1	8	.154	.083
Jaime Navarro	.400	10	4	2	0	0	1	1	0	.455	.600	Randy Johnson	.083	12	1	0	0	0	0	2	4	.214	.083
Melido Perez	.364	11	4	0	1	0	2	0	2	.364	.545	Greg Maddux	.091	11	1	0	0	0	0	0	1	.091	.091
Bryn Smith	.333	12	4	1	0	1	2	1	2	.385	.667	Rheal Cormier	.143	14	2	1	0	0	0	0	3	.143	.214

Paul Miller — Pirates

Age 29 – Pitches Right

	ERA	W	L	Sv	G	GS	IP	BB	SO	Avg	H	2B	3B	HR	RBI	OBP	SLG	CG	ShO	Sup	QS	#P/S	SB	CS	GB	FB	G/F
1993 Season	5.40	0	0	0	3	2	10.0	2	2	.349	15	3	0	2	6	.378	.558	0	0	3.60	0	69	1	0	17	14	1.21
Career (1991-1993)	4.10	1	0	0	10	3	26.1	6	9	.288	30	10	0	2	12	.324	.442	0	0	4.44	0	73	1	1	42	35	1.20

1993 Season

	ERA	W	L	Sv	G	GS	IP	H	HR	BB	SO		Avg	AB	H	2B	3B	HR	RBI	BB	SO	OBP	SLG
Home	7.11	0	0	0	2	1	6.1	10	1	0	0	vs. Left	.278	18	5	1	0	1	1	0	2	.278	.500
Away	2.45	0	0	0	1	1	3.2	5	1	2	2	vs. Right	.400	25	10	2	0	1	5	2	0	.444	.600

Joe Millette — Phillies

Age 27 – Bats Right (groundball hitter)

	Avg	G	AB	R	H	2B	3B	HR	RBI	BB	SO	HBP	GDP	SB	CS	OBP	SLG	IBB	SH	SF	#Pit	#P/PA	GB	FB	G/F
1993 Season	.200	10	10	3	2	0	0	0	2	1	2	0	1	0	0	.273	.200	0	3	0	51	3.64	5	3	1.67
Career (1992-1993)	.205	43	88	8	18	0	0	0	4	6	12	2	9	1	0	.271	.205	2	5	0	303	3.00	38	24	1.58

1993 Season

	Avg	AB	H	2B	3B	HR	RBI	BB	SO	OBP	SLG		Avg	AB	H	2B	3B	HR	RBI	BB	SO	OBP	SLG
vs. Left	.000	5	0	0	0	0	0	0	0	.000	.000	Scoring Posn	.333	3	1	0	0	0	2	1	0	.500	.333
vs. Right	.400	5	2	0	0	0	2	1	2	.500	.400	Close & Late	1.000	1	1	0	0	0	1	0	0	1.000	1.000

Randy Milligan — Indians

Age 32 – Bats Right

	Avg	G	AB	R	H	2B	3B	HR	RBI	BB	SO	HBP	GDP	SB	CS	OBP	SLG	IBB	SH	SF	#Pit	#P/PA	GB	FB	G/F
1993 Season	.299	102	281	37	84	18	1	6	36	60	53	1	3	0	2	.423	.434	0	0	1	1329	3.87	94	72	1.31
Last Five Years	.264	613	1953	285	516	99	10	65	264	412	385	12	64	15	16	.393	.425	9	0	14	9863	4.13	651	573	1.14

1993 Season

	Avg	AB	H	2B	3B	HR	RBI	BB	SO	OBP	SLG		Avg	AB	H	2B	3B	HR	RBI	BB	SO	OBP	SLG
vs. Left	.383	133	51	13	1	4	21	26	17	.484	.586	Scoring Posn	.315	73	23	4	0	1	29	13	14	.414	.411
vs. Right	.223	148	33	5	0	2	15	34	36	.370	.297	Close & Late	.209	43	9	2	0	0	6	12	9	.382	.256
Groundball	.252	107	27	5	1	1	13	23	18	.385	.346	None on/out	.329	76	25	5	1	3	3	23	14	.485	.539
Flyball	.273	55	15	2	0	3	6	9	13	.369	.473	Batting #5	.384	86	33	9	0	2	11	23	9	.514	.558
Home	.308	130	40	7	0	5	19	38	30	.465	.477	Batting #6	.277	119	33	5	1	3	14	23	24	.399	.412
Away	.291	151	44	11	1	1	17	22	23	.382	.397	Other	.237	76	18	4	0	1	11	14	20	.352	.329

1993 Season

	Avg	AB	H	2B	3B	HR	RBI	BB	SO	OBP	SLG
Day	.278	90	25	7	0	0	8	23	19	.425	.356
Night	.309	191	59	11	1	6	28	37	34	.422	.471
Grass	.316	117	37	12	0	0	12	22	17	.424	.419
Turf	.287	164	47	6	1	6	24	38	36	.422	.445
First Pitch	.400	50	20	7	0	2	10	0	0	.400	.660
Ahead in Count	.362	69	25	5	1	1	8	32	0	.564	.507
Behind in Count	.229	105	24	2	0	2	8	0	39	.236	.305
Two Strikes	.180	122	22	2	0	2	6	28	53	.338	.246

	Avg	AB	H	2B	3B	HR	RBI	BB	SO	OBP	SLG
April	.314	70	22	1	1	0	4	16	15	.442	.357
May	.207	87	18	4	0	3	12	16	16	.337	.356
June	.371	35	13	3	0	2	7	3	6	.421	.629
July	.290	31	9	3	0	1	5	6	8	.405	.484
August	.367	30	11	4	0	0	5	12	6	.535	.500
September/October	.393	28	11	3	0	0	3	7	2	.514	.500
Pre-All Star	.278	212	59	10	1	6	26	36	42	.386	.420
Post-All Star	.362	69	25	8	0	0	10	24	11	.521	.478

1993 By Position

Position	Avg	AB	H	2B	3B	HR	RBI	BB	SO	OBP	SLG	G	GS	Innings	PO	A	E	DP	Fld Pct	Rng Fctr	In Zone	Outs	Zone Rtg	MLB Zone
As Pinch Hitter	.389	18	7	2	0	0	5	4	6	.500	.500	22	0	---	---	---	---	---	---	---	---	---	---	---
As 1b	.299	241	72	15	1	6	28	45	41	.411	.444	79	71	603.2	569	63	3	64	.995	---	120	100	.833	.834

Last Five Years

	Avg	AB	H	2B	3B	HR	RBI	BB	SO	OBP	SLG
vs. Left	.284	649	184	40	4	26	98	148	116	.416	.478
vs. Right	.255	1304	332	59	6	39	166	264	269	.381	.399
Groundball	.255	554	141	30	3	10	82	106	96	.377	.374
Flyball	.277	401	111	18	2	22	54	106	85	.428	.496
Home	.253	944	239	40	4	37	128	235	179	.403	.422
Away	.275	1009	277	59	6	28	136	177	206	.383	.428
Day	.279	526	147	28	2	14	71	111	96	.405	.420
Night	.259	1427	369	71	8	51	193	301	289	.389	.427
Grass	.258	1533	396	75	7	50	199	327	295	.390	.414
Turf	.286	420	120	24	3	15	65	85	90	.405	.464
First Pitch	.328	247	81	19	1	12	42	6	0	.342	.559
Ahead in Count	.319	423	135	29	4	19	72	223	0	.551	.541
Behind in Count	.206	830	171	24	4	15	74	0	278	.213	.299
Two Strikes	.202	1002	202	28	4	21	98	182	385	.329	.300

	Avg	AB	H	2B	3B	HR	RBI	BB	SO	OBP	SLG
Scoring Posn	.270	504	136	23	1	15	199	113	109	.399	.409
Close & Late	.248	310	77	15	1	10	46	73	57	.393	.400
None on/out	.264	451	119	21	3	20	20	110	87	.409	.457
Batting #5	.262	939	246	51	4	31	123	200	167	.391	.424
Batting #6	.280	346	97	18	3	10	42	62	74	.396	.436
Other	.259	668	173	30	3	24	99	150	144	.395	.421
April	.245	269	66	9	1	5	29	54	67	.370	.342
May	.251	382	96	25	3	11	49	92	79	.402	.419
June	.318	358	114	20	0	23	74	69	59	.430	.567
July	.241	369	89	13	2	16	53	80	66	.376	.417
August	.271	291	79	16	2	4	35	71	56	.413	.381
September/October	.254	284	72	16	2	6	24	46	58	.357	.387
Pre-All Star	.270	1132	306	59	4	44	166	245	225	.402	.446
Post-All Star	.256	821	210	40	6	21	98	167	160	.381	.396

Batter vs. Pitcher (career)

Hits Best Against	Avg	AB	H	2B	3B	HR	RBI	BB	SO	OBP	SLG
Kenny Rogers	.444	9	4	3	0	0	1	4	2	.615	.778
Mark Gubicza	.417	12	5	1	1	2	7	1	4	.462	1.167
Greg Swindell	.406	32	13	1	0	6	10	3	4	.457	1.000
Terry Leach	.400	10	4	1	0	2	4	1	1	.455	1.100
Joe Slusarski	.400	10	4	0	0	1	2	4	1	.571	.700

Hits Worst Against	Avg	AB	H	2B	3B	HR	RBI	BB	SO	OBP	SLG
Nolan Ryan	.000	13	0	0	0	0	0	2	8	.133	.000
Bud Black	.000	13	0	0	0	0	0	3	0	.188	.000
Jack Morris	.053	19	1	1	0	0	0	0	6	.053	.105
Dave Stewart	.091	11	1	0	0	0	1	1	1	.167	.091
Rod Nichols	.118	17	2	0	0	0	0	0	3	.118	.118

Alan Mills — Orioles

Age 27 – Pitches Right

	ERA	W	L	Sv	G	GS	IP	BB	SO	Avg	H	2B	3B	HR	RBI	OBP	SLG	GF	IR	IRS	Hld	SvOp	SB	CS	GB	FB	G/F
1993 Season	3.23	5	4	4	45	0	100.1	51	68	.225	80	11	3	14	49	.324	.390	18	53	20	4	7	6	3	102	129	0.79
Career (1990-1993)	3.20	17	14	6	122	5	261.2	146	163	.236	222	39	7	24	120	.338	.368	51	116	40	9	12	25	8	316	310	1.02

1993 Season

	ERA	W	L	Sv	G	GS	IP	H	HR	BB	SO
Home	3.31	3	3	3	26	0	54.1	43	10	29	28
Away	3.13	2	1	1	19	0	46.0	37	4	22	40
Starter	0.00	0	0	0	0	0	0.0	0	0	0	0
Reliever	3.23	5	4	4	45	0	100.1	80	14	51	68
0 Days rest	3.09	0	1	2	5	0	11.2	10	1	3	11
1 or 2 Days rest	1.05	1	0	2	13	0	25.2	16	1	13	20
3+ Days rest	4.14	4	3	0	27	0	63.0	54	12	35	37
Pre-All Star	4.32	1	3	0	25	0	58.1	51	11	31	38
Post-All Star	1.71	4	1	4	20	0	42.0	29	3	20	30

	Avg	AB	H	2B	3B	HR	RBI	BB	SO	OBP	SLG
vs. Left	.285	137	39	2	1	5	19	20	16	.377	.423
vs. Right	.187	219	41	9	2	9	30	31	52	.291	.370
Scoring Posn	.184	98	18	1	0	4	36	17	25	.301	.316
Close & Late	.245	98	24	4	2	3	14	16	24	.350	.418
None on/out	.301	83	25	4	1	4	4	15	13	.408	.518
First Pitch	.264	53	14	2	0	2	11	4	0	.310	.415
Ahead in Count	.160	144	23	2	0	4	14	0	54	.178	.257
Behind in Count	.256	78	20	3	1	3	10	22	0	.420	.436
Two Strikes	.160	162	26	2	2	6	19	25	68	.278	.309

Career (1990-1993)

	ERA	W	L	Sv	G	GS	IP	H	HR	BB	SO
Home	3.08	8	9	5	63	1	134.1	115	13	70	74
Away	3.32	9	5	1	59	4	127.1	107	11	76	89
Day	4.01	2	7	1	42	3	85.1	82	4	54	62
Night	2.81	15	7	5	80	2	176.1	140	20	92	101
Grass	2.89	15	13	6	106	3	227.1	185	20	128	138
Turf	5.24	2	1	0	16	2	34.1	37	4	18	25
April	2.43	1	1	0	15	0	33.1	21	3	19	18
May	2.13	1	2	0	20	0	42.1	35	1	20	27
June	2.42	5	3	0	21	0	44.2	42	5	22	27
July	4.91	2	1	1	26	0	44.0	40	7	30	23
August	3.16	3	3	2	17	3	51.1	44	5	29	34
September/October	3.91	5	4	3	23	2	46.0	40	3	26	34
Starter	5.64	1	2	0	5	5	22.1	26	2	12	11
Reliever	2.97	16	12	6	117	0	239.1	196	22	134	152
0 Days rest	2.38	1	1	3	14	0	22.2	19	3	8	19
1 or 2 Days rest	1.58	4	2	3	39	0	74.0	52	3	46	50
3+ Days rest	3.79	11	9	0	64	0	142.2	125	16	80	83
Pre-All Star	2.75	9	6	1	68	0	140.2	117	15	73	84
Post-All Star	3.72	8	8	5	54	5	121.0	105	9	73	79

	Avg	AB	H	2B	3B	HR	RBI	BB	SO	OBP	SLG
vs. Left	.274	423	116	18	2	9	48	66	50	.372	.390
vs. Right	.204	519	106	21	5	15	72	80	113	.310	.351
Inning 1-6	.223	426	95	15	1	14	58	58	76	.318	.362
Inning 7+	.246	516	127	24	6	10	62	88	87	.354	.374
None on	.260	473	123	27	3	14	14	71	67	.359	.419
Runners on	.211	469	99	12	4	10	106	75	96	.317	.318
Scoring Posn	.200	290	58	8	3	7	97	59	68	.329	.321
Close & Late	.232	254	59	12	4	4	30	50	50	.360	.358
None on/out	.284	215	61	12	1	7	7	33	27	.382	.447
vs. 1st Batr (relief)	.260	104	27	7	0	4	23	8	14	.313	.442
First Inning Pitched	.233	386	90	17	2	8	69	61	71	.337	.350
First 15 Pitches	.228	347	79	15	2	8	56	51	61	.328	.352
Pitch 16-30	.271	255	69	10	2	9	34	40	43	.365	.431
Pitch 31-45	.235	179	42	8	2	4	13	24	33	.328	.369
Pitch 46+	.199	161	32	6	1	3	17	31	26	.328	.304
First Pitch	.303	132	40	7	1	3	22	17	0	.380	.439
Ahead in Count	.184	385	71	10	1	4	35	0	128	.194	.247
Behind in Count	.271	218	59	12	2	8	32	66	0	.434	.454
Two Strikes	.173	427	74	9	4	10	49	63	163	.281	.283

Pitcher vs. Batter (career)

Pitches Best Vs.	Avg	AB	H	2B	3B	HR	RBI	BB	SO	OBP	SLG
Lou Whitaker	.000	9	0	0	0	0	1	2	1	.182	.000
George Bell	.071	14	1	0	0	0	0	1	1	.133	.071
Kevin Seitzer	.091	11	1	1	0	0	0	0	1	.091	.182
Carlos Baerga	.091	11	1	0	0	0	0	2	2	.231	.091
Frank Thomas	.091	11	1	0	0	0	1	4	3	.313	.091

Pitches Worst Vs.	Avg	AB	H	2B	3B	HR	RBI	BB	SO	OBP	SLG
Robin Yount	.333	9	3	0	0	0	0	2	2	.455	.333

Nate Minchey — Red Sox

Age 24 – Pitches Right

	ERA	W	L	Sv	G	GS	IP	BB	SO	Avg	H	2B	3B	HR	RBI	OBP	SLG	CG	ShO	Sup	QS	#P/S	SB	CS	GB	FB	G/F
1993 Season	3.55	1	2	0	5	5	33.0	8	18	.265	35	8	1	5	14	.307	.455	1	0	5.73	3	103	1	1	51	34	1.50

1993 Season

	ERA	W	L	Sv	G	GS	IP	H	HR	BB	SO
Home	4.63	0	1	0	2	2	11.2	14	1	4	7
Away	2.95	1	1	0	3	3	21.1	21	4	4	11

	Avg	AB	H	2B	3B	HR	RBI	BB	SO	OBP	SLG
vs. Left	.238	63	15	1	1	3	7	7	3	.314	.429
vs. Right	.290	69	20	7	0	2	7	1	15	.300	.478

Blas Minor — Pirates

Age 28 – Pitches Right

	ERA	W	L	Sv	G	GS	IP	BB	SO	Avg	H	2B	3B	HR	RBI	OBP	SLG	GF	IR	IRS	Hld	SvOp	SB	CS	GB	FB	G/F
1993 Season	4.10	8	6	2	65	0	94.1	26	84	.263	94	12	4	8	43	.316	.385	18	37	15	7	3	5	4	126	86	1.47
Career (1992-1993)	4.11	8	6	2	66	0	96.1	26	84	.264	97	13	5	8	43	.317	.392	18	37	15	7	3	5	4	130	88	1.48

1993 Season

	ERA	W	L	Sv	G	GS	IP	H	HR	BB	SO
Home	4.35	5	3	1	37	0	49.2	51	2	15	44
Away	3.83	3	3	1	28	0	44.2	43	6	11	40
Day	3.86	3	2	0	17	0	23.1	25	1	4	17
Night	4.18	5	4	2	48	0	71.0	69	7	22	67
Grass	2.79	2	3	1	18	0	29.0	24	3	8	28
Turf	4.68	6	3	1	47	0	65.1	70	5	18	56
April	1.26	3	0	0	11	0	14.1	8	1	2	15
May	6.43	1	2	0	11	0	14.0	17	1	6	14
June	3.92	0	1	2	12	0	20.2	22	3	5	15
July	4.05	2	1	0	13	0	20.0	20	1	6	16
August	8.25	1	1	0	10	0	12.0	17	2	4	12
September/October	1.35	1	1	0	8	0	13.1	10	0	3	12
Starter	0.00	0	0	0	0	0	0.0	0	0	0	0
Reliever	4.10	8	6	2	65	0	94.1	94	8	26	84
0 Days rest	4.72	3	4	0	13	0	13.1	12	0	4	10
1 or 2 Days rest	3.50	3	2	2	39	0	64.1	58	6	18	53
3+ Days rest	5.94	2	0	0	13	0	16.2	24	2	4	21
Pre-All Star	3.84	5	3	2	39	0	58.2	55	6	15	53
Post-All Star	4.54	3	3	0	26	0	35.2	39	2	11	31

	Avg	AB	H	2B	3B	HR	RBI	BB	SO	OBP	SLG
vs. Left	.286	140	40	5	2	5	23	15	25	.350	.457
vs. Right	.248	218	54	7	2	3	20	11	59	.294	.339
Inning 1-6	.295	122	36	5	0	3	21	10	26	.353	.410
Inning 7+	.246	236	58	7	4	5	22	16	58	.297	.373
None on	.239	205	49	7	3	5	5	13	50	.291	.376
Runners on	.294	153	45	5	1	3	38	13	34	.349	.399
Scoring Posn	.316	95	30	3	0	2	34	10	27	.373	.411
Close & Late	.228	123	28	2	1	2	11	9	31	.281	.309
None on/out	.224	85	19	3	3	1	1	5	20	.275	.365
vs. 1st Batr (relief)	.241	58	14	2	2	0	8	3	14	.281	.345
First Inning Pitched	.284	211	60	8	2	6	36	22	42	.356	.427
First 15 Pitches	.270	204	55	6	3	4	26	15	39	.321	.387
Pitch 16-30	.292	96	28	5	1	2	15	9	28	.355	.427
Pitch 31-45	.206	34	7	1	0	1	1	1	10	.250	.324
Pitch 46+	.167	24	4	0	0	1	1	1	7	.200	.292
First Pitch	.308	52	16	2	0	3	6	2	0	.327	.519
Ahead in Count	.186	167	31	2	3	1	11	0	69	.195	.251
Behind in Count	.373	75	28	4	0	4	21	18	0	.485	.587
Two Strikes	.179	168	30	5	2	1	10	6	84	.216	.250

Gino Minutelli — Giants

Age 30 – Pitches Left (flyball pitcher)

	ERA	W	L	Sv	G	GS	IP	BB	SO	Avg	H	2B	3B	HR	RBI	OBP	SLG	GF	IR	IRS	Hld	SvOp	SB	CS	GB	FB	G/F
1993 Season	3.77	0	1	0	9	0	14.1	15	10	.152	7	1	1	2	7	.349	.348	4	3	2	1	1	2	0	10	27	0.37
Career (1990-1993)	5.31	0	3	0	27	3	40.2	35	31	.242	37	6	3	7	21	.378	.458	6	13	6	2	1	4	0	33	62	0.53

1993 Season

	ERA	W	L	Sv	G	GS	IP	H	HR	BB	SO
Home	4.22	0	0	0	5	0	10.2	3	1	11	6
Away	2.45	0	1	0	4	0	3.2	4	1	4	4

	Avg	AB	H	2B	3B	HR	RBI	BB	SO	OBP	SLG
vs. Left	.091	11	1	0	0	0	0	2	3	.231	.091
vs. Right	.171	35	6	1	1	2	7	13	7	.380	.429

Angel Miranda — Brewers

Age 24 – Pitches Left

	ERA	W	L	Sv	G	GS	IP	BB	SO	Avg	H	2B	3B	HR	RBI	OBP	SLG	CG	ShO	Sup	QS	#P/S	SB	CS	GB	FB	G/F
1993 Season	3.30	4	5	0	22	17	120.0	52	88	.226	100	23	3	12	44	.309	.373	2	0	4.43	11	105	7	3	149	140	1.06

1993 Season

	ERA	W	L	Sv	G	GS	IP	H	HR	BB	SO
Home	3.07	3	2	0	12	10	70.1	63	3	26	52
Away	3.62	1	3	0	10	7	49.2	37	9	26	36
Starter	3.28	4	5	0	17	17	112.2	95	11	44	85
Reliever	3.68	0	0	0	5	0	7.1	5	1	8	3
0-3 Days Rest	0.00	0	0	0	0	0	0.0	0	0	0	0
4 Days Rest	4.00	1	4	0	10	10	63.0	60	7	32	45
5+ Days Rest	2.36	3	1	0	7	7	49.2	35	4	12	40
Pre-All Star	3.72	0	1	0	7	3	19.1	17	1	11	9
Post-All Star	3.22	4	4	0	15	14	100.2	83	11	41	79

	Avg	AB	H	2B	3B	HR	RBI	BB	SO	OBP	SLG
vs. Left	.210	81	17	7	0	0	6	15	16	.330	.296
vs. Right	.230	361	83	16	3	12	38	37	72	.303	.391
Scoring Posn	.187	91	17	7	1	0	24	18	20	.313	.286
Close & Late	.220	41	9	4	0	1	3	8	7	.340	.390
None on/out	.232	125	29	8	0	3	3	8	21	.284	.368
First Pitch	.271	59	16	8	0	1	6	3	0	.313	.458
Ahead in Count	.146	185	27	5	1	2	12	0	74	.150	.216
Behind in Count	.333	120	40	7	1	8	17	24	0	.441	.608
Two Strikes	.149	194	29	6	1	2	14	25	88	.249	.222

Kevin Mitchell — Reds

Age 32 – Bats Right (flyball hitter)

	Avg	G	AB	R	H	2B	3B	HR	RBI	BB	SO	HBP	GDP	SB	CS	OBP	SLG	IBB	SH	SF	#Pit	#P/PA	GB	FB	G/F
1993 Season	.341	93	323	56	110	21	3	19	64	25	48	1	14	1	0	.385	.601	4	0	4	1195	3.39	107	105	1.02
Last Five Years	.291	599	2121	346	618	116	12	137	418	248	353	14	39	10	16	.366	.551	57	0	24	8417	3.50	636	797	0.80

1993 Season

	Avg	AB	H	2B	3B	HR	RBI	BB	SO	OBP	SLG		Avg	AB	H	2B	3B	HR	RBI	BB	SO	OBP	SLG
vs. Left	.394	94	37	7	1	8	16	5	7	.424	.745	Scoring Posn	.330	103	34	11	1	3	45	12	24	.387	.544
vs. Right	.319	229	73	14	2	11	48	20	41	.370	.541	Close & Late	.283	46	13	3	0	4	14	5	6	.346	.609
Groundball	.431	123	53	13	1	10	29	10	12	.470	.797	None on/out	.325	77	25	2	1	7	7	6	7	.373	.649
Flyball	.210	62	13	2	1	3	7	1	15	.222	.419	Batting #3	.333	9	3	0	0	2	2	0	1	.333	1.000
Home	.349	186	65	15	2	10	35	13	26	.386	.613	Batting #4	.344	311	107	21	3	17	62	21	45	.383	.595
Away	.328	137	45	6	1	9	29	12	22	.384	.584	Other	.000	3	0	0	0	0	0	4	2	.571	.000
Day	.365	96	35	6	0	7	19	8	15	.410	.646	April	.357	42	15	2	0	2	10	2	1	.378	.548
Night	.330	227	75	15	3	12	45	17	33	.375	.581	May	.333	93	31	5	1	4	19	8	16	.379	.538
Grass	.323	96	31	3	1	7	19	10	18	.387	.594	June	.421	76	32	7	1	5	16	5	9	.457	.737
Turf	.348	227	79	18	2	12	45	15	30	.385	.604	July	.318	44	14	4	0	4	11	3	7	.375	.682
First Pitch	.323	62	20	3	1	2	19	3	0	.348	.500	August	.269	67	18	3	1	4	8	7	14	.333	.522
Ahead in Count	.462	78	36	6	0	10	16	8	0	.506	.923	September/October	.000	1	0	0	0	0	0	0	1	.000	.000
Behind in Count	.290	124	36	9	2	3	19	0	39	.290	.468	Pre-All Star	.357	241	86	16	2	15	52	16	32	.392	.627
Two Strikes	.292	120	35	8	1	4	19	14	48	.366	.475	Post-All Star	.293	82	24	5	1	4	12	9	16	.366	.524

1993 By Position

Position	Avg	AB	H	2B	3B	HR	RBI	BB	SO	OBP	SLG	G	GS	Innings	PO	A	E	DP	Fld Pct	Rng Fctr	In Zone	Outs	Zone Rtg	MLB Zone
As lf	.340	312	106	20	3	17	62	22	45	.381	.587	86	85	640.2	141	6	7	2	.955	2.07	165	140	.848	.818

Last Five Years

	Avg	AB	H	2B	3B	HR	RBI	BB	SO	OBP	SLG		Avg	AB	H	2B	3B	HR	RBI	BB	SO	OBP	SLG
vs. Left	.323	641	207	38	3	49	134	96	75	.409	.621	Scoring Posn	.271	609	165	38	2	26	261	116	106	.379	.468
vs. Right	.278	1480	411	78	9	88	284	152	278	.346	.521	Close & Late	.283	329	93	16	0	20	58	47	62	.370	.514
Groundball	.316	697	220	45	6	49	148	70	106	.381	.608	None on/out	.297	512	152	23	5	42	42	45	77	.358	.607
Flyball	.265	502	133	23	3	33	91	64	94	.347	.520	Batting #4	.292	2082	608	114	12	134	411	240	344	.365	.551
Home	.297	1079	320	66	9	61	211	125	160	.367	.544	Batting #9	.125	8	1	1	0	0	0	5	5	.462	.250
Away	.286	1042	298	50	3	76	207	123	193	.364	.559	Other	.290	31	9	1	0	3	7	3	4	.353	.613
Day	.295	759	224	45	2	48	137	99	136	.376	.549	April	.293	345	101	23	2	19	69	31	53	.348	.536
Night	.289	1362	394	71	10	89	281	149	217	.360	.552	May	.279	426	119	19	3	26	73	56	71	.360	.521
Grass	.280	1273	357	58	8	86	251	154	224	.359	.541	June	.337	365	123	26	2	28	81	41	37	.403	.649
Turf	.308	848	261	58	4	51	167	94	129	.375	.566	July	.296	361	107	21	0	27	87	43	74	.374	.579
First Pitch	.312	375	117	25	1	30	95	35	0	.374	.624	August	.286	402	115	18	4	24	76	49	76	.367	.530
Ahead in Count	.407	487	198	30	7	50	133	111	0	.513	.805	September/October	.239	222	53	9	1	13	32	28	42	.325	.464
Behind in Count	.231	876	202	39	4	34	129	0	293	.231	.401	Pre-All Star	.302	1250	377	73	7	86	251	140	182	.370	.578
Two Strikes	.202	866	175	38	2	28	111	93	353	.278	.348	Post-All Star	.277	871	241	43	5	51	167	108	171	.359	.513

Batter vs. Pitcher (career)

Hits Best Against	Avg	AB	H	2B	3B	HR	RBI	BB	SO	OBP	SLG	Hits Worst Against	Avg	AB	H	2B	3B	HR	RBI	BB	SO	OBP	SLG
Joe Hesketh	.600	15	9	2	0	1	3	2	2	.647	.933	Mike Morgan	.077	13	1	0	0	0	0	2	3	.200	.077
Rick Honeycutt	.538	13	7	2	0	2	3	0	0	.538	1.154	Jim Gott	.077	13	1	0	0	0	0	1	2	.143	.077
Mike Harkey	.500	10	5	1	0	1	3	1	2	.545	.900	Pete Harnisch	.083	12	1	0	0	0	1	2	4	.214	.083
Darryl Kile	.500	10	5	1	0	2	5	3	0	.571	1.200	Frank Tanana	.133	15	2	1	0	0	0	1	2	.188	.200
Bruce Hurst	.333	21	7	1	0	5	8	5	2	.462	1.095	Shawn Boskie	.182	11	2	0	0	0	1	0	1	.182	.182

Dave Mlicki — Indians

Age 26 – Pitches Right (flyball pitcher)

	ERA	W	L	Sv	G	GS	IP	BB	SO	Avg	H	2B	3B	HR	RBI	OBP	SLG	CG	ShO	Sup	QS	#P/S	SB	CS	GB	FB	G/F
1993 Season	3.38	0	0	0	3	3	13.1	6	7	.220	11	3	0	2	5	.328	.400	0	0	2.03	0	80	2	2	14	19	0.74
Career (1992-1993)	4.37	0	2	0	7	7	35.0	22	23	.258	34	6	1	5	13	.376	.432	0	0	4.11	2	91	9	3	34	45	0.76

1993 Season

	ERA	W	L	Sv	G	GS	IP	H	HR	BB	SO		Avg	AB	H	2B	3B	HR	RBI	BB	SO	OBP	SLG
Home	3.38	0	0	0	3	3	13.1	11	2	6	7	vs. Left	.182	33	6	1	0	1	3	4	4	.308	.303
Away	0.00	0	0	0	0	0	0.0	0	0	0	0	vs. Right	.294	17	5	2	0	1	2	2	3	.368	.588

Dennis Moeller — Pirates

Age 26 – Pitches Left

	ERA	W	L	Sv	G	GS	IP	BB	SO	Avg	H	2B	3B	HR	RBI	OBP	SLG	GF	IR	IRS	Hld	SvOp	SB	CS	GB	FB	G/F
1993 Season	9.92	1	0	0	10	0	16.1	7	13	.356	26	4	0	2	19	.420	.493	3	2	2	0	0	2	1	25	17	1.47
Career (1992-1993)	8.39	1	3	0	15	4	34.1	18	19	.345	50	8	0	7	34	.413	.545	4	2	2	0	0	4	1	50	44	1.14

1993 Season

	ERA	W	L	Sv	G	GS	IP	H	HR	BB	SO		Avg	AB	H	2B	3B	HR	RBI	BB	SO	OBP	SLG
Home	7.71	0	0	0	4	0	7.0	10	0	2	5	vs. Left	.348	23	8	0	0	1	7	3	2	.444	.478
Away	11.57	1	0	0	6	0	9.1	16	2	5	8	vs. Right	.360	50	18	4	0	1	12	4	11	.407	.500

Mike Mohler — Athletics

Age 25 – Pitches Left (flyball pitcher)

	ERA	W	L	Sv	G	GS	IP	BB	SO	Avg	H	2B	3B	HR	RBI	OBP	SLG	GF	IR	IRS	Hld	SvOp	SB	CS	GB	FB	G/F
1993 Season	5.60	1	6	0	42	9	64.1	44	42	.241	57	11	0	10	43	.361	.414	4	38	9	1	1	8	3	75	82	0.91

1993 Season

	ERA	W	L	Sv	G	GS	IP	H	HR	BB	SO		Avg	AB	H	2B	3B	HR	RBI	BB	SO	OBP	SLG
Home	5.40	0	3	0	20	4	28.1	28	5	16	25	vs. Left	.192	73	14	4	0	0	12	13	16	.314	.247

1993 Season	ERA	W	L	Sv	G	GS	IP	H	HR	BB	SO		Avg	AB	H	2B	3B	HR	RBI	BB	SO	OBP	SLG
Away	5.75	1	3	0	22	5	36.0	29	5	28	17	vs. Right	.262	164	43	7	0	10	31	31	26	.382	.488
Starter	6.88	0	5	0	9	9	34.0	36	7	18	21	Scoring Posn	.242	66	16	2	0	6	35	17	12	.388	.545
Reliever	4.15	1	1	0	33	0	30.1	21	3	26	21	Close & Late	.250	16	4	1	0	0	4	5	4	.455	.313
0 Days rest	1.80	0	1	0	5	0	5.0	2	0	5	3	None on/out	.214	56	12	2	0	1	1	5	9	.279	.304
1 or 2 Days rest	2.61	0	0	0	15	0	10.1	7	0	10	8	First Pitch	.286	28	8	1	0	2	5	4	0	.375	.536
3+ Days rest	6.00	1	0	0	13	0	15.0	12	3	11	10	Ahead in Count	.154	91	14	5	0	2	10	0	34	.163	.275
Pre-All Star	4.94	0	1	0	30	2	27.1	26	2	22	25	Behind in Count	.328	58	19	1	0	6	23	20	0	.500	.655
Post-All Star	6.08	1	5	0	12	7	37.0	31	8	22	17	Two Strikes	.185	108	20	5	0	1	8	20	42	.313	.259

Paul Molitor — Blue Jays

Age 37 – Bats Right

	Avg	G	AB	R	H	2B	3B	HR	RBI	BB	SO	HBP	GDP	SB	CS	OBP	SLG	IBB	SH	SF	#Pit	#P/PA	GB	FB	G/F
1993 Season	.332	160	636	121	211	37	5	22	111	77	71	3	13	22	4	.402	.509	3	1	8	2712	3.74	248	179	1.39
Last Five Years	.318	734	2943	491	935	167	35	74	376	328	317	17	54	117	32	.386	.474	39	9	31	11945	3.58	1130	844	1.34

1993 Season	Avg	AB	H	2B	3B	HR	RBI	BB	SO	OBP	SLG		Avg	AB	H	2B	3B	HR	RBI	BB	SO	OBP	SLG
vs. Left	.363	171	62	13	2	7	32	26	23	.446	.585	Scoring Posn	.384	190	73	13	1	5	88	34	15	.468	.542
vs. Right	.320	465	149	24	3	15	79	51	48	.385	.482	Close & Late	.411	90	37	6	0	2	21	15	12	.486	.544
Groundball	.316	98	31	3	1	5	19	11	7	.378	.520	None on/out	.365	104	38	8	1	6	6	13	14	.436	.635
Flyball	.398	93	37	10	2	5	24	9	14	.452	.710	Batting #3	.328	515	169	28	4	18	89	67	55	.404	.503
Home	.364	316	115	23	2	13	68	37	30	.431	.573	Batting #6	.343	102	35	9	1	4	21	6	13	.375	.569
Away	.300	320	96	14	3	9	43	40	41	.374	.447	Other	.368	19	7	0	0	0	1	4	3	.478	.368
Day	.308	211	65	10	3	6	30	31	25	.398	.469	April	.292	89	26	3	1	2	13	14	10	.388	.416
Night	.344	425	146	27	2	16	81	46	46	.404	.529	May	.374	115	43	2	1	5	22	13	8	.442	.539
Grass	.325	249	81	11	2	9	40	33	28	.399	.494	June	.284	109	31	9	0	2	16	14	11	.363	.422
Turf	.336	387	130	26	3	13	71	44	43	.404	.519	July	.347	98	34	4	0	6	17	15	13	.435	.571
First Pitch	.365	85	31	5	1	5	21	2	0	.375	.624	August	.355	110	39	9	2	3	24	14	18	.419	.555
Ahead in Count	.432	185	80	13	0	8	46	49	0	.544	.632	September/October	.330	115	38	10	1	4	19	7	11	.363	.539
Behind in Count	.259	247	64	10	2	6	32	0	60	.265	.389	Pre-All Star	.307	348	107	15	2	10	55	47	33	.390	.448
Two Strikes	.242	248	60	8	2	7	28	26	71	.319	.375	Post-All Star	.361	288	104	22	3	12	56	30	38	.416	.583

1993 By Position

Position	Avg	AB	H	2B	3B	HR	RBI	BB	SO	OBP	SLG	G	GS	Innings	PO	A	E	DP	Fld Pct	Rng Fctr	In Zone	Outs	Zone Rtg	MLB Zone
As Designated Hitter	.311	543	169	32	4	17	90	68	60	.386	.479	137	137	---	---	---	---	---	---	---	---	---	---	---
As 1b	.452	93	42	5	1	5	21	9	11	.500	.688	23	23	206.0	179	14	3	16	.985	---	47	39	.830	.834

Last Five Years	Avg	AB	H	2B	3B	HR	RBI	BB	SO	OBP	SLG		Avg	AB	H	2B	3B	HR	RBI	BB	SO	OBP	SLG
vs. Left	.349	746	260	50	10	27	108	98	76	.421	.551	Scoring Posn	.340	691	235	41	6	13	293	130	77	.434	.473
vs. Right	.307	2197	675	117	25	47	268	230	241	.373	.447	Close & Late	.319	389	124	18	0	9	59	67	46	.418	.434
Groundball	.326	711	232	33	11	16	97	88	72	.401	.471	None on/out	.319	914	292	55	16	25	25	69	94	.370	.497
Flyball	.319	601	192	47	6	20	94	64	72	.381	.517	Batting #1	.307	1633	501	84	24	37	163	180	178	.377	.456
Home	.318	1398	444	81	16	36	189	173	140	.392	.476	Batting #3	.331	1186	392	74	10	33	191	138	122	.398	.493
Away	.318	1545	491	86	19	38	187	155	177	.380	.472	Other	.339	124	42	9	1	4	22	10	17	.384	.524
Day	.321	910	292	54	6	22	116	111	101	.395	.466	April	.296	311	92	14	1	9	40	33	34	.364	.434
Night	.316	2033	643	113	29	52	260	217	216	.381	.477	May	.335	552	185	28	8	17	66	57	58	.397	.507
Grass	.307	2150	661	112	27	51	246	255	224	.380	.456	June	.309	489	151	35	5	13	65	63	49	.388	.481
Turf	.346	793	274	55	8	23	130	73	93	.400	.522	July	.309	424	131	13	5	11	51	57	57	.392	.441
First Pitch	.352	460	162	31	5	18	68	27	0	.386	.559	August	.320	588	188	36	8	13	81	63	70	.384	.474
Ahead in Count	.364	774	282	50	4	22	120	185	0	.483	.525	September/October	.325	579	188	41	8	11	73	55	49	.382	.480
Behind in Count	.270	1164	314	54	15	20	123	0	268	.275	.393	Pre-All Star	.311	1493	465	81	14	43	186	170	158	.382	.471
Two Strikes	.247	1134	280	44	13	19	108	114	317	.319	.359	Post-All Star	.324	1450	470	86	21	31	190	158	159	.389	.477

Batter vs. Pitcher (since 1984)

Hits Best Against	Avg	AB	H	2B	3B	HR	RBI	BB	SO	OBP	SLG	Hits Worst Against	Avg	AB	H	2B	3B	HR	RBI	BB	SO	OBP	SLG
Dave Fleming	.875	8	7	0	0	0	2	2	0	.818	.875	Mike Jackson	.000	12	0	0	0	0	0	1	4	.077	.000
Eric Plunk	.600	15	9	1	0	1	5	4	2	.684	.867	Luis Aquino	.071	14	1	0	0	0	0	0	3	.071	.071
Neal Heaton	.467	15	7	3	1	1	3	2	2	.500	1.000	John Habyan	.083	12	1	0	0	0	0	1	4	.154	.083
Greg Cadaret	.385	13	5	2	0	1	5	5	2	.556	.769	Doug Jones	.100	20	2	0	0	0	0	0	3	.100	.100
Scott Aldred	.333	9	3	1	0	2	3	2	1	.417	1.111	Mark Guthrie	.143	14	2	0	0	0	1	0	3	.143	.143

Raul Mondesi — Dodgers

Age 23 – Bats Right

	Avg	G	AB	R	H	2B	3B	HR	RBI	BB	SO	HBP	GDP	SB	CS	OBP	SLG	IBB	SH	SF	#Pit	#P/PA	GB	FB	G/F
1993 Season	.291	42	86	13	25	3	1	4	10	4	16	0	1	4	1	.322	.488	0	1	0	293	3.22	27	27	1.00

1993 Season	Avg	AB	H	2B	3B	HR	RBI	BB	SO	OBP	SLG		Avg	AB	H	2B	3B	HR	RBI	BB	SO	OBP	SLG
vs. Left	.315	54	17	3	1	2	5	2	7	.339	.519	Scoring Posn	.208	24	5	0	1	3	9	1	5	.240	.667
vs. Right	.250	32	8	0	0	2	5	2	9	.294	.438	Close & Late	.235	17	4	0	0	0	0	2	6	.316	.235

Rich Monteleone — Yankees

Age 31 – Pitches Right

	ERA	W	L	Sv	G	GS	IP	BB	SO	Avg	H	2B	3B	HR	RBI	OBP	SLG	GF	IR	IRS	Hld	SvOp	SB	CS	GB	FB	G/F
1993 Season	4.94	7	4	0	42	0	85.2	35	50	.262	85	13	6	14	49	.329	.468	11	41	10	1	1	5	1	120	99	1.21
Last Five Years	3.93	19	11	0	144	0	272.1	96	181	.248	256	44	11	29	141	.309	.396	38	111	39	9	5	10	9	357	324	1.10

1993 Season

	ERA	W	L	Sv	G	GS	IP	H	HR	BB	SO
Home	5.13	1	1	0	18	0	33.1	38	7	12	21
Away	4.82	6	3	0	24	0	52.1	47	7	23	29
Starter	0.00	0	0	0	0	0	0.0	0	0	0	0
Reliever	4.94	7	4	0	42	0	85.2	85	14	35	50
0 Days rest	0.00	0	0	0	3	0	5.0	0	0	1	4
1 or 2 Days rest	6.65	3	2	0	14	0	23.0	32	6	12	10
3+ Days rest	4.68	4	2	0	25	0	57.2	53	8	22	36
Pre-All Star	4.80	5	4	0	23	0	54.1	49	6	22	29
Post-All Star	5.17	2	0	0	19	0	31.1	36	8	13	21

	Avg	AB	H	2B	3B	HR	RBI	BB	SO	OBP	SLG
vs. Left	.273	139	38	4	3	10	25	21	26	.364	.581
vs. Right	.253	186	47	9	3	4	24	14	24	.300	.398
Scoring Posn	.256	82	21	2	2	4	35	18	6	.371	.476
Close & Late	.261	46	12	3	0	1	6	11	5	.397	.391
None on/out	.276	76	21	4	1	3	3	9	10	.353	.474
First Pitch	.178	45	8	1	0	2	3	8	0	.302	.333
Ahead in Count	.229	157	36	7	1	5	18	0	45	.226	.382
Behind in Count	.379	66	25	3	3	3	12	19	0	.512	.652
Two Strikes	.223	157	35	6	0	7	18	8	50	.259	.395

Last Five Years

	ERA	W	L	Sv	G	GS	IP	H	HR	BB	SO
Home	3.85	7	5	0	72	0	131.0	122	16	41	86
Away	4.01	12	6	0	72	0	141.1	134	13	55	95
Day	3.46	4	4	0	49	0	88.1	85	9	33	56
Night	4.16	15	7	0	95	0	184.0	171	20	63	125
Grass	3.95	17	9	0	119	0	228.0	214	24	77	152
Turf	3.86	2	2	0	25	0	44.1	42	5	19	29
April	3.48	4	1	0	17	0	31.0	21	3	9	24
May	2.21	3	4	0	21	0	40.2	33	3	22	25
June	3.29	4	0	0	23	0	54.2	46	5	15	35
July	7.06	1	2	0	17	0	29.1	39	2	12	15
August	3.49	3	1	0	33	0	59.1	54	8	20	39
September/October	4.87	4	3	0	33	0	57.1	63	8	18	43
Starter	0.00	0	0	0	0	0	0.0	0	0	0	0
Reliever	3.93	19	11	0	144	0	272.1	256	29	96	181
0 Days rest	0.49	0	0	0	10	0	18.1	8	0	4	11
1 or 2 Days rest	5.05	7	4	0	54	0	82.0	92	13	31	60
3+ Days rest	3.77	12	7	0	80	0	172.0	156	16	61	110
Pre-All Star	3.37	12	7	0	68	0	136.1	111	11	50	89
Post-All Star	4.50	7	4	0	76	0	136.0	145	18	46	92

	Avg	AB	H	2B	3B	HR	RBI	BB	SO	OBP	SLG
vs. Left	.263	449	118	21	6	14	55	44	63	.327	.430
vs. Right	.236	585	138	23	5	15	86	52	118	.296	.369
Inning 1-6	.242	380	92	21	6	9	60	34	67	.301	.400
Inning 7+	.251	654	164	23	5	20	81	62	114	.314	.393
None on	.229	598	137	27	5	15	15	38	116	.275	.366
Runners on	.273	436	119	17	6	14	126	58	65	.352	.436
Scoring Posn	.291	254	74	11	3	9	111	46	34	.387	.465
Close & Late	.245	245	60	13	1	6	27	31	40	.330	.380
None on/out	.224	246	55	8	2	7	7	21	40	.285	.358
vs. 1st Batr (relief)	.264	125	33	7	2	6	28	15	21	.338	.496
First Inning Pitched	.271	479	130	24	7	12	87	52	87	.338	.426
First 15 Pitches	.287	443	127	26	6	11	71	39	71	.340	.447
Pitch 16-30	.205	303	62	8	2	6	34	34	57	.283	.304
Pitch 31-45	.234	201	47	6	2	7	22	16	38	.289	.388
Pitch 46+	.230	87	20	4	1	5	14	7	15	.292	.471
First Pitch	.242	132	32	6	1	3	17	13	0	.308	.371
Ahead in Count	.211	513	108	17	3	12	57	0	149	.211	.326
Behind in Count	.345	197	68	12	4	8	38	50	0	.472	.569
Two Strikes	.201	497	100	16	1	14	57	33	181	.250	.322

Pitcher vs. Batter (career)

Pitches Best Vs.	Avg	AB	H	2B	3B	HR	RBI	BB	SO	OBP	SLG
Juan Gonzalez	.077	13	1	1	0	0	0	0	3	.077	.154

Pitches Worst Vs.	Avg	AB	H	2B	3B	HR	RBI	BB	SO	OBP	SLG
Manuel Lee	.364	11	4	1	0	0	3	0	2	.364	.455
Jose Canseco	.333	12	4	1	0	1	6	1	3	.385	.667
Ruben Sierra	.333	9	3	2	0	0	1	3	1	.500	.556
Cal Ripken	.308	13	4	0	0	0	0	0	1	.308	.308

Jeff Montgomery — Royals

Age 32 – Pitches Right

	ERA	W	L	Sv	G	GS	IP	BB	SO	Avg	H	2B	3B	HR	RBI	OBP	SLG	GF	IR	IRS	Hld	SvOp	SB	CS	GB	FB	G/F
1993 Season	2.27	7	5	45	69	0	87.1	23	66	.206	65	14	2	3	29	.263	.291	63	30	8	0	51	7	1	107	86	1.24
Last Five Years	2.22	25	23	159	337	0	446.1	137	400	.217	356	60	6	23	167	.282	.303	239	153	58	21	194	38	11	565	421	1.34

1993 Season

	ERA	W	L	Sv	G	GS	IP	H	HR	BB	SO
Home	2.49	5	4	16	33	0	43.1	30	0	8	29
Away	2.05	2	1	29	36	0	44.0	35	3	15	37
Day	2.45	2	2	15	24	0	29.1	24	1	11	25
Night	2.17	5	3	30	45	0	58.0	41	2	12	41
Grass	2.16	2	1	22	28	0	33.1	27	3	13	27
Turf	2.33	5	4	23	41	0	54.0	38	0	10	39
April	2.08	1	1	6	10	0	13.0	10	1	3	10
May	2.95	1	1	10	14	0	18.1	16	0	7	12
June	0.69	0	0	7	10	0	13.0	7	0	1	11
July	0.66	1	0	8	10	0	13.2	7	0	1	11
August	3.38	0	3	10	14	0	16.0	12	1	7	12
September/October	3.38	4	0	4	11	0	13.1	13	1	4	10
Starter	0.00	0	0	0	0	0	0.0	0	0	0	0
Reliever	2.27	7	5	45	69	0	87.1	65	3	23	66
0 Days rest	1.25	0	1	16	18	0	21.2	11	0	9	14
1 or 2 Days rest	2.14	3	2	24	34	0	42.0	29	1	10	37
3+ Days rest	3.42	4	2	5	17	0	23.2	25	2	4	15
Pre-All Star	1.80	3	2	25	38	0	50.0	35	1	11	38
Post-All Star	2.89	4	3	20	31	0	37.1	30	2	12	28

	Avg	AB	H	2B	3B	HR	RBI	BB	SO	OBP	SLG
vs. Left	.234	158	37	8	2	1	17	13	24	.297	.329
vs. Right	.177	158	28	6	0	2	12	10	42	.229	.253
Inning 1-6	.000	0	0	0	0	0	0	0	0	.000	.000
Inning 7+	.206	316	65	14	2	3	29	23	66	.263	.291
None on	.214	173	37	8	0	2	2	9	40	.253	.295
Runners on	.196	143	28	6	2	1	27	14	26	.275	.287
Scoring Posn	.189	90	17	3	2	1	25	7	15	.260	.300
Close & Late	.210	257	54	9	1	2	27	21	53	.271	.276
None on/out	.257	74	19	5	0	0	0	2	14	.276	.324
vs. 1st Batr (relief)	.258	66	17	5	0	0	6	3	13	.290	.333
First Inning Pitched	.210	243	51	12	1	3	23	19	44	.269	.305
First 15 Pitches	.195	210	41	10	0	2	17	13	40	.244	.271
Pitch 16-30	.247	85	21	4	2	1	11	7	19	.312	.376
Pitch 31-45	.150	20	3	0	0	0	1	3	6	.261	.150
Pitch 46+	.000	1	0	0	0	0	0	0	1	.000	.000
First Pitch	.167	30	5	2	0	0	2	4	0	.257	.233
Ahead in Count	.170	171	29	8	2	1	13	0	59	.179	.257
Behind in Count	.333	57	19	4	0	1	9	9	0	.424	.456
Two Strikes	.150	167	25	7	2	0	12	10	66	.207	.216

Last Five Years

	ERA	W	L	Sv	G	GS	IP	H	HR	BB	SO
Home	2.05	18	15	78	179	0	242.0	198	10	54	224
Away	2.42	7	8	81	158	0	204.1	158	13	83	176
Day	2.83	5	9	41	91	0	121.0	102	8	45	114
Night	1.99	20	14	118	246	0	325.1	254	15	92	286
Grass	2.46	7	7	60	118	0	157.1	120	11	64	131

	Avg	AB	H	2B	3B	HR	RBI	BB	SO	OBP	SLG
vs. Left	.240	800	192	34	4	13	89	76	150	.309	.341
vs. Right	.195	841	164	26	2	10	78	61	250	.255	.266
Inning 1-6	.216	37	8	3	0	1	7	5	6	.310	.378
Inning 7+	.217	1604	348	57	6	22	160	132	394	.281	.301
None on	.228	865	197	38	3	12	12	67	208	.289	.320

Last Five Years	ERA	W	L	Sv	G	GS	IP	H	HR	BB	SO		Avg	AB	H	2B	3B	HR	RBI	BB	SO	OBP	SLG
Turf	2.09	18	16	99	219	0	289.0	236	12	73	269	Runners on	.205	776	159	22	3	11	155	70	192	.274	.284
April	2.39	5	6	13	45	0	60.1	53	3	13	52	Scoring Posn	.199	463	92	11	3	7	140	52	118	.281	.281
May	2.63	8	5	24	58	0	85.2	64	4	26	77	Close & Late	.231	1038	240	37	4	16	133	90	236	.294	.321
June	2.29	0	2	28	57	0	74.2	65	4	20	69	None on/out	.217	369	80	16	0	5	5	31	87	.283	.301
July	1.73	3	2	32	56	0	83.0	62	4	25	76	vs. 1st Batr (relief)	.238	307	73	16	0	5	35	21	75	.295	.339
August	2.06	3	5	36	62	0	70.0	50	4	26	68	First Inning Pitched	.223	1190	265	50	4	19	139	100	276	.286	.319
September/October	2.23	6	3	26	59	0	72.2	62	4	27	58	First 15 Pitches	.232	1051	244	48	4	18	116	79	230	.290	.337
Starter	0.00	0	0	0	0	0	0.0	0	0	0	0	Pitch 16-30	.187	443	83	10	2	2	34	46	134	.270	.233
Reliever	2.22	25	23	159	337	0	446.1	356	23	137	400	Pitch 31-45	.189	122	23	1	0	2	13	11	33	.256	.246
0 Days rest	1.60	4	4	61	85	0	106.2	73	5	38	93	Pitch 46+	.240	25	6	1	0	1	4	1	3	.269	.400
1 or 2 Days rest	2.82	11	15	68	161	0	210.2	185	11	66	196	First Pitch	.264	208	55	11	1	4	32	16	0	.326	.385
3+ Days rest	1.74	10	4	30	91	0	129.0	98	7	33	111	Ahead in Count	.166	885	147	23	4	9	71	0	349	.174	.232
Pre-All Star	2.37	15	14	71	179	0	250.2	204	13	66	231	Behind in Count	.311	267	83	16	1	6	38	75	0	.459	.446
Post-All Star	2.02	10	9	88	158	0	195.2	152	10	71	169	Two Strikes	.141	874	123	18	2	6	53	45	400	.188	.186

Pitcher vs. Batter (career)

Pitches Best Vs.	Avg	AB	H	2B	3B	HR	RBI	BB	SO	OBP	SLG	Pitches Worst Vs.	Avg	AB	H	2B	3B	HR	RBI	BB	SO	OBP	SLG
Joe Carter	.000	12	0	0	0	0	1	0	3	.000	.000	Lou Whitaker	.600	10	6	1	0	1	3	2	0	.667	1.000
Gene Larkin	.000	12	0	0	0	0	0	1	5	.077	.000	Kent Hrbek	.429	14	6	1	0	1	4	2	0	.500	.714
Darryl Hamilton	.000	12	0	0	0	0	0	1	0	.077	.000	Mike Greenwell	.429	14	6	1	0	1	2	0	0	.429	.714
Greg Gagne	.100	10	1	0	0	0	0	1	1	.182	.100	Don Mattingly	.400	15	6	2	0	1	4	1	0	.438	.733
Steve Sax	.125	16	2	0	0	0	1	0	5	.125	.125	Frank Thomas	.333	9	3	1	0	1	3	2	3	.455	.778

Charlie Montoyo — Expos

Age 28 – Bats Right

	Avg	G	AB	R	H	2B	3B	HR	RBI	BB	SO	HBP	GDP	SB	CS	OBP	SLG	IBB	SH	SF	#Pit	#P/PA	GB	FB	G/F
1993 Season	.400	4	5	1	2	1	0	0	3	0	0	0	0	0	0	.400	.600	0	0	0	20	4.00	0	2	0.00

1993 Season

	Avg	AB	H	2B	3B	HR	RBI	BB	SO	OBP	SLG		Avg	AB	H	2B	3B	HR	RBI	BB	SO	OBP	SLG
vs. Left	.500	4	2	1	0	0	3	0	0	.500	.750	Scoring Posn	.500	4	2	1	0	0	3	0	0	.500	.750
vs. Right	.000	1	0	0	0	0	0	0	0	.000	.000	Close & Late	.500	2	1	0	0	0	1	0	0	.500	.500

Marcus Moore — Rockies

Age 23 – Pitches Right (flyball pitcher)

	ERA	W	L	Sv	G	GS	IP	BB	SO	Avg	H	2B	3B	HR	RBI	OBP	SLG	GF	IR	IRS	Hld	SvOp	SB	CS	GB	FB	G/F
1993 Season	6.84	3	1	0	27	0	26.1	20	13	.291	30	5	2	4	23	.398	.495	8	22	8	3	2	2	0	36	38	0.95

1993 Season

	ERA	W	L	Sv	G	GS	IP	H	HR	BB	SO		Avg	AB	H	2B	3B	HR	RBI	BB	SO	OBP	SLG
Home	4.40	1	0	0	14	0	14.1	13	3	12	8	vs. Left	.265	49	13	1	1	2	12	12	9	.394	.449
Away	9.75	2	1	0	13	0	12.0	17	1	8	5	vs. Right	.315	54	17	4	1	2	11	8	4	.403	.537
Starter	0.00	0	0	0	0	0	0.0	0	0	0	0	Scoring Posn	.314	35	11	1	0	2	19	5	4	.378	.514
Reliever	6.84	3	1	0	27	0	26.1	30	4	20	13	Close & Late	.342	38	13	2	1	1	8	7	7	.426	.526
0 Days rest	4.15	2	0	0	12	0	13.0	13	2	9	7	None on/out	.238	21	5	1	0	1	1	5	3	.385	.429
1 or 2 Days rest	10.29	0	1	0	9	0	7.0	11	1	3	3	First Pitch	.385	13	5	0	0	1	5	0	0	.333	.615
3+ Days rest	8.53	1	0	0	6	0	6.1	6	1	8	3	Ahead in Count	.189	37	7	1	1	0	5	0	9	.184	.270
Pre-All Star	0.00	1	0	0	1	0	0.2	1	0	0	0	Behind in Count	.226	31	7	3	1	0	3	12	0	.432	.387
Post-All Star	7.01	2	1	0	26	0	25.2	29	4	20	13	Two Strikes	.229	48	11	2	1	1	10	8	13	.333	.375

Mike Moore — Tigers

Age 34 – Pitches Right

	ERA	W	L	Sv	G	GS	IP	BB	SO	Avg	H	2B	3B	HR	RBI	OBP	SLG	CG	ShO	Sup	QS	#P/S	SB	CS	GB	FB	G/F
1993 Season	5.22	13	9	0	36	36	213.2	89	89	.271	227	40	4	35	119	.340	.453	4	3	6.32	15	95	23	8	347	234	1.48
Last Five Years	3.87	79	55	0	173	173	1087.2	464	604	.251	1029	188	19	94	453	.327	.375	18	7	4.82	95	102	85	49	1640	1106	1.48

1993 Season

	ERA	W	L	Sv	G	GS	IP	H	HR	BB	SO		Avg	AB	H	2B	3B	HR	RBI	BB	SO	OBP	SLG
Home	5.12	6	4	0	15	15	91.1	88	14	36	41	vs. Left	.271	432	117	20	4	15	54	49	35	.346	.440
Away	5.30	7	5	0	21	21	122.1	139	21	53	48	vs. Right	.271	406	110	20	0	20	65	40	54	.334	.468
Day	5.29	5	2	0	11	11	66.1	67	14	27	33	Inning 1-6	.277	716	198	38	4	28	107	77	72	.345	.458
Night	5.19	8	7	0	25	25	147.1	160	21	62	56	Inning 7+	.238	122	29	2	0	7	12	12	17	.311	.426
Grass	5.17	11	8	0	30	30	177.2	185	27	75	76	None on	.270	481	130	24	1	15	15	42	49	.333	.418
Turf	5.50	2	1	0	6	6	36.0	42	8	14	13	Runners on	.272	357	97	16	3	20	104	47	40	.350	.501
April	6.25	2	1	0	6	6	31.2	36	3	18	11	Scoring Posn	.245	200	49	10	1	10	80	32	22	.338	.455
May	4.60	1	0	0	5	5	29.1	28	4	14	10	Close & Late	.176	34	6	0	0	1	1	2	5	.222	.265
June	7.64	2	4	0	6	6	33.0	36	9	15	12	None on/out	.290	210	61	10	0	7	7	25	17	.366	.438
July	5.74	2	0	0	6	6	31.1	42	4	7	16	vs. 1st Batr (relief)	.000	0	0	0	0	0	0	0	0	.000	.000
August	2.45	4	1	0	6	6	47.2	36	7	16	22	First Inning Pitched	.272	147	40	6	0	11	33	19	9	.355	.537
September/October	5.75	2	3	0	7	7	40.2	49	8	19	18	First 75 Pitches	.278	607	169	34	2	25	92	70	63	.351	.465
Starter	5.22	13	9	0	36	36	213.2	227	35	89	89	Pitch 76-90	.231	104	24	4	1	2	7	5	9	.264	.346
Reliever	0.00	0	0	0	0	0	0.0	0	0	0	0	Pitch 91-105	.232	82	19	2	1	5	14	4	11	.267	.463
0-3 Days Rest	6.75	1	2	0	6	6	34.2	43	9	15	12	Pitch 106+	.333	45	15	0	0	3	6	10	6	.464	.533
4 Days Rest	4.84	11	5	0	24	24	147.0	147	21	60	62	First Pitch	.350	123	43	9	1	6	24	7	0	.381	.585
5+ Days Rest	5.34	1	2	0	6	6	32.0	37	5	14	15	Ahead in Count	.223	341	76	9	1	9	28	0	75	.222	.334
Pre-All Star	6.53	5	5	0	19	19	100.2	117	17	49	34	Behind in Count	.304	214	65	17	0	12	43	51	0	.433	.551
Post-All Star	4.06	8	4	0	17	17	113.0	110	18	40	55	Two Strikes	.199	336	67	7	1	8	26	31	89	.267	.298

Last Five Years

	ERA	W	L	Sv	G	GS	IP	H	HR	BB	SO
Home	3.41	41	25	0	87	87	557.1	497	47	227	304
Away	4.36	38	30	0	86	86	530.1	532	47	237	300
Day	3.80	35	19	0	67	67	428.1	390	40	176	246
Night	3.92	44	36	0	106	106	659.1	639	54	288	358
Grass	3.79	68	47	0	146	146	922.2	864	77	391	509
Turf	4.31	11	8	0	27	27	165.0	165	17	73	95
April	3.50	13	3	0	24	24	149.0	132	8	73	80
May	4.28	13	10	0	29	29	180.2	172	16	86	95
June	4.74	9	17	0	31	31	188.0	185	23	87	96
July	3.84	14	6	0	28	28	168.2	170	13	62	98
August	3.03	14	8	0	29	29	202.0	182	17	66	123
September/October	3.84	16	11	0	32	32	199.1	188	17	90	112
Starter	3.87	79	55	0	173	173	1087.2	1029	94	464	604
Reliever	0.00	0	0	0	0	0	0.0	0	0	0	0
0-3 Days Rest	3.95	12	6	0	25	25	157.1	143	17	71	74
4 Days Rest	4.08	51	38	0	115	115	719.2	699	58	307	429
5+ Days Rest	3.12	16	11	0	33	33	210.2	187	19	86	101
Pre-All Star	4.13	42	30	0	94	94	578.0	546	53	266	312
Post-All Star	3.58	37	25	0	79	79	509.2	483	41	198	292

	Avg	AB	H	2B	3B	HR	RBI	BB	SO	OBP	SLG
vs. Left	.248	2101	521	96	10	35	220	239	267	.324	.353
vs. Right	.254	2001	508	92	9	59	233	225	337	.331	.397
Inning 1-6	.255	3550	904	162	18	79	412	411	522	.332	.377
Inning 7+	.226	552	125	26	1	15	41	53	82	.296	.359
None on	.249	2406	598	108	9	57	57	236	371	.320	.372
Runners on	.254	1696	431	80	10	37	396	228	233	.338	.379
Scoring Posn	.249	947	236	49	7	21	348	161	132	.349	.382
Close & Late	.237	274	65	17	0	5	21	23	42	.298	.354
None on/out	.236	1061	250	45	6	24	24	109	172	.310	.357
vs. 1st Batr (relief)	.000	0	0	0	0	0	0	0	0	.000	.000
First Inning Pitched	.255	646	165	32	2	17	93	83	94	.338	.390
First 75 Pitches	.253	2897	733	141	14	62	322	332	429	.330	.376
Pitch 76-90	.250	517	129	21	2	14	67	58	60	.326	.379
Pitch 91-105	.223	382	85	7	1	12	38	40	69	.296	.340
Pitch 106+	.268	306	82	19	2	6	26	34	46	.343	.402
First Pitch	.299	558	167	33	4	16	89	15	0	.315	.459
Ahead in Count	.210	1701	358	50	6	31	122	0	490	.215	.302
Behind in Count	.291	982	286	65	5	30	150	245	0	.430	.459
Two Strikes	.201	1765	355	58	8	23	116	204	604	.286	.282

Pitcher vs. Batter (since 1984)

Pitches Best Vs.	Avg	AB	H	2B	3B	HR	RBI	BB	SO	OBP	SLG
Carlos Quintana	.000	10	0	0	0	0	0	1	1	.091	.000
Troy Neel	.000	10	0	0	0	0	0	1	2	.091	.000
Dante Bichette	.000	9	0	0	0	0	0	2	2	.182	.000
Ivan Rodriguez	.063	16	1	1	0	0	0	1	2	.118	.125
Daryl Boston	.087	23	2	2	0	0	2	0	6	.083	.174

Pitches Worst Vs.	Avg	AB	H	2B	3B	HR	RBI	BB	SO	OBP	SLG
Mark Lewis	.636	11	7	3	0	0	3	0	1	.636	.909
Pat Kelly	.636	11	7	1	0	0	3	0	2	.636	.727
Darnell Coles	.467	15	7	1	1	3	10	3	0	.556	1.267
Sammy Sosa	.462	13	6	2	1	1	3	1	1	.500	1.000
Rob Deer	.415	41	17	2	0	6	13	8	8	.500	.902

Mickey Morandini — Phillies

Age 28 – Bats Left (groundball hitter)

	Avg	G	AB	R	H	2B	3B	HR	RBI	BB	SO	HBP	GDP	SB	CS	OBP	SLG	IBB	SH	SF	#Pit	#P/PA	GB	FB	G/F
1993 Season	.247	120	425	57	105	19	9	3	33	34	73	5	6	13	2	.309	.355	2	4	2	1701	3.62	160	105	1.52
Career (1990-1993)	.253	370	1251	151	317	42	21	8	86	94	201	7	18	37	7	.308	.340	4	18	6	5080	3.69	512	280	1.83

1993 Season

	Avg	AB	H	2B	3B	HR	RBI	BB	SO	OBP	SLG
vs. Left	.212	99	21	2	2	1	6	9	10	.284	.303
vs. Right	.258	326	84	17	7	2	27	25	63	.317	.371
Groundball	.262	145	38	5	4	2	11	14	21	.333	.393
Flyball	.212	66	14	5	0	0	3	3	14	.246	.288
Home	.262	225	59	10	3	2	19	15	33	.311	.360
Away	.230	200	46	9	6	1	14	19	40	.306	.350
Day	.260	131	34	5	4	1	14	13	24	.331	.382
Night	.241	294	71	14	5	2	19	21	49	.299	.344
Grass	.202	124	25	6	3	0	8	10	22	.267	.298
Turf	.266	301	80	13	6	3	25	24	51	.326	.379
First Pitch	.387	75	29	1	4	1	11	2	0	.403	.547
Ahead in Count	.322	87	28	4	2	0	7	15	0	.425	.414
Behind in Count	.184	185	34	10	2	1	10	0	59	.197	.276
Two Strikes	.155	181	28	8	2	1	9	17	73	.231	.238

	Avg	AB	H	2B	3B	HR	RBI	BB	SO	OBP	SLG
Scoring Posn	.223	103	23	2	3	1	28	16	17	.339	.330
Close & Late	.174	69	12	3	2	2	9	5	12	.237	.362
None on/out	.313	83	26	2	2	0	0	8	11	.374	.386
Batting #2	.264	265	70	17	5	2	23	19	47	.316	.389
Batting #8	.217	129	28	2	4	0	8	8	21	.275	.295
Other	.226	31	7	0	0	1	2	7	5	.385	.323
April	.222	72	16	5	1	1	3	7	14	.291	.361
May	.211	90	19	4	1	0	5	4	14	.245	.278
June	.287	94	27	4	4	0	7	5	22	.337	.415
July	.198	91	18	1	0	2	10	10	10	.284	.275
August	.323	31	10	1	3	0	5	4	5	.400	.548
September/October	.319	47	15	4	0	0	3	4	8	.385	.404
Pre-All Star	.243	309	75	14	6	2	23	21	55	.296	.346
Post-All Star	.259	116	30	5	3	1	10	13	18	.344	.379

1993 By Position

Position	Avg	AB	H	2B	3B	HR	RBI	BB	SO	OBP	SLG	G	GS	Innings	PO	A	E	DP	Fld Pct	Rng Fctr	In Zone	Outs	Zone Rtg	MLB Zone
As Pinch Hitter	.273	11	3	0	0	1	2	3	1	.429	.545	14	0	---	---	---	---	---	---	---	---	---	---	---
As 2b	.246	414	102	19	9	2	31	31	72	.305	.350	111	101	928.0	208	287	5	48	.990	4.80	324	290	.895	.895

Career (1990-1993)

	Avg	AB	H	2B	3B	HR	RBI	BB	SO	OBP	SLG
vs. Left	.197	300	59	4	3	2	17	20	45	.248	.250
vs. Right	.271	951	258	38	18	6	69	74	156	.326	.368
Groundball	.277	469	130	13	11	4	32	36	64	.332	.377
Flyball	.216	236	51	8	1	1	13	18	49	.271	.271
Home	.261	640	167	20	10	6	48	44	100	.310	.352
Away	.245	611	150	22	11	2	38	50	101	.306	.327
Day	.268	339	91	13	7	1	25	27	52	.323	.357
Night	.248	912	226	29	14	7	61	67	149	.302	.333
Grass	.273	341	93	15	6	1	29	24	51	.321	.361
Turf	.246	910	224	27	15	7	57	70	150	.303	.332
First Pitch	.287	195	56	2	5	1	15	3	0	.298	.364
Ahead in Count	.320	253	81	8	4	3	26	50	0	.432	.419
Behind in Count	.218	563	123	24	9	3	34	0	165	.223	.309
Two Strikes	.194	561	109	22	9	2	28	41	201	.251	.276

	Avg	AB	H	2B	3B	HR	RBI	BB	SO	OBP	SLG
Scoring Posn	.238	281	67	3	7	3	74	35	54	.323	.331
Close & Late	.248	210	52	8	3	2	16	18	31	.310	.343
None on/out	.287	293	84	9	3	1	1	23	40	.341	.348
Batting #2	.265	623	165	24	9	4	47	47	90	.318	.352
Batting #8	.247	328	81	10	7	2	21	18	63	.290	.338
Other	.237	300	71	8	5	2	18	29	48	.307	.317
April	.288	153	44	6	3	2	8	12	29	.339	.405
May	.232	190	44	6	1	1	14	14	34	.288	.289
June	.235	243	57	10	6	1	21	21	44	.299	.337
July	.243	230	56	7	3	2	20	18	30	.300	.326
August	.254	130	33	3	5	0	7	11	17	.317	.354
September/October	.272	305	83	10	3	2	16	18	47	.314	.344
Pre-All Star	.252	702	177	25	10	5	53	54	122	.308	.338
Post-All Star	.255	549	140	17	11	3	33	40	79	.308	.342

Batter vs. Pitcher (career)

Hits Best Against	Avg	AB	H	2B	3B	HR	RBI	BB	SO	OBP	SLG
Willie Blair	.545	11	6	1	1	0	1	0	1	.545	.818
Mike Bielecki	.417	12	5	2	0	0	2	1	1	.462	.583
Dwight Gooden	.370	27	10	1	1	0	3	3	5	.433	.481

Hits Worst Against	Avg	AB	H	2B	3B	HR	RBI	BB	SO	OBP	SLG
Dennis Martinez	.045	22	1	0	0	0	0	1	3	.087	.045
Omar Olivares	.059	17	1	0	0	0	0	1	1	.111	.059
Donovan Osborne	.091	11	1	0	0	0	0	0	0	.091	.091

Batter vs. Pitcher (career)											
Hits Best Against	Avg	AB	H	2B	3B	HR	RBI	BB	SO	OBP	SLG
Bob Walk	.368	19	7	1	0	1	2	2	1	.429	.579
Bryn Smith	.333	9	3	2	0	0	1	2	0	.455	.556

Hits Worst Against	Avg	AB	H	2B	3B	HR	RBI	BB	SO	OBP	SLG
Bob Tewksbury	.120	25	3	0	0	0	0	0	3	.120	.120
Pete Harnisch	.143	14	2	0	0	0	1	0	6	.143	.143

Mike Morgan — Cubs

Age 34 – Pitches Right (groundball pitcher)

	ERA	W	L	Sv	G	GS	IP	BB	SO	Avg	H	2B	3B	HR	RBI	OBP	SLG	CG	ShO	Sup	QS	#P/S	SB	CS	GB	FB	G/F
1993 Season	4.03	10	15	0	32	32	207.2	74	111	.262	206	31	5	15	87	.329	.372	1	1	3.42	19	95	17	14	356	158	2.25
Last Five Years	3.14	59	59	1	173	151	1047.2	307	552	.245	952	150	22	66	363	.302	.345	18	7	3.69	104	95	70	47	1887	764	2.47

1993 Season

	ERA	W	L	Sv	G	GS	IP	H	HR	BB	SO
Home	3.12	5	6	0	15	15	104.0	97	6	32	60
Away	4.95	5	9	0	17	17	103.2	109	9	42	51
Day	3.05	5	9	0	19	19	130.0	120	6	44	68
Night	5.68	5	6	0	13	13	77.2	86	9	00	40
Grass	3.99	8	10	0	24	24	158.0	159	13	48	85
Turf	4.17	2	5	0	8	8	49.2	47	2	26	26
April	4.65	1	4	0	5	5	31.0	30	1	17	14
May	2.94	2	2	0	5	5	33.2	31	0	10	12
June	4.45	2	2	0	4	4	28.1	31	3	10	16
July	2.77	2	2	0	6	6	39.0	35	2	10	22
August	5.12	1	3	0	6	6	38.2	52	3	13	25
September/October	4.38	2	2	0	6	6	37.0	27	6	14	22
Starter	4.03	10	15	0	32	32	207.2	206	15	74	111
Reliever	0.00	0	0	0	0	0	0.0	0	0	0	0
0-3 Days Rest	0.00	0	0	0	0	0	0.0	0	0	0	0
4 Days Rest	4.27	6	10	0	21	21	139.0	141	11	53	75
5+ Days Rest	3.54	4	5	0	11	11	68.2	65	4	21	36
Pre-All Star	3.86	6	9	0	16	16	107.1	105	5	40	49
Post-All Star	4.22	4	6	0	16	16	100.1	101	10	34	62

	Avg	AB	H	2B	3B	HR	RBI	BB	SO	OBP	SLG
vs. Left	.245	424	104	16	4	7	41	51	63	.330	.351
vs. Right	.282	362	102	15	1	8	46	23	48	.328	.395
Inning 1-6	.262	682	179	27	4	13	79	67	98	.333	.371
Inning 7+	.200	104	27	4	1	2	8	7	13	.304	.375
None on	.248	467	116	18	3	7	7	38	64	.310	.345
Runners on	.282	319	90	13	2	8	80	36	47	.355	.411
Scoring Posn	.289	187	54	7	2	4	70	27	26	.378	.412
Close & Late	.300	60	18	3	0	2	5	3	7	.333	.450
None on/out	.267	202	54	7	2	3	3	17	31	.330	.366
vs. 1st Batr (relief)	.000	0	0	0	0	0	0	0	0	.000	.000
First Inning Pitched	.279	129	36	5	2	2	21	11	22	.343	.395
First 75 Pitches	.271	601	163	24	4	12	75	54	87	.337	.384
Pitch 76-90	.204	93	19	3	0	2	6	11	10	.283	.301
Pitch 91-105	.243	74	18	3	1	1	4	5	11	.291	.351
Pitch 106+	.333	18	6	1	0	0	2	4	3	.455	.389
First Pitch	.280	143	40	6	2	0	15	6	0	.314	.350
Ahead in Count	.225	316	71	13	0	6	30	0	96	.234	.323
Behind in Count	.342	187	64	9	3	7	27	39	0	.454	.535
Two Strikes	.177	300	53	8	0	3	23	29	111	.250	.233

Last Five Years

	ERA	W	L	Sv	G	GS	IP	H	HR	BB	SO
Home	2.74	29	25	1	84	75	546.0	475	37	145	288
Away	3.57	30	34	0	89	76	501.2	477	29	162	264
Day	2.54	29	21	1	70	63	456.1	393	20	139	232
Night	3.59	30	38	0	103	88	591.1	559	46	168	320
Grass	2.91	46	36	1	124	109	780.2	696	53	206	402
Turf	3.81	13	23	0	49	42	267.0	256	13	101	150
April	2.87	8	10	0	23	20	141.1	114	7	41	65
May	2.64	15	7	0	27	27	187.2	158	8	57	117
June	2.96	10	11	0	27	26	188.1	176	12	42	89
July	3.25	8	12	1	31	28	174.2	165	7	60	89
August	3.31	7	11	0	34	24	182.0	192	10	57	94
September/October	3.78	11	8	0	31	26	173.2	147	22	50	98
Starter	3.19	57	59	0	151	151	1014.0	933	66	301	537
Reliever	1.60	2	0	1	22	0	33.2	19	0	6	15
0-3 Days Rest	2.00	2	2	0	4	4	27.0	25	0	4	10
4 Days Rest	3.11	35	35	0	97	97	656.0	602	48	192	330
5+ Days Rest	3.43	20	22	0	50	50	331.0	306	18	105	197
Pre-All Star	2.82	35	32	1	88	83	581.1	516	30	157	306
Post-All Star	3.53	24	27	0	85	68	466.1	436	36	150	246

	Avg	AB	H	2B	3B	HR	RBI	BB	SO	OBP	SLG
vs. Left	.252	2165	546	93	12	38	197	209	292	.319	.359
vs. Right	.235	1726	406	57	10	28	166	98	260	.278	.329
Inning 1-6	.243	3200	778	125	16	54	313	266	469	.303	.343
Inning 7+	.252	691	174	25	6	12	50	41	83	.295	.357
None on	.235	2409	567	86	13	38	38	152	345	.284	.329
Runners on	.260	1482	385	64	9	28	325	155	207	.329	.372
Scoring Posn	.248	823	204	37	6	12	281	121	143	.341	.351
Close & Late	.259	352	91	14	4	6	30	25	40	.310	.372
None on/out	.237	1027	243	36	5	15	15	67	139	.287	.325
vs. 1st Batr (relief)	.200	20	4	2	0	0	3	1	1	.238	.300
First Inning Pitched	.232	624	145	27	3	6	68	52	101	.294	.314
First 75 Pitches	.243	2964	720	115	16	46	279	230	433	.300	.339
Pitch 76-90	.235	489	115	18	2	11	43	39	62	.289	.348
Pitch 91-105	.255	321	82	12	2	5	29	24	42	.308	.352
Pitch 106+	.299	117	35	5	2	4	12	14	15	.376	.479
First Pitch	.279	685	191	33	4	14	77	28	0	.310	.400
Ahead in Count	.188	1537	289	46	6	16	109	0	449	.192	.257
Behind in Count	.302	947	286	38	6	25	110	167	0	.405	.434
Two Strikes	.178	1506	268	43	10	12	100	110	552	.235	.244

Pitcher vs. Batter (since 1984)

Pitches Best Vs.	Avg	AB	H	2B	3B	HR	RBI	BB	SO	OBP	SLG
Gerald Young	.000	11	0	0	0	0	1	0	1	.000	.000
Greg Olson	.000	11	0	0	0	0	0	0	3	.000	.000
Dennis Martinez	.063	16	1	0	0	0	0	0	4	.063	.063
Andujar Cedeno	.067	15	1	1	0	0	1	0	6	.067	.133
Cal Ripken	.091	22	2	0	0	0	0	0	4	.091	.091

Pitches Worst Vs.	Avg	AB	H	2B	3B	HR	RBI	BB	SO	OBP	SLG
Danny Tartabull	.727	11	8	0	0	1	4	1	0	.750	1.000
Randy Bush	.478	23	11	2	0	2	8	3	1	.538	.826
Wally Joyner	.417	12	5	2	0	1	4	0	1	.417	.833
Rickey Henderson	.400	10	4	0	0	2	2	1	2	.455	1.000
Dan Pasqua	.385	13	5	0	0	2	2	2	4	.467	.846

Hal Morris — Reds

Age 29 – Bats Left (groundball hitter)

	Avg	G	AB	R	H	2B	3B	HR	RBI	BB	SO	HBP	GDP	SB	CS	OBP	SLG	IBB	SH	SF	#Pit	#P/PA	GB	FB	G/F
1993 Season	.317	101	379	48	120	18	0	7	49	34	51	2	5	2	2	.371	.420	4	0	6	1473	3.50	152	88	1.73
Last Five Years	.310	474	1579	213	489	94	7	34	201	147	201	6	35	27	15	.367	.443	23	10	17	6338	3.60	649	397	1.63

1993 Season

	Avg	AB	H	2B	3B	HR	RBI	BB	SO	OBP	SLG
vs. Left	.244	86	21	4	0	0	8	7	20	.305	.291
vs. Right	.338	293	99	14	0	7	41	27	31	.390	.457
Groundball	.306	124	38	11	0	1	14	10	15	.362	.419
Flyball	.292	72	21	0	0	0	10	8	10	.354	.292
Home	.321	184	59	12	0	2	20	17	23	.376	.418
Away	.313	195	61	6	0	5	29	17	28	.366	.421
Day	.393	89	35	3	0	5	17	12	11	.462	.596
Night	.293	290	85	15	0	2	32	22	40	.340	.366
Grass	.303	119	36	2	0	4	20	12	22	.358	.420

	Avg	AB	H	2B	3B	HR	RBI	BB	SO	OBP	SLG
Scoring Posn	.280	100	28	5	0	1	40	14	18	.350	.360
Close & Late	.283	60	17	3	0	1	5	5	13	.338	.383
None on/out	.305	82	25	3	0	2	2	5	12	.345	.415
Batting #2	.278	133	37	6	0	0	11	10	20	.331	.323
Batting #3	.323	189	61	7	0	7	32	19	24	.379	.471
Other	.386	57	22	5	0	0	6	5	7	.435	.474
April	.000	0	0	0	0	0	0	0	0	.000	.000
May	.000	0	0	0	0	0	0	0	0	.000	.000
June	.284	81	23	1	0	0	8	4	10	.307	.296

1993 Season

	Avg	AB	H	2B	3B	HR	RBI	BB	SO	OBP	SLG
Turf	.323	260	84	16	0	3	29	22	29	.376	.419
First Pitch	.425	73	31	5	0	2	12	4	0	.449	.575
Ahead in Count	.375	88	33	3	0	2	13	16	0	.467	.477
Behind in Count	.215	149	32	6	0	2	13	0	37	.225	.295
Two Strikes	.193	150	29	8	0	2	13	14	51	.267	.287

	Avg	AB	H	2B	3B	HR	RBI	BB	SO	OBP	SLG
July	.305	95	29	6	0	1	9	10	13	.377	.400
August	.330	100	33	5	0	3	17	9	14	.387	.470
September/October	.340	103	35	6	0	3	15	11	14	.397	.485
Pre-All Star	.274	113	31	1	0	1	10	9	13	.325	.310
Post-All Star	.335	266	89	17	0	6	39	25	38	.390	.466

1993 By Position

Position	Avg	AB	H	2B	3B	HR	RBI	BB	SO	OBP	SLG	G	GS	Innings	PO	A	E	DP	Fld Pct	Rng Fctr	In Zone	Outs	Zone Rtg	MLB Zone
As 1b	.320	375	120	18	0	7	49	32	51	.371	.424	98	94	834.1	745	76	5	61	.994	---	170	145	.853	.834

Last Five Years

	Avg	AB	H	2B	3B	HR	RBI	BB	SO	OBP	SLG
vs. Left	.244	405	99	17	1	2	36	33	89	.304	.306
vs. Right	.332	1174	390	77	6	32	165	114	112	.389	.490
Groundball	.307	524	161	38	1	8	67	41	58	.358	.429
Flyball	.294	361	106	21	1	10	46	35	48	.353	.440
Home	.309	779	241	56	3	17	104	67	96	.363	.454
Away	.310	800	248	38	4	17	97	80	105	.371	.431
Day	.318	475	151	33	2	16	72	51	50	.383	.497
Night	.306	1104	338	61	5	18	129	96	151	.360	.419
Grass	.300	467	140	23	3	10	61	48	68	.362	.426
Turf	.314	1112	349	71	4	24	140	99	133	.369	.450
First Pitch	.377	265	100	22	2	8	44	15	0	.408	.566
Ahead in Count	.377	403	152	30	0	14	67	70	0	.466	.556
Behind in Count	.228	624	142	25	3	7	59	0	162	.232	.311
Two Strikes	.218	638	139	24	3	7	56	59	201	.286	.298

	Avg	AB	H	2B	3B	HR	RBI	BB	SO	OBP	SLG
Scoring Posn	.299	418	125	25	1	5	160	63	65	.378	.400
Close & Late	.282	255	72	15	3	3	17	19	48	.337	.400
None on/out	.316	348	110	20	3	7	7	20	43	.353	.451
Batting #2	.297	401	119	24	1	6	37	39	59	.359	.406
Batting #3	.295	471	139	20	2	12	66	36	58	.341	.423
Other	.327	707	231	50	4	16	98	72	84	.389	.477
April	.307	101	31	8	1	2	12	4	14	.336	.465
May	.311	151	47	10	2	2	26	16	17	.376	.444
June	.309	265	82	13	1	3	38	21	36	.356	.400
July	.328	354	116	21	2	9	41	39	44	.392	.475
August	.298	329	98	20	0	10	40	23	42	.344	.450
September/October	.303	379	115	22	1	8	44	44	48	.375	.430
Pre-All Star	.316	624	197	35	4	11	90	59	76	.374	.438
Post-All Star	.306	955	292	59	3	23	111	88	125	.363	.446

Batter vs. Pitcher (career)

Hits Best Against	Avg	AB	H	2B	3B	HR	RBI	BB	SO	OBP	SLG
Jimmy Jones	.636	11	7	0	0	1	2	0	0	.636	.909
Mel Rojas	.538	13	7	2	0	1	1	0	1	.538	.923
Greg Maddux	.520	25	13	3	0	0	2	1	1	.538	.640
Kevin Gross	.500	14	7	0	0	0	1	2	1	.563	.500
John Burkett	.423	26	11	1	0	2	4	4	1	.500	.692

Hits Worst Against	Avg	AB	H	2B	3B	HR	RBI	BB	SO	OBP	SLG
Frank Seminara	.000	9	0	0	0	0	2	2	1	.167	.000
Al Osuna	.091	11	1	0	0	0	1	0	2	.083	.091
Jeff Innis	.111	9	1	0	0	0	1	1	0	.182	.111
Bruce Hurst	.125	16	2	1	0	0	2	0	2	.125	.188
Butch Henry	.182	11	2	1	0	0	0	0	1	.182	.273

Jack Morris — Blue Jays

Age 39 – Pitches Right

	ERA	W	L	Sv	G	GS	IP	BB	SO	Avg	H	2B	3B	HR	RBI	OBP	SLG	CG	ShO	Sup	QS	#P/S	SB	CS	GB	FB	G/F
1993 Season	6.19	7	12	0	27	27	152.2	65	103	.302	189	31	6	18	98	.368	.458	4	1	4.78	8	95	17	10	249	152	1.64
Last Five Years	4.45	67	62	0	156	156	1060.0	393	675	.260	1057	175	23	103	517	.326	.390	41	7	5.04	76	104	140	46	1505	1105	1.36

1993 Season

	ERA	W	L	Sv	G	GS	IP	H	HR	BB	SO
Home	7.34	3	6	0	14	14	76.0	102	11	36	59
Away	5.05	4	6	0	13	13	76.2	87	7	29	44
Starter	6.19	7	12	0	27	27	152.2	189	18	65	103
Reliever	0.00	0	0	0	0	0	0.0	0	0	0	0
0-3 Days Rest	0.00	0	0	0	0	0	0.0	0	0	0	0
4 Days Rest	5.84	6	6	0	16	16	89.1	104	7	40	60
5+ Days Rest	6.68	1	6	0	11	11	63.1	85	11	25	43
Pre-All Star	7.41	5	9	0	16	16	88.2	115	10	38	57
Post-All Star	4.50	2	3	0	11	11	64.0	74	8	27	46

	Avg	AB	H	2B	3B	HR	RBI	BB	SO	OBP	SLG
vs. Left	.318	321	102	17	4	9	50	37	41	.385	.480
vs. Right	.286	304	87	14	2	9	48	28	62	.350	.434
Scoring Posn	.331	175	58	10	2	6	78	17	33	.381	.514
Close & Late	.256	39	10	1	0	2	6	3	7	.302	.436
None on/out	.268	149	40	5	1	3	3	16	27	.343	.376
First Pitch	.386	83	32	7	2	1	18	1	0	.400	.554
Ahead in Count	.275	287	79	12	3	7	31	0	83	.273	.411
Behind in Count	.347	124	43	4	0	6	28	43	0	.509	.524
Two Strikes	.243	280	68	9	3	8	30	21	103	.295	.382

Last Five Years

	ERA	W	L	Sv	G	GS	IP	H	HR	BB	SO
Home	4.22	39	25	0	77	77	535.2	525	49	181	333
Away	4.69	28	37	0	79	79	524.1	532	54	212	342
Day	4.19	27	19	0	52	52	343.2	351	30	131	209
Night	4.57	40	43	0	104	104	716.1	706	73	262	466
Grass	4.46	34	45	0	89	89	605.0	602	65	231	391
Turf	4.43	33	17	0	67	67	455.0	455	38	162	284
April	5.66	8	14	0	25	25	154.1	187	17	70	113
May	5.12	9	13	0	27	27	181.0	182	22	83	101
June	4.12	16	4	0	22	22	148.2	145	15	49	87
July	4.57	7	11	0	23	23	149.2	143	14	42	102
August	4.44	13	10	0	30	30	202.2	207	15	80	128
September/October	3.22	14	10	0	29	29	223.2	193	20	69	144
Starter	4.45	67	62	0	156	156	1060.0	1057	103	393	675
Reliever	0.00	0	0	0	0	0	0.0	0	0	0	0
0-3 Days Rest	3.89	4	0	0	6	6	39.1	37	2	19	31
4 Days Rest	4.40	45	44	0	105	105	720.2	710	72	262	468
5+ Days Rest	4.65	18	18	0	45	45	300.0	310	29	112	176
Pre-All Star	4.93	36	34	0	81	81	534.2	555	58	217	331
Post-All Star	3.96	31	28	0	75	75	525.1	502	45	176	344

	Avg	AB	H	2B	3B	HR	RBI	BB	SO	OBP	SLG
vs. Left	.282	2010	567	91	15	52	264	228	290	.353	.420
vs. Right	.238	2061	490	84	8	51	252	165	385	.299	.361
Inning 1-6	.264	3339	881	141	21	86	442	340	549	.333	.396
Inning 7+	.240	732	176	34	2	17	74	53	126	.292	.362
None on	.245	2357	577	99	16	55	55	218	404	.312	.370
Runners on	.280	1714	480	76	7	48	461	175	271	.345	.417
Scoring Posn	.283	987	279	47	4	29	400	127	190	.358	.427
Close & Late	.251	435	109	17	1	10	52	32	66	.302	.363
None on/out	.254	1033	262	43	7	30	30	94	172	.318	.396
vs. 1st Batr (relief)	.000	0	0	0	0	0	0	0	0	.000	.000
First Inning Pitched	.279	621	173	25	4	16	95	56	91	.339	.409
First 75 Pitches	.266	2831	753	117	18	78	365	280	455	.333	.403
Pitch 76-90	.263	506	133	25	1	13	71	56	91	.339	.393
Pitch 91-105	.237	431	102	20	4	3	48	36	69	.295	.323
Pitch 106+	.228	303	69	13	0	9	33	21	60	.280	.360
First Pitch	.303	636	193	40	5	22	107	14	0	.324	.486
Ahead in Count	.212	1820	386	63	5	28	178	0	579	.214	.298
Behind in Count	.324	877	284	41	6	38	149	229	0	.461	.514
Two Strikes	.192	1728	332	51	7	26	156	149	675	.258	.275

Pitcher vs. Batter (since 1984)

Pitches Best Vs.	Avg	AB	H	2B	3B	HR	RBI	BB	SO	OBP	SLG
Randy Milligan	.053	19	1	1	0	0	0	0	6	.053	.105
Walt Weiss	.071	14	1	0	0	0	1	2	3	.176	.071

Pitches Worst Vs.	Avg	AB	H	2B	3B	HR	RBI	BB	SO	OBP	SLG
Darnell Coles	.600	10	6	1	0	0	1	1	2	.636	.700
Kenny Lofton	.526	19	10	1	1	0	1	1	2	.550	.684

Pitcher vs. Batter (since 1984)

Pitches Best Vs.	Avg	AB	H	2B	3B	HR	RBI	BB	SO	OBP	SLG
Steve Sax	.100	20	2	0	0	0	0	0	1	.100	.100
Tony Pena	.125	16	2	0	0	0	2	0	2	.125	.125
Dave Gallagher	.125	16	2	0	0	0	1	0	2	.125	.125

Pitches Worst Vs.	Avg	AB	H	2B	3B	HR	RBI	BB	SO	OBP	SLG
Henry Cotto	.500	16	8	2	0	1	1	0	2	.500	.813
Thomas Howard	.500	12	6	1	0	1	5	0	1	.500	.833
Chad Curtis	.455	11	5	2	0	1	5	1	1	.500	.909

Jamie Moyer — Orioles

Age 31 – Pitches Left

	ERA	W	L	Sv	G	GS	IP	BB	SO	Avg	H	2B	3B	HR	RBI	OBP	SLG	CG	ShO	Sup	QS	#P/S	SB	CS	GB	FB	G/F
1993 Season	3.43	12	9	0	25	25	152.0	38	90	.265	154	30	1	11	53	.316	.376	3	1	4.32	16	90	5	6	235	157	1.50
Last Five Years	4.28	18	29	0	81	57	361.2	126	212	.280	391	86	6	32	163	.343	.420	5	1	3.91	27	87	28	20	539	393	1.37

1993 Season

	ERA	W	L	Sv	G	GS	IP	H	HR	BB	SO
Home	4.68	3	5	0	12	12	67.1	73	8	24	45
Away	2.44	9	4	0	13	13	84.2	81	3	14	45
Starter	3.43	12	9	0	25	25	152.0	154	11	38	90
Reliever	0.00	0	0	0	0	0	0.0	0	0	0	0
0-3 Days Rest	36.00	0	0	0	1	1	1.0	3	0	2	1
4 Days Rest	3.07	8	5	0	14	14	88.0	86	6	18	49
5+ Days Rest	3.43	4	4	0	10	10	63.0	65	5	18	40
Pre-All Star	3.60	5	4	0	11	11	65.0	71	4	21	28
Post-All Star	3.31	7	5	0	14	14	87.0	83	7	17	62

	Avg	AB	H	2B	3B	HR	RBI	BB	SO	OBP	SLG
vs. Left	.304	102	31	8	0	3	9	10	13	.377	.471
vs. Right	.256	480	123	22	1	8	44	28	77	.302	.356
Scoring Posn	.245	110	27	7	0	3	40	14	22	.333	.391
Close & Late	.394	33	13	2	0	1	5	1	3	.412	.545
None on/out	.222	162	36	5	0	3	3	3	26	.246	.309
First Pitch	.375	88	33	6	0	2	11	1	0	.389	.511
Ahead in Count	.198	263	52	10	0	3	17	0	75	.213	.270
Behind in Count	.319	116	37	5	1	6	13	13	0	.385	.534
Two Strikes	.193	238	46	5	0	2	14	24	90	.278	.239

Last Five Years

	ERA	W	L	Sv	G	GS	IP	H	HR	BB	SO
Home	4.40	8	12	0	40	28	188.0	197	16	67	128
Away	4.15	10	17	0	41	29	173.2	194	16	59	84
Day	5.27	6	4	0	17	14	85.1	103	6	28	51
Night	3.97	12	25	0	64	43	276.1	288	26	98	161
Grass	4.25	15	22	0	62	43	279.2	298	23	97	166
Turf	4.39	3	7	0	19	14	82.0	93	9	29	46
April	3.73	3	5	0	13	11	62.2	65	7	27	37
May	5.69	0	11	0	19	12	68.0	83	7	28	43
June	4.05	3	0	0	13	5	40.0	48	3	17	21
July	4.58	4	2	0	12	7	55.0	53	5	17	35
August	3.53	4	4	0	12	12	74.0	66	1	21	42
September/October	4.06	4	7	0	12	10	62.0	76	9	16	34
Starter	4.25	17	28	0	57	57	313.2	337	28	110	176
Reliever	4.50	1	1	0	24	0	48.0	54	4	16	36
0-3 Days Rest	10.50	0	1	0	2	2	6.0	9	0	3	5
4 Days Rest	3.34	11	11	0	24	24	145.1	136	9	44	72
5+ Days Rest	4.82	6	16	0	31	31	162.1	192	19	63	99
Pre-All Star	4.38	8	17	0	50	31	199.1	221	19	80	114
Post-All Star	4.16	10	12	0	31	26	162.1	170	13	46	98

	Avg	AB	H	2B	3B	HR	RBI	BB	SO	OBP	SLG
vs. Left	.284	250	71	16	1	8	33	24	32	.357	.452
vs. Right	.280	1144	320	70	5	24	130	102	180	.339	.413
Inning 1-6	.276	1172	323	74	6	26	141	108	182	.339	.416
Inning 7+	.306	222	68	12	0	6	22	18	30	.362	.441
None on	.266	839	223	44	5	21	21	64	125	.324	.405
Runners on	.303	555	168	42	1	11	142	62	87	.369	.441
Scoring Posn	.284	313	89	22	0	6	121	43	54	.360	.412
Close & Late	.338	65	22	5	0	3	9	7	7	.403	.554
None on/out	.270	371	100	20	3	8	8	29	55	.331	.404
vs. 1st Batr (relief)	.250	20	5	1	0	0	3	4	0	.375	.300
First Inning Pitched	.271	295	80	19	0	6	40	31	45	.342	.397
First 75 Pitches	.281	1113	313	75	6	27	140	106	173	.346	.432
Pitch 76-90	.323	161	52	10	0	4	17	8	20	.363	.460
Pitch 91-105	.213	89	19	0	0	1	6	6	11	.263	.247
Pitch 106+	.226	31	7	1	0	0	0	6	8	.351	.258
First Pitch	.373	193	72	18	0	5	36	5	0	.388	.544
Ahead in Count	.217	585	127	23	1	6	40	0	168	.227	.291
Behind in Count	.359	326	117	29	2	13	51	58	0	.452	.580
Two Strikes	.201	571	115	20	3	5	38	63	212	.286	.273

Pitcher vs. Batter (career)

Pitches Best Vs.	Avg	AB	H	2B	3B	HR	RBI	BB	SO	OBP	SLG
Mike Macfarlane	.077	13	1	0	0	0	0	1	4	.143	.077
Robby Thompson	.091	11	1	0	0	0	1	1	2	.167	.091
Tim Teufel	.100	20	2	0	0	0	0	1	2	.143	.100
Glenn Wilson	.120	25	3	0	0	0	0	0	6	.120	.120
Luis Rivera	.130	23	3	0	0	0	1	0	3	.130	.130

Pitches Worst Vs.	Avg	AB	H	2B	3B	HR	RBI	BB	SO	OBP	SLG
Randy Ready	.500	14	7	2	1	0	2	0	0	.500	.786
Pat Borders	.500	10	5	0	1	1	2	1	1	.545	1.000
Ken Griffey Jr	.500	10	5	2	0	0	2	2	4	.583	.700
Dale Murphy	.429	14	6	1	0	2	5	5	2	.579	.929
Darnell Coles	.375	16	6	1	0	3	5	1	2	.412	1.000

Terry Mulholland — Phillies

Age 31 – Pitches Left

	ERA	W	L	Sv	G	GS	IP	BB	SO	Avg	H	2B	3B	HR	RBI	OBP	SLG	CG	ShO	Sup	QS	#P/S	SB	CS	GB	FB	G/F
1993 Season	3.25	12	9	0	29	28	191.0	40	116	.241	177	38	2	20	73	.282	.380	7	2	4.99	18	95	1	5	292	185	1.58
Last Five Years	3.69	54	50	0	153	138	948.0	213	524	.259	944	192	16	72	386	.301	.380	35	9	4.48	78	96	16	21	1423	1013	1.40

1993 Season

	ERA	W	L	Sv	G	GS	IP	H	HR	BB	SO
Home	3.62	6	4	0	14	14	92.0	88	10	19	73
Away	2.91	6	5	0	15	14	99.0	89	10	21	43
Day	2.67	4	3	0	9	9	64.0	50	5	15	30
Night	3.54	8	6	0	20	19	127.0	127	15	25	86
Grass	3.65	4	5	0	9	9	61.2	61	8	13	27
Turf	3.06	8	4	0	20	19	129.1	116	12	27	89
April	3.00	2	3	0	5	5	36.0	30	4	7	22
May	2.83	4	1	0	5	5	35.0	30	2	10	16
June	2.06	3	1	0	5	5	39.1	36	2	6	31
July	4.41	1	3	0	5	5	32.2	34	4	9	19
August	4.76	1	1	0	5	5	34.0	38	7	5	22
September/October	1.93	1	0	0	4	3	14.0	9	1	3	6
Starter	3.27	12	9	0	28	28	190.0	176	20	40	116
Reliever	0.00	0	0	0	1	0	1.0	1	0	0	0
0-3 Days Rest	0.00	0	0	0	1	1	4.0	1	0	0	3
4 Days Rest	3.36	6	4	0	13	13	88.1	82	13	18	48
5+ Days Rest	3.32	6	5	0	14	14	97.2	93	7	22	65
Pre-All Star	2.72	9	6	0	17	17	122.1	109	8	26	75

	Avg	AB	H	2B	3B	HR	RBI	BB	SO	OBP	SLG
vs. Left	.216	134	29	7	1	3	16	10	15	.271	.351
vs. Right	.247	600	148	31	1	17	57	30	101	.284	.387
Inning 1-6	.239	593	142	30	2	17	59	34	95	.283	.383
Inning 7+	.248	141	35	8	0	3	14	6	21	.277	.369
None on	.235	455	107	22	1	12	12	20	81	.272	.367
Runners on	.251	279	70	16	1	8	61	20	35	.297	.401
Scoring Posn	.266	143	38	11	1	5	53	9	16	.301	.462
Close & Late	.292	89	26	8	0	2	13	5	13	.326	.449
None on/out	.232	190	44	6	0	7	7	11	40	.284	.374
vs. 1st Batr (relief)	.000	1	0	0	0	0	0	0	0	.000	.000
First Inning Pitched	.248	117	29	6	0	2	16	13	17	.323	.350
First 75 Pitches	.229	532	122	25	2	16	50	28	88	.270	.374
Pitch 76-90	.278	97	27	6	0	1	8	3	14	.304	.371
Pitch 91-105	.257	70	18	3	0	2	8	4	11	.293	.386
Pitch 106+	.286	35	10	4	0	1	7	5	3	.375	.486
First Pitch	.280	118	33	8	0	3	15	2	0	.289	.424
Ahead in Count	.179	336	60	12	1	5	20	0	99	.183	.265
Behind in Count	.335	158	53	11	0	8	27	22	0	.415	.557

1993 Season	ERA	W	L	Sv	G	GS	IP	H	HR	BB	SO		Avg	AB	H	2B	3B	HR	RBI	BB	SO	OBP	SLG
Post-All Star	4.19	3	3	0	12	11	68.2	68	12	14	41	Two Strikes	.142	303	43	12	1	4	13	16	116	.189	.228

Last Five Years	ERA	W	L	Sv	G	GS	IP	H	HR	BB	SO		Avg	AB	H	2B	3B	HR	RBI	BB	SO	OBP	SLG
Home	3.35	31	19	0	77	69	499.1	467	34	112	293	vs. Left	.234	638	149	26	4	15	75	35	91	.273	.357
Away	4.07	23	31	0	76	69	448.2	477	38	101	231	vs. Right	.265	3002	795	166	12	57	311	178	433	.306	.385
Day	3.85	15	21	0	47	41	285.0	285	25	66	168	Inning 1-6	.260	2957	768	155	11	58	323	187	442	.304	.378
Night	3.62	39	29	0	106	97	663.0	659	47	147	356	Inning 7+	.258	683	176	37	5	14	63	26	82	.287	.388
Grass	4.60	13	22	0	45	38	246.2	285	26	58	141	None on	.253	2190	553	110	11	41	41	101	320	.289	.369
Turf	3.38	41	28	0	108	100	701.1	659	46	155	383	Runners on	.270	1450	391	82	5	31	345	112	204	.318	.397
April	4.31	5	8	0	19	19	119.0	121	9	34	61	Scoring Posn	.288	773	223	51	4	18	306	68	101	.336	.435
May	2.74	15	5	0	25	21	160.2	149	11	37	71	Close & Late	.271	373	101	26	3	8	42	12	51	.298	.421
June	4.54	7	9	0	25	21	134.2	145	10	36	83	None on/out	.266	948	252	46	4	22	22	48	137	.307	.392
July	2.96	9	12	0	28	25	194.1	183	16	32	110	vs. 1st Batr (relief)	.400	10	4	2	0	0	5	0	1	.364	.600
August	4.15	10	8	0	30	27	184.1	202	17	41	115	First Inning Pitched	.276	577	159	31	2	12	88	52	84	.334	.399
September/October	3.83	8	8	0	26	25	155.0	144	9	33	84	First 75 Pitches	.256	2700	690	137	9	49	282	167	410	.299	.367
Starter	3.70	54	50	0	138	138	928.2	921	71	207	516	Pitch 76-90	.261	459	120	27	4	9	45	19	59	.295	.397
Reliever	3.26	0	0	0	15	0	19.1	23	1	6	8	Pitch 91-105	.286	322	92	18	3	9	38	14	41	.316	.444
0-3 Days Rest	4.81	2	3	0	8	8	48.2	50	4	14	20	Pitch 106+	.264	159	42	10	0	5	21	13	14	.320	.421
4 Days Rest	3.71	33	29	0	82	82	553.2	544	45	111	319	First Pitch	.304	595	181	45	3	17	84	13	0	.317	.476
5+ Days Rest	3.53	19	18	0	48	48	326.1	327	22	82	177	Ahead in Count	.218	1674	365	75	7	17	130	0	462	.222	.302
Pre-All Star	3.59	29	25	0	78	68	473.1	465	33	120	254	Behind in Count	.300	809	243	38	3	27	121	123	0	.390	.455
Post-All Star	3.79	25	25	0	75	70	474.2	479	39	93	270	Two Strikes	.196	1529	299	66	7	13	97	76	524	.237	.273

Pitcher vs. Batter (career)

Pitches Best Vs.	Avg	AB	H	2B	3B	HR	RBI	BB	SO	OBP	SLG	Pitches Worst Vs.	Avg	AB	H	2B	3B	HR	RBI	BB	SO	OBP	SLG
Darrin Jackson	.087	23	2	0	1	0	3	1	5	.125	.174	Chris Jones	.545	11	6	1	0	0	1	0	1	.545	.636
Todd Benzinger	.118	17	2	0	0	0	1	1	2	.167	.118	Bernard Gilkey	.500	24	12	1	2	1	4	2	0	.538	.833
Sammy Sosa	.118	17	2	1	0	0	1	0	7	.118	.176	Fred McGriff	.464	28	13	1	1	3	8	4	3	.531	.893
Mark Lemke	.125	16	2	1	0	0	0	0	0	.125	.188	Bobby Bonilla	.400	25	10	3	0	3	9	1	1	.423	.880
Doug Dascenzo	.158	19	3	0	0	0	0	0	1	.158	.158	Barry Bonds	.324	34	11	2	1	6	12	2	2	.361	.971

Bobby Munoz — Yankees

Age 26 – Pitches Right (groundball pitcher)

	ERA	W	L	Sv	G	GS	IP	BB	SO	Avg	H	2B	3B	HR	RBI	OBP	SLG	GF	IR	IRS	Hld	SvOp	SB	CS	GB	FB	G/F
1993 Season	5.32	3	3	0	38	0	45.2	26	33	.270	48	9	0	1	19	.357	.337	12	33	6	6	2	6	0	76	41	1.85

1993 Season	ERA	W	L	Sv	G	GS	IP	H	HR	BB	SO		Avg	AB	H	2B	3B	HR	RBI	BB	SO	OBP	SLG
Home	3.70	3	1	0	18	0	24.1	20	0	11	18	vs. Left	.203	59	12	3	0	0	4	10	10	.314	.254
Away	7.17	0	2	0	20	0	21.1	28	1	15	15	vs. Right	.303	119	36	6	0	1	15	16	23	.380	.378
Starter	0.00	0	0	0	0	0	0.0	0	0	0	0	Scoring Posn	.222	54	12	1	0	0	16	13	13	.357	.241
Reliever	5.32	3	3	0	38	0	45.2	48	1	26	33	Close & Late	.321	84	27	6	0	0	12	15	17	.420	.393
0 Days rest	6.14	0	0	0	6	0	7.1	9	0	8	5	None on/out	.231	39	9	2	0	0	0	5	8	.318	.282
1 or 2 Days rest	5.06	3	1	0	19	0	26.2	24	1	10	19	First Pitch	.318	22	7	2	0	0	2	4	0	.423	.409
3+ Days rest	5.40	0	2	0	13	0	11.2	15	0	8	9	Ahead in Count	.256	78	20	3	0	0	9	0	25	.250	.295
Pre-All Star	4.22	2	1	0	17	0	21.1	19	0	12	19	Behind in Count	.340	47	16	2	0	1	8	13	0	.475	.447
Post-All Star	6.29	1	2	0	21	0	24.1	29	1	14	14	Two Strikes	.173	81	14	3	0	0	2	9	33	.253	.210

Mike Munoz — Rockies

Age 28 – Pitches Left (groundball pitcher)

	ERA	W	L	Sv	G	GS	IP	BB	SO	Avg	H	2B	3B	HR	RBI	OBP	SLG	GF	IR	IRS	Hld	SvOp	SB	CS	GB	FB	G/F
1993 Season	4.71	2	2	0	29	0	21.0	15	17	.309	25	6	2	2	19	.408	.506	10	21	9	2	2	1	1	31	18	1.72
Career (1989-1993)	4.57	3	5	2	111	0	86.2	50	48	.283	94	15	3	6	55	.372	.401	32	87	25	19	6	4	4	157	65	2.42

1993 Season	ERA	W	L	Sv	G	GS	IP	H	HR	BB	SO		Avg	AB	H	2B	3B	HR	RBI	BB	SO	OBP	SLG
Home	5.79	2	0	0	12	0	9.1	13	0	5	10	vs. Left	.316	38	12	3	0	2	7	3	8	.357	.553
Away	3.86	0	2	0	17	0	11.2	12	2	10	7	vs. Right	.302	43	13	3	2	0	12	12	9	.446	.465
Starter	0.00	0	0	0	0	0	0.0	0	0	0	0	Scoring Posn	.345	29	10	3	1	1	17	12	5	.512	.621
Reliever	4.71	2	2	0	29	0	21.0	25	2	15	17	Close & Late	.400	30	12	3	2	1	5	6	2	.486	.733
0 Days rest	1.74	1	0	0	12	0	10.1	13	0	7	6	None on/out	.167	18	3	1	0	0	0	3	4	.286	.222
1 or 2 Days rest	9.00	0	2	0	10	0	7.0	8	1	6	8	First Pitch	.500	14	7	2	0	1	2	4	0	.611	.857
3+ Days rest	4.91	1	0	0	7	0	3.2	4	1	2	3	Ahead in Count	.207	29	6	0	2	0	5	0	10	.200	.345
Pre-All Star	6.00	0	1	0	8	0	3.0	4	1	6	1	Behind in Count	.364	22	8	2	0	1	8	5	0	.481	.591
Post-All Star	4.50	2	1	0	21	0	18.0	21	1	9	16	Two Strikes	.194	36	7	0	2	0	8	6	17	.295	.306

Career (1989-1993)	ERA	W	L	Sv	G	GS	IP	H	HR	BB	SO		Avg	AB	H	2B	3B	HR	RBI	BB	SO	OBP	SLG
Home	5.03	2	2	0	48	0	39.1	50	2	19	28	vs. Left	.254	138	35	7	0	2	19	13	21	.314	.348
Away	4.18	1	3	2	63	0	47.1	44	4	31	20	vs. Right	.304	194	59	8	3	4	36	37	27	.410	.438
Day	5.79	2	2	0	40	0	28.0	29	2	20	15	Inning 1-6	.292	48	14	0	0	1	14	13	8	.429	.354
Night	3.99	1	3	2	71	0	58.2	65	4	30	33	Inning 7+	.282	284	80	15	3	5	41	37	40	.361	.408
Grass	4.91	2	3	2	81	0	62.1	67	4	38	39	None on	.310	158	49	6	1	5	5	14	26	.366	.456
Turf	3.70	1	2	0	30	0	24.1	27	2	12	9	Runners on	.259	174	45	9	2	1	50	36	22	.377	.351
April	2.77	0	1	0	19	0	13.0	14	2	14	7	Scoring Posn	.270	111	30	8	1	1	49	32	18	.419	.387
May	4.60	0	1	0	17	0	15.2	18	0	7	6	Close & Late	.290	93	27	5	2	3	16	13	10	.370	.484
June	6.10	1	1	0	13	0	10.1	10	2	8	7	None on/out	.308	78	24	4	0	3	3	7	12	.365	.474
July	6.55	0	1	0	17	0	11.0	14	0	5	3	vs. 1st Batr (relief)	.280	93	26	5	0	3	14	15	15	.376	.430

Career (1989-1993)	ERA	W	L	Sv	G	GS	IP	H	HR	BB	SO
August	3.55	1	0	1	14	0	12.2	15	0	4	2
September/October	4.50	1	1	1	31	0	24.0	23	2	12	23
Starter	0.00	0	0	0	0	0	0.0	0	0	0	0
Reliever	4.57	3	5	2	111	0	86.2	94	6	50	48
0 Days rest	2.59	1	1	1	39	0	31.1	31	1	17	17
1 or 2 Days rest	6.86	0	3	0	30	0	19.2	25	1	15	14
3+ Days rest	5.05	2	1	1	42	0	35.2	38	4	18	12
Pre-All Star	4.21	1	3	0	59	0	47.0	49	4	33	23
Post-All Star	4.99	2	2	2	52	0	39.2	45	2	17	25

	Avg	AB	H	2B	3B	HR	RBI	BB	SO	OBP	SLG
First Inning Pitched	.263	266	70	11	3	5	44	42	43	.359	.383
First 15 Pitches	.278	241	67	9	3	5	34	31	33	.356	.402
Pitch 16-30	.324	74	24	6	0	1	19	16	13	.435	.446
Pitch 31-45	.200	15	3	0	0	0	2	3	2	.333	.200
Pitch 46+	.000	2	0	0	0	0	0	0	0	.000	.000
First Pitch	.439	41	18	2	0	2	4	8	0	.531	.634
Ahead in Count	.200	120	24	3	2	2	17	0	35	.195	.308
Behind in Count	.313	96	30	5	1	1	16	24	0	.446	.417
Two Strikes	.176	136	24	4	2	2	24	18	48	.266	.279

Pedro Munoz — Twins

Age 25 – Bats Right (groundball hitter)

	Avg	G	AB	R	H	2B	3B	HR	RBI	BB	SO	HBP	GDP	SB	CS	OBP	SLG	IBB	SH	SF	#Pit	#P/PA	GB	FB	G/F
1993 Season	.233	104	326	34	76	11	1	13	38	25	97	3	7	1	2	.294	.303	2	0	0	1348	3.81	96	75	1.28
Career (1990-1993)	.260	304	967	106	251	38	6	32	140	53	234	5	30	11	7	.299	.411	3	2	7	3825	3.70	359	218	1.65

1993 Season

	Avg	AB	H	2B	3B	HR	RBI	BB	SO	OBP	SLG
vs. Left	.255	102	26	3	0	6	19	9	26	.321	.461
vs. Right	.223	224	50	8	1	7	19	16	71	.281	.362
Groundball	.243	70	17	1	0	3	10	3	17	.274	.386
Flyball	.138	65	9	4	0	1	4	4	26	.188	.246
Home	.196	168	33	6	1	2	12	16	55	.274	.280
Away	.272	158	43	5	0	11	26	9	42	.315	.513
Day	.190	84	16	2	0	0	3	4	24	.244	.214
Night	.248	242	60	9	1	13	35	21	73	.311	.455
Grass	.294	126	37	3	0	10	22	8	30	.341	.556
Turf	.195	200	39	8	1	3	16	17	67	.265	.290
First Pitch	.314	51	16	4	0	3	7	1	0	.327	.569
Ahead in Count	.357	56	20	2	1	3	11	11	0	.463	.589
Behind in Count	.132	159	21	2	0	4	10	0	84	.143	.220
Two Strikes	.129	170	22	4	0	3	11	13	97	.196	.206

	Avg	AB	H	2B	3B	HR	RBI	BB	SO	OBP	SLG
Scoring Posn	.264	72	19	1	0	3	26	8	25	.338	.403
Close & Late	.273	44	12	0	0	2	7	6	12	.360	.409
None on/out	.253	83	21	6	0	4	4	5	17	.295	.470
Batting #6	.301	143	43	7	1	5	23	11	32	.359	.469
Batting #7	.172	116	20	3	0	4	7	7	40	.226	.302
Other	.194	67	13	1	0	4	8	7	25	.270	.388
April	.306	49	15	5	1	2	2	3	13	.346	.571
May	.231	65	15	1	0	2	7	3	20	.275	.338
June	.232	56	13	0	0	4	6	8	17	.328	.446
July	.071	14	1	1	0	0	1	0	3	.071	.143
August	.140	43	6	0	0	1	2	4	17	.229	.209
September/October	.263	99	26	4	0	4	20	7	27	.318	.424
Pre-All Star	.253	170	43	6	1	8	15	14	50	.314	.441
Post-All Star	.212	156	33	5	0	5	23	11	47	.272	.340

1993 By Position

Position	Avg	AB	H	2B	3B	HR	RBI	BB	SO	OBP	SLG	G	GS	Innings	PO	A	E	DP	Fld Pct	Rng Fctr	In Zone	Outs	Zone Rtg	MLB Zone
As lf	.230	200	46	6	0	6	27	13	63	.284	.350	64	55	494.1	123	3	2	2	.984	2.29	151	116	.768	.818
As rf	.244	123	30	5	1	7	11	12	33	.316	.472	41	38	316.0	49	2	1	0	.981	1.45	58	48	.828	.826

Career (1990-1993)

	Avg	AB	H	2B	3B	HR	RBI	BB	SO	OBP	SLG
vs. Left	.289	291	84	12	3	12	58	19	62	.330	.474
vs. Right	.247	676	167	26	3	20	82	34	172	.286	.383
Groundball	.247	239	59	8	1	7	38	13	50	.282	.377
Flyball	.240	208	50	10	2	7	27	12	61	.281	.409
Home	.247	470	116	22	3	14	65	31	118	.296	.396
Away	.272	497	135	16	3	18	75	22	116	.302	.425
Day	.236	297	70	10	1	10	40	14	76	.275	.377
Night	.270	670	181	28	5	22	100	39	158	.310	.425
Grass	.272	397	108	12	2	15	64	20	82	.305	.426
Turf	.251	570	143	26	4	17	76	33	152	.296	.400
First Pitch	.288	163	47	9	0	8	24	1	0	.291	.491
Ahead in Count	.368	182	67	8	1	8	34	27	0	.443	.555
Behind in Count	.189	440	83	14	2	9	52	0	198	.195	.291
Two Strikes	.178	466	83	15	4	8	48	25	234	.221	.279

	Avg	AB	H	2B	3B	HR	RBI	BB	SO	OBP	SLG
Scoring Posn	.286	245	70	9	2	12	113	19	61	.331	.486
Close & Late	.279	129	36	4	0	4	16	11	38	.333	.403
None on/out	.254	252	64	12	1	9	9	12	52	.288	.417
Batting #6	.296	247	73	13	2	9	45	16	62	.343	.474
Batting #7	.234	346	81	11	1	11	37	15	91	.266	.367
Other	.259	374	97	14	3	12	58	22	81	.300	.409
April	.314	118	37	8	1	5	15	6	26	.347	.525
May	.243	181	44	5	1	5	24	12	46	.292	.365
June	.294	160	47	7	0	9	30	11	36	.337	.506
July	.216	102	22	4	0	2	11	4	20	.250	.314
August	.196	97	19	2	1	2	8	5	32	.240	.299
September/October	.265	309	82	12	3	9	52	15	74	.301	.411
Pre-All Star	.275	505	139	21	2	21	75	32	119	.319	.450
Post-All Star	.242	462	112	17	4	11	65	21	115	.278	.368

Batter vs. Pitcher (career)

Hits Best Against	Avg	AB	H	2B	3B	HR	RBI	BB	SO	OBP	SLG
Ricky Bones	.583	12	7	3	1	1	2	0	0	.583	1.250
Erik Hanson	.455	11	5	0	0	1	4	0	1	.455	.727
Kenny Rogers	.417	12	5	0	0	0	2	0	3	.417	.417
Dave Stewart	.400	15	6	0	0	1	5	1	7	.438	.600
Jim Abbott	.348	23	8	1	0	2	6	0	3	.348	.652

Hits Worst Against	Avg	AB	H	2B	3B	HR	RBI	BB	SO	OBP	SLG
Jack McDowell	.067	15	1	0	0	0	0	2	4	.176	.067
Bobby Witt	.071	14	1	0	0	0	1	0	7	.071	.071
Tim Leary	.091	11	1	0	0	0	1	0	1	.091	.091
Mark Leiter	.100	10	1	1	0	0	0	1	4	.182	.200
Mike Mussina	.154	13	2	0	0	0	0	0	2	.154	.154

Dale Murphy — Rockies

Age 38 – Bats Right

	Avg	G	AB	R	H	2B	3B	HR	RBI	BB	SO	HBP	GDP	SB	CS	OBP	SLG	IBB	SH	SF	#Pit	#P/PA	GB	FB	G/F
1993 Season	.143	26	42	1	6	1	0	0	7	5	15	0	5	0	0	.224	.167	1	0	2	176	3.59	16	11	1.45
Last Five Years	.236	505	1785	192	422	74	2	64	262	180	393	3	65	13	5	.304	.388	28	0	19	6927	3.49	655	498	1.32

1993 Season

	Avg	AB	H	2B	3B	HR	RBI	BB	SO	OBP	SLG
vs. Left	.143	28	4	1	0	0	6	4	8	.235	.179
vs. Right	.143	14	2	0	0	0	1	1	7	.200	.143

	Avg	AB	H	2B	3B	HR	RBI	BB	SO	OBP	SLG
Scoring Posn	.250	12	3	1	0	0	7	3	3	.353	.333
Close & Late	.000	10	0	0	0	0	2	1	9	.083	.000

Last Five Years

	Avg	AB	H	2B	3B	HR	RBI	BB	SO	OBP	SLG
vs. Left	.274	603	165	30	1	25	91	89	104	.364	.451
vs. Right	.217	1182	257	44	1	39	171	91	289	.272	.355
Groundball	.220	624	137	21	1	13	73	62	133	.287	.319

	Avg	AB	H	2B	3B	HR	RBI	BB	SO	OBP	SLG
Scoring Posn	.270	470	127	19	0	21	197	77	118	.362	.445
Close & Late	.196	311	61	10	0	10	46	35	89	.274	.325
None on/out	.208	452	94	20	1	11	11	24	100	.248	.330

Last Five Years

	Avg	AB	H	2B	3B	HR	RBI	BB	SO	OBP	SLG
Flyball	.248	412	102	19	0	20	65	43	85	.316	.439
Home	.247	904	223	38	1	29	138	96	193	.317	.387
Away	.226	881	199	36	1	35	124	84	200	.292	.388
Day	.226	421	95	19	0	11	61	44	97	.296	.349
Night	.240	1364	327	55	2	53	201	136	296	.307	.400
Grass	.231	930	215	27	1	39	141	98	215	.303	.388
Turf	.242	855	207	47	1	25	121	82	178	.307	.387
First Pitch	.307	332	102	17	1	15	61	8	0	.324	.500
Ahead in Count	.310	378	117	21	0	17	58	89	0	.436	.500
Behind in Count	.154	740	114	21	0	21	85	0	324	.155	.268
Two Strikes	.140	763	107	22	0	12	67	66	393	.207	.216

	Avg	AB	H	2B	3B	HR	RBI	BB	SO	OBP	SLG
Batting #4	.242	921	223	34	1	33	131	86	216	.305	.389
Batting #5	.240	600	144	32	1	23	96	68	119	.315	.412
Other	.208	264	55	8	0	8	35	26	58	.279	.330
April	.243	276	67	7	0	11	48	22	70	.297	.388
May	.237	342	81	20	0	10	37	36	73	.307	.383
June	.230	291	67	10	1	9	42	21	68	.282	.364
July	.213	268	57	8	0	12	43	36	55	.303	.377
August	.218	308	67	12	0	13	45	31	70	.289	.383
September/October	.277	300	83	17	1	9	47	34	57	.347	.430
Pre-All Star	.235	990	233	38	1	33	138	92	232	.299	.376
Post-All Star	.238	795	189	36	1	31	124	88	161	.311	.403

Batter vs. Pitcher (since 1984)

Hits Best Against	Avg	AB	H	2B	3B	HR	RBI	BB	SO	OBP	SLG
Bobby Ojeda	.500	26	13	5	1	1	3	9	2	.629	.885
Bob Tewksbury	.500	14	7	2	0	1	3	0	1	.500	.857
Frank Viola	.429	21	9	2	0	2	2	1	4	.455	.810
Jamie Moyer	.429	14	6	1	0	2	5	5	2	.579	.929
Mark Davis	.393	28	11	0	0	4	10	6	4	.486	.821

Hits Worst Against	Avg	AB	H	2B	3B	HR	RBI	BB	SO	OBP	SLG
Rob Murphy	.000	14	0	0	0	0	0	1	4	.067	.000
Ken Hill	.000	12	0	0	0	0	1	1	3	.077	.000
Greg Maddux	.059	34	2	0	0	0	0	1	12	.086	.059
Jeff Russell	.100	10	1	0	0	0	1	1	1	.182	.100
Rob Dibble	.150	20	3	0	0	0	2	0	11	.150	.150

Rob Murphy — Cardinals

Age 34 – Pitches Left

	ERA	W	L	Sv	G	GS	IP	BB	SO	Avg	H	2B	3B	HR	RBI	OBP	SLG	GF	IR	IRS	Hld	SvOp	SB	CS	GB	FB	G/F
1993 Season	4.87	5	7	1	73	0	64.2	20	41	.290	73	7	2	8	28	.342	.429	23	33	4	24	4	3	1	83	75	1.11
Last Five Years	4.03	13	22	21	331	0	330.1	133	278	.279	358	63	10	31	184	.345	.416	75	244	67	72	36	26	7	430	359	1.20

1993 Season

	ERA	W	L	Sv	G	GS	IP	H	HR	BB	SO
Home	4.22	2	2	1	35	0	32.0	37	4	8	19
Away	5.51	3	5	0	38	0	32.2	36	4	12	22
Day	6.38	1	2	0	23	0	18.1	23	5	9	10
Night	4.27	4	5	1	50	0	46.1	50	3	11	31
Grass	5.59	3	3	0	24	0	19.1	19	3	7	14
Turf	4.57	2	4	1	49	0	45.1	54	5	13	27
April	1.86	1	2	0	11	0	9.2	9	2	5	9
May	4.91	0	2	0	12	0	11.0	9	2	4	4
June	2.53	0	0	0	14	0	10.2	4	0	0	9
July	8.53	0	1	0	14	0	12.2	20	2	7	5
August	3.38	2	0	1	12	0	13.1	18	1	3	8
September/October	8.59	2	2	0	10	0	7.1	13	1	1	6
Starter	0.00	0	0	0	0	0	0.0	0	0	0	0
Reliever	4.87	5	7	1	73	0	64.2	73	8	20	41
0 Days rest	2.12	2	1	1	21	0	17.0	15	1	5	10
1 or 2 Days rest	5.88	3	4	0	38	0	33.2	41	5	9	21
3+ Days rest	5.79	0	2	0	14	0	14.0	17	2	6	10
Pre-All Star	3.22	1	4	0	42	0	36.1	27	5	10	25
Post-All Star	6.99	4	3	1	31	0	28.1	46	3	10	16

	Avg	AB	H	2B	3B	HR	RBI	BB	SO	OBP	SLG
vs. Left	.293	82	24	3	0	2	10	4	14	.326	.402
vs. Right	.288	170	49	4	2	6	18	16	27	.349	.441
Inning 1-6	.600	5	3	0	0	0	0	0	0	.600	.600
Inning 7+	.283	247	70	7	2	8	28	20	41	.337	.425
None on	.300	150	45	5	2	5	5	4	23	.318	.460
Runners on	.275	102	28	2	0	3	23	16	18	.372	.382
Scoring Posn	.300	60	18	1	0	2	20	13	15	.413	.417
Close & Late	.248	149	37	2	1	5	16	13	25	.313	.376
None on/out	.309	68	21	3	1	2	2	2	9	.329	.471
vs. 1st Batr (relief)	.239	71	17	3	1	1	3	2	15	.260	.352
First Inning Pitched	.282	216	61	7	2	6	26	18	35	.338	.417
First 15 Pitches	.295	200	59	7	2	6	22	15	30	.344	.440
Pitch 16-30	.275	51	14	0	0	2	6	4	10	.327	.392
Pitch 31-45	.000	1	0	0	0	0	0	1	1	.500	.000
Pitch 46+	.000	0	0	0	0	0	0	0	0	.000	.000
First Pitch	.341	44	15	0	1	3	4	4	0	.396	.591
Ahead in Count	.168	101	17	2	1	0	3	0	35	.168	.208
Behind in Count	.429	56	24	3	0	2	12	10	0	.507	.589
Two Strikes	.158	95	15	1	1	1	6	6	41	.206	.221

Last Five Years

	ERA	W	L	Sv	G	GS	IP	H	HR	BB	SO
Home	3.57	5	7	8	159	0	166.1	167	13	60	141
Away	4.50	8	15	13	172	0	164.0	191	18	73	137
Day	4.49	6	9	8	109	0	106.1	119	13	50	93
Night	3.82	7	13	13	222	0	224.0	239	18	83	185
Grass	4.13	9	13	13	187	0	189.2	207	24	78	184
Turf	3.90	4	9	8	144	0	140.2	151	7	55	94
April	3.44	1	5	1	46	0	55.0	58	6	26	50
May	3.72	0	4	2	51	0	55.2	52	8	29	38
June	3.15	1	3	5	66	0	60.0	55	4	14	56
July	4.40	2	5	6	60	0	61.1	72	4	22	52
August	4.89	6	1	5	58	0	53.1	68	5	30	45
September/October	4.80	3	4	2	50	0	45.0	53	4	12	37
Starter	0.00	0	0	0	0	0	0.0	0	0	0	0
Reliever	4.03	13	22	21	331	0	330.1	358	31	133	278
0 Days rest	3.03	4	5	10	97	0	101.0	102	7	40	90
1 or 2 Days rest	4.50	6	12	10	153	0	144.0	151	15	51	122
3+ Days rest	4.43	3	5	1	81	0	85.1	105	9	42	66
Pre-All Star	3.39	4	13	10	184	0	191.0	186	19	75	161
Post-All Star	4.91	9	9	11	147	0	139.1	172	12	58	117

	Avg	AB	H	2B	3B	HR	RBI	BB	SO	OBP	SLG
vs. Left	.251	438	110	21	1	6	52	32	84	.304	.345
vs. Right	.293	847	248	42	9	25	132	101	194	.366	.452
Inning 1-6	[illegible]	106	26	5	2	1	19	6	20	.287	.358
Inning 7+	.282	1179	332	58	8	30	165	127	258	.350	.421
None on	.271	641	174	34	3	19	19	52	122	.327	.423
Runners on	.286	644	184	29	7	12	165	81	156	.362	.408
Scoring Posn	.295	410	121	14	3	9	150	60	109	.378	.410
Close & Late	.281	501	141	17	3	13	77	65	109	.363	.405
None on/out	.289	291	84	19	2	10	10	25	54	.345	.471
vs. 1st Batr (relief)	.289	305	88	15	1	7	43	18	63	.324	.413
First Inning Pitched	.284	978	278	49	9	26	163	89	203	.343	.433
First 15 Pitches	.284	883	251	43	9	25	129	77	173	.341	.438
Pitch 16-30	.262	332	87	17	1	5	44	47	84	.351	.364
Pitch 31-45	.298	57	17	3	0	1	9	9	16	.394	.404
Pitch 46+	.231	13	3	0	0	0	2	0	5	.231	.231
First Pitch	.329	207	68	10	3	9	31	19	0	.383	.536
Ahead in Count	.215	595	128	27	4	4	62	0	236	.216	.294
Behind in Count	.371	259	96	14	3	11	56	56	0	.481	.575
Two Strikes	.184	591	109	18	4	5	59	58	278	.255	.254

Pitcher vs. Batter (career)

Pitches Best Vs.	Avg	AB	H	2B	3B	HR	RBI	BB	SO	OBP	SLG
Dale Murphy	.000	14	0	0	0	0	0	1	4	.067	.000
Andy Van Slyke	.000	11	0	0	0	0	0	1	4	.083	.000
Billy Doran	.077	13	1	0	0	0	2	3	0	.250	.077
Darryl Strawberry	.083	12	1	0	0	0	1	0	7	.077	.083
Mitch Webster	.182	11	2	0	0	0	1	0	2	.182	.182

Pitches Worst Vs.	Avg	AB	H	2B	3B	HR	RBI	BB	SO	OBP	SLG
Don Mattingly	.364	11	4	0	0	1	4	0	1	.364	.636
Lenny Dykstra	.364	11	4	1	0	0	3	0	3	.364	.455
Fred McGriff	.357	14	5	0	0	1	2	1	5	.375	.571
Barry Bonds	.357	14	5	2	0	1	2	3	4	.471	.714
Chili Davis	.308	13	4	2	0	0	2	3	5	.438	.462

Eddie Murray — Mets

Age 38 – Bats Both

	Avg	G	AB	R	H	2B	3B	HR	RBI	BB	SO	HBP	GDP	SB	CS	OBP	SLG	IBB	SH	SF	#Pit	#P/PA	GB	FB	G/F
1993 Season	.285	154	610	77	174	28	1	27	100	40	61	0	24	2	2	.325	.467	4	0	9	2277	3.46	244	177	1.38
Last Five Years	.277	778	2889	372	799	139	8	108	472	330	358	3	86	31	14	.347	.442	74	0	36	11491	3.53	1081	927	1.17

1993 Season

	Avg	AB	H	2B	3B	HR	RBI	BB	SO	OBP	SLG		Avg	AB	H	2B	3B	HR	RBI	BB	SO	OBP	SLG
vs. Left	.311	183	57	10	0	8	25	12	17	.352	.497	Scoring Posn	.319	135	43	8	0	9	74	15	15	.365	.578
vs. Right	.274	427	117	18	1	19	75	28	44	.313	.454	Close & Late	.265	102	27	4	1	4	14	7	15	.312	.441
Groundball	.243	206	50	15	1	7	28	12	23	.282	.427	None on/out	.242	120	29	3	0	4	4	5	13	.272	.367
Flyball	.319	91	29	4	0	5	20	6	11	.361	.527	Batting #3	.285	592	169	28	1	24	96	39	59	.325	.458
Home	.290	314	91	11	1	15	52	16	33	.320	.475	Batting #4	.278	18	5	0	0	3	4	1	2	.316	.778
Away	.280	296	83	17	0	12	48	24	28	.329	.459	Other	.000	0	0	0	0	0	0	0	0	.000	.000
Day	.295	217	64	12	0	13	48	12	25	.326	.530	April	.296	81	24	2	0	4	15	9	15	.367	.469
Night	.280	393	110	16	1	14	52	28	36	.324	.433	May	.256	90	23	6	0	1	10	3	9	.271	.356
Grass	.288	483	139	21	1	23	85	30	50	.324	.478	June	.250	100	25	4	0	4	17	6	14	.284	.410
Turf	.276	127	35	7	0	4	15	10	11	.328	.425	July	.333	105	35	5	0	6	26	5	8	.354	.552
First Pitch	.371	116	43	10	0	8	26	3	0	.380	.664	August	.210	119	25	6	1	5	11	4	7	.236	.403
Ahead in Count	.351	151	53	8	0	12	36	18	0	.410	.642	September/October	.365	115	42	5	0	7	21	13	8	.430	.591
Behind in Count	.201	229	46	5	1	2	16	0	48	.200	.258	Pre-All Star	.269	312	84	12	0	11	53	19	41	.304	.413
Two Strikes	.193	218	42	5	1	3	15	19	61	.255	.266	Post-All Star	.302	298	90	16	1	16	47	21	20	.347	.523

1993 By Position

Position	Avg	AB	H	2B	3B	HR	RBI	BB	SO	OBP	SLG	G	GS	Innings	PO	A	E	DP	Fld Pct	Rng Fctr	In Zone	Outs	Zone Rtg	MLB Zone
As 1b	.285	610	174	28	1	27	100	40	61	.325	.467	154	154	1321.0	1320	109	18	116	.988	---	243	205	.844	.834

Last Five Years

	Avg	AB	H	2B	3B	HR	RBI	BB	SO	OBP	SLG		Avg	AB	H	2B	3B	HR	RBI	BB	SO	OBP	SLG
vs. Left	.255	1055	269	54	2	29	157	105	113	.319	.392	Scoring Posn	.285	730	208	47	2	36	366	168	100	.403	.503
vs. Right	.289	1834	530	85	6	79	315	225	245	.363	.471	Close & Late	.248	479	119	20	2	13	70	72	76	.343	.380
Groundball	.271	1000	271	56	1	28	147	117	117	.344	.413	None on/out	.257	725	186	28	3	22	22	38	87	.295	.394
Flyball	.266	582	155	23	3	26	104	77	74	.349	.450	Batting #3	.271	802	217	34	2	32	124	67	94	.323	.438
Home	.276	1425	394	60	6	49	228	170	188	.352	.430	Batting #4	.277	1837	509	89	6	67	300	232	233	.355	.441
Away	.277	1464	405	79	2	59	244	160	170	.343	.454	Other	.292	250	73	16	0	9	48	31	31	.369	.464
Day	.288	855	246	41	0	43	156	89	104	.351	.487	April	.285	379	108	24	0	14	68	49	51	.363	.459
Night	.272	2034	553	98	8	65	316	241	254	.346	.424	May	.272	437	119	25	1	13	70	55	62	.348	.423
Grass	.282	2127	599	93	6	89	360	245	265	.353	.457	June	.235	494	116	22	2	14	81	59	72	.312	.372
Turf	.262	762	200	46	2	19	112	85	93	.333	.403	July	.273	498	136	26	0	20	84	47	67	.333	.446
First Pitch	.334	533	178	37	3	27	100	43	0	.380	.567	August	.262	542	142	18	3	20	74	52	54	.327	.417
Ahead in Count	.331	661	219	42	2	36	138	152	0	.452	.564	September/October	.330	539	178	24	2	27	95	68	52	.403	.532
Behind in Count	.213	1162	248	31	2	23	129	0	287	.213	.303	Pre-All Star	.264	1474	389	79	3	48	251	181	204	.340	.419
Two Strikes	.204	1159	237	36	2	21	131	118	358	.277	.293	Post-All Star	.290	1415	410	60	5	60	221	149	154	.356	.466

Batter vs. Pitcher (since 1984)

Hits Best Against	Avg	AB	H	2B	3B	HR	RBI	BB	SO	OBP	SLG	Hits Worst Against	Avg	AB	H	2B	3B	HR	RBI	BB	SO	OBP	SLG
Roger McDowell	.600	10	6	2	0	0	2	2	0	.667	.800	Curt Schilling	.077	26	2	0	0	0	0	2	6	.143	.077
Frank Castillo	.588	17	10	2	0	1	8	1	1	.579	.882	Jimmy Key	.083	24	2	0	0	0	1	1	4	.120	.083
Joe Boever	.556	9	5	1	0	1	6	3	0	.667	1.000	Larry Andersen	.083	12	1	0	0	0	1	1	4	.154	.083
Jack Armstrong	.538	13	7	1	0	2	4	1	1	.571	1.077	Mike Stanton	.083	12	1	0	0	0	0	0	1	.083	.083
Mark Grant	.500	8	4	0	0	2	6	3	0	.636	1.250	Al Osuna	.083	12	1	0	0	0	3	1	3	.133	.083

Mike Mussina — Orioles

Age 25 – Pitches Right (flyball pitcher)

	ERA	W	L	Sv	G	GS	IP	BB	SO	Avg	H	2B	3B	HR	RBI	OBP	SLG	CG	ShO	Sup	QS	#P/S	SB	CS	GB	FB	G/F
1993 Season	4.46	14	6	0	25	25	167.2	44	117	.256	163	34	2	20	78	.306	.410	3	2	6.12	14	105	3	6	211	191	1.10
Career (1991-1993)	3.25	36	16	0	69	69	496.1	113	299	.245	452	87	8	43	172	.289	.371	13	6	5.08	47	107	16	19	576	620	0.93

1993 Season

	ERA	W	L	Sv	G	GS	IP	H	HR	BB	SO		Avg	AB	H	2B	3B	HR	RBI	BB	SO	OBP	SLG
Home	4.72	5	2	0	12	12	74.1	77	10	21	50	vs. Left	.256	285	73	13	1	4	32	21	56	.307	.351
Away	4.24	9	4	0	13	13	93.1	86	10	23	67	vs. Right	.256	351	90	21	1	16	46	23	61	.304	.459
Day	3.37	7	1	0	9	9	69.1	57	5	16	55	Inning 1-6	.260	520	135	29	2	17	66	35	99	.306	.421
Night	5.22	7	5	0	16	16	98.1	106	15	28	62	Inning 7+	.241	116	28	5	0	3	12	9	18	.305	.362
Grass	4.83	11	6	0	22	22	143.1	149	19	39	107	None on	.253	387	98	21	2	12	12	28	76	.307	.411
Turf	2.22	3	0	0	3	3	24.1	14	1	5	10	Runners on	.261	249	65	13	0	8	66	16	41	.304	.410
April	3.12	3	1	0	5	5	40.1	31	5	8	20	Scoring Posn	.298	131	39	8	0	6	61	14	22	.356	.496
May	2.68	4	1	0	6	6	43.2	35	5	10	35	Close & Late	.212	52	11	1	0	0	4	5	6	.281	.231
June	7.48	2	1	0	4	4	21.2	29	2	6	21	None on/out	.282	170	48	12	1	7	7	11	33	.326	.488
July	7.48	2	1	0	4	4	21.2	30	3	8	15	vs. 1st Batr (relief)	.000	0	0	0	0	0	0	0	0	.000	.000
August	2.78	2	1	0	3	3	22.2	17	3	6	15	First Inning Pitched	.222	90	20	4	0	3	11	10	22	.300	.367
September/October	6.62	1	1	0	3	3	17.2	21	2	6	11	First 75 Pitches	.252	441	111	21	2	13	50	32	83	.302	.397
Starter	4.46	14	6	0	25	25	167.2	163	20	44	117	Pitch 76-90	.329	79	26	8	0	7	18	5	11	.379	.696
Reliever	0.00	0	0	0	0	0	0.0	0	0	0	0	Pitch 91-105	.225	71	16	2	0	0	4	0	16	.233	.254
0-3 Days Rest	0.00	0	0	0	0	0	0.0	0	0	0	0	Pitch 106+	.222	45	10	3	0	0	6	7	7	.321	.289
4 Days Rest	4.55	6	5	0	14	14	93.0	98	8	21	60	First Pitch	.324	74	24	5	1	4	10	1	0	.342	.581
5+ Days Rest	4.34	8	1	0	11	11	74.2	65	12	23	57	Ahead in Count	.215	311	67	12	1	5	32	0	94	.219	.309
Pre-All Star	4.10	10	4	0	17	17	116.1	107	13	28	83	Behind in Count	.360	139	50	15	0	6	22	22	0	.447	.597
Post-All Star	5.26	4	2	0	8	8	51.1	56	7	16	34	Two Strikes	.205	308	63	9	1	8	30	21	117	.258	.318

Career (1991-1993)	ERA	W	L	Sv	G	GS	IP	H	HR	BB	SO		Avg	AB	H	2B	3B	HR	RBI	BB	SO	OBP	SLG
Home	3.33	15	6	0	33	33	232.2	213	21	51	146	vs. Left	.231	889	205	38	3	8	66	64	149	.282	.307
Away	3.17	21	10	0	36	36	263.2	239	22	62	153	vs. Right	.258	957	247	49	5	35	106	49	150	.295	.429
Day	3.01	11	5	0	21	21	152.2	133	11	39	91	Inning 1-6	.249	1467	365	70	7	35	141	88	249	.291	.378
Night	3.35	25	11	0	48	48	343.2	319	32	74	208	Inning 7+	.230	379	87	17	1	8	31	25	50	.280	.343
Grass	3.19	30	14	0	59	59	421.0	377	35	96	273	None on	.247	1150	284	59	4	25	25	78	196	.297	.370
Turf	3.58	6	2	0	10	10	75.1	75	8	17	26	Runners on	.241	696	168	28	4	18	147	35	103	.275	.371
April	2.80	6	1	0	9	9	70.2	58	7	16	30	Scoring Posn	.238	340	81	17	2	8	121	25	47	.283	.371
May	2.82	8	2	0	10	10	73.1	59	6	14	49	Close & Late	.244	176	43	9	0	2	15	13	16	.293	.330
June	3.80	5	3	0	10	10	66.1	62	5	14	45	None on/out	.252	500	126	26	2	11	11	27	89	.292	.378
July	4.57	4	2	0	10	10	63.0	74	7	14	38	vs. 1st Batr (relief)	.000	0	0	0	0	0	0	0	0	.000	.000
August	3.70	7	6	0	15	15	104.2	102	13	31	70	First Inning Pitched	.202	243	49	10	0	6	19	21	50	.265	.317
September/October	2.36	8	2	0	15	15	118.1	97	5	24	67	First 75 Pitches	.249	1261	314	59	6	28	111	81	214	.294	.372
Starter	3.25	36	16	0	69	69	496.1	452	43	113	299	Pitch 76-90	.254	232	59	13	1	10	34	9	37	.286	.448
Reliever	0.00	0	0	0	0	0	0.0	0	0	0	0	Pitch 91-105	.254	201	51	6	1	3	13	6	29	.276	.338
0-3 Days Rest	4.50	0	1	0	1	1	8.0	10	2	1	5	Pitch 106+	.184	152	28	9	0	2	14	17	19	.265	.283
4 Days Rest	3.49	20	11	0	42	42	299.1	287	24	60	177	First Pitch	.293	256	75	17	2	7	20	2	0	.305	.457
5+ Days Rest	2.81	16	4	0	26	26	189.0	155	17	52	117	Ahead in Count	.217	900	195	32	3	13	70	0	250	.218	.302
Pre-All Star	3.24	19	7	0	33	33	236.1	211	20	50	134	Behind in Count	.315	378	119	25	3	16	54	45	0	.386	.524
Post-All Star	3.25	17	9	0	36	36	260.0	241	23	63	165	Two Strikes	.193	861	166	26	2	15	51	66	299	.252	.280

Pitcher vs. Batter (career)

Pitches Best Vs.	Avg	AB	H	2B	3B	HR	RBI	BB	SO	OBP	SLG	Pitches Worst Vs.	Avg	AB	H	2B	3B	HR	RBI	BB	SO	OBP	SLG
Dan Pasqua	.000	14	0	0	0	0	0	0	3	.000	.000	Scott Cooper	.700	10	7	1	0	1	2	2	0	.750	1.100
Harold Baines	.000	10	0	0	0	0	0	1	3	.091	.000	Frank Thomas	.588	17	10	3	0	3	5	4	1	.667	1.294
Jose Canseco	.071	14	1	0	0	0	1	0	2	.071	.071	Mike Greenwell	.500	10	5	2	0	0	1	4	1	.643	.700
Robin Yount	.077	13	1	0	0	0	1	0	2	.077	.077	Carlos Baerga	.455	11	5	4	0	0	2	0	0	.455	.818
Rafael Palmeiro	.091	22	2	1	0	0	1	1	3	.125	.136	Juan Gonzalez	.304	23	7	0	0	5	8	0	7	.304	.957

Jeff Mutis — Indians

Age 27 – Pitches Left

	ERA	W	L	Sv	G	GS	IP	BB	SO	Avg	H	2B	3B	HR	RBI	OBP	SLG	CG	ShO	Sup	QS	#P/S	SB	CS	GB	FB	G/F
1993 Season	5.78	3	6	0	17	13	81.0	33	29	.289	93	16	1	14	52	.365	.475	1	1	4.67	3	83	6	3	130	98	1.33
Career (1991-1993)	6.88	3	11	0	23	18	104.2	46	43	.321	140	24	5	19	75	.391	.530	1	1	4.47	3	82	6	3	174	129	1.35

1993 Season	ERA	W	L	Sv	G	GS	IP	H	HR	BB	SO		Avg	AB	H	2B	3B	HR	RBI	BB	SO	OBP	SLG
Home	3.70	3	1	0	7	5	41.1	41	3	14	16	vs. Left	.320	75	24	1	1	5	17	4	5	.363	.560
Away	7.94	0	5	0	10	8	39.2	52	11	19	13	vs. Right	.279	247	69	15	0	9	35	29	24	.366	.449
Starter	5.87	3	6	0	13	13	69.0	77	12	26	27	Scoring Posn	.357	70	25	6	1	2	35	7	8	.413	.557
Reliever	5.25	0	0	0	4	0	12.0	16	2	7	2	Close & Late	.300	20	6	2	0	0	2	2	1	.391	.400
0-3 Days Rest	0.00	0	0	0	0	0	0.0	0	0	0	0	None on/out	.192	78	15	3	0	4	4	11	6	.308	.385
4 Days Rest	8.18	2	4	0	7	7	33.0	44	7	13	13	First Pitch	.357	56	20	1	0	2	9	2	0	.410	.482
5+ Days Rest	3.75	1	2	0	6	6	36.0	33	5	13	14	Ahead in Count	.250	116	29	5	0	4	15	0	26	.267	.397
Pre-All Star	5.93	1	2	0	5	5	27.1	33	4	9	13	Behind in Count	.299	87	26	7	1	3	17	16	0	.408	.506
Post-All Star	5.70	2	4	0	12	8	53.2	60	10	24	16	Two Strikes	.205	112	23	3	0	4	13	15	29	.310	.339

Greg Myers — Angels

Age 28 – Bats Left

	Avg	G	AB	R	H	2B	3B	HR	RBI	BB	SO	HBP	GDP	SB	CS	OBP	SLG	IBB	SH	SF	#Pit	#P/PA	GB	FB	G/F
1993 Season	.255	108	290	27	74	10	0	7	40	17	47	2	8	3	3	.298	.362	2	3	3	1090	3.46	117	73	1.60
Last Five Years	.244	349	971	89	237	48	1	21	112	67	145	2	36	3	5	.291	.360	6	5	12	3540	3.35	378	273	1.38

1993 Season	Avg	AB	H	2B	3B	HR	RBI	BB	SO	OBP	SLG		Avg	AB	H	2B	3B	HR	RBI	BB	SO	OBP	SLG
vs. Left	.375	24	9	3	0	0	4	0	4	.400	.500	Scoring Posn	.271	85	23	2	0	1	32	6	13	.316	.329
vs. Right	.244	266	65	7	0	7	36	17	43	.289	.350	Close & Late	.241	54	13	2	0	1	6	3	6	.293	.333
Home	.266	143	38	6	0	4	22	7	26	.296	.392	None on/out	.194	62	12	3	0	1	1	1	8	.206	.290
Away	.245	147	36	4	0	3	18	10	21	.300	.333	Batting #5	.244	78	19	1	0	0	8	3	15	.286	.256
First Pitch	.263	57	15	1	0	1	7	1	0	.271	.333	Batting #6	.254	118	30	4	0	5	9	5	21	.285	.415
Ahead in Count	.333	72	24	2	0	4	14	10	0	.412	.528	Other	.266	94	25	5	0	2	23	9	11	.324	.383
Behind in Count	.196	112	22	4	0	2	12	0	38	.204	.286	Pre-All Star	.247	150	37	6	0	4	18	12	22	.302	.367
Two Strikes	.177	113	20	4	0	2	12	6	47	.225	.265	Post-All Star	.264	140	37	4	0	3	22	5	25	.293	.357

Last Five Years	Avg	AB	H	2B	3B	HR	RBI	BB	SO	OBP	SLG		Avg	AB	H	2B	3B	HR	RBI	BB	SO	OBP	SLG
vs. Left	.222	90	20	4	0	1	9	5	17	.265	.300	Scoring Posn	.224	272	61	10	1	7	94	23	41	.276	.346
vs. Right	.246	881	217	44	1	20	103	62	128	.294	.367	Close & Late	.279	154	43	11	0	2	15	10	20	.327	.390
Groundball	.236	271	64	18	1	3	40	18	36	.280	.343	None on/out	.276	192	53	18	0	6	6	8	23	.305	.464
Flyball	.267	202	54	8	0	8	25	11	35	.305	.426	Batting #6	.240	263	63	11	0	6	21	13	46	.273	.350
Home	.258	466	120	26	0	12	61	38	74	.309	.391	Batting #7	.244	349	85	20	1	7	39	31	50	.301	.367
Away	.232	505	117	22	1	9	51	29	71	.274	.333	Other	.248	359	89	17	0	8	52	23	49	.294	.362
Day	.242	265	64	12	0	4	28	21	46	.298	.332	April	.248	125	31	5	0	4	17	12	14	.307	.384
Night	.245	706	173	36	1	17	84	46	99	.288	.371	May	.261	134	35	12	0	2	13	16	18	.338	.396
Grass	.225	488	110	19	1	11	50	29	80	.266	.336	June	.255	200	51	9	0	6	23	13	26	.300	.390
Turf	.263	483	127	29	0	10	62	38	65	.315	.385	July	.226	212	48	13	1	2	25	6	38	.242	.325
First Pitch	.306	229	70	15	0	4	29	4	0	.312	.424	August	.269	145	39	4	0	4	15	7	27	.305	.379
Ahead in Count	.286	227	65	11	0	9	32	39	0	.387	.454	September/October	.213	155	33	5	0	3	19	13	22	.275	.303
Behind in Count	.179	364	65	10	0	5	28	0	120	.180	.247	Pre-All Star	.253	530	134	31	0	12	58	43	65	.307	.379

Last Five Years

	Avg	AB	H	2B	3B	HR	RBI	BB	SO	OBP	SLG		Avg	AB	H	2B	3B	HR	RBI	BB	SO	OBP	SLG
Two Strikes	.171	362	62	13	1	5	30	24	145	.224	.254	Post-All Star	.234	441	103	17	1	9	54	24	80	.272	.338

Batter vs. Pitcher (career)

Hits Best Against	Avg	AB	H	2B	3B	HR	RBI	BB	SO	OBP	SLG	Hits Worst Against	Avg	AB	H	2B	3B	HR	RBI	BB	SO	OBP	SLG
Storm Davis	.375	8	3	3	0	0	1	2	1	.455	.750	Nolan Ryan	.115	26	3	0	0	1	1	2	11	.179	.231
Tim Leary	.368	19	7	1	0	1	8	2	1	.409	.579	Mike Moore	.118	17	2	1	0	0	1	4	3	.286	.176
Kevin Appier	.353	17	6	0	0	0	3	2	1	.400	.353	Tom Gordon	.133	15	2	0	0	0	1	0	4	.133	.133
Kevin Tapani	.350	20	7	1	0	0	0	1	2	.381	.400	Dave Stewart	.200	10	2	0	0	0	0	1	4	.273	.200
												Roger Clemens	.211	19	4	0	0	0	0	0	3	.211	.211

Randy Myers — Cubs

Age 31 – Pitches Left (flyball pitcher)

	ERA	W	L	Sv	G	GS	IP	BB	SO	Avg	H	2B	3B	HR	RBI	OBP	SLG	GF	IR	IRS	Hld	SvOp	SB	CS	GB	FB	G/F
1993 Season	3.11	2	4	53	73	0	75.1	26	86	.230	65	15	1	7	28	.295	.364	69	24	4	0	59	1	1	81	71	1.14
Last Five Years	3.10	22	33	152	328	12	458.0	218	446	.231	386	65	10	32	193	.319	.330	203	188	41	10	181	15	10	473	481	0.98

1993 Season

	ERA	W	L	Sv	G	GS	IP	H	HR	BB	SO		Avg	AB	H	2B	3B	HR	RBI	BB	SO	OBP	SLG
Home	3.16	1	2	25	36	0	37.0	35	4	17	40	vs. Left	.178	45	8	0	1	1	2	8	17	.302	.289
Away	3.05	1	2	28	37	0	38.1	30	3	9	46	vs. Right	.239	238	57	15	0	6	26	18	69	.293	.378
Day	3.55	1	2	27	37	0	38.0	36	4	17	40	Inning 1-6	.000	0	0	0	0	0	0	0	0	.000	.000
Night	2.65	1	2	26	36	0	37.1	29	3	9	46	Inning 7+	.230	283	65	15	1	7	28	26	86	.295	.364
Grass	3.20	2	4	39	56	0	56.1	51	5	21	66	None on	.252	147	37	12	1	5	5	15	46	.321	.449
Turf	2.84	0	0	14	17	0	19.0	14	2	5	20	Runners on	.206	136	28	3	0	2	23	11	40	.267	.272
April	0.00	0	0	6	10	0	9.2	3	0	5	12	Scoring Posn	.205	73	15	1	0	2	21	9	23	.294	.301
May	3.55	0	1	9	12	0	12.2	12	1	6	15	Close & Late	.245	192	47	10	0	5	22	19	53	.313	.375
June	1.46	1	0	9	11	0	12.1	10	1	1	16	None on/out	.242	62	15	5	1	0	0	6	16	.309	.355
July	6.94	0	1	8	12	0	11.2	14	2	5	10	vs. 1st Batr (relief)	.231	65	15	5	1	0	1	7	15	.315	.338
August	4.63	1	2	5	11	0	11.2	12	2	6	12	First Inning Pitched	.236	259	61	14	1	6	27	23	76	.298	.367
September/October	2.08	0	0	16	17	0	17.1	14	1	3	21	First 15 Pitches	.233	210	49	13	1	6	20	18	59	.296	.390
Starter	0.00	0	0	0	0	0	0.0	0	0	0	0	Pitch 16-30	.214	70	15	2	0	1	7	7	26	.282	.286
Reliever	3.11	2	4	53	73	0	75.1	65	7	26	86	Pitch 31-45	.333	3	1	0	0	0	1	1	1	.500	.333
0 Days rest	5.29	0	3	13	18	0	17.0	18	4	9	17	Pitch 46+	.000	0	0	0	0	0	0	0	0	.000	.000
1 or 2 Days rest	2.56	1	1	34	44	0	45.2	36	2	13	52	First Pitch	.379	29	11	2	1	0	4	1	0	.400	.517
3+ Days rest	2.13	1	0	6	11	0	12.2	11	1	4	17	Ahead in Count	.141	149	21	4	0	2	8	0	77	.146	.208
Pre-All Star	2.37	1	2	27	37	0	38.0	29	2	14	49	Behind in Count	.347	49	17	4	0	2	9	11	0	.467	.551
Post-All Star	3.86	1	2	26	36	0	37.1	36	5	12	37	Two Strikes	.115	157	18	5	0	1	5	14	86	.186	.166

Last Five Years

	ERA	W	L	Sv	G	GS	IP	H	HR	BB	SO		Avg	AB	H	2B	3B	HR	RBI	BB	SO	OBP	SLG
Home	2.88	12	12	82	176	5	240.2	207	14	114	220	vs. Left	.227	375	85	15	3	8	42	67	135	.340	.347
Away	3.35	10	21	70	152	7	217.1	179	18	104	226	vs. Right	.232	1296	301	50	7	24	151	151	311	.313	.337
Day	3.11	7	8	51	115	2	147.2	127	10	67	147	Inning 1-6	.237	236	56	6	2	4	28	36	54	.335	.331
Night	3.10	15	25	101	213	10	310.1	259	22	151	299	Inning 7+	.230	1435	330	59	8	28	165	182	392	.316	.341
Grass	3.08	12	14	95	185	5	236.1	202	18	98	233	None on	.234	851	199	34	5	20	20	101	235	.315	.356
Turf	3.13	10	19	57	143	7	221.2	184	14	120	213	Runners on	.228	820	187	31	5	12	173	117	211	.323	.322
April	2.92	3	3	23	45	0	52.1	46	1	27	65	Scoring Posn	.213	489	104	17	3	7	153	80	135	.319	.303
May	2.75	6	3	26	60	0	72.0	56	3	31	77	Close & Late	.232	988	229	38	3	21	120	126	269	.317	.340
June	2.61	7	7	20	60	0	82.2	68	8	39	81	None on/out	.245	372	91	18	4	7	7	38	97	.315	.371
July	3.84	0	6	25	52	2	70.1	59	7	37	57	vs. 1st Batr (relief)	.223	282	63	16	3	4	19	29	81	.296	.344
August	3.08	2	9	27	53	5	84.2	77	8	41	66	First Inning Pitched	.230	1103	254	54	8	18	145	139	297	.316	.343
September/October	3.38	4	5	31	58	5	96.0	80	5	43	100	First 15 Pitches	.231	901	208	45	7	16	92	104	239	.310	.350
Starter	3.45	2	6	0	12	12	70.1	62	5	43	55	Pitch 16-30	.228	457	104	11	1	6	58	67	129	.325	.295
Reliever	3.04	20	27	152	316	0	387.2	324	27	175	391	Pitch 31-45	.236	144	34	5	0	6	27	20	44	.327	.396
0 Days rest	2.49	8	8	46	77	0	90.1	73	8	34	86	Pitch 46+	.237	169	40	4	2	4	16	27	34	.342	.355
1 or 2 Days rest	3.09	7	14	79	164	0	203.2	171	12	91	216	First Pitch	.371	167	62	9	5	3	40	17	0	.428	.539
3+ Days rest	3.46	5	5	27	75	0	93.2	80	7	50	89	Ahead in Count	.175	872	153	22	1	8	57	0	373	.178	.231
Pre-All Star	2.76	16	15	77	180	0	222.0	181	13	104	237	Behind in Count	.313	297	93	17	2	9	54	88	0	.465	.475
Post-All Star	3.43	6	18	75	148	12	236.0	205	19	114	209	Two Strikes	.157	951	149	28	2	8	58	111	446	.245	.216

Pitcher vs. Batter (career)

Pitches Best Vs.	Avg	AB	H	2B	3B	HR	RBI	BB	SO	OBP	SLG	Pitches Worst Vs.	Avg	AB	H	2B	3B	HR	RBI	BB	SO	OBP	SLG
Craig Biggio	.067	15	1	0	0	0	0	0	3	.067	.067	Andre Dawson	.467	15	7	2	0	1	4	0	1	.467	.800
Hubie Brooks	.077	13	1	0	0	0	0	0	5	.077	.077	Jeff Bagwell	.455	11	5	3	0	2	5	0	3	.455	1.273
Todd Zeile	.083	12	1	0	0	0	0	1	5	.154	.083	Sid Bream	.444	9	4	2	0	1	4	2	3	.462	1.000
Jose Lind	.095	21	2	0	0	0	0	4	7	.240	.095	Mark Grace	.429	14	6	0	2	1	6	1	3	.467	.929
Eddie Murray	.111	18	2	0	0	0	1	2	3	.200	.111	Jay Bell	.333	12	4	1	1	1	6	3	4	.467	.833

Chris Nabholz — Expos

Age 27 – Pitches Left

	ERA	W	L	Sv	G	GS	IP	BB	SO	Avg	H	2B	3B	HR	RBI	OBP	SLG	CG	ShO	Sup	QS	#P/S	SB	CS	GB	FB	G/F
1993 Season	4.09	9	8	0	26	21	116.2	63	74	.236	100	18	1	9	47	.343	.348	1	0	5.71	10	81	15	9	163	118	1.38
Career (1990-1993)	3.51	34	29	0	93	88	535.1	226	356	.232	453	90	13	31	180	.315	.338	4	2	4.67	47	89	60	29	750	525	1.43

1993 Season

	ERA	W	L	Sv	G	GS	IP	H	HR	BB	SO
Home	2.71	6	2	0	15	10	73.0	52	2	35	45
Away	6.39	3	6	0	11	11	43.2	48	7	28	29
Starter	4.04	9	8	0	21	21	111.1	96	9	58	69
Reliever	5.06	0	0	0	5	0	5.1	4	0	5	5
0-3 Days Rest	1.50	2	0	0	2	2	12.0	5	0	7	5
4 Days Rest	4.02	3	5	0	9	9	47.0	40	6	23	32
5+ Days Rest	4.64	4	3	0	10	10	52.1	51	3	28	32
Pre-All Star	4.99	5	5	0	15	14	70.1	67	6	44	49
Post-All Star	2.72	4	3	0	11	7	46.1	33	3	19	25

	Avg	AB	H	2B	3B	HR	RBI	BB	SO	OBP	SLG
vs. Left	.243	70	17	2	1	1	3	10	17	.354	.343
vs. Right	.235	353	83	16	0	8	44	53	57	.341	.348
Scoring Posn	.250	104	26	5	0	5	42	17	21	.359	.442
Close & Late	.240	25	6	0	0	0	0	3	7	.321	.240
None on/out	.272	103	28	7	0	1	1	22	19	.405	.369
First Pitch	.313	64	20	3	0	0	3	4	0	.366	.359
Ahead in Count	.213	183	39	6	1	4	23	0	60	.222	.322
Behind in Count	.192	104	20	3	0	3	14	40	0	.421	.308
Two Strikes	.186	177	33	4	1	5	21	19	74	.272	.305

Career (1990-1993)

	ERA	W	L	Sv	G	GS	IP	H	HR	BB	SO
Home	3.01	17	16	0	47	42	286.2	212	14	115	183
Away	4.09	17	13	0	46	46	248.2	241	17	111	173
Day	3.02	10	6	0	24	23	149.0	112	6	63	94
Night	3.70	24	23	0	69	65	386.1	341	25	163	262
Grass	4.40	7	9	0	21	21	120.2	114	8	52	78
Turf	3.26	27	20	0	72	67	414.2	339	23	174	278
April	4.58	2	7	0	14	14	76.2	78	6	40	49
May	4.63	6	4	0	13	13	70.0	58	5	38	54
June	4.52	3	4	0	14	13	71.2	69	1	37	59
July	3.01	3	3	0	10	10	68.2	59	5	22	32
August	3.09	7	6	0	17	17	110.2	82	8	38	62
September/October	2.42	13	5	0	25	21	137.2	107	6	51	100
Starter	3.50	34	29	0	88	88	530.0	449	31	221	351
Reliever	5.06	0	0	0	5	0	5.1	4	0	5	5
0-3 Days Rest	1.50	2	0	0	2	2	12.0	5	0	7	5
4 Days Rest	3.51	17	19	0	48	48	294.2	255	18	120	193
5+ Days Rest	3.59	15	10	0	38	38	223.1	189	13	94	153
Pre-All Star	4.28	12	15	0	45	44	248.1	225	13	125	178
Post-All Star	2.85	22	14	0	48	44	287.0	228	18	101	178

	Avg	AB	H	2B	3B	HR	RBI	BB	SO	OBP	SLG
vs. Left	.232	341	79	11	4	7	28	41	90	.322	.349
vs. Right	.232	1615	374	79	9	24	152	185	266	.313	.336
Inning 1-6	.231	1733	401	81	12	30	173	195	324	.312	.344
Inning 7+	.233	223	52	9	1	1	7	31	32	.332	.296
None on	.233	1140	266	51	10	18	18	140	207	.321	.343
Runners on	.229	816	187	39	3	13	162	86	149	.305	.332
Scoring Posn	.244	426	104	25	1	6	143	58	85	.332	.350
Close & Late	.214	117	25	2	0	1	4	18	16	.324	.256
None on/out	.245	510	125	25	5	10	10	66	97	.335	.373
vs. 1st Batr (relief)	.500	4	2	0	0	0	0	1	1	.600	.500
First Inning Pitched	.221	326	72	12	2	5	40	40	65	.311	.316
First 75 Pitches	.234	1566	366	73	9	25	157	175	292	.314	.340
Pitch 76-90	.210	252	53	10	4	4	17	31	40	.299	.329
Pitch 91-105	.273	110	30	5	0	2	6	18	21	.380	.373
Pitch 106+	.143	28	4	2	0	0	0	2	3	.200	.214
First Pitch	.269	294	79	16	2	3	26	11	0	.297	.367
Ahead in Count	.189	835	158	26	2	9	61	0	309	.197	.257
Behind in Count	.274	474	130	30	8	13	60	142	0	.440	.454
Two Strikes	.166	801	133	25	3	8	61	73	356	.242	.235

Pitcher vs. Batter (career)

Pitches Best Vs.	Avg	AB	H	2B	3B	HR	RBI	BB	SO	OBP	SLG
Will Clark	.000	17	0	0	0	0	1	1	1	.056	.000
Tony Fernandez	.000	12	0	0	0	0	1	1	0	.077	.000
Lloyd McClendon	.071	14	1	0	0	0	0	2	1	.188	.071
Ken Caminiti	.125	16	2	0	0	0	1	0	1	.125	.125
Benito Santiago	.133	15	2	0	0	0	1	0	3	.133	.133

Pitches Worst Vs.	Avg	AB	H	2B	3B	HR	RBI	BB	SO	OBP	SLG
Felix Jose	.636	11	7	2	0	0	3	1	3	.667	.818
Chris Sabo	.500	14	7	3	1	2	5	2	0	.563	1.286
Fred McGriff	.500	12	6	0	1	2	4	4	1	.625	1.167
Ray Lankford	.471	17	8	1	1	0	2	1	5	.500	.647
Matt D. Williams	.353	17	6	1	0	3	7	2	4	.400	.941

Tim Naehring — Red Sox

Age 27 – Bats Right

	Avg	G	AB	R	H	2B	3B	HR	RBI	BB	SO	HBP	GDP	SB	CS	OBP	SLG	IBB	SH	SF	#Pit	#P/PA	GB	FB	G/F
1993 Season	.331	39	127	14	42	10	0	1	17	10	26	0	3	1	0	.377	.433	0	3	1	556	3.94	38	36	1.06
Career (1990-1993)	.252	155	453	37	114	25	0	6	46	42	87	3	6	1	0	.318	.347	1	13	2	1955	3.81	157	129	1.22

1993 Season

	Avg	AB	H	2B	3B	HR	RBI	BB	SO	OBP	SLG
vs. Left	.395	43	17	4	0	0	4	4	6	.447	.488
vs. Right	.298	84	25	6	0	1	13	6	20	.341	.405
Home	.311	74	23	6	0	0	10	7	18	.366	.392
Away	.358	53	19	4	0	1	7	3	8	.393	.491
First Pitch	.286	7	2	0	0	0	0	0	0	.286	.286
Ahead in Count	.515	33	17	4	0	1	7	9	0	.619	.727
Behind in Count	.232	56	13	5	0	0	8	0	21	.228	.321
Two Strikes	.227	66	15	4	0	0	6	1	26	.235	.288

	Avg	AB	H	2B	3B	HR	RBI	BB	SO	OBP	SLG
Scoring Posn	.345	29	10	3	0	0	15	5	4	.429	.448
Close & Late	.222	18	4	1	0	0	0	2	6	.300	.278
None on/out	.250	24	6	1	0	1	1	3	5	.333	.417
Batting #3	.412	51	21	6	0	0	12	3	9	.444	.529
Batting #7	.294	17	5	0	0	0	2	2	2	.368	.294
Other	.271	59	16	4	0	1	3	5	15	.323	.390
Pre-All Star	.000	0	0	0	0	0	0	0	0	.000	.000
Post-All Star	.331	127	42	10	0	1	17	10	26	.377	.433

Career (1990-1993)

	Avg	AB	H	2B	3B	HR	RBI	BB	SO	OBP	SLG
vs. Left	.301	156	47	10	0	3	20	14	28	.364	.423
vs. Right	.226	297	67	15	0	3	26	28	59	.294	.306
Groundball	.235	119	28	5	0	2	13	8	12	.281	.328
Flyball	.235	85	20	9	0	2	11	9	17	.316	.412
Home	.239	209	50	11	0	2	21	26	49	.322	.321
Away	.262	244	64	14	0	4	25	16	38	.314	.369
Day	.266	173	46	9	0	2	18	26	36	.366	.353
Night	.243	280	68	16	0	4	28	16	51	.285	.343
Grass	.273	362	99	23	0	6	41	38	71	.342	.387
Turf	.165	91	15	2	0	0	5	4	16	.216	.187
First Pitch	.227	44	10	0	0	0	5	0	0	.222	.227
Ahead in Count	.325	120	39	9	0	2	13	27	0	.449	.450
Behind in Count	.196	194	38	9	0	4	23	0	71	.207	.304
Two Strikes	.184	207	38	10	0	3	20	15	87	.248	.275

	Avg	AB	H	2B	3B	HR	RBI	BB	SO	OBP	SLG
Scoring Posn	.290	100	29	9	0	1	38	15	12	.376	.410
Close & Late	.225	80	18	3	0	2	4	8	19	.295	.338
None on/out	.202	114	23	4	0	3	3	12	28	.289	.316
Batting #7	.207	87	18	2	0	0	6	4	15	.242	.230
Batting #9	.255	149	38	10	0	5	18	13	30	.317	.423
Other	.267	217	58	13	0	1	22	25	42	.347	.341
April	.176	74	13	2	0	1	6	8	19	.256	.243
May	.160	50	8	2	0	0	1	3	14	.236	.200
June	.190	21	4	0	0	1	1	3	0	.320	.333
July	.196	97	19	5	0	1	9	6	13	.243	.278
August	.258	62	16	1	0	1	7	5	13	.313	.323
September/October	.362	149	54	15	0	2	22	17	28	.423	.503
Pre-All Star	.182	170	31	4	0	2	10	15	35	.261	.241
Post-All Star	.293	283	83	21	0	4	36	27	52	.353	.410

Batter vs. Pitcher (career)

Hits Best Against	Avg	AB	H	2B	3B	HR	RBI	BB	SO	OBP	SLG	Hits Worst Against	Avg	AB	H	2B	3B	HR	RBI	BB	SO	OBP	SLG
Frank Tanana	.545	11	6	1	0	1	2	1	1	.583	.909	Kevin Appier	.083	12	1	0	0	0	1	0	3	.083	.083
Jimmy Key	.364	11	4	0	0	0	0	0	3	.364	.364	Todd Stottlemyre	.091	11	1	1	0	0	2	0	5	.091	.182
												Bill Krueger	.200	10	2	1	0	0	0	1	2	.273	.300

Charles Nagy — Indians

Age 27 – Pitches Right (groundball pitcher)

	ERA	W	L	Sv	G	GS	IP	BB	SO	Avg	H	2B	3B	HR	RBI	OBP	SLG	CG	ShO	Sup	QS	#P/S	SB	CS	GB	FB	G/F
1993 Season	6.29	2	6	0	9	9	48.2	13	30	.322	66	11	0	6	33	.367	.463	1	0	6.47	2	90	10	2	96	35	2.74
Career (1990-1993)	3.94	31	35	0	84	83	557.2	157	334	.276	597	106	12	39	230	.326	.391	17	4	4.24	49	101	47	26	963	462	2.08

1993 Season

	ERA	W	L	Sv	G	GS	IP	H	HR	BB	SO		Avg	AB	H	2B	3B	HR	RBI	BB	SO	OBP	SLG
Home	4.37	2	2	0	4	4	22.2	24	2	8	11	vs. Left	.288	104	30	4	0	2	14	6	14	.324	.385
Away	7.96	0	4	0	5	5	26.0	42	4	5	19	vs. Right	.350	101	36	7	0	4	19	7	16	.409	.545

Career (1990-1993)

	ERA	W	L	Sv	G	GS	IP	H	HR	BB	SO		Avg	AB	H	2B	3B	HR	RBI	BB	SO	OBP	SLG
Home	3.27	18	14	0	41	40	288.2	289	15	76	182	vs. Left	.277	1094	303	48	8	17	115	82	162	.326	.382
Away	4.65	13	21	0	43	43	269.0	308	24	81	152	vs. Right	.276	1067	294	58	4	22	115	75	172	.326	.399
Day	4.37	9	15	0	30	30	191.2	212	19	56	135	Inning 1-6	.276	1774	490	89	12	33	200	141	282	.330	.396
Night	3.71	22	20	0	54	53	366.0	385	20	101	199	Inning 7+	.276	387	107	17	0	6	30	16	52	.303	.367
Grass	3.72	29	24	0	68	67	452.2	472	31	118	266	None on	.280	1249	350	70	9	18	18	82	209	.326	.394
Turf	4.89	2	11	0	16	16	105.0	125	8	39	68	Runners on	.271	912	247	36	3	21	212	75	125	.326	.386
April	3.12	5	6	0	14	14	101.0	94	6	25	65	Scoring Posn	.273	524	143	19	2	15	193	49	93	.329	.403
May	4.95	4	7	0	15	15	91.0	109	7	29	49	Close & Late	.277	188	52	7	0	2	10	11	27	.317	.346
June	2.96	5	6	0	12	12	82.0	91	2	20	49	None on/out	.271	558	151	32	4	7	7	35	93	.315	.380
July	2.93	5	5	0	12	12	83.0	85	3	25	35	vs. 1st Batr (relief)	.000	0	0	0	0	0	0	1	0	1.000	.000
August	5.34	4	5	0	13	13	86.0	101	9	27	63	First Inning Pitched	.296	335	99	22	3	6	52	38	54	.371	.433
September/October	4.24	8	6	0	18	17	114.2	117	12	31	73	First 75 Pitches	.275	1513	416	78	11	29	165	122	239	.330	.399
Starter	3.92	31	35	0	83	83	556.0	594	38	156	332	Pitch 76-90	.293	283	83	12	1	7	39	15	43	.327	.417
Reliever	10.80	0	0	0	1	0	1.2	3	1	1	2	Pitch 91-105	.260	231	60	10	0	2	18	9	34	.285	.329
0-3 Days Rest	0.00	0	0	0	0	0	0.0	0	0	0	0	Pitch 106+	.284	134	38	6	0	1	8	11	18	.338	.351
4 Days Rest	4.49	9	20	0	39	39	256.1	310	19	75	162	First Pitch	.302	308	93	11	4	6	42	9	0	.323	.422
5+ Days Rest	3.42	22	15	0	44	44	299.2	284	19	81	170	Ahead in Count	.212	925	196	35	2	12	71	0	294	.215	.293
Pre-All Star	3.52	17	20	0	45	45	304.0	319	17	80	172	Behind in Count	.357	558	199	38	5	11	74	87	0	.439	.502
Post-All Star	4.43	14	15	0	39	38	253.2	278	22	77	162	Two Strikes	.196	890	174	32	3	9	53	61	334	.250	.269

Pitcher vs. Batter (career)

Pitches Best Vs.	Avg	AB	H	2B	3B	HR	RBI	BB	SO	OBP	SLG	Pitches Worst Vs.	Avg	AB	H	2B	3B	HR	RBI	BB	SO	OBP	SLG
Jose Canseco	.000	12	0	0	0	0	0	2	2	.143	.000	Greg Gagne	.529	17	9	3	0	0	1	0	2	.529	.706
Kent Hrbek	.067	15	1	0	0	0	0	2	4	.176	.067	Tim Raines	.429	14	6	2	0	1	2	2	3	.471	.786
Manuel Lee	.067	15	1	0	0	0	0	2	5	.176	.067	Kelly Gruber	.400	20	8	3	0	2	6	2	2	.455	.850
Chuck Knoblauch	.091	11	1	0	0	0	1	0	0	.083	.091	Ken Griffey Jr	.381	21	8	3	1	2	5	3	6	.458	.905
Leo Gomez	.154	13	2	0	0	0	0	0	3	.154	.154	Mickey Tettleton	.313	16	5	0	0	3	4	3	5	.421	.875

Bob Natal — Marlins

Age 28 – Bats Right

	Avg	G	AB	R	H	2B	3B	HR	RBI	BB	SO	HBP	GDP	SB	CS	OBP	SLG	IBB	SH	SF	#Pit	#P/PA	GB	FB	G/F
1993 Season	.214	41	117	3	25	4	1	1	6	6	22	4	5	1	0	.273	.291	0	3	1	488	3.73	45	35	1.29
Career (1992-1993)	.203	46	123	3	25	4	1	1	6	7	23	4	6	1	0	.267	.276	0	3	1	512	3.71	49	36	1.36

1993 Season

	Avg	AB	H	2B	3B	HR	RBI	BB	SO	OBP	SLG		Avg	AB	H	2B	3B	HR	RBI	BB	SO	OBP	SLG
vs. Left	.219	32	7	1	0	0	1	2	5	.265	.250	Scoring Posn	.129	31	4	1	0	0	4	1	6	.200	.161
vs. Right	.212	85	18	3	1	1	5	4	17	.277	.306	Close & Late	.192	26	5	0	1	0	1	1	6	.222	.269
Home	.177	62	11	2	1	0	2	4	14	.268	.242	None on/out	.154	26	4	2	0	0	0	1	5	.241	.231
Away	.255	55	14	2	0	1	4	2	8	.281	.345	Batting #6	.091	11	1	0	0	0	0	2	2	.231	.091
First Pitch	.500	4	2	0	1	0	1	0	0	.600	1.000	Batting #7	.234	77	18	3	0	1	5	4	16	.302	.312
Ahead in Count	.296	27	8	1	0	1	2	1	0	.345	.444	Other	.207	29	6	1	1	0	1	0	4	.207	.310
Behind in Count	.162	68	11	1	0	0	1	0	20	.186	.176	Pre-All Star	.167	18	3	0	0	1	2	0	8	.167	.333
Two Strikes	.164	61	10	1	0	0	1	5	22	.250	.180	Post-All Star	.222	99	22	4	1	0	4	6	14	.291	.283

Jaime Navarro — Brewers

Age 26 – Pitches Right

	ERA	W	L	Sv	G	GS	IP	BB	SO	Avg	H	2B	3B	HR	RBI	OBP	SLG	CG	ShO	Sup	QS	#P/S	SB	CS	GB	FB	G/F
1993 Season	5.33	11	12	0	35	34	214.1	73	114	.300	254	38	9	21	121	.356	.440	5	1	5.16	15	100	23	6	320	241	1.33
Career (1989-1993)	4.08	58	50	1	154	141	953.1	283	459	.273	1010	160	25	70	407	.326	.387	24	6	4.77	75	100	86	33	1470	1071	1.37

1993 Season

	ERA	W	L	Sv	G	GS	IP	H	HR	BB	SO		Avg	AB	H	2B	3B	HR	RBI	BB	SO	OBP	SLG
Home	5.03	5	5	0	16	15	98.1	112	5	38	55	vs. Left	.317	448	142	20	9	11	66	38	60	.367	.475
Away	5.59	6	7	0	19	19	116.0	142	16	35	59	vs. Right	.280	400	112	18	0	10	55	35	54	.344	.400
Day	5.02	5	4	0	13	13	80.2	97	5	25	41	Inning 1-6	.308	741	228	34	9	18	114	63	98	.362	.451
Night	5.52	6	8	0	22	21	133.2	157	16	48	73	Inning 7+	.243	107	26	4	0	3	7	10	16	.317	.364
Grass	5.34	8	10	0	28	27	168.2	190	17	65	94	None on	.283	494	140	21	5	12	12	34	68	.336	.419
Turf	5.32	3	2	0	7	7	45.2	64	4	8	20	Runners on	.322	354	114	17	4	9	109	39	46	.382	.469
April	6.11	0	2	0	5	5	28.0	31	4	13	18	Scoring Posn	.285	207	59	15	1	4	94	27	37	.350	.425
May	3.18	3	1	0	5	5	34.0	38	2	10	12	Close & Late	.300	40	12	3	0	1	3	5	4	.383	.450

1993 Season

	ERA	W	L	Sv	G	GS	IP	H	HR	BB	SO		Avg	AB	H	2B	3B	HR	RBI	BB	SO	OBP	SLG
June	4.24	2	1	0	7	7	46.2	45	5	16	23	None on/out	.275	218	60	11	2	5	5	17	28	.333	.413
July	8.16	1	4	0	5	5	28.2	43	3	9	7	vs. 1st Batr (relief)	.000	1	0	0	0	0	0	0	0	.000	.000
August	6.35	2	1	0	7	6	39.2	54	5	14	26	First Inning Pitched	.354	144	51	8	4	2	31	12	24	.393	.507
September/October	4.82	3	3	0	6	6	37.1	43	2	11	28	First 75 Pitches	.307	618	190	30	8	12	91	48	84	.356	.440
Starter	5.30	11	12	0	34	34	212.1	250	21	72	111	Pitch 76-90	.282	117	33	2	0	6	20	13	11	.358	.453
Reliever	9.00	0	0	0	1	0	2.0	4	0	1	3	Pitch 91-105	.312	77	24	5	1	3	6	7	12	.386	.519
0-3 Days Rest	5.79	0	1	0	3	3	18.2	14	2	9	12	Pitch 106+	.194	36	7	1	0	0	4	5	7	.286	.222
4 Days Rest	4.52	9	5	0	21	21	139.1	159	15	40	70	First Pitch	.423	123	52	7	0	2	22	3	0	.446	.528
5+ Days Rest	7.12	2	6	0	10	10	54.1	77	4	23	29	Ahead in Count	.233	348	81	13	3	3	31	0	97	.240	.313
Pre-All Star	4.78	5	6	0	19	19	118.2	130	12	41	55	Behind in Count	.347	213	74	13	4	10	46	38	0	.438	.587
Post-All Star	6.02	6	6	0	16	15	95.2	124	9	32	59	Two Strikes	.223	349	78	12	5	5	35	32	114	.292	.330

Career (1989-1993)

	ERA	W	L	Sv	G	GS	IP	H	HR	BB	SO		Avg	AB	H	2B	3B	HR	RBI	BB	SO	OBP	SLG
Home	3.79	33	20	1	74	66	460.1	473	25	141	230	vs. Left	.284	1878	533	80	15	36	211	154	221	.335	.400
Away	4.34	25	30	0	80	75	493.0	537	45	142	229	vs. Right	.262	1820	477	80	10	34	196	129	238	.316	.373
Day	3.84	21	16	0	53	45	306.2	324	16	95	152	Inning 1-6	.270	3023	817	129	21	53	339	238	375	.325	.379
Night	4.19	37	34	1	101	96	646.2	686	54	188	307	Inning 7+	.286	675	193	31	4	17	68	45	84	.331	.419
Grass	3.87	46	38	1	125	113	775.0	792	52	245	370	None on	.264	2184	576	92	16	42	42	149	280	.315	.378
Turf	5.00	12	12	0	29	28	178.1	218	18	38	89	Runners on	.287	1514	434	68	9	28	365	134	179	.341	.399
April	5.48	2	4	0	17	17	93.2	117	7	37	45	Scoring Posn	.268	848	227	42	4	13	319	91	115	.329	.373
May	3.86	11	6	0	21	21	142.1	156	12	29	60	Close & Late	.288	299	86	14	3	7	32	21	32	.331	.425
June	3.94	10	6	0	23	23	157.2	155	15	57	74	None on/out	.250	956	239	39	5	19	19	65	120	.303	.361
July	3.80	6	11	1	29	20	154.0	155	6	46	67	vs. 1st Batr (relief)	.000	12	0	0	0	0	0	0	5	.000	.000
August	4.69	14	12	0	32	28	186.1	200	16	52	102	First Inning Pitched	.266	571	152	21	7	5	67	55	85	.327	.354
September/October	3.41	15	11	0	32	32	219.1	227	14	62	111	First 75 Pitches	.266	2692	715	109	20	43	275	203	339	.318	.369
Starter	4.14	57	50	0	141	141	926.0	987	69	278	439	Pitch 76-90	.287	478	137	24	2	14	70	35	59	.337	.433
Reliever	1.98	1	0	1	13	0	27.1	23	1	5	20	Pitch 91-105	.284	335	95	15	2	5	23	26	40	.345	.385
0-3 Days Rest	3.86	2	3	0	8	8	56.0	48	3	15	31	Pitch 106+	.326	193	63	12	1	8	39	19	21	.376	.523
4 Days Rest	4.04	45	27	0	91	91	610.1	649	49	170	284	First Pitch	.363	545	198	31	3	9	76	13	0	.381	.481
5+ Days Rest	4.44	10	20	0	42	42	259.2	290	17	93	124	Ahead in Count	.207	1564	323	45	8	14	115	0	398	.211	.272
Pre-All Star	4.37	24	21	0	70	68	440.1	484	37	139	194	Behind in Count	.342	896	306	53	11	29	140	138	0	.423	.522
Post-All Star	3.82	34	29	1	84	73	513.0	526	33	144	265	Two Strikes	.196	1495	293	44	8	18	114	131	459	.263	.272

Pitcher vs. Batter (career)

Pitches Best Vs.	Avg	AB	H	2B	3B	HR	RBI	BB	SO	OBP	SLG	Pitches Worst Vs.	Avg	AB	H	2B	3B	HR	RBI	BB	SO	OBP	SLG
Ron Karkovice	.000	12	0	0	0	0	0	0	6	.000	.000	Danny Tartabull	.571	21	12	1	0	3	8	4	5	.640	1.048
Gary DiSarcina	.071	14	1	0	0	0	1	0	0	.071	.071	Roberto Alomar	.550	20	11	2	1	0	0	0	0	.550	.750
Kelly Gruber	.100	20	2	0	0	0	2	1	1	.143	.100	Jose Canseco	.500	14	7	1	0	1	9	4	3	.611	.786
Ernest Riles	.100	10	1	0	0	0	0	1	3	.182	.100	John Valentin	.500	10	5	1	0	1	2	2	1	.583	.900
Chad Curtis	.133	15	2	0	0	0	0	0	4	.133	.133	Dave Winfield	.478	23	11	2	0	4	13	1	3	.500	1.087

Tito Navarro — Mets

Age 23 – Bats Both

	Avg	G	AB	R	H	2B	3B	HR	RBI	BB	SO	HBP	GDP	SB	CS	OBP	SLG	IBB	SH	SF	#Pit	#P/PA	GB	FB	G/F
1993 Season	.059	12	17	1	1	0	0	0	1	0	4	0	1	0	0	.059	.059	0	1	0	60	3.33	9	0	0.00

1993 Season

	Avg	AB	H	2B	3B	HR	RBI	BB	SO	OBP	SLG		Avg	AB	H	2B	3B	HR	RBI	BB	SO	OBP	SLG
vs. Left	.000	4	0	0	0	0	0	0	0	.000	.000	Scoring Posn	.200	5	1	0	0	0	1	0	1	.200	.200
vs. Right	.077	13	1	0	0	0	1	0	4	.077	.077	Close & Late	.250	4	1	0	0	0	1	0	0	.250	.250

Denny Neagle — Pirates

Age 25 – Pitches Left (flyball pitcher)

	ERA	W	L	Sv	G	GS	IP	BB	SO	Avg	H	2B	3B	HR	RBI	OBP	SLG	GF	IR	IRS	Hld	SvOp	SB	CS	GB	FB	G/F
1993 Season	5.31	3	5	1	50	7	81.1	37	73	.258	82	18	2	10	54	.340	.421	13	28	11	6	1	16	5	69	123	0.56
Career (1991-1993)	4.80	7	12	3	112	16	187.2	87	164	.261	191	43	4	22	100	.342	.421	23	54	15	11	5	32	9	187	246	0.76

1993 Season

	ERA	W	L	Sv	G	GS	IP	H	HR	BB	SO		Avg	AB	H	2B	3B	HR	RBI	BB	SO	OBP	SLG
Home	4.86	1	1	0	25	3	37.0	37	5	14	35	vs. Left	.223	94	21	4	1	3	18	10	29	.305	.383
Away	5.68	2	4	1	25	4	44.1	45	5	23	38	vs. Right	.272	224	61	14	1	7	36	27	44	.354	.438
Starter	6.61	2	3	0	7	7	32.2	35	6	21	29	Scoring Posn	.321	84	27	9	1	2	39	16	22	.437	.524
Reliever	4.44	1	2	1	43	0	48.2	47	4	16	44	Close & Late	.222	63	14	6	0	2	16	6	16	.310	.413
0 Days rest	5.68	0	0	0	6	0	6.1	7	1	2	7	None on/out	.213	75	16	2	0	0	0	11	20	.314	.240
1 or 2 Days rest	5.02	1	2	0	24	0	28.2	32	2	12	26	First Pitch	.548	31	17	5	0	2	12	2	0	.588	.903
3+ Days rest	2.63	0	0	1	13	0	13.2	8	1	2	11	Ahead in Count	.183	164	30	6	1	2	16	0	61	.192	.268
Pre-All Star	6.12	2	4	0	27	7	57.1	67	7	29	54	Behind in Count	.397	58	23	5	1	4	18	15	0	.521	.724
Post-All Star	3.38	1	1	1	23	0	24.0	15	3	8	19	Two Strikes	.175	177	31	6	0	3	18	20	73	.265	.260

Career (1991-1993)

	ERA	W	L	Sv	G	GS	IP	H	HR	BB	SO		Avg	AB	H	2B	3B	HR	RBI	BB	SO	OBP	SLG
Home	5.28	2	7	0	58	9	93.2	111	14	42	87	vs. Left	.227	207	47	13	1	5	33	25	61	.316	.372
Away	4.31	5	5	3	54	7	94.0	80	8	45	77	vs. Right	.275	524	144	30	3	17	67	62	103	.352	.441
Day	4.13	2	2	1	32	2	48.0	40	5	20	40	Inning 1-6	.286	385	110	25	2	15	58	48	76	.363	.478
Night	5.03	5	10	2	80	14	139.2	151	17	67	124	Inning 7+	.234	346	81	18	2	7	42	39	88	.319	.358
Grass	2.74	4	2	1	29	2	42.2	34	1	20	39	None on	.249	418	104	21	2	11	11	42	90	.322	.388
Turf	5.40	3	10	2	83	14	145.0	157	21	67	125	Runners on	.278	313	87	22	2	11	89	45	74	.368	.466
April	4.18	0	1	0	13	2	23.2	24	2	7	22	Scoring Posn	.303	185	56	17	1	6	77	40	53	.424	.503

Career (1991-1993)

	ERA	W	L	Sv	G	GS	IP	H	HR	BB	SO
May	3.77	2	2	0	18	3	28.2	32	1	8	22
June	7.14	3	4	1	17	7	46.2	50	9	30	43
July	5.02	0	2	0	17	2	28.2	28	4	17	32
August	2.35	2	2	2	21	0	30.2	22	3	13	21
September/October	4.91	0	1	0	26	2	29.1	35	3	12	24
Starter	5.80	3	7	0	16	16	71.1	85	11	32	57
Reliever	4.18	4	5	3	96	0	116.1	106	11	55	107
0 Days rest	4.91	1	0	0	10	0	11.0	10	1	6	10
1 or 2 Days rest	5.14	2	4	2	55	0	70.0	67	9	35	68
3+ Days rest	2.04	1	1	1	31	0	35.1	29	1	14	29
Pre-All Star	5.37	5	8	1	55	13	114.0	120	13	55	104
Post-All Star	3.91	2	4	2	57	3	73.2	71	9	32	60

	Avg	AB	H	2B	3B	HR	RBI	BB	SO	OBP	SLG
Close & Late	.205	166	34	7	0	5	21	18	49	.294	.337
None on/out	.233	180	42	7	1	3	3	23	37	.327	.333
vs. 1st Batr (relief)	.141	85	12	1	1	1	10	11	18	.240	.212
First Inning Pitched	.244	357	87	19	3	7	52	45	81	.331	.373
First 15 Pitches	.231	295	68	16	3	5	35	38	67	.321	.356
Pitch 16-30	.297	202	60	13	1	8	38	18	47	.353	.490
Pitch 31-45	.226	84	19	3	0	1	6	14	23	.350	.298
Pitch 46+	.293	150	44	11	0	8	21	17	27	.365	.527
First Pitch	.389	72	28	6	0	5	22	8	0	.458	.681
Ahead in Count	.196	368	72	15	3	5	25	0	139	.202	.293
Behind in Count	.404	136	55	13	1	8	35	36	0	.526	.691
Two Strikes	.181	393	71	13	1	8	31	42	164	.264	.280

Pitcher vs. Batter (career)

Pitches Best Vs.	Avg	AB	H	2B	3B	HR	RBI	BB	SO	OBP	SLG
Delino DeShields	.091	11	1	0	0	0	0	2	2	.231	.091
Tony Gwynn	.100	10	1	0	0	0	0	1	0	.182	.100

Pitches Worst Vs.	Avg	AB	H	2B	3B	HR	RBI	BB	SO	OBP	SLG
Larry Walker	.400	10	4	0	0	2	6	2	2	.500	1.000
Eddie Murray	.333	9	3	0	1	0	2	1	0	.364	.556

Troy Neel — Athletics

Age 28 – Bats Left

	Avg	G	AB	R	H	2B	3B	HR	RBI	BB	SO	HBP	GDP	SB	CS	OBP	SLG	IBB	SH	SF	#Pit	#P/PA	GB	FB	G/F
1993 Season	.290	123	427	59	124	21	0	19	63	49	101	4	7	3	5	.367	.473	5	0	2	1841	3.82	142	99	1.43
Career (1992-1993)	.288	147	480	67	138	24	0	22	72	54	116	5	8	3	6	.364	.475	5	0	2	2091	3.87	158	115	1.37

1993 Season

	Avg	AB	H	2B	3B	HR	RBI	BB	SO	OBP	SLG
vs. Left	.357	98	35	6	0	4	15	10	22	.427	.541
vs. Right	.271	329	89	15	0	15	48	39	79	.349	.453
Groundball	.293	99	29	9	0	4	15	12	21	.369	.505
Flyball	.330	100	33	4	0	7	20	11	20	.398	.580
Home	.312	199	62	7	0	11	32	21	51	.388	.513
Away	.272	228	62	14	0	8	31	28	50	.349	.439
Day	.278	176	49	6	0	8	30	19	43	.347	.449
Night	.299	251	75	15	0	11	33	30	58	.381	.490
Grass	.281	363	102	15	0	15	51	41	89	.359	.446
Turf	.344	64	22	6	0	4	12	8	12	.411	.625
First Pitch	.200	55	11	5	0	0	3	4	0	.279	.291
Ahead in Count	.478	115	55	10	0	10	34	29	0	.579	.826
Behind in Count	.178	180	32	2	0	5	16	0	81	.186	.272
Two Strikes	.171	205	35	4	0	6	20	16	101	.233	.278

	Avg	AB	H	2B	3B	HR	RBI	BB	SO	OBP	SLG
Scoring Posn	.235	115	27	3	0	5	48	20	29	.348	.391
Close & Late	.266	64	17	5	0	2	13	11	16	.373	.438
None on/out	.381	113	43	8	0	9	9	12	22	.440	.690
Batting #4	.316	256	81	11	0	12	42	29	61	.389	.500
Batting #6	.316	76	24	6	0	2	8	8	15	.381	.474
Other	.200	95	19	4	0	5	13	12	25	.300	.400
April	.260	50	13	3	0	2	4	4	11	.315	.440
May	.149	67	10	2	0	2	9	7	16	.227	.269
June	.371	35	13	3	0	2	7	3	9	.410	.629
July	.333	87	29	4	0	5	19	12	20	.414	.552
August	.318	88	28	4	0	5	14	13	23	.412	.534
September/October	.310	100	31	5	0	3	10	10	22	.389	.450
Pre-All Star	.279	190	53	9	0	11	33	16	43	.332	.500
Post-All Star	.300	237	71	12	0	8	30	33	58	.394	.451

1993 By Position

Position	Avg	AB	H	2B	3B	HR	RBI	BB	SO	OBP	SLG	G	GS	Innings	PO	A	E	DP	Fld Pct	Rng Fctr	In Zone	Outs	Zone Rtg	MLB Zone
As Designated Hitter	.274	318	87	15	0	15	44	34	79	.346	.462	85	84	---	---	---	---	---	---	---	---	---	---	---
As 1b	.350	103	36	6	0	4	16	14	21	.437	.524	34	31	252.2	236	21	5	25	.981	---	54	48	.889	.834

Gene Nelson — Rangers

Age 33 – Pitches Right

	ERA	W	L	Sv	G	GS	IP	BB	SO	Avg	H	2B	3B	HR	RBI	OBP	SLG	GF	IR	IRS	Hld	SvOp	SB	CS	GB	FB	G/F
1993 Season	3.12	0	5	5	52	0	60.2	24	35	.259	60	12	1	3	31	.328	.358	22	40	10	9	8	3	1	81	76	1.07
Last Five Years	3.91	10	19	13	225	2	315.2	116	189	.254	303	46	11	30	172	.320	.387	58	195	58	49	26	16	7	410	383	1.07

1993 Season

	ERA	W	L	Sv	G	GS	IP	H	HR	BB	SO
Home	2.23	0	2	4	28	0	32.1	32	1	10	21
Away	4.13	0	3	1	24	0	28.1	28	2	14	14
Starter	0.00	0	0	0	0	0	0.0	0	0	0	0
Reliever	3.12	0	5	5	52	0	60.2	60	3	24	35
0 Days rest	1.98	0	2	1	12	0	13.2	10	0	5	10
1 or 2 Days rest	2.89	0	2	2	19	0	18.2	20	1	9	13
3+ Days rest	3.81	0	1	2	21	0	28.1	30	2	10	12
Pre-All Star	1.30	0	2	3	32	0	34.2	27	2	16	22
Post-All Star	5.54	0	3	2	20	0	26.0	33	1	8	13

	Avg	AB	H	2B	3B	HR	RBI	BB	SO	OBP	SLG
vs. Left	.320	75	24	8	1	1	13	18	5	.442	.493
vs. Right	.229	157	36	4	0	2	18	6	30	.263	.293
Scoring Posn	.317	60	19	6	0	0	27	10	7	.392	.417
Close & Late	.327	98	32	8	0	0	18	14	14	.404	.408
None on/out	.321	56	18	3	0	3	3	3	8	.356	.536
First Pitch	.152	33	5	1	0	0	4	5	0	.263	.182
Ahead in Count	.250	100	25	6	0	1	15	0	26	.257	.340
Behind in Count	.333	51	17	4	1	2	9	9	0	.426	.569
Two Strikes	.236	106	25	5	0	1	11	10	35	.305	.311

Last Five Years

	ERA	W	L	Sv	G	GS	IP	H	HR	BB	SO
Home	3.55	6	8	7	105	1	154.2	136	15	50	105
Away	4.25	4	11	6	120	1	161.0	167	15	66	84
Day	4.47	2	5	4	69	1	110.2	101	10	43	71
Night	3.60	8	14	9	156	1	205.0	202	20	73	118
Grass	3.71	9	17	12	189	2	276.1	257	25	98	178
Turf	5.26	1	2	1	36	0	39.1	46	5	18	11
April	3.10	2	2	1	22	0	29.0	26	1	11	17
May	2.94	1	2	4	40	0	52.0	39	5	17	32
June	4.91	2	4	2	45	0	66.0	66	5	29	40
July	5.72	3	6	1	40	2	67.2	88	11	30	36
August	2.91	1	3	2	38	0	52.2	44	3	15	31
September/October	2.61	1	2	3	40	0	48.1	40	5	14	33

	Avg	AB	H	2B	3B	HR	RBI	BB	SO	OBP	SLG
vs. Left	.292	466	136	24	8	9	64	67	56	.373	.436
vs. Right	.230	726	167	22	3	21	108	49	133	.284	.355
Inning 1-6	.280	296	83	8	4	9	65	36	48	.349	.426
Inning 7+	.246	896	220	38	7	21	107	80	141	.310	.374
None on	.260	634	165	25	3	17	17	49	110	.320	.390
Runners on	.247	558	138	21	8	13	155	67	79	.320	.384
Scoring Posn	.251	307	77	12	6	7	137	52	46	.344	.397
Close & Late	.283	375	106	19	3	11	64	39	52	.351	.437
None on/out	.278	281	78	12	0	8	8	21	48	.332	.406
vs. 1st Batr (relief)	.217	203	44	3	0	8	36	12	42	.261	.350
First Inning Pitched	.255	706	180	25	5	18	124	65	113	.316	.381
First 15 Pitches	.250	721	180	25	7	19	103	56	110	.304	.383

Last Five Years	ERA	W	L	Sv	G	GS	IP	H	HR	BB	SO
Starter	3.12	1	0	0	2	2	8.2	12	0	4	6
Reliever	3.93	9	19	13	223	0	307.0	291	30	112	183
0 Days rest	4.78	1	6	2	34	0	37.2	38	2	14	17
1 or 2 Days rest	3.87	3	8	6	87	0	111.2	109	13	38	69
3+ Days rest	3.77	5	5	5	102	0	157.2	144	15	60	97
Pre-All Star	3.95	5	11	7	120	1	171.0	165	14	67	105
Post-All Star	3.86	5	8	6	105	1	144.2	138	16	49	84

	Avg	AB	H	2B	3B	HR	RBI	BB	SO	OBP	SLG
Pitch 16-30	.254	299	76	16	3	3	50	37	56	.333	.358
Pitch 31-45	.276	116	32	3	1	8	15	13	16	.354	.526
Pitch 46+	.268	56	15	2	0	0	4	10	7	.379	.304
First Pitch	.288	191	55	8	3	8	36	14	0	.333	.487
Ahead in Count	.212	513	109	16	2	8	59	0	160	.219	.298
Behind in Count	.293	280	82	15	4	9	48	55	0	.399	.471
Two Strikes	.202	500	101	15	2	8	52	47	189	.273	.288

Pitcher vs. Batter (since 1984)

Pitches Best Vs.	Avg	AB	H	2B	3B	HR	RBI	BB	SO	OBP	SLG
Tom Brunansky	.063	16	1	0	0	0	0	1	4	.118	.063
Don Slaught	.077	13	1	0	0	0	0	0	2	.077	.077
Cecil Fielder	.087	23	2	0	0	0	1	1	5	.125	.087
Billy Ripken	.091	11	1	1	0	0	0	0	1	.091	.182
Dan Gladden	.190	21	4	0	0	0	2	0	2	.190	.190

Pitches Worst Vs.	Avg	AB	H	2B	3B	HR	RBI	BB	SO	OBP	SLG
Randy Bush	.545	11	6	1	0	1	3	1	2	.583	.909
Don Mattingly	.458	24	11	4	0	1	2	2	1	.500	.750
Gary Gaetti	.444	27	12	2	0	1	8	2	5	.483	.630
Paul Molitor	.400	15	6	0	1	1	3	0	1	.375	.733
George Brett	.350	20	7	0	0	4	5	1	0	.381	.950

Jeff Nelson — Mariners

Age 27 – Pitches Right (groundball pitcher)

	ERA	W	L	Sv	G	GS	IP	BB	SO	Avg	H	2B	3B	HR	RBI	OBP	SLG	GF	IR	IRS	Hld	SvOp	SB	CS	GB	FB	G/F
1993 Season	4.35	5	3	1	71	0	60.0	34	61	.258	57	8	0	5	49	.371	.362	13	95	32	17	11	10	1	92	40	2.30
Career (1992-1993)	3.83	6	10	7	137	0	141.0	78	107	.250	128	18	3	12	89	.361	.368	40	158	50	23	25	14	4	202	132	1.53

1993 Season

	ERA	W	L	Sv	G	GS	IP	H	HR	BB	SO
Home	3.57	3	0	1	36	0	35.1	29	2	16	38
Away	5.47	2	3	0	35	0	24.2	28	3	18	23
Day	4.32	1	3	0	16	0	16.2	13	1	14	20
Night	4.36	4	0	1	55	0	43.1	44	4	20	41
Grass	4.50	2	3	0	29	0	22.0	22	3	17	20
Turf	4.26	3	0	1	42	0	38.0	35	2	17	41
April	1.50	0	0	0	5	0	6.0	8	0	4	6
May	4.15	1	1	0	14	0	13.0	9	0	9	14
June	2.89	1	0	0	12	0	9.1	12	0	4	8
July	3.29	1	1	1	14	0	13.2	8	3	5	12
August	8.68	2	1	0	12	0	9.1	11	1	5	14
September/October	5.19	0	0	0	14	0	8.2	9	1	7	7
Starter	0.00	0	0	0	0	0	0.0	0	0	0	0
Reliever	4.35	5	3	1	71	0	60.0	57	5	34	61
0 Days rest	4.50	1	1	0	22	0	18.0	13	1	11	22
1 or 2 Days rest	4.06	3	1	1	36	0	31.0	30	3	19	28
3+ Days rest	4.91	1	1	0	13	0	11.0	14	1	4	11
Pre-All Star	3.09	2	1	0	36	0	32.0	31	1	18	32
Post-All Star	5.79	3	2	1	35	0	28.0	26	4	16	29

	Avg	AB	H	2B	3B	HR	RBI	BB	SO	OBP	SLG
vs. Left	.354	48	17	4	0	3	17	10	12	.484	.625
vs. Right	.231	173	40	4	0	2	32	24	49	.337	.289
Inning 1-6	.263	19	5	1	0	0	3	4	8	.391	.316
Inning 7+	.257	202	52	7	0	5	46	30	53	.369	.366
None on	.226	93	21	4	0	3	3	8	31	.301	.366
Runners on	.281	128	36	4	0	2	46	26	30	.415	.359
Scoring Posn	.307	88	27	2	0	2	45	22	18	.458	.398
Close & Late	.239	117	28	2	0	2	30	22	25	.366	.308
None on/out	.244	41	10	2	0	1	1	3	13	.311	.366
vs. 1st Batr (relief)	.283	60	17	1	0	3	18	8	16	.357	.450
First Inning Pitched	.276	181	50	7	0	4	46	22	47	.366	.381
First 15 Pitches	.273	165	45	7	0	4	42	21	47	.367	.388
Pitch 16-30	.217	46	10	1	0	0	5	10	10	.368	.239
Pitch 31-45	.125	8	1	0	0	1	2	2	4	.300	.500
Pitch 46+	.500	2	1	0	0	0	0	1	0	.750	.500
First Pitch	.250	24	6	1	0	1	10	8	0	.444	.417
Ahead in Count	.189	111	21	1	0	0	16	0	54	.216	.198
Behind in Count	.356	59	21	5	0	2	12	14	0	.493	.542
Two Strikes	.152	112	17	1	0	1	16	12	61	.250	.188

Career (1992-1993)

	ERA	W	L	Sv	G	GS	IP	H	HR	BB	SO
Home	3.51	4	2	6	66	0	77.0	63	4	30	61
Away	4.22	2	8	1	71	0	64.0	65	8	48	46
Day	3.06	2	5	2	42	0	53.0	39	3	27	38
Night	4.30	4	5	5	95	0	88.0	89	9	51	69
Grass	4.25	2	7	1	56	0	53.0	54	8	43	35
Turf	3.58	4	3	6	81	0	88.0	74	4	35	72
April	2.51	0	1	0	11	0	14.1	14	0	8	9
May	4.50	1	2	0	27	0	24.0	21	1	12	20
June	3.60	1	1	0	24	0	25.0	29	2	14	16
July	3.58	1	2	2	23	0	27.2	23	5	11	20
August	3.42	3	1	3	24	0	26.1	17	1	12	25
September/October	4.94	0	3	2	28	0	23.2	24	3	21	17
Starter	0.00	0	0	0	0	0	0.0	0	0	0	0
Reliever	3.83	6	10	7	137	0	141.0	128	12	78	107
0 Days rest	4.55	1	4	0	35	0	29.2	29	2	19	28
1 or 2 Days rest	2.96	3	3	6	75	0	82.0	65	7	46	57
3+ Days rest	5.52	2	3	1	27	0	29.1	34	3	13	22
Pre-All Star	3.70	2	5	0	71	0	73.0	72	5	37	53
Post-All Star	3.97	4	5	7	66	0	68.0	56	7	41	54

	Avg	AB	H	2B	3B	HR	RBI	BB	SO	OBP	SLG
vs. Left	.308	156	48	8	1	5	27	35	30	.439	.468
vs. Right	.225	355	80	10	2	7	62	43	77	.324	.324
Inning 1-6	.288	59	17	1	0	0	9	8	12	.391	.305
Inning 7+	.246	452	111	17	3	12	80	70	95	.357	.376
None on	.245	229	56	8	2	8	8	21	54	.327	.402
Runners on	.255	282	72	10	1	4	81	57	53	.385	.340
Scoring Posn	.257	191	49	4	1	3	78	48	34	.409	.335
Close & Late	.242	244	59	6	1	5	52	47	46	.369	.336
None on/out	.277	101	28	5	2	1	1	8	22	.348	.396
vs. 1st Batr (relief)	.269	119	32	4	1	4	30	14	25	.341	.420
First Inning Pitched	.268	384	103	15	2	9	79	53	82	.362	.388
First 15 Pitches	.272	367	100	15	3	9	72	41	79	.350	.403
Pitch 16-30	.193	114	22	2	0	1	13	33	20	.396	.237
Pitch 31-45	.192	26	5	1	0	2	4	3	8	.300	.462
Pitch 46+	.250	4	1	0	0	0	0	1	0	.500	.250
First Pitch	.254	71	18	3	2	2	13	16	0	.415	.437
Ahead in Count	.188	234	44	3	0	4	28	0	93	.207	.252
Behind in Count	.351	134	47	9	0	3	28	34	0	.486	.485
Two Strikes	.166	229	38	3	1	5	28	28	107	.267	.253

Robb Nen — Marlins

Age 24 – Pitches Right

	ERA	W	L	Sv	G	GS	IP	BB	SO	Avg	H	2B	3B	HR	RBI	OBP	SLG	GF	IR	IRS	Hld	SvOp	SB	CS	GB	FB	G/F
1993 Season	6.75	2	1	0	24	4	56.0	46	39	.283	63	17	2	6	39	.402	.457	5	11	4	0	0	5	2	80	62	1.29

1993 Season

	ERA	W	L	Sv	G	GS	IP	H	HR	BB	SO
Home	6.28	2	0	0	15	2	38.2	42	5	25	28
Away	7.79	0	1	0	9	2	17.1	21	1	21	11

	Avg	AB	H	2B	3B	HR	RBI	BB	SO	OBP	SLG
vs. Left	.216	97	21	3	2	0	9	18	17	.339	.289
vs. Right	.333	126	42	14	0	6	30	28	22	.449	.587

Marc Newfield — Mariners

Age 21 – Bats Right (groundball hitter)

	Avg	G	AB	R	H	2B	3B	HR	RBI	BB	SO	HBP	GDP	SB	CS	OBP	SLG	IBB	SH	SF	#Pit	#P/PA	GB	FB	G/F
1993 Season	.227	22	66	5	15	3	0	1	7	2	8	1	2	0	1	.257	.318	0	0	1	256	3.66	33	15	2.20

1993 Season

	Avg	AB	H	2B	3B	HR	RBI	BB	SO	OBP	SLG		Avg	AB	H	2B	3B	HR	RBI	BB	SO	OBP	SLG
vs. Left	.259	27	7	2	0	1	5	2	4	.300	.444	Scoring Posn	.222	18	4	1	0	0	5	0	2	.211	.278
vs. Right	.205	39	8	1	0	0	2	0	4	.225	.231	Close & Late	.111	9	1	0	0	0	0	1	4	.200	.111

Warren Newson — White Sox

Age 29 – Bats Left (groundball hitter)

	Avg	G	AB	R	H	2B	3B	HR	RBI	BB	SO	HBP	GDP	SB	CS	OBP	SLG	IBB	SH	SF	#Pit	#P/PA	GB	FB	G/F
1993 Season	.300	26	40	9	12	0	0	2	6	9	12	0	2	0	0	.429	.450	1	0	0	211	4.31	17	5	3.40
Career (1991-1993)	.263	160	308	48	81	8	0	7	42	74	84	0	10	5	2	.406	.357	4	0	0	1587	4.15	119	48	2.48

1993 Season

	Avg	AB	H	2B	3B	HR	RBI	BB	SO	OBP	SLG		Avg	AB	H	2B	3B	HR	RBI	BB	SO	OBP	SLG
vs. Left	.667	3	2	0	0	0	0	2	0	.800	.667	Scoring Posn	.556	9	5	0	0	0	4	4	2	.692	.556
vs. Right	.270	37	10	0	0	2	6	7	12	.386	.432	Close & Late	.364	11	4	0	0	0	3	2	4	.462	.364

Career (1991-1993)

	Avg	AB	H	2B	3B	HR	RBI	BB	SO	OBP	SLG		Avg	AB	H	2B	3B	HR	RBI	BB	SO	OBP	SLG
vs. Left	.286	14	4	0	0	0	0	6	5	.500	.286	Scoring Posn	.306	85	26	5	0	1	36	27	28	.473	.400
vs. Right	.262	294	77	8	0	7	42	68	79	.401	.361	Close & Late	.324	71	23	4	0	0	11	16	22	.448	.380
Groundball	.219	96	21	1	0	2	11	21	20	.359	.292	None on/out	.237	76	18	2	0	1	1	21	17	.402	.303
Flyball	.286	56	16	2	0	1	9	23	17	.494	.375	Batting #5	.264	110	29	5	0	3	19	30	26	.421	.391
Home	.248	157	39	2	0	4	24	35	38	.385	.338	Batting #6	.247	85	21	0	0	2	8	13	30	.347	.318
Away	.278	151	42	6	0	3	18	39	46	.426	.377	Other	.274	113	31	3	0	2	15	31	28	.431	.354
Day	.277	101	28	2	0	3	19	27	24	.430	.386	April	.286	7	2	0	0	0	1	3	1	.500	.286
Night	.256	207	53	6	0	4	23	47	60	.394	.343	May	.179	28	5	0	0	0	3	4	8	.281	.179
Grass	.260	265	69	5	0	7	39	66	74	.408	.358	June	.282	71	20	2	0	1	8	16	17	.414	.352
Turf	.279	43	12	3	0	0	3	8	10	.392	.349	July	.208	72	15	3	0	1	13	24	23	.406	.292
First Pitch	.262	42	11	4	0	1	8	2	0	.295	.429	August	.295	61	18	1	0	4	6	12	18	.411	.508
Ahead in Count	.485	66	32	1	0	0	15	24	0	.622	.500	September/October	.304	69	21	2	0	1	11	15	17	.429	.377
Behind in Count	.174	132	23	1	0	5	13	0	62	.174	.295	Pre-All Star	.258	128	33	3	0	1	15	30	35	.399	.305
Two Strikes	.136	154	21	0	0	3	11	48	84	.342	.195	Post-All Star	.267	180	48	5	0	6	27	44	49	.411	.394

Batter vs. Pitcher (career)

Hits Best Against	Avg	AB	H	2B	3B	HR	RBI	BB	SO	OBP	SLG	Hits Worst Against	Avg	AB	H	2B	3B	HR	RBI	BB	SO	OBP	SLG
Kevin Tapani	.500	10	5	1	0	0	2	1	5	.545	.600	Mike Gardiner	.125	8	1	0	0	0	0	3	3	.364	.125

Rod Nichols — Dodgers

Age 29 – Pitches Right (flyball pitcher)

	ERA	W	L	Sv	G	GS	IP	BB	SO	Avg	H	2B	3B	HR	RBI	OBP	SLG	GF	IR	IRS	Hld	SvOp	SB	CS	GB	FB	G/F
1993 Season	5.68	0	1	0	4	0	6.1	2	3	.360	9	2	0	1	7	.407	.560	2	4	3	0	1	0	0	6	7	0.86
Last Five Years	4.28	10	24	1	84	38	336.2	93	180	.281	373	54	11	34	177	.331	.415	11	46	26	2	3	30	14	431	437	0.99

1993 Season

	ERA	W	L	Sv	G	GS	IP	H	HR	BB	SO		Avg	AB	H	2B	3B	HR	RBI	BB	SO	OBP	SLG
Home	0.00	0	0	0	0	0	0.0	0	0	0	0	vs. Left	.417	12	5	2	0	1	6	1	0	.462	.833
Away	5.68	0	1	0	4	0	6.1	9	1	2	3	vs. Right	.308	13	4	0	0	0	1	1	3	.357	.308

Last Five Years

	ERA	W	L	Sv	G	GS	IP	H	HR	BB	SO		Avg	AB	H	2B	3B	HR	RBI	BB	SO	OBP	SLG
Home	4.44	5	12	0	41	21	176.1	196	16	51	96	vs. Left	.308	613	189	31	5	16	91	47	75	.361	.454
Away	4.10	5	12	1	43	17	160.1	177	18	42	84	vs. Right	.257	715	184	23	6	18	86	46	105	.305	.382
Day	5.27	1	6	0	21	10	80.1	94	11	18	52	Inning 1-6	.284	1010	287	43	9	24	139	77	140	.338	.416
Night	3.97	9	18	1	63	28	256.1	279	23	75	128	Inning 7+	.270	318	86	11	2	10	38	16	40	.309	.412
Grass	4.34	10	21	1	74	35	304.2	335	32	82	162	None on	.281	744	209	30	4	19	19	45	103	.331	.409
Turf	3.66	0	3	0	10	3	32.0	38	2	11	18	Runners on	.281	584	164	24	7	15	158	48	77	.331	.423
April	6.38	0	2	0	12	0	24.0	34	4	8	14	Scoring Posn	.283	315	89	14	5	6	130	30	46	.336	.416
May	2.98	1	4	0	11	4	45.1	42	2	13	25	Close & Late	.234	175	41	7	1	7	22	8	21	.272	.406
June	4.50	0	3	1	7	4	34.0	38	4	9	18	None on/out	.286	339	97	18	2	5	5	15	45	.326	.395
July	4.15	3	6	0	14	10	65.0	71	7	13	33	vs. 1st Batr (relief)	.390	41	16	2	1	1	16	3	3	.444	.561
August	4.46	4	5	0	20	13	101.0	115	10	30	45	First Inning Pitched	.294	326	96	12	3	10	65	25	55	.345	.442
September/October	4.14	2	4	0	20	7	67.1	73	7	20	45	First 15 Pitches	.310	271	84	11	2	6	46	19	41	.354	.432
Starter	4.36	8	17	0	38	38	223.0	249	23	60	125	Pitch 16-30	.239	285	68	10	2	9	38	15	41	.284	.382
Reliever	4.12	2	7	1	46	0	113.2	124	11	33	55	Pitch 31-45	.317	208	66	9	2	4	25	20	28	.383	.438
0 Days rest	10.13	0	1	0	4	0	5.1	7	2	2	4	Pitch 46+	.275	564	155	24	5	15	68	39	70	.324	.415
1 or 2 Days rest	4.01	1	2	0	16	0	33.2	37	4	9	16	First Pitch	.361	194	70	9	1	11	39	4	0	.381	.588
3+ Days rest	3.74	1	4	1	26	0	74.2	80	5	22	35	Ahead in Count	.238	583	139	22	6	9	56	0	156	.245	.343
Pre-All Star	4.29	1	11	1	34	9	113.1	125	11	34	61	Behind in Count	.322	301	97	10	3	9	47	49	0	.409	.465
Post-All Star	4.27	9	13	0	50	29	223.1	248	23	59	119	Two Strikes	.218	583	127	22	5	7	51	40	180	.272	.309

Pitcher vs. Batter (career)

Pitches Best Vs.	Avg	AB	H	2B	3B	HR	RBI	BB	SO	OBP	SLG	Pitches Worst Vs.	Avg	AB	H	2B	3B	HR	RBI	BB	SO	OBP	SLG
Brady Anderson	.000	11	0	0	0	0	0	0	4	.000	.000	Dave Winfield	.714	7	5	1	0	0	4	4	2	.818	.857
George Bell	.083	12	1	1	0	0	2	0	0	.071	.167	Jody Reed	.545	11	6	0	0	0	0	1	0	.583	.545
Randy Milligan	.118	17	2	0	0	0	0	0	3	.118	.118	Pete O'Brien	.500	12	6	1	0	0	4	3	1	.600	.583
Dante Bichette	.154	13	2	0	0	0	2	1	3	.214	.154	Steve Lyons	.444	9	4	0	1	0	2	2	0	.545	.667
Brian Harper	.182	11	2	0	0	0	0	0	0	.182	.182	Cal Ripken	.368	19	7	0	0	3	4	0	4	.368	.842

Dave Nied — Rockies

Age 25 – Pitches Right

	ERA	W	L	Sv	G	GS	IP	BB	SO	Avg	H	2B	3B	HR	RBI	OBP	SLG	CG	ShO	Sup	QS	#P/S	SB	CS	GB	FB	G/F
1993 Season	5.17	5	9	0	16	16	87.0	42	46	.296	99	19	1	8	52	.369	.430	1	0	5.59	3	87	16	2	118	102	1.16
Career (1992-1993)	4.34	8	9	0	22	18	110.0	47	65	.265	109	24	1	8	55	.336	.386	1	0	5.56	5	90	18	2	139	125	1.11

1993 Season

	ERA	W	L	Sv	G	GS	IP	H	HR	BB	SO
Home	3.60	4	3	0	7	7	45.0	47	1	13	27
Away	6.86	1	6	0	9	9	42.0	52	7	29	19
Starter	5.17	5	9	0	16	16	87.0	99	8	42	46
Reliever	0.00	0	0	0	0	0	0.0	0	0	0	0
0-3 Days Rest	0.00	0	0	0	0	0	0.0	0	0	0	0
4 Days Rest	5.34	4	6	0	11	11	60.2	69	3	32	36
5+ Days Rest	4.78	1	3	0	5	5	26.1	30	5	10	10
Pre-All Star	5.68	3	7	0	11	11	65.0	76	6	32	35
Post-All Star	3.68	2	2	0	5	5	22.0	23	2	10	11

	Avg	AB	H	2B	3B	HR	RBI	BB	SO	OBP	SLG
vs. Left	.314	169	53	11	0	5	21	25	19	.394	.467
vs. Right	.277	166	46	8	1	3	31	17	27	.342	.392
Scoring Posn	.287	87	25	2	1	4	45	19	12	.389	.471
Close & Late	.222	9	2	0	0	0	2	0	2	.222	.222
None on/out	.195	82	16	6	0	2	2	8	15	.267	.341
First Pitch	.328	58	19	8	0	2	11	3	0	.355	.569
Ahead in Count	.259	143	37	4	1	5	23	0	40	.260	.406
Behind in Count	.301	83	25	5	0	1	13	26	0	.455	.398
Two Strikes	.248	141	35	3	1	3	14	13	46	.308	.348

Jerry Nielsen — Angels

Age 27 – Pitches Left

	ERA	W	L	Sv	G	GS	IP	BB	SO	Avg	H	2B	3B	HR	RBI	OBP	SLG	GF	IR	IRS	Hld	SvOp	SB	CS	GB	FB	G/F
1993 Season	8.03	0	0	0	10	0	12.1	4	8	.340	18	2	0	1	11	.377	.434	3	3	1	0	0	1	0	23	16	1.44
Career (1992-1993)	5.91	1	0	0	30	0	32.0	22	20	.285	35	4	1	2	17	.387	.382	15	11	3	0	0	3	2	50	40	1.25

1993 Season

	ERA	W	L	Sv	G	GS	IP	H	HR	BB	SO
Home	9.64	0	0	0	6	0	9.1	14	1	3	6
Away	3.00	0	0	0	4	0	3.0	4	0	1	2

	Avg	AB	H	2B	3B	HR	RBI	BB	SO	OBP	SLG
vs. Left	.261	23	6	2	0	0	4	0	3	.261	.348
vs. Right	.400	30	12	0	0	1	7	4	5	.447	.500

Melvin Nieves — Padres

Age 22 – Bats Both (groundball hitter)

	Avg	G	AB	R	H	2B	3B	HR	RBI	BB	SO	HBP	GDP	SB	CS	OBP	SLG	IBB	SH	SF	#Pit	#P/PA	GB	FB	G/F
1993 Season	.191	19	47	4	9	0	0	2	3	3	21	1	0	0	0	.255	.319	0	0	0	209	4.10	12	7	1.71
Career (1992-1993)	.197	31	66	4	13	1	0	2	4	5	28	1	0	0	0	.264	.303	0	0	0	298	4.14	18	11	1.64

1993 Season

	Avg	AB	H	2B	3B	HR	RBI	BB	SO	OBP	SLG
vs. Left	.167	6	1	0	0	1	1	0	4	.167	.667
vs. Right	.195	41	8	0	0	1	2	3	17	.267	.268

	Avg	AB	H	2B	3B	HR	RBI	BB	SO	OBP	SLG
Scoring Posn	.143	7	1	0	0	0	1	0	4	.143	.143
Close & Late	.000	11	0	0	0	0	0	1	7	.083	.000

Dave Nilsson — Brewers

Age 24 – Bats Left

	Avg	G	AB	R	H	2B	3B	HR	RBI	BB	SO	HBP	GDP	SB	CS	OBP	SLG	IBB	SH	SF	#Pit	#P/PA	GB	FB	G/F
1993 Season	.257	100	296	35	76	10	2	7	40	37	36	0	9	3	6	.336	.375	5	4	3	1240	3.65	105	86	1.22
Career (1992-1993)	.248	151	460	50	114	18	2	11	65	54	54	0	10	5	8	.325	.367	6	6	3	1914	3.66	153	152	1.01

1993 Season

	Avg	AB	H	2B	3B	HR	RBI	BB	SO	OBP	SLG
vs. Left	.272	81	22	5	2	2	19	12	15	.358	.457
vs. Right	.251	215	54	5	0	5	21	25	21	.328	.344
Groundball	.259	58	15	0	0	1	8	5	8	.308	.310
Flyball	.240	50	12	1	0	1	3	4	7	.296	.320
Home	.274	164	45	9	1	5	26	19	19	.344	.433
Away	.235	132	31	1	1	2	14	18	17	.327	.303
Day	.227	88	20	3	0	2	13	7	11	.281	.330
Night	.269	208	56	7	2	5	27	30	25	.358	.394
Grass	.262	271	71	10	2	7	39	34	33	.341	.391
Turf	.200	25	5	0	0	0	1	3	3	.286	.200
First Pitch	.306	36	11	2	0	1	5	4	0	.375	.444
Ahead in Count	.259	81	21	5	2	2	15	16	0	.374	.444
Behind in Count	.250	124	31	2	0	2	13	0	30	.248	.315
Two Strikes	.205	117	24	0	0	4	11	17	36	.306	.308

	Avg	AB	H	2B	3B	HR	RBI	BB	SO	OBP	SLG
Scoring Posn	.263	80	21	3	1	2	33	17	3	.380	.400
Close & Late	.245	49	12	1	0	0	5	4	6	.302	.265
None on/out	.288	66	19	2	0	1	1	8	5	.365	.364
Batting #6	.293	58	17	2	0	3	13	10	8	.397	.483
Batting #7	.242	95	23	5	1	1	13	13	13	.324	.347
Other	.252	143	36	3	1	3	14	14	15	.318	.350
April	.172	29	5	0	0	1	2	2	1	.226	.276
May	.160	25	4	1	0	0	0	0	2	.160	.200
June	.143	21	3	0	0	0	1	2	4	.217	.143
July	.308	65	20	1	1	1	12	10	9	.395	.400
August	.293	82	24	5	1	2	13	9	10	.355	.451
September/October	.270	74	20	3	0	3	12	14	10	.386	.432
Pre-All Star	.223	103	23	2	1	2	12	4	8	.250	.320
Post-All Star	.275	193	53	8	1	5	28	33	28	.377	.404

1993 By Position

Position	Avg	AB	H	2B	3B	HR	RBI	BB	SO	OBP	SLG	G	GS	Innings	PO	A	E	DP	Fld Pct	Rng Fctr	In Zone	Outs	Zone Rtg	MLB Zone
As c	.254	268	68	10	2	7	36	35	31	.337	.384	91	85	719.0	430	30	9	3	.981	---	---	---	---	---

Otis Nixon — Braves

Age 35 – Bats Both (groundball hitter)

	Avg	G	AB	R	H	2B	3B	HR	RBI	BB	SO	HBP	GDP	SB	CS	OBP	SLG	IBB	SH	SF	#Pit	#P/PA	GB	FB	G/F
1993 Season	.269	134	461	77	124	12	3	1	24	61	63	0	9	47	13	.351	.315	2	5	5	1922	3.61	217	85	2.55
Last Five Years	.272	623	1807	324	491	49	10	4	113	208	226	2	24	247	77	.346	.317	6	22	11	7069	3.45	785	358	2.19

1993 Season

	Avg	AB	H	2B	3B	HR	RBI	BB	SO	OBP	SLG
vs. Left	.263	152	40	1	2	1	6	18	21	.339	.316
vs. Right	.272	309	84	11	1	0	18	43	42	.357	.314
Groundball	.258	178	46	7	3	0	6	19	22	.327	.331
Flyball	.254	71	18	1	0	0	4	14	14	.368	.268
Home	.287	216	62	9	2	1	12	34	22	.379	.361
Away	.253	245	62	3	1	0	12	27	41	.325	.273

	Avg	AB	H	2B	3B	HR	RBI	BB	SO	OBP	SLG
Scoring Posn	.196	97	19	2	0	0	22	15	10	.291	.216
Close & Late	.230	74	17	3	0	0	5	13	14	.341	.270
None on/out	.280	200	56	4	1	1	1	28	31	.368	.325
Batting #1	.273	447	122	11	3	1	22	61	57	.357	.318
Batting #9	.100	10	1	1	0	0	2	0	5	.100	.200
Other	.250	4	1	0	0	0	0	0	1	.250	.250

1993 Season

	Avg	AB	H	2B	3B	HR	RBI	BB	SO	OBP	SLG
Day	.273	143	39	2	0	0	5	19	22	.356	.287
Night	.267	318	85	10	3	1	19	42	41	.349	.327
Grass	.279	351	98	9	2	1	17	50	46	.365	.325
Turf	.236	110	26	3	1	0	7	11	17	.306	.282
First Pitch	.329	79	26	3	0	0	6	1	0	.333	.367
Ahead in Count	.246	114	28	4	0	0	7	33	0	.409	.281
Behind in Count	.278	187	52	5	0	1	9	0	52	.278	.321
Two Strikes	.219	192	42	4	2	1	7	27	63	.314	.276

	Avg	AB	H	2B	3B	HR	RBI	BB	SO	OBP	SLG
April	.247	89	22	2	0	0	9	14	13	.346	.270
May	.240	96	23	4	0	0	5	14	11	.330	.281
June	.227	22	5	0	0	0	0	2	4	.292	.227
July	.224	58	13	3	1	1	3	5	7	.281	.362
August	.289	76	22	0	0	0	1	4	15	.325	.289
September/October	.325	120	39	3	2	0	6	22	13	.427	.383
Pre-All Star	.237	228	54	8	0	0	15	32	29	.327	.272
Post-All Star	.300	233	70	4	3	1	9	29	34	.375	.356

1993 By Position

Position	Avg	AB	H	2B	3B	HR	RBI	BB	SO	OBP	SLG	G	GS	Innings	PO	A	E	DP	Fld Pct	Rng Fctr	In Zone	Outs	Zone Rtg	MLB Zone
As Pinch Hitter	.154	13	2	1	0	0	2	0	6	.154	.231	14	0	---	---	---	---	---	---	---	---	---	---	---
As cf	.273	447	122	11	3	1	22	61	57	.357	.318	115	111	994.2	308	4	3	1	.990	2.80	333	286	.859	.829

Last Five Years

	Avg	AB	H	2B	3B	HR	RBI	BB	SO	OBP	SLG
vs. Left	.277	726	201	21	6	4	52	72	77	.342	.339
vs. Right	.268	1081	290	28	4	0	61	136	149	.348	.302
Groundball	.283	651	184	18	5	0	35	72	67	.353	.326
Flyball	.223	426	95	11	1	0	32	61	70	.319	.254
Home	.283	884	250	29	6	2	58	114	105	.364	.336
Away	.261	923	241	20	4	2	55	94	121	.328	.298
Day	.298	523	156	14	5	1	45	48	68	.357	.350
Night	.261	1284	335	35	5	3	68	160	158	.341	.303
Grass	.290	1071	311	33	2	4	68	129	135	.364	.336
Turf	.245	736	180	16	8	0	45	79	91	.318	.288
First Pitch	.314	344	108	8	2	0	25	4	0	.320	.349
Ahead in Count	.273	451	123	13	1	0	27	123	0	.427	.306
Behind in Count	.241	677	163	17	1	4	36	0	185	.241	.287
Two Strikes	.205	673	138	18	4	3	30	81	226	.290	.257

	Avg	AB	H	2B	3B	HR	RBI	BB	SO	OBP	SLG
Scoring Posn	.250	372	93	12	2	1	104	42	42	.319	.301
Close & Late	.292	318	93	12	1	0	28	42	48	.374	.336
None on/out	.286	734	210	22	2	1	1	88	100	.363	.326
Batting #1	.275	1547	425	42	7	3	86	183	186	.349	.317
Batting #2	.275	120	33	2	2	1	16	10	15	.331	.350
Other	.236	140	33	5	1	0	11	15	25	.318	.286
April	.246	183	45	5	1	0	19	26	23	.338	.284
May	.309	304	94	11	1	0	16	38	33	.382	.352
June	.266	282	75	6	1	2	24	34	35	.348	.316
July	.282	347	98	15	1	1	16	33	37	.344	.340
August	.251	343	86	6	2	1	19	32	52	.314	.289
September/October	.267	348	93	6	4	0	19	45	46	.348	.307
Pre-All Star	.273	874	239	27	3	2	61	109	102	.353	.318
Post-All Star	.270	933	252	22	7	2	52	99	124	.338	.315

Batter vs. Pitcher (since 1984)

Hits Best Against	Avg	AB	H	2B	3B	HR	RBI	BB	SO	OBP	SLG
Randy Tomlin	.583	12	7	2	2	0	1	1	0	.615	1.083
Ken Hill	.556	18	10	2	0	0	0	4	1	.636	.667
Mike Bielecki	.545	11	6	0	1	0	2	1	3	.583	.727
Trevor Wilson	.462	13	6	0	0	2	5	0	1	.429	.923
Danny Cox	.444	9	4	1	0	0	0	3	1	.583	.556

Hits Worst Against	Avg	AB	H	2B	3B	HR	RBI	BB	SO	OBP	SLG
Charlie Hough	.071	14	1	0	0	0	1	2	0	.176	.071
Dennis Martinez	.071	14	1	0	0	0	1	0	0	.071	.071
Tom Browning	.091	33	3	0	0	0	4	3	3	.167	.091
Danny Darwin	.091	11	1	0	0	0	0	0	3	.091	.091
Xavier Hernandez	.100	10	1	0	0	0	1	0	1	.091	.100

Matt Nokes — Yankees

Age 30 – Bats Left (flyball hitter)

	Avg	G	AB	R	H	2B	3B	HR	RBI	BB	SO	HBP	GDP	SB	CS	OBP	SLG	IBB	SH	SF	#Pit	#P/PA	GB	FB	G/F
1993 Season	.249	76	217	25	54	8	0	10	35	16	31	2	4	0	0	.303	.424	2	0	3	808	3.39	59	85	0.69
Last Five Years	.248	555	1676	167	416	56	2	76	250	119	226	18	42	6	5	.302	.420	25	1	19	6127	3.34	524	633	0.83

1993 Season

	Avg	AB	H	2B	3B	HR	RBI	BB	SO	OBP	SLG
vs. Left	.100	30	3	0	0	2	3	0	6	.129	.300
vs. Right	.273	187	51	8	0	8	32	16	25	.329	.444
Home	.245	102	25	4	0	4	14	6	10	.294	.402
Away	.252	115	29	4	0	6	21	10	21	.310	.443
First Pitch	.268	41	11	3	0	5	11	2	0	.318	.707
Ahead in Count	.292	48	14	1	0	1	6	7	0	.362	.375
Behind in Count	.205	88	18	3	0	1	11	0	28	.213	.273
Two Strikes	.165	85	14	2	0	2	9	7	31	.237	.259

	Avg	AB	H	2B	3B	HR	RBI	BB	SO	OBP	SLG
Scoring Posn	.203	59	12	0	0	4	26	8	15	.306	.407
Close & Late	.286	28	8	1	0	2	5	2	8	.333	.536
None on/out	.226	53	12	2	0	1	1	1	2	.241	.321
Batting #6	.225	111	25	3	0	4	14	3	15	.252	.360
Batting #7	.246	57	14	3	0	1	7	7	8	.323	.351
Other	.306	49	15	2	0	5	14	6	8	.379	.653
Pre-All Star	.260	146	38	6	0	9	25	6	20	.297	.486
Post-All Star	.225	71	16	2	0	1	10	10	11	.313	.296

Last Five Years

	Avg	AB	H	2B	3B	HR	RBI	BB	SO	OBP	SLG
vs. Left	.219	269	59	7	0	16	52	15	54	.269	.424
vs. Right	.254	1407	357	49	2	60	198	104	172	.308	.419
Groundball	.247	474	117	19	0	15	68	33	67	.300	.382
Flyball	.226	336	76	10	1	17	57	32	55	.299	.414
Home	.260	763	198	23	0	46	138	58	97	.314	.471
Away	.239	913	218	33	2	30	112	61	129	.292	.378
Day	.272	577	157	15	0	38	110	40	63	.320	.496
Night	.236	1099	259	41	2	38	140	79	163	.293	.380
Grass	.242	1375	333	40	1	64	207	102	181	.298	.412
Turf	.276	301	83	16	1	12	43	17	45	.321	.455
First Pitch	.275	327	90	14	0	18	57	19	0	.321	.483
Ahead in Count	.291	413	120	12	0	21	61	52	0	.364	.472
Behind in Count	.199	652	130	20	0	19	86	0	190	.210	.317
Two Strikes	.185	628	116	21	0	19	79	43	226	.243	.309

	Avg	AB	H	2B	3B	HR	RBI	BB	SO	OBP	SLG
Scoring Posn	.240	429	103	13	0	21	171	51	69	.318	.417
Close & Late	.253	265	67	6	0	14	48	28	49	.329	.434
None on/out	.260	384	100	16	0	17	17	22	43	.307	.435
Batting #6	.253	675	171	21	1	29	92	42	84	.301	.416
Batting #7	.216	342	74	11	1	13	49	33	56	.286	.368
Other	.259	659	171	24	0	34	109	44	86	.311	.451
April	.269	271	73	13	0	11	37	17	32	.315	.439
May	.252	330	83	12	1	18	53	19	44	.296	.458
June	.236	276	65	6	0	13	42	16	39	.281	.399
July	.245	216	53	5	0	14	41	19	35	.317	.463
August	.246	293	72	8	0	13	41	24	35	.301	.406
September/October	.241	290	70	12	1	7	36	24	41	.304	.362
Pre-All Star	.252	943	238	32	1	49	153	58	129	.299	.444
Post-All Star	.243	733	178	24	1	27	97	61	97	.305	.389

Batter vs. Pitcher (career)

Hits Best Against	Avg	AB	H	2B	3B	HR	RBI	BB	SO	OBP	SLG
Jeff Russell	.417	12	5	0	0	1	3	1	1	.462	.667
Scott Bankhead	.417	12	5	1	0	2	7	0	2	.417	1.000
Bobby Thigpen	.400	15	6	0	0	1	2	1	2	.438	.600
Mike Witt	.385	13	5	1	0	2	2	1	1	.429	.923

Hits Worst Against	Avg	AB	H	2B	3B	HR	RBI	BB	SO	OBP	SLG
Jose Mesa	.000	15	0	0	0	0	0	2	2	.118	.000
Juan Guzman	.071	14	1	0	0	0	0	1	4	.133	.071
Tom Henke	.091	11	1	0	0	0	0	1	4	.167	.091
Edwin Nunez	.091	11	1	0	0	0	0	0	3	.091	.091

Batter vs. Pitcher (career)

Hits Best Against	Avg	AB	H	2B	3B	HR	RBI	BB	SO	OBP	SLG
Todd Stottlemyre	.377	53	20	3	0	7	19	3	4	.404	.830

Hits Worst Against	Avg	AB	H	2B	3B	HR	RBI	BB	SO	OBP	SLG
Nolan Ryan	.105	19	2	1	0	0	1	1	8	.150	.158

Rafael Novoa — Brewers

Age 26 – Pitches Left (flyball pitcher)

	ERA	W	L	Sv	G	GS	IP	BB	SO	Avg	H	2B	3B	HR	RBI	OBP	SLG	GF	IR	IRS	Hld	SvOp	SB	CS	GB	FB	G/F
1993 Season	4.50	0	3	0	15	7	56.0	22	17	.267	58	14	0	7	33	.343	.429	0	6	4	0	0	3	1	68	85	0.80
Career (1990-1993)	5.06	0	4	1	22	9	74.2	35	31	.271	79	14	1	10	47	.354	.430	2	13	6	0	1	6	3	92	111	0.83

1993 Season

	ERA	W	L	Sv	G	GS	IP	H	HR	BB	SO
Home	4.78	0	1	0	7	4	26.1	32	3	13	8
Away	4.25	0	2	0	8	3	29.2	26	4	9	9

	Avg	AB	H	2B	3B	HR	RBI	BB	SO	OBP	SLG
vs. Left	.227	44	10	2	0	2	9	0	3	.271	.409
vs. Right	.277	173	48	12	0	5	24	22	14	.360	.434

Edwin Nunez — Athletics

Age 31 – Pitches Right

	ERA	W	L	Sv	G	GS	IP	BB	SO	Avg	H	2B	3B	HR	RBI	OBP	SLG	GF	IR	IRS	Hld	SvOp	SB	CS	GB	FB	G/F
1993 Season	3.81	3	6	1	56	0	75.2	29	58	.298	89	17	3	2	43	.369	.395	16	43	15	16	4	5	3	110	77	1.43
Last Five Years	3.85	12	15	19	197	0	294.2	137	238	.261	294	60	8	24	170	.343	.393	65	161	49	29	27	20	10	347	340	1.02

1993 Season

	ERA	W	L	Sv	G	GS	IP	H	HR	BB	SO
Home	3.64	1	2	1	26	0	29.2	35	0	13	24
Away	3.91	2	4	0	30	0	46.0	54	2	16	34
Starter	0.00	0	0	0	0	0	0.0	0	0	0	0
Reliever	3.81	3	6	1	56	0	75.2	89	2	29	58
0 Days rest	2.35	1	0	0	7	0	7.2	9	0	3	7
1 or 2 Days rest	3.55	2	1	1	28	0	38.0	38	1	18	29
3+ Days rest	4.50	0	5	0	21	0	30.0	42	1	8	22
Pre-All Star	2.58	3	3	1	32	0	45.1	48	1	15	37
Post-All Star	5.64	0	3	0	24	0	30.1	41	1	14	21

	Avg	AB	H	2B	3B	HR	RBI	BB	SO	OBP	SLG
vs. Left	.270	137	37	9	1	0	15	12	28	.325	.350
vs. Right	.321	162	52	8	2	2	28	17	30	.405	.432
Scoring Posn	.278	108	30	4	2	2	43	10	21	.344	.407
Close & Late	.323	167	54	10	2	2	25	16	31	.385	.443
None on/out	.311	61	19	7	1	0	0	7	15	.391	.459
First Pitch	.406	32	13	1	1	0	6	1	0	.474	.500
Ahead in Count	.231	147	34	6	1	2	14	0	51	.242	.327
Behind in Count	.392	51	20	4	0	0	10	9	0	.475	.471
Two Strikes	.256	160	41	8	0	2	19	19	58	.339	.344

Last Five Years

	ERA	W	L	Sv	G	GS	IP	H	HR	BB	SO
Home	4.08	5	7	9	96	0	143.1	148	14	72	122
Away	3.63	7	8	10	101	0	151.1	146	10	65	116
Day	4.35	5	3	4	55	0	72.1	91	3	35	64
Night	3.68	7	12	15	142	0	222.1	203	21	102	174
Grass	3.97	9	13	17	162	0	244.2	246	19	118	203
Turf	3.24	3	2	2	35	0	50.0	48	5	19	35
April	3.69	1	1	2	30	0	39.0	40	2	21	37
May	2.61	3	3	2	27	0	41.1	38	3	14	24
June	2.87	3	3	2	28	0	53.1	47	3	23	42
July	2.34	2	4	3	33	0	50.0	37	1	23	41
August	4.82	1	2	8	46	0	65.1	69	9	31	54
September/October	6.50	2	2	2	33	0	45.2	63	6	25	40
Starter	0.00	0	0	0	0	0	0.0	0	0	0	0
Reliever	3.85	12	15	19	197	0	294.2	294	24	137	238
0 Days rest	3.11	1	1	5	27	0	37.2	33	5	14	31
1 or 2 Days rest	2.93	9	6	9	92	0	129.0	114	6	67	100
3+ Days rest	4.99	2	8	5	78	0	128.0	147	13	56	107
Pre-All Star	2.87	9	7	7	98	0	153.2	141	8	64	123
Post-All Star	4.91	3	8	12	99	0	141.0	153	16	73	115

	Avg	AB	H	2B	3B	HR	RBI	BB	SO	OBP	SLG
vs. Left	.250	476	119	27	4	9	73	67	107	.338	.380
vs. Right	.269	650	175	33	4	15	97	70	131	.347	.402
Inning 1-6	.253	225	57	12	0	3	32	26	54	.332	.347
Inning 7+	.263	901	237	48	8	21	138	111	184	.346	.404
None on	.263	540	142	30	2	14	14	63	122	.343	.404
Runners on	.259	586	152	30	6	10	156	74	116	.343	.382
Scoring Posn	.277	357	99	16	6	8	148	57	76	.372	.423
Close & Late	.292	424	124	26	2	11	73	61	78	.379	.441
None on/out	.253	245	62	11	1	6	6	29	58	.337	.380
vs. 1st Batr (relief)	.270	163	44	8	0	6	31	30	36	.381	.429
First Inning Pitched	.260	646	168	30	3	15	116	78	129	.340	.385
First 15 Pitches	.261	568	148	26	2	14	85	71	109	.342	.387
Pitch 16-30	.257	378	97	19	3	9	56	39	87	.329	.394
Pitch 31-45	.281	139	39	12	2	1	20	20	31	.377	.417
Pitch 46+	.244	41	10	3	1	0	9	7	11	.380	.366
First Pitch	.347	144	50	4	1	4	27	16	0	.423	.472
Ahead in Count	.197	554	109	21	3	11	59	0	210	.204	.305
Behind in Count	.301	206	62	15	2	5	45	63	0	.453	.466
Two Strikes	.201	567	114	27	2	8	62	56	238	.278	.298

Pitcher vs. Batter (since 1984)

Pitches Best Vs.	Avg	AB	H	2B	3B	HR	RBI	BB	SO	OBP	SLG
Steve Balboni	.000	12	0	0	0	0	0	0	7	.000	.000
Mike Pagliarulo	.000	11	0	0	0	0	1	0	4	.000	.000
Rob Deer	.091	11	1	0	0	0	0	1	6	.167	.091
Matt Nokes	.091	11	1	0	0	0	0	0	3	.091	.091
Luis Polonia	.091	11	1	0	0	0	2	0	3	.091	.091

Pitches Worst Vs.	Avg	AB	H	2B	3B	HR	RBI	BB	SO	OBP	SLG
Harold Baines	.583	12	7	2	0	2	7	1	2	.615	1.250
Mickey Tettleton	.467	15	7	0	0	2	10	2	4	.529	.867
Brian Harper	.455	11	5	1	0	1	3	2	1	.538	.818
George Brett	.417	12	5	1	0	2	5	1	1	.462	1.000
Devon White	.400	15	6	1	0	2	5	3	5	.500	.867

Charlie O'Brien — Mets

Age 33 – Bats Right (flyball hitter)

	Avg	G	AB	R	H	2B	3B	HR	RBI	BB	SO	HBP	GDP	SB	CS	OBP	SLG	IBB	SH	SF	#Pit	#P/PA	GB	FB	G/F
1993 Season	.255	67	188	15	48	11	0	4	23	14	14	2	4	1	1	.312	.378	1	3	1	724	3.48	60	72	0.83
Last Five Years	.212	340	913	85	194	49	2	14	105	89	102	19	28	1	4	.294	.317	7	25	5	3899	3.71	300	344	0.87

1993 Season

	Avg	AB	H	2B	3B	HR	RBI	BB	SO	OBP	SLG
vs. Left	.271	118	32	8	0	1	13	7	5	.310	.364
vs. Right	.229	70	16	3	0	3	10	7	9	.316	.400
Home	.200	85	17	1	0	1	4	4	9	.250	.247
Away	.301	103	31	10	0	3	19	10	5	.363	.485
First Pitch	.279	43	12	2	0	1	3	0	0	.295	.395
Ahead in Count	.280	50	14	3	0	2	7	7	0	.362	.460
Behind in Count	.155	71	11	5	0	0	9	0	12	.155	.225
Two Strikes	.167	66	11	4	0	0	6	7	14	.257	.227

	Avg	AB	H	2B	3B	HR	RBI	BB	SO	OBP	SLG
Scoring Posn	.378	37	14	4	0	0	18	6	2	.455	.486
Close & Late	.323	31	10	3	0	2	10	2	2	.364	.613
None on/out	.340	47	16	5	0	3	3	2	3	.367	.638
Batting #2	.270	63	17	3	0	1	8	2	6	.292	.365
Batting #7	.257	74	19	6	0	2	9	7	2	.337	.419
Other	.235	51	12	2	0	1	6	5	6	.298	.333
Pre-All Star	.231	78	18	4	0	0	7	5	8	.286	.282
Post-All Star	.273	110	30	7	0	4	16	9	6	.331	.445

Last Five Years

	Avg	AB	H	2B	3B	HR	RBI	BB	SO	OBP	SLG
vs. Left	.216	486	105	29	1	6	42	39	46	.281	.317
vs. Right	.208	427	89	20	1	8	63	50	56	.309	.316
Groundball	.226	266	60	13	0	2	26	33	29	.318	.297
Flyball	.199	171	34	17	1	2	25	15	21	.270	.345
Home	.202	410	83	14	2	7	40	45	38	.290	.298
Away	.221	503	111	35	0	7	65	44	64	.298	.332
Day	.185	330	61	16	0	5	31	31	39	.270	.279
Night	.228	583	133	33	2	9	74	58	63	.308	.338
Grass	.214	645	138	30	2	11	79	67	66	.300	.318
Turf	.209	268	56	19	0	3	26	22	36	.281	.313
First Pitch	.240	154	37	11	1	2	16	1	0	.269	.364
Ahead in Count	.257	191	49	13	1	3	30	58	0	.437	.382
Behind in Count	.153	404	62	16	0	3	30	0	86	.169	.215
Two Strikes	.162	414	67	16	0	5	33	28	102	.226	.237

	Avg	AB	H	2B	3B	HR	RBI	BB	SO	OBP	SLG
Scoring Posn	.256	207	53	14	2	4	89	33	26	.359	.401
Close & Late	.272	114	31	9	0	2	16	9	14	.331	.404
None on/out	.209	220	46	14	0	7	7	19	27	.281	.368
Batting #7	.233	240	56	15	0	5	31	19	22	.306	.358
Batting #8	.197	483	95	26	2	4	50	56	60	.289	.284
Other	.226	190	43	8	0	5	24	14	20	.293	.347
April	.185	119	22	8	0	0	12	18	17	.312	.252
May	.216	134	29	6	1	2	16	7	19	.264	.321
June	.186	113	21	6	1	1	8	12	7	.264	.283
July	.221	136	30	7	0	3	20	12	15	.301	.338
August	.223	197	44	10	0	5	23	17	25	.305	.350
September/October	.224	214	48	12	0	3	26	23	19	.305	.322
Pre-All Star	.202	406	82	24	2	3	39	30	49	.281	.293
Post-All Star	.221	507	112	25	0	11	66	51	53	.305	.335

Batter vs. Pitcher (career)

Hits Best Against	Avg	AB	H	2B	3B	HR	RBI	BB	SO	OBP	SLG
Tom Glavine	.389	18	7	4	0	0	2	1	1	.421	.611
Rheal Cormier	.353	17	6	2	0	0	0	1	1	.389	.471
Danny Jackson	.333	21	7	2	0	0	2	1	1	.364	.429
Bud Black	.333	12	4	0	2	0	3	1	2	.385	.667

Hits Worst Against	Avg	AB	H	2B	3B	HR	RBI	BB	SO	OBP	SLG
Zane Smith	.091	11	1	0	0	0	0	0	1	.091	.091
Chris Hammond	.100	10	1	0	0	0	1	1	1	.182	.100
Randy Tomlin	.125	16	2	0	0	0	0	0	1	.125	.125
Terry Mulholland	.133	15	2	0	0	0	1	1	2	.188	.133
Greg Hibbard	.167	12	2	1	0	0	2	0	2	.167	.250

Pete O'Brien — Mariners

Age 36 – Bats Left

	Avg	G	AB	R	H	2B	3B	HR	RBI	BB	SO	HBP	GDP	SB	CS	OBP	SLG	IBB	SH	SF	#Pit	#P/PA	GB	FB	G/F
1993 Season	.257	72	210	30	54	7	0	7	27	26	21	0	8	0	0	.335	.390	4	0	3	887	3.71	91	66	1.38
Last Five Years	.243	621	2086	235	507	93	5	55	249	237	190	5	52	5	3	.318	.372	37	7	28	8356	3.54	803	740	1.09

1993 Season

	Avg	AB	H	2B	3B	HR	RBI	BB	SO	OBP	SLG
vs. Left	.200	25	5	0	0	0	0	3	4	.286	.200
vs. Right	.265	185	49	7	0	7	27	23	17	.341	.416
Home	.222	99	22	3	0	1	13	13	11	.310	.283
Away	.288	111	32	4	0	6	14	13	10	.357	.486
First Pitch	.200	15	3	0	0	0	1	3	0	.316	.200
Ahead in Count	.383	60	23	3	0	6	17	18	0	.519	.733
Behind in Count	.244	86	21	2	0	1	8	0	16	.241	.302
Two Strikes	.202	84	17	2	0	0	5	5	21	.244	.226

	Avg	AB	H	2B	3B	HR	RBI	BB	SO	OBP	SLG
Scoring Posn	.200	60	12	1	0	2	21	12	13	.320	.317
Close & Late	.294	34	10	1	0	2	4	5	3	.385	.500
None on/out	.368	38	14	2	0	2	2	3	3	.415	.579
Batting #4	.268	112	30	4	0	4	17	10	14	.323	.411
Batting #5	.270	37	10	2	0	0	5	8	2	.391	.324
Other	.230	61	14	1	0	3	5	8	5	.319	.393
Pre-All Star	.260	200	52	7	0	7	27	24	20	.335	.400
Post-All Star	.200	10	2	0	0	0	0	2	1	.333	.200

Last Five Years

	Avg	AB	H	2B	3B	HR	RBI	BB	SO	OBP	SLG
vs. Left	.241	557	134	25	1	10	66	55	63	.309	.343
vs. Right	.244	1529	373	68	4	45	183	182	127	.321	.382
Groundball	.240	509	122	21	0	13	55	62	46	.321	.358
Flyball	.240	487	117	20	0	19	66	64	49	.327	.398
Home	.250	1010	252	51	5	27	140	120	84	.327	.390
Away	.237	1076	255	42	0	28	109	117	106	.310	.354
Day	.252	595	150	25	1	19	71	58	53	.317	.393
Night	.239	1491	357	68	4	36	178	179	137	.318	.363
Grass	.248	1076	267	36	1	28	117	127	101	.326	.362
Turf	.238	1010	240	57	4	27	132	110	89	.309	.382
First Pitch	.265	279	74	11	0	5	32	22	0	.317	.358
Ahead in Count	.284	617	175	36	3	27	94	123	0	.400	.483
Behind in Count	.196	776	152	25	1	10	78	0	160	.197	.269
Two Strikes	.183	731	134	13	2	14	64	88	190	.269	.264

	Avg	AB	H	2B	3B	HR	RBI	BB	SO	OBP	SLG
Scoring Posn	.236	550	130	26	0	16	200	100	66	.339	.371
Close & Late	.235	358	84	16	1	10	50	51	34	.329	.369
None on/out	.278	504	140	27	2	19	19	47	37	.341	.452
Batting #4	.258	643	166	29	1	19	96	73	68	.329	.395
Batting #5	.256	758	194	34	3	20	84	97	60	.339	.388
Other	.215	685	147	30	1	16	69	67	62	.283	.331
April	.276	348	96	18	0	14	54	33	22	.336	.448
May	.216	375	81	14	2	19	58	40	31	.287	.416
June	.247	368	91	19	0	5	32	51	43	.343	.340
July	.239	380	91	17	2	5	39	47	27	.320	.334
August	.234	303	71	11	0	5	30	28	33	.296	.320
September/October	.247	312	77	14	1	7	36	38	34	.323	.365
Pre-All Star	.241	1217	293	55	3	40	153	141	106	.319	.389
Post-All Star	.246	869	214	38	2	15	96	96	84	.317	.346

Batter vs. Pitcher (since 1984)

Hits Best Against	Avg	AB	H	2B	3B	HR	RBI	BB	SO	OBP	SLG
Dave Righetti	.533	15	8	2	0	0	3	4	1	.600	.667
Rod Nichols	.500	12	6	1	0	0	4	3	1	.600	.583
Jose Mesa	.385	13	5	0	0	2	5	3	0	.500	.846
Mike Morgan	.375	16	6	0	0	2	5	1	1	.412	.750
Eric Plunk	.333	9	3	0	0	1	2	8	2	.647	.667

Hits Worst Against	Avg	AB	H	2B	3B	HR	RBI	BB	SO	OBP	SLG
Mark Williamson	.000	11	0	0	0	0	0	1	1	.083	.000
Kenny Rogers	.067	15	1	0	0	0	2	2	3	.167	.067
Gregg Olson	.067	15	1	0	0	0	1	0	3	.067	.067
Greg Hibbard	.083	12	1	0	0	0	0	0	1	.083	.083
Dennis Rasmussen	.118	17	2	0	0	0	1	0	4	.118	.118

John O'Donoghue — Orioles

Age 25 – Pitches Left

	ERA	W	L	Sv	G	GS	IP	BB	SO	Avg	H	2B	3B	HR	RBI	OBP	SLG	GF	IR	IRS	Hld	SvOp	SB	CS	GB	FB	G/F
1993 Season	4.58	0	1	0	11	1	19.2	10	16	.278	22	7	0	4	13	.367	.519	3	7	3	0	0	3	0	30	23	1.30

1993 Season

	ERA	W	L	Sv	G	GS	IP	H	HR	BB	SO
Home	6.23	0	1	0	5	1	13.0	16	4	8	9
Away	1.35	0	0	0	6	0	6.2	6	0	2	7

	Avg	AB	H	2B	3B	HR	RBI	BB	SO	OBP	SLG
vs. Left	.217	23	5	1	0	0	2	5	4	.379	.261
vs. Right	.304	56	17	6	0	4	11	5	12	.361	.625

Troy O'Leary — Brewers

Age 24 – Bats Left

	Avg	G	AB	R	H	2B	3B	HR	RBI	BB	SO	HBP	GDP	SB	CS	OBP	SLG	IBB	SH	SF	#Pit	#P/PA	GB	FB	G/F
1993 Season	.293	19	41	3	12	3	0	0	3	5	9	0	1	0	0	.370	.366	0	3	0	176	3.59	16	5	3.20

1993 Season

	Avg	AB	H	2B	3B	HR	RBI	BB	SO	OBP	SLG		Avg	AB	H	2B	3B	HR	RBI	BB	SO	OBP	SLG
vs. Left	.111	9	1	0	0	0	0	2	2	.273	.111	Scoring Posn	.100	10	1	1	0	0	3	1	2	.182	.200
vs. Right	.344	32	11	3	0	0	3	3	7	.400	.438	Close & Late	.200	10	2	2	0	0	2	3	2	.385	.400

Paul O'Neill — Yankees

Age 31 – Bats Left

	Avg	G	AB	R	H	2B	3B	HR	RBI	BB	SO	HBP	GDP	SB	CS	OBP	SLG	IBB	SH	SF	#Pit	#P/PA	GB	FB	G/F
1993 Season	.311	141	498	71	155	34	1	20	75	44	69	2	13	2	4	.367	.504	5	0	3	1971	3.60	182	128	1.42
Last Five Years	.271	703	2457	309	667	141	4	93	384	293	428	9	51	53	30	.349	.446	55	4	19	10112	3.63	854	720	1.19

1993 Season

	Avg	AB	H	2B	3B	HR	RBI	BB	SO	OBP	SLG		Avg	AB	H	2B	3B	HR	RBI	BB	SO	OBP	SLG
vs. Left	.230	135	31	6	0	2	15	9	29	.279	.319	Scoring Posn	.262	141	37	11	0	0	48	17	26	.340	.340
vs. Right	.342	363	124	28	1	18	60	35	40	.400	.573	Close & Late	.355	62	22	6	0	3	17	9	9	.425	.597
Groundball	.319	91	29	6	0	0	9	7	14	.367	.385	None on/out	.296	108	32	2	0	7	7	7	15	.345	.509
Flyball	.325	117	38	5	0	7	14	10	13	.383	.547	Batting #5	.325	372	121	28	1	16	57	33	48	.380	.535
Home	.325	249	81	17	1	8	39	20	32	.377	.498	Batting #7	.250	64	16	4	0	2	10	7	12	.329	.406
Away	.297	249	74	17	0	12	36	24	37	.358	.510	Other	.290	62	18	2	0	2	8	4	9	.333	.419
Day	.311	164	51	11	1	7	25	12	23	.358	.518	April	.296	54	16	3	1	1	10	3	8	.328	.444
Night	.311	334	104	23	0	13	50	32	46	.372	.497	May	.340	103	35	9	0	3	11	8	9	.387	.515
Grass	.319	420	134	29	1	15	61	39	61	.378	.500	June	.343	102	35	6	0	7	18	5	11	.374	.608
Turf	.269	78	21	5	0	5	14	5	8	.310	.526	July	.313	83	26	9	0	3	13	10	17	.389	.530
First Pitch	.414	87	36	9	0	2	17	4	0	.441	.586	August	.260	77	20	2	0	2	14	12	13	.363	.364
Ahead in Count	.398	98	39	7	0	10	21	16	0	.483	.776	September/October	.291	79	23	5	0	4	9	6	11	.341	.506
Behind in Count	.291	196	57	16	0	4	26	0	54	.289	.434	Pre-All Star	.329	283	93	21	1	11	40	22	36	.376	.527
Two Strikes	.243	202	49	10	1	4	25	24	69	.322	.361	Post-All Star	.288	215	62	13	0	9	35	22	33	.357	.474

1993 By Position

Position	Avg	AB	H	2B	3B	HR	RBI	BB	SO	OBP	SLG	G	GS	Innings	PO	A	E	DP	Fld Pct	Rng Fctr	In Zone	Outs	Zone Rtg	MLB Zone
As Pinch Hitter	.083	12	1	0	0	0	1	1	3	.154	.083	13	0	---	---	---	---	---	---	---	---	---	---	---
As lf	.333	150	50	13	1	4	22	11	15	.380	.513	46	40	351.0	65	3	0	0	1.000	1.74	81	63	.778	.818
As rf	.310	332	103	20	0	16	52	32	50	.371	.515	103	81	759.1	165	4	2	1	.988	2.00	190	160	.842	.826

Last Five Years

	Avg	AB	H	2B	3B	HR	RBI	BB	SO	OBP	SLG		Avg	AB	H	2B	3B	HR	RBI	BB	SO	OBP	SLG
vs. Left	.218	772	168	38	1	14	106	59	208	.273	.324	Scoring Posn	.268	684	183	44	1	19	277	143	118	.387	.418
vs. Right	.296	1685	499	103	3	79	278	234	220	.382	.501	Close & Late	.261	376	98	21	1	10	54	67	80	.371	.402
Groundball	.289	754	218	43	1	20	112	101	108	.374	.428	None on/out	.257	568	146	24	1	31	31	48	97	.319	.467
Flyball	.252	572	144	27	2	33	100	71	114	.334	.479	Batting #4	.274	660	181	33	1	27	104	89	98	.361	.450
Home	.290	1234	358	76	3	55	212	141	192	.364	.490	Batting #5	.270	925	250	53	2	36	138	100	158	.340	.449
Away	.253	1223	309	65	1	38	172	152	236	.334	.401	Other	.271	872	236	55	1	30	142	104	172	.349	.439
Day	.271	774	210	46	1	29	114	83	132	.340	.446	April	.290	324	94	20	1	13	55	41	56	.367	.478
Night	.272	1683	457	95	3	64	270	210	296	.353	.446	May	.283	456	129	27	0	17	77	52	77	.359	.454
Grass	.286	993	284	53	2	35	140	110	180	.357	.449	June	.284	465	132	26	1	27	85	50	64	.356	.518
Turf	.262	1464	383	88	2	58	244	183	248	.344	.443	July	.258	380	98	23	0	10	47	46	76	.339	.397
First Pitch	.368	399	147	38	0	16	80	37	0	.421	.584	August	.278	349	97	22	0	12	59	57	69	.376	.444
Ahead in Count	.343	577	198	41	0	40	125	124	0	.458	.622	September/October	.242	483	117	23	2	14	61	47	86	.307	.385
Behind in Count	.204	998	204	45	3	13	107	0	350	.206	.295	Pre-All Star	.282	1364	384	79	2	58	230	164	225	.359	.470
Two Strikes	.176	1063	187	42	3	19	111	121	428	.260	.275	Post-All Star	.259	1093	283	62	2	35	154	129	203	.336	.415

Batter vs. Pitcher (career)

Hits Best Against	Avg	AB	H	2B	3B	HR	RBI	BB	SO	OBP	SLG	Hits Worst Against	Avg	AB	H	2B	3B	HR	RBI	BB	SO	OBP	SLG
Jay Howell	.727	11	8	2	1	2	10	2	1	.769	1.636	Jeff Parrett	.000	15	0	0	0	0	0	1	6	.063	.000
Shawn Boskie	.600	10	6	1	0	2	2	2	1	.667	1.300	Bob Patterson	.000	13	0	0	0	0	0	0	5	.000	.000
Frank DiPino	.545	11	6	3	1	0	5	3	3	.643	1.000	Tom Glavine	.050	20	1	0	0	0	0	0	7	.050	.050
Mike Harkey	.500	10	5	0	0	2	4	3	0	.615	1.100	Paul Assenmacher	.071	14	1	0	0	0	1	1	7	.133	.071
Jeff Brantley	.364	11	4	0	0	2	6	6	1	.588	.909	Bob Welch	.083	12	1	0	0	0	0	0	1	.083	.083

Sherman Obando — Orioles

Age 24 – Bats Right

	Avg	G	AB	R	H	2B	3B	HR	RBI	BB	SO	HBP	GDP	SB	CS	OBP	SLG	IBB	SH	SF	#Pit	#P/PA	GB	FB	G/F
1993 Season	.272	31	92	8	25	2	0	3	15	4	26	1	1	0	0	.309	.391	0	0	0	396	4.08	25	22	1.14

1993 Season

	Avg	AB	H	2B	3B	HR	RBI	BB	SO	OBP	SLG		Avg	AB	H	2B	3B	HR	RBI	BB	SO	OBP	SLG
vs. Left	.295	44	13	2	0	2	10	3	11	.340	.477	Scoring Posn	.385	26	10	1	0	1	12	1	7	.407	.538
vs. Right	.250	48	12	0	0	1	5	1	15	.280	.313	Close & Late	.188	16	3	0	0	0	1	0	6	.188	.188

Jose Offerman — Dodgers

Age 25 – Bats Both (groundball hitter)

	Avg	G	AB	R	H	2B	3B	HR	RBI	BB	SO	HBP	GDP	SB	CS	OBP	SLG	IBB	SH	SF	#Pit	#P/PA	GB	FB	G/F
1993 Season	.269	158	590	77	159	21	6	1	62	71	75	2	12	30	13	.346	.331	7	25	8	2519	3.62	255	136	1.88
Career (1990-1993)	.254	388	1295	161	329	43	14	3	102	157	219	3	23	57	31	.334	.316	14	32	10	5540	3.70	527	263	2.00

1993 Season

	Avg	AB	H	2B	3B	HR	RBI	BB	SO	OBP	SLG
vs. Left	.250	184	46	7	2	1	19	21	18	.327	.326
vs. Right	.278	406	113	14	4	0	43	50	57	.354	.333
Groundball	.292	137	40	3	3	0	22	19	24	.366	.358
Flyball	.282	103	29	1	1	0	11	9	11	.336	.311
Home	.326	288	94	13	0	1	27	40	34	.409	.382
Away	.215	302	65	8	6	0	35	31	41	.284	.281
Day	.288	160	46	7	2	0	21	17	22	.350	.356
Night	.263	430	113	14	4	1	41	54	53	.344	.321
Grass	.283	459	130	17	2	1	49	60	55	.364	.330
Turf	.221	131	29	4	4	0	13	11	20	.281	.313
First Pitch	.338	77	26	4	1	0	11	6	0	.381	.416
Ahead in Count	.291	151	44	7	3	1	17	32	0	.406	.397
Behind in Count	.208	240	50	6	1	0	21	0	66	.212	.242
Two Strikes	.208	250	52	6	1	0	21	33	75	.304	.240

	Avg	AB	H	2B	3B	HR	RBI	BB	SO	OBP	SLG
Scoring Posn	.308	146	45	3	2	0	60	30	17	.408	.356
Close & Late	.218	101	22	0	0	0	12	17	13	.320	.218
None on/out	.264	110	29	3	1	1	1	13	16	.341	.336
Batting #2	.264	417	110	18	3	0	43	50	50	.339	.321
Batting #8	.330	88	29	1	1	0	10	11	13	.406	.364
Other	.235	85	20	2	2	1	9	10	12	.316	.341
April	.215	79	17	0	0	0	5	7	13	.287	.215
May	.358	95	34	5	3	0	14	13	13	.431	.474
June	.232	99	23	3	1	0	8	13	16	.319	.283
July	.295	112	33	6	0	0	15	6	16	.322	.348
August	.277	101	28	3	1	0	12	16	8	.370	.327
September/October	.231	104	24	4	1	1	8	16	9	.336	.317
Pre-All Star	.276	322	89	12	4	0	34	36	49	.348	.339
Post-All Star	.261	268	70	9	2	1	28	35	26	.343	.321

1993 By Position

Position	Avg	AB	H	2B	3B	HR	RBI	BB	SO	OBP	SLG	G	GS	Innings	PO	A	E	DP	Fld Pct	Rng Fctr	In Zone	Outs	Zone Rtg	MLB Zone
As ss	.270	589	159	21	6	1	62	71	74	.346	.331	158	156	1406.2	251	455	37	96	.950	4.52	564	494	.876	.880

Career (1990-1993)

	Avg	AB	H	2B	3B	HR	RBI	BB	SO	OBP	SLG
vs. Left	.260	461	120	16	3	2	30	48	60	.329	.321
vs. Right	.251	834	209	27	11	1	72	109	159	.336	.313
Groundball	.289	360	104	13	4	2	44	47	68	.366	.364
Flyball	.247	291	72	3	4	0	17	32	54	.322	.285
Home	.285	667	190	29	5	3	51	89	101	.370	.357
Away	.221	628	139	14	9	0	51	68	118	.295	.272
Day	.273	362	99	12	5	1	29	39	59	.342	.343
Night	.247	933	230	31	9	2	73	118	160	.331	.305
Grass	.259	997	258	33	7	3	84	124	156	.340	.315
Turf	.238	298	71	10	7	0	18	33	63	.313	.319
First Pitch	.307	179	55	6	5	0	21	11	0	.344	.397
Ahead in Count	.296	291	86	14	4	1	26	64	0	.417	.381
Behind in Count	.200	560	112	12	3	1	34	0	188	.202	.237
Two Strikes	.185	595	110	12	1	1	36	81	219	.284	.213

	Avg	AB	H	2B	3B	HR	RBI	BB	SO	OBP	SLG
Scoring Posn	.280	279	78	6	4	0	95	62	46	.399	.330
Close & Late	.220	232	51	1	1	0	18	25	41	.291	.233
None on/out	.261	329	86	9	4	2	2	36	54	.334	.331
Batting #2	.262	420	110	18	3	0	44	51	51	.338	.319
Batting #8	.248	495	123	12	6	0	32	66	95	.339	.297
Other	.253	380	96	13	5	3	26	40	73	.322	.337
April	.216	153	33	3	2	0	9	14	27	.286	.261
May	.300	200	60	7	4	0	19	30	35	.390	.375
June	.258	190	49	6	3	0	13	22	31	.333	.321
July	.269	227	61	11	1	0	18	17	43	.316	.326
August	.267	281	75	8	3	2	24	42	46	.362	.338
September/October	.209	244	51	8	1	1	19	32	37	.300	.262
Pre-All Star	.262	642	168	23	9	0	51	75	109	.338	.326
Post-All Star	.247	653	161	20	5	3	51	82	110	.329	.306

Batter vs. Pitcher (career)

Hits Best Against	Avg	AB	H	2B	3B	HR	RBI	BB	SO	OBP	SLG
Willie Blair	.500	12	6	4	0	0	1	1	0	.538	.833
Terry Mulholland	.429	21	9	3	0	0	1	2	3	.478	.571
Chris Hammond	.429	14	6	0	0	0	2	2	3	.500	.429
Dennis Martinez	.412	17	7	1	0	1	2	0	2	.389	.647
Tom Glavine	.368	19	7	2	0	1	3	2	1	.429	.632

Hits Worst Against	Avg	AB	H	2B	3B	HR	RBI	BB	SO	OBP	SLG
David Cone	.059	17	1	0	0	0	0	0	6	.059	.059
Steve Avery	.059	17	1	0	0	0	0	0	1	.059	.059
Curt Schilling	.083	12	1	0	0	0	0	1	5	.154	.083
Pete Smith	.091	11	1	0	0	0	0	0	0	.091	.091
John Smoltz	.095	21	2	0	0	0	0	1	4	.136	.095

Bobby Ojeda — Indians

Age 36 – Pitches Left (groundball pitcher)

	ERA	W	L	Sv	G	GS	IP	BB	SO	Avg	H	2B	3B	HR	RBI	OBP	SLG	CG	ShO	Sup	QS	#P/S	SB	CS	GB	FB	G/F
1993 Season	4.40	2	1	0	9	7	43.0	21	27	.289	48	13	1	5	22	.363	.470	0	0	5.44	3	95	2	1	52	56	0.93
Last Five Years	3.52	40	36	0	138	110	708.2	290	398	.261	700	131	17	54	293	.331	.382	9	4	4.14	64	94	87	52	1048	686	1.53

1993 Season

	ERA	W	L	Sv	G	GS	IP	H	HR	BB	SO
Home	4.22	1	1	0	4	4	21.1	22	3	15	8
Away	4.57	1	0	0	5	3	21.2	26	2	6	19

	Avg	AB	H	2B	3B	HR	RBI	BB	SO	OBP	SLG
vs. Left	.278	36	10	2	1	1	5	4	7	.341	.472
vs. Right	.292	130	38	11	0	4	17	17	20	.369	.469

Last Five Years

	ERA	W	L	Sv	G	GS	IP	H	HR	BB	SO
Home	3.01	21	13	0	65	51	352.1	342	22	136	209
Away	4.02	19	23	0	73	59	356.1	358	32	154	189
Day	3.87	11	14	0	44	36	223.1	235	15	84	110
Night	3.36	29	22	0	94	74	485.1	465	39	206	288
Grass	3.39	28	23	0	99	78	511.2	512	40	198	294
Turf	3.84	12	13	0	39	32	197.0	188	14	92	104
April	4.62	2	8	0	17	12	76.0	97	9	33	44
May	2.56	8	7	0	22	19	137.1	104	10	57	73
June	3.37	9	4	0	20	20	125.2	127	9	49	75
July	4.24	4	8	0	22	19	108.1	122	8	47	58
August	3.19	9	2	0	32	19	132.2	122	5	57	70
September/October	3.78	8	7	0	25	21	128.2	128	13	47	78
Starter	3.62	37	35	0	110	110	654.1	654	52	270	367
Reliever	2.32	3	1	0	28	0	54.1	46	2	20	31
0-3 Days Rest	4.24	2	4	0	6	6	34.0	37	4	14	15
4 Days Rest	3.31	17	14	0	51	51	315.2	326	27	119	188
5+ Days Rest	3.87	18	17	0	53	53	304.2	291	21	137	164

	Avg	AB	H	2B	3B	HR	RBI	BB	SO	OBP	SLG
vs. Left	.226	562	127	21	4	9	47	52	119	.294	.326
vs. Right	.270	2123	573	110	13	45	246	238	279	.341	.398
Inning 1-6	.260	2271	591	106	16	44	262	241	342	.329	.379
Inning 7+	.263	414	109	25	1	10	31	49	56	.344	.401
None on	.270	1536	415	80	11	39	39	148	229	.336	.413
Runners on	.248	1149	285	51	6	15	254	142	169	.325	.342
Scoring Posn	.249	666	166	28	5	6	226	105	112	.339	.333
Close & Late	.253	166	42	9	1	3	14	25	26	.354	.373
None on/out	.256	691	177	36	5	22	22	67	87	.325	.418
vs. 1st Batr (relief)	.346	26	9	3	0	0	0	2	3	.393	.462
First Inning Pitched	.277	530	147	33	4	8	73	51	80	.339	.400
First 75 Pitches	.259	2114	548	107	13	41	232	209	313	.324	.380
Pitch 76-90	.254	283	72	11	2	4	27	42	41	.352	.350
Pitch 91-105	.263	175	46	10	1	5	22	25	29	.356	.417
Pitch 106+	.301	113	34	3	1	4	12	14	15	.378	.451
First Pitch	.282	415	117	23	2	6	49	18	0	.314	.390
Ahead in Count	.191	984	188	33	5	16	73	0	306	.192	.284

Last Five Years

	ERA	W	L	Sv	G	GS	IP	H	HR	BB	SO
Pre-All Star	3.44	21	20	0	65	57	369.1	369	31	151	214
Post-All Star	3.61	19	16	0	73	53	339.1	331	23	139	184

	Avg	AB	H	2B	3B	HR	RBI	BB	SO	OBP	SLG
Behind in Count	.336	717	241	45	6	20	107	152	0	.448	.499
Two Strikes	.175	1040	182	36	6	22	77	120	398	.260	.285

Pitcher vs. Batter (since 1984)

Pitches Best Vs.	Avg	AB	H	2B	3B	HR	RBI	BB	SO	OBP	SLG
Darren Daulton	.000	11	0	0	0	0	0	0	5	.000	.000
Eddie Murray	.034	29	1	1	0	0	1	5	4	.176	.069
Joe Oliver	.071	28	2	1	0	0	3	1	7	.103	.107
Robin Yount	.091	11	1	0	0	0	0	1	2	.167	.091
Gerald Perry	.091	11	1	0	0	0	1	1	1	.167	.091

Pitches Worst Vs.	Avg	AB	H	2B	3B	HR	RBI	BB	SO	OBP	SLG
Ken Caminiti	.611	18	11	2	0	1	4	4	1	.682	.889
Dale Murphy	.500	26	13	5	1	1	3	9	2	.629	.885
Dave Winfield	.444	9	4	1	1	0	1	2	0	.545	.778
Reggie Sanders	.429	14	6	2	0	1	1	1	2	.467	.786
Carlton Fisk	.417	12	5	2	0	1	2	0	1	.417	.833

John Olerud — Blue Jays

Age 25 – Bats Left

	Avg	G	AB	R	H	2B	3B	HR	RBI	BB	SO	HBP	GDP	SB	CS	OBP	SLG	IBB	SH	SF	#Pit	#P/PA	GB	FB	G/F
1993 Season	.363	158	551	109	200	54	2	24	107	114	65	7	12	0	2	.473	.599	33	0	7	2375	3.50	189	173	1.09
Career (1989-1993)	.297	552	1829	286	544	127	4	71	289	309	286	15	44	1	6	.398	.488	59	5	28	8139	3.72	688	502	1.37

1993 Season

	Avg	AB	H	2B	3B	HR	RBI	BB	SO	OBP	SLG
vs. Left	.291	172	50	11	0	4	28	34	23	.413	.424
vs. Right	.396	379	150	43	2	20	79	80	42	.500	.678
Groundball	.352	88	31	7	1	0	8	22	13	.478	.455
Flyball	.345	87	30	7	1	6	22	17	7	.457	.655
Home	.346	269	93	24	2	9	48	56	28	.464	.550
Away	.379	282	107	30	0	15	59	58	37	.481	.645
Day	.387	181	70	18	0	10	37	41	20	.502	.652
Night	.351	370	130	36	2	14	70	73	45	.458	.573
Grass	.400	225	90	23	0	14	48	50	28	.509	.689
Turf	.337	326	110	31	2	10	59	64	37	.448	.537
First Pitch	.500	88	44	16	0	4	20	30	0	.628	.818
Ahead in Count	.442	154	68	17	0	10	34	50	0	.577	.747
Behind in Count	.285	207	59	12	1	6	37	0	46	.286	.440
Two Strikes	.258	209	54	14	2	3	35	34	65	.359	.388

	Avg	AB	H	2B	3B	HR	RBI	BB	SO	OBP	SLG
Scoring Posn	.371	140	52	13	1	3	76	54	19	.532	.543
Close & Late	.308	78	24	4	0	3	12	22	16	.455	.474
None on/out	.375	168	63	23	0	9	9	22	24	.450	.673
Batting #4	.360	50	18	4	0	3	10	7	7	.439	.620
Batting #5	.364	500	182	50	2	21	97	107	58	.477	.598
Other	.000	1	0	0	0	0	0	0	0	.000	.000
April	.450	80	36	7	0	3	18	13	7	.527	.650
May	.348	92	32	8	1	6	16	21	10	.470	.652
June	.427	96	41	17	0	5	30	22	8	.525	.760
July	.389	90	35	10	0	6	19	18	11	.491	.700
August	.310	100	31	4	1	3	14	19	17	.421	.460
September/October	.269	93	25	8	0	1	10	21	12	.414	.387
Pre-All Star	.395	304	120	37	1	15	69	59	29	.492	.671
Post-All Star	.324	247	80	17	1	9	38	55	36	.450	.510

1993 By Position

Position	Avg	AB	H	2B	3B	HR	RBI	BB	SO	OBP	SLG	G	GS	Innings	PO	A	E	DP	Fld Pct	Rng Fctr	In Zone	Outs	Zone Rtg	MLB Zone
As Designated Hitter	.315	73	23	4	0	1	9	12	12	.409	.411	20	20	---	---	---	---	---	---	---	---	---	---	---
As 1b	.371	477	177	50	2	23	98	102	53	.483	.629	137	137	1205.1	1159	97	10	107	.992	---	257	225	.875	.834

Career (1989-1993)

	Avg	AB	H	2B	3B	HR	RBI	BB	SO	OBP	SLG
vs. Left	.277	426	118	23	1	13	74	88	77	.402	.427
vs. Right	.304	1403	426	104	3	58	215	221	209	.397	.506
Groundball	.293	482	141	37	1	10	65	83	74	.396	.436
Flyball	.297	353	105	22	2	20	66	60	66	.397	.541
Home	.292	920	269	64	4	31	141	160	137	.399	.472
Away	.303	909	275	63	0	40	148	149	149	.396	.504
Day	.302	553	167	39	0	22	95	105	90	.413	.492
Night	.295	1276	377	88	4	49	194	204	196	.391	.486
Grass	.320	697	223	53	0	35	121	127	111	.422	.547
Turf	.284	1132	321	74	4	36	168	182	175	.383	.451
First Pitch	.381	273	104	27	0	12	49	49	0	.476	.612
Ahead in Count	.370	449	166	41	1	29	98	152	0	.524	.659
Behind in Count	.246	728	179	40	2	16	96	0	214	.248	.372
Two Strikes	.224	798	179	38	3	13	87	105	286	.314	.328

	Avg	AB	H	2B	3B	HR	RBI	BB	SO	OBP	SLG
Scoring Posn	.282	464	131	31	1	11	196	129	83	.424	.425
Close & Late	.307	309	95	22	0	11	54	55	61	.408	.485
None on/out	.340	438	149	48	1	23	23	63	71	.425	.612
Batting #5	.329	989	325	80	2	40	163	183	132	.433	.535
Batting #6	.254	480	122	21	2	18	71	73	86	.351	.419
Other	.269	360	97	26	0	13	55	53	68	.363	.450
April	.316	256	81	17	0	9	37	48	31	.425	.488
May	.244	308	75	14	2	12	40	56	58	.361	.419
June	.343	329	113	31	1	17	74	48	48	.420	.599
July	.352	310	109	24	0	15	42	41	43	.431	.574
August	.269	312	84	18	1	11	53	52	49	.370	.439
September/October	.261	314	82	23	0	7	43	64	57	.386	.401
Pre-All Star	.301	999	301	71	3	44	166	164	151	.399	.511
Post-All Star	.293	830	243	56	1	27	123	145	135	.397	.460

Batter vs. Pitcher (career)

Hits Best Against	Avg	AB	H	2B	3B	HR	RBI	BB	SO	OBP	SLG
Melido Perez	.500	14	7	3	0	0	1	8	3	.682	.714
Kevin Brown	.478	23	11	4	0	1	6	3	4	.538	.783
Tim Leary	.467	15	7	4	0	0	3	4	3	.579	.733
Danny Darwin	.462	13	6	3	0	0	6	3	0	.563	.692
Fernando Valenzuela	.444	9	4	0	0	1	1	3	0	.583	.778

Hits Worst Against	Avg	AB	H	2B	3B	HR	RBI	BB	SO	OBP	SLG
Cal Eldred	.000	11	0	0	0	0	0	0	1	.000	.000
Tom Gordon	.050	20	1	0	0	1	1	1	5	.095	.200
Dave Fleming	.100	10	1	0	0	0	1	1	1	.167	.100
Nolan Ryan	.105	19	2	1	0	0	1	2	4	.190	.158
Kirk McCaskill	.174	23	4	0	0	0	3	1	3	.200	.174

Omar Olivares — Cardinals

Age 26 – Pitches Right (groundball pitcher)

	ERA	W	L	Sv	G	GS	IP	BB	SO	Avg	H	2B	3B	HR	RBI	OBP	SLG	GF	IR	IRS	Hld	SvOp	SB	CS	GB	FB	G/F
1993 Season	4.17	5	3	1	58	9	118.2	54	63	.288	134	29	2	10	66	.370	.423	11	38	18	2	5	12	5	228	91	2.51
Career (1990-1993)	3.79	26	20	2	127	69	532.1	195	298	.259	516	93	10	45	218	.329	.384	14	41	19	3	6	35	32	857	481	1.78

1993 Season

	ERA	W	L	Sv	G	GS	IP	H	HR	BB	SO
Home	4.71	2	3	1	27	5	63.0	73	5	26	37
Away	3.56	3	0	0	31	4	55.2	61	5	28	26
Starter	4.47	2	3	0	9	9	48.1	53	3	25	31
Reliever	3.97	3	0	1	49	0	70.1	81	7	29	32
0 Days rest	8.40	1	0	0	13	0	15.0	26	4	8	7
1 or 2 Days rest	3.15	2	0	1	26	0	40.0	36	2	16	19
3+ Days rest	1.76	0	0	0	10	0	15.1	19	1	5	6

	Avg	AB	H	2B	3B	HR	RBI	BB	SO	OBP	SLG
vs. Left	.276	232	64	18	2	6	42	28	35	.361	.448
vs. Right	.299	234	70	11	0	4	24	26	28	.378	.397
Scoring Posn	.273	150	41	6	2	4	56	25	26	.383	.420
Close & Late	.273	77	21	7	0	2	13	12	12	.378	.442
None on/out	.321	106	34	7	0	1	1	8	12	.374	.415
First Pitch	.364	77	28	7	0	0	10	6	0	.433	.455
Ahead in Count	.229	170	39	10	1	1	15	0	52	.243	.318

1993 Season

	ERA	W	L	Sv	G	GS	IP	H	HR	BB	SO
Pre-All Star	4.78	2	2	1	26	7	69.2	83	8	29	38
Post-All Star	3.31	3	1	0	32	2	49.0	51	2	25	25

	Avg	AB	H	2B	3B	HR	RBI	BB	SO	OBP	SLG
Behind in Count	.328	128	42	5	1	9	29	29	0	.453	.594
Two Strikes	.201	169	34	12	1	0	13	19	63	.293	.284

Career (1990-1993)

	ERA	W	L	Sv	G	GS	IP	H	HR	BB	SO
Home	3.84	14	14	2	65	38	293.1	283	24	97	168
Away	3.73	12	6	0	62	31	239.0	233	21	98	130
Day	4.75	6	6	0	29	19	130.2	133	19	53	81
Night	3.47	20	14	2	98	50	401.2	383	26	142	217
Grass	4.23	7	3	0	35	17	127.2	129	13	61	68
Turf	3.65	19	17	2	92	52	404.2	387	32	134	230
April	3.21	3	2	2	16	7	70.0	57	4	21	42
May	6.56	0	3	0	11	9	48.0	59	9	23	27
June	4.28	4	1	0	16	11	75.2	74	6	34	28
July	4.54	5	5	0	26	9	73.1	81	12	30	39
August	2.69	6	4	0	28	15	124.0	115	5	36	65
September/October	3.44	8	5	0	30	18	141.1	130	9	51	97
Starter	3.80	23	20	0	69	69	440.2	418	38	158	254
Reliever	3.73	3	0	2	58	0	91.2	98	7	37	44
0 Days rest	8.40	1	0	0	13	0	15.0	26	4	8	7
1 or 2 Days rest	3.15	2	0	1	26	0	40.0	36	2	16	19
3+ Days rest	2.45	0	0	1	19	0	36.2	36	1	13	18
Pre-All Star	4.41	9	7	2	54	30	224.1	219	23	87	114
Post-All Star	3.33	17	13	0	73	39	308.0	297	22	108	184

	Avg	AB	H	2B	3B	HR	RBI	BB	SO	OBP	SLG
vs. Left	.260	1093	284	57	7	24	127	123	159	.338	.391
vs. Right	.258	899	232	36	3	21	91	72	139	.319	.375
Inning 1-6	.254	1556	395	64	7	34	167	148	234	.323	.370
Inning 7+	.278	436	121	29	3	11	51	47	64	.352	.433
None on	.259	1158	300	53	5	26	26	107	175	.329	.381
Runners on	.259	834	216	40	5	19	192	88	123	.329	.387
Scoring Posn	.246	464	114	19	3	10	157	62	69	.333	.364
Close & Late	.258	240	62	16	1	5	24	32	38	.349	.396
None on/out	.278	521	145	28	2	9	9	33	65	.324	.392
vs. 1st Batr (relief)	.365	52	19	4	0	1	10	6	3	.431	.500
First Inning Pitched	.282	447	126	25	3	14	75	48	60	.356	.445
First 15 Pitches	.286	392	112	21	3	13	56	36	46	.355	.454
Pitch 16-30	.281	342	96	17	3	8	44	34	48	.348	.418
Pitch 31-45	.248	303	75	13	1	6	26	22	55	.302	.356
Pitch 46+	.244	955	233	42	3	18	92	103	149	.320	.351
First Pitch	.316	313	99	18	1	4	36	11	0	.347	.419
Ahead in Count	.215	820	176	27	5	17	78	0	248	.223	.322
Behind in Count	.301	509	153	31	1	18	70	104	0	.420	.472
Two Strikes	.186	801	149	29	6	9	52	80	298	.267	.271

Pitcher vs. Batter (career)

Pitches Best Vs.	Avg	AB	H	2B	3B	HR	RBI	BB	SO	OBP	SLG
Wes Chamberlain	.000	11	0	0	0	0	0	0	2	.000	.000
Mickey Morandini	.059	17	1	0	0	0	0	1	1	.111	.059
John VanderWal	.067	15	1	0	0	0	0	0	2	.067	.067
Mark Lemke	.077	13	1	0	0	0	0	1	2	.143	.077
Tom Foley	.083	12	1	0	0	0	0	0	1	.083	.083

Pitches Worst Vs.	Avg	AB	H	2B	3B	HR	RBI	BB	SO	OBP	SLG
Ryne Sandberg	.478	23	11	1	0	2	3	4	1	.556	.783
Dwight Smith	.471	17	8	3	1	1	6	1	3	.500	.941
Ron Gant	.444	18	8	3	0	2	3	4	3	.545	.944
Andre Dawson	.429	14	6	0	0	2	7	0	1	.429	.857
Terry Pendleton	.421	19	8	1	0	2	2	2	4	.476	.789

Darren Oliver — Rangers

Age 23 – Pitches Left

	ERA	W	L	Sv	G	GS	IP	BB	SO	Avg	H	2B	3B	HR	RBI	OBP	SLG	GF	IR	IRS	Hld	SvOp	SB	CS	GB	FB	G/F
1993 Season	2.70	0	0	0	2	0	3.1	1	4	.154	2	0	0	1	1	.214	.385	0	1	0	0	0	1	0	4	4	1.00

1993 Season

	ERA	W	L	Sv	G	GS	IP	H	HR	BB	SO
Home	2.70	0	0	0	1	0	3.1	2	1	0	4
Away	0.00	0	0	0	1	0	0.0	0	0	1	0

	Avg	AB	H	2B	3B	HR	RBI	BB	SO	OBP	SLG
vs. Left	.167	6	1	0	0	0	0	1	3	.286	.167
vs. Right	.143	7	1	0	0	1	1	0	1	.143	.571

Joe Oliver — Reds

Age 28 – Bats Right

	Avg	G	AB	R	H	2B	3B	HR	RBI	BB	SO	HBP	GDP	SB	CS	OBP	SLG	IBB	SH	SF	#Pit	#P/PA	GB	FB	G/F
1993 Season	.239	139	482	40	115	28	0	14	75	27	91	1	13	0	0	.276	.384	2	2	9	1841	3.53	167	149	1.12
Career (1989-1993)	.245	546	1751	150	429	95	1	46	248	123	322	5	48	3	4	.293	.379	42	18	19	6526	3.41	578	565	1.02

1993 Season

	Avg	AB	H	2B	3B	HR	RBI	BB	SO	OBP	SLG
vs. Left	.291	134	39	11	0	6	25	10	17	.338	.507
vs. Right	.218	348	76	17	0	8	50	17	74	.251	.336
Groundball	.228	167	38	8	0	5	22	11	28	.273	.365
Flyball	.264	87	23	7	0	3	16	4	16	.297	.448
Home	.250	232	58	17	0	7	38	12	41	.283	.414
Away	.228	250	57	11	0	7	37	15	50	.269	.356
Day	.227	110	25	7	0	3	24	8	18	.283	.373
Night	.242	372	90	21	0	11	51	19	73	.273	.387
Grass	.188	144	27	8	0	4	23	8	29	.229	.326
Turf	.260	338	88	20	0	10	52	19	62	.295	.408
First Pitch	.352	71	25	5	0	3	16	2	0	.354	.549
Ahead in Count	.378	90	34	10	0	3	16	12	0	.442	.589
Behind in Count	.145	228	33	7	0	5	30	0	78	.143	.241
Two Strikes	.154	208	32	9	0	3	28	13	91	.202	.240

	Avg	AB	H	2B	3B	HR	RBI	BB	SO	OBP	SLG
Scoring Posn	.277	148	41	9	0	6	63	10	26	.305	.459
Close & Late	.269	78	21	4	0	3	16	4	10	.298	.436
None on/out	.235	98	23	4	0	0	0	8	17	.299	.276
Batting #7	.268	183	49	7	0	7	40	8	36	.296	.421
Batting #8	.217	180	39	15	0	3	22	14	33	.269	.350
Other	.227	119	27	6	0	4	13	5	22	.254	.378
April	.263	80	21	6	0	2	13	6	13	.314	.413
May	.213	94	20	7	0	3	16	6	19	.265	.383
June	.214	70	15	5	0	1	8	4	12	.244	.329
July	.302	86	26	3	0	3	14	2	17	.315	.442
August	.200	75	15	6	0	3	15	6	13	.256	.400
September/October	.234	77	18	1	0	2	9	3	17	.256	.325
Pre-All Star	.250	276	69	19	0	8	44	16	47	.288	.406
Post-All Star	.223	206	46	9	0	6	31	11	44	.259	.354

1993 By Position

Position	Avg	AB	H	2B	3B	HR	RBI	BB	SO	OBP	SLG	G	GS	Innings	PO	A	E	DP	Fld Pct	Rng Fctr	In Zone	Outs	Zone Rtg	MLB Zone
As c	.241	456	110	27	0	14	72	27	86	.278	.393	133	128	1102.2	791	66	7	8	.992	---	---	---	---	---
As 1b	.211	19	4	0	0	0	2	0	3	.250	.211	12	3	46.0	34	2	0	5	1.000	---	3	4	1.333	.834

Career (1989-1993)

	Avg	AB	H	2B	3B	HR	RBI	BB	SO	OBP	SLG
vs. Left	.288	699	201	45	0	24	117	63	114	.344	.455
vs. Right	.217	1052	228	50	1	22	131	60	208	.259	.329
Groundball	.251	646	162	32	1	15	82	37	104	.291	.373
Flyball	.200	355	71	18	0	11	46	34	84	.267	.344
Home	.246	873	215	56	0	25	130	60	157	.293	.396
Away	.244	878	214	39	1	21	118	63	165	.294	.362

	Avg	AB	H	2B	3B	HR	RBI	BB	SO	OBP	SLG
Scoring Posn	.249	478	119	30	0	18	203	62	91	.326	.425
Close & Late	.260	285	74	15	0	5	33	23	45	.312	.365
None on/out	.239	401	96	21	0	8	8	19	77	.277	.352
Batting #7	.268	523	140	30	1	13	90	23	88	.297	.403
Batting #8	.224	870	195	46	0	25	119	85	173	.292	.363
Other	.263	358	94	19	0	8	39	15	61	.291	.383

Career (1989-1993)

	Avg	AB	H	2B	3B	HR	RBI	BB	SO	OBP	SLG		Avg	AB	H	2B	3B	HR	RBI	BB	SO	OBP	SLG
Day	.273	428	117	28	0	8	69	33	75	.325	.395	April	.234	222	52	14	1	3	25	22	39	.303	.347
Night	.236	1323	312	67	1	38	179	90	247	.283	.374	May	.221	271	60	14	0	9	36	28	53	.300	.373
Grass	.232	512	119	27	1	14	78	26	100	.268	.371	June	.229	253	58	13	0	5	28	21	46	.283	.340
Turf	.250	1239	310	68	0	32	170	97	222	.304	.383	July	.271	325	88	17	0	8	47	19	57	.307	.397
First Pitch	.293	317	93	19	0	10	59	24	0	.341	.448	August	.248	343	85	20	0	14	67	19	67	.285	.429
Ahead in Count	.338	302	102	25	1	13	56	46	0	.420	.556	September/October	.255	337	86	17	0	7	45	14	60	.285	.368
Behind in Count	.183	818	150	31	0	13	83	0	277	.183	.269	Pre-All Star	.242	855	207	49	1	21	111	74	152	.302	.375
Two Strikes	.162	766	124	28	0	8	68	38	322	.200	.230	Post-All Star	.248	896	222	46	0	25	137	49	170	.285	.383

Batter vs. Pitcher (career)

Hits Best Against	Avg	AB	H	2B	3B	HR	RBI	BB	SO	OBP	SLG	Hits Worst Against	Avg	AB	H	2B	3B	HR	RBI	BB	SO	OBP	SLG
Pete Schourek	.545	11	6	3	0	1	4	0	2	.545	1.091	Bill Swift	.063	16	1	0	0	0	0	0	1	.063	.063
Bob Walk	.444	9	4	1	0	0	1	1	0	.455	.556	Bobby Ojeda	.071	28	2	1	0	0	3	1	7	.103	.107
Ben Rivera	.444	9	4	1	0	0	0	2	1	.545	.556	John Burkett	.083	12	1	0	0	0	0	0	3	.083	.083
Zane Smith	.367	30	11	1	0	3	3	0	4	.367	.700	Joe Boever	.091	11	1	0	0	0	0	1	3	.167	.091
Bud Black	.313	16	5	1	0	2	5	1	3	.353	.750	Joe Magrane	.133	15	2	0	0	0	0	0	2	.133	.133

Greg Olson — Braves

Age 33 – Bats Right

	Avg	G	AB	R	H	2B	3B	HR	RBI	BB	SO	HBP	GDP	SB	CS	OBP	SLG	IBB	SH	SF	#Pit	#P/PA	GB	FB	G/F
1993 Season	.225	83	262	23	59	10	0	4	24	29	27	1	11	1	0	.304	.309	0	2	1	1090	3.69	115	81	1.42
Career (1989-1993)	.242	414	1275	132	309	61	3	20	131	137	157	7	40	5	3	.317	.342	11	6	8	5076	3.54	535	372	1.44

1993 Season

	Avg	AB	H	2B	3B	HR	RBI	BB	SO	OBP	SLG		Avg	AB	H	2B	3B	HR	RBI	BB	SO	OBP	SLG
vs. Left	.237	97	23	3	0	3	15	6	5	.282	.361	Scoring Posn	.200	60	12	1	0	2	18	5	11	.258	.317
vs. Right	.218	165	36	7	0	1	9	23	22	.316	.279	Close & Late	.190	42	8	1	0	1	4	7	6	.300	.286
Home	.198	126	25	4	0	3	13	14	15	.277	.302	None on/out	.194	67	13	2	0	0	0	4	2	.250	.224
Away	.250	136	34	6	0	1	11	15	12	.329	.316	Batting #7	.224	254	57	10	0	3	21	28	25	.303	.299
First Pitch	.316	38	12	1	0	1	5	0	0	.316	.421	Batting #9	.200	5	1	0	0	1	3	1	2	.333	.800
Ahead in Count	.253	75	19	5	0	0	8	16	0	.385	.320	Other	.333	3	1	0	0	0	0	0	0	.333	.333
Behind in Count	.157	102	16	2	0	2	8	0	23	.165	.235	Pre-All Star	.212	193	41	7	0	2	15	22	20	.292	.280
Two Strikes	.133	105	14	2	0	1	4	13	27	.235	.181	Post-All Star	.261	69	18	3	0	2	9	7	7	.338	.391

Career (1989-1993)

	Avg	AB	H	2B	3B	HR	RBI	BB	SO	OBP	SLG		Avg	AB	H	2B	3B	HR	RBI	BB	SO	OBP	SLG
vs. Left	.278	468	130	25	3	11	67	37	50	.329	.415	Scoring Posn	.228	307	70	10	0	6	98	51	50	.331	.319
vs. Right	.222	807	179	36	0	9	64	100	107	.311	.300	Close & Late	.202	218	44	9	0	4	24	30	32	.298	.298
Groundball	.223	400	89	15	0	8	41	38	53	.291	.320	None on/out	.230	330	76	16	0	4	4	30	28	.298	.315
Flyball	.285	316	90	23	1	8	42	42	34	.373	.440	Batting #7	.235	796	187	41	1	9	74	90	95	.315	.323
Home	.258	616	159	27	1	13	76	60	64	.320	.369	Batting #8	.254	284	72	10	1	7	33	28	41	.323	.370
Away	.228	659	150	34	2	7	55	77	93	.315	.317	Other	.256	195	50	10	1	4	24	19	21	.321	.379
Day	.254	342	87	16	1	5	33	35	46	.325	.351	April	.273	128	35	6	0	1	7	18	16	.363	.344
Night	.238	933	222	45	2	15	98	102	111	.315	.339	May	.234	231	54	7	0	6	28	21	31	.305	.342
Grass	.244	932	227	42	2	16	96	99	108	.315	.344	June	.260	265	69	14	0	5	29	27	26	.329	.370
Turf	.239	343	82	19	1	4	35	38	49	.324	.335	July	.221	235	52	9	2	4	22	28	29	.303	.328
First Pitch	.319	191	61	11	1	1	19	6	0	.342	.403	August	.283	205	58	14	1	4	32	19	28	.342	.420
Ahead in Count	.268	380	102	22	2	7	49	77	0	.391	.392	September/October	.194	211	41	11	0	0	13	24	27	.282	.246
Behind in Count	.177	469	83	16	0	6	39	0	132	.182	.249	Pre-All Star	.256	696	178	29	1	14	70	77	83	.332	.361
Two Strikes	.146	471	69	14	0	7	31	51	157	.232	.221	Post-All Star	.226	579	131	32	2	6	61	60	74	.300	.320

Batter vs. Pitcher (career)

Hits Best Against	Avg	AB	H	2B	3B	HR	RBI	BB	SO	OBP	SLG	Hits Worst Against	Avg	AB	H	2B	3B	HR	RBI	BB	SO	OBP	SLG
Mark Gardner	.556	9	5	0	0	0	3	2	2	.636	.556	Mike Morgan	.000	11	0	0	0	0	0	0	3	.000	.000
Jack Armstrong	.438	16	7	2	0	0	2	1	1	.471	.563	Bruce Ruffin	.154	13	2	1	0	0	0	0	3	.154	.231
Donovan Osborne	.364	11	4	1	1	0	2	0	0	.364	.636	Andy Benes	.194	31	6	1	0	0	0	3	4	.265	.226
Pete Harnisch	.350	20	7	4	0	1	4	0	1	.350	.700	John Burkett	.200	25	5	0	0	0	1	2	4	.259	.200
Bud Black	.333	15	5	1	1	0	0	2	1	.412	.533	Greg W. Harris	.200	10	2	0	0	0	0	1	1	.273	.200

Gregg Olson — Orioles

Age 27 – Pitches Right

	ERA	W	L	Sv	G	GS	IP	BB	SO	Avg	H	2B	3B	HR	RBI	OBP	SLG	GF	IR	IRS	Hld	SvOp	SB	CS	GB	FB	G/F
1993 Season	1.60	0	2	29	50	0	45.0	18	44	.223	37	9	0	1	23	.296	.295	45	31	15	0	35	1	1	64	34	1.88
Last Five Years	2.23	16	20	160	310	0	339.1	148	338	.219	271	41	3	9	122	.303	.279	221	173	52	2	193	50	5	425	291	1.46

1993 Season

	ERA	W	L	Sv	G	GS	IP	H	HR	BB	SO		Avg	AB	H	2B	3B	HR	RBI	BB	SO	OBP	SLG
Home	1.96	0	2	16	25	0	23.0	17	1	10	30	vs. Left	.212	85	18	4	0	1	13	9	24	.281	.294
Away	1.23	0	0	13	25	0	22.0	20	0	8	14	vs. Right	.235	81	19	5	0	0	10	9	20	.311	.296
Starter	0.00	0	0	0	0	0	0.0	0	0	0	0	Scoring Posn	.237	59	14	3	0	1	23	9	18	.329	.339
Reliever	1.60	0	2	29	50	0	45.0	37	1	18	44	Close & Late	.236	123	29	7	0	1	23	13	34	.304	.317
0 Days rest	2.16	0	0	5	9	0	8.1	10	0	4	8	None on/out	.281	32	9	1	0	0	0	4	9	.361	.313
1 or 2 Days rest	1.50	0	1	18	26	0	24.0	20	0	9	30	First Pitch	.300	20	6	2	0	0	3	1	0	.318	.400
3+ Days rest	1.42	0	1	6	15	0	12.2	7	1	5	6	Ahead in Count	.127	79	10	3	0	0	3	0	40	.127	.165
Pre-All Star	1.24	0	1	23	38	0	36.1	26	1	12	31	Behind in Count	.310	42	13	2	0	1	10	7	0	.408	.429
Post-All Star	3.12	0	1	6	12	0	8.2	11	0	6	13	Two Strikes	.122	82	10	2	0	0	9	10	44	.215	.146

Last Five Years

	ERA	W	L	Sv	G	GS	IP	H	HR	BB	SO		Avg	AB	H	2B	3B	HR	RBI	BB	SO	OBP	SLG
Home	1.94	12	4	71	155	0	167.1	117	6	77	184	vs. Left	.193	623	120	16	0	3	55	74	166	.280	.233

Last Five Years

	ERA	W	L	Sv	G	GS	IP	H	HR	BB	SO
Away	2.51	4	16	89	155	0	172.0	154	3	71	154
Day	3.65	1	11	44	81	0	93.2	91	5	42	85
Night	1.69	15	9	116	229	0	245.2	180	4	106	253
Grass	1.85	14	11	140	255	0	277.1	194	8	119	283
Turf	3.92	2	9	20	55	0	62.0	77	1	29	55
April	1.94	3	2	16	42	0	55.2	47	3	21	43
May	1.48	2	2	27	56	0	67.0	46	2	31	74
June	2.28	4	4	40	57	0	59.1	38	2	21	64
July	3.12	1	7	29	57	0	57.2	59	0	31	65
August	2.92	2	2	25	50	0	49.1	44	2	24	39
September/October	1.79	4	3	23	48	0	50.1	37	0	20	53
Starter	0.00	0	0	0	0	0	0.0	0	0	0	0
Reliever	2.23	16	20	160	310	0	339.1	271	9	148	338
0 Days rest	2.54	4	5	45	70	0	74.1	70	1	28	71
1 or 2 Days rest	2.16	9	10	80	148	0	158.1	120	5	79	166
3+ Days rest	2.11	3	5	35	92	0	106.2	81	3	41	101
Pre-All Star	1.94	9	10	92	173	0	199.0	147	7	81	197
Post-All Star	2.63	7	10	68	137	0	140.1	124	2	67	141

	Avg	AB	H	2B	3B	HR	RBI	BB	SO	OBP	SLG
vs. Right	.246	615	151	25	3	6	67	74	172	.327	.325
Inning 1-6	.417	12	5	2	0	0	4	2	1	.500	.583
Inning 7+	.217	1226	266	39	3	9	118	146	337	.301	.276
None on	.223	602	134	26	2	5	5	60	162	.296	.297
Runners on	.215	636	137	15	1	4	117	88	176	.309	.261
Scoring Posn	.207	410	85	10	1	2	112	71	123	.320	.251
Close & Late	.230	781	180	24	3	8	99	102	216	.319	.300
None on/out	.193	254	49	5	2	3	3	28	63	.278	.264
vs. 1st Batr (relief)	.223	274	61	9	1	3	27	31	68	.304	.296
First Inning Pitched	.233	1015	236	33	2	6	109	110	269	.308	.287
First 15 Pitches	.234	870	204	31	2	6	84	84	230	.303	.295
Pitch 16-30	.176	290	51	7	0	2	30	47	88	.293	.221
Pitch 31-45	.214	70	15	3	1	1	7	14	19	.345	.329
Pitch 46+	.125	8	1	0	0	0	1	3	1	.333	.125
First Pitch	.283	152	43	4	0	1	19	14	0	.343	.329
Ahead in Count	.151	602	91	17	2	2	34	0	292	.157	.196
Behind in Count	.314	258	81	13	1	4	38	61	0	.441	.419
Two Strikes	.144	640	92	14	2	3	45	70	338	.231	.186

Pitcher vs. Batter (career)

Pitches Best Vs.	Avg	AB	H	2B	3B	HR	RBI	BB	SO	OBP	SLG
Ruben Sierra	.000	10	0	0	0	0	0	1	3	.091	.000
Pete O'Brien	.067	15	1	0	0	0	1	0	3	.067	.067
Don Mattingly	.091	11	1	0	0	0	0	2	1	.231	.091
Steve Sax	.154	13	2	0	0	0	0	0	0	.154	.154
Wally Joyner	.167	12	2	0	0	0	2	0	3	.154	.167

Pitches Worst Vs.	Avg	AB	H	2B	3B	HR	RBI	BB	SO	OBP	SLG
Mark McGwire	.444	9	4	0	0	1	4	3	3	.583	.778
Danny Tartabull	.417	12	5	0	0	0	4	2	4	.500	.417

Steve Ontiveros — Mariners

Age 33 – Pitches Right (groundball pitcher)

	ERA	W	L	Sv	G	GS	IP	BB	SO	Avg	H	2B	3B	HR	RBI	OBP	SLG	GF	IR	IRS	Hld	SvOp	SB	CS	GB	FB	G/F
1993 Season	1.00	0	2	0	14	0	18.0	6	13	.277	18	4	0	0	7	.338	.338	8	9	5	0	0	1	0	31	12	2.58
Last Five Years	2.76	2	3	0	25	5	58.2	24	31	.274	61	10	0	3	24	.344	.359	9	11	7	1	0	6	1	110	41	2.68

1993 Season

	ERA	W	L	Sv	G	GS	IP	H	HR	BB	SO
Home	0.00	0	1	0	7	0	10.2	9	0	6	6
Away	2.45	0	1	0	7	0	7.1	9	0	0	7

	Avg	AB	H	2B	3B	HR	RBI	BB	SO	OBP	SLG
vs. Left	.226	31	7	1	0	0	0	3	9	.294	.258
vs. Right	.324	34	11	3	0	0	7	3	4	.378	.412

Jose Oquendo — Cardinals

Age 30 – Bats Both

	Avg	G	AB	R	H	2B	3B	HR	RBI	BB	SO	HBP	GDP	SB	CS	OBP	SLG	IBB	SH	SF	#Pit	#P/PA	GB	FB	G/F
1993 Season	.205	46	73	7	15	0	0	0	4	12	8	0	5	0	0	.314	.205	1	3	1	333	3.74	33	19	1.74
Last Five Years	.262	506	1499	144	392	59	17	3	118	237	164	1	29	5	8	.359	.330	30	19	17	6474	3.65	558	483	1.16

1993 Season

	Avg	AB	H	2B	3B	HR	RBI	BB	SO	OBP	SLG
vs. Left	.125	24	3	0	0	0	0	1	2	.160	.125
vs. Right	.245	49	12	0	0	0	4	11	6	.377	.245

	Avg	AB	H	2B	3B	HR	RBI	BB	SO	OBP	SLG
Scoring Posn	.200	15	3	0	0	0	4	2	0	.278	.200
Close & Late	.364	11	4	0	0	0	1	2	1	.462	.364

Last Five Years

	Avg	AB	H	2B	3B	HR	RBI	BB	SO	OBP	SLG
vs. Left	.238	579	138	27	6	2	37	84	67	.334	.316
vs. Right	.276	920	254	32	11	1	81	153	97	.375	.338
Groundball	.292	531	155	17	12	2	46	85	51	.388	.380
Flyball	.250	356	89	20	2	1	30	54	39	.346	.326
Home	.266	729	194	26	10	1	59	109	70	.359	.333
Away	.257	770	198	33	7	2	59	128	94	.359	.326
Day	.232	462	107	15	5	1	45	70	49	.328	.292
Night	.275	1037	285	44	12	2	73	167	115	.373	.346
Grass	.265	411	109	12	3	0	31	64	58	.360	.309
Turf	.260	1088	283	47	14	3	87	173	106	.359	.337
First Pitch	.308	266	82	16	2	2	24	14	0	.340	.406
Ahead in Count	.304	375	114	13	5	0	38	120	0	.465	.365
Behind in Count	.233	563	131	19	6	0	30	0	134	.232	.288
Two Strikes	.218	620	135	20	7	1	41	93	164	.318	.277

	Avg	AB	H	2B	3B	HR	RBI	BB	SO	OBP	SLG
Scoring Posn	.254	362	92	14	6	0	114	82	42	.377	.326
Close & Late	.298	258	77	11	1	1	17	48	32	.409	.360
None on/out	.241	377	91	18	3	0	0	50	43	.330	.305
Batting #7	.282	387	109	14	4	2	28	61	40	.375	.354
Batting #8	.253	731	185	26	9	1	58	127	74	.362	.317
Other	.257	381	98	19	4	0	32	49	50	.337	.328
April	.243	210	51	7	4	0	20	39	29	.359	.314
May	.209	249	52	6	1	1	6	31	31	.294	.253
June	.268	272	73	9	2	1	27	52	25	.381	.327
July	.309	285	88	15	6	0	21	38	31	.387	.404
August	.283	279	79	19	0	0	28	42	24	.373	.351
September/October	.240	204	49	3	4	1	16	35	24	.349	.309
Pre-All Star	.255	812	207	27	11	2	63	132	94	.356	.323
Post-All Star	.269	687	185	32	6	1	55	105	70	.363	.338

Batter vs. Pitcher (since 1984)

Hits Best Against	Avg	AB	H	2B	3B	HR	RBI	BB	SO	OBP	SLG
Paul Assenmacher	.556	9	5	0	0	0	1	2	1	.636	.556
Norm Charlton	.417	12	5	1	0	1	3	3	0	.533	.750
Tom Browning	.400	25	10	4	0	2	3	4	0	.483	.800
Frank Viola	.389	18	7	0	1	1	3	5	1	.500	.667
Jose Rijo	.364	11	4	1	1	0	1	3	2	.500	.636

Hits Worst Against	Avg	AB	H	2B	3B	HR	RBI	BB	SO	OBP	SLG
Mark Portugal	.000	11	0	0	0	0	0	2	4	.154	.000
Dwight Gooden	.077	26	2	0	0	0	0	1	3	.111	.077
Mark Gardner	.091	11	1	0	0	0	1	2	2	.214	.091
Kelly Downs	.100	10	1	0	0	0	1	2	2	.250	.100
Andy Benes	.111	9	1	0	0	0	0	2	1	.273	.111

Mike Oquist — Orioles

Age 26 – Pitches Right (flyball pitcher)

	ERA	W	L	Sv	G	GS	IP	BB	SO	Avg	H	2B	3B	HR	RBI	OBP	SLG	GF	IR	IRS	Hld	SvOp	SB	CS	GB	FB	G/F
1993 Season	3.86	0	0	0	5	0	11.2	4	8	.261	12	3	0	0	3	.320	.326	2	5	1	0	0	0	1	12	16	0.75

1993 Season

	ERA	W	L	Sv	G	GS	IP	H	HR	BB	SO		Avg	AB	H	2B	3B	HR	RBI	BB	SO	OBP	SLG
Home	7.94	0	0	0	2	0	5.2	10	0	4	4	vs. Left	.267	15	4	0	0	0	2	2	0	.353	.267
Away	0.00	0	0	0	3	0	6.0	2	0	0	4	vs. Right	.258	31	8	3	0	0	1	2	8	.303	.355

Jesse Orosco — Brewers

Age 37 – Pitches Left (flyball pitcher)

	ERA	W	L	Sv	G	GS	IP	BB	SO	Avg	H	2B	3B	HR	RBI	OBP	SLG	GF	IR	IRS	Hld	SvOp	SB	CS	GB	FB	G/F
1993 Season	3.18	3	5	8	57	0	56.2	17	67	.224	47	9	1	2	24	.289	.305	27	41	11	11	13	2	5	71	40	1.78
Last Five Years	3.14	16	14	14	287	0	284.0	109	277	.232	244	43	5	27	146	.305	.360	89	273	77	39	25	18	13	300	307	0.98

1993 Season

	ERA	W	L	Sv	G	GS	IP	H	HR	BB	SO		Avg	AB	H	2B	3B	HR	RBI	BB	SO	OBP	SLG
Home	4.60	0	5	5	29	0	29.1	30	2	11	39	vs. Left	.313	64	20	5	0	1	8	3	15	.353	.438
Away	1.65	3	0	3	28	0	27.1	17	0	6	28	vs. Right	.185	146	27	4	1	1	16	14	52	.262	.247
Starter	0.00	0	0	0	0	0	0.0	0	0	0	0	Scoring Posn	.220	59	13	2	0	1	20	8	15	.304	.305
Reliever	3.18	3	5	8	57	0	56.2	47	2	17	67	Close & Late	.203	143	29	6	1	2	17	12	48	.275	.301
0 Days rest	2.77	0	1	2	12	0	13.0	13	2	4	20	None on/out	.295	44	13	3	0	1	1	3	10	.340	.432
1 or 2 Days rest	2.38	1	0	4	24	0	22.2	17	0	6	24	First Pitch	.321	28	9	3	0	0	3	2	0	.387	.429
3+ Days rest	4.29	2	4	2	21	0	21.0	17	0	7	23	Ahead in Count	.141	99	14	2	1	0	6	0	55	.140	.182
Pre-All Star	5.18	0	2	1	32	0	24.1	27	1	6	28	Behind in Count	.308	39	12	2	0	1	7	6	0	.391	.436
Post-All Star	1.67	3	3	7	25	0	32.1	20	1	11	39	Two Strikes	.133	105	14	3	1	0	6	9	67	.202	.181

Last Five Years

	ERA	W	L	Sv	G	GS	IP	H	HR	BB	SO		Avg	AB	H	2B	3B	HR	RBI	BB	SO	OBP	SLG
Home	2.85	9	11	8	147	0	157.2	131	15	54	159	vs. Left	.238	336	80	17	0	6	46	31	91	.302	.342
Away	3.49	7	3	6	140	0	126.1	113	12	55	118	vs. Right	.230	714	164	26	5	21	100	78	186	.307	.368
Day	3.43	6	5	7	93	0	81.1	61	14	28	73	Inning 1-6	.379	58	22	4	1	2	19	5	12	.422	.586
Night	3.02	10	9	7	194	0	202.2	183	13	81	204	Inning 7+	.224	992	222	39	4	25	127	104	265	.299	.347
Grass	3.06	14	13	13	241	0	244.1	205	25	91	239	None on	.240	521	125	22	3	15	15	51	140	.315	.380
Turf	3.63	2	1	1	46	0	39.2	39	2	18	38	Runners on	.225	529	119	21	2	12	131	58	137	.296	.340
April	2.45	0	3	2	33	0	22.0	17	1	17	15	Scoring Posn	.231	321	74	12	1	5	113	48	88	.321	.321
May	4.04	4	2	3	53	0	49.0	43	6	16	47	Close & Late	.211	454	96	18	1	8	56	46	129	.288	.308
June	3.88	1	2	0	48	0	51.0	43	2	17	55	None on/out	.267	225	60	10	2	9	9	24	52	.343	.449
July	2.41	3	2	1	54	0	52.1	49	3	26	43	vs. 1st Batr (relief)	.245	253	62	10	0	6	41	23	61	.307	.356
August	3.05	2	3	4	52	0	59.0	50	10	15	57	First Inning Pitched	.234	782	183	33	4	17	125	85	188	.309	.352
September/October	2.66	6	2	4	47	0	50.2	42	5	18	60	First 15 Pitches	.226	722	163	29	3	18	106	75	175	.299	.349
Starter	0.00	0	0	0	0	0	0.0	0	0	0	0	Pitch 16-30	.240	258	62	9	2	7	31	27	84	.313	.372
Reliever	3.14	16	14	14	287	0	284.0	244	27	109	277	Pitch 31-45	.267	60	16	5	0	2	8	7	17	.353	.450
0 Days rest	2.47	4	3	5	67	0	54.2	51	7	18	63	Pitch 46+	.300	10	3	0	0	0	1	0	1	.273	.300
1 or 2 Days rest	3.55	7	5	7	122	0	132.0	114	14	52	120	First Pitch	.329	140	46	9	2	6	25	17	0	.400	.550
3+ Days rest	2.96	5	6	2	98	0	97.1	79	6	39	94	Ahead in Count	.163	522	85	11	2	6	49	0	239	.164	.226
Pre-All Star	3.56	5	9	5	153	0	144.0	125	11	58	137	Behind in Count	.341	205	70	12	1	10	38	49	0	.467	.556
Post-All Star	2.70	11	5	9	134	0	140.0	119	16	51	140	Two Strikes	.136	522	71	15	2	5	46	43	277	.201	.201

Pitcher vs. Batter (since 1984)

Pitches Best Vs.	Avg	AB	H	2B	3B	HR	RBI	BB	SO	OBP	SLG	Pitches Worst Vs.	Avg	AB	H	2B	3B	HR	RBI	BB	SO	OBP	SLG
Chili Davis	.000	14	0	0	0	0	0	4	7	.222	.000	Andre Dawson	.600	10	6	1	0	1	3	1	1	.636	1.000
Terry Pendleton	.063	16	1	0	0	0	0	4	4	.250	.063	Harold Reynolds	.600	10	6	1	0	0	3	1	2	.636	.700
Steve Sax	.071	14	1	1	0	0	0	2	0	.188	.143	Candy Maldonado	.333	9	3	0	0	2	4	1	2	.364	1.000
Cal Ripken	.083	12	1	0	0	0	1	0	3	.083	.083	Robin Ventura	.333	9	3	1	0	2	3	3	3	.500	1.111
Bobby Bonilla	.182	11	2	0	0	0	0	1	1	.250	.182	Kevin McReynolds	.308	13	4	0	0	2	2	4	3	.471	.769

Joe Orsulak — Mets

Age 32 – Bats Left

	Avg	G	AB	R	H	2B	3B	HR	RBI	BB	SO	HBP	GDP	SB	CS	OBP	SLG	IBB	SH	SF	#Pit	#P/PA	GB	FB	G/F
1993 Season	.284	134	409	59	116	15	4	8	35	28	25	2	6	5	4	.331	.399	1	0	2	1464	3.32	168	125	1.34
Last Five Years	.281	641	2089	269	586	91	16	35	229	171	187	13	34	27	21	.337	.390	22	15	13	7751	3.37	813	628	1.29

1993 Season

	Avg	AB	H	2B	3B	HR	RBI	BB	SO	OBP	SLG		Avg	AB	H	2B	3B	HR	RBI	BB	SO	OBP	SLG
vs. Left	.357	42	15	1	1	0	7	1	5	.364	.429	Scoring Posn	.286	84	24	2	1	0	27	7	5	.340	.333
vs. Right	.275	367	101	14	3	8	28	27	20	.327	.395	Close & Late	.282	78	22	3	0	1	7	6	3	.341	.359
Groundball	.233	120	28	2	2	2	10	8	5	.281	.333	None on/out	.296	108	32	7	1	3	3	7	5	.345	.463
Flyball	.259	58	15	2	1	1	5	8	4	.358	.379	Batting #1	.241	87	21	2	2	2	9	5	2	.283	.379
Home	.285	179	51	8	0	5	12	19	5	.350	.413	Batting #5	.319	113	36	6	1	2	13	8	8	.366	.442
Away	.283	230	65	7	4	3	23	9	20	.315	.387	Other	.282	209	59	7	1	4	13	15	15	.332	.383
Day	.230	135	31	1	1	2	9	16	13	.316	.296	April	.282	39	11	1	0	0	2	1	3	.300	.308
Night	.310	274	85	14	3	6	26	12	12	.339	.449	May	.292	72	21	1	0	2	6	4	5	.338	.389
Grass	.280	300	84	11	2	6	25	25	14	.335	.390	June	.313	67	21	4	0	2	8	5	3	.365	.463
Turf	.294	109	32	4	2	2	10	3	11	.319	.422	July	.292	65	19	4	0	2	6	6	2	.347	.446
First Pitch	.290	69	20	2	1	0	2	1	0	.300	.348	August	.300	80	24	4	2	2	7	3	5	.325	.475
Ahead in Count	.304	92	28	4	1	5	12	20	0	.421	.533	September/October	.233	86	20	1	2	0	6	9	7	.305	.291
Behind in Count	.255	165	42	5	1	1	10	0	20	.259	.315	Pre-All Star	.310	203	63	10	0	4	18	14	11	.357	.419
Two Strikes	.263	137	36	6	1	1	9	7	25	.303	.343	Post-All Star	.257	206	53	5	4	4	17	14	14	.305	.379

1993 By Position

Position	Avg	AB	H	2B	3B	HR	RBI	BB	SO	OBP	SLG	G	GS	Innings	PO	A	E	DP	Fld Pct	Rng Fctr	In Zone	Outs	Zone Rtg	MLB Zone
As Pinch Hitter	.323	31	10	1	0	0	4	2	0	.364	.355	33	0	---	---	---	---	---	---	---	---	---	---	---
As lf	.246	203	50	7	4	3	15	16	15	.300	.365	66	49	458.1	114	4	5	0	.959	2.32	136	112	.824	.818
As cf	.312	125	39	4	0	5	11	9	7	.363	.464	40	35	291.1	79	2	0	0	1.000	2.50	83	75	.904	.829
As rf	.326	46	15	2	0	0	5	0	3	.333	.370	23	10	103.2	22	3	0	0	1.000	2.17	27	22	.815	.826

Last Five Years

	Avg	AB	H	2B	3B	HR	RBI	BB	SO	OBP	SLG		Avg	AB	H	2B	3B	HR	RBI	BB	SO	OBP	SLG
vs. Left	.249	342	85	14	3	0	36	22	39	.298	.307	Scoring Posn	.280	490	137	23	4	7	190	72	51	.370	.386
vs. Right	.287	1747	501	77	13	35	193	149	148	.344	.406	Close & Late	.254	346	88	13	2	5	31	42	31	.341	.347
Groundball	.263	616	162	23	5	7	71	57	45	.325	.351	None on/out	.283	487	138	26	3	9	9	33	30	.333	.405
Flyball	.280	393	110	22	3	8	47	39	37	.350	.412	Batting #2	.273	578	158	22	5	12	63	42	58	.322	.391
Home	.277	990	274	40	6	19	109	94	87	.340	.387	Batting #5	.286	412	118	16	5	4	45	32	31	.341	.379
Away	.284	1099	312	51	10	16	120	77	100	.334	.392	Other	.282	1099	310	53	6	19	121	97	98	.343	.393
Day	.244	565	138	21	3	9	48	56	58	.316	.340	April	.267	243	65	13	1	3	23	14	32	.310	.366
Night	.294	1524	448	70	13	26	181	115	129	.345	.408	May	.289	322	93	13	3	8	45	31	32	.356	.422
Grass	.279	1719	479	73	9	31	185	152	148	.339	.386	June	.272	423	115	16	3	5	51	33	33	.327	.359
Turf	.289	370	107	18	7	4	44	19	39	.326	.408	July	.302	427	129	25	4	7	41	29	28	.343	.429
First Pitch	.293	345	101	17	2	6	31	11	0	.318	.406	August	.299	371	111	19	3	7	46	35	39	.362	.423
Ahead in Count	.333	493	164	27	4	15	80	103	0	.444	.495	September/October	.241	303	73	5	2	5	23	29	23	.313	.320
Behind in Count	.239	863	206	30	6	8	69	0	162	.244	.315	Pre-All Star	.284	1146	326	54	10	19	131	87	106	.337	.399
Two Strikes	.213	756	161	24	6	7	64	49	187	.264	.288	Post-All Star	.276	943	260	37	6	16	98	84	81	.337	.379

Batter vs. Pitcher (since 1984)

Hits Best Against	Avg	AB	H	2B	3B	HR	RBI	BB	SO	OBP	SLG	Hits Worst Against	Avg	AB	H	2B	3B	HR	RBI	BB	SO	OBP	SLG
Rick Sutcliffe	.500	22	11	3	1	0	1	2	3	.542	.727	Greg Swindell	.091	11	1	0	0	0	0	0	1	.091	.091
Curt Schilling	.500	14	7	0	0	1	2	1	4	.533	.714	Mike Morgan	.111	9	1	0	0	0	1	2	1	.273	.111
Alex Fernandez	.467	15	7	1	2	0	2	0	0	.467	.800	Greg Maddux	.125	16	2	0	0	0	0	0	2	.125	.125
Jack McDowell	.458	24	11	2	0	2	5	1	1	.480	.792	Kevin Appier	.167	18	3	0	0	0	0	1	1	.211	.167
Bill Gullickson	.417	24	10	5	0	1	4	2	1	.462	.750	Jeff Reardon	.167	12	2	0	0	0	0	0	0	.167	.167

Junior Ortiz — Indians

Age 34 – Bats Right (groundball hitter)

	Avg	G	AB	R	H	2B	3B	HR	RBI	BB	SO	HBP	GDP	SB	CS	OBP	SLG	IBB	SH	SF	#Pit	#P/PA	GB	FB	G/F
1993 Season	.221	95	249	19	55	13	0	0	20	11	26	5	10	1	0	.267	.273	1	4	1	959	3.55	115	57	2.02
Last Five Years	.244	404	1027	82	251	38	3	1	95	70	97	14	36	4	10	.300	.290	5	12	5	3898	3.46	526	224	2.35

1993 Season

	Avg	AB	H	2B	3B	HR	RBI	BB	SO	OBP	SLG		Avg	AB	H	2B	3B	HR	RBI	BB	SO	OBP	SLG
vs. Left	.192	99	19	7	0	0	10	3	12	.231	.263	Scoring Posn	.268	56	15	5	0	0	19	6	3	.344	.357
vs. Right	.240	150	36	6	0	0	10	8	14	.290	.280	Close & Late	.222	27	6	1	0	0	3	2	2	.276	.259
Home	.205	117	24	5	0	0	10	6	11	.260	.248	None on/out	.224	67	15	1	0	0	0	2	8	.268	.239
Away	.235	132	31	8	0	0	10	5	15	.273	.295	Total	.221	249	55	13	0	0	20	11	26	.267	.273
First Pitch	.326	43	14	6	0	0	4	0	0	.341	.465	Batting #9	.221	249	55	13	0	0	20	11	26	.267	.273
Ahead in Count	.234	64	15	4	0	0	7	5	0	.296	.297	Other	.000	0	0	0	0	0	0	0	0	.000	.000
Behind in Count	.184	103	19	2	0	0	6	0	23	.200	.204	Pre-All Star	.228	158	36	10	0	0	14	5	18	.265	.291
Two Strikes	.147	95	14	2	0	0	5	6	26	.214	.168	Post-All Star	.209	91	19	3	0	0	6	6	8	.270	.242

Last Five Years

	Avg	AB	H	2B	3B	HR	RBI	BB	SO	OBP	SLG		Avg	AB	H	2B	3B	HR	RBI	BB	SO	OBP	SLG
vs. Left	.232	353	82	13	2	1	36	29	36	.299	.289	Scoring Posn	.272	268	73	11	0	1	91	29	29	.342	.325
vs. Right	.251	674	169	25	1	0	59	41	61	.301	.291	Close & Late	.247	150	37	6	0	0	12	6	15	.283	.287
Groundball	.200	255	51	7	1	0	20	22	39	.277	.235	None on/out	.227	255	58	8	1	0	0	16	23	.284	.267
Flyball	.259	216	56	9	0	1	17	13	20	.308	.315	Batting #8	.256	324	83	11	1	0	28	29	27	.324	.296
Home	.270	507	137	16	2	0	61	43	44	.335	.310	Batting #9	.241	482	116	23	0	0	41	19	49	.280	.288
Away	.219	520	114	22	1	1	34	27	53	.264	.271	Other	.235	221	52	4	2	1	26	22	21	.306	.285
Day	.239	355	85	14	2	1	32	23	34	.298	.299	April	.202	109	22	0	0	0	12	13	8	.286	.202
Night	.247	672	166	24	1	0	63	47	63	.301	.286	May	.231	216	50	14	0	0	19	11	21	.275	.296
Grass	.248	569	141	21	0	0	43	32	55	.299	.285	June	.279	172	48	8	2	0	20	10	14	.324	.349
Turf	.240	458	110	17	3	1	52	38	42	.302	.297	July	.296	213	63	8	1	1	24	10	24	.335	.357
First Pitch	.286	182	52	13	1	0	17	4	0	.307	.368	August	.204	147	30	3	0	0	9	17	13	.295	.224
Ahead in Count	.280	236	66	10	0	1	28	36	0	.377	.335	September/October	.224	170	38	5	0	0	11	9	17	.279	.253
Behind in Count	.203	429	87	10	1	0	32	0	80	.217	.231	Pre-All Star	.244	553	135	24	2	0	55	41	50	.304	.295
Two Strikes	.196	418	82	11	1	0	26	30	97	.261	.227	Post-All Star	.245	474	116	14	1	1	40	29	47	.296	.285

Batter vs. Pitcher (since 1984)

Hits Best Against	Avg	AB	H	2B	3B	HR	RBI	BB	SO	OBP	SLG	Hits Worst Against	Avg	AB	H	2B	3B	HR	RBI	BB	SO	OBP	SLG
Zane Smith	.563	16	9	2	0	0	1	1	1	.588	.688	Orel Hershiser	.000	11	0	0	0	0	1	0	0	.000	.000
Bobby Witt	.455	11	5	0	0	0	2	0	2	.455	.455	Joe Magrane	.091	11	1	0	0	0	0	0	0	.091	.091
Scott Sanderson	.444	18	8	1	0	0	0	0	1	.444	.500	Tom Gordon	.100	10	1	0	0	0	1	1	1	.182	.100
Jaime Navarro	.375	8	3	1	0	0	0	3	0	.545	.500	Chuck Finley	.111	18	2	0	0	0	1	1	0	.158	.111
Bill Gullickson	.357	14	5	2	0	0	1	1	1	.400	.500	Sid Fernandez	.143	21	3	0	0	0	0	1	5	.182	.143

Luis Ortiz — Red Sox

Age 24 – Bats Right

	Avg	G	AB	R	H	2B	3B	HR	RBI	BB	SO	HBP	GDP	SB	CS	OBP	SLG	IBB	SH	SF	#Pit	#P/PA	GB	FB	G/F
1993 Season	.250	9	12	0	3	0	0	0	1	0	2	0	0	0	0	.250	.250	0	0	0	33	2.75	4	4	1.00

1993 Season

	Avg	AB	H	2B	3B	HR	RBI	BB	SO	OBP	SLG
vs. Left	.500	6	3	0	0	0	1	0	1	.500	.500
vs. Right	.000	6	0	0	0	0	0	0	1	.000	.000

	Avg	AB	H	2B	3B	HR	RBI	BB	SO	OBP	SLG
Scoring Posn	.286	7	2	0	0	0	1	0	1	.286	.286
Close & Late	.000	3	0	0	0	0	0	0	1	.000	.000

John Orton — Angels

Age 28 – Bats Right

	Avg	G	AB	R	H	2B	3B	HR	RBI	BB	SO	HBP	GDP	SB	CS	OBP	SLG	IBB	SH	SF	#Pit	#P/PA	GB	FB	G/F
1993 Season	.189	37	95	5	18	5	0	1	4	7	24	1	1	1	2	.252	.274	0	2	0	420	4.00	35	21	1.67
Career (1989-1993)	.200	156	401	35	80	18	0	4	29	31	121	5	6	2	5	.265	.274	0	11	0	1748	3.90	127	98	1.30

1993 Season

	Avg	AB	H	2B	3B	HR	RBI	BB	SO	OBP	SLG
vs. Left	.054	37	2	0	0	0	0	4	9	.146	.054
vs. Right	.276	58	16	5	0	1	4	3	15	.323	.414

	Avg	AB	H	2B	3B	HR	RBI	BB	SO	OBP	SLG
Scoring Posn	.130	23	3	0	0	0	2	2	7	.200	.130
Close & Late	.000	12	0	0	0	0	0	1	1	.143	.000

Career (1989-1993)

	Avg	AB	H	2B	3B	HR	RBI	BB	SO	OBP	SLG
vs. Left	.143	119	17	3	0	1	7	10	36	.221	.193
vs. Right	.223	282	63	15	0	3	22	21	85	.284	.309
Groundball	.269	93	25	4	0	1	9	6	26	.313	.344
Flyball	.134	97	13	6	0	0	3	8	29	.208	.196
Home	.172	198	34	7	0	1	12	12	62	.226	.222
Away	.227	203	46	11	0	3	17	19	59	.302	.325
Day	.167	114	19	4	0	0	8	4	35	.202	.202
Night	.213	287	61	14	0	4	21	27	86	.289	.303
Grass	.206	306	63	13	0	4	23	21	88	.264	.288
Turf	.179	95	17	5	0	0	6	10	33	.271	.232
First Pitch	.246	65	16	4	0	1	8	0	0	.246	.354
Ahead in Count	.329	82	27	4	0	1	7	14	0	.427	.415
Behind in Count	.129	178	23	5	0	1	6	0	99	.153	.174
Two Strikes	.112	214	24	6	0	0	8	17	121	.185	.140

	Avg	AB	H	2B	3B	HR	RBI	BB	SO	OBP	SLG
Scoring Posn	.216	88	19	5	0	1	25	10	28	.310	.307
Close & Late	.146	48	7	2	0	0	0	6	11	.255	.188
None on/out	.240	104	25	5	0	2	2	9	26	.301	.346
Batting #8	.174	144	25	3	0	1	9	13	47	.242	.215
Batting #9	.242	207	50	14	0	3	19	13	56	.296	.353
Other	.100	50	5	1	0	0	1	5	18	.211	.120
April	.221	68	15	4	0	2	4	1	20	.243	.368
May	.162	74	12	4	0	0	3	4	22	.205	.216
June	.210	81	17	1	0	0	4	9	22	.304	.222
July	.067	15	1	0	0	0	0	1	5	.125	.067
August	.389	18	7	1	0	0	3	3	7	.476	.444
September/October	.193	145	28	8	0	2	15	13	45	.269	.290
Pre-All Star	.189	238	45	9	0	2	11	15	69	.246	.252
Post-All Star	.215	163	35	9	0	2	18	16	52	.293	.307

Batter vs. Pitcher (career)

Hits Best Against	Avg	AB	H	2B	3B	HR	RBI	BB	SO	OBP	SLG

Hits Worst Against	Avg	AB	H	2B	3B	HR	RBI	BB	SO	OBP	SLG
Nolan Ryan	.000	10	0	0	0	0	0	2	6	.167	.000

Donovan Osborne — Cardinals

Age 25 – Pitches Left

	ERA	W	L	Sv	G	GS	IP	BB	SO	Avg	H	2B	3B	HR	RBI	OBP	SLG	CG	ShO	Sup	QS	#P/S	SB	CS	GB	FB	G/F
1993 Season	3.76	10	7	0	26	26	155.2	47	83	.257	153	27	5	18	61	.318	.410	1	0	4.45	17	92	4	5	202	189	1.07
Career (1992-1993)	3.76	21	16	0	60	55	334.2	85	187	.267	346	66	10	32	137	.315	.407	1	0	4.01	33	90	19	8	459	404	1.14

1993 Season

	ERA	W	L	Sv	G	GS	IP	H	HR	BB	SO
Home	2.50	7	3	0	13	13	86.1	85	9	20	46
Away	5.32	3	4	0	13	13	69.1	68	9	27	37
Starter	3.76	10	7	0	26	26	155.2	153	18	47	83
Reliever	0.00	0	0	0	0	0	0.0	0	0	0	0
0-3 Days Rest	11.25	0	0	0	1	1	4.0	6	2	2	6
4 Days Rest	4.01	7	4	0	16	16	94.1	92	9	27	52
5+ Days Rest	2.83	3	3	0	9	9	57.1	55	7	18	25
Pre-All Star	3.57	8	3	0	18	18	113.1	109	14	33	60
Post-All Star	4.25	2	4	0	8	8	42.1	44	4	14	23

	Avg	AB	H	2B	3B	HR	RBI	BB	SO	OBP	SLG
vs. Left	.207	116	24	5	0	2	10	9	15	.264	.302
vs. Right	.269	479	129	22	5	16	51	38	68	.331	.436
Scoring Posn	.261	119	31	3	0	5	44	15	14	.353	.412
Close & Late	.220	41	9	3	1	0	3	1	3	.238	.341
None on/out	.261	161	42	9	1	4	4	9	17	.304	.404
First Pitch	.302	86	26	3	1	2	9	4	0	.330	.430
Ahead in Count	.196	250	49	7	1	8	27	0	73	.212	.328
Behind in Count	.312	141	44	9	2	6	18	25	0	.417	.532
Two Strikes	.162	260	42	6	1	8	16	18	83	.227	.285

Career (1992-1993)

	ERA	W	L	Sv	G	GS	IP	H	HR	BB	SO
Home	2.94	12	6	0	29	25	165.1	169	13	37	95
Away	4.57	9	10	0	31	30	169.1	177	19	48	92
Day	3.94	5	5	0	20	18	109.2	111	12	29	71
Night	3.68	16	11	0	40	37	225.0	235	20	56	116
Grass	4.72	6	6	0	18	18	97.1	104	12	27	53
Turf	3.38	15	10	0	42	37	237.1	242	20	58	134
April	2.68	3	0	0	9	9	50.1	41	4	16	22
May	2.85	4	4	0	11	11	75.2	73	9	17	41
June	4.02	4	3	0	11	11	69.1	74	8	16	40
July	5.96	5	3	0	12	10	54.1	62	7	16	35
August	3.42	3	4	0	11	8	50.0	50	4	11	35
September/October	3.86	2	2	0	6	6	35.0	46	0	9	14
Starter	3.77	20	15	0	55	55	324.2	336	32	84	181
Reliever	3.60	1	1	0	5	0	10.0	10	0	1	6
0-3 Days Rest	5.40	1	0	0	3	3	15.0	16	3	7	13
4 Days Rest	3.82	14	8	0	31	31	186.1	192	18	43	113
5+ Days Rest	3.50	5	7	0	21	21	123.1	128	11	34	55
Pre-All Star	3.39	15	8	0	36	36	223.1	215	24	56	120
Post-All Star	4.53	6	8	0	24	19	111.1	131	8	29	67

	Avg	AB	H	2B	3B	HR	RBI	BB	SO	OBP	SLG
vs. Left	.270	267	72	18	0	5	33	17	38	.311	.393
vs. Right	.266	1031	274	48	10	27	104	68	149	.316	.410
Inning 1-6	.268	1143	306	55	9	31	128	79	170	.319	.413
Inning 7+	.258	155	40	11	1	1	9	6	17	.286	.361
None on	.249	803	200	43	6	21	21	37	127	.284	.396
Runners on	.295	495	146	23	4	11	116	48	60	.362	.424
Scoring Posn	.283	290	82	11	2	7	101	28	42	.346	.407
Close & Late	.229	105	24	8	1	1	7	3	13	.250	.352
None on/out	.261	345	90	23	1	9	9	20	40	.305	.412
vs. 1st Batr (relief)	.200	5	1	1	0	0	0	0	0	.200	.400
First Inning Pitched	.267	236	63	11	2	7	35	21	42	.326	.419
First 75 Pitches	.270	1027	277	49	8	29	115	67	155	.316	.418
Pitch 76-90	.267	161	43	11	1	2	13	10	17	.314	.385
Pitch 91-105	.259	85	22	5	1	1	6	5	12	.308	.376
Pitch 106+	.160	25	4	1	0	0	3	3	3	.276	.200
First Pitch	.332	196	65	9	2	3	16	5	0	.343	.444
Ahead in Count	.225	551	124	24	1	11	56	0	153	.234	.332
Behind in Count	.299	301	90	20	4	12	42	46	0	.393	.512
Two Strikes	.188	564	106	16	2	12	43	34	187	.240	.287

Pitcher vs. Batter (career)

Pitches Best Vs.	Avg	AB	H	2B	3B	HR	RBI	BB	SO	OBP	SLG
Jerald Clark	.000	14	0	0	0	0	0	1	3	.067	.000
Mickey Morandini	.091	11	1	0	0	0	0	0	0	.091	.091
Jeff Bagwell	.111	9	1	0	0	0	3	1	2	.182	.111
Fred McGriff	.118	17	2	0	0	0	0	1	3	.167	.118
Jeff King	.133	15	2	0	0	0	0	0	0	.133	.133

Pitches Worst Vs.	Avg	AB	H	2B	3B	HR	RBI	BB	SO	OBP	SLG
Craig Biggio	.545	11	6	1	0	1	2	1	2	.583	.909
Brian Hunter	.545	11	6	0	0	2	2	0	1	.545	1.091
Darrin Jackson	.467	15	7	0	0	1	2	1	2	.500	.667
Darren Daulton	.444	9	4	1	0	1	4	3	2	.583	.889
Andy Van Slyke	.429	14	6	3	0	0	1	0	2	.429	.643

Al Osuna — Astros

Age 28 – Pitches Left (flyball pitcher)

	ERA	W	L	Sv	G	GS	IP	BB	SO	Avg	H	2B	3B	HR	RBI	OBP	SLG	GF	IR	IRS	Hld	SvOp	SB	CS	GB	FB	G/F
1993 Season	3.20	1	1	2	44	0	25.1	13	21	.200	17	1	0	3	10	.301	.318	6	44	5	11	2	0	0	24	29	0.83
Career (1990-1993)	3.75	16	10	14	193	0	180.0	103	132	.217	138	24	2	17	78	.326	.342	57	144	31	28	26	6	2	185	244	0.76

1993 Season

	ERA	W	L	Sv	G	GS	IP	H	HR	BB	SO
Home	3.00	1	0	1	17	0	9.0	7	1	4	7
Away	3.31	0	1	1	27	0	16.1	10	2	9	14
Starter	0.00	0	0	0	0	0	0.0	0	0	0	0
Reliever	3.20	1	1	2	44	0	25.1	17	3	13	21
0 Days rest	5.06	0	1	0	15	0	10.2	11	2	6	7
1 or 2 Days rest	3.86	0	0	1	10	0	4.2	4	1	3	3
3+ Days rest	0.90	1	0	1	19	0	10.0	2	0	4	11
Pre-All Star	3.68	1	1	2	21	0	14.2	11	2	5	10
Post-All Star	2.53	0	0	0	23	0	10.2	6	1	8	11

	Avg	AB	H	2B	3B	HR	RBI	BB	SO	OBP	SLG
vs. Left	.222	36	8	1	0	2	5	11	8	.400	.417
vs. Right	.184	49	9	0	0	1	5	2	13	.208	.245
Scoring Posn	.130	23	3	0	0	0	6	8	5	.314	.130
Close & Late	.220	41	9	1	0	1	4	9	9	.353	.317
None on/out	.211	19	4	0	0	2	2	4	6	.375	.526
First Pitch	.250	8	2	0	0	0	0	2	0	.400	.250
Ahead in Count	.162	37	6	0	0	1	4	0	20	.154	.243
Behind in Count	.148	27	4	1	0	1	3	8	0	.333	.296
Two Strikes	.158	38	6	0	0	1	3	3	21	.209	.237

Career (1990-1993)

	ERA	W	L	Sv	G	GS	IP	H	HR	BB	SO
Home	3.63	11	4	6	97	0	86.2	66	8	42	60
Away	3.86	5	6	8	96	0	93.1	72	9	61	72
Day	2.88	2	1	4	59	0	59.1	41	8	28	43
Night	4.18	14	9	10	134	0	120.2	97	9	75	89
Grass	3.71	4	0	6	54	0	51.0	40	6	27	41
Turf	3.77	12	10	8	139	0	129.0	98	11	76	91
April	0.48	3	0	0	19	0	18.2	12	0	10	10
May	4.40	1	5	4	29	0	28.2	18	4	18	20
June	4.20	5	1	3	34	0	30.0	30	2	16	22
July	1.87	3	1	2	37	0	33.2	22	3	19	25
August	3.77	1	2	2	33	0	28.2	26	1	16	19
September/October	6.02	3	1	3	41	0	40.1	30	7	24	36
Starter	0.00	0	0	0	0	0	0.0	0	0	0	0
Reliever	3.75	16	10	14	193	0	180.0	138	17	103	132
0 Days rest	3.93	6	5	4	56	0	50.1	39	6	30	28
1 or 2 Days rest	4.17	7	4	6	80	0	73.1	60	8	44	61
3+ Days rest	3.04	3	1	4	57	0	56.1	39	3	29	43
Pre-All Star	3.24	10	6	7	96	0	89.0	70	7	47	59
Post-All Star	4.25	6	4	7	97	0	91.0	68	10	56	73

	Avg	AB	H	2B	3B	HR	RBI	BB	SO	OBP	SLG
vs. Left	.235	234	55	8	0	7	34	36	52	.340	.359
vs. Right	.207	401	83	16	2	10	44	67	80	.318	.332
Inning 1-6	.208	53	11	0	0	5	11	5	15	.279	.491
Inning 7+	.218	582	127	24	2	12	67	98	117	.330	.328
None on	.201	328	66	9	1	12	12	51	73	.316	.345
Runners on	.235	307	72	15	1	5	66	52	59	.337	.339
Scoring Posn	.224	170	38	5	1	4	62	43	38	.358	.335
Close & Late	.223	337	75	15	1	10	49	65	61	.346	.362
None on/out	.205	146	30	3	1	5	5	29	33	.345	.342
vs. 1st Batr (relief)	.233	159	37	6	1	5	15	24	28	.335	.377
First Inning Pitched	.227	484	110	21	1	11	60	67	88	.319	.343
First 15 Pitches	.224	447	100	18	1	11	51	58	84	.310	.342
Pitch 16-30	.188	149	28	5	0	1	10	34	37	.346	.242
Pitch 31-45	.200	35	7	1	1	3	12	11	11	.375	.543
Pitch 46+	.750	4	3	0	0	2	5	0	0	.800	2.250
First Pitch	.291	79	23	6	0	4	13	10	0	.372	.519
Ahead in Count	.156	282	44	7	1	3	24	0	104	.155	.220
Behind in Count	.289	135	39	6	1	3	17	52	0	.487	.415
Two Strikes	.137	300	41	8	1	3	28	41	132	.236	.200

Pitcher vs. Batter (career)

Pitches Best Vs.	Avg	AB	H	2B	3B	HR	RBI	BB	SO	OBP	SLG
Brett Butler	.000	7	0	0	0	0	0	5	3	.417	.000
Eddie Murray	.083	12	1	0	0	0	3	1	3	.133	.083
Hal Morris	.091	11	1	0	0	0	1	0	2	.083	.091
Paul O'Neill	.100	10	1	1	0	0	0	2	5	.250	.200
Bobby Bonilla	.111	9	1	0	0	1	2	2	0	.250	.444

Pitches Worst Vs.	Avg	AB	H	2B	3B	HR	RBI	BB	SO	OBP	SLG
Barry Bonds	.385	13	5	0	0	2	2	5	2	.556	.846
Tony Gwynn	.333	12	4	0	0	0	1	0	0	.333	.333
Fred McGriff	.333	9	3	2	0	0	1	2	4	.455	.556

Dave Otto — Pirates

Age 29 – Pitches Left (groundball pitcher)

	ERA	W	L	Sv	G	GS	IP	BB	SO	Avg	H	2B	3B	HR	RBI	OBP	SLG	GF	IR	IRS	Hld	SvOp	SB	CS	GB	FB	G/F
1993 Season	5.03	3	4	0	28	8	68.0	28	30	.317	85	14	2	9	34	.387	.485	7	6	2	1	0	8	2	126	67	1.88
Last Five Years	5.32	10	21	0	67	39	257.1	93	115	.308	312	48	6	28	139	.369	.450	9	14	7	1	0	24	9	469	239	1.96

1993 Season

	ERA	W	L	Sv	G	GS	IP	H	HR	BB	SO
Home	2.97	0	1	0	13	3	30.1	39	1	14	16
Away	6.69	3	3	0	15	5	37.2	46	8	14	14
Starter	4.53	2	3	0	8	8	43.2	49	5	18	20
Reliever	5.92	1	1	0	20	0	24.1	36	4	10	10
0 Days rest	1.80	0	0	0	4	0	5.0	3	1	0	3
1 or 2 Days rest	10.29	1	1	0	5	0	7.0	14	2	2	2
3+ Days rest	5.11	0	0	0	11	0	12.1	19	1	8	5
Pre-All Star	4.43	3	4	0	21	8	61.0	66	7	25	28
Post-All Star	10.29	0	0	0	7	0	7.0	19	2	3	2

	Avg	AB	H	2B	3B	HR	RBI	BB	SO	OBP	SLG
vs. Left	.348	69	24	3	0	1	10	6	7	.416	.435
vs. Right	.307	199	61	11	2	8	24	22	23	.377	.503
Scoring Posn	.234	77	18	2	0	3	28	9	6	.310	.377
Close & Late	.324	34	11	1	1	1	3	2	4	.361	.500
None on/out	.400	70	28	5	1	3	3	8	8	.462	.629
First Pitch	.465	43	20	2	1	0	4	0	0	.477	.558
Ahead in Count	.221	95	21	3	0	5	10	0	22	.235	.411
Behind in Count	.390	82	32	7	1	2	13	13	0	.474	.573
Two Strikes	.218	101	22	4	0	3	8	15	30	.331	.347

Last Five Years

	ERA	W	L	Sv	G	GS	IP	H	HR	BB	SO
Home	4.47	4	9	0	32	19	133.0	157	14	42	69
Away	6.23	6	12	0	35	20	124.1	155	14	51	46
Day	5.69	0	5	0	18	8	61.2	73	7	26	36
Night	5.20	10	16	0	49	31	195.2	239	21	67	79
Grass	5.18	8	17	0	42	31	191.0	223	18	66	87

	Avg	AB	H	2B	3B	HR	RBI	BB	SO	OBP	SLG
vs. Left	.317	202	64	9	0	2	30	16	14	.374	.391
vs. Right	.306	811	248	39	6	26	109	77	101	.367	.465
Inning 1-6	.301	835	251	40	4	21	113	74	95	.360	.434
Inning 7+	.343	178	61	8	2	7	26	19	20	.410	.528
None on	.316	560	177	34	4	12	12	45	66	.369	.455

Last Five Years

	ERA	W	L	Sv	G	GS	IP	H	HR	BB	SO
Turf	5.70	2	4	0	25	8	66.1	89	10	27	28
April	5.44	3	4	0	11	9	46.1	54	6	17	21
May	5.90	2	2	0	8	7	39.2	52	5	18	21
June	4.95	1	5	0	15	5	43.2	47	3	18	20
July	5.14	1	1	0	14	3	35.0	44	3	14	14
August	5.86	2	6	0	13	9	55.1	70	8	16	23
September/October	4.34	1	3	0	6	6	37.1	45	3	10	16
Starter	5.06	9	20	0	39	39	220.2	257	23	74	100
Reliever	6.87	1	1	0	28	0	36.2	55	5	19	15
0 Days rest	1.80	0	0	0	4	0	5.0	3	1	0	3
1 or 2 Days rest	12.86	1	1	0	6	0	7.0	16	2	3	2
3+ Days rest	6.20	0	0	0	18	0	24.2	36	2	16	10
Pre-All Star	5.40	7	11	0	39	21	138.1	162	15	57	64
Post-All Star	5.22	3	10	0	28	18	119.0	150	13	36	51

	Avg	AB	H	2B	3B	HR	RBI	BB	SO	OBP	SLG
Runners on	.298	453	135	14	2	16	127	48	49	.368	.444
Scoring Posn	.312	269	84	12	2	10	115	30	24	.374	.483
Close & Late	.337	95	32	3	2	5	14	9	11	.396	.568
None on/out	.322	261	84	18	1	6	6	23	29	.381	.467
vs. 1st Batr (relief)	.480	25	12	2	0	1	6	3	2	.536	.680
First Inning Pitched	.341	246	84	11	2	7	46	29	25	.411	.488
First 15 Pitches	.350	214	75	9	2	7	32	24	16	.419	.509
Pitch 16-30	.314	185	58	6	2	4	27	21	26	.384	.432
Pitch 31-45	.287	167	48	8	0	2	20	10	20	.331	.371
Pitch 46+	.293	447	131	25	2	15	60	38	53	.351	.459
First Pitch	.363	157	57	8	2	3	21	3	0	.378	.497
Ahead in Count	.218	353	77	8	2	7	36	0	97	.231	.312
Behind in Count	.358	313	112	20	2	11	55	44	0	.435	.540
Two Strikes	.238	361	86	15	2	6	32	46	115	.331	.341

Pitcher vs. Batter (career)

Pitches Best Vs.	Avg	AB	H	2B	3B	HR	RBI	BB	SO	OBP	SLG
Randy Milligan	.000	9	0	0	0	0	0	4	1	.308	.000
Tom Brunansky	.182	11	2	1	0	0	1	1	1	.250	.273
Wade Boggs	.214	14	3	0	0	0	2	1	0	.267	.214

Pitches Worst Vs.	Avg	AB	H	2B	3B	HR	RBI	BB	SO	OBP	SLG
Gary Thurman	.556	9	5	1	0	0	3	2	3	.636	.667
Jody Reed	.438	16	7	2	0	0	4	0	1	.438	.563
Don Mattingly	.364	11	4	2	0	0	2	0	0	.364	.545
George Brett	.333	12	4	0	0	0	0	0	1	.333	.333
Bobby Kelly	.308	13	4	0	0	2	3	0	3	.308	.769

Spike Owen — Yankees

Age 33 – Bats Both

	Avg	G	AB	R	H	2B	3B	HR	RBI	BB	SO	HBP	GDP	SB	CS	OBP	SLG	IBB	SH	SF	#Pit	#P/PA	GB	FB	G/F
1993 Season	.234	103	334	41	78	16	2	2	20	29	30	0	5	3	2	.294	.311	2	3	1	1251	3.41	125	118	1.06
Last Five Years	.245	655	2034	239	498	95	22	23	162	267	225	4	43	25	20	.331	.347	53	19	19	8736	3.73	791	659	1.20

1993 Season

	Avg	AB	H	2B	3B	HR	RBI	BB	SO	OBP	SLG
vs. Left	.248	137	34	6	1	1	8	8	14	.290	.328
vs. Right	.223	197	44	10	1	1	12	21	16	.297	.299
Groundball	.214	56	12	1	0	1	7	4	9	.267	.286
Flyball	.270	63	17	7	0	0	5	7	4	.343	.381
Home	.210	157	33	6	1	1	9	10	17	.256	.280
Away	.254	177	45	10	1	1	11	19	13	.327	.339
Day	.304	102	31	4	1	2	10	11	10	.368	.422
Night	.203	232	47	12	1	0	10	18	20	.260	.263
Grass	.241	278	67	12	1	2	17	24	26	.300	.313
Turf	.196	56	11	4	1	0	3	5	4	.262	.304
First Pitch	.235	51	12	2	0	0	3	2	0	.259	.275
Ahead in Count	.283	99	28	6	1	1	12	20	0	.403	.394
Behind in Count	.168	119	20	2	0	1	5	0	28	.168	.210
Two Strikes	.148	108	16	2	0	1	4	7	30	.200	.194

	Avg	AB	H	2B	3B	HR	RBI	BB	SO	OBP	SLG
Scoring Posn	.188	85	16	4	0	1	19	7	10	.247	.271
Close & Late	.200	45	9	3	1	0	0	6	4	.294	.311
None on/out	.297	74	22	6	1	1	1	7	9	.358	.446
Batting #2	.169	59	10	2	0	0	2	3	11	.210	.203
Batting #8	.275	204	56	11	2	2	14	24	16	.351	.377
Other	.169	71	12	3	0	0	4	2	3	.189	.211
April	.296	71	21	3	0	0	3	8	7	.367	.338
May	.234	94	22	6	0	1	8	9	10	.301	.330
June	.257	74	19	3	1	1	5	10	6	.345	.365
July	.164	61	10	1	1	0	2	2	4	.188	.213
August	.211	19	4	2	0	0	0	0	2	.211	.316
September/October	.133	15	2	1	0	0	2	0	1	.133	.200
Pre-All Star	.254	264	67	12	1	2	17	29	25	.328	.330
Post-All Star	.157	70	11	4	1	0	3	0	5	.155	.243

1993 By Position

Position	Avg	AB	H	2B	3B	HR	RBI	BB	SO	OBP	SLG	G	GS	Innings	PO	A	E	DP	Fld Pct	Rng Fctr	In Zone	Outs	Zone Rtg	MLB Zone
As ss	.236	330	78	16	2	2	20	28	28	.295	.315	96	88	797.0	116	310	14	45	.968	4.81	387	332	.858	.880

Last Five Years

	Avg	AB	H	2B	3B	HR	RBI	BB	SO	OBP	SLG
vs. Left	.276	830	229	57	7	11	74	80	92	.338	.401
vs. Right	.223	1204	269	38	15	12	88	187	133	.326	.310
Groundball	.231	653	151	30	7	4	63	92	71	.324	.317
Flyball	.225	476	107	26	4	11	38	63	59	.315	.366
Home	.235	907	213	40	7	12	78	122	101	.323	.334
Away	.253	1127	285	55	15	11	84	145	124	.337	.358
Day	.268	590	158	27	10	11	55	81	75	.354	.403
Night	.235	1444	340	68	12	12	107	186	150	.321	.324
Grass	.234	772	181	27	6	8	56	96	92	.318	.316
Turf	.251	1262	317	68	16	15	106	171	133	.339	.366
First Pitch	.278	209	58	12	1	5	20	33	0	.376	.416
Ahead in Count	.318	557	177	37	9	7	64	147	0	.459	.454
Behind in Count	.207	810	168	26	8	5	49	0	191	.212	.278
Two Strikes	.192	845	162	26	8	6	51	75	225	.256	.263

	Avg	AB	H	2B	3B	HR	RBI	BB	SO	OBP	SLG
Scoring Posn	.234	471	110	19	4	3	128	106	61	.363	.310
Close & Late	.262	363	95	15	4	7	36	50	49	.347	.383
None on/out	.246	480	118	24	9	5	5	61	45	.333	.365
Batting #2	.270	345	93	19	3	3	25	29	47	.323	.368
Batting #8	.245	1431	350	66	18	17	118	212	152	.341	.352
Other	.213	258	55	10	1	3	19	26	26	.282	.295
April	.284	320	91	19	6	3	32	32	33	.346	.409
May	.217	396	86	16	0	9	35	66	47	.329	.326
June	.232	384	89	22	4	5	30	70	38	.348	.349
July	.226	274	62	10	3	2	15	35	29	.314	.307
August	.274	303	83	15	4	2	29	35	40	.347	.370
September/October	.244	357	87	13	5	2	21	29	38	.299	.325
Pre-All Star	.245	1231	301	62	11	19	106	186	134	.343	.359
Post-All Star	.245	803	197	33	11	4	56	81	91	.312	.329

Batter vs. Pitcher (since 1984)

Hits Best Against	Avg	AB	H	2B	3B	HR	RBI	BB	SO	OBP	SLG
Juan Agosto	.545	11	6	2	1	1	3	0	0	.545	1.182
Tom Browning	.500	24	12	4	1	1	2	1	1	.520	.875
Greg Swindell	.500	12	6	1	0	0	1	1	0	.538	.583
Ken Hill	.357	14	5	0	2	0	2	3	1	.471	.643
Paul Assenmacher	.333	12	4	1	0	1	1	2	3	.429	.667

Hits Worst Against	Avg	AB	H	2B	3B	HR	RBI	BB	SO	OBP	SLG
Orel Hershiser	.000	13	0	0	0	0	0	2	2	.133	.000
Bill Wegman	.000	10	0	0	0	0	0	1	1	.091	.000
Tom Candiotti	.034	29	1	0	0	0	0	2	2	.097	.034
Mike Bielecki	.042	24	1	0	0	0	0	1	5	.080	.042
Joe Boever	.067	15	1	0	0	0	1	0	3	.063	.067

Jayhawk Owens — Rockies

Age 25 – Bats Right (groundball hitter)

	Avg	G	AB	R	H	2B	3B	HR	RBI	BB	SO	HBP	GDP	SB	CS	OBP	SLG	IBB	SH	SF	#Pit	#P/PA	GB	FB	G/F
1993 Season	.209	33	86	12	18	5	0	3	6	6	30	2	1	1	0	.277	.372	1	0	0	317	3.37	24	13	1.85

1993 Season

	Avg	AB	H	2B	3B	HR	RBI	BB	SO	OBP	SLG
vs. Left	.217	23	5	1	0	1	2	2	4	.280	.391
vs. Right	.206	63	13	4	0	2	4	4	26	.275	.365

	Avg	AB	H	2B	3B	HR	RBI	BB	SO	OBP	SLG
Scoring Posn	.231	13	3	0	0	0	3	5	7	.444	.231
Close & Late	.182	11	2	1	0	0	1	1	3	.250	.273

Mike Pagliarulo — Orioles

Age 34 – Bats Left

	Avg	G	AB	R	H	2B	3B	HR	RBI	BB	SO	HBP	GDP	SB	CS	OBP	SLG	IBB	SH	SF	#Pit	#P/PA	GB	FB	G/F
1993 Season	.303	116	370	55	112	25	4	9	44	26	49	6	7	6	6	.357	.465	2	2	1	1419	3.50	145	107	1.36
Last Five Years	.254	531	1609	163	409	89	6	29	157	124	269	16	34	12	12	.312	.371	12	7	8	6236	3.54	585	469	1.25

1993 Season

	Avg	AB	H	2B	3B	HR	RBI	BB	SO	OBP	SLG
vs. Left	.417	36	15	2	0	0	2	2	4	.462	.472
vs. Right	.290	334	97	23	4	9	42	24	45	.346	.464
Groundball	.309	81	25	4	0	2	7	5	15	.349	.432
Flyball	.267	86	23	8	0	5	14	6	15	.344	.535
Home	.343	169	58	14	3	5	23	12	22	.393	.550
Away	.269	201	54	11	1	4	21	14	27	.327	.393
Day	.331	127	42	10	0	1	8	8	17	.386	.433
Night	.288	243	70	15	4	8	36	18	32	.342	.481
Grass	.293	215	63	13	1	7	31	15	22	.349	.460
Turf	.316	155	49	12	3	2	13	11	27	.369	.471
First Pitch	.343	70	24	6	0	1	6	2	0	.373	.471
Ahead in Count	.398	93	37	9	1	2	13	13	0	.472	.581
Behind in Count	.232	138	32	8	0	4	13	0	43	.254	.377
Two Strikes	.228	145	33	6	3	3	16	11	49	.291	.372

	Avg	AB	H	2B	3B	HR	RBI	BB	SO	OBP	SLG
Scoring Posn	.303	99	30	4	0	7	39	8	14	.358	.556
Close & Late	.279	61	17	3	0	0	2	4	9	.328	.328
None on/out	.286	77	22	5	0	0	0	6	10	.360	.351
Batting #7	.210	105	22	3	0	0	6	7	14	.263	.238
Batting #8	.331	139	46	12	3	2	14	8	17	.376	.504
Other	.349	126	44	10	1	7	24	11	18	.414	.611
April	.269	52	14	1	4	0	5	2	3	.296	.442
May	.328	58	19	5	0	2	6	4	10	.371	.517
June	.273	33	9	4	0	1	7	3	2	.351	.485
July	.282	71	20	4	0	0	1	4	14	.346	.338
August	.333	69	23	5	0	3	13	7	12	.397	.536
September/October	.310	87	27	6	0	3	12	6	8	.362	.483
Pre-All Star	.282	181	51	12	4	3	18	9	24	.319	.442
Post-All Star	.323	189	61	13	0	6	26	17	25	.392	.487

1993 By Position

Position	Avg	AB	H	2B	3B	HR	RBI	BB	SO	OBP	SLG	G	GS	Innings	PO	A	E	DP	Fld Pct	Rng Fctr	In Zone	Outs	Zone Rtg	MLB Zone
As Pinch Hitter	.222	9	2	0	0	1	3	1	4	.364	.556	11	0	---	---	---	---	---	---	---	---	---	---	---
As 3b	.307	349	107	24	4	8	41	25	42	.361	.467	107	98	861.0	69	184	8	17	.969	2.64	251	208	.829	.834

Last Five Years

	Avg	AB	H	2B	3B	HR	RBI	BB	SO	OBP	SLG
vs. Left	.257	218	56	9	0	4	21	24	46	.337	.353
vs. Right	.254	1391	353	80	6	25	136	100	223	.308	.374
Groundball	.238	484	115	24	0	8	40	33	103	.288	.337
Flyball	.244	349	85	26	1	9	37	26	64	.309	.401
Home	.270	756	204	42	4	15	87	62	140	.331	.396
Away	.240	853	205	47	2	14	70	62	129	.296	.349
Day	.263	491	129	31	1	8	36	42	81	.329	.379
Night	.250	1118	280	58	5	21	121	82	188	.305	.368
Grass	.242	976	236	51	3	20	91	81	160	.306	.362
Turf	.273	633	173	38	3	9	66	43	109	.322	.385
First Pitch	.324	287	93	26	1	5	35	8	0	.348	.474
Ahead in Count	.328	369	121	22	1	9	47	59	0	.421	.466
Behind in Count	.186	671	125	27	1	10	38	0	237	.197	.274
Two Strikes	.183	677	124	29	4	6	43	54	269	.246	.264

	Avg	AB	H	2B	3B	HR	RBI	BB	SO	OBP	SLG
Scoring Posn	.239	393	94	16	1	9	123	40	73	.309	.354
Close & Late	.255	255	65	16	1	2	15	23	49	.317	.349
None on/out	.246	374	92	18	1	8	8	30	69	.311	.364
Batting #6	.257	474	122	29	0	12	50	36	84	.313	.395
Batting #7	.228	499	114	22	0	8	41	44	82	.295	.321
Other	.272	636	173	38	6	9	66	44	103	.326	.393
April	.188	170	32	3	4	0	10	7	21	.223	.253
May	.288	264	76	22	0	7	28	27	39	.357	.451
June	.239	238	57	15	1	5	24	19	37	.303	.374
July	.279	283	79	17	1	2	19	26	57	.350	.367
August	.241	353	85	15	0	6	39	23	70	.287	.334
September/October	.266	301	80	17	0	9	37	22	45	.322	.412
Pre-All Star	.246	773	190	48	5	13	64	60	120	.305	.371
Post-All Star	.262	836	219	41	1	16	93	64	149	.319	.371

Batter vs. Pitcher (career)

Hits Best Against	Avg	AB	H	2B	3B	HR	RBI	BB	SO	OBP	SLG
Jeff Russell	.455	11	5	0	0	2	9	2	2	.538	1.000
Alex Fernandez	.444	9	4	1	0	0	3	2	2	.500	.556
Tim Leary	.400	25	10	1	0	1	2	1	3	.423	.560
Steve Ontiveros	.308	13	4	0	0	2	3	2	4	.400	.769
Mike Henneman	.308	13	4	2	0	1	2	0	4	.308	.692

Hits Worst Against	Avg	AB	H	2B	3B	HR	RBI	BB	SO	OBP	SLG
Edwin Nunez	.000	11	0	0	0	0	1	0	4	.000	.000
Curt Young	.063	16	1	0	0	0	0	1	4	.118	.063
Bob Welch	.074	27	2	0	0	0	0	3	9	.167	.074
David Cone	.091	11	1	0	0	0	0	0	1	.091	.091
Jimmy Key	.111	18	2	0	0	0	0	1	7	.158	.111

Tom Pagnozzi — Cardinals

Age 31 – Bats Right

	Avg	G	AB	R	H	2B	3B	HR	RBI	BB	SO	HBP	GDP	SB	CS	OBP	SLG	IBB	SH	SF	#Pit	#P/PA	GB	FB	G/F
1993 Season	.258	92	330	31	85	15	1	7	41	19	30	1	7	1	0	.296	.373	6	0	5	1203	3.39	110	141	0.78
Last Five Years	.254	492	1574	125	400	82	9	18	168	103	213	8	39	13	19	.300	.352	24	12	16	5769	3.37	575	492	1.17

1993 Season

	Avg	AB	H	2B	3B	HR	RBI	BB	SO	OBP	SLG
vs. Left	.280	75	21	2	0	2	12	5	4	.313	.387
vs. Right	.251	255	64	13	1	5	29	14	26	.290	.369
Groundball	.290	93	27	5	0	2	13	6	8	.330	.409
Flyball	.200	65	13	2	1	1	8	4	7	.246	.308
Home	.238	143	34	6	1	1	16	10	10	.287	.315
Away	.273	187	51	9	0	6	25	9	20	.303	.417
Day	.294	109	32	4	0	4	18	3	8	.316	.440
Night	.240	221	53	11	1	3	23	16	22	.286	.339
Grass	.347	124	43	7	0	4	21	7	7	.376	.500
Turf	.204	206	42	8	1	3	20	12	23	.248	.296

	Avg	AB	H	2B	3B	HR	RBI	BB	SO	OBP	SLG
Scoring Posn	.250	100	25	3	1	1	34	11	7	.310	.330
Close & Late	.213	61	13	1	0	1	8	2	4	.242	.279
None on/out	.342	76	26	6	0	1	1	1	4	.351	.461
Batting #7	.214	42	9	0	0	0	2	0	4	.214	.214
Batting #8	.262	286	75	15	1	7	38	19	26	.305	.395
Other	.500	2	1	0	0	0	1	0	0	.500	.500
April	.164	61	10	1	0	1	4	6	3	.235	.230
May	.211	19	4	2	0	1	3	2	0	.286	.474
June	.353	34	12	0	1	2	9	1	4	.361	.588
July	.268	71	19	3	0	0	5	3	10	.293	.310

1993 Season

	Avg	AB	H	2B	3B	HR	RBI	BB	SO	OBP	SLG
First Pitch	.265	49	13	3	0	2	6	5	0	.316	.449
Ahead in Count	.217	83	18	3	0	1	8	7	0	.278	.289
Behind in Count	.263	137	36	3	1	4	21	0	28	.264	.387
Two Strikes	.244	119	29	4	1	3	16	7	30	.289	.370

	Avg	AB	H	2B	3B	HR	RBI	BB	SO	OBP	SLG
August	.250	88	22	5	0	3	12	2	5	.272	.409
September/October	.316	57	18	4	0	0	8	5	8	.365	.386
Pre-All Star	.231	147	34	4	1	4	19	10	12	.277	.354
Post-All Star	.279	183	51	11	0	3	22	9	18	.311	.388

1993 By Position

Position	Avg	AB	H	2B	3B	HR	RBI	BB	SO	OBP	SLG	G	GS	Innings	PO	A	E	DP	Fld Pct	Rng Fctr	In Zone	Outs	Zone Rtg	MLB Zone
As c	.258	329	85	15	1	7	41	19	30	.297	.374	92	90	787.0	421	44	4	4	.991	---	---	---	---	---

Last Five Years

	Avg	AB	H	2B	3B	HR	RBI	BB	SO	OBP	SLG
vs. Left	.249	571	142	29	3	10	63	45	88	.301	.363
vs. Right	.257	1003	258	53	6	8	105	58	125	.300	.346
Groundball	.242	561	136	29	1	6	53	42	69	.297	.330
Flyball	.221	317	70	17	3	2	30	25	56	.279	.312
Home	.239	727	174	31	5	8	72	60	95	.301	.329
Away	.267	847	226	51	4	10	96	43	118	.300	.372
Day	.273	487	133	29	3	8	71	35	58	.321	.394
Night	.246	1087	267	53	6	10	97	68	155	.291	.333
Grass	.291	454	132	30	3	5	61	23	56	.323	.403
Turf	.239	1120	268	52	6	13	107	80	157	.291	.331
First Pitch	.284	264	75	18	4	3	30	22	0	.338	.417
Ahead in Count	.308	325	100	20	2	6	44	48	0	.394	.437
Behind in Count	.218	719	157	28	2	8	64	0	194	.221	.296
Two Strikes	.197	635	125	25	1	6	53	33	213	.241	.268

	Avg	AB	H	2B	3B	HR	RBI	BB	SO	OBP	SLG
Scoring Posn	.248	436	108	24	4	3	140	47	73	.313	.342
Close & Late	.196	306	60	10	0	3	26	17	50	.245	.258
None on/out	.247	368	91	17	2	3	3	20	44	.288	.329
Batting #7	.254	782	199	44	6	6	86	47	107	.298	.349
Batting #8	.260	724	188	34	3	12	74	53	88	.311	.365
Other	.191	68	13	4	0	0	8	3	18	.219	.250
April	.238	214	51	7	1	1	16	12	24	.275	.294
May	.266	229	61	14	2	3	25	19	28	.328	.384
June	.255	239	61	9	2	6	36	14	32	.295	.385
July	.243	267	65	11	3	3	30	22	44	.301	.341
August	.230	326	75	23	1	3	28	18	43	.269	.334
September/October	.291	299	87	18	0	2	33	18	42	.334	.371
Pre-All Star	.258	780	201	34	6	11	88	47	99	.300	.359
Post-All Star	.251	794	199	48	3	7	80	56	114	.300	.345

Batter vs. Pitcher (career)

Hits Best Against	Avg	AB	H	2B	3B	HR	RBI	BB	SO	OBP	SLG
Terry Mulholland	.458	24	11	2	0	1	6	0	3	.440	.667
Tom Browning	.455	11	5	2	0	0	0	2	1	.538	.636
Frank Castillo	.417	12	5	1	1	1	5	0	1	.417	.917
John Smiley	.368	19	7	3	0	1	3	2	5	.429	.684
Pete Schourek	.357	14	5	3	0	1	4	0	1	.357	.786

Hits Worst Against	Avg	AB	H	2B	3B	HR	RBI	BB	SO	OBP	SLG
John Franco	.000	13	0	0	0	0	0	2	5	.133	.000
Mark Portugal	.000	12	0	0	0	0	0	1	1	.077	.000
Bill Landrum	.000	11	0	0	0	0	0	0	2	.000	.000
Norm Charlton	.000	10	0	0	0	0	0	1	2	.091	.000
Mel Rojas	.083	12	1	0	0	0	0	0	2	.083	.083

Lance Painter — Rockies

Age 26 – Pitches Left

	ERA	W	L	Sv	G	GS	IP	BB	SO	Avg	H	2B	3B	HR	RBI	OBP	SLG	CG	ShO	Sup	QS	#P/S	SB	CS	GB	FB	G/F
1993 Season	6.00	2	2	0	10	6	39.0	9	16	.333	52	10	3	5	24	.370	.532	1	0	5.08	1	86	2	4	51	51	1.00

1993 Season

	ERA	W	L	Sv	G	GS	IP	H	HR	BB	SO
Home	7.63	1	1	0	4	2	15.1	24	3	4	9
Away	4.94	1	1	0	6	4	23.2	28	2	5	7

	Avg	AB	H	2B	3B	HR	RBI	BB	SO	OBP	SLG
vs. Left	.226	31	7	0	2	1	6	5	4	.333	.452
vs. Right	.360	125	45	10	1	4	18	4	12	.380	.552

Donn Pall — Phillies

Age 32 – Pitches Right (groundball pitcher)

	ERA	W	L	Sv	G	GS	IP	BB	SO	Avg	H	2B	3B	HR	RBI	OBP	SLG	GF	IR	IRS	Hld	SvOp	SB	CS	GB	FB	G/F
1993 Season	3.07	3	3	1	47	0	76.1	14	40	.260	77	11	0	6	37	.297	.358	11	34	15	9	2	4	0	114	89	1.28
Last Five Years	3.40	22	17	10	246	0	383.1	104	204	.254	368	59	5	38	188	.311	.381	41	205	74	41	18	28	9	634	372	1.70

1993 Season

	ERA	W	L	Sv	G	GS	IP	H	HR	BB	SO
Home	4.50	2	2	1	26	0	34.0	41	3	9	20
Away	1.91	1	1	0	21	0	42.1	36	3	5	20
Starter	0.00	0	0	0	0	0	0.0	0	0	0	0
Reliever	3.07	3	3	1	47	0	76.1	77	6	14	40
0 Days rest	2.25	2	0	0	5	0	8.0	8	1	2	7
1 or 2 Days rest	5.11	0	1	0	20	0	24.2	29	3	4	11
3+ Days rest	2.06	1	2	1	22	0	43.2	40	2	8	22
Pre-All Star	2.30	2	2	1	23	0	43.0	35	3	7	21
Post-All Star	4.05	1	1	0	24	0	33.1	42	3	7	19

	Avg	AB	H	2B	3B	HR	RBI	BB	SO	OBP	SLG
vs. Left	.263	152	40	8	0	3	19	8	18	.300	.375
vs. Right	.257	144	37	3	0	3	18	6	22	.294	.340
Scoring Posn	.289	90	26	1	0	1	30	6	11	.330	.333
Close & Late	.253	87	22	4	0	0	7	3	13	.286	.299
None on/out	.250	72	18	2	0	4	4	3	8	.280	.444
First Pitch	.297	37	11	1	0	0	8	3	0	.341	.324
Ahead in Count	.203	143	29	4	0	3	13	0	35	.208	.294
Behind in Count	.404	52	21	3	0	2	9	6	0	.466	.577
Two Strikes	.215	130	28	5	0	3	15	5	40	.250	.323

Last Five Years

	ERA	W	L	Sv	G	GS	IP	H	HR	BB	SO
Home	3.99	12	7	6	127	0	191.2	193	18	54	112
Away	2.82	10	10	4	119	0	191.2	175	20	50	92
Day	3.18	6	6	3	69	0	119.0	109	14	33	49
Night	3.51	16	11	7	177	0	264.1	259	24	71	155
Grass	3.57	20	13	9	206	0	315.1	307	33	91	174
Turf	2.65	2	4	1	40	0	68.0	61	5	13	30
April	2.16	2	1	2	37	0	58.1	53	4	10	38
May	3.25	4	4	0	46	0	63.2	53	3	21	38
June	3.06	3	3	2	44	0	61.2	57	7	17	23
July	3.89	6	3	4	43	0	71.2	75	5	21	32
August	3.86	4	6	1	40	0	65.1	69	9	16	38
September/October	4.02	3	0	1	36	0	62.2	61	10	19	35
Starter	0.00	0	0	0	0	0	0.0	0	0	0	0
Reliever	3.40	22	17	10	246	0	383.1	368	38	104	204
0 Days rest	4.78	4	1	0	25	0	32.0	34	5	10	18

	Avg	AB	H	2B	3B	HR	RBI	BB	SO	OBP	SLG
vs. Left	.256	633	162	26	4	11	70	53	94	.315	.362
vs. Right	.253	813	206	33	1	27	118	51	110	.308	.396
Inning 1-6	.228	413	94	17	1	7	66	26	65	.279	.324
Inning 7+	.265	1033	274	42	4	31	122	78	139	.324	.404
None on	.243	769	187	30	4	23	23	47	116	.298	.382
Runners on	.267	677	181	29	1	15	165	57	88	.326	.380
Scoring Posn	.271	414	112	13	1	10	149	48	60	.343	.379
Close & Late	.256	468	120	16	3	10	44	45	62	.328	.368
None on/out	.257	331	85	12	2	13	13	18	44	.305	.423
vs. 1st Batr (relief)	.230	222	51	4	2	5	33	12	30	.279	.333
First Inning Pitched	.257	791	203	24	5	19	138	62	107	.318	.372
First 15 Pitches	.259	803	208	28	5	20	118	48	98	.311	.381
Pitch 16-30	.240	434	104	15	0	11	46	37	80	.303	.350
Pitch 31-45	.280	175	49	13	0	7	23	17	22	.345	.474
Pitch 46+	.206	34	7	3	0	0	1	2	4	.250	.294

Last Five Years

	ERA	W	L	Sv	G	GS	IP	H	HR	BB	SO
1 or 2 Days rest	3.51	10	10	3	114	0	164.0	172	17	44	97
3+ Days rest	3.07	8	6	7	107	0	187.1	162	16	50	89
Pre-All Star	2.93	10	8	5	142	0	206.0	182	15	56	107
Post-All Star	3.96	12	9	5	104	0	177.1	186	23	48	97

	Avg	AB	H	2B	3B	HR	RBI	BB	SO	OBP	SLG
First Pitch	.302	232	70	10	1	3	36	21	0	.371	.392
Ahead in Count	.205	634	130	21	0	18	78	0	178	.215	.323
Behind in Count	.315	298	94	16	1	12	48	44	0	.406	.497
Two Strikes	.185	607	112	22	2	15	58	38	204	.237	.301

Pitcher vs. Batter (career)

Pitches Best Vs.	Avg	AB	H	2B	3B	HR	RBI	BB	SO	OBP	SLG
Gary Gaetti	.091	11	1	0	0	0	0	0	1	.091	.091
Joe Carter	.091	11	1	0	0	0	0	1	1	.167	.091
Terry Steinbach	.091	11	1	0	0	0	0	1	2	.167	.091
Travis Fryman	.091	11	1	0	0	0	1	0	0	.091	.091
Robin Yount	.154	13	2	0	0	0	0	0	0	.154	.154

Pitches Worst Vs.	Avg	AB	H	2B	3B	HR	RBI	BB	SO	OBP	SLG
Rickey Henderson	.455	11	5	1	0	1	6	1	0	.500	.818
Mark McGwire	.417	12	5	1	0	1	2	2	1	.500	.750
Mike Greenwell	.400	10	4	1	0	1	1	1	1	.455	.800
Rob Deer	.385	13	5	0	0	3	9	0	4	.385	1.077
Rafael Palmeiro	.364	11	4	2	0	1	2	3	0	.500	.818

Rafael Palmeiro — Rangers

Age 29 – Bats Left

	Avg	G	AB	R	H	2B	3B	HR	RBI	BB	SO	HBP	GDP	SB	CS	OBP	SLG	IBB	SH	SF	#Pit	#P/PA	GB	FB	G/F
1993 Season	.295	160	597	124	176	40	2	37	105	73	85	5	8	22	3	.371	.554	22	2	9	2445	3.56	171	230	0.74
Last Five Years	.296	788	2993	471	887	174	19	107	431	316	347	30	78	35	15	.366	.474	49	13	32	12181	3.60	1016	1004	1.01

1993 Season

	Avg	AB	H	2B	3B	HR	RBI	BB	SO	OBP	SLG
vs. Left	.268	149	40	7	0	2	18	12	24	.323	.356
vs. Right	.304	448	136	33	2	35	87	61	61	.387	.621
Groundball	.330	109	36	8	1	7	19	11	11	.387	.615
Flyball	.288	111	32	7	1	10	28	17	16	.377	.640
Home	.282	294	83	19	1	22	58	36	42	.360	.578
Away	.307	303	93	21	1	15	47	37	43	.382	.531
Day	.290	138	40	12	1	4	24	20	14	.374	.478
Night	.296	459	136	28	1	33	81	53	71	.370	.577
Grass	.290	511	148	34	2	32	90	66	72	.370	.552
Turf	.326	86	28	6	0	5	15	7	13	.381	.570
First Pitch	.273	77	21	5	0	5	13	19	0	.420	.532
Ahead in Count	.361	155	56	16	0	11	31	25	0	.446	.677
Behind in Count	.252	238	60	13	1	9	37	0	71	.255	.429
Two Strikes	.202	228	46	7	0	14	33	29	85	.293	.417

	Avg	AB	H	2B	3B	HR	RBI	BB	SO	OBP	SLG
Scoring Posn	.266	124	33	7	2	4	57	44	19	.435	.452
Close & Late	.292	72	21	3	0	6	15	11	14	.376	.583
None on/out	.372	137	51	16	0	9	9	9	15	.419	.686
Batting #3	.316	376	119	29	0	28	74	53	60	.403	.617
Batting #5	.289	97	28	7	0	7	18	11	13	.355	.577
Other	.234	124	29	4	2	2	13	9	12	.281	.347
April	.183	82	15	3	1	1	8	7	7	.242	.280
May	.286	105	30	5	1	6	17	9	14	.339	.524
June	.348	92	32	6	0	6	14	7	15	.396	.609
July	.426	108	46	13	0	11	34	14	10	.484	.852
August	.257	101	26	5	0	8	16	18	18	.385	.545
September/October	.248	109	27	8	0	5	16	18	21	.349	.459
Pre-All Star	.301	326	98	18	2	16	52	28	39	.353	.515
Post-All Star	.288	271	78	22	0	21	53	45	46	.392	.601

1993 By Position

Position	Avg	AB	H	2B	3B	HR	RBI	BB	SO	OBP	SLG	G	GS	Innings	PO	A	E	DP	Fld Pct	Rng Fctr	In Zone	Outs	Zone Rtg	MLB Zone
As 1b	.295	596	176	40	2	37	105	72	85	.371	.555	160	158	1395.0	1388	143	5	135	.997	---	295	249	.844	.834

Last Five Years

	Avg	AB	H	2B	3B	HR	RBI	BB	SO	OBP	SLG
vs. Left	.284	867	246	39	5	23	123	65	107	.338	.420
vs. Right	.302	2126	641	135	14	84	308	251	240	.377	.497
Groundball	.293	782	229	41	7	25	96	72	90	.356	.459
Flyball	.306	656	201	34	6	29	118	81	64	.384	.509
Home	.287	1447	415	80	12	55	209	174	172	.365	.473
Away	.305	1546	472	94	7	52	222	142	175	.366	.476
Day	.297	589	175	37	4	16	100	63	61	.364	.455
Night	.296	2404	712	137	15	91	331	253	286	.366	.479
Grass	.295	2530	746	137	18	95	376	275	287	.366	.476
Turf	.305	463	141	37	1	12	55	41	60	.367	.467
First Pitch	.322	376	121	24	3	13	54	35	0	.384	.505
Ahead in Count	.345	803	277	65	4	40	132	168	0	.454	.585
Behind in Count	.253	1218	308	51	6	30	146	0	300	.260	.378
Two Strikes	.231	1173	271	51	6	34	150	107	347	.300	.372

	Avg	AB	H	2B	3B	HR	RBI	BB	SO	OBP	SLG
Scoring Posn	.275	695	191	39	7	12	281	142	92	.389	.403
Close & Late	.257	459	118	21	3	20	64	47	63	.325	.447
None on/out	.298	604	180	37	3	24	24	42	61	.350	.488
Batting #2	.285	877	250	48	8	29	103	82	109	.350	.457
Batting #3	.301	1735	523	109	10	61	273	182	190	.370	.481
Other	.299	381	114	17	1	17	55	52	48	.381	.483
April	.273	385	105	23	4	12	60	39	44	.343	.447
May	.318	534	170	32	4	14	70	46	57	.374	.472
June	.292	517	151	31	0	16	66	44	62	.353	.445
July	.332	500	166	27	4	29	97	49	51	.392	.576
August	.270	540	146	26	4	18	67	64	68	.353	.433
September/October	.288	517	149	35	3	18	71	74	65	.376	.472
Pre-All Star	.302	1612	487	95	11	50	228	149	181	.363	.468
Post-All Star	.290	1381	400	79	8	57	203	167	166	.368	.482

Batter vs. Pitcher (career)

Hits Best Against	Avg	AB	H	2B	3B	HR	RBI	BB	SO	OBP	SLG
Mike Jackson	.778	9	7	1	0	2	3	2	1	.818	1.556
Mark Leiter	.647	17	11	2	0	3	7	4	0	.714	1.294
Bob Milacki	.600	15	9	2	0	2	5	5	0	.700	1.133
Rick Sutcliffe	.545	11	6	2	0	2	7	3	1	.643	1.273
Bill Gullickson	.471	17	8	1	0	4	7	0	1	.471	1.235

Hits Worst Against	Avg	AB	H	2B	3B	HR	RBI	BB	SO	OBP	SLG
Steve Bedrosian	.000	10	0	0	0	0	0	2	1	.167	.000
John Smiley	.050	20	1	0	0	0	0	4	2	.208	.050
Randy Johnson	.059	17	1	0	0	0	0	0	2	.059	.059
Mike Mussina	.091	22	2	1	0	0	1	1	3	.125	.136
Rick Honeycutt	.100	20	2	0	0	0	0	0	2	.100	.100

Dean Palmer — Rangers

Age 25 – Bats Right (flyball hitter)

	Avg	G	AB	R	H	2B	3B	HR	RBI	BB	SO	HBP	GDP	SB	CS	OBP	SLG	IBB	SH	SF	#Pit	#P/PA	GB	FB	G/F
1993 Season	.245	148	519	88	127	31	2	33	96	53	154	8	5	11	10	.321	.503	4	0	5	2279	3.90	103	176	0.59
Career (1989-1993)	.225	397	1347	200	303	67	4	74	206	147	418	15	17	21	16	.306	.445	6	3	10	6103	4.01	288	441	0.65

1993 Season

	Avg	AB	H	2B	3B	HR	RBI	BB	SO	OBP	SLG
vs. Left	.257	101	26	4	0	6	17	16	32	.372	.475
vs. Right	.242	418	101	27	2	27	79	37	122	.308	.510
Groundball	.184	98	18	3	1	6	26	14	30	.296	.418
Flyball	.236	110	26	8	0	9	17	9	30	.306	.555
Home	.246	252	62	12	0	12	32	28	78	.329	.437
Away	.243	267	65	19	2	21	64	25	76	.314	.566

	Avg	AB	H	2B	3B	HR	RBI	BB	SO	OBP	SLG
Scoring Posn	.200	140	28	8	1	6	55	21	41	.304	.400
Close & Late	.167	78	13	4	0	4	9	12	28	.278	.372
None on/out	.357	115	41	8	1	10	10	10	26	.408	.704
Batting #6	.271	199	54	13	1	16	50	21	64	.339	.588
Batting #7	.258	159	41	10	1	11	28	18	43	.343	.541
Other	.199	161	32	8	0	6	18	14	47	.278	.360

1993 Season

	Avg	AB	H	2B	3B	HR	RBI	BB	SO	OBP	SLG		Avg	AB	H	2B	3B	HR	RBI	BB	SO	OBP	SLG
Day	.273	143	39	13	0	12	40	12	39	.333	.615	April	.286	70	20	7	0	7	15	8	13	.370	.686
Night	.234	376	88	18	2	21	56	41	115	.317	.460	May	.210	105	22	7	0	6	18	13	42	.297	.448
Grass	.257	443	114	27	2	28	80	47	129	.335	.517	June	.213	75	16	6	1	3	12	11	22	.307	.440
Turf	.171	76	13	4	0	5	16	6	25	.238	.421	July	.247	93	23	2	1	5	20	5	26	.311	.452
First Pitch	.277	65	18	5	0	5	17	3	0	.333	.585	August	.253	91	23	4	0	7	19	8	27	.324	.527
Ahead in Count	.362	94	34	6	1	7	23	27	0	.504	.670	September/October	.271	85	23	5	0	5	12	8	24	.333	.506
Behind in Count	.180	250	45	10	0	13	34	0	133	.188	.376	Pre-All Star	.238	286	68	21	2	21	65	34	86	.323	.545
Two Strikes	.157	280	44	9	0	11	27	23	154	.222	.307	Post-All Star	.253	233	59	10	0	12	31	19	68	.319	.451

1993 By Position

Position	Avg	AB	H	2B	3B	HR	RBI	BB	SO	OBP	SLG	G	GS	Innings	PO	A	E	DP	Fld Pct	Rng Fctr	In Zone	Outs	Zone Rtg	MLB Zone
As 3b	.245	518	127	31	2	33	96	53	153	.322	.504	148	144	1259.0	86	256	29	21	.922	2.44	348	279	.802	.834

Career (1989-1993)

	Avg	AB	H	2B	3B	HR	RBI	BB	SO	OBP	SLG		Avg	AB	H	2B	3B	HR	RBI	BB	SO	OBP	SLG
vs. Left	.250	336	84	16	0	23	53	45	108	.342	.503	Scoring Posn	.198	324	64	12	1	15	118	44	101	.295	.380
vs. Right	.217	1011	219	51	4	51	153	102	310	.294	.426	Close & Late	.213	221	47	10	1	14	32	31	73	.308	.457
Groundball	.222	297	66	10	3	19	59	39	86	.321	.468	None on/out	.290	317	92	23	1	19	19	35	81	.364	.549
Flyball	.220	322	71	22	0	21	52	36	103	.305	.484	Batting #6	.237	451	107	25	2	26	77	53	149	.317	.475
Home	.223	641	143	28	1	29	78	82	205	.319	.406	Batting #7	.214	378	81	17	2	23	55	36	119	.288	.452
Away	.227	706	160	39	3	45	128	65	213	.294	.482	Other	.222	518	115	25	0	25	74	58	150	.310	.415
Day	.241	324	78	23	1	19	62	27	99	.304	.494	April	.267	146	39	9	0	12	28	22	39	.366	.575
Night	.220	1023	225	44	3	55	144	120	319	.307	.430	May	.214	206	44	17	0	9	30	16	76	.276	.427
Grass	.223	1136	253	55	3	58	160	131	349	.308	.430	June	.255	188	48	11	1	9	39	27	50	.345	.468
Turf	.237	211	50	12	1	16	46	16	69	.293	.531	July	.227	256	58	6	2	14	39	27	69	.314	.430
First Pitch	.318	129	41	10	1	11	29	5	0	.360	.667	August	.221	249	55	10	1	14	32	21	77	.288	.438
Ahead in Count	.311	241	75	15	1	15	46	76	0	.478	.568	September/October	.195	302	59	14	0	16	38	34	107	.278	.401
Behind in Count	.163	692	113	23	0	28	80	0	357	.168	.318	Pre-All Star	.245	636	156	38	2	40	129	77	194	.331	.500
Two Strikes	.135	750	101	21	0	23	66	67	418	.207	.255	Post-All Star	.207	711	147	29	2	34	77	70	224	.284	.397

Batter vs. Pitcher (career)

Hits Best Against	Avg	AB	H	2B	3B	HR	RBI	BB	SO	OBP	SLG	Hits Worst Against	Avg	AB	H	2B	3B	HR	RBI	BB	SO	OBP	SLG
Bill Wegman	.429	14	6	2	0	3	6	1	4	.467	1.214	Cal Eldred	.000	10	0	0	0	0	0	1	5	.091	.000
Dave Fleming	.400	20	8	2	0	2	4	0	2	.400	.800	Duane Ward	.000	9	0	0	0	0	0	3	5	.250	.000
Jim Abbott	.389	18	7	0	0	2	5	5	3	.522	.722	John Smiley	.091	11	1	0	0	0	0	0	3	.091	.091
Chuck Finley	.375	16	6	2	0	1	1	1	4	.412	.688	Chris Bosio	.105	19	2	1	0	0	0	1	8	.150	.158
Bill Krueger	.333	9	3	1	0	1	5	3	1	.462	.778	Kevin Appier	.167	12	2	0	0	0	1	0	3	.167	.167

Erik Pappas — Cardinals

Age 28 – Bats Right

	Avg	G	AB	R	H	2B	3B	HR	RBI	BB	SO	HBP	GDP	SB	CS	OBP	SLG	IBB	SH	SF	#Pit	#P/PA	GB	FB	G/F
1993 Season	.276	82	228	25	63	12	0	1	28	35	35	0	7	1	3	.368	.342	2	0	3	1097	4.12	86	70	1.23
Career (1991-1993)	.269	89	245	26	66	12	0	1	30	36	40	0	7	1	3	.359	.331	2	0	3	1162	4.09	90	76	1.18

1993 Season

	Avg	AB	H	2B	3B	HR	RBI	BB	SO	OBP	SLG		Avg	AB	H	2B	3B	HR	RBI	BB	SO	OBP	SLG
vs. Left	.319	69	22	3	0	1	9	14	13	.434	.406	Scoring Posn	.281	64	18	5	0	0	26	13	16	.388	.359
vs. Right	.258	159	41	9	0	0	19	21	22	.339	.314	Close & Late	.295	44	13	4	0	0	4	8	5	.404	.386
Home	.216	116	25	4	0	1	15	13	19	.292	.276	None on/out	.271	48	13	2	0	0	0	5	3	.340	.313
Away	.339	112	38	8	0	0	13	22	16	.441	.411	Batting #7	.289	97	28	5	0	0	7	12	19	.364	.340
First Pitch	.238	21	5	2	0	1	5	1	0	.273	.476	Batting #8	.270	115	31	6	0	1	16	16	15	.353	.348
Ahead in Count	.254	59	15	4	0	0	5	15	0	.400	.322	Other	.250	16	4	1	0	0	5	7	1	.478	.313
Behind in Count	.259	108	28	5	0	0	15	0	29	.255	.306	Pre-All Star	.302	116	35	5	0	1	19	19	11	.394	.371
Two Strikes	.267	116	31	5	0	0	12	19	35	.365	.310	Post-All Star	.250	112	28	7	0	0	9	16	24	.341	.313

Craig Paquette — Athletics

Age 25 – Bats Right

	Avg	G	AB	R	H	2B	3B	HR	RBI	BB	SO	HBP	GDP	SB	CS	OBP	SLG	IBB	SH	SF	#Pit	#P/PA	GB	FB	G/F
1993 Season	.219	105	393	35	86	20	4	12	46	14	108	0	7	4	2	.245	.382	2	1	1	1451	3.55	125	98	1.28

1993 Season

	Avg	AB	H	2B	3B	HR	RBI	BB	SO	OBP	SLG		Avg	AB	H	2B	3B	HR	RBI	BB	SO	OBP	SLG
vs. Left	.228	136	31	4	2	5	15	9	43	.276	.397	Scoring Posn	.229	105	24	5	1	4	35	5	31	.261	.410
vs. Right	.214	257	55	16	2	7	31	5	65	.228	.374	Close & Late	.238	63	15	4	0	3	12	1	23	.250	.444
Groundball	.147	68	10	2	0	1	7	2	16	.171	.221	None on/out	.234	94	22	3	2	3	3	3	22	.258	.404
Flyball	.235	81	19	4	0	4	12	2	21	.250	.432	Batting #6	.297	91	27	7	1	4	14	7	21	.347	.527
Home	.229	170	39	5	2	8	14	8	56	.264	.424	Batting #7	.222	162	36	7	2	4	14	4	49	.241	.364
Away	.211	223	47	15	2	4	32	6	52	.230	.350	Other	.164	140	23	6	1	4	18	3	38	.181	.307
Day	.227	132	30	7	1	4	11	4	39	.248	.386	April	.000	0	0	0	0	0	0	0	0	.000	.000
Night	.215	261	56	13	3	8	35	10	69	.244	.379	May	.000	0	0	0	0	0	0	0	0	.000	.000
Grass	.219	302	66	14	2	9	24	11	84	.246	.368	June	.292	96	28	8	1	4	19	1	28	.296	.521
Turf	.220	91	20	6	2	3	22	3	24	.242	.429	July	.220	91	20	5	0	1	6	3	20	.245	.308
First Pitch	.255	55	14	8	2	0	8	2	0	.276	.473	August	.181	105	19	4	2	5	13	7	33	.232	.400
Ahead in Count	.347	75	26	4	0	5	12	6	0	.395	.600	September/October	.188	101	19	3	1	2	8	3	27	.212	.297
Behind in Count	.123	195	24	3	1	4	19	0	92	.123	.210	Pre-All Star	.271	129	35	9	1	5	22	2	39	.280	.473
Two Strikes	.122	189	23	4	0	2	10	6	108	.149	.175	Post-All Star	.193	264	51	11	3	7	24	12	69	.228	.337

1993 By Position																							
Position	Avg	AB	H	2B	3B	HR	RBI	BB	SO	OBP	SLG	G	GS	Innings	PO	A	E	DP	Fld Pct	Rng Fctr	In Zone	Outs	Zone Rtg	MLB Zone
As 3b	.219	389	85	19	4	12	46	14	108	.245	.380	104	100	888.2	81	165	13	17	.950	2.49	216	182	.843	.834

Mark Parent — Orioles

Age 32 – Bats Right (flyball hitter)

	Avg	G	AB	R	H	2B	3B	HR	RBI	BB	SO	HBP	GDP	SB	CS	OBP	SLG	IBB	SH	SF	#Pit	#P/PA	GB	FB	G/F
1993 Season	.259	22	54	7	14	2	0	4	12	3	14	0	1	0	0	.293	.519	0	3	1	208	3.41	15	18	0.83
Last Five Years	.217	159	419	36	91	18	0	16	53	30	85	1	8	2	0	.268	.375	5	9	5	1559	3.36	134	136	0.99

1993 Season

	Avg	AB	H	2B	3B	HR	RBI	BB	SO	OBP	SLG		Avg	AB	H	2B	3B	HR	RBI	BB	SO	OBP	SLG
vs. Left	.364	22	8	1	0	2	6	1	4	.391	.682	Scoring Posn	.200	20	4	0	0	1	7	1	5	.227	.350
vs. Right	.188	32	6	1	0	2	6	2	10	.229	.406	Close & Late	.250	8	2	0	0	1	3	0	3	.250	.625

Last Five Years

	Avg	AB	H	2B	3B	HR	RBI	BB	SO	OBP	SLG		Avg	AB	H	2B	3B	HR	RBI	BB	SO	OBP	SLG
vs. Left	.268	168	45	9	0	7	18	19	30	.340	.446	Scoring Posn	.190	105	20	5	0	2	36	13	25	.268	.295
vs. Right	.183	251	46	9	0	9	35	11	55	.217	.327	Close & Late	.197	66	13	2	0	1	3	6	14	.264	.273
Groundball	.176	153	27	6	0	2	10	9	25	.223	.255	None on/out	.281	89	25	6	0	8	8	4	13	.312	.618
Flyball	.200	100	20	5	0	5	13	8	24	.257	.400	Batting #7	.218	165	36	9	0	5	18	7	33	.247	.364
Home	.251	179	45	8	0	8	29	13	43	.296	.430	Batting #8	.210	143	30	4	0	4	17	15	22	.281	.322
Away	.192	240	46	10	0	8	24	17	42	.247	.333	Other	.225	111	25	5	0	7	18	8	30	.281	.459
Day	.192	198	38	7	0	5	21	12	41	.241	.303	April	.258	31	8	1	0	2	3	2	7	.303	.484
Night	.240	221	53	11	0	11	32	18	44	.292	.439	May	.182	44	8	2	0	1	9	2	9	.208	.295
Grass	.232	315	73	13	0	14	45	22	68	.279	.406	June	.171	82	14	2	0	3	5	7	18	.236	.305
Turf	.173	104	18	5	0	2	8	8	17	.237	.279	July	.204	93	19	5	0	2	6	7	12	.257	.323
First Pitch	.309	81	25	1	0	5	13	3	0	.333	.506	August	.248	113	28	5	0	5	23	9	22	.304	.425
Ahead in Count	.313	83	26	7	0	5	11	12	0	.388	.578	September/October	.250	56	14	3	0	3	7	3	17	.288	.464
Behind in Count	.136	191	26	5	0	3	14	0	73	.135	.209	Pre-All Star	.180	189	34	5	0	7	19	15	41	.238	.317
Two Strikes	.119	176	21	4	0	2	12	13	85	.183	.176	Post-All Star	.248	230	57	13	0	9	34	15	44	.293	.422

Batter vs. Pitcher (career)

Hits Best Against	Avg	AB	H	2B	3B	HR	RBI	BB	SO	OBP	SLG	Hits Worst Against	Avg	AB	H	2B	3B	HR	RBI	BB	SO	OBP	SLG
Jim Deshaies	.357	14	5	1	0	1	2	0	2	.357	.643	Tom Glavine	.050	20	1	0	0	0	0	0	2	.050	.050
												Tom Browning	.154	13	2	1	0	0	2	0	3	.154	.231
												Joe Magrane	.200	10	2	1	0	0	0	2	0	.333	.300

Rick Parker — Astros

Age 31 – Bats Right

	Avg	G	AB	R	H	2B	3B	HR	RBI	BB	SO	HBP	GDP	SB	CS	OBP	SLG	IBB	SH	SF	#Pit	#P/PA	GB	FB	G/F
1993 Season	.333	45	45	11	15	3	0	0	4	3	8	0	2	1	2	.375	.400	0	1	0	183	3.73	20	8	2.50
Career (1990-1993)	.253	112	166	30	42	8	0	2	19	14	28	1	3	7	3	.315	.337	0	4	0	616	3.33	60	45	1.33

1993 Season

	Avg	AB	H	2B	3B	HR	RBI	BB	SO	OBP	SLG		Avg	AB	H	2B	3B	HR	RBI	BB	SO	OBP	SLG
vs. Left	.375	32	12	3	0	0	4	3	4	.429	.469	Scoring Posn	.500	10	5	1	0	0	4	0	2	.500	.600
vs. Right	.231	13	3	0	0	0	0	0	4	.231	.231	Close & Late	.429	7	3	1	0	0	1	0	2	.429	.571

Derek Parks — Twins

Age 25 – Bats Right

	Avg	G	AB	R	H	2B	3B	HR	RBI	BB	SO	HBP	GDP	SB	CS	OBP	SLG	IBB	SH	SF	#Pit	#P/PA	GB	FB	G/F
1993 Season	.200	7	20	3	4	0	0	0	1	1	2	0	0	0	0	.238	.200	0	0	0	80	3.81	6	8	0.75
Career (1992-1993)	.231	14	26	4	6	0	0	0	1	2	3	1	0	0	0	.310	.231	0	0	0	106	3.66	8	10	0.80

1993 Season

	Avg	AB	H	2B	3B	HR	RBI	BB	SO	OBP	SLG		Avg	AB	H	2B	3B	HR	RBI	BB	SO	OBP	SLG
vs. Left	.143	7	1	0	0	0	1	1	1	.250	.143	Scoring Posn	.200	5	1	0	0	0	1	0	1	.200	.200
vs. Right	.231	13	3	0	0	0	0	0	1	.231	.231	Close & Late	.000	3	0	0	0	0	0	0	0	.000	.000

Jeff Parrett — Rockies

Age 32 – Pitches Right (flyball pitcher)

	ERA	W	L	Sv	G	GS	IP	BB	SO	Avg	H	2B	3B	HR	RBI	OBP	SLG	GF	IR	IRS	Hld	SvOp	SB	CS	GB	FB	G/F
1993 Season	5.38	3	3	1	40	6	73.2	45	66	.274	78	13	1	6	51	.371	.389	13	20	13	1	4	11	2	87	84	1.04
Last Five Years	4.04	30	22	10	263	11	407.2	198	342	.260	399	79	12	32	225	.343	.389	55	165	70	37	26	40	16	453	463	0.98

1993 Season

	ERA	W	L	Sv	G	GS	IP	H	HR	BB	SO		Avg	AB	H	2B	3B	HR	RBI	BB	SO	OBP	SLG
Home	6.18	3	2	0	20	4	43.2	55	3	30	38	vs. Left	.295	149	44	7	0	1	28	21	35	.383	.362
Away	4.20	0	1	1	20	2	30.0	23	3	15	28	vs. Right	.250	136	34	6	1	5	23	24	31	.358	.419
Starter	5.87	2	1	0	6	6	23.0	26	3	11	18	Scoring Posn	.296	98	29	6	0	2	46	22	23	.408	.418
Reliever	5.15	1	2	1	34	0	50.2	52	3	34	48	Close & Late	.329	73	24	3	0	1	14	8	16	.390	.411
0 Days rest	9.00	0	0	1	6	0	6.0	8	0	4	4	None on/out	.210	62	13	2	1	1	1	8	21	.300	.323
1 or 2 Days rest	4.78	0	2	0	23	0	37.2	38	2	23	34	First Pitch	.444	27	12	1	0	0	5	5	0	.531	.481
3+ Days rest	3.86	1	0	0	5	0	7.0	6	1	7	10	Ahead in Count	.204	142	29	7	0	1	19	0	55	.201	.275
Pre-All Star	4.54	3	2	1	36	3	67.1	67	4	38	60	Behind in Count	.328	67	22	3	0	5	20	26	0	.505	.597
Post-All Star	14.21	0	1	0	4	3	6.1	11	2	7	6	Two Strikes	.184	147	27	5	0	1	18	14	66	.252	.238

Last Five Years

	ERA	W	L	Sv	G	GS	IP	H	HR	BB	SO		Avg	AB	H	2B	3B	HR	RBI	BB	SO	OBP	SLG
Home	4.45	17	9	5	131	7	218.2	225	18	115	170	vs. Left	.269	751	202	36	8	10	117	116	154	.366	.378

Last Five Years

	ERA	W	L	Sv	G	GS	IP	H	HR	BB	SO
Away	3.57	13	13	5	132	4	189.0	174	14	83	172
Day	4.79	9	7	2	81	6	124.0	133	9	72	105
Night	3.71	21	15	8	182	5	283.2	266	23	126	237
Grass	4.28	16	10	3	154	5	222.2	229	18	111	189
Turf	3.75	14	12	7	109	6	185.0	170	14	87	153
April	3.12	5	3	2	51	0	78.0	76	3	36	64
May	6.14	2	4	1	50	0	66.0	62	8	39	54
June	4.32	6	5	2	53	1	83.1	90	6	33	61
July	3.38	10	6	2	39	10	85.1	73	7	39	71
August	3.12	5	1	2	38	0	57.2	50	6	28	55
September/October	4.58	2	3	1	32	0	37.1	48	2	23	37
Starter	5.11	3	4	0	11	11	49.1	54	5	24	37
Reliever	3.89	27	18	10	252	0	358.1	345	27	174	305
0 Days rest	3.75	7	5	4	59	0	72.0	72	3	32	75
1 or 2 Days rest	4.61	13	9	5	137	0	199.0	204	19	100	166
3+ Days rest	2.37	7	4	1	56	0	87.1	69	5	42	64
Pre-All Star	4.13	16	13	6	166	5	261.1	257	19	123	209
Post-All Star	3.87	14	9	4	97	6	146.1	142	13	75	133

	Avg	AB	H	2B	3B	HR	RBI	BB	SO	OBP	SLG
vs. Right	.251	785	197	43	4	22	108	82	188	.319	.400
Inning 1-6	.262	389	102	24	4	7	67	54	79	.347	.398
Inning 7+	.259	1147	297	55	8	25	158	144	263	.341	.386
None on	.255	783	200	43	4	19	19	84	176	.329	.393
Runners on	.264	753	199	36	8	13	206	114	166	.356	.385
Scoring Posn	.273	484	132	26	5	5	181	94	107	.381	.378
Close & Late	.273	542	148	17	5	11	79	70	124	.355	.384
None on/out	.268	355	95	16	3	12	12	38	81	.340	.431
vs. 1st Batr (relief)	.250	216	54	9	2	3	30	27	48	.333	.352
First Inning Pitched	.252	878	221	38	6	19	159	128	192	.344	.374
First 15 Pitches	.258	764	197	32	7	16	111	97	151	.339	.381
Pitch 16-30	.238	491	117	26	3	12	71	59	133	.321	.377
Pitch 31-45	.280	157	44	11	1	3	19	24	38	.377	.420
Pitch 46+	.331	124	41	10	1	1	24	18	20	.410	.452
First Pitch	.298	191	57	10	3	4	30	27	0	.381	.445
Ahead in Count	.212	744	158	31	4	13	101	0	300	.212	.317
Behind in Count	.320	322	103	24	2	10	55	97	0	.475	.500
Two Strikes	.195	771	150	26	3	11	94	72	342	.263	.279

Pitcher vs. Batter (career)

Pitches Best Vs.	Avg	AB	H	2B	3B	HR	RBI	BB	SO	OBP	SLG
Paul O'Neill	.000	15	0	0	0	0	0	1	6	.063	.000
Sid Bream	.083	12	1	1	0	0	3	2	4	.200	.167
Chris Sabo	.154	13	2	1	0	0	1	0	4	.154	.231
Jay Bell	.200	10	2	0	0	0	1	0	3	.182	.200
Ryne Sandberg	.211	19	4	0	0	0	0	1	2	.250	.211

Pitches Worst Vs.	Avg	AB	H	2B	3B	HR	RBI	BB	SO	OBP	SLG
Tim Raines	.538	13	7	1	1	0	6	0	2	.538	.769
Glenn Davis	.455	11	5	2	0	2	4	4	3	.600	1.182
John Kruk	.444	9	4	0	0	1	2	3	1	.583	.778
Todd Zeile	.400	15	6	0	0	2	7	1	3	.412	.800
Kevin McReynolds	.375	24	9	1	1	3	8	4	2	.464	.875

Lance Parrish — Indians

Age 38 – Bats Right (flyball hitter)

	Avg	G	AB	R	H	2B	3B	HR	RBI	BB	SO	HBP	GDP	SB	CS	OBP	SLG	IBB	SH	SF	#Pit	#P/PA	GB	FB	G/F
1993 Season	.200	10	20	2	4	1	0	1	2	4	5	0	2	1	0	.333	.400	0	0	0	110	4.58	4	9	0.44
Last Five Years	.240	479	1600	168	384	52	2	73	205	151	403	13	39	5	5	.309	.412	15	2	12	6762	3.80	483	494	0.98

1993 Season

	Avg	AB	H	2B	3B	HR	RBI	BB	SO	OBP	SLG
vs. Left	.000	5	0	0	0	0	0	0	2	.000	.000
vs. Right	.267	15	4	1	0	1	2	4	3	.421	.533

	Avg	AB	H	2B	3B	HR	RBI	BB	SO	OBP	SLG
Scoring Posn	.000	2	0	0	0	0	0	1	1	.333	.000
Close & Late	.000	4	0	0	0	0	0	1	1	.200	.000

Last Five Years

	Avg	AB	H	2B	3B	HR	RBI	BB	SO	OBP	SLG
vs. Left	.247	474	117	12	1	21	57	55	96	.323	.409
vs. Right	.237	1126	267	40	1	52	148	96	307	.302	.413
Groundball	.258	388	100	14	1	18	54	36	99	.326	.438
Flyball	.253	392	99	16	1	21	54	35	99	.314	.459
Home	.248	806	200	27	0	39	109	67	186	.307	.427
Away	.232	794	184	25	2	34	96	84	217	.310	.397
Day	.240	354	85	11	0	17	51	32	94	.302	.415
Night	.240	1246	299	41	2	56	154	119	309	.310	.411
Grass	.236	1268	299	37	2	55	166	119	313	.305	.398
Turf	.256	332	85	15	0	18	39	32	90	.321	.464
First Pitch	.292	195	57	7	0	12	36	9	0	.332	.513
Ahead in Count	.339	375	127	19	0	22	73	53	0	.414	.565
Behind in Count	.172	738	127	14	0	26	63	0	327	.180	.297
Two Strikes	.160	789	126	15	1	26	61	85	403	.244	.280

	Avg	AB	H	2B	3B	HR	RBI	BB	SO	OBP	SLG
Scoring Posn	.229	385	88	13	0	15	126	54	103	.319	.379
Close & Late	.182	286	52	5	0	9	25	28	100	.254	.294
None on/out	.230	370	85	12	0	22	22	25	92	.282	.441
Batting #6	.217	460	100	12	0	22	60	45	129	.294	.387
Batting #7	.258	605	156	15	2	31	81	56	142	.322	.443
Other	.239	535	128	25	0	20	64	50	132	.306	.398
April	.239	238	57	9	1	10	28	25	61	.321	.412
May	.257	269	69	11	0	15	46	31	58	.334	.465
June	.256	211	54	7	0	10	27	17	43	.316	.431
July	.268	302	81	7	1	17	51	34	72	.343	.467
August	.201	298	60	8	0	13	28	23	96	.265	.359
September/October	.223	282	63	10	0	8	25	21	73	.275	.344
Pre-All Star	.256	812	208	29	1	42	118	86	177	.332	.450
Post-All Star	.223	788	176	23	1	31	87	65	226	.284	.373

Batter vs. Pitcher (since 1984)

Hits Best Against	Avg	AB	H	2B	3B	HR	RBI	BB	SO	OBP	SLG
Greg Hibbard	.500	18	9	0	0	2	3	2	1	.550	.833
Tom Browning	.455	11	5	1	0	1	3	1	1	.500	.818
Jose Rijo	.444	9	4	0	0	1	1	2	1	.545	.778
Kirk McCaskill	.412	17	7	1	0	3	4	0	5	.412	1.000
Bruce Hurst	.385	13	5	0	0	3	7	3	4	.500	1.077

Hits Worst Against	Avg	AB	H	2B	3B	HR	RBI	BB	SO	OBP	SLG
Dennis Eckersley	.000	12	0	0	0	0	0	0	5	.000	.000
Todd Worrell	.000	11	0	0	0	0	0	2	4	.154	.000
Scott Sanderson	.048	21	1	1	0	0	2	2	7	.125	.095
David Wells	.063	16	1	0	0	0	0	1	7	.118	.063
Ben McDonald	.071	14	1	0	0	0	0	1	5	.133	.071

Dan Pasqua — White Sox

Age 32 – Bats Left (flyball hitter)

	Avg	G	AB	R	H	2B	3B	HR	RBI	BB	SO	HBP	GDP	SB	CS	OBP	SLG	IBB	SH	SF	#Pit	#P/PA	GB	FB	G/F
1993 Season	.205	78	176	22	36	10	1	5	20	26	51	0	3	2	2	.302	.358	1	1	3	855	4.15	53	52	1.02
Last Five Years	.245	490	1429	188	350	84	11	53	224	186	318	7	20	4	8	.332	.430	14	4	16	6343	3.86	405	484	0.84

1993 Season

	Avg	AB	H	2B	3B	HR	RBI	BB	SO	OBP	SLG
vs. Left	.400	10	4	1	0	2	4	2	4	.500	1.100
vs. Right	.193	166	32	9	1	3	16	24	47	.290	.313
Home	.263	76	20	4	0	2	10	15	26	.380	.395
Away	.160	100	16	6	1	3	10	11	25	.239	.330
First Pitch	.360	25	9	2	1	1	5	0	0	.360	.640
Ahead in Count	.250	44	11	3	0	1	4	15	0	.433	.386
Behind in Count	.129	70	9	3	0	2	6	0	35	.129	.257
Two Strikes	.115	87	10	3	0	1	4	11	51	.212	.184

	Avg	AB	H	2B	3B	HR	RBI	BB	SO	OBP	SLG
Scoring Posn	.109	46	5	0	0	2	13	11	13	.267	.239
Close & Late	.250	20	5	1	0	1	3	6	4	.407	.450
None on/out	.205	39	8	3	0	0	0	4	14	.279	.282
Batting #6	.220	91	20	5	1	5	14	9	28	.287	.462
Batting #7	.184	38	7	0	0	0	4	8	10	.313	.184
Other	.191	47	9	5	0	0	2	9	13	.321	.298
Pre-All Star	.191	94	18	3	0	3	13	17	31	.310	.319
Post-All Star	.220	82	18	7	1	2	7	9	20	.293	.402

Last Five Years	Avg	AB	H	2B	3B	HR	RBI	BB	SO	OBP	SLG
vs. Left	.228	184	42	7	1	8	29	19	44	.302	.408
vs. Right	.247	1245	308	77	10	45	195	167	274	.336	.434
Groundball	.254	394	100	29	1	8	54	47	79	.333	.393
Flyball	.214	336	72	12	6	18	59	55	78	.327	.446
Home	.269	670	180	38	7	23	97	101	145	.364	.449
Away	.224	759	170	46	4	30	127	85	173	.302	.414
Day	.293	376	110	28	5	15	76	52	86	.377	.513
Night	.228	1053	240	56	6	38	148	134	232	.315	.401
Grass	.242	1208	292	69	10	43	180	166	265	.334	.422
Turf	.262	221	58	15	1	10	44	20	53	.320	.475
First Pitch	.347	190	66	16	2	10	38	3	0	.357	.611
Ahead in Count	.317	350	111	22	3	13	63	100	0	.468	.509
Behind in Count	.171	592	101	29	3	18	71	0	243	.173	.321
Two Strikes	.147	661	97	30	4	10	65	80	318	.239	.250

	Avg	AB	H	2B	3B	HR	RBI	BB	SO	OBP	SLG
Scoring Posn	.243	383	93	23	6	11	158	65	90	.343	.420
Close & Late	.234	222	52	9	2	9	34	29	50	.324	.414
None on/out	.241	353	85	23	1	16	16	35	79	.313	.448
Batting #4	.274	536	147	37	6	24	97	68	105	.359	.500
Batting #6	.218	450	98	24	1	13	57	51	108	.296	.362
Other	.237	443	105	23	4	16	70	67	105	.334	.415
April	.260	123	32	5	1	5	23	17	37	.340	.439
May	.227	220	50	14	1	8	31	38	49	.337	.409
June	.252	270	68	15	3	13	48	30	57	.329	.474
July	.268	313	84	17	2	12	54	39	66	.351	.450
August	.212	259	55	16	1	6	27	31	60	.301	.351
September/October	.250	244	61	17	3	9	41	31	49	.332	.455
Pre-All Star	.249	712	177	41	5	31	114	99	166	.337	.451
Post-All Star	.241	717	173	43	6	22	110	87	152	.326	.410

Batter vs. Pitcher (career)

Hits Best Against	Avg	AB	H	2B	3B	HR	RBI	BB	SO	OBP	SLG
Dave Johnson	.667	9	6	1	0	3	6	2	1	.727	1.778
Luis Aquino	.400	15	6	1	0	2	3	1	2	.438	.867
Mike Morgan	.385	13	5	0	0	2	2	2	4	.467	.846
Scott Erickson	.368	19	7	2	0	3	5	0	4	.368	.947
Steve Ontiveros	.333	15	5	0	0	3	5	2	6	.412	.933

Hits Worst Against	Avg	AB	H	2B	3B	HR	RBI	BB	SO	OBP	SLG
Mike Mussina	.000	14	0	0	0	0	0	0	3	.000	.000
Jose Guzman	.000	10	0	0	0	0	0	2	2	.167	.000
Curt Young	.077	13	1	0	0	0	2	0	2	.077	.077
Doug Jones	.077	13	1	0	0	0	1	0	5	.077	.077
Nolan Ryan	.107	28	3	1	0	0	1	0	13	.107	.143

Bob Patterson — Rangers

Age 35 – Pitches Left (flyball pitcher)

	ERA	W	L	Sv	G	GS	IP	BB	SO	Avg	H	2B	3B	HR	RBI	OBP	SLG	GF	IR	IRS	Hld	SvOp	SB	CS	GB	FB	G/F
1993 Season	4.78	2	4	1	52	0	52.2	11	46	.282	59	9	1	8	33	.318	.450	29	29	12	6	2	3	2	50	71	0.70
Last Five Years	3.61	24	18	18	233	9	304.1	78	236	.257	296	50	6	34	149	.304	.399	93	141	48	37	27	11	16	315	393	0.80

1993 Season

	ERA	W	L	Sv	G	GS	IP	H	HR	BB	SO
Home	6.14	1	2	0	25	0	22.0	32	4	5	18
Away	3.82	1	2	1	27	0	30.2	27	4	6	28
Starter	0.00	0	0	0	0	0	0.0	0	0	0	0
Reliever	4.78	2	4	1	52	0	52.2	59	8	11	46
0 Days rest	11.57	1	1	0	7	0	7.0	11	2	2	10
1 or 2 Days rest	3.90	0	3	1	25	0	27.2	26	5	4	20
3+ Days rest	3.50	1	0	0	20	0	18.0	22	1	5	16
Pre-All Star	4.30	2	3	1	28	0	29.1	35	4	8	29
Post-All Star	5.40	0	1	0	24	0	23.1	24	4	3	17

	Avg	AB	H	2B	3B	HR	RBI	BB	SO	OBP	SLG
vs. Left	.247	73	18	4	0	1	9	2	18	.263	.342
vs. Right	.301	136	41	5	1	7	24	9	28	.347	.507
Scoring Posn	.346	52	18	1	0	3	26	3	11	.368	.538
Close & Late	.293	58	17	0	0	3	11	4	15	.339	.448
None on/out	.333	45	15	4	1	0	0	2	8	.362	.467
First Pitch	.444	18	8	0	1	1	7	0	0	.429	.722
Ahead in Count	.195	113	22	3	0	3	10	0	40	.195	.301
Behind in Count	.400	35	14	4	0	2	9	7	0	.500	.686
Two Strikes	.160	94	15	1	0	4	9	4	46	.194	.298

Last Five Years

	ERA	W	L	Sv	G	GS	IP	H	HR	BB	SO
Home	3.98	13	9	9	110	6	158.1	155	21	42	127
Away	3.21	11	9	9	123	3	146.0	141	13	36	109
Day	4.73	5	6	7	67	2	72.1	70	12	20	51
Night	3.26	19	12	11	166	7	232.0	226	22	58	185
Grass	3.32	7	5	6	96	2	114.0	117	11	27	92
Turf	3.78	17	13	12	137	7	190.1	179	23	51	144
April	3.00	5	1	0	30	0	36.0	33	3	7	28
May	5.20	2	2	2	35	1	45.0	55	8	12	39
June	2.38	4	2	4	38	4	53.0	48	4	13	34
July	3.49	4	2	6	42	0	56.2	50	5	14	48
August	3.21	2	4	2	40	1	47.2	45	7	15	32
September/October	4.23	7	7	4	48	3	66.0	65	7	17	55
Starter	4.33	3	4	0	9	9	43.2	44	5	12	28
Reliever	3.49	21	14	18	224	0	260.2	252	29	66	208
0 Days rest	4.37	7	4	4	37	0	45.1	39	5	14	42
1 or 2 Days rest	3.81	7	7	7	108	0	118.0	115	17	30	91
3+ Days rest	2.68	7	3	7	79	0	97.1	98	7	22	75
Pre-All Star	3.49	13	7	8	118	5	152.0	147	17	37	121
Post-All Star	3.72	11	11	10	115	4	152.1	149	17	41	115

	Avg	AB	H	2B	3B	HR	RBI	BB	SO	OBP	SLG
vs. Left	.213	362	77	14	2	4	36	23	93	.260	.296
vs. Right	.277	790	219	36	4	30	113	55	143	.324	.447
Inning 1-6	.246	297	73	10	1	6	34	19	56	.290	.347
Inning 7+	.261	855	223	40	5	28	115	59	180	.309	.418
None on	.246	659	162	37	4	15	15	41	137	.294	.382
Runners on	.272	493	134	13	2	19	134	37	99	.317	.422
Scoring Posn	.295	268	79	8	1	15	123	29	51	.352	.500
Close & Late	.260	365	95	15	1	14	56	32	86	.320	.422
None on/out	.285	281	80	17	1	7	7	17	55	.330	.427
vs. 1st Batr (relief)	.290	207	60	10	1	5	26	12	49	.327	.420
First Inning Pitched	.267	722	193	26	4	22	116	47	162	.312	.406
First 15 Pitches	.261	681	178	27	2	20	94	41	147	.303	.395
Pitch 16-30	.245	306	75	13	4	9	39	28	61	.309	.402
Pitch 31-45	.213	80	17	5	0	2	8	5	15	.256	.350
Pitch 46+	.306	85	26	5	0	3	8	4	13	.337	.471
First Pitch	.311	183	57	12	1	7	31	15	0	.358	.503
Ahead in Count	.200	581	116	16	1	12	49	0	209	.203	.293
Behind in Count	.337	184	62	15	1	9	32	34	0	.436	.576
Two Strikes	.166	541	90	14	1	12	46	29	236	.211	.262

Pitcher vs. Batter (career)

Pitches Best Vs.	Avg	AB	H	2B	3B	HR	RBI	BB	SO	OBP	SLG
Paul O'Neill	.000	13	0	0	0	0	0	0	5	.000	.000
Darren Daulton	.077	13	1	0	0	0	0	1	2	.143	.077
Dave Magadan	.111	9	1	1	0	0	3	2	4	.273	.222
Eddie Murray	.143	14	2	0	0	0	1	0	3	.133	.143
Milt Thompson	.182	11	2	1	0	0	1	0	2	.182	.273

Pitches Worst Vs.	Avg	AB	H	2B	3B	HR	RBI	BB	SO	OBP	SLG
Casey Candaele	.583	12	7	2	0	0	1	0	0	.583	.750
Tim Teufel	.444	18	8	2	0	1	6	3	3	.524	.722
Dickie Thon	.385	13	5	0	0	1	2	1	3	.429	.615
Kevin McReynolds	.368	19	7	1	0	2	5	0	2	.368	.737
Todd Zeile	.333	12	4	2	0	1	4	0	2	.333	.750

John Patterson — Giants

Age 27 – Bats Both

	Avg	G	AB	R	H	2B	3B	HR	RBI	BB	SO	HBP	GDP	SB	CS	OBP	SLG	IBB	SH	SF	#Pit	#P/PA	GB	FB	G/F
1993 Season	.188	16	16	1	3	0	0	1	2	0	5	0	0	0	1	.188	.375	0	0	0	57	3.56	3	7	0.43
Career (1992-1993)	.185	48	119	11	22	1	1	1	6	5	29	1	2	5	2	.224	.235	0	0	0	461	3.69	43	31	1.39

1993 Season

	Avg	AB	H	2B	3B	HR	RBI	BB	SO	OBP	SLG
vs. Left	.200	5	1	0	0	0	1	0	1	.200	.200
vs. Right	.182	11	2	0	0	1	1	0	4	.182	.455

	Avg	AB	H	2B	3B	HR	RBI	BB	SO	OBP	SLG
Scoring Posn	.333	3	1	0	0	0	1	0	1	.333	.333
Close & Late	.200	5	1	0	0	1	1	0	1	.200	.800

Ken Patterson — Angels

Age 29 – Pitches Left (flyball pitcher)

	ERA	W	L	Sv	G	GS	IP	BB	SO	Avg	H	2B	3B	HR	RBI	OBP	SLG	GF	IR	IRS	Hld	SvOp	SB	CS	GB	FB	G/F
1993 Season	4.58	1	1	1	46	0	59.0	35	36	.249	54	9	0	7	28	.352	.387	9	53	10	4	2	7	3	85	53	1.60
Last Five Years	3.83	14	6	4	214	2	296.1	159	174	.245	265	44	9	36	159	.340	.402	41	220	58	14	9	23	14	337	383	0.88

1993 Season

	ERA	W	L	Sv	G	GS	IP	H	HR	BB	SO
Home	4.93	1	0	1	26	0	34.2	28	3	21	23
Away	4.07	0	1	0	20	0	24.1	26	4	14	13
Starter	0.00	0	0	0	0	0	0.0	0	0	0	0
Reliever	4.58	1	1	1	46	0	59.0	54	7	35	36
0 Days rest	7.50	0	0	1	6	0	6.0	5	0	4	7
1 or 2 Days rest	4.66	0	0	0	16	0	19.1	19	3	14	7
3+ Days rest	4.01	1	1	0	24	0	33.2	30	4	17	22
Pre-All Star	6.12	0	1	0	23	0	32.1	36	6	19	14
Post-All Star	2.70	1	0	1	23	0	26.2	18	1	16	22

	Avg	AB	H	2B	3B	HR	RBI	BB	SO	OBP	SLG
vs. Left	.276	76	21	4	0	3	13	14	10	.389	.447
vs. Right	.234	141	33	5	0	4	15	21	26	.331	.355
Scoring Posn	.227	66	15	1	0	4	24	15	11	.366	.424
Close & Late	.297	37	11	2	0	2	5	9	10	.426	.514
None on/out	.229	48	11	3	0	0	0	8	8	.339	.292
First Pitch	.314	35	11	1	0	1	8	4	0	.375	.429
Ahead in Count	.164	67	11	1	0	0	2	0	26	.164	.179
Behind in Count	.333	69	23	4	0	6	14	14	0	.446	.652
Two Strikes	.146	82	12	2	0	0	2	17	36	.293	.171

Last Five Years

	ERA	W	L	Sv	G	GS	IP	H	HR	BB	SO
Home	3.88	6	3	3	107	1	150.2	132	18	77	96
Away	3.77	8	3	1	107	1	145.2	133	18	82	78
Day	2.84	5	1	0	65	2	88.2	66	10	48	59
Night	4.25	9	5	4	149	0	207.2	199	26	111	115
Grass	3.67	13	5	3	174	2	245.0	213	29	129	155
Turf	4.56	1	1	1	40	0	51.1	52	7	30	19
April	4.79	1	0	0	32	0	41.1	43	10	21	19
May	3.70	3	1	0	34	0	56.0	45	6	37	36
June	5.34	2	2	1	32	1	55.2	54	9	31	26
July	1.51	4	1	2	34	0	47.2	34	2	16	35
August	3.95	4	2	0	47	0	57.0	55	6	29	38
September/October	3.49	0	0	1	35	1	38.2	34	3	25	20
Starter	11.81	0	0	0	2	2	5.1	12	2	4	4
Reliever	3.68	14	6	4	212	0	291.0	253	34	155	170
0 Days rest	4.81	1	1	1	37	0	48.2	47	10	24	42
1 or 2 Days rest	3.54	4	2	2	73	0	89.0	80	6	53	41
3+ Days rest	3.40	9	3	1	102	0	153.1	126	18	78	87
Pre-All Star	4.41	7	4	1	108	1	165.1	154	26	91	91
Post-All Star	3.09	7	2	3	106	1	131.0	111	10	68	83

	Avg	AB	H	2B	3B	HR	RBI	BB	SO	OBP	SLG
vs. Left	.260	334	87	11	3	8	55	54	54	.360	.383
vs. Right	.238	749	178	33	6	28	104	105	120	.331	.410
Inning 1-6	.249	461	115	21	5	18	88	69	65	.344	.434
Inning 7+	.241	622	150	23	4	18	71	90	109	.337	.378
None on	.265	574	152	30	5	16	16	74	94	.351	.418
Runners on	.222	509	113	14	4	20	143	85	80	.329	.383
Scoring Posn	.232	314	73	10	3	13	127	65	52	.353	.408
Close & Late	.279	136	38	7	1	6	23	30	28	.402	.478
None on/out	.264	258	68	16	2	6	6	26	44	.333	.411
vs. 1st Batr (relief)	.287	178	51	8	1	8	47	27	28	.376	.478
First Inning Pitched	.254	630	160	25	9	24	121	94	103	.348	.437
First 15 Pitches	.251	581	146	22	7	20	91	78	78	.339	.417
Pitch 16-30	.237	295	70	17	2	7	37	49	54	.341	.380
Pitch 31-45	.228	127	29	4	0	3	15	20	26	.340	.331
Pitch 46+	.250	80	20	1	0	6	16	12	16	.348	.488
First Pitch	.276	163	45	10	0	5	30	11	0	.317	.429
Ahead in Count	.217	428	93	10	1	13	55	0	138	.219	.336
Behind in Count	.271	266	72	14	3	12	44	73	0	.422	.481
Two Strikes	.196	459	90	10	3	13	56	75	174	.310	.316

Pitcher vs. Batter (career)

Pitches Best Vs.	Avg	AB	H	2B	3B	HR	RBI	BB	SO	OBP	SLG
Jody Reed	.200	10	2	0	0	0	1	1	1	.273	.200

Pitches Worst Vs.	Avg	AB	H	2B	3B	HR	RBI	BB	SO	OBP	SLG
Cecil Fielder	.625	8	5	0	0	3	8	3	3	.727	1.750
Ruben Sierra	.375	8	3	0	0	1	3	3	0	.545	.750
Mike Greenwell	.353	17	6	0	0	0	1	1	1	.389	.353
Lou Whitaker	.308	13	4	2	0	0	1	3	2	.438	.462

Roger Pavlik — Rangers

Age 26 – Pitches Right

	ERA	W	L	Sv	G	GS	IP	BB	SO	Avg	H	2B	3B	HR	RBI	OBP	SLG	CG	ShO	Sup	QS	#P/S	SB	CS	GB	FB	G/F
1993 Season	3.41	12	6	0	26	26	166.1	80	131	.245	151	25	3	18	56	.334	.382	2	0	4.55	18	105	15	6	205	171	1.20
Career (1992-1993)	3.63	16	10	0	39	38	228.1	114	176	.254	217	32	7	21	79	.346	.382	3	0	4.38	25	100	18	14	275	243	1.13

1993 Season

	ERA	W	L	Sv	G	GS	IP	H	HR	BB	SO
Home	2.73	7	2	0	14	14	92.1	70	7	42	77
Away	4.26	5	4	0	12	12	74.0	81	11	38	54
Day	3.23	4	1	0	5	5	30.2	32	2	18	25
Night	3.45	8	5	0	21	21	135.2	119	16	62	106
Grass	3.38	10	4	0	21	21	133.1	117	14	63	108
Turf	3.55	2	2	0	5	5	33.0	34	4	17	23
April	0.00	0	0	0	0	0	0.0	0	0	0	0
May	2.84	1	1	0	2	2	12.2	11	1	7	10
June	4.62	2	3	0	6	6	39.0	36	5	22	29
July	5.06	3	1	0	5	5	26.2	39	2	10	24
August	2.66	3	1	0	6	6	44.0	39	7	15	39
September/October	2.25	3	0	0	7	7	44.0	26	3	26	29
Starter	3.41	12	6	0	26	26	166.1	151	18	80	131
Reliever	0.00	0	0	0	0	0	0.0	0	0	0	0
0-3 Days Rest	2.45	1	0	0	3	3	18.1	12	1	11	8
4 Days Rest	3.50	7	4	0	14	14	92.2	82	10	47	72

	Avg	AB	H	2B	3B	HR	RBI	BB	SO	OBP	SLG
vs. Left	.228	329	75	13	2	8	23	46	71	.324	.353
vs. Right	.264	288	76	12	1	10	33	34	60	.347	.417
Inning 1-6	.247	534	132	21	3	15	50	72	112	.340	.382
Inning 7+	.229	83	19	4	0	3	6	8	19	.293	.386
None on	.246	370	91	17	3	12	12	45	79	.331	.405
Runners on	.243	247	60	8	0	6	44	35	52	.339	.348
Scoring Posn	.223	139	31	4	0	5	41	22	32	.321	.360
Close & Late	.227	44	10	1	0	1	4	5	13	.300	.318
None on/out	.230	161	37	7	1	5	5	20	33	.319	.379
vs. 1st Batr (relief)	.000	0	0	0	0	0	0	0	0	.000	.000
First Inning Pitched	.268	97	26	6	2	0	8	10	24	.339	.371
First 75 Pitches	.251	426	107	16	3	11	39	59	87	.344	.380
Pitch 76-90	.230	87	20	3	0	5	11	15	26	.343	.437
Pitch 91-105	.211	71	15	2	0	2	4	1	11	.240	.324
Pitch 106+	.273	33	9	4	0	0	2	5	7	.368	.394
First Pitch	.402	82	33	6	0	4	12	2	0	.419	.622

1993 Season

	ERA	W	L	Sv	G	GS	IP	H	HR	BB	SO
5+ Days Rest	3.58	4	2	0	9	9	55.1	57	7	22	51
Pre-All Star	3.90	5	4	0	10	10	64.2	62	6	34	49
Post-All Star	3.10	7	2	0	16	16	101.2	89	12	46	82

	Avg	AB	H	2B	3B	HR	RBI	BB	SO	OBP	SLG
Ahead in Count	.180	272	49	7	0	9	20	0	114	.188	.305
Behind in Count	.269	156	42	9	3	4	17	44	0	.426	.442
Two Strikes	.171	281	48	8	0	7	15	34	131	.264	.274

Bill Pecota — Braves

Age 34 – Bats Right

	Avg	G	AB	R	H	2B	3B	HR	RBI	BB	SO	HBP	GDP	SB	CS	OBP	SLG	IBB	SH	SF	#Pit	#P/PA	GB	FB	G/F
1993 Season	.323	72	62	17	20	2	1	0	5	2	5	0	0	1	1	.344	.387	0	1	0	227	3.49	25	17	1.47
Last Five Years	.257	466	1052	162	270	57	7	16	101	108	138	5	27	39	16	.328	.370	10	20	2	4375	3.69	406	310	1.31

1993 Season

	Avg	AB	H	2B	3B	HR	RBI	BB	SO	OBP	SLG
vs. Left	.412	34	14	2	1	0	5	1	1	.429	.529
vs. Right	.214	28	6	0	0	0	0	1	4	.241	.214

	Avg	AB	H	2B	3B	HR	RBI	BB	SO	OBP	SLG
Scoring Posn	.385	13	5	1	1	0	5	0	1	.385	.615
Close & Late	.400	15	6	1	0	0	2	0	3	.400	.467

Last Five Years

	Avg	AB	H	2B	3B	HR	RBI	BB	SO	OBP	SLG
vs. Left	.294	394	116	31	3	6	41	44	40	.364	.434
vs. Right	.234	658	154	26	4	10	60	64	98	.306	.331
Groundball	.252	369	93	18	0	7	43	40	49	.326	.358
Flyball	.262	229	60	15	3	4	19	19	38	.320	.406
Home	.259	499	129	28	2	8	52	57	59	.338	.371
Away	.255	553	141	29	5	8	49	51	79	.319	.369
Day	.281	320	90	16	2	5	31	38	45	.359	.391
Night	.246	732	180	41	5	11	70	70	93	.314	.361
Grass	.266	482	128	29	3	8	56	46	72	.328	.388
Turf	.249	570	142	28	4	8	45	62	66	.328	.354
First Pitch	.293	92	27	5	0	1	13	5	0	.337	.380
Ahead in Count	.295	278	82	21	3	11	31	69	0	.437	.511
Behind in Count	.214	454	97	18	1	4	41	0	114	.216	.284
Two Strikes	.198	430	85	19	2	1	39	34	138	.258	.258

	Avg	AB	H	2B	3B	HR	RBI	BB	SO	OBP	SLG
Scoring Posn	.246	240	59	11	1	3	78	49	28	.373	.338
Close & Late	.257	179	46	10	0	0	14	21	28	.340	.313
None on/out	.253	241	61	15	0	3	3	16	31	.302	.353
Batting #2	.258	198	51	12	2	1	11	23	29	.338	.354
Batting #6	.289	301	87	15	2	3	37	29	39	.354	.382
Other	.239	553	132	30	3	12	53	56	70	.310	.369
April	.186	70	13	2	1	0	5	8	9	.269	.243
May	.238	126	30	7	0	2	20	8	14	.289	.341
June	.339	127	43	9	0	2	13	14	25	.404	.457
July	.271	277	75	13	3	4	24	26	44	.340	.383
August	.229	231	53	15	2	6	20	23	23	.301	.390
September/October	.253	221	56	11	1	2	19	29	23	.339	.339
Pre-All Star	.268	388	104	23	1	4	43	36	57	.332	.363
Post-All Star	.250	664	166	34	6	12	58	72	81	.326	.373

Batter vs. Pitcher (career)

Hits Best Against	Avg	AB	H	2B	3B	HR	RBI	BB	SO	OBP	SLG
David Wells	.462	13	6	3	0	0	1	0	1	.462	.692
Matt Young	.417	12	5	2	0	0	0	1	2	.462	.583
Mike Witt	.364	11	4	2	0	0	2	1	0	.417	.545
Randy Johnson	.364	11	4	1	0	2	2	5	0	.563	1.000
Greg Swindell	.304	23	7	2	0	0	2	3	2	.385	.391

Hits Worst Against	Avg	AB	H	2B	3B	HR	RBI	BB	SO	OBP	SLG
Jack Morris	.091	11	1	0	0	0	0	1	1	.167	.091
Jose DeLeon	.091	11	1	1	0	0	0	0	3	.091	.182
Roger Clemens	.091	11	1	1	0	0	0	1	4	.167	.182
Tom Bolton	.091	11	1	0	0	0	1	0	2	.091	.091
Tom Candiotti	.154	13	2	0	0	0	1	1	6	.214	.154

Dan Peltier — Rangers

Age 26 – Bats Left (groundball hitter)

	Avg	G	AB	R	H	2B	3B	HR	RBI	BB	SO	HBP	GDP	SB	CS	OBP	SLG	IBB	SH	SF	#Pit	#P/PA	GB	FB	G/F
1993 Season	.269	65	160	23	43	7	1	1	17	20	27	1	3	0	4	.352	.344	0	1	1	664	3.63	63	36	1.75
Career (1992-1993)	.255	77	184	24	47	7	1	1	19	20	30	1	3	0	4	.330	.321	0	1	1	744	3.59	73	45	1.62

1993 Season

	Avg	AB	H	2B	3B	HR	RBI	BB	SO	OBP	SLG
vs. Left	.125	8	1	0	0	0	1	1	1	.222	.125
vs. Right	.276	152	42	7	1	1	16	19	26	.358	.355
Home	.314	86	27	4	0	1	10	8	12	.379	.395
Away	.216	74	16	3	1	0	7	12	15	.322	.284
First Pitch	.333	33	11	0	0	0	0	0	0	.333	.333
Ahead in Count	.417	36	15	2	1	1	6	10	0	.543	.611
Behind in Count	.191	68	13	3	0	0	6	0	22	.191	.235
Two Strikes	.212	66	14	5	0	0	9	10	27	.325	.288

	Avg	AB	H	2B	3B	HR	RBI	BB	SO	OBP	SLG
Scoring Posn	.196	51	10	2	1	1	15	6	11	.276	.333
Close & Late	.167	18	3	1	0	0	2	2	5	.286	.222
None on/out	.297	37	11	0	0	0	0	2	3	.333	.297
Batting #7	.333	45	15	3	0	1	8	3	8	.375	.467
Batting #8	.333	48	16	2	0	0	4	8	9	.439	.375
Other	.179	67	12	2	1	0	5	9	10	.273	.239
Pre-All Star	.315	73	23	4	1	1	11	8	9	.378	.438
Post-All Star	.230	87	20	3	0	0	6	12	18	.330	.264

Geronimo Pena — Cardinals

Age 27 – Bats Both

	Avg	G	AB	R	H	2B	3B	HR	RBI	BB	SO	HBP	GDP	SB	CS	OBP	SLG	IBB	SH	SF	#Pit	#P/PA	GB	FB	G/F
1993 Season	.256	74	254	34	65	19	2	5	30	25	71	4	3	13	5	.330	.406	0	4	2	1108	3.83	65	68	0.96
Career (1990-1993)	.266	258	687	108	183	41	6	17	80	71	167	15	4	42	19	.344	.418	1	5	10	2946	3.74	205	194	1.06

1993 Season

	Avg	AB	H	2B	3B	HR	RBI	BB	SO	OBP	SLG
vs. Left	.333	93	31	9	0	3	14	9	19	.385	.527
vs. Right	.211	161	34	10	2	2	16	16	52	.298	.335
Home	.306	108	33	10	0	2	14	11	25	.385	.454
Away	.219	146	32	9	2	3	16	14	46	.288	.370
First Pitch	.333	30	10	5	0	2	8	0	0	.355	.700
Ahead in Count	.373	59	22	4	0	2	6	10	0	.451	.542
Behind in Count	.173	110	19	4	1	1	8	0	54	.180	.255
Two Strikes	.189	122	23	7	2	0	11	15	71	.288	.279

	Avg	AB	H	2B	3B	HR	RBI	BB	SO	OBP	SLG
Scoring Posn	.246	61	15	5	1	2	27	6	22	.324	.459
Close & Late	.283	46	13	3	1	1	6	6	17	.365	.457
None on/out	.217	83	18	9	0	2	2	10	25	.309	.398
Batting #1	.264	121	32	8	0	3	12	14	29	.345	.405
Batting #7	.272	92	25	11	1	1	14	8	26	.343	.446
Other	.195	41	8	0	1	1	4	3	16	.250	.317
Pre-All Star	.254	193	49	14	1	2	19	21	52	.333	.368
Post-All Star	.262	61	16	5	1	3	11	4	19	.318	.525

Career (1990-1993)

	Avg	AB	H	2B	3B	HR	RBI	BB	SO	OBP	SLG
vs. Left	.320	266	85	19	1	10	38	26	56	.388	.511
vs. Right	.233	421	98	22	5	7	42	45	111	.315	.359
Groundball	.253	217	55	10	1	4	21	21	63	.325	.364

	Avg	AB	H	2B	3B	HR	RBI	BB	SO	OBP	SLG
Scoring Posn	.247	170	42	10	3	2	61	15	51	.320	.376
Close & Late	.254	138	35	10	1	2	12	12	35	.325	.384
None on/out	.267	217	58	14	1	9	9	27	49	.351	.465

Career (1990-1993)	Avg	AB	H	2B	3B	HR	RBI	BB	SO	OBP	SLG
Flyball	.293	150	44	11	2	5	21	16	32	.374	.493
Home	.274	318	87	19	3	7	30	40	71	.366	.418
Away	.260	369	96	22	3	10	50	31	96	.324	.417
Day	.276	196	54	14	2	7	32	11	51	.311	.474
Night	.263	491	129	27	4	10	48	60	116	.356	.395
Grass	.286	213	61	14	3	5	33	16	58	.330	.451
Turf	.257	474	122	27	3	12	47	55	109	.349	.403
First Pitch	.330	94	31	7	1	6	17	1	0	.347	.617
Ahead in Count	.399	168	67	13	3	5	25	33	0	.488	.601
Behind in Count	.182	307	56	12	1	4	21	0	140	.199	.267
Two Strikes	.185	324	60	14	2	5	28	37	167	.279	.287

	Avg	AB	H	2B	3B	HR	RBI	BB	SO	OBP	SLG
Batting #1	.260	246	64	13	1	5	21	26	52	.341	.382
Batting #7	.293	246	72	18	4	7	39	28	55	.369	.484
Other	.241	195	47	10	1	5	20	17	60	.315	.379
April	.239	88	21	4	0	2	7	14	24	.358	.352
May	.270	100	27	7	1	1	8	8	20	.324	.390
June	.276	170	47	15	1	3	21	16	39	.349	.429
July	.167	42	7	1	1	2	7	2	17	.213	.381
August	.250	36	9	2	0	2	5	2	8	.293	.472
September/October	.287	251	72	12	3	7	32	29	59	.370	.442
Pre-All Star	.257	378	97	26	2	6	37	39	89	.336	.384
Post-All Star	.278	309	86	15	4	11	43	32	78	.353	.460

Batter vs. Pitcher (career)

Hits Best Against	Avg	AB	H	2B	3B	HR	RBI	BB	SO	OBP	SLG
Danny Jackson	.600	10	6	2	0	1	3	1	0	.636	1.100
Frank Castillo	.500	6	3	1	0	0	5	4	1	.636	.667
Sid Fernandez	.364	11	4	0	0	1	1	0	2	.364	.636
Pete Schourek	.333	18	6	1	0	0	2	1	3	.368	.389

Hits Worst Against	Avg	AB	H	2B	3B	HR	RBI	BB	SO	OBP	SLG
Doug Drabek	.071	14	1	0	0	0	1	0	4	.071	.071
Terry Mulholland	.071	14	1	1	0	0	1	2	5	.176	.143
Dwight Gooden	.167	12	2	0	0	0	0	0	5	.167	.167
John Burkett	.182	11	2	0	0	0	0	1	3	.250	.182
Curt Schilling	.200	10	2	0	0	0	0	1	1	.273	.200

Tony Pena — Red Sox

Age 37 – Bats Right (groundball hitter)

	Avg	G	AB	R	H	2B	3B	HR	RBI	BB	SO	HBP	GDP	SB	CS	OBP	SLG	IBB	SH	SF	#Pit	#P/PA	GB	FB	G/F
1993 Season	.181	126	304	20	55	11	0	4	19	25	46	2	12	1	3	.246	.257	0	13	3	1264	3.64	128	79	1.62
Last Five Years	.239	684	2093	202	500	91	6	21	198	164	264	10	88	25	17	.296	.318	23	34	12	7971	3.45	973	481	2.02

1993 Season

	Avg	AB	H	2B	3B	HR	RBI	BB	SO	OBP	SLG
vs. Left	.253	83	21	4	0	2	6	2	10	.264	.373
vs. Right	.154	221	34	7	0	2	13	23	36	.239	.213
Groundball	.139	36	5	1	0	0	4	5	7	.244	.167
Flyball	.152	66	10	3	0	2	5	5	15	.219	.288
Home	.155	155	24	6	0	2	12	14	23	.227	.232
Away	.208	149	31	5	0	2	7	11	23	.265	.282
Day	.178	101	18	4	0	1	2	9	15	.245	.248
Night	.182	203	37	7	0	3	17	16	31	.246	.261
Grass	.160	256	41	7	0	4	18	24	39	.235	.234
Turf	.292	48	14	4	0	0	1	1	7	.306	.375
First Pitch	.231	52	12	1	0	0	3	0	0	.222	.250
Ahead in Count	.219	64	14	3	0	1	3	14	0	.359	.313
Behind in Count	.152	132	20	5	0	1	9	0	37	.163	.212
Two Strikes	.121	132	16	5	0	1	7	11	46	.194	.182

	Avg	AB	H	2B	3B	HR	RBI	BB	SO	OBP	SLG
Scoring Posn	.143	70	10	2	0	1	16	8	13	.232	.214
Close & Late	.256	31	8	3	0	0	0	3	6	.324	.355
None on/out	.183	71	13	1	0	0	0	6	6	.247	.197
Batting #8	.180	133	24	2	0	1	6	8	17	.225	.218
Batting #9	.182	170	31	9	0	3	12	17	29	.262	.288
Other	.000	1	0	0	0	0	1	0	0	.000	.000
April	.180	50	9	1	0	0	1	0	5	.176	.200
May	.167	60	10	3	0	0	2	8	10	.265	.217
June	.188	48	9	2	0	1	3	5	9	.264	.292
July	.155	58	9	3	0	1	3	6	10	.246	.259
August	.204	49	10	0	0	1	5	3	5	.250	.265
September/October	.205	39	8	2	0	1	5	3	7	.267	.333
Pre-All Star	.178	180	32	8	0	1	6	16	28	.244	.239
Post-All Star	.185	124	23	3	0	3	13	9	18	.248	.282

1993 By Position

Position	Avg	AB	H	2B	3B	HR	RBI	BB	SO	OBP	SLG	G	GS	Innings	PO	A	E	DP	Fld Pct	Rng Fctr	In Zone	Outs	Zone Rtg	MLB Zone
As c	.181	304	55	11	0	4	19	25	46	.246	.257	125	102	915.1	698	53	4	6	.995	---	---	---	---	---

Last Five Years

	Avg	AB	H	2B	3B	HR	RBI	BB	SO	OBP	SLG
vs. Left	.278	625	174	23	1	14	73	43	58	.325	.386
vs. Right	.222	1468	326	68	5	7	125	121	206	.283	.290
Groundball	.247	559	138	23	2	1	54	42	61	.304	.301
Flyball	.246	505	124	27	1	6	44	47	83	.309	.339
Home	.236	1036	245	50	3	11	99	93	136	.301	.322
Away	.241	1057	255	41	3	10	99	71	128	.290	.314
Day	.244	611	149	30	3	3	59	50	82	.303	.318
Night	.237	1482	351	61	3	18	139	114	182	.293	.318
Grass	.239	1528	365	69	5	14	160	130	207	.300	.318
Turf	.239	565	135	22	1	7	38	34	57	.285	.319
First Pitch	.314	392	123	18	2	5	53	18	0	.341	.408
Ahead in Count	.304	448	136	21	2	7	53	83	0	.411	.406
Behind in Count	.168	903	152	35	2	3	57	0	238	.177	.221
Two Strikes	.169	856	145	35	0	3	54	61	264	.230	.221

	Avg	AB	H	2B	3B	HR	RBI	BB	SO	OBP	SLG
Scoring Posn	.239	556	133	22	1	3	171	57	70	.307	.299
Close & Late	.239	356	85	12	2	2	24	29	56	.297	.301
None on/out	.234	474	111	20	2	7	7	46	53	.305	.329
Batting #8	.244	1354	331	59	4	12	131	112	161	.304	.321
Batting #9	.206	306	63	14	0	4	23	28	46	.276	.291
Other	.245	433	106	18	2	5	44	24	57	.283	.330
April	.260	319	83	17	0	5	28	5	35	.270	.361
May	.230	391	90	17	1	4	29	28	51	.288	.309
June	.253	336	85	14	4	2	42	31	47	.314	.336
July	.201	369	74	15	0	4	25	36	46	.276	.274
August	.238	340	81	9	0	3	39	29	48	.298	.291
September/October	.257	338	87	19	1	3	35	35	37	.327	.346
Pre-All Star	.243	1172	285	53	5	11	105	77	148	.292	.325
Post-All Star	.233	921	215	38	1	10	93	87	116	.301	.309

Batter vs. Pitcher (since 1984)

Hits Best Against	Avg	AB	H	2B	3B	HR	RBI	BB	SO	OBP	SLG
Kenny Rogers	.545	11	6	2	0	0	1	0	0	.545	.727
Jimmy Key	.467	30	14	2	0	2	6	0	1	.467	.733
Greg Hibbard	.462	13	6	0	0	1	3	1	1	.500	.692
Ben McDonald	.455	11	5	2	0	0	3	6	3	.647	.636
Dennis Rasmussen	.400	10	4	2	0	0	2	3	1	.538	.600

Hits Worst Against	Avg	AB	H	2B	3B	HR	RBI	BB	SO	OBP	SLG
Duane Ward	.000	11	0	0	0	0	1	2	1	.154	.000
Bob Walk	.053	19	1	1	0	0	1	1	1	.100	.105
Chris Bosio	.053	19	1	0	0	0	1	0	2	.053	.053
Kirk McCaskill	.053	19	1	0	0	0	1	1	4	.100	.053
Jose Guzman	.083	12	1	0	0	0	0	0	1	.083	.083

Terry Pendleton — Braves

Age 33 – Bats Both

	Avg	G	AB	R	H	2B	3B	HR	RBI	BB	SO	HBP	GDP	SB	CS	OBP	SLG	IBB	SH	SF	#Pit	#P/PA	GB	FB	G/F
1993 Season	.272	161	633	81	172	33	1	17	84	36	97	3	18	5	1	.311	.408	5	3	7	2436	3.57	236	188	1.26
Last Five Years	.282	757	2919	402	823	154	17	79	407	190	373	5	78	36	15	.324	.428	32	17	29	10792	3.42	1160	849	1.37

1993 Season

	Avg	AB	H	2B	3B	HR	RBI	BB	SO	OBP	SLG		Avg	AB	H	2B	3B	HR	RBI	BB	SO	OBP	SLG
vs. Left	.297	175	52	9	1	4	27	9	20	.326	.429	Scoring Posn	.229	170	39	7	0	4	60	14	24	.281	.341
vs. Right	.262	458	120	24	0	13	57	27	77	.305	.400	Close & Late	.276	87	24	5	0	2	10	11	18	.354	.402
Groundball	.239	205	49	15	0	5	30	13	32	.283	.385	None on/out	.238	122	29	5	0	4	4	5	21	.268	.377
Flyball	.374	107	40	4	1	4	19	7	20	.419	.542	Batting #3	.277	292	81	14	0	5	34	11	34	.300	.377
Home	.281	310	87	19	1	9	46	18	47	.314	.435	Batting #6	.290	186	54	9	1	9	36	14	37	.342	.495
Away	.263	323	85	14	0	8	38	18	50	.307	.381	Other	.239	155	37	10	0	3	14	11	26	.293	.361
Day	.263	160	42	4	1	5	22	9	27	.295	.394	April	.158	101	16	3	0	2	7	10	20	.234	.248
Night	.275	473	130	29	0	12	62	27	70	.316	.412	May	.279	104	29	8	0	0	14	3	11	.291	.350
Grass	.276	485	104	25	1	13	67	29	71	.316	.412	June	.324	102	33	4	0	3	11	1	13	.336	.451
Turf	.257	148	38	8	0	4	17	7	26	.293	.392	July	.291	110	32	8	0	3	15	7	12	.336	.445
First Pitch	.283	92	26	5	0	4	26	5	0	.313	.467	August	.293	99	29	3	0	2	12	6	21	.330	.384
Ahead in Count	.308	130	40	9	0	3	15	16	0	.381	.446	September/October	.282	117	33	7	1	7	25	9	20	.333	.538
Behind in Count	.221	298	66	8	1	4	28	0	88	.224	.295	Pre-All Star	.259	352	91	18	0	5	36	17	47	.293	.352
Two Strikes	.187	283	53	9	1	4	23	15	97	.229	.269	Post-All Star	.288	281	81	15	1	12	48	19	50	.333	.477

1993 By Position

Position	Avg	AB	H	2B	3B	HR	RBI	BB	SO	OBP	SLG	G	GS	Innings	PO	A	E	DP	Fld Pct	Rng Fctr	In Zone	Outs	Zone Rtg	MLB Zone
As 3b	.273	631	172	33	1	17	84	36	96	.312	.409	161	160	1392.2	129	318	19	32	.959	2.89	427	359	.841	.834

Last Five Years

	Avg	AB	H	2B	3B	HR	RBI	BB	SO	OBP	SLG		Avg	AB	H	2B	3B	HR	RBI	BB	SO	OBP	SLG
vs. Left	.291	964	281	56	6	22	134	55	77	.327	.430	Scoring Posn	.289	788	228	45	5	25	325	76	110	.341	.454
vs. Right	.277	1955	542	98	11	57	273	135	296	.323	.426	Close & Late	.266	448	119	20	2	10	55	44	68	.329	.386
Groundball	.308	1009	311	57	5	24	144	69	121	.350	.446	None on/out	.309	596	184	34	5	15	15	25	62	.337	.458
Flyball	.256	671	172	38	3	22	87	45	99	.304	.420	Batting #3	.296	1268	375	70	5	30	179	77	146	.334	.430
Home	.290	1447	419	84	11	49	224	99	177	.332	.464	Batting #5	.252	654	165	36	3	14	88	44	99	.297	.381
Away	.274	1472	404	70	6	30	183	91	196	.316	.391	Other	.284	997	283	48	9	35	140	69	128	.329	.455
Day	.292	818	239	32	3	27	122	51	109	.331	.438	April	.232	370	86	23	0	5	49	36	49	.297	.335
Night	.278	2101	584	122	14	52	285	139	264	.321	.424	May	.290	489	142	24	3	14	69	31	51	.328	.438
Grass	.300	1651	495	92	7	52	246	107	204	.340	.459	June	.293	509	149	23	4	14	73	25	69	.325	.436
Turf	.259	1268	328	62	10	27	161	83	169	.303	.387	July	.270	515	139	27	2	13	65	23	65	.300	.406
First Pitch	.322	488	157	31	2	15	84	23	0	.349	.486	August	.278	540	150	26	2	15	73	35	74	.321	.417
Ahead in Count	.320	644	206	42	4	28	94	99	0	.408	.528	September/October	.317	496	157	31	6	18	78	40	65	.367	.512
Behind in Count	.238	1313	312	52	5	19	151	0	330	.237	.328	Pre-All Star	.274	1544	423	80	8	37	206	100	188	.316	.408
Two Strikes	.229	1194	273	47	5	21	140	60	373	.265	.329	Post-All Star	.291	1375	400	74	9	42	201	90	185	.333	.449

Batter vs. Pitcher (career)

Hits Best Against	Avg	AB	H	2B	3B	HR	RBI	BB	SO	OBP	SLG	Hits Worst Against	Avg	AB	H	2B	3B	HR	RBI	BB	SO	OBP	SLG
Bryan Hickerson	.692	13	9	1	0	1	3	0	0	.692	1.000	Jesse Orosco	.063	16	1	0	0	0	0	4	4	.250	.063
Shawn Boskie	.615	13	8	4	0	1	1	1	1	.643	1.154	Lee Smith	.067	15	1	1	0	0	0	2	6	.176	.133
Jose DeLeon	.542	24	13	3	2	0	3	3	2	.593	.833	Juan Agosto	.083	12	1	0	0	0	0	1	0	.154	.083
Brian Williams	.538	13	7	0	0	1	6	0	3	.538	.769	Rod Beck	.083	12	1	0	0	0	0	0	4	.083	.083
Norm Charlton	.500	18	9	1	1	1	6	1	1	.526	.833	John Smoltz	.105	19	2	0	0	0	2	3	6	.227	.105

Brad Pennington — Orioles

Age 25 – Pitches Left (flyball pitcher)

	ERA	W	L	Sv	G	GS	IP	BB	SO	Avg	H	2B	3B	HR	RBI	OBP	SLG	GF	IR	IRS	Hld	SvOp	SB	CS	GB	FB	G/F
1993 Season	6.55	3	2	4	34	0	33.0	25	39	.266	34	4	1	7	35	.391	.477	16	45	13	5	7	3	1	33	38	0.87

1993 Season

	ERA	W	L	Sv	G	GS	IP	H	HR	BB	SO		Avg	AB	H	2B	3B	HR	RBI	BB	SO	OBP	SLG
Home	8.00	1	1	3	18	0	18.0	23	3	16	19	vs. Left	.342	38	13	1	0	1	9	4	5	.419	.447
Away	4.80	2	1	1	16	0	15.0	11	4	9	20	vs. Right	.233	90	21	3	1	6	26	21	34	.381	.489
Starter	0.00	0	0	0	0	0	0.0	0	0	0	0	Scoring Posn	.246	65	16	2	0	3	29	12	23	.359	.415
Reliever	6.55	3	2	4	34	0	33.0	34	7	25	39	Close & Late	.212	52	11	1	1	2	9	6	19	.305	.385
0 Days rest	4.50	1	0	0	4	0	4.0	4	1	2	4	None on/out	.278	18	5	0	0	1	1	6	4	.480	.444
1 or 2 Days rest	6.23	1	1	1	12	0	8.2	11	3	5	13	First Pitch	.500	10	5	1	0	1	9	0	0	.500	.900
3+ Days rest	7.08	1	1	3	18	0	20.1	19	3	18	22	Ahead in Count	.200	70	14	0	0	2	9	0	33	.211	.286
Pre-All Star	4.44	3	2	4	25	0	24.1	21	4	13	30	Behind in Count	.500	20	10	2	0	4	11	9	0	.667	1.200
Post-All Star	12.46	0	0	0	9	0	8.2	13	3	12	9	Two Strikes	.171	70	12	1	1	1	10	16	39	.333	.257

William Pennyfeather — Pirates

Age 26 – Bats Right

	Avg	G	AB	R	H	2B	3B	HR	RBI	BB	SO	HBP	GDP	SB	CS	OBP	SLG	IBB	SH	SF	#Pit	#P/PA	GB	FB	G/F
1993 Season	.206	21	34	4	7	1	0	0	2	0	6	0	1	0	1	.206	.235	0	0	0	109	3.21	14	12	1.17
Career (1992-1993)	.209	36	43	6	9	1	0	0	2	0	6	0	2	0	1	.209	.233	0	1	0	132	3.00	18	15	1.20

1993 Season

	Avg	AB	H	2B	3B	HR	RBI	BB	SO	OBP	SLG		Avg	AB	H	2B	3B	HR	RBI	BB	SO	OBP	SLG
vs. Left	.150	20	3	1	0	0	1	0	2	.150	.200	Scoring Posn	.167	6	1	0	0	0	2	0	2	.167	.167
vs. Right	.286	14	4	0	0	0	1	0	4	.286	.286	Close & Late	.000	4	0	0	0	0	0	0	0	.000	.000

Eduardo Perez — Angels

Age 24 – Bats Right

	Avg	G	AB	R	H	2B	3B	HR	RBI	BB	SO	HBP	GDP	SB	CS	OBP	SLG	IBB	SH	SF	#Pit	#P/PA	GB	FB	G/F
1993 Season	.250	52	180	16	45	6	2	4	30	9	39	2	4	5	4	.292	.372	0	0	1	700	3.65	60	56	1.07

1993 Season

	Avg	AB	H	2B	3B	HR	RBI	BB	SO	OBP	SLG
vs. Left	.268	41	11	2	1	0	9	2	8	.318	.366
vs. Right	.245	139	34	4	1	4	21	7	31	.284	.374
Home	.183	82	15	1	2	2	13	5	15	.236	.317
Away	.306	98	30	5	0	2	17	4	24	.340	.418
First Pitch	.250	20	5	1	0	1	2	0	0	.286	.450
Ahead in Count	.381	21	8	2	0	0	6	6	0	.519	.476
Behind in Count	.198	101	20	3	1	2	12	0	36	.204	.307
Two Strikes	.163	92	15	3	1	2	11	3	39	.188	.283

	Avg	AB	H	2B	3B	HR	RBI	BB	SO	OBP	SLG
Scoring Posn	.300	50	15	2	2	3	28	2	13	.333	.600
Close & Late	.257	35	9	2	0	1	6	1	7	.297	.400
None on/out	.211	38	8	2	0	0	0	2	10	.250	.263
Batting #5	.234	107	25	2	1	1	15	2	20	.252	.299
Batting #6	.292	65	19	4	1	3	15	7	16	.361	.523
Other	.125	8	1	0	0	0	0	0	3	.222	.125
Pre-All Star	.000	0	0	0	0	0	0	0	0	.000	.000
Post-All Star	.250	180	45	6	2	4	30	9	39	.292	.372

Melido Perez — Yankees

Age 28 – Pitches Right

	ERA	W	L	Sv	G	GS	IP	BB	SO	Avg	H	2B	3B	HR	RBI	OBP	SLG	CG	ShO	Sup	QS	#P/S	SB	CS	GB	FB	G/F
1993 Season	5.19	6	14	0	25	25	163.0	64	148	.267	173	34	3	22	86	.333	.431	0	0	3.48	8	107	11	6	203	178	1.14
Last Five Years	4.11	51	65	1	173	132	926.2	385	796	.247	860	146	26	90	394	.322	.381	15	4	4.27	67	102	74	52	1094	991	1.10

1993 Season

	ERA	W	L	Sv	G	GS	IP	H	HR	BB	SO
Home	6.26	3	9	0	14	14	83.1	98	12	34	75
Away	4.07	3	5	0	11	11	79.2	75	10	30	73
Day	7.23	3	4	0	8	8	42.1	63	10	11	33
Night	4.48	3	10	0	17	17	120.2	110	12	53	115
Grass	5.58	6	14	0	23	23	146.2	162	21	62	137
Turf	1.65	0	0	0	2	2	16.1	11	1	2	11
April	2.05	1	1	0	3	3	22.0	13	0	8	22
May	4.11	2	3	0	6	6	46.0	41	5	17	39
June	5.66	2	2	0	5	5	35.0	45	7	15	35
July	6.75	0	3	0	5	5	28.0	34	5	11	20
August	6.67	1	4	0	5	5	27.0	31	4	12	28
September/October	9.00	0	1	0	1	1	5.0	9	1	1	4
Starter	5.19	6	14	0	25	25	163.0	173	22	64	148
Reliever	0.00	0	0	0	0	0	0.0	0	0	0	0
0-3 Days Rest	0.00	0	0	0	0	0	0.0	0	0	0	0
4 Days Rest	5.38	4	7	0	14	14	93.2	99	13	37	84
5+ Days Rest	4.93	2	7	0	11	11	69.1	74	9	27	64
Pre-All Star	4.38	5	8	0	16	16	117.0	111	15	46	104
Post-All Star	7.24	1	6	0	9	9	46.0	62	7	18	44

	Avg	AB	H	2B	3B	HR	RBI	BB	SO	OBP	SLG
vs. Left	.281	342	96	15	1	9	38	40	81	.354	.409
vs. Right	.252	305	77	19	2	13	48	24	67	.309	.456
Inning 1-6	.274	551	151	29	2	19	77	52	133	.337	.437
Inning 7+	.229	96	22	5	1	3	9	12	15	.315	.396
None on	.236	373	88	19	2	10	10	39	88	.308	.378
Runners on	.310	274	85	15	1	12	76	25	60	.368	.504
Scoring Posn	.347	147	51	8	1	9	69	14	32	.402	.599
Close & Late	.232	69	16	4	0	0	4	6	12	.293	.290
None on/out	.256	164	42	7	1	4	4	13	27	.311	.384
vs. 1st Batr (relief)	.000	0	0	0	0	0	0	0	0	.000	.000
First Inning Pitched	.298	104	31	3	1	7	21	13	21	.373	.548
First 75 Pitches	.263	426	112	21	1	14	55	40	104	.326	.415
Pitch 76-90	.250	88	22	5	0	1	4	5	24	.290	.341
Pitch 91-105	.312	77	24	5	1	4	19	12	7	.404	.558
Pitch 106+	.268	56	15	3	1	3	8	7	13	.349	.518
First Pitch	.309	94	29	7	3	3	10	5	0	.343	.543
Ahead in Count	.204	299	61	12	0	5	30	0	127	.203	.294
Behind in Count	.361	147	53	10	0	10	29	28	0	.463	.633
Two Strikes	.194	320	62	11	0	6	32	31	148	.264	.284

Last Five Years

	ERA	W	L	Sv	G	GS	IP	H	HR	BB	SO
Home	4.59	19	30	0	80	58	403.2	397	41	166	347
Away	3.73	32	35	1	93	74	523.0	463	49	219	449
Day	4.66	15	18	0	47	43	259.0	266	32	123	214
Night	3.90	36	47	1	126	89	667.2	594	58	262	582
Grass	4.15	46	54	1	145	110	779.0	716	75	325	672
Turf	3.90	5	11	0	28	22	147.2	144	15	60	124
April	3.90	5	8	0	19	19	110.2	98	7	51	102
May	4.21	10	13	0	29	28	186.0	170	21	88	161
June	4.23	11	11	0	33	24	170.1	164	17	70	130
July	3.88	10	9	0	28	19	148.1	129	19	59	112
August	4.42	5	14	0	33	23	167.0	161	13	62	147
September/October	3.87	10	10	1	31	19	144.1	138	13	55	144
Starter	4.31	44	62	0	132	132	837.2	788	84	361	711
Reliever	2.22	7	3	1	41	0	89.0	72	6	24	85
0-3 Days Rest	6.86	0	4	0	4	4	21.0	21	1	13	11
4 Days Rest	4.10	25	32	0	73	73	467.1	436	42	207	392
5+ Days Rest	4.43	19	26	0	55	55	349.1	331	41	141	308
Pre-All Star	4.12	29	36	0	90	77	513.1	472	51	226	427
Post-All Star	4.09	22	29	1	83	55	413.1	388	39	159	369

	Avg	AB	H	2B	3B	HR	RBI	BB	SO	OBP	SLG
vs. Left	.252	1744	439	74	16	41	188	204	394	.329	.383
vs. Right	.242	1742	421	72	10	49	206	181	402	.314	.379
Inning 1-6	.248	2763	686	116	22	72	337	311	634	.325	.384
Inning 7+	.241	723	174	30	4	18	57	74	162	.311	.368
None on	.237	2041	483	87	12	54	54	223	477	.313	.370
Runners on	.261	1445	377	59	14	36	340	162	319	.334	.396
Scoring Posn	.261	804	210	30	6	23	299	102	192	.339	.399
Close & Late	.236	373	88	17	1	7	31	37	83	.306	.343
None on/out	.254	887	225	38	7	22	22	98	176	.329	.387
vs. 1st Batr (relief)	.371	35	13	3	0	1	9	2	8	.395	.543
First Inning Pitched	.280	646	181	25	6	16	106	78	147	.355	.412
First 75 Pitches	.247	2502	619	98	18	64	284	271	579	.322	.378
Pitch 76-90	.248	419	104	21	1	10	42	37	96	.308	.375
Pitch 91-105	.233	330	77	16	4	9	38	41	66	.319	.388
Pitch 106+	.255	235	60	11	3	7	30	36	55	.352	.417
First Pitch	.325	517	168	32	8	12	56	10	0	.337	.487
Ahead in Count	.175	1539	269	44	9	16	120	0	686	.178	.246
Behind in Count	.307	791	243	44	7	33	116	212	0	.450	.506
Two Strikes	.171	1648	281	40	8	27	135	163	796	.247	.254

Pitcher vs. Batter (career)

Pitches Best Vs.	Avg	AB	H	2B	3B	HR	RBI	BB	SO	OBP	SLG
Albert Belle	.000	16	0	0	0	0	0	5	6	.238	.000
Wally Backman	.000	9	0	0	0	0	0	3	4	.250	.000
Travis Fryman	.050	20	1	0	0	0	0	0	7	.050	.050
Carlos Quintana	.071	14	1	0	0	0	0	1	4	.133	.071
Scott Leius	.077	13	1	1	0	0	3	0	4	.077	.154

Pitches Worst Vs.	Avg	AB	H	2B	3B	HR	RBI	BB	SO	OBP	SLG
Rene Gonzales	.583	12	7	1	0	0	2	2	3	.643	.667
John Olerud	.500	14	7	3	0	0	1	8	3	.682	.714
Gary DiSarcina	.500	14	7	1	0	1	6	3	0	.588	.786
Fred McGriff	.368	19	7	0	1	4	7	2	2	.429	1.105
Tim Salmon	.333	12	4	1	0	2	4	1	5	.385	.917

Mike Perez — Cardinals

Age 29 – Pitches Right

	ERA	W	L	Sv	G	GS	IP	BB	SO	Avg	H	2B	3B	HR	RBI	OBP	SLG	GF	IR	IRS	Hld	SvOp	SB	CS	GB	FB	G/F
1993 Season	2.48	7	2	7	65	0	72.2	20	58	.244	65	8	3	4	27	.295	.342	25	22	7	13	10	8	2	83	78	1.06
Career (1990-1993)	2.57	17	7	8	169	0	196.1	62	116	.232	166	23	6	9	67	.292	.319	56	82	22	26	15	17	5	253	225	1.12

1993 Season

	ERA	W	L	Sv	G	GS	IP	H	HR	BB	SO
Home	2.65	7	0	3	30	0	37.1	32	2	9	27
Away	2.29	0	2	4	35	0	35.1	33	2	11	31
Day	3.75	3	1	3	25	0	24.0	24	3	8	21
Night	1.85	4	1	4	40	0	48.2	41	1	12	37
Grass	2.42	0	1	2	24	0	26.0	22	2	9	26
Turf	2.51	7	1	5	41	0	46.2	43	2	11	32
April	3.31	2	1	0	12	0	16.1	18	2	4	16
May	1.65	2	1	2	14	0	16.1	12	0	4	14
June	2.03	0	0	1	14	0	13.1	8	0	0	11
July	0.00	0	0	0	3	0	1.1	4	0	0	0
August	1.13	1	0	0	7	0	8.0	6	1	1	7
September/October	3.63	2	0	4	15	0	17.1	17	1	3	10
Starter	0.00	0	0	0	0	0	0.0	0	0	0	0
Reliever	2.48	7	2	7	65	0	72.2	65	4	20	58
0 Days rest	1.88	1	0	5	25	0	28.2	27	0	7	27
1 or 2 Days rest	2.10	4	1	2	30	0	34.1	24	2	10	28
3+ Days rest	5.59	2	1	0	10	0	9.2	14	2	3	3
Pre-All Star	2.28	4	2	3	43	0	47.1	42	2	16	41
Post-All Star	2.84	3	0	4	22	0	25.1	23	2	4	17

	Avg	AB	H	2B	3B	HR	RBI	BB	SO	OBP	SLG
vs. Left	.272	114	31	4	1	2	13	10	21	.328	.377
vs. Right	.224	152	34	4	2	2	14	10	37	.269	.316
Inning 1-6	.286	7	2	0	0	0	1	1	3	.375	.286
Inning 7+	.243	259	63	8	3	4	26	19	55	.292	.344
None on	.242	161	39	4	2	2	2	8	34	.278	.329
Runners on	.248	105	26	4	1	2	25	12	24	.317	.362
Scoring Posn	.266	64	17	3	0	1	22	8	14	.325	.359
Close & Late	.234	145	34	2	2	4	15	9	33	.277	.359
None on/out	.221	68	15	2	2	1	1	5	12	.274	.353
vs. 1st Batr (relief)	.237	59	14	2	0	0	4	4	13	.277	.271
First Inning Pitched	.231	208	48	6	1	3	21	18	45	.290	.313
First 15 Pitches	.233	193	45	5	1	3	16	13	42	.278	.316
Pitch 16-30	.297	64	19	3	2	1	10	7	12	.365	.453
Pitch 31-45	.111	9	1	0	0	0	1	0	4	.111	.111
Pitch 46+	.000	0	0	0	0	0	0	0	0	.000	.000
First Pitch	.368	38	14	2	1	2	8	0	0	.368	.632
Ahead in Count	.185	130	24	2	2	1	6	0	52	.183	.254
Behind in Count	.319	47	15	3	0	1	6	7	0	.400	.447
Two Strikes	.165	127	21	1	2	1	7	13	58	.245	.228

Career (1990-1993)

	ERA	W	L	Sv	G	GS	IP	H	HR	BB	SO
Home	2.08	13	3	4	77	0	99.2	78	2	26	53
Away	3.07	4	4	4	92	0	96.2	88	7	36	63
Day	3.93	5	3	3	58	0	66.1	61	6	24	45
Night	1.87	12	4	5	111	0	130.0	105	3	38	71
Grass	2.56	4	2	2	49	0	52.2	47	3	21	41
Turf	2.57	13	5	6	120	0	143.2	119	6	41	75
April	2.42	4	2	0	31	0	48.1	43	2	12	32
May	3.03	4	2	2	31	0	32.2	31	1	11	24
June	2.15	1	1	1	30	0	29.1	19	1	14	21
July	1.13	1	1	0	14	0	16.0	17	0	5	6
August	1.96	2	1	0	19	0	23.0	17	4	11	11
September/October	3.45	5	0	5	44	0	47.0	39	1	9	22
Starter	0.00	0	0	0	0	0	0.0	0	0	0	0
Reliever	2.57	17	7	8	169	0	196.1	166	9	62	116
0 Days rest	2.14	5	2	5	56	0	63.0	53	0	15	40
1 or 2 Days rest	2.69	7	3	3	81	0	93.2	74	6	30	58
3+ Days rest	2.95	5	2	0	32	0	39.2	39	3	17	18
Pre-All Star	2.50	10	5	3	99	0	115.1	102	4	40	80
Post-All Star	2.67	7	2	5	70	0	81.0	64	5	22	36

	Avg	AB	H	2B	3B	HR	RBI	BB	SO	OBP	SLG
vs. Left	.262	321	84	12	2	4	34	37	45	.335	.349
vs. Right	.208	394	82	11	4	5	33	25	71	.255	.294
Inning 1-6	.200	90	18	3	0	0	7	7	16	.257	.233
Inning 7+	.237	625	148	20	6	9	60	55	100	.297	.331
None on	.225	436	98	14	5	6	6	23	73	.265	.321
Runners on	.244	279	68	9	1	3	61	39	43	.329	.315
Scoring Posn	.244	164	40	6	0	2	57	31	24	.348	.317
Close & Late	.238	340	81	8	4	7	32	37	55	.313	.347
None on/out	.217	184	40	4	3	4	4	8	21	.254	.337
vs. 1st Batr (relief)	.236	157	37	5	0	2	15	7	22	.268	.306
First Inning Pitched	.225	515	116	16	2	7	57	46	87	.287	.305
First 15 Pitches	.217	498	108	14	3	7	44	39	81	.271	.299
Pitch 16-30	.280	189	53	9	3	2	22	20	28	.352	.392
Pitch 31-45	.179	28	5	0	0	0	1	3	7	.258	.179
Pitch 46+	.000	0	0	0	0	0	0	0	0	.000	.000
First Pitch	.292	106	31	6	1	3	14	7	0	.333	.453
Ahead in Count	.196	331	65	9	3	3	22	0	97	.198	.269
Behind in Count	.268	142	38	7	1	1	17	28	0	.382	.352
Two Strikes	.162	315	51	5	2	1	19	27	116	.231	.200

Pitcher vs. Batter (career)

Pitches Best Vs.	Avg	AB	H	2B	3B	HR	RBI	BB	SO	OBP	SLG
Tim Wallach	.000	12	0	0	0	0	1	2	2	.133	.000
Ryne Sandberg	.182	11	2	0	0	0	3	0	0	.167	.182

Pitches Worst Vs.	Avg	AB	H	2B	3B	HR	RBI	BB	SO	OBP	SLG

Gerald Perry — Cardinals

Age 33 – Bats Left

	Avg	G	AB	R	H	2B	3B	HR	RBI	BB	SO	HBP	GDP	SB	CS	OBP	SLG	IBB	SH	SF	#Pit	#P/PA	GB	FB	G/F
1993 Season	.337	96	98	21	33	5	0	4	16	18	23	0	4	1	1	.440	.510	2	0	0	455	3.92	37	21	1.76
Last Five Years	.255	497	1214	144	310	54	6	23	148	126	164	7	29	46	25	.326	.367	16	0	12	4786	3.52	510	344	1.48

1993 Season

	Avg	AB	H	2B	3B	HR	RBI	BB	SO	OBP	SLG
vs. Left	.250	8	2	0	0	0	0	2	1	.400	.250
vs. Right	.344	90	31	5	0	4	16	16	22	.443	.533

	Avg	AB	H	2B	3B	HR	RBI	BB	SO	OBP	SLG
Scoring Posn	.357	28	10	2	0	1	12	9	6	.514	.536
Close & Late	.333	30	10	2	0	1	8	13	9	.535	.500

Last Five Years

	Avg	AB	H	2B	3B	HR	RBI	BB	SO	OBP	SLG
vs. Left	.253	375	95	13	2	6	39	27	50	.306	.347
vs. Right	.256	839	215	41	4	17	109	99	114	.334	.375
Groundball	.254	390	99	18	2	4	39	45	35	.330	.341
Flyball	.264	296	78	11	3	7	39	31	54	.333	.392
Home	.262	615	161	28	5	10	73	63	77	.330	.372
Away	.249	599	149	26	1	13	75	63	87	.321	.361
Day	.298	322	96	15	2	11	48	35	39	.363	.460
Night	.240	892	214	39	4	12	100	91	125	.313	.333
Grass	.270	514	139	25	1	11	64	54	62	.341	.387
Turf	.244	700	171	29	5	12	84	72	102	.315	.351
First Pitch	.282	195	55	11	3	3	26	10	0	.317	.415
Ahead in Count	.260	315	82	15	2	9	54	70	0	.391	.406
Behind in Count	.222	495	110	15	1	5	33	0	133	.229	.287
Two Strikes	.184	489	90	12	1	6	33	44	164	.256	.249

	Avg	AB	H	2B	3B	HR	RBI	BB	SO	OBP	SLG
Scoring Posn	.263	342	90	25	3	3	117	61	51	.367	.380
Close & Late	.229	258	59	8	2	7	40	40	42	.334	.357
None on/out	.244	262	64	9	0	7	7	17	24	.295	.359
Batting #3	.248	471	117	18	2	7	45	47	56	.322	.340
Batting #5	.293	205	60	13	2	3	26	15	29	.338	.420
Other	.247	538	133	23	2	13	77	64	79	.325	.370
April	.285	193	55	8	1	6	31	37	21	.400	.430
May	.235	272	64	15	1	3	32	25	36	.299	.331
June	.252	214	54	10	1	3	21	12	25	.293	.350
July	.248	250	62	11	0	8	28	21	43	.304	.388
August	.296	162	48	5	3	1	23	17	21	.363	.383
September/October	.220	123	27	5	0	2	13	14	18	.309	.309
Pre-All Star	.250	752	188	34	3	16	96	80	95	.322	.367
Post-All Star	.264	462	122	20	3	7	52	46	69	.333	.366

Batter vs. Pitcher (since 1984)

Hits Best Against	Avg	AB	H	2B	3B	HR	RBI	BB	SO	OBP	SLG	Hits Worst Against	Avg	AB	H	2B	3B	HR	RBI	BB	SO	OBP	SLG
Danny Cox	.550	20	11	2	0	0	2	2	1	.591	.650	Steve Avery	.000	11	0	0	0	0	0	2	1	.154	.000
Dennis Rasmussen	.438	16	7	0	1	2	5	1	2	.444	.938	Dave Stewart	.000	10	0	0	0	0	0	1	2	.091	.000
Tom Browning	.429	21	9	2	0	1	2	0	2	.429	.667	Roger McDowell	.063	16	1	1	0	0	0	2	3	.167	.125
Larry Andersen	.357	14	5	2	0	1	3	1	0	.375	.714	Bobby Ojeda	.091	11	1	0	0	0	1	1	1	.167	.091
Dennis Martinez	.353	17	6	3	0	1	5	1	0	.389	.706	Goose Gossage	.100	10	1	0	0	0	2	0	2	.091	.100

Mark Petkovsek — Pirates

Age 28 – Pitches Right

	ERA	W	L	Sv	G	GS	IP	BB	SO	Avg	H	2B	3B	HR	RBI	OBP	SLG	GF	IR	IRS	Hld	SvOp	SB	CS	GB	FB	G/F
1993 Season	6.96	3	0	0	26	0	32.1	9	14	.328	43	7	4	7	31	.369	.603	8	20	9	0	0	7	0	64	35	1.83
Career (1991-1993)	8.64	3	1	0	30	1	41.2	13	20	.358	64	10	4	11	47	.397	.642	9	22	10	0	0	8	0	80	54	1.48

1993 Season

	ERA	W	L	Sv	G	GS	IP	H	HR	BB	SO		Avg	AB	H	2B	3B	HR	RBI	BB	SO	OBP	SLG
Home	4.50	1	0	0	13	0	18.0	18	3	6	4	vs. Left	.409	44	18	3	2	2	8	3	6	.447	.705
Away	10.05	2	0	0	13	0	14.1	25	4	3	10	vs. Right	.287	87	25	4	2	5	23	6	8	.330	.552
Starter	0.00	0	0	0	0	0	0.0	0	0	0	0	Scoring Posn	.389	54	21	4	1	3	27	7	6	.452	.667
Reliever	6.96	3	0	0	26	0	32.1	43	7	9	14	Close & Late	.150	20	3	0	0	0	0	4	1	.292	.150
0 Days rest	24.00	0	0	0	3	0	3.0	11	1	3	0	None on/out	.346	26	9	1	1	3	3	0	2	.346	.808
1 or 2 Days rest	3.80	2	0	0	16	0	21.1	20	5	3	8	First Pitch	.455	22	10	1	2	3	9	2	0	.500	1.091
3+ Days rest	9.00	1	0	0	7	0	8.0	12	1	3	6	Ahead in Count	.286	42	12	2	1	1	7	0	12	.286	.452
Pre-All Star	3.75	1	0	0	9	0	12.0	14	0	3	6	Behind in Count	.348	46	16	4	1	2	13	4	0	.392	.609
Post-All Star	8.85	2	0	0	17	0	20.1	29	7	6	8	Two Strikes	.205	44	9	2	1	0	5	3	14	.255	.295

Geno Petralli — Rangers

Age 34 – Bats Both

	Avg	G	AB	R	H	2B	3B	HR	RBI	BB	SO	HBP	GDP	SB	CS	OBP	SLG	IBB	SH	SF	#Pit	#P/PA	GB	FB	G/F
1993 Season	.241	59	133	16	32	5	0	1	13	22	17	0	5	2	0	.348	.301	3	1	0	583	3.74	51	36	1.42
Last Five Years	.255	443	1033	94	263	45	2	8	95	130	149	5	34	4	3	.339	.325	10	11	5	4455	3.76	358	291	1.23

1993 Season

	Avg	AB	H	2B	3B	HR	RBI	BB	SO	OBP	SLG		Avg	AB	H	2B	3B	HR	RBI	BB	SO	OBP	SLG
vs. Left	.267	15	4	1	0	0	0	2	1	.353	.333	Scoring Posn	.222	36	8	1	0	0	11	9	4	.378	.250
vs. Right	.237	118	28	4	0	1	13	20	16	.348	.297	Close & Late	.261	23	6	1	0	0	3	7	2	.433	.304
Home	.185	54	10	1	0	1	3	6	10	.267	.259	None on/out	.174	23	4	2	0	0	0	5	3	.321	.261
Away	.278	79	22	4	0	0	10	16	7	.400	.329	Batting #5	.321	28	9	0	0	1	6	10	4	.500	.429
First Pitch	.400	25	10	2	0	0	2	2	0	.444	.480	Batting #6	.261	46	12	2	0	0	3	4	7	.320	.304
Ahead in Count	.200	40	8	0	0	1	2	12	0	.385	.275	Other	.186	59	11	3	0	0	4	8	6	.284	.237
Behind in Count	.217	46	10	3	0	0	7	0	14	.217	.283	Pre-All Star	.309	55	17	1	0	1	8	12	4	.433	.382
Two Strikes	.208	53	11	1	0	0	4	8	17	.311	.226	Post-All Star	.192	78	15	4	0	0	5	10	13	.284	.244

Last Five Years

	Avg	AB	H	2B	3B	HR	RBI	BB	SO	OBP	SLG		Avg	AB	H	2B	3B	HR	RBI	BB	SO	OBP	SLG
vs. Left	.200	75	15	1	0	0	5	13	17	.311	.213	Scoring Posn	.244	246	60	10	2	3	86	45	38	.355	.337
vs. Right	.259	958	248	44	2	8	90	117	132	.342	.334	Close & Late	.226	186	42	8	0	1	12	31	27	.335	.285
Groundball	.317	284	90	13	1	2	30	35	30	.393	.391	None on/out	.249	233	58	12	0	1	1	32	37	.345	.313
Flyball	.225	244	55	11	0	1	20	33	37	.321	.283	Batting #6	.266	297	79	12	0	3	20	31	38	.343	.337
Home	.229	497	114	19	0	2	34	56	81	.310	.280	Batting #7	.247	373	92	18	0	0	26	51	54	.336	.295
Away	.278	536	149	26	2	6	61	74	68	.366	.368	Other	.253	363	92	15	2	5	49	48	57	.339	.347
Day	.283	219	62	15	0	1	26	35	28	.380	.365	April	.264	159	42	6	1	1	12	20	25	.344	.333
Night	.247	814	201	30	2	7	69	95	121	.328	.314	May	.232	211	49	7	1	2	22	24	23	.312	.303
Grass	.250	873	218	35	2	7	79	103	124	.330	.318	June	.240	175	42	10	0	3	17	18	25	.320	.349
Turf	.281	160	45	10	0	1	16	27	25	.388	.363	July	.241	112	27	4	0	0	10	24	22	.370	.277
First Pitch	.333	186	62	13	0	1	17	5	0	.351	.419	August	.298	198	59	7	0	2	25	19	30	.359	.364
Ahead in Count	.296	267	79	13	1	4	33	59	0	.422	.397	September/October	.247	178	44	11	0	0	9	25	24	.343	.309
Behind in Count	.195	389	76	11	0	1	19	0	129	.201	.231	Pre-All Star	.250	584	146	25	2	6	55	71	79	.334	.330
Two Strikes	.179	446	80	11	0	2	23	65	149	.289	.217	Post-All Star	.261	449	117	20	0	2	40	59	70	.346	.318

Batter vs. Pitcher (since 1984)

Hits Best Against	Avg	AB	H	2B	3B	HR	RBI	BB	SO	OBP	SLG	Hits Worst Against	Avg	AB	H	2B	3B	HR	RBI	BB	SO	OBP	SLG
Jaime Navarro	.500	10	5	0	0	0	2	1	1	.545	.500	Tom Gordon	.000	11	0	0	0	0	0	3	2	.214	.000
Dave Stieb	.476	21	10	2	0	0	1	5	1	.577	.571	Mark Gubicza	.050	20	1	0	0	0	1	2	7	.130	.050
Mike Boddicker	.444	36	16	4	0	2	3	4	5	.500	.722	Dave Stewart	.095	21	2	1	0	0	1	2	4	.167	.143
Melido Perez	.333	30	10	1	2	2	4	3	6	.394	.700	Bobby Thigpen	.111	18	2	0	0	0	1	0	5	.111	.111
Eric Plunk	.333	15	5	2	0	1	6	1	2	.375	.667	Kevin Appier	.167	12	2	0	0	0	0	1	3	.231	.167

J.R. Phillips — Giants

Age 24 – Bats Left

	Avg	G	AB	R	H	2B	3B	HR	RBI	BB	SO	HBP	GDP	SB	CS	OBP	SLG	IBB	SH	SF	#Pit	#P/PA	GB	FB	G/F
1993 Season	.313	11	16	1	5	1	1	1	4	0	5	0	0	0	0	.313	.688	0	0	0	57	3.56	4	5	0.80

1993 Season

	Avg	AB	H	2B	3B	HR	RBI	BB	SO	OBP	SLG		Avg	AB	H	2B	3B	HR	RBI	BB	SO	OBP	SLG
vs. Left	.000	2	0	0	0	0	0	0	1	.000	.000	Scoring Posn	.400	5	2	1	0	1	4	0	2	.400	1.200
vs. Right	.357	14	5	1	1	1	4	0	4	.357	.786	Close & Late	.500	2	1	0	0	0	0	0	0	.500	.500

Tony Phillips — Tigers

Age 35 – Bats Both (groundball hitter)

	Avg	G	AB	R	H	2B	3B	HR	RBI	BB	SO	HBP	GDP	SB	CS	OBP	SLG	IBB	SH	SF	#Pit	#P/PA	GB	FB	G/F
1993 Season	.313	151	566	113	177	27	0	7	57	132	102	4	11	16	11	.443	.398	5	1	4	2938	4.16	247	104	2.38
Last Five Years	.278	751	2760	459	766	125	18	46	295	482	441	15	59	60	43	.385	.386	14	23	26	13189	3.99	1095	682	1.61

1993 Season

	Avg	AB	H	2B	3B	HR	RBI	BB	SO	OBP	SLG		Avg	AB	H	2B	3B	HR	RBI	BB	SO	OBP	SLG
vs. Left	.316	171	54	8	0	1	10	40	28	.444	.380	Scoring Posn	.301	133	40	6	0	2	52	36	28	.446	.391
vs. Right	.311	395	123	19	0	6	47	92	74	.443	.405	Close & Late	.275	69	19	4	0	1	9	17	19	.419	.377
Groundball	.328	119	39	2	0	2	10	28	24	.459	.395	None on/out	.313	227	71	11	0	3	3	48	42	.433	.401
Flyball	.324	111	36	8	0	2	20	21	19	.425	.450	Batting #1	.311	559	174	27	0	7	56	131	101	.443	.397
Home	.309	256	79	12	0	3	23	67	56	.452	.391	Batting #8	.250	4	1	0	0	0	0	0	1	.250	.250
Away	.316	310	98	15	0	4	34	65	46	.436	.403	Other	.667	3	2	0	0	0	1	1	0	.750	.667
Day	.328	189	62	12	0	3	26	52	29	.469	.439	April	.348	89	31	2	0	2	13	20	12	.464	.438
Night	.305	377	115	15	0	4	31	80	73	.430	.377	May	.287	94	27	5	0	1	14	23	20	.427	.372
Grass	.314	472	148	23	0	4	40	109	87	.444	.388	June	.274	95	26	7	0	1	9	23	17	.412	.379
Turf	.309	94	29	4	0	3	17	23	15	.442	.447	July	.337	101	34	7	0	1	9	29	22	.485	.436
First Pitch	.403	67	27	2	0	1	9	4	0	.459	.478	August	.286	98	28	2	0	1	8	22	16	.423	.337
Ahead in Count	.409	115	47	8	0	2	21	58	0	.600	.530	September/October	.348	89	31	4	0	1	4	15	15	.448	.427
Behind in Count	.231	247	57	7	0	1	17	0	76	.233	.271	Pre-All Star	.313	319	100	17	0	4	42	81	56	.450	.404
Two Strikes	.231	286	66	10	0	3	20	70	102	.383	.297	Post-All Star	.312	247	77	10	0	3	15	51	46	.434	.389

1993 By Position

Position	Avg	AB	H	2B	3B	HR	RBI	BB	SO	OBP	SLG	G	GS	Innings	PO	A	E	DP	Fld Pct	Rng Fctr	In Zone	Outs	Zone Rtg	MLB Zone
As 2b	.352	182	64	12	0	1	20	39	29	.466	.434	51	47	403.2	106	158	4	33	.985	5.89	181	165	.912	.895
As lf	.278	234	65	10	0	4	22	52	45	.410	.372	70	61	522.2	130	3	2	0	.985	2.29	144	124	.861	.818
As rf	.276	105	29	4	0	0	7	26	19	.422	.314	34	27	246.0	69	2	4	1	.947	2.60	79	65	.823	.826

Last Five Years

	Avg	AB	H	2B	3B	HR	RBI	BB	SO	OBP	SLG		Avg	AB	H	2B	3B	HR	RBI	BB	SO	OBP	SLG
vs. Left	.288	840	242	41	7	19	87	158	108	.402	.421	Scoring Posn	.290	600	174	30	7	9	242	118	97	.397	.408
vs. Right	.273	1920	524	84	11	27	208	324	333	.377	.370	Close & Late	.253	384	97	22	2	8	45	74	76	.376	.383
Groundball	.282	733	207	25	2	13	77	123	104	.387	.375	None on/out	.272	990	269	43	4	17	17	163	162	.376	.375
Flyball	.274	650	178	35	5	13	76	110	114	.376	.403	Batting #1	.282	2064	582	102	12	33	219	367	330	.391	.391
Home	.277	1337	371	50	4	21	142	262	223	.395	.368	Batting #2	.293	263	77	11	2	6	28	49	38	.403	.418
Away	.278	1423	395	75	14	25	153	220	218	.374	.403	Other	.247	433	107	12	4	7	48	66	73	.345	.342
Day	.282	909	256	39	3	15	98	157	138	.386	.381	April	.284	387	110	13	3	6	41	65	60	.386	.380
Night	.276	1851	510	86	15	31	197	325	303	.384	.388	May	.265	456	121	20	5	10	70	93	70	.391	.397
Grass	.275	2317	637	97	13	33	228	415	377	.385	.371	June	.253	455	115	24	3	9	50	91	79	.375	.378
Turf	.291	443	129	28	5	13	67	67	64	.383	.465	July	.287	484	139	27	3	8	43	88	81	.397	.405
First Pitch	.332	371	123	14	5	9	46	10	0	.353	.469	August	.280	472	132	18	2	8	47	72	77	.374	.377
Ahead in Count	.355	681	242	45	3	20	114	240	0	.519	.518	September/October	.294	506	149	23	2	5	44	73	74	.384	.377
Behind in Count	.217	1136	247	39	6	9	82	0	347	.220	.286	Pre-All Star	.275	1479	406	71	13	25	171	283	237	.391	.391
Two Strikes	.209	1290	269	42	7	12	93	231	441	.330	.280	Post-All Star	.281	1281	360	54	5	21	124	199	204	.378	.380

Batter vs. Pitcher (since 1984)

Hits Best Against	Avg	AB	H	2B	3B	HR	RBI	BB	SO	OBP	SLG	Hits Worst Against	Avg	AB	H	2B	3B	HR	RBI	BB	SO	OBP	SLG
Wilson Alvarez	.500	10	5	1	0	0	0	2	1	.583	.600	John Habyan	.083	12	1	0	0	0	0	1	1	.154	.083
Carl Willis	.417	12	5	2	1	0	0	0	2	.417	.750	David Wells	.100	20	2	1	0	0	1	1	5	.143	.150
Todd Burns	.417	12	5	1	0	1	2	1	1	.462	.750	Chuck Cary	.143	14	2	0	0	0	1	1	3	.200	.143
Storm Davis	.400	25	10	1	0	2	8	6	3	.516	.680	Cal Eldred	.143	14	2	0	0	0	2	1	2	.188	.143
Edwin Nunez	.400	10	4	1	1	0	5	2	2	.500	.700	Jeff Montgomery	.167	12	2	0	0	0	1	0	4	.167	.167

Mike Piazza — Dodgers

Age 25 – Bats Right

	Avg	G	AB	R	H	2B	3B	HR	RBI	BB	SO	HBP	GDP	SB	CS	OBP	SLG	IBB	SH	SF	#Pit	#P/PA	GB	FB	G/F
1993 Season	.318	149	547	81	174	24	2	35	112	46	86	3	10	3	4	.370	.561	6	0	6	2243	3.73	211	157	1.34
Career (1992-1993)	.308	170	616	86	190	27	2	36	119	50	98	4	11	3	4	.361	.534	6	0	6	2502	3.70	240	169	1.42

1993 Season

	Avg	AB	H	2B	3B	HR	RBI	BB	SO	OBP	SLG		Avg	AB	H	2B	3B	HR	RBI	BB	SO	OBP	SLG
vs. Left	.324	142	46	8	0	13	36	13	19	.377	.655	Scoring Posn	.324	148	48	2	0	7	73	16	22	.380	.480
vs. Right	.316	405	128	16	2	22	76	33	67	.368	.528	Close & Late	.237	97	23	4	1	2	6	7	18	.288	.361
Groundball	.291	134	39	5	0	5	24	13	20	.355	.440	None on/out	.363	124	45	6	0	12	12	8	16	.410	.702
Flyball	.330	91	30	2	1	12	27	5	20	.361	.769	Batting #3	.328	125	41	6	0	8	30	14	24	.397	.568
Home	.313	281	88	11	1	21	63	25	48	.370	.584	Batting #5	.320	278	89	10	2	18	55	18	46	.363	.565
Away	.323	266	86	13	1	14	49	21	38	.371	.538	Other	.306	144	44	8	0	9	27	14	16	.360	.549
Day	.370	135	50	8	0	10	29	14	20	.425	.652	April	.307	75	23	4	0	4	13	6	17	.354	.520
Night	.301	412	124	16	2	25	83	32	66	.352	.532	May	.344	96	33	3	0	4	19	5	18	.385	.500
Grass	.319	430	137	19	1	30	94	34	69	.369	.577	June	.302	96	29	4	1	7	20	5	15	.333	.583
Turf	.316	117	37	5	1	5	18	12	17	.377	.504	July	.290	93	27	3	1	6	15	8	12	.347	.538
First Pitch	.426	54	23	1	0	9	25	5	0	.452	.944	August	.333	84	28	4	0	7	18	10	8	.402	.631
Ahead in Count	.394	137	54	8	1	11	29	28	0	.497	.708	September/October	.330	103	34	6	0	7	27	12	16	.397	.592
Behind in Count	.259	247	64	10	1	11	34	0	69	.262	.441	Pre-All Star	.317	306	97	12	1	18	58	20	56	.360	.539
Two Strikes	.250	244	61	8	1	8	30	13	86	.291	.389	Post-All Star	.320	241	77	12	1	17	54	26	30	.384	.589

1993 By Position

Position	Avg	AB	H	2B	3B	HR	RBI	BB	SO	OBP	SLG	G	GS	Innings	PO	A	E	DP	Fld Pct	Rng Fctr	In Zone	Outs	Zone Rtg	MLB Zone
As c	.321	542	174	24	2	35	112	46	84	.374	.566	146	141	1243.1	898	99	11	11	.989	---	---	---	---	---

Hipolito Pichardo — Royals

Age 24 – Pitches Right (groundball pitcher)

	ERA	W	L	Sv	G	GS	IP	BB	SO	Avg	H	2B	3B	HR	RBI	OBP	SLG	CG	ShO	Sup	QS	#P/S	SB	CS	GB	FB	G/F
1993 Season	4.04	7	8	0	30	25	165.0	53	70	.282	183	46	0	10	76	.338	.398	2	0	5.02	8	100	8	7	309	139	2.22
Career (1992-1993)	3.99	16	14	0	61	49	308.2	102	129	.275	331	77	2	19	131	.333	.390	3	1	5.34	20	91	19	10	550	293	1.88

1993 Season

	ERA	W	L	Sv	G	GS	IP	H	HR	BB	SO		Avg	AB	H	2B	3B	HR	RBI	BB	SO	OBP	SLG
Home	3.90	4	4	0	17	14	90.0	105	7	26	38	vs. Left	.303	333	101	22	0	5	44	30	24	.358	.414
Away	4.20	3	4	0	13	11	75.0	78	3	27	32	vs. Right	.259	317	82	24	0	5	32	23	46	.316	.382
Day	3.95	3	3	0	11	8	57.0	58	2	18	29	Inning 1-6	.289	582	168	43	0	9	73	47	61	.343	.409
Night	4.08	4	5	0	19	17	108.0	125	8	35	41	Inning 7+	.221	68	15	3	0	1	3	6	9	.293	.309
Grass	4.09	2	1	0	8	7	44.0	45	1	16	15	None on	.299	341	102	26	0	6	6	28	33	.359	.428
Turf	4.02	5	7	0	22	18	121.0	138	9	37	55	Runners on	.262	309	81	20	0	4	70	25	37	.314	.366
April	4.28	1	1	0	5	4	27.1	30	1	7	16	Scoring Posn	.281	178	50	13	0	2	63	21	27	.346	.388
May	4.26	2	1	0	5	5	31.2	37	1	14	12	Close & Late	.257	35	9	2	0	1	3	3	4	.316	.400
June	4.55	1	2	0	5	5	31.2	31	2	17	13	None on/out	.277	159	44	11	0	4	4	13	14	.335	.421
July	4.67	1	3	0	6	5	34.2	44	6	5	12	vs. 1st Batr (relief)	.400	5	2	1	0	0	1	0	0	.400	.600
August	2.70	1	0	0	3	3	16.2	16	0	7	7	First Inning Pitched	.311	122	38	8	0	0	18	12	19	.368	.377
September/October	2.74	1	1	0	6	3	23.0	25	0	3	10	First 75 Pitches	.294	489	144	35	0	7	59	38	56	.346	.409
Starter	4.00	7	7	0	25	25	155.1	170	10	52	64	Pitch 76-90	.239	88	21	6	0	1	6	4	6	.277	.341
Reliever	4.66	0	1	0	5	0	9.2	13	0	1	6	Pitch 91-105	.231	52	12	4	0	2	6	8	6	.333	.423
0-3 Days Rest	1.80	0	0	0	1	1	5.0	3	0	2	3	Pitch 106+	.286	21	6	1	0	0	5	3	2	.400	.333
4 Days Rest	5.04	4	4	0	12	12	69.2	88	5	22	27	First Pitch	.274	95	26	6	0	1	13	2	0	.293	.368
5+ Days Rest	3.24	3	3	0	12	12	80.2	79	5	28	34	Ahead in Count	.259	228	59	17	0	1	17	0	54	.264	.346
Pre-All Star	4.06	4	5	0	18	16	106.1	112	6	40	47	Behind in Count	.335	170	57	11	0	5	32	25	0	.421	.488
Post-All Star	3.99	3	3	0	12	9	58.2	71	4	13	23	Two Strikes	.228	250	57	10	0	2	16	26	70	.301	.292

Greg Pirkl — Mariners

Age 23 – Bats Right

	Avg	G	AB	R	H	2B	3B	HR	RBI	BB	SO	HBP	GDP	SB	CS	OBP	SLG	IBB	SH	SF	#Pit	#P/PA	GB	FB	G/F
1993 Season	.174	7	23	1	4	0	0	1	4	0	4	0	2	0	0	.174	.304	0	0	0	68	2.96	7	11	0.64

1993 Season

	Avg	AB	H	2B	3B	HR	RBI	BB	SO	OBP	SLG		Avg	AB	H	2B	3B	HR	RBI	BB	SO	OBP	SLG
vs. Left	.214	14	3	0	0	1	4	0	1	.214	.429	Scoring Posn	.333	6	2	0	0	1	4	0	1	.333	.833
vs. Right	.111	9	1	0	0	0	0	0	3	.111	.111	Close & Late	.000	1	0	0	0	0	0	0	0	.000	.000

Erik Plantenberg — Mariners

Age 25 – Pitches Left (groundball pitcher)

	ERA	W	L	Sv	G	GS	IP	BB	SO	Avg	H	2B	3B	HR	RBI	OBP	SLG	GF	IR	IRS	Hld	SvOp	SB	CS	GB	FB	G/F
1993 Season	6.52	0	0	1	20	0	9.2	12	3	.282	11	2	0	0	5	.462	.333	4	21	5	6	1	0	0	24	6	4.00

1993 Season

	ERA	W	L	Sv	G	GS	IP	H	HR	BB	SO		Avg	AB	H	2B	3B	HR	RBI	BB	SO	OBP	SLG
Home	9.00	0	0	1	11	0	5.0	8	0	9	3	vs. Left	.211	19	4	1	0	0	3	5	2	.400	.263
Away	3.86	0	0	0	9	0	4.2	3	0	3	0	vs. Right	.350	20	7	1	0	0	2	7	1	.519	.400

Phil Plantier — Padres

Age 25 – Bats Left (flyball hitter)

	Avg	G	AB	R	H	2B	3B	HR	RBI	BB	SO	HBP	GDP	SB	CS	OBP	SLG	IBB	SH	SF	#Pit	#P/PA	GB	FB	G/F
1993 Season	.240	138	462	67	111	20	1	34	100	61	124	7	4	4	5	.335	.509	7	1	5	2136	3.99	99	154	0.64
Career (1990-1993)	.255	313	974	141	248	47	2	52	168	132	251	11	16	7	8	.347	.467	17	3	10	4517	3.99	230	311	0.74

1993 Season

	Avg	AB	H	2B	3B	HR	RBI	BB	SO	OBP	SLG		Avg	AB	H	2B	3B	HR	RBI	BB	SO	OBP	SLG
vs. Left	.185	119	22	2	0	7	21	13	39	.277	.378	Scoring Posn	.274	135	37	9	1	12	70	24	40	.372	.622
vs. Right	.259	343	89	18	1	27	79	48	85	.354	.554	Close & Late	.205	88	18	0	0	6	8	10	28	.286	.409
Groundball	.272	151	41	5	1	12	26	19	37	.360	.556	None on/out	.163	104	17	4	0	3	3	11	29	.263	.288
Flyball	.227	75	17	4	0	6	17	9	25	.326	.520	Batting #4	.247	186	46	8	0	16	45	36	46	.377	.548
Home	.224	237	53	7	1	16	47	27	62	.307	.464	Batting #5	.255	161	41	9	1	9	30	13	45	.315	.491
Away	.258	225	58	13	0	18	53	34	62	.362	.556	Other	.209	115	24	3	0	9	25	12	33	.287	.470
Day	.308	156	48	8	0	16	47	21	35	.391	.667	April	.260	50	13	3	0	3	8	3	13	.296	.500
Night	.206	306	63	12	1	18	53	40	99	.306	.428	May	.232	56	13	5	0	3	13	5	16	.323	.482
Grass	.215	367	79	13	1	22	71	43	97	.304	.436	June	.267	90	24	3	1	6	15	7	23	.320	.522
Turf	.337	95	32	7	0	12	29	18	27	.447	.789	July	.211	90	19	2	0	6	14	10	24	.287	.433
First Pitch	.265	34	9	2	0	1	9	6	0	.381	.412	August	.298	84	25	3	0	11	30	18	15	.433	.726
Ahead in Count	.358	120	43	9	0	18	46	31	0	.494	.883	September/October	.185	92	17	4	0	5	20	18	33	.325	.391
Behind in Count	.181	215	39	5	1	10	33	0	96	.190	.353	Pre-All Star	.247	231	57	12	1	14	40	18	60	.307	.489
Two Strikes	.145	241	35	3	1	8	26	24	124	.227	.266	Post-All Star	.234	231	54	8	0	20	60	43	64	.359	.528

1993 By Position

Position	Avg	AB	H	2B	3B	HR	RBI	BB	SO	OBP	SLG	G	GS	Innings	PO	A	E	DP	Fld Pct	Rng Fctr	In Zone	Outs	Zone Rtg	MLB Zone
As lf	.243	457	111	20	1	34	100	60	122	.336	.514	134	131	1103.0	271	14	3	3	.990	2.33	295	260	.881	.818

Career (1990-1993)

	Avg	AB	H	2B	3B	HR	RBI	BB	SO	OBP	SLG		Avg	AB	H	2B	3B	HR	RBI	BB	SO	OBP	SLG
vs. Left	.191	215	41	4	0	10	35	23	72	.275	.349	Scoring Posn	.251	275	69	19	2	16	119	55	74	.368	.509
vs. Right	.273	759	207	43	2	42	133	109	179	.367	.501	Close & Late	.225	191	43	5	0	8	22	27	68	.321	.377
Groundball	.278	291	81	10	1	16	43	34	75	.363	.485	None on/out	.216	213	46	9	0	7	7	22	55	.298	.357
Flyball	.277	206	57	13	0	13	40	23	44	.355	.529	Batting #4	.251	187	47	8	0	16	46	37	46	.383	.551

Career (1990-1993)

	Avg	AB	H	2B	3B	HR	RBI	BB	SO	OBP	SLG
Home	.252	516	130	20	2	27	91	59	126	.330	.455
Away	.258	458	118	27	0	25	77	73	125	.365	.480
Day	.281	352	99	14	1	24	76	51	86	.373	.531
Night	.240	622	149	33	1	28	92	81	165	.332	.431
Grass	.243	820	199	35	2	39	134	110	210	.335	.433
Turf	.318	154	49	12	0	13	34	22	41	.408	.649
First Pitch	.371	70	26	8	0	5	25	13	0	.465	.700
Ahead in Count	.382	241	92	20	0	25	64	69	0	.519	.776
Behind in Count	.175	474	83	10	2	15	59	0	208	.182	.300
Two Strikes	.152	513	78	11	1	12	47	49	251	.231	.248

	Avg	AB	H	2B	3B	HR	RBI	BB	SO	OBP	SLG
Batting #5	.251	295	74	19	1	16	51	32	72	.325	.485
Other	.258	492	127	20	1	20	71	63	133	.345	.425
April	.248	117	29	8	0	4	17	11	31	.315	.419
May	.200	130	26	12	0	3	15	17	33	.303	.362
June	.257	167	43	5	1	10	30	16	44	.321	.479
July	.266	177	47	5	0	7	19	16	42	.328	.412
August	.294	160	47	5	1	14	40	35	33	.430	.600
September/October	.251	223	56	12	0	14	47	37	68	.357	.493
Pre-All Star	.242	487	118	27	1	20	69	49	123	.316	.425
Post-All Star	.267	487	130	20	1	32	99	83	128	.376	.509

Batter vs. Pitcher (career)

Hits Best Against	Avg	AB	H	2B	3B	HR	RBI	BB	SO	OBP	SLG
Bill Swift	.467	15	7	2	0	1	3	2	1	.529	.800
Kevin Appier	.400	10	4	3	0	0	0	3	2	.538	.700
Willie Blair	.308	13	4	0	0	0	0	1	4	.357	.308

Hits Worst Against	Avg	AB	H	2B	3B	HR	RBI	BB	SO	OBP	SLG
Kevin Gross	.000	12	0	0	0	0	0	1	5	.077	.000

Dan Plesac — Cubs

Age 32 – Pitches Left (flyball pitcher)

	ERA	W	L	Sv	G	GS	IP	BB	SO	Avg	H	2B	3B	HR	RBI	OBP	SLG	GF	IR	IRS	Hld	SvOp	SB	CS	GB	FB	G/F
1993 Season	4.74	2	1	0	57	0	62.2	21	47	.298	74	9	2	10	44	.349	.472	12	38	19	12	2	3	2	74	72	1.03
Last Five Years	3.78	15	23	66	264	14	364.1	143	279	.253	344	66	5	38	209	.324	.393	102	178	62	16	91	19	13	407	435	0.94

1993 Season

	ERA	W	L	Sv	G	GS	IP	H	HR	BB	SO
Home	5.85	1	1	0	28	0	32.1	40	7	13	29
Away	3.56	1	0	0	29	0	30.1	34	3	8	18
Starter	0.00	0	0	0	0	0	0.0	0	0	0	0
Reliever	4.74	2	1	0	57	0	62.2	74	10	21	47
0 Days rest	3.31	1	1	0	17	0	16.1	19	1	5	15
1 or 2 Days rest	3.99	1	0	0	24	0	29.1	29	4	10	18
3+ Days rest	7.41	0	0	0	16	0	17.0	26	5	6	14
Pre-All Star	4.76	0	0	0	26	0	39.2	45	9	10	29
Post-All Star	4.70	2	1	0	31	0	23.0	29	1	11	18

	Avg	AB	H	2B	3B	HR	RBI	BB	SO	OBP	SLG
vs. Left	.258	89	23	4	1	2	12	6	29	.305	.393
vs. Right	.321	159	51	5	1	8	32	15	18	.373	.516
Scoring Posn	.317	63	20	1	1	3	34	10	11	.395	.508
Close & Late	.333	54	18	2	1	2	13	9	10	.415	.519
None on/out	.246	57	14	3	1	2	2	0	11	.246	.439
First Pitch	.325	40	13	2	1	0	6	6	0	.413	.425
Ahead in Count	.211	114	24	3	0	5	17	0	39	.209	.368
Behind in Count	.447	47	21	3	0	4	13	8	0	.518	.766
Two Strikes	.220	118	26	3	1	5	20	7	47	.264	.390

Last Five Years

	ERA	W	L	Sv	G	GS	IP	H	HR	BB	SO
Home	4.50	7	11	31	126	6	174.0	174	19	66	144
Away	3.12	8	12	35	138	8	190.1	170	19	77	135
Day	3.25	3	8	20	96	3	130.1	125	9	45	115
Night	4.08	12	15	46	168	11	234.0	219	29	98	164
Grass	4.04	14	19	55	213	12	296.1	288	35	120	240
Turf	2.65	1	4	11	51	2	68.0	56	3	23	39
April	3.70	3	4	6	33	1	48.2	49	6	12	41
May	4.88	1	3	15	36	3	55.1	52	7	24	50
June	3.82	1	3	16	56	0	66.0	63	9	24	40
July	2.88	3	4	11	47	0	59.1	59	4	28	47
August	2.89	5	5	9	47	3	65.1	47	8	25	47
September/October	4.52	2	4	9	45	7	69.2	74	4	30	54
Starter	4.83	3	4	0	14	14	69.0	70	7	32	51
Reliever	3.53	12	19	66	250	0	295.1	274	31	111	228
0 Days rest	3.45	2	4	10	44	0	44.1	45	5	19	32
1 or 2 Days rest	3.26	5	7	34	113	0	132.2	120	13	45	100
3+ Days rest	3.88	5	8	22	93	0	118.1	109	13	47	96
Pre-All Star	3.80	5	10	43	140	4	192.0	178	23	69	147
Post-All Star	3.76	10	13	23	124	10	172.1	166	15	74	132

	Avg	AB	H	2B	3B	HR	RBI	BB	SO	OBP	SLG
vs. Left	.242	330	80	13	2	9	60	28	88	.304	.376
vs. Right	.256	1030	264	53	3	29	149	115	191	.330	.398
Inning 1-6	.256	429	110	27	3	12	64	47	79	.328	.417
Inning 7+	.251	931	234	39	2	26	145	96	200	.322	.381
None on	.247	687	170	29	2	21	21	77	152	.326	.387
Runners on	.259	673	174	37	3	17	188	66	127	.322	.398
Scoring Posn	.277	386	107	23	3	10	169	48	72	.347	.430
Close & Late	.268	426	114	18	2	13	87	52	82	.349	.411
None on/out	.276	301	83	12	2	10	10	29	59	.345	.429
vs. 1st Batr (relief)	.268	224	60	11	2	6	39	20	44	.333	.415
First Inning Pitched	.251	818	205	44	3	24	143	83	157	.320	.400
First 15 Pitches	.261	751	196	38	3	24	116	74	141	.329	.415
Pitch 16-30	.220	322	71	15	0	7	45	39	73	.304	.332
Pitch 31-45	.231	134	31	4	1	2	20	15	28	.307	.321
Pitch 46+	.301	153	46	9	1	5	28	15	37	.354	.471
First Pitch	.302	212	64	14	1	6	39	16	0	.358	.462
Ahead in Count	.195	650	127	27	0	12	81	0	240	.199	.292
Behind in Count	.341	246	84	12	1	14	55	81	0	.494	.569
Two Strikes	.200	676	135	27	2	17	86	46	279	.252	.321

Pitcher vs. Batter (career)

Pitches Best Vs.	Avg	AB	H	2B	3B	HR	RBI	BB	SO	OBP	SLG
Rob Deer	.000	11	0	0	0	0	0	0	5	.000	.000
Kent Hrbek	.000	8	0	0	0	0	2	1	1	.091	.000
Pete Incaviglia	.056	18	1	0	0	0	2	1	4	.105	.056
Roberto Alomar	.077	13	1	0	0	0	1	1	2	.143	.077
Steve Balboni	.083	12	1	0	0	0	0	0	8	.083	.083

Pitches Worst Vs.	Avg	AB	H	2B	3B	HR	RBI	BB	SO	OBP	SLG
Brian Harper	.545	11	6	0	0	3	8	1	0	.583	1.364
Julio Franco	.455	11	5	0	0	1	1	2	1	.538	.727
Cory Snyder	.455	11	5	1	0	2	8	0	1	.455	1.091
Lou Whitaker	.444	9	4	0	0	1	3	2	2	.500	.778
Wade Boggs	.375	16	6	2	1	0	5	1	5	.412	.625

Eric Plunk — Indians

Age 30 – Pitches Right (flyball pitcher)

	ERA	W	L	Sv	G	GS	IP	BB	SO	Avg	H	2B	3B	HR	RBI	OBP	SLG	GF	IR	IRS	Hld	SvOp	SB	CS	GB	FB	G/F
1993 Season	2.79	4	5	15	70	0	71.0	30	77	.226	61	17	1	5	32	.301	.352	40	56	14	16	18	6	1	78	77	1.01
Last Five Years	3.55	29	25	20	268	15	431.1	237	382	.241	390	65	12	44	219	.338	.378	82	205	70	35	30	51	22	468	506	0.92

1993 Season

	ERA	W	L	Sv	G	GS	IP	H	HR	BB	SO
Home	2.25	3	1	7	35	0	36.0	28	2	8	37
Away	3.34	1	4	8	35	0	35.0	33	3	22	40
Day	1.59	1	2	4	22	0	22.2	19	1	10	31
Night	3.35	3	3	11	48	0	48.1	42	4	20	46
Grass	3.20	4	4	11	58	0	59.0	52	5	22	64
Turf	0.75	0	1	4	12	0	12.0	9	0	8	13

	Avg	AB	H	2B	3B	HR	RBI	BB	SO	OBP	SLG
vs. Left	.238	105	25	8	1	2	9	15	26	.333	.390
vs. Right	.218	165	36	9	0	3	23	15	51	.280	.327
Inning 1-6	.000	0	0	0	0	0	0	0	0	.000	.000
Inning 7+	.226	270	61	17	1	5	32	30	77	.301	.352
None on	.238	126	30	11	1	3	3	10	30	.294	.413
Runners on	.215	144	31	6	0	2	29	20	47	.307	.299

1993 Season

	ERA	W	L	Sv	G	GS	IP	H	HR	BB	SO
April	4.22	1	2	0	10	0	10.2	13	1	5	14
May	1.50	0	0	3	12	0	12.0	8	0	5	17
June	2.45	2	0	4	11	0	11.0	7	1	2	11
July	3.24	1	1	3	11	0	8.1	10	1	7	4
August	4.50	0	2	3	13	0	14.0	9	2	5	16
September/October	1.20	0	0	2	13	0	15.0	14	0	6	15
Starter	0.00	0	0	0	0	0	0.0	0	0	0	0
Reliever	2.79	4	5	15	70	0	71.0	61	5	30	77
0 Days rest	1.83	1	1	6	18	0	19.2	18	0	7	23
1 or 2 Days rest	2.20	2	1	4	33	0	32.2	23	3	18	31
3+ Days rest	4.82	1	3	5	19	0	18.2	20	2	5	23
Pre-All Star	3.11	4	3	9	37	0	37.2	33	3	17	44
Post-All Star	2.43	0	2	6	33	0	33.1	28	2	13	33

	Avg	AB	H	2B	3B	HR	RBI	BB	SO	OBP	SLG
Scoring Posn	.200	105	21	4	0	2	28	13	32	.283	.295
Close & Late	.261	161	42	10	1	4	23	21	40	.342	.410
None on/out	.259	54	14	5	0	1	1	5	10	.322	.407
vs. 1st Batr (relief)	.226	62	14	7	0	1	9	6	14	.294	.387
First Inning Pitched	.201	209	42	10	0	5	26	21	60	.274	.321
First 15 Pitches	.208	183	38	11	0	3	20	18	50	.279	.317
Pitch 16-30	.222	72	16	4	1	2	9	11	22	.325	.389
Pitch 31-45	.467	15	7	2	0	0	3	1	5	.444	.600
Pitch 46+	.000	0	0	0	0	0	0	0	0	.000	.000
First Pitch	.310	29	9	3	0	0	6	3	0	.364	.414
Ahead in Count	.156	141	22	7	1	1	9	0	67	.155	.241
Behind in Count	.352	54	19	5	0	3	11	12	0	.470	.611
Two Strikes	.159	151	24	7	1	2	11	15	77	.234	.258

Last Five Years

	ERA	W	L	Sv	G	GS	IP	H	HR	BB	SO
Home	3.39	19	8	9	124	9	212.1	197	22	110	181
Away	3.70	10	17	11	144	6	219.0	193	22	127	201
Day	2.51	12	7	5	85	3	122.0	104	6	82	111
Night	3.96	17	18	15	183	12	309.1	286	38	155	271
Grass	3.62	25	21	15	227	13	373.1	340	40	201	326
Turf	3.10	4	4	5	41	2	58.0	50	4	36	56
April	4.06	4	3	0	31	0	37.2	46	6	26	36
May	4.04	0	3	4	47	0	64.2	54	3	35	58
June	2.17	4	1	5	44	0	58.0	42	1	25	56
July	3.48	7	3	4	46	0	64.2	70	5	38	47
August	4.02	6	6	4	51	6	96.1	79	17	55	90
September/October	3.44	8	9	3	49	9	110.0	99	12	58	95
Starter	4.34	4	6	0	15	15	87.0	83	13	50	69
Reliever	3.35	25	19	20	253	0	344.1	307	31	187	313
0 Days rest	3.52	5	4	9	48	0	64.0	58	5	30	56
1 or 2 Days rest	3.32	11	8	6	123	0	152.0	135	17	93	137
3+ Days rest	3.30	9	7	5	82	0	128.1	114	9	64	120
Pre-All Star	3.46	13	8	12	137	0	177.0	153	12	98	158
Post-All Star	3.61	16	17	8	131	15	254.1	237	32	139	224

	Avg	AB	H	2B	3B	HR	RBI	BB	SO	OBP	SLG
vs. Left	.257	703	181	27	10	20	75	112	158	.358	.410
vs. Right	.229	912	209	38	2	24	144	125	224	.322	.354
Inning 1-6	.258	650	168	31	5	22	104	99	146	.355	.423
Inning 7+	.230	965	222	34	7	22	115	138	236	.326	.348
None on	.249	843	210	34	9	25	25	112	174	.338	.400
Runners on	.233	772	180	31	3	19	194	125	208	.338	.355
Scoring Posn	.233	498	116	24	2	10	171	93	134	.350	.349
Close & Late	.248	467	116	18	3	14	65	67	100	.340	.390
None on/out	.238	369	88	18	3	10	10	52	69	.334	.385
vs. 1st Batr (relief)	.246	199	49	12	0	6	37	24	45	.326	.397
First Inning Pitched	.231	756	175	30	7	17	119	114	198	.331	.357
First 15 Pitches	.231	710	164	29	8	16	103	91	170	.319	.362
Pitch 16-30	.216	412	89	16	1	9	43	64	117	.321	.325
Pitch 31-45	.295	200	59	11	2	5	33	40	43	.408	.445
Pitch 46+	.266	293	78	9	1	14	40	42	52	.357	.447
First Pitch	.330	203	67	14	2	8	48	11	0	.361	.537
Ahead in Count	.168	752	126	20	6	6	53	0	319	.169	.234
Behind in Count	.341	320	109	16	2	19	65	110	0	.506	.581
Two Strikes	.164	853	140	24	7	9	61	116	382	.265	.240

Pitcher vs. Batter (career)

Pitches Best Vs.	Avg	AB	H	2B	3B	HR	RBI	BB	SO	OBP	SLG
Cory Snyder	.000	11	0	0	0	0	0	1	4	.083	.000
Joe Carter	.050	20	1	1	0	0	0	3	4	.174	.100
Candy Maldonado	.083	12	1	0	0	0	2	2	4	.214	.083
Ozzie Guillen	.083	12	1	0	0	0	1	1	0	.143	.083
Alan Trammell	.091	22	2	0	0	0	1	3	5	.200	.091

Pitches Worst Vs.	Avg	AB	H	2B	3B	HR	RBI	BB	SO	OBP	SLG
Wally Joyner	.625	16	10	2	0	3	8	3	1	.684	1.313
Paul Molitor	.600	15	9	1	0	1	5	4	2	.684	.867
Kirk Gibson	.500	12	6	0	0	3	5	3	3	.600	1.250
Carlton Fisk	.462	13	6	0	0	2	6	2	2	.533	.923
Pete O'Brien	.333	9	3	0	0	1	2	8	2	.647	.667

Gus Polidor — Marlins

Age 32 – Bats Right

	Avg	G	AB	R	H	2B	3B	HR	RBI	BB	SO	HBP	GDP	SB	CS	OBP	SLG	IBB	SH	SF	#Pit	#P/PA	GB	FB	G/F
1993 Season	.167	7	6	0	1	1	0	0	0	0	2	0	0	0	0	.167	.333	0	0	0	25	4.17	0	3	0.00
Last Five Years	.184	104	196	15	36	8	0	0	15	6	21	2	6	3	0	.216	.224	0	3	0	667	3.22	85	59	1.44

1993 Season

	Avg	AB	H	2B	3B	HR	RBI	BB	SO	OBP	SLG
vs. Left	.500	2	1	1	0	0	0	0	0	.500	1.000
vs. Right	.000	4	0	0	0	0	0	0	2	.000	.000

	Avg	AB	H	2B	3B	HR	RBI	BB	SO	OBP	SLG
Scoring Posn	.000	0	0	0	0	0	0	0	0	.000	.000
Close & Late	.000	0	0	0	0	0	0	0	0	.000	.000

Luis Polonia — Angels

Age 29 – Bats Left (groundball hitter)

	Avg	G	AB	R	H	2B	3B	HR	RBI	BB	SO	HBP	GDP	SB	CS	OBP	SLG	IBB	SH	SF	#Pit	#P/PA	GB	FB	G/F
1993 Season	.271	152	576	75	156	17	6	1	32	48	53	2	7	55	24	.328	.326	7	8	3	2188	3.43	278	137	2.03
Last Five Years	.295	696	2593	372	765	86	33	8	198	195	278	7	57	197	90	.344	.363	19	23	18	9803	3.46	1207	535	2.26

1993 Season

	Avg	AB	H	2B	3B	HR	RBI	BB	SO	OBP	SLG
vs. Left	.232	112	26	1	0	0	7	3	10	.248	.241
vs. Right	.280	464	130	16	6	1	25	45	43	.346	.347
Groundball	.286	119	34	3	0	1	11	11	9	.346	.336
Flyball	.275	131	36	2	3	0	9	6	14	.314	.336
Home	.229	288	66	6	3	0	16	20	23	.282	.271
Away	.313	288	90	11	3	1	16	28	30	.372	.382
Day	.316	171	54	10	1	0	6	16	18	.378	.386
Night	.252	405	102	7	5	1	26	32	35	.306	.301
Grass	.262	478	125	13	5	0	24	39	41	.319	.310
Turf	.316	98	31	4	1	1	8	9	12	.370	.408
First Pitch	.344	93	32	1	1	0	5	5	0	.374	.376
Ahead in Count	.327	110	36	4	0	0	11	27	0	.457	.364
Behind in Count	.244	262	64	9	3	1	11	0	46	.249	.313
Two Strikes	.225	222	50	9	3	1	11	16	53	.279	.306

	Avg	AB	H	2B	3B	HR	RBI	BB	SO	OBP	SLG
Scoring Posn	.336	119	40	5	1	0	30	12	11	.388	.395
Close & Late	.253	95	24	2	2	0	6	8	11	.311	.316
None on/out	.256	246	63	8	2	0	0	19	21	.312	.305
Batting #1	.272	567	154	17	6	1	32	47	51	.328	.328
Batting #9	.500	4	2	0	0	0	0	0	0	.500	.500
Other	.000	5	0	0	0	0	0	1	2	.167	.000
April	.289	76	22	2	2	0	7	3	7	.313	.368
May	.257	105	27	4	1	1	3	12	15	.333	.343
June	.218	87	19	2	0	0	2	6	8	.277	.241
July	.274	113	31	3	1	0	6	4	6	.299	.319
August	.341	82	28	4	1	0	6	10	6	.415	.415
September/October	.257	113	29	2	1	0	8	13	11	.331	.292
Pre-All Star	.258	318	82	10	3	1	15	23	32	.309	.318
Post-All Star	.287	258	74	7	3	0	17	25	21	.350	.337

1993 By Position

Position	Avg	AB	H	2B	3B	HR	RBI	BB	SO	OBP	SLG	G	GS	Innings	PO	A	E	DP	Fld Pct	Rng Fctr	In Zone	Outs	Zone Rtg	MLB Zone
As If	.274	552	151	17	6	1	32	47	48	.331	.332	141	135	1181.0	284	12	5	4	.983	2.26	346	271	.783	.818

Last Five Years

	Avg	AB	H	2B	3B	HR	RBI	BB	SO	OBP	SLG
vs. Left	.249	534	133	14	3	0	38	30	80	.289	.287
vs. Right	.307	2059	632	72	30	8	160	165	198	.358	.383
Groundball	.281	648	182	19	4	4	64	50	67	.331	.341
Flyball	.301	591	178	22	10	1	44	46	75	.350	.377
Home	.291	1263	368	38	17	4	104	92	132	.341	.358
Away	.298	1330	397	48	16	4	94	103	146	.346	.368
Day	.324	744	241	37	12	1	53	59	79	.375	.410
Night	.283	1849	524	49	21	7	145	136	199	.331	.344
Grass	.290	2168	629	69	30	7	165	165	221	.340	.359
Turf	.320	425	136	17	3	1	33	30	57	.362	.381
First Pitch	.323	409	132	12	2	1	35	13	0	.342	.369
Ahead in Count	.357	485	173	20	2	0	41	116	0	.478	.406
Behind in Count	.268	1253	336	32	20	5	89	0	253	.270	.338
Two Strikes	.260	1097	285	33	17	5	83	65	278	.302	.335

	Avg	AB	H	2B	3B	HR	RBI	BB	SO	OBP	SLG
Scoring Posn	.317	552	175	19	8	2	184	47	58	.360	.391
Close & Late	.275	385	106	12	3	1	27	24	48	.317	.330
None on/out	.285	969	276	37	13	3	3	82	114	.342	.359
Batting #1	.293	2278	667	74	29	6	165	178	236	.343	.359
Batting #2	.333	213	71	10	3	1	27	12	26	.368	.423
Other	.265	102	27	2	1	1	6	5	16	.299	.333
April	.288	302	87	7	5	0	30	26	22	.342	.344
May	.287	464	133	14	10	2	31	32	54	.331	.373
June	.284	454	129	12	3	1	37	20	52	.326	.330
July	.297	468	139	18	5	3	32	30	48	.341	.376
August	.314	442	139	17	6	2	41	38	45	.368	.394
September/October	.298	463	138	18	4	0	27	40	57	.353	.354
Pre-All Star	.286	1379	394	39	19	4	110	101	145	.334	.350
Post-All Star	.306	1214	371	47	14	4	88	94	133	.355	.377

Batter vs. Pitcher (career)

Hits Best Against	Avg	AB	H	2B	3B	HR	RBI	BB	SO	OBP	SLG
Mike Henneman	.600	10	6	0	0	0	2	1	0	.636	.600
Ricky Bones	.545	11	6	1	0	0	1	2	0	.571	.636
Jose DeLeon	.538	13	7	0	1	0	1	1	0	.571	.692
Tim Leary	.471	17	8	3	0	2	7	2	1	.526	1.000
Steve Farr	.471	17	8	4	0	0	0	2	2	.526	.706

Hits Worst Against	Avg	AB	H	2B	3B	HR	RBI	BB	SO	OBP	SLG
Kenny Rogers	.000	14	0	0	0	0	0	1	3	.067	.000
Teddy Higuera	.000	10	0	0	0	0	0	1	3	.091	.000
Rick Sutcliffe	.056	18	1	0	1	0	1	0	1	.056	.167
Edwin Nunez	.091	11	1	0	0	0	2	0	3	.091	.091
Greg Hibbard	.091	11	1	0	0	0	1	1	2	.167	.091

Jim Poole — Orioles

Age 28 – Pitches Left

	ERA	W	L	Sv	G	GS	IP	BB	SO	Avg	H	2B	3B	HR	RBI	OBP	SLG	GF	IR	IRS	Hld	SvOp	SB	CS	GB	FB	G/F
1993 Season	2.15	2	1	2	55	0	50.1	21	29	.175	30	5	0	2	20	.263	.240	11	65	14	14	3	2	1	60	60	1.00
Career (1990-1993)	2.37	5	3	3	106	0	106.1	42	76	.186	69	11	0	6	46	.266	.265	21	118	29	20	5	4	3	134	110	1.22

1993 Season

	ERA	W	L	Sv	G	GS	IP	H	HR	BB	SO
Home	2.28	2	0	0	30	0	27.2	18	0	11	15
Away	1.99	0	1	2	25	0	22.2	12	2	10	14
Starter	0.00	0	0	0	0	0	0.0	0	0	0	0
Reliever	2.15	2	1	2	55	0	50.1	30	2	21	29
0 Days rest	1.65	1	0	0	11	0	16.1	4	0	5	9
1 or 2 Days rest	4.34	1	1	1	26	0	18.2	17	2	11	10
3+ Days rest	0.00	0	0	1	18	0	15.1	9	0	5	10
Pre-All Star	2.03	1	0	0	31	0	31.0	17	1	12	22
Post-All Star	2.33	1	1	2	24	0	19.1	13	1	9	7

	Avg	AB	H	2B	3B	HR	RBI	BB	SO	OBP	SLG
vs. Left	.177	79	14	3	0	0	9	6	15	.233	.215
vs. Right	.174	92	16	2	0	2	11	15	14	.287	.261
Scoring Posn	.220	50	11	2	0	1	19	13	10	.369	.320
Close & Late	.177	62	11	2	0	0	10	5	11	.235	.210
None on/out	.219	32	7	0	0	0	0	6	5	.342	.219
First Pitch	.240	25	6	1	0	0	3	5	0	.367	.280
Ahead in Count	.141	64	9	1	0	1	9	0	23	.138	.203
Behind in Count	.125	40	5	1	0	0	3	10	0	.300	.150
Two Strikes	.088	57	5	1	0	0	6	6	29	.172	.105

Mark Portugal — Astros

Age 31 – Pitches Right

	ERA	W	L	Sv	G	GS	IP	BB	SO	Avg	H	2B	3B	HR	RBI	OBP	SLG	CG	ShO	Sup	QS	#P/S	SB	CS	GB	FB	G/F
1993 Season	2.77	18	4	0	33	33	208.0	77	131	.248	194	26	1	10	63	.318	.323	1	1	4.98	21	97	14	4	305	202	1.51
Last Five Years	3.34	52	30	1	135	123	782.1	281	535	.244	711	111	10	64	279	.312	.355	6	3	4.27	79	94	63	33	1124	764	1.47

1993 Season

	ERA	W	L	Sv	G	GS	IP	H	HR	BB	SO
Home	2.37	10	1	0	15	15	95.0	97	4	30	72
Away	3.11	8	3	0	18	18	113.0	97	6	47	59
Day	2.33	6	1	0	9	9	58.0	53	1	19	32
Night	2.94	12	3	0	24	24	150.0	141	9	58	99
Grass	3.18	4	2	0	12	12	76.1	63	5	35	40
Turf	2.53	14	2	0	21	21	131.2	131	5	42	91
April	3.69	2	2	0	5	5	31.2	31	1	7	14
May	1.91	2	0	0	5	5	28.1	25	1	15	18
June	4.66	1	1	0	5	5	29.0	28	3	16	22
July	2.39	4	1	0	6	6	37.2	47	2	10	27
August	2.92	4	0	0	6	6	37.0	34	3	18	19
September/October	1.62	5	0	0	6	6	44.1	29	0	11	31
Starter	2.77	18	4	0	33	33	208.0	194	10	77	131
Reliever	0.00	0	0	0	0	0	0.0	0	0	0	0
0-3 Days Rest	1.29	1	0	0	1	1	7.0	2	0	5	4
4 Days Rest	3.14	10	3	0	19	19	117.2	121	9	38	72
5+ Days Rest	2.38	7	1	0	13	13	83.1	71	1	34	55
Pre-All Star	3.47	7	4	0	18	18	106.1	104	6	46	70
Post-All Star	2.04	11	0	0	15	15	101.2	90	4	31	61

	Avg	AB	H	2B	3B	HR	RBI	BB	SO	OBP	SLG
vs. Left	.234	411	96	11	1	4	30	42	71	.305	.294
vs. Right	.265	370	98	15	0	6	33	35	60	.332	.354
Inning 1-6	.241	688	166	20	1	8	57	67	118	.311	.308
Inning 7+	.301	93	28	6	0	2	6	10	13	.365	.430
None on	.240	454	109	16	0	4	4	47	74	.313	.302
Runners on	.260	327	85	10	1	6	59	30	57	.325	.352
Scoring Posn	.265	166	44	5	1	3	51	21	34	.349	.361
Close & Late	.319	47	15	2	0	1	4	3	7	.353	.426
None on/out	.250	200	50	9	0	1	1	22	31	.324	.310
vs. 1st Batr (relief)	.000	0	0	0	0	0	0	0	0	.000	.000
First Inning Pitched	.254	126	32	4	0	2	15	13	21	.326	.333
First 75 Pitches	.233	589	137	17	1	6	45	51	102	.298	.295
Pitch 76-90	.287	108	31	4	0	4	13	11	14	.350	.435
Pitch 91-105	.311	61	19	2	0	0	3	10	11	.408	.344
Pitch 106+	.304	23	7	3	0	0	2	5	4	.414	.435
First Pitch	.330	103	34	5	0	5	15	2	0	.340	.524
Ahead in Count	.209	350	73	9	1	1	19	0	116	.213	.249
Behind in Count	.285	193	55	9	0	3	17	50	0	.433	.378
Two Strikes	.173	341	59	4	1	1	17	25	131	.232	.199

Last Five Years

	ERA	W	L	Sv	G	GS	IP	H	HR	BB	SO
Home	2.38	30	9	1	67	57	385.2	333	20	125	284
Away	4.27	22	21	0	68	66	396.2	378	44	156	251
Day	3.60	18	12	1	41	37	240.0	229	20	88	154

	Avg	AB	H	2B	3B	HR	RBI	BB	SO	OBP	SLG
vs. Left	.234	1624	380	57	9	32	150	172	322	.308	.339
vs. Right	.257	1290	331	54	1	32	129	109	213	.316	.374
Inning 1-6	.238	2507	597	90	10	51	238	240	473	.306	.343

Last Five Years	ERA	W	L	Sv	G	GS	IP	H	HR	BB	SO		Avg	AB	H	2B	3B	HR	RBI	BB	SO	OBP	SLG
Night	3.22	34	18	0	94	86	542.1	482	44	193	381	Inning 7+	.280	407	114	21	0	13	41	41	62	.345	.428
Grass	4.70	13	16	0	46	44	262.1	269	31	107	170	None on	.243	1738	422	70	6	35	35	161	322	.309	.350
Turf	2.65	39	14	1	89	79	520.0	442	33	174	365	Runners on	.246	1176	289	41	4	29	244	120	213	.316	.361
April	3.90	7	7	0	17	17	101.2	102	5	30	62	Scoring Posn	.258	632	163	22	3	16	208	78	123	.336	.378
May	3.47	7	4	0	21	21	127.0	114	12	53	83	Close & Late	.288	222	64	9	0	6	20	21	35	.348	.410
June	3.61	4	7	0	22	20	132.0	114	13	43	91	None on/out	.256	762	195	30	5	22	22	82	127	.331	.395
July	2.89	10	4	0	22	21	121.1	126	12	43	90	vs. 1st Batr (relief)	.444	9	4	1	0	0	1	3	1	.583	.556
August	2.96	11	1	0	22	20	133.2	123	9	51	98	First Inning Pitched	.281	505	142	22	3	10	72	60	88	.356	.396
September/October	3.29	13	7	1	31	24	166.2	132	13	61	111	First 75 Pitches	.241	2224	535	83	9	43	209	216	423	.309	.344
Starter	3.27	51	28	0	123	123	768.1	695	63	271	526	Pitch 76-90	.234	381	89	13	1	12	34	29	58	.287	.367
Reliever	7.07	1	2	1	12	0	14.0	16	1	10	9	Pitch 91-105	.270	226	61	10	0	5	20	29	40	.353	.381
0-3 Days Rest	1.96	4	0	0	7	7	46.0	35	2	16	38	Pitch 106+	.313	83	26	5	0	4	16	7	14	.370	.518
4 Days Rest	3.34	27	17	0	73	73	457.2	419	42	150	307	First Pitch	.312	433	135	26	2	10	57	7	0	.324	.450
5+ Days Rest	3.37	20	11	0	43	43	264.2	241	19	105	181	Ahead in Count	.180	1279	230	33	1	14	75	0	455	.182	.240
Pre-All Star	3.64	23	20	0	69	67	410.1	380	37	148	274	Behind in Count	.301	701	211	31	3	24	83	172	0	.439	.456
Post-All Star	3.00	29	10	1	66	56	372.0	331	27	133	261	Two Strikes	.158	1258	199	26	1	14	78	102	535	.223	.214

Pitcher vs. Batter (career)

Pitches Best Vs.	Avg	AB	H	2B	3B	HR	RBI	BB	SO	OBP	SLG	Pitches Worst Vs.	Avg	AB	H	2B	3B	HR	RBI	BB	SO	OBP	SLG
Tom Pagnozzi	.000	12	0	0	0	0	0	1	1	.077	.000	Vince Coleman	.545	11	6	1	1	0	0	1	2	.583	.818
Jose Oquendo	.000	11	0	0	0	0	0	2	4	.154	.000	Orlando Merced	.526	19	10	2	1	1	7	1	3	.550	.895
Larry Walker	.000	11	0	0	0	0	0	2	4	.154	.000	Rickey Henderson	.500	8	4	1	0	1	3	2	0	.545	1.000
Jose Uribe	.067	15	1	0	0	0	0	2	6	.176	.067	Darryl Strawberry	.421	19	8	1	0	3	6	3	7	.500	.947
Matt D. Williams	.070	43	3	0	0	0	0	2	13	.111	.070	Jeff Blauser	.389	18	7	0	0	3	5	3	3	.476	.889

Scott Pose — Marlins

Age 27 – Bats Left

	Avg	G	AB	R	H	2B	3B	HR	RBI	BB	SO	HBP	GDP	SB	CS	OBP	SLG	IBB	SH	SF	#Pit	#P/PA	GB	FB	G/F
1993 Season	.195	15	41	0	8	2	0	0	3	2	4	0	0	0	2	.233	.244	0	0	0	151	3.51	25	4	6.25

1993 Season

	Avg	AB	H	2B	3B	HR	RBI	BB	SO	OBP	SLG		Avg	AB	H	2B	3B	HR	RBI	BB	SO	OBP	SLG
vs. Left	.167	6	1	0	0	0	0	0	0	.167	.167	Scoring Posn	.182	11	2	0	0	0	3	1	1	.250	.182
vs. Right	.200	35	7	2	0	0	3	2	4	.243	.257	Close & Late	.111	9	1	0	0	0	0	1	1	.200	.111

Dennis Powell — Mariners

Age 30 – Pitches Left

	ERA	W	L	Sv	G	GS	IP	BB	SO	Avg	H	2B	3B	HR	RBI	OBP	SLG	GF	IR	IRS	Hld	SvOp	SB	CS	GB	FB	G/F
1993 Season	4.15	0	0	0	33	2	47.2	24	32	.255	42	7	0	7	23	.349	.424	7	30	9	11	0	4	3	71	39	1.82
Last Five Years	5.11	6	8	2	136	10	192.0	95	117	.279	204	37	5	18	106	.365	.418	20	116	26	27	2	17	8	287	193	1.49

1993 Season

	ERA	W	L	Sv	G	GS	IP	H	HR	BB	SO		Avg	AB	H	2B	3B	HR	RBI	BB	SO	OBP	SLG
Home	4.26	0	0	0	19	1	25.1	23	5	8	18	vs. Left	.159	63	10	2	0	1	7	5	17	.217	.238
Away	4.03	0	0	0	14	1	22.1	19	2	16	14	vs. Right	.314	102	32	5	0	6	16	19	15	.423	.539
Starter	4.50	0	0	0	2	2	10.0	11	2	6	5	Scoring Posn	.289	38	11	1	0	0	13	10	6	.420	.316
Reliever	4.06	0	0	0	31	0	37.2	31	5	18	27	Close & Late	.333	33	11	0	0	0	4	5	7	.421	.333
0 Days rest	5.68	0	0	0	8	0	12.2	14	1	5	8	None on/out	.250	44	11	3	0	1	1	2	9	.283	.386
1 or 2 Days rest	5.11	0	0	0	12	0	12.1	10	3	4	13	First Pitch	.313	32	10	2	0	2	5	2	0	.371	.563
3+ Days rest	1.42	0	0	0	11	0	12.2	7	1	9	6	Ahead in Count	.190	58	11	1	0	1	7	0	23	.190	.259
Pre-All Star	3.66	0	0	0	23	2	39.1	33	6	18	26	Behind in Count	.275	40	11	2	0	2	6	14	0	.446	.475
Post-All Star	6.48	0	0	0	10	0	8.1	9	1	6	6	Two Strikes	.152	66	10	2	0	1	4	8	32	.243	.227

Last Five Years

	ERA	W	L	Sv	G	GS	IP	H	HR	BB	SO		Avg	AB	H	2B	3B	HR	RBI	BB	SO	OBP	SLG
Home	4.80	2	2	1	71	4	93.2	95	12	47	63	vs. Left	.236	237	56	11	1	7	43	19	50	.293	.380
Away	5.40	4	6	1	65	6	98.1	109	6	48	54	vs. Right	.300	493	148	26	4	11	63	76	67	.398	.436
Day	4.54	3	3	1	42	5	77.1	74	2	33	41	Inning 1-6	.270	344	93	21	2	6	56	44	51	.356	.395
Night	5.49	3	5	1	94	5	114.2	130	16	62	76	Inning 7+	.288	386	111	16	3	12	50	51	66	.374	.438
Grass	5.23	2	6	1	54	7	93.0	96	4	47	51	None on	.276	380	105	16	2	12	12	48	67	.360	.424
Turf	5.00	4	2	1	82	3	99.0	108	14	48	66	Runners on	.283	350	99	21	3	6	94	47	50	.371	.411
April	3.20	0	0	0	17	0	19.2	13	1	12	9	Scoring Posn	.278	209	58	8	1	3	84	32	37	.371	.368
May	4.55	3	3	1	36	3	55.1	54	5	23	34	Close & Late	.306	144	44	8	0	3	13	17	29	.383	.424
June	5.81	1	2	0	34	3	52.2	63	5	28	38	None on/out	.267	180	48	9	1	3	3	16	24	.330	.378
July	4.91	0	1	1	28	2	33.0	32	4	17	15	vs. 1st Batr (relief)	.231	104	24	4	1	3	17	14	19	.331	.375
August	8.55	1	2	0	11	2	20.0	34	1	12	11	First Inning Pitched	.273	363	99	22	1	6	55	51	59	.363	.388
September/October	2.38	1	0	0	10	0	11.1	8	2	3	10	First 15 Pitches	.284	327	93	19	1	7	44	43	52	.370	.413
Starter	6.44	0	5	0	10	10	50.1	69	2	25	27	Pitch 16-30	.295	173	51	8	1	7	25	26	25	.389	.474
Reliever	4.64	6	3	2	126	0	141.2	135	16	70	90	Pitch 31-45	.247	97	24	2	2	2	19	13	21	.333	.371
0 Days rest	5.84	2	1	1	22	0	24.2	29	1	11	14	Pitch 46+	.271	133	36	8	1	2	18	13	19	.345	.391
1 or 2 Days rest	5.00	0	1	0	56	0	54.0	56	7	26	37	First Pitch	.361	119	43	7	2	3	20	4	0	.386	.529
3+ Days rest	3.86	4	1	1	48	0	63.0	50	8	33	39	Ahead in Count	.231	299	69	10	2	4	42	0	96	.237	.318
Pre-All Star	4.70	4	5	1	99	8	145.2	147	12	73	88	Behind in Count	.335	179	60	14	0	8	33	55	0	.492	.547
Post-All Star	6.41	2	3	1	37	2	46.1	57	6	22	29	Two Strikes	.162	296	48	6	3	3	28	36	117	.257	.233

Pitcher vs. Batter (career)

Pitches Best Vs.	Avg	AB	H	2B	3B	HR	RBI	BB	SO	OBP	SLG	Pitches Worst Vs.	Avg	AB	H	2B	3B	HR	RBI	BB	SO	OBP	SLG
Robin Ventura	.182	11	2	0	0	0	1	1	3	.250	.182	Don Mattingly	.375	24	9	2	0	1	5	2	0	.407	.583
George Brett	.231	13	3	1	0	0	4	0	3	.231	.308												

Ross Powell — Reds

Age 26 – Pitches Left

	ERA	W	L	Sv	G	GS	IP	BB	SO	Avg	H	2B	3B	HR	RBI	OBP	SLG	GF	IR	IRS	Hld	SvOp	SB	CS	GB	FB	G/F
1993 Season	4.41	0	3	0	9	1	16.1	6	17	.224	13	1	1	1	4	.297	.328	1	2	0	0	0	2	1	18	14	1.29

1993 Season

	ERA	W	L	Sv	G	GS	IP	H	HR	BB	SO
Home	2.45	0	1	0	5	0	7.1	5	0	2	8
Away	6.00	0	2	0	4	1	9.0	8	1	4	9

	Avg	AB	H	2B	3B	HR	RBI	BB	SO	OBP	SLG
vs. Left	.154	13	2	0	0	0	0	2	3	.267	.154
vs. Right	.244	45	11	1	1	1	4	4	14	.306	.378

Ted Power — Mariners

Age 39 – Pitches Right

	ERA	W	L	Sv	G	GS	IP	BB	SO	Avg	H	2B	3B	HR	RBI	OBP	SLG	GF	IR	IRS	Hld	SvOp	SB	CS	GB	FB	G/F
1993 Season	5.36	2	4	13	45	0	45.1	17	27	.310	57	11	1	3	29	.365	.429	24	42	13	6	16	1	1	61	63	0.97
Last Five Years	3.57	18	20	29	240	15	380.1	121	214	.263	378	70	8	28	183	.319	.381	87	102	56	92	38	31	11	497	466	1.07

1993 Season

	ERA	W	L	Sv	G	GS	IP	H	HR	BB	SO
Home	6.98	0	1	8	25	0	19.1	27	2	8	8
Away	4.15	2	3	5	20	0	26.0	30	1	9	19
Starter	0.00	0	0	0	0	0	0.0	0	0	0	0
Reliever	5.36	2	4	13	45	0	45.1	57	3	17	27
0 Days rest	12.71	0	1	3	8	0	5.2	9	0	5	2
1 or 2 Days rest	5.40	1	3	8	24	0	26.2	34	3	7	18
3+ Days rest	2.08	1	0	2	13	0	13.0	14	0	5	7
Pre-All Star	7.20	0	2	0	20	0	20.0	30	2	8	11
Post-All Star	3.91	2	2	13	25	0	25.1	27	1	9	16

	Avg	AB	H	2B	3B	HR	RBI	BB	SO	OBP	SLG
vs. Left	.314	70	22	3	1	2	11	9	11	.392	.471
vs. Right	.307	114	35	8	0	1	18	8	16	.347	.404
Scoring Posn	.257	74	19	4	1	1	27	11	13	.345	.378
Close & Late	.295	88	26	4	1	1	19	10	13	.364	.398
None on/out	.286	35	10	3	0	0	0	3	5	.342	.371
First Pitch	.269	26	7	2	0	0	3	2	0	.300	.346
Ahead in Count	.291	79	23	4	0	1	14	0	25	.291	.380
Behind in Count	.391	46	18	3	1	1	7	12	0	.517	.565
Two Strikes	.233	73	17	6	0	1	10	3	27	.263	.356

Last Five Years

	ERA	W	L	Sv	G	GS	IP	H	HR	BB	SO
Home	3.28	11	5	18	129	5	192.0	181	12	64	109
Away	3.87	7	15	11	111	10	188.1	197	16	57	105
Day	3.49	5	7	7	74	3	108.1	111	8	38	75
Night	3.61	13	13	22	166	12	272.0	267	20	83	139
Grass	3.50	7	9	8	108	5	177.1	173	19	60	98
Turf	3.64	11	11	21	132	10	203.0	205	9	61	116
April	2.70	3	2	3	34	0	43.1	31	1	22	26
May	4.24	0	4	4	38	1	46.2	54	4	16	26
June	4.63	1	3	0	33	2	46.2	65	2	14	34
July	3.36	4	2	5	34	4	72.1	65	6	18	41
August	2.44	3	4	9	49	6	96.0	82	6	26	51
September/October	4.66	7	5	8	52	2	75.1	81	9	25	36
Starter	4.07	5	7	0	15	15	84.0	89	7	18	38
Reliever	3.43	13	13	29	225	0	296.1	289	21	103	176
0 Days rest	4.22	2	3	6	48	0	53.1	61	4	17	26
1 or 2 Days rest	3.75	6	8	15	111	0	146.1	136	13	47	89
3+ Days rest	2.51	5	2	8	66	0	96.2	92	4	39	61
Pre-All Star	3.81	5	10	8	113	4	160.2	175	11	57	101
Post-All Star	3.40	13	10	21	127	11	219.2	203	17	64	113

	Avg	AB	H	2B	3B	HR	RBI	BB	SO	OBP	SLG
vs. Left	.272	659	179	36	5	13	71	73	100	.345	.401
vs. Right	.255	781	199	34	3	15	112	48	114	.296	.364
Inning 1-6	.243	498	121	27	3	12	69	37	64	.297	.382
Inning 7+	.273	942	257	43	5	16	114	84	150	.330	.380
None on	.265	752	199	40	4	13	13	45	113	.310	.380
Runners on	.260	688	179	30	4	15	170	76	101	.328	.381
Scoring Posn	.258	426	110	18	3	10	155	61	66	.339	.385
Close & Late	.264	428	113	16	4	6	61	40	65	.326	.362
None on/out	.295	336	99	19	2	4	4	18	49	.332	.399
vs. 1st Batr (relief)	.256	199	51	7	0	2	21	14	36	.308	.322
First Inning Pitched	.259	789	204	32	3	15	120	69	134	.317	.364
First 15 Pitches	.260	716	186	35	3	11	92	57	119	.314	.363
Pitch 16-30	.271	376	102	13	0	8	45	38	57	.339	.370
Pitch 31-45	.250	160	40	8	3	5	25	13	24	.305	.431
Pitch 46+	.266	188	50	14	2	4	21	13	14	.307	.426
First Pitch	.306	193	59	14	2	6	29	22	0	.373	.492
Ahead in Count	.224	718	161	26	2	15	83	0	187	.228	.329
Behind in Count	.312	276	86	16	3	2	38	57	0	.428	.413
Two Strikes	.208	668	139	25	3	12	77	42	214	.257	.308

Pitcher vs. Batter (since 1984)

Pitches Best Vs.	Avg	AB	H	2B	3B	HR	RBI	BB	SO	OBP	SLG
Benito Santiago	.063	16	1	0	0	0	1	0	3	.063	.063
Charlie Hayes	.100	10	1	0	0	0	1	0	4	.091	.100
Hubie Brooks	.143	28	4	0	0	0	1	1	4	.172	.143
Sid Bream	.167	18	3	0	0	0	2	0	1	.167	.167
Rafael Belliard	.176	17	3	0	0	0	1	0	3	.176	.176

Pitches Worst Vs.	Avg	AB	H	2B	3B	HR	RBI	BB	SO	OBP	SLG
John Kruk	.556	18	10	3	1	0	6	2	0	.600	.833
Dan Gladden	.545	11	6	2	0	1	5	3	0	.643	1.000
Will Clark	.467	15	7	1	0	2	5	3	1	.556	.933
Willie McGee	.462	13	6	2	1	0	5	0	2	.462	.769
Gregg Jefferies	.417	12	5	1	0	2	4	1	0	.462	1.000

Todd Pratt — Phillies

Age 27 – Bats Right

	Avg	G	AB	R	H	2B	3B	HR	RBI	BB	SO	HBP	GDP	SB	CS	OBP	SLG	IBB	SH	SF	#Pit	#P/PA	GB	FB	G/F
1993 Season	.287	33	87	8	25	6	0	5	13	5	19	1	2	0	0	.330	.529	0	1	1	387	4.07	26	27	0.96
Career (1992-1993)	.286	49	133	14	38	7	0	7	23	9	31	1	4	0	0	.333	.496	0	1	1	580	4.00	41	36	1.14

1993 Season

	Avg	AB	H	2B	3B	HR	RBI	BB	SO	OBP	SLG
vs. Left	.400	25	10	4	0	4	9	2	4	.464	1.040
vs. Right	.242	62	15	2	0	1	4	3	15	.273	.323
Scoring Posn	.318	22	7	3	0	1	8	1	6	.360	.591
Close & Late	.389	18	7	2	0	2	5	0	3	.368	.833

Curtis Pride — Expos

Age 25 – Bats Left

	Avg	G	AB	R	H	2B	3B	HR	RBI	BB	SO	HBP	GDP	SB	CS	OBP	SLG	IBB	SH	SF	#Pit	#P/PA	GB	FB	G/F
1993 Season	.444	10	9	3	4	1	1	1	5	0	3	0	0	1	0	.444	1.111	0	0	0	29	3.22	1	2	0.50

1993 Season

	Avg	AB	H	2B	3B	HR	RBI	BB	SO	OBP	SLG
vs. Left	.000	0	0	0	0	0	0	0	0	.000	.000
vs. Right	.444	9	4	1	1	1	5	0	3	.444	1.111
Scoring Posn	.667	3	2	1	0	0	2	0	1	.667	1.000
Close & Late	1.000	2	2	1	0	1	4	0	0	1.000	3.000

Tom Prince — Pirates

Age 29 – Bats Right (flyball hitter)

	Avg	G	AB	R	H	2B	3B	HR	RBI	BB	SO	HBP	GDP	SB	CS	OBP	SLG	IBB	SH	SF	#Pit	#P/PA	GB	FB	G/F
1993 Season	.196	66	179	14	35	14	0	2	24	13	38	7	5	1	1	.272	.307	2	2	3	731	3.58	47	70	0.67
Last Five Years	.176	144	319	21	56	23	0	3	36	33	64	8	11	3	4	.265	.276	3	2	6	1311	3.56	98	121	0.81

1993 Season

	Avg	AB	H	2B	3B	HR	RBI	BB	SO	OBP	SLG		Avg	AB	H	2B	3B	HR	RBI	BB	SO	OBP	SLG
vs. Left	.229	70	16	8	0	0	4	4	9	.280	.343	Scoring Posn	.326	46	15	4	0	2	24	5	6	.404	.543
vs. Right	.174	109	19	6	0	2	20	9	29	.268	.284	Close & Late	.182	33	6	1	0	0	1	3	13	.270	.212
Home	.165	79	13	5	0	2	13	7	18	.239	.304	None on/out	.063	48	3	3	0	0	0	4	9	.151	.125
Away	.220	100	22	9	0	0	11	6	20	.298	.310	Batting #7	.158	38	6	2	0	0	5	2	7	.233	.211
First Pitch	.217	23	5	2	0	1	6	0	0	.269	.435	Batting #8	.195	128	25	9	0	2	18	10	30	.276	.313
Ahead in Count	.308	39	12	4	0	0	8	6	0	.396	.410	Other	.308	13	4	3	0	0	1	1	1	.357	.538
Behind in Count	.136	81	11	6	0	0	2	0	35	.157	.210	Pre-All Star	.202	89	18	6	0	1	14	5	14	.260	.303
Two Strikes	.141	78	11	6	0	0	4	7	38	.230	.218	Post-All Star	.189	90	17	8	0	1	10	8	24	.284	.311

Kirby Puckett — Twins

Age 33 – Bats Right (groundball hitter)

	Avg	G	AB	R	H	2B	3B	HR	RBI	BB	SO	HBP	GDP	SB	CS	OBP	SLG	IBB	SH	SF	#Pit	#P/PA	GB	FB	G/F
1993 Season	.296	156	622	89	184	39	3	22	89	47	93	7	15	8	6	.349	.474	7	1	5	2179	3.20	224	181	1.24
Last Five Years	.317	773	3058	442	968	191	20	77	453	220	400	23	95	52	26	.364	.468	44	11	26	10352	3.10	1333	744	1.79

1993 Season

	Avg	AB	H	2B	3B	HR	RBI	BB	SO	OBP	SLG		Avg	AB	H	2B	3B	HR	RBI	BB	SO	OBP	SLG
vs. Left	.295	139	41	8	1	7	20	18	19	.371	.518	Scoring Posn	.263	160	42	12	1	6	65	26	27	.369	.463
vs. Right	.296	483	143	31	2	15	69	29	74	.343	.462	Close & Late	.358	95	34	6	1	1	12	7	15	.398	.474
Groundball	.273	110	30	6	0	4	14	9	8	.325	.436	None on/out	.325	120	39	11	2	2	2	3	19	.341	.500
Flyball	.273	128	35	9	1	6	17	13	28	.354	.500	Batting #3	.301	585	176	38	3	21	83	45	86	.355	.484
Home	.322	320	103	22	3	12	53	32	44	.392	.522	Batting #4	.212	33	7	1	0	1	6	1	6	.235	.333
Away	.268	302	81	17	0	10	36	15	49	.302	.424	Other	.250	4	1	0	0	0	0	1	1	.400	.250
Day	.292	192	56	12	0	10	25	16	32	.357	.510	April	.295	78	23	4	0	4	14	9	15	.385	.500
Night	.298	430	128	27	3	12	64	31	61	.346	.458	May	.250	96	24	2	1	3	12	9	11	.314	.385
Grass	.291	230	67	13	0	6	28	10	36	.321	.426	June	.321	106	34	9	0	3	18	5	13	.348	.491
Turf	.298	392	117	26	3	16	61	37	57	.365	.503	July	.287	108	31	11	0	1	11	9	9	.345	.417
First Pitch	.396	154	61	9	0	8	26	5	0	.414	.610	August	.322	115	37	8	1	5	17	4	23	.350	.539
Ahead in Count	.339	124	42	10	0	2	18	18	0	.423	.468	September/October	.294	119	35	5	1	6	17	11	22	.359	.504
Behind in Count	.233	245	57	14	1	8	29	0	80	.247	.396	Pre-All Star	.298	326	97	22	1	11	50	26	40	.355	.472
Two Strikes	.180	222	40	9	1	2	12	24	93	.269	.257	Post-All Star	.294	296	87	17	2	11	39	21	53	.344	.476

1993 By Position

Position	Avg	AB	H	2B	3B	HR	RBI	BB	SO	OBP	SLG	G	GS	Innings	PO	A	E	DP	Fld Pct	Rng Fctr	In Zone	Outs	Zone Rtg	MLB Zone
As Designated Hitter	.254	63	16	6	0	1	4	5	5	.309	.397	17	17	---	---	---	---	---	---	---	---	---	---	---
As cf	.298	372	111	23	1	13	58	28	56	.354	.470	95	94	807.0	215	9	2	1	.991	2.50	266	208	.782	.829
As rf	.295	183	54	9	2	6	25	13	32	.343	.464	47	44	408.1	96	4	0	1	1.000	2.20	114	91	.798	.826

Last Five Years

	Avg	AB	H	2B	3B	HR	RBI	BB	SO	OBP	SLG		Avg	AB	H	2B	3B	HR	RBI	BB	SO	OBP	SLG
vs. Left	.326	774	252	48	8	22	107	72	102	.380	.494	Scoring Posn	.317	815	258	50	6	21	351	110	126	.393	.470
vs. Right	.313	2284	716	143	12	55	346	148	298	.358	.459	Close & Late	.325	453	147	28	3	10	70	40	71	.381	.466
Groundball	.304	774	235	42	4	11	99	64	94	.358	.411	None on/out	.319	571	182	43	3	13	13	25	76	.352	.473
Flyball	.303	644	195	43	5	24	96	53	114	.359	.497	Batting #3	.318	2894	919	184	20	74	422	206	369	.364	.472
Home	.346	1574	545	107	14	41	251	111	208	.390	.510	Batting #4	.290	155	45	7	0	3	31	11	29	.343	.394
Away	.285	1484	423	84	6	36	202	109	192	.336	.423	Other	.444	9	4	0	0	0	0	3	2	.583	.444
Day	.321	921	296	68	9	27	138	81	121	.381	.503	April	.311	402	125	26	5	14	58	34	50	.366	.505
Night	.314	2137	672	123	11	50	315	139	279	.356	.453	May	.336	530	178	36	5	18	87	37	51	.379	.525
Grass	.290	1131	328	62	5	29	157	83	149	.341	.431	June	.308	545	168	34	4	17	87	34	72	.354	.479
Turf	.332	1927	640	129	15	48	296	137	251	.377	.489	July	.323	517	167	33	3	7	75	42	61	.375	.439
First Pitch	.389	764	297	54	4	26	138	26	0	.411	.572	August	.316	526	166	32	1	11	70	25	93	.350	.443
Ahead in Count	.369	620	229	51	5	14	104	112	0	.465	.535	September/October	.305	538	164	30	2	10	76	48	73	.361	.424
Behind in Count	.245	1198	293	56	8	20	132	0	348	.249	.355	Pre-All Star	.318	1651	525	111	14	51	250	119	192	.366	.495
Two Strikes	.215	1061	228	45	5	15	97	72	400	.265	.309	Post-All Star	.315	1407	443	80	6	26	203	101	208	.362	.436

Batter vs. Pitcher (career)

Hits Best Against	Avg	AB	H	2B	3B	HR	RBI	BB	SO	OBP	SLG	Hits Worst Against	Avg	AB	H	2B	3B	HR	RBI	BB	SO	OBP	SLG
Mark Knudson	.727	11	8	1	0	1	3	1	1	.750	1.091	Todd Frohwirth	.000	16	0	0	0	0	0	1	4	.059	.000
Jose DeLeon	.571	14	8	1	0	2	3	0	2	.571	1.071	David Cone	.077	13	1	0	0	0	0	3	7	.250	.077
Jeff Ballard	.563	16	9	2	0	1	3	1	0	.556	.875	Bryan Harvey	.100	10	1	0	0	0	0	1	4	.182	.100
Kenny Rogers	.545	11	6	2	0	2	3	3	1	.643	1.273	Dennis Eckersley	.105	19	2	0	1	0	1	0	5	.100	.211
Jeff Johnson	.444	9	4	1	0	1	3	2	1	.545	.889	Danny Darwin	.125	32	4	0	0	0	2	0	9	.121	.125

Tim Pugh — Reds

Age 27 – Pitches Right

	ERA	W	L	Sv	G	GS	IP	BB	SO	Avg	H	2B	3B	HR	RBI	OBP	SLG	CG	ShO	Sup	QS	#P/S	SB	CS	GB	FB	G/F
1993 Season	5.26	10	15	0	31	27	164.1	59	94	.303	200	20	6	19	92	.363	.437	3	1	5.26	12	88	19	7	264	173	1.53
Career (1992-1993)	4.68	14	17	0	38	34	209.2	72	112	.297	247	31	8	21	104	.357	.430	3	1	4.72	17	89	20	8	331	224	1.48

1993 Season

	ERA	W	L	Sv	G	GS	IP	H	HR	BB	SO		Avg	AB	H	2B	3B	HR	RBI	BB	SO	OBP	SLG
Home	4.76	6	5	0	14	12	79.1	89	10	28	44	vs. Left	.348	325	113	15	4	12	55	35	40	.410	.529
Away	5.72	4	10	0	17	15	85.0	111	9	31	50	vs. Right	.259	336	87	5	2	7	37	24	54	.317	.348

1993 Season

	ERA	W	L	Sv	G	GS	IP	H	HR	BB	SO
Day	6.12	3	6	0	12	10	60.1	73	11	17	40
Night	4.76	7	9	0	19	17	104.0	127	8	42	54
Grass	5.17	3	6	0	12	10	62.2	75	9	22	40
Turf	5.31	7	9	0	19	17	101.2	125	10	37	54
April	2.77	2	1	0	5	4	26.0	25	2	6	13
May	6.52	1	4	0	5	5	29.0	41	4	14	12
June	6.94	0	4	0	6	3	23.1	35	3	5	14
July	3.55	3	1	0	5	5	33.0	36	3	6	18
August	7.76	2	3	0	6	6	29.0	40	5	14	18
September/October	4.13	2	2	0	4	4	24.0	23	2	14	19
Starter	5.28	10	14	0	27	27	155.0	189	18	56	87
Reliever	4.82	0	1	0	4	0	9.1	11	1	3	7
0-3 Days Rest	1.29	1	0	0	1	1	7.0	4	0	1	2
4 Days Rest	5.28	6	8	0	16	16	93.2	124	8	32	54
5+ Days Rest	5.80	3	6	0	10	10	54.1	61	10	23	31
Pre-All Star	4.94	5	9	0	18	14	93.0	113	12	27	44
Post-All Star	5.68	5	6	0	13	13	71.1	87	7	32	50

	Avg	AB	H	2B	3B	HR	RBI	BB	SO	OBP	SLG
Inning 1-6	.307	574	176	19	6	18	86	53	78	.369	.455
Inning 7+	.276	87	24	1	0	1	6	6	16	.323	.322
None on	.270	378	102	16	3	8	8	32	56	.332	.392
Runners on	.346	283	98	4	3	11	84	27	38	.404	.498
Scoring Posn	.327	162	53	3	2	5	70	17	21	.384	.463
Close & Late	.318	22	7	0	0	0	1	1	6	.348	.318
None on/out	.271	166	45	8	2	4	4	12	26	.324	.416
vs. 1st Batr (relief)	.500	4	2	1	0	0	0	0	1	.500	.750
First Inning Pitched	.360	125	45	4	2	3	23	14	18	.429	.496
First 75 Pitches	.286	549	157	17	6	16	73	46	78	.347	.426
Pitch 76-90	.358	67	24	2	0	2	10	7	13	.413	.478
Pitch 91-105	.436	39	17	1	0	0	7	4	3	.488	.462
Pitch 106+	.333	6	2	0	0	1	2	2	0	.500	.833
First Pitch	.383	128	49	4	1	9	34	0	0	.389	.641
Ahead in Count	.215	284	61	1	1	5	27	0	84	.217	.278
Behind in Count	.392	153	60	10	3	4	24	33	0	.497	.575
Two Strikes	.205	254	52	4	0	2	16	26	94	.281	.244

Harvey Pulliam — Royals

Age 26 – Bats Right

	Avg	G	AB	R	H	2B	3B	HR	RBI	BB	SO	HBP	GDP	SB	CS	OBP	SLG	IBB	SH	SF	#Pit	#P/PA	GB	FB	G/F
1993 Season	.258	27	62	7	16	5	0	1	6	2	14	1	3	0	0	.292	.387	0	0	0	234	3.60	19	15	1.27
Career (1991-1993)	.260	49	100	13	26	7	0	4	10	6	26	1	4	0	0	.308	.450	1	1	0	406	3.76	30	26	1.15

1993 Season

	Avg	AB	H	2B	3B	HR	RBI	BB	SO	OBP	SLG
vs. Left	.333	45	15	5	0	1	6	1	9	.362	.511
vs. Right	.059	17	1	0	0	0	0	1	5	.111	.059
Scoring Posn	.545	11	6	2	0	1	6	1	2	.615	1.000
Close & Late	.308	13	4	2	0	1	3	1	3	.357	.692

Paul Quantrill — Red Sox

Age 25 – Pitches Right

	ERA	W	L	Sv	G	GS	IP	BB	SO	Avg	H	2B	3B	HR	RBI	OBP	SLG	GF	IR	IRS	Hld	SvOp	SB	CS	GB	FB	G/F
1993 Season	3.91	6	12	1	49	14	138.0	44	66	.279	151	29	6	13	62	.334	.426	8	36	5	3	2	12	1	183	161	1.14
Career (1992-1993)	3.46	8	15	2	76	14	187.1	59	90	.281	206	35	7	14	75	.335	.405	18	53	12	6	7	15	3	257	211	1.22

1993 Season

	ERA	W	L	Sv	G	GS	IP	H	HR	BB	SO
Home	3.67	4	6	1	26	8	83.1	90	7	27	35
Away	4.28	2	6	0	23	6	54.2	61	6	17	31
Starter	3.87	2	7	0	14	14	81.1	89	10	18	32
Reliever	3.97	4	5	1	35	0	56.2	62	3	26	34
0 Days rest	0.00	1	0	0	1	0	3.1	2	0	0	3
1 or 2 Days rest	4.06	3	3	0	20	0	31.0	31	2	17	13
3+ Days rest	4.43	0	2	1	14	0	22.1	29	1	9	18
Pre-All Star	2.92	4	6	0	25	10	86.1	85	8	19	46
Post-All Star	5.57	2	6	1	24	4	51.2	66	5	25	20

	Avg	AB	H	2B	3B	HR	RBI	BB	SO	OBP	SLG
vs. Left	.271	247	67	15	3	7	24	28	29	.350	.441
vs. Right	.285	295	84	14	3	6	38	16	37	.319	.414
Scoring Posn	.277	141	39	5	2	4	51	25	19	.385	.426
Close & Late	.377	69	26	7	2	1	10	9	9	.443	.580
None on/out	.259	135	35	12	0	2	2	4	19	.286	.393
First Pitch	.355	93	33	5	0	3	9	12	0	.429	.505
Ahead in Count	.208	231	48	13	3	3	25	0	58	.208	.329
Behind in Count	.351	114	40	7	1	6	13	18	0	.444	.588
Two Strikes	.223	238	53	11	4	3	31	14	66	.265	.340

Carlos Quintana — Red Sox

Age 28 – Bats Right (groundball hitter)

	Avg	G	AB	R	H	2B	3B	HR	RBI	BB	SO	HBP	GDP	SB	CS	OBP	SLG	IBB	SH	SF	#Pit	#P/PA	GB	FB	G/F
1993 Season	.244	101	303	31	74	5	0	1	19	31	52	2	13	1	0	.317	.271	2	5	2	1300	3.79	153	42	3.64
Last Five Years	.276	433	1370	162	378	59	1	19	163	151	204	6	54	3	2	.349	.362	4	15	7	5691	3.67	672	260	2.58

1993 Season

	Avg	AB	H	2B	3B	HR	RBI	BB	SO	OBP	SLG
vs. Left	.250	104	26	1	0	0	9	15	18	.342	.260
vs. Right	.241	199	48	4	0	1	10	16	34	.303	.276
Groundball	.240	50	12	0	0	0	4	3	5	.273	.240
Flyball	.259	81	21	3	0	1	6	6	14	.318	.333
Home	.264	148	39	4	0	0	10	15	23	.329	.291
Away	.226	155	35	1	0	1	9	16	29	.305	.252
Day	.243	107	26	4	0	1	5	10	20	.308	.308
Night	.245	196	48	1	0	0	14	21	32	.321	.250
Grass	.249	249	62	5	0	0	18	23	37	.315	.269
Turf	.222	54	12	0	0	1	1	8	15	.323	.278
First Pitch	.238	42	10	1	0	0	2	2	0	.304	.262
Ahead in Count	.313	83	26	1	0	1	10	17	0	.422	.361
Behind in Count	.179	123	22	0	0	0	4	0	42	.179	.179
Two Strikes	.133	135	18	0	0	0	2	12	52	.204	.133

	Avg	AB	H	2B	3B	HR	RBI	BB	SO	OBP	SLG
Scoring Posn	.203	79	16	2	0	0	18	11	13	.301	.228
Close & Late	.283	46	13	0	0	0	1	4	9	.340	.283
None on/out	.302	63	19	1	0	0	0	10	7	.397	.317
Batting #5	.298	47	14	1	0	1	6	8	6	.400	.383
Batting #6	.189	106	20	2	0	0	5	12	23	.275	.208
Other	.267	150	40	2	0	0	8	11	23	.319	.280
April	.339	59	20	1	0	0	4	7	9	.409	.356
May	.261	92	24	1	0	0	3	10	12	.330	.272
June	.261	46	12	0	0	1	5	1	9	.286	.326
July	.176	68	12	3	0	0	3	9	14	.282	.221
August	.105	19	2	0	0	0	1	0	5	.105	.105
September/October	.211	19	4	0	0	0	3	4	3	.348	.211
Pre-All Star	.268	224	60	3	0	1	12	24	35	.341	.295
Post-All Star	.177	79	14	2	0	0	7	7	17	.244	.203

1993 By Position

Position	Avg	AB	H	2B	3B	HR	RBI	BB	SO	OBP	SLG	G	GS	Innings	PO	A	E	DP	Fld Pct	Rng Fctr	In Zone	Outs	Zone Rtg	MLB Zone
As Pinch Hitter	.182	11	2	0	0	0	0	0	2	.182	.182	11	0	---	---	---	---	---	---	---	---	---	---	---
As 1b	.220	127	28	2	0	0	9	9	25	.270	.236	53	32	314.0	320	21	3	30	.991	---	60	51	.850	.834
As rf	.262	164	43	3	0	1	10	22	25	.354	.299	50	46	383.1	91	4	0	1	1.000	2.23	106	86	.811	.826

Last Five Years

	Avg	AB	H	2B	3B	HR	RBI	BB	SO	OBP	SLG
vs. Left	.317	473	150	23	0	8	64	59	65	.393	.416
vs. Right	.254	897	228	36	1	11	99	92	139	.325	.333
Groundball	.264	364	96	11	0	4	36	37	53	.333	.327
Flyball	.276	319	88	15	0	9	44	36	50	.352	.408
Home	.285	650	185	26	0	5	71	76	92	.361	.348
Away	.268	720	193	33	1	14	92	75	112	.338	.375
Day	.294	432	127	28	1	7	65	55	63	.373	.412
Night	.268	938	251	31	0	12	98	96	141	.337	.339
Grass	.286	1122	321	52	1	12	136	124	153	.358	.366
Turf	.230	248	57	7	0	7	27	27	51	.305	.343
First Pitch	.330	233	77	12	1	2	36	4	0	.347	.416
Ahead in Count	.335	334	112	16	0	11	54	80	0	.460	.482
Behind in Count	.200	555	111	17	0	2	43	0	172	.204	.241
Two Strikes	.187	579	108	16	0	1	40	67	204	.272	.219

	Avg	AB	H	2B	3B	HR	RBI	BB	SO	OBP	SLG
Scoring Posn	.265	366	97	17	0	5	134	49	54	.348	.352
Close & Late	.324	210	68	7	0	2	25	18	36	.376	.386
None on/out	.309	275	85	12	0	4	4	24	33	.369	.396
Batting #2	.274	336	92	13	0	5	40	40	52	.353	.357
Batting #7	.295	302	89	12	0	4	31	26	47	.355	.374
Other	.269	732	197	34	1	10	92	85	105	.345	.359
April	.329	140	46	6	0	1	11	12	22	.386	.393
May	.297	269	80	10	0	3	26	24	27	.356	.368
June	.283	244	69	9	0	5	32	25	45	.353	.381
July	.250	256	64	15	0	6	38	36	39	.341	.379
August	.260	204	53	8	1	3	24	27	38	.349	.353
September/October	.257	257	66	11	0	1	32	27	33	.325	.311
Pre-All Star	.298	726	216	30	0	11	80	71	102	.363	.384
Post-All Star	.252	644	162	29	1	8	83	80	102	.333	.337

Batter vs. Pitcher (career)

Hits Best Against	Avg	AB	H	2B	3B	HR	RBI	BB	SO	OBP	SLG
Jim Abbott	.476	21	10	1	0	0	0	2	3	.522	.524
Frank Tanana	.455	11	5	2	0	0	2	2	1	.538	.636
Jack McDowell	.400	10	4	1	0	0	1	3	2	.538	.500
Dave Stewart	.348	23	8	3	1	1	6	1	1	.375	.696
David Wells	.333	21	7	0	0	2	3	1	1	.364	.619

Hits Worst Against	Avg	AB	H	2B	3B	HR	RBI	BB	SO	OBP	SLG
Mike Moore	.000	10	0	0	0	0	0	1	1	.091	.000
Melido Perez	.071	14	1	0	0	0	0	1	4	.133	.071
Todd Stottlemyre	.083	12	1	0	0	0	0	0	2	.083	.083
Duane Ward	.091	11	1	0	0	0	1	0	8	.091	.091
Dave Johnson	.091	11	1	0	0	0	0	1	0	.167	.091

Scott Radinsky — White Sox

Age 26 – Pitches Left

	ERA	W	L	Sv	G	GS	IP	BB	SO	Avg	H	2B	3B	HR	RBI	OBP	SLG	GF	IR	IRS	Hld	SvOp	SB	CS	GB	FB	G/F
1993 Season	4.28	8	2	4	73	0	54.2	19	44	.268	61	6	0	3	27	.327	.333	24	50	13	12	5	2	0	78	58	1.34
Career (1990-1993)	3.33	22	15	31	270	0	237.2	112	187	.238	215	32	3	11	112	.324	.317	94	237	65	53	48	6	3	305	236	1.29

1993 Season

	ERA	W	L	Sv	G	GS	IP	H	HR	BB	SO
Home	5.70	3	2	2	36	0	30.0	35	3	11	26
Away	2.55	5	0	2	37	0	24.2	26	0	8	18
Day	2.33	5	0	1	21	0	19.1	20	1	5	15
Night	5.35	3	2	3	52	0	35.1	41	2	14	29
Grass	4.30	7	2	3	59	0	46.0	53	3	16	39
Turf	4.15	1	0	1	14	0	8.2	8	0	3	5
April	3.18	0	0	1	9	0	11.1	10	0	4	8
May	10.13	2	0	0	11	0	8.0	15	2	2	5
June	2.16	0	0	0	16	0	8.1	10	0	3	10
July	1.08	4	0	2	12	0	8.1	2	0	1	5
August	5.79	0	2	1	13	0	9.1	10	1	5	8
September/October	3.86	2	0	0	12	0	9.1	14	0	4	8
Starter	0.00	0	0	0	0	0	0.0	0	0	0	0
Reliever	4.28	8	2	4	73	0	54.2	61	3	19	44
0 Days rest	5.40	2	0	1	22	0	10.0	13	0	4	8
1 or 2 Days rest	3.77	5	2	1	34	0	28.2	36	1	10	23
3+ Days rest	4.50	1	0	2	17	0	16.0	12	2	5	13
Pre-All Star	4.55	2	0	1	39	0	29.2	36	2	10	24
Post-All Star	3.96	6	2	3	34	0	25.0	25	1	9	20

	Avg	AB	H	2B	3B	HR	RBI	BB	SO	OBP	SLG
vs. Left	.239	88	21	2	0	0	7	6	29	.287	.261
vs. Right	.286	140	40	4	0	3	20	13	15	.351	.379
Inning 1-6	.000	0	0	0	0	0	0	0	0	.000	.000
Inning 7+	.268	228	61	6	0	3	27	19	44	.327	.333
None on	.279	111	31	3	0	1	1	5	18	.310	.333
Runners on	.256	117	30	3	0	2	26	14	26	.341	.333
Scoring Posn	.280	75	21	1	0	2	26	7	19	.349	.373
Close & Late	.239	113	27	2	0	1	7	9	20	.295	.283
None on/out	.224	49	11	0	0	0	0	1	8	.240	.224
vs. 1st Batr (relief)	.221	68	15	2	0	0	5	5	18	.274	.250
First Inning Pitched	.281	192	54	5	0	3	27	17	38	.343	.354
First 15 Pitches	.281	178	50	5	0	3	22	15	28	.340	.360
Pitch 16-30	.262	42	11	1	0	0	5	3	12	.311	.286
Pitch 31-45	.000	7	0	0	0	0	0	1	3	.125	.000
Pitch 46+	.000	1	0	0	0	0	0	0	1	.000	.000
First Pitch	.333	21	7	1	0	0	3	3	0	.440	.381
Ahead in Count	.192	104	20	2	0	1	7	0	37	.192	.240
Behind in Count	.429	49	21	1	0	2	11	5	0	.481	.571
Two Strikes	.170	100	17	1	0	0	8	11	44	.252	.180

Career (1990-1993)

	ERA	W	L	Sv	G	GS	IP	H	HR	BB	SO
Home	3.02	9	7	20	135	0	128.1	109	6	47	110
Away	3.70	13	8	11	135	0	109.1	106	5	65	77
Day	3.27	10	5	7	79	0	77.0	79	2	36	56
Night	3.36	12	10	24	191	0	160.2	136	9	76	131
Grass	2.98	18	11	28	223	0	199.1	173	7	90	166
Turf	5.17	4	4	3	47	0	38.1	42	4	22	21
April	2.05	2	2	2	33	0	30.2	25	0	12	26
May	3.61	8	1	2	48	0	47.1	39	3	21	42
June	2.68	1	4	6	50	0	40.1	31	4	18	32
July	3.77	6	3	7	52	0	43.0	39	3	21	40
August	2.72	2	3	10	42	0	39.2	37	1	17	26
September/October	4.91	3	2	4	45	0	36.2	44	0	23	21
Starter	0.00	0	0	0	0	0	0.0	0	0	0	0
Reliever	3.33	22	15	31	270	0	237.2	215	11	112	187
0 Days rest	3.17	6	5	11	83	0	59.2	48	2	33	44
1 or 2 Days rest	2.77	13	7	15	118	0	107.1	98	4	48	88
3+ Days rest	4.33	3	3	5	69	0	70.2	69	5	31	55
Pre-All Star	2.88	11	8	11	148	0	131.1	103	8	61	112
Post-All Star	3.89	11	7	20	122	0	106.1	112	3	51	75

	Avg	AB	H	2B	3B	HR	RBI	BB	SO	OBP	SLG
vs. Left	.204	294	60	6	2	5	34	23	91	.264	.289
vs. Right	.255	608	155	26	1	6	78	89	96	.352	.331
Inning 1-6	.207	29	6	1	0	0	9	6	8	.342	.241
Inning 7+	.239	873	209	31	3	11	103	106	179	.324	.320
None on	.255	415	106	13	1	6	6	40	78	.325	.335
Runners on	.224	487	109	19	2	5	106	72	109	.323	.302
Scoring Posn	.210	309	65	9	2	3	96	50	80	.318	.282
Close & Late	.216	504	109	18	1	6	48	63	98	.306	.292
None on/out	.243	189	46	7	0	3	3	19	35	.319	.328
vs. 1st Batr (relief)	.236	237	56	10	0	2	36	27	64	.315	.304
First Inning Pitched	.244	730	178	25	2	10	101	85	162	.324	.325
First 15 Pitches	.245	669	164	25	2	9	82	73	131	.321	.329
Pitch 16-30	.223	206	46	6	1	2	26	33	49	.333	.291
Pitch 31-45	.192	26	5	1	0	0	4	6	6	.333	.231
Pitch 46+	.000	1	0	0	0	0	0	0	1	.000	.000
First Pitch	.281	121	34	11	0	0	19	11	0	.348	.372
Ahead in Count	.164	456	75	7	0	3	33	0	164	.169	.200
Behind in Count	.354	161	57	9	1	6	38	54	0	.509	.534
Two Strikes	.163	443	72	6	1	3	38	47	187	.247	.201

Pitcher vs. Batter (career)

Pitches Best Vs.	Avg	AB	H	2B	3B	HR	RBI	BB	SO	OBP	SLG
Ken Griffey Jr	.071	14	1	1	0	0	0	0	6	.071	.143
Lou Whitaker	.091	11	1	0	0	0	0	1	6	.167	.091
George Brett	.111	18	2	0	0	0	0	0	3	.111	.111
Don Mattingly	.200	15	3	0	0	0	2	0	2	.200	.200

Pitches Worst Vs.	Avg	AB	H	2B	3B	HR	RBI	BB	SO	OBP	SLG
Ruben Sierra	.375	8	3	0	0	0	1	5	0	.615	.375

Pitcher vs. Batter (career)																						
Pitches Best Vs.	Avg	AB	H	2B	3B	HR	RBI	BB	SO	OBP	SLG	Pitches Worst Vs.	Avg	AB	H	2B	3B	HR	RBI	BB	SO	OBP	SLG
Wally Joyner	.231	13	3	0	0	0	1	0	3	.231	.231												

Tim Raines — White Sox

Age 34 – Bats Both

	Avg	G	AB	R	H	2B	3B	HR	RBI	BB	SO	HBP	GDP	SB	CS	OBP	SLG	IBB	SH	SF	#Pit	#P/PA	GB	FB	G/F
1993 Season	.306	115	415	75	127	16	4	16	54	64	35	3	7	21	7	.401	.480	4	2	2	1831	3.77	151	138	1.09
Last Five Years	.287	689	2549	420	731	98	30	46	280	391	242	14	36	207	53	.381	.403	43	15	26	10915	3.64	1017	740	1.37

1993 Season

	Avg	AB	H	2B	3B	HR	RBI	BB	SO	OBP	SLG		Avg	AB	H	2B	3B	HR	RBI	BB	SO	OBP	SLG
vs. Left	.348	112	39	5	0	3	18	19	9	.439	.473	Scoring Posn	.325	77	25	3	0	2	36	23	5	.471	.442
vs. Right	.290	303	88	11	4	13	36	45	26	.386	.482	Close & Late	.361	61	22	3	0	1	6	14	3	.480	.459
Groundball	.324	71	23	1	1	0	10	15	5	.448	.366	None on/out	.318	179	57	7	3	9	9	20	11	.396	.542
Flyball	.308	91	28	0	1	5	10	14	8	.408	.527	Batting #1	.308	413	127	16	4	16	54	62	35	.400	.482
Home	.291	196	57	5	1	7	25	26	15	.378	.434	Batting #6	.000	1	0	0	0	0	0	1	0	.500	.000
Away	.320	219	70	11	3	9	29	38	20	.421	.521	Other	.000	1	0	0	0	0	0	1	0	.500	.000
Day	.319	113	36	5	2	1	7	17	9	.412	.425	April	.250	12	3	0	0	2	5	2	2	.400	.750
Night	.301	302	91	11	2	15	47	47	26	.397	.500	May	.321	28	9	1	0	1	2	5	0	.424	.464
Grass	.313	345	108	11	4	12	42	50	28	.401	.472	June	.306	72	22	4	0	4	10	20	4	.452	.528
Turf	.271	70	19	5	0	4	12	14	7	.400	.514	July	.323	99	32	2	4	4	15	8	6	.380	.545
First Pitch	.279	61	17	1	0	4	10	2	0	.302	.492	August	.292	106	31	3	0	4	15	14	13	.372	.434
Ahead in Count	.331	142	47	9	1	6	19	37	0	.467	.535	September/October	.306	98	30	6	0	1	7	15	10	.404	.398
Behind in Count	.287	129	37	4	1	3	15	0	30	.301	.403	Pre-All Star	.308	156	48	6	2	8	25	28	11	.414	.526
Two Strikes	.303	145	44	5	0	5	19	25	35	.414	.441	Post-All Star	.305	259	79	10	2	8	29	36	24	.393	.452

1993 By Position

Position	Avg	AB	H	2B	3B	HR	RBI	BB	SO	OBP	SLG	G	GS	Innings	PO	A	E	DP	Fld Pct	Rng Fctr	In Zone	Outs	Zone Rtg	MLB Zone
As lf	.307	411	126	16	4	16	54	60	35	.397	.482	112	102	913.2	201	5	0	1	1.000	2.03	228	189	.829	.818

Last Five Years

	Avg	AB	H	2B	3B	HR	RBI	BB	SO	OBP	SLG		Avg	AB	H	2B	3B	HR	RBI	BB	SO	OBP	SLG
vs. Left	.288	768	221	21	5	11	87	108	65	.374	.371	Scoring Posn	.323	527	170	24	10	7	225	166	47	.470	.446
vs. Right	.286	1781	510	77	25	35	193	283	177	.384	.417	Close & Late	.296	456	135	15	3	9	60	87	41	.407	.401
Groundball	.281	805	226	37	9	7	80	120	78	.375	.375	None on/out	.281	907	255	33	11	20	20	96	88	.356	.408
Flyball	.298	574	171	17	6	13	61	105	46	.406	.416	Batting #1	.280	1679	470	66	21	26	162	253	160	.375	.391
Home	.287	1203	345	45	12	24	128	178	107	.378	.404	Batting #3	.285	383	109	10	4	8	53	60	37	.380	.394
Away	.287	1346	386	53	18	22	152	213	135	.384	.402	Other	.312	487	152	22	5	12	65	78	45	.405	.452
Day	.272	683	186	23	11	11	66	122	76	.380	.387	April	.244	295	72	11	6	2	41	44	25	.340	.342
Night	.292	1866	545	75	19	35	214	269	166	.382	.409	May	.310	422	131	19	8	11	43	81	50	.422	.472
Grass	.294	1613	474	54	18	27	159	243	155	.386	.400	June	.276	388	107	20	2	4	48	71	35	.383	.369
Turf	.275	936	257	44	12	19	121	148	87	.374	.408	July	.280	425	119	9	7	8	52	54	34	.366	.391
First Pitch	.302	407	123	10	3	9	40	25	0	.339	.408	August	.293	525	154	22	3	12	54	79	61	.383	.415
Ahead in Count	.329	835	275	41	10	21	108	195	0	.451	.478	September/October	.300	494	148	17	4	9	42	62	37	.380	.405
Behind in Count	.237	815	193	31	6	8	70	0	196	.245	.319	Pre-All Star	.279	1225	342	52	20	19	146	209	120	.383	.401
Two Strikes	.240	897	215	34	7	12	87	158	242	.360	.333	Post-All Star	.294	1324	389	46	10	27	134	182	122	.380	.405

Batter vs. Pitcher (since 1984)

Hits Best Against	Avg	AB	H	2B	3B	HR	RBI	BB	SO	OBP	SLG	Hits Worst Against	Avg	AB	H	2B	3B	HR	RBI	BB	SO	OBP	SLG
Ken Hill	.714	14	10	3	1	0	4	7	1	.810	1.071	Jack Armstrong	.063	16	1	0	0	0	1	1	2	.118	.063
Mark Leiter	.583	12	7	0	0	3	4	3	1	.667	1.333	Chris Bosio	.071	14	1	0	0	0	0	2	0	.188	.071
Craig Lefferts	.500	20	10	3	1	1	5	3	2	.542	.900	Luis Aquino	.091	11	1	0	0	0	1	2	1	.214	.091
Bill Gullickson	.432	37	16	2	1	4	8	6	1	.512	.865	Jose Mesa	.091	11	1	0	0	0	0	0	0	.091	.091
Cris Carpenter	.429	7	3	0	1	0	1	4	0	.636	.714	Jim Deshaies	.095	21	2	0	0	0	1	0	2	.091	.095

Manny Ramirez — Indians

Age 22 – Bats Right (flyball hitter)

	Avg	G	AB	R	H	2B	3B	HR	RBI	BB	SO	HBP	GDP	SB	CS	OBP	SLG	IBB	SH	SF	#Pit	#P/PA	GB	FB	G/F
1993 Season	.170	22	53	5	9	1	0	2	5	2	8	0	3	0	0	.200	.302	0	0	0	196	3.56	13	23	0.57

1993 Season

	Avg	AB	H	2B	3B	HR	RBI	BB	SO	OBP	SLG		Avg	AB	H	2B	3B	HR	RBI	BB	SO	OBP	SLG
vs. Left	.115	26	3	0	0	1	1	0	5	.115	.231	Scoring Posn	.133	15	2	0	0	0	2	1	1	.188	.133
vs. Right	.222	27	6	1	0	1	4	2	3	.276	.370	Close & Late	.286	7	2	0	0	0	1	1	1	.375	.286

Pat Rapp — Marlins

Age 26 – Pitches Right

	ERA	W	L	Sv	G	GS	IP	BB	SO	Avg	H	2B	3B	HR	RBI	OBP	SLG	CG	ShO	Sup	QS	#P/S	SB	CS	GB	FB	G/F
1993 Season	4.02	4	6	0	16	16	94.0	39	57	.281	101	21	4	7	44	.351	.421	1	0	4.02	8	95	3	6	133	96	1.39
Career (1992-1993)	4.33	4	8	0	19	18	104.0	45	60	.277	109	24	5	7	51	.353	.417	1	0	3.72	8	92	7	7	150	104	1.44

1993 Season

	ERA	W	L	Sv	G	GS	IP	H	HR	BB	SO		Avg	AB	H	2B	3B	HR	RBI	BB	SO	OBP	SLG
Home	4.64	4	1	0	7	7	42.2	49	4	19	28	vs. Left	.269	175	47	11	2	3	20	26	17	.363	.406
Away	3.51	0	5	0	9	9	51.1	52	3	20	29	vs. Right	.293	184	54	10	2	4	24	13	40	.340	.435
Starter	4.02	4	6	0	16	16	94.0	101	7	39	57	Scoring Posn	.245	102	25	5	1	2	36	11	15	.314	.373
Reliever	0.00	0	0	0	0	0	0.0	0	0	0	0	Close & Late	.286	14	4	2	1	1	2	2	1	.375	.786
0-3 Days Rest	0.00	0	0	0	0	0	0.0	0	0	0	0	None on/out	.279	86	24	3	1	1	1	13	11	.374	.372
4 Days Rest	4.37	3	2	0	10	10	55.2	63	5	26	40	First Pitch	.455	55	25	5	2	1	11	1	0	.456	.673
5+ Days Rest	3.52	1	4	0	6	6	38.1	38	2	13	17	Ahead in Count	.204	152	31	7	2	3	12	0	46	.208	.336

1993 Season

	ERA	W	L	Sv	G	GS	IP	H	HR	BB	SO
Pre-All Star	4.76	0	1	0	1	1	5.2	5	0	1	4
Post-All Star	3.97	4	5	0	15	15	88.1	96	7	38	53

	Avg	AB	H	2B	3B	HR	RBI	BB	SO	OBP	SLG
Behind in Count	.341	88	30	5	0	2	11	18	0	.450	.466
Two Strikes	.201	154	31	8	2	3	16	20	57	.295	.338

Dennis Rasmussen — Royals

Age 35 – Pitches Left

	ERA	W	L	Sv	G	GS	IP	BB	SO	Avg	H	2B	3B	HR	RBI	OBP	SLG	GF	IR	IRS	Hld	SvOp	SB	CS	GB	FB	G/F
1993 Season	7.45	1	2	0	9	4	29.0	14	12	.328	40	7	2	4	22	.399	.516	3	6	0	1	0	1	4	27	49	0.55
Last Five Years	4.24	32	41	0	106	99	589.2	205	272	.277	634	90	15	64	274	.336	.414	4	6	0	1	0	55	39	820	718	1.14

1993 Season

	ERA	W	L	Sv	G	GS	IP	H	HR	BB	SO
Home	6.14	1	0	0	3	2	14.2	18	2	7	4
Away	8.79	0	2	0	6	2	14.1	22	2	7	8

	Avg	AB	H	2B	3B	HR	RBI	BB	SO	OBP	SLG
vs. Left	.316	19	6	1	0	0	3	1	2	.333	.368
vs. Right	.330	103	34	6	2	4	19	13	10	.410	.544

Last Five Years

	ERA	W	L	Sv	G	GS	IP	H	HR	BB	SO
Home	3.98	17	19	0	47	46	278.0	290	33	91	132
Away	4.48	15	22	0	59	53	311.2	344	31	114	140
Day	4.67	9	14	0	35	32	175.1	208	25	71	74
Night	4.06	23	27	0	71	67	414.1	426	39	134	198
Grass	4.35	22	35	0	77	73	428.1	465	53	144	195
Turf	3.96	10	6	0	29	26	161.1	169	11	61	77
April	6.80	2	5	0	10	9	46.1	68	9	16	20
May	2.56	6	3	0	17	14	91.1	83	8	31	47
June	3.11	5	4	0	17	15	101.1	106	12	31	45
July	5.78	2	14	0	20	20	109.0	134	10	51	46
August	3.89	6	9	0	19	19	111.0	102	9	43	52
September/October	4.41	11	6	0	23	22	130.2	141	16	33	62
Starter	4.15	32	40	0	99	99	579.1	619	62	200	268
Reliever	9.58	0	1	0	7	0	10.1	15	2	5	4
0 Days rest	0.00	0	0	0	0	0	0.0	0	0	0	0
1 or 2 Days rest	15.43	0	1	0	3	0	2.1	5	1	3	2
3+ Days rest	7.88	0	0	0	4	0	8.0	10	1	2	2
Pre-All Star	4.08	13	16	0	51	45	271.0	296	34	98	126
Post-All Star	4.38	19	25	0	55	54	318.2	338	30	107	146

	Avg	AB	H	2B	3B	HR	RBI	BB	SO	OBP	SLG
vs. Left	.268	385	103	11	4	11	54	30	52	.323	.403
vs. Right	.279	1902	531	79	11	53	220	175	220	.339	.416
Inning 1-6	.279	2001	559	82	15	57	250	175	235	.337	.421
Inning 7+	.262	286	75	8	0	7	24	30	37	.334	.364
None on	.270	1329	359	58	9	35	35	107	157	.328	.406
Runners on	.287	958	275	32	6	29	239	98	115	.348	.424
Scoring Posn	.287	495	142	17	5	13	199	69	72	.363	.420
Close & Late	.277	130	36	3	0	3	13	20	19	.373	.369
None on/out	.303	595	180	33	5	17	17	48	55	.359	.461
vs. 1st Batr (relief)	.200	5	1	0	0	1	1	2	1	.429	.800
First Inning Pitched	.338	438	148	21	2	20	86	47	59	.400	.532
First 15 Pitches	.345	333	115	14	1	16	47	34	36	.406	.538
Pitch 16-30	.256	387	99	14	1	10	50	28	61	.306	.375
Pitch 31-45	.274	379	104	15	5	9	44	31	50	.331	.412
Pitch 46+	.266	1188	316	47	8	29	133	112	125	.328	.392
First Pitch	.345	374	129	20	1	12	46	12	0	.365	.500
Ahead in Count	.235	918	216	33	4	10	71	0	225	.238	.313
Behind in Count	.309	605	187	23	7	33	114	114	0	.417	.534
Two Strikes	.212	888	188	34	5	11	68	77	272	.277	.298

Pitcher vs. Batter (since 1984)

Pitches Best Vs.	Avg	AB	H	2B	3B	HR	RBI	BB	SO	OBP	SLG
Vince Coleman	.083	12	1	0	0	0	0	0	5	.083	.083
Lance Parrish	.087	23	2	0	0	0	0	2	7	.160	.087
Glenn Wilson	.091	11	1	0	0	0	0	1	1	.167	.091
Spike Owen	.100	30	3	0	0	0	2	3	7	.182	.100
Pete O'Brien	.118	17	2	0	0	0	1	0	4	.118	.118

Pitches Worst Vs.	Avg	AB	H	2B	3B	HR	RBI	BB	SO	OBP	SLG
Matt D. Williams	.600	20	12	2	0	3	11	2	3	.583	1.150
Andres Galarraga	.500	10	5	1	0	2	4	2	1	.583	1.200
Lloyd McClendon	.478	23	11	3	0	2	5	3	1	.538	.870
Ruben Sierra	.455	11	5	0	1	1	3	3	1	.533	.909
Ivan Calderon	.400	15	6	0	0	3	6	2	3	.471	1.000

Randy Ready — Expos

Age 34 – Bats Right (flyball hitter)

	Avg	G	AB	R	H	2B	3B	HR	RBI	BB	SO	HBP	GDP	SB	CS	OBP	SLG	IBB	SH	SF	#Pit	#P/PA	GB	FB	G/F
1993 Season	.254	40	134	22	34	8	1	1	10	23	8	1	4	2	1	.367	.351	0	1	0	587	3.69	56	44	1.27
Last Five Years	.246	378	935	134	230	42	5	14	99	166	128	5	17	12	7	.358	.347	4	8	13	4592	4.07	313	327	0.96

1993 Season

	Avg	AB	H	2B	3B	HR	RBI	BB	SO	OBP	SLG
vs. Left	.186	43	8	1	0	0	4	4	2	.255	.209
vs. Right	.286	91	26	7	1	1	6	19	6	.414	.418
Home	.209	67	14	5	1	0	5	12	5	.329	.313
Away	.299	67	20	3	0	1	5	11	3	.405	.388
First Pitch	.471	17	8	2	0	1	5	0	0	.500	.765
Ahead in Count	.270	37	10	4	1	0	2	13	0	.460	.432
Behind in Count	.161	56	9	2	0	0	3	0	5	.161	.196
Two Strikes	.173	52	9	2	0	0	3	10	8	.306	.212

	Avg	AB	H	2B	3B	HR	RBI	BB	SO	OBP	SLG
Scoring Posn	.222	36	8	3	0	0	8	11	2	.404	.306
Close & Late	.286	14	4	0	0	0	0	5	2	.474	.286
None on/out	.314	35	11	1	0	1	1	3	0	.368	.429
Batting #2	.182	33	6	1	0	0	0	5	3	.289	.212
Batting #7	.286	70	20	5	1	0	7	11	3	.390	.386
Other	.258	31	8	2	0	1	3	7	2	.395	.419
Pre-All Star	.000	0	0	0	0	0	0	0	0	.000	.000
Post-All Star	.254	134	34	8	1	1	10	23	8	.367	.351

Last Five Years

	Avg	AB	H	2B	3B	HR	RBI	BB	SO	OBP	SLG
vs. Left	.260	527	137	26	4	10	64	95	70	.370	.381
vs. Right	.228	408	93	16	1	4	35	71	58	.344	.301
Groundball	.255	357	91	14	1	6	36	58	42	.359	.350
Flyball	.222	185	41	10	0	3	17	34	30	.342	.324
Home	.236	479	113	22	3	5	45	95	65	.361	.326
Away	.257	456	117	20	2	9	54	71	63	.355	.368
Day	.241	278	67	13	1	4	29	61	38	.376	.338
Night	.248	657	163	29	4	10	70	105	90	.351	.350
Grass	.216	305	66	9	1	4	31	60	48	.341	.292
Turf	.260	630	164	33	4	10	68	106	80	.367	.373
First Pitch	.404	52	21	4	0	1	9	2	0	.448	.538
Ahead in Count	.226	226	51	9	2	3	20	92	0	.445	.323
Behind in Count	.240	454	109	18	2	5	41	0	105	.239	.322
Two Strikes	.202	435	88	14	2	3	39	72	128	.313	.264

	Avg	AB	H	2B	3B	HR	RBI	BB	SO	OBP	SLG
Scoring Posn	.242	252	61	11	0	2	79	60	35	.372	.310
Close & Late	.304	168	51	7	0	3	22	41	26	.441	.399
None on/out	.244	209	51	11	1	4	4	29	21	.344	.364
Batting #2	.249	309	77	14	2	2	37	52	35	.355	.327
Batting #7	.214	126	27	6	1	0	10	26	16	.351	.278
Other	.252	500	126	22	2	12	52	88	77	.362	.376
April	.288	111	32	3	0	1	13	19	12	.391	.342
May	.281	96	27	3	1	1	14	24	11	.425	.365
June	.241	137	33	9	0	2	12	16	26	.327	.350
July	.214	140	30	6	1	5	23	27	25	.341	.379
August	.218	216	47	7	2	3	19	40	26	.336	.310
September/October	.260	235	61	14	1	2	18	40	28	.363	.353
Pre-All Star	.272	375	102	18	1	6	45	66	53	.382	.373
Post-All Star	.229	560	128	24	4	8	54	100	75	.343	.329

Batter vs. Pitcher (since 1984)											
Hits Best Against	Avg	AB	H	2B	3B	HR	RBI	BB	SO	OBP	SLG
Jamie Moyer	.500	14	7	2	1	0	2	0	0	.500	.786
Dwight Gooden	.500	12	6	1	1	0	0	1	2	.538	.750
Bryn Smith	.450	20	9	2	0	1	1	0	2	.450	.700
Jim Deshaies	.429	14	6	2	0	1	7	6	1	.571	.786
Fernando Valenzuela	.370	27	10	1	1	2	5	8	3	.514	.704

Hits Worst Against	Avg	AB	H	2B	3B	HR	RBI	BB	SO	OBP	SLG
Orel Hershiser	.000	11	0	0	0	0	0	1	1	.083	.000
Dennis Martinez	.154	13	2	0	0	0	1	0	4	.143	.154
Brian Barnes	.176	17	3	0	0	0	1	3	3	.300	.176
Greg Maddux	.182	11	2	2	0	0	0	0	2	.182	.364
Mark Langston	.231	13	3	0	0	0	3	0	3	.231	.231

Jeff Reardon — Reds

Age 38 – Pitches Right (flyball pitcher)

	ERA	W	L	Sv	G	GS	IP	BB	SO	Avg	H	2B	3B	HR	RBI	OBP	SLG	GF	IR	IRS	Hld	SvOp	SB	CS	GB	FB	G/F
1993 Season	4.09	4	6	8	58	0	61.2	10	35	.270	66	15	2	4	29	.308	.398	32	28	1	9	12	6	1	58	103	0.56
Last Five Years	3.59	20	19	130	287	0	303.1	66	197	.252	294	62	5	32	161	.295	.396	170	144	43	10	171	27	3	294	479	0.61

1993 Season

	ERA	W	L	Sv	G	GS	IP	H	HR	BB	SO
Home	3.34	4	3	5	29	0	29.2	27	2	8	20
Away	4.78	0	3	3	29	0	32.0	39	2	2	15
Starter	0.00	0	0	0	0	0	0.0	0	0	0	0
Reliever	4.09	4	6	8	58	0	61.2	66	4	10	35
0 Days rest	0.73	1	0	3	11	0	12.1	6	0	1	8
1 or 2 Days rest	4.82	1	5	3	26	0	28.0	38	2	5	19
3+ Days rest	5.06	2	1	2	21	0	21.1	22	2	4	8
Pre-All Star	2.08	2	2	7	35	0	34.2	31	0	3	18
Post-All Star	6.67	2	4	1	23	0	27.0	35	4	7	17

	Avg	AB	H	2B	3B	HR	RBI	BB	SO	OBP	SLG
vs. Left	.297	118	35	9	1	0	11	8	10	.351	.390
vs. Right	.246	126	31	6	1	4	18	2	25	.265	.405
Scoring Posn	.227	75	17	6	1	1	24	3	15	.262	.373
Close & Late	.303	145	44	8	1	4	20	4	21	.325	.455
None on/out	.132	53	7	1	0	1	1	1	9	.164	.208
First Pitch	.436	39	17	6	1	1	7	0	0	.463	.718
Ahead in Count	.220	127	28	7	0	3	14	0	30	.225	.346
Behind in Count	.319	47	15	1	0	0	4	5	0	.370	.340
Two Strikes	.205	122	25	5	0	2	12	5	35	.240	.295

Last Five Years

	ERA	W	L	Sv	G	GS	IP	H	HR	BB	SO
Home	3.42	17	9	74	157	0	163.0	150	19	36	109
Away	3.78	3	10	56	130	0	140.1	144	13	30	88
Day	4.41	3	7	30	83	0	83.2	85	9	14	44
Night	3.28	17	12	100	204	0	219.2	209	23	52	153
Grass	3.29	12	9	90	186	0	194.1	177	22	40	130
Turf	4.13	8	10	40	101	0	109.0	117	10	26	67
April	2.11	1	1	18	40	0	42.2	33	2	11	22
May	4.06	2	3	26	51	0	51.0	47	6	8	32
June	3.45	5	3	23	54	0	57.1	50	6	12	39
July	3.44	2	4	22	51	0	55.0	55	8	11	38
August	3.61	3	4	26	47	0	52.1	58	5	11	39
September/October	4.80	7	4	15	44	0	45.0	51	5	13	27
Starter	0.00	0	0	0	0	0	0.0	0	0	0	0
Reliever	3.59	20	19	130	287	0	303.1	294	32	66	197
0 Days rest	3.64	9	8	45	84	0	84.0	82	5	21	44
1 or 2 Days rest	3.62	7	8	56	110	0	119.1	122	15	22	93
3+ Days rest	3.51	4	3	29	93	0	100.0	90	12	23	60
Pre-All Star	3.24	9	8	74	163	0	172.0	150	16	34	109
Post-All Star	4.04	11	11	56	124	0	131.1	144	16	32	88

	Avg	AB	H	2B	3B	HR	RBI	BB	SO	OBP	SLG
vs. Left	.264	573	151	32	3	18	71	41	69	.316	.424
vs. Right	.240	595	143	30	2	14	90	25	128	.275	.368
Inning 1-6	.000	5	0	0	0	0	0	0	1	.000	.000
Inning 7+	.253	1163	294	62	5	32	161	66	196	.297	.397
None on	.224	642	144	27	3	19	19	27	107	.261	.364
Runners on	.285	526	150	35	2	13	142	39	90	.335	.433
Scoring Posn	.266	338	90	22	1	10	131	33	60	.326	.426
Close & Late	.250	719	180	33	4	22	109	47	126	.299	.399
None on/out	.152	244	37	11	1	4	4	10	42	.195	.254
vs. 1st Batr (relief)	.205	268	55	12	1	3	27	12	46	.244	.291
First Inning Pitched	.254	985	250	52	4	25	140	50	172	.293	.391
First 15 Pitches	.256	878	225	46	5	22	106	45	135	.294	.395
Pitch 16-30	.235	264	62	14	0	9	48	19	56	.298	.390
Pitch 31-45	.269	26	7	2	0	1	7	2	6	.310	.462
Pitch 46+	.000	0	0	0	0	0	0	0	0	.000	.000
First Pitch	.289	180	52	18	2	5	25	9	0	.338	.494
Ahead in Count	.213	586	125	21	1	16	63	0	173	.215	.334
Behind in Count	.321	209	67	12	0	5	37	33	0	.409	.450
Two Strikes	.205	562	115	19	1	14	63	23	197	.237	.317

Pitcher vs. Batter (since 1984)

Pitches Best Vs.	Avg	AB	H	2B	3B	HR	RBI	BB	SO	OBP	SLG
Jay Buhner	.000	10	0	0	0	0	0	1	2	.091	.000
Ryne Sandberg	.071	14	1	0	0	0	2	0	4	.071	.071
Fred McGriff	.100	10	1	0	0	0	1	1	2	.182	.100
Ozzie Guillen	.100	10	1	0	0	0	1	1	1	.167	.100
Joe Orsulak	.167	12	2	0	0	0	0	0	0	.167	.167

Pitches Worst Vs.	Avg	AB	H	2B	3B	HR	RBI	BB	SO	OBP	SLG
Kelly Gruber	.500	12	6	2	0	1	2	2	1	.571	.917
Dan Pasqua	.429	7	3	1	0	0	1	4	1	.636	.571
Jim Eisenreich	.417	12	5	3	0	0	2	1	1	.462	.667
Danny Tartabull	.375	8	3	0	1	1	4	3	3	.545	1.000
Carlton Fisk	.333	15	5	2	0	2	5	0	5	.333	.867

Jeff Reboulet — Twins

Age 30 – Bats Right (groundball hitter)

	Avg	G	AB	R	H	2B	3B	HR	RBI	BB	SO	HBP	GDP	SB	CS	OBP	SLG	IBB	SH	SF	#Pit	#P/PA	GB	FB	G/F
1993 Season	.258	109	240	33	62	8	0	1	15	35	37	2	6	5	5	.356	.304	0	5	1	1182	4.18	104	63	1.65
Career (1992-1993)	.233	182	377	48	88	15	1	2	31	58	63	3	6	8	7	.339	.294	0	12	1	1871	4.15	156	94	1.66

1993 Season

	Avg	AB	H	2B	3B	HR	RBI	BB	SO	OBP	SLG
vs. Left	.290	93	27	5	0	0	5	13	13	.380	.344
vs. Right	.238	147	35	3	0	1	10	22	24	.341	.279
Home	.183	126	23	2	0	0	2	12	24	.264	.198
Away	.342	114	39	6	0	1	13	23	13	.449	.421
First Pitch	.368	19	7	2	0	0	1	0	0	.368	.474
Ahead in Count	.283	46	13	1	0	0	4	23	0	.522	.304
Behind in Count	.178	107	19	2	0	0	4	0	32	.183	.196
Two Strikes	.229	131	30	4	0	1	10	12	37	.297	.282

	Avg	AB	H	2B	3B	HR	RBI	BB	SO	OBP	SLG
Scoring Posn	.235	51	12	3	0	1	15	12	7	.375	.353
Close & Late	.290	31	9	2	0	0	5	2	3	.333	.355
None on/out	.327	49	16	3	0	0	0	7	9	.411	.388
Batting #2	.282	85	24	2	0	1	5	16	14	.396	.341
Batting #9	.224	116	26	5	0	0	10	13	19	.311	.267
Other	.308	39	12	1	0	0	0	6	4	.400	.333
Pre-All Star	.176	119	21	3	0	0	3	15	21	.279	.202
Post-All Star	.339	121	41	5	0	1	12	20	16	.430	.405

Gary Redus — Rangers

Age 37 – Bats Right (flyball hitter)

	Avg	G	AB	R	H	2B	3B	HR	RBI	BB	SO	HBP	GDP	SB	CS	OBP	SLG	IBB	SH	SF	#Pit	#P/PA	GB	FB	G/F
1993 Season	.288	77	222	28	64	12	4	6	31	23	35	0	3	4	4	.351	.459	1	0	3	971	3.92	67	72	0.93
Last Five Years	.265	445	1156	173	306	64	19	28	123	141	188	6	10	68	22	.344	.426	6	3	15	5035	3.81	366	426	0.86

1993 Season

	Avg	AB	H	2B	3B	HR	RBI	BB	SO	OBP	SLG		Avg	AB	H	2B	3B	HR	RBI	BB	SO	OBP	SLG
vs. Left	.302	86	26	7	2	2	10	8	12	.358	.500	Scoring Posn	.310	58	18	1	1	3	26	9	7	.386	.517
vs. Right	.279	136	38	5	2	4	21	15	23	.346	.434	Close & Late	.279	43	12	1	0	1	8	2	8	.311	.372
Home	.275	109	30	2	2	2	18	11	14	.339	.385	None on/out	.311	61	19	4	1	3	3	6	8	.373	.557
Away	.301	113	34	10	2	4	13	12	21	.362	.531	Batting #1	.275	102	28	8	2	2	12	9	14	.330	.451
First Pitch	.567	30	17	3	0	2	12	1	0	.563	.867	Batting #2	.364	55	20	3	1	2	9	6	4	.413	.564
Ahead in Count	.291	55	16	5	2	2	6	8	0	.381	.564	Other	.246	65	16	1	1	2	10	8	17	.329	.385
Behind in Count	.159	82	13	1	1	1	6	0	27	.159	.232	Pre-All Star	.241	83	20	3	1	3	11	8	16	.304	.410
Two Strikes	.170	100	17	1	1	1	6	14	35	.270	.230	Post-All Star	.317	139	44	9	3	3	20	15	19	.378	.489

Last Five Years

	Avg	AB	H	2B	3B	HR	RBI	BB	SO	OBP	SLG		Avg	AB	H	2B	3B	HR	RBI	BB	SO	OBP	SLG
vs. Left	.268	725	194	43	16	18	73	85	112	.341	.446	Scoring Posn	.254	240	61	2	5	10	100	41	41	.353	.429
vs. Right	.260	431	112	21	3	10	50	56	76	.349	.392	Close & Late	.301	216	65	12	2	6	27	24	39	.369	.458
Groundball	.288	365	105	25	5	7	37	45	54	.367	.441	None on/out	.277	408	113	24	6	12	12	45	56	.350	.453
Flyball	.253	273	69	10	4	10	34	32	51	.327	.429	Batting #1	.255	638	163	40	7	15	56	67	98	.326	.411
Home	.265	567	150	33	8	11	65	73	85	.350	.409	Batting #6	.288	184	53	8	3	4	22	26	31	.380	.429
Away	.265	589	156	31	11	17	58	68	103	.338	.441	Other	.269	334	90	16	9	9	45	48	59	.356	.452
Day	.220	328	72	16	6	8	39	43	55	.307	.378	April	.234	128	30	4	3	2	12	16	13	.331	.359
Night	.283	828	234	48	13	20	84	98	133	.359	.444	May	.222	171	38	8	2	0	11	18	26	.292	.292
Grass	.252	448	113	17	8	13	48	51	78	.323	.413	June	.288	177	51	13	1	5	19	24	27	.367	.458
Turf	.273	708	193	47	11	15	75	90	110	.356	.434	July	.259	224	58	11	5	7	26	27	50	.343	.446
First Pitch	.351	134	47	10	1	5	31	6	0	.377	.552	August	.292	233	68	13	4	9	29	26	38	.364	.498
Ahead in Count	.362	312	113	21	10	14	48	69	0	.476	.628	September/October	.274	223	61	15	4	5	26	28	32	.352	.444
Behind in Count	.192	452	87	18	5	6	25	0	145	.197	.294	Pre-All Star	.249	543	135	28	8	10	49	64	88	.327	.385
Two Strikes	.171	496	85	24	2	6	25	66	188	.271	.264	Post-All Star	.279	613	171	36	11	18	74	77	100	.358	.462

Batter vs. Pitcher (since 1984)

Hits Best Against	Avg	AB	H	2B	3B	HR	RBI	BB	SO	OBP	SLG	Hits Worst Against	Avg	AB	H	2B	3B	HR	RBI	BB	SO	OBP	SLG
Randy Myers	.429	7	3	1	0	0	1	5	2	.667	.571	Danny Jackson	.000	18	0	0	0	0	1	4	2	.182	.000
Joe Magrane	.409	22	9	4	2	0	4	1	3	.417	.773	Greg Swindell	.000	16	0	0	0	0	0	2	3	.111	.000
Chris Hammond	.368	19	7	2	2	0	2	4	2	.478	.684	Danny Cox	.059	17	1	0	0	0	1	0	2	.059	.059
Paul Kilgus	.364	11	4	2	1	0	2	1	1	.417	.727	Rick Sutcliffe	.063	16	1	0	0	0	1	3	3	.200	.063
Mike Boddicker	.357	14	5	2	1	1	3	0	4	.333	.857	Dwight Gooden	.067	15	1	1	0	0	1	1	5	.118	.133

Jeff Reed — Giants

Age 31 – Bats Left (groundball hitter)

	Avg	G	AB	R	H	2B	3B	HR	RBI	BB	SO	HBP	GDP	SB	CS	OBP	SLG	IBB	SH	SF	#Pit	#P/PA	GB	FB	G/F
1993 Season	.261	66	119	10	31	3	0	6	12	16	22	0	2	0	1	.346	.437	4	0	1	531	3.90	34	45	0.76
Last Five Years	.245	346	876	60	215	37	3	15	84	98	136	3	19	0	2	.320	.346	18	9	11	3716	3.73	351	230	1.53

1993 Season

	Avg	AB	H	2B	3B	HR	RBI	BB	SO	OBP	SLG		Avg	AB	H	2B	3B	HR	RBI	BB	SO	OBP	SLG
vs. Left	.375	8	3	0	0	2	2	2	2	.500	1.125	Scoring Posn	.138	29	4	0	0	0	5	8	11	.316	.138
vs. Right	.252	111	28	3	0	4	10	14	20	.333	.387	Close & Late	.129	31	4	1	0	1	1	2	6	.182	.258
Home	.274	73	20	1	0	5	9	4	9	.308	.493	None on/out	.333	30	10	1	0	1	1	0	2	.333	.467
Away	.239	46	11	2	0	1	3	12	13	.397	.348	Batting #7	.273	33	9	1	0	1	1	3	6	.333	.394
First Pitch	.250	12	3	0	0	1	1	3	0	.400	.500	Batting #8	.288	59	17	2	0	3	8	9	9	.377	.475
Ahead in Count	.438	32	14	2	0	3	8	9	0	.548	.781	Other	.185	27	5	0	0	2	3	4	7	.290	.407
Behind in Count	.184	49	9	0	0	1	1	0	16	.184	.245	Pre-All Star	.247	81	20	1	0	6	10	11	19	.333	.481
Two Strikes	.172	58	10	0	0	1	2	4	22	.226	.224	Post-All Star	.289	38	11	2	0	0	2	5	3	.372	.342

Last Five Years

	Avg	AB	H	2B	3B	HR	RBI	BB	SO	OBP	SLG		Avg	AB	H	2B	3B	HR	RBI	BB	SO	OBP	SLG
vs. Left	.231	104	24	6	0	4	17	16	23	.341	.404	Scoring Posn	.216	208	45	4	1	2	64	44	47	.341	.274
vs. Right	.247	772	191	31	3	11	67	82	113	.317	.338	Close & Late	.152	138	21	4	0	1	6	16	22	.236	.203
Groundball	.233	301	70	7	0	4	28	38	35	.318	.296	None on/out	.246	224	55	8	2	2	2	17	26	.299	.326
Flyball	.247	190	47	10	0	5	25	18	41	.310	.379	Batting #7	.249	470	117	23	0	5	42	49	84	.318	.330
Home	.251	410	103	20	2	9	43	45	62	.323	.376	Batting #8	.248	307	76	11	3	8	34	33	35	.319	.381
Away	.240	466	112	17	1	6	41	53	74	.317	.320	Other	.222	99	22	3	0	2	8	16	17	.331	.313
Day	.272	331	90	11	3	7	37	45	51	.356	.387	April	.250	132	33	5	0	3	14	16	24	.327	.356
Night	.229	545	125	26	0	8	47	53	85	.297	.321	May	.252	163	41	4	0	4	16	12	27	.307	.350
Grass	.245	363	89	10	0	9	30	35	58	.313	.347	June	.224	156	35	7	0	4	17	19	22	.307	.346
Turf	.246	513	126	27	3	6	54	63	78	.325	.345	July	.287	101	29	6	1	1	11	13	19	.371	.396
First Pitch	.322	115	37	7	0	2	13	11	0	.378	.435	August	.243	152	37	4	0	2	13	14	20	.302	.309
Ahead in Count	.310	239	74	13	1	5	31	56	0	.440	.435	September/October	.233	172	40	11	2	1	13	24	24	.323	.337
Behind in Count	.199	366	73	9	2	4	26	0	119	.199	.268	Pre-All Star	.235	476	112	17	1	11	47	50	80	.309	.345
Two Strikes	.177	396	70	8	1	4	25	26	136	.227	.232	Post-All Star	.258	400	103	20	2	4	37	48	56	.333	.348

Batter vs. Pitcher (career)

Hits Best Against	Avg	AB	H	2B	3B	HR	RBI	BB	SO	OBP	SLG	Hits Worst Against	Avg	AB	H	2B	3B	HR	RBI	BB	SO	OBP	SLG
Bob Tewksbury	.500	12	6	0	0	0	1	0	1	.500	.500	David Cone	.095	21	2	0	0	0	2	3	7	.208	.095
Andy Benes	.476	21	10	1	0	2	6	3	3	.520	.810	Mike Morgan	.125	16	2	0	0	0	0	0	1	.125	.125
Tim Leary	.385	13	5	2	0	0	1	1	4	.429	.538	Mike Bielecki	.125	16	2	0	0	0	1	3	3	.250	.125
Danny Darwin	.333	15	5	3	1	0	2	2	1	.412	.667	Rick Sutcliffe	.160	25	4	0	0	0	2	3	4	.241	.160
Greg Maddux	.314	35	11	0	0	1	7	4	1	.385	.400	Doug Drabek	.167	18	3	0	0	0	1	2	2	.250	.167

Jody Reed — Dodgers

Age 31 – Bats Right

	Avg	G	AB	R	H	2B	3B	HR	RBI	BB	SO	HBP	GDP	SB	CS	OBP	SLG	IBB	SH	SF	#Pit	#P/PA	GB	FB	G/F
1993 Season	.276	132	445	48	123	21	2	2	31	38	40	1	16	1	3	.333	.346	10	17	3	1748	3.47	167	130	1.28
Last Five Years	.277	729	2735	345	758	177	7	18	222	308	246	13	79	22	25	.351	.367	18	62	18	11672	3.72	1023	842	1.21

1993 Season

	Avg	AB	H	2B	3B	HR	RBI	BB	SO	OBP	SLG
vs. Left	.325	123	40	8	0	0	7	11	9	.381	.390
vs. Right	.258	322	83	13	2	2	24	27	31	.314	.329
Groundball	.303	132	40	10	1	0	11	9	8	.347	.394
Flyball	.302	63	19	2	0	0	4	5	6	.348	.333
Home	.292	233	68	13	0	0	19	23	19	.357	.348
Away	.259	212	55	8	2	2	12	15	21	.306	.344
Day	.227	128	29	4	1	1	5	12	12	.291	.297
Night	.297	317	94	17	1	1	26	26	28	.350	.366
Grass	.295	353	104	17	1	2	26	34	35	.357	.365
Turf	.207	92	19	4	1	0	5	4	5	.235	.272
First Pitch	.282	39	11	3	0	0	0	6	0	.378	.359
Ahead in Count	.361	122	44	10	1	2	18	19	0	.441	.508
Behind in Count	.251	195	49	6	1	0	8	0	34	.251	.292
Two Strikes	.200	165	33	3	0	0	5	13	40	.258	.218

	Avg	AB	H	2B	3B	HR	RBI	BB	SO	OBP	SLG
Scoring Posn	.308	104	32	4	0	0	26	20	9	.414	.346
Close & Late	.253	83	21	5	0	0	5	6	9	.300	.313
None on/out	.235	119	28	5	0	0	0	8	15	.283	.277
Batting #2	.285	130	37	6	1	1	6	7	5	.324	.369
Batting #8	.272	290	79	13	1	1	24	30	33	.340	.334
Other	.280	25	7	2	0	0	1	1	2	.296	.360
April	.225	80	18	2	0	0	3	5	8	.279	.250
May	.306	85	26	3	2	1	12	9	4	.368	.424
June	.364	44	16	2	0	1	5	4	5	.417	.477
July	.278	54	15	3	0	0	4	5	7	.339	.333
August	.227	88	20	5	0	0	3	5	7	.266	.284
September/October	.298	94	28	6	0	0	4	10	9	.362	.362
Pre-All Star	.287	209	60	7	2	2	20	18	17	.345	.368
Post-All Star	.267	236	63	14	0	0	11	20	23	.322	.326

1993 By Position

Position	Avg	AB	H	2B	3B	HR	RBI	BB	SO	OBP	SLG	G	GS	Innings	PO	A	E	DP	Fld Pct	Rng Fctr	In Zone	Outs	Zone Rtg	MLB Zone
As 2b	.275	444	122	21	2	2	31	38	40	.331	.345	132	129	1134.2	278	412	5	74	.993	5.47	461	416	.902	.895

Last Five Years

	Avg	AB	H	2B	3B	HR	RBI	BB	SO	OBP	SLG
vs. Left	.292	766	224	58	2	2	51	91	59	.366	.381
vs. Right	.271	1969	534	119	5	16	171	217	187	.345	.361
Groundball	.281	744	209	44	3	3	70	74	74	.349	.360
Flyball	.296	581	172	35	2	7	45	79	49	.377	.399
Home	.284	1405	399	106	2	10	128	166	132	.361	.384
Away	.270	1330	359	71	5	8	94	142	114	.341	.349
Day	.270	863	233	56	1	5	71	107	76	.349	.355
Night	.280	1872	525	121	6	13	151	201	170	.352	.372
Grass	.281	2326	654	154	5	18	202	270	210	.356	.375
Turf	.254	409	104	23	2	0	20	38	36	.322	.320
First Pitch	.295	237	70	20	0	4	18	9	0	.327	.430
Ahead in Count	.318	741	236	70	2	9	91	186	0	.450	.455
Behind in Count	.250	1163	291	52	5	2	65	0	196	.254	.309
Two Strikes	.224	1117	250	48	2	2	50	109	246	.295	.276

	Avg	AB	H	2B	3B	HR	RBI	BB	SO	OBP	SLG
Scoring Posn	.275	593	163	36	1	0	190	116	57	.388	.339
Close & Late	.250	432	108	22	0	1	41	58	48	.339	.308
None on/out	.268	702	188	44	1	3	3	66	63	.332	.346
Batting #1	.270	755	204	45	2	4	50	85	70	.346	.351
Batting #2	.290	1271	368	96	3	8	111	140	102	.361	.389
Other	.262	709	186	36	2	6	61	83	74	.338	.344
April	.232	349	81	14	0	3	25	40	33	.314	.298
May	.308	500	154	37	4	2	47	48	40	.368	.410
June	.257	443	114	34	0	2	34	45	41	.325	.348
July	.287	439	126	35	0	4	36	52	46	.361	.394
August	.274	507	139	30	1	4	37	50	41	.340	.361
September/October	.290	497	144	27	2	3	43	73	45	.385	.370
Pre-All Star	.276	1422	392	96	4	8	118	147	125	.343	.366
Post-All Star	.279	1313	366	81	3	10	104	161	121	.359	.368

Batter vs. Pitcher (career)

Hits Best Against	Avg	AB	H	2B	3B	HR	RBI	BB	SO	OBP	SLG
Willie Blair	.571	14	8	1	0	2	5	0	2	.571	1.071
Tom Henke	.556	9	5	1	0	0	1	2	0	.636	.667
Randy Johnson	.500	10	5	4	0	0	0	6	3	.688	.900
Curt Young	.462	13	6	2	0	0	2	3	0	.563	.615
Scott Sanderson	.448	29	13	3	0	2	3	2	1	.484	.759

Hits Worst Against	Avg	AB	H	2B	3B	HR	RBI	BB	SO	OBP	SLG
Steve Farr	.091	11	1	0	0	0	0	1	1	.167	.091
Frank Viola	.100	10	1	0	0	0	0	2	4	.250	.100
Duane Ward	.111	18	2	1	0	0	1	0	2	.111	.167
David Wells	.143	21	3	0	0	0	0	2	0	.217	.143
Tom Candiotti	.150	20	3	1	0	0	0	0	4	.150	.200

Rick Reed — Rangers

Age 29 – Pitches Right

	ERA	W	L	Sv	G	GS	IP	BB	SO	Avg	H	2B	3B	HR	RBI	OBP	SLG	GF	IR	IRS	Hld	SvOp	SB	CS	GB	FB	G/F
1993 Season	5.87	1	0	0	3	0	7.2	2	5	.375	12	3	0	1	4	.444	.563	0	1	1	0	0	0	1	16	7	2.29
Last Five Years	4.53	7	14	1	51	34	220.2	46	117	.285	249	51	4	23	105	.324	.431	2	5	3	1	1	22	5	308	282	1.09

1993 Season

	ERA	W	L	Sv	G	GS	IP	H	HR	BB	SO
Home	6.75	1	0	0	2	0	5.1	7	0	1	5
Away	3.86	0	0	0	1	0	2.1	5	1	1	0

	Avg	AB	H	2B	3B	HR	RBI	BB	SO	OBP	SLG
vs. Left	.222	9	2	1	0	0	2	1	1	.364	.333
vs. Right	.435	23	10	2	0	1	2	1	4	.480	.652

Last Five Years

	ERA	W	L	Sv	G	GS	IP	H	HR	BB	SO
Home	4.17	3	6	0	25	16	103.2	120	6	19	49
Away	4.85	4	8	1	26	18	117.0	129	17	27	68
Day	3.92	2	4	0	14	9	59.2	65	10	12	36
Night	4.75	5	10	1	37	25	161.0	184	13	34	81
Grass	4.16	5	5	0	17	12	80.0	86	10	12	47
Turf	4.73	2	9	1	34	22	140.2	163	13	34	70
April	0.00	0	0	0	0	0	0.0	0	0	0	0
May	0.00	0	0	0	0	0	0.0	0	0	0	0
June	2.93	2	3	1	11	5	46.0	44	7	8	28
July	5.94	2	4	0	13	12	66.2	75	6	17	33
August	4.39	1	5	0	12	11	55.1	60	5	10	29
September/October	4.27	2	2	0	15	6	52.2	70	5	11	27
Starter	4.56	5	14	0	34	34	181.2	201	19	38	96
Reliever	4.38	2	0	1	17	0	39.0	48	4	8	21
0 Days rest	9.00	0	0	0	1	0	2.0	4	1	0	1

	Avg	AB	H	2B	3B	HR	RBI	BB	SO	OBP	SLG
vs. Left	.239	440	105	27	3	10	55	29	56	.285	.382
vs. Right	.331	435	144	24	1	13	50	17	61	.365	.480
Inning 1-6	.286	749	214	40	4	18	89	42	102	.328	.422
Inning 7+	.278	126	35	11	0	5	16	4	15	.305	.484
None on	.267	529	141	24	2	16	16	21	75	.300	.410
Runners on	.312	346	108	27	2	7	89	25	42	.360	.462
Scoring Posn	.305	200	61	10	1	6	77	21	27	.362	.455
Close & Late	.412	17	7	3	0	2	5	1	2	.444	.941
None on/out	.275	229	63	13	1	7	7	6	24	.303	.432
vs. 1st Batr (relief)	.313	16	5	0	0	1	2	0	1	.353	.500
First Inning Pitched	.313	201	63	9	1	4	31	18	27	.371	.428
First 15 Pitches	.315	181	57	9	1	3	16	11	21	.361	.425
Pitch 16-30	.318	179	57	10	1	3	28	12	23	.360	.436
Pitch 31-45	.242	153	37	6	1	6	16	7	23	.282	.412
Pitch 46+	.271	362	98	26	1	11	45	16	50	.306	.439

Last Five Years

	ERA	W	L	Sv	G	GS	IP	H	HR	BB	SO		Avg	AB	H	2B	3B	HR	RBI	BB	SO	OBP	SLG
1 or 2 Days rest	1.00	0	0	1	5	0	9.0	8	1	0	3	First Pitch	.364	132	48	10	0	3	28	11	0	.420	.508
3+ Days rest	5.14	2	0	0	11	0	28.0	36	2	8	17	Ahead in Count	.259	413	107	19	1	14	43	0	101	.261	.412
Pre-All Star	3.82	4	4	1	14	8	66.0	61	8	14	38	Behind in Count	.326	187	61	13	3	2	22	19	0	.389	.460
Post-All Star	4.83	3	10	0	37	26	154.2	188	15	32	79	Two Strikes	.217	355	77	16	0	13	37	16	117	.251	.372

Pitcher vs. Batter (career)

Pitches Best Vs.	Avg	AB	H	2B	3B	HR	RBI	BB	SO	OBP	SLG	Pitches Worst Vs.	Avg	AB	H	2B	3B	HR	RBI	BB	SO	OBP	SLG
Lenny Dykstra	.222	18	4	2	0	0	1	1	0	.263	.333	Charlie Hayes	.556	18	10	1	0	2	6	0	3	.556	.944
												Hubie Brooks	.333	15	5	0	0	1	4	0	2	.333	.533

Steve Reed — Rockies

Age 28 – Pitches Right (groundball pitcher)

	ERA	W	L	Sv	G	GS	IP	BB	SO	Avg	H	2B	3B	HR	RBI	OBP	SLG	GF	IR	IRS	Hld	SvOp	SB	CS	GB	FB	G/F
1993 Season	4.48	9	5	3	64	0	84.1	30	51	.259	80	13	2	13	43	.328	.440	14	44	9	9	6	8	7	119	86	1.38
Career (1992-1993)	4.14	10	5	3	82	0	100.0	33	62	.253	93	17	2	15	55	.319	.432	16	66	17	10	6	9	7	150	96	1.56

1993 Season

	ERA	W	L	Sv	G	GS	IP	H	HR	BB	SO		Avg	AB	H	2B	3B	HR	RBI	BB	SO	OBP	SLG
Home	6.39	7	3	1	39	0	50.2	58	13	18	24	vs. Left	.336	122	41	8	2	7	21	13	16	.410	.607
Away	1.60	2	2	2	25	0	33.2	22	0	12	27	vs. Right	.209	187	39	5	0	6	22	17	35	.272	.332
Day	7.36	2	2	2	19	0	22.0	24	6	9	17	Inning 1-6	.253	95	24	5	0	2	14	8	16	.317	.368
Night	3.47	7	3	1	45	0	62.1	56	7	21	34	Inning 7+	.262	214	56	8	2	11	29	22	35	.332	.472
Grass	4.90	9	4	2	54	0	71.2	75	13	25	38	None on	.250	200	50	7	2	8	8	14	35	.302	.425
Turf	2.13	0	1	1	10	0	12.2	5	0	5	13	Runners on	.275	109	30	6	0	5	35	16	16	.369	.468
April	8.68	1	0	0	8	0	9.1	12	4	4	4	Scoring Posn	.304	69	21	4	0	3	30	12	8	.400	.493
May	16.88	0	2	0	3	0	2.2	6	1	3	2	Close & Late	.180	100	18	4	1	2	10	11	17	.265	.300
June	1.50	2	0	0	8	0	12.0	9	1	2	6	None on/out	.284	81	23	4	1	4	4	8	16	.356	.506
July	4.57	2	2	1	15	0	21.2	25	3	7	14	vs. 1st Batr (relief)	.254	59	15	4	0	1	8	4	12	.297	.373
August	2.50	2	0	2	13	0	18.0	15	1	7	10	First Inning Pitched	.273	205	56	9	1	9	33	18	35	.333	.459
September/October	4.35	2	1	0	17	0	20.2	13	3	7	15	First 15 Pitches	.279	190	53	8	1	10	29	14	30	.327	.489
Starter	0.00	0	0	0	0	0	0.0	0	0	0	0	Pitch 16-30	.232	95	22	4	1	2	11	13	18	.336	.358
Reliever	4.48	9	5	3	64	0	84.1	80	13	30	51	Pitch 31-45	.250	20	5	1	0	1	3	3	3	.348	.450
0 Days rest	2.92	4	1	1	18	0	24.2	20	4	3	14	Pitch 46+	.000	4	0	0	0	0	0	0	0	.000	.000
1 or 2 Days rest	4.81	4	3	2	37	0	48.2	48	7	23	32	First Pitch	.389	36	14	2	0	1	5	4	0	.450	.528
3+ Days rest	6.55	1	1	0	9	0	11.0	12	2	4	5	Ahead in Count	.189	127	24	3	1	2	11	0	45	.208	.276
Pre-All Star	4.59	5	2	1	25	0	33.1	32	6	12	19	Behind in Count	.291	79	23	3	0	6	14	12	0	.380	.557
Post-All Star	4.41	4	3	2	39	0	51.0	48	7	18	32	Two Strikes	.194	129	25	5	1	2	14	14	51	.281	.295

Kevin Reimer — Brewers

Age 30 – Bats Left

	Avg	G	AB	R	H	2B	3B	HR	RBI	BB	SO	HBP	GDP	SB	CS	OBP	SLG	IBB	SH	SF	#Pit	#P/PA	GB	FB	G/F
1993 Season	.249	125	437	53	109	22	1	13	60	30	72	5	12	5	4	.303	.394	4	1	4	1709	3.58	169	123	1.37
Last Five Years	.261	476	1430	160	373	85	4	51	202	115	291	23	36	7	12	.324	.433	15	1	11	5860	3.71	462	425	1.09

1993 Season

	Avg	AB	H	2B	3B	HR	RBI	BB	SO	OBP	SLG		Avg	AB	H	2B	3B	HR	RBI	BB	SO	OBP	SLG
vs. Left	.208	106	22	5	0	1	15	8	18	.277	.283	Scoring Posn	.218	110	24	4	1	2	41	11	14	.286	.327
vs. Right	.263	331	87	17	1	12	45	22	54	.311	.429	Close & Late	.225	71	16	3	0	1	5	8	16	.296	.310
Groundball	.306	98	30	6	0	1	11	6	15	.355	.398	None on/out	.259	85	22	4	0	1	1	10	16	.351	.341
Flyball	.176	91	16	4	0	4	12	3	8	.198	.352	Batting #4	.247	154	38	7	0	6	22	14	25	.320	.409
Home	.240	217	52	10	1	8	27	18	37	.310	.406	Batting #5	.252	274	69	15	1	7	38	13	43	.288	.391
Away	.259	220	57	12	0	5	33	12	35	.295	.382	Other	.222	9	2	0	0	0	0	3	4	.417	.222
Day	.206	126	26	6	0	5	23	9	26	.261	.373	April	.327	52	17	2	1	3	12	3	5	.362	.577
Night	.267	311	83	16	1	8	37	21	46	.320	.402	May	.240	104	25	4	0	5	22	2	20	.255	.423
Grass	.257	354	91	18	1	13	51	25	62	.313	.424	June	.265	98	26	3	0	3	13	9	18	.327	.388
Turf	.217	83	18	4	0	0	9	5	10	.256	.265	July	.203	79	16	5	0	2	6	6	14	.267	.342
First Pitch	.244	82	20	3	0	3	10	3	0	.264	.390	August	.263	80	21	8	0	0	5	6	12	.314	.363
Ahead in Count	.310	100	31	6	0	5	18	13	0	.391	.520	September/October	.167	24	4	0	0	0	2	4	3	.333	.167
Behind in Count	.258	182	47	10	1	5	24	0	58	.273	.407	Pre-All Star	.266	286	76	12	1	13	52	16	47	.305	.451
Two Strikes	.223	188	42	11	1	5	23	14	72	.284	.372	Post-All Star	.219	151	33	10	0	0	8	14	25	.298	.285

1993 By Position

Position	Avg	AB	H	2B	3B	HR	RBI	BB	SO	OBP	SLG	G	GS	Innings	PO	A	E	DP	Fld Pct	Rng Fctr	In Zone	Outs	Zone Rtg	MLB Zone
As Designated Hitter	.261	307	80	19	1	9	36	19	48	.312	.417	83	80	---	---	---	---	---	---	---	---	---	---	---
As Pinch Hitter	.182	11	2	0	0	0	0	2	4	.308	.182	13	0	---	---	---	---	---	---	---	---	---	---	---
As lf	.245	98	24	3	0	4	22	6	18	.283	.398	28	25	214.1	57	1	2	0	.967	2.44	67	59	.881	.818
As rf	.208	24	5	0	0	0	2	3	2	.296	.208	10	6	49.0	18	0	1	0	.947	3.31	21	17	.810	.826

Last Five Years

	Avg	AB	H	2B	3B	HR	RBI	BB	SO	OBP	SLG		Avg	AB	H	2B	3B	HR	RBI	BB	SO	OBP	SLG
vs. Left	.220	236	52	10	0	4	27	22	58	.302	.314	Scoring Posn	.239	373	89	17	3	12	141	47	89	.328	.397
vs. Right	.269	1194	321	75	4	47	175	93	233	.328	.456	Close & Late	.290	245	71	17	1	7	28	29	56	.366	.453
Groundball	.309	369	114	25	1	12	51	24	72	.360	.480	None on/out	.271	303	82	20	1	12	12	24	59	.338	.462
Flyball	.226	336	76	19	0	17	54	26	67	.286	.435	Batting #5	.238	719	171	37	2	21	90	45	149	.288	.382
Home	.265	691	183	45	3	31	111	58	156	.333	.473	Batting #6	.303	290	88	18	0	13	43	24	52	.366	.500
Away	.257	739	190	40	1	20	91	57	135	.314	.395	Other	.271	421	114	30	2	17	69	46	90	.353	.473
Day	.255	329	84	20	0	15	53	27	69	.318	.453	April	.308	169	52	13	1	7	30	12	27	.355	.521
Night	.262	1101	289	65	4	36	149	88	222	.325	.427	May	.266	271	72	17	0	8	43	11	55	.296	.417

Last Five Years

	Avg	AB	H	2B	3B	HR	RBI	BB	SO	OBP	SLG
Grass	.262	1172	307	68	4	47	178	96	247	.327	.447
Turf	.256	258	66	17	0	4	24	19	44	.310	.368
First Pitch	.329	252	83	12	2	14	37	13	0	.364	.560
Ahead in Count	.331	314	104	22	0	18	52	44	0	.416	.573
Behind in Count	.207	619	128	32	2	14	77	0	244	.224	.333
Two Strikes	.186	667	124	34	1	15	77	58	291	.262	.307

	Avg	AB	H	2B	3B	HR	RBI	BB	SO	OBP	SLG
June	.262	267	70	10	1	9	41	24	48	.328	.408
July	.261	234	61	21	0	7	23	21	51	.335	.440
August	.264	296	78	17	1	14	43	23	63	.329	.470
September/October	.207	193	40	7	1	6	22	24	47	.306	.347
Pre-All Star	.277	805	223	49	2	28	126	54	149	.326	.447
Post-All Star	.240	625	150	36	2	23	76	61	142	.320	.414

Batter vs. Pitcher (career)

Hits Best Against	Avg	AB	H	2B	3B	HR	RBI	BB	SO	OBP	SLG
Tom Gordon	.467	15	7	2	0	2	4	2	4	.529	1.000
Mark Leiter	.462	13	6	0	0	2	2	3	2	.563	.923
Rick Sutcliffe	.400	10	4	1	0	1	1	2	2	.500	.800
Kevin Appier	.313	16	5	2	0	2	8	3	2	.400	.813
Kirk McCaskill	.308	13	4	1	0	2	4	0	3	.308	.846

Hits Worst Against	Avg	AB	H	2B	3B	HR	RBI	BB	SO	OBP	SLG
Jack McDowell	.074	27	2	1	1	0	1	1	5	.107	.185
Juan Guzman	.083	12	1	0	0	0	1	1	5	.154	.083
Charlie Hough	.100	10	1	1	0	0	0	1	0	.182	.200
Chris Bosio	.103	29	3	1	0	0	0	1	9	.133	.138
Ben McDonald	.143	14	2	0	0	0	2	1	3	.200	.143

Rich Renteria — Marlins

Age 32 – Bats Right

	Avg	G	AB	R	H	2B	3B	HR	RBI	BB	SO	HBP	GDP	SB	CS	OBP	SLG	IBB	SH	SF	#Pit	#P/PA	GB	FB	G/F
1993 Season	.255	103	263	27	67	9	2	2	30	21	31	2	8	0	2	.314	.327	1	3	1	1091	3.76	104	81	1.28

1993 Season

	Avg	AB	H	2B	3B	HR	RBI	BB	SO	OBP	SLG
vs. Left	.211	95	20	3	1	1	12	6	13	.255	.295
vs. Right	.280	168	47	6	1	1	18	15	18	.346	.345
Home	.292	144	42	5	2	2	20	14	19	.358	.396
Away	.210	119	25	4	0	0	10	7	12	.258	.244
First Pitch	.333	21	7	1	0	0	3	1	0	.364	.381
Ahead in Count	.387	62	24	4	0	2	13	14	0	.494	.548
Behind in Count	.173	127	22	3	1	0	10	0	26	.180	.213
Two Strikes	.198	121	24	2	1	0	9	6	31	.248	.231

	Avg	AB	H	2B	3B	HR	RBI	BB	SO	OBP	SLG
Scoring Posn	.351	74	26	4	1	1	29	6	8	.402	.473
Close & Late	.212	66	14	2	1	1	10	6	10	.288	.318
None on/out	.302	63	19	5	1	0	0	3	6	.343	.413
Batting #2	.251	179	45	6	0	2	18	13	20	.304	.318
Batting #9	.219	32	7	0	1	0	5	4	5	.306	.281
Other	.288	52	15	3	1	0	7	4	6	.351	.385
Pre-All Star	.299	134	40	7	2	2	21	10	16	.352	.425
Post-All Star	.209	129	27	2	0	0	9	11	15	.275	.225

Harold Reynolds — Orioles

Age 33 – Bats Both

	Avg	G	AB	R	H	2B	3B	HR	RBI	BB	SO	HBP	GDP	SB	CS	OBP	SLG	IBB	SH	SF	#Pit	#P/PA	GB	FB	G/F
1993 Season	.252	145	485	64	122	20	4	4	47	66	47	4	4	12	11	.343	.334	3	10	5	2122	3.72	191	151	1.26
Last Five Years	.262	759	2829	401	741	137	27	15	235	319	248	18	40	111	65	.338	.345	10	43	24	11773	3.64	1121	844	1.33

1993 Season

	Avg	AB	H	2B	3B	HR	RBI	BB	SO	OBP	SLG
vs. Left	.179	134	24	4	0	0	12	6	17	.213	.209
vs. Right	.279	351	98	16	4	4	35	60	30	.387	.382
Groundball	.282	103	29	8	0	3	15	13	10	.362	.447
Flyball	.292	89	26	6	1	1	14	12	6	.373	.416
Home	.249	261	65	13	3	2	24	32	28	.331	.345
Away	.254	224	57	7	1	2	23	34	19	.356	.321
Day	.284	134	38	5	0	1	16	13	16	.345	.343
Night	.239	351	84	15	4	3	31	53	31	.342	.330
Grass	.251	426	107	18	4	3	39	52	41	.333	.333
Turf	.254	59	15	2	0	1	8	14	6	.408	.339
First Pitch	.255	51	13	2	0	0	8	2	0	.304	.294
Ahead in Count	.260	146	38	4	1	3	20	36	0	.398	.363
Behind in Count	.260	192	50	10	1	0	11	0	36	.268	.323
Two Strikes	.272	184	50	8	1	0	9	28	47	.371	.326

	Avg	AB	H	2B	3B	HR	RBI	BB	SO	OBP	SLG
Scoring Posn	.319	116	37	10	1	1	43	23	13	.417	.448
Close & Late	.355	76	27	4	0	1	7	10	8	.425	.447
None on/out	.228	136	31	6	1	2	2	14	9	.305	.331
Batting #8	.297	138	41	7	1	3	19	27	16	.410	.428
Batting #9	.229	192	44	6	3	1	18	20	16	.309	.307
Other	.239	155	37	7	0	0	10	19	15	.322	.284
April	.228	57	13	2	1	0	5	5	6	.297	.298
May	.253	95	24	2	0	0	6	13	9	.339	.274
June	.295	95	28	8	0	0	7	11	7	.374	.379
July	.244	78	19	2	0	1	5	13	7	.351	.308
August	.215	79	17	1	0	3	13	14	9	.330	.342
September/October	.259	81	21	5	3	0	11	10	9	.348	.395
Pre-All Star	.267	288	77	13	1	0	21	37	24	.352	.319
Post-All Star	.228	197	45	7	3	4	26	29	23	.329	.355

1993 By Position

Position	Avg	AB	H	2B	3B	HR	RBI	BB	SO	OBP	SLG	G	GS	Innings	PO	A	E	DP	Fld Pct	Rng Fctr	In Zone	Outs	Zone Rtg	MLB Zone
As 2b	.251	482	121	20	4	4	47	66	46	.343	.334	141	138	1225.2	306	395	10	111	.986	5.15	422	382	.905	.895

Last Five Years

	Avg	AB	H	2B	3B	HR	RBI	BB	SO	OBP	SLG
vs. Left	.266	801	213	41	3	2	76	72	55	.325	.332
vs. Right	.260	2028	528	96	24	13	159	247	193	.343	.351
Groundball	.260	708	184	45	2	6	54	82	73	.342	.355
Flyball	.253	588	149	25	8	3	42	68	42	.330	.338
Home	.274	1416	388	76	17	5	116	164	118	.351	.362
Away	.250	1413	353	61	10	10	119	155	130	.325	.328
Day	.250	727	182	30	6	4	67	81	69	.328	.325
Night	.266	2102	559	107	21	11	168	238	179	.341	.353
Grass	.250	1354	339	58	10	9	122	146	123	.323	.328
Turf	.273	1475	402	79	17	6	113	173	125	.351	.361
First Pitch	.278	324	90	18	3	2	37	3	0	.294	.370
Ahead in Count	.290	894	259	52	11	10	88	194	0	.412	.406
Behind in Count	.230	1056	243	45	5	1	64	0	203	.237	.285
Two Strikes	.226	1036	234	36	7	2	67	120	248	.308	.280

	Avg	AB	H	2B	3B	HR	RBI	BB	SO	OBP	SLG
Scoring Posn	.302	605	183	44	3	5	213	80	54	.373	.410
Close & Late	.294	439	129	18	2	4	61	49	60	.361	.371
None on/out	.240	933	224	45	12	3	3	111	83	.325	.324
Batting #1	.264	1669	441	81	15	7	133	189	132	.340	.343
Batting #2	.263	594	156	28	7	3	48	58	66	.331	.348
Other	.254	566	144	28	5	5	54	72	50	.340	.348
April	.243	404	98	13	7	2	39	30	30	.297	.324
May	.289	519	150	31	4	0	43	66	46	.364	.364
June	.251	475	119	25	4	2	35	61	42	.341	.333
July	.264	488	129	18	2	4	42	61	37	.345	.334
August	.249	473	118	25	1	3	32	56	44	.334	.326
September/October	.270	470	127	25	9	4	44	45	49	.335	.387
Pre-All Star	.263	1564	411	76	15	5	132	177	127	.338	.340
Post-All Star	.261	1265	330	61	12	10	103	142	121	.338	.352

Batter vs. Pitcher (since 1984)

Hits Best Against	Avg	AB	H	2B	3B	HR	RBI	BB	SO	OBP	SLG
Jesse Orosco	.600	10	6	1	0	0	3	1	2	.636	.700
Chris Bosio	.538	26	14	2	0	0	1	2	1	.571	.615

Hits Worst Against	Avg	AB	H	2B	3B	HR	RBI	BB	SO	OBP	SLG
Danny Darwin	.053	19	1	1	0	0	1	0	1	.053	.105
Bobby Thigpen	.077	13	1	0	0	0	0	2	1	.200	.077

Batter vs. Pitcher (since 1984)																						
Hits Best Against	Avg	AB	H	2B	3B	HR	RBI	BB	SO	OBP	SLG	**Hits Worst Against**	Avg	AB	H	2B	3B	HR	RBI	BB	SO	OBP	SLG
Mike Henneman	.529	17	9	3	1	1	5	2	3	.579	1.000	Scott Kamieniecki	.133	15	2	0	0	0	2	0	1	.133	.133
Steve Farr	.500	22	11	2	1	0	0	2	2	.542	.682	Mike Gardiner	.143	14	2	0	0	0	1	1	2	.200	.143
Bob Milacki	.364	11	4	1	1	1	2	2	2	.462	.909	David Wells	.148	27	4	0	0	0	1	1	5	.172	.148

Shane Reynolds — Astros

Age 26 – Pitches Right (groundball pitcher)

	ERA	W	L	Sv	G	GS	IP	BB	SO	Avg	H	2B	3B	HR	RBI	OBP	SLG	GF	IR	IRS	Hld	SvOp	SB	CS	GB	FB	G/F
1993 Season	0.82	0	0	0	5	1	11.0	6	10	.256	11	1	0	0	4	.347	.279	0	4	1	0	0	0	0	21	5	4.20
Career (1992-1993)	5.20	1	3	0	13	6	36.1	12	20	.349	53	12	3	2	23	.394	.507	0	6	3	0	0	6	1	64	32	2.00

1993 Season

	ERA	W	L	Sv	G	GS	IP	H	HR	BB	SO		Avg	AB	H	2B	3B	HR	RBI	BB	SO	OBP	SLG
Home	0.00	0	0	0	1	0	0.1	1	0	0	0	vs. Left	.292	24	7	0	0	0	2	4	5	.393	.292
Away	0.84	0	0	0	4	1	10.2	10	0	6	10	vs. Right	.211	19	4	1	0	0	2	2	5	.286	.263

Armando Reynoso — Rockies

Age 28 – Pitches Right

	ERA	W	L	Sv	G	GS	IP	BB	SO	Avg	H	2B	3B	HR	RBI	OBP	SLG	CG	ShO	Sup	QS	#P/S	SB	CS	GB	FB	G/F
1993 Season	4.00	12	11	0	30	30	189.0	63	117	.277	206	35	10	22	91	.337	.439	4	0	4.76	13	103	11	5	264	213	1.24
Career (1991-1993)	4.25	15	12	1	39	36	220.0	75	129	.283	243	43	13	28	113	.346	.460	4	0	4.99	15	98	12	7	309	246	1.26

1993 Season

	ERA	W	L	Sv	G	GS	IP	H	HR	BB	SO		Avg	AB	H	2B	3B	HR	RBI	BB	SO	OBP	SLG
Home	4.36	7	3	0	14	14	88.2	103	11	28	51	vs. Left	.277	379	105	23	7	10	47	32	64	.342	.454
Away	3.68	5	8	0	16	16	100.1	103	11	35	66	vs. Right	.276	366	101	12	3	12	44	31	53	.332	.423
Day	3.69	5	4	0	10	10	61.0	64	4	22	39	Inning 1-6	.278	658	183	29	9	20	83	53	102	.336	.441
Night	4.15	7	7	0	20	20	128.0	142	18	41	78	Inning 7+	.264	87	23	6	1	2	8	10	15	.347	.425
Grass	4.01	11	8	0	24	24	152.2	170	17	47	96	None on	.289	418	121	20	7	18	18	27	66	.339	.500
Turf	3.96	1	3	0	6	6	36.1	36	5	16	21	Runners on	.260	327	85	15	3	4	73	36	51	.335	.361
April	1.00	1	0	0	1	1	9.0	6	0	2	4	Scoring Posn	.226	208	47	10	3	1	64	28	35	.316	.317
May	3.32	2	2	0	6	6	43.1	49	5	13	30	Close & Late	.256	39	10	4	0	1	6	6	7	.370	.436
June	3.53	2	1	0	5	5	35.2	32	5	14	23	None on/out	.311	193	60	12	5	9	9	11	27	.348	.565
July	4.06	2	3	0	6	6	37.2	38	5	9	21	vs. 1st Batr (relief)	.000	0	0	0	0	0	0	0	0	.000	.000
August	4.28	2	3	0	6	6	33.2	41	3	15	21	First Inning Pitched	.323	127	41	7	2	4	19	6	14	.360	.504
September/October	6.07	3	2	0	6	6	29.2	40	4	10	18	First 75 Pitches	.270	540	146	23	8	15	60	42	79	.329	.426
Starter	4.00	12	11	0	30	30	189.0	206	22	63	117	Pitch 76-90	.314	86	27	6	0	3	9	7	17	.365	.488
Reliever	0.00	0	0	0	0	0	0.0	0	0	0	0	Pitch 91-105	.266	64	17	2	1	2	16	10	10	.355	.422
0-3 Days Rest	0.00	0	0	0	0	0	0.0	0	0	0	0	Pitch 106+	.291	55	16	4	1	2	6	4	11	.350	.509
4 Days Rest	3.63	9	8	0	20	20	134.0	141	16	41	81	First Pitch	.395	114	45	3	3	5	26	2	0	.403	.605
5+ Days Rest	4.91	3	3	0	10	10	55.0	65	6	22	36	Ahead in Count	.176	295	52	9	1	3	17	0	99	.195	.244
Pre-All Star	3.03	7	4	0	15	15	107.0	104	12	34	65	Behind in Count	.380	184	70	19	4	8	31	37	0	.480	.658
Post-All Star	5.27	5	7	0	15	15	82.0	102	10	29	52	Two Strikes	.159	320	51	7	2	6	22	24	117	.233	.250

Arthur Rhodes — Orioles

Age 24 – Pitches Left (flyball pitcher)

	ERA	W	L	Sv	G	GS	IP	BB	SO	Avg	H	2B	3B	HR	RBI	OBP	SLG	CG	ShO	Sup	QS	#P/S	SB	CS	GB	FB	G/F
1993 Season	6.51	5	6	0	17	17	85.2	49	49	.274	91	20	5	16	55	.366	.509	0	0	5.25	2	90	5	4	100	125	0.80
Career (1991-1993)	5.50	12	14	0	40	40	216.0	110	149	.272	225	48	10	26	113	.356	.449	2	1	5.04	14	94	16	10	255	280	0.91

1993 Season

	ERA	W	L	Sv	G	GS	IP	H	HR	BB	SO		Avg	AB	H	2B	3B	HR	RBI	BB	SO	OBP	SLG
Home	7.36	2	4	0	7	7	36.2	37	12	23	23	vs. Left	.300	40	12	4	0	1	5	7	2	.404	.475
Away	5.88	3	2	0	10	10	49.0	54	4	26	26	vs. Right	.271	292	79	16	5	15	50	42	47	.361	.514
Starter	6.51	5	6	0	17	17	85.2	91	16	49	49	Scoring Posn	.305	82	25	4	1	3	39	11	10	.381	.488
Reliever	0.00	0	0	0	0	0	0.0	0	0	0	0	Close & Late	.333	6	2	0	1	1	2	2	3	.500	1.167
0-3 Days Rest	10.80	0	1	0	1	1	5.0	10	0	4	1	None on/out	.232	82	19	3	2	5	5	15	12	.351	.500
4 Days Rest	3.86	2	1	0	6	6	37.1	27	5	16	21	First Pitch	.333	33	11	2	0	2	6	1	0	.343	.576
5+ Days Rest	8.31	3	4	0	10	10	43.1	54	11	29	27	Ahead in Count	.241	116	28	5	2	4	17	0	35	.246	.422
Pre-All Star	9.36	1	2	0	6	6	25.0	37	7	12	18	Behind in Count	.277	101	28	6	1	5	18	31	0	.447	.505
Post-All Star	5.34	4	4	0	11	11	60.2	54	9	37	31	Two Strikes	.222	135	30	5	2	5	21	17	49	.312	.400

Karl Rhodes — Cubs

Age 25 – Bats Left

	Avg	G	AB	R	H	2B	3B	HR	RBI	BB	SO	HBP	GDP	SB	CS	OBP	SLG	IBB	SH	SF	#Pit	#P/PA	GB	FB	G/F
1993 Season	.278	20	54	12	15	2	1	3	7	11	9	0	0	2	0	.400	.519	0	0	0	276	4.25	15	19	0.79
Career (1990-1993)	.232	107	280	31	65	11	3	5	22	38	49	1	4	8	3	.324	.346	6	1	2	1258	3.91	103	78	1.32

1993 Season

	Avg	AB	H	2B	3B	HR	RBI	BB	SO	OBP	SLG		Avg	AB	H	2B	3B	HR	RBI	BB	SO	OBP	SLG
vs. Left	.250	8	2	0	0	2	3	4	3	.500	1.000	Scoring Posn	.556	9	5	0	1	1	5	5	0	.714	1.111
vs. Right	.283	46	13	2	1	1	4	7	6	.377	.435	Close & Late	.375	8	3	0	0	1	2	0	1	.375	.750

Jeff Richardson — Red Sox

Age 28 – Bats Right (flyball hitter)

	Avg	G	AB	R	H	2B	3B	HR	RBI	BB	SO	HBP	GDP	SB	CS	OBP	SLG	IBB	SH	SF	#Pit	#P/PA	GB	FB	G/F
1993 Season	.208	15	24	3	5	2	0	0	2	1	3	0	0	0	0	.240	.292	0	2	0	93	3.44	6	7	0.86
Career (1989-1993)	.176	74	153	13	27	6	0	2	13	11	29	1	3	1	0	.235	.255	0	5	1	590	3.45	47	50	0.94

1993 Season

	Avg	AB	H	2B	3B	HR	RBI	BB	SO	OBP	SLG
vs. Left	.000	1	0	0	0	0	0	0	0	.000	.000
vs. Right	.217	23	5	2	0	0	2	1	3	.250	.304

	Avg	AB	H	2B	3B	HR	RBI	BB	SO	OBP	SLG
Scoring Posn	.200	5	1	0	0	0	1	0	0	.200	.200
Close & Late	.200	5	1	1	0	0	1	0	0	.200	.400

Dave Righetti — Giants

Age 35 – Pitches Left

	ERA	W	L	Sv	G	GS	IP	BB	SO	Avg	H	2B	3B	HR	RBI	OBP	SLG	GF	IR	IRS	Hld	SvOp	SB	CS	GB	FB	G/F
1993 Season	5.70	1	1	1	51	0	47.1	17	31	.305	58	6	2	11	31	.365	.532	15	23	9	6	3	1	4	54	66	0.82
Last Five Years	4.09	8	22	89	274	4	319.1	133	223	.264	322	49	8	30	156	.337	.391	134	118	29	13	110	23	10	424	309	1.15

1993 Season

	ERA	W	L	Sv	G	GS	IP	H	HR	BB	SO
Home	3.57	0	1	1	24	0	22.2	21	5	11	15
Away	7.66	1	0	0	27	0	24.2	37	6	6	16
Starter	0.00	0	0	0	0	0	0.0	0	0	0	0
Reliever	5.70	1	1	1	51	0	47.1	58	11	17	31
0 Days rest	3.00	0	0	0	9	0	9.0	6	2	2	5
1 or 2 Days rest	3.54	1	1	1	21	0	20.1	23	5	8	12
3+ Days rest	9.50	0	0	0	21	0	18.0	29	4	7	14
Pre-All Star	3.94	1	1	0	33	0	32.0	32	4	13	21
Post-All Star	9.39	0	0	1	18	0	15.1	26	7	4	10

	Avg	AB	H	2B	3B	HR	RBI	BB	SO	OBP	SLG
vs. Left	.288	59	17	3	1	4	12	2	11	.311	.576
vs. Right	.313	131	41	3	1	7	19	15	20	.388	.511
Scoring Posn	.289	45	13	2	0	4	21	2	3	.319	.600
Close & Late	.268	41	11	2	1	3	9	4	6	.333	.585
None on/out	.340	47	16	3	0	1	1	4	10	.404	.468
First Pitch	.414	29	12	0	0	2	3	0	0	.414	.621
Ahead in Count	.259	81	21	3	1	2	12	0	28	.268	.395
Behind in Count	.317	41	13	2	0	3	9	8	0	.429	.585
Two Strikes	.261	88	23	2	0	3	11	9	31	.337	.386

Last Five Years

	ERA	W	L	Sv	G	GS	IP	H	HR	BB	SO
Home	3.25	3	10	49	138	2	163.1	151	9	59	119
Away	4.96	5	12	40	136	2	156.0	171	21	74	104
Day	4.46	5	9	26	104	1	119.0	119	13	58	87
Night	3.86	3	13	63	170	3	200.1	203	17	75	136
Grass	4.04	7	19	69	212	3	245.0	248	23	100	167
Turf	4.24	1	3	20	62	1	74.1	74	7	33	56
April	4.23	3	3	10	40	0	44.2	51	4	20	32
May	4.22	1	4	11	45	0	49.0	55	2	22	37
June	4.14	3	4	23	51	4	74.0	67	6	36	41
July	3.17	0	3	13	44	0	48.1	40	5	17	36
August	4.01	0	4	16	53	0	60.2	58	9	18	45
September/October	4.85	1	4	16	41	0	42.2	51	4	20	32
Starter	8.68	0	2	0	4	4	18.2	20	2	9	5
Reliever	3.80	8	20	89	270	0	300.2	302	28	124	218
0 Days rest	3.80	0	3	23	45	0	47.1	49	5	15	38
1 or 2 Days rest	3.88	3	13	48	125	0	139.0	141	10	56	87
3+ Days rest	3.70	5	4	18	100	0	114.1	112	13	53	93
Pre-All Star	4.10	7	12	47	150	4	184.1	189	14	84	124
Post-All Star	4.07	1	10	42	124	0	135.0	133	16	49	99

	Avg	AB	H	2B	3B	HR	RBI	BB	SO	OBP	SLG
vs. Left	.238	323	77	11	3	7	46	26	63	.297	.356
vs. Right	.273	897	245	38	5	23	110	107	160	.352	.404
Inning 1-6	.261	111	29	6	1	3	19	10	11	.320	.414
Inning 7+	.264	1109	293	43	7	27	137	123	212	.339	.389
None on	.257	630	162	22	5	15	15	66	116	.333	.379
Runners on	.271	590	160	27	3	15	141	67	107	.342	.403
Scoring Posn	.248	343	85	16	1	8	120	47	59	.333	.370
Close & Late	.253	561	142	15	2	16	72	70	114	.338	.373
None on/out	.231	277	64	14	1	5	5	29	59	.313	.343
vs. 1st Batr (relief)	.201	244	49	9	0	8	23	21	56	.269	.336
First Inning Pitched	.249	927	231	34	6	21	117	102	176	.325	.367
First 15 Pitches	.247	810	200	30	6	21	88	75	148	.314	.377
Pitch 16-30	.294	306	90	14	1	5	48	46	61	.385	.395
Pitch 31-45	.292	72	21	3	0	2	11	7	11	.350	.417
Pitch 46+	.344	32	11	2	1	2	9	5	3	.432	.656
First Pitch	.346	188	65	12	0	8	35	14	0	.390	.537
Ahead in Count	.226	549	124	18	5	7	53	0	192	.231	.315
Behind in Count	.306	265	81	12	1	8	39	69	0	.447	.449
Two Strikes	.188	549	103	12	3	6	44	49	223	.258	.253

Pitcher vs. Batter (since 1984)

Pitches Best Vs.	Avg	AB	H	2B	3B	HR	RBI	BB	SO	OBP	SLG
Don Slaught	.000	13	0	0	0	0	0	1	6	.071	.000
Darnell Coles	.000	12	0	0	0	0	0	2	4	.143	.000
Dave Henderson	.000	10	0	0	0	0	1	0	0	.000	.000
Ivan Calderon	.133	15	2	0	0	0	0	1	6	.188	.133
Kelly Gruber	.154	13	2	0	0	0	1	2	1	.267	.154

Pitches Worst Vs.	Avg	AB	H	2B	3B	HR	RBI	BB	SO	OBP	SLG
Lou Whitaker	.583	12	7	1	0	1	3	4	1	.688	.917
Pete O'Brien	.533	15	8	2	0	0	3	4	1	.600	.667
Terry Pendleton	.455	11	5	1	0	1	4	0	1	.455	.818
George Bell	.400	25	10	3	1	3	10	0	3	.400	.960
Pete Incaviglia	.364	11	4	2	0	2	6	3	4	.500	1.091

Jose Rijo — Reds

Age 29 – Pitches Right (groundball pitcher)

	ERA	W	L	Sv	G	GS	IP	BB	SO	Avg	H	2B	3B	HR	RBI	OBP	SLG	CG	ShO	Sup	QS	#P/S	SB	CS	GB	FB	G/F
1993 Season	2.48	14	9	0	36	36	257.1	62	227	.230	218	32	9	19	73	.278	.342	2	1	4.23	28	113	22	10	361	211	1.71
Last Five Years	2.59	65	39	0	147	147	980.2	287	808	.228	820	141	22	58	283	.286	.328	15	4	4.43	106	102	87	38	1328	855	1.55

1993 Season

	ERA	W	L	Sv	G	GS	IP	H	HR	BB	SO
Home	2.60	8	6	0	19	19	135.0	117	13	38	117
Away	2.35	6	3	0	17	17	122.1	101	6	24	110
Day	2.25	6	2	0	9	9	68.0	55	4	16	47
Night	2.57	8	7	0	27	27	189.1	163	15	46	180
Grass	2.06	3	3	0	10	10	74.1	57	6	8	69
Turf	2.66	11	6	0	26	26	183.0	161	13	54	158
April	2.31	2	1	0	5	5	35.0	25	2	8	30
May	3.32	4	0	0	6	6	40.2	36	6	11	32
June	3.80	0	2	0	6	6	42.2	38	4	7	38
July	1.87	3	2	0	7	7	53.0	46	3	12	49
August	1.50	3	2	0	6	6	42.0	37	2	13	40
September/October	2.25	2	2	0	6	6	44.0	36	2	11	38
Starter	2.48	14	9	0	36	36	257.1	218	19	62	227
Reliever	0.00	0	0	0	0	0	0.0	0	0	0	0
0-3 Days Rest	0.00	0	0	0	0	0	0.0	0	0	0	0

	Avg	AB	H	2B	3B	HR	RBI	BB	SO	OBP	SLG
vs. Left	.242	520	126	20	6	10	48	40	110	.297	.362
vs. Right	.214	429	92	12	3	9	25	22	117	.253	.319
Inning 1-6	.237	799	189	30	9	17	66	52	197	.284	.360
Inning 7+	.193	150	29	2	0	2	7	10	30	.242	.247
None on	.253	589	149	21	6	18	18	28	134	.289	.401
Runners on	.192	360	69	11	3	1	55	34	93	.259	.247
Scoring Posn	.188	202	38	8	2	0	51	25	58	.274	.248
Close & Late	.200	75	15	2	0	1	4	3	17	.231	.267
None on/out	.264	254	67	8	2	8	8	12	53	.300	.406
vs. 1st Batr (relief)	.000	0	0	0	0	0	0	0	0	.000	.000
First Inning Pitched	.169	124	21	2	1	1	6	9	38	.224	.226
First 75 Pitches	.226	620	140	21	9	14	44	36	148	.269	.356
Pitch 76-90	.242	124	30	7	0	1	14	10	33	.299	.323
Pitch 91-105	.250	116	29	3	0	2	8	5	29	.287	.328
Pitch 106+	.213	89	19	1	0	2	7	11	17	.297	.292

1993 Season

	ERA	W	L	Sv	G	GS	IP	H	HR	BB	SO
4 Days Rest	2.47	12	7	0	31	31	222.1	190	17	53	198
5+ Days Rest	2.57	2	2	0	5	5	35.0	28	2	9	29
Pre-All Star	3.27	6	5	0	20	20	140.1	122	14	31	120
Post-All Star	1.54	8	4	0	16	16	117.0	96	5	31	107

	Avg	AB	H	2B	3B	HR	RBI	BB	SO	OBP	SLG
First Pitch	.264	125	33	4	4	0	12	2	0	.276	.360
Ahead in Count	.153	444	68	9	2	3	18	0	187	.157	.203
Behind in Count	.331	181	60	9	2	10	26	25	0	.411	.569
Two Strikes	.153	491	75	10	3	5	18	35	227	.210	.216

Last Five Years

	ERA	W	L	Sv	G	GS	IP	H	HR	BB	SO
Home	2.68	33	16	0	71	71	474.0	380	33	157	406
Away	2.50	32	23	0	76	76	506.2	440	25	130	402
Day	2.27	21	12	0	45	45	297.0	235	16	76	245
Night	2.73	44	27	0	102	102	683.2	585	42	211	563
Grass	2.44	18	16	0	45	45	309.1	269	19	71	246
Turf	2.65	47	23	0	102	102	671.1	551	39	216	562
April	2.59	5	6	0	20	20	132.0	109	5	40	109
May	3.20	14	3	0	29	29	174.1	159	17	58	149
June	3.47	9	10	0	28	28	186.2	163	15	46	159
July	2.26	10	5	0	20	20	131.1	118	8	36	101
August	2.15	12	8	0	23	23	159.1	122	9	50	134
September/October	1.78	15	7	0	27	27	197.0	149	4	57	156
Starter	2.59	65	39	0	147	147	980.2	820	58	287	808
Reliever	0.00	0	0	0	0	0	0.0	0	0	0	0
0-3 Days Rest	1.45	5	2	0	8	8	62.0	37	2	16	44
4 Days Rest	2.48	46	26	0	103	103	707.0	596	43	199	588
5+ Days Rest	3.27	14	11	0	36	36	211.2	187	13	72	176
Pre-All Star	3.11	30	22	0	84	84	539.0	473	41	158	455
Post-All Star	1.96	35	17	0	63	63	441.2	347	17	129	353

	Avg	AB	H	2B	3B	HR	RBI	BB	SO	OBP	SLG
vs. Left	.248	2036	505	89	15	33	178	208	421	.318	.355
vs. Right	.202	1561	315	52	7	25	105	79	387	.242	.292
Inning 1-6	.229	3111	711	125	19	48	251	250	705	.287	.327
Inning 7+	.224	486	109	16	3	10	32	37	103	.278	.331
None on	.232	2224	517	94	13	49	49	155	477	.284	.353
Runners on	.221	1373	303	47	9	9	234	132	331	.288	.288
Scoring Posn	.213	785	167	30	5	2	209	98	221	.296	.271
Close & Late	.241	237	57	8	1	6	18	15	54	.285	.359
None on/out	.232	949	220	35	4	26	26	69	188	.287	.359
vs. 1st Batr (relief)	.000	0	0	0	0	0	0	0	0	.000	.000
First Inning Pitched	.235	537	126	27	3	4	44	57	122	.312	.318
First 75 Pitches	.231	2580	595	103	18	43	200	203	569	.288	.334
Pitch 76-90	.219	466	102	22	0	4	43	39	109	.276	.292
Pitch 91-105	.228	325	74	7	2	8	23	21	79	.277	.335
Pitch 106+	.217	226	49	9	2	3	17	24	51	.291	.314
First Pitch	.303	502	152	24	10	4	57	9	0	.319	.414
Ahead in Count	.160	1683	269	42	5	13	83	0	673	.163	.214
Behind in Count	.346	700	242	44	6	32	100	136	0	.448	.563
Two Strikes	.145	1748	253	43	5	14	73	141	808	.210	.199

Pitcher vs. Batter (career)

Pitches Best Vs.	Avg	AB	H	2B	3B	HR	RBI	BB	SO	OBP	SLG
Doug Dascenzo	.000	13	0	0	0	0	0	1	3	.071	.000
Gary Sheffield	.000	12	0	0	0	0	0	1	4	.077	.000
Tom Foley	.067	15	1	0	0	0	1	0	4	.067	.067
Dave Hollins	.083	12	1	0	0	0	1	0	4	.083	.083
Jeff King	.091	11	1	0	0	0	1	0	4	.083	.091

Pitches Worst Vs.	Avg	AB	H	2B	3B	HR	RBI	BB	SO	OBP	SLG
Bernard Gilkey	.583	12	7	1	0	0	2	1	1	.615	.667
George Brett	.500	12	6	1	0	2	7	5	2	.647	1.083
Joe Girardi	.455	11	5	1	0	1	2	1	1	.500	.818
Lance Parrish	.444	9	4	0	0	1	1	2	1	.545	.778
Dave Martinez	.438	16	7	2	0	3	5	0	2	.438	1.125

Ernest Riles — Red Sox

Age 33 – Bats Left

	Avg	G	AB	R	H	2B	3B	HR	RBI	BB	SO	HBP	GDP	SB	CS	OBP	SLG	IBB	SH	SF	#Pit	#P/PA	GB	FB	G/F
1993 Season	.189	94	143	15	27	8	0	5	20	20	40	2	3	1	3	.292	.350	3	2	3	746	4.39	47	41	1.15
Last Five Years	.231	455	942	115	218	32	7	26	117	107	169	5	20	5	11	.309	.363	12	9	13	4180	3.88	358	286	1.25

1993 Season

	Avg	AB	H	2B	3B	HR	RBI	BB	SO	OBP	SLG
vs. Left	.143	7	1	0	0	1	2	2	3	.300	.571
vs. Right	.191	136	26	8	0	4	18	18	37	.291	.338
Home	.220	59	13	4	0	2	9	9	17	.324	.390
Away	.167	84	14	4	0	3	11	11	23	.268	.321
First Pitch	.143	7	1	1	0	0	0	3	0	.400	.286
Ahead in Count	.206	34	7	0	0	2	4	8	0	.349	.382
Behind in Count	.134	67	9	3	0	1	7	0	32	.147	.224
Two Strikes	.174	86	15	7	0	1	12	9	40	.263	.291

	Avg	AB	H	2B	3B	HR	RBI	BB	SO	OBP	SLG
Scoring Posn	.167	42	7	1	0	1	14	9	12	.296	.262
Close & Late	.190	42	8	4	0	2	8	4	13	.255	.429
None on/out	.229	35	8	2	0	2	2	2	7	.289	.457
Batting #2	.209	43	9	2	0	2	3	9	14	.346	.395
Batting #9	.273	33	9	3	0	2	7	5	9	.359	.545
Other	.134	67	9	3	0	1	10	6	17	.221	.224
Pre-All Star	.210	100	21	8	0	2	13	12	29	.296	.350
Post-All Star	.140	43	6	0	0	3	7	8	11	.283	.349

Last Five Years

	Avg	AB	H	2B	3B	HR	RBI	BB	SO	OBP	SLG
vs. Left	.160	81	13	2	1	2	8	9	21	.242	.284
vs. Right	.238	861	205	30	6	24	109	98	148	.316	.370
Groundball	.230	322	74	9	1	7	42	40	56	.313	.329
Flyball	.245	212	52	10	1	7	26	19	40	.312	.401
Home	.236	433	102	19	4	17	58	61	75	.331	.416
Away	.228	509	116	13	3	9	59	46	94	.290	.318
Day	.215	349	75	12	3	7	32	37	70	.294	.327
Night	.241	593	143	20	4	19	85	70	99	.318	.384
Grass	.231	722	167	24	6	24	93	84	115	.312	.381
Turf	.232	220	51	8	1	2	24	23	54	.300	.305
First Pitch	.247	89	22	1	0	2	12	7	0	.309	.326
Ahead in Count	.258	213	55	9	2	12	45	54	0	.399	.488
Behind in Count	.206	451	93	11	4	6	38	0	146	.210	.288
Two Strikes	.200	456	91	13	3	7	35	43	169	.271	.287

	Avg	AB	H	2B	3B	HR	RBI	BB	SO	OBP	SLG
Scoring Posn	.238	239	57	9	2	9	94	42	47	.343	.406
Close & Late	.235	183	43	7	3	7	29	26	41	.327	.421
None on/out	.237	232	55	5	3	7	7	19	37	.298	.375
Batting #2	.184	185	34	4	0	3	15	20	38	.264	.254
Batting #5	.258	221	57	11	2	4	29	22	33	.324	.380
Other	.237	536	127	17	5	19	73	65	98	.319	.394
April	.239	117	28	3	1	4	8	15	21	.321	.385
May	.254	213	54	8	4	7	36	26	37	.335	.427
June	.271	166	45	12	1	1	22	20	35	.347	.373
July	.186	161	30	2	0	6	15	14	23	.253	.311
August	.205	112	23	4	0	4	19	14	22	.289	.348
September/October	.220	173	38	3	1	4	17	18	31	.297	.318
Pre-All Star	.250	543	136	23	6	12	66	67	100	.332	.381
Post-All Star	.206	399	82	9	1	14	51	40	69	.277	.338

Batter vs. Pitcher (career)

Hits Best Against	Avg	AB	H	2B	3B	HR	RBI	BB	SO	OBP	SLG
John Smoltz	.440	25	11	2	0	1	1	1	1	.462	.640
Bill Gullickson	.421	19	8	0	0	3	3	2	4	.476	.895
Mike Bielecki	.375	8	3	0	0	0	0	3	0	.545	.375
Tim Leary	.364	11	4	0	1	0	2	1	0	.417	.545
David Cone	.364	11	4	1	0	1	1	1	1	.417	.727

Hits Worst Against	Avg	AB	H	2B	3B	HR	RBI	BB	SO	OBP	SLG
Mark Portugal	.053	19	1	0	0	0	1	4	5	.217	.053
Ramon Martinez	.077	13	1	0	0	0	0	2	2	.200	.077
Scott Sanderson	.091	11	1	0	0	0	1	0	1	.091	.091
Jaime Navarro	.100	10	1	0	0	0	0	1	3	.182	.100
Kirk McCaskill	.136	22	3	0	0	0	3	2	6	.208	.136

Billy Ripken — Rangers

Age 29 – Bats Right (groundball hitter)

	Avg	G	AB	R	H	2B	3B	HR	RBI	BB	SO	HBP	GDP	SB	CS	OBP	SLG	IBB	SH	SF	#Pit	#P/PA	GB	FB	G/F
1993 Season	.189	50	132	12	25	4	0	0	11	11	19	4	6	0	2	.270	.220	0	5	1	578	3.78	60	36	1.67
Last Five Years	.242	509	1473	150	357	69	4	9	125	94	172	11	49	8	10	.291	.313	3	62	11	5588	3.38	656	369	1.78

1993 Season

	Avg	AB	H	2B	3B	HR	RBI	BB	SO	OBP	SLG		Avg	AB	H	2B	3B	HR	RBI	BB	SO	OBP	SLG
vs. Left	.222	45	10	2	0	0	3	4	7	.280	.267	Scoring Posn	.154	39	6	1	0	0	11	0	8	.209	.179
vs. Right	.172	87	15	2	0	0	8	7	12	.265	.195	Close & Late	.357	14	5	1	0	0	3	3	2	.500	.429
Home	.192	52	10	1	0	0	8	7	7	.306	.212	None on/out	.212	33	7	2	0	0	0	3	3	.278	.273
Away	.188	80	15	3	0	0	3	4	12	.244	.225	Batting #8	.240	25	6	1	0	0	2	2	4	.321	.280
First Pitch	.333	15	5	2	0	0	2	0	0	.412	.467	Batting #9	.172	99	17	2	0	0	8	9	14	.259	.192
Ahead in Count	.308	26	8	1	0	0	5	9	0	.472	.346	Other	.250	8	2	1	0	0	1	0	1	.250	.375
Behind in Count	.138	58	8	1	0	0	3	0	14	.153	.155	Pre-All Star	.193	114	22	2	0	0	10	10	17	.279	.211
Two Strikes	.097	62	6	0	0	0	1	2	19	.138	.097	Post-All Star	.167	18	3	2	0	0	1	1	2	.211	.278

Last Five Years

	Avg	AB	H	2B	3B	HR	RBI	BB	SO	OBP	SLG		Avg	AB	H	2B	3B	HR	RBI	BB	SO	OBP	SLG
vs. Left	.270	497	134	26	1	2	39	36	54	.317	.338	Scoring Posn	.258	357	92	12	0	1	109	17	47	.294	.300
vs. Right	.228	976	223	43	3	7	86	58	118	.277	.300	Close & Late	.277	166	46	7	0	1	16	17	17	.349	.337
Groundball	.234	380	89	16	0	3	40	21	54	.278	.300	None on/out	.233	348	81	19	2	2	2	23	35	.282	.316
Flyball	.259	301	78	18	0	3	28	21	33	.310	.349	Batting #8	.259	243	63	11	0	2	25	17	19	.312	.329
Home	.244	692	169	33	2	5	70	52	78	.301	.319	Batting #9	.238	1111	264	51	4	6	89	70	133	.285	.307
Away	.241	781	188	36	2	4	55	42	94	.281	.307	Other	.252	119	30	7	0	1	11	7	20	.297	.336
Day	.227	370	84	15	0	3	23	26	41	.281	.292	April	.202	213	43	9	0	1	16	14	27	.258	.258
Night	.248	1103	273	54	4	6	102	68	131	.294	.320	May	.249	265	66	10	1	2	23	18	27	.299	.317
Grass	.236	1256	297	59	2	8	103	80	145	.285	.306	June	.234	325	76	15	1	2	31	12	41	.267	.305
Turf	.276	217	60	10	2	1	22	14	27	.326	.355	July	.267	232	62	11	1	2	15	18	19	.319	.349
First Pitch	.306	271	83	14	0	3	25	2	0	.319	.391	August	.262	195	51	8	0	0	19	17	31	.319	.303
Ahead in Count	.270	289	78	18	3	4	34	65	0	.398	.394	September/October	.243	243	59	16	1	2	21	15	27	.292	.342
Behind in Count	.212	647	137	21	1	1	54	0	151	.215	.252	Pre-All Star	.239	879	210	36	3	6	77	53	98	.286	.307
Two Strikes	.181	614	111	22	0	2	43	26	172	.218	.226	Post-All Star	.247	594	147	33	1	3	48	41	74	.297	.322

Batter vs. Pitcher (career)

Hits Best Against	Avg	AB	H	2B	3B	HR	RBI	BB	SO	OBP	SLG	Hits Worst Against	Avg	AB	H	2B	3B	HR	RBI	BB	SO	OBP	SLG
Bill Wegman	.647	17	11	0	0	1	5	1	1	.632	.824	Mark Gubicza	.059	17	1	0	0	0	0	4	3	.238	.059
Storm Davis	.462	13	6	1	1	0	0	1	0	.500	.692	Dave Stewart	.071	14	1	1	0	0	1	0	3	.071	.143
Charlie Leibrandt	.429	14	6	1	0	0	1	1	3	.467	.500	Jack McDowell	.077	13	1	0	0	0	1	0	2	.077	.077
David Wells	.412	17	7	2	0	1	1	3	0	.500	.706	Gene Nelson	.091	11	1	1	0	0	0	0	1	.091	.182
Scott Bankhead	.333	12	4	0	0	1	3	0	1	.333	.583	Roger Clemens	.133	15	2	0	0	0	0	0	0	.133	.133

Cal Ripken — Orioles

Age 33 – Bats Right

	Avg	G	AB	R	H	2B	3B	HR	RBI	BB	SO	HBP	GDP	SB	CS	OBP	SLG	IBB	SH	SF	#Pit	#P/PA	GB	FB	G/F
1993 Season	.257	162	641	87	165	26	3	24	90	65	58	6	17	1	4	.329	.420	19	0	6	2428	3.38	263	219	1.20
Last Five Years	.268	809	3174	417	851	159	13	114	453	321	292	26	83	17	11	.337	.434	71	1	35	12395	3.48	1286	1040	1.24

1993 Season

	Avg	AB	H	2B	3B	HR	RBI	BB	SO	OBP	SLG		Avg	AB	H	2B	3B	HR	RBI	BB	SO	OBP	SLG
vs. Left	.282	177	50	7	0	7	31	21	18	.355	.441	Scoring Posn	.262	149	39	8	1	8	66	35	13	.393	.490
vs. Right	.248	464	115	19	3	17	59	44	40	.318	.412	Close & Late	.239	92	22	4	0	4	14	19	8	.374	.413
Groundball	.307	114	35	5	0	4	15	12	7	.369	.456	None on/out	.252	151	38	5	0	9	9	11	13	.302	.464
Flyball	.214	131	28	6	2	3	17	10	13	.283	.359	Batting #3	.239	318	76	15	3	9	39	34	25	.319	.390
Home	.273	311	85	7	1	14	53	40	28	.360	.437	Batting #5	.298	218	65	9	0	10	37	17	27	.350	.477
Away	.242	330	80	19	2	10	37	25	30	.297	.403	Other	.229	105	24	2	0	5	14	14	6	.314	.390
Day	.258	182	47	8	1	7	28	21	15	.337	.429	April	.239	88	21	4	3	2	11	10	8	.316	.420
Night	.257	459	118	18	2	17	62	44	43	.325	.416	May	.200	110	22	5	0	3	11	17	8	.318	.327
Grass	.263	540	142	21	1	23	80	57	49	.337	.433	June	.248	109	27	5	0	4	17	11	9	.320	.404
Turf	.228	101	23	5	2	1	10	8	9	.282	.347	July	.235	98	23	2	0	7	19	13	11	.319	.469
First Pitch	.250	84	21	3	1	5	12	16	0	.373	.488	August	.324	111	36	2	0	7	22	8	8	.366	.532
Ahead in Count	.261	199	52	9	1	9	29	28	0	.348	.452	September/October	.288	125	36	8	0	1	10	6	14	.331	.376
Behind in Count	.259	251	65	9	0	7	33	0	44	.267	.378	Pre-All Star	.229	353	81	16	3	12	45	40	29	.312	.394
Two Strikes	.245	216	53	8	1	4	24	21	58	.320	.347	Post-All Star	.292	288	84	10	0	12	45	25	29	.349	.451

1993 By Position

Position	Avg	AB	H	2B	3B	HR	RBI	BB	SO	OBP	SLG	G	GS	Innings	PO	A	E	DP	Fld Pct	Rng Fctr	In Zone	Outs	Zone Rtg	MLB Zone
As ss	.257	641	165	26	3	24	90	65	58	.329	.420	162	162	1425.1	227	494	17	101	.977	4.55	571	507	.888	.880

Last Five Years

	Avg	AB	H	2B	3B	HR	RBI	BB	SO	OBP	SLG		Avg	AB	H	2B	3B	HR	RBI	BB	SO	OBP	SLG
vs. Left	.270	884	239	48	4	35	121	99	79	.342	.452	Scoring Posn	.261	775	202	39	4	26	317	157	82	.376	.422
vs. Right	.267	2290	612	111	9	79	332	222	213	.335	.427	Close & Late	.273	455	124	28	1	17	63	69	44	.367	.451
Groundball	.275	811	223	40	2	14	95	77	71	.336	.381	None on/out	.263	650	171	28	1	32	32	44	46	.316	.457
Flyball	.256	677	173	41	4	29	109	58	68	.316	.456	Batting #3	.267	2360	631	117	12	87	338	238	217	.336	.438
Home	.252	1550	390	69	5	56	220	166	155	.325	.411	Batting #5	.285	424	121	20	1	16	66	38	49	.347	.450
Away	.284	1624	461	90	8	58	233	155	137	.348	.456	Other	.254	390	99	22	0	11	49	45	26	.330	.395
Day	.273	858	234	34	2	35	121	90	77	.344	.439	April	.266	403	107	22	6	12	67	51	36	.356	.439
Night	.266	2316	617	125	11	79	332	231	215	.334	.432	May	.263	517	136	23	1	21	64	69	40	.352	.433
Grass	.267	2681	716	127	10	102	379	271	255	.336	.436	June	.306	563	172	31	1	19	77	53	44	.367	.465
Turf	.274	493	135	32	3	12	74	50	37	.341	.424	July	.235	523	123	22	0	20	77	59	48	.315	.392
First Pitch	.296	409	121	27	1	22	60	45	0	.370	.528	August	.278	561	156	25	3	22	93	44	59	.327	.451

Last Five Years

	Avg	AB	H	2B	3B	HR	RBI	BB	SO	OBP	SLG		Avg	AB	H	2B	3B	HR	RBI	BB	SO	OBP	SLG
Ahead in Count	.279	858	239	40	2	46	147	152	0	.383	.491	September/October	.259	607	157	36	2	20	75	45	65	.310	.423
Behind in Count	.256	1317	337	57	4	30	166	0	240	.262	.374	Pre-All Star	.272	1668	454	81	8	60	229	188	137	.350	.438
Two Strikes	.228	1162	265	51	8	19	133	112	292	.299	.335	Post-All Star	.264	1506	397	78	5	54	224	133	155	.322	.430

Batter vs. Pitcher (since 1984)

Hits Best Against	Avg	AB	H	2B	3B	HR	RBI	BB	SO	OBP	SLG	Hits Worst Against	Avg	AB	H	2B	3B	HR	RBI	BB	SO	OBP	SLG
Doug Jones	.556	18	10	3	0	1	6	2	2	.600	.889	Bob Wickman	.000	11	0	0	0	0	0	0	2	.000	.000
Scott Aldred	.545	11	6	0	1	2	4	1	1	.583	1.273	Jose DeLeon	.000	10	0	0	0	0	0	3	4	.231	.000
Chuck Crim	.529	17	9	1	0	1	6	1	1	.556	.765	Steve Ontiveros	.000	10	0	0	0	0	0	1	2	.091	.000
David Wells	.409	22	9	2	0	3	6	1	2	.435	.909	Jesse Orosco	.083	12	1	0	0	0	1	0	3	.083	.083
John Candelaria	.400	10	4	1	0	1	2	1	1	.455	.800	Mike Morgan	.091	22	2	0	0	0	0	0	4	.091	.091

Bill Risley — Expos

Age 27 – Pitches Right

	ERA	W	L	Sv	G	GS	IP	BB	SO	Avg	H	2B	3B	HR	RBI	OBP	SLG	GF	IR	IRS	Hld	SvOp	SB	CS	GB	FB	G/F
1993 Season	6.00	0	0	0	2	0	3.0	2	2	.200	2	0	0	1	2	.385	.500	1	0	0	0	0	0	0	2	4	0.50
Career (1992-1993)	3.38	1	0	0	3	1	8.0	3	4	.222	6	1	0	1	3	.323	.370	1	0	0	0	0	2	0	5	10	0.50

1993 Season

	ERA	W	L	Sv	G	GS	IP	H	HR	BB	SO		Avg	AB	H	2B	3B	HR	RBI	BB	SO	OBP	SLG
Home	0.00	0	0	0	1	0	1.0	1	0	1	1	vs. Left	.333	6	2	0	0	1	2	2	2	.500	.833
Away	9.00	0	0	0	1	0	2.0	1	1	1	1	vs. Right	.000	4	0	0	0	0	0	0	0	.200	.000

Ben Rivera — Phillies

Age 25 – Pitches Right

	ERA	W	L	Sv	G	GS	IP	BB	SO	Avg	H	2B	3B	HR	RBI	OBP	SLG	CG	ShO	Sup	QS	#P/S	SB	CS	GB	FB	G/F
1993 Season	5.02	13	9	0	30	28	163.0	85	123	.273	175	19	10	16	83	.361	.409	1	1	6.90	11	101	15	3	218	170	1.28
Career (1992-1993)	4.21	20	13	0	58	42	280.1	130	200	.256	274	37	15	25	125	.340	.388	5	2	6.49	20	100	30	7	377	296	1.27

1993 Season

	ERA	W	L	Sv	G	GS	IP	H	HR	BB	SO		Avg	AB	H	2B	3B	HR	RBI	BB	SO	OBP	SLG
Home	5.74	4	6	0	16	15	80.0	90	8	38	71	vs. Left	.301	316	95	13	6	7	45	43	52	.384	.446
Away	4.34	9	3	0	14	13	83.0	85	8	47	52	vs. Right	.246	325	80	6	4	9	38	42	71	.339	.372
Day	5.02	3	4	0	8	7	43.0	44	9	18	34	Inning 1-6	.271	576	156	17	10	14	79	81	114	.364	.408
Night	5.03	10	5	0	22	21	120.0	131	7	67	89	Inning 7+	.292	65	19	2	0	2	4	4	9	.333	.415
Grass	3.48	6	2	0	8	8	51.2	50	3	31	22	None on	.270	341	92	6	5	9	9	41	72	.352	.396
Turf	5.74	7	7	0	22	20	111.1	125	13	54	101	Runners on	.277	300	83	13	5	7	74	44	51	.371	.423
April	6.55	1	1	0	3	3	11.0	14	2	12	12	Scoring Posn	.222	176	39	6	3	4	63	30	38	.336	.358
May	3.60	2	1	0	5	5	30.0	35	1	18	11	Close & Late	.250	24	6	0	0	1	2	0	3	.250	.375
June	3.69	5	1	0	6	6	39.0	39	3	11	34	None on/out	.261	161	42	3	3	4	4	13	31	.320	.391
July	9.45	1	3	0	4	4	20.0	26	3	14	17	vs. 1st Batr (relief)	.000	1	0	0	0	0	0	1	0	.500	.000
August	4.72	3	1	0	6	5	34.1	35	4	12	23	First Inning Pitched	.284	116	33	4	3	3	20	21	25	.393	.448
September/October	5.02	1	2	0	6	5	28.2	26	3	18	26	First 75 Pitches	.262	454	119	14	8	11	60	60	91	.350	.401
Starter	5.12	13	9	0	28	28	160.0	175	16	83	121	Pitch 76-90	.247	77	19	1	1	4	12	12	16	.356	.442
Reliever	0.00	0	0	0	2	0	3.0	0	0	2	2	Pitch 91-105	.339	59	20	2	0	0	6	10	5	.443	.373
0-3 Days Rest	0.00	1	0	0	1	1	9.0	4	0	4	9	Pitch 106+	.333	51	17	2	1	1	5	3	11	.370	.471
4 Days Rest	4.43	7	4	0	14	14	83.1	89	10	38	66	First Pitch	.344	93	32	4	2	1	12	2	0	.365	.462
5+ Days Rest	6.65	5	5	0	13	13	67.2	82	6	41	46	Ahead in Count	.184	282	52	6	4	2	21	0	106	.189	.255
Pre-All Star	4.91	9	4	0	16	16	88.0	102	8	48	64	Behind in Count	.397	146	58	5	3	7	31	49	0	.545	.616
Post-All Star	5.16	4	5	0	14	12	75.0	73	8	37	59	Two Strikes	.162	309	50	3	3	4	22	34	123	.251	.230

Luis Rivera — Red Sox

Age 30 – Bats Right

	Avg	G	AB	R	H	2B	3B	HR	RBI	BB	SO	HBP	GDP	SB	CS	OBP	SLG	IBB	SH	SF	#Pit	#P/PA	GB	FB	G/F
1993 Season	.208	62	130	13	27	8	1	1	7	11	36	1	2	1	2	.273	.308	0	2	1	555	3.83	29	47	0.62
Last Five Years	.238	504	1501	167	357	78	6	21	150	117	296	9	34	15	15	.296	.340	1	35	7	5936	3.56	462	454	1.02

1993 Season

	Avg	AB	H	2B	3B	HR	RBI	BB	SO	OBP	SLG		Avg	AB	H	2B	3B	HR	RBI	BB	SO	OBP	SLG
vs. Left	.239	46	11	3	0	0	0	3	12	.286	.304	Scoring Posn	.071	28	2	0	0	0	5	3	10	.156	.071
vs. Right	.190	84	16	5	1	1	7	8	24	.266	.310	Close & Late	.111	9	1	0	0	0	0	2	3	.273	.111
Home	.241	54	13	3	0	1	5	3	15	.281	.352	None on/out	.222	36	8	2	0	0	0	3	11	.282	.278
Away	.184	76	14	5	1	0	2	8	21	.267	.276	Batting #8	.188	16	3	1	0	1	3	1	5	.235	.438
First Pitch	.250	16	4	0	0	0	3	0	0	.235	.250	Batting #9	.188	101	19	5	1	0	3	9	28	.259	.257
Ahead in Count	.286	21	6	0	0	1	3	8	0	.483	.429	Other	.385	13	5	2	0	0	1	1	3	.429	.538
Behind in Count	.113	62	7	4	1	0	0	0	28	.127	.210	Pre-All Star	.208	96	20	6	1	0	4	9	23	.280	.292
Two Strikes	.129	70	9	4	0	0	0	3	36	.164	.186	Post-All Star	.206	34	7	2	0	1	3	2	13	.250	.353

Last Five Years

	Avg	AB	H	2B	3B	HR	RBI	BB	SO	OBP	SLG		Avg	AB	H	2B	3B	HR	RBI	BB	SO	OBP	SLG
vs. Left	.238	450	107	26	2	8	50	32	95	.290	.358	Scoring Posn	.224	411	92	18	2	5	126	42	82	.293	.314
vs. Right	.238	1051	250	52	4	13	100	85	201	.298	.332	Close & Late	.176	210	37	10	1	2	14	21	50	.250	.262
Groundball	.255	381	97	18	0	7	49	23	56	.299	.357	None on/out	.220	373	82	19	0	3	3	29	77	.281	.295
Flyball	.207	352	73	16	1	5	32	23	98	.256	.301	Batting #8	.239	322	77	12	1	3	34	21	60	.287	.311
Home	.243	725	176	45	0	13	86	58	133	.303	.359	Batting #9	.239	919	220	45	4	12	81	74	175	.298	.336
Away	.233	776	181	33	6	8	64	59	163	.288	.322	Other	.231	260	60	21	1	6	35	22	61	.296	.388
Day	.259	478	124	32	0	12	62	46	90	.325	.402	April	.204	108	22	6	0	0	4	13	24	.289	.259
Night	.228	1023	233	46	6	9	88	71	206	.281	.311	May	.278	237	66	12	2	4	32	28	40	.354	.397
Grass	.241	1235	298	60	4	19	132	98	253	.300	.343	June	.240	337	81	16	1	3	29	24	67	.300	.320

Last Five Years

	Avg	AB	H	2B	3B	HR	RBI	BB	SO	OBP	SLG		Avg	AB	H	2B	3B	HR	RBI	BB	SO	OBP	SLG
Turf	.222	266	59	18	2	2	18	19	43	.274	.327	July	.241	295	71	22	1	6	28	22	54	.292	.383
First Pitch	.240	246	59	11	1	6	25	0	0	.242	.366	August	.232	259	60	9	1	6	32	14	54	.275	.344
Ahead in Count	.284	345	98	24	1	10	58	53	0	.377	.446	September/October	.215	265	57	13	1	2	25	16	57	.261	.294
Behind in Count	.204	653	133	21	4	5	44	0	253	.212	.271	Pre-All Star	.246	772	190	40	3	8	74	73	145	.315	.337
Two Strikes	.190	647	123	26	3	4	49	64	296	.267	.258	Post-All Star	.229	729	167	38	3	13	76	44	151	.274	.343

Batter vs. Pitcher (career)

Hits Best Against	Avg	AB	H	2B	3B	HR	RBI	BB	SO	OBP	SLG	Hits Worst Against	Avg	AB	H	2B	3B	HR	RBI	BB	SO	OBP	SLG
Tim Leary	.615	13	8	2	0	1	3	1	0	.643	1.000	Nolan Ryan	.000	12	0	0	0	0	1	0	6	.000	.000
Kenny Rogers	.500	12	6	3	1	0	3	0	2	.500	.917	Sid Fernandez	.000	12	0	0	0	0	0	2	3	.143	.000
Jaime Navarro	.462	13	6	0	0	1	4	1	0	.500	.692	Jim Deshaies	.000	12	0	0	0	0	0	0	5	.000	.000
Bruce Ruffin	.429	14	6	1	0	0	2	1	0	.467	.500	Chuck Cary	.000	12	0	0	0	0	0	1	4	.077	.000
Randy Johnson	.400	10	4	1	0	0	2	4	4	.571	.500	Kevin Tapani	.000	11	0	0	0	0	0	0	3	.000	.000

Kevin Roberson — Cubs

Age 26 – Bats Both (flyball hitter)

	Avg	G	AB	R	H	2B	3B	HR	RBI	BB	SO	HBP	GDP	SB	CS	OBP	SLG	IBB	SH	SF	#Pit	#P/PA	GB	FB	G/F
1993 Season	.189	62	180	23	34	4	1	9	27	12	48	3	2	0	1	.251	.372	0	0	0	702	3.60	48	58	0.83

1993 Season

	Avg	AB	H	2B	3B	HR	RBI	BB	SO	OBP	SLG		Avg	AB	H	2B	3B	HR	RBI	BB	SO	OBP	SLG
vs. Left	.156	64	10	1	0	2	6	1	14	.169	.266	Scoring Posn	.200	45	9	1	1	3	17	1	14	.234	.467
vs. Right	.207	116	24	3	1	7	21	11	34	.292	.431	Close & Late	.216	37	8	1	1	4	10	3	7	.293	.622
Home	.159	88	14	1	0	4	11	8	26	.245	.307	None on/out	.086	35	3	1	0	0	0	3	9	.179	.114
Away	.217	92	20	3	1	5	16	4	22	.258	.435	Batting #7	.194	98	19	2	0	6	13	6	21	.262	.398
First Pitch	.250	36	9	2	0	1	2	0	0	.270	.389	Batting #8	.260	50	13	1	0	3	10	2	16	.288	.460
Ahead in Count	.235	34	8	1	0	3	7	8	0	.381	.529	Other	.063	32	2	1	1	0	4	4	11	.167	.156
Behind in Count	.175	80	14	1	1	5	18	0	38	.185	.400	Pre-All Star	.000	0	0	0	0	0	0	0	0	.000	.000
Two Strikes	.135	89	12	1	1	4	16	4	48	.181	.303	Post-All Star	.189	180	34	4	1	9	27	12	48	.251	.372

Bip Roberts — Reds

Age 30 – Bats Both (groundball hitter)

	Avg	G	AB	R	H	2B	3B	HR	RBI	BB	SO	HBP	GDP	SB	CS	OBP	SLG	IBB	SH	SF	#Pit	#P/PA	GB	FB	G/F
1993 Season	.240	83	292	46	70	13	0	1	18	38	46	3	2	26	6	.330	.295	1	0	3	1281	3.81	124	65	1.91
Last Five Years	.296	613	2133	389	632	111	20	20	164	241	281	16	26	163	56	.369	.395	6	19	16	9008	3.71	957	435	2.20

1993 Season

	Avg	AB	H	2B	3B	HR	RBI	BB	SO	OBP	SLG		Avg	AB	H	2B	3B	HR	RBI	BB	SO	OBP	SLG
vs. Left	.179	84	15	5	0	0	5	8	10	.258	.238	Scoring Posn	.181	72	13	2	0	1	17	5	10	.235	.250
vs. Right	.264	208	55	8	0	1	13	30	36	.358	.317	Close & Late	.171	41	7	1	0	0	2	9	6	.327	.195
Groundball	.256	117	30	8	0	0	8	16	17	.341	.325	None on/out	.294	109	32	6	0	0	0	14	17	.374	.349
Flyball	.122	49	6	0	0	1	6	4	9	.185	.184	Batting #1	.233	249	58	10	0	1	16	35	42	.329	.285
Home	.221	140	31	4	0	0	12	17	21	.313	.250	Batting #2	.324	37	12	3	0	0	2	1	1	.359	.405
Away	.257	152	39	9	0	1	6	21	25	.347	.336	Other	.000	6	0	0	0	0	0	2	3	.250	.000
Day	.222	90	20	2	0	1	10	9	12	.290	.278	April	.169	77	13	2	0	1	6	10	13	.261	.234
Night	.248	202	50	11	0	0	8	29	34	.347	.302	May	.305	82	25	2	0	0	8	15	13	.422	.329
Grass	.255	94	24	3	0	1	4	12	14	.340	.319	June	.267	101	27	8	0	0	4	7	8	.315	.347
Turf	.232	198	46	10	0	0	14	26	32	.326	.283	July	.179	28	5	1	0	0	0	6	11	.324	.214
First Pitch	.321	53	17	2	0	1	9	1	0	.327	.415	August	.000	4	0	0	0	0	0	0	1	.000	.000
Ahead in Count	.261	69	18	6	0	0	3	26	0	.463	.348	September/October	.000	0	0	0	0	0	0	0	0	.000	.000
Behind in Count	.192	120	23	3	0	0	5	0	38	.208	.217	Pre-All Star	.249	261	65	12	0	1	18	32	34	.334	.307
Two Strikes	.163	135	22	3	0	0	4	11	46	.238	.185	Post-All Star	.161	31	5	1	0	0	0	6	12	.297	.194

1993 By Position

Position	Avg	AB	H	2B	3B	HR	RBI	BB	SO	OBP	SLG	G	GS	Innings	PO	A	E	DP	Fld Pct	Rng Fctr	In Zone	Outs	Zone Rtg	MLB Zone
As 2b	.249	257	64	12	0	1	18	32	36	.336	.307	65	63	525.1	137	173	5	31	.984	5.31	194	174	.897	.895
As lf	.150	20	3	1	0	0	0	2	4	.227	.200	12	5	47.2	12	0	1	0	.923	2.27	20	12	.600	.818

Last Five Years

	Avg	AB	H	2B	3B	HR	RBI	BB	SO	OBP	SLG		Avg	AB	H	2B	3B	HR	RBI	BB	SO	OBP	SLG
vs. Left	.278	726	202	37	5	10	57	61	87	.339	.384	Scoring Posn	.283	406	115	28	5	8	141	41	52	.343	.436
vs. Right	.306	1407	430	74	15	10	107	180	194	.385	.401	Close & Late	.275	335	92	10	3	3	32	41	52	.358	.349
Groundball	.313	793	248	45	8	6	64	84	94	.377	.412	None on/out	.305	924	282	46	9	7	7	103	128	.379	.397
Flyball	.293	457	134	20	4	6	36	53	70	.369	.394	Batting #1	.297	1963	583	105	17	18	150	220	257	.369	.395
Home	.295	1061	313	51	10	12	84	105	134	.362	.396	Batting #2	.310	87	27	4	2	1	6	10	8	.388	.437
Away	.298	1072	319	60	10	8	80	136	147	.377	.395	Other	.265	83	22	2	1	1	8	11	16	.351	.349
Day	.303	624	189	28	5	9	53	79	94	.385	.407	April	.238	315	75	11	5	3	23	36	40	.317	.333
Night	.294	1509	443	83	15	11	111	162	187	.363	.390	May	.307	398	122	19	5	2	33	56	57	.395	.394
Grass	.287	1237	355	47	13	13	89	120	160	.353	.378	June	.289	433	125	27	4	1	28	36	60	.349	.376
Turf	.309	896	277	64	7	7	75	121	121	.392	.420	July	.277	314	87	13	1	2	26	43	48	.363	.344
First Pitch	.371	340	126	21	4	6	42	6	0	.377	.509	August	.313	335	105	22	2	7	24	31	45	.369	.454
Ahead in Count	.347	392	136	34	5	4	43	168	0	.542	.490	September/October	.349	338	118	19	3	5	30	39	31	.418	.467
Behind in Count	.252	986	248	36	6	6	49	0	243	.259	.318	Pre-All Star	.277	1235	342	58	15	6	89	144	171	.356	.363
Two Strikes	.232	957	222	33	9	7	44	66	281	.287	.307	Post-All Star	.323	898	290	53	5	14	75	97	110	.388	.440

Batter vs. Pitcher (career)

Hits Best Against	Avg	AB	H	2B	3B	HR	RBI	BB	SO	OBP	SLG	Hits Worst Against	Avg	AB	H	2B	3B	HR	RBI	BB	SO	OBP	SLG
Brian Williams	.556	9	5	0	0	0	0	3	1	.667	.556	Wally Whitehurst	.000	12	0	0	0	0	1	0	3	.000	.000
Gil Heredia	.538	13	7	3	0	0	3	0	1	.538	.769	Rick Honeycutt	.000	11	0	0	0	0	0	1	2	.083	.000

Batter vs. Pitcher (career)																						
Hits Best Against	Avg	AB	H	2B	3B	HR	RBI	BB	SO	OBP	SLG	Hits Worst Against	Avg	AB	H	2B	3B	HR	RBI	BB	SO	OBP	SLG
Greg Maddux	.480	25	12	3	0	0	3	7	4	.594	.600	Tim Belcher	.067	15	1	0	0	0	0	2	2	.176	.067
John Smoltz	.406	32	13	2	1	0	1	10	3	.548	.531	Scott Scudder	.083	12	1	0	0	0	1	0	2	.083	.083
Jose DeLeon	.400	10	4	0	0	1	3	3	2	.500	.700	Pete Schourek	.125	16	2	0	0	0	1	0	0	.125	.125

Rich Robertson — Pirates

Age 25 – Pitches Left

	ERA	W	L	Sv	G	GS	IP	BB	SO	Avg	H	2B	3B	HR	RBI	OBP	SLG	GF	IR	IRS	Hld	SvOp	SB	CS	GB	FB	G/F
1993 Season	6.00	0	1	0	9	0	9.0	4	5	.385	15	3	0	0	4	.442	.462	2	2	1	0	1	1	0	17	7	2.43

1993 Season																						
	ERA	W	L	Sv	G	GS	IP	H	HR	BB	SO		Avg	AB	H	2B	3B	HR	RBI	BB	SO	OBP	SLG
Home	9.00	0	1	0	4	0	5.0	8	0	3	2	vs. Left	.333	15	5	0	0	0	2	3	4	.444	.333
Away	2.25	0	0	0	5	0	4.0	7	0	1	3	vs. Right	.417	24	10	3	0	0	2	1	1	.440	.542

Henry Rodriguez — Dodgers

Age 26 – Bats Left (flyball hitter)

	Avg	G	AB	R	H	2B	3B	HR	RBI	BB	SO	HBP	GDP	SB	CS	OBP	SLG	IBB	SH	SF	#Pit	#P/PA	GB	FB	G/F
1993 Season	.222	76	176	20	39	10	0	8	23	11	39	0	1	1	0	.266	.415	2	0	1	675	3.59	46	69	0.67
Career (1992-1993)	.220	129	322	31	71	17	0	11	37	19	69	0	3	1	0	.262	.376	2	1	2	1233	3.58	86	119	0.72

1993 Season																						
	Avg	AB	H	2B	3B	HR	RBI	BB	SO	OBP	SLG		Avg	AB	H	2B	3B	HR	RBI	BB	SO	OBP	SLG
vs. Left	.000	6	0	0	0	0	0	0	3	.000	.000	Scoring Posn	.184	49	9	1	0	3	15	4	11	.241	.388
vs. Right	.229	170	39	10	0	8	23	11	36	.275	.429	Close & Late	.211	38	8	3	0	0	1	1	8	.231	.289
Home	.237	97	23	5	0	5	14	7	24	.288	.443	None on/out	.256	43	11	6	0	1	1	3	12	.304	.465
Away	.203	79	16	5	0	3	9	4	15	.238	.380	Batting #6	.132	53	7	2	0	1	3	6	16	.220	.226
First Pitch	.267	30	8	4	0	2	4	2	0	.313	.600	Batting #7	.218	55	12	2	0	3	9	3	9	.259	.418
Ahead in Count	.250	36	9	1	0	5	12	7	0	.372	.694	Other	.294	68	20	6	0	4	11	2	14	.310	.559
Behind in Count	.200	85	17	3	0	1	7	0	31	.198	.271	Pre-All Star	.211	38	8	2	0	1	4	1	10	.231	.342
Two Strikes	.181	83	15	4	0	1	6	2	39	.200	.265	Post-All Star	.225	138	31	8	0	7	19	10	29	.275	.435

Ivan Rodriguez — Rangers

Age 22 – Bats Right (groundball hitter)

	Avg	G	AB	R	H	2B	3B	HR	RBI	BB	SO	HBP	GDP	SB	CS	OBP	SLG	IBB	SH	SF	#Pit	#P/PA	GB	FB	G/F
1993 Season	.273	137	473	56	129	28	4	10	66	29	70	4	16	8	7	.315	.412	3	5	8	1745	3.36	182	133	1.37
Career (1991-1993)	.266	348	1173	119	312	60	5	21	130	58	185	5	41	8	8	.301	.379	5	14	11	4270	3.39	472	304	1.55

1993 Season																						
	Avg	AB	H	2B	3B	HR	RBI	BB	SO	OBP	SLG		Avg	AB	H	2B	3B	HR	RBI	BB	SO	OBP	SLG
vs. Left	.278	108	30	6	0	2	16	9	18	.325	.389	Scoring Posn	.270	126	34	8	0	3	52	10	24	.324	.405
vs. Right	.271	365	99	22	4	8	50	20	52	.312	.419	Close & Late	.318	66	21	1	2	1	10	3	11	.343	.439
Groundball	.293	92	27	5	1	0	10	5	16	.330	.370	None on/out	.317	104	33	10	2	2	2	4	12	.343	.510
Flyball	.242	95	23	8	0	3	11	3	20	.263	.421	Batting #6	.245	196	48	12	0	5	28	14	27	.294	.383
Home	.244	242	59	15	3	7	36	15	36	.286	.417	Batting #7	.295	139	41	10	1	3	30	13	24	.350	.446
Away	.303	231	70	13	1	3	30	14	34	.345	.407	Other	.290	138	40	6	3	2	8	2	19	.308	.420
Day	.382	110	42	7	1	2	18	6	12	.412	.518	April	.349	63	22	6	0	1	19	8	9	.425	.492
Night	.240	363	87	21	3	8	48	23	58	.286	.380	May	.303	99	30	6	3	0	7	2	12	.320	.424
Grass	.266	402	107	24	4	8	58	24	60	.308	.405	June	.216	74	16	2	0	3	9	3	13	.244	.365
Turf	.310	71	22	4	0	2	8	5	10	.355	.451	July	.269	67	18	4	0	2	8	7	10	.342	.418
First Pitch	.307	88	27	6	0	5	24	2	0	.323	.545	August	.279	86	24	9	0	3	17	5	8	.312	.488
Ahead in Count	.375	96	36	8	3	2	11	10	0	.426	.583	September/October	.226	84	19	1	1	1	6	4	18	.264	.298
Behind in Count	.204	226	46	11	0	1	18	0	58	.208	.265	Pre-All Star	.272	265	72	14	3	5	39	16	39	.316	.404
Two Strikes	.177	198	35	7	0	1	17	17	70	.245	.227	Post-All Star	.274	208	57	14	1	5	27	13	31	.314	.423

1993 By Position																								
Position	Avg	AB	H	2B	3B	HR	RBI	BB	SO	OBP	SLG	G	GS	Innings	PO	A	E	DP	Fld Pct	Rng Fctr	In Zone	Outs	Zone Rtg	MLB Zone
As c	.272	464	126	28	4	10	64	29	68	.315	.414	134	130	1116.2	800	74	8	7	.991	---	---	---	---	---

Career (1991-1993)																						
	Avg	AB	H	2B	3B	HR	RBI	BB	SO	OBP	SLG		Avg	AB	H	2B	3B	HR	RBI	BB	SO	OBP	SLG
vs. Left	.268	284	76	16	0	5	34	18	41	.307	.377	Scoring Posn	.269	279	75	14	0	6	103	21	54	.317	.384
vs. Right	.265	889	236	44	5	16	96	40	144	.299	.380	Close & Late	.297	195	58	2	2	2	20	11	31	.332	.359
Groundball	.244	262	64	13	1	2	30	9	33	.272	.324	None on/out	.300	257	77	16	2	6	6	11	27	.331	.447
Flyball	.242	273	66	17	1	7	23	15	64	.279	.388	Batting #7	.269	416	112	21	2	9	56	31	70	.318	.394
Home	.240	588	141	29	4	14	73	27	104	.272	.374	Batting #8	.284	278	79	14	0	3	22	4	42	.293	.367
Away	.292	585	171	31	1	7	57	31	81	.329	.385	Other	.253	479	121	25	3	9	52	23	73	.290	.374
Day	.316	231	73	14	1	4	29	12	30	.350	.437	April	.331	133	44	11	0	2	27	11	18	.385	.459
Night	.254	942	239	46	4	17	101	46	155	.289	.365	May	.280	182	51	6	3	4	20	7	31	.307	.412
Grass	.263	975	256	49	5	17	111	44	157	.294	.375	June	.269	130	35	5	0	5	17	6	21	.297	.423
Turf	.283	198	56	11	0	4	19	14	28	.332	.399	July	.259	224	58	12	1	3	18	14	33	.304	.362
First Pitch	.359	195	70	13	0	7	35	3	0	.371	.533	August	.258	260	67	18	0	4	31	9	36	.280	.373
Ahead in Count	.330	230	76	15	4	4	27	23	0	.387	.483	September/October	.234	244	57	8	1	3	17	11	46	.267	.311
Behind in Count	.213	574	122	24	0	6	50	0	161	.213	.286	Pre-All Star	.285	537	153	25	4	13	76	30	84	.324	.419
Two Strikes	.175	497	87	15	0	6	44	32	185	.226	.241	Post-All Star	.250	636	159	35	1	8	54	28	101	.281	.346

Batter vs. Pitcher (career)																						
Hits Best Against	Avg	AB	H	2B	3B	HR	RBI	BB	SO	OBP	SLG	Hits Worst Against	Avg	AB	H	2B	3B	HR	RBI	BB	SO	OBP	SLG
Ben McDonald	.545	11	6	3	0	0	2	1	2	.583	.818	Mike Moore	.063	16	1	1	0	0	0	1	2	.118	.125
Alex Fernandez	.471	17	8	1	0	0	0	2	1	.526	.529	Randy Johnson	.077	13	1	1	0	0	0	2	3	.200	.154

Batter vs. Pitcher (career)																						
Hits Best Against	Avg	AB	H	2B	3B	HR	RBI	BB	SO	OBP	SLG	Hits Worst Against	Avg	AB	H	2B	3B	HR	RBI	BB	SO	OBP	SLG
Dave Stewart	.438	16	7	1	0	1	3	0	3	.438	.688	Mark Langston	.176	17	3	0	0	0	2	0	6	.176	.176
Jimmy Key	.417	12	5	0	0	1	3	0	1	.417	.667	Kevin Appier	.182	11	2	0	0	0	0	0	3	.182	.182
Bill Wegman	.308	13	4	1	1	1	4	1	2	.357	.769	Kevin Tapani	.182	11	2	0	0	0	0	0	0	.182	.182

Rich Rodriguez — Marlins

Age 31 – Pitches Left (groundball pitcher)

	ERA	W	L	Sv	G	GS	IP	BB	SO	Avg	H	2B	3B	HR	RBI	OBP	SLG	GF	IR	IRS	Hld	SvOp	SB	CS	GB	FB	G/F
1993 Season	3.79	2	4	3	70	0	76.0	33	43	.251	73	10	1	10	40	.331	.395	21	51	14	10	7	5	2	107	82	1.30
Career (1990-1993)	3.05	12	9	4	227	2	294.2	122	169	.246	268	45	3	24	129	.322	.359	70	163	44	26	11	21	13	426	260	1.64

1993 Season

	ERA	W	L	Sv	G	GS	IP	H	HR	BB	SO		Avg	AB	H	2B	3B	HR	RBI	BB	SO	OBP	SLG
Home	3.50	2	1	2	34	0	36.0	37	4	16	22	vs. Left	.263	99	26	3	1	3	13	12	7	.348	.404
Away	4.05	0	3	1	36	0	40.0	36	6	17	21	vs. Right	.245	192	47	7	0	7	27	21	36	.322	.391
Day	1.06	0	0	1	18	0	17.0	9	1	7	14	Inning 1-6	.237	38	9	0	0	2	11	6	5	.341	.395
Night	4.58	2	4	2	52	0	59.0	64	9	26	29	Inning 7+	.253	253	64	10	1	8	29	27	38	.330	.395
Grass	3.40	2	1	2	52	0	53.0	52	8	23	30	None on	.234	158	37	5	1	4	4	16	25	.309	.354
Turf	4.70	0	3	1	18	0	23.0	21	2	10	13	Runners on	.271	133	36	5	0	6	36	17	18	.358	.444
April	3.09	1	0	2	13	0	11.2	11	0	6	10	Scoring Posn	.271	85	23	3	0	4	30	14	9	.380	.447
May	7.56	1	3	0	12	0	8.1	14	2	1	4	Close & Late	.276	116	32	3	0	5	16	16	12	.368	.431
June	1.54	0	0	0	11	0	11.2	12	1	2	8	None on/out	.268	71	19	2	1	2	2	7	15	.333	.408
July	6.00	0	0	0	9	0	9.0	10	3	3	4	vs. 1st Batr (relief)	.266	64	17	1	1	4	10	6	13	.329	.500
August	3.15	0	0	0	13	0	20.0	11	2	15	8	First Inning Pitched	.279	208	58	7	1	8	34	27	33	.367	.438
September/October	3.52	0	1	1	12	0	15.1	15	2	6	9	First 15 Pitches	.280	207	58	8	1	8	32	18	29	.341	.444
Starter	0.00	0	0	0	0	0	0.0	0	0	0	0	Pitch 16-30	.138	65	9	1	0	2	3	12	12	.282	.246
Reliever	3.79	2	4	3	70	0	76.0	73	10	33	43	Pitch 31-45	.278	18	5	1	0	0	5	3	2	.381	.333
0 Days rest	5.23	1	0	1	12	0	10.1	8	3	9	0	Pitch 46+	1.000	1	1	0	0	0	0	0	0	1.000	1.000
1 or 2 Days rest	3.26	1	3	2	42	0	47.0	46	4	20	32	First Pitch	.300	40	12	1	1	3	7	7	0	.417	.600
3+ Days rest	4.34	0	1	0	16	0	18.2	19	3	4	11	Ahead in Count	.198	126	25	2	0	2	10	0	37	.198	.262
Pre-All Star	3.89	2	3	2	40	0	37.0	42	6	10	23	Behind in Count	.318	66	21	6	0	5	18	12	0	.423	.636
Post-All Star	3.69	0	1	1	30	0	39.0	31	4	23	20	Two Strikes	.207	121	25	2	0	2	12	14	43	.289	.273

Career (1990-1993)

	ERA	W	L	Sv	G	GS	IP	H	HR	BB	SO		Avg	AB	H	2B	3B	HR	RBI	BB	SO	OBP	SLG
Home	3.07	8	3	2	118	0	152.2	147	10	67	95	vs. Left	.239	364	87	12	1	8	45	46	53	.325	.343
Away	3.04	4	6	2	109	2	142.0	121	14	55	74	vs. Right	.249	726	181	33	2	16	84	76	116	.321	.366
Day	2.50	3	2	1	60	0	79.1	66	5	35	60	Inning 1-6	.230	304	70	14	2	8	42	25	49	.290	.368
Night	3.26	9	7	3	167	2	215.1	202	19	87	109	Inning 7+	.252	786	198	31	1	16	87	97	120	.334	.355
Grass	3.03	8	3	3	165	1	214.0	196	17	87	124	None on	.242	578	140	21	2	14	14	59	102	.315	.358
Turf	3.12	4	6	1	62	1	80.2	72	7	35	45	Runners on	.250	512	128	24	1	10	115	63	67	.330	.359
April	2.98	2	1	2	32	0	45.1	45	3	23	23	Scoring Posn	.245	314	77	16	1	6	103	55	38	.355	.360
May	2.36	5	4	0	33	1	42.0	35	4	14	20	Close & Late	.234	312	73	7	0	9	35	49	41	.339	.343
June	4.10	0	1	0	31	1	37.1	39	4	19	23	None on/out	.250	260	65	6	2	7	7	20	51	.304	.369
July	3.13	2	0	0	41	0	54.2	49	3	20	33	vs. 1st Batr (relief)	.259	205	53	8	2	6	30	18	31	.317	.405
August	3.11	2	0	0	44	0	55.0	43	5	25	30	First Inning Pitched	.245	681	167	28	3	11	93	87	108	.331	.344
September/October	2.83	1	3	2	46	0	60.1	57	5	21	40	First 15 Pitches	.249	679	169	28	3	13	78	72	100	.321	.356
Starter	3.00	0	1	0	2	2	9.0	7	1	4	6	Pitch 16-30	.231	286	66	11	0	10	36	41	48	.328	.374
Reliever	3.06	12	8	4	225	0	285.2	261	23	118	163	Pitch 31-45	.261	92	24	5	0	1	12	6	16	.306	.348
0 Days rest	3.67	4	1	1	50	0	61.1	44	7	29	28	Pitch 46+	.273	33	9	1	0	0	3	3	5	.333	.303
1 or 2 Days rest	3.05	4	6	2	113	0	138.2	142	10	58	84	First Pitch	.277	148	41	10	2	5	23	20	0	.363	.473
3+ Days rest	2.63	4	1	1	62	0	85.2	75	6	31	51	Ahead in Count	.179	476	85	10	0	4	33	0	146	.180	.225
Pre-All Star	3.03	8	6	2	111	2	148.1	139	14	66	78	Behind in Count	.323	263	85	17	1	14	55	62	0	.450	.555
Post-All Star	3.08	4	3	2	116	0	146.1	129	10	56	91	Two Strikes	.183	470	86	9	0	5	34	39	169	.246	.234

Pitcher vs. Batter (career)

Pitches Best Vs.	Avg	AB	H	2B	3B	HR	RBI	BB	SO	OBP	SLG	Pitches Worst Vs.	Avg	AB	H	2B	3B	HR	RBI	BB	SO	OBP	SLG
Steve Finley	.000	10	0	0	0	0	0	1	1	.091	.000	Craig Biggio	.545	11	6	3	0	0	2	3	0	.643	.818
John Kruk	.000	9	0	0	0	0	0	2	1	.182	.000	Lenny Dykstra	.500	8	4	0	0	1	3	3	1	.636	.875
Jay Bell	.071	14	1	0	0	0	0	0	5	.071	.071	Brett Butler	.467	15	7	0	0	0	0	3	0	.556	.467
Jeff Bagwell	.100	10	1	0	0	0	0	2	4	.250	.100	Mike Sharperson	.417	12	5	1	0	1	1	0	2	.417	.750
Will Clark	.167	12	2	0	0	0	3	1	2	.231	.167	Jeff Blauser	.333	12	4	3	0	0	1	2	0	.429	.583

Kenny Rogers — Rangers

Age 29 – Pitches Left

	ERA	W	L	Sv	G	GS	IP	BB	SO	Avg	H	2B	3B	HR	RBI	OBP	SLG	CG	ShO	Sup	QS	#P/S	SB	CS	GB	FB	G/F
1993 Season	4.10	16	10	0	35	33	208.1	71	140	.263	210	46	7	18	91	.325	.406	5	0	6.09	22	99	4	11	270	239	1.13
Career (1989-1993)	3.90	42	36	28	321	45	568.0	242	420	.260	564	119	14	47	290	.336	.393	5	0	4.75	25	96	16	24	724	636	1.14

1993 Season

	ERA	W	L	Sv	G	GS	IP	H	HR	BB	SO		Avg	AB	H	2B	3B	HR	RBI	BB	SO	OBP	SLG
Home	5.00	9	4	0	17	16	93.2	100	8	32	64	vs. Left	.222	90	20	6	2	0	6	5	20	.271	.333
Away	3.38	7	6	0	18	17	114.2	110	10	39	76	vs. Right	.268	708	190	40	5	18	85	66	120	.331	.415
Day	7.97	1	1	0	4	4	20.1	26	5	8	16	Inning 1-6	.269	677	182	38	7	16	84	65	115	.334	.417
Night	3.69	15	9	0	31	29	188.0	184	13	63	124	Inning 7+	.231	121	28	8	0	2	7	6	25	.268	.347
Grass	4.52	14	9	0	31	29	177.1	182	16	64	119	None on	.234	483	113	27	3	12	12	36	88	.291	.377
Turf	1.74	2	1	0	4	4	31.0	28	2	7	21	Runners on	.308	315	97	19	4	6	79	35	52	.374	.451
April	2.51	2	1	0	6	4	28.2	15	1	11	21	Scoring Posn	.277	191	53	9	1	6	72	24	37	.353	.429
May	11.17	1	3	0	5	5	19.1	32	3	13	16	Close & Late	.179	39	7	0	0	0	2	2	8	.220	.179

1993 Season

	ERA	W	L	Sv	G	GS	IP	H	HR	BB	SO
June	4.97	2	2	0	6	6	38.0	42	1	15	27
July	3.16	3	0	0	5	5	31.1	37	3	8	23
August	3.19	6	1	0	7	7	48.0	43	5	16	29
September/October	2.93	2	3	0	6	6	43.0	41	5	8	24
Starter	4.14	16	10	0	33	33	206.2	210	18	71	138
Reliever	0.00	0	0	0	2	0	1.2	0	0	0	2
0-3 Days Rest	2.41	4	1	0	5	5	41.0	30	4	6	25
4 Days Rest	4.20	9	4	0	18	18	109.1	115	11	38	69
5+ Days Rest	5.27	3	5	0	10	10	56.1	65	3	27	44
Pre-All Star	5.24	6	6	0	19	17	99.2	102	8	42	78
Post-All Star	3.06	10	4	0	16	16	108.2	108	10	29	62

	Avg	AB	H	2B	3B	HR	RBI	BB	SO	OBP	SLG
None on/out	.250	208	52	13	1	7	7	19	31	.316	.423
vs. 1st Batr (relief)	.000	2	0	0	0	0	0	0	1	.000	.000
First Inning Pitched	.295	139	41	8	1	2	17	13	27	.351	.410
First 75 Pitches	.276	584	161	37	5	13	72	59	95	.344	.423
Pitch 76-90	.190	100	19	4	1	2	8	4	20	.219	.310
Pitch 91-105	.276	76	21	2	1	3	9	6	12	.329	.447
Pitch 106+	.237	38	9	3	0	0	2	2	13	.275	.316
First Pitch	.360	111	40	8	0	1	14	2	0	.368	.459
Ahead in Count	.163	344	56	12	1	2	22	0	117	.168	.221
Behind in Count	.330	215	71	14	4	10	36	36	0	.426	.572
Two Strikes	.187	342	64	18	3	2	29	33	140	.263	.275

Career (1989-1993)

	ERA	W	L	Sv	G	GS	IP	H	HR	BB	SO
Home	4.03	28	17	14	170	20	283.1	285	19	124	209
Away	3.76	14	19	14	151	25	284.2	279	28	118	211
Day	5.09	4	6	7	52	7	81.1	93	12	40	65
Night	3.70	38	30	21	269	38	486.2	471	35	202	355
Grass	4.02	37	30	26	270	38	479.1	473	40	210	360
Turf	3.25	5	6	2	51	7	88.2	91	7	32	60
April	4.42	4	5	2	36	8	71.1	69	6	31	52
May	5.50	7	6	1	54	10	103.0	120	11	59	76
June	4.76	3	8	8	54	7	96.1	109	8	44	70
July	3.20	7	3	8	56	5	84.1	82	8	29	78
August	3.01	11	5	3	64	7	107.2	93	7	42	75
September/October	2.65	10	9	6	57	8	105.1	91	7	37	69
Starter	4.58	21	16	0	45	45	265.0	291	25	107	168
Reliever	3.30	21	20	28	276	0	303.0	273	22	135	252
0-3 Days Rest	3.61	5	2	0	8	8	52.1	49	7	18	30
4 Days Rest	4.33	10	5	0	20	20	120.2	133	12	42	73
5+ Days Rest	5.48	6	9	0	17	17	92.0	109	6	47	65
Pre-All Star	4.86	17	21	13	161	27	298.1	329	31	145	222
Post-All Star	2.84	25	15	15	160	18	269.2	235	16	97	198

	Avg	AB	H	2B	3B	HR	RBI	BB	SO	OBP	SLG
vs. Left	.221	457	101	25	3	5	55	43	101	.297	.322
vs. Right	.271	1710	463	94	11	42	235	199	319	.346	.412
Inning 1-6	.283	964	273	56	10	23	131	108	157	.357	.434
Inning 7+	.242	1203	291	63	4	24	159	134	263	.320	.361
None on	.246	1132	279	60	7	25	25	103	221	.313	.378
Runners on	.275	1035	285	59	7	22	265	139	199	.361	.410
Scoring Posn	.270	640	173	34	3	20	252	105	134	.371	.427
Close & Late	.243	614	149	35	2	11	84	72	131	.324	.360
None on/out	.245	489	120	25	2	9	9	48	83	.315	.360
vs. 1st Batr (relief)	.246	240	59	9	1	2	33	25	59	.317	.317
First Inning Pitched	.250	980	245	49	6	19	156	121	217	.334	.370
First 75 Pitches	.260	1893	493	105	12	40	262	226	368	.341	.392
Pitch 76-90	.254	134	34	6	1	3	15	7	25	.289	.381
Pitch 91-105	.264	91	24	4	1	3	9	7	13	.316	.429
Pitch 106+	.265	49	13	4	0	1	4	2	14	.294	.408
First Pitch	.342	284	97	20	0	7	52	28	0	.396	.486
Ahead in Count	.184	957	176	39	5	9	87	0	345	.191	.263
Behind in Count	.343	534	183	30	7	22	100	118	0	.459	.549
Two Strikes	.181	997	180	46	7	10	87	96	420	.257	.271

Pitcher vs. Batter (career)

Pitches Best Vs.	Avg	AB	H	2B	3B	HR	RBI	BB	SO	OBP	SLG
Luis Polonia	.000	14	0	0	0	0	0	1	3	.067	.000
Gary DiSarcina	.000	11	0	0	0	0	0	0	0	.000	.000
Gary Thurman	.000	9	0	0	0	0	1	2	3	.167	.000
Mike Greenwell	.063	16	1	1	0	0	0	0	3	.063	.125
Ozzie Guillen	.071	14	1	0	0	0	2	0	0	.071	.071

Pitches Worst Vs.	Avg	AB	H	2B	3B	HR	RBI	BB	SO	OBP	SLG
Kirby Puckett	.545	11	6	2	0	2	3	3	1	.643	1.273
Luis Rivera	.500	12	6	3	1	0	3	0	2	.500	.917
Craig Grebeck	.500	10	5	1	0	2	7	2	2	.583	1.200
Bo Jackson	.400	10	4	0	0	2	5	3	2	.538	1.000
Mark McGwire	.375	8	3	1	0	1	6	3	3	.545	.875

Kevin Rogers — Giants

Age 25 – Pitches Left

	ERA	W	L	Sv	G	GS	IP	BB	SO	Avg	H	2B	3B	HR	RBI	OBP	SLG	GF	IR	IRS	Hld	SvOp	SB	CS	GB	FB	G/F
1993 Season	2.68	2	2	0	64	0	80.2	28	62	.236	71	10	0	3	25	.308	.299	24	41	11	17	2	6	2	110	80	1.38
Career (1992-1993)	3.14	2	4	0	70	6	114.2	41	88	.249	108	12	0	7	39	.321	.326	24	41	11	17	2	7	4	149	125	1.19

1993 Season

	ERA	W	L	Sv	G	GS	IP	H	HR	BB	SO
Home	2.55	1	0	0	30	0	42.1	37	2	18	32
Away	2.82	1	2	0	34	0	38.1	34	1	10	30
Day	2.49	2	1	0	37	0	47.0	44	2	16	36
Night	2.94	0	1	0	27	0	33.2	27	1	12	26
Grass	2.18	2	1	0	50	0	66.0	57	2	22	52
Turf	4.91	0	1	0	14	0	14.2	14	1	6	10
April	4.67	0	1	0	10	0	17.1	15	2	15	12
May	0.60	0	0	0	11	0	15.0	10	0	0	14
June	2.53	0	1	0	9	0	10.2	10	0	3	8
July	3.38	0	0	0	10	0	13.1	12	0	2	8
August	0.87	2	0	0	10	0	10.1	9	1	3	11
September/October	3.21	0	0	0	14	0	14.0	15	0	5	9
Starter	0.00	0	0	0	0	0	0.0	0	0	0	0
Reliever	2.68	2	2	0	64	0	80.2	71	3	28	62
0 Days rest	2.20	1	0	0	13	0	16.1	13	2	6	13
1 or 2 Days rest	2.98	0	1	0	31	0	42.1	38	1	15	28
3+ Days rest	2.45	1	1	0	20	0	22.0	20	0	7	21
Pre-All Star	3.06	0	2	0	34	0	47.0	40	2	19	36
Post-All Star	2.14	2	0	0	30	0	33.2	31	1	9	26

	Avg	AB	H	2B	3B	HR	RBI	BB	SO	OBP	SLG
vs. Left	.230	87	20	2	0	0	7	9	26	.323	.253
vs. Right	.238	214	51	8	0	3	18	19	36	.302	.318
Inning 1-6	.129	31	4	0	0	1	4	4	5	.222	.226
Inning 7+	.248	270	67	10	0	2	21	24	57	.319	.307
None on	.265	151	40	6	0	2	2	14	32	.335	.344
Runners on	.207	150	31	4	0	1	23	14	30	.281	.253
Scoring Posn	.270	74	20	2	0	1	21	11	16	.375	.338
Close & Late	.306	134	41	6	0	2	14	12	24	.363	.396
None on/out	.250	68	17	1	0	0	0	6	18	.320	.265
vs. 1st Batr (relief)	.267	60	16	1	0	1	7	3	14	.313	.333
First Inning Pitched	.196	204	40	4	0	1	16	17	47	.267	.230
First 15 Pitches	.226	186	42	4	0	1	15	14	39	.286	.263
Pitch 16-30	.274	84	23	4	0	2	6	8	18	.351	.393
Pitch 31-45	.182	22	4	1	0	0	3	3	4	.280	.227
Pitch 46+	.222	9	2	1	0	0	1	3	1	.417	.333
First Pitch	.200	30	6	2	0	0	3	5	0	.351	.267
Ahead in Count	.156	154	24	3	0	1	9	0	56	.160	.195
Behind in Count	.397	63	25	3	0	2	9	13	0	.506	.540
Two Strikes	.179	151	27	3	0	0	6	10	62	.233	.199

Mel Rojas — Expos

Age 27 – Pitches Right

	ERA	W	L	Sv	G	GS	IP	BB	SO	Avg	H	2B	3B	HR	RBI	OBP	SLG	GF	IR	IRS	Hld	SvOp	SB	CS	GB	FB	G/F
1993 Season	2.95	5	8	10	66	0	88.1	30	48	.242	80	24	2	6	49	.308	.382	25	37	19	14	19	8	1	129	102	1.26
Career (1990-1993)	2.63	18	13	27	194	0	277.0	101	181	.223	227	55	7	17	111	.297	.342	69	131	38	35	41	29	7	373	311	1.20

1993 Season

	ERA	W	L	Sv	G	GS	IP	H	HR	BB	SO		Avg	AB	H	2B	3B	HR	RBI	BB	SO	OBP	SLG
Home	3.07	4	3	4	31	0	44.0	28	5	16	21	vs. Left	.270	185	50	13	2	4	28	21	26	.338	.427
Away	2.84	1	5	6	35	0	44.1	52	1	14	27	vs. Right	.207	145	30	11	0	2	21	9	22	.269	.324
Day	3.86	1	4	3	20	0	25.2	25	1	15	12	Inning 1-6	.273	22	6	4	0	0	11	5	4	.387	.455
Night	2.59	4	4	7	46	0	62.2	55	5	15	36	Inning 7+	.240	308	74	20	2	6	38	25	44	.301	.377
Grass	2.42	1	1	3	18	0	26.0	27	0	6	17	None on	.263	175	46	12	1	4	4	11	27	.314	.411
Turf	3.18	4	7	7	48	0	62.1	53	6	24	31	Runners on	.219	155	34	12	1	2	45	19	21	.302	.348
April	5.00	0	1	5	10	0	9.0	11	0	4	6	Scoring Posn	.245	98	24	9	1	2	43	17	15	.350	.418
May	3.44	1	2	1	14	0	18.1	21	1	7	5	Close & Late	.239	184	44	11	2	4	18	18	28	.307	.386
June	3.71	2	3	0	11	0	17.0	12	3	8	5	None on/out	.316	79	25	5	0	2	2	6	7	.365	.456
July	2.84	1	1	2	8	0	12.2	13	0	3	11	vs. 1st Batr (relief)	.321	56	18	3	0	2	7	6	6	.385	.482
August	0.96	0	1	2	10	0	18.2	10	0	5	15	First Inning Pitched	.271	218	59	17	0	4	41	23	29	.337	.404
September/October	2.84	1	0	0	13	0	12.2	13	2	3	6	First 15 Pitches	.268	209	56	16	0	4	33	20	29	.328	.402
Starter	0.00	0	0	0	0	0	0.0	0	0	0	0	Pitch 16-30	.208	106	22	8	2	1	15	9	16	.286	.349
Reliever	2.95	5	8	10	66	0	88.1	80	6	30	48	Pitch 31-45	.133	15	2	0	0	1	1	1	3	.188	.333
0 Days rest	5.84	1	3	2	12	0	12.1	18	2	7	5	Pitch 46+	.000	0	0	0	0	0	0	0	0	.000	.000
1 or 2 Days rest	2.56	4	5	6	40	0	56.1	47	3	17	34	First Pitch	.206	63	13	5	0	1	9	3	0	.246	.333
3+ Days rest	2.29	0	0	2	14	0	19.2	15	1	6	9	Ahead in Count	.197	152	30	9	1	2	15	0	45	.206	.309
Pre-All Star	3.70	4	6	6	37	0	48.2	47	4	20	23	Behind in Count	.333	63	21	6	1	2	13	14	0	.443	.556
Post-All Star	2.04	1	2	4	29	0	39.2	33	2	10	25	Two Strikes	.197	142	28	8	0	3	17	13	48	.266	.317

Career (1990-1993)

	ERA	W	L	Sv	G	GS	IP	H	HR	BB	SO		Avg	AB	H	2B	3B	HR	RBI	BB	SO	OBP	SLG
Home	2.90	10	5	10	92	0	127.1	96	10	41	81	vs. Left	.230	565	130	30	5	10	64	69	95	.310	.354
Away	2.41	8	8	17	102	0	149.2	131	7	60	100	vs. Right	.215	451	97	25	2	7	47	32	86	.279	.326
Day	2.84	7	4	6	55	0	76.0	62	6	28	44	Inning 1-6	.258	186	48	14	1	7	34	20	29	.336	.457
Night	2.55	11	9	21	139	0	201.0	165	11	73	137	Inning 7+	.216	830	179	41	6	10	77	81	152	.287	.316
Grass	2.70	5	3	11	50	0	73.1	63	2	27	49	None on	.268	518	139	35	4	10	10	41	96	.326	.409
Turf	2.61	13	10	16	144	0	203.2	164	15	74	132	Runners on	.177	498	88	20	3	7	101	60	85	.268	.271
April	4.50	0	2	5	19	0	24.0	30	1	13	13	Scoring Posn	.184	315	58	14	3	4	92	52	60	.301	.286
May	2.00	2	2	2	27	0	36.0	31	1	14	19	Close & Late	.223	452	101	16	4	6	43	52	80	.305	.316
June	2.65	2	3	2	24	0	34.0	25	4	12	15	None on/out	.306	232	71	16	3	4	4	22	38	.366	.453
July	2.06	3	3	6	25	0	39.1	36	0	7	31	vs. 1st Batr (relief)	.256	168	43	7	1	4	15	16	32	.326	.381
August	2.21	4	3	6	49	0	77.1	49	5	28	61	First Inning Pitched	.222	632	140	36	4	9	87	64	119	.296	.334
September/October	3.12	7	0	6	50	0	66.1	56	6	27	42	First 15 Pitches	.222	604	134	33	2	8	67	57	112	.291	.323
Starter	0.00	0	0	0	0	0	0.0	0	0	0	0	Pitch 16-30	.211	308	65	17	5	3	32	38	54	.305	.328
Reliever	2.63	18	13	27	194	0	277.0	227	17	101	181	Pitch 31-45	.244	86	21	5	0	3	6	6	13	.293	.407
0 Days rest	2.45	7	4	6	43	0	58.2	49	7	27	41	Pitch 46+	.389	18	7	0	0	3	6	0	2	.368	.889
1 or 2 Days rest	2.71	8	8	14	103	0	152.2	123	5	51	101	First Pitch	.252	151	38	11	0	5	18	13	0	.311	.424
3+ Days rest	2.60	3	1	7	48	0	65.2	55	5	23	39	Ahead in Count	.167	484	81	19	1	5	37	0	162	.177	.242
Pre-All Star	2.63	6	7	12	77	0	106.0	94	6	42	59	Behind in Count	.305	213	65	15	4	6	36	47	0	.423	.498
Post-All Star	2.63	12	6	15	117	0	171.0	133	11	59	122	Two Strikes	.156	462	72	17	1	5	33	41	181	.231	.229

Pitcher vs. Batter (career)

Pitches Best Vs.	Avg	AB	H	2B	3B	HR	RBI	BB	SO	OBP	SLG	Pitches Worst Vs.	Avg	AB	H	2B	3B	HR	RBI	BB	SO	OBP	SLG
Jeff King	.000	12	0	0	0	0	0	1	1	.077	.000	Hal Morris	.538	13	7	2	0	1	1	0	1	.538	.923
Todd Zeile	.000	8	0	0	0	0	2	1	1	.091	.000	Barry Bonds	.455	11	5	1	0	1	2	2	2	.538	.818
Tom Pagnozzi	.083	12	1	0	0	0	0	0	2	.083	.083	John Kruk	.400	10	4	1	0	0	1	2	1	.500	.500
Mariano Duncan	.154	13	2	1	0	1	4	0	2	.154	.462	Bobby Bonilla	.385	13	5	1	0	2	2	1	3	.429	.923
Mickey Morandini	.182	11	2	1	0	0	1	1	0	.250	.273	Barry Larkin	.364	11	4	1	0	0	2	0	0	.364	.455

Marc Ronan — Cardinals

Age 24 – Bats Left

	Avg	G	AB	R	H	2B	3B	HR	RBI	BB	SO	HBP	GDP	SB	CS	OBP	SLG	IBB	SH	SF	#Pit	#P/PA	GB	FB	G/F
1993 Season	.083	6	12	0	1	0	0	0	0	0	5	0	0	0	0	.083	.083	0	0	0	49	4.08	2	4	0.50

1993 Season

	Avg	AB	H	2B	3B	HR	RBI	BB	SO	OBP	SLG		Avg	AB	H	2B	3B	HR	RBI	BB	SO	OBP	SLG
vs. Left	.000	1	0	0	0	0	0	0	1	.000	.000	Scoring Posn	.000	4	0	0	0	0	0	0	2	.000	.000
vs. Right	.091	11	1	0	0	0	0	0	4	.091	.091	Close & Late	.000	2	0	0	0	0	0	0	1	.000	.000

John Roper — Reds

Age 22 – Pitches Right

	ERA	W	L	Sv	G	GS	IP	BB	SO	Avg	H	2B	3B	HR	RBI	OBP	SLG	CG	ShO	Sup	QS	#P/S	SB	CS	GB	FB	G/F
1993 Season	5.63	2	5	0	16	15	80.0	36	54	.295	92	14	4	10	44	.372	.462	0	0	6.97	5	89	10	4	112	88	1.27

1993 Season

	ERA	W	L	Sv	G	GS	IP	H	HR	BB	SO		Avg	AB	H	2B	3B	HR	RBI	BB	SO	OBP	SLG
Home	4.84	2	4	0	9	9	48.1	46	7	20	34	vs. Left	.362	149	54	6	4	5	22	18	24	.435	.557
Away	6.82	0	1	0	7	6	31.2	46	3	16	20	vs. Right	.233	163	38	8	0	5	22	18	30	.314	.374
Starter	5.70	2	5	0	15	15	79.0	90	10	34	53	Scoring Posn	.310	71	22	4	1	6	37	12	8	.409	.648
Reliever	0.00	0	0	0	1	0	1.0	2	0	2	1	Close & Late	.444	9	4	0	0	0	0	2	1	.545	.444
0-3 Days Rest	14.54	0	1	0	1	1	4.1	8	1	2	1	None on/out	.333	78	26	2	1	1	1	10	15	.416	.423
4 Days Rest	4.75	0	3	0	8	8	41.2	46	5	17	27	First Pitch	.282	39	11	1	0	0	9	2	0	.295	.308
5+ Days Rest	5.73	2	1	0	6	6	33.0	36	4	15	25	Ahead in Count	.227	154	35	5	2	2	12	0	49	.242	.325

1993 Season	ERA	W	L	Sv	G	GS	IP	H	HR	BB	SO		Avg	AB	H	2B	3B	HR	RBI	BB	SO	OBP	SLG
Pre-All Star	5.14	1	1	0	4	3	14.0	15	1	5	7	Behind in Count	.434	76	33	5	2	5	18	18	0	.543	.750
Post-All Star	5.73	1	4	0	12	12	66.0	77	9	31	47	Two Strikes	.203	148	30	5	1	1	7	16	54	.293	.270

Rico Rossy — Royals

Age 30 – Bats Right

	Avg	G	AB	R	H	2B	3B	HR	RBI	BB	SO	HBP	GDP	SB	CS	OBP	SLG	IBB	SH	SF	#Pit	#P/PA	GB	FB	G/F
1993 Season	.221	46	86	10	19	4	0	2	12	9	11	1	0	0	0	.302	.337	0	1	0	321	3.31	37	22	1.68
Career (1991-1993)	.216	110	236	31	51	12	1	3	24	29	32	2	6	0	3	.306	.314	1	8	1	984	3.57	96	69	1.39

1993 Season	Avg	AB	H	2B	3B	HR	RBI	BB	SO	OBP	SLG		Avg	AB	H	2B	3B	HR	RBI	BB	SO	OBP	SLG
vs. Left	.333	27	9	3	0	2	6	2	3	.400	.667	Scoring Posn	.217	23	5	1	0	0	9	4	4	.333	.261
vs. Right	.169	59	10	1	0	0	6	7	8	.258	.186	Close & Late	.250	12	3	0	0	1	3	3	1	.400	.500

Rich Rowland — Tigers

Age 27 – Bats Right

	Avg	G	AB	R	H	2B	3B	HR	RBI	BB	SO	HBP	GDP	SB	CS	OBP	SLG	IBB	SH	SF	#Pit	#P/PA	GB	FB	G/F
1993 Season	.217	21	46	2	10	3	0	0	4	5	16	0	1	0	0	.294	.283	0	1	0	198	3.81	14	9	1.56
Career (1990-1993)	.205	38	83	7	17	4	0	0	5	11	25	0	3	0	0	.295	.253	1	1	1	373	3.89	26	18	1.44

1993 Season	Avg	AB	H	2B	3B	HR	RBI	BB	SO	OBP	SLG		Avg	AB	H	2B	3B	HR	RBI	BB	SO	OBP	SLG
vs. Left	.229	35	8	3	0	0	4	3	10	.289	.314	Scoring Posn	.133	15	2	1	0	0	3	1	4	.188	.200
vs. Right	.182	11	2	0	0	0	0	2	6	.308	.182	Close & Late	.000	3	0	0	0	0	0	0	2	.000	.000

Stan Royer — Cardinals

Age 26 – Bats Right

	Avg	G	AB	R	H	2B	3B	HR	RBI	BB	SO	HBP	GDP	SB	CS	OBP	SLG	IBB	SH	SF	#Pit	#P/PA	GB	FB	G/F
1993 Season	.304	24	46	4	14	2	0	1	8	2	14	0	2	0	1	.333	.413	0	0	0	180	3.75	9	12	0.75
Career (1991-1993)	.306	46	98	11	30	5	0	3	18	4	20	0	2	0	1	.330	.449	0	0	1	351	3.41	30	28	1.07

1993 Season	Avg	AB	H	2B	3B	HR	RBI	BB	SO	OBP	SLG		Avg	AB	H	2B	3B	HR	RBI	BB	SO	OBP	SLG
vs. Left	.294	17	5	0	0	0	3	2	7	.368	.294	Scoring Posn	.600	10	6	1	0	0	7	1	0	.636	.700
vs. Right	.310	29	9	2	0	1	5	0	7	.310	.483	Close & Late	.200	15	3	1	0	0	2	1	8	.250	.267

Kirk Rueter — Expos

Age 23 – Pitches Left

	ERA	W	L	Sv	G	GS	IP	BB	SO	Avg	H	2B	3B	HR	RBI	OBP	SLG	CG	ShO	Sup	QS	#P/S	SB	CS	GB	FB	G/F
1993 Season	2.73	8	0	0	14	14	85.2	18	31	.264	85	20	0	5	30	.303	.373	1	0	5.78	7	91	4	7	115	111	1.04

1993 Season	ERA	W	L	Sv	G	GS	IP	H	HR	BB	SO		Avg	AB	H	2B	3B	HR	RBI	BB	SO	OBP	SLG
Home	2.82	4	0	0	6	6	38.1	37	1	11	16	vs. Left	.250	48	12	1	0	0	4	2	5	.280	.271
Away	2.66	4	0	0	8	8	47.1	48	4	7	15	vs. Right	.266	274	73	19	0	5	26	16	26	.307	.391
Starter	2.73	8	0	0	14	14	85.2	85	5	18	31	Scoring Posn	.353	68	24	6	0	1	25	5	13	.397	.485
Reliever	0.00	0	0	0	0	0	0.0	0	0	0	0	Close & Late	.219	32	7	2	0	0	1	2	3	.265	.281
0-3 Days Rest	0.00	0	0	0	0	0	0.0	0	0	0	0	None on/out	.295	88	26	5	0	3	3	5	5	.333	.455
4 Days Rest	4.04	4	0	0	7	7	42.1	51	3	7	13	First Pitch	.256	39	10	0	0	1	2	1	0	.275	.333
5+ Days Rest	1.45	4	0	0	7	7	43.1	34	2	11	18	Ahead in Count	.196	153	30	8	0	1	9	0	29	.196	.268
Pre-All Star	0.00	1	0	0	1	1	8.1	2	0	3	5	Behind in Count	.329	70	23	7	0	1	8	8	0	.397	.471
Post-All Star	3.03	7	0	0	13	13	77.1	83	5	15	26	Two Strikes	.211	142	30	6	0	1	9	9	31	.258	.275

Scott Ruffcorn — White Sox

Age 24 – Pitches Right

	ERA	W	L	Sv	G	GS	IP	BB	SO	Avg	H	2B	3B	HR	RBI	OBP	SLG	CG	ShO	Sup	QS	#P/S	SB	CS	GB	FB	G/F
1993 Season	8.10	0	2	0	3	2	10.0	10	2	.265	9	2	0	2	10	.422	.500	0	0	1.80	0	87	5	0	14	11	1.27

1993 Season	ERA	W	L	Sv	G	GS	IP	H	HR	BB	SO		Avg	AB	H	2B	3B	HR	RBI	BB	SO	OBP	SLG
Home	8.31	0	1	0	1	1	4.1	4	2	3	1	vs. Left	.250	16	4	0	0	1	4	6	0	.455	.438
Away	7.94	0	1	0	2	1	5.2	5	0	7	1	vs. Right	.278	18	5	2	0	1	6	4	2	.391	.556

Bruce Ruffin — Rockies

Age 30 – Pitches Left (groundball pitcher)

	ERA	W	L	Sv	G	GS	IP	BB	SO	Avg	H	2B	3B	HR	RBI	OBP	SLG	GF	IR	IRS	Hld	SvOp	SB	CS	GB	FB	G/F
1993 Season	3.87	6	5	2	59	12	139.2	69	126	.269	145	24	3	10	65	.350	.380	8	25	6	3	3	14	9	234	95	2.46
Last Five Years	4.63	23	41	2	171	81	591.1	272	405	.286	666	136	16	47	309	.359	.419	17	60	22	9	5	40	28	969	530	1.83

1993 Season	ERA	W	L	Sv	G	GS	IP	H	HR	BB	SO		Avg	AB	H	2B	3B	HR	RBI	BB	SO	OBP	SLG
Home	3.81	3	3	1	29	8	80.1	79	4	44	75	vs. Left	.233	120	28	5	0	3	13	25	28	.360	.350
Away	3.94	3	2	1	30	4	59.1	66	6	25	51	vs. Right	.279	419	117	19	3	7	52	44	98	.347	.389
Starter	6.08	3	4	0	12	12	53.1	73	4	31	46	Scoring Posn	.237	152	36	5	0	2	51	28	36	.349	.309
Reliever	2.50	3	1	2	47	0	86.1	72	6	38	80	Close & Late	.182	66	12	0	0	1	4	7	17	.260	.227
0 Days rest	4.76	0	1	0	8	0	11.1	14	2	6	10	None on/out	.280	125	35	5	2	1	1	14	30	.353	.376
1 or 2 Days rest	2.42	3	0	2	33	0	67.0	53	4	30	65	First Pitch	.275	69	19	3	0	2	16	8	0	.346	.406
3+ Days rest	0.00	0	0	0	6	0	8.0	5	0	2	5	Ahead in Count	.171	252	43	5	3	2	12	0	107	.174	.238
Pre-All Star	5.11	3	4	0	20	12	74.0	94	5	41	60	Behind in Count	.393	117	46	8	0	1	17	39	0	.535	.487

1993 Season	ERA	W	L	Sv	G	GS	IP	H	HR	BB	SO
Post-All Star	2.47	3	1	2	39	0	65.2	51	5	28	66

1993 Season	Avg	AB	H	2B	3B	HR	RBI	BB	SO	OBP	SLG
Two Strikes	.160	257	41	6	3	4	16	22	126	.226	.253

Last Five Years

	ERA	W	L	Sv	G	GS	IP	H	HR	BB	SO
Home	4.50	16	23	1	90	48	325.2	358	24	156	232
Away	4.78	7	18	1	81	33	265.2	308	23	116	173
Day	5.15	8	11	1	56	24	185.1	217	15	80	127
Night	4.39	15	30	1	115	57	406.0	449	32	192	278
Grass	5.31	7	16	1	85	27	235.2	270	25	121	186
Turf	4.18	16	25	1	86	54	355.2	396	22	151	219
April	6.05	3	6	0	16	10	58.0	85	4	31	33
May	5.29	2	5	0	20	8	64.2	78	6	37	34
June	4.88	5	5	0	29	17	118.0	131	7	48	76
July	4.21	6	8	0	32	20	132.2	139	13	66	88
August	4.81	2	11	0	36	15	112.1	120	11	49	78
September/October	3.49	5	6	2	38	11	105.2	113	6	41	96
Starter	5.05	18	38	0	81	81	417.1	502	36	191	259
Reliever	3.62	5	3	2	90	0	174.0	164	11	81	146
0 Days rest	5.52	1	2	0	16	0	31.0	42	3	12	21
1 or 2 Days rest	3.46	3	1	2	47	0	91.0	85	5	44	82
3+ Days rest	2.77	1	0	0	27	0	52.0	37	3	25	43
Pre-All Star	4.78	13	20	0	77	43	295.2	349	20	144	183
Post-All Star	4.47	10	21	2	94	38	295.2	317	27	128	222

	Avg	AB	H	2B	3B	HR	RBI	BB	SO	OBP	SLG
vs. Left	.257	483	124	24	2	6	72	74	89	.352	.352
vs. Right	.294	1844	542	112	14	41	237	198	316	.361	.437
Inning 1-6	.295	1897	559	116	15	44	279	221	329	.366	.441
Inning 7+	.249	430	107	20	1	3	30	51	76	.329	.321
None on	.278	1230	342	72	6	25	25	130	225	.348	.407
Runners on	.295	1097	324	64	10	22	284	142	180	.371	.432
Scoring Posn	.292	623	182	39	5	13	252	101	104	.383	.433
Close & Late	.253	182	46	9	0	1	11	23	32	.340	.319
None on/out	.293	556	163	36	4	11	11	64	99	.367	.432
vs. 1st Batr (relief)	.174	69	12	1	0	1	8	16	21	.330	.232
First Inning Pitched	.283	622	176	32	2	13	113	88	135	.369	.404
First 15 Pitches	.272	540	147	26	1	13	69	68	115	.352	.396
Pitch 16-30	.291	460	134	29	6	7	76	62	86	.374	.426
Pitch 31-45	.293	393	115	29	4	6	47	45	76	.365	.433
Pitch 46+	.289	934	270	52	5	21	117	97	128	.353	.423
First Pitch	.347	343	119	21	3	8	73	22	0	.380	.496
Ahead in Count	.218	1026	224	42	5	13	90	0	357	.219	.307
Behind in Count	.341	549	187	43	4	11	71	165	0	.491	.494
Two Strikes	.208	986	205	37	5	19	86	85	405	.270	.313

Pitcher vs. Batter (career)

Pitches Best Vs.	Avg	AB	H	2B	3B	HR	RBI	BB	SO	OBP	SLG
Fred McGriff	.000	10	0	0	0	0	0	1	5	.091	.000
Ray Lankford	.143	14	2	0	0	0	0	2	2	.250	.143
Greg Olson	.154	13	2	1	0	0	0	0	3	.154	.231
Kevin Bass	.182	22	4	1	0	0	0	0	4	.182	.227
Jose Uribe	.188	16	3	0	0	0	0	0	0	.188	.188

Pitches Worst Vs.	Avg	AB	H	2B	3B	HR	RBI	BB	SO	OBP	SLG
Mitch Webster	.556	18	10	2	1	0	0	2	0	.600	.778
Keith Miller	.500	16	8	4	1	0	1	4	3	.600	.875
Joe Girardi	.500	12	6	2	0	1	4	1	2	.538	.917
Ron Gant	.450	20	9	4	1	1	7	3	2	.522	.900
Matt D. Williams	.375	16	6	0	0	3	5	3	2	.474	.938

Johnny Ruffin — Reds

Age 22 – Pitches Right

	ERA	W	L	Sv	G	GS	IP	BB	SO	Avg	H	2B	3B	HR	RBI	OBP	SLG	GF	IR	IRS	Hld	SvOp	SB	CS	GB	FB	G/F
1993 Season	3.58	2	1	2	21	0	37.2	11	30	.247	36	7	4	4	20	.304	.432	5	10	5	2	3	4	0	48	47	1.02

1993 Season

	ERA	W	L	Sv	G	GS	IP	H	HR	BB	SO
Home	1.86	0	0	1	11	0	19.1	18	1	5	15
Away	5.40	2	1	1	10	0	18.1	18	3	6	15

	Avg	AB	H	2B	3B	HR	RBI	BB	SO	OBP	SLG
vs. Left	.295	78	23	3	4	1	9	5	15	.337	.474
vs. Right	.191	68	13	4	0	3	11	6	15	.267	.382

Scott Ruskin — Reds

Age 31 – Pitches Left

	ERA	W	L	Sv	G	GS	IP	BB	SO	Avg	H	2B	3B	HR	RBI	OBP	SLG	GF	IR	IRS	Hld	SvOp	SB	CS	GB	FB	G/F
1993 Season	18.00	0	0	0	4	0	1.0	2	0	.500	3	1	0	1	4	.625	1.167	0	6	3	0	0	0	0	1	2	0.50
Career (1990-1993)	3.95	11	9	8	192	0	193.2	90	146	.260	191	37	3	15	94	.343	.379	55	125	36	27	22	32	8	259	208	1.25

1993 Season

	ERA	W	L	Sv	G	GS	IP	H	HR	BB	SO
Home	27.00	0	0	0	2	0	0.1	1	0	1	0
Away	13.50	0	0	0	2	0	0.2	2	1	1	0

	Avg	AB	H	2B	3B	HR	RBI	BB	SO	OBP	SLG
vs. Left	.500	2	1	0	0	1	1	0	0	.500	2.000
vs. Right	.500	4	2	1	0	0	3	2	0	.667	.750

Career (1990-1993)

	ERA	W	L	Sv	G	GS	IP	H	HR	BB	SO
Home	2.34	7	4	4	89	0	96.0	86	5	41	71
Away	5.53	4	5	4	103	0	97.2	105	10	49	75
Day	3.43	2	3	2	56	0	65.2	51	4	22	52
Night	4.22	9	6	6	136	0	128.0	140	11	68	94
Grass	4.07	3	0	3	57	0	55.1	56	3	19	42
Turf	3.90	8	9	5	135	0	138.1	135	12	71	104
April	2.70	1	1	0	27	0	26.2	24	0	11	22
May	4.94	1	1	4	27	0	31.0	33	3	15	24
June	3.26	4	2	3	35	0	30.1	25	1	12	18
July	3.00	3	0	1	31	0	33.0	30	2	15	27
August	4.71	0	2	0	33	0	36.1	42	3	15	24
September/October	4.71	2	3	0	39	0	36.1	37	6	22	31
Starter	0.00	0	0	0	0	0	0.0	0	0	0	0
Reliever	3.95	11	9	8	192	0	193.2	191	15	90	146
0 Days rest	3.28	3	4	2	46	0	49.1	44	0	19	31
1 or 2 Days rest	3.80	6	3	4	93	0	87.2	93	8	49	79
3+ Days rest	4.76	2	2	2	53	0	56.2	54	7	22	36
Pre-All Star	3.54	7	4	7	98	0	96.2	92	5	40	74
Post-All Star	4.36	4	5	1	94	0	97.0	99	10	50	72

	Avg	AB	H	2B	3B	HR	RBI	BB	SO	OBP	SLG
vs. Left	.273	275	75	12	1	5	38	32	67	.347	.378
vs. Right	.252	461	116	25	2	10	56	58	79	.341	.380
Inning 1-6	.241	116	28	5	0	2	16	14	17	.323	.336
Inning 7+	.263	620	163	32	3	13	78	76	129	.347	.387
None on	.238	395	94	19	2	5	5	42	83	.314	.334
Runners on	.284	341	97	18	1	10	89	48	63	.375	.431
Scoring Posn	.252	210	53	11	1	5	76	40	42	.374	.386
Close & Late	.290	334	97	20	0	7	48	40	68	.368	.413
None on/out	.255	184	47	8	2	3	3	18	41	.322	.370
vs. 1st Batr (relief)	.246	171	42	9	1	3	21	18	40	.316	.363
First Inning Pitched	.256	550	141	25	3	9	69	62	115	.335	.362
First 15 Pitches	.258	519	134	23	2	10	60	56	107	.332	.368
Pitch 16-30	.259	174	45	9	1	3	22	28	36	.366	.374
Pitch 31-45	.300	40	12	5	0	2	12	5	2	.391	.575
Pitch 46+	.000	3	0	0	0	0	0	1	1	.250	.000
First Pitch	.272	92	25	4	1	2	11	7	0	.323	.402
Ahead in Count	.208	361	75	11	1	6	39	0	128	.215	.294
Behind in Count	.336	152	51	11	1	5	21	48	0	.495	.520
Two Strikes	.187	364	68	13	1	6	46	34	146	.261	.277

Pitcher vs. Batter (career)

Pitches Best Vs.	Avg	AB	H	2B	3B	HR	RBI	BB	SO	OBP	SLG
Brett Butler	.182	11	2	2	0	0	0	1	3	.250	.364
Tony Gwynn	.200	15	3	0	0	0	0	0	0	.200	.200
Bobby Thompson	.200	10	2	1	0	0	0	1	3	.273	.300

Pitches Worst Vs.	Avg	AB	H	2B	3B	HR	RBI	BB	SO	OBP	SLG
John Kruk	.500	8	4	1	0	0	1	3	0	.636	.625
Barry Bonds	.462	13	6	0	0	1	2	2	2	.533	.692
Bobby Bonilla	.333	12	4	3	0	1	2	2	1	.429	.833

Jeff Russell — Red Sox

Age 32 – Pitches Right

	ERA	W	L	Sv	G	GS	IP	BB	SO	Avg	H	2B	3B	HR	RBI	OBP	SLG	GF	IR	IRS	Hld	SvOp	SB	CS	GB	FB	G/F
1993 Season	2.70	1	4	33	51	0	46.2	14	45	.231	39	11	0	1	23	.287	.314	48	24	10	1	37	1	1	61	39	1.56
Last Five Years	2.57	18	20	141	276	0	290.1	105	238	.221	233	44	2	20	151	.292	.324	172	201	67	3	172	11	6	381	279	1.37

1993 Season

	ERA	W	L	Sv	G	GS	IP	H	HR	BB	SO
Home	1.99	0	1	15	25	0	22.2	21	0	8	19
Away	3.38	1	3	18	26	0	24.0	18	1	6	26
Starter	0.00	0	0	0	0	0	0.0	0	0	0	0
Reliever	2.70	1	4	33	51	0	46.2	39	1	14	45
0 Days rest	1.59	0	1	10	12	0	11.1	8	0	9	11
1 or 2 Days rest	3.72	1	2	14	21	0	19.1	15	1	4	22
3+ Days rest	2.25	0	1	9	18	0	16.0	16	0	1	12
Pre-All Star	3.03	0	2	20	32	0	29.2	25	0	4	32
Post-All Star	2.12	1	2	13	19	0	17.0	14	1	10	13

	Avg	AB	H	2B	3B	HR	RBI	BB	SO	OBP	SLG
vs. Left	.269	93	25	9	0	0	12	5	20	.307	.366
vs. Right	.184	76	14	2	0	1	11	9	25	.264	.250
Scoring Posn	.304	46	14	1	0	0	20	6	7	.368	.326
Close & Late	.210	124	26	7	0	1	17	10	34	.261	.290
None on/out	.231	39	9	6	0	0	0	1	10	.250	.385
First Pitch	.263	19	5	2	0	0	4	0	0	.238	.368
Ahead in Count	.184	98	18	3	0	1	11	0	41	.192	.245
Behind in Count	.448	29	13	5	0	0	6	6	0	.528	.621
Two Strikes	.088	91	8	2	0	0	5	8	45	.162	.110

Last Five Years

	ERA	W	L	Sv	G	GS	IP	H	HR	BB	SO
Home	2.20	6	8	79	143	0	151.1	105	11	45	129
Away	2.98	12	12	62	133	0	139.0	128	9	60	109
Day	2.82	8	10	33	77	0	83.0	74	4	33	69
Night	2.47	10	10	108	199	0	207.1	159	16	72	169
Grass	2.30	12	15	122	233	0	246.0	186	16	87	207
Turf	4.06	6	5	19	43	0	44.1	47	4	18	31
April	1.47	4	2	24	43	0	49.0	30	2	11	42
May	3.32	3	6	31	62	0	65.0	60	5	21	44
June	2.74	1	3	21	40	0	42.2	33	2	19	43
July	2.34	3	5	26	45	0	50.0	39	3	17	46
August	2.93	1	4	22	43	0	43.0	38	5	20	35
September/October	2.43	6	0	17	43	0	40.2	33	3	17	28
Starter	0.00	0	0	0	0	0	0.0	0	0	0	0
Reliever	2.57	18	20	141	276	0	290.1	233	20	105	238
0 Days rest	2.55	6	5	41	68	0	67.0	58	6	29	62
1 or 2 Days rest	2.72	6	12	67	127	0	139.0	114	9	57	111
3+ Days rest	2.35	6	3	33	81	0	84.1	61	5	19	65
Pre-All Star	2.68	10	13	86	162	0	178.0	141	10	59	148
Post-All Star	2.40	8	7	55	114	0	112.1	92	10	46	90

	Avg	AB	H	2B	3B	HR	RBI	BB	SO	OBP	SLG
vs. Left	.230	499	115	23	1	4	67	52	97	.306	.305
vs. Right	.213	555	118	21	1	16	84	53	141	.280	.341
Inning 1-6	.143	7	1	0	0	0	0	0	0	.143	.143
Inning 7+	.222	1047	232	44	2	20	151	105	238	.293	.325
None on	.194	510	99	18	0	7	7	43	134	.262	.271
Runners on	.246	544	134	26	2	13	144	62	104	.319	.373
Scoring Posn	.226	354	80	15	2	2	118	44	71	.304	.297
Close & Late	.229	686	157	30	2	15	114	72	146	.301	.344
None on/out	.197	198	39	10	0	2	2	18	44	.271	.278
vs. 1st Batr (relief)	.259	247	64	14	0	6	42	23	52	.318	.389
First Inning Pitched	.232	876	203	38	2	16	138	83	190	.298	.334
First 15 Pitches	.224	784	176	34	2	17	115	70	176	.288	.338
Pitch 16-30	.224	241	54	10	0	3	32	25	49	.300	.303
Pitch 31-45	.120	25	3	0	0	0	4	10	12	.371	.120
Pitch 46+	.000	4	0	0	0	0	0	0	1	.000	.000
First Pitch	.274	146	40	9	1	2	25	9	0	.311	.390
Ahead in Count	.186	547	102	20	0	7	67	0	205	.191	.261
Behind in Count	.287	188	54	11	1	6	43	52	0	.431	.452
Two Strikes	.146	533	78	12	0	4	45	44	238	.213	.191

Pitcher vs. Batter (since 1984)

Pitches Best Vs.	Avg	AB	H	2B	3B	HR	RBI	BB	SO	OBP	SLG
Gary Gaetti	.048	21	1	0	0	0	1	0	6	.045	.048
Mark McGwire	.071	14	1	0	0	0	0	1	3	.133	.071
Dale Murphy	.100	10	1	0	0	0	1	1	1	.182	.100
Joe Carter	.125	16	2	0	0	0	2	0	4	.118	.125
Dan Gladden	.129	31	4	0	0	0	2	0	8	.125	.129

Pitches Worst Vs.	Avg	AB	H	2B	3B	HR	RBI	BB	SO	OBP	SLG
Mike Greenwell	.615	13	8	1	0	2	11	2	2	.667	1.154
Mike Pagliarulo	.455	11	5	0	0	2	9	2	2	.538	1.000
Ellis Burks	.450	20	9	2	0	2	6	2	3	.500	.850
Kelly Gruber	.429	14	6	1	0	2	6	0	0	.400	.929
George Brett	.400	15	6	0	0	3	10	5	2	.500	1.000

John Russell — Rangers

Age 33 – Bats Right

	Avg	G	AB	R	H	2B	3B	HR	RBI	BB	SO	HBP	GDP	SB	CS	OBP	SLG	IBB	SH	SF	#Pit	#P/PA	GB	FB	G/F
1993 Season	.227	18	22	1	5	1	0	1	3	2	10	0	0	0	0	.292	.409	0	0	0	89	3.71	3	5	0.60
Last Five Years	.211	189	346	35	73	7	0	5	23	23	115	2	7	1	0	.262	.275	3	1	3	1377	3.67	94	94	1.00

1993 Season

	Avg	AB	H	2B	3B	HR	RBI	BB	SO	OBP	SLG
vs. Left	.300	10	3	1	0	0	2	1	3	.364	.400
vs. Right	.167	12	2	0	0	1	1	1	7	.231	.417

	Avg	AB	H	2B	3B	HR	RBI	BB	SO	OBP	SLG
Scoring Posn	.286	7	2	1	0	0	2	1	4	.375	.429
Close & Late	.333	3	1	0	0	0	0	1	2	.500	.333

Last Five Years

	Avg	AB	H	2B	3B	HR	RBI	BB	SO	OBP	SLG
vs. Left	.198	187	37	4	0	2	10	11	60	.246	.251
vs. Right	.226	159	36	3	0	3	13	12	55	.280	.302
Groundball	.247	97	24	3	0	1	8	5	29	.288	.309
Flyball	.226	93	21	2	0	3	7	8	31	.291	.344
Home	.210	157	33	3	0	2	10	9	50	.253	.268
Away	.212	189	40	4	0	3	13	14	65	.270	.280
Day	.158	76	12	2	0	0	2	7	30	.229	.184
Night	.226	270	61	5	0	5	21	16	85	.271	.300
Grass	.200	265	53	3	0	4	17	17	88	.248	.257
Turf	.247	81	20	4	0	1	6	6	27	.307	.333
First Pitch	.415	53	22	2	0	1	4	1	0	.426	.509
Ahead in Count	.347	49	17	2	0	1	8	13	0	.469	.449
Behind in Count	.125	176	22	1	0	1	7	0	91	.135	.148
Two Strikes	.103	194	20	1	0	2	6	7	115	.143	.139

	Avg	AB	H	2B	3B	HR	RBI	BB	SO	OBP	SLG
Scoring Posn	.200	80	16	3	0	0	17	9	26	.280	.238
Close & Late	.187	75	14	2	0	0	5	5	30	.238	.213
None on/out	.153	85	13	1	0	4	4	3	26	.182	.306
Batting #7	.241	87	21	2	0	3	6	2	23	.267	.368
Batting #8	.192	130	25	3	0	2	12	9	38	.246	.262
Other	.209	129	27	2	0	0	5	12	54	.275	.225
April	.175	40	7	0	0	1	1	0	16	.175	.250
May	.231	26	6	0	0	0	0	1	7	.259	.231
June	.213	80	17	2	0	2	6	6	23	.270	.313
July	.204	54	11	2	0	0	5	1	22	.232	.241
August	.236	89	21	2	0	1	7	11	24	.317	.292
September/October	.193	57	11	1	0	1	4	4	23	.246	.263
Pre-All Star	.209	158	33	2	0	3	7	8	51	.249	.278
Post-All Star	.213	188	40	5	0	2	16	15	64	.273	.271

Batter vs. Pitcher (career)

Hits Best Against	Avg	AB	H	2B	3B	HR	RBI	BB	SO	OBP	SLG
Joe Hesketh	.357	14	5	3	0	0	2	0	2	.357	.571
Zane Smith	.308	13	4	2	0	0	3	1	4	.357	.462

Hits Worst Against	Avg	AB	H	2B	3B	HR	RBI	BB	SO	OBP	SLG
Sid Fernandez	.000	14	0	0	0	0	0	6	8	.300	.000
Rick Sutcliffe	.059	17	1	0	0	1	2	1	7	.111	.235
Bobby Ojeda	.100	10	1	0	0	0	1	1	3	.182	.100

Batter vs. Pitcher (career)											
Hits Best Against	Avg	AB	H	2B	3B	HR	RBI	BB	SO	OBP	SLG

Hits Worst Against	Avg	AB	H	2B	3B	HR	RBI	BB	SO	OBP	SLG
Mike Bielecki	.111	9	1	0	0	0	0	3	4	.333	.111
Bob Walk	.143	14	2	0	0	0	0	0	5	.143	.143

Ken Ryan — Red Sox

Age 25 – Pitches Right (groundball pitcher)

	ERA	W	L	Sv	G	GS	IP	BB	SO	Avg	H	2B	3B	HR	RBI	OBP	SLG	GF	IR	IRS	Hld	SvOp	SB	CS	GB	FB	G/F
1993 Season	3.60	7	2	1	47	0	50.0	29	49	.235	43	10	1	2	29	.342	.333	26	41	16	3	4	3	2	60	36	1.67
Career (1992-1993)	3.95	7	2	2	54	0	57.0	34	54	.228	47	10	1	4	34	.339	.345	32	48	20	3	5	3	2	73	41	1.78

1993 Season

	ERA	W	L	Sv	G	GS	IP	H	HR	BB	SO
Home	5.55	3	2	0	23	0	24.1	26	0	13	23
Away	1.75	4	0	1	24	0	25.2	17	2	16	26
Starter	0.00	0	0	0	0	0	0.0	0	0	0	0
Reliever	3.60	7	2	1	47	0	50.0	43	2	29	49
0 Days rest	2.08	0	1	0	7	0	8.2	10	0	1	7
1 or 2 Days rest	4.30	5	1	1	28	0	29.1	25	2	16	34
3+ Days rest	3.00	2	0	0	12	0	12.0	8	0	12	8
Pre-All Star	2.86	2	0	0	26	0	28.1	23	1	13	24
Post-All Star	4.57	5	2	1	21	0	21.2	20	1	16	25

	Avg	AB	H	2B	3B	HR	RBI	BB	SO	OBP	SLG
vs. Left	.232	82	19	6	0	0	11	18	29	.366	.305
vs. Right	.238	101	24	4	1	2	18	11	20	.322	.356
Scoring Posn	.242	62	15	6	0	0	26	15	13	.378	.339
Close & Late	.247	77	19	3	1	0	13	14	22	.347	.312
None on/out	.200	40	8	2	0	2	2	5	12	.289	.400
First Pitch	.364	22	8	1	1	0	6	3	0	.462	.500
Ahead in Count	.143	84	12	4	0	0	5	0	44	.153	.190
Behind in Count	.357	42	15	5	0	1	10	11	0	.491	.548
Two Strikes	.144	97	14	3	0	0	8	15	49	.263	.175

Nolan Ryan — Rangers

Age 47 – Pitches Right (flyball pitcher)

	ERA	W	L	Sv	G	GS	IP	BB	SO	Avg	H	2B	3B	HR	RBI	OBP	SLG	CG	ShO	Sup	QS	#P/S	SB	CS	GB	FB	G/F
1993 Season	4.88	5	5	0	13	13	66.1	40	46	.220	54	13	1	5	39	.329	.341	0	0	4.48	5	89	13	4	94	76	1.24
Last Five Years	3.43	51	39	0	129	129	840.0	353	939	.197	593	113	21	61	302	.286	.309	15	6	4.55	76	109	124	39	794	906	0.88

1993 Season

	ERA	W	L	Sv	G	GS	IP	H	HR	BB	SO
Home	4.12	4	2	0	7	7	39.1	33	3	21	31
Away	6.00	1	3	0	6	6	27.0	21	2	19	15
Starter	4.88	5	5	0	13	13	66.1	54	5	40	46
Reliever	0.00	0	0	0	0	0	0.0	0	0	0	0
0-3 Days Rest	0.00	0	0	0	0	0	0.0	0	0	0	0
4 Days Rest	4.06	2	3	0	6	6	31.0	24	1	17	22
5+ Days Rest	5.60	3	2	0	7	7	35.1	30	4	23	24
Pre-All Star	4.50	1	2	0	3	3	14.0	19	0	8	10
Post-All Star	4.99	4	3	0	10	10	52.1	35	5	32	36

	Avg	AB	H	2B	3B	HR	RBI	BB	SO	OBP	SLG
vs. Left	.188	133	25	4	1	2	20	30	22	.339	.278
vs. Right	.257	113	29	9	0	3	19	10	24	.315	.416
Scoring Posn	.265	68	18	3	1	3	36	14	14	.381	.471
Close & Late	.400	5	2	0	0	0	0	1	0	.500	.400
None on/out	.222	63	14	4	0	2	2	9	16	.319	.381
First Pitch	.263	38	10	2	0	1	5	0	0	.282	.395
Ahead in Count	.200	110	22	7	1	2	18	0	38	.200	.336
Behind in Count	.200	50	10	1	0	1	8	16	0	.382	.280
Two Strikes	.192	125	24	7	1	2	21	24	46	.322	.312

Last Five Years

	ERA	W	L	Sv	G	GS	IP	H	HR	BB	SO
Home	3.43	34	23	0	80	80	533.0	363	46	215	617
Away	3.43	17	16	0	49	49	307.0	230	15	138	322
Day	2.31	10	2	0	21	21	144.0	93	3	67	153
Night	3.66	41	37	0	108	108	696.0	500	58	286	786
Grass	3.45	45	34	0	111	111	730.2	511	58	303	822
Turf	3.29	6	5	0	18	18	109.1	82	3	50	117
April	3.21	10	5	0	17	17	109.1	78	5	47	135
May	5.08	3	7	0	19	19	108.0	86	12	50	125
June	2.32	9	5	0	20	20	135.2	88	12	44	146
July	3.39	15	4	0	25	25	169.2	115	15	75	199
August	4.05	8	12	0	23	23	146.2	109	10	67	151
September/October	2.90	6	6	0	25	25	170.2	117	7	70	183
Starter	3.43	51	39	0	129	129	840.0	593	61	353	939
Reliever	0.00	0	0	0	0	0	0.0	0	0	0	0
0-3 Days Rest	4.63	0	0	0	2	2	11.2	9	0	2	16
4 Days Rest	3.68	21	21	0	59	59	381.1	292	33	155	407
5+ Days Rest	3.18	30	18	0	68	68	447.0	292	28	196	516
Pre-All Star	3.28	27	17	0	63	63	406.1	282	34	157	477
Post-All Star	3.57	24	22	0	66	66	433.2	311	27	196	462

	Avg	AB	H	2B	3B	HR	RBI	BB	SO	OBP	SLG
vs. Left	.201	1580	318	53	16	28	147	201	432	.292	.308
vs. Right	.192	1436	275	60	5	33	155	152	507	.279	.309
Inning 1-6	.197	2537	499	94	19	53	271	317	788	.291	.311
Inning 7+	.196	479	94	19	2	8	31	36	151	.257	.294
None on	.173	1923	333	71	14	38	38	212	666	.262	.284
Runners on	.238	1093	260	42	7	23	264	141	273	.326	.352
Scoring Posn	.219	679	149	23	3	17	237	104	189	.323	.337
Close & Late	.195	246	48	9	1	3	18	20	83	.259	.276
None on/out	.176	803	141	31	6	16	16	79	264	.257	.289
vs. 1st Batr (relief)	.000	0	0	0	0	0	0	0	0	.000	.000
First Inning Pitched	.223	475	106	19	10	13	81	80	153	.343	.387
First 75 Pitches	.193	1997	386	68	17	48	211	225	606	.281	.316
Pitch 76-90	.202	351	71	18	1	3	28	54	120	.308	.285
Pitch 91-105	.195	323	63	10	2	3	28	35	109	.277	.266
Pitch 106+	.212	345	73	17	1	7	35	39	104	.296	.328
First Pitch	.298	325	97	20	4	10	53	3	0	.320	.477
Ahead in Count	.146	1586	231	45	5	17	91	0	770	.152	.212
Behind in Count	.276	551	152	33	7	20	95	148	0	.427	.470
Two Strikes	.130	1749	228	42	7	19	106	201	939	.223	.195

Pitcher vs. Batter (since 1984)

Pitches Best Vs.	Avg	AB	H	2B	3B	HR	RBI	BB	SO	OBP	SLG
Sammy Sosa	.000	16	0	0	0	0	0	2	8	.111	.000
Rob Deer	.000	14	0	0	0	0	0	0	10	.000	.000
Randy Milligan	.000	13	0	0	0	0	0	2	8	.133	.000
Luis Rivera	.000	12	0	0	0	0	1	0	6	.000	.000
Tom Brunansky	.000	9	0	0	0	0	1	1	5	.091	.000

Pitches Worst Vs.	Avg	AB	H	2B	3B	HR	RBI	BB	SO	OBP	SLG
Carlos Baerga	.600	10	6	0	0	1	2	2	0	.667	.900
Lance Blankenship	.556	9	5	1	0	0	2	3	1	.667	.667
Larry Sheets	.467	15	7	2	0	2	5	2	3	.529	1.000
Harold Baines	.364	22	8	1	0	4	6	3	4	.440	.955
Joe Carter	.353	17	6	3	1	2	7	2	6	.421	1.000

Bret Saberhagen — Mets

Age 30 – Pitches Right

	ERA	W	L	Sv	G	GS	IP	BB	SO	Avg	H	2B	3B	HR	RBI	OBP	SLG	CG	ShO	Sup	QS	#P/S	SB	CS	GB	FB	G/F
1993 Season	3.29	7	7	0	19	19	139.1	17	93	.250	131	20	4	11	50	.275	.366	4	1	4.65	12	104	9	7	188	144	1.31
Last Five Years	2.90	51	35	0	120	117	830.2	160	590	.238	735	127	23	51	262	.277	.343	29	8	4.28	82	104	31	35	1082	896	1.21

1993 Season

	ERA	W	L	Sv	G	GS	IP	H	HR	BB	SO
Home	2.41	3	3	0	8	8	59.2	47	4	6	41
Away	3.95	4	4	0	11	11	79.2	84	7	11	52

	Avg	AB	H	2B	3B	HR	RBI	BB	SO	OBP	SLG
vs. Left	.264	250	66	8	4	7	29	11	49	.298	.412
vs. Right	.237	274	65	12	0	4	21	6	44	.253	.325

1993 Season

	ERA	W	L	Sv	G	GS	IP	H	HR	BB	SO
Starter	3.29	7	7	0	19	19	139.1	131	11	17	93
Reliever	0.00	0	0	0	0	0	0.0	0	0	0	0
0-3 Days Rest	0.00	0	0	0	0	0	0.0	0	0	0	0
4 Days Rest	2.78	3	5	0	10	10	74.1	62	6	8	54
5+ Days Rest	3.88	4	2	0	9	9	65.0	69	5	9	39
Pre-All Star	3.17	5	7	0	16	16	116.1	110	9	13	80
Post-All Star	3.91	2	0	0	3	3	23.0	21	2	4	13

	Avg	AB	H	2B	3B	HR	RBI	BB	SO	OBP	SLG
Scoring Posn	.274	84	23	6	0	3	37	7	12	.309	.452
Close & Late	.338	65	22	5	0	0	10	4	11	.375	.415
None on/out	.214	145	31	4	3	2	2	4	26	.235	.324
First Pitch	.320	75	24	5	0	1	12	4	0	.346	.427
Ahead in Count	.213	282	60	10	1	2	16	0	82	.221	.277
Behind in Count	.326	86	28	2	0	6	14	6	0	.362	.558
Two Strikes	.188	261	49	8	2	1	14	7	93	.214	.245

Last Five Years

	ERA	W	L	Sv	G	GS	IP	H	HR	BB	SO
Home	2.45	25	14	0	59	59	419.0	345	19	75	306
Away	3.37	26	21	0	61	58	411.2	390	32	85	284
Day	3.28	10	16	0	37	36	252.1	217	21	57	193
Night	2.74	41	19	0	83	81	578.1	518	30	103	397
Grass	2.85	22	17	0	56	55	394.1	347	31	76	281
Turf	2.95	29	18	0	64	62	436.1	388	20	84	309
April	3.92	7	12	0	26	25	167.2	171	14	35	108
May	2.18	14	5	0	25	25	190.0	154	8	34	134
June	3.18	4	6	0	18	18	124.2	120	6	18	97
July	4.47	6	4	0	16	16	98.2	113	7	32	69
August	1.32	11	1	0	14	14	109.0	68	6	15	72
September/October	2.56	9	7	0	21	19	140.2	109	10	26	110
Starter	2.85	51	33	0	117	117	823.2	724	48	156	586
Reliever	9.00	0	2	0	3	0	7.0	11	3	4	4
0-3 Days Rest	1.25	5	2	0	8	8	65.0	45	2	10	46
4 Days Rest	2.44	32	19	0	66	66	476.1	384	26	82	347
5+ Days Rest	3.92	14	12	0	43	43	282.1	295	20	64	193
Pre-All Star	3.01	27	23	0	73	72	508.1	474	29	94	363
Post-All Star	2.74	24	12	0	47	45	322.1	261	22	66	227

	Avg	AB	H	2B	3B	HR	RBI	BB	SO	OBP	SLG
vs. Left	.226	1562	353	53	17	32	141	103	332	.273	.343
vs. Right	.250	1531	382	74	6	19	121	57	258	.282	.343
Inning 1-6	.231	2459	569	98	22	36	207	131	489	.272	.333
Inning 7+	.262	634	166	29	1	15	55	29	101	.297	.382
None on	.233	1956	456	72	15	32	32	82	379	.269	.334
Runners on	.245	1137	279	55	8	19	230	78	211	.292	.358
Scoring Posn	.244	587	143	31	5	13	203	51	112	.299	.380
Close & Late	.250	368	92	17	1	9	41	20	68	.295	.375
None on/out	.235	823	193	35	8	13	13	41	156	.273	.344
vs. 1st Batr (relief)	.000	3	0	0	0	0	0	0	0	.000	.000
First Inning Pitched	.238	450	107	23	5	6	45	32	94	.294	.351
First 75 Pitches	.231	2113	489	84	18	30	169	115	416	.274	.331
Pitch 76-90	.219	425	93	24	2	9	37	19	80	.251	.348
Pitch 91-105	.272	334	91	11	2	4	28	17	55	.306	.353
Pitch 106+	.281	221	62	8	1	8	28	9	39	.319	.434
First Pitch	.276	446	123	27	1	12	48	16	0	.299	.422
Ahead in Count	.202	1557	314	53	11	15	91	0	514	.207	.279
Behind in Count	.284	560	159	23	5	16	72	59	0	.351	.429
Two Strikes	.185	1512	279	48	7	16	86	85	590	.230	.257

Pitcher vs. Batter (career)

Pitches Best Vs.	Avg	AB	H	2B	3B	HR	RBI	BB	SO	OBP	SLG
Dave Valle	.000	9	0	0	0	0	0	2	2	.182	.000
Glenallen Hill	.063	16	1	0	0	0	0	0	7	.063	.063
Junior Felix	.063	16	1	0	0	0	1	2	7	.167	.063
Mike Devereaux	.077	13	1	0	0	0	1	0	3	.077	.077
Craig Biggio	.091	11	1	0	0	0	0	0	3	.091	.091

Pitches Worst Vs.	Avg	AB	H	2B	3B	HR	RBI	BB	SO	OBP	SLG
Alvaro Espinoza	.529	17	9	2	1	0	1	0	0	.529	.765
Delino DeShields	.462	13	6	1	1	0	1	4	3	.588	.692
Sam Horn	.421	19	8	1	0	4	9	0	7	.421	1.105
Albert Belle	.385	13	5	2	0	1	4	0	3	.385	.769
George Bell	.372	43	16	4	0	5	13	1	1	.378	.814

Chris Sabo — Reds

Age 32 – Bats Right (flyball hitter)

	Avg	G	AB	R	H	2B	3B	HR	RBI	BB	SO	HBP	GDP	SB	CS	OBP	SLG	IBB	SH	SF	#Pit	#P/PA	GB	FB	G/F
1993 Season	.259	148	552	86	143	33	2	21	82	43	105	6	10	6	4	.315	.440	5	2	8	2338	3.83	163	209	0.78
Last Five Years	.270	627	2349	354	634	146	11	90	313	203	329	18	45	68	34	.330	.456	18	13	22	9436	3.62	716	915	0.78

1993 Season

	Avg	AB	H	2B	3B	HR	RBI	BB	SO	OBP	SLG
vs. Left	.252	135	34	9	0	4	20	16	21	.333	.407
vs. Right	.261	417	109	24	2	17	62	27	84	.309	.451
Groundball	.295	200	59	13	0	10	35	14	43	.347	.510
Flyball	.208	96	20	4	0	1	7	7	22	.260	.281
Home	.281	263	74	19	1	12	47	27	52	.346	.498
Away	.239	289	69	14	1	9	35	16	53	.286	.388
Day	.279	165	46	11	1	7	22	15	32	.341	.485
Night	.251	387	97	22	1	14	60	28	73	.304	.421
Grass	.239	180	43	3	0	7	24	8	32	.281	.372
Turf	.269	372	100	30	2	14	58	35	73	.331	.473
First Pitch	.349	63	22	5	0	6	18	4	0	.406	.714
Ahead in Count	.339	121	41	11	1	4	23	18	0	.423	.545
Behind in Count	.182	258	47	8	1	6	22	0	83	.189	.291
Two Strikes	.160	269	43	10	1	6	21	21	105	.224	.271

	Avg	AB	H	2B	3B	HR	RBI	BB	SO	OBP	SLG
Scoring Posn	.257	140	36	11	1	7	63	17	31	.329	.500
Close & Late	.221	86	19	5	1	2	6	6	17	.277	.372
None on/out	.267	131	35	10	1	5	5	12	18	.347	.473
Batting #4	.240	175	42	9	1	6	16	10	34	.280	.406
Batting #5	.249	277	69	17	1	12	50	22	53	.308	.448
Other	.320	100	32	7	0	3	16	11	18	.391	.480
April	.221	86	19	5	0	4	14	3	11	.258	.419
May	.243	107	26	5	0	3	18	5	15	.287	.374
June	.308	52	16	1	0	1	7	3	7	.351	.385
July	.337	101	34	9	0	4	16	15	21	.417	.545
August	.250	100	25	7	2	4	16	9	27	.309	.480
September/October	.217	106	23	6	0	5	11	8	24	.272	.415
Pre-All Star	.277	285	79	17	0	9	46	20	39	.329	.432
Post-All Star	.240	267	64	16	2	12	36	23	66	.300	.449

1993 By Position

Position	Avg	AB	H	2B	3B	HR	RBI	BB	SO	OBP	SLG	G	GS	Innings	PO	A	E	DP	Fld Pct	Rng Fctr	In Zone	Outs	Zone Rtg	MLB Zone
As 3b	.259	552	143	33	2	21	82	43	105	.315	.440	148	148	1265.1	79	241	11	17	.967	2.28	303	255	.842	.834

Last Five Years

	Avg	AB	H	2B	3B	HR	RBI	BB	SO	OBP	SLG
vs. Left	.302	788	238	54	4	33	109	84	90	.372	.506
vs. Right	.254	1561	396	92	7	57	204	119	239	.308	.431
Groundball	.294	856	252	59	2	33	129	61	116	.343	.484
Flyball	.239	447	107	27	1	14	48	48	76	.313	.398
Home	.284	1142	324	85	4	53	173	111	156	.347	.504
Away	.257	1207	310	61	7	37	140	92	173	.313	.411
Day	.249	650	162	37	3	22	74	68	95	.323	.417
Night	.278	1699	472	109	8	68	239	135	234	.333	.471
Grass	.255	737	188	33	2	24	86	51	104	.307	.403
Turf	.277	1612	446	113	9	66	227	152	225	.340	.481
First Pitch	.343	329	113	28	3	18	56	10	0	.369	.611

	Avg	AB	H	2B	3B	HR	RBI	BB	SO	OBP	SLG
Scoring Posn	.262	591	155	37	2	25	229	75	92	.341	.459
Close & Late	.226	345	78	14	1	11	36	37	51	.303	.368
None on/out	.271	649	176	38	3	29	29	62	76	.341	.473
Batting #1	.278	561	156	34	2	23	64	61	66	.353	.469
Batting #5	.256	546	140	32	3	26	90	37	88	.306	.469
Other	.272	1242	338	80	6	41	159	105	175	.330	.445
April	.251	339	85	21	0	11	35	30	38	.316	.410
May	.256	489	125	26	2	18	66	44	68	.319	.427
June	.303	433	131	27	5	18	64	40	61	.365	.513
July	.275	342	94	22	1	12	45	35	48	.342	.450
August	.280	371	104	29	3	17	49	25	56	.326	.512

Last Five Years

	Avg	AB	H	2B	3B	HR	RBI	BB	SO	OBP	SLG		Avg	AB	H	2B	3B	HR	RBI	BB	SO	OBP	SLG
Ahead in Count	.333	573	191	49	2	25	82	100	0	.431	.557	September/October	.253	375	95	21	0	14	54	29	58	.309	.421
Behind in Count	.215	989	213	40	4	29	108	0	261	.219	.352	Pre-All Star	.273	1385	378	82	8	50	181	126	183	.335	.452
Two Strikes	.186	971	181	39	3	23	91	86	329	.254	.304	Post-All Star	.266	964	256	64	3	40	132	77	146	.322	.463

Batter vs. Pitcher (career)

Hits Best Against	Avg	AB	H	2B	3B	HR	RBI	BB	SO	OBP	SLG	Hits Worst Against	Avg	AB	H	2B	3B	HR	RBI	BB	SO	OBP	SLG
Frank Viola	.545	11	6	1	0	1	2	4	2	.667	.909	Sid Fernandez	.037	27	1	1	0	0	0	2	6	.103	.074
Kelly Downs	.545	11	6	3	0	1	3	1	0	.583	1.091	Pete Harnisch	.059	17	1	0	0	0	0	3	7	.200	.059
Chris Nabholz	.500	14	7	3	1	2	5	2	0	.563	1.286	John Wetteland	.091	11	1	1	0	0	1	0	1	.091	.182
Steve Avery	.419	31	13	3	0	1	7	3	5	.457	.613	Larry Andersen	.125	16	2	0	0	0	1	1	6	.176	.125
Paul Assenmacher	.417	12	5	0	0	1	2	3	2	.533	.667	Mike Maddux	.154	13	2	0	0	0	0	0	2	.154	.154

Roger Salkeld — Mariners

Age 23 – Pitches Right (flyball pitcher)

	ERA	W	L	Sv	G	GS	IP	BB	SO	Avg	H	2B	3B	HR	RBI	OBP	SLG	CG	ShO	Sup	QS	#P/S	SB	CS	GB	FB	G/F
1993 Season	2.51	0	0	0	3	2	14.1	4	13	.232	13	5	1	0	3	.295	.357	0	0	2.51	1	87	0	0	14	16	0.88

1993 Season

	ERA	W	L	Sv	G	GS	IP	H	HR	BB	SO		Avg	AB	H	2B	3B	HR	RBI	BB	SO	OBP	SLG
Home	0.00	0	0	0	0	0	0.0	0	0	0	0	vs. Left	.300	30	9	3	1	0	2	1	5	.323	.467
Away	2.51	0	0	0	3	2	14.1	13	0	4	13	vs. Right	.154	26	4	2	0	0	1	3	8	.267	.231

Tim Salmon — Angels

Age 25 – Bats Right

	Avg	G	AB	R	H	2B	3B	HR	RBI	BB	SO	HBP	GDP	SB	CS	OBP	SLG	IBB	SH	SF	#Pit	#P/PA	GB	FB	G/F
1993 Season	.283	142	515	93	146	35	1	31	95	82	135	5	6	5	6	.382	.536	5	0	8	2520	4.13	153	158	0.97
Career (1992-1993)	.269	165	594	101	160	36	1	33	101	93	158	6	7	6	7	.369	.500	6	0	9	2906	4.14	178	176	1.01

1993 Season

	Avg	AB	H	2B	3B	HR	RBI	BB	SO	OBP	SLG		Avg	AB	H	2B	3B	HR	RBI	BB	SO	OBP	SLG
vs. Left	.230	122	28	2	1	7	24	25	31	.368	.434	Scoring Posn	.282	131	37	10	0	8	64	33	37	.414	.542
vs. Right	.300	393	118	33	0	24	71	57	104	.386	.567	Close & Late	.286	84	24	4	0	4	10	12	27	.384	.476
Groundball	.323	96	31	10	0	6	25	16	18	.421	.615	None on/out	.325	114	37	8	0	7	7	9	27	.379	.579
Flyball	.224	116	26	8	0	5	15	27	36	.365	.422	Batting #3	.278	392	109	26	1	23	71	63	103	.379	.526
Home	.314	258	81	14	0	23	58	41	62	.406	.636	Batting #5	.277	94	26	6	0	6	19	16	25	.377	.532
Away	.253	257	65	21	1	8	37	41	73	.358	.436	Other	.379	29	11	3	0	2	5	3	7	.438	.690
Day	.286	161	46	10	0	5	23	17	41	.352	.441	April	.254	59	15	3	0	5	14	14	12	.392	.559
Night	.282	354	100	25	1	26	72	65	94	.395	.579	May	.294	102	30	6	0	4	18	16	30	.388	.471
Grass	.291	446	130	28	1	31	90	70	113	.387	.567	June	.273	88	24	7	0	5	15	16	22	.380	.523
Turf	.232	69	16	7	0	0	5	12	22	.349	.333	July	.283	106	30	6	0	9	24	17	26	.384	.594
First Pitch	.419	31	13	4	0	2	8	2	0	.447	.742	August	.250	112	28	6	1	6	15	11	30	.320	.482
Ahead in Count	.406	133	54	16	0	12	32	37	0	.532	.797	September/October	.396	48	19	7	0	2	9	8	15	.491	.667
Behind in Count	.204	226	46	7	0	11	35	0	104	.210	.381	Pre-All Star	.282	291	82	18	0	17	58	55	76	.393	.519
Two Strikes	.170	264	45	8	1	10	36	43	135	.290	.322	Post-All Star	.286	224	64	17	1	14	37	27	59	.366	.558

1993 By Position

Position	Avg	AB	H	2B	3B	HR	RBI	BB	SO	OBP	SLG	G	GS	Innings	PO	A	E	DP	Fld Pct	Rng Fctr	In Zone	Outs	Zone Rtg	MLB Zone
As rf	.281	509	143	33	1	31	94	81	132	.380	.532	141	141	1219.2	333	12	7	2	.980	2.55	362	314	.867	.826

Bill Sampen — Royals

Age 31 – Pitches Right

	ERA	W	L	Sv	G	GS	IP	BB	SO	Avg	H	2B	3B	HR	RBI	OBP	SLG	GF	IR	IRS	Hld	SvOp	SB	CS	GB	FB	G/F
1993 Season	5.89	2	2	0	18	0	18.1	9	9	.338	25	3	1	1	14	.437	.446	3	16	6	3	4	4	2	29	17	1.71
Career (1990-1993)	3.58	24	20	2	172	14	284.0	120	167	.276	298	47	4	25	145	.352	.396	50	107	36	15	8	50	15	403	317	1.27

1993 Season

	ERA	W	L	Sv	G	GS	IP	H	HR	BB	SO		Avg	AB	H	2B	3B	HR	RBI	BB	SO	OBP	SLG
Home	5.11	0	1	0	8	0	12.1	16	0	4	6	vs. Left	.514	37	19	2	0	1	9	3	4	.571	.649
Away	7.50	2	1	0	10	0	6.0	9	1	5	3	vs. Right	.162	37	6	1	1	0	5	6	5	.311	.243

Career (1990-1993)

	ERA	W	L	Sv	G	GS	IP	H	HR	BB	SO		Avg	AB	H	2B	3B	HR	RBI	BB	SO	OBP	SLG
Home	3.25	11	8	0	81	5	130.1	139	9	55	89	vs. Left	.287	533	153	24	2	12	75	74	66	.373	.407
Away	3.87	13	12	2	91	9	153.2	159	16	65	78	vs. Right	.265	547	145	23	2	13	70	46	101	.332	.386
Day	3.86	9	5	0	59	6	95.2	107	10	24	42	Inning 1-6	.249	466	116	18	1	13	55	44	71	.321	.376
Night	3.44	15	15	2	113	8	188.1	191	15	96	125	Inning 7+	.296	614	182	29	3	12	90	76	96	.376	.412
Grass	3.74	10	6	1	58	5	91.1	99	12	32	52	None on	.278	562	156	24	1	16	16	65	102	.358	.409
Turf	3.50	14	14	1	114	9	192.2	199	13	88	115	Runners on	.274	518	142	23	3	9	129	55	65	.347	.382
April	3.21	1	2	0	20	4	42.0	34	6	23	20	Scoring Posn	.264	326	86	16	3	7	123	46	47	.354	.396
May	3.64	6	1	0	39	2	54.1	57	6	22	39	Close & Late	.307	326	100	12	3	5	49	43	52	.391	.408
June	3.60	6	4	1	38	1	55.0	57	4	25	36	None on/out	.284	257	73	12	1	7	7	23	42	.350	.420
July	4.71	2	3	0	25	1	36.1	52	1	19	19	vs. 1st Batr (relief)	.301	146	44	6	1	5	31	12	25	.354	.459
August	3.34	4	5	1	22	0	32.1	30	4	11	18	First Inning Pitched	.278	543	151	28	1	15	90	70	88	.364	.416
September/October	3.23	5	5	0	28	6	64.0	68	4	20	35	First 15 Pitches	.279	519	145	24	1	14	68	54	71	.351	.410
Starter	3.88	4	5	0	14	14	62.2	63	8	29	35	Pitch 16-30	.274	307	84	14	2	5	45	36	54	.353	.381
Reliever	3.50	20	15	2	158	0	221.1	235	17	91	132	Pitch 31-45	.295	139	41	6	0	3	16	14	24	.361	.403
0 Days rest	3.80	5	4	1	30	0	42.2	56	4	16	20	Pitch 46+	.243	115	28	3	1	3	16	16	18	.346	.365
1 or 2 Days rest	4.63	7	9	0	74	0	91.1	104	8	44	60	First Pitch	.297	175	52	11	1	2	28	16	0	.366	.406
3+ Days rest	2.16	8	2	1	54	0	87.1	75	5	31	52	Ahead in Count	.219	493	108	15	2	10	44	0	148	.226	.318

Career (1990-1993)	ERA	W	L	Sv	G	GS	IP	H	HR	BB	SO		Avg	AB	H	2B	3B	HR	RBI	BB	SO	OBP	SLG
Pre-All Star	3.59	14	8	1	108	7	168.0	173	17	72	102	Behind in Count	.378	217	82	12	1	7	46	58	0	.505	.539
Post-All Star	3.57	10	12	1	64	7	116.0	125	8	48	65	Two Strikes	.204	461	94	12	2	11	47	46	167	.282	.310

Pitcher vs. Batter (career)

Pitches Best Vs.	Avg	AB	H	2B	3B	HR	RBI	BB	SO	OBP	SLG	Pitches Worst Vs.	Avg	AB	H	2B	3B	HR	RBI	BB	SO	OBP	SLG
Andre Dawson	.091	11	1	0	0	0	0	1	2	.167	.091	Sid Bream	.500	10	5	0	0	1	3	0	2	.455	.800
Howard Johnson	.125	8	1	1	0	0	2	4	2	.417	.250	Barry Bonds	.429	7	3	0	0	2	4	4	1	.636	1.286
Ozzie Smith	.167	12	2	1	0	0	1	1	0	.214	.250	Ryne Sandberg	.333	15	5	0	0	2	3	2	4	.412	.733
Jose Lind	.167	12	2	0	0	0	1	2	5	.286	.167	Ron Gant	.333	9	3	0	0	1	1	2	2	.455	.667
Terry Pendleton	.200	10	2	0	0	0	1	1	1	.273	.200	Mark Grace	.308	13	4	2	0	1	4	1	1	.333	.692

Juan Samuel — Reds

Age 33 – Bats Right (groundball hitter)

	Avg	G	AB	R	H	2B	3B	HR	RBI	BB	SO	HBP	GDP	SB	CS	OBP	SLG	IBB	SH	SF	#Pit	#P/PA	GB	FB	G/F
1993 Season	.230	103	261	31	60	10	4	4	26	23	53	3	2	9	7	.298	.345	3	0	2	1082	3.74	98	71	1.38
Last Five Years	.250	612	2103	258	526	80	19	40	207	179	481	24	27	120	50	.314	.363	18	21	14	8895	3.80	782	485	1.61

1993 Season

	Avg	AB	H	2B	3B	HR	RBI	BB	SO	OBP	SLG		Avg	AB	H	2B	3B	HR	RBI	BB	SO	OBP	SLG
vs. Left	.265	98	26	4	4	1	9	10	21	.339	.418	Scoring Posn	.348	46	16	2	1	2	24	12	4	.475	.565
vs. Right	.209	163	34	6	0	3	17	13	32	.272	.301	Close & Late	.273	44	12	1	0	1	6	5	11	.347	.364
Home	.224	98	22	2	2	1	9	12	18	.310	.316	None on/out	.187	75	14	1	3	0	0	3	20	.228	.280
Away	.233	163	38	8	2	3	17	11	35	.290	.362	Batting #1	.200	75	15	2	3	0	3	5	17	.250	.307
First Pitch	.351	37	13	2	1	2	6	2	0	.400	.622	Batting #7	.259	85	22	6	1	1	11	8	12	.337	.388
Ahead in Count	.291	55	16	5	1	2	9	10	0	.400	.527	Other	.228	101	23	2	0	3	12	10	24	.298	.337
Behind in Count	.161	124	20	1	1	0	7	0	47	.175	.185	Pre-All Star	.222	99	22	2	3	2	10	4	26	.260	.364
Two Strikes	.143	126	18	2	1	0	9	11	53	.216	.175	Post-All Star	.235	162	38	8	1	2	16	19	27	.319	.333

Last Five Years

	Avg	AB	H	2B	3B	HR	RBI	BB	SO	OBP	SLG		Avg	AB	H	2B	3B	HR	RBI	BB	SO	OBP	SLG
vs. Left	.268	829	222	34	11	24	92	70	180	.329	.422	Scoring Posn	.237	490	116	13	5	6	157	66	124	.329	.320
vs. Right	.239	1274	304	46	8	16	115	109	301	.305	.325	Close & Late	.295	322	95	15	3	7	48	33	84	.366	.425
Groundball	.264	675	178	23	6	12	69	57	152	.328	.369	None on/out	.254	544	138	20	7	12	12	45	113	.316	.382
Flyball	.229	476	109	20	4	6	38	43	123	.297	.326	Batting #2	.276	651	180	25	4	11	66	53	145	.339	.378
Home	.247	991	245	32	9	16	101	89	221	.315	.346	Batting #7	.259	482	125	30	1	13	58	55	108	.344	.407
Away	.253	1112	281	48	10	24	106	90	260	.313	.379	Other	.228	970	221	25	14	16	83	71	228	.282	.332
Day	.247	571	141	23	6	8	43	45	115	.308	.350	April	.243	280	68	10	2	7	30	24	69	.304	.368
Night	.251	1532	385	57	13	32	164	134	366	.317	.368	May	.263	315	83	12	1	7	28	24	74	.320	.375
Grass	.252	1311	331	51	11	24	131	109	300	.314	.363	June	.260	335	87	8	2	9	38	31	88	.321	.376
Turf	.246	792	195	29	8	16	76	70	181	.314	.364	July	.246	390	96	13	4	7	37	26	68	.299	.354
First Pitch	.344	247	85	14	4	8	38	11	0	.383	.530	August	.224	380	85	12	6	2	27	44	95	.313	.303
Ahead in Count	.365	417	152	25	5	19	66	85	0	.472	.585	September/October	.266	403	107	25	4	8	47	30	87	.327	.407
Behind in Count	.183	1053	193	27	4	11	74	0	410	.192	.248	Pre-All Star	.258	1068	276	35	8	26	116	84	252	.314	.379
Two Strikes	.167	1084	181	23	8	8	66	79	481	.230	.225	Post-All Star	.242	1035	250	45	11	14	91	95	229	.314	.347

Batter vs. Pitcher (since 1984)

Hits Best Against	Avg	AB	H	2B	3B	HR	RBI	BB	SO	OBP	SLG	Hits Worst Against	Avg	AB	H	2B	3B	HR	RBI	BB	SO	OBP	SLG
Bud Black	.526	19	10	1	1	2	3	2	0	.571	1.000	Mark Langston	.063	16	1	0	0	0	1	3	5	.211	.063
Mike Bielecki	.474	19	9	2	0	2	8	2	2	.478	.895	Bob Tewksbury	.083	12	1	0	0	0	0	1	2	.154	.083
Jim Gott	.417	12	5	1	0	1	3	0	2	.417	.750	Kent Mercker	.100	10	1	0	0	0	0	1	3	.182	.100
Rob Dibble	.400	10	4	1	0	1	7	0	4	.364	.800	Steve Avery	.129	31	4	1	0	0	2	0	6	.129	.161
John Dopson	.333	12	4	0	2	1	3	0	1	.333	.917	Danny Darwin	.133	15	2	0	0	0	1	1	3	.176	.133

Rey Sanchez — Cubs

Age 26 – Bats Right (groundball hitter)

	Avg	G	AB	R	H	2B	3B	HR	RBI	BB	SO	HBP	GDP	SB	CS	OBP	SLG	IBB	SH	SF	#Pit	#P/PA	GB	FB	G/F
1993 Season	.282	105	344	35	97	11	2	0	28	15	22	3	8	1	1	.316	.326	7	9	2	1068	2.86	157	76	2.07
Career (1991-1993)	.268	192	622	60	167	25	5	1	49	29	42	6	15	3	2	.306	.330	8	14	4	1961	2.91	283	137	2.07

1993 Season

	Avg	AB	H	2B	3B	HR	RBI	BB	SO	OBP	SLG		Avg	AB	H	2B	3B	HR	RBI	BB	SO	OBP	SLG
vs. Left	.297	118	35	1	0	0	8	3	5	.314	.305	Scoring Posn	.339	59	20	3	1	0	28	8	6	.414	.424
vs. Right	.274	226	62	10	2	0	20	12	17	.317	.336	Close & Late	.269	67	18	0	0	0	4	0	6	.279	.269
Groundball	.225	120	27	3	0	0	9	7	7	.277	.250	None on/out	.262	107	28	2	1	0	0	4	5	.295	.299
Flyball	.300	50	15	1	1	0	8	2	3	.327	.360	Batting #1	.286	105	30	5	0	0	4	5	5	.324	.333
Home	.308	159	49	7	1	0	18	8	11	.345	.365	Batting #2	.260	123	32	1	0	0	9	2	7	.272	.268
Away	.259	185	48	4	1	0	10	7	11	.291	.292	Other	.302	116	35	5	2	0	15	8	10	.352	.379
Day	.274	197	54	7	0	0	22	9	11	.309	.310	April	.256	86	22	1	0	0	6	2	5	.273	.267
Night	.293	147	43	4	2	0	6	6	11	.325	.347	May	.344	32	11	1	0	0	2	1	4	.364	.375
Grass	.304	263	80	9	2	0	24	9	19	.330	.354	June	.395	86	34	5	2	0	10	4	4	.419	.500
Turf	.210	81	17	2	0	0	4	6	3	.273	.235	July	.250	44	11	3	0	0	4	5	3	.327	.318
First Pitch	.266	79	21	3	0	0	9	5	0	.306	.304	August	.195	77	15	1	0	0	4	3	5	.244	.208
Ahead in Count	.268	97	26	2	0	0	10	6	0	.308	.289	September/October	.211	19	4	0	0	0	2	0	1	.211	.211
Behind in Count	.255	110	28	4	1	0	5	0	20	.274	.309	Pre-All Star	.324	210	68	7	2	0	18	7	13	.345	.376
Two Strikes	.255	94	24	3	2	0	2	4	22	.293	.330	Post-All Star	.216	134	29	4	0	0	10	8	9	.271	.246

1993 By Position

Position	Avg	AB	H	2B	3B	HR	RBI	BB	SO	OBP	SLG	G	GS	Innings	PO	A	E	DP	Fld Pct	Rng Fctr	In Zone	Outs	Zone Rtg	MLB Zone
As Pinch Hitter	.400	10	4	0	0	0	1	0	3	.400	.400	10	0	---	---	---	---	---	---	---	---	---	---	---

1993 By Position

Position	Avg	AB	H	2B	3B	HR	RBI	BB	SO	OBP	SLG	G	GS	Innings	PO	A	E	DP	Fld Pct	Rng Fctr	In Zone	Outs	Zone Rtg	MLB Zone
As ss	.278	334	93	11	2	0	27	15	19	.314	.323	98	82	762.1	158	317	15	62	.969	5.61	326	308	.945	.880

Ryne Sandberg — Cubs

Age 34 – Bats Right

	Avg	G	AB	R	H	2B	3B	HR	RBI	BB	SO	HBP	GDP	SB	CS	OBP	SLG	IBB	SH	SF	#Pit	#P/PA	GB	FB	G/F
1993 Season	.309	117	456	67	141	20	0	9	45	37	62	2	12	9	2	.359	.412	1	2	6	1961	3.90	191	118	1.62
Last Five Years	.300	745	2874	491	861	139	18	131	408	301	393	10	51	88	28	.364	.497	25	4	32	11975	3.72	1118	844	1.32

1993 Season

	Avg	AB	H	2B	3B	HR	RBI	BB	SO	OBP	SLG
vs. Left	.385	109	42	5	0	1	7	8	11	.427	.459
vs. Right	.285	347	99	15	0	8	38	29	51	.339	.398
Groundball	.341	173	59	9	0	2	16	17	21	.396	.428
Flyball	.313	67	21	2	0	0	1	3	9	.352	.343
Home	.296	243	72	10	0	5	30	22	34	.352	.399
Away	.324	213	69	10	0	4	15	15	28	.368	.427
Day	.287	244	70	8	0	4	28	18	37	.331	.369
Night	.335	212	71	12	0	5	17	19	25	.391	.462
Grass	.304	349	106	13	0	6	37	27	43	.352	.393
Turf	.327	107	35	7	0	3	8	10	19	.381	.477
First Pitch	.385	13	5	1	0	0	3	1	0	.400	.462
Ahead in Count	.358	95	34	5	0	5	14	21	0	.462	.568
Behind in Count	.298	248	74	9	0	2	21	0	52	.301	.359
Two Strikes	.276	221	61	8	0	1	18	15	62	.322	.326

	Avg	AB	H	2B	3B	HR	RBI	BB	SO	OBP	SLG
Scoring Posn	.282	103	29	5	0	0	34	13	15	.344	.330
Close & Late	.250	68	17	2	0	0	2	8	14	.333	.279
None on/out	.347	75	26	6	0	1	1	6	7	.395	.453
Batting #2	.316	215	68	15	0	5	17	18	25	.374	.456
Batting #3	.323	124	40	2	0	1	15	6	17	.348	.363
Other	.282	117	33	3	0	3	13	13	20	.343	.385
April	.000	3	0	0	0	0	0	2	2	.400	.000
May	.274	95	26	3	0	3	12	11	16	.336	.400
June	.341	91	31	3	0	1	11	3	9	.365	.407
July	.280	107	30	8	0	3	12	7	18	.322	.439
August	.348	112	39	5	0	2	7	9	10	.402	.446
September/October	.313	48	15	1	0	0	3	5	7	.377	.333
Pre-All Star	.293	232	68	7	0	5	28	19	33	.341	.388
Post-All Star	.326	224	73	13	0	4	17	18	29	.379	.438

1993 By Position

Position	Avg	AB	H	2B	3B	HR	RBI	BB	SO	OBP	SLG	G	GS	Innings	PO	A	E	DP	Fld Pct	Rng Fctr	In Zone	Outs	Zone Rtg	MLB Zone
As 2b	.309	453	140	20	0	9	45	37	61	.359	.413	115	114	989.0	209	347	7	77	.988	5.06	368	347	.943	.895

Last Five Years

	Avg	AB	H	2B	3B	HR	RBI	BB	SO	OBP	SLG
vs. Left	.324	910	295	60	6	30	101	121	102	.402	.502
vs. Right	.288	1964	566	79	12	101	307	180	291	.347	.495
Groundball	.311	1060	330	48	6	45	146	100	138	.370	.495
Flyball	.290	659	191	31	5	30	84	69	76	.358	.489
Home	.314	1442	453	73	12	77	242	156	193	.379	.542
Away	.285	1432	408	66	6	54	166	145	200	.350	.453
Day	.316	1493	472	72	8	72	231	153	196	.377	.520
Night	.282	1381	389	67	10	59	177	148	197	.351	.473
Grass	.305	2047	625	97	15	98	312	206	274	.367	.511
Turf	.285	827	236	42	3	33	96	95	119	.358	.463
First Pitch	.404	188	76	12	1	17	39	13	0	.444	.750
Ahead in Count	.351	730	256	53	7	48	128	166	0	.466	.640
Behind in Count	.249	1361	339	46	6	37	151	0	333	.250	.373
Two Strikes	.235	1243	292	39	3	37	130	113	393	.298	.360

	Avg	AB	H	2B	3B	HR	RBI	BB	SO	OBP	SLG
Scoring Posn	.290	618	179	28	7	24	250	104	88	.376	.474
Close & Late	.285	478	136	15	2	17	65	57	86	.359	.431
None on/out	.288	534	154	27	3	32	32	56	78	.357	.530
Batting #2	.308	1700	523	88	12	90	232	168	215	.368	.532
Batting #3	.297	906	269	42	5	32	140	99	129	.366	.460
Other	.257	268	69	9	1	9	36	34	49	.334	.399
April	.241	319	77	12	1	6	32	28	41	.301	.342
May	.320	522	167	30	1	25	73	52	70	.379	.525
June	.311	508	158	23	5	29	88	52	61	.375	.547
July	.276	489	135	25	4	16	60	55	73	.348	.442
August	.297	558	166	24	4	27	72	59	78	.363	.500
September/October	.331	478	158	25	3	28	83	55	70	.397	.571
Pre-All Star	.295	1510	445	72	8	64	214	155	197	.359	.480
Post-All Star	.305	1364	416	67	10	67	194	146	196	.370	.516

Batter vs. Pitcher (since 1984)

Hits Best Against	Avg	AB	H	2B	3B	HR	RBI	BB	SO	OBP	SLG
Eric Hillman	.545	11	6	0	0	1	2	0	0	.545	.818
Randy Tomlin	.500	28	14	2	2	1	5	2	1	.533	.821
Charlie Leibrandt	.500	16	8	1	0	2	3	3	1	.579	.938
Jeff Brantley	.500	10	5	1	0	1	3	3	3	.615	.900
Darryl Kile	.375	8	3	2	0	1	4	3	1	.500	1.000

Hits Worst Against	Avg	AB	H	2B	3B	HR	RBI	BB	SO	OBP	SLG
Ken Dayley	.000	10	0	0	0	0	0	4	1	.286	.000
Mark Langston	.000	8	0	0	0	0	0	3	3	.273	.000
Jeff Reardon	.071	14	1	0	0	0	2	0	4	.071	.071
Larry Andersen	.091	33	3	0	0	0	3	0	8	.088	.091
Mike Perez	.182	11	2	0	0	0	3	0	0	.167	.182

Deion Sanders — Braves

Age 26 – Bats Left

	Avg	G	AB	R	H	2B	3B	HR	RBI	BB	SO	HBP	GDP	SB	CS	OBP	SLG	IBB	SH	SF	#Pit	#P/PA	GB	FB	G/F
1993 Season	.276	95	272	42	75	18	6	6	28	16	42	3	3	19	7	.321	.452	3	1	2	996	3.39	104	71	1.46
Career (1989-1993)	.254	317	865	143	220	29	24	23	85	62	152	6	11	65	21	.307	.423	4	3	4	3200	3.40	330	229	1.44

1993 Season

	Avg	AB	H	2B	3B	HR	RBI	BB	SO	OBP	SLG
vs. Left	.143	35	5	0	0	0	2	0	8	.167	.143
vs. Right	.295	237	70	18	6	6	26	16	34	.342	.498
Home	.289	135	39	12	4	1	11	6	19	.319	.459
Away	.263	137	36	6	2	5	17	10	23	.322	.445
First Pitch	.339	56	19	4	1	3	10	3	0	.373	.607
Ahead in Count	.407	54	22	6	1	1	10	6	0	.460	.611
Behind in Count	.165	121	20	3	3	1	5	0	39	.179	.264
Two Strikes	.176	108	19	1	3	1	5	7	42	.239	.269

	Avg	AB	H	2B	3B	HR	RBI	BB	SO	OBP	SLG
Scoring Posn	.340	50	17	3	2	1	23	6	5	.407	.540
Close & Late	.262	42	11	4	1	0	4	4	3	.326	.405
None on/out	.257	113	29	9	2	2	2	7	18	.306	.425
Batting #1	.263	228	60	12	6	5	22	13	37	.303	.434
Batting #9	.474	19	9	3	0	1	3	3	1	.545	.789
Other	.240	25	6	3	0	0	3	0	4	.296	.360
Pre-All Star	.256	172	44	16	4	1	14	7	35	.295	.413
Post-All Star	.310	100	31	2	2	5	14	9	7	.364	.520

Career (1989-1993)

	Avg	AB	H	2B	3B	HR	RBI	BB	SO	OBP	SLG
vs. Left	.191	131	25	2	5	2	9	6	37	.232	.328
vs. Right	.266	734	195	27	19	21	76	56	115	.320	.440
Groundball	.279	297	83	8	9	9	37	22	45	.329	.458
Flyball	.286	192	55	4	6	8	19	15	39	.344	.495
Home	.249	410	102	14	10	9	40	34	75	.309	.398

	Avg	AB	H	2B	3B	HR	RBI	BB	SO	OBP	SLG
Scoring Posn	.289	187	54	5	7	4	64	28	32	.377	.455
Close & Late	.228	127	29	7	5	3	14	16	19	.324	.433
None on/out	.262	325	85	12	7	9	9	16	51	.300	.425
Batting #1	.267	606	162	17	22	17	57	40	101	.313	.452
Batting #2	.216	116	25	5	2	2	12	9	24	.289	.345

Career (1989-1993)

	Avg	AB	H	2B	3B	HR	RBI	BB	SO	OBP	SLG
Away	.259	455	118	15	14	14	45	28	77	.305	.446
Day	.241	212	51	6	5	4	15	21	35	.314	.373
Night	.259	653	169	23	19	19	70	41	117	.305	.440
Grass	.243	633	154	18	16	16	55	50	116	.301	.398
Turf	.284	232	66	11	8	7	30	12	36	.325	.491
First Pitch	.299	164	49	4	5	6	20	4	0	.315	.494
Ahead in Count	.328	195	64	13	5	4	27	26	0	.407	.508
Behind in Count	.182	362	66	7	8	9	26	0	132	.191	.320
Two Strikes	.167	336	56	3	7	7	23	32	152	.245	.280

	Avg	AB	H	2B	3B	HR	RBI	BB	SO	OBP	SLG
Other	.231	143	33	7	0	4	16	13	27	.297	.364
April	.271	177	48	8	8	5	16	15	30	.332	.492
May	.276	127	35	5	4	1	10	9	23	.328	.402
June	.210	224	47	7	3	5	16	17	42	.267	.335
July	.268	194	52	3	6	8	28	13	39	.316	.469
August	.262	103	27	3	3	3	13	5	13	.303	.437
September/October	.275	40	11	3	0	1	4	3	5	.326	.425
Pre-All Star	.246	598	147	22	19	13	50	45	111	.301	.411
Post-All Star	.273	267	73	7	5	10	35	17	41	.322	.449

Batter vs. Pitcher (career)

Hits Best Against	Avg	AB	H	2B	3B	HR	RBI	BB	SO	OBP	SLG
John Burkett	.600	15	9	1	2	0	3	0	2	.600	.933
David Cone	.600	10	6	0	0	1	1	1	1	.636	.900
Curt Schilling	.400	10	4	0	1	0	3	2	1	.500	.600
Tim Belcher	.385	26	10	2	2	1	1	2	4	.429	.731
Orel Hershiser	.348	23	8	1	1	2	3	1	3	.375	.739

Hits Worst Against	Avg	AB	H	2B	3B	HR	RBI	BB	SO	OBP	SLG
Jack Armstrong	.083	12	1	0	0	1	1	0	4	.083	.333
Doug Drabek	.133	15	2	1	0	0	1	1	2	.188	.200
Dennis Martinez	.158	19	3	1	0	0	2	0	5	.158	.211
Darryl Kile	.182	11	2	0	0	0	1	1	1	.250	.182
Frank Castillo	.182	11	2	1	0	0	0	1	2	.250	.273

Reggie Sanders — Reds

Age 26 – Bats Right

	Avg	G	AB	R	H	2B	3B	HR	RBI	BB	SO	HBP	GDP	SB	CS	OBP	SLG	IBB	SH	SF	#Pit	#P/PA	GB	FB	G/F
1993 Season	.274	138	496	90	136	16	4	20	83	51	118	5	10	27	10	.343	.444	7	3	8	2130	3.78	160	144	1.11
Career (1991-1993)	.269	263	921	158	248	42	10	33	122	99	225	9	17	44	18	.343	.444	9	3	9	3955	3.80	280	263	1.06

1993 Season

	Avg	AB	H	2B	3B	HR	RBI	BB	SO	OBP	SLG
vs. Left	.310	129	40	6	0	6	22	12	24	.366	.496
vs. Right	.262	367	96	10	4	14	61	39	94	.335	.425
Groundball	.313	176	55	5	1	9	36	25	42	.401	.506
Flyball	.222	72	16	1	1	2	10	5	28	.266	.347
Home	.287	237	68	12	1	8	43	25	58	.357	.447
Away	.263	259	68	4	3	12	40	26	60	.330	.440
Day	.259	139	36	4	1	5	29	13	32	.316	.410
Night	.280	357	100	12	3	15	54	38	86	.353	.457
Grass	.261	161	42	3	2	9	28	20	34	.344	.472
Turf	.281	335	94	13	2	11	55	31	84	.342	.430
First Pitch	.344	61	21	1	1	4	13	6	0	.400	.590
Ahead in Count	.435	115	50	6	1	10	38	23	0	.529	.765
Behind in Count	.213	230	49	8	2	3	19	0	94	.222	.304
Two Strikes	.171	245	42	6	2	2	20	21	118	.238	.237

	Avg	AB	H	2B	3B	HR	RBI	BB	SO	OBP	SLG
Scoring Posn	.322	149	48	6	3	5	65	27	40	.414	.503
Close & Late	.254	71	18	2	1	2	9	10	21	.349	.394
None on/out	.253	91	23	3	1	4	4	11	24	.333	.440
Batting #6	.302	169	51	6	1	7	34	14	37	.353	.473
Batting #7	.279	147	41	5	1	8	22	18	35	.357	.490
Other	.244	180	44	5	2	5	27	19	46	.322	.378
April	.240	75	18	2	1	2	8	6	21	.294	.373
May	.308	91	28	3	0	6	15	15	19	.404	.538
June	.239	92	22	2	0	3	14	8	23	.311	.359
July	.278	90	25	4	0	4	19	6	16	.330	.456
August	.311	61	19	3	1	2	14	8	13	.386	.492
September/October	.276	87	24	2	2	3	13	8	26	.333	.448
Pre-All Star	.270	296	80	9	1	13	45	30	71	.339	.439
Post-All Star	.280	200	56	7	3	7	38	21	47	.348	.450

1993 By Position

Position	Avg	AB	H	2B	3B	HR	RBI	BB	SO	OBP	SLG	G	GS	Innings	PO	A	E	DP	Fld Pct	Rng Fctr	In Zone	Outs	Zone Rtg	MLB Zone
As rf	.279	481	134	14	4	20	83	50	113	.347	.449	135	133	1161.1	302	4	7	0	.978	2.37	336	281	.836	.826

Career (1991-1993)

	Avg	AB	H	2B	3B	HR	RBI	BB	SO	OBP	SLG
vs. Left	.303	320	97	21	4	13	41	31	57	.369	.516
vs. Right	.251	601	151	21	6	20	81	68	168	.329	.406
Groundball	.298	309	92	14	3	12	50	40	82	.379	.479
Flyball	.196	153	30	3	1	3	14	27	54	.324	.288
Home	.260	453	118	26	4	14	65	57	112	.347	.428
Away	.278	468	130	16	6	19	57	42	113	.338	.459
Day	.251	267	67	14	2	7	41	33	71	.331	.397
Night	.277	654	181	28	8	26	81	66	154	.348	.463
Grass	.263	300	79	9	4	13	38	28	62	.329	.450
Turf	.272	621	169	33	6	20	84	71	163	.349	.441
First Pitch	.313	128	40	3	2	8	20	8	0	.353	.555
Ahead in Count	.409	193	79	11	1	13	49	45	0	.523	.679
Behind in Count	.202	440	89	21	5	6	31	0	184	.213	.314
Two Strikes	.168	459	77	17	5	2	28	45	225	.245	.240

	Avg	AB	H	2B	3B	HR	RBI	BB	SO	OBP	SLG
Scoring Posn	.270	252	68	9	4	6	87	38	78	.363	.409
Close & Late	.277	141	39	7	1	4	18	19	44	.364	.426
None on/out	.236	199	47	8	1	6	6	25	51	.321	.377
Batting #6	.305	223	68	9	2	9	40	22	55	.365	.484
Batting #7	.269	160	43	5	1	9	23	19	40	.346	.481
Other	.255	538	137	28	7	15	59	58	130	.333	.416
April	.277	148	41	6	3	4	14	12	37	.329	.439
May	.310	129	40	7	0	6	22	21	28	.406	.504
June	.237	173	41	7	1	5	22	14	44	.300	.376
July	.288	118	34	7	2	4	19	8	25	.339	.483
August	.273	161	44	8	2	8	22	24	38	.372	.497
September/October	.250	192	48	7	2	6	23	20	53	.322	.401
Pre-All Star	.276	515	142	25	5	17	66	50	126	.341	.443
Post-All Star	.261	406	106	17	5	16	56	49	99	.345	.446

Batter vs. Pitcher (career)

Hits Best Against	Avg	AB	H	2B	3B	HR	RBI	BB	SO	OBP	SLG
Armando Reynoso	.700	10	7	0	1	3	5	1	1	.727	1.800
Bruce Hurst	.500	14	7	2	0	1	3	0	3	.500	.857
Bobby Ojeda	.429	14	6	2	0	1	1	1	2	.467	.786
Doug Drabek	.417	12	5	0	0	1	1	1	2	.462	.667
Dwight Gooden	.375	8	3	0	0	1	3	2	3	.455	.750

Hits Worst Against	Avg	AB	H	2B	3B	HR	RBI	BB	SO	OBP	SLG
Kevin Gross	.071	14	1	0	0	0	0	2	5	.188	.071
Pete Harnisch	.091	11	1	0	0	0	0	1	7	.167	.091
John Smoltz	.100	20	2	0	0	1	2	0	9	.100	.250
Charlie Leibrandt	.133	15	2	0	0	0	0	0	3	.133	.133
Bill Swift	.188	16	3	0	0	0	0	1	7	.235	.188

Scott Sanders — Padres

Age 25 – Pitches Right (groundball pitcher)

	ERA	W	L	Sv	G	GS	IP	BB	SO	Avg	H	2B	3B	HR	RBI	OBP	SLG	CG	ShO	Sup	QS	#P/S	SB	CS	GB	FB	G/F
1993 Season	4.13	3	3	0	9	9	52.1	23	37	.265	54	6	1	4	29	.339	.363	0	0	4.99	3	92	4	4	86	42	2.05

1993 Season

	ERA	W	L	Sv	G	GS	IP	H	HR	BB	SO
Home	4.33	2	1	0	5	5	27.0	30	2	12	17
Away	3.91	1	2	0	4	4	25.1	24	2	11	20

	Avg	AB	H	2B	3B	HR	RBI	BB	SO	OBP	SLG
vs. Left	.333	93	31	4	0	3	15	18	10	.446	.473
vs. Right	.207	111	23	2	1	1	14	5	27	.237	.270

Scott Sanderson — Giants

Age 37 – Pitches Right (flyball pitcher)

	ERA	W	L	Sv	G	GS	IP	BB	SO	Avg	H	2B	3B	HR	RBI	OBP	SLG	CG	ShO	Sup	QS	#P/S	SB	CS	GB	FB	G/F
1993 Season	4.21	11	13	0	32	29	184.0	34	102	.280	201	34	3	27	89	.314	.448	4	1	4.16	16	90	7	6	219	268	0.82
Last Five Years	4.15	67	54	0	170	153	938.0	224	550	.269	981	183	25	120	436	.311	.431	12	5	5.12	74	90	69	31	1111	1339	0.83

1993 Season

	ERA	W	L	Sv	G	GS	IP	H	HR	BB	SO
Home	4.85	5	5	0	15	14	85.1	89	17	18	50
Away	3.65	6	8	0	17	15	98.2	112	10	16	52
Day	3.50	4	5	0	13	11	72.0	68	9	11	42
Night	4.66	7	8	0	19	18	112.0	133	18	23	60
Grass	4.54	9	10	0	26	24	148.2	162	23	30	84
Turf	2.80	2	3	0	6	5	35.1	39	4	4	18
April	3.00	3	0	0	4	4	27.0	19	2	8	19
May	2.70	4	2	0	6	6	43.1	40	4	4	22
June	6.00	0	6	0	6	6	35.2	51	5	10	16
July	6.44	0	3	0	5	5	29.1	43	4	5	9
August	4.30	2	1	0	5	4	23.0	26	6	3	13
September/October	2.81	2	1	0	6	4	25.2	22	6	4	23
Starter	4.28	11	13	0	29	29	178.2	198	26	34	100
Reliever	1.69	0	0	0	3	0	5.1	3	1	0	2
0-3 Days Rest	5.40	1	1	0	2	2	11.2	18	1	1	7
4 Days Rest	4.30	5	7	0	15	15	96.1	106	11	22	45
5+ Days Rest	4.08	5	5	0	12	12	70.2	74	14	11	48
Pre-All Star	4.04	7	8	0	18	18	118.0	123	13	24	57
Post-All Star	4.50	4	5	0	14	11	66.0	78	14	10	45

	Avg	AB	H	2B	3B	HR	RBI	BB	SO	OBP	SLG
vs. Left	.271	354	96	14	1	17	47	24	55	.317	.460
vs. Right	.288	364	105	20	2	10	42	10	47	.311	.437
Inning 1-6	.272	633	172	30	3	25	82	32	94	.307	.447
Inning 7+	.341	85	29	4	0	2	7	2	8	.364	.459
None on	.265	449	119	25	1	16	16	14	62	.293	.432
Runners on	.305	269	82	9	2	11	73	20	40	.346	.476
Scoring Posn	.284	141	40	3	1	6	61	15	22	.339	.447
Close & Late	.429	35	15	2	0	1	5	1	1	.444	.571
None on/out	.296	189	56	12	0	6	6	5	22	.325	.455
vs. 1st Batr (relief)	.333	3	1	0	0	0	1	0	0	.333	.333
First Inning Pitched	.262	122	32	6	1	4	17	7	24	.303	.426
First 75 Pitches	.268	574	154	26	2	21	71	28	86	.302	.430
Pitch 76-90	.318	85	27	7	1	4	10	4	10	.356	.565
Pitch 91-105	.311	45	14	1	0	2	8	1	5	.333	.467
Pitch 106+	.429	14	6	0	0	0	0	1	1	.467	.429
First Pitch	.288	104	30	3	1	7	18	7	0	.342	.538
Ahead in Count	.236	347	82	17	1	7	30	0	83	.240	.352
Behind in Count	.370	138	51	9	0	5	19	12	0	.409	.543
Two Strikes	.211	313	66	8	2	10	32	15	102	.252	.345

Last Five Years

	ERA	W	L	Sv	G	GS	IP	H	HR	BB	SO
Home	4.40	29	27	0	81	71	441.1	466	71	110	258
Away	3.93	38	27	0	89	82	496.2	515	49	114	292
Day	3.96	20	21	0	66	54	352.0	345	43	89	223
Night	4.27	47	33	0	104	99	586.0	636	77	135	327
Grass	4.29	55	46	0	139	127	771.2	823	104	186	457
Turf	3.52	12	8	0	31	26	166.1	158	16	38	93
April	4.58	10	5	0	22	22	125.2	131	21	34	69
May	3.13	17	6	0	27	27	172.2	168	14	32	103
June	4.06	11	15	0	29	29	179.2	194	18	49	94
July	5.41	7	12	0	28	28	166.1	199	25	29	87
August	3.87	11	7	0	33	24	163.0	155	25	48	114
September/October	3.99	11	9	0	31	23	130.2	134	17	32	83
Starter	4.19	66	52	0	153	153	906.0	948	115	215	526
Reliever	3.09	1	2	0	17	0	32.0	33	5	9	24
0-3 Days Rest	3.86	4	2	0	8	8	44.1	49	4	10	19
4 Days Rest	4.28	41	36	0	98	98	597.0	629	78	155	351
5+ Days Rest	4.05	21	14	0	47	47	264.2	270	33	50	156
Pre-All Star	4.03	41	28	0	87	87	533.1	563	64	124	290
Post-All Star	4.31	26	26	0	83	66	404.2	418	56	100	260

	Avg	AB	H	2B	3B	HR	RBI	BB	SO	OBP	SLG
vs. Left	.270	1903	514	86	14	66	236	139	269	.319	.434
vs. Right	.267	1748	467	97	11	54	200	85	281	.303	.428
Inning 1-6	.268	3272	877	166	22	110	410	200	497	.310	.433
Inning 7+	.274	379	104	17	3	10	26	24	53	.321	.414
None on	.264	2227	589	114	14	70	70	112	329	.303	.423
Runners on	.275	1424	392	69	11	50	366	112	221	.324	.445
Scoring Posn	.276	749	207	37	6	22	296	81	128	.337	.430
Close & Late	.291	148	43	6	1	2	10	13	19	.352	.385
None on/out	.285	964	275	51	8	26	26	42	126	.319	.436
vs. 1st Batr (relief)	.375	16	6	1	0	0	4	1	2	.412	.438
First Inning Pitched	.277	667	185	30	5	18	89	47	127	.325	.418
First 75 Pitches	.269	2895	778	140	18	94	350	169	449	.309	.427
Pitch 76-90	.284	419	119	24	5	20	58	26	49	.327	.508
Pitch 91-105	.238	240	57	11	1	5	22	17	35	.290	.354
Pitch 106+	.278	97	27	8	1	1	6	12	17	.358	.412
First Pitch	.308	522	161	29	6	25	83	18	0	.335	.531
Ahead in Count	.221	1753	387	68	8	33	166	0	478	.224	.325
Behind in Count	.345	754	260	58	7	33	110	108	0	.421	.572
Two Strikes	.203	1669	339	57	8	35	157	98	550	.249	.310

Pitcher vs. Batter (since 1984)

Pitches Best Vs.	Avg	AB	H	2B	3B	HR	RBI	BB	SO	OBP	SLG
Greg Briley	.000	21	0	0	0	0	0	0	3	.000	.000
Cory Snyder	.000	11	0	0	0	0	0	0	4	.000	.000
Rob Deer	.056	18	1	0	0	0	0	2	8	.150	.056
Brian McRae	.077	13	1	0	0	0	1	0	2	.077	.077
Ernest Riles	.091	11	1	0	0	0	1	0	1	.091	.091

Pitches Worst Vs.	Avg	AB	H	2B	3B	HR	RBI	BB	SO	OBP	SLG
Shane Mack	.533	15	8	0	0	3	6	1	1	.563	1.133
Roberto Alomar	.524	21	11	2	1	1	5	3	3	.560	.857
Scott Fletcher	.516	31	16	2	1	2	12	0	2	.516	.839
Julio Franco	.500	18	9	1	0	2	4	3	0	.571	.889
Robin Ventura	.471	17	8	1	0	2	8	3	2	.550	.882

Mo Sanford — Rockies

Age 27 – Pitches Right (flyball pitcher)

	ERA	W	L	Sv	G	GS	IP	BB	SO	Avg	H	2B	3B	HR	RBI	OBP	SLG	CG	ShO	Sup	QS	#P/S	SB	CS	GB	FB	G/F
1993 Season	5.30	1	2	0	11	6	35.2	27	36	.278	37	6	3	4	23	.395	.459	0	0	3.79	1	92	8	1	38	36	1.06
Career (1991-1993)	4.66	2	4	0	16	11	63.2	42	67	.238	56	8	3	7	35	.354	.387	0	0	4.38	3	93	12	1	57	63	0.90

1993 Season

	ERA	W	L	Sv	G	GS	IP	H	HR	BB	SO
Home	5.54	0	1	0	6	2	13.0	14	1	10	14
Away	5.16	1	1	0	5	4	22.2	23	3	17	22

	Avg	AB	H	2B	3B	HR	RBI	BB	SO	OBP	SLG
vs. Left	.349	63	22	4	2	2	14	17	13	.481	.571
vs. Right	.214	70	15	2	1	2	9	10	23	.309	.357

Benito Santiago — Marlins

Age 29 – Bats Right

	Avg	G	AB	R	H	2B	3B	HR	RBI	BB	SO	HBP	GDP	SB	CS	OBP	SLG	IBB	SH	SF	#Pit	#P/PA	GB	FB	G/F
1993 Season	.230	139	469	49	108	19	6	13	50	37	88	5	9	10	7	.291	.380	2	0	4	1744	3.38	157	146	1.08
Last Five Years	.251	626	2241	238	562	86	17	67	294	134	398	13	57	36	33	.294	.394	16	4	24	8087	3.35	716	698	1.03

1993 Season

	Avg	AB	H	2B	3B	HR	RBI	BB	SO	OBP	SLG
vs. Left	.276	123	34	8	3	4	15	15	15	.355	.488
vs. Right	.214	346	74	11	3	9	35	22	73	.268	.341
Groundball	.232	155	36	8	2	6	18	11	24	.288	.426

	Avg	AB	H	2B	3B	HR	RBI	BB	SO	OBP	SLG
Scoring Posn	.223	121	27	5	3	2	36	13	12	.295	.364
Close & Late	.148	88	13	3	0	2	5	5	26	.202	.250
None on/out	.264	106	28	3	3	5	5	8	24	.322	.491

1993 Season	Avg	AB	H	2B	3B	HR	RBI	BB	SO	OBP	SLG		Avg	AB	H	2B	3B	HR	RBI	BB	SO	OBP	SLG
Flyball	.229	96	22	3	3	2	7	8	22	.288	.385	Batting #5	.222	117	26	4	1	4	14	13	24	.303	.376
Home	.227	233	53	11	4	6	29	18	52	.291	.386	Batting #6	.247	194	48	9	4	7	25	13	40	.300	.443
Away	.233	236	55	8	2	7	21	19	36	.292	.373	Other	.215	158	34	6	1	2	11	11	24	.272	.304
Day	.286	70	20	2	0	1	6	11	10	.373	.357	April	.253	79	20	4	0	3	9	8	17	.322	.418
Night	.221	399	88	17	6	12	44	26	78	.275	.383	May	.189	90	17	5	0	1	10	8	17	.257	.278
Grass	.216	361	78	14	4	9	39	30	72	.281	.352	June	.281	89	25	3	4	2	13	7	17	.354	.472
Turf	.278	108	30	5	2	4	11	7	16	.325	.472	July	.183	82	15	3	0	2	7	6	20	.236	.293
First Pitch	.330	94	31	5	3	3	10	1	0	.351	.543	August	.230	87	20	3	1	2	2	4	11	.264	.356
Ahead in Count	.298	84	25	5	0	3	10	15	0	.400	.464	September/October	.262	42	11	1	1	3	9	4	6	.333	.548
Behind in Count	.156	211	33	8	2	3	17	0	78	.164	.256	Pre-All Star	.234	291	68	13	4	7	34	27	59	.306	.378
Two Strikes	.129	194	25	7	1	3	17	21	88	.220	.222	Post-All Star	.225	178	40	6	2	6	16	10	29	.267	.382

1993 By Position

Position	Avg	AB	H	2B	3B	HR	RBI	BB	SO	OBP	SLG	G	GS	Innings	PO	A	E	DP	Fld Pct	Rng Fctr	In Zone	Outs	Zone Rtg	MLB Zone
As c	.231	463	107	19	6	13	49	36	86	.292	.382	136	125	1095.0	741	63	11	4	.987	---	---	---	---	---

Last Five Years

	Avg	AB	H	2B	3B	HR	RBI	BB	SO	OBP	SLG		Avg	AB	H	2B	3B	HR	RBI	BB	SO	OBP	SLG
vs. Left	.272	690	188	33	6	22	91	52	117	.322	.433	Scoring Posn	.250	627	157	21	7	20	231	48	114	.296	.402
vs. Right	.241	1551	374	53	11	45	203	82	281	.281	.377	Close & Late	.275	411	113	16	3	13	51	26	81	.321	.423
Groundball	.255	801	204	33	7	20	107	41	114	.292	.388	None on/out	.258	511	132	18	5	17	17	31	99	.305	.413
Flyball	.249	506	126	19	4	19	66	25	120	.281	.415	Batting #5	.246	905	223	34	3	24	133	56	160	.289	.370
Home	.263	1116	293	41	10	33	149	64	203	.304	.406	Batting #6	.258	792	204	35	9	26	97	46	144	.297	.423
Away	.239	1125	269	45	7	34	145	70	195	.284	.382	Other	.248	544	135	17	5	17	64	32	94	.297	.392
Day	.284	440	125	13	3	17	67	34	82	.337	.443	April	.273	396	108	16	1	13	54	19	59	.308	.417
Night	.243	1801	437	73	14	50	227	100	316	.283	.382	May	.227	450	102	18	2	9	58	22	79	.261	.336
Grass	.259	1670	432	58	13	56	233	102	305	.303	.410	June	.291	302	88	11	6	9	43	22	61	.345	.457
Turf	.228	571	130	28	4	11	61	32	93	.269	.349	July	.239	280	67	12	1	7	32	19	57	.289	.364
First Pitch	.325	437	142	21	3	18	76	12	0	.340	.510	August	.235	421	99	15	5	12	36	23	67	.276	.380
Ahead in Count	.298	466	139	22	3	19	73	52	0	.365	.481	September/October	.250	392	98	14	2	17	71	29	75	.301	.426
Behind in Count	.188	954	179	28	7	19	95	0	334	.194	.291	Pre-All Star	.253	1229	311	46	9	35	160	68	218	.294	.391
Two Strikes	.159	898	143	28	5	16	80	67	398	.222	.255	Post-All Star	.248	1012	251	40	8	32	134	66	180	.294	.398

Batter vs. Pitcher (career)

Hits Best Against	Avg	AB	H	2B	3B	HR	RBI	BB	SO	OBP	SLG	Hits Worst Against	Avg	AB	H	2B	3B	HR	RBI	BB	SO	OBP	SLG
Paul Assenmacher	.500	10	5	1	0	0	2	2	2	.583	.600	Dave Burba	.000	11	0	0	0	0	0	1	1	.083	.000
John Burkett	.462	26	12	0	0	1	2	1	2	.481	.577	Doug Drabek	.045	22	1	0	1	0	3	1	4	.087	.136
Trevor Wilson	.462	13	6	2	1	1	7	2	2	.533	1.000	Ted Power	.063	16	1	0	0	0	1	0	3	.063	.063
Zane Smith	.419	31	13	4	0	5	10	2	3	.455	1.032	Larry Andersen	.071	14	1	0	0	0	2	1	3	.133	.071
Rick Sutcliffe	.385	13	5	1	0	1	2	2	2	.467	.692	Tim Pugh	.071	14	1	0	0	0	0	1	3	.133	.071

Nelson Santovenia — Royals

Age 32 – Bats Right

	Avg	G	AB	R	H	2B	3B	HR	RBI	BB	SO	HBP	GDP	SB	CS	OBP	SLG	IBB	SH	SF	#Pit	#P/PA	GB	FB	G/F
1993 Season	.125	4	8	0	1	0	0	0	0	1	2	0	0	0	0	.222	.125	0	0	0	39	4.33	1	3	0.33
Last Five Years	.232	203	574	51	133	22	2	14	75	35	88	3	21	2	4	.274	.350	4	2	13	2122	3.38	202	195	1.04

1993 Season

	Avg	AB	H	2B	3B	HR	RBI	BB	SO	OBP	SLG		Avg	AB	H	2B	3B	HR	RBI	BB	SO	OBP	SLG
vs. Left	.000	1	0	0	0	0	0	1	0	.500	.000	Scoring Posn	.000	2	0	0	0	0	0	0	0	.000	.000
vs. Right	.143	7	1	0	0	0	0	0	2	.143	.143	Close & Late	.000	1	0	0	0	0	0	0	1	.000	.000

Last Five Years

	Avg	AB	H	2B	3B	HR	RBI	BB	SO	OBP	SLG		Avg	AB	H	2B	3B	HR	RBI	BB	SO	OBP	SLG
vs. Left	.241	216	52	9	1	5	24	13	24	.281	.361	Scoring Posn	.253	158	40	5	1	4	60	14	24	.292	.373
vs. Right	.226	358	81	13	1	9	51	22	64	.269	.344	Close & Late	.267	120	32	8	1	1	19	7	18	.305	.375
Groundball	.277	224	62	9	1	4	36	13	21	.314	.379	None on/out	.131	130	17	3	0	3	3	7	23	.181	.223
Flyball	.194	155	30	5	1	3	11	7	30	.236	.297	Batting #6	.217	69	15	2	0	1	6	3	10	.253	.290
Home	.277	249	69	11	1	9	43	21	34	.325	.438	Batting #7	.224	411	92	15	1	9	52	29	66	.273	.331
Away	.197	325	64	11	1	5	32	14	54	.232	.283	Other	.277	94	26	5	1	4	17	3	12	.293	.479
Day	.270	148	40	6	1	4	17	8	24	.310	.405	April	.219	128	28	5	0	3	15	9	19	.275	.328
Night	.218	426	93	16	1	10	58	27	64	.261	.331	May	.247	81	20	4	0	1	8	8	15	.312	.333
Grass	.203	138	28	3	0	3	12	4	27	.225	.290	June	.264	91	24	5	0	4	16	6	22	.309	.451
Turf	.241	436	105	19	2	11	63	31	61	.288	.369	July	.250	72	18	3	1	4	15	4	4	.282	.486
First Pitch	.258	93	24	3	0	1	11	4	0	.293	.323	August	.222	54	12	2	0	0	3	4	6	.271	.259
Ahead in Count	.243	140	34	8	0	6	23	19	0	.329	.429	September/October	.209	148	31	3	1	2	18	4	22	.224	.284
Behind in Count	.208	259	54	10	2	4	25	0	75	.208	.309	Pre-All Star	.239	331	79	16	0	9	47	24	59	.290	.369
Two Strikes	.183	235	43	6	1	3	27	12	88	.218	.255	Post-All Star	.222	243	54	6	2	5	28	11	29	.251	.325

Batter vs. Pitcher (career)

Hits Best Against	Avg	AB	H	2B	3B	HR	RBI	BB	SO	OBP	SLG	Hits Worst Against	Avg	AB	H	2B	3B	HR	RBI	BB	SO	OBP	SLG
Joe Magrane	.429	14	6	1	0	0	5	2	1	.500	.500	Tim Belcher	.077	13	1	1	0	0	2	1	2	.143	.154
Zane Smith	.364	11	4	0	0	0	0	0	0	.364	.364	Jose DeLeon	.100	20	2	0	0	0	2	1	10	.143	.100
Bobby Ojeda	.333	12	4	2	0	0	1	0	2	.333	.500	David Cone	.167	12	2	0	0	0	0	0	4	.167	.167
Tom Glavine	.308	13	4	1	0	1	4	1	2	.333	.615	Sid Fernandez	.188	16	3	0	0	1	1	0	5	.188	.375
												Greg Maddux	.200	15	3	0	0	0	1	0	4	.188	.200

Mackey Sasser — Mariners

Age 31 – Bats Left

	Avg	G	AB	R	H	2B	3B	HR	RBI	BB	SO	HBP	GDP	SB	CS	OBP	SLG	IBB	SH	SF	#Pit	#P/PA	GB	FB	G/F
1993 Season	.218	83	188	18	41	10	2	1	21	15	30	1	7	1	0	.274	.309	6	0	4	658	3.16	74	48	1.54
Last Five Years	.271	443	1009	91	273	58	6	15	137	49	93	3	27	1	3	.302	.385	21	2	16	3109	2.88	366	327	1.12

1993 Season

	Avg	AB	H	2B	3B	HR	RBI	BB	SO	OBP	SLG		Avg	AB	H	2B	3B	HR	RBI	BB	SO	OBP	SLG
vs. Left	.286	7	2	0	0	0	1	0	0	.286	.286	Scoring Posn	.208	48	10	3	1	0	18	7	7	.288	.313
vs. Right	.215	181	39	10	2	1	20	15	30	.274	.309	Close & Late	.194	36	7	2	0	0	7	7	7	.311	.250
Home	.225	102	23	7	1	0	11	11	15	.302	.314	None on/out	.256	43	11	3	0	0	0	2	6	.289	.326
Away	.209	86	18	3	1	1	10	4	15	.239	.302	Batting #2	.208	53	11	2	1	0	9	2	9	.246	.283
First Pitch	.333	45	15	5	1	0	5	4	0	.380	.489	Batting #7	.200	50	10	2	1	0	6	6	7	.281	.280
Ahead in Count	.324	34	11	1	1	1	7	6	0	.425	.500	Other	.235	85	20	6	0	1	6	7	14	.287	.341
Behind in Count	.092	76	7	2	0	0	3	0	26	.104	.118	Pre-All Star	.248	117	29	7	2	0	15	6	17	.286	.342
Two Strikes	.125	72	9	3	0	0	4	5	30	.179	.167	Post-All Star	.169	71	12	3	0	1	6	9	13	.256	.254

Last Five Years

	Avg	AB	H	2B	3B	HR	RBI	BB	SO	OBP	SLG		Avg	AB	H	2B	3B	HR	RBI	BB	SO	OBP	SLG
vs. Left	.206	131	27	7	0	1	13	5	22	.232	.282	Scoring Posn	.278	270	75	17	3	7	120	27	30	.328	.441
vs. Right	.280	878	246	51	6	14	124	44	71	.312	.400	Close & Late	.206	223	46	13	0	3	32	14	27	.246	.305
Groundball	.310	306	95	19	1	5	49	11	21	.334	.428	None on/out	.290	231	67	17	1	2	2	4	15	.305	.398
Flyball	.241	232	56	13	3	4	35	7	25	.261	.375	Batting #7	.283	364	103	25	2	5	52	21	24	.321	.404
Home	.267	521	139	33	3	8	78	30	46	.304	.388	Batting #8	.269	182	49	11	1	3	25	8	18	.297	.390
Away	.275	488	134	25	3	7	59	19	47	.300	.381	Other	.261	463	121	22	3	7	60	20	51	.289	.367
Day	.301	329	99	20	5	5	51	11	30	.322	.438	April	.157	70	11	2	0	0	4	5	7	.211	.186
Night	.256	680	174	38	1	10	86	38	63	.292	.359	May	.339	127	43	9	1	4	17	6	12	.366	.520
Grass	.283	636	180	36	3	11	95	23	54	.306	.401	June	.281	224	63	13	2	1	30	15	19	.325	.371
Turf	.249	373	93	22	3	4	42	26	39	.295	.357	July	.340	200	68	18	2	6	46	4	15	.351	.540
First Pitch	.335	281	94	28	3	3	46	8	0	.347	.488	August	.227	207	47	10	1	2	19	9	23	.256	.314
Ahead in Count	.313	224	70	12	2	4	35	20	0	.366	.438	September/October	.227	181	41	6	0	2	21	10	17	.264	.293
Behind in Count	.204	348	71	12	1	4	32	0	83	.208	.279	Pre-All Star	.279	494	138	30	5	6	65	28	46	.318	.397
Two Strikes	.201	294	59	10	0	5	31	12	93	.234	.286	Post-All Star	.262	515	135	28	1	9	72	21	47	.286	.373

Batter vs. Pitcher (career)

Hits Best Against	Avg	AB	H	2B	3B	HR	RBI	BB	SO	OBP	SLG	Hits Worst Against	Avg	AB	H	2B	3B	HR	RBI	BB	SO	OBP	SLG
Mark Portugal	.444	18	8	1	1	1	5	1	2	.474	.778	Tim Belcher	.167	12	2	0	0	0	0	0	0	.167	.167
Ramon Martinez	.438	16	7	2	0	1	1	0	1	.438	.750	Pete Smith	.182	11	2	0	0	0	1	0	0	.167	.182
Bob Tewksbury	.385	13	5	1	0	0	1	0	1	.385	.462	Lee Smith	.200	15	3	1	1	0	3	0	2	.200	.400
Doug Drabek	.333	18	6	1	0	1	4	2	0	.381	.556	John Smoltz	.211	19	4	1	0	0	5	0	2	.200	.263
Jose DeLeon	.333	15	5	1	0	1	5	0	0	.333	.600	Greg Maddux	.214	28	6	1	0	0	4	1	3	.241	.250

Doug Saunders — Mets

Age 24 – Bats Right

	Avg	G	AB	R	H	2B	3B	HR	RBI	BB	SO	HBP	GDP	SB	CS	OBP	SLG	IBB	SH	SF	#Pit	#P/PA	GB	FB	G/F
1993 Season	.209	28	67	8	14	2	0	0	0	3	4	0	2	0	0	.243	.239	0	3	0	232	3.18	28	20	1.40

1993 Season

	Avg	AB	H	2B	3B	HR	RBI	BB	SO	OBP	SLG		Avg	AB	H	2B	3B	HR	RBI	BB	SO	OBP	SLG
vs. Left	.217	23	5	1	0	0	0	1	0	.250	.261	Scoring Posn	.000	15	0	0	0	0	0	2	2	.118	.000
vs. Right	.205	44	9	1	0	0	0	2	4	.239	.227	Close & Late	.167	6	1	1	0	0	0	0	1	.167	.333

Steve Sax — White Sox

Age 34 – Bats Right (groundball hitter)

	Avg	G	AB	R	H	2B	3B	HR	RBI	BB	SO	HBP	GDP	SB	CS	OBP	SLG	IBB	SH	SF	#Pit	#P/PA	GB	FB	G/F
1993 Season	.235	57	119	20	28	5	0	1	8	8	6	0	1	7	3	.283	.303	0	2	0	482	3.74	59	31	1.90
Last Five Years	.278	671	2604	337	725	119	11	24	216	193	176	10	64	154	52	.328	.360	11	33	23	10052	3.51	1437	531	2.71

1993 Season

	Avg	AB	H	2B	3B	HR	RBI	BB	SO	OBP	SLG		Avg	AB	H	2B	3B	HR	RBI	BB	SO	OBP	SLG
vs. Left	.239	67	16	4	0	0	5	4	3	.282	.299	Scoring Posn	.172	29	5	2	0	0	7	2	2	.226	.241
vs. Right	.231	52	12	1	0	1	3	4	3	.286	.308	Close & Late	.350	20	7	1	0	0	1	0	1	.350	.400
Home	.250	60	15	2	0	1	4	3	4	.286	.333	None on/out	.279	43	12	1	0	1	1	3	2	.326	.372
Away	.220	59	13	3	0	0	4	5	2	.281	.271	Batting #1	.222	63	14	3	0	1	3	5	3	.279	.317
First Pitch	.167	6	1	0	0	0	0	0	0	.167	.167	Batting #7	.391	23	9	1	0	0	1	1	1	.417	.435
Ahead in Count	.265	34	9	1	0	1	6	5	0	.359	.382	Other	.152	33	5	1	0	0	4	2	2	.200	.182
Behind in Count	.232	56	13	3	0	0	2	0	6	.232	.286	Pre-All Star	.214	56	12	3	0	1	3	4	3	.267	.321
Two Strikes	.239	46	11	3	0	0	2	3	6	.286	.304	Post-All Star	.254	63	16	2	0	0	5	4	3	.299	.286

Last Five Years

	Avg	AB	H	2B	3B	HR	RBI	BB	SO	OBP	SLG		Avg	AB	H	2B	3B	HR	RBI	BB	SO	OBP	SLG
vs. Left	.302	818	247	49	2	8	60	69	34	.355	.396	Scoring Posn	.262	588	154	19	6	7	191	54	51	.317	.350
vs. Right	.268	1786	478	70	9	16	156	124	142	.315	.344	Close & Late	.276	398	110	15	3	3	40	30	29	.324	.352
Groundball	.276	725	200	26	0	8	68	52	60	.324	.345	None on/out	.275	767	211	35	2	9	9	47	43	.319	.361
Flyball	.279	569	159	29	6	4	52	51	33	.339	.373	Batting #1	.287	1151	330	56	3	13	90	78	75	.332	.374
Home	.275	1297	357	66	8	13	116	104	88	.328	.369	Batting #2	.276	1248	345	54	7	9	105	101	90	.330	.353
Away	.282	1307	368	53	3	11	100	89	88	.328	.352	Other	.244	205	50	9	1	2	21	14	11	.293	.327
Day	.284	751	213	36	7	4	70	61	42	.337	.366	April	.283	314	89	9	1	3	34	26	20	.336	.347
Night	.276	1853	512	83	4	20	146	132	134	.324	.358	May	.249	425	106	18	2	1	26	43	25	.317	.308
Grass	.276	2196	606	103	10	21	176	168	147	.327	.361	June	.308	448	138	19	2	4	40	31	32	.353	.386
Turf	.292	408	119	16	1	3	40	25	29	.335	.358	July	.277	430	119	25	2	8	45	31	32	.325	.400
First Pitch	.311	244	76	11	2	3	27	8	0	.340	.410	August	.270	500	135	25	2	1	34	38	39	.322	.334

Last Five Years

	Avg	AB	H	2B	3B	HR	RBI	BB	SO	OBP	SLG
Ahead in Count	.330	669	221	45	5	11	73	119	0	.428	.462
Behind in Count	.238	1154	275	36	2	7	78	0	157	.240	.291
Two Strikes	.235	987	232	35	2	6	58	64	176	.281	.293

	Avg	AB	H	2B	3B	HR	RBI	BB	SO	OBP	SLG
September/October	.283	487	138	23	2	7	37	24	28	.318	.382
Pre-All Star	.278	1336	372	53	5	12	113	111	88	.333	.353
Post-All Star	.278	1268	353	66	6	12	103	82	88	.323	.368

Batter vs. Pitcher (since 1984)

Hits Best Against	Avg	AB	H	2B	3B	HR	RBI	BB	SO	OBP	SLG
Todd Worrell	.600	10	6	2	1	0	1	1	0	.636	1.000
Ben McDonald	.571	14	8	1	1	1	3	0	1	.533	1.000
Paul Gibson	.545	11	6	2	0	0	1	0	0	.545	.727
Dave Fleming	.500	14	7	4	0	0	1	1	0	.533	.786
Neal Heaton	.471	17	8	4	0	0	1	2	1	.526	.706

Hits Worst Against	Avg	AB	H	2B	3B	HR	RBI	BB	SO	OBP	SLG
Randy Johnson	.038	26	1	1	0	0	0	2	4	.107	.077
John Dopson	.087	23	2	0	0	0	0	3	1	.192	.087
Jack Morris	.100	20	2	0	0	0	0	0	1	.100	.100
Bob Walk	.105	19	2	0	0	0	0	0	2	.105	.105
Jeff Montgomery	.125	16	2	0	0	0	1	0	5	.125	.125

Bob Scanlan — Cubs

Age 27 – Pitches Right (groundball pitcher)

	ERA	W	L	Sv	G	GS	IP	BB	SO	Avg	H	2B	3B	HR	RBI	OBP	SLG	GF	IR	IRS	Hld	SvOp	SB	CS	GB	FB	G/F
1993 Season	4.54	4	5	0	70	0	75.1	28	44	.278	79	25	2	6	48	.343	.444	13	59	19	25	3	5	4	124	52	2.38
Career (1991-1993)	3.75	14	19	15	179	13	273.2	98	130	.261	269	57	8	15	136	.325	.375	70	115	36	34	23	16	14	484	210	2.30

1993 Season

	ERA	W	L	Sv	G	GS	IP	H	HR	BB	SO
Home	5.80	2	4	0	36	0	35.2	39	5	15	23
Away	3.40	2	1	0	34	0	39.2	40	1	13	21
Day	5.68	3	4	0	32	0	31.2	36	5	10	16
Night	3.71	1	1	0	38	0	43.2	43	1	18	28
Grass	4.62	3	5	0	58	0	60.1	64	5	23	36
Turf	4.20	1	0	0	12	0	15.0	15	1	5	8
April	4.35	0	2	0	12	0	10.1	11	2	5	9
May	4.38	1	1	0	13	0	12.1	9	0	2	6
June	2.87	0	1	0	14	0	15.2	14	1	7	8
July	8.36	1	1	0	11	0	14.0	23	2	5	7
August	5.11	1	0	0	13	0	12.1	16	1	5	9
September/October	1.69	1	0	0	7	0	10.2	6	0	4	5
Starter	0.00	0	0	0	0	0	0.0	0	0	0	0
Reliever	4.54	4	5	0	70	0	75.1	79	6	28	44
0 Days rest	5.24	2	2	0	24	0	22.1	26	2	7	14
1 or 2 Days rest	4.03	2	3	0	32	0	38.0	32	3	14	21
3+ Days rest	4.80	0	0	0	14	0	15.0	21	1	7	9
Pre-All Star	4.01	1	4	0	44	0	42.2	43	3	17	25
Post-All Star	5.23	3	1	0	26	0	32.2	36	3	11	19

	Avg	AB	H	2B	3B	HR	RBI	BB	SO	OBP	SLG
vs. Left	.305	118	36	11	1	2	23	13	22	.368	.466
vs. Right	.259	166	43	14	1	4	25	15	22	.324	.428
Inning 1-6	.250	20	5	1	0	0	2	1	2	.318	.300
Inning 7+	.280	264	74	24	2	6	46	27	42	.344	.455
None on	.279	129	36	12	1	1	1	14	25	.359	.411
Runners on	.277	155	43	13	1	5	47	14	19	.330	.471
Scoring Posn	.286	91	26	8	1	3	41	12	12	.355	.495
Close & Late	.293	150	44	14	2	2	29	13	20	.345	.453
None on/out	.286	56	16	5	1	0	0	6	8	.365	.411
vs. 1st Batr (relief)	.213	61	13	3	0	1	11	5	9	.275	.311
First Inning Pitched	.273	220	60	17	0	4	37	21	38	.335	.405
First 15 Pitches	.269	197	53	16	1	4	31	20	31	.338	.421
Pitch 16-30	.286	77	22	8	1	0	12	7	13	.341	.416
Pitch 31-45	.444	9	4	1	0	2	5	1	0	.500	1.222
Pitch 46+	.000	1	0	0	0	0	0	0	0	.000	.000
First Pitch	.261	46	12	5	0	1	9	7	0	.345	.435
Ahead in Count	.235	136	32	7	1	2	15	0	38	.248	.346
Behind in Count	.340	50	17	9	0	2	12	12	0	.453	.640
Two Strikes	.207	121	25	8	1	3	19	9	44	.269	.364

Career (1991-1993)

	ERA	W	L	Sv	G	GS	IP	H	HR	BB	SO
Home	4.72	8	11	4	89	8	135.1	151	11	49	65
Away	2.80	6	8	11	90	5	138.1	118	4	49	65
Day	4.65	7	10	6	87	7	127.2	133	10	44	56
Night	2.96	7	9	9	92	6	146.0	136	5	54	74
Grass	3.84	11	13	9	133	10	201.2	203	11	69	96
Turf	3.50	3	6	6	46	3	72.0	66	4	29	34
April	3.05	0	3	0	22	0	20.2	18	3	7	13
May	3.05	4	2	1	29	5	59.0	50	1	19	32
June	4.08	1	6	2	32	6	57.1	66	2	25	21
July	5.13	3	4	3	29	0	40.1	39	3	10	20
August	3.12	3	2	6	31	2	52.0	46	2	20	24
September/October	4.06	3	2	3	36	0	44.1	50	4	17	20
Starter	4.28	2	4	0	13	13	69.1	83	2	26	25
Reliever	3.57	12	15	15	166	0	204.1	186	13	72	105
0 Days rest	3.98	3	4	7	54	0	54.1	54	5	17	28
1 or 2 Days rest	3.55	7	10	5	72	0	101.1	86	7	42	56
3+ Days rest	3.14	2	1	3	40	0	48.2	46	1	13	21
Pre-All Star	3.35	6	12	3	96	11	156.0	150	7	55	76
Post-All Star	4.28	8	7	12	83	2	117.2	119	8	43	54

	Avg	AB	H	2B	3B	HR	RBI	BB	SO	OBP	SLG
vs. Left	.260	503	131	30	5	7	70	54	62	.332	.382
vs. Right	.261	528	138	27	3	8	66	44	68	.319	.369
Inning 1-6	.281	320	90	16	5	3	45	29	32	.346	.391
Inning 7+	.252	711	179	41	3	12	91	69	98	.316	.368
None on	.255	526	134	30	3	6	6	49	68	.323	.357
Runners on	.267	505	135	27	5	9	130	49	62	.327	.394
Scoring Posn	.274	317	87	19	3	5	118	40	42	.344	.401
Close & Late	.258	419	108	23	2	5	57	39	53	.318	.358
None on/out	.272	232	63	12	3	1	1	21	24	.340	.362
vs. 1st Batr (relief)	.238	147	35	6	0	2	16	13	19	.299	.320
First Inning Pitched	.255	588	150	33	1	10	84	58	87	.320	.366
First 15 Pitches	.245	530	130	29	2	7	63	52	71	.311	.347
Pitch 16-30	.265	260	69	14	2	4	34	24	40	.329	.381
Pitch 31-45	.337	89	30	7	2	3	19	9	9	.406	.562
Pitch 46+	.263	152	40	7	2	1	20	13	10	.320	.355
First Pitch	.252	163	41	9	0	1	24	15	0	.314	.325
Ahead in Count	.245	441	108	16	6	5	44	0	114	.252	.342
Behind in Count	.289	235	68	25	1	7	39	46	0	.401	.494
Two Strikes	.220	410	90	16	5	5	50	37	130	.286	.320

Pitcher vs. Batter (career)

Pitches Best Vs.	Avg	AB	H	2B	3B	HR	RBI	BB	SO	OBP	SLG
Tom Pagnozzi	.100	10	1	0	0	0	0	1	1	.182	.100
Matt D. Williams	.125	16	2	1	0	0	2	0	2	.125	.188
Tim Wallach	.200	15	3	1	0	0	1	0	3	.188	.267
Bret Barberie	.200	10	2	1	0	0	2	3	2	.385	.300
Delino DeShields	.222	9	2	0	0	0	2	4	1	.429	.222

Pitches Worst Vs.	Avg	AB	H	2B	3B	HR	RBI	BB	SO	OBP	SLG
Todd Zeile	.600	10	6	2	0	0	3	1	0	.636	.800
Andres Galarraga	.429	14	6	1	0	0	3	0	0	.429	.500
Eddie Murray	.364	11	4	1	0	0	0	0	0	.364	.455
Willie McGee	.364	11	4	2	0	0	4	0	0	.364	.545
Marquis Grissom	.348	23	8	2	2	0	7	0	2	.333	.609

Steve Scarsone — Giants

Age 28 – Bats Right (flyball hitter)

	Avg	G	AB	R	H	2B	3B	HR	RBI	BB	SO	HBP	GDP	SB	CS	OBP	SLG	IBB	SH	SF	#Pit	#P/PA	GB	FB	G/F
1993 Season	.252	44	103	16	26	9	0	2	15	4	32	0	0	0	1	.278	.398	0	4	1	403	3.60	22	35	0.63
Career (1992-1993)	.233	62	133	19	31	9	0	2	15	6	44	0	0	0	1	.264	.346	0	5	1	520	3.59	27	42	0.64

1993 Season

	Avg	AB	H	2B	3B	HR	RBI	BB	SO	OBP	SLG
vs. Left	.256	39	10	4	0	0	3	2	11	.286	.359

	Avg	AB	H	2B	3B	HR	RBI	BB	SO	OBP	SLG
Scoring Posn	.304	23	7	5	0	1	12	0	5	.292	.652

1993 Season	Avg	AB	H	2B	3B	HR	RBI	BB	SO	OBP	SLG
vs. Right	.250	64	16	5	0	2	12	2	21	.273	.422
Close & Late	.222	9	2	0	0	0	0	0	4	.222	.222

Curt Schilling — Phillies

Age 27 – Pitches Right

	ERA	W	L	Sv	G	GS	IP	BB	SO	Avg	H	2B	3B	HR	RBI	OBP	SLG	CG	ShO	Sup	QS	#P/S	SB	CS	GB	FB	G/F
1993 Season	4.02	16	7	0	34	34	235.1	57	186	.259	234	40	6	23	100	.303	.392	7	2	4.97	23	108	11	11	315	225	1.40
Last Five Years	3.27	34	26	13	172	61	592.0	177	442	.237	526	95	13	39	227	.293	.345	17	6	3.94	45	107	22	22	756	614	1.23

1993 Season

	ERA	W	L	Sv	G	GS	IP	H	HR	BB	SO
Home	3.90	9	4	0	16	16	113.0	111	8	28	100
Away	4.12	7	3	0	18	18	122.1	123	15	29	86
Day	5.77	5	4	0	12	12	73.1	86	10	18	61
Night	3.22	11	3	0	22	22	162.0	148	13	39	125
Grass	3.44	4	1	0	10	10	73.1	68	11	15	52
Turf	4.28	12	6	0	24	24	162.0	166	12	42	134
April	2.54	4	1	0	5	5	39.0	31	2	9	26
May	3.00	2	0	0	6	6	48.0	37	6	12	34
June	5.52	2	2	0	5	5	29.1	32	4	6	18
July	6.62	1	3	0	6	6	34.0	47	4	10	26
August	4.01	2	0	0	6	6	42.2	44	3	11	42
September/October	3.40	5	1	0	6	6	42.1	43	4	9	40
Starter	4.02	16	7	0	34	34	235.1	234	23	57	186
Reliever	0.00	0	0	0	0	0	0.0	0	0	0	0
0-3 Days Rest	0.00	0	0	0	0	0	0.0	0	0	0	0
4 Days Rest	4.06	10	5	0	21	21	144.0	155	11	31	116
5+ Days Rest	3.94	6	2	0	13	13	91.1	79	12	26	70
Pre-All Star	4.51	8	6	0	19	19	127.2	131	13	33	86
Post-All Star	3.43	8	1	0	15	15	107.2	103	10	24	100

	Avg	AB	H	2B	3B	HR	RBI	BB	SO	OBP	SLG
vs. Left	.259	490	127	23	4	13	59	37	105	.310	.402
vs. Right	.258	415	107	17	2	10	41	20	81	.295	.381
Inning 1-6	.255	734	187	34	4	18	82	50	155	.303	.386
Inning 7+	.275	171	47	0	2	5	18	7	31	.304	.421
None on	.243	571	139	23	4	16	16	30	115	.282	.382
Runners on	.284	334	95	17	2	7	84	27	71	.337	.410
Scoring Posn	.311	177	55	10	2	5	77	19	43	.368	.475
Close & Late	.257	105	27	4	1	3	14	6	20	.298	.400
None on/out	.252	238	60	14	2	6	6	11	45	.288	.403
vs. 1st Batr (relief)	.000	0	0	0	0	0	0	0	0	.000	.000
First Inning Pitched	.260	131	34	10	1	2	17	13	29	.331	.397
First 75 Pitches	.250	607	152	32	3	14	64	45	126	.303	.382
Pitch 76-90	.281	114	32	3	2	3	15	5	22	.317	.421
Pitch 91-105	.260	100	26	3	0	4	12	3	18	.282	.410
Pitch 106+	.286	84	24	2	1	2	9	4	20	.311	.405
First Pitch	.333	123	41	3	2	5	15	5	0	.357	.512
Ahead in Count	.175	451	79	13	2	9	34	0	168	.180	.273
Behind in Count	.370	165	61	19	2	5	26	23	0	.445	.600
Two Strikes	.190	447	85	12	2	8	42	29	186	.238	.280

Last Five Years

	ERA	W	L	Sv	G	GS	IP	H	HR	BB	SO
Home	3.23	21	15	5	90	32	323.2	284	18	101	249
Away	3.32	13	11	8	82	29	268.1	242	21	76	193
Day	4.42	6	10	4	43	19	159.0	164	13	46	128
Night	2.85	28	16	9	129	42	433.0	362	26	131	314
Grass	3.41	9	7	6	73	16	187.1	169	17	61	136
Turf	3.20	25	19	7	99	45	404.2	357	22	116	306
April	2.81	6	3	4	24	5	67.1	52	4	22	55
May	3.21	4	4	3	26	9	92.2	80	8	29	75
June	3.76	7	6	1	20	11	83.2	76	5	21	59
July	3.94	5	4	1	21	11	89.0	94	5	17	62
August	2.96	4	3	1	36	12	124.2	110	9	51	95
September/October	3.07	8	6	3	45	13	134.2	114	8	37	96
Starter	3.28	28	17	0	61	61	435.2	387	32	106	307
Reliever	3.22	6	9	13	111	0	156.1	139	7	71	135
0-3 Days Rest	0.00	0	0	0	0	0	0.0	0	0	0	0
4 Days Rest	3.31	17	11	0	38	38	272.0	254	17	55	201
5+ Days Rest	3.24	11	6	0	23	23	163.2	133	15	51	106
Pre-All Star	3.77	17	17	8	78	30	272.0	254	19	79	209
Post-All Star	2.84	17	9	5	94	31	320.0	272	20	98	233

	Avg	AB	H	2B	3B	HR	RBI	BB	SO	OBP	SLG
vs. Left	.237	1175	279	51	8	22	113	111	230	.301	.351
vs. Right	.237	1041	247	44	5	17	114	66	212	.283	.338
Inning 1-6	.238	1387	330	56	7	28	142	106	270	.292	.349
Inning 7+	.236	829	196	39	6	11	85	71	172	.295	.338
None on	.228	1332	304	53	7	24	24	90	255	.278	.333
Runners on	.251	884	222	42	6	15	203	87	187	.315	.363
Scoring Posn	.259	483	125	25	3	8	179	65	123	.337	.373
Close & Late	.249	393	98	16	5	8	54	37	84	.312	.377
None on/out	.238	568	135	22	4	11	11	36	100	.284	.349
vs. 1st Batr (relief)	.309	97	30	7	0	2	11	11	20	.382	.443
First Inning Pitched	.247	587	145	33	3	7	80	65	128	.321	.349
First 75 Pitches	.238	1676	399	76	8	29	179	153	344	.301	.345
Pitch 76-90	.239	222	53	7	2	3	17	12	41	.281	.329
Pitch 91-105	.239	180	43	7	2	5	20	5	29	.258	.383
Pitch 106+	.225	138	31	5	1	2	11	7	28	.259	.319
First Pitch	.300	293	88	14	3	6	28	15	0	.330	.430
Ahead in Count	.173	1101	191	36	4	10	72	0	395	.175	.241
Behind in Count	.332	407	135	29	4	11	67	88	0	.448	.504
Two Strikes	.175	1082	189	37	3	14	80	74	442	.226	.253

Pitcher vs. Batter (career)

Pitches Best Vs.	Avg	AB	H	2B	3B	HR	RBI	BB	SO	OBP	SLG
Darrin Fletcher	.000	22	0	0	0	0	2	0	3	.000	.000
Eddie Murray	.077	26	2	0	0	0	0	2	6	.143	.077
Jose Offerman	.083	12	1	0	0	0	0	1	5	.154	.083
Rick Wilkins	.083	12	1	0	0	0	0	1	2	.154	.083
Chico Walker	.133	15	2	0	0	0	0	0	2	.133	.133

Pitches Worst Vs.	Avg	AB	H	2B	3B	HR	RBI	BB	SO	OBP	SLG
Marquis Grissom	.519	27	14	2	0	1	6	0	2	.519	.704
Joe Orsulak	.500	14	7	0	0	1	2	1	4	.533	.714
Mark Lemke	.471	17	8	0	0	2	3	2	2	.526	.824
Tony Gwynn	.438	16	7	3	0	1	3	0	1	.438	.813
Dave Justice	.375	16	6	1	0	3	8	6	5	.545	1.000

Dick Schofield — Blue Jays

Age 31 – Bats Right

	Avg	G	AB	R	H	2B	3B	HR	RBI	BB	SO	HBP	GDP	SB	CS	OBP	SLG	IBB	SH	SF	#Pit	#P/PA	GB	FB	G/F
1993 Season	.191	36	110	11	21	1	2	0	5	16	25	0	1	3	0	.294	.236	0	2	0	515	4.02	25	42	0.60
Last Five Years	.224	503	1572	190	352	47	10	9	116	207	284	13	22	34	15	.318	.284	9	43	7	7043	3.82	517	483	1.07

1993 Season

	Avg	AB	H	2B	3B	HR	RBI	BB	SO	OBP	SLG
vs. Left	.171	35	6	0	0	0	1	6	8	.293	.171
vs. Right	.200	75	15	1	2	0	4	10	17	.294	.267
Home	.255	55	14	1	2	0	5	12	16	.388	.345
Away	.127	55	7	0	0	0	0	4	9	.186	.127
First Pitch	.273	11	3	0	0	0	0	0	0	.273	.273
Ahead in Count	.278	18	5	0	0	0	0	12	0	.567	.278
Behind in Count	.180	61	11	0	2	0	3	0	21	.180	.246
Two Strikes	.138	58	8	0	1	0	3	4	25	.194	.172

	Avg	AB	H	2B	3B	HR	RBI	BB	SO	OBP	SLG
Scoring Posn	.240	25	6	1	0	0	5	4	7	.345	.280
Close & Late	.143	14	2	0	0	0	1	3	3	.294	.143
None on/out	.095	21	2	0	0	0	0	7	4	.321	.095
Batting #2	.091	11	1	0	0	0	0	0	1	.091	.091
Batting #9	.200	95	19	1	2	0	5	15	24	.309	.253
Other	.250	4	1	0	0	0	0	1	0	.400	.250
Pre-All Star	.211	90	19	1	2	0	5	14	23	.317	.267
Post-All Star	.100	20	2	0	0	0	0	2	2	.182	.100

Last Five Years

	Avg	AB	H	2B	3B	HR	RBI	BB	SO	OBP	SLG
vs. Left	.223	511	114	15	3	4	39	76	78	.327	.288
vs. Right	.224	1061	238	32	7	5	77	131	206	.313	.282
Groundball	.249	453	113	13	2	2	32	52	71	.331	.300
Flyball	.166	307	51	10	1	3	19	40	73	.265	.235
Home	.226	771	174	21	6	5	65	111	132	.324	.288
Away	.222	801	178	26	4	4	51	96	152	.312	.280
Day	.229	410	94	11	4	2	41	57	65	.329	.290
Night	.222	1162	258	36	6	7	75	150	219	.314	.281
Grass	.231	1221	282	36	8	8	95	153	203	.321	.293
Turf	.199	351	70	11	2	1	21	54	81	.308	.251
First Pitch	.232	181	42	5	0	2	14	4	0	.255	.293
Ahead in Count	.325	335	109	15	2	3	40	121	0	.503	.409
Behind in Count	.181	728	132	17	5	3	38	0	239	.188	.231
Two Strikes	.161	731	118	16	4	1	32	82	284	.252	.198

	Avg	AB	H	2B	3B	HR	RBI	BB	SO	OBP	SLG
Scoring Posn	.243	354	86	12	3	2	104	73	64	.371	.311
Close & Late	.213	249	53	4	1	1	16	34	57	.314	.249
None on/out	.215	423	91	12	2	3	3	47	75	.300	.274
Batting #8	.213	296	63	14	2	3	29	35	56	.293	.304
Batting #9	.223	731	163	16	6	2	56	99	143	.319	.269
Other	.231	545	126	17	2	4	31	73	85	.330	.292
April	.247	190	47	7	1	0	10	29	44	.356	.295
May	.237	228	54	9	3	2	22	26	35	.320	.329
June	.200	310	62	7	0	1	16	42	50	.296	.232
July	.222	302	67	8	1	5	28	34	58	.305	.305
August	.236	271	64	7	1	0	19	41	46	.344	.269
September/October	.214	271	58	9	4	1	21	35	51	.302	.288
Pre-All Star	.221	825	182	26	5	3	50	109	153	.316	.275
Post-All Star	.228	747	170	21	5	6	66	98	131	.320	.293

Batter vs. Pitcher (since 1984)

Hits Best Against	Avg	AB	H	2B	3B	HR	RBI	BB	SO	OBP	SLG
Jose Bautista	.500	12	6	0	0	0	0	1	4	.538	.500
Jeff Ballard	.450	20	9	1	0	1	3	0	0	.450	.650
Bill Swift	.421	19	8	1	0	1	7	1	2	.450	.632
Bill Krueger	.400	15	6	2	1	0	4	3	2	.500	.667
Matt Young	.357	14	5	1	0	1	2	4	0	.500	.643

Hits Worst Against	Avg	AB	H	2B	3B	HR	RBI	BB	SO	OBP	SLG
Mark Gubicza	.000	27	0	0	0	0	0	1	5	.036	.000
Nolan Ryan	.000	13	0	0	0	0	0	3	9	.188	.000
Tom Henke	.000	11	0	0	0	0	0	1	4	.083	.000
Mitch Williams	.000	10	0	0	0	0	0	2	3	.167	.000
Jose DeLeon	.077	13	1	1	0	0	0	0	2	.077	.154

Mike Schooler — Rangers

Age 31 – Pitches Right

	ERA	W	L	Sv	G	GS	IP	BB	SO	Avg	H	2B	3B	HR	RBI	OBP	SLG	GF	IR	IRS	Hld	SvOp	SB	CS	GB	FB	G/F
1993 Season	5.55	3	0	0	17	0	24.1	10	16	.303	30	7	1	3	17	.367	.485	0	23	7	4	0	5	1	31	33	0.94
Last Five Years	3.48	10	21	83	220	0	243.1	79	194	.254	238	36	7	19	134	.313	.369	104	129	49	9	102	28	5	321	253	1.27

1993 Season

	ERA	W	L	Sv	G	GS	IP	H	HR	BB	SO
Home	5.40	0	0	0	6	0	8.1	11	2	3	4
Away	5.63	3	0	0	11	0	16.0	19	1	7	12

	Avg	AB	H	2B	3B	HR	RBI	BB	SO	OBP	SLG
vs. Left	.382	34	13	1	1	1	8	5	4	.462	.559
vs. Right	.262	65	17	6	0	2	9	5	12	.314	.446

Last Five Years

	ERA	W	L	Sv	G	GS	IP	H	HR	BB	SO
Home	3.21	4	12	46	116	0	129.0	123	7	37	101
Away	3.78	6	9	37	104	0	114.1	115	12	42	93
Day	3.28	3	6	20	61	0	71.1	80	7	22	50
Night	3.56	7	15	63	159	0	172.0	158	12	57	144
Grass	3.53	6	5	28	84	0	97.0	98	12	34	72
Turf	3.44	4	16	55	136	0	146.1	140	7	45	122
April	3.33	0	1	12	23	0	27.0	26	2	13	23
May	2.51	1	2	24	42	0	43.0	36	4	13	30
June	2.53	1	4	14	40	0	42.2	40	2	11	36
July	3.55	4	1	13	41	0	50.2	48	3	19	40
August	4.70	1	9	10	40	0	44.0	52	7	10	34
September/October	4.25	3	4	10	34	0	36.0	36	1	13	31
Starter	0.00	0	0	0	0	0	0.0	0	0	0	0
Reliever	3.48	10	21	83	220	0	243.1	238	19	79	194
0 Days rest	4.04	2	8	27	52	0	55.2	52	5	21	48
1 or 2 Days rest	3.05	4	9	35	98	0	106.1	102	7	31	86
3+ Days rest	3.65	4	4	21	70	0	81.1	84	7	27	60
Pre-All Star	2.77	6	7	55	119	0	130.0	118	9	46	103
Post-All Star	4.29	4	14	28	101	0	113.1	120	10	33	91

	Avg	AB	H	2B	3B	HR	RBI	BB	SO	OBP	SLG
vs. Left	.257	420	108	18	6	8	69	50	70	.337	.386
vs. Right	.252	516	130	18	1	11	65	29	124	.292	.355
Inning 1-6	.345	87	30	7	1	3	24	7	14	.389	.552
Inning 7+	.245	849	208	29	6	16	110	72	180	.305	.350
None on	.239	464	111	15	5	8	8	39	101	.301	.345
Runners on	.269	472	127	21	2	11	126	40	93	.324	.392
Scoring Posn	.296	291	86	12	1	10	121	31	54	.356	.447
Close & Late	.273	462	126	17	2	14	82	39	104	.327	.409
None on/out	.250	196	49	10	3	1	1	12	43	.293	.347
vs. 1st Batr (relief)	.222	207	46	9	2	5	26	6	45	.247	.357
First Inning Pitched	.245	731	179	27	5	13	111	59	155	.303	.349
First 15 Pitches	.255	652	166	26	4	11	85	53	131	.313	.357
Pitch 16-30	.236	216	51	7	2	4	36	22	45	.304	.343
Pitch 31-45	.300	60	18	2	1	2	8	4	17	.338	.467
Pitch 46+	.375	8	3	1	0	2	5	0	1	.375	1.250
First Pitch	.321	134	43	8	2	1	17	15	0	.387	.433
Ahead in Count	.185	466	86	15	3	9	58	0	177	.186	.288
Behind in Count	.343	175	60	7	0	7	40	34	0	.453	.503
Two Strikes	.162	451	73	10	4	4	34	30	194	.216	.228

Pitcher vs. Batter (career)

Pitches Best Vs.	Avg	AB	H	2B	3B	HR	RBI	BB	SO	OBP	SLG
Rob Deer	.182	11	2	0	0	0	0	0	4	.182	.182
Gary Gaetti	.214	14	3	0	0	0	0	0	4	.214	.214
Dan Gladden	.214	14	3	1	0	0	1	0	6	.214	.286

Pitches Worst Vs.	Avg	AB	H	2B	3B	HR	RBI	BB	SO	OBP	SLG
Ruben Sierra	.500	12	6	1	0	1	6	1	1	.538	.833
Terry Steinbach	.462	13	6	1	0	0	3	0	2	.429	.538
Alan Trammell	.417	12	5	1	0	0	1	1	2	.462	.500
Lou Whitaker	.417	12	5	0	0	1	4	3	1	.533	.667
Randy Bush	.385	13	5	0	0	2	7	1	2	.429	.846

Pete Schourek — Mets

Age 25 – Pitches Left

	ERA	W	L	Sv	G	GS	IP	BB	SO	Avg	H	2B	3B	HR	RBI	OBP	SLG	GF	IR	IRS	Hld	SvOp	SB	CS	GB	FB	G/F
1993 Season	5.96	5	12	0	41	18	128.1	45	72	.319	168	41	4	13	83	.370	.486	6	10	4	2	1	10	4	192	129	1.49
Career (1991-1993)	4.65	16	24	2	98	47	350.2	132	199	.280	387	83	15	29	187	.342	.425	13	31	13	5	4	37	9	460	420	1.10

1993 Season

	ERA	W	L	Sv	G	GS	IP	H	HR	BB	SO
Home	6.46	1	8	0	20	8	62.2	89	7	19	32
Away	5.48	4	4	0	21	10	65.2	79	6	26	40
Starter	5.47	5	11	0	18	18	102.0	131	10	33	52
Reliever	7.86	0	1	0	23	0	26.1	37	3	12	20
0 Days rest	0.00	0	0	0	2	0	2.0	2	0	1	1
1 or 2 Days rest	8.59	0	1	0	11	0	14.2	24	1	3	12
3+ Days rest	8.38	0	0	0	10	0	9.2	11	2	8	7

	Avg	AB	H	2B	3B	HR	RBI	BB	SO	OBP	SLG
vs. Left	.315	124	39	6	2	1	15	11	17	.368	.419
vs. Right	.320	403	129	35	2	12	68	34	55	.371	.506
Scoring Posn	.341	126	43	15	1	2	63	22	20	.424	.524
Close & Late	.393	61	24	6	0	4	17	4	8	.424	.689
None on/out	.286	133	38	7	1	1	1	6	17	.317	.376
First Pitch	.357	70	25	6	1	3	18	6	0	.403	.600
Ahead in Count	.217	217	47	12	1	2	20	0	64	.225	.309

1993 Season

	ERA	W	L	Sv	G	GS	IP	H	HR	BB	SO		Avg	AB	H	2B	3B	HR	RBI	BB	SO	OBP	SLG
Pre-All Star	6.16	2	10	0	18	13	76.0	109	10	25	43	Behind in Count	.428	145	62	15	2	7	28	21	0	.491	.703
Post-All Star	5.68	3	2	0	23	5	52.1	59	3	20	29	Two Strikes	.243	218	53	12	0	2	21	18	72	.310	.326

Career (1991-1993)

	ERA	W	L	Sv	G	GS	IP	H	HR	BB	SO		Avg	AB	H	2B	3B	HR	RBI	BB	SO	OBP	SLG
Home	4.10	10	12	0	51	25	202.0	214	14	75	108	vs. Left	.280	354	99	14	5	5	41	40	49	.348	.390
Away	5.39	6	12	2	47	22	148.2	173	15	57	91	vs. Right	.280	1028	288	69	10	24	146	92	150	.340	.437
Day	4.93	8	7	0	33	17	131.1	137	11	48	74	Inning 1-6	.279	1070	298	68	12	19	135	96	153	.338	.418
Night	4.47	8	17	2	65	30	219.1	250	18	84	125	Inning 7+	.285	312	89	15	3	10	52	36	46	.356	.449
Grass	4.38	12	17	1	69	33	253.0	270	23	94	142	None on	.261	783	204	43	8	17	17	59	105	.315	.401
Turf	5.34	4	7	1	29	14	97.2	117	6	38	57	Runners on	.306	599	183	40	7	12	170	73	94	.376	.456
April	5.00	2	2	1	11	3	27.0	38	1	12	16	Scoring Posn	.305	357	109	25	2	5	148	60	57	.394	.429
May	5.29	2	5	1	15	7	49.1	59	4	25	29	Close & Late	.263	152	40	9	0	7	26	15	23	.327	.461
June	4.39	1	5	0	13	8	53.1	63	7	16	34	None on/out	.256	348	89	10	2	8	8	21	54	.302	.388
July	4.23	2	3	0	13	8	55.1	55	3	15	24	vs. 1st Batr (relief)	.244	41	10	1	0	2	8	6	8	.320	.415
August	5.68	1	4	0	25	6	58.2	71	8	27	36	First Inning Pitched	.274	332	91	17	2	8	57	43	54	.352	.410
September/October	4.04	8	5	0	21	15	107.0	101	6	37	60	First 15 Pitches	.275	291	80	12	3	6	33	31	46	.339	.399
Starter	4.43	13	22	0	47	47	280.1	303	22	95	152	Pitch 16-30	.300	263	79	18	2	6	48	31	37	.371	.452
Reliever	5.50	3	2	2	51	0	70.1	84	7	37	47	Pitch 31-45	.266	207	55	12	4	4	22	22	40	.338	.420
0 Days rest	7.36	0	1	0	5	0	7.1	11	1	6	3	Pitch 46+	.279	621	173	41	6	13	84	48	76	.332	.427
1 or 2 Days rest	7.18	1	1	1	23	0	31.1	46	3	14	24	First Pitch	.321	212	68	15	5	5	31	14	0	.362	.509
3+ Days rest	3.41	2	0	1	23	0	31.2	27	3	17	20	Ahead in Count	.206	557	115	22	3	6	49	0	179	.213	.289
Pre-All Star	4.89	5	13	2	44	21	151.0	186	12	58	84	Behind in Count	.339	369	125	29	5	12	61	65	0	.435	.542
Post-All Star	4.46	11	11	0	54	26	199.2	201	17	74	115	Two Strikes	.219	562	123	26	3	6	62	53	199	.291	.308

Pitcher vs. Batter (career)

Pitches Best Vs.	Avg	AB	H	2B	3B	HR	RBI	BB	SO	OBP	SLG	Pitches Worst Vs.	Avg	AB	H	2B	3B	HR	RBI	BB	SO	OBP	SLG
Bip Roberts	.125	16	2	0	0	0	1	0	0	.125	.125	Joe Oliver	.545	11	6	3	0	1	4	0	2	.545	1.091
Jeff Bagwell	.154	13	2	0	1	0	3	2	2	.250	.308	Luis Gonzalez	.500	14	7	2	0	0	4	1	1	.533	.643
Ryne Sandberg	.182	11	2	0	0	0	0	2	2	.308	.182	Ken Caminiti	.500	12	6	0	0	2	5	2	1	.571	1.000
Chuck Carr	.200	10	2	0	0	0	0	1	2	.273	.200	Jay Bell	.435	23	10	5	0	0	5	6	1	.552	.652
Steve Finley	.231	13	3	0	0	0	0	1	0	.286	.231	Tom Pagnozzi	.357	14	5	3	0	1	4	0	1	.357	.786

Jeff Schwarz — White Sox

Age 30 – Pitches Right

	ERA	W	L	Sv	G	GS	IP	BB	SO	Avg	H	2B	3B	HR	RBI	OBP	SLG	GF	IR	IRS	Hld	SvOp	SB	CS	GB	FB	G/F
1993 Season	3.71	2	2	0	41	0	51.0	38	41	.201	35	9	2	1	18	.349	.293	10	22	7	6	0	8	5	62	44	1.41

1993 Season

	ERA	W	L	Sv	G	GS	IP	H	HR	BB	SO		Avg	AB	H	2B	3B	HR	RBI	BB	SO	OBP	SLG
Home	1.69	1	1	0	18	0	21.1	13	1	13	19	vs. Left	.216	74	16	4	1	1	9	20	19	.385	.338
Away	5.16	1	1	0	23	0	29.2	22	0	25	22	vs. Right	.190	100	19	5	1	0	9	18	22	.320	.260
Starter	0.00	0	0	0	0	0	0.0	0	0	0	0	Scoring Posn	.180	61	11	1	1	0	17	12	17	.312	.230
Reliever	3.71	2	2	0	41	0	51.0	35	1	38	41	Close & Late	.167	66	11	3	0	1	8	12	19	.305	.258
0 Days rest	6.00	0	0	0	4	0	3.0	2	0	2	1	None on/out	.200	40	8	2	0	1	1	8	5	.333	.325
1 or 2 Days rest	5.31	1	1	0	18	0	20.1	15	0	18	17	First Pitch	.158	19	3	0	0	0	1	1	0	.238	.158
3+ Days rest	2.28	1	1	0	19	0	27.2	18	1	18	23	Ahead in Count	.111	63	7	1	1	0	4	0	31	.123	.159
Pre-All Star	3.38	1	1	0	25	0	32.0	19	1	21	25	Behind in Count	.292	48	14	4	1	0	9	26	0	.532	.417
Post-All Star	4.26	1	1	0	16	0	19.0	16	0	17	16	Two Strikes	.107	84	9	2	0	0	4	11	41	.211	.131

Darryl Scott — Angels

Age 25 – Pitches Right (flyball pitcher)

	ERA	W	L	Sv	G	GS	IP	BB	SO	Avg	H	2B	3B	HR	RBI	OBP	SLG	GF	IR	IRS	Hld	SvOp	SB	CS	GB	FB	G/F
1993 Season	5.85	1	2	0	16	0	20.0	11	13	.250	19	6	0	1	18	.344	.368	2	15	10	2	0	4	0	18	25	0.72

1993 Season

	ERA	W	L	Sv	G	GS	IP	H	HR	BB	SO		Avg	AB	H	2B	3B	HR	RBI	BB	SO	OBP	SLG
Home	2.89	1	0	0	8	0	9.1	9	0	2	7	vs. Left	.171	35	6	3	0	0	5	4	6	.256	.257
Away	8.44	0	2	0	8	0	10.2	10	1	9	6	vs. Right	.317	41	13	3	0	1	13	7	7	.412	.463

Tim Scott — Expos

Age 27 – Pitches Right

	ERA	W	L	Sv	G	GS	IP	BB	SO	Avg	H	2B	3B	HR	RBI	OBP	SLG	GF	IR	IRS	Hld	SvOp	SB	CS	GB	FB	G/F
1993 Season	3.01	7	2	1	56	0	71.2	34	65	.253	69	13	2	4	35	.342	.359	18	31	17	3	4	18	2	73	84	0.87
Career (1991-1993)	3.83	11	3	1	92	0	110.1	55	96	.259	110	19	5	8	56	.349	.384	34	41	19	7	5	24	4	133	118	1.13

1993 Season

	ERA	W	L	Sv	G	GS	IP	H	HR	BB	SO		Avg	AB	H	2B	3B	HR	RBI	BB	SO	OBP	SLG
Home	2.41	4	1	1	27	0	37.1	32	2	14	29	vs. Left	.180	128	23	2	0	1	13	20	39	.291	.219
Away	3.67	3	1	0	29	0	34.1	37	2	20	36	vs. Right	.317	145	46	11	2	3	22	14	26	.388	.483
Starter	0.00	0	0	0	0	0	0.0	0	0	0	0	Scoring Posn	.282	85	24	2	0	1	31	17	19	.394	.341
Reliever	3.01	7	2	1	56	0	71.2	69	4	34	65	Close & Late	.256	78	20	3	1	1	8	13	18	.376	.359
0 Days rest	7.04	1	1	0	7	0	7.2	10	1	6	5	None on/out	.197	61	12	2	1	0	0	6	11	.269	.262
1 or 2 Days rest	2.27	4	1	1	31	0	39.2	39	2	15	36	First Pitch	.364	33	12	2	0	0	5	1	0	.389	.424
3+ Days rest	2.96	2	0	0	18	0	24.1	20	1	13	24	Ahead in Count	.223	139	31	8	1	0	12	0	51	.229	.295
Pre-All Star	2.93	2	1	0	31	0	43.0	44	1	20	32	Behind in Count	.275	51	14	0	1	3	10	14	0	.433	.490
Post-All Star	3.14	5	1	1	25	0	28.2	25	3	14	33	Two Strikes	.186	145	27	8	1	1	14	19	65	.285	.276

Scott Scudder — Indians

Age 26 – Pitches Right

	ERA	W	L	Sv	G	GS	IP	BB	SO	Avg	H	2B	3B	HR	RBI	OBP	SLG	CG	ShO	Sup	QS	#P/S	SB	CS	GB	FB	G/F
1993 Season	9.00	0	1	0	2	1	4.0	4	1	.333	5	3	0	0	4	.500	.533	0	0	0.00	0	75	2	1	3	10	0.30
Career (1989-1993)	4.80	21	34	1	96	64	386.1	206	226	.266	395	75	10	42	189	.358	.415	0	0	4.03	32	89	53	19	503	468	1.07

1993 Season

	ERA	W	L	Sv	G	GS	IP	H	HR	BB	SO
Home	0.00	0	0	0	1	0	1.0	0	0	0	0
Away	12.00	0	1	0	1	1	3.0	5	0	4	1

	Avg	AB	H	2B	3B	HR	RBI	BB	SO	OBP	SLG
vs. Left	.250	8	2	2	0	0	2	2	0	.400	.500
vs. Right	.429	7	3	1	0	0	2	2	1	.600	.571

Career (1989-1993)

	ERA	W	L	Sv	G	GS	IP	H	HR	BB	SO
Home	5.15	10	17	0	51	31	194.0	214	24	94	120
Away	4.45	11	17	1	45	33	192.1	181	18	112	106
Day	4.87	8	11	0	35	21	142.1	140	14	78	75
Night	4.76	13	23	1	61	43	244.0	255	28	128	151
Grass	4.84	11	16	1	41	33	182.1	194	18	102	108
Turf	4.76	10	18	0	55	31	204.0	201	24	104	118
April	4.97	1	3	1	9	3	29.0	33	4	9	16
May	3.77	4	6	0	20	10	71.2	69	5	43	34
June	4.65	6	4	0	13	13	69.2	73	6	38	44
July	5.98	2	7	0	17	11	61.2	73	9	28	45
August	3.93	4	4	0	15	11	71.0	62	10	35	36
September/October	5.62	4	10	0	22	16	83.1	85	8	53	51
Starter	4.96	19	31	0	64	64	326.1	335	35	182	193
Reliever	3.90	2	3	1	32	0	60.0	60	7	24	33
0-3 Days Rest	2.59	3	2	0	5	5	31.1	23	7	7	22
4 Days Rest	5.09	12	17	0	36	36	187.1	190	20	115	107
5+ Days Rest	5.43	4	12	0	23	23	107.2	122	8	60	64
Pre-All Star	5.02	12	17	1	47	31	184.2	202	18	102	105
Post-All Star	4.60	9	17	0	49	33	201.2	193	24	104	121

	Avg	AB	H	2B	3B	HR	RBI	BB	SO	OBP	SLG
vs. Left	.268	829	222	44	8	16	98	117	107	.360	.398
vs. Right	.263	657	173	31	2	26	91	89	119	.355	.435
Inning 1-6	.252	1255	316	62	8	36	161	180	198	.349	.400
Inning 7+	.342	231	79	13	2	6	28	26	28	.406	.494
None on	.264	825	218	41	6	21	21	105	131	.352	.405
Runners on	.268	661	177	34	4	21	168	101	95	.365	.427
Scoring Posn	.249	381	95	17	3	8	137	77	63	.372	.373
Close & Late	.323	124	40	7	1	2	14	18	14	.406	.444
None on/out	.241	377	91	14	2	5	5	40	57	.319	.329
vs. 1st Batr (relief)	.300	30	9	2	0	2	5	2	4	.344	.567
First Inning Pitched	.315	368	116	20	4	17	76	63	57	.420	.530
First 75 Pitches	.259	1184	307	60	9	34	154	168	185	.355	.411
Pitch 76-90	.309	139	43	8	0	6	25	25	14	.416	.496
Pitch 91-105	.202	109	22	3	0	1	1	6	19	.243	.257
Pitch 106+	.426	54	23	4	1	1	9	7	8	.476	.593
First Pitch	.294	201	59	11	1	9	42	15	0	.344	.493
Ahead in Count	.210	615	129	19	1	9	44	0	192	.217	.288
Behind in Count	.329	371	122	23	4	14	60	113	0	.485	.526
Two Strikes	.213	661	141	23	2	17	60	78	226	.302	.331

Pitcher vs. Batter (career)

Pitches Best Vs.	Avg	AB	H	2B	3B	HR	RBI	BB	SO	OBP	SLG
Darryl Strawberry	.000	9	0	0	0	0	1	3	2	.231	.000
Tommy Gregg	.077	13	1	0	0	0	1	1	3	.143	.077
Alfredo Griffin	.083	12	1	0	0	0	1	1	0	.143	.083
Bip Roberts	.083	12	1	0	0	0	1	0	2	.083	.083
Lenny Harris	.100	10	1	0	0	0	0	2	1	.250	.100

Pitches Worst Vs.	Avg	AB	H	2B	3B	HR	RBI	BB	SO	OBP	SLG
Howard Johnson	.833	6	5	3	0	2	6	4	0	.818	2.333
Brian McRae	.556	9	5	0	1	0	2	3	0	.667	.778
Will Clark	.444	18	8	3	0	0	2	4	1	.545	.611
Willie McGee	.364	11	4	2	0	0	0	2	0	.462	.545
Dale Murphy	.313	16	5	1	0	2	3	0	3	.313	.750

Rudy Seanez — Padres

Age 25 – Pitches Right

	ERA	W	L	Sv	G	GS	IP	BB	SO	Avg	H	2B	3B	HR	RBI	OBP	SLG	GF	IR	IRS	Hld	SvOp	SB	CS	GB	FB	G/F
1993 Season	13.50	0	0	0	3	0	3.1	2	1	.471	8	1	0	1	6	.526	.706	3	3	3	0	0	0	0	10	2	5.00
Career (1989-1993)	7.30	2	1	0	37	0	40.2	38	39	.261	41	5	1	5	38	.402	.401	15	27	12	3	1	7	1	51	44	1.16

1993 Season

	ERA	W	L	Sv	G	GS	IP	H	HR	BB	SO
Home	15.00	0	0	0	2	0	3.0	7	1	2	1
Away	0.00	0	0	0	1	0	0.1	1	0	0	0

	Avg	AB	H	2B	3B	HR	RBI	BB	SO	OBP	SLG
vs. Left	.500	8	4	1	0	0	3	1	0	.556	.625
vs. Right	.444	9	4	0	0	1	3	1	1	.500	.778

David Segui — Orioles

Age 27 – Bats Both

	Avg	G	AB	R	H	2B	3B	HR	RBI	BB	SO	HBP	GDP	SB	CS	OBP	SLG	IBB	SH	SF	#Pit	#P/PA	GB	FB	G/F
1993 Season	.273	146	450	54	123	27	0	10	60	58	53	0	18	2	1	.351	.400	4	3	8	1757	3.39	173	146	1.18
Career (1990-1993)	.263	387	974	104	256	50	0	15	114	101	110	1	41	4	2	.330	.360	11	9	9	3724	3.40	400	277	1.44

1993 Season

	Avg	AB	H	2B	3B	HR	RBI	BB	SO	OBP	SLG
vs. Left	.292	144	42	7	0	5	15	17	18	.364	.444
vs. Right	.265	306	81	20	0	5	45	41	35	.345	.379
Groundball	.176	91	16	4	0	1	12	7	13	.228	.253
Flyball	.306	85	26	7	0	2	11	14	11	.400	.459
Home	.280	236	66	19	0	6	36	31	29	.357	.436
Away	.266	214	57	8	0	4	24	27	24	.344	.360
Day	.265	132	35	7	0	2	15	15	15	.336	.364
Night	.277	318	88	20	0	8	45	43	38	.357	.415
Grass	.277	404	112	24	0	10	57	51	46	.352	.411
Turf	.239	46	11	3	0	0	3	7	7	.340	.304
First Pitch	.281	96	27	4	0	2	7	3	0	.300	.385
Ahead in Count	.259	108	28	4	0	4	22	30	0	.408	.407
Behind in Count	.247	182	45	7	0	3	14	0	49	.246	.335
Two Strikes	.231	160	37	9	0	2	18	25	53	.332	.325

	Avg	AB	H	2B	3B	HR	RBI	BB	SO	OBP	SLG
Scoring Posn	.297	118	35	8	0	0	46	12	18	.341	.364
Close & Late	.152	79	12	1	0	2	10	9	13	.233	.241
None on/out	.288	111	32	5	0	4	4	15	8	.373	.441
Batting #7	.292	192	56	13	0	4	25	29	23	.379	.422
Batting #8	.262	168	44	13	0	5	24	16	16	.319	.429
Other	.256	90	23	1	0	1	11	13	14	.346	.300
April	.292	24	7	1	0	0	4	6	5	.433	.333
May	.270	74	20	7	0	2	10	11	6	.360	.446
June	.403	77	31	6	0	2	16	9	6	.444	.558
July	.275	91	25	5	0	3	9	10	11	.343	.429
August	.242	91	22	3	0	1	4	14	14	.343	.308
September/October	.194	93	18	5	0	2	17	8	11	.252	.312
Pre-All Star	.330	212	70	14	0	5	33	32	20	.410	.467
Post-All Star	.223	238	53	13	0	5	27	26	33	.296	.340

1993 By Position

Position	Avg	AB	H	2B	3B	HR	RBI	BB	SO	OBP	SLG	G	GS	Innings	PO	A	E	DP	Fld Pct	Rng Fctr	In Zone	Outs	Zone Rtg	MLB Zone
As 1b	.275	448	123	27	0	10	60	57	52	.351	.402	144	127	1155.0	1152	94	5	122	.996	—	232	179	.772	.834

Career (1990-1993)

	Avg	AB	H	2B	3B	HR	RBI	BB	SO	OBP	SLG
vs. Left	.281	360	101	18	0	7	42	29	45	.333	.389

	Avg	AB	H	2B	3B	HR	RBI	BB	SO	OBP	SLG
Scoring Posn	.279	258	72	13	0	2	95	27	35	.337	.353

Career (1990-1993)

	Avg	AB	H	2B	3B	HR	RBI	BB	SO	OBP	SLG
vs. Right	.252	614	155	32	0	8	72	72	65	.328	.344
Groundball	.223	242	54	8	0	2	25	20	35	.279	.281
Flyball	.309	181	56	12	0	4	19	22	19	.385	.442
Home	.258	496	128	27	0	9	67	51	63	.324	.367
Away	.268	478	128	23	0	6	47	50	47	.336	.354
Day	.256	281	72	13	0	2	25	32	31	.330	.324
Night	.266	693	184	37	0	13	89	69	79	.330	.375
Grass	.266	836	222	42	0	13	100	90	95	.334	.362
Turf	.246	138	34	8	0	2	14	11	15	.302	.348
First Pitch	.293	164	48	8	0	4	23	8	0	.324	.415
Ahead in Count	.309	236	73	12	0	5	36	50	0	.424	.424
Behind in Count	.210	404	85	15	0	4	28	0	97	.212	.277
Two Strikes	.206	364	75	17	0	3	31	41	110	.287	.277

	Avg	AB	H	2B	3B	HR	RBI	BB	SO	OBP	SLG
Close & Late	.210	176	37	3	0	5	23	22	25	.295	.313
None on/out	.293	229	67	11	0	5	5	23	18	.357	.406
Batting #7	.257	334	86	20	0	6	37	41	45	.336	.371
Batting #8	.278	334	93	26	0	8	53	32	34	.337	.428
Other	.252	306	77	4	0	1	24	28	31	.315	.275
April	.246	69	17	4	0	0	8	11	8	.350	.304
May	.237	190	45	14	0	3	23	19	17	.308	.358
June	.328	177	58	10	0	3	26	17	16	.377	.435
July	.268	153	41	8	0	4	15	13	18	.323	.399
August	.256	164	42	3	0	1	12	20	22	.337	.293
September/October	.240	221	53	11	0	4	30	21	29	.303	.344
Pre-All Star	.280	490	137	29	0	8	65	53	48	.347	.388
Post-All Star	.246	484	119	21	0	7	49	48	62	.312	.333

Batter vs. Pitcher (career)

Hits Best Against	Avg	AB	H	2B	3B	HR	RBI	BB	SO	OBP	SLG
Danny Darwin	.455	11	5	3	0	0	1	0	1	.417	.727
Roger Clemens	.455	11	5	1	0	0	3	1	0	.500	.545
Jack Morris	.381	21	8	1	0	0	1	2	1	.435	.429
Mike Moore	.353	17	6	0	0	0	4	2	0	.421	.353
Mark Langston	.353	17	6	1	0	1	3	3	2	.450	.588

Hits Worst Against	Avg	AB	H	2B	3B	HR	RBI	BB	SO	OBP	SLG
Jimmy Key	.118	17	2	1	0	0	0	0	5	.118	.176
Greg Harris	.143	14	2	1	0	0	4	2	5	.235	.214
Frank Tanana	.200	10	2	1	0	0	1	1	3	.273	.300
Wilson Alvarez	.231	13	3	0	0	0	0	2	0	.333	.231
Cal Eldred	.231	13	3	1	0	0	0	1	2	.286	.308

Kevin Seitzer — Brewers

Age 32 – Bats Right (groundball hitter)

	Avg	G	AB	R	H	2B	3B	HR	RBI	BB	SO	HBP	GDP	SB	CS	OBP	SLG	IBB	SH	SF	#Pit	#P/PA	GB	FB	G/F
1993 Season	.269	120	417	45	112	16	2	11	57	44	48	2	14	7	7	.338	.396	1	3	5	1830	3.89	174	126	1.38
Last Five Years	.273	671	2410	316	659	110	13	27	239	299	255	13	61	48	32	.354	.363	17	19	24	10426	3.77	1050	680	1.54

1993 Season

	Avg	AB	H	2B	3B	HR	RBI	BB	SO	OBP	SLG
vs. Left	.280	143	40	5	0	4	25	17	12	.356	.399
vs. Right	.263	274	72	11	2	7	32	27	36	.328	.394
Groundball	.284	88	25	2	2	1	13	6	8	.330	.386
Flyball	.214	70	15	1	0	1	5	7	13	.282	.271
Home	.266	207	55	7	0	6	27	30	18	.363	.386
Away	.271	210	57	9	2	5	30	14	30	.311	.405
Day	.272	180	49	9	0	4	26	22	24	.346	.389
Night	.266	237	63	7	2	7	31	22	24	.331	.401
Grass	.274	358	98	14	2	11	51	37	37	.343	.416
Turf	.237	59	14	2	0	0	6	7	11	.309	.271
First Pitch	.306	36	11	1	0	2	7	1	0	.324	.500
Ahead in Count	.356	104	37	6	0	5	24	27	0	.489	.558
Behind in Count	.232	207	48	8	2	3	18	0	38	.233	.333
Two Strikes	.207	198	41	8	0	2	16	16	48	.266	.278

	Avg	AB	H	2B	3B	HR	RBI	BB	SO	OBP	SLG
Scoring Posn	.269	104	28	3	1	4	47	15	11	.347	.433
Close & Late	.282	85	24	6	0	2	12	4	15	.304	.424
None on/out	.185	92	17	2	0	3	3	9	15	.257	.304
Batting #2	.260	123	32	4	0	4	19	5	11	.295	.390
Batting #6	.330	100	33	4	0	1	10	11	8	.389	.400
Other	.242	194	47	8	2	6	28	28	29	.336	.397
April	.226	53	12	2	0	3	4	4	5	.281	.434
May	.233	103	24	2	2	0	12	11	14	.307	.291
June	.275	69	19	4	0	1	11	8	10	.341	.377
July	.313	32	10	2	0	0	0	4	4	.389	.375
August	.288	73	21	1	0	5	21	12	7	.391	.507
September/October	.299	87	26	5	0	2	9	5	8	.337	.425
Pre-All Star	.256	250	64	10	2	4	27	26	32	.324	.360
Post-All Star	.287	167	48	6	0	7	30	18	16	.358	.449

1993 By Position

Position	Avg	AB	H	2B	3B	HR	RBI	BB	SO	OBP	SLG	G	GS	Innings	PO	A	E	DP	Fld Pct	Rng Fctr	In Zone	Outs	Zone Rtg	MLB Zone
As Pinch Hitter	.154	13	2	0	0	0	1	1	4	.214	.154	14	0	---	---	---	---	---	---	---	---	---	---	---
As 1b	.297	91	27	6	0	1	14	12	10	.361	.396	31	24	216.1	210	19	0	28	1.000	---	42	39	.929	.834
As 3b	.267	285	76	10	2	9	37	30	30	.339	.411	79	73	659.1	53	125	12	15	.937	2.43	178	143	.803	.834

Last Five Years

	Avg	AB	H	2B	3B	HR	RBI	BB	SO	OBP	SLG
vs. Left	.284	721	205	41	5	14	84	107	64	.376	.413
vs. Right	.269	1689	454	69	8	13	155	192	191	.344	.342
Groundball	.288	622	179	27	6	3	57	69	59	.358	.365
Flyball	.261	537	140	24	3	7	60	73	60	.347	.356
Home	.283	1190	337	55	7	15	122	153	114	.367	.379
Away	.264	1220	322	55	6	12	117	146	141	.341	.348
Day	.265	709	188	39	1	6	77	97	79	.355	.348
Night	.277	1701	471	71	12	21	162	202	176	.353	.370
Grass	.255	1387	353	55	7	18	142	163	139	.333	.343
Turf	.299	1023	306	55	6	9	97	136	116	.381	.391
First Pitch	.329	277	91	15	1	6	38	12	0	.361	.455
Ahead in Count	.321	655	210	47	4	9	88	160	0	.452	.446
Behind in Count	.226	997	225	23	5	7	70	0	209	.228	.280
Two Strikes	.212	1010	214	25	2	5	68	123	255	.298	.255

	Avg	AB	H	2B	3B	HR	RBI	BB	SO	OBP	SLG
Scoring Posn	.275	579	159	29	5	4	203	111	59	.381	.363
Close & Late	.295	387	114	22	1	4	47	42	50	.359	.388
None on/out	.244	618	151	29	3	6	6	58	76	.317	.330
Batting #1	.278	618	172	32	8	5	39	72	67	.356	.380
Batting #2	.266	1016	270	38	1	12	112	131	116	.349	.341
Other	.280	776	217	40	4	10	88	96	72	.357	.380
April	.243	345	84	17	0	5	35	28	35	.303	.336
May	.303	416	126	20	3	4	43	50	48	.381	.394
June	.289	467	135	23	3	4	49	59	39	.364	.377
July	.257	377	97	12	4	3	31	60	46	.358	.334
August	.260	393	102	17	1	5	45	55	44	.349	.346
September/October	.279	412	115	21	2	6	36	47	43	.356	.383
Pre-All Star	.280	1363	381	64	8	14	142	158	140	.355	.369
Post-All Star	.266	1047	278	46	5	13	97	141	115	.352	.356

Batter vs. Pitcher (career)

Hits Best Against	Avg	AB	H	2B	3B	HR	RBI	BB	SO	OBP	SLG
Bill Gullickson	.500	12	6	1	0	0	1	0	0	.500	.583
Erik Hanson	.450	20	9	2	0	0	2	7	2	.593	.550
Greg Cadaret	.421	19	8	2	0	1	3	2	0	.476	.684
Jose Guzman	.389	18	7	3	0	0	4	5	4	.522	.556
Alex Fernandez	.375	8	3	0	0	2	3	3	1	.545	1.125

Hits Worst Against	Avg	AB	H	2B	3B	HR	RBI	BB	SO	OBP	SLG
Scott Erickson	.000	12	0	0	0	0	1	0	0	.000	.000
Scott Bankhead	.000	11	0	0	0	0	0	2	2	.154	.000
Jack McDowell	.045	22	1	0	0	0	2	3	3	.148	.045
Paul Kilgus	.091	11	1	1	0	0	0	1	2	.167	.182
Alan Mills	.091	11	1	1	0	0	0	0	1	.091	.182

Aaron Sele — Red Sox

Age 24 – Pitches Right (groundball pitcher)

	ERA	W	L	Sv	G	GS	IP	BB	SO	Avg	H	2B	3B	HR	RBI	OBP	SLG	CG	ShO	Sup	QS	#P/S	SB	CS	GB	FB	G/F
1993 Season	2.74	7	2	0	18	18	111.2	48	93	.237	100	24	1	5	37	.322	.334	0	0	5.24	12	107	8	1	157	90	1.74

1993 Season

	ERA	W	L	Sv	G	GS	IP	H	HR	BB	SO
Home	2.81	4	2	0	9	9	57.2	49	3	26	50
Away	2.67	3	0	0	9	9	54.0	51	2	22	43
Starter	2.74	7	2	0	18	18	111.2	100	5	48	93
Reliever	0.00	0	0	0	0	0	0.0	0	0	0	0
0-3 Days Rest	3.18	0	0	0	1	1	5.2	4	0	1	5
4 Days Rest	2.63	3	1	0	8	8	48.0	46	3	18	33
5+ Days Rest	2.79	4	1	0	9	9	58.0	50	2	29	55
Pre-All Star	1.05	2	0	0	4	4	25.2	16	0	12	25
Post-All Star	3.24	5	2	0	14	14	86.0	84	5	36	68

	Avg	AB	H	2B	3B	HR	RBI	BB	SO	OBP	SLG
vs. Left	.229	218	50	12	0	2	16	33	44	.328	.312
vs. Right	.245	204	50	12	1	3	21	15	49	.314	.358
Scoring Posn	.226	106	24	7	1	0	29	15	29	.320	.311
Close & Late	.290	31	9	3	0	1	2	4	5	.405	.484
None on/out	.198	111	22	4	0	1	1	9	28	.270	.261
First Pitch	.259	54	14	3	0	0	4	0	0	.255	.315
Ahead in Count	.191	178	34	11	0	0	9	0	76	.203	.253
Behind in Count	.358	95	34	5	0	4	16	31	0	.508	.537
Two Strikes	.153	202	31	11	1	0	10	17	93	.236	.218

Frank Seminara — Padres

Age 27 – Pitches Right (groundball pitcher)

	ERA	W	L	Sv	G	GS	IP	BB	SO	Avg	H	2B	3B	HR	RBI	OBP	SLG	GF	IR	IRS	Hld	SvOp	SB	CS	GB	FB	G/F
1993 Season	4.47	3	3	0	18	7	46.1	21	22	.294	53	7	3	5	27	.374	.450	0	8	3	1	1	3	3	81	43	1.88
Career (1992-1993)	3.93	12	7	0	37	25	146.2	67	83	.270	151	19	6	10	65	.352	.379	0	10	5	1	1	13	9	235	124	1.90

1993 Season

	ERA	W	L	Sv	G	GS	IP	H	HR	BB	SO
Home	5.61	1	3	0	11	4	25.2	38	4	11	14
Away	3.05	2	0	0	7	3	20.2	15	1	10	8

	Avg	AB	H	2B	3B	HR	RBI	BB	SO	OBP	SLG
vs. Left	.287	101	29	5	1	3	21	13	13	.368	.446
vs. Right	.304	79	24	2	2	2	6	8	9	.382	.456

Scott Servais — Astros

Age 27 – Bats Right

	Avg	G	AB	R	H	2B	3B	HR	RBI	BB	SO	HBP	GDP	SB	CS	OBP	SLG	IBB	SH	SF	#Pit	#P/PA	GB	FB	G/F
1993 Season	.244	85	258	24	63	11	0	11	32	22	45	5	6	0	0	.313	.415	2	3	3	1054	3.62	99	72	1.38
Career (1991-1993)	.236	178	500	36	118	23	0	11	53	37	78	10	13	0	0	.300	.348	4	10	3	1960	3.50	192	145	1.32

1993 Season

	Avg	AB	H	2B	3B	HR	RBI	BB	SO	OBP	SLG
vs. Left	.297	138	41	10	0	7	24	12	21	.357	.522
vs. Right	.183	120	22	1	0	4	8	10	24	.261	.292
Home	.246	134	33	10	0	5	19	10	20	.311	.433
Away	.242	124	30	1	0	6	13	12	25	.314	.395
First Pitch	.317	41	13	0	0	2	5	1	0	.318	.463
Ahead in Count	.328	64	21	5	0	5	12	13	0	.436	.641
Behind in Count	.196	107	21	5	0	2	10	0	39	.225	.299
Two Strikes	.144	104	15	3	0	3	8	8	45	.226	.260

	Avg	AB	H	2B	3B	HR	RBI	BB	SO	OBP	SLG
Scoring Posn	.258	62	16	1	0	2	21	9	11	.347	.371
Close & Late	.286	42	12	3	0	1	4	0	5	.286	.429
None on/out	.267	60	16	3	0	2	2	2	12	.313	.417
Batting #6	.143	28	4	1	0	0	1	1	6	.172	.179
Batting #7	.257	226	58	10	0	11	31	21	37	.329	.447
Other	.250	4	1	0	0	0	0	0	2	.250	.250
Pre-All Star	.281	171	48	8	0	8	24	13	27	.339	.468
Post-All Star	.172	87	15	3	0	3	8	9	18	.263	.310

Scott Service — Reds

Age 26 – Pitches Right

	ERA	W	L	Sv	G	GS	IP	BB	SO	Avg	H	2B	3B	HR	RBI	OBP	SLG	GF	IR	IRS	Hld	SvOp	SB	CS	GB	FB	G/F
1993 Season	4.30	2	2	2	29	0	46.0	16	43	.254	44	7	4	6	23	.318	.445	7	19	4	3	2	2	1	50	50	1.00
Last Five Years	5.60	2	2	2	34	0	53.0	21	54	.282	59	8	5	7	34	.347	.469	7	23	6	4	2	4	1	63	54	1.17

1993 Season

	ERA	W	L	Sv	G	GS	IP	H	HR	BB	SO
Home	4.95	0	0	2	12	0	20.0	25	3	5	17
Away	3.81	2	2	0	17	0	26.0	19	3	11	26
Starter	0.00	0	0	0	0	0	0.0	0	0	0	0
Reliever	4.30	2	2	2	29	0	46.0	44	6	16	43
0 Days rest	8.31	0	1	0	5	0	8.2	10	0	5	10
1 or 2 Days rest	4.74	0	0	1	12	0	19.0	18	4	6	20
3+ Days rest	1.96	2	1	1	12	0	18.1	16	2	5	13
Pre-All Star	5.87	1	0	0	4	0	7.2	8	1	1	6
Post-All Star	3.99	1	2	2	25	0	38.1	36	5	15	37

	Avg	AB	H	2B	3B	HR	RBI	BB	SO	OBP	SLG
vs. Left	.231	65	15	2	4	1	10	13	9	.357	.431
vs. Right	.269	108	29	5	0	5	13	3	34	.288	.454
Scoring Posn	.178	45	8	2	0	0	15	7	12	.281	.222
Close & Late	.303	33	10	3	1	2	8	7	4	.425	.636
None on/out	.220	41	9	0	2	2	2	4	10	.304	.463
First Pitch	.391	23	9	2	0	2	10	2	0	.393	.739
Ahead in Count	.172	87	15	3	2	2	5	0	40	.180	.322
Behind in Count	.257	35	9	1	0	1	4	4	0	.333	.371
Two Strikes	.182	88	16	2	3	2	5	10	43	.270	.341

Mike Sharperson — Dodgers

Age 32 – Bats Right

	Avg	G	AB	R	H	2B	3B	HR	RBI	BB	SO	HBP	GDP	SB	CS	OBP	SLG	IBB	SH	SF	#Pit	#P/PA	GB	FB	G/F
1993 Season	.256	73	90	13	23	4	0	2	10	5	17	1	2	2	0	.299	.367	0	0	1	378	3.90	40	15	2.67
Last Five Years	.289	462	1008	129	291	53	4	10	107	127	120	3	19	20	12	.367	.379	8	24	8	4326	3.70	391	264	1.48

1993 Season

	Avg	AB	H	2B	3B	HR	RBI	BB	SO	OBP	SLG
vs. Left	.253	79	20	4	0	2	9	2	15	.277	.380
vs. Right	.273	11	3	0	0	0	1	3	2	.429	.273

	Avg	AB	H	2B	3B	HR	RBI	BB	SO	OBP	SLG
Scoring Posn	.240	25	6	1	0	0	7	2	7	.286	.280
Close & Late	.250	28	7	1	0	1	3	0	4	.250	.393

Last Five Years

	Avg	AB	H	2B	3B	HR	RBI	BB	SO	OBP	SLG
vs. Left	.309	657	203	36	3	8	67	75	77	.379	.409
vs. Right	.251	351	88	17	1	2	40	52	43	.346	.322
Groundball	.337	300	101	18	0	1	31	43	29	.420	.407
Flyball	.233	253	59	10	2	0	14	24	32	.297	.289
Home	.306	496	152	22	1	5	51	56	57	.376	.385
Away	.271	512	139	31	3	5	56	71	63	.359	.373

	Avg	AB	H	2B	3B	HR	RBI	BB	SO	OBP	SLG
Scoring Posn	.249	269	67	10	1	0	88	50	42	.360	.294
Close & Late	.262	210	55	12	2	3	31	28	32	.344	.381
None on/out	.297	219	65	12	1	1	1	16	23	.345	.374
Batting #2	.326	389	127	26	2	2	43	50	41	.401	.419
Batting #7	.331	157	52	7	0	4	19	20	17	.406	.452
Other	.242	462	112	20	2	4	45	57	62	.326	.320

Last Five Years

	Avg	AB	H	2B	3B	HR	RBI	BB	SO	OBP	SLG
Day	.291	285	83	17	0	5	36	39	35	.373	.404
Night	.288	723	208	36	4	5	71	88	85	.365	.369
Grass	.304	784	238	43	1	8	86	96	95	.379	.392
Turf	.237	224	53	10	3	2	21	31	25	.327	.335
First Pitch	.307	140	43	11	1	1	15	2	0	.324	.421
Ahead in Count	.346	228	79	11	0	7	37	65	0	.483	.487
Behind in Count	.254	449	114	15	0	1	36	0	101	.254	.294
Two Strikes	.238	454	108	21	2	2	35	54	120	.318	.306

	Avg	AB	H	2B	3B	HR	RBI	BB	SO	OBP	SLG
April	.257	109	28	5	0	0	9	14	10	.344	.303
May	.316	114	36	7	0	1	14	18	15	.403	.404
June	.311	180	56	10	1	2	27	26	18	.396	.411
July	.302	189	57	10	1	3	24	24	23	.379	.413
August	.274	179	49	7	1	2	11	23	25	.356	.358
September/October	.274	237	65	14	1	2	22	22	29	.337	.367
Pre-All Star	.304	480	146	26	1	5	61	67	52	.388	.394
Post-All Star	.275	528	145	27	3	5	46	60	68	.348	.366

Batter vs. Pitcher (career)

Hits Best Against	Avg	AB	H	2B	3B	HR	RBI	BB	SO	OBP	SLG
Butch Henry	.600	10	6	0	0	0	0	2	1	.667	.600
Rich Rodriguez	.417	12	5	1	0	1	1	0	2	.417	.750
Craig Lefferts	.400	10	4	0	0	2	5	2	1	.500	1.000
Tom Glavine	.393	28	11	6	0	0	0	2	3	.433	.607
Randy Myers	.353	17	6	2	2	0	3	5	5	.478	.706

Hits Worst Against	Avg	AB	H	2B	3B	HR	RBI	BB	SO	OBP	SLG
Greg Swindell	.000	14	0	0	0	0	0	0	4	.000	.000
Chris Hammond	.100	10	1	0	0	0	0	2	2	.250	.100
Jim Deshaies	.105	19	2	0	0	0	0	0	1	.105	.105
Bud Black	.208	24	5	0	0	0	0	1	1	.240	.208
Dennis Rasmussen	.222	18	4	0	0	0	1	0	0	.222	.222

Jon Shave — Rangers

Age 26 – Bats Right (groundball hitter)

	Avg	G	AB	R	H	2B	3B	HR	RBI	BB	SO	HBP	GDP	SB	CS	OBP	SLG	IBB	SH	SF	#Pit	#P/PA	GB	FB	G/F
1993 Season	.319	17	47	3	15	2	0	0	7	0	8	0	0	1	3	.306	.362	0	3	2	182	3.50	18	9	2.00

1993 Season

	Avg	AB	H	2B	3B	HR	RBI	BB	SO	OBP	SLG
vs. Left	.545	11	6	1	0	0	3	0	1	.545	.636
vs. Right	.250	36	9	1	0	0	4	0	7	.237	.278

	Avg	AB	H	2B	3B	HR	RBI	BB	SO	OBP	SLG
Scoring Posn	.364	11	4	2	0	0	7	0	1	.308	.545
Close & Late	.200	5	1	0	0	0	0	0	1	.200	.200

Jeff Shaw — Expos

Age 27 – Pitches Right (groundball pitcher)

	ERA	W	L	Sv	G	GS	IP	BB	SO	Avg	H	2B	3B	HR	RBI	OBP	SLG	GF	IR	IRS	Hld	SvOp	SB	CS	GB	FB	G/F
1993 Season	4.14	2	7	0	55	8	95.2	32	50	.254	91	22	1	12	46	.326	.422	13	32	7	4	1	5	2	155	84	1.85
Career (1990-1993)	4.57	5	17	1	98	19	224.1	83	109	.281	243	48	3	31	122	.348	.451	23	75	28	4	5	11	6	358	236	1.52

1993 Season

	ERA	W	L	Sv	G	GS	IP	H	HR	BB	SO
Home	3.07	1	3	0	26	6	55.2	50	5	20	28
Away	5.63	1	4	0	29	2	40.0	41	7	12	22
Starter	3.96	1	4	0	8	8	36.1	38	3	15	14
Reliever	4.25	1	3	0	47	0	59.1	53	9	17	36
0 Days rest	4.72	1	2	0	12	0	13.1	12	4	4	2
1 or 2 Days rest	3.81	0	1	0	22	0	28.1	23	1	9	26
3+ Days rest	4.58	0	0	0	13	0	17.2	18	4	4	8
Pre-All Star	3.66	1	5	0	26	8	64.0	57	7	20	34
Post-All Star	5.12	1	2	0	29	0	31.2	34	5	12	16

	Avg	AB	H	2B	3B	HR	RBI	BB	SO	OBP	SLG
vs. Left	.312	173	54	11	0	7	23	20	18	.383	.497
vs. Right	.200	185	37	11	1	5	23	12	32	.271	.351
Scoring Posn	.216	88	19	5	1	1	30	12	17	.304	.330
Close & Late	.244	45	11	1	0	4	7	6	8	.340	.533
None on/out	.209	86	18	4	0	2	2	7	15	.277	.326
First Pitch	.313	67	21	4	1	3	11	1	0	.333	.537
Ahead in Count	.210	143	30	7	0	3	12	0	43	.235	.322
Behind in Count	.264	72	19	5	0	4	11	20	0	.430	.500
Two Strikes	.182	137	25	6	0	1	9	11	50	.261	.248

Danny Sheaffer — Rockies

Age 32 – Bats Right (groundball hitter)

	Avg	G	AB	R	H	2B	3B	HR	RBI	BB	SO	HBP	GDP	SB	CS	OBP	SLG	IBB	SH	SF	#Pit	#P/PA	GB	FB	G/F
1993 Season	.278	82	216	26	60	9	1	4	32	8	15	1	9	2	3	.299	.384	0	2	6	731	3.14	115	51	2.25
Last Five Years	.263	89	232	27	61	9	1	4	32	10	17	1	9	2	3	.289	.362	0	3	6	801	3.18	124	54	2.30

1993 Season

	Avg	AB	H	2B	3B	HR	RBI	BB	SO	OBP	SLG
vs. Left	.396	48	19	2	0	1	7	1	1	.400	.500
vs. Right	.244	168	41	7	1	3	25	7	14	.271	.351
Home	.295	122	36	7	1	2	22	2	9	.302	.418
Away	.255	94	24	2	0	2	10	6	6	.295	.340
First Pitch	.419	43	18	2	0	1	12	0	0	.409	.535
Ahead in Count	.271	48	13	2	1	1	11	5	0	.316	.417
Behind in Count	.198	96	19	5	0	0	5	0	15	.204	.250
Two Strikes	.250	84	21	4	0	2	6	3	15	.284	.369

	Avg	AB	H	2B	3B	HR	RBI	BB	SO	OBP	SLG
Scoring Posn	.365	52	19	1	0	1	29	5	5	.391	.442
Close & Late	.357	28	10	1	0	1	7	1	2	.355	.500
None on/out	.324	37	12	2	1	1	1	1	2	.342	.514
Batting #7	.235	85	20	3	0	1	17	5	4	.277	.306
Batting #8	.263	76	20	2	0	3	9	2	5	.275	.408
Other	.364	55	20	4	1	0	6	1	6	.368	.473
Pre-All Star	.261	115	30	5	0	4	14	2	7	.269	.409
Post-All Star	.297	101	30	4	1	0	18	6	8	.330	.356

Larry Sheets — Mariners

Age 34 – Bats Left

	Avg	G	AB	R	H	2B	3B	HR	RBI	BB	SO	HBP	GDP	SB	CS	OBP	SLG	IBB	SH	SF	#Pit	#P/PA	GB	FB	G/F
1993 Season	.118	11	17	0	2	1	0	0	1	2	1	1	2	0	0	.250	.176	0	0	0	79	3.95	8	5	1.60
Last Five Years	.250	244	681	73	170	30	3	17	86	52	101	6	18	2	4	.305	.377	12	0	9	2654	3.55	242	198	1.22

1993 Season

	Avg	AB	H	2B	3B	HR	RBI	BB	SO	OBP	SLG
vs. Left	.000	0	0	0	0	0	0	0	0	.000	.000
vs. Right	.118	17	2	1	0	0	1	2	1	.250	.176

	Avg	AB	H	2B	3B	HR	RBI	BB	SO	OBP	SLG
Scoring Posn	.333	6	2	1	0	0	1	0	1	.333	.500
Close & Late	.000	2	0	0	0	0	0	1	1	.333	.000

Last Five Years

	Avg	AB	H	2B	3B	HR	RBI	BB	SO	OBP	SLG
vs. Left	.179	56	10	1	0	0	2	3	16	.230	.196
vs. Right	.256	625	160	29	3	17	84	49	85	.311	.394
Groundball	.264	208	55	12	1	4	21	15	28	.316	.389
Flyball	.299	127	38	4	2	3	23	10	21	.352	.433

	Avg	AB	H	2B	3B	HR	RBI	BB	SO	OBP	SLG
Scoring Posn	.261	184	48	7	1	7	71	25	25	.335	.424
Close & Late	.266	94	25	7	0	2	13	12	20	.349	.404
None on/out	.298	151	45	7	0	3	3	9	16	.350	.404
Batting #5	.229	210	48	10	3	3	27	15	35	.281	.348

Last Five Years

	Avg	AB	H	2B	3B	HR	RBI	BB	SO	OBP	SLG
Home	.235	319	75	14	1	8	44	26	54	.294	.361
Away	.262	362	95	16	2	9	42	26	47	.314	.392
Day	.280	164	46	6	2	5	21	14	19	.335	.433
Night	.240	517	124	24	1	12	65	38	82	.295	.360
Grass	.248	556	138	27	2	16	70	42	82	.303	.390
Turf	.256	125	32	3	1	1	16	10	19	.312	.320
First Pitch	.292	137	40	10	1	3	14	8	0	.329	.445
Ahead in Count	.262	145	38	4	0	8	34	18	0	.337	.455
Behind in Count	.190	263	50	9	1	2	20	0	80	.206	.255
Two Strikes	.194	289	56	10	1	5	25	24	101	.262	.287

	Avg	AB	H	2B	3B	HR	RBI	BB	SO	OBP	SLG
Batting #7	.271	207	56	10	0	7	23	15	24	.317	.420
Other	.250	264	66	10	0	7	36	22	42	.314	.367
April	.246	126	31	6	1	1	12	10	18	.293	.333
May	.304	102	31	2	0	6	14	10	13	.374	.500
June	.229	109	25	7	1	3	13	9	13	.283	.394
July	.240	125	30	5	1	3	20	8	23	.281	.368
August	.303	119	36	5	0	3	19	7	17	.346	.420
September/October	.170	100	17	5	0	1	8	8	17	.252	.250
Pre-All Star	.255	377	96	17	2	10	42	33	50	.312	.390
Post-All Star	.243	304	74	13	1	7	44	19	51	.296	.362

Batter vs. Pitcher (career)

Hits Best Against	Avg	AB	H	2B	3B	HR	RBI	BB	SO	OBP	SLG
Paul Kilgus	.600	10	6	0	0	2	5	1	0	.636	1.200
Steve Farr	.545	11	6	3	0	1	1	1	2	.583	1.091
Nolan Ryan	.467	15	7	2	0	2	5	2	3	.529	1.000
Todd Stottlemyre	.417	12	5	0	0	2	5	0	0	.417	.917
Bobby Witt	.357	14	5	0	1	2	6	3	3	.444	.929

Hits Worst Against	Avg	AB	H	2B	3B	HR	RBI	BB	SO	OBP	SLG
Storm Davis	.083	12	1	0	0	0	1	0	3	.083	.083
Tom Henke	.083	12	1	0	0	0	0	1	5	.154	.083
Curt Young	.083	12	1	0	0	0	0	0	0	.083	.083
Bob Welch	.100	20	2	2	0	0	2	0	3	.095	.200
Chris Bosio	.150	20	3	0	0	0	1	0	2	.150	.150

Gary Sheffield — Marlins

Age 25 – Bats Right (flyball hitter)

	Avg	G	AB	R	H	2B	3B	HR	RBI	BB	SO	HBP	GDP	SB	CS	OBP	SLG	IBB	SH	SF	#Pit	#P/PA	GB	FB	G/F
1993 Season	.294	140	494	67	145	20	5	20	73	47	64	9	11	17	5	.361	.476	6	0	7	1898	3.41	143	165	0.87
Last Five Years	.287	556	2061	280	597	114	11	70	294	185	193	25	48	62	32	.348	.453	13	8	31	7645	3.28	682	748	0.91

1993 Season

	Avg	AB	H	2B	3B	HR	RBI	BB	SO	OBP	SLG
vs. Left	.326	135	44	4	0	4	23	16	10	.400	.444
vs. Right	.281	359	101	16	5	16	50	31	54	.346	.487
Groundball	.256	164	42	5	3	8	27	15	24	.330	.470
Flyball	.247	77	19	2	0	0	9	5	14	.310	.273
Home	.315	241	76	12	2	10	40	24	24	.382	.506
Away	.273	253	69	8	3	10	33	23	40	.340	.447
Day	.316	114	36	4	3	5	21	11	13	.386	.535
Night	.287	380	109	16	2	15	52	36	51	.353	.458
Grass	.318	384	122	16	5	16	61	38	48	.383	.510
Turf	.209	110	23	4	0	4	12	9	16	.281	.355
First Pitch	.367	79	29	3	0	2	9	5	0	.414	.481
Ahead in Count	.348	112	39	7	2	6	20	25	0	.465	.607
Behind in Count	.224	214	48	7	2	5	26	0	49	.234	.346
Two Strikes	.227	194	44	5	1	3	18	17	64	.294	.309

	Avg	AB	H	2B	3B	HR	RBI	BB	SO	OBP	SLG
Scoring Posn	.263	114	30	1	3	4	44	22	16	.372	.430
Close & Late	.326	86	28	2	2	4	18	15	14	.429	.535
None on/out	.284	102	29	7	1	1	1	3	10	.318	.402
Batting #3	.296	287	85	13	2	13	41	27	39	.359	.491
Batting #4	.287	202	58	7	3	7	32	18	24	.357	.455
Other	.400	5	2	0	0	0	0	2	1	.571	.400
April	.286	84	24	2	0	5	13	6	11	.330	.488
May	.245	98	24	5	1	3	12	10	10	.318	.408
June	.354	96	34	5	1	3	14	4	9	.388	.521
July	.288	80	23	6	1	4	13	11	12	.370	.538
August	.292	89	26	2	0	4	16	6	12	.356	.449
September/October	.298	47	14	0	2	1	5	10	10	.433	.447
Pre-All Star	.298	305	91	13	2	13	42	27	35	.358	.482
Post-All Star	.286	189	54	7	3	7	31	20	29	.365	.466

1993 By Position

Position	Avg	AB	H	2B	3B	HR	RBI	BB	SO	OBP	SLG	G	GS	Innings	PO	A	E	DP	Fld Pct	Rng Fctr	In Zone	Outs	Zone Rtg	MLB Zone
As 3b	.294	490	144	20	5	20	73	45	63	.359	.478	134	133	1129.2	79	224	34	14	.899	2.41	329	237	.720	.834

Last Five Years

	Avg	AB	H	2B	3B	HR	RBI	BB	SO	OBP	SLG
vs. Left	.307	615	189	35	4	23	97	63	46	.370	.489
vs. Right	.278	1466	408	79	7	47	197	122	147	.338	.438
Groundball	.282	667	188	36	3	21	93	62	63	.350	.439
Flyball	.263	433	114	19	1	11	53	33	48	.318	.388
Home	.304	1040	316	64	6	40	145	103	94	.369	.492
Away	.270	1041	281	50	5	30	149	82	99	.326	.414
Day	.275	636	175	32	6	18	79	53	57	.331	.429
Night	.292	1445	422	82	5	52	215	132	136	.355	.464
Grass	.298	1643	490	95	11	61	229	157	157	.362	.481
Turf	.244	438	107	19	0	9	65	28	36	.292	.349
First Pitch	.342	401	137	29	3	14	55	10	0	.360	.534
Ahead in Count	.323	446	144	25	3	20	84	108	0	.453	.527
Behind in Count	.240	854	205	38	3	19	96	0	157	.249	.358
Two Strikes	.219	736	161	25	3	12	72	65	193	.286	.310

	Avg	AB	H	2B	3B	HR	RBI	BB	SO	OBP	SLG
Scoring Posn	.284	507	144	22	6	16	210	70	54	.359	.446
Close & Late	.339	310	105	12	4	11	53	39	29	.413	.510
None on/out	.274	390	107	24	2	10	10	24	30	.323	.423
Batting #2	.295	305	90	21	1	7	37	20	27	.335	.439
Batting #3	.287	1341	385	68	7	51	200	126	122	.350	.462
Other	.280	435	122	25	3	12	57	39	44	.347	.434
April	.282	373	105	24	2	12	51	40	35	.350	.453
May	.291	399	116	19	2	13	56	34	37	.348	.446
June	.283	413	117	25	1	11	64	29	42	.330	.429
July	.294	377	111	28	3	11	50	31	21	.353	.472
August	.290	290	84	10	0	16	54	24	32	.347	.490
September/October	.279	229	64	8	3	7	19	27	26	.364	.432
Pre-All Star	.289	1323	382	76	7	42	194	116	124	.346	.452
Post-All Star	.284	758	215	38	4	28	100	69	69	.349	.455

Batter vs. Pitcher (career)

Hits Best Against	Avg	AB	H	2B	3B	HR	RBI	BB	SO	OBP	SLG
Jack McDowell	.545	11	6	2	0	0	2	2	0	.615	.727
Greg Harris	.444	9	4	1	0	1	3	2	0	.545	.889
Ken Hill	.429	14	6	1	0	1	2	2	0	.500	.714
John Burkett	.417	12	5	1	0	3	6	1	0	.462	1.250
Bob Walk	.316	19	6	0	0	5	8	0	1	.316	1.105

Hits Worst Against	Avg	AB	H	2B	3B	HR	RBI	BB	SO	OBP	SLG
Jose Rijo	.000	12	0	0	0	0	0	1	4	.077	.000
Bob Tewksbury	.000	12	0	0	0	0	0	0	2	.000	.000
Greg Hibbard	.083	12	1	0	0	0	1	1	2	.154	.083
Tim Pugh	.083	12	1	0	0	0	0	0	1	.083	.083
Dave Stieb	.118	17	2	0	0	0	0	0	2	.118	.118

Ben Shelton — Pirates

Age 24 – Bats Right

	Avg	G	AB	R	H	2B	3B	HR	RBI	BB	SO	HBP	GDP	SB	CS	OBP	SLG	IBB	SH	SF	#Pit	#P/PA	GB	FB	G/F
1993 Season	.250	15	24	3	6	1	0	2	7	3	3	0	2	0	0	.333	.542	0	0	0	97	3.59	7	11	0.64

1993 Season

	Avg	AB	H	2B	3B	HR	RBI	BB	SO	OBP	SLG
vs. Left	.200	10	2	1	0	0	3	2	1	.333	.300

	Avg	AB	H	2B	3B	HR	RBI	BB	SO	OBP	SLG
Scoring Posn	.500	4	2	1	0	0	5	1	1	.600	.750

1993 Season	Avg	AB	H	2B	3B	HR	RBI	BB	SO	OBP	SLG
vs. Right	.286	14	4	0	0	2	4	1	2	.333	.714
Close & Late	.000	4	0	0	0	0	0	0	2	.000	.000

Keith Shepherd — Rockies

Age 26 – Pitches Right

	ERA	W	L	Sv	G	GS	IP	BB	SO	Avg	H	2B	3B	HR	RBI	OBP	SLG	GF	IR	IRS	Hld	SvOp	SB	CS	GB	FB	G/F
1993 Season	6.98	1	3	1	14	1	19.1	4	7	.333	26	4	0	4	15	.369	.538	3	7	1	2	2	0	2	32	18	1.78
Career (1992-1993)	5.01	2	4	3	26	1	41.1	10	17	.290	45	10	0	4	26	.329	.432	9	13	5	2	8	3	5	59	42	1.40

1993 Season

	ERA	W	L	Sv	G	GS	IP	H	HR	BB	SO
Home	10.45	1	2	0	8	1	10.1	18	4	3	4
Away	3.00	0	1	1	6	0	9.0	8	0	1	3

	Avg	AB	H	2B	3B	HR	RBI	BB	SO	OBP	SLG
vs. Left	.286	35	10	0	0	0	2	1	3	.306	.286
vs. Right	.372	43	16	4	0	4	13	3	4	.417	.744

Darrell Sherman — Padres

Age 26 – Bats Left (groundball hitter)

	Avg	G	AB	R	H	2B	3B	HR	RBI	BB	SO	HBP	GDP	SB	CS	OBP	SLG	IBB	SH	SF	#Pit	#P/PA	GB	FB	G/F
1993 Season	.222	37	63	8	14	1	0	0	2	6	8	3	0	2	1	.315	.238	0	1	1	294	3.97	26	12	2.17

1993 Season

	Avg	AB	H	2B	3B	HR	RBI	BB	SO	OBP	SLG
vs. Left	.091	11	1	0	0	0	0	1	1	.167	.091
vs. Right	.250	52	13	1	0	0	2	5	7	.344	.269
Scoring Posn	.091	11	1	0	0	0	2	2	1	.267	.091
Close & Late	.222	18	4	0	0	0	0	1	1	.333	.222

Tommy Shields — Cubs

Age 29 – Bats Right

	Avg	G	AB	R	H	2B	3B	HR	RBI	BB	SO	HBP	GDP	SB	CS	OBP	SLG	IBB	SH	SF	#Pit	#P/PA	GB	FB	G/F
1993 Season	.176	20	34	4	6	1	0	0	1	2	10	0	1	0	0	.222	.206	0	0	0	134	3.72	12	6	2.00

1993 Season

	Avg	AB	H	2B	3B	HR	RBI	BB	SO	OBP	SLG
vs. Left	.188	16	3	0	0	0	0	1	6	.235	.188
vs. Right	.167	18	3	1	0	0	1	1	4	.211	.222
Scoring Posn	.250	12	3	1	0	0	1	1	4	.308	.333
Close & Late	.333	6	2	0	0	0	0	0	1	.333	.333

Zak Shinall — Mariners

Age 25 – Pitches Right

	ERA	W	L	Sv	G	GS	IP	BB	SO	Avg	H	2B	3B	HR	RBI	OBP	SLG	GF	IR	IRS	Hld	SvOp	SB	CS	GB	FB	G/F
1993 Season	3.38	0	0	0	1	0	2.2	2	0	.333	4	1	1	1	1	.429	.833	0	1	0	0	0	0	0	5	6	0.83

1993 Season

	ERA	W	L	Sv	G	GS	IP	H	HR	BB	SO
Home	3.38	0	0	0	1	0	2.2	4	1	2	0
Away	0.00	0	0	0	0	0	0.0	0	0	0	0

	Avg	AB	H	2B	3B	HR	RBI	BB	SO	OBP	SLG
vs. Left	.250	4	1	0	1	0	0	1	0	.400	.750
vs. Right	.375	8	3	1	0	1	1	1	0	.444	.875

Craig Shipley — Padres

Age 31 – Bats Right

	Avg	G	AB	R	H	2B	3B	HR	RBI	BB	SO	HBP	GDP	SB	CS	OBP	SLG	IBB	SH	SF	#Pit	#P/PA	GB	FB	G/F
1993 Season	.235	105	230	25	54	9	0	4	22	10	31	3	3	12	3	.275	.326	0	1	1	677	2.76	89	68	1.31
Last Five Years	.245	198	433	41	106	18	0	5	35	14	67	4	6	13	5	.274	.321	1	3	1	1350	2.97	158	124	1.27

1993 Season

	Avg	AB	H	2B	3B	HR	RBI	BB	SO	OBP	SLG
vs. Left	.229	96	22	3	0	1	7	7	10	.282	.292
vs. Right	.239	134	32	6	0	3	15	3	21	.270	.351
Home	.222	108	24	4	0	2	11	6	8	.270	.315
Away	.246	122	30	5	0	2	11	4	23	.279	.336
First Pitch	.197	71	14	3	0	0	1	0	0	.219	.239
Ahead in Count	.400	40	16	1	0	3	9	8	0	.500	.650
Behind in Count	.209	91	19	4	0	1	9	0	30	.215	.286
Two Strikes	.147	68	10	2	0	1	7	2	31	.171	.221
Scoring Posn	.256	43	11	2	0	1	18	4	5	.313	.372
Close & Late	.214	56	12	3	0	1	5	1	5	.241	.321
None on/out	.188	69	13	4	0	0	0	2	11	.211	.246
Batting #2	.305	59	18	2	0	2	10	1	5	.328	.441
Batting #7	.318	44	14	2	0	1	6	2	3	.348	.432
Other	.173	127	22	5	0	1	6	7	23	.226	.236
Pre-All Star	.223	139	31	7	0	2	14	4	19	.248	.317
Post-All Star	.253	91	23	2	0	2	8	6	12	.313	.341

Brian Shouse — Pirates

Age 25 – Pitches Left

	ERA	W	L	Sv	G	GS	IP	BB	SO	Avg	H	2B	3B	HR	RBI	OBP	SLG	GF	IR	IRS	Hld	SvOp	SB	CS	GB	FB	G/F
1993 Season	9.00	0	0	0	6	0	4.0	2	3	.368	7	1	0	1	3	.409	.579	1	1	0	0	0	0	0	9	4	2.25

1993 Season

	ERA	W	L	Sv	G	GS	IP	H	HR	BB	SO
Home	13.50	0	0	0	2	0	1.1	3	1	0	1
Away	6.75	0	0	0	4	0	2.2	4	0	2	2

	Avg	AB	H	2B	3B	HR	RBI	BB	SO	OBP	SLG
vs. Left	.556	9	5	1	0	1	3	0	2	.500	1.000
vs. Right	.200	10	2	0	0	0	0	2	1	.333	.200

Terry Shumpert — Royals

Age 27 – Bats Right (flyball hitter)

	Avg	G	AB	R	H	2B	3B	HR	RBI	BB	SO	HBP	GDP	SB	CS	OBP	SLG	IBB	SH	SF	#Pit	#P/PA	GB	FB	G/F
1993 Season	.100	8	10	0	1	0	0	0	0	2	2	0	0	1	0	.250	.100	0	0	0	42	3.50	1	5	0.20
Career (1990-1993)	.213	220	564	58	120	27	6	6	53	37	111	6	16	23	16	.266	.314	0	12	5	2204	3.53	162	201	0.81

1993 Season

	Avg	AB	H	2B	3B	HR	RBI	BB	SO	OBP	SLG
vs. Left	.000	1	0	0	0	0	0	0	0	.000	.000
Scoring Posn	.000	1	0	0	0	0	0	1	0	.500	.000

1993 Season

	Avg	AB	H	2B	3B	HR	RBI	BB	SO	OBP	SLG		Avg	AB	H	2B	3B	HR	RBI	BB	SO	OBP	SLG
vs. Right	.111	9	1	0	0	0	0	2	2	.273	.111	Close & Late	.000	3	0	0	0	0	0	0	1	.000	.000

Career (1990-1993)

	Avg	AB	H	2B	3B	HR	RBI	BB	SO	OBP	SLG		Avg	AB	H	2B	3B	HR	RBI	BB	SO	OBP	SLG
vs. Left	.231	195	45	12	0	3	21	10	32	.281	.338	Scoring Posn	.264	144	38	8	2	1	45	12	35	.323	.368
vs. Right	.203	369	75	15	6	3	32	27	79	.259	.301	Close & Late	.273	77	21	4	3	1	7	6	12	.321	.442
Groundball	.174	161	28	5	3	0	13	11	36	.234	.242	None on/out	.210	138	29	6	2	2	2	12	29	.288	.326
Flyball	.230	148	34	7	1	4	11	10	31	.281	.372	Batting #8	.219	96	21	3	0	1	5	9	17	.299	.281
Home	.206	272	56	12	5	1	23	15	50	.256	.298	Batting #9	.218	449	98	23	6	5	48	27	88	.266	.330
Away	.219	292	64	15	1	5	30	22	61	.276	.329	Other	.053	19	1	1	0	0	0	1	6	.100	.105
Day	.164	146	24	4	3	1	10	11	38	.228	.253	April	.169	83	14	3	1	0	7	4	23	.205	.229
Night	.230	418	96	23	3	5	43	26	73	.280	.335	May	.261	176	46	12	3	1	19	6	27	.285	.381
Grass	.220	227	50	11	0	5	26	19	47	.280	.335	June	.164	73	12	1	0	3	8	7	14	.235	.301
Turf	.208	337	70	16	6	1	27	18	64	.257	.300	July	.244	82	20	3	1	1	9	6	10	.303	.341
First Pitch	.267	90	24	6	3	0	4	0	0	.283	.400	August	.260	77	20	5	1	0	5	11	19	.360	.351
Ahead in Count	.264	91	24	9	1	4	17	22	0	.400	.516	September/October	.110	73	8	3	0	1	5	3	18	.177	.192
Behind in Count	.179	290	52	8	2	2	24	0	100	.198	.241	Pre-All Star	.222	352	78	17	4	5	37	19	65	.260	.335
Two Strikes	.167	270	45	8	2	2	23	15	111	.217	.233	Post-All Star	.198	212	42	10	2	1	16	18	46	.277	.278

Batter vs. Pitcher (career)

Hits Best Against	Avg	AB	H	2B	3B	HR	RBI	BB	SO	OBP	SLG	Hits Worst Against	Avg	AB	H	2B	3B	HR	RBI	BB	SO	OBP	SLG
												Chuck Finley	.000	14	0	0	0	0	0	0	1	.000	.000
												Bill Gullickson	.182	11	2	0	0	0	2	0	2	.167	.182
												Kevin Brown	.214	14	3	0	0	0	0	0	3	.214	.214

Joe Siddall — Expos

Age 26 – Bats Left

	Avg	G	AB	R	H	2B	3B	HR	RBI	BB	SO	HBP	GDP	SB	CS	OBP	SLG	IBB	SH	SF	#Pit	#P/PA	GB	FB	G/F
1993 Season	.100	19	20	0	2	1	0	0	1	1	5	0	0	0	0	.143	.150	1	0	0	73	3.48	7	4	1.75

1993 Season

	Avg	AB	H	2B	3B	HR	RBI	BB	SO	OBP	SLG		Avg	AB	H	2B	3B	HR	RBI	BB	SO	OBP	SLG
vs. Left	.143	7	1	0	0	0	0	0	3	.143	.143	Scoring Posn	.333	3	1	0	0	0	0	1	2	.500	.333
vs. Right	.077	13	1	1	0	0	1	1	2	.143	.154	Close & Late	.500	2	1	1	0	0	1	0	0	.500	1.000

Ruben Sierra — Athletics

Age 28 – Bats Both

	Avg	G	AB	R	H	2B	3B	HR	RBI	BB	SO	HBP	GDP	SB	CS	OBP	SLG	IBB	SH	SF	#Pit	#P/PA	GB	FB	G/F
1993 Season	.233	158	630	77	147	23	5	22	101	52	97	0	17	25	5	.288	.390	16	0	10	2448	3.54	229	218	1.05
Last Five Years	.281	791	3134	441	881	173	33	109	519	245	424	3	67	72	15	.329	.462	51	0	47	12099	3.53	1162	1011	1.15

1993 Season

	Avg	AB	H	2B	3B	HR	RBI	BB	SO	OBP	SLG		Avg	AB	H	2B	3B	HR	RBI	BB	SO	OBP	SLG
vs. Left	.231	199	46	8	0	8	32	20	29	.297	.392	Scoring Posn	.243	173	42	5	0	11	83	30	26	.338	.462
vs. Right	.234	431	101	15	5	14	69	32	68	.283	.390	Close & Late	.252	103	26	1	1	4	19	19	16	.363	.398
Groundball	.233	129	30	7	3	3	19	6	19	.263	.403	None on/out	.233	116	27	6	1	2	2	6	14	.270	.353
Flyball	.236	127	30	1	0	7	21	11	21	.295	.409	Batting #3	.238	551	131	22	5	20	94	44	81	.289	.405
Home	.222	306	68	9	2	9	49	26	58	.280	.353	Batting #4	.205	73	15	1	0	2	7	8	14	.284	.301
Away	.244	324	79	14	3	13	52	26	39	.295	.426	Other	.167	6	1	0	0	0	0	0	2	.167	.167
Day	.226	257	58	8	4	5	30	20	44	.280	.346	April	.296	71	21	7	0	4	15	3	9	.316	.563
Night	.239	373	89	15	1	17	71	32	53	.293	.421	May	.200	120	24	5	1	3	22	7	18	.240	.333
Grass	.242	516	125	19	4	19	84	38	80	.290	.405	June	.255	106	27	3	0	4	13	12	15	.331	.396
Turf	.193	114	22	4	1	3	17	14	17	.277	.325	July	.306	108	33	4	1	5	23	11	12	.361	.500
First Pitch	.296	54	16	3	1	2	9	12	0	.412	.500	August	.190	116	22	2	2	1	6	8	26	.242	.267
Ahead in Count	.292	185	54	8	4	10	49	24	0	.370	.541	September/October	.183	109	20	2	1	5	22	11	17	.252	.358
Behind in Count	.185	259	48	5	0	6	25	0	83	.184	.274	Pre-All Star	.247	344	85	17	2	12	55	26	49	.297	.413
Two Strikes	.151	245	37	2	0	6	21	16	97	.202	.233	Post-All Star	.217	286	62	6	3	10	46	26	48	.277	.364

1993 By Position

Position	Avg	AB	H	2B	3B	HR	RBI	BB	SO	OBP	SLG	G	GS	Innings	PO	A	E	DP	Fld Pct	Rng Fctr	In Zone	Outs	Zone Rtg	MLB Zone
As Designated Hitter	.216	102	22	3	1	4	17	6	20	.255	.382	25	25	---	---	---	---	---	---	---	---	---	---	---
As rf	.238	526	125	20	4	18	84	46	76	.295	.394	133	131	1150.0	291	9	7	3	.977	2.35	351	280	.798	.826

Last Five Years

	Avg	AB	H	2B	3B	HR	RBI	BB	SO	OBP	SLG		Avg	AB	H	2B	3B	HR	RBI	BB	SO	OBP	SLG
vs. Left	.314	979	307	64	9	33	172	82	107	.362	.498	Scoring Posn	.305	852	260	44	9	39	405	105	116	.364	.515
vs. Right	.266	2155	574	109	24	76	347	163	317	.314	.445	Close & Late	.272	496	135	20	4	19	90	61	70	.348	.444
Groundball	.307	833	256	51	7	24	139	54	105	.346	.472	None on/out	.282	716	202	49	10	25	25	44	85	.326	.483
Flyball	.275	706	194	38	10	24	99	67	95	.333	.459	Batting #3	.266	1203	320	57	8	41	199	93	162	.314	.429
Home	.274	1538	422	80	16	62	269	109	241	.319	.468	Batting #4	.291	1900	553	115	25	68	317	151	256	.340	.485
Away	.288	1596	459	93	17	47	250	136	183	.339	.456	Other	.258	31	8	1	0	0	3	1	6	.281	.290
Day	.263	745	196	37	5	22	114	65	89	.319	.415	April	.302	388	117	32	2	18	76	29	59	.344	.534
Night	.287	2389	685	136	28	87	405	180	335	.332	.476	May	.276	551	152	25	7	16	89	40	68	.323	.434
Grass	.275	2613	719	138	23	96	436	195	358	.322	.456	June	.322	540	174	37	9	19	91	49	72	.378	.530
Turf	.311	521	162	35	10	13	83	50	66	.367	.491	July	.266	511	136	26	4	19	86	36	66	.310	.444
First Pitch	.308	344	106	10	9	21	84	30	0	.353	.573	August	.255	572	146	28	7	14	69	37	92	.296	.402
Ahead in Count	.338	902	305	56	8	41	187	128	0	.415	.554	September/October	.273	572	156	25	4	23	108	54	67	.329	.451
Behind in Count	.230	1260	290	61	10	29	152	0	353	.229	.363	Pre-All Star	.296	1650	488	100	20	60	278	130	220	.345	.490
Two Strikes	.193	1201	232	48	8	26	122	77	424	.241	.311	Post-All Star	.265	1484	393	73	13	49	241	115	204	.312	.431

Batter vs. Pitcher (career)																							
Hits Best Against	Avg	AB	H	2B	3B	HR	RBI	BB	SO	OBP	SLG	Hits Worst Against	Avg	AB	H	2B	3B	HR	RBI	BB	SO	OBP	SLG
Bud Black	.667	21	14	4	0	2	7	1	0	.682	1.143	Todd Frohwirth	.000	11	0	0	0	0	0	0	0	.000	.000
Mark Knudson	.556	9	5	2	0	3	7	0	0	.455	1.778	Gregg Olson	.000	10	0	0	0	0	0	1	3	.091	.000
Mike Schooler	.500	12	6	1	0	1	6	1	1	.538	.833	Jeff Shaw	.000	10	0	0	0	0	0	1	1	.091	.000
Julio Valera	.500	6	3	1	0	0	2	5	1	.727	.667	Teddy Higuera	.059	17	1	0	0	0	0	0	2	.059	.059
Dennis Rasmussen	.455	11	5	0	1	1	3	3	1	.533	.909	Doug Jones	.071	14	1	0	0	0	0	0	2	.071	.071

Dave Silvestri — Yankees

Age 26 – Bats Right (flyball hitter)

	Avg	G	AB	R	H	2B	3B	HR	RBI	BB	SO	HBP	GDP	SB	CS	OBP	SLG	IBB	SH	SF	#Pit	#P/PA	GB	FB	G/F
1993 Season	.286	7	21	4	6	1	0	1	4	5	3	0	1	0	0	.423	.476	0	0	0	109	4.19	7	7	1.00
Career (1992-1993)	.294	14	34	7	10	1	2	1	5	5	6	0	2	0	0	.385	.529	0	0	0	151	3.87	11	12	0.92

1993 Season																							
	Avg	AB	H	2B	3B	HR	RBI	BB	SO	OBP	SLG		Avg	AB	H	2B	3B	HR	RBI	BB	SO	OBP	SLG
vs. Left	.444	9	4	0	0	1	3	3	1	.583	.778	Scoring Posn	.400	5	2	0	0	0	2	2	1	.571	.400
vs. Right	.167	12	2	1	0	0	1	2	2	.286	.250	Close & Late	.000	1	0	0	0	0	0	0	0	.000	.000

Don Slaught — Pirates

Age 35 – Bats Right

	Avg	G	AB	R	H	2B	3B	HR	RBI	BB	SO	HBP	GDP	SB	CS	OBP	SLG	IBB	SH	SF	#Pit	#P/PA	GB	FB	G/F
1993 Season	.300	116	377	34	113	19	2	10	55	29	56	6	13	2	1	.356	.440	2	4	4	1472	3.50	131	99	1.32
Last Five Years	.295	481	1432	140	423	92	12	24	188	124	195	19	36	6	5	.355	.427	13	20	19	5364	3.32	490	445	1.10

1993 Season																							
	Avg	AB	H	2B	3B	HR	RBI	BB	SO	OBP	SLG		Avg	AB	H	2B	3B	HR	RBI	BB	SO	OBP	SLG
vs. Left	.333	120	40	5	2	2	13	6	14	.374	.458	Scoring Posn	.347	101	35	4	0	2	38	12	15	.412	.446
vs. Right	.284	257	73	14	0	8	42	23	42	.347	.432	Close & Late	.321	81	26	3	0	3	12	10	11	.396	.469
Groundball	.305	131	40	3	0	4	19	11	16	.354	.420	None on/out	.304	79	24	5	1	3	3	7	15	.375	.506
Flyball	.233	60	14	4	1	3	8	6	10	.313	.483	Batting #6	.263	118	31	9	1	5	23	10	22	.321	.483
Home	.284	183	52	12	2	1	20	13	28	.333	.388	Batting #7	.298	238	71	8	1	3	27	17	32	.355	.378
Away	.314	194	61	7	0	9	35	16	28	.377	.490	Other	.524	21	11	2	0	2	5	2	2	.565	.905
Day	.247	81	20	7	0	2	9	9	10	.337	.407	April	.383	60	23	3	1	0	10	7	8	.464	.467
Night	.314	296	93	12	2	8	46	20	46	.361	.449	May	.274	73	20	1	0	1	5	3	9	.303	.329
Grass	.319	119	38	6	0	4	19	11	19	.382	.471	June	.261	69	18	3	0	3	10	5	12	.325	.435
Turf	.291	258	75	13	2	6	36	18	37	.344	.426	July	.296	71	21	4	1	3	15	7	14	.358	.507
First Pitch	.424	66	28	6	2	3	18	2	0	.443	.712	August	.279	68	19	8	0	1	9	4	10	.324	.441
Ahead in Count	.380	100	38	8	0	2	19	15	0	.462	.520	September/October	.333	36	12	0	0	2	6	3	3	.385	.500
Behind in Count	.211	152	32	5	0	3	12	0	50	.226	.303	Pre-All Star	.301	229	69	8	2	7	35	19	37	.362	.445
Two Strikes	.207	150	31	5	0	4	15	12	56	.268	.320	Post-All Star	.297	148	44	11	0	3	20	10	19	.346	.432

1993 By Position																								
Position	Avg	AB	H	2B	3B	HR	RBI	BB	SO	OBP	SLG	G	GS	Innings	PO	A	E	DP	Fld Pct	Rng Fctr	In Zone	Outs	Zone Rtg	MLB Zone
As Pinch Hitter	.462	13	6	0	0	1	3	2	0	.533	.692	15	0	---	---	---	---	---	---	---	---	---	---	---
As c	.294	364	107	19	2	9	52	27	56	.349	.431	105	99	874.2	540	50	4	9	.993	---	---	---	---	---

Last Five Years																							
	Avg	AB	H	2B	3B	HR	RBI	BB	SO	OBP	SLG		Avg	AB	H	2B	3B	HR	RBI	BB	SO	OBP	SLG
vs. Left	.297	715	212	47	8	9	75	66	90	.357	.422	Scoring Posn	.311	376	117	24	1	2	147	51	51	.384	.396
vs. Right	.294	717	211	45	4	15	113	58	105	.353	.431	Close & Late	.296	280	83	14	3	5	44	29	43	.370	.421
Groundball	.309	469	145	27	1	7	64	38	69	.365	.416	None on/out	.309	346	107	27	4	10	10	28	40	.374	.497
Flyball	.272	265	72	18	3	9	35	28	38	.346	.464	Batting #6	.290	335	97	28	3	6	51	24	53	.336	.445
Home	.297	714	212	57	8	7	92	63	100	.354	.429	Batting #7	.291	900	262	52	6	13	105	87	117	.359	.406
Away	.294	718	211	35	4	17	96	61	95	.356	.425	Other	.325	197	64	12	3	5	32	13	25	.371	.492
Day	.258	337	87	23	2	7	47	43	48	.345	.401	April	.351	202	71	15	4	3	32	13	27	.394	.510
Night	.307	1095	336	69	10	17	141	81	147	.358	.435	May	.301	289	87	14	5	4	32	28	32	.364	.426
Grass	.300	590	177	37	1	13	80	45	87	.353	.432	June	.308	279	86	17	0	5	31	20	43	.358	.423
Turf	.292	842	246	55	11	11	108	79	108	.356	.423	July	.221	213	47	10	1	5	32	23	39	.300	.347
First Pitch	.382	304	116	29	3	7	48	11	0	.406	.566	August	.275	255	70	24	1	3	34	17	33	.326	.412
Ahead in Count	.377	361	136	25	4	7	58	57	0	.459	.526	September/October	.320	194	62	12	1	4	27	23	21	.397	.454
Behind in Count	.192	525	101	22	1	6	51	0	167	.205	.272	Pre-All Star	.307	836	257	48	10	16	110	70	119	.363	.446
Two Strikes	.173	510	88	18	2	7	45	54	195	.255	.257	Post-All Star	.279	596	166	44	2	8	78	54	76	.344	.399

Batter vs. Pitcher (since 1984)																							
Hits Best Against	Avg	AB	H	2B	3B	HR	RBI	BB	SO	OBP	SLG	Hits Worst Against	Avg	AB	H	2B	3B	HR	RBI	BB	SO	OBP	SLG
Matt Young	.600	15	9	3	0	0	2	1	1	.625	.800	Dave Stewart	.000	19	0	0	0	0	2	2	5	.091	.000
Jim Deshaies	.583	12	7	3	0	0	3	3	1	.625	.833	Dave Righetti	.000	13	0	0	0	0	0	1	6	.071	.000
Joe Magrane	.455	11	5	0	0	1	1	0	1	.455	.727	Mike Henneman	.000	10	0	0	0	0	0	1	3	.091	.000
Pete Harnisch	.455	11	5	2	0	2	7	1	1	.500	1.182	Gene Nelson	.077	13	1	0	0	0	0	0	2	.077	.077
Dennis Martinez	.400	20	8	2	1	1	3	1	0	.429	.750	Craig Lefferts	.091	11	1	0	0	0	0	0	0	.091	.091

Heathcliff Slocumb — Indians

Age 28 – Pitches Right (groundball pitcher)

	ERA	W	L	Sv	G	GS	IP	BB	SO	Avg	H	2B	3B	HR	RBI	OBP	SLG	GF	IR	IRS	Hld	SvOp	SB	CS	GB	FB	G/F
1993 Season	4.03	4	1	0	30	0	38.0	20	22	.250	35	3	0	3	25	.337	.336	9	32	13	3	2	4	0	58	44	1.32
Career (1991-1993)	4.41	6	5	2	112	0	136.2	71	83	.271	140	16	1	9	84	.357	.358	41	94	32	10	6	20	5	218	129	1.69

1993 Season																							
	ERA	W	L	Sv	G	GS	IP	H	HR	BB	SO		Avg	AB	H	2B	3B	HR	RBI	BB	SO	OBP	SLG
Home	2.49	1	0	0	18	0	21.2	22	1	10	15	vs. Left	.239	46	11	0	0	1	9	10	5	.368	.304

1993 Season	ERA	W	L	Sv	G	GS	IP	H	HR	BB	SO		Avg	AB	H	2B	3B	HR	RBI	BB	SO	OBP	SLG
Away	6.06	3	1	0	12	0	16.1	13	2	10	7	vs. Right	.255	94	24	3	0	2	16	10	17	.321	.351
Starter	0.00	0	0	0	0	0	0.0	0	0	0	0	Scoring Posn	.250	48	12	0	0	2	24	10	11	.361	.375
Reliever	4.03	4	1	0	30	0	38.0	35	3	20	22	Close & Late	.359	39	14	1	0	1	8	8	1	.458	.462
0 Days rest	0.00	0	0	0	3	0	3.1	3	0	1	2	None on/out	.200	30	6	0	0	1	1	2	4	.250	.300
1 or 2 Days rest	5.67	3	1	0	20	0	27.0	30	3	18	16	First Pitch	.211	19	4	0	0	0	3	2	0	.261	.211
3+ Days rest	0.00	1	0	0	7	0	7.2	2	0	1	4	Ahead in Count	.185	65	12	1	0	1	2	0	18	.185	.246
Pre-All Star	4.32	4	1	0	26	0	33.1	33	2	18	17	Behind in Count	.323	31	10	1	0	1	9	10	0	.488	.452
Post-All Star	1.93	0	0	0	4	0	4.2	2	1	2	5	Two Strikes	.213	75	16	1	0	1	8	8	22	.286	.267

Career (1991-1993)	ERA	W	L	Sv	G	GS	IP	H	HR	BB	SO		Avg	AB	H	2B	3B	HR	RBI	BB	SO	OBP	SLG
Home	3.27	3	2	2	57	0	74.1	73	3	32	51	vs. Left	.320	228	73	5	1	7	40	35	29	.410	.443
Away	5.78	3	3	0	55	0	62.1	67	6	39	32	vs. Right	.232	289	67	11	0	2	44	36	54	.313	.291
Day	6.11	2	3	2	55	0	66.1	79	4	36	46	Inning 1-6	.283	159	45	7	1	3	35	23	29	.366	.396
Night	2.82	4	2	0	57	0	70.1	61	5	35	37	Inning 7+	.265	358	95	9	0	6	49	48	54	.353	.341
Grass	4.13	5	3	2	83	0	102.1	104	6	54	67	None on	.236	242	57	7	0	2	2	27	37	.320	.289
Turf	5.24	1	2	0	29	0	34.1	36	3	17	16	Runners on	.302	275	83	9	1	7	82	44	46	.387	.418
April	4.38	2	2	1	21	0	24.2	19	2	11	13	Scoring Posn	.272	191	52	6	0	5	76	31	36	.359	.382
May	2.91	0	0	1	20	0	21.2	13	1	10	9	Close & Late	.296	125	37	4	0	3	22	27	14	.418	.400
June	2.04	2	1	0	31	0	35.1	27	1	23	20	None on/out	.229	109	25	3	0	1	1	11	16	.311	.284
July	9.00	2	0	0	11	0	15.0	31	2	6	10	vs. 1st Batr (relief)	.242	91	22	4	0	0	12	15	14	.357	.286
August	5.94	0	0	0	9	0	16.2	24	0	6	14	First Inning Pitched	.273	348	95	11	1	7	67	57	56	.372	.371
September/October	5.40	0	2	0	20	0	23.1	26	3	15	17	First 15 Pitches	.253	292	74	10	1	6	50	45	43	.350	.356
Starter	0.00	0	0	0	0	0	0.0	0	0	0	0	Pitch 16-30	.266	158	42	4	0	2	22	18	29	.345	.329
Reliever	4.41	6	5	2	112	0	136.2	140	9	71	83	Pitch 31-45	.270	37	10	2	0	0	5	6	7	.372	.324
0 Days rest	7.36	1	0	0	30	0	29.1	49	2	14	16	Pitch 46+	.467	30	14	0	0	1	7	2	4	.471	.567
1 or 2 Days rest	4.04	4	4	1	51	0	64.2	57	7	38	32	First Pitch	.309	68	21	0	0	1	10	8	0	.375	.353
3+ Days rest	2.95	1	1	1	31	0	42.2	34	0	19	35	Ahead in Count	.250	240	60	8	1	3	32	0	65	.252	.329
Pre-All Star	3.83	5	3	2	77	0	89.1	79	6	47	49	Behind in Count	.252	115	29	4	0	3	23	44	0	.453	.365
Post-All Star	5.51	1	2	0	35	0	47.1	61	3	24	34	Two Strikes	.214	238	51	6	1	3	30	18	83	.270	.286

Joe Slusarski — Athletics

Age 27 – Pitches Right

	ERA	W	L	Sv	G	GS	IP	BB	SO	Avg	H	2B	3B	HR	RBI	OBP	SLG	CG	ShO	Sup	QS	#P/S	SB	CS	GB	FB	G/F
1993 Season	5.19	0	0	0	2	1	8.2	11	1	.300	9	1	0	1	5	.488	.433	0	0	4.15	1	106	0	0	12	11	1.09
Career (1991-1993)	5.34	10	12	0	37	34	194.0	90	99	.284	215	35	6	30	98	.365	.466	1	0	5.15	11	87	11	9	266	231	1.15

1993 Season	ERA	W	L	Sv	G	GS	IP	H	HR	BB	SO		Avg	AB	H	2B	3B	HR	RBI	BB	SO	OBP	SLG
Home	0.00	0	0	0	0	0	0.0	0	0	0	0	vs. Left	.375	16	6	1	0	1	4	5	0	.524	.625
Away	5.19	0	0	0	2	1	8.2	9	1	11	1	vs. Right	.214	14	3	0	0	0	1	6	1	.450	.214

Career (1991-1993)	ERA	W	L	Sv	G	GS	IP	H	HR	BB	SO		Avg	AB	H	2B	3B	HR	RBI	BB	SO	OBP	SLG
Home	5.14	5	7	0	17	16	96.1	106	16	34	56	vs. Left	.290	403	117	19	6	14	47	39	47	.350	.471
Away	5.53	5	5	0	20	18	97.2	109	14	56	43	vs. Right	.278	353	98	16	0	16	51	51	52	.380	.459
Day	5.15	4	4	0	14	14	78.2	79	9	42	42	Inning 1-6	.283	692	196	34	6	28	93	79	93	.361	.471
Night	5.46	6	8	0	23	20	115.1	136	21	48	57	Inning 7+	.297	64	19	1	0	2	5	11	6	.400	.406
Grass	5.24	9	10	0	30	27	156.1	172	23	73	83	None on	.278	457	127	20	5	18	18	46	56	.350	.462
Turf	5.73	1	2	0	7	7	37.2	43	7	17	16	Runners on	.294	299	88	15	1	12	80	44	43	.385	.472
April	4.32	3	0	0	8	8	41.2	42	7	24	18	Scoring Posn	.293	164	48	10	1	8	69	28	29	.389	.512
May	6.22	2	5	0	10	9	50.2	59	11	15	31	Close & Late	.278	18	5	0	0	1	3	5	2	.435	.444
June	5.76	2	3	0	9	8	45.1	51	3	28	24	None on/out	.245	196	48	5	3	7	7	19	25	.327	.408
July	0.75	1	0	0	2	1	12.0	8	0	3	3	vs. 1st Batr (relief)	.667	3	2	1	0	1	3	0	0	.667	2.000
August	7.71	0	2	0	4	4	23.1	29	5	9	9	First Inning Pitched	.248	137	34	8	2	6	18	10	17	.298	.467
September/October	4.29	2	2	0	4	4	21.0	26	4	11	14	First 75 Pitches	.278	633	176	24	6	22	79	64	85	.350	.439
Starter	5.45	10	12	0	34	34	185.0	203	29	85	95	Pitch 76-90	.293	82	24	8	0	7	16	19	11	.426	.646
Reliever	3.00	0	0	0	3	0	9.0	12	1	5	4	Pitch 91-105	.368	38	14	3	0	1	3	6	2	.455	.526
0-3 Days Rest	4.91	0	0	0	1	1	3.2	7	0	2	4	Pitch 106+	.333	3	1	0	0	0	0	1	1	.500	.333
4 Days Rest	5.88	4	6	0	18	18	98.0	103	17	42	52	First Pitch	.360	114	41	5	0	8	25	4	0	.383	.614
5+ Days Rest	4.97	6	6	0	15	15	83.1	93	12	41	39	Ahead in Count	.226	314	71	13	1	6	23	0	79	.238	.331
Pre-All Star	5.37	7	8	0	28	25	140.2	158	21	68	74	Behind in Count	.311	183	57	10	1	9	25	53	0	.461	.525
Post-All Star	5.23	3	4	0	9	9	53.1	57	9	22	25	Two Strikes	.216	296	64	15	2	6	22	33	99	.299	.341

Pitcher vs. Batter (career)

Pitches Best Vs.	Avg	AB	H	2B	3B	HR	RBI	BB	SO	OBP	SLG	Pitches Worst Vs.	Avg	AB	H	2B	3B	HR	RBI	BB	SO	OBP	SLG
Brady Anderson	.077	13	1	0	0	1	2	0	3	.077	.308	Randy Milligan	.400	10	4	0	0	1	2	4	1	.571	.700
Chris Hoiles	.167	12	2	1	0	0	0	1	1	.231	.250	Darryl Hamilton	.400	10	4	1	0	0	1	1	0	.455	.500
Mike Devereaux	.214	14	3	0	0	1	2	1	4	.267	.429	Omar Vizquel	.375	8	3	1	0	0	0	3	1	.545	.500
												Robin Yount	.364	11	4	1	0	0	2	0	0	.364	.455

John Smiley — Reds

Age 29 – Pitches Left (flyball pitcher)

	ERA	W	L	Sv	G	GS	IP	BB	SO	Avg	H	2B	3B	HR	RBI	OBP	SLG	CG	ShO	Sup	QS	#P/S	SB	CS	GB	FB	G/F
1993 Season	5.62	3	9	0	18	18	105.2	31	60	.286	117	17	3	15	63	.337	.452	2	0	4.51	8	86	13	4	135	136	0.99
Last Five Years	3.60	60	44	0	139	137	909.0	225	561	.249	851	164	20	86	358	.296	.383	19	4	4.36	84	94	98	48	1119	1141	0.98

1993 Season

	ERA	W	L	Sv	G	GS	IP	H	HR	BB	SO
Home	4.81	1	5	0	8	8	48.2	49	5	14	21
Away	6.32	2	4	0	10	10	57.0	68	10	17	39
Starter	5.62	3	9	0	18	18	105.2	117	15	31	60
Reliever	0.00	0	0	0	0	0	0.0	0	0	0	0
0-3 Days Rest	0.00	0	0	0	0	0	0.0	0	0	0	0
4 Days Rest	5.36	3	7	0	16	16	95.2	105	11	27	56
5+ Days Rest	8.10	0	2	0	2	2	10.0	12	4	4	4
Pre-All Star	5.62	3	9	0	18	18	105.2	117	15	31	60
Post-All Star	0.00	0	0	0	0	0	0.0	0	0	0	0

	Avg	AB	H	2B	3B	HR	RBI	BB	SO	OBP	SLG
vs. Left	.275	51	14	2	1	1	7	9	5	.383	.412
vs. Right	.288	358	103	15	2	14	56	22	55	.330	.458
Scoring Posn	.378	98	37	4	0	6	51	9	12	.423	.602
Close & Late	.273	22	6	0	0	2	3	0	3	.273	.545
None on/out	.248	109	27	6	0	3	3	5	13	.281	.385
First Pitch	.346	78	27	4	1	4	15	0	0	.342	.577
Ahead in Count	.237	186	44	4	1	5	24	0	53	.245	.349
Behind in Count	.329	82	27	6	1	3	16	21	0	.457	.537
Two Strikes	.222	176	39	5	1	5	21	10	60	.263	.347

Last Five Years

	ERA	W	L	Sv	G	GS	IP	H	HR	BB	SO
Home	3.16	32	22	0	69	67	458.0	410	41	125	286
Away	4.05	28	22	0	70	70	451.0	441	45	100	275
Day	3.58	22	14	0	45	45	294.1	288	20	61	160
Night	3.62	38	30	0	94	92	614.2	563	66	164	401
Grass	3.64	18	16	0	44	44	287.0	262	30	66	164
Turf	3.59	42	28	0	95	93	622.0	589	56	159	397
April	3.72	8	8	0	23	23	145.0	120	7	49	83
May	4.08	13	7	0	24	24	154.1	156	18	32	101
June	3.38	9	7	0	23	23	154.1	149	19	31	108
July	3.67	8	10	0	23	23	162.0	143	19	53	100
August	3.10	12	5	0	23	23	156.2	157	11	32	93
September/October	3.69	10	7	0	23	21	136.2	126	12	28	76
Starter	3.63	59	44	0	137	137	903.2	847	86	222	559
Reliever	0.00	1	0	0	2	0	5.1	4	0	3	2
0-3 Days Rest	0.00	0	0	0	0	0	0.0	0	0	0	0
4 Days Rest	3.44	40	27	0	91	91	609.2	564	58	146	376
5+ Days Rest	4.01	19	17	0	46	46	294.0	283	28	76	183
Pre-All Star	3.77	32	26	0	78	78	508.1	480	48	128	322
Post-All Star	3.39	28	18	0	61	59	400.2	371	38	97	239

	Avg	AB	H	2B	3B	HR	RBI	BB	SO	OBP	SLG
vs. Left	.247	539	133	23	8	9	52	39	75	.298	.369
vs. Right	.249	2885	718	141	12	77	306	186	486	.296	.386
Inning 1-6	.246	2870	707	132	19	69	314	191	487	.295	.378
Inning 7+	.260	554	144	32	1	17	44	34	74	.303	.413
None on	.243	2142	520	110	10	51	51	135	365	.291	.375
Runners on	.258	1282	331	54	10	35	307	90	196	.304	.398
Scoring Posn	.283	722	204	35	4	21	264	57	114	.329	.429
Close & Late	.213	287	61	12	0	9	20	21	49	.267	.348
None on/out	.249	918	229	52	6	22	22	52	142	.294	.391
vs. 1st Batr (relief)	.000	2	0	0	0	0	0	0	0	.000	.000
First Inning Pitched	.256	531	136	24	4	18	73	44	91	.313	.418
First 75 Pitches	.245	2631	645	119	18	63	272	172	439	.293	.376
Pitch 76-90	.274	424	116	25	1	12	49	25	65	.314	.422
Pitch 91-105	.229	245	56	11	0	7	26	19	41	.284	.359
Pitch 106+	.274	124	34	9	1	4	11	9	16	.323	.460
First Pitch	.324	584	189	34	3	18	80	6	0	.331	.485
Ahead in Count	.200	1703	340	62	10	24	129	0	497	.205	.290
Behind in Count	.308	603	186	43	4	25	85	136	0	.432	.517
Two Strikes	.171	1539	263	48	7	22	99	83	561	.216	.254

Pitcher vs. Batter (career)

Pitches Best Vs.	Avg	AB	H	2B	3B	HR	RBI	BB	SO	OBP	SLG
Rafael Palmeiro	.050	20	1	0	0	0	0	4	2	.208	.050
Howard Johnson	.091	44	4	1	0	0	1	1	12	.111	.114
George Brett	.091	11	1	0	0	0	0	0	1	.091	.091
Glenn Wilson	.091	11	1	0	0	0	1	0	3	.083	.091
Dean Palmer	.091	11	1	0	0	0	0	0	3	.091	.091

Pitches Worst Vs.	Avg	AB	H	2B	3B	HR	RBI	BB	SO	OBP	SLG
Mark McGwire	.500	10	5	2	0	2	2	3	2	.615	1.300
Matt D. Williams	.464	28	13	2	0	6	14	1	5	.483	1.179
Andre Dawson	.447	38	17	1	1	4	9	0	4	.447	.842
Wes Chamberlain	.400	15	6	0	0	2	6	0	3	.400	.800
Glenn Davis	.333	24	8	0	0	4	9	3	3	.379	.833

Bryn Smith — Rockies

Age 38 – Pitches Right (groundball pitcher)

	ERA	W	L	Sv	G	GS	IP	BB	SO	Avg	H	2B	3B	HR	RBI	OBP	SLG	GF	IR	IRS	Hld	SvOp	SB	CS	GB	FB	G/F
1993 Season	8.49	2	4	0	11	5	29.2	11	9	.362	47	4	1	2	22	.412	.454	2	0	0	0	1	4	1	62	28	2.21
Last Five Years	3.84	37	34	0	114	94	606.2	145	319	.256	592	95	17	48	252	.303	.374	5	1	0	4	1	72	17	942	608	1.55

1993 Season

	ERA	W	L	Sv	G	GS	IP	H	HR	BB	SO
Home	4.63	1	3	0	6	4	23.1	31	1	5	7
Away	22.74	1	1	0	5	1	6.1	16	1	6	2

	Avg	AB	H	2B	3B	HR	RBI	BB	SO	OBP	SLG
vs. Left	.371	70	26	2	1	1	14	5	4	.392	.471
vs. Right	.350	60	21	2	0	1	8	6	5	.435	.433

Last Five Years

	ERA	W	L	Sv	G	GS	IP	H	HR	BB	SO
Home	3.45	19	16	0	62	53	352.2	333	23	89	191
Away	4.39	18	18	0	52	41	254.0	259	25	56	128
Day	3.88	11	12	0	38	30	197.0	180	15	48	107
Night	3.82	26	22	0	76	64	409.2	412	33	97	212
Grass	3.96	9	15	0	34	28	175.0	178	18	34	87
Turf	3.79	28	19	0	80	66	431.2	414	30	111	232
April	3.31	8	5	0	17	17	100.2	101	6	26	37
May	4.27	8	6	0	24	18	126.1	124	9	31	72
June	3.87	5	6	0	17	16	100.0	98	10	22	55
July	3.34	6	6	0	17	17	105.0	94	6	24	64
August	4.83	3	5	0	12	11	69.0	70	8	15	35
September/October	3.66	7	6	0	27	15	105.2	105	9	27	56
Starter	3.69	32	32	0	94	94	580.1	559	44	137	306
Reliever	7.18	5	2	0	20	0	26.1	33	4	8	13
0 Days rest	10.80	1	0	0	3	0	1.2	1	0	3	0
1 or 2 Days rest	8.40	2	2	0	11	0	15.0	21	2	3	5
3+ Days rest	4.66	2	0	0	6	0	9.2	11	2	2	8
Pre-All Star	3.60	23	18	0	63	56	360.0	343	26	85	179
Post-All Star	4.20	14	16	0	51	38	246.2	249	22	60	140

	Avg	AB	H	2B	3B	HR	RBI	BB	SO	OBP	SLG
vs. Left	.266	1333	354	60	13	17	141	82	148	.310	.368
vs. Right	.243	980	238	35	4	31	111	63	171	.294	.382
Inning 1-6	.258	1980	510	85	14	40	231	129	274	.306	.375
Inning 7+	.246	333	82	10	3	8	21	16	45	.288	.366
None on	.243	1413	344	47	9	27	27	77	185	.288	.347
Runners on	.276	900	248	48	8	21	225	68	134	.326	.417
Scoring Posn	.261	524	137	24	8	13	199	52	94	.323	.412
Close & Late	.320	128	41	5	1	5	10	5	18	.351	.492
None on/out	.262	618	162	23	7	14	14	26	72	.295	.390
vs. 1st Batr (relief)	.222	18	4	0	0	1	1	1	0	.300	.389
First Inning Pitched	.301	438	132	16	5	11	66	38	49	.359	.436
First 15 Pitches	.300	400	120	15	3	10	36	28	36	.350	.428
Pitch 16-30	.220	422	93	11	2	5	35	23	72	.265	.291
Pitch 31-45	.251	399	100	19	5	11	46	26	53	.299	.406
Pitch 46+	.255	1092	279	50	7	22	135	68	158	.302	.375
First Pitch	.346	407	141	19	2	8	64	8	0	.355	.462
Ahead in Count	.196	1049	206	26	6	16	74	0	276	.206	.278
Behind in Count	.326	481	157	34	4	19	81	75	0	.417	.532
Two Strikes	.177	928	164	17	5	14	57	62	319	.237	.251

Pitcher vs. Batter (since 1984)

Pitches Best Vs.	Avg	AB	H	2B	3B	HR	RBI	BB	SO	OBP	SLG	Pitches Worst Vs.	Avg	AB	H	2B	3B	HR	RBI	BB	SO	OBP	SLG
Tim Teufel	.000	10	0	0	0	0	0	2	4	.167	.000	Daryl Boston	.700	10	7	1	1	0	3	3	0	.769	1.000
Larry Walker	.067	15	1	0	0	0	1	0	1	.067	.067	Randy Ready	.450	20	9	2	0	1	1	0	2	.450	.700
Luis Gonzalez	.083	12	1	0	0	0	1	0	3	.083	.083	Chili Davis	.429	14	6	1	0	2	3	1	2	.467	.929
Casey Candaele	.091	11	1	0	0	0	0	1	1	.167	.091	Andy Van Slyke	.425	40	17	4	0	1	7	5	4	.489	.600
Gregg Jefferies	.111	18	2	0	0	0	1	0	1	.111	.111	Orlando Merced	.400	15	6	2	0	1	7	0	0	.375	.733

Dwight Smith — Cubs

Age 30 – Bats Left (groundball hitter)

	Avg	G	AB	R	H	2B	3B	HR	RBI	BB	SO	HBP	GDP	SB	CS	OBP	SLG	IBB	SH	SF	#Pit	#P/PA	GB	FB	G/F
1993 Season	.300	111	310	51	93	17	5	11	35	25	51	3	3	8	6	.355	.494	1	1	3	1296	3.78	102	76	1.34
Career (1989-1993)	.285	536	1327	181	378	68	16	32	159	108	220	9	16	39	27	.341	.433	5	6	8	5371	3.68	520	314	1.66

1993 Season

	Avg	AB	H	2B	3B	HR	RBI	BB	SO	OBP	SLG		Avg	AB	H	2B	3B	HR	RBI	BB	SO	OBP	SLG
vs. Left	.364	11	4	3	0	0	3	0	3	.462	.636	Scoring Posn	.241	58	14	4	1	1	23	7	11	.309	.397
vs. Right	.298	299	89	14	5	11	32	25	48	.351	.488	Close & Late	.279	43	12	1	0	1	7	4	8	.333	.372
Groundball	.326	129	42	6	2	4	14	11	17	.378	.496	None on/out	.326	135	44	8	2	5	5	11	19	.381	.526
Flyball	.146	41	6	1	1	1	2	4	9	.255	.293	Batting #1	.300	247	74	11	3	10	23	17	38	.349	.490
Home	.377	146	55	12	4	6	21	16	22	.440	.637	Batting #9	.409	22	9	2	1	1	7	3	2	.462	.727
Away	.232	164	38	5	1	5	14	9	29	.274	.366	Other	.244	41	10	4	1	0	5	5	11	.326	.390
Day	.296	152	45	8	2	4	16	13	26	.355	.454	April	.400	35	14	4	1	2	2	4	7	.462	.743
Night	.304	158	48	9	3	7	19	12	25	.355	.532	May	.325	80	26	4	2	4	10	2	10	.345	.575
Grass	.311	241	75	13	5	9	30	25	36	.379	.519	June	.218	87	19	2	0	2	8	5	12	.266	.310
Turf	.261	69	18	4	0	2	5	0	15	.261	.406	July	.444	9	4	0	1	0	3	0	1	.400	.667
First Pitch	.357	42	15	3	1	1	5	1	0	.396	.548	August	.319	47	15	2	0	3	3	7	6	.407	.553
Ahead in Count	.444	99	44	8	1	7	18	14	0	.513	.758	September/October	.288	52	15	5	1	0	9	7	15	.383	.423
Behind in Count	.117	103	12	3	1	2	7	0	42	.115	.223	Pre-All Star	.299	211	63	10	4	8	23	11	30	.335	.498
Two Strikes	.164	128	21	5	3	2	9	10	51	.223	.297	Post-All Star	.303	99	30	7	1	3	12	14	21	.395	.485

1993 By Position

Position	Avg	AB	H	2B	3B	HR	RBI	BB	SO	OBP	SLG	G	GS	Innings	PO	A	E	DP	Fld Pct	Rng Fctr	In Zone	Outs	Zone Rtg	MLB Zone
As Pinch Hitter	.375	24	9	3	1	0	5	3	4	.444	.583	28	0	---	---	---	---	---	---	---	---	---	---	---
As lf	.172	29	5	1	1	0	6	2	7	.242	.276	14	7	63.1	12	1	1	0	.929	1.85	15	13	.867	.818
As cf	.304	191	58	9	3	9	22	9	30	.338	.524	53	49	400.1	112	3	6	0	.950	2.59	132	108	.818	.829
As rf	.318	66	21	4	0	2	2	11	10	.416	.470	28	20	154.1	39	1	1	1	.976	2.33	47	38	.809	.826

Career (1989-1993)

	Avg	AB	H	2B	3B	HR	RBI	BB	SO	OBP	SLG		Avg	AB	H	2B	3B	HR	RBI	BB	SO	OBP	SLG
vs. Left	.228	101	23	5	1	3	15	6	29	.288	.386	Scoring Posn	.293	314	92	19	2	5	118	33	65	.356	.414
vs. Right	.290	1226	355	63	15	29	144	102	191	.345	.436	Close & Late	.250	252	63	11	2	5	29	16	44	.297	.369
Groundball	.303	541	164	27	7	12	72	33	86	.345	.445	None on/out	.265	381	101	23	4	12	12	28	58	.319	.441
Flyball	.267	266	71	12	6	5	29	29	48	.347	.414	Batting #1	.294	402	118	16	4	13	37	27	59	.339	.450
Home	.315	629	198	36	8	19	90	57	95	.374	.488	Batting #5	.291	234	68	16	1	7	31	18	34	.345	.457
Away	.258	698	180	32	8	13	69	51	125	.311	.383	Other	.278	691	192	36	11	12	91	63	127	.341	.414
Day	.293	697	204	34	9	15	86	58	108	.349	.432	April	.264	125	33	9	2	3	9	14	22	.343	.440
Night	.276	630	174	34	7	17	73	50	112	.331	.433	May	.316	263	83	15	5	7	29	13	39	.351	.490
Grass	.301	928	279	45	11	25	110	77	142	.356	.454	June	.267	300	80	14	1	8	34	25	49	.324	.400
Turf	.248	399	99	23	5	7	49	31	78	.306	.383	July	.288	153	44	11	2	4	20	9	22	.329	.464
First Pitch	.338	222	75	13	3	3	19	2	0	.349	.464	August	.258	221	57	7	1	7	29	14	45	.301	.394
Ahead in Count	.352	378	133	30	3	16	64	52	0	.430	.574	September/October	.306	265	81	12	5	3	38	33	43	.386	.423
Behind in Count	.184	479	88	12	6	6	41	0	186	.188	.271	Pre-All Star	.291	749	218	41	9	19	78	56	115	.342	.446
Two Strikes	.195	558	109	21	8	6	52	52	220	.265	.294	Post-All Star	.277	578	160	27	7	13	81	52	105	.339	.415

Batter vs. Pitcher (career)

Hits Best Against	Avg	AB	H	2B	3B	HR	RBI	BB	SO	OBP	SLG	Hits Worst Against	Avg	AB	H	2B	3B	HR	RBI	BB	SO	OBP	SLG
Omar Olivares	.471	17	8	3	1	1	6	1	3	.500	.941	John Smoltz	.000	19	0	0	0	0	0	0	2	.000	.000
David Cone	.462	13	6	1	1	1	3	2	1	.533	.923	Roger McDowell	.083	12	1	0	0	0	0	0	0	.083	.083
Cris Carpenter	.455	11	5	3	0	0	1	1	2	.500	.727	Mike Morgan	.125	16	2	0	0	0	0	1	4	.176	.125
Jose DeLeon	.429	28	12	1	1	1	6	6	4	.529	.643	John Burkett	.167	18	3	0	0	0	0	0	2	.167	.167
Mark Gardner	.429	14	6	1	1	1	3	2	2	.471	.857	Andy Ashby	.200	10	2	0	0	0	1	0	3	.182	.200

Lee Smith — Yankees

Age 36 – Pitches Right (flyball pitcher)

	ERA	W	L	Sv	G	GS	IP	BB	SO	Avg	H	2B	3B	HR	RBI	OBP	SLG	GF	IR	IRS	Hld	SvOp	SB	CS	GB	FB	G/F
1993 Season	3.88	2	4	46	63	0	58.0	14	60	.239	53	9	3	11	29	.280	.455	56	25	5	0	53	12	2	52	78	0.67
Last Five Years	2.93	23	22	192	328	0	359.2	115	370	.229	309	47	11	29	151	.288	.345	225	140	36	5	224	57	13	337	422	0.80

1993 Season

	ERA	W	L	Sv	G	GS	IP	H	HR	BB	SO		Avg	AB	H	2B	3B	HR	RBI	BB	SO	OBP	SLG
Home	4.18	1	3	23	31	0	28.0	27	5	6	31	vs. Left	.225	120	27	3	1	6	14	9	31	.275	.417
Away	3.60	1	1	23	32	0	30.0	26	6	8	29	vs. Right	.255	102	26	6	2	5	15	5	29	.287	.500
Day	3.66	2	1	15	24	0	19.2	13	4	7	19	Inning 1-6	.000	0	0	0	0	0	0	0	0	.000	.000
Night	3.99	0	3	31	39	0	38.1	40	7	7	41	Inning 7+	.239	222	53	9	3	11	29	14	60	.280	.455
Grass	2.55	0	0	21	26	0	24.2	22	2	7	24	None on	.256	129	33	7	3	5	5	6	30	.289	.473
Turf	4.86	2	4	25	37	0	33.1	31	9	7	36	Runners on	.215	93	20	2	0	6	24	8	30	.269	.430
April	0.90	0	0	10	11	0	10.0	5	0	3	10	Scoring Posn	.172	58	10	0	0	4	19	6	25	.239	.379
May	5.87	2	1	4	8	0	7.2	6	4	3	9	Close & Late	.254	169	43	4	2	11	27	9	43	.289	.497
June	4.30	0	0	15	15	0	14.2	17	2	1	11	None on/out	.245	53	13	4	1	2	2	3	10	.286	.472

1993 Season

	ERA	W	L	Sv	G	GS	IP	H	HR	BB	SO
July	6.97	0	1	7	12	0	10.1	11	3	0	13
August	4.91	0	2	7	9	0	7.1	10	2	2	6
September/October	0.00	0	0	3	8	0	8.0	4	0	5	11
Starter	0.00	0	0	0	0	0	0.0	0	0	0	0
Reliever	3.88	2	4	46	63	0	58.0	53	11	14	60
0 Days rest	3.43	0	1	19	23	0	21.0	17	3	1	18
1 or 2 Days rest	2.70	1	1	13	18	0	16.2	15	3	7	22
3+ Days rest	5.31	1	2	14	22	0	20.1	21	5	6	20
Pre-All Star	4.08	2	2	30	38	0	35.1	31	8	7	33
Post-All Star	3.57	0	2	16	25	0	22.2	22	3	7	27

	Avg	AB	H	2B	3B	HR	RBI	BB	SO	OBP	SLG
vs. 1st Batr (relief)	.193	57	11	4	0	2	3	5	14	.258	.368
First Inning Pitched	.227	211	48	8	3	10	26	14	58	.272	.436
First 15 Pitches	.242	186	45	9	3	9	25	12	48	.284	.468
Pitch 16-30	.222	36	8	0	0	2	4	2	12	.263	.389
Pitch 31-45	.000	0	0	0	0	0	0	0	0	.000	.000
Pitch 46+	.000	0	0	0	0	0	0	0	0	.000	.000
First Pitch	.500	28	14	2	2	3	8	2	0	.533	1.036
Ahead in Count	.156	122	19	5	0	3	11	0	56	.153	.270
Behind in Count	.293	41	12	1	1	3	5	6	0	.383	.585
Two Strikes	.110	109	12	4	0	3	9	6	60	.155	.229

Last Five Years

	ERA	W	L	Sv	G	GS	IP	H	HR	BB	SO
Home	2.93	19	15	91	179	0	202.2	181	13	65	219
Away	3.02	4	7	101	149	0	157.0	128	16	50	151
Day	2.92	10	5	63	112	0	123.1	96	11	45	141
Night	2.93	13	17	129	216	0	236.1	213	18	70	229
Grass	2.68	10	2	75	131	0	144.1	108	9	57	159
Turf	3.09	13	20	117	197	0	215.1	201	20	58	211
April	2.47	5	3	31	47	0	54.2	40	1	19	57
May	3.96	7	4	22	50	0	50.0	45	7	14	56
June	3.71	2	3	35	60	0	70.1	69	6	21	69
July	2.22	6	1	34	54	0	65.0	51	7	14	66
August	2.82	1	6	39	60	0	60.2	58	4	19	58
September/October	2.44	2	5	31	57	0	59.0	46	4	28	64
Starter	0.00	0	0	0	0	0	0.0	0	0	0	0
Reliever	2.93	23	22	192	328	0	359.2	309	29	115	370
0 Days rest	2.45	1	8	67	96	0	99.1	81	5	33	105
1 or 2 Days rest	2.73	12	5	82	137	0	154.2	130	15	44	156
3+ Days rest	3.66	10	9	43	95	0	105.2	98	9	38	109
Pre-All Star	3.17	16	11	103	179	0	199.0	166	17	63	201
Post-All Star	2.63	7	11	89	149	0	160.2	143	12	52	169

	Avg	AB	H	2B	3B	HR	RBI	BB	SO	OBP	SLG
vs. Left	.230	748	172	25	7	19	92	81	212	.303	.359
vs. Right	.229	599	137	22	4	10	59	34	158	.268	.329
Inning 1-6	.000	0	0	0	0	0	0	0	0	.000	.000
Inning 7+	.229	1347	309	47	11	29	151	115	370	.288	.345
None on	.221	732	162	25	10	14	14	49	180	.270	.340
Runners on	.239	615	147	22	1	15	137	66	190	.308	.351
Scoring Posn	.225	396	89	12	1	8	118	52	133	.308	.321
Close & Late	.231	977	226	30	5	24	113	78	262	.286	.346
None on/out	.228	311	71	12	3	7	7	19	70	.273	.354
vs. 1st Batr (relief)	.232	306	71	14	1	6	25	20	68	.278	.343
First Inning Pitched	.231	1121	259	39	10	24	131	98	312	.290	.348
First 15 Pitches	.237	955	226	38	10	20	92	70	233	.287	.360
Pitch 16-30	.216	329	71	5	1	8	48	39	118	.296	.310
Pitch 31-45	.193	57	11	3	0	1	10	6	17	.270	.298
Pitch 46+	.167	6	1	1	0	0	1	0	2	.167	.333
First Pitch	.290	155	45	6	3	5	26	20	0	.369	.465
Ahead in Count	.177	739	131	17	4	11	62	0	309	.176	.256
Behind in Count	.318	198	63	7	2	7	31	42	0	.434	.480
Two Strikes	.160	749	120	18	5	10	56	52	370	.214	.238

Pitcher vs. Batter (since 1984)

Pitches Best Vs.	Avg	AB	H	2B	3B	HR	RBI	BB	SO	OBP	SLG
John Kruk	.000	15	0	0	0	0	0	1	6	.063	.000
Jay Bell	.000	10	0	0	0	0	0	1	5	.091	.000
Dickie Thon	.091	11	1	0	0	0	0	0	1	.091	.091
Ivan Calderon	.100	10	1	0	0	0	0	1	3	.182	.100
Kevin Bass	.105	19	2	0	0	0	0	0	5	.105	.105

Pitches Worst Vs.	Avg	AB	H	2B	3B	HR	RBI	BB	SO	OBP	SLG
Mariano Duncan	.500	16	8	0	2	1	7	0	1	.500	.938
Tim Raines	.455	11	5	1	0	0	0	0	0	.455	.545
Barry Bonds	.400	10	4	1	0	2	4	1	3	.455	1.100
Dwight Smith	.400	10	4	0	0	1	3	2	3	.462	.700
Bobby Bonilla	.308	13	4	0	0	2	3	0	2	.308	.769

Lonnie Smith — Orioles

Age 38 – Bats Right (flyball hitter)

	Avg	G	AB	R	H	2B	3B	HR	RBI	BB	SO	HBP	GDP	SB	CS	OBP	SLG	IBB	SH	SF	#Pit	#P/PA	GB	FB	G/F
1993 Season	.278	103	223	43	62	6	4	8	27	51	52	5	3	9	4	.420	.448	2	3	2	1076	3.79	50	84	0.60
Last Five Years	.293	578	1682	285	492	94	20	51	225	252	317	34	17	57	31	.391	.463	12	7	21	7492	3.75	478	565	0.85

1993 Season

	Avg	AB	H	2B	3B	HR	RBI	BB	SO	OBP	SLG
vs. Left	.303	132	40	3	1	5	20	28	30	.426	.455
vs. Right	.242	91	22	3	3	3	7	23	22	.412	.440
Home	.313	99	31	1	1	6	13	23	26	.447	.525
Away	.250	124	31	5	3	2	14	28	26	.399	.387
First Pitch	.282	39	11	0	1	2	5	0	0	.300	.487
Ahead in Count	.352	54	19	2	1	1	6	28	0	.566	.481
Behind in Count	.220	91	20	2	1	3	10	0	45	.250	.363
Two Strikes	.242	99	24	3	1	3	11	23	52	.392	.384

	Avg	AB	H	2B	3B	HR	RBI	BB	SO	OBP	SLG
Scoring Posn	.245	49	12	1	0	0	16	16	11	.435	.265
Close & Late	.265	49	13	2	1	2	6	15	16	.446	.469
None on/out	.291	79	23	2	1	5	5	15	18	.411	.532
Batting #1	.250	84	21	0	2	1	9	13	15	.354	.333
Batting #3	.375	40	15	2	0	2	5	10	12	.500	.575
Other	.263	99	26	4	2	5	13	28	25	.439	.495
Pre-All Star	.244	123	30	1	3	2	13	26	22	.379	.350
Post-All Star	.320	100	32	5	1	6	14	25	30	.469	.570

Last Five Years

	Avg	AB	H	2B	3B	HR	RBI	BB	SO	OBP	SLG
vs. Left	.309	674	208	43	9	21	91	103	116	.404	.493
vs. Right	.282	1008	284	51	11	30	134	149	201	.383	.443
Groundball	.309	553	171	35	9	14	76	84	113	.406	.481
Flyball	.246	394	97	20	4	17	52	65	78	.361	.447
Home	.313	820	257	48	9	27	119	118	155	.403	.493
Away	.273	862	235	46	11	24	106	134	162	.380	.435
Day	.312	407	127	22	4	16	50	65	85	.411	.504
Night	.286	1275	365	72	16	35	175	187	232	.385	.450
Grass	.300	1189	357	67	14	40	167	175	218	.395	.481
Turf	.274	493	135	27	6	11	58	77	99	.382	.420
First Pitch	.375	317	119	26	6	13	45	6	0	.402	.618
Ahead in Count	.332	380	126	24	3	19	64	127	0	.492	.561
Behind in Count	.229	652	149	28	8	12	81	0	240	.252	.351
Two Strikes	.211	726	153	31	9	7	67	118	317	.332	.307

	Avg	AB	H	2B	3B	HR	RBI	BB	SO	OBP	SLG
Scoring Posn	.308	380	117	16	3	9	163	78	78	.419	.437
Close & Late	.258	275	71	13	3	9	30	51	65	.390	.425
None on/out	.279	519	145	22	7	18	18	62	92	.366	.453
Batting #1	.316	642	203	33	10	17	66	87	94	.404	.478
Batting #3	.289	512	148	29	4	15	79	78	113	.387	.449
Other	.267	528	141	32	6	19	80	87	110	.380	.458
April	.267	202	54	7	3	5	24	34	42	.379	.406
May	.261	238	62	14	3	6	30	40	53	.375	.420
June	.304	247	75	10	5	9	31	32	33	.388	.494
July	.313	300	94	14	4	11	41	58	58	.431	.497
August	.326	334	109	30	2	8	50	32	53	.394	.500
September/October	.271	361	98	19	3	12	49	56	78	.374	.440
Pre-All Star	.278	776	216	37	11	24	94	121	146	.382	.447
Post-All Star	.305	906	276	57	9	27	131	131	171	.399	.477

Batter vs. Pitcher (since 1984)

Hits Best Against	Avg	AB	H	2B	3B	HR	RBI	BB	SO	OBP	SLG
Bob Walk	.714	14	10	2	0	2	7	0	0	.714	1.286
Ken Hill	.545	11	6	3	0	0	2	4	0	.667	.818

Hits Worst Against	Avg	AB	H	2B	3B	HR	RBI	BB	SO	OBP	SLG
Greg Swindell	.063	16	1	0	0	0	0	0	2	.063	.063
Joe Magrane	.071	14	1	1	0	0	0	3	2	.235	.143

Batter vs. Pitcher (since 1984)

Hits Best Against	Avg	AB	H	2B	3B	HR	RBI	BB	SO	OBP	SLG	Hits Worst Against	Avg	AB	H	2B	3B	HR	RBI	BB	SO	OBP	SLG
Norm Charlton	.412	17	7	1	1	2	3	2	4	.474	.941	Ramon Martinez	.071	14	1	0	0	0	1	0	6	.067	.071
Dennis Cook	.412	17	7	1	0	3	6	0	1	.412	1.000	Neal Heaton	.111	18	2	0	0	0	1	2	2	.200	.111
Mitch Williams	.400	5	2	1	1	0	3	8	2	.769	1.000	Teddy Higuera	.125	24	3	0	0	0	1	2	6	.185	.125

Ozzie Smith — Cardinals

Age 39 – Bats Both (groundball hitter)

	Avg	G	AB	R	H	2B	3B	HR	RBI	BB	SO	HBP	GDP	SB	CS	OBP	SLG	IBB	SH	SF	#Pit	#P/PA	GB	FB	G/F
1993 Season	.288	141	545	75	157	22	6	1	53	43	18	1	11	21	8	.337	.356	1	7	7	2087	3.46	282	152	1.86
Last Five Years	.279	721	2718	387	759	123	20	7	234	301	158	6	48	160	39	.350	.347	14	43	22	10901	3.53	1357	690	1.97

1993 Season

	Avg	AB	H	2B	3B	HR	RBI	BB	SO	OBP	SLG		Avg	AB	H	2B	3B	HR	RBI	BB	SO	OBP	SLG
vs. Left	.320	150	48	9	1	1	16	9	4	.354	.413	Scoring Posn	.307	137	42	9	2	0	47	9	6	.338	.401
vs. Right	.276	395	109	13	5	0	37	34	14	.331	.334	Close & Late	.323	93	30	5	3	0	13	4	4	.347	.441
Groundball	.250	164	41	3	0	0	11	14	5	.304	.268	None on/out	.258	97	25	1	1	0	0	12	5	.339	.289
Flyball	.384	99	38	6	2	0	14	3	4	.394	.485	Batting #2	.290	538	156	22	6	1	53	42	17	.338	.359
Home	.299	288	86	11	4	1	29	28	9	.357	.375	Batting #8	.000	4	0	0	0	0	0	0	1	.000	.000
Away	.276	257	71	11	2	0	24	15	9	.314	.335	Other	.333	3	1	0	0	0	0	1	0	.500	.333
Day	.285	144	41	7	1	1	19	10	4	.323	.368	April	.274	84	23	1	2	0	10	5	5	.311	.333
Night	.289	401	116	15	5	0	34	33	14	.342	.352	May	.253	95	24	2	1	1	9	7	2	.308	.326
Grass	.313	144	45	8	1	0	18	9	3	.346	.382	June	.309	97	30	8	1	0	15	9	2	.364	.412
Turf	.279	401	112	14	5	1	35	34	15	.334	.347	July	.311	103	32	5	0	0	6	6	4	.345	.359
First Pitch	.279	86	24	0	1	0	9	0	0	.281	.302	August	.283	92	26	1	1	0	4	7	3	.330	.315
Ahead in Count	.322	149	48	9	2	0	15	27	0	.426	.409	September/October	.297	74	22	5	1	0	9	9	2	.365	.392
Behind in Count	.264	208	55	7	1	0	19	0	15	.259	.308	Pre-All Star	.281	313	88	13	4	1	35	23	9	.329	.358
Two Strikes	.238	206	49	7	1	0	21	16	18	.289	.282	Post-All Star	.297	232	69	9	2	0	18	20	9	.348	.353

1993 By Position

Position	Avg	AB	H	2B	3B	HR	RBI	BB	SO	OBP	SLG	G	GS	Innings	PO	A	E	DP	Fld Pct	Rng Fctr	In Zone	Outs	Zone Rtg	MLB Zone
As ss	.291	540	157	22	6	1	52	42	18	.340	.359	134	131	1138.1	251	450	19	98	.974	5.54	514	483	.940	.880

Last Five Years

	Avg	AB	H	2B	3B	HR	RBI	BB	SO	OBP	SLG		Avg	AB	H	2B	3B	HR	RBI	BB	SO	OBP	SLG
vs. Left	.283	1049	297	66	7	6	93	109	66	.349	.377	Scoring Posn	.273	675	184	30	4	1	211	95	39	.355	.333
vs. Right	.277	1669	462	57	13	1	141	192	92	.351	.328	Close & Late	.276	446	123	18	7	0	54	59	26	.357	.348
Groundball	.271	932	253	34	4	0	72	86	38	.330	.317	None on/out	.257	502	129	23	6	1	1	68	29	.348	.333
Flyball	.290	597	173	31	6	3	48	65	43	.360	.377	Batting #2	.283	2354	666	103	17	7	197	264	133	.354	.350
Home	.295	1410	416	65	12	4	129	168	80	.368	.367	Batting #3	.275	142	39	7	3	0	14	15	8	.342	.366
Away	.262	1308	343	58	8	3	105	133	78	.330	.326	Other	.243	222	54	13	0	0	23	22	17	.307	.302
Day	.289	743	215	40	6	2	65	62	35	.345	.367	April	.264	322	85	6	2	1	34	40	20	.341	.304
Night	.275	1975	544	83	14	5	169	239	123	.352	.339	May	.284	496	141	23	4	1	44	51	26	.354	.353
Grass	.260	705	183	37	5	0	54	61	46	.317	.326	June	.284	430	122	25	4	0	57	59	23	.369	.360
Turf	.286	2013	576	86	15	7	180	240	112	.361	.354	July	.309	463	143	24	1	0	31	53	33	.377	.365
First Pitch	.296	392	116	24	1	1	41	6	0	.304	.370	August	.259	502	130	15	5	3	34	53	28	.327	.327
Ahead in Count	.315	785	247	45	10	2	82	181	0	.443	.405	September/October	.273	505	138	30	4	2	34	45	28	.331	.360
Behind in Count	.239	1009	241	28	4	2	61	0	130	.238	.280	Pre-All Star	.285	1407	401	63	11	2	147	168	77	.361	.350
Two Strikes	.235	1004	236	27	2	1	68	109	158	.308	.269	Post-All Star	.273	1311	358	60	9	5	87	133	81	.337	.344

Batter vs. Pitcher (since 1984)

Hits Best Against	Avg	AB	H	2B	3B	HR	RBI	BB	SO	OBP	SLG	Hits Worst Against	Avg	AB	H	2B	3B	HR	RBI	BB	SO	OBP	SLG
Frank Castillo	.529	17	9	1	0	0	1	4	1	.619	.588	Mike Morgan	.091	22	2	0	0	0	0	3	1	.200	.091
Mark Davis	.500	20	10	1	0	1	2	3	2	.565	.700	Mark Grant	.100	20	2	0	0	0	2	3	2	.217	.100
Bud Black	.455	11	5	1	0	1	2	0	0	.455	.818	Mark Portugal	.111	18	2	0	0	0	2	1	1	.158	.111
Jimmy Jones	.429	14	6	1	0	0	3	6	0	.600	.500	Jim Gott	.143	14	2	0	0	0	1	0	2	.133	.143
Rick Honeycutt	.412	17	7	3	0	0	0	3	2	.500	.588	Jeff Fassero	.143	14	2	0	0	0	0	1	1	.200	.143

Pete Smith — Braves

Age 28 – Pitches Right

	ERA	W	L	Sv	G	GS	IP	BB	SO	Avg	H	2B	3B	HR	RBI	OBP	SLG	CG	ShO	Sup	QS	#P/S	SB	CS	GB	FB	G/F
1993 Season	4.37	4	8	0	20	14	90.2	36	53	.270	92	17	3	15	39	.339	.469	0	0	4.86	5	91	8	8	118	109	1.08
Last Five Years	4.23	22	31	0	87	75	436.2	167	296	.256	424	71	9	47	184	.322	.395	6	1	4.37	35	87	55	23	583	500	1.17

1993 Season

	ERA	W	L	Sv	G	GS	IP	H	HR	BB	SO		Avg	AB	H	2B	3B	HR	RBI	BB	SO	OBP	SLG
Home	4.31	3	7	0	12	9	54.1	57	9	21	29	vs. Left	.275	178	49	5	2	8	22	21	25	.348	.461
Away	4.46	1	1	0	8	5	36.1	35	6	15	24	vs. Right	.264	163	43	12	1	7	17	15	28	.328	.479
Starter	4.63	3	8	0	14	14	79.2	86	14	32	46	Scoring Posn	.194	72	14	2	0	3	21	10	18	.284	.347
Reliever	2.45	1	0	0	6	0	11.0	6	1	4	7	Close & Late	.200	20	4	0	0	1	3	1	2	.238	.350
0-3 Days Rest	1.13	0	1	0	1	1	8.0	4	0	1	4	None on/out	.298	94	28	7	2	3	3	4	9	.327	.511
4 Days Rest	6.20	0	3	0	5	5	24.2	33	7	11	17	First Pitch	.327	55	18	4	0	3	8	2	0	.356	.564
5+ Days Rest	4.40	3	4	0	8	8	47.0	49	7	20	25	Ahead in Count	.217	152	33	4	3	1	11	0	47	.217	.303
Pre-All Star	4.31	3	7	0	15	12	79.1	77	11	32	47	Behind in Count	.375	80	30	8	0	6	13	15	0	.474	.700
Post-All Star	4.76	1	1	0	5	2	11.1	15	4	4	6	Two Strikes	.182	159	29	3	1	5	13	19	53	.268	.308

Last Five Years

	ERA	W	L	Sv	G	GS	IP	H	HR	BB	SO		Avg	AB	H	2B	3B	HR	RBI	BB	SO	OBP	SLG
Home	4.76	11	19	0	44	39	217.1	238	29	90	140	vs. Left	.271	947	257	40	6	22	100	115	128	.347	.396
Away	3.69	11	12	0	43	36	219.1	186	18	77	156	vs. Right	.235	710	167	31	3	25	84	52	168	.286	.393
Day	4.30	5	6	0	19	16	98.1	91	14	38	70	Inning 1-6	.258	1470	379	63	9	45	172	145	264	.322	.405

Last Five Years

	ERA	W	L	Sv	G	GS	IP	H	HR	BB	SO		Avg	AB	H	2B	3B	HR	RBI	BB	SO	OBP	SLG
Night	4.20	17	25	0	68	59	338.1	333	33	129	226	Inning 7+	.241	187	45	8	0	2	12	22	32	.319	.316
Grass	4.00	18	25	0	67	59	351.0	330	40	129	247	None on	.254	1002	255	41	6	26	26	101	185	.323	.385
Turf	5.15	4	6	0	20	16	85.2	94	7	38	49	Runners on	.258	655	169	30	3	21	158	66	111	.320	.409
April	2.85	4	6	0	14	13	85.1	77	5	27	82	Scoring Posn	.251	371	93	18	3	9	128	46	70	.321	.388
May	5.17	3	9	0	17	16	95.2	92	15	39	58	Close & Late	.216	102	22	3	0	1	8	11	16	.289	.275
June	5.53	3	7	0	18	17	81.1	88	8	35	50	None on/out	.261	440	115	21	4	14	14	34	74	.314	.423
July	6.36	1	6	0	12	10	46.2	62	11	21	29	vs. 1st Batr (relief)	.273	11	3	1	0	1	3	1	1	.333	.636
August	3.16	6	2	0	10	10	62.2	53	4	21	33	First Inning Pitched	.286	336	96	15	3	9	53	37	63	.351	.429
September/October	2.49	5	1	0	16	9	65.0	52	4	24	44	First 75 Pitches	.250	1322	331	57	9	36	148	136	251	.317	.389
Starter	4.36	21	31	0	75	75	416.2	413	46	161	283	Pitch 76-90	.267	191	51	9	0	7	21	16	25	.322	.424
Reliever	1.35	1	0	0	12	0	20.0	11	1	6	13	Pitch 91-105	.311	103	32	5	0	3	11	12	15	.385	.447
0-3 Days Rest	1.13	0	1	0	1	1	8.0	4	0	1	4	Pitch 106+	.244	41	10	0	0	1	4	3	5	.295	.317
4 Days Rest	3.88	9	15	0	35	35	201.2	188	20	74	152	First Pitch	.332	241	80	16	1	12	42	8	0	.353	.556
5+ Days Rest	4.96	12	15	0	39	39	207.0	221	26	86	127	Ahead in Count	.197	792	156	21	5	9	63	0	261	.196	.270
Pre-All Star	4.62	11	25	0	54	50	284.2	287	32	111	203	Behind in Count	.333	345	115	21	1	14	46	93	0	.472	.522
Post-All Star	3.49	11	6	0	33	25	152.0	137	15	56	93	Two Strikes	.183	772	141	21	1	12	59	65	296	.244	.259

Pitcher vs. Batter (career)

Pitches Best Vs.	Avg	AB	H	2B	3B	HR	RBI	BB	SO	OBP	SLG	Pitches Worst Vs.	Avg	AB	H	2B	3B	HR	RBI	BB	SO	OBP	SLG
Milt Thompson	.000	13	0	0	0	0	0	2	1	.133	.000	Bobby Bonilla	.529	17	9	2	0	3	8	4	3	.591	1.176
Jose Offerman	.091	11	1	0	0	0	0	0	0	.091	.091	Paul O'Neill	.524	21	11	3	0	0	3	2	3	.565	.667
Mitch Webster	.100	10	1	1	0	0	0	1	2	.182	.200	Will Clark	.414	29	12	0	0	4	7	5	4	.500	.828
Benito Santiago	.139	36	5	0	0	0	1	1	5	.162	.139	Andre Dawson	.368	19	7	2	0	4	8	0	1	.350	1.105
Mackey Sasser	.182	11	2	0	0	0	1	0	0	.167	.182	Darryl Strawberry	.357	14	5	0	0	3	4	5	3	.526	1.000

Zane Smith — Pirates

Age 33 – Pitches Left (groundball pitcher)

	ERA	W	L	Sv	G	GS	IP	BB	SO	Avg	H	2B	3B	HR	RBI	OBP	SLG	CG	ShO	Sup	QS	#P/S	SB	CS	GB	FB	G/F
1993 Season	4.55	3	7	0	14	14	83.0	22	32	.298	97	18	8	5	42	.343	.449	1	0	3.04	7	90	7	2	145	94	1.54
Last Five Years	3.19	40	47	2	153	119	814.1	172	431	.261	806	123	28	50	315	.301	.368	15	8	3.70	76	91	83	25	1525	655	2.33

1993 Season

	ERA	W	L	Sv	G	GS	IP	H	HR	BB	SO		Avg	AB	H	2B	3B	HR	RBI	BB	SO	OBP	SLG
Home	3.48	1	3	0	7	7	44.0	50	1	11	16	vs. Left	.222	54	12	2	0	0	4	4	8	.276	.259
Away	5.77	2	4	0	7	7	39.0	47	4	11	16	vs. Right	.314	271	85	16	8	5	38	18	24	.356	.487
Starter	4.55	3	7	0	14	14	83.0	97	5	22	32	Scoring Posn	.306	85	26	5	4	1	33	7	9	.359	.494
Reliever	0.00	0	0	0	0	0	0.0	0	0	0	0	Close & Late	.231	26	6	1	0	0	2	3	5	.310	.269
0-3 Days Rest	0.00	0	0	0	0	0	0.0	0	0	0	0	None on/out	.287	87	25	5	1	2	2	2	12	.303	.437
4 Days Rest	5.30	3	4	0	9	9	52.2	65	4	13	22	First Pitch	.364	44	16	2	0	2	5	2	0	.391	.545
5+ Days Rest	3.26	0	3	0	5	5	30.1	32	1	9	10	Ahead in Count	.215	130	28	7	2	0	7	0	26	.215	.300
Pre-All Star	6.23	0	3	0	5	5	26.0	33	3	9	8	Behind in Count	.443	79	35	3	3	2	22	9	0	.500	.633
Post-All Star	3.79	3	4	0	9	9	57.0	64	2	13	24	Two Strikes	.219	128	28	7	4	0	8	11	32	.281	.336

Last Five Years

	ERA	W	L	Sv	G	GS	IP	H	HR	BB	SO		Avg	AB	H	2B	3B	HR	RBI	BB	SO	OBP	SLG
Home	2.73	26	18	1	76	60	432.1	423	22	81	256	vs. Left	.200	546	109	10	4	5	44	31	126	.242	.260
Away	3.72	14	29	1	77	59	382.0	383	28	91	175	vs. Right	.274	2541	697	113	24	45	271	141	305	.313	.391
Day	3.34	10	14	0	40	30	202.1	207	13	52	93	Inning 1-6	.262	2477	649	102	26	38	263	141	340	.302	.370
Night	3.15	30	33	2	113	89	612.0	599	37	120	338	Inning 7+	.257	610	157	21	2	12	52	31	91	.294	.357
Grass	4.09	5	20	0	42	32	206.2	213	14	53	104	None on	.252	1903	479	75	14	27	27	86	273	.285	.348
Turf	2.89	35	27	2	111	87	607.2	593	36	119	327	Runners on	.276	1184	327	48	14	23	288	86	158	.325	.399
April	2.78	8	6	0	18	18	116.2	110	7	21	61	Scoring Posn	.298	664	198	35	9	17	264	59	88	.352	.455
May	3.81	7	10	0	22	22	141.2	155	8	34	74	Close & Late	.255	369	94	12	0	6	35	20	57	.294	.336
June	3.77	3	16	0	26	26	160.0	166	10	47	78	None on/out	.276	822	227	43	5	14	14	31	122	.303	.392
July	3.16	7	7	1	27	18	131.0	127	9	33	65	vs. 1st Batr (relief)	.233	30	7	2	0	1	3	3	7	.303	.400
August	3.43	8	5	1	32	20	144.1	153	9	22	74	First Inning Pitched	.247	503	124	23	6	6	48	37	79	.300	.352
September/October	1.86	7	3	0	28	15	120.2	95	7	15	79	First 75 Pitches	.260	2430	631	101	25	36	241	138	340	.300	.366
Starter	3.29	40	46	0	119	119	762.1	765	48	151	394	Pitch 76-90	.273	355	97	12	3	7	42	20	50	.311	.383
Reliever	1.73	0	1	2	34	0	52.0	41	2	21	37	Pitch 91-105	.247	223	55	7	0	4	22	12	29	.285	.332
0-3 Days Rest	3.02	4	2	0	10	10	62.2	60	4	10	44	Pitch 106+	.291	79	23	3	0	3	10	2	12	.309	.443
4 Days Rest	3.15	28	24	0	68	68	459.2	445	33	92	216	First Pitch	.300	486	146	24	4	10	62	17	0	.325	.428
5+ Days Rest	3.64	8	20	0	41	41	240.0	260	11	49	134	Ahead in Count	.198	1297	257	34	9	12	77	0	381	.201	.266
Pre-All Star	3.42	23	34	1	76	74	476.1	484	30	113	236	Behind in Count	.339	711	241	30	9	17	111	87	0	.408	.478
Post-All Star	2.88	17	13	1	77	45	338.0	322	20	59	195	Two Strikes	.204	1251	255	36	11	15	91	67	431	.246	.286

Pitcher vs. Batter (career)

Pitches Best Vs.	Avg	AB	H	2B	3B	HR	RBI	BB	SO	OBP	SLG	Pitches Worst Vs.	Avg	AB	H	2B	3B	HR	RBI	BB	SO	OBP	SLG
Kirt Manwaring	.000	14	0	0	0	0	0	0	1	.000	.000	Junior Ortiz	.563	16	9	2	0	0	1	1	1	.588	.688
Charlie O'Brien	.091	11	1	0	0	0	0	0	1	.091	.091	Barry Larkin	.450	40	18	2	0	4	11	2	2	.465	.800
Jerome Walton	.091	11	1	0	0	0	0	0	3	.091	.091	Glenn Wilson	.433	30	13	5	0	1	4	4	2	.500	.700
Greg Litton	.091	11	1	0	0	0	1	0	1	.091	.091	Benito Santiago	.419	31	13	4	0	5	10	2	3	.455	1.032
Andy Van Slyke	.100	20	2	0	0	0	0	0	8	.100	.100	Chris James	.389	18	7	1	1	2	5	1	2	.421	.889

Roger Smithberg — Athletics

Age 28 – Pitches Right (groundball pitcher)

	ERA	W	L	Sv	G	GS	IP	BB	SO	Avg	H	2B	3B	HR	RBI	OBP	SLG	GF	IR	IRS	Hld	SvOp	SB	CS	GB	FB	G/F
1993 Season	2.75	1	2	3	13	0	19.2	7	4	.197	13	3	0	2	9	.284	.333	9	3	2	0	4	1	0	35	13	2.69

1993 Season

	ERA	W	L	Sv	G	GS	IP	H	HR	BB	SO
Home	1.69	0	1	2	6	0	10.2	5	2	1	1
Away	4.00	1	1	1	7	0	9.0	8	0	6	3

	Avg	AB	H	2B	3B	HR	RBI	BB	SO	OBP	SLG
vs. Left	.231	26	6	0	0	2	4	3	1	.310	.462
vs. Right	.175	40	7	3	0	0	5	4	3	.267	.250

John Smoltz — Braves

Age 27 – Pitches Right

	ERA	W	L	Sv	G	GS	IP	BB	SO	Avg	H	2B	3B	HR	RBI	OBP	SLG	CG	ShO	Sup	QS	#P/S	SB	CS	GB	FB	G/F
1993 Season	3.62	15	11	0	35	35	243.2	100	208	.230	208	45	6	23	93	.309	.369	3	1	5.28	19	106	12	5	278	265	1.05
Last Five Years	3.42	70	58	0	169	169	1159.1	419	909	.230	986	183	26	91	421	.299	.348	28	6	4.56	104	105	82	41	1383	1305	1.06

1993 Season

	ERA	W	L	Sv	G	GS	IP	H	HR	BB	SO
Home	3.92	4	5	0	15	15	101.0	92	11	44	88
Away	3.41	11	6	0	20	20	142.2	116	12	56	120
Day	3.21	3	4	0	10	10	70.0	65	5	31	71
Night	3.78	12	7	0	25	25	173.2	143	18	69	137
Grass	3.36	12	9	0	27	27	190.0	152	21	77	160
Turf	4.53	3	2	0	8	8	53.2	56	2	23	48
April	2.15	2	2	0	5	5	37.2	29	2	16	35
May	5.54	2	2	0	6	6	37.1	40	5	18	21
June	2.25	3	3	0	6	6	44.0	26	2	20	47
July	3.71	2	1	0	5	5	34.0	32	2	18	35
August	3.95	4	1	0	6	6	43.1	36	8	9	27
September/October	4.18	2	2	0	7	7	47.1	45	4	19	43
Starter	3.62	15	11	0	35	35	243.2	208	23	100	208
Reliever	0.00	0	0	0	0	0	0.0	0	0	0	0
0-3 Days Rest	7.11	0	0	0	1	1	6.1	11	0	0	7
4 Days Rest	3.31	12	7	0	27	27	190.1	157	17	82	161
5+ Days Rest	4.40	3	4	0	7	7	47.0	40	6	18	40
Pre-All Star	3.09	8	7	0	19	19	134.0	107	10	59	119
Post-All Star	4.27	7	4	0	16	16	109.2	101	13	41	89

	Avg	AB	H	2B	3B	HR	RBI	BB	SO	OBP	SLG
vs. Left	.260	458	119	29	5	10	51	55	72	.345	.410
vs. Right	.199	447	89	16	1	13	42	45	136	.272	.327
Inning 1-6	.214	758	162	36	4	18	73	79	186	.291	.343
Inning 7+	.313	147	46	9	2	5	20	21	22	.402	.503
None on	.236	535	126	30	1	13	13	50	115	.304	.368
Runners on	.222	370	82	15	5	10	80	50	93	.316	.370
Scoring Posn	.232	207	48	11	3	6	69	42	60	.358	.401
Close & Late	.330	115	38	8	2	3	15	17	20	.421	.513
None on/out	.255	239	61	15	1	7	7	20	47	.313	.414
vs. 1st Batr (relief)	.000	0	0	0	0	0	0	0	0	.000	.000
First Inning Pitched	.264	140	37	6	1	3	17	20	32	.364	.386
First 75 Pitches	.209	626	131	27	2	16	51	67	147	.289	.335
Pitch 76-90	.264	121	32	6	0	4	20	15	31	.348	.413
Pitch 91-105	.250	96	24	8	2	1	11	7	19	.301	.406
Pitch 106+	.339	62	21	4	2	2	11	11	11	.446	.565
First Pitch	.313	150	47	10	0	6	23	9	0	.350	.500
Ahead in Count	.163	417	68	14	5	5	32	0	179	.171	.257
Behind in Count	.283	184	52	10	1	7	18	46	0	.429	.462
Two Strikes	.165	437	72	11	5	6	28	45	208	.247	.254

Last Five Years

	ERA	W	L	Sv	G	GS	IP	H	HR	BB	SO
Home	3.29	33	26	0	81	81	563.2	474	54	190	443
Away	3.54	37	32	0	88	88	595.2	512	37	229	466
Day	2.95	17	14	0	39	39	280.1	229	20	95	241
Night	3.56	53	44	0	130	130	879.0	757	71	324	668
Grass	3.41	52	40	0	124	124	855.1	712	81	302	653
Turf	3.43	18	18	0	45	45	304.0	274	10	117	256
April	3.57	8	11	0	24	24	153.2	139	11	64	124
May	3.52	13	10	0	29	29	207.1	172	14	75	156
June	3.71	11	13	0	29	29	196.2	176	13	72	174
July	3.18	13	7	0	28	28	195.0	152	18	71	148
August	3.29	16	10	0	31	31	221.2	185	22	66	163
September/October	3.26	9	7	0	28	28	185.0	162	13	71	144
Starter	3.42	70	58	0	169	169	1159.1	986	91	419	909
Reliever	0.00	0	0	0	0	0	0.0	0	0	0	0
0-3 Days Rest	5.29	3	4	0	10	10	63.0	64	5	25	39
4 Days Rest	3.28	51	37	0	117	117	812.2	701	67	301	630
5+ Days Rest	3.39	16	17	0	42	42	283.2	221	19	93	240
Pre-All Star	3.51	37	36	0	91	91	619.2	532	43	240	499
Post-All Star	3.30	33	22	0	78	78	539.2	454	48	179	410

	Avg	AB	H	2B	3B	HR	RBI	BB	SO	OBP	SLG
vs. Left	.255	2452	625	112	21	45	241	274	403	.330	.373
vs. Right	.197	1837	361	71	5	46	180	145	506	.255	.316
Inning 1-6	.231	3552	821	150	21	75	356	349	777	.300	.349
Inning 7+	.224	737	165	33	5	16	65	70	132	.292	.347
None on	.227	2568	582	116	11	51	51	232	540	.293	.340
Runners on	.235	1721	404	67	15	40	370	187	369	.307	.361
Scoring Posn	.231	941	217	35	13	22	318	145	241	.326	.366
Close & Late	.233	404	94	21	3	7	39	37	84	.299	.351
None on/out	.235	1120	263	47	6	19	19	97	224	.298	.338
vs. 1st Batr (relief)	.000	0	0	0	0	0	0	0	0	.000	.000
First Inning Pitched	.244	639	156	21	4	13	76	80	147	.329	.351
First 75 Pitches	.232	2946	684	119	15	58	275	286	654	.300	.342
Pitch 76-90	.248	553	137	25	5	19	70	54	105	.316	.414
Pitch 91-105	.178	456	81	21	3	7	35	38	88	.242	.283
Pitch 106+	.251	334	84	18	3	7	41	41	62	.335	.386
First Pitch	.301	632	190	33	3	23	88	19	0	.323	.472
Ahead in Count	.164	1930	317	54	10	22	147	0	753	.166	.237
Behind in Count	.301	957	288	62	6	29	96	210	0	.425	.469
Two Strikes	.154	1975	304	45	12	24	136	189	909	.230	.225

Pitcher vs. Batter (career)

Pitches Best Vs.	Avg	AB	H	2B	3B	HR	RBI	BB	SO	OBP	SLG
Dwight Smith	.000	19	0	0	0	0	0	0	2	.000	.000
Sammy Sosa	.000	16	0	0	0	0	0	1	9	.059	.000
Kurt Stillwell	.000	13	0	0	0	0	1	0	3	.000	.000
Orestes Destrade	.000	10	0	0	0	0	1	1	2	.091	.000
Jerald Clark	.071	14	1	0	0	0	1	0	5	.071	.071

Pitches Worst Vs.	Avg	AB	H	2B	3B	HR	RBI	BB	SO	OBP	SLG
Al Martin	.625	8	5	2	0	0	1	3	3	.727	.875
Mike LaValliere	.550	20	11	2	0	1	3	5	0	.640	.800
Eric Davis	.500	26	13	2	0	4	6	5	3	.581	1.038
Mike Aldrete	.500	8	4	1	1	0	1	3	0	.636	.875
Rick Wilkins	.389	18	7	0	0	3	3	1	3	.421	.889

J.T. Snow — Angels

Age 26 – Bats Both (flyball hitter)

	Avg	G	AB	R	H	2B	3B	HR	RBI	BB	SO	HBP	GDP	SB	CS	OBP	SLG	IBB	SH	SF	#Pit	#P/PA	GB	FB	G/F
1993 Season	.241	129	419	60	101	18	2	16	57	55	88	2	10	3	0	.328	.408	4	7	6	1846	3.78	124	133	0.93
Career (1992-1993)	.238	136	433	61	103	19	2	16	59	60	93	2	10	3	0	.329	.402	5	7	6	1922	3.78	126	136	0.93

1993 Season

	Avg	AB	H	2B	3B	HR	RBI	BB	SO	OBP	SLG
vs. Left	.218	87	19	3	1	2	10	10	18	.306	.345
vs. Right	.247	332	82	15	1	14	47	45	70	.333	.425
Groundball	.293	75	22	4	1	3	12	12	14	.398	.493
Flyball	.250	92	23	5	0	5	15	10	16	.324	.467
Home	.286	196	56	6	1	10	35	24	38	.359	.480
Away	.202	223	45	12	1	6	22	31	50	.301	.345
Day	.213	136	29	4	1	6	17	15	34	.290	.390
Night	.254	283	72	14	1	10	40	40	54	.346	.417
Grass	.246	358	88	14	2	15	53	44	74	.325	.422
Turf	.213	61	13	4	0	1	4	11	14	.342	.328
First Pitch	.289	45	13	6	1	4	9	4	0	.373	.733
Ahead in Count	.377	122	46	8	0	6	20	22	0	.466	.590
Behind in Count	.167	168	28	3	0	4	16	0	76	.165	.256
Two Strikes	.108	185	20	2	1	4	20	29	88	.225	.195

	Avg	AB	H	2B	3B	HR	RBI	BB	SO	OBP	SLG
Scoring Posn	.216	97	21	4	0	4	39	13	21	.293	.381
Close & Late	.219	64	14	2	1	0	7	14	17	.350	.281
None on/out	.207	82	17	1	1	6	6	11	16	.309	.463
Batting #3	.277	137	38	5	1	11	29	15	30	.348	.569
Batting #7	.238	122	29	7	0	2	12	12	28	.301	.344
Other	.213	160	34	6	1	3	16	28	30	.330	.319
April	.343	67	23	1	2	6	17	4	11	.389	.687
May	.124	89	11	1	0	4	11	15	21	.252	.270
June	.292	72	21	5	0	0	11	12	10	.379	.361
July	.159	63	10	3	0	1	4	8	20	.254	.254
August	.222	27	6	2	0	1	2	5	5	.344	.407
September/October	.297	101	30	6	0	4	12	11	21	.363	.475
Pre-All Star	.236	259	61	9	2	11	41	36	53	.328	.413
Post-All Star	.250	160	40	9	0	5	16	19	35	.328	.400

1993 By Position

Position	Avg	AB	H	2B	3B	HR	RBI	BB	SO	OBP	SLG	G	GS	Innings	PO	A	E	DP	Fld Pct	Rng Fctr	In Zone	Outs	Zone Rtg	MLB Zone
As 1b	.242	417	101	18	2	16	57	55	88	.329	.410	129	119	1059.0	1010	78	6	103	.995	---	198	151	.763	.834

Cory Snyder — Dodgers

Age 31 – Bats Right

	Avg	G	AB	R	H	2B	3B	HR	RBI	BB	SO	HBP	GDP	SB	CS	OBP	SLG	IBB	SH	SF	#Pit	#P/PA	GB	FB	G/F
1993 Season	.266	143	516	61	137	33	1	11	56	47	147	4	8	4	1	.331	.397	3	2	1	2103	3.69	151	128	1.18
Last Five Years	.239	593	1999	218	478	103	7	60	244	123	555	10	46	15	14	.285	.388	10	9	15	7595	3.52	583	574	1.02

1993 Season

	Avg	AB	H	2B	3B	HR	RBI	BB	SO	OBP	SLG
vs. Left	.265	151	40	11	0	3	13	15	36	.333	.397
vs. Right	.266	365	97	22	1	8	43	32	111	.330	.397
Groundball	.239	138	33	8	1	3	21	9	42	.284	.377
Flyball	.318	88	28	6	0	1	10	11	18	.394	.420
Home	.266	256	68	14	0	5	26	24	71	.335	.379
Away	.265	260	69	19	1	6	30	23	76	.327	.415
Day	.274	146	40	10	1	3	18	4	40	.293	.418
Night	.262	370	97	23	0	8	38	43	107	.344	.389
Grass	.269	387	104	26	1	7	43	34	109	.333	.395
Turf	.256	129	33	7	0	4	13	13	38	.324	.403
First Pitch	.310	87	27	8	0	2	6	2	0	.333	.471
Ahead in Count	.388	85	33	11	0	5	20	24	0	.527	.694
Behind in Count	.221	263	58	12	0	4	21	0	126	.226	.312
Two Strikes	.178	264	47	7	1	3	19	21	147	.244	.246

	Avg	AB	H	2B	3B	HR	RBI	BB	SO	OBP	SLG
Scoring Posn	.260	131	34	9	1	1	41	18	45	.347	.366
Close & Late	.267	90	24	6	1	1	13	11	30	.353	.389
None on/out	.190	121	23	6	0	2	2	6	37	.228	.289
Batting #3	.206	102	21	9	0	0	9	4	28	.234	.294
Batting #6	.311	212	66	9	0	5	21	14	62	.362	.425
Other	.248	202	50	15	1	6	26	29	57	.345	.421
April	.200	15	3	1	0	0	1	3	5	.333	.267
May	.321	81	26	5	0	2	14	10	26	.409	.457
June	.320	97	31	7	0	4	12	10	28	.394	.515
July	.197	117	23	10	1	0	11	4	32	.221	.299
August	.276	98	27	7	0	2	9	10	27	.343	.408
September/October	.250	108	27	3	0	3	9	10	29	.314	.361
Pre-All Star	.286	248	71	18	0	6	31	26	75	.363	.431
Post-All Star	.246	268	66	15	1	5	25	21	72	.300	.366

1993 By Position

Position	Avg	AB	H	2B	3B	HR	RBI	BB	SO	OBP	SLG	G	GS	Innings	PO	A	E	DP	Fld Pct	Rng Fctr	In Zone	Outs	Zone Rtg	MLB Zone
As 1b	.200	10	2	0	1	0	2	2	3	.333	.400	12	0	29.2	22	3	0	1	1.000	---	5	5	1.000	.834
As 3b	.193	83	16	6	0	0	4	6	26	.244	.265	23	21	202.1	12	26	5	3	.884	1.69	35	28	.800	.834
As rf	.287	401	115	25	0	10	45	38	112	.354	.424	113	108	926.1	168	11	4	1	.978	1.74	198	163	.823	.826

Last Five Years

	Avg	AB	H	2B	3B	HR	RBI	BB	SO	OBP	SLG
vs. Left	.244	737	180	38	1	26	84	54	184	.298	.404
vs. Right	.236	1262	298	65	6	34	160	69	371	.277	.378
Groundball	.251	630	158	33	4	18	96	34	160	.287	.402
Flyball	.249	397	99	19	2	14	50	22	109	.289	.413
Home	.244	953	233	56	1	24	109	65	263	.295	.381
Away	.234	1046	245	47	6	36	135	58	292	.275	.394
Day	.241	640	154	33	1	21	92	27	172	.273	.394
Night	.238	1359	324	70	6	39	152	96	383	.290	.385
Grass	.243	1608	390	81	6	48	201	98	438	.288	.390
Turf	.225	391	88	22	1	12	43	25	117	.272	.379
First Pitch	.311	357	111	22	1	14	54	4	0	.323	.496
Ahead in Count	.362	309	112	25	1	20	71	66	0	.474	.644
Behind in Count	.177	1013	179	38	2	21	79	0	470	.179	.280
Two Strikes	.147	991	146	28	3	14	68	50	555	.190	.224

	Avg	AB	H	2B	3B	HR	RBI	BB	SO	OBP	SLG
Scoring Posn	.237	519	123	26	2	8	168	49	169	.297	.341
Close & Late	.216	384	83	20	4	6	34	25	115	.265	.336
None on/out	.211	483	102	24	0	18	18	22	144	.247	.373
Batting #4	.251	486	122	23	0	18	76	35	120	.305	.409
Batting #5	.224	464	104	26	3	11	53	23	134	.262	.364
Other	.240	1049	252	54	4	31	115	65	301	.285	.388
April	.264	235	62	13	0	7	35	12	65	.300	.409
May	.220	364	80	18	0	9	43	25	109	.277	.343
June	.295	414	122	28	3	23	70	21	106	.330	.543
July	.207	362	75	19	3	4	34	17	102	.241	.309
August	.215	335	72	15	1	8	33	25	95	.270	.337
September/October	.232	289	67	10	0	9	29	23	78	.287	.360
Pre-All Star	.253	1154	292	67	3	40	159	67	315	.297	.420
Post-All Star	.220	845	186	36	4	20	85	56	240	.268	.343

Batter vs. Pitcher (career)

Hits Best Against	Avg	AB	H	2B	3B	HR	RBI	BB	SO	OBP	SLG
Tim Leary	.583	12	7	0	0	2	8	0	2	.583	1.083
Dan Plesac	.455	11	5	1	0	2	8	0	1	.455	1.091
Mark Williamson	.455	11	5	0	1	2	4	0	2	.455	1.182
John Candelaria	.438	16	7	4	0	0	2	1	4	.471	.688
Chris Nabholz	.385	13	5	0	0	1	4	2	2	.467	.615

Hits Worst Against	Avg	AB	H	2B	3B	HR	RBI	BB	SO	OBP	SLG
John Burkett	.000	12	0	0	0	0	0	1	7	.077	.000
Scott Sanderson	.000	11	0	0	0	0	0	0	4	.000	.000
Eric Plunk	.000	11	0	0	0	0	0	1	4	.083	.000
Chuck Crim	.063	16	1	0	0	0	0	0	5	.063	.063
Todd Stottlemyre	.063	16	1	0	0	0	1	1	5	.111	.063

Luis Sojo — Blue Jays

Age 28 – Bats Right

	Avg	G	AB	R	H	2B	3B	HR	RBI	BB	SO	HBP	GDP	SB	CS	OBP	SLG	IBB	SH	SF	#Pit	#P/PA	GB	FB	G/F
1993 Season	.170	19	47	5	8	2	0	0	6	4	2	0	3	0	0	.231	.213	0	2	1	200	3.70	19	18	1.06
Career (1990-1993)	.256	271	859	94	220	31	4	11	78	37	57	6	30	12	14	.291	.340	0	28	2	3078	3.30	341	279	1.22

1993 Season

	Avg	AB	H	2B	3B	HR	RBI	BB	SO	OBP	SLG		Avg	AB	H	2B	3B	HR	RBI	BB	SO	OBP	SLG
vs. Left	.071	14	1	1	0	0	2	3	0	.235	.143	Scoring Posn	.273	11	3	1	0	0	6	2	0	.357	.364
vs. Right	.212	33	7	1	0	0	4	1	2	.229	.242	Close & Late	.000	8	0	0	0	0	1	1	0	.111	.000

Career (1990-1993)

	Avg	AB	H	2B	3B	HR	RBI	BB	SO	OBP	SLG		Avg	AB	H	2B	3B	HR	RBI	BB	SO	OBP	SLG
vs. Left	.247	259	64	12	1	0	15	16	19	.291	.301	Scoring Posn	.284	229	65	12	2	3	69	11	12	.317	.393
vs. Right	.260	600	156	19	3	11	63	21	38	.291	.357	Close & Late	.295	132	39	2	1	2	13	8	7	.345	.371
Groundball	.241	232	56	8	0	4	27	4	12	.256	.328	None on/out	.251	175	44	9	0	1	1	13	11	.311	.320
Flyball	.252	202	51	11	2	3	19	6	16	.274	.371	Batting #2	.238	407	97	16	4	8	45	17	29	.272	.356
Home	.245	400	98	12	0	3	36	23	21	.287	.298	Batting #8	.263	190	50	11	0	2	17	7	13	.300	.353
Away	.266	459	122	19	4	8	42	14	36	.294	.377	Other	.279	262	73	4	0	1	16	13	15	.313	.305
Day	.275	211	58	10	1	5	25	9	14	.306	.403	April	.258	62	16	2	1	0	5	1	4	.281	.323
Night	.250	648	162	21	3	6	53	28	43	.286	.319	May	.213	75	16	4	0	0	5	2	5	.234	.267
Grass	.262	671	176	23	3	8	58	29	41	.297	.341	June	.232	125	29	5	0	2	13	7	4	.281	.320
Turf	.234	188	44	8	1	3	20	8	16	.269	.335	July	.301	206	62	9	0	3	20	4	16	.318	.388
First Pitch	.294	102	30	4	1	1	13	0	0	.314	.382	August	.253	217	55	6	3	5	21	10	16	.286	.378
Ahead in Count	.326	190	62	11	1	5	21	28	0	.413	.474	September/October	.241	174	42	5	0	1	14	13	12	.300	.287
Behind in Count	.188	382	72	8	1	3	27	0	53	.194	.238	Pre-All Star	.246	317	78	14	1	4	28	10	21	.275	.334
Two Strikes	.174	322	56	6	0	2	19	9	57	.201	.211	Post-All Star	.262	542	142	17	3	7	50	27	36	.300	.343

Batter vs. Pitcher (career)

Hits Best Against	Avg	AB	H	2B	3B	HR	RBI	BB	SO	OBP	SLG	Hits Worst Against	Avg	AB	H	2B	3B	HR	RBI	BB	SO	OBP	SLG
Scott Sanderson	.400	15	6	3	0	0	1	0	0	.400	.600	Greg Hibbard	.091	11	1	0	0	0	1	0	1	.091	.091
Greg Swindell	.400	15	6	2	0	0	2	0	2	.400	.533	Kevin Tapani	.143	14	2	0	0	0	0	0	0	.143	.143
Charlie Hough	.375	16	6	1	0	0	1	0	1	.375	.438	Frank Tanana	.154	13	2	1	0	0	0	0	0	.154	.231
Ben McDonald	.333	15	5	0	0	0	0	0	1	.333	.333	Randy Johnson	.176	17	3	1	0	0	1	1	4	.222	.235
												Chris Bosio	.182	11	2	0	0	0	0	0	3	.182	.182

Paul Sorrento — Indians

Age 28 – Bats Left

	Avg	G	AB	R	H	2B	3B	HR	RBI	BB	SO	HBP	GDP	SB	CS	OBP	SLG	IBB	SH	SF	#Pit	#P/PA	GB	FB	G/F
1993 Season	.257	148	463	75	119	26	1	18	65	58	121	2	10	3	1	.340	.434	11	0	4	2077	3.94	144	115	1.25
Career (1989-1993)	.256	369	1110	146	284	56	3	45	152	130	256	4	29	4	5	.334	.433	21	1	9	4778	3.81	368	292	1.26

1993 Season

	Avg	AB	H	2B	3B	HR	RBI	BB	SO	OBP	SLG		Avg	AB	H	2B	3B	HR	RBI	BB	SO	OBP	SLG
vs. Left	.241	87	21	2	0	2	11	7	31	.305	.333	Scoring Posn	.226	115	26	4	0	4	43	26	34	.359	.365
vs. Right	.261	376	98	24	1	16	54	51	90	.347	.457	Close & Late	.306	72	22	3	0	2	12	6	22	.354	.431
Groundball	.333	81	27	4	0	5	14	6	19	.379	.568	None on/out	.297	111	33	12	0	4	4	6	26	.339	.514
Flyball	.185	81	15	3	0	3	11	9	21	.272	.333	Batting #5	.245	388	95	25	0	16	59	49	98	.328	.433
Home	.281	217	61	13	0	8	29	38	54	.389	.452	Batting #6	.321	56	18	1	1	2	6	4	17	.367	.482
Away	.236	246	58	13	1	10	36	20	67	.293	.419	Other	.316	19	6	0	0	0	0	5	6	.480	.316
Day	.265	162	43	9	1	10	21	21	49	.348	.519	April	.278	79	22	7	0	5	14	6	22	.329	.557
Night	.252	301	76	17	0	8	44	37	72	.335	.389	May	.282	71	20	5	0	6	13	15	18	.402	.606
Grass	.274	383	105	22	1	13	51	53	96	.363	.439	June	.235	81	19	2	0	2	11	9	23	.311	.333
Turf	.175	80	14	4	0	5	14	5	25	.221	.413	July	.152	66	10	1	0	1	8	4	21	.197	.212
First Pitch	.367	49	18	5	0	4	12	8	0	.448	.714	August	.267	86	23	6	0	3	12	12	18	.360	.442
Ahead in Count	.367	128	47	12	0	6	25	29	0	.478	.602	September/October	.313	80	25	5	1	1	7	12	19	.404	.438
Behind in Count	.180	189	34	6	1	5	19	0	88	.183	.302	Pre-All Star	.256	258	66	15	0	14	44	30	71	.331	.477
Two Strikes	.147	232	34	8	1	6	18	21	121	.220	.267	Post-All Star	.259	205	53	11	1	4	21	28	50	.350	.380

1993 By Position

Position	Avg	AB	H	2B	3B	HR	RBI	BB	SO	OBP	SLG	G	GS	Innings	PO	A	E	DP	Fld Pct	Rng Fctr	In Zone	Outs	Zone Rtg	MLB Zone
As Pinch Hitter	.231	13	3	1	0	0	0	2	6	.333	.308	15	0	---	---	---	---	---	---	---	---	---	---	---
As 1b	.260	443	115	25	1	18	65	55	112	.341	.442	144	119	1083.0	1012	86	6	106	.995	---	229	184	.803	.834

Career (1989-1993)

	Avg	AB	H	2B	3B	HR	RBI	BB	SO	OBP	SLG		Avg	AB	H	2B	3B	HR	RBI	BB	SO	OBP	SLG
vs. Left	.218	142	31	4	0	3	17	15	51	.296	.310	Scoring Posn	.211	280	59	11	1	10	102	46	65	.315	.364
vs. Right	.261	968	253	52	3	42	135	115	205	.339	.451	Close & Late	.293	198	58	11	1	9	37	22	50	.359	.495
Groundball	.290	241	70	13	1	8	40	23	42	.352	.452	None on/out	.304	263	80	19	0	12	12	20	54	.358	.513
Flyball	.222	261	58	9	0	11	30	24	66	.287	.383	Batting #5	.253	718	182	45	1	27	94	84	158	.330	.432
Home	.279	544	152	31	1	23	73	73	121	.365	.467	Batting #6	.259	193	50	6	1	8	23	23	50	.341	.425
Away	.233	566	132	25	2	22	79	57	135	.303	.401	Other	.261	199	52	5	1	10	35	23	48	.338	.447
Day	.272	379	103	15	1	22	55	44	83	.346	.491	April	.245	163	40	8	0	6	21	12	42	.299	.405
Night	.248	731	181	41	2	23	97	86	173	.327	.404	May	.250	140	35	6	0	11	28	25	38	.361	.529
Grass	.270	838	226	44	3	34	115	104	188	.350	.451	June	.287	164	47	6	0	5	18	18	34	.357	.415
Turf	.213	272	58	12	0	11	37	26	68	.281	.379	July	.239	205	49	9	1	7	26	19	49	.301	.395
First Pitch	.300	150	45	8	1	10	26	18	0	.371	.567	August	.261	176	46	11	0	8	25	20	34	.340	.460
Ahead in Count	.334	299	100	20	0	16	54	56	0	.436	.562	September/October	.256	262	67	16	2	8	34	36	59	.344	.424
Behind in Count	.195	446	87	16	2	13	44	0	204	.200	.327	Pre-All Star	.254	555	141	24	0	25	79	62	134	.328	.432
Two Strikes	.152	513	78	18	2	11	37	57	256	.239	.259	Post-All Star	.258	555	143	32	3	20	73	68	122	.339	.434

Batter vs. Pitcher (career)

Hits Best Against	Avg	AB	H	2B	3B	HR	RBI	BB	SO	OBP	SLG
Jaime Navarro	.533	15	8	1	0	0	1	4	1	.632	.600
Bobby Witt	.500	12	6	1	0	1	1	5	3	.647	.833
Kevin Tapani	.438	16	7	2	0	2	4	2	5	.500	.938
Todd Stottlemyre	.391	23	9	0	0	3	7	2	5	.440	.783
Jack McDowell	.333	24	8	2	0	3	6	3	7	.407	.792

Hits Worst Against	Avg	AB	H	2B	3B	HR	RBI	BB	SO	OBP	SLG
Danny Darwin	.091	11	1	0	0	0	0	1	2	.167	.091
David Cone	.091	11	1	0	0	0	0	1	3	.167	.091
Jack Morris	.120	25	3	1	0	0	1	3	7	.214	.160
Ben McDonald	.143	21	3	0	0	0	1	0	5	.143	.143
Cal Eldred	.182	11	2	0	0	0	0	0	0	.182	.182

Sammy Sosa — Cubs

Age 25 – Bats Right

	Avg	G	AB	R	H	2B	3B	HR	RBI	BB	SO	HBP	GDP	SB	CS	OBP	SLG	IBB	SH	SF	#Pit	#P/PA	GB	FB	G/F
1993 Season	.261	159	598	92	156	25	5	33	93	38	135	4	13	36	11	.309	.485	6	0	1	2327	3.63	158	189	0.84
Career (1989-1993)	.243	553	1891	271	459	76	18	70	234	115	493	18	38	103	45	.291	.413	15	16	12	7512	3.66	571	507	1.13

1993 Season

	Avg	AB	H	2B	3B	HR	RBI	BB	SO	OBP	SLG
vs. Left	.287	150	43	8	2	10	33	13	33	.344	.567
vs. Right	.252	448	113	17	3	23	60	25	102	.297	.458
Groundball	.315	197	62	11	2	16	40	15	39	.372	.635
Flyball	.215	93	20	6	0	3	8	7	26	.270	.376
Home	.272	298	81	14	1	23	57	21	61	.323	.557
Away	.250	300	75	11	4	10	36	17	74	.295	.413
Day	.241	319	77	8	3	22	52	23	77	.296	.492
Night	.283	279	79	17	2	11	41	15	58	.324	.477
Grass	.282	458	129	21	2	30	80	34	102	.336	.533
Turf	.193	140	27	4	3	3	13	4	33	.215	.329
First Pitch	.290	100	29	6	1	4	16	6	0	.330	.490
Ahead in Count	.381	105	40	8	1	9	31	11	0	.440	.733
Behind in Count	.187	289	54	8	1	13	29	0	115	.189	.356
Two Strikes	.198	288	57	8	0	14	32	21	135	.257	.372

	Avg	AB	H	2B	3B	HR	RBI	BB	SO	OBP	SLG
Scoring Posn	.213	164	35	7	1	4	50	16	39	.286	.341
Close & Late	.214	103	22	1	0	2	8	7	29	.264	.282
None on/out	.265	155	41	7	1	8	8	5	29	.292	.477
Batting #5	.259	305	79	11	4	15	43	19	66	.309	.469
Batting #7	.246	142	35	6	0	11	27	9	31	.296	.521
Other	.278	151	42	8	1	7	23	10	38	.321	.483
April	.229	83	19	4	1	4	11	3	19	.256	.446
May	.284	95	27	5	0	5	15	6	21	.327	.495
June	.277	101	28	2	2	7	20	7	21	.330	.545
July	.252	107	27	5	1	4	13	4	17	.277	.430
August	.270	111	30	5	0	9	18	10	28	.341	.559
September/October	.248	101	25	4	1	4	16	8	29	.309	.426
Pre-All Star	.264	322	85	12	4	17	51	18	67	.305	.484
Post-All Star	.257	276	71	13	1	16	42	20	68	.313	.486

1993 By Position

Position	Avg	AB	H	2B	3B	HR	RBI	BB	SO	OBP	SLG	G	GS	Innings	PO	A	E	DP	Fld Pct	Rng Fctr	In Zone	Outs	Zone Rtg	MLB Zone
As cf	.276	239	66	13	2	14	38	15	54	.324	.523	70	61	527.0	144	5	5	2	.968	2.54	162	136	.840	.829
As rf	.249	357	89	12	3	19	55	22	80	.296	.459	114	92	836.1	200	12	4	2	.981	2.28	222	191	.860	.826

Career (1989-1993)

	Avg	AB	H	2B	3B	HR	RBI	BB	SO	OBP	SLG
vs. Left	.273	664	181	35	5	29	95	56	169	.328	.471
vs. Right	.227	1227	278	41	13	41	139	59	324	.270	.381
Groundball	.277	575	159	28	6	28	86	37	132	.329	.492
Flyball	.226	421	95	17	4	13	37	27	125	.275	.378
Home	.253	892	226	42	10	41	118	66	229	.309	.461
Away	.233	999	233	34	8	29	116	49	264	.274	.370
Day	.226	698	158	27	6	32	91	44	188	.280	.420
Night	.252	1193	301	49	12	38	143	71	305	.297	.409
Grass	.244	1514	370	63	14	59	186	101	397	.297	.421
Turf	.236	377	89	13	4	11	48	14	96	.267	.379
First Pitch	.343	303	104	18	3	18	59	10	0	.360	.601
Ahead in Count	.340	300	102	21	4	16	65	38	0	.415	.597
Behind in Count	.168	934	157	20	5	19	57	0	420	.177	.261
Two Strikes	.163	956	156	25	6	21	68	62	493	.220	.268

	Avg	AB	H	2B	3B	HR	RBI	BB	SO	OBP	SLG
Scoring Posn	.228	470	107	22	5	15	154	39	125	.287	.391
Close & Late	.218	331	72	10	2	6	21	24	88	.275	.314
None on/out	.232	539	125	19	5	17	17	27	133	.276	.380
Batting #1	.270	422	114	21	5	14	54	25	105	.310	.443
Batting #5	.250	412	103	17	4	19	51	27	90	.300	.449
Other	.229	1057	242	38	9	37	129	63	298	.280	.387
April	.237	274	65	10	4	9	29	18	70	.287	.401
May	.247	393	97	13	1	13	39	21	109	.288	.384
June	.255	364	93	12	8	16	50	17	89	.295	.464
July	.226	279	63	18	3	8	35	10	65	.252	.398
August	.255	278	71	10	0	14	40	25	71	.324	.442
September/October	.231	303	70	13	2	10	41	24	89	.297	.386
Pre-All Star	.246	1139	280	42	14	40	128	59	289	.287	.413
Post-All Star	.238	752	179	34	4	30	106	56	204	.297	.414

Batter vs. Pitcher (career)

Hits Best Against	Avg	AB	H	2B	3B	HR	RBI	BB	SO	OBP	SLG
Randy Tomlin	.583	12	7	1	0	1	3	0	2	.583	.917
Mike Moore	.462	13	6	2	1	1	3	1	1	.500	1.000
Dennis Martinez	.429	14	6	0	0	1	3	1	4	.467	.643
David West	.429	14	6	2	1	1	2	2	5	.500	.929
Jeff Ballard	.308	13	4	0	0	2	4	1	2	.357	.769

Hits Worst Against	Avg	AB	H	2B	3B	HR	RBI	BB	SO	OBP	SLG
Nolan Ryan	.000	16	0	0	0	0	0	2	8	.111	.000
John Smoltz	.000	16	0	0	0	0	0	1	9	.059	.000
Tim Belcher	.000	13	0	0	0	0	0	0	1	.000	.000
Dave Burba	.000	13	0	0	0	0	0	0	3	.000	.000
Bob Walk	.063	16	1	0	0	0	0	0	2	.063	.063

Tim Spehr — Expos

Age 27 – Bats Right

	Avg	G	AB	R	H	2B	3B	HR	RBI	BB	SO	HBP	GDP	SB	CS	OBP	SLG	IBB	SH	SF	#Pit	#P/PA	GB	FB	G/F
1993 Season	.230	53	87	14	20	6	0	2	10	6	20	1	0	2	0	.281	.368	1	3	2	390	3.94	34	23	1.48
Career (1991-1993)	.211	90	161	21	34	11	0	5	24	15	38	2	2	3	0	.282	.373	1	6	3	741	3.96	54	48	1.13

1993 Season

	Avg	AB	H	2B	3B	HR	RBI	BB	SO	OBP	SLG
vs. Left	.245	53	13	5	0	1	5	4	7	.310	.396
vs. Right	.206	34	7	1	0	1	5	2	13	.237	.324

	Avg	AB	H	2B	3B	HR	RBI	BB	SO	OBP	SLG
Scoring Posn	.235	17	4	1	0	0	7	3	3	.348	.294
Close & Late	.231	13	3	2	0	0	1	1	3	.286	.385

Bill Spiers — Brewers

Age 28 – Bats Left (groundball hitter)

	Avg	G	AB	R	H	2B	3B	HR	RBI	BB	SO	HBP	GDP	SB	CS	OBP	SLG	IBB	SH	SF	#Pit	#P/PA	GB	FB	G/F
1993 Season	.238	113	340	43	81	8	4	2	36	29	51	4	10	9	8	.302	.303	2	9	4	1417	3.67	162	65	2.49
Career (1989-1993)	.256	484	1478	204	379	47	16	16	161	101	218	8	33	45	25	.305	.342	3	30	13	5665	3.48	622	355	1.75

1993 Season

	Avg	AB	H	2B	3B	HR	RBI	BB	SO	OBP	SLG		Avg	AB	H	2B	3B	HR	RBI	BB	SO	OBP	SLG
vs. Left	.176	68	12	2	1	0	4	7	17	.273	.235	Scoring Posn	.242	95	23	2	1	0	33	10	13	.303	.284
vs. Right	.254	272	69	6	3	2	32	22	34	.310	.320	Close & Late	.250	56	14	1	1	0	6	4	7	.311	.304
Groundball	.209	67	14	2	1	0	4	8	12	.312	.269	None on/out	.264	72	19	0	1	2	2	4	12	.321	.375
Flyball	.182	77	14	2	0	1	9	7	9	.244	.247	Batting #2	.233	159	37	3	2	0	17	14	24	.302	.277
Home	.277	166	46	5	2	2	25	18	23	.344	.367	Batting #9	.258	97	25	3	1	2	6	5	16	.291	.371
Away	.201	174	35	3	2	0	11	11	28	.262	.241	Other	.226	84	19	2	1	0	13	10	11	.316	.274
Day	.226	93	21	1	2	0	6	13	15	.321	.280	April	.245	49	12	0	1	0	4	5	8	.315	.286
Night	.243	247	60	7	2	2	30	16	36	.295	.312	May	.244	82	20	2	1	0	8	7	15	.312	.293
Grass	.257	280	72	7	2	2	30	26	42	.325	.318	June	.198	81	16	2	1	0	8	9	10	.275	.247
Turf	.150	60	9	1	2	0	6	3	9	.197	.233	July	.263	57	15	2	1	1	10	2	8	.300	.386
First Pitch	.189	37	7	1	0	0	1	1	0	.250	.216	August	.349	43	15	2	0	1	3	2	6	.370	.465
Ahead in Count	.235	68	16	0	1	2	13	19	0	.393	.353	September/October	.107	28	3	0	0	0	3	4	4	.242	.107
Behind in Count	.240	154	37	5	1	0	17	0	44	.248	.286	Pre-All Star	.234	231	54	5	4	0	27	22	38	.302	.290
Two Strikes	.205	146	30	4	0	0	12	9	51	.258	.233	Post-All Star	.248	109	27	3	0	2	9	7	13	.303	.330

1993 By Position

Position	Avg	AB	H	2B	3B	HR	RBI	BB	SO	OBP	SLG	G	GS	Innings	PO	A	E	DP	Fld Pct	Rng Fctr	In Zone	Outs	Zone Rtg	MLB Zone
As 2b	.229	327	75	8	3	2	33	28	50	.293	.291	104	92	804.0	210	226	13	52	.971	4.88	265	229	.864	.895

Career (1989-1993)

	Avg	AB	H	2B	3B	HR	RBI	BB	SO	OBP	SLG		Avg	AB	H	2B	3B	HR	RBI	BB	SO	OBP	SLG
vs. Left	.224	339	76	8	3	3	33	26	66	.285	.292	Scoring Posn	.275	375	103	16	7	5	146	34	59	.325	.395
vs. Right	.266	1139	303	39	13	13	128	75	152	.311	.357	Close & Late	.280	250	70	6	4	1	30	18	38	.330	.348
Groundball	.264	416	110	15	7	5	61	37	64	.327	.370	None on/out	.226	385	87	13	3	4	4	16	52	.262	.306
Flyball	.261	280	73	9	2	6	26	22	41	.311	.371	Batting #2	.256	223	57	5	4	3	26	17	35	.313	.354
Home	.283	707	200	27	8	6	89	55	106	.333	.369	Batting #9	.266	997	265	36	9	11	108	63	143	.309	.353
Away	.232	771	179	20	8	10	72	46	112	.279	.318	Other	.221	258	57	6	3	2	27	21	40	.281	.291
Day	.245	444	109	18	5	5	46	36	78	.302	.342	April	.242	132	32	1	1	4	19	14	21	.313	.356
Night	.261	1034	270	29	11	11	115	65	140	.306	.342	May	.225	227	51	10	1	0	17	18	41	.288	.278
Grass	.269	1256	338	41	14	14	142	86	188	.317	.357	June	.247	259	64	11	3	1	23	23	35	.310	.324
Turf	.185	222	41	6	2	2	19	15	30	.236	.257	July	.265	257	68	6	2	4	34	10	41	.289	.350
First Pitch	.279	244	68	8	1	4	26	2	0	.294	.369	August	.268	287	77	9	3	2	35	22	36	.319	.341
Ahead in Count	.317	312	99	12	3	4	41	69	0	.435	.413	September/October	.275	316	87	10	6	5	33	14	44	.309	.392
Behind in Count	.207	646	134	15	6	4	58	0	193	.211	.268	Pre-All Star	.245	678	166	25	6	6	74	58	107	.305	.326
Two Strikes	.205	614	126	17	6	6	65	30	218	.245	.282	Post-All Star	.266	800	213	22	10	10	87	43	111	.305	.356

Batter vs. Pitcher (career)

Hits Best Against	Avg	AB	H	2B	3B	HR	RBI	BB	SO	OBP	SLG	Hits Worst Against	Avg	AB	H	2B	3B	HR	RBI	BB	SO	OBP	SLG
Dave Johnson	.500	16	8	3	0	0	4	0	0	.500	.688	Jose Mesa	.000	12	0	0	0	0	1	1	3	.071	.000
Mark Gubicza	.455	11	5	0	1	0	2	0	2	.455	.636	Tom Candiotti	.100	20	2	0	0	0	3	1	5	.136	.100
Mark Leiter	.375	8	3	0	0	1	1	3	2	.545	.750	Erik Hanson	.100	20	2	0	0	0	0	0	5	.100	.100
Roger Clemens	.353	17	6	1	1	1	1	0	4	.353	.706	Bill Swift	.111	9	1	0	0	0	0	2	1	.273	.111
Mike Witt	.333	12	4	1	2	0	5	0	1	.333	.750	Kevin Tapani	.158	19	3	1	0	0	4	0	7	.158	.211

Jerry Spradlin — Reds

Age 27 – Pitches Right

	ERA	W	L	Sv	G	GS	IP	BB	SO	Avg	H	2B	3B	HR	RBI	OBP	SLG	GF	IR	IRS	Hld	SvOp	SB	CS	GB	FB	G/F
1993 Season	3.49	2	1	2	37	0	49.0	9	24	.249	44	7	4	4	26	.279	.401	16	22	10	0	3	4	2	72	60	1.20

1993 Season

	ERA	W	L	Sv	G	GS	IP	H	HR	BB	SO		Avg	AB	H	2B	3B	HR	RBI	BB	SO	OBP	SLG
Home	3.75	1	0	2	20	0	24.0	21	2	7	12	vs. Left	.261	69	18	2	3	4	14	4	10	.297	.551
Away	3.24	1	1	0	17	0	25.0	23	2	2	12	vs. Right	.241	108	26	5	1	0	12	5	14	.267	.306
Starter	0.00	0	0	0	0	0	0.0	0	0	0	0	Scoring Posn	.250	44	11	2	2	1	20	1	6	.245	.455
Reliever	3.49	2	1	2	37	0	49.0	44	4	9	24	Close & Late	.200	35	7	1	2	1	3	1	3	.222	.429
0 Days rest	1.04	0	0	1	6	0	8.2	4	0	2	4	None on/out	.262	42	11	2	0	0	0	3	5	.311	.310
1 or 2 Days rest	3.81	2	1	1	23	0	28.1	28	3	3	15	First Pitch	.429	35	15	1	1	3	11	0	0	.417	.771
3+ Days rest	4.50	0	0	0	8	0	12.0	12	1	4	5	Ahead in Count	.150	80	12	0	2	0	9	0	22	.148	.200
Pre-All Star	2.25	0	0	1	4	0	8.0	6	0	1	3	Behind in Count	.281	32	9	4	1	1	6	5	0	.359	.563
Post-All Star	3.73	2	1	1	33	0	41.0	38	4	8	21	Two Strikes	.158	76	12	1	2	0	6	4	24	.198	.224

Ed Sprague — Blue Jays

Age 26 – Bats Right

	Avg	G	AB	R	H	2B	3B	HR	RBI	BB	SO	HBP	GDP	SB	CS	OBP	SLG	IBB	SH	SF	#Pit	#P/PA	GB	FB	G/F
1993 Season	.260	150	546	50	142	31	1	12	73	32	85	10	23	1	0	.310	.386	1	2	6	2161	3.63	185	174	1.06
Career (1991-1993)	.262	233	753	73	197	40	1	17	100	54	135	13	25	1	3	.319	.385	3	2	7	2976	3.59	242	235	1.03

1993 Season

	Avg	AB	H	2B	3B	HR	RBI	BB	SO	OBP	SLG
vs. Left	.247	146	36	11	0	2	11	12	20	.304	.363
vs. Right	.265	400	106	20	1	10	62	20	65	.312	.395
Groundball	.338	80	27	4	0	2	17	4	14	.376	.463
Flyball	.272	81	22	6	0	2	14	2	13	.292	.420
Home	.291	268	78	20	1	8	46	14	41	.328	.463
Away	.230	278	64	11	0	4	27	18	44	.293	.313
Day	.306	183	56	14	0	9	43	9	23	.340	.530
Night	.237	363	86	17	1	3	30	23	62	.295	.314
Grass	.242	211	51	8	0	4	20	16	27	.309	.336
Turf	.272	335	91	23	1	8	53	16	58	.310	.418
First Pitch	.375	80	30	12	1	2	12	1	0	.412	.625
Ahead in Count	.360	139	50	7	0	5	28	15	0	.429	.518
Behind in Count	.159	233	37	5	0	3	22	0	72	.158	.219
Two Strikes	.152	237	36	7	0	3	18	16	85	.203	.219

	Avg	AB	H	2B	3B	HR	RBI	BB	SO	OBP	SLG
Scoring Posn	.225	169	38	11	0	1	60	14	31	.294	.308
Close & Late	.257	70	18	1	1	0	9	2	18	.303	.300
None on/out	.273	132	36	7	0	7	7	5	19	.304	.485
Batting #7	.225	284	64	16	0	6	34	12	52	.263	.345
Batting #8	.277	137	38	9	0	1	21	13	11	.346	.365
Other	.320	125	40	6	1	5	18	7	22	.372	.504
April	.244	82	20	6	0	2	17	3	17	.264	.390
May	.282	85	24	3	0	4	13	6	14	.340	.459
June	.260	104	27	6	0	3	14	4	21	.319	.404
July	.250	100	25	5	1	1	5	5	18	.286	.350
August	.250	96	24	5	0	1	14	6	7	.291	.333
September/October	.278	79	22	6	0	1	10	8	8	.360	.392
Pre-All Star	.266	308	82	18	1	10	46	15	60	.313	.429
Post-All Star	.252	238	60	13	0	2	27	17	25	.306	.332

1993 By Position

Position	Avg	AB	H	2B	3B	HR	RBI	BB	SO	OBP	SLG	G	GS	Innings	PO	A	E	DP	Fld Pct	Rng Fctr	In Zone	Outs	Zone Rtg	MLB Zone
As 3b	.260	546	142	31	1	12	73	32	85	.310	.386	150	150	1291.1	128	231	17	20	.955	2.50	300	250	.833	.834

Russ Springer — Angels

Age 25 – Pitches Right (flyball pitcher)

	ERA	W	L	Sv	G	GS	IP	BB	SO	Avg	H	2B	3B	HR	RBI	OBP	SLG	CG	ShO	Sup	QS	#P/S	SB	CS	GB	FB	G/F
1993 Season	7.20	1	6	0	14	9	60.0	32	31	.303	73	10	0	11	41	.390	.481	1	0	3.75	2	103	11	1	56	106	0.53
Career (1992-1993)	6.99	1	6	0	28	9	76.0	42	43	.298	91	14	1	11	54	.389	.459	1	0	3.55	2	103	14	1	74	131	0.56

1993 Season

	ERA	W	L	Sv	G	GS	IP	H	HR	BB	SO
Home	6.75	1	2	0	7	5	32.0	45	5	21	15
Away	7.71	0	4	0	7	4	28.0	28	6	11	16
Starter	7.62	1	6	0	9	9	52.0	64	9	31	25
Reliever	4.50	0	0	0	5	0	8.0	9	2	1	6
0-3 Days Rest	0.00	0	0	0	0	0	0.0	0	0	0	0
4 Days Rest	8.39	1	5	0	8	8	44.0	60	8	29	22
5+ Days Rest	3.38	0	1	0	1	1	8.0	4	1	2	3
Pre-All Star	6.69	1	3	0	10	5	37.2	51	6	16	23
Post-All Star	8.06	0	3	0	4	4	22.1	22	5	16	8

	Avg	AB	H	2B	3B	HR	RBI	BB	SO	OBP	SLG
vs. Left	.301	123	37	4	0	5	16	15	20	.386	.455
vs. Right	.305	118	36	6	0	6	25	17	11	.394	.508
Scoring Posn	.348	66	23	4	0	7	36	6	8	.397	.727
Close & Late	.250	12	3	2	0	1	2	3	1	.438	.667
None on/out	.357	56	20	5	0	2	2	12	6	.471	.554
First Pitch	.182	22	4	0	0	0	1	1	0	.217	.182
Ahead in Count	.229	105	24	5	0	3	12	0	26	.250	.362
Behind in Count	.347	72	25	5	0	4	15	17	0	.467	.583
Two Strikes	.250	100	25	4	0	2	11	14	31	.342	.350

Scott Stahoviak — Twins

Age 24 – Bats Left (flyball hitter)

	Avg	G	AB	R	H	2B	3B	HR	RBI	BB	SO	HBP	GDP	SB	CS	OBP	SLG	IBB	SH	SF	#Pit	#P/PA	GB	FB	G/F
1993 Season	.193	20	57	1	11	4	0	0	1	3	22	0	2	0	2	.233	.263	0	0	0	242	4.03	13	14	0.93

1993 Season

	Avg	AB	H	2B	3B	HR	RBI	BB	SO	OBP	SLG
vs. Left	.333	3	1	1	0	0	0	0	1	.333	.667
vs. Right	.185	54	10	3	0	0	1	3	21	.228	.241

	Avg	AB	H	2B	3B	HR	RBI	BB	SO	OBP	SLG
Scoring Posn	.077	13	1	0	0	0	1	0	7	.077	.077
Close & Late	.111	9	1	0	0	0	1	0	3	.111	.111

Matt Stairs — Expos

Age 25 – Bats Left (groundball hitter)

	Avg	G	AB	R	H	2B	3B	HR	RBI	BB	SO	HBP	GDP	SB	CS	OBP	SLG	IBB	SH	SF	#Pit	#P/PA	GB	FB	G/F
1993 Season	.375	6	8	1	3	1	0	0	2	0	1	0	1	0	0	.375	.500	0	0	0	27	3.38	3	3	1.00
Career (1992-1993)	.211	19	38	3	8	3	0	0	7	7	8	0	1	0	0	.326	.289	0	0	1	169	3.67	16	10	1.60

1993 Season

	Avg	AB	H	2B	3B	HR	RBI	BB	SO	OBP	SLG
vs. Left	.500	2	1	1	0	0	1	0	1	.500	1.000
vs. Right	.333	6	2	0	0	0	1	0	0	.333	.333

	Avg	AB	H	2B	3B	HR	RBI	BB	SO	OBP	SLG
Scoring Posn	.333	3	1	0	0	0	1	0	1	.333	.333
Close & Late	.500	4	2	1	0	0	1	0	1	.500	.750

Andy Stankiewicz — Yankees

Age 29 – Bats Right

	Avg	G	AB	R	H	2B	3B	HR	RBI	BB	SO	HBP	GDP	SB	CS	OBP	SLG	IBB	SH	SF	#Pit	#P/PA	GB	FB	G/F
1993 Season	.000	16	9	5	0	0	0	0	0	1	1	0	0	0	0	.100	.000	0	0	0	28	2.80	1	6	0.17
Career (1992-1993)	.262	132	409	57	107	22	2	2	25	39	43	5	13	9	5	.333	.340	0	7	1	1631	3.54	154	122	1.26

1993 Season

	Avg	AB	H	2B	3B	HR	RBI	BB	SO	OBP	SLG		Avg	AB	H	2B	3B	HR	RBI	BB	SO	OBP	SLG
vs. Left	.000	5	0	0	0	0	0	1	0	.167	.000	Scoring Posn	.000	1	0	0	0	0	0	0	1	.000	.000
vs. Right	.000	4	0	0	0	0	0	0	1	.000	.000	Close & Late	.000	1	0	0	0	0	0	0	0	.000	.000

Career (1992-1993)

	Avg	AB	H	2B	3B	HR	RBI	BB	SO	OBP	SLG		Avg	AB	H	2B	3B	HR	RBI	BB	SO	OBP	SLG
vs. Left	.262	141	37	5	1	0	10	11	11	.329	.312	Scoring Posn	.300	70	21	4	1	0	21	8	12	.367	.386
vs. Right	.261	268	70	17	1	2	15	28	32	.334	.354	Close & Late	.250	72	18	5	0	0	6	6	7	.325	.319
Groundball	.254	114	29	6	1	0	7	6	15	.298	.325	None on/out	.252	143	36	5	0	1	1	15	18	.327	.308
Flyball	.269	119	32	9	0	0	8	10	10	.328	.345	Batting #1	.274	259	71	15	1	2	17	23	34	.337	.363
Home	.284	215	61	13	1	2	15	20	19	.345	.381	Batting #8	.238	80	19	3	1	0	5	9	3	.330	.300
Away	.237	194	46	9	1	0	10	19	24	.320	.294	Other	.243	70	17	4	0	0	3	7	6	.321	.300
Day	.285	137	39	9	0	1	6	11	13	.342	.372	April	.308	39	12	2	0	1	4	8	7	.438	.436
Night	.250	272	68	13	2	1	19	28	30	.328	.324	May	.353	34	12	5	0	0	4	1	0	.371	.500
Grass	.251	359	90	17	2	2	23	34	42	.322	.326	June	.284	109	31	7	1	1	7	12	16	.363	.394
Turf	.340	50	17	5	0	0	2	5	1	.411	.440	July	.188	101	19	2	0	0	3	7	13	.241	.208
First Pitch	.311	61	19	3	0	1	3	0	0	.306	.410	August	.290	62	18	3	0	0	3	3	4	.343	.339
Ahead in Count	.267	116	31	6	1	1	11	25	0	.397	.362	September/October	.234	64	15	3	1	0	4	8	3	.319	.313
Behind in Count	.194	144	28	2	0	0	5	0	38	.216	.208	Pre-All Star	.285	228	65	15	1	2	16	26	28	.364	.386
Two Strikes	.196	153	30	5	1	0	7	14	43	.276	.242	Post-All Star	.232	181	42	7	1	0	9	13	15	.291	.282

Batter vs. Pitcher (career)

Hits Best Against	Avg	AB	H	2B	3B	HR	RBI	BB	SO	OBP	SLG	Hits Worst Against	Avg	AB	H	2B	3B	HR	RBI	BB	SO	OBP	SLG
Randy Johnson	.333	12	4	1	0	0	0	2	1	.429	.417												

Mike Stanley — Yankees

Age 31 – Bats Right (flyball hitter)

	Avg	G	AB	R	H	2B	3B	HR	RBI	BB	SO	HBP	GDP	SB	CS	OBP	SLG	IBB	SH	SF	#Pit	#P/PA	GB	FB	G/F
1993 Season	.305	130	423	70	129	17	1	26	84	57	85	5	10	1	1	.389	.534	4	0	6	1950	3.97	105	168	0.63
Last Five Years	.270	463	1088	149	294	48	4	40	166	166	228	10	27	3	1	.369	.432	7	12	8	5088	3.96	317	356	0.89

1993 Season

	Avg	AB	H	2B	3B	HR	RBI	BB	SO	OBP	SLG		Avg	AB	H	2B	3B	HR	RBI	BB	SO	OBP	SLG
vs. Left	.307	166	51	6	0	14	38	30	27	.415	.596	Scoring Posn	.308	104	32	6	0	8	60	25	22	.431	.596
vs. Right	.304	257	78	11	1	12	46	27	58	.371	.494	Close & Late	.369	65	24	3	0	2	10	7	12	.432	.508
Groundball	.352	71	25	5	0	3	13	7	22	.420	.549	None on/out	.310	116	36	3	0	6	6	9	26	.365	.491
Flyball	.282	110	31	1	0	7	26	9	17	.341	.482	Batting #5	.324	170	55	6	0	14	41	23	28	.411	.606
Home	.312	199	62	8	0	17	56	30	34	.408	.608	Batting #7	.279	190	53	8	0	8	32	23	41	.359	.447
Away	.299	224	67	9	1	9	28	27	51	.372	.469	Other	.333	63	21	3	1	4	11	11	16	.416	.603
Day	.361	122	44	4	0	9	30	24	21	.470	.615	April	.250	32	8	0	0	1	5	4	4	.333	.344
Night	.282	301	85	13	1	17	54	33	64	.353	.502	May	.382	76	29	8	0	3	12	12	19	.456	.605
Grass	.300	363	109	14	1	21	70	52	70	.391	.518	June	.271	85	23	2	0	6	18	10	19	.347	.506
Turf	.333	60	20	3	0	5	14	5	15	.379	.633	July	.378	82	31	2	1	9	27	8	13	.452	.756
First Pitch	.420	50	21	5	0	2	12	3	0	.455	.640	August	.194	72	14	1	0	3	9	9	14	.289	.333
Ahead in Count	.394	94	37	3	0	14	43	27	0	.520	.872	September/October	.316	76	24	4	0	4	13	14	16	.415	.526
Behind in Count	.215	186	40	5	0	4	14	0	69	.226	.306	Pre-All Star	.316	228	72	12	1	11	41	28	48	.388	.522
Two Strikes	.192	213	41	5	1	4	15	27	85	.288	.282	Post-All Star	.292	195	57	5	0	15	43	29	37	.391	.549

1993 By Position

Position	Avg	AB	H	2B	3B	HR	RBI	BB	SO	OBP	SLG	G	GS	Innings	PO	A	E	DP	Fld Pct	Rng Fctr	In Zone	Outs	Zone Rtg	MLB Zone
As Pinch Hitter	.273	11	3	1	0	0	0	2	5	.385	.364	15	0	---	---	---	---	---	---	---	---	---	---	---
As c	.307	410	126	16	1	26	82	55	80	.392	.541	122	112	1001.1	652	46	3	5	.996	---	---	---	---	---

Last Five Years

	Avg	AB	H	2B	3B	HR	RBI	BB	SO	OBP	SLG		Avg	AB	H	2B	3B	HR	RBI	BB	SO	OBP	SLG
vs. Left	.276	587	162	25	3	25	91	103	112	.384	.457	Scoring Posn	.266	282	75	13	0	11	122	61	55	.393	.429
vs. Right	.263	501	132	23	1	15	75	63	116	.352	.403	Close & Late	.284	169	48	7	0	5	27	29	35	.391	.414
Groundball	.264	250	66	9	2	5	37	30	55	.347	.376	None on/out	.281	285	80	9	0	12	12	33	61	.363	.439
Flyball	.252	258	65	13	0	12	45	40	57	.359	.442	Batting #5	.318	198	63	7	0	15	47	28	31	.407	.581
Home	.292	528	154	25	2	25	108	83	100	.392	.489	Batting #7	.272	470	128	21	1	14	68	64	110	.363	.411
Away	.250	560	140	23	2	15	58	83	128	.348	.379	Other	.245	420	103	20	3	11	51	74	87	.359	.386
Day	.275	280	77	9	2	14	50	54	60	.399	.471	April	.237	93	22	1	0	2	12	18	17	.366	.312
Night	.269	808	217	39	2	26	116	112	168	.359	.418	May	.260	192	50	12	1	7	27	30	38	.356	.443
Grass	.271	919	249	41	4	33	141	140	191	.371	.432	June	.233	219	51	8	0	7	31	27	53	.319	.365
Turf	.266	169	45	7	0	7	25	26	37	.362	.432	July	.342	187	64	8	2	13	41	17	33	.406	.615
First Pitch	.319	144	46	10	1	3	27	4	0	.344	.465	August	.263	160	42	8	0	3	16	29	34	.377	.369
Ahead in Count	.372	226	84	12	0	20	73	85	0	.538	.690	September/October	.274	237	65	11	1	8	39	45	53	.394	.430
Behind in Count	.197	503	99	15	1	9	36	0	184	.207	.284	Pre-All Star	.257	568	146	25	3	18	83	79	117	.348	.407
Two Strikes	.172	541	93	13	2	8	34	75	228	.278	.248	Post-All Star	.285	520	148	23	1	22	83	87	111	.393	.460

Batter vs. Pitcher (career)																							
Hits Best Against	Avg	AB	H	2B	3B	HR	RBI	BB	SO	OBP	SLG	**Hits Worst Against**	Avg	AB	H	2B	3B	HR	RBI	BB	SO	OBP	SLG
Tom Bolton	.500	10	5	1	1	1	2	2	2	.583	1.100	Kirk McCaskill	.000	11	0	0	0	0	0	1	5	.083	.000
Chuck Finley	.415	41	17	4	0	1	8	5	7	.478	.585	Rick Honeycutt	.100	10	1	1	0	0	0	1	3	.182	.200
Dave Fleming	.357	14	5	0	0	2	5	1	1	.400	.786	Bret Saberhagen	.154	13	2	0	0	0	1	1	2	.214	.154
Charlie Leibrandt	.353	17	6	0	0	2	8	1	1	.389	.706	Greg Swindell	.158	19	3	1	0	0	0	2	9	.238	.211
Wilson Alvarez	.333	12	4	0	0	2	2	5	4	.529	.833	John Candelaria	.182	11	2	0	0	0	1	1	2	.250	.182

Mike Stanton — Braves

Age 27 – Pitches Left

	ERA	W	L	Sv	G	GS	IP	BB	SO	Avg	H	2B	3B	HR	RBI	OBP	SLG	GF	IR	IRS	Hld	SvOp	SB	CS	GB	FB	G/F
1993 Season	4.67	4	6	27	63	0	52.0	29	43	.255	51	11	0	4	33	.346	.370	41	25	10	5	33	5	1	66	60	1.10
Career (1989-1993)	3.97	14	19	51	229	0	224.2	82	175	.243	205	33	4	17	117	.312	.352	88	147	44	37	65	18	4	280	243	1.15

1993 Season

	ERA	W	L	Sv	G	GS	IP	H	HR	BB	SO		Avg	AB	H	2B	3B	HR	RBI	BB	SO	OBP	SLG
Home	2.25	4	3	14	31	0	28.0	22	2	17	27	vs. Left	.218	55	12	2	0	1	9	13	15	.357	.309
Away	7.50	0	3	13	32	0	24.0	29	2	12	16	vs. Right	.269	145	39	9	0	3	24	16	28	.342	.393
Day	9.53	1	2	8	15	0	11.1	17	1	3	5	Inning 1-6	.000	3	0	0	0	0	0	2	1	.400	.000
Night	3.32	3	4	19	48	0	40.2	34	3	26	38	Inning 7+	.259	197	51	11	0	4	33	27	42	.345	.376
Grass	4.35	4	5	21	47	0	39.1	40	3	22	37	None on	.224	98	22	5	0	2	2	16	18	.333	.337
Turf	5.68	0	1	6	16	0	12.2	11	1	7	6	Runners on	.284	102	29	6	0	2	31	13	25	.359	.402
April	3.48	1	1	8	13	0	10.1	9	0	5	6	Scoring Posn	.295	61	18	5	0	1	28	10	13	.384	.426
May	3.38	0	0	10	12	0	10.2	10	0	3	8	Close & Late	.277	130	36	7	0	4	29	20	30	.371	.423
June	2.57	2	1	3	7	0	7.0	5	1	4	7	None on/out	.200	40	8	3	0	0	0	8	7	.333	.275
July	5.59	1	1	6	12	0	9.2	10	1	6	8	vs. 1st Batr (relief)	.167	54	9	3	0	1	5	9	10	.286	.278
August	12.15	0	2	0	10	0	6.2	9	2	9	10	First Inning Pitched	.251	191	48	11	0	4	32	26	41	.338	.372
September/October	2.35	0	1	0	9	0	7.2	8	0	2	4	First 15 Pitches	.241	166	40	9	0	4	25	22	37	.328	.367
Starter	0.00	0	0	0	0	0	0.0	0	0	0	0	Pitch 16-30	.355	31	11	2	0	0	8	7	4	.462	.419
Reliever	4.67	4	6	27	63	0	52.0	51	4	29	43	Pitch 31-45	.000	3	0	0	0	0	0	0	2	.000	.000
0 Days rest	4.91	0	1	8	15	0	11.0	8	0	4	8	Pitch 46+	.000	0	0	0	0	0	0	0	0	.000	.000
1 or 2 Days rest	5.96	2	3	12	28	0	22.2	21	2	16	18	First Pitch	.364	22	8	2	0	1	10	5	0	.464	.591
3+ Days rest	2.95	2	2	7	20	0	18.1	22	2	9	17	Ahead in Count	.168	107	18	3	0	0	7	0	39	.167	.196
Pre-All Star	3.45	4	3	23	36	0	31.1	28	1	14	26	Behind in Count	.325	40	13	3	0	3	10	11	0	.471	.625
Post-All Star	6.53	0	3	4	27	0	20.2	23	3	15	17	Two Strikes	.139	101	14	5	0	0	8	13	43	.235	.188

Career (1989-1993)

	ERA	W	L	Sv	G	GS	IP	H	HR	BB	SO		Avg	AB	H	2B	3B	HR	RBI	BB	SO	OBP	SLG
Home	3.15	7	7	25	109	0	117.0	102	7	36	88	vs. Left	.215	256	55	6	1	6	29	36	73	.313	.316
Away	4.85	7	12	26	120	0	107.2	103	10	46	87	vs. Right	.256	587	150	27	3	11	88	46	102	.311	.368
Day	5.64	2	4	12	59	0	52.2	49	6	19	42	Inning 1-6	.081	37	3	0	0	0	1	4	10	.171	.081
Night	3.45	12	15	39	170	0	172.0	156	11	63	133	Inning 7+	.251	806	202	33	4	17	116	78	165	.318	.365
Grass	3.83	10	15	39	166	0	166.2	151	11	58	123	None on	.241	440	106	17	0	9	9	34	86	.300	.341
Turf	4.34	4	4	12	63	0	58.0	54	6	24	52	Runners on	.246	403	99	16	4	8	108	48	89	.325	.365
April	5.91	1	5	11	37	0	32.0	35	1	16	22	Scoring Posn	.254	256	65	10	3	5	99	32	59	.334	.375
May	6.00	1	1	13	33	0	30.0	30	8	7	20	Close & Late	.246	505	124	21	4	9	78	51	102	.317	.356
June	4.50	5	4	5	31	0	28.0	25	3	10	23	None on/out	.262	191	50	10	0	3	3	15	39	.319	.361
July	3.26	2	2	7	30	0	30.1	18	2	16	20	vs. 1st Batr (relief)	.198	207	41	8	1	1	21	21	46	.275	.261
August	3.56	0	2	7	41	0	43.0	34	3	20	36	First Inning Pitched	.239	682	163	27	3	14	101	68	149	.310	.349
September/October	2.35	5	5	8	57	0	61.1	63	0	13	54	First 15 Pitches	.238	629	150	25	3	12	79	59	128	.307	.345
Starter	0.00	0	0	0	0	0	0.0	0	0	0	0	Pitch 16-30	.268	183	49	8	1	5	35	20	37	.335	.404
Reliever	3.97	14	19	51	229	0	224.2	205	17	82	175	Pitch 31-45	.214	28	6	0	0	0	3	3	9	.290	.214
0 Days rest	4.45	4	6	14	66	0	58.2	55	3	24	49	Pitch 46+	.000	3	0	0	0	0	0	0	1	.000	.000
1 or 2 Days rest	3.96	7	10	25	107	0	102.1	92	6	39	74	First Pitch	.294	126	37	6	1	2	24	14	0	.371	.405
3+ Days rest	3.53	3	3	12	56	0	63.2	58	8	19	52	Ahead in Count	.190	406	77	9	1	5	35	0	153	.188	.254
Pre-All Star	5.12	9	11	31	113	0	102.0	95	12	37	76	Behind in Count	.308	169	52	11	2	8	36	39	0	.438	.538
Post-All Star	3.01	5	8	20	116	0	122.2	110	5	45	99	Two Strikes	.177	413	73	12	1	6	37	29	175	.230	.254

Pitcher vs. Batter (career)																							
Pitches Best Vs.	Avg	AB	H	2B	3B	HR	RBI	BB	SO	OBP	SLG	**Pitches Worst Vs.**	Avg	AB	H	2B	3B	HR	RBI	BB	SO	OBP	SLG
Luis Gonzalez	.000	8	0	0	0	0	1	3	3	.250	.000	Darren Daulton	.400	10	4	2	0	1	1	2	3	.500	.900
Eddie Murray	.083	12	1	0	0	0	0	0	1	.083	.083	Barry Bonds	.375	8	3	2	0	0	1	4	1	.583	.625
Brett Butler	.100	10	1	0	0	0	1	2	1	.250	.100	Mark Grace	.364	11	4	0	0	0	1	4	1	.533	.364
Ken Caminiti	.133	15	2	1	0	0	2	0	3	.133	.200	Steve Finley	.364	11	4	1	0	0	0	2	3	.462	.455
Craig Biggio	.143	14	2	0	0	0	1	1	3	.200	.143	Hal Morris	.333	9	3	0	0	0	0	3	3	.500	.333

Dave Staton — Padres

Age 26 – Bats Right

	Avg	G	AB	R	H	2B	3B	HR	RBI	BB	SO	HBP	GDP	SB	CS	OBP	SLG	IBB	SH	SF	#Pit	#P/PA	GB	FB	G/F
1993 Season	.262	17	42	7	11	3	0	5	9	3	12	1	2	0	0	.326	.690	0	0	0	180	3.91	15	8	1.88

1993 Season

	Avg	AB	H	2B	3B	HR	RBI	BB	SO	OBP	SLG		Avg	AB	H	2B	3B	HR	RBI	BB	SO	OBP	SLG
vs. Left	.286	7	2	1	0	0	0	0	3	.286	.429	Scoring Posn	.500	4	2	1	0	0	3	0	0	.500	.750
vs. Right	.257	35	9	2	0	5	9	3	9	.333	.743	Close & Late	.000	4	0	0	0	0	0	0	1	.000	.000

Terry Steinbach — Athletics

Age 32 – Bats Right

	Avg	G	AB	R	H	2B	3B	HR	RBI	BB	SO	HBP	GDP	SB	CS	OBP	SLG	IBB	SH	SF	#Pit	#P/PA	GB	FB	G/F
1993 Season	.285	104	389	47	111	19	1	10	43	25	65	3	13	3	3	.333	.416	1	0	1	1426	3.40	153	104	1.47
Last Five Years	.273	605	2116	214	577	98	6	44	262	141	325	17	73	8	11	.321	.387	11	7	19	8001	3.47	809	596	1.36

1993 Season

	Avg	AB	H	2B	3B	HR	RBI	BB	SO	OBP	SLG
vs. Left	.296	108	32	4	0	6	13	9	19	.350	.500
vs. Right	.281	281	79	15	1	4	30	16	46	.326	.384
Groundball	.247	97	24	4	1	1	6	3	18	.277	.340
Flyball	.329	73	24	4	0	1	9	6	10	.388	.425
Home	.326	184	60	13	1	5	26	13	31	.377	.489
Away	.249	205	51	6	0	5	17	12	34	.292	.351
Day	.244	160	39	9	1	3	20	12	28	.305	.369
Night	.314	229	72	10	0	7	23	13	37	.352	.450
Grass	.280	321	90	14	1	9	37	20	52	.328	.414
Turf	.309	68	21	5	0	1	6	5	13	.351	.426
First Pitch	.370	73	27	4	0	2	4	1	0	.378	.507
Ahead in Count	.341	91	31	8	0	4	12	14	0	.429	.560
Behind in Count	.194	170	33	3	1	3	21	0	60	.207	.276
Two Strikes	.199	156	31	4	1	3	18	10	65	.250	.295

	Avg	AB	H	2B	3B	HR	RBI	BB	SO	OBP	SLG
Scoring Posn	.194	98	19	4	1	3	33	12	19	.286	.347
Close & Late	.209	67	14	3	0	1	8	6	11	.284	.299
None on/out	.318	107	34	7	0	2	2	3	16	.336	.439
Batting #5	.270	263	71	15	1	4	26	16	47	.318	.380
Batting #6	.323	62	20	3	0	1	6	3	6	.354	.419
Other	.313	64	20	1	0	5	11	6	12	.371	.563
April	.300	70	21	5	0	2	8	4	5	.338	.457
May	.315	89	28	5	0	2	11	7	11	.371	.438
June	.271	96	26	6	1	1	8	7	25	.317	.385
July	.279	86	24	0	0	3	12	4	15	.311	.384
August	.250	48	12	3	0	2	4	3	9	.321	.438
September/October	.000	0	0	0	0	0	0	0	0	.000	.000
Pre-All Star	.301	289	87	16	1	7	34	19	48	.345	.436
Post-All Star	.240	100	24	3	0	3	9	6	17	.296	.360

1993 By Position

Position	Avg	AB	H	2B	3B	HR	RBI	BB	SO	OBP	SLG	G	GS	Innings	PO	A	E	DP	Fld Pct	Rng Fctr	In Zone	Outs	Zone Rtg	MLB Zone
As c	.281	320	90	18	1	5	34	19	51	.325	.391	86	82	707.2	422	38	5	9	.989	---	---	---	---	---
As 1b	.255	47	12	1	0	4	5	5	11	.340	.532	15	12	112.1	102	9	2	9	.982	---	23	16	.696	.834

Last Five Years

	Avg	AB	H	2B	3B	HR	RBI	BB	SO	OBP	SLG
vs. Left	.278	625	174	32	1	20	80	44	84	.326	.429
vs. Right	.270	1491	403	66	5	24	182	97	241	.318	.370
Groundball	.259	626	162	27	2	9	73	29	96	.294	.351
Flyball	.272	460	125	18	2	13	60	31	74	.317	.404
Home	.274	1019	279	47	3	17	127	73	146	.323	.376
Away	.272	1097	298	51	3	27	135	68	179	.318	.397
Day	.265	785	208	44	2	14	104	54	125	.313	.380
Night	.277	1331	369	54	4	30	158	87	200	.325	.391
Grass	.270	1757	474	75	4	36	217	122	254	.319	.378
Turf	.287	359	103	23	2	8	45	19	71	.329	.429
First Pitch	.319	354	113	16	1	7	54	4	0	.327	.429
Ahead in Count	.324	516	167	36	2	15	71	78	0	.409	.488
Behind in Count	.219	887	194	27	2	12	91	0	287	.226	.294
Two Strikes	.205	868	178	31	3	15	92	56	325	.257	.300

	Avg	AB	H	2B	3B	HR	RBI	BB	SO	OBP	SLG
Scoring Posn	.276	533	147	24	3	12	217	51	81	.335	.400
Close & Late	.238	328	78	9	0	3	40	24	54	.295	.293
None on/out	.255	494	126	21	2	8	8	35	77	.307	.354
Batting #5	.292	1016	297	46	5	23	131	58	156	.332	.415
Batting #6	.263	555	146	28	0	12	72	38	89	.313	.378
Other	.246	545	134	24	1	9	59	45	80	.307	.343
April	.279	283	79	19	0	6	36	23	44	.338	.410
May	.279	408	114	18	1	10	45	27	57	.327	.402
June	.292	411	120	16	4	10	48	24	67	.333	.423
July	.311	347	108	22	1	6	55	17	52	.342	.432
August	.235	371	87	15	0	8	38	27	61	.292	.340
September/October	.233	296	69	8	0	4	40	23	44	.290	.301
Pre-All Star	.289	1224	354	59	5	29	145	80	188	.335	.417
Post-All Star	.250	892	223	39	1	15	117	61	137	.301	.346

Batter vs. Pitcher (career)

Hits Best Against	Avg	AB	H	2B	3B	HR	RBI	BB	SO	OBP	SLG
Scott Erickson	.583	12	7	1	0	0	0	0	0	.583	.667
Chuck Finley	.474	38	18	3	0	4	17	1	4	.487	.868
Kevin Tapani	.471	17	8	4	0	1	4	1	2	.500	.882
Dave Fleming	.417	12	5	1	0	1	1	2	1	.500	.750
Danny Darwin	.389	18	7	0	0	3	4	1	2	.421	.889

Hits Worst Against	Avg	AB	H	2B	3B	HR	RBI	BB	SO	OBP	SLG
Jeff Ballard	.063	16	1	0	0	0	0	1	1	.118	.063
Donn Pall	.091	11	1	0	0	0	0	1	2	.167	.091
Jaime Navarro	.100	10	1	0	0	0	2	1	2	.182	.100
Bobby Witt	.133	15	2	0	0	0	1	0	5	.133	.133
Ben McDonald	.133	15	2	0	0	0	0	0	3	.133	.133

Dave Stewart — Blue Jays

Age 37 – Pitches Right (flyball pitcher)

	ERA	W	L	Sv	G	GS	IP	BB	SO	Avg	H	2B	3B	HR	RBI	OBP	SLG	CG	ShO	Sup	QS	#P/S	SB	CS	GB	FB	G/F
1993 Season	4.44	12	8	0	26	26	162.0	72	96	.242	146	30	4	23	82	.325	.419	0	0	5.83	11	102	13	12	172	232	0.74
Last Five Years	3.74	78	49	0	164	164	1112.0	408	691	.251	1052	193	25	111	469	.319	.389	23	5	5.26	93	107	75	45	1290	1428	0.90

1993 Season

	ERA	W	L	Sv	G	GS	IP	H	HR	BB	SO
Home	4.01	6	4	0	13	13	85.1	69	14	35	56
Away	4.93	6	4	0	13	13	76.2	77	9	37	40
Day	3.64	5	2	0	7	7	47.0	33	8	16	27
Night	4.77	7	6	0	19	19	115.0	113	15	56	69
Grass	5.27	5	3	0	10	10	56.1	60	5	26	25
Turf	4.00	7	5	0	16	16	105.2	86	18	46	71
April	0.00	0	0	0	0	0	0.0	0	0	0	0
May	7.27	2	1	0	4	4	17.1	18	1	11	9
June	3.89	1	2	0	6	6	41.2	38	5	17	29
July	5.40	3	2	0	5	5	31.2	39	7	13	16
August	4.62	2	3	0	6	6	39.0	27	7	19	21
September/October	2.51	4	0	0	5	5	32.1	24	3	12	21
Starter	4.44	12	8	0	26	26	162.0	146	23	72	96
Reliever	0.00	0	0	0	0	0	0.0	0	0	0	0
0-3 Days Rest	0.00	0	0	0	0	0	0.0	0	0	0	0
4 Days Rest	3.70	8	5	0	15	15	97.1	83	14	36	55

	Avg	AB	H	2B	3B	HR	RBI	BB	SO	OBP	SLG
vs. Left	.245	269	66	16	2	8	36	36	44	.332	.409
vs. Right	.239	335	80	14	2	15	46	36	52	.318	.427
Inning 1-6	.234	521	122	24	4	18	69	66	89	.323	.399
Inning 7+	.289	83	24	6	0	5	13	6	7	.333	.542
None on	.233	356	83	17	4	13	13	44	52	.324	.413
Runners on	.254	248	63	13	0	10	69	28	44	.325	.427
Scoring Posn	.262	126	33	8	0	3	53	21	20	.358	.397
Close & Late	.250	24	6	0	0	2	5	0	4	.240	.500
None on/out	.220	150	33	10	1	4	4	20	20	.316	.380
vs. 1st Batr (relief)	.000	0	0	0	0	0	0	0	0	.000	.000
First Inning Pitched	.253	95	24	6	1	4	16	16	18	.363	.463
First 75 Pitches	.226	412	93	20	3	14	56	56	70	.321	.391
Pitch 76-90	.253	75	19	5	0	3	6	7	16	.317	.440
Pitch 91-105	.237	76	18	3	1	1	9	5	7	.280	.342
Pitch 106+	.390	41	16	2	0	5	11	4	3	.447	.805
First Pitch	.185	65	12	2	2	2	8	0	0	.185	.369

1993 Season

	ERA	W	L	Sv	G	GS	IP	H	HR	BB	SO
5+ Days Rest	5.57	4	3	0	11	11	64.2	63	9	36	41
Pre-All Star	4.69	4	4	0	12	12	71.0	68	9	32	42
Post-All Star	4.25	8	4	0	14	14	91.0	78	14	40	54

	Avg	AB	H	2B	3B	HR	RBI	BB	SO	OBP	SLG
Ahead in Count	.230	291	67	9	1	9	38	0	85	.237	.361
Behind in Count	.309	123	38	12	0	11	26	41	0	.482	.675
Two Strikes	.208	279	58	9	0	5	28	31	96	.292	.294

Last Five Years

	ERA	W	L	Sv	G	GS	IP	H	HR	BB	SO
Home	3.15	40	20	0	82	82	580.1	500	54	192	370
Away	4.38	38	29	0	82	82	531.2	552	57	216	321
Day	3.33	35	15	0	57	57	408.1	357	37	122	262
Night	3.98	43	34	0	107	107	703.2	695	74	286	429
Grass	3.58	61	33	0	124	124	850.0	794	77	304	531
Turf	4.26	17	16	0	40	40	262.0	258	34	104	160
April	3.59	13	4	0	21	21	145.1	137	11	55	70
May	3.80	12	8	0	26	26	166.0	158	16	67	103
June	4.34	12	10	0	30	30	201.1	188	21	78	130
July	4.18	12	7	0	26	26	174.1	186	24	55	116
August	3.77	14	13	0	31	31	217.0	196	25	81	133
September/October	2.81	15	7	0	30	30	208.0	187	14	72	139
Starter	3.74	78	49	0	164	164	1112.0	1052	111	408	691
Reliever	0.00	0	0	0	0	0	0.0	0	0	0	0
0-3 Days Rest	2.74	9	4	0	14	14	101.2	93	7	28	53
4 Days Rest	3.95	52	35	0	115	115	777.2	742	78	297	490
5+ Days Rest	3.48	17	10	0	35	35	232.2	217	26	83	148
Pre-All Star	3.92	41	25	0	85	85	565.1	533	57	213	331
Post-All Star	3.56	37	24	0	79	79	546.2	519	54	195	360

	Avg	AB	H	2B	3B	HR	RBI	BB	SO	OBP	SLG
vs. Left	.256	2053	526	98	12	47	240	219	284	.325	.384
vs. Right	.246	2134	526	95	13	64	229	189	407	.313	.393
Inning 1-6	.249	3474	864	164	24	88	406	340	585	.317	.386
Inning 7+	.264	713	188	29	1	23	63	68	106	.328	.404
None on	.247	2466	609	108	14	66	66	233	397	.317	.382
Runners on	.257	1721	443	85	11	45	403	175	294	.322	.398
Scoring Posn	.245	940	230	49	8	22	344	116	162	.319	.384
Close & Late	.272	305	83	9	1	9	30	37	46	.349	.397
None on/out	.250	1090	272	56	5	33	33	100	183	.317	.401
vs. 1st Batr (relief)	.000	0	0	0	0	0	0	0	0	.000	.000
First Inning Pitched	.282	628	177	35	5	16	88	74	96	.360	.430
First 75 Pitches	.244	2810	685	134	18	65	300	278	480	.314	.374
Pitch 76-90	.267	544	145	29	5	19	68	46	90	.321	.443
Pitch 91-105	.252	477	120	13	2	15	59	40	79	.311	.382
Pitch 106+	.287	356	102	17	0	12	42	44	42	.365	.435
First Pitch	.312	602	188	39	6	16	75	3	0	.324	.477
Ahead in Count	.207	1941	401	64	8	37	181	0	590	.211	.305
Behind in Count	.298	884	263	45	8	37	140	223	0	.437	.492
Two Strikes	.198	1912	378	66	8	33	155	182	691	.269	.292

Pitcher vs. Batter (since 1984)

Pitches Best Vs.	Avg	AB	H	2B	3B	HR	RBI	BB	SO	OBP	SLG
Don Slaught	.000	19	0	0	0	0	2	2	5	.091	.000
Gary DiSarcina	.000	12	0	0	0	0	0	1	3	.077	.000
Mike Macfarlane	.000	11	0	0	0	0	0	1	2	.083	.000
Gerald Perry	.000	10	0	0	0	0	0	1	2	.091	.000
Dave Clark	.059	17	1	1	0	0	1	0	4	.059	.118

Pitches Worst Vs.	Avg	AB	H	2B	3B	HR	RBI	BB	SO	OBP	SLG
Gregg Jefferies	.556	9	5	1	0	1	1	2	1	.636	1.000
Edgar Martinez	.500	18	9	3	0	0	1	6	1	.625	.667
Ken Griffey Jr	.400	35	14	4	0	4	9	3	1	.447	.857
Pat Kelly	.400	10	4	0	1	1	3	1	3	.455	.900
Danny Tartabull	.395	38	15	1	0	5	9	9	11	.511	.816

Dave Stieb — Royals

Age 36 – Pitches Right

	ERA	W	L	Sv	G	GS	IP	BB	SO	Avg	H	2B	3B	HR	RBI	OBP	SLG	CG	ShO	Sup	QS	#P/S	SB	CS	GB	FB	G/F
1993 Season	6.04	1	3	0	4	4	22.1	14	11	.300	27	1	1	1	15	.390	.367	0	0	3.63	2	103	3	1	36	27	1.33
Last Five Years	3.56	44	26	0	100	93	593.2	220	311	.238	520	91	10	37	232	.314	.339	7	4	4.40	55	95	28	26	867	624	1.39

1993 Season

	ERA	W	L	Sv	G	GS	IP	H	HR	BB	SO
Home	6.06	1	2	0	3	3	16.1	19	1	11	10
Away	6.00	0	1	0	1	1	6.0	8	0	3	1

	Avg	AB	H	2B	3B	HR	RBI	BB	SO	OBP	SLG
vs. Left	.222	45	10	1	0	0	6	10	5	.357	.244
vs. Right	.378	45	17	0	1	1	9	4	6	.429	.489

Last Five Years

	ERA	W	L	Sv	G	GS	IP	H	HR	BB	SO
Home	3.99	20	17	0	50	47	288.2	269	19	110	163
Away	3.16	24	9	0	50	46	305.0	251	18	110	148
Day	4.21	15	11	0	38	35	218.0	196	15	88	115
Night	3.19	29	15	0	62	58	375.2	324	22	132	196
Grass	3.15	21	8	0	42	39	259.2	210	16	101	134
Turf	3.88	23	18	0	58	54	334.0	310	21	119	177
April	4.10	8	5	0	17	17	101.0	96	8	36	58
May	3.94	9	10	0	24	24	155.1	141	9	54	68
June	5.42	8	4	0	16	16	83.0	90	8	42	38
July	2.01	7	2	0	17	11	85.0	57	3	35	41
August	3.22	7	4	0	14	13	86.2	67	4	30	53
September/October	2.29	5	1	0	12	12	82.2	69	5	23	53
Starter	3.61	43	26	0	93	93	576.1	505	37	214	304
Reliever	2.08	1	0	0	7	0	17.1	15	0	6	7
0-3 Days Rest	9.00	0	1	0	3	3	11.0	16	1	7	5
4 Days Rest	3.51	22	17	0	48	48	307.2	247	23	101	175
5+ Days Rest	3.49	21	8	0	42	42	257.2	242	13	106	124
Pre-All Star	4.06	27	20	0	63	60	368.1	343	25	142	182
Post-All Star	2.76	17	6	0	37	33	225.1	177	12	78	129

	Avg	AB	H	2B	3B	HR	RBI	BB	SO	OBP	SLG
vs. Left	.253	1124	284	47	3	21	131	121	133	.328	.356
vs. Right	.222	1063	236	44	7	16	101	99	178	.299	.322
Inning 1-6	.243	1904	463	83	8	33	209	193	273	.319	.347
Inning 7+	.201	283	57	8	2	4	23	27	38	.282	.286
None on	.218	1279	279	45	6	24	24	140	188	.306	.319
Runners on	.265	908	241	46	4	13	208	80	123	.325	.368
Scoring Posn	.273	498	136	29	2	7	190	51	64	.336	.382
Close & Late	.181	138	25	5	0	2	10	13	19	.266	.261
None on/out	.210	553	116	16	3	11	11	63	72	.301	.309
vs. 1st Batr (relief)	.200	5	1	0	0	0	0	2	0	.429	.200
First Inning Pitched	.234	359	84	14	2	6	44	41	50	.313	.334
First 75 Pitches	.236	1667	394	74	6	30	181	172	231	.315	.342
Pitch 76-90	.262	271	71	11	3	5	27	22	48	.324	.380
Pitch 91-105	.229	188	43	3	1	1	18	23	22	.311	.271
Pitch 106+	.197	61	12	3	0	1	6	3	10	.258	.295
First Pitch	.267	315	84	10	3	4	36	3	0	.283	.356
Ahead in Count	.200	917	183	31	3	11	77	0	262	.213	.276
Behind in Count	.295	508	150	31	1	17	80	130	0	.440	.461
Two Strikes	.172	918	158	26	3	12	73	87	311	.255	.246

Pitcher vs. Batter (since 1984)

Pitches Best Vs.	Avg	AB	H	2B	3B	HR	RBI	BB	SO	OBP	SLG
Brady Anderson	.000	15	0	0	0	0	0	3	6	.167	.000
Carlos Baerga	.000	9	0	0	0	0	0	2	0	.182	.000
Steve Lyons	.040	25	1	1	0	0	0	1	7	.077	.080
Rob Deer	.043	23	1	0	0	0	0	3	10	.154	.043
Darnell Coles	.077	13	1	0	0	0	2	1	1	.143	.077

Pitches Worst Vs.	Avg	AB	H	2B	3B	HR	RBI	BB	SO	OBP	SLG
Geno Petralli	.476	21	10	2	0	0	1	5	1	.577	.571
Rene Gonzales	.385	13	5	1	0	1	4	0	1	.385	.692
Gene Larkin	.385	13	5	1	0	1	1	0	3	.385	.692
Wally Joyner	.375	40	15	3	0	4	8	4	3	.432	.750
Jose Canseco	.364	33	12	8	0	2	9	3	9	.405	.788

Kurt Stillwell — Angels

Age 29 – Bats Both

	Avg	G	AB	R	H	2B	3B	HR	RBI	BB	SO	HBP	GDP	SB	CS	OBP	SLG	IBB	SH	SF	#Pit	#P/PA	GB	FB	G/F
1993 Season	.231	79	182	11	42	6	2	1	14	15	33	1	4	6	3	.290	.302	2	3	2	792	3.90	69	43	1.60
Last Five Years	.249	589	1915	202	477	93	17	19	194	155	271	10	32	22	16	.305	.345	19	21	22	7495	3.53	722	577	1.25

1993 Season

	Avg	AB	H	2B	3B	HR	RBI	BB	SO	OBP	SLG		Avg	AB	H	2B	3B	HR	RBI	BB	SO	OBP	SLG
vs. Left	.160	25	4	0	0	0	0	3	5	.276	.160	Scoring Posn	.237	38	9	2	0	0	13	8	5	.354	.289
vs. Right	.242	157	38	6	2	1	14	12	28	.292	.325	Close & Late	.125	48	6	0	0	1	4	4	14	.189	.188
Home	.250	84	21	4	0	1	9	9	16	.326	.333	None on/out	.209	43	9	2	1	1	1	2	9	.244	.372
Away	.214	98	21	2	2	0	5	6	17	.257	.276	Batting #7	.230	87	20	6	0	1	8	7	14	.287	.333
First Pitch	.333	12	4	1	0	0	0	1	0	.385	.417	Batting #8	.229	48	11	0	1	0	3	3	9	.264	.271
Ahead in Count	.304	46	14	2	1	1	8	10	0	.429	.457	Other	.234	47	11	0	1	0	3	5	10	.321	.277
Behind in Count	.190	84	16	1	0	0	3	0	28	.198	.202	Pre-All Star	.217	115	25	4	0	1	9	10	22	.286	.278
Two Strikes	.159	88	14	2	0	0	1	4	33	.204	.182	Post-All Star	.254	67	17	2	2	0	5	5	11	.297	.343

Last Five Years

	Avg	AB	H	2B	3B	HR	RBI	BB	SO	OBP	SLG		Avg	AB	H	2B	3B	HR	RBI	BB	SO	OBP	SLG
vs. Left	.242	495	120	19	8	3	55	44	67	.307	.331	Scoring Posn	.256	469	120	20	8	5	168	63	65	.330	.365
vs. Right	.251	1420	357	74	9	16	139	111	204	.305	.350	Close & Late	.202	336	68	11	1	2	17	35	60	.277	.259
Groundball	.264	607	160	27	6	6	59	46	83	.316	.357	None on/out	.249	429	107	29	6	7	7	35	67	.309	.394
Flyball	.213	394	84	19	5	5	35	35	62	.274	.325	Batting #2	.255	440	112	31	3	1	44	48	50	.332	.345
Home	.244	929	227	46	9	8	111	84	137	.305	.339	Batting #8	.249	547	136	21	3	6	46	42	89	.299	.331
Away	.254	986	250	47	8	11	83	71	134	.306	.351	Other	.247	928	229	41	11	12	104	65	132	.296	.353
Day	.258	523	135	32	2	4	44	51	70	.322	.350	April	.297	236	70	17	2	2	23	17	42	.342	.411
Night	.246	1392	342	61	15	15	150	104	201	.299	.343	May	.260	419	109	18	2	5	41	44	61	.330	.348
Grass	.240	954	229	43	5	8	76	78	133	.297	.321	June	.241	382	92	18	3	2	36	29	58	.296	.319
Turf	.258	961	248	50	12	11	118	77	138	.314	.369	July	.196	245	48	9	3	4	28	17	27	.245	.306
First Pitch	.313	233	73	16	2	4	33	13	0	.357	.451	August	.263	293	77	11	5	3	32	19	43	.304	.365
Ahead in Count	.314	516	162	35	7	7	73	89	0	.411	.450	September/October	.238	340	81	20	2	3	34	29	40	.303	.335
Behind in Count	.177	802	142	22	3	5	46	0	241	.180	.231	Pre-All Star	.254	1147	291	57	8	9	114	97	169	.311	.341
Two Strikes	.166	782	130	26	5	3	48	50	271	.217	.224	Post-All Star	.242	768	186	36	9	10	80	58	102	.296	.352

Batter vs. Pitcher (career)

Hits Best Against	Avg	AB	H	2B	3B	HR	RBI	BB	SO	OBP	SLG	Hits Worst Against	Avg	AB	H	2B	3B	HR	RBI	BB	SO	OBP	SLG
Barry Jones	.545	11	6	1	0	0	2	0	1	.545	.636	John Smoltz	.000	13	0	0	0	0	1	0	3	.000	.000
Jose Rijo	.455	11	5	1	0	0	0	0	2	.455	.545	Bud Black	.000	12	0	0	0	0	0	0	5	.000	.000
Doug Drabek	.400	10	4	2	1	0	2	1	1	.455	.800	Jack McDowell	.000	10	0	0	0	0	1	2	1	.154	.000
Orel Hershiser	.391	23	9	3	1	0	2	3	2	.462	.609	Doug Jones	.000	9	0	0	0	0	0	2	3	.182	.000
Mark Williamson	.308	13	4	0	1	1	2	1	1	.357	.692	Jim Gott	.091	11	1	0	0	0	0	0	3	.091	.091

Kevin Stocker — Phillies

Age 24 – Bats Both

	Avg	G	AB	R	H	2B	3B	HR	RBI	BB	SO	HBP	GDP	SB	CS	OBP	SLG	IBB	SH	SF	#Pit	#P/PA	GB	FB	G/F
1993 Season	.324	70	259	46	84	12	3	2	31	30	43	8	8	5	0	.409	.417	11	4	1	1041	3.45	80	65	1.23

1993 Season

	Avg	AB	H	2B	3B	HR	RBI	BB	SO	OBP	SLG		Avg	AB	H	2B	3B	HR	RBI	BB	SO	OBP	SLG
vs. Left	.395	81	32	5	0	0	7	13	9	.479	.457	Scoring Posn	.229	70	16	2	1	1	28	16	13	.402	.329
vs. Right	.292	178	52	7	3	2	24	17	34	.377	.399	Close & Late	.292	48	14	2	1	0	8	3	5	.358	.375
Home	.302	126	38	4	1	1	10	15	24	.395	.373	None on/out	.387	62	24	4	0	0	0	9	9	.472	.452
Away	.346	133	46	8	2	1	21	15	19	.424	.459	Batting #2	.500	10	5	0	1	0	1	0	1	.500	.700
First Pitch	.293	41	12	0	0	0	3	10	0	.444	.293	Batting #8	.317	249	79	12	2	2	30	30	42	.406	.406
Ahead in Count	.483	60	29	1	2	1	7	14	0	.592	.617	Other	.000	0	0	0	0	0	0	0	0	.000	.000
Behind in Count	.219	105	23	7	0	0	9	0	39	.241	.286	Pre-All Star	.375	24	9	0	1	1	2	2	3	.423	.583
Two Strikes	.200	110	22	8	1	0	13	6	43	.261	.291	Post-All Star	.319	235	75	12	2	1	29	28	40	.408	.400

Todd Stottlemyre — Blue Jays

Age 29 – Pitches Right

	ERA	W	L	Sv	G	GS	IP	BB	SO	Avg	H	2B	3B	HR	RBI	OBP	SLG	CG	ShO	Sup	QS	#P/S	SB	CS	GB	FB	G/F
1993 Season	4.84	11	12	0	30	28	176.2	69	98	.292	204	45	7	11	92	.353	.424	1	1	5.40	9	98	24	7	240	211	1.14
Last Five Years	4.27	58	55	0	152	140	900.1	320	490	.267	924	167	24	81	408	.332	.399	12	3	5.12	66	97	109	34	1245	1077	1.16

1993 Season

	ERA	W	L	Sv	G	GS	IP	H	HR	BB	SO		Avg	AB	H	2B	3B	HR	RBI	BB	SO	OBP	SLG
Home	4.18	6	5	0	15	14	92.2	91	6	36	57	vs. Left	.305	374	114	28	3	7	50	45	48	.375	.452
Away	5.57	5	7	0	15	14	84.0	113	5	33	41	vs. Right	.278	324	90	17	4	4	42	24	50	.328	.392
Day	3.90	5	2	0	10	9	64.2	60	6	25	37	Inning 1-6	.302	610	184	42	6	10	85	64	82	.366	.439
Night	5.38	6	10	0	20	19	112.0	144	5	44	61	Inning 7+	.227	88	20	3	1	1	7	5	16	.263	.318
Grass	5.86	4	5	0	12	11	63.0	88	4	30	26	None on	.299	361	108	24	6	5	5	31	51	.356	.440
Turf	4.28	7	7	0	18	17	113.2	116	7	39	72	Runners on	.285	337	96	21	1	6	87	38	47	.351	.407
April	4.33	3	2	0	5	5	35.1	44	2	10	18	Scoring Posn	.275	200	55	14	1	5	81	32	27	.361	.430
May	5.00	1	2	0	4	4	18.0	25	3	10	13	Close & Late	.200	25	5	1	0	0	1	2	2	.259	.240
June	3.94	1	1	0	4	2	16.0	19	0	4	13	None on/out	.345	174	60	13	3	3	3	12	26	.390	.506
July	5.13	0	2	0	5	5	33.1	35	2	13	15	vs. 1st Batr (relief)	.000	2	0	0	0	0	0	0	0	.000	.000
August	5.77	3	2	0	6	6	34.1	44	3	13	14	First Inning Pitched	.254	114	29	3	2	3	17	15	23	.338	.395

1993 Season

	ERA	W	L	Sv	G	GS	IP	H	HR	BB	SO
September/October	4.54	3	3	0	6	6	39.2	37	1	19	25
Starter	4.93	11	12	0	28	28	171.2	201	11	69	92
Reliever	1.80	0	0	0	2	0	5.0	3	0	0	6
0-3 Days Rest	0.00	0	0	0	0	0	0.0	0	0	0	0
4 Days Rest	5.25	7	8	0	17	17	104.2	134	8	47	52
5+ Days Rest	4.43	4	4	0	11	11	67.0	67	3	22	40
Pre-All Star	4.45	5	7	0	15	13	83.0	101	6	28	53
Post-All Star	5.19	6	5	0	15	15	93.2	103	5	41	45

	Avg	AB	H	2B	3B	HR	RBI	BB	SO	OBP	SLG
First 75 Pitches	.297	509	151	30	5	9	70	49	78	.356	.428
Pitch 76-90	.304	92	28	8	2	1	10	12	9	.381	.467
Pitch 91-105	.271	70	19	5	0	0	9	6	6	.325	.343
Pitch 106+	.222	27	6	2	0	1	3	2	5	.276	.407
First Pitch	.316	98	31	8	0	5	24	3	0	.324	.551
Ahead in Count	.288	264	76	15	2	1	26	0	75	.293	.371
Behind in Count	.357	185	66	15	1	3	26	40	0	.467	.497
Two Strikes	.240	267	64	13	3	2	24	26	98	.310	.333

Last Five Years

	ERA	W	L	Sv	G	GS	IP	H	HR	BB	SO
Home	4.15	33	24	0	75	70	473.1	473	43	152	261
Away	4.41	25	31	0	77	70	427.0	451	38	168	229
Day	4.59	16	18	0	47	43	272.2	282	31	104	144
Night	4.13	42	37	0	105	97	627.2	642	50	216	346
Grass	4.09	20	21	0	57	53	323.1	323	32	127	177
Turf	4.37	38	34	0	95	87	577.0	601	49	193	313
April	4.48	11	8	0	28	21	142.2	149	10	62	82
May	4.61	6	9	0	22	20	125.0	125	15	53	75
June	3.71	10	7	0	20	18	128.2	138	12	33	56
July	4.50	6	9	0	23	23	134.0	143	8	56	79
August	4.17	12	10	0	29	29	183.2	187	17	56	95
September/October	4.20	13	12	0	30	29	186.1	182	19	60	103
Starter	4.28	57	54	0	140	140	875.1	900	81	310	476
Reliever	3.96	1	1	0	12	0	25.0	24	0	10	14
0-3 Days Rest	2.19	0	0	0	2	2	12.1	10	1	5	4
4 Days Rest	4.54	37	32	0	82	82	507.1	534	56	184	279
5+ Days Rest	3.97	20	22	0	56	56	355.2	356	24	121	193
Pre-All Star	4.29	29	28	0	77	66	436.2	462	40	164	241
Post-All Star	4.25	29	27	0	75	74	463.2	462	41	156	249

	Avg	AB	H	2B	3B	HR	RBI	BB	SO	OBP	SLG
vs. Left	.285	1696	484	85	13	39	193	171	180	.352	.420
vs. Right	.249	1764	440	82	11	42	215	149	310	.313	.380
Inning 1-6	.268	2987	801	144	22	76	372	290	422	.336	.407
Inning 7+	.260	473	123	20	2	5	36	30	68	.306	.349
None on	.267	1969	525	102	15	38	38	168	272	.331	.392
Runners on	.268	1491	399	65	9	43	370	152	218	.334	.410
Scoring Posn	.268	824	221	46	4	21	311	110	116	.348	.410
Close & Late	.253	198	50	8	1	2	15	16	34	.312	.333
None on/out	.296	888	263	45	7	21	21	63	111	.348	.434
vs. 1st Batr (relief)	.000	10	0	0	0	0	0	2	0	.167	.000
First Inning Pitched	.254	558	142	21	3	24	86	61	92	.331	.432
First 75 Pitches	.267	2583	689	121	18	64	312	246	375	.334	.402
Pitch 76-90	.271	447	121	23	5	10	54	42	53	.337	.412
Pitch 91-105	.271	329	89	18	1	6	33	26	38	.326	.386
Pitch 106+	.248	101	25	5	0	1	9	6	24	.294	.327
First Pitch	.320	500	160	25	2	20	93	16	0	.351	.498
Ahead in Count	.220	1493	328	52	11	17	109	0	407	.228	.303
Behind in Count	.317	805	255	56	4	30	129	173	0	.433	.508
Two Strikes	.199	1418	282	53	8	14	97	131	490	.272	.277

Pitcher vs. Batter (career)

Pitches Best Vs.	Avg	AB	H	2B	3B	HR	RBI	BB	SO	OBP	SLG
Joe Carter	.000	11	0	0	0	0	0	0	2	.000	.000
Jeff Huson	.000	9	0	0	0	0	0	2	1	.182	.000
Cory Snyder	.063	16	1	0	0	0	1	1	5	.111	.063
Carlos Quintana	.083	12	1	0	0	0	0	0	2	.083	.083
Dante Bichette	.091	11	1	0	0	0	0	0	2	.091	.091

Pitches Worst Vs.	Avg	AB	H	2B	3B	HR	RBI	BB	SO	OBP	SLG
Mark McLemore	.538	13	7	2	1	0	3	0	0	.538	.846
Albert Belle	.500	22	11	2	0	2	7	2	4	.542	.864
Jose Canseco	.423	26	11	0	0	8	15	4	6	.500	1.346
Rafael Palmeiro	.414	29	12	3	2	3	8	6	3	.514	.966
Rickey Henderson	.364	11	4	0	0	2	2	7	2	.611	.909

Doug Strange — Rangers

Age 30 – Bats Both

	Avg	G	AB	R	H	2B	3B	HR	RBI	BB	SO	HBP	GDP	SB	CS	OBP	SLG	IBB	SH	SF	#Pit	#P/PA	GB	FB	G/F
1993 Season	.256	145	484	58	124	29	0	7	60	43	69	3	12	6	4	.318	.360	3	8	4	1783	3.29	173	143	1.21
Career (1989-1993)	.236	264	783	81	185	35	1	9	80	70	121	5	20	11	7	.301	.318	5	13	5	2943	3.36	289	225	1.28

1993 Season

	Avg	AB	H	2B	3B	HR	RBI	BB	SO	OBP	SLG
vs. Left	.248	109	27	6	0	0	13	6	19	.282	.303
vs. Right	.259	375	97	23	0	7	47	37	50	.329	.376
Groundball	.239	88	21	5	0	0	8	10	12	.316	.295
Flyball	.280	93	26	6	0	1	17	5	11	.314	.376
Home	.296	257	76	20	0	4	37	23	34	.358	.420
Away	.211	227	48	9	0	3	23	20	35	.273	.291
Day	.175	103	18	5	0	0	12	8	16	.237	.223
Night	.278	381	106	24	0	7	48	35	53	.340	.396
Grass	.279	402	112	25	0	6	54	39	58	.344	.386
Turf	.146	82	12	4	0	1	6	4	11	.186	.232
First Pitch	.279	104	29	7	0	0	9	3	0	.306	.346
Ahead in Count	.292	106	31	8	0	5	24	21	0	.406	.509
Behind in Count	.227	194	44	13	0	1	20	0	61	.232	.309
Two Strikes	.156	173	27	7	0	1	10	19	69	.246	.214

	Avg	AB	H	2B	3B	HR	RBI	BB	SO	OBP	SLG
Scoring Posn	.270	126	34	11	0	3	52	15	18	.342	.429
Close & Late	.329	70	23	4	0	2	10	9	7	.400	.471
None on/out	.319	119	38	7	0	2	2	9	20	.367	.429
Batting #7	.223	139	31	9	0	1	9	12	17	.289	.309
Batting #8	.297	192	57	10	0	2	26	23	25	.367	.380
Other	.235	153	36	10	0	4	25	8	27	.280	.379
April	.280	25	7	2	0	1	4	0	6	.296	.480
May	.278	79	22	6	0	1	11	5	6	.329	.392
June	.281	96	27	3	0	2	11	7	14	.327	.375
July	.198	91	18	3	0	0	9	10	11	.282	.231
August	.215	107	23	7	0	2	12	10	21	.280	.336
September/October	.314	86	27	8	0	1	13	11	11	.392	.442
Pre-All Star	.267	232	62	12	0	4	29	15	31	.313	.371
Post-All Star	.246	252	62	17	0	3	31	28	38	.323	.349

1993 By Position

Position	Avg	AB	H	2B	3B	HR	RBI	BB	SO	OBP	SLG	G	GS	Innings	PO	A	E	DP	Fld Pct	Rng Fctr	In Zone	Outs	Zone Rtg	MLB Zone
As Pinch Hitter	.333	12	4	1	0	1	3	0	4	.333	.667	13	0	---	---	---	---	---	---	---	---	---	---	---
As 2b	.258	446	115	26	0	6	54	41	62	.320	.357	135	122	1101.0	272	361	13	81	.980	5.17	388	345	.889	.895

Career (1989-1993)

	Avg	AB	H	2B	3B	HR	RBI	BB	SO	OBP	SLG
vs. Left	.229	175	40	7	0	0	14	12	29	.275	.269
vs. Right	.238	608	145	28	1	9	66	58	92	.309	.332
Groundball	.230	174	40	5	0	0	12	18	25	.306	.259
Flyball	.242	161	39	7	1	2	25	11	26	.292	.335
Home	.258	414	107	24	0	5	50	40	60	.329	.353
Away	.211	369	78	11	1	4	30	30	61	.269	.279
Day	.187	214	40	7	0	2	21	20	38	.259	.248

	Avg	AB	H	2B	3B	HR	RBI	BB	SO	OBP	SLG
Scoring Posn	.262	191	50	12	1	3	70	23	28	.339	.382
Close & Late	.252	135	34	4	1	2	14	14	16	.322	.341
None on/out	.293	188	55	9	0	3	3	16	31	.348	.388
Batting #7	.221	213	47	10	1	2	18	15	27	.275	.305
Batting #8	.249	333	83	14	0	3	36	38	53	.324	.318
Other	.232	237	55	11	0	4	26	17	41	.291	.329
April	.286	28	8	2	0	1	4	1	6	.323	.464

Career (1989-1993)	Avg	AB	H	2B	3B	HR	RBI	BB	SO	OBP	SLG		Avg	AB	H	2B	3B	HR	RBI	BB	SO	OBP	SLG
Night	.255	569	145	28	1	7	59	50	83	.317	.344	May	.231	143	33	7	0	2	16	11	15	.290	.322
Grass	.247	647	160	29	1	8	72	63	101	.317	.332	June	.277	101	28	3	0	2	11	9	14	.333	.366
Turf	.184	136	25	6	0	1	8	7	20	.224	.250	July	.196	138	27	4	0	0	11	10	20	.253	.225
First Pitch	.266	158	42	9	0	0	13	5	0	.293	.323	August	.212	184	39	8	1	2	17	15	35	.270	.299
Ahead in Count	.313	160	50	11	0	6	31	37	0	.439	.494	September/October	.265	189	50	11	0	2	21	24	31	.352	.354
Behind in Count	.196	332	65	13	1	2	28	0	104	.199	.259	Pre-All Star	.244	307	75	13	0	5	34	24	41	.301	.336
Two Strikes	.139	303	42	7	0	2	15	28	121	.216	.182	Post-All Star	.231	476	110	22	1	4	46	46	80	.302	.307

Batter vs. Pitcher (career)																							
Hits Best Against	Avg	AB	H	2B	3B	HR	RBI	BB	SO	OBP	SLG	Hits Worst Against	Avg	AB	H	2B	3B	HR	RBI	BB	SO	OBP	SLG
Todd Stottlemyre	.444	9	4	0	0	0	0	2	0	.545	.444	Alex Fernandez	.077	13	1	0	0	0	0	0	2	.077	.077
												Jose Mesa	.200	10	2	0	0	0	1	1	1	.273	.200

Darryl Strawberry — Dodgers

Age 32 – Bats Left (flyball hitter)

	Avg	G	AB	R	H	2B	3B	HR	RBI	BB	SO	HBP	GDP	SB	CS	OBP	SLG	IBB	SH	SF	#Pit	#P/PA	GB	FB	G/F
1993 Season	.140	32	100	12	14	2	0	5	12	16	19	2	1	1	0	.267	.310	1	0	2	476	3.97	33	41	0.80
Last Five Years	.248	500	1779	279	442	76	6	104	321	241	393	11	20	40	21	.339	.473	37	0	16	7927	3.87	541	554	0.98

1993 Season	Avg	AB	H	2B	3B	HR	RBI	BB	SO	OBP	SLG		Avg	AB	H	2B	3B	HR	RBI	BB	SO	OBP	SLG
vs. Left	.143	21	3	1	0	0	1	8	5	.367	.190	Scoring Posn	.083	24	2	0	0	1	7	10	4	.333	.208
vs. Right	.139	79	11	1	0	5	11	8	14	.233	.342	Close & Late	.067	15	1	0	0	0	0	5	3	.333	.067

Last Five Years	Avg	AB	H	2B	3B	HR	RBI	BB	SO	OBP	SLG		Avg	AB	H	2B	3B	HR	RBI	BB	SO	OBP	SLG
vs. Left	.245	710	174	31	2	31	116	82	171	.323	.425	Scoring Posn	.266	526	140	20	3	32	220	104	121	.381	.498
vs. Right	.251	1069	268	45	4	73	205	159	222	.350	.505	Close & Late	.206	301	62	10	0	13	44	47	80	.316	.369
Groundball	.259	580	150	26	2	36	117	71	116	.342	.497	None on/out	.230	405	93	14	0	22	22	43	88	.307	.427
Flyball	.245	383	94	19	0	30	79	53	116	.337	.530	Batting #3	.240	396	95	18	3	21	67	55	95	.332	.460
Home	.265	859	228	37	4	59	182	110	177	.349	.524	Batting #4	.245	1264	310	53	2	78	233	171	279	.337	.475
Away	.233	920	214	39	2	45	139	131	216	.330	.426	Other	.311	119	37	5	1	5	21	15	19	.380	.496
Day	.257	537	138	25	3	25	99	70	108	.345	.454	April	.247	352	87	19	2	15	50	59	75	.359	.440
Night	.245	1242	304	51	3	79	222	171	285	.337	.481	May	.199	297	59	9	0	19	48	38	84	.290	.421
Grass	.247	1314	325	59	5	78	237	170	278	.335	.478	June	.280	200	56	5	0	16	43	31	35	.385	.545
Turf	.252	465	117	17	1	26	84	71	115	.351	.460	July	.248	310	77	13	2	20	57	38	72	.331	.497
First Pitch	.300	220	66	9	2	20	56	20	0	.363	.632	August	.267	311	83	16	1	18	63	45	60	.357	.498
Ahead in Count	.352	421	148	24	0	38	113	123	0	.495	.679	September/October	.259	309	80	14	1	16	60	30	67	.321	.466
Behind in Count	.169	785	133	28	2	23	79	0	326	.175	.298	Pre-All Star	.245	937	230	40	3	56	161	136	208	.344	.474
Two Strikes	.169	885	150	28	2	29	99	82	393	.243	.304	Post-All Star	.252	842	212	36	3	48	160	105	185	.333	.473

Batter vs. Pitcher (since 1984)																							
Hits Best Against	Avg	AB	H	2B	3B	HR	RBI	BB	SO	OBP	SLG	Hits Worst Against	Avg	AB	H	2B	3B	HR	RBI	BB	SO	OBP	SLG
Bill Gullickson	.433	30	13	3	0	4	10	6	5	.500	.933	Trevor Wilson	.000	16	0	0	0	0	1	2	5	.111	.000
Mark Portugal	.421	19	8	1	0	3	6	3	7	.500	.947	Mitch Williams	.000	12	0	0	0	0	0	2	7	.143	.000
Bob Walk	.381	21	8	1	0	4	12	5	4	.464	1.000	Rob Dibble	.000	10	0	0	0	0	0	2	6	.167	.000
Pete Smith	.357	14	5	0	0	3	4	5	3	.526	1.000	Rob Murphy	.083	12	1	0	0	0	1	0	7	.077	.083
Neal Heaton	.316	19	6	1	0	4	8	1	2	.350	1.000	Ramon Martinez	.083	12	1	0	0	0	1	0	4	.083	.083

William Suero — Brewers

Age 27 – Bats Right (flyball hitter)

	Avg	G	AB	R	H	2B	3B	HR	RBI	BB	SO	HBP	GDP	SB	CS	OBP	SLG	IBB	SH	SF	#Pit	#P/PA	GB	FB	G/F
1993 Season	.286	15	14	0	4	0	0	0	0	1	3	0	1	0	1	.333	.286	0	0	0	56	3.73	4	5	0.80
Career (1992-1993)	.233	33	30	4	7	1	0	0	0	3	4	1	3	1	2	.324	.267	0	0	0	119	3.50	10	12	0.83

1993 Season	Avg	AB	H	2B	3B	HR	RBI	BB	SO	OBP	SLG		Avg	AB	H	2B	3B	HR	RBI	BB	SO	OBP	SLG
vs. Left	.364	11	4	0	0	0	0	1	1	.417	.364	Scoring Posn	.000	2	0	0	0	0	0	1	1	.333	.000
vs. Right	.000	3	0	0	0	0	0	0	2	.000	.000	Close & Late	.333	3	1	0	0	0	0	0	0	.333	.333

B.J. Surhoff — Brewers

Age 29 – Bats Left (groundball hitter)

	Avg	G	AB	R	H	2B	3B	HR	RBI	BB	SO	HBP	GDP	SB	CS	OBP	SLG	IBB	SH	SF	#Pit	#P/PA	GB	FB	G/F
1993 Season	.274	148	552	66	151	38	3	7	79	36	47	2	7	12	9	.318	.391	5	4	5	2003	3.34	215	186	1.16
Last Five Years	.268	691	2447	283	657	114	16	27	323	174	187	8	52	63	44	.314	.361	21	32	41	8936	3.31	1070	696	1.54

1993 Season	Avg	AB	H	2B	3B	HR	RBI	BB	SO	OBP	SLG		Avg	AB	H	2B	3B	HR	RBI	BB	SO	OBP	SLG
vs. Left	.274	186	51	13	1	3	33	14	15	.328	.403	Scoring Posn	.338	130	44	13	2	1	71	14	16	.389	.492
vs. Right	.273	366	100	25	2	4	46	22	32	.312	.385	Close & Late	.253	91	23	4	0	0	10	7	9	.300	.297
Groundball	.290	124	36	11	1	2	20	4	9	.313	.444	None on/out	.278	126	35	7	0	4	4	7	11	.326	.429
Flyball	.168	107	18	2	0	0	7	4	8	.198	.187	Batting #3	.279	233	65	20	1	5	39	19	16	.327	.438
Home	.289	263	76	19	2	4	40	15	25	.325	.422	Batting #6	.232	142	33	7	2	2	14	4	17	.253	.352

1993 Season

	Avg	AB	H	2B	3B	HR	RBI	BB	SO	OBP	SLG		Avg	AB	H	2B	3B	HR	RBI	BB	SO	OBP	SLG
Away	.260	289	75	19	1	3	39	21	22	.311	.363	Other	.299	177	53	11	0	0	26	13	14	.354	.362
Day	.275	182	50	13	1	1	24	18	14	.337	.374	April	.203	59	12	3	0	0	7	7	9	.288	.254
Night	.273	370	101	25	2	6	55	18	33	.308	.400	May	.163	80	13	3	0	0	7	6	8	.221	.200
Grass	.270	466	126	33	3	6	64	33	42	.319	.393	June	.275	102	28	4	1	0	11	4	8	.312	.333
Turf	.291	86	25	5	0	1	15	3	5	.311	.384	July	.347	101	35	9	2	2	14	3	10	.365	.535
First Pitch	.363	80	29	5	2	0	21	2	0	.373	.475	August	.290	107	31	7	0	3	22	11	6	.353	.439
Ahead in Count	.276	163	45	11	0	2	20	22	0	.358	.380	September/October	.311	103	32	12	0	2	18	5	6	.333	.485
Behind in Count	.223	206	46	11	1	5	24	0	39	.229	.359	Pre-All Star	.250	280	70	13	1	1	33	17	27	.297	.314
Two Strikes	.242	182	44	11	1	4	27	12	47	.294	.379	Post-All Star	.298	272	81	25	2	6	46	19	20	.339	.471

1993 By Position

Position	Avg	AB	H	2B	3B	HR	RBI	BB	SO	OBP	SLG	G	GS	Innings	PO	A	E	DP	Fld Pct	Rng Fctr	In Zone	Outs	Zone Rtg	MLB Zone
As 3b	.266	443	118	28	3	5	62	29	38	.312	.377	121	116	1013.2	101	217	17	19	.949	2.82	277	243	.877	.834
As lf	.286	35	10	4	0	0	7	4	1	.059	.400	12	8	75.0	17	1	1	0	.947	2.16	19	18	.947	.818
As rf	.320	50	16	3	0	2	10	1	6	.315	.500	14	12	106.0	20	1	0	0	1.000	1.78	24	20	.833	.826

Last Five Years

	Avg	AB	H	2B	3B	HR	RBI	BB	SO	OBP	SLG		Avg	AB	H	2B	3B	HR	RBI	BB	SO	OBP	SLG
vs. Left	.282	602	170	28	4	9	98	39	60	.325	.387	Scoring Posn	.301	615	185	35	9	7	290	61	49	.347	.421
vs. Right	.264	1845	487	86	12	18	225	135	127	.311	.353	Close & Late	.258	411	106	16	1	5	56	29	43	.301	.338
Groundball	.293	639	187	39	4	4	104	41	38	.332	.385	None on/out	.246	560	138	22	0	9	9	35	44	.293	.334
Flyball	.274	514	141	19	6	5	52	42	41	.328	.364	Batting #3	.264	512	135	28	4	6	89	32	34	.299	.369
Home	.277	1190	330	54	8	17	167	96	92	.330	.379	Batting #7	.259	634	164	31	4	3	75	50	51	.312	.334
Away	.260	1257	327	60	8	10	156	78	95	.300	.344	Other	.275	1301	358	55	8	18	159	92	102	.321	.371
Day	.270	749	202	37	3	5	93	61	57	.323	.347	April	.184	294	54	8	1	5	39	24	32	.241	.269
Night	.268	1698	455	77	13	22	230	113	130	.310	.367	May	.232	366	85	11	1	4	44	25	28	.278	.301
Grass	.272	2079	565	99	14	25	265	155	155	.320	.369	June	.285	467	133	22	3	3	53	22	33	.318	.364
Turf	.250	368	92	15	2	2	58	19	32	.280	.318	July	.298	406	121	22	3	3	49	24	28	.334	.389
First Pitch	.339	342	116	12	5	4	74	9	0	.348	.439	August	.287	436	125	22	3	6	63	37	34	.341	.392
Ahead in Count	.281	733	206	38	4	15	111	99	0	.361	.405	September/October	.291	478	139	29	5	6	75	42	32	.342	.410
Behind in Count	.234	932	218	35	5	7	93	0	160	.236	.305	Pre-All Star	.253	1264	320	50	5	13	152	81	100	.296	.331
Two Strikes	.231	796	184	30	3	4	75	66	187	.292	.291	Post-All Star	.285	1183	337	64	11	14	171	93	87	.334	.393

Batter vs. Pitcher (career)

Hits Best Against	Avg	AB	H	2B	3B	HR	RBI	BB	SO	OBP	SLG	Hits Worst Against	Avg	AB	H	2B	3B	HR	RBI	BB	SO	OBP	SLG
Joe Grahe	.556	9	5	1	0	0	2	3	0	.667	.667	Bud Black	.000	10	0	0	0	0	1	0	0	.000	.000
Hipolito Pichardo	.545	11	6	3	0	0	2	0	0	.545	.818	Nolan Ryan	.053	19	1	0	0	0	0	1	3	.100	.053
Jim Abbott	.529	17	9	2	0	0	2	1	0	.556	.647	Bill Gullickson	.077	13	1	0	0	0	1	1	0	.133	.077
Charles Nagy	.500	10	5	1	0	0	3	1	0	.545	.600	Greg Swindell	.077	13	1	0	0	0	1	0	1	.077	.077
Scott Sanderson	.400	15	6	2	0	1	3	0	2	.375	.733	Kevin Appier	.077	13	1	0	0	0	0	2	2	.200	.077

Rick Sutcliffe — Orioles

Age 38 – Pitches Right

	ERA	W	L	Sv	G	GS	IP	BB	SO	Avg	H	2B	3B	HR	RBI	OBP	SLG	CG	ShO	Sup	QS	#P/S	SB	CS	GB	FB	G/F
1993 Season	5.75	10	10	0	29	28	166.0	74	80	.314	212	44	5	23	102	.385	.496	3	0	5.37	12	98	17	8	231	221	1.05
Last Five Years	4.50	48	43	0	124	121	750.1	274	401	.273	786	138	22	67	335	.335	.405	13	3	4.71	62	98	88	24	1052	889	1.18

1993 Season

	ERA	W	L	Sv	G	GS	IP	H	HR	BB	SO		Avg	AB	H	2B	3B	HR	RBI	BB	SO	OBP	SLG
Home	4.50	6	6	0	16	15	100.0	121	10	32	48	vs. Left	.307	342	105	19	3	11	43	42	35	.386	.477
Away	7.64	4	4	0	13	13	66.0	91	13	42	32	vs. Right	.320	334	107	25	2	12	59	32	45	.384	.515
Day	6.20	1	2	0	5	4	24.2	36	6	9	11	Inning 1-6	.305	568	173	38	5	21	90	68	71	.383	.500
Night	5.67	9	8	0	24	24	141.1	176	17	65	69	Inning 7+	.361	108	39	6	0	2	12	6	9	.395	.472
Grass	5.36	8	8	0	24	23	137.2	179	18	54	68	None on	.303	370	112	23	3	9	9	38	41	.372	.454
Turf	7.62	2	2	0	5	5	28.1	33	5	20	12	Runners on	.327	306	100	21	2	14	93	36	39	.399	.546
April	5.13	2	2	0	5	5	33.1	36	4	21	19	Scoring Posn	.337	163	55	12	1	9	77	28	20	.431	.589
May	4.10	3	0	0	6	6	37.1	39	6	16	16	Close & Late	.303	33	10	0	0	1	3	3	3	.361	.394
June	5.18	3	1	0	5	5	33.0	41	4	14	16	None on/out	.277	166	46	9	0	5	5	17	18	.348	.422
July	7.61	0	3	0	5	5	23.2	35	5	9	14	vs. 1st Batr (relief)	.000	1	0	0	0	0	0	0	0	.000	.000
August	7.77	1	3	0	5	4	22.0	34	2	11	7	First Inning Pitched	.383	128	49	12	0	7	34	17	11	.459	.641
September/October	6.48	1	1	0	3	3	16.2	27	2	3	8	First 75 Pitches	.319	476	152	34	4	19	78	59	54	.396	.527
Starter	5.66	10	10	0	28	28	163.2	207	23	72	79	Pitch 76-90	.270	74	20	3	0	0	5	8	9	.360	.311
Reliever	11.57	0	0	0	1	0	2.1	5	0	2	1	Pitch 91-105	.273	77	21	4	1	2	8	4	14	.309	.429
0-3 Days Rest	0.00	0	0	0	0	0	0.0	0	0	0	0	Pitch 106+	.388	49	19	3	0	2	11	3	3	.423	.571
4 Days Rest	6.80	7	7	0	18	18	98.0	140	13	45	44	First Pitch	.415	82	34	6	1	3	15	4	0	.442	.622
5+ Days Rest	3.97	3	3	0	10	10	65.2	67	10	27	35	Ahead in Count	.235	243	57	9	2	4	23	0	68	.247	.337
Pre-All Star	5.27	8	4	0	18	18	107.2	127	17	55	56	Behind in Count	.341	214	73	13	1	12	37	38	0	.443	.579
Post-All Star	6.63	2	6	0	11	10	58.1	85	6	19	24	Two Strikes	.221	249	55	10	3	4	21	32	80	.312	.333

Last Five Years

	ERA	W	L	Sv	G	GS	IP	H	HR	BB	SO		Avg	AB	H	2B	3B	HR	RBI	BB	SO	OBP	SLG
Home	4.41	23	23	0	66	63	398.0	401	36	129	225	vs. Left	.272	1545	420	71	15	39	177	165	195	.339	.413
Away	4.60	25	20	0	58	58	352.1	385	31	145	176	vs. Right	.273	1339	366	67	7	28	158	109	206	.330	.397
Day	4.33	14	19	0	49	46	280.2	296	24	96	168	Inning 1-6	.266	2435	648	119	21	56	288	246	337	.333	.401
Night	4.60	34	24	0	75	75	469.2	490	43	178	233	Inning 7+	.307	449	138	19	1	11	47	28	64	.346	.428
Grass	4.88	30	34	0	92	89	542.2	586	56	188	294	None on	.272	1669	454	80	12	36	36	143	223	.333	.399

Last Five Years

	ERA	W	L	Sv	G	GS	IP	H	HR	BB	SO
Turf	3.51	18	9	0	32	32	207.2	200	11	86	107
April	3.87	10	7	0	18	18	125.2	117	8	44	77
May	5.22	10	6	0	24	23	139.2	150	18	49	62
June	3.94	9	5	0	16	16	109.2	117	6	35	53
July	5.15	2	12	0	18	17	108.1	120	11	38	65
August	3.33	9	6	0	25	24	148.2	141	10	63	81
September/October	5.70	8	7	0	23	23	118.1	141	14	45	63
Starter	4.48	48	43	0	121	121	746.0	778	67	272	399
Reliever	8.31	0	0	0	3	0	4.1	8	0	2	2
0-3 Days Rest	6.75	3	4	0	9	9	49.1	52	7	20	33
4 Days Rest	4.62	28	28	0	78	78	487.1	521	43	167	247
5+ Days Rest	3.61	17	11	0	34	34	209.1	205	17	85	119
Pre-All Star	4.44	30	22	0	65	63	411.2	428	36	139	213
Post-All Star	4.57	18	21	0	59	58	338.2	358	31	135	188

	Avg	AB	H	2B	3B	HR	RBI	BB	SO	OBP	SLG
Runners on	.273	1215	332	58	10	31	299	131	178	.338	.414
Scoring Posn	.266	662	176	28	6	21	263	103	114	.352	.421
Close & Late	.267	180	48	5	0	5	18	12	30	.308	.378
None on/out	.288	754	217	34	3	19	19	61	83	.344	.416
vs. 1st Batr (relief)	.667	3	2	0	0	0	1	0	0	.667	.667
First Inning Pitched	.310	500	155	29	6	13	91	52	61	.370	.470
First 75 Pitches	.268	2082	559	103	16	46	229	206	294	.334	.400
Pitch 76-90	.263	334	88	14	2	6	43	35	39	.339	.371
Pitch 91-105	.279	290	81	9	3	9	36	16	46	.313	.424
Pitch 106+	.326	178	58	12	1	6	27	17	22	.380	.506
First Pitch	.317	391	124	19	3	8	58	15	0	.337	.442
Ahead in Count	.220	1092	240	34	10	14	84	0	342	.223	.308
Behind in Count	.306	831	254	50	4	26	109	137	0	.402	.469
Two Strikes	.206	1143	236	34	10	18	90	122	401	.284	.301

Pitcher vs. Batter (since 1984)

Pitches Best Vs.	Avg	AB	H	2B	3B	HR	RBI	BB	SO	OBP	SLG
Mariano Duncan	.000	14	0	0	0	0	0	0	4	.000	.000
George Brett	.000	12	0	0	0	0	0	0	0	.000	.000
Thomas Howard	.000	10	0	0	0	0	1	0	1	.000	.000
Luis Polonia	.056	18	1	0	1	0	1	0	1	.056	.167
Cecil Fielder	.083	12	1	0	0	0	1	0	0	.083	.083

Pitches Worst Vs.	Avg	AB	H	2B	3B	HR	RBI	BB	SO	OBP	SLG
Scott Livingstone	.636	11	7	2	0	0	3	0	0	.636	.818
Rickey Henderson	.583	12	7	0	0	1	3	7	2	.737	.833
Edgar Martinez	.571	14	8	3	1	0	1	3	2	.611	.929
Rafael Palmeiro	.545	11	6	2	0	2	7	3	1	.643	1.273
Larry Walker	.375	8	3	1	0	1	1	5	0	.615	.875

Dale Sveum — Athletics

Age 30 – Bats Both (flyball hitter)

	Avg	G	AB	R	H	2B	3B	HR	RBI	BB	SO	HBP	GDP	SB	CS	OBP	SLG	IBB	SH	SF	#Pit	#P/PA	GB	FB	G/F
1993 Season	.177	30	79	12	14	2	1	2	6	16	21	0	2	0	0	.316	.304	1	1	0	403	4.20	24	27	0.89
Last Five Years	.211	262	711	88	150	41	2	11	89	88	197	3	18	3	6	.296	.321	5	8	11	3333	4.06	194	219	0.89

1993 Season

	Avg	AB	H	2B	3B	HR	RBI	BB	SO	OBP	SLG
vs. Left	.133	15	2	0	0	0	1	3	5	.278	.133
vs. Right	.188	64	12	2	1	2	5	13	16	.325	.344
Scoring Posn	.158	19	3	1	1	0	4	5	5	.333	.316
Close & Late	.211	19	4	0	1	0	2	2	5	.286	.316

Last Five Years

	Avg	AB	H	2B	3B	HR	RBI	BB	SO	OBP	SLG
vs. Left	.215	260	56	15	1	3	25	35	80	.310	.315
vs. Right	.208	451	94	26	1	8	64	53	117	.289	.324
Groundball	.271	207	56	16	1	2	25	30	39	.358	.386
Flyball	.156	147	23	4	0	3	20	15	58	.229	.245
Home	.187	364	68	19	0	5	42	48	93	.279	.280
Away	.236	347	82	22	2	6	47	40	104	.315	.363
Day	.218	239	52	14	0	4	25	24	66	.288	.326
Night	.208	472	98	27	2	7	64	64	131	.300	.318
Grass	.224	539	121	29	0	9	70	64	136	.305	.328
Turf	.169	172	29	12	2	2	19	24	61	.270	.297
First Pitch	.314	70	22	6	0	0	11	5	0	.364	.400
Ahead in Count	.362	138	50	11	0	5	29	44	0	.511	.551
Behind in Count	.126	341	43	15	1	2	26	0	152	.127	.194
Two Strikes	.113	389	44	15	0	5	34	39	197	.193	.190
Scoring Posn	.242	194	47	16	2	2	77	23	54	.313	.376
Close & Late	.237	156	37	7	2	1	20	13	46	.294	.327
None on/out	.201	159	32	12	0	3	3	26	45	.317	.333
Batting #8	.201	154	31	4	0	4	12	29	44	.328	.305
Batting #9	.217	299	65	25	1	2	43	33	86	.294	.328
Other	.209	258	54	12	1	5	34	26	67	.279	.322
April	.152	66	10	1	0	0	5	6	18	.237	.167
May	.214	173	37	9	2	3	24	31	53	.332	.341
June	.157	140	22	6	0	2	12	22	46	.270	.243
July	.247	93	23	7	0	3	13	5	21	.287	.419
August	.215	65	14	4	0	1	11	5	16	.268	.323
September/October	.253	174	44	14	0	2	24	19	43	.320	.368
Pre-All Star	.192	432	83	18	2	7	47	60	129	.291	.292
Post-All Star	.240	279	67	23	0	4	42	28	68	.305	.366

Batter vs. Pitcher (career)

Hits Best Against	Avg	AB	H	2B	3B	HR	RBI	BB	SO	OBP	SLG
Mark Eichhorn	.500	14	7	1	0	1	6	0	1	.500	.786
Paul Kilgus	.364	11	4	0	0	1	3	0	1	.364	.636
Greg Cadaret	.364	11	4	2	0	0	2	2	6	.462	.545
Mark Gubicza	.333	12	4	1	1	0	3	5	4	.529	.583
John Farrell	.333	12	4	1	0	1	4	0	2	.333	.667

Hits Worst Against	Avg	AB	H	2B	3B	HR	RBI	BB	SO	OBP	SLG
Bud Black	.000	12	0	0	0	0	0	2	4	.143	.000
Randy Johnson	.000	8	0	0	0	0	0	3	4	.273	.000
Roger Clemens	.083	24	2	1	0	0	0	2	12	.154	.125
John Candelaria	.091	11	1	0	0	0	0	2	3	.231	.091
Jose Guzman	.125	24	3	1	0	0	2	0	8	.125	.167

Russ Swan — Mariners

Age 30 – Pitches Left (groundball pitcher)

	ERA	W	L	Sv	G	GS	IP	BB	SO	Avg	H	2B	3B	HR	RBI	OBP	SLG	GF	IR	IRS	Hld	SvOp	SB	CS	GB	FB	G/F
1993 Season	9.15	3	3	0	23	0	19.2	18	10	.316	25	3	0	2	14	.455	.430	6	20	1	5	0	1	1	37	15	2.47
Career (1989-1993)	4.63	14	21	11	156	20	258.2	117	106	.271	269	52	6	25	142	.348	.412	43	128	26	25	16	18	5	515	209	2.46

1993 Season

	ERA	W	L	Sv	G	GS	IP	H	HR	BB	SO
Home	3.72	2	2	0	12	0	9.2	8	0	7	5
Away	14.40	1	1	0	11	0	10.0	17	2	11	5

	Avg	AB	H	2B	3B	HR	RBI	BB	SO	OBP	SLG
vs. Left	.231	26	6	1	0	0	5	7	3	.412	.269
vs. Right	.358	53	19	2	0	2	9	11	7	.477	.509

Career (1989-1993)

	ERA	W	L	Sv	G	GS	IP	H	HR	BB	SO
Home	5.42	5	11	4	74	8	111.1	140	16	44	55
Away	4.03	9	10	7	82	12	147.1	129	9	73	51
Day	4.17	5	5	2	45	5	77.2	67	9	34	37

	Avg	AB	H	2B	3B	HR	RBI	BB	SO	OBP	SLG
vs. Left	.203	266	54	5	0	1	27	27	33	.278	.233
vs. Right	.297	725	215	47	6	24	115	90	73	.374	.477
Inning 1-6	.257	470	121	29	5	12	76	56	48	.337	.417

Career (1989-1993)

	ERA	W	L	Sv	G	GS	IP	H	HR	BB	SO
Night	4.82	9	16	9	111	15	181.0	202	16	83	69
Grass	3.84	7	8	7	65	9	117.1	101	10	58	42
Turf	5.29	7	13	4	91	11	141.1	168	15	59	64
April	4.61	3	5	2	21	6	52.2	48	2	23	22
May	6.00	3	4	0	28	4	48.0	56	6	27	22
June	3.33	3	2	2	33	4	54.0	57	4	18	22
July	3.15	2	4	6	24	1	34.1	30	5	10	15
August	8.19	0	4	1	20	2	29.2	42	7	19	11
September/October	3.38	3	2	0	30	3	40.0	36	1	20	14
Starter	5.27	4	11	0	20	20	100.2	100	11	44	38
Reliever	4.22	10	10	11	136	0	158.0	169	14	73	68
0 Days rest	2.21	4	2	2	33	0	36.2	25	0	21	16
1 or 2 Days rest	4.32	4	5	6	57	0	66.2	74	7	26	31
3+ Days rest	5.43	2	3	3	46	0	54.2	70	7	26	21
Pre-All Star	4.42	10	13	7	95	15	171.0	174	14	72	70
Post-All Star	5.03	4	8	4	61	5	87.2	95	11	45	36

	Avg	AB	H	2B	3B	HR	RBI	BB	SO	OBP	SLG
Inning 7+	.284	521	148	23	1	13	66	61	58	.359	.407
None on	.264	518	137	25	1	12	12	58	51	.340	.386
Runners on	.279	473	132	27	5	13	130	59	55	.358	.440
Scoring Posn	.267	296	79	13	3	8	113	39	42	.347	.412
Close & Late	.240	304	73	10	0	8	33	32	37	.311	.352
None on/out	.267	236	63	6	1	6	6	22	22	.332	.377
vs. 1st Batr (relief)	.303	119	36	5	0	2	21	9	14	.346	.395
First Inning Pitched	.278	475	132	20	2	8	65	50	56	.347	.379
First 15 Pitches	.279	455	127	20	2	9	56	45	42	.344	.391
Pitch 16-30	.259	232	60	12	0	4	31	35	30	.354	.362
Pitch 31-45	.282	110	31	6	1	4	23	17	14	.377	.464
Pitch 46+	.263	194	51	14	3	8	32	20	20	.333	.490
First Pitch	.286	161	46	9	1	4	28	11	0	.335	.429
Ahead in Count	.227	384	87	16	3	5	50	0	87	.230	.323
Behind in Count	.313	246	77	11	2	11	36	63	0	.450	.508
Two Strikes	.224	366	82	19	2	5	44	42	106	.308	.328

Pitcher vs. Batter (career)

Pitches Best Vs.	Avg	AB	H	2B	3B	HR	RBI	BB	SO	OBP	SLG
Lou Whitaker	.000	12	0	0	0	0	1	2	1	.143	.000
Don Mattingly	.091	11	1	0	0	0	1	3	2	.286	.091
Mike Greenwell	.154	13	2	0	0	0	1	1	3	.200	.154
Mickey Tettleton	.222	9	2	1	0	0	2	2	1	.333	.333
Wade Boggs	.231	13	3	0	0	0	3	0	0	.231	.231

Pitches Worst Vs.	Avg	AB	H	2B	3B	HR	RBI	BB	SO	OBP	SLG
Ruben Sierra	.417	12	5	1	0	0	1	0	1	.417	.500
Alan Trammell	.333	15	5	2	0	0	2	1	1	.353	.467
Dan Gladden	.333	12	4	1	1	0	3	1	0	.385	.583
Travis Fryman	.333	12	4	2	0	0	0	1	0	.385	.500
Cecil Fielder	.313	16	5	2	0	0	4	2	1	.389	.438

Bill Swift — Giants

Age 32 – Pitches Right (groundball pitcher)

	ERA	W	L	Sv	G	GS	IP	BB	SO	Avg	H	2B	3B	HR	RBI	OBP	SLG	CG	ShO	Sup	QS	#P/S	SB	CS	GB	FB	G/F
1993 Season	2.82	21	8	0	34	34	232.2	55	157	.226	195	30	1	18	72	.277	.326	1	1	5.88	23	92	12	11	440	141	3.12
Last Five Years	2.76	45	21	25	227	80	745.2	183	369	.246	688	102	9	38	260	.296	.330	4	3	4.67	52	88	23	21	1547	446	3.47

1993 Season

	ERA	W	L	Sv	G	GS	IP	H	HR	BB	SO
Home	2.35	11	4	0	16	16	111.0	86	7	29	75
Away	3.25	10	4	0	18	18	121.2	109	11	26	82
Day	3.39	12	5	0	19	19	130.0	113	13	31	84
Night	2.10	9	3	0	15	15	102.2	82	5	24	73
Grass	3.03	16	8	0	27	27	184.1	157	17	48	124
Turf	2.05	5	0	0	7	7	48.1	38	1	7	33
April	2.90	2	1	0	5	5	31.0	23	2	6	19
May	3.03	4	1	0	5	5	35.2	33	5	11	20
June	2.66	4	2	0	6	6	44.0	31	1	8	32
July	2.08	5	1	0	6	6	39.0	36	2	10	32
August	4.42	2	2	0	6	6	38.2	40	8	8	26
September/October	2.03	4	1	0	6	6	44.1	32	0	12	28
Starter	2.82	21	8	0	34	34	232.2	195	18	55	157
Reliever	0.00	0	0	0	0	0	0.0	0	0	0	0
0-3 Days Rest	1.20	2	0	0	2	2	15.0	5	0	5	6
4 Days Rest	2.74	14	4	0	21	21	144.1	120	14	36	100
5+ Days Rest	3.31	5	4	0	11	11	73.1	70	4	14	51
Pre-All Star	2.93	11	5	0	18	18	123.0	102	9	29	80
Post-All Star	2.71	10	3	0	16	16	109.2	93	9	26	77

	Avg	AB	H	2B	3B	HR	RBI	BB	SO	OBP	SLG
vs. Left	.268	471	126	20	0	12	47	42	64	.331	.386
vs. Right	.177	390	69	10	1	6	25	13	93	.209	.254
Inning 1-6	.220	723	159	23	1	15	59	51	135	.277	.317
Inning 7+	.261	138	36	7	0	3	13	4	22	.280	.377
None on	.227	534	121	13	1	13	13	32	103	.275	.328
Runners on	.226	327	74	17	0	5	59	23	54	.280	.324
Scoring Posn	.218	165	36	10	0	2	50	17	34	.292	.315
Close & Late	.216	74	16	4	0	1	6	3	11	.247	.311
None on/out	.187	225	42	4	0	1	1	13	41	.241	.218
vs. 1st Batr (relief)	.000	0	0	0	0	0	0	0	0	.000	.000
First Inning Pitched	.217	115	25	3	0	3	10	13	17	.302	.322
First 75 Pitches	.214	678	145	23	1	14	50	51	129	.273	.313
Pitch 76-90	.252	119	30	5	0	1	14	4	19	.274	.319
Pitch 91-105	.352	54	19	2	0	2	7	0	6	.364	.500
Pitch 106+	.100	10	1	0	0	1	1	0	3	.100	.400
First Pitch	.350	143	50	4	0	5	18	4	0	.362	.483
Ahead in Count	.144	369	53	9	1	6	26	0	136	.157	.222
Behind in Count	.292	209	61	13	0	4	18	34	0	.391	.411
Two Strikes	.141	341	48	7	1	4	22	17	157	.193	.202

Last Five Years

	ERA	W	L	Sv	G	GS	IP	H	HR	BB	SO
Home	2.68	22	12	10	109	40	366.0	330	19	93	175
Away	2.84	23	9	15	118	40	379.2	358	19	90	194
Day	2.68	25	9	6	77	36	305.1	269	19	69	144
Night	2.82	20	12	19	150	44	440.1	419	19	114	225
Grass	2.82	28	16	14	115	53	447.1	408	27	120	247
Turf	2.68	17	5	11	112	27	298.1	280	11	63	122
April	2.13	6	1	1	21	10	88.2	81	3	20	44
May	3.51	10	4	5	41	15	133.1	132	10	40	69
June	3.50	7	4	1	36	14	118.1	109	6	29	54
July	2.26	12	5	4	37	18	147.2	144	7	34	71
August	2.69	3	5	4	38	15	127.1	114	11	30	60
September/October	2.42	7	2	10	54	8	130.1	108	1	30	71
Starter	2.96	38	16	0	80	80	514.0	471	33	127	264
Reliever	2.33	7	5	25	147	0	231.2	217	5	56	105
0-3 Days Rest	1.73	3	0	0	4	4	26.0	14	0	7	10
4 Days Rest	2.80	24	11	0	47	47	302.1	279	24	79	167
5+ Days Rest	3.39	11	5	0	29	29	185.2	178	9	41	87
Pre-All Star	3.26	26	11	7	110	45	384.0	375	23	104	184
Post-All Star	2.24	19	10	18	117	35	361.2	313	15	79	185

	Avg	AB	H	2B	3B	HR	RBI	BB	SO	OBP	SLG
vs. Left	.275	1424	391	61	4	25	145	116	146	.331	.376
vs. Right	.217	1369	297	41	5	13	115	67	223	.258	.283
Inning 1-6	.247	1890	466	72	6	27	184	136	249	.301	.334
Inning 7+	.246	903	222	30	3	11	76	47	120	.286	.322
None on	.245	1590	389	52	3	21	21	99	230	.294	.321
Runners on	.249	1203	299	50	6	17	239	84	139	.298	.342
Scoring Posn	.221	643	142	28	3	7	206	67	84	.295	.306
Close & Late	.247	466	115	14	0	6	41	31	63	.298	.315
None on/out	.235	697	164	17	1	4	4	34	99	.277	.280
vs. 1st Batr (relief)	.218	133	29	6	1	0	14	7	16	.261	.278
First Inning Pitched	.251	766	192	30	3	6	101	62	98	.309	.321
First 75 Pitches	.243	2415	587	89	7	31	222	168	314	.296	.324
Pitch 76-90	.254	236	60	8	1	2	21	12	36	.295	.322
Pitch 91-105	.324	105	34	3	1	3	11	2	12	.343	.457
Pitch 106+	.189	37	7	2	0	2	6	1	7	.211	.405
First Pitch	.313	501	157	13	2	10	55	16	0	.334	.407
Ahead in Count	.184	1098	202	38	3	11	82	0	322	.193	.254
Behind in Count	.288	701	202	34	2	11	75	95	0	.374	.389
Two Strikes	.173	1002	173	27	4	10	68	71	369	.234	.238

Pitcher vs. Batter (career)																						
Pitches Best Vs.	Avg	AB	H	2B	3B	HR	RBI	BB	SO	OBP	SLG	Pitches Worst Vs.	Avg	AB	H	2B	3B	HR	RBI	BB	SO	OBP	SLG
Joe Oliver	.063	16	1	0	0	0	0	0	1	.063	.063	Dave Henderson	.615	13	8	1	0	0	2	1	0	.600	.692
Mariano Duncan	.067	15	1	0	0	0	1	0	3	.067	.067	Dave Magadan	.600	10	6	1	0	0	3	3	0	.692	.700
Marquis Grissom	.077	13	1	0	0	0	0	0	1	.077	.077	Kent Hrbek	.500	26	13	3	0	1	5	5	1	.581	.731
Tim Teufel	.125	16	2	0	0	0	0	0	1	.125	.125	Darren Daulton	.500	14	7	3	0	2	5	1	2	.533	1.143
Darrin Fletcher	.133	15	2	0	0	0	0	0	1	.133	.133	Phil Plantier	.467	15	7	2	0	1	3	2	1	.529	.800

Greg Swindell — Astros

Age 29 – Pitches Left (flyball pitcher)

	ERA	W	L	Sv	G	GS	IP	BB	SO	Avg	H	2B	3B	HR	RBI	OBP	SLG	CG	ShO	Sup	QS	#P/S	SB	CS	GB	FB	G/F
1993 Season	4.16	12	13	0	31	30	190.1	40	124	.283	215	43	8	24	90	.318	.455	1	1	4.35	16	95	16	11	239	224	1.07
Last Five Years	3.61	58	52	0	157	155	1041.0	210	695	.269	1081	195	28	102	411	.304	.407	21	6	4.33	92	98	63	56	1237	1282	0.96

1993 Season																						
	ERA	W	L	Sv	G	GS	IP	H	HR	BB	SO		Avg	AB	H	2B	3B	HR	RBI	BB	SO	OBP	SLG
Home	4.90	3	9	0	14	13	82.2	98	12	17	48	vs. Left	.318	129	41	11	3	3	11	8	20	.355	.519
Away	3.59	9	4	0	17	17	107.2	117	12	23	76	vs. Right	.275	632	174	32	5	21	79	32	104	.310	.441
Day	5.35	6	5	0	13	13	74.0	91	15	15	45	Inning 1-6	.270	664	179	34	8	21	78	39	107	.310	.440
Night	3.40	6	8	0	18	17	116.1	124	9	25	79	Inning 7+	.371	97	36	9	0	3	12	1	17	.378	.557
Grass	4.34	7	1	0	11	11	66.1	77	9	15	52	None on	.281	445	125	28	5	12	12	20	70	.313	.447
Turf	4.06	5	12	0	20	19	124.0	138	15	25	72	Runners on	.285	316	90	15	3	12	78	20	54	.324	.465
April	3.08	4	1	0	5	5	38.0	35	2	4	19	Scoring Posn	.259	185	48	7	1	7	65	13	29	.303	.422
May	7.71	1	3	0	6	6	30.1	44	7	9	25	Close & Late	.327	49	16	3	0	0	3	1	14	.340	.388
June	3.82	1	3	0	6	6	37.2	41	5	9	16	None on/out	.277	195	54	15	3	6	6	9	28	.312	.477
July	6.75	0	1	0	2	1	8.0	12	1	3	4	vs. 1st Batr (relief)	1.000	1	1	0	0	0	0	0	0	1.000	1.000
August	2.41	4	2	0	6	6	37.1	35	4	5	30	First Inning Pitched	.282	124	35	5	3	6	16	5	22	.310	.516
September/October	3.92	2	3	0	6	6	39.0	48	5	10	30	First 75 Pitches	.282	575	162	28	6	19	64	32	93	.320	.450
Starter	4.23	12	13	0	30	30	187.1	213	24	40	121	Pitch 76-90	.184	87	16	3	2	3	9	5	16	.228	.368
Reliever	0.00	0	0	0	1	0	3.0	2	0	0	3	Pitch 91-105	.371	70	26	10	0	2	11	1	7	.375	.600
0-3 Days Rest	7.20	0	1	0	1	1	5.0	7	2	0	5	Pitch 106+	.379	29	11	2	0	0	6	2	8	.419	.448
4 Days Rest	4.03	6	6	0	16	16	96.0	121	10	24	57	First Pitch	.275	131	36	8	0	3	15	3	0	.289	.405
5+ Days Rest	4.27	6	6	0	13	13	86.1	85	12	16	59	Ahead in Count	.233	374	87	14	5	9	37	0	109	.235	.369
Pre-All Star	4.95	6	8	0	18	18	111.0	130	15	25	61	Behind in Count	.336	125	42	10	1	7	19	14	0	.397	.600
Post-All Star	3.06	6	5	0	13	12	79.1	85	9	15	63	Two Strikes	.218	348	76	11	3	9	28	23	124	.269	.345

Last Five Years																						
	ERA	W	L	Sv	G	GS	IP	H	HR	BB	SO		Avg	AB	H	2B	3B	HR	RBI	BB	SO	OBP	SLG
Home	3.42	30	28	0	81	80	553.0	556	49	109	354	vs. Left	.269	683	184	37	6	11	59	37	111	.307	.389
Away	3.84	28	24	0	76	75	488.0	525	53	101	341	vs. Right	.268	3342	897	158	22	91	352	173	584	.303	.411
Day	3.56	18	14	0	43	42	285.1	301	35	47	184	Inning 1-6	.264	3333	880	159	25	88	362	181	583	.301	.406
Night	3.63	40	38	0	114	113	755.2	780	67	163	511	Inning 7+	.290	692	201	36	3	14	49	29	112	.317	.412
Grass	3.75	40	30	0	103	103	679.0	712	70	137	477	None on	.263	2482	653	125	19	62	62	115	443	.298	.404
Turf	3.36	18	22	0	54	52	362.0	369	32	73	218	Runners on	.277	1543	428	70	9	40	349	95	252	.314	.412
April	3.43	9	7	0	23	23	155.0	149	10	32	106	Scoring Posn	.264	845	223	31	5	19	290	64	151	.306	.380
May	3.80	9	9	0	28	28	187.1	195	22	37	120	Close & Late	.272	360	98	18	1	6	25	22	69	.313	.378
June	3.48	11	6	0	30	30	209.2	227	25	46	134	None on/out	.266	1082	288	66	13	35	35	39	189	.295	.448
July	2.94	11	8	0	23	22	156.0	141	12	33	107	vs. 1st Batr (relief)	.500	2	1	0	0	0	0	0	0	.500	.500
August	3.45	13	10	0	24	24	159.0	172	12	26	111	First Inning Pitched	.262	600	157	29	7	20	76	36	108	.304	.433
September/October	4.50	5	12	0	29	28	174.0	197	21	36	117	First 75 Pitches	.261	2943	767	134	21	72	291	168	519	.300	.394
Starter	3.63	58	52	0	155	155	1037.0	1079	102	210	690	Pitch 76-90	.286	539	154	31	4	20	64	19	86	.308	.469
Reliever	0.00	0	0	0	2	0	4.0	2	0	0	5	Pitch 91-105	.282	369	104	18	1	7	33	14	55	.304	.393
0-3 Days Rest	3.94	0	2	0	3	3	16.0	20	3	2	14	Pitch 106+	.322	174	56	12	2	3	23	9	35	.353	.466
4 Days Rest	3.72	36	29	0	96	96	631.2	678	68	143	423	First Pitch	.307	671	206	37	5	19	85	8	0	.313	.462
5+ Days Rest	3.47	22	21	0	56	56	389.1	381	31	65	253	Ahead in Count	.217	1979	429	76	14	28	153	0	622	.218	.312
Pre-All Star	3.53	34	24	0	89	89	609.1	620	61	126	398	Behind in Count	.320	723	231	43	4	36	105	98	0	.398	.539
Post-All Star	3.73	24	28	0	68	66	431.2	461	41	84	297	Two Strikes	.201	1798	362	68	8	27	126	104	695	.246	.293

Pitcher vs. Batter (career)																						
Pitches Best Vs.	Avg	AB	H	2B	3B	HR	RBI	BB	SO	OBP	SLG	Pitches Worst Vs.	Avg	AB	H	2B	3B	HR	RBI	BB	SO	OBP	SLG
Gary Redus	.000	16	0	0	0	0	0	2	3	.111	.000	Andres Galarraga	.545	11	6	2	0	1	5	1	2	.583	1.000
Mike Sharperson	.000	14	0	0	0	0	0	0	4	.000	.000	Carlton Fisk	.478	23	11	1	0	4	9	1	3	.500	1.043
Kirt Manwaring	.000	11	0	0	0	0	0	2	3	.154	.000	Marquis Grissom	.438	16	7	0	1	4	7	0	2	.438	1.313
Lonnie Smith	.063	16	1	0	0	0	0	0	2	.063	.063	Randy Milligan	.406	32	13	1	0	6	10	3	4	.457	1.000
B.J. Surhoff	.077	13	1	0	0	0	1	0	1	.077	.077	Dave Justice	.400	10	4	0	0	2	2	1	1	.455	1.000

Paul Swingle — Angels

Age 27 – Pitches Right

	ERA	W	L	Sv	G	GS	IP	BB	SO	Avg	H	2B	3B	HR	RBI	OBP	SLG	GF	IR	IRS	Hld	SvOp	SB	CS	GB	FB	G/F
1993 Season	8.38	0	1	0	9	0	9.2	6	6	.357	15	4	0	2	7	.429	.595	2	7	2	0	0	3	0	9	15	0.60

1993 Season																						
	ERA	W	L	Sv	G	GS	IP	H	HR	BB	SO		Avg	AB	H	2B	3B	HR	RBI	BB	SO	OBP	SLG
Home	13.50	0	0	0	4	0	3.1	5	0	4	1	vs. Left	.286	14	4	0	0	2	2	0	3	.286	.714
Away	5.68	0	1	0	5	0	6.1	10	2	2	5	vs. Right	.393	28	11	4	0	0	5	6	3	.486	.536

Jeff Tackett — Orioles

Age 28 – Bats Right (groundball hitter)

	Avg	G	AB	R	H	2B	3B	HR	RBI	BB	SO	HBP	GDP	SB	CS	OBP	SLG	IBB	SH	SF	#Pit	#P/PA	GB	FB	G/F
1993 Season	.172	38	87	8	15	3	0	0	9	13	28	0	5	0	0	.277	.207	0	2	1	419	4.07	34	13	2.62
Career (1991-1993)	.215	109	274	30	59	11	1	5	33	32	58	2	16	0	0	.297	.318	1	9	5	1252	3.89	115	67	1.72

1993 Season

	Avg	AB	H	2B	3B	HR	RBI	BB	SO	OBP	SLG		Avg	AB	H	2B	3B	HR	RBI	BB	SO	OBP	SLG
vs. Left	.263	19	5	0	0	0	2	3	6	.364	.263	Scoring Posn	.188	32	6	2	0	0	9	9	11	.357	.250
vs. Right	.147	68	10	3	0	0	7	10	22	.253	.191	Close & Late	.222	9	2	0	0	0	1	3	3	.417	.222

Frank Tanana — Yankees

Age 40 – Pitches Left

	ERA	W	L	Sv	G	GS	IP	BB	SO	Avg	H	2B	3B	HR	RBI	OBP	SLG	CG	ShO	Sup	QS	#P/S	SB	CS	GB	FB	G/F
1993 Season	4.35	7	17	0	32	32	202.2	55	116	.273	216	41	4	28	95	.326	.441	0	0	4.09	20	98	15	6	254	247	1.03
Last Five Years	4.23	52	62	1	164	158	1006.2	363	575	.270	1038	182	12	122	466	.335	.418	13	3	4.43	89	102	84	58	1300	1175	1.11

1993 Season

	ERA	W	L	Sv	G	GS	IP	H	HR	BB	SO		Avg	AB	H	2B	3B	HR	RBI	BB	SO	OBP	SLG
Home	4.62	3	8	0	15	15	99.1	112	13	25	64	vs. Left	.245	159	39	8	0	4	11	10	35	.292	.371
Away	4.09	4	9	0	17	17	103.1	104	15	30	52	vs. Right	.280	633	177	33	4	24	84	45	81	.334	.458
Day	3.91	3	8	0	12	12	78.1	76	11	23	40	Inning 1-6	.265	701	186	36	3	24	87	50	102	.321	.428
Night	4.63	4	9	0	20	20	124.1	140	17	32	76	Inning 7+	.330	91	30	5	1	4	8	5	14	.361	.538
Grass	4.25	5	11	0	22	22	144.0	158	19	38	89	None on	.270	500	135	28	3	17	17	19	69	.301	.440
Turf	4.60	2	6	0	10	10	58.2	58	9	17	27	Runners on	.277	292	81	13	1	11	78	36	47	.364	.442
April	1.71	2	0	0	3	3	21.0	22	0	8	10	Scoring Posn	.265	166	44	6	1	6	62	29	32	.376	.422
May	5.79	1	3	0	6	6	32.2	44	5	16	21	Close & Late	.383	47	18	2	0	2	4	2	6	.408	.553
June	5.35	1	4	0	6	6	33.2	43	3	10	23	None on/out	.237	215	51	8	0	9	9	4	25	.255	.400
July	4.67	1	3	0	5	5	34.2	30	7	7	15	vs. 1st Batr (relief)	.000	0	0	0	0	0	0	0	0	.000	.000
August	3.68	1	3	0	6	6	44.0	38	6	5	23	First Inning Pitched	.246	122	30	8	1	0	19	7	24	.306	.328
September/October	4.17	1	4	0	6	6	36.2	39	7	9	24	First 75 Pitches	.273	594	162	31	2	20	70	42	83	.328	.433
Starter	4.35	7	17	0	32	32	202.2	216	28	55	116	Pitch 76-90	.296	98	29	8	1	5	19	9	17	.349	.551
Reliever	0.00	0	0	0	0	0	0.0	0	0	0	0	Pitch 91-105	.253	75	19	2	0	2	4	3	10	.291	.360
0-3 Days Rest	3.86	0	1	0	1	1	7.0	7	2	2	3	Pitch 106+	.240	25	6	0	1	1	2	1	6	.269	.440
4 Days Rest	5.14	3	11	0	19	19	117.1	142	18	32	64	First Pitch	.243	115	28	6	0	5	17	6	0	.287	.426
5+ Days Rest	3.22	4	5	0	12	12	78.1	67	8	21	49	Ahead in Count	.224	344	77	11	2	8	35	0	95	.240	.337
Pre-All Star	5.02	4	8	0	17	17	100.1	127	12	38	61	Behind in Count	.363	182	66	14	2	14	32	26	0	.440	.692
Post-All Star	3.69	3	9	0	15	15	102.1	89	16	17	55	Two Strikes	.216	333	72	12	2	5	30	23	116	.273	.309

Last Five Years

	ERA	W	L	Sv	G	GS	IP	H	HR	BB	SO		Avg	AB	H	2B	3B	HR	RBI	BB	SO	OBP	SLG
Home	4.56	25	30	0	83	82	515.2	539	68	186	325	vs. Left	.247	651	161	28	1	14	63	49	106	.303	.358
Away	3.89	27	32	1	81	76	491.0	499	54	177	250	vs. Right	.274	3197	877	154	11	108	403	314	469	.341	.431
Day	4.10	18	27	1	56	55	358.0	361	44	131	186	Inning 1-6	.269	3302	888	152	9	102	408	300	498	.332	.413
Night	4.30	34	35	0	108	103	648.2	677	78	232	389	Inning 7+	.275	546	150	30	3	20	58	63	77	.353	.451
Grass	4.32	47	52	1	142	137	864.1	905	109	311	509	None on	.274	2306	632	115	7	77	77	172	328	.330	.430
Turf	3.67	5	10	0	22	21	142.1	133	13	52	66	Runners on	.263	1542	406	67	5	45	389	191	247	.342	.401
April	4.52	7	8	0	21	21	129.1	152	12	45	61	Scoring Posn	.258	814	210	32	2	22	324	137	141	.355	.383
May	4.78	9	10	0	29	28	171.1	184	27	72	96	Close & Late	.280	250	70	12	1	9	25	39	30	.380	.444
June	3.94	12	12	0	29	29	185.0	189	22	66	128	None on/out	.269	1019	274	48	2	38	38	64	142	.314	.432
July	4.58	5	9	0	25	24	145.1	147	12	54	71	vs. 1st Batr (relief)	.500	4	2	1	0	0	4	1	0	.667	.750
August	4.04	10	9	1	30	26	178.0	179	25	55	93	First Inning Pitched	.300	637	191	34	4	17	118	73	119	.373	.446
September/October	3.73	9	14	0	30	30	197.2	187	24	71	126	First 75 Pitches	.276	2731	755	126	7	88	337	251	409	.340	.424
Starter	4.21	51	62	0	158	158	994.0	1021	121	352	566	Pitch 76-90	.259	471	122	27	1	13	64	49	69	.328	.403
Reliever	5.68	1	0	1	6	0	12.2	17	1	11	9	Pitch 91-105	.263	384	101	14	2	12	38	31	51	.320	.404
0-3 Days Rest	3.86	0	1	0	1	1	7.0	7	2	2	3	Pitch 106+	.229	262	60	15	2	9	27	32	46	.321	.405
4 Days Rest	4.42	36	45	0	108	108	669.2	708	86	236	393	First Pitch	.294	472	139	24	1	18	64	20	0	.327	.464
5+ Days Rest	3.77	15	16	0	49	49	317.1	306	33	114	170	Ahead in Count	.206	1654	340	52	6	32	133	0	457	.213	.302
Pre-All Star	4.40	30	34	0	88	87	539.2	586	67	206	312	Behind in Count	.352	922	325	58	4	52	167	186	0	.458	.593
Post-All Star	4.03	22	28	1	76	71	467.0	452	55	157	263	Two Strikes	.200	1716	343	54	6	31	141	155	575	.269	.293

Pitcher vs. Batter (since 1984)

Pitches Best Vs.	Avg	AB	H	2B	3B	HR	RBI	BB	SO	OBP	SLG	Pitches Worst Vs.	Avg	AB	H	2B	3B	HR	RBI	BB	SO	OBP	SLG
Nelson Liriano	.000	10	0	0	0	0	0	1	3	.091	.000	Tim Naehring	.545	11	6	1	0	1	2	1	1	.583	.909
Rene Gonzales	.063	16	1	0	0	0	0	2	4	.167	.063	Alan Trammell	.444	9	4	0	0	1	1	2	0	.545	.778
Michael Huff	.077	13	1	0	0	0	0	1	2	.143	.077	George Brett	.410	39	16	5	0	4	9	3	5	.452	.846
Jim Leyritz	.077	13	1	0	0	0	0	0	1	.077	.077	Mickey Tettleton	.375	24	9	2	0	3	5	5	7	.467	.833
Stan Javier	.095	21	2	1	0	0	4	0	4	.095	.143	Rickey Henderson	.356	73	26	6	0	10	15	12	5	.447	.849

Kevin Tapani — Twins

Age 30 – Pitches Right

	ERA	W	L	Sv	G	GS	IP	BB	SO	Avg	H	2B	3B	HR	RBI	OBP	SLG	CG	ShO	Sup	QS	#P/S	SB	CS	GB	FB	G/F
1993 Season	4.43	12	15	0	36	35	225.2	57	150	.272	243	56	6	21	106	.318	.419	3	1	4.23	20	99	42	13	324	252	1.29
Career (1989-1993)	3.83	58	45	0	140	136	889.0	186	547	.262	897	192	24	76	354	.301	.399	12	4	5.13	79	95	100	36	1260	985	1.28

1993 Season

	ERA	W	L	Sv	G	GS	IP	H	HR	BB	SO		Avg	AB	H	2B	3B	HR	RBI	BB	SO	OBP	SLG
Home	4.39	3	9	0	14	14	98.1	102	8	28	66	vs. Left	.280	528	148	34	5	13	65	34	93	.322	.438
Away	4.45	9	6	0	22	21	127.1	141	13	29	84	vs. Right	.260	365	95	22	1	8	41	23	57	.313	.392
Day	3.23	6	5	0	14	13	86.1	85	6	18	64	Inning 1-6	.268	754	202	45	6	17	92	47	133	.314	.411
Night	5.17	6	10	0	22	22	139.1	158	15	39	86	Inning 7+	.295	139	41	11	0	4	14	10	17	.342	.460
Grass	4.19	8	4	0	16	15	92.1	99	10	24	65	None on	.270	523	141	30	2	14	14	31	90	.315	.415

1993 Season

	ERA	W	L	Sv	G	GS	IP	H	HR	BB	SO
Turf	4.59	4	11	0	20	20	133.1	144	11	33	85
April	7.85	0	3	0	5	5	28.2	34	5	10	17
May	3.95	2	3	0	7	7	41.0	50	3	11	30
June	6.00	1	3	0	5	5	30.0	40	2	12	21
July	5.45	2	2	0	7	6	34.2	40	5	6	20
August	3.11	2	2	0	5	5	37.2	32	4	8	24
September/October	2.35	5	2	0	7	7	53.2	47	2	10	38
Starter	4.47	12	15	0	35	35	223.2	241	21	57	149
Reliever	0.00	0	0	0	1	0	2.0	2	0	0	1
0-3 Days Rest	3.32	1	0	0	3	3	19.0	19	2	2	8
4 Days Rest	4.47	7	12	0	23	23	145.0	159	12	44	108
5+ Days Rest	4.83	4	3	0	9	9	59.2	63	7	11	33
Pre-All Star	5.79	3	11	0	20	19	110.1	139	11	36	77
Post-All Star	3.12	9	4	0	16	16	115.1	104	10	21	73

	Avg	AB	H	2B	3B	HR	RBI	BB	SO	OBP	SLG
Runners on	.276	370	102	26	4	7	92	26	60	.323	.424
Scoring Posn	.266	233	62	17	1	4	80	19	43	.320	.399
Close & Late	.264	72	19	6	0	1	8	6	7	.321	.389
None on/out	.276	232	64	14	1	7	7	11	48	.314	.435
vs. 1st Batr (relief)	.000	1	0	0	0	0	0	0	0	.000	.000
First Inning Pitched	.274	146	40	9	1	0	22	13	30	.338	.349
First 75 Pitches	.275	648	178	41	6	14	80	39	111	.319	.421
Pitch 76-90	.261	115	30	6	0	4	13	5	18	.292	.417
Pitch 91-105	.295	95	28	9	0	3	12	9	17	.356	.484
Pitch 106+	.200	35	7	0	0	0	1	4	4	.282	.200
First Pitch	.335	155	52	17	0	4	24	0	0	.342	.523
Ahead in Count	.216	402	87	20	4	7	34	0	127	.223	.338
Behind in Count	.315	168	53	9	1	9	29	29	0	.412	.542
Two Strikes	.200	390	78	17	4	4	26	28	150	.256	.295

Career (1989-1993)

	ERA	W	L	Sv	G	GS	IP	H	HR	BB	SO
Home	3.56	33	22	0	67	66	450.1	458	28	100	286
Away	4.10	25	23	0	73	70	438.2	439	48	86	261
Day	3.24	19	10	0	41	38	255.2	244	22	49	173
Night	4.06	39	35	0	99	98	633.1	653	54	137	374
Grass	3.98	22	15	0	53	50	312.1	311	35	63	190
Turf	3.75	36	30	0	87	86	576.2	586	41	123	357
April	4.46	5	7	0	17	17	105.0	108	8	26	69
May	4.65	10	12	0	25	25	153.0	181	19	35	111
June	3.68	9	7	0	22	22	149.1	148	10	24	90
July	3.51	12	3	0	28	24	156.1	157	12	28	77
August	3.42	9	6	0	19	19	137.0	116	15	33	75
September/October	3.49	13	10	0	29	29	188.1	187	12	40	125
Starter	3.84	58	45	0	136	136	879.2	890	75	182	544
Reliever	2.89	0	0	0	4	0	9.1	7	1	4	3
0-3 Days Rest	3.93	1	1	0	6	6	36.2	40	3	5	22
4 Days Rest	3.78	36	32	0	89	89	583.1	575	45	131	363
5+ Days Rest	3.95	21	12	0	41	41	259.2	275	27	46	159
Pre-All Star	4.14	27	28	0	75	72	465.1	496	41	101	296
Post-All Star	3.48	31	17	0	65	64	423.2	401	35	85	251

	Avg	AB	H	2B	3B	HR	RBI	BB	SO	OBP	SLG
vs. Left	.268	1889	507	113	20	41	203	103	304	.305	.415
vs. Right	.254	1535	390	79	4	35	151	83	243	.295	.379
Inning 1-6	.262	2900	760	167	21	64	313	155	470	.300	.400
Inning 7+	.261	524	137	25	3	12	41	31	77	.305	.389
None on	.256	2122	544	116	13	54	54	110	358	.296	.400
Runners on	.271	1302	353	76	11	22	300	76	189	.308	.397
Scoring Posn	.265	766	203	42	6	11	259	53	125	.306	.379
Close & Late	.256	262	67	14	2	5	27	21	37	.310	.382
None on/out	.254	914	232	54	10	27	27	37	156	.286	.423
vs. 1st Batr (relief)	.000	3	0	0	0	0	0	1	1	.250	.000
First Inning Pitched	.242	508	123	22	5	6	53	33	99	.288	.341
First 75 Pitches	.261	2584	675	153	18	56	267	135	410	.298	.399
Pitch 76-90	.271	421	114	17	5	14	48	18	62	.305	.435
Pitch 91-105	.273	308	84	17	1	6	32	22	59	.319	.393
Pitch 106+	.216	111	24	5	0	0	7	11	16	.285	.261
First Pitch	.318	591	188	55	5	17	78	2	0	.321	.514
Ahead in Count	.212	1578	334	66	10	23	134	0	469	.215	.310
Behind in Count	.325	658	214	43	2	26	84	100	0	.412	.515
Two Strikes	.204	1509	308	57	12	20	115	84	547	.248	.298

Pitcher vs. Batter (career)

Pitches Best Vs.	Avg	AB	H	2B	3B	HR	RBI	BB	SO	OBP	SLG
Candy Maldonado	.000	11	0	0	0	0	0	1	5	.083	.000
Luis Rivera	.000	11	0	0	0	0	0	0	3	.000	.000
Jeff Huson	.048	21	1	1	0	0	1	0	3	.048	.095
Albert Belle	.059	17	1	0	0	0	2	2	5	.158	.059
Gary DiSarcina	.067	15	1	0	0	0	0	0	3	.067	.067

Pitches Worst Vs.	Avg	AB	H	2B	3B	HR	RBI	BB	SO	OBP	SLG
Travis Fryman	.643	14	9	1	0	1	2	0	1	.643	.929
Dion James	.526	19	10	3	1	2	5	0	2	.526	1.105
Brady Anderson	.500	14	7	0	0	2	5	2	3	.563	.929
Terry Steinbach	.471	17	8	4	0	1	4	1	2	.500	.882
Paul Sorrento	.438	16	7	2	0	2	4	2	5	.500	.938

Tony Tarasco — Braves

Age 23 – Bats Left

	Avg	G	AB	R	H	2B	3B	HR	RBI	BB	SO	HBP	GDP	SB	CS	OBP	SLG	IBB	SH	SF	#Pit	#P/PA	GB	FB	G/F
1993 Season	.229	24	35	6	8	2	0	0	2	0	5	1	1	0	1	.243	.286	0	0	1	118	3.19	7	15	0.47

1993 Season

	Avg	AB	H	2B	3B	HR	RBI	BB	SO	OBP	SLG
vs. Left	.500	6	3	1	0	0	1	0	0	.500	.667
vs. Right	.172	29	5	1	0	0	1	0	5	.194	.207
Scoring Posn	.000	6	0	0	0	0	1	0	1	.125	.000
Close & Late	.500	12	6	1	0	0	0	0	0	.500	.583

Danny Tartabull — Yankees

Age 31 – Bats Right

	Avg	G	AB	R	H	2B	3B	HR	RBI	BB	SO	HBP	GDP	SB	CS	OBP	SLG	IBB	SH	SF	#Pit	#P/PA	GB	FB	G/F
1993 Season	.250	138	513	87	128	33	2	31	102	92	156	2	8	0	0	.363	.503	9	0	4	2404	3.93	146	140	1.04
Last Five Years	.274	614	2172	332	595	128	5	120	409	365	608	8	45	13	8	.378	.503	31	0	16	10204	3.98	686	565	1.21

1993 Season

	Avg	AB	H	2B	3B	HR	RBI	BB	SO	OBP	SLG
vs. Left	.200	175	35	11	1	7	23	38	50	.341	.394
vs. Right	.275	338	93	22	1	24	79	54	106	.375	.559
Groundball	.376	85	32	9	0	5	20	19	19	.490	.659
Flyball	.211	114	24	7	0	8	24	19	43	.321	.482
Home	.210	229	48	13	0	11	42	47	70	.343	.410
Away	.282	284	80	20	2	20	60	45	86	.381	.577
Day	.215	177	38	13	1	9	36	35	56	.340	.452
Night	.268	336	90	20	1	22	66	57	100	.376	.530
Grass	.230	439	101	26	1	28	89	71	137	.337	.485
Turf	.365	74	27	7	1	3	13	21	19	.505	.608
First Pitch	.362	69	25	3	0	7	19	8	0	.429	.710
Ahead in Count	.365	104	38	11	1	8	25	45	0	.556	.721
Behind in Count	.168	226	38	15	1	9	32	0	120	.167	.363
Two Strikes	.138	261	36	10	1	8	36	39	156	.249	.276

	Avg	AB	H	2B	3B	HR	RBI	BB	SO	OBP	SLG
Scoring Posn	.281	139	39	7	0	8	72	38	46	.425	.504
Close & Late	.348	69	24	9	0	3	13	18	14	.483	.609
None on/out	.246	130	32	10	0	12	12	12	36	.310	.600
Batting #4	.250	513	128	33	2	31	102	91	156	.362	.503
Batting #6	.000	0	0	0	0	0	0	1	0	1.000	.000
Other	.000	0	0	0	0	0	0	0	0	.000	.000
April	.247	73	18	4	1	4	13	16	22	.378	.493
May	.183	82	15	7	0	3	13	15	32	.303	.378
June	.260	50	13	3	0	4	11	6	15	.339	.560
July	.340	97	33	5	0	10	27	16	22	.430	.701
August	.229	105	24	9	0	7	20	17	29	.336	.514
September/October	.236	106	25	5	1	3	18	22	36	.377	.387
Pre-All Star	.244	246	60	17	1	14	43	39	80	.344	.492
Post-All Star	.255	267	68	16	1	17	59	53	76	.381	.513

1993 By Position

Position	Avg	AB	H	2B	3B	HR	RBI	BB	SO	OBP	SLG	G	GS	Innings	PO	A	E	DP	Fld Pct	Rng Fctr	In Zone	Outs	Zone Rtg	MLB Zone
As Designated Hitter	.260	327	85	21	0	20	70	58	94	.374	.508	88	88	---	---	---	---	---	---	---	---	---	---	---
As rf	.231	186	43	12	2	11	32	33	62	.342	.495	50	49	434.0	88	3	2	2	.978	1.89	104	84	.808	.826

Last Five Years

	Avg	AB	H	2B	3B	HR	RBI	BB	SO	OBP	SLG
vs. Left	.276	667	184	39	2	39	119	159	169	.413	.516
vs. Right	.273	1505	411	89	3	81	290	206	439	.361	.498
Groundball	.290	542	157	37	0	19	86	86	131	.387	.463
Flyball	.274	514	141	30	1	39	109	89	163	.380	.564
Home	.267	1015	271	54	2	49	181	180	277	.375	.469
Away	.280	1157	324	74	3	71	228	185	331	.381	.533
Day	.260	624	162	37	1	31	121	101	178	.361	.471
Night	.280	1548	433	91	4	89	288	264	430	.385	.516
Grass	.266	1291	343	77	2	80	262	231	378	.377	.514
Turf	.286	881	252	51	3	40	147	134	230	.379	.487
First Pitch	.370	270	100	19	2	21	56	26	0	.433	.689
Ahead in Count	.363	465	169	36	1	35	112	168	0	.526	.671
Behind in Count	.188	970	182	39	2	31	131	0	471	.188	.328
Two Strikes	.184	1128	207	39	2	46	170	170	608	.290	.344

	Avg	AB	H	2B	3B	HR	RBI	BB	SO	OBP	SLG
Scoring Posn	.285	596	170	39	1	33	289	152	176	.424	.520
Close & Late	.327	343	112	30	1	19	72	60	80	.428	.586
None on/out	.267	581	155	38	2	34	34	61	160	.337	.515
Batting #4	.283	1594	451	101	5	91	314	263	425	.384	.524
Batting #5	.225	236	53	8	0	12	42	47	78	.350	.411
Other	.266	342	91	19	0	17	53	55	105	.369	.471
April	.292	267	78	18	2	8	46	46	77	.391	.464
May	.230	379	87	18	0	16	57	52	114	.323	.404
June	.283	343	97	17	0	24	70	52	98	.377	.542
July	.302	324	98	21	0	29	80	60	86	.409	.636
August	.281	438	123	28	1	24	76	71	118	.381	.514
September/October	.266	421	112	26	2	19	80	84	115	.391	.473
Pre-All Star	.265	1130	299	61	2	64	204	167	333	.358	.492
Post-All Star	.284	1042	296	67	3	56	205	198	275	.399	.515

Batter vs. Pitcher (career)

Hits Best Against	Avg	AB	H	2B	3B	HR	RBI	BB	SO	OBP	SLG
Mike Morgan	.727	11	8	0	0	1	4	1	0	.750	1.000
Jaime Navarro	.571	21	12	1	0	3	8	4	5	.640	1.048
Mark Guthrie	.545	11	6	0	0	2	5	6	2	.706	1.091
Tim Leary	.409	22	9	2	1	2	5	4	5	.500	.864
Jeff Reardon	.375	8	3	0	1	1	4	3	3	.545	1.000

Hits Worst Against	Avg	AB	H	2B	3B	HR	RBI	BB	SO	OBP	SLG
David Cone	.000	12	0	0	0	0	0	2	3	.143	.000
John Farrell	.059	17	1	0	0	0	0	0	6	.059	.059
Tom Henke	.067	15	1	1	0	0	1	2	7	.176	.133
Eric Plunk	.083	24	2	2	0	0	2	3	7	.185	.167
Doug Jones	.167	12	2	0	0	0	0	0	4	.167	.167

Jimmy Tatum — Rockies

Age 26 – Bats Right (flyball hitter)

	Avg	G	AB	R	H	2B	3B	HR	RBI	BB	SO	HBP	GDP	SB	CS	OBP	SLG	IBB	SH	SF	#Pit	#P/PA	GB	FB	G/F
1993 Season	.204	92	98	7	20	5	0	1	12	5	27	1	0	0	0	.245	.286	0	0	2	397	3.75	24	32	0.75
Career (1992-1993)	.198	97	106	7	21	5	0	1	12	6	29	1	0	0	0	.243	.274	0	0	2	429	3.73	27	34	0.79

1993 Season

	Avg	AB	H	2B	3B	HR	RBI	BB	SO	OBP	SLG
vs. Left	.250	32	8	2	0	1	5	1	8	.294	.406
vs. Right	.182	66	12	3	0	0	7	4	19	.222	.227

	Avg	AB	H	2B	3B	HR	RBI	BB	SO	OBP	SLG
Scoring Posn	.176	17	3	1	0	1	10	1	5	.200	.412
Close & Late	.208	24	5	2	0	1	6	3	6	.296	.417

Eddie Taubensee — Astros

Age 25 – Bats Left

	Avg	G	AB	R	H	2B	3B	HR	RBI	BB	SO	HBP	GDP	SB	CS	OBP	SLG	IBB	SH	SF	#Pit	#P/PA	GB	FB	G/F
1993 Season	.250	94	288	26	72	11	1	9	42	21	44	0	8	1	0	.299	.389	5	1	2	1084	3.47	112	86	1.30
Career (1991-1993)	.237	224	651	54	154	28	2	14	78	57	138	2	13	3	1	.298	.350	9	1	5	2531	3.53	217	184	1.18

1993 Season

	Avg	AB	H	2B	3B	HR	RBI	BB	SO	OBP	SLG
vs. Left	.200	50	10	1	0	1	6	1	9	.216	.280
vs. Right	.261	238	62	10	1	8	36	20	35	.315	.412
Home	.243	136	33	7	1	4	17	11	19	.297	.397
Away	.257	152	39	4	0	5	25	10	25	.301	.382
First Pitch	.327	49	16	3	0	3	12	3	0	.365	.571
Ahead in Count	.328	58	19	3	1	3	12	9	0	.412	.569
Behind in Count	.189	127	24	4	0	1	11	0	38	.188	.244
Two Strikes	.160	119	19	3	0	1	10	9	44	.217	.210

	Avg	AB	H	2B	3B	HR	RBI	BB	SO	OBP	SLG
Scoring Posn	.216	88	19	2	1	1	27	11	14	.297	.295
Close & Late	.234	47	11	3	0	1	3	2	8	.265	.362
None on/out	.349	63	22	2	0	3	3	3	4	.379	.524
Batting #7	.229	118	27	5	0	3	14	6	20	.262	.347
Batting #8	.276	156	43	6	1	6	28	15	22	.339	.442
Other	.143	14	2	0	0	0	0	0	2	.143	.143
Pre-All Star	.242	128	31	3	1	5	25	13	19	.310	.398
Post-All Star	.256	160	41	8	0	4	17	8	25	.290	.381

Career (1991-1993)

	Avg	AB	H	2B	3B	HR	RBI	BB	SO	OBP	SLG
vs. Left	.234	107	25	4	0	3	11	8	23	.293	.355
vs. Right	.237	544	129	24	2	11	67	49	115	.299	.349
Groundball	.207	256	53	10	0	5	25	21	58	.264	.305
Flyball	.252	123	31	6	1	3	11	9	28	.303	.390
Home	.237	333	79	19	1	6	36	32	67	.304	.354
Away	.236	318	75	9	1	8	42	25	71	.292	.346
Day	.216	176	38	8	0	7	25	19	40	.289	.381
Night	.244	475	116	20	2	7	53	38	98	.301	.339
Grass	.225	249	56	7	1	5	32	19	55	.280	.321
Turf	.244	402	98	21	1	9	46	38	83	.309	.368
First Pitch	.333	108	36	8	0	4	22	6	0	.368	.519
Ahead in Count	.313	134	42	10	1	5	23	21	0	.405	.515
Behind in Count	.174	316	55	7	1	2	19	0	119	.175	.222
Two Strikes	.157	286	45	6	1	2	19	30	138	.238	.206

	Avg	AB	H	2B	3B	HR	RBI	BB	SO	OBP	SLG
Scoring Posn	.216	176	38	5	1	1	53	27	38	.316	.273
Close & Late	.205	112	23	4	0	2	11	8	26	.258	.295
None on/out	.306	144	44	6	1	4	4	11	24	.355	.444
Batting #7	.212	297	63	12	0	4	27	20	66	.262	.293
Batting #8	.252	322	81	16	2	10	50	36	64	.327	.407
Other	.313	32	10	0	0	0	1	1	8	.333	.313
April	.206	102	21	4	1	2	12	9	24	.268	.324
May	.176	119	21	4	0	1	8	16	23	.272	.235
June	.179	39	7	1	0	0	10	4	12	.256	.205
July	.382	68	26	5	0	4	11	3	10	.408	.632
August	.211	142	30	6	0	7	17	9	35	.266	.401
September/October	.271	181	49	8	1	0	20	16	34	.327	.326
Pre-All Star	.197	274	54	9	1	5	36	31	61	.277	.292
Post-All Star	.265	377	100	19	1	9	42	26	77	.314	.393

Batter vs. Pitcher (career)

Hits Best Against	Avg	AB	H	2B	3B	HR	RBI	BB	SO	OBP	SLG
John Smoltz	.353	17	6	0	0	0	1	3	5	.450	.353
Bob Tewksbury	.333	12	4	0	0	1	2	0	2	.308	.583

Hits Worst Against	Avg	AB	H	2B	3B	HR	RBI	BB	SO	OBP	SLG
Dennis Martinez	.182	11	2	1	0	0	0	0	5	.182	.273
Greg W. Harris	.182	11	2	0	0	0	0	0	1	.182	.182
Ken Hill	.188	16	3	1	0	0	0	1	4	.235	.250
John Burkett	.227	22	5	2	0	0	5	0	5	.227	.318

Batter vs. Pitcher (career)																							
Hits Best Against	Avg	AB	H	2B	3B	HR	RBI	BB	SO	OBP	SLG	Hits Worst Against	Avg	AB	H	2B	3B	HR	RBI	BB	SO	OBP	SLG
												Curt Schilling	.231	13	3	0	0	0	2	1	1	.267	.231

Julian Tavarez — Indians

Age 21 – Pitches Right (groundball pitcher)

	ERA	W	L	Sv	G	GS	IP	BB	SO	Avg	H	2B	3B	HR	RBI	OBP	SLG	CG	ShO	Sup	QS	#P/S	SB	CS	GB	FB	G/F
1993 Season	6.57	2	2	0	8	7	37.0	13	19	.340	53	8	0	7	26	.395	.526	0	0	8.27	2	81	2	2	63	40	1.58

1993 Season	ERA	W	L	Sv	G	GS	IP	H	HR	BB	SO		Avg	AB	H	2B	3B	HR	RBI	BB	SO	OBP	SLG
Home	4.30	1	0	0	3	2	14.2	19	3	2	4	vs. Left	.343	70	24	3	0	2	11	6	7	.397	.471
Away	8.06	1	2	0	5	5	22.1	34	4	11	15	vs. Right	.337	86	29	5	0	5	15	7	12	.394	.570

Kerry Taylor — Padres

Age 23 – Pitches Right

	ERA	W	L	Sv	G	GS	IP	BB	SO	Avg	H	2B	3B	HR	RBI	OBP	SLG	GF	IR	IRS	Hld	SvOp	SB	CS	GB	FB	G/F
1993 Season	6.45	0	5	0	36	7	68.1	49	45	.277	72	11	1	5	45	.396	.385	9	16	7	0	0	13	3	77	74	1.04

1993 Season	ERA	W	L	Sv	G	GS	IP	H	HR	BB	SO		Avg	AB	H	2B	3B	HR	RBI	BB	SO	OBP	SLG
Home	3.89	0	2	0	20	4	41.2	26	5	25	31	vs. Left	.308	117	36	6	1	3	20	23	15	.418	.453
Away	10.46	0	3	0	16	3	26.2	46	0	24	14	vs. Right	.252	143	36	5	0	2	25	26	30	.377	.329
Starter	9.21	0	5	0	7	7	28.1	28	5	23	18	Scoring Posn	.353	85	30	6	1	1	39	18	13	.458	.482
Reliever	4.50	0	0	0	29	0	40.0	44	0	26	27	Close & Late	.000	3	0	0	0	0	0	0	1	.000	.000
0 Days rest	1.74	0	0	0	6	0	10.1	6	0	8	7	None on/out	.194	62	12	0	0	0	0	9	12	.296	.194
1 or 2 Days rest	0.00	0	0	0	5	0	5.2	5	0	3	6	First Pitch	.292	24	7	1	1	0	4	0	0	.292	.417
3+ Days rest	6.75	0	0	0	18	0	24.0	33	0	15	14	Ahead in Count	.215	107	23	3	0	2	18	0	37	.241	.299
Pre-All Star	7.59	0	5	0	17	7	40.1	42	5	32	24	Behind in Count	.338	71	24	7	0	1	13	24	0	.500	.479
Post-All Star	4.82	0	0	0	19	0	28.0	30	0	17	21	Two Strikes	.188	117	22	3	0	3	17	25	45	.340	.291

Scott Taylor — Red Sox

Age 26 – Pitches Left

	ERA	W	L	Sv	G	GS	IP	BB	SO	Avg	H	2B	3B	HR	RBI	OBP	SLG	GF	IR	IRS	Hld	SvOp	SB	CS	GB	FB	G/F
1993 Season	8.18	0	1	0	16	0	11.0	12	8	.311	14	6	0	1	13	.466	.511	3	19	8	2	0	0	0	20	9	2.22
Career (1992-1993)	6.31	1	2	0	20	1	25.2	16	15	.276	27	8	2	5	25	.383	.551	4	26	12	2	0	0	1	39	32	1.22

1993 Season	ERA	W	L	Sv	G	GS	IP	H	HR	BB	SO		Avg	AB	H	2B	3B	HR	RBI	BB	SO	OBP	SLG
Home	13.50	0	1	0	10	0	5.1	12	0	10	4	vs. Left	.313	16	5	2	0	1	5	4	3	.450	.625
Away	3.18	0	0	0	6	0	5.2	2	1	2	4	vs. Right	.310	29	9	4	0	0	8	8	5	.474	.448

Anthony Telford — Orioles

Age 28 – Pitches Right

	ERA	W	L	Sv	G	GS	IP	BB	SO	Avg	H	2B	3B	HR	RBI	OBP	SLG	GF	IR	IRS	Hld	SvOp	SB	CS	GB	FB	G/F
1993 Season	9.82	0	0	0	3	0	7.1	1	6	.344	11	1	0	3	8	.382	.656	2	2	0	0	0	1	0	10	13	0.77
Career (1990-1993)	5.12	3	3	0	20	9	70.1	26	50	.289	81	15	0	10	40	.350	.450	6	11	3	0	0	5	3	93	87	1.07

1993 Season	ERA	W	L	Sv	G	GS	IP	H	HR	BB	SO		Avg	AB	H	2B	3B	HR	RBI	BB	SO	OBP	SLG
Home	0.00	0	0	0	1	0	2.0	2	0	1	1	vs. Left	.353	17	6	0	0	1	2	1	3	.389	.529
Away	13.50	0	0	0	2	0	5.1	9	3	0	5	vs. Right	.333	15	5	1	0	2	6	0	3	.375	.800

Dave Telgheder — Mets

Age 27 – Pitches Right

	ERA	W	L	Sv	G	GS	IP	BB	SO	Avg	H	2B	3B	HR	RBI	OBP	SLG	GF	IR	IRS	Hld	SvOp	SB	CS	GB	FB	G/F
1993 Season	4.76	6	2	0	24	7	75.2	21	35	.276	82	19	2	10	39	.331	.455	7	5	3	1	0	4	5	98	98	1.00

1993 Season	ERA	W	L	Sv	G	GS	IP	H	HR	BB	SO		Avg	AB	H	2B	3B	HR	RBI	BB	SO	OBP	SLG
Home	5.54	3	1	0	11	4	37.1	40	5	11	15	vs. Left	.281	153	43	12	1	4	17	12	19	.335	.451
Away	3.99	3	1	0	13	3	38.1	42	5	10	20	vs. Right	.271	144	39	7	1	6	22	9	16	.327	.458
Starter	4.60	5	2	0	7	7	45.0	51	6	17	18	Scoring Posn	.333	69	23	7	1	2	27	5	5	.390	.551
Reliever	4.99	1	0	0	17	0	30.2	31	4	4	17	Close & Late	.094	32	3	1	0	0	0	0	3	.094	.125
0 Days rest	0.00	0	0	0	0	0	0.0	0	0	0	0	None on/out	.233	73	17	4	1	3	3	6	11	.291	.438
1 or 2 Days rest	6.60	1	0	0	7	0	15.0	18	3	1	9	First Pitch	.268	56	15	4	0	2	9	2	0	.300	.446
3+ Days rest	3.45	0	0	0	10	0	15.2	13	1	3	8	Ahead in Count	.269	130	35	9	1	4	18	0	34	.286	.446
Pre-All Star	5.67	3	1	0	8	3	27.0	31	5	7	9	Behind in Count	.302	63	19	4	0	3	9	10	0	.397	.508
Post-All Star	4.25	3	1	0	16	4	48.2	51	5	14	26	Two Strikes	.259	112	29	7	1	5	16	9	35	.325	.473

Mickey Tettleton — Tigers

Age 33 – Bats Both (flyball hitter)

	Avg	G	AB	R	H	2B	3B	HR	RBI	BB	SO	HBP	GDP	SB	CS	OBP	SLG	IBB	SH	SF	#Pit	#P/PA	GB	FB	G/F
1993 Season	.245	152	522	79	128	25	4	32	110	109	139	0	5	3	7	.372	.492	12	0	6	2733	4.29	133	166	0.80
Last Five Years	.246	715	2403	386	590	109	10	136	398	511	684	9	37	11	22	.377	.469	46	1	23	12478	4.23	642	714	0.90

1993 Season	Avg	AB	H	2B	3B	HR	RBI	BB	SO	OBP	SLG		Avg	AB	H	2B	3B	HR	RBI	BB	SO	OBP	SLG
vs. Left	.260	123	32	9	1	7	28	32	28	.408	.520	Scoring Posn	.311	132	41	4	3	8	77	45	31	.470	.568
vs. Right	.241	399	96	16	3	25	82	77	111	.360	.484	Close & Late	.320	75	24	0	1	5	19	14	17	.422	.547
Groundball	.207	116	24	5	0	8	23	20	32	.321	.457	None on/out	.244	156	38	8	0	12	12	23	41	.341	.526

1993 Season

	Avg	AB	H	2B	3B	HR	RBI	BB	SO	OBP	SLG
Flyball	.248	109	27	5	2	4	20	16	20	.339	.440
Home	.230	256	59	14	1	16	52	54	68	.360	.480
Away	.259	266	69	11	3	16	58	55	71	.384	.504
Day	.253	190	48	12	1	10	39	37	48	.373	.484
Night	.241	332	80	13	3	22	71	72	91	.372	.497
Grass	.252	445	112	22	4	27	93	89	114	.374	.501
Turf	.208	77	16	3	0	5	17	20	25	.364	.442
First Pitch	.333	30	10	2	0	1	8	6	0	.432	.500
Ahead in Count	.350	157	55	10	2	20	61	51	0	.502	.822
Behind in Count	.175	194	34	10	0	5	21	0	100	.173	.304
Two Strikes	.161	255	41	10	2	7	34	52	139	.301	.298

	Avg	AB	H	2B	3B	HR	RBI	BB	SO	OBP	SLG
Batting #5	.214	126	27	7	1	9	21	24	36	.338	.500
Batting #6	.268	284	76	15	3	18	69	58	76	.388	.532
Other	.223	112	25	3	0	5	20	27	27	.369	.384
April	.185	65	12	3	0	5	19	21	17	.375	.462
May	.258	93	24	5	2	4	19	11	27	.337	.484
June	.271	96	26	2	0	11	25	11	22	.343	.635
July	.218	101	22	7	0	6	15	20	30	.341	.465
August	.253	91	23	3	1	4	21	22	22	.395	.440
September/October	.276	76	21	5	1	2	11	24	21	.450	.447
Pre-All Star	.250	296	74	13	2	24	73	50	79	.355	.551
Post-All Star	.239	226	54	12	2	8	37	59	60	.392	.416

1993 By Position

Position	Avg	AB	H	2B	3B	HR	RBI	BB	SO	OBP	SLG	G	GS	Innings	PO	A	E	DP	Fld Pct	Rng Fctr	In Zone	Outs	Zone Rtg	MLB Zone
As c	.259	174	45	9	1	10	41	41	42	.394	.494	56	51	430.0	267	20	1	1	.997	---	---	---	---	---
As 1b	.286	147	42	8	2	8	32	27	32	.397	.531	59	35	363.0	364	24	3	41	.992	---	71	56	.789	.834
As lf	.207	58	12	3	0	4	10	10	18	.319	.466	18	16	135.1	23	3	0	1	1.000	1.73	35	24	.686	.818
As rf	.200	130	26	5	1	9	25	25	44	.325	.462	39	38	313.0	68	1	2	0	.972	1.98	79	68	.861	.826

Last Five Years

	Avg	AB	H	2B	3B	HR	RBI	BB	SO	OBP	SLG
vs. Left	.252	634	160	39	1	39	114	117	185	.366	.502
vs. Right	.243	1769	430	70	9	97	284	394	499	.381	.457
Groundball	.265	635	168	30	0	38	99	127	163	.386	.491
Flyball	.221	543	120	19	3	38	93	112	163	.352	.477
Home	.261	1168	305	60	7	72	205	258	330	.392	.509
Away	.231	1235	285	49	3	64	193	253	354	.362	.431
Day	.252	749	189	36	3	37	112	161	224	.383	.457
Night	.242	1654	401	73	7	99	286	350	460	.374	.475
Grass	.253	2017	510	91	10	121	354	433	568	.384	.488
Turf	.207	386	80	18	0	15	44	78	116	.341	.370
First Pitch	.324	170	55	10	2	12	37	34	0	.433	.618
Ahead in Count	.353	665	235	51	4	66	188	238	0	.518	.740
Behind in Count	.169	1003	170	30	2	24	88	0	521	.170	.275
Two Strikes	.160	1231	197	26	4	41	124	237	684	.296	.288

	Avg	AB	H	2B	3B	HR	RBI	BB	SO	OBP	SLG
Scoring Posn	.235	595	140	19	3	36	268	202	175	.420	.459
Close & Late	.253	387	98	8	1	23	65	66	118	.365	.457
None on/out	.247	659	163	35	3	38	38	107	183	.354	.483
Batting #4	.247	563	139	26	4	25	74	133	176	.390	.440
Batting #5	.245	1198	293	53	3	76	197	252	331	.375	.484
Other	.246	642	158	30	3	35	127	126	177	.368	.466
April	.215	312	67	16	0	19	58	68	98	.352	.449
May	.262	432	113	18	3	25	75	68	113	.363	.491
June	.273	469	128	18	4	37	102	100	128	.399	.565
July	.241	453	109	23	1	20	58	94	138	.368	.428
August	.219	360	79	14	1	15	47	95	91	.380	.389
September/October	.249	377	94	20	1	20	58	86	116	.391	.467
Pre-All Star	.252	1371	346	60	7	89	258	267	386	.373	.501
Post-All Star	.236	1032	244	49	3	47	140	244	298	.382	.426

Batter vs. Pitcher (career)

Hits Best Against	Avg	AB	H	2B	3B	HR	RBI	BB	SO	OBP	SLG
Greg Hibbard	.500	16	8	3	0	2	4	1	3	.529	1.063
Edwin Nunez	.467	15	7	0	0	2	10	2	4	.529	.867
Cal Eldred	.467	15	7	1	1	1	4	2	1	.529	.867
Mark Eichhorn	.400	15	6	0	0	4	7	2	5	.444	1.200
Joe Hesketh	.400	15	6	2	0	2	3	2	3	.471	.933

Hits Worst Against	Avg	AB	H	2B	3B	HR	RBI	BB	SO	OBP	SLG
Todd Burns	.000	16	0	0	0	0	0	2	6	.111	.000
Erik Hanson	.048	21	1	0	0	1	1	3	11	.167	.190
Scott Bankhead	.059	17	1	0	0	0	1	1	4	.105	.059
Steve Farr	.067	15	1	0	0	0	0	2	10	.176	.067
Frank Viola	.091	22	2	0	1	0	3	3	6	.200	.182

Tim Teufel — Padres

Age 35 – Bats Right

	Avg	G	AB	R	H	2B	3B	HR	RBI	BB	SO	HBP	GDP	SB	CS	OBP	SLG	IBB	SH	SF	#Pit	#P/PA	GB	FB	G/F
1993 Season	.250	96	200	26	50	11	2	7	31	27	39	0	9	2	2	.338	.430	0	3	1	955	4.13	68	55	1.24
Last Five Years	.235	477	1181	145	278	55	4	37	139	156	244	3	33	14	9	.324	.383	9	8	7	5481	4.05	389	318	1.22

1993 Season

	Avg	AB	H	2B	3B	HR	RBI	BB	SO	OBP	SLG
vs. Left	.286	133	38	9	2	6	23	21	22	.381	.519
vs. Right	.179	67	12	2	0	1	8	6	17	.247	.254
Home	.273	99	27	5	1	5	17	14	20	.360	.495
Away	.228	101	23	6	1	2	14	13	19	.316	.366
First Pitch	.500	12	6	4	0	1	4	0	0	.500	1.083
Ahead in Count	.320	50	16	2	0	4	11	15	0	.477	.600
Behind in Count	.198	86	17	3	1	2	12	0	31	.195	.326
Two Strikes	.168	95	16	2	0	2	11	12	39	.259	.253

	Avg	AB	H	2B	3B	HR	RBI	BB	SO	OBP	SLG
Scoring Posn	.310	42	13	2	0	0	15	9	9	.423	.357
Close & Late	.233	30	7	1	0	1	6	5	10	.343	.367
None on/out	.103	39	4	1	0	1	1	5	12	.205	.205
Batting #2	.214	56	12	1	0	1	5	9	9	.323	.286
Batting #6	.274	62	17	3	1	3	9	6	11	.333	.500
Other	.256	82	21	7	1	3	17	12	19	.351	.476
Pre-All Star	.243	115	28	6	1	5	22	16	22	.333	.443
Post-All Star	.259	85	22	5	1	2	9	11	17	.344	.412

Last Five Years

	Avg	AB	H	2B	3B	HR	RBI	BB	SO	OBP	SLG
vs. Left	.264	598	158	33	3	23	83	89	102	.358	.445
vs. Right	.206	583	120	22	1	14	56	67	142	.289	.319
Groundball	.226	416	94	17	3	8	35	59	90	.321	.339
Flyball	.310	271	84	12	0	17	50	41	53	.398	.542
Home	.242	541	131	24	1	18	74	81	102	.342	.390
Away	.230	640	147	31	3	19	65	75	142	.309	.377
Day	.247	377	93	19	1	17	55	36	87	.314	.438
Night	.230	804	185	36	3	20	84	120	157	.329	.357
Grass	.236	819	193	36	1	23	101	118	159	.332	.366
Turf	.235	362	85	19	3	14	38	38	85	.306	.420
First Pitch	.315	92	29	10	0	4	14	6	0	.360	.554
Ahead in Count	.312	308	96	16	1	19	52	74	0	.442	.555
Behind in Count	.173	515	89	20	2	8	45	0	202	.174	.266
Two Strikes	.170	578	98	17	1	10	45	75	244	.265	.254

	Avg	AB	H	2B	3B	HR	RBI	BB	SO	OBP	SLG
Scoring Posn	.232	293	68	12	0	9	91	49	69	.335	.365
Close & Late	.223	229	51	11	0	7	27	35	47	.323	.362
None on/out	.219	269	59	9	0	10	10	29	55	.298	.364
Batting #6	.228	302	69	14	1	10	36	31	62	.299	.381
Batting #7	.232	237	55	13	2	8	26	40	55	.343	.405
Other	.240	642	154	28	1	19	77	85	127	.329	.375
April	.261	134	35	5	2	4	16	16	20	.344	.418
May	.224	165	37	5	0	4	17	24	43	.321	.327
June	.259	189	49	8	0	4	30	28	32	.353	.365
July	.227	203	46	10	0	3	17	27	42	.319	.320
August	.253	217	55	10	1	12	33	31	41	.343	.475
September/October	.205	273	56	17	1	10	26	30	66	.285	.385
Pre-All Star	.252	556	140	23	2	15	74	79	110	.346	.381
Post-All Star	.221	625	138	32	2	22	65	77	134	.305	.384

Batter vs. Pitcher (since 1984)

Hits Best Against	Avg	AB	H	2B	3B	HR	RBI	BB	SO	OBP	SLG
Tom Browning	.458	48	22	3	0	5	8	5	5	.509	.833
Bob Patterson	.444	18	8	2	0	1	6	3	3	.524	.722
Bob McClure	.444	9	4	0	0	1	4	4	2	.615	.778
Dave Stewart	.400	10	4	3	0	0	1	2	3	.500	.700
Sid Fernandez	.333	12	4	0	0	2	4	1	2	.385	.833

Hits Worst Against	Avg	AB	H	2B	3B	HR	RBI	BB	SO	OBP	SLG
Bryn Smith	.000	10	0	0	0	0	0	2	4	.167	.000
Roger Clemens	.000	10	0	0	0	0	1	1	3	.083	.000
Mark Davis	.000	8	0	0	0	0	0	3	3	.273	.000
Jamie Moyer	.100	20	2	0	0	0	0	1	2	.143	.100
Bill Swift	.125	16	2	0	0	0	0	0	1	.125	.125

Bob Tewksbury — Cardinals

Age 33 – Pitches Right (groundball pitcher)

	ERA	W	L	Sv	G	GS	IP	BB	SO	Avg	H	2B	3B	HR	RBI	OBP	SLG	CG	ShO	Sup	QS	#P/S	SB	CS	GB	FB	G/F
1993 Season	3.83	17	10	0	32	32	213.2	20	97	.301	258	42	4	15	87	.318	.412	2	0	5.85	22	91	21	6	367	221	1.66
Last Five Years	3.13	55	36	1	130	118	813.0	103	330	.273	857	165	19	52	295	.297	.387	14	3	4.75	81	86	48	25	1355	853	1.59

1993 Season

	ERA	W	L	Sv	G	GS	IP	H	HR	BB	SO
Home	3.35	11	7	0	19	19	131.2	150	9	10	57
Away	4.61	6	3	0	13	13	82.0	108	6	10	40
Day	3.09	7	3	0	11	11	81.2	90	5	1	44
Night	4.30	10	7	0	21	21	132.0	168	10	19	53
Grass	3.68	5	1	0	7	7	44.0	59	5	3	27
Turf	3.87	12	9	0	25	25	169.2	199	10	17	70
April	3.80	1	3	0	4	4	23.2	34	1	1	11
May	3.68	3	2	0	6	6	44.0	48	3	2	18
June	4.65	4	1	0	5	5	31.0	40	2	3	16
July	3.43	2	1	0	6	6	42.0	44	3	4	23
August	3.59	4	1	0	6	6	42.2	54	4	7	15
September/October	4.15	3	2	0	5	5	30.1	38	2	3	14
Starter	3.83	17	10	0	32	32	213.2	258	15	20	97
Reliever	0.00	0	0	0	0	0	0.0	0	0	0	0
0-3 Days Rest	2.45	2	0	0	2	2	14.2	17	1	0	6
4 Days Rest	4.08	10	7	0	21	21	136.2	173	9	14	69
5+ Days Rest	3.61	5	3	0	9	9	62.1	68	5	6	22
Pre-All Star	3.73	9	7	0	18	18	120.2	143	6	6	56
Post-All Star	3.97	8	3	0	14	14	93.0	115	9	14	41

	Avg	AB	H	2B	3B	HR	RBI	BB	SO	OBP	SLG
vs. Left	.313	431	135	19	4	6	41	10	47	.326	.418
vs. Right	.289	426	123	23	0	9	46	10	50	.311	.406
Inning 1-6	.304	718	218	36	4	14	75	17	82	.321	.423
Inning 7+	.288	139	40	6	0	1	12	3	15	.303	.353
None on	.310	496	154	21	0	11	11	8	55	.324	.419
Runners on	.288	361	104	21	4	4	76	12	42	.311	.402
Scoring Posn	.239	197	47	6	4	1	65	8	34	.271	.325
Close & Late	.313	64	20	5	0	0	6	2	5	.338	.391
None on/out	.323	217	70	9	0	5	5	5	18	.344	.433
vs. 1st Batr (relief)	.000	0	0	0	0	0	0	0	0	.000	.000
First Inning Pitched	.341	132	45	6	2	3	19	4	13	.367	.485
First 75 Pitches	.301	674	203	34	4	14	71	16	76	.319	.426
Pitch 76-90	.298	114	34	3	0	1	10	3	10	.317	.351
Pitch 91-105	.333	51	17	4	0	0	6	1	5	.346	.412
Pitch 106+	.222	18	4	1	0	0	0	0	6	.222	.278
First Pitch	.369	141	52	10	0	2	13	1	0	.368	.482
Ahead in Count	.261	383	100	15	3	6	27	0	92	.272	.363
Behind in Count	.358	201	72	12	1	6	33	13	0	.394	.517
Two Strikes	.242	322	78	15	2	3	20	6	97	.262	.329

Last Five Years

	ERA	W	L	Sv	G	GS	IP	H	HR	BB	SO
Home	2.85	31	17	0	68	61	435.2	422	26	49	174
Away	3.46	24	19	1	62	57	377.1	435	26	54	156
Day	3.17	18	12	0	39	36	252.1	259	15	35	107
Night	3.11	37	24	1	91	82	560.2	598	37	68	223
Grass	3.09	14	10	0	34	31	215.1	244	19	26	99
Turf	3.15	41	26	1	96	87	597.2	613	33	77	231
April	3.27	5	4	1	19	12	88.0	100	3	13	41
May	3.03	8	4	0	18	16	116.0	119	7	12	41
June	2.69	13	4	0	20	20	140.1	142	9	16	56
July	2.57	6	9	0	21	21	140.1	144	9	19	68
August	3.06	13	5	0	23	23	162.0	170	7	17	52
September/October	4.06	10	10	0	29	26	166.1	182	17	26	72
Starter	3.07	54	36	0	118	118	791.2	829	51	98	319
Reliever	5.48	1	0	1	12	0	21.1	28	1	5	11
0-3 Days Rest	1.68	5	0	0	8	8	53.2	58	3	4	15
4 Days Rest	3.02	30	24	0	67	67	453.0	471	26	52	200
5+ Days Rest	3.41	19	12	0	43	43	285.0	300	22	42	104
Pre-All Star	2.84	28	16	1	65	56	399.0	412	21	44	162
Post-All Star	3.41	27	20	0	65	62	414.0	445	31	59	168

	Avg	AB	H	2B	3B	HR	RBI	BB	SO	OBP	SLG
vs. Left	.275	1743	480	89	10	25	160	68	166	.300	.381
vs. Right	.269	1399	377	76	9	27	135	35	164	.293	.395
Inning 1-6	.278	2605	723	135	16	44	266	82	270	.300	.392
Inning 7+	.250	537	134	30	3	8	29	21	60	.280	.361
None on	.274	1929	528	103	10	34	34	51	209	.296	.390
Runners on	.271	1213	329	62	9	18	261	52	121	.298	.382
Scoring Posn	.258	682	176	31	6	13	237	40	76	.291	.378
Close & Late	.241	216	52	11	1	4	13	11	23	.279	.356
None on/out	.262	821	215	42	5	12	12	24	87	.289	.369
vs. 1st Batr (relief)	.364	11	4	0	0	0	1	0	2	.333	.364
First Inning Pitched	.336	529	178	34	5	9	83	21	57	.357	.471
First 75 Pitches	.272	2622	714	135	16	50	256	83	269	.296	.393
Pitch 76-90	.270	363	98	20	1	2	29	15	45	.301	.347
Pitch 91-105	.292	130	38	9	2	0	9	4	10	.313	.392
Pitch 106+	.259	27	7	1	0	0	1	1	6	.276	.296
First Pitch	.329	601	198	42	1	7	61	8	0	.337	.438
Ahead in Count	.221	1375	304	50	11	20	99	0	309	.229	.317
Behind in Count	.330	691	228	49	5	18	78	63	0	.381	.493
Two Strikes	.200	1127	225	40	7	15	72	31	330	.225	.287

Pitcher vs. Batter (career)

Pitches Best Vs.	Avg	AB	H	2B	3B	HR	RBI	BB	SO	OBP	SLG
Gary Sheffield	.000	12	0	0	0	0	0	0	2	.000	.000
Chico Walker	.000	11	0	0	0	0	0	0	1	.000	.000
Joe Girardi	.063	16	1	0	0	0	0	0	1	.063	.063
Todd Benzinger	.071	14	1	0	0	0	0	1	3	.133	.071
Kevin Bass	.118	17	2	0	0	0	0	0	1	.118	.118

Pitches Worst Vs.	Avg	AB	H	2B	3B	HR	RBI	BB	SO	OBP	SLG
Lenny Harris	.583	12	7	2	0	0	1	0	0	.583	.750
Dale Murphy	.500	14	7	2	0	1	3	0	1	.500	.857
Joe Carter	.455	11	5	0	0	2	3	1	0	.500	1.000
Rick Wilkins	.421	19	8	2	0	2	7	0	3	.421	.842
Ryne Sandberg	.333	39	13	3	1	4	9	1	1	.341	.769

Bobby Thigpen — Phillies

Age 30 – Pitches Right

	ERA	W	L	Sv	G	GS	IP	BB	SO	Avg	H	2B	3B	HR	RBI	OBP	SLG	GF	IR	IRS	Hld	SvOp	SB	CS	GB	FB	G/F
1993 Season	5.83	3	1	1	42	0	54.0	21	29	.335	74	12	1	7	45	.401	.493	16	18	10	1	4	4	4	78	69	1.13
Last Five Years	3.69	17	21	144	302	0	346.1	164	238	.247	317	48	6	36	193	.335	.379	187	167	52	4	180	23	9	414	384	1.08

1993 Season

	ERA	W	L	Sv	G	GS	IP	H	HR	BB	SO
Home	6.75	1	1	0	17	0	22.2	23	5	10	15
Away	5.17	2	0	1	25	0	31.1	51	2	11	14
Starter	0.00	0	0	0	0	0	0.0	0	0	0	0
Reliever	5.83	3	1	1	42	0	54.0	74	7	21	29
0 Days rest	11.57	0	0	0	2	0	2.1	7	2	0	0
1 or 2 Days rest	8.55	1	1	0	19	0	20.0	34	1	10	12

	Avg	AB	H	2B	3B	HR	RBI	BB	SO	OBP	SLG
vs. Left	.333	108	36	7	1	4	22	13	15	.403	.528
vs. Right	.336	113	38	5	0	3	23	8	14	.398	.460
Scoring Posn	.365	63	23	4	1	2	39	7	4	.421	.556
Close & Late	.237	38	9	1	0	0	3	5	9	.318	.263
None on/out	.275	51	14	2	0	3	3	5	13	.351	.490
First Pitch	.306	36	11	1	0	0	10	1	0	.359	.333

1993 Season

	ERA	W	L	Sv	G	GS	IP	H	HR	BB	SO
3+ Days rest	3.69	2	0	1	21	0	31.2	33	4	11	17
Pre-All Star	4.24	0	0	1	19	0	23.1	34	3	9	11
Post-All Star	7.04	3	1	0	23	0	30.2	40	4	12	18

	Avg	AB	H	2B	3B	HR	RBI	BB	SO	OBP	SLG
Ahead in Count	.274	95	26	5	0	2	19	0	27	.290	.389
Behind in Count	.417	48	20	5	0	3	10	15	0	.547	.708
Two Strikes	.261	88	23	5	0	2	17	5	29	.320	.386

Last Five Years

	ERA	W	L	Sv	G	GS	IP	H	HR	BB	SO
Home	3.79	11	10	66	150	0	171.0	163	17	77	128
Away	3.59	6	11	78	152	0	175.1	154	19	87	110
Day	4.03	2	8	44	87	0	98.1	94	8	56	71
Night	3.56	15	13	100	215	0	248.0	223	28	108	167
Grass	3.42	13	15	127	256	0	292.1	256	29	142	204
Turf	5.17	4	6	17	46	0	54.0	61	7	22	34
April	3.33	1	1	19	40	0	46.0	39	6	28	31
May	4.14	4	6	26	54	0	63.0	58	10	30	50
June	2.68	2	2	29	49	0	53.2	42	6	26	40
July	3.02	8	4	25	57	0	73.0	67	8	31	48
August	4.30	3	5	22	53	0	60.2	65	5	22	43
September/October	3.60	1	3	23	49	0	50.0	46	1	27	26
Starter	0.00	0	0	0	0	0	0.0	0	0	0	0
Reliever	3.69	17	21	144	302	0	346.1	317	36	164	238
0 Days rest	3.13	4	5	53	72	0	72.0	59	9	32	55
1 or 2 Days rest	3.67	9	12	63	135	0	162.0	147	14	89	122
3+ Days rest	4.09	4	4	28	95	0	112.1	111	13	43	61
Pre-All Star	3.36	10	10	80	163	0	190.0	169	25	95	141
Post-All Star	4.09	7	11	64	139	0	156.1	148	11	69	97

	Avg	AB	H	2B	3B	HR	RBI	BB	SO	OBP	SLG
vs. Left	.256	606	155	20	5	19	95	92	96	.350	.399
vs. Right	.240	675	162	28	1	17	98	72	142	.322	.360
Inning 1-6	.395	38	15	4	0	2	17	3	4	.455	.658
Inning 7+	.243	1243	302	44	6	34	176	161	234	.332	.370
None on	.244	606	148	22	3	15	15	84	125	.343	.365
Runners on	.250	675	169	26	3	21	178	80	113	.329	.391
Scoring Posn	.250	380	95	16	3	12	157	55	66	.339	.403
Close & Late	.224	709	159	24	3	19	111	103	158	.320	.347
None on/out	.202	257	52	7	0	7	7	45	56	.326	.311
vs. 1st Batr (relief)	.213	258	55	9	0	10	33	30	47	.306	.364
First Inning Pitched	.246	1003	247	36	5	32	151	109	179	.325	.388
First 15 Pitches	.249	865	215	30	4	33	125	89	148	.324	.407
Pitch 16-30	.242	343	83	15	2	2	49	65	78	.359	.315
Pitch 31-45	.267	60	16	3	0	1	18	9	9	.356	.367
Pitch 46+	.231	13	3	0	0	0	1	1	3	.286	.231
First Pitch	.238	181	43	3	1	4	28	16	0	.309	.331
Ahead in Count	.210	618	130	26	3	13	74	0	201	.217	.325
Behind in Count	.361	238	86	9	0	16	56	89	0	.530	.601
Two Strikes	.187	614	115	25	2	11	62	58	238	.262	.288

Pitcher vs. Batter (career)

Pitches Best Vs.	Avg	AB	H	2B	3B	HR	RBI	BB	SO	OBP	SLG
Tony Fernandez	.000	12	0	0	0	0	0	1	1	.077	.000
Joe Carter	.063	16	1	1	0	0	2	0	5	.063	.125
George Brett	.067	15	1	0	0	0	1	2	0	.176	.067
Harold Reynolds	.077	13	1	0	0	0	0	2	1	.200	.077
Geno Petralli	.111	18	2	0	0	0	1	0	5	.111	.111

Pitches Worst Vs.	Avg	AB	H	2B	3B	HR	RBI	BB	SO	OBP	SLG
Randy Bush	.667	9	6	2	0	1	6	3	0	.750	1.222
Julio Franco	.643	14	9	2	0	1	1	0	1	.643	1.000
Alan Trammell	.600	10	6	0	0	0	3	3	0	.692	.600
Rafael Palmeiro	.500	4	2	1	0	0	2	6	0	.727	.750
Dave Winfield	.462	13	6	0	0	2	3	0	1	.462	.923

Frank Thomas — White Sox

Age 26 – Bats Right (flyball hitter)

	Avg	G	AB	R	H	2B	3B	HR	RBI	BB	SO	HBP	GDP	SB	CS	OBP	SLG	IBB	SH	SF	#Pit	#P/PA	GB	FB	G/F
1993 Season	.317	153	549	106	174	36	0	41	128	112	54	2	10	4	2	.426	.607	23	0	13	2501	3.70	188	204	0.92
Career (1990-1993)	.321	531	1872	357	600	124	7	104	383	416	308	10	54	11	8	.441	.561	42	0	29	9431	4.05	583	621	0.94

1993 Season

	Avg	AB	H	2B	3B	HR	RBI	BB	SO	OBP	SLG
vs. Left	.311	151	47	9	0	14	38	33	14	.419	.649
vs. Right	.319	398	127	27	0	27	90	79	40	.429	.590
Groundball	.337	104	35	5	0	9	27	17	15	.435	.644
Flyball	.322	118	38	8	0	11	30	24	6	.425	.669
Home	.326	279	91	21	0	26	66	54	24	.432	.681
Away	.307	270	83	15	0	15	62	58	30	.420	.530
Day	.305	154	47	12	0	9	34	31	21	.417	.558
Night	.322	395	127	24	0	32	94	81	33	.429	.625
Grass	.318	466	148	31	0	35	108	90	44	.423	.609
Turf	.313	83	26	5	0	6	20	22	10	.444	.590
First Pitch	.420	81	34	7	0	10	29	19	0	.520	.877
Ahead in Count	.375	184	69	19	0	16	47	49	0	.502	.739
Behind in Count	.244	160	39	8	0	6	24	0	39	.241	.406
Two Strikes	.226	195	44	7	0	8	29	44	54	.368	.385

	Avg	AB	H	2B	3B	HR	RBI	BB	SO	OBP	SLG
Scoring Posn	.297	158	47	8	0	14	91	48	17	.436	.614
Close & Late	.304	69	21	4	0	5	20	19	5	.456	.580
None on/out	.354	113	40	5	0	7	7	8	11	.397	.584
Total	.317	549	174	36	0	41	128	112	54	.426	.607
Batting #3	.317	549	174	36	0	41	128	112	54	.426	.607
Other	.000	0	0	0	0	0	0	0	0	.000	.000
April	.269	78	21	7	0	3	21	12	12	.362	.474
May	.290	93	27	7	0	5	16	17	14	.393	.527
June	.350	103	36	5	0	8	23	21	8	.456	.631
July	.345	87	30	4	0	11	25	27	5	.496	.770
August	.333	102	34	7	0	10	26	16	8	.413	.696
September/October	.302	86	26	6	0	4	17	19	7	.422	.512
Pre-All Star	.302	311	94	20	0	20	68	60	37	.410	.559
Post-All Star	.336	238	80	16	0	21	60	52	17	.446	.668

1993 By Position

Position	Avg	AB	H	2B	3B	HR	RBI	BB	SO	OBP	SLG	G	GS	Innings	PO	A	E	DP	Fld Pct	Rng Fctr	In Zone	Outs	Zone Rtg	MLB Zone
As 1b	.314	532	167	33	0	40	121	109	50	.424	.602	150	149	1300.2	1222	82	15	127	.989	---	234	175	.748	.834

Career (1990-1993)

	Avg	AB	H	2B	3B	HR	RBI	BB	SO	OBP	SLG
vs. Left	.357	532	190	39	2	38	111	124	78	.471	.652
vs. Right	.306	1340	410	85	5	66	272	292	230	.429	.525
Groundball	.348	485	169	28	2	24	98	107	76	.463	.563
Flyball	.324	414	134	37	3	27	89	95	80	.446	.623
Home	.334	911	304	64	5	62	194	220	153	.461	.619
Away	.308	961	296	60	2	42	189	196	155	.421	.506
Day	.313	496	155	36	1	28	103	110	83	.433	.558
Night	.323	1376	445	88	6	76	280	306	225	.444	.562
Grass	.328	1560	512	105	7	91	331	354	255	.450	.579
Turf	.282	312	88	19	0	13	52	62	53	.395	.468
First Pitch	.429	212	91	21	0	16	58	33	0	.504	.755
Ahead in Count	.393	550	216	45	3	46	145	206	0	.553	.736
Behind in Count	.249	678	169	39	2	17	90	0	220	.250	.388
Two Strikes	.222	839	186	38	4	25	112	177	308	.355	.366

	Avg	AB	H	2B	3B	HR	RBI	BB	SO	OBP	SLG
Scoring Posn	.320	532	170	32	3	27	274	149	94	.452	.543
Close & Late	.303	300	91	18	2	14	72	66	58	.430	.517
None on/out	.322	367	118	28	1	22	22	61	62	.421	.583
Batting #3	.326	1401	457	96	2	85	297	301	199	.442	.580
Batting #4	.292	342	100	20	3	13	60	85	76	.430	.482
Other	.333	129	43	8	2	6	26	30	33	.456	.566
April	.265	204	54	14	2	7	41	42	40	.389	.456
May	.316	275	87	19	0	16	62	70	50	.449	.560
June	.313	310	97	17	1	17	64	67	50	.435	.539
July	.340	285	97	16	0	23	58	72	32	.471	.639
August	.346	399	138	27	4	26	88	81	54	.453	.629
September/October	.318	399	127	31	0	15	70	84	82	.433	.509
Pre-All Star	.304	886	269	55	3	47	183	206	150	.432	.532
Post-All Star	.336	986	331	69	4	57	200	210	158	.449	.587

Batter vs. Pitcher (career)

Hits Best Against	Avg	AB	H	2B	3B	HR	RBI	BB	SO	OBP	SLG	Hits Worst Against	Avg	AB	H	2B	3B	HR	RBI	BB	SO	OBP	SLG
Mike Gardiner	.643	14	9	1	0	2	5	2	1	.688	1.143	Nolan Ryan	.000	12	0	0	0	0	0	2	11	.143	.000
Mike Mussina	.588	17	10	3	0	3	5	4	1	.667	1.294	Danny Darwin	.000	12	0	0	0	0	0	2	1	.143	.000
Joe Hesketh	.556	9	5	2	0	2	4	5	3	.714	1.444	Alan Mills	.091	11	1	0	0	0	1	4	3	.313	.091
Luis Aquino	.545	11	6	1	0	3	6	2	0	.615	1.455	Greg Harris	.133	15	2	0	0	0	1	2	4	.222	.133
Cal Eldred	.500	12	6	2	0	2	3	1	1	.538	1.167	Jose Mesa	.182	11	2	0	0	0	1	2	1	.286	.182

Jim Thome — Indians

Age 23 – Bats Left (groundball hitter)

	Avg	G	AB	R	H	2B	3B	HR	RBI	BB	SO	HBP	GDP	SB	CS	OBP	SLG	IBB	SH	SF	#Pit	#P/PA	GB	FB	G/F
1993 Season	.266	47	154	28	41	11	0	7	22	29	36	4	3	2	1	.385	.474	1	0	5	771	4.02	57	39	1.46
Career (1991-1993)	.244	114	369	43	90	18	3	10	43	44	86	7	10	5	2	.330	.390	4	0	7	1639	3.84	140	92	1.52

1993 Season

	Avg	AB	H	2B	3B	HR	RBI	BB	SO	OBP	SLG		Avg	AB	H	2B	3B	HR	RBI	BB	SO	OBP	SLG
vs. Left	.302	43	13	5	0	2	11	11	4	.456	.558	Scoring Posn	.243	37	9	3	0	0	14	11	10	.377	.324
vs. Right	.252	111	28	6	0	5	11	18	32	.356	.441	Close & Late	.321	28	9	3	0	1	5	3	5	.394	.536
Home	.247	81	20	5	0	5	15	12	15	.350	.494	None on/out	.250	40	10	0	0	2	2	6	14	.348	.400
Away	.288	73	21	6	0	2	7	17	21	.424	.452	Batting #5	.235	34	8	1	0	3	6	9	8	.413	.529
First Pitch	.444	18	8	3	0	1	8	1	0	.522	.778	Batting #7	.308	78	24	10	0	3	12	12	16	.394	.551
Ahead in Count	.429	35	15	5	0	2	6	16	0	.604	.743	Other	.214	42	9	0	0	1	4	8	12	.346	.286
Behind in Count	.169	71	12	2	0	1	4	0	31	.164	.239	Pre-All Star	.000	0	0	0	0	0	0	0	0	.000	.000
Two Strikes	.177	79	14	2	0	3	7	12	36	.277	.316	Post-All Star	.266	154	41	11	0	7	22	29	36	.385	.474

Milt Thompson — Phillies

Age 35 – Bats Left (groundball hitter)

	Avg	G	AB	R	H	2B	3B	HR	RBI	BB	SO	HBP	GDP	SB	CS	OBP	SLG	IBB	SH	SF	#Pit	#P/PA	GB	FB	G/F
1993 Season	.262	129	340	42	89	14	2	4	44	40	57	2	8	9	4	.341	.350	9	3	2	1308	3.38	185	57	3.25
Last Five Years	.272	643	1837	230	499	81	23	24	193	166	300	13	31	95	32	.335	.380	29	6	6	7062	3.48	901	328	2.75

1993 Season

	Avg	AB	H	2B	3B	HR	RBI	BB	SO	OBP	SLG		Avg	AB	H	2B	3B	HR	RBI	BB	SO	OBP	SLG
vs. Left	.175	57	10	0	0	0	2	6	9	.250	.175	Scoring Posn	.293	92	27	5	0	1	36	23	18	.427	.380
vs. Right	.279	283	79	14	2	4	42	34	48	.359	.385	Close & Late	.212	66	14	2	0	0	8	9	13	.307	.242
Groundball	.238	126	30	5	1	0	20	11	20	.307	.294	None on/out	.315	73	23	2	1	1	1	8	8	.390	.411
Flyball	.316	57	18	4	0	1	8	8	12	.400	.439	Batting #6	.209	67	14	3	0	1	9	7	13	.293	.299
Home	.252	159	40	7	1	2	19	22	25	.341	.346	Batting #7	.277	195	54	4	0	2	24	20	34	.346	.328
Away	.271	181	49	7	1	2	25	18	32	.342	.354	Other	.269	78	21	7	2	1	11	13	10	.370	.449
Day	.232	99	23	2	0	3	13	9	19	.297	.343	April	.210	62	13	1	0	0	9	6	12	.279	.226
Night	.274	241	66	12	2	1	31	31	38	.359	.353	May	.250	52	13	0	0	0	9	5	10	.310	.250
Grass	.279	122	34	2	1	1	12	12	24	.350	.336	June	.289	38	11	3	0	1	7	9	4	.438	.447
Turf	.252	218	55	12	1	3	32	28	33	.336	.358	July	.268	82	22	8	1	3	13	9	11	.348	.500
First Pitch	.277	47	13	5	0	0	12	9	0	.379	.383	August	.313	48	15	2	1	0	2	7	11	.393	.396
Ahead in Count	.295	95	28	5	0	2	11	15	0	.391	.411	September/October	.259	58	15	0	0	0	4	4	9	.306	.259
Behind in Count	.183	131	24	2	2	0	10	0	48	.195	.229	Pre-All Star	.254	189	48	8	1	3	33	24	29	.340	.354
Two Strikes	.162	117	19	3	1	0	7	16	57	.274	.205	Post-All Star	.272	151	41	6	1	1	11	16	28	.343	.344

1993 By Position

Position	Avg	AB	H	2B	3B	HR	RBI	BB	SO	OBP	SLG	G	GS	Innings	PO	A	E	DP	Fld Pct	Rng Fctr	In Zone	Outs	Zone Rtg	MLB Zone
As Pinch Hitter	.320	25	8	2	1	0	3	3	5	.379	.480	30	0	---	---	---	---	---	---	---	---	---	---	---
As lf	.260	311	81	12	1	4	41	37	51	.342	.344	102	79	754.0	162	6	1	1	.994	2.01	181	152	.840	.818

Last Five Years

	Avg	AB	H	2B	3B	HR	RBI	BB	SO	OBP	SLG		Avg	AB	H	2B	3B	HR	RBI	BB	SO	OBP	SLG
vs. Left	.228	483	110	24	5	2	40	25	109	.270	.311	Scoring Posn	.268	459	123	18	8	5	159	74	94	.369	.375
vs. Right	.287	1354	389	57	18	22	153	141	191	.358	.405	Close & Late	.264	367	97	22	4	3	41	41	73	.336	.371
Groundball	.298	650	194	27	9	3	75	53	93	.355	.382	None on/out	.290	421	122	19	3	7	7	34	51	.347	.399
Flyball	.247	417	103	17	3	6	41	34	85	.307	.345	Batting #6	.257	404	104	17	5	9	42	39	65	.327	.391
Home	.266	915	243	39	16	12	108	80	133	.326	.383	Batting #7	.292	469	137	18	6	4	53	37	94	.346	.382
Away	.278	922	256	42	7	12	85	86	167	.344	.377	Other	.268	964	258	46	12	11	98	90	141	.334	.374
Day	.261	591	154	31	6	9	63	49	97	.324	.379	April	.272	250	68	11	2	2	29	25	40	.341	.356
Night	.277	1246	345	50	17	15	130	117	203	.341	.380	May	.264	250	66	5	3	5	27	28	38	.344	.368
Grass	.281	533	150	24	7	6	42	54	94	.354	.386	June	.296	334	99	18	9	5	48	35	49	.363	.449
Turf	.268	1304	349	57	16	18	151	112	206	.328	.377	July	.243	350	85	14	5	4	32	28	56	.306	.346
First Pitch	.354	294	104	19	0	5	43	18	0	.389	.469	August	.299	314	94	16	3	5	28	31	61	.365	.417
Ahead in Count	.308	467	144	28	7	8	59	79	0	.411	.450	September/October	.257	339	87	17	1	3	29	19	56	.298	.339
Behind in Count	.209	761	159	16	10	7	60	0	254	.214	.284	Pre-All Star	.272	967	263	40	15	15	115	99	144	.344	.391
Two Strikes	.176	726	128	15	6	2	47	64	300	.248	.222	Post-All Star	.271	870	236	41	8	9	78	67	156	.326	.368

Batter vs. Pitcher (career)

Hits Best Against	Avg	AB	H	2B	3B	HR	RBI	BB	SO	OBP	SLG	Hits Worst Against	Avg	AB	H	2B	3B	HR	RBI	BB	SO	OBP	SLG
Neal Heaton	.429	14	6	3	0	0	1	0	0	.429	.643	Pete Smith	.000	13	0	0	0	0	0	2	1	.133	.000
Jeff Parrett	.417	12	5	1	1	0	5	3	4	.533	.667	Paul Assenmacher	.053	19	1	1	0	0	1	1	2	.100	.105
Bill Gullickson	.409	22	9	3	1	1	2	1	0	.435	.773	Tom Browning	.071	14	1	0	0	0	0	1	3	.133	.071
Jim Gott	.400	10	4	0	1	0	2	1	2	.455	.600	Frank Castillo	.083	12	1	0	0	0	0	2	3	.214	.083
Les Lancaster	.393	28	11	2	1	1	4	3	0	.452	.643	Tommy Greene	.133	15	2	1	0	0	1	0	1	.133	.200

Robby Thompson — Giants

Age 32 – Bats Right

	Avg	G	AB	R	H	2B	3B	HR	RBI	BB	SO	HBP	GDP	SB	CS	OBP	SLG	IBB	SH	SF	#Pit	#P/PA	GB	FB	G/F
1993 Season	.312	128	494	85	154	30	2	19	65	45	97	7	7	10	4	.375	.496	0	9	4	2174	3.89	154	157	0.98
Last Five Years	.264	692	2474	371	652	127	22	80	268	236	496	40	35	55	26	.336	.430	4	44	12	10633	3.79	803	772	1.04

1993 Season

	Avg	AB	H	2B	3B	HR	RBI	BB	SO	OBP	SLG
vs. Left	.352	145	51	12	0	5	20	14	21	.409	.538
vs. Right	.295	349	103	18	2	14	45	31	76	.361	.479
Groundball	.314	153	48	8	1	5	25	12	25	.363	.477
Flyball	.329	70	23	9	0	1	7	6	15	.390	.500
Home	.309	223	69	13	2	13	31	26	43	.389	.561
Away	.314	271	85	17	0	6	34	19	54	.362	.443
Day	.333	231	77	13	1	11	38	22	39	.396	.541
Night	.293	263	77	17	1	8	27	23	58	.355	.456
Grass	.329	386	127	26	2	18	51	35	74	.388	.547
Turf	.250	108	27	4	0	1	14	10	23	.325	.315
First Pitch	[illegible]	52	19	4	2	2	12	0	0	.370	.635
Ahead in Count	.373	118	44	9	0	9	23	21	0	.469	.678
Behind in Count	.243	218	53	8	0	7	21	0	78	.252	.376
Two Strikes	.222	234	52	7	0	5	19	24	97	.299	.316

	Avg	AB	H	2B	3B	HR	RBI	BB	SO	OBP	SLG
Scoring Posn	.304	125	38	10	0	1	41	17	29	.381	.408
Close & Late	.239	71	17	4	1	1	7	2	19	.263	.366
None on/out	.322	87	28	7	0	7	7	7	18	.385	.644
Batting #2	.327	382	125	23	2	18	49	36	76	.392	.539
Batting #6	.259	108	28	7	0	0	15	9	20	.317	.324
Other	.250	4	1	0	0	1	1	0	1	.250	1.000
April	.250	64	16	3	0	0	11	5	11	.296	.297
May	.320	103	33	8	0	4	12	7	22	.368	.515
June	.398	98	39	6	0	5	15	8	16	.443	.612
July	.250	48	12	2	1	0	3	3	11	.294	.333
August	.394	99	39	7	1	8	18	11	16	.464	.727
September/October	.183	82	15	4	0	2	6	11	21	.302	.305
Pre-All Star	.325	277	90	17	0	9	40	20	51	.370	.484
Post-All Star	.295	217	64	13	2	10	25	25	46	.381	.512

1993 By Position

Position	Avg	AB	H	2B	3B	HR	RBI	BB	SO	OBP	SLG	G	GS	Innings	PO	A	E	DP	Fld Pct	Rng Fctr	In Zone	Outs	Zone Rtg	MLB Zone
As 2b	.311	492	153	29	2	19	63	45	97	.374	.494	128	124	1094.2	274	384	8	95	.988	5.41	409	379	.927	.895

Last Five Years

	Avg	AB	H	2B	3B	HR	RBI	BB	SO	OBP	SLG
vs. Left	.297	821	244	57	9	26	91	87	138	.368	.484
vs. Right	.247	1653	408	70	13	54	177	149	358	.320	.403
Groundball	.246	866	213	39	9	20	86	73	149	.316	.381
Flyball	.241	506	122	28	3	19	55	42	117	.308	.421
Home	.280	1234	346	71	14	47	150	133	235	.359	.475
Away	.247	1240	306	56	8	33	118	103	261	.313	.385
Day	.278	1012	281	54	10	37	127	106	192	.355	.460
Night	.254	1462	371	73	12	43	141	130	304	.323	.408
Grass	.279	1875	524	106	18	66	216	185	362	.351	.461
Turf	.214	599	128	21	4	14	52	51	134	.288	.332
First Pitch	.333	273	91	19	4	8	42	2	0	.360	.520
Ahead in Count	.344	573	197	39	8	35	97	125	0	.461	.623
Behind in Count	.207	1155	239	44	7	23	78	0	417	.219	.317
Two Strikes	.173	1165	201	38	6	20	66	106	496	.248	.267

	Avg	AB	H	2B	3B	HR	RBI	BB	SO	OBP	SLG
Scoring Posn	.234	556	130	28	3	14	176	70	132	.323	.371
Close & Late	.230	413	95	17	3	10	48	34	92	.295	.358
None on/out	.259	505	131	31	4	20	20	48	103	.337	.455
Batting #2	.261	1352	353	73	13	44	139	119	277	.331	.432
Batting #6	.270	578	156	27	4	18	67	61	116	.346	.424
Other	.263	544	143	27	5	18	62	56	103	.338	.430
April	.259	370	96	17	4	8	39	39	73	.332	.392
May	.282	394	111	25	3	15	40	34	75	.344	.475
June	.272	445	121	21	5	16	57	45	86	.353	.449
July	.240	396	95	19	3	12	37	32	76	.310	.394
August	.298	473	141	26	5	19	57	45	89	.366	.495
September/October	.222	396	88	19	2	10	38	41	97	.302	.356
Pre-All Star	.269	1336	359	68	12	44	156	133	253	.343	.436
Post-All Star	.257	1138	293	59	10	36	112	103	243	.328	.422

Batter vs. Pitcher (career)

Hits Best Against	Avg	AB	H	2B	3B	HR	RBI	BB	SO	OBP	SLG
Paul Assenmacher	.545	11	6	2	0	0	3	0	1	.545	.727
Chris Hammond	.500	16	8	2	0	0	2	3	0	.579	.625
Mike Maddux	.471	17	8	1	1	2	6	0	2	.471	1.000
Butch Henry	.455	11	5	2	0	0	1	2	2	.538	.636
Tom Glavine	.452	42	19	7	1	3	6	4	6	.500	.881

Hits Worst Against	Avg	AB	H	2B	3B	HR	RBI	BB	SO	OBP	SLG
Jimmy Jones	.053	19	1	0	0	0	0	3	3	.182	.053
Ken Hill	.071	14	1	0	0	0	0	1	2	.133	.071
Todd Worrell	.077	13	1	0	0	0	0	0	3	.077	.077
Norm Charlton	.091	11	1	0	0	0	1	0	4	.091	.091
Jay Howell	.118	17	2	0	0	0	3	0	9	.111	.118

Ryan Thompson — Mets

Age 26 – Bats Right (flyball hitter)

	Avg	G	AB	R	H	2B	3B	HR	RBI	BB	SO	HBP	GDP	SB	CS	OBP	SLG	IBB	SH	SF	#Pit	#P/PA	GB	FB	G/F
1993 Season	.250	80	288	34	72	19	2	11	26	19	81	3	5	2	7	.302	.444	4	5	1	1105	3.50	79	80	0.99
Career (1992-1993)	.242	110	396	49	96	26	3	14	36	27	105	3	7	4	9	.294	.429	4	5	2	1509	3.48	113	118	0.96

1993 Season

	Avg	AB	H	2B	3B	HR	RBI	BB	SO	OBP	SLG
vs. Left	.217	92	20	4	0	1	2	3	28	.258	.293
vs. Right	.265	196	52	15	2	10	24	16	53	.322	.515
Home	.259	135	35	7	1	5	16	8	39	.310	.437
Away	.242	153	37	12	1	6	10	11	42	.295	.451
First Pitch	.500	38	19	5	1	2	6	3	0	.548	.842
Ahead in Count	.419	43	18	6	1	2	4	11	0	.537	.744
Behind in Count	.147	163	24	6	0	3	10	0	73	.157	.239
Two Strikes	.136	154	21	6	0	3	8	5	81	.168	.234

	Avg	AB	H	2B	3B	HR	RBI	BB	SO	OBP	SLG
Scoring Posn	.155	58	9	4	1	2	16	6	25	.254	.362
Close & Late	.277	47	13	2	0	4	6	3	18	.327	.574
None on/out	.245	98	24	5	0	3	3	6	23	.295	.388
Batting #1	.253	186	47	12	1	5	14	8	49	.293	.409
Batting #8	.421	38	16	5	0	5	7	6	11	.500	.947
Other	.141	64	9	2	1	1	5	5	21	.203	.250
Pre-All Star	.125	40	5	1	1	0	1	2	13	.167	.200
Post-All Star	.270	248	67	18	1	11	25	17	68	.323	.484

Dickie Thon — Brewers

Age 36 – Bats Right

	Avg	G	AB	R	H	2B	3B	HR	RBI	BB	SO	HBP	GDP	SB	CS	OBP	SLG	IBB	SH	SF	#Pit	#P/PA	GB	FB	G/F
1993 Season	.269	85	245	23	66	10	1	1	33	22	39	0	4	6	5	.324	.331	3	3	5	900	3.27	80	76	1.05
Last Five Years	.259	611	2046	196	529	81	16	37	222	137	321	3	35	47	20	.303	.368	26	10	19	6876	3.10	758	602	1.26

1993 Season

	Avg	AB	H	2B	3B	HR	RBI	BB	SO	OBP	SLG
vs. Left	.270	122	33	3	0	1	15	13	21	.336	.320
vs. Right	.268	123	33	7	1	0	18	9	18	.311	.341
Home	.280	118	33	5	0	0	14	10	19	.333	.322
Away	.260	127	33	5	1	1	19	12	20	.315	.339

	Avg	AB	H	2B	3B	HR	RBI	BB	SO	OBP	SLG
Scoring Posn	.351	74	26	3	1	0	31	12	8	.418	.419
Close & Late	.184	49	9	2	0	0	8	5	10	.250	.224
None on/out	.206	63	13	4	0	1	1	6	17	.275	.317
Batting #5	.269	52	14	3	0	0	8	4	6	.316	.327

1993 Season

	Avg	AB	H	2B	3B	HR	RBI	BB	SO	OBP	SLG
First Pitch	.277	47	13	2	1	0	9	2	0	.300	.362
Ahead in Count	.392	51	20	0	0	1	7	16	0	.529	.451
Behind in Count	.241	108	26	6	0	0	11	0	30	.236	.296
Two Strikes	.222	99	22	6	0	0	10	4	39	.248	.283

	Avg	AB	H	2B	3B	HR	RBI	BB	SO	OBP	SLG
Batting #6	.300	70	21	1	0	1	9	6	8	.355	.357
Other	.252	123	31	6	1	0	16	12	25	.309	.317
Pre-All Star	.292	185	54	9	1	1	30	14	29	.333	.368
Post-All Star	.200	60	12	1	0	0	3	8	10	.294	.217

Last Five Years

	Avg	AB	H	2B	3B	HR	RBI	BB	SO	OBP	SLG
vs. Left	.269	804	216	32	8	17	89	68	114	.323	.392
vs. Right	.252	1242	313	49	8	20	133	69	207	.290	.353
Groundball	.244	684	167	22	0	11	66	52	98	.296	.325
Flyball	.271	450	122	29	5	13	61	35	68	.323	.444
Home	.263	992	261	35	7	17	114	66	161	.307	.364
Away	.254	1054	268	46	9	20	108	71	160	.300	.372
Day	.239	577	138	24	3	7	54	39	83	.286	.328
Night	.266	1469	391	57	13	30	168	98	238	.310	.384
Grass	.259	865	224	39	6	8	85	67	138	.310	.346
Turf	.258	1181	305	42	10	29	137	70	183	.298	.384
First Pitch	.306	448	137	22	5	17	76	11	0	.318	.491
Ahead in Count	.316	424	134	17	3	10	51	77	0	.417	.441
Behind in Count	.200	879	176	30	3	7	68	0	292	.201	.265
Two Strikes	.183	766	140	25	4	4	52	39	321	.223	.242

	Avg	AB	H	2B	3B	HR	RBI	BB	SO	OBP	SLG
Scoring Posn	.283	513	145	28	2	8	175	53	78	.338	.392
Close & Late	.267	374	100	12	3	5	38	28	60	.315	.356
None on/out	.254	519	132	17	4	10	10	27	89	.294	.360
Batting #7	.250	663	166	30	4	11	68	45	112	.298	.357
Batting #8	.265	548	145	21	4	12	64	41	80	.312	.383
Other	.261	835	218	30	8	14	90	51	129	.302	.366
April	.256	301	77	11	2	1	34	25	51	.307	.316
May	.264	368	97	12	3	6	49	26	55	.309	.361
June	.237	388	92	15	3	9	38	33	61	.295	.361
July	.269	323	87	12	4	6	33	13	50	.299	.387
August	.259	347	90	19	2	6	38	26	54	.310	.378
September/October	.270	319	86	12	2	9	30	14	50	.300	.404
Pre-All Star	.250	1173	293	46	10	17	134	88	189	.299	.350
Post-All Star	.270	873	236	35	6	20	88	49	132	.310	.393

Batter vs. Pitcher (since 1984)

Hits Best Against	Avg	AB	H	2B	3B	HR	RBI	BB	SO	OBP	SLG
Neal Heaton	.421	19	8	1	0	2	8	1	2	.450	.789
Mark Davis	.400	10	4	0	1	2	4	3	2	.538	1.200
Bob Patterson	.385	13	5	0	0	1	2	1	3	.429	.615
Jim Deshaies	.378	37	14	2	2	2	6	2	9	.400	.703
Omar Olivares	.333	12	4	1	1	0	2	1	3	.385	.583

Hits Worst Against	Avg	AB	H	2B	3B	HR	RBI	BB	SO	OBP	SLG
Norm Charlton	.083	12	1	0	0	0	0	1	3	.154	.083
Charlie Leibrandt	.091	11	1	0	0	0	1	0	1	.083	.091
Lee Smith	.091	11	1	0	0	0	0	0	1	.091	.091
Danny Darwin	.100	10	1	0	0	0	1	1	4	.182	.100
Brian Barnes	.125	16	2	0	0	0	0	0	4	.125	.125

Gary Thurman — Tigers

Age 29 – Bats Right (groundball hitter)

	Avg	G	AB	R	H	2B	3B	HR	RBI	BB	SO	HBP	GDP	SB	CS	OBP	SLG	IBB	SH	SF	#Pit	#P/PA	GB	FB	G/F
1993 Season	.213	75	89	22	19	2	2	0	13	11	30	0	2	7	0	.297	.281	0	1	1	410	4.02	23	17	1.35
Last Five Years	.242	337	620	100	150	22	6	2	54	48	144	2	11	48	12	.297	.306	0	13	3	2522	3.68	235	120	1.96

1993 Season

	Avg	AB	H	2B	3B	HR	RBI	BB	SO	OBP	SLG
vs. Left	.276	58	16	2	1	0	8	5	15	.328	.345
vs. Right	.097	31	3	0	1	0	5	6	15	.243	.161

	Avg	AB	H	2B	3B	HR	RBI	BB	SO	OBP	SLG
Scoring Posn	.290	31	9	0	2	0	13	5	11	.378	.419
Close & Late	.375	8	3	0	0	0	2	1	3	.444	.375

Last Five Years

	Avg	AB	H	2B	3B	HR	RBI	BB	SO	OBP	SLG
vs. Left	.265	374	99	18	5	1	38	24	71	.308	.348
vs. Right	.207	246	51	4	1	1	16	24	73	.281	.244
Groundball	.318	154	49	4	3	1	20	11	29	.365	.403
Flyball	.241	158	38	7	1	1	8	15	39	.309	.316
Home	.211	308	65	12	3	1	24	23	68	.269	.279
Away	.272	312	85	10	3	1	30	25	76	.324	.333
Day	.233	180	42	5	3	0	20	15	44	.294	.294
Night	.245	440	108	17	3	2	34	33	100	.298	.311
Grass	.253	273	69	8	4	0	33	21	74	.304	.311
Turf	.233	347	81	14	2	2	21	27	70	.292	.303
First Pitch	.312	93	29	8	1	1	8	0	0	.312	.452
Ahead in Count	.348	112	39	5	4	1	22	19	0	.436	.491
Behind in Count	.184	305	56	5	1	0	15	0	120	.188	.207
Two Strikes	.168	303	51	6	1	0	16	29	144	.246	.195

	Avg	AB	H	2B	3B	HR	RBI	BB	SO	OBP	SLG
Scoring Posn	.271	170	46	3	3	0	50	18	46	.335	.324
Close & Late	.279	86	24	2	1	0	9	7	26	.337	.326
None on/out	.220	186	41	10	1	2	2	15	38	.279	.317
Batting #1	.280	232	65	10	1	2	15	21	48	.343	.358
Batting #9	.195	113	22	1	2	0	7	12	30	.270	.239
Other	.229	275	63	11	3	0	32	15	66	.270	.291
April	.208	72	15	1	2	0	8	8	21	.288	.278
May	.273	110	30	5	1	1	15	11	25	.339	.364
June	.195	82	16	2	1	0	5	1	16	.205	.244
July	.268	112	30	5	1	1	7	10	29	.331	.357
August	.258	93	24	4	1	0	13	8	19	.317	.323
September/October	.232	151	35	5	0	0	6	10	34	.280	.265
Pre-All Star	.240	308	74	10	4	2	31	23	74	.295	.318
Post-All Star	.244	312	76	12	2	0	23	25	70	.299	.295

Batter vs. Pitcher (career)

Hits Best Against	Avg	AB	H	2B	3B	HR	RBI	BB	SO	OBP	SLG
Dave Otto	.556	9	5	1	0	0	3	2	3	.636	.667
Greg Swindell	.333	12	4	1	0	0	0	0	3	.333	.417

Hits Worst Against	Avg	AB	H	2B	3B	HR	RBI	BB	SO	OBP	SLG
Kenny Rogers	.000	9	0	0	0	0	1	2	3	.167	.000
Curt Young	.067	15	1	0	0	0	1	1	5	.125	.067
Jim Abbott	.136	22	3	0	0	0	0	3	3	.240	.136
Mark Langston	.143	28	4	0	0	0	0	2	8	.200	.143
Dave Fleming	.182	11	2	0	0	0	1	0	1	.182	.182

Mike Timlin — Blue Jays

Age 28 – Pitches Right (groundball pitcher)

	ERA	W	L	Sv	G	GS	IP	BB	SO	Avg	H	2B	3B	HR	RBI	OBP	SLG	GF	IR	IRS	Hld	SvOp	SB	CS	GB	FB	G/F
1993 Season	4.69	4	2	1	54	0	55.2	27	49	.284	63	6	0	7	36	.360	.405	27	32	12	9	4	9	0	95	37	2.57
Career (1991-1993)	3.77	15	10	5	143	3	207.2	97	169	.255	202	18	1	13	117	.336	.330	58	99	40	19	13	24	8	366	125	2.93

1993 Season

	ERA	W	L	Sv	G	GS	IP	H	HR	BB	SO
Home	4.15	2	1	0	31	0	30.1	34	4	14	30
Away	5.33	2	1	1	23	0	25.1	29	3	13	19
Starter	0.00	0	0	0	0	0	0.0	0	0	0	0
Reliever	4.69	4	2	1	54	0	55.2	63	7	27	49
0 Days rest	9.35	0	0	0	10	0	8.2	13	1	8	8
1 or 2 Days rest	4.94	1	1	0	25	0	27.1	28	3	8	28

	Avg	AB	H	2B	3B	HR	RBI	BB	SO	OBP	SLG
vs. Left	.275	102	28	5	0	4	16	15	19	.361	.441
vs. Right	.292	120	35	1	0	3	20	12	30	.358	.375
Scoring Posn	.294	68	20	4	0	1	29	10	14	.370	.397
Close & Late	.290	69	20	4	0	2	12	7	12	.354	.435
None on/out	.300	50	15	0	0	3	3	7	13	.386	.480
First Pitch	.357	28	10	1	0	3	5	3	0	.419	.714

1993 Season

	ERA	W	L	Sv	G	GS	IP	H	HR	BB	SO
3+ Days rest	2.29	3	1	1	19	0	19.2	22	3	11	13
Pre-All Star	5.54	1	1	0	35	0	37.1	46	4	18	38
Post-All Star	2.95	3	1	1	19	0	18.1	17	3	9	11

	Avg	AB	H	2B	3B	HR	RBI	BB	SO	OBP	SLG
Ahead in Count	.205	117	24	2	0	2	15	0	42	.208	.274
Behind in Count	.386	44	17	3	0	2	13	14	0	.525	.591
Two Strikes	.190	105	20	2	0	1	12	10	49	.265	.238

Career (1991-1993)

	ERA	W	L	Sv	G	GS	IP	H	HR	BB	SO
Home	3.56	9	5	2	78	2	116.1	119	6	53	92
Away	4.04	6	5	3	65	1	91.1	83	7	44	77
Day	2.43	6	3	1	55	1	77.2	58	4	36	61
Night	4.57	9	7	4	88	2	130.0	144	9	61	108
Grass	4.34	4	4	2	51	1	74.2	65	6	39	70
Turf	3.45	11	6	3	92	2	133.0	137	7	58	99
April	3.90	3	1	0	20	0	27.2	27	5	8	22
May	4.45	1	2	2	26	0	30.1	29	2	19	25
June	4.01	3	3	0	23	3	42.2	46	0	24	33
July	3.70	6	0	1	23	0	41.1	36	4	17	40
August	4.60	0	0	0	16	0	29.1	32	1	14	24
September/October	2.23	2	1	2	35	0	36.1	32	1	15	25
Starter	1.84	1	1	0	3	3	14.2	14	0	7	10
Reliever	3.92	14	9	5	140	0	193.0	188	13	90	159
0 Days rest	4.26	3	0	0	25	0	31.2	30	1	17	23
1 or 2 Days rest	3.71	6	7	2	65	0	97.0	88	7	38	80
3+ Days rest	4.06	5	2	3	50	0	64.1	70	5	35	56
Pre-All Star	3.73	8	6	2	76	3	115.2	111	8	54	97
Post-All Star	3.82	7	4	3	67	0	92.0	91	5	43	72

	Avg	AB	H	2B	3B	HR	RBI	BB	SO	OBP	SLG
vs. Left	.293	345	101	12	1	7	55	54	57	.386	.394
vs. Right	.226	447	101	6	0	6	62	43	112	.296	.280
Inning 1-6	.288	240	69	3	0	3	49	33	49	.375	.338
Inning 7+	.241	552	133	15	1	10	68	64	120	.319	.326
None on	.222	414	92	7	0	7	7	40	94	.291	.290
Runners on	.291	378	110	11	1	6	110	57	75	.383	.373
Scoring Posn	.283	244	69	9	0	3	103	47	56	.395	.357
Close & Late	.256	250	64	8	0	5	36	33	49	.341	.348
None on/out	.215	177	38	3	0	3	3	19	41	.291	.282
vs. 1st Batr (relief)	.235	119	28	3	0	1	19	19	23	.345	.286
First Inning Pitched	.275	491	135	13	0	9	84	60	96	.354	.356
First 15 Pitches	.280	439	123	13	1	7	68	45	71	.347	.362
Pitch 16-30	.220	223	49	3	0	4	28	34	62	.323	.287
Pitch 31-45	.238	84	20	2	0	2	16	12	23	.333	.333
Pitch 46+	.217	46	10	0	0	0	5	6	13	.308	.217
First Pitch	.316	95	30	1	0	5	18	16	0	.414	.484
Ahead in Count	.225	413	93	8	1	3	57	0	143	.229	.271
Behind in Count	.320	153	49	5	0	2	26	48	0	.478	.392
Two Strikes	.199	381	76	6	1	4	50	33	169	.266	.252

Pitcher vs. Batter (career)

Pitches Best Vs.	Avg	AB	H	2B	3B	HR	RBI	BB	SO	OBP	SLG
Rob Deer	.111	9	1	0	0	1	2	2	6	.273	.444
Rafael Palmeiro	.182	11	2	0	0	1	2	0	0	.182	.455

Pitches Worst Vs.	Avg	AB	H	2B	3B	HR	RBI	BB	SO	OBP	SLG

Ron Tingley — Angels

Age 35 – Bats Right (groundball hitter)

	Avg	G	AB	R	H	2B	3B	HR	RBI	BB	SO	HBP	GDP	SB	CS	OBP	SLG	IBB	SH	SF	#Pit	#P/PA	GB	FB	G/F
1993 Season	.200	58	90	7	18	7	0	0	12	9	22	1	4	1	2	.277	.278	0	3	1	386	3.71	42	19	2.21
Last Five Years	.198	183	338	33	67	16	1	4	33	32	92	4	10	2	4	.275	.287	0	12	1	1511	3.90	127	78	1.63

1993 Season

	Avg	AB	H	2B	3B	HR	RBI	BB	SO	OBP	SLG
vs. Left	.167	54	9	2	0	0	7	5	14	.233	.204
vs. Right	.250	36	9	5	0	0	5	4	8	.341	.389
Scoring Posn	.421	19	8	3	0	0	11	3	4	.500	.579
Close & Late	.000	12	0	0	0	0	0	3	4	.200	.000

Lee Tinsley — Mariners

Age 25 – Bats Both

	Avg	G	AB	R	H	2B	3B	HR	RBI	BB	SO	HBP	GDP	SB	CS	OBP	SLG	IBB	SH	SF	#Pit	#P/PA	GB	FB	G/F
1993 Season	.158	11	19	2	3	1	0	1	2	2	9	0	1	0	0	.238	.368	0	0	0	91	4.33	3	5	0.60

1993 Season

	Avg	AB	H	2B	3B	HR	RBI	BB	SO	OBP	SLG
vs. Left	.000	5	0	0	0	0	0	1	2	.167	.000
vs. Right	.214	14	3	1	0	1	2	1	7	.267	.500
Scoring Posn	.125	8	1	0	0	1	2	2	4	.300	.500
Close & Late	.143	7	1	0	0	0	0	1	4	.250	.143

Fred Toliver — Pirates

Age 33 – Pitches Right (groundball pitcher)

	ERA	W	L	Sv	G	GS	IP	BB	SO	Avg	H	2B	3B	HR	RBI	OBP	SLG	GF	IR	IRS	Hld	SvOp	SB	CS	GB	FB	G/F
1993 Season	3.74	1	0	0	12	0	21.2	8	14	.267	20	2	0	2	13	.341	.373	3	16	4	1	0	2	0	29	20	1.45
Last Five Years	6.26	2	3	0	28	5	64.2	32	39	.303	76	16	0	9	43	.385	.474	3	20	5	1	0	5	1	108	62	1.74

1993 Season

	ERA	W	L	Sv	G	GS	IP	H	HR	BB	SO
Home	0.00	1	0	0	4	0	3.0	0	0	1	5
Away	4.34	0	0	0	8	0	18.2	20	2	7	9

	Avg	AB	H	2B	3B	HR	RBI	BB	SO	OBP	SLG
vs. Left	.286	42	12	1	0	1	7	1	9	.311	.381
vs. Right	.242	33	8	1	0	1	6	7	5	.372	.364

Andy Tomberlin — Pirates

Age 27 – Bats Left

	Avg	G	AB	R	H	2B	3B	HR	RBI	BB	SO	HBP	GDP	SB	CS	OBP	SLG	IBB	SH	SF	#Pit	#P/PA	GB	FB	G/F
1993 Season	.286	27	42	4	12	0	1	1	5	2	14	1	0	0	0	.333	.405	0	0	0	181	4.02	15	7	2.14

1993 Season

	Avg	AB	H	2B	3B	HR	RBI	BB	SO	OBP	SLG
vs. Left	.167	6	1	0	0	0	0	0	4	.167	.167
vs. Right	.306	36	11	0	1	1	5	2	10	.359	.444
Scoring Posn	.188	16	3	0	1	0	4	1	7	.235	.313
Close & Late	.333	6	2	0	0	0	1	1	2	.429	.333

Randy Tomlin — Pirates

Age 28 – Pitches Left (groundball pitcher)

	ERA	W	L	Sv	G	GS	IP	BB	SO	Avg	H	2B	3B	HR	RBI	OBP	SLG	CG	ShO	Sup	QS	#P/S	SB	CS	GB	FB	G/F
1993 Season	4.85	4	8	0	18	18	98.1	15	44	.291	109	30	5	11	52	.320	.485	1	0	4.58	9	80	7	4	148	115	1.29
Career (1990-1993)	3.41	30	28	0	96	90	559.2	123	280	.267	567	120	19	36	210	.310	.392	8	3	4.20	55	89	47	30	899	568	1.58

1993 Season

	ERA	W	L	Sv	G	GS	IP	H	HR	BB	SO
Home	4.13	2	4	0	10	10	56.2	65	5	8	27
Away	5.83	2	4	0	8	8	41.2	44	6	7	17
Starter	4.85	4	8	0	18	18	98.1	109	11	15	44
Reliever	0.00	0	0	0	0	0	0.0	0	0	0	0
0-3 Days Rest	0.00	0	0	0	0	0	0.0	0	0	0	0
4 Days Rest	4.31	4	3	0	11	11	64.2	62	10	12	26
5+ Days Rest	5.88	0	5	0	7	7	33.2	47	1	3	18
Pre-All Star	4.96	2	5	0	10	10	52.2	57	3	7	29
Post-All Star	4.73	2	3	0	8	8	45.2	52	8	8	15

	Avg	AB	H	2B	3B	HR	RBI	BB	SO	OBP	SLG
vs. Left	.315	73	23	7	2	1	13	2	10	.338	.507
vs. Right	.285	302	86	23	3	10	39	13	34	.316	.480
Scoring Posn	.330	88	29	9	1	1	38	2	13	.343	.489
Close & Late	.160	25	4	0	0	1	1	1	1	.192	.280
None on/out	.327	104	34	10	3	4	4	4	13	.358	.596
First Pitch	.391	46	18	4	0	3	13	0	0	.396	.674
Ahead in Count	.190	153	29	7	1	4	13	0	37	.201	.327
Behind in Count	.352	108	38	13	2	2	11	10	0	.405	.565
Two Strikes	.162	136	22	5	1	4	16	5	44	.197	.301

Career (1990-1993)

	ERA	W	L	Sv	G	GS	IP	H	HR	BB	SO
Home	2.94	16	14	0	50	48	309.2	302	17	50	173
Away	4.00	14	14	0	46	42	250.0	265	19	73	107
Day	3.81	6	11	0	30	26	170.0	187	14	39	79
Night	3.23	24	17	0	66	64	389.2	380	22	84	201
Grass	3.74	8	6	0	25	22	134.2	134	12	35	46
Turf	3.30	22	22	0	71	68	425.0	433	24	88	234
April	2.88	7	1	0	11	11	68.2	57	6	18	27
May	4.84	3	8	0	16	14	70.2	87	3	21	36
June	2.62	5	3	0	11	10	68.2	62	4	14	40
July	4.07	4	6	0	15	14	86.1	101	6	21	35
August	3.27	7	4	0	22	22	146.0	134	12	25	74
September/October	3.02	4	6	0	21	19	119.1	126	5	24	68
Starter	3.46	30	28	0	90	90	551.2	563	36	121	274
Reliever	0.00	0	0	0	6	0	8.0	4	0	2	6
0-3 Days Rest	3.38	1	2	0	3	3	16.0	21	1	5	11
4 Days Rest	3.53	19	14	0	56	56	349.0	353	28	72	167
5+ Days Rest	3.33	10	12	0	31	31	186.2	189	7	44	96
Pre-All Star	3.64	15	13	0	43	39	229.2	238	16	57	113
Post-All Star	3.25	15	15	0	53	51	330.0	329	20	66	167

	Avg	AB	H	2B	3B	HR	RBI	BB	SO	OBP	SLG
vs. Left	.239	402	96	17	2	6	37	27	77	.294	.336
vs. Right	.273	1723	471	103	17	30	173	96	203	.314	.405
Inning 1-6	.267	1849	494	109	19	28	187	104	242	.309	.392
Inning 7+	.264	276	73	11	0	8	23	19	38	.315	.391
None on	.263	1262	332	66	10	23	23	76	161	.309	.386
Runners on	.272	863	235	54	9	13	187	47	119	.311	.401
Scoring Posn	.282	479	135	31	5	5	159	37	67	.331	.399
Close & Late	.253	162	41	9	0	5	12	11	25	.309	.401
None on/out	.289	558	161	32	5	11	11	35	64	.337	.423
vs. 1st Batr (relief)	.200	5	1	0	0	0	1	1	1	.333	.200
First Inning Pitched	.256	355	91	20	2	6	38	26	41	.307	.375
First 75 Pitches	.262	1703	447	103	14	26	157	91	219	.302	.385
Pitch 76-90	.322	239	77	10	4	5	36	20	36	.380	.460
Pitch 91-105	.211	128	27	4	1	4	11	8	19	.261	.352
Pitch 106+	.291	55	16	3	0	1	6	4	6	.350	.400
First Pitch	.341	290	99	23	1	4	42	7	0	.362	.469
Ahead in Count	.222	918	204	36	7	15	76	0	235	.229	.326
Behind in Count	.283	508	144	40	5	9	50	77	0	.377	.435
Two Strikes	.189	874	165	29	3	15	64	39	280	.228	.280

Pitcher vs. Batter (career)

Pitches Best Vs.	Avg	AB	H	2B	3B	HR	RBI	BB	SO	OBP	SLG
Fred McGriff	.000	23	0	0	0	0	1	3	8	.111	.000
Darrin Jackson	.000	11	0	0	0	0	0	1	2	.083	.000
Vince Coleman	.043	23	1	0	0	0	0	0	5	.043	.043
Andres Galarraga	.083	12	1	0	0	0	0	0	4	.083	.083
Charlie O'Brien	.125	16	2	0	0	0	0	0	1	.125	.125

Pitches Worst Vs.	Avg	AB	H	2B	3B	HR	RBI	BB	SO	OBP	SLG
Barry Larkin	.692	13	9	4	1	0	2	0	0	.692	1.154
Otis Nixon	.583	12	7	2	2	0	1	1	0	.615	1.083
Sammy Sosa	.583	12	7	1	0	1	3	0	2	.583	.917
Pete Incaviglia	.538	13	7	3	0	1	5	0	1	.538	1.000
Ryne Sandberg	.500	28	14	2	2	1	5	2	1	.533	.821

Salomon Torres — Giants

Age 22 – Pitches Right

	ERA	W	L	Sv	G	GS	IP	BB	SO	Avg	H	2B	3B	HR	RBI	OBP	SLG	CG	ShO	Sup	QS	#P/S	SB	CS	GB	FB	G/F
1993 Season	4.03	3	5	0	8	8	44.2	27	23	.231	37	7	0	5	18	.344	.369	0	0	3.63	5	87	5	3	62	49	1.27

1993 Season

	ERA	W	L	Sv	G	GS	IP	H	HR	BB	SO
Home	3.42	1	3	0	4	4	23.2	15	4	17	15
Away	4.71	2	2	0	4	4	21.0	22	1	10	8

	Avg	AB	H	2B	3B	HR	RBI	BB	SO	OBP	SLG
vs. Left	.169	83	14	2	0	4	11	17	12	.307	.337
vs. Right	.299	77	23	5	0	1	7	10	11	.386	.403

Steve Trachsel — Cubs

Age 23 – Pitches Right (flyball pitcher)

	ERA	W	L	Sv	G	GS	IP	BB	SO	Avg	H	2B	3B	HR	RBI	OBP	SLG	CG	ShO	Sup	QS	#P/S	SB	CS	GB	FB	G/F
1993 Season	4.58	0	2	0	3	3	19.2	3	14	.219	16	3	1	4	8	.247	.452	0	0	2.75	2	99	2	0	21	22	0.95

1993 Season

	ERA	W	L	Sv	G	GS	IP	H	HR	BB	SO
Home	2.57	0	1	0	1	1	7.0	4	1	1	5
Away	5.68	0	1	0	2	2	12.2	12	3	2	9

	Avg	AB	H	2B	3B	HR	RBI	BB	SO	OBP	SLG
vs. Left	.150	40	6	1	0	1	2	2	8	.190	.250
vs. Right	.303	33	10	2	1	3	6	1	6	.314	.697

Alan Trammell — Tigers

Age 36 – Bats Right

	Avg	G	AB	R	H	2B	3B	HR	RBI	BB	SO	HBP	GDP	SB	CS	OBP	SLG	IBB	SH	SF	#Pit	#P/PA	GB	FB	G/F
1993 Season	.329	112	401	72	132	25	3	12	60	38	38	2	7	12	8	.388	.496	2	4	2	1637	3.66	140	135	1.04
Last Five Years	.282	509	1886	265	532	109	8	41	258	203	181	11	40	47	24	.353	.414	11	16	15	7609	3.57	661	612	1.08

1993 Season

	Avg	AB	H	2B	3B	HR	RBI	BB	SO	OBP	SLG
vs. Left	.289	135	39	8	0	7	21	21	13	.386	.504
vs. Right	.350	266	93	17	3	5	39	17	25	.389	.492
Groundball	.315	89	28	1	1	2	9	6	8	.365	.416
Flyball	.360	86	31	7	1	3	9	10	6	.433	.570
Home	.330	203	67	12	2	6	28	21	19	.396	.498
Away	.328	198	65	13	1	6	32	17	19	.380	.495

	Avg	AB	H	2B	3B	HR	RBI	BB	SO	OBP	SLG
Scoring Posn	.319	116	37	4	0	4	48	11	13	.377	.457
Close & Late	.245	53	13	1	0	0	7	3	7	.298	.264
None on/out	.337	89	30	9	1	3	3	9	8	.398	.562
Batting #5	.336	110	37	8	0	2	13	10	13	.390	.464
Batting #7	.327	110	36	9	2	2	16	8	8	.378	.500
Other	.326	181	59	8	1	8	31	20	17	.393	.514

1993 Season

	Avg	AB	H	2B	3B	HR	RBI	BB	SO	OBP	SLG		Avg	AB	H	2B	3B	HR	RBI	BB	SO	OBP	SLG
Day	.340	141	48	8	1	8	26	16	16	.405	.582	April	.200	30	6	2	0	1	6	6	2	.333	.367
Night	.323	260	84	17	2	4	34	22	22	.379	.450	May	.323	62	20	1	1	1	8	5	5	.373	.419
Grass	.317	338	107	20	3	10	46	32	33	.377	.482	June	.324	68	22	7	0	1	10	5	5	.378	.471
Turf	.397	63	25	5	0	2	14	6	5	.449	.571	July	.312	77	24	4	0	1	7	5	11	.349	.403
First Pitch	.418	55	23	4	0	6	22	2	0	.433	.818	August	.405	84	34	6	2	3	18	9	7	.457	.631
Ahead in Count	.333	114	38	11	1	3	15	23	0	.445	.526	September/October	.325	80	26	5	0	5	11	8	8	.393	.575
Behind in Count	.296	162	48	9	1	2	19	0	34	.301	.401	Pre-All Star	.321	190	61	13	1	4	27	18	15	.383	.463
Two Strikes	.319	166	53	9	2	3	19	13	38	.372	.452	Post-All Star	.336	211	71	12	2	8	33	20	23	.393	.526

1993 By Position

Position	Avg	AB	H	2B	3B	HR	RBI	BB	SO	OBP	SLG	G	GS	Innings	PO	A	E	DP	Fld Pct	Rng Fctr	In Zone	Outs	Zone Rtg	MLB Zone
As Pinch Hitter	.182	11	2	1	0	0	2	1	2	.250	.273	12	0	---	---	---	---	---	---	---	---	---	---	---
As 3b	.293	116	34	8	0	2	12	12	11	.364	.414	35	27	260.2	19	56	5	7	.938	2.59	74	66	.802	.834
As ss	.350	226	79	13	2	10	40	20	19	.402	.558	63	58	508.2	00	181	3	24	.989	4.62	206	186	.903	.880

Last Five Years

	Avg	AB	H	2B	3B	HR	RBI	BB	SO	OBP	SLG		Avg	AB	H	2B	3B	HR	RBI	BB	SO	OBP	SLG
vs. Left	.278	612	170	40	1	19	89	68	45	.349	.440	Scoring Posn	.320	494	158	29	1	12	215	63	43	.389	.455
vs. Right	.284	1274	362	69	7	22	169	135	136	.354	.401	Close & Late	.254	264	67	15	0	2	32	34	35	.348	.333
Groundball	.287	527	151	29	2	10	76	40	47	.338	.406	None on/out	.256	359	92	20	2	10	10	26	32	.306	.407
Flyball	.292	391	114	25	3	8	46	51	38	.374	.432	Batting #2	.249	511	127	26	3	7	63	59	51	.330	.352
Home	.289	976	282	55	6	23	154	112	84	.364	.428	Batting #3	.295	765	226	51	1	22	124	86	65	.366	.451
Away	.275	910	250	54	2	18	104	91	97	.340	.398	Other	.293	610	179	32	4	12	71	58	65	.355	.418
Day	.294	635	187	35	3	16	88	71	64	.366	.435	April	.275	324	89	23	1	6	42	41	30	.363	.407
Night	.276	1251	345	74	5	25	170	132	117	.346	.403	May	.273	377	103	17	2	4	42	50	33	.356	.361
Grass	.279	1615	451	94	8	34	225	177	154	.351	.411	June	.277	300	83	12	0	8	46	29	33	.341	.397
Turf	.299	271	81	15	0	7	33	26	27	.361	.432	July	.284	282	80	17	2	4	26	30	31	.353	.401
First Pitch	.313	227	71	10	0	8	42	3	0	.316	.463	August	.298	329	98	23	3	10	57	27	27	.346	.477
Ahead in Count	.327	542	177	48	3	18	99	135	0	.460	.526	September/October	.288	274	79	17	0	9	45	26	27	.354	.449
Behind in Count	.249	766	191	34	2	11	73	0	157	.256	.342	Pre-All Star	.276	1085	299	57	3	19	136	130	106	.355	.386
Two Strikes	.248	710	176	37	3	12	78	58	181	.308	.359	Post-All Star	.291	801	233	52	5	22	122	73	75	.350	.451

Batter vs. Pitcher (since 1984)

Hits Best Against	Avg	AB	H	2B	3B	HR	RBI	BB	SO	OBP	SLG	Hits Worst Against	Avg	AB	H	2B	3B	HR	RBI	BB	SO	OBP	SLG
Bobby Thigpen	.600	10	6	0	0	0	3	3	0	.692	.600	Luis Aquino	.059	17	1	0	0	0	0	1	0	.111	.059
Greg Harris	.462	26	12	4	0	1	6	4	2	.533	.731	Bob Milacki	.067	30	2	0	0	0	0	5	5	.200	.067
Frank Tanana	.444	9	4	0	0	1	1	2	0	.545	.778	Bobby Ojeda	.067	15	1	0	0	0	0	3	3	.222	.067
Tom Gordon	.429	14	6	1	0	2	3	3	1	.529	.929	Scott Sanderson	.071	14	1	1	0	0	0	1	0	.133	.143
Dennis Rasmussen	.385	26	10	2	1	2	4	3	3	.448	.769	Jose Rijo	.091	11	1	0	0	0	0	0	0	.091	.091

Jeff Treadway — Indians

Age 31 – Bats Left (flyball hitter)

	Avg	G	AB	R	H	2B	3B	HR	RBI	BB	SO	HBP	GDP	SB	CS	OBP	SLG	IBB	SH	SF	#Pit	#P/PA	GB	FB	G/F
1993 Season	.303	97	221	25	67	14	1	2	27	14	21	2	6	1	1	.347	.403	2	1	2	761	3.17	73	87	0.84
Last Five Years	.286	526	1600	185	458	75	9	24	163	101	136	7	36	10	11	.329	.389	11	15	14	5565	3.20	554	555	1.00

1993 Season

	Avg	AB	H	2B	3B	HR	RBI	BB	SO	OBP	SLG		Avg	AB	H	2B	3B	HR	RBI	BB	SO	OBP	SLG
vs. Left	.105	19	2	0	0	0	0	2	2	.227	.105	Scoring Posn	.356	59	21	6	1	1	26	4	7	.385	.542
vs. Right	.322	202	65	14	1	2	27	12	19	.359	.431	Close & Late	.289	45	13	3	0	1	6	4	6	.347	.422
Home	.265	102	27	3	1	0	13	4	10	.290	.314	None on/out	.263	57	15	3	0	1	1	2	6	.288	.368
Away	.336	119	40	11	0	2	14	10	11	.394	.479	Batting #2	.455	22	10	1	0	1	3	2	1	.500	.636
First Pitch	.325	40	13	4	0	0	8	2	0	.372	.425	Batting #7	.294	136	40	10	1	1	21	8	14	.338	.404
Ahead in Count	.302	43	13	3	1	1	7	9	0	.423	.488	Other	.270	63	17	3	0	0	3	4	6	.313	.317
Behind in Count	.260	100	26	5	0	1	6	0	18	.265	.340	Pre-All Star	.310	126	39	9	0	0	10	7	10	.356	.381
Two Strikes	.263	76	20	3	0	1	6	3	21	.288	.342	Post-All Star	.295	95	28	5	1	2	17	7	11	.337	.432

Last Five Years

	Avg	AB	H	2B	3B	HR	RBI	BB	SO	OBP	SLG		Avg	AB	H	2B	3B	HR	RBI	BB	SO	OBP	SLG
vs. Left	.237	274	65	6	0	4	30	22	32	.298	.303	Scoring Posn	.309	363	112	15	4	6	136	34	29	.357	.421
vs. Right	.296	1326	393	69	9	20	133	79	104	.335	.407	Close & Late	.254	256	65	7	2	4	35	17	28	.297	.344
Groundball	.286	528	151	23	4	4	40	31	44	.324	.367	None on/out	.269	353	95	17	2	6	6	15	31	.301	.380
Flyball	.277	372	103	16	0	7	35	28	34	.328	.376	Batting #2	.296	915	271	39	5	19	105	56	69	.336	.412
Home	.271	778	211	31	5	8	77	53	59	.319	.355	Batting #7	.274	277	76	14	2	4	37	16	24	.315	.383
Away	.300	822	247	44	4	16	86	48	77	.338	.422	Other	.272	408	111	22	2	1	21	29	43	.321	.343
Day	.291	437	127	18	2	5	43	29	49	.333	.375	April	.297	185	55	4	2	4	17	6	8	.318	.405
Night	.285	1163	331	57	7	19	120	72	87	.327	.395	May	.323	251	81	11	3	4	27	15	15	.365	.438
Grass	.277	1143	317	49	6	13	106	76	102	.324	.365	June	.299	311	93	20	0	4	27	18	35	.340	.402
Turf	.309	457	141	26	3	11	57	25	34	.342	.451	July	.263	274	72	12	0	6	31	19	26	.311	.372
First Pitch	.321	327	105	14	3	5	43	10	0	.341	.428	August	.285	323	92	11	1	5	24	22	27	.328	.372
Ahead in Count	.310	397	123	22	2	8	40	71	0	.413	.436	September/October	.254	256	65	17	3	1	37	21	25	.308	.355
Behind in Count	.243	646	157	25	3	4	47	0	123	.247	.310	Pre-All Star	.294	849	250	37	5	14	81	44	75	.331	.399
Two Strikes	.222	550	122	21	3	8	49	19	136	.250	.315	Post-All Star	.277	751	208	38	4	10	82	57	61	.326	.378

Batter vs. Pitcher (career)

Hits Best Against	Avg	AB	H	2B	3B	HR	RBI	BB	SO	OBP	SLG	Hits Worst Against	Avg	AB	H	2B	3B	HR	RBI	BB	SO	OBP	SLG
Wally Whitehurst	.500	12	6	3	0	0	1	0	0	.500	.750	John Burkett	.143	28	4	1	1	0	2	1	4	.172	.250
Bob Tewksbury	.500	10	5	0	0	0	2	2	0	.583	.500	Jimmy Jones	.176	17	3	0	0	0	1	0	2	.176	.176
Rick Sutcliffe	.471	17	8	2	1	0	2	0	2	.471	.706	Mark Grant	.182	11	2	0	0	0	1	1	1	.231	.182

Batter vs. Pitcher (career)

Hits Best Against	Avg	AB	H	2B	3B	HR	RBI	BB	SO	OBP	SLG
Mark Gardner	.462	13	6	2	0	0	1	0	0	.462	.615
Orel Hershiser	.350	20	7	2	0	1	2	3	0	.435	.600

Hits Worst Against	Avg	AB	H	2B	3B	HR	RBI	BB	SO	OBP	SLG
Paul Assenmacher	.182	11	2	0	0	0	2	0	1	.182	.182
Greg Maddux	.188	32	6	0	0	0	1	1	1	.212	.188

Ricky Trlicek — Dodgers

Age 25 – Pitches Right (groundball pitcher)

	ERA	W	L	Sv	G	GS	IP	BB	SO	Avg	H	2B	3B	HR	RBI	OBP	SLG	GF	IR	IRS	Hld	SvOp	SB	CS	GB	FB	G/F
1993 Season	4.08	1	2	1	41	0	64.0	21	41	.244	59	13	3	3	35	.309	.360	18	37	11	1	1	6	1	122	37	3.30
Career (1992-1993)	4.25	1	2	1	43	0	65.2	23	42	.245	61	13	3	3	37	.314	.357	18	39	12	1	1	6	1	124	38	3.26

1993 Season

	ERA	W	L	Sv	G	GS	IP	H	HR	BB	SO
Home	2.03	1	1	0	18	0	26.2	21	1	7	17
Away	5.54	0	1	1	23	0	37.1	38	2	14	24
Starter	0.00	0	0	0	0	0	0.0	0	0	0	0
Reliever	4.08	1	2	1	41	0	64.0	59	3	21	41
0 Days rest	1.29	1	1	0	5	0	7.0	6	0	2	5
1 or 2 Days rest	3.14	0	1	0	19	0	28.2	21	1	11	18
3+ Days rest	5.72	0	0	1	17	0	28.1	32	2	8	18
Pre-All Star	5.18	0	2	0	25	0	40.0	36	2	15	24
Post-All Star	2.25	1	0	1	16	0	24.0	23	1	6	17

	Avg	AB	H	2B	3B	HR	RBI	BB	SO	OBP	SLG
vs. Left	.308	117	36	9	1	1	20	9	14	.362	.427
vs. Right	.184	125	23	4	2	2	15	12	27	.261	.296
Scoring Posn	.253	91	23	6	2	0	31	10	14	.327	.363
Close & Late	.182	33	6	0	0	1	5	5	4	.289	.273
None on/out	.278	54	15	5	1	1	1	2	10	.304	.463
First Pitch	.371	35	13	3	1	1	8	1	0	.389	.600
Ahead in Count	.192	104	20	2	2	0	8	0	37	.200	.250
Behind in Count	.211	57	12	3	0	2	7	16	0	.392	.368
Two Strikes	.137	95	13	0	0	0	5	4	41	.172	.137

Mike Trombley — Twins

Age 27 – Pitches Right

	ERA	W	L	Sv	G	GS	IP	BB	SO	Avg	H	2B	3B	HR	RBI	OBP	SLG	GF	IR	IRS	Hld	SvOp	SB	CS	GB	FB	G/F
1993 Season	4.88	6	6	2	44	10	114.1	41	85	.290	131	33	6	15	73	.349	.490	8	29	11	8	5	7	6	149	136	1.10
Career (1992-1993)	4.43	9	8	2	54	17	160.2	58	123	.278	174	45	6	20	91	.340	.466	8	29	11	8	5	9	9	208	184	1.13

1993 Season

	ERA	W	L	Sv	G	GS	IP	H	HR	BB	SO
Home	4.28	2	4	2	23	4	61.0	60	8	10	48
Away	5.57	4	2	0	21	6	53.1	71	7	31	37
Starter	5.86	3	5	0	10	10	50.2	69	4	23	34
Reliever	4.10	3	1	2	34	0	63.2	62	11	18	51
0 Days rest	2.45	2	0	0	5	0	7.1	4	0	2	5
1 or 2 Days rest	6.23	0	1	0	15	0	21.2	26	9	7	16
3+ Days rest	3.12	1	0	2	14	0	34.2	32	2	9	30
Pre-All Star	4.88	4	3	1	25	3	59.0	57	12	22	45
Post-All Star	4.88	2	3	1	19	7	55.1	74	3	19	40

	Avg	AB	H	2B	3B	HR	RBI	BB	SO	OBP	SLG
vs. Left	.320	222	71	18	3	9	40	31	40	.396	.550
vs. Right	.262	229	60	15	3	6	33	10	45	.298	.432
Scoring Posn	.296	125	37	8	3	2	54	18	27	.367	.456
Close & Late	.255	47	12	1	1	2	10	2	9	.288	.447
None on/out	.315	111	35	9	2	3	3	6	15	.350	.514
First Pitch	.457	46	21	7	0	1	12	3	0	.490	.674
Ahead in Count	.228	215	49	12	3	5	30	0	72	.228	.381
Behind in Count	.336	125	42	12	2	6	24	25	0	.447	.608
Two Strikes	.209	206	43	11	4	5	25	13	85	.258	.374

George Tsamis — Twins

Age 27 – Pitches Left

	ERA	W	L	Sv	G	GS	IP	BB	SO	Avg	H	2B	3B	HR	RBI	OBP	SLG	GF	IR	IRS	Hld	SvOp	SB	CS	GB	FB	G/F
1993 Season	6.19	1	2	1	41	0	68.1	27	30	.317	86	17	1	9	51	.378	.487	18	39	13	2	2	0	4	106	86	1.23

1993 Season

	ERA	W	L	Sv	G	GS	IP	H	HR	BB	SO
Home	7.50	0	1	0	22	0	30.0	39	4	15	15
Away	5.17	1	1	1	19	0	38.1	47	5	12	15
Starter	0.00	0	0	0	0	0	0.0	0	0	0	0
Reliever	6.19	1	2	1	41	0	68.1	86	9	27	30
0 Days rest	13.00	0	0	0	7	0	9.0	20	2	6	1
1 or 2 Days rest	5.19	0	2	0	14	0	26.0	29	2	11	13
3+ Days rest	5.13	1	0	1	20	0	33.1	37	5	10	16
Pre-All Star	5.51	1	1	0	18	0	32.2	36	4	10	16
Post-All Star	6.81	0	1	1	23	0	35.2	50	5	17	14

	Avg	AB	H	2B	3B	HR	RBI	BB	SO	OBP	SLG
vs. Left	.348	89	31	5	0	4	22	6	9	.408	.539
vs. Right	.302	182	55	12	1	5	29	21	21	.364	.462
Scoring Posn	.286	84	24	4	1	0	36	14	14	.371	.357
Close & Late	.371	35	13	1	0	1	8	6	3	.463	.486
None on/out	.397	63	25	4	0	5	5	8	5	.465	.698
First Pitch	.333	39	13	1	0	1	8	3	0	.386	.436
Ahead in Count	.262	103	27	7	0	2	17	0	25	.269	.388
Behind in Count	.301	73	22	4	1	1	10	15	0	.411	.425
Two Strikes	.316	114	36	8	0	3	18	9	30	.370	.465

Greg Tubbs — Reds

Age 31 – Bats Right (flyball hitter)

	Avg	G	AB	R	H	2B	3B	HR	RBI	BB	SO	HBP	GDP	SB	CS	OBP	SLG	IBB	SH	SF	#Pit	#P/PA	GB	FB	G/F
1993 Season	.186	35	59	10	11	0	0	1	2	14	10	1	0	3	1	.351	.237	0	0	0	312	4.22	19	20	0.95

1993 Season

	Avg	AB	H	2B	3B	HR	RBI	BB	SO	OBP	SLG
vs. Left	.048	21	1	0	0	0	0	2	5	.130	.048
vs. Right	.263	38	10	0	0	1	2	12	5	.451	.342

	Avg	AB	H	2B	3B	HR	RBI	BB	SO	OBP	SLG
Scoring Posn	.100	10	1	0	0	0	1	3	0	.308	.100
Close & Late	.111	9	1	0	0	0	0	2	1	.273	.111

Scooter Tucker — Astros

Age 27 – Bats Right (flyball hitter)

	Avg	G	AB	R	H	2B	3B	HR	RBI	BB	SO	HBP	GDP	SB	CS	OBP	SLG	IBB	SH	SF	#Pit	#P/PA	GB	FB	G/F
1993 Season	.192	9	26	1	5	1	0	0	3	2	3	0	0	0	0	.250	.231	0	0	0	116	4.14	9	9	1.00
Career (1992-1993)	.145	29	76	6	11	2	0	0	6	5	16	2	2	1	1	.217	.171	0	1	0	339	4.04	25	27	0.93

1993 Season

	Avg	AB	H	2B	3B	HR	RBI	BB	SO	OBP	SLG
vs. Left	.250	8	2	0	0	0	1	1	2	.333	.250
vs. Right	.167	18	3	1	0	0	2	1	1	.211	.222

	Avg	AB	H	2B	3B	HR	RBI	BB	SO	OBP	SLG
Scoring Posn	.333	3	1	1	0	0	3	2	0	.600	.667
Close & Late	.000	2	0	0	0	0	0	0	0	.000	.000

Brian Turang — Mariners

Age 27 – Bats Right

	Avg	G	AB	R	H	2B	3B	HR	RBI	BB	SO	HBP	GDP	SB	CS	OBP	SLG	IBB	SH	SF	#Pit	#P/PA	GB	FB	G/F
1993 Season	.250	40	140	22	35	11	1	0	7	17	20	2	3	6	2	.340	.343	0	1	0	560	3.50	48	45	1.07

1993 Season

	Avg	AB	H	2B	3B	HR	RBI	BB	SO	OBP	SLG		Avg	AB	H	2B	3B	HR	RBI	BB	SO	OBP	SLG
vs. Left	.302	63	19	6	0	0	5	7	3	.371	.397	Scoring Posn	.231	26	6	2	0	0	7	4	1	.333	.308
vs. Right	.208	77	16	5	1	0	2	10	17	.315	.299	Close & Late	.083	12	1	1	0	0	0	2	0	.267	.167
Home	.247	81	20	7	0	0	3	8	9	.322	.333	None on/out	.283	53	15	5	1	0	0	7	12	.367	.415
Away	.254	59	15	4	1	0	4	9	11	.362	.356	Batting #1	.256	86	22	6	1	0	4	10	14	.347	.349
First Pitch	.250	16	4	1	0	0	0	0	0	.250	.313	Batting #2	.255	47	12	5	0	0	2	6	5	.340	.362
Ahead in Count	.313	16	5	2	0	0	3	13	0	.633	.438	Other	.143	7	1	0	0	0	1	1	1	.250	.143
Behind in Count	.192	73	14	4	0	0	4	0	20	.203	.247	Pre-All Star	.000	0	0	0	0	0	0	0	0	.000	.000
Two Strikes	.159	63	10	3	1	0	3	4	20	.209	.238	Post-All Star	.250	140	35	11	1	0	7	17	20	.340	.343

Chris Turner — Angels

Age 25 – Bats Right (flyball hitter)

	Avg	G	AB	R	H	2B	3B	HR	RBI	BB	SO	HBP	GDP	SB	CS	OBP	SLG	IBB	SH	SF	#Pit	#P/PA	GB	FB	G/F
1993 Season	.280	25	75	9	21	5	0	1	13	9	16	1	1	1	1	.360	.387	0	0	1	342	3.98	18	28	0.64

1993 Season

	Avg	AB	H	2B	3B	HR	RBI	BB	SO	OBP	SLG		Avg	AB	H	2B	3B	HR	RBI	BB	SO	OBP	SLG
vs. Left	.500	12	6	2	0	0	2	5	3	.647	.667	Scoring Posn	.455	22	10	2	0	1	12	3	1	.500	.682
vs. Right	.238	63	15	3	0	1	11	4	13	.290	.333	Close & Late	.556	9	5	0	0	0	1	2	2	.636	.556

Matt Turner — Marlins

Age 27 – Pitches Right (flyball pitcher)

	ERA	W	L	Sv	G	GS	IP	BB	SO	Avg	H	2B	3B	HR	RBI	OBP	SLG	GF	IR	IRS	Hld	SvOp	SB	CS	GB	FB	G/F
1993 Season	2.91	4	5	0	55	0	68.0	26	59	.227	55	10	1	7	33	.300	.364	26	40	14	9	1	1	2	72	79	0.91

1993 Season

	ERA	W	L	Sv	G	GS	IP	H	HR	BB	SO		Avg	AB	H	2B	3B	HR	RBI	BB	SO	OBP	SLG
Home	3.12	2	2	0	31	0	40.1	31	3	15	34	vs. Left	.254	114	29	7	1	3	16	16	23	.344	.412
Away	2.60	2	3	0	24	0	27.2	24	4	11	25	vs. Right	.203	128	26	3	0	4	17	10	36	.261	.320
Starter	0.00	0	0	0	0	0	0.0	0	0	0	0	Scoring Posn	.262	61	16	3	0	1	25	11	14	.355	.361
Reliever	2.91	4	5	0	55	0	68.0	55	7	26	59	Close & Late	.253	150	38	7	1	3	20	19	35	.337	.373
0 Days rest	1.59	2	1	0	11	0	11.1	8	1	5	9	None on/out	.183	60	11	1	1	1	1	3	20	.222	.283
1 or 2 Days rest	2.80	1	4	0	27	0	35.1	31	3	16	31	First Pitch	.350	40	14	2	0	3	8	7	0	.447	.625
3+ Days rest	3.80	1	0	0	17	0	21.1	16	3	5	19	Ahead in Count	.171	105	18	2	0	3	12	0	50	.168	.276
Pre-All Star	3.08	1	2	0	20	0	26.1	22	3	8	27	Behind in Count	.317	60	19	5	1	1	10	9	0	.403	.483
Post-All Star	2.81	3	3	0	35	0	41.2	33	4	18	32	Two Strikes	.131	107	14	1	0	3	12	10	59	.202	.224

Tom Urbani — Cardinals

Age 26 – Pitches Left (groundball pitcher)

	ERA	W	L	Sv	G	GS	IP	BB	SO	Avg	H	2B	3B	HR	RBI	OBP	SLG	CG	ShO	Sup	QS	#P/S	SB	CS	GB	FB	G/F
1993 Season	4.65	1	3	0	18	9	62.0	26	33	.296	73	16	3	4	35	.355	.433	0	0	3.48	6	88	1	6	105	68	1.54

1993 Season

	ERA	W	L	Sv	G	GS	IP	H	HR	BB	SO		Avg	AB	H	2B	3B	HR	RBI	BB	SO	OBP	SLG
Home	5.50	0	3	0	9	5	34.1	47	1	14	15	vs. Left	.175	40	7	0	0	1	8	6	8	.277	.250
Away	3.58	1	0	0	9	4	27.2	26	3	12	18	vs. Right	.319	207	66	16	3	3	27	20	25	.371	.469
Starter	3.73	1	2	0	9	9	50.2	54	2	20	24	Scoring Posn	.269	67	18	3	0	2	32	7	9	.313	.403
Reliever	8.74	0	1	0	9	0	11.1	19	2	6	9	Close & Late	.250	12	3	2	0	0	1	1	0	.308	.417
0-3 Days Rest	6.35	0	0	0	1	1	5.2	6	0	4	1	None on/out	.267	60	16	5	1	1	1	6	7	.333	.433
4 Days Rest	3.71	1	0	0	5	5	26.2	31	1	11	12	First Pitch	.341	41	14	4	0	1	8	2	0	.348	.512
5+ Days Rest	2.95	0	2	0	3	3	18.1	17	1	5	11	Ahead in Count	.200	100	20	2	2	1	6	0	28	.198	.290
Pre-All Star	8.74	0	1	0	9	0	11.1	19	2	6	9	Behind in Count	.381	63	24	7	1	1	11	17	0	.506	.571
Post-All Star	3.73	1	2	0	9	9	50.2	54	2	20	24	Two Strikes	.170	94	16	3	1	1	6	7	33	.225	.255

Jose Uribe — Astros

Age 35 – Bats Both

	Avg	G	AB	R	H	2B	3B	HR	RBI	BB	SO	HBP	GDP	SB	CS	OBP	SLG	IBB	SH	SF	#Pit	#P/PA	GB	FB	G/F
1993 Season	.245	45	53	4	13	1	0	0	3	8	5	1	1	1	0	.355	.264	4	4	0	210	3.18	16	22	0.73
Last Five Years	.233	490	1314	120	306	38	17	5	82	105	186	1	21	17	21	.289	.299	38	19	5	4678	3.24	507	415	1.22

1993 Season

	Avg	AB	H	2B	3B	HR	RBI	BB	SO	OBP	SLG		Avg	AB	H	2B	3B	HR	RBI	BB	SO	OBP	SLG
vs. Left	.294	17	5	1	0	0	2	2	1	.400	.353	Scoring Posn	.250	12	3	1	0	0	3	5	3	.471	.333
vs. Right	.222	36	8	0	0	0	1	6	4	.333	.222	Close & Late	.100	10	1	0	0	0	0	0	0	.100	.100

Last Five Years

	Avg	AB	H	2B	3B	HR	RBI	BB	SO	OBP	SLG		Avg	AB	H	2B	3B	HR	RBI	BB	SO	OBP	SLG
vs. Left	.256	422	108	13	5	1	31	34	54	.310	.318	Scoring Posn	.250	296	74	8	4	2	75	54	44	.361	.324
vs. Right	.222	892	198	25	12	4	51	71	132	.279	.290	Close & Late	.215	191	41	6	2	0	5	22	34	.296	.267
Groundball	.271	491	133	19	6	4	38	36	62	.322	.358	None on/out	.240	329	79	9	3	2	2	18	49	.280	.304
Flyball	.216	287	62	7	5	1	14	23	47	.272	.286	Batting #8	.234	1264	296	36	17	5	78	99	174	.289	.301
Home	.234	610	143	20	7	0	34	53	92	.294	.290	Batting #9	.147	34	5	1	0	0	1	4	10	.256	.176
Away	.232	704	163	18	10	5	48	52	94	.285	.307	Other	.313	16	5	1	0	0	3	2	2	.389	.375
Day	.224	554	124	19	8	1	26	40	77	.275	.292	April	.228	167	38	3	4	0	14	13	29	.282	.293
Night	.239	760	182	19	9	4	56	65	109	.299	.304	May	.264	254	67	8	2	3	17	25	41	.329	.346
Grass	.224	896	201	26	9	0	58	73	130	.281	.273	June	.236	263	62	6	5	1	17	16	30	.278	.308

Last Five Years

	Avg	AB	H	2B	3B	HR	RBI	BB	SO	OBP	SLG
Turf	.251	418	105	12	8	5	24	32	56	.306	.354
First Pitch	.277	238	66	5	1	2	21	19	0	.329	.332
Ahead in Count	.296	318	94	10	7	2	23	44	0	.379	.390
Behind in Count	.194	541	105	13	7	1	30	0	165	.196	.250
Two Strikes	.172	518	89	8	7	1	24	29	186	.216	.220

	Avg	AB	H	2B	3B	HR	RBI	BB	SO	OBP	SLG
July	.227	251	57	9	4	0	15	19	30	.283	.295
August	.238	240	57	10	2	1	16	22	34	.302	.308
September/October	.180	139	25	2	0	0	3	10	22	.235	.194
Pre-All Star	.250	765	191	21	14	4	54	60	109	.303	.329
Post-All Star	.209	549	115	17	3	1	28	45	77	.270	.257

Batter vs. Pitcher (career)

Hits Best Against	Avg	AB	H	2B	3B	HR	RBI	BB	SO	OBP	SLG
Danny Jackson	.462	26	12	0	0	0	0	2	0	.500	.462
Jose DeLeon	.455	22	10	0	2	0	2	4	3	.538	.636
Terry Leach	.417	12	5	1	0	0	1	0	0	.417	.500
Ted Power	.313	16	5	0	1	0	0	3	1	.421	.438
Larry Andersen	.313	16	5	1	0	1	3	1	4	.353	.563

Hits Worst Against	Avg	AB	H	2B	3B	HR	RBI	BB	SO	OBP	SLG
Joe Boever	.000	11	0	0	0	0	0	0	2	.000	.000
Shawn Boskie	.000	11	0	0	0	0	0	0	2	.000	.000
Mark Portugal	.067	15	1	0	0	0	0	2	6	.176	.067
Doug Drabek	.095	21	2	0	0	0	0	1	4	.136	.095
Tim Belcher	.095	21	2	0	0	0	0	0	4	.095	.095

Sergio Valdez — Expos

Age 28 – Pitches Right

	ERA	W	L	Sv	G	GS	IP	BB	SO	Avg	H	2B	3B	HR	RBI	OBP	SLG	GF	IR	IRS	Hld	SvOp	SB	CS	GB	FB	G/F
1993 Season	9.00	0	0	0	4	0	3.0	1	2	.308	4	1	0	1	4	.357	.615	1	3	1	0	0	1	1	6	2	3.00
Last Five Years	4.71	8	10	0	86	14	197.0	73	137	.252	190	42	2	28	108	.317	.424	18	55	18	1	1	19	7	282	214	1.32

1993 Season

	ERA	W	L	Sv	G	GS	IP	H	HR	BB	SO
Home	0.00	0	0	0	2	0	1.2	1	0	0	1
Away	20.25	0	0	0	2	0	1.1	3	1	1	1

	Avg	AB	H	2B	3B	HR	RBI	BB	SO	OBP	SLG
vs. Left	.429	7	3	1	0	0	2	1	0	.500	.571
vs. Right	.167	6	1	0	0	1	2	0	2	.167	.667

Last Five Years

	ERA	W	L	Sv	G	GS	IP	H	HR	BB	SO
Home	3.94	4	3	0	42	5	98.1	88	12	26	63
Away	5.47	4	7	0	44	9	98.2	102	16	47	74
Day	6.35	2	4	0	25	5	45.1	53	10	14	34
Night	4.21	6	6	0	61	9	151.2	137	18	59	103
Grass	5.08	6	9	0	51	11	140.0	140	23	50	100
Turf	3.79	2	1	0	35	3	57.0	50	5	23	37
April	6.75	0	0	0	6	0	5.1	6	0	3	3
May	5.68	2	1	0	12	2	31.2	36	5	11	21
June	5.67	1	3	0	15	2	39.2	36	8	15	29
July	6.75	0	4	0	15	2	22.2	22	6	13	19
August	2.55	1	0	0	16	2	35.1	32	3	12	22
September/October	3.90	4	2	0	22	6	62.1	58	6	19	43
Starter	5.63	5	6	0	14	14	76.2	91	13	30	41
Reliever	4.11	3	4	0	72	0	120.1	99	15	43	96
0 Days rest	5.54	0	1	0	10	0	13.0	12	1	5	11
1 or 2 Days rest	3.48	1	2	0	27	0	41.1	31	5	19	30
3+ Days rest	4.23	2	1	0	35	0	66.0	56	9	19	55
Pre-All Star	5.58	3	6	0	40	5	88.2	88	18	32	63
Post-All Star	3.99	5	4	0	46	9	108.1	102	10	41	74

	Avg	AB	H	2B	3B	HR	RBI	BB	SO	OBP	SLG
vs. Left	.226	359	81	14	2	10	43	46	57	.312	.359
vs. Right	.276	395	109	28	0	18	65	27	80	.321	.484
Inning 1-6	.267	472	126	31	0	16	76	44	85	.327	.434
Inning 7+	.227	282	64	11	2	12	32	29	52	.299	.408
None on	.235	434	102	20	1	18	18	41	85	.303	.410
Runners on	.275	320	88	22	1	10	90	32	52	.335	.444
Scoring Posn	.249	181	45	14	0	3	72	26	35	.333	.376
Close & Late	.282	85	24	3	0	2	11	9	18	.351	.388
None on/out	.239	188	45	8	0	9	9	16	29	.302	.426
vs. 1st Batr (relief)	.159	63	10	2	0	3	10	8	10	.250	.333
First Inning Pitched	.223	300	67	20	1	10	53	35	65	.303	.397
First 15 Pitches	.222	266	59	16	0	12	44	28	56	.295	.417
Pitch 16-30	.224	192	43	7	1	2	14	20	41	.297	.302
Pitch 31-45	.276	98	27	4	0	6	24	14	17	.363	.500
Pitch 46+	.308	198	61	15	1	8	26	11	23	.341	.515
First Pitch	.309	152	47	17	0	5	31	4	0	.325	.520
Ahead in Count	.181	310	56	11	2	7	22	0	119	.178	.297
Behind in Count	.333	174	58	8	0	10	31	33	0	.438	.552
Two Strikes	.127	306	39	6	2	4	20	36	137	.217	.199

Pitcher vs. Batter (career)

Pitches Best Vs.	Avg	AB	H	2B	3B	HR	RBI	BB	SO	OBP	SLG
Steve Finley	.222	9	2	0	0	0	0	2	1	.364	.222

Pitches Worst Vs.	Avg	AB	H	2B	3B	HR	RBI	BB	SO	OBP	SLG

John Valentin — Red Sox

Age 27 – Bats Right (flyball hitter)

	Avg	G	AB	R	H	2B	3B	HR	RBI	BB	SO	HBP	GDP	SB	CS	OBP	SLG	IBB	SH	SF	#Pit	#P/PA	GB	FB	G/F
1993 Season	.278	144	468	50	130	40	3	11	66	49	77	2	9	3	4	.346	.447	2	16	4	2009	3.73	136	171	0.80
Career (1992-1993)	.277	202	653	71	181	53	3	16	91	69	94	4	14	4	4	.347	.441	2	20	5	2750	3.66	202	228	0.89

1993 Season

	Avg	AB	H	2B	3B	HR	RBI	BB	SO	OBP	SLG
vs. Left	.248	129	32	11	1	3	10	13	20	.319	.419
vs. Right	.289	339	98	29	2	8	56	36	57	.356	.457
Groundball	.349	83	29	7	0	1	16	9	8	.413	.470
Flyball	.277	112	31	9	1	1	13	13	19	.346	.402
Home	.293	242	71	23	1	7	39	31	47	.376	.483
Away	.261	226	59	17	2	4	27	18	30	.313	.407
Day	.286	154	44	11	2	2	24	17	29	.355	.422
Night	.274	314	86	29	1	9	42	32	48	.342	.459
Grass	.291	395	115	34	2	10	57	43	68	.361	.463
Turf	.205	73	15	6	1	1	9	6	9	.263	.356
First Pitch	.417	48	20	8	0	2	12	2	0	.451	.708
Ahead in Count	.349	129	45	18	2	5	19	25	0	.449	.636
Behind in Count	.202	188	38	8	1	2	22	0	62	.204	.287
Two Strikes	.192	198	38	7	1	1	21	22	77	.274	.253

	Avg	AB	H	2B	3B	HR	RBI	BB	SO	OBP	SLG
Scoring Posn	.301	123	37	9	1	1	49	15	21	.371	.415
Close & Late	.253	79	20	9	0	5	15	8	18	.326	.557
None on/out	.264	110	29	10	1	3	3	17	13	.367	.455
Batting #8	.306	206	63	20	0	4	29	22	38	.372	.461
Batting #9	.313	96	30	7	2	3	19	8	13	.362	.521
Other	.223	166	37	13	1	4	18	19	26	.305	.386
April	.143	28	4	0	0	3	7	2	4	.194	.464
May	.258	93	24	5	1	0	8	8	19	.317	.333
June	.256	78	20	4	0	2	14	9	14	.333	.385
July	.273	88	24	11	1	0	9	7	13	.323	.420
August	.311	90	28	10	1	3	11	9	15	.374	.544
September/October	.330	91	30	10	0	3	17	14	12	.425	.538
Pre-All Star	.243	235	57	15	1	5	36	21	41	.300	.379
Post-All Star	.313	233	73	25	2	6	30	28	36	.392	.515

1993 By Position

Position	Avg	AB	H	2B	3B	HR	RBI	BB	SO	OBP	SLG	G	GS	Innings	PO	A	E	DP	Fld Pct	Rng Fctr	In Zone	Outs	Zone Rtg	MLB Zone
As ss	.278	467	130	40	3	11	66	48	77	.345	.448	144	138	1221.2	237	431	20	96	.971	4.92	507	449	.886	.880

Jose Valentin — Brewers

Age 24 – Bats Both (flyball hitter)

	Avg	G	AB	R	H	2B	3B	HR	RBI	BB	SO	HBP	GDP	SB	CS	OBP	SLG	IBB	SH	SF	#Pit	#P/PA	GB	FB	G/F
1993 Season	.245	19	53	10	13	1	2	1	7	7	16	1	1	1	0	.344	.396	1	2	0	248	3.94	14	18	0.78
Career (1992-1993)	.232	23	56	11	13	1	2	1	8	7	16	1	1	1	0	.323	.375	1	2	1	257	3.84	16	20	0.80

1993 Season

	Avg	AB	H	2B	3B	HR	RBI	BB	SO	OBP	SLG
vs. Left	.263	19	5	0	1	0	1	1	6	.333	.368
vs. Right	.235	34	8	1	1	1	6	6	10	.350	.412

	Avg	AB	H	2B	3B	HR	RBI	BB	SO	OBP	SLG
Scoring Posn	.308	13	4	1	0	1	7	2	3	.400	.615
Close & Late	.182	11	2	0	1	0	0	2	5	.308	.364

Fernando Valenzuela — Orioles

Age 33 – Pitches Left

	ERA	W	L	Sv	G	GS	IP	BB	SO	Avg	H	2B	3B	HR	RBI	OBP	SLG	CG	ShO	Sup	QS	#P/S	SB	CS	GB	FB	G/F
1993 Season	4.94	8	10	0	32	31	178.2	79	78	.266	179	44	6	18	87	.343	.429	5	2	4.58	15	97	10	14	256	221	1.16
Last Five Years	4.39	31	38	0	98	97	586.0	257	314	.267	601	139	7	51	270	.341	.403	13	4	4.75	52	102	44	36	787	714	1.10

1993 Season

	ERA	W	L	Sv	G	GS	IP	H	HR	BB	SO
Home	4.40	5	3	0	15	15	88.0	89	6	33	37
Away	5.46	3	7	0	17	16	90.2	90	12	46	41
Day	4.76	3	3	0	8	8	45.1	44	1	23	18
Night	5.00	5	7	0	24	23	133.1	135	17	56	60
Grass	5.68	7	10	0	26	26	139.1	152	15	65	64
Turf	2.29	1	0	0	6	5	39.1	27	3	14	14
April	11.05	0	2	0	3	2	7.1	11	2	3	3
May	3.54	1	3	0	6	6	40.2	34	5	16	21
June	3.79	2	2	0	6	6	38.0	33	2	18	16
July	1.56	3	0	0	5	5	40.1	24	1	14	13
August	13.95	0	2	0	6	6	20.0	39	5	11	10
September/October	5.29	2	1	0	6	6	32.1	38	3	17	15
Starter	4.96	8	10	0	31	31	177.2	179	18	79	78
Reliever	0.00	0	0	0	1	0	1.0	0	0	0	0
0-3 Days Rest	23.14	0	1	0	1	1	2.1	5	1	2	1
4 Days Rest	4.34	5	5	0	18	18	110.0	106	10	46	51
5+ Days Rest	5.37	3	4	0	12	12	65.1	68	7	31	26
Pre-All Star	3.67	4	7	0	17	16	100.2	83	9	45	46
Post-All Star	6.58	4	3	0	15	15	78.0	96	9	34	32

	Avg	AB	H	2B	3B	HR	RBI	BB	SO	OBP	SLG
vs. Left	.283	120	34	10	1	4	19	19	22	.379	.483
vs. Right	.262	554	145	34	5	14	68	60	56	.335	.417
Inning 1-6	.276	569	157	35	6	18	82	67	70	.353	.453
Inning 7+	.210	105	22	9	0	0	5	12	8	.288	.295
None on	.240	392	94	29	2	9	9	47	50	.324	.393
Runners on	.301	282	85	15	4	9	78	32	28	.368	.479
Scoring Posn	.321	165	53	11	2	5	67	18	18	.380	.503
Close & Late	.235	34	8	2	0	0	3	7	1	.366	.294
None on/out	.273	183	50	15	1	6	6	17	17	.335	.464
vs. 1st Batr (relief)	.000	1	0	0	0	0	0	0	0	.000	.000
First Inning Pitched	.346	133	46	12	3	7	30	10	15	.389	.639
First 75 Pitches	.291	478	139	33	5	16	71	57	58	.363	.481
Pitch 76-90	.211	76	16	2	0	1	6	8	8	.310	.276
Pitch 91-105	.191	68	13	3	1	1	8	10	6	.295	.309
Pitch 106+	.212	52	11	6	0	0	2	4	6	.263	.327
First Pitch	.364	88	32	8	0	3	18	1	0	.363	.557
Ahead in Count	.223	265	59	13	1	7	20	0	51	.230	.358
Behind in Count	.338	157	53	14	4	4	30	40	0	.472	.554
Two Strikes	.162	296	48	12	1	3	15	38	78	.260	.240

Last Five Years

	ERA	W	L	Sv	G	GS	IP	H	HR	BB	SO
Home	3.96	17	16	0	51	51	311.2	313	21	130	159
Away	4.89	14	22	0	47	46	274.1	288	30	127	155
Day	4.36	10	8	0	24	24	140.1	143	10	64	74
Night	4.40	21	30	0	74	73	445.2	458	41	193	240
Grass	4.69	23	30	0	75	75	437.1	460	41	196	248
Turf	3.51	8	8	0	23	22	148.2	141	10	61	66
April	4.28	1	6	0	12	11	61.0	62	5	25	37
May	4.55	4	7	0	16	16	95.0	90	11	45	50
June	3.81	8	8	0	20	20	127.2	123	11	55	72
July	3.25	6	6	0	15	15	105.1	95	4	40	43
August	5.13	8	6	0	18	18	100.0	116	13	40	57
September/October	5.57	4	5	0	17	17	97.0	115	7	52	55
Starter	4.40	31	38	0	97	97	585.0	601	51	257	314
Reliever	0.00	0	0	0	1	0	1.0	0	0	0	0
0-3 Days Rest	6.75	1	1	0	2	2	9.1	9	2	6	7
4 Days Rest	4.61	17	24	0	58	58	347.2	373	31	148	186
5+ Days Rest	3.99	13	13	0	37	37	228.0	219	18	103	121
Pre-All Star	4.00	14	24	0	53	52	315.1	299	29	138	175
Post-All Star	4.85	17	14	0	45	45	270.2	302	22	119	139

	Avg	AB	H	2B	3B	HR	RBI	BB	SO	OBP	SLG
vs. Left	.289	381	110	25	1	10	45	47	62	.363	.438
vs. Right	.263	1870	491	114	6	41	225	210	252	.337	.396
Inning 1-6	.268	1952	524	116	7	48	247	226	286	.343	.409
Inning 7+	.258	299	77	23	0	3	23	31	28	.326	.365
None on	.251	1277	321	78	3	25	25	131	191	.323	.376
Runners on	.287	974	280	61	4	26	245	126	123	.364	.438
Scoring Posn	.278	579	161	36	2	14	210	81	84	.358	.420
Close & Late	.285	123	35	6	0	1	11	15	9	.362	.358
None on/out	.271	580	157	37	1	8	8	45	82	.324	.379
vs. 1st Batr (relief)	.000	1	0	0	0	0	0	0	0	.000	.000
First Inning Pitched	.294	388	114	27	3	13	64	43	57	.359	.479
First 75 Pitches	.271	1597	432	98	5	40	195	182	228	.343	.413
Pitch 76-90	.276	254	70	15	1	5	31	35	28	.369	.402
Pitch 91-105	.208	221	46	14	1	2	23	22	37	.279	.308
Pitch 106+	.296	179	53	12	0	4	21	18	21	.359	.430
First Pitch	.353	337	119	26	0	11	53	6	0	.362	.528
Ahead in Count	.205	874	179	38	2	12	67	0	232	.206	.294
Behind in Count	.340	533	181	47	4	15	88	126	0	.463	.527
Two Strikes	.180	990	178	41	2	12	70	124	314	.271	.262

Pitcher vs. Batter (since 1984)

Pitches Best Vs.	Avg	AB	H	2B	3B	HR	RBI	BB	SO	OBP	SLG
Mike Aldrete	.000	8	0	0	0	0	1	3	2	.250	.000
Wally Backman	.071	14	1	0	0	0	0	1	3	.133	.071
Tom Foley	.077	13	1	0	0	0	0	0	4	.077	.077
Ed Sprague	.083	12	1	0	0	0	0	0	1	.083	.083
Lloyd McClendon	.091	11	1	0	0	0	1	0	2	.083	.091

Pitches Worst Vs.	Avg	AB	H	2B	3B	HR	RBI	BB	SO	OBP	SLG
Kenny Lofton	.500	8	4	3	0	0	1	3	1	.636	.875
Casey Candaele	.476	21	10	2	0	2	4	2	1	.522	.857
John Olerud	.444	9	4	0	0	1	1	3	0	.583	.778
Dale Murphy	.379	66	25	4	0	7	20	16	8	.500	.758
Randy Ready	.370	27	10	1	1	2	5	8	3	.514	.704

Julio Valera — Angels

Age 25 – Pitches Right

	ERA	W	L	Sv	G	GS	IP	BB	SO	Avg	H	2B	3B	HR	RBI	OBP	SLG	GF	IR	IRS	Hld	SvOp	SB	CS	GB	FB	G/F
1993 Season	6.62	3	6	4	19	5	53.0	15	28	.344	77	14	1	8	37	.388	.522	8	10	2	2	7	2	1	96	56	1.71
Career (1990-1993)	4.46	12	18	4	54	36	256.0	90	148	.284	286	57	4	24	116	.345	.420	9	13	3	2	7	17	7	368	309	1.19

1993 Season

	ERA	W	L	Sv	G	GS	IP	H	HR	BB	SO
Home	5.85	2	3	2	11	3	32.1	51	6	10	21
Away	7.84	1	3	2	8	2	20.2	26	2	5	7

	Avg	AB	H	2B	3B	HR	RBI	BB	SO	OBP	SLG
vs. Left	.396	106	42	6	1	4	20	12	8	.458	.585
vs. Right	.297	118	35	8	0	4	17	3	20	.320	.466

Career (1990-1993)

	ERA	W	L	Sv	G	GS	IP	H	HR	BB	SO
Home	3.31	9	6	2	28	18	141.1	148	11	40	80
Away	5.89	3	12	2	26	18	114.2	138	13	50	68
Day	3.44	5	5	1	16	12	86.1	88	6	31	51
Night	4.99	7	13	3	38	24	169.2	198	18	59	97
Grass	3.56	12	12	4	45	30	225.0	236	17	72	133
Turf	11.03	0	6	0	9	6	31.0	50	7	18	15
April	3.76	2	2	2	8	1	26.1	25	2	10	15
May	3.62	3	4	2	13	7	54.2	54	3	17	34
June	5.97	2	7	0	14	9	60.1	72	7	21	35
July	3.86	1	1	0	6	6	39.2	48	6	10	25
August	4.50	1	1	0	5	5	30.0	32	3	15	14
September/October	4.40	3	3	0	8	8	45.0	55	3	17	25
Starter	4.31	10	15	0	36	36	219.1	240	19	75	128
Reliever	5.40	2	3	4	18	0	36.2	46	5	15	20
0 Days rest	0.00	0	0	0	0	0	0.0	0	0	0	0
1 or 2 Days rest	5.59	0	0	4	9	0	19.1	25	3	6	8
3+ Days rest	5.19	2	3	0	9	0	17.1	21	2	9	12
Pre-All Star	4.58	8	14	4	37	19	155.1	164	15	52	99
Post-All Star	4.29	4	4	0	17	17	100.2	122	9	38	49

	Avg	AB	H	2B	3B	HR	RBI	BB	SO	OBP	SLG
vs. Left	.321	480	154	28	2	8	50	46	43	.380	.438
vs. Right	.251	526	132	29	2	16	66	44	105	.312	.405
Inning 1-6	.282	779	220	43	3	18	89	69	117	.343	.415
Inning 7+	.291	227	66	14	1	6	27	21	31	.349	.441
None on	.281	565	159	37	2	14	14	45	86	.337	.428
Runners on	.288	441	127	20	2	10	102	45	62	.354	.410
Scoring Posn	.275	255	70	11	0	5	85	36	33	.363	.376
Close & Late	.304	115	35	8	1	2	17	11	19	.365	.443
None on/out	.313	252	79	16	0	6	6	24	35	.375	.448
vs. 1st Batr (relief)	.118	17	2	0	0	0	3	1	2	.167	.118
First Inning Pitched	.310	210	65	12	0	7	27	21	27	.371	.467
First 15 Pitches	.316	174	55	11	0	5	19	15	19	.368	.466
Pitch 16-30	.264	163	43	6	0	4	16	17	26	.337	.374
Pitch 31-45	.295	166	49	9	1	2	13	13	27	.348	.398
Pitch 46+	.276	503	139	31	3	13	68	45	76	.338	.427
First Pitch	.331	145	48	10	0	4	20	8	0	.368	.483
Ahead in Count	.232	414	96	18	2	4	30	0	120	.236	.314
Behind in Count	.354	240	85	16	2	10	35	41	0	.447	.563
Two Strikes	.199	433	86	17	1	6	37	41	148	.269	.284

Pitcher vs. Batter (career)

Pitches Best Vs.	Avg	AB	H	2B	3B	HR	RBI	BB	SO	OBP	SLG
Rickey Henderson	.091	11	1	0	0	0	0	1	3	.167	.091
Harold Baines	.154	13	2	1	0	0	0	1	2	.214	.231
Brian McRae	.182	11	2	0	0	0	0	1	5	.250	.182
Chris Hoiles	.222	9	2	0	0	0	0	3	0	.417	.222
Brady Anderson	.231	13	3	0	0	0	1	0	3	.231	.231

Pitches Worst Vs.	Avg	AB	H	2B	3B	HR	RBI	BB	SO	OBP	SLG
George Brett	.727	11	8	1	1	0	2	0	0	.727	1.000
Kirby Puckett	.500	10	5	1	0	0	2	2	2	.583	.600
Ruben Sierra	.500	6	3	1	0	0	2	5	1	.727	.667
Roberto Alomar	.417	12	5	0	0	2	4	1	1	.462	.917
Wally Joyner	.364	11	4	0	0	1	1	1	1	.417	.636

Dave Valle — Mariners

Age 33 – Bats Right

	Avg	G	AB	R	H	2B	3B	HR	RBI	BB	SO	HBP	GDP	SB	CS	OBP	SLG	IBB	SH	SF	#Pit	#P/PA	GB	FB	G/F
1993 Season	.258	135	423	48	109	19	0	13	63	48	56	17	18	1	0	.354	.395	4	8	4	1761	3.52	148	148	1.00
Last Five Years	.231	592	1738	194	401	68	5	44	192	183	243	47	68	2	4	.319	.352	7	26	11	7225	3.60	716	525	1.36

1993 Season

	Avg	AB	H	2B	3B	HR	RBI	BB	SO	OBP	SLG
vs. Left	.280	118	33	6	0	5	17	13	12	.370	.458
vs. Right	.249	305	76	13	0	8	46	35	44	.347	.370
Groundball	.227	66	15	2	0	1	11	8	8	.346	.303
Flyball	.250	88	22	2	0	6	16	15	14	.380	.477
Home	.265	219	58	10	0	4	34	17	34	.340	.365
Away	.250	204	51	9	0	9	29	31	22	.368	.426
Day	.287	94	27	7	0	5	10	12	10	.391	.521
Night	.249	329	82	12	0	8	53	36	46	.343	.359
Grass	.280	157	44	6	0	9	27	27	19	.399	.490
Turf	.244	266	65	13	0	4	36	21	37	.326	.338
First Pitch	.288	52	15	5	0	2	14	3	0	.333	.500
Ahead in Count	.302	116	35	5	0	5	24	28	0	.453	.474
Behind in Count	.230	183	42	6	0	2	17	0	46	.254	.295
Two Strikes	.260	173	45	9	0	2	19	17	56	.347	.347

	Avg	AB	H	2B	3B	HR	RBI	BB	SO	OBP	SLG
Scoring Posn	.267	116	31	6	0	3	49	13	20	.350	.397
Close & Late	.267	75	20	2	0	2	15	6	9	.341	.373
None on/out	.330	91	30	6	0	4	4	13	7	.425	.527
Batting #7	.184	38	7	1	0	0	0	2	4	.244	.211
Batting #8	.264	382	101	18	0	13	63	46	52	.364	.414
Other	.333	3	1	0	0	0	0	0	0	.333	.333
April	.258	62	16	2	0	2	11	9	10	.351	.387
May	.266	79	21	1	0	2	5	11	9	.385	.354
June	.254	63	16	3	0	2	9	6	6	.356	.397
July	.259	58	15	3	0	4	10	4	10	.348	.517
August	.221	68	15	4	0	1	10	9	7	.316	.324
September/October	.280	93	26	6	0	2	18	9	14	.356	.409
Pre-All Star	.261	226	59	8	0	7	27	27	26	.366	.389
Post-All Star	.254	197	50	11	0	6	36	21	30	.339	.401

1993 By Position

Position	Avg	AB	H	2B	3B	HR	RBI	BB	SO	OBP	SLG	G	GS	Innings	PO	A	E	DP	Fld Pct	Rng Fctr	In Zone	Outs	Zone Rtg	MLB Zone
As c	.258	423	109	19	0	13	63	48	56	.354	.395	135	133	1131.1	880	71	5	13	.995	---	---	---	---	---

Last Five Years

	Avg	AB	H	2B	3B	HR	RBI	BB	SO	OBP	SLG
vs. Left	.248	560	139	18	1	21	65	60	64	.334	.396
vs. Right	.222	1178	262	50	4	23	127	123	179	.312	.330
Groundball	.278	425	118	18	1	11	52	38	60	.352	.402
Flyball	.216	408	88	15	2	16	48	54	59	.319	.380
Home	.229	884	202	42	3	13	91	84	127	.310	.327
Away	.233	854	199	26	2	31	101	99	116	.328	.377
Day	.234	406	95	15	0	14	35	39	56	.315	.374
Night	.230	1332	306	53	5	30	157	144	187	.320	.345
Grass	.239	673	161	18	2	27	89	80	105	.331	.392
Turf	.225	1065	240	50	3	17	103	103	138	.311	.326
First Pitch	.272	184	50	14	0	9	36	4	0	.317	.495
Ahead in Count	.299	461	138	18	3	18	66	115	0	.445	.469
Behind in Count	.193	791	153	22	2	11	61	0	205	.213	.268
Two Strikes	.183	744	136	28	2	9	56	63	243	.261	.262

	Avg	AB	H	2B	3B	HR	RBI	BB	SO	OBP	SLG
Scoring Posn	.219	457	100	22	1	6	143	43	70	.298	.311
Close & Late	.213	282	60	7	2	5	29	26	42	.299	.305
None on/out	.234	419	98	21	2	11	11	42	51	.323	.372
Batting #7	.217	272	59	11	0	8	28	24	32	.287	.346
Batting #8	.238	1211	288	49	4	27	138	135	180	.331	.352
Other	.212	255	54	8	1	9	26	24	31	.294	.357
April	.251	295	74	8	1	11	40	30	50	.328	.397
May	.244	275	67	11	1	5	19	35	33	.344	.345
June	.207	222	46	9	0	7	22	17	30	.287	.342
July	.193	275	53	7	2	7	26	18	35	.262	.309
August	.226	310	70	13	0	7	31	41	46	.322	.335
September/October	.252	361	91	20	1	7	54	42	49	.348	.371
Pre-All Star	.233	884	206	31	4	25	88	88	124	.317	.362
Post-All Star	.228	854	195	37	1	19	104	95	119	.320	.341

Batter vs. Pitcher (career)

Hits Best Against	Avg	AB	H	2B	3B	HR	RBI	BB	SO	OBP	SLG
Joe Hesketh	.545	11	6	0	0	1	5	2	1	.571	.818
Mark Guthrie	.462	13	6	0	0	1	4	0	2	.462	.692
Jeff Ballard	.458	24	11	0	0	3	10	3	1	.500	.833
John Candelaria	.400	10	4	2	0	1	3	1	0	.455	.900

Hits Worst Against	Avg	AB	H	2B	3B	HR	RBI	BB	SO	OBP	SLG
Scott Erickson	.000	14	0	0	0	0	1	4	5	.222	.000
Bret Saberhagen	.000	9	0	0	0	0	0	2	2	.182	.000
Teddy Higuera	.074	27	2	1	0	0	1	4	5	.188	.111
Tom Gordon	.083	12	1	0	0	0	0	3	6	.267	.083

Batter vs. Pitcher (career)

Hits Best Against	Avg	AB	H	2B	3B	HR	RBI	BB	SO	OBP	SLG	Hits Worst Against	Avg	AB	H	2B	3B	HR	RBI	BB	SO	OBP	SLG
Nolan Ryan	.333	12	4	2	0	1	2	2	5	.400	.750	Jeff Russell	.154	13	2	0	0	0	4	0	0	.143	.154

Ty Van Burkleo — Angels

Age 30 – Bats Left

	Avg	G	AB	R	H	2B	3B	HR	RBI	BB	SO	HBP	GDP	SB	CS	OBP	SLG	IBB	SH	SF	#Pit	#P/PA	GB	FB	G/F
1993 Season	.152	12	33	2	5	3	0	1	1	6	9	0	0	1	0	.282	.333	0	0	0	149	3.82	12	9	1.33

1993 Season

	Avg	AB	H	2B	3B	HR	RBI	BB	SO	OBP	SLG		Avg	AB	H	2B	3B	HR	RBI	BB	SO	OBP	SLG
vs. Left	.333	3	1	1	0	0	0	0	1	.333	.667	Scoring Posn	.000	4	0	0	0	0	0	2	2	.333	.000
vs. Right	.133	30	4	2	0	1	1	6	8	.278	.300	Close & Late	.400	5	2	2	0	0	0	0	1	.400	.800

Todd Van Poppel — Athletics

Age 22 – Pitches Right (flyball pitcher)

	ERA	W	L	Sv	G	GS	IP	BB	SO	Avg	H	2B	3B	HR	RBI	OBP	SLG	CG	ShO	Sup	QS	#P/S	SB	CS	GB	FB	G/F
1993 Season	5.04	6	6	0	16	16	84.0	62	47	.243	76	17	2	10	45	.369	.406	0	0	6.00	4	95	5	5	81	124	0.65
Career (1991-1993)	5.28	6	6	0	17	17	88.2	64	53	.250	83	17	3	11	50	.373	.419	0	0	5.89	4	95	6	6	83	129	0.64

1993 Season

	ERA	W	L	Sv	G	GS	IP	H	HR	BB	SO		Avg	AB	H	2B	3B	HR	RBI	BB	SO	OBP	SLG
Home	5.91	3	2	0	6	6	32.0	28	6	25	18	vs. Left	.241	166	40	8	2	5	29	39	25	.386	.404
Away	4.50	3	4	0	10	10	52.0	48	4	37	29	vs. Right	.245	147	36	9	0	5	16	23	22	.349	.408
Starter	5.04	6	6	0	16	16	84.0	76	10	62	47	Scoring Posn	.268	71	19	6	2	3	30	14	16	.386	.535
Reliever	0.00	0	0	0	0	0	0.0	0	0	0	0	Close & Late	.375	8	3	1	0	0	0	0	0	.375	.500
0-3 Days Rest	3.52	1	0	0	2	2	7.2	5	1	7	2	None on/out	.160	75	12	2	0	1	1	17	8	.315	.227
4 Days Rest	3.56	5	2	0	8	8	48.0	41	4	28	27	First Pitch	.364	33	12	0	0	3	6	0	0	.353	.636
5+ Days Rest	7.94	0	4	0	6	6	28.1	30	5	27	18	Ahead in Count	.190	121	23	6	0	2	9	0	41	.202	.289
Pre-All Star	21.00	0	1	0	1	1	3.0	5	2	5	3	Behind in Count	.256	86	22	4	1	5	20	39	0	.488	.500
Post-All Star	4.44	6	5	0	15	15	81.0	71	8	57	44	Two Strikes	.174	132	23	7	0	2	12	23	47	.299	.273

Andy Van Slyke — Pirates

Age 33 – Bats Left

	Avg	G	AB	R	H	2B	3B	HR	RBI	BB	SO	HBP	GDP	SB	CS	OBP	SLG	IBB	SH	SF	#Pit	#P/PA	GB	FB	G/F
1993 Season	.310	83	323	42	100	13	4	8	50	24	40	2	13	11	2	.357	.449	5	0	4	1271	3.59	149	76	1.96
Last Five Years	.285	641	2397	363	682	126	38	65	352	266	413	14	46	63	16	.355	.450	15	4	32	10318	3.80	824	741	1.11

1993 Season

	Avg	AB	H	2B	3B	HR	RBI	BB	SO	OBP	SLG		Avg	AB	H	2B	3B	HR	RBI	BB	SO	OBP	SLG
vs. Left	.308	117	36	3	1	1	14	7	14	.347	.376	Scoring Posn	.341	85	29	2	2	4	39	12	14	.412	.553
vs. Right	.311	206	64	10	3	7	36	17	26	.362	.490	Close & Late	.274	62	17	2	0	2	8	5	8	.328	.403
Groundball	.349	109	38	6	1	4	23	8	13	.393	.532	None on/out	.146	41	6	0	0	0	0	2	5	.186	.146
Flyball	.244	45	11	0	1	1	8	5	7	.308	.356	Batting #3	.315	317	100	13	4	8	50	24	39	.363	.457
Home	.255	153	39	7	1	5	26	9	22	.297	.412	Batting #9	.000	4	0	0	0	0	0	0	1	.000	.000
Away	.359	170	61	6	3	3	24	15	18	.410	.482	Other	.000	2	0	0	0	0	0	0	0	.000	.000
Day	.318	66	21	1	0	2	7	8	10	.400	.424	April	.267	90	24	4	1	2	17	8	11	.327	.400
Night	.307	257	79	12	4	6	43	16	30	.345	.455	May	.362	105	38	7	3	3	17	11	16	.425	.571
Grass	.368	125	46	6	2	3	22	11	14	.420	.520	June	.340	47	16	0	0	1	5	1	6	.340	.404
Turf	.273	198	54	7	2	5	28	13	26	.316	.404	July	.000	0	0	0	0	0	0	0	0	.000	.000
First Pitch	.391	46	18	1	0	1	13	4	0	.442	.478	August	.000	4	0	0	0	0	0	0	1	.000	.000
Ahead in Count	.300	100	30	4	2	3	11	13	0	.374	.470	September/October	.286	77	22	2	0	2	11	4	6	.321	.390
Behind in Count	.265	113	30	5	2	1	14	0	29	.270	.372	Pre-All Star	.322	242	78	11	4	6	39	20	33	.373	.475
Two Strikes	.209	115	24	3	1	1	8	7	40	.258	.278	Post-All Star	.272	81	22	2	0	2	11	4	7	.306	.370

1993 By Position

Position	Avg	AB	H	2B	3B	HR	RBI	BB	SO	OBP	SLG	G	GS	Innings	PO	A	E	DP	Fld Pct	Rng Fctr	In Zone	Outs	Zone Rtg	MLB Zone
As cf	.315	317	100	13	4	8	50	24	39	.363	.457	78	76	675.0	204	2	1	1	.995	2.75	255	193	.757	.829

Last Five Years

	Avg	AB	H	2B	3B	HR	RBI	BB	SO	OBP	SLG		Avg	AB	H	2B	3B	HR	RBI	BB	SO	OBP	SLG
vs. Left	.262	921	241	46	12	15	125	97	168	.332	.387	Scoring Posn	.304	615	187	34	16	11	249	96	109	.385	.465
vs. Right	.299	1476	441	80	26	50	227	169	245	.370	.490	Close & Late	.259	417	108	16	5	9	55	43	92	.323	.386
Groundball	.276	815	225	41	11	19	119	114	141	.364	.423	None on/out	.251	434	109	27	1	8	8	46	82	.329	.373
Flyball	.256	507	130	25	10	16	81	61	104	.333	.440	Batting #3	.288	2265	653	123	37	63	334	247	388	.357	.459
Home	.265	1168	309	60	18	30	169	126	195	.334	.424	Batting #6	.186	59	11	2	1	1	9	9	12	.290	.305
Away	.303	1229	373	66	20	35	183	140	218	.375	.475	Other	.247	73	18	1	0	1	9	10	13	.337	.301
Day	.296	692	205	39	10	23	101	69	134	.358	.481	April	.271	321	87	16	4	10	58	42	53	.351	.439
Night	.280	1705	477	87	28	42	251	197	279	.354	.438	May	.328	430	141	24	8	9	67	62	69	.414	.484
Grass	.303	671	203	29	10	22	97	80	116	.377	.474	June	.277	415	115	17	8	5	44	37	76	.337	.393
Turf	.278	1726	479	97	28	43	255	186	297	.347	.441	July	.265	355	94	17	8	13	54	46	54	.345	.468
First Pitch	.362	354	128	20	6	9	73	10	0	.381	.528	August	.274	368	101	18	4	15	63	36	71	.340	.467
Ahead in Count	.334	574	192	36	9	27	98	147	0	.466	.570	September/October	.283	508	144	34	6	13	66	43	90	.338	.451
Behind in Count	.226	1026	232	39	18	14	109	0	335	.226	.340	Pre-All Star	.295	1302	384	65	21	31	193	157	223	.369	.449
Two Strikes	.204	1076	219	44	18	18	107	105	413	.272	.328	Post-All Star	.272	1095	298	61	17	34	159	109	190	.338	.452

Batter vs. Pitcher (since 1984)

Hits Best Against	Avg	AB	H	2B	3B	HR	RBI	BB	SO	OBP	SLG	Hits Worst Against	Avg	AB	H	2B	3B	HR	RBI	BB	SO	OBP	SLG
Ben Rivera	.625	16	10	0	2	1	2	1	0	.647	1.063	Rob Murphy	.000	11	0	0	0	0	0	1	4	.083	.000
Frank Castillo	.526	19	10	0	1	2	5	1	3	.550	.947	Jeff Fassero	.083	12	1	1	0	0	1	1	5	.154	.167
Shawn Boskie	.462	13	6	0	1	2	3	1	2	.467	1.077	Zane Smith	.100	20	2	0	0	0	0	0	8	.100	.100

Batter vs. Pitcher (since 1984)																							
Hits Best Against	Avg	AB	H	2B	3B	HR	RBI	BB	SO	OBP	SLG	Hits Worst Against	Avg	AB	H	2B	3B	HR	RBI	BB	SO	OBP	SLG
Jimmy Jones	.448	29	13	1	2	3	10	3	2	.485	.931	Neal Heaton	.167	12	2	0	0	0	0	0	3	.167	.167
Steve Wilson	.421	19	8	1	1	2	5	4	2	.522	.895	Tom Candiotti	.167	12	2	0	0	0	1	0	1	.154	.167

John VanderWal — Expos

Age 28 – Bats Left

	Avg	G	AB	R	H	2B	3B	HR	RBI	BB	SO	HBP	GDP	SB	CS	OBP	SLG	IBB	SH	SF	#Pit	#P/PA	GB	FB	G/F
1993 Season	.233	106	215	34	50	7	4	5	30	27	30	1	4	6	3	.320	.372	2	0	1	920	3.77	92	65	1.42
Career (1991-1993)	.233	232	489	59	114	19	7	10	58	52	84	1	8	9	3	.307	.362	4	0	2	1984	3.65	194	139	1.40

1993 Season																							
	Avg	AB	H	2B	3B	HR	RBI	BB	SO	OBP	SLG		Avg	AB	H	2B	3B	HR	RBI	BB	SO	OBP	SLG
vs. Left	.118	17	2	1	0	0	0	4	1	.286	.176	Scoring Posn	.262	65	17	3	2	2	26	9	10	.347	.462
vs. Right	.242	198	48	6	4	5	30	23	29	.323	.389	Close & Late	.231	39	9	0	0	1	5	6	12	.333	.308
Home	.241	79	19	4	0	1	11	13	7	.355	.329	None on/out	.245	49	12	2	1	0	0	3	5	.302	.327
Away	.228	136	31	3	4	4	19	14	23	.298	.397	Batting #2	.228	57	13	0	1	3	9	7	11	.313	.421
First Pitch	.455	22	10	2	1	1	6	2	0	.480	.773	Batting #4	.276	29	8	3	0	1	6	5	7	.382	.483
Ahead in Count	.242	66	16	2	2	1	7	13	0	.367	.379	Other	.225	129	29	4	3	1	15	15	12	.308	.326
Behind in Count	.148	81	12	1	1	2	8	0	23	.159	.259	Pre-All Star	.261	119	31	2	3	3	19	12	15	.331	.403
Two Strikes	.148	88	13	1	0	1	11	12	30	.257	.193	Post-All Star	.198	96	19	5	1	2	11	15	15	.306	.333

Gary Varsho — Reds

Age 33 – Bats Left

	Avg	G	AB	R	H	2B	3B	HR	RBI	BB	SO	HBP	GDP	SB	CS	OBP	SLG	IBB	SH	SF	#Pit	#P/PA	GB	FB	G/F
1993 Season	.232	77	95	8	22	6	0	2	11	9	19	1	1	1	0	.302	.358	0	3	1	377	3.46	31	29	1.07
Last Five Years	.237	386	579	73	137	31	7	10	63	43	104	3	6	20	4	.291	.366	5	4	3	2171	3.44	203	172	1.18

1993 Season																							
	Avg	AB	H	2B	3B	HR	RBI	BB	SO	OBP	SLG		Avg	AB	H	2B	3B	HR	RBI	BB	SO	OBP	SLG
vs. Left	.400	5	2	0	0	0	0	0	2	.400	.400	Scoring Posn	.240	25	6	1	0	1	10	2	7	.310	.400
vs. Right	.222	90	20	6	0	2	11	9	17	.297	.356	Close & Late	.333	24	8	2	0	0	4	1	4	.346	.417

Last Five Years																							
	Avg	AB	H	2B	3B	HR	RBI	BB	SO	OBP	SLG		Avg	AB	H	2B	3B	HR	RBI	BB	SO	OBP	SLG
vs. Left	.200	35	7	2	0	1	4	0	10	.222	.343	Scoring Posn	.226	146	33	9	0	5	49	17	33	.310	.390
vs. Right	.239	544	130	29	7	9	59	43	94	.296	.368	Close & Late	.210	162	34	11	1	0	13	10	31	.257	.290
Groundball	.232	228	53	12	3	3	20	18	28	.291	.351	None on/out	.256	156	40	10	2	1	1	8	29	.297	.365
Flyball	.254	134	34	7	2	4	16	5	30	.284	.425	Batting #6	.225	129	29	6	2	2	13	11	22	.284	.349
Home	.224	281	63	15	5	5	30	20	46	.280	.367	Batting #9	.234	167	39	8	1	4	19	11	35	.282	.365
Away	.248	298	74	16	2	5	33	23	58	.302	.366	Other	.244	283	69	17	4	4	31	21	47	.301	.375
Day	.296	223	66	21	3	5	36	11	30	.326	.484	April	.289	76	22	6	2	1	10	9	14	.375	.461
Night	.199	356	71	10	4	5	27	32	74	.270	.292	May	.218	101	22	5	2	0	7	5	20	.255	.307
Grass	.250	224	56	15	2	3	22	16	41	.299	.375	June	.219	114	25	6	1	1	11	10	21	.282	.316
Turf	.228	355	81	16	5	7	41	27	63	.287	.361	July	.235	132	31	7	2	4	19	11	19	.292	.409
First Pitch	.281	96	27	4	0	3	13	4	0	.307	.417	August	.193	57	11	2	0	0	5	1	16	.207	.228
Ahead in Count	.302	149	45	10	4	1	21	24	0	.402	.443	September/October	.263	99	26	5	0	4	11	7	14	.315	.434
Behind in Count	.177	254	45	14	2	4	19	0	93	.180	.295	Pre-All Star	.253	352	89	21	7	5	40	26	62	.306	.395
Two Strikes	.172	233	40	9	2	2	15	14	104	.222	.253	Post-All Star	.211	227	48	10	0	5	23	17	42	.268	.322

Batter vs. Pitcher (career)																							
Hits Best Against	Avg	AB	H	2B	3B	HR	RBI	BB	SO	OBP	SLG	Hits Worst Against	Avg	AB	H	2B	3B	HR	RBI	BB	SO	OBP	SLG
David Cone	.471	17	8	3	0	0	3	0	2	.471	.647	John Smoltz	.053	19	1	0	0	0	0	4	4	.217	.053
Andy Benes	.455	11	5	2	0	0	2	0	2	.455	.636	Tommy Greene	.143	14	2	0	0	1	2	0	4	.143	.357
Mike Morgan	.417	12	5	1	1	0	3	0	1	.417	.667	Mark Gardner	.167	12	2	0	0	0	0	0	1	.167	.167
Bill Sampen	.364	11	4	1	0	0	1	0	1	.364	.455	Jose Rijo	.200	10	2	1	0	0	0	1	1	.273	.300
Jimmy Jones	.333	12	4	0	0	0	0	1	2	.385	.333	Dennis Martinez	.208	24	5	1	0	0	3	2	2	.269	.250

Greg Vaughn — Brewers

Age 28 – Bats Right (flyball hitter)

	Avg	G	AB	R	H	2B	3B	HR	RBI	BB	SO	HBP	GDP	SB	CS	OBP	SLG	IBB	SH	SF	#Pit	#P/PA	GB	FB	G/F
1993 Season	.267	154	569	97	152	28	2	30	97	89	118	5	6	10	7	.369	.482	14	0	4	2422	3.63	167	207	0.81
Career (1989-1993)	.243	598	2107	324	512	99	11	102	357	257	480	12	30	38	29	.325	.446	18	11	24	8990	3.73	584	735	0.79

1993 Season																							
	Avg	AB	H	2B	3B	HR	RBI	BB	SO	OBP	SLG		Avg	AB	H	2B	3B	HR	RBI	BB	SO	OBP	SLG
vs. Left	.319	166	53	10	1	7	22	37	29	.443	.518	Scoring Posn	.299	147	44	9	0	5	65	38	26	.434	.463
vs. Right	.246	403	99	18	1	23	75	52	89	.336	.467	Close & Late	.226	93	21	4	0	2	12	16	24	.339	.333
Groundball	.252	107	27	3	0	6	22	20	23	.372	.449	None on/out	.232	138	32	8	2	9	9	14	23	.312	.514
Flyball	.250	108	27	5	0	6	16	19	25	.367	.463	Batting #3	.268	149	40	7	0	6	22	11	35	.325	.436
Home	.284	271	77	12	1	12	47	46	52	.389	.469	Batting #4	.268	418	112	21	2	24	75	78	82	.384	.500
Away	.252	298	75	16	1	18	50	43	66	.350	.493	Other	.000	2	0	0	0	0	0	0	1	.000	.000
Day	.280	200	56	11	2	9	28	35	44	.396	.490	April	.292	65	19	3	1	4	11	16	13	.432	.554
Night	.260	369	96	17	0	21	69	54	74	.354	.477	May	.290	100	29	2	0	8	25	17	23	.395	.550
Grass	.250	484	121	21	2	23	77	72	100	.348	.444	June	.279	111	31	9	0	5	23	5	24	.310	.495
Turf	.365	85	31	7	0	7	20	17	18	.481	.694	July	.290	93	27	7	1	3	14	5	17	.337	.484
First Pitch	.275	102	28	7	0	2	13	11	0	.351	.402	August	.252	111	28	5	0	7	16	29	16	.410	.486
Ahead in Count	.380	158	60	9	2	13	42	35	0	.487	.709	September/October	.202	89	18	2	0	3	8	17	25	.330	.326
Behind in Count	.175	206	36	8	0	3	17	0	89	.182	.257	Pre-All Star	.308	318	98	18	1	19	68	41	66	.390	.550
Two Strikes	.172	233	40	8	0	9	28	43	118	.300	.322	Post-All Star	.215	251	54	10	1	11	29	48	52	.344	.394

1993 By Position

Position	Avg	AB	H	2B	3B	HR	RBI	BB	SO	OBP	SLG	G	GS	Innings	PO	A	E	DP	Fld Pct	Rng Fctr	In Zone	Outs	Zone Rtg	MLB Zone
As Designated Hitter	.251	219	55	9	0	11	38	39	57	.365	.443	58	58	---	---	---	---	---	---	---	---	---	---	---
As lf	.279	348	97	19	2	19	59	50	60	.373	.509	94	93	813.0	214	1	3	1	.986	2.38	236	206	.873	.818

Career (1989-1993)

	Avg	AB	H	2B	3B	HR	RBI	BB	SO	OBP	SLG		Avg	AB	H	2B	3B	HR	RBI	BB	SO	OBP	SLG
vs. Left	.251	574	144	30	4	22	84	93	117	.352	.432	Scoring Posn	.285	564	161	32	1	28	257	99	139	.381	.495
vs. Right	.240	1533	368	69	7	80	273	164	363	.315	.451	Close & Late	.211	327	69	9	0	11	47	45	79	.306	.339
Groundball	.247	542	134	25	5	18	90	56	117	.316	.411	None on/out	.222	546	121	26	5	30	30	54	102	.295	.452
Flyball	.218	454	99	16	1	28	74	57	124	.305	.443	Batting #4	.239	838	200	36	3	41	136	119	191	.333	.436
Home	.246	1014	249	49	4	49	180	138	222	.335	.447	Batting #5	.251	466	117	24	3	24	92	52	109	.325	.470
Away	.241	1093	263	50	7	53	177	119	258	.316	.445	Other	.243	803	195	39	5	37	129	86	180	.318	.442
Day	.239	623	149	26	5	29	102	93	145	.339	.437	April	.277	224	62	15	2	14	43	37	50	.379	.549
Night	.245	1484	363	73	6	73	255	164	335	.320	.449	May	.227	330	75	13	1	19	62	49	78	.327	.445
Grass	.242	1815	440	83	9	90	312	218	407	.323	.447	June	.241	332	80	20	2	14	66	25	72	.296	.440
Turf	.247	292	72	16	2	12	45	39	73	.343	.438	July	.234	367	86	17	4	14	51	26	97	.288	.417
First Pitch	.287	356	102	17	2	19	72	14	0	.311	.506	August	.232	379	88	12	1	18	51	60	78	.336	.412
Ahead in Count	.313	504	158	32	6	35	125	120	0	.439	.609	September/October	.255	475	121	22	1	23	84	60	105	.337	.451
Behind in Count	.178	854	154	27	2	23	83	0	374	.183	.295	Pre-All Star	.252	1019	257	56	6	51	188	120	232	.333	.469
Two Strikes	.163	957	156	33	2	29	102	122	480	.259	.293	Post-All Star	.234	1088	255	43	5	51	169	137	248	.319	.424

Batter vs. Pitcher (career)

Hits Best Against	Avg	AB	H	2B	3B	HR	RBI	BB	SO	OBP	SLG	Hits Worst Against	Avg	AB	H	2B	3B	HR	RBI	BB	SO	OBP	SLG
Doug Jones	.500	12	6	4	0	1	3	0	1	.500	1.083	Tim Leary	.000	11	0	0	0	0	1	2	3	.143	.000
Scott Erickson	.455	11	5	0	0	2	3	2	3	.538	1.000	Mark Guthrie	.000	11	0	0	0	0	0	1	3	.083	.000
Paul Quantrill	.417	12	5	1	0	2	3	0	0	.417	1.000	Chuck Finley	.050	20	1	0	0	0	1	2	8	.136	.050
Ron Darling	.350	20	7	1	0	3	5	4	1	.458	.850	Roger Clemens	.056	18	1	0	0	0	0	0	10	.056	.056
Mike Moore	.313	16	5	1	1	2	3	5	1	.476	.875	Mike Gardiner	.100	10	1	0	0	0	1	0	1	.091	.100

Mo Vaughn — Red Sox

Age 26 – Bats Left

	Avg	G	AB	R	H	2B	3B	HR	RBI	BB	SO	HBP	GDP	SB	CS	OBP	SLG	IBB	SH	SF	#Pit	#P/PA	GB	FB	G/F
1993 Season	.297	152	539	86	160	34	1	29	101	79	130	8	14	4	3	.390	.525	23	0	7	2372	3.75	177	128	1.38
Career (1991-1993)	.270	339	1113	149	300	62	3	46	190	152	240	13	29	9	7	.360	.455	32	0	14	4843	3.75	383	293	1.31

1993 Season

	Avg	AB	H	2B	3B	HR	RBI	BB	SO	OBP	SLG		Avg	AB	H	2B	3B	HR	RBI	BB	SO	OBP	SLG
vs. Left	.268	164	44	9	0	12	39	16	48	.351	.543	Scoring Posn	.351	134	47	7	0	10	78	39	32	.484	.627
vs. Right	.309	375	116	25	1	17	62	63	82	.407	.517	Close & Late	.262	84	22	3	1	5	12	7	19	.326	.500
Groundball	.241	79	19	5	0	3	16	12	19	.344	.418	None on/out	.282	156	44	12	1	7	7	11	40	.329	.506
Flyball	.299	127	38	8	0	6	22	23	34	.413	.504	Batting #4	.265	204	54	8	0	13	35	31	56	.361	.495
Home	.332	277	92	23	1	13	56	39	63	.418	.563	Batting #5	.302	291	88	22	1	16	58	40	63	.394	.550
Away	.260	262	68	11	0	16	45	40	67	.361	.485	Other	.409	44	18	4	0	0	8	8	11	.491	.500
Day	.331	178	59	12	0	9	44	26	37	.413	.551	April	.412	68	28	10	0	4	16	9	10	.474	.735
Night	.280	361	101	22	1	20	57	53	93	.379	.512	May	.288	104	30	3	1	3	15	15	23	.383	.423
Grass	.300	454	136	29	1	25	87	72	108	.399	.533	June	.250	88	22	7	0	3	13	17	24	.385	.432
Turf	.282	85	24	5	0	4	14	7	22	.340	.482	July	.362	69	25	3	0	8	27	9	15	.439	.754
First Pitch	.394	66	26	3	0	4	13	20	0	.535	.621	August	.256	90	23	5	0	3	8	13	24	.349	.411
Ahead in Count	.420	119	50	13	0	9	29	37	0	.547	.756	September/October	.267	120	32	6	0	8	22	16	34	.355	.517
Behind in Count	.202	248	50	9	1	9	35	0	104	.220	.355	Pre-All Star	.308	289	89	21	1	13	56	44	67	.405	.522
Two Strikes	.169	267	45	9	0	7	27	22	130	.243	.281	Post-All Star	.284	250	71	13	0	16	45	35	63	.373	.528

1993 By Position

Position	Avg	AB	H	2B	3B	HR	RBI	BB	SO	OBP	SLG	G	GS	Innings	PO	A	E	DP	Fld Pct	Rng Fctr	In Zone	Outs	Zone Rtg	MLB Zone
As Designated Hitter	.239	67	16	4	0	3	11	12	19	.346	.433	19	19	---	---	---	---	---	---	---	---	---	---	---
As 1b	.306	470	144	30	1	26	89	66	110	.397	.540	131	130	1129.1	1110	67	16	103	.987	---	240	196	.817	.834

Career (1991-1993)

	Avg	AB	H	2B	3B	HR	RBI	BB	SO	OBP	SLG		Avg	AB	H	2B	3B	HR	RBI	BB	SO	OBP	SLG
vs. Left	.239	276	66	14	0	17	60	28	73	.321	.475	Scoring Posn	.311	293	91	19	0	15	150	68	74	.427	.529
vs. Right	.280	837	234	48	3	29	130	124	167	.372	.448	Close & Late	.242	186	45	4	2	6	24	18	45	.314	.382
Groundball	.268	198	53	8	0	7	36	28	36	.364	.414	None on/out	.247	287	71	19	1	12	12	32	60	.325	.446
Flyball	.240	283	68	11	0	13	40	35	67	.328	.417	Batting #4	.254	256	65	10	0	13	41	35	66	.346	.445
Home	.306	579	177	42	3	22	109	81	121	.393	.503	Batting #5	.283	492	139	36	2	21	83	60	92	.369	.492
Away	.230	534	123	20	0	24	81	71	119	.324	.403	Other	.263	365	96	16	1	12	66	57	82	.358	.411
Day	.294	367	108	21	0	15	72	64	71	.399	.474	April	.325	117	38	11	0	6	23	21	25	.421	.573
Night	.257	746	192	41	3	31	118	88	169	.340	.445	May	.267	120	32	3	1	3	19	23	30	.389	.383
Grass	.272	965	262	55	3	39	166	135	203	.364	.456	June	.268	127	34	9	0	5	18	22	28	.383	.457
Turf	.257	148	38	7	0	7	24	17	37	.333	.446	July	.273	227	62	9	1	13	53	28	46	.354	.493
First Pitch	.357	140	50	8	0	8	26	29	0	.474	.586	August	.263	236	62	12	0	8	31	30	40	.346	.415
Ahead in Count	.374	273	102	25	1	13	65	72	0	.494	.615	September/October	.252	286	72	18	1	11	46	28	71	.326	.437
Behind in Count	.193	492	95	20	2	14	62	0	190	.206	.327	Pre-All Star	.278	457	127	25	2	21	89	78	108	.386	.479
Two Strikes	.162	525	85	17	0	14	56	51	240	.245	.274	Post-All Star	.264	656	173	37	1	25	101	74	132	.341	.438

Batter vs. Pitcher (career)

Hits Best Against	Avg	AB	H	2B	3B	HR	RBI	BB	SO	OBP	SLG	Hits Worst Against	Avg	AB	H	2B	3B	HR	RBI	BB	SO	OBP	SLG
Kirk McCaskill	.500	12	6	1	0	1	4	2	0	.571	.833	Wilson Alvarez	.000	9	0	0	0	0	2	3	3	.250	.000
David Cone	.400	15	6	2	0	1	1	3	2	.500	.733	Cal Eldred	.091	11	1	1	0	0	0	0	4	.091	.182
Scott Kamieniecki	.385	13	5	2	0	1	2	4	1	.529	.769	Jack McDowell	.095	21	2	0	0	0	1	2	4	.174	.095

Batter vs. Pitcher (career)

Hits Best Against	Avg	AB	H	2B	3B	HR	RBI	BB	SO	OBP	SLG	Hits Worst Against	Avg	AB	H	2B	3B	HR	RBI	BB	SO	OBP	SLG
Jimmy Key	.364	11	4	0	0	3	4	1	1	.417	1.182	Pat Hentgen	.143	14	2	0	0	0	1	0	2	.143	.143
David Wells	.333	9	3	0	0	1	2	4	5	.538	.667	Bill Gullickson	.158	19	3	0	0	0	2	0	5	.158	.158

Randy Velarde — Yankees

Age 31 – Bats Right (groundball hitter)

	Avg	G	AB	R	H	2B	3B	HR	RBI	BB	SO	HBP	GDP	SB	CS	OBP	SLG	IBB	SH	SF	#Pit	#P/PA	GB	FB	G/F
1993 Season	.301	85	226	28	68	13	2	7	24	18	39	4	12	2	2	.360	.469	2	3	2	932	3.68	97	47	2.06
Last Five Years	.267	414	1151	137	307	58	8	22	115	101	227	11	37	12	11	.330	.388	3	17	8	4771	3.70	471	270	1.74

1993 Season

	Avg	AB	H	2B	3B	HR	RBI	BB	SO	OBP	SLG		Avg	AB	H	2B	3B	HR	RBI	BB	SO	OBP	SLG
vs. Left	.345	116	40	7	2	6	13	10	15	.402	.595	Scoring Posn	.273	55	15	2	1	0	15	11	14	.408	.345
vs. Right	.255	110	28	6	0	1	11	8	24	.317	.336	Close & Late	.276	29	8	2	0	0	1	4	6	.364	.345
Home	.313	115	36	8	0	4	13	9	19	.365	.487	None on/out	.313	48	15	5	0	3	3	2	13	.340	.604
Away	.288	111	32	5	2	3	11	9	20	.355	.450	Batting #2	.277	83	23	5	1	1	6	4	8	.318	.398
First Pitch	.292	24	7	2	0	0	1	1	0	.308	.375	Batting #9	.436	55	24	5	1	2	10	2	7	.441	.673
Ahead in Count	.355	62	22	3	2	3	10	8	0	.438	.613	Other	.239	88	21	3	0	4	8	12	24	.350	.409
Behind in Count	.298	104	31	7	0	3	6	0	31	.311	.452	Pre-All Star	.261	92	24	6	0	3	11	13	17	.370	.424
Two Strikes	.248	101	25	4	0	2	3	9	39	.321	.347	Post-All Star	.328	134	44	7	2	4	13	5	22	.352	.500

Last Five Years

	Avg	AB	H	2B	3B	HR	RBI	BB	SO	OBP	SLG		Avg	AB	H	2B	3B	HR	RBI	BB	SO	OBP	SLG
vs. Left	.301	425	128	24	4	11	43	40	77	.365	.454	Scoring Posn	.262	267	70	16	1	6	92	35	61	.349	.397
vs. Right	.247	726	179	34	4	11	72	61	150	.309	.350	Close & Late	.249	185	46	10	1	3	11	18	37	.315	.362
Groundball	.269	309	83	18	1	4	29	26	44	.334	.372	None on/out	.297	279	83	18	3	5	5	18	58	.344	.437
Flyball	.267	273	73	12	1	8	39	31	59	.340	.407	Batting #2	.259	239	62	15	2	3	20	24	35	.330	.377
Home	.279	551	154	28	2	8	64	53	98	.348	.381	Batting #6	.267	217	58	9	0	4	31	23	45	.340	.364
Away	.255	600	153	30	6	14	51	48	129	.312	.395	Other	.269	695	187	34	6	15	64	54	147	.326	.400
Day	.288	371	107	19	2	8	32	24	63	.337	.415	April	.221	136	30	7	0	4	12	10	31	.287	.360
Night	.256	780	200	39	6	14	83	77	164	.326	.376	May	.222	185	41	8	1	0	11	18	44	.304	.276
Grass	.268	965	259	42	3	21	100	88	180	.334	.383	June	.253	95	24	3	1	3	10	8	16	.317	.400
Turf	.258	186	48	16	5	1	15	13	47	.308	.414	July	.292	130	38	12	2	3	7	13	26	.357	.485
First Pitch	.307	140	43	9	3	0	13	2	0	.324	.414	August	.278	255	71	9	2	4	32	27	48	.345	.376
Ahead in Count	.338	284	96	19	3	7	38	48	0	.436	.500	September/October	.294	350	103	19	2	8	43	25	62	.342	.429
Behind in Count	.199	508	101	18	1	7	27	0	193	.206	.280	Pre-All Star	.223	440	98	19	2	7	33	40	97	.299	.323
Two Strikes	.185	509	94	18	0	8	33	51	227	.262	.267	Post-All Star	.294	711	209	39	6	15	82	61	130	.349	.429

Batter vs. Pitcher (career)

Hits Best Against	Avg	AB	H	2B	3B	HR	RBI	BB	SO	OBP	SLG	Hits Worst Against	Avg	AB	H	2B	3B	HR	RBI	BB	SO	OBP	SLG
Joe Hesketh	.545	11	6	3	0	0	0	1	0	.583	.818	Greg Hibbard	.063	16	1	1	0	0	2	0	2	.063	.125
Randy Johnson	.500	14	7	2	0	0	6	2	4	.563	.643	Kirk McCaskill	.083	12	1	1	0	0	0	0	1	.083	.167
Jaime Navarro	.444	9	4	0	0	0	1	2	2	.545	.444	David Wells	.091	11	1	0	0	0	0	1	5	.167	.091
Mike Boddicker	.417	12	5	1	0	0	3	0	5	.417	.500	Erik Hanson	.091	11	1	0	0	0	0	0	3	.091	.091
Jimmy Key	.400	15	6	2	0	0	0	0	2	.400	.533	Frank Viola	.143	14	2	1	0	0	0	0	2	.143	.214

Guillermo Velasquez — Padres

Age 26 – Bats Left

	Avg	G	AB	R	H	2B	3B	HR	RBI	BB	SO	HBP	GDP	SB	CS	OBP	SLG	IBB	SH	SF	#Pit	#P/PA	GB	FB	G/F
1993 Season	.210	79	143	7	30	2	0	3	20	13	35	0	3	0	0	.274	.287	2	0	1	602	3.83	45	42	1.07
Career (1992-1993)	.223	94	166	8	37	2	0	4	25	14	42	0	3	0	0	.282	.307	2	0	1	682	3.77	50	46	1.09

1993 Season

	Avg	AB	H	2B	3B	HR	RBI	BB	SO	OBP	SLG		Avg	AB	H	2B	3B	HR	RBI	BB	SO	OBP	SLG
vs. Left	.143	14	2	0	0	1	2	0	8	.143	.357	Scoring Posn	.293	41	12	1	0	1	18	8	7	.400	.390
vs. Right	.217	129	28	2	0	2	18	13	27	.287	.279	Close & Late	.200	35	7	0	0	0	8	2	13	.237	.200
Home	.242	66	16	1	0	1	11	11	15	.346	.303	None on/out	.067	30	2	0	0	0	0	0	6	.067	.067
Away	.182	77	14	1	0	2	9	2	20	.203	.273	Batting #5	.276	29	8	0	0	0	6	2	4	.323	.276
First Pitch	.190	21	4	0	0	0	2	1	0	.227	.190	Batting #6	.188	69	13	1	0	1	4	8	18	.273	.246
Ahead in Count	.364	22	8	0	0	1	8	5	0	.464	.500	Other	.200	45	9	1	0	2	10	3	13	.245	.356
Behind in Count	.137	73	10	1	0	2	4	0	29	.137	.233	Pre-All Star	.161	31	5	0	0	0	9	3	7	.229	.161
Two Strikes	.158	76	12	1	0	2	6	7	35	.229	.250	Post-All Star	.223	112	25	2	0	3	11	10	28	.287	.321

Robin Ventura — White Sox

Age 26 – Bats Left

	Avg	G	AB	R	H	2B	3B	HR	RBI	BB	SO	HBP	GDP	SB	CS	OBP	SLG	IBB	SH	SF	#Pit	#P/PA	GB	FB	G/F
1993 Season	.262	157	554	85	145	27	1	22	94	105	82	3	15	1	6	.379	.433	16	1	6	2772	4.14	187	177	1.06
Career (1989-1993)	.269	637	2290	315	615	110	4	66	348	341	279	9	59	6	18	.362	.407	30	24	27	10476	3.89	880	698	1.26

1993 Season

	Avg	AB	H	2B	3B	HR	RBI	BB	SO	OBP	SLG		Avg	AB	H	2B	3B	HR	RBI	BB	SO	OBP	SLG
vs. Left	.267	176	47	12	0	5	29	26	42	.361	.420	Scoring Posn	.273	161	44	11	0	4	68	43	21	.420	.416
vs. Right	.259	378	98	15	1	17	65	79	40	.387	.439	Close & Late	.289	83	24	4	0	3	12	11	12	.368	.446
Groundball	.200	95	19	3	0	1	14	19	19	.328	.263	None on/out	.242	128	31	7	1	5	5	22	23	.353	.430
Flyball	.270	111	30	8	1	9	27	28	14	.423	.604	Batting #4	.258	279	72	14	0	11	51	47	43	.367	.427
Home	.248	254	63	12	0	12	50	59	40	.386	.437	Batting #5	.252	218	55	5	1	10	34	49	31	.385	.422
Away	.273	300	82	15	1	10	44	46	42	.372	.430	Other	.316	57	18	8	0	1	9	9	8	.412	.509
Day	.261	165	43	7	0	7	24	27	29	.363	.430	April	.289	76	22	3	0	2	6	17	8	.415	.408
Night	.262	389	102	20	1	15	70	78	53	.385	.434	May	.265	83	22	2	1	7	21	23	17	.421	.566
Grass	.252	453	114	20	0	19	84	96	64	.382	.422	June	.202	104	21	3	0	4	13	13	23	.288	.346

1993 Season

	Avg	AB	H	2B	3B	HR	RBI	BB	SO	OBP	SLG
Turf	.307	101	31	7	1	3	10	9	18	.364	.485
First Pitch	.333	36	12	0	0	1	10	13	0	.520	.417
Ahead in Count	.268	164	44	10	0	6	29	63	0	.470	.439
Behind in Count	.229	214	49	9	1	7	27	0	66	.230	.379
Two Strikes	.239	264	63	13	1	13	45	29	82	.313	.443

	Avg	AB	H	2B	3B	HR	RBI	BB	SO	OBP	SLG
July	.240	96	23	4	0	4	19	18	9	.365	.406
August	.283	92	26	8	0	2	14	13	10	.380	.435
September/October	.301	103	31	7	0	3	21	21	15	.413	.456
Pre-All Star	.247	304	75	10	1	14	49	57	50	.363	.424
Post-All Star	.280	250	70	17	0	8	45	48	32	.398	.444

1993 By Position

Position	Avg	AB	H	2B	3B	HR	RBI	BB	SO	OBP	SLG	G	GS	Innings	PO	A	E	DP	Fld Pct	Rng Fctr	In Zone	Outs	Zone Rtg	MLB Zone
As 3b	.261	551	144	27	1	22	94	105	82	.379	.434	155	155	1367.0	112	277	14	23	.965	2.56	345	303	.878	.834

Career (1989-1993)

	Avg	AB	H	2B	3B	HR	RBI	BB	SO	OBP	SLG
vs. Left	.253	711	180	32	2	12	89	107	132	.350	.354
vs. Right	.275	1579	435	78	2	54	259	234	147	.367	.430
Groundball	.262	583	153	33	1	11	90	82	57	.350	.379
Flyball	.265	536	142	38	1	18	86	75	65	.356	.440
Home	.275	1104	304	49	2	37	186	176	134	.373	.424
Away	.262	1186	311	61	2	29	162	165	145	.351	.390
Day	.287	613	176	32	1	19	84	88	90	.373	.436
Night	.262	1677	439	78	3	47	264	253	189	.358	.396
Grass	.267	1936	517	91	3	60	313	292	235	.362	.410
Turf	.277	354	98	19	1	6	35	49	44	.361	.387
First Pitch	.271	214	58	9	0	4	35	22	0	.343	.369
Ahead in Count	.327	710	232	46	2	28	141	203	0	.473	.515
Behind in Count	.225	863	194	31	1	17	97	0	223	.226	.322
Two Strikes	.222	947	210	35	2	25	122	114	279	.304	.342

	Avg	AB	H	2B	3B	HR	RBI	BB	SO	OBP	SLG
Scoring Posn	.305	594	181	33	0	15	264	123	74	.411	.436
Close & Late	.267	375	100	17	1	9	54	43	48	.340	.389
None on/out	.220	479	109	21	2	13	13	58	61	.312	.361
Batting #2	.292	881	257	37	2	28	136	104	100	.366	.434
Batting #5	.266	478	127	24	1	17	87	91	60	.379	.427
Other	.248	931	231	49	1	21	125	146	119	.349	.371
April	.272	246	67	13	1	6	29	51	28	.397	.407
May	.238	357	85	11	1	11	48	59	54	.344	.367
June	.291	406	118	19	1	10	52	53	58	.371	.416
July	.263	426	112	18	0	19	71	45	39	.335	.439
August	.275	375	103	22	1	10	69	49	39	.356	.419
September/October	.271	480	130	27	0	10	79	84	61	.376	.390
Pre-All Star	.266	1157	308	48	3	32	149	176	153	.362	.396
Post-All Star	.271	1133	307	62	1	34	199	165	126	.362	.417

Batter vs. Pitcher (career)

Hits Best Against	Avg	AB	H	2B	3B	HR	RBI	BB	SO	OBP	SLG
Scott Sanderson	.471	17	8	1	0	2	8	3	2	.550	.882
Dave Johnson	.462	13	6	2	0	1	4	2	0	.533	.846
Cal Eldred	.385	13	5	1	0	1	3	2	1	.467	.692
David Cone	.364	11	4	1	0	2	3	4	2	.533	1.000
Jesse Orosco	.333	9	3	1	0	2	3	3	3	.500	1.111

Hits Worst Against	Avg	AB	H	2B	3B	HR	RBI	BB	SO	OBP	SLG
Tom Gordon	.000	16	0	0	0	0	0	4	5	.200	.000
Kirk McCaskill	.091	11	1	0	0	0	0	1	2	.167	.091
Bob Welch	.095	21	2	0	0	0	0	3	2	.208	.095
Jose Guzman	.100	10	1	0	0	0	1	1	1	.182	.100
Tom Bolton	.176	17	3	0	0	0	0	1	3	.222	.176

Hector Villanueva — Cardinals

Age 29 – Bats Right

	Avg	G	AB	R	H	2B	3B	HR	RBI	BB	SO	HBP	GDP	SB	CS	OBP	SLG	IBB	SH	SF	#Pit	#P/PA	GB	FB	G/F
1993 Season	.145	17	55	7	8	1	0	3	9	4	17	0	3	0	0	.203	.327	1	0	0	251	4.25	14	15	0.93
Career (1990-1993)	.230	191	473	53	109	21	2	25	72	40	98	2	13	1	0	.293	.442	6	0	1	1960	3.80	149	143	1.04

1993 Season

	Avg	AB	H	2B	3B	HR	RBI	BB	SO	OBP	SLG
vs. Left	.167	12	2	0	0	2	5	0	4	.167	.667
vs. Right	.140	43	6	1	0	1	4	4	13	.213	.233

	Avg	AB	H	2B	3B	HR	RBI	BB	SO	OBP	SLG
Scoring Posn	.231	13	3	1	0	1	6	1	3	.286	.538
Close & Late	.077	13	1	0	0	1	2	0	4	.077	.308

Career (1990-1993)

	Avg	AB	H	2B	3B	HR	RBI	BB	SO	OBP	SLG
vs. Left	.240	221	53	9	2	14	40	25	45	.317	.489
vs. Right	.222	252	56	12	0	11	32	15	53	.270	.401
Groundball	.257	136	35	10	1	7	22	14	27	.336	.500
Flyball	.252	111	28	4	0	8	18	8	25	.300	.505
Home	.256	242	62	8	1	17	46	21	49	.320	.508
Away	.203	231	47	13	1	8	26	19	49	.264	.372
Day	.257	214	55	7	1	14	35	21	39	.328	.495
Night	.208	259	54	14	1	11	37	19	59	.263	.398
Grass	.256	305	78	13	1	18	50	25	64	.315	.482
Turf	.185	168	31	8	1	7	22	15	34	.251	.369
First Pitch	.194	67	13	2	0	5	8	1	0	.206	.448
Ahead in Count	.300	100	30	5	1	6	22	21	0	.421	.550
Behind in Count	.180	222	40	8	1	9	28	0	83	.187	.347
Two Strikes	.167	239	40	8	0	10	30	16	98	.225	.326

	Avg	AB	H	2B	3B	HR	RBI	BB	SO	OBP	SLG
Scoring Posn	.239	117	28	5	0	8	45	12	22	.318	.487
Close & Late	.210	105	22	2	1	4	14	4	30	.239	.362
None on/out	.200	110	22	9	1	2	2	9	28	.261	.355
Batting #6	.235	196	46	10	1	10	28	14	39	.284	.449
Batting #7	.269	104	28	4	0	7	16	11	16	.350	.510
Other	.202	173	35	7	1	8	28	15	43	.266	.393
April	.179	67	12	3	0	4	15	7	18	.257	.403
May	.146	103	15	2	0	3	7	8	23	.205	.252
June	.235	119	28	5	1	8	22	10	16	.305	.496
July	.360	50	18	2	0	2	6	3	12	.396	.520
August	.280	25	7	2	1	2	7	1	6	.308	.680
September/October	.266	109	29	7	0	6	15	11	23	.333	.495
Pre-All Star	.213	315	67	11	1	17	48	26	63	.276	.416
Post-All Star	.266	158	42	10	1	8	24	14	35	.326	.494

Batter vs. Pitcher (career)

Hits Best Against	Avg	AB	H	2B	3B	HR	RBI	BB	SO	OBP	SLG
Randy Tomlin	.364	11	4	1	0	0	1	1	0	.417	.455
Dennis Rasmussen	.333	15	5	1	0	2	4	1	0	.375	.800

Hits Worst Against	Avg	AB	H	2B	3B	HR	RBI	BB	SO	OBP	SLG
Terry Mulholland	.125	16	2	1	0	0	4	2	4	.222	.188
Zane Smith	.182	11	2	0	0	1	2	0	0	.182	.455

Fernando Vina — Mets

Age 25 – Bats Left (flyball hitter)

	Avg	G	AB	R	H	2B	3B	HR	RBI	BB	SO	HBP	GDP	SB	CS	OBP	SLG	IBB	SH	SF	#Pit	#P/PA	GB	FB	G/F
1993 Season	.222	24	45	5	10	2	0	0	2	4	3	3	0	6	0	.327	.267	0	1	0	140	2.64	14	17	0.82

1993 Season

	Avg	AB	H	2B	3B	HR	RBI	BB	SO	OBP	SLG
vs. Left	.000	2	0	0	0	0	0	0	0	.000	.000
vs. Right	.233	43	10	2	0	0	2	4	3	.340	.279

	Avg	AB	H	2B	3B	HR	RBI	BB	SO	OBP	SLG
Scoring Posn	.182	11	2	0	0	0	2	2	1	.400	.182
Close & Late	.294	17	5	1	0	0	0	2	2	.400	.353

Frank Viola — Red Sox

Age 34 – Pitches Left

	ERA	W	L	Sv	G	GS	IP	BB	SO	Avg	H	2B	3B	HR	RBI	OBP	SLG	CG	ShO	Sup	QS	#P/S	SB	CS	GB	FB	G/F
1993 Season	3.14	11	8	0	29	29	183.2	72	91	.259	180	32	5	12	63	.331	.372	2	1	4.80	16	100	11	11	269	201	1.34
Last Five Years	3.38	70	64	0	170	170	1163.2	349	737	.255	1126	192	17	87	427	.311	.366	27	7	4.18	105	105	70	58	1690	1161	1.46

1993 Season

	ERA	W	L	Sv	G	GS	IP	H	HR	BB	SO
Home	2.26	5	3	0	14	14	91.2	93	2	30	48
Away	4.01	6	5	0	15	15	92.0	87	10	42	43
Day	2.17	5	0	0	10	10	66.1	64	3	23	31
Night	3.68	6	8	0	19	19	117.1	116	9	49	60
Grass	3.17	8	7	0	24	24	150.1	151	9	55	77
Turf	2.97	3	1	0	5	5	33.1	29	3	17	14
April	1.47	4	1	0	5	5	36.2	31	0	7	15
May	4.45	0	3	0	5	5	30.1	32	2	17	16
June	4.55	0	3	0	5	5	29.2	33	3	12	18
July	4.58	2	1	0	6	6	35.1	47	4	20	18
August	1.64	4	0	0	5	5	33.0	23	2	11	13
September/October	1.93	1	0	0	3	3	18.2	14	1	5	11
Starter	3.14	11	8	0	29	29	183.2	180	12	72	91
Reliever	0.00	0	0	0	0	0	0.0	0	0	0	0
0-3 Days Rest	1.23	1	0	0	1	1	7.1	5	0	2	3
4 Days Rest	2.79	4	5	0	15	15	96.2	95	6	39	51
5+ Days Rest	3.73	6	3	0	13	13	79.2	80	6	31	37
Pre-All Star	3.68	5	7	0	17	17	107.2	113	7	41	54
Post-All Star	2.37	6	1	0	12	12	76.0	67	5	31	37

	Avg	AB	H	2B	3B	HR	RBI	BB	SO	OBP	SLG
vs. Left	.272	114	31	8	2	1	8	13	11	.341	.404
vs. Right	.257	580	149	24	3	11	55	59	80	.329	.366
Inning 1-6	.263	608	160	31	5	12	62	68	81	.340	.390
Inning 7+	.233	86	20	1	0	0	1	4	10	.264	.244
None on	.274	401	110	15	4	11	11	42	64	.346	.414
Runners on	.239	293	70	17	1	1	52	30	27	.311	.314
Scoring Posn	.209	153	32	6	1	1	49	19	14	.297	.281
Close & Late	.210	62	13	1	0	0	0	3	9	.246	.226
None on/out	.261	180	47	3	3	7	7	21	30	.338	.428
vs. 1st Batr (relief)	.000	0	0	0	0	0	0	0	0	.000	.000
First Inning Pitched	.217	106	23	6	0	0	7	9	16	.276	.274
First 75 Pitches	.270	514	139	28	3	10	48	51	70	.340	.395
Pitch 76-90	.244	78	19	3	1	1	6	9	9	.322	.346
Pitch 91-105	.250	52	13	1	1	1	8	10	4	.365	.365
Pitch 106+	.180	50	9	0	0	0	1	2	8	.208	.180
First Pitch	.320	122	39	5	0	7	18	4	0	.351	.533
Ahead in Count	.224	263	59	8	1	1	11	0	72	.226	.274
Behind in Count	.298	151	45	11	1	1	15	40	0	.440	.404
Two Strikes	.229	293	67	11	3	1	15	28	91	.298	.297

Last Five Years

	ERA	W	L	Sv	G	GS	IP	H	HR	BB	SO
Home	3.35	39	32	0	85	85	585.0	588	38	156	384
Away	3.41	31	32	0	85	85	578.2	538	49	193	353
Day	3.00	30	20	0	60	60	417.0	391	30	106	270
Night	3.59	40	44	0	110	110	746.2	735	57	243	467
Grass	3.42	49	48	0	122	122	824.2	815	65	241	519
Turf	3.29	21	16	0	48	48	339.0	311	22	108	218
April	2.53	13	7	0	24	24	167.0	151	10	37	108
May	3.52	12	11	0	27	27	186.2	190	14	48	126
June	3.50	11	10	0	29	29	203.1	207	13	64	123
July	3.10	12	10	0	30	30	206.1	185	19	79	117
August	4.01	12	17	0	31	31	206.1	204	16	61	135
September/October	3.48	10	9	0	29	29	194.0	189	15	60	128
Starter	3.38	70	64	0	170	170	1163.2	1126	87	349	737
Reliever	0.00	0	0	0	0	0	0.0	0	0	0	0
0-3 Days Rest	2.91	6	5	0	12	12	80.1	68	3	21	56
4 Days Rest	3.51	42	45	0	112	112	776.1	767	63	230	495
5+ Days Rest	3.17	22	14	0	46	46	307.0	291	21	98	186
Pre-All Star	3.08	43	29	0	91	91	640.0	618	42	176	400
Post-All Star	3.75	27	35	0	79	79	523.2	508	45	173	337

	Avg	AB	H	2B	3B	HR	RBI	BB	SO	OBP	SLG
vs. Left	.249	771	192	45	4	11	68	57	126	.302	.361
vs. Right	.257	3638	934	147	13	76	359	292	611	.313	.367
Inning 1-6	.262	3687	966	172	16	75	397	302	629	.319	.378
Inning 7+	.222	722	160	20	1	12	30	47	108	.270	.302
None on	.258	2594	668	105	12	57	57	193	425	.311	.373
Runners on	.252	1815	458	87	5	30	370	156	312	.311	.355
Scoring Posn	.241	979	236	45	2	18	327	111	183	.314	.346
Close & Late	.226	421	95	6	1	7	22	29	51	.276	.295
None on/out	.262	1149	301	48	7	27	27	81	169	.311	.386
vs. 1st Batr (relief)	.000	0	0	0	0	0	0	0	0	.000	.000
First Inning Pitched	.202	520	105	22	0	4	34	42	104	.261	.267
First 75 Pitches	.262	3046	797	144	12	54	291	233	536	.315	.370
Pitch 76-90	.267	577	154	23	3	13	68	47	81	.325	.385
Pitch 91-105	.219	424	93	14	2	10	41	39	68	.283	.333
Pitch 106+	.227	362	82	11	0	10	27	30	52	.285	.340
First Pitch	.338	704	238	40	2	25	100	14	0	.353	.507
Ahead in Count	.189	1880	355	56	3	20	114	0	608	.192	.254
Behind in Count	.317	943	299	45	7	25	109	185	0	.427	.459
Two Strikes	.183	1965	359	66	4	16	127	150	737	.243	.245

Pitcher vs. Batter (since 1984)

Pitches Best Vs.	Avg	AB	H	2B	3B	HR	RBI	BB	SO	OBP	SLG
Glenn Wilson	.000	11	0	0	0	0	0	0	2	.000	.000
Greg Gagne	.000	11	0	0	0	0	0	1	5	.083	.000
Albert Belle	.059	17	1	1	0	0	3	1	4	.095	.118
Steve Lyons	.083	12	1	1	0	0	1	0	5	.083	.167
Brian McRae	.125	16	2	0	0	0	3	0	2	.125	.125

Pitches Worst Vs.	Avg	AB	H	2B	3B	HR	RBI	BB	SO	OBP	SLG
Chris Sabo	.545	11	6	1	0	1	2	4	2	.667	.909
Brian Harper	.500	10	5	1	0	1	1	3	0	.615	.900
Dale Murphy	.429	21	9	2	0	2	2	1	4	.455	.810
Randy Milligan	.429	14	6	1	0	1	6	4	1	.556	.714
Ryne Sandberg	.375	24	9	1	0	3	5	7	6	.500	.792

Jose Vizcaino — Cubs

Age 26 – Bats Both (groundball hitter)

	Avg	G	AB	R	H	2B	3B	HR	RBI	BB	SO	HBP	GDP	SB	CS	OBP	SLG	IBB	SH	SF	#Pit	#P/PA	GB	FB	G/F
1993 Season	.287	151	551	74	158	19	4	4	54	46	71	3	9	12	9	.340	.358	2	8	9	2142	3.47	245	110	2.23
Career (1989-1993)	.265	374	1042	111	276	35	9	5	83	69	133	3	15	18	11	.309	.330	5	16	12	3803	3.33	464	206	2.25

1993 Season

	Avg	AB	H	2B	3B	HR	RBI	BB	SO	OBP	SLG
vs. Left	.297	128	38	4	0	0	8	14	15	.364	.328
vs. Right	.284	423	120	15	4	4	46	32	56	.333	.366
Groundball	.246	203	50	6	0	0	12	14	26	.290	.276
Flyball	.329	85	28	2	0	2	9	5	11	.363	.424
Home	.338	278	94	10	2	1	26	23	34	.384	.399
Away	.234	273	64	9	2	3	28	23	37	.296	.315
Day	.316	294	93	10	2	1	22	24	34	.366	.374
Night	.253	257	65	9	2	3	32	22	37	.311	.339
Grass	.307	423	130	17	3	3	47	34	55	.355	.383
Turf	.219	128	28	2	1	1	7	12	16	.289	.273
First Pitch	.374	99	37	5	1	0	15	1	0	.373	.444
Ahead in Count	.336	119	40	6	1	0	13	31	0	.474	.403
Behind in Count	.247	243	60	5	2	2	18	0	65	.246	.309
Two Strikes	.242	236	57	7	1	3	22	14	71	.282	.318

	Avg	AB	H	2B	3B	HR	RBI	BB	SO	OBP	SLG
Scoring Posn	.280	107	30	4	0	3	48	13	9	.344	.402
Close & Late	.244	86	21	0	0	1	11	6	16	.298	.279
None on/out	.308	130	40	4	1	1	1	16	12	.384	.377
Batting #1	.248	129	32	3	0	0	12	12	12	.310	.271
Batting #2	.295	308	91	12	4	2	22	23	40	.344	.380
Other	.307	114	35	4	0	2	20	11	19	.362	.395
April	.347	75	26	2	1	1	13	5	9	.383	.440
May	.372	94	35	1	0	0	5	6	6	.416	.383
June	.253	99	25	6	2	0	3	5	17	.286	.354
July	.230	87	20	4	1	1	15	13	12	.327	.333
August	.210	81	17	2	0	0	5	7	12	.273	.235
September/October	.304	115	35	4	0	2	13	10	15	.354	.391
Pre-All Star	.309	307	95	11	4	1	27	20	36	.350	.381
Post-All Star	.258	244	63	8	0	3	27	26	35	.327	.328

1993 By Position

Position	Avg	AB	H	2B	3B	HR	RBI	BB	SO	OBP	SLG	G	GS	Innings	PO	A	E	DP	Fld Pct	Rng Fctr	In Zone	Outs	Zone Rtg	MLB Zone
As Pinch Hitter	.250	8	2	0	0	0	0	2	2	.400	.250	11	0	---	---	---	---	---	---	---	---	---	---	---
As 2b	.295	105	31	3	0	1	11	6	15	.336	.352	34	27	245.2	67	75	2	23	.986	5.20	86	79	.919	.895
As 3b	.250	124	31	5	2	2	13	13	19	.314	.371	44	29	286.2	25	68	2	6	.979	2.92	95	75	.789	.834
As ss	.299	314	94	11	2	1	30	25	35	.350	.357	81	79	680.1	126	264	13	44	.968	5.16	294	272	.925	.880

Career (1989-1993)

	Avg	AB	H	2B	3B	HR	RBI	BB	SO	OBP	SLG		Avg	AB	H	2B	3B	HR	RBI	BB	SO	OBP	SLG
vs. Left	.264	273	72	7	3	0	16	22	30	.316	.311	Scoring Posn	.261	203	53	6	0	3	74	22	23	.322	.335
vs. Right	.265	769	204	28	6	5	67	47	103	.306	.337	Close & Late	.234	184	43	5	0	1	19	13	26	.284	.277
Groundball	.243	391	95	12	2	0	17	20	50	.277	.284	None on/out	.252	286	72	9	3	2	2	25	35	.312	.325
Flyball	.273	205	56	5	1	2	17	12	28	.311	.337	Batting #1	.225	302	68	12	0	0	18	18	37	.269	.265
Home	.292	520	152	19	4	1	40	35	64	.333	.350	Batting #2	.293	368	108	13	7	2	28	24	43	.336	.383
Away	.238	522	124	16	5	4	43	34	69	.285	.310	Other	.269	372	100	10	2	3	37	27	53	.315	.331
Day	.273	560	153	20	5	1	39	35	77	.313	.332	April	.286	105	30	2	1	1	15	7	12	.322	.352
Night	.255	482	123	15	4	4	44	34	56	.304	.328	May	.300	180	54	2	2	0	7	11	14	.344	.333
Grass	.279	811	226	29	7	4	70	52	100	.320	.346	June	.244	238	58	13	2	0	10	12	37	.278	.315
Turf	.216	231	50	6	2	1	13	17	33	.272	.273	July	.246	199	49	12	2	1	21	19	29	.311	.342
First Pitch	.328	201	66	7	2	0	24	3	0	.333	.383	August	.244	168	41	2	2	1	17	10	23	.287	.298
Ahead in Count	.320	222	71	10	2	0	24	44	0	.432	.383	September/October	.289	152	44	4	0	2	13	10	18	.329	.355
Behind in Count	.217	438	95	12	5	3	22	0	116	.216	.288	Pre-All Star	.265	618	164	23	6	1	40	36	74	.304	.327
Two Strikes	.218	413	90	14	2	4	26	21	133	.255	.291	Post-All Star	.264	424	112	12	3	4	43	33	59	.316	.335

Batter vs. Pitcher (career)

Hits Best Against	Avg	AB	H	2B	3B	HR	RBI	BB	SO	OBP	SLG	Hits Worst Against	Avg	AB	H	2B	3B	HR	RBI	BB	SO	OBP	SLG
Tim Belcher	.615	13	8	1	1	0	4	1	2	.643	.846	Charlie Leibrandt	.083	12	1	1	0	0	0	0	0	.083	.167
Orel Hershiser	.455	11	5	1	1	0	0	1	1	.500	.727	Bob Walk	.133	15	2	0	0	0	0	2	1	.235	.133
Doug Drabek	.412	17	7	1	0	0	2	1	2	.444	.471	Greg W. Harris	.154	13	2	0	0	0	1	0	1	.154	.154
Tom Glavine	.364	11	4	0	0	0	1	3	0	.500	.364	Pete Harnisch	.167	12	2	0	0	0	0	1	1	.231	.167
John Burkett	.313	16	5	1	1	0	0	0	1	.313	.500	Ken Hill	.182	11	2	0	0	0	0	0	2	.182	.182

Omar Vizquel — Mariners

Age 27 – Bats Both (groundball hitter)

	Avg	G	AB	R	H	2B	3B	HR	RBI	BB	SO	HBP	GDP	SB	CS	OBP	SLG	IBB	SH	SF	#Pit	#P/PA	GB	FB	G/F
1993 Season	.255	158	560	68	143	14	2	2	31	50	71	4	7	12	14	.319	.298	2	13	3	2373	3.77	231	143	1.62
Career (1989-1993)	.252	660	2111	223	531	60	15	6	131	173	208	7	42	39	34	.309	.303	2	53	11	8406	3.57	902	554	1.63

1993 Season

	Avg	AB	H	2B	3B	HR	RBI	BB	SO	OBP	SLG		Avg	AB	H	2B	3B	HR	RBI	BB	SO	OBP	SLG
vs. Left	.197	132	26	6	0	0	6	11	16	.264	.242	Scoring Posn	.227	132	30	3	1	1	29	11	18	.291	.288
vs. Right	.273	428	117	8	2	2	25	39	55	.336	.315	Close & Late	.267	101	27	1	0	0	5	11	10	.351	.277
Groundball	.258	89	23	3	1	0	3	12	8	.353	.315	None on/out	.268	157	42	6	0	1	1	24	27	.365	.325
Flyball	.283	113	32	4	0	0	7	13	16	.349	.319	Batting #1	.254	283	72	8	1	1	11	29	42	.325	.300
Home	.266	274	73	7	0	1	14	27	29	.333	.303	Batting #9	.255	275	70	6	1	1	20	21	29	.312	.295
Away	.245	286	70	7	2	1	17	23	42	.306	.294	Other	.500	2	1	0	0	0	0	0	0	.500	.500
Day	.258	159	41	6	0	0	6	13	14	.316	.296	April	.225	80	18	1	0	1	8	14	11	.340	.275
Night	.254	401	102	8	2	2	25	37	57	.321	.299	May	.309	110	34	1	0	0	5	8	13	.353	.318
Grass	.222	230	51	5	0	0	10	15	39	.273	.243	June	.333	99	33	3	1	0	5	11	14	.405	.384
Turf	.279	330	92	9	2	2	21	35	32	.351	.336	July	.267	101	27	6	0	1	4	8	16	.324	.356
First Pitch	.397	68	27	0	0	0	2	2	0	.417	.397	August	.128	78	10	0	0	0	2	3	9	.160	.128
Ahead in Count	.288	104	30	3	0	0	9	24	0	.423	.317	September/October	.228	92	21	3	1	0	7	6	8	.287	.283
Behind in Count	.205	278	57	9	2	1	14	0	66	.210	.263	Pre-All Star	.292	332	97	6	1	2	19	36	46	.362	.334
Two Strikes	.175	257	45	8	2	2	15	24	71	.251	.245	Post-All Star	.202	228	46	8	1	0	12	14	25	.255	.246

1993 By Position

Position	Avg	AB	H	2B	3B	HR	RBI	BB	SO	OBP	SLG	G	GS	Innings	PO	A	E	DP	Fld Pct	Rng Fctr	In Zone	Outs	Zone Rtg	MLB Zone
As ss	.254	559	142	14	2	2	31	50	71	.318	.297	155	150	1330.2	247	476	15	108	.980	4.89	558	519	.930	.880

Career (1989-1993)

	Avg	AB	H	2B	3B	HR	RBI	BB	SO	OBP	SLG		Avg	AB	H	2B	3B	HR	RBI	BB	SO	OBP	SLG
vs. Left	.215	507	109	20	0	2	36	33	39	.264	.266	Scoring Posn	.245	502	123	14	4	2	122	40	47	.299	.301
vs. Right	.263	1604	422	40	15	4	95	140	169	.323	.314	Close & Late	.252	357	90	11	4	0	13	27	29	.308	.305
Groundball	.241	498	120	11	4	1	23	47	46	.310	.285	None on/out	.265	566	150	19	5	3	3	61	71	.337	.332
Flyball	.268	437	117	15	2	1	33	41	35	.328	.318	Batting #1	.287	550	158	19	4	1	24	45	67	.344	.342
Home	.258	1024	264	37	9	3	68	82	111	.313	.320	Batting #9	.243	1181	287	27	8	4	77	100	107	.303	.290
Away	.246	1087	267	23	6	3	63	91	97	.305	.286	Other	.226	380	86	14	3	1	30	28	34	.277	.287
Day	.260	581	151	19	2	1	38	50	48	.320	.305	April	.191	199	38	2	1	1	13	24	17	.278	.226
Night	.248	1530	380	41	13	5	93	123	160	.305	.302	May	.277	292	81	5	5	0	22	20	28	.320	.329
Grass	.243	841	204	17	2	1	44	61	77	.294	.271	June	.291	337	98	15	1	0	16	38	36	.363	.341
Turf	.257	1270	327	43	13	5	87	112	131	.319	.324	July	.293	427	125	20	2	4	30	28	39	.338	.377
First Pitch	.304	283	86	9	3	1	19	2	0	.309	.367	August	.204	411	84	5	2	1	21	26	46	.252	.234
Ahead in Count	.295	441	130	16	3	2	37	98	0	.421	.358	September/October	.236	445	105	13	4	0	29	37	42	.298	.283
Behind in Count	.214	996	213	25	8	2	49	0	191	.216	.261	Pre-All Star	.269	967	260	29	9	3	59	92	95	.332	.327
Two Strikes	.186	872	162	24	7	3	46	73	208	.250	.240	Post-All Star	.237	1144	271	31	6	3	72	81	113	.289	.282

Batter vs. Pitcher (career)

Hits Best Against	Avg	AB	H	2B	3B	HR	RBI	BB	SO	OBP	SLG	Hits Worst Against	Avg	AB	H	2B	3B	HR	RBI	BB	SO	OBP	SLG
Chuck Crim	.500	10	5	0	0	0	3	1	0	.545	.500	David Wells	.077	13	1	0	0	0	0	1	3	.143	.077
Hipolito Pichardo	.500	10	5	0	0	0	0	2	0	.583	.500	Jeff Ballard	.083	12	1	0	0	0	1	1	0	.154	.083

Batter vs. Pitcher (career)																							
Hits Best Against	Avg	AB	H	2B	3B	HR	RBI	BB	SO	OBP	SLG	Hits Worst Against	Avg	AB	H	2B	3B	HR	RBI	BB	SO	OBP	SLG
John Dopson	.462	13	6	1	1	0	2	0	1	.462	.692	Dave Stieb	.091	11	1	0	0	0	1	1	1	.167	.091
Mike Gardiner	.400	10	4	0	1	0	2	1	0	.455	.600	Bob Welch	.095	21	2	0	0	0	1	3	2	.200	.095
Joe Slusarski	.375	8	3	1	0	0	0	3	1	.545	.500	Roger Clemens	.133	30	4	0	0	0	1	1	6	.161	.133

Jack Voigt — Orioles

Age 28 – Bats Right (flyball hitter)

	Avg	G	AB	R	H	2B	3B	HR	RBI	BB	SO	HBP	GDP	SB	CS	OBP	SLG	IBB	SH	SF	#Pit	#P/PA	GB	FB	G/F
1993 Season	.296	64	152	32	45	11	1	6	23	25	33	0	3	1	0	.395	.500	0	0	0	692	3.91	40	53	0.75

1993 Season																							
	Avg	AB	H	2B	3B	HR	RBI	BB	SO	OBP	SLG		Avg	AB	H	2B	3B	HR	RBI	BB	SO	OBP	SLG
vs. Left	.352	91	32	8	0	6	19	9	15	.410	.637	Scoring Posn	.295	44	13	2	0	2	17	3	8	.340	.477
vs. Right	.213	61	13	3	1	0	4	16	18	.377	.295	Close & Late	.296	27	8	2	0	1	3	4	5	.387	.481
Home	.314	86	27	6	0	5	14	15	19	.416	.558	None on/out	.361	36	13	2	1	2	2	8	11	.477	.639
Away	.273	66	18	5	1	1	9	10	14	.368	.424	Batting #8	.400	50	20	6	1	3	8	4	7	.444	.740
First Pitch	.500	24	12	2	1	1	5	0	0	.500	.792	Batting #9	.317	41	13	3	0	1	9	10	9	.451	.463
Ahead in Count	.375	40	15	4	0	4	9	13	0	.528	.775	Other	.197	61	12	2	0	2	6	11	17	.319	.328
Behind in Count	.210	62	13	3	0	1	6	0	28	.210	.306	Pre-All Star	.244	45	11	0	0	1	6	7	9	.346	.311
Two Strikes	.203	69	14	5	0	1	9	12	33	.321	.319	Post-All Star	.318	107	34	11	1	5	17	18	24	.416	.579

Paul Wagner — Pirates

Age 26 – Pitches Right

	ERA	W	L	Sv	G	GS	IP	BB	SO	Avg	H	2B	3B	HR	RBI	OBP	SLG	GF	IR	IRS	Hld	SvOp	SB	CS	GB	FB	G/F
1993 Season	4.27	8	8	2	44	17	141.1	42	114	.263	143	21	2	15	65	.314	.392	9	21	11	4	5	18	7	174	172	1.01
Career (1992-1993)	3.97	10	8	2	50	18	154.1	47	119	.258	152	24	2	15	66	.310	.381	10	23	11	4	5	18	8	193	189	1.02

1993 Season																							
	ERA	W	L	Sv	G	GS	IP	H	HR	BB	SO		Avg	AB	H	2B	3B	HR	RBI	BB	SO	OBP	SLG
Home	4.31	4	4	0	21	7	62.2	67	6	10	55	vs. Left	.301	266	80	13	2	7	35	25	48	.356	.444
Away	4.23	4	4	2	23	10	78.2	76	9	32	59	vs. Right	.227	277	63	8	0	8	30	17	66	.272	.343
Starter	3.96	6	5	0	17	17	104.2	102	11	28	75	Scoring Posn	.254	138	35	4	0	5	52	10	30	.295	.391
Reliever	5.15	2	3	2	27	0	36.2	41	4	14	39	Close & Late	.333	87	29	3	0	3	18	7	19	.371	.471
0 Days rest	10.38	0	0	1	5	0	4.1	7	1	2	4	None on/out	.254	138	35	5	1	2	2	8	24	.295	.348
1 or 2 Days rest	4.55	2	2	1	18	0	27.2	28	2	11	28	First Pitch	.312	77	24	1	1	1	8	2	0	.329	.390
3+ Days rest	3.86	0	1	0	4	0	4.2	6	1	1	7	Ahead in Count	.166	223	37	5	0	6	20	0	103	.164	.269
Pre-All Star	4.86	4	6	2	32	7	74.0	79	8	22	61	Behind in Count	.318	151	48	6	1	3	23	23	0	.401	.430
Post-All Star	3.61	4	2	0	12	10	67.1	64	7	20	53	Two Strikes	.175	240	42	8	0	6	24	17	114	.229	.283

David Wainhouse — Mariners

Age 26 – Pitches Right

	ERA	W	L	Sv	G	GS	IP	BB	SO	Avg	H	2B	3B	HR	RBI	OBP	SLG	GF	IR	IRS	Hld	SvOp	SB	CS	GB	FB	G/F
1993 Season	27.00	0	0	0	3	0	2.1	5	2	.500	7	1	0	1	9	.650	.786	0	2	2	0	0	2	0	3	5	0.60
Career (1991-1993)	16.20	0	1	0	5	0	5.0	9	3	.391	9	1	0	1	11	.559	.565	1	2	2	0	0	2	0	7	7	1.00

1993 Season																							
	ERA	W	L	Sv	G	GS	IP	H	HR	BB	SO		Avg	AB	H	2B	3B	HR	RBI	BB	SO	OBP	SLG
Home	0.00	0	0	0	2	0	1.1	2	0	1	1	vs. Left	.500	6	3	0	0	1	5	1	2	.571	1.000
Away	63.00	0	0	0	1	0	1.0	5	1	4	1	vs. Right	.500	8	4	1	0	0	4	4	0	.692	.625

Tim Wakefield — Pirates

Age 27 – Pitches Right (flyball pitcher)

	ERA	W	L	Sv	G	GS	IP	BB	SO	Avg	H	2B	3B	HR	RBI	OBP	SLG	CG	ShO	Sup	QS	#P/S	SB	CS	GB	FB	G/F
1993 Season	5.61	6	11	0	24	20	128.1	75	59	.291	145	34	3	14	75	.390	.456	3	2	4.49	8	99	8	5	150	191	0.79
Career (1992-1993)	4.17	14	12	0	37	33	220.1	110	110	.268	221	46	5	17	100	.357	.398	7	3	4.41	18	99	12	14	264	296	0.89

1993 Season																							
	ERA	W	L	Sv	G	GS	IP	H	HR	BB	SO		Avg	AB	H	2B	3B	HR	RBI	BB	SO	OBP	SLG
Home	3.15	4	3	0	12	10	74.1	63	4	48	36	vs. Left	.270	211	57	14	2	5	35	46	26	.413	.427
Away	9.00	2	8	0	12	10	54.0	82	10	27	23	vs. Right	.307	287	88	20	1	9	40	29	33	.372	.477
Starter	5.86	5	11	0	20	20	122.1	139	14	74	55	Scoring Posn	.312	138	43	12	2	3	60	26	13	.425	.493
Reliever	4.50	1	0	0	4	0	6.0	6	0	1	4	Close & Late	.232	56	13	2	0	3	5	7	6	.323	.429
0-3 Days Rest	5.40	1	1	0	2	2	15.0	12	2	9	4	None on/out	.262	122	32	3	1	6	6	18	16	.362	.451
4 Days Rest	5.40	1	4	0	8	8	50.0	62	7	29	12	First Pitch	.398	83	33	7	1	3	17	1	0	.414	.614
5+ Days Rest	5.97	3	6	0	10	10	57.1	65	5	36	39	Ahead in Count	.227	211	48	13	0	4	22	0	48	.228	.346
Pre-All Star	6.35	4	8	0	19	15	95.0	112	12	61	43	Behind in Count	.318	110	35	10	2	5	24	52	0	.539	.582
Post-All Star	3.51	2	3	0	5	5	33.1	33	2	14	16	Two Strikes	.191	188	36	12	0	1	21	22	59	.282	.271

Matt Walbeck — Cubs

Age 24 – Bats Both

	Avg	G	AB	R	H	2B	3B	HR	RBI	BB	SO	HBP	GDP	SB	CS	OBP	SLG	IBB	SH	SF	#Pit	#P/PA	GB	FB	G/F
1993 Season	.200	11	30	2	6	2	0	1	6	1	6	0	0	0	0	.226	.367	0	0	0	129	4.16	12	10	1.20

1993 Season																							
	Avg	AB	H	2B	3B	HR	RBI	BB	SO	OBP	SLG		Avg	AB	H	2B	3B	HR	RBI	BB	SO	OBP	SLG
vs. Left	.091	11	1	0	0	0	2	1	0	.167	.091	Scoring Posn	.600	5	3	1	0	1	5	0	0	.600	1.400
vs. Right	.263	19	5	2	0	1	4	0	6	.263	.526	Close & Late	.286	7	2	0	0	1	4	0	2	.286	.714

Jim Walewander — Angels

Age 33 – Bats Both

	Avg	G	AB	R	H	2B	3B	HR	RBI	BB	SO	HBP	GDP	SB	CS	OBP	SLG	IBB	SH	SF	#Pit	#P/PA	GB	FB	G/F
1993 Season	.125	12	8	2	1	0	0	0	3	5	1	0	0	1	1	.429	.125	0	0	1	54	3.86	3	5	0.60
Last Five Years	.154	21	13	3	2	1	0	0	4	5	1	0	0	2	2	.368	.231	0	0	1	71	3.74	4	8	0.50

1993 Season

	Avg	AB	H	2B	3B	HR	RBI	BB	SO	OBP	SLG		Avg	AB	H	2B	3B	HR	RBI	BB	SO	OBP	SLG
vs. Left	.500	2	1	0	0	0	2	1	0	.500	.500	Scoring Posn	.250	4	1	0	0	0	3	2	0	.429	.250
vs. Right	.000	6	0	0	0	0	1	4	1	.400	.000	Close & Late	.000	0	0	0	0	0	0	0	0	.000	.000

Bob Walk — Pirates

Age 37 – Pitches Right (groundball pitcher)

	ERA	W	L	Sv	G	GS	IP	BB	SO	Avg	H	2B	3B	HR	RBI	OBP	SLG	CG	ShO	Sup	QS	#P/S	SB	CS	GB	FB	G/F
1993 Season	5.68	13	14	0	32	32	187.0	70	80	.294	214	36	5	23	108	.356	.452	3	0	5.05	10	90	19	6	306	211	1.45
Last Five Years	4.27	52	37	3	152	126	762.2	249	363	.270	794	142	15	75	344	.330	.405	7	1	5.24	52	88	82	35	1232	814	1.51

1993 Season

	ERA	W	L	Sv	G	GS	IP	H	HR	BB	SO		Avg	AB	H	2B	3B	HR	RBI	BB	SO	OBP	SLG
Home	5.35	9	6	0	17	17	101.0	115	13	32	40	vs. Left	.276	384	106	25	3	12	56	45	44	.349	.451
Away	6.07	4	8	0	15	15	86.0	99	10	38	40	vs. Right	.314	344	108	11	2	11	52	25	36	.364	.453
Day	6.94	3	3	0	9	9	48.0	60	4	23	24	Inning 1-6	.288	649	187	33	3	20	91	66	77	.353	.441
Night	5.24	10	11	0	23	23	139.0	154	19	47	56	Inning 7+	.342	79	27	3	2	3	17	4	3	.381	.544
Grass	6.00	3	5	0	9	9	51.0	59	5	22	20	None on	.274	423	116	20	2	12	12	37	46	.335	.416
Turf	5.56	10	9	0	23	23	136.0	155	18	48	60	Runners on	.321	305	98	16	3	11	96	33	34	.383	.502
April	5.17	2	2	0	5	5	31.1	35	6	9	20	Scoring Posn	.315	178	56	8	3	7	85	24	24	.382	.511
May	4.41	4	1	0	5	5	32.2	38	1	10	7	Close & Late	.378	45	17	1	2	1	11	3	3	.417	.556
June	5.12	3	2	0	6	6	38.2	36	5	13	13	None on/out	.268	190	51	6	1	7	7	14	16	.319	.421
July	5.22	2	3	0	5	5	29.1	38	4	10	18	vs. 1st Batr (relief)	.000	0	0	0	0	0	0	0	0	.000	.000
August	7.92	1	4	0	6	6	30.2	36	6	12	14	First Inning Pitched	.310	129	40	9	1	4	25	17	18	.384	.488
September/October	6.66	1	2	0	5	5	24.1	31	1	16	8	First 75 Pitches	.294	568	167	27	3	19	83	56	70	.358	.452
Starter	5.68	13	14	0	32	32	187.0	214	23	70	80	Pitch 76-90	.238	80	19	6	0	2	9	8	5	.300	.388
Reliever	0.00	0	0	0	0	0	0.0	0	0	0	0	Pitch 91-105	.302	53	16	0	2	1	6	4	4	.351	.434
0-3 Days Rest	0.00	0	0	0	0	0	0.0	0	0	0	0	Pitch 106+	.444	27	12	3	0	1	10	2	1	.483	.667
4 Days Rest	6.52	8	10	0	19	19	106.1	127	15	38	45	First Pitch	.298	104	31	6	0	5	15	5	0	.336	.500
5+ Days Rest	4.57	5	4	0	13	13	80.2	87	8	32	35	Ahead in Count	.255	290	74	12	4	4	34	0	65	.259	.366
Pre-All Star	4.83	10	6	0	18	18	113.2	124	12	34	44	Behind in Count	.335	206	69	9	0	9	41	37	0	.433	.510
Post-All Star	7.00	3	8	0	14	14	73.1	90	11	36	36	Two Strikes	.227	264	60	8	4	1	25	28	80	.303	.299

Last Five Years

	ERA	W	L	Sv	G	GS	IP	H	HR	BB	SO		Avg	AB	H	2B	3B	HR	RBI	BB	SO	OBP	SLG
Home	3.85	31	18	1	75	64	390.1	403	33	117	189	vs. Left	.276	1647	454	84	11	41	194	160	166	.342	.415
Away	4.71	21	19	2	77	62	372.1	391	42	132	174	vs. Right	.262	1297	340	58	4	34	150	89	197	.314	.392
Day	4.46	15	8	2	45	35	216.0	224	17	76	103	Inning 1-6	.264	2553	674	121	12	65	296	223	333	.326	.397
Night	4.20	37	29	1	107	91	546.2	570	58	173	260	Inning 7+	.307	391	120	21	3	10	48	26	30	.356	.453
Grass	4.80	11	12	1	41	35	200.2	214	23	74	88	None on	.256	1753	449	83	7	39	39	136	203	.315	.378
Turf	4.08	41	25	2	111	91	562.0	580	52	175	275	Runners on	.290	1191	345	59	8	36	305	113	160	.351	.443
April	4.14	6	8	0	21	20	119.2	123	14	41	64	Scoring Posn	.289	705	204	36	7	21	266	81	105	.360	.450
May	3.47	11	4	0	23	21	132.1	129	6	43	58	Close & Late	.316	187	59	10	2	3	25	12	14	.363	.439
June	4.68	10	4	1	24	20	117.1	121	17	42	59	None on/out	.252	771	194	28	3	20	20	50	82	.299	.374
July	4.42	7	9	0	27	22	130.1	145	13	41	64	vs. 1st Batr (relief)	.500	24	12	0	0	1	3	1	3	.538	.625
August	4.44	9	6	2	25	17	119.2	119	13	35	44	First Inning Pitched	.304	592	180	28	4	15	86	61	64	.370	.441
September/October	4.52	9	6	0	32	26	143.1	157	12	47	74	First 75 Pitches	.269	2347	632	108	10	58	260	192	315	.328	.398
Starter	4.41	46	37	0	126	126	722.2	747	73	240	346	Pitch 76-90	.275	320	88	22	3	8	49	28	24	.335	.438
Reliever	1.80	6	0	3	26	0	40.0	47	2	9	17	Pitch 91-105	.240	196	47	6	2	6	16	19	19	.310	.383
0-3 Days Rest	6.40	3	1	0	6	6	32.1	39	4	15	9	Pitch 106+	.333	81	27	6	0	3	19	10	5	.407	.519
4 Days Rest	5.02	23	24	0	69	69	394.1	438	43	136	179	First Pitch	.292	377	110	16	1	11	52	14	0	.319	.427
5+ Days Rest	3.38	20	12	0	51	51	296.0	270	26	89	158	Ahead in Count	.221	1162	257	44	7	17	102	0	302	.228	.315
Pre-All Star	4.05	29	19	1	78	66	406.1	423	38	131	194	Behind in Count	.329	815	268	49	4	30	128	143	0	.428	.509
Post-All Star	4.52	23	18	2	74	60	356.1	371	37	118	169	Two Strikes	.206	1118	230	43	7	17	91	92	363	.270	.302

Pitcher vs. Batter (since 1984)

Pitches Best Vs.	Avg	AB	H	2B	3B	HR	RBI	BB	SO	OBP	SLG	Pitches Worst Vs.	Avg	AB	H	2B	3B	HR	RBI	BB	SO	OBP	SLG
Tony Pena	.053	19	1	1	0	0	1	1	1	.100	.105	Lonnie Smith	.714	14	10	2	0	2	7	0	0	.714	1.286
Matt D. Williams	.063	16	1	0	0	0	1	1	5	.111	.063	Daryl Boston	.545	11	6	1	0	2	9	3	0	.643	1.182
Sammy Sosa	.063	16	1	0	0	0	0	0	2	.063	.063	Bernard Gilkey	.444	9	4	1	0	1	2	3	0	.583	.889
Casey Candaele	.083	12	1	0	0	0	0	1	0	.154	.083	Darryl Strawberry	.381	21	8	1	0	4	12	5	4	.464	1.000
Steve Sax	.105	19	2	0	0	0	0	0	2	.105	.105	Gary Sheffield	.316	19	6	0	0	5	8	0	1	.316	1.105

Chico Walker — Mets

Age 35 – Bats Both (groundball hitter)

	Avg	G	AB	R	H	2B	3B	HR	RBI	BB	SO	HBP	GDP	SB	CS	OBP	SLG	IBB	SH	SF	#Pit	#P/PA	GB	FB	G/F
1993 Season	.225	115	213	18	48	7	1	5	19	14	29	0	3	7	0	.271	.338	0	0	2	772	3.36	85	61	1.39
Last Five Years	.258	365	840	95	217	29	3	15	91	74	136	0	14	35	6	.315	.354	5	1	10	3355	3.62	329	214	1.54

1993 Season

	Avg	AB	H	2B	3B	HR	RBI	BB	SO	OBP	SLG		Avg	AB	H	2B	3B	HR	RBI	BB	SO	OBP	SLG
vs. Left	.319	72	23	6	1	2	11	3	4	.347	.514	Scoring Posn	.174	46	8	2	1	2	14	5	8	.245	.391
vs. Right	.177	141	25	1	0	3	8	11	25	.234	.248	Close & Late	.122	74	9	1	1	1	6	7	11	.198	.203
Home	.208	96	20	2	0	1	5	5	9	.245	.260	None on/out	.216	51	11	4	0	0	0	3	5	.259	.294
Away	.239	117	28	5	1	4	14	9	20	.291	.402	Batting #5	.258	62	16	3	0	1	4	2	7	.281	.355
First Pitch	.341	41	14	1	0	1	1	0	0	.341	.439	Batting #9	.196	51	10	1	0	1	4	3	12	.241	.275

1993 Season

	Avg	AB	H	2B	3B	HR	RBI	BB	SO	OBP	SLG		Avg	AB	H	2B	3B	HR	RBI	BB	SO	OBP	SLG
Ahead in Count	.263	57	15	1	0	2	5	5	0	.317	.386	Other	.220	100	22	3	1	3	11	9	10	.279	.360
Behind in Count	.171	70	12	3	1	0	4	0	23	.169	.243	Pre-All Star	.232	99	23	4	0	3	10	8	14	.287	.364
Two Strikes	.137	73	10	3	1	0	3	9	29	.232	.205	Post-All Star	.219	114	25	3	1	2	9	6	15	.256	.316

Last Five Years

	Avg	AB	H	2B	3B	HR	RBI	BB	SO	OBP	SLG		Avg	AB	H	2B	3B	HR	RBI	BB	SO	OBP	SLG
vs. Left	.274	281	77	12	2	5	36	15	34	.306	.384	Scoring Posn	.260	200	52	7	2	6	78	38	40	.363	.405
vs. Right	.250	559	140	17	1	10	55	59	102	.319	.338	Close & Late	.239	243	58	8	1	2	30	30	43	.320	.305
Groundball	.272	290	79	9	1	5	35	16	37	.304	.362	None on/out	.217	244	53	9	0	2	2	17	36	.268	.279
Flyball	.246	191	47	7	0	3	17	26	38	.332	.330	Batting #1	.248	298	74	7	1	5	24	24	44	.302	.329
Home	.268	400	107	12	1	5	42	36	62	.324	.340	Batting #9	.233	120	28	3	0	2	17	15	25	.316	.308
Away	.250	440	110	17	2	10	49	38	74	.307	.366	Other	.273	422	115	19	2	8	50	35	67	.324	.384
Day	.261	356	93	11	2	7	35	32	54	.318	.362	April	.163	49	8	1	0	0	3	4	5	.222	.184
Night	.256	484	124	18	1	8	56	42	82	.313	.347	May	.268	112	30	2	0	2	11	9	22	.317	.339
Grass	.273	600	164	18	3	12	75	51	94	.326	.373	June	.244	119	29	6	0	3	15	11	20	.308	.370
Turf	.221	240	53	11	0	3	16	23	42	.287	.304	July	.333	147	49	6	1	3	18	15	21	.388	.449
First Pitch	.380	142	54	8	0	6	24	3	0	.393	.563	August	.254	193	49	5	2	2	19	15	23	.306	.332
Ahead in Count	.303	178	54	7	0	6	26	26	0	.388	.444	September/October	.236	220	52	9	0	5	25	20	45	.296	.345
Behind in Count	.181	342	62	9	2	0	17	0	114	.179	.219	Pre-All Star	.256	332	85	12	0	8	38	30	58	.315	.364
Two Strikes	.169	360	61	8	2	1	20	45	136	.259	.211	Post-All Star	.260	508	132	17	3	7	53	44	78	.315	.346

Batter vs. Pitcher (since 1984)

Hits Best Against	Avg	AB	H	2B	3B	HR	RBI	BB	SO	OBP	SLG	Hits Worst Against	Avg	AB	H	2B	3B	HR	RBI	BB	SO	OBP	SLG
Dennis Martinez	.471	17	8	0	0	1	2	0	2	.471	.647	Andy Benes	.000	13	0	0	0	0	0	0	4	.000	.000
Pete Harnisch	.417	12	5	0	0	0	0	3	1	.533	.417	Bob Tewksbury	.000	11	0	0	0	0	0	0	1	.000	.000
Ken Hill	.333	12	4	0	0	0	0	1	2	.385	.333	Dwight Gooden	.063	16	1	0	0	0	0	1	1	.118	.063
Greg Maddux	.313	16	5	1	0	0	0	2	3	.389	.375	Brian Barnes	.067	15	1	0	0	0	0	1	3	.125	.067
Mark Gardner	.313	16	5	1	0	2	4	0	5	.294	.750	Tom Browning	.077	13	1	0	0	0	0	0	1	.077	.077

Larry Walker — Expos

Age 27 – Bats Left

	Avg	G	AB	R	H	2B	3B	HR	RBI	BB	SO	HBP	GDP	SB	CS	OBP	SLG	IBB	SH	SF	#Pit	#P/PA	GB	FB	G/F
1993 Season	.265	138	490	85	130	24	5	22	86	80	76	6	8	29	7	.371	.469	20	0	6	1997	3.43	192	149	1.29
Career (1989-1993)	.273	571	1971	292	539	103	14	80	298	217	400	23	32	83	30	.349	.462	37	7	20	7652	3.42	759	511	1.49

1993 Season

	Avg	AB	H	2B	3B	HR	RBI	BB	SO	OBP	SLG		Avg	AB	H	2B	3B	HR	RBI	BB	SO	OBP	SLG
vs. Left	.238	185	44	5	2	7	27	24	28	.336	.400	Scoring Posn	.254	142	36	7	4	2	58	42	27	.420	.401
vs. Right	.282	305	86	19	3	15	59	56	48	.391	.511	Close & Late	.235	81	19	2	2	2	7	15	11	.361	.383
Groundball	.261	153	40	11	0	3	18	16	23	.341	.392	None on/out	.240	129	31	6	0	8	8	14	22	.315	.473
Flyball	.235	68	16	2	2	3	15	19	13	.404	.456	Batting #1	.000	1	0	0	0	0	0	0	1	.000	.000
Home	.307	241	74	18	2	13	56	41	36	.410	.560	Batting #4	.266	488	130	24	5	22	86	80	75	.372	.471
Away	.225	249	56	6	3	9	30	39	40	.333	.382	Other	.000	1	0	0	0	0	0	0	0	.000	.000
Day	.255	145	37	3	1	9	22	18	27	.349	.476	April	.364	55	20	4	1	5	13	10	10	.463	.745
Night	.270	345	93	21	4	13	64	62	49	.380	.467	May	.238	84	20	4	0	2	11	11	13	.340	.357
Grass	.213	141	30	1	3	4	17	23	23	.321	.348	June	.262	65	17	5	0	3	13	8	12	.355	.477
Turf	.287	349	100	23	2	18	69	57	53	.391	.519	July	.261	92	24	3	1	3	8	17	14	.376	.413
First Pitch	.344	122	42	7	1	5	31	12	0	.404	.541	August	.252	103	26	6	1	3	24	17	14	.347	.417
Ahead in Count	.309	81	25	6	0	8	16	41	0	.540	.679	September/October	.253	91	23	2	2	6	17	17	13	.376	.516
Behind in Count	.200	200	40	4	4	7	22	0	66	.209	.365	Pre-All Star	.266	241	64	13	1	12	41	37	40	.372	.477
Two Strikes	.191	199	38	6	3	6	24	27	76	.292	.342	Post-All Star	.265	249	66	11	4	10	45	43	36	.370	.462

1993 By Position

Position	Avg	AB	H	2B	3B	HR	RBI	BB	SO	OBP	SLG	G	GS	Innings	PO	A	E	DP	Fld Pct	Rng Fctr	In Zone	Outs	Zone Rtg	MLB Zone
As rf	.260	473	123	22	4	21	81	77	71	.367	.457	132	132	1145.0	273	13	6	2	.979	2.25	299	259	.866	.826

Career (1989-1993)

	Avg	AB	H	2B	3B	HR	RBI	BB	SO	OBP	SLG		Avg	AB	H	2B	3B	HR	RBI	BB	SO	OBP	SLG
vs. Left	.267	674	180	28	4	27	112	55	136	.332	.441	Scoring Posn	.261	540	141	28	5	14	203	104	116	.375	.409
vs. Right	.277	1297	359	75	10	53	186	162	264	.358	.473	Close & Late	.260	365	95	15	4	12	42	51	76	.355	.422
Groundball	.272	665	181	38	2	19	88	61	119	.340	.421	None on/out	.288	504	145	28	4	27	27	39	103	.341	.520
Flyball	.251	399	100	17	5	20	66	51	104	.341	.469	Batting #4	.284	1015	288	55	9	45	179	121	173	.363	.489
Home	.278	918	255	52	7	40	154	104	188	.357	.480	Batting #5	.272	486	132	28	1	12	52	41	108	.333	.407
Away	.270	1053	284	51	7	40	144	113	212	.342	.445	Other	.253	470	119	20	4	23	67	55	119	.335	.460
Day	.238	568	135	21	6	25	86	63	135	.321	.428	April	.262	252	66	17	2	11	36	30	60	.346	.476
Night	.288	1403	404	82	8	55	212	154	265	.361	.475	May	.260	315	82	14	2	12	40	37	63	.340	.432
Grass	.277	570	158	20	6	27	90	69	118	.355	.475	June	.268	276	74	16	0	15	49	34	61	.351	.489
Turf	.272	1401	381	83	8	53	208	148	282	.347	.456	July	.250	308	77	8	3	13	41	26	72	.310	.422
First Pitch	.353	417	147	26	1	23	97	24	0	.397	.585	August	.307	397	122	27	2	14	66	41	63	.374	.491
Ahead in Count	.392	362	142	24	3	27	73	90	0	.509	.699	September/October	.279	423	118	21	5	15	66	49	81	.361	.459
Behind in Count	.182	878	160	30	8	22	86	0	352	.189	.310	Pre-All Star	.258	970	250	50	5	44	141	114	214	.339	.456
Two Strikes	.178	837	149	30	6	19	73	99	400	.268	.296	Post-All Star	.289	1001	289	53	9	36	157	103	186	.359	.468

Batter vs. Pitcher (career)

Hits Best Against	Avg	AB	H	2B	3B	HR	RBI	BB	SO	OBP	SLG	Hits Worst Against	Avg	AB	H	2B	3B	HR	RBI	BB	SO	OBP	SLG
Kent Mercker	.556	9	5	2	0	0	3	2	1	.636	.778	Wally Whitehurst	.000	12	0	0	0	0	0	0	5	.000	.000
Charlie Leibrandt	.500	14	7	2	1	1	4	1	1	.500	1.000	Mark Portugal	.000	11	0	0	0	0	0	2	4	.154	.000
Greg W. Harris	.478	23	11	1	0	3	7	5	3	.571	.913	Bryn Smith	.067	15	1	0	0	0	1	0	1	.067	.067
Denny Neagle	.400	10	4	0	0	2	6	2	2	.500	1.000	Frank Viola	.083	12	1	1	0	0	0	0	5	.083	.167

Batter vs. Pitcher (career)

Hits Best Against	Avg	AB	H	2B	3B	HR	RBI	BB	SO	OBP	SLG	Hits Worst Against	Avg	AB	H	2B	3B	HR	RBI	BB	SO	OBP	SLG
Rick Sutcliffe	.375	8	3	1	0	1	1	5	0	.615	.875	Zane Smith	.118	17	2	0	0	0	2	0	1	.118	.118

Tim Wallach — Dodgers

Age 36 – Bats Right (flyball hitter)

	Avg	G	AB	R	H	2B	3B	HR	RBI	BB	SO	HBP	GDP	SB	CS	OBP	SLG	IBB	SH	SF	#Pit	#P/PA	GB	FB	G/F
1993 Season	.222	133	477	42	106	19	1	12	62	32	70	3	9	0	2	.271	.342	2	1	9	1867	3.58	164	168	0.98
Last Five Years	.251	749	2790	300	700	149	8	68	369	232	421	21	64	13	24	.310	.383	33	1	34	10934	3.55	945	949	1.00

1993 Season

	Avg	AB	H	2B	3B	HR	RBI	BB	SO	OBP	SLG		Avg	AB	H	2B	3B	HR	RBI	BB	SO	OBP	SLG
vs. Left	.194	139	27	5	0	5	21	6	23	.223	.338	Scoring Posn	.240	129	31	8	0	1	50	11	18	.287	.326
vs. Right	.234	338	79	14	1	7	41	26	47	.290	.343	Close & Late	.174	86	15	3	0	2	9	12	13	.283	.279
Groundball	.263	133	35	6	1	6	22	8	18	.301	.459	None on/out	.206	131	27	6	1	5	5	7	14	.252	.382
Flyball	.234	64	15	3	0	0	9	5	10	.282	.281	Batting #4	.223	175	39	8	0	6	33	11	25	.266	.371
Home	.253	217	55	8	0	4	28	12	30	.297	.346	Batting #7	.255	102	26	2	0	1	14	8	12	.313	.304
Away	.196	260	51	11	1	8	34	20	40	.249	.338	Other	.205	200	41	9	1	5	15	13	33	.253	.335
Day	.197	117	23	4	0	6	12	10	23	.266	.385	April	.190	84	16	4	1	2	6	6	10	.239	.333
Night	.231	360	83	15	1	6	50	22	47	.272	.328	May	.273	99	27	4	0	4	22	8	18	.318	.434
Grass	.230	361	83	13	1	9	48	25	55	.280	.346	June	.154	78	12	4	0	2	11	3	8	.188	.282
Turf	.198	116	23	6	0	3	14	7	15	.242	.328	July	.250	52	13	3	0	2	8	5	8	.328	.423
First Pitch	.200	80	16	4	0	1	4	1	0	.217	.288	August	.288	73	21	4	0	2	11	5	7	.329	.425
Ahead in Count	.204	98	20	3	0	4	23	20	0	.331	.357	September/October	.187	91	17	0	0	0	4	5	19	.237	.187
Behind in Count	.190	216	41	7	0	6	21	0	64	.186	.306	Pre-All Star	.214	304	65	15	1	10	46	22	42	.263	.368
Two Strikes	.177	209	37	5	0	7	27	11	70	.219	.301	Post-All Star	.237	173	41	4	0	2	16	10	28	.285	.295

1993 By Position

Position	Avg	AB	H	2B	3B	HR	RBI	BB	SO	OBP	SLG	G	GS	Innings	PO	A	E	DP	Fld Pct	Rng Fctr	In Zone	Outs	Zone Rtg	MLB Zone
As 3b	.222	468	104	19	1	11	61	32	69	.271	.338	130	121	1084.2	112	227	15	14	.958	2.81	294	244	.830	.834

Last Five Years

	Avg	AB	H	2B	3B	HR	RBI	BB	SO	OBP	SLG		Avg	AB	H	2B	3B	HR	RBI	BB	SO	OBP	SLG
vs. Left	.254	886	225	46	3	31	125	80	115	.317	.418	Scoring Posn	.259	749	194	40	4	17	287	109	128	.348	.391
vs. Right	.249	1904	475	103	5	37	244	152	306	.306	.367	Close & Late	.241	528	127	28	1	11	61	67	76	.331	.360
Groundball	.278	1009	280	55	3	30	153	78	149	.329	.427	None on/out	.254	755	192	54	1	17	17	41	94	.294	.396
Flyball	.238	602	143	34	0	16	76	65	92	.315	.374	Batting #4	.252	1185	299	53	3	28	164	86	184	.305	.373
Home	.268	1296	347	80	5	29	180	117	198	.332	.404	Batting #5	.247	949	234	60	5	28	124	80	132	.306	.409
Away	.236	1494	353	69	3	39	189	115	223	.290	.365	Other	.255	656	167	36	0	12	81	66	105	.325	.364
Day	.261	777	203	42	3	25	106	67	136	.321	.420	April	.250	400	100	26	1	8	36	32	63	.306	.380
Night	.247	2013	497	107	5	43	263	165	285	.305	.369	May	.257	486	125	30	1	18	79	40	78	.316	.434
Grass	.243	996	242	42	2	27	133	73	150	.295	.370	June	.255	498	127	30	1	8	71	48	68	.324	.367
Turf	.255	1794	458	107	6	41	236	159	271	.318	.390	July	.256	430	110	24	2	15	66	46	68	.328	.426
First Pitch	.309	453	140	33	0	15	61	19	0	.342	.481	August	.265	487	129	21	2	9	51	34	68	.312	.372
Ahead in Count	.287	620	178	40	3	17	109	111	0	.389	.444	September/October	.223	489	109	18	1	10	66	32	76	.273	.325
Behind in Count	.196	1245	244	53	3	22	131	0	373	.203	.296	Pre-All Star	.251	1561	392	95	3	41	208	143	240	.316	.395
Two Strikes	.178	1214	216	40	3	25	125	93	421	.242	.278	Post-All Star	.251	1229	308	54	5	27	161	89	181	.301	.369

Batter vs. Pitcher (since 1984)

Hits Best Against	Avg	AB	H	2B	3B	HR	RBI	BB	SO	OBP	SLG	Hits Worst Against	Avg	AB	H	2B	3B	HR	RBI	BB	SO	OBP	SLG
Mark Grant	.500	20	10	2	0	2	7	1	4	.500	.900	Mike Perez	.000	12	0	0	0	0	1	2	2	.133	.000
Bruce Ruffin	.429	28	12	3	1	2	8	1	2	.448	.821	Mark Davis	.000	11	0	0	0	0	0	1	5	.083	.000
Jeff Parrett	.400	10	4	3	0	0	2	1	1	.455	.700	Jay Howell	.000	9	0	0	0	0	1	1	1	.091	.000
Bob Welch	.391	23	9	2	0	2	3	2	4	.440	.739	Andy Benes	.074	27	2	0	0	0	1	4	8	.188	.074
Tom Glavine	.352	54	19	4	1	5	11	5	2	.407	.741	Tim Leary	.118	17	2	0	0	0	0	0	8	.118	.118

Dan Walters — Padres

Age 27 – Bats Right (groundball hitter)

	Avg	G	AB	R	H	2B	3B	HR	RBI	BB	SO	HBP	GDP	SB	CS	OBP	SLG	IBB	SH	SF	#Pit	#P/PA	GB	FB	G/F
1993 Season	.202	27	94	6	19	3	0	1	10	7	13	0	2	0	0	.255	.266	2	0	1	333	3.26	41	23	1.78
Career (1992-1993)	.234	84	273	20	64	14	1	5	32	17	41	2	5	1	0	.281	.348	2	1	3	977	3.30	115	71	1.62

1993 Season

	Avg	AB	H	2B	3B	HR	RBI	BB	SO	OBP	SLG		Avg	AB	H	2B	3B	HR	RBI	BB	SO	OBP	SLG
vs. Left	.324	37	12	3	0	0	5	4	2	.390	.405	Scoring Posn	.263	19	5	1	0	0	8	3	3	.348	.316
vs. Right	.123	57	7	0	0	1	5	3	11	.164	.175	Close & Late	.120	25	3	0	0	0	1	2	6	.179	.120

Bruce Walton — Expos

Age 31 – Pitches Right

	ERA	W	L	Sv	G	GS	IP	BB	SO	Avg	H	2B	3B	HR	RBI	OBP	SLG	GF	IR	IRS	Hld	SvOp	SB	CS	GB	FB	G/F
1993 Season	9.53	0	0	0	4	0	5.2	3	0	.407	11	1	0	1	5	.467	.556	3	2	0	0	0	0	0	16	6	2.67
Career (1991-1993)	8.16	1	0	0	23	0	28.2	12	17	.325	39	7	0	5	24	.385	.508	10	16	3	3	1	2	0	46	34	1.35

1993 Season

	ERA	W	L	Sv	G	GS	IP	H	HR	BB	SO		Avg	AB	H	2B	3B	HR	RBI	BB	SO	OBP	SLG
Home	6.00	0	0	0	2	0	3.0	4	1	1	0	vs. Left	.308	13	4	0	0	1	2	0	0	.308	.538
Away	13.50	0	0	0	2	0	2.2	7	0	2	0	vs. Right	.500	14	7	1	0	0	3	3	0	.588	.571

Jerome Walton — Angels

Age 28 – Bats Right (groundball hitter)

	Avg	G	AB	R	H	2B	3B	HR	RBI	BB	SO	HBP	GDP	SB	CS	OBP	SLG	IBB	SH	SF	#Pit	#P/PA	GB	FB	G/F
1993 Season	.000	5	2	2	0	0	0	0	0	1	2	0	0	1	0	.333	.000	0	0	0	17	5.67	0	0	0.00
Career (1989-1993)	.258	375	1194	178	308	52	7	12	85	106	217	15	18	47	19	.324	.343	2	9	10	4747	3.56	471	247	1.91

1993 Season

	Avg	AB	H	2B	3B	HR	RBI	BB	SO	OBP	SLG
vs. Left	.000	1	0	0	0	0	0	1	1	.500	.000
vs. Right	.000	1	0	0	0	0	0	0	1	.000	.000
Scoring Posn	.000	0	0	0	0	0	0	0	0	.000	.000
Close & Late	.000	0	0	0	0	0	0	0	0	.000	.000

Career (1989-1993)

	Avg	AB	H	2B	3B	HR	RBI	BB	SO	OBP	SLG
vs. Left	.256	450	115	18	4	3	38	47	78	.330	.333
vs. Right	.259	744	193	34	3	9	47	59	139	.320	.349
Groundball	.228	451	103	18	1	2	31	31	88	.282	.286
Flyball	.229	262	60	7	2	5	15	36	44	.330	.328
Home	.277	571	158	21	5	8	39	50	88	.336	.373
Away	.241	623	150	31	2	4	46	56	129	.313	.316
Day	.280	604	169	25	5	5	50	55	98	.343	.363
Night	.236	590	139	27	2	7	35	51	119	.304	.324
Grass	.272	793	216	33	5	9	48	73	132	.340	.361
Turf	.229	401	92	19	2	3	37	33	85	.292	.309
First Pitch	.298	178	53	9	0	3	9	1	0	.324	.399
Ahead in Count	.329	277	91	14	2	4	27	68	0	.457	.437
Behind in Count	.213	539	115	21	3	4	34	0	193	.218	.286
Two Strikes	.179	530	95	18	4	2	26	36	217	.235	.240
Scoring Posn	.256	227	58	9	3	0	72	25	51	.325	.322
Close & Late	.210	186	39	5	2	1	18	18	41	.286	.274
None on/out	.284	510	145	28	2	11	11	42	83	.345	.412
Batting #1	.262	1077	282	45	6	10	75	92	194	.326	.343
Batting #7	.182	33	6	1	1	0	1	2	5	.229	.273
Other	.238	84	20	6	0	2	9	12	18	.337	.381
April	.254	209	53	11	1	3	13	17	39	.322	.359
May	.247	178	44	9	2	0	8	17	31	.313	.320
June	.260	223	58	11	0	2	14	26	43	.345	.336
July	.287	143	41	10	0	2	16	5	26	.316	.399
August	.277	235	65	5	2	3	22	23	36	.346	.353
September/October	.228	206	47	6	2	2	12	18	42	.290	.306
Pre-All Star	.259	664	172	37	3	6	43	61	124	.327	.351
Post-All Star	.257	530	136	15	4	6	42	45	93	.319	.334

Batter vs. Pitcher (career)

Hits Best Against	Avg	AB	H	2B	3B	HR	RBI	BB	SO	OBP	SLG
Bruce Hurst	.500	12	6	0	0	0	2	2	1	.571	.500
Dennis Rasmussen	.474	19	9	2	0	0	0	1	2	.500	.579
John Smiley	.400	20	8	0	0	2	4	0	5	.400	.700
Dennis Martinez	.364	11	4	2	0	1	1	0	1	.364	.818
Bill Landrum	.364	11	4	0	0	2	3	1	3	.417	.909

Hits Worst Against	Avg	AB	H	2B	3B	HR	RBI	BB	SO	OBP	SLG
Bud Black	.091	11	1	0	0	0	0	2	1	.231	.091
Zane Smith	.091	11	1	0	0	0	0	0	3	.091	.091
Jose Rijo	.167	18	3	1	0	0	0	1	2	.211	.222
Dwight Gooden	.188	16	3	0	0	0	1	2	4	.278	.188
Mike Morgan	.231	13	3	0	0	0	0	0	0	.231	.231

Duane Ward — Blue Jays

Age 30 – Pitches Right (groundball pitcher)

	ERA	W	L	Sv	G	GS	IP	BB	SO	Avg	H	2B	3B	HR	RBI	OBP	SLG	GF	IR	IRS	Hld	SvOp	SB	CS	GB	FB	G/F
1993 Season	2.13	2	3	45	71	0	71.2	25	97	.193	49	6	0	4	24	.266	.264	70	26	9	0	51	3	0	70	50	1.40
Last Five Years	2.91	22	31	106	370	0	522.2	197	566	.214	400	53	8	25	204	.289	.291	190	188	62	58	139	48	16	671	371	1.81

1993 Season

	ERA	W	L	Sv	G	GS	IP	H	HR	BB	SO
Home	2.73	1	2	21	33	0	33.0	25	2	14	45
Away	1.63	1	1	24	38	0	38.2	24	2	11	52
Day	1.16	0	1	15	23	0	23.1	13	0	5	34
Night	2.61	2	2	30	48	0	48.1	36	4	20	63
Grass	1.38	1	1	21	32	0	32.2	20	1	11	42
Turf	2.77	1	2	24	39	0	39.0	29	3	14	55
April	2.00	0	0	8	10	0	9.0	5	1	1	12
May	2.57	1	2	7	13	0	14.0	11	0	8	19
June	1.46	0	0	7	12	0	12.1	6	0	2	13
July	1.74	1	0	6	10	0	10.1	5	1	4	21
August	1.59	0	0	10	12	0	11.1	12	1	3	14
September/October	3.07	0	1	7	14	0	14.2	10	1	7	18
Starter	0.00	0	0	0	0	0	0.0	0	0	0	0
Reliever	2.13	2	3	45	71	0	71.2	49	4	25	97
0 Days rest	1.48	0	0	23	24	0	24.1	14	2	7	31
1 or 2 Days rest	2.67	1	2	18	31	0	30.1	25	2	13	40
3+ Days rest	2.12	1	1	4	16	0	17.0	10	0	5	26
Pre-All Star	2.17	1	2	22	37	0	37.1	24	1	11	50
Post-All Star	2.10	1	1	23	34	0	34.1	25	3	14	47

	Avg	AB	H	2B	3B	HR	RBI	BB	SO	OBP	SLG
vs. Left	.211	123	26	3	0	2	11	18	47	.310	.285
vs. Right	.176	131	23	3	0	2	13	7	50	.221	.244
Inning 1-6	.000	0	0	0	0	0	0	0	0	.000	.000
Inning 7+	.193	254	49	6	0	4	24	25	97	.266	.264
None on	.166	145	24	3	0	3	3	13	57	.239	.248
Runners on	.229	109	25	3	0	1	21	12	40	.301	.284
Scoring Posn	.243	70	17	1	0	1	21	8	28	.313	.300
Close & Late	.156	154	24	2	0	2	19	17	64	.237	.208
None on/out	.175	63	11	3	0	1	1	3	23	.212	.270
vs. 1st Batr (relief)	.227	66	15	4	0	2	9	5	23	.282	.379
First Inning Pitched	.188	240	45	6	0	4	20	22	90	.257	.263
First 15 Pitches	.207	203	42	6	0	4	18	17	68	.269	.296
Pitch 16-30	.143	49	7	0	0	0	6	8	28	.263	.143
Pitch 31-45	.000	2	0	0	0	0	0	0	1	.000	.000
Pitch 46+	.000	0	0	0	0	0	0	0	0	.000	.000
First Pitch	.227	22	5	1	0	0	2	1	0	.261	.273
Ahead in Count	.136	154	21	4	0	3	13	0	92	.135	.221
Behind in Count	.340	50	17	1	0	1	5	15	0	.492	.420
Two Strikes	.092	152	14	2	0	0	3	9	97	.143	.105

Last Five Years

	ERA	W	L	Sv	G	GS	IP	H	HR	BB	SO
Home	2.89	14	17	54	188	0	267.2	202	12	91	292
Away	2.93	8	14	52	182	0	255.0	198	13	106	274
Day	2.86	10	10	38	122	0	169.2	120	8	63	198
Night	2.93	12	21	68	248	0	353.0	280	17	134	368
Grass	3.08	6	12	40	141	0	196.0	154	10	85	204
Turf	2.81	16	19	66	229	0	326.2	246	15	112	362
April	2.94	2	5	21	52	0	64.1	52	3	24	76
May	2.72	3	9	19	64	0	89.1	72	1	50	90
June	3.32	5	5	15	62	0	100.1	72	3	40	100
July	2.33	5	4	17	56	0	89.0	70	8	23	111
August	3.06	5	4	17	63	0	85.1	78	3	21	86
September/October	3.05	2	4	17	73	0	94.1	56	7	39	103
Starter	0.00	0	0	0	0	0	0.0	0	0	0	0
Reliever	2.91	22	31	106	370	0	522.2	400	25	197	566
0 Days rest	2.63	6	6	37	80	0	99.1	68	6	30	113
1 or 2 Days rest	2.95	14	18	57	225	0	335.2	264	15	136	343

	Avg	AB	H	2B	3B	HR	RBI	BB	SO	OBP	SLG
vs. Left	.225	854	192	30	4	17	98	132	279	.328	.329
vs. Right	.204	1018	208	23	4	8	106	65	287	.253	.258
Inning 1-6	.233	60	14	2	0	2	18	13	18	.365	.367
Inning 7+	.213	1812	386	51	8	23	186	184	548	.286	.288
None on	.201	1051	211	33	3	11	11	86	351	.263	.269
Runners on	.230	821	189	20	5	14	193	111	215	.319	.318
Scoring Posn	.245	514	126	9	4	12	185	74	141	.334	.348
Close & Late	.214	1015	217	31	4	15	127	119	306	.296	.297
None on/out	.193	440	85	15	1	3	3	40	149	.260	.252
vs. 1st Batr (relief)	.206	339	70	10	0	5	34	25	113	.261	.280
First Inning Pitched	.209	1251	261	33	5	20	158	129	373	.282	.291
First 15 Pitches	.213	1099	234	29	4	17	111	96	309	.276	.293
Pitch 16-30	.212	547	116	16	2	5	69	75	190	.306	.276
Pitch 31-45	.237	186	44	8	2	2	21	21	57	.314	.333
Pitch 46+	.150	40	6	0	0	1	3	5	10	.261	.225
First Pitch	.327	208	68	11	2	4	36	22	0	.388	.457

Last Five Years

	ERA	W	L	Sv	G	GS	IP	H	HR	BB	SO
3+ Days rest	3.08	2	7	12	65	0	87.2	68	4	31	110
Pre-All Star	2.78	13	19	59	198	0	285.0	212	9	120	307
Post-All Star	3.07	9	12	47	172	0	237.2	188	16	77	259

	Avg	AB	H	2B	3B	HR	RBI	BB	SO	OBP	SLG
Ahead in Count	.145	1055	153	16	4	15	84	0	518	.146	.210
Behind in Count	.332	298	99	13	1	4	40	91	0	.486	.423
Two Strikes	.140	1065	149	17	4	10	74	83	566	.202	.192

Pitcher vs. Batter (career)

Pitches Best Vs.	Avg	AB	H	2B	3B	HR	RBI	BB	SO	OBP	SLG
Jose Canseco	.000	17	0	0	0	0	2	0	10	.000	.000
Tony Pena	.000	11	0	0	0	0	1	2	1	.154	.000
Steve Buechele	.000	10	0	0	0	0	0	2	6	.167	.000
Dean Palmer	.000	9	0	0	0	0	0	3	5	.250	.000
Carlos Quintana	.091	11	1	0	0	0	1	0	8	.091	.091

Pitches Worst Vs.	Avg	AB	H	2B	3B	HR	RBI	BB	SO	OBP	SLG
Mike Greenwell	.500	16	8	2	0	0	0	2	1	.556	.625
Rickey Henderson	.458	24	11	1	1	0	3	3	3	.519	.583
Alan Trammell	.455	11	5	2	0	0	0	3	1	.571	.636
Ken Griffey Jr	.385	13	5	1	0	1	1	2	2	.467	.692
Tom Brunansky	.333	12	4	0	0	1	5	2	1	.429	.583

Turner Ward — Blue Jays

Age 29 – Bats Both

	Avg	G	AB	R	H	2B	3B	HR	RBI	BB	SO	HBP	GDP	SB	CS	OBP	SLG	IBB	SH	SF	#Pit	#P/PA	GB	FB	G/F
1993 Season	.192	72	167	20	32	4	2	4	28	23	26	1	7	3	3	.287	.311	2	3	4	764	3.86	68	51	1.33
Career (1990-1993)	.239	152	355	49	85	16	3	6	48	41	56	1	11	6	4	.317	.352	2	7	4	1552	3.80	131	102	1.28

1993 Season

	Avg	AB	H	2B	3B	HR	RBI	BB	SO	OBP	SLG
vs. Left	.367	30	11	2	1	1	6	3	5	.424	.600
vs. Right	.153	137	21	2	1	3	22	20	21	.259	.248
Home	.132	76	10	1	2	2	10	7	13	.212	.276
Away	.242	91	22	3	0	2	18	16	13	.345	.341
First Pitch	.269	26	7	1	0	1	8	1	0	.286	.423
Ahead in Count	.132	38	5	0	0	1	4	12	0	.327	.211
Behind in Count	.138	65	9	0	0	1	6	0	21	.149	.185
Two Strikes	.190	84	16	2	1	2	13	10	26	.277	.310

	Avg	AB	H	2B	3B	HR	RBI	BB	SO	OBP	SLG
Scoring Posn	.234	47	11	2	1	1	22	9	9	.333	.383
Close & Late	.152	33	5	0	0	1	3	5	7	.275	.242
None on/out	.243	37	9	0	1	1	1	4	3	.317	.378
Batting #7	.256	39	10	1	1	2	13	5	5	.326	.487
Batting #9	.204	54	11	1	1	1	8	9	8	.313	.315
Other	.149	74	11	2	0	1	7	9	13	.247	.216
Pre-All Star	.194	108	21	2	2	4	17	14	20	.290	.361
Post-All Star	.186	59	11	2	0	0	11	9	6	.282	.220

Allen Watson — Cardinals

Age 23 – Pitches Left

	ERA	W	L	Sv	G	GS	IP	BB	SO	Avg	H	2B	3B	HR	RBI	OBP	SLG	CG	ShO	Sup	QS	#P/S	SB	CS	GB	FB	G/F
1993 Season	4.60	6	7	0	16	15	86.0	28	49	.271	90	18	3	11	42	.330	.443	0	0	5.65	8	83	11	4	114	101	1.13

1993 Season

	ERA	W	L	Sv	G	GS	IP	H	HR	BB	SO
Home	3.13	3	2	0	8	8	46.0	42	4	17	25
Away	6.30	3	5	0	8	7	40.0	48	7	11	24
Starter	4.77	6	6	0	15	15	83.0	87	11	27	48
Reliever	0.00	0	1	0	1	0	3.0	3	0	1	1
0-3 Days Rest	0.00	0	0	0	0	0	0.0	0	0	0	0
4 Days Rest	5.16	4	5	0	11	11	61.0	67	10	18	38
5+ Days Rest	3.68	2	1	0	4	4	22.0	20	1	9	10
Pre-All Star	1.50	1	0	0	1	1	6.0	4	0	3	2
Post-All Star	4.84	5	7	0	15	14	80.0	86	11	25	47

	Avg	AB	H	2B	3B	HR	RBI	BB	SO	OBP	SLG
vs. Left	.240	50	12	1	0	1	5	8	7	.345	.320
vs. Right	.277	282	78	17	3	10	37	20	42	.327	.465
Scoring Posn	.268	82	22	5	0	3	29	9	15	.340	.439
Close & Late	.273	22	6	1	0	0	2	1	2	.280	.318
None on/out	.284	81	23	4	1	1	1	11	12	.370	.395
First Pitch	.367	60	22	5	1	2	8	2	0	.375	.583
Ahead in Count	.188	128	24	5	1	2	10	0	41	.192	.289
Behind in Count	.247	77	19	3	1	6	17	17	0	.385	.545
Two Strikes	.208	125	26	7	1	0	8	9	49	.267	.280

Gary Wayne — Rockies

Age 31 – Pitches Left (flyball pitcher)

	ERA	W	L	Sv	G	GS	IP	BB	SO	Avg	H	2B	3B	HR	RBI	OBP	SLG	GF	IR	IRS	Hld	SvOp	SB	CS	GB	FB	G/F
1993 Season	5.05	5	3	1	65	0	62.1	26	49	.276	68	14	6	8	46	.339	.480	21	58	20	3	3	3	1	78	75	1.04
Career (1989-1993)	3.87	13	11	4	212	0	232.1	98	154	.249	218	52	10	20	137	.324	.400	48	185	56	29	12	15	4	281	296	0.95

1993 Season

	ERA	W	L	Sv	G	GS	IP	H	HR	BB	SO
Home	7.15	0	1	0	32	0	34.0	48	7	14	33
Away	2.54	5	2	1	33	0	28.1	20	1	12	16
Day	6.00	0	3	0	22	0	18.0	24	4	6	13
Night	4.67	5	0	1	43	0	44.1	44	4	20	36
Grass	6.09	1	1	0	44	0	44.1	54	8	21	38
Turf	2.50	4	2	1	21	0	18.0	14	0	5	11
April	3.86	0	2	0	8	0	7.0	7	0	3	6
May	5.17	2	0	0	15	0	15.2	17	4	7	10
June	8.00	0	0	1	10	0	9.0	12	1	6	6
July	6.14	0	1	0	9	0	7.1	10	0	2	5
August	2.19	2	0	0	11	0	12.1	11	0	6	13
September/October	5.73	1	0	0	12	0	11.0	11	3	2	9
Starter	0.00	0	0	0	0	0	0.0	0	0	0	0
Reliever	5.05	5	3	1	65	0	62.1	68	8	26	49
0 Days rest	7.07	0	0	0	14	0	14.0	20	4	4	9
1 or 2 Days rest	4.59	3	2	1	33	0	33.1	34	3	13	29
3+ Days rest	4.20	2	1	0	18	0	15.0	14	1	9	11
Pre-All Star	5.45	2	2	1	37	0	34.2	39	5	18	22
Post-All Star	4.55	3	1	0	28	0	27.2	29	3	8	27

	Avg	AB	H	2B	3B	HR	RBI	BB	SO	OBP	SLG
vs. Left	.277	101	28	4	5	3	22	7	23	.319	.505
vs. Right	.276	145	40	10	1	5	24	19	26	.353	.462
Inning 1-6	.192	52	10	5	1	0	5	6	14	.271	.327
Inning 7+	.299	194	58	9	5	8	41	20	35	.357	.521
None on	.307	101	31	10	1	6	6	10	21	.375	.604
Runners on	.255	145	37	4	5	2	40	16	28	.315	.393
Scoring Posn	.223	103	23	3	4	0	35	14	22	.298	.330
Close & Late	.341	41	14	0	2	2	9	5	6	.426	.585
None on/out	.288	52	15	4	1	3	3	5	15	.351	.577
vs. 1st Batr (relief)	.304	56	17	1	4	2	17	4	13	.333	.571
First Inning Pitched	.263	179	47	6	5	6	37	20	34	.325	.453
First 15 Pitches	.277	148	41	5	5	5	31	17	31	.337	.480
Pitch 16-30	.253	75	19	6	0	3	10	9	13	.341	.453
Pitch 31-45	.364	22	8	3	1	0	5	0	5	.364	.591
Pitch 46+	.000	1	0	0	0	0	0	0	0	.000	.000
First Pitch	.185	27	5	1	0	0	2	5	0	.303	.222
Ahead in Count	.272	114	31	4	5	3	23	0	39	.271	.474
Behind in Count	.404	57	23	6	0	4	17	11	0	.479	.719
Two Strikes	.195	118	23	5	4	0	16	10	49	.258	.305

Career (1989-1993)

	ERA	W	L	Sv	G	GS	IP	H	HR	BB	SO
Home	4.50	5	3	2	108	0	122.0	120	13	56	92
Away	3.18	8	8	2	104	0	110.1	98	7	42	62
Day	5.04	1	6	0	64	0	64.1	77	9	24	38

	Avg	AB	H	2B	3B	HR	RBI	BB	SO	OBP	SLG
vs. Left	.232	289	67	14	5	8	56	24	64	.292	.398
vs. Right	.257	587	151	38	5	12	81	74	90	.340	.400
Inning 1-6	.213	136	29	9	1	2	23	19	31	.310	.338

Career (1989-1993)

	ERA	W	L	Sv	G	GS	IP	H	HR	BB	SO		Avg	AB	H	2B	3B	HR	RBI	BB	SO	OBP	SLG
Night	3.43	12	5	4	148	0	168.0	141	11	74	116	Inning 7+	.255	740	189	43	9	18	114	79	123	.327	.411
Grass	4.47	3	5	0	101	0	108.2	111	13	48	78	None on	.254	422	107	33	2	10	10	44	73	.331	.412
Turf	3.35	10	6	4	111	0	123.2	107	7	50	76	Runners on	.244	454	111	19	8	10	127	54	81	.318	.388
April	4.01	0	3	0	32	0	33.2	33	3	21	27	Scoring Posn	.251	295	74	14	6	7	119	42	60	.331	.410
May	2.93	3	0	0	43	0	55.1	45	6	18	28	Close & Late	.221	240	53	8	3	3	25	30	45	.316	.317
June	5.65	3	1	1	39	0	43.0	50	3	24	29	None on/out	.261	199	52	19	2	5	5	21	37	.338	.452
July	4.44	0	3	0	26	0	26.1	26	1	8	17	vs. 1st Batr (relief)	.237	186	44	7	4	6	43	16	42	.292	.414
August	2.48	3	2	1	26	0	29.0	24	2	12	21	First Inning Pitched	.234	576	135	30	9	11	104	70	99	.314	.375
September/October	3.80	4	2	2	46	0	45.0	40	5	15	32	First 15 Pitches	.234	522	122	24	8	11	87	57	93	.307	.374
Starter	0.00	0	0	0	0	0	0.0	0	0	0	0	Pitch 16-30	.248	246	61	18	1	7	34	34	45	.343	.415
Reliever	3.87	13	11	4	212	0	232.1	218	20	98	154	Pitch 31-45	.309	81	25	7	1	1	12	7	15	.364	.457
0 Days rest	6.07	1	4	1	45	0	46.0	58	7	20	30	Pitch 46+	.370	27	10	3	0	1	4	0	1	.393	.593
1 or 2 Days rest	3.64	7	4	2	99	0	113.2	102	11	46	73	First Pitch	.298	114	34	9	1	2	16	12	0	.362	.447
3+ Days rest	2.85	5	3	1	68	0	72.2	58	2	32	51	Ahead in Count	.209	402	84	16	7	6	55	0	130	.218	.328
Pre-All Star	4.13	6	5	1	127	0	141.2	140	12	68	88	Behind in Count	.310	216	67	17	1	7	44	50	0	.433	.495
Post-All Star	3.47	7	6	3	85	0	90.2	78	8	30	66	Two Strikes	.175	405	71	18	6	3	44	36	154	.246	.272

Pitcher vs. Batter (career)

Pitches Best Vs.	Avg	AB	H	2B	3B	HR	RBI	BB	SO	OBP	SLG	Pitches Worst Vs.	Avg	AB	H	2B	3B	HR	RBI	BB	SO	OBP	SLG
Wally Joyner	.200	10	2	1	0	0	3	0	0	.182	.300												

Dave Weathers — Marlins

Age 24 – Pitches Right (groundball pitcher)

	ERA	W	L	Sv	G	GS	IP	BB	SO	Avg	H	2B	3B	HR	RBI	OBP	SLG	GF	IR	IRS	Hld	SvOp	SB	CS	GB	FB	G/F
1993 Season	5.12	2	3	0	14	6	45.2	13	34	.306	57	14	1	3	23	.355	.441	2	5	1	0	0	7	0	69	46	1.50
Career (1991-1993)	5.23	3	3	0	31	6	63.2	32	50	.301	77	18	1	5	36	.384	.438	6	25	9	1	0	11	1	93	59	1.58

1993 Season

	ERA	W	L	Sv	G	GS	IP	H	HR	BB	SO		Avg	AB	H	2B	3B	HR	RBI	BB	SO	OBP	SLG
Home	7.20	0	3	0	5	3	20.0	30	1	6	14	vs. Left	.309	97	30	10	1	1	7	7	15	.356	.464
Away	3.51	2	0	0	9	3	25.2	27	2	7	20	vs. Right	.303	89	27	4	0	2	16	6	19	.354	.416

Lenny Webster — Twins

Age 29 – Bats Right (groundball hitter)

	Avg	G	AB	R	H	2B	3B	HR	RBI	BB	SO	HBP	GDP	SB	CS	OBP	SLG	IBB	SH	SF	#Pit	#P/PA	GB	FB	G/F
1993 Season	.198	49	106	14	21	2	0	1	8	11	8	0	1	1	0	.274	.245	1	0	0	386	3.30	44	31	1.42
Career (1989-1993)	.254	136	284	35	72	16	1	5	30	30	32	0	6	1	2	.324	.370	1	2	1	1088	3.43	123	79	1.56

1993 Season

	Avg	AB	H	2B	3B	HR	RBI	BB	SO	OBP	SLG		Avg	AB	H	2B	3B	HR	RBI	BB	SO	OBP	SLG
vs. Left	.267	30	8	1	0	0	4	4	2	.353	.300	Scoring Posn	.172	29	5	1	0	0	7	3	4	.250	.207
vs. Right	.171	76	13	1	0	1	4	7	6	.241	.224	Close & Late	.333	15	5	1	0	0	0	3	1	.444	.400

Mitch Webster — Dodgers

Age 35 – Bats Both (flyball hitter)

	Avg	G	AB	R	H	2B	3B	HR	RBI	BB	SO	HBP	GDP	SB	CS	OBP	SLG	IBB	SH	SF	#Pit	#P/PA	GB	FB	G/F
1993 Season	.244	88	172	26	42	6	2	2	14	11	24	2	3	4	6	.293	.337	2	4	3	622	3.24	49	68	0.72
Last Five Years	.248	556	1346	180	334	58	22	25	142	109	250	8	15	53	22	.305	.380	12	28	16	5144	3.41	362	486	0.74

1993 Season

	Avg	AB	H	2B	3B	HR	RBI	BB	SO	OBP	SLG		Avg	AB	H	2B	3B	HR	RBI	BB	SO	OBP	SLG
vs. Left	.275	69	19	4	2	0	6	2	8	.292	.391	Scoring Posn	.255	47	12	1	1	1	13	4	10	.309	.383
vs. Right	.223	103	23	2	0	2	8	9	16	.293	.301	Close & Late	.242	62	15	3	0	2	4	3	9	.277	.387
Home	.221	77	17	1	1	1	6	6	12	.279	.299	None on/out	.333	36	12	1	0	1	1	2	4	.385	.444
Away	.263	95	25	5	1	1	8	5	12	.304	.368	Batting #3	.290	69	20	2	1	0	5	4	6	.333	.348
First Pitch	.282	39	11	3	0	0	1	0	0	.300	.359	Batting #9	.167	42	7	0	0	1	2	4	7	.239	.238
Ahead in Count	.231	39	9	2	0	0	2	7	0	.333	.282	Other	.246	61	15	4	1	1	7	3	11	.281	.393
Behind in Count	.209	67	14	1	1	1	6	0	23	.209	.299	Pre-All Star	.268	123	33	3	2	1	10	9	17	.316	.350
Two Strikes	.129	62	8	1	1	0	3	4	24	.182	.177	Post-All Star	.184	49	9	3	0	1	4	2	7	.231	.306

Last Five Years

	Avg	AB	H	2B	3B	HR	RBI	BB	SO	OBP	SLG		Avg	AB	H	2B	3B	HR	RBI	BB	SO	OBP	SLG
vs. Left	.282	556	157	28	9	14	70	40	76	.330	.441	Scoring Posn	.238	336	80	14	5	7	114	37	73	.306	.372
vs. Right	.224	790	177	30	13	11	72	69	174	.288	.337	Close & Late	.246	301	74	11	5	8	38	39	68	.333	.395
Groundball	.267	430	115	20	9	8	48	30	85	.316	.412	None on/out	.297	300	89	19	6	4	4	25	53	.359	.440
Flyball	.227	344	78	12	6	9	42	28	58	.285	.375	Batting #2	.256	442	113	22	6	11	49	31	61	.305	.407
Home	.233	631	147	21	7	11	71	59	106	.299	.341	Batting #3	.284	232	66	9	4	3	21	15	41	.329	.397
Away	.262	715	187	37	15	14	71	50	144	.310	.414	Other	.231	672	155	27	12	11	72	63	148	.297	.356
Day	.256	481	123	24	7	6	51	32	102	.303	.372	April	.283	180	51	9	2	2	18	14	36	.333	.389
Night	.244	865	211	34	15	19	91	77	148	.306	.384	May	.210	290	61	6	8	6	27	24	60	.272	.348
Grass	.238	999	238	34	17	16	104	71	178	.290	.354	June	.245	286	70	8	4	5	30	26	58	.308	.353
Turf	.277	347	96	24	5	9	38	38	72	.348	.452	July	.289	249	72	16	5	4	26	13	33	.330	.442
First Pitch	.331	278	92	15	6	8	36	7	0	.347	.514	August	.225	191	43	10	0	5	24	18	36	.286	.356
Ahead in Count	.298	302	90	21	7	3	40	59	0	.410	.444	September/October	.247	150	37	9	3	3	17	14	27	.313	.407
Behind in Count	.172	551	95	14	5	5	29	0	214	.171	.243	Pre-All Star	.244	848	207	27	17	14	86	67	164	.300	.366
Two Strikes	.133	549	73	11	5	7	33	41	250	.192	.209	Post-All Star	.255	498	127	31	5	11	56	42	86	.313	.404

Batter vs. Pitcher (since 1984)

Hits Best Against	Avg	AB	H	2B	3B	HR	RBI	BB	SO	OBP	SLG	Hits Worst Against	Avg	AB	H	2B	3B	HR	RBI	BB	SO	OBP	SLG
Bruce Ruffin	.556	18	10	2	1	0	0	2	0	.600	.778	Tim Belcher	.059	17	1	0	0	0	0	1	5	.111	.059
Zane Smith	.462	26	12	4	1	0	2	2	1	.500	.692	Pete Harnisch	.071	14	1	0	0	0	0	1	3	.133	.071
Danny Darwin	.435	23	10	3	1	0	1	2	5	.480	.652	Randy Johnson	.071	14	1	0	0	0	1	2	2	.188	.071
Ron Darling	.350	40	14	1	2	2	4	6	10	.426	.625	Tom Glavine	.125	16	2	0	0	0	1	1	3	.176	.125
Randy Myers	.333	12	4	0	0	1	7	2	3	.429	.583	Bob Murphy	.182	11	2	0	0	0	1	0	2	.182	.182

Eric Wedge — Rockies

Age 26 – Bats Right (flyball hitter)

	Avg	G	AB	R	H	2B	3B	HR	RBI	BB	SO	HBP	GDP	SB	CS	OBP	SLG	IBB	SH	SF	#Pit	#P/PA	GB	FB	G/F
1993 Season	.182	9	11	2	2	0	0	0	1	0	4	0	0	0	0	.182	.182	0	0	0	43	3.91	2	4	0.50
Career (1991-1993)	.250	37	80	13	20	2	0	5	12	13	22	0	0	0	0	.355	.463	0	0	0	375	4.03	16	26	0.62

1993 Season

	Avg	AB	H	2B	3B	HR	RBI	BB	SO	OBP	SLG		Avg	AB	H	2B	3B	HR	RBI	BB	SO	OBP	SLG
vs. Left	.000	2	0	0	0	0	0	0	2	.000	.000	Scoring Posn	.333	3	1	0	0	0	1	0	1	.333	.333
vs. Right	.222	9	2	0	0	0	1	0	2	.222	.222	Close & Late	.000	1	0	0	0	0	0	0	1	.000	.000

Bill Wegman — Brewers

Age 31 – Pitches Right (groundball pitcher)

	ERA	W	L	Sv	G	GS	IP	BB	SO	Avg	H	2B	3B	HR	RBI	OBP	SLG	CG	ShO	Sup	QS	#P/S	SB	CS	GB	FB	G/F
1993 Season	4.48	4	14	0	20	18	120.2	34	50	.291	135	35	5	13	61	.335	.472	5	0	3.13	10	94	10	7	193	130	1.48
Last Five Years	3.67	36	43	0	102	94	656.1	156	313	.264	668	136	13	69	270	.308	.409	20	3	4.51	51	100	44	20	1042	679	1.53

1993 Season

	ERA	W	L	Sv	G	GS	IP	H	HR	BB	SO		Avg	AB	H	2B	3B	HR	RBI	BB	SO	OBP	SLG
Home	3.88	3	6	0	9	9	62.2	70	6	15	27	vs. Left	.326	221	72	14	4	5	28	13	18	.358	.493
Away	5.12	1	8	0	11	9	58.0	65	7	19	23	vs. Right	.259	243	63	21	1	8	33	21	32	.313	.453
Starter	4.34	4	14	0	18	18	118.1	132	13	33	49	Scoring Posn	.265	113	30	7	0	3	44	10	13	.299	.407
Reliever	11.57	0	0	0	2	0	2.1	3	0	1	1	Close & Late	.465	43	20	4	0	0	7	7	2	.519	.558
0-3 Days Rest	4.76	0	2	0	2	2	11.1	10	1	3	3	None on/out	.370	127	47	12	3	6	6	10	11	.420	.654
4 Days Rest	4.28	3	9	0	12	12	82.0	91	8	25	32	First Pitch	.354	82	29	12	1	7	20	4	0	.382	.780
5+ Days Rest	4.32	1	3	0	4	4	25.0	31	4	5	14	Ahead in Count	.199	161	32	10	0	1	10	0	43	.200	.280
Pre-All Star	4.34	4	14	0	18	18	118.1	132	13	33	49	Behind in Count	.324	139	45	7	2	4	19	17	0	.385	.489
Post-All Star	11.57	0	0	0	2	0	2.1	3	0	1	1	Two Strikes	.155	155	24	7	1	1	10	13	50	.218	.232

Last Five Years

	ERA	W	L	Sv	G	GS	IP	H	HR	BB	SO		Avg	AB	H	2B	3B	HR	RBI	BB	SO	OBP	SLG
Home	2.88	20	17	0	50	47	340.1	327	30	80	158	vs. Left	.251	1244	312	58	7	25	119	75	99	.291	.369
Away	4.53	16	26	0	52	47	316.0	341	39	76	155	vs. Right	.276	1291	356	78	6	44	151	81	214	.324	.448
Day	4.09	12	17	0	40	36	240.0	276	33	60	113	Inning 1-6	.261	2011	525	107	11	58	223	130	244	.307	.412
Night	3.44	24	26	0	62	58	416.1	392	36	96	200	Inning 7+	.273	524	143	29	2	11	47	26	69	.311	.399
Grass	3.48	32	34	0	86	80	564.1	564	61	131	270	None on	.263	1558	409	88	10	41	41	84	199	.304	.411
Turf	4.89	4	9	0	16	14	92.0	104	8	25	43	Runners on	.265	977	259	48	3	28	229	72	114	.314	.406
April	3.30	5	7	0	16	15	111.2	107	7	32	52	Scoring Posn	.258	550	142	23	1	14	191	53	67	.315	.380
May	4.30	9	13	0	29	24	163.1	179	23	42	80	Close & Late	.302	258	78	18	0	8	34	19	37	.356	.465
June	4.88	4	9	0	17	17	97.2	108	13	27	46	None on/out	.276	682	188	33	7	28	28	33	78	.313	.468
July	3.72	5	6	0	13	13	96.2	105	12	16	38	vs. 1st Batr (relief)	.375	8	3	1	1	0	1	0	0	.375	.750
August	2.87	6	5	0	12	12	81.2	85	8	16	38	First Inning Pitched	.267	393	105	16	5	10	61	30	60	.319	.410
September/October	2.56	7	3	0	15	13	105.1	84	6	23	59	First 75 Pitches	.257	1801	463	86	10	53	200	119	227	.304	.404
Starter	3.63	36	42	0	94	94	639.0	644	67	152	301	Pitch 76-90	.269	338	91	27	1	9	24	14	37	.303	.435
Reliever	5.19	0	1	0	8	0	17.1	24	2	4	12	Pitch 91-105	.288	236	68	15	2	3	31	13	30	.332	.407
0-3 Days Rest	4.58	0	3	0	3	3	17.2	19	3	4	6	Pitch 106+	.288	160	46	8	0	4	15	10	19	.331	.413
4 Days Rest	3.68	23	26	0	61	61	430.2	434	45	91	201	First Pitch	.299	411	123	24	3	20	56	10	0	.315	.518
5+ Days Rest	3.45	13	13	0	30	30	190.2	191	19	57	94	Ahead in Count	.225	1006	226	45	2	18	89	0	263	.233	.327
Pre-All Star	4.22	20	32	0	67	61	405.2	441	50	105	190	Behind in Count	.308	623	192	43	4	18	76	79	0	.383	.477
Post-All Star	2.80	16	11	0	35	33	250.2	227	19	51	123	Two Strikes	.194	993	193	37	4	20	83	67	313	.251	.300

Pitcher vs. Batter (career)

Pitches Best Vs.	Avg	AB	H	2B	3B	HR	RBI	BB	SO	OBP	SLG	Pitches Worst Vs.	Avg	AB	H	2B	3B	HR	RBI	BB	SO	OBP	SLG
Spike Owen	.000	10	0	0	0	0	0	1	1	.091	.000	Billy Ripken	.647	17	11	0	0	1	5	1	1	.632	.824
Brett Butler	.056	18	1	1	0	0	1	0	0	.056	.111	Mike Greenwell	.500	20	10	2	0	1	4	6	1	.615	.750
Steve Buechele	.059	17	1	0	0	0	2	1	2	.111	.059	Sam Horn	.500	16	8	2	0	2	4	2	0	.556	1.000
Alex Cole	.077	13	1	0	0	0	1	2	1	.200	.077	Darnell Coles	.455	11	5	2	0	1	3	3	3	.571	.909
Pat Kelly	.083	12	1	0	0	0	0	0	0	.083	.083	Dean Palmer	.429	14	6	2	0	3	6	1	4	.467	1.214

John Wehner — Pirates

Age 27 – Bats Right (groundball hitter)

	Avg	G	AB	R	H	2B	3B	HR	RBI	BB	SO	HBP	GDP	SB	CS	OBP	SLG	IBB	SH	SF	#Pit	#P/PA	GB	FB	G/F
1993 Season	.143	29	35	3	5	0	0	0	0	6	10	0	0	0	0	.268	.143	1	2	0	162	3.77	13	10	1.30
Career (1991-1993)	.239	121	264	29	63	13	0	0	11	25	49	0	4	6	0	.304	.288	3	4	0	1060	3.62	113	66	1.71

1993 Season

	Avg	AB	H	2B	3B	HR	RBI	BB	SO	OBP	SLG		Avg	AB	H	2B	3B	HR	RBI	BB	SO	OBP	SLG
vs. Left	.050	20	1	0	0	0	0	5	6	.240	.050	Scoring Posn	.000	12	0	0	0	0	0	2	4	.143	.000
vs. Right	.267	15	4	0	0	0	0	1	4	.313	.267	Close & Late	.000	9	0	0	0	0	0	1	2	.100	.000

Walt Weiss — Marlins

Age 30 – Bats Both (groundball hitter)

	Avg	G	AB	R	H	2B	3B	HR	RBI	BB	SO	HBP	GDP	SB	CS	OBP	SLG	IBB	SH	SF	#Pit	#P/PA	GB	FB	G/F
1993 Season	.266	158	500	50	133	14	2	1	39	79	73	3	5	7	3	.367	.308	13	5	4	2186	3.70	199	119	1.67
Last Five Years	.247	523	1630	181	403	53	6	6	129	201	218	9	31	34	10	.331	.298	19	28	14	6918	3.68	675	410	1.65

1993 Season

	Avg	AB	H	2B	3B	HR	RBI	BB	SO	OBP	SLG
vs. Left	.234	128	30	6	0	0	11	23	19	.353	.281
vs. Right	.277	372	103	8	2	1	28	56	54	.372	.317
Groundball	.258	159	41	4	1	0	8	25	21	.367	.296
Flyball	.232	99	23	3	0	0	7	14	22	.322	.263
Home	.250	244	61	6	1	0	19	44	37	.362	.283
Away	.281	256	72	8	1	1	20	35	36	.372	.332
Day	.253	99	25	5	1	0	9	18	19	.370	.323
Night	.269	401	108	9	1	1	30	61	54	.366	.304
Grass	.264	382	101	12	1	1	28	66	57	.373	.309
Turf	.271	118	32	2	1	0	11	13	16	.348	.305
First Pitch	.378	82	31	6	1	1	12	11	0	.452	.512
Ahead in Count	.275	138	38	0	0	0	9	36	0	.424	.275
Behind in Count	.202	198	40	7	1	0	16	0	61	.208	.247
Two Strikes	.193	202	39	5	0	0	10	32	73	.307	.218

	Avg	AB	H	2B	3B	HR	RBI	BB	SO	OBP	SLG
Scoring Posn	.299	107	32	4	1	0	37	28	15	.440	.355
Close & Late	.255	106	27	2	0	0	8	20	16	.370	.274
None on/out	.211	123	26	4	0	0	0	18	26	.312	.244
Batting #2	.294	34	10	2	0	0	1	7	6	.415	.353
Batting #8	.267	435	116	11	2	1	38	65	65	.363	.308
Other	.226	31	7	1	0	0	0	7	2	.368	.258
April	.254	67	17	0	1	0	8	13	11	.378	.284
May	.333	84	28	5	1	0	6	12	10	.423	.417
June	.278	90	25	1	0	1	5	8	10	.337	.322
July	.188	85	16	3	0	0	9	9	15	.268	.224
August	.299	87	26	3	0	0	6	16	13	.408	.333
September/October	.241	87	21	2	0	0	5	21	14	.385	.264
Pre-All Star	.271	277	75	7	2	1	23	36	37	.358	.321
Post-All Star	.260	223	58	7	0	0	16	43	36	.378	.291

1993 By Position

Position	Avg	AB	H	2B	3B	HR	RBI	BB	SO	OBP	SLG	G	GS	Innings	PO	A	E	DP	Fld Pct	Rng Fctr	In Zone	Outs	Zone Rtg	MLB Zone
As ss	.269	494	133	14	2	1	39	78	72	.370	.312	153	149	1322.1	231	407	15	79	.977	4.34	477	423	.887	.880

Last Five Years

	Avg	AB	H	2B	3B	HR	RBI	BB	SO	OBP	SLG
vs. Left	.220	405	89	16	1	0	30	39	41	.289	.264
vs. Right	.256	1225	314	37	5	6	99	162	177	.344	.309
Groundball	.232	499	116	17	1	1	40	50	72	.307	.277
Flyball	.272	364	99	14	1	4	34	55	51	.365	.349
Home	.220	821	181	20	2	3	57	106	123	.310	.261
Away	.274	809	222	33	4	3	72	95	95	.352	.336
Day	.240	550	132	20	3	2	44	68	81	.326	.298
Night	.251	1080	271	33	3	4	85	133	137	.333	.298
Grass	.248	1340	332	45	4	6	102	165	183	.331	.301
Turf	.245	290	71	8	2	0	27	36	35	.327	.286
First Pitch	.329	252	83	13	2	3	34	12	0	.359	.433
Ahead in Count	.285	459	131	16	0	2	33	89	0	.400	.333
Behind in Count	.175	627	110	18	2	1	36	0	194	.178	.215
Two Strikes	.181	659	119	17	1	1	36	96	218	.286	.214

	Avg	AB	H	2B	3B	HR	RBI	BB	SO	OBP	SLG
Scoring Posn	.226	390	88	9	2	1	118	68	56	.335	.267
Close & Late	.285	270	77	7	2	0	27	41	32	.377	.326
None on/out	.237	409	97	18	1	0	0	42	64	.310	.286
Batting #8	.250	1126	281	36	4	3	94	136	158	.332	.297
Batting #9	.229	350	80	11	2	3	29	39	42	.304	.297
Other	.273	154	42	6	0	0	6	26	18	.381	.312
April	.264	227	60	10	1	4	22	26	29	.340	.370
May	.264	303	80	13	1	0	23	32	34	.337	.314
June	.255	271	69	7	2	1	18	27	33	.326	.306
July	.223	265	59	7	1	0	23	30	35	.299	.257
August	.265	294	78	11	1	1	25	38	45	.347	.320
September/October	.211	270	57	5	0	0	18	48	42	.333	.230
Pre-All Star	.256	895	229	32	5	5	73	97	105	.330	.320
Post-All Star	.237	735	174	21	1	1	56	104	113	.331	.272

Batter vs. Pitcher (career)

Hits Best Against	Avg	AB	H	2B	3B	HR	RBI	BB	SO	OBP	SLG
Tim Leary	.583	12	7	1	0	0	0	4	1	.688	.667
Scott Bankhead	.545	11	6	1	1	1	4	1	0	.583	1.091
Charles Nagy	.462	13	6	2	0	0	2	0	1	.462	.615
Mark Williamson	.444	9	4	1	0	1	3	2	1	.545	.889
Orel Hershiser	.333	9	3	0	1	0	2	2	2	.455	.556

Hits Worst Against	Avg	AB	H	2B	3B	HR	RBI	BB	SO	OBP	SLG
Pete Harnisch	.000	9	0	0	0	0	0	2	2	.182	.000
Jack McDowell	.048	21	1	0	0	0	1	0	4	.048	.048
Jack Morris	.071	14	1	0	0	0	1	2	3	.176	.071
Bill Krueger	.091	11	1	0	0	0	2	1	0	.167	.091
David Wells	.091	11	1	0	0	0	2	1	1	.167	.091

Bob Welch — Athletics

Age 37 – Pitches Right

	ERA	W	L	Sv	G	GS	IP	BB	SO	Avg	H	2B	3B	HR	RBI	OBP	SLG	CG	ShO	Sup	QS	#P/S	SB	CS	GB	FB	G/F
1993 Season	5.29	9	11	0	30	28	166.2	56	63	.310	208	36	5	25	91	.368	.491	0	0	4.05	12	93	8	12	251	223	1.13
Last Five Years	3.79	76	45	0	153	151	958.0	345	475	.260	947	164	22	102	392	.327	.401	10	3	4.94	83	97	60	47	1317	1149	1.15

1993 Season

	ERA	W	L	Sv	G	GS	IP	H	HR	BB	SO
Home	5.61	5	6	0	15	14	85.0	117	13	25	36
Away	4.96	4	5	0	15	14	81.2	91	12	31	27
Day	6.08	4	6	0	13	12	71.0	98	12	24	36
Night	4.70	5	5	0	17	16	95.2	110	13	32	27
Grass	5.23	9	10	0	27	25	151.1	192	24	48	61
Turf	5.87	0	1	0	3	3	15.1	16	1	8	2
April	5.00	2	2	0	5	4	27.0	33	4	5	8
May	4.58	2	2	0	6	6	35.1	45	4	13	16
June	4.15	1	2	0	5	5	34.2	41	3	9	9
July	5.40	3	1	0	6	5	28.1	37	3	10	11
August	5.23	1	0	0	4	4	20.2	21	4	8	14
September/October	8.71	0	4	0	4	4	20.2	31	7	11	5
Starter	5.34	8	11	0	28	28	161.2	202	25	54	61
Reliever	3.60	1	0	0	2	0	5.0	6	0	2	2
0-3 Days Rest	4.15	1	2	0	4	4	21.2	23	2	8	7
4 Days Rest	4.75	6	2	0	12	12	72.0	86	5	25	36
5+ Days Rest	6.35	1	7	0	12	12	68.0	93	18	21	18
Pre-All Star	4.84	6	6	0	18	17	106.0	135	11	31	37
Post-All Star	6.08	3	5	0	12	11	60.2	73	14	25	26

	Avg	AB	H	2B	3B	HR	RBI	BB	SO	OBP	SLG
vs. Left	.307	371	114	23	3	11	50	30	35	.360	.474
vs. Right	.314	299	94	13	2	14	41	26	28	.378	.512
Inning 1-6	.305	614	187	31	5	23	82	51	62	.364	.484
Inning 7+	.375	56	21	5	0	2	9	5	1	.419	.571
None on	.321	383	123	17	3	17	17	32	31	.376	.514
Runners on	.296	287	85	19	2	8	74	24	32	.357	.460
Scoring Posn	.295	149	44	9	2	4	62	14	14	.365	.463
Close & Late	.348	23	8	0	0	0	1	0	1	.348	.348
None on/out	.278	176	49	8	1	6	6	8	16	.310	.438
vs. 1st Batr (relief)	.500	2	1	0	0	0	0	0	0	.500	.500
First Inning Pitched	.336	125	42	5	1	7	21	8	10	.385	.560
First 75 Pitches	.328	525	172	29	5	22	77	46	51	.388	.528
Pitch 76-90	.177	79	14	2	0	2	5	4	7	.217	.278
Pitch 91-105	.304	46	14	3	0	0	4	3	5	.347	.370
Pitch 106+	.400	20	8	2	0	1	5	3	0	.458	.650
First Pitch	.300	110	33	11	2	4	20	4	0	.330	.545
Ahead in Count	.288	264	76	14	2	6	23	0	49	.299	.424
Behind in Count	.360	189	68	8	1	11	35	22	0	.423	.587
Two Strikes	.265	260	69	11	1	7	27	30	63	.345	.396

Last Five Years

	ERA	W	L	Sv	G	GS	IP	H	HR	BB	SO
Home	3.29	41	20	0	75	74	486.1	463	39	151	266
Away	4.29	35	25	0	78	77	471.2	484	63	194	209
Day	3.31	33	16	0	57	56	364.1	343	35	132	202
Night	4.08	43	29	0	96	95	593.2	604	67	213	273
Grass	3.55	64	35	0	125	123	786.1	765	82	274	407
Turf	4.88	12	10	0	28	28	171.2	182	20	71	68
April	2.38	11	6	0	20	19	136.0	110	10	33	58
May	4.01	12	10	0	29	29	191.0	191	26	78	89
June	3.28	16	5	0	24	24	162.0	150	14	55	69
July	4.52	12	6	0	27	26	151.1	176	19	57	89
August	3.58	16	6	0	25	25	163.1	160	14	54	100
September/October	4.78	9	12	0	28	28	154.1	160	19	68	70
Starter	3.79	75	45	0	151	151	953.0	941	102	343	473
Reliever	3.60	1	0	0	2	0	5.0	6	0	2	2
0-3 Days Rest	4.16	7	5	0	15	15	88.2	102	13	21	43
4 Days Rest	3.52	53	21	0	91	91	586.1	553	52	223	291
5+ Days Rest	4.24	15	19	0	45	45	278.0	286	37	99	139
Pre-All Star	3.52	44	22	0	82	81	535.0	518	60	175	240
Post-All Star	4.13	32	23	0	71	70	423.0	429	42	170	235

	Avg	AB	H	2B	3B	HR	RBI	BB	SO	OBP	SLG
vs. Left	.261	1924	502	88	16	40	192	197	226	.331	.386
vs. Right	.259	1720	445	76	6	62	200	148	249	.323	.418
Inning 1-6	.261	3160	824	143	19	86	350	304	422	.329	.400
Inning 7+	.254	484	123	21	3	16	42	41	53	.317	.409
None on	.262	2181	572	98	13	64	64	191	245	.326	.407
Runners on	.256	1463	375	66	9	38	328	154	230	.330	.392
Scoring Posn	.269	796	214	36	7	22	283	99	142	.349	.415
Close & Late	.226	252	57	7	1	5	18	21	38	.293	.321
None on/out	.254	971	247	42	3	32	32	70	106	.307	.403
vs. 1st Batr (relief)	.500	2	1	0	0	0	0	0	0	.500	.500
First Inning Pitched	.263	586	154	25	2	18	67	40	80	.314	.404
First 75 Pitches	.268	2726	730	126	15	77	299	247	357	.332	.410
Pitch 76-90	.211	432	91	17	2	10	34	52	50	.301	.329
Pitch 91-105	.231	312	72	11	3	8	33	26	52	.291	.343
Pitch 106+	.310	174	54	10	2	9	26	20	16	.381	.546
First Pitch	.295	586	173	32	5	29	86	13	0	.316	.515
Ahead in Count	.231	1551	358	62	7	25	123	0	374	.239	.328
Behind in Count	.306	814	249	39	8	34	130	174	0	.427	.499
Two Strikes	.205	1509	310	52	5	25	116	158	475	.286	.296

Pitcher vs. Batter (since 1984)

Pitches Best Vs.	Avg	AB	H	2B	3B	HR	RBI	BB	SO	OBP	SLG
Darryl Strawberry	.053	19	1	0	0	0	0	2	7	.143	.053
Pete Incaviglia	.056	18	1	0	0	0	0	1	7	.105	.056
Steve Finley	.063	16	1	0	0	0	0	1	0	.118	.063
Paul O'Neill	.083	12	1	0	0	0	0	0	1	.083	.083
Vince Coleman	.095	21	2	0	0	0	1	1	9	.136	.095

Pitches Worst Vs.	Avg	AB	H	2B	3B	HR	RBI	BB	SO	OBP	SLG
Carlos Baerga	.560	25	14	3	0	1	3	0	1	.560	.800
Glenn Davis	.455	33	15	3	0	2	7	3	3	.500	.727
Kelly Gruber	.412	17	7	2	0	1	2	4	2	.500	.706
Juan Gonzalez	.385	13	5	2	0	1	5	2	2	.467	.769
Kenny Lofton	.364	11	4	2	1	1	3	0	0	.364	1.000

David Wells — Tigers

Age 31 – Pitches Left (flyball pitcher)

	ERA	W	L	Sv	G	GS	IP	BB	SO	Avg	H	2B	3B	HR	RBI	OBP	SLG	CG	ShO	Sup	QS	#P/S	SB	CS	GB	FB	G/F
1993 Season	4.19	11	9	0	32	30	187.0	42	139	.254	183	33	3	26	78	.300	.416	0	0	5.05	17	96	14	10	227	206	1.10
Last Five Years	3.80	51	38	8	210	97	780.2	200	500	.249	740	154	16	85	316	.300	.398	2	0	4.83	55	95	58	43	956	975	0.98

1993 Season

	ERA	W	L	Sv	G	GS	IP	H	HR	BB	SO
Home	2.74	8	3	0	16	15	108.1	90	9	18	78
Away	6.18	3	6	0	16	15	78.2	93	17	24	61
Day	4.82	3	4	0	12	11	71.0	73	9	18	44
Night	3.80	8	5	0	20	19	116.0	110	17	24	95
Grass	3.78	11	7	0	26	24	157.1	145	20	32	109
Turf	6.37	0	2	0	6	6	29.2	38	6	10	30
April	1.47	4	0	0	5	5	30.2	20	2	5	16
May	2.45	2	1	0	6	6	44.0	29	3	10	35
June	5.68	3	2	0	6	6	38.0	42	8	11	33
July	8.28	1	4	0	6	6	29.1	41	7	10	23
August	2.16	0	0	0	3	1	8.1	10	1	0	8
September/October	4.17	1	2	0	6	6	36.2	41	5	6	24
Starter	4.17	11	9	0	30	30	183.2	178	25	42	136
Reliever	5.40	0	0	0	2	0	3.1	5	1	0	3
0-3 Days Rest	2.16	1	1	0	3	3	16.2	15	3	2	14
4 Days Rest	4.09	8	5	0	20	20	127.2	121	16	31	94
5+ Days Rest	5.26	2	3	0	7	7	39.1	42	6	9	28
Pre-All Star	3.97	9	4	0	19	19	120.0	105	17	30	89
Post-All Star	4.57	2	5	0	13	11	67.0	78	9	12	50

	Avg	AB	H	2B	3B	HR	RBI	BB	SO	OBP	SLG
vs. Left	.250	108	27	4	1	2	7	9	20	.328	.361
vs. Right	.254	613	156	29	2	24	71	33	119	.295	.426
Inning 1-6	.248	638	158	27	2	23	69	36	128	.292	.404
Inning 7+	.301	83	25	6	1	3	9	6	11	.359	.506
None on	.259	448	116	19	2	13	13	20	84	.300	.397
Runners on	.245	273	67	14	1	13	65	22	55	.301	.447
Scoring Posn	.223	139	31	8	0	5	46	17	37	.306	.388
Close & Late	.390	59	23	6	1	3	9	5	6	.431	.678
None on/out	.296	196	58	12	0	5	5	6	36	.320	.434
vs. 1st Batr (relief)	.500	2	1	0	0	1	1	0	0	.500	2.000
First Inning Pitched	.211	114	24	5	0	3	11	8	27	.260	.333
First 75 Pitches	.245	559	137	21	2	21	59	34	107	.291	.403
Pitch 76-90	.253	75	19	4	0	2	5	4	17	.309	.387
Pitch 91-105	.352	54	19	5	0	1	8	2	8	.386	.500
Pitch 106+	.242	33	8	3	1	2	6	2	7	.297	.576
First Pitch	.261	88	23	4	0	2	7	5	0	.301	.375
Ahead in Count	.188	314	59	10	1	10	29	0	119	.202	.322
Behind in Count	.353	184	65	10	2	9	29	18	0	.412	.576
Two Strikes	.190	332	63	15	1	9	28	19	139	.245	.322

Last Five Years

	ERA	W	L	Sv	G	GS	IP	H	HR	BB	SO
Home	3.27	26	15	4	105	43	385.2	350	45	92	247
Away	4.33	25	23	4	105	54	395.0	390	40	108	253
Day	4.92	12	14	1	65	28	223.0	226	26	67	125
Night	3.36	39	24	7	145	69	557.2	514	59	133	375
Grass	4.11	28	21	3	95	56	403.0	387	39	104	269
Turf	3.48	23	17	5	115	41	377.2	353	46	96	231
April	3.20	7	5	3	31	11	98.1	79	9	23	56
May	2.39	11	4	1	43	14	135.2	96	8	34	108
June	3.80	10	6	3	36	18	149.1	146	17	44	115
July	4.04	12	7	0	31	23	153.2	145	22	36	86
August	6.25	5	10	0	27	17	112.1	144	16	40	56
September/October	3.36	6	6	1	42	14	131.1	130	13	23	79
Starter	4.03	41	31	0	97	97	607.1	589	71	152	363
Reliever	3.01	10	7	8	113	0	173.1	151	14	48	137
0-3 Days Rest	2.12	3	1	0	5	5	29.2	21	5	8	29
4 Days Rest	4.36	23	20	0	60	60	378.0	379	48	97	231
5+ Days Rest	3.70	15	10	0	32	32	199.2	189	18	47	103
Pre-All Star	3.40	30	18	7	122	51	437.0	379	45	115	307
Post-All Star	4.32	21	20	1	88	46	343.2	361	40	85	193

	Avg	AB	H	2B	3B	HR	RBI	BB	SO	OBP	SLG
vs. Left	.248	517	128	27	4	11	54	34	70	.308	.379
vs. Right	.250	2449	612	127	12	74	262	166	430	.298	.402
Inning 1-6	.250	2185	547	121	12	65	244	143	354	.299	.406
Inning 7+	.247	781	193	33	4	20	72	57	146	.301	.376
None on	.248	1793	445	88	6	47	47	111	319	.296	.383
Runners on	.251	1173	295	66	10	38	269	89	181	.305	.422
Scoring Posn	.251	622	156	41	5	13	207	74	110	.328	.395
Close & Late	.281	427	120	20	3	11	42	31	75	.330	.419
None on/out	.253	767	194	38	1	19	19	48	138	.299	.379
vs. 1st Batr (relief)	.225	102	23	3	0	3	12	8	21	.286	.343
First Inning Pitched	.233	711	166	40	3	17	77	44	138	.278	.370
First 75 Pitches	.240	2416	579	115	13	67	239	163	415	.289	.381
Pitch 76-90	.299	291	87	15	1	14	38	21	40	.351	.502
Pitch 91-105	.319	188	60	18	1	2	31	11	30	.365	.457
Pitch 106+	.197	71	14	6	1	2	8	5	15	.266	.394
First Pitch	.287	383	110	20	3	17	49	17	0	.319	.488
Ahead in Count	.185	1302	241	49	5	19	94	0	437	.193	.274
Behind in Count	.328	762	250	48	6	36	119	97	0	.402	.549
Two Strikes	.177	1305	231	61	6	17	92	85	500	.232	.272

Pitcher vs. Batter (career)																							
Pitches Best Vs.	Avg	AB	H	2B	3B	HR	RBI	BB	SO	OBP	SLG	Pitches Worst Vs.	Avg	AB	H	2B	3B	HR	RBI	BB	SO	OBP	SLG
Bo Jackson	.000	11	0	0	0	0	0	1	6	.083	.000	Albert Belle	.462	13	6	2	0	1	5	1	1	.467	.846
Lance Parrish	.063	16	1	0	0	0	0	1	7	.118	.063	Frank Thomas	.444	18	8	0	1	3	5	6	3	.583	1.056
Omar Vizquel	.077	13	1	0	0	0	0	1	3	.143	.077	Cal Ripken	.409	22	9	2	0	3	6	1	2	.435	.909
Jim Eisenreich	.091	11	1	0	0	0	0	0	0	.091	.091	Cecil Fielder	.385	13	5	0	0	2	5	5	2	.556	.846
Michael Huff	.091	11	1	0	0	0	1	1	1	.154	.091	Juan Gonzalez	.385	13	5	0	0	2	6	2	1	.467	.846

Turk Wendell — Cubs

Age 27 – Pitches Right (groundball pitcher)

	ERA	W	L	Sv	G	GS	IP	BB	SO	Avg	H	2B	3B	HR	RBI	OBP	SLG	CG	ShO	Sup	QS	#P/S	SB	CS	GB	FB	G/F
1993 Season	4.37	1	2	0	7	4	22.2	8	15	.273	24	4	0	0	7	.333	.318	0	0	3.18	2	77	1	0	36	19	1.89

1993 Season																						
	ERA	W	L	Sv	G	GS	IP	H	HR	BB	SO		Avg	AB	H	2B	3B	HR	RBI	BB	SO	OBP	SLG
Home	8.44	0	1	0	3	1	5.1	9	0	3	2	vs. Left	.372	43	16	4	0	0	5	4	7	.426	.465
Away	3.12	1	1	0	4	3	17.1	15	0	5	13	vs. Right	.178	45	8	0	0	0	2	4	8	.245	.178

Bill Wertz — Indians

Age 27 – Pitches Right (flyball pitcher)

	ERA	W	L	Sv	G	GS	IP	BB	SO	Avg	H	2B	3B	HR	RBI	OBP	SLG	GF	IR	IRS	Hld	SvOp	SB	CS	GB	FB	G/F
1993 Season	3.62	2	3	0	34	0	59.2	32	53	.238	54	9	0	5	28	.333	.344	7	29	8	3	2	1	0	62	70	0.89

1993 Season																						
	ERA	W	L	Sv	G	GS	IP	H	HR	BB	SO		Avg	AB	H	2B	3B	HR	RBI	BB	SO	OBP	SLG
Home	5.28	0	3	0	18	0	30.2	27	5	17	24	vs. Left	.214	103	22	5	0	2	13	15	21	.314	.320
Away	1.86	2	0	0	16	0	29.0	27	0	15	29	vs. Right	.258	124	32	4	0	3	15	17	32	.350	.363
Starter	0.00	0	0	0	0	0	0.0	0	0	0	0	Scoring Posn	.315	54	17	5	0	1	23	8	13	.397	.463
Reliever	3.62	2	3	0	34	0	59.2	54	5	32	53	Close & Late	.222	72	16	1	0	2	8	9	18	.305	.319
0 Days rest	3.97	0	1	0	7	0	11.1	9	2	7	9	None on/out	.145	55	8	2	0	2	2	5	11	.217	.291
1 or 2 Days rest	3.82	1	2	0	17	0	33.0	30	1	19	29	First Pitch	.308	26	8	1	0	0	6	2	0	.345	.346
3+ Days rest	2.93	1	0	0	10	0	15.1	15	2	6	15	Ahead in Count	.157	115	18	3	0	0	4	0	45	.157	.183
Pre-All Star	4.50	0	0	0	7	0	8.0	8	0	8	12	Behind in Count	.378	45	17	4	0	3	11	14	0	.533	.667
Post-All Star	3.48	2	3	0	27	0	51.2	46	5	24	41	Two Strikes	.123	114	14	3	0	0	3	16	53	.231	.149

David West — Phillies

Age 29 – Pitches Left (flyball pitcher)

	ERA	W	L	Sv	G	GS	IP	BB	SO	Avg	H	2B	3B	HR	RBI	OBP	SLG	GF	IR	IRS	Hld	SvOp	SB	CS	GB	FB	G/F
1993 Season	2.92	6	4	3	76	0	86.1	51	87	.194	60	11	1	6	45	.316	.294	27	52	18	21	9	5	3	89	95	0.94
Last Five Years	4.93	21	24	3	150	49	396.0	210	300	.248	373	81	8	52	230	.343	.417	28	63	23	23	10	16	11	436	503	0.87

1993 Season																						
	ERA	W	L	Sv	G	GS	IP	H	HR	BB	SO		Avg	AB	H	2B	3B	HR	RBI	BB	SO	OBP	SLG
Home	2.93	3	1	2	36	0	43.0	31	3	27	52	vs. Left	.193	83	16	2	1	2	12	23	25	.385	.313
Away	2.91	3	3	1	40	0	43.1	29	3	24	35	vs. Right	.195	226	44	9	0	4	33	28	62	.287	.288
Day	2.53	2	0	2	25	0	21.1	12	1	14	23	Inning 1-6	.174	23	4	0	0	0	4	6	11	.345	.174
Night	3.05	4	4	1	51	0	65.0	48	5	37	64	Inning 7+	.196	286	56	11	1	6	41	45	76	.314	.304
Grass	3.18	2	2	1	24	0	28.1	22	2	10	25	None on	.214	159	34	5	0	1	1	18	47	.302	.264
Turf	2.79	4	2	2	52	0	58.0	38	4	41	62	Runners on	.173	150	26	6	1	5	44	33	40	.330	.327
April	1.46	0	0	1	9	0	12.1	5	1	7	17	Scoring Posn	.174	109	19	4	1	4	41	19	29	.298	.339
May	1.29	0	1	1	12	0	14.0	15	0	6	12	Close & Late	.173	156	27	5	1	3	26	32	45	.323	.276
June	7.43	1	1	0	11	0	13.1	13	3	8	12	None on/out	.279	68	19	4	0	0	0	9	18	.380	.338
July	0.87	2	0	0	15	0	20.2	14	1	10	20	vs. 1st Batr (relief)	.250	64	16	3	0	1	5	11	15	.368	.344
August	4.50	3	1	0	14	0	14.0	9	1	6	15	First Inning Pitched	.202	228	46	10	0	3	33	36	60	.320	.285
September/October	3.00	0	1	1	15	0	12.0	4	0	14	11	First 15 Pitches	.217	184	40	7	0	2	25	31	43	.338	.288
Starter	0.00	0	0	0	0	0	0.0	0	0	0	0	Pitch 16-30	.161	87	14	4	0	3	14	16	31	.305	.310
Reliever	2.92	6	4	3	76	0	86.1	60	6	51	87	Pitch 31-45	.158	38	6	0	1	1	6	4	13	.233	.289
0 Days rest	5.00	3	3	3	27	0	27.0	24	4	15	24	Pitch 46+	.000	0	0	0	0	0	0	0	0	.000	.000
1 or 2 Days rest	2.34	2	0	0	35	0	42.1	25	1	29	40	First Pitch	.313	32	10	2	0	2	8	4	0	.436	.563
3+ Days rest	1.06	1	1	0	14	0	17.0	11	1	7	23	Ahead in Count	.158	152	24	6	0	2	22	0	69	.162	.237
Pre-All Star	2.70	1	2	2	38	0	50.0	39	4	26	51	Behind in Count	.233	60	14	2	0	0	5	23	0	.452	.267
Post-All Star	3.22	5	2	1	38	0	36.1	21	2	25	36	Two Strikes	.143	175	25	6	0	3	25	24	87	.248	.229

Last Five Years																						
	ERA	W	L	Sv	G	GS	IP	H	HR	BB	SO		Avg	AB	H	2B	3B	HR	RBI	BB	SO	OBP	SLG
Home	5.99	9	13	2	72	25	183.1	177	26	102	169	vs. Left	.224	277	62	9	4	5	34	50	63	.349	.339
Away	4.02	12	11	1	78	24	212.2	196	26	108	131	vs. Right	.254	1226	311	72	4	47	196	160	237	.341	.434
Day	5.10	5	5	2	46	13	95.1	83	13	58	78	Inning 1-6	.259	1050	272	60	5	43	168	148	196	.351	.449
Night	4.88	16	19	1	104	36	300.2	290	39	152	222	Inning 7+	.223	453	101	21	3	9	62	62	104	.323	.342
Grass	5.35	7	10	1	56	21	153.0	165	25	80	100	None on	.228	854	195	44	5	20	20	110	167	.319	.362
Turf	4.67	14	14	2	94	28	243.0	208	27	130	200	Runners on	.274	649	178	37	3	32	210	100	133	.373	.488
April	2.80	1	3	1	13	4	35.1	25	6	18	29	Scoring Posn	.264	397	105	26	3	15	173	59	85	.356	.458
May	4.58	1	1	1	17	5	37.1	36	5	22	24	Close & Late	.206	204	42	6	2	4	32	36	53	.332	.314
June	4.58	2	4	0	22	6	55.0	54	5	23	47	None on/out	.241	381	92	20	2	13	13	39	68	.317	.407
July	5.12	6	5	0	32	13	95.0	97	13	50	74	vs. 1st Batr (relief)	.260	77	20	4	0	2	8	14	16	.380	.390
August	5.71	10	7	0	38	15	121.1	114	20	59	79	First Inning Pitched	.242	463	112	22	3	15	79	78	106	.357	.400
September/October	4.85	1	4	1	28	6	52.0	47	3	38	47	First 15 Pitches	.239	401	96	16	2	12	54	61	81	.345	.379
Starter	5.39	14	20	0	49	49	257.1	263	40	127	172	Pitch 16-30	.215	288	62	16	1	13	49	57	75	.350	.413
Reliever	4.09	7	4	3	101	0	138.2	110	12	83	128	Pitch 31-45	.260	246	64	11	1	9	36	30	52	.336	.423
0 Days rest	5.00	3	3	3	27	0	27.0	24	4	15	24	Pitch 46+	.266	568	151	38	4	18	91	62	92	.339	.442

Last Five Years

	ERA	W	L	Sv	G	GS	IP	H	HR	BB	SO
1 or 2 Days rest	3.45	2	0	0	42	0	57.1	45	3	40	53
3+ Days rest	4.31	2	1	0	32	0	54.1	41	5	28	51
Pre-All Star	3.82	6	9	2	63	19	165.0	142	20	79	130
Post-All Star	5.73	15	15	1	87	30	231.0	231	32	131	170

	Avg	AB	H	2B	3B	HR	RBI	BB	SO	OBP	SLG
First Pitch	.303	198	60	17	2	11	51	8	0	.349	.576
Ahead in Count	.210	709	149	33	4	19	87	0	243	.213	.348
Behind in Count	.311	315	98	19	0	13	54	111	0	.488	.495
Two Strikes	.185	735	136	31	4	17	81	90	300	.275	.307

Pitcher vs. Batter (career)

Pitches Best Vs.	Avg	AB	H	2B	3B	HR	RBI	BB	SO	OBP	SLG
Manuel Lee	.091	11	1	0	0	0	0	3	4	.286	.091
Cory Snyder	.091	11	1	0	0	0	0	2	5	.231	.091
Kelly Gruber	.154	13	2	0	0	0	0	1	4	.214	.154
Tony Fernandez	.182	11	2	0	0	0	1	0	0	.182	.182
Devon White	.188	16	3	0	0	0	1	0	5	.188	.188

Pitches Worst Vs.	Avg	AB	H	2B	3B	HR	RBI	BB	SO	OBP	SLG
Sammy Sosa	.429	14	6	2	1	1	2	2	5	.500	.929
Ken Griffey Jr	.400	15	6	1	0	2	3	1	3	.438	.867
Tony Phillips	.364	11	4	1	0	1	3	0	1	.364	.727
Ron Karkovice	.364	11	4	1	0	1	5	1	2	.417	.727
Ruben Sierra	.364	11	4	2	0	0	2	3	1	.500	.545

Mickey Weston — Mets

Age 33 – Pitches Right (groundball pitcher)

	ERA	W	L	Sv	G	GS	IP	BB	SO	Avg	H	2B	3B	HR	RBI	OBP	SLG	GF	IR	IRS	Hld	SvOp	SB	CS	GB	FB	G/F
1993 Season	7.94	0	0	0	4	0	5.2	1	2	.393	11	1	0	0	5	.433	.429	0	4	3	0	0	1	0	17	2	8.50
Career (1989-1993)	7.15	1	2	1	23	3	45.1	11	19	.340	65	8	1	8	38	.385	.518	6	15	8	2	1	2	0	86	47	1.83

1993 Season

	ERA	W	L	Sv	G	GS	IP	H	HR	BB	SO
Home	5.06	0	0	0	3	0	5.1	9	0	1	1
Away	54.00	0	0	0	1	0	0.1	2	0	0	1

	Avg	AB	H	2B	3B	HR	RBI	BB	SO	OBP	SLG
vs. Left	.273	11	3	1	0	0	2	1	2	.333	.364
vs. Right	.471	17	8	0	0	0	3	0	0	.500	.471

John Wetteland — Expos

Age 27 – Pitches Right (flyball pitcher)

	ERA	W	L	Sv	G	GS	IP	BB	SO	Avg	H	2B	3B	HR	RBI	OBP	SLG	GF	IR	IRS	Hld	SvOp	SB	CS	GB	FB	G/F
1993 Season	1.37	9	3	43	70	0	85.1	28	113	.188	58	10	4	3	23	.260	.276	58	33	6	0	49	13	2	59	97	0.61
Career (1989-1993)	2.95	21	19	81	196	17	323.1	118	353	.214	252	40	6	23	132	.290	.317	126	93	25	1	97	43	11	302	353	0.86

1993 Season

	ERA	W	L	Sv	G	GS	IP	H	HR	BB	SO
Home	1.44	6	1	22	38	0	43.2	31	1	10	57
Away	1.30	3	2	21	32	0	41.2	27	2	18	56
Day	2.66	3	1	9	19	0	23.2	18	2	8	31
Night	0.88	6	2	34	51	0	61.2	40	1	20	82
Grass	1.48	1	1	12	18	0	24.1	19	1	7	35
Turf	1.33	8	2	31	52	0	61.0	39	2	21	78
April	2.70	0	0	1	3	0	3.1	6	1	2	3
May	2.08	2	0	7	15	0	17.1	11	1	3	21
June	0.51	1	0	8	12	0	17.2	9	0	10	21
July	2.76	4	1	6	13	0	16.1	13	1	4	24
August	1.15	1	2	9	12	0	15.2	15	0	6	22
September/October	0.00	1	0	12	15	0	15.0	4	0	3	22
Starter	0.00	0	0	0	0	0	0.0	0	0	0	0
Reliever	1.37	9	3	43	70	0	85.1	58	3	28	113
0 Days rest	1.33	1	1	12	20	0	20.1	18	1	4	18
1 or 2 Days rest	1.21	7	0	21	34	0	44.2	26	0	17	64
3+ Days rest	1.77	1	2	10	16	0	20.1	14	2	7	31
Pre-All Star	1.40	4	0	20	36	0	45.0	30	2	15	55
Post-All Star	1.34	5	3	23	34	0	40.1	28	1	13	58

	Avg	AB	H	2B	3B	HR	RBI	BB	SO	OBP	SLG
vs. Left	.175	177	31	5	1	3	15	18	69	.254	.266
vs. Right	.206	131	27	5	3	0	8	10	44	.268	.290
Inning 1-6	.000	0	0	0	0	0	0	0	0	.000	.000
Inning 7+	.188	308	58	10	4	3	23	28	113	.260	.276
None on	.212	151	32	3	3	2	2	14	48	.283	.311
Runners on	.166	157	26	7	1	1	21	14	65	.237	.242
Scoring Posn	.146	103	15	5	0	0	16	11	50	.226	.194
Close & Late	.183	268	49	9	3	3	21	24	94	.254	.272
None on/out	.226	62	14	2	3	1	1	8	25	.314	.403
vs. 1st Batr (relief)	.217	60	13	3	2	1	3	8	18	.309	.383
First Inning Pitched	.177	226	40	8	3	2	16	22	87	.253	.265
First 15 Pitches	.193	187	36	8	2	2	11	18	68	.267	.289
Pitch 16-30	.192	104	20	2	2	1	10	8	38	.254	.279
Pitch 31-45	.118	17	2	0	0	0	2	2	7	.211	.118
Pitch 46+	.000	0	0	0	0	0	0	0	0	.000	.000
First Pitch	.308	26	8	1	1	1	4	1	0	.333	.538
Ahead in Count	.134	187	25	4	2	1	10	0	98	.143	.193
Behind in Count	.366	41	15	1	1	1	4	12	0	.500	.512
Two Strikes	.132	197	26	6	1	1	13	15	113	.201	.188

Career (1989-1993)

	ERA	W	L	Sv	G	GS	IP	H	HR	BB	SO
Home	3.04	14	9	44	104	7	154.0	123	11	46	167
Away	2.87	7	10	37	92	10	169.1	129	12	72	186
Day	4.44	6	7	19	62	7	105.1	99	13	40	115
Night	2.23	15	12	62	134	10	218.0	153	10	78	238
Grass	3.06	10	11	20	75	13	158.2	131	11	54	153
Turf	2.84	11	8	61	121	4	164.2	121	12	64	200
April	6.98	1	3	4	17	1	19.1	30	4	7	20
May	4.60	2	2	12	32	3	45.0	41	7	16	54
June	1.97	3	1	13	37	2	64.0	39	1	24	67
July	2.29	7	4	16	34	2	55.0	41	1	17	60
August	2.55	4	6	16	30	4	60.0	47	3	28	65
September/October	2.59	4	3	20	46	5	80.0	54	7	26	87
Starter	5.49	2	9	0	17	17	82.0	79	10	31	74
Reliever	2.09	19	10	81	179	0	241.1	173	13	87	279
0 Days rest	1.74	3	4	25	47	0	62.0	50	3	18	71
1 or 2 Days rest	2.45	13	4	33	81	0	106.1	74	5	45	129
3+ Days rest	1.85	3	2	23	51	0	73.0	49	5	24	79
Pre-All Star	3.35	10	8	37	102	6	153.0	129	12	54	170
Post-All Star	2.59	11	11	44	94	11	170.1	123	11	64	183

	Avg	AB	H	2B	3B	HR	RBI	BB	SO	OBP	SLG
vs. Left	.210	649	136	19	3	12	68	67	201	.288	.304
vs. Right	.219	529	116	21	3	11	64	51	152	.293	.333
Inning 1-6	.234	393	92	18	0	10	59	39	101	.308	.356
Inning 7+	.204	785	160	22	6	13	73	79	252	.281	.297
None on	.214	622	133	15	5	13	13	64	181	.291	.317
Runners on	.214	556	119	25	1	10	119	54	172	.289	.317
Scoring Posn	.229	345	79	18	0	8	108	45	111	.317	.351
Close & Late	.215	558	120	17	5	11	60	57	181	.291	.323
None on/out	.245	274	67	9	5	9	9	30	84	.319	.412
vs. 1st Batr (relief)	.253	158	40	8	3	4	17	18	46	.328	.418
First Inning Pitched	.202	655	132	22	5	11	71	68	204	.280	.301
First 15 Pitches	.214	543	116	19	3	9	48	58	149	.293	.309
Pitch 16-30	.189	334	63	7	3	7	37	26	123	.255	.290
Pitch 31-45	.185	130	24	4	0	0	5	12	42	.259	.215
Pitch 46+	.287	171	49	10	0	7	42	22	39	.369	.468
First Pitch	.317	120	38	3	1	3	11	8	0	.369	.433
Ahead in Count	.149	646	96	13	2	6	46	0	299	.157	.203
Behind in Count	.350	200	70	15	1	10	48	58	0	.494	.585
Two Strikes	.151	688	104	13	3	9	54	51	353	.215	.218

Pitcher vs. Batter (career)

Pitches Best Vs.	Avg	AB	H	2B	3B	HR	RBI	BB	SO	OBP	SLG
Jeff King	.000	13	0	0	0	0	0	1	5	.071	.000
Bobby Bonilla	.083	12	1	0	0	0	1	0	2	.083	.083
Barry Larkin	.091	11	1	1	0	0	2	0	0	.091	.182

Pitches Worst Vs.	Avg	AB	H	2B	3B	HR	RBI	BB	SO	OBP	SLG
Craig Biggio	.455	11	5	0	0	2	6	3	4	.571	1.000
Benito Santiago	.429	14	6	1	0	0	1	1	4	.467	.500
Billy Doran	.400	10	4	0	0	1	5	2	1	.500	.700

Pitches Best Vs.	Avg	AB	H	2B	3B	HR	RBI	BB	SO	OBP	SLG	Pitches Worst Vs.	Avg	AB	H	2B	3B	HR	RBI	BB	SO	OBP	SLG
Pitcher vs. Batter (career)																							
Chris Sabo	.091	11	1	1	0	0	1	0	1	.091	.182	Matt D. Williams	.333	15	5	1	0	1	4	1	4	.375	.600
Mike Pagliarulo	.182	11	2	0	0	0	0	0	2	.182	.182	Kevin Bass	.333	12	4	0	1	0	0	1	1	.385	.500

Lou Whitaker — Tigers

Age 37 – Bats Left (flyball hitter)

	Avg	G	AB	R	H	2B	3B	HR	RBI	BB	SO	HBP	GDP	SB	CS	OBP	SLG	IBB	SH	SF	#Pit	#P/PA	GB	FB	G/F
1993 Season	.290	119	383	72	111	32	1	9	67	78	46	4	5	3	3	.412	.449	4	7	4	1913	4.02	128	131	0.98
Last Five Years	.266	667	2287	395	608	127	6	97	361	412	267	10	34	27	14	.376	.454	28	16	30	10592	3.84	713	838	0.85

1993 Season

	Avg	AB	H	2B	3B	HR	RBI	BB	SO	OBP	SLG		Avg	AB	H	2B	3B	HR	RBI	BB	SO	OBP	SLG
vs. Left	.122	49	6	1	0	0	8	7	10	.254	.143	Scoring Posn	.289	114	33	9	0	5	56	17	12	.375	.500
vs. Right	.314	334	105	31	1	9	59	71	36	.434	.494	Close & Late	.271	59	16	3	0	2	14	8	7	.357	.424
Groundball	.295	78	23	10	1	1	13	19	4	.436	.487	None on/out	.269	52	14	1	0	2	2	10	7	.387	.404
Flyball	.292	96	28	9	0	3	16	11	12	.370	.479	Batting #2	.292	363	106	30	1	9	62	78	44	.419	.455
Home	.269	193	52	18	0	5	35	36	20	.388	.440	Batting #9	.182	11	2	1	0	0	1	0	2	.182	.273
Away	.311	190	59	14	1	4	32	42	26	.435	.458	Other	.333	9	3	1	0	0	4	0	0	.333	.444
Day	.222	135	30	10	0	0	10	28	14	.361	.296	April	.353	51	18	6	0	2	16	12	7	.493	.588
Night	.327	248	81	22	1	9	57	50	32	.439	.532	May	.247	85	21	4	1	1	11	10	11	.320	.353
Grass	.272	320	87	25	0	7	52	66	37	.398	.416	June	.394	71	28	9	0	4	13	17	5	.506	.690
Turf	.381	63	24	7	1	2	15	12	9	.481	.619	July	.226	53	12	3	0	1	8	10	6	.349	.340
First Pitch	.394	33	13	3	0	1	12	2	0	.417	.576	August	.288	59	17	5	0	0	9	20	6	.468	.373
Ahead in Count	.320	122	39	12	1	3	21	44	0	.497	.508	September/October	.234	64	15	5	0	1	10	9	11	.338	.359
Behind in Count	.234	154	36	10	0	2	20	0	35	.242	.338	Pre-All Star	.319	210	67	19	1	7	40	40	24	.428	.519
Two Strikes	.200	160	32	10	0	0	16	32	46	.342	.263	Post-All Star	.254	173	44	13	0	2	27	38	22	.392	.364

1993 By Position

Position	Avg	AB	H	2B	3B	HR	RBI	BB	SO	OBP	SLG	G	GS	Innings	PO	A	E	DP	Fld Pct	Rng Fctr	In Zone	Outs	Zone Rtg	MLB Zone
As Pinch Hitter	.313	16	5	2	0	0	5	0	2	.313	.438	18	0	---	---	---	---	---	---	---	---	---	---	---
As 2b	.289	367	106	30	1	9	62	78	44	.415	.450	110	97	864.0	236	320	11	76	.981	5.79	360	323	.897	.895

Last Five Years

	Avg	AB	H	2B	3B	HR	RBI	BB	SO	OBP	SLG		Avg	AB	H	2B	3B	HR	RBI	BB	SO	OBP	SLG
vs. Left	.211	456	96	18	2	11	58	77	73	.330	.331	Scoring Posn	.292	571	167	32	1	29	256	108	66	.390	.504
vs. Right	.280	1831	512	109	4	86	303	335	194	.387	.484	Close & Late	.229	353	81	14	0	17	63	67	52	.350	.414
Groundball	.279	619	173	42	3	20	101	107	51	.384	.454	None on/out	.259	464	120	22	1	12	12	65	48	.350	.388
Flyball	.264	492	130	31	0	24	74	98	59	.384	.474	Batting #2	.286	1271	363	80	3	52	211	240	129	.398	.476
Home	.275	1112	306	67	2	56	195	223	128	.395	.490	Batting #3	.239	698	167	27	1	36	110	124	91	.352	.436
Away	.257	1175	302	60	4	41	166	189	139	.357	.420	Other	.245	318	78	20	2	9	40	48	47	.341	.406
Day	.261	720	188	45	1	26	101	133	71	.374	.435	April	.257	276	71	12	0	15	47	61	31	.392	.464
Night	.268	1567	420	82	5	71	260	279	196	.377	.463	May	.243	432	105	17	3	18	65	69	61	.346	.421
Grass	.266	1924	511	102	5	85	307	361	220	.380	.456	June	.284	419	119	30	1	19	57	79	45	.393	.496
Turf	.267	363	97	25	1	12	54	51	47	.357	.441	July	.303	356	108	22	2	12	51	52	30	.388	.478
First Pitch	.285	302	86	20	1	13	55	16	0	.313	.487	August	.277	401	111	22	0	22	84	93	51	.409	.496
Ahead in Count	.323	607	196	40	3	37	125	241	0	.512	.582	September/October	.233	403	94	24	0	11	57	58	49	.331	.375
Behind in Count	.220	915	201	42	2	20	105	0	211	.222	.336	Pre-All Star	.267	1241	331	64	6	57	188	230	147	.380	.466
Two Strikes	.216	970	210	40	1	30	114	149	267	.323	.353	Post-All Star	.265	1046	277	63	0	40	173	182	120	.372	.440

Batter vs. Pitcher (since 1984)

Hits Best Against	Avg	AB	H	2B	3B	HR	RBI	BB	SO	OBP	SLG	Hits Worst Against	Avg	AB	H	2B	3B	HR	RBI	BB	SO	OBP	SLG
Jeff Montgomery	.600	10	6	1	0	1	3	2	0	.667	1.000	Russ Swan	.000	12	0	0	0	0	1	2	1	.143	.000
Dave Righetti	.583	12	7	1	0	1	3	4	1	.688	.917	Rick Aguilera	.000	11	0	0	0	0	0	1	2	.083	.000
Dave Johnson	.529	17	9	0	0	2	4	0	2	.529	.882	Alan Mills	.000	9	0	0	0	0	1	2	1	.182	.000
Scott Kamieniecki	.500	12	6	2	0	1	3	1	1	.538	.917	Jeff Ballard	.063	16	1	0	0	0	1	0	5	.063	.063
John Farrell	.438	16	7	1	0	3	6	1	1	.471	1.063	Tom Henke	.074	27	2	0	0	0	0	1	6	.107	.074

Derrick White — Expos

Age 24 – Bats Right (groundball hitter)

	Avg	G	AB	R	H	2B	3B	HR	RBI	BB	SO	HBP	GDP	SB	CS	OBP	SLG	IBB	SH	SF	#Pit	#P/PA	GB	FB	G/F
1993 Season	.224	17	49	6	11	3	0	2	4	2	12	1	1	2	0	.269	.408	1	0	0	174	3.35	20	13	1.54

1993 Season

	Avg	AB	H	2B	3B	HR	RBI	BB	SO	OBP	SLG		Avg	AB	H	2B	3B	HR	RBI	BB	SO	OBP	SLG
vs. Left	.348	23	8	2	0	2	3	1	6	.400	.696	Scoring Posn	.063	16	1	0	0	0	1	2	6	.167	.063
vs. Right	.115	26	3	1	0	0	1	1	6	.148	.154	Close & Late	.200	10	2	0	0	1	1	0	2	.200	.500

Devon White — Blue Jays

Age 31 – Bats Both

	Avg	G	AB	R	H	2B	3B	HR	RBI	BB	SO	HBP	GDP	SB	CS	OBP	SLG	IBB	SH	SF	#Pit	#P/PA	GB	FB	G/F
1993 Season	.273	146	598	116	163	42	6	15	52	57	127	7	3	34	4	.341	.438	1	3	3	2530	3.79	208	144	1.44
Last Five Years	.255	736	2960	467	755	143	39	72	272	234	640	24	35	169	40	.313	.403	10	25	17	12428	3.81	1069	724	1.48

1993 Season

	Avg	AB	H	2B	3B	HR	RBI	BB	SO	OBP	SLG		Avg	AB	H	2B	3B	HR	RBI	BB	SO	OBP	SLG
vs. Left	.254	185	47	15	1	3	16	15	37	.324	.395	Scoring Posn	.256	117	30	8	1	3	37	16	27	.353	.419
vs. Right	.281	413	116	27	5	12	36	42	90	.349	.458	Close & Late	.247	73	18	4	2	1	8	11	20	.360	.397
Groundball	.305	82	25	7	0	4	9	7	20	.367	.537	None on/out	.308	211	65	15	2	11	11	13	38	.357	.555
Flyball	.256	90	23	2	2	2	6	8	16	.320	.389	Batting #1	.276	434	120	30	4	13	38	38	87	.343	.454
Home	.290	307	89	24	5	10	31	30	62	.361	.498	Batting #2	.262	164	43	12	2	2	14	18	40	.333	.396

1993 Season	Avg	AB	H	2B	3B	HR	RBI	BB	SO	OBP	SLG		Avg	AB	H	2B	3B	HR	RBI	BB	SO	OBP	SLG
Away	.254	291	74	18	1	5	21	27	65	.321	.375	Other	.000	0	0	0	0	0	0	1	0	1.000	.000
Day	.342	202	69	15	3	11	24	20	41	.406	.609	April	.385	52	20	1	1	1	4	5	11	.439	.500
Night	.237	396	94	27	3	4	28	37	86	.308	.351	May	.290	124	36	13	0	5	13	7	26	.333	.516
Grass	.250	236	59	13	1	4	17	18	51	.304	.364	June	.265	117	31	10	2	4	9	12	25	.333	.487
Turf	.287	362	104	29	5	11	35	39	76	.365	.486	July	.183	93	17	3	1	1	7	10	19	.296	.269
First Pitch	.390	77	30	7	1	5	9	0	0	.405	.701	August	.279	122	34	10	2	3	9	11	24	.341	.467
Ahead in Count	.343	102	35	13	3	4	18	41	0	.527	.647	September/October	.278	90	25	5	0	1	10	12	22	.356	.367
Behind in Count	.207	300	62	15	0	6	20	0	111	.216	.317	Pre-All Star	.289	325	94	26	3	11	28	29	66	.355	.489
Two Strikes	.200	310	62	15	0	4	19	16	127	.239	.287	Post-All Star	.253	273	69	16	3	4	24	28	61	.326	.377

1993 By Position

Position	Avg	AB	H	2B	3B	HR	RBI	BB	SO	OBP	SLG	G	GS	Innings	PO	A	E	DP	Fld Pct	Rng Fctr	In Zone	Outs	Zone Rtg	MLB Zone
As cf	.273	598	163	42	6	15	52	56	127	.340	.438	145	144	1265.2	399	6	3	2	.993	2.88	444	383	.863	.829

Last Five Years

	Avg	AB	H	2B	3B	HR	RBI	BB	SO	OBP	SLG		Avg	AB	H	2B	3B	HR	RBI	BB	SO	OBP	SLG
vs. Left	.254	907	230	49	7	21	82	69	174	.311	.393	Scoring Posn	.216	629	136	27	6	10	186	72	155	.295	.326
vs. Right	.256	2053	525	94	32	51	190	165	466	.314	.407	Close & Late	.239	443	106	15	5	7	39	53	117	.325	.343
Groundball	.258	732	189	40	6	16	68	48	160	.307	.395	None on/out	.289	984	284	52	13	35	35	55	196	.332	.475
Flyball	.242	637	154	30	11	15	59	48	130	.298	.394	Batting #1	.260	1917	499	102	22	49	163	148	403	.318	.413
Home	.265	1475	391	81	26	40	144	116	309	.323	.437	Batting #3	.248	513	127	18	10	11	49	30	114	.292	.386
Away	.245	1485	364	62	13	32	128	118	331	.304	.369	Other	.243	530	129	23	7	12	60	56	123	.317	.381
Day	.290	837	243	50	12	21	72	61	190	.344	.454	April	.281	384	108	23	5	7	43	26	85	.334	.422
Night	.241	2123	512	93	27	51	200	173	450	.301	.382	May	.259	544	141	33	8	15	57	48	104	.323	.432
Grass	.240	1638	393	62	17	39	139	119	362	.293	.370	June	.257	518	133	26	8	15	42	39	116	.311	.425
Turf	.274	1322	362	81	22	33	133	115	278	.338	.443	July	.235	460	108	15	6	6	38	37	99	.298	.333
First Pitch	.323	350	113	27	6	14	49	1	0	.330	.554	August	.250	544	136	24	9	21	51	43	113	.307	.443
Ahead in Count	.349	576	201	45	12	33	93	129	0	.463	.641	September/October	.253	510	129	22	3	8	41	41	123	.310	.355
Behind in Count	.195	1458	285	48	8	16	77	0	540	.205	.272	Pre-All Star	.261	1604	418	90	24	41	162	126	340	.319	.423
Two Strikes	.180	1543	277	44	14	13	83	98	640	.232	.251	Post-All Star	.249	1356	337	53	15	31	110	108	300	.306	.378

Batter vs. Pitcher (career)

Hits Best Against	Avg	AB	H	2B	3B	HR	RBI	BB	SO	OBP	SLG	Hits Worst Against	Avg	AB	H	2B	3B	HR	RBI	BB	SO	OBP	SLG
John Dopson	.538	13	7	0	0	2	4	0	1	.538	1.000	Paul Gibson	.077	13	1	1	0	0	1	1	4	.143	.154
Jeff Johnson	.455	11	5	1	0	1	3	1	2	.462	.818	Bret Saberhagen	.114	35	4	2	0	0	0	0	9	.114	.171
Shawn Hillegas	.429	14	6	2	1	0	2	2	0	.500	.714	Kevin Brown	.115	26	3	1	0	0	2	2	5	.179	.154
Edwin Nunez	.400	15	6	1	0	2	5	3	5	.500	.867	Fernando Valenzuela	.143	14	2	1	0	0	1	0	2	.133	.214
Rick Sutcliffe	.313	16	5	2	0	2	2	2	2	.389	.813	Chuck Crim	.143	14	2	1	0	0	1	0	4	.143	.214

Rondell White — Expos

Age 22 – Bats Right (groundball hitter)

	Avg	G	AB	R	H	2B	3B	HR	RBI	BB	SO	HBP	GDP	SB	CS	OBP	SLG	IBB	SH	SF	#Pit	#P/PA	GB	FB	G/F
1993 Season	.260	23	73	9	19	3	1	2	15	7	16	0	2	1	2	.321	.411	0	2	1	312	3.76	33	17	1.94

1993 Season

	Avg	AB	H	2B	3B	HR	RBI	BB	SO	OBP	SLG		Avg	AB	H	2B	3B	HR	RBI	BB	SO	OBP	SLG
vs. Left	.296	27	8	1	0	2	8	2	6	.345	.556	Scoring Posn	.333	27	9	2	0	0	11	3	4	.387	.407
vs. Right	.239	46	11	2	1	0	7	5	10	.308	.326	Close & Late	.167	6	1	0	1	0	2	3	1	.444	.500

Wally Whitehurst — Padres

Age 30 – Pitches Right (groundball pitcher)

	ERA	W	L	Sv	G	GS	IP	BB	SO	Avg	H	2B	3B	HR	RBI	OBP	SLG	CG	ShO	Sup	QS	#P/S	SB	CS	GB	FB	G/F
1993 Season	3.83	4	7	0	21	19	105.2	30	57	.276	109	20	3	11	44	.326	.425	0	0	3.24	7	84	3	7	142	103	1.38
Career (1989-1993)	3.83	15	29	3	148	51	415.2	102	269	.269	430	79	13	34	189	.315	.399	0	0	3.92	15	79	26	21	677	352	1.92

1993 Season

	ERA	W	L	Sv	G	GS	IP	H	HR	BB	SO		Avg	AB	H	2B	3B	HR	RBI	BB	SO	OBP	SLG
Home	4.11	1	5	0	10	9	46.0	49	8	12	25	vs. Left	.278	187	52	8	2	6	23	22	23	.347	.439
Away	3.62	3	2	0	11	10	59.2	60	3	18	32	vs. Right	.274	208	57	12	1	5	21	8	34	.305	.413
Starter	3.86	4	7	0	19	19	102.2	107	11	28	57	Scoring Posn	.272	81	22	5	0	2	31	15	11	.368	.407
Reliever	3.00	0	0	0	2	0	3.0	2	0	2	0	Close & Late	.176	17	3	0	1	0	1	2	1	.250	.294
0-3 Days Rest	0.00	0	0	0	0	0	0.0	0	0	0	0	None on/out	.294	109	32	7	1	5	5	5	17	.330	.514
4 Days Rest	4.03	3	6	0	15	15	82.2	82	8	26	45	First Pitch	.300	60	18	3	0	4	14	4	0	.324	.550
5+ Days Rest	3.15	1	1	0	4	4	20.0	25	3	2	12	Ahead in Count	.229	157	36	5	1	3	9	0	50	.238	.331
Pre-All Star	3.28	3	5	0	13	13	74.0	73	4	24	40	Behind in Count	.299	97	29	7	2	1	13	16	0	.388	.443
Post-All Star	5.12	1	2	0	8	6	31.2	36	7	6	17	Two Strikes	.228	167	38	6	1	6	13	10	57	.274	.383

Career (1989-1993)

	ERA	W	L	Sv	G	GS	IP	H	HR	BB	SO		Avg	AB	H	2B	3B	HR	RBI	BB	SO	OBP	SLG
Home	3.58	7	16	1	73	23	196.0	193	16	47	129	vs. Left	.271	812	220	43	7	17	90	64	143	.324	.404
Away	4.06	8	13	2	75	28	219.2	237	18	55	140	vs. Right	.268	785	210	36	6	17	99	38	126	.305	.394
Day	4.75	2	11	1	51	16	121.1	147	17	30	77	Inning 1-6	.275	1188	327	64	12	26	137	75	196	.319	.415
Night	3.46	13	18	2	97	35	294.1	283	17	72	192	Inning 7+	.252	409	103	15	1	8	52	27	73	.303	.352
Grass	3.93	11	22	3	103	39	304.1	315	28	76	205	None on	.265	932	247	44	8	17	17	46	156	.303	.384
Turf	3.56	4	7	0	45	12	111.1	115	6	26	64	Runners on	.275	665	183	35	5	17	172	56	113	.330	.420
April	3.47	1	3	0	17	3	36.1	34	2	5	15	Scoring Posn	.271	391	106	16	4	8	142	46	78	.344	.394
May	3.42	2	4	2	28	8	73.2	73	3	20	62	Close & Late	.276	185	51	9	1	2	24	12	24	.327	.368
June	2.73	4	5	0	25	12	89.0	87	9	28	54	None on/out	.277	411	114	23	5	11	11	18	51	.311	.438
July	4.61	3	7	0	23	13	95.2	96	11	18	51	vs. 1st Batr (relief)	.261	88	23	4	0	1	14	7	9	.320	.341

Career (1989-1993)

	ERA	W	L	Sv	G	GS	IP	H	HR	BB	SO
August	4.53	2	5	0	20	9	55.2	68	3	13	34
September/October	4.27	3	5	1	35	6	65.1	72	6	18	53
Starter	4.24	10	24	0	51	51	263.1	293	23	62	160
Reliever	3.13	5	5	3	97	0	152.1	137	11	40	109
0-3 Days Rest	5.09	0	4	0	8	8	35.1	46	2	10	25
4 Days Rest	4.50	5	14	0	28	28	152.0	164	13	42	91
5+ Days Rest	3.32	5	6	0	15	15	76.0	83	8	10	44
Pre-All Star	3.07	10	13	2	75	27	231.1	221	15	58	151
Post-All Star	4.78	5	16	1	73	24	184.1	209	19	44	118

	Avg	AB	H	2B	3B	HR	RBI	BB	SO	OBP	SLG
First Inning Pitched	.259	536	139	23	4	8	67	36	95	.310	.362
First 75 Pitches	.269	1466	395	66	11	31	164	89	255	.313	.393
Pitch 76-90	.258	93	24	11	1	2	19	9	10	.327	.462
Pitch 91-105	.306	36	11	2	1	1	6	4	4	.357	.500
Pitch 106+	.000	2	0	0	0	0	0	0	0	.000	.000
First Pitch	.310	271	84	17	1	8	49	12	0	.336	.469
Ahead in Count	.193	658	127	23	1	10	45	0	230	.200	.277
Behind in Count	.361	382	138	27	10	8	60	59	0	.444	.547
Two Strikes	.190	695	132	22	2	14	57	31	269	.228	.288

Pitcher vs. Batter (career)

Pitches Best Vs.	Avg	AB	H	2B	3B	HR	RBI	BB	SO	OBP	SLG
Bip Roberts	.000	12	0	0	0	0	1	0	3	.000	.000
Larry Walker	.000	12	0	0	0	0	0	0	5	.000	.000
Steve Buechele	.100	10	1	0	0	0	1	2	2	.250	.100
Robby Thompson	.100	10	1	0	0	0	0	1	2	.182	.100
Andres Galarraga	.133	15	2	0	0	0	0	0	2	.133	.133

Pitches Worst Vs.	Avg	AB	H	2B	3B	HR	RBI	BB	SO	OBP	SLG
John Kruk	.500	12	6	1	0	1	3	0	1	.500	.833
Mark Lemke	.500	10	5	0	2	0	0	1	0	.545	.900
Ryne Sandberg	.423	26	11	2	2	2	5	2	3	.464	.885
Andre Dawson	.400	15	6	1	0	2	6	1	1	.412	.867
Rick Wilkins	.385	13	5	1	0	2	4	2	2	.467	.923

Mark Whiten — Cardinals

Age 27 – Bats Both (groundball hitter)

	Avg	G	AB	R	H	2B	3B	HR	RBI	BB	SO	HBP	GDP	SB	CS	OBP	SLG	IBB	SH	SF	#Pit	#P/PA	GB	FB	G/F
1993 Season	.253	152	562	81	142	13	4	25	99	58	110	2	11	15	8	.323	.423	9	0	4	2155	3.44	250	136	1.84
Career (1990-1993)	.252	449	1565	212	394	51	16	45	194	167	311	7	37	37	23	.324	.391	21	3	13	6263	3.57	626	383	1.63

1993 Season

	Avg	AB	H	2B	3B	HR	RBI	BB	SO	OBP	SLG
vs. Left	.231	160	37	2	0	8	26	15	22	.296	.394
vs. Right	.261	402	105	11	4	17	73	43	88	.333	.435
Groundball	.268	190	51	6	0	5	35	10	39	.307	.379
Flyball	.212	104	22	3	2	3	10	14	24	.303	.365
Home	.237	262	62	6	0	12	52	24	54	.302	.397
Away	.267	300	80	7	4	13	47	34	56	.340	.447
Day	.266	169	45	6	0	6	32	21	31	.342	.408
Night	.247	393	97	7	4	19	67	37	79	.314	.430
Grass	.254	193	49	6	2	6	25	26	42	.342	.399
Turf	.252	369	93	7	2	19	74	32	68	.312	.436
First Pitch	.314	118	37	3	0	8	26	6	0	.344	.542
Ahead in Count	.328	128	42	2	2	9	33	27	0	.442	.586
Behind in Count	.199	216	43	3	0	5	23	0	79	.205	.282
Two Strikes	.178	230	41	6	1	4	23	25	110	.264	.265

	Avg	AB	H	2B	3B	HR	RBI	BB	SO	OBP	SLG
Scoring Posn	.266	169	45	5	1	8	74	24	36	.357	.450
Close & Late	.204	98	20	2	0	3	14	14	24	.298	.316
None on/out	.239	142	34	5	1	3	3	11	28	.294	.352
Batting #5	.251	323	81	8	3	12	47	36	67	.325	.406
Batting #6	.267	180	48	2	1	11	40	14	27	.322	.472
Other	.220	59	13	3	0	2	12	8	16	.313	.373
April	.253	87	22	1	1	5	12	10	20	.330	.460
May	.242	99	24	2	0	1	16	8	17	.299	.293
June	.238	101	24	2	1	4	15	10	23	.313	.396
July	.323	65	21	2	2	6	19	11	11	.410	.692
August	.207	92	19	2	0	2	10	6	17	.250	.293
September/October	.271	118	32	4	0	7	27	13	22	.348	.483
Pre-All Star	.247	299	74	5	3	11	47	29	64	.316	.395
Post-All Star	.259	263	68	8	1	14	52	29	46	.330	.456

1993 By Position

Position	Avg	AB	H	2B	3B	HR	RBI	BB	SO	OBP	SLG	G	GS	Innings	PO	A	E	DP	Fld Pct	Rng Fctr	In Zone	Outs	Zone Rtg	MLB Zone
As cf	.371	70	26	3	0	8	26	5	10	.413	.757	22	18	149.2	52	1	1	0	.981	3.19	57	49	.860	.829
As rf	.235	486	114	10	4	17	70	53	99	.310	.377	138	128	1149.2	277	8	9	1	.969	2.23	317	264	.833	.826

Career (1990-1993)

	Avg	AB	H	2B	3B	HR	RBI	BB	SO	OBP	SLG
vs. Left	.260	434	113	17	3	14	48	50	78	.337	.410
vs. Right	.248	1131	281	34	13	31	146	117	233	.319	.384
Groundball	.239	477	114	17	5	10	61	38	105	.296	.358
Flyball	.259	324	84	8	3	12	43	50	54	.360	.414
Home	.251	748	188	26	8	23	96	74	155	.321	.400
Away	.252	817	206	25	8	22	98	93	156	.327	.383
Day	.255	458	117	18	3	9	54	50	96	.326	.367
Night	.250	1107	277	33	13	36	140	117	215	.323	.401
Grass	.257	947	243	36	10	21	97	111	186	.334	.382
Turf	.244	618	151	15	6	24	97	56	125	.308	.405
First Pitch	.307	283	87	8	0	12	38	16	0	.343	.463
Ahead in Count	.321	380	122	11	6	14	63	74	0	.429	.492
Behind in Count	.195	630	123	20	4	14	63	0	241	.202	.306
Two Strikes	.172	675	116	22	5	10	54	79	311	.262	.264

	Avg	AB	H	2B	3B	HR	RBI	BB	SO	OBP	SLG
Scoring Posn	.238	395	94	13	2	11	142	66	88	.340	.365
Close & Late	.219	283	62	8	1	8	33	39	60	.313	.339
None on/out	.261	403	105	16	4	10	10	29	78	.315	.395
Batting #5	.244	614	150	26	7	15	68	69	135	.321	.383
Batting #6	.268	489	131	11	6	17	70	42	85	.329	.419
Other	.245	462	113	14	3	13	56	56	91	.324	.372
April	.276	228	63	3	3	9	38	21	54	.333	.434
May	.251	255	64	11	3	3	28	30	55	.332	.353
June	.217	198	43	6	2	5	19	22	45	.299	.343
July	.260	304	79	12	5	12	42	30	52	.330	.451
August	.244	308	75	14	2	8	32	32	56	.311	.380
September/October	.257	272	70	5	1	8	35	32	49	.336	.371
Pre-All Star	.257	756	194	24	9	22	101	80	165	.328	.399
Post-All Star	.247	809	200	27	7	23	93	87	146	.320	.383

Batter vs. Pitcher (career)

Hits Best Against	Avg	AB	H	2B	3B	HR	RBI	BB	SO	OBP	SLG
Chuck Finley	.500	16	8	3	1	0	1	2	3	.556	.813
Todd Stottlemyre	.400	10	4	2	0	0	1	1	0	.455	.600
Jack McDowell	.381	21	8	2	1	0	1	3	2	.458	.571
Kevin Brown	.333	18	6	1	0	2	6	4	4	.455	.722
Chris Bosio	.333	9	3	0	0	1	3	1	2	.364	.667

Hits Worst Against	Avg	AB	H	2B	3B	HR	RBI	BB	SO	OBP	SLG
Matt Young	.077	13	1	1	0	0	1	2	3	.200	.154
Nolan Ryan	.100	10	1	0	0	0	1	1	2	.167	.100
Mike Moore	.143	14	2	0	0	0	0	0	3	.143	.143
Jaime Navarro	.143	14	2	0	0	0	2	0	3	.143	.143
Bob Welch	.154	13	2	0	0	0	0	0	3	.154	.154

Matt Whiteside — Rangers

Age 26 – Pitches Right

	ERA	W	L	Sv	G	GS	IP	BB	SO	Avg	H	2B	3B	HR	RBI	OBP	SLG	GF	IR	IRS	Hld	SvOp	SB	CS	GB	FB	G/F
1993 Season	4.32	2	1	1	60	0	73.0	23	39	.281	78	10	1	7	33	.337	.399	10	59	15	14	5	4	6	116	75	1.55
Career (1992-1993)	3.65	3	2	5	80	0	101.0	34	52	.271	104	16	1	8	43	.330	.380	18	77	17	14	9	5	6	156	110	1.42

1993 Season

	ERA	W	L	Sv	G	GS	IP	H	HR	BB	SO
Home	3.23	1	1	0	28	0	39.0	35	4	11	19
Away	5.56	1	0	1	32	0	34.0	43	3	12	20
Day	5.40	1	0	0	15	0	15.0	25	0	7	5
Night	4.03	1	1	1	45	0	58.0	53	7	16	34
Grass	3.45	2	1	1	49	0	62.2	63	7	19	32
Turf	9.58	0	0	0	11	0	10.1	15	0	4	7
April	2.53	0	0	0	8	0	10.2	9	0	2	7
May	2.30	1	0	0	13	0	15.2	16	0	2	8
June	4.58	1	1	0	13	0	19.2	20	4	7	10
July	5.40	0	0	1	10	0	8.1	13	1	3	3
August	2.08	0	0	0	4	0	4.1	5	0	1	2
September/October	7.53	0	0	0	12	0	14.1	15	2	8	9
Starter	0.00	0	0	0	0	0	0.0	0	0	0	0
Reliever	4.32	2	1	1	60	0	73.0	78	7	23	39
0 Days rest	4.20	1	0	1	14	0	15.0	19	2	6	5
1 or 2 Days rest	3.20	0	1	0	31	0	39.1	37	4	7	23
3+ Days rest	6.75	1	0	0	15	0	18.2	22	1	10	11
Pre-All Star	3.60	2	1	1	40	0	50.0	53	5	13	26
Post-All Star	5.87	0	0	0	20	0	23.0	25	2	10	13

	Avg	AB	H	2B	3B	HR	RBI	BB	SO	OBP	SLG
vs. Left	.298	84	25	5	0	0	6	7	9	.355	.357
vs. Right	.273	194	53	5	1	7	27	16	30	.329	.418
Inning 1-6	.217	60	13	3	0	1	8	6	10	.299	.317
Inning 7+	.298	218	65	7	1	6	25	17	29	.347	.422
None on	.297	148	44	4	0	5	5	8	20	.338	.426
Runners on	.262	130	34	6	1	2	28	15	19	.336	.369
Scoring Posn	.225	80	18	4	1	1	26	13	14	.330	.338
Close & Late	.263	114	30	3	1	3	12	5	16	.294	.386
None on/out	.309	68	21	2	0	2	2	4	7	.347	.426
vs. 1st Batr (relief)	.185	54	10	1	0	1	8	5	10	.254	.259
First Inning Pitched	.253	194	49	7	1	3	26	17	27	.313	.345
First 15 Pitches	.265	185	49	6	1	4	25	17	23	.327	.373
Pitch 16-30	.282	78	22	4	0	3	8	5	15	.329	.449
Pitch 31-45	.467	15	7	0	0	0	0	1	1	.500	.467
Pitch 46+	.000	0	0	0	0	0	0	0	0	.000	.000
First Pitch	.405	42	17	0	0	4	7	5	0	.468	.690
Ahead in Count	.259	135	35	5	0	3	14	0	31	.265	.363
Behind in Count	.294	51	15	2	1	0	5	9	0	.400	.373
Two Strikes	.242	132	32	5	0	3	14	9	39	.296	.348

Darrell Whitmore — Marlins

Age 25 – Bats Left

	Avg	G	AB	R	H	2B	3B	HR	RBI	BB	SO	HBP	GDP	SB	CS	OBP	SLG	IBB	SH	SF	#Pit	#P/PA	GB	FB	G/F
1993 Season	.204	76	250	24	51	8	2	4	19	10	72	5	8	4	2	.249	.300	0	2	0	958	3.59	85	59	1.44

1993 Season

	Avg	AB	H	2B	3B	HR	RBI	BB	SO	OBP	SLG
vs. Left	.128	39	5	3	0	0	2	1	16	.209	.205
vs. Right	.218	211	46	5	2	4	17	9	56	.257	.318
Home	.227	132	30	2	1	3	13	5	42	.271	.326
Away	.178	118	21	6	1	1	6	5	30	.224	.271
First Pitch	.238	42	10	3	0	1	4	0	0	.256	.381
Ahead in Count	.321	53	17	2	0	1	6	4	0	.368	.415
Behind in Count	.127	118	15	2	2	1	7	0	60	.156	.203
Two Strikes	.120	125	15	1	2	1	7	6	72	.173	.184

	Avg	AB	H	2B	3B	HR	RBI	BB	SO	OBP	SLG
Scoring Posn	.161	56	9	1	0	0	12	1	18	.203	.179
Close & Late	.262	42	11	3	0	0	5	4	10	.340	.333
None on/out	.177	62	11	3	0	2	2	2	24	.215	.323
Batting #6	.135	52	7	1	1	0	4	1	17	.167	.192
Batting #7	.225	120	27	5	0	2	6	7	38	.290	.317
Other	.218	78	17	2	1	2	9	2	17	.238	.346
Pre-All Star	.207	58	12	3	2	0	3	2	21	.246	.328
Post-All Star	.203	192	39	5	0	4	16	8	51	.250	.292

Kevin Wickander — Reds

Age 29 – Pitches Left (flyball pitcher)

	ERA	W	L	Sv	G	GS	IP	BB	SO	Avg	H	2B	3B	HR	RBI	OBP	SLG	GF	IR	IRS	Hld	SvOp	SB	CS	GB	FB	G/F
1993 Season	6.09	1	0	0	44	0	34.0	22	23	.324	47	6	2	8	33	.420	.559	9	46	15	2	1	3	1	40	49	0.82
Career (1989-1993)	4.30	3	1	1	100	0	90.0	56	71	.299	106	14	4	9	54	.401	.438	22	99	30	10	5	6	2	96	109	0.88

1993 Season

	ERA	W	L	Sv	G	GS	IP	H	HR	BB	SO
Home	8.10	0	0	0	23	0	20.0	32	5	15	13
Away	3.21	1	0	0	21	0	14.0	15	3	7	10
Starter	0.00	0	0	0	0	0	0.0	0	0	0	0
Reliever	6.09	1	0	0	44	0	34.0	47	8	22	23
0 Days rest	3.86	0	0	0	9	0	4.2	4	1	3	3
1 or 2 Days rest	7.62	0	0	0	18	0	13.0	22	3	9	10
3+ Days rest	5.51	1	0	0	17	0	16.1	21	4	10	10
Pre-All Star	3.93	1	0	0	21	0	18.1	22	4	7	9
Post-All Star	8.62	0	0	0	23	0	15.2	25	4	15	14

	Avg	AB	H	2B	3B	HR	RBI	BB	SO	OBP	SLG
vs. Left	.263	57	15	1	0	2	11	13	13	.408	.386
vs. Right	.364	88	32	5	2	6	22	9	10	.429	.670
Scoring Posn	.283	53	15	0	1	3	25	9	14	.397	.491
Close & Late	.421	19	8	1	0	0	5	2	5	.476	.474
None on/out	.207	29	6	1	0	2	2	2	2	.281	.448
First Pitch	.296	27	8	2	0	0	0	0	0	.321	.370
Ahead in Count	.246	69	17	2	0	2	11	0	22	.257	.362
Behind in Count	.440	25	11	0	0	5	9	12	0	.622	1.040
Two Strikes	.265	68	18	2	1	1	14	10	23	.367	.368

Bob Wickman — Yankees

Age 25 – Pitches Right (groundball pitcher)

	ERA	W	L	Sv	G	GS	IP	BB	SO	Avg	H	2B	3B	HR	RBI	OBP	SLG	GF	IR	IRS	Hld	SvOp	SB	CS	GB	FB	G/F
1993 Season	4.63	14	4	4	41	19	140.0	69	70	.284	156	31	4	13	76	.368	.425	9	24	6	2	8	20	9	261	121	2.16
Career (1992-1993)	4.49	20	5	4	49	27	190.1	89	91	.281	207	40	7	15	99	.362	.415	9	24	6	2	8	28	10	359	158	2.27

1993 Season

	ERA	W	L	Sv	G	GS	IP	H	HR	BB	SO
Home	2.75	9	0	1	21	8	68.2	56	3	29	38
Away	6.43	5	4	3	20	11	71.1	100	10	40	32
Starter	4.78	8	4	0	19	19	111.0	130	12	54	49
Reliever	4.03	6	0	4	22	0	29.0	26	1	15	21
0 Days rest	0.00	1	0	2	3	0	3.0	1	0	1	3
1 or 2 Days rest	6.94	1	0	1	11	0	11.2	13	0	10	8
3+ Days rest	2.51	4	0	1	8	0	14.1	12	1	4	10
Pre-All Star	4.63	8	3	0	16	16	95.1	107	9	50	39
Post-All Star	4.63	6	1	4	25	3	44.2	49	4	19	31

	Avg	AB	H	2B	3B	HR	RBI	BB	SO	OBP	SLG
vs. Left	.283	247	70	19	0	6	34	37	30	.379	.433
vs. Right	.284	303	86	12	4	7	42	32	40	.359	.419
Scoring Posn	.270	152	41	10	3	5	66	26	25	.385	.474
Close & Late	.344	61	21	3	1	2	12	3	7	.394	.525
None on/out	.291	141	41	9	0	4	4	10	13	.338	.440
First Pitch	.265	98	26	6	0	2	9	4	0	.294	.388
Ahead in Count	.238	206	49	13	0	3	27	0	57	.248	.345
Behind in Count	.315	149	47	7	2	3	24	36	0	.452	.450
Two Strikes	.266	203	54	13	2	4	31	29	70	.359	.409

Curt Wilkerson — Royals

Age 33 – Bats Both (groundball hitter)

	Avg	G	AB	R	H	2B	3B	HR	RBI	BB	SO	HBP	GDP	SB	CS	OBP	SLG	IBB	SH	SF	#Pit	#P/PA	GB	FB	G/F
1993 Season	.143	12	28	1	4	0	0	0	0	1	6	0	1	2	0	.172	.143	0	0	0	106	3.66	14	4	3.50
Last Five Years	.225	362	861	87	194	28	5	5	73	49	162	1	14	28	12	.265	.287	5	11	9	2993	3.21	347	205	1.69

1993 Season

	Avg	AB	H	2B	3B	HR	RBI	BB	SO	OBP	SLG		Avg	AB	H	2B	3B	HR	RBI	BB	SO	OBP	SLG
vs. Left	.000	7	0	0	0	0	0	0	1	.000	.000	Scoring Posn	.125	8	1	0	0	0	0	0	1	.125	.125
vs. Right	.190	21	4	0	0	0	0	1	5	.227	.190	Close & Late	.000	7	0	0	0	0	0	0	1	.000	.000

Last Five Years

	Avg	AB	H	2B	3B	HR	RBI	BB	SO	OBP	SLG		Avg	AB	H	2B	3B	HR	RBI	BB	SO	OBP	SLG
vs. Left	.233	223	52	8	1	2	22	16	35	.282	.305	Scoring Posn	.189	222	42	5	3	2	70	17	41	.241	.266
vs. Right	.223	638	142	20	4	3	51	33	127	.259	.281	Close & Late	.239	176	42	7	0	2	19	10	36	.282	.313
Groundball	.217	281	61	6	0	0	20	16	40	.259	.238	None on/out	.243	210	51	10	1	3	3	7	37	.267	.343
Flyball	.237	224	53	8	2	3	30	16	48	.286	.330	Batting #8	.232	224	52	7	1	1	26	14	49	.272	.286
Home	.255	428	109	16	4	5	44	28	71	.301	.346	Batting #9	.233	189	44	4	2	2	14	9	36	.265	.307
Away	.196	433	85	12	1	0	29	21	91	.230	.229	Other	.219	448	98	17	2	2	33	26	77	.262	.279
Day	.226	371	84	14	3	1	25	16	76	.256	.288	April	.200	105	21	4	1	1	6	5	22	.232	.286
Night	.224	490	110	14	2	4	48	33	86	.272	.286	May	.241	191	46	7	1	1	18	7	33	.265	.304
Grass	.252	412	104	16	2	1	32	18	80	.280	.308	June	.213	174	37	4	2	0	11	10	31	.255	.259
Turf	.200	449	90	12	3	4	41	31	82	.252	.267	July	.250	132	33	3	0	1	14	7	23	.282	.295
First Pitch	.292	185	54	10	0	1	21	3	0	.298	.362	August	.239	113	27	4	1	0	12	10	27	.298	.292
Ahead in Count	.284	176	50	7	3	1	17	27	0	.379	.375	September/October	.205	146	30	6	0	2	12	10	26	.259	.288
Behind in Count	.171	386	66	10	1	2	24	0	153	.169	.218	Pre-All Star	.221	521	115	15	4	3	39	25	98	.255	.282
Two Strikes	.129	349	45	4	1	2	13	18	162	.171	.163	Post-All Star	.232	340	79	13	1	2	34	24	64	.281	.294

Batter vs. Pitcher (since 1984)

Hits Best Against	Avg	AB	H	2B	3B	HR	RBI	BB	SO	OBP	SLG	Hits Worst Against	Avg	AB	H	2B	3B	HR	RBI	BB	SO	OBP	SLG
Jack McDowell	.500	8	4	0	0	0	0	3	0	.636	.500	Doug Drabek	.000	11	0	0	0	0	0	0	4	.000	.000
Bill Krueger	.462	13	6	1	0	0	1	3	1	.563	.538	Danny Darwin	.000	10	0	0	0	0	1	1	1	.083	.000
Ron Darling	.455	11	5	1	0	0	0	0	3	.455	.545	Dennis Martinez	.059	17	1	0	0	0	0	0	7	.059	.059
Kirk McCaskill	.391	23	9	2	1	0	1	2	3	.440	.565	Matt Young	.071	14	1	0	0	0	2	0	2	.071	.071
Mike Moore	.357	28	10	2	0	0	3	1	5	.379	.429	Mark Gardner	.091	11	1	0	0	0	0	1	3	.167	.091

Rick Wilkins — Cubs

Age 27 – Bats Left

	Avg	G	AB	R	H	2B	3B	HR	RBI	BB	SO	HBP	GDP	SB	CS	OBP	SLG	IBB	SH	SF	#Pit	#P/PA	GB	FB	G/F
1993 Season	.303	136	446	78	135	23	1	30	73	50	99	3	6	2	1	.376	.561	13	0	1	1879	3.76	131	113	1.16
Career (1991-1993)	.275	305	893	119	246	41	2	44	117	97	208	9	14	5	6	.352	.474	22	8	2	3793	3.76	248	246	1.01

1993 Season

	Avg	AB	H	2B	3B	HR	RBI	BB	SO	OBP	SLG		Avg	AB	H	2B	3B	HR	RBI	BB	SO	OBP	SLG
vs. Left	.224	67	15	3	0	3	10	8	22	.325	.403	Scoring Posn	.283	113	32	5	0	6	43	28	32	.427	.487
vs. Right	.317	379	120	20	1	27	63	42	77	.385	.588	Close & Late	.282	78	22	3	0	6	14	11	19	.371	.551
Groundball	.314	153	48	6	0	10	27	17	25	.391	.549	None on/out	.245	110	27	3	0	5	5	6	28	.291	.409
Flyball	.254	67	17	2	0	6	14	8	22	.333	.552	Batting #6	.366	202	74	15	1	15	40	19	40	.423	.673
Home	.256	238	61	11	0	10	31	19	61	.317	.429	Batting #8	.353	102	36	4	0	10	15	13	27	.436	.686
Away	.356	208	74	12	1	20	42	31	38	.440	.712	Other	.176	142	25	4	0	5	18	18	32	.267	.310
Day	.220	232	51	12	0	10	20	20	59	.285	.401	April	.122	41	5	0	0	1	2	6	6	.234	.195
Night	.393	214	84	11	1	20	53	30	40	.470	.734	May	.299	77	23	4	0	5	6	7	23	.357	.545
Grass	.292	353	103	18	0	25	62	35	84	.361	.555	June	.414	87	36	7	1	8	20	11	15	.485	.793
Turf	.344	93	32	5	1	5	11	15	15	.431	.581	July	.256	86	22	2	0	6	15	10	19	.340	.488
First Pitch	.233	60	14	1	1	4	10	9	0	.343	.483	August	.286	84	24	7	0	5	16	6	21	.330	.548
Ahead in Count	.484	95	46	7	0	11	25	17	0	.558	.905	September/October	.352	71	25	3	0	5	14	10	15	.439	.606
Behind in Count	.216	204	44	11	0	8	24	0	82	.223	.387	Pre-All Star	.310	239	74	12	1	17	33	26	51	.382	.582
Two Strikes	.181	221	40	9	0	8	20	24	99	.267	.330	Post-All Star	.295	207	61	11	0	13	40	24	48	.369	.536

1993 By Position

Position	Avg	AB	H	2B	3B	HR	RBI	BB	SO	OBP	SLG	G	GS	Innings	PO	A	E	DP	Fld Pct	Rng Fctr	In Zone	Outs	Zone Rtg	MLB Zone
As Pinch Hitter	.444	9	4	0	0	2	2	0	3	.444	1.111	10	0	---	---	---	---	---	---	---	---	---	---	---
As c	.300	437	131	23	1	28	71	50	96	.375	.549	133	118	1077.1	717	89	3	8	.996	---	---	---	---	---

Career (1991-1993)

	Avg	AB	H	2B	3B	HR	RBI	BB	SO	OBP	SLG		Avg	AB	H	2B	3B	HR	RBI	BB	SO	OBP	SLG
vs. Left	.245	155	38	7	0	4	16	16	46	.331	.368	Scoring Posn	.263	209	55	9	1	10	76	50	55	.409	.459
vs. Right	.282	738	208	34	2	40	101	81	162	.356	.496	Close & Late	.272	173	47	9	0	9	23	24	44	.364	.480
Groundball	.298	312	93	14	0	16	44	35	60	.376	.497	None on/out	.257	218	56	9	0	5	5	13	55	.311	.367
Flyball	.210	186	39	5	0	9	24	20	55	.293	.382	Batting #6	.319	310	99	17	1	17	48	23	67	.370	.545
Home	.240	470	113	20	0	15	49	44	116	.312	.379	Batting #7	.231	290	67	13	1	9	30	38	69	.319	.376
Away	.314	423	133	21	2	29	68	53	92	.394	.579	Other	.273	293	80	11	0	18	39	36	72	.365	.495
Day	.218	478	104	18	1	16	44	44	117	.286	.360	April	.137	51	7	0	0	1	2	7	8	.241	.196
Night	.342	415	142	23	1	28	73	53	91	.423	.605	May	.299	77	23	4	0	5	6	7	23	.357	.545
Grass	.267	681	182	31	0	33	92	68	162	.339	.458	June	.368	163	60	11	1	13	36	15	32	.432	.687
Turf	.302	212	64	10	2	11	25	29	46	.392	.524	July	.255	216	55	7	0	10	24	18	52	.318	.426
First Pitch	.300	120	36	6	1	7	18	18	0	.400	.542	August	.233	210	49	9	0	6	23	23	55	.314	.362
Ahead in Count	.409	193	79	12	0	14	35	40	0	.509	.689	September/October	.295	176	52	10	1	9	26	27	38	.392	.517
Behind in Count	.194	418	81	17	1	14	45	0	181	.207	.340	Pre-All Star	.306	379	116	17	1	23	54	33	78	.370	.538
Two Strikes	.171	444	76	16	1	12	36	42	208	.253	.293	Post-All Star	.253	514	130	24	1	21	63	64	130	.338	.426

Batter vs. Pitcher (career)																							
Hits Best Against	Avg	AB	H	2B	3B	HR	RBI	BB	SO	OBP	SLG	Hits Worst Against	Avg	AB	H	2B	3B	HR	RBI	BB	SO	OBP	SLG
Kevin Gross	.571	14	8	3	0	2	4	1	2	.600	1.214	Curt Schilling	.083	12	1	0	0	0	0	1	2	.154	.083
Ken Hill	.533	15	8	3	0	1	4	2	2	.556	.933	Dennis Martinez	.100	10	1	1	0	0	0	2	3	.250	.200
Bob Walk	.500	18	9	1	0	2	3	1	2	.526	.889	David Cone	.154	13	2	1	0	0	1	1	6	.214	.231
Jack Armstrong	.500	8	4	1	0	2	3	3	0	.636	1.375	Doug Drabek	.182	22	4	0	0	1	1	2	4	.250	.318
Wally Whitehurst	.385	13	5	1	0	2	4	2	2	.467	.923	Mark Portugal	.231	13	3	1	0	0	0	0	0	.231	.308

Bernie Williams — Yankees

Age 25 – Bats Both (groundball hitter)

	Avg	G	AB	R	H	2B	3B	HR	RBI	BB	SO	HBP	GDP	SB	CS	OBP	SLG	IBB	SH	SF	#Pit	#P/PA	GB	FB	G/F
1993 Season	.268	139	567	67	152	31	4	12	68	53	106	4	17	9	9	.333	.400	4	1	3	2327	3.71	219	138	1.59
Career (1991-1993)	.262	286	1148	149	301	64	10	20	128	130	199	6	26	26	20	.339	.388	5	5	6	4805	3.71	451	290	1.56

1993 Season																							
	Avg	AB	H	2B	3B	HR	RBI	BB	SO	OBP	SLG		Avg	AB	H	2B	3B	HR	RBI	BB	SO	OBP	SLG
vs. Left	.325	191	62	13	0	7	29	26	33	.402	.503	Scoring Posn	.270	148	40	8	0	4	58	14	20	.327	.405
vs. Right	.239	376	90	18	4	5	39	27	73	.297	.348	Close & Late	.262	84	22	1	0	3	10	8	21	.326	.381
Groundball	.237	93	22	4	0	2	11	7	15	.290	.344	None on/out	.254	173	44	12	2	6	6	10	32	.303	.451
Flyball	.220	127	28	5	2	5	17	9	18	.272	.409	Batting #1	.239	289	69	11	4	9	40	27	56	.306	.398
Home	.266	256	68	14	2	5	32	28	40	.339	.395	Batting #6	.310	242	75	17	0	3	26	24	38	.375	.417
Away	.270	311	84	17	2	7	36	25	66	.328	.405	Other	.222	36	8	3	0	0	2	2	12	.263	.306
Day	.253	194	49	14	1	3	16	17	37	.315	.381	April	.264	87	23	6	1	2	12	12	17	.356	.425
Night	.276	373	103	17	3	9	52	36	69	.343	.410	May	.220	50	11	1	1	0	3	6	12	.316	.280
Grass	.279	476	133	28	3	10	62	46	80	.346	.414	June	.255	102	26	4	2	5	20	6	20	.294	.480
Turf	.209	91	19	3	1	2	6	7	26	.265	.330	July	.280	107	30	6	0	3	15	13	13	.358	.421
First Pitch	.309	81	25	8	0	3	19	2	0	.333	.519	August	.349	109	38	9	0	1	11	6	22	.385	.459
Ahead in Count	.321	137	44	8	2	2	14	26	0	.422	.453	September/October	.214	112	24	5	0	1	7	10	22	.285	.286
Behind in Count	.236	242	57	7	2	5	26	0	85	.245	.343	Pre-All Star	.239	285	68	11	4	9	39	27	56	.307	.400
Two Strikes	.184	245	45	5	2	6	20	25	106	.262	.294	Post-All Star	.298	282	84	20	0	3	29	26	50	.360	.401

1993 By Position																								
Position	Avg	AB	H	2B	3B	HR	RBI	BB	SO	OBP	SLG	G	GS	Innings	PO	A	E	DP	Fld Pct	Rng Fctr	In Zone	Outs	Zone Rtg	MLB Zone
As cf	.268	567	152	31	4	12	68	53	106	.333	.400	139	139	1225.0	367	5	4	1	.989	2.73	423	355	.839	.829

Career (1991-1993)																							
	Avg	AB	H	2B	3B	HR	RBI	BB	SO	OBP	SLG		Avg	AB	H	2B	3B	HR	RBI	BB	SO	OBP	SLG
vs. Left	.285	379	108	25	1	10	51	53	55	.371	.435	Scoring Posn	.279	280	78	16	2	5	107	30	42	.342	.404
vs. Right	.251	769	193	39	9	10	77	77	144	.322	.364	Close & Late	.232	185	43	6	1	3	23	19	45	.307	.324
Groundball	.261	264	69	14	1	4	28	31	42	.341	.367	None on/out	.250	380	95	20	3	8	8	40	64	.325	.382
Flyball	.239	255	61	12	3	8	34	23	38	.304	.404	Batting #1	.246	759	187	39	8	15	86	89	138	.328	.378
Home	.271	549	149	32	5	9	64	68	82	.353	.397	Batting #6	.310	242	75	17	0	3	26	24	38	.375	.417
Away	.254	599	152	32	5	11	64	62	117	.326	.379	Other	.265	147	39	8	2	2	16	17	23	.335	.388
Day	.277	383	106	28	3	4	45	36	71	.341	.397	April	.261	92	24	6	1	2	12	12	19	.349	.413
Night	.255	765	195	36	7	16	83	94	128	.338	.383	May	.220	50	11	1	1	0	3	6	12	.316	.280
Grass	.268	973	261	54	9	17	116	111	153	.345	.395	June	.255	102	26	4	2	5	20	6	20	.294	.480
Turf	.229	175	40	10	1	3	12	19	46	.304	.349	July	.270	178	48	10	1	5	26	28	27	.370	.421
First Pitch	.294	163	48	14	0	3	25	3	0	.315	.436	August	.276	359	99	25	1	6	37	42	63	.354	.401
Ahead in Count	.323	285	92	21	3	6	34	74	0	.457	.481	September/October	.253	367	93	18	4	2	30	36	58	.320	.341
Behind in Count	.217	471	102	15	5	7	45	0	156	.223	.314	Pre-All Star	.239	293	70	11	4	9	41	27	58	.305	.396
Two Strikes	.192	496	95	16	5	8	40	53	199	.270	.292	Post-All Star	.270	855	231	53	6	11	87	103	141	.350	.385

Batter vs. Pitcher (career)																							
Hits Best Against	Avg	AB	H	2B	3B	HR	RBI	BB	SO	OBP	SLG	Hits Worst Against	Avg	AB	H	2B	3B	HR	RBI	BB	SO	OBP	SLG
Mark Gubicza	.417	12	5	1	0	0	3	1	0	.462	.500	Ricky Bones	.083	12	1	0	0	0	1	0	0	.083	.083
Cal Eldred	.400	10	4	0	0	0	0	2	1	.500	.400	Bob Milacki	.091	11	1	0	0	0	0	1	0	.167	.091
Brian Bohanon	.364	11	4	1	0	0	3	1	1	.417	.455	Tom Gordon	.100	10	1	1	0	0	1	0	4	.091	.200
Alex Fernandez	.357	14	5	1	0	1	1	1	1	.400	.643	Erik Hanson	.133	15	2	0	0	0	0	0	3	.133	.133
Bill Krueger	.333	12	4	0	0	1	1	2	0	.429	.583	Ben McDonald	.182	11	2	0	0	0	0	0	3	.182	.182

Brian Williams — Astros

Age 25 – Pitches Right

	ERA	W	L	Sv	G	GS	IP	BB	SO	Avg	H	2B	3B	HR	RBI	OBP	SLG	GF	IR	IRS	Hld	SvOp	SB	CS	GB	FB	G/F
1993 Season	4.83	4	4	3	42	5	82.0	38	56	.248	76	14	2	7	39	.335	.375	12	22	5	2	6	6	2	131	77	1.70
Career (1991-1993)	4.30	11	11	3	60	23	190.1	84	114	.251	179	30	4	19	86	.332	.385	12	22	5	2	6	14	7	283	196	1.44

1993 Season																						
	ERA	W	L	Sv	G	GS	IP	H	HR	BB	SO		Avg	AB	H	2B	3B	HR	RBI	BB	SO	OBP	SLG
Home	4.33	2	2	2	19	3	43.2	41	4	14	35	vs. Left	.241	133	32	5	0	4	15	19	32	.344	.368
Away	5.40	2	2	1	23	2	38.1	35	3	24	21	vs. Right	.253	174	44	9	2	3	24	19	24	.328	.379
Starter	4.40	3	1	0	5	5	30.2	25	4	15	26	Scoring Posn	.259	85	22	5	1	0	28	12	14	.340	.341
Reliever	5.08	1	3	3	37	0	51.1	51	3	23	30	Close & Late	.314	70	22	2	0	3	13	11	12	.415	.471
0 Days rest	6.52	0	1	0	8	0	9.2	17	0	5	7	None on/out	.273	77	21	3	0	4	4	8	19	.341	.468
1 or 2 Days rest	5.40	0	1	2	10	0	15.0	11	2	5	11	First Pitch	.396	53	21	6	0	3	15	2	0	.421	.679
3+ Days rest	4.39	1	1	1	19	0	26.2	23	1	13	12	Ahead in Count	.163	129	21	5	1	1	7	0	41	.174	.240
Pre-All Star	4.35	2	2	3	29	2	51.2	43	3	20	33	Behind in Count	.239	67	16	0	0	2	12	26	0	.447	.328
Post-All Star	5.64	2	2	0	13	3	30.1	33	4	18	23	Two Strikes	.157	127	20	6	1	0	5	10	56	.225	.220

Gerald Williams — Yankees

Age 27 – Bats Right (flyball hitter)

	Avg	G	AB	R	H	2B	3B	HR	RBI	BB	SO	HBP	GDP	SB	CS	OBP	SLG	IBB	SH	SF	#Pit	#P/PA	GB	FB	G/F
1993 Season	.149	42	67	11	10	2	3	0	6	1	14	2	2	2	0	.183	.269	0	0	1	252	3.55	20	28	0.71
Career (1992-1993)	.191	57	94	18	18	4	3	3	12	1	17	2	2	4	0	.214	.394	0	0	1	329	3.36	30	39	0.77

1993 Season

	Avg	AB	H	2B	3B	HR	RBI	BB	SO	OBP	SLG
vs. Left	.139	36	5	0	1	0	2	1	6	.179	.194
vs. Right	.161	31	5	2	2	0	4	0	8	.188	.355

	Avg	AB	H	2B	3B	HR	RBI	BB	SO	OBP	SLG
Scoring Posn	.158	19	3	0	2	0	6	0	1	.190	.368
Close & Late	.333	9	3	1	0	0	1	0	4	.333	.444

Matt D. Williams — Giants

Age 28 – Bats Right (flyball hitter)

	Avg	G	AB	R	H	2B	3B	HR	RBI	BB	SO	HBP	GDP	SB	CS	OBP	SLG	IBB	SH	SF	#Pit	#P/PA	GB	FB	G/F
1993 Season	.294	145	579	105	170	33	4	38	110	27	80	4	12	1	3	.325	.561	4	0	9	2076	3.35	185	217	0.85
Last Five Years	.260	691	2606	353	678	115	17	143	446	146	527	25	56	21	21	.303	.482	31	3	25	9425	3.36	811	888	0.91

1993 Season

	Avg	AB	H	2B	3B	HR	RBI	BB	SO	OBP	SLG
vs. Left	.328	186	61	11	2	17	42	11	19	.363	.683
vs. Right	.277	393	109	22	2	21	68	16	61	.306	.504
Groundball	.337	181	61	9	0	10	30	11	23	.378	.552
Flyball	.304	92	28	7	0	5	12	5	16	.340	.543
Home	.293	287	84	17	3	19	61	15	42	.330	.571
Away	.295	292	86	16	1	19	49	12	38	.319	.551
Day	.299	294	88	16	1	24	60	14	44	.330	.605
Night	.288	285	82	17	3	14	50	13	36	.319	.516
Grass	.296	452	134	24	4	26	81	22	63	.330	.540
Turf	.283	127	36	9	0	12	29	5	17	.306	.638
First Pitch	.257	113	29	3	0	9	19	4	0	.280	.522
Ahead in Count	.333	123	41	9	1	10	27	13	0	.388	.667
Behind in Count	.273	242	66	16	3	9	40	0	65	.277	.475
Two Strikes	.231	225	52	14	2	8	33	10	80	.269	.418

	Avg	AB	H	2B	3B	HR	RBI	BB	SO	OBP	SLG
Scoring Posn	.323	155	50	9	1	10	74	12	19	.352	.587
Close & Late	.262	84	22	1	1	7	16	4	12	.289	.548
None on/out	.331	151	50	15	0	14	14	4	17	.348	.709
Batting #4	.292	566	165	31	4	37	108	25	79	.319	.557
Batting #5	.455	11	5	2	0	1	2	2	0	.600	.909
Other	.000	2	0	0	0	0	0	0	1	.000	.000
April	.330	94	31	7	0	8	18	11	11	.396	.660
May	.284	116	33	5	1	7	25	3	22	.308	.526
June	.250	80	20	5	0	6	21	0	13	.247	.538
July	.293	58	17	3	0	3	10	3	6	.338	.500
August	.312	109	34	8	1	3	11	5	15	.342	.486
September/October	.287	122	35	5	2	11	25	5	13	.310	.631
Pre-All Star	.290	290	84	17	1	21	64	14	46	.322	.572
Post-All Star	.298	289	86	16	3	17	46	13	34	.328	.550

1993 By Position

Position	Avg	AB	H	2B	3B	HR	RBI	BB	SO	OBP	SLG	G	GS	Innings	PO	A	E	DP	Fld Pct	Rng Fctr	In Zone	Outs	Zone Rtg	MLB Zone
As 3b	.294	578	170	33	4	38	110	27	80	.325	.562	144	143	1275.2	117	264	12	35	.969	2.69	316	287	.908	.834

Last Five Years

	Avg	AB	H	2B	3B	HR	RBI	BB	SO	OBP	SLG
vs. Left	.279	810	226	36	4	55	157	55	136	.325	.537
vs. Right	.252	1796	452	79	13	88	289	91	391	.293	.457
Groundball	.266	898	239	38	2	38	140	51	175	.310	.440
Flyball	.243	518	126	26	5	28	74	32	109	.297	.475
Home	.265	1292	342	59	13	75	232	70	259	.306	.505
Away	.256	1314	336	56	4	68	214	76	268	.300	.460
Day	.274	1094	300	52	7	74	209	54	216	.311	.537
Night	.250	1512	378	63	10	69	237	92	311	.297	.442
Grass	.267	1969	525	90	14	104	333	100	388	.305	.485
Turf	.240	637	153	25	3	39	113	46	139	.296	.473
First Pitch	.300	470	141	28	1	28	97	19	0	.331	.543
Ahead in Count	.346	500	173	28	5	47	137	61	0	.412	.704
Behind in Count	.208	1228	255	45	8	41	142	0	464	.214	.357
Two Strikes	.178	1118	199	39	8	36	120	57	527	.222	.324

	Avg	AB	H	2B	3B	HR	RBI	BB	SO	OBP	SLG
Scoring Posn	.263	689	181	29	4	38	297	66	149	.323	.482
Close & Late	.220	419	92	14	2	16	57	29	89	.275	.377
None on/out	.272	658	179	31	6	44	44	33	116	.312	.538
Batting #4	.271	900	244	46	7	52	177	42	152	.305	.511
Batting #5	.256	1392	356	54	10	77	225	81	305	.302	.475
Other	.248	314	78	15	0	14	44	23	70	.301	.430
April	.251	383	96	15	2	20	69	25	73	.300	.457
May	.248	420	104	15	3	22	69	25	86	.292	.455
June	.263	369	97	19	1	18	70	12	79	.286	.466
July	.281	356	100	14	4	20	60	25	78	.338	.511
August	.247	527	130	26	4	28	70	24	110	.281	.471
September/October	.274	551	151	26	3	35	108	35	101	.321	.523
Pre-All Star	.257	1262	324	51	8	64	223	66	262	.297	.462
Post-All Star	.263	1344	354	64	9	79	223	80	265	.309	.501

Batter vs. Pitcher (career)

Hits Best Against	Avg	AB	H	2B	3B	HR	RBI	BB	SO	OBP	SLG
Dennis Rasmussen	.600	20	12	2	0	3	11	2	3	.583	1.150
John Smiley	.464	28	13	2	0	6	14	1	5	.483	1.179
Danny Cox	.455	11	5	1	0	3	5	1	0	.500	1.364
Mike Harkey	.438	16	7	0	0	3	5	0	2	.438	1.000
Ryan Bowen	.385	13	5	2	0	3	7	3	2	.500	1.231

Hits Worst Against	Avg	AB	H	2B	3B	HR	RBI	BB	SO	OBP	SLG
Greg W. Harris	.000	20	0	0	0	0	0	0	3	.000	.000
Bob Walk	.063	16	1	0	0	0	1	1	5	.111	.063
Rob Dibble	.067	15	1	0	0	0	0	0	9	.067	.067
Mark Portugal	.070	43	3	0	0	0	0	2	13	.111	.070
Mark Grant	.143	14	2	0	0	0	1	0	4	.133	.143

Mike Williams — Phillies

Age 25 – Pitches Right

	ERA	W	L	Sv	G	GS	IP	BB	SO	Avg	H	2B	3B	HR	RBI	OBP	SLG	GF	IR	IRS	Hld	SvOp	SB	CS	GB	FB	G/F
1993 Season	5.29	1	3	0	17	4	51.0	22	33	.253	50	12	2	5	29	.327	.409	2	11	5	0	0	6	3	76	61	1.25
Career (1992-1993)	5.31	2	4	0	22	9	79.2	29	38	.255	79	21	3	8	45	.318	.419	2	11	5	0	0	7	4	118	102	1.16

1993 Season

	ERA	W	L	Sv	G	GS	IP	H	HR	BB	SO
Home	4.50	1	2	0	11	2	32.0	33	3	9	22
Away	6.63	0	1	0	6	2	19.0	17	2	13	11

	Avg	AB	H	2B	3B	HR	RBI	BB	SO	OBP	SLG
vs. Left	.234	94	22	5	1	4	13	14	12	.333	.436
vs. Right	.269	104	28	7	1	1	16	8	21	.321	.385

Mitch Williams — Phillies

Age 29 – Pitches Left (flyball pitcher)

	ERA	W	L	Sv	G	GS	IP	BB	SO	Avg	H	2B	3B	HR	RBI	OBP	SLG	GF	IR	IRS	Hld	SvOp	SB	CS	GB	FB	G/F
1993 Season	3.34	3	7	43	65	0	62.0	44	60	.245	56	9	0	3	29	.368	.323	57	9	5	1	49	9	0	63	64	0.98
Last Five Years	3.16	25	32	154	335	2	379.1	272	340	.227	312	68	8	21	178	.361	.334	212	145	49	9	191	40	10	351	457	0.77

1993 Season

	ERA	W	L	Sv	G	GS	IP	H	HR	BB	SO
Home	4.18	1	3	19	32	0	28.0	26	1	16	27
Away	2.65	2	4	24	33	0	34.0	30	2	28	33
Day	3.20	2	3	12	19	0	19.2	20	2	15	20
Night	3.40	1	4	31	46	0	42.1	36	1	29	40
Grass	2.41	2	0	14	17	0	18.2	17	1	13	15
Turf	3.74	1	7	29	48	0	43.1	39	2	31	45
April	3.00	1	0	10	12	0	12.0	11	1	4	13
May	5.68	0	2	4	7	0	6.1	8	0	4	4
June	2.08	0	1	9	10	0	8.2	7	1	4	9
July	2.08	1	0	5	13	0	13.0	7	0	9	7
August	4.35	1	1	8	10	0	10.1	12	0	11	13
September/October	3.86	0	3	7	13	0	11.2	11	1	12	14
Starter	0.00	0	0	0	0	0	0.0	0	0	0	0
Reliever	3.34	3	7	43	65	0	62.0	56	3	44	60
0 Days rest	1.69	1	2	13	21	0	21.1	17	0	14	16
1 or 2 Days rest	4.35	0	4	17	22	0	20.2	20	1	17	24
3+ Days rest	4.05	2	1	13	22	0	20.0	19	2	13	20
Pre-All Star	3.55	2	3	23	35	0	33.0	31	2	16	31
Post-All Star	3.10	1	4	20	30	0	29.0	25	1	28	29

	Avg	AB	H	2B	3B	HR	RBI	BB	SO	OBP	SLG
vs. Left	.231	39	9	0	0	0	4	5	12	.326	.231
vs. Right	.247	190	47	9	0	3	25	39	48	.377	.342
Inning 1-6	.000	0	0	0	0	0	0	0	0	.000	.000
Inning 7+	.245	229	56	9	0	3	29	44	60	.368	.323
None on	.252	107	27	5	0	1	1	20	24	.375	.327
Runners on	.238	122	29	4	0	2	28	24	36	.362	.320
Scoring Posn	.221	77	17	2	0	1	26	14	20	.340	.286
Close & Late	.260	169	44	4	0	2	25	37	46	.392	.320
None on/out	.235	51	12	2	0	1	1	10	14	.371	.000
vs. 1st Batr (relief)	.204	54	11	2	0	1	1	10	14	.338	.296
First Inning Pitched	.242	219	53	8	0	3	28	43	58	.370	.320
First 15 Pitches	.255	161	41	5	0	3	16	30	38	.378	.342
Pitch 16-30	.227	66	15	4	0	0	12	13	21	.350	.288
Pitch 31-45	.000	2	0	0	0	0	1	1	1	.250	.000
Pitch 46+	.000	0	0	0	0	0	0	0	0	.000	.000
First Pitch	.188	16	3	0	0	0	4	1	0	.235	.188
Ahead in Count	.186	129	24	5	0	2	10	0	48	.185	.271
Behind in Count	.409	44	18	2	0	1	13	26	0	.625	.523
Two Strikes	.190	126	24	6	0	2	11	17	60	.285	.286

Last Five Years

	ERA	W	L	Sv	G	GS	IP	H	HR	BB	SO
Home	3.51	17	13	71	169	1	187.1	167	9	135	179
Away	2.81	8	19	83	166	1	192.0	145	12	137	161
Day	3.01	9	9	51	129	0	140.2	127	11	103	119
Night	3.24	16	23	103	206	2	238.2	185	10	169	221
Grass	3.37	9	12	59	141	1	163.0	146	16	114	129
Turf	3.00	16	20	95	194	1	216.1	166	5	158	211
April	2.51	3	4	30	54	0	61.0	51	3	38	55
May	2.91	0	7	22	52	0	58.2	46	5	47	56
June	2.41	3	4	29	53	0	56.0	43	4	39	52
July	2.75	2	2	23	48	0	55.2	41	3	34	42
August	3.30	12	6	22	64	0	76.1	64	1	55	71
September/October	4.65	5	9	28	64	2	71.2	67	5	59	64
Starter	9.95	0	1	0	2	2	6.1	11	0	4	2
Reliever	3.04	25	31	154	333	0	373.0	301	21	268	338
0 Days rest	2.42	4	12	51	98	0	107.2	80	6	81	92
1 or 2 Days rest	3.42	16	12	67	144	0	163.1	134	9	128	157
3+ Days rest	3.09	5	7	36	91	0	102.0	87	6	59	89
Pre-All Star	2.56	7	15	84	173	0	193.1	148	13	136	177
Post-All Star	3.77	18	17	70	162	2	186.0	164	8	136	163

	Avg	AB	H	2B	3B	HR	RBI	BB	SO	OBP	SLG
vs. Left	.232	293	68	13	2	2	43	51	82	.356	.311
vs. Right	.226	1080	244	55	6	19	135	221	258	.362	.341
Inning 1-6	.325	40	13	4	3	1	11	7	4	.426	.650
Inning 7+	.224	1333	299	64	5	20	167	265	336	.359	.325
None on	.241	605	146	31	0	9	9	124	127	.381	.337
Runners on	.216	768	166	37	8	12	169	148	213	.345	.332
Scoring Posn	.207	488	101	18	6	8	152	95	131	.336	.318
Close & Late	.226	848	192	38	3	13	122	181	226	.366	.324
None on/out	.210	286	60	9	0	5	5	54	64	.345	.294
vs. 1st Batr (relief)	.224	263	59	10	0	4	20	61	63	.373	.308
First Inning Pitched	.217	1067	232	51	5	16	146	224	264	.359	.320
First 15 Pitches	.233	803	187	40	4	14	89	173	185	.377	.345
Pitch 16-30	.217	448	97	24	1	6	73	77	117	.337	.315
Pitch 31-45	.202	99	20	3	2	1	11	18	30	.317	.303
Pitch 46+	.348	23	8	1	1	0	5	4	8	.444	.478
First Pitch	.278	133	37	3	2	2	23	17	0	.374	.376
Ahead in Count	.202	693	140	43	3	10	75	0	264	.207	.316
Behind in Count	.290	252	73	10	2	7	50	134	0	.541	.429
Two Strikes	.196	772	151	44	3	10	80	120	340	.306	.299

Pitcher vs. Batter (career)

Pitches Best Vs.	Avg	AB	H	2B	3B	HR	RBI	BB	SO	OBP	SLG
Darryl Strawberry	.000	12	0	0	0	0	0	2	7	.143	.000
Dick Schofield	.000	10	0	0	0	0	0	2	3	.167	.000
Mark Grace	.077	13	1	0	0	0	0	0	2	.077	.077
Dave Justice	.091	11	1	0	0	0	0	1	4	.167	.091
Chico Walker	.100	10	1	0	0	0	1	1	3	.167	.100

Pitches Worst Vs.	Avg	AB	H	2B	3B	HR	RBI	BB	SO	OBP	SLG
Ray Lankford	.500	10	5	1	1	0	2	3	3	.615	.800
Delino DeShields	.429	7	3	1	0	0	2	4	1	.583	.571
Ken Caminiti	.417	12	5	0	0	1	3	3	4	.533	.667
Lonnie Smith	.400	5	2	1	1	0	3	8	2	.769	1.000
Kevin Bass	.333	15	5	2	0	2	5	0	4	.333	.867

Woody Williams — Blue Jays

Age 27 – Pitches Right (flyball pitcher)

	ERA	W	L	Sv	G	GS	IP	BB	SO	Avg	H	2B	3B	HR	RBI	OBP	SLG	GF	IR	IRS	Hld	SvOp	SB	CS	GB	FB	G/F
1993 Season	4.38	3	1	0	30	0	37.0	22	24	.274	40	7	0	2	19	.371	.363	9	20	9	4	2	0	0	43	55	0.78

1993 Season

	ERA	W	L	Sv	G	GS	IP	H	HR	BB	SO
Home	4.34	3	0	0	15	0	18.2	19	1	13	13
Away	4.42	0	1	0	15	0	18.1	21	1	9	11
Starter	0.00	0	0	0	0	0	0.0	0	0	0	0
Reliever	4.38	3	1	0	30	0	37.0	40	2	22	24
0 Days rest	4.09	0	1	0	7	0	11.0	13	2	5	7
1 or 2 Days rest	6.75	0	0	0	9	0	8.0	10	0	4	6
3+ Days rest	3.50	3	0	0	14	0	18.0	17	0	13	11
Pre-All Star	4.18	3	0	0	16	0	23.2	31	0	11	16
Post-All Star	4.72	0	1	0	14	0	13.1	9	2	11	8

	Avg	AB	H	2B	3B	HR	RBI	BB	SO	OBP	SLG
vs. Left	.246	57	14	2	0	0	4	12	7	.377	.281
vs. Right	.292	89	26	5	0	2	15	10	17	.366	.416
Scoring Posn	.304	46	14	5	0	1	18	9	11	.421	.478
Close & Late	.280	50	14	2	0	2	7	9	6	.390	.440
None on/out	.188	32	6	0	0	1	1	3	5	.257	.281
First Pitch	.368	19	7	1	0	0	4	3	0	.455	.421
Ahead in Count	.263	76	20	2	0	1	10	0	22	.269	.329
Behind in Count	.226	31	7	2	0	1	4	10	0	.415	.387
Two Strikes	.282	71	20	4	0	1	11	9	24	.366	.380

Mark Williamson — Orioles

Age 34 – Pitches Right

	ERA	W	L	Sv	G	GS	IP	BB	SO	Avg	H	2B	3B	HR	RBI	OBP	SLG	GF	IR	IRS	Hld	SvOp	SB	CS	GB	FB	G/F
1993 Season	4.91	7	5	0	48	1	88.0	25	45	.304	106	25	0	5	47	.345	.418	12	43	10	10	2	3	4	146	81	1.80
Last Five Years	3.46	30	17	15	239	1	379.2	128	227	.264	379	73	7	27	205	.321	.381	53	244	86	41	30	22	13	557	377	1.48

1993 Season

	ERA	W	L	Sv	G	GS	IP	H	HR	BB	SO
Home	4.76	5	1	0	21	0	34.0	44	3	9	9
Away	5.00	2	4	0	27	1	54.0	62	2	16	36
Starter	7.36	0	0	0	1	1	3.2	5	0	1	2
Reliever	4.80	7	5	0	47	0	84.1	101	5	24	43
0 Days rest	5.06	0	1	0	4	0	5.1	9	0	6	7
1 or 2 Days rest	5.50	5	4	0	21	0	36.0	41	3	8	19
3+ Days rest	4.19	2	0	0	22	0	43.0	51	2	10	17
Pre-All Star	3.88	5	1	0	25	1	53.1	61	2	11	28
Post-All Star	6.49	2	4	0	23	0	34.2	45	3	14	17

	Avg	AB	H	2B	3B	HR	RBI	BB	SO	OBP	SLG
vs. Left	.255	141	36	7	0	3	16	12	22	.314	.369
vs. Right	.337	208	70	18	0	2	31	13	23	.366	.452
Scoring Posn	.293	92	27	6	0	1	38	12	12	.355	.391
Close & Late	.300	110	33	8	0	2	7	10	20	.358	.427
None on/out	.305	82	25	5	0	2	2	4	7	.337	.439
First Pitch	.477	44	21	5	0	1	7	8	0	.537	.659
Ahead in Count	.202	168	34	6	0	0	15	0	41	.200	.238
Behind in Count	.392	79	31	8	0	2	16	8	0	.438	.570
Two Strikes	.172	151	26	4	0	2	15	9	45	.216	.238

Last Five Years

	ERA	W	L	Sv	G	GS	IP	H	HR	BB	SO
Home	2.58	20	7	5	119	0	191.2	166	13	58	106
Away	4.36	10	10	10	120	1	188.0	213	14	70	121
Day	4.28	9	6	8	70	1	103.0	108	10	38	63
Night	3.16	21	11	7	169	0	276.2	271	17	90	164
Grass	3.31	28	9	12	208	1	318.1	311	21	104	188
Turf	4.26	2	8	3	31	0	61.1	68	6	24	39
April	3.00	1	2	5	31	0	54.0	52	3	20	37
May	3.42	7	3	1	46	1	76.1	66	5	26	40
June	2.39	8	1	3	45	0	75.1	68	5	18	41
July	4.31	7	5	1	40	0	62.2	68	4	25	34
August	4.80	4	2	1	35	0	50.2	66	7	16	33
September/October	3.26	3	4	4	42	0	60.2	59	3	23	42
Starter	7.36	0	0	0	1	1	3.2	5	0	1	2
Reliever	3.42	30	17	15	238	0	376.0	374	27	127	225
0 Days rest	3.41	9	6	4	52	0	74.0	71	4	37	44
1 or 2 Days rest	3.40	15	10	8	116	0	190.2	179	17	50	113
3+ Days rest	3.48	6	1	3	70	0	111.1	124	6	40	68
Pre-All Star	3.04	18	6	10	135	1	228.1	208	13	68	129
Post-All Star	4.10	12	11	5	104	0	151.1	171	14	60	98

	Avg	AB	H	2B	3B	HR	RBI	BB	SO	OBP	SLG
vs. Left	.244	610	149	21	4	11	75	47	99	.296	.346
vs. Right	.278	827	230	52	3	16	130	81	128	.338	.406
Inning 1-6	.270	296	80	15	2	4	61	23	46	.318	.375
Inning 7+	.262	1141	299	58	5	23	144	105	181	.321	.382
None on	.245	744	182	37	3	13	13	47	104	.290	.355
Runners on	.284	693	197	36	4	14	192	81	123	.351	.408
Scoring Posn	.272	408	111	20	3	9	173	66	81	.359	.402
Close & Late	.265	544	144	29	4	11	76	62	81	.338	.393
None on/out	.266	323	86	18	2	7	7	15	42	.299	.399
vs. 1st Batr (relief)	.276	210	58	11	2	4	46	17	27	.325	.405
First Inning Pitched	.262	768	201	42	6	18	149	69	120	.318	.402
First 15 Pitches	.273	728	199	41	6	19	129	67	100	.330	.424
Pitch 16-30	.259	452	117	24	1	3	53	39	78	.315	.336
Pitch 31-45	.245	192	47	5	0	4	15	15	39	.298	.333
Pitch 46+	.246	65	16	3	0	1	8	7	10	.311	.338
First Pitch	.338	210	71	13	0	5	41	22	0	.389	.471
Ahead in Count	.183	617	113	19	2	4	57	0	196	.184	.240
Behind in Count	.347	354	123	24	3	13	69	58	0	.433	.542
Two Strikes	.174	628	109	19	4	7	61	47	227	.232	.250

Pitcher vs. Batter (career)

Pitches Best Vs.	Avg	AB	H	2B	3B	HR	RBI	BB	SO	OBP	SLG
Pete O'Brien	.000	11	0	0	0	0	0	1	1	.083	.000
Mark McLemore	.091	11	1	0	0	0	0	1	1	.167	.091
Rafael Palmeiro	.100	10	1	0	0	0	1	1	0	.182	.100
Ozzie Guillen	.118	17	2	0	0	0	3	0	2	.118	.118
Carlos Martinez	.143	14	2	0	0	0	1	0	0	.143	.143

Pitches Worst Vs.	Avg	AB	H	2B	3B	HR	RBI	BB	SO	OBP	SLG
Mike Macfarlane	.538	13	7	1	0	1	4	1	0	.571	.846
Mickey Tettleton	.500	12	6	0	0	1	3	2	2	.571	.750
Cory Snyder	.455	11	5	0	1	2	4	0	2	.455	1.182
Mark McGwire	.444	18	8	2	0	3	7	4	4	.545	1.056
Walt Weiss	.444	9	4	1	0	1	3	2	1	.545	.889

Carl Willis — Twins

Age 33 – Pitches Right (groundball pitcher)

	ERA	W	L	Sv	G	GS	IP	BB	SO	Avg	H	2B	3B	HR	RBI	OBP	SLG	GF	IR	IRS	Hld	SvOp	SB	CS	GB	FB	G/F
1993 Season	3.10	3	0	5	53	0	58.0	17	44	.259	56	20	1	2	39	.312	.389	21	59	22	14	9	4	1	81	54	1.50
Last Five Years	2.78	18	6	8	152	0	226.1	47	142	.244	205	44	5	10	105	.282	.344	51	137	49	29	15	11	5	332	215	1.54

1993 Season

	ERA	W	L	Sv	G	GS	IP	H	HR	BB	SO
Home	5.00	1	0	1	26	0	27.0	29	0	8	19
Away	1.45	2	0	4	27	0	31.0	27	2	9	25
Starter	0.00	0	0	0	0	0	0.0	0	0	0	0
Reliever	3.10	3	0	5	53	0	58.0	56	2	17	44
0 Days rest	8.38	0	0	3	11	0	9.2	14	0	2	7
1 or 2 Days rest	2.36	1	0	2	29	0	26.2	25	0	9	19
3+ Days rest	1.66	2	0	0	13	0	21.2	17	2	6	18
Pre-All Star	7.52	2	0	1	22	0	20.1	30	2	7	15
Post-All Star	0.72	1	0	4	31	0	37.2	26	0	10	29

	Avg	AB	H	2B	3B	HR	RBI	BB	SO	OBP	SLG
vs. Left	.292	89	26	8	0	2	16	10	15	.364	.449
vs. Right	.236	127	30	12	1	0	23	7	29	.274	.346
Scoring Posn	.282	85	24	10	1	0	35	11	19	.361	.424
Close & Late	.224	107	24	9	0	0	11	11	24	.297	.308
None on/out	.385	39	15	3	0	1	1	4	6	.442	.538
First Pitch	.353	34	12	3	0	0	10	5	0	.436	.441
Ahead in Count	.240	121	29	11	1	2	16	0	40	.240	.397
Behind in Count	.278	36	10	6	0	0	10	6	0	.372	.444
Two Strikes	.234	107	25	10	0	1	13	6	44	.274	.355

Last Five Years

	ERA	W	L	Sv	G	GS	IP	H	HR	BB	SO
Home	3.36	12	4	2	78	0	120.2	113	6	16	73
Away	2.13	6	2	6	74	0	105.2	92	4	31	69
Day	3.31	4	0	3	43	0	54.1	54	3	12	30
Night	2.62	14	6	5	109	0	172.0	151	7	35	112
Grass	2.08	6	2	4	59	0	86.2	74	3	22	56
Turf	3.22	12	4	4	93	0	139.2	131	7	25	86
April	4.85	1	1	0	9	0	13.0	13	2	4	5
May	5.52	1	1	1	25	0	31.0	39	0	10	16
June	3.09	2	1	2	27	0	35.0	34	1	9	23
July	2.01	8	2	1	30	0	49.1	38	3	4	29
August	1.50	3	1	3	26	0	54.0	44	1	6	28
September/October	2.45	3	0	1	35	0	44.0	37	3	14	41
Starter	0.00	0	0	0	0	0	0.0	0	0	0	0
Reliever	2.78	18	6	8	152	0	226.1	205	10	47	142

	Avg	AB	H	2B	3B	HR	RBI	BB	SO	OBP	SLG
vs. Left	.269	327	88	17	3	4	36	25	45	.320	.376
vs. Right	.228	514	117	27	2	6	69	22	97	.257	.323
Inning 1-6	.253	249	63	11	2	2	35	10	48	.277	.337
Inning 7+	.240	592	142	33	3	8	70	37	94	.284	.346
None on	.242	447	108	20	2	7	7	19	84	.274	.342
Runners on	.246	394	97	24	3	3	98	28	58	.291	.345
Scoring Posn	.258	244	63	18	2	1	89	24	44	.315	.361
Close & Late	.231	277	64	14	0	3	25	23	46	.288	.314
None on/out	.288	191	55	9	2	2	2	11	29	.330	.387
vs. 1st Batr (relief)	.272	136	37	7	0	1	31	11	25	.316	.346
First Inning Pitched	.254	465	118	24	3	5	80	29	76	.294	.351
First 15 Pitches	.242	471	114	26	2	5	69	27	71	.280	.338
Pitch 16-30	.248	230	57	14	3	2	23	15	45	.294	.361
Pitch 31-45	.235	102	24	4	0	1	8	4	22	.262	.304

Last Five Years

	ERA	W	L	Sv	G	GS	IP	H	HR	BB	SO
0 Days rest	5.00	3	0	3	18	0	18.0	23	0	2	11
1 or 2 Days rest	2.65	7	2	2	80	0	102.0	90	4	21	68
3+ Days rest	2.54	8	4	3	54	0	106.1	92	6	24	63
Pre-All Star	4.35	8	4	3	71	0	97.1	102	6	24	55
Post-All Star	1.60	10	2	5	81	0	129.0	103	4	23	87

	Avg	AB	H	2B	3B	HR	RBI	BB	SO	OBP	SLG
Pitch 46+	.263	38	10	0	0	2	5	1	4	.293	.421
First Pitch	.310	145	45	10	1	0	20	7	0	.342	.393
Ahead in Count	.207	416	86	19	2	6	43	0	132	.206	.305
Behind in Count	.263	171	45	11	2	2	26	20	0	.339	.386
Two Strikes	.187	375	70	18	1	3	33	20	142	.227	.264

Pitcher vs. Batter (career)

Pitches Best Vs.	Avg	AB	H	2B	3B	HR	RBI	BB	SO	OBP	SLG
Travis Fryman	.000	12	0	0	0	0	1	0	2	.000	.000
Jose Canseco	.100	10	1	0	0	0	0	3	5	.308	.100
Cecil Fielder	.143	14	2	0	0	0	0	0	3	.143	.143
Mark McGwire	.167	12	2	0	0	0	0	1	0	.231	.167
Rob Deer	.231	13	3	2	0	0	2	0	6	.231	.385

Pitches Worst Vs.	Avg	AB	H	2B	3B	HR	RBI	BB	SO	OBP	SLG
Wade Boggs	.583	12	7	1	0	0	4	3	0	.667	.667
Tony Phillips	.417	12	5	2	1	0	0	0	2	.417	.750
Don Mattingly	.364	11	4	0	0	1	2	0	0	.364	.636
Frank Thomas	.364	11	4	0	0	1	2	0	1	.364	.636
Terry Steinbach	.333	12	4	1	0	0	1	1	3	.385	.417

Craig Wilson — Royals

Age 29 – Bats Right (groundball hitter)

	Avg	G	AB	R	H	2B	3B	HR	RBI	BB	SO	HBP	GDP	SB	CS	OBP	SLG	IBB	SH	SF	#Pit	#P/PA	GB	FB	G/F
1993 Season	.265	21	49	6	13	1	0	1	3	7	6	0	0	1	1	.357	.347	0	1	0	203	3.56	25	12	2.08
Career (1989-1993)	.251	203	362	31	91	11	0	1	37	32	50	0	13	2	5	.308	.290	4	3	5	1349	3.36	162	95	1.71

1993 Season

	Avg	AB	H	2B	3B	HR	RBI	BB	SO	OBP	SLG
vs. Left	.250	12	3	0	0	1	2	2	1	.357	.500
vs. Right	.270	37	10	1	0	0	1	5	5	.357	.297
Scoring Posn	.308	13	4	0	0	1	3	2	2	.400	.538
Close & Late	.000	10	0	0	0	0	0	1	1	.091	.000

Career (1989-1993)

	Avg	AB	H	2B	3B	HR	RBI	BB	SO	OBP	SLG
vs. Left	.260	192	50	5	0	1	26	19	29	.319	.302
vs. Right	.241	170	41	6	0	0	11	13	21	.295	.276
Groundball	.281	121	34	6	0	1	15	7	16	.320	.355
Flyball	.282	78	22	1	0	0	7	10	12	.360	.295
Home	.215	191	41	7	0	1	19	21	27	.291	.267
Away	.292	171	50	4	0	0	18	11	23	.328	.316
Day	.277	119	33	6	0	0	12	9	14	.326	.328
Night	.239	243	58	5	0	1	25	23	36	.300	.272
Grass	.256	86	22	2	0	0	12	3	14	.278	.279
Turf	.250	276	69	9	0	1	25	29	36	.317	.293
First Pitch	.333	48	16	2	0	0	9	2	0	.353	.375
Ahead in Count	.212	104	22	3	0	0	10	22	0	.346	.240
Behind in Count	.272	151	41	6	0	1	14	0	45	.268	.331
Two Strikes	.214	126	27	3	0	1	12	8	50	.257	.262

	Avg	AB	H	2B	3B	HR	RBI	BB	SO	OBP	SLG
Scoring Posn	.238	130	31	4	0	1	36	12	24	.293	.292
Close & Late	.311	122	38	4	0	0	14	14	17	.380	.344
None on/out	.292	65	19	0	0	0	0	5	3	.343	.292
Batting #6	.179	95	17	2	0	0	7	5	11	.220	.200
Batting #7	.280	75	21	4	0	0	5	6	14	.333	.333
Other	.276	192	53	5	0	1	25	21	25	.339	.318
April	.233	30	7	0	0	0	3	6	5	.351	.233
May	.240	25	6	2	0	0	8	2	5	.286	.320
June	.296	81	24	4	0	0	8	4	9	.329	.346
July	.177	62	11	2	0	0	4	9	10	.282	.210
August	.325	83	27	1	0	0	6	2	8	.333	.337
September/October	.198	81	16	2	0	1	8	9	13	.275	.259
Pre-All Star	.264	159	42	6	0	0	21	13	24	.316	.302
Post-All Star	.241	203	49	5	0	1	16	19	26	.302	.281

Batter vs. Pitcher (career)

Hits Best Against	Avg	AB	H	2B	3B	HR	RBI	BB	SO	OBP	SLG

Hits Worst Against	Avg	AB	H	2B	3B	HR	RBI	BB	SO	OBP	SLG
Zane Smith	.154	13	2	0	0	0	1	0	1	.154	.154

Dan Wilson — Reds

Age 25 – Bats Right (groundball hitter)

	Avg	G	AB	R	H	2B	3B	HR	RBI	BB	SO	HBP	GDP	SB	CS	OBP	SLG	IBB	SH	SF	#Pit	#P/PA	GB	FB	G/F
1993 Season	.224	36	76	6	17	3	0	0	8	9	16	0	2	0	0	.302	.263	4	2	1	311	3.53	25	19	1.32
Career (1992-1993)	.257	48	101	8	26	4	0	0	11	12	24	0	4	0	0	.333	.297	4	2	1	436	3.76	34	20	1.70

1993 Season

	Avg	AB	H	2B	3B	HR	RBI	BB	SO	OBP	SLG
vs. Left	.167	18	3	0	0	0	1	1	3	.211	.167
vs. Right	.241	58	14	3	0	0	7	8	13	.328	.293
Scoring Posn	.286	21	6	2	0	0	8	6	4	.429	.381
Close & Late	.231	13	3	0	0	0	2	1	3	.286	.231

Glenn Wilson — Pirates

Age 35 – Bats Right

	Avg	G	AB	R	H	2B	3B	HR	RBI	BB	SO	HBP	GDP	SB	CS	OBP	SLG	IBB	SH	SF	#Pit	#P/PA	GB	FB	G/F
1993 Season	.143	10	14	0	2	0	0	0	0	0	9	0	0	0	0	.143	.143	0	1	0	58	3.87	3	1	3.00
Last Five Years	.254	256	814	92	207	40	4	21	119	63	126	2	27	1	8	.306	.391	6	1	10	3016	3.38	327	235	1.39

1993 Season

	Avg	AB	H	2B	3B	HR	RBI	BB	SO	OBP	SLG
vs. Left	.167	12	2	0	0	0	0	0	7	.167	.167
vs. Right	.000	2	0	0	0	0	0	0	2	.000	.000
Scoring Posn	.000	3	0	0	0	0	0	0	3	.000	.000
Close & Late	.000	4	0	0	0	0	0	0	2	.000	.000

Last Five Years

	Avg	AB	H	2B	3B	HR	RBI	BB	SO	OBP	SLG
vs. Left	.285	319	91	24	1	6	50	26	48	.334	.423
vs. Right	.234	495	116	16	3	15	69	37	78	.288	.370
Groundball	.265	287	76	18	2	4	46	18	30	.307	.383
Flyball	.250	180	45	9	0	6	28	18	29	.315	.400
Home	.257	377	97	23	1	9	64	34	55	.317	.395
Away	.252	437	110	17	3	12	55	29	71	.297	.387
Day	.276	246	68	15	3	7	39	27	39	.345	.447
Night	.245	568	139	25	1	14	80	36	87	.288	.366
Grass	.253	217	55	7	0	11	33	17	40	.304	.438
Turf	.255	597	152	33	4	10	86	46	86	.307	.374

	Avg	AB	H	2B	3B	HR	RBI	BB	SO	OBP	SLG
Scoring Posn	.296	226	67	15	1	5	98	21	41	.347	.438
Close & Late	.275	153	42	7	1	4	29	17	29	.341	.412
None on/out	.247	194	48	10	0	5	5	16	26	.305	.376
Batting #5	.281	442	124	24	4	12	65	32	54	.325	.434
Batting #6	.199	191	38	8	0	3	19	17	35	.265	.288
Other	.249	181	45	8	0	6	35	14	37	.303	.392
April	.209	129	27	3	0	5	17	13	19	.283	.349
May	.301	156	47	9	1	5	23	10	23	.337	.468
June	.246	138	34	3	1	4	21	8	27	.286	.370
July	.225	142	32	11	0	3	22	21	27	.325	.366

Last Five Years

	Avg	AB	H	2B	3B	HR	RBI	BB	SO	OBP	SLG		Avg	AB	H	2B	3B	HR	RBI	BB	SO	OBP	SLG
First Pitch	.219	146	32	8	3	4	18	3	0	.242	.397	August	.288	191	55	11	2	3	27	8	21	.315	.414
Ahead in Count	.301	176	53	11	0	6	31	29	0	.394	.466	September/October	.207	58	12	3	0	1	9	3	9	.242	.310
Behind in Count	.240	350	84	14	1	9	50	0	98	.240	.363	Pre-All Star	.249	466	116	17	2	14	63	34	77	.299	.384
Two Strikes	.209	311	65	10	0	8	36	30	126	.276	.318	Post-All Star	.261	348	91	23	2	7	56	29	49	.316	.399

Batter vs. Pitcher (since 1984)

Hits Best Against	Avg	AB	H	2B	3B	HR	RBI	BB	SO	OBP	SLG	Hits Worst Against	Avg	AB	H	2B	3B	HR	RBI	BB	SO	OBP	SLG
Frank DiPino	.667	12	8	1	0	2	5	3	0	.733	1.250	Frank Viola	.000	11	0	0	0	0	0	0	2	.000	.000
John Candelaria	.526	19	10	2	0	2	3	1	3	.550	.947	Paul Assenmacher	.000	11	0	0	0	0	0	0	4	.000	.000
Roger McDowell	.500	18	9	1	0	1	5	1	4	.526	.722	John Smiley	.091	11	1	0	0	0	1	0	3	.083	.091
Zane Smith	.433	30	13	5	0	1	4	4	2	.500	.700	Craig Lefferts	.105	19	2	0	0	0	1	0	2	.105	.105
Les Lancaster	.400	10	4	1	0	1	2	1	2	.455	.800	Jamie Moyer	.120	25	3	0	0	0	0	0	6	.120	.120

Nigel Wilson — Marlins

Age 24 – Bats Left

	Avg	G	AB	R	H	2B	3B	HR	RBI	BB	SO	HBP	GDP	SB	CS	OBP	SLG	IBB	SH	SF	#Pit	#P/PA	GB	FB	G/F
1993 Season	.000	7	16	0	0	0	0	0	0	0	11	0	0	0	0	.000	.000	0	0	0	66	4.13	2	3	0.67

1993 Season

	Avg	AB	H	2B	3B	HR	RBI	BB	SO	OBP	SLG		Avg	AB	H	2B	3B	HR	RBI	BB	SO	OBP	SLG
vs. Left	.000	2	0	0	0	0	0	0	2	.000	.000	Scoring Posn	.000	4	0	0	0	0	0	0	2	.000	.000
vs. Right	.000	14	0	0	0	0	0	0	9	.000	.000	Close & Late	.000	5	0	0	0	0	0	0	2	.000	.000

Steve Wilson — Dodgers

Age 29 – Pitches Left (flyball pitcher)

	ERA	W	L	Sv	G	GS	IP	BB	SO	Avg	H	2B	3B	HR	RBI	OBP	SLG	GF	IR	IRS	Hld	SvOp	SB	CS	GB	FB	G/F
1993 Season	4.56	1	0	1	25	0	25.2	14	23	.288	30	5	1	2	14	.378	.413	4	25	5	1	1	5	1	36	29	1.24
Last Five Years	4.37	13	18	6	202	23	337.2	126	251	.262	341	58	16	32	174	.327	.405	32	173	34	30	12	22	16	386	417	0.93

1993 Season

	ERA	W	L	Sv	G	GS	IP	H	HR	BB	SO		Avg	AB	H	2B	3B	HR	RBI	BB	SO	OBP	SLG
Home	4.08	1	0	1	14	0	17.2	20	2	5	14	vs. Left	.311	45	14	2	1	0	4	6	9	.404	.400
Away	5.63	0	0	0	11	0	8.0	10	0	9	9	vs. Right	.271	59	16	3	0	2	10	8	14	.358	.424
Starter	0.00	0	0	0	0	0	0.0	0	0	0	0	Scoring Posn	.241	29	7	1	0	0	7	10	9	.436	.276
Reliever	4.56	1	0	1	25	0	25.2	30	2	14	23	Close & Late	.333	12	4	1	0	1	2	3	1	.467	.667
0 Days rest	1.69	0	0	0	4	0	5.1	3	0	3	8	None on/out	.261	23	6	0	0	0	0	0	6	.261	.261
1 or 2 Days rest	3.46	0	0	1	14	0	13.0	14	0	11	11	First Pitch	.176	17	3	1	0	1	3	3	0	.300	.412
3+ Days rest	8.59	1	0	0	7	0	7.1	13	2	0	4	Ahead in Count	.267	45	12	3	1	0	6	0	19	.283	.378
Pre-All Star	4.85	1	0	1	16	0	13.0	17	2	8	9	Behind in Count	.520	25	13	1	0	1	4	9	0	.647	.680
Post-All Star	4.26	0	0	0	9	0	12.2	13	0	6	14	Two Strikes	.217	46	10	2	1	0	4	2	23	.265	.304

Last Five Years

	ERA	W	L	Sv	G	GS	IP	H	HR	BB	SO		Avg	AB	H	2B	3B	HR	RBI	BB	SO	OBP	SLG
Home	4.84	8	10	5	97	15	169.1	183	22	61	133	vs. Left	.247	396	98	14	7	6	54	38	88	.314	.364
Away	3.90	5	8	1	105	8	168.1	158	10	65	118	vs. Right	.269	904	243	44	9	26	120	88	163	.333	.424
Day	4.72	7	10	2	92	15	160.1	168	17	65	130	Inning 1-6	.246	757	186	32	9	21	104	67	146	.307	.395
Night	4.06	6	8	4	110	8	177.1	173	15	61	121	Inning 7+	.285	543	155	26	7	11	70	59	105	.355	.420
Grass	4.34	11	12	6	141	18	238.1	247	26	84	181	None on	.260	711	185	28	5	19	19	60	139	.320	.394
Turf	4.44	2	6	0	61	5	99.1	94	6	42	70	Runners on	.265	589	156	30	11	13	155	66	112	.336	.419
April	4.67	1	5	2	32	4	44.1	56	3	21	26	Scoring Posn	.266	354	94	18	7	3	123	48	76	.346	.381
May	5.06	3	2	0	30	1	37.1	40	6	16	28	Close & Late	.311	180	56	9	2	3	28	23	31	.389	.433
June	3.38	4	2	1	31	4	72.0	62	6	24	44	None on/out	.257	319	82	14	1	5	5	19	59	.299	.354
July	3.81	1	2	1	31	3	52.0	53	5	17	42	vs. 1st Batr (relief)	.200	155	31	5	2	0	22	17	36	.275	.258
August	4.79	3	3	0	30	3	56.1	58	7	16	45	First Inning Pitched	.246	577	142	25	5	8	82	72	117	.328	.348
September/October	4.88	1	4	2	48	8	75.2	72	5	32	66	First 15 Pitches	.249	522	130	25	4	8	68	65	101	.332	.358
Starter	5.50	5	9	0	23	23	113.0	127	16	36	75	Pitch 16-30	.297	293	87	12	3	9	41	31	59	.365	.451
Reliever	3.81	8	9	6	179	0	224.2	214	16	90	176	Pitch 31-45	.225	187	42	9	3	6	25	10	45	.264	.401
0 Days rest	3.60	2	1	3	41	0	50.0	42	4	18	33	Pitch 46+	.275	298	82	12	6	9	40	20	46	.320	.446
1 or 2 Days rest	3.40	3	4	2	81	0	95.1	88	2	42	78	First Pitch	.296	159	47	11	2	5	28	21	0	.374	.484
3+ Days rest	4.42	3	4	1	57	0	79.1	84	10	30	65	Ahead in Count	.219	606	133	22	8	9	58	0	213	.224	.327
Pre-All Star	4.01	8	9	4	104	9	170.2	172	17	68	114	Behind in Count	.320	278	89	13	3	10	58	61	0	.437	.496
Post-All Star	4.74	5	9	2	98	14	167.0	169	15	58	137	Two Strikes	.205	638	131	23	9	14	59	43	251	.258	.335

Pitcher vs. Batter (career)

Pitches Best Vs.	Avg	AB	H	2B	3B	HR	RBI	BB	SO	OBP	SLG	Pitches Worst Vs.	Avg	AB	H	2B	3B	HR	RBI	BB	SO	OBP	SLG
Dave Magadan	.091	11	1	0	0	0	1	0	1	.091	.091	Willie McGee	.500	10	5	0	0	0	2	1	4	.545	.500
Dave Martinez	.100	10	1	0	0	0	0	1	0	.182	.100	John Kruk	.467	15	7	0	0	0	2	2	2	.500	.467
Gregg Jefferies	.133	15	2	0	1	0	1	2	1	.235	.267	Andy Van Slyke	.421	19	8	1	1	2	5	4	2	.522	.895
Jose Oquendo	.167	12	2	1	0	0	0	0	3	.167	.250	Jay Bell	.417	12	5	0	1	0	1	3	2	.533	.583
Gary Redus	.182	11	2	0	0	0	1	1	0	.250	.182	Jeff King	.333	15	5	1	0	2	4	2	2	.412	.800

Trevor Wilson — Giants

Age 28 – Pitches Left (groundball pitcher)

	ERA	W	L	Sv	G	GS	IP	BB	SO	Avg	H	2B	3B	HR	RBI	OBP	SLG	CG	ShO	Sup	QS	#P/S	SB	CS	GB	FB	G/F
1993 Season	3.60	7	5	0	22	18	110.0	40	57	.275	110	14	2	8	41	.347	.380	1	0	3.68	8	84	4	4	157	105	1.50
Last Five Years	3.86	38	40	0	133	94	615.2	254	372	.245	550	87	13	52	249	.325	.364	7	4	3.84	47	90	22	32	909	574	1.58

1993 Season

	ERA	W	L	Sv	G	GS	IP	H	HR	BB	SO		Avg	AB	H	2B	3B	HR	RBI	BB	SO	OBP	SLG
Home	2.76	4	2	0	11	10	62.0	61	2	26	32	vs. Left	.179	84	15	4	0	1	6	4	12	.231	.262

1993 Season

	ERA	W	L	Sv	G	GS	IP	H	HR	BB	SO
Away	4.69	3	3	0	11	8	48.0	49	6	14	25
Starter	3.65	7	5	0	18	18	106.0	105	8	38	55
Reliever	2.25	0	0	0	4	0	4.0	5	0	2	2
0-3 Days Rest	0.00	0	0	0	0	0	0.0	0	0	0	0
4 Days Rest	3.32	4	2	0	10	10	59.2	60	3	24	31
5+ Days Rest	4.08	3	3	0	8	8	46.1	45	5	14	24
Pre-All Star	3.60	5	4	0	15	15	90.0	89	8	33	47
Post-All Star	3.60	2	1	0	7	3	20.0	21	0	7	10

	Avg	AB	H	2B	3B	HR	RBI	BB	SO	OBP	SLG
vs. Right	.301	316	95	10	2	7	35	36	45	.377	.411
Scoring Posn	.279	86	24	1	0	3	31	8	11	.337	.395
Close & Late	.273	22	6	0	0	0	1	1	0	.333	.273
None on/out	.314	102	32	5	1	1	1	12	19	.391	.412
First Pitch	.328	64	21	3	0	1	12	3	0	.386	.422
Ahead in Count	.223	175	39	6	0	2	14	0	49	.228	.291
Behind in Count	.263	99	26	2	2	4	9	20	0	.392	.444
Two Strikes	.207	150	31	3	0	1	8	17	57	.294	.247

Last Five Years

	ERA	W	L	Sv	G	GS	IP	H	HR	BB	SO
Home	3.17	22	19	0	65	53	355.1	299	25	142	201
Away	4.81	16	21	0	68	41	260.1	251	27	112	171
Day	3.32	20	10	0	50	37	236.0	205	21	95	158
Night	4.20	18	30	0	83	57	379.2	345	31	159	214
Grass	3.53	30	29	0	99	70	472.1	407	38	100	275
Turf	4.96	8	11	0	34	24	143.1	143	14	74	97
April	4.75	1	5	0	17	8	60.2	67	7	34	34
May	3.61	6	6	0	19	14	89.2	70	7	38	55
June	3.44	11	8	0	28	23	149.1	134	14	56	87
July	4.16	7	10	0	25	22	129.2	114	12	59	83
August	4.09	8	8	0	21	19	116.2	110	7	42	71
September/October	3.36	5	3	0	23	8	69.2	55	5	25	42
Starter	3.81	36	35	0	94	94	555.0	501	46	222	331
Reliever	4.30	2	5	0	39	0	60.2	49	6	32	41
0-3 Days Rest	3.57	7	5	0	15	15	85.2	76	6	25	52
4 Days Rest	4.04	19	20	0	53	53	307.2	281	26	133	190
5+ Days Rest	3.51	10	10	0	26	26	161.2	144	14	64	89
Pre-All Star	3.65	22	22	0	72	53	347.1	307	31	147	206
Post-All Star	4.13	16	18	0	61	41	268.1	243	21	107	166

	Avg	AB	H	2B	3B	HR	RBI	BB	SO	OBP	SLG
vs. Left	.207	469	97	14	2	6	47	48	96	.289	.284
vs. Right	.255	1779	453	73	11	46	202	206	276	.334	.386
Inning 1-6	.253	1894	479	79	13	47	226	220	305	.333	.383
Inning 7+	.201	354	71	8	0	5	23	34	67	.283	.266
None on	.234	1276	299	46	5	24	24	162	222	.326	.335
Runners on	.258	972	251	41	8	28	225	92	150	.324	.403
Scoring Posn	.280	496	139	20	4	19	196	65	78	.362	.452
Close & Late	.202	173	35	6	0	1	7	16	34	.281	.254
None on/out	.242	563	136	19	3	6	6	78	96	.338	.318
vs. 1st Batr (relief)	.286	35	10	2	0	1	3	4	6	.359	.429
First Inning Pitched	.259	467	121	18	1	13	69	62	69	.348	.385
First 75 Pitches	.252	1816	458	74	12	44	214	212	296	.333	.379
Pitch 76-90	.226	234	53	9	1	8	27	20	35	.296	.376
Pitch 91-105	.219	151	33	3	0	0	4	13	28	.283	.238
Pitch 106+	.128	47	6	1	0	0	4	9	13	.293	.149
First Pitch	.297	313	93	15	1	9	52	9	0	.329	.438
Ahead in Count	.196	1037	203	32	8	15	93	0	310	.201	.285
Behind in Count	.297	505	150	18	3	20	65	150	0	.459	.463
Two Strikes	.174	973	169	23	6	11	71	95	372	.252	.244

Pitcher vs. Batter (career)

Pitches Best Vs.	Avg	AB	H	2B	3B	HR	RBI	BB	SO	OBP	SLG
Darryl Strawberry	.000	16	0	0	0	0	1	2	5	.111	.000
Lloyd McClendon	.000	13	0	0	0	0	0	5	1	.278	.000
Eric Yelding	.071	14	1	0	0	0	0	3	4	.235	.071
Eric Anthony	.077	13	1	0	0	0	0	0	5	.077	.077
Roberto Alomar	.091	11	1	0	0	0	0	0	1	.091	.091

Pitches Worst Vs.	Avg	AB	H	2B	3B	HR	RBI	BB	SO	OBP	SLG
Fred McGriff	.529	17	9	1	0	2	6	4	1	.619	.941
Otis Nixon	.462	13	6	0	0	2	5	0	1	.429	.923
Benito Santiago	.462	13	6	2	1	1	7	2	2	.533	1.000
Marquis Grissom	.350	20	7	1	0	3	4	2	1	.409	.850
George Bell	.333	9	3	1	0	2	4	2	0	.417	1.111

Willie Wilson — Cubs

Age 38 – Bats Both (groundball hitter)

	Avg	G	AB	R	H	2B	3B	HR	RBI	BB	SO	HBP	GDP	SB	CS	OBP	SLG	IBB	SH	SF	#Pit	#P/PA	GB	FB	G/F
1993 Season	.258	105	221	29	57	11	3	1	11	11	40	3	2	7	2	.301	.348	1	1	1	907	3.83	88	50	1.76
Last Five Years	.262	577	1601	212	420	70	22	6	161	121	283	11	36	103	27	.316	.345	5	13	14	6532	3.71	666	365	1.82

1993 Season

	Avg	AB	H	2B	3B	HR	RBI	BB	SO	OBP	SLG
vs. Left	.235	102	24	4	0	0	4	3	12	.257	.275
vs. Right	.277	119	33	7	3	1	7	8	28	.336	.412
Home	.289	114	33	6	3	0	4	6	21	.331	.395
Away	.224	107	24	5	0	1	7	5	19	.270	.299
First Pitch	.281	32	9	1	0	0	4	1	0	.324	.313
Ahead in Count	.297	37	11	5	0	0	2	6	0	.395	.432
Behind in Count	.257	105	27	4	3	0	3	0	28	.262	.352
Two Strikes	.209	110	23	3	2	0	3	4	40	.241	.273

	Avg	AB	H	2B	3B	HR	RBI	BB	SO	OBP	SLG
Scoring Posn	.205	39	8	1	0	0	10	3	7	.273	.231
Close & Late	.286	56	16	2	1	0	3	3	11	.322	.357
None on/out	.213	89	19	4	1	0	0	4	22	.255	.281
Batting #1	.248	145	36	7	1	0	3	4	23	.273	.310
Batting #9	.263	38	10	2	2	0	2	3	9	.317	.421
Other	.289	38	11	2	0	1	6	4	8	.378	.421
Pre-All Star	.248	161	40	8	2	0	6	5	31	.284	.323
Post-All Star	.283	60	17	3	1	1	5	6	9	.343	.417

Last Five Years

	Avg	AB	H	2B	3B	HR	RBI	BB	SO	OBP	SLG
vs. Left	.257	548	141	29	3	1	59	34	100	.299	.327
vs. Right	.265	1053	279	41	19	5	102	87	183	.325	.354
Groundball	.268	421	113	15	6	1	41	25	66	.309	.340
Flyball	.285	362	103	23	4	2	41	27	72	.338	.387
Home	.282	808	228	36	11	2	74	64	139	.336	.361
Away	.242	793	192	34	11	4	87	57	144	.296	.328
Day	.246	499	123	23	6	1	40	38	85	.303	.323
Night	.270	1102	297	47	16	5	121	83	198	.322	.355
Grass	.252	965	243	41	12	2	89	75	167	.308	.325
Turf	.278	636	177	29	10	4	72	46	116	.328	.374
First Pitch	.297	229	68	9	5	0	23	4	0	.318	.380
Ahead in Count	.339	304	103	19	1	2	35	67	0	.453	.428
Behind in Count	.211	776	164	25	8	2	66	0	235	.214	.272
Two Strikes	.194	782	152	23	8	3	66	50	283	.244	.256

	Avg	AB	H	2B	3B	HR	RBI	BB	SO	OBP	SLG
Scoring Posn	.264	394	104	19	7	1	148	31	69	.315	.355
Close & Late	.246	264	65	9	2	2	29	25	53	.313	.318
None on/out	.232	435	101	14	6	1	1	39	87	.300	.299
Batting #1	.252	496	125	23	7	2	37	30	78	.296	.339
Batting #7	.288	423	122	20	6	1	46	43	67	.353	.371
Other	.254	682	173	27	9	3	78	48	138	.307	.333
April	.262	309	81	21	4	1	40	26	36	.321	.366
May	.210	272	57	8	3	1	20	23	53	.269	.272
June	.267	225	60	8	1	0	20	22	46	.333	.311
July	.305	308	94	9	6	1	44	26	55	.363	.383
August	.244	234	57	10	5	2	19	12	44	.282	.355
September/October	.281	253	71	14	3	1	18	12	49	.317	.372
Pre-All Star	.244	923	225	39	10	2	91	82	163	.307	.314
Post-All Star	.288	678	195	31	12	4	70	39	120	.328	.386

Batter vs. Pitcher (since 1984)

Hits Best Against	Avg	AB	H	2B	3B	HR	RBI	BB	SO	OBP	SLG
Bud Black	.600	10	6	1	0	0	1	1	3	.636	.700
Doug Drabek	.583	12	7	0	0	0	0	0	0	.583	.583
Neal Heaton	.522	23	12	1	1	0	3	3	0	.577	.652
Tom Gordon	.500	10	5	1	0	0	1	2	2	.583	.600

Hits Worst Against	Avg	AB	H	2B	3B	HR	RBI	BB	SO	OBP	SLG
Steve Ontiveros	.000	14	0	0	0	0	0	1	2	.067	.000
Jack McDowell	.000	13	0	0	0	0	0	0	4	.000	.000
Chris Bosio	.045	22	1	0	0	0	2	0	6	.043	.045
Jim Abbott	.091	11	1	0	0	0	3	0	2	.083	.091

Batter vs. Pitcher (since 1984)

Hits Best Against	Avg	AB	H	2B	3B	HR	RBI	BB	SO	OBP	SLG
Rich DeLucia	.455	11	5	2	0	0	4	1	0	.500	.636

Hits Worst Against	Avg	AB	H	2B	3B	HR	RBI	BB	SO	OBP	SLG
Mike Morgan	.120	25	3	0	0	0	0	0	2	.120	.120

Dave Winfield — Twins

Age 42 – Bats Right

	Avg	G	AB	R	H	2B	3B	HR	RBI	BB	SO	HBP	GDP	SB	CS	OBP	SLG	IBB	SH	SF	#Pit	#P/PA	GB	FB	G/F
1993 Season	.271	143	547	72	148	27	2	21	76	45	106	0	15	2	3	.325	.442	2	0	2	2254	3.79	214	139	1.54
Last Five Years	.273	581	2173	309	593	108	11	96	348	235	385	4	64	11	9	.342	.465	19	4	18	9171	3.77	857	592	1.45

1993 Season

	Avg	AB	H	2B	3B	HR	RBI	BB	SO	OBP	SLG
vs. Left	.292	137	40	9	1	4	19	11	21	.345	.460
vs. Right	.263	410	108	18	1	17	57	34	85	.318	.437
Groundball	.276	105	29	6	0	2	11	8	19	.327	.390
Flyball	.260	104	27	5	1	8	17	10	14	.325	.558
Home	.255	278	71	13	1	12	47	24	60	.313	.439
Away	.286	269	77	14	1	9	29	21	46	.338	.446
Day	.224	156	35	6	1	6	17	14	37	.287	.391
Night	.289	391	113	21	1	15	59	31	69	.340	.463
Grass	.301	209	63	10	1	6	22	18	32	.357	.445
Turf	.251	338	85	17	1	15	54	27	74	.305	.441
First Pitch	.254	59	15	5	0	1	8	2	0	.279	.390
Ahead in Count	.336	113	38	7	1	6	21	21	0	.440	.575
Behind in Count	.206	267	55	9	1	10	30	0	89	.206	.360
Two Strikes	.201	259	52	9	1	6	25	22	106	.261	.313

	Avg	AB	H	2B	3B	HR	RBI	BB	SO	OBP	SLG
Scoring Posn	.220	168	37	6	0	8	55	20	35	.300	.399
Close & Late	.242	91	22	3	1	2	10	8	17	.300	.363
None on/out	.291	134	39	8	1	2	2	8	23	.331	.410
Batting #4	.275	222	61	10	2	9	34	18	36	.328	.459
Batting #5	.272	298	81	17	0	12	42	26	62	.329	.450
Other	.222	27	6	0	0	0	0	1	8	.250	.222
April	.230	74	17	3	0	4	16	4	19	.269	.432
May	.276	87	24	5	0	3	12	7	17	.330	.437
June	.220	82	18	0	1	1	6	5	19	.264	.280
July	.355	107	38	9	1	9	25	10	17	.410	.710
August	.239	113	27	3	0	2	6	10	19	.298	.319
September/October	.286	84	24	7	0	2	11	9	15	.351	.440
Pre-All Star	.267	288	77	11	1	13	46	21	59	.317	.448
Post-All Star	.274	259	71	16	1	8	30	24	47	.333	.436

1993 By Position

Position	Avg	AB	H	2B	3B	HR	RBI	BB	SO	OBP	SLG	G	GS	Innings	PO	A	E	DP	Fld Pct	Rng Fctr	In Zone	Outs	Zone Rtg	MLB Zone
As Designated Hitter	.258	414	107	23	1	12	49	33	79	.313	.406	105	104	---	---	---	---	---	---	---	---	---	---	---
As rf	.277	112	31	3	1	7	22	12	22	.344	.509	31	29	253.0	62	2	0	0	1.000	2.28	77	61	.792	.826

Last Five Years

	Avg	AB	H	2B	3B	HR	RBI	BB	SO	OBP	SLG
vs. Left	.295	599	177	34	5	28	106	75	88	.373	.509
vs. Right	.264	1574	416	74	6	68	242	160	297	.331	.449
Groundball	.301	552	166	26	4	24	80	65	98	.373	.493
Flyball	.264	473	125	22	4	25	90	47	73	.328	.486
Home	.265	1055	280	45	5	51	168	123	195	.339	.463
Away	.280	1118	313	63	6	45	180	112	190	.345	.468
Day	.252	583	147	26	2	23	85	65	118	.325	.422
Night	.281	1590	446	82	9	73	263	170	267	.349	.481
Grass	.264	1331	352	67	6	53	186	141	232	.334	.443
Turf	.286	842	241	41	5	43	162	94	153	.356	.500
First Pitch	.346	208	72	18	3	13	50	14	0	.389	.649
Ahead in Count	.359	529	190	36	2	35	105	123	0	.478	.633
Behind in Count	.191	988	189	27	4	30	113	0	323	.190	.318
Two Strikes	.196	988	194	33	4	27	111	96	385	.266	.320

	Avg	AB	H	2B	3B	HR	RBI	BB	SO	OBP	SLG
Scoring Posn	.262	596	156	30	3	26	246	97	97	.356	.453
Close & Late	.252	317	80	12	2	13	43	37	65	.328	.426
None on/out	.270	570	154	31	3	19	19	49	99	.332	.435
Batting #4	.273	1429	390	70	8	60	243	173	247	.350	.459
Batting #5	.269	468	126	24	0	25	69	42	89	.329	.481
Other	.279	276	77	14	3	11	36	20	49	.327	.471
April	.272	265	72	12	0	13	47	16	54	.310	.464
May	.255	349	89	18	3	15	46	36	56	.324	.453
June	.283	364	103	19	4	18	62	42	62	.355	.505
July	.277	393	109	23	2	19	59	37	58	.341	.491
August	.268	396	106	18	1	15	59	49	82	.348	.432
September/October	.281	406	114	18	1	16	75	55	73	.362	.448
Pre-All Star	.275	1111	306	55	7	55	176	106	191	.337	.486
Post-All Star	.270	1062	287	53	4	41	172	129	194	.348	.444

Batter vs. Pitcher (since 1984)

Hits Best Against	Avg	AB	H	2B	3B	HR	RBI	BB	SO	OBP	SLG
Lee Guetterman	.900	10	9	0	1	1	4	1	0	.909	1.400
Rod Nichols	.714	7	5	1	0	0	4	4	2	.818	.857
John Habyan	.667	12	8	3	0	0	4	2	1	.714	.917
Jaime Navarro	.478	23	11	2	0	4	13	1	3	.500	1.087
Scott Bankhead	.474	19	9	4	0	2	6	3	3	.545	1.000

Hits Worst Against	Avg	AB	H	2B	3B	HR	RBI	BB	SO	OBP	SLG
Kenny Rogers	.071	14	1	0	0	0	0	2	5	.188	.071
Juan Guzman	.077	13	1	0	0	0	0	1	4	.143	.077
Mike Henneman	.083	12	1	0	0	0	0	0	5	.083	.083
Arthur Rhodes	.083	12	1	0	0	0	1	0	3	.083	.083
Nolan Ryan	.143	14	2	0	0	0	3	0	6	.125	.143

Bobby Witt — Athletics

Age 30 – Pitches Right

	ERA	W	L	Sv	G	GS	IP	BB	SO	Avg	H	2B	3B	HR	RBI	OBP	SLG	CG	ShO	Sup	QS	#P/S	SB	CS	GB	FB	G/F
1993 Season	4.21	14	13	0	35	33	220.0	91	131	.269	226	47	4	16	96	.340	.392	5	1	4.34	18	103	19	9	320	224	1.43
Last Five Years	4.40	56	57	0	147	143	918.0	503	725	.253	872	150	17	62	414	.347	.360	18	4	4.54	70	106	125	34	1208	941	1.28

1993 Season

	ERA	W	L	Sv	G	GS	IP	H	HR	BB	SO
Home	3.30	7	6	0	17	17	125.1	108	7	53	79
Away	5.42	7	7	0	18	16	94.2	118	9	38	52
Day	4.78	5	8	0	15	15	96.0	104	6	44	57
Night	3.77	9	5	0	20	18	124.0	122	10	47	74
Grass	4.46	11	12	0	31	29	193.2	206	14	82	112
Turf	2.39	3	1	0	4	4	26.1	20	2	9	19
April	3.04	1	0	0	4	4	26.2	22	1	11	13
May	4.31	4	2	0	6	6	39.2	43	3	20	21
June	4.11	2	3	0	6	6	35.0	38	5	16	22
July	7.31	1	4	0	7	5	32.0	47	3	7	25
August	4.24	1	3	0	6	6	40.1	41	1	22	16
September/October	2.72	5	1	0	6	6	46.1	35	3	15	34
Starter	4.29	14	13	0	33	33	212.0	217	16	91	125
Reliever	2.25	0	0	0	2	0	8.0	9	0	0	6
0-3 Days Rest	10.69	1	3	0	4	4	16.0	31	3	7	8

	Avg	AB	H	2B	3B	HR	RBI	BB	SO	OBP	SLG
vs. Left	.280	428	120	32	3	7	48	45	56	.351	.418
vs. Right	.258	411	106	15	1	9	48	46	75	.329	.365
Inning 1-6	.270	692	187	40	4	13	86	81	104	.346	.396
Inning 7+	.265	147	39	7	0	3	10	10	27	.312	.374
None on	.259	468	121	24	1	9	9	53	67	.335	.372
Runners on	.283	371	105	23	3	7	87	38	64	.346	.418
Scoring Posn	.266	207	55	12	2	5	79	24	41	.331	.415
Close & Late	.231	91	21	4	0	1	5	6	18	.278	.308
None on/out	.306	216	66	13	0	4	4	21	27	.370	.421
vs. 1st Batr (relief)	.000	2	0	0	0	0	0	0	1	.000	.000
First Inning Pitched	.319	141	45	10	0	3	23	23	21	.416	.454
First 75 Pitches	.286	594	170	35	4	12	78	65	85	.355	.419
Pitch 76-90	.202	99	20	3	0	1	5	8	19	.262	.263
Pitch 91-105	.264	72	19	3	0	3	10	12	10	.369	.431
Pitch 106+	.230	74	17	6	0	0	3	6	17	.288	.311

1993 Season

	ERA	W	L	Sv	G	GS	IP	H	HR	BB	SO		Avg	AB	H	2B	3B	HR	RBI	BB	SO	OBP	SLG
4 Days Rest	4.10	8	8	0	18	18	120.2	114	11	54	78	First Pitch	.299	137	41	8	0	3	14	4	0	.324	.423
5+ Days Rest	3.23	5	2	0	11	11	75.1	72	2	30	39	Ahead in Count	.231	390	90	23	1	4	44	0	112	.231	.326
Pre-All Star	3.77	8	6	0	18	18	119.1	117	10	50	71	Behind in Count	.339	165	56	7	2	4	17	48	0	.488	.479
Post-All Star	4.74	6	7	0	17	15	100.2	109	6	41	60	Two Strikes	.203	374	76	17	1	6	35	39	131	.278	.302

Last Five Years

	ERA	W	L	Sv	G	GS	IP	H	HR	BB	SO		Avg	AB	H	2B	3B	HR	RBI	BB	SO	OBP	SLG
Home	3.96	26	31	0	74	73	479.2	446	29	246	370	vs. Left	.251	1616	405	76	13	28	203	265	328	.354	.366
Away	4.89	30	26	0	73	70	438.1	426	33	257	355	vs. Right	.255	1831	467	74	4	34	211	238	397	.340	.356
Day	4.44	11	15	0	33	32	209.0	207	10	121	152	Inning 1-6	.256	2917	747	137	14	55	377	433	620	.351	.369
Night	4.39	45	42	0	114	111	709.0	665	52	382	573	Inning 7+	.236	530	125	13	3	7	37	70	105	.326	.311
Grass	4.45	46	49	0	127	124	790.1	759	52	432	620	None on	.243	1910	464	76	4	40	40	278	399	.341	.350
Turf	4.09	10	8	0	20	19	127.2	113	10	71	105	Runners on	.265	1537	408	74	13	22	374	225	326	.355	.373
April	3.83	7	7	0	20	19	122.1	114	11	69	88	Scoring Posn	.256	882	226	45	6	12	337	145	210	.351	.362
May	4.90	12	13	0	28	28	185.2	181	13	112	143	Close & Late	.225	276	62	8	2	3	22	43	58	.331	.301
June	4.46	8	11	0	23	23	139.1	141	10	78	100	None on/out	.263	867	228	41	2	17	17	118	168	.353	.374
July	4.13	11	6	0	23	21	146.0	131	13	63	126	vs. 1st Batr (relief)	.000	4	0	0	0	0	1	0	1	.000	.000
August	5.35	6	14	0	28	28	170.0	173	9	102	125	First Inning Pitched	.265	559	148	33	0	7	81	99	119	.373	.361
September/October	3.43	12	6	0	25	24	154.2	132	6	79	143	First 75 Pitches	.261	2345	612	107	13	43	296	346	494	.354	.373
Starter	4.47	56	57	0	143	143	901.0	859	62	497	709	Pitch 76-90	.234	441	103	17	0	6	49	52	84	.313	.313
Reliever	1.06	0	0	0	4	0	17.0	13	0	6	16	Pitch 91-105	.220	332	73	13	1	10	32	50	80	.324	.355
0-3 Days Rest	7.32	3	4	0	8	8	39.1	53	5	22	30	Pitch 106+	.255	329	84	13	3	3	37	55	67	.361	.340
4 Days Rest	4.22	29	24	0	67	67	437.0	402	31	240	353	First Pitch	.315	496	156	26	3	9	74	11	0	.331	.433
5+ Days Rest	4.45	24	29	0	68	68	424.2	404	26	235	326	Ahead in Count	.185	1594	295	56	3	16	150	0	584	.186	.254
Pre-All Star	4.29	31	32	0	78	77	497.2	474	38	282	373	Behind in Count	.347	733	254	37	8	24	113	279	0	.521	.517
Post-All Star	4.54	25	25	0	69	66	420.1	398	24	221	352	Two Strikes	.163	1613	263	53	3	18	142	213	725	.261	.233

Pitcher vs. Batter (career)

Pitches Best Vs.	Avg	AB	H	2B	3B	HR	RBI	BB	SO	OBP	SLG	Pitches Worst Vs.	Avg	AB	H	2B	3B	HR	RBI	BB	SO	OBP	SLG
Bo Jackson	.000	11	0	0	0	0	0	2	8	.154	.000	Felix Fermin	.571	21	12	2	0	0	5	4	0	.640	.667
Sam Horn	.000	10	0	0	0	0	1	2	7	.154	.000	Paul Sorrento	.500	12	6	1	0	1	1	5	3	.647	.833
Andy Allanson	.071	14	1	0	0	0	1	0	4	.071	.071	Mark McLemore	.455	11	5	1	1	0	4	3	1	.533	.727
Pedro Munoz	.071	14	1	0	0	0	1	0	7	.071	.071	Frank Thomas	.409	22	9	2	0	2	6	4	4	.500	.773
Pat Borders	.077	13	1	0	0	0	0	0	0	.077	.077	Larry Sheets	.357	14	5	0	1	2	6	3	3	.444	.929

Mike Witt — Yankees

Age 33 – Pitches Right (groundball pitcher)

	ERA	W	L	Sv	G	GS	IP	BB	SO	Avg	H	2B	3B	HR	RBI	OBP	SLG	CG	ShO	Sup	QS	#P/S	SB	CS	GB	FB	G/F
1993 Season	5.27	3	2	0	9	9	41.0	22	30	.248	39	5	0	7	22	.352	.414	0	0	7.24	3	82	3	3	57	41	1.39
Last Five Years	4.53	17	27	1	70	60	383.1	118	227	.273	405	68	4	43	184	.327	.411	7	1	4.74	27	96	25	14	631	364	1.73

1993 Season

	ERA	W	L	Sv	G	GS	IP	H	HR	BB	SO		Avg	AB	H	2B	3B	HR	RBI	BB	SO	OBP	SLG
Home	4.78	2	2	0	7	7	32.0	29	6	15	21	vs. Left	.213	75	16	2	0	2	11	16	10	.359	.320
Away	7.00	1	0	0	2	2	9.0	10	1	7	9	vs. Right	.280	82	23	3	0	5	11	6	20	.344	.500

Last Five Years

	ERA	W	L	Sv	G	GS	IP	H	HR	BB	SO		Avg	AB	H	2B	3B	HR	RBI	BB	SO	OBP	SLG
Home	4.44	9	14	1	35	30	196.2	200	30	50	108	vs. Left	.281	737	207	32	2	17	84	63	92	.335	.399
Away	4.63	8	13	0	35	30	186.2	205	13	68	119	vs. Right	.265	748	198	36	2	26	100	55	135	.318	.422
Day	3.64	10	8	0	25	24	158.1	152	14	47	94	Inning 1-6	.269	1205	324	54	4	35	150	95	186	.322	.407
Night	5.16	7	19	1	45	36	225.0	253	29	71	133	Inning 7+	.289	280	81	14	0	8	34	23	41	.346	.425
Grass	4.55	15	24	1	58	50	320.1	338	39	94	192	None on	.260	886	230	41	0	25	25	66	126	.315	.391
Turf	4.43	2	3	0	12	10	63.0	67	4	24	35	Runners on	.292	599	175	27	4	18	159	52	101	.344	.441
April	4.60	2	6	1	13	7	58.2	66	8	18	34	Scoring Posn	.261	329	86	11	2	12	138	27	71	.309	.416
May	3.57	4	3	0	18	14	93.1	94	12	35	55	Close & Late	.307	137	42	5	0	4	20	6	24	.331	.431
June	5.30	3	5	0	11	11	54.1	57	8	15	25	None on/out	.281	398	112	21	0	11	11	19	57	.317	.417
July	4.31	1	1	0	6	6	39.2	45	2	8	27	vs. 1st Batr (relief)	.250	8	2	0	0	0	0	1	0	.333	.250
August	4.90	4	5	0	10	10	60.2	64	7	19	37	First Inning Pitched	.267	258	69	9	1	9	34	31	47	.348	.415
September/October	4.93	3	7	0	12	12	76.2	79	6	23	49	First 75 Pitches	.270	1091	295	50	3	31	135	93	167	.328	.407
Starter	4.69	17	24	0	60	60	363.0	386	42	105	213	Pitch 76-90	.267	176	47	8	0	5	19	10	28	.309	.398
Reliever	1.77	0	3	1	10	0	20.1	19	1	13	14	Pitch 91-105	.288	132	38	6	1	3	15	8	13	.331	.417
0-3 Days Rest	0.00	0	0	0	0	0	0.0	0	0	0	0	Pitch 106+	.291	86	25	4	0	4	15	7	19	.340	.477
4 Days Rest	5.09	10	12	0	34	34	205.0	224	24	53	126	First Pitch	.379	195	74	19	1	5	41	4	0	.390	.564
5+ Days Rest	4.16	7	12	0	26	26	158.0	162	18	52	87	Ahead in Count	.204	545	111	18	1	15	47	0	187	.210	.323
Pre-All Star	4.23	10	14	1	44	34	219.1	229	29	70	120	Behind in Count	.296	456	135	22	1	12	56	63	0	.380	.428
Post-All Star	4.94	7	13	0	26	26	164.0	176	14	48	107	Two Strikes	.192	608	117	19	1	14	52	51	227	.253	.296

Pitcher vs. Batter (since 1984)

Pitches Best Vs.	Avg	AB	H	2B	3B	HR	RBI	BB	SO	OBP	SLG	Pitches Worst Vs.	Avg	AB	H	2B	3B	HR	RBI	BB	SO	OBP	SLG
Kelly Gruber	.059	17	1	1	0	0	2	2	0	.158	.118	Jerry Browne	.429	21	9	4	0	1	3	3	1	.500	.762
Ivan Calderon	.071	28	2	0	0	0	1	2	6	.129	.071	Dan Pasqua	.412	34	14	3	0	2	8	3	10	.447	.676
Bo Jackson	.071	14	1	0	0	0	0	0	8	.071	.071	Lonnie Smith	.400	20	8	3	1	0	2	2	3	.455	.650
Alvaro Espinoza	.083	12	1	0	0	0	0	0	4	.083	.083	Matt Nokes	.385	13	5	1	0	2	2	1	1	.429	.923
Curt Wilkerson	.136	22	3	0	0	0	0	0	9	.136	.136	Eddie Murray	.333	45	15	4	0	3	13	15	5	.492	.622

Mark Wohlers — Braves

Age 24 – Pitches Right (groundball pitcher)

	ERA	W	L	Sv	G	GS	IP	BB	SO	Avg	H	2B	3B	HR	RBI	OBP	SLG	GF	IR	IRS	Hld	SvOp	SB	CS	GB	FB	G/F
1993 Season	4.50	6	2	0	46	0	48.0	22	45	.218	37	7	0	2	24	.309	.294	13	21	8	12	0	3	0	60	35	1.71
Career (1991-1993)	3.58	10	5	6	95	0	103.0	49	75	.228	82	15	1	3	43	.325	.300	33	43	14	16	10	11	1	137	82	1.67

1993 Season

	ERA	W	L	Sv	G	GS	IP	H	HR	BB	SO
Home	4.91	4	2	0	26	0	29.1	23	2	14	26
Away	3.86	2	0	0	20	0	18.2	14	0	8	19
Starter	0.00	0	0	0	0	0	0.0	0	0	0	0
Reliever	4.50	6	2	0	46	0	48.0	37	2	22	45
0 Days rest	6.39	1	0	0	13	0	12.2	15	0	8	9
1 or 2 Days rest	3.65	3	2	0	23	0	24.2	14	2	8	25
3+ Days rest	4.22	2	0	0	10	0	10.2	8	0	6	11
Pre-All Star	2.45	3	0	0	14	0	14.2	10	0	3	18
Post-All Star	5.40	3	2	0	32	0	33.1	27	2	19	27

	Avg	AB	H	2B	3B	HR	RBI	BB	SO	OBP	SLG
vs. Left	.225	71	16	1	0	1	9	12	18	.337	.282
vs. Right	.212	99	21	6	0	1	15	10	27	.288	.303
Scoring Posn	.234	47	11	2	0	0	20	8	10	.351	.277
Close & Late	.204	93	19	3	0	1	8	13	28	.302	.269
None on/out	.167	42	7	0	0	1	1	3	11	.222	.238
First Pitch	.438	16	7	1	0	0	1	3	0	.526	.500
Ahead in Count	.106	85	9	3	0	0	10	0	38	.105	.141
Behind in Count	.375	32	12	1	0	2	10	6	0	.474	.594
Two Strikes	.100	90	9	1	0	0	8	13	45	.212	.111

Tony Womack — Pirates

Age 24 – Bats Left

	Avg	G	AB	R	H	2B	3B	HR	RBI	BB	SO	HBP	GDP	SB	CS	OBP	SLG	IBB	SH	SF	#Pit	#P/PA	GB	FB	G/F
1993 Season	.083	15	24	5	2	0	0	0	0	3	3	0	0	2	0	.185	.083	0	1	0	106	3.79	10	10	1.00

1993 Season

	Avg	AB	H	2B	3B	HR	RBI	BB	SO	OBP	SLG
vs. Left	.000	5	0	0	0	0	0	0	1	.000	.000
vs. Right	.105	19	2	0	0	0	0	3	2	.227	.105
Scoring Posn	.000	3	0	0	0	0	0	0	0	.000	.000
Close & Late	.000	4	0	0	0	0	0	0	2	.000	.000

Ted Wood — Expos

Age 27 – Bats Left (groundball hitter)

	Avg	G	AB	R	H	2B	3B	HR	RBI	BB	SO	HBP	GDP	SB	CS	OBP	SLG	IBB	SH	SF	#Pit	#P/PA	GB	FB	G/F
1993 Season	.192	13	26	4	5	1	0	0	3	3	3	0	0	0	0	.276	.231	1	3	0	112	3.50	15	2	7.50
Career (1991-1993)	.183	47	109	9	20	3	0	1	7	11	29	1	4	0	0	.264	.239	1	6	0	503	3.96	42	24	1.75

1993 Season

	Avg	AB	H	2B	3B	HR	RBI	BB	SO	OBP	SLG
vs. Left	.000	1	0	0	0	0	0	1	0	.500	.000
vs. Right	.200	25	5	1	0	0	3	2	3	.259	.240
Scoring Posn	.286	7	2	1	0	0	3	1	1	.375	.429
Close & Late	.000	1	0	0	0	0	0	0	0	.000	.000

Tracy Woodson — Cardinals

Age 31 – Bats Right (groundball hitter)

	Avg	G	AB	R	H	2B	3B	HR	RBI	BB	SO	HBP	GDP	SB	CS	OBP	SLG	IBB	SH	SF	#Pit	#P/PA	GB	FB	G/F
1993 Season	.208	62	77	4	16	2	0	0	2	1	14	0	1	0	0	.215	.234	0	0	1	260	3.29	30	21	1.43
Last Five Years	.259	97	197	13	51	10	0	1	24	4	25	1	4	0	0	.276	.325	0	1	1	640	3.14	89	50	1.78

1993 Season

	Avg	AB	H	2B	3B	HR	RBI	BB	SO	OBP	SLG
vs. Left	.208	53	11	2	0	0	2	1	10	.218	.245
vs. Right	.208	24	5	0	0	0	0	0	4	.208	.208
Scoring Posn	.071	14	1	0	0	0	2	0	4	.067	.071
Close & Late	.211	19	4	1	0	0	0	1	3	.250	.263

Tim Worrell — Padres

Age 26 – Pitches Right

	ERA	W	L	Sv	G	GS	IP	BB	SO	Avg	H	2B	3B	HR	RBI	OBP	SLG	CG	ShO	Sup	QS	#P/S	SB	CS	GB	FB	G/F
1993 Season	4.92	2	7	0	21	16	100.2	43	52	.269	104	16	2	11	58	.338	.406	0	0	4.92	6	92	10	9	149	118	1.26

1993 Season

	ERA	W	L	Sv	G	GS	IP	H	HR	BB	SO
Home	3.82	2	3	0	12	10	68.1	62	6	23	40
Away	7.24	0	4	0	9	6	32.1	42	5	20	12
Starter	5.40	2	7	0	16	16	88.1	95	10	39	40
Reliever	1.46	0	0	0	5	0	12.1	9	1	4	12
0-3 Days Rest	6.35	0	1	0	2	2	11.1	16	1	4	5
4 Days Rest	4.62	1	4	0	9	9	50.2	53	6	19	22
5+ Days Rest	6.49	1	2	0	5	5	26.1	26	3	16	13
Pre-All Star	8.83	0	3	0	4	3	17.1	26	5	9	6
Post-All Star	4.10	2	4	0	17	13	83.1	78	6	34	46

	Avg	AB	H	2B	3B	HR	RBI	BB	SO	OBP	SLG
vs. Left	.270	189	51	5	1	5	26	27	19	.356	.386
vs. Right	.268	198	53	11	1	6	32	16	33	.319	.424
Scoring Posn	.309	97	30	5	1	4	47	15	15	.385	.505
Close & Late	.400	20	8	0	0	1	2	0	1	.400	.550
None on/out	.296	98	29	4	0	2	2	8	7	.349	.398
First Pitch	.185	54	10	1	0	2	9	3	0	.228	.315
Ahead in Count	.217	161	35	4	2	1	15	0	44	.212	.286
Behind in Count	.315	92	29	4	0	4	18	22	0	.447	.489
Two Strikes	.206	165	34	3	2	2	13	18	52	.283	.285

Todd Worrell — Dodgers

Age 34 – Pitches Right (flyball pitcher)

	ERA	W	L	Sv	G	GS	IP	BB	SO	Avg	H	2B	3B	HR	RBI	OBP	SLG	GF	IR	IRS	Hld	SvOp	SB	CS	GB	FB	G/F
1993 Season	6.05	1	1	5	35	0	38.2	11	31	.313	46	8	0	6	28	.348	.490	22	13	3	4	8	9	1	38	52	0.73
Last Five Years	3.38	9	9	28	149	0	154.1	62	136	.236	133	28	1	14	65	.310	.364	36	51	13	32	38	28	2	156	184	0.85

1993 Season

	ERA	W	L	Sv	G	GS	IP	H	HR	BB	SO
Home	7.23	0	1	0	16	0	18.2	25	2	8	13
Away	4.95	1	0	5	19	0	20.0	21	4	3	18
Starter	0.00	0	0	0	0	0	0.0	0	0	0	0
Reliever	6.05	1	1	5	35	0	38.2	46	6	11	31
0 Days rest	7.94	0	0	2	7	0	5.2	7	1	3	8
1 or 2 Days rest	6.98	1	1	0	18	0	19.1	24	3	6	13
3+ Days rest	3.95	0	0	3	10	0	13.2	15	2	2	10

	Avg	AB	H	2B	3B	HR	RBI	BB	SO	OBP	SLG
vs. Left	.313	80	25	6	0	4	18	8	19	.359	.538
vs. Right	.313	67	21	2	0	2	10	3	12	.333	.433
Scoring Posn	.302	43	13	3	0	1	20	5	7	.333	.442
Close & Late	.315	73	23	4	0	0	13	7	19	.357	.370
None on/out	.265	34	9	2	0	1	1	1	9	.286	.412
First Pitch	.467	30	14	2	0	0	5	1	0	.469	.533
Ahead in Count	.268	71	19	5	0	3	13	0	27	.257	.465

1993 Season

	ERA	W	L	Sv	G	GS	IP	H	HR	BB	SO
Pre-All Star	10.80	0	1	1	7	0	6.2	13	3	1	6
Post-All Star	5.06	1	0	4	28	0	32.0	33	3	10	25

	Avg	AB	H	2B	3B	HR	RBI	BB	SO	OBP	SLG
Behind in Count	.318	22	7	1	0	2	7	4	0	.393	.636
Two Strikes	.239	71	17	5	0	2	10	6	31	.291	.394

Last Five Years

	ERA	W	L	Sv	G	GS	IP	H	HR	BB	SO
Home	3.02	4	5	14	78	0	80.1	61	3	35	72
Away	3.77	5	4	14	71	0	74.0	72	11	27	64
Day	3.59	4	0	5	46	0	42.2	37	6	16	39
Night	3.30	5	9	23	103	0	111.2	96	8	46	97
Grass	4.19	1	2	7	53	0	58.0	58	7	23	43
Turf	2.90	8	7	21	96	0	96.1	75	7	39	93
April	0.69	1	1	4	22	0	26.0	13	2	9	24
May	4.76	1	1	3	18	0	17.0	16	3	8	19
June	6.63	2	4	4	19	0	19.0	29	4	12	11
July	2.55	0	0	6	25	0	24.2	21	1	5	20
August	4.19	4	3	5	39	0	38.2	38	2	18	35
September/October	2.48	1	0	6	26	0	29.0	16	2	10	27
Starter	0.00	0	0	0	0	0	0.0	0	0	0	0
Reliever	3.38	9	9	28	149	0	154.1	133	14	62	136
0 Days rest	2.17	2	1	8	34	0	29.0	28	3	7	26
1 or 2 Days rest	4.35	4	6	11	73	0	78.2	66	6	36	67
3+ Days rest	2.51	3	2	9	42	0	46.2	39	5	19	43
Pre-All Star	3.34	4	6	12	65	0	67.1	62	9	29	59
Post-All Star	3.41	5	3	16	84	0	87.0	71	5	33	77

	Avg	AB	H	2B	3B	HR	RBI	BB	SO	OBP	SLG
vs. Left	.234	291	68	15	1	10	40	34	78	.311	.395
vs. Right	.239	272	65	13	0	4	25	28	58	.308	.331
Inning 1-6	.000	0	0	0	0	0	0	0	0	.000	.000
Inning 7+	.236	563	133	28	1	14	65	62	136	.310	.364
None on	.243	304	74	18	0	6	6	27	83	.307	.362
Runners on	.228	259	59	10	1	8	59	35	53	.312	.367
Scoring Posn	.200	175	35	8	1	3	48	29	39	.303	.309
Close & Late	.224	326	73	16	1	4	39	40	82	.307	.316
None on/out	.238	130	31	6	0	4	4	9	30	.288	.377
vs. 1st Batr (relief)	.209	139	29	5	0	4	8	5	27	.233	.331
First Inning Pitched	.227	476	108	22	1	11	54	52	115	.301	.347
First 15 Pitches	.246	415	102	22	0	11	40	43	90	.315	.378
Pitch 16-30	.213	136	29	6	1	2	21	19	40	.304	.316
Pitch 31-45	.167	12	2	0	0	1	4	0	6	.167	.417
Pitch 46+	.000	0	0	0	0	0	0	0	0	.000	.000
First Pitch	.299	87	26	3	0	3	13	17	0	.410	.437
Ahead in Count	.197	295	58	14	1	6	31	0	116	.197	.312
Behind in Count	.263	80	21	5	0	4	12	22	0	.413	.475
Two Strikes	.185	298	55	14	1	4	24	22	136	.241	.279

Pitcher vs. Batter (career)

Pitches Best Vs.	Avg	AB	H	2B	3B	HR	RBI	BB	SO	OBP	SLG
Eric Davis	.000	12	0	0	0	0	0	3	2	.200	.000
Lance Parrish	.000	11	0	0	0	0	0	2	4	.154	.000
Robby Thompson	.077	13	1	0	0	0	0	0	3	.077	.077
Kevin Bass	.091	11	1	0	0	0	1	0	1	.091	.091
Shawon Dunston	.133	15	2	0	0	0	2	0	4	.133	.133

Pitches Worst Vs.	Avg	AB	H	2B	3B	HR	RBI	BB	SO	OBP	SLG
Steve Sax	.600	10	6	2	1	0	1	1	0	.636	1.000
Will Clark	.600	10	6	2	0	1	3	3	2	.692	1.100
Howard Johnson	.556	9	5	0	0	4	8	6	1	.733	1.889
Andres Galarraga	.421	19	8	3	1	0	3	1	4	.450	.684
Juan Samuel	.368	19	7	3	1	1	7	0	3	.368	.789

Rick Wrona — White Sox

Age 30 – Bats Right (groundball hitter)

	Avg	G	AB	R	H	2B	3B	HR	RBI	BB	SO	HBP	GDP	SB	CS	OBP	SLG	IBB	SH	SF	#Pit	#P/PA	GB	FB	G/F
1993 Season	.125	4	8	0	1	0	0	0	1	0	4	0	0	0	0	.125	.125	0	0	0	32	4.00	1	3	0.33
Last Five Years	.237	69	152	14	36	2	1	2	15	4	39	1	3	1	0	.258	.303	2	1	2	522	3.26	60	30	2.00

1993 Season

	Avg	AB	H	2B	3B	HR	RBI	BB	SO	OBP	SLG
vs. Left	.333	3	1	0	0	0	0	0	1	.333	.333
vs. Right	.000	5	0	0	0	0	1	0	3	.000	.000

	Avg	AB	H	2B	3B	HR	RBI	BB	SO	OBP	SLG
Scoring Posn	.000	1	0	0	0	0	1	0	0	.000	.000
Close & Late	.000	1	0	0	0	0	0	0	0	.000	.000

Eric Yelding — Cubs

Age 29 – Bats Right (groundball hitter)

	Avg	G	AB	R	H	2B	3B	HR	RBI	BB	SO	HBP	GDP	SB	CS	OBP	SLG	IBB	SH	SF	#Pit	#P/PA	GB	FB	G/F
1993 Season	.204	69	108	14	22	5	1	1	10	11	22	0	3	3	2	.277	.296	2	4	0	474	3.85	38	29	1.31
Career (1989-1993)	.244	368	993	122	242	27	7	3	67	70	177	1	21	89	41	.292	.294	6	13	8	3919	3.61	378	238	1.59

1993 Season

	Avg	AB	H	2B	3B	HR	RBI	BB	SO	OBP	SLG
vs. Left	.313	32	10	2	0	0	1	3	3	.371	.375
vs. Right	.158	76	12	3	1	1	9	8	19	.238	.263

	Avg	AB	H	2B	3B	HR	RBI	BB	SO	OBP	SLG
Scoring Posn	.172	29	5	2	1	0	8	3	4	.250	.310
Close & Late	.214	14	3	0	0	0	0	0	2	.214	.214

Career (1989-1993)

	Avg	AB	H	2B	3B	HR	RBI	BB	SO	OBP	SLG
vs. Left	.280	410	115	12	4	0	26	30	58	.326	.329
vs. Right	.218	583	127	15	3	3	41	40	119	.268	.269
Groundball	.254	346	88	13	1	1	13	19	52	.293	.306
Flyball	.205	176	36	1	2	0	17	14	35	.258	.233
Home	.235	477	112	6	4	1	27	36	85	.286	.270
Away	.252	516	130	21	3	2	40	34	92	.298	.316
Day	.252	305	77	8	2	2	22	26	54	.313	.311
Night	.240	688	165	19	5	1	45	44	123	.282	.286
Grass	.255	353	90	15	1	1	27	31	63	.314	.312
Turf	.238	640	152	12	6	2	40	39	114	.279	.284
First Pitch	.278	151	42	5	2	2	24	3	0	.287	.377
Ahead in Count	.236	203	48	3	1	1	11	33	0	.342	.276
Behind in Count	.234	478	112	15	2	0	21	0	164	.234	.274
Two Strikes	.193	488	94	14	1	0	17	34	177	.245	.225

	Avg	AB	H	2B	3B	HR	RBI	BB	SO	OBP	SLG
Scoring Posn	.241	216	52	6	3	0	60	14	27	.277	.296
Close & Late	.265	166	44	2	0	0	12	13	31	.320	.277
None on/out	.233	356	83	7	1	1	1	30	66	.295	.267
Batting #1	.246	633	156	16	5	1	34	43	113	.294	.292
Batting #8	.275	153	42	7	1	2	18	14	22	.333	.373
Other	.213	207	44	4	1	0	15	13	42	.256	.242
April	.218	119	26	3	2	0	6	3	19	.234	.277
May	.288	198	57	5	1	1	16	9	32	.319	.338
June	.246	187	46	3	1	1	13	20	29	.317	.289
July	.261	184	48	4	1	0	13	13	35	.305	.293
August	.180	133	24	5	0	0	6	8	22	.229	.218
September/October	.238	172	41	7	2	1	13	17	40	.307	.320
Pre-All Star	.251	566	142	11	4	2	37	37	92	.295	.295
Post-All Star	.234	427	100	16	3	1	30	33	85	.288	.293

Batter vs. Pitcher (career)

Hits Best Against	Avg	AB	H	2B	3B	HR	RBI	BB	SO	OBP	SLG
Frank Viola	.600	15	9	0	0	0	1	2	2	.647	.600
Steve Avery	.455	11	5	3	0	0	2	3	1	.571	.727
Fernando Valenzuela	.385	13	5	0	0	0	1	0	2	.385	.385
Mike Bielecki	.375	16	6	2	0	0	0	0	3	.375	.500
Doug Drabek	.357	14	5	1	0	0	2	0	3	.357	.429

Hits Worst Against	Avg	AB	H	2B	3B	HR	RBI	BB	SO	OBP	SLG
Trevor Wilson	.071	14	1	0	0	0	0	3	4	.235	.071
Jose DeLeon	.091	11	1	0	0	0	0	0	5	.091	.091
Greg Maddux	.115	26	3	1	0	0	0	1	6	.148	.154
Mark Gardner	.154	13	2	0	0	0	0	0	4	.154	.154
Chris Hammond	.154	13	2	0	0	0	0	0	0	.154	.154

Anthony Young — Mets

Age 28 – Pitches Right (groundball pitcher)

	ERA	W	L	Sv	G	GS	IP	BB	SO	Avg	H	2B	3B	HR	RBI	OBP	SLG	GF	IR	IRS	Hld	SvOp	SB	CS	GB	FB	G/F
1993 Season	3.77	1	16	3	39	10	100.1	42	62	.265	103	12	1	8	60	.336	.363	19	7	2	2	5	15	2	162	83	1.95
Career (1991-1993)	3.82	5	35	18	101	31	270.2	85	146	.273	285	43	11	20	137	.327	.392	47	26	6	4	25	28	9	467	247	1.89

1993 Season

	ERA	W	L	Sv	G	GS	IP	H	HR	BB	SO		Avg	AB	H	2B	3B	HR	RBI	BB	SO	OBP	SLG
Home	4.65	1	10	1	20	7	60.0	66	5	26	40	vs. Left	.263	186	49	9	0	5	31	27	33	.353	.392
Away	2.45	0	6	2	19	3	40.1	37	3	16	22	vs. Right	.267	202	54	3	1	3	29	15	29	.320	.337
Starter	3.52	0	8	0	10	10	64.0	60	5	21	43	Scoring Posn	.278	115	32	5	0	2	50	18	18	.368	.374
Reliever	4.21	1	8	3	29	0	36.1	43	3	21	19	Close & Late	.319	91	29	3	0	4	22	12	15	.398	.484
0 Days rest	3.60	0	2	1	4	0	5.0	6	0	2	3	None on/out	.236	89	21	2	0	1	1	11	20	.320	.292
1 or 2 Days rest	4.91	0	5	1	15	0	18.1	25	1	14	7	First Pitch	.226	62	14	1	0	2	9	8	0	.314	.339
3+ Days rest	3.46	1	1	1	10	0	13.0	12	2	5	9	Ahead in Count	.254	173	44	5	0	3	27	0	52	.256	.335
Pre-All Star	4.56	0	12	0	26	8	73.0	79	6	31	45	Behind in Count	.318	88	28	4	0	2	16	20	0	.440	.432
Post-All Star	1.65	1	4	3	13	2	27.1	24	2	11	17	Two Strikes	.211	166	35	3	0	1	17	14	62	.275	.247

Career (1991-1993)

	ERA	W	L	Sv	G	GS	IP	H	HR	BB	SO		Avg	AB	H	2B	3B	HR	RBI	BB	SO	OBP	SLG
Home	4.21	2	20	9	51	18	141.0	166	11	48	83	vs. Left	.298	557	166	28	8	11	76	51	74	.354	.436
Away	3.40	3	15	9	50	13	129.2	119	9	37	63	vs. Right	.244	488	119	15	3	9	61	34	72	.295	.342
Day	3.02	3	13	7	39	13	113.1	99	5	32	56	Inning 1-6	.282	685	193	31	7	12	84	50	99	.329	.400
Night	4.40	2	22	11	62	18	157.1	186	15	53	90	Inning 7+	.256	360	92	12	4	8	53	35	47	.322	.378
Grass	3.65	3	25	14	76	25	209.1	223	14	69	121	None on	.254	587	149	23	7	8	8	46	96	.311	.358
Turf	4.40	2	10	4	25	6	61.1	62	6	16	25	Runners on	.297	458	136	20	4	12	129	39	50	.347	.437
April	3.25	2	3	0	12	3	36.0	37	1	13	17	Scoring Posn	.295	261	77	14	1	8	112	31	32	.360	.448
May	5.53	0	5	0	16	5	42.1	52	4	13	31	Close & Late	.286	217	62	5	2	8	40	23	28	.354	.438
June	4.57	0	10	0	12	11	63.0	76	5	22	34	None on/out	.254	260	66	9	2	3	3	20	41	.307	.338
July	3.03	1	4	8	19	2	32.2	30	1	8	21	vs. 1st Batr (relief)	.194	62	12	1	0	0	2	6	11	.265	.210
August	1.73	0	3	6	22	1	36.1	24	2	16	15	First Inning Pitched	.266	357	95	12	0	6	50	40	47	.340	.350
September/October	3.88	2	10	4	20	9	60.1	66	7	13	28	First 15 Pitches	.254	319	81	8	0	5	30	35	43	.328	.326
Starter	3.96	3	20	0	31	31	182.0	201	14	47	106	Pitch 16-30	.243	218	53	8	2	2	26	17	28	.301	.326
Reliever	3.55	2	15	18	70	0	88.2	84	6	38	40	Pitch 31-45	.224	152	34	4	3	3	21	7	26	.258	.349
0 Days rest	4.26	0	4	6	14	0	12.2	13	0	6	5	Pitch 46+	.329	356	117	23	6	10	60	26	49	.371	.511
1 or 2 Days rest	3.24	0	8	7	32	0	41.2	42	2	19	20	First Pitch	.292	168	49	5	3	5	32	13	0	.344	.446
3+ Days rest	3.67	2	3	5	24	0	34.1	29	4	13	15	Ahead in Count	.233	468	109	16	2	7	48	0	126	.235	.321
Pre-All Star	4.58	2	21	3	48	21	159.1	183	11	52	95	Behind in Count	.321	237	76	14	3	5	33	45	0	.425	.468
Post-All Star	2.75	3	14	15	53	10	111.1	102	9	33	51	Two Strikes	.220	432	95	13	3	6	37	27	146	.267	.306

Pitcher vs. Batter (career)

Pitches Best Vs.	Avg	AB	H	2B	3B	HR	RBI	BB	SO	OBP	SLG	Pitches Worst Vs.	Avg	AB	H	2B	3B	HR	RBI	BB	SO	OBP	SLG
Ron Gant	.000	8	0	0	0	0	0	3	2	.273	.000	John Kruk	.500	10	5	2	0	0	2	1	1	.545	.700
Luis Alicea	.083	12	1	1	0	0	0	0	1	.083	.167	Larry Walker	.467	15	7	1	0	2	4	0	2	.467	.933
Wes Chamberlain	.167	12	2	0	0	0	2	0	1	.167	.167	Delino DeShields	.438	16	7	1	2	0	4	0	1	.438	.750
Dwight Smith	.176	17	3	0	0	0	0	4	2	.333	.176	Rick Wilkins	.400	15	6	1	0	2	6	1	3	.438	.867
Jose Vizcaino	.200	15	3	1	0	0	2	0	2	.188	.267	Dave Justice	.364	11	4	0	0	2	4	1	2	.417	.909

Cliff Young — Indians

Age 29 – Pitches Left (groundball pitcher)

	ERA	W	L	Sv	G	GS	IP	BB	SO	Avg	H	2B	3B	HR	RBI	OBP	SLG	GF	IR	IRS	Hld	SvOp	SB	CS	GB	FB	G/F
1993 Season	4.62	3	3	1	21	7	60.1	18	31	.298	74	12	0	9	38	.352	.456	3	23	10	0	2	4	4	98	68	1.44
Career (1990-1993)	4.25	5	4	1	49	7	103.2	28	56	.302	126	20	1	14	67	.348	.456	14	58	21	0	4	5	7	171	110	1.55

1993 Season

	ERA	W	L	Sv	G	GS	IP	H	HR	BB	SO		Avg	AB	H	2B	3B	HR	RBI	BB	SO	OBP	SLG
Home	2.41	2	0	1	9	4	33.2	33	2	7	19	vs. Left	.316	57	18	2	0	0	8	1	5	.339	.351
Away	7.43	1	3	0	12	3	26.2	41	7	11	12	vs. Right	.293	191	56	10	0	9	30	17	26	.355	.487
Starter	5.02	1	2	0	7	7	37.2	46	4	11	18	Scoring Posn	.279	68	19	1	0	2	29	8	10	.351	.382
Reliever	3.97	2	1	1	14	0	22.2	28	5	7	13	Close & Late	.280	25	7	1	0	1	2	1	1	.333	.440
0 Days rest	4.91	1	0	0	4	0	7.1	11	1	0	2	None on/out	.323	65	21	5	0	4	4	1	4	.333	.585
1 or 2 Days rest	1.80	1	0	1	5	0	10.0	9	2	2	7	First Pitch	.367	30	11	5	0	1	6	0	0	.406	.633
3+ Days rest	6.75	0	1	0	5	0	5.1	8	2	5	4	Ahead in Count	.255	102	26	1	0	1	12	0	28	.262	.294
Pre-All Star	4.56	2	3	1	19	5	51.1	60	8	18	24	Behind in Count	.357	70	25	4	0	5	15	10	0	.438	.629
Post-All Star	5.00	1	0	0	2	2	9.0	14	1	0	7	Two Strikes	.177	96	17	1	0	1	10	8	31	.245	.219

Curt Young — Athletics

Age 34 – Pitches Left

	ERA	W	L	Sv	G	GS	IP	BB	SO	Avg	H	2B	3B	HR	RBI	OBP	SLG	CG	ShO	Sup	QS	#P/S	SB	CS	GB	FB	G/F
1993 Season	4.30	1	1	0	3	3	14.2	6	4	.241	14	1	0	5	6	.313	.517	0	0	4.91	1	85	2	1	27	15	1.80
Last Five Years	4.38	23	20	0	118	52	386.0	157	162	.272	409	78	5	42	171	.343	.414	1	0	4.36	17	86	31	19	554	490	1.13

1993 Season

	ERA	W	L	Sv	G	GS	IP	H	HR	BB	SO		Avg	AB	H	2B	3B	HR	RBI	BB	SO	OBP	SLG
Home	3.38	1	1	0	2	2	10.2	8	3	5	2	vs. Left	.333	12	4	1	0	0	0	1	2	.385	.417
Away	6.75	0	0	0	1	1	4.0	6	2	1	2	vs. Right	.217	46	10	0	0	5	6	5	2	.294	.543

Last Five Years

	ERA	W	L	Sv	G	GS	IP	H	HR	BB	SO		Avg	AB	H	2B	3B	HR	RBI	BB	SO	OBP	SLG
Home	3.95	13	9	0	63	29	211.2	214	19	87	95	vs. Left	.261	348	91	14	1	3	41	23	48	.313	.333
Away	4.90	10	11	0	55	23	174.1	195	23	70	67	vs. Right	.275	1156	318	64	4	39	130	134	114	.352	.439
Day	3.90	12	5	0	50	22	166.0	159	19	69	69	Inning 1-6	.278	1248	347	65	4	36	153	132	136	.348	.423

Last Five Years

	ERA	W	L	Sv	G	GS	IP	H	HR	BB	SO
Night	4.75	11	15	0	68	30	220.0	250	23	88	93
Grass	3.72	20	14	0	96	42	324.0	311	32	132	141
Turf	7.84	3	6	0	22	10	62.0	98	10	25	21
April	6.84	1	5	0	17	6	51.1	63	11	24	19
May	4.06	6	3	0	23	10	77.2	82	11	31	30
June	4.50	2	5	0	15	9	56.0	47	5	28	28
July	3.81	6	4	0	23	13	87.1	89	6	27	40
August	2.61	4	1	0	14	7	51.2	55	6	18	22
September/October	4.94	4	2	0	26	7	62.0	73	3	29	23
Starter	4.26	19	18	0	52	52	274.1	292	33	111	120
Reliever	4.67	4	2	0	66	0	111.2	117	9	46	42
0-3 Days Rest	4.02	1	1	0	3	3	15.2	19	0	3	5
4 Days Rest	6.14	4	9	0	18	18	85.0	112	14	41	49
5+ Days Rest	3.37	14	8	0	31	31	173.2	161	19	67	66
Pre-All Star	4.71	10	15	0	63	29	210.0	219	28	89	82
Post-All Star	3.99	13	5	0	55	23	176.0	190	14	68	80

	Avg	AB	H	2B	3B	HR	RBI	BB	SO	OBP	SLG
Inning 7+	.242	256	62	13	1	6	18	25	26	.317	.371
None on	.265	868	230	49	3	28	28	86	102	.334	.425
Runners on	.281	636	179	29	2	14	143	71	60	.355	.399
Scoring Posn	.259	352	91	12	1	9	127	49	38	.349	.375
Close & Late	.244	82	20	5	0	1	6	14	8	.360	.341
None on/out	.227	383	87	20	0	8	8	35	48	.292	.342
vs. 1st Batr (relief)	.217	60	13	4	0	0	3	6	7	.288	.283
First Inning Pitched	.277	422	117	23	1	11	62	44	44	.349	.415
First 75 Pitches	.271	1308	354	72	3	35	147	133	138	.341	.411
Pitch 76-90	.266	109	29	4	1	1	10	8	15	.316	.349
Pitch 91-105	.279	68	19	1	1	4	7	9	9	.364	.500
Pitch 106+	.368	19	7	1	0	2	7	7	0	.538	.737
First Pitch	.297	182	54	11	0	6	22	6	0	.338	.456
Ahead in Count	.218	588	128	24	2	12	60	0	138	.218	.327
Behind in Count	.319	420	134	29	2	17	62	91	0	.440	.519
Two Strikes	.228	596	136	26	0	16	64	60	162	.299	.352

Pitcher vs. Batter (since 1984)

Pitches Best Vs.	Avg	AB	H	2B	3B	HR	RBI	BB	SO	OBP	SLG
Mike Pagliarulo	.063	16	1	0	0	0	0	1	4	.118	.063
Gary Thurman	.067	15	1	0	0	0	1	1	5	.125	.067
Dan Pasqua	.077	13	1	0	0	0	2	0	2	.077	.077
Larry Sheets	.083	12	1	0	0	0	0	0	0	.083	.083
Carlton Fisk	.097	31	3	0	0	0	1	1	4	.121	.097

Pitches Worst Vs.	Avg	AB	H	2B	3B	HR	RBI	BB	SO	OBP	SLG
Dante Bichette	.625	8	5	0	0	2	3	4	1	.750	1.375
Bobby Kelly	.600	10	6	1	0	1	1	1	2	.636	1.000
Chili Davis	.455	11	5	1	0	1	2	1	2	.500	.818
Jay Buhner	.455	11	5	1	0	1	4	5	1	.588	.818
Kirby Puckett	.441	34	15	4	1	2	7	1	2	.457	.794

Eric Young — Rockies

Age 27 – Bats Right (groundball hitter)

	Avg	G	AB	R	H	2B	3B	HR	RBI	BB	SO	HBP	GDP	SB	CS	OBP	SLG	IBB	SH	SF	#Pit	#P/PA	GB	FB	G/F
1993 Season	.269	144	490	82	132	16	8	3	42	63	41	4	9	42	19	.355	.353	3	4	4	2107	3.73	230	114	2.02
Career (1992-1993)	.267	193	622	91	166	17	8	4	53	71	50	4	12	48	20	.344	.339	3	8	4	2609	3.68	284	147	1.93

1993 Season

	Avg	AB	H	2B	3B	HR	RBI	BB	SO	OBP	SLG
vs. Left	.289	128	37	5	3	0	13	16	12	.372	.375
vs. Right	.262	362	95	11	5	3	29	47	29	.349	.345
Groundball	.236	157	37	5	0	1	9	19	15	.326	.287
Flyball	.321	84	27	4	2	0	8	13	7	.418	.417
Home	.303	238	72	5	7	3	33	41	14	.401	.420
Away	.238	252	60	11	1	0	9	22	27	.307	.290
Day	.297	172	51	5	2	3	14	23	14	.385	.401
Night	.255	318	81	11	6	0	28	40	27	.338	.327
Grass	.279	358	100	11	7	3	35	53	26	.373	.374
Turf	.242	132	32	5	1	0	7	10	15	.301	.295
First Pitch	.250	52	13	1	0	0	5	3	0	.304	.269
Ahead in Count	.292	137	40	2	0	1	17	41	0	.453	.328
Behind in Count	.255	208	53	10	4	1	11	0	33	.261	.356
Two Strikes	.241	203	49	8	5	2	9	19	41	.308	.360

	Avg	AB	H	2B	3B	HR	RBI	BB	SO	OBP	SLG
Scoring Posn	.307	88	27	3	3	0	39	17	7	.414	.409
Close & Late	.333	69	23	3	2	0	6	9	6	.405	.435
None on/out	.251	207	52	6	4	2	2	23	17	.332	.348
Batting #1	.254	414	105	15	7	1	29	51	33	.339	.331
Batting #7	.342	38	13	1	0	0	5	4	3	.395	.368
Other	.368	38	14	0	1	2	8	8	5	.478	.579
April	.259	81	21	2	2	1	8	13	5	.365	.370
May	.255	106	27	3	3	0	7	7	7	.308	.340
June	.265	68	18	1	0	0	7	10	9	.359	.279
July	.272	92	25	6	1	0	6	8	8	.330	.359
August	.169	59	10	1	1	0	1	10	5	.300	.220
September/October	.369	84	31	3	1	2	13	15	7	.460	.500
Pre-All Star	.260	296	77	9	5	1	23	33	24	.337	.334
Post-All Star	.284	194	55	7	3	2	19	30	17	.381	.381

1993 By Position

Position	Avg	AB	H	2B	3B	HR	RBI	BB	SO	OBP	SLG	G	GS	Innings	PO	A	E	DP	Fld Pct	Rng Fctr	In Zone	Outs	Zone Rtg	MLB Zone
As Pinch Hitter	.357	14	5	0	0	0	0	2	3	.438	.357	16	0	---	---	---	---	---	---	---	---	---	---	---
As 2b	.259	293	76	9	5	1	23	32	23	.335	.334	79	74	650.1	154	227	15	43	.962	5.27	268	239	.892	.895
As lf	.288	153	44	6	3	2	16	21	12	.375	.405	46	39	351.0	88	2	2	1	.978	2.31	103	84	.816	.818
As cf	.233	30	7	1	0	0	3	8	3	.395	.267	10	8	66.1	13	0	1	0	.929	1.76	20	13	.650	.829

Gerald Young — Rockies

Age 29 – Bats Both (groundball hitter)

	Avg	G	AB	R	H	2B	3B	HR	RBI	BB	SO	HBP	GDP	SB	CS	OBP	SLG	IBB	SH	SF	#Pit	#P/PA	GB	FB	G/F
1993 Season	.053	19	19	5	1	0	0	0	1	4	1	0	2	0	1	.217	.053	0	0	0	87	3.78	9	8	1.13
Last Five Years	.213	404	924	131	197	25	6	2	58	132	112	2	17	62	36	.311	.260	4	15	8	4001	3.70	407	264	1.54

1993 Season

	Avg	AB	H	2B	3B	HR	RBI	BB	SO	OBP	SLG
vs. Left	.000	3	0	0	0	0	0	0	0	.000	.000
vs. Right	.063	16	1	0	0	0	1	4	1	.250	.063

	Avg	AB	H	2B	3B	HR	RBI	BB	SO	OBP	SLG
Scoring Posn	.000	4	0	0	0	0	1	0	0	.000	.000
Close & Late	.143	7	1	0	0	0	0	0	1	.143	.143

Last Five Years

	Avg	AB	H	2B	3B	HR	RBI	BB	SO	OBP	SLG
vs. Left	.220	309	68	8	2	2	23	43	41	.315	.278
vs. Right	.210	615	129	17	4	0	35	89	71	.308	.250
Groundball	.188	336	63	6	2	1	21	44	34	.279	.226
Flyball	.233	227	53	10	1	0	14	40	31	.348	.286
Home	.229	481	110	15	4	1	30	68	51	.323	.283
Away	.196	443	87	10	2	1	28	64	61	.297	.235
Day	.192	260	50	4	1	0	18	41	34	.303	.215
Night	.221	664	147	21	5	2	40	91	78	.314	.277
Grass	.188	276	52	6	0	0	22	44	42	.298	.210
Turf	.224	648	145	19	6	2	36	88	70	.316	.281

	Avg	AB	H	2B	3B	HR	RBI	BB	SO	OBP	SLG
Scoring Posn	.239	188	45	7	2	0	56	41	25	.368	.298
Close & Late	.175	200	35	5	1	0	11	24	31	.263	.210
None on/out	.196	311	61	7	3	2	2	40	40	.288	.257
Batting #1	.208	456	95	16	3	2	27	56	49	.296	.270
Batting #2	.234	209	49	4	1	0	14	27	31	.317	.263
Other	.205	259	53	5	2	0	17	49	32	.330	.239
April	.191	162	31	5	1	1	4	19	20	.275	.253
May	.178	169	30	3	2	0	10	28	18	.294	.219
June	.250	132	33	6	0	1	13	19	17	.338	.318
July	.211	142	30	4	1	0	14	21	23	.313	.254

Last Five Years	Avg	AB	H	2B	3B	HR	RBI	BB	SO	OBP	SLG		Avg	AB	H	2B	3B	HR	RBI	BB	SO	OBP	SLG
First Pitch	.208	144	30	4	1	0	6	3	0	.223	.250	August	.257	148	38	3	1	0	7	16	12	.331	.291
Ahead in Count	.235	251	59	7	1	2	22	75	0	.405	.295	September/October	.205	171	35	4	1	0	10	29	22	.320	.240
Behind in Count	.162	334	54	5	4	0	12	0	98	.164	.201	Pre-All Star	.204	509	104	15	4	2	33	74	61	.303	.261
Two Strikes	.175	372	65	5	2	0	13	54	112	.279	.199	Post-All Star	.224	415	93	10	2	0	25	58	51	.320	.258

Batter vs. Pitcher (career)

Hits Best Against	Avg	AB	H	2B	3B	HR	RBI	BB	SO	OBP	SLG	Hits Worst Against	Avg	AB	H	2B	3B	HR	RBI	BB	SO	OBP	SLG
Jamie Moyer	.615	13	8	0	0	0	0	2	0	.667	.615	Roger McDowell	.000	12	0	0	0	0	0	2	2	.143	.000
Ramon Martinez	.462	13	6	0	0	0	1	1	1	.500	.462	Mike Morgan	.000	11	0	0	0	0	1	0	1	.000	.000
Joe Boever	.444	9	4	0	1	0	3	3	0	.583	.667	John Smiley	.056	18	1	0	0	0	0	4	2	.227	.056
Pete Smith	.409	22	9	1	0	0	1	3	0	.480	.455	Greg W. Harris	.071	14	1	0	0	0	0	0	1	.071	.071
Mike Bielecki	.375	16	6	1	0	0	1	1	2	.412	.438	Ron Darling	.083	12	1	0	0	0	1	1	3	.154	.083

Kevin Young — Pirates

Age 25 – Bats Right (flyball hitter)

	Avg	G	AB	R	H	2B	3B	HR	RBI	BB	SO	HBP	GDP	SB	CS	OBP	SLG	IBB	SH	SF	#Pit	#P/PA	GB	FB	G/F
1993 Season	.236	141	449	38	106	24	3	6	47	36	82	9	9	2	2	.300	.343	3	5	9	1899	3.74	132	161	0.82
Career (1992-1993)	.241	151	456	40	110	24	3	6	51	38	82	9	9	3	2	.307	.346	3	5	9	1942	3.76	135	163	0.83

1993 Season

	Avg	AB	H	2B	3B	HR	RBI	BB	SO	OBP	SLG		Avg	AB	H	2B	3B	HR	RBI	BB	SO	OBP	SLG
vs. Left	.237	169	40	11	0	3	14	16	31	.303	.355	Scoring Posn	.192	120	23	4	0	2	40	19	28	.289	.275
vs. Right	.236	280	66	13	3	3	33	20	51	.298	.336	Close & Late	.217	83	18	4	0	2	14	9	17	.296	.337
Groundball	.221	149	33	5	1	2	12	8	27	.276	.309	None on/out	.231	108	25	3	0	2	2	5	18	.278	.315
Flyball	.277	65	18	3	1	1	11	5	8	.319	.400	Batting #6	.230	183	42	5	2	3	27	20	28	.318	.328
Home	.240	229	55	13	1	6	35	24	38	.317	.384	Batting #8	.252	143	36	12	1	1	9	12	27	.310	.371
Away	.232	220	51	11	2	0	12	12	44	.282	.300	Other	.228	123	28	7	0	2	11	4	27	.260	.333
Day	.198	126	25	4	1	1	9	9	26	.259	.270	April	.239	67	16	1	1	1	13	7	14	.321	.328
Night	.251	323	81	20	2	5	38	27	56	.316	.372	May	.194	72	14	2	1	3	8	8	8	.306	.375
Grass	.228	127	29	5	2	0	8	6	22	.279	.299	June	.244	78	19	5	0	0	7	5	14	.291	.308
Turf	.239	322	77	19	1	6	39	30	60	.309	.360	July	.230	87	20	5	0	0	6	10	22	.313	.287
First Pitch	.348	66	23	5	0	1	9	3	0	.397	.470	August	.243	70	17	4	0	0	5	3	11	.280	.300
Ahead in Count	.204	98	20	4	1	1	8	16	0	.313	.296	September/October	.267	75	20	7	1	2	8	3	13	.288	.467
Behind in Count	.202	203	41	8	1	3	22	0	70	.215	.296	Pre-All Star	.229	262	60	10	2	4	31	21	49	.297	.328
Two Strikes	.201	209	42	11	1	3	22	17	82	.271	.306	Post-All Star	.246	187	46	14	1	2	16	15	33	.304	.364

1993 By Position

Position	Avg	AB	H	2B	3B	HR	RBI	BB	SO	OBP	SLG	G	GS	Innings	PO	A	E	DP	Fld Pct	Rng Fctr	In Zone	Outs	Zone Rtg	MLB Zone
As 1b	.237	431	102	24	3	6	44	35	77	.301	.348	135	121	1056.2	1115	100	3	111	.998	---	203	180	.887	.834

Matt Young — Blue Jays

Age 35 – Pitches Left (groundball pitcher)

	ERA	W	L	Sv	G	GS	IP	BB	SO	Avg	H	2B	3B	HR	RBI	OBP	SLG	GF	IR	IRS	Hld	SvOp	SB	CS	GB	FB	G/F
1993 Season	5.21	1	6	0	22	8	74.1	57	65	.266	75	11	0	8	35	.394	.390	2	13	4	0	0	9	7	102	63	1.62
Last Five Years	4.46	13	39	0	129	69	496.1	290	394	.253	476	66	6	36	225	.355	.352	7	73	25	5	1	55	27	809	357	2.27

1993 Season

	ERA	W	L	Sv	G	GS	IP	H	HR	BB	SO		Avg	AB	H	2B	3B	HR	RBI	BB	SO	OBP	SLG
Home	5.04	0	3	0	9	3	30.1	31	5	22	22	vs. Left	.236	55	13	0	0	1	6	10	17	.364	.291
Away	5.32	1	3	0	13	5	44.0	44	3	35	43	vs. Right	.273	227	62	11	0	7	29	47	48	.401	.414
Starter	6.87	0	4	0	8	8	38.0	46	5	25	25	Scoring Posn	.266	79	21	5	0	0	23	17	18	.404	.329
Reliever	3.47	1	2	0	14	0	36.1	29	3	32	40	Close & Late	1.000	2	2	0	0	0	1	1	0	1.000	1.000
0 Days rest	4.15	0	0	0	1	0	4.1	3	2	3	4	None on/out	.324	74	24	2	0	2	2	8	16	.390	.432
1 or 2 Days rest	4.91	0	2	0	6	0	11.0	12	0	13	10	First Pitch	.297	37	11	2	0	0	2	0	0	.333	.351
3+ Days rest	2.57	1	0	0	7	0	21.0	14	1	16	26	Ahead in Count	.183	115	21	5	0	2	12	0	51	.190	.278
Pre-All Star	5.34	1	6	0	17	8	60.2	65	5	44	48	Behind in Count	.325	77	25	2	0	2	13	35	0	.531	.429
Post-All Star	4.61	0	0	0	5	0	13.2	10	3	13	17	Two Strikes	.157	127	20	3	0	2	8	22	65	.287	.228

Last Five Years

	ERA	W	L	Sv	G	GS	IP	H	HR	BB	SO		Avg	AB	H	2B	3B	HR	RBI	BB	SO	OBP	SLG
Home	4.01	7	21	0	59	36	258.1	242	22	145	200	vs. Left	.220	305	67	8	0	3	37	44	79	.326	.275
Away	4.95	6	18	0	70	33	238.0	234	14	145	194	vs. Right	.260	1575	409	58	6	33	188	246	315	.360	.367
Day	4.04	7	14	0	45	22	164.2	157	11	92	135	Inning 1-6	.250	1581	396	53	4	29	194	239	323	.351	.344
Night	4.67	6	25	0	84	47	331.2	319	25	198	259	Inning 7+	.268	299	80	13	2	7	31	51	71	.377	.395
Grass	5.49	7	29	0	90	41	290.1	308	24	191	244	None on	.251	1011	254	31	3	21	21	152	219	.351	.350
Turf	3.01	6	10	0	39	28	206.0	168	12	99	150	Runners on	.255	869	222	35	3	15	204	138	175	.359	.354
April	3.95	0	6	0	12	12	68.1	56	3	44	43	Scoring Posn	.261	517	135	22	1	9	186	89	112	.370	.360
May	5.68	4	7	0	22	20	101.1	114	10	61	74	Close & Late	.323	130	42	10	0	4	14	20	26	.421	.492
June	3.86	2	6	0	22	9	79.1	70	4	44	69	None on/out	.255	463	118	16	0	9	9	73	95	.358	.348
July	3.73	4	7	0	24	8	79.2	62	7	58	60	vs. 1st Batr (relief)	.333	48	16	2	0	1	12	8	9	.424	.438
August	3.64	1	5	0	23	10	94.0	88	7	34	77	First Inning Pitched	.253	443	112	12	2	9	75	60	113	.344	.350
September/October	5.74	2	8	0	26	10	73.2	86	5	49	71	First 15 Pitches	.251	370	93	9	1	8	45	48	88	.340	.346
Starter	4.54	11	34	0	69	69	398.1	389	29	218	295	Pitch 16-30	.251	346	87	12	3	8	42	51	77	.350	.373
Reliever	4.13	2	5	0	60	0	98.0	87	7	72	99	Pitch 31-45	.223	314	70	7	1	4	34	38	64	.308	.290
0 Days rest	3.60	0	0	0	3	0	5.0	5	2	3	6	Pitch 46+	.266	850	226	38	1	16	104	153	165	.379	.369
1 or 2 Days rest	4.88	1	2	0	23	0	31.1	33	2	29	24	First Pitch	.332	262	87	13	1	3	29	7	0	.364	.424
3+ Days rest	3.79	1	3	0	34	0	61.2	49	3	40	69	Ahead in Count	.181	786	142	27	1	10	78	0	334	.185	.256
Pre-All Star	4.74	7	23	0	64	44	275.1	268	18	170	208	Behind in Count	.313	479	150	15	2	13	68	171	0	.491	.434

Last Five Years

	ERA	W	L	Sv	G	GS	IP	H	HR	BB	SO		Avg	AB	H	2B	3B	HR	RBI	BB	SO	OBP	SLG
Post-All Star	4.11	6	16	0	65	25	221.0	208	18	120	186	Two Strikes	.176	830	146	20	0	10	77	110	394	.275	.236

Pitcher vs. Batter (since 1984)

Pitches Best Vs.	Avg	AB	H	2B	3B	HR	RBI	BB	SO	OBP	SLG	Pitches Worst Vs.	Avg	AB	H	2B	3B	HR	RBI	BB	SO	OBP	SLG
Ron Karkovice	.000	12	0	0	0	0	0	0	7	.000	.000	Ellis Burks	.556	9	5	0	0	1	2	3	2	.667	.889
Ozzie Guillen	.048	21	1	0	0	0	0	0	6	.048	.048	Jay Buhner	.556	9	5	0	0	1	3	2	3	.636	.889
Curt Wilkerson	.071	14	1	0	0	0	2	0	2	.071	.071	Juan Gonzalez	.500	12	6	3	0	1	1	0	3	.500	1.000
Brian McRae	.071	14	1	0	0	0	0	0	3	.071	.071	Frank Thomas	.357	14	5	0	0	3	6	7	3	.571	1.000
Wade Boggs	.091	22	2	0	0	0	3	1	5	.130	.091	Cecil Fielder	.313	16	5	0	0	4	11	5	5	.476	1.063

Pete Young — Expos

Age 26 – Pitches Right

	ERA	W	L	Sv	G	GS	IP	BB	SO	Avg	H	2B	3B	HR	RBI	OBP	SLG	GF	IR	IRS	Hld	SvOp	SB	CS	GB	FB	G/F
1993 Season	3.38	1	0	0	4	0	5.1	0	3	.211	4	1	0	1	2	.211	.421	2	0	0	0	0	0	0	1	11	0.09
Career (1992-1993)	3.86	1	0	0	17	0	25.2	9	14	.239	22	6	2	1	16	.308	.380	8	10	5	0	0	2	1	30	30	1.00

1993 Season

	ERA	W	L	Sv	G	GS	IP	H	HR	BB	SO		Avg	AB	H	2B	3B	HR	RBI	BB	SO	OBP	SLG
Home	4.15	1	0	0	3	0	4.1	4	1	0	3	vs. Left	.333	6	2	0	0	1	1	0	2	.333	.833
Away	0.00	0	0	0	1	0	1.0	0	0	0	0	vs. Right	.154	13	2	1	0	0	1	0	1	.154	.231

Robin Yount — Brewers

Age 38 – Bats Right

	Avg	G	AB	R	H	2B	3B	HR	RBI	BB	SO	HBP	GDP	SB	CS	OBP	SLG	IBB	SH	SF	#Pit	#P/PA	GB	FB	G/F
1993 Season	.258	127	454	62	117	25	3	8	51	44	93	5	12	9	2	.326	.379	5	5	6	1890	3.68	135	137	0.99
Last Five Years	.271	725	2715	398	735	140	24	64	385	292	413	24	50	64	23	.342	.411	37	17	39	11079	3.59	911	891	1.02

1993 Season

	Avg	AB	H	2B	3B	HR	RBI	BB	SO	OBP	SLG		Avg	AB	H	2B	3B	HR	RBI	BB	SO	OBP	SLG
vs. Left	.262	122	32	5	1	2	14	19	23	.362	.369	Scoring Posn	.236	110	26	5	3	0	40	15	22	.328	.336
vs. Right	.256	332	85	20	2	6	37	25	70	.313	.383	Close & Late	.233	73	17	0	0	0	8	8	18	.301	.233
Groundball	.183	82	15	4	1	0	7	10	17	.287	.256	None on/out	.283	92	26	4	0	2	2	8	16	.340	.391
Flyball	.288	104	30	7	0	5	18	7	19	.327	.500	Batting #2	.250	216	54	9	0	4	20	18	38	.305	.347
Home	.256	234	60	9	3	1	25	31	44	.344	.333	Batting #5	.326	95	31	8	3	2	18	11	23	.393	.537
Away	.259	220	57	16	0	7	26	13	49	.305	.427	Other	.224	143	32	8	0	2	13	15	32	.313	.322
Day	.336	143	48	9	2	3	26	14	28	.395	.490	April	.245	49	12	2	0	0	4	4	15	.304	.286
Night	.222	311	69	16	1	5	25	30	65	.294	.328	May	.308	52	16	3	0	2	7	5	10	.373	.481
Grass	.242	376	91	16	3	6	42	38	76	.314	.348	June	.244	82	20	4	0	3	10	7	17	.315	.402
Turf	.333	78	26	9	0	2	9	6	17	.388	.526	July	.301	93	28	4	0	2	12	8	12	.353	.409
First Pitch	.267	60	16	4	0	2	3	5	0	.343	.433	August	.196	107	21	5	2	1	10	11	21	.277	.308
Ahead in Count	.293	99	29	6	0	3	19	17	0	.387	.444	September/October	.282	71	20	7	1	0	8	9	18	.358	.408
Behind in Count	.199	201	40	9	2	2	17	0	78	.205	.294	Pre-All Star	.281	221	62	12	0	5	27	20	47	.345	.403
Two Strikes	.183	202	37	6	2	1	15	22	93	.269	.248	Post-All Star	.236	233	55	13	3	3	24	24	46	.308	.356

1993 By Position

Position	Avg	AB	H	2B	3B	HR	RBI	BB	SO	OBP	SLG	G	GS	Innings	PO	A	E	DP	Fld Pct	Rng Fctr	In Zone	Outs	Zone Rtg	MLB Zone
As cf	.252	413	104	23	1	7	40	42	85	.325	.363	114	111	949.1	297	6	1	1	.997	2.87	354	291	.822	.829

Last Five Years

	Avg	AB	H	2B	3B	HR	RBI	BB	SO	OBP	SLG		Avg	AB	H	2B	3B	HR	RBI	BB	SO	OBP	SLG
vs. Left	.285	699	199	40	7	17	95	98	112	.371	.435	Scoring Posn	.282	731	206	34	10	18	310	107	114	.363	.430
vs. Right	.266	2016	536	100	17	47	290	194	301	.332	.402	Close & Late	.261	391	102	14	3	6	62	45	69	.337	.358
Groundball	.265	703	186	34	4	8	103	75	103	.335	.358	None on/out	.277	591	164	29	3	15	15	40	79	.329	.413
Flyball	.285	603	172	33	7	20	94	58	106	.345	.463	Batting #3	.256	769	197	26	7	15	105	92	120	.339	.367
Home	.259	1346	348	64	16	34	196	154	207	.336	.406	Batting #4	.299	715	214	40	7	20	122	79	98	.369	.459
Away	.283	1369	387	76	8	30	189	138	206	.349	.416	Other	.263	1231	324	74	10	29	158	121	195	.329	.410
Day	.294	853	251	47	7	23	133	91	123	.359	.447	April	.275	342	94	15	5	7	43	35	56	.349	.409
Night	.260	1862	484	93	17	41	252	201	290	.335	.394	May	.272	467	127	25	2	15	69	47	65	.341	.430
Grass	.267	2283	610	109	22	57	334	250	351	.340	.409	June	.267	486	130	23	1	12	65	56	75	.344	.393
Turf	.289	432	125	31	2	7	51	42	62	.353	.419	July	.286	413	118	26	6	10	56	41	53	.351	.450
First Pitch	.300	380	114	27	1	8	67	24	0	.341	.439	August	.247	518	128	24	8	7	70	56	87	.320	.365
Ahead in Count	.352	659	232	43	8	26	140	139	0	.458	.560	September/October	.282	489	138	27	2	13	82	57	77	.354	.425
Behind in Count	.210	1184	249	45	9	18	112	0	340	.219	.309	Pre-All Star	.272	1457	396	74	10	36	197	153	211	.343	.410
Two Strikes	.203	1120	227	38	8	18	107	124	413	.288	.299	Post-All Star	.269	1258	339	66	14	28	188	139	202	.341	.411

Batter vs. Pitcher (since 1984)

Hits Best Against	Avg	AB	H	2B	3B	HR	RBI	BB	SO	OBP	SLG	Hits Worst Against	Avg	AB	H	2B	3B	HR	RBI	BB	SO	OBP	SLG
Dave Fleming	.600	10	6	2	0	0	1	3	1	.692	.800	Juan Guzman	.059	17	1	0	0	0	1	1	8	.111	.059
Kenny Rogers	.444	9	4	1	0	0	2	4	1	.615	.556	Mike Mussina	.077	13	1	0	0	0	1	0	2	.077	.077
Lee Guetterman	.429	14	6	0	0	1	1	3	1	.529	.643	Bobby Ojeda	.091	11	1	0	0	0	0	1	2	.167	.091
Shawn Hillegas	.389	18	7	1	0	2	4	1	2	.421	.778	Jeff Montgomery	.143	14	2	0	0	0	2	0	6	.143	.143
Bud Black	.387	31	12	4	1	2	8	7	3	.500	.774	Donn Pall	.154	13	2	0	0	0	0	0	0	.154	.154

Eddie Zambrano — Cubs

Age 28 – Bats Right

	Avg	G	AB	R	H	2B	3B	HR	RBI	BB	SO	HBP	GDP	SB	CS	OBP	SLG	IBB	SH	SF	#Pit	#P/PA	GB	FB	G/F
1993 Season	.294	8	17	1	5	0	0	0	2	1	3	0	1	0	0	.333	.294	0	0	0	65	3.61	4	6	0.67

1993 Season

	Avg	AB	H	2B	3B	HR	RBI	BB	SO	OBP	SLG		Avg	AB	H	2B	3B	HR	RBI	BB	SO	OBP	SLG
vs. Left	.167	6	1	0	0	0	0	0	0	.167	.167	Scoring Posn	.400	5	2	0	0	0	2	1	1	.500	.400
vs. Right	.364	11	4	0	0	0	2	1	3	.417	.364	Close & Late	.000	2	0	0	0	0	0	0	1	.000	.000

Todd Zeile — Cardinals

Age 28 – Bats Right

	Avg	G	AB	R	H	2B	3B	HR	RBI	BB	SO	HBP	GDP	SB	CS	OBP	SLG	IBB	SH	SF	#Pit	#P/PA	GB	FB	G/F
1993 Season	.277	157	571	82	158	36	1	17	103	70	76	0	15	5	4	.352	.433	5	0	6	2533	3.91	195	192	1.02
Career (1989-1993)	.265	610	2152	278	571	118	12	51	297	276	331	7	53	31	29	.347	.402	16	1	26	9764	3.97	795	662	1.20

1993 Season

	Avg	AB	H	2B	3B	HR	RBI	BB	SO	OBP	SLG		Avg	AB	H	2B	3B	HR	RBI	BB	SO	OBP	SLG
vs. Left	.271	133	36	7	1	4	24	18	19	.355	.429	Scoring Posn	.271	188	51	12	0	7	85	38	24	.384	.447
vs. Right	.279	438	122	29	0	13	79	52	57	.352	.434	Close & Late	.229	96	22	6	0	1	14	11	17	.306	.323
Groundball	.273	183	50	12	0	3	25	24	20	.356	.388	None on/out	.289	135	39	11	0	5	5	8	17	.329	.481
Flyball	.245	102	25	2	1	5	20	10	17	.307	.431	Batting #4	.297	367	109	21	1	16	76	45	55	.369	.490
Home	.304	280	85	18	0	8	49	35	35	.376	.454	Batting #6	.273	132	36	8	0	1	19	18	12	.358	.356
Away	.251	291	73	18	1	9	54	35	41	.329	.412	Other	.181	72	13	7	0	0	8	7	9	.253	.278
Day	.329	158	52	14	1	2	26	24	24	.415	.468	April	.286	84	24	5	0	0	8	11	7	.365	.345
Night	.257	413	106	22	0	15	77	46	52	.328	.419	May	.213	94	20	7	0	1	12	8	11	.275	.319
Grass	.249	173	43	11	0	7	39	24	22	.338	.434	June	.247	89	22	6	0	1	15	7	9	.299	.348
Turf	.289	398	115	25	1	10	64	46	54	.359	.432	July	.363	102	37	8	1	7	30	11	19	.417	.667
First Pitch	.333	42	14	3	0	1	11	5	0	.396	.476	August	.287	108	31	5	0	3	16	16	20	.376	.417
Ahead in Count	.289	142	41	8	0	8	31	42	0	.444	.514	September/October	.255	94	24	5	0	5	22	17	10	.366	.468
Behind in Count	.245	249	61	14	0	5	41	0	67	.244	.361	Pre-All Star	.261	306	80	20	1	3	43	29	36	.322	.363
Two Strikes	.223	256	57	14	0	4	37	23	76	.287	.324	Post-All Star	.294	265	78	16	0	14	60	41	40	.385	.513

1993 By Position

Position	Avg	AB	H	2B	3B	HR	RBI	BB	SO	OBP	SLG	G	GS	Innings	PO	A	E	DP	Fld Pct	Rng Fctr	In Zone	Outs	Zone Rtg	MLB Zone
As 3b	.276	568	157	36	1	17	102	68	76	.350	.433	153	149	1299.2	83	309	33	26	.922	2.71	414	328	.792	.834

Career (1989-1993)

	Avg	AB	H	2B	3B	HR	RBI	BB	SO	OBP	SLG		Avg	AB	H	2B	3B	HR	RBI	BB	SO	OBP	SLG
vs. Left	.283	715	202	40	4	16	99	96	106	.368	.417	Scoring Posn	.245	628	154	38	1	11	230	126	107	.361	.361
vs. Right	.257	1437	369	78	8	35	198	180	225	.337	.395	Close & Late	.233	404	94	16	3	3	33	52	76	.320	.309
Groundball	.252	718	181	41	5	12	92	98	101	.342	.373	None on/out	.287	536	154	29	1	20	20	54	79	.354	.457
Flyball	.241	448	108	17	3	14	68	49	74	.311	.386	Batting #4	.275	673	185	33	2	22	108	87	102	.353	.428
Home	.274	1057	290	58	6	27	158	143	147	.360	.417	Batting #6	.277	523	145	30	3	10	63	61	84	.354	.403
Away	.257	1095	281	60	6	24	139	133	184	.335	.388	Other	.252	956	241	55	7	19	126	128	145	.339	.384
Day	.292	568	166	38	3	14	80	82	94	.377	.444	April	.279	287	80	15	3	6	39	38	40	.360	.415
Night	.256	1584	405	80	9	37	217	194	237	.336	.388	May	.229	350	80	22	1	4	39	44	64	.313	.331
Grass	.253	589	149	37	2	13	75	70	103	.330	.389	June	.252	369	93	20	3	7	43	40	45	.324	.379
Turf	.270	1563	422	81	10	38	222	206	228	.353	.408	July	.290	365	106	18	2	15	61	43	58	.363	.474
First Pitch	.330	191	63	11	1	7	32	12	0	.364	.508	August	.291	357	104	12	2	8	46	34	56	.351	.403
Ahead in Count	.309	541	167	32	3	17	86	158	0	.459	.473	September/October	.255	424	108	31	1	11	69	77	68	.368	.410
Behind in Count	.214	910	195	34	6	14	106	0	279	.218	.311	Pre-All Star	.260	1138	296	64	8	20	139	134	171	.336	.383
Two Strikes	.198	994	197	40	5	15	103	106	331	.278	.294	Post-All Star	.271	1014	275	54	4	31	158	142	160	.359	.424

Batter vs. Pitcher (career)

Hits Best Against	Avg	AB	H	2B	3B	HR	RBI	BB	SO	OBP	SLG	Hits Worst Against	Avg	AB	H	2B	3B	HR	RBI	BB	SO	OBP	SLG
Bob Scanlan	.600	10	6	2	0	0	3	1	0	.636	.800	Mel Rojas	.000	8	0	0	0	0	2	1	1	.091	.000
Pete Harnisch	.412	17	7	2	0	1	6	1	0	.444	.706	Jose Rijo	.063	16	1	0	0	0	0	5	3	.286	.063
Roger McDowell	.400	15	6	4	0	0	4	1	4	.438	.667	Randy Myers	.083	12	1	0	0	0	0	1	5	.154	.083
Jeff Parrett	.400	15	6	0	0	2	7	1	3	.412	.800	Greg W. Harris	.083	12	1	1	0	0	2	1	3	.154	.167
Mike Bielecki	.308	13	4	2	1	0	0	5	4	.500	.615	Bobby Ojeda	.111	18	2	0	0	0	2	1	4	.158	.111

Bob Zupcic — Red Sox

Age 27 – Bats Right (flyball hitter)

	Avg	G	AB	R	H	2B	3B	HR	RBI	BB	SO	HBP	GDP	SB	CS	OBP	SLG	IBB	SH	SF	#Pit	#P/PA	GB	FB	G/F
1993 Season	.241	141	286	40	69	24	2	2	26	27	54	2	7	5	2	.308	.360	2	8	3	1217	3.73	77	104	0.74
Career (1991-1993)	.257	283	703	89	181	43	3	6	72	53	120	6	13	7	4	.312	.353	3	16	7	2817	3.59	200	254	0.79

1993 Season

	Avg	AB	H	2B	3B	HR	RBI	BB	SO	OBP	SLG		Avg	AB	H	2B	3B	HR	RBI	BB	SO	OBP	SLG
vs. Left	.216	97	21	6	2	2	6	11	14	.303	.381	Scoring Posn	.321	53	17	10	0	0	23	8	13	.391	.509
vs. Right	.254	189	48	18	0	0	20	16	40	.311	.349	Close & Late	.244	45	11	6	0	0	6	5	10	.314	.378
Groundball	.487	39	19	8	0	1	8	2	7	.524	.769	None on/out	.119	67	8	4	0	1	1	3	9	.157	.224
Flyball	.194	72	14	2	0	1	7	6	12	.250	.264	Batting #2	.357	56	20	5	1	0	5	6	6	.422	.482
Home	.279	154	43	17	1	1	17	13	30	.337	.422	Batting #6	.310	84	26	9	0	1	13	6	14	.352	.452
Away	.197	132	26	7	1	1	9	14	24	.275	.288	Other	.158	146	23	10	1	1	8	15	34	.239	.260
Day	.276	127	35	9	2	2	14	16	27	.359	.425	April	.296	27	8	2	0	0	3	5	4	.394	.370
Night	.214	159	34	15	0	0	12	11	27	.266	.308	May	.229	48	11	5	0	0	3	3	14	.275	.333
Grass	.255	247	63	22	2	1	23	25	48	.325	.372	June	.333	42	14	4	1	1	4	6	6	.440	.548
Turf	.154	39	6	2	0	1	3	2	6	.195	.282	July	.238	63	15	6	0	0	8	7	10	.306	.333
First Pitch	.209	43	9	3	0	0	3	2	0	.239	.279	August	.184	49	9	2	0	1	2	1	12	.200	.286

1993 Season

	Avg	AB	H	2B	3B	HR	RBI	BB	SO	OBP	SLG		Avg	AB	H	2B	3B	HR	RBI	BB	SO	OBP	SLG
Ahead in Count	.250	60	15	4	1	1	7	10	0	.357	.400	September/October	.211	57	12	5	1	0	6	5	8	.274	.333
Behind in Count	.215	135	29	15	0	0	14	0	47	.223	.326	Pre-All Star	.274	135	37	12	1	1	11	15	27	.351	.400
Two Strikes	.213	141	30	11	1	1	13	15	54	.296	.326	Post-All Star	.212	151	32	12	1	1	15	12	27	.268	.325

1993 By Position

Position	Avg	AB	H	2B	3B	HR	RBI	BB	SO	OBP	SLG	G	GS	Innings	PO	A	E	DP	Fld Pct	Rng Fctr	In Zone	Outs	Zone Rtg	MLB Zone
As lf	.224	85	19	8	0	0	8	9	17	.295	.318	48	20	223.1	48	3	1	0	.981	2.06	67	46	.687	.818
As cf	.244	86	21	5	1	1	6	9	15	.316	.360	37	23	224.1	51	1	1	0	.981	2.09	65	51	.785	.829
As rf	.257	105	27	10	1	1	12	9	21	.322	.400	54	29	294.1	78	4	2	0	.976	2.51	85	74	.871	.826

Career (1991-1993)

	Avg	AB	H	2B	3B	HR	RBI	BB	SO	OBP	SLG		Avg	AB	H	2B	3B	HR	RBI	BB	SO	OBP	SLG
vs. Left	.257	241	62	14	3	2	23	25	29	.330	.365	Scoring Posn	.297	155	46	13	1	2	65	14	32	.341	.432
vs. Right	.258	462	119	29	0	4	49	28	91	.303	.346	Close & Late	.286	119	34	10	0	2	22	12	18	.353	.420
Groundball	.338	154	52	15	0	3	22	9	21	.386	.494	None on/out	.179	151	27	7	0	3	3	9	23	.230	.285
Flyball	.223	188	42	7	0	3	19	14	38	.272	.309	Batting #2	.306	134	41	7	1	2	12	12	12	.369	.418
Home	.270	356	96	28	2	5	44	24	65	.321	.402	Batting #6	.337	172	58	15	1	2	26	11	30	.371	.471
Away	.245	347	85	15	1	1	28	29	55	.303	.303	Other	.207	397	82	21	1	2	34	30	78	.267	.280
Day	.284	271	77	17	3	4	30	25	59	.351	.413	April	.313	32	10	3	0	0	4	5	5	.395	.406
Night	.241	432	104	26	0	2	42	28	61	.287	.315	May	.277	94	26	10	0	0	6	7	20	.333	.383
Grass	.265	604	160	39	3	5	66	48	107	.321	.364	June	.315	92	29	7	1	2	11	7	15	.369	.478
Turf	.212	99	21	4	0	1	6	5	13	.255	.283	July	.273	143	39	10	0	2	18	14	20	.331	.385
First Pitch	.260	96	25	5	0	2	8	3	0	.277	.375	August	.209	158	33	5	0	1	13	8	30	.260	.259
Ahead in Count	.290	162	47	7	2	2	20	20	0	.372	.395	September/October	.239	184	44	8	2	1	20	12	30	.284	.321
Behind in Count	.209	325	68	21	0	1	29	0	108	.214	.283	Pre-All Star	.301	272	82	23	1	4	30	26	47	.364	.438
Two Strikes	.197	314	62	19	1	2	30	30	120	.272	.283	Post-All Star	.230	431	99	20	2	2	42	27	73	.278	.299

Batter vs. Pitcher (career)

Hits Best Against	Avg	AB	H	2B	3B	HR	RBI	BB	SO	OBP	SLG	Hits Worst Against	Avg	AB	H	2B	3B	HR	RBI	BB	SO	OBP	SLG
Mark Langston	.538	13	7	3	0	0	0	2	3	.600	.769	Cal Eldred	.000	11	0	0	0	0	0	0	2	.000	.000
Jack McDowell	.400	10	4	1	0	0	1	2	2	.500	.500	Chuck Finley	.100	10	1	0	0	0	0	1	2	.182	.100
Scott Kamieniecki	.357	14	5	1	0	0	4	0	3	.357	.429	Wilson Alvarez	.111	9	1	0	0	0	1	3	2	.333	.111
Bill Gullickson	.353	17	6	1	0	0	0	1	3	.389	.412	Scott Sanderson	.154	13	2	0	0	0	3	0	1	.133	.154
												Jaime Navarro	.154	13	2	0	0	0	0	0	2	.154	.154

Team/League Profiles

By far, the most suggested change from last year's Player Profiles book was the addition of Team and League Profiles. Considering we include every single player who made an appearance during the 1993 season in this book (even Paul Fletcher and his six pitches), it seemed right to include teams and leagues as well.

This section includes all 28 team profiles, an American League profile, a National League profile and a Major League profile.

Major League Baseball Batting

	Avg	G	AB	R	H	2B	3B	HR	RBI	BB	SO	HBP	GDP	SB	CS	OBP	SLG	IBB	SH	SF	#Pit	#P/PA	GB	FB	G/F
1993 Season	.265	4538	154995	20864	41088	7449	940	4030	19596	15110	26310	1200	3431	3263	1660	.332	.403	1477	1811	1430	634672	3.64	56450	43611	1.29

1993 Batting

	Avg	AB	H	2B	3B	HR	RBI	BB	SO	OBP	SLG
vs. Left	.268	45161	12118	2271	241	1193	5716	4402	7404	.335	.409
vs. Right	.264	109834	28970	5178	699	2837	13880	10708	18906	.331	.401
Groundball	.268	39226	10529	1880	226	857	4879	3581	6362	.332	.393
Flyball	.258	28371	7325	1373	177	858	3735	2857	5208	.328	.410
Home	.270	75707	20446	3689	487	2019	10026	7659	12519	.339	.412
Away	.260	79288	20642	3760	453	2011	9570	7451	13791	.326	.395
Day	.265	50343	13345	2448	312	1364	6385	4948	8638	.333	.407
Night	.265	104652	27743	5001	628	2666	13211	10162	17672	.332	.401
Grass	.265	99547	26428	4521	564	2728	12650	9776	16863	.333	.404
Turf	.264	55448	14660	2920	376	1302	6946	5334	9447	.331	.401
First Pitch	.322	22462	7233	1329	164	705	3512	1135	0	.357	.490
Ahead in Count	.332	35588	11824	2218	276	1456	6187	7710	0	.448	.533
Behind in Count	.205	67937	13957	2429	308	1055	6090	0	22221	.211	.297
Two Strikes	.189	67840	12832	2247	302	1072	5871	6263	26310	.261	.279

	Avg	AB	H	2B	3B	HR	RBI	BB	SO	OBP	SLG
Scoring Posn	.267	39404	10522	1895	268	987	15083	5630	7148	.353	.404
Close & Late	.259	24848	6439	1050	129	559	3201	2717	4727	.334	.379
None on/out	.267	38685	10332	1971	255	1034	1034	3131	6205	.326	.411
Leadoff	.276	18858	5201	873	190	273	1605	2063	2619	.350	.386
Batting #3	.290	18009	5231	962	98	635	2776	1928	2582	.359	.461
Cleanup	.271	17507	4743	902	75	808	3052	2024	3138	.348	.469
April	.258	20777	5369	969	132	486	2604	2137	3518	.329	.388
May	.264	26124	6896	1221	161	645	3231	2528	4375	.331	.397
June	.267	25052	6895	1275	161	675	3266	2429	4347	.331	.407
July	.274	26171	7179	1328	155	748	3482	2430	4246	.338	.423
August	.264	27353	7214	1282	159	784	3433	2640	4661	.330	.408
September/October	.262	28718	7535	1374	172	692	3580	2946	5163	.333	.394
Pre-All Star	.266	83441	22160	4036	517	2113	10575	8031	13925	.332	.402
Post-All Star	.265	71554	18928	3413	423	1917	9021	7079	12385	.333	.404

Major League Baseball Pitching

	ERA	W	L	Sv	Opp	G	IP	BB	SO	Avg	H	2B	3B	HR	RBI	OBP	SLG	CG	ShO	Sup	QS	#P/S	SB	CS	GB	FB	G/F
1993 Season	4.18	2268	2268	1192	1728	4538	40507.0	15110	26310	.265	41088	7449	940	4030	19596	.332	.403	371	220	4.64	2285	96	3263	1660	56450	43611	1.29

1993 Pitching

	ERA	W	L	Sv	G	GS	IP	H	HR	BB	SO
Home	3.97	1221	1047	573	7456	2269	20818.1	20642	2011	7451	13791
Away	4.43	1047	1221	619	7383	2269	19688.2	20446	2019	7659	12519
Day	4.17	738	738	388	4867	1478	13161.1	13345	1364	4948	8638
Night	4.20	1530	1530	804	9972	3060	27345.2	27743	2666	10162	17672
Grass	4.18	1458	1458	766	9541	2918	26028.1	26428	2728	9776	16863
Turf	4.20	810	810	426	5298	1620	14478.2	14660	1302	5334	9447
April	4.07	307	307	167	1968	614	5486.2	5369	486	2137	3518
May	4.10	381	381	190	2487	764	6823.2	6896	645	2528	4375
June	4.22	382	382	208	2457	764	6751.1	6895	675	2429	4347
July	4.47	381	381	208	2483	762	6762.1	7179	748	2430	4246
August	4.16	398	398	216	2566	796	7162.1	7214	784	2640	4661
September/October	4.12	419	419	203	2878	838	7520.2	7535	692	2946	5163
Starters	4.26	1619	1640	0	4538	4538	27730.0	28480	2838	9708	16934
Relievers	4.04	649	628	1192	10301	0	12777.0	12608	1192	5402	9376
0-3 Days Rest (SP)	4.17	77	91	0	238	238	1374.0	1386	145	467	792
4 Days Rest	4.28	943	943	0	2569	2569	15972.2	16497	1650	5457	9862
5+ Days Rest	4.24	599	606	0	1731	1731	10383.1	10597	1043	3784	6280
Pre-All Star	4.20	1223	1223	638	7924	2448	21791.2	22160	2113	8031	13925
Post-All Star	4.18	1045	1045	554	6915	2090	18715.1	18928	1917	7079	12385

	Avg	AB	H	2B	3B	HR	RBI	BB	SO	OBP	SLG
vs. Left	.270	63857	17243	3011	473	1569	7989	7145	10144	.344	.406
vs. Right	.262	91138	23845	4438	467	2461	11607	7965	16166	.324	.402
Inning 1-6	.267	104298	27866	5176	667	2803	13395	9926	16953	.333	.410
Inning 7+	.261	50697	13222	2273	273	1227	6201	5184	9357	.331	.389
None on	.259	87471	22673	4215	511	2292	2292	7458	14985	.322	.398
Runners on	.273	67524	18415	3234	429	1738	17304	7652	11325	.345	.411
Scoring Posn	.267	39404	10522	1895	268	987	15083	5630	7148	.353	.404
Close & Late	.259	24848	6439	1050	129	559	3201	2717	4727	.334	.379
None on/out	.267	38685	10332	1971	255	1034	1034	3131	6205	.326	.411
vs. 1st Batr (relief)	.258	9112	2351	421	56	222	1316	919	1757	.328	.390
First Inning Pitched	.263	49736	13096	2273	324	1244	7807	5521	9271	.338	.397
First 75 Pits (SP)	.264	127920	33804	6048	817	3265	16292	12554	21983	.332	.401
Pitch 76-90	.271	13131	3555	721	53	410	1673	1190	2006	.333	.427
Pitch 91-105	.271	8902	2416	425	50	242	1073	806	1379	.333	.412
Pitch 106+	.260	5042	1313	255	20	113	558	560	942	.336	.386
First Pitch	.322	22462	7233	1329	164	705	3512	1135	0	.357	.490
Ahead in Count	.205	67937	13957	2429	308	1055	6090	0	22221	.211	.297
Behind in Count	.332	35588	11824	2218	276	1456	6187	7710	0	.448	.533
Two Strikes	.189	67840	12832	2247	302	1072	5871	6263	26310	.261	.279

Games Finished: 4167 Inherited Runners: 7183 Inherited Runners Scored: 2311 Holds: 1258

National League Batting

	Avg	G	AB	R	H	2B	3B	HR	RBI	BB	SO	HBP	GDP	SB	CS	OBP	SLG	IBB	SH	SF	#Pit	#P/PA	GB	FB	G/F
1993 Season	.264	2270	77489	10190	20427	3588	513	1956	9533	7104	13358	567	1638	1714	788	.327	.399	743	1110	701	311568	3.58	28556	21217	1.35

1993 Batting

	Avg	AB	H	2B	3B	HR	RBI	BB	SO	OBP	SLG
vs. Left	.272	22808	6209	1155	146	588	2843	2059	3655	.333	.413
vs. Right	.260	54681	14218	2433	367	1368	6690	5045	9703	.325	.393
Groundball	.265	25460	6742	1182	159	551	3031	2208	4184	.326	.389
Flyball	.255	12624	3225	585	86	348	1610	1232	2468	.323	.398
Home	.268	37813	10135	1755	257	981	4857	3565	6370	.333	.406
Away	.259	39676	10292	1833	256	975	4676	3539	6988	.322	.392
Day	.262	25290	6630	1181	169	678	3080	2303	4356	.326	.403
Night	.264	52199	13797	2407	344	1278	6453	4801	9002	.328	.397
Grass	.265	44445	11773	1943	285	1190	5477	4022	7681	.328	.402
Turf	.262	33044	8654	1645	228	766	4056	3082	5677	.327	.395
First Pitch	.321	11744	3773	648	99	368	1832	570	0	.354	.487
Ahead in Count	.332	17426	5791	1058	146	698	2957	3623	0	.444	.530
Behind in Count	.202	34331	6941	1162	178	519	2977	0	11403	.208	.292
Two Strikes	.186	33798	6275	1065	161	504	2784	2910	13358	.254	.271

	Avg	AB	H	2B	3B	HR	RBI	BB	SO	OBP	SLG
Scoring Posn	.264	19656	5191	925	149	461	7307	2741	3636	.348	.397
Close & Late	.254	12807	3250	514	72	294	1597	1330	2499	.325	.374
None on/out	.266	19459	5183	951	144	500	500	1458	3158	.321	.407
Leadoff	.274	9464	2589	430	99	140	756	964	1289	.343	.384
Batting #3	.292	9035	2640	456	49	270	1321	924	1277	.357	.443
Cleanup	.276	8780	2421	463	49	371	1483	958	1442	.347	.466
April	.252	10705	2702	460	70	237	1246	1089	1809	.323	.375
May	.266	12867	3423	609	77	300	1597	1190	2113	.331	.395
June	.266	12881	3429	607	87	314	1550	1079	2237	.324	.400
July	.271	13182	3570	650	88	359	1693	1157	2220	.331	.415
August	.264	13528	3576	605	89	405	1691	1206	2320	.327	.412
September/October	.260	14326	3727	657	102	341	1756	1383	2659	.327	.392
Pre-All Star	.265	41955	11098	1978	273	1005	5146	3802	7076	.327	.397
Post-All Star	.263	35534	9329	1610	240	951	4387	3302	6282	.327	.402

National League Pitching

	ERA	W	L	Sv	Opp	G	IP	BB	SO	Avg	H	2B	3B	HR	RBI	OBP	SLG	CG	ShO	Sup	QS	#P/S	SB	CS	GB	FB	G/F
1993 Season	4.04	1134	1134	599	860	2270	20284.2	7104	13358	.264	20427	3588	513	1956	9533	.327	.399	162	110	4.52	1197	93	1714	788	28556	21217	1.35

1993 Pitching

	ERA	W	L	Sv	G	GS	IP	H	HR	BB	SO
Home	3.84	602	532	278	3808	1135	10418.0	10292	975	3539	6988
Away	4.26	532	602	321	3794	1135	9866.2	10135	981	3565	6370
Day	3.96	372	372	208	2521	746	6637.0	6630	678	2303	4356
Night	4.09	762	762	391	5081	1524	13647.2	13797	1278	4801	9002
Grass	4.02	648	648	340	4365	1298	11635.1	11773	1190	4022	7681
Turf	4.09	486	486	259	3237	972	8649.1	8654	766	3082	5677
April	3.75	158	158	95	1049	316	2843.1	2702	237	1089	1809
May	4.11	188	188	86	1243	378	3363.0	3423	300	1190	2113
June	4.04	190	190	101	1224	380	3361.0	3429	314	1079	2237
July	4.25	192	192	104	1275	384	3422.2	3570	359	1157	2220
August	4.08	196	196	108	1315	392	3534.0	3576	405	1206	2320
September/October	4.01	210	210	105	1496	420	3760.2	3727	341	1383	2659
Starters	4.08	808	813	0	2270	2270	13851.0	14193	1347	4507	8502
Relievers	3.98	326	321	599	5332	0	6433.2	6234	609	2597	4856
0-3 Days Rest (SP)	3.67	36	34	0	104	104	597.2	597	51	198	376
4 Days Rest	4.14	466	468	0	1290	1290	7964.0	8231	813	2499	4913
5+ Days Rest	4.03	306	311	0	876	876	5289.1	5365	483	1810	3213
Pre-All Star	4.06	615	615	320	4046	1232	10970.1	11098	1005	3802	7076
Post-All Star	4.03	519	519	279	3556	1038	9314.1	9329	951	3302	6282

	Avg	AB	H	2B	3B	HR	RBI	BB	SO	OBP	SLG
vs. Left	.266	32279	8577	1436	244	797	3981	3586	5394	.340	.399
vs. Right	.262	45210	11850	2152	269	1159	5552	3518	7964	.318	.399
Inning 1-6	.267	52089	13894	2494	354	1340	6489	4643	8600	.329	.405
Inning 7+	.257	25400	6533	1094	159	616	3044	2461	4758	.324	.386
None on	.258	44125	11385	2036	280	1123	1123	3494	7681	.317	.393
Runners on	.271	33364	9042	1552	233	833	8410	3610	5677	.341	.406
Scoring Posn	.264	19656	5191	925	149	461	7307	2741	3636	.348	.397
Close & Late	.254	12807	3250	514	72	294	1597	1330	2499	.325	.374
None on/out	.266	19459	5183	951	144	500	500	1458	3158	.321	.407
vs. 1st Batr (relief)	.251	4735	1188	199	34	105	565	461	920	.318	.374
First Inning Pitched	.263	25639	6733	1112	182	630	3837	2764	4818	.335	.394
First 75 Pits (SP)	.262	65029	17036	2946	448	1598	7946	5975	11385	.326	.395
Pitch 76-90	.276	6444	1777	344	32	206	870	581	1002	.337	.435
Pitch 91-105	.271	4028	1092	191	23	108	488	341	615	.329	.410
Pitch 106+	.263	1988	522	107	10	44	229	207	356	.333	.393
First Pitch	.321	11744	3773	648	99	368	1832	570	0	.354	.487
Ahead in Count	.202	34331	6941	1162	178	519	2977	0	11403	.208	.292
Behind in Count	.332	17426	5791	1058	146	698	2957	3623	0	.444	.530
Two Strikes	.186	33798	6275	1065	161	504	2784	2910	13358	.254	.271

Games Finished: 2108   Inherited Runners: 3170   Inherited Runners Scored: 1025   Holds: 618

American League Batting

	Avg	G	AB	R	H	2B	3B	HR	RBI	BB	SO	HBP	GDP	SB	CS	OBP	SLG	IBB	SH	SF	#Pit	#P/PA	GB	FB	G/F
1993 Season	.267	2268	77506	10674	20661	3861	427	2074	10063	8006	12952	633	1793	1549	872	.337	.408	734	701	729	323104	3.69	27894	22394	1.25

1993 Batting

	Avg	AB	H	2B	3B	HR	RBI	BB	SO	OBP	SLG		Avg	AB	H	2B	3B	HR	RBI	BB	SO	OBP	SLG
vs. Left	.264	22353	5909	1116	95	605	2873	2343	3749	.336	.404	Scoring Posn	.270	19748	5331	970	119	526	7776	2889	3512	.357	.411
vs. Right	.267	55153	14752	2745	332	1469	7190	5663	9203	.338	.409	Close & Late	.265	12041	3189	536	57	265	1604	1387	2228	.342	.385
Groundball	.275	13766	3787	698	67	306	1848	1373	2178	.344	.402	None on/out	.268	19226	5149	1020	111	534	534	1673	3047	.330	.416
Flyball	.260	15747	4100	788	91	510	2125	1625	2740	.332	.419	Leadoff	.278	9394	2612	443	91	133	849	1099	1330	.356	.387
Home	.272	37894	10311	1934	230	1038	5169	4094	6149	.345	.417	Batting #3	.289	8974	2591	506	49	365	1455	1004	1305	.361	.478
Away	.261	39612	10350	1927	197	1036	4894	3912	6803	.330	.398	Cleanup	.266	8727	2322	439	26	437	1569	1066	1696	.348	.473
Day	.268	25053	6715	1267	143	686	3305	2645	4282	.340	.412	April	.265	10072	2667	509	62	249	1358	1048	1709	.336	.402
Night	.266	52453	13946	2594	284	1388	6758	5361	8670	.336	.406	May	.262	13257	3473	612	84	345	1634	1338	2262	.332	.300
Grass	.266	55102	14655	2578	279	1538	7173	5754	9182	.337	.407	June	.207	12971	3466	668	74	361	1716	1350	2110	.338	.414
Turf	.268	22404	6006	1203	148	536	2890	2252	3770	.338	.410	July	.278	12989	3609	678	67	389	1789	1273	2026	.345	.430
First Pitch	.323	10718	3460	681	65	337	1680	565	0	.361	.493	August	.263	13825	3638	677	70	379	1742	1434	2341	.334	.404
Ahead in Count	.332	18162	6033	1160	130	758	3230	4087	0	.452	.536	September/October	.265	14392	3808	717	70	351	1824	1563	2504	.339	.397
Behind in Count	.209	33606	7016	1267	130	536	3113	0	10818	.215	.302	Pre-All Star	.267	41486	11062	2058	244	1108	5429	4229	6849	.337	.408
Two Strikes	.193	34042	6557	1182	141	568	3087	3353	12952	.268	.286	Post-All Star	.266	36020	9599	1803	183	966	4634	3777	6103	.338	.407

American League Pitching

	ERA	W	L	Sv	Opp	G	IP	BB	SO	Avg	H	2B	3B	HR	RBI	OBP	SLG	CG	ShO	Sup	QS	#P/S	SB	CS	GB	FB	G/F
1993 Season	4.32	1134	1134	593	868	2268	20222.1	8006	12952	.267	20661	3861	427	2074	10063	.337	.408	209	110	4.75	1088	98	1549	872	27894	22394	1.25

1993 Pitching

	ERA	W	L	Sv	G	GS	IP	H	HR	BB	SO		Avg	AB	H	2B	3B	HR	RBI	BB	SO	OBP	SLG
Home	4.09	619	515	295	3648	1134	10400.1	10350	1036	3912	6803	vs. Left	.274	31578	8666	1575	229	772	4008	3559	4750	.349	.412
Away	4.59	515	619	298	3589	1134	9822.0	10311	1038	4094	6149	vs. Right	.261	45928	11995	2286	198	1302	6055	4447	8202	.329	.405
Day	4.39	366	366	180	2346	732	6524.1	6715	686	2645	4282	Inning 1-6	.268	52209	13972	2682	313	1463	6906	5283	8353	.337	.415
Night	4.31	768	768	413	4891	1536	13698.0	13946	1388	5361	8670	Inning 7+	.264	25297	6689	1179	114	611	3157	2723	4599	.338	.392
Grass	4.32	810	810	426	5176	1620	14393.0	14655	1538	5754	9182	None on	.260	43346	11288	2179	231	1169	1169	3964	7304	.327	.402
Turf	4.37	324	324	167	2061	648	5829.1	6006	536	2252	3770	Runners on	.274	34160	9373	1682	196	905	8894	4042	5648	.350	.415
April	4.42	149	149	72	919	298	2643.1	2667	249	1048	1709	Scoring Posn	.270	19748	5331	970	119	526	7776	2889	3512	.357	.411
May	4.09	193	193	104	1244	386	3460.2	3473	345	1338	2262	Close & Late	.265	12041	3189	536	57	265	1604	1387	2228	.342	.385
June	4.40	192	192	107	1233	384	3390.1	3466	361	1350	2110	None on/out	.268	19226	5149	1020	111	534	534	1673	3047	.330	.416
July	4.69	189	189	104	1208	378	3339.2	3609	389	1273	2026	vs. 1st Batr (relief)	.266	4377	1163	222	22	117	751	458	837	.338	.407
August	4.23	202	202	108	1251	404	3628.1	3638	379	1434	2341	First Inning Pitched	.264	24097	6363	1161	142	614	3970	2757	4453	.341	.400
September/October	4.23	209	209	98	1382	418	3760.0	3808	351	1563	2504	First 75 Pits (SP)	.267	62891	16768	3102	369	1667	8346	6579	10598	.338	.407
Starters	4.44	811	827	0	2268	2268	13879.0	14287	1491	5201	8432	Pitch 76-90	.266	6687	1778	377	21	204	803	609	1004	.330	.420
Relievers	4.10	323	307	593	4969	0	6343.1	6374	583	2805	4520	Pitch 91-105	.272	4874	1324	234	27	134	585	465	764	.337	.413
0-3 Days Rest (SP)	4.56	41	57	0	134	134	776.1	789	94	269	416	Pitch 106+	.259	3054	791	148	10	69	329	353	586	.338	.382
4 Days Rest	4.43	477	475	0	1279	1279	8008.2	8266	837	2958	4949	First Pitch	.323	10718	3460	681	65	337	1680	565	0	.361	.493
5+ Days Rest	4.45	293	295	0	855	855	5094.0	5232	560	1974	3067	Ahead in Count	.209	33606	7016	1267	130	536	3113	0	10818	.215	.302
Pre-All Star	4.35	608	608	318	3878	1216	10821.1	11062	1108	4229	6849	Behind in Count	.332	18162	6033	1160	130	758	3230	4087	0	.452	.536
Post-All Star	4.32	526	526	275	3359	1052	9401.0	9599	966	3777	6103	Two Strikes	.193	34042	6557	1182	141	568	3087	3353	12952	.268	.286

Games Finished: 2059 Inherited Runners: 4013 Inherited Runners Scored: 1286 Holds: 640

Baltimore Orioles

1993 Record: 85 – 77

	Avg	G	AB	R	H	2B	3B	HR	RBI	BB	SO	HBP	GDP	SB	CS	OBP	SLG	IBB	SH	SF	#Pit	#P/PA	GB	FB	G/F
1993 Season	.267	162	5508	786	1470	287	24	157	744	655	930	41	131	73	54	.346	.413	52	49	56	23902	3.79	1956	1691	1.16

1993 Batting

	Avg	AB	H	2B	3B	HR	RBI	BB	SO	OBP	SLG		Avg	AB	H	2B	3B	HR	RBI	BB	SO	OBP	SLG
vs. Left	.268	1650	442	83	2	47	216	182	288	.342	.406	Scoring Posn	.282	1434	404	91	6	37	573	214	255	.366	.431
vs. Right	.266	3858	1028	204	22	110	528	473	642	.348	.416	Close & Late	.247	853	211	37	4	21	108	110	171	.333	.374
Groundball	.271	1048	284	65	2	23	134	116	165	.344	.403	None on/out	.257	1348	346	60	5	49	49	152	229	.335	.418
Flyball	.246	1063	261	65	5	34	153	126	200	.329	.412	Leadoff	.261	652	170	41	8	13	70	94	106	.359	.408
Home	.278	2722	757	148	11	87	414	348	469	.360	.436	Batting #3	.245	658	161	27	4	18	89	68	93	.317	.380
Away	.256	2786	713	139	13	70	330	307	461	.332	.391	Cleanup	.265	623	165	25	0	28	99	81	87	.346	.440
Day	.271	1588	430	83	7	44	200	174	292	.344	.415	April	.258	740	191	43	7	11	85	80	138	.335	.380
Night	.265	3920	1040	204	17	113	544	481	638	.347	.413	May	.238	960	228	42	2	21	93	121	188	.326	.351
Grass	.266	4665	1241	238	18	137	638	555	772	.345	.413	June	.279	927	259	59	2	28	133	110	141	.356	.438
Turf	.272	843	229	49	6	20	106	100	158	.351	.415	July	.290	887	257	51	3	30	137	95	131	.358	.455
First Pitch	.318	686	218	35	4	25	99	40	0	.357	.490	August	.268	964	258	39	3	36	147	131	157	.352	.426
Ahead in Count	.324	1397	452	85	4	64	250	337	0	.451	.528	September/October	.269	1030	277	53	7	31	149	118	175	.347	.424
Behind in Count	.218	2304	502	97	5	39	238	0	754	.223	.315	Pre-All Star	.260	2995	780	162	11	71	369	350	507	.340	.393
Two Strikes	.207	2425	502	101	9	38	238	278	930	.291	.303	Post-All Star	.275	2513	690	125	13	86	375	305	423	.353	.437

	ERA	W	L	Sv	Opp	G	IP	BB	SO	Avg	H	2B	3B	HR	RBI	OBP	SLG	CG	ShO	Sup	QS	#P/S	SB	CS	GB	FB	G/F
1993 Season	4.31	85	77	42	61	162	1442.2	579	900	.261	1427	284	30	153	710	.333	.407	21	10	4.90	82	98	96	64	1988	1628	1.22

1993 Pitching

	ERA	W	L	Sv	G	GS	IP	H	HR	BB	SO		Avg	AB	H	2B	3B	HR	RBI	BB	SO	OBP	SLG
Home	4.18	48	33	23	251	81	747.0	737	81	296	457	vs. Left	.262	2005	526	93	12	44	237	231	321	.340	.387
Away	4.48	37	44	19	240	81	695.2	690	72	283	443	vs. Right	.260	3468	901	191	18	109	473	348	579	.329	.420
Day	4.39	22	24	10	137	46	407.2	418	39	166	269	Inning 1-6	.260	3689	960	198	24	117	495	382	594	.332	.422
Night	4.30	63	53	32	354	116	1035.0	1009	114	413	631	Inning 7+	.262	1784	467	86	6	36	215	197	306	.335	.377
Grass	4.31	75	63	37	426	138	1235.1	1227	132	495	783	None on	.249	3096	771	165	18	83	83	304	518	.320	.394
Turf	4.38	10	14	5	65	24	207.1	200	21	84	117	Runners on	.276	2377	656	119	12	70	627	275	382	.350	.424
April	4.32	8	13	6	65	21	191.2	183	23	81	123	Scoring Posn	.272	1370	372	68	6	46	551	207	231	.362	.431
May	3.77	13	16	7	86	29	257.2	253	27	89	165	Close & Late	.256	828	212	34	4	14	100	97	157	.334	.357
June	3.62	20	7	14	87	27	241.0	227	20	105	151	None on/out	.266	1363	363	73	8	41	41	133	209	.334	.422
July	4.57	14	12	6	77	26	228.1	217	25	78	133	vs. 1st Batr (relief)	.258	291	75	13	0	6	52	31	52	.331	.364
August	5.41	15	14	5	91	29	256.0	281	36	113	156	First Inning Pitched	.255	1587	405	70	7	42	274	172	284	.328	.388
September/October	4.23	15	15	4	85	30	268.0	266	22	113	172	First 75 Pitches (SP)	.259	4386	1135	223	27	126	583	491	736	.334	.408
Starters	4.57	62	56	0	162	162	977.1	993	108	373	589	Pitch 76-90	.293	461	135	33	0	16	60	37	65	.358	.469
Relievers	3.81	23	21	42	329	0	465.1	434	45	206	311	Pitch 91-105	.233	395	92	13	3	8	43	27	64	.283	.342
0-3 Days Rest (SP)	17.28	0	2	0	3	3	8.1	18	1	8	3	Pitch 106+	.281	231	65	15	0	3	24	24	35	.349	.385
4 Days Rest	4.48	35	33	0	91	91	560.2	578	51	196	327	First Pitch	.351	676	237	53	2	22	120	35	0	.381	.533
5+ Days Rest	4.43	27	21	0	68	68	408.1	397	56	169	259	Ahead in Count	.195	2326	454	79	8	40	194	0	733	.203	.288
Pre-All Star	4.04	47	41	29	273	88	786.1	755	85	311	485	Behind in Count	.330	1333	440	90	9	58	233	287	0	.449	.542
Post-All Star	4.66	38	36	13	218	74	656.1	672	68	268	415	Two Strikes	.173	2379	412	68	11	42	197	257	900	.258	.264

Games Finished: 141 Inherited Runners: 339 Inherited Runners Scored: 100 Holds: 47

Boston Red Sox

1993 Record: 80 – 82

	Avg	G	AB	R	H	2B	3B	HR	RBI	BB	SO	HBP	GDP	SB	CS	OBP	SLG	IBB	SH	SF	#Pit	#P/PA	GB	FB	G/F
1993 Season	.264	162	5496	686	1451	319	29	114	644	508	871	62	146	73	38	.330	.395	69	80	49	22144	3.57	2000	1595	1.25

1993 Batting

	Avg	AB	H	2B	3B	HR	RBI	BB	SO	OBP	SLG		Avg	AB	H	2B	3B	HR	RBI	BB	SO	OBP	SLG
vs. Left	.263	1515	399	82	10	42	188	120	230	.323	.414	Scoring Posn	.278	1353	376	79	7	32	525	191	222	.364	.418
vs. Right	.264	3981	1052	237	19	72	456	388	641	.333	.388	Close & Late	.269	845	227	51	4	23	110	76	149	.333	.420
Groundball	.281	864	243	53	3	13	114	70	119	.340	.395	None on/out	.254	1382	351	84	12	26	26	100	195	.309	.389
Flyball	.273	1298	354	84	9	30	162	114	223	.335	.421	Leadoff	.264	686	181	37	6	8	60	51	60	.323	.370
Home	.281	2743	770	193	14	54	367	269	432	.349	.420	Batting #3	.285	635	181	45	4	9	75	59	78	.350	.411
Away	.247	2753	681	126	15	60	277	239	439	.312	.369	Cleanup	.279	637	178	35	1	26	103	52	106	.340	.460
Day	.274	1907	522	107	12	38	239	191	305	.343	.402	April	.261	733	191	40	5	13	87	62	107	.322	.382
Night	.259	3589	929	212	17	76	405	317	566	.324	.391	May	.276	947	261	52	6	10	105	85	146	.338	.375
Grass	.268	4624	1238	269	23	98	554	440	723	.336	.399	June	.255	885	226	47	3	21	109	99	146	.336	.386
Turf	.244	872	213	50	6	16	90	68	148	.303	.370	July	.279	904	252	59	3	27	133	88	127	.347	.440
First Pitch	.331	816	270	54	5	22	115	58	0	.380	.490	August	.245	918	225	60	6	14	76	62	141	.298	.369
Ahead in Count	.325	1334	434	106	12	38	189	245	0	.428	.508	September/October	.267	1109	296	61	6	29	134	112	204	.338	.411
Behind in Count	.199	2327	463	104	9	30	212	0	716	.209	.290	Pre-All Star	.265	2909	772	158	15	55	351	280	447	.334	.387
Two Strikes	.179	2324	417	90	8	26	184	205	871	.254	.259	Post-All Star	.262	2587	679	161	14	59	293	228	424	.327	.404

Boston Red Sox

	ERA	W	L	Sv	Opp	G	IP	BB	SO	Avg	H	2B	3B	HR	RBI	OBP	SLG	CG	ShO	Sup	QS	#P/S	SB	CS	GB	FB	G/F
1993 Season	3.77	80	82	44	67	162	1452.1	552	997	.252	1379	281	33	127	650	.322	.384	9	11	4.25	84	96	92	44	2010	1465	1.37

1993 Pitching

	ERA	W	L	Sv	G	GS	IP	H	HR	BB	SO
Home	3.74	43	38	22	279	81	750.0	739	53	286	516
Away	3.87	37	44	22	272	81	702.1	640	74	266	481
Day	3.55	29	26	16	195	55	502.1	475	44	193	371
Night	3.94	51	56	28	356	107	950.0	904	83	359	626
Grass	3.73	67	70	37	458	137	1229.2	1164	105	447	858
Turf	4.20	13	12	7	93	25	222.2	215	22	105	139
April	3.20	13	9	4	65	22	194.0	169	20	62	118
May	3.11	14	14	8	95	28	249.0	222	15	90	191
June	3.95	11	16	6	86	27	237.0	233	21	81	167
July	3.62	20	7	14	90	27	241.1	226	22	83	169
August	3.68	11	16	7	89	27	244.1	232	20	99	155
September/October	4.96	11	20	5	126	31	286.2	297	29	137	197
Starters	3.81	55	56	0	162	162	1001.0	966	98	332	623
Relievers	3.79	25	26	44	389	0	451.1	413	29	220	374
0-3 Days Rest (SP)	3.86	3	6	0	13	13	77.0	73	9	24	41
4 Days Rest	4.05	27	34	0	88	88	541.2	543	58	184	334
5+ Days Rest	3.46	25	16	0	61	61	382.1	350	31	124	248
Pre-All Star	3.50	45	42	23	279	87	769.2	705	66	263	544
Post-All Star	4.15	35	40	21	272	75	682.2	674	61	289	453

	Avg	AB	H	2B	3B	HR	RBI	BB	SO	OBP	SLG
vs. Left	.256	2502	640	137	22	55	288	292	416	.333	.394
vs. Right	.248	2981	739	144	11	72	362	260	581	.313	.376
Inning 1-6	.252	3679	926	188	21	93	429	331	606	.315	.390
Inning 7+	.251	1804	453	93	12	34	221	221	391	.336	.373
None on	.244	3170	775	167	15	83	83	254	579	.305	.385
Runners on	.261	2313	604	114	18	44	567	298	418	.345	.383
Scoring Posn	.254	1355	344	62	10	25	502	226	264	.355	.370
Close & Late	.249	912	227	45	5	14	110	103	209	.327	.355
None on/out	.256	1393	356	85	6	41	41	106	265	.012	.413
vs. 1st Batr (relief)	.251	346	87	24	1	8	61	28	72	.313	.396
First Inning Pitched	.248	1715	426	85	10	31	253	186	363	.323	.364
First 75 Pitches (SP)	.251	4597	1154	240	26	98	546	458	835	.322	.379
Pitch 76-90	.262	439	115	26	4	16	54	50	76	.335	.449
Pitch 91-105	.254	272	69	10	3	11	38	27	50	.317	.434
Pitch 106+	.234	175	41	5	0	2	12	17	36	.308	.297
First Pitch	.322	822	265	53	6	29	128	62	0	.373	.507
Ahead in Count	.205	2442	501	108	11	34	220	0	847	.210	.300
Behind in Count	.314	1140	358	73	5	42	187	268	0	.441	.497
Two Strikes	.183	2491	456	96	13	31	206	222	997	.253	.269

Games Finished: 153 Inherited Runners: 331 Inherited Runners Scored: 100 Holds: 44

California Angels

1993 Record: 71 – 91

	Avg	G	AB	R	H	2B	3B	HR	RBI	BB	SO	HBP	GDP	SB	CS	OBP	SLG	IBB	SH	SF	#Pit	#P/PA	GB	FB	G/F
1993 Season	.260	162	5391	684	1399	259	24	114	644	564	930	38	129	169	100	.331	.380	39	50	46	22582	3.71	2060	1478	1.39

1993 Batting

	Avg	AB	H	2B	3B	HR	RBI	BB	SO	OBP	SLG
vs. Left	.261	1332	348	61	6	24	149	143	216	.336	.370
vs. Right	.259	4059	1051	198	18	90	495	421	714	.330	.383
Groundball	.272	1012	275	53	7	18	137	101	149	.341	.391
Flyball	.247	1207	298	59	5	27	147	129	219	.322	.371
Home	.264	2654	701	118	12	64	345	270	437	.334	.390
Away	.255	2737	698	141	12	50	299	294	493	.329	.370
Day	.272	1603	436	88	5	35	199	167	284	.342	.399
Night	.254	3788	963	171	19	79	445	397	646	.327	.372
Grass	.260	4452	1156	205	19	98	544	470	775	.332	.380
Turf	.259	939	243	54	5	16	100	94	155	.330	.378
First Pitch	.323	719	232	45	4	21	113	28	0	.354	.484
Ahead in Count	.338	1271	429	91	2	40	201	285	0	.456	.507
Behind in Count	.200	2363	472	70	9	28	192	0	789	.206	.273
Two Strikes	.177	2366	419	67	11	31	203	251	930	.259	.254

	Avg	AB	H	2B	3B	HR	RBI	BB	SO	OBP	SLG
Scoring Posn	.281	1335	375	68	6	33	514	176	245	.360	.415
Close & Late	.245	897	220	26	5	14	97	111	164	.333	.332
None on/out	.244	1354	330	63	7	20	20	120	218	.308	.345
Leadoff	.266	668	178	22	7	1	42	61	67	.328	.325
Batting #3	.276	616	170	36	2	35	106	85	149	.364	.511
Cleanup	.248	624	155	35	0	28	119	73	144	.328	.439
April	.266	612	163	27	5	18	87	51	104	.323	.415
May	.257	958	246	47	3	18	113	133	174	.350	.368
June	.250	891	223	50	3	18	113	99	137	.325	.374
July	.258	943	243	41	2	20	101	91	145	.325	.369
August	.266	956	254	47	3	16	105	86	179	.329	.371
September/October	.262	1031	270	47	8	24	125	104	191	.331	.393
Pre-All Star	.258	2854	736	142	12	61	359	325	473	.335	.380
Post-All Star	.261	2537	663	117	12	53	285	239	457	.327	.380

	ERA	W	L	Sv	Opp	G	IP	BB	SO	Avg	H	2B	3B	HR	RBI	OBP	SLG	CG	ShO	Sup	QS	#P/S	SB	CS	GB	FB	G/F
1993 Season	4.34	71	91	41	55	162	1430.1	550	843	.270	1482	268	15	153	732	.339	.408	26	6	4.30	89	100	122	52	1938	1699	1.14

1993 Pitching

	ERA	W	L	Sv	G	GS	IP	H	HR	BB	SO
Home	4.39	44	37	23	248	81	744.0	761	84	278	464
Away	4.33	27	54	18	234	81	686.1	721	69	272	379
Day	4.44	19	28	10	141	47	411.1	437	45	173	249
Night	4.33	52	63	31	341	115	1019.0	1045	108	377	594
Grass	4.30	63	72	36	398	135	1200.1	1226	132	449	735
Turf	4.70	8	19	5	84	27	230.0	256	21	101	108
April	3.48	13	6	5	48	19	168.0	137	16	69	121
May	3.62	14	15	11	94	29	261.0	265	30	90	153
June	5.73	10	17	6	90	27	235.2	284	28	91	136
July	4.20	11	17	5	79	28	251.0	270	29	85	135
August	4.34	11	17	7	85	28	247.0	243	25	111	151
September/October	4.61	12	19	7	86	31	267.2	283	25	104	147
Starters	4.32	57	71	0	162	162	1039.1	1080	111	371	612
Relievers	4.47	14	20	41	320	0	391.0	402	42	179	231
0-3 Days Rest (SP)	5.16	2	2	0	4	4	22.2	35	1	8	21
4 Days Rest	4.28	40	43	0	107	107	705.0	742	76	250	420
5+ Days Rest	4.36	15	26	0	51	51	311.2	303	34	113	171
Pre-All Star	4.22	43	43	23	265	86	771.2	799	85	287	466
Post-All Star	4.52	28	48	18	217	76	658.2	683	68	263	377

	Avg	AB	H	2B	3B	HR	RBI	BB	SO	OBP	SLG
vs. Left	.280	1719	481	88	7	48	233	206	222	.360	.423
vs. Right	.266	3769	1001	180	8	105	499	344	621	.329	.401
Inning 1-6	.272	3726	1014	196	10	108	515	359	565	.339	.417
Inning 7+	.266	1762	468	72	5	45	217	191	278	.339	.389
None on	.262	3048	798	164	8	73	73	283	511	.330	.393
Runners on	.280	2440	684	104	7	80	659	267	332	.349	.427
Scoring Posn	.282	1385	391	62	4	52	588	181	200	.357	.445
Close & Late	.265	840	223	38	0	17	110	107	133	.348	.371
None on/out	.285	1350	385	78	2	36	36	121	217	.350	.426
vs. 1st Batr (relief)	.274	285	78	11	0	12	51	25	45	.341	.439
First Inning Pitched	.273	1630	445	81	5	52	296	190	259	.350	.425
First 75 Pitches (SP)	.272	4367	1188	221	13	122	604	435	675	.340	.412
Pitch 76-90	.251	495	124	30	1	12	64	48	62	.319	.388
Pitch 91-105	.262	362	95	10	0	12	43	38	56	.334	.390
Pitch 106+	.284	264	75	7	1	7	21	29	50	.357	.398
First Pitch	.284	795	226	37	3	24	106	25	0	.311	.429
Ahead in Count	.220	2312	508	97	5	37	224	0	711	.226	.314
Behind in Count	.330	1364	450	89	4	60	242	294	0	.446	.533
Two Strikes	.197	2296	453	82	6	35	226	231	843	.273	.284

Games Finished: 136 Inherited Runners: 265 Inherited Runners Scored: 78 Holds: 34

Chicago White Sox

1993 Record: 94 – 68

	Avg	G	AB	R	H	2B	3B	HR	RBI	BB	SO	HBP	GDP	SB	CS	OBP	SLG	IBB	SH	SF	#Pit	#P/PA	GB	FB	G/F
1993 Season	.265	162	5483	776	1454	228	44	162	731	604	834	33	126	106	57	.338	.411	52	72	61	23040	3.68	1969	1624	1.21

1993 Batting

	Avg	AB	H	2B	3B	HR	RBI	BB	SO	OBP	SLG
vs. Left	.254	1674	425	64	6	53	209	182	280	.326	.394
vs. Right	.270	3809	1029	164	38	109	522	422	554	.344	.419
Groundball	.260	1002	261	33	9	25	131	108	168	.335	.386
Flyball	.251	1179	296	53	12	38	153	136	184	.331	.413
Home	.270	2657	718	109	20	82	369	300	385	.345	.419
Away	.260	2826	736	119	24	80	362	304	449	.332	.404
Day	.254	1578	401	64	13	40	201	174	255	.329	.387
Night	.270	3905	1053	164	31	122	530	430	579	.342	.421
Grass	.264	4611	1219	183	32	138	615	509	670	.338	.408
Turf	.269	872	235	45	12	24	116	95	164	.339	.431
First Pitch	.313	774	242	26	8	27	121	41	0	.347	.472
Ahead in Count	.310	1415	438	72	15	59	261	318	0	.434	.507
Behind in Count	.215	2228	479	88	10	43	210	0	696	.220	.321
Two Strikes	.205	2288	470	82	12	52	214	245	834	.284	.320

	Avg	AB	H	2B	3B	HR	RBI	BB	SO	OBP	SLG
Scoring Posn	.270	1357	367	57	11	42	553	210	205	.358	.422
Close & Late	.258	790	204	34	6	14	101	93	130	.336	.370
None on/out	.267	1380	368	54	11	42	42	121	199	.329	.413
Leadoff	.292	664	194	24	9	18	79	88	58	.376	.437
Batting #3	.306	591	181	40	0	43	131	120	65	.417	.592
Cleanup	.233	634	148	28	2	18	92	70	93	.311	.369
April	.268	750	201	34	7	13	102	86	120	.342	.384
May	.259	842	218	29	8	32	116	102	129	.336	.426
June	.268	946	254	36	6	31	125	102	141	.340	.418
July	.279	917	256	36	11	34	138	107	123	.356	.454
August	.268	974	261	47	5	30	130	85	160	.327	.419
September/October	.250	1054	264	46	7	22	120	122	161	.331	.370
Pre-All Star	.268	2914	780	111	26	89	400	329	438	.341	.415
Post-All Star	.262	2569	674	117	18	73	331	275	396	.335	.407

	ERA	W	L	Sv	Opp	G	IP	BB	SO	Avg	H	2B	3B	HR	RBI	OBP	SLG	CG	ShO	Sup	QS	#P/S	SB	CS	GB	FB	G/F
1993 Season	3.70	94	68	48	58	162	1454.0	566	974	.255	1398	217	22	125	625	.328	.372	16	11	4.80	93	105	82	82	1848	1565	1.18

1993 Pitching

	ERA	W	L	Sv	G	GS	IP	H	HR	BB	SO
Home	3.70	45	36	22	246	81	737.0	705	70	283	492
Away	3.74	49	32	26	238	81	717.0	693	55	283	482
Day	3.65	26	21	13	138	47	419.2	406	42	164	289
Night	3.75	68	47	35	346	115	1034.1	992	83	402	685
Grass	3.76	77	61	38	412	138	1234.1	1182	112	485	833
Turf	3.52	17	7	10	72	24	219.2	216	13	81	141
April	3.79	13	9	5	60	22	197.0	197	11	73	115
May	4.61	11	14	6	77	25	222.1	234	29	85	149
June	3.69	15	13	7	85	28	251.0	234	19	113	175
July	4.26	18	9	10	85	27	241.0	240	24	107	147
August	3.40	17	12	9	86	29	259.2	239	20	85	187
September/October	2.83	20	11	11	91	31	283.0	254	22	103	201
Starters	3.72	76	55	0	162	162	1067.1	1006	97	425	708
Relievers	3.72	18	13	48	322	0	386.2	392	28	141	266
0-3 Days Rest (SP)	0.00	0	0	0	0	0	0.0	0	0	0	0
4 Days Rest	3.35	43	27	0	90	90	617.0	564	55	230	395
5+ Days Rest	4.22	33	28	0	72	72	450.1	442	42	195	313
Pre-All Star	4.09	45	41	21	254	86	766.1	760	69	314	479
Post-All Star	3.31	49	27	27	230	76	687.2	638	56	252	495

	Avg	AB	H	2B	3B	HR	RBI	BB	SO	OBP	SLG
vs. Left	.264	2311	610	101	8	49	255	265	392	.340	.378
vs. Right	.249	3161	788	116	14	76	370	301	582	.318	.367
Inning 1-6	.252	3623	914	150	15	89	419	393	656	.327	.376
Inning 7+	.262	1849	484	67	7	36	206	173	318	.329	.364
None on	.251	3064	769	120	14	72	72	318	559	.326	.370
Runners on	.261	2408	629	97	8	53	553	248	415	.329	.374
Scoring Posn	.255	1311	334	50	5	21	468	175	240	.336	.349
Close & Late	.243	857	208	28	2	17	89	82	153	.312	.340
None on/out	.251	1364	343	54	7	38	38	132	230	.321	.385
vs. 1st Batr (relief)	.244	287	70	11	1	7	42	26	55	.319	.362
First Inning Pitched	.256	1649	422	57	9	34	236	179	314	.333	.363
First 75 Pitches (SP)	.254	4165	1059	161	19	95	477	430	750	.327	.370
Pitch 76-90	.227	528	120	17	0	9	47	58	94	.304	.311
Pitch 91-105	.294	446	131	24	1	10	54	43	74	.358	.419
Pitch 106+	.264	333	88	15	2	11	47	35	56	.336	.420
First Pitch	.307	737	226	37	4	18	121	30	0	.340	.441
Ahead in Count	.194	2516	487	67	5	33	199	0	822	.198	.264
Behind in Count	.335	1138	381	72	8	46	172	294	0	.469	.533
Two Strikes	.187	2529	472	70	6	36	205	242	974	.259	.262

Games Finished: 146 Inherited Runners: 198 Inherited Runners Scored: 75 Holds: 37

Cleveland Indians

1993 Record: 76 – 86

	Avg	G	AB	R	H	2B	3B	HR	RBI	BB	SO	HBP	GDP	SB	CS	OBP	SLG	IBB	SH	SF	#Pit	#P/PA	GB	FB	G/F
1993 Season	.275	162	5619	790	1547	264	31	141	747	488	843	49	131	159	55	.335	.409	57	39	72	22441	3.58	2198	1502	1.46

1993 Batting

	Avg	AB	H	2B	3B	HR	RBI	BB	SO	OBP	SLG
vs. Left	.270	1792	484	84	9	39	228	163	294	.334	.392
vs. Right	.278	3827	1063	180	22	102	519	325	549	.335	.416
Groundball	.273	858	234	36	3	13	113	92	136	.347	.367
Flyball	.237	1013	240	40	3	32	124	85	154	.298	.377
Home	.272	2667	726	106	19	69	366	264	384	.338	.404
Away	.278	2952	821	158	12	72	381	224	459	.331	.413
Day	.275	1936	532	79	11	54	262	168	290	.334	.411
Night	.276	3683	1015	185	20	87	485	320	553	.335	.408
Grass	.276	4729	1303	215	29	124	633	426	701	.337	.412
Turf	.274	890	244	49	2	17	114	62	142	.320	.391
First Pitch	.311	859	267	44	3	18	138	41	0	.344	.432
Ahead in Count	.351	1329	467	76	10	56	227	243	0	.448	.550
Behind in Count	.215	2400	517	92	13	36	236	0	710	.220	.310
Two Strikes	.206	2393	492	85	12	46	229	204	843	.271	.309

	Avg	AB	H	2B	3B	HR	RBI	BB	SO	OBP	SLG
Scoring Posn	.281	1426	401	62	11	40	598	187	233	.353	.424
Close & Late	.286	878	251	39	2	22	135	91	138	.354	.410
None on/out	.270	1386	374	74	10	30	30	104	200	.327	.403
Leadoff	.317	666	211	30	10	2	56	89	104	.398	.401
Batting #3	.315	667	210	28	6	22	117	38	75	.351	.474
Cleanup	.290	610	177	36	3	39	133	81	99	.373	.551
April	.284	779	221	42	5	24	103	56	138	.335	.443
May	.262	968	254	36	5	22	117	71	136	.315	.378
June	.267	886	237	46	8	24	123	74	128	.326	.419
July	.268	895	240	41	2	21	119	81	124	.330	.389
August	.290	1055	306	51	7	26	150	99	150	.351	.426
September/October	.279	1036	289	48	4	24	135	107	167	.347	.403
Pre-All Star	.274	3010	824	146	18	82	397	225	460	.327	.416
Post-All Star	.277	2609	723	118	13	59	350	263	383	.343	.400

Cleveland Indians

	ERA	W	L	Sv	Opp	G	IP	BB	SO	Avg	H	2B	3B	HR	RBI	OBP	SLG	CG	ShO	Sup	QS	#P/S	SB	CS	GB	FB	G/F
1993 Season	4.58	76	86	45	72	162	1445.2	591	888	.281	1591	278	21	182	759	.351	.434	7	8	4.92	52	90	113	68	1985	1692	1.17

1993 Pitching

	ERA	W	L	Sv	G	GS	IP	H	HR	BB	SO
Home	3.83	46	35	24	283	81	737.0	756	83	284	435
Away	5.35	30	51	21	289	81	708.2	835	99	307	453
Day	4.99	24	32	12	188	56	496.1	575	69	212	312
Night	4.36	52	54	33	384	106	949.1	1016	113	379	576
Grass	4.44	69	69	38	481	138	1230.0	1323	155	496	752
Turf	5.34	7	17	7	91	24	215.2	268	27	95	136
April	5.57	7	15	3	83	22	192.1	235	30	52	136
May	4.76	12	17	7	96	29	249.1	277	29	94	156
June	3.63	17	10	10	94	27	238.0	225	29	95	135
July	4.72	12	14	8	06	26	220.0	251	05	97	132
August	4.97	14	14	8	101	28	266.0	296	34	133	155
September/October	4.02	14	16	9	102	30	271.0	307	25	120	174
Starters	5.25	42	54	0	162	162	884.1	1002	119	341	481
Relievers	3.51	34	32	45	410	0	561.1	589	63	250	407
0-3 Days Rest (SP)	4.34	3	2	0	10	10	58.0	61	10	21	39
4 Days Rest	5.59	23	34	0	85	85	466.2	531	64	189	257
5+ Days Rest	4.95	16	18	0	67	67	359.2	410	45	131	185
Pre-All Star	4.68	40	48	24	314	88	768.2	844	100	289	478
Post-All Star	4.45	36	38	21	258	74	677.0	747	82	302	410

	Avg	AB	H	2B	3B	HR	RBI	BB	SO	OBP	SLG
vs. Left	.283	2270	642	86	8	65	288	253	324	.356	.414
vs. Right	.280	3394	949	192	13	117	471	338	564	.347	.447
Inning 1-6	.281	3788	1064	185	18	130	537	399	559	.352	.442
Inning 7+	.281	1876	527	93	3	52	222	192	329	.347	.417
None on	.284	3066	871	163	13	112	112	288	467	.349	.455
Runners on	.277	2598	720	115	8	70	647	303	421	.352	.408
Scoring Posn	.282	1521	429	68	5	43	576	211	259	.364	.418
Close & Late	.274	942	258	42	2	21	123	107	149	.349	.390
None on/out	.285	1389	396	74	8	51	51	121	182	.347	.460
vs. 1st Batr (relief)	.313	364	114	24	2	11	66	37	65	.379	.481
First Inning Pitched	.268	1958	524	81	9	62	329	221	348	.342	.413
First 75 Pitches (SP)	.273	4900	1340	232	20	147	651	517	787	.345	.419
Pitch 76-90	.322	422	136	28	0	18	51	37	59	.379	.517
Pitch 91-105	.354	246	87	13	1	14	44	30	32	.427	.585
Pitch 106+	.292	96	28	5	0	3	13	7	10	.340	.438
First Pitch	.349	745	260	49	5	23	119	42	0	.392	.521
Ahead in Count	.213	2458	524	96	8	41	233	0	757	.218	.309
Behind in Count	.329	1369	450	80	6	61	232	308	0	.449	.530
Two Strikes	.204	2505	510	85	8	50	226	240	888	.276	.304

Games Finished: 155   Inherited Runners: 349   Inherited Runners Scored: 120   Holds: 57

Detroit Tigers

1993 Record: 85 – 77

	Avg	G	AB	R	H	2B	3B	HR	RBI	BB	SO	HBP	GDP	SB	CS	OBP	SLG	IBB	SH	SF	#Pit	#P/PA	GB	FB	G/F
1993 Season	.275	162	5620	899	1546	282	38	178	853	765	1122	35	101	104	63	.362	.434	50	33	52	25385	3.90	1812	1613	1.12

1993 Batting

	Avg	AB	H	2B	3B	HR	RBI	BB	SO	OBP	SLG
vs. Left	.259	1555	403	74	6	54	239	236	292	.357	.419
vs. Right	.281	4065	1143	208	32	124	614	529	830	.365	.440
Groundball	.284	1197	340	52	7	39	183	153	208	.366	.437
Flyball	.284	1179	335	65	7	45	191	137	239	.358	.466
Home	.273	2728	746	137	20	103	436	381	526	.363	.452
Away	.277	2892	800	145	18	75	417	384	596	.362	.417
Day	.282	2049	577	111	16	62	311	284	397	.371	.442
Night	.271	3571	969	171	22	116	542	481	725	.358	.429
Grass	.270	4695	1268	221	34	145	695	645	920	.358	.424
Turf	.301	925	278	61	4	33	158	120	202	.383	.482
First Pitch	.366	659	241	47	3	24	126	33	0	.400	.555
Ahead in Count	.344	1327	457	93	16	73	311	376	0	.485	.604
Behind in Count	.210	2443	513	86	10	39	232	0	907	.214	.301
Two Strikes	.190	2616	496	82	13	42	231	355	1122	.288	.279

	Avg	AB	H	2B	3B	HR	RBI	BB	SO	OBP	SLG
Scoring Posn	.278	1579	439	67	13	52	662	257	316	.373	.436
Close & Late	.281	720	202	31	4	21	122	108	163	.375	.422
None on/out	.270	1326	358	66	8	45	45	167	267	.354	.434
Leadoff	.310	641	199	29	3	11	69	137	119	.433	.417
Batting #3	.308	656	202	42	6	23	106	80	130	.384	.495
Cleanup	.271	630	171	26	1	32	129	95	140	.367	.468
April	.298	768	229	46	5	29	160	127	160	.397	.484
May	.270	919	248	35	13	24	127	124	195	.356	.415
June	.249	971	242	49	5	38	137	115	182	.327	.427
July	.271	995	270	62	4	30	124	122	210	.352	.432
August	.290	994	288	47	7	30	178	153	187	.386	.442
September/October	.276	973	269	43	4	27	127	124	188	.361	.412
Pre-All Star	.272	3073	836	159	23	105	480	415	625	.358	.441
Post-All Star	.279	2547	710	123	15	73	373	350	497	.367	.425

	ERA	W	L	Sv	Opp	G	IP	BB	SO	Avg	H	2B	3B	HR	RBI	OBP	SLG	CG	ShO	Sup	QS	#P/S	SB	CS	GB	FB	G/F
1993 Season	4.65	85	77	36	54	162	1436.2	542	828	.276	1547	263	35	188	783	.342	.436	11	7	5.63	70	90	102	57	2056	1599	1.29

1993 Pitching

	ERA	W	L	Sv	G	GS	IP	H	HR	BB	SO
Home	4.45	44	37	14	263	81	737.0	762	99	263	443
Away	4.98	41	40	22	274	81	699.2	785	89	279	385
Day	4.93	32	28	14	202	60	529.0	575	76	211	287
Night	4.57	53	49	22	335	102	907.2	972	112	331	541
Grass	4.69	72	65	31	445	137	1217.1	1287	164	464	714
Turf	4.80	13	12	5	92	25	219.1	260	24	78	114
April	3.82	15	7	5	80	22	195.1	196	19	79	82
May	4.10	15	11	7	94	26	239.0	243	29	93	145
June	5.18	13	16	4	89	29	252.0	283	44	101	148
July	5.65	10	18	5	86	28	248.1	312	38	87	140
August	4.03	18	11	6	82	29	252.2	227	26	92	144
September/October	5.23	14	14	9	106	28	249.1	286	32	90	169
Starters	4.78	64	51	0	162	162	940.1	1012	128	304	473
Relievers	4.57	21	26	36	375	0	496.1	535	60	238	355
0-3 Days Rest (SP)	4.09	9	7	0	22	22	136.1	138	20	41	58
4 Days Rest	4.97	41	34	0	103	103	601.2	652	83	198	304
5+ Days Rest	4.67	14	10	0	37	37	202.1	222	25	65	111
Pre-All Star	4.63	48	40	18	301	88	785.2	857	107	300	422
Post-All Star	4.80	37	37	18	236	74	651.0	690	81	242	406

	Avg	AB	H	2B	3B	HR	RBI	BB	SO	OBP	SLG
vs. Left	.290	2238	649	101	23	83	317	241	277	.359	.467
vs. Right	.267	3367	898	162	12	105	466	301	551	.330	.416
Inning 1-6	.274	3790	1038	180	20	128	541	346	530	.336	.433
Inning 7+	.280	1815	509	83	15	60	242	196	298	.354	.442
None on	.282	3142	885	141	20	100	100	230	452	.335	.435
Runners on	.269	2463	662	122	15	88	683	312	376	.350	.438
Scoring Posn	.260	1379	359	63	7	47	567	232	222	.361	.418
Close & Late	.303	766	232	33	7	25	114	87	114	.377	.462
None on/out	.294	1390	408	62	9	38	38	106	197	.345	.433
vs. 1st Batr (relief)	.259	320	83	14	3	12	53	47	71	.352	.434
First Inning Pitched	.271	1799	488	83	13	63	317	212	302	.349	.437
First 75 Pitches (SP)	.275	4764	1310	221	31	156	670	475	709	.343	.433
Pitch 76-90	.261	418	109	20	1	14	51	28	61	.310	.414
Pitch 91-105	.314	290	91	16	2	12	47	22	39	.363	.507
Pitch 106+	.278	133	37	6	1	6	15	17	19	.366	.474
First Pitch	.340	804	273	58	4	36	128	66	0	.393	.556
Ahead in Count	.217	2354	511	71	11	53	235	0	709	.224	.324
Behind in Count	.327	1378	451	85	10	62	263	280	0	.436	.538
Two Strikes	.207	2352	488	75	12	57	257	196	828	.273	.322

Games Finished: 151   Inherited Runners: 298   Inherited Runners Scored: 95   Holds: 48

Kansas City Royals

1993 Record: 84 – 78

	Avg	G	AB	R	H	2B	3B	HR	RBI	BB	SO	HBP	GDP	SB	CS	OBP	SLG	IBB	SH	SF	#Pit	#P/PA	GB	FB	G/F
1993 Season	.263	162	5522	675	1455	294	35	125	641	428	936	52	107	100	75	.320	.397	50	48	51	21808	3.57	1987	1615	1.23

1993 Batting

	Avg	AB	H	2B	3B	HR	RBI	BB	SO	OBP	SLG
vs. Left	.258	1561	403	94	8	31	189	122	259	.316	.388
vs. Right	.266	3961	1052	200	27	94	452	306	677	.321	.401
Groundball	.307	808	248	50	4	15	114	73	111	.369	.434
Flyball	.245	1145	281	56	6	30	120	74	208	.292	.383
Home	.283	2785	788	183	23	50	355	205	401	.336	.419
Away	.244	2737	667	111	12	75	286	223	535	.304	.375
Day	.261	1745	455	85	13	43	211	146	316	.322	.398
Night	.265	3777	1000	209	22	82	430	282	620	.319	.397
Grass	.247	2118	524	77	9	62	229	166	399	.304	.380
Turf	.274	3404	931	217	26	63	412	262	537	.329	.408
First Pitch	.314	885	278	55	11	26	121	37	0	.347	.489
Ahead in Count	.318	1180	375	81	13	36	190	201	0	.415	.500
Behind in Count	.210	2467	517	96	9	34	199	0	813	.218	.297
Two Strikes	.193	2407	464	103	9	36	192	190	936	.256	.288

	Avg	AB	H	2B	3B	HR	RBI	BB	SO	OBP	SLG
Scoring Posn	.260	1362	354	69	10	27	490	161	260	.334	.385
Close & Late	.254	1034	263	44	5	26	123	93	194	.318	.382
None on/out	.278	1386	385	90	10	27	27	91	216	.327	.416
Leadoff	.275	691	190	44	6	9	51	41	124	.319	.395
Batting #3	.273	653	178	38	3	24	86	47	79	.320	.450
Cleanup	.282	611	172	40	2	22	93	68	122	.360	.462
April	.253	770	195	40	5	11	84	61	116	.309	.361
May	.270	879	237	43	5	18	103	57	137	.321	.391
June	.283	972	275	58	5	18	117	74	161	.337	.408
July	.283	958	271	56	11	26	129	66	156	.333	.446
August	.244	987	241	52	5	26	95	79	178	.303	.386
September/October	.247	956	236	45	4	26	113	91	188	.314	.384
Pre-All Star	.272	2964	806	163	18	56	345	216	462	.325	.396
Post-All Star	.254	2558	649	131	17	69	296	212	474	.314	.399

	ERA	W	L	Sv	Opp	G	IP	BB	SO	Avg	H	2B	3B	HR	RBI	OBP	SLG	CG	ShO	Sup	QS	#P/S	SB	CS	GB	FB	G/F
1993 Season	4.04	84	78	48	67	162	1445.1	571	985	.254	1379	292	28	105	651	.327	.376	16	6	4.20	89	105	119	71	1942	1526	1.27

1993 Pitching

	ERA	W	L	Sv	G	GS	IP	H	HR	BB	SO
Home	3.94	43	38	19	244	81	747.1	728	49	270	471
Away	4.15	41	40	29	221	81	698.0	651	56	301	514
Day	3.77	28	23	16	145	51	451.2	418	26	176	335
Night	4.17	56	55	32	320	111	993.2	961	79	395	650
Grass	4.01	31	31	22	174	62	534.1	492	45	223	400
Turf	4.06	53	47	26	291	100	911.0	887	60	348	585
April	4.60	9	14	6	59	23	203.2	204	11	84	141
May	3.68	16	9	11	73	25	227.2	207	14	109	161
June	4.35	13	15	7	82	28	250.1	233	29	85	161
July	4.27	16	12	9	79	28	249.0	245	22	95	173
August	3.28	15	14	11	88	29	260.1	242	14	87	176
September/October	4.18	15	14	4	84	29	254.1	248	15	111	173
Starters	4.03	59	55	0	162	162	1040.0	979	81	404	682
Relievers	4.06	25	23	48	303	0	405.1	400	24	167	303
0-3 Days Rest (SP)	4.15	1	1	0	3	3	17.1	16	1	8	10
4 Days Rest	4.05	33	33	0	90	90	590.2	560	41	219	415
5+ Days Rest	4.00	25	21	0	69	69	432.0	403	39	177	257
Pre-All Star	4.18	44	42	26	246	86	773.2	733	60	313	527
Post-All Star	3.89	40	36	22	219	76	671.2	646	45	258	458

	Avg	AB	H	2B	3B	HR	RBI	BB	SO	OBP	SLG
vs. Left	.266	2451	653	121	14	47	307	272	377	.340	.385
vs. Right	.243	2985	726	171	14	58	344	299	608	.316	.368
Inning 1-6	.246	3613	890	197	18	69	417	379	634	.319	.368
Inning 7+	.268	1823	489	95	10	36	234	192	351	.342	.391
None on	.248	3074	761	162	8	67	67	300	554	.318	.371
Runners on	.262	2362	618	130	20	38	584	271	431	.337	.382
Scoring Posn	.264	1399	369	79	17	22	526	198	285	.350	.392
Close & Late	.270	1020	275	47	6	17	134	106	184	.342	.377
None on/out	.249	1371	342	78	4	41	41	115	220	.311	.402
vs. 1st Batr (relief)	.272	268	73	14	4	9	45	32	48	.351	.455
First Inning Pitched	.255	1578	403	90	11	30	228	176	303	.331	.383
First 75 Pitches (SP)	.254	4242	1079	230	25	77	504	434	771	.326	.375
Pitch 76-90	.252	457	115	27	0	13	55	51	67	.328	.396
Pitch 91-105	.227	405	92	22	3	10	44	45	84	.303	.370
Pitch 106+	.280	332	93	13	0	5	48	41	63	.363	.364
First Pitch	.312	638	199	50	2	16	95	32	0	.346	.472
Ahead in Count	.205	2421	497	99	12	24	214	0	783	.212	.286
Behind in Count	.318	1254	399	84	9	39	221	270	0	.437	.493
Two Strikes	.188	2498	469	85	13	31	218	269	985	.271	.269

Games Finished: 146 Inherited Runners: 192 Inherited Runners Scored: 63 Holds: 31

Milwaukee Brewers

1993 Record: 69 – 93

	Avg	G	AB	R	H	2B	3B	HR	RBI	BB	SO	HBP	GDP	SB	CS	OBP	SLG	IBB	SH	SF	#Pit	#P/PA	GB	FB	G/F
1993 Season	.258	162	5525	733	1426	240	25	125	688	555	932	40	117	138	93	.328	.378	52	57	45	23030	3.70	1983	1572	1.26

1993 Batting

	Avg	AB	H	2B	3B	HR	RBI	BB	SO	OBP	SLG
vs. Left	.256	1872	480	78	11	38	235	203	305	.332	.371
vs. Right	.259	3653	946	162	14	87	453	352	627	.326	.382
Groundball	.253	1127	285	52	4	16	136	102	190	.319	.349
Flyball	.251	1080	271	47	2	31	127	102	171	.315	.384
Home	.268	2704	724	112	17	53	353	302	442	.343	.381
Away	.249	2821	702	128	8	72	335	253	490	.313	.376
Day	.252	2017	508	80	12	42	253	217	346	.327	.366
Night	.262	3508	918	160	13	83	435	338	586	.328	.386
Grass	.258	4645	1197	191	23	104	576	471	796	.328	.376
Turf	.260	880	229	49	2	21	112	84	136	.328	.392
First Pitch	.300	741	222	38	3	14	105	36	0	.340	.416
Ahead in Count	.313	1326	415	63	7	51	226	285	0	.431	.486
Behind in Count	.213	2389	508	86	10	32	214	0	772	.218	.297
Two Strikes	.200	2424	485	87	8	42	236	234	932	.273	.295

	Avg	AB	H	2B	3B	HR	RBI	BB	SO	OBP	SLG
Scoring Posn	.277	1370	379	66	9	21	540	214	231	.367	.384
Close & Late	.253	932	236	35	3	11	105	99	178	.325	.333
None on/out	.255	1382	352	58	7	36	36	117	229	.318	.385
Leadoff	.281	672	189	27	2	9	61	73	108	.354	.368
Batting #3	.280	651	182	40	1	17	93	60	97	.342	.422
Cleanup	.260	607	158	28	2	31	100	95	115	.364	.466
April	.257	650	167	19	4	8	76	67	105	.330	.335
May	.234	932	218	37	4	23	111	74	174	.293	.356
June	.255	976	249	44	4	18	116	93	168	.322	.364
July	.272	891	242	43	5	21	109	73	143	.329	.402
August	.267	1107	296	54	5	35	158	138	167	.349	.420
September/October	.262	969	254	43	3	20	118	110	175	.340	.375
Pre-All Star	.256	2920	748	122	14	57	361	262	490	.320	.366
Post-All Star	.260	2605	678	118	11	68	327	293	442	.337	.392

Milwaukee Brewers

	ERA	W	L	Sv	Opp	G	IP	BB	SO	Avg	H	2B	3B	HR	RBI	OBP	SLG	CG	ShO	Sup	QS	#P/S	SB	CS	GB	FB	G/F
1993 Season	4.45	69	93	29	52	162	1447.0	522	810	.271	1511	290	48	153	758	.336	.422	26	6	4.56	76	101	115	51	1985	1729	1.15

1993 Pitching

	ERA	W	L	Sv	G	GS	IP	H	HR	BB	SO
Home	4.09	38	43	13	264	81	741.0	764	65	247	425
Away	4.86	31	50	16	251	81	706.0	747	88	275	385
Day	4.49	25	35	11	191	60	533.1	564	56	187	297
Night	4.45	44	58	18	324	102	913.2	947	97	335	513
Grass	4.50	58	79	25	446	137	1229.1	1284	135	452	704
Turf	4.26	11	14	4	69	25	217.2	227	18	70	106
April	5.53	9	11	6	66	20	174.0	192	17	68	109
May	3.47	13	14	5	89	27	248.2	261	22	79	133
June	4.38	10	19	5	95	29	250.2	243	34	75	108
July	5.04	9	17	4	82	26	227.0	246	32	84	100
August	4.17	16	16	4	86	32	291.2	303	26	110	187
September/October	4.62	12	16	5	97	28	255.0	266	22	106	173
Starters	4.63	50	70	0	162	162	1036.0	1100	122	349	554
Relievers	4.05	19	23	29	353	0	411.0	411	31	173	256
0-3 Days Rest (SP)	5.42	2	10	0	16	16	98.0	95	15	31	37
4 Days Rest	4.34	36	42	0	96	96	638.1	672	74	213	340
5+ Days Rest	4.99	12	18	0	50	50	299.2	333	33	105	177
Pre-All Star	4.45	37	49	18	285	86	761.2	801	84	251	389
Post-All Star	4.48	32	44	11	230	76	685.1	710	69	271	421

	Avg	AB	H	2B	3B	HR	RBI	BB	SO	OBP	SLG
vs. Left	.281	2377	669	118	30	60	317	213	278	.341	.432
vs. Right	.263	3200	842	172	18	93	441	309	532	.332	.415
Inning 1-6	.279	3792	1057	213	40	117	558	352	532	.343	.449
Inning 7+	.254	1785	454	77	8	36	200	170	278	.321	.367
None on	.268	3143	843	178	26	80	80	243	451	.327	.418
Runners on	.274	2434	668	112	22	73	678	279	359	.346	.429
Scoring Posn	.256	1435	368	68	10	38	577	204	230	.339	.397
Close & Late	.270	889	240	43	6	19	117	107	148	.349	.396
None on/out	.284	1402	398	94	15	34	34	97	189	.335	.445
vs. 1st Batr (relief)	.318	314	100	23	3	7	56	31	40	.379	.478
First Inning Pitched	.279	1752	488	95	20	41	318	178	268	.346	.426
First 75 Pitches (SP)	.275	4405	1210	224	40	116	623	425	649	.341	.423
Pitch 76-90	.272	533	145	34	4	20	79	50	58	.336	.463
Pitch 91-105	.280	372	104	22	3	11	36	21	58	.323	.444
Pitch 106+	.195	267	52	10	1	6	20	26	45	.264	.307
First Pitch	.335	840	281	58	6	31	143	46	0	.375	.529
Ahead in Count	.196	2235	439	87	13	36	204	0	667	.204	.295
Behind in Count	.346	1429	495	87	17	59	272	247	0	.438	.555
Two Strikes	.177	2291	406	77	15	34	200	229	810	.255	.268

Games Finished: 136 Inherited Runners: 285 Inherited Runners Scored: 99 Holds: 34

Minnesota Twins

1993 Record: 71 – 91

	Avg	G	AB	R	H	2B	3B	HR	RBI	BB	SO	HBP	GDP	SB	CS	OBP	SLG	IBB	SH	SF	#Pit	#P/PA	GB	FB	G/F
1993 Season	.264	162	5601	693	1480	261	27	121	642	493	850	51	150	83	59	.327	.385	35	27	37	22032	3.55	2181	1562	1.40

1993 Batting

	Avg	AB	H	2B	3B	HR	RBI	BB	SO	OBP	SLG
vs. Left	.275	1345	370	67	5	32	160	113	191	.334	.404
vs. Right	.261	4256	1110	194	22	89	482	380	659	.325	.379
Groundball	.283	1040	294	50	1	21	129	93	135	.343	.393
Flyball	.265	1175	311	61	10	35	162	123	200	.343	.423
Home	.270	2768	746	141	17	56	330	265	423	.337	.393
Away	.259	2833	734	120	10	65	312	228	427	.318	.377
Day	.263	1780	468	96	8	40	206	161	272	.330	.393
Night	.265	3821	1012	165	19	81	436	332	578	.326	.382
Grass	.269	2182	586	91	8	52	249	187	305	.330	.389
Turf	.261	3419	894	170	19	69	393	306	545	.326	.383
First Pitch	.316	916	289	60	6	24	121	29	0	.342	.473
Ahead in Count	.319	1265	404	67	9	38	185	260	0	.434	.477
Behind in Count	.209	2403	503	94	6	37	207	0	713	.218	.300
Two Strikes	.192	2333	447	80	9	24	198	204	850	.262	.264

	Avg	AB	H	2B	3B	HR	RBI	BB	SO	OBP	SLG
Scoring Posn	.257	1380	354	60	6	38	506	182	231	.343	.391
Close & Late	.278	911	253	51	3	12	102	92	138	.344	.380
None on/out	.266	1403	373	73	6	23	23	85	192	.312	.376
Leadoff	.274	680	186	33	4	4	49	68	73	.347	.351
Batting #3	.293	651	191	39	5	26	98	58	101	.355	.488
Cleanup	.258	623	161	24	3	37	125	74	97	.336	.485
April	.240	726	174	40	6	13	83	69	109	.309	.365
May	.278	869	242	42	4	20	110	79	128	.343	.405
June	.263	901	237	31	8	20	94	75	135	.324	.382
July	.279	939	262	57	2	22	113	68	118	.334	.414
August	.261	1085	283	42	4	24	116	91	182	.320	.373
September/October	.261	1081	282	49	3	22	126	111	178	.331	.373
Pre-All Star	.265	2886	766	136	18	64	337	252	412	.329	.392
Post-All Star	.263	2715	714	125	9	57	305	241	438	.326	.379

	ERA	W	L	Sv	Opp	G	IP	BB	SO	Avg	H	2B	3B	HR	RBI	OBP	SLG	CG	ShO	Sup	QS	#P/S	SB	CS	GB	FB	G/F
1993 Season	4.71	71	91	44	63	162	1444.1	514	901	.283	1591	349	39	148	781	.344	.438	5	3	4.32	69	97	137	66	2007	1721	1.17

1993 Pitching

	ERA	W	L	Sv	G	GS	IP	H	HR	BB	SO
Home	4.73	36	45	19	262	81	750.0	804	70	255	480
Away	4.73	35	46	25	256	81	694.1	787	78	259	421
Day	4.59	23	29	17	171	52	462.2	495	46	150	315
Night	4.79	48	62	27	347	110	981.2	1096	102	364	586
Grass	4.75	28	34	19	204	62	534.1	608	60	219	327
Turf	4.72	43	57	25	314	100	910.0	983	88	295	574
April	6.06	8	14	6	69	22	193.0	216	23	98	125
May	4.87	12	13	8	88	25	218.0	234	24	72	145
June	4.66	12	15	11	86	27	235.2	255	24	86	141
July	5.01	11	16	8	85	27	233.2	279	28	74	130
August	3.52	13	17	4	81	30	281.0	277	27	68	177
September/October	4.74	15	16	7	109	31	283.0	330	22	116	183
Starters	4.92	50	78	0	162	162	966.0	1086	104	338	581
Relievers	4.35	21	13	44	356	0	478.1	505	44	176	320
0-3 Days Rest (SP)	4.97	5	5	0	14	14	83.1	92	11	26	50
4 Days Rest	5.10	23	53	0	92	92	552.2	643	50	189	313
5+ Days Rest	4.61	22	20	0	56	56	330.0	351	43	123	218
Pre-All Star	5.23	36	49	26	277	85	743.0	836	83	282	458
Post-All Star	4.20	35	42	18	241	77	701.1	755	65	232	443

	Avg	AB	H	2B	3B	HR	RBI	BB	SO	OBP	SLG
vs. Left	.297	2559	760	158	23	64	343	245	401	.357	.452
vs. Right	.272	3059	831	191	16	84	438	269	500	.333	.427
Inning 1-6	.288	3799	1095	232	30	108	535	342	593	.347	.450
Inning 7+	.273	1819	496	117	9	40	246	172	308	.339	.413
None on	.274	3095	847	183	16	93	93	267	503	.337	.433
Runners on	.295	2523	744	166	23	55	688	247	398	.354	.444
Scoring Posn	.291	1509	439	106	14	28	602	189	257	.361	.435
Close & Late	.263	791	208	47	3	14	108	85	131	.338	.383
None on/out	.280	1377	386	88	6	42	42	114	217	.339	.444
vs. 1st Batr (relief)	.239	314	75	19	1	6	59	30	61	.311	.363
First Inning Pitched	.282	1770	499	112	5	44	316	176	325	.346	.425
First 75 Pitches (SP)	.280	4662	1307	287	32	125	664	422	770	.341	.436
Pitch 76-90	.294	480	141	28	5	16	64	36	60	.344	.473
Pitch 91-105	.304	342	104	27	2	6	36	39	47	.379	.447
Pitch 106+	.291	134	39	7	0	1	17	17	24	.385	.366
First Pitch	.344	823	283	66	5	23	139	21	0	.367	.520
Ahead in Count	.228	2447	558	114	16	47	270	0	758	.233	.345
Behind in Count	.346	1347	466	108	13	54	237	279	0	.453	.566
Two Strikes	.213	2426	517	113	13	44	237	214	901	.280	.325

Games Finished: 157 Inherited Runners: 291 Inherited Runners Scored: 97 Holds: 54

New York Yankees

1993 Record: 88 – 74

	Avg	G	AB	R	H	2B	3B	HR	RBI	BB	SO	HBP	GDP	SB	CS	OBP	SLG	IBB	SH	SF	#Pit	#P/PA	GB	FB	G/F
1993 Season	.279	162	5615	821	1568	294	24	178	793	629	910	43	149	39	35	.353	.435	47	22	50	23840	3.75	1930	1679	1.15

1993 Batting

	Avg	AB	H	2B	3B	HR	RBI	BB	SO	OBP	SLG
vs. Left	.266	1930	514	98	7	61	256	233	317	.347	.419
vs. Right	.286	3685	1054	196	17	117	537	396	593	.357	.444
Groundball	.296	965	286	59	2	21	130	100	154	.366	.427
Flyball	.265	1241	329	58	6	48	183	126	197	.333	.438
Home	.280	2674	750	139	10	88	374	309	395	.357	.439
Away	.278	2941	818	155	14	90	419	320	515	.350	.432
Day	.293	1855	544	105	9	67	289	222	299	.371	.468
Night	.272	3760	1024	189	15	111	504	407	611	.345	.419
Grass	.279	4757	1328	244	17	147	668	535	759	.354	.430
Turf	.280	858	240	50	7	31	125	94	151	.351	.463
First Pitch	.340	724	246	51	2	29	132	36	0	.374	.536
Ahead in Count	.354	1363	482	89	12	67	275	336	0	.479	.584
Behind in Count	.224	2390	535	102	6	46	238	0	747	.230	.329
Two Strikes	.200	2441	488	81	8	48	231	257	910	.280	.299

	Avg	AB	H	2B	3B	HR	RBI	BB	SO	OBP	SLG
Scoring Posn	.273	1438	393	74	5	43	609	224	262	.366	.421
Close & Late	.291	784	228	40	2	20	118	88	142	.363	.423
None on/out	.263	1367	359	73	5	50	50	122	221	.326	.433
Leadoff	.281	690	194	32	8	12	85	77	92	.354	.403
Batting #3	.295	648	191	33	3	17	99	79	49	.372	.434
Cleanup	.247	611	151	35	2	35	120	105	174	.361	.483
April	.275	738	203	38	3	21	101	79	119	.345	.420
May	.276	1041	287	62	4	31	145	120	174	.354	.432
June	.284	969	275	48	8	39	154	107	156	.356	.471
July	.301	923	278	45	4	38	144	91	137	.367	.482
August	.272	937	255	50	2	24	120	114	159	.350	.407
September/October	.268	1007	270	51	3	25	129	118	165	.347	.399
Pre-All Star	.275	3107	854	162	16	101	436	336	519	.348	.435
Post-All Star	.285	2508	714	132	8	77	357	293	391	.361	.436

	ERA	W	L	Sv	Opp	G	IP	BB	SO	Avg	H	2B	3B	HR	RBI	OBP	SLG	CG	ShO	Sup	QS	#P/S	SB	CS	GB	FB	G/F
1993 Season	4.35	88	74	38	57	162	1438.1	552	899	.266	1467	262	30	170	730	.333	.416	11	13	5.14	81	98	115	47	2235	1437	1.56

1993 Pitching

	ERA	W	L	Sv	G	GS	IP	H	HR	BB	SO
Home	3.85	50	31	19	233	81	732.0	676	85	256	474
Away	4.91	38	43	19	261	81	706.1	791	85	296	425
Day	4.28	36	18	10	168	54	485.1	473	59	194	296
Night	4.41	52	56	28	326	108	953.0	994	111	358	603
Grass	4.24	77	61	33	410	138	1231.0	1227	149	480	787
Turf	5.12	11	13	5	84	24	207.1	240	21	72	112
April	4.21	12	9	7	60	21	186.0	180	20	63	108
May	3.74	17	13	6	77	30	274.2	240	32	112	186
June	4.73	17	11	9	86	28	245.2	273	26	98	151
July	4.53	14	12	5	80	26	230.2	245	31	84	140
August	4.40	15	13	8	90	28	249.1	259	32	84	148
September/October	4.64	13	16	3	101	29	252.0	270	29	111	166
Starters	4.26	60	55	0	162	162	1011.2	1038	117	358	627
Relievers	4.62	28	19	38	332	0	426.2	429	53	194	272
0-3 Days Rest (SP)	6.30	0	1	0	2	2	10.0	16	2	1	6
4 Days Rest	4.26	36	26	0	86	86	542.2	549	58	198	367
5+ Days Rest	4.22	24	28	0	74	74	459.0	473	57	159	254
Pre-All Star	4.25	48	41	23	254	89	794.0	785	88	315	487
Post-All Star	4.51	40	33	15	240	73	644.1	682	82	237	412

	Avg	AB	H	2B	3B	HR	RBI	BB	SO	OBP	SLG
vs. Left	.265	1886	500	89	13	54	235	233	304	.347	.412
vs. Right	.266	3636	967	173	17	116	495	319	595	.326	.419
Inning 1-6	.265	3737	992	181	21	114	485	359	614	.330	.417
Inning 7+	.266	1785	475	81	9	56	245	193	285	.339	.416
None on	.254	3149	800	148	15	93	93	283	513	.319	.399
Runners on	.281	2373	667	114	15	77	637	269	386	.351	.439
Scoring Posn	.285	1331	379	63	9	49	556	187	231	.365	.456
Close & Late	.284	753	214	37	3	22	119	89	129	.358	.429
None on/out	.257	1372	352	63	5	40	40	123	201	.320	.397
vs. 1st Batr (relief)	.257	284	73	13	1	8	54	33	54	.335	.394
First Inning Pitched	.263	1615	424	83	12	51	282	210	294	.347	.424
First 75 Pitches (SP)	.263	4422	1164	208	26	136	590	460	722	.333	.414
Pitch 76-90	.285	537	153	36	0	12	60	36	84	.334	.419
Pitch 91-105	.284	366	104	11	2	16	60	33	51	.345	.456
Pitch 106+	.234	197	46	7	2	6	20	23	42	.315	.381
First Pitch	.304	812	247	49	7	26	118	48	0	.344	.478
Ahead in Count	.211	2360	498	92	4	42	220	0	750	.214	.307
Behind in Count	.322	1328	427	67	10	65	243	287	0	.441	.534
Two Strikes	.203	2375	482	89	5	49	237	217	899	.270	.307

Games Finished: 151 Inherited Runners: 292 Inherited Runners Scored: 91 Holds: 33

Oakland Athletics

1993 Record: 68 – 94

	Avg	G	AB	R	H	2B	3B	HR	RBI	BB	SO	HBP	GDP	SB	CS	OBP	SLG	IBB	SH	SF	#Pit	#P/PA	GB	FB	G/F
1993 Season	.254	162	5543	715	1408	260	21	158	679	622	1048	33	125	131	59	.330	.394	45	46	49	24000	3.81	1947	1595	1.22

1993 Batting

	Avg	AB	H	2B	3B	HR	RBI	BB	SO	OBP	SLG
vs. Left	.255	1653	422	75	2	62	206	201	343	.338	.416
vs. Right	.253	3890	986	185	19	96	473	421	705	.327	.385
Groundball	.259	1140	295	61	8	25	137	112	193	.328	.392
Flyball	.260	1145	298	49	0	37	145	139	219	.341	.400
Home	.252	2675	674	105	5	78	313	309	533	.331	.382
Away	.256	2868	734	155	16	80	366	313	515	.329	.405
Day	.233	2229	519	93	8	50	227	266	452	.315	.349
Night	.268	3314	889	167	13	108	452	356	596	.340	.424
Grass	.249	4572	1138	193	15	135	531	490	856	.323	.386
Turf	.278	971	270	67	6	23	148	132	192	.363	.430
First Pitch	.308	620	191	46	3	16	78	36	0	.350	.469
Ahead in Count	.335	1267	425	93	6	62	242	334	0	.471	.565
Behind in Count	.190	2511	476	70	7	41	210	0	871	.195	.272
Two Strikes	.177	2612	462	67	5	44	213	252	1048	.251	.257

	Avg	AB	H	2B	3B	HR	RBI	BB	SO	OBP	SLG
Scoring Posn	.236	1414	334	58	6	42	518	233	298	.337	.375
Close & Late	.239	930	222	40	3	21	130	133	203	.335	.356
None on/out	.267	1367	365	74	6	47	47	148	242	.343	.433
Leadoff	.280	640	179	32	3	19	64	120	102	.396	.428
Batting #3	.237	658	156	23	5	25	110	57	101	.295	.401
Cleanup	.276	616	170	25	1	33	101	80	146	.359	.481
April	.257	596	153	30	0	23	76	70	89	.337	.423
May	.237	961	228	44	6	24	114	128	195	.328	.370
June	.267	894	239	46	3	23	119	121	172	.353	.403
July	.272	980	267	38	2	32	130	107	174	.342	.413
August	.235	1014	238	44	7	28	99	95	214	.303	.375
September/October	.258	1098	283	58	3	28	141	101	204	.323	.393
Pre-All Star	.256	2842	728	132	10	86	362	360	531	.340	.400
Post-All Star	.252	2701	680	128	11	72	317	262	517	.320	.387

Oakland A's

	ERA	W	L	Sv	Opp	G	IP	BB	SO	Avg	H	2B	3B	HR	RBI	OBP	SLG	CG	ShO	Sup	QS	#P/S	SB	CS	GB	FB	G/F
1993 Season	4.90	68	94	42	64	162	1452.1	680	864	.276	1551	283	35	157	801	.356	.422	8	2	4.43	63	93	120	71	1956	1737	1.13

1993 Pitching

	ERA	W	L	Sv	G	GS	IP	H	HR	BB	SO
Home	4.34	38	43	24	284	81	743.0	752	78	314	479
Away	5.49	30	51	18	302	81	709.1	799	79	366	385
Day	4.95	23	45	17	245	68	605.0	662	65	289	379
Night	4.86	45	49	25	341	94	847.1	889	92	391	485
Grass	5.08	52	84	33	487	136	1207.1	1315	136	572	717
Turf	4.04	16	10	9	99	26	245.0	236	21	108	147
April	5.22	7	11	3	70	18	160.1	173	14	76	96
May	4.88	12	16	8	104	28	250.2	269	23	124	141
June	4.61	12	14	7	94	26	234.1	253	25	112	122
July	5.01	12	17	8	108	29	251.2	307	28	107	153
August	4.91	9	21	6	105	30	267.2	278	33	136	164
September/October	4.35	16	15	10	105	31	287.2	271	34	125	188
Starters	5.19	41	63	0	162	162	904.0	987	113	415	476
Relievers	4.43	27	31	42	424	0	548.1	564	44	265	388
0-3 Days Rest (SP)	5.77	5	11	0	23	23	107.2	125	13	50	54
4 Days Rest	5.04	25	25	0	75	75	437.2	461	49	200	253
5+ Days Rest	5.19	11	27	0	64	64	358.2	401	51	165	169
Pre-All Star	4.84	38	46	24	308	84	753.1	814	71	349	438
Post-All Star	4.97	30	48	18	278	78	699.0	737	86	331	426

	Avg	AB	H	2B	3B	HR	RBI	BB	SO	OBP	SLG
vs. Left	.289	2730	788	153	22	63	398	354	356	.370	.430
vs. Right	.264	2893	763	130	13	94	403	326	508	.343	.415
Inning 1-6	.277	3784	1050	193	20	123	545	440	529	.356	.437
Inning 7+	.272	1839	501	90	15	34	256	240	335	.358	.393
None on	.272	3053	830	152	19	74	74	322	449	.345	.407
Runners on	.281	2570	721	131	16	83	727	358	415	.369	.441
Scoring Posn	.282	1466	414	71	10	51	628	242	243	.379	.449
Close & Late	.280	896	251	40	10	14	127	105	174	.357	.394
None on/out	.265	1380	366	65	12	32	32	123	187	.328	.399
vs. 1st Batr (relief)	.271	377	102	14	5	8	53	39	69	.341	.398
First Inning Pitched	.270	1948	526	88	13	48	341	260	349	.357	.402
First 75 Pitches (SP)	.280	4764	1333	237	30	141	714	578	750	.360	.431
Pitch 76-90	.231	428	99	21	1	6	29	39	54	.296	.327
Pitch 91-105	.281	260	73	13	3	7	36	36	31	.370	.435
Pitch 106+	.269	171	46	12	1	3	22	27	29	.363	.404
First Pitch	.309	802	248	40	5	24	123	52	0	.359	.461
Ahead in Count	.220	2427	534	107	12	37	235	0	733	.227	.320
Behind in Count	.345	1322	456	76	8	61	270	333	0	.474	.553
Two Strikes	.207	2476	513	95	9	47	251	295	864	.294	.310

Games Finished: 154 Inherited Runners: 297 Inherited Runners Scored: 91 Holds: 62

Seattle Mariners

1993 Record: 82 – 80

	Avg	G	AB	R	H	2B	3B	HR	RBI	BB	SO	HBP	GDP	SB	CS	OBP	SLG	IBB	SH	SF	#Pit	#P/PA	GB	FB	G/F
1993 Season	.260	162	5494	734	1429	272	24	161	681	624	901	56	132	91	68	.339	.406	73	63	51	23070	3.67	1984	1648	1.20

1993 Batting

	Avg	AB	H	2B	3B	HR	RBI	BB	SO	OBP	SLG
vs. Left	.281	1670	470	105	6	52	231	179	252	.356	.445
vs. Right	.251	3824	959	167	18	109	450	445	649	.332	.389
Groundball	.276	832	230	36	2	25	115	94	131	.354	.415
Flyball	.261	1143	298	61	9	42	149	145	203	.346	.440
Home	.259	2698	699	141	10	74	353	356	445	.350	.401
Away	.261	2796	730	131	14	87	328	268	456	.328	.411
Day	.270	1609	434	82	5	61	210	165	246	.342	.441
Night	.256	3885	995	190	19	100	471	459	655	.338	.392
Grass	.259	2140	555	93	7	78	245	201	351	.325	.419
Turf	.261	3354	874	179	17	83	436	423	550	.347	.398
First Pitch	.315	712	224	57	3	23	118	60	0	.370	.500
Ahead in Count	.329	1251	412	74	8	63	234	311	0	.463	.552
Behind in Count	.203	2447	497	89	8	44	209	0	761	.210	.300
Two Strikes	.191	2434	466	87	8	46	221	253	901	.271	.290

	Avg	AB	H	2B	3B	HR	RBI	BB	SO	OBP	SLG
Scoring Posn	.246	1372	338	62	7	37	500	233	238	.350	.383
Close & Late	.267	937	250	45	2	19	122	121	158	.352	.380
None on/out	.269	1378	371	79	6	36	36	125	234	.332	.414
Leadoff	.259	688	178	29	5	1	48	60	96	.321	.320
Batting #3	.300	609	183	36	2	48	113	102	96	.403	.603
Cleanup	.258	605	156	28	1	25	97	98	133	.359	.431
April	.255	732	187	30	1	21	95	101	128	.348	.385
May	.273	1020	278	41	6	30	115	95	158	.339	.413
June	.270	911	246	49	5	26	110	102	145	.346	.420
July	.283	903	256	51	3	32	136	96	134	.357	.453
August	.224	861	193	40	4	28	91	104	152	.308	.377
September/October	.252	1067	269	61	5	24	134	126	184	.334	.386
Pre-All Star	.269	3003	809	140	14	87	374	343	473	.348	.412
Post-All Star	.249	2491	620	132	10	74	307	281	428	.328	.399

	ERA	W	L	Sv	Opp	G	IP	BB	SO	Avg	H	2B	3B	HR	RBI	OBP	SLG	CG	ShO	Sup	QS	#P/S	SB	CS	GB	FB	G/F
1993 Season	4.20	82	80	41	64	162	1453.2	605	1083	.259	1421	276	31	135	697	.337	.395	22	10	4.54	89	102	105	68	2021	1467	1.38

1993 Pitching

	ERA	W	L	Sv	G	GS	IP	H	HR	BB	SO
Home	3.91	46	35	22	274	81	755.0	709	66	297	607
Away	4.52	36	45	19	241	81	698.2	712	69	308	476
Day	4.61	21	25	8	140	46	413.2	427	44	185	331
Night	4.04	61	55	33	375	116	1040.0	994	91	420	752
Grass	4.57	26	36	13	190	62	535.2	544	52	257	369
Turf	3.99	56	44	28	325	100	918.0	877	83	348	714
April	4.27	11	11	4	64	22	198.1	193	15	91	165
May	3.77	14	15	6	92	29	262.2	243	27	97	208
June	4.26	13	14	7	85	27	240.2	242	20	110	173
July	5.03	13	13	7	90	26	231.0	251	27	88	134
August	4.97	14	13	11	86	27	235.1	239	25	103	191
September/October	3.21	17	14	6	98	31	285.2	253	21	116	212
Starters	3.99	62	54	0	162	162	1043.2	1023	98	381	754
Relievers	4.74	20	26	41	353	0	410.0	398	37	224	329
0-3 Days Rest (SP)	2.82	3	2	0	6	6	38.1	27	3	11	29
4 Days Rest	3.84	36	33	0	97	97	652.1	634	65	229	498
5+ Days Rest	4.41	23	19	0	59	59	353.0	362	30	141	227
Pre-All Star	4.13	44	44	19	274	88	793.2	769	76	321	606
Post-All Star	4.30	38	36	22	241	74	660.0	652	59	284	477

	Avg	AB	H	2B	3B	HR	RBI	BB	SO	OBP	SLG
vs. Left	.266	1923	511	108	20	42	240	208	331	.341	.408
vs. Right	.256	3560	910	168	11	93	457	397	752	.336	.387
Inning 1-6	.260	3682	958	192	25	82	444	358	671	.330	.393
Inning 7+	.257	1801	463	84	6	53	253	247	412	.352	.399
None on	.248	3109	770	161	17	78	78	280	632	.316	.386
Runners on	.274	2374	651	115	14	57	619	325	451	.364	.406
Scoring Posn	.265	1420	377	66	9	37	559	226	304	.365	.403
Close & Late	.262	924	242	39	5	29	154	137	215	.361	.409
None on/out	.262	1369	358	75	9	31	31	124	265	.329	.397
vs. 1st Batr (relief)	.283	297	84	17	0	6	63	41	64	.370	.401
First Inning Pitched	.258	1594	412	86	8	30	257	205	331	.346	.379
First 75 Pitches (SP)	.260	4315	1122	216	27	101	566	485	836	.340	.393
Pitch 76-90	.264	478	126	23	1	21	74	44	87	.332	.448
Pitch 91-105	.277	382	106	17	2	9	35	36	66	.344	.403
Pitch 106+	.218	308	67	20	1	4	22	40	94	.310	.328
First Pitch	.285	761	217	44	3	19	104	42	0	.327	.426
Ahead in Count	.197	2379	468	87	9	35	218	0	906	.207	.285
Behind in Count	.338	1262	427	92	13	45	220	311	0	.469	.539
Two Strikes	.181	2467	446	81	10	40	216	252	1083	.262	.270

Games Finished: 140 Inherited Runners: 335 Inherited Runners Scored: 106 Holds: 60

Texas Rangers

1993 Record: 86 – 76

	Avg	G	AB	R	H	2B	3B	HR	RBI	BB	SO	HBP	GDP	SB	CS	OBP	SLG	IBB	SH	SF	#Pit	#P/PA	GB	FB	G/F
1993 Season	.267	162	5510	835	1472	284	39	181	780	483	984	48	111	113	67	.329	.431	56	69	56	22582	3.66	1935	1532	1.26

1993 Batting

	Avg	AB	H	2B	3B	HR	RBI	BB	SO	OBP	SLG
vs. Left	.270	1217	328	61	8	32	163	100	225	.326	.412
vs. Right	.266	4293	1144	223	31	149	617	383	759	.329	.437
Groundball	.260	1022	266	56	9	28	151	76	188	.312	.415
Flyball	.270	1068	288	45	8	52	179	92	181	.331	.473
Home	.273	2685	734	141	22	90	381	234	473	.334	.443
Away	.261	2825	738	143	17	91	399	249	511	.323	.421
Day	.280	1322	370	88	11	38	210	114	220	.341	.449
Night	.263	4188	1102	196	28	143	570	369	764	.325	.426
Grass	.272	4666	1268	241	35	154	678	413	821	.333	.437
Turf	.242	844	204	43	4	27	102	70	163	.302	.398
First Pitch	.321	792	254	52	3	31	141	45	0	.362	.511
Ahead in Count	.335	1157	388	77	9	58	218	227	0	.441	.568
Behind in Count	.213	2492	531	104	15	53	263	0	831	.219	.331
Two Strikes	.185	2503	464	82	14	55	239	211	984	.252	.295

	Avg	AB	H	2B	3B	HR	RBI	BB	SO	OBP	SLG
Scoring Posn	.270	1417	383	73	9	45	570	184	263	.348	.430
Close & Late	.271	745	202	31	6	23	111	76	150	.339	.421
None on/out	.301	1393	419	93	11	44	44	96	213	.351	.478
Leadoff	.271	693	188	26	15	8	60	50	106	.318	.387
Batting #3	.295	634	187	42	2	38	118	67	125	.366	.547
Cleanup	.298	647	193	38	3	46	129	38	117	.349	.580
April	.252	705	178	39	3	25	105	61	127	.319	.423
May	.255	982	250	54	11	30	124	63	190	.301	.424
June	.267	875	234	37	7	28	121	76	151	.325	.422
July	.287	969	278	52	9	35	162	97	163	.354	.467
August	.260	969	252	50	3	37	141	92	160	.331	.432
September/October	.277	1010	280	52	6	26	127	94	193	.337	.418
Pre-All Star	.265	2966	786	150	27	99	431	238	527	.322	.434
Post-All Star	.270	2544	686	134	12	82	349	245	457	.336	.428

	ERA	W	L	Sv	Opp	G	IP	BB	SO	Avg	H	2B	3B	HR	RBI	OBP	SLG	CG	ShO	Sup	QS	#P/S	SB	CS	GB	FB	G/F
1993 Season	4.28	86	76	45	65	162	1438.1	562	957	.267	1476	278	29	144	692	.337	.405	20	6	5.22	82	97	95	67	2002	1557	1.29

1993 Pitching

	ERA	W	L	Sv	G	GS	IP	H	HR	BB	SO
Home	3.73	50	31	30	258	81	738.0	703	72	261	521
Away	4.86	36	45	15	263	81	700.1	773	72	301	436
Day	4.82	21	16	10	126	37	330.1	350	33	140	197
Night	4.12	65	60	35	395	125	1108.0	1126	111	422	760
Grass	4.08	76	61	39	438	137	1227.1	1227	122	475	834
Turf	5.46	10	15	6	83	25	211.0	249	22	87	123
April	3.13	11	10	4	61	21	187.0	175	12	66	126
May	4.54	14	14	6	85	28	254.0	269	24	90	154
June	4.99	10	16	6	87	26	225.2	244	27	96	151
July	4.76	17	11	9	97	28	247.2	275	21	109	182
August	4.13	17	12	10	87	29	257.1	260	31	98	170
September/October	3.95	17	13	10	104	30	266.2	253	29	103	174
Starters	4.39	63	59	0	162	162	968.2	992	92	378	623
Relievers	4.06	23	17	45	359	0	469.2	484	52	184	334
0-3 Days Rest (SP)	2.95	7	7	0	16	16	110.0	87	8	34	62
4 Days Rest	4.49	34	28	0	83	83	509.0	519	49	204	335
5+ Days Rest	4.68	22	24	0	63	63	349.2	386	35	140	226
Pre-All Star	4.32	44	42	20	272	86	765.1	791	73	296	503
Post-All Star	4.24	42	34	25	249	76	673.0	685	71	266	454

	Avg	AB	H	2B	3B	HR	RBI	BB	SO	OBP	SLG
vs. Left	.258	1997	515	94	10	39	225	232	340	.337	.374
vs. Right	.272	3538	961	184	19	105	467	330	617	.336	.423
Inning 1-6	.271	3759	1019	203	23	89	482	409	619	.346	.408
Inning 7+	.257	1776	457	75	6	55	210	153	338	.318	.399
None on	.260	3129	814	150	17	87	87	274	553	.324	.402
Runners on	.275	2406	662	128	12	57	605	288	404	.352	.409
Scoring Posn	.264	1418	374	72	9	36	537	198	254	.351	.403
Close & Late	.261	813	212	33	4	24	106	73	159	.322	.400
None on/out	.260	1363	355	73	9	36	36	121	240	.324	.406
vs. 1st Batr (relief)	.252	325	82	11	1	8	39	28	74	.315	.366
First Inning Pitched	.269	1761	473	85	11	43	280	194	325	.343	.403
First 75 Pitches (SP)	.273	4533	1236	220	26	122	594	477	768	.344	.413
Pitch 76-90	.224	491	110	26	1	14	55	48	94	.293	.367
Pitch 91-105	.253	340	86	18	1	6	30	17	53	.298	.365
Pitch 106+	.257	171	44	14	1	2	13	20	42	.337	.386
First Pitch	.370	771	285	50	4	24	122	34	0	.397	.538
Ahead in Count	.194	2449	476	74	7	41	203	0	797	.200	.281
Behind in Count	.341	1252	427	87	14	53	223	286	0	.463	.560
Two Strikes	.183	2443	448	85	11	38	200	242	957	.261	.274

Games Finished: 142 Inherited Runners: 310 Inherited Runners Scored: 90 Holds: 53

Toronto Blue Jays

1993 Record: 95 – 67

	Avg	G	AB	R	H	2B	3B	HR	RBI	BB	SO	HBP	GDP	SB	CS	OBP	SLG	IBB	SH	SF	#Pit	#P/PA	GB	FB	G/F
1993 Season	.279	162	5579	847	1556	317	42	159	796	588	861	52	138	170	49	.350	.436	57	46	54	23248	3.68	1952	1688	1.16

1993 Batting

	Avg	AB	H	2B	3B	HR	RBI	BB	SO	OBP	SLG
vs. Left	.265	1587	421	90	9	38	204	166	257	.338	.405
vs. Right	.284	3992	1135	227	33	121	592	422	604	.355	.449
Groundball	.289	851	246	42	6	24	124	83	131	.356	.437
Flyball	.296	811	240	45	9	29	130	97	142	.373	.481
Home	.285	2734	778	161	30	90	413	282	404	.355	.464
Away	.273	2845	778	156	12	69	383	306	457	.345	.409
Day	.283	1835	519	106	13	72	287	196	308	.355	.472
Night	.277	3744	1037	211	29	87	509	392	553	.348	.419
Grass	.282	2246	634	117	10	66	318	246	334	.354	.431
Turf	.277	3333	922	200	32	93	478	342	527	.348	.440
First Pitch	.351	815	286	71	7	37	152	45	0	.392	.591
Ahead in Count	.355	1280	455	93	7	53	221	329	0	.486	.563
Behind in Count	.206	2442	503	89	13	34	253	0	738	.210	.295
Two Strikes	.196	2476	485	88	15	38	258	214	861	.261	.290

	Avg	AB	H	2B	3B	HR	RBI	BB	SO	OBP	SLG
Scoring Posn	.287	1511	434	84	13	37	618	223	253	.375	.433
Close & Late	.280	785	220	32	8	18	120	96	150	.362	.410
None on/out	.290	1374	398	79	7	59	59	125	192	.352	.486
Leadoff	.264	663	175	37	5	18	55	90	115	.358	.416
Batting #3	.337	647	218	37	6	20	114	84	67	.413	.505
Cleanup	.257	649	167	36	5	37	129	56	123	.320	.499
April	.277	773	214	41	6	19	114	78	149	.342	.419
May	.284	979	278	48	7	42	141	86	138	.345	.476
June	.279	967	270	68	7	29	145	103	147	.355	.454
July	.268	885	237	46	6	21	114	91	141	.339	.405
August	.287	1004	288	54	9	25	136	105	155	.355	.433
September/October	.277	971	269	60	7	23	146	125	131	.362	.424
Pre-All Star	.275	3043	837	175	22	95	427	298	485	.343	.441
Post-All Star	.284	2536	719	142	20	64	369	290	376	.358	.431

Toronto Blue Jays

	ERA	W	L	Sv	Opp	G	IP	BB	SO	Avg	H	2B	3B	HR	RBI	OBP	SLG	CG	ShO	Sup	QS	#P/S	SB	CS	GB	FB	G/F
1993 Season	4.21	95	67	50	69	162	1441.1	620	1023	.261	1441	240	31	134	694	.336	.388	11	11	5.29	69	102	136	64	1921	1572	1.22

1993 Pitching

	ERA	W	L	Sv	G	GS	IP	H	HR	BB	SO
Home	4.40	48	33	21	259	81	742.0	754	81	322	539
Away	4.03	47	34	29	247	81	699.1	687	53	298	484
Day	3.91	37	16	16	159	53	476.0	440	42	205	355
Night	4.37	58	51	34	347	109	965.1	1001	92	415	668
Grass	4.17	39	24	25	207	63	546.2	549	39	240	369
Turf	4.26	56	43	25	299	99	894.2	892	95	380	654
April	4.80	13	10	8	69	23	202.2	217	18	86	144
May	4.50	16	12	8	94	28	246.0	256	20	114	175
June	3.88	19	9	8	87	28	252.2	237	15	102	191
July	4.42	12	14	6	74	26	230.0	245	27	96	158
August	4.12	17	12	12	94	29	260.0	262	30	115	180
September/October	3.74	18	10	8	88	28	250.0	224	24	108	175
Starters	4.63	70	50	0	162	162	999.1	1023	103	432	649
Relievers	3.30	25	17	50	344	0	442.0	418	31	188	374
0-3 Days Rest (SP)	3.86	1	1	0	2	2	9.1	6	0	6	6
4 Days Rest	4.68	45	30	0	96	96	592.2	618	64	259	391
5+ Days Rest	4.58	24	19	0	64	64	397.1	399	39	167	252
Pre-All Star	4.42	49	40	24	276	89	788.1	813	61	338	567
Post-All Star	3.98	46	27	26	230	73	653.0	628	73	282	456

	Avg	AB	H	2B	3B	HR	RBI	BB	SO	OBP	SLG
vs. Left	.277	2610	722	128	17	59	325	314	411	.353	.407
vs. Right	.246	2917	719	112	14	75	369	306	612	.321	.372
Inning 1-6	.265	3748	995	174	28	96	504	434	651	.343	.404
Inning 7+	.251	1779	446	66	3	38	190	186	372	.321	.355
None on	.251	3008	754	125	25	74	74	318	563	.326	.383
Runners on	.273	2519	687	115	6	60	620	302	460	.347	.395
Scoring Posn	.264	1449	382	72	4	31	539	213	292	.350	.383
Close & Late	.231	810	187	30	0	18	93	102	173	.315	.335
None on/out	.254	1343	341	58	11	33	33	138	238	.328	.387
vs. 1st Batr (relief)	.220	305	67	14	0	9	57	30	67	.288	.354
First Inning Pitched	.246	1741	428	65	9	43	243	198	388	.322	.368
First 75 Pitches (SP)	.259	4369	1131	182	27	105	560	492	840	.335	.385
Pitch 76-90	.288	520	150	28	3	17	60	47	83	.348	.452
Pitch 91-105	.227	396	90	18	1	2	39	51	59	.312	.293
Pitch 106+	.289	242	70	12	0	10	35	30	41	.372	.463
First Pitch	.308	692	213	37	9	22	114	30	0	.339	.483
Ahead in Count	.226	2480	561	89	9	36	244	0	845	.230	.313
Behind in Count	.326	1246	406	70	4	53	215	343	0	.468	.516
Two Strikes	.193	2514	485	81	9	34	211	247	1023	.267	.273

Games Finished: 151 Inherited Runners: 231 Inherited Runners Scored: 81 Holds: 46

Atlanta Braves

1993 Record: 104 – 58

	Avg	G	AB	R	H	2B	3B	HR	RBI	BB	SO	HBP	GDP	SB	CS	OBP	SLG	IBB	SH	SF	#Pit	#P/PA	GB	FB	G/F
1993 Season	.262	162	5515	767	1444	239	29	169	712	560	946	36	127	125	48	.331	.408	46	73	50	22714	3.64	2014	1568	1.28

1993 Batting

	Avg	AB	H	2B	3B	HR	RBI	BB	SO	OBP	SLG
vs. Left	.273	1521	415	63	12	47	215	146	223	.335	.423
vs. Right	.258	3994	1029	176	17	122	497	414	723	.330	.402
Groundball	.262	1860	488	84	13	46	232	188	314	.329	.396
Flyball	.263	916	241	42	4	27	131	116	180	.349	.406
Home	.262	2693	705	116	15	78	340	279	432	.331	.403
Away	.262	2822	739	123	14	91	372	281	514	.331	.412
Day	.266	1437	382	50	11	39	172	160	256	.340	.397
Night	.260	4078	1062	189	18	130	540	400	690	.328	.411
Grass	.261	4235	1107	174	23	134	543	430	715	.330	.408
Turf	.263	1280	337	65	6	35	169	130	231	.336	.405
First Pitch	.325	904	294	42	3	34	158	35	0	.350	.491
Ahead in Count	.326	1193	389	75	5	63	215	296	0	.457	.556
Behind in Count	.192	2407	461	69	13	40	196	0	796	.197	.281
Two Strikes	.187	2469	461	66	16	39	207	229	946	.260	.274

	Avg	AB	H	2B	3B	HR	RBI	BB	SO	OBP	SLG
Scoring Posn	.257	1397	359	66	5	44	524	202	247	.343	.406
Close & Late	.248	876	217	34	5	31	116	96	167	.323	.404
None on/out	.243	1375	334	48	7	36	36	116	212	.304	.367
Leadoff	.270	675	182	23	9	6	44	74	94	.339	.357
Batting #3	.270	663	179	22	2	23	103	51	109	.320	.413
Cleanup	.270	623	168	32	3	36	115	78	100	.354	.504
April	.229	839	192	33	0	19	80	102	150	.314	.336
May	.264	900	238	49	5	25	112	89	147	.333	.413
June	.249	873	217	43	6	21	95	70	147	.306	.384
July	.279	959	268	41	7	40	142	92	139	.342	.462
August	.268	898	241	26	4	37	124	79	165	.329	.430
September/October	.275	1046	288	47	7	27	159	128	198	.356	.411
Pre-All Star	.248	2980	739	143	14	78	332	297	498	.318	.384
Post-All Star	.278	2535	705	96	15	91	380	263	448	.346	.436

	ERA	W	L	Sv	Opp	G	IP	BB	SO	Avg	H	2B	3B	HR	RBI	OBP	SLG	CG	ShO	Sup	QS	#P/S	SB	CS	GB	FB	G/F
1993 Season	3.14	104	58	46	60	162	1455.0	480	1036	.240	1297	240	21	101	524	.303	.349	18	16	4.74	107	97	121	53	2001	1436	1.39

1993 Pitching

	ERA	W	L	Sv	G	GS	IP	H	HR	BB	SO
Home	3.11	51	30	22	273	81	747.0	689	52	247	505
Away	3.17	53	28	24	242	81	708.0	608	49	233	531
Day	3.42	27	15	14	136	42	374.0	364	27	134	277
Night	3.04	77	43	32	379	120	1081.0	933	74	346	759
Grass	3.10	82	43	36	400	125	1135.1	1027	84	356	799
Turf	3.27	22	15	10	115	37	319.2	270	17	124	237
April	2.91	12	13	8	76	25	229.0	199	14	83	147
May	3.66	17	10	10	81	27	238.2	218	17	84	160
June	2.97	15	11	3	72	26	230.2	199	12	79	167
July	3.17	19	9	8	96	28	247.0	234	20	88	187
August	3.27	19	7	9	86	26	237.0	205	20	73	153
September/October	2.87	22	8	8	104	30	272.2	242	18	73	222
Starters	3.13	79	42	0	162	162	1083.0	997	82	327	719
Relievers	3.15	25	16	46	353	0	372.0	300	19	153	317
0-3 Days Rest (SP)	3.24	6	3	0	10	10	66.2	58	5	14	56
4 Days Rest	3.22	54	28	0	112	112	747.0	682	58	229	500
5+ Days Rest	2.87	19	11	0	40	40	269.1	257	19	84	163
Pre-All Star	3.21	50	39	23	266	89	793.2	712	50	274	557
Post-All Star	3.05	54	19	23	249	73	661.1	585	51	206	479

	Avg	AB	H	2B	3B	HR	RBI	BB	SO	OBP	SLG
vs. Left	.241	2011	485	85	10	32	196	215	381	.315	.341
vs. Right	.240	3383	812	155	11	69	328	265	655	.296	.354
Inning 1-6	.246	3621	890	167	16	70	344	301	663	.304	.359
Inning 7+	.230	1773	407	73	5	31	180	179	373	.301	.329
None on	.242	3162	765	143	13	65	65	258	605	.302	.357
Runners on	.238	2232	532	97	8	36	459	222	431	.305	.337
Scoring Posn	.233	1259	293	59	5	18	400	175	272	.320	.330
Close & Late	.244	989	241	40	2	21	106	102	207	.315	.352
None on/out	.257	1391	358	73	8	34	34	100	243	.309	.395
vs. 1st Batr (relief)	.181	304	55	10	1	3	24	38	73	.274	.250
First Inning Pitched	.241	1703	411	74	5	26	218	177	368	.313	.336
First 75 Pitches (SP)	.237	4368	1035	188	15	80	415	386	850	.299	.342
Pitch 76-90	.268	508	136	28	2	10	63	50	95	.333	.390
Pitch 91-105	.208	360	75	16	2	6	24	24	63	.260	.314
Pitch 106+	.323	158	51	8	2	5	22	20	28	.402	.494
First Pitch	.300	834	250	51	1	21	105	39	0	.330	.439
Ahead in Count	.174	2478	430	81	13	28	175	0	897	.177	.251
Behind in Count	.318	1139	362	62	4	37	151	240	0	.434	.477
Two Strikes	.159	2456	391	74	10	24	161	201	1036	.225	.227

Games Finished: 144 Inherited Runners: 163 Inherited Runners Scored: 61 Holds: 45

Chicago Cubs

1993 Record: 84 – 78 – 1

	Avg	G	AB	R	H	2B	3B	HR	RBI	BB	SO	HBP	GDP	SB	CS	OBP	SLG	IBB	SH	SF	#Pit	#P/PA	GB	FB	G/F
1993 Season	.270	163	5627	738	1521	259	32	161	706	446	923	34	131	100	43	.325	.414	61	67	42	21762	3.50	2050	1449	1.41

1993 Batting

	Avg	AB	H	2B	3B	HR	RBI	BB	SO	OBP	SLG
vs. Left	.276	1532	423	71	4	45	199	118	230	.329	.416
vs. Right	.268	4095	1098	188	28	116	507	328	693	.324	.413
Groundball	.273	1999	545	94	13	55	257	154	303	.327	.415
Flyball	.259	831	215	25	4	26	102	59	149	.311	.392
Home	.283	2769	784	131	16	76	366	223	453	.338	.424
Away	.258	2858	737	128	16	85	340	223	470	.313	.403
Day	.262	2939	770	114	13	74	327	230	483	.317	.385
Night	.279	2688	751	145	19	87	379	216	440	.335	.445
Grass	.279	4314	1202	203	24	125	566	346	707	.334	.424
Turf	.243	1313	319	56	8	36	140	100	216	.297	.380
First Pitch	.304	911	277	51	6	24	138	48	0	.341	.452
Ahead in Count	.340	1310	446	83	7	57	234	219	0	.433	.545
Behind in Count	.210	2429	511	87	11	45	207	0	786	.214	.311
Two Strikes	.194	2379	462	68	10	49	207	179	923	.253	.293

	Avg	AB	H	2B	3B	HR	RBI	BB	SO	OBP	SLG
Scoring Posn	.268	1365	366	69	10	34	510	181	244	.349	.408
Close & Late	.272	891	242	27	4	25	127	74	181	.329	.395
None on/out	.267	1407	375	61	6	38	38	90	216	.314	.399
Leadoff	.275	695	191	29	5	13	49	51	89	.328	.387
Batting #3	.321	647	208	32	4	15	102	67	52	.381	.453
Cleanup	.289	647	187	34	2	20	105	51	88	.338	.440
April	.258	760	196	31	4	20	88	50	118	.304	.388
May	.285	887	253	42	6	23	106	56	152	.327	.424
June	.277	974	270	47	7	28	122	67	131	.325	.426
July	.261	928	242	41	6	26	114	80	154	.321	.402
August	.262	1044	274	46	1	32	123	89	167	.323	.400
September/October	.277	1034	286	52	8	32	153	104	201	.345	.435
Pre-All Star	.274	2986	817	131	21	79	358	198	463	.319	.411
Post-All Star	.267	2641	704	128	11	82	348	248	460	.332	.417

	ERA	W	L	Sv	Opp	G	IP	BB	SO	Avg	H	2B	3B	HR	RBI	OBP	SLG	CG	ShO	Sup	QS	#P/S	SB	CS	GB	FB	G/F
1993 Season	4.18	84	78	56	74	163	1449.2	470	905	.273	1514	285	38	153	691	.332	.421	8	5	4.58	86	89	84	69	2106	1373	1.53

1993 Pitching

	ERA	W	L	Sv	G	GS	IP	H	HR	BB	SO
Home	4.10	43	38	26	302	82	748.0	761	94	252	472
Away	4.26	41	40	30	283	81	701.2	753	59	218	433
Day	3.96	41	46	28	312	88	785.0	800	86	254	479
Night	4.44	43	32	28	273	75	664.2	714	67	216	426
Grass	4.06	66	58	41	450	125	1125.2	1177	125	344	714
Turf	4.58	18	20	15	135	38	324.0	337	28	126	191
April	3.78	11	11	6	76	22	195.0	186	25	82	117
May	4.01	13	12	9	96	26	229.0	233	17	71	131
June	4.65	13	15	9	103	28	244.0	273	25	83	161
July	3.83	15	12	8	95	27	244.1	248	20	66	158
August	4.31	12	18	7	106	30	273.1	301	32	90	165
September/October	4.36	20	10	17	109	30	264.0	273	34	78	173
Starters	4.45	58	62	0	163	163	981.1	1051	106	304	566
Relievers	3.61	26	16	56	422	0	468.1	463	47	166	339
0-3 Days Rest (SP)	4.86	0	5	0	7	7	37.0	46	7	16	24
4 Days Rest	4.71	30	41	0	92	92	552.1	599	60	188	305
5+ Days Rest	4.04	28	16	0	64	64	392.0	406	39	100	237
Pre-All Star	4.15	41	45	27	311	87	765.1	800	77	262	477
Post-All Star	4.21	43	33	29	274	76	684.1	714	76	208	428

	Avg	AB	H	2B	3B	HR	RBI	BB	SO	OBP	SLG
vs. Left	.265	2342	621	106	16	72	303	251	397	.338	.416
vs. Right	.279	3203	893	179	22	81	388	219	508	.327	.424
Inning 1-6	.276	3738	1032	191	29	108	475	300	579	.332	.429
Inning 7+	.267	1807	482	94	9	45	216	170	326	.332	.403
None on	.268	3206	858	162	22	88	88	233	520	.322	.414
Runners on	.280	2339	656	123	16	65	603	237	385	.344	.430
Scoring Posn	.283	1344	380	68	12	38	522	178	233	.360	.436
Close & Late	.264	879	232	44	5	20	115	89	159	.334	.394
None on/out	.277	1392	386	69	12	36	36	98	195	.331	.422
vs. 1st Batr (relief)	.266	376	100	16	4	8	62	33	56	.329	.394
First Inning Pitched	.269	1940	522	87	11	52	280	172	355	.331	.406
First 75 Pitches (SP)	.276	4789	1323	246	34	137	620	395	781	.334	.428
Pitch 76-90	.260	420	109	22	2	13	46	40	70	.321	.414
Pitch 91-105	.222	243	54	11	2	1	15	24	38	.294	.296
Pitch 106+	.301	93	28	6	0	2	10	11	16	.387	.430
First Pitch	.298	887	264	51	11	21	109	50	0	.337	.451
Ahead in Count	.216	2402	519	93	4	46	231	0	775	.223	.316
Behind in Count	.359	1221	438	84	15	58	212	234	0	.460	.595
Two Strikes	.193	2338	452	90	5	41	220	186	905	.255	.289

Games Finished: 155 Inherited Runners: 273 Inherited Runners Scored: 90 Holds: 71

Cincinnati Reds

1993 Record: 73 – 89

	Avg	G	AB	R	H	2B	3B	HR	RBI	BB	SO	HBP	GDP	SB	CS	OBP	SLG	IBB	SH	SF	#Pit	#P/PA	GB	FB	G/F
1993 Season	.264	162	5517	722	1457	261	28	137	669	485	1025	32	104	142	59	.324	.396	42	63	66	22394	3.63	2009	1522	1.32

1993 Batting

	Avg	AB	H	2B	3B	HR	RBI	BB	SO	OBP	SLG
vs. Left	.271	1534	415	89	7	43	184	124	263	.326	.422
vs. Right	.262	3983	1042	172	21	94	485	361	762	.323	.386
Groundball	.280	2003	561	106	6	50	253	177	342	.339	.414
Flyball	.231	956	221	38	6	20	95	80	230	.290	.346
Home	.265	2659	705	134	10	69	344	252	494	.328	.401
Away	.263	2858	752	127	18	68	325	233	531	.319	.392
Day	.265	1573	417	75	10	47	210	157	285	.330	.415
Night	.264	3944	1040	186	18	90	459	328	740	.321	.388
Grass	.254	1746	443	66	14	47	204	149	333	.313	.388
Turf	.269	3771	1014	195	14	90	465	336	692	.328	.400
First Pitch	.323	799	258	40	5	27	136	31	0	.347	.487
Ahead in Count	.350	1217	426	83	10	44	194	259	0	.460	.543
Behind in Count	.196	2490	487	86	8	40	207	0	844	.201	.285
Two Strikes	.182	2510	458	88	8	37	208	194	1025	.243	.268

	Avg	AB	H	2B	3B	HR	RBI	BB	SO	OBP	SLG
Scoring Posn	.271	1400	379	71	8	35	530	189	271	.347	.408
Close & Late	.251	818	205	32	4	15	94	83	164	.319	.355
None on/out	.270	1376	371	67	11	37	37	107	241	.326	.415
Leadoff	.250	684	171	36	7	9	40	68	103	.319	.363
Batting #3	.298	631	188	32	3	15	88	79	87	.373	.429
Cleanup	.284	638	181	34	5	27	99	54	117	.338	.480
April	.251	742	186	28	5	14	77	77	134	.321	.358
May	.281	973	273	51	2	25	134	105	170	.352	.414
June	.277	966	268	42	3	21	119	66	170	.323	.392
July	.279	955	266	56	5	30	126	82	172	.337	.442
August	.242	926	224	45	6	26	114	85	191	.305	.388
September/October	.251	955	240	39	7	21	99	70	188	.301	.373
Pre-All Star	.277	3105	859	150	13	79	390	277	537	.336	.410
Post-All Star	.248	2412	598	111	15	58	279	208	488	.307	.379

Cincinnati Reds

	ERA	W	L	Sv	Opp	G	IP	BB	SO	Avg	H	2B	3B	HR	RBI	OBP	SLG	CG	ShO	Sup	QS	#P/S	SB	CS	GB	FB	G/F
1993 Season	4.51	73	89	37	55	162	1434.0	508	996	.272	1510	239	54	158	743	.336	.420	11	8	4.53	84	94	134	56	1934	1596	1.21

1993 Pitching

	ERA	W	L	Sv	G	GS	IP	H	HR	BB	SO
Home	4.33	41	40	21	267	81	730.0	747	81	266	497
Away	4.70	32	49	16	270	81	704.0	763	77	242	499
Day	4.47	21	26	11	148	47	412.1	436	50	132	269
Night	4.53	52	63	26	389	115	1021.2	1074	108	376	727
Grass	4.60	20	30	9	159	50	434.0	467	55	134	296
Turf	4.47	53	59	28	378	112	1000.0	1043	103	374	700
April	3.84	8	14	5	71	22	194.2	190	13	66	130
May	3.92	17	12	7	88	29	250.0	251	25	91	152
June	4.66	13	14	6	90	27	247.0	268	31	60	166
July	3.89	15	13	11	88	28	245.1	249	21	78	178
August	4.66	13	15	5	96	28	247.1	265	35	91	183
September/October	5.95	7	21	3	104	28	249.2	287	33	122	187
Starters	4.50	49	62	0	162	162	969.0	1042	104	314	652
Relievers	4.55	24	27	37	375	0	465.0	468	54	194	344
0-3 Days Rest (SP)	6.35	1	1	0	2	2	11.1	12	1	3	3
4 Days Rest	4.24	35	41	0	113	113	689.2	748	66	209	472
5+ Days Rest	5.07	13	20	0	47	47	268.0	282	37	102	177
Pre-All Star	4.18	45	45	24	285	90	797.0	820	80	245	522
Post-All Star	4.93	28	44	13	252	72	637.0	690	78	263	474

	Avg	AB	H	2B	3B	HR	RBI	BB	SO	OBP	SLG
vs. Left	.278	2381	661	103	31	66	318	294	392	.358	.430
vs. Right	.268	3168	849	136	23	92	425	214	604	.318	.413
Inning 1-6	.276	3761	1038	170	39	110	521	329	683	.337	.430
Inning 7+	.264	1788	472	69	15	48	222	179	313	.332	.400
None on	.264	3163	835	138	24	83	83	239	581	.320	.402
Runners on	.283	2386	675	101	30	75	660	269	415	.355	.445
Scoring Posn	.282	1420	400	63	16	45	573	189	260	.361	.444
Close & Late	.266	777	207	28	7	20	101	85	132	.340	.398
None on/out	.269	1381	372	65	10	36	36	102	235	.325	.409
vs. 1st Batr (relief)	.242	322	78	16	4	6	34	40	59	.331	.373
First Inning Pitched	.267	1832	490	85	23	50	291	213	354	.346	.421
First 75 Pitches (SP)	.268	4656	1250	204	52	136	625	436	838	.334	.422
Pitch 76-90	.313	457	143	23	1	10	65	37	84	.366	.433
Pitch 91-105	.289	287	83	9	0	7	38	19	50	.335	.394
Pitch 106+	.228	149	34	3	1	5	15	16	24	.301	.362
First Pitch	.355	884	314	50	11	32	168	25	0	.376	.545
Ahead in Count	.210	2505	525	73	19	43	231	0	847	.216	.305
Behind in Count	.342	1188	406	67	17	56	227	261	0	.457	.568
Two Strikes	.195	2481	483	71	15	36	195	222	996	.265	.279

Games Finished: 151 Inherited Runners: 219 Inherited Runners Scored: 59 Holds: 32

Houston Astros

1993 Record: 85 – 77

	Avg	G	AB	R	H	2B	3B	HR	RBI	BB	SO	HBP	GDP	SB	CS	OBP	SLG	IBB	SH	SF	#Pit	#P/PA	GB	FB	G/F
1993 Season	.267	162	5464	716	1459	288	37	138	656	497	911	40	125	103	60	.330	.409	58	82	47	21957	3.58	2031	1542	1.32

1993 Batting

	Avg	AB	H	2B	3B	HR	RBI	BB	SO	OBP	SLG
vs. Left	.273	1819	497	109	11	54	249	182	284	.342	.434
vs. Right	.264	3645	962	179	26	84	407	315	627	.324	.396
Groundball	.264	1867	492	103	15	40	208	143	314	.319	.399
Flyball	.266	766	204	42	6	29	121	90	148	.347	.450
Home	.267	2625	700	142	19	62	332	244	436	.332	.406
Away	.267	2839	759	146	18	76	324	253	475	.329	.412
Day	.264	1747	461	92	13	48	208	158	290	.328	.414
Night	.268	3717	998	196	24	90	448	339	621	.331	.407
Grass	.269	1809	486	93	15	56	217	174	301	.333	.430
Turf	.266	3655	973	195	22	82	439	323	610	.329	.399
First Pitch	.327	829	271	44	8	27	132	44	0	.362	.497
Ahead in Count	.353	1178	416	85	13	42	184	247	0	.463	.554
Behind in Count	.204	2401	489	102	8	39	224	0	779	.211	.302
Two Strikes	.180	2349	423	84	6	44	199	206	911	.250	.277

	Avg	AB	H	2B	3B	HR	RBI	BB	SO	OBP	SLG
Scoring Posn	.262	1385	363	68	12	28	490	168	250	.337	.389
Close & Late	.260	865	225	47	2	19	94	77	145	.325	.385
None on/out	.273	1380	377	65	12	39	39	104	212	.328	.422
Leadoff	.288	649	187	45	5	22	68	80	95	.372	.475
Batting #3	.318	626	199	44	4	22	97	72	84	.385	.506
Cleanup	.266	627	167	29	4	16	82	63	110	.333	.402
April	.266	741	197	46	5	19	97	70	106	.333	.418
May	.273	912	249	48	4	31	118	84	136	.336	.436
June	.248	866	215	39	7	18	84	70	145	.306	.372
July	.274	971	266	55	8	23	129	85	152	.337	.418
August	.271	962	261	49	6	27	114	97	181	.338	.419
September/October	.268	1012	271	51	7	20	114	91	191	.329	.391
Pre-All Star	.265	2923	775	160	21	81	365	265	449	.329	.417
Post-All Star	.269	2541	684	128	16	57	291	232	462	.332	.399

	ERA	W	L	Sv	Opp	G	IP	BB	SO	Avg	H	2B	3B	HR	RBI	OBP	SLG	CG	ShO	Sup	QS	#P/S	SB	CS	GB	FB	G/F
1993 Season	3.49	85	77	42	63	162	1441.1	476	1056	.251	1363	226	25	117	590	.313	.366	18	14	4.47	100	100	110	42	1969	1454	1.35

1993 Pitching

	ERA	W	L	Sv	G	GS	IP	H	HR	BB	SO
Home	3.11	44	37	17	229	81	734.0	664	56	213	570
Away	3.88	41	40	25	257	81	707.1	699	61	263	486
Day	3.47	28	23	15	162	51	457.0	431	41	158	322
Night	3.50	57	54	27	324	111	984.1	932	76	318	734
Grass	4.05	27	24	17	164	51	450.2	457	38	164	305
Turf	3.23	58	53	25	322	111	990.2	906	79	312	751
April	3.06	14	8	6	58	22	197.0	162	10	58	130
May	3.60	13	14	7	87	27	242.2	239	19	80	173
June	4.61	11	15	8	85	26	224.2	249	25	74	148
July	3.38	16	13	7	89	29	260.2	247	21	89	200
August	3.00	15	13	8	84	28	251.2	213	23	82	189
September/October	3.33	16	14	6	83	30	264.2	253	19	93	216
Starters	3.48	72	53	0	162	162	1049.1	997	87	339	764
Relievers	3.51	13	24	42	324	0	392.0	366	30	137	292
0-3 Days Rest (SP)	1.88	6	1	0	9	9	57.1	40	3	21	56
4 Days Rest	3.51	42	29	0	87	87	572.1	567	48	163	417
5+ Days Rest	3.67	24	23	0	66	66	419.2	390	36	155	291
Pre-All Star	3.73	46	41	22	263	87	771.1	750	62	239	529
Post-All Star	3.21	39	36	20	223	75	670.0	613	55	237	527

	Avg	AB	H	2B	3B	HR	RBI	BB	SO	OBP	SLG
vs. Left	.254	2462	625	92	15	56	255	272	448	.330	.372
vs. Right	.248	2978	738	134	10	61	335	204	608	.299	.361
Inning 1-6	.247	3641	898	153	21	78	389	317	679	.310	.364
Inning 7+	.258	1799	465	73	4	39	201	159	377	.319	.369
None on	.238	3146	750	122	17	63	63	251	630	.299	.348
Runners on	.267	2294	613	104	8	54	527	225	426	.333	.390
Scoring Posn	.259	1325	343	60	6	27	452	168	264	.338	.374
Close & Late	.278	914	254	33	1	24	118	83	208	.341	.395
None on/out	.239	1382	330	49	11	36	36	104	264	.294	.368
vs. 1st Batr (relief)	.271	292	79	12	0	4	27	23	59	.322	.353
First Inning Pitched	.259	1629	422	65	10	33	217	148	298	.323	.372
First 75 Pitches (SP)	.250	4372	1093	177	23	94	475	372	850	.312	.366
Pitch 76-90	.239	510	122	18	2	12	55	53	96	.317	.353
Pitch 91-105	.272	367	100	21	0	10	42	31	71	.324	.411
Pitch 106+	.251	191	48	10	0	1	18	20	39	.324	.319
First Pitch	.292	831	243	49	2	20	126	42	0	.328	.428
Ahead in Count	.191	2488	475	71	9	33	186	0	913	.197	.266
Behind in Count	.316	1192	377	62	6	45	176	242	0	.430	.492
Two Strikes	.176	2484	438	61	12	35	171	192	1056	.239	.253

Games Finished: 144 Inherited Runners: 194 Inherited Runners Scored: 53 Holds: 47

Los Angeles Dodgers

1993 Record: 81 – 81

	Avg	G	AB	R	H	2B	3B	HR	RBI	BB	SO	HBP	GDP	SB	CS	OBP	SLG	IBB	SH	SF	#Pit	#P/PA	GB	FB	G/F
1993 Season	.261	162	5588	675	1458	234	28	130	639	492	937	27	105	126	61	.321	.383	48	107	47	22481	3.59	2086	1488	1.40

1993 Batting

	Avg	AB	H	2B	3B	HR	RBI	BB	SO	OBP	SLG
vs. Left	.269	1613	434	79	8	35	184	136	244	.324	.393
vs. Right	.258	3975	1024	155	20	95	455	356	693	.320	.378
Groundball	.269	1507	405	64	10	29	164	127	251	.326	.382
Flyball	.271	905	245	40	4	20	113	78	158	.326	.390
Home	.275	2716	747	104	7	66	318	258	437	.339	.391
Away	.248	2872	711	130	21	64	321	234	500	.304	.374
Day	.256	1532	392	78	12	40	162	123	275	.312	.401
Night	.263	4056	1066	156	16	90	477	369	662	.325	.376
Grass	.267	4276	1142	176	17	106	510	397	714	.330	.391
Turf	.241	1312	316	58	11	24	129	95	223	.293	.357
First Pitch	.309	806	249	48	3	27	111	36	0	.342	.476
Ahead in Count	.327	1218	398	75	9	53	221	248	0	.437	.534
Behind in Count	.213	2556	545	77	8	32	188	0	806	.215	.287
Two Strikes	.191	2502	479	67	7	32	181	208	937	.255	.262

	Avg	AB	H	2B	3B	HR	RBI	BB	SO	OBP	SLG
Scoring Posn	.271	1414	383	49	9	28	499	192	259	.351	.378
Close & Late	.240	1063	255	40	6	20	107	112	198	.314	.345
None on/out	.266	1433	381	65	8	47	47	95	232	.314	.421
Leadoff	.298	657	196	22	11	2	49	85	78	.380	.374
Batting #3	.241	643	155	29	3	20	91	66	126	.312	.389
Cleanup	.228	640	146	33	0	27	106	59	85	.293	.406
April	.227	761	173	24	2	12	68	78	128	.300	.311
May	.289	896	259	39	8	20	126	80	158	.346	.417
June	.269	905	243	37	4	25	111	72	168	.323	.401
July	.254	989	251	51	7	20	110	73	152	.305	.380
August	.260	931	242	42	4	26	104	81	141	.322	.397
September/October	.262	1106	290	41	3	27	120	108	190	.327	.378
Pre-All Star	.264	3012	795	124	15	66	356	263	526	.323	.381
Post-All Star	.257	2576	663	110	13	64	283	229	411	.319	.385

	ERA	W	L	Sv	Opp	G	IP	BB	SO	Avg	H	2B	3B	HR	RBI	OBP	SLG	CG	ShO	Sup	QS	#P/S	SB	CS	GB	FB	G/F
1993 Season	3.50	81	81	36	47	162	1472.2	567	1043	.254	1406	223	33	103	613	.324	.361	17	9	4.13	95	99	129	66	2132	1388	1.54

1993 Pitching

	ERA	W	L	Sv	G	GS	IP	H	HR	BB	SO
Home	3.17	41	40	15	246	81	747.0	703	48	273	530
Away	3.84	40	41	21	262	81	725.2	703	55	294	513
Day	3.60	21	24	8	136	45	402.1	362	25	177	279
Night	3.46	60	57	28	372	117	1070.1	1044	78	390	764
Grass	3.38	64	61	26	388	125	1143.0	1102	76	427	806
Turf	3.93	17	20	10	120	37	329.2	304	27	140	237
April	3.71	8	15	5	74	23	204.0	185	13	106	136
May	3.36	18	8	5	82	26	233.1	228	11	73	170
June	3.45	14	13	7	80	27	240.0	227	20	82	170
July	3.58	14	13	7	84	27	256.1	241	20	105	168
August	3.09	12	15	6	83	27	247.2	245	19	96	177
September/October	3.80	15	17	6	105	32	291.1	280	20	105	222
Starters	3.55	57	59	0	162	162	1033.2	990	72	390	700
Relievers	3.38	24	22	36	346	0	439.0	416	31	177	343
0-3 Days Rest (SP)	4.80	2	1	0	5	5	30.0	31	2	10	18
4 Days Rest	3.21	17	24	0	58	58	387.0	361	24	138	248
5+ Days Rest	3.71	38	34	0	99	99	616.2	598	46	242	434
Pre-All Star	3.57	46	41	21	277	87	785.2	745	53	311	549
Post-All Star	3.42	35	40	15	231	75	687.0	661	50	256	494

	Avg	AB	H	2B	3B	HR	RBI	BB	SO	OBP	SLG
vs. Left	.252	2902	732	121	16	52	330	352	529	.332	.359
vs. Right	.255	2642	674	102	17	51	283	215	514	.316	.364
Inning 1-6	.257	3685	946	153	25	70	430	374	681	.328	.369
Inning 7+	.247	1859	460	70	8	33	183	193	362	.318	.347
None on	.247	3127	773	125	18	60	60	279	588	.314	.356
Runners on	.262	2417	633	98	15	43	553	288	455	.337	.368
Scoring Posn	.248	1417	351	59	11	21	488	216	294	.340	.349
Close & Late	.241	1035	249	35	3	18	112	116	231	.318	.332
None on/out	.253	1388	351	64	8	26	26	116	244	.316	.367
vs. 1st Batr (relief)	.245	318	78	11	0	4	28	22	61	.297	.318
First Inning Pitched	.270	1725	465	69	10	31	246	195	332	.344	.375
First 75 Pitches (SP)	.257	4483	1152	173	29	87	522	449	858	.326	.367
Pitch 76-90	.251	479	120	26	2	9	45	48	81	.323	.370
Pitch 91-105	.233	344	80	11	1	6	27	37	65	.311	.323
Pitch 106+	.227	238	54	13	1	1	19	33	39	.318	.303
First Pitch	.304	850	258	40	10	21	123	46	0	.338	.448
Ahead in Count	.206	2393	494	63	15	33	203	0	854	.212	.287
Behind in Count	.316	1184	374	63	4	34	173	286	0	.447	.462
Two Strikes	.174	2407	419	54	10	26	169	235	1043	.251	.237

Games Finished: 145 Inherited Runners: 230 Inherited Runners Scored: 64 Holds: 40

Montreal Expos

1993 Record: 94 – 68 – 1

	Avg	G	AB	R	H	2B	3B	HR	RBI	BB	SO	HBP	GDP	SB	CS	OBP	SLG	IBB	SH	SF	#Pit	#P/PA	GB	FB	G/F
1993 Season	.257	163	5493	732	1410	270	36	122	682	542	860	48	95	228	56	.326	.386	65	100	50	22481	3.61	2152	1608	1.34

1993 Batting

	Avg	AB	H	2B	3B	HR	RBI	BB	SO	OBP	SLG
vs. Left	.258	1723	444	86	11	40	203	168	264	.328	.390
vs. Right	.256	3770	966	184	25	82	479	374	596	.325	.384
Groundball	.259	1667	431	74	5	25	188	151	243	.325	.354
Flyball	.262	844	221	39	5	25	120	110	129	.349	.409
Home	.261	2640	689	139	13	62	349	281	403	.334	.394
Away	.253	2853	721	131	23	60	333	261	457	.319	.378
Day	.254	1746	444	91	12	35	201	146	300	.315	.380
Night	.258	3747	966	179	24	87	481	396	560	.331	.388
Grass	.252	1723	434	68	12	40	202	164	294	.319	.375
Turf	.259	3770	976	202	24	82	480	378	566	.329	.390
First Pitch	.303	745	226	44	9	18	111	50	0	.353	.459
Ahead in Count	.296	1366	405	85	9	46	226	297	0	.419	.473
Behind in Count	.211	2388	503	81	16	36	210	0	747	.219	.303
Two Strikes	.205	2349	482	81	13	34	222	195	860	.270	.294

	Avg	AB	H	2B	3B	HR	RBI	BB	SO	OBP	SLG
Scoring Posn	.240	1520	365	83	10	30	537	237	261	.339	.367
Close & Late	.264	887	234	41	6	12	112	104	163	.343	.364
None on/out	.269	1386	373	70	13	32	32	100	186	.322	.408
Leadoff	.307	681	209	24	8	12	64	76	88	.376	.419
Batting #3	.285	653	186	30	3	18	98	55	83	.342	.423
Cleanup	.252	602	152	30	5	26	104	91	95	.356	.449
April	.278	774	215	43	7	23	111	80	118	.346	.441
May	.256	910	233	49	3	16	102	82	143	.325	.369
June	.226	906	205	41	2	18	100	90	137	.301	.336
July	.269	936	252	36	6	21	111	95	151	.338	.388
August	.251	991	249	47	7	20	126	99	156	.319	.373
September/October	.262	976	256	54	11	24	132	96	155	.330	.414
Pre-All Star	.255	2953	753	145	13	69	357	292	455	.326	.383
Post-All Star	.259	2540	657	125	23	53	325	250	405	.326	.389

Montreal Expos

	ERA	W	L	Sv	Opp	G	IP	BB	SO	Avg	H	2B	3B	HR	RBI	OBP	SLG	CG	ShO	Sup	QS	#P/S	SB	CS	GB	FB	G/F
1993 Season	3.55	94	68	61	85	163	1456.2	521	934	.249	1369	287	30	119	626	.317	.377	8	7	4.52	80	87	172	51	2164	1459	1.48

1993 Pitching

	ERA	W	L	Sv	G	GS	IP	H	HR	BB	SO
Home	3.18	55	26	32	269	81	751.0	662	50	268	463
Away	3.94	39	42	29	279	82	705.2	707	69	253	471
Day	4.13	22	28	14	184	51	450.2	469	46	173	279
Night	3.28	72	40	47	364	112	1006.0	900	73	348	655
Grass	3.77	24	25	16	162	50	427.0	425	35	123	287
Turf	3.45	70	43	45	386	113	1029.2	944	84	398	647
April	4.25	13	10	8	74	23	201.0	199	19	75	110
May	3.81	14	12	9	101	27	240.2	220	24	101	142
June	3.63	14	14	9	89	28	250.1	237	21	110	149
July	3.50	15	12	10	94	27	242.0	233	17	72	159
August	2.83	17	12	11	85	29	261.0	240	19	81	184
September/October	3.44	21	8	14	105	29	261.2	240	19	82	190
Starters	3.61	64	44	0	163	163	944.1	909	73	319	540
Relievers	3.43	30	24	61	385	0	512.1	460	46	202	394
0-3 Days Rest (SP)	3.29	3	3	0	8	8	41.0	37	1	16	19
4 Days Rest	3.78	34	23	0	86	86	500.1	491	48	158	291
5+ Days Rest	3.44	27	18	0	69	69	403.0	381	24	145	230
Pre-All Star	3.85	48	40	31	303	89	793.0	748	70	313	472
Post-All Star	3.19	46	28	30	245	74	663.2	621	49	208	462

	Avg	AB	H	2B	3B	HR	RBI	BB	SO	OBP	SLG
vs. Left	.257	2249	579	126	16	53	263	250	366	.332	.398
vs. Right	.243	3252	790	161	14	66	363	271	568	.307	.362
Inning 1-6	.252	3681	927	196	18	78	428	362	583	.322	.378
Inning 7+	.243	1820	442	91	12	41	198	159	351	.307	.374
None on	.256	3102	795	160	20	69	69	258	498	.318	.387
Runners on	.239	2399	574	127	10	50	557	263	436	.316	.363
Scoring Posn	.235	1475	346	77	5	29	487	215	302	.330	.353
Close & Late	.222	1002	222	42	6	17	90	100	222	.295	.326
None on/out	.270	1372	370	81	10	26	26	121	204	.333	.400
vs. 1st Batr (relief)	.238	324	77	17	4	7	32	45	63	.328	.380
First Inning Pitched	.260	1873	487	89	10	45	281	214	360	.338	.390
First 75 Pitches (SP)	.246	4767	1173	246	27	99	533	462	829	.316	.371
Pitch 76-90	.276	427	118	17	1	13	57	42	55	.341	.412
Pitch 91-105	.252	218	55	17	2	6	29	14	37	.302	.431
Pitch 106+	.258	89	23	7	0	1	7	3	13	.287	.371
First Pitch	.311	832	259	49	5	19	116	30	0	.337	.451
Ahead in Count	.190	2520	480	105	10	29	192	0	819	.197	.275
Behind in Count	.307	1176	361	70	12	50	200	270	0	.435	.514
Two Strikes	.174	2435	423	93	8	30	185	221	934	.247	.255

Games Finished: 155 Inherited Runners: 222 Inherited Runners Scored: 72 Holds: 32

New York Mets

1993 Record: 59 – 103

	Avg	G	AB	R	H	2B	3B	HR	RBI	BB	SO	HBP	GDP	SB	CS	OBP	SLG	IBB	SH	SF	#Pit	#P/PA	GB	FB	G/F
1993 Season	.248	162	5448	672	1350	228	37	158	632	448	879	24	108	79	50	.305	.390	43	89	47	21267	3.51	1858	1581	1.18

1993 Batting

	Avg	AB	H	2B	3B	HR	RBI	BB	SO	OBP	SLG
vs. Left	.251	1601	402	76	10	30	158	114	226	.301	.367
vs. Right	.246	3847	948	152	27	128	474	334	653	.307	.400
Groundball	.244	1797	438	80	10	40	188	136	275	.298	.366
Flyball	.235	837	197	38	6	25	106	88	156	.310	.385
Home	.245	2668	653	102	17	75	306	196	424	.297	.380
Away	.251	2780	697	126	20	83	326	252	455	.313	.400
Day	.246	1949	480	88	12	67	233	181	310	.312	.407
Night	.249	3499	870	140	25	91	399	267	569	.302	.381
Grass	.251	4155	1042	163	28	124	495	342	661	.308	.393
Turf	.238	1293	308	65	9	34	137	106	218	.298	.381
First Pitch	.288	902	260	49	7	29	105	35	0	.316	.455
Ahead in Count	.320	1240	397	60	13	62	227	227	0	.422	.540
Behind in Count	.184	2326	427	68	16	34	164	0	747	.187	.270
Two Strikes	.171	2267	388	66	12	37	161	186	879	.235	.260

	Avg	AB	H	2B	3B	HR	RBI	BB	SO	OBP	SLG
Scoring Posn	.256	1191	305	44	13	35	467	149	213	.332	.403
Close & Late	.227	1008	229	36	8	25	113	95	195	.292	.353
None on/out	.256	1424	365	68	12	43	43	88	212	.301	.412
Leadoff	.256	688	176	28	11	9	50	36	122	.295	.368
Batting #3	.276	652	180	28	2	24	99	44	71	.319	.436
Cleanup	.260	601	156	28	3	37	98	83	105	.344	.501
April	.229	690	158	24	6	15	84	82	118	.313	.346
May	.236	905	214	42	4	24	103	72	140	.294	.371
June	.257	930	239	37	6	22	97	53	145	.298	.381
July	.264	904	239	34	4	32	117	84	143	.324	.417
August	.243	971	236	43	12	34	117	80	143	.302	.417
September/October	.252	1048	264	48	5	31	114	77	190	.304	.396
Pre-All Star	.249	2906	723	119	19	73	344	246	467	.308	.378
Post-All Star	.247	2542	627	109	18	85	288	202	412	.302	.404

	ERA	W	L	Sv	Opp	G	IP	BB	SO	Avg	H	2B	3B	HR	RBI	OBP	SLG	CG	ShO	Sup	QS	#P/S	SB	CS	GB	FB	G/F
1993 Season	4.05	59	103	22	43	162	1438.0	434	867	.269	1483	275	29	139	700	.324	.404	16	8	4.21	94	97	143	56	2058	1435	1.43

1993 Pitching

	ERA	W	L	Sv	G	GS	IP	H	HR	BB	SO
Home	3.95	28	53	9	221	81	739.0	746	72	220	454
Away	4.16	31	50	13	238	81	699.0	737	67	214	413
Day	3.64	21	37	8	161	58	516.1	486	45	152	292
Night	4.28	38	66	14	298	104	921.2	997	94	282	575
Grass	4.04	47	77	14	341	124	1110.2	1147	107	335	679
Turf	4.07	12	26	8	118	38	327.1	336	32	99	188
April	3.69	8	13	3	58	21	187.2	189	19	55	94
May	4.03	9	18	2	84	27	238.2	272	15	87	155
June	4.75	6	21	1	81	27	237.0	264	28	70	157
July	4.36	12	16	6	72	28	243.2	264	25	58	141
August	4.12	11	18	7	81	29	257.2	237	31	63	161
September/October	3.36	13	17	3	83	30	273.1	257	21	101	159
Starters	3.88	45	76	0	162	162	1064.1	1069	108	281	634
Relievers	4.53	14	27	22	297	0	373.2	414	31	153	233
0-3 Days Rest (SP)	2.93	4	4	0	11	11	70.2	68	6	21	36
4 Days Rest	4.05	26	44	0	94	94	622.1	624	65	164	372
5+ Days Rest	3.78	15	28	0	57	57	371.1	377	37	96	226
Pre-All Star	4.42	27	60	8	253	87	767.1	861	74	236	465
Post-All Star	3.62	32	43	14	206	75	670.2	622	65	198	402

	Avg	AB	H	2B	3B	HR	RBI	BB	SO	OBP	SLG
vs. Left	.267	2027	542	99	12	41	234	207	347	.336	.389
vs. Right	.269	3495	941	176	17	98	466	227	520	.317	.413
Inning 1-6	.265	3727	989	190	22	97	461	274	583	.319	.406
Inning 7+	.275	1795	494	85	7	42	239	160	284	.336	.401
None on	.256	3230	827	155	16	81	81	199	517	.304	.389
Runners on	.286	2292	656	120	13	58	619	235	350	.352	.426
Scoring Posn	.282	1378	388	74	7	29	531	188	225	.363	.409
Close & Late	.292	870	254	42	2	25	138	88	136	.358	.431
None on/out	.257	1404	361	73	9	33	33	82	205	.302	.392
vs. 1st Batr (relief)	.248	262	65	12	2	5	31	21	43	.307	.366
First Inning Pitched	.264	1608	424	83	7	32	245	158	254	.332	.384
First 75 Pitches (SP)	.268	4466	1199	216	23	109	559	356	698	.325	.400
Pitch 76-90	.278	489	136	33	4	17	76	42	80	.337	.466
Pitch 91-105	.259	351	91	18	2	7	38	21	49	.303	.382
Pitch 106+	.264	216	57	8	0	6	27	15	40	.315	.384
First Pitch	.304	863	262	48	3	30	139	51	0	.341	.470
Ahead in Count	.213	2450	521	98	11	39	242	0	751	.224	.309
Behind in Count	.345	1269	438	85	8	58	217	202	0	.432	.562
Two Strikes	.199	2320	461	81	8	30	207	181	867	.264	.279

Games Finished: 146 Inherited Runners: 146 Inherited Runners Scored: 60 Holds: 19

Philadelphia Phillies

1993 Record: 97 – 65

	Avg	G	AB	R	H	2B	3B	HR	RBI	BB	SO	HBP	GDP	SB	CS	OBP	SLG	IBB	SH	SF	#Pit	#P/PA	GB	FB	G/F
1993 Season	.274	162	5685	877	1555	297	51	156	811	665	1049	42	107	91	32	.351	.426	70	84	51	23774	3.64	2133	1426	1.50

1993 Batting

	Avg	AB	H	2B	3B	HR	RBI	BB	SO	OBP	SLG
vs. Left	.280	1889	528	93	18	66	271	202	345	.350	.453
vs. Right	.271	3796	1027	204	33	90	540	463	704	.352	.413
Groundball	.272	1945	530	102	19	53	285	229	346	.351	.426
Flyball	.266	922	245	48	6	29	142	106	194	.341	.425
Home	.276	2793	771	143	26	80	407	322	499	.353	.432
Away	.271	2892	784	154	25	76	404	343	550	.349	.420
Day	.282	1619	456	80	13	46	235	184	328	.355	.432
Night	.270	4066	1099	217	38	110	576	481	721	.350	.424
Grass	.274	1761	483	89	12	55	257	204	329	.350	.432
Turf	.273	3924	1072	208	39	101	554	461	720	.351	.423
First Pitch	.337	810	273	63	8	26	149	60	0	.379	.531
Ahead in Count	.367	1265	464	80	19	64	259	343	0	.499	.612
Behind in Count	.197	2557	504	89	15	36	242	0	893	.205	.286
Two Strikes	.187	2534	473	88	15	31	234	262	1049	.268	.270

	Avg	AB	H	2B	3B	HR	RBI	BB	SO	OBP	SLG
Scoring Posn	.261	1632	426	76	16	41	632	278	325	.364	.403
Close & Late	.258	888	229	38	5	28	150	122	179	.346	.407
None on/out	.300	1367	410	84	9	41	41	152	239	.373	.465
Leadoff	.301	655	197	45	6	19	67	131	66	.416	.475
Batting #3	.314	640	201	36	6	19	99	112	106	.415	.478
Cleanup	.268	630	169	36	4	19	105	95	131	.365	.429
April	.246	759	187	43	4	22	102	99	142	.337	.401
May	.271	936	254	58	5	30	153	110	170	.347	.440
June	.279	950	265	51	15	25	135	110	197	.356	.443
July	.279	1021	285	40	7	27	139	116	171	.355	.411
August	.287	963	276	54	14	36	150	112	182	.364	.484
September/October	.273	1056	288	51	6	16	132	118	187	.345	.378
Pre-All Star	.269	3108	835	175	27	90	454	367	580	.347	.429
Post-All Star	.279	2577	720	122	24	66	357	298	469	.356	.422

	ERA	W	L	Sv	Opp	G	IP	BB	SO	Avg	H	2B	3B	HR	RBI	OBP	SLG	CG	ShO	Sup	QS	#P/S	SB	CS	GB	FB	G/F
1993 Season	3.95	97	65	46	70	162	1472.2	573	1117	.252	1419	247	39	129	673	.322	.378	24	11	5.36	92	101	101	49	1936	1549	1.25

1993 Pitching

	ERA	W	L	Sv	G	GS	IP	H	HR	BB	SO
Home	3.89	52	29	21	257	81	755.0	725	57	268	629
Away	4.05	45	36	25	255	81	717.2	694	72	305	488
Day	4.25	26	20	14	153	46	406.1	394	43	167	311
Night	3.86	71	45	32	359	116	1066.1	1025	86	406	806
Grass	3.68	30	19	15	143	49	435.2	415	44	171	271
Turf	4.09	67	46	31	369	113	1037.0	1004	85	402	846
April	3.25	17	5	11	75	22	205.0	173	18	86	165
May	3.55	17	10	5	68	27	241.0	224	14	93	155
June	3.90	18	10	9	82	28	249.0	242	22	82	187
July	4.50	14	14	5	93	28	262.0	278	26	106	183
August	4.37	16	11	8	90	27	245.1	249	26	88	202
September/October	4.06	15	15	8	104	30	270.1	253	23	118	225
Starters	3.95	69	42	0	162	162	1040.2	1027	88	346	749
Relievers	4.00	28	23	46	350	0	432.0	392	41	227	368
0-3 Days Rest (SP)	0.72	2	0	0	4	4	25.0	11	2	5	23
4 Days Rest	3.93	39	22	0	83	83	543.0	557	46	164	383
5+ Days Rest	4.15	28	20	0	75	75	472.2	459	40	177	343
Pre-All Star	3.91	57	32	25	270	89	814.0	794	65	309	591
Post-All Star	4.03	40	33	21	242	73	658.2	625	64	264	526

	Avg	AB	H	2B	3B	HR	RBI	BB	SO	OBP	SLG
vs. Left	.261	2109	550	92	16	51	268	246	406	.340	.392
vs. Right	.246	3533	869	155	23	78	405	327	711	.312	.369
Inning 1-6	.254	3732	949	165	30	92	448	358	723	.321	.389
Inning 7+	.246	1910	470	82	9	37	225	215	394	.326	.357
None on	.245	3195	784	136	19	76	76	280	637	.310	.371
Runners on	.260	2447	635	111	20	53	597	293	480	.337	.386
Scoring Posn	.257	1429	367	72	14	36	541	204	300	.345	.402
Close & Late	.245	989	242	41	3	19	143	131	218	.336	.350
None on/out	.243	1393	338	69	7	34	34	119	279	.307	.375
vs. 1st Batr (relief)	.219	297	65	13	0	5	25	49	76	.334	.313
First Inning Pitched	.248	1782	442	83	14	39	270	262	394	.348	.376
First 75 Pitches (SP)	.246	4447	1094	191	30	100	532	482	910	.322	.370
Pitch 76-90	.262	519	136	23	5	14	58	41	88	.322	.407
Pitch 91-105	.287	394	113	17	1	11	52	30	62	.336	.419
Pitch 106+	.270	282	76	16	3	4	31	20	57	.315	.390
First Pitch	.314	780	245	40	11	25	121	28	0	.342	.490
Ahead in Count	.193	2726	526	92	17	36	229	0	971	.197	.279
Behind in Count	.327	1164	381	70	7	36	184	290	0	.460	.492
Two Strikes	.178	2692	478	85	14	41	236	255	1117	.251	.265

Games Finished: 138   Inherited Runners: 192   Inherited Runners Scored: 63   Holds: 59

Pittsburgh Pirates

1993 Record: 75 – 87

	Avg	G	AB	R	H	2B	3B	HR	RBI	BB	SO	HBP	GDP	SB	CS	OBP	SLG	IBB	SH	SF	#Pit	#P/PA	GB	FB	G/F
1993 Season	.267	162	5549	707	1482	267	50	110	664	536	972	55	129	92	55	.335	.393	50	76	52	22585	3.60	2057	1613	1.28

1993 Batting

	Avg	AB	H	2B	3B	HR	RBI	BB	SO	OBP	SLG
vs. Left	.271	1756	475	98	14	23	182	176	280	.339	.382
vs. Right	.265	3793	1007	169	36	87	482	360	692	.333	.398
Groundball	.268	1796	482	72	13	26	200	155	304	.329	.366
Flyball	.241	854	206	44	11	25	103	92	163	.315	.406
Home	.260	2719	708	131	25	64	346	277	485	.330	.398
Away	.273	2830	774	136	25	46	318	259	487	.340	.388
Day	.260	1467	382	76	10	26	158	137	242	.328	.379
Night	.269	4082	1100	191	40	84	506	399	730	.337	.398
Grass	.283	1773	502	77	17	31	211	169	298	.350	.398
Turf	.260	3776	980	190	33	79	453	367	674	.327	.390
First Pitch	.341	810	276	35	10	25	146	40	0	.375	.501
Ahead in Count	.319	1287	411	78	14	34	188	264	0	.435	.481
Behind in Count	.208	2429	505	87	18	30	203	0	827	.216	.296
Two Strikes	.192	2371	455	90	15	29	183	232	972	.268	.279

	Avg	AB	H	2B	3B	HR	RBI	BB	SO	OBP	SLG
Scoring Posn	.261	1442	377	69	12	22	520	221	270	.355	.372
Close & Late	.266	987	263	37	5	19	121	117	209	.346	.372
None on/out	.267	1370	366	68	13	30	30	119	228	.332	.401
Leadoff	.261	702	183	24	10	16	58	43	100	.308	.392
Batting #3	.287	649	186	27	5	15	84	75	116	.362	.413
Cleanup	.288	626	180	43	2	8	100	79	61	.367	.401
April	.271	780	211	34	9	8	94	73	132	.336	.368
May	.259	895	232	42	11	19	113	87	156	.329	.394
June	.257	921	237	39	5	18	103	90	159	.323	.369
July	.268	947	254	53	6	15	100	94	185	.338	.384
August	.291	988	288	54	7	25	133	82	159	.352	.436
September/October	.255	1018	260	45	12	25	121	110	181	.329	.397
Pre-All Star	.265	3013	799	147	27	55	366	277	529	.329	.387
Post-All Star	.269	2536	683	120	23	55	298	259	443	.341	.400

Pittsburgh Pirates

	ERA	W	L	Sv	Opp	G	IP	BB	SO	Avg	H	2B	3B	HR	RBI	OBP	SLG	CG	ShO	Sup	QS	#P/S	SB	CS	GB	FB	G/F
1993 Season	4.77	75	87	34	50	162	1445.2	485	832	.280	1557	317	50	153	767	.339	.437	12	5	4.40	74	90	148	51	2044	1738	1.18

1993 Pitching

	ERA	W	L	Sv	G	GS	IP	H	HR	BB	SO
Home	4.36	40	41	13	277	81	751.0	791	67	240	419
Away	5.21	35	46	21	269	81	694.2	766	86	245	413
Day	4.42	21	22	9	140	43	382.2	405	41	106	232
Night	4.89	54	65	25	406	119	1063.0	1152	112	379	600
Grass	4.69	26	24	16	167	50	436.0	462	46	146	263
Turf	4.80	49	63	18	379	112	1009.2	1095	107	339	569
April	4.72	11	11	8	79	22	204.0	204	23	83	136
May	4.92	12	14	5	84	26	234.1	268	18	82	141
June	4.33	14	14	6	85	28	243.0	234	22	82	148
July	5.35	10	18	5	90	28	244.0	290	32	82	126
August	5.39	15	13	5	100	28	254.0	293	40	68	140
September/October	3.95	13	17	5	108	30	266.1	268	18	88	141
Starters	4.78	46	64	0	162	162	954.0	1046	101	323	483
Relievers	4.74	29	23	34	384	0	491.2	511	52	162	349
0-3 Days Rest (SP)	5.21	1	3	0	9	9	46.2	57	4	22	16
4 Days Rest	5.16	23	34	0	78	78	464.0	520	62	143	211
5+ Days Rest	4.34	22	27	0	75	75	443.1	469	35	158	256
Pre-All Star	4.85	42	46	22	287	88	783.1	834	78	280	485
Post-All Star	4.67	33	41	12	259	74	662.1	723	75	205	347

	Avg	AB	H	2B	3B	HR	RBI	BB	SO	OBP	SLG
vs. Left	.283	1948	552	103	18	52	291	215	306	.356	.435
vs. Right	.278	3619	1005	214	32	101	476	270	526	.330	.438
Inning 1-6	.286	3751	1072	226	31	108	530	328	522	.344	.449
Inning 7+	.267	1816	485	91	19	45	237	157	310	.329	.412
None on	.270	3143	849	180	25	89	89	251	481	.328	.428
Runners on	.292	2424	708	137	25	64	678	234	351	.354	.448
Scoring Posn	.294	1461	430	90	19	38	600	180	238	.366	.460
Close & Late	.255	912	233	45	8	24	131	84	153	.320	.401
None on/out	.274	1403	385	82	15	46	46	105	203	.328	.453
vs. 1st Batr (relief)	.267	344	92	11	5	8	38	28	64	.323	.398
First Inning Pitched	.275	1831	504	80	16	49	293	170	302	.337	.417
First 75 Pitches (SP)	.279	4733	1321	260	44	119	637	413	734	.340	.428
Pitch 76-90	.279	430	120	37	2	17	64	31	48	.323	.493
Pitch 91-105	.291	261	76	12	3	12	45	21	30	.344	.498
Pitch 106+	.280	143	40	8	1	5	21	20	20	.370	.455
First Pitch	.347	804	279	53	6	33	129	33	0	.378	.551
Ahead in Count	.202	2287	462	90	15	39	212	0	705	.208	.306
Behind in Count	.349	1455	508	108	19	48	281	258	0	.443	.548
Two Strikes	.189	2267	429	91	14	37	213	194	832	.258	.291

Games Finished: 150 Inherited Runners: 215 Inherited Runners Scored: 73 Holds: 31

St. Louis Cardinals

1993 Record: 87 – 75

	Avg	G	AB	R	H	2B	3B	HR	RBI	BB	SO	HBP	GDP	SB	CS	OBP	SLG	IBB	SH	SF	#Pit	#P/PA	GB	FB	G/F
1993 Season	.272	162	5551	758	1508	262	34	118	724	588	882	27	128	153	72	.341	.395	50	59	54	23071	3.67	2113	1613	1.31

1993 Batting

	Avg	AB	H	2B	3B	HR	RBI	BB	SO	OBP	SLG
vs. Left	.284	1477	419	65	7	41	202	144	209	.347	.420
vs. Right	.267	4074	1089	197	27	77	522	444	673	.339	.386
Groundball	.281	1784	502	83	5	27	228	186	267	.348	.379
Flyball	.252	979	247	40	8	25	116	104	180	.323	.386
Home	.279	2660	741	125	18	59	359	280	394	.348	.406
Away	.265	2891	767	137	16	59	365	308	488	.335	.385
Day	.275	1707	469	96	12	29	227	183	276	.345	.396
Night	.270	3844	1039	166	22	89	497	405	606	.340	.394
Grass	.272	1792	488	91	7	36	230	202	301	.344	.391
Turf	.271	3759	1020	171	27	82	494	386	581	.340	.397
First Pitch	.309	741	229	32	5	20	120	30	0	.337	.447
Ahead in Count	.321	1360	436	76	12	39	224	308	0	.442	.480
Behind in Count	.224	2381	533	81	10	34	248	0	746	.226	.309
Two Strikes	.206	2415	497	90	11	31	244	250	882	.282	.291

	Avg	AB	H	2B	3B	HR	RBI	BB	SO	OBP	SLG
Scoring Posn	.286	1502	430	78	10	36	599	233	258	.374	.423
Close & Late	.272	963	262	46	8	15	123	121	171	.352	.383
None on/out	.270	1362	368	73	9	28	28	125	218	.334	.399
Leadoff	.290	679	197	48	4	14	67	71	105	.359	.434
Batting #3	.332	645	214	28	5	22	98	72	51	.397	.493
Cleanup	.277	613	170	31	2	19	106	91	113	.371	.427
April	.245	773	189	18	7	15	82	87	127	.319	.344
May	.253	882	223	27	4	8	99	90	138	.322	.320
June	.297	930	276	63	8	21	141	89	146	.359	.449
July	.298	940	280	48	6	27	140	90	155	.358	.448
August	.259	964	250	44	5	23	114	112	133	.336	.387
September/October	.273	1062	290	62	4	24	148	120	183	.348	.407
Pre-All Star	.271	2964	804	125	23	53	378	292	481	.336	.383
Post-All Star	.272	2587	704	137	11	65	346	296	401	.347	.409

	ERA	W	L	Sv	Opp	G	IP	BB	SO	Avg	H	2B	3B	HR	RBI	OBP	SLG	CG	ShO	Sup	QS	#P/S	SB	CS	GB	FB	G/F
1993 Season	4.09	87	75	54	78	162	1453.0	383	775	.276	1553	282	44	152	693	.324	.422	5	7	4.70	92	87	112	54	2198	1602	1.37

1993 Pitching

	ERA	W	L	Sv	G	GS	IP	H	HR	BB	SO
Home	3.51	49	32	26	274	81	733.0	751	59	171	388
Away	4.70	38	43	28	311	81	720.0	802	93	212	387
Day	3.85	31	19	20	182	50	446.2	470	51	95	260
Night	4.21	56	56	34	403	112	1006.1	1083	101	288	515
Grass	4.43	27	23	22	199	50	449.1	491	63	133	254
Turf	3.95	60	52	32	386	112	1003.2	1062	89	250	521
April	3.41	13	10	11	80	23	211.1	209	18	55	121
May	3.63	12	14	6	86	26	233.1	231	26	62	122
June	3.84	20	7	16	98	27	239.0	254	18	51	129
July	5.49	14	13	8	102	27	237.2	294	35	67	127
August	4.25	13	16	8	98	29	260.2	284	31	67	119
September/October	3.92	15	15	5	121	30	271.0	281	24	81	157
Starters	4.03	61	49	0	162	162	973.1	1051	99	226	475
Relievers	4.24	26	26	54	423	0	479.2	502	53	157	300
0-3 Days Rest (SP)	3.72	2	1	0	8	8	48.1	49	6	10	27
4 Days Rest	4.24	38	31	0	101	101	598.1	662	63	139	305
5+ Days Rest	3.69	21	17	0	53	53	326.2	340	30	77	143
Pre-All Star	3.69	51	36	34	302	87	779.2	793	75	187	422
Post-All Star	4.57	36	39	20	283	75	673.1	760	77	196	353

	Avg	AB	H	2B	3B	HR	RBI	BB	SO	OBP	SLG
vs. Left	.274	1968	540	87	15	47	235	148	275	.326	.405
vs. Right	.276	3664	1013	195	29	105	458	235	500	.322	.431
Inning 1-6	.280	3781	1057	199	24	102	465	244	504	.326	.426
Inning 7+	.268	1851	496	83	20	50	228	139	271	.320	.415
None on	.273	3273	895	175	26	87	87	174	458	.313	.423
Runners on	.279	2359	658	107	18	65	606	209	317	.338	.422
Scoring Posn	.264	1402	370	58	13	42	536	166	224	.339	.414
Close & Late	.252	994	250	38	12	27	119	77	155	.305	.395
None on/out	.284	1420	403	73	10	31	31	79	171	.324	.415
vs. 1st Batr (relief)	.271	388	105	17	3	11	49	30	64	.321	.415
First Inning Pitched	.287	1968	564	90	19	60	307	170	301	.342	.443
First 75 Pitches (SP)	.274	4901	1343	239	39	134	606	335	701	.323	.421
Pitch 76-90	.280	447	125	23	1	12	58	32	45	.325	.416
Pitch 91-105	.319	216	69	14	4	3	21	10	17	.351	.463
Pitch 106+	.235	68	16	6	0	3	8	6	12	.307	.456
First Pitch	.345	940	324	64	10	32	133	45	0	.375	.536
Ahead in Count	.212	2352	498	86	19	35	189	0	683	.218	.309
Behind in Count	.329	1350	444	79	11	61	239	192	0	.411	.539
Two Strikes	.198	2230	441	84	17	34	174	145	775	.251	.296

Games Finished: 157 Inherited Runners: 252 Inherited Runners Scored: 82 Holds: 61

San Diego Padres

1993 Record: 61 – 101

	Avg	G	AB	R	H	2B	3B	HR	RBI	BB	SO	HBP	GDP	SB	CS	OBP	SLG	IBB	SH	SF	#Pit	#P/PA	GB	FB	G/F
1993 Season	.252	162	5503	679	1386	239	28	153	633	443	1046	59	111	92	41	.312	.389	43	80	50	22101	3.60	1973	1334	1.48

1993 Batting

	Avg	AB	H	2B	3B	HR	RBI	BB	SO	OBP	SLG
vs. Left	.268	1692	453	79	6	49	202	150	287	.328	.408
vs. Right	.245	3811	933	160	22	104	431	293	759	.305	.380
Groundball	.245	1858	456	83	12	49	207	160	327	.311	.382
Flyball	.255	928	237	43	3	33	120	64	194	.309	.415
Home	.255	2748	701	105	14	87	322	223	526	.316	.398
Away	.249	2755	685	134	14	66	311	220	520	.308	.379
Day	.251	1788	449	80	9	58	206	130	327	.309	.403
Night	.252	3715	937	159	19	95	427	313	719	.313	.382
Grass	.258	4257	1097	176	19	121	499	335	796	.316	.393
Turf	.232	1246	289	63	9	32	134	108	250	.298	.374
First Pitch	.314	795	250	48	4	30	116	31	0	.340	.498
Ahead in Count	.328	1215	398	68	7	60	204	211	0	.426	.543
Behind in Count	.184	2520	464	68	14	36	208	0	894	.195	.265
Two Strikes	.168	2458	414	66	8	34	178	201	1046	.237	.243

	Avg	AB	H	2B	3B	HR	RBI	BB	SO	OBP	SLG
Scoring Posn	.256	1288	330	60	8	33	457	159	268	.335	.392
Close & Late	.234	997	233	30	1	27	119	94	228	.307	.347
None on/out	.251	1394	350	64	8	29	29	95	253	.305	.371
Leadoff	.266	661	176	39	5	4	46	70	114	.347	.359
Batting #3	.299	662	198	42	3	17	89	43	80	.343	.449
Cleanup	.265	600	159	23	1	39	107	84	115	.359	.502
April	.251	760	191	33	3	24	82	58	151	.307	.397
May	.264	938	248	44	2	23	105	80	145	.327	.389
June	.246	947	233	33	6	20	85	75	179	.305	.357
July	.257	927	238	47	8	29	120	82	171	.319	.419
August	.283	963	273	48	3	34	133	76	164	.340	.445
September/October	.210	968	203	34	6	23	108	72	236	.273	.329
Pre-All Star	.254	3027	768	133	15	75	321	238	542	.311	.382
Post-All Star	.250	2476	618	106	13	78	312	205	504	.312	.397

	ERA	W	L	Sv	Opp	G	IP	BB	SO	Avg	H	2B	3B	HR	RBI	OBP	SLG	CG	ShO	Sup	QS	#P/S	SB	CS	GB	FB	G/F
1993 Season	4.23	61	101	32	51	162	1437.2	558	957	.266	1470	238	40	148	716	.334	.404	8	6	4.25	67	91	142	68	1942	1474	1.32

1993 Pitching

	ERA	W	L	Sv	G	GS	IP	H	HR	BB	SO
Home	3.81	34	47	12	289	81	752.0	725	79	258	527
Away	4.69	27	54	20	270	81	685.2	745	69	300	430
Day	4.10	19	33	13	176	52	463.1	475	55	174	309
Night	4.29	42	68	19	383	110	974.1	995	93	384	648
Grass	4.15	50	75	22	435	125	1126.0	1136	126	421	762
Turf	4.50	11	26	10	124	37	311.2	334	22	137	195
April	3.91	10	12	7	84	22	202.2	196	12	78	119
May	4.48	10	18	3	93	28	243.0	258	24	87	150
June	3.80	9	19	4	92	28	249.0	258	27	74	184
July	4.36	11	16	7	84	27	239.1	236	27	110	155
August	4.11	12	15	6	96	27	241.0	242	25	97	152
September/October	4.63	9	21	5	110	30	262.2	280	33	112	197
Starters	4.53	42	72	0	162	162	939.0	973	111	341	559
Relievers	3.65	19	29	32	397	0	498.2	497	37	217	398
0-3 Days Rest (SP)	5.91	0	5	0	7	7	35.0	53	3	14	17
4 Days Rest	4.25	29	46	0	105	105	638.0	637	77	213	402
5+ Days Rest	5.04	13	21	0	50	50	266.0	283	31	114	140
Pre-All Star	4.19	33	56	17	305	89	788.1	820	73	286	503
Post-All Star	4.27	28	45	15	254	73	649.1	650	75	272	454

	Avg	AB	H	2B	3B	HR	RBI	BB	SO	OBP	SLG
vs. Left	.271	2633	713	99	20	73	349	316	399	.348	.407
vs. Right	.262	2887	757	139	20	75	367	242	558	.321	.402
Inning 1-6	.263	3717	976	163	23	104	489	367	615	.329	.403
Inning 7+	.274	1803	494	75	17	44	227	191	342	.344	.408
None on	.265	3065	811	143	25	94	94	257	536	.326	.420
Runners on	.268	2455	659	95	15	54	622	301	421	.344	.385
Scoring Posn	.264	1479	391	60	9	33	557	235	258	.356	.384
Close & Late	.279	838	234	35	7	17	101	96	154	.354	.399
None on/out	.284	1392	396	72	11	45	45	97	218	.335	.449
vs. 1st Batr (relief)	.273	362	99	19	4	10	57	29	66	.325	.431
First Inning Pitched	.253	1882	477	71	14	39	277	226	362	.332	.368
First 75 Pitches (SP)	.264	4720	1247	195	32	106	581	473	836	.332	.386
Pitch 76-90	.254	445	113	23	4	23	78	47	68	.325	.479
Pitch 91-105	.318	274	87	15	3	16	45	26	40	.375	.569
Pitch 106+	.284	81	23	5	1	3	12	12	13	.368	.481
First Pitch	.319	795	254	34	7	23	132	49	0	.358	.467
Ahead in Count	.209	2435	508	80	13	42	226	0	795	.213	.304
Behind in Count	.340	1239	421	78	12	52	223	280	0	.458	.548
Two Strikes	.185	2440	452	72	15	45	207	229	957	.258	.282

Games Finished: 154 Inherited Runners: 265 Inherited Runners Scored: 89 Holds: 30

San Francisco Giants

1993 Record: 103 – 59

	Avg	G	AB	R	H	2B	3B	HR	RBI	BB	SO	HBP	GDP	SB	CS	OBP	SLG	IBB	SH	SF	#Pit	#P/PA	GB	FB	G/F
1993 Season	.276	162	5557	808	1534	269	33	168	759	516	930	46	121	120	65	.340	.427	88	102	50	22084	3.52	2034	1600	1.27

1993 Batting

	Avg	AB	H	2B	3B	HR	RBI	BB	SO	OBP	SLG
vs. Left	.296	1798	532	101	10	56	258	164	282	.353	.457
vs. Right	.267	3759	1002	168	23	112	501	352	648	.333	.413
Groundball	.290	1751	507	74	5	52	239	143	273	.346	.427
Flyball	.269	887	239	56	9	24	132	83	165	.333	.434
Home	.266	2663	708	127	13	82	338	227	433	.326	.416
Away	.285	2894	826	142	20	86	421	289	497	.352	.437
Day	.271	2717	735	133	15	95	384	250	442	.334	.435
Night	.281	2840	799	136	18	73	375	266	488	.345	.419
Grass	.273	4232	1157	197	24	129	549	386	707	.336	.423
Turf	.285	1325	377	72	9	39	210	130	223	.351	.441
First Pitch	.324	882	286	45	7	31	146	76	0	.376	.497
Ahead in Count	.343	1220	419	86	7	58	222	251	0	.455	.568
Behind in Count	.229	2492	570	97	13	50	266	0	792	.234	.338
Two Strikes	.196	2392	470	75	12	42	208	189	930	.259	.291

	Avg	AB	H	2B	3B	HR	RBI	BB	SO	OBP	SLG
Scoring Posn	.280	1468	411	80	12	34	560	206	249	.362	.420
Close & Late	.252	811	204	33	4	26	95	57	152	.301	.398
None on/out	.284	1392	395	81	8	45	45	100	212	.338	.450
Leadoff	.252	707	178	21	5	4	53	44	75	.301	.313
Batting #3	.287	635	182	35	2	24	98	84	97	.372	.461
Cleanup	.288	660	190	39	4	45	132	40	90	.327	.564
April	.265	829	220	42	6	20	110	85	141	.332	.403
May	.294	950	279	43	11	26	128	85	154	.356	.444
June	.278	935	260	48	0	32	126	83	157	.338	.432
July	.296	903	267	51	4	27	143	78	130	.357	.451
August	.270	919	248	38	7	32	133	82	167	.332	.431
September/October	.255	1021	260	47	5	31	119	103	181	.324	.402
Pre-All Star	.288	3087	890	159	18	89	439	289	504	.351	.438
Post-All Star	.261	2470	644	110	15	79	320	227	426	.325	.413

San Francisco Giants

	ERA	W	L	Sv	Opp	G	IP	BB	SO	Avg	H	2B	3B	HR	RBI	OBP	SLG	CG	ShO	Sup	QS	#P/S	SB	CS	GB	FB	G/F
1993 Season	3.61	103	59	50	67	162	1456.2	442	982	.253	1385	185	23	168	605	.313	.387	4	9	4.99	86	88	81	66	1942	1601	1.21

1993 Pitching

	ERA	W	L	Sv	G	GS	IP	H	HR	BB	SO
Home	3.27	50	31	23	284	81	748.0	673	81	235	526
Away	4.00	53	28	27	292	81	708.2	712	87	207	456
Day	3.63	54	27	28	294	81	734.0	697	90	247	518
Night	3.62	49	32	22	282	81	722.2	688	78	195	464
Grass	3.59	78	47	41	448	125	1132.1	1062	133	357	781
Turf	3.75	25	12	9	128	37	324.1	323	35	85	201
April	3.70	15	9	8	90	24	216.2	192	22	85	142
May	3.32	18	9	6	96	27	247.0	224	28	71	151
June	2.85	19	9	10	91	28	249.2	228	16	61	175
July	3.80	18	8	8	89	26	232.0	227	28	70	153
August	4.64	15	11	8	93	26	234.2	254	47	58	168
September/October	3.55	18	13	10	117	31	276.2	260	27	97	193
Starters	3.72	82	43	0	162	162	980.2	972	111	277	583
Relievers	3.44	21	16	50	414	0	476.0	413	57	165	399
0-3 Days Rest (SP)	3.21	8	3	0	13	13	70.0	63	8	29	45
4 Days Rest	3.54	46	17	0	84	84	533.1	507	62	147	321
5+ Days Rest	4.05	28	23	0	65	65	377.1	402	41	101	217
Pre-All Star	3.42	59	30	25	313	89	796.1	742	80	242	522
Post-All Star	3.87	44	29	25	263	73	660.1	643	88	200	460

	Avg	AB	H	2B	3B	HR	RBI	BB	SO	OBP	SLG
vs. Left	.263	2279	599	79	10	71	263	195	384	.322	.400
vs. Right	.246	3193	786	106	13	97	342	247	598	.306	.379
Inning 1-6	.260	3641	948	129	16	112	409	297	596	.320	.397
Inning 7+	.239	1831	437	56	7	56	196	145	386	.298	.369
None on	.252	3214	811	111	11	97	97	246	603	.312	.384
Runners on	.254	2258	574	74	12	71	508	196	379	.313	.392
Scoring Posn	.250	1169	292	33	5	40	419	144	231	.329	.389
Close & Late	.226	893	202	27	4	20	101	73	188	.287	.333
None on/out	.262	1397	366	54	6	35	35	92	242	.315	.384
vs. 1st Batr (relief)	.236	382	90	9	1	11	50	24	92	.284	.351
First Inning Pitched	.237	1904	451	47	10	59	234	171	402	.304	.365
First 75 Pitches (SP)	.248	4763	1181	154	21	136	501	403	876	.310	.375
Pitch 76-90	.284	458	130	22	2	21	69	19	73	.316	.478
Pitch 91-105	.306	206	63	8	0	10	33	17	25	.363	.490
Pitch 106+	.244	45	11	1	0	1	2	3	8	.292	.333
First Pitch	.319	834	266	30	3	33	119	42	0	.362	.481
Ahead in Count	.185	2437	450	53	7	43	186	0	842	.192	.265
Behind in Count	.315	1209	381	62	8	55	187	225	0	.419	.516
Two Strikes	.176	2368	417	44	5	43	169	175	982	.238	.253

Games Finished: 158 Inherited Runners: 234 Inherited Runners Scored: 74 Holds: 84

Colorado Rockies

1993 Record: 67 – 95

	Avg	G	AB	R	H	2B	3B	HR	RBI	BB	SO	HBP	GDP	SB	CS	OBP	SLG	IBB	SH	SF	#Pit	#P/PA	GB	FB	G/F
1993 Season	.273	162	5517	758	1507	278	59	142	704	388	944	46	125	146	90	.323	.422	40	70	52	20619	3.40	2086	1423	1.47

1993 Batting

	Avg	AB	H	2B	3B	HR	RBI	BB	SO	OBP	SLG
vs. Left	.289	1282	370	78	17	31	170	79	216	.332	.449
vs. Right	.268	4235	1137	200	42	111	534	309	728	.321	.414
Groundball	.258	1878	484	100	20	33	218	115	326	.304	.385
Flyball	.261	955	249	49	8	24	108	69	177	.312	.404
Home	.306	2754	843	158	48	77	449	228	410	.361	.482
Away	.240	2763	664	120	11	65	255	160	534	.285	.362
Day	.266	1843	491	91	22	53	234	135	312	.320	.426
Night	.277	3674	1016	187	37	89	470	253	632	.325	.420
Grass	.278	4219	1174	218	52	111	573	308	698	.329	.434
Turf	.257	1298	333	60	7	31	131	80	246	.303	.385
First Pitch	.351	962	338	69	16	34	163	31	0	.375	.562
Ahead in Count	.337	1159	391	68	15	37	189	203	0	.432	.518
Behind in Count	.211	2502	527	101	17	46	246	0	845	.216	.320
Two Strikes	.183	2338	429	77	17	43	199	154	944	.238	.286

	Avg	AB	H	2B	3B	HR	RBI	BB	SO	OBP	SLG
Scoring Posn	.283	1327	376	71	16	39	558	148	249	.349	.449
Close & Late	.279	768	214	42	7	21	121	59	133	.330	.434
None on/out	.272	1414	385	78	18	37	37	73	230	.311	.431
Leadoff	.255	651	166	23	11	4	51	76	71	.334	.343
Batting #3	.294	656	193	47	3	25	105	36	113	.338	.489
Cleanup	.345	646	223	46	8	32	126	39	109	.383	.590
April	.274	734	201	34	8	16	97	59	99	.328	.407
May	.251	993	249	39	8	20	105	72	142	.308	.367
June	.298	853	254	51	6	23	126	64	172	.347	.453
July	.272	903	246	55	11	26	111	47	160	.310	.444
August	.248	1029	255	40	9	27	107	62	204	.293	.383
September/October	.300	1005	302	59	17	30	158	84	167	.358	.483
Pre-All Star	.273	2943	802	149	25	68	374	206	468	.323	.409
Post-All Star	.274	2574	705	129	34	74	330	182	476	.324	.437

	ERA	W	L	Sv	Opp	G	IP	BB	SO	Avg	H	2B	3B	HR	RBI	OBP	SLG	CG	ShO	Sup	QS	#P/S	SB	CS	GB	FB	G/F
1993 Season	5.41	67	95	35	55	162	1431.1	609	913	.294	1664	280	54	181	913	.362	.458	9	0	4.77	53	89	119	56	2116	1547	1.37

1993 Pitching

	ERA	W	L	Sv	G	GS	IP	H	HR	BB	SO
Home	5.87	39	42	16	322	81	733.0	907	107	320	483
Away	4.99	28	53	19	293	81	698.1	757	74	289	430
Day	5.24	24	32	14	211	56	487.1	551	54	207	319
Night	5.54	43	63	21	404	106	944.0	1113	127	402	594
Grass	5.50	53	72	24	469	125	1110.1	1316	149	462	713
Turf	5.24	14	23	11	146	37	321.0	348	32	147	200
April	4.78	8	14	1	75	22	192.0	219	15	92	116
May	7.03	7	22	4	110	29	258.2	343	38	119	164
June	5.89	11	14	5	89	25	218.2	271	31	85	136
July	5.91	10	17	6	105	27	236.0	286	37	88	145
August	4.29	14	16	11	108	30	266.2	276	28	122	161
September/October	4.72	17	12	8	128	29	259.1	269	32	103	191
Starters	5.49	37	73	0	162	162	878.2	1072	113	348	492
Relievers	5.36	30	22	35	453	0	552.2	592	68	261	421
0-3 Days Rest (SP)	5.51	0	2	0	7	7	32.2	46	3	8	23
4 Days Rest	5.66	25	48	0	99	99	547.0	671	75	216	320
5+ Days Rest	5.18	12	23	0	56	56	299.0	355	35	124	149
Pre-All Star	5.83	33	54	14	318	87	766.1	941	96	325	476
Post-All Star	4.99	34	41	21	297	75	665.0	723	85	284	437

	Avg	AB	H	2B	3B	HR	RBI	BB	SO	OBP	SLG
vs. Left	.296	2462	729	121	33	66	383	297	374	.372	.452
vs. Right	.292	3198	935	159	21	115	530	312	539	.355	.463
Inning 1-6	.300	3853	1155	202	32	121	624	406	582	.367	.463
Inning 7+	.282	1807	509	78	22	60	289	203	331	.353	.449
None on	.280	3038	851	150	25	95	95	273	502	.344	.440
Runners on	.310	2622	813	130	29	86	818	336	411	.383	.480
Scoring Posn	.292	1625	475	87	20	42	709	254	269	.376	.448
Close & Late	.270	730	197	28	8	21	113	85	135	.345	.416
None on/out	.292	1365	398	74	16	46	46	127	233	.355	.470
vs. 1st Batr (relief)	.258	391	101	18	5	9	53	50	77	.341	.399
First Inning Pitched	.283	2113	599	105	25	66	406	255	370	.357	.451
First 75 Pitches (SP)	.290	4909	1423	242	48	147	770	518	806	.357	.449
Pitch 76-90	.363	383	139	21	2	23	76	46	50	.429	.608
Pitch 91-105	.300	237	71	10	3	7	49	33	33	.382	.456
Pitch 106+	.237	131	31	7	1	4	18	12	24	.303	.397
First Pitch	.351	826	290	49	12	30	178	46	0	.382	.548
Ahead in Count	.224	2396	536	80	15	36	253	0	760	.230	.315
Behind in Count	.369	1373	506	95	15	67	294	324	0	.483	.606
Two Strikes	.211	2446	516	77	16	41	256	239	913	.284	.306

Games Finished: 153 Inherited Runners: 279 Inherited Runners Scored: 99 Holds: 29

Florida Marlins

1993 Record: 64 – 98

	Avg	G	AB	R	H	2B	3B	HR	RBI	BB	SO	HBP	GDP	SB	CS	OBP	SLG	IBB	SH	SF	#Pit	#P/PA	GB	FB	G/F
1993 Season	.248	162	5475	581	1356	197	31	94	542	498	1054	51	122	117	56	.314	.346	39	58	43	22278	3.64	1960	1450	1.35

1993 Batting

	Avg	AB	H	2B	3B	HR	RBI	BB	SO	OBP	SLG
vs. Left	.256	1571	402	68	11	28	166	156	302	.325	.367
vs. Right	.244	3904	954	129	20	66	376	342	752	.310	.338
Groundball	.241	1748	421	63	13	26	164	144	299	.303	.336
Flyball	.247	1044	258	41	6	16	101	93	245	.312	.344
Home	.251	2706	680	98	16	44	281	275	544	.324	.348
Away	.244	2769	676	99	15	50	261	223	510	.304	.345
Day	.246	1226	302	37	5	21	123	129	230	.321	.336
Night	.248	4249	1054	160	26	73	419	369	824	.312	.349
Grass	.245	4153	1016	152	21	75	421	416	827	.317	.346
Turf	.257	1322	340	45	10	19	121	82	227	.304	.349
First Pitch	.337	848	286	38	8	16	101	23	0	.361	.458
Ahead in Count	.330	1198	395	56	6	39	170	250	0	.442	.484
Behind in Count	.169	2453	415	69	11	21	168	0	901	.178	.232
Two Strikes	.156	2465	384	59	11	22	153	225	1054	.232	.215

	Avg	AB	H	2B	3B	HR	RBI	BB	SO	OBP	SLG
Scoring Posn	.242	1325	321	41	8	22	424	178	272	.331	.335
Close & Late	.242	985	238	31	7	11	105	119	214	.327	.321
None on/out	.241	1379	333	59	10	18	18	94	267	.296	.338
Leadoff	.265	680	180	23	2	6	50	59	89	.323	.331
Batting #3	.270	633	171	24	4	11	70	68	102	.343	.373
Cleanup	.276	627	173	25	6	20	100	51	123	.333	.431
April	.244	763	186	27	4	10	74	89	145	.324	.329
May	.246	890	219	36	4	10	93	98	162	.326	.329
June	.267	925	247	36	12	22	106	80	184	.326	.403
July	.240	899	216	42	3	16	91	59	185	.289	.347
August	.265	979	259	29	4	26	99	70	167	.318	.382
September/October	.225	1019	229	27	4	10	79	102	211	.302	.289
Pre-All Star	.251	2948	739	118	22	50	312	295	577	.322	.357
Post-All Star	.244	2527	617	79	9	44	230	203	477	.305	.335

	ERA	W	L	Sv	Opp	G	IP	BB	SO	Avg	H	2B	3B	HR	RBI	OBP	SLG	CG	ShO	Sup	QS	#P/S	SB	CS	GB	FB	G/F
1993 Season	4.13	64	98	48	62	162	1440.1	598	945	.261	1437	264	33	135	679	.334	.395	4	5	3.63	87	93	118	51	2014	1565	1.29

1993 Pitching

	ERA	W	L	Sv	G	GS	IP	H	HR	BB	SO
Home	4.16	35	46	25	298	81	750.0	748	72	308	525
Away	4.13	29	52	23	273	81	690.1	689	63	290	420
Day	3.16	16	20	12	126	36	319.0	290	24	127	210
Night	4.43	48	78	36	445	126	1121.1	1147	111	471	735
Grass	3.92	54	70	41	440	124	1119.1	1089	109	449	751
Turf	4.96	10	28	7	131	38	321.0	348	26	149	194
April	3.63	10	13	8	79	23	203.1	199	16	85	146
May	4.06	11	15	8	87	26	232.2	214	24	89	147
June	3.39	13	14	8	87	27	239.0	225	16	86	160
July	4.49	9	18	8	94	27	232.1	243	30	78	140
August	4.82	12	16	9	109	28	256.0	272	29	130	166
September/October	4.35	9	22	7	115	31	277.0	284	20	130	186
Starters	4.33	47	72	0	162	162	959.2	997	92	372	586
Relievers	3.78	17	26	48	409	0	480.2	440	43	226	359
0-3 Days Rest (SP)	3.12	1	2	0	4	4	26.0	26	0	9	13
4 Days Rest	4.60	28	40	0	98	98	569.1	605	59	228	366
5+ Days Rest	4.00	18	30	0	60	60	364.1	366	33	135	207
Pre-All Star	3.87	37	50	27	293	87	769.0	738	72	293	506
Post-All Star	4.46	27	48	21	278	75	671.1	699	63	305	439

	Avg	AB	H	2B	3B	HR	RBI	BB	SO	OBP	SLG
vs. Left	.259	2506	649	123	16	65	293	328	390	.345	.399
vs. Right	.263	2995	788	141	17	70	386	270	555	.326	.392
Inning 1-6	.270	3760	1017	190	28	90	476	386	607	.339	.408
Inning 7+	.241	1741	420	74	5	45	203	212	338	.324	.367
None on	.255	3061	781	136	19	76	76	296	525	.324	.386
Runners on	.269	2440	656	128	14	59	603	302	420	.346	.405
Scoring Posn	.248	1473	365	65	7	23	492	229	266	.343	.348
Close & Late	.237	985	233	36	4	21	109	121	201	.321	.345
None on/out	.268	1379	369	53	11	36	36	116	222	.328	.400
vs. 1st Batr (relief)	.279	373	104	18	1	14	55	29	67	.329	.445
First Inning Pitched	.257	1849	475	84	8	49	272	233	366	.339	.390
First 75 Pitches (SP)	.258	4655	1202	215	31	114	570	495	818	.330	.391
Pitch 76-90	.275	472	130	28	2	12	60	53	69	.353	.419
Pitch 91-105	.278	270	75	12	0	6	30	34	35	.363	.389
Pitch 106+	.288	104	30	9	0	3	19	16	23	.379	.462
First Pitch	.338	784	265	40	7	28	134	44	0	.375	.514
Ahead in Count	.210	2462	517	97	11	37	222	0	791	.213	.303
Behind in Count	.311	1267	394	73	8	41	193	319	0	.447	.478
Two Strikes	.195	2434	475	88	12	41	221	235	945	.268	.292

Games Finished: 158 Inherited Runners: 286 Inherited Runners Scored: 86 Holds: 38

Leader Boards

Here are the Leader Boards! We added a new feature this year, minimum cutoffs for each stat split. The minimums vary from stat to stat, but the cutoff level for each one is designed to keep all but regulars out of the list, but also take into account the frequency that the stat occurs. That is why the cutoff for "1st Pitch" is much higher than "Full Count".

One item to keep in mind is that, like last year, "Batting #9" includes American League players only. Orel Hershiser had a remarkable season at the plate in 1993, but don't expect to find him in this section.

1993 Batting Leaders

Overall
(Minimum 502 PA)

Player, Team	AB	H	AVG
A GALARRAGA, Col	**470**	**174**	**.370**
J Olerud, Tor	551	200	.363
T Gwynn, SD	489	175	.358
G Jefferies, StL	544	186	.342
B Bonds, SF	539	181	.336
P Molitor, Tor	636	211	.332
R Alomar, Tor	589	192	.326
K Lofton, Cle	569	185	.325
M Grace, ChN	594	193	.325
C Baerga, Cle	624	200	.321

LHP
(Minimum 150 PA)

Player, Team	AB	H	AVG
R MILLIGAN, Cle	**133**	**51**	**.383**
R Amaral, Sea	148	55	.372
P Molitor, Tor	171	62	.363
T Gwynn, SD	192	69	.359
M Blowers, Sea	154	55	.357
M Grace, ChN	193	68	.352
R Thompson, SF	145	51	.352
G Jefferies, StL	148	52	.351
J Bell, Pit	190	65	.342
A Cedeno, Hou	164	56	.341

RHP
(Minimum 200 PA)

Player, Team	AB	H	AVG
J OLERUD, Tor	**379**	**150**	**.396**
A Galarraga, Col	353	133	.377
R Alomar, Tor	423	152	.359
T Gwynn, SD	297	106	.357
A Trammell, Det	266	93	.350
B Kelly, Cin	224	78	.348
B Bonds, SF	321	110	.343
K Lofton, Cle	374	128	.342
P O'Neill, NYA	363	124	.342
C Hale, Min	179	61	.341

Home
(Minimum 175 PA)

Player, Team	AB	H	AVG
A GALARRAGA, Col	**266**	**107**	**.402**
T Gwynn, SD	254	97	.382
D Bichette, Col	260	97	.373
P Molitor, Tor	316	115	.364
D James, NYA	181	65	.359
M Grace, ChN	300	106	.353
K Mitchell, Cin	186	65	.349
B Butler, LA	291	101	.347
J Olerud, Tor	269	93	.346
H Baines, Bal	197	68	.345

Away
(Minimum 175 PA)

Player, Team	AB	H	AVG
J OLERUD, Tor	**282**	**107**	**.379**
B Bonds, SF	273	98	.359
A Van Slyke, Pit	170	61	.359
R Wilkins, ChN	208	74	.356
G Jefferies, StL	295	101	.342
B Kelly, Cin	168	57	.339
B Larkin, Cin	189	64	.339
K Lofton, Cle	291	98	.337
B Barberie, Fla	176	59	.335
T Gwynn, SD	235	78	.332

Groundball Pitchers
(Minimum 125 PA)

Player, Team	AB	H	AVG
K MITCHELL, Cin	**123**	**53**	**.431**
B Kelly, Cin	123	45	.366
B Bonds, SF	162	59	.364
J Blauser, Atl	212	75	.354
L Gonzalez, Hou	186	65	.349
R Sandberg, ChN	173	59	.341
G Jefferies, StL	168	57	.339
M Williams, SF	181	61	.337
B Larkin, Cin	150	50	.333
J Bagwell, Hou	181	60	.331

Grass
(Minimum 150 PA)

Player, Team	AB	H	AVG
J OLERUD, Tor	**225**	**90**	**.400**
T Gwynn, SD	371	141	.380
A Galarraga, Col	379	135	.356
G Jefferies, StL	189	66	.349
M Grace, ChN	451	156	.346
R Alomar, Tor	239	81	.339
J Bagwell, Hou	166	56	.337
B Bonds, SF	408	136	.333
J Bell, Pit	207	69	.333
D James, NYA	285	94	.330

Turf
(Minimum 150 PA)

Player, Team	AB	H	AVG
K MITCHELL, Cin	**227**	**79**	**.348**
B Bonds, SF	131	45	.344
G Jefferies, StL	355	120	.338
J Olerud, Tor	326	110	.337
P Molitor, Tor	387	130	.336
K Griffey Jr, Sea	347	115	.331
J King, Pit	415	135	.325
H Morris, Cin	260	84	.323
B Harper, Min	326	105	.322
J Kruk, Phi	356	113	.317

Flyball Pitchers
(Minimum 125 PA)

Player, Team	AB	H	AVG
B HATCHER, Bos	**121**	**46**	**.380**
K Griffey Jr, Sea	126	43	.341
J Buhner, Sea	124	42	.339
S Cooper, Bos	125	42	.336
D Mattingly, NYA	117	39	.333
P O'Neill, NYA	117	38	.325
T Phillips, Det	111	36	.324
F Thomas, ChA	118	38	.322
M McLemore, Bal	113	36	.319
J Cora, ChA	128	40	.313

Day
(Minimum 150 PA)

Player, Team	AB	H	AVG
D DeSHIELDS, Mon	**133**	**54**	**.406**
J Olerud, Tor	181	70	.387
D Justice, Atl	150	56	.373
M Piazza, LA	135	50	.370
A Galarraga, Col	163	59	.362
M Stanley, NYA	122	44	.361
T Gwynn, SD	165	58	.352
D White, Tor	202	69	.342
A Trammell, Det	141	48	.340
C Baerga, Cle	197	67	.340

Night
(Minimum 200 PA)

Player, Team	AB	H	AVG
R WILKINS, ChN	**214**	**84**	**.393**
A Galarraga, Col	307	115	.375
T Gwynn, SD	324	117	.361
B Bonds, SF	276	99	.359
J Olerud, Tor	370	130	.351
G Jefferies, StL	374	130	.348
R Alomar, Tor	405	140	.346
P Molitor, Tor	425	146	.344
J Bagwell, Hou	373	127	.340
J Eisenreich, Phi	274	92	.336

Scoring Position
(Minimum 100 PA)

Player, Team	AB	H	AVG
A GALARRAGA, Col	**128**	**54**	**.422**
P Molitor, Tor	190	73	.384
G Jefferies, StL	146	56	.384
J Olerud, Tor	140	52	.371
D Mattingly, NYA	125	46	.368
T Gwynn, SD	87	32	.368
L Johnson, ChA	118	43	.364
B Harper, Min	134	48	.358
B Bonds, SF	123	44	.358
M Greenwell, Bos	121	43	.355

1993 Batting Leaders

April
(Minimum 75 PA)

Player, Team	AB	H	AVG
J OLERUD, Tor	**80**	**36**	**.450**
B Bonds, SF	72	31	.431
A Galarraga, Col	85	35	.412
M Vaughn, Bos	68	28	.412
K Gibson, Det	59	24	.407
S Cooper, Bos	80	28	.350
T Phillips, Det	89	31	.348
J Vizcaino, ChN	75	26	.347
D Hamilton, Mil	78	27	.346
O Merced, Pit	67	23	.343

May
(Minimum 100 PA)

Player, Team	AB	H	AVG
J BAGWELL, Hou	**102**	**42**	**.412**
J Kruk, Phi	91	35	.385
W McGee, SF	96	36	.375
B Hatcher, Bos	104	39	.375
P Molitor, Tor	115	43	.374
K Lofton, Cle	102	38	.373
J Vizcaino, ChN	94	35	.372
B Bonds, SF	98	36	.367
M Grace, ChN	99	36	.364
A Van Slyke, Pit	105	38	.362

June
(Minimum 100 PA)

Player, Team	AB	H	AVG
G JEFFERIES, StL	**108**	**48**	**.444**
J Olerud, Tor	96	41	.427
A Galarraga, Col	100	42	.420
R Thompson, SF	98	39	.398
R Alomar, Tor	103	38	.369
J King, Pit	105	38	.362
G Sheffield, Fla	96	34	.354
K Griffey Jr, Sea	102	36	.353
F Thomas, ChA	103	36	.350
R Palmeiro, Tex	92	32	.348

July
(Minimum 100 PA)

Player, Team	AB	H	AVG
R PALMEIRO, Tex	**108**	**46**	**.426**
D DeShields, Mon	117	46	.393
S Mack, Min	102	40	.392
J Olerud, Tor	90	35	.389
R Henderson, Tor	91	35	.385
T Gwynn, SD	105	40	.381
W Joyner, KC	93	35	.376
L Dykstra, Phi	107	40	.374
L Gonzalez, Hou	95	35	.368
J Kruk, Phi	85	31	.365

August
(Minimum 100 PA)

Player, Team	AB	H	AVG
T GWYNN, SD	**105**	**47**	**.448**
R Thompson, SF	99	39	.394
J Bell, Pit	114	44	.386
R Alomar, Tor	111	40	.360
P Molitor, Tor	110	39	.355
B Bonds, SF	85	30	.353
J Bagwell, Hou	108	38	.352
J Blauser, Atl	103	36	.350
B Williams, NYA	109	38	.349
R Sandberg, ChN	112	39	.348

September-October
(Minimum 100 PA)

Player, Team	AB	H	AVG
M GREENWELL, Bos	**111**	**43**	**.387**
T Naehring, Bos	99	37	.374
C Hoiles, Bal	91	34	.374
K Lofton, Cle	92	34	.370
E Young, Col	84	31	.369
E Murray, NYN	115	42	.365
A Galarraga, Col	122	44	.361
R Alomar, Tor	84	30	.357
T Phillips, Det	89	31	.348
C Baerga, Cle	92	32	.348

1st Pitch
(Minimum 125 PA)

Player, Team	AB	H	AVG
J OLERUD, Tor	**88**	**44**	**.500**
A Galarraga, Col	119	55	.462
D Bichette, Col	109	47	.431
F Thomas, ChA	81	34	.420
M Greenwell, Bos	137	57	.416
L Johnson, ChA	140	57	.407
D Bell, SD	98	39	.398
K Puckett, Min	154	61	.396
J Conine, Fla	118	46	.390
W McGee, SF	92	35	.380

Ahead in Count
(Minimum 150 PA)

Player, Team	AB	H	AVG
J KRUK, Phi	**132**	**61**	**.462**
K Lofton, Cle	161	73	.453
T Gwynn, SD	132	59	.447
J Olerud, Tor	154	68	.442
P Molitor, Tor	185	80	.432
L Gonzalez, Hou	122	52	.426
B Bonds, SF	157	66	.420
M Vaughn, Bos	119	50	.420
C Fielder, Det	109	45	.413
K Griffey Jr, Sea	143	59	.413

Behind in Count
(Minimum 150 PA)

Player, Team	AB	H	AVG
G JEFFERIES, StL	**210**	**69**	**.329**
B Bonds, SF	195	59	.303
R Sandberg, ChN	248	74	.298
A Trammell, Det	162	48	.296
B Gilkey, StL	191	56	.293
P O'Neill, NYA	196	57	.291
T Gwynn, SD	187	54	.289
B Gates, Oak	247	71	.287
R Alomar, Tor	242	69	.285
J Olerud, Tor	207	59	.285

Two Strikes
(Minimum 150 PA)

Player, Team	AB	H	AVG
T GWYNN, SD	**146**	**47**	**.322**
A Trammell, Det	166	53	.319
T Raines, ChA	145	44	.303
G Jefferies, StL	182	55	.302
L Johnson, ChA	158	45	.285
D Mattingly, NYA	185	52	.281
D Hamilton, Mil	253	71	.281
R Sandberg, ChN	221	61	.276
H Reynolds, Bal	184	50	.272
B Gates, Oak	257	69	.268

Full Count
(Minimum 40 PA)

Player, Team	AB	H	AVG
L DYKSTRA, Phi	**69**	**28**	**.406**
S Javier, Cal	30	12	.400
T Raines, ChA	43	17	.395
M Lemke, Atl	41	16	.390
D Magadan, Sea	54	20	.370
T Brunansky, Mil	33	12	.364
B Surhoff, Mil	33	12	.364
M Macfarlane, KC	33	12	.364
R Amaral, Sea	25	9	.360
D Fletcher, Mon	31	11	.355

Close & Late
(Minimum 75 PA)

Player, Team	AB	H	AVG
M GRACE, ChN	**86**	**39**	**.453**
P Molitor, Tor	90	37	.411
G Jefferies, StL	87	35	.402
W McGee, SF	75	30	.400
M Greenwell, Bos	83	32	.386
T Gwynn, SD	89	33	.371
B Bonds, SF	81	30	.370
F Fermin, Cle	65	24	.369
T Raines, ChA	61	22	.361
K Puckett, Min	95	34	.358

1993 Batting Leaders

Batting #1
(Minimum 175 PA)

Player, Team	AB	H	AVG
R AMARAL, Sea	**158**	**56**	**.354**
D Hamilton, Mil	304	99	.326
K Lofton, Cle	566	184	.325
W Boggs, NYA	253	80	.316
B Gilkey, StL	395	123	.311
T Phillips, Det	559	174	.311
B McRae, KC	190	59	.311
T Raines, ChA	413	127	.308
L Dykstra, Phi	637	194	.305
B Butler, LA	584	176	.301

Batting #2
(Minimum 175 PA)

Player, Team	AB	H	AVG
D JAMES, NYA	**193**	**70**	**.363**
R Thompson, SF	382	125	.327
B Gates, Oak	288	92	.319
R Sandberg, ChN	215	68	.316
R Alomar, Tor	401	126	.314
J Blauser, Atl	561	174	.310
J Bell, Pit	604	187	.310
B Hatcher, Bos	312	93	.298
B Barberie, Fla	255	76	.298
J Vizcaino, ChN	308	91	.295

Batting #3
(Minimum 175 PA)

Player, Team	AB	H	AVG
T GWYNN, SD	**217**	**86**	**.396**
G Jefferies, StL	523	180	.344
P Molitor, Tor	515	169	.328
M Grace, ChN	497	163	.328
D Bichette, Col	359	116	.323
H Morris, Cin	189	61	.323
C Baerga, Cle	624	200	.321
J Bagwell, Hou	519	165	.318
J Kruk, Phi	529	168	.318
F Thomas, ChA	549	174	.317

Batting #4
(Minimum 150 PA)

Player, Team	AB	H	AVG
A GALARRAGA, Col	**392**	**152**	**.388**
O Merced, Pit	133	46	.346
K Mitchell, Cin	311	107	.344
W Joyner, KC	178	57	.320
T Neel, Oak	256	81	.316
H Baines, Bal	385	121	.314
J Gonzalez, Tex	535	165	.308
D May, ChN	252	77	.306
T Zeile, StL	367	109	.297
F McGriff, Atl	535	157	.293

Batting #5
(Minimum 150 PA)

Player, Team	AB	H	AVG
J OLERUD, Tor	**500**	**182**	**.364**
O Merced, Pit	159	55	.346
B Bonds, SF	404	139	.344
J Buhner, Sea	143	47	.329
P O'Neill, NYA	372	121	.325
J Franco, Tex	213	69	.324
M Stanley, NYA	170	55	.324
M Piazza, LA	278	89	.320
C Hayes, Col	350	111	.317
M Vaughn, Bos	291	88	.302

Batting #6
(Minimum 150 PA)

Player, Team	AB	H	AVG
R WILKINS, ChN	**202**	**74**	**.366**
W McGee, SF	187	64	.342
J Eisenreich, Phi	248	84	.339
B Harper, Min	245	78	.318
S Cooper, Bos	151	48	.318
C Snyder, LA	212	66	.311
B Williams, NYA	242	75	.310
L Gonzalez, Hou	223	68	.305
C Hoiles, Bal	184	56	.304
J Clark, Col	307	93	.303

Batting #7
(Minimum 100 PA)

Player, Team	AB	H	AVG
C HOILES, Bal	**122**	**45**	**.369**
T Fernandez, Tor	148	50	.338
A Trammell, Det	110	36	.327
D Easley, Cal	108	35	.324
S Buechele, ChN	84	27	.321
A Cedeno, Hou	166	52	.313
T Hulett, Bal	99	31	.313
K Manwaring, SF	112	35	.313
A Arias, Fla	96	30	.313
E Karros, LA	129	40	.310

Batting #8
(Minimum 100 PA)

Player, Team	AB	H	AVG
R WILKINS, ChN	**102**	**36**	**.353**
M Pagliarulo, Bal	139	46	.331
J Offerman, LA	88	29	.330
K Stocker, Phi	249	79	.317
J Valentin, Bos	206	63	.306
M Gallego, NYA	233	70	.300
H Reynolds, Bal	138	41	.297
D Strange, Tex	192	57	.297
J Brumfield, Cin	90	26	.289
T Lovullo, Cal	94	27	.287

Batting #9
(Minimum 100 PA)

Player, Team	AB	H	AVG
J VALENTIN, Bos	**96**	**30**	**.313**
S Alomar Jr, Cle	171	53	.310
M Bordick, Oak	107	32	.299
M Diaz, Tex	104	31	.298
P Borders, Tor	165	47	.285
O Guillen, ChA	457	128	.280
S Hemond, Oak	157	43	.274
P Kelly, NYA	403	110	.273
J Bell, Mil	99	27	.273
G DiSarcina, Cal	194	52	.268

None On/None Out
(Minimum 100 PA)

Player, Team	AB	H	AVG
J KRUK, Phi	**99**	**43**	**.434**
T Neel, Oak	113	43	.381
J Olerud, Tor	168	63	.375
L Gonzalez, Hou	110	41	.373
R Palmeiro, Tex	137	51	.372
J Gonzalez, Tex	141	52	.369
P Molitor, Tor	104	38	.365
M Piazza, LA	124	45	.363
C Curtis, Cal	105	38	.362
O Merced, Pit	86	31	.360

Pre-All Star
(Minimum 175 PA)

Player, Team	AB	H	AVG
J OLERUD, Tor	**304**	**120**	**.395**
A Galarraga, Col	271	106	.391
O Merced, Pit	265	96	.362
K Mitchell, Cin	241	86	.357
J Kruk, Phi	294	103	.350
B Bonds, SF	299	104	.348
J Eisenreich, Phi	171	59	.345
G Jefferies, StL	327	112	.343
W McGee, SF	275	93	.338
M Grace, ChN	307	102	.332

Post-All Star
(Minimum 175 PA)

Player, Team	AB	H	AVG
T GWYNN, SD	**190**	**76**	**.400**
P Molitor, Tor	288	104	.361
D James, NYA	189	68	.360
C Baerga, Cle	276	97	.351
R Alomar, Tor	264	92	.348
A Galarraga, Col	199	68	.342
G Jefferies, StL	217	74	.341
A Trammell, Det	211	71	.336
F Thomas, ChA	238	80	.336
H Morris, Cin	266	89	.335

5-Year Batting Leaders

Overall
(Minimum 2000 PA)

Player	AB	H	AVG
T GWYNN	**2716**	**888**	**.327**
F Thomas	1872	600	.321
P Molitor	2943	935	.318
K Puckett	3058	968	.317
B Larkin	2320	719	.310
J Franco	2358	725	.307
B Harper	2337	718	.307
W Boggs	2860	875	.306
J Kruk	2380	727	.305
S Mack	1858	567	.305

LHP
(Minimum 600 PA)

Player	AB	H	AVG
F THOMAS	**532**	**190**	**.357**
P Molitor	746	260	.349
B Larkin	754	248	.329
K Puckett	774	252	.326
R Sandberg	910	295	.324
K Mitchell	641	207	.323
C Baerga	651	210	.323
E Martinez	558	179	.321
M Duncan	856	269	.314
R Jordan	646	203	.314

RHP
(Minimum 800 PA)

Player	AB	H	AVG
T GWYNN	**1680**	**565**	**.336**
H Morris	1174	390	.332
W Boggs	1928	619	.321
R Alomar	2094	671	.320
D Hamilton	1184	378	.319
J Kruk	1565	494	.316
K Puckett	2284	716	.313
M Grace	1901	591	.311
W Clark	1709	529	.310
P Molitor	2197	675	.307

Home
(Minimum 700 PA)

Player	AB	H	AVG
K PUCKETT	**1574**	**545**	**.346**
W Boggs	1383	468	.338
J Franco	1192	399	.335
F Thomas	911	304	.334
T Gwynn	1321	431	.326
C Baerga	1077	347	.322
B Butler	1461	469	.321
S Mack	858	273	.318
M Grace	1473	468	.318
P Molitor	1398	444	.318

Away
(Minimum 700 PA)

Player	AB	H	AVG
T GWYNN	**1395**	**457**	**.328**
P Molitor	1545	491	.318
B Bonds	1365	429	.314
B Larkin	1187	372	.313
E Martinez	969	301	.311
H Morris	800	248	.310
F Thomas	961	296	.308
R Palmeiro	1546	472	.305
A Van Slyke	1229	373	.303
W Clark	1374	417	.303

Groundball Pitchers
(Minimum 500 PA)

Player	AB	H	AVG
F THOMAS	**485**	**169**	**.348**
T Gwynn	953	312	.327
P Molitor	711	232	.326
W McGee	766	246	.321
B Harper	614	197	.321
K Griffey Jr	649	208	.320
W Boggs	740	237	.320
B Larkin	831	266	.320
J Kruk	852	272	.319
B Bonds	904	286	.316

Grass
(Minimum 600 PA)

Player	AB	H	AVG
F THOMAS	**1560**	**512**	**.328**
T Gwynn	1979	641	.324
J Olerud	697	223	.320
J Franco	1962	620	.316
E Martinez	741	231	.312
M Grace	2119	660	.311
W Boggs	2401	744	.310
B Butler	2234	690	.309
B Bonds	992	306	.308
W Clark	2050	631	.308

Turf
(Minimum 600 PA)

Player	AB	H	AVG
P MOLITOR	**793**	**274**	**.346**
T Gwynn	737	247	.335
K Puckett	1927	640	.332
B Harper	1429	452	.316
B Larkin	1645	519	.316
H Morris	1112	349	.314
R Alomar	1399	438	.313
W McGee	924	288	.312
J Kruk	1679	523	.311
K Griffey Jr	1672	518	.310

Flyball Pitchers
(Minimum 500 PA)

Player	AB	H	AVG
F THOMAS	**414**	**134**	**.324**
P Molitor	601	192	.319
D Mattingly	606	192	.317
K Griffey Jr	627	195	.311
R Alomar	670	208	.310
B Butler	649	201	.310
L Dykstra	466	144	.309
J Franco	513	158	.308
A Dawson	590	181	.307
R Palmeiro	656	201	.306

Day
(Minimum 600 PA)

Player	AB	H	AVG
W McGEE	**813**	**267**	**.328**
B Harper	619	203	.328
H Baines	679	222	.327
L Polonia	744	241	.324
K Puckett	921	296	.321
P Molitor	910	292	.321
K Griffey Jr	730	233	.319
R Sandberg	1493	472	.316
M Greenwell	791	250	.316
F Thomas	496	155	.313

Night
(Minimum 800 PA)

Player	AB	H	AVG
T GWYNN	**1901**	**635**	**.334**
F Thomas	1376	445	.323
D Hamilton	1045	335	.321
B Larkin	1670	533	.319
P Molitor	2033	643	.316
K Puckett	2137	672	.314
S Mack	1279	400	.313
J Franco	1913	598	.313
B Butler	2008	624	.311
W Boggs	1890	584	.309

Scoring Position
(Minimum 400 PA)

Player	AB	H	AVG
P MOLITOR	**691**	**235**	**.340**
T Gwynn	588	198	.337
J Franco	603	201	.333
B Bonds	624	206	.330
D Hamilton	396	129	.326
T Raines	527	170	.323
A Trammell	494	158	.320
D Mattingly	691	221	.320
F Thomas	532	170	.320
W Boggs	583	186	.319

5-Year Batting Leaders

April
(Minimum 300 PA)

Player	AB	H	AVG
B BUTLER	**421**	**139**	**.330**
T Gwynn	452	146	.323
J Olerud	256	81	.316
B Kelly	360	112	.311
K Puckett	402	125	.311
W Clark	421	130	.309
K Griffey Jr	392	121	.309
W McGee	322	99	.307
J Kruk	335	102	.304
B Harper	277	84	.303

May
(Minimum 400 PA)

Player	AB	H	AVG
T GWYNN	**531**	**183**	**.345**
B Larkin	417	141	.338
K Puckett	530	178	.336
P Molitor	552	185	.335
W Joyner	435	143	.329
A Van Slyke	430	141	.328
J Franco	405	132	.326
J Kruk	368	119	.323
R Sandberg	522	167	.320
H Baines	344	110	.320

June
(Minimum 400 PA)

Player	AB	H	AVG
T GWYNN	**486**	**164**	**.337**
K Mitchell	365	123	.337
G Jefferies	469	158	.337
W McGee	361	120	.332
M Grace	441	143	.324
R Sierra	540	174	.322
L Dykstra	388	125	.322
W Clark	446	143	.321
R Milligan	358	114	.318
B Harper	398	125	.314

July
(Minimum 400 PA)

Player	AB	H	AVG
S MACK	**350**	**127**	**.363**
H Baines	369	127	.344
D DeShields	385	130	.338
W Boggs	457	153	.335
R Palmeiro	500	166	.332
K Griffey Jr	470	156	.332
R Henderson	395	130	.329
H Morris	354	116	.328
B Harper	410	133	.324
K Puckett	517	167	.323

August
(Minimum 400 PA)

Player	AB	H	AVG
T GWYNN	**522**	**185**	**.354**
F Thomas	399	138	.346
M Grace	576	188	.326
J Franco	390	127	.326
P Molitor	588	188	.320
K Griffey Jr	444	141	.318
B Bonilla	475	150	.316
K Puckett	526	166	.316
M Greenwell	387	122	.315
L Polonia	442	139	.314

September-October
(Minimum 400 PA)

Player	AB	H	AVG
R SANDBERG	**478**	**158**	**.331**
E Murray	539	178	.330
M Greenwell	411	135	.328
P Molitor	579	188	.325
J Franco	402	130	.323
R Alomar	481	154	.320
F Thomas	399	127	.318
C Baerga	435	138	.317
T Pendleton	496	157	.317
T Fernandez	528	166	.314

1st Pitch
(Minimum 500 PA)

Player	AB	H	AVG
H BAINES	**477**	**186**	**.390**
K Puckett	764	297	.389
K Griffey Jr	438	164	.374
T Gwynn	363	134	.369
P O'Neill	399	147	.368
W Clark	478	172	.360
A Galarraga	383	137	.358
F Jose	392	139	.355
F McGriff	396	140	.354
L Walker	417	147	.353

Ahead in Count
(Minimum 600 PA)

Player	AB	H	AVG
K MITCHELL	**487**	**198**	**.407**
J Kruk	612	247	.404
F McGriff	700	281	.401
F Thomas	550	216	.393
W Clark	592	232	.392
C Fielder	473	184	.389
J Franco	591	222	.376
K Griffey Jr	617	231	.374
C Baerga	553	205	.371
J Olerud	449	166	.370

Behind in Count
(Minimum 600 PA)

Player	AB	H	AVG
T GWYNN	**1076**	**330**	**.307**
G Jefferies	1100	302	.275
C Baerga	1001	272	.272
P Molitor	1164	314	.270
L Polonia	1253	336	.268
B Harper	1013	271	.268
B Larkin	993	263	.265
D Hamilton	710	186	.262
E Martinez	803	208	.259
C Ripken	1317	337	.256

Two Strikes
(Minimum 600 PA)

Player	AB	H	AVG
T GWYNN	**860**	**255**	**.297**
D Hamilton	687	179	.261
L Polonia	1097	285	.260
G Jefferies	997	258	.259
B Harper	820	210	.256
E Martinez	856	218	.255
W Boggs	1358	345	.254
D Magadan	914	232	.254
R Henderson	1255	318	.253
C Knoblauch	645	161	.250

Full Count
(Minimum 160 PA)

Player	AB	H	AVG
T GWYNN	**155**	**50**	**.323**
D Hamilton	155	50	.323
S Javier	149	47	.315
W Boggs	347	108	.311
E Martinez	216	67	.310
L Dykstra	233	71	.305
D Mattingly	135	41	.304
C Knoblauch	119	36	.303
J Franco	233	70	.300
R Palmeiro	260	78	.300

Close & Late
(Minimum 300 PA)

Player	AB	H	AVG
T GWYNN	**453**	**154**	**.340**
G Sheffield	310	105	.339
W McGee	388	130	.335
M Grace	479	159	.332
E Martinez	283	93	.329
D Tartabull	343	112	.327
L Dykstra	363	118	.325
K Puckett	453	147	.325
M Greenwell	371	119	.321
P Molitor	389	124	.319

5-Year Batting Leaders

Batting #1
(Minimum 700 PA)

Player	AB	H	AVG
L SMITH	**642**	**203**	**.316**
W Boggs	1748	537	.307
P Molitor	1633	501	.307
B Roberts	1963	583	.297
K Lofton	1189	353	.297
S Mack	694	206	.297
B Butler	2733	803	.294
L Dykstra	2294	674	.294
L Polonia	2278	667	.293
R Henderson	2346	678	.289

Batting #2
(Minimum 700 PA)

Player	AB	H	AVG
T GWYNN	**808**	**263**	**.325**
J Franco	673	216	.321
R Sandberg	1700	523	.308
W McGee	894	267	.299
R Alomar	2288	680	.297
J Treadway	915	271	.296
C Knoblauch	1070	315	.294
D Magadan	894	262	.293
J Blauser	1060	310	.292
R Ventura	881	257	.292

Batting #3
(Minimum 700 PA)

Player	AB	H	AVG
P MOLITOR	**1186**	**392**	**.331**
T Gwynn	1731	572	.330
F Thomas	1401	457	.326
K Puckett	2894	919	.318
B Larkin	1554	490	.315
W Boggs	881	276	.313
K Griffey Jr	1971	608	.308
C Baerga	1834	560	.305
W Clark	2732	832	.305
M Grace	1813	550	.303

Batting #4
(Minimum 600 PA)

Player	AB	H	AVG
J KRUK	**845**	**274**	**.324**
A Galarraga	734	236	.322
M Greenwell	701	216	.308
R Yount	715	214	.299
W Joyner	817	244	.299
K Mitchell	2082	608	.292
R Sierra	1900	553	.291
J Gonzalez	835	237	.284
L Walker	1015	288	.284
F McGriff	1873	531	.284

Batting #5
(Minimum 600 PA)

Player	AB	H	AVG
J OLERUD	**989**	**325**	**.329**
M Greenwell	694	216	.311
J Franco	971	301	.310
B Bonds	1628	499	.307
F Jose	605	185	.306
C Davis	728	220	.302
B Harper	881	266	.302
F McGriff	778	229	.294
T Steinbach	1016	297	.292
C Fisk	604	176	.291

Batting #6
(Minimum 600 PA)

Player	AB	H	AVG
B HARPER	**970**	**304**	**.313**
J Eisenreich	627	187	.298
E Burks	657	184	.280
R Thompson	578	156	.270
J Clark	602	159	.264
T Steinbach	555	146	.263
C Hayes	727	190	.261
S Bream	749	193	.258
B Santiago	792	204	.258
M Nokes	675	171	.253

Batting #7
(Minimum 400 PA)

Player	AB	H	AVG
L JOHNSON	**890**	**260**	**.292**
M Thompson	469	137	.292
D Slaught	900	262	.291
W Wilson	423	122	.288
J Oquendo	387	109	.282
M LaValliere	939	261	.278
S Buechele	473	131	.277
M Stanley	470	128	.272
A Cedeno	437	118	.270
I Rodriguez	416	112	.269

Batting #8
(Minimum 400 PA)

Player	AB	H	AVG
J REED	**403**	**115**	**.285**
S Livingstone	416	117	.281
C Hayes	485	134	.276
M Bordick	626	172	.275
C Candaele	383	105	.274
M Pagliarulo	453	124	.274
M Gallego	643	176	.274
F Fermin	520	142	.273
S Alomar Jr	366	99	.270
K Manwaring	398	107	.269

Batting #9
(Minimum 400 PA)

Player	AB	H	AVG
B KELLY	**377**	**124**	**.329**
S Fletcher	403	112	.278
O Guillen	1693	466	.275
M Bordick	380	102	.268
B Spiers	997	265	.266
G Gagne	1291	328	.254
M Lee	965	244	.253
F Fermin	933	235	.252
P Kelly	1008	253	.251
H Reynolds	395	99	.251

None On/None Out
(Minimum 400 PA)

Player	AB	H	AVG
J OLERUD	**438**	**149**	**.340**
J Kruk	544	185	.340
F Thomas	367	118	.322
E Martinez	461	148	.321
P Molitor	914	292	.319
K Puckett	571	182	.319
R Alomar	661	210	.318
B Harper	543	170	.313
J Eisenreich	530	165	.311
B Bonilla	732	226	.309

Pre-All Star
(Minimum 700 PA)

Player	AB	H	AVG
T GWYNN	**1622**	**544**	**.335**
K Puckett	1651	525	.318
H Morris	624	197	.316
W McGee	1240	390	.315
B Harper	1189	371	.312
B Larkin	1446	451	.312
P Molitor	1493	465	.311
D Slaught	836	257	.307
J Kruk	1271	390	.307
D Hamilton	673	206	.306

Post-All Star
(Minimum 700 PA)

Player	AB	H	AVG
F THOMAS	**986**	**331**	**.336**
S Mack	987	330	.334
P Molitor	1450	470	.324
B Roberts	898	290	.323
J Franco	1064	338	.318
K Puckett	1407	443	.315
T Gwynn	1094	344	.314
M Greenwell	1054	331	.314
E Martinez	825	259	.314
C Baerga	1066	334	.313

1993 Pitching Leaders

Overall
(Minimum 162 IP)

Pitcher, Team	IP	ER	ERA
G MADDUX, Atl	**267.0**	**70**	**2.36**
J Rijo, Cin	257.1	71	2.48
K Appier, KC	238.2	68	2.56
M Portugal, Hou	208.0	64	2.77
B Swift, SF	232.2	73	2.82
S Avery, Atl	223.1	73	2.94
W Alvarez, ChA	207.2	68	2.95
P Harnisch, Hou	217.2	72	2.98
J Key, NYA	236.2	79	3.00
T Candiotti, LA	213.2	74	3.12

Home
(Minimum 75 IP)

Pitcher, Team	IP	ER	ERA
T CANDIOTTI, LA	**115.2**	**25**	**1.95**
G Maddux, Atl	123.1	30	2.19
F Viola, Bos	91.2	23	2.26
D Kile, Hou	92.0	24	2.35
B Swift, SF	111.0	29	2.35
M Portugal, Hou	95.0	25	2.37
K Appier, KC	116.2	31	2.39
K Brown, Tex	124.1	34	2.46
D Osborne, StL	86.1	24	2.50
P Harnisch, Hou	128.2	36	2.52

Away
(Minimum 75 IP)

Pitcher, Team	IP	ER	ERA
J RIJO, Cin	**122.1**	**32**	**2.35**
J Moyer, Bal	84.2	23	2.44
W Alvarez, ChA	101.0	28	2.50
G Maddux, Atl	143.2	40	2.51
J McDowell, ChA	125.2	35	2.51
J Fassero, Mon	82.0	23	2.52
D Cone, KC	127.1	37	2.62
M Langston, Cal	121.0	36	2.68
R Martinez, LA	100.2	30	2.68
K Appier, KC	122.0	37	2.73

April
(Minimum 25 IP)

Pitcher, Team	IP	ER	ERA
J KEY, NYA	**38.2**	**4**	**0.93**
K Brown, Tex	31.2	4	1.14
D Wells, Det	30.2	5	1.47
F Viola, Bos	36.2	6	1.47
E Hanson, Sea	35.1	6	1.53
R Clemens, Bos	38.1	7	1.64
K Hill, Mon	40.0	8	1.80
D Drabek, Hou	41.0	9	1.98
O Olivares, StL	26.0	6	2.08
J Doherty, Det	34.2	8	2.08

May
(Minimum 25 IP)

Pitcher, Team	IP	ER	ERA
D DARWIN, Bos	**40.2**	**6**	**1.33**
T Greene, Phi	43.1	7	1.45
L Aquino, Fla	29.2	6	1.82
M Leiter, Det	38.1	8	1.88
M Portugal, Hou	28.1	6	1.91
B Saberhagen, NYN	31.1	7	2.01
P Quantrill, Bos	25.1	6	2.13
D Cone, KC	46.0	11	2.15
T Belcher, ChA	32.2	8	2.20
M Langston, Cal	44.0	11	2.25

June
(Minimum 25 IP)

Pitcher, Team	IP	ER	ERA
J HERNANDEZ, Cle	**25.0**	**3**	**1.08**
D Kile, Hou	31.0	4	1.16
B Black, SF	33.0	5	1.36
B McDonald, Bal	37.1	7	1.69
K Gross, LA	35.1	7	1.78
T Candiotti, LA	35.0	7	1.80
W Whitehurst, SD	33.0	7	1.91
C Finley, Cal	37.2	8	1.91
T Mulholland, Phi	39.1	9	2.06
S Avery, Atl	41.2	10	2.16

July
(Minimum 25 IP)

Pitcher, Team	IP	ER	ERA
J FASSERO, Mon	**25.0**	**2**	**0.72**
T Candiotti, LA	42.1	7	1.49
F Valenzuela, Bal	40.1	7	1.56
J Rijo, Cin	53.0	11	1.87
B Swift, SF	39.0	9	2.08
R Clemens, Bos	29.0	7	2.17
M Portugal, Hou	37.2	10	2.39
K Appier, KC	29.2	8	2.43
C Nabholz, Mon	36.0	10	2.50
O Hershiser, LA	35.0	10	2.57

August
(Minimum 25 IP)

Pitcher, Team	IP	ER	ERA
D JACKSON, Phi	**26.2**	**4**	**1.35**
T Candiotti, LA	37.0	6	1.46
J Rijo, Cin	42.0	7	1.50
G Maddux, Atl	47.0	8	1.53
F Viola, Bos	33.0	6	1.64
J McDowell, ChA	51.2	10	1.74
J Fassero, Mon	41.0	10	2.20
S Avery, Atl	44.2	11	2.22
D Darwin, Bos	44.1	11	2.23
R Martinez, LA	38.0	10	2.37

September-October
(Minimum 25 IP)

Pitcher, Team	IP	ER	ERA
K APPIER, KC	**44.0**	**5**	**1.02**
W Alvarez, ChA	43.2	5	1.03
P Harnisch, Hou	38.2	5	1.16
P Astacio, LA	47.1	7	1.33
G Maddux, Atl	45.1	7	1.39
M Portugal, Hou	44.1	8	1.62
B Ruffin, Col	27.2	5	1.63
R Johnson, Sea	52.0	10	1.73
K Brown, Tex	47.2	10	1.89
D Boucher, Mon	28.1	6	1.91

Grass
(Minimum 75 IP)

Pitcher, Team	IP	ER	ERA
J BAUTISTA, ChN	**91.1**	**22**	**2.17**
G Maddux, Atl	202.0	54	2.41
T Candiotti, LA	155.0	42	2.44
A Sele, Bos	91.2	27	2.65
P Martinez, LA	80.0	24	2.70
D Cone, KC	99.2	30	2.71
S Avery, Atl	185.1	56	2.72
T Wilson, SF	84.2	26	2.76
J Key, NYA	212.0	67	2.84
D Darwin, Bos	212.2	68	2.88

Turf
(Minimum 75 IP)

Pitcher, Team	IP	ER	ERA
K APPIER, KC	**140.2**	**36**	**2.30**
M Portugal, Hou	131.2	37	2.53
J Fassero, Mon	98.2	28	2.55
R Johnson, Sea	185.0	54	2.63
J Rijo, Cin	183.0	54	2.66
E Hanson, Sea	134.1	41	2.75
T Gordon, KC	80.1	25	2.80
D Kile, Hou	115.2	36	2.80
K Hill, Mon	142.1	47	2.97
D Osborne, StL	111.1	37	2.99

1st Batter
(Minimum 50 BFP)

Pitcher, Team	AB	H	AVG
L ANDERSEN, Phi	**58**	**7**	**.121**
L Lancaster, StL	47	7	.149
B MacDonald, Det	57	9	.158
R Beck, SF	69	11	.159
M Stanton, Atl	54	9	.167
L Casian, Min	48	8	.167
R Aguilera, Min	62	11	.177
M Whiteside, Tex	54	10	.185
L Smith, NYA	57	11	.193
J Howell, Atl	46	9	.196

1993 Pitching Leaders

Overall

(Minimum 625 BFP)

Pitcher, Team	AB	H	AVG
R JOHNSON, Sea	**913**	**185**	**.203**
K Appier, KC	863	183	.212
P Harnisch, Hou	798	171	.214
T Gordon, KC	561	125	.223
D Cone, KC	920	205	.223
B Swift, SF	861	195	.226
B McDonald, Bal	812	185	.228
C Bosio, Sea	602	138	.229
J Rijo, Cin	949	218	.230
J Smoltz, Atl	905	208	.230

LHB

(Minimum 125 BFP)

Pitcher, Team	AB	H	AVG
B HARVEY, Fla	**121**	**16**	**.132**
J Wetteland, Mon	177	31	.175
M Langston, Cal	136	24	.176
T Scott, Mon	128	23	.180
R Beck, SF	161	29	.180
J Fassero, Mon	115	21	.183
N Ryan, Tex	133	25	.188
G McMichael, Atl	155	30	.194
R Aguilera, Min	145	29	.200
T Henke, Tex	132	27	.205

RHB

(Minimum 225 BFP)

Pitcher, Team	AB	H	AVG
B SWIFT, SF	**390**	**69**	**.177**
K Appier, KC	425	78	.184
P Harnisch, Hou	370	69	.186
A Mills, Bal	219	41	.187
S Fernandez, NYN	345	67	.194
D West, Phi	226	44	.195
J Smoltz, Atl	447	89	.199
C Bosio, Sea	303	61	.201
D Darwin, Bos	377	77	.204
R Johnson, Sea	842	172	.204

None On/None Out

(Minimum 150 BFP)

Pitcher, Team	AB	H	AVG
K APPIER, KC	**226**	**37**	**.164**
B Swift, SF	225	42	.187
R Johnson, Sea	238	47	.197
J Fassero, Mon	145	30	.207
P Harnisch, Hou	213	45	.211
T Belcher, ChA	201	43	.214
T Candiotti, LA	208	45	.216
D Stewart, Tor	150	33	.220
B McDonald, Bal	218	48	.220
K Brown, Tex	231	51	.221

None On

(Minimum 250 BFP)

Pitcher, Team	AB	H	AVG
S FERNANDEZ, NYN	**303**	**56**	**.185**
R Johnson, Sea	566	107	.189
K Appier, KC	539	104	.193
P Harnisch, Hou	484	99	.205
B McDonald, Bal	516	106	.205
J Fassero, Mon	334	69	.207
J Bere, ChA	279	60	.215
M Langston, Cal	569	123	.216
O Hershiser, LA	502	109	.217
T Belcher, ChA	480	106	.221

Runners On

(Minimum 250 BFP)

Pitcher, Team	AB	H	AVG
J RIJO, Cin	**360**	**69**	**.192**
D Martinez, Mon	339	67	.198
J Bere, ChA	239	49	.205
W Alvarez, ChA	311	65	.209
G Maddux, Atl	392	86	.219
D Cone, KC	378	83	.220
J Smoltz, Atl	370	82	.222
T Gordon, KC	243	54	.222
P Astacio, LA	260	58	.223
R Johnson, Sea	347	78	.225

1st Pitch

(Minimum 125 BFP)

Pitcher, Team	AB	H	AVG
F TANANA, NYA	**115**	**28**	**.243**
J Rijo, Cin	125	33	.264
T Leary, Sea	119	32	.269
R Bones, Mil	144	39	.271
G Hibbard, ChN	139	38	.273
G Swindell, Hou	131	36	.275
G Maddux, Atl	171	47	.275
T Belcher, ChA	123	34	.276
M Morgan, ChN	143	40	.280
D Drabek, Hou	171	48	.281

Two Strikes

(Minimum 150 BFP)

Pitcher, Team	AB	H	AVG
D WARD, Tor	**152**	**14**	**.092**
J Fassero, Mon	262	29	.111
M Jackson, SF	144	16	.111
P Martinez, LA	195	22	.113
A Leiter, Tor	175	20	.114
R Myers, ChN	157	18	.115
X Hernandez, Hou	165	20	.121
T Frohwirth, Bal	138	17	.123
K Mercker, Atl	134	17	.127
T Gordon, KC	272	35	.129

Scoring Position

(Minimum 125 BFP)

Pitcher, Team	AB	H	AVG
R LEWIS, Fla	**99**	**17**	**.172**
D Martinez, Mon	207	36	.174
D West, Phi	109	19	.174
D Cone, KC	225	40	.178
J Bere, ChA	112	20	.179
R Martinez, LA	197	36	.183
A Mills, Bal	98	18	.184
J Rijo, Cin	202	38	.188
W Alvarez, ChA	159	32	.201
F Viola, Bos	153	32	.209

Ahead in Count

(Minimum 150 BFP)

Pitcher, Team	AB	H	AVG
J FASSERO, Mon	**268**	**33**	**.123**
X Hernandez, Hou	167	21	.126
P Martinez, LA	165	21	.127
B McDonald, Bal	337	45	.134
J Wetteland, Mon	187	25	.134
G McMichael, Atl	179	24	.134
R Johnson, Sea	504	68	.135
D Ward, Tor	154	21	.136
R Myers, ChN	149	21	.141
S Fernandez, NYN	210	30	.143

Behind in Count

(Minimum 150 BFP)

Pitcher, Team	AB	H	AVG
D DARWIN, Bos	**147**	**32**	**.218**
D Cone, KC	192	47	.245
T Greene, Phi	153	38	.248
P Astacio, LA	180	46	.256
J Mesa, Cle	186	48	.258
R Pavlik, Tex	156	42	.269
M Langston, Cal	201	56	.279
A Benes, SD	153	43	.281
T Gordon, KC	142	40	.282
J Smoltz, Atl	184	52	.283

Close & Late

(Minimum 50 BFP)

Pitcher, Team	AB	H	AVG
B BREWER, KC	**44**	**6**	**.136**
T Candiotti, LA	97	15	.155
D Ward, Tor	154	24	.156
R Clemens, Bos	63	10	.159
R Johnson, Sea	107	17	.159
R Beck, SF	176	29	.165
P Harnisch, Hou	48	8	.167
J Schwarz, ChA	66	11	.167
B Barnes, Mon	82	14	.171
D West, Phi	156	27	.173

5-Year Pitching Leaders

Overall
(Minimum 650 IP)

Pitcher	IP	ER	ERA
J RIJO	**980.2**	**282**	**2.59**
B Swift	745.2	229	2.76
G Maddux	1273.1	402	2.84
R Clemens	1191.1	377	2.85
B Saberhagen	830.2	268	2.90
K Appier	862.0	283	2.95
S Fernandez	777.0	256	2.97
D Martinez	1131.0	373	2.97
D Drabek	1204.2	406	3.03
T Candiotti	1063.1	365	3.09

Home
(Minimum 300 IP)

Pitcher	IP	ER	ERA
M PORTUGAL	**385.2**	**102**	**2.38**
B Saberhagen	419.0	114	2.45
S Fernandez	411.0	116	2.54
D Drabek	640.0	181	2.55
J Rijo	474.0	141	2.68
C Finley	598.0	178	2.68
B Swift	366.0	109	2.68
Z Smith	432.1	131	2.73
M Morgan	546.0	166	2.74
K Appier	407.1	125	2.76

Away
(Minimum 300 IP)

Pitcher	IP	ER	ERA
J RIJO	**506.2**	**141**	**2.50**
R Clemens	598.0	182	2.74
B Swift	379.2	120	2.84
G Maddux	656.2	210	2.88
D Cone	582.1	187	2.89
M Langston	578.2	191	2.97
D Martinez	557.2	193	3.11
K Appier	454.2	158	3.13
D Darwin	370.2	130	3.16
D Stieb	305.0	107	3.16

April
(Minimum 100 IP)

Pitcher	IP	ER	ERA
R CLEMENS	**190.1**	**36**	**1.70**
C Bosio	170.2	44	2.32
B Welch	136.0	36	2.38
K Hill	124.0	34	2.47
F Viola	167.0	47	2.53
C Finley	132.1	38	2.58
D Drabek	174.0	50	2.59
J Rijo	132.0	38	2.59
T Glavine	160.0	48	2.70
J Key	156.0	47	2.71

May
(Minimum 100 IP)

Pitcher	IP	ER	ERA
B SABERHAGEN	**190.0**	**46**	**2.18**
D Wells	135.2	36	2.39
D Darwin	101.2	27	2.39
B Ojeda	137.1	39	2.56
M Morgan	187.2	55	2.64
T Mulholland	160.2	49	2.74
T Glavine	192.0	59	2.77
D Cone	186.1	58	2.80
D Martinez	192.0	60	2.81
G Maddux	212.2	69	2.92

June
(Minimum 100 IP)

Pitcher	IP	ER	ERA
N RYAN	**135.2**	**35**	**2.32**
D Martinez	220.0	58	2.37
J McDowell	169.1	48	2.55
B Tewksbury	140.1	42	2.69
R Martinez	152.1	46	2.72
M Langston	211.1	65	2.77
T Candiotti	192.1	60	2.81
O Hershiser	155.0	50	2.90
J Magrane	125.1	41	2.94
M Morgan	188.1	62	2.96

July
(Minimum 100 IP)

Pitcher	IP	ER	ERA
T CANDIOTTI	**185.2**	**45**	**2.18**
B Swift	147.2	37	2.26
M Gardner	127.2	32	2.26
J Rijo	131.1	33	2.26
L Aquino	124.2	33	2.38
B Tewksbury	140.1	40	2.57
D Darwin	131.1	38	2.60
Ju Guzman	100.0	30	2.70
J Abbott	170.1	52	2.75
S Fernandez	124.0	38	2.76

August
(Minimum 100 IP)

Pitcher	IP	ER	ERA
B SABERHAGEN	**109.0**	**16**	**1.32**
J Rijo	159.1	38	2.15
G Maddux	253.0	64	2.28
D Darwin	144.2	38	2.36
J McDowell	194.0	56	2.60
M Boddicker	128.0	37	2.60
T Candiotti	184.2	54	2.63
O Olivares	124.0	37	2.69
B Swift	127.1	38	2.69
K Appier	157.2	49	2.80

September-October
(Minimum 100 IP)

Pitcher	IP	ER	ERA
J RIJO	**197.0**	**39**	**1.78**
Z Smith	120.2	25	1.86
M Mussina	118.1	31	2.36
B Swift	130.1	35	2.42
C Nabholz	137.2	37	2.42
K Appier	137.0	37	2.43
O Hershiser	145.0	41	2.54
B Saberhagen	140.2	40	2.56
B Wegman	105.1	30	2.56
S Fernandez	167.2	48	2.58

Grass
(Minimum 300 IP)

Pitcher	IP	ER	ERA
J RIJO	**309.1**	**84**	**2.44**
B Swift	447.1	140	2.82
S Fernandez	556.2	176	2.85
B Saberhagen	394.1	125	2.85
GW Harris	550.0	177	2.90
M Morgan	780.2	252	2.91
G Maddux	916.1	296	2.91
T Belcher	617.1	201	2.93
R Clemens	1003.0	332	2.98
T Candiotti	790.2	269	3.06

Turf
(Minimum 300 IP)

Pitcher	IP	ER	ERA
D DRABEK	**913.2**	**247**	**2.43**
M Portugal	520.0	153	2.65
J Rijo	671.1	198	2.65
G Maddux	357.0	106	2.67
K Appier	491.2	152	2.78
D Ward	326.2	102	2.81
D Martinez	852.1	272	2.87
Z Smith	607.2	195	2.89
B Saberhagen	436.1	143	2.95
N Charlton	339.0	112	2.97

1st Batter
(Minimum 200 BFP)

Pitcher	AB	H	AVG
R AGUILERA	**259**	**50**	**.193**
R Honeycutt	253	49	.194
P Assenmacher	271	53	.196
S Belinda	214	42	.196
S Bedrosian	188	37	.197
M Stanton	207	41	.198
J Brantley	235	47	.200
D Righetti	244	49	.201
L Andersen	243	49	.202
T Fossas	245	50	.204

5-Year Pitching Leaders

Overall
(Minimum 2500 BFP)

Pitcher	AB	H	AVG
N RYAN	**3016**	**593**	**.197**
S Fernandez	2803	567	.202
R Johnson	3769	811	.215
D Cone	4310	970	.225
J DeLeon	2810	640	.228
J Rijo	3597	820	.228
R Clemens	4394	1005	.229
J Smoltz	4289	986	.230
P Harnisch	3486	808	.232
M Langston	4412	1029	.233

LHB
(Minimum 500 BFP)

Pitcher	AB	H	AVG
B HARVEY	**549**	**94**	**.171**
G Olson	623	120	.193
M Langston	626	121	.193
R Dibble	719	139	.193
T Henke	619	122	.197
Z Smith	546	109	.200
N Ryan	1580	318	.201
T Wilson	469	97	.207
S Fernandez	511	107	.209
J Wetteland	649	136	.210

RHB
(Minimum 900 BFP)

Pitcher	AB	H	AVG
J DeLEON	**1232**	**232**	**.188**
N Ryan	1436	275	.192
J Montgomery	841	164	.195
J Smoltz	1837	361	.197
S Fernandez	2292	460	.201
J Rijo	1561	315	.202
M Jackson	877	177	.202
D Ward	1018	208	.204
D Darwin	1286	269	.209
P Harnisch	1519	318	.209

None On/None Out
(Minimum 600 BFP)

Pitcher	AB	H	AVG
N RYAN	**803**	**141**	**.176**
S Fernandez	780	159	.204
D Stieb	553	116	.210
J DeLeon	722	155	.215
B McDonald	706	154	.218
T Belcher	1006	222	.221
K Appier	833	185	.222
R Johnson	959	216	.225
B Hurst	900	203	.226
GA Harris	608	138	.227

None On
(Minimum 1000 BFP)

Pitcher	AB	H	AVG
N RYAN	**1923**	**333**	**.173**
S Fernandez	1857	361	.194
D Ward	1051	211	.201
R Johnson	2154	444	.206
N Charlton	991	211	.213
J DeLeon	1684	360	.214
D Stieb	1279	279	.218
B McDonald	1658	362	.218
M Gardner	1426	314	.220
Ju Guzman	1135	252	.222

Runners On
(Minimum 1000 BFP)

Pitcher	AB	H	AVG
S FERNANDEZ	**946**	**206**	**.218**
D Martinez	1590	349	.219
J Rijo	1373	303	.221
D Cone	1743	387	.222
R Johnson	1615	367	.227
R Clemens	1697	392	.231
J Boever	869	201	.231
T Gordon	1301	303	.233
D Darwin	1086	254	.234
J Smoltz	1721	404	.235

1st Pitch
(Minimum 500 BFP)

Pitcher	AB	H	AVG
J MCDOWELL	**541**	**149**	**.275**
M Morgan	685	191	.279
C Hough	479	134	.280
T Glavine	670	188	.281
B Black	576	163	.283
M Langston	643	182	.283
J Key	521	149	.286
G Hibbard	583	167	.286
G Maddux	792	227	.287
D Darwin	457	131	.287

Two Strikes
(Minimum 600 BFP)

Pitcher	AB	H	AVG
R DIBBLE	**846**	**90**	**.106**
B Harvey	637	74	.116
N Ryan	1749	228	.130
N Charlton	774	103	.133
R Johnson	2076	278	.134
D Eckersley	776	106	.137
T Henke	698	97	.139
M Jackson	798	111	.139
D Ward	1065	149	.140
T Frohwirth	549	77	.140

Scoring Position
(Minimum 500 BFP)

Pitcher	AB	H	AVG
R DIBBLE	**492**	**95**	**.193**
J Montgomery	463	92	.199
D Cone	1034	206	.199
D Martinez	945	190	.201
J Brantley	494	100	.202
Mitch Williams	488	101	.207
Ju Guzman	472	99	.210
R Myers	489	104	.213
J Rijo	785	167	.213
R Clemens	928	203	.219

Ahead in Count
(Minimum 600 BFP)

Pitcher	AB	H	AVG
B HARVEY	**629**	**82**	**.130**
R Dibble	834	109	.131
D Ward	1055	153	.145
N Ryan	1586	231	.146
R Johnson	1944	284	.146
J Wetteland	646	96	.149
G Olson	602	91	.151
S Fernandez	1478	229	.155
T Henke	673	105	.156
M Jackson	767	121	.158

Behind in Count
(Minimum 600 BFP)

Pitcher	AB	H	AVG
D MARTINEZ	**853**	**221**	**.259**
S Fernandez	508	139	.274
C Nabholz	474	130	.274
N Ryan	551	152	.276
J Deshaies	743	208	.280
R Tomlin	508	144	.283
B Saberhagen	560	159	.284
P Harnisch	640	182	.284
B Swift	701	202	.288
C Hough	891	257	.288

Close & Late
(Minimum 200 BFP)

Pitcher	AB	H	AVG
R BECK	**395**	**73**	**.185**
PJ Martinez	235	44	.187
R Johnson	346	65	.188
B Harvey	714	137	.192
N Ryan	246	48	.195
D Eckersley	886	173	.195
P Harnisch	254	50	.197
R Clemens	504	100	.198
M Fetters	197	40	.203
M Boddicker	215	44	.205

About STATS, Inc.

READ THIS. REALLY. It's new this year. Those of you who've been buying our books faithfully for more than one season know that this little description of our company never changes. At least you think it never changes. Anyway, since that first About STATS, Inc. was written four years ago, unlike the article, the company has changed quite a bit.

Back then, we were the hotshot new kids on the baseball block, with three reporters tracking all kinds of interesting, new data on every major league game. That data took us a long way. We found that baseball fans were very interested in that data. We worked with major league teams. We worked with the media. (We revolutionized the boxscore business, both in timeliness and accuracy. Everything from boxscores to same day pitching matchup details to feature articles led to interaction with television, newspaper, and magazine accounts.) We worked with the individual baseball fan. (Our Major League Handbook allowed fans to begin reviewing the past season in November, and not have to wait for the Spring. Our Bill James Fantasy Baseball game became undoubtedly the most realistic, intense fantasy baseball game available. Our STATS On-Line allowed baseball fanatics not only access to boxscores, but In-Progress boxscores, half-inning by half- inning. Our year-end reports on disk let fans do their own number crunching, without the hassle of data entry.)

But it's time to move on to new horizons. Let's face it, knowing that Bryan Harvey rarely blows a save and that Mile High Stadium outrageously favors hitters isn't exactly ground-breaking information anymore.

Where do we go from here? Well, in case you haven't noticed there are three other major professional sports out there which could use a bit of revolutionary data analysis. For example, what gets Steve Young most of his passing yards, his arm or his receivers' legs? I bet you'd have a guess, but do you really know? Or how about the NBA? All the games are basically decided in the last two minutes, right? But what makes you so sure? Perhaps the last three games you watched on TV? We're well into the answers already. Although a couple years worth of data may not be definitive, it makes for good hypotheses and two years turns into five years in three years (revolutionary!). In fact, you can phone us or walk over to your nearest bookstore and purchase a new product we're extremely proud of: the *STATS Basketball Scoreboard 1993-1994*, our first non-baseball book. You'll find the answer above in there (a first quarter lead has held up 57 percent of the time over the last two seasons) and the customary "many, many more." In football there's no book yet, but we have football data on STATS On-Line, which, for computer users, is far better, since the data is always current. If you're not an On-Line customer already, you have twice as many reasons to sign up now. As for hockey, we'll be gathering data for the first time this year, so by next Handbook, we'll be able to tell you about hockey also.

Do we need help collecting all this data? You bet we do. For baseball, although we're fairly stocked in some cities at this point, we're always looking for new reporters. For football, we have numerous openings. We have no reporter network yet in basketball or hockey, but things could change in the near future. You won't be able to quit your job reporting for STATS, but you'll have some fun and learn lots about the sports you love.

For more information write to:

STATS, Inc.
7366 North Lincoln Ave.
Lincolnwood, IL 60646-1708

. . .or call us at 1-708-676-3322. We can send you a STATS brochure, a free information kit on Bill James Fantasy Baseball, the BJFB Winter Game, STATS Fantasy Football, or info on our brand new game, STATS Fantasy Hoops.

And, by the way, we haven't forgotten baseball (as if you thought we ever could). You'll definitely want a copy of our brand new *Batter versus Pitcher MATCH-UPS!* book which will give you the scoop on how every active pitcher has done against every active batter. The perfect ballpark or TV companion, it will be pocket-sized (another STATS first) and will be out in February.

Turn to the last pages in this book to find a handy order form and additional information about the fine products from STATS.

Glossary

There are quite a few abbreviations in the book, with which most of you are probably familiar. But for the sake of completeness, here is a rundown of all the abbreviations, plus descriptions of many of the categories for the stat splits and some of the formulas used.

For Hitters:

Avg=batting average, G=games played, AB=at bats, R=runs scored, H=hits, 2B=doubles, 3B=triples, HR=home runs, RBI=runs batted in, BB=walks, SO=strikeouts, HBP=times hit by pitch, GDP=times grounded into double play, SB=stolen bases, CS=caught stealing, OBP=on base percentage, SLG=slugging percentage, IBB=intentional walks received, SH=sacrifice hits, SF=sacrifice flies, #Pit=number of pitches offered to the hitter, #P/PA=average number of pitches per plate appearance, GB=number of fair ground balls hit (hits, outs and errors), FB=number of fly balls hit (excludes line drives), G/F=ratio of grounders to fly balls.

For Fielders:

G=number of games the player appeared at that position, GS=number of starts the player made, Innings=number of innings played at that position, PO=putouts, A=assists, E=errors, DP=double plays turned, Fld.Pct=fielding percentage, Rng.Fctr=Range Factor, In Zone=balls hit in the player's area, Outs=number of outs resulting from a ball hit to a player, Zone Rtg=Zone Rating (see below), MLB Zone=major league average zone rating for that position.

For Pitchers:

ERA=earned run average, W=wins, L=losses, Sv=saves, G=games pitched, GS=games started, IP=innings pitched, BB=walks issued, SO=strikeouts, Avg.=opposition batting average against the pitcher, H=hits allowed, 2B=doubles allowed, 3B=triples allowed, HR=homers allowed, RBI=RBI's allowed, OBP=on base percentage against the pitcher, SLG=slugging percentage against the pitcher, CG=complete games, ShO=shutouts, Sup=run support per nine innings, GF=games finished, IR=inherited runners, IRS=inherited runners who scored, QS=quality starts, Hld=holds, SvOp=save opportunities, SB=stolen bases against the pitcher, CS=times runners were caught stealing while the pitcher was on the mound, GB=groundballs hit against the pitcher (hits, outs and errors), FB=fly balls hit against the pitcher (excludes line drives), G/F=ratio of grounders to flies.

Formulas and Definitions

OBP = (H + BB + HBP) / (AB + BB + HBP + SF) SLG = Total Bases / At Bats Fld.Pct. = (PO + A) / (PO + A + E) Rng.Fctr. = (PO + A) * 9 / defensive innings played, or the average number of plays a fielder makes over a nine-inning game. Zone Rating = The Zone Rating measures all the balls hit in the area where a fielder can reasonably be expected to record an out, then counts the percentage of outs actually made. Thus, a zone rating of .895, like Mickey Morandini had last year, means that he got 290 outs on the 324 balls hit into his general area last year, or 89.5%. GF = games in which the pitcher was the last reliever in the game. Hold = A pitcher gets a hold when he enters the game in a save situation, records at least one out, and leaves the game having never relinquished the lead. A player cannot finish the game and get a hold, nor can he get credit for a hold and a save in the same game.

Player Breakdowns

There are three styles of player breakdowns in this book. The first is for all the Regulars, the second is for Subs and the final type is for the "Cup-of-Coffee" players. We defined Regulars as being any batters with 325 or more plate appearances last season or pitchers with either 162+ innings or 60 appearances. Subs are hitters with between 126 and 324 plate appearances or pitchers who threw between 60 and 161.2 innings last year or appeared in between 25 and 59 games. The final type of player includes everyone else who appeared in a game in 1993. What this means is that the Regulars have stat splits in every category, the Subs have splits in most categories and the fringe players have just a couple of listings. There are only so many ways you can only breakdown Jim Walewander's lone single last year.

The multi-year section (career or five-year) is shown for any hitter whose career exceeds his 1993 playing time by 325+ appearances or for any pitcher whose career exceeds his 1993 playing time by 162 innings or 60 games.

Starting pitchers have slightly different formats than relief pitchers. In the top section, starters have stats for CG, ShO, Sup, QS and #P/S. For relievers, defined as pitchers with more games relieved than started, we show GF, IR,

IRS, Hld and SvOp. In the stat breakdowns, starters have statistics based on longer rest between starts and higher pitch levels per outing.

Breakdown Categories

Most of the categories are fairly straight forward, but below is some information that could make a few of them a little less ambiguous.

The "1993 Season" label refers to his total stats for last year, even if he got traded midway through the season. So Bobby Thigpen's line is for both the White Sox and the Phillies. The next line is either the pitcher's performance since 1989 or his career if he debuted since 1989.

AGE indicates how old the player will be on July 1, 1994, or midway through next season.

GROUNDBALL and FLYBALL are a hitter's stats against pitchers that induce mostly grounders or flies, respectively. So Travis Fryman's "Groundball" line is his performance against pitchers like Jim Abbott, who throw mostly grounders. If a player's Groundball/Flyball ratio is less than 1.00, then he is a Flyball hitter. If the ratio is greater then 1.50, then he is a Groundball hitter. Anything else is classified as neutral. The same cutoffs are used for pitchers in classifying them as flyball/groundball pitchers. Also, anybody with less then 50 plate appearances is automatically called neutral.

DAY/NIGHT designations differ between the leagues. Officially, night games in the National League are those that start after 5:00 p.m., while night games in the AL are those that begin after 6:00 p.m. So a game starting at 5:30 in Yankee Stadium is a day game while one in Shea Stadium at the same time is a night contest. We avoid this silliness by calling all games starting after 5:00 p.m. night games. GRASS is grass and TURF is artificial turf.

FIRST PITCH refers to the first pitch of a given at bat, and any walks listed here are intentional walks. For hitters, AHEAD IN COUNT includes 1-0, 2-0, 3-0, 2-1, and 3-1. BEHIND IN COUNT includes 0-1, 0-2, 1-2, and 2-2. For pitchers, it's the opposite.

SCORING POSITION is having at least one runner at either second or third base. CLOSE AND LATE occurs when a) the game is in the seventh inning or later and b) the batting team is either leading by one run, tied, or has the potential tying run on base, at bat or on deck. NONE ON/OUT is when there are no outs and the bases are empty (generally leadoff situations).

INNING 1-6 and INNING 7+ refer to the actual innings in which a pitcher worked. NONE ON/RUNNERS ON is the status of the baserunners.

VS. 1ST BATR (RELIEF) is what happened to the first batter a reliever faced. FIRST INNING PITCHED is the result of the pitcher's work until he recorded three outs.

The NUMBER OF PITCHES section shows the results of balls put into play while his pitch count was in that range.

All of the above is the same for the multi-year data as well.

In the PITCHER/BATTER MATCHUPS, the following conditions must be met before a player is added to the list: a) There must be greater than 10 plate appearances between the batter and the pitcher; and b) Batters must have a .300 average against a pitcher to be considered as a "Hits Best Against" candidate, and pitchers must limit hitters to under .250 to be listed under "Pitches Best Vs.". Thus, not all hitters will have five pitchers that qualify, and not all pitchers will have five batters that qualify.

— *Allan Spear*

Bill James and STATS, Inc. Present a Star-Studded Line-up

Six Essential Books Perfect for Any Baseball Fan!

- Best Seller–the earliest and most complete stats
- Exclusive **Bill James** 1994 projections
- **Career** data for every active major leaguer
- Exclusive 1994 pitcher projections
- **Lefty/Righty** stats for every hitter and pitcher
- Available Nov 1, 1993

- **All minor leaguers**, AAA through rookie leagues
- Careeer stats for AAA and AA minor leaguers
- **Bill James' exclusive major league equivalencies**
- Team batting and pitching
- First time in print–**AAA lefty/righty data**
- Available Nov 1, 1993

THE DEFINITIVE STATISTICAL EVALUATION GUIDE
STATS 1994
PLAYER
PROFILES
Available
November 1st

- The most complete player breakdowns ever printed, over 27 in all, includes:
- Against lefty/righty pitchers
- Ahead/behind in the count
- Month by month breakdown
- NEW for 1994 – Team and League Profiles!
- Includes 1993 and last 5 years
- Available Nov 1, 1993

- The unique STATS analysis used by teams, networks and now YOU!
- Find out the answers to questions like:
  "Why play for one run?"
  "Who are baseballs tablesetters?"
  "What makes for an efficient defense?"
- Available Mar 15, 1994

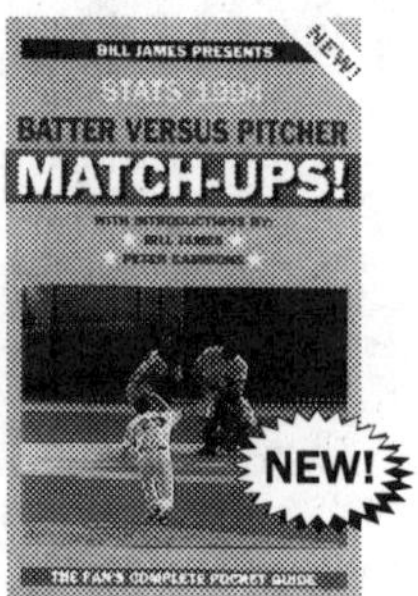

- Includes all 1993 Major Leaguers
- Complete stats for batters vs. pitchers.
- Most and least dominating match-ups
- Available Feb 1, 1994

- The most in-depth, easy-to-use, professional quality scouting reports ever made available to the public.
- Complete scouting reports on over 700 players
- Essential information on each teams hottest prospects
- Available Feb 1, 1994

To Order, Fill Out the Order Form in This Book
Or Call 1-800-63-STATS.

Bill James FANTASY BASEBALL

If You Like Fantasy Baseball, You'll Love Bill James Fantasy Baseball...

"Hi, This is Bill James. A few years ago I designed a set of rules for a new fantasy baseball league, which has been updated with the benefit of experience and the input of a few thousand owners.

The idea of a fantasy league, of course, is that it forges a link between you and your ballplayers; YOU win or lose based on how the players that you picked have performed. My goal was to develop a fantasy league based on the simplest and yet most realistic principles possible — a league in which the values are as nearly as possible what they ought to be, without being distorted by artificial category values or rankings, but which at the same time are so simple that you can keep track of how you've done just by checking the boxscores. There are a lot of different rules around for fantasy leagues, but none of them before this provided exactly what I was looking for. Here's what we want:

1) We want it to be realistic. We don't want the rules to make Randy Johnson the MVP just because of his strikeouts. We don't want Chuck Carr to be worth more than Fred McGriff because he steals lots of bases. We want good ballplayers to be good ballplayers.

2) We prefer it simple. We want you to be able to look up your players in the morning paper, and know how you've done.

3) We want you to have to develop a real team. We don't want somebody to win by stacking up starting pitchers and leadoff men. We don't want somebody to corner the market on home run hitters.

I made up the rules and I'll be playing the game with you. STATS, Inc. is running the leagues. They'll run the draft, man the computers, keep the rosters straight and provide you with weekly updates. Of course you can make trades, pick up free agents and move players on and off the inactive list; that not my department, but there are rules for that, too. It all starts with a draft . . ."

- Draft Your Own Team and Play vs. Other Owners! Play by Mail or With a Computer On-Line!
- Manage Your Roster All Season With Daily Transactions! Live Fantasy Phone Lines Every Day of the Baseball Season!
- Realistic Team and Individual Player Totals That Even Take Fielding Into Account!
- The Best Weekly Reports in the Business!
- Play Against Bill James' Own Drafted Teams!
- Get Discounted Prices by Forming Your Own Private League of 11 or 12 owners! (Call or write for more information)
- Money-Back Guarantee! Play one month, and if not satisfied, we'll return your franchise fee!

All This, All Summer Long — For Less Than An Average of $5 per week.

Reserve your BJFB team now! Sign up with the STATS Order Form in this book, or send for additional Free Information.

Product (Date Available)	Quantity	Your Price	Total
Bill James/STATS 1994 Major League Handbook (11/1/93)		$17.95	
Player Projections Update (3/1/94)		9.95	
Bill James/STATS 1994 Minor League Handbook (11/1/93)		17.95	
STATS 1994 Player Profiles (11/1/93)		17.95	
Bill James/STATS 1994 BVSP Match-Ups! (2/1/94)		6.99	
STATS 1994 Baseball Scoreboard (3/1/94)		15.00	
The Scouting Report: 1994 (3/1/94)		16.00	
STATS Basketball Scoreboard 1993-1994 (10/1/93)		15.00	
Discounts on previous editions while supplies last:			
Major League Handbook 1990 (#) 1991 (#) 1992 (#) 1993 (#)		9.95	
Minor League Handbook 1992 (#) 1993 (#)		9.95	
Player Profiles 1993		9.95	
Baseball Scoreboard 1991 (#) 1992 (#) 1993 (#)		9.95	
The Scouting Report 1992 (#) 1993 (#)		9.95	
U.S.—For first class mailing—add $2.50 per book		2.50	
Canada—all orders—add $3.50 per book		3.50	
Order 2 or more books—subtract $1 per book		–1.00	
SUBTOTAL			
Illinois Residents Include 7.75% Sales Tax			
TOTAL			

☐ Yes, I can't wait! Sign me up to play **Bill James Fantasy Baseball** in 1994. Enclosed is my deposit of $25.00 on the franchise fee of $89.00. A processing fee of $1.00 per player is charged during the season for roster moves.

☐ Yes, I can't wait! Sign me up to play **BJFB: The Winter Game** in 1994. Enclosed is my deposit of $50.00 on the franchise fee of $129.00. A processing fee between 50 cents to $1.00 per player is charged during the season for roster moves and changes to manager profiles.

Team Nickname:______________________ ______________________ (example: San Francisco Crab)

Would you like to play in a league with a team drafted by Bill James? Yes No (circle one)

Would you like to receive information on playing fantasy games on-line by computer? Yes No (circle one)

Please Rush Me These Free Informational Brochures:

- ☐ **Bill James Fantasy Baseball Info Kit**
- ☐ **STATS Fantasy Football Info Kit**
- ☐ **STATS Baseball Reporter Brochure**
- ☐ **STATS Football Reporter Brochure**
- ☐ **STATS Product Guide (Including Year-End-Reports information)**
- ☐ **Pro-Line Brochure**
- ☐ **STATS Fantasy Hoops Info Kit (NEW!)**
- ☐ **BJFB: The Wnter Game Info Kit**
- ☐ **STATSfax Brochure (sent via fax)**
- ☐ **STATS On-Line Brochure**

Return this form (don't tear your book; copy this page) to:

STATS, Inc.
7366 N. Lincoln Ave.
Lincolnwood, IL
60646-1708

Please Print:

Name______________________________ Phone______________________________

Address______________________________ Fax______________________________

City____________________State__________ Zip______________________________

Method of Payment (U.S. Funds only):

☐ Check (no Canadian checks)

☐ Money Order

☐ Visa

☐ MasterCard

Credit Card Information:

Cardholder Name______________________________

Visa/MasterCard No.______________________________

Exp. Date______________________________

Signature______________________________

For faster credit card service: call 1-800-63-STATS (1-800-637-8287) to place your order, or fax this form to 1-708-676-0821.

PP94